THE COMPLETE RESOURCE GUIDE FOR PEOPLE WITH DISABILITIES

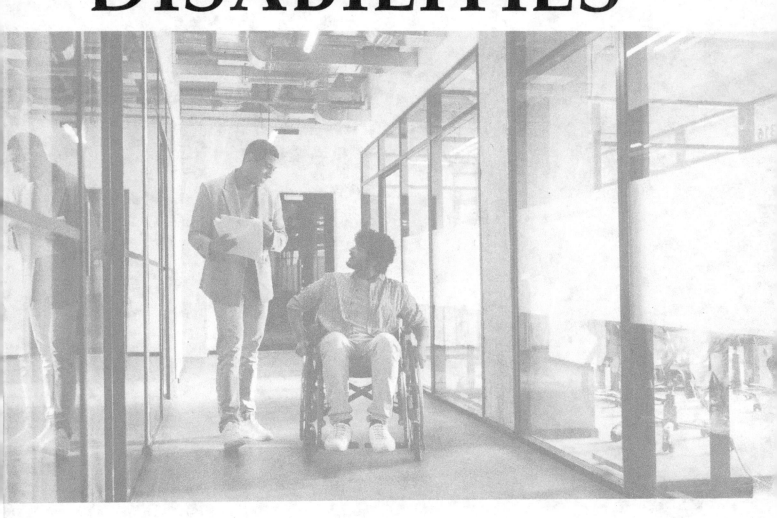

2024
THIRTY-SECOND
EDITION

THE COMPLETE RESOURCE GUIDE FOR PEOPLE WITH DISABILITIES

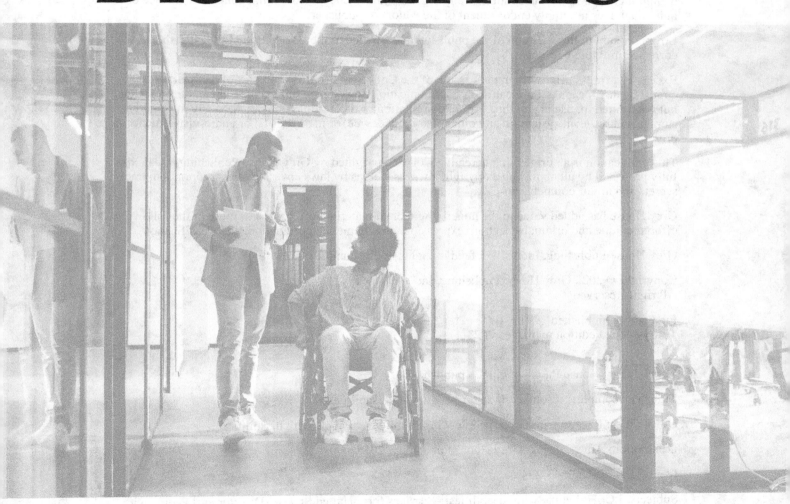

GREY HOUSE PUBLISHING

PUBLISHER: Leslie Mackenzie
EDITORIAL DIRECTOR: Stuart Paterson
STATISTICS: David Garoogian
MARKETING DIRECTOR: Jessica Moody

Grey House Publishing, Inc.
4919 Route 22
Amenia, NY 12501
518.789.8700
Fax: 845.373.6390
www.greyhouse.com
books@greyhouse.com

First edition published 1991
Thirty-second edition published 2023

Names: Grey House Publishing, Inc., publisher.

Title: The complete resource guide for people with disabilities.

Other Titles: Resource guide for people with disabilities | People with disabilities

Description: Amenia, NY : Grey House Publishing, 2018-

Identifiers: ISSN: 2643-234X

Subjects: LCSH: People with disabilities—Services for—United States—Directories. | People with disabilities—Services for—United States—Periodicals. | People with disabilities—Services for—United States—Bibliography—Periodicals.

Classification: LCC HV1553 .C58 | DDC 362.4—dc23

Printed in Canada
ISBN 13: 978-1-63700-550-7 Softcover

Table of Contents

Table of Contents

Table of Contents

Introduction

This 32nd edition of the award-winning *Complete Resource Guide for People with Disabilities* is invaluable for all those living with a disability, their personal and professional community, and all those committed to empowering these individuals. It offers thousands of ways for people with disabilities to succeed at work, in school, and in their community.

Careful research and compilation of the best data available maintains the reputation of *The Complete Resource Guide for People with Disabilities* among educators, librarians and the disability community. This resource is a repeat recipient of the **National Mature Media Award** and the **National Health Information Award**.

This comprehensive resource opens with the following valuable front matter:
- An in-depth report on the impact of extreme weather events on people living with disabilities, including the following sections: Laws and Regulations; Healthcare; Housing; Employment; Education; and Emergency Management
- User Guide and Key
- Glossary of Disability-Related Terms

Coverage continues with subject-specific listing sections (i.e. Arts, Assistive Devices, Camps, Vocational Programs), Rehabilitation Facilities, and disability-specific sections (i.e. Aging, Cognitive, Mobility, Speech). Each disability section includes a range of resources from Associations to Support Groups. The comprehensive Table of Contents guides you through the 33 chapters and more than 100 subchapters contained in this rich resource.

Following the listing chapters is a 2023 Annual Disability Statistics Compendium: a robust section of easy-to-read tables featuring the latest available data. The first part of the compendium features numbers of disabled individuals by both state and disability—hearing, vision, cognitive, ambulatory, and self-care and independent-living disabilities—and the second part features individuals who are employed, broken down by the categories listed above.

Sure to save hours of Internet research time, *The Complete Resource Guide for People with Disabilities* provides comprehensive, critical and immediate information in one source that can be accessed quickly and easily. This edition provides 9,192 descriptive listings, 23,397 key contacts, 7,206 fax numbers, 5,796 email addresses, and 8,193 web sites.

Indexes
Three indexes provide quick, easy access to the data.
- **Subject Index** alphabetically organizes directory listings by relevant topics, i.e. autism, language disorders.
- **Geographic Index** organizes listings alphabetically by state.
- **Entry & Publisher Index** lists all directory listings alphabetically.

In addition to the print work, The Complete Resource Guide for People with Disabilities is available by subscription on G.O.L.D., Grey House OnLine Databases. This gives you immediate access to the most valuable disability community contacts in the United States, plus offers easy-to-use keyword searches, organization type and subject searches, hotlinks to web sites and emails, and so much more. Call 800-562-2139 for a free trial or visit http://gold.greyhouse.com for more information.

Praise for previous editions:

> *"This comprehensive directory is an excellent starting point...a very useful resource for public, hospital, and consumer-health libraries as well as social-service agencies and nonprofits serving the disabled."*

—Booklist

> *"The strength of this source is in the information referral portion for each entry: the wide range of resources and organizations presented that can assist with additional information and support."*

—ARBA

> *"...thousands of resources...covering a diverse range of services...separate section for specific disabilities...from aging to mobility and from the blind and deaf to speech and language disorders. Libraries...will want to consider..."*

—Against the Grain

We welcome your comments, and look forward to another year of serving the disability community.

The Impacts of Extreme Weather Events on
People with Disabilities

National Council on Disability
May 4, 2023

Introduction

The global mortality rate of people with disabilities in natural disasters is up to four times higher than that of people without disabilities.[20] People with disabilities are far more likely than anyone else to face major hardships including displacement from their homes due to a major disaster. If they evacuate, people with disabilities face dangerous levels of isolation, squalid living conditions, shortages of food and water and electricity, and permanent dislocation.[21] The increased frequency and severity of extreme weather events and environmental hazards adversely and disproportionately impact people with disabilities in the United States and its territories. Despite this, the needs of people with disabilities are being overlooked in disaster management policy and planning. Federal and state emergency management planning often fails to include people with disabilities.

The global mortality rate of people with disabilities in natural disasters is up to four times higher than that of people without disabilities.

According to a 2022 comprehensive review and analysis of disability inclusion in national climate commitments and policies, few countries make provisions for the needs of people with disabilities when they make plans for adapting to the effects of climate change and none mention disabled people in their programs.

Recent research shows that people with disabilities are being "systematically ignored" by governments around the world when it comes to planning for extreme weather events. According to a 2022 comprehensive review and analysis of disability inclusion in national climate commitments and policies, few countries make provisions for the needs of people with disabilities when they make plans for adapting to the effects of climate change and none mention people with disabilities in their programs.[22]

Extreme weather events are occurrences of unusually severe weather or climate conditions that can be disruptive and deadly[23] and cause devastating impacts on communities and agricultural and natural ecosystems.[24] In the United States, when extreme weather events occur, the governor of a state or territory may request that the president declare a major disaster or emergency. Extreme weather events such as severe storms, hurricanes, floods, tornadoes, drought, extreme heat events, wildfires, or other weather-related emergencies and disasters can strike quickly and without warning, forcing people to quickly evacuate or be confined in their homes unexpectedly.[25] For the 61 million (26 percent or 1 in 4) adults in the United States who live with a disability,[26] emergencies such as fires and floods present a real challenge.[27]

During an emergency or major disaster, people who live with physical, sensory, mental, or cognitive disabilities are disproportionately affected. When an emergency occurs, people with disabilities typically have fewer reserves to draw upon, their options for housing and healthcare are more limited, and it can be harder to recover once the immediate emergency has passed.[28] The increased prevalence of extreme weather events will further destroy these reserves and further hinder people with disabilities' ability to "rebound" after an extreme weather event.

In the United States, weather-related events are happening more often: breaking records, claiming lives, and costing billions of dollars. These events include record-breaking heat waves, increased number and intensity of hurricanes, more precipitation and floods, more wildfires, more intense droughts, and increasingly severe storms.[29] Projections indicate that the occurrence and severity of some extreme events will continue to increase.[30]

Extreme weather events can damage or destroy critical infrastructure and facilities. The disruption to critical services disproportionately and negatively impacts people with disabilities and puts individuals at increased risk. Temperature increases and heatwaves can lead to brownouts or blackouts. Power outages can jeopardize the health and safety of people with disabilities, older adults, and people with serious health conditions, who often depend on equipment powered by electricity.

Extreme weather events are expected to further disrupt many areas of life, exacerbating existing challenges posed by aging and deteriorating infrastructure, stressed ecosystems, and economic inequality. Impacts within and across regions will not be distributed equally.[31] People with disabilities and those who are already vulnerable, including lower-income and other marginalized communities, have lower capacity to prepare for and cope with extreme weather and climate-related events and are expected to experience greater impacts.[32]

Some regions are prone to extreme weather and face disasters year after year, compounding the impacts of previous disasters. Certain types of extreme weather events are increasing in frequency as well as intensity. The rise in vulnerability to drought is lengthening wildfire seasons in the Western states, and the potential for extremely heavy rainfall is becoming more common in the Eastern states. A rise in sea levels is worsening the hurricane and storm surge flooding that coastal communities experience.[33] With 23 of the 25 most densely populated U.S. counties located on the coasts,

> *When an emergency occurs, people with disabilities typically have fewer reserves to draw upon, their options for housing and healthcare are more limited, and it can be harder to recover once the immediate emergency has passed.*

a rise in sea levels is a big issue for millions of people in the United States.[34]

As the U.S. population ages, disabilities are becoming more prevalent. In addition, studies have not yet determined how many citizens who contracted COVID-19 will become disabled because of long-haul COVID. The increase in the number of people with disabilities will increase demand for resources and services, place an added strain on support systems (e.g., healthcare, housing, transportation, employment, education, and emergency management), and exacerbate the drivers of insecurity. As the number of people with disabilities increases, so too will the demand for accessible services, resources, and assistive technologies during a disaster, the lack of which increases the risk to people with disabilities.

Furthermore, the United States is facing staffing shortages in healthcare providers and direct care workers;[35] affordable, accessible housing; special education providers and other workers; accessible places of employment; and other support systems. The increase in the number of people with disabilities paired with the shortage of support systems will create a "perfect storm" or critical situation to exacerbate the drivers of insecurity and increase the risk to people with disabilities, including during an extreme weather event where individuals are already vulnerable and emergency services are already stretched.

> *The increase in the number of people with disabilities paired with the shortage of support systems will create a "perfect storm" or critical situation to exacerbate the drivers of insecurity and increase the risk to people with disabilities, including during an extreme weather event where individuals are already vulnerable and emergency services are already stretched.*

There is little data collection on the impact of people with disabilities during disasters, especially during extreme weather events. With an increase in population of people with disabilities, all federal agencies who play a role in emergency management planning, response or recovery should collect bifurcated data on the impact extreme weather events have on people with disabilities, and then utilize that data to improve processes, programs, and plans to mitigate the detrimental impact of extreme weather events on people with disabilities.

During and after an extreme weather event, federal fund recipients must comply with the Rehab Act and the ADA by making appropriate and reasonable accommodations to ensure that people with disabilities have equal physical and communications access to services and programs, as defined by federal law. Unfortunately, the mechanisms in place to enforce disability laws are underutilized. Despite numerous reports and recommendations concerning people with disabilities, significant improvements have not been made.

Extreme Weather Events are Increasing in Frequency and Severity

Recent studies describe a significant rise in the number of extreme weather event disasters.[36] For the purposes of this report, the term *disaster* will be reserved for natural hazard–related disasters, excluding biological and technological disasters. Extreme weather event disasters include disasters categorized as meteorological, climatological, or hydrological.

A 2021 World Meteorological Organization (WMO) report found that a disaster related to a weather, climate, or water hazard occurred, on average, every day over the past 50 years.[37] Much of the United States has seen increases in prolonged periods of excessively high temperatures, heavy downpours, and, in some regions, severe floods and droughts.[38] These types of records are expected to continue to be broken in the future.

A 2021 World Meteorological Organization (WMO) report found that a disaster related to a weather, climate, or water hazard occurred, on average, every day over the past 50 years.

Globally, from 2000 to 2019, there were 7,348 major recorded disaster events claiming 1.23 million lives, affecting 4.2 billion people (many on more than one occasion), and resulting in approximately $2.97 trillion in global economic losses. This is a sharp increase over the previous 20 years. Between 1980 and 1999, 4,212 disasters were linked to natural hazards worldwide, claiming approximately 1.19 million lives, affecting 3.25 billion people, and resulting in approximately $1.63 trillion in economic losses.[39]

The last 20 years have seen the number of major floods more than double, from 1,389 to 3,254, while the incidence of storms grew from 1,457 to 2,034. Floods and storms were the most prevalent events.[40]

The last 20 years have seen the number of major floods more than double, from 1,389 to 3,254, while the incidence of storms grew from 1,457 to 2,034. Floods and storms were the most prevalent events.

In 2022, the United States experienced 18 separate billion-dollar weather and climate disasters, tying 2017 and 2011 as the 3rd highest number of billion-dollar disasters.[41] 2021 holds 2nd place for the most disasters in a calendar year behind the record 22 separate billion-dollar events in 2020.[42] What made 2022 stand out was the diversity of disasters: 1 drought event, 1 flooding event, 9 severe storm events, 3 tropical cyclone events, 1 wildfire event, and 1 winter storm event.[43] The 18 events in 2022 caused at least 474 direct or indirect fatalities-the 8th most disaster-related fatalities for the contiguous U.S. since 1980.[44] The year 2021 was also unusually deadly. The 20 events of 2021 caused at least 688 direct or indirect fatalities—the most disaster-related fatalities for the contiguous United States since 2011, and more than double 2020's 262 deaths.[45]

The increasing frequency and intensity of certain types of extreme weather include the rise in vulnerability to drought, lengthening wildfire seasons in the Western states, and the potential for extremely heavy rainfall becoming more common in the Eastern states. Sea level rise is worsening hurricane storm surge flooding.[46] Severe storms have caused the most billion-dollar disaster events (143), while hurricanes and flooding represent the second and third most frequent event types (56 and 35), respectively.[47]

Recent examples of severe weather events include the powerful billion-dollar Hurricane Harvey (2017),[48] which resulted in devastating flooding that inundated Harris County, Texas, with 1 trillion gallons of water over a four-day period,[49] and Winter Storm Uri (2021), a historic cold wave and winter storm that impacted many Northwest, Central, and Eastern states in February 2021. The prolonged Arctic air caused widespread power outages in Texas, as well as other southern states, with multiple days of sustained below-freezing temperatures. At the peak of the outage, nearly 10 million people were without power.[50] Additional impacts included frozen water pipes that burst upon thawing, causing water damage to buildings. The extreme conditions also caused or contributed to the direct and indirect deaths of more than 210 people in Texas alone.[51] During the Western wildfires (2020–2021),[52] severe drought conditions and periods of extreme heat provided conditions favorable for wildfires,[53] which impacted the states of California, Oregon, Washington, Idaho, and Montana. The Southern and Central U.S. also experienced remarkable late autumn tornadoes in 2021.[54]

Extreme Weather Events are Increasing in Cost

As extreme weather events accelerate in frequency and grow in intensity, the impacts are costly. In 2014, the U.S. National Climate Assessment (2014 NCA) found that rising temperatures, the resulting increases in the frequency or intensity of some extreme weather events, rising sea levels, and melting snow and ice were already disrupting people's lives and damaging some sectors of the U.S. economy.[55] The money spent on disaster recovery efforts can mean a loss to productive investments and gross domestic product (GDP). Consequently, real disaster costs are high and growing faster than the U.S. GDP.[56]

The National Oceanic and Atmospheric Administration (NOAA), NCEI U.S. Billion-Dollar Weather and Climate Disasters (2022) report calculates the costs of disasters. The report found that from 1980 to 2021, the U.S. has sustained 323 distinct billion-dollar disasters (weather and climate events) where overall damages/costs reached or exceeded at least $1 billion in direct losses (CPI-adjusted, 2022).[57] The direct losses from these 323 events exceed $2.199 trillion (CPI-adjusted, 2022).[58]

The disaster costs for 2022 ($165 billion) surpassed the disaster costs for 2021 ($155.3 billion)[59] by $10 billion and 2022 had $2 less billion-dollar events. The total cost for the last 5 years ($595.5 billion) is almost one third of the disaster cost total of the last 42 years (1980 to 2022) at $2.476 trillion (inflation-adjusted to $2022).[60] This reflects a 5 year average cost of nearly $161.5 billion per year—a new record.[61] The 1980–2022

> *In 2021, the U.S. experienced 20 separate billion-dollar weather and climate disasters, putting 2021 in second place for the most disasters in a calendar year, behind the record 22 separate billion-dollar events in 2020.*

> *[R]eal disaster costs are high and growing faster than the U.S. GDP.*

annual average cost per year is $57.6 billion (CPI-adjusted); the annual average for the most recent 5 years (2018–2022) is $119.1 billion (CPI-adjusted).[62]

Between 1980 and 2022, 21 wildfire, 30 drought, 163 severe storm, 60 tropical cyclone, 37 flooding, 21 winter storm, and 9 freeze billion-dollar disaster events affected the United States (CPI adjusted).[63] The distribution of damage from U.S. billion-dollar disaster events from 1980 to 2022 is dominated by tropical cyclones. Hurricanes have caused the most damage ($1,333.6 billion, CPI-adjusted) and also have the highest average event cost ($22.2 billion, CPI-adjusted). Drought ($327.7 billion, CPI-adjusted), severe storms ($383.7 billion, CPI-adjusted), and inland flooding ($177.9 billion, CPI-adjusted) have also caused considerable damage.[65]

The total cost for the last 5 years ($595.5 billion) is almost one third of the disaster cost total of the last 42 years (1980 to 2022) at $2.476 trillion (inflation-adjusted to $2022).[64]

Severe storms have caused the highest number of billion-dollar disaster events (143), but have the lowest average event cost ($2.3 billion, CPI-adjusted). Hurricanes and flooding represent the second and third most frequent event types (56 and 35), respectively. Hurricanes are responsible for the highest number of deaths (6,697), followed by drought/heat wave events (4,139) and severe storms (1,880).[66]

As hurricanes and flooding tend to occur in the southern part of the U.S., from 1980–2022, the U.S. South, Central, and Southeast regions experienced higher costs from billion-dollar disaster events (this was also the case for California, New York, New Jersey, Puerto Rico, and the U.S. Virgin Islands). The top three most impacted states were Texas ($349 billion), Louisiana ($278 billion), and Florida ($249 billion).[67] The relative costs were more acute in Louisiana, which has a smaller population and economy than Texas and Florida. Louisiana also has a high frequency of disaster events, which can lead to compounding, cascading socioeconomic impacts.[68]

Regional Impact and Rural Communities

While each region of the United States faces a unique combination of weather and climate events, every state in the country, as well as Puerto Rico and the Virgin Islands, has been impacted by at least one, billion-dollar disaster since 1980. Since 1980, there have been more than 100 of these events that have affected at

While each region of the United States faces a unique combination of weather and climate events, every state in the country, as well as Puerto Rico and the Virgin Islands, has been impacted by at least one billion-dollar disaster since 1980.

least some part of Texas, while only one event has impacted Hawaii (Hurricane Iniki in 1992).[69]

The U.S. Central, South, and Southeast regions typically experience a higher frequency of billion-dollar disasters than other regions.[70] These same U.S. regions are also projected to have the most negative future impacts across several socioeconomic metrics.[71] Severe local storm events are common across the Plains, Southeast, and Ohio River Valley states. Winter storm impacts are concentrated in the Northeastern states, while tropical cyclone impacts range from Texas to New England, but also impact many inland states. Inland flood events—not caused by tropical cyclones—often occur in states near large rivers or the Gulf of Mexico, which is a warm source of moisture to fuel rainstorms. Drought impacts are mostly focused in the Southern and Plains states, where crop and livestock assets are densely populated. Wildfires are most common west of the Plains states and in several Southeastern states. Concurrent or consecutive extreme weather events will continue to pose unprecedented challenges and test federal and SLTT government EMAs' preparedness and coordination efforts and complicate response and recovery efforts. Concurrent or consecutive extreme weather events will stress critical systems (e.g., healthcare, housing, transportation, education) and support services upon which people with disabilities rely and heighten risks, compound impacts, and have far-reaching consequences for people with disabilities. Some

The U.S. Central, South, and Southeast regions typically experience a higher frequency of billion-dollar disasters than other regions.

By 2050, "moderate" (typically damaging) flooding is expected to occur, on average, more than 10 times as often as it does today; this flooding can be intensified by local factors. "Major" (often destructive) flooding is expected to occur 5 times as often in 2050 (0.2 events/year) as it does today (0.04 events/year).

U.S. regions experience multiple disasters occurring at the same time, much like Louisiana faced in 2020 as its local government leaders and their emergency managers responded to the COVID-19 pandemic and an "epidemic" of landfalling hurricanes during the 2020 season.[72] Some U.S. regions are prone to and are well known for experiencing consecutive extreme weather events, which compound the impacts of previous disasters.

According to the FEMA NRI – All Hazards data, there is a particularly high risk of natural hazards along the West Coast (specifically in Southern California), the Gulf Coast, and Florida. The Gulf Coast states will be especially susceptible to sea levels rising. States such as Texas, Louisiana, Mississippi, Alabama, and Florida may experience increased storm surges and flooding due to rising sea levels.

NOAA's Sea Level Rise Technical Report projects sea levels along the coastline will rise an additional 10 to 12 inches by 2050, with specific amounts varying regionally, mainly due to land height changes. Sea level rise will create a profound shift in coastal flooding over the next 30 years by causing tide and storm surge heights to increase and reach further inland. By 2050, "moderate" (typically damaging) flooding is expected to occur, on average, more than 10 times as often as it does today; this flooding can be intensified by local factors. "Major" (often destructive) flooding is expected to occur 5 times as often in 2050 (0.2 events/year) as it does today (0.04 events/year).[73] This is especially troubling for people with disabilities living in these areas, and especially those with mobility disabilities who do not have the funds to raise the elevation of their home to mitigate the risk of flood or those who are trapped in their home during a flood event with no option to evacuate.

U.S. Territories

In September 2017 Hurricane Maria made landfall in Puerto Rico and decimated its infrastructure. In Maria's aftermath, some 3.4 million American citizens found themselves in a humanitarian crisis, facing destroyed infrastructure; power outages lasting for over six months; shortages of water, food, and fuel; and an uncertain future.[74] In January 2020, Puerto Rico suffered a 6.4 magnitude earthquake and continuing aftershocks in the southwestern part of the island that destroyed homes and businesses, further weakening an already dire economy and creating significant impact to the health and well-being of the residents of Puerto Rico. In March 2020, Puerto Rico, along with the rest of the world, was hit with the COVID-19 pandemic, which strained health and medical systems. The government took early precautions by shuttering all businesses, except for essential services. These restrictions, though necessary, saddled the island with further economic burdens, leaving thousands unemployed, resulting in increased poverty rates and further widening the gap to accessible services for people with

disabilities. As a result of these conditions and threats, the island experienced an exodus of residents to the mainland United States. This migration created a shortage of medical doctors, educators, and other professionals, further exacerbating availability of services for people with disabilities.[75]

Regional Impacts

Some states, counties, and cities are more likely than others to have residents with disabilities. The percentage of people living with disabilities is highest in the South.[76] West Virginia has the highest share of people with disabilities of any state, at 19.4 percent. In Arkansas, Kentucky, and Alabama, about 17 percent of residents said they had a disability. In contrast, Utah was among the lowest, with 9.9 percent of the population reporting a disability in 2015.[77]

Among counties with populations of 65,000 or more, three had a quarter or more of residents reporting a disability: Pike County, Kentucky (28.7 percent), and Calhoun (25.2 percent) and Walker (25.1 percent) counties, both in Alabama. The share of residents with a disability varied widely at the county level, with Kendall County in Illinois (4.9 percent) among the lowest rates in the country. Few of the cities with the largest shares of disabled residents in 2015are in the South (among places with a minimum population of 65,000). In Flint, Michigan; Hemet, California; and Pueblo, Colorado, roughly 22 percent of residents reported having a disability. The town of Fishers, Indiana, had one of the lowest shares in the nation, with 3.5 percent of residents having a disability.[78]

People with disabilities are more likely to live in poverty, be unemployed, and have limited access to healthcare before a disaster, which compounds these difficulties.[79] In the U.S., according to the CDC, 61 million adults in the U.S. live with a disability—that is 26 percent of (or 1 in 4) adults. The CDC data (2020) report that disabilities are especially common in older adults, women, and people from diverse cultures or backgrounds.

Older Adults

The population is getting older and disabilities become more prevalent with age. According to CDC data (2020), two in five adults aged 65 years and older have disabilities.[80] According to the American Community Survey, about half of Americans ages 75 and older (49.8 percent) reported living with a disability in 2015, as did about a quarter (25.4 percent) of those 65 to 74. In contrast, just 6 percent of Americans ages 18 to 34 and 13 percent of those 35 to 64 said they had a disability. In absolute numbers, however, ages 35 to 64 accounted for more disabled Americans— nearly 16 million in 2015—than any other age group.[81]

The number of adults over age 65 in the U.S. is estimated to reach 84 million, or over 20 percent of the population, by 2050.[82] As people grow older and the probability of disabilities increases, the use of assistive technology—that is, alternate and augmentative communication equipment, devices, strategies, tools, and

> *People with disabilities are more likely to live in poverty, be unemployed, and have limited access to healthcare before a disaster, which compounds these difficulties.*

supportive services that allow individuals to live in their homes with dignity and autonomy—may increase.[83] Using a conservative estimate of 20 percent of the population age 60 and over requiring assistive devices leads to a worldwide estimate of at least 800 million items being used by older adults by 2050. To meet the needs of this population, assistive devices and technology need to be available and accessible for this population, affordable and appropriate for their needs, and safe for their use.[84] This need becomes even more important when disasters occur, as these devices may be lost, damaged, or unavailable without services such as electrical power and refrigeration.[85]

Using a conservative estimate of 20 percent of the population age 60 and over requiring assistive devices leads to a worldwide estimate of at least 800 million items being used by older adults by 2050.

People from Marginalized or Underserved Communities Including American Indians or Alaska Natives

People from marginalized or underserved communities, including Black and American Indians or Alaska Natives, are more likely to have disabilities than other populations. At the high end of the scale, American Indians or Alaskan Natives are most likely to report a disability: 17.7 percent,[86] or two in five of American Indians or Alaska Natives have a disability.[87] For comparison, 13.9 percent of white people and 14.1 percent of Black people reported living with a disability, followed by 8.8 percent of Hispanic people and 6.9 percent of Asian people.[88]

Minority populations, including Black and American Indians or Alaska Natives, are more likely to have disabilities than other populations.

There are shortages in healthcare, housing, education, employment, and other support systems, which will increase the risk to people with disabilities.

While the number of people with disabilities is increasing, there is a health care worker shortage. The increase in demand for support and growing gap in supply will strain the U.S. healthcare system and impact access to healthcare. The shortage of care workers (e.g., direct support professionals (DSPs) and personal care assistants (PCAs)) places people with disabilities at additional risk of harm and puts an additional burden on the people who care for them.

In addition, it has become harder than ever for middle-income Americans to rent or buy a home as the U.S. faces a housing shortage. The Census Bureau reported that despite the strong demand for rentals, the national vacancy rate was at 6.8 percent in 2019. Still, the increase in the number of households paying more than 30 percent of their income for rent and utilities grew by 261,000 to 20.8 million in 2018. In 2018, one in four renters spent more than half their income on housing, especially individuals earning between $45,000 and $74,999.[89] There is also a nationwide shortage of qualified special education teachers and related service providers.[90] Qualified staff for in-home education can be wholly unavailable.[91] The COVID-19 pandemic has only exacerbated these challenges.[92]

The mechanisms in place to enforce disability laws are underutilized. Despite numerous reports and recommendations submitted by NCD and other organizations, significant improvements have not been made.

Key federal laws such as the ADA,[93] the Rehab Act,[94] and IDEA[95] have helped people with disabilities increase their presence in the workforce, receive improved educational services, and live independently in the community. These and other laws, such as the Fair Housing Amendments Act of 1988 and the Telecommunications Act of 1996, seek to ensure that people with disabilities have the opportunity to access housing, education, employment, effective communications and other activities without discrimination.[96] During emergencies or disasters, any SLTT partners who accept federal emergency/disaster funding must comply with the ADA and the Rehab Act; however, the mechanisms in place to enforce disability rights laws are underutilized.

This report examines the federal and SLTT government policies and programs (specifically disaster prevention and preparedness and response and recovery programs) in place to support people with disabilities before, during, and after a disaster and endeavors to determine whether those policies and programs ensure accessibility and safety and protect the civil right of people with disabilities.

In 2018, one in four renters spent more than half their income on housing, especially individuals earning between $45,000 and $74,999.

Chapter 1: Laws and Regulations

During extreme weather events, the rights of people with disabilities must not be ignored and recipients of federal funds must comply with federal disability laws. In federally declared emergencies and disasters,[97] federal and SLTT government EMAs are responsible for ensuring equal access to facilities and programs. Key federal laws, including the ADA,[98] and the Rehab Act,[99] were enacted to ensure that people with disabilities have access to the same opportunities as those without disabilities. Section 504 of the Rehabilitation Act specifically states that any program or activity that receives federal financial assistance cannot deny benefits to people with disabilities.[100] Other laws, such as IDEA (reauthorized in 2004),[101] the Fair Housing Amendments Act of 1988,[102] and the Telecommunications Act of 1996,[103] seek to ensure that individuals with disabilities have the opportunity to access housing, education, employment, and other activities without discrimination.[104] In 2010, Congress passed the Twenty-First Century Communications and Video Accessibility Act (CVAA) to ensure accessibility to people with disabilities to the rapidly changing telecommunications and information technology sector.

In *Saving Lives: Including People with Disabilities in Emergency Planning* (2005), NCD reported that "all too often in emergency situations the legitimate concerns of people with disabilities are overlooked or swept aside."[105] Seventeen years later, we find that emergency management planning still does not sufficiently account for the needs of people with disabilities and does not afford equal access to people with disabilities (PWDs) during emergencies and disasters. In other words, disability rights continue to be violated and federal laws are not applied consistently. People with disabilities will continue to be disproportionately impacted by extreme weather events unless emergency planners address the specific needs and include people with disabilities in all emergency management

> *People with disabilities will continue to be disproportionately impacted by extreme weather events unless emergency planners address the specific needs and include people with disabilities in all emergency management activities including mitigation, preparedness, response, and recovery and entities that receive federal funding comply with federal civil rights and disability laws.*

activities including mitigation, preparedness, response, and recovery and entities that receive federal funding comply with federal civil rights and disability laws.

Preparedness and Response

Federally Assisted Programs Must Be ADA and Rehabilitation Act Compliant

Some SLTTs do not comply with federal rules and regulations, even though those rules and regulations clearly state that programs and services funded with federal dollars must be compliant with federal disability rights laws. SLTTs and their contractors are legally required to comply with Title II of the ADA provision of

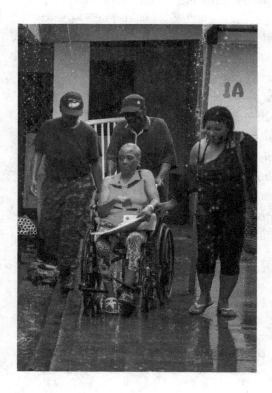

"emergency-and disaster-related programs, services, and activities they provide"[106] and with Section 504 of the Rehabilitation Act, to ensure federally funded programs allow for equal access. Even during the most challenging notice or no-notice disasters, SLTTs, and third parties have a legal obligation to ensure that people with disabilities who are impacted by extreme weather events do not face unlawful discrimination in the provision of services before, during, and after disasters.[107] Title II of the ADA,[108] which covers all activities of SLTTs, requires that SLTTs give people with disabilities an equal opportunity to benefit from all programs, services, and activities (e.g., public education, employment, transportation, recreation, healthcare, social services, courts, voting, and town meetings).[109] During disasters, people with disabilities have the right to access emergency information in clear, plain, and actionable language; the right to be included in community evacuation transportation plans; the right to independent living supports in community shelters; the right to accessible temporary housing; and the right to healthcare.[110] In terms of shelter, in the landmark case, *Olmstead v. L.C.* (1999), the U.S. Supreme Court ruled that unjustified segregation of people with disabilities constitutes discrimination in violation of Title II of the ADA. The court held that public entities must provide community-based services to people with disabilities when "(1) such services are appropriate; (2) the affected persons do not oppose community-based treatment; and (3) community-based services can be reasonably accommodated, taking into account the resources available to the public entity and the needs of others who are receiving disability services from the entity." This case had a significant impact on the opportunities for people with disabilities to live and fully participate in their communities.[111] Even with the abundance of laws and regulations prohibiting the discrimination of people with disabilities in emergency management activities, people with disabilities continue to face discriminatory practices before, during and after disasters.

FEMA *Developing and Maintaining Emergency Operations Plans* (2021)[112] guide for SLTT planners, recommends using demographic data and information on the number of individuals in the community with disabilities; identifying mechanisms to disseminate timely and accessible emergency public information using multiple methods to reach individuals with sensory, intellectual and cognitive disabilities, as well as individuals with limited English proficiency; identifying accessible transportation resources (including paratransit service vehicles, school buses, municipal surface transit vehicles, drivers and/or trained attendants) that can provide needed services during an evacuation; allocating adequate shelter space for individuals with disabilities who may need additional space for assistive devices (e.g., wheelchairs, walkers); and planning for sufficient staff, medicines, durable medical equipment and supplies during an emergency, among other recommendations.[113] In addition, SLTT's should provide in-home assistance or sheltering options for individuals with disabilities whose survival depends on electrically powered equipment during a shelter-in-place response, such as during a power outage.[114]

Research has shown that SLTT's continue to neglect the needs of people with disabilities. In *The Impact of COVID-19 on People with Disabilities* (2021), NCD reported that during the COVID-19 pandemic, civil rights concerns continued to impact the lives of people with disabilities, in relation to congregate care facilities (CCFs) specifically and regarding healthcare discrimination more broadly. The report stated that the "disregard for the safety of people with disabilities was another example of the degree to which people with disabilities were discounted in the pandemic"—they were "left out of basic data gathering on death certificates, left out of emergency planning and distribution of supplies, and subjected to ongoing stereotypes and assumptions about their health and quality of life by healthcare providers, which led to further deadly consequences for those people with disabilities who needed urgent intensive care at the height of the pandemic."[115]

Following Hurricane Irene (2011) and Hurricane Sandy (2012), in *Brooklyn Center for Independence of the Disabled et al. v. Bloomberg et al.* (2012),[116] the plaintiffs by way of federal class action, sued the City of New York—regarding the applicability of certain

> *The plaintiffs demonstrated that [New York City] failed to create a system to evacuate a large number of people with disabilities many of whom were trapped in high-rise buildings during disasters. . . . [T]he court ruled in favor of the plaintiffs, holding that New York City had violated the rights of about 900,000 of its residents with disabilities . . .*

portions of Title II of the ADA,[117] Section 504 of the Rehab Act, and the New York City Human Rights Law—for the city's systemic failure to incorporate the unique needs of people with disabilities in its emergency and disaster planning, which resulted in the exclusion of those individuals from equal participation in emergency services. At the time, New York City's nearly 900,000 residents with disabilities, made up about 11 percent of its population. The plaintiffs demonstrated that the city failed to create a system to evacuate a large number of people with disabilities many of whom were trapped in high-rise buildings during disasters. The city's limited options to accessible transportation, communication, and housing, and individuals reliance on the availability of specialized equipment, disability-related assistance, consumable medical supplies, durable medical equipment, and food, interfered with the ability of individuals with a variety of disabilities to equally respond to and recover from the city's emergencies and disasters.[118] In November 2013, following a bench trial, under federal Judge Jesse M. Furman, the

The court further held that "because of [Los Angeles's] failure to address their unique needs, individuals with disabilities are disproportionately vulnerable to harm in the event of an emergency or disaster."

court ruled[119] in favor of the plaintiffs, holding that New York City had violated the rights of about 900,000 of its residents with disabilities by failing to accommodate their needs during emergencies.[120]

In 2010, in *Communities Actively Living Independently and Free, et al., v. City of Los Angeles and County of Los Angeles*, the plaintiffs alleged that the County and City of Los Angeles, California discriminated against individuals with disabilities in their emergency management programs in violation of federal law, including Title II of the ADA and Section 504 of the Rehab Act. The plaintiffs contended that Los Angeles failed to conduct the planning required to meet the needs of individuals with disabilities and ensure access for those individuals across the full spectrum of its emergency programs, services, and activities.[121] In 2011, the court held that the plaintiffs were "denied the benefits of the city's emergency preparedness program because the city's practice of failing to address the needs of individuals with disabilities discriminates against such individuals by denying them meaningful access to the city's emergency preparedness program." The court further held that "because of the city's failure to address their unique needs, individuals with disabilities are disproportionately vulnerable to harm in the event of an emergency or disaster."[122] To support SLTTs to better comply with civil rights and disability rights DOJ's ADA Best Practices Tool Kit for State and Local Governments (March 9, 2017),[123] may be useful but may need updating.

Federal agencies have oversight roles and can monitor how grant funding is spent but may not have the authority to ensure equitable outcomes. Once grant funding is distributed, it is incumbent upon the SLTTs to ensure compliance with disability law.

Also, HHS, under the Stafford Act, has a role in disaster response. But the relevant component, the Administration for Community Living (ACL), does not specifically work on disaster planning or emergency management.

Recovery

Federal Agencies that Administer Funding May Not Have Enforcement

Authorities

Federal agencies responsible for administering disaster recovery funding may not have enforcement authority and have no mechanism to ensure that states and public entities that receive federal disaster funding comply with federal disability law. In disasters, if a state is "overwhelmed," under the Robert T. Stafford Disaster Relief and Emergency Assistance Act, 42 U.S.C. §§ 5121-5206 (1988),[124] a governor may request a disaster declaration from the President. As part of the request, the governor must take appropriate action under state law and direct execution of the state's emergency plan. Based on the governor's request, the President may declare a major disaster or emergency,[125] activating an array of federal programs to assist in the response and recovery effort. States or public entities may receive funding via FEMA's Public Assistance (PA) program[126] to fund the repair, restoration, reconstruction, or replacement of a public facility or infrastructure damaged or destroyed by a disaster. States may also receive funding through the U.S. HUD CDBG program[127] or other federal programs.

Any federal funds received by state and local governments, and other entities, must comply with all federal and applicable SLTT

Although DOJ can file civil judicial actions against noncompliant states and entities, settlements may take years, leaving people with disabilities without basic access to programs and supports such as to accessible shelter and housing.

disability rights laws. This requirement applies to programs, services, and activities provided directly by state and local governments, as well as those provided through third parties, such as the American Red Cross, private nonprofit organizations, and religious entities.[128] The ADA also requires reasonable modifications to policies, practices, and procedures when necessary to avoid discrimination against a person with a disability[129] and taking the steps necessary to ensure effective communication for people with disabilities.[130]

Disability stakeholders shared that federal agencies responsible for administering federal disaster grants do not have the power to enforce federal disability law. Federal agencies have oversight roles and can monitor how grant funding is spent but may not have the authority to ensure equitable outcomes. Once grant funding is distributed, it is incumbent upon the SLTTs to ensure compliance with disability law. some federal agencies can revoke funds when projects or programs do not comply with agency requirements or applicable laws and regulations. DOJ is responsible for the enforcement of numerous federal laws which impact people with disabilities. These laws include Title II of the ADA which applies to state and local governments. DOJ enforces the Civil Rights of Institutionalized Persons Act (CRIPA), which requires compliance with the rights of people residing in facilities such as intermediate care facilities and nursing homes; and Section 504 of the Rehab Act, which includes rights for people with disabilities similar to the ADA in regard to federal contractors, entities that receive federal financial assistance, and Federal Government agencies. Similarly, DOJ shares responsibilities with HUD to enforce the Fair Housing Act when certain cases are brought to federal court.[131] For example, HUD CDBG funding is distributed though states to local governments and local programs. If HUD receives complaints of civil rights violations or other civil rights complaints, the agency can investigate and work with the state or local government to ensure that they are complying with the federal requirements and report noncompliance to DOJ. In these instances, interagency coordination is critical to ensure people with disabilities do not have long wait times for recovery support such as accessible housing.

Also, the U.S. HHS, under the Stafford Act, has a role in disaster response. But the relevant component, HHS Administration for Community Living (ACL), does not specifically work on disaster planning or emergency management. ACL primarily distributes grant money to nonprofit organizations. According to disability stakeholders, although the ACL provides funding support to nonprofit organizations, the agency has no enforcement ability and cannot ensure that funding recipients comply with disability law. Similarly, the U.S. Environmental Protection Agency (EPA) creates water and wastewater regulations and is responsible for oversight of the implementation of the Public Notification Rule (PN),[132] which is part of the Safe Drinking Water Act (SDWA).[133] The PN ensures that consumers will know if there is a problem with their drinking water. These notices alert consumers about risks to public health.[134] Although the EPA creates and oversees implantation of the regulation, it is the states and public water systems that are responsible for meeting drinking water standards (including monitoring requirements) and notifying their consumers. If noncompliance is found, the EPA can take civil administrative actions, which are nonjudicial enforcement actions in the form of a notice of violation or an order. If the violation requires judicial action, DOJ files a case on behalf of the EPA.[135] Although DOJ can file civil judicial actions against noncompliant states and entities, settlements may take years, leaving people with disabilities without basic access to programs and supports such as to accessible shelter and housing.

Rather than rely on litigation, federal agencies administering federal disaster grants must better coordinate across agencies and with disability rights organizations to identify ways to track and monitor noncompliance with federal disability laws. Proper enforcement of federal disability laws means redefining enforcement during all phases of the disaster life cycle, including (and especially) the preparedness phase. It is critical that enforcement includes a new approach to disaster with a greater emphasis on universal design—one that includes people with disabilities and implementation/enforcement of disability laws before disaster strikes.

Recommendations

- Congress should request the Government Accountability Office (GAO) commission a study of which states have developed and maintain state-level emergency management plans and guidance that fully integrate people with disabilities.

- DOJ, in coordination with other relevant federal agencies, should provide updated comprehensive guidance (similar to its 2022 new Guidance on Web Accessibility[136]) and technical assistance to SLTT governments to better comply with federal civil rights and disability laws during emergency preparedness, response, and recovery.

- DOJ should reissue its Advance Notice of Proposed Rulemaking regarding Nondiscrimination on the Basis of Disability; Accessibility of Web Information and Services of State and Local Government Entities.

- DOJ Disability Rights Section (DRS) should update the ADA Best Practices Tool Kit for State and Local Governments (March 9, 2017)[137] to ensure that SLTT governments have the latest information on ADA best practices.

- Department of Homeland Security (DHS) Civil Rights and Civil Liberties (CRCL) and/or DOJ DRS and other appropriate governing bodies should prioritize and strengthen oversight and enforcement capabilities to ensure recipients and sub recipients of federal funds comply with the scope of their obligations to people with disabilities.

- DHS CRCL and DOJ DRS, should provide guidance to SLTTs emergency management operations frontline efforts to ensure nondiscrimination in the provision of emergency and disaster-relief services, benefits, and activities.

Chapter 2: Healthcare

The global mortality rate of people with disabilities in natural disasters is up to four times higher than that of people without disabilities.[138] People with disabilities face dangerous levels of isolation, squalid living conditions, shortages of food and water and electricity, and permanent dislocation.[139] This is due to a combination of factors, including a scarcity of inclusive planning, lack of accessible disaster information, early warning systems that do not reach everyone, lack of accessible transportation, and discriminatory attitudes toward people with disabilities.

The global mortality rate of people with disabilities in natural disasters is up to four times higher than that of people without disabilities.

Extreme weather events such as extreme heat, flooding, severe storms, tornadoes, winter weather, wildfires, and hurricanes, and environmental hazards negatively impact communities in the U.S. and its territories. everyone is vulnerable to health impacts associated with extreme weather events, however, people with disabilities or with preexisting physical, behavioral, or chronic health conditions are disproportionately impacted.[140] According to HHS *Climate Action Plan* (2021), other susceptible groups include communities of color, older adults, children, pregnant women, people with lower incomes, and those who live or work in areas with greater exposure, such as people with outdoor jobs.[141] Additionally, individuals affected by poverty, communities near contaminated waste sites or industrial areas, and rural areas with limited health systems may be more impacted by extreme weather events.[142] The health effects of extreme weather are worsened when events disrupt critical infrastructure.[143] Extreme weather events can damage roads, bridges, and transportation systems disrupting access to hospitals, pharmacies, and healthcare services. Extreme weather events can interrupt utilities, (e.g., power), water and wastewater services, and communications systems (e.g., Internet, telehealth, and other communications systems) that people with disabilities rely on to maintain access to health care.[144] Research shows that serious health risks can arise from utility outages; infrastructure and housing damage; and disruption or loss of access to sanitation, safe food and water supplies, health care, communication, and transportation.[145] Disruption of essential infrastructure and services after extreme events can increase population exposure to health hazards and reduce their ability to adapt.

Hurricane Maria's Impact on Puerto Rico

In 2017 during Hurricane Maria, Puerto Rico experienced a significant loss of basic infrastructure including electricity and access to food and clean water. Hurricane Maria cut nearly all communication across the island and destroyed the power grid.[146] "The storm disrupted medical services across the island and many households were left for weeks without water, electricity, or cell phone coverage. The average household went approximately 41 days without cell phone service, 68 days without water, and 84 days without electricity following the storm. More than 30 percent of surveyed households reported interruptions to medical care. Trouble accessing medications and powering respiratory equipment was the most cited challenge."[147]

Emergency response actions can impact an individual's physical health by injuries and premature death and a person's mental health due to trauma or displacement.[148] People with disabilities are among the most vulnerable in an emergency, sustaining disproportionately high rates of morbidity and mortality; they are also among those least able to access emergency support.[149]

Other impacts from extreme weather and climate-related events include a reduction in the availability of safe drinking water; a threat to food safety, nutrition, and distribution; waterborne-related illness; vector-borne disease (transmitted through insects and pests); and poor air quality[150] which increasingly threaten the health and well-being of people, particularly populations who are already vulnerable.[151] Extreme weather events have immediate and long-term impacts on people with disabilities and their caregivers as they disrupt access to health care, housing, education, employment, community, and other facets of life.[152]

Preparedness

An Increase in People with Disabilities

The World Health Organization (WHO) reports that the number of people with disabilities is increasing globally. The increase is due to demographic trends including an aging population,[153] increases in chronic health conditions,[154] increasing poverty,[155] and the disabilities caused by COVID-19.[156] According to the CDC, in 2020, 61 million adults in the United States live with a disability—that is 26 percent of, or one in four, adults.[157] This is compared to just three years before, in 2017, where people with disabilities made up approximately 12 percent of the U.S. working-age population.[158] The CDC reports that disabilities are especially common in older adults, women, and people from diverse cultures or backgrounds.[159] An increase in the number of people with disabilities will strengthen the need for accessible healthcare services and providers. It will increase demand on resources and strain critical systems, including the healthcare system, and emergency management agencies. In 2022, half of people with disabilities

> An increase in the number of people with disabilities will strengthen the need for accessible healthcare services and providers.

were age 65 and over. Overall, women were slightly more likely to have a disability than men, partly reflecting the greater life expectancy of women. In 2022, the prevalence of disability continued to be higher for Blacks and Whites than for Hispanics and Asians.[160]

Older Adults with Disabilities

The number of adults over age 65 in the United States is estimated to reach 80 million (or over 20 percent of the U.S. population) by 2040 and nearly 95 million by 2060.[161] With age, disability becomes more common. The increase in the older adult population with disabilities will increase demand for resources and services, including prescription medication, necessary medical equipment, and accessible healthcare facilities, support services, and caregivers. The increase in older adults will also put those who they care for at risk. Older adults often provide care to younger family members. In 2019, among the 5.37 million people with intellectual and developmental disabilities (IDD) living with a family caregiver, 24 percent had caregivers who were age 60 and older. In 2019, 19 percent of adults aged 65 and older reported they could not function at all or had a lot of difficulty with at least one of six activities of daily living. The percentage

In 2019, among the 5.37 million people with intellectual and developmental disabilities (IDD) living with a family caregiver, 24 percent had caregivers who were age 60 and older.

reporting any level of difficulty varied. Specifically, 22 percent reported trouble seeing (even if wearing glasses), 31 percent reported difficulty hearing (even if wearing hearing aids), 40 percent reported trouble with mobility (walking or climbing stairs), 8 percent reported difficulty with communication (understanding or being understood by others), 27 percent reported trouble with cognition (remembering or concentrating), and 9 percent reported difficulty with self-care (such as washing or dressing).[162] In addition, older adults also tend to live in states with high disaster risk, such as coastal cities at risk for flooding or warmer climates at risk for hurricanes and wildfires (e.g., California, Florida, Texas, North Carolina), which puts them at heightened risk.

Poverty is associated with malnutrition, inadequate access to public health services (e.g., immunization), poor living conditions (e.g., lack of safe water), and environmental exposures (e.g., unsafe work environments), which can lead to health conditions which result in disability.

Chronic Health Conditions, Poverty, and "Long COVID"

The increase in older adults with disabilities and chronic conditions will increase demand for health care to address chronic conditions such as chronic obstructive pulmonary disease (COPD), emphysema, or chronic bronchitis or diagnosed and undiagnosed diabetes.[163] Poverty increases the likelihood of disability. Chronically poor people are often at risk of ill health and injuries, which may lead to disability.[164] Poverty is associated with malnutrition, inadequate access to public health services (e.g., immunization), poor living conditions (e.g., lack of safe water), and environmental exposures (e.g., unsafe work environments), which can lead to health conditions which result in disability.[165] The poor who become disabled are likely to descend further into poverty, with a significant effect on their entire household.[166] According to the CDC, some people who have been infected with COVID-19 can experience long-term effects from their infection, known as post COVID conditions (PCC) or "long COVID." "Long COVID" is considered a disability under the ADA.[167]

An Increased Population Will Strain Emergency Management Capabilities

An increase in the number of people with disabilities will increase demand for federal and SLTT government emergency management capability and resources including accessible information; accessible evacuations; accessible transportation; accessible shelters; sign language interpreters; PCAs, access to durable medical equipment (DME) (e.g., oxygen equipment and accessories, wheelchairs); ATs; and other health supports. Emergency management will also require more human resources such as FEMAs Regional Disability Integration Specialists (RDIS) and other disability experts. People with disabilities are at increased risk to extreme weather events and coastal flooding because of their specific needs. Dependence on caregivers and others for assistance, and potential reliance on medical equipment that could be damaged or inoperable during power outages. Individuals with disabilities are likely to need special assistance during evacuations.

Evacuation challenges following Hurricanes Harvey, Irma, and Maria

In 2017, three sequential hurricanes—Harvey, Irma, and Maria—affected more than 28 million people. Survivors aged 65 and older and those with disabilities faced particular challenges evacuating to safe shelter, accessing medicine, and obtaining recovery assistance. "A range of officials from entities that partner with FEMA—including states, territories, localities, and nonprofits)—reported challenges providing assistance to individuals who are older or have disabilities following the 2017 hurricanes. For example, officials said that many of these individuals required specialized assistance obtaining food, water, medicine, and oxygen, but aid was sometimes difficult to provide. Officials in Puerto Rico and the U.S. Virgin Islands cited particular difficulties providing this assistance due to damaged roads and communication systems, as well as a lack of documentation of nursing home locations."[168]

Public health agencies should create inclusive emergency preparedness and response plans that incorporate people with disabilities[169] and disability organizations as stakeholders in inclusive health adaptation and disaster planning. EMAs should engage the disability community by using an all-hazards planning process that includes stakeholders from the disability community. Federal and state agencies should offer trainings that empower people with disabilities to participate in the disaster risk management process.

Limited Data on Extreme Weather Impacts on People With Disabilities

There is limited research and data at the national and local levels documenting the impacts of extreme weather events on people with disabilities. Data collection is key to creating a clearer picture of how extreme weather events impact people with disabilities and the specific vulnerabilities of people with disabilities to environmental justice issues. Reliable data serve as a starting point for developing better policies, programs, and initiatives to support people with disabilities. Data can help SLTTs better understand the needs of their communities to better prepare, respond, and support people with disabilities as they recover from disasters. Historically, there has been a lack of data on disability.[170] Federal and state healthcare data collection practices fail to capture baseline information about functional disability status of patients, leaving people with disabilities uncounted during and after emergencies.[171] The U.S. Census Bureau ACS[172] does provide disability data across a wide range of variables and geographies. In fact, the ACS provides county-level disability data for variables such as gender, race, veteran status, poverty status and employment for people with disabilities. However, according to a University of Montana Rural Institute report (2017),[173] the ACS data "is not without limitations." The ACS provides data estimates for disability in rural counties and estimates are drawn from smaller sample sizes, resulting in higher margins of error. These high margins of error make data less reliable at smaller geographies and forces researchers to aggregate the data to increase data validity. This limits the ability to analyze county-level disability data, particularly for subgroups like race and ethnicity.[174] Other concerns previously raised about ACS data included the ability of the question sets to adequately represent the population with disabilities, because the data do not capture all those eligible for certain benefit programs such as Social Security Income/Social Security Disability Insurance (SSI/SSDI).[175] Disability stakeholders stated that data should account for where people with disabilities are clustered. For example, Gallaudet University in Washington, DC, has a Deaf community where students live and learn using American Sign Language (ASL).

Federal and state healthcare data collection practices fail to capture baseline information about functional disability status of patients, leaving people with disabilities uncounted during and after emergencies.

Convening participants said that data sets often do not include all disability types. For example, Deaf individuals are excluded from phone surveys; Deafblind individuals, multiply marginalized people with disabilities, or those who are in carceral or institutional settings or are unhoused are often not included in data collection or research studies.

In our 2021 Progress Report: *The Impact of Covid-19 on People with Disabilities*,[176] NCD reported that the COVID-19 pandemic exposed gaps in disability data collection and antidiscrimination laws that need to be rectified before the next pandemic or public health emergency.[177] The report stated that a decades-long dearth in the collection of detailed disability and functional status information has left people with disabilities overlooked. The report also noted that there is a complete lack of standardized or historical gathering of death rates among LTCFs,[178] and that disability status is not a recognized component of mortality data. The report points to the need for state collection of healthcare demographic data relating to functional disability and HCBS use for all Medicaid enrollees, including better data collection across the full range of long-term care, group homes, and congregate settings licensed, certified, or approved by the state. Without these data and analyses, it is extremely hard to get a full picture of how much emergency Medicaid and other measures developed as a response to the pandemic benefited people with disabilities. It is even more difficult to see, for example, whether other populations within the disability community, such as Black or Brown people, face discernible compound discrimination.[179] According to FEMA's *National Preparedness Report* (2021)[180] during initial response efforts of the COVID-19 pandemic, "GAO found that the Federal Government did not have a process to systematically define and ensure the collection of standardized data across relevant federal agencies and related stakeholders to support the response to COVID-19, communicate the status of the pandemic with citizens, or prepare for future pandemics."[181] Federal and SLTT government planning will benefit from more accurate data as extreme weather events increase in intensity and severity and as the number of people with disabilities increases. Policymakers can use improved disability data

to promote the health and safety of this long-understudied population.

The health staffing shortage is placing pressure on an already overwhelmed U.S. healthcare system by reducing access to healthcare providers, including DSPs. People with disabilities and chronic health conditions, and persons who rely on DSPs for day-to-day support are often more vulnerable to health complications and are disproportionately impacted by the shortages of healthcare and DSP. Without support, PWDs can experience decline in health status, face unnecessary hospitalizations due to compromised care, or have increased need for emergency services. Existing shortages in healthcare workers exacerbate risks to individuals who require immediate care during disasters and are not able to get the assistance they require and leaves those individuals and their caregivers with reduced support during and after disasters.

The growing shortage of DSPs that existed prior to the pandemic became worse during the pandemic. In our Progress Report: *The Impact of Covid-19 on People with Disabilities* (2021),[182] NCD reported that well before the pandemic, the direct care workforce was subject to frequent turnover and a shortage of providers who could supply personal care services.[183] A Mercer report (2018)[184] projects that by 2025 demand for healthcare workers will outpace supply. In its analysis of the U.S. health workforce, Mercer estimated that by 2025, there will be a shortage of 446,000 home health aides, nearly 100,000 medical and laboratory technicians, 95,000 nursing assistants, and 30,000 nurse practitioners.[185] Even in 2018, prior to the pandemic, this shortage was of concern to maintaining health care quality; it has since contributed to increases in doctors and nurses leaving their jobs, with 8 percent of doctors closing their practices altogether in 2020—an estimated loss of 16,000 practices. This reduction in healthcare providers amid the pandemic only worsened the shortage. Staffing shortages also further exacerbated the vulnerabilities of CCF residents and staff.[186]

The United States is also facing crisis-level shortages of life-saving medical supplies and pharmaceuticals, such as pain medications. Common classes of drugs affected by shortages include anesthesia medications, antibiotics, pain medications, nutrition and electrolyte products, and chemotherapy agents. Clinically, patients have been harmed by the lack of drugs or inferior alternatives, resulting in more than 15 documented deaths.[187] The sum of these shortages is placing an unprecedented strain on the U.S. health care system and impacting those who depend on it.

People with Disabilities and Healthcare Disparities and Barriers

People with disabilities experience decades of health care disparities and systemic barriers to healthcare and treatment. Compromised health makes people with disabilities more vulnerable to extreme weather events, which are likely to exacerbate existing health conditions and increase barriers to health care. Research shows that adults with disabilities are three times more likely than adults without disabilities to have heart disease, diabetes, cancer, or stroke.[188] In our *Health Equity Framework on People with Disabilities* (2022), NCD reported that people with disabilities are "more than three times as likely to have arthritis, diabetes, and a heart attack; five times more likely to report a stroke, COPD, and depression; and more likely to be obese."[189] Adults with any level of hearing loss are three to five times more likely to have heart disease and are more likely to report fair or poor health compared to those who do not have hearing impairments.[190] People with IDD have a shorter life expectancy than people without IDD.[191] These underlying medical conditions put adults with disabilities at higher risk for severe infection, hospitalization, or even death. In addition, factors such as race and ethnicity, age, language, sex or gender, poverty, and low education can compound the effects of having a disability.[192]

These disparities are exacerbated if you are a person with a disability and a person of color. Studies have found that adults with disabilities in underserved racial and ethnic groups are more likely to report fair to poor health or that their health has worsened over the past year,

> *In its analysis of the U.S. health workforce, Mercer estimated that by 2025, there will be a shortage of 446,000 home health aides, nearly 100,000 medical and laboratory technicians, 95,000 nursing assistants, and 30,000 nurse practitioners.*

> *Compromised health makes people with disabilities more vulnerable to extreme weather events, which are likely to exacerbate existing health conditions and increase barriers to health care.*

compared with people without disabilities in the same racial/ethnic groups and with non-Hispanic Caucasians with disabilities.[193] Indigenous people in the United States also have an increased risk of chronic conditions including diabetes and heart disease. Many tribal nations may have limited access to clean water, a key component of infection control. In the Navajo Nation, about 15 percent of the population does not have access to piped water in their homes.[194] Older adults, as a result of chronic health conditions and limitations, experience general "frailty."[195] Women with disabilities are likely to receive poorer maternity care,[196] and pregnant women with disabilities have a much higher risk for severe pregnancy- and birth-related complications, including 11 times the risk of maternal death.[197]

Many tribal nations may have limited access to clean water, a key component of infection control. In the Navajo Nation, about 15 percent of the population does not have access to piped water in their homes.

Extreme Weather Events Exacerbate Underlying Health Conditions

Extreme weather events exacerbate underlying health conditions, can lead to injury, illness, or death, and can have long-term adverse effects on mental health. People with disabilities are two to four times more likely to be injured or killed in a natural disaster.[198] Extreme weather events can disrupt critical infrastructure, including roads and bridges, power/electricity, water and wastewater, communications systems, which are essential to maintaining access to healthcare and emergency

People with disabilities are two to four times more likely to be injured or killed in a natural disaster.

response services. Limited access to healthcare services includes loss of access to hospitals and pharmacies, medication, oxygen, personal care assistance, and medical devices. Extreme weather events can limit access to food and water. People with disabilities, those with preexisting health conditions, are especially vulnerable to the health impacts of power outages due to their reliance on electrically powered medical equipment such as ventilators oxygen, BiPAP machines and power wheelchairs. Extreme weather often causes utility interruptions. Between the 2000s and the 2010s, the U.S. saw a 67% increase in significant power outages due to weather-related incidents. In 2020, U.S. electricity consumers experienced over eight hours of power interruptions on average, the longest interruption time since the U.S. Energy Information Administration began collecting data in 2013.[199] Children with chronic illnesses who use medical equipment and services that require a functioning electrical power grid are also at significantly higher risk for poor outcomes after disasters. In rural communities, power and communications can take longer to restore after damage from an extreme event, placing people in rural communities at high risk.

Extreme temperature days, or days that are substantially hotter than the average seasonal temperature in summer, or substantially colder than the average seasonal temperature in winter, cause increases in illnesses and death by compromising the body's ability to regulate its temperature.[200] Exposure to extreme temperature may result in more severe health responses or death because it exacerbates preexisting conditions, including cerebral, respiratory, and cardiovascular diseases, and because it has a greater impact on those who are taking prescription or other drugs that may affect the body's ability to regulate its temperature.[201] People whose disabilities are affected by temperature sensitivity or thermoregulation are negatively impacted by high ambient temperatures. People with spinal cord injuries (SCIs) are especially at risk during extreme weather, both hot and cold, because of their inability to control their body temperature.[202] Socially vulnerable populations are disproportionately affected by extreme heat, particularly those who live with disabilities, communities of color, low-income individuals, individuals lacking a high school diploma, and populations 65 or older.[14] These groups often live in areas with increasing childhood asthma diagnoses from climate-driven changes, higher labor hour losses from extreme heat exposure, and growing climate driven mortality rates."[203] High temperatures in the summer are conclusively linked to an increased risk of a range of illnesses and death.[204] The National Weather Service

People with disabilities, those with preexisting health conditions, are especially vulnerable to the health impacts of power outages due to their reliance on electrically powered medical equipment such as ventilators oxygen, BiPAP machines and power wheelchairs.

Heat waves triple the risk of death for people with preexisting psychosocial disabilities.

(NWS) confirmed that extreme heat is now the leading weather-related killer in America. Rising temperatures pose an imminent threat to millions of American workers exposed to the elements, to students in schools without air-conditioning, to seniors in nursing homes without cooling resources, and particularly to disadvantaged communities.[205] Extreme heat is linked to elevated emergency room visits, hospital admissions, and mortality for individuals with mental health issues, cardiovascular and respiratory complications, and other disabilities. Rising temperatures will lead to an increase in heat-related illnesses and deaths.[206] Heat waves triple the risk of death for people with preexisting psychosocial disabilities. With continued warming, cold-related deaths are projected to decrease and heat-related deaths are projected to increase; in most regions, increases in heat-related deaths are expected to outpace reductions in cold-related deaths.[207]

Droughts are associated with reduced water quality and quantity; respiratory impacts related to reduced air quality; and mental health impacts.[208] Long periods of record high temperatures are associated with droughts that contribute to dry conditions and drive wildfires in some areas. Wildfires are directly linked to air pollution. Wildfire smoke contains particulate matter, carbon monoxide, nitrogen oxides, and various volatile organic compounds and can significantly reduce air quality, both locally and in areas downwind of fires.[209] Smoke exposure and inhalation increases respiratory and cardiovascular hospitalizations; medication dispensations for asthma, bronchitis, chest pain, COPD, and respiratory infections; and medical visits for lung illnesses. Wildfires are associated with burns or other traumatic injury, and mental health impacts.[210] Wildfires are also associated with hundreds of thousands of deaths annually. For people with disabilities, wildfires are especially dangerous because mobility limitations can make it difficult to evacuate in an emergency if accessible transportation is not available. During wildfires, people with disabilities often lose critical AT, tools, and devices.

Floods can cause power, water, and gas outages; disrupt transportation routes; pollute drinking water systems; damage homes, buildings, and roads; and cause severe environmental problems including landslides and mudslides.[211] Flooding related to extreme precipitation, hurricanes, and coastal storms can lead to fatalities and serious injuries when people do not (or cannot) evacuate areas that are flooded.[222] Flooding is also associated with mental health impacts; disease spread; contaminated water; and carbon monoxide poisoning related to power outages.[223] People with disabilities who

California Wildfires

During the 2017 California Wildfire season, there were 9,270 wildfires, the largest of which was the Thomas Fire.[212] The wildfires led to mass evacuations, displaced over 100,000 people, caused $12 billion in damages, exceeding the total losses from the previous 10 costliest fires combined, and took 47 lives.[213] People with disabilities struggled to receive evacuation information and find adequate transportation and shelter. In addition, professional caregivers were ordered to evacuate and unable to work.[214] The fires burned rapidly and unpredictably, aided by strong winds.[215] The speed and unpredictability of the wildfires quickly overcame communities while trying to evacuate.[216] In California, most people rely on personal vehicles for evacuations because there is minimal public transportation for wildfire evacuees and some areas have little to no access to public transit.[217] People with disabilities evacuating from rural areas face particularly steep challenges. In Northern California, many people with disabilities live in rural areas and lack the resources to evacuate during disasters. Roughly twice as many people with disabilities live in rural areas in Northern California versus the rest of the state, and they lack critical infrastructure for safe evacuations.[218] After an evacuation occurs, there is still the risk of inhaling polluted air from wildfires. After the Thomas Fire, Ventura and Santa Barbara counties had extended periods of air quality categorized as "hazardous."[219] This led to an increase in hospital visits related to the dangerous air quality.[220] While the impact of air pollution is usually temporary, underlying health conditions and long-term exposure can lead to severe impacts.[221]

live in flood zones, coastal areas, and drought prone areas face greater vulnerability to health impacts.[224]

Winter storms and severe thunderstorms are associated with traumatic injury and death; carbon monoxide poisoning related to power outages; hypothermia and frostbite; and mental health impacts.[225] Freezing temperatures and winter storms leave people with disabilities and chronic health conditions without power for life-saving medical supplies and a way to charge ATs or other dependent devices.

> *People with disabilities in rural communities, U.S. territories, and tribal nations are less likely to have access to broadband and the Internet which limits access to national weather warnings and alerts and limits access to telehealth options.*

Limited Internet Access Puts Communities at Risk

People with disabilities in rural communities, U.S. territories, and tribal nations are less likely to have access to broadband and the Internet which limits access to national weather warnings and alerts and limits access to telehealth options. Limited access to the Internet puts these communities at a disadvantage before, during, and after disasters. Analysis of 2019 ACS data established that people with disabilities,

Winter Storm Uri in Texas

According to the Disability Rights Texas report (2021),[226] during Winter Storm Uri in Texas (2020), 75 percent of people surveyed lost power for 24 hours or longer (22 percent for 4 days or longer); 45 percent of those who lost power believed they were in danger; 80 percent lost water for 24 hours or longer (32 percent for 4 days or longer). The loss of power and lack of refrigeration resulted in spoilage of life-saving medication and food; lack of access to medications and in-home healthcare assistance; the inability to use breathing devices or mobility equipment that depend on electric power; and trauma impacting mental health.[227]

Case Study – Proximity to Pollution

A University of Texas at El Paso study observed that Houston neighborhoods located near pollution sources—like Superfund sites and hazardous waste facilities—were home to a significantly higher proportion of people with disabilities than the rest of the city. In addition, race, ethnicity, and age all further amplified these inequalities—people with disabilities of color and those aged 75 years or older both lived in even closer proximity to polluted areas, likely decreasing their quality of life.[228]

older adults, and people of color including Native Americans, Black, and Latino people lacked Internet access in higher proportions when compared to their White and Asian counterparts. In all groups between the ages of 18 and 74, Native Americans (non-Latino) had the highest percentage of people without household Internet access. When grouped by age and disability, 34 percent of people age 75 and older were without household Internet access, the highest percentage of all the groups.

Native Americans (non-Latino) had the highest percentage of people without household Internet access. When grouped by age and disability, 34 percent of people age 75 and older were without household Internet access.

According to a June 2021 AARP study, "rural residents are much more likely than suburban or urban residents to say that access to high-speed internet is a problem—more than half, 58 percent, vs. about a third of urban and suburban residents."[229] About 14.5 million Americans live in areas without broadband Internet access, and the "urban-rural divide is vast. At the end of 2019, 17 percent of rural residents and 21 percent who live on tribal lands lacked even the slowest definition of high-speed internet access compared with about 1 percent in urban areas, according to a Federal Communications Commission (FCC) report released in January 2021."[230] The lack of reliable Internet access for many rural communities can mean limited access to healthcare, specifically telehealth.

At the end of 2019, 17 percent of rural residents and 21 percent who live on tribal lands lacked even the slowest definition of high-speed internet access compared with about 1 percent in urban areas.

Telehealth can provide medical assistance to those who lack reliable transportation. Lack of transportation is a recurring problem for people with disabilities who live in rural communities or are sheltering in place during a disaster.

Tribal nations and Indigenous peoples are disproportionately vulnerable to the impacts of extreme weather events, due in part to their dependence on specific geographic areas for their livelihoods; unique cultural, economic, and political characteristics; and limited resources to prepare for, respond to, and recover from extreme weather hazards.[231] The 2021 $1.2 trillion Bipartisan Infrastructure Law[232] allocates over $13 billion in new tribal infrastructure projects is the largest investment in tribal nation infrastructure projects. It includes $214 million to bring running water to 40 percent of Navajo families from the Navajo Utah Water Rights Settlement, $2 billion for a tribal broadband connectivity program to expand broadband Internet access, and $11.2 billion in grants for abandoned coal mine land and water reclamation projects. However, according to tribal stakeholders NCD spoke with, not enough progress has been made to improve Internet access on tribal lands, leaving tribes still at risk for the next disaster.

Assistive Technology, Durable Medical Equipment, and Electronic Equipment

Extreme weather events can interrupt utilities. Resulting power outages place people with disabilities, some who are power dependent and require AT or DME at a disproportionate health risk. These populations often have more health problems, medication needs, and/or limited mobility.[233] As previously discussed, during a power outage people with disabilities lose access to medications, DME, and ATs. During a power outage, the lack of refrigeration can result in the spoilage of life-saving medications, such as insulin, which needs to be kept cold, impacting people with diabetes. Power outages mean the inability to use breathing devices or mobility equipment that depend on electric power.[234] People who depend on electric medical devices[235] (e.g., require oxygen equipment and accessories (ventilators), require heat to regulate their body temperature due to an SCI, require dialysis, or require power for wheelchairs are disproportionately at risk during a power outage.

People with spinal cord injuries as well as mental health disabilities on medication will find it difficult to regulate their body temperatures. Given the extreme uptick in summer temperatures and colder temperatures in the winter, provisions have to be available for people with disabilities who are unable to regulate their body heat, meaning portable generators to assist those who are power dependent in the winter and portable air-conditioning units available to those who are unable to access cooling stations.

The loss of power also means the loss of access to AT—that is, alternate and augmentative communication equipment,

Case Study – Winter Storm Uri in Texas, 2021

During Winter Storm Uri in 2021, 4.5 million homes and business were without power at its peak.[236] Nearly 70 percent of Texans lost power at some point during the storm.[237] In a Disability Rights Texas survey of 600 people with disabilities, 75 percent lost power for 24 hours or longer.[238] One resident lost power and heat, and was in danger because she can't control her body temperature, stating "cold temperatures are more severe for a person with a spinal cord injury." Another resident who lost electricity, struggled with utilizing a ventilator (via battery) because the humidifier was blowing cold air from the house into her lungs, "I could barely use it," she said.

Hearing by keeping them informed. However, loss of power makes it difficult to charge devices and disrupts services, rendering the devices useless.[239]

People with disabilities use AT to maintain their independence. A conservative estimate of 20 percent of the population age 60 and over require an assistive technology device leads to a worldwide estimate of at least 800 million items being used by older adults with disabilities by 2050. During disasters, assistive products may not function properly or may be lost or damaged, increasing the likelihood that people with disabilities and at-risk populations face threats, vulnerabilities, and severe health complications.[240] The loss of power can affect any assistive devices that need electricity, and backup batteries may not always be at hand. Medication access and pharmacy refills (or refrigeration for some types of medications) may also not be present after a disaster.[241] According to disability stakeholders, people with disabilities require appropriate ATs but developers have struggled to get new ATs in the market due to lack of investment.

devices, strategies, tools, and supportive services that allow individuals to live in their homes. Mobile devices for accessing the Internet or receiving texts are generally the most common way information would be obtained during a power outage. Other AT products such as video-remote interpreting (VRI), transcription services, Communication Access Realtime Translation (CART), and assistive listening devices; or low-tech solutions such as communication boards; can assist individuals who are Deaf or Hard of

The loss of power also means the loss of access to AT—that is, alternate and augmentative communication equipment, devices, strategies, tools, and supportive services that allow individuals to live in their homes.

Recovery

Those Forced to Relocate Out of State Lose Access to Medicaid Services

People with disabilities forced to relocate out of state due to a disaster lose their Medicaid health benefits, which means a disruption in their health care regimen which includes access to medicines, medical services, and supports. During extreme weather events, people with disabilities may lose access to proof of identification and medical records. They may also lose access to their medicines and medical services and supports. They may be separated from their AT and DME, increasing the risk of severe health complications. During recovery, people with disabilities who do not have access to medical records and other key paperwork will struggle to access healthcare, services, and programs because of limited knowledge and a complex application process. When an individual with a disability moves out of state, state supports rarely move with them. In the case of students, individual education plans do not transfer to new schools. In the case of adults, state-run Medicaid benefits do not transfer out of state.

The Centers for Medicare & Medicaid Services (CMS) issued (2021) a final rule "to strengthen Medicare by expanding access to certain durable medical equipment, such as continuous glucose monitors that increase diabetes treatment choices for people with Medicare. The Durable Medical Equipment, Prosthetics, Orthotics and Supplies (DMEPOS) final rule could help to improve accessibility, quality, affordability, empowerment and innovation."[242] According to disability stakeholders, Medicaid has historically had

People with disabilities forced to relocate out of state due to a disaster lose their Medicaid health benefits, which means a disruption in their health care regimen which includes access to medicines, medical services, and supports.

When an individual with a disability moves out of state, state supports rarely move with them. In the case of students, individual education plans do not transfer to new schools.

issues maintaining coverage when disaster survivors evacuate across state lines and the rule will need to be tested and updated over time to ensure that services are transportable and can easily be transferred to new providers in the event of disaster.

DRMA, S.2646,[243] would ensure that individuals receiving Medicaid, who are forced to relocate due to a disaster, are able to continue to access their Medicaid-supported services, making coverage transportable across state lines for disaster survivors. DRMA would provide states with resources to support the Medicaid needs of individuals forced to relocate following a disaster. This legislation would designate an individual who resides in an area covered under a presidential disaster declaration as a relief-eligible survivor and allow them to continue to access their Medicaid services if they are forced to relocate to another state as a result of a disaster. DRMA helps states meet the needs of relief-eligible survivors through a limited-time 100 percent federal match for displaced individuals and technical assistance and support to develop innovative state strategies to respond to an influx of out-of-state individuals. The bill also creates a grant to help states develop an emergency response corps to provide HCBS. The legislation also guarantees a 100 percent federal matching payment for medical assistance to states in disaster areas.[244]

Extreme Weather Events Contribute to Mental Health Issues

Experiencing severe or repeated extreme weather events can contribute to anxiety, depression, and other mental health impacts. In the Strategy to Address Our National Mental Health Crisis, President Biden stated that "the U.S. faces an unprecedented mental health crisis among people of all ages. "Two out of five adults report symptoms of anxiety or depression."[245] Research has found correlations between disaster exposure and psychological distress. While a person with a disability experiences the same natural disasters as anyone else, the disaster is likely to exacerbate daily challenges and increase stress.[246] The health impacts following Hurricanes Irma and Maria in Puerto Rico were wide ranging, and increases in anxiety, depression, and PTSD were widely reported.[247]

> *The Durable Medical Equipment, Prosthetics, Orthotics and Supplies (DMEPOS) final rule could help to improve accessibility, quality, affordability, empowerment and innovation.*

> *A study of wildfire survivors showed that 10 to 30 percent developed diagnosable mental health conditions, including PTSD and depression.*

A study of wildfire survivors showed that 10 to 30 percent developed diagnosable mental health conditions, including PTSD and depression.[248] Another study found that children with disabilities that evacuated during the 2017 wildfire season exhibited stress, grief, emotional and behavioral reactions one year post-disaster.[249] While wildfires have been causing stress, California has also been experiencing a shortage of mental health professionals.[250] While it is well documented that wildfires contribute to physical health effects such as lung conditions like asthma, COPD, other respiratory conditions, and can be life-threatening, studies now show that air pollution resulting from wildfires can also contribute to mental health issues.[251] There is limited mental health support after a disaster, and it is often not included in the planning process. Communities and organizations need structures in place to mentally prepare residents for disasters and after disasters, those organizations should include trauma-informed responses.

Recommendations

- Congress should pass legislation such as the REAADI in Disasters Act to address gaps in meeting civil rights obligations to people with disabilities impacted by disasters. The bill would establish a research center to be defined in legislation, to conduct research to determine recommended practices for including people with disabilities and older adults in planning during and following disasters; Establish a "projects of national significance" program to increase the involvement of people with disabilities and older adults in the planning and response to disasters and identify strategies for reducing deaths, injuries, and losses to those groups as a result of disasters; Establish a National Commission on Disability Rights and Disasters that will provide recommendations on how to ensure effective emergency preparedness, disaster response, recovery, and community resilience efforts for people with disabilities and older adults; Establish Training and Technical Assistance Disability and Disaster Centers that provide comprehensive training, technical assistance, development of funding sources, and support to state, tribal, and local disaster relief; public health entities; social service agencies; and stakeholder groups.

- Congress should appropriate funds to FEMA for the express purpose to advise SLTTs EMAs and state health departments to conduct reviews and update emergency management plans and guidance to prepare for an increase of people with disabilities. The plans should be data-driven, inclusive, and compliant with disability laws to ensure equal access including effective communication, evacuations, and shelters that provide accommodations and modifications to ensure the safety of people with disabilities.

- HHS Office of Civil Rights (OCR) should develop additional guidance for healthcare providers to actively prepare and plan for an increase of people with disabilities requiring healthcare services during disasters.

- HHS and the National Advisory Council on Innovation & Entrepreneurship (NACIE) should launch a multiagency national emergency management strategy to help states plan for an increase in the number of people with disabilities to mitigate risks during disasters.

- Federal and SLTT EMAs and state health departments should request congressional funding to surge medical resources (equipment and supplies) for disasters.

- HHS should provide guidance to SLTTs on standardized disability categories and levels to inform emergency management planning. The methodology should be used at all levels of government to ensure complete and consistent data collection.

(continued)

Recommendations: *continued*

- Congress should require state collection of health care demographic data relating to functional disability and HCBS use for all Medicaid enrollees, including better data collection across the full range of long-term care, group homes, and congregate settings, licensed, certified, or approved by the state.

- FEMA should resurrect the Interagency Coordinating Council to include the U.S. Census Bureau, CMS, and DOT, to identify methods to efficiently, collect disability information to identify how many people with disabilities are affected during specific disasters, where they live or work in the community, and whether they have HCBS needs. This information should be used to inform emergency management policies and anonymized data should be regularly updated and shared with SLTTs.

- Congress should pass legislation to address the shortage of primary care doctors and other health care providers. The legislation should address shortfalls in the nation's supply of health care providers and include inclusive recruitment for a diverse health care workforce, loan forgiveness that encourages health care providers to work with underserved populations, and other innovative targeted incentive measures.

- Congress should provide funding to HHS for the Secretary to implement section 5307 of the Patient Protection and Affordable Care Act. Funding section 5307 would allow for the development, evaluation and dissemination of research, demonstration projects, and model curricula for cultural competency, prevention, public health proficiency, reducing health disparities, and aptitude for working with people with disabilities, training for use in health professions schools and continuing education programs.[252]

- FEMA, in coordination with SLTT Department of Public Works, should identify people with disabilities in the community at risk of heat-related illnesses and death and ensure such individuals have access to cooling stations. If, because of their disabilities they are unable to access cooling stations, portable air-conditioning units should be made available to mitigate the risk of heat-related illness or death.

- HHS should commission a study to identify health disparities and gaps in access to healthcare in relation to extreme weather impacts on people with disabilities, older adults, tribal nations, and other impacted communities. HHS should also identify strategies to mitigate those gaps.

Recommendations: *continued*

- State health departments, in coordination with state EMAs, should plan and track medical infrastructure and medical equipment and equipment stockpiles, (e.g., medications, generators, PPE, and necessary medical equipment like oxygen, dialysis machines, wheelchairs, and other DME) to ensure availability and distribution in a disaster, especially in U.S. territories.

- HHS Office of the Assistant Secretary for Preparedness and Response (ASPR), when replenishing the Strategic National Stockpile (SNS), should coordinate with SLTT partners on available equipment that can be requested from the SNS and provide or update guidelines on how to request such equipment.

- Congress should make R&D investments that promote assistive technology. This should involve: (a) Greater investments for R&D of accessible apps and devices to incentivize developers to create innovative technology, which can help people with disabilities enhance functional performance to improve outcomes in areas such as education, employment, and independent living. (b) Increase the R&D budget for NIDILRR, the Medical Research and Development Program. (c.) Provide funding to a federal unit such as the Administration for Community Living (ACL) to design and fund technical assistance on R&D for the technology industry to support accessible design of emerging technology. And (d) Provide funding to ACL to establish and expand peer support programs on accessible assistive technology. These programs could be provided through independent living centers and grassroots experts and should involve a community of practice platform for exchanging information and managing requests for peer consultation.

- The Federal Energy Regulatory Commission (FERC) should work with utility companies to improve their power outage notification programs and create public awareness campaigns to build knowledge. They should improve power resiliency programs and enhance power restoration priority for people with disabilities who are power dependent. Additionally, utility companies should invest in portable generators to be made available to people with disabilities who are power dependent and unable to evacuate in the event of extended power outages.

- Congress should pass the Disaster Relief Medicaid Act (DRMA). Upon passage, states should immediately implement DRMA to ensure that individuals who are eligible for Medicaid and are forced to relocate due to a disaster, are able to continue to access their Medicaid-supported services.

(continued)

Recommendations: *continued*

- CMS should clarify and promote its new rules and regulations about replacing ATs and DME damaged or lost in a disaster.
- FEMA should more broadly publicize its mental health programs and the Substance Abuse and Mental Health Services Administration (SAMHSA) Disaster Distress Helpline, which provide crisis counseling and support to people experiencing emotional distress related to natural or human-caused disasters. FEMA should monitor SLTTs execution and accessibility of its crisis care hotline and provide guidance as needed to ensure programs are accessible to all disabilities.

Chapter 3: Housing

People with disabilities face significant challenges securing affordable, accessible housing. The U.S. housing shortage, low vacancy rates, high prices, limited availability of accessible units, and increasing extreme weather events that damage or destroy homes are increasing risks for people with disabilities who are more likely to be low income and live in areas affected by disasters.

Poverty rates for people with disabilities is more than twice the rate of people without disabilities.[253] Extreme weather events are exacerbating the housing crisis as disasters damage and destroy homes with increased frequency within the same community. People with disabilities are more likely to live in low-income areas and areas affected by disasters, including flood zones where low-income housing is often built. In the event of evacuation, some SLTTs offer a registration program for people with disabilities to register who may need assistance evacuating their home during emergency. However, the majority of these registries provide a false sense of hope for the person with a disability. The city of Houston had such a registry. During Hurricane Harvey less than 5 percent of registrants were contacted and even less were provided evacuation assistance.[254] Some SLTTs operate special needs or medical needs shelters which are segregated from the general population shelters. These shelters are often underfunded, separates families, typically only allow one other person to accompany the PWD, are costly to run, and often do not have the amenities required to accommodate a PWD. After leaving shelters, people with disabilities, if their home is damaged or destroyed, often cannot afford to move to another location or rebuild without assistance and may be forced to return to an uninhabitable

> *People with disabilities are more likely to live in low-income areas and areas affected by disasters, including flood zones where low-income housing is often built.*

> *[T]he majority of these registries provide a false sense of hope for the person with a disability. The city of Houston had such a registry. During Hurricane Harvey less than 5 percent of registrants were contacted and even less were provided evacuation assistance.*

home. In addition, there is a scarcity of accessible temporary housing and personal care assistance placing people with disabilities at an increased risk of institutionalization or homelessness. Finally, government assistance programs are complex, confusing, and sometimes inaccessible to people with disabilities.

Preparedness

The Shortage of Affordable, Accessible Housing is a Serious Concern

Living independently and as part of a community are goals shared by all families and an affordable, accessible home is key to achieving those goals. However, people with disabilities face significant challenges securing affordable, accessible housing. The U.S. housing shortage, low vacancy rates, high prices, limited availability of accessible units, and increasing extreme weather events that damage or destroy homes are increasing risks for people with disabilities who are more likely to be low income and live in areas affected by disasters. The White House "*Housing Supply Action Plan" To Help Close the Housing Supply Gap in Five Years (2022)* states that the housing supply shortfall is more than 1.5 million homes nationwide (2021).[255] The low housing stock correlates with low vacancy rates. A U.S. Census Bureau report (2020) showed that the

> *One report showed that the average rent for a basic one-bedroom apartment is $1,063 per month, or about 128 percent of an individual with a disability's income, leaving no money for food, transportation, and other necessities.*

"national vacancy rate decreased from 11.4 percent in 2010 to 9.7 percent in 2020."[256]

In 2020, more than 37 million people were living in poverty, approximately 3.3 million more than in 2019.[257] For adults with disabilities, the poverty rate is more than twice the rate of adults without a disability.[258] These factors contribute to a housing affordability crisis for people with disabilities. Housing is the largest expense for families: more than 38 million U.S. households live in housing that they cannot afford.[259] The Federal Government considers housing unaffordable if it costs more than 30 percent of a household's income. More than 23 million people (in over 10 million low-income households) pay more than half their income for rent, often forgoing food or medicine to keep a roof over their heads. Of the 23 million, 18 percent have a disability.[260] As of July 2020, Census data shows that 13.8 million adults in rental housing—one in five renters—report being behind on rent, with households of color reporting far higher rates of missed payments than the national average.[261] One report showed that the average rent for a basic one-bedroom apartment is $1,063 per month, or about 128 percent of an individual with a disability's income, leaving no money for food, transportation, and other necessities.[262] Moreover, with the end of the eviction moratorium (August 26, 2021),[263] 4.2 million renters reported being at risk of losing their homes.

In the United States, an individual living solely on SSI cannot afford a safe, decent apartment without rental assistance.[264] But the available assistance is not enough. Of more than 10 million people (5 million households) who use federal rental assistance to afford modest housing, 25 percent (2.5 million) have a disability.[265] Approximately 4.7 million noninstitutionalized people with disabilities who rely on federal monthly SSI have incomes averaging only about $9,156 per year, in other words, not enough to afford rent. Many people with an IDD live with aging caregivers (60 and older). As this generation of caregivers ages, their adult children with IDD may be at risk of institutionalization or homelessness.[266] More than 397,000 individuals live on the street or in shelters; many others in expensive institutions at a cost of $232 to $1,467 per person per day.[267] Renters with disabilities struggle to find affordable and accessible homes. In 18 percent of extremely low-income renter households, at least one adult member is a person with a disability. This accounts for over 5 million households, which are likely to need accessibility features like grab-bars, extra-wide hallways, or entry-level bedrooms, further limiting their housing options. As of 2011, just 3.5 percent of all homes had these basic accessibility features.[268] While homeowners and higher-income households can add such features, the lowest-income renters often cannot afford to do so. Thus, extremely low-income renters with disabilities often face severe difficulties in finding affordable, available, and accessible housing.[269]

Increasing Extreme Weather Events Exacerbates the Housing Crisis

As extreme weather events increase, they will damage or destroy more and more homes or make them uninhabitable. In 2021, about 1 in 10 U.S. homes (or 14.5 million homes) were impacted by natural disasters, totaling nearly $57 billion in property damage.[270] People with disabilities are more likely because of their income, to live in areas affected by disasters. Unaffordable and insecure housing leaves

> *In 2021, about 1 in 10 U.S. homes (or 14.5 million homes) were impacted by natural disasters, totaling nearly $57 billion in property damage.*

Impact of Recent Disasters on Housing

Hurricane Harvey (2017) flooded 154,170 homes in Harris County, Texas of which only 36 percent had flood insurance.[271] Hurricane Irma (2017) destroyed about 25 percent of homes in the Florida Keys.[272] During Hurricane Laura (2020), Grand Isle, Louisiana took a direct hit with 100 percent of its homes damaged and nearly 40 percent were destroyed.[273]

California's wildfire season (2017) burned over 1.2 million acres, a 112 percent increase over the previous year, destroyed or damaged 32,000 homes, and displaced 100,000 people.[274] The Marshall Fire in Boulder County, Colorado (2021) damaged or destroyed more than 1,000 homes and businesses.[275]

families less able to cope with extensive repairs or rebuilding after extreme weather events such as flooding or wildfires. As disasters increase, they will have devastating impacts damaging or destroying homes or making them uninhabitable.

Communities affected by extreme weather events are often impacted by multiple natural disasters in a relatively short period. In 2015 and 2016, Harris County, Texas suffered four Presidential Declared Disasters before Hurricane Harvey (2017). The county was impacted by six Presidentially Declared Disasters in 10 years.[276] In Fall 2020, two hurricanes hit Southwest Louisiana within a month, affecting working-class residents the most. Homes that survived the high winds of the first hurricane were damaged by the flooding of the second. In addition, the COVID-19 pandemic limited private aid and public assistance, thereby slowing the recovery. Two months later, many families were still rebuilding, often living in rented trailers or tents as their homes were repaired by a limited supply of contractors.[277]

> *Currently, fewer than 200,000 housing units in the U.S. are universally accessible, and only a fraction are affordable.*

Section 504 Requirements For Federally Assisted New Construction

HUD's 5 percent accessibility requirement for federally assisted new construction housing developments[278] does not meet the needs of people with disabilities, who represent 25 percent of the population. The Section 504 requirements for federally assisted new construction[279] state that all federally assisted new construction housing developments with five or more units must ensure that 5 percent of the dwelling units, or at least one unit, are accessible to people with mobility disabilities. An additional 2 percent of the dwelling units, or at least one unit, must be accessible for people with hearing or visual disabilities. The project must also meet all Section 504 requirements in HUD's implementing regulation.[280] In the United States, of the 61 million adults with disabilities many require accessible housing, which includes such features as lowered kitchen counters and sinks, widened doorways to allow passage by persons in wheelchairs, and wheel-in showers. Currently, fewer than 200,000 housing units in the United States are universally accessible, and only a fraction are affordable.[281] Neither the aging population nor the impact of long COVID has yet to be realized. The need for accessible housing will increase because of our aging population and persons newly disabled from long COVID. The percentage of accessible houses must be increased to accommodate for the newly disabled as well as existing accessible units damaged by extreme weather events.

Tribal nations also face a shortage in accessible units. In the United States there are 574 federally recognized tribal entities (347 federally recognized American Indian tribes within the contiguous 48 states and 227 federally recognized tribal entities within the state of Alaska).[282] According to the U.S. Census, an estimated 24 percent of American Indians and Alaska Natives live with disabilities, compared to 19 percent of the general population.[283] According to tribal stakeholders NCD spoke with, in the Navajo Nation, housing is a top priority for people with disabilities. Although the Navajo Nation receives HUD funding, it does not meet the needs of the Navajo disability community.

Low-Income People with Disabilities in Flood Zones are at High Risk

In the United States, affordable housing units tend to be built in flood-prone and coastal areas leaving people with disabilities who may be low-income, unsafe, and at risk of environmental contamination, to contend with expensive reconstruction or homeless in the aftermath of a natural disaster. The sea level rise has increased the damage caused by hurricane storm surge flooding.[284] Between 1990 and 2000, affordable housing was often built in floodplains where property values are lower and developed for multifamily housing, mobile homes, and single-family housing in the very low-income neighborhoods. Harris County, Texas has an estimated 184,546 homes in a 100-year floodplain; over 26 percent of these homes were affected by Hurricane Harvey (2017).[285] Households of color are more likely to live in a floodplain, exacerbating inequalities after a disaster strikes and making it harder for these communities to recover.[286] Some of the low-income complexes are privately-owned buildings with a U.S. Department of Housing and Urban Development (HUD) contract. The landlord receives payment from the government in exchange for renting to low-income tenants. During disasters, residents who are often recipients of housing vouchers, cannot afford to move to another location without a housing choice voucher.[287] There appears to be limitations preventing individuals to be able to "transfer/

transport" their housing voucher to a new location leaving them no choice but to return to a property that may be un-livable. Some disability stakeholders suggested HUD issue "climate vouchers" for individuals whose home is damaged or destroyed in a disaster.

Scenarios like the one described above because of the increased prevalence of extreme weather events will also become more prevalent. In the United States, the frequency of coastal flooding has increased sharply over the last few decades, and rising sea levels indicate further acceleration. Estimates put 14.6 million properties at substantial risk of flooding (2020), and 7.1 million single-family homes and 253,000 multifamily units under threat from storm

Case Study

In 2018, tenants of Arbor Court Apartments in Houston, Texas filed a federal lawsuit against HUD and the owners of Arbor Court Apartments, an HUD-funded low-income rental housing project. After the complex had flooded several times, including in 2016 and during Hurricane Harvey in 2017, the plaintiffs cited "dangerous," "uninhabitable," and "life-threatening" conditions. The City of Houston Fire Marshall deemed it a fire hazard. But tenants could not afford to leave without voucher assistance which HUD allegedly refused to provide. Several of the residents identified as living with disabilities. One resident, whose sole income was SSDI, was unable to move to a more secure, less flood-prone residence without the assistance of a housing voucher.[288]

surges, with a total reconstruction cost of $2.65 trillion.[289] The risk of coastal floods damaging or destroying low-income homes will triple over the next 30 years as rising tides and storm surges encroach on low-lying developed areas. By 2050, more than 25,000 affordable housing units are expected to see coastal flooding at least once in a typical year with the largest number of at-risk housing units in three states: New Jersey, New York, and Massachusetts.[290] As extreme weather events increase and continue to impact low-income people with disabilities living in flood zones, federal funding, including housing choice vouchers and CDBG, are needed. According to the Joint Center for Housing Studies at Harvard University's "the State of the Nation's Housing 2020 Report," "funding for Housing for Persons with Disabilities has been reduced by 43 percent over the decade and critical programs (e.g., CDBG funding down 34 percent in 2020) have lost funding."[291]

Congregate Care Facilities (CCFs) Have Insufficient Evacuation Plans

Many states either do not prepare evacuation plans for CCFs, or requirements are not robust enough to ensure an actionable, executable evacuation plan that maintains appropriate care during and after an evacuation. The reliance on CCFs for lower-income people with disabilities increases when housing expenses rise. The approximately 4.7 million people with disabilities who rely on SSI cannot afford to live in their own homes, even where home-based care might be available,[292] and may live in CCFs. In addition, a large, aging population will continue to expand the need for accessible and integrated housing solutions and health care infrastructure.[293] The pandemic highlighted the tragic impact of substandard conditions at CCFs and nursing homes, which are home to many of the most at-risk community members. The recent CMS Emergency Preparedness Rule was designed in part to increase the mitigation and preparedness activities of long-term care facilities to reduce these risks.[294] Assisted living communities are not regulated nationally like nursing homes. Instead, each state has its own laws, regulations, and licensing standards for assisted living communities. In some states, as many as 25 hours of training are required for caregiving staff; other states have no training requirements. Even where states require robust, actionable evacuation plans, they have historically overcommitted resources, impacting the ability of all CCFs to execute their plans (e.g., multiple CCFs will have a contract with the same transport service that only has the capacity to evacuate one or two CCFs.

The pandemic highlighted the tragic impact of substandard conditions at CCFs and nursing homes, which are home to many of the most at-risk community members.

Response

Special Needs Registries Cause Confusion and Are Unreliable

Special needs registries . . . are not consistently used by local emergency management agencies, and create a false sense of security for people with disabilities that emergency responders will alert and inform them and ensure their safety during disasters.

Special needs registries (or emergency assistance) are not consistently used by local emergency management agencies, and create a false sense of security for people with disabilities that emergency responders will alert and inform

them and ensure their safety during disasters. Some states do not have plans in place for how they will use registries and do not address that people with disabilities may move or may not be home during a disaster. Prior to disasters, people with disabilities can sign up on registries which are designed to identify individuals who may require special assistance during emergencies. Disability stakeholders said that people with disabilities expect that, during a disaster, individuals who have signed up on a registry can remain in their homes and state emergency responders will contact them and ensure their safety. In reality, when local municipalities are in the midst of a disaster, most municipalities have no plan on how to utilize the registry list to assist people with disabilities.

A GAO report (2019) found that[295] Texas and Florida operate registries to help local governments prepare to assist residents with disabilities during evacuations and sheltering, but state, local, and nonprofit officials in those locations reported confusion about the registries limited effectiveness.

State officials in Texas created a state registry to provide local emergency management officials with information about the needs of community members with disabilities. According to representatives of state, local, and nonprofit agencies, it created a misconception among residents who thought being on the Texas registry guaranteed direct evacuation or transportation assistance. Prior to Hurricane Harvey, officials from Texas expressed concerns that confusion about the registry would lead to residents' overreliance on public disaster services.[296] People who registered with the State of Texas Emergency Assistance Registry (STEAR) erroneously assumed that by registering they would receive assistance during a natural disaster. It was quite the opposite, Texas' purpose for the registry was to collect data to better inform SLTTs on the disability population in their jurisdiction. Very few STEAR registrants received assistance or wellness checks during or in the days following Hurricane Harvey.[297]

The state of Florida has a similar registry program. However, in addition to providing registrant data to local emergency managers to use as a tool for disaster preparation, their registry is also used to register people with disabilities for special needs shelters. Florida, by statute, requires special needs shelters and uses the registry to determine eligibility. Disability stakeholders assert that even though persons with disabilities registered for a special needs shelter, their names were never shared with the county and they were denied admittance.

> In reality, when local municipalities are in the midst of a disaster, most municipalities have no plan on how to utilize the registry list to assist people with disabilities.

> Registries do not guarantee assistance, such as accessible transportation to shelters.

Registries are managed by individual states and are not standardized across regions or the country. Registries do not guarantee assistance, such as accessible transportation to shelters.

Mass Population Shelters Are Underprepared for People With Disabilities

Some mass population shelters do not meet the accessibility needs of people with disabilities as required by law, breaking the trust of people with disabilities and increasing the risk to their safety during disasters. SLTTs are obligated to ensure equal opportunity for individuals with disabilities when providing mass care services.[298] The Robert T. Stafford Disaster Relief and Emergency Assistance Act (Stafford Act) Section 308 prohibits disability-related discrimination during disaster relief and assistance activities.[299]

However, mass population shelters are often not ADA compliant. Disability stakeholders reported that shelters are often set up in schools or houses of worship with basic design that may not physically accommodate people with disabilities, like wide aisles for navigation and accessible bathroom and bathing facilities. During Hurricane Florence (2019), Pender County, North Carolina, experienced more than 40 inches of rain, and officials opened shelters in four middle and elementary schools. The Pender County After-Action Report

(AAR), identified areas for improvement, including developing shelter plans with roles and responsibilities, completing Red Cross site approval of primary pre-storm shelters, and developing a plan to manage special need citizens.[300] Developing a plan to "manage special needs citizens" a.k.a. people with disabilities should not be an item that is consistently an item to address in an after action report.

Because of the inconsistencies of shelter access, people with disabilities often wait out a storm in their accessible homes than evacuate to an inaccessible shelter. Some feel that shelters marginalize people with disabilities. People with disabilities going to shelters should know that their needs will be met (e.g., they will be able to use the restroom, with or without assistance).

FEMA's Mass Care/Emergency Assistance Pandemic Planning Considerations for State, Local, Tribal, Territorial and Nongovernment Organizational Planners, Providers and Support Agencies (2020) states that congregate sheltering facilities must ensure that facilities can accommodate people with disabilities, and provide support for household pets, service animals, and support animals. Messaging should be provided in various languages and forms to reach survivors with disabilities.[301] Emergency managers and shelter operators should identify the disability-related needs of a shelter and make advance arrangements to meet

those needs. EMAs must involve community members with a variety of disabilities in the advance planning process to ensure that their needs will be accommodated in the aftermath of a community disasters.[302]

Medical/Special Needs Shelters Are Underperforming

Medical and special needs shelters are often not fully accessible and fail to meet the needs of people with disabilities. They are often designed only for individuals who are power dependent, rather than for all people with disabilities. People with disabilities get separated from their family, friends, and neighbors when they enter "special needs" or "special medical needs" shelters, who may not know when their loved one with a disability left the shelter or where they went.[303]

in 2007, DOJ instructed state and local governments in their ADA Best Practices Toolkit for State and Local Governments, Chapter 7, that "the ADA requires people with disabilities to be accommodated in the most integrated setting appropriate to their needs, and the disability-related needs of people who are not medically fragile can typically be met in a mass care shelter. For this reason, people with disabilities should generally be housed with their families, friends, and neighbors in mass care shelters and not be diverted to special needs or medical shelters."[304]

FEMA estimates that more than 50 percent of individuals visiting disaster recovery centers have disabilities that limit their ability.[305] As history

has taught us and is discussed in more detail in NCD's 2019 report, Preserving our Freedom: Ending the Institutionalization of People with Disabilities, stand-alone "special needs" shelters do not provide equivalent provisions to people with disabilities. When at least half of the shelter population may be people with disabilities, a best practice should be to ensure that mass shelters are accessible to all and not segregate people with disabilities.

Shelters Lack Supplies and Staffing

During a disaster, people with disabilities must bring their own medications and equipment to shelters and many have limited access to support staff, putting them at risk. Emergencies can strike quickly and force people to evacuate promptly. During disaster evacuations, people with disabilities may lose essential medications or assistive devices.[306] Some private nonprofits have programs in place to replace lost medications and provide equipment for people with disabilities.

Historically, shelter operators fail to plan and meet the need for personal attendant services (PAS), attendant care services, and personal care services in shelters. Although PAS is required by federal law, this gap has persisted, leading to the denial of full and equal services[307] increasing the risk of institutionalization to people with disabilities. In 2021, FEMA updated its Guidance on Planning for Personal Assistant Services in General Population Shelters and recommended that SLTTs incorporate PAS as a natural part of

> *. . . [A] best practice should be to ensure that mass shelters are accessible to all and not segregate people with disabilities.*

shelter preparations and that contracts for PAS services be established well before an extreme weather event.[308]

Shelter staff and FEMA personnel require additional training and resources to provide aid and assistance to people with disabilities. According to the GAO (2022) FEMA has faced long-standing challenges with its workforce staffing including providing timely, program-specific training.[309] Staff who work in shelters must be trained on disability competency awareness to meet the needs in the field. FEMA previously offered a two-day disability integration course to its nonfederal partners but canceled the course in 2017. In 2018, FEMA required all staff to take a 30-minute training on basic disability integration principles and offered targeted 'just-in-time' training to deployed staff. FEMA's disability integration specialists are also critical to ensuring that people with disabilities are adequately supported.

Due to a lack of accessible shelters, or when PAS care is not made available, people with disabilities are at risk of being institutionalized.

While disability rights laws protect against people with disabilities from being placed in long-term care facilities, these requirements are often waived during disasters allowing for institutionalization.

People with Disabilities Face 'Institutionalization' During Disasters

Due to a lack of accessible shelters, or when PAS care is not made available, people with disabilities are at risk of being institutionalized.[310] While disability rights laws protect against people with disabilities from being placed in long-term care facilities, these requirements are often waived during disasters allowing for institutionalization. Emergency managers often consider hospitals and CCFs as appropriate locations for short-term housing for people with disabilities. Individuals may be placed in nursing homes, psychiatric institutions, assisted living facilities and other long-term care facilities. Oftentimes, this occurs when a person with a disability does not require medical care but just accessible facilities. When a shelter is not made accessible for all, it places people with disabilities at a higher risk of being institutionalized in order to attain the needed physical access or services required. Such institutionalization is detrimental to people with disabilities who were living independently and is also a violation of their civil rights. As NCD reported in *Preserving Our Freedom: Ending Institutionalization of People with Disabilities During and After Disasters*,[311] once someone is in an institution, they are likely to remain even after the threat of the disaster has passed. The DOJ ADA Tool Kit (2007) says "people should receive services in the most integrated setting appropriate to the needs of the person, and only persons who require the type and level of medical care that would ordinarily be provided by trained medical personnel in a nursing home or hospital" can be placed in a restrictive setting.

However, HHS CMS issues waivers to these rules during disasters, allowing states to place people with disabilities in institutions. Some states to combat institutionalization have used Appendix K waivers to pay legally responsible relatives to provide care that is *extraordinary* and is necessary in order to prevent institutionalization.[312]

HHS must approve the waivers for states to cover services that are ordinarily not covered.

Recovery

Federal Reimbursement Programs Favor Property Owners

Federal housing assistance programs favor individuals who own property. Individuals recovering from disasters will often require documentation to verify their eligibility, such as proof of homeownership and insurance information, to qualify for federal or other assistance. This requirement places a significant burden of proof on the applicant to prove home ownership if property records are destroyed in a disaster and limits assistance to those who rent. FEMA's Individuals and Households Program (IHP) provides financial and direct services to eligible individuals and households affected by a disaster who have uninsured or underinsured necessary expenses and serious needs. Federal reimbursement

[O]nce someone is in an institution, they are likely to remain even after the threat of the disaster has passed.

This requirement places a significant burden of proof on the applicant to prove home ownership if property records are destroyed in a disaster and limits assistance to those who rent.

programs use property tax data to determine property value, favoring homeowners and leaving out a huge population, including individuals with disabilities who often are not homeowners. In Puerto Rico, post Hurricane Maria, some individuals did not have titles or deeds to their homes, which created a significant barrier to receiving assistance.

Finding Accessible Housing Post-Disaster is Difficult for People with Disabilities

Relocation creates challenges for people with disabilities, including separation from their support services and community and finding affordable, accessible housing. Some individuals have difficulty understanding FEMA's IHP application process, including required documentation, supporting applications, and approval processes. Some low-income families do not qualify for disaster loans.

After a disaster, some individuals leave shelters to find their home has been destroyed and they must find accessible, safe housing which sometimes requires relocating. Individuals may land in temporary housing far from their support services and community. In addition, they may need to replace lost resources such as their DME or AT which may have been lost or destroyed. People with disabilities may need financial assistance, in the form of rental or relocation assistance or to replace assistive technologies.

Several federal assistance programs are typically activated to support large-scale disaster recovery. Unfortunately, these programs fail to provide needed assistance to the most vulnerable people. Through the Emergency Housing Voucher program, HUD can provide housing choice vouchers to local public housing authorities (PHAs) to assist individuals and families. As mentioned in an earlier section, there appears to be limitations preventing individuals to be able to "transfer/transport" their housing voucher to a new location requiring them to return to a property that may be unlivable.

FEMA IHP process allows FEMA, in coordination with states, to provide financial assistance and direct services to individuals and households that have disaster-related expenses and serious needs that cannot be met through other organizations and programs. However, FEMA's IHP application process is complicated, may require assistance or AT that might not be available in the immediate aftermath of a disaster, and the approval process is lengthy, leaving people without housing and support for extended periods. Research has highlighted barriers faced such as lack of knowledge of disaster-aid processes, discomfort with these processes, and difficulty accessing disaster assistance facilities because of transportation, childcare, and work challenges.[313] For some low-income individuals and families, FEMA's IHP grants may not be enough to fund rebuilding (e.g., homes that have specific accessibility requirements) and HUD funding takes months or even years to reach families. A GAO report (2021), "found that FEMA requires that certain survivors first be denied a U.S. Small Business Administration (SBA) disaster loan before receiving certain Individual Assistance (IA) grants, and survivors did not understand and were frustrated by this requirement."[314] Some FEMA programs require applicants to complete the SBA application, even if the applicant does not want or cannot qualify for the SBA loan. Many applicants will fail to apply for SBA disaster loans, not realizing that the loan application is a prerequisite for most IHP programs. Disability stakeholders said, many lower-income families do not qualify for disaster loans, the FEMA IA grants are insufficient to fund rebuilding, and funding from HUD takes months or even years to reach families.

> *People with disabilities may need financial assistance, in the form of rental or relocation assistance or to replace assistive technologies.*

> *FEMA's IHP application process is complicated, may require assistance or AT that might not be available in the immediate aftermath of a disaster, and the approval process is lengthy, leaving people without housing and support for extended periods.*

HUD CDBG-DR Programs Are Not Permanently Authorized

HUD's Community Development Block Grant-Disaster Recovery (CDBG-DR) programs are supplemental appropriations typically tied to a presidentially declared disaster. Unlike other recovery assistance programs administered by FEMA and SBA, CDBG-DR assistance is not permanently authorized leaving communities and people with disabilities waiting for years for accessible housing to be rebuilt. HUD's CDBG program provides disaster recovery grants to rebuild areas impacted by extreme weather and provide crucial seed money to start the recovery process. The grants help states, cities, and counties recover from presidentially declared disasters, especially in low-income areas.

HUD's CDBG Mitigation (CDBG-MIT) program funds can be used by grantees in areas impacted by disasters to carry out strategic and high-impact activities to mitigate disaster risks and reduce future losses. The CDBG-DR assistance can be used to help communities recover from disaster.[315] This may include building accessible facilities in the community. CDBG MIT and DR, are not standing programs but supplemental appropriations tied to a specific disaster. CDBG-DR funds are appropriated by Congress in response to a specific disaster or series of disasters—there is no standing authority for HUD to grant DR funds without an act of Congress.[316] Statutory requirements of CDBG-DR appropriations, recovery needs of grantees, and waivers granted by HUD may change from one disaster to the next, thus, causing grantees to seek clarifying guidance each disaster about which activities are covered by the funding. For people with disabilities who require accessible homes, schools, places of work and worship, waiting years is unacceptable. Reinvestment must be part of the disaster recovery process—not only in getting people back into apartments and houses but in rebuilding accessible, habitable communities. Restoring communities after disasters presents SLTTs opportunities to review accessibility standards and requirements and to update inaccessible public facilities and infrastructure. The recovery process is an opportunity to ensure that ADA and other disability laws, and federal rebuild standards are met and to build resilient communities accessible to all.

> *A GAO report (2021), "found that FEMA requires that certain survivors first be denied a U.S. Small Business Administration (SBA) disaster loan before receiving certain Individual Assistance (IA) grants, and survivors did not understand and were frustrated by this requirement."*

> *Statutory requirements of CDBG-DR appropriations, recovery needs of grantees, and waivers granted by HUD may change from one disaster to the next, thus, causing grantees to seek clarifying guidance each disaster about which activities are covered by the funding.*

Recommendations

- Congress should pass legislation to spur affordable housing production and measures to preserve existing homes so that people with disabilities can return to their homes post an extreme weather event as outlined in the White House Actions to Ease the Burden of Housing Costs. Doing so would expand and improve existing forms of federal financing for affordable multifamily development and allocate a percentage of the housing development units to be accessible to people with disabilities.

- Congress should pass legislation to ease rising costs for renters and prospective homebuyers and encourage construction of new affordable and accessible housing units.

- SLTTs should encourage the construction of universally designed accessible units by passing universal design ordinances that go beyond the ADA and require that builders offer accessibility features to buyers as upgrades.[317]

- HUD should increase the number of accessible units from the 5 percent accessibility requirement for federally assisted new construction housing developments to 25 percent, which represents the percentage of people with disabilities in the United States.

- HUD Office of Public and Indian Housing (PIH) should expand its housing voucher program[318] to offer climate vouchers for families affected by extreme weather events to relocate in the event their home is not habitable.

- HUD should initiate a policy that will not approve funding of federal financed housing in floodplains.

- HUD should require developers use materials that are more resilient to extreme weather events indicative of the area, for instance, metal shingles in California to mitigate wildfires, or a safe room in units designed for people with disabilities that should withstand high winds from hurricanes or tornadoes.

- HUD should establish and implement a Federal Flood Risk Management Standard (FFRMS); update/modernize HUD's floodplain management regulations in 24 CFR part 55; extend increased flood protection across all HUD programs; increase flood resilience; and clarify processes and standards, and promote environmental justice concerns in floodplain decision-making.

- CMS should examine and consider changes to emergency preparedness plans to bolster the resiliency of the health care sector as part of an administration-wide effort to be ready for the next weather-related emergency.

Recommendations: *continued*

- HHS ASPR should require that states develop written emergency evacuation plans and response procedures for CCFs that include situation assessment and plans for protecting residents, staff, volunteers, visitors, equipment, medications, and vital records as part of the states' assisted living licensing and regulation requirements.

- No federal funds—including but not limited to federal funds from DHS and HHS—should be used in development, deployment, and maintenance of emergency "special needs" registries exclusively created for people with disabilities. Instead of registries, SLTTs should take an innovative, holistic, and inclusive approach to include people with disabilities in their overall emergency management plans.

- SLTTs should develop/update shelter management plans with clear roles and responsibilities that fully integrate the needs of people with disabilities to meet legal requirements.

- DOJ and HUD should monitor and enforce compliance obligations for emergency sheltering in a disaster consistent with emergency sheltering requirements under the Fair Housing Amendments Act. Whether the disaster shelter is considered transient or long-term, the rights of people with disabilities in these shelters should be seamlessly protected.

- The federal entity (typically FEMA and DHS) providing funds ultimately received by local emergency management departments should require the participation of local staff in training on the scope of obligations under the Rehab Act.

- HHS and DOJ should issue joint guidance and provide technical assistance to SLTTs and shelter planners on the ADA and other legal requirements as well as Crisis Standards of Care (CSC) requirements for all shelters.

- SLTTs and emergency planners should involve people with disabilities and disability organizations in emergency evacuation planning, ensure that shelters are physically accessible, and provide guidance on post-evacuation residency for individuals with disabilities.

- FEMA, SLTTs, and shelter providers should join private nonprofits to develop contingency plans to replace lost medications and DME equipment.

- FEMA should continue outreach to SLTTs on the requirement to provide PAS in shelters and advise the importance of acquiring a contract for PAS services prior to a shelter opening and advise SLTTs of the proper method for reimbursement following disasters.

Recommendations: *continued*

- FEMA, SLTTs and NGOs (e.g., the Red Cross or religious organizations) should provide adequate planning and training, to include disability cultural competency training and resources, including supplies and equipment, to staff working in shelters, health care professionals, first responders, and search-and-rescue teams to better support people with disabilities in shelters. Expand training to individuals and community groups and recruit, train, and provide clearance for volunteers with specific skill sets, such as interpreters, mental health professionals, counselors, behavioral therapists, and PCAs.

- The FEMA Administrator should develop a plan for delivering training to FEMA staff that promotes competency in disability awareness. The plan should include milestones and performance measures and outline how performance will be monitored. (GAO Recommendation 6).[319] The plan should include FEMA Disability Integration Cadre. NCD recommends FEMA should ensure its emergency management workforce receives formal training on guidance related to supporting people with disabilities prior to their deployment in a disaster response role.[320] FEMA should lengthen its two-hour course (IS-368: Including People With Disabilities and Others With Access & Functional Needs in Disaster Operations (2014))[321] and ensure that people with disabilities are consulted during course development.

- SLTT EMAs should ensure that shelter staff receives specific training to address the needs of people with IDD and mental/behavioral health issues.

- FEMA should ensure emergency shelter providers plan for and ensure all shelters are accessible and compliant with the ADA and the Rehab Act to avoid the threat of institutionalization. Employing local disability organizations to collaborate on shelter operations will assist to ensure shelter facilities are more accessible to people with disabilities

- HHS CMS should cease issuing waivers that allow people with disabilities to be institutionalized in the absence of accessible shelters and services. Absent an alternative, if waivers are issued, SLTTs should require EMA's to immediately remedy or face severe penalties with a stipulation that the people institutionalized be moved into other accessible accommodations within a specified short timeframe or additional penalties will be applied.

- HHS should approve Appendix K waivers for SLTT partners to pay legally responsible relatives to provide care during disasters.

(continued)

Recommendations: *continued*

- Congress should fund legislation to enable states to increase accessibility to HCBS and to expand access to assistive technologies in order to promote independence and community integration.

- FEMA should revise and provide technical assistance in plain language to its IHP application process

- which would include enhancing and publishing guidance for requesting and receiving such services and removing any challenges related to language accessibility, literacy, technical expertise, or disability and the prerequisite to apply for SBA disaster loans.[322]

- Congress should permanently authorize HUD Community Development Block Grant (CDBG) funding or in the alternative, streamline the authorization process after a disaster so that subsidies reach recovering communities earlier, so rebuilding can begin immediately following a disaster.

- HUD should authorize CDBG-DR and CDBG-MIT grants to be used toward long-term relocation of housing projects and other infrastructure including building in safer zones or retrofitting buildings to be more resilient to expected weather events. HUD should work with and offer guidance to local leaders to help community planning and development.

- HUD should provide guidance to CDBG recipients of the requirement to comply with federal disability rights laws and require the incorporation of universal design in any rebuild to ensure accessibility for PWDs.

- HUD should update its CDBG-DR Policy Guidance for Grantees (2019) and include references to people with disabilities and use the CDBG to advance equity, access, and inclusion.

- FEMA should provide guidance and training to SLTT partners on the legal requirements for Functional Needs Support Services (FNSS) for general population shelters and the potential loss of shelter reimbursement funds and propensity for lawsuits should they not provide accessible sheltering.

Chapter 4: Employment

Extreme weather events disrupt access to employment for people with disabilities and yet there is limited public research and data about how disasters impact job rates for people with disabilities.[323] Employees with disabilities are displaced at a disproportionate rate to people without disabilities outside of extreme weather events. The employment rate of people with disabilities is 19.1 percent compared to 63 percent of people without disabilities.[324]

During COVID, unemployment rates were 12 percent for people with disabilities and only 9.5 percent for people without disabilities.[325] Employees with disabilities are 89 percent more likely to experience an involuntary job loss than those without disabilities in the United States.[326] Data shows people with disabilities are more likely to experience an involuntary job loss absent of extreme weather events. Extreme weather events disrupt the job market, therefore, it is easy to hypothesize that since the unemployment rate of employees with disabilities is consistently higher than those without disabilities. Extreme weather events exacerbate the unemployment rate of people with disabilities.

People with disabilities are 89 percent more likely to experience an involuntary job loss than people without disabilities.

Preparedness

Measuring the Impact of Extreme Weather on Employment of People with Disabilities

Extreme weather events often involve temporary disruptions to the local economy through direct and indirect effects on local infrastructure, business structures, homes, and the workforce, and limit access to reliable employment. After a natural disaster, the labor demand tends to decrease because businesses are forced to close or relocate. Even businesses with long-term viability will have difficulty operating immediately after a disaster because of disruptions to the supply chain, power grid, communications, and other infrastructure.[327] Businesses that are damaged in a disaster may take weeks or months to reopen or may never reopen due to many factors including the loss of customers. In 2017, the California Wildfires "destroyed or damaged more than 10,000 structures in the state (destroyed 9,470, damaged 810), a higher tally than the previous nine years combined." According to CalFire, "in terms of property damage, 2017 was the most destructive wildfire season on record in California at the time."[328] In 2012, Hurricane Sandy, which was one of the deadliest hurricanes to make landfall on the continental U.S., struck the northeastern region of the United States resulting in over $19 billion in losses and the deaths of at least 53 people in New York City. A decade later, New York City has rebounded. However, there is still a void as to the labor outcomes of people affected by Hurricane Sandy.[329]

Recent COVID-19 pandemic-related layoffs have disproportionately impacted people with disabilities. From March to April 2020, the number of employed working-age people with disabilities fell by 20 percent (950,000 people), while the number of employed working-age people without disabilities decreased by 14 percent.[330]

> *One of the difficulties of measuring employment after a disaster is the inability to run standard surveys in disaster-affected areas.*

One of the difficulties of measuring employment after a disaster is the inability to run standard surveys in disaster-affected areas.[331] While there is some information about how the labor market and employment in general are impacted by natural hazards, and while DOL produces labor force statistics on people with disabilities, it is unclear whether there are Federal Government efforts underway to measure how extreme weather events impact the employment outcomes for people with disabilities. Although DOL tracks the impacts of disasters on people with disabilities in terms of employment, the agency primarily focuses on large disasters or crises, such as the COVID-19 pandemic and its economic impact. DOL does not track how individual disasters impact people with disabilities in terms of

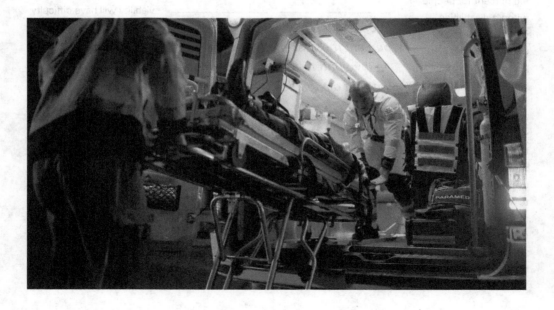

employment and it does not track real-time data. The limited data on how extreme weather impacts people with disabilities makes it difficult to measure and build capacity.

Recovery

Extreme Weather Events Exacerbate Mental Health Issues

Extreme weather events impact the labor market by loss of life, injury, and the evacuation of people to areas outside the disaster zone. After a disaster, individuals may require mental health support and other accommodations at work that were not previously required. Natural disasters can have cascading impacts on people with disabilities, further limiting employment opportunities Disasters can affect stress levels, labor productivity, and mental health. Disasters may lead to or exacerbate mental health issues. People who become unemployed after a disaster must take care of their basic life and safety requirements before seeking employment.[332] It is critical that employees are educated and made aware of their rights, especially after a disaster. During disaster recovery, federal crisis counseling programs provide funding and infrastructure for individual states to administer and implement guidance. DOL provides information on available mental health services on its Office of Disability Employment Policy website at https://www.whatcanyoudocampaign.org/psa-campaigns/mental-health-psa/.

Displaced Employees Require Vocational Assistance Programs

People with disabilities displaced after a disaster may need access to assistance programs such as vocational rehabilitation (VR) services

to find new employment. The Rehabilitation Services Administration (RSA) provides four programs that service people with disabilities to achieve successful employment outcomes. The VR Service Program and the Supported Employment Service (SE), both state formula grant programs; the American Indian Vocational Rehabilitation Service Program (AIVR); and the Demonstration and Training programs, which are discretionary grant programs with up to five years of competitive awards.[333]

Approximately 1.2 million youths and adults are served by the 100-year-old VR Service Program each year. The system is designed to assist people with disabilities, including those with the most significant disabilities, who have visual, auditory, physical, intellectual, and learning disabilities, and psychosocial or psychological disabilities, to achieve and maintain employment. The VR Service Program performance data from the last decade—FYs 2010 through 2019—revealed that each year, there were approximately one million people with disabilities receiving VR services under an individual plan for employment.[334]

In our 2020 report, *Progress Report on National Disability Policy: Increasing Disability Employment*, NCD reported that, "historically, American Job Centers (AJCs) have been found to be physically and programmatically inaccessible to people with disabilities and not well coordinated with the other parts of the adult employment system,[335] although several identified steps are being taken to remedy these barriers." In its 2018 report, GAO found "some gaps exist in federal guidance intended to enhance coordination. Employers GAO spoke with cited challenges navigating workforce programs, yet few agencies reported

documenting roles and responsibilities of the agencies they partner with to work with employers. While Education and the Department of Labor (DOL) have provided some related technical assistance, they have not provided examples of documentation of roles and responsibilities. GAO's prior work has found that such documentation can help improve coordination by clarifying who does what in a partnership."[336] In addition to schools, VR, and Medicaid, the public workforce system also provides employment services to people with disabilities, albeit to a smaller share of self-identified people with disabilities, through AJCs.[337]

Access to Transportation is Necessary for Returning to Work

The process of finding employment is significantly disrupted if the employee relies on accessible public transportation or paratransit.

As mentioned in previous chapters, disruption or damage to critical infrastructure such as public facilities, roads, bridges, and public transportation systems limits options for people with disabilities to get to work. People with disabilities face significant obstacles to employment because accessible and affordable transportation often cannot be found.[338] This obstacle is often exacerbated after a disaster. Lack of public transportation because of damaged infrastructure is a common barrier for people with disabilities to return to work.[339]

Employees staffing these services may also be displaced during disasters. Many businesses may not be able to recover no matter the amount of support. In this instance, employees should be provided support and job placement assistance for alternative employment. Displaced employees could benefit from job-search assistance or new training if needed.[340]

Recommendations

- DOL Bureau of Labor Statistics should collaborate with the National Institute on Disability, Independent Living, and Rehabilitation Research to commission a study on how individual disasters impact people with disabilities in terms of employment and economic impacts.

- Given the dearth of data on employment losses due to natural disasters, DOL should create a system to collect and share data on how individual disasters impact people with disabilities in terms of employment.

- Rehabilitation counselors should work with disability program navigators (DPNs) (people trained to utilize the One-Stop Career Centers to help people with disabilities) to help navigate the web of career services.

- Federal agencies and private sector employers should offer remote work as an option, especially after a disaster where people with disabilities who rely on public transportation may not have access to transportation or paratransit services.

Chapter 5: Education

Eighteen extreme weather events affected the United States in 2022 with losses exceeding $1 billion each.[341] As these events have shown, extreme weather events affect communities, school districts, and institutions of higher education.[342] Students with disabilities face extra risks and challenges to their academic, physical, and mental well-being when extreme weather events disrupt education. U.S. public schools provide special education services to more than 7.2 million, or 15 percent of all public school students[343] ages 3 to 21.[344] Since 2017, more than 341 presidentially declared major disasters have occurred across all 50 states and U.S. territories,[345] with devastating effects on K-12 schools, including those in socially vulnerable communities where disaster recovery is more challenging.[346] During the 2018–2019 school year in California, more than one million students were impacted by school closures because of wildfires, specifically

During the 2018–2019 school year in California, more than one million students were impacted by school closures because of wildfires...

After Hurricanes Maria and Irma (2017), Puerto Rican students missed an average of 78 days of school because of infrastructure damage and transportation disruption; the storms also accelerated declines in school enrollment.

the Camp Fire (2018), which impacted more than 2,200 schools.[347] After Hurricanes Maria and Irma (2017), Puerto Rican students missed an average of 78 days of school because of infrastructure damage and transportation disruption; the storms also accelerated declines in school enrollment. One year later, 1 in 10 students with special needs were still not receiving special education services.[348] Hurricane Harvey impacted 181 school districts in Texas, including the Houston school district, one of the nation's largest, with more than 200,000 students.[349] Hurricane Harvey kept 1.4 million students out of public schools for at least one week.[350]

Nearly 1 in 10 U.S. schools are located in a floodplain, placing 4 million students at risk of being flooded out of school.[351] Students with disabilities face challenges during response and evacuation and disasters have long-term impacts on students' physical and mental health, and on academic outcomes. More research, data, and preparedness planning on how to protect students with disabilities during disasters is needed.

Preparedness

Students with Disabilities in Rural, Tribal, and Low-Income Areas

The special education system lacks resilience, or capacity to quickly recover, and students with disabilities living in rural, tribal and low-income areas are especially susceptible to educational disruption because the present shortage of special education professionals, which is exacerbated when an extreme weather event occurs.

Hurricane Harvey kept 1.4 million students out of public schools for at least one week.

Students with disabilities already face multiple and substantial barriers to accessing a quality inclusive education. Their education is resource-intensive, requiring access to specialized equipment, educators with unique training,[352] and accessible transportation. Even before the COVID-19 pandemic, the United States was facing a nationwide shortage of qualified special education teachers and related service providers.[353] Research shows that these shortages disproportionately impact students with disabilities, students of color, students from low-income backgrounds, and students from rural communities.[354] Students in rural, territorial, or tribal areas may have access to just one occupational therapist,[355] a single adapted school vehicle, or a few nurses capable

Nearly 1 in 10 U.S. schools are located in a floodplain, placing 4 million students at risk of being flooded out of school.

of tending to specialized needs.[356] If a disaster puts these assets out of commission, students lose services with no alternative.

Multiply Marginalized

Research shows that socially vulnerable groups are particularly susceptible to the adverse effects of disasters, such as increased housing instability, food insecurity, parental job loss, and social disconnection.[357] In our 2021 report, *The Impact of COVID-19 on People with Disabilities*,[358] NCD reported that many students with disabilities face additional barriers to equal educational opportunity as they are multiply marginalized.[359] For example, students with disabilities are more likely to be low-income,[360] are disproportionately Black,[361] and may be in foster care or juvenile justice systems, or both. (About 32 percent of children in foster care have disabilities,[362] and, as noted, up to 85 percent of children in juvenile detention have disabilities.) Disabled students also may be homeless[363] and may be English language learners.[364] Many experience intersectional discrimination based on disability, sex, race, ethnicity, and size. These additional burdens exacerbate the vulnerabilities of students already struggling with academics, behavior, planning, speech, motor skills, and other areas essential to long-term success.[365] Because of their marginalization, parents of these children may not be aware of the required processes and procedures for securing services and accessing programs and opportunities.

Poverty and Academic Impacts

In the United States, a higher percentage of children (18.3 percent) and individuals with severe disabilities (26 percent) live in poverty than does the population as a whole (13.3 percent; U.S. Census Bureau, 2006).[366] A January 2022 GAO report, *Disaster Recovery: School Districts in Socially Vulnerable Communities Faced Heightened Challenges after Recent Natural Disasters*, reported that most school districts that received key federal disaster recovery grants following 2017–2019 presidentially declared major disasters had elevated proportions of students from socially vulnerable groups.[367]

Academic achievement may be particularly disrupted by disasters in districts with high proportions of socially vulnerable students, including those with disabilities. One recent study found that lower-income school districts' academic achievement tended to be adversely affected by natural disasters, whereas higher-income districts did not see extended declines in academic achievement.[368] For example, one county education official noted that, over the last decade, school districts in his county had narrowed the gap between White and Hispanic students in high school graduation rates and college attendance. However, after natural disasters, both rates declined for Hispanic students.

Limited Research and Data

Limited research exists on the specific educational impacts of natural disasters on children with disabilities.[369] We do know that globally, 86 percent of children with disabilities did not participate in national disaster management; thus, their fatality rates during disasters are 4.3 percent higher than those of children without disabilities.[370] To impact policy on how to better prepare children with a disability in disasters data collection on the subject is needed. Although research has reported that children are particularly vulnerable to the impact of extreme weather events,[371] few studies examined the impacts of extreme weather events on children with disabilities and their families and how disasters impact physical and mental health, and interrupt children's educational achievement.

Few studies address how to support young people's feelings regarding extreme weather events.[372] Although some studies have examined the threats to children's physical health, the psychological and mental health impacts of extreme weather events have been less well-researched; however, evidence from extreme weather event disasters shows that they can be equally devastating. Impacts include significant increases in PTSD, depression and anxiety, sleep problems, cognitive deficits, and learning problems.[373] Further, few studies have examined the intersection of psychological and mental health impacts of extreme weather events on children with disabilities and how they disrupt students' academic achievement.

Research on and collection of high-quality data concerning children with disabilities is critical for

> *One recent study found that lower-income school districts' academic achievement tended to be adversely affected by natural disasters, whereas higher-income districts did not see extended declines in academic achievement.*

mitigation, preparedness, response, and recovery efforts related to disasters. Without research and data, the needs of children with disabilities fail to be included as an appropriate and significant part of nations' overall discussion of disaster management planning.

In the United States, federal, and SLTT EMAs and school districts must improve processes for collecting data about and including children with disabilities and their families in disaster management planning. This means identifying and then eliminating the challenges faced by children with disabilities during disasters.[374] These challenges could include the need for accommodations such as screen reader access to computers, or a sign language interpreter,[375] during or after a disaster.

An accurate assessment of people with disabilities allows for a proper distribution of project resources and provides a greater understanding of inclusion needs to local officials. It may also be valuable to collect data following a disaster to better inform future prevention initiatives.[376]

States and Territories Face Special Education Funding Challenges

States and territories faced challenges acquiring specialized services and personnel needed to comply with federal IDEA requirements. IDEA Part B was designed to ensure that all children with disabilities are provided a FAPE[377] in the least restrictive environment. However, many states and territories do not have nonfederal funding to cover the costs for these services and personnel.[378] In addition, school districts have historically found it challenging to meet federal special education requirements after natural disasters. Section 504 of the Rehabilitation Act of 1973 guarantees that no student "shall, solely by reason of her or his disability, be excluded from the participation in, be denied the benefits of, or be subjected to discrimination under any program or activity receiving Federal financial assistance."[379] Per Section 504, for students with disabilities who do not require special education services, school districts must provide students with disabilities with related aids and services (including reasonable accommodations) to meet their individual needs as adequately as students without disabilities.[380] One way to meet FAPE requirements under Section 504 is the creation of an individualized education program (IEP)[381] per IDEA. An IEP includes details about the students' education goals and the supports and services that student will receive to meet those goals.[382]

Some estimates indicate that 12 percent of the displaced students have disabilities.

IDEA Continues to Be Underfunded

Multiple factors impact the quality of education provided to students with disabilities, including a school district's access to funding. The lack of financial resources and the impact of natural disasters can delay recovery and directly impact educational services to all students, but especially for students with disabilities. Under the 1975 IDEA legislation, the Federal Government committed to pay 40 percent of the excess cost of special education. However, that pledge has never been met, and current funding is at just 15.7 percent. The Federal Government provides no additional funds to comply with Section 504. The IDEA Full Funding Act (S.3213)[383]—bipartisan, bicameral legislation to ensure Congress's commitment to fully fund IDEA—was reintroduced on November 16, 2021. It would require regular increases in IDEA spending, increasing direct support for public schools and students with disabilities so Congress can meet its commitment to schools and children and help provide every American student with a quality education.[384] This legislation is imperative, as its passage would ensure ample funding to accommodate any additional students requiring special education services because of the impact of climate change on the student. According to the National Education Association, the IDEA nationwide shortfall in 2021 was $23.58 billion.[385] There is no non legislative mechanism to ensure that IDEA funding commitments are met and that additional funds are appropriated for compliance with Section 504 of the Rehab Act.

Response

Evacuation and Transferring Schools

For student disaster evacuees with disabilities, transferring between school systems presents unique challenges. Although there is limited data about these student transfers, what data is available provides information on population movements. Some estimates indicate that 12 percent of the displaced students have disabilities.[386] One of the most crucial challenges for disaster-recovery efforts is to continue the education of student-evacuees while rebuilding educational services.[387]

Studies indicate that the average child requires between four and six months to "catch up" academically each time they transfer schools.[388] Students with disabilities likely require even longer. First, families with students with disabilities may need extra time to secure accessible housing, meaning they may linger in shelters or require multiple transfers between school districts. Without secure housing, students may lack the residency documentation they need to register for school. Second, families may not have the educational records (e.g., IEPs, 504 plans) for the supports and services the student requires in their new school district. The lack of records may require additional evaluations to determine a student's eligibility, which may delay the provision of services. Finally, the new school district may require time to procure additional equipment or hire additional personnel, particularly troublesome if a student transfers to a rural, tribal, territorial, or low-income school district where resources are already scarce.

> Studies indicate that the average child requires between four and six months to "catch up" academically each time they transfer schools. Students with disabilities likely require even longer.

Recovery

Limited Functionality and Services After School Reopening

When schools reopen after an extreme weather event, limited school facilities and services can deny students with disabilities who remain in the disaster-affected district equal access to an education. Extreme weather events

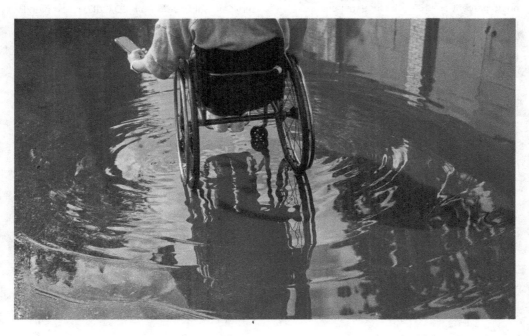

Hurricane Maria's Impact on Students with Disabilities in Puerto Rico

In 2017, Hurricane Maria, a Category 5 hurricane, disrupted the lives of some 350,000 Puerto Rican public school students. It took nearly five weeks before the first public schools began to reopen, though most were still operating without power. Since the hurricane, some schools have been converted into community centers and shelters, requiring students to relocate and find alternate routes to resume their studies. Economic trouble exacerbated by the storm forced the closure of 265 schools—roughly a quarter of all of the island's public schools, affecting an estimated 60,000 students. These school closures had cascading impacts on 35 percent or ~103,318 students between the ages of 3 and 21 that receive special education services in Puerto Rico. One of these cascading impacts is that as of March 2020, ~9,800 special education students did not have access to transportation, placing the burden on the parents to transport their children to school.[389]

can result in extensive damage to homes, education infrastructure, and transportation networks. School rebuilding and reopening tends to be prioritized by actions that help the greatest number of students and staff return to learning, which means students who have more specialized needs tend to be left behind. For example, some students require in-person services or supports such as physical therapy or behavior intervention strategies to receive FAPE.[390] If a district's Braille printer is damaged, blind students may not be able to read their schoolwork. School personnel who provide related services like occupational therapy or adapted transportation may be unable to return to work because of damaged homes or road networks, and schools may experience delays hiring new personnel for the same reasons.[391]

Legal guidance from the U.S. Department of Education (ED) OCR is clear: school districts owe compensatory services to students with disabilities who are denied FAPE, even for "situations outside of a district's control or where the district is not at fault."[392] To ensure these students' rights are protected, school districts must have a way of recording which services were not delivered and for how long, in order to provide appropriate resources for compensatory services. Guidance[393] from ED (2017) recommends that IEP or 504 teams meet after a natural disaster to determine and document which services can and cannot be provided during the period of limited functionality, e.g., if trained and certified personnel are not available, or if a student cannot access school facilities or adapted technology. After full functionality is reached, school districts must assess students with disabilities for regression or loss of skills during the period of limited functionality, and these losses must also be accounted for during the determination of the type, duration, and amount of compensatory services. Finally, school districts must track delays in eligibility evaluations or starting new special education services or accommodations, so students can receive appropriate compensatory services for those delays.

In addition to this documentation following the extreme weather event, school districts should assess their risk factors for educational disruption and work with federal and SLTT governments to mitigate them. For example, some areas may have private service providers such as speech or occupational therapists who substitute temporarily for school personnel who are affected by extreme weather events. School districts should consider identifying and pre-contracting with these private providers to shorten the period during which special education services are disrupted. School districts should consider making more of their transportation fleet accessible to students with disabilities. During disasters, available school buses are used as public transport rather than for schools. Having only a few accessible vehicles presents risk to disabled students.

School rebuilding and reopening tends to be prioritized by actions that help the greatest number of students and staff return to learning, which means students who have more specialized needs tend to be left behind.

Limited Special Education Staffing

There is a chronic shortage of special education teachers in the United States and replacing qualified educators after a disaster can be challenging. It has been noted that, after extreme weather events, some communities lack sufficient housing for educators and their families. Thus teachers, including special education teachers, cannot serve their students, compounding an already significant shortage of special education professionals.

Several studies have found special education teachers provide critical psychological support to children with disabilities and their families post-disaster, even when schools are closed and students have been displaced from their school districts.[394] School districts must consider working with their state and local governments to prioritize educational staff for access to housing close to their schools.

Disruption to College-Aged Students

Extreme weather events, such as heat waves, are impacting college-aged students with disabilities. At the University of California, Los Angeles (UCLA), the growing number of heat waves is impacting students—either through the increased risk of wildfires or more difficulty in learning. UCLA's campus is located near high fire hazard zones, according to data from the California Department of Forestry and Fire Protection. In 2019, UCLA administrators canceled classes when the Getty Fire spread less than two miles from campus.

Recommendations

- Congress should enact legislation to combat special education and rural teacher shortages across the United States and appropriate funding for programs to assist in recruitment of special education teachers.

- Congress should require ED to conduct a study assessing the impact of extreme weather events on students with and without disabilities. The study should assess the physical, psychological, and mental health impacts of extreme weather events, the impact on academic achievement and utilize collected data to inform school districts in disaster management planning.

- ED should commission a study to examine the impacts of extreme weather events and adaptation strategies on children with disabilities and their families. The study should include findings to support disaster planning.

- Congress should take action to strengthen the safety net for socially vulnerable groups, such as students with disabilities, school staff with disabilities, and their families.

- Congress should provide funding to ED to develop information technology standards for secure, interoperable electronic education records. These records must include the supports and services a student receives under IDEA and Section 504, and the standards must interoperate with electronic health record systems to allow school districts, students, and parents to access their IEPs, 504 plans, and supporting medical documentation. Once the information technology standards are established, ED should strongly encourage and provide technical assistance for local school districts to avail themselves of the technology to mitigate delays in special education services because of relocation or loss of records due to extreme weather events.

- Congress should amend the IDEA funding formula to mitigate the high incidence of poverty in rural and low-income communities, including U.S. territories.

- ED should collect standardized tracking and reporting of educational services and supports that are unable to be provided to students with disabilities during and after a disaster.

- Congress should require ED to track and report on post-disaster compensatory services provided to students in any school district located in a presidentially declared major natural disaster area to better prepare and develop best practices for recovery after extreme weather events.

Chapter 6: Emergency Management

Emergency management planning is critical to prevent, protect against, mitigate, respond to, and recover from the extreme weather events that pose a risk to communities. As the scope, scale, and frequency of weather-related incidents increases, the capabilities of FEMA and SLTTs EMAs will be tested. Emergency management cannot be reactionary. Climate change directly impacts the frequency and intensity of natural disasters and our ability to ensure the safety of our communities. Building community-wide resilience to climate change through targeted mitigation investments and leveraging future risk data needs to be a primary focus for all levels of government and partners.[395] Resilience cannot be achieved without equitable consideration for, and participation of, all community members. Ensuring equitable disaster risk reduction for all marginalized populations, including people with disabilities, should remain a high priority for emergency managers nationwide.[396] People with disabilities, especially those living in underserved populations, are disproportionately impacted by disasters and more than ever, federal and SLTTs must include people with disabilities in all facets of emergency management to ensure that they can participate in, and benefit from, programs and services during all phases of emergency management.[397]

Preparedness

Concurrent Extreme Weather Events Pose Unprecedented Challenges to Federal Agencies and SLTTs

Concurrent extreme weather events pose unprecedented challenges to federal and SLTT EMAs, reducing capacity, testing capabilities, straining resources, and complicating and potentially delaying response and recovery efforts, all which impact people with disabilities. Concurrent disasters of unparalleled nature are becoming more common, and climate change will likely continue to increase disaster activity in the coming years.[398] According to the DHS *National Preparedness Report* (2021), disasters are lasting longer, are increasingly complex, and are happening simultaneously. In 2020, the number of disasters that were either declared in, or still open at the end of the year made up almost 20 percent of all federally declared disasters since 1953.[399] The increased severity, duration, and occurrence rate of climate-related disasters puts immense strain

> *In 2020, the number of disasters that were either declared in, or still open at the end of the year made up almost 20 percent of all federally declared disasters since 1953.*

on emergency responders. It continues to cause delays in recovery efforts which can take weeks, months, or even decades.[400] At the height of the COVID-19 pandemic, the United States experienced an unprecedented number of disasters, including one of the most active wildfire seasons on record across the western U.S., a record of 30 named tropical storms and hurricanes, and severe weather, including hailstorms and flooding, across the Midwest.[401] According to the CDC, 47 million people were impacted by Hurricanes Harvey, Irma, and Maria, and of those, an estimated 12 million were people with disabilities. Communities and individuals are impacted differently by disasters, which often magnify existing social and economic trends that drive inequities in recovery. As the frequency of natural disasters continues to increase, so does the disproportionate risk exposure to, and consequences for, individuals and communities who are likely to be rendered most vulnerable. Several factors, including poverty, lack of access to transportation, and crowded housing may weaken an individual and community ability to prevent financial loss, injury, and fatalities in a disaster.[402] Concurrent disasters disproportionately impact people with disabilities. One of the myriad of reasons is the failure to provide reasonable accommodations in the form of supports and services during the recovery phase of a disaster.

Reducing Capacity

When concurrent disasters overwhelm a community's capacity to provide critical services, state and federal resources may be available to support local emergency response and recovery

> *In 2020, the COVID-19 pandemic, coupled with the active wildfire and hurricane seasons, taxed the capabilities of the emergency management community at all levels of the government.*

Concurrent disasters in Louisiana

In 2020, changing climate dynamics led to a confluence of disaster events that Louisiana local government leaders and emergency managers had not faced previously: a global pandemic and an "epidemic" of landfalling hurricanes during the 2020 season, including two hurricanes (Marco and Laura) passing over the same location within 36 hours with 150-mile-per-hour winds. The two storms in direct succession created difficulties in forecasting the magnitude of storm surge and wind speeds. The resulting initial reporting errors led to issues in immediate response and delayed long-term recovery efforts. The impacts were later compounded by Hurricane Zeta, which passed directly over a densely populated area.

efforts. When multiple large-scale incidents require simultaneous support, however, state and federal capability may be strained, reducing capacity to enable ongoing recovery efforts and respond to additional incidents. In 2020, the COVID-19 pandemic, coupled with the active wildfire and hurricane seasons, taxed the capabilities of the emergency management community at all levels of the government. FEMA's National Response Coordination Center (NRCC) was not intended to be staffed full-time. The NRCC has been activated for the longest period in FEMA's history—606 days since activating the Response

Operations Cell on March 5, 2020, as of November 1, 2021. It was activated to the highest operating level (Level 1) for 168 days, starting on March 19, 2020. Comparatively, during the 2017 hurricane season, for hurricanes Harvey, Irma, and Maria, and concurrent wildfires, the NRCC was activated at Level 1 for only 76 days (the previous record).[403]

Testing Capabilities

The concurrent disasters of 2020 overwhelmed federal, regional, and local governments and tested capabilities. In its *COVID-19 Initial Assessment Report* (2020), FEMA reported being unable to "anticipate SLTT requirements due to insufficient understanding of SLTT projected consequences and capabilities; regional pandemic plans either did not exist or did not account for jurisdiction-specific capabilities or deficiencies; and pandemic plans lacked the specificity and guidance to establish data collection and reporting mechanisms for effective decision-making for a national event. Thus, decision-makers initially did not have all the information they needed to make the most informed decisions about scarce resource allocation and prioritization of medical supplies."[404]

Straining Resources

Concurrent disasters strain resources including staffing resources. According to the *National Advisory Council Report to the FEMA Administrator* (2020), during disasters, SLTTs

> *"At the federal level, the National Response Coordination Center (NRCC) was not designed or intended to be staffed full-time and as a result FEMA was not prepared to staff the NRCC for a long-duration pandemic incident of national scale..."*

> *[D]uring disasters, SLTTs may not be aware of each other's resource capabilities, potentially resulting in duplicate, inadequate, or poorly distributed resources.*

may not be aware of each other's resource capabilities, potentially resulting in duplicate, inadequate, or poorly distributed resources. SLTTs may become overly dependent upon federal resources, which limits the ability of FEMA and other agencies to prepare for and respond to simultaneous extreme weather events. Just-in-time delivery supply chains are not designed to accommodate a large-scale disaster. Material and equipment may not be available in large enough quantities, and the transportation network may be compromised by the disaster, due to vulnerable interdependencies and cascading effects. Government stockpiles may be outdated or quickly exhausted by a large event or simultaneous events.[405] In addition, mutual aid agreements may be impacted by reducing the viability of those lending and receiving assistance. California's 2020 wildfire season stressed local capacity due to the timing and severity of the fires. The large wildfires occurred earlier than expected and impeded standard patterns of state-to-state mutual aid.[406]

FEMA's *Hurricane AAR* (2017)[407] states that during Hurricanes Harvey, Irma, and Maria, FEMA faced multiple challenges. The sequential and overlapping timing of the hurricanes caused staffing shortages and required FEMA to shift staff who were already deployed. There were

Response Coordination to Alabama Tornadoes (2011)

Following the devastating tornadoes in Alabama during the spring of 2011, various agencies, organizations, and volunteers united to locate recovery resources in the community and communicate information about those resources to the public. Two days after the tornadoes, they formed the Alabama Interagency Emergency Response Coordinating Committee. The committee was led by representatives from Independent Living Resources of Greater Birmingham, United Cerebral Palsy of Greater Birmingham, and the Alabama Governor's Office on Disability. The committee also included representatives from FEMA and the American Red Cross. A daily conference call was attended by as many as 60 individuals representing agencies that serve people with disabilities and chronic illnesses. Volunteers with disabilities scanned media and called agency contacts to obtain the latest information on disaster recovery resources. For instance, volunteers called local hospitals, clinics, faith-based organizations, and organizations representing clinical professionals to request help with crisis counseling. Recovery resource information was compiled in a database and information was disseminated in multiple formats.[408]

also logistic challenges that complicated efforts to deploy federal resources and personnel quickly. There was also limited preparedness by the U.S. Virgin Islands and Puerto Rico for a Category 5 hurricane; and incapacitation of local response because of loss of power and communications, which led FEMA to assume response functions that SLTTs would usually perform themselves.

FEMA's strategic plan states that the agency should coordinate with other federal agencies and SLTTs to foster a common understanding of how concurrent disasters are reshaping emergency management. Federal and state agencies should build better resources and tools to drive understanding of future risk and enhance agencies' ability to act.[409] In recent years, FEMA has called up its surge capacity force – Other Federal Agencies (OFAs) personnel supplementing FEMA personnel – much more frequently than in the past.[410] In 2019, a FEMA National Advisory Council convened to address the future vision of emergency management and FEMA, coordination between FEMA and nonfederal partners in an outlook of increasing disasters; ways to build capacity and response, recovery, preparedness, and mitigation at the local, tribal, territorial, and state levels and actions FEMA should take to ensure marginalized and vulnerable communities recover quickly. Over 20 recommendations were proffered to the FEMA Administrator in November 2020. Disability was mentioned only four times in the 52-page report.

The needs of people with disabilities are not well integrated in emergency management planning. People with disabilities face a unique set of barriers during disasters, and EMAs consistently fail to account for people with disabilities or coordinate with disability organizations and CBOs to mitigate the risk. Excluding people with disabilities in plan development can lead to increased injury and death during disasters. People with disabilities have unique needs that EMAs must plan for before a disaster occurs. Despite the documented importance of accounting for the unique needs of people with disabilities in planning for emergencies, many state and local emergency plans throughout the United States fail to do so.[411] NCD has released multiple reports on the outcomes of people with disabilities when emergency planning does not incorporate the needs of people with disabilities. The negative outcomes highlighted in NCD's prior reports will increase because of the increased prevalence of extreme weather events. During disasters, people with disabilities may have accessibility needs that must be met for evacuation and/or sheltering. For example, during disasters, people with disabilities may need emergency information in clear, plain, and actionable language. People who are Deaf or Hard of Hearing may need systems in place to receive messages about the need to evacuate or shelter in place. People with disabilities may need accessible transportation for those who use wheelchairs and need evacuation assistance; emergency shelters with accessible entrances and bathrooms, accessible temporary housing, life-sustaining medications, consumable medical supplies, durable medical equipment, or assistance in eating, dressing, or toileting for people with disabilities who require these things to survive in an emergency shelter, or in-home assistance or sheltering options for people with disabilities whose survival depends on electrically powered equipment during a shelter-in-place response, such as during a power outage.

Over 20 recommendations were proffered to the FEMA Administrator in November 2020. Disability was mentioned only four times in the 52-page report.

Federal, state, and local officials often fail to engage disability led organizations when planning for disasters. As a result, required resources and programs to assist people with disabilities during and after disasters is inadequate.[412]

Although there is some engagement and collaboration with people with disabilities, inclusive disaster management collaboration is not happening at scale. Many SLTTs do not conduct inclusive planning to meet the needs of people with disabilities and ensure access for these individuals across the full spectrum of its emergency programs, services, and activities.[413] During a federal, state, and local government convening, participants shared that it is often not until a disaster happens that federal, state and local agencies plan for people with disabilities. Relationships with the disability community should start well before disasters.

Convening participants shared that state and local government EMAs and State Homeland Security Advisory Council (HSAC) need to gain a better understanding of their communities. FEMA's 2022-2026 Strategic Plan[414] speaks to the goals of instilling equity as a foundation of emergency management and leading the whole community in climate resilience. EMAs and HSAC teams should engage people with disabilities during steady state conditions and plan for communications and accommodations before disasters. Federal and SLTT emergency managers should conduct outreach to determine the unique needs of people with disabilities, such as who will need assistance evacuating their homes and take a people-first, whole-of-community approach to emergency management by collaborating and planning with people with disabilities and organizations representing people with disabilities to create fully integrated emergency management policies, plans, and programs.

Underrepresentation in Emergency Management Leadership Roles

During convenings with stakeholder organizations and separately with federal, state, and local governments, participants said that people with disabilities are not represented in emergency management agencies in leadership and key decision-making roles nor on planning committees in relation to emergency management policy, planning, and program development While decision-makers come with a host of different qualifications and backgrounds, it is not possible to replace lived experience. One example a participant gave was of a state whose emergency management division lacks expertise on disability but has not hired disability coordinators, although encouraged to do so. Although a few states' EMAs may have disability integration roles or disability integration coordinators, this approach is not adopted nationwide. During disasters, because of the lack of preparedness for response and recovery, the state's Office for People with Disabilities representative (or ADA coordinator) has had to step into the emergency management role. Hiring people with lived experience would go a long way to improve emergency planning and safety.

Some Tribal Nations' emergency management plans are out of date and/or do not specifically include the needs of people with disabilities.

GAO identified that not all Tribal Nations have sufficient funding to develop emergency management departments, which can be a barrier to accessing federal resources.

Gap in Tribal Nations Emergency Management Plans

The status of tribal emergency management planning is generally unknown. Some Tribal Nations' emergency management plans are out of date and/or do not specifically include the needs of people with disabilities. There are 574 federally recognized Tribal Nations in the United States and its territories and they all have individual concerns and challenges.[415] Some Tribal Nations are well resourced and have robust emergency management programs (e.g., Seminole Tribe emergency management program), while other Tribal Nations do not have any plan in place. It is unclear which Tribal Nations have emergency management plans, how many of those plans are current, and how many specifically are inclusive of people with disabilities. One indicator of community planning is FEMA's Threat and Hazard Identification and Risk Assessment (THIRA) process. FEMA requires states, territories, Tribal Nations, and urban areas that receive federal preparedness grant funding to report their threats and hazards of greatest concern and set preparedness goals through the THIRA process. According to the National Preparedness Report (2021), many Tribal Nations have not completed a THIRA/Stakeholder Preparedness Review.[416]

In a GAO report (2021), GAO identified that not all Tribal Nations have sufficient funding to develop emergency management departments, which can be a barrier to accessing federal resources.[417] Remote Tribal Nations face specific challenges in recovery planning and receiving assistance after a disaster, such as a lack of access to transportation, which makes it difficult for Tribal Nation members to get to disaster recovery centers where they can learn about and apply for assistance. The November 2020 National Advisory Council report suggests that if low-resource communities continue to face barriers to accessing funding for preparedness and disaster resilience, there is a potential for a compounding effect.[418] The November 2020 National Advisory Council report included multiple recommendations to the FEMA Administrator. The recommendations NCD believes would improve the outcome of people with disabilities before, during, and after disasters has been incorporated through reference herein.[419]

A Tribal Nations representative told NCD that although they have emergency operations plans, the plans are not "disability specific." However, the representative also said that although people with disabilities may not be specifically identified in emergency management plans, the concept of taking care of seniors or people with special needs is inherent in Native American culture. The representative

[A]lthough people with disabilities may not be specifically identified in emergency management plans, the concept of taking care of seniors or people with special needs is inherent in Native American culture.

Tribal Nations are exceptionally underserved and underrepresented when it comes to emergency management planning.

said that funding should be set aside for Tribal Nations to plan for people with disabilities during disasters.

While the Bureau of Indian Affairs (BIA) works with Tribes, BIA does not provide guidance on emergency management plans or conduct emergency management exercises or response. Tribal Nations are responsible for emergency management planning for disaster events on Tribal lands. Tribal Nations have requested or applied for Federal Government funding for planning. They also coordinate with states and FEMA for funding after a disaster. Tribal Nations have access to FEMA's Tribal Homeland Security Grant Program (THSGP),[420] which provides $15 million for all 574 federally recognized tribes to enhance their ability to prevent, protect against, respond to and recover from potential terrorist attacks and other hazards.[421] The vast majority of tribes do not participate in the THSGP because the money is given to states to distribute and while some states share the grants with tribes, others may only give small amounts or none. Tribal Nations are exceptionally underserved and underrepresented when it comes to emergency management planning. Tribal Nations do not receive services and support needed to build resilience. FEMA and other federal agencies should dedicate more staff to help tribes plan for the next disaster.[422]

Response

Provide Accessible Communication During Disasters

Limited effective communications during extreme weather events means people with disabilities do not have equal access to information, which increases the risk to their safety and infringes on their civil rights protections.

Websites

People with disabilities need access to information.[423] Some weather and emergency management websites are not interoperable with AT such as screen readers used by people who are blind or have low vision. For example, there are parts of the National Hurricane Center (NHC) website that some people have difficulty accessing. NOAA's website is currently updating its site for 508 compliance.[424]

> Some weather and emergency management websites are not interoperable with AT such as screen readers used by people who are blind or have low vision.

ASL, Plain Language and Multiple Languages

The way information is transmitted and communicated in response to natural disasters is not accessible to all people with disabilities. During disasters, federal and SLTTs are required to provide accessible communications to people with disabilities in accordance with the ADA. However, information is not always provided in accessible, plain language or in different languages or in different forms and formats and via multiple methods or platforms. Federal and SLTT governments must ensure that public warning and alert systems are accessible to people who are Deaf, Hard of Hearing, blind, low vision, or have sensory and cognitive disabilities. Federal and SLTT governments must improve communications to ensure disaster information is accessible to people with disabilities and must integrate additional technologies and encourage industry innovation to meet the needs of all people. Community organizations also provide lifesaving and life-sustaining support related to advocacy and communication. It is critical that people with various communication disabilities, people who are Deaf or Hard of Hearing have different means of effective communication to stay safe and stay alive.

Traditional Alert and Warning Systems Do Not Reach Everyone

Many SLTTs continue to rely primarily on the traditional EAS that interrupt television or radio programming to provide disaster notifications. Also used are sirens, loudspeakers, and public address systems. More than half (55.1 percent) of U.S. consumers have "cut the cord" from cable and rely on streaming and web-based services rather than television.[425] EAS in addition, auditory alert systems are ineffective for individuals who are Deaf and Hard of Hearing and place the Deaf community at a high risk of being left behind during an emergency. Executive Order 13407 mandates that the Federal Government "include in the public alert and warning system the capability to alert and warn all Americans, including those with disabilities and those without an understanding of the English language." Although some EMAs are improving disaster warnings by sending warnings directly to cellphones.

FEMA's Common Alerting Protocol

Best Practice

FEMA developed the Common Alerting Protocol (CAP), a digital format for exchanging emergency alerts, that allows a consistent alert message to be disseminated simultaneously over multiple communications pathways, an Integrated Public Alert and Warning System (IPAWS) standard. FEMA's IPAWS office has identified emerging technologies and assistive technology products that support or provide direct alert and warning capabilities for people with disabilities, including braille readers, wall beacons, sign language interpretation, and video remote interpreting.[426]

It is unclear whether the warnings reach all people, including individuals without access to power sources or internet, people who do not have smart phones or social media accounts, or those who rely on alternative forms of communication. People with sensory and cognitive disabilities are specifically among those excluded from traditional media. FEMA's IPAWS is available for SLTTs to sign up and use to alert their communities. IPAWS send alerts through the EAS, Wireless Emergency Alerts (WEA), NOAA Weather Radio, and an Internet-Based Services and Unique Systems.[427]

During disasters people who are Deaf and Hard of Hearing may not have equal access to warning alerts.[428] Video Relay Service (VRS) is a good way to reach Deaf people who sign. For Deaf people who do not sign, and Hard of Hearing people who use residual hearing and augmented hearing for the phone, there are captioned relay services. However, many jurisdictions do not know who in their community requires these services and risk leaving these members of the community behind during disasters. SLTT EMAs must review their EASs to ensure they know the needs of their community and that emergency alerts are reaching everyone.

The National Oceanic and Atmospheric Administration (NOAA) supports a nationwide network of NOAA weather radio stations (NWR). The stations broadcast continuously and provide local weather service warnings, watches, forecasts, and hazard information. NOAA collaborates with the Federal Communication Commissions (FCC) Emergency Alert System. Federal, state, and local EMAs may also access NWR to broadcast warnings and post event information on natural, environmental and public safety events.[429]

A benefit of many of the All-Hazards Radios is the visual and vibrating alarm feature & text readouts to ensure that people who are deaf and hard of hearing receive timely alerts.[430]

Emergency Communications Need to Be Inclusive

Some SLTTs do not use ASL interpreters when broadcasting announcements or emergency weather alerts. SLTTs that do not have sign language interpreters as part of their emergency

Some states and counties do not provide qualified sign language when providing public information about emergencies and disasters (e.g., during press conferences) where vital information is shared about emergencies or disasters.

preparedness plan may unwittingly hire unqualified sign language interpreters; And local news stations also fail to use sign language interpreters for weather alerts. The national shortage of ASL interpreters[431] may play a small part as to availability, but SLTTs must ensure that effective communication, a.k.a. sign language interpreters are baked into their emergency management preparedness plans to ensure that the entire community has access to all emergency weather alerts and updates. Convening participants stated that Florida's governor and counties have a list of qualified interpreters. NCD recommends that all SLTTs should create a database of sign language interpreters and share that database with neighboring SLTTs to help mitigate the usage of unqualified or no sign language interpreters during broadcast announcements and press conferences.

Of additional concern, even if sign language interpretation is integrated into an SLTTs emergency preparedness plan, often times other languages are not provided. For example, in Puerto Rico, most Deaf individuals use Puerto Rican Sign Language (PRSL) not ASL. However, during Hurricane Maria (2017) in Puerto Rico, FEMA brought in ASL interpreters who were not able to effectively communicate with people who were Deaf or Hard-of-Hearing. There are also

> *[I]n Puerto Rico, most Deaf individuals use Puerto Rican Sign Language (PRSL) not ASL. However, during Hurricane Maria (2017) in Puerto Rico, FEMA brought in ASL interpreters who were not able to effectively communicate with people who were Deaf or Hard of Hearing.*

> *[S]ome jurisdictions do not have enough vehicles to evacuate everyone during disasters.*

many communities in the United States who use PRSL and other international sign languages.

The Need of Accessible Transportation for Evacuation is High

Jurisdictions face transportation resource gaps for emergency evacuations. The need for accessible transportation during disaster response and evacuation often surpasses the resources of the local community, forcing jurisdictions to be creative, dependent on volunteers, and with a patchwork approach to provide accessible transportation to safely evacuate people with disabilities during disasters. Accessible transportation is critical for evacuating during a disaster. During a disaster there may be individuals who do not have access to personal or public transportation. In rural and tribal communities, some people do not have consistent access to public transportation during blue sky days. During a convening of federal, state, and local government representatives, participants said that there are more people who need accessible transportation than many local jurisdictions can accommodate. In other words, some jurisdictions do not have enough vehicles to evacuate everyone during disasters. With limited resources and capabilities, local

jurisdictions have to be creative to determine where resources are available and how to work with other federal agencies and SLTTs to "braid" their services together. SLTTs often work with mutual aid disability organizations and other organizations to identify accessible transportation options. Community organizations who have wheelchair accessible vehicles and know where people with disabilities live in their community provide transportation support during disasters. However, such organizations have experienced difficulties attaining reimbursements, and when reimbursed, being sufficiently compensated to fully cover the costs of the services provided.

Some local jurisdictions set up agreements with outside jurisdictions to "surge" transportation supplies during disasters.

Although some local jurisdictions' emergency operation plans state that they will provide accessible transportation, not all have identified the resources to provide such accessible transportation. Where contracts, agreements, and memorandum of understanding (MOUs) with accessible transportation providers exist, not all contain the types of emergency services provisions one might need. For example, they may not explicitly require that the providers must be available 24 hours a day, 7 days a week, or that the transport is free for those being transported.

Paratransit Needs Workers and Improvement

Given the limited availability of paratransit services, and constraints on such services, SLTT

EMAs do not consistently incorporate paratransit agencies into emergency management plans. According to the U.S. DOT, paratransit systems provide transportation in areas served by fixed-route public transit systems, for people with disabilities who cannot use the fixed-route transit, in an equivalent manner to the users of the fixed-route transit. They only provide services within ¾ mile of fixed-route transit lines, and only during the hours of operation of those transit lines. With few exceptions, paratransit does not provide services outside of the specified service requirements. The level of service capacity is sized to meet the limited demand constrained by these service requirements. Seventy-five percent of paratransit across the U.S. is provided by contractors.

The contracts with the providers are constrained by these requirements and it is unclear whether the constraints can be waived during an emergency. During disasters, people with disabilities may need transportation to a safe location outside of the evacuation area. It is also unclear whether paratransit can provide services to evacuees outside of the ¾ mile constraints or outside of the normal operating hours.

Disability stakeholders recommended a review of how paratransit is used during an emergency. They said that paratransit needs funding and improvement and DOT should provide additional funding to contract paratransit workers. The DOT Coordinating Council on Access and Mobility (CCAM),[432] is a multiagency group with 11 federal agencies. The purpose of CCAM is to coordinate funding and provide expertise on human services transportation for three targeted populations: people with disabilities, older adults, and people of lower income[433]. CCAM-issued transportation coordination guidance aims to reduce overlap between the 130 CCAM programs across nine agencies that may fund human services transportation and incentivize collaboration by clarifying eligible reporting into the National Transit Database (NTD). CCAM reviews components of transportation including access to employment, access to health care, and access to community living. CCAM was not authorized by Congress to review the role of paratransit during a disaster.[434]

Public Law 117-58, the Infrastructure Investment and Jobs Act[435] promises to rebuild America's roads, bridges, and rails; expand access to clean drinking water; ensure every American has access to high-speed Internet; tackle the climate crisis; advance environmental justice; and invest in communities that have too often been left behind. The legislation includes $39 billion of new investment to modernize transit, in addition to continuing the existing transit programs for five years as part of surface transportation reauthorization. In total, the new investments and reauthorization provide $89.9 billion in guaranteed funding for public transit over the next five years—the largest federal investment in public transit in history. The legislation will expand public transit options across every state in the country; replace thousands of deficient transit vehicles (including buses) with clean, zero-emission vehicles. Since paratransit service must be provided within three quarters of a mile of a bus route or rail station and

> *The contracts with the [paratransit] providers are constrained by these requirements and it is unclear whether the constraints can be waived during an emergency.*

during the same hours of operation, passengers with disabilities who rely on paratransit will reap the benefits of the expanded service. A.

FEMA Regional Disability Integration Specialists (RDIS) Play a Critical Role

Before disasters, RDIS provide essential support to SLTT partners in their planning and preparedness efforts. During a disaster, FEMA RDIS and other FEMA Disability Integration Advisors are critical to adequately support people with disabilities. SLTT partners should engage and collaborate with FEMA RDIS, state-designated disability integration coordinators, and members of the disability community to better understand the needs of people with disabilities in disasters. RDIS may also be able to help identify resources for shelter, housing, and

other disaster services. Accessible resources, accommodations, and reasonable modifications ensure that housing plans and operations include people with disabilities. For example, survivors with disabilities must often stay near their established support systems, which restricts accessible housing options.[436]

Recovery

Community Organizations Have Difficulty Getting Compensated

Volunteer organizations play key roles in disaster response. They, and other disability-led nonprofit organizations, respond to disasters on the ground and play a pivotal role in emergency response to meet the needs of the disability community. However, many disability-led nonprofit organizations have reported difficulty in applying for reimbursement or do not know how to be reimbursed for their services. Some disability organizations reported that they have to prove value to receive reimbursements for the life-sustaining and lifesaving work they do. FEMA PA funding is available for other emergency protective measures (Category B), when authorized for a new incident, for work necessary to meet immediate threats to life and property.[437] Some community disability organizations provide services that should be covered under FEMA PA Category B funds but have reported reimbursement for services is onerous. The application process may be unclear or there may be a lack of understanding for how disability organizations can receive FEMA PA Category B Funding support. FEMA has convened a federal working group to create a document to assist SLTTs and nonprofits on federal disaster assistance for people with disabilities. The final document will simplify the different disaster relief funding programs available to SLTTs and nonprofit agencies. FEMA's strategic plan for 2022 to 2026 includes removing barriers to FEMA programs through a people-first approach and include community outreach to make sure that FEMA programs are accessible to the whole community, including people with disabilities. This is also required under Executive Order

[M]any disability-led nonprofit organizations have reported difficulty in applying for reimbursement or do not know how to be reimbursed for their services.

Disability lessons learned should be incorporated into overarching Emergency Management lessons learned, rather than a side issue.

13985, Advancing Racial Equity and Support for Underserved Communities Through the Federal Government, which requires community engagement.

Sharing Lessons Learned Will Enhance Emergency Planning

Following disasters, SLTT EMAs and other responders do not sufficiently share lessons learned among responders and with disability organizations and CBOs. While FEMA develops and publishes Disaster AARs, it is unclear how the agency shares the best practices and lessons learned with OFAs, SLTT EMAs, NGOs, and CBOs working with people with disabilities and other stakeholders. Efforts by the Partnership for Inclusive Disaster Strategies and the National State Level Disability Coordinators have resulted in the sharing and implementing of numerous best practices across the state coordinators and nonprofit partners. It is important to ensure the resources are made available to incorporate the lessons from CBOs working with people with disabilities. FEMA and SLTT EMAs should proactively share best practices and lessons learned with key stakeholders. Disability lessons learned should be incorporated into overarching Emergency Management lessons learned, rather than a side issue.

Recommendations

- FEMA and emergency managers at all levels of government should develop strategies to manage multiple concurrent disasters. Federal entities and SLTTs should adjust planning and response protocols developed for "standard" events to satisfy new response needs. These strategies could include a list of anticipated gaps, prioritizations for which gaps to invest in, and proactive planning to manage those gaps through other means when investments are not available. This recommendation works both for the overarching issues and the specifics around disability inclusion.

- FEMA should prioritize the implementation of the FEMA 2020 National Advisory Council recommendations (2020-01, 2020-02 2020-03 2020-05, 2020-06, 2020-07, 2020-08, 2020-09, 2020-11, 2020-12, 2020-13, 2020-15, 2020-18, 2020-19, 2020-20, 2020-21, 2020-22, 2020-25a).[438] Implementation should ensure that the needs of people with disabilities are integrated into the final policy, plans and services.

- FEMA should determine what steps are needed to address the nation's emergency management capability gaps across all levels of government and inform federal partners, such as the Office of Management and Budget, and Congress, about what level of resources would be necessary to address the known gaps.[439]

- SLTTs should put in place state HSAC teams. State HSAC teams meet regularly with and coordinate with public health, NGOs, and other area agencies to plan and better understand how to work together during response.

- FEMA should enhance its stakeholder engagement strategy to intentionally include people with disabilities and disability-led organizations in emergency management planning and exercises. FEMA should then encourage and share this strategy with SLTT EMAs.

- Federal agencies responsible for emergency preparedness, community resilience, and disaster-related services, programs, supports, or activities should engage with national, state, and local coalitions of disability-led organizations and stakeholders. These federal agencies include but are not limited to: DHS, FEMA, CRCL, HHS, ASPR, ACL, CDC, HUD, DOT, DOJ, DRS, ED, OSERS, DOL, the Office of Disability Employment (ODEP), DOD, Veterans Affairs, and U.S. Access Board.

(continued)

Recommendations: *continued*

- FEMA Administrator should communicate to Regional Administrators and RDIS a written plan for implementing its new disability integration staffing approach, consistent with the objectives established for disability integration. Such a plan should include an implementation timeline and details on staff responsibilities, which regions could use to evaluate staff performance.[440]

- All federal and SLTT EMA's should engage people with disabilities, disability organizations, and CBO's in disaster management planning. Ensuring that recommendations and concerns from people with disabilities are prioritized and incorporated into any disaster management plan.

- The federal and SLTT EMAs should hire people with disabilities to help inform emergency management policy and planning.

- Congress should authorize additional funding and FEMA should provide guidance to Tribal Nations to strengthen/establish an emergency preparedness plan inclusive of people with disabilities.

- Tribal Nations should form Disability Advisory Councils to liaise with federal, state, and local EMAs.

- State EMAs should work with Tribal Nations to develop emergency management plans that specifically include people with disabilities. FEMA, the Indian Health Service (IHS), and BIA should advise and support these efforts.

- Tribal Nations should put in place personal preparedness plans and create Communication, Maintaining Health, Independence, Support, and Transportation (CMIST)[441] response teams to prepare their communities. Examples of personal preparedness plans are found at https://www.ready.gov/disability.

- Congress should appropriate funds and require DOJ, in collaboration with OFAs to increase monitoring and enforcement of federal disability laws, which requires that emergency communications be fully accessible to people with disabilities.

- DOJ should review websites such as the National Hurricane Center (NHC) to ensure that it is 508 compliant and that all federal webpages are accessible to people who use screen readers or other assistive technology devices.

- FEMA, FCC, and SLTT partners should inform and encourage all SLTT emergency managers to utilize the full IPAWS alerting system, since IPAWs includes EAS, along with numerous other, more accessible, communications methods.

Recommendations: *continued*

- Federal and SLTT EMAs should activate alerts via IPAWS simultaneously when they activate alert sirens and public address systems, to ensure alerts are accessible for people who are Deaf and Hard of Hearing.

- NOAA, FEMA and/or HHS ASPR and/or ACL should promote the availability and distribution of adapted weather radios for people who are Deaf and Hard of Hearing though SLTT, Center for Independent Living (CIL), and NGO partners.

- NOAA, NCEI and the NWS should collaborate with FEMA, state EMAs, and public health agencies to share data and develop agile strategies to manage multiple concurrent disasters.

- FEMA, DOJ, and the FCC should review, consolidate, and enhance existing guidance for effective communications before, during, and after disasters, compiling these materials into a comprehensive guide that is distributed, and promoted, across federal, SLTT, and NGO partners.

- FEMA should hire multilingual sign language interpreters and contract for VRI services for all major sign languages, to meet the needs of specific communities such as Puerto Rican Spanish Sign Language in the U.S. and its territories.

- FEMA should better inform SLTT and OFA partners that providing sign language interpreters is required for any activities funded by FEMA. Also, FEMA should make its VRI services available to all SLTT and OFA partners to ensure that SLTT partners have access to such services, whenever needed to support stakeholders and disaster workers who are Deaf or Hard of Hearing.

- All SLTT partners should incorporate provisions for accessible transportation in their Emergency Operations Plans. Such incorporation should include analysis of the required demand for such services and appropriate contracts, agreements, and MOUs to support that demand in an emergency. Appropriate contracts should include emergency requirements such as ensuring 24/7 availability on short notice, with costs being charged to the jurisdiction, rather than passengers. Such agreements do not need to be commercial contracts. In fact, mutual aid agreements with other jurisdictions and/or NGOs may be the most effective and cost-effective options, provided that both partners are not impacted by the same disaster.

(continued)

Recommendations: *continued*

- FEMA should assess the resource needs of RDIS to ensure that they are fully resourced to meet the needs of their SLTT partners for planning and preparedness. FEMA should assess the resource needs to ensure that there is a sufficient cadre of trained disability integration advisors (DIA), including reservists to staff all disaster operations.

- FEMA should conduct outreach to, and training for, community organizations, to ensure that all interested community organizations know how to prepare for and apply for PA program Category B public assistance funds, when performing essential services.

- FEMA and SLTT partners should share their processes for capturing and disseminating disability-related lessons learned and best practices.

- The President should sign an executive order (EO) charging federal agencies to develop/update emergency management plans to anticipate an increase in extreme weather events, address the impact to agency functions, and provide guidance to the SLTTs. The EO should specifically address how each agency will integrate people with disabilities into the emergency management plan to ensure services for people with disabilities are available before, during, and after disaster.

"The Impacts of Extreme Weather Events on People with Disabilities." National Council on Disability, May 4, 2023. Accessed May 25, 2023. The full report can be accessed online at https://ncd.gov/publications/2023/impacts-extreme-weather-events-people-disabilities.

User Guide

Descriptive listings in *The Complete Resource Guide for People with Disabilities* are organized into 31 chapters, by either resource type or disability category type. You will find the following types of listings throughout the book:

- National Agencies & Associations
- State Agencies & Associations
- Camps & Exchanges Programs
- Manufacturers of Assistive Devices, Clothing, Computer Equipment & Supplies
- Print & Electronic Media
- Living Centers & Facilities
- Libraries & Research Centers
- Conferences & Trade Shows

Below is a sample listing illustrating the kind of information that is or might be included in an Association entry. Each numbered item of information is described in the paragraphs on the following page.

---

1 ➔ 1234
2 ➔ **Advocacy Center for Seniors with Disabilities**
3 ➔ 1762 South Major Drive
New Orleans, LA 98087

4 ➔ **800-000-0000**

5 ➔ **058-884-0709**

6 ➔ **Fax: 058-884-0568**

7 ➔ **TDD: 800-000-0001**

8 ➔ **email: info@sadvoc.com**

9 ➔ **www.sadvoc.com**

10 ➔ Barbara Pierce, Executive Director
Diane Watkins, Marketing Director
Robert Goldfarb, Administrative Assistant

11 ➔ The mission of the Center is to advance the dignity, equality, self-determination and choices of senior citizens with disabilities. It provides referrals, publishes information, including a monthly newsletter, offers workshops and consultation on legal, social, travel, and medical issues. The Center works with various local organizations to help seniors with disabilities stay active in their community.

12 ➔ Founded 1964

13 ➔ 18 pages

14 ➔ Monthly

User Key

1 ➤ **Record Number**: Entries are listed alphabetically within each category and numbered sequentially. The entry numbers, rather than page numbers, are used in the indexes to refer to listings.

2 ➤ **Organization Name**: Formal name of company or organization. Where organization names are completely capitalized, the listing will appear at the beginning of the alphabetized section. In the case of publications, the title of the publication will appear first, followed by the publisher.

3 ➤ **Address**: Location or permanent address of the organization.

4 ➤ **Toll Free Number**: This is listed when provided by the organization.

5 ➤ **Phone Number**: The listed phone number is usually for the main office of the organization, but may also be for the sales, marketing, or public relations office as provided by the organization.

6 ➤ **Fax Number**: This is listed when provided by the organization.

7 ➤ **TDD Number**: This is listed when provided. It refers to Telephone Device for the Deaf.

8 ➤ **E-Mail**: This is listed when provided by the organization and is generally the main office e-mail.

9 ➤ **Web Site**: This is also referred to as an URL address. These web sites are accessed through the Internet by typing *http://* before the URL address.

10 ➤ **Key Personnel**: Name and titles of department heads of the organization.

11 ➤ **Organization Description**: This paragraph contains a brief description of the organization and their services.

12 ➤ **Year Founded:** The year in which the organization was established or founded. If the organization has changed its name, the founding date is usually for the earliest name under which it was known.

13 ➤ **Number of Pages**: Number of pages if the listing is a publication.

14 ➤ **Frequency:** The frequency of the listing if it is a publication.

Glossary of Disability-Related Terms

Accessible: In the case of a facility, readily usable by a particular individual; in the case of a program or activity, presented or provided in such a way that a particular individual can participate, with or without auxiliary aids(s); in the case of electronic resources, accessible with or without the use of adaptive computer technology.

Access barrier: Any obstruction that prevents people with disabilities from using standard facilities, equipment and resources.

Accessible Web design: Creating World Wide Web pages according to universal design principles to eliminate or reduce barriers, including those that affect people with disabilities.

Accommodation: An adjustment to make a workstation, job, program, facility, or resource accessible to a person with a disability.

Adaptive technology: Hardware or software products that provide access to a computer that is otherwise inaccessible to an individual with a disability.

ALT attribute: HTML code that works in combination with graphical tags to provide alternative text for graphical elements.

Americans with Disabilities Act of 1990 (ADA): A comprehensive Federal law that prohibits discrimination on the basis of disability in employment, telecommunications, public services, public accommodations and services.

American Standard Code for Information Interchange (ASCII): Standard for unformatted text which enables transfer of data between platforms and computer systems.

Assistive technology: Technology used to assist a person with a disability (e.g., a handsplint or computer-related equipment).

Auxiliary aids and services: May include qualified interpreters or other effective methods of making aurally delivered materials available to individuals with hearing impairments; qualified readers, taped texts, or other effective methods of making visually delivered materials available to individuals with visual impairments; acquisition or modification of equipment or devices; and other similar services and actions.

Braille: A system of embossed characters formed by using a Braille cell, a combination of six dots consisting of two vertical columns of three dots each. Each simple Braille character is formed by one or more of these dots and occupies a full cell or space.

Browser: A program that runs on an Internet-connected computer and provides access to the World Wide Web. Web browsers may be text-only, such as Lynx, or graphical, such as Internet Explorer and Netscape Navigator.

Captioned film or videos: Transcription of the verbal portion of films or videos is displayed to make them accessible to people who have hearing impairments.

Closed Circuit TV Magnifier (CCTV): A camera used to magnify books or other materials on a monitor.

Cooperative education: Programs that work with students, faculty, staff, and employers to help students clarify career and academic goals, and expand classroom study by allowing students to participate in paid, practical work experiences.

Compensatory tools: Adaptive computing systems that allow people with disabilities to use computers to complete tasks that would be difficult without a computer (e.g., reading, writing, communicating, accessing information).

Disability: A physical or mental impairment that substantially limits one or more major life activities; a record of such an impairment; or being regarded as having such an impairment (Americans with Disabilities Act of 1990).

Discrimination: The act of treating a person differently in a negative manner based on factors other than individual merit.

Dymo Labeller: A device used to create raised print or Braille labels.

Electronic information: Any digital data for use with computers or computer networks, including disks, CD-ROMs, and World Wide Web resources.

Essential job functions: Those functions of a job or task which must be completed with or without an accommodation.

Facility: All or any portion of a physical complex, including buildings, structures, equipment, grounds, roads, and parking lots.

FM sound amplification system: An electronic amplification system consisting of three components: a microphone/transmitter, monaural FM receiver and a combination charger/carrying case. It provides wireless FM broadcasts from a speaker to a listener who has a hearing impairment.

Frame tags: A means of displaying Web pages. The browser reads the frame tags and produces an output that subdivides output within a browser into discrete windows.

Graphical user interface (GUI): Program interface that presents digital information and software programs in an image-based format as compared to a character-based format.

Hardware: Physical equipment related to computers.

Hearing impairment: Complete or partial loss of the ability to hear, caused by a variety of injuries or diseases, including congenital causes. Limitations, including difficulties in understanding language or other auditory messages and/or in production of understandable speech, are possible.

Independent study: A student works one-on-one with individual faculty members to develop projects for credit.

Informational interview: An activity where students meet with people working in careers to ask questions about their jobs and companies, allowing students to gain personal perspectives on career interests.

Input: Any method by which information is entered into a computer.

Internet: Computer network connecting governmental, educational, commercial, other organizations, and individual computer systems.

Internship: A time-limited, intensive learning experience outside of the typical classroom.

Interpreter: Professional person who assists a person who is deaf in communicating with hearing people.

Job shadowing: A short work-based learning experience where students visit businesses to observe one or more specific jobs to provide them with a realistic view of occupations in a variety of settings.

Keyboard emulation: Uses hardware and/or software in place of a standard keyboard.

Kinesthetic: Refers to touch-based feedback.

Large-print: Most ordinary print is six to ten points in height (about 1/16 to 1/8 of an inch). Large-print type is fourteen to eighteen points (about 1/8 to 1/4 of an inch) and sometimes larger.

Link: a connection between two electronic files or data items.

Lynx: A text-based World Wide Web browser.

Macro: A mini-program that, when run within an application, executes a series of predetermined keystrokes and commands to accomplish a specific task. Macros can automate tedious and often-repeated tasks or create special menus to speed data entry.

Mainstreaming: The inclusion of people with disabilities, with or without special accommodations, in programs, activities, and facilities with non-disabled people.

Major life activities: Functions such as caring for oneself, performing manual tasks, walking, seeing, hearing, speaking, breathing, learning, working, and participating in community activities (Americans with Disabilities Act of 1990).

Multimedia: A computer-based method of presenting information by using more than one medium of communication, such as text, graphics, and sound.

Optical Character Recognition (OCR): Machine recognition of printed or typed text. Using OCR software with a scanner, a printed page can be scanned and the characters converted into text in an electronic format.

Output: Any method of displaying or presenting electronic information to the user through a computer monitor or other device (e.g., speech synthesizer).

Portable Document Format (PDF): The file format for representing documents in a manner that is independent of the original application software, hardware and operating system used to create the documents.

Physical or mental impairment: Any physiological disorder or condition, cosmetic disfigurement, or anatomical loss affecting one or more, but not necessarily limited to, the following body systems: neurological; musculoskeletal; special sense organs; respiratory, including speech organs; cardiovascular; reproductive; digestive; genitourinary; hemic and lymphatic; skin and endocrine; or any mental or psychological disorder, such as mental retardation, organic brain syndrome, emotional or mental illness, and specific learning disabilities (Americans with Disabilities Act of 1990).

Plug-ins: Programs that work within a browser to alter, enhance, or extend the browser,s operation. They are often used for viewing video, animation or listening to audio files.

Proprietary software: Privately owned software based on trade secrets, privately developed technology, or specifications that the owner refuses to divulge, thus preventing others from duplicating a product or program unless an explicit license is purchased. The opposite of proprietary is open (publicly published and available for emulation by others).

Qualified individual with a disability: An individual with a disability who, with or without reasonable modification to rules, policies or practices, the removal of architectural, communication, or transportation barriers, or the provision of auxiliary aids and services, meets the essential eligibility requirements for the receipt of services or participation in programs or activities provided by a public entity (Americans with Disabilities Act of 1990).

Reader: Volunteer or employee of a blind or partially sighted individual who reads printed material in person or records to audiotape.

Relay service: A third-party service (usually free) that allows a hearing person without a TTY/TDD device to communicate over the telephone with a person who has a hearing impairment. The system also allows a person with a hearing impairment who has a TTY/TDD to communicate in voice through a third party, with a hearing person or business.

Screen reader: A text-to-speech system intended for use by computer users who are blind or have low vision that speaks the text content of a computer display using a speech synthesizer.

Service learning: A structured, volunteer work experience where students provide community service in non-paid, volunteer positions to give them opportunities to apply knowledge and skills learned in school while making a contribution to local communities.

Sign language: Manual communication commonly used by people who are deaf. Sign language is not universal; deaf people from different countries speak different sign languages. The gestures or symbols in sign language are organized in a linguistic way. Each individual gesture is called a sign. Each sign has three distinct parts: the hand shape, the position of the hands, and the movement of the hands. American Sign Language (ASL) is the most commonly used sign language in the United States.

Specific learning disability (SLD): A disorder of one or more of the basic psychological processes involved in understanding or in using language, spoken or written, which may manifest itself in difficulties listening, thinking, speaking, reading, writing, spelling, or doing mathematical calculations. Limitations may include hyperactivity, distractibility, emotional instability, visual and/or auditory perception difficulties and/or motor limitations, depending on the type(s) of learning disability.

Speech output system: A system that provides the user with a voice alternative to the text presented on the computer screen.

Speech impairment: A problem in communication and related areas, such as oral motor function, ranging from simple sound substitutions to the inability to understand or use language or use the oral-motor mechanism for functional speech and feeding. Some causes of speech and language disorders include hearing loss; neurological disorders; brain injury; mental retardation; drug abuse; physical impairments, such as cleft lip or palate; and vocal abuse or misuse.

Speech input system: A computer-based system that allows the operator to control the system using his/her voice.

Sticky keys: Enables a computer user to do multiple key combinations on a keyboard using only one finger at a time. The sticky keys function is usually used with the Ctrl, Alt, and Shift keys. Simultaneous keystrokes can be entered sequentially.

Telecommunications Device for the Deaf (TDD) or Teletypewriter (TTY): A device which enables someone who has a speech or hearing impairment to use a telephone when communicating with someone else who has a TDD/TTY. TDD/TTYs can be used with any telephone, and one needs only a basic typing ability to use them.

Trackball: A pointing device consisting of a ball housed in a socket containing sensors to detect the rotation of the ball " like an upside down mouse. The user rolls the ball with his thumb or the palm of his hand to move the pointer.

Traumatic Brain Injury (TBI): An open or closed head injury resulting in impairments in one or more areas, such as cognition; language; memory; attention; reasoning; abstract thinking; judgment; problem-solving; sensory, perceptual, and motor abilities; psychosocial behavior; physical functions; information processing; and speech. The term does not apply to brain injuries that are congenital or degenerative, or brain injuries induced by birth trauma.

Undue hardship: An action that requires significant difficulty or expense in relation to the size of the employer, the resources available, and the nature of the operation (Americans with Disabilities Act of 1990).

Universal design: Designing programs, services, tools, and facilities so that they are usable, without additional modification, by the widest range of users possible, taking into account a variety of abilities and disabilities.

Vocational Rehabilitation Act of 1973: An act prohibiting discrimination on the basis of disability which applies to any program that receives federal financial assistance. Section 504 of the act is aimed at making educational programs and facilities accessible to all people with disabilities. Section 508 of the act requires that electronic office equipment purchased through federal procurement meets disability access guidelines.

Voice input system: A computer-based system that allows the operator to control the system using his/her voice.

Vision impairments: A complete or partial loss of the ability to see, caused by a variety of injuries or diseases including congenital causes. Legal blindness is defined as visual acuity of 20/200 or less in the better eye with correcting lenses, on the widest diameter of the visual field subtending an angular distance no greater than 20 degrees.

World Wide Web (WWW, W3, or Web): Hypertext and multimedia gateway to the Internet.

DO-IT
University of Washington
Box 354842
Seattle, WA 98195-4842
doit@uw.edu
http://www.washington.edu/doit/
206-685-DOIT (3648) (voice/TTY)
888-972-DOIT (3648) (toll free voice/TTY)
206-221-4171 (FAX)
509-328-9331 (voice/TTY) Spokane

Director: Sheryl Burgstahler, Ph.D.

Arts & Entertainment

Resources for the Disabled

1 AbleArts
P.O. Box 831
Bear, DE 19701   302-368-7477
AbleArts is a nonprofit, community based performing arts organization composed of people with and without disabilities. Their mission is to entertain and inform the public of the abilities and talents possessed by individuals with disabilities. Performances include dance, poetry, comedy skits, and satire.

2 American Art Therapy Association (AATA)
4875 Eisenhower Ave.
Suite 240
Alexandria, VA 22304   703-548-5860
                                                    888-290-0878
                                              FAX: 703-783-8468
                                              info@arttherapy.org
                                                  arttherapy.org
Cynthia Woodruff, Executive Director
Barbara Florence, Director, Events & Education
Kat Michel, Senior Manager, Member Services
Not-for-profit organization dedicated to advancing the art therapy profession.

3 American Council of the Blind
1703 N Beauregard St
Suite 420
Alexandria, VA 22311   202-467-5081
                                                    800-424-8666
                                              FAX: 703-465-5085
                                                   info@acb.org
                                                   www.acb.org
Eric Bridges, Executive Director
Sharon Lovering, Editor
Tony Stephens, Director, Advocacy and Governmental Affairs
The American Council of the Blind (ACB) is an association working to increase the independence, security, and opportunity for all blind or visually impaired individuals. The Council primarily focuses on developing and maintaining policies to implement the services needed for the blind or visually impaired.

4 American Dance Therapy Association (ADTA)
230 Washington Ave.
Suite 101
Albany, NY 12203-3539   518-704-3636
                                              FAX: 518-463-8656
                                                  info@adta.org
                                                  www.adta.org
Michelle Lavoy, Manager, Operations
Lora Wilson, Continuing Education Administrator
Lauren Hoyt, Office Administrator
Supports the dance and movement therapy profession by promoting education, training, practice and research.

5 American Music Therapy Association (AMTA)
8455 Colesville Rd.
Suite 1000
Silver Spring, MD 20910   301-589-3300
                                              FAX: 301-589-5175
                                            info@musictherapy.org
                                            www.musictherapy.org
Adonia Calhoun Coates, Chief Executive Officer
Jane P. Creagan, Director, Professional Programs
Angie K. Elkins, Director, Membership Services & Information Systems
AMTA's purpose is the progressive development of the therapeutic use of music in rehabilitation, special education and community settings. Predecessors to the American Music Therapy Association included the National Association for Music Therapy founded in 1950 and the American Association for Music Therapy founded in 1971. AMTA supports the music therapy profession through the advancement of education, training, professional standards, credentialing, and research.

6 Arena Stage
The Mead Center for American Theater
1101 Sixth St. SW
Washington, DC 20024   202-554-9066
                                              FAX: 202-488-4056
                                              TTY:202-484-0247
                                             info@arenastage.org
                                                 arenastage.org
Edgar Dobie, Executive Director
Molly Smith, Artistic Director
Joseph Berardelli, CFO
Arena Stage has played a pioneering role in providing access to all productions for people with disabilities. Access services and programs include wheelchair accessible seating; infrared assistive listening devices; Braille, large print, audio description and sign interpretation at designated performances.

7 Art Therapy SourceBook
McGraw-Hill Company
2 Penn Plaza
New York, NY 10121-101   212-904-2000
                                         www.mhhe.com/hper/physed
Cathy Malchiodi, Author
An overview of the uses of art as a mentally therapeutic tool.
$18.00
272 pages
ISBN 1-565658-84-1

8 Art and Disabilities
Brookline Books
8 Trumbull Rd
Suite B-001
Northampton, MA 01060   413-584-0184
                                                    800-666-2665
                                              FAX: 413-584-6184
                                            brbooks@yahoo.com
                                          www.brooklinebooks.com
Florence Ludins-Katz, Author
A step-by-step guide to establishing creative arts centers for people with disabilities. Includes philosophy and making creative arts centers happen.

9 Art and Healing: Using Expressive Art to Heal Your Body, Mind, and Soul
Three Rivers Press/Crown Publishing-Random House
1745 Broadway
New York, NY 10019   212-782-9000
                                     crownpublicity@randomhouse.com
                                    www.randomhouse.com/crown/trp.html
Barbara Ganim, Author
Markus Dohle, Chairman & CEO
Melanie Fallon-Houska, Dir., Corporate Contributions
The author believes creating a visual image through any medium can produce physical and emotional benefits for both the creator as well as those who view it. *$17.00*
256 pages
ISBN 0-609803-16-6

10 Art for All the Children: Approaches to Art Therapy for Children with Disabilities
Charles C. Thomas
2600 S First St
Springfield, IL 62704-4730   217-789-8980
                                                    800-258-8980
                                              FAX: 217-789-9130
                                            books@ccthomas.com
                                              www.ccthomas.com
Frances E Anderson, Author
Sharon Moorman, Editorial Assistant
This second edition is for art therapists in training and for in-service professionals in art therapy, art education and special education who have children with disabilities as a part of their case/class load. *$56.95*
398 pages Paperback
ISBN 0-398060-07-7

11   Arts Unbound
542/544 Freeman Street
Orange, NJ 07050   973-675-2787
                                         FAX: 973-678-4408
                                         www.artsunbound.org
Margaret Mikkelsen, Executive Director
Catherine Lazen, Founder and Board Chair
Alan Hirsh, Executive Vice President
Arts Unbound is a nonprofit organization dedicated to the artistic
achievement of youth, adults, and senior citizens with disabili-
ties.

**12   Association of Mouth and Foot Painting Artists
(AMPFA)**
2070 Peachtree Court
Suite 101
Atlanta, GA 30341   770-986-7764
                                         877-637- 872
                                         FAX: 770-986-8563
                                         mfpausa@bellsouth.net
                                         www.mfpausa.com
Erich Stegmann, Founder
The AMPF is an international, for-profit association wholly
owned and run by disabled artists to help them meet their financial needs. Members paint with brushes held in their mouths or
feet as a result of a disability sustained at birth or through an accident or illness that prohibits them from using their hands.

13   Awakenings Project, The
PO Box 177
Wheaton, IL 60187   www.awakeningsproject.org
Robert Lundin, Co-Director
Irene O'Neill, President and Co-Director
Mary Lou Lowry, Secretary
The Awakenings Project is an organization whose mission is to
assist those artists with psychiatric illnesses in developing their
talent and finding an outlet for their creative abilities through art
in all forms.

14   Brookline Books
8 Trumbull Rd
Suite B-001
Northampton, MA 01060   413-584-0184
                                         800-666-2665
                                         FAX: 413-584-6184
                                         brbooks@yahoo.com
                                         www.brooklinebooks.com
Brookline Books has been publishing reader-friendly and informative education literature for more than 20 years, with a mission
to reach both a specialized and non-specialized audience. They
have a strong list of books for people with disabilities, including
general information on advocacy, assistive technology, parent involvement, professional resources, early childhood intervention,
as well as on specific disabilities.

**15   Clinical Applications of Music Therapy in
Developmental Disability, Pediatrics and Neurolog**
Taylor & Francis
400 Market Street
Suite 400
Philadelphia, PA 19106-4738   215-922-1161
                                         866-416-1078
                                         FAX: 215-922-1474
                                         hello.usa@jkp.com
                                         www.jkp.com
Tony Wigram, Editor
Jessica Kingsley, Chairman, Managing Director
Jemima Kingsley, Director
More and more, music therapy is being practiced as an interven-
tion in medical and special educational settings. This book describes and explains the planning and evaluation of music
therapy intervention and how it can be used for assessing complex organic and emotional disabilities. *$34.95*
312 pages
ISBN 1-853027-34-0

16   Contemporary Art Therapy with Adolescents
Taylor & Francis
400 Market Street
Suite 400
Philadelphia, PA 19106-4738   215-922-1161
                                         866-416-1078
                                         FAX: 215-922-1474
                                         hello.usa@jkp.com
                                         www.jkp.com
Shirley Riley, Author
Jessica Kingsley, Chairman, Managing Director
Jemima Kingsley, Director
Reviews contemporary theories on adolescent development and
therapy and offers solutions to the treatment of young people.
$26.95
285 pages
ISBN 1-853026-37-9

17   Creative Arts Resources Catalog
MMB Music
9051 Watson Road
Ste 161
St. Louis, MO 63126   314-531-9635
                                         FAX: 314-531-8384
                                         info@mmbmusic.com
                                         www.mmbmusic.com
Norm Goldberg, Founder & Chair
Publisher and distributor of creative arts therapy materials in the
areas of music, dance, art, drama, and poetry. Free catalog con-
tains hundreds of books, recordings, and videos.

18   Creative Growth Art Center
355 - 24th St
Oakland, CA 94612   510-836-2340
                                         FAX: 510-836-0769
                                         info@creativegrowth.org
                                         www.creativegrowth.org
Becki Couch-Alvarado, Executive Director
Tom Di Maria, Director
Jennifer Strate O'Neal, Partnerships & Communications Manager
Creative Growth Art Center serves adult artists with developmen-
tal, mental and physical disabilities, providing a professional stu-
dio environment for artistic development, gallery exhibition and
representation and a social atmosphere among peers.

19   Creativity Explored
3245 16th St.
San Francisco, CA 94103   415-863-2108
                                         FAX: 415-863-1655
                                         info@creativityexplored.org
                                         www.creativityexplored.org
Linda Johnson, Executive Director
Creativity Explored is a nonprofit visual arts center giving artists
with developmental disabilities the means to create and share
their work with the community, celebrating the power of art to
change lives.

20   Dancing from the Inside Out
Fanlight Productions
c/o Icarus Films
32 Court Street, 21st Floor
Brooklyn, NY 11201   718-488-8900
                                         800-876-1710
                                         FAX: 718-488-8642
                                         info@fanlight.com
                                         www.fanlight.com
Ben Achtenberg, Founder
This eloquent video looks at the lives and work of three talented
dancers who dance professionally with the acclaimed AXIS
Dance Troupe, which includes both disabled and non-disabled
dancers. They discuss the process they went through in adapting
to their disability and how they came to re-discover physical expression through dance.

21 Deaf West Theatre
5114 Lankershim Blvd.
Los Angeles, CA 91601   818-762-2998
                                    FAX: 818-762-2981
                                    info@deafwest.org
                                        deafwest.org

Ed Waterstreet, Founding Artistic Director
David Kurs, Artistic Director
Mark Freund, President
Deaf West Theatre, Inc., was founded in 1991 to directly improve and enrich the cultural lives of the 1.2 million deaf and hard-of-hearing individuals who live in the Los Angeles area. DWT provides exposure and access to professional theatre, filling a void for deaf artists and audiences.

22 Disability and Social Performance: Using Drama to Achieve Successful Acts
Brookline Books
8 Trumbull Rd
Suite B-001
Northampton, MA 01060   413-584-0184
                                        800-666-2665
                                    FAX: 413-584-6184
                                    brbooks@yahoo.com
                                    www.brooklinebooks.com

Bernie Warren, Author
This book makes a major contribution to the understanding of disability, people with disabilities and the creative power they possess which can be unleashed through performance. The books name is Disability and Social Performance: Using Drama to Achieve Successful Acts of Being. *$17.95*

23 Expressive Arts for the Very Disabled and Handicapped of All Ages
Charles C. Thomas
2600 S First St
Springfield, IL 62704-4730   217-789-8980
                                        800-258-8980
                                    FAX: 217-789-9130
                                    books@ccthomas.com
                                    www.ccthomas.com

Marilyn Wannamaker, Co-Author
Jane G. Cohen, Co-Author
The ideas presented are not only designed to hold the interest of the children and adults, but to meet the needs of professionals and volunteers working with the disabled artists. All crafts are rated on a sliding scale, are of a low difficulty rating, use inexpensive and safe materials, and include explicit instructions. *$49.95*
236 pages Spiral-Paper 1996
ISBN 0-398067-04-5

24 Fanlight Productions
c/o Icarus Films
32 Court Street, 21st Floor
Brooklyn, NY 11201   718-488-8900
                                        800-876-1710
                                    FAX: 718-488-8642
                                    info@fanlight.com
                                    www.fanlight.com

Ben Achtenberg, Founder
Fanlight Productions is a leading distributor of innovative film and video works on the social issues of our time, with a special focus on healthcare, mental health, professional ethics, aging and gerontology, disabilities, the workplace, and gender and family issues. Select titles include Acting Blind, Autism: A World Apart, Dancing from the Inside Out, and Able to Laugh.

25 Fountain House Gallery
702 Ninth Ave at 48th St
New York, NY 10019   212-262-2756
                                    fountaingallerynyc.com

Ariel Wilmott, Director
Camille Tibaldeo, Communications Director
Fountain House Gallery provides an environment for artists living and working with mental illness to pursue their personal visions and to challenge the stigma that surrounds mental illness.

26 Friends In Art (FIA)
4317 Vermont Court
Columbia, MO 65203   573-445-5564
                                    www.friendsinart.com

Peter Altschul, President
Lynn Hedl, Vice President
Don Horn, Corresponding Secretary
Friends in Art is a national organization for blind, visually impaired, and deaf-blind artists, musicians and writers, and art enthusiasts. The organization is dedicated to enhancing the skills and broadening the opportunities of the individuals involved with the organization.

27 Future Horizons
721 West Abram Street
Arlington, TX 76013-6995   817-277-0727
                                        800-489-0727
                                    FAX: 817-277-2270
                                    www.fhautism.com

R. Wayne Gilpin, President
Jennifer Gilpin, VP, Foreign Translations
Kelly Gilpin, Editorial Dir.
Founded in 1996, Future Horizons is devoted to supporting and fostering works and programs for those who live and work with autism and asperger's syndrome.

28 Guide to the Selection of Musical Instruments
MMB Music
9051 Watson Road
Ste 161
St. Louis, MO 63126   314-531-9635
                                        800-543-3771
                                    FAX: 314-531-8384
                                    info@mmbmusic.com
                                    www.mmbmusic.com

Norm Goldberg, Founder & Chair
A marvelous resource book to aid therapists teaching those who are disabled to play musical instruments. *$7.75*

29 In-Definite Arts Society
8038 Fairmount Drive SE
Calgary, AB T2H0Y   403-253-3174
                                    FAX: 403-255-2234
                                    www.indefinitearts.com

Darlene Murphy, Executive Director
Dijana Andric, Client Services Manager
Peter Kelsch, Accountant
Promotes opportunities for people with developmental disabilities to express themselves and to grow and develop through their involvement in art.

30 Infinity Dance Theater
220 W 93rd St
New York, NY 10025   212-877-3490
                                    info@infinitydance.com
                                        infinitydance.com

Kitty Lunn, RDE, Founder/Artistic Director
Michael A. Fitch, Executive Director
Infinity Dance Theater is a non-traditional dance company committed to expanding the boundaries of dance by featuring dancers with and without disabilities. The company aims to inspire people with and without disabilities, encourage their artistic and other professional aspirations, and empower them through the organization's educational and performance programs.

31 Instrumental Music for Dyslexics: A Teaching Handbook
Wiley & Sons
111 River Street
Hoboken, NJ 07030-5774   201-748-6000
                                    FAX: 201-748-6088
                                    info@wiley.com
                                    www.wiley.com

Sheila Oglethorpe, Author
Stephen M. Smith, President and CEO
Ellis E. Cousens, Executive Vice President, Chief Operations Officer
Describes dyslexia in layman's terms and explains how the various problems that a dyslexic may have can affect all aspects of learning to play a musical instrument. It alerts the music teacher with a problem pupil to the possibilities of that pupil having some form of dyslexia. It offers suggestions as to how to teach dyslex-

ics, with particular reference to piano teaching, and it suggests ways in which the music teacher may contribute to the welfare of a dyslexic pupil. *$34.95*
200 pages
ISBN 1-861562-91-8

32 Interact Center for the Visual and Performing Arts
Interact Center
1860 Minnehaha Ave W
St. Paul, MN 55401
651-209-3575
FAX: 651-209-3579
info@interactcenter.com
interactcenter.com

Jeanne Calvit, Artistic & Executive Director
Shannon Forney, Managing Director
Beth Bowman, Director, Advancement
Creates art in a spirit of radical inclusion; Inspires artists and audiences to explore the full spectrum of human potential; Transforms lives by expanding ideas of what is possible.

33 Kaleidoscope: Exploring the Experience of Disability through Literature & the Fine Arts
United Disability Services
701 South Main St
Akron, OH 44311-1019
330-762-9755
FAX: 330-762-0912
kaleidoscope@udsakron.org
www.udsakron.org/services/kaleidoscope
Howard Taylor, President & CEO
Lisa Armstrong, Director of Community Relations & Managing Editor
Gail Willmott, Editor in Chief
Kaleidoscope is a magazine published by United Disability Services. Kaleidoscope challenges and transcends stereotypical, patronizing and sentimental attitudes about disability, looking at the experience of actually living with a disability from a more personal/individual perspective rather than a clinical, sociological or rehabilitative point of view. Included are a variety of articles, fiction, art and poetry relating to issues of disability, literature and the fine arts. *$10.00*
64 pages BiAnnually

34 Keshet Dance and Center for the Arts
4121 Cutler Ave NE
Albuquerque, NM 87110
505-224-9808
info@keshetarts.org
keshetarts.org

Shira Greenberg, Artistic Director
Adrian Moore Trask, Director of Business Advancement
Emily Dunkin, Events Director
Keshet offers youth and adult classes and workshops for individuals with varying levels of physical disabilities and dance experience. Within the Adaptive Dance programming, Keshet pairs dancers with disabilities with able-bodied dancers, which often include siblings, parents, and peers, to create professional-quality dance works.

35 Learning Disabilities Sourcebook, 3rd Ed.
Omnigraphics
615 Griswold Street
Suite 520
Detroit, MI 48226
610-461-3548
800-234-1340
FAX: 800-875-1340
contact@omnigraphics.com
www.omnigraphics.com
Peter Ruffner, Co-Founder
Fred Ruffner, Co-Founder
Learning Disabilities Sourcebook, Third Edition provides updated information about specific learning disabilities and other conditions that make learning difficult. These include dyscalculia, dysgraphia, dyslexia, auditory and visual processing, communication disorders, autism spectrum disorders, attention deficit and hyperactivity disorder, hearing and visual impairments, and brain injury. *$84.00*
600 pages Hard cover
ISBN 0-780810-39-6

36 Manual of Sequential Art Activities for Classified Children and Adolescents
Charles C. Thomas
2600 S First St
Springfield, IL 62704-4730
217-789-8980
800-258-8980
FAX: 217-789-9130
books@ccthomas.com
www.ccthomas.com

Rocco A L Fugaro, Author
Offers information to the special education professional on art therapy and management. *$41.95*
246 pages Softcover
ISBN 0-39805 -85-6

37 Mozart Effect: Tapping the Power of Music to Heal the Body, Strengthen the Mind
Harper Collins Publishers
10 E 53rd St
New York, NY 10022-5244
212-207-7000
www.harpercollins.com

Don Campbell, Author
Brian Murray, President and CEO
Michael Morrison, President and Publisher, U.S. General Books and Canada
Offers dramatic accounts of how doctors, shamans, musicians, and others use music to deal with everything from anxiety, cancer, and chronic pain, to dyslexia and mental illness. *$14.95*
352 pages
ISBN 0-060937-20-3

38 Music Therapy
Future Horizons, Inc.
721 West Abram St
Arlington, TX 76013-6995
817-277-0727
800-489-0727
FAX: 817-277-2270
www.fhautism.com

Betsey King Brunk, Author
R. Wayne Gilpin, President
Jennifer Gilpin, VP, Foreign Translations
Music therapy is the use of music to address non-musical goals. Parents and professionals are finding that music can break down barriers for children with autism in areas such as cognition, socialization, and communication. *$19.95*
123 pages
ISBN 1-885477-53-8

39 Music Therapy and Leisure for Persons with Disabilities
Sagamore Publishing
1807 N Federal Drive
Urbana, IL 61801
217-359-5940
800-327-5557
FAX: 217-359-5975
books@sagamorepub.com
www.sagamorepub.com

Alicia L. Barksdale, Author
Joseph J. Bannon, Sr., Ph.D., Publisher & CEO
Peter L. Bannon, MBA, President
Explores the use of musical therapy in order to enhance the development of independent leisure skills with a variety of special populations. Suggestions are provided for alternative avenues through musical experiences enabling individuals to achieve their greatest potential for independence and a high quality of life. *$19.95*
ISBN 1-571675-11-6

40 Music Therapy for the Developmentally Disabled
Sage Publications
2455 Teller Road
Thousand Oaks, CA 91320
805-499-9774
800-818-7243
FAX: 800-583-2665
info@sagepub.com
www.sagepub.com

S. Venkatesan, Author
Included are practical guidelines, case samples and step-by-step instructions that enable a music therapist to bring about dramatic

improvements in developmentally disabled adults and children.
$40.00
269 pages Hardcover
ISBN 0-890791-90-2

41 Music Therapy in Dementia Care
Jessica Kingsley Publishers
400 Market Street
Suite 400
Philadelphia, PA 19106-4738   215-922-1161
866-416-1078
FAX: 215-922-1474
hello.usa@jkp.com
www.jkp.com

David Aldridge, Editor
Jessica Kingsley, Chairman, Managing Director
Jemima Kingsley, Director
A comprehensive look at music therapy as a means of improving memory, health, and identity in those suffering from dementia, particularly Alzheimer's. For music therapists and those involved in psychogeriatry. *$29.95*
256 pages
ISBN 1-853027-76-6

42 Music Therapy, Sensory Integration and the Autistic Child
Jessica Kingsley Publishers
400 Market Street
Suite 400
Philadelphia, PA 19106-4738   215-922-1161
866-416-1078
FAX: 215-922-1474
hello.usa@jkp.com
www.jkp.com

Dorita S. Berger, Author
Jessica Kingsley, Chairman, Managing Director
Jemima Kingsley, Director
Examines the human physiologic function, the brain, information processing, functional adaption, and how that might be affected by music interventions in persons with sensory integration difficulties. *$23.95*
256 pages
ISBN 1-843107-00-7

43 Music and Dyslexia: A Positive Approach
Wiley & Sons
111 River Street
Hoboken, NJ 07030-5774   201-748-6000
FAX: 201-748-6088
info@wiley.com
www.wiley.com

John Westcombe, Editor
Stephen M. Smith, President and CEO
Ellis E. Cousens, Executive Vice President, Chief Operations Officer
This book shows how some people who have Dyslexia can be gifted musicians. The main point this books makes is that Dyslexic musicians can succeed provided only that they are given sufficient encouragement and understanding. *$34.95*
200 pages
ISBN 1-861562-05-5

44 Music for the Hearing Impaired
MMB Music
9051 Watson Road
Ste 161
St. Louis, MO 63126   314-531-9635
800-543-3771
FAX: 314-531-8384
info@mmbmusic.com
www.mmbmusic.com
Norm Goldberg, Founder & Chair
A resource manual and curriculum guide. It is the product of a four-year developmental music program, placing emphasis on the needs of those with severe and profound losses. *$29.95*

45 Music: Physician for Times to Come
Quest Books
P.O.Box 270
Wheaton, IL 60187-270   630-665-0130
800-669-9425
FAX: 630-665-8791
submissions@questbooks.net
www.questbooks.net

Don Campbell, Author
A resource guide for various types of music and their therapeutic outcome.
365 pages
ISBN 0-835607-88-7

46 NIAD Art Center (Nurturing Independence through Artistic Development)
551 23rd St.
Richmond, CA 94804-1626   510-620-0290
FAX: 510-620-0326
admin@niadart.org
www.niadart.org

Deborah Dyer, Executive Director
NIAD Art Center promotes creativity, independence, dignity, and community integration for people with developmental and other disabilities. The visual arts studio supports artists with disabilities by providing materials, space to make art and facilitators to teach skills in drawing, painting, printmaking, ceramics, fiber arts and mixed media. The work that they make is exhibited in the Richmond gallery as well as in other galleries, on-line and other exhibition spaces.

47 National Arts and Disability Center (NADC)
Tarjan Center at UCLA
760 Westwood Plaza
Los Angeles, CA 90095-1759   310-825-5054
FAX: 310-794-1143
bstoffmacher@mednet.ucla.edu
www.semel.ucla.edu/nadc

Olivia Raynor, Director
Beth Stoffmacher, Center Coordinator
NADC has a database and website advocating for access to and participation in the arts by people with disabilities.

48 National Association for Drama Therapy
1450 Western Avenue
Suite 101
Albany, NY 12203   571-223-6440
888-416-7167
FAX: 518-463-8656
office@nadta.org
www.nadt.org

Nadya Trytan, MA, RDT/BCT, President
Jeremy Segall, MA, RDT, LCAT, Vice President
Jason Butler, RDT/BCT, LCAT, President-Elect
The National Association for Drama Therapy (NADT) was incorporated in 1979 to establish and uphold rigorous standards of professional competence for drama therapists. The NADT promotes drama therapy through information and advocacy.

49 National Endowment for the Arts: Office for AccessAbility
1100 Pennsylvania Ave NW
Washington, DC 20506-0001   202-682-5034
FAX: 202-682-5666
TTY:202-682-5496
webmgr@arts.gov
www.arts.gov/

Jane Chu, Chairman
Beth Bienvenu, Accessibility Director
Wendy Clark, Director of Museums, Visual Arts, and Indemnity
The National Endowment for the Arts Office for AccessAbility is the advocacy-technical assistance arm of the Arts Endowment to make the arts accessible for people with disabilities, older adults, veterans, and people living in institutions.

50   **National Library Service for the Blind and Physically Handicapped (NLS)**
1291 Taylor St NW
Washington, DC 20011   202-707-5100
                                          800-424-8567
                                      FAX: 202-707-0712
                                          nls@loc.gov
                                          www.loc.gov/nls
Administers a national library service that provides Braille and recorded books and magazines on free loan to anyone who cannot read standard print because of visual or physical disabilities.
Annual

51   **National Theatre Workshop of the Handicapped (NTWH)**
535 Greenwich Street
New York, NY 10013-1004   212-206-7789
                                      FAX: 212-206-0200
                                          www.ntwh.org

Jason Matthews, Director of Admissions
Rick Curry, President & CEO
John Spalla, General Manager
A non-profit organization that provides individuals within the disabled community with the communication skills and the artistic discipline necessary to pursue a life in professional theatre.

52   **National Theatre of the Deaf**
139 N Main St
West Hartford, CT 06107-1264   860-236-4193
                                      FAX: 860-574-9107
                                          Info@NTD.org
                                          www.ntd.org
Betty Beekman, Executive Director
William C. Martin, Marketing/PR Director
George Ghista, Accountant
The mission of the National Theatre of the Deaf is to produce theatrically challenging work of the highest quality, drawing from as wide a range of the world's literature as possible and to perform these original works in a style that links American Sign Language with the spoken word.

53   **New Music Therapist's Handbook, 2nd Ed. Berklee School of Music**
Berklee Press Publications
1140 Boylston Street
Boston, MA 02215   617-747-2146
                                          866-237-5533
                                      www.berkleepress.com
Suzanne B. Hanser, Author
Dr. Hanser's well-respected Music Therapist's Handbook has been revised and thoroughly updated to reflect the latest developments in the field of music therapy. *$29.95*
256 pages
ISBN 0-634006-45-2

54   **No Limits**
9801 Washington Blvd
2nd Fl
Culver City, CA 90232   310-280-0878
                                      FAX: 310-280-0872
                           michelle@nolimitsfordeafchildren.org
                                nolimitsfordeafchildren.org
Michelle Christie, Founder & Executive Director
Juliana Scott, Director, Operations & Development
The mission of No Limits is to meet the auditory, speech and language needs of deaf children and enhance their confidence through the theatrical arts and individual therapy as well as provide family support and community awareness on the needs and talents of deaf children who are learning to speak.

55   **Non-Traditional Casting Project**
Ste 1600
1560 Broadway
New York, NY 10036-1518   212-730-4750
                                      FAX: 212-730-4820
                                      TTY:212-730-4913
                                          www.ntcp.org/
Nancy Kim, Manager
The Non-Traditional Casting Project (NTCP) is a not-for-profit advocacy organization whose purpose is to address and seek solu-

tions to the problems of racism and exclusion in theatre, film and television. NTCP's principal concerns are those of artists of color, female artists, Deaf and hard of hearing artists, and artists with disabilities.

56   **Nuvisions For Disabled Artists, Inc.**
C/O Rose Marcus
1319 Magee Street
Philadelphia, PA 19111
Kaye E Schonbach, Executive Director
Nuvisions was established to enable physically challenged artists to pursue professional and semi-professional artistic opportunities. Nuvisions supports these artists by sponsoring accessible exhibitions, special projects and educational opportunities in Southeastern Pennsylvania and Southern New Jersey.

57   **Open Circle Theatre**
102-500 King Farm Blvd
Rockville, MD 20850   240-683-8934
                                   info@opencircletheatre.org
                                       opencircletheatre.org
Suzanne Richard, Artistic Director
Ian Armstrong, Executive Producer
Open Circle Theatre is a professional theatre dedicated to producing productions that integrate the considerable talents of artists with disabilities. OCT was formed by a group of people with and without disabilities, who possess professional theater experience, love of the theater, and a commitment to full access for all persons in every opportunity our community has to offer.

58   **Pied Piper: Musical Activities to Develop Basic Skills**
Jessica Kingsley Publishers
400 Market Street
Suite 400
Philadelphia, PA 19106-4738   215-922-1161
                                          866-416-1078
                                      FAX: 215-922-1474
                                          hello.usa@jkp.com
                                          www.jkp.com
John Bean, Author
Jessica Kingsley, Chairman, Managing Director
Jemima Kingsley, Director
Describes 78 enjoyable music activities for groups of children or adults who may have learning difficulties. The emphasis is on using music, rather than learning songs or rhythms, so group members do not need any special skills to be able to participate. Full details are given about any equipment required for the games, as well as suggestions for variations or modifications. *$21.95*
96 pages
ISBN 1-853029-94-

59   **Project Onward Gallery**
Bridgeport Art Center
1200 W. 35th St
4th Fl
Chicago, IL 60609   773-940-2992
                                   info@projectonward.org
                                       projectonward.org
Project Onward is dedicated to supporting the career development of artists with mental and developmental disabilities. Operating as both a studio and gallery, Project Onward supports the work of visual artists who have exceptional talents but face challenges ranging from autism to mental illness.

60   **Pure Vision Arts**
The Shield Institute
114 W 17th St
3rd Fl
New York, NY 10011   212-366-4263
                                      FAX: 718-269-2059
                                          progers@shield.org
                                          purevisionarts.org
Pamala Rogers, Director
Pure Vision Arts mission is to provide people with autism and developmental disabilities opportunities for artistic expression and to build public awareness of their important creative contributions.

61 Reaching the Child with Autism Through Art
Future Horizons, Inc.
721 W Abram St
Arlington, TX 76013-6995   817-277-0727
800-489-0727
FAX: 817-277-2270
www.fhautism.com
Toni Flowers, Author
R. Wayne Gilpin, President
Jennifer Gilpin Yacio, Vice President and Editorial Director
This book uncovers how art encourages communication, positive self-image, concept development, spatial relationships, fine-motor skills, and many more facets of health child development. *$19.95*
130 pages

62 Survivors Art Foundation
PO Box 383
Westhampton, NY 11977   www.survivorsartfoundation.org
Michael Herships, Ph.D, Project Leader & Board President
Candyce Brokaw, Art Director
Candyce M. Brokaw, Executive Director
Dedicated to encourage healing through the arts, committed to empowering Trauma-Survivors with Effective Expressive Outlets via Internet Art Gallery, Outreach Programs, National Exhibitions, Publications and Development of Employment Skills.

63 Teaching Asperger's Students Social Skills Through Acting
Future Horizons, Inc.
721 W Abram St
Arlington, TX 76013-6995   817-277-0727
800-489-0727
FAX: 817-277-2270
www.fhautism.com
Amelia Davies, Author
R. Wayne Gilpin, President
Jennifer Gilpin Yacio, Vice President and Editorial Director
This book provides the theories and activities needed for setting up acting classes that double as social skills groups for individuals with Asperger's or high-functioning autism. Using these skills, students will be able to develop social understanding through repetition and generalization. *$19.95*
211 pages

64 Teaching Basic Guitar Skills to Special Learners
MMB Music
9051 Watson Road
Ste 161
St. Louis, MO 63126   314-531-9635
800-543-3771
FAX: 314-531-8384
info@mmbmusic.com
www.mmbmusic.com
Norm Goldberg, Founder & Chair
The first-of-its-kind guitar book for use with persons who have difficulty learning to play via traditional methods. *$16.00*

65 The Arts of Life
2010 W. Carroll Ave
Chicago, IL 60612   312-829-2787
info@artsoflife.org
artsoflife.org
Denise Fisher, Co-Founder & Executive Director
Sara Bemer, Development Coordinator
An organization comprised of people with and without disabilities seeking to promote artistic expression, community building, self-respect, and independence.

66 Theatre Without Limits
P.O.Box 4002
Portland, ME 04101   207-607-4016
FAX: 207-761-4740
www.vsartsmaine.org
Kippy Rudy, Executive Director
VSA Maine is a 501(c)(3) non-profit organization providing educational, arts, and cultural opportunities to children and adults with disabilities in Maine.

67 VSA - The International Organization on Arts and Disability
2700 F Street, NW
Washington, DC 20566   202-467-4600
800-444-1324
FAX: 202-429-0868
TTY: 202-737-0645
www.kennedy-center.org/education/vsa/
Ambassador J Kennedy Smith, Founder
David M. Rubenstein, Chair
Michael M. Kaiser, President
VSA offers a large selection of guides, publications, and other resources dealing with a wide variety of subject matter in education, arts, and disabilities.

68 VSA arts
2700 F Street, NW
Washington, DC 20566   202-467-4600
800-444-1324
FAX: 202-429-0868
TTY: 202-737-0645
www.kennedy-center.org/education/vsa/
Ambassador J Kennedy Smith, Founder
David M. Rubenstein, Chair
Michael M. Kaiser, President
VSA arts is an international, nonprofit organization founded in 1974 by Ambassador Jean Kennedy Smith whose mission is to create a society where all people with disabilities learn through, participate in, and enjoy the arts. Most states offer local programs, such as Arts in Action, that showcases the accomplishments of artists with disabilities and promotes increased access to the arts for people with disabilities.

69 We Are PHAMALY
Fanlight Productions
c/o Icarus Films
32 Court Street, 21st Floor
Brooklyn, NY 11201   718-488-8900
800-876-1710
FAX: 718-488-8642
info@fanlight.com
www.fanlight.com
Ben Achtenberg, Owner
Stands for Physically Handicapped Musical Actors League. This dynamic troupe doesn't cut any corners or make any compromises. The musicals they perform are chosen for their appeal to the audience, not because they are easy for the performers, who have a variety of sensory and mobility handicaps. *$199.00*
ISBN 1-572954-08-6

Assistive Devices

Automobile

70 AUT Secondary Control
Ace Mobility, LLC
9850 E 30th St.
Indianapolis, IN 46229
317-241-2444
877-223-5301
info@acemobility.us
www.acemobility.us

Doron Mishor, President & CEO
Zvika Amir, Vice President, Marketing & Sales
Controls up to 35 secondary functions.

71 AUTone
Ace Mobility, LLC
9850 E 30th St.
Indianapolis, IN 46229
317-241-2444
877-223-5301
info@acemobility.us
www.acemobility.us

Doron Mishor, President & CEO
Zvika Amir, Vice President, Marketing & Sales
Sound-activated signal device that allows drivers to momentarily activate a secondary function by pressing a button, which will play one to eight tones.

72 Ability Center
4797 Ruffner St.
San Diego, CA 92111
858-541-0552
833-919-2581
FAX: 858-541-1941
www.abilitycenter.com

Terry Barton, General Manager
Specializes in accessible vehicles and mobility products; the company has more than 100 employees in 14 locations across the western U.S.
1994

73 Accelerator Shield
Handicaps, Inc.
4335 S Santa Fe Dr.
Englewood, CO 80110-5417
303-781-2062
800-782-4335
info@handicapsinc.com
www.handicapsinc.com
Designed to help prevent vehicles from accelerating during leg spasms.

74 Accelerator/Brake Foot Control
Ace Mobility, LLC
9850 E 30th St.
Indianapolis, IN 46229
317-241-2444
877-223-5301
info@acemobility.us
www.acemobility.us

Doron Mishor, President & CEO
Zvika Amir, Vice President, Marketing & Sales
Electronic foot pedals designed for drivers with adaptive driving needs. The pedals can be mounted at any height, spacing, and angle.

75 Accelerator/Brake Hand Control
Ace Mobility, LLC
9850 E 30th St.
Indianapolis, IN 46229
317-241-2444
877-223-5301
info@acemobility.us
www.acemobility.us

Doron Mishor, President & CEO
Zvika Amir, Vice President, Marketing & Sales
Hand control device that controls the vehicle's acceleration and brakes. The device can be modified to the needs of the client through the push and pull functions.

76 Automobile Lifts for Scooters, Wheelchairs and Powerchairs
Bruno Independent Living Aids, Inc.
1780 Executive Dr.
PO Box 84
Oconomowoc, WI 53066
262-567-4990
800-454-4355
FAX: 262-953-5501
www.bruno.com

Michael R. Bruno, II, President & CEO
Offers automobile lifts for scooters, wheelchairs and powerchairs for nearly any car, van, truck or sport utility vehicle that can raise scooters or wheelchairs under 200 pounds and power chairs up to 300 pounds.

77 BraunAbility
645 W Carmel Dr.
Carmel, IN 46032
800-488-0359
888-365-9417
questions@braunability.com
www.braunability.com

Staci Kroon, President & CEO
Manufactures wheelchair lifts and lowered floor minivans as well as many other mobility products.

78 COM Hand Control
Ace Mobility, LLC
9850 E 30th St.
Indianapolis, IN 46229
317-241-2444
877-223-5301
info@acemobility.us
www.acemobility.us

Doron Mishor, President & CEO
Zvika Amir, Vice President, Marketing & Sales
A hand control device that integrates Ace Mobility's Hand Control and JoySpinner devices.

79 Car Cane with Transfer Swivel Cushion
Maxi Aids
42 Executive Blvd.
Farmingdale, NY 11735-4710
631-752-0521
800-522-6294
FAX: 631-752-0689
TTY: 631-752-0738
sales@maxiaids.com
www.maxiaids.com

Elliot Zaretsky, Founder, President & CEO
This device is designed for those who have trouble getting in and out of a car. The portable handle slides into any car door and can be easily stored in the door or glove box. *$64.90*

80 DW Auto & Home Mobility
1208 N Garth Ave.
Columbia, MO 65203-4056
573-449-3859
800-568-2271
contactus@dwauto.com
www.dwauto.com

Shawn Bright, Owner
DW manufactures paratransit conversions and personalized conversions for the physically challenged. Products include home elevators and lifts, scooters, and wheelchairs.
1967

81 Digital Shifter
Ace Mobility, LLC
9850 E 30th St.
Indianapolis, IN 46229
317-241-2444
877-223-5301
info@acemobility.us
www.acemobility.us

Doron Mishor, President & CEO
Zvika Amir, Vice President, Marketing & Sales
Enables drivers with limited arm strength and range of motion to use buttons to switch between the vehicle's gears. The switch console can be placed at any location to suit the needs of the driver.

82 **Drive Master Company**
37 Daniel Rd. W
Fairfield, NJ 07004-2521   973-808-9709
FAX: 973-808-9713
info@drivemastermobility.com
www.drivemastermobility.com
Peter B. Ruprecht, President
The Drive Master Company offers a full service mobility center, raised tops/doors, drop floors, custom driving equipment. Distributor of name brand devices and systems for full sized and mini vans.

83 **Driving Systems Inc.**
16139 Runnymede St.
Van Nuys, CA 91406-2913   818-782-6793
www.drivingsystems.com
DSI is the manufacturer of the Scott Driving System for disabled drivers. DSI manufactures the 'Wave Grip' grab rails and bathroom accessories for the disabled and elderly. DSI is also the importer of the Carospeed Menox Hand Controls, Left Foot Pedals and other disability driving aids.

84 **Dual Brake Control**
Kroepke Kontrols
104 Hawkins St.
Bronx, NY 10464   718-885-1100
This product includes one lever fingertip brake controls and precision steel machines. Does not take up lots of legroom. *$105.00*

85 **Entervan**
BraunAbility
645 W Carmel Dr.
Carmel, IN 46032   800-488-0359
888-365-9417
questions@braunability.com
www.braunability.com
Staci Kroon, President & CEO
The Entervan's accessible features include a power sliding door, ramp, and auto-kneel system, allowing for easier entry and exit for wheelchair and scooter users.

86 **Foot Steering Systems**
Drive Master Company
37 Daniel Rd. W
Fairfield, NJ 07004-2521   973-808-9709
FAX: 973-808-9713
info@drivemastermobility.com
www.drivemastermobility.com
Peter B. Ruprecht, President
Custom installed foot steering systems for drivers without the use of their arms.

87 **Four Way Switches**
Gresham Driving Aids
30800 S Wixom Rd.
Wixom, MI 48393-2418   248-624-1533
800-521-8930
FAX: 248-624-6358
www.greshamdrivingaids.com
David Ohrt, General Manager
Craig Wigginton, Sales Consultant
Joyce Martell, Customer Service
Multi-function switches for hand controls. Up to four functions can be added, including left turn signal, right turn signal, horn and dimmer.

88 **Freedom Motors USA, Inc.**
740 Watkins Rd.
Battle Creek, MI 49015   269-244-3497
866-581-7463
FAX: 269-580-8291
www.freedommotors.com
Sieto van Dillen, Chief Executive Officer
Freedom Motors offers van conversions with equipment that is easily installed and accessible for the physically challenged.

89 **Gas and Brake Pedal Guard**
Gresham Driving Aids
30800 S Wixom Rd.
Wixom, MI 48393-2418   248-624-1533
800-521-8930
FAX: 248-624-6358
www.greshamdrivingaids.com
David Ohrt, General Manager
Craig Wigginton, Sales Consultant
Joyce Martell, Customer Service
Designed for drivers who use hand controls, this device guards gas and brake pedals so they do not get accidentally pushed.

90 **Gear Shift Adaptor**
Handicaps, Inc.
4335 S Santa Fe Dr.
Englewood, CO 80110-5417   303-781-2062
FAX: 303-782-4335
info@handicapsinc.com
www.handicapsinc.com
This device allows column mounted gear shift to be used with the left hand.

91 **Gear Shift Extension**
Gresham Driving Aids
30800 S Wixom Rd.
Wixom, MI 48393-2418   248-624-1533
800-521-8930
FAX: 248-624-6358
www.greshamdrivingaids.com
David Ohrt, General Manager
Craig Wigginton, Sales Consultant
Joyce Martell, Customer Service
Allows for easier gear shift operation.

92 **Gresham Driving Aids**
30800 S Wixom Rd.
Wixom, MI 48393-2418   248-624-1533
800-521-8930
FAX: 248-624-6358
www.greshamdrivingaids.com
David Ohrt, General Manager
Craig Wigginton, Sales Consultant
Joyce Martell, Customer Service
Gresham Driving Aids offers mobility solutions to physically challenged individuals including lowered floors, raised roofs and doors and high-quad driver control systems. Dealer for Braun, Ricon, Crow River and Bruno wheelchair lifts.

93 **Hand Brake Control Only**
Kroepke Kontrols
104 Hawkins St.
Bronx, NY 10464   718-885-2100
These devices include one-lever, fingertip-operated brake controls that are custom designed to fit each car, are completely adjustable, and offer positioning operation at your fingertips. *$130.00*

94 **Hand Control Multi-Function Buttons**
Gresham Driving Aids
30800 S Wixom Rd.
Wixom, MI 48393-2418   248-624-1533
800-521-8930
FAX: 248-624-6358
www.greshamdrivingaids.com
David Ohrt, General Manager
Craig Wigginton, Sales Consultant
Joyce Martell, Customer Service
Enables the driver to operate multiple vehicle controls using only one hand.

95 **Hand Gas & Brake Control**
Kroepke Kontrols
104 Hawkins St.
Bronx, NY 10464   718-885-2100
Driving controls that are attached by a control level right on to the gas and brake pedals for easy maneuvering and convenience. *$220.00*

96   Hand Parking Brake
Kroepke Kontrols
104 Hawkins St.
Bronx, NY 10464   718-885-2100
These devices include one lever, fingertip-operated brake controls that are custom designed to fit each car. *$25.00*

97   HandBrake
Ace Mobility, LLC
9850 E 30th St.
Indianapolis, IN 46229   317-241-2444
                                         877-223-5301
                                         info@acemobility.us
                                         www.acemobility.us

Doron Mishor, President & CEO
Zvika Amir, Vice President, Marketing & Sales
Electrical power parking brake aid device for drivers with limited arm or hand strength.

98   Handicaps, Inc.
4335 S Santa Fe Dr.
Englewood, CO 80110-5417   303-781-2062
                                         800-782-4335
                                         info@handicapsinc.com
                                         www.handicapsinc.com
Handicaps, Inc. is a manufacturer of 'SuperArm' wheelchair lifts, hand driving controls, and left foot gas pedals for vans and motor homes.

99   Headlight Dimmer Switch
Kroepke Kontrols
104 Hawkins St.
Bronx, NY 10464   718-885-2100
This device is a one lever, fingertip controls for disabled drivers. *$23.00*

100   Horizontal Steering Systems
Drive Master Company
37 Daniel Rd. W
Fairfield, NJ 07004-2521   973-808-9709
                                         FAX: 973-808-9713
                                         info@drivemastermobility.com
                                         www.drivemastermobility.com
Peter B. Ruprecht, President
The Horizontal Steering System is designed to meet the needs of drivers with spinal cord injuries and other individuals with limited arm strength and range of motion.

101   Horn Control Switch
Kroepke Kontrols
104 Hawkins St.
Bronx, NY 10464   718-885-2100
This device is one lever, fingertip control for disabled drivers that does not interfere with the regular operation of the vehicle. *$23.00*

102   JoySpinner
Ace Mobility, LLC
9850 E 30th St.
Indianapolis, IN 46229   317-241-2444
                                         877-223-5301
                                         info@acemobility.us
                                         www.acemobility.us
Doron Mishor, President & CEO
Zvika Amir, Vice President, Marketing & Sales
An ergonomic built-in remote-control joystick for secondary driving operations, including turn signals, beams, wipers, and hazard signals.

103   Kersey Mobility
6015 160th Ave. E
Sumner, WA 98390   253-863-4744
                                         www.kerseymobility.com
Mike Kersey, Owner
Kersey Mobility is a wheelchair van dealer serving the Pacific Northwest. Also offers a line of mobility products and accessories, including lifts, wheelchair restraints, vehicle transfer seating, and adaptive driving aids.

104   Kessler Institute for Rehabilitation
1199 Pleasant Valley Way
West Orange, NJ 07052   973-731-3600
                                         877-322-2580
                                         FAX: 973-243-6819
                                         www.kessler-rehab.com
Sue Kida, President
Driver evaluation training for the physically/mentally challenged. Offers state certified driving instructors. Door-to-door pickup at home, work or rehab centers are available.

105   Left Foot Gas Pedal
Kroepke Kontrols
104 Hawkins St.
Bronx, NY 10464   718-885-2100
This device is one lever, fingertip control for disabled drivers that does not interfere with the regular operation of the vehicle. *$90.00*

106   Left Foot Gas Pedal, The
Handicaps, Inc.
4335 S Santa Fe Dr.
Englewood, CO 80110-5417   303-781-2062
                                         800-782-4335
                                         info@handicapsinc.com
                                         www.handicapsinc.com
Designed for drivers with limited use of the right foot.

107   MobilityWorks
4199 Kinross Lakes Pkwy.
Suite 300
Richfield, OH 44286   877-275-4907
                                         www.mobilityworks.com
Bryan Everett, Chief Executive Officer
Offers a selection of wheelchair accessible vehicles, mobility equipment, adaptive systems, and seating solutions.

108   Multi-Function Spinner Knobs
Gresham Driving Aids
30800 S Wixom Rd.
Wixom, MI 48393-2418   248-624-1533
                                         800-521-8930
                                         FAX: 248-624-6358
                                         www.greshamdrivingaids.com
David Ohrt, General Manager
Craig Wigginton, Sales Consultant
Joyce Martell, Customer Service
Spinner knobs that can include up to six vehicle accessory controls.

109   Park Brake Extension
Handicaps, Inc.
4335 S Santa Fe Dr.
Englewood, CO 80110-5417   303-781-2062
                                         800-782-4335
                                         info@handicapsinc.com
                                         www.handicapsinc.com
This is designed for cars with foot operated parking brake, to operate with hand.

110   Parking Brake Extension
Gresham Driving Aids
30800 S Wixom Rd.
Wixom, MI 48393-2418   248-624-1533
                                         800-521-8930
                                         FAX: 248-624-6358
                                         www.greshamdrivingaids.com
David Ohrt, General Manager
Craig Wigginton, Sales Consultant
Joyce Martell, Customer Service
Enables drivers to operate the foot parking/emergency brake by hand.

111   Portable Hand Controls by Handicaps, Inc.
Handicaps, Inc.
4335 S Santa Fe Dr.
Englewood, CO 80110-5417   303-781-2062
                                         800-782-4335
                                         info@handicapsinc.com
                                         www.handicapsinc.com

To be used on a temporary basis only. Must be used on vehicles with automatic transmission, power brakes, and power steering. Unimpaired hand use is required.

112   Power Transfer Seat Base (6-Way)
Ricon
1135 Aviation Pl.
San Fernando, CA 91340   818-267-3000
                                          800-322-2884
                                     FAX: 800-962-1201
                                     ricinsales@wabtec.com
                                     www.riconcorp.com
Facilitates a driver's self-transfer from a wheelchair to the driving seat and allows optimal driving positioning.

113   Push Pull Hand Controls
Gresham Driving Aids
30800 S Wixom Rd.
Wixom, MI 48393-2418   248-624-1533
                                          800-521-8930
                                     FAX: 248-624-6358
                                     www.greshamdrivingaids.com

David Ohrt, General Manager
Craig Wigginton, Sales Consultant
Joyce Martell, Customer Service
These controls are operated by pushing for brake and pulling back for acceleration.

114   Push Rock Hand Controls
Gresham Driving Aids
30800 S Wixom Rd.
Wixom, MI 48393-2418   248-624-1533
                                          800-521-8930
                                     FAX: 248-624-6358
                                     www.greshamdrivingaids.com

David Ohrt, General Manager
Craig Wigginton, Sales Consultant
Joyce Martell, Customer Service
These controls allow the driver to apply the accelerator and brakes by hand.

115   Rampvan
BraunAbility
645 W Carmel Dr.
Carmel, IN 46032   800-488-0359
                                          888-365-9417
                                     questions@braunability.com
                                     www.braunability.com

Staci Kroon, President & CEO
Fully accessible minivan conversions with automatic doors and ramps.

116   Reduced Effort Steering
Drive Master Company
37 Daniel Rd. W
Fairfield, NJ 07004-2521   973-808-9709
                                     FAX: 973-808-9713
                                     info@drivemastermobility.com
                                     www.drivemastermobility.com
Peter B. Ruprecht, President
Reduced effort steering modifications available for nearly all vehicles. Additional products are pedal extensions which are 1 inch to 4 inch clamp-on aluminum blocks and 6 inch to 12 inch adjustable fold-down pedals.

117   Right Angle Hand Controls
Gresham Driving Aids
30800 S Wixom Rd.
Wixom, MI 48393-2418   248-624-1533
                                          800-521-8930
                                     FAX: 248-624-6358
                                     www.greshamdrivingaids.com

David Ohrt, General Manager
Craig Wigginton, Sales Consultant
Joyce Martell, Customer Service
These controls apply the gas and accelerator at a right angle to the brake.

118   Right Hand Gas and Brake Control
Gresham Driving Aids
30800 S Wixom Rd.
Wixom, MI 48393-2418   248-624-1533
                                          800-521-8930
                                     FAX: 248-624-6358
                                     www.greshamdrivingaids.com

David Ohrt, General Manager
Craig Wigginton, Sales Consultant
Joyce Martell, Customer Service
Floor-mounted hand control that allows drivers to accelerate and brake using their right hand.

119   SWAB Steering Wheel
Ace Mobility, LLC
9850 E 30th St.
Indianapolis, IN 46229   317-241-2444
                                          877-223-5301
                                     info@acemobility.us
                                     www.acemobility.us

Doron Mishor, President & CEO
Zvika Amir, Vice President, Marketing & Sales
The SWAB (Steering Wheel Accelerator-Brake) allows drivers to steer the vehicle and control gas and brake functions with low effort.

120   Spider Network Systems
Ace Mobility, LLC
9850 E 30th St.
Indianapolis, IN 46229   317-241-2444
                                          877-223-5301
                                     info@acemobility.us
                                     www.acemobility.us

Doron Mishor, President & CEO
Zvika Amir, Vice President, Marketing & Sales
Modular control network system that allows drivers with disabilities to activate secondary driving functions, including gear-shift, hand-brake, signaling, lights, and more. Also available in touch screen format.

121   Spinner Knobs
Ace Mobility, LLC
9850 E 30th St.
Indianapolis, IN 46229   317-241-2444
                                          877-223-5301
                                     info@acemobility.us
                                     www.acemobility.us

Doron Mishor, President & CEO
Zvika Amir, Vice President, Marketing & Sales
Knobs designed to maximize the comfort of drivers with disabilities who have difficulty turning the steering wheel.

122   Steering Device
Handicaps, Inc.
4335 S Santa Fe Dr.
Englewood, CO 80110-5417   303-781-2062
                                          800-782-4335
                                     info@handicapsinc.com
                                     www.handicapsinc.com
Mounts to one side of steering wheel. Allows for easier steering using only one hand.

123   Steering Wheel Devices
Drive Master Company
37 Daniel Rd. W
Fairfield, NJ 07004-2521   973-808-9709
                                     FAX: 973-808-9713
                                     info@drivemastermobility.com
                                     www.drivemastermobility.com

Peter B. Ruprecht, President
Steering devices for disabled drivers, including steering knobs, steering cuffs, amputee rings, tri-pins, and grips.

124   Super Grade IV Hand Controls
Handicaps, Inc.
4335 S Santa Fe Dr.
Englewood, CO 80110-5417   303-781-2062
                                          800-782-4335
                                     info@handicapsinc.com
                                     www.handicapsinc.com

Hand controls the operation of accelerator and brakes. VA tested. Right angle style.

125 TapGear
Ace Mobility, LLC
9850 E 30th St.
Indianapolis, IN 46229   317-241-2444
                                                                        877-223-5301
                                                                  info@acemobility.us
                                                                  www.acemobility.us

Doron Mishor, President & CEO
Zvika Amir, Vice President, Marketing & Sales
Electronic device that allows the driver to control gear positions.

126 Tim's Trim
25 Bermar Park
Rochester, NY 14624-1542   585-429-6270
                                                                        888-468-6784
                                                                  info@timstrim.com
                                                                  www.timstrim.com

Tim Miller, Owner
Offers vehicle modifications, drop floors, raised tops/doors, driving equipment, touch pads and lifts.

127 Transportation Equipment for People with Disabilities
Gresham Driving Aids
30800 S Wixom Rd.
Wixom, MI 48393-2418   248-624-1533
                                                                        800-521-8930
                                                             FAX: 248-624-6358
                                                       www.greshamdrivingaids.com

David Ohrt, General Manager
Craig Wigginton, Sales Consultant
Joyce Martell, Customer Service
Wheelchair lifts and ramps, hand and foot controls, steering and braking modifications, complete van conversions, home modifications, wheelchairs and scooters and wheelchair accessible van rentals.

128 Turn Signal Cross-Over
Gresham Driving Aids
30800 S Wixom Rd.
Wixom, MI 48393-2418   248-624-1533
                                                                        800-521-8930
                                                             FAX: 248-624-6358
                                                       www.greshamdrivingaids.com

David Ohrt, General Manager
Craig Wigginton, Sales Consultant
Joyce Martell, Customer Service
This device enables the driver to operate the turn signal lever using the right hand.

129 United Access
9389 Natural Bridge Rd.
St. Louis, MO 63134   877-578-1962
                                                                  www.unitedaccess.com

John Beering, President
Various automobile control systems that use hand, foot and steering aids for the disabled, including complete vehicle modifications.

130 Vantage Mobility International
5202 S 28th Pl.
Phoenix, AZ 85040   855-864-8267
                                                                  www.vantagemobility.com

Mark Shaughnessy, Chief Executive Officer
Manufacturer and distributor of accessible vehicles and mobility products.

131 Vehicle Access Remote Control
Ace Mobility, LLC
9850 E 30th St.
Indianapolis, IN 46229   317-241-2444
                                                                        877-223-5301
                                                                  info@acemobility.us
                                                                  www.acemobility.us

Doron Mishor, President & CEO
Zvika Amir, Vice President, Marketing & Sales
Universal remote control that opens and closes vehicle doors, raises and lowers hoist and chair elevators, and includes full lift control.

132 Wheelers Accessible Van Rentals
6614 W Sweetwater Ave.
Glendale, AZ 85304   623-776-8830
                                                                        800-456-1371
                                                             FAX: 623-900-2708
                                                       corporate@wheelersavr.com
                                                       www.wheelersvanrentals.com
Offers daily, weekly and monthly rentals to accommodate various disabilities at locations across the U.S.
1987

Bath

133 Adjustable Raised Toilet Seat & Guard
Invacare
1 Invacare Way
Elyria, OH 44035-4190   800-333-6900
                                                                  www.invacare.com

Matthew E. Monaghan, Chairman of the Board & Chief Executive Officer
Rick A. Cassiday, Senior Vice President & Chief Human Resources Officer
Kathleen P. Leneghan, Senior Vice President & Chief Financial Officer
The seat features an exclusive pivot locking system so it won't slip or tip and the adjustable guard rail fits all toilets.

134 ArjoHuntleigh
ArjoHuntleigh
2349 W Lake St.
Suite 250
Addison, IL 60101   800-323-1245
                                                                  us.cc@arjohuntleigh.com
                                                                  www.arjohuntleigh.us

Joacim Lindoff, President & CEO
Daniel Faldt, Chief Financial Officer
ARJO offers a complete line of patient bathing, showering and lift/transport systems, bariatric solutions, and accompanying skin care products for long-term and acute care facilities.

135 Bath Fixtures
Fiat Products
41 Cairns Rd.
Mansfield, OH 44904   833-549-2887
                                                             FAX: 816-763-9244
                                                                  www.fiatproducts.com
Manufacturers plumbing fixtures for the disabled. Products include toilets, lavatories, showers and tub/shower units.

136 Bath Products
R82, Inc.
13137 Bleinheim Lane
Matthews, NC 28105   844-876-6245
                                                             FAX: 704-882-0751
                                                                  sales.us@etac.com
                                                                  www.etac.com

Michael Wirzberger, Chief Executive Officer
Johan Nylander, Chief Financial Officer
Kim Ankj'r, Vie President, Quality Assurance & Regulatory Affairs
Offers a wide range of products to meet the transportation, mobility, seating and bath aid needs for people of all ages. From car seats and standers for children with special needs to versatile wheelchairs that offer adults customized options and the freedom to go anywhere with confidence.

137 Bath Shower & Commode Chair
Clarke Health Care Products
7830 Steubenville Pike
Oakdale, PA 15071-9226   724-695-2122
                                                                        888-347-4537
                                                             FAX: 724-695-2922
                                                                  info@clarkehealthcare.com
                                                                  www.clarkehealthcare.com
Aquatic Stainless steel shower/commode chairs and powered bathlifts. Mobeli portable grab bars, Dolomite rollators, Arco bed rails, Care bags for hygiene collection, DecPac portable ramps, Ableware eating, hygiene and dressing aids.

138 Bath and Shower Bench 3301B
Mada Medical Products
625 Washington Ave.
Carlstadt, NJ 07072-2901   201-460-0454
800-526-6370
FAX: 201-460-3509
saragannon@madamedical.com
www.madamedical.com
The bath and shower bench is corrosion-resistant, has a cross brace design and angled legs to prevent tipping, and seat height adjustments.

139 Bathroom Transfer Systems
Inspired By Drive
11724 Willake St.
Santa Fe Springs, CA 90670-5032   800-454-6612
info@inspiredbydrive.com
www.inspiredbydrive.com
Michael Gipson, Senior Director
Offers a complete line of bathroom transfer systems, bath lifts, reclining bath chairs, bath/shower/commode chairs, wrap-around bath supports, toilet supports, positioning commodes, premium air, foam and gel seat cushions, giant trainers and positioning restraint car seats that accommodate individuals from 20-130 pounds.

140 Bathtub Safety Rail
AliMed, Inc.
297 High Street
Dedham, MA 02026-2852   781-329-2900
800-437-2966
FAX: 781-437-2966
customerservice@alimed.com
www.alimed.com
Adam S. Epstein, Chief Executive Officer
Made of stainless steel, this safety rail fits in any size bathtub and offers safety and independence at bathing time. *$55.00*

141 Can-Do Products Catalog
Independent Living Aids
137 Rano Rd.
Buffalo, NY 14207   716-332-2970
800-537-2118
FAX: 877-498-1482
can-do@independentliving.com
www.independentliving.com
Can-Do Products Catalogue provides aids and products for the blind and visually impairments.
84 pages Quarterly

142 Clarke Healthcare Products, Inc.
7830 Steubenville Pike
Oakdale, PA 15071-9226   724-695-2122
888-347-4537
FAX: 724-695-2922
info@clarkehealthcare.com
www.clarkehealthcare.com
Aquatic Stainless steel shower/commode chairs and powered bathlifts. Mobeli portable grab bars, Dolomite rollators, Arco bed rails, Care bags for hygiene collection, DecPac portable ramps, clarke aluminum ramps.

143 Commode
Maxi Aids
42 Executive Blvd.
Farmingdale, NY 11735-4710   631-752-0521
800-522-6294
FAX: 631-752-0689
TTY: 631-752-0738
sales@maxiaids.com
www.maxiaids.com
Elliot Zaretsky, Founder, President & CEO
Adjustable seat height for patient comfort. Easily assembled, aluminum frame.

144 Deluxe Bath Bench with Adjustable Legs
Maxi Aids
42 Executive Blvd.
Farmingdale, NY 11735-4710   631-752-0521
800-522-6294
FAX: 631-752-0689
TTY: 631-752-0738
sales@maxiaids.com
www.maxiaids.com
Elliot Zaretsky, Founder, President & CEO
Bath bench with back support and adjustable legs. *$69.95*

145 Electric Leg Bag Emptier
RD Equipment, Inc.
230 Percival Dr.
West Barnstable, MA 02668-1244   508-362-7498
FAX: 508-362-1458
r_dag@hotmail.com
www.rdequipment.com
Richard Dagostino, Owner and Founder
Designed for independence, this small, lightweight, battery-operated valve attaches to the bottom of the leg bag. A simple flip of the switch empties the leg bag, allowing the user to take in unlimited amounts of fluids. *$550.00*

146 Freedom Bath
ArjoHuntleigh
2349 W Lake St.
Suite 250
Addison, IL 60101   800-323-1245
us.cc@arjohuntleigh.com
www.arjohuntleigh.us
Joacim Lindoff, President & CEO
Daniel Faldt, Chief Financial Officer
Residents can relax on a semi-reclining seat and enjoy the soothing deluxe whirlpool system. Freedom Bath offers a revolutionary solution with its unique Roll-Door. Includes head cushion and safety belt.

147 Heavy-Duty Bath and Shower Seat
AliMed, Inc.
297 High Street
Dedham, MA 02026-2852   781-329-2900
800-437-2966
FAX: 781-437-2966
customerservice@alimed.com
www.alimed.com
Adam S. Epstein, Chief Executive Officer
Bath and shower seat that fits easily in any tub or shower. Includes easy-to-grip handles for safety and convenience. *$59.25*

148 Long Handled Bath Sponges
Therapro, Inc.
225 Arlington St
Framingham, MA 01702-8723   508-872-9494
800-257-5376
FAX: 508-268-6624
info@therapro.com
www.therapro.com
Karen Conrad Weihrauch, President & Owner
Plastic-handled, 18-inch bath sponge. Handle may be heated and bent for easy reach. *$2.50*

149 Modular Wall Grab Bars
Invacare
1 Invacare Way
Elyria, OH 44035-4190   800-333-6900
www.invacare.com
Matthew E. Monaghan, Chairman of the Board & Chief Executive Officer
Rick A. Cassiday, Senior Vice President & Chief Human Resources Officer
Kathleen P. Leneghan, Senior Vice President & Chief Financial Officer
Engineered for strength and beauty, these bars can be assembled in various combinations to fit any bath or shower.

150 P.T. Rail
Maxi Aids
42 Executive Blvd.
Farmingdale, NY 11735-4710 631-752-0521
  800-522-6294
  FAX: 631-752-0689
  TTY: 631-752-0738
  sales@maxiaids.com
  www.maxiaids.com
Elliot Zaretsky, Founder, President & CEO
Wall-mounted support rail for safer transfer to and from the toilet.
Left side and right side rails available.

151 Portable Shampoo Bowl
JK Designs
4500 Williams Dr.
Suite 212-140
Georgetown, TX 78633- 1332 206-999-8226
  info@portableshampoobowl.com
  www.portableshampoobowl.com
A bowl designed to allow a person who is in a wheelchair or sitting on a regular chair to shampoo hair; useful for assisted living environments.

152 Prelude
ArjoHuntleigh
2349 W Lake St.
Suite 250
Addison, IL 60101 800-323-1245
  us.cc@arjohuntleigh.com
  www.arjohuntleigh.us
Joacim Lindoff, President & CEO
Daniel Faldt, Chief Financial Officer
Prelude shower cabinet allows patients to be showered in comfort and privacy, at the same time as protecting staff from excessive splashing.

153 Shower Bathtub Mat
Maxi Aids
42 Executive Blvd.
Farmingdale, NY 11735-4710 631-752-0521
  800-522-6294
  FAX: 631-752-0689
  TTY: 631-752-0738
  sales@maxiaids.com
  www.maxiaids.com
Elliot Zaretsky, Founder, President & CEO
Tub mat provides security against falls in the bath and shower.
$22.95

154 Superior Clear Voice Talking Scale
Independent Living Aids
137 Rano Rd.
Buffalo, NY 14207 716-332-2970
  800-537-2118
  FAX: 877-498-1482
  can-do@independentliving.com
  www.independentliving.com
Speaks in a clear voice. Automatically calibrates when stepped on and turns off once weight is announced. Maximum weight of 550 lbs. *$69.95*

155 Suregrip Bathtub Rail
Invacare
1 Invacare Way
Elyria, OH 44035-4190 800-333-6900
  www.invacare.com
Matthew E. Monaghan, Chairman of the Board & Chief Executive Officer
Rick A. Cassiday, Senior Vice President & Chief Human Resources Officer
Kathleen P. Leneghan, Senior Vice President & Chief Financial Officer
Compact and versatile, the bars have a soft-touch, contoured, white vinyl gripping area for added safety.

156 Transfer Tub Bench
Arista Surgical Supply Company/AliMed
297 High Street
Dedham, MA 02026-2852 781-329-2900
  800-437-2966
  FAX: 781-437-2966
  customerservice@alimed.com
  www.alimed.com
Adam S. Epstein, Chief Executive Officer
Curved padded backrest for comfortable support. Backrest also assists patient during lateral transfer. *$64.00*

157 Tri-Grip Bathtub Rail
Maxi Aids
42 Executive Blvd.
Farmingdale, NY 11735-4710 631-752-0521
  800-522-6294
  FAX: 631-752-0689
  TTY: 631-752-0738
  sales@maxiaids.com
  www.maxiaids.com
Elliot Zaretsky, Founder, President & CEO
Two gripping heights for easy bathtub entrance or exit. *$54.95*

Bed

158 ASSISTECH Special Needs
42 Executive Blvd.
Farmingdale, NY 11735 631-752-0521
  800-522-6294
  FAX: 631-752-0689
  TTY: 800-281-3555
  www.assistech.com
ASSISTECH is a division of Maxi-Aids that sells hearing, visual, and mobility aid devices.

159 Bye-Bye Decubiti Air Mattress Overlay
Rand-Scot, Inc.
209 Christman Drive
Fort Collins, CO 80524 970-484-7967
  800-467-7967
  FAX: 970-484-3800
  info@randscot.com
  www.randscot.com
Joel Lerich, Co-Founder
Barbara Lerich, Co-Founder
Originally designed for hospital beds, the overlay converts any bed into a therapeutic flotation unit when used between the conventional mattress and pad. The complete overlay is comprised of five individually inflatable, 100 percent natural rubber, ventilated sections enclosed within separate pockets of a soft fleece cover. Conforms to any configuration of electric or manual beds. The overlay comes in a kit that includes an overlay cover, overlay sections, air pump, and patch kit. *$1588.00*

160 Dual Security Bed Rail
Maxi Aids
42 Executive Blvd.
Farmingdale, NY 11735-4710 631-752-0521
  800-522-6294
  FAX: 631-752-0689
  TTY: 631-752-0738
  sales@maxiaids.com
  www.maxiaids.com
Elliot Zaretsky, Founder, President & CEO
Bed safety rails for the injured or elderly to help getting in and out of bed, and to prevent falling out of bed. The rails are made of steel with a powder coat. *$150.00*

161 Foam Decubitus Bed Pads
Profex Medical Products
P.O. Box 140188
Memphis, TN 38114 800-325-0196
  FAX: 901-454-9850
  customercare@ProfexMed.com
  www.profexmed.com
Robert Gates Watel, Founder
Convoluted foam provides extra back support and comfort for wheelchair users.

162 Hard Manufacturing Company
230 Grider Street
Buffalo, NY 14215   800-873-4273
                                    www.hardmfg.com
Manufacturer of pediatric cribs and age-appropriate youth beds.

163 Hausmann Industries
130 Union Street
Northvale, NJ 07647   201-767-0255
                                    888-428-7626
                                    info@hausmann.com
                                    hausmann.com
David Hausmann, Chief Executive Officer
Lori Picano, Sales & Marketing Administrator
Wheelchair accessible exam tables, treatment tables and mat platforms. Hausmann Industries has been in the healthcare sector for over 60 years.

164 Home Bed Side Helper
Maxi Aids
42 Executive Blvd.
Farmingdale, NY 11735-4710   631-752-0521
                                    800-522-6294
                                    FAX: 631-752-0689
                                    TTY: 631-752-0738
                                    sales@maxiaids.com
                                    www.maxiaids.com
Elliot Zaretsky, Founder, President & CEO
The rail attaches to home bed frames and provides support for those who require assistance getting in and out of bed. *$149.95*

165 SleepSafe Beds
3629 Reed Creek Drive
Bassett, VA 24055   276-627-0088
                                    866-852-2337
                                    FAX: 276-627-0234
                                    SleepSafeBed@SleepSafeBed.com
                                    www.sleepsafebed.com
Gregg Weinschreider, President
Edward Hettig, Marketing Director
Rachel Markwood, Marketing Director
Perfect for adult home or home care use. SleepSafe offers twin or full size bed frames in classic style. The beds offer an attractive alternative to a hospital bed. SleepSafe beds keeps the user safe during rest and electrically adjusts smoothly for user comfort and caregiver ease of use.

166 Sonic Alert Alarm Clock with Bed Shaker
ASSISTECH
42 Executive Blvd.
Farmingdale, NY 11735   631-752-0521
                                    800-522-6294
                                    FAX: 631-752-0689
                                    TTY: 800-281-3555
                                    www.assistech.com
A vibrator that is put under the pillow or between the mattress and box spring that helps to wake heavy sleepers or individuals who are hard of hearing and/or have hearing impairments. The Sonic Alert Alarm Clock features a large and easy-to-read display. *$47.95*

167 iLuv SmartShaker 2
ASSISTECH
42 Executive Blvd.
Farmingdale, NY 11735   631-752-0521
                                    800-522-6294
                                    FAX: 631-752-0689
                                    TTY: 800-281-3555
                                    www.assistech.com
The iLuv SmartShaker 2 is a smartphone-controlled bed shaker for individuals with hearing loss. The alarm comes with three vibration settings and works with a variety of smartphones. *$29.99*

Communication

168 Accent 1400
Prentke Romich Company
1022 Heyl Road
Wooster, OH 44691   330-262-1984
                                    800-262-1984
                                    FAX: 330-263-4829
                                    info@prc-saltillo.com
                                    www.prentrom.com
Dave Hershberger, President & CEO
Barry Romich, Co-Founder
A portable electronic communication device that uses Minspeak so that symbols are used to represent words, sentences, or phrases. Accent 1400 can be accessed by touching the screen or optical/head tracking. Other versions of the Accent are also available. *$7595.00*

169 Access Control Systems: NHX Nurse Call System
Aiphone Corporation
6670 185th Ave NE
Redmond, WA 98052   425-455-0510
                                    800-692-0200
                                    FAX: 800-525-3372
                                    info@aiphone.com
                                    www.aiphone.com
Toshiki Yamazaki, President/CEO
AIPHONE manufactures audio and video intercom systems for home or business to help the physically disabled answer doors and communicate through physical barriers; also ADA-compliant emergency call intercom stations for use in public facilities and an Environmental Control System for persons with limited mobility. NHX Nurse Call System provides staff alert in nursing homes, assisted-living facilities, clinics, wards, and hospitals.

170 Adaptek Systems
14224 Plank Street
Fort Wayne, IN 46818   260-637-8660
                                    FAX: 260-637-8597
                                    sales@adapteksystems.com
                                    www.adapteksystems.com
Developers of a voice output module designed to work with the Kurzweil voice-recognition system. The device provides voice output of what the computer hears for persons with visual impairments.

171 Amplified Handsets
HARC Mercantile
5413 S Westnedge Ave.
Suite A
Portage, MI 49002   800-445-9968
                                    TTY:269-324-1615
                                    info@harc.com
                                    www.harc.com
Michael Martinson, Owner
Amplified handsets are phones for individuals who are hard of hearing. The phones are louder than other headsets, and can also include extra loud ringers, larger press keypads, and designated speed dial buttons.

172 Amplified Phones
HARC Mercantile
5413 S Westnedge Ave.
Suite A
Portage, MI 49002   800-445-9968
                                    TTY:269-324-1615
                                    info@harc.com
                                    www.harc.com
Michael Martinson, Owner
Amplified phones are phones for individuals who are hard of hearing. Amplified phones enhance and/or amplify sound, and can have a low frequency ringer, an indicator light, and lighted easy-to-read dial pads.

173 Amplified Portable Phone
HARC Mercantile
5413 S Westnedge Ave.
Suite A
Portage, MI 49002
800-445-9968
TTY:269-324-1615
info@harc.com
www.harc.com

Michael Martinson, Owner
Cordless phones with amplified or enhanced sound for individuals with hearing loss.

174 Assistive Technology
Tobii Dynavox
2100 Wharton Street
Suite 400
Pittsburgh, PA 15203
800-344-1778
FAX: 866-804-1267
www.tobii.com

Anand Srivatsa, Chief Executive Officer
Magdalena Rodell Andersson, Chief Financial Officer & Vice President
Ann Emilson, Executive Vice President, Sales & Marketing
A premiere developer of innovative touch and eye-tracking technology solutions for people with physical and learning disabilities. Breakthrough products enable people of all ages and abilities to live and learn independently. Supportive material for teachers, clinicians, and those with disabilities.

175 Big Red Switch
AbleNet, Inc.
2625 Patton Road
Roseville, MN 55113-1137
651-294-2200
800-322-0956
customerservice@ablenetinc.com
www.ablenetinc.com

Jennifer Thalhuber, President & CEO
Paul Sugden, CFO & Trustee
Five inches across the top and activates no matter where on its surface it is touched. It is made of shatterproof plastic and contains a cord storage compartment. The Big Red Switch provides auditory, visual, and tactile feedback. Also available in green, yellow, and blue.

176 Closed Caption Decoder
HARC Mercantile
5413 S Westnedge Ave.
Suite A
Portage, MI 49002
800-445-9968
TTY:269-324-1615
info@harc.com
www.harc.com

Michael Martinson, Owner
Provides closed captions for TV programs, with text displayed as white letters on a black background. *$50.00*

177 Cornell Communications
7915 North 81st Street
Milwaukee, WI 53223
414-351-4660
800-558-8957
FAX: 414-351-4657
www.cornell.com

Cornell's Rescue Assistance Systems allow personnel to request emergency assistance. Applications include handicapped evacuations, parking garages, and elevators. Voice, intercom, and visual only signaling systems are available.

178 Harc Mercantile, Ltd.
HARC Mercantile
5413 S Westnedge Ave.
Suite A
Portage, MI 49002
800-445-9968
TTY:269-324-1615
info@harc.com
www.harc.com

Michael Martinson, Owner
HARC sells assistive devices for the hard of hearing and deaf, such as amplified telephones, personal amplifiers, personal and large area fm systems, induction hearing loops, signaling systems for wake-up, smoke/fire door and telephone, and hearing aid batteries and supplies.

179 InfoLoop Induction Receiver
HARC Mercantile
5413 S Westnedge Ave.
Suite A
Portage, MI 49002
800-445-9968
TTY:269-324-1615
info@harc.com
www.harc.com

Michael Martinson, Owner
Sound-induction receiver to be used with any loop system (a length of wire around the perimeter of a room and connected to an amplifier). *$99.00*

180 Large Button Speaker Phone
HARC Mercantile
5413 S Westnedge Ave.
Suite A
Portage, MI 49002
800-445-9968
TTY:269-324-1615
info@harc.com
www.harc.com

Michael Martinson, Owner
HARC Mercantile amplified phones have large, easy-to-read buttons for individuals who have visual impairments. Most phones also have a speakerphone option.

181 Metropolitan Washington Ear
12061 Tech Rd.
Silver Spring, MD 20904
301-681-6636
FAX: 301-625-1986
information@washear.org
www.washear.org

Terry Pacheco, President
Amir Rahimi, Secretary
John F. Anderschat, Treasurer
Multi-media reading service for the blind and visually impaired. Offering 24-hour audio radio reading, dial-in newspapers and webcasting, as well as audio description at theaters, museums and films.

182 Microloop III Basic
HARC Mercantile
5413 S Westnedge Ave.
Suite A
Portage, MI 49002
800-445-9968
TTY:269-324-1615
info@harc.com
www.harc.com

Michael Martinson, Owner
Home induction loop amplifier for use with hearing aids equipped with T-Coil. Small and compact, the Microloop is also suitable for use in a vehicle. *$198.00*

183 MyAlert Body Worn Multifunction Receiver
HARC Mercantile
5413 S Westnedge Ave.
Suite A
Portage, MI 49002
800-445-9968
TTY:269-324-1615
info@harc.com
www.harc.com

Michael Martinson, Owner
Composed of a small wireless personal device that receives coded signals and a group of transmitters that send them. Transmitters can send alert signals for telephone, smartphone, door, and window. *$39.00*

184 PLA240 Room Loop System
HARC Mercantile
5413 S Westnedge Ave.
Suite A
Portage, MI 49002
800-445-9968
TTY:269-324-1615
info@harc.com
www.harc.com

Michael Martinson, Owner
Helps hearing aid users listen to TV or audio equipment via the "T" or "Loop" programs of their hearing aids. *$325.00*

185 Personal FM Systems
HARC Mercantile
5413 S Westnedge Ave.
Suite A
Portage, MI 49002   800-445-9968
                                       TTY:269-324-1615
                                          info@harc.com
                                           www.harc.com

Michael Martinson, Owner
Wireless FM systems transmit sound via a radio carrier wave.

186 Phone Ringers
HARC Mercantile
5413 S Westnedge Ave.
Suite A
Portage, MI 49002   800-445-9968
                                       TTY:269-324-1615
                                          info@harc.com
                                           www.harc.com

Michael Martinson, Owner
Uses loud ringers and/or bright flashers to signal phone rings and messages.

187 Phone Strobe Flasher
Independent Living Aids
137 Rano Rd.
Buffalo, NY 14207   716-332-2970
                                           800-537-2118
                                      FAX: 877-498-1482
                         can-do@independentliving.com
                            www.independentliving.com
Once the phone is plugged into the Phone Strobe Flasher, the light will flash with each ring, alerting individials that there is a phone call. *$23.95*

188 Pocketalker Personal Amplifier
HARC Mercantile
5413 S Westnedge Ave.
Suite A
Portage, MI 49002   800-445-9968
                                       TTY:269-324-1615
                                          info@harc.com
                                           www.harc.com

Michael Martinson, Owner
Amplifies sounds and voices for better understanding.

189 Prentke Romich Company
1022 Heyl Road
Wooster, OH 44691   330-262-1984
                                           800-262-1984
                                      FAX: 330-263-4829
                                      info@prentrom.com
                                        www.prentrom.com

Dave Hershberger, President & CEO
Barry Romich, Co-Founder
The Prentke Romich Company is a full-service company offering easy yet powerful communication aids. The company believes in supporting customers before and after the sale by providing funding assistance, distance learning training, extended warranty, service assistance, etc.

190 Silent Call Communications
5095 Williams Lake Rd.
Waterford, MI 48329   800-572-5227
                                       TTY:800-572-5227
                           customerservice@silentcall.com
                                        www.silentcall.com

George J. Elwell, President
Diana Elwell, President
Lisa DeLeuil, Director of Sales & Marketing
Alerting devices such as paging systems and smoke detectors for deaf and deaf-blind people.

191 Sonic Alert
Harris Communications
15155 Technology Dr
Eden Prairie, MN 55344   800-825-6758
                                      FAX: 952-906-1099
                                      TTY:952-388-2152
                                      info@harriscomm.com
                                       www.harriscomm.com

Ray Harris, CEO
Offers visual alerting devices that provide safety and convenience by turning vital sound into flashing light: telephone ring signalers, doorbell signalers, baby cry signalers, and wake up alarms. Free catalog available.

192 Speech Adjust-A-Tone Basic
Maxi Aids
42 Executive Blvd.
Farmingdale, NY 11735-4710   631-752-0521
                                           800-522-6294
                                      FAX: 631-752-0689
                                      TTY: 631-752-0738
                                       sales@maxiaids.com
                                         www.maxiaids.com

Elliot Zaretsky, Founder, President & CEO
Speech Adjust-A-Tone improves speech amplification for use with telephone, TV, radio, tape recorder, or computer sound card. *$155.00*

193 Step-by-Step Communicator
AbleNet, Inc.
2625 Patton Road
Roseville, MN 55113-1137   651-294-2200
                                           800-322-0956
                                      FAX: 651-294-2259
                          customerservice@ablenetinc.com
                                       www.ablenetinc.com

Jennifer Thalhuber, President & CEO
Paul Sugden, CFO & Trustee
Allows individuals to record a series of messages for later communication. It has a 2 1/2 inches diameter switch surface and is 3 inches at its tallest point. The Step-by-Step Communicator includes 2 minutes of record time, and comes in yellow, green, blue, or red.

194 TTYs: Telephone Device for the Deaf
HARC Mercantile
5413 S Westnedge Ave.
Suite A
Portage, MI 49002   800-445-9968
                                       TTY:269-324-1615
                                          info@harc.com
                                           www.harc.com

Michael Martinson, Owner
A telecommunications device for individuals who are deaf. The device is a teleprinter that creates text communication over a telephone line. *$239.00*

195 TalkTrac Wearable Communicator
AbleNet, Inc.
2625 Patton Road
Roseville, MN 55113-1137   651-294-2200
                                           800-322-0956
                                      FAX: 651-294-2259
                          customerservice@ablenetinc.com
                                       www.ablenetinc.com

Jennifer Thalhuber, President & CEO
Paul Sugden, CFO & Trustee
The TalkTrac Wearable Communicator is a personal, portable communication aid that is wearable on the wrist. TalkTrac features simple to use, 80 seconds of recording time, as well as four message locations, rechargeable battery, water resistant coating, and adjustable band. *$145.00*

196 Talking Calculators
ASSISTECH
42 Executive Blvd.
Farmingdale, NY 11735   631-752-0521
                                           800-522-6294
                                      FAX: 631-752-0689
                                      TTY: 800-281-3555
                                        www.assistech.com

Calculators for blind and low vision users that announce numbers and calculation results.

197   Talking Watches
Maxi Aids
42 Executive Blvd.
Farmingdale, NY 11735-4710

631-752-0521
800-522-6294
FAX: 631-752-0689
TTY: 631-752-0738
sales@maxiaids.com
www.maxiaids.com

Elliot Zaretsky, Founder, President & CEO
Digital display watches that announce the time at the touch of a button.

198   Unity Language System
Prentke Romich Company
1022 Heyl Road
Wooster, OH 44691

330-262-1984
800-262-1984
FAX: 330-263-4829
info@prentrom.com
www.prentrom.com

Dave Hershberger, President & CEO
Barry Romich, Co-Founder
A Minspeak application program designed for adolescent and adult individuals with developmental disabilities and associated learning difficulties. The software is used with Prentke Romich Company augmentative communication devices.

199   Voice Amplified Handsets
HARC Mercantile
5413 S Westnedge Ave.
Suite A
Portage, MI 49002

800-445-9968
TTY:269-324-1615
info@harc.com
www.harc.com

Michael Martinson, Owner
Designed for the person who has a weak speaking voice. Control increases the level of the user's voice and can increase as much as 30%.

Chairs

200   Adjustable Chair
Bailey Manufacturing Company
P.O. Box 130
Lodi, OH 44254-0130

330-948-1080
800-321-8372
FAX: 330-948-4439
baileymfg@baileymfg.com
www.baileymfg.com

The seat and footboard of this versatile chair can be adjusted to accommodate children of various sizes. A classroom-suitable variation of this model is also available.

201   Adjustable Clear Acrylic Tray
Bailey Manufacturing Company
P.O. Box 130
Lodi, OH 44254-0130

330-948-1080
800-321-8372
FAX: 330-948-4439
baileymfg@baileymfg.com
www.baileymfg.com

An clear tray that adjusts for heigh and depth, and is equipped with a spill rim for easy to clean edges.

202   Adjustable Tee Stool
Bailey Manufacturing Company
P.O. Box 130
Lodi, OH 44254-0130

330-948-1080
800-321-8372
FAX: 330-948-4439
baileymfg@baileymfg.com
www.baileymfg.com

May be used to encourage balance as well as develop integrative and perceptual motor skills. The stool has five adjustable height ranges.

203   BackSaver
BackSaver Products Company
3000 East Imperial Highway
Lynwood, CA 90262

310-661-3044
800-251-2225
www.backsaver.com

A recliner desinged to relieve the pressure on the spine and reduce muscle tension. The recliner aids in expanding lung capacity, increasing circulation, and increasing blood oxygen levels.
$1999.00

204   Carendo
Arjo Inc
2349 West Lake Street
Suite 250
Addison, IL 60101

800-323-1245
888-594-2756
www.arjo.com

Joacim Lindoff, President & CEO
The Carendo hygiene chair has been designed for caregivers. The chair is battery powered, and allows for easy access to most parts of the body for sensitive hygiene tasks. Its innovative, ergonomic design makes for better grooming and hygiene routines.

205   Century Bath System
Arjo Inc
2349 West Lake Street
Suite 250
Addison, IL 60101

800-323-1245
888-594-2756
www.arjo.com

Joacim Lindoff, President & CEO
This bathing system is used with a hygiene lift chair and has a built-in cleaning/disinfectant injection system with adjustable flowmeter. The incorporation of an automatic hot water alarm/shut-off system, and digital temperature monitors, helps to assure resident safety and comfort.

206   Convert-Able Table
REAL Design
187 S. Main St.
Dolgeville, NY 13329

315-429-3071
800-696-7041
rdesign@twcny.rr.com
www.realdesigninc.com

Sam Camardello, Owner
Kris Wohnsen, Vice President
This table has push button height adjustment and interchangeable tops so it can become a desk, art easel, or a sensory stimulation bowl.

207   Drive DeVilbiss Healthcare
99 Seaview Boulevard
Port Washington, NY 11050

877-224-0946
FAX: 516-998-4601
customerSupport@drivemedical.com
www.drivemedical.com

Derek Lampbert, Chief Executive Officer
Jeffrey Schwartz, Executive Vice President, Commerical Operations
Nora Coleman, Executive Vice President, General Counsel
Supplies durable medical equipment, including those dealing with mobility, wheelchairs, beds and sleeping surfaces, personal care products, and electrotherapy devices. Company's goals are to promote independence and improve people's quality of life.

208   Evac + Chair Emergency Evacuation Chair
Evac + Chair North America LLC
3000 Marcus Ave.
Suite 3E6
Lake Success, NY 11042-1012

516-502-4240
FAX: 516-327-8220
sales@evac-chair.com
www.evac-chair.com

David Egen, Founder
Gravity-driven evaluation chair allows one nondisabled person to smoothly glide a seated passenger down fire stairs and across landings to exit on a combination of wheels and track belts. Pivots

in own width for tight landing turns. Features include ability to compactly store on wall mount, a maximum capacity of 400 pounds, and braking features. No installation needed and works on all fire exit stairs.

209   Golden Technologies
401 Bridge Street
Old Forge, PA 18518

570-451-7477
800-624-6374
FAX: 800-628-5165
www.goldentech.com

Richard Golden, CEO
Robert Golden, Chair
Fred Kiwak, Vice President, Research & Development
The largest facility in the world dedicated to the manufacture of lift chairs, scooters, and power chairs.

210   High-Low Chair
REAL Design
187 S. Main St.
Dolgeville, NY 13329

315-429-3071
800-696-7041
rdesign@twcny.rr.com
www.realdesigninc.com

Sam Camardello, Owner
Kris Wohnsen, Vice President
A high chair and mobile floor sitter in one. The High-Low Chair comes with colorful upholstered wipe clean seat and height adjustable tray. The chair has a single lever adjustment to change the seat height. Lateral and head supports are available as options. *$1720.00*

211   Ladybug Corner Chair
REAL Design
187 S. Main St.
Dolgeville, NY 13329

315-429-3071
800-696-7041
rdesign@twcny.rr.com
www.realdesigninc.com

Sam Camardello, Owner
Kris Wohnsen, Vice President
For children 0-3 years. This chair is adjustable for long leg or conventional sitting positions. The back can also be removed for independent sitting. The Ladybug Chair is upholstered in padded vinyl, and includes an H-strap harness, hip belt, abductor, and removable tray.

212   Lumex Recliner
Graham-Field Health Products
One Graham-Field Way
Atlanta, GA 30340-4700

770-368-4700
FAX: 770-368-4932
cs@grahamfield.com
www.grahamfield.com

Kenneth Spett, President & CEO
Cherie Antoniazzi, Senior Vice President, Quality, Regulatory & Risk Management
Marc Bernstein, Senior Vice President, Consumer Sales
A recliner designed to improve the mobility of residents in extended care facilities. This chair combines therapeutic benefits of position change with attractive appearance.

213   Prime Engineering
Prime Engineering
4202 W Sierra Madre Ave.
Fresno, CA 93722

559-276-0991
800-827-8263
FAX: 800-800-3355
info@primeengineering.com
www.primeengineering.com

Bruce Boegel, CFO
Mary Boegel, President
Mark Allen, Vice President
Prime Engineering is a leading manufacturer of adult and pediatric standing devices and patient transfer equipment. Products include Superstand HLT, Granstand III MSS Standing System, Kidstand III MSS Standing System, Superstand Standing System, Symmetry Youth Standing Systen, UpRite Standing System, and the Symmetry Standing System.

214   Rifton Equipment
P.O. Box 260
Rifton, NY 12471-0260

845-658-7750
800-571-8198
FAX: 845-658-7751
sales@rifton.com
www.rifton.com

A leader in manufacturing furniture and equipment for children with special needs.

215   Roll Chair
Bailey Manufacturing Company
P.O. Box 130
Lodi, OH 44254-0130

330-948-1080
800-321-8372
FAX: 330-948-4439
baileymfg@baileymfg.com
www.baileymfg.com

A chair with a padded roll seat that helps maintain proper hip abduction and prevents scissoring of the legs.

216   Safari Tilt
Convaid
2830 California Street
Torrance, CA 90503

888-266-8243
FAX: 310-618-2166
convaidsales.us@etac.com
www.convaid.com

Chris Braun, President
A semi-contour seat provides positioning with 5-45 degree tilt adjustment. One step design folds compactly into a lightweight chair.

217   Transfer Bench with Back
Invacare
1 Invacare Way
Elyria, OH 44035-4190

800-333-6900
www.invacare.com

Matthew E. Monaghan, Chairman of the Board & Chief Executive Officer
Rick A. Cassiday, Senior Vice President & Chief Human Resources Officer
Kathleen P. Leneghan, Senior Vice President & Chief Financial Officer
A shower bench with back rest designed to help individuals get in and out of the bathtub. Features a textured seat with drain holes, built-in soap dish, and hand-held shower holder. *$268.84*

Cushions & Wedges

218   Action Products
954 Sweeney Dr.
Hagerstown, MD 21740

301-797-1414
800-228-7763
service@actionproducts.com
www.actionproducts.com

Mistie Witt, President
Janet Kaplan, Marketing Director
Wheelchair pads, mattress pads, positioning cushions, and insoles that aid in the prevention and cure of pressure sores by reducing pressure. All products are made of Akton viscoelastic polymer that does not leak, flow, or bottom out. Manufacturer of the Xact line of positioning cushions for patients with high risk of skin breakdown.

219   Adjustable Wedge
Bailey Manufacturing Company
P.O. Box 130
Lodi, OH 44254-0130

330-948-1080
800-321-8372
FAX: 330-948-4439
baileymfg@baileymfg.com
www.baileymfg.com

Orthopedically and neurologically disabled children can freely move arms and hands while lying on this adjustable wedge.

220 **Back-Huggar Pillow**
Bodyline Comfort Systems
3730 Kori Rd.
Jacksonville, FL 32257
904-262-4068
800-874-7715
FAX: 800-323-2225
info@bodyline.com
www.bodyline.com

Dr. John W. Fiore, Owner
Exclusive design makes almost any seat more comfortable by exerting soothing pressure against back muscles and discs. *$32.95*

221 **Bye-Bye Decubiti (BBD)**
Rand-Scot, Inc.
209 Christman Drive
Fort Collins, CO 80524
970-484-7967
800-467-7967
FAX: 970-484-3800
info@randscot.com
www.randscot.com

Joel Lerich, Co-Founder
Barbara Lerich, Co-Founder
The BBD therapeutic wheelchair cushions have been market-proven since 1951 in the prevention and cure of pressure sores (decubiti). These natural rubber inflatable products have recently been expanded to include pediatric, sports, and double-valve models.

222 **Dynamic Systems, Inc.**
Dynamic Systems, Inc.
104 Morrow Branch Road
Leicester, NC 28748
828-683-3523
855-786-6283
FAX: 844-270-6478
dsi@sunmatecushions.com
www.sunmatecushions.com

Mardi Norman, President & CEO
Dynamic Systems, Inc. manufactures high-performance, medical-grade, orthopedic cushion materials for applications where pressure relief, body support, and skin health are critical. Molding seat inserts.

223 **Geo-Matt for High Risk Patients**
Span-America Medical Systems
70 Commerce Ctr
Greenville, SC 29615
864-288-8877
800-888-6752
FAX: 864-288-8692
www.spanamerica.com

James Ferguson, President & CEO
Provides a line of healthcare products concerned with pressure management and patient positioning, including therapeutic mattress systems, overlay and seat cushions, wound-care seating, and skincare. Helps prevent pressure sores in high-risk patients.

224 **Inflatable Back Pillow**
Corflex Inc.
669 East Industrial Park Dr
Manchester, NH 03109-5625
603-623-3344
800-426-7353
FAX: 603-623-4111
sales@corflex.com
www.corflex.com

Paul Lorenzetti, President & CEO
Corflex specializes in orthopedic rehabilitation products. ReFolds flat to fit into its own carrying case, this inflatable back pillow ensures comfort while at home or traveling.

225 **Jobri**
Jobri
510 Fountain Pkwy
Grand Prairie, TX 75050
972-641-9680
Sales@AlexOrthopedic.com
www.jobri.com

Brian Gourley, CEO
Jobri manufactures ergonomic back supports, ergonomic chairs, orthopedic soft goods and sleep products.

226 **Lumbar Cushions**
Graham-Field Health Products
One Graham-Field Way
Atlanta, GA 30340-3140
770-368-4700
FAX: 770-368-4932
cs@grahamfield.com
www.grahamfield.com

Kenneth Spett, President & CEO
Cherie Antoniazzi, Senior Vice President, Quality, Regulatory & Risk Management
Marc Bernstein, Senior Vice President, Consumer Sales
Line of cushions and pillows give comfort and independence to the physically challenged.

227 **Medpro Static Air Chair Cushion**
Medpro
1950 Rutgers Blvd
Lakewood, NJ 08701-4537
732-905-9001
800-257-5145
FAX: 732-905-9899

Jody Gorran, President
Provides a protective layer of air beneath the patient helping prevent and treat pressure ulcers. *$94.95*

228 **Medpro Static Air Mattress Overlay**
Medpro
1950 Rutgers Blvd
Lakewood, NJ 08701-4537
732-905-9001
800-257-5145
FAX: 732-905-9899

Jody Gorran, President
Supports the patient on a cushioned network of air designed to redistribute the patient's weight reducing tissue interface pressure. Medpro's design incorporates a series of 65 air-breather vents that maintain air circulation. Medpro effectively reduces pressure and helps prevent and treat pressure ulcers. *$164.95*

229 **Silicone Padding**
Spenco Medical Group
P.O.Box 2501
Waco, TX 76702-2501
254-772-6000
800-877-3626
spenco@spenco.com
www.spenco.com

For the management of pressure sores, this padding provides a special support system which allows even distribution of pressure and cool, comfortable, well-ventilated support.

230 **Spenco Medical Group**
Spenco Medical Group
P.O.Box 2501
Waco, TX 76702-2501
254-772-6000
800-877-3626
spenco@spenco.com
www.spenco.com

Wheelchair cushions, silicone mattress pads, wound dressings, second skin blister and burn pads, polysorb insoles, elbow, knee and wrist supports and walking shoes.

231 **Stryker**
2825 Airview Boulevard
Kalamazoo, MI 49002
269-385-2600
FAX: 269-385-1062
www.stryker.com/us/en/about.html

Kevin A. Lobo, Chair & CEO
Yin C. Becker, Vice President & Chief Corporate Affairs Officer
William E. Berry Jr., Vice President & Chief Accounting Officer
Leader in medical technology companies, with the drive to improve healthcare. Provides services and products in Orthopaedics, Medical and Surgical, and Neurotechnology and Spine.

232 **Sun-Mate Seat Cushions**
Dynamic Systems, Inc.
104 Morrow Branch Road
Leicester, NC 28748
828-683-3523
855-786-6283
FAX: 844-270-6478
dsi@sunmatecushions.com
www.sunmatecushions.com

Mardi Norman, President & CEO

Line of cushions, pads and accessory items for personal comfort of the disabled. SunMate Orthopedic foam cushions and sheets that contours slowly to give uniform pressure distribution and soft spring back. Liquid SunMate for Foam-in-Place Seating (FIPS) to make custom molded seat inserts.

Dressing Aids

233 **Button Aid**
Maxi Aids
42 Executive Blvd.
Farmingdale, NY 11735-4710

631-752-0521
800-522-6294
FAX: 631-752-0689
TTY: 631-752-0738
sales@maxiaids.com
www.maxiaids.com

Elliot Zaretsky, Founder, President & CEO
Makes buttoning possible with the use of only one hand. *$10.95*

234 **Dressing Stick**
Maxi Aids
42 Executive Blvd.
Farmingdale, NY 11735-4710

631-752-0521
800-522-6294
FAX: 631-752-0689
TTY: 631-752-0738
sales@maxiaids.com
www.maxiaids.com

Elliot Zaretsky, Founder, President & CEO
Helps put on coats, sweaters and garments even when arm and shoulder movement is limited. *$16.95*

235 **Elastic Shoelaces**
Therapro, Inc.
225 Arlington St
Framingham, MA 01702-8723

508-872-9494
800-257-5376
FAX: 508-268-6624
info@therapro.com
www.therapro.com

Karen Conrad Weihrauch, President & Owner
The elastic laces allow the wearer to slip tied shoes on and off. *$8.75*

236 **Mirror Go Lightly**
AbleNet, Inc.
2625 Patton Road
Roseville, MN 55113-1137

651-294-2200
800-322-0956
FAX: 651-294-2259
customerservice@ablenetinc.com
www.ablenetinc.com

Jennifer Thalhuber, President & CEO
Paul Sugden, CFO & Trustee
Framed in plastic, the mirror can be tilted to provide either a normal or magnified image or to direct its lights at, or away from, the user. *$22.00*

237 **Molded Sock and Stocking Aid**
Therapro, Inc.
225 Arlington St
Framingham, MA 01702-8723

508-872-9494
800-257-5376
FAX: 508-268-6624
info@therapro.com
www.therapro.com

Karen Conrad Weihrauch, President & Owner
Sock or stocking is pulled over the molded plastic and then can be put on more easily. *$13.00*

238 **Say What Clothing Identifier**
Maxi Aids
42 Executive Blvd.
Farmingdale, NY 11735-4710

631-752-0521
800-522-6294
FAX: 631-752-0689
TTY: 631-752-0738
sales@maxiaids.com
www.maxiaids.com

Elliot Zaretsky, Founder, President & CEO
Braille the tag with information that the wearer wants on the tag and place the tag on a hanger. The custom-identification program makes it easier for the user to remember and identify the right clothes. *$4.95*

239 **Shoe Horn and Sock Remover**
Maxi Aids
42 Executive Blvd.
Farmingdale, NY 11735-4710

631-752-0521
800-522-6294
FAX: 631-752-0689
TTY: 631-752-0738
sales@maxiaids.com
www.maxiaids.com

Elliot Zaretsky, Founder, President & CEO
Helps with the removal of socks and shoes. Designed for those with arthritic or weak hands. Easily assembled and taken apart. The handle is 28" (13.75" when disassembled). *$11.95*

Health Aids

240 **AMI**
Aqua Massage International
P.O.Box 808
Groton, CT 06340-0808

860-536-3735
800-248-4031
FAX: 860-536-4362
sales@aquamassage.com
www.aquamassage.com

The Aqua PT provides the major benefits of Hydrotherapy, Massage Therapy and Dry Heat Therapy. 36 water jets provide continuous full body or localized massage while the user remains clothed and dry. Adjustable water pressure, temperature and pulsation frequency can massage in either a two direction travel mode for musculoskeletal pain management or a one direction mode, flowing water from head to foot for a contrast massage-relax therapy.

241 **American Medical Industries**
EZ Healthcare
19550 N. 10th Street
Covington, LA 70433

504-717-4884
www.ezhealthcare.com

Rick Martin, CEO
Software solutions that allow for healthcare providers to cut back on operational expenses through the automation of office procedures. Tailored to physicians in managing office practices and procedures.

242 **BIPAP S/T Ventilatory Support System**
Respironics
1010 Murry Ridge Ln
Murrysville, PA 15668-8517

724-733-0200
www.respironics.com

John L. Miclot, CEO
Gerald McGinnis, Chair
Daniel Bevevino, Vice President & CFO
Respironics, a recognized resource in the medical device market, provides innovative products and unique designs to the health care provider while helping them to grow and manage their business efficiently. As a global leader in the sleep and respiratory fields, Respironics provides innovative products that deal with sleep apnea management, oxygen therapy, noninvasive ventilation, and respiratory drug delivery.

243 Coast to Coast Home Medical
Coast to Coast Home Medical
100 Waldron Rd.
Fall River, MA 02720   774-888-1000
                                          c2cmed.com

Keri Suess, Owner
Home-delivered medical supplies for diabetes, respiratory, arthritis and impotence.

244 Compass Health
6753 Engle Road
Middleburg Heights, OH 44130   440-572-1962
                                        800-376-7263
                                   FAX: 440-572-4261
                corporate@compasshealthbrands.com
                             www.roscoemedical.com
For over 20 years, Compass Health Brands has been offering Pain Management, Respiratory and Home Medical Equipment. Delivers products of high quality in addition to unparalleled personal service.

245 Drew Karol Industries
Drew Karol Industries
633 Highway 1 North
P.O.box 1066
Greenville, MS 38702- 1066   662-378-2188
                                  FAX: 601-378-3188
Andrew K. Hoszowski, Owner
Orally operated toothbrush and dental care system for persons with limited or complete loss of hand or arm use - wheelchair accessible. *$600.00*

246 Duraline Medical Products Inc.
Duraline Medical Products Inc.
P.O.Box 67
324 Werner Street
Leipsic, OH 45856-1039   419-943-2044
                                        800-654-3376
                                  FAX: 419-943-3637
                             duraline@fairpoint.net
                                www.dmponline.com
An assortment of quality incontinence products for adults and children.

247 Duro-Med Industries
Duro-Med Industries
128 Rockingham Road
Suite 1
Windham, NH 03087   800-563-0433
                                  FAX: 603-898-9348
                                       hello@hpms.com
           www.hpms.com/Duro-Med-Industries-s/184.htm
Mike Mazza, President
Tony D'Antonio, Senior Vice President of Sales
Alan Yefsky, Exec Vice President, Sales & Marketing
Manufacturers of a complete line of home health care products. Featured products are patient gowns, back and seat cushions, pillows and a complete line of aids for daily living.

248 Ekso Bionics
1414 Harbour Way S.
Suite 1201
Richmond, CA 94804   510-984-1761
                                  hello@eksobionics.com
                                       eksobionics.com
Steven Sherman, Chairman & CEO
Scott Davis, President & COO
Jack CFO, CFO
Develops and manufactures exoskeleton solutions to enhance the mobility of users with paralysis. Provides research for the U.S. defense capabilities.

249 Electronic Amplified Stethoscopes
HARC Mercantile
5413 S Westnedge Ave.
Suite A
Portage, MI 49002   800-445-9968
                                   TTY:269-324-1615
                                       info@harc.com
                                       www.harc.com

Michael Martinson, Owner

A stethoscope designed for hearing aid users. Amplifies heart, breath, and Korotkoff sounds. *$335.00*

250 Healing Dressing for Pressure Sores
Baxter Healthcare Corporation
1 Baxter Pkwy
Deerfield, IL 60015-4625   224-948-1812
                                        800-422-9837
                                     media@baxter.com
                                       www.baxter.com
Jos, E. Almeida, Chairman, President & CEO
A dressing specifically designed to promote healing of pressure sores and other dermal ulcers.

251 Invacare Corporation
Invacare
1 Invacare Way
Elyria, OH 44035-4190   800-333-6900
                                       www.invacare.com
Matthew E. Monaghan, Chairman of the Board & Chief Executive Officer
Rick A. Cassiday, Senior Vice President & Chief Human Resources Officer
Kathleen P. Leneghan, Senior Vice President & Chief Financial Officer
The world's leading manufacturer and distributor of innovative home and long-term care medical products which promote recovery and active lifestyles.

252 MedDev Corporation
MedDev Corporation
730 N Pastoria Ave
Sunnyvale, CA 94085-3522   408-730-9702
                                        800-543-2789
                                  FAX: 408-730-9732
                               info@meddev-corp.com
                              www.meddev-corp.com
Aids to rehabilitate hands following injury or illness, including patented complementary FingerHelper, ThumbHelper and Iso HandHelper models. MedDev also manufactures Soft Touch foam exercisers and the FiddlLink exerciser for digital dexterity. The Ultimate Hand Helper, an ergonomically designed hand exerciser, is curved to conform to the shape of the hand.

253 Osborn Medical Corporation
Osborn Medical Corporation
9800 E. Easter Ave.
Suite 130
Centennial, CO 80112   303-223-1800
                                        800-535-5865
                                  FAX: 507-932-5044
                             www.rookeproducts.com
Bill Davis, President & CEO
Keith Walli-Ware, Vice President, Sales & Marketing
Strider allows the user to exercise in most chairs found in at home. No more small, uncomfortable bicycle seats to sit on while exercising. A hands-free exercising experience.

254 Talking Digital Cooking Thermometer
Maxi Aids
42 Executive Blvd.
Farmingdale, NY 11735-4710   631-752-0521
                                        800-522-6294
                                  FAX: 631-752-0689
                                  TTY: 631-752-0738
                                  sales@maxiaids.com
                                     www.maxiaids.com
Elliot Zaretsky, Founder, President & CEO
Clearly announces temperature in Fahrenheit or Celsius. *$24.95*

255 Talking Digital Thermometer
Maxi Aids
42 Executive Blvd.
Farmingdale, NY 11735-4710   631-752-0521
                                        800-522-6294
                                  FAX: 631-752-0689
                                  TTY: 631-752-0738
                                  sales@maxiaids.com
                                     www.maxiaids.com
Elliot Zaretsky, Founder, President & CEO

Talking and large print thermometer. Announces and displays temperature in Fahrenheit or Celsius. *$16.95*

256   Thinklabs One Stethoscope
HARC Mercantile
5413 S Westnedge Ave.
Suite A
Portage, MI 49002
800-445-9968
TTY:269-324-1615
info@harc.com
www.harc.com

Michael Martinson, Owner
Stethoscope that amplifies sounds by more than 100x. Works with any headphones or hearing aid streamer.

Hearing Aids

257   Auditech: Personal PA Value Pack System
Auditech
P.O.Box 510476
St. Louis, MO 63151
314-416-1050
800-669-9065
auditecinfo@auditec.com
www.auditec.com
Reliable hearing assistance. This wireless FM system broadcasts to listeners with a hearing assistance system, helping them overcome background noise at a distance from the sound source. *$899.00*

258   Battery Device Adapter
AbleNet, Inc.
2625 Patton Road
Roseville, MN 55113-1137
651-294-2200
800-322-0956
FAX: 651-294-2259
customerservice@ablenetinc.com
www.ablenetinc.com

Jennifer Thalhuber, President & CEO
Paul Sugden, CFO & Trustee
A cable which connects to and adapts battery-operated devices for external switch control. Two sizes are available to adapt devices with either AA or C and D size batteries. *$8.00*

259   Cochlear
10350 Park Meadows Drive
Lone Tree, CO 80124
303-790-9010
800-523-5798
FAX: 303-790-1157
www.cochlear.com/us/en/home
Dig Howitt, President & CEO
Stuart Sayers, Chief Financial Officer
Jan Janssen, Chief Technology Officer
For over three decades, Cochlear has been delivering hearing implant innovation worldwide. Cochlear helps with the communication of implant recipients.

260   Custom Earmolds
Lloyd Hearing Aid Corporation
P.O.Box 1645
4435 Manchester Drive
Rockford, IL 61109
815-964-4191
800-323-4212
FAX: 815-964-8378
info@lloydhearingaid.com
www.lloydhearingaid.com

Andrew Palmquist, President
Hearing aid molds, custom built to the exact fit of the customer. *$29.95*

261   Digital Hearing Aids
Lloyd Hearing Aid Corporation
P.O.Box 1645
4435 Manchester Drive
Rockford, IL 61109
815-964-4191
800-323-4212
FAX: 815-964-8378
info@lloydhearingaid.com
www.lloydhearingaid.com

Andrew Palmquist, President

Latest hearing technology. *$7.50*

262   Duracell & Rayovac Hearing Aid Batteries
Lloyd Hearing Aid Corporation
P.O.Box 1645
4435 Manchester Drive
Rockford, IL 61109
815-964-4191
800-323-4212
FAX: 815-964-8378
info@lloydhearingaid.com
www.lloydhearingaid.com

Andrew Palmquist, President
Reliable and long-lasting, these batteries power the user's hearing aid. Easy to insert into hearing aid.

263   Harris Communications
Harris Communications
15155 Technology Dr
Eden Prairie, MN 55344
800-825-6758
FAX: 952-906-1099
TTY:952-388-2152
info@harriscomm.com
www.harriscomm.com

Ray Harris, CEO
A national distributor of assistive devices for the deaf and hard-of-hearing with many manufacturers represented. Catalog includes a wide range of assistive devices as well as a variety of books and video tapes related to deaf and hard-of-hearing issues. Products available for children, teachers, hearing professionals, interpreters and anyone interested in deaf culture, hearing loss and sign language.
180 pages Yearly

264   Hearing Aid Batteries
HARC Mercantile
5413 S Westnedge Ave.
Suite A
Portage, MI 49002
800-445-9968
TTY:269-324-1615
info@harc.com
www.harc.com

Michael Martinson, Owner
Hearing aid batteries in all popular sizes in mercury, zinc air, silver as well as Nicad and Varta and batteries for electrolarynx and infrared systems.

265   Hearing Aid Battery Testers
HARC Mercantile
5413 S Westnedge Ave.
Suite A
Portage, MI 49002
800-445-9968
TTY:269-324-1615
info@harc.com
www.harc.com

Michael Martinson, Owner
From pocket size to professional type battery testers which test mercury, zinc air, silver, specialty and general usage batteries. *$7.00*

266   Hearing Aid Care Kit
HARC Mercantile
5413 S Westnedge Ave.
Suite A
Portage, MI 49002
800-445-9968
TTY:269-324-1615
info@harc.com
www.harc.com

Michael Martinson, Owner
Includes a hearing aid dehumidifer, stethoset, and cleaning tools. *$40.00*

267   MED-EL Corporation, USA
2645 Meridian Parkway
Suite 100
Durham, NC 27713
919-572-2222
888-633-3524
FAX: 919-484-9229
www.medel.com/us

Ingeborg Hochmair, CEO

MED-EL is the leader in implantable hearing solutions. In 2017, the company launched the RONDO 2, a revolutionary cochlear implant powered by wireless charging technology.

268 Micro Audiometrics Corporation
Micro Audiometrics
1901 Mason Ave
Suite 104
Daytona Beach, FL 32117
386-888-7878
866-327-7226
FAX: 866-683-4447
sales@microaud.com
www.microaud.com

Jason Keller, President
Manufacturer and distributor of hearing testing instruments, including the complete line of Earscan.

269 Mushroom Inserts
Lloyd Hearing Aid Corporation
P.O.Box 1645
4435 Manchester Drive
Rockford, IL 61109
815-964-4191
800-323-4212
FAX: 815-964-8378
info@lloydhearingaid.com
www.lloydhearingaid.com

Andrew Palmquist, President
A universal earplug useful in wearing behind the ear type hearing instruments. *$2.50*

270 Oval Window Audio
33 Wildflower Ct
Nederland, CO 80466
303-447-3607
FAX: 303-447-3607
TTY:303-447-3607
info@ovalwindowaudio.com
www.ovalwindowaudio.com

Norman Lederman, Director of Research & Development
Paula Hendricks, Educational Director
Manufacturer of induction loop hearing assistance technologies compatible with telecoil-equipped hearing aids used by many hard of hearing people. The company also makes multisensory sound systems for use in speech and music therapy and science classes.

271 Sonova USA Inc.
Phonak
4520 Weaver Parkway
Warrenville, IL 60555-3927
800-679-4871
Info@Phonak.com
www.sonova.com/usa/en-us

Provides innovative technology and solutions to every form of hearing loss. Hearing aid brands Sonova carries aside from Phonak are Unitron, Advanced Bionics, and Connect Hearing.

272 Starkey Hearing Foundation
P.O. Box 41514
Minneapolis, MN 55441
866-354-3254
info@starkeyfoundation.org
www.starkeyhearingfoundation.org

Richard S. Brown, President
Brady Forseth, Executive Director
Keith Becker, Senior Director of Operations
The Starkey Hearing Foundation works to assist those with hearing impairments by offering hearing aids and aftercare services.
Quarterly

273 Ultratec
450 Science Dr
Madison, WI 53711
800-482-2424
FAX: 608-204-6167
TTY:800-482-2424
service@ultratec.com
www.ultratec.com

Jackie Morgan, Marketing Director
Ultratec works to make telephone access more convenient and reliable for people with hearing loss by providing assistive devices such as amplified phones and text phones.

274 Widex USA, Inc.
185 Commerce Drive
Hauppauge, NY 11788
800-221-0188
www.widex.com/en-us

Provider and producer of hearing aids, Widex's design combines technology with functionality and aesthetics.

Kitchen & Eating Aids

275 Bagel Holder
Maxi Aids
42 Executive Blvd.
Farmingdale, NY 11735-4710
631-752-0521
800-522-6294
FAX: 631-752-0689
TTY: 631-752-0738
sales@maxiaids.com
www.maxiaids.com

Elliot Zaretsky, Founder, President & CEO
Holds bagels in place for easy slicing. *$4.95*

276 Big and Bold Low Vision Timer
Maxi Aids
42 Executive Blvd.
Farmingdale, NY 11735-4710
631-752-0521
800-522-6294
FAX: 631-752-0689
TTY: 631-752-0738
sales@maxiaids.com
www.maxiaids.com

Elliot Zaretsky, Founder, President & CEO
Sixty-minute mechanical timer with large, easy-to-read numbers for the visually impaired. *$14.75*

277 Big-Grip Cutlery
Therapro, Inc.
225 Arlington St
Framingham, MA 01702-8723
508-872-9494
800-257-5376
FAX: 508-268-6624
info@therapro.com
www.therapro.com

Karen Conrad Weihrauch, President & Owner
Stainless steel utensils have a special twist built into the metal to facilitate bending of a spoon or fork at any angle for right or left handed people. *$11.95*

278 Box Top Opener
Performance Health
28100 Torch Parkway
Suite 700
Warrenville, IL 60555-3938
630-393-6000
800-323-5547
FAX: 630-547-4333
customersupport@performancehealth.com
www.performancehealth.com

Francis Dirksmeier, Chief Executive Officer
Greg Nulty, Chief Financial Officer
Jim Plewa, Chief Sales Officer
This handy device exerts the pressure on those hard-to-open boxes of laundry/dishwasher soap, rice and prepared dinners. *$2.95*

279 Braille Timer
Maxi Aids
42 Executive Blvd.
Farmingdale, NY 11735-4710
631-752-0521
800-522-6294
FAX: 631-752-0689
TTY: 631-752-0738
sales@maxiaids.com
www.maxiaids.com

Elliot Zaretsky, Founder, President & CEO
Three raised dots at 15, 30 and 45, two raised dots at 0, and one raised dot on all other numbers.

280 Cordless Receiver
AbleNet, Inc.
2625 Patton Road
Roseville, MN 55113-1137

651-294-2200
800-322-0956
FAX: 651-294-2259
customerservice@ablenetinc.com
www.ablenetinc.com

Jennifer Thalhuber, President & CEO
Paul Sugden, CFO & Trustee
The Cordless Receiver in conjunction with the Cordless Big Red Switch, can be used anywhere a switch is currently used to control battery or electrically-operated toys, games or appliances; augmentative communication systems; and computers (through a computer switch interface). *$79.00*

281 Deluxe Roller Knife
Performance Health
28100 Torch Parkway
Suite 700
Warrenville, IL 60555-3938

630-393-6000
FAX: 630-393-7600
customersupport@performancehealth.com
www.performancehealth.com

Francis Dirksmeier, Chief Executive Officer
Greg Nulty, Chief Financial Officer
Jim Plewa, Chief Sales Officer
Stainless steel blade rolls smoothly, cutting food cleanly. *$10.95*

282 Dual Brush with Suction Base
Performance Health
28100 Torch Parkway
Suite 700
Warrenville, IL 60555-3938

630-393-6000
FAX: 630-393-7600
customersupport@performancehealth.com
www.performancehealth.com

Francis Dirksmeier, Chief Executive Officer
Greg Nulty, Chief Financial Officer
Jim Plewa, Chief Sales Officer
Two brushes clean the inside and outside of bottles and glasses at the same time using just one hand. *$14.50*

283 Etac Relieve Angled Table Knife
R82, Inc.
13137 Bleinheim Lane
Matthews, NC 28105

844-876-6245
FAX: 704-882-0751
sales.us@etac.com
www.r82.com

The design of these knives allows a better working posture and makes optimal use of strength in the arms and hands.

284 Folding Pot Stabilizer
Maxi Aids
42 Executive Blvd.
Farmingdale, NY 11735-4710

631-752-0521
800-522-6294
FAX: 631-752-0689
TTY: 631-752-0738
sales@maxiaids.com
www.maxiaids.com

Elliot Zaretsky, Founder, President & CEO
This device holds onto the pot handle and secures the pot in place, allowing for easier use for those with physical challenges. *$35.95*

285 H.E.L.P. Knife
Maxi Aids
42 Executive Blvd.
Farmingdale, NY 11735-4710

631-752-0521
800-522-6294
FAX: 631-752-0689
TTY: 631-752-0738
sales@maxiaids.com
www.maxiaids.com

Elliot Zaretsky, Founder, President & CEO
Adjustable food slicing system guides the knife for even, uniform slices while protecting the user. *$22.95*

286 Innerlip Plates
Therapro, Inc.
225 Arlington St
Framingham, MA 01702-8723

508-872-9494
800-257-5376
FAX: 508-268-6624
info@therapro.com
www.therapro.com

Karen Conrad Weihrauch, President & Owner
Food may be pushed to the side of the plate, then scooped up with a fork and spoon. Available in beige or blue. *$8.50*

287 Long Oven Mitts
Performance Health
28100 Torch Parkway
Suite 700
Warrenville, IL 60555-3938

630-393-6000
FAX: 630-393-7600
customersupport@performancehealth.com
www.performancehealth.com

Francis Dirksmeier, Chief Executive Officer
Greg Nulty, Chief Financial Officer
Jim Plewa, Chief Sales Officer
Protect hands and forearms from heat, flames and oven grates with these practical mitts that allow a longer reach and less bending. *$8.95*

288 Nosey Cup
Therapro, Inc.
225 Arlington St
Framingham, MA 01702-8723

508-872-9494
800-257-5376
FAX: 508-268-6624
info@therapro.com
www.therapro.com

Karen Conrad Weihrauch, President & Owner
For those with a stiff neck or persons who can't tip their head back while drinking. *$5.95*

289 Performance Health
Performance Health
28100 Torch Parkway
Suite 700
Warrenville, IL 60555-3938

630-393-6000
FAX: 630-393-7600
customersupport@performancehealth.com
www.performancehealth.com

Francis Dirksmeier, Chief Executive Officer
Greg Nulty, Chief Financial Officer
Jim Plewa, Chief Sales Officer
Performance Health is a leading provider of rehabilitation and assistive devices to help those with disabilities meet daily physical challenges and achieve their greatest level of independence. With one of the industry's largest catalogs, Sammons Preston Rolyan offers a wide range of products available.
Annually

290 PowerLink 4 Control Unit
AbleNet, Inc.
2625 Patton Road
Roseville, MN 55113-1137

651-294-2200
800-322-0956
FAX: 651-294-2259
customerservice@ablenetinc.com
www.ablenetinc.com

Jennifer Thalhuber, President & CEO
Paul Sugden, CFO & Trustee
The PowerLink 4 Control Unit allows switch operation of electrical appliances. It can be used to activate 1 or 2 appliances (up to 1700 watts combined). If 2 appliances are used, they will activate simultaneously. There are four modes of control on the PowerLink 2; direct mode, timed (seconds) mode, timed (minutes) mode and latch mode. Meets safety standards from Underwriters Laboratory (UL) and Canadian Standards Association (CSA) for electrical appliances. *$330.00*

291 **Steel Food Bumper**
Maxi Aids
42 Executive Blvd.
Farmingdale, NY 11735-4710
631-752-0521
800-522-6294
FAX: 631-752-0689
TTY: 631-752-0738
sales@maxiaids.com
www.maxiaids.com

Elliot Zaretsky, Founder, President & CEO
Provides stable area to push against while eating. *$16.95*

292 **Stove Knob Turner**
Maxi Aids
42 Executive Blvd.
Farmingdale, NY 11735-4710
631-752-0521
800-522-6294
FAX: 631-752-0689
TTY: 631-752-0738
sales@maxiaids.com
www.maxiaids.com

Elliot Zaretsky, Founder, President & CEO
Lightweight aluminum rod for turning stove knobs. Designed for wheelchair users. *$34.95*

293 **Talking Food Cans**
Maxi Aids
42 Executive Blvd.
Farmingdale, NY 11735-4710
631-752-0521
800-522-6294
FAX: 631-752-0689
TTY: 631-752-0738
sales@maxiaids.com
www.maxiaids.com

Elliot Zaretsky, Founder, President & CEO
Voice recording device for recording descriptions of hard to identify objects, such as food cans, bottles and storage containers. *$25.95*

294 **Undercounter Lid Opener**
Performance Health
28100 Torch Parkway
Suite 700
Warrenville, IL 60555-3938
630-393-6000
FAX: 630-393-7600
customersupport@performancehealth.com
www.performancehealth.com

Francis Dirksmeier, Chief Executive Officer
Greg Nulty, Chief Financial Officer
Jim Plewa, Chief Sales Officer
The gripper of this unit which installs under the counter can help unscrew any cap. *$5.75*

295 **Uni-Turner**
Performance Health
28100 Torch Parkway
Suite 700
Warrenville, IL 60555-3938
630-393-6000
FAX: 630-393-7600
customersupport@performancehealth.com
www.performancehealth.com

Francis Dirksmeier, Chief Executive Officer
Greg Nulty, Chief Financial Officer
Jim Plewa, Chief Sales Officer
Odd-shaped handles can be turned easily with one-handed, L-shaped Uni-Turner. *$16.50*

296 **Universal Hand Cuff**
Therapro, Inc.
225 Arlington St
Framingham, MA 01702-8723
508-872-9494
800-257-5376
FAX: 508-268-6624
info@therapro.com
www.therapro.com

Karen Conrad Weihrauch, President & Owner
Comfortable cuff with Velcro strap holds utensils, toothbrushes, etc. Washable and adjustable to the user's condition and hand size. *$8.50*

Lifts, Ramps & Elevators

297 **Accessibility Lift**
Inclinator Company of America
601 Gibson Blvd
Harrisburg, PA 17104
800-343-9007
info@inclinator.com
www.inclinator.com

Cliff Warner, President & CEO
Mark Crispen, Director of Marketing, Corporate Secretary & Board Member
Marcia Cleland, Human Resource Manager/Accounting
An economical lift for restricted usage that provides barrier-free access that can be used by churches, schools, lodging halls and meeting halls to meet compliance requirements, with the dignified convenience and freedom they deserve.

298 **Adjustable Incline Board**
Bailey Manufacturing Company
P.O. Box 130
Lodi, OH 44254-0130
330-948-1080
800-321-8372
FAX: 330-948-4439
baileymfg@baileymfg.com
www.baileymfg.com

Incline board for the physically challenged with a foot board with non-slip tread.

299 **AlumiRamp**
AlumiRamp, Inc.
855 East Chicago Road
Quincy, MI 49082-9450
517-639-8777
800-800-3864
FAX: 517-639-4314
sales@alumiramp.com
www.alumiramp.com

Doug Cannon, Sales & Customer Service
Complete line of modular, aluminum and portable ramps for both home and vehicle use. Welded construction and non-skid extruded surfaces are featured on all our ramps.

300 **Area Access**
Area Access
7131 Gateway Court
Manassas, VA 20109-1015
703-396-4949
www.areaaccess.com

Serving the entire Mid-Atlantic with scooters, stairway lifts and elevators. Large inventory and fully stocked showrooms.

301 **Back-Saver**
Bruno Independent Living Aids, Inc.
1780 Executive Dr.
PO Box 84
Oconomowoc, WI 53066
262-567-4990
800-454-4355
FAX: 262-953-5501
webinfo@bruno.com
www.bruno.com

Michael R. Bruno, II, President & CEO
Exterior platform lift for transporting manual folding wheelchairs. 100 lb lift capacity.

302 **Basement Motorhome Lift**
Handicaps, Inc.
4335 S Santa Fe Dr.
Englewood, CO 80110-5417
303-781-2062
800-782-4335
info@handicapsinc.com
www.handicapsinc.com

Wheelchair lifts made for vans and motor homes. Lift is made without a platform so no doorways are blocked.

303   Big Lifter
Bruno Independent Living Aids, Inc.
1780 Executive Dr.
PO Box 84
Oconomowoc, WI 53066

262-567-4990
800-454-4355
FAX: 262-953-5501
webinfo@bruno.com
www.bruno.com

Michael R. Bruno, II, President & CEO
Hoist-style lift for scooters and power chairs. Can be manually rotated; 400 lb lift capacity.

304   BraunAbility
645 W Carmel Dr.
Carmel, IN 46032

800-488-0359
888-365-9417
questions@braunability.com
www.braunability.com

Staci Kroon, President & CEO
Manufactures wheelchair and mobility scooter lifts and ramps for vehicles.

305   Bruno Independent Living Aids
Bruno Independent Living Aids, Inc.
1780 Executive Dr.
PO Box 84
Oconomowoc, WI 53066

262-567-4990
800-454-4355
FAX: 262-953-5501
webinfo@bruno.com
www.bruno.com

Michael R. Bruno, II, President & CEO
An ISO 9001 Certified Manufacturer of automotive lifts for scooter, wheelchairs, powerchairs, three and four wheel scooters, and straight and custom curve stairlifts.

306   Butlers Wheelchair Lifts
Butler Mobility Products
571 Industrial Drive
Lewisberry, PA 17339

717-938-4253
888-847-0804
FAX: 717-938-4238
www.butlermobility.com

Wheelchair lift can be equipped with a ramp and guard. Automatically retractable, it locks firmly into place when the lift is in operation.

307   Chariot
Bruno Independent Living Aids, Inc.
1780 Executive Dr.
PO Box 84
Oconomowoc, WI 53066

262-567-4990
800-454-4355
FAX: 262-953-5501
webinfo@bruno.com
www.bruno.com

Michael R. Bruno, II, President & CEO
Exterior lift for transporting scooters and power chairs. The lift includes 360-degree spinning wheels and has a 350 lb lift capacity.

308   Clearway
Ricon
1135 Aviation Pl.
San Fernando, CA 91340

818-267-3000
800-322-2884
FAX: 800-962-1201
ricinsales@wabtec.com
www.riconcorp.com

Wheelchair lift featuring an automatic split platform that allows for clear access to the vehicle.

309   Columbus McKinnon Corporation
Columbus Mckinnon Corporation
205 Crosspoint Parkway
Getzville, NY 14068

716-689-5400
800-888-0985
www.cmworks.com

David J. Wilson, President & CEO

Supplies various lift and transfer systems for independent or attended applications including ceiling mounted or freestanding overhead track lifts and mobile floorbase units for homes, schools and healthcare facilities. Lift Systems for transferring between bed, chair, commode or bath are available with a variety of slings, scales and accessories.

310   Curb-Sider
Bruno Independent Living Aids, Inc.
1780 Executive Dr.
PO Box 84
Oconomowoc, WI 53066

262-567-4990
800-454-4355
FAX: 262-953-5501
webinfo@bruno.com
www.bruno.com

Michael R. Bruno, II, President & CEO
A hoist lift that stores fully or partially assembled scooters or power chairs weighing up to 450 pounds in the rear of a van, minivan, SUV, pickup truck, or some station wagon applications.

311   Custom Lift Residential Elevators
Waupaca Elevator Company
1726 N. Ballard Road
Suite 1
Appleton, WI 54911-2404

800-238-8739
info@waupacaelevator.com
waupacaelevator.com

Bill Mc Michael, Owner
Waupaca Elevator residential elevators and dumbwaiters add value, convenience and reliability to today's homes.

312   Deluxe Convertible Exercise Staircase
Performance Health
28100 Torch Parkway
Suite 700
Warrenville, IL 60555-3938

630-393-6000
FAX: 630-393-7600
customersupport@performancehealth.com
www.performancehealth.com

Francis Dirksmeier, Chief Executive Officer
Greg Nulty, Chief Financial Officer
Jim Plewa, Chief Sales Officer
An exercise staircase to fit any department configuration. Just reposition a few nuts and bolts to change from a straight to a corner type staircase.

313   Digital Wheelchair Ramp Scale
Graham-Field Health Products
One Graham-Field Way
Atlanta, GA 30340-3140

770-368-4700
FAX: 770-368-4932
cs@grahamfield.com
www.grahamfield.com

Kenneth Spett, President & CEO
Cherie Antoniazzi, Senior Vice President, Quality, Regulatory &
Risk Management
Marc Bernstein, Senior Vice President, Consumer Sales
Weight capacity of 1,000 lbs; 270 patient memory; platform with wheels for mobility.

314   Easy Pivot Transfer Machine
Rand-Scot, Inc.
209 Christman Drive
Fort Collins, CO 80524

970-484-7967
800-467-7967
FAX: 970-484-3800
info@randscot.com
www.randscot.com

Joel Lerich, Co-Founder
Barbara Lerich, Co-Founder
The Easy Pivot Patient Lifting System allows for strain-free, one-caregiver transfers of the disabled individual.

315 Easy Stand
Altimate Medical
262 W. 1st St.
Morton, MN 56270-180
507-697-6393
800-342-8968
FAX: 507-697-6900
info@easystand.com
www.easystand.com

Designed to make standing fast and simple. The easy-to-operate, hydraulic lift system provides controlled lifting and lowering. With the convenience of simply transferring to the chair and reaching a standing position in seconds with no straps to struggle with.

316 Elan Stair Lift
Bruno Independent Living Aids, Inc.
1780 Executive Dr.
PO Box 84
Oconomowoc, WI 53066
262-567-4990
800-454-4355
FAX: 262-953-5501
webinfo@bruno.com
www.bruno.com

Michael R. Bruno, II, President & CEO
Indoor stairlift; vertical rail design; 300 lb lift capacity.

317 Elite Curved Stair Lift
Bruno Independent Living Aids, Inc.
1780 Executive Dr.
PO Box 84
Oconomowoc, WI 53066
262-567-4990
800-454-4355
FAX: 262-953-5501
webinfo@bruno.com
www.bruno.com

Michael R. Bruno, II, President & CEO
Curved stairlift with 400 lb lift capacity; indoor and outdoor stairlifts available.

318 Elite Stair Lift
Bruno Independent Living Aids, Inc.
1780 Executive Dr.
PO Box 84
Oconomowoc, WI 53066
262-567-4990
800-454-4355
FAX: 262-953-5501
webinfo@bruno.com
www.bruno.com

Michael R. Bruno, II, President & CEO
Stairlift with 400 lb lift capacity; indoor and outdoor stairlifts available.

319 Freedom Wheels
Freedom Wheels
580 TC Jester Blvd
Houston, TX 77007
713-864-1460
FAX: 713-864-1469
info@freedomwheels.com
www.freedomwheels.com

Carlos Saez, Owner
Assistive technology and mobility-equipment provider committed to people with disabilities and personal transportation options for an independent lifestyle.

320 Handi Lift
Handi-Lift
730 Garden St
Carlstadt, NJ 07072
201-933-0111
800-432-5438
sales@handi-lift.com
www.handi-lift.com

Douglas Boydston, Founder
Accessibility with Dignity. Solutions that enable users with mobility impairments to live freely with products like wheelchair lifts and home elevators.

321 Handi Prolift
Handi-Lift
730 Garden St
Carlstadt, NJ 07072
201-933-0111
800-432-5438
sales@handi-lift.com
www.handi-lift.com

Douglas Boydston, Founder
Provides dependable vertical transportation for multi-level buildings.

322 Handi-Ramp
Handi-Ramp
5600 99th Ave
Unit A1
Kenosha, WI 53144
847-876-7267
info@handiramp.com
www.handiramp.com

Thomas Disch, President & CEO
Provides a complete line of economic, ADA-compliant access ramping products. Line includes van attachable and wheelchair tie-downs; aluminum or expanded metal folding portables; aluminum channels; portable, sectional ramp systems; semi-permanent ramps, platforms and systems. All ramp series are available in varied lengths and widths combined with platforms, optional hand railing, and single or double bar construction with return ends. Special Order ramps and ramp systems.

323 Home Elevators
Handi-Lift
730 Garden St
Carlstadt, NJ 07072
201-933-0111
800-432-5438
sales@handi-lift.com
www.handi-lift.com

Douglas Boydston, Founder
Home Elevators answers access problems in churches, schools and small offices.

324 Homewaiter
Inclinator Company of America
601 Gibson Blvd
Harrisburg, PA 17104
800-343-9007
info@inclinator.com
www.inclinator.com

Cliff Warner, President & CEO
Mark Crispen, Director of Marketing, Corporate Secretary & Board Member
Marcia Cleland, Human Resource Manager/Accounting
Easy to install and highly adaptable to existing conditions. Can travel up to 35 feet, opening on any or all three sides at different stations, whether at counter level or floor level.

325 Horcher Lifting Systems
Horcher Medical Systems
324 Cypress Rd
Ocala, FL 34472-3102
352-687-8020
800-582-8732
FAX: 866-378-3318
info@horcherlifts.com
www.horcherlifts.com

Barrier Free Lifts by Horcher leads the industry for excellence in patient transfers and technology for over 18 years. They offer state of the art ceiling track systems, floor base lifts and bathing systems such as the Unilift, PC-2, Diana, Lexa, and Raisa to achieve greater mobility.

326 Inclinette
Inclinator Company of America
601 Gibson Blvd
Harrisburg, PA 17104
800-343-9007
info@inclinator.com
www.inclinator.com

Cliff Warner, President & CEO
Mark Crispen, Director of Marketing, Corporate Secretary & Board Member
Marcia Cleland, Human Resource Manager/Accounting
Inclinette provides comfort and convenience in providing multi-floor access to persons who have difficulty climbing stairs.

327 **Independent Driving Systems**
Independent Driving Systems
580 T.C. Jester
Houston, TX 77007   713-864-1460
            info@independentdrivingsystems.com
            www.independentdrivingsystems.com
Chad Donnelly, Owner
Provides adaptive driving systems for individuals with disabilities with more severe higher levels of injury that require more sophisticated types of assistive technology to enable them to drive safely.

328 **Joey Interior Platform Lift**
Bruno Independent Living Aids, Inc.
1780 Executive Dr.
PO Box 84
Oconomowoc, WI 53066   262-567-4990
                                    800-454-4355
                            FAX: 262-953-5501
                            webinfo@bruno.com
                            www.bruno.com
Michael R. Bruno, II, President & CEO
Lifts and stores unoccupied scooters or powerchairs in the back of a minivan at the touch of a button.

329 **KlearVue**
Ricon
1135 Aviation Pl.
San Fernando, CA 91340   818-267-3000
                                    800-322-2884
                            FAX: 800-962-1201
                            ricinsales@wabtec.com
                            www.riconcorp.com
Wheelchair lift and folding platform with an unobstructed view from inside the vehicle.

330 **Lift-All**
Amigo Mobility International
6693 Dixie Highway
Bridgeport, MI 48722   989-777-0910
                            service@myamigo.com
                            www.myamigo.com
Al Thieme, Chair & Founder
Beth Thieme, President & CEO
Leading manufacturer of electric mobility; Amigo's Lift-All transports your wheelchair easily into the trunk of an automobile and neatly stores it for easy access. *$965.00*

331 **Lifter**
Bruno Independent Living Aids, Inc.
1780 Executive Dr.
PO Box 84
Oconomowoc, WI 53066   262-567-4990
                                    800-454-4355
                            FAX: 262-953-5501
                            webinfo@bruno.com
                            www.bruno.com
Michael R. Bruno, II, President & CEO
Raises and stows folding manual wheelchairs, travel scooters, and travel power chairs. 200 lb lift capacity.

332 **Lifts for Swimming Pools and Spas**
Aquatic Access
1921 Production Dr
Louisville, KY 40299-2110   502-425-5817
                                    800-325-5438
                            FAX: 502-425-9607
                            info@AquaticAccess.com
                            www.aquaticaccess.com
Linda Nolan, President
David Nolan, Vice President & CEO
Aquatic Access manufacturers and sells water-powered lifts providing access to in-ground and above-ground swimming pools, spas, boats and docks. *$2310.00*

333 **Mac's Lift Gate**
Mac's Lift Gate, Inc.
2801 South Street
Long Beach, CA 90805   800-795-6227
                            FAX: 562-529-3466
                            sales@macsliftgate.com
                            www.macsliftgate.com
Rick Pearce, Contact
Paul Hemmingway, Contact
Sales and service of van and truck lifts. Sales and service of wheel chair lifts for vans and automobiles. Sales, installation and service of vertical home lifts, scooter lifts and pool lifts. Sales of scooters.

334 **Mecalift Sling Lifter**
Arjo Inc
2349 West Lake Street
Suite 250
Addison, IL 60101   800-323-1245
                                    888-594-2756
                            www.arjo.com
Joacim Lindoff, President & CEO
Tailored to the mobility level and needs of the resident and patient for the purpose of lifting manoeuvers.

335 **Motorhome Lift**
Handicaps, Inc.
4335 S Santa Fe Dr.
Englewood, CO 80110-5417   303-781-2062
                                    800-782-4335
                            info@handicapsinc.com
                            www.handicapsinc.com
Wheelchair lifts made for vans and motor homes. Lift is made without a platform so no doorways are blocked.

336 **Out-Sider III**
Bruno Independent Living Aids, Inc.
1780 Executive Dr.
PO Box 84
Oconomowoc, WI 53066   262-567-4990
                                    800-454-4355
                            FAX: 262-953-5501
                            webinfo@bruno.com
                            www.bruno.com
Michael R. Bruno, II, President & CEO
Exterior platform lift. Maintains seating and cargo space. Designed specifically for rear-view visibility. Platform folds automatically when not being used. 350 lb lift capacity.

337 **Parker Bath**
Arjo Inc
2349 West Lake Street
Suite 250
Addison, IL 60101   800-323-1245
                                    888-594-2756
                            www.arjo.com
Joacim Lindoff, President & CEO
This product involves no manual lifting, strain or stress for the caregiver.

338 **Patient Lifting & Injury Prevention**
Arjo Inc
2349 West Lake Street
Suite 250
Addison, IL 60101   800-323-1245
                                    888-594-2756
                            www.arjo.com
Joacim Lindoff, President & CEO
Aids in patient lifting while protecting the caregiver from the risk of backstrain.

339 **Platform Lifts**
Handi-Lift
730 Garden St
Carlstadt, NJ 07072   201-933-0111
                                    800-432-5438
                            sales@handi-lift.com
                            www.handi-lift.com
Douglas Boydston, Founder
Designed to provide access over stairs that impede movement.

340 Portable Wheelchair Ramp
Maxi Aids
42 Executive Blvd.
Farmingdale, NY 11735-4710
631-752-0521
800-522-6294
FAX: 631-752-0689
TTY: 631-752-0738
sales@maxiaids.com
www.maxiaids.com

Elliot Zaretsky, Founder, President & CEO
Single-fold ramp designed to help wheelchair or scooter users easily transition from one surface level to another.

341 Rickshaw Exerciser
Access to Recreation
8 Sandra Ct
Newbury Park, CA 91320-4302
805-498-7535
800-634-4351
FAX: 805-498-8186
customerservice@accesstr.com
www.accesstr.com

Don Krebs, President & Founder
This Exerciser develops the muscle used most by those in wheelchairs. It develops the strength you need to lift yourself for pressure relief, doing transfers and pushing your wheelchair.

342 Ricon Classic
Ricon
1135 Aviation Pl.
San Fernando, CA 91340
818-267-3000
800-322-2884
FAX: 800-962-1201
ricinsales@wabtec.com
www.riconcorp.com

Wheelchair lift featuring Ricon Safety Zone, an occupant restraint belt system, as well as Sto-Loc, a design that prevents lift drift.

343 Ricon Corporation
1135 Aviation Pl.
San Fernando, CA 91340
818-267-3000
800-322-2884
FAX: 800-962-1201
ricinsales@wabtec.com
www.riconcorp.com

Ricon Corporation is a manufacturer of lifts and other mobility products for people with disabilities. It is a subsidiary of Wabtec Corporation and Faiveley Transport.

344 Smart Leg
Invacare
1 Invacare Way
Elyria, OH 44035-4190
800-333-6900
www.invacare.com

Matthew E. Monaghan, Chairman of the Board & Chief Executive Officer
Rick A. Cassiday, Senior Vice President & Chief Human Resources Officer
Kathleen P. Leneghan, Senior Vice President & Chief Financial Officer
An elevating leg rest that automatically extends to correctly fit every outstretched leg.

345 Smooth Mover
Dixie EMS
300 Liberty Ave
Brooklyn, NY 11207
718-257-6400
800-347-3494
FAX: 718-257-6401
info@dixieems.com
www.dixieems.com

Eva Silverstein, President
Patient mover is a board designed to transfer patients from bed to stretcher or table with one or two people. Being radio-translucent makes it suitable for x-ray procedures. *$199.95*

346 SpectraLift
Inclinator Company of America
601 Gibson Blvd
Harrisburg, PA 17104
800-343-9007
info@inclinator.com
www.inclinator.com

Cliff Warner, President & CEO
Mark Crispen, Director of Marketing, Corporate Secretary & Board Member
Marcia Cleland, Human Resource Manager/Accounting
A newly designed hydraulic wheelchair lift made of fiberglass construction suitable for commercial and residential use.

347 Spectrum Products
Spectrum Aquatics
7100 Spectrum Lane
Missoula, MT 59808
800-791-8056
www.spectrumproducts.com

Manufacturers of swimming pool disabled access products such as lifts, ramps, railings, ladders, and stainless steel hydrotherapy tanks for the swimming pool and medical therapy markets.

348 Spectrum Products Catalog
Spectrum Aquatics
7100 Spectrum Lane
Missoula, MT 59808
800-791-8056
www.spectrumproducts.com

Manufacturers of swimming pool disabled access products such as lifts, ramps, railings, ladders, and stainless steel hydrotherapy tanks for the swimming pool and medical therapy markets.

349 StairLIFT SC & SL
Inclinator Company of America
601 Gibson Blvd
Harrisburg, PA 17104
800-343-9007
info@inclinator.com
www.inclinator.com

Cliff Warner, President & CEO
Mark Crispen, Director of Marketing, Corporate Secretary & Board Member
Marcia Cleland, Human Resource Manager/Accounting
Simple, self-contained and efficient stair units.

350 Superarm Lift for Vans
Handicaps, Inc.
4335 S Santa Fe Dr.
Englewood, CO 80110-5417
303-781-2062
800-782-4335
info@handicapsinc.com
www.handicapsinc.com

Wheelchair lifts made for vans and motor homes. Lift is made without a platform so no doorways are blocked.

351 SureHands Lift & Care Systems
982 County Route 1
Pine Island, NY 10969-1205
800-724-5305
info@surehands.com
www.surehands.com

Thomas Herceg, President
SureHands specializes in lift & care systems for both homecare and professional settings where safety is most important, to assist an individual in overcoming physical and architectural barriers. Some of their products include lifting and body support systems, handi-slides, accessories and bathing equipment.

352 Vangater, Vangater II, Mini-Vangater
BraunAbility
645 W Carmel Dr.
Carmel, IN 46032
800-488-0359
888-365-9417
questions@braunability.com
www.braunability.com

Staci Kroon, President & CEO
Tri-fold and fold-in-half lifts for adapted van transportation.

353 Versatrainer
Pro- Max/ Division Of Bow- Flex Of America
800-605-3369
customerservice@bowflex.com
www.bowflex.com

One exercise system for the disabled person that does everything. Incorporates full-body strength, muscle development, and cardiovascular conditioning, giving full muscle movement and balanced muscle development.

354   Vestibular Board
Bailey Manufacturing Company
P.O. Box 130
Lodi, OH 44254-0130   330-948-1080
                                        800-321-8372
                              FAX: 330-948-4439
                              baileymfg@baileymfg.com
                              www.baileymfg.com

Creates tilting in a rolling motion for reclining patients who need help developing balance.

355   Wheelchair Carrier
Wheelchair Carrier
5254 Jackman Road
Unit B
Toledo, OH 43613   800-541-3213
                              admin@WheelChairCarrier.com
                              wheelchaircarrier.com

David Makulinsky, President
Wheelchair, scooter and powerchair carriers for hitch mount on vehicles, both manual and electric, making it easy and simple to transport the user's mobility device.

356   Williams Lift Company
24 S Ave.
Fanwood, NJ 07023   908-325-3648
                              FAX: 308-322-8020
                              contact@williamslifts.com
                              www.williamslifts.com

Barry Williams, Owner
A division of Williams Surgical, Williams Lift Company offers stairlifts, wheelchair ramps, and power lift recliners. Services include installation, repairs, and rentals.

Major Catalogs

357   Access to Recreation
Access to Recreation
8 Sandra Ct
Newbury Park, CA 91320-4302   805-498-7535
                                        800-634-4351
                              FAX: 805-498-8186
                              customerservice@accessstr.com
                              www.accesstr.com

Don Krebs, President & Founder
The Access to Recreation catalog is full of recreation and exercise equipment. One can find items such as electric fishing reels and other fishing and hunting equipment for the disabled sportsman. There are also adapted golf clubs, swimming pool lifts, wheelchair gloves and cuffs and bowling equipment. There are devices to help with embroidery, knitting and card playing, videos, books and practical aides such as wheelchair ramps and book.
64 pages Bi-Annually

358   Adaptive Technology Catalog
Synapse Adaptive
14 Lynn Ct
San Rafael, CA 94901-5114   415-455-9700
                                        800-317-9611
                              FAX: 415-455-9801
                              info@synapse-ada.com
                              www.synapseadaptive.com

Martin Tibor, President
Adaptive technology for individuals with disabilities, ADA compliant workstations, and ergonomic furniture. Products accommodate blindness, low vision, mobility impairments or learning differences.

359   AliMed
Alimed, Inc.
297 High Street
Dedham, MA 02026   781-329-2900
                                        800-437-2966
                              FAX: 781-437-2966
                              customerservice@alimed.com
                              www.alimed.com

Adam S. Epstein, Chief Executive Officer
AliMed is a leading provider of medical and healthcare products serving all segments of the healthcare market, including hospitals and clinics, nursing homes and care facilities, private medical practices, therapists and more.

360   Apria Healthcare
Apria Healthcare Group, Inc.
1975 Wehrle Dr
Buffalo, NY 14221   716-631-8726
Lifts, chairs, bathroom aids, bedroom aids, eating utensils and independent living aids for the physically challenged.

361   Armstrong Medical
American Medical Industries, Inc.
575 Knightsbridge Parkway
P.O. Box 700
Lincolnshire, IL 60069-0700   847-913-0101
                                        800-323-4220
                              FAX: 847-913-0138
                              csr@armstrongmedical.com
                              www.armstrongmedical.com

John Armstrong, Founder
Jim Armstrong, Vice President
Training aids, anatomical models, medical equipment, pediatrics equipment and rehabilitation equipment.

362   Assistive Technology Journal
Technologists, Inc.
3120 Fairview Park Drive
Suite 610
Falls Church, VA 22042   202-681-3851
                              email@technologistsinc.com
                              www.technologistsinc.com

Sayed "Aziz" Azimi, President & CEO
Integrates technical and management in difficult environments. Various disciplines include architecture, engineering, construction management, etc. *$32.50*
Bi-Annually

363   Bailey
Bailey Manufacturing Company
P.O. Box 130
Lodi, OH 44254-0130   330-948-1080
                                        800-321-8372
                              FAX: 330-948-4439
                              baileymfg@baileymfg.com
                              www.baileymfg.com

Ambulation aids, balance aids, benches, chairs, exercise devices, tables, stools, rehabilitation and physical therapy equipment for the physically challenged.
70 pages

364   Cambridge Career Products Catalog
Cambridge Educational
132 West 31st Street
16th Floor
New York, NY 10001   800-322-8755
                              FAX: 800-678-3633
                              custserv@films.com
                              cambridge.films.com

A full-color catalog featuring hundreds of products designed to aid people in career exploration, selecting specific occupations and obtaining these jobs through resume and interview preparation.
64 pages BiAnnual

365   Carex Health Brands
Carex Health Brands   800-526-8051
                              carex.com

Duane Wagner, CEO

The Carex brand provides a full line of home healthCare mobility, bath safety and personal care products that improve quality of life and increase independence. Consistently provides innovative, high-quality, safe and reliable products that exceed customer expectations.

366 Carolyn's Low Vision Products
3938 S. Tamiami Trail
Sarasota, FL 34231-3622
941-373-9100
800-648-2266
info@carolynscatalog.com
www.carolynscatalog.com

John Colton, Owner
A trusted leader in low-vision products. Free national mail-order catalog of items for visually impaired and blind people. Well versed in a variety of eye diseases that damage vision and have an expertise in helping customers making product purchasing decisions for their needs.

367 Connect Hearing
Hearing Center
750 N Commons Dr
Suite 200
Aurora, IL 60504
630-303-5380
info@connecthearing.com
www.connecthearing.com

Marcello J. Celentano, President & CEO
Specializes in products for the hard of hearing and deaf as required under ADA including visual alerting products for fire, phone, door, wake up, phone amplification, TTY, FM and infrared listening systems. Provides expertise on diagnosing hearing loss.

368 Danmar Products
221 Jackson Industrial Dr
Ann Arbor, MI 48103
800-783-1998
FAX: 734-761-8977
sales@danmarproducts.com
www.danmarproducts.com

Dan Russo, President & COO
Manufactures adaptive equipment for persons with physical and mental disabilities. Products include seating and positioning equipment, flotation devices, toileting aids, and hard and soft shell helmets.

369 Disabilities Sourcebook
Omnigraphics
132 West 31st Street
16th Floor
New York, NY 10001
800-322-8755
FAX: 800-678-3633
contact@omnigraphics.com
www.omnigraphics.com

Peter Ruffner, Co-Founder
Fred Ruffner, Co-Founder
For people with disabilities and caregivers, this product gives general information concerning birth defects, loss in hearing and vision, speech disorders, learning disorders,intellectual and cognitive disabilities, and other impairments due to illness, injury, and trauma. *$78.00*
616 pages
ISBN 0-780803-89-2

370 Enrichments Catalog
Performance Health
28100 Torch Parkway
Suite 700
Warrenville, IL 60555-3938
630-393-6000
FAX: 630-393-7600
customersupport@performancehealth.com
www.performancehealth.com

Francis Dirksmeier, Chief Executive Officer
Greg Nulty, Chief Financial Officer
Jim Plewa, Chief Sales Officer
Provides people with physical challenges with the products they need to help live their lives to the fullest. Includes items for everyday tasks and personal care; assistive products for home use; toileting and bathing aids; grooming and dressing devices; kitchen and dining aids. Also items for range of motion, mobility and exercise such as weights, therapy putty and exercise equip-ment; ergonomic gloves and supports; canes, crutches, walkers and wheelchair accessories. 36-page catalog.

371 Equipment Shop
34 Hartford Street
P.O. Box 33
Bedford, MA 01730
781-275-7681
800-525-7681
FAX: 781-275-4094
sales@equipmentshop.com
www.equipmentshop.com

Ken Larson, President
Carrie Larson, Manager
Specializing in oral motor therapy equipment, including Flexi Cut Cups, Maroon Spoons, Chewy Tubes, ARK grabbers and z-vibes. Also tricycle foot peal attachments and trike back supports as well as fat wheels.

372 Essential Medical Supply, Inc.
6420 Hazeltine National Drive
Orlando, FL 32822
407-770-0710
essentialmedicalsupply.com

John Hoepner, President
Carol Ann Hoepner, Secretary & Treasurer
Michael J. Hoepner, Vice President & COO
A broad based supplier of home medical and health related products designed with the needs of the user in mind.

373 Express Medical Supply
218 Seebold Spur
Fenton, MO 63026
800-633-2139
customerservice@exmed.net
www.exmed.net

William Nahm, President
Offers a full line of high quality medical and ostomy supplies to individuals, clinics, and medical institutions.

374 FlagHouse, Inc.
601 Flaghouse Drive
Hasbrouck Heights, NJ 07604-3116
201-288-7600
800-793-7900
FAX: 800-793-7922
sales@flaghouse.com
www.flaghouse.com

George Carmel, President
Global supplier of products for physical activity, recreation, education and special needs with the mantra of improving the lives of everyone.
Bi-Annually

375 Freedom Rider
Freedom Rider
5225 Tudor Court
Naples, FL 34112
603-540-0933
888-253-8811
FAX: 866-522-4708
info@freedomrider.com
www.freedomrider.com

Victoria Surr, President
A catalog of equipment for people with disabilities who ride and drive horses which includes instructional aids, vaulting equipment, and lots of hard to find items. Provides safety in their prod for riders, horses, instructors, and trainers.

376 Graham Field
One Graham-Field Way
Atlanta, GA 30340-4700
770-368-4700
FAX: 770-368-4932
cs@grahamfield.com
www.grahamfield.com

Kenneth Spett, President & CEO
Cherie Antoniazzi, Senior Vice President, Quality, Regulatory & Risk Management
Marc Bernstein, Senior Vice President, Consumer Sales
Manufactures more than 200 items for persons with physical disabilities, including wheelchairs, seat cushions, shower chairs, grab bars and more.

377   Health and Rehabilitation Products
Luminaud, Inc.
8688 Tyler Blvd
Mentor, OH 44060
440-255-9082
800-255-3408
FAX: 440-255-2250
info@luminaud.com
www.luminaud.com
Thomas M. Lennox, President
Dorothy Lennox, Vice President
Switches for limited capability, stoma and trach covers, shower protectors and thermo-stim oral motor stimulator. Personal voice amplifiers for people with weak voices. Artificial larynges for people with no voices. Small electronic communication boards. Books for laryngectomies and speech pathologists.

378   Huntleigh Healthcare
2349 W. Lake Street
Suite 250
Addison, IL 60101
800-323-1245
FAX: 888-594-2756
www.huntleigh-healthcare.us
Offers quality products including support surfaces, seating surfaces, fetal monitoring, vascular Assessment and treatment, and intermittent pneumatic compression devices.

379   Invacare Corporation
1 Invacare Way
Elyria, OH 44035-4190
800-333-6900
invacare.com
Matthew E. Monaghan, Chairman of the Board & Chief Executive Officer
Rick A. Cassiday, Senior Vice President & Chief Human Resources Officer
Kathleen P. Leneghan, Senior Vice President & Chief Financial Officer
A global leader in the manufacture and distribution of innovative home and long-term care medical products that promote recovery and active lifestyles.

380   Kleinert's
433 Newton St
Elba, AL 36323
800-498-7051
FAX: 305-937-0825
customercare@kleinerts.com
www.kleinerts.com
Michael Brier, President
Offers a complete line of sweat and odor protection products, incontinence products, and skin care products consisting of disposable and reusable panties for women and pants for men. Also disposable liners, diapers, underpads,antiperspirant wipes, deodorants, bedding, underpads, and cleaning solutions.

381   LS&S
145 River Rock Drive
Buffalo, NY 14207
716-348-3500
800-468-4789
FAX: 877-498-1482
LSSInfo@LSSproducts.com
www.LSSproducts.com
Melissa Balbach, President
John K. Bace, Executive Vice President
Specializes in products for the blind, visually impaired, hearing impaired, and deaf. A variety of hearing helpers, daily living aids, and vision aids. LS&S aids in the adjustment of alterations in life.

382   Lighthouse Low Vision Products
Lighthouse Guild
250 West 64th Street
New York, NY 10023
800-284-4422
www.lighthouseguild.org
Calvin W. Roberts, President & CEO
James M. Dubin, Chairman
Lawrence E. Goldschmidt, Vice Chairman & Treasurer
This organization provides health care services related to vision loss; Career and academic services for people with vision loss; Music instruction and pre K curriculum for visually impaired students.

383   Luminaud, Inc.
8688 Tyler Blvd
Mentor, OH 44060
440-255-9082
800-255-3408
FAX: 440-255-2250
info@luminaud.com
www.luminaud.com
Thomas M. Lennox, President
Dorothy Lennox, Vice President
Offers a line of artificial larynx, personal voice amplifiers, special switches, stoma covers and other communication, health and safety items.

384   MOMS Catalog
Home Delivery Incontinent Supplies
9385 Dielman Ind Dr
Saint Louis, MO 63132
800-269-4663
custcare@hdis.com
www.hdis.com
Bruce Grench, President
MOMS catalog features high quality, incontinence supplies, mobility products, bath safety products urological products, aids for daily living products, ostomy supplies and many other adaptive items. MOMS offers low prices, excellent customer service and convenient home delivery to your doorstep.
52 pages

385   Maddak Inc.
661 Route 23 South
Wayne, NJ 07470
973-628-7600
FAX: 973-305-0841
custservice@maddak.com
maddak.com
Brian Larkin, President & CEO
Maddak is proud to be a leading manufacturer of home healthcare products for seniors, people with disabilities and people recovering from injuries and illnesses. Marketed under the Ableware brand name, our products make daily living activities easier enabling you to remain active and independent.

386   Maxi Aids
Maxi Aids
42 Executive Blvd.
Farmingdale, NY 11735-4710
631-752-0521
800-522-6294
FAX: 631-752-0689
TTY: 631-752-0738
sales@maxiaids.com
www.maxiaids.com
Elliot Zaretsky, Founder, President & CEO
Products specially designed for blind, low vision, visually impaired, deaf, deaf-blind, hard of hearing, arthritic, diabetic, and disabled persons.

387   Memory Tips for Making Life Easier
Attainment Company
504 Commerce Parkway
P.O. Box 930160
Verona, WI 53593- 160
608-845-7880
800-327-4269
FAX: 800-942-3865
info@attainmentcompany.com
www.attainmentcompany.com
Autumn Garza, President
Don Bastian, CEO
Offers more than 100 resources specially designed or easy-on/easy-off clothing for men, women, children and wheelchair users. An invaluable resource for older adults on mild impairments or advanced memory loss. *$25.00*
167 pages 2006
ISBN 1-578615-72-0

388   Performance Health
28100 Torch Parkway
Suite 700
Warrenville, IL 60555-3938   630-393-6000
                                              800-323-5547
                                         FAX: 630-393-7600
customersupport@performancehealth.com
www.performancehealth.com
Francis Dirksmeier, Chief Executive Officer
Greg Nulty, Chief Financial Officer
Jim Plewa, Chief Sales Officer
Performance Health is a global provider of rehabilitation,
assistive, and splinting products, working with occupational
therapists, physical therapists, long-term care facilities, and
clinics.

389   Performance Health Enrichments Catalog
Performance Health
28100 Torch Parkway
Suite 700
Warrenville, IL 60555-3938   630-393-6000
                                         FAX: 630-393-7600
customersupport@performancehealth.com
www.performancehealth.com
Francis Dirksmeier, Chief Executive Officer
Greg Nulty, Chief Financial Officer
Jim Plewa, Chief Sales Officer
Performance Health Enrichments Catalog offers products that
make the tasks and challenges of living at home - bathing, getting
dressed, getting around - a little easier. Choose from personal
care items to kitchen and dining aids, household helpers to mobility devices, plus a complete selection of pain-reducing products,
exercise items, health monitoring equipment and more.
40 pages Yearly

390   Prentke Romich Company Product Catalog
1022 Heyl Road
Wooster, OH 44691   330-262-1984
                                              800-262-1984
                                         FAX: 330-263-4829
info@prentrom.com
www.prentrom.com
Dave Hershberger, President & CEO
Barry Romich, Co-Founder
A full-line product catalog containing information on
speech-output communication devices, environmental controls
and computer access products.

391   Products for People with Disabilities
LS&S
145 River Rock Drive
Buffalo, NY 14207   716-348-3500
                                              800-468-4789
                                         FAX: 877-498-1482
LSSInfo@LSSproducts.com
www.LSSproducts.com
Melissa Balbach, President
John K. Bace, Executive Vice President
LS&S, LLC has a free catalog of products for the blind, deaf, vi-
sually and hearing impaired including: TTYs, computer adaptive
devices, CCTVs, talking blood pressure, blood glucose and talk-
ing scales.

**392   Rehabilitation Engineering and AssistiveTechnology
Society of North America (RESNA)**
2001 K Street NW
3rd Floor North
Washington, DC 20006   202-367-1121
                                         FAX: 202-367-2121
info@resna.org
www.resna.org
Maureen Linden, President
Andrea Van Hook, Interim Executive Director
RESNA improves the potential of people with disabilities to
achieve their goals through technology. RESNA promotes research, development, education, advocacy and provision of
technology.

393   SafePath Products
SafePath Products
                                              530-893-1596
                                              800-497-2003
info@safepathproducts.com
www.safepathproducts.com
Tim Vander Heiden, Owner
As a ramp manufacturer, Safe Path solves vertical rises with a variety of product solutions. One of the largest online ADA Compliance Catalogs available. Offers everything from innovative
barrier removal products to survey equipment, to unique
specialty products.

394   Sportaid
78 Bay Creek Rd
Loganville, GA 30052   770-554-5033
                                              800-743-7203
                                         FAX: 770-554-5944
stuff@sportaid.com
www.sportaid.com
Stacy Green, Co-Owner
Jimmy Green, Co-Owner
Offers an assortment of wheelchairs (everyday and racing),
wheelchair sports equipment, replacement tires, hubs, spokes,
pushrims, cushions and more.
68 pages Yearly

395   Store @ HDSC Product Catalog
Hearing, Speech & Deafness Center (HDSC)
1625 19th Ave.
Seattle, WA 98122   206-323-5770
                                              888-222-5036
                                         FAX: 206-328-6871
TTY:800-761-2821
clinics@hsdc.org
www.hsdc.org
Lindsay Klarman, Executive Director
Hearing, Speech & Deaf Center (HSDC) is a nonprofit for clients
who are deaf, hard of hearing, or who face other communication
barriers such as speech challenges. Their mission is to foster inclusive and accessible communities through communication, advocacy, and education.
32 pages Yearly

396   Walgreens Home Medical Center
200 Wilmot Rd.
MS #2002
Deerfield, IL 60015   800-925-4733
www.walgreens.com
John Standley, Executive Vice President, WBA & President
Hospital supplies and home medical equipment with nationwide
direct mail delivery.

397   Weitbrecht Communications, Inc. (WCI)
                                              310-656-4924
                                              800-233-9130
                                         FAX: 310-450-9918
www.weitbrecht.com
Robert Weitbrecht, Co-Founder
James C. Marsters, Co-Founder
This catalog offers a variety of products for the deaf and hard of
hearing, such as wake-up devices, alarm clocks, alerting systems,
assistive listening devices, signalers, smoke detectors, TTY, captioned telephones and telephone amplifiers. Novelties and educational books and videos are also available.
24 pages

Miscellaneous

398   Access-USA
242 James St.
P.O. Box 160
Clayton, NY 13624-160   800-263-2750
                                         FAX: 800-563-1687
info@access-usa.com
www.access-usa.com
Deborah Webster, Manager
Produces Braille business Cards. Access-USA also provides Alternate Format transcription services for documentation, i.e., re-

ports, schedules, menus, statements, brochures, and more. submissions accepted via email or hard copy. AF formats include Braille, Large Print, Accessible Audio as well as Captioning Audio Description. Accessible products are also available for custom projects.

399   Access-USA: Transcription Services
242 James St.
P.O. Box 160
Clayton, NY 13624-160   800-263-2750
                                     FAX: 800-563-1687
                                     info@access-usa.com
                                     www.access-usa.com

Deborah Webster, Manager
Access-USA produces Braille business cards as well as offering alternate format services and products to enhance accessibility. Braille, large print, captioning, audio-descriptive forms are available.

400   BeOK Key Lever
Performance Health
28100 Torch Parkway
Suite 700
Warrenville, IL 60555-3938   630-393-6000
                                     FAX: 630-393-7600
                        customersupport@performancehealth.com
                                     www.performancehealth.com
Francis Dirksmeier, Chief Executive Officer
Greg Nulty, Chief Financial Officer
Jim Plewa, Chief Sales Officer
Handy accessory helps position key to provide maximum leverage enabling the user to work the most stubborn lock. *$11.50*

401   Big Lamp Switch
Maxi Aids
42 Executive Blvd.
Farmingdale, NY 11735-4710   631-752-0521
                                     800-522-6294
                                     FAX: 631-752-0689
                                     TTY: 631-752-0738
                                     sales@maxiaids.com
                                     www.maxiaids.com

Elliot Zaretsky, Founder, President & CEO
This three-spoked knob replaces small rotating knobs which are a problem for those with arthritis or other limitations of the fingers. *$10.95*

402   Bookholder: Roberts
Therapro, Inc.
225 Arlington St
Framingham, MA 01702-8723   508-872-9494
                                     800-257-5376
                                     FAX: 508-268-6624
                                     info@therapro.com
                                     www.therapro.com
Karen Conrad Weihrauch, President & Owner
Gray plastic, ideal for hands-free reading, adjusts to all sizes of books and prevents pages from flipping for the physically challenged. *$32.90*

403   Brandt Industries
4461 Bronx Blvd.
Bronx, NY 10470-1496   718-994-0800
                                     800-221-8031
                                     FAX: 718-325-7995
                                     brandtequip@yahoo.com
                                     www.brandtind.com
Shaun Semple, President
Family-owned, Brandt Industries is a provider of Wholesale Medical Equipment desgined for maintaining and operating healthcare facilities. Carries and manufactures medical equipment widely used across the medical industry.

404   Child Convertible Balance Beam Set
Bailey Manufacturing Company
P.O. Box 130
Lodi, OH 44254-0130   330-948-1080
                                     800-321-8372
                                     FAX: 330-948-4439
                                     baileymfg@baileymfg.com
                                     www.baileymfg.com

This convertible set is used to develop balance in two stages.

405   Child Variable Balance Beam
Bailey Manufacturing Company
P.O. Box 130
Lodi, OH 44254-0130   330-948-1080
                                     800-321-8372
                                     FAX: 330-948-4439
                                     baileymfg@baileymfg.com
                                     www.baileymfg.com
The four walking beams can be arranged in several different ways for variable balance training.

406   Child's Mobility Crawler
Bailey Manufacturing Company
P.O. Box 130
Lodi, OH 44254-0130   330-948-1080
                                     800-321-8372
                                     FAX: 330-948-4439
                                     baileymfg@baileymfg.com
                                     www.baileymfg.com
Neurologically delayed or orthopedically impaired small children can perform crawling and coordination exercises while being comfortably supported by the crawler.

407   Dazor Lighting Technology
2360 Chaffee Drive
St. Louis, MO 63146   314-652-2400
                                     800-345-9103
                                     info@dazor.com
                                     www.dazor.com
Dazor is a U.S. manufacturer of quality task lighting. Products include fluorescent, incandescent and halogen lighting fixtures. Illuminated magnifiers combine light and magnification to greatly enhance activities such as reading and make hobbies more enjoyable. All lamps come in various mounting options, including desk bases, floor stands and wall tracks.

408   Digi-Flex
Therapro, Inc.
225 Arlington St
Framingham, MA 01702-8723   508-872-9494
                                     800-257-5376
                                     FAX: 508-268-6624
                                     info@therapro.com
                                     www.therapro.com
Karen Conrad Weihrauch, President & Owner
This is a unique hand and finger exercise unit. Recommended for use of individuation of fingers, web space and general strengthening of work hands. Available in a variety of resistances. *$20.00*

409   Digital Talking Compass
Maxi Aids
42 Executive Blvd.
Farmingdale, NY 11735-4710   631-752-0521
                                     800-522-6294
                                     FAX: 631-752-0689
                                     TTY: 631-752-0738
                                     sales@maxiaids.com
                                     www.maxiaids.com
Elliot Zaretsky, Founder, President & CEO
Compass that speaks the direction it is pointed to. Includes eight points for noisy conditions for hard of hearing users. *$89.95*

410   Door Knock Signaler
HARC Mercantile
5413 S Westnedge Ave.
Suite A
Portage, MI 49002   800-445-9968
                                     TTY:269-324-1615
                                     info@harc.com
                                     www.harc.com
Michael Martinson, Owner
Flashes light to signal a knock on the door. *$31.00*

411 Doorbell Signalers
HARC Mercantile
5413 S Westnedge Ave.
Suite A
Portage, MI 49002
800-445-9968
TTY:269-324-1615
info@harc.com
www.harc.com

Michael Martinson, Owner
Doorbell signalers to alert with either louder chime or flashing light.

412 Dormakaba USA Inc.
1 DORMA Drive, AC Drawer
Reamstown, PA 17567
717-336-3881
866-401-6063
FAX: 717-336-2106
archdw@dorma-usa.com
www.dormakaba.com/en

Riet Cadonau, CEO
Bernd Brinker, CFO
Alwin Berninger, COO Access Solutions DACH
DORMA provides a complete line of door controls, including barrier-free units that comply with the Americans with Disabilities Act. A wide variety of surface-applied and concealed closers, low-energy operators, exit devices and electronic access control systems are available to address this equipment.

413 Dual Switch Latch and Timer
AbleNet, Inc.
2625 Patton Road
Roseville, MN 55113-1137
651-294-2200
800-322-0956
FAX: 651-294-2259
customerservice@ablenetinc.com
www.ablenetinc.com

Jennifer Thalhuber, President & CEO
Paul Sugden, CFO & Trustee
A Dual Switch Latch and Timer allows two users to activate two devices at a time in the latch. Timed seconds or timed minutes mode of control. *$235.00*

414 Enabling Devices
50 Broadway
Hawthorne, NY 10532
914-747-3070
800-832-8697
FAX: 914-747-3480
sales@enablingdevices.com
www.enablingdevices.com

Seth Kanor, President & CEO
For more than 25 years, Enabling Devices has been dedicated to providing affordable learning and assistive devices for the physically challenged. Products include augmentative communicators, adapted toys, capability switches, training and sensory devices and activity centers.

415 Foot Inversion Tread
Bailey Manufacturing Company
P.O. Box 130
Lodi, OH 44254-0130
330-948-1080
800-321-8372
FAX: 330-948-4439
baileymfg@baileymfg.com
www.baileymfg.com

Effective for correcting flat feet. These angled boards require the patient to walk on the outside of the foot instead of the arch.

416 Foot Placement Ladder
Bailey Manufacturing Company
P.O. Box 130
Lodi, OH 44254-0130
330-948-1080
800-321-8372
FAX: 330-948-4439
baileymfg@baileymfg.com
www.baileymfg.com

Adjustable cross bars for different length steps. Reinforced metal crosses for easier climbing for the physically disabled.

417 HealthCraft SuperPole
Maxi Aids
42 Executive Blvd.
Farmingdale, NY 11735-4710
631-752-0521
800-522-6294
FAX: 631-752-0689
TTY: 631-752-0738
sales@maxiaids.com
www.maxiaids.com

Elliot Zaretsky, Founder, President & CEO
A floor-to-ceiling grab bar designed for those who require assistance with standing, transferring, or moving. Can be used beside a bed, bath, toilet or chair.

418 Hocoma AG
77 Accord Park Drive
Suite D-1
Norwell, MA 02061
877-944-220
FAX: 781-792-0104
service.usa@hocoma.com
www.hocoma.com

Dr. Gery Colombo, President & CEO
Mark Faris, CFO
Leader in developing, manufacturing and marketing robotic and sensor-based products for functional movement therapy on a global level.

419 Home Alerting Systems
HARC Mercantile
5413 S Westnedge Ave.
Suite A
Portage, MI 49002
800-445-9968
TTY:269-324-1615
info@harc.com
www.harc.com

Michael Martinson, Owner
Alerting systems featuring bright flasher, loud speaker, and/or bedshaker signals.

420 Hospital Environmental Control System
Prentke Romich Company
1022 Heyl Road
Wooster, OH 44691
330-262-1984
800-262-1984
FAX: 330-263-4829
info@prentrom.com
www.prentrom.com

Dave Hershberger, President & CEO
Barry Romich, Co-Founder
Permits the non-ambulatory patient to operate a variety of electrical items in a single room. A large liquid crystal display is mounted in front of the user and they scan through the menu of operations and make a selection using a sip-puff switch. Options include nurse call, standard telephone functions, electric bed control, hospital television operation and electrical appliance on and off. *$3860.00*

421 Identity Group
10 Burton Hills Blvd
Suite 101
Nashville, TN 37215
800-237-9447
help@identitygroup.com
www.identitygroup.com

Sam Richardson, President & CEO
Bob Tate, CFO
Manufacturer of signs and visual decor for office and personal use.

422 Leg Elevation Board
Bailey Manufacturing Company
P.O. Box 130
Lodi, OH 44254-0130
330-948-1080
800-321-8372
FAX: 330-948-4439
baileymfg@baileymfg.com
www.baileymfg.com

Includes seven positions to a 30 degree incline, three pillows with Velcro, easy carry hand slot and a natural finish.

423   **Leveron Door Lever**
Lindustries
440 E. Southern Ave.
Tempe, AZ 85282   877-794-9511
customer.service@trademarkia.com
www.trademarkia.com/leveron-73486756.ht ml
Dave Lind, Jr., President & CEO
Leveron is a doorknob lever handle for ease of operation. Leveron converts standard doorknobs to lever action without removing existing hardware. No gripping, twisting or pinching when hands are wet, arthritic or arms are full. Leveron provides convenience. ADA access requirements in public and private places. *$16.95*

424   **Loop Scissors**
Therapro, Inc.
225 Arlington St
Framingham, MA 01702-8723   508-872-9494
800-257-5376
FAX: 508-268-6624
info@therapro.com
www.therapro.com
Karen Conrad Weihrauch, President & Owner
Pliable, plastic handles that allow for easy and controlled cutting. Extra finger room provides better control when cutting. *$17.95*

425   **Pacific Rehab, Inc.**
36805 N Never Mind Tr.
P.O. Box 5406
Carefree, AZ 85377-5406   888-222-9040
FAX: 480-575-7907
information@pacificrehabinc.com
pacificrehabinc.com

426   **Pet Partners**
Delta Society National Service Dog Center
345 118th Ave SE
Suite 100
Bellevue, WA 98005   425-679-5550
FAX: 425-379-5539
www.petpartners.org
C. Annie Peters, President & CEO
Jenn Gilbertson, Chief Marketing & Technology Officer
Linda Dicus, Executive Assistant
Pet Partners, formerly Delta Society, is a non-profit organization that helps people live healthier and happier lives by incorporating therapy, service and companion animals into their lives.

427   **Plastic Card Holder**
Therapro, Inc.
225 Arlington St
Framingham, MA 01702-8723   508-872-9494
800-257-5376
FAX: 508-268-6624
info@therapro.com
www.therapro.com
Karen Conrad Weihraucher, President & Owner
For those with reduced finger control. Front extension for pencils and coins.

428   **ProtectaCap, ProtectaCap+PLUS, ProtectaChin Guard and ProtectaHip**
Plum Enterprises

800-321-7586
info@plument.com
www.plument.com
Janice Carrington, Founder & CEO
Plum Enterprises award winning, exquisite, ergonomic protective wear keeps you safe from the dangers of falls. ProtectCap+Plus and ProtectHips are engineered for superior shock-absorption and designed for exquisite simplicity and amazing lightweight comfort.

429   **Real Design Inc.**
187 S. Main Street
Dolgeville, NY 13329   800-696-7041
FAX: 315-429-3071
rdesign@twcny.rr.com
sites.google.com/site/realdesign95/

Real Design inc. (Rehab and Educational Aids for Living) specializes in rehabilitation products for children with disabilities. To understand the needs of child with disabilities, the company deals with therapists, parents, and caregivers.

430   **Rex Bionics, Ltd.**
50 Milk Street
Floor 16
Boston, MA 02109   info@rexbionics.com
www.rexbionics.com
Rex Bionics develops and manufactures exoskeletons, capable of performing exercises in multiple positions: upright, backward, sideways, lunge, or ssquat. REX exoskeletons. Permits both at home or gym exercises and stretches for the upper and lower body, accessing different groups of muscles.

431   **Rocker Balance Square**
Bailey Manufacturing Company
P.O. Box 130
Lodi, OH 44254-0130   330-948-1080
800-321-8372
FAX: 330-948-4439
baileymfg@baileymfg.com
www.baileymfg.com
The rocker is used in developing activity, balance control and co-ordination.

432   **Room Valet Visual-Tactile Alerting System**
HARC Mercantile
5413 S Westnedge Ave.
Suite A
Portage, MI 49002   800-445-9968
TTY:269-324-1615
info@harc.com
www.harc.com
Michael Martinson, Owner
ADA compliant built-in visual-tactile alerting system. The Room Valet is fully supervised and has power failure back up. Alerts to in-room smoke, building alarm, door, phone, and alarm clock. Designed for permanent installation.

433   **Series Adapter**
AbleNet, Inc.
2625 Patton Road
Roseville, MN 55113-1137   651-294-2200
800-322-0956
FAX: 651-294-2259
customerservice@ablenetinc.com
www.ablenetinc.com
Jennifer Thalhuber, President & CEO
Paul Sugden, CFO & Trustee
Allows two-switch operation of any battery-operated device or electrical devices. *$20.00*

434   **Signaling Wake-Up Devices**
HARC Mercantile
5413 S Westnedge Ave.
Suite A
Portage, MI 49002   800-445-9968
TTY:269-324-1615
info@harc.com
www.harc.com
Michael Martinson, Owner
Wake up devices. Vibrating alarm clocks, available with flashing lights, louder alarm noises and more.

435   **Smoke Detector with Strobe**
HARC Mercantile
5413 S Westnedge Ave.
Suite A
Portage, MI 49002   800-445-9968
TTY:269-324-1615
info@harc.com
www.harc.com
Michael Martinson, Owner
Detects smoke within a radius of 100' and flashes a strobe as a signal.

436 Spinal Network: The Total Wheelchair Resource Book
No Limits Communications & New Mobility
120-34 Queens Blvd.
Suite 330
Kew Gardens, NY 11415   800-404-2898
                                  www.newmobility.com

Jean Dobbs, Publisher & Editorial Director
Josie Byzek, Executive Editor
Ian Ruder, Editor
Nearly 600 pages of profiles, articles and resources on every
topic of interest to wheelchair users. Subjects include health,
coping, relationships, sexuality, parenthood, computers, sports,
recreation, travel, personal assistance services, legal rights, financial strategies, employment, and media images. *$34.95*
400 pages

437 SteeleVest
Steele
P.O. Box 7304
Kingston, WA 98346   888-783-3538
                                  FAX: 360-297-2816
                                  steelevest@gmail.com
                                  www.steelevest.com

Lynn Steele, Owner
Vest developed by NASA provides an external cooling system.
Cooling Vests are tailored to industrial workers while operating
in warm environments to keep cool and safe.

438 Strobe Light Signalers
HARC Mercantile
5413 S Westnedge Ave.
Suite A
Portage, MI 49002   800-445-9968
                                  TTY:269-324-1615
                                  info@harc.com
                                  www.harc.com

Michael Martinson, Owner
Strobe alerts that plug into receivers for signaling systems. A
strobe light on the device will flash to alert for calls, visitors, and
home alarms.

439 Tactile Braille Signs
Maxi Aids
42 Executive Blvd.
Farmingdale, NY 11735-4710   631-752-0521
                                  800-522-6294
                                  FAX: 631-752-0689
                                  TTY: 631-752-0738
                                  sales@maxiaids.com
                                  www.maxiaids.com

Elliot Zaretsky, Founder, President & CEO
Contains raised text and pictograms, Grade 2 braille, and contrasting colors. Stairs, No Smoking, and various Restroom signs
available. *$19.95*

440 Tactile Thermostat
ASB
919 Walnut Street
Philadelphia, PA 19107-5237   215-627-0600
                                  FAX: 215-922-0692
                                  asbinfo@asb.org
                                  www.asb.org

Karla S. McCaney, President & CEO
Beth Deering, Chief Program Officer
Sylvia Purnell, Director of Learning & Development
Large embossed numbers on cover ring and raised temperature
setting knob. *$31.50*

441 Therapy Putty
Therapro, Inc.
225 Arlington St
Framingham, MA 01702-8723   508-872-9494
                                  800-257-5376
                                  FAX: 508-268-6624
                                  info@therapro.com
                                  www.therapro.com

Karen Conrad Weihrauch, President & Owner
Designed to exercise and strengthen hands, ranging from soft to
firm, for developing a stronger grasp. Available in two, four and
six-ounce sizes. Three-ounce putty in a clear fist-shaped con-
tainer.

442 Window-Ease
A-Solution
1331 Wind Ridge Dr NW
Albuquerque, NM 87120   505-856-6632
                                  FAX: 505-856-6652
                                  www.windowease.com
Device adapts horizontally and vertically sliding windows to
ANSI A117.1 standards. 10:1 mechanical advantage at the crank
arm opens a 50lb window with 5lbs force.

Office Devices & Workstations

443 BAT Personal Keyboard
Infogrip
Ventura, CA 93001   503-828-1221
                                  866-606-8551
                                  support@infogrip.com
                                  www.infogrip.com

Liza Jacobs, President
Aaron Gaston, Vice President
Infogrip has creative computer access solutions for people with
all types of disabilities. Alternative keyboards and mice,
switches, screen readers, magnifiers and educational software.
$200.00

444 Computer Workstation and Activity Table
Maxi Aids
42 Executive Blvd.
Farmingdale, NY 11735-4710   631-752-0521
                                  800-522-6294
                                  FAX: 631-752-0689
                                  TTY: 631-752-0738
                                  sales@maxiaids.com
                                  www.maxiaids.com

Elliot Zaretsky, Founder, President & CEO
Height-adjustable wheelchair accessible table. Adjusts with a
hand crank. ADA compliant. *$989.00*

445 Desk-Top Talking Calculator
Maxi Aids
42 Executive Blvd.
Farmingdale, NY 11735-4710   631-752-0521
                                  800-522-6294
                                  FAX: 631-752-0689
                                  TTY: 631-752-0738
                                  sales@maxiaids.com
                                  www.maxiaids.com

Elliot Zaretsky, Founder, President & CEO
Full-function calculator that announces results in a clear voice.
Also features a large 8-digit display. *$13.85*

446 Don Johnston
26799 West Commerce Drive
Volo, IL 60073   847-740-0749
                                  800-999-4660
                                  FAX: 847-740-7326
                                  info@donjohnston.com
                                  www.donjohnston.com

Don Johnston, Founder
Ruth Ziolkowski, President
Kevin Johnston, Director of Product Design
A provider of quality products and services that enable people
with special needs to discover their potential and experience suc-
cess. Products are developed for the areas of Physical Access,
Augmentative Communication and for those who struggle with
reading and writing.

447 Freedom Ryder Handcycles
Brike International
20589 SW Elk Horn Ct
Tualatin, OR 97062-9518   503-692-1029
                                  michaelslofgren@gmail.com
                                  www.freedomryder.com

The finest handcycle in the world. The cycles incorporate body,
lean steering and the finest bicycle components to make this a
three-wheeled vehicle without equal. Suitable for both recreation
and competition. *$1995.00*

448 Golf Xpress
Emotorsports
4400 West M-61
Standish, MI 48658
989-846-6255
mitch@golfxpress.com
www.golfxpress.com
Patented single-rider adaptive golf cart allows users to play golf, seated or supported. Hit woods, irons, and putt from the car. Drives onto tees and greens and into traps without damaging the course.

449 Pencil/Pen Weighted Holders
Therapro, Inc.
225 Arlington St
Framingham, MA 01702-8723
508-872-9494
800-257-5376
FAX: 508-268-6624
info@therapro.com
www.therapro.com
Karen Conrad Weihrauch, President & Owner
Securely hold any pencil or pen. These weighted holders allow for more control along with proprioceptive feedback to encourage better writing skills.

450 Perkins Electric Brailler
Maxi Aids
42 Executive Blvd.
Farmingdale, NY 11735-4710
631-752-0521
800-522-6294
FAX: 631-752-0689
TTY: 631-752-0738
sales@maxiaids.com
www.maxiaids.com
Elliot Zaretsky, Founder, President & CEO
Can emboss 25 lines with 42 cells on an 11 x 11 1/2 sheet. *$1035.00*

451 Raised Line Drawing Kit
Maxi Aids
42 Executive Blvd.
Farmingdale, NY 11735-4710
631-752-0521
800-522-6294
FAX: 631-752-0689
TTY: 631-752-0738
sales@maxiaids.com
www.maxiaids.com
Elliot Zaretsky, Founder, President & CEO
For writing script or drawing graphs by the use of special plastic paper. *$34.95*

452 Reizen RL-350 Braille Labeler
Maxi Aids
42 Executive Blvd.
Farmingdale, NY 11735-4710
631-752-0521
800-522-6294
FAX: 631-752-0689
TTY: 631-752-0738
sales@maxiaids.com
www.maxiaids.com
Elliot Zaretsky, Founder, President & CEO
For labeling in braille with 3/8 or 1/2 wide labeling tape. *$32.87*

453 SciPlus 3200 Low Vision Scientific Vision
Independent Living Aids
137 Rano Rd.
Buffalo, NY 14207
716-332-2970
800-537-2118
FAX: 877-498-1482
can-do@independentliving.com
www.independentliving.com
Large scientific calculator with large illuminated numbers, full color display, and large buttons/display for visually impaired users. *$405.00*

454 Steady Write
Maxi Aids
42 Executive Blvd.
Farmingdale, NY 11735-4710
631-752-0521
800-522-6294
FAX: 631-752-0689
TTY: 631-752-0738
sales@maxiaids.com
www.maxiaids.com
Elliot Zaretsky, Founder, President & CEO
Furnishes the writer with increased holding capacity and stabilizes the hand. *$8.95*

455 Television Remote Controls with Large Numbers
Independent Living Aids
137 Rano Rd.
Buffalo, NY 14207
716-332-2970
800-537-2118
FAX: 877-498-1482
can-do@independentliving.com
www.independentliving.com
Television remote control with large, easy-to-see, and color-coded buttons. *$49.95*

456 Touch-Dots
Maxi Aids
42 Executive Blvd.
Farmingdale, NY 11735-4710
631-752-0521
800-522-6294
FAX: 631-752-0689
TTY: 631-752-0738
sales@maxiaids.com
www.maxiaids.com
Elliot Zaretsky, Founder, President & CEO
Adhesive-backed dots for identification. Can be used with keyboards, telephones, calculators and more. *$1.95*

Scooters

457 Ability Center
4797 Ruffner St.
San Diego, CA 92111
858-541-0552
833-919-2581
FAX: 858-541-1941
www.abilitycenter.com
Terry Barton, General Manager
Specializes in accessible vehicles and mobility products; the company has more than 100 employees in 14 locations across the western U.S.
1994

458 Aerospace Compadre
Aerospace America, Inc.
900 Parkway Drive
Bay City, MI 48706
989-684-2121
800-237-6414
sales@aerospaceamerica.com
www.aerospaceamerica.com
Mike Alley, President
Fully customized golf-cart type vehicle for the physically impaired person. Fully equipped with hand controls, wheelchair rack, storage racks, head and tail lights and full safety belts. *$2500.00*

459 Alante
Golden Technologies
401 Bridge Street
Old Forge, PA 18518
570-451-7477
800-624-6374
FAX: 800-628-5165
www.goldentech.com
Richard Golden, CEO
Robert Golden, Chair
Fred Kiwak, Vice President, Research & Development
Rear-wheel-drive vehicle that represents the best in powered mobility.

460   Amigo Mobility International
Amigo Mobility International
6693 Dixie Highway
Bridgeport, MI 48722   989-777-0910
service@myamigo.com
www.myamigo.com
Al Thieme, Chair & Founder
Beth Thieme, President & CEO
An industry leader in power operated vehicles and scooters, Amigo provides innovative, durable, and customized mobility solutions for the disabled, injured, and seniors worldwide. Other services include healthcare, travel and transportation services. *$1295.00*

461   Amigo Mobility International Inc.
6693 Dixie Highway
Bridgeport, MI 48722   989-777-0910
service@myamigo.com
www.myamigo.com
Al Thieme, Chair & Founder
Beth Thieme, President & CEO
Amigo Mobility designs and manufactures a complete line of power operated vehicles/mobility scooters and accessories.

462   Cruiser Bus Buggy 4MB
Convaid
2830 California Street
Torrance, CA 90503   888-266-8243
FAX: 310-618-2166
convaidsales.us@etac.com
www.convaid.com
Chris Braun, President
In sizes from infant through young adult, this positioning buggy is crash-tested.

463   E-Wheels Electric Senior Mobility Scooter
Maxi Aids
42 Executive Blvd.
Farmingdale, NY 11735-4710   631-752-0521
800-522-6294
FAX: 631-752-0689
TTY: 631-752-0738
sales@maxiaids.com
www.maxiaids.com
Elliot Zaretsky, Founder, President & CEO
Three-wheel, high-powered scooter for seniors. Travels up to 45 miles on a single charge.

464   EMS 2000 - Analog Muscle Stimulator
BioMedical Life Systems
1954 Kellogg Avenue
Calsbad, CA 92008-6581   760-579-0801
800-726-8367
FAX: 760-929-9953
information@bmls.com
www.bmls.com
This three-mode device has four adjustable modulations and is powered by one 9-volt battery.

465   Electric Power Scooter
Electro Kinetic Technologies
W194 N11301 McCormick Drive
Germantown, WI 53022   262-250-7740
800-824-1068
FAX: 262-250-7741
info@ek-tech.com
www.ek-tech.com
Designed to increase your mobility indoors. Features up to 20 hours of continuous operation between charges. Weight capacity: 750 lbs.

466   Espree Atlas
PaceSaver
1800 Merriam Lane
Kansas City, KS 66106   913-722-5658
FAX: 913-722-2614
leisure-lift@leisure-lift.com
www.pacesaver.com
Bill Burke, Founder
This easily maneuverable scooter boasts the industry's best incline stability rating. Weight capacity: 500 lbs. *$2695.00*

467   Invacare Fulfillment Center
Invacare
1 Invacare Way
Elyria, OH 44035-4190   800-333-6900
www.invacare.com
Matthew E. Monaghan, Chairman of the Board & Chief Executive Officer
Rick A. Cassiday, Senior Vice President & Chief Human Resources Officer
Kathleen P. Leneghan, Senior Vice President & Chief Financial Officer
Invacare Corporation is a leading manufacturer and distributor of non-acute medical products which promote recovery and active lifestyles for people requiring home and other non-acute health care.

468   Outdoor Independence
Palmer Industries
71 Cyrpress St
Warwick, RI 02888
Electric, outdoor scotter. Includes bench seat, push button control panel, headlight and stop light, horn, on-off key, rear basket, moped/motorcycle tires, and stainless steel foot platform.

469   PaceSaver Power Scooter
PaceSaver
1800 Merriam Lane
Kansas City, KS 66106   913-722-5658
FAX: 913-722-2614
leisure-lift@leisure-lift.com
www.pacesaver.com
Bill Burke, Founder
The scooter combines outdoor ruggedness with indoor maneuverability at a low price.

470   Polaris Trail Blazer
Polaris Industries
2100 Highway 55
Medina, MN 55340-9770   763-542-0500
888-704-5290
FAX: 763-542-0599
www.polarisindustries.com
Michael T. Speetzen, CEO
Michael F. Donoughe, SVP, Chief Technical Officer & Head of Electrification
Lucy Clark Dougherty, SVP, General Counsel & Corporate Secretary
A four-wheeler that has many engineered innovations, features such as: full floorboards for full comfort, single lever breaking with auxiliary foot brake, electronic throttle control, parking brake and adjustable handlebars.

471   Quickie LXI/LX
Sunrise Medical
2842 Business Park Avenue
Fresno, CA 93727   800-333-4000
FAX: 800-300-7502
www.sunrisemedical.com
Thomas Babacan, President & CEO
Roxane Cromwell, Chief Operating Officer
Adrian Platt, Chief Financial Officer
This custom, ultralight, folding, everyday wheelchair offers portability and performance.

472   Rascal Scooter
Mobility Parts and Service
1501 Grandview Avenue
Suite 400
West Deptford, NJ 08066   800-257-7955
info@mobilitypartsandservice.com
mobilitypartsandservice.com
An electric vehicle that serves as both a compact mobile chair and a rugged outdoor scooter. Usable in both indoors and outdoor environments. Also available with joystick controls.

473 **Regent**
Golden Technologies
401 Bridge Street
Old Forge, PA 18518
570-451-7477
800-624-6374
FAX: 800-628-5165
info@goldentech.com
www.goldentech.com

Richard Golden, CEO
Robert Golden, Chair
Fred Kiwak, Vice President, Research & Development
Top-rated performance scooter, with extra features and economically priced.

474 **Scoota Bug**
Golden Technologies
401 Bridge Street
Old Forge, PA 18518
570-451-7477
800-624-6374
FAX: 800-628-5165
www.goldentech.com

Richard Golden, CEO
Robert Golden, Chair
Fred Kiwak, Vice President, Research & Development
A lightweight, completely modular scooter that disassembles and fits into most auto trunks.

475 **SoloRider Industries**
Regal Research & Manufacturing Company
1200 East Plano Parkway
Plano, TX 75074
800-898-3353
info@solorider.com
www.solorider.com

Roger Pretekin, Founder
Manufacturer and distributor of the Solorider Golf Cart. This revolutionary single rider adaptive cart is specifically designed to meet the needs of individuals with mobility impairments.

476 **Terra-Jet: Utility Vehicle**
TERRA-JET USA
P.O. Box 918
Innis, LA 70747
225-492-2249
800-864-5000
FAX: 225-492-2226
Terrajet@Yahoo.com
www.terra-jet.com

Larry Rabalais, President & CEO
TERRA-JET utility vehicles are unique in their ability to traverse many different types of terrain in remote areas otherwise inaccessible. It has a multitude of uses for industry, sportsmen or the whole family. Uniquely designed, industrial duty construction of low-maintenance and low-fuel consumption.

477 **Terrier Tricycle**
TRIAID
P.O. Box 1364
Cumberland, MD 21501
301-759-3525
FAX: 301-759-3525
sales@triaid.com
www.triaid.com

Provides fun therapy and actively encourages participation, awareness and the building of self-confidence. Designed for children from about five years, it features ATB styling, 16-inch wheels, an adjustable steering stop and a supportive saddle. Handlebar and seat adjustments combine with a broad wheelbase to ensure the rider is in the optimum position to pedal, and the tricycle gives good stability and confident handling.

478 **Tracer Tricycle**
TRIAID
P.O. Box 1364
Cumberland, MD 21501
301-759-3525
FAX: 301-759-3525
sales@triaid.com
www.triaid.com

These tricycles provide fun therapy for teenagers and adults. Highly recommended by therapists for users whose use of the lower limbs is restricted. *$740.00*

Stationery

479 **Access-USA**
242 James St.
P.O. Box 160
Clayton, NY 13624-160
800-263-2750
FAX: 800-563-1687
www.access-usa.com

Deborah Webster, Manager
Access-USA provides one-stop alternate format transcription services for almost any type of document-reports, schedules, menus, monthly statements, brochures, reports, etc. Items may be submitted on computer disk, hard copy or email. Alternate formats include Braille, large print, Braille and print, audio recordings, adapted disks as well as video services-open/closed captioning and video descriptions. Accessible products also include Braille Business Cards and ADA signage.

480 **Address Book**
ASB
919 Walnut Street
Philadelphia, PA 19107-5237
215-627-0600
FAX: 215-922-0692
asbinfo@asb.org
www.asb.org

Karla S. McCaney, President & CEO
Beth Deering, Chief Program Officer
Sylvia Purnell, Director of Learning & Development
The big print address book is the first personal book to provide enlarged writing spaces, making it easier to write down and retrieve information. *$12.50*

481 **Bold Line Paper**
ASB
919 Walnut Street
Philadelphia, PA 19107-5237
215-627-0600
FAX: 215-922-0692
asbinfo@asb.org
www.asb.org

Karla S. McCaney, President & CEO
Beth Deering, Chief Program Officer
Sylvia Purnell, Director of Learning & Development
This pad consists of 100 sheets of paper with bold lines to help guide the writing of an individual with limited vision. *$2.50*

482 **Braille Calendar**
Maxi Aids
42 Executive Blvd.
Farmingdale, NY 11735-4710
631-752-0521
800-522-6294
FAX: 631-752-0689
TTY: 631-752-0738
sales@maxiaids.com
www.maxiaids.com

Elliot Zaretsky, Founder, President & CEO
Calendar with braille markings for touch reading. *$14.99*

483 **Braille Notebook**
Maxi Aids
42 Executive Blvd.
Farmingdale, NY 11735-4710
631-752-0521
800-522-6294
FAX: 631-752-0689
TTY: 631-752-0738
sales@maxiaids.com
www.maxiaids.com

Elliot Zaretsky, Founder, President & CEO
Made of heavy-duty board, covered with waterproof plastic and contains three rings for binding. *$18.95*

484 **Braille: Greeting Cards**
ASB
919 Walnut Street
Philadelphia, PA 19107-5237
215-627-0600
FAX: 215-922-0692
asbinfo@asb.org
www.asb.org

Karla S. McCaney, President & CEO
Beth Deering, Chief Program Officer
Sylvia Purnell, Director of Learning & Development

Birthday, anniversary, get well, sympathy and Christmas cards offering Braille print for the blind. *$.95*

485   Clip Board Notebook
ASB
919 Walnut Street
Philadelphia, PA 19107-5237   215-627-0600
                                               FAX: 215-922-0692
                                               asbinfo@asb.org
                                               www.asb.org

Karla S. McCaney, President & CEO
Beth Deering, Chief Program Officer
Sylvia Purnell, Director of Learning & Development
Kit includes a pack of Bold Line paper and black ink pen. *$5.95*

486   Deluxe Signature Guide
Maxi Aids
42 Executive Blvd.
Farmingdale, NY 11735-4710   631-752-0521
                                               800-522-6294
                                               FAX: 631-752-0689
                                               TTY: 631-752-0738
                                               sales@maxiaids.com
                                               www.maxiaids.com

Elliot Zaretsky, Founder, President & CEO
Consisting of rods supported by two rubber blocks, this device helps to facilitate writing. *$1.95*

487   Giant Print Address Book
Maxi Aids
42 Executive Blvd.
Farmingdale, NY 11735-4710   631-752-0521
                                               800-522-6294
                                               FAX: 631-752-0689
                                               TTY: 631-752-0738
                                               sales@maxiaids.com
                                               www.maxiaids.com

Elliot Zaretsky, Founder, President & CEO
Large print address book for storing up to 360 names. Three-ring hardcover binder with removable pages. *$16.95*

488   Letter Writing Guide
Independent Living Aids
137 Rano Rd.
Buffalo, NY 14207   716-332-2970
                                               800-537-2118
                                               FAX: 877-498-1482
                                               can-do@independentliving.com
                                               www.independentliving.com
Sturdy plastic sheet with 13 apertures corresponding to standard line spacing. *$3.95*

489   Ottobock
11501 Alterra Parkway
Suite 600
Austin, TX 78758   800-328-4058
                                               supportUS@OttoBock.com
                                               www.ottobockus.com

Provides prosthetic devices to people with amputations. Assists users in maintaining and gaining their freedom of movement.

490   Writing Guide Value Kit
Independent Living Aids
137 Rano Rd.
Buffalo, NY 14207   716-332-2970
                                               800-537-2118
                                               855-746-7452
                                               FAX: 516-937-3906
                                               can-do@independentliving.com
                                               www.independentliving.com
Included in this useful pack are four durable plastic lettering and number guides for tracing letters when the individual is unable to write letters unassisted. *$9.95*

Visual Aids

491   Adjustable Folding Support Cane for the Blind
Maxi Aids
42 Executive Blvd.
Farmingdale, NY 11735-4710   631-752-0521
                                               800-522-6294
                                               FAX: 631-752-0689
                                               TTY: 631-752-0738
                                               sales@maxiaids.com
                                               www.maxiaids.com

Elliot Zaretsky, Founder, President & CEO
Adjustable canes for the visually impaired. *$21.95*

492   All Terrain Cane
Maxi Aids
42 Executive Blvd.
Farmingdale, NY 11735-4710   631-752-0521
                                               800-522-6294
                                               FAX: 631-752-0689
                                               TTY: 631-752-0738
                                               sales@maxiaids.com
                                               www.maxiaids.com

Elliot Zaretsky, Founder, President & CEO
A rigid aluminum cane with a curved nylon tip and golf grip with hook handle. Designed to help blind and visually impaired persons navigate unpaved areas. *$49.95*

493   Audio Book Contractors
P.O. Box 96
Riverdale, MD 20738-0096   301-439-5830
                                        audiobookcontractors@verizon.net
                                        www.audiobookcontractors.com

Flo Gibson, Founder
Over 950 titles of unabridged classic books in a variety of genres on audio cassettes in sturdy vinyl covers with picture and spine windows. Discounted prices for disabled patrons.

494   Beyond Sight, Inc.
5650 S Windermere St
Littleton, CO 80120   303-795-6455
                                               www.beyondsight.com
Products for the blind and visually impaired, including talking clocks, watches and calculators. Beyond Sight, Inc. also carries a large selection of Braille products, magnifiers, reading machines and computer equipment.
Site is under construction.

495   Big Button Talking Calculator with Function Replay
Independent Living Aids
137 Rano Rd.
Buffalo, NY 14207   716-332-2970
                                               800-537-2118
                                               FAX: 877-498-1482
                                               can-do@independentliving.com
                                               www.independentliving.com

Big Button Talking Calculator features color-coded buttons ideal for hard of hearing and low vision users. New repeat function lets you listen to the most recent entry. *$15.95*

496   Braille Elevator Plates
Maxi Aids
42 Executive Blvd.
Farmingdale, NY 11735-4710   631-752-0521
                                               800-522-6294
                                               FAX: 631-752-0689
                                               TTY: 631-752-0738
                                               sales@maxiaids.com
                                               www.maxiaids.com

Elliot Zaretsky, Founder, President & CEO
The plates have curing type pressure sensitive material applied for metal to metal bonding. *$49.95*

497 **Braille Touch-Time Watches**
Independent Living Aids
137 Rano Rd.
Buffalo, NY 14207
716-332-2970
800-537-2118
FAX: 877-498-1482
can-do@independentliving.com
www.independentliving.com
White dial with black numerals and hands makes telling time possible quickly and easily for the visually impaired. *$44.95*

498 **Circline Illuminated Magnifer**
Dazor Lighting Technology
2360 Chaffee Drive
St. Louis, MO 63146
314-652-2400
800-345-9103
info@dazor.com
www.dazor.com
Provides even, shadow-free light under the magnifying lens with a 22-watt circline fluorescent. The magnifier is mounted on a floating arm that allows you to position the light source and lens with the touch of a finger.

499 **Large Display Alarm Clock**
HARC Mercantile
5413 S Westnedge Ave.
Suite A
Portage, MI 49002
800-445-9968
TTY:269-324-1615
info@harc.com
www.harc.com

Michael Martinson, Owner
Features a large, easy-to-read display, as well as an extra-loud alarm and bedshaker. *$54.00*

500 **Low Vision Watches & Clocks**
Maxi Aids
42 Executive Blvd.
Farmingdale, NY 11735-4710
631-752-0521
800-522-6294
FAX: 631-752-0689
TTY: 631-752-0738
sales@maxiaids.com
www.maxiaids.com

Elliot Zaretsky, Founder, President & CEO
Offers a wide range of watches and clocks, including braille watches, talking watches, and large display clocks.

501 **Magni-Cam & Primer**
Innoventions

Magni-Cam and Primer are hand-held, light weight, inexpensive auto-focus electronic magnification systems designed to meet the reading and writing needs of those with low vision. The systems present the image in black and white or in color with three different view modes. Connects to any TV monitor in minutes. Systems read any surface with no distortion. A battery powered system is available, providing total portability and flexibility. *$25.00*

502 **Magnifier Paperweight**
Levenger
420 S Congress Ave
Delray Beach, FL 33445-4693
800-544-0880
FAX: 800-544-6910
Cservice@levenger.com
www.levenger.com

Margaret Moraskie, CEO
The Magnifier Paperweight features an optical quality magnifier and is long enough to enlarge the entire width of most book pages while holding the pages open. *$25.00*

503 **Man's Low-Vision Quartz Watches**
Independent Living Aids
137 Rano Rd.
Buffalo, NY 14207
716-332-2970
800-537-2118
FAX: 877-498-1482
can-do@independentliving.com
www.independentliving.com
An inexpensive, easy-to-read watch with chrome case. *$27.95*

504 **MonoMouse Electronic Magnifiers**
Maxi Aids
42 Executive Blvd.
Farmingdale, NY 11735-4710
631-752-0521
800-522-6294
FAX: 631-752-0689
TTY: 631-752-0738
sales@maxiaids.com
www.maxiaids.com

Elliot Zaretsky, Founder, President & CEO
Portable magnifier for people with low vision. Just about the size of a standard computer mouse. Compatible with any desktop or notebook PC. Variable magnification from 3x to 100x.

505 **Stretch-View Wide-View Rectangular Illuminated Magnifier**
Dazor Lighting Technology
2360 Chaffee Drive
St. Louis, MO 63146
314-652-2400
800-345-9103
info@dazor.com
www.dazor.com
Provides even, shadow-free light under the magnifying lens with a 22-watt circline fluorescent. The magnifier is mounted on a floating arm that allows you to position the light source and lens with the touch of a finger.

506 **Unisex Low Vision Watch**
Independent Living Aids
137 Rano Rd.
Buffalo, NY 14207
716-332-2970
800-537-2118
FAX: 877-498-1482
can-do@independentliving.com
www.independentliving.com
Unisex watch with large numbers and wide hands. Gold-toned case with either expansion or leather band. *$31.95*

Walking Aids: Canes, Crutches & Walkers

507 **Aluminum Kiddie Canes**
Maxi Aids
42 Executive Blvd.
Farmingdale, NY 11735-4710
631-752-0521
800-522-6294
FAX: 631-752-0689
TTY: 631-752-0738
sales@maxiaids.com
www.maxiaids.com

Elliot Zaretsky, Founder, President & CEO
Rigid and folding canes for children.

508 **Aluminum Walking Canes**
Maxi Aids
42 Executive Blvd.
Farmingdale, NY 11735-4710
631-752-0521
800-522-6294
FAX: 631-752-0689
TTY: 631-752-0738
sales@maxiaids.com
www.maxiaids.com

Elliot Zaretsky, Founder, President & CEO
Lightweight walking canes made of a heavy gauge aluminum tube with safety locknuts and heavy-duty rubber tips.

509 **Axillary Crutches**
Arista Surgical Supply Company
297 High Street
Dedham, MA 02026-2852
781-329-2900
800-437-2966
FAX: 781-437-2966
customerservice@alimed.com
www.alimed.com

Adam S. Epstein, Chief Executive Officer
Lightweight crutches with wood underarms and handgrips. Adjusts to custom fit any user. *$43.25*

510   Days Hemi Walker
Performance Health
28100 Torch Parkway
Suite 700
Warrenville, IL 60555-3938   630-393-6000
                                          FAX: 630-393-7600
            CustomerSupport@performancehealth.com
                    www.performancehealth.com
Francis Dirksmeier, Chief Executive Officer
Greg Nulty, Chief Financial Officer
Jim Plewa, Chief Sales Officer
For upper extremity trauma. An alternative to crutches that allows safe, stable ambulation for elderly or disabled individuals with the use of only one arm. *$74.50*

511   Deluxe Nova Wheeled Walker & Avant Wheeled Walker
Performance Health
28100 Torch Parkway
Suite 700
Warrenville, IL 60555-3938   630-393-6000
                                          FAX: 630-393-7600
            CustomerSupport@performancehealth.com
                    www.performancehealth.com
Francis Dirksmeier, Chief Executive Officer
Greg Nulty, Chief Financial Officer
Jim Plewa, Chief Sales Officer
Lightweight and simple to handle with an easy-to-operate braking system. *$425.40*

512   Equalizer 6000 Single Stack Gym
Access To Recreation
8 Sandra Ct
Newbury Park, CA 91320-4302   805-498-7535
                                               800-634-4351
                                          FAX: 805-498-8186
                customerservice@accesstr.com
                        www.accesstr.com
Don Krebs, President & Founder
Provides dynamic leg motion for individuals who are unable to stand upright or walk on their own.

513   Europa Superior Folding Cane
Maxi Aids
42 Executive Blvd.
Farmingdale, NY 11735-4710   631-752-0521
                                               800-522-6294
                                          FAX: 631-752-0689
                                          TTY: 631-752-0738
                    sales@maxiaids.com
                        www.maxiaids.com
Elliot Zaretsky, Founder, President & CEO
Aluminum folding cane with tapered joints, golf grip with wrist loop, and screw-on glide tip. *$23.95*

514   Foot Harness
Consumer Care Products, LLC
W282 N7109 Main Street
Merton, WI 53056   262-820-2300
                    info@consumercarellc.com
                        www.consumercarellc.com
This sandle-like Foot Harness is designed for wheelchair plates and pedals. Available in small, medium, and large sizes.

515   Mobility Aid Trike
Consumer Care Products, LLC
W282 N7109 Main Street
Merton, WI 53056   262-820-2300
                    info@consumercarellc.com
                        www.consumercarellc.com
This mobility aid promotes postural alignment, balance, exercise and coordination.

516   Rand-Scot
Rand-Scot, Inc.
209 Christman Drive
Fort Collins, CO 80524   970-484-7967
                                               800-467-7967
                                          FAX: 970-484-3800
                    info@randscot.com
                        www.randscot.com
Joel Lerich, Co-Founder
Barbara Lerich, Co-Founder
Manufactures the Easy Pivot patient lift, the BBD wheelchair cushion line and Saratoga Exercise products for the disabled. Offers a line of patient lifts and standers for the disabled. Rand-scot products are designed to help the disabled achieve independence, comfort, and stamina.

517   Rollators
Maxi Aids
42 Executive Blvd.
Farmingdale, NY 11735-4710   631-752-0521
                                               800-522-6294
                                          FAX: 631-752-0689
                                          TTY: 631-752-0738
                    sales@maxiaids.com
                        www.maxiaids.com
Elliot Zaretsky, Founder, President & CEO
Offers a wide range of rolling walkers.

518   Stable Base Quad Cane
Arista Surgical Supply Company/AliMed
297 High Street
Dedham, MA 02026-2852   781-329-2900
                                               800-437-2966
                                          FAX: 781-437-2966
                    info@alimed.com
                        www.alimed.com
Adam S. Epstein, Chief Executive Officer
A reliable walking cane offering independence to the physically challenged user. *$29.75*

519   T-Handle Cane
Arista Surgical Supply Company/AliMed
297 High Street
Dedham, MA 02026-2852   781-329-2900
                                               800-437-2966
                                          FAX: 781-437-2966
                    info@alimed.com
                        www.alimed.com
Adam S. Epstein, Chief Executive Officer
A standard old-fashioned wooden cane for the physically challenged. Ideal for those with arthritis. *$33.00*

520   TIDI Products, LLC
570 Enterprise Drive
Neenaha, WI 54956   920-751-4300
                                               800-521-1314
                                          FAX: 920-751-4370
                    excellence@tidiproducts.com
                        www.tidiproducts.com
Kevin McNamara, President & CEO
Jeff Hebbard, Vice President & COO
Jennifer Jones, Vice President, Marketing
TIDI Products meets the needs of caregivers for job optimization and providing solutions to other healthcare professionals. Supplies Brand name medical equipment and devices including: POSEY patient safety devices, TIDISHIELD eyewear and devices, C-AMOR drapes, STERILE-Z drapes, GRIP-LOK securement items, and ZERO-GRAVITY radiation protection.

521   U-Step Walking Stabilizer: Walker
Maxi Aids
42 Executive Blvd.
Farmingdale, NY 11735-4710   631-752-0521
                                               800-522-6294
                                          FAX: 631-752-0689
                                          TTY: 631-752-0738
                    sales@maxiaids.com
                        www.maxiaids.com
Elliot Zaretsky, Founder, President & CEO

Stabilizing walker with braking system, seat and basket. Easily foldable. Weight capacity is 375 lbs. Suitable for users 5'1 to 6'1 tall. *$539.95*

522 Ventura Enterprises
4431 S. Eastern Avenue
Las Vegas, NV 89119
702-457-7676
info@venturaenterprises.com
www.venturaenterprises.com

Sam Ventura, President & CEO
Ron Ventura, Vice President of Development
Galit Rozen, Vice President of Acquisitions
Manufacturer of everyday living mobility aids. Products include carrying aids for walkers and wheelchairs and also wheelchair cushions.

523 WCIB Heavy-Duty Folding Cane
Maxi Aids
42 Executive Blvd.
Farmingdale, NY 11735-4710
631-752-0521
800-522-6294
FAX: 631-752-0689
TTY: 631-752-0738
sales@maxiaids.com
www.maxiaids.com

Elliot Zaretsky, Founder, President & CEO
A four section aluminum folding cane with a golf-type grip handle and flexible wrist loop. *$27.95*

Wheelchairs: Accessories

524 Advantage Wheelchair & Walker Bags
Advantage Bag Company
310-540-8197
advantagebag@verizon.net
www.advantagebag.com
Wheelchairs with and without push handles. Pac slips over back of almost any wheelchair.

525 Automatic Wheelchair Rollback Lock
Alzheimer's Store
3197 Trout Place Rd
Cumming, GA 30041-8260
678-947-4001
800-752-3238
FAX: 678-947-8411
contact@alzstore.com
www.alzstore.com

Ellen Warner, President & Co-Founder
Mark Warner, Co-Founder
Automatic anti-rollback safety device automatically locks the wheels whenever the user stands or sits.

526 Battery Operated Cushion
DA Schulman
3827 Creekside Lane
Holmen, WI 54636
608-782-0031
866-782-9658
FAX: 608-782-0488
aquila@aquilacorp.com
www.aquilacorp.com

Steve Kohlman, Owner & President
Justine Kohlman, Vice President
Battery-operated, dynamic cushion for wheelchairs. The Airpulse PK wheelchair cushion system is Aquila Corporation's most dynamic cushion system. It was designed to be the most advanced solution to help prevent and heal pressure ulcers.

527 Dual-Mode Charger
Lester Electrical
625 West A Street
Lincoln, NE 68522-1794
402-477-8988
sales@lesterelectrical.com
www.lesterelectrical.com

Spencer Stock, President & CEO
Fully automatic battery charger.

528 Equalizer 1000 Series
Helm Distributing
Deer Park P.O.
PO Box 25105
Red Deer, Alberta, Canada, T4R-2M2
403-309-5551
FAX: 403-342-5509
james@equalizerexercise.com
www.equalizerexercise.com
Weight training equipment designed for wheelchair users. Features 7 stations targeting different major muscle parts: Vertical Bench Press, Seated Military Press, High/Low Pulleys, Lat Pull Down, Vertical Butterfly, Leg Curl and Extension, Lateral Deltoid, and Seated Leg Press/Calf Extension, in addition to a variety of accessories. *$7050.00*

529 Equalizer 6000 Series
Helm Distributing
Deer Park P.O.
PO Box 25105
Red Deer, Alberta, Canada, T4R-2M2
403-309-5551
FAX: 403-342-5509
james@equalizerexercise.com
www.equalizerexercise.com
Weight training equipment designed for wheelchair users. Includes Vertical Bench Press, Rowing/Long Pull, Lat Pull Down, Vertical Butterfly, Low Pulley/Prchr. Bench, Gripless Bicep Curl, Gripless Tricep Extension, Mid Pulley, and Removable Rolling Stool. *$4250.00*

530 Featherspring Shoe Inserts
Luxis International, Inc.
1292 South 7th St.
DeKalb, IL 60115
815-981-3793
800-628-4693
FAX: 800-261-1164
www.luxis.com
Foot supports for wheelchair users to prevent and treat cold feet, sore heels, swollen feet and weak ankles. *$199.95*

531 Gem Wheelchair & Scooter Service: Mobility & Homecare
176-39 Union Turnpike
Flushing, NY 11366
718-969-8600
800-943-3578
help@gemwheelchairservice.com
www.gemwheelchairservice.com
GEM sells, repairs and rents all models of manual and motorized wheelchairs, power scooters, ramps, stairway lifts, and homecare products including diapers, chux, and bathroom safety equipment.

532 MAT Factory, Inc.
6726 North Figueroa Street
Los Angeles, CA 90042
800-628-7626
888-266-7590
FAX: 888-266-9555
sales@matfactoryinc.com
www.matfactoryinc.com
Wheelchair access mats for pathways, walkways, trails and playgrounds.

533 Permobil
300 Duke Dr
Lebanon, TN 37090
800-736-0925
www.permobilus.com

Bengt Thorsson, President & CEO
Charlotta Nyberg, Chief Financial Officer
Jonas Cederhage, Executive Vice President, Group Supply Chain
Develops and manufactures wheelchairs, communication systems, and seating and positioning systems for users with disabilities. Offers a full line of standing wheelchairs for manual operation. *$7000.00*

534 Safety Deck II
MAT Factory, Inc.
6726 North Figueroa Street
Los Angeles, CA 90042
800-628-7626
888-266-7590
FAX: 888-266-9555
sales@matfactoryinc.com
www.matfactoryinc.com

The Safety Deck II is an interlocking grid system made from recycled rubber tires and recycled PVC. The tiles are set directly on top of the ground and permit grass to grow through the holes and cover the surface. The system provides safe, non-barrier access for wheelchairs over grass. Once the grass has covered the tiles the only maintenance required is watering and mowing. Safety Deck II also allows for beach and sand access. *$7.80*

535   Scooter & Wheelchair Battery Fuel Gauges and Motor Speed Controllers
Curtis Instruments, Inc.
200 Kisco Ave.
Mount Kisco, NY 10549   914-666-2971
                                    www.curtisinst.com
Provides a readable, accurate indication of battery in easy to read type of display. Innovative, efficient motor speed controllers for single or dual PM motor vehicles.

536   Softfoot Ergomatta
MAT Factory, Inc.
6726 North Figueroa Street
Los Angeles, CA 90042   800-628-7626
                                    888-266-7590
                              FAX: 888-266-9555
                           sales@matfactoryinc.com
                           www.matfactoryinc.com
Interlocking roll-up mat system with antimicrobial additive. Allows wheelchairs and walkers to move easily and safely along wet and potentially hazardous surfaces. *$9.90*

537   Wheelchair Accessories
Diestco Manufacturing Company
370 Ryan Ave.
Chico, CA 95973   800-795-2392
                                    www.diestco.com
Diestco makes innovative accessories for wheelchairs, scooters and walkers. Products include canopies, backpacks, cupholders, pouches, threshold ramps, laptrays and others.

538   Wheelchair Back Pack and Tote Bag
Med Covers
321 Route 59
Suite 147
Tallman, NY 10982   718-302-1923
                                    800-320-7140
                              FAX: 866-522-6967
                           info@1800wheelchair.com
                           www.1800wheelchair.com
Accessories are specifically designed with the wheelchair user in mind. The Back Pack has a main roomy pouch for larger items and has a full length zipper with four sliders for convenient access.

539   Wheelchair Positioning Tray
Graham-Field
One Graham-Field Way
Atlanta, GA 30340-4700   770-368-4700
                              FAX: 770-368-4932
                           cs@grahamfield.com
                           www.grahamfield.com
Kenneth Spett, President & CEO
Cherie Antoniazzi, Senior Vice President, Quality, Regulatory & Risk Management
Marc Bernstein, Senior Vice President, Consumer Sales
This is a heavy-duty wheelchair comfort tray which surrounds the wheelchair user and provides a large, smooth surface for dining, writing, hobbies or work. Includes washable nylon cover with zippered pockets.

540   Wheelchair Roller
Access To Recreation
8 Sandra Ct
Newbury Park, CA 91320-4302   805-498-7535
                                    800-634-4351
                              FAX: 805-498-8186
                       customerservice@accesstr.com
                           www.accesstr.com
Don Krebs, President & Founder
The McClain Wheelchair Roller allows you to build strength and stamina in the comfort of your own home.

541   Wheelchair Work Table
Bailey Manufacturing Company
P.O. Box 130
Lodi, OH 44254-0130   330-948-1080
                                    800-321-8372
                              FAX: 330-948-4439
                           baileymfg@baileymfg.com
                           www.baileymfg.com
An adjustable height, functional, individual cut-out work table featuring a wood-grain laminate, scratch resistant top with chrome plated steel legs.

Wheelchairs: General

542   21st Century Scientific, Inc. - Bounder Power Wheelchair
4931 N Manufacturing Way
Coeur D Alene, ID 83815-8931   208-667-8800
                                    800-448-3680
                              FAX: 208-667-6600
                           21st@wheelchairs.com
                           wheelchairs.com
Ronald E. Prior, Ph.D., President & Founder
High-performance power chairs for active individuals. High-speed (11 + MPH), OFF-ROAD, and Bariatric options are available. Power seating options include tilt, recline, 13-inch seat elevator, reverse tilt, leg rests, standing, and front load (latitude). 6-drive programmable electronics standard; lights, horn, electric bag emptier and many other options available.

543   Ability Center
4797 Ruffner St.
San Diego, CA 92111   858-541-0552
                                    833-919-2581
                              FAX: 858-541-1941
                           www.abilitycenter.com
Terry Barton, General Manager
Specializes in accessible vehicles and mobility products; the company has more than 100 employees in 14 locations across the western U.S.
1994

544   Advantage Wheelchair
Sizewise
8601 Monrovia Street
Lenexa, KS 66215   800-814-9389
                           info@sizewise.com
                           www.sizewise.com
A large-frame wheelchair constructed of high-quality, stress-tested stainless steel to ensure durability and peak performance.

545   Breezy
Sunrise Medical
2842 Business Park Avenue
Fresno, CA 93727   800-333-4000
                              FAX: 800-300-7502
                           www.sunrisemedical.com
Thomas Babacan, President & CEO
Roxane Cromwell, Chief Operating Officer
Adrian Platt, Chief Financial Officer
This lightweight chair is durable, comfortable and flexible enough to meet the needs of a wide range of wheelchair users.

546   Breezy Elegance
Sunrise Medical
2842 Business Park Avenue
Fresno, CA 93727   800-333-4000
                              FAX: 800-300-7502
                           www.sunrisemedical.com
Thomas Babacan, President & CEO
Roxane Cromwell, Chief Operating Officer
Adrian Platt, Chief Financial Officer
A lightweight, portable folding wheelchair. *$750.00*

547   Champion
Kuschall of America
                                    kuschall.com

46

The ultra-light, compact, foldable Champion wheelchair has the feel and performance of a rigid chair.

548 **Choosing a Wheelchair: A Guide for Optimal Independence**
Patient-Centered Guides
1005 Gravenstein Highway North
Sebastopol, CA 95472
707-827-7000
FAX: 707-829-0104
support@oreilly.com
www.oreilly.com

Linda Lamb, Series Editor
Shawnde Paull, Marketing
Tim O'Reilly, Publisher
With the right wheelchair, quality of life increases dramatically and even people with severe disabilities can have a considerable degree of independence and activity. Choosing the wrong chair can indeed the tantamount to confinement. This book describes technology, options, and the selection process to help you identify the chair than can provide you with optimal independence.
$11.19
186 pages Paperback
ISBN 1-565924-11-8

549 **Compact**
Kuschall of America

kuschall.com
The Compact wheelchair is lightweight, foldable and features new, ergonomic bended knee shape for maximum convenience.

550 **Convaid**
2830 California Street
Torrance, CA 90503
888-266-8243
FAX: 310-618-2166
convaidsales.us@etac.com
www.convaid.com

Chris Braun, President
Five different styles of wheelchairs.

551 **Etac USA**
P.O. Box 1739
Matthews, NC 28106-1739
262-717-9910
800-678-3822
FAX: 262-796-4605
sales.us@etac.com
www.etac.com/en-us/us/
Offers wheelchairs designed to provide function, comfort and flexibility. Seat frame and upholstery are adjustable to fit each individual. Swing away, detachable footrests are standard. Numerous accessories are available in order to individualize each chair. Lifetime warranty on frame for original user.

552 **Evacu-Trac**
Garaventa Lift Canada
18920 - 36th
Surrey, BC, Canada, V3Z-0P6
604-594-0422
800-663-6556
info@garaventalift.com
www.garaventalift.com
This emergency evacuation chair is designed for safety and fast operation.

553 **Gem Wheelchair & Scooter Service: Mobility & Homecare**
176-39 Union Turnpike
Flushing, NY 11366
718-969-8600
800-943-3578
help@gemwheelchairservice.com
www.gemwheelchairservice.com
GEM sells, repairs and rents all models of manual and motorized wheelchairs, power scooters, ramps, stairway lifts, and homecare products including diapers, chux, and bathroom safety equipment.

554 **Gendron**
GF Health Products, Inc.
P.O. Box 47510
Doraville, GA 30362-0510
770-368-4700
cs@grahamfield.com
www.gendroninc.com
Katie Johnson, Director of Customer Service & Technical Support

Manufacturer of wheelchairs for a variety of other applications, specializing in bariatric mobility products.

555 **K-Series**
Kuschall of America

kuschall.com
Fully-adjustable wheelchair that can be modified independently from the frame.

556 **Lounge Chairs**
Graham-Field Health Products
One Graham-Field Way
Atlanta, GA 30340-4700
770-368-4700
FAX: 770-368-4932
cs@grahamfield.com
www.grahamfield.com

Kenneth Spett, President & CEO
Cherie Antoniazzi, Senior Vice President, Quality, Regulatory & Risk Management
Marc Bernstein, Senior Vice President, Consumer Sales
Provides all-day comfort and safe, independent mobilization with feet or hands. The ergonomically engineered seat back provides correct support.

557 **Majors Medical Service**
2601 W Mockingbird Ln
Suite 101
Dallas, TX 75235
214-951-9710
FAX: 214-951-9720
www.majorsmedicalservice.com

Pat Metz, Owner
Offers selection of wheelchairs and homecare medical equipment for safety and mobility needs.

558 **Pride Mobility**
401 York Avenue
Duryea, PA 18642
800-522-7391
info@pridemobility.com
www.pridemobility.com

Scott Meuser, Chair & CEO
Dan Meuser, Owner
Pride Mobility manufacturers a variety of electric wheelchairs, mobility scooters, and lift chairs for users of all sizes. As a global innovator, Pride Mobility is dedicated to improving the lives of users through mobility solutions.

559 **Regency XL 2002**
GF Health Products, Inc.
P.O. Box 47510
Doraville, GA 30362-0510
770-368-4700
cs@grahamfield.com
www.gendroninc.com
Katie Johnson, Director of Customer Service & Technical Support
Bariatric wheelchairs for users weighing up to 600 pounds.

560 **Rock-King X3000 Wheel Chair Kit**
Maxi Aids
42 Executive Blvd.
Farmingdale, NY 11735-4710
631-752-0521
800-522-6294
FAX: 631-752-0689
TTY: 631-752-0738
sales@maxiaids.com
www.maxiaids.com

Elliot Zaretsky, Founder, President & CEO
Wheelchair that can turn into a rocking chair with the flip of a lever. The kit includes wheels, footrests, lateral supports, black frame finish, heal-leg strap, cushion and standard head pillow.
$1995.00

561 **Rolls 2000 Series**
Invacare
1 Invacare Way
Elyria, OH 44035-4190
800-333-6900
www.invacare.com

Matthew E. Monaghan, Chairman of the Board & Chief Executive Officer
Rick A. Cassiday, Senior Vice President & Chief Human Resources Officer
Kathleen P. Leneghan, Senior Vice President & Chief Financial Officer

The first light-weight wheelchairs designed for rental use. Comes with optional elevating footrests.

562 Skyway
Skyway Machine
4451 Caterpillar Rd
Redding, CA 96003
530-243-5151
800-332-3357
FAX: 530-243-5104
www.skywaywheels.com

Ken Coster, Sales Department
Parrey Cremeans, Sales Department
Rein Stolz, Engineering Department
Supplies wheel combinations for wheelchairs, lawn and garden products, bicycles, and a large assortment of wheeled devices to serve the Health Care industry. Wheel sizes range from 4-inch to 24-inch diameter.

563 The KSL
Kuschall of America
kuschall.com
Ultralight wheelchair designed to improve mobility.

564 Vista Wheelchair
Arista Surgical Supply Company/AliMed
297 High Street
Dedham, MA 02026-2852
781-329-2900
800-437-2966
FAX: 781-437-2966
info@alimed.com
www.alimed.com

Adam S. Epstein, Chief Executive Officer
Vista has a rugged cold-rolled steel frame, durable vinyl upholstery and steel bearings to assure a smooth ride. *$220.00*

565 Wheelchairs and Transport Chairs
Maxi Aids
42 Executive Blvd.
Farmingdale, NY 11735-4710
631-752-0521
800-522-6294
FAX: 631-752-0689
TTY: 631-752-0738
sales@maxiaids.com
www.maxiaids.com

Elliot Zaretsky, Founder, President & CEO
Offers a wide range of wheelchairs, including lightweight transport chairs, full-reclining wheelchairs, bariatric wheelchairs, and more.

Wheelchairs: Pediatric

566 Convaid
2830 California Street
Torrance, CA 90503
888-266-8243
FAX: 310-618-2166
convaidsales.us@etac.com
www.convaid.com

Chris Braun, President
Convaid manufactures Mobile Positioning Systems for children. The Expedition, Safari Tilt, Cruiser, EZ Rider and Metro offer a non-institutional styling and are lightweight and compact-folding. The steel/aluminum structure is engineered for maximum comfort and durability. The mobile positioning lines come with more than 20 positioning features and a full range of positioning adaptations.

567 Imp Tricycle
TRIAID
P.O. Box 1364
Cumberland, MD 21501
301-759-3525
FAX: 301-759-3525
sales@triaid.com
www.triaid.com

Provides fun therapy and actively encourages participation, awareness and the building of self confidence. Designed for children from 2 1/2 years, it features ATB styling, 12 1/2 inch wheels, an adjustable steering stop and a supportive saddle. Handlebar and seat adjustments combine with a broad wheelbase to ensure

the rider is in the optimum position to pedal, and the tricycle gives good stability and confident handling. Support accessories are available. *$590.00*

568 Koala R-Net
Permobil USA
300 Duke Dr
Lebanon, TN 37090
800-736-0925
www.permobilus.com

Bengt Thorsson, President & CEO
Charlotta Nyberg, Chief Financial Officer
Jonas Cederhage, Executive Vice President, Group Supply Chain
The Koala Miniflex is a powered wheelchair designed for use by children with lower extremity, mobility, or neurological disabilities or spinal cord injury.

569 TMX Tricycle
TRIAID
P.O. Box 1364
Cumberland, MD 21501
301-759-3525
FAX: 301-759-3525
sales@triaid.com
www.triaid.com

Provides fun therapy and actively encourages participation, awareness and the building of self confidence. Designed for children from about eight years, it features ATB styling, 20-inch wheels, adjustable steering stop and a supportive saddle. Handlebar and seat adjustments combine with a broad wheelbase to ensure the rider is in the optimum position to pedal and the tricycle gives good stability and confident handling. Support accessories are available. *$795.00*

Wheelchairs: Powered

570 Bounder 450
21st Century Scientific
4931 N Manufacturing Way
Coeur D Alene, ID 83815-8931
208-667-8800
800-448-3680
FAX: 208-667-6600
21st@wheelchairs.com
wheelchairs.com

Ronald E. Prior, Ph.D., President & Founder
The Heavy Duty Bounder 450 Power Wheelchair is designed for users up to 450 lbs.

571 Bounder Power Wheelchair
21st Century Scientific
4931 N Manufacturing Way
Coeur D Alene, ID 83815-8931
208-667-8800
800-448-3680
FAX: 208-667-6600
21st@wheelchairs.com
wheelchairs.com

Ronald E. Prior, Ph.D., President & Founder
The Bounder Power Wheelchair is designed for users up to 300 lbs. *$8695.00*

572 Chief 107-ZRx
Redman Powerchair
1601 S Pantano Rd
Suite 107
Tucson, AZ 85710
800-727-6684
Info@RedmanPowerChair.com
www.redmanpowerchair.com

Don Redman, Co-Founder
Paula Redman, Co-Founder
Motorized standing chair which allows you to stand, recline, and tilt comfortably. Custom sizing is available for power chairs from 3'8 40 lbs. to 6'8 350 lbs.

573 Damaco D90 Biomedical Battery
Damaco
28381 Constellation Rd.
Valencia, CA 91355
877-528-2288
FAX: 661-775-2025
www.atbatt.com

Sealed Lead Acid battery for Damaco D90 Power Wheelchair. Nominal voltage of 12.0V/rated capacity of 26.0Ah. 2/Unit Required. *$2495.00*

574 Folding Lightweight Power Wheelchair
Maxi Aids
42 Executive Blvd.
Farmingdale, NY 11735-4710　　　631-752-0521
　　　　　　　　　　　　　　　　800-522-6294
　　　　　　　　　　　　　FAX: 631-752-0689
　　　　　　　　　　　　　TTY: 631-752-0738
　　　　　　　　　　　　　sales@maxiaids.com
　　　　　　　　　　　　　www.maxiaids.com
Elliot Zaretsky, Founder, President & CEO
Folding power wheelchair with large foot platform, foam seat design and back seat pocket for storage. Weight capacity is 400 lbs. *$2579.00*

575 Gem Wheelchair & Scooter Service: Mobility & Homecare
176-39 Union Turnpike
Flushing, NY 11366　　　　　　　718-969-8600
　　　　　　　　　　　　　　　　800-943-3578
　　　　　　　　help@gemwheelchairservice.com
　　　　　　　　www.gemwheelchairservice.com
GEM sells, repairs and rents all models of manual and motorized wheelchairs, power scooters, ramps, stairway lifts, and homecare products including diapers, chux, and bathroom safety equipment.

576 Permobil F3 Corpus
Permobil
　　　　　　　　　　　　　　　　800-736-0925
　　　　　　　　　　　　www.permobil.com/en-us
An easily maneuverable power wheelchair featuring the smallest footprint of the Permobil F-series.

577 Permobil M300 Corpus HD
Permobil
　　　　　　　　　　　　　　　　800-736-0925
　　　　　　　　　　　　www.permobil.com/en-us
The power wheelchair is designed for users up to 450 lbs.

578 Power Wheelchairs
LaBac Systems
8245 Quebec St
Commerce City, CO 80022　　　　800-370-6808
　　　　　　　　　　　　　FAX: 303-340-3863
　　　　　　　　　　　　　www.falconrehab.net
Power tilt and recline seating systems for wheelchairs, offering more comfort and dependability for the physically challenged.

Wheelchairs: Racing

579 Eagle Sportschairs, LLC
2351 Parkwood Road
Snellville, GA 30039-4003　　　　770-972-0763
　　　　　　　　　　　　　FAX: 770-985-4885
　　　　　　　　　eaglesportschairs@gmail.com
　　　　　　　　　www.eaglesportschairs.com
Barry Ewing, Owner
The Eagle line of custom lightweight performance chairs includes various options to fit all racing and sports needs, including track, baseball, quad-rugby, tennis, field events and waterskiing. Also popular for daily use. Ability to customize any chair to accommodate size and disability.

580 East Penn Manufacturing Company
East Penn Manufacturing Company
102 Deka Rd.
Lyons, PA 19536　　　　　　　　610-682-6361
　　　　　　　　　　　　　FAX: 610-682-4781
　　　　　　　　　contactus@eastpenn-deka.com
　　　　　　　　　www.eastpennmanufacturing.com
Daniel Langdon, President & CEO
DeLight Breidegam, Co-Founder & Chair
David Byrne, Director of Finance & Accounting

Specially engineered for demanding deep-cycle applications, Gelled electrolyte Deka Dominator Batteries provide maintenance-free operation and longer battery life.

581 Invacare Top End
Invacare
1 Invacare Way
Elyria, OH 44035-4107　　　　　800-333-6900
　　　　　　　　　　　　　www.invacare.com
Matthew E. Monaghan, Chairman of the Board & Chief Executive Officer
Rick A. Cassiday, Senior Vice President & Chief Human Resources Officer
Kathleen P. Leneghan, Senior Vice President & Chief Financial Officer
Manufacturers of lightweight, rigid, sport-specific wheelchairs, such as the Eliminator line of racing chairs, T-3 tennis and softball chairs, and the Terminator for quad rugby and basketball. The Excelerator, XLT three-wheel hand cycle for adults and juniors.

Associations

General Disabilities

582 A Loving Spoonful
1449 Powell St.
Vancouver, BC, Canada V5L-1G8   604-682-6325
                                       FAX: 604-682-6327
                                       info@alovingspoonful.org
                                       alovingspoonful.org

Gerald Regio, President
Quinn Newcomb, Vice President
Ken Channon, Treasurer
A Loving Spoonful is a volunteer-driven, non-partisan Society that provides free, nutritious meals to people living with HIV/AIDS in Greater Vancouver. Every week volunteers deliver frozen meals and snack packs to men, women, and children who are primarily homebound with AIDS.
1989

583 ADA National Network
ADA Knowledge Translation Center
University of Washington
Seattle, WA 98382   800-949-4232
                                       adakt@uw.edu
                                       adata.org

The Network offers information and training on how to implement the Americans with Disabilities Act (ADA). It consists of 10 regional centers across the U.S., plus an ADA Knowledge Translation Center, and is funded by the National Institute on Disability, Independent Living, and Rehabilitation Research (NIDILRR).

584 AHF Federation
AIDS Healthcare Foundation
6255 Sunset Blvd.
21st Floor
Los Angeles, CA 90028   323-860-5200
                                       www.aidshealth.org

Michael Weinstein, President
Peter Reis, Senior Vice President
Scott Carruthers, Chief Pharmacy Officer
A consortium of AIDS Service Organizations under the umbrella of the AIDS Healthcare Foundation.

585 AIDS Healthcare Foundation
6255 Sunset Blvd.
21st Floor
Los Angeles, CA 90028   323-860-5200
                                       www.aidshealth.org

Michael Weinstein, President
Peter Reis, Senior Vice President
Scott Carruthers, Chief Pharmacy Officer
The Los Angeles-based AIDS Healthcare Foundation (AHF) is a global nonprofit organization providing medicine and advocacy to people all around the world. AHF is currently the largest provider of HIV/AIDS medical care in the U.S.
1987

586 AIDS Vancouver
1101 Seymour St.
4th Floor
Vancouver, BC, Canada V6B-0R1   604-893-2201
                                       FAX: 604-893-2205
                                       contact@aidsvancouver.org
                                       aidsvancouver.org

Sarah Chown, Executive Director
Janet Cheng, Director of Finance
Laura Imayoshi, Director of Programs & Services
AIDS Vancouver strives to create a community with no new HIV infections while ensuring support for those who are affected through case management services, financial assistance, grocery and nutrition support, and confidential helplines.
1983

587 Abilities, Inc.
The Viscardi Center
201 I.U. Willets Rd.
Albertson, NY 11507   516-465-1400
                                       info@viscardicenter.org
                                       viscardicenter.org/services/abilities-inc
Dr. Chris Rosa, President & Chief Executive Officer
Sheryl P. Buchel, Executive Vice President & Chief Financial Officer
Michael Caprara, Chief Information Officer
The Viscardi Center is a network of nonprofit organizations that provides a lifespan of services for children and adults with disabilities. The Abilities, Inc. program prepares adolescents and adults with disabilities for entering the workforce.
1952

588 Academy of Integrative Health & Medicine (AIHM)
6919 La Jolla Blvd.
San Diego, CA 92037   aihm.org
Tabatha Parker, Executive Director
Erika Cappelluti, Fellowship Director
April Gruzinsky, Fellowship Admissions Director
The Academy of Integrative Health & Medicine unites health care professionals from family doctors to psychologists, acupuncturists to nurses, to build bridges between disciplines and offer credible educational and certification programs for licensed health care providers.
1996

589 Access & Information Network
2600 N. Stemmons Fwy.
Suite 151
Dallas, TX 75207   214-943-4444
                                       FAX: 469-329-0717
                                       info@aindallas.org
                                       aindallas.org

Steven Pace, President & Chief Executive Officer
Joni Wysocki, Chief Operating Officer
Zachariah Skariah, Director of Programs
AIN is a nonprofit organization providing services for individuals with chronic health conditions and prevention programs for at-risk communities.

590 Accreditation Commission for Acupuncture & Herbal Medicine
500 Lake Street
Suite 204
Excelsior, MN 55331   952-212-2434
                                       info@acahm.org
                                       acahm.org

Mark McKenzie, Executive Director
Karl Gauby, Director, Regulatory Affairs
Jason Wright, Director, Accreditation Services
National accrediting agency of programs in acupuncture and herbal medicine.

591 Accreditation Commission for Midwifery Education (ACME)
American College of Nurse Midwives
8403 Colesville Rd.
Suite 1230
Silver Spring, MD 20910   240-485-1803
                                       asmith@acnm.org
                                       midwife.org/acme

Eva Fried, Chair
Pamela Reis, Vice Chair
Mavis Schorn, Commissioner
Commission of the American College of Nurse Midwives responsible for overseeing all aspects of the accreditation review process.

592 Advocacy Centre for the Elderly (ACE)
2 Carlton St.
Suite 701
Toronto, ON, Canada M5B-1J3   416-598-2656
                                     855-598-2656
                                FAX: 416-598-7924
                    www.advocacycentreelderly.org
Graham Webb, Executive Director
Shelley Hobbs, Chair
Alexander Henderson, Vice Chair
The Advocacy Centre for the Elderly is a specialty community legal clinic that provides a range of legal services to low-income seniors in Ontario. Legal services include advice and representation to individual and group clients, public legal education, law reform, and community development activities.
1984

593 Advocates for Children of New York (AFC)
151 West 30th St.
5th Floor
New York, NY 10001   212-947-9779
                                FAX: 212-947-9790
                    info@advocatesforchildren.org
                    www.advocatesforchildren.org
Kim Sweet, Executive Director
Matthew Lenaghan, Deputy Director
Kimberley D. Harris, President
AFC works on behalf of children from infancy to age 21 who are at risk for school-based discrimination and/or academic failure. These include children with disabilities, ethnic minorities, immigrants, homeless children, foster care children, English language learners, and those living in poverty.

594 Advocates for Developmental Disabilities
1301 Lincoln Ave. S.
Owatonna, MN 55060   597-451-9769
Advocates for Developmental Disabilities is a local agency that advocates for the dissemination of information regarding developmental disabilities, the enhancement of existing services, and the development of new programs on behalf of individuals with developmental disabilities. Its goal is to develop a better understanding of developmental disabilities by families and others interested in the welfare of individuals with developmental disabilities.

595 American Academy of Audiology (AAA)
11480 Commerce Park Dr.
Suite 220
Reston, VA 20191   703-790-8466
                                FAX: 703-790-8631
                         infoaud@audiology.org
                             www.audiology.org
Patrick E. Gallagher, Executive Director
Kathryn Werner, Chief Operating Officer
Amy Miedema, VP, Communications & Membership
The American Academy of Audiology is the world's largest professional organization for audiologists. The Academy is dedicated to providing quality hearing care services through professional development, education, research, and increased public awareness of hearing and balance disorders.

596 American Academy of Environmental Medicine (AAEM)
717 Kreutzberg Rd.
Boerne, TX 78006   316-684-5500
                                FAX: 888-411-1206
                             www.aaemonline.org
Diego Saporta, President
Barry Smeltzer, Executive Director
Renee Grandi, Secretary
The Academy is an association of physicians and other professionals engaged in investigating and coming up with preventive strategies for medical care relating to environmentally triggered illnesses.
1965

597 American Academy of Medical Acupuncture
2512 Artesia Blvd.
Suite 200
Redondo Beach, CA 90278   310-379-8261
                    info@medicalacupuncture.org
                    www.medicalacupuncture.org
Donna Pittman, President
Joseph Audette, Vice President
Michael Freedman, Secretary
Professional organization for physicians in North America who have incorporated acupuncture into their traditional medical practice.
1987

598 American Academy of Pain Medicine (AAPM)
4380-B Montgomery Road
Suite 1025
Ellicott City, MD 20143   800-917-1619
                                FAX: 407-749-0714
                                       painmed.org
Farshad M. Ahadian, President
Charles E. Argoff, President-Elect
Eduardo Fraifield, Treasurer
AAPM is an organization created for physicians practicing the specialty of pain medicine in the United States. AAPM works to provide the most up-to-date information available on the practice of pain medicine, advocate for its members, and bring visibility and credibility to the specialty of pain medicine.
1983

599 American Academy of Pain Medicine Foundation
American Academy of Pain Medicine
4380-B Montgomery Road
Suite 1025
Ellicott City, MD 20143   800-917-1619
                                FAX: 407-749-0714
                         painmed.org/aapm-foundation
Farshad M. Ahadian, President
The Foundation supports AAPM's core purpose to optimize the health of patients in pain and eliminate the major health problem of pain by advancing the practice and the specialty of pain medicine.
1911

600 American Academy of Pediatrics (AAP)
345 Park Blvd.
Itasca, IL 60143   800-433-9016
                                FAX: 847-434-8000
                                       www.aap.org
Mark Del Monte, Chief Executive Officer & Executive Vice President
Christine Bork, Chief Development Officer & Sr. Vice President, Development
Roberta Bosak, Chief Administrative Officer & Sr. Vice President, HR
An organization of pediatricians committed to attaining the best physical, mental, and social health and well-being for all infants, children, adolescents, and young adults.
1930

601 American Acupuncture Council
1100 W Town & Country Rd.
Suite 1400
Orange, CA 92868   800-838-0383
                                FAX: 714-571-1863
                    info@acupuncturecouncil.com
                       acupuncturecouncil.com
Marilyn Allen, Contact
Provides acupuncture malpractice insurance across the country.

602 American Association of Acupuncture and Oriental Medicine (AAAOM)
PO Box 96503
Suite 44114
Washington, DC 20090-6503   admin@aaaomonline.org
                                 www.aaaomonline.org
Carlos Chapa, President
Drea Miller, Vice President
Fotios Sardelis, Treasurer

A national professional organization that is dedicated to the promotion and advancement of high ethical, educational, and professional standards in the practice of acupuncture and Oriental medicine (AOM) in the U.S.

603 American Association of People with Disabilities (AAPD)
2020 Pennsylvania Ave.
Mailbox 263
Washington, DC 20006 202-521-4316
800-840-8844
communications@aapd.com
www.aapd.com
Maria Town, President & Chief Executive Officer
Jasmin Bailey, Operations Director
Christine Liao, Programs Director
Nonprofit cross-disability member organization dedicated to ensuring economic self-sufficiency and political empowerment for Americans with disabilities. AAPD works in coalition with other disability organizations for the full implementation and enforcement of disability nondiscrimination laws, particularly the Americans With Disabilities Act (ADA) of 1990 and the Rehabilitation Act of 1973.

604 American Association on Health and Disability (AAHD)
110 N Washington St.
Suite 407
Rockville, MD 20850 301-545-6140
FAX: 301-545-6144
contact@aahd.us
www.aahd.us
Roberta Carlin, Executive Director
Karl Cooper, Director, Public Health Programs
E. Clarke Ross, Director, Public Policy
The American Association on Health and Disability is a cross-disability national nonprofit organization committed to promoting health and wellness initiatives for children and adults with disabilities.

605 American Association on Intellectual and Developmental Disabilities (AAIDD)
8403 Colesville Rd.
Suite 900
Silver Spring, MD 20910 202-387-1968
FAX: 202-387-2193
aaidd.org
Margaret A. Nygren, Executive Director & Chief Executive Officer
Paul D. Aitken, Director, Finance & Administration
Ravita Maharaj, Director, Supports Intensity Scale Program
The organization focuses on intellectual and developmental disabilities, advocating for quality of life and rights for individuals with such disabilities.

606 American Board of Disability Analysts (ABDA)
1483 N. Mt. Juliet Rd.
Suite 175
Nashville, TN 37122 629-255-0870
FAX: 615-296-9980
office@eventsm3.com
www.americandisability.org
Certifies physicians, psychologists, attorneys, and counselors as specialists in disability and personal injury.

607 American Board of Medical Psychotherapists and Psychodiagnosticians
American Board of Disability Analysts
1483 N. Mt. Juliet Rd.
Suite 175
Nashville, TN 37122 629-255-0870
FAX: 615-296-9980
office@eventsm3.com
www.americandisability.org
Affiliated organization of the American Board of Disability Analysts (ABDA).

608 American Board of Professional Disability Consultants
American Board of Disability Analysts
1483 N. Mt. Juliet Rd.
Suite 175
Nashville, TN 37122 629-255-0870
FAX: 615-296-9980
office@eventsm3.com
www.americandisability.org
Affiliated organization of the American Board of Disability Analysts (ABDA).

609 American Botanical Council (ABC)
6200 Manor Rd.
Austin, TX 78723-4345 512-926-4900
800-373-7105
FAX: 512-926-2345
abc@herbalgram.org
herbalgram.org
Mark Blumenthal, Founder & Executive Director
Stefan Gafner, Chief Science Officer
Denise Meikel, Development Director
The American Botanical Council is an independent, nonprofit, international member-based organization providing education using science-based and traditional information to promote the responsible use of herbal medicine.
1988

610 American Camp Association (ACA)
5000 State Rd. 67 North
Martinsville, IN 46151-7902 765-342-8456
800-428-2267
FAX: 765-342-2065
www.acacamps.org
Tom Rosenberg, President & Chief Executive Officer
Lizabeth Fogel, Chair
Dayna Hardin, Vice Chair
The American Camp Association is a community of camp professionals who have joined together to share their knowledge and experience and to ensure the quality of camp programs. Children and adults have the opportunity to engage with a community, developing character building and other skills.

611 American Chiropractic Association (ACA)
1701 Clarendon Blvd.
Suite 200
Arlington, VA 22209 703-276-8800
FAX: 703-243-2593
memberinfo@acatoday.org
www.acatoday.org
Michele R. Martin, President
Marcus Nynas, Vice President
Eric A. Benson, Board Member
The ACA is a professional organization representing chiropractors. Its mission is to preserve, protect, improve, and promote the chiropractic profession. The purpose of the ACA is to provide leadership in health care and a positive vision for the chiropractic profession and its natural approach to health and wellness.

612 American College of Advancement in Medicine (ACAM)
380 Ice Center Lane
Suite C
Bozeman, MT 59718 800-532-3688
members@acam.org
www.acam.org
Ahvie Herskowitz, President
Allen Green, Treasurer
Neal Speight, Secretary
The American College for Advancement in Medicine is a nonprofit society dedicated to educating physicians and other health care professionals on the latest findings and emerging procedures in integrative medicine. ACAM's goals are to improve skills, knowledge, and diagnostic procedures as they relate to integrative medicine; to support research; and to develop awareness of alternative methods of medical treatment.

613 American College of Nurse Midwives (ACNM)
8403 Colesville Rd.
Suite 1230
Silver Spring, MD 20910   240-485-1800
                                         FAX: 240-485-1818
                                        membership@acnm.org
                                              midwife.org

Katrina H. Holland, Chief Executive Officer
Heather Clarke, President
Jessica Brumley, Vice President
The American College of Nurse-Midwives is the oldest women's health care organization in the U.S. ACNM provides research, accredits midwifery education programs, administers and promotes continuing education programs, establishes clinical practice standards, and creates liaisons with state and federal agencies and members of Congress.

614 American Counseling Association (ACA)
P.O. Box 31110
Alexandria, VA 22310-9998   800-347-6647
                                         FAX: 800-473-2329
                                          www.counseling.org

Kimberly N. Frazier, President
Edil Torres-Rivera, President-Elect
Michele Kerulis, Treasurer
The American Counseling Association is a not-for-profit, professional and educational organization dedicated to advancing the counseling profession.
1952

615 American Disabled Golfers Association (ADGA)
United States Golf Teachers Federation
200 S Indian River Dr.
Suite 206
Fort Pierce, FL 34950   772-888-7483
                                           info@usgtf.com
                                            www.usgtf.com

Brandon Lee, President
The American Disabled Golfers Association helps create accessibility to golf courses for disabled golfers.
1989

616 American Disabled for Attendant Programs Today (ADAPT)
                                               adapt.org
National organization fighting for the rights of disabled people through non-violent activism tactics and advocacy. The national body is made up of local groups and individuals.

617 American Foundation for Suicide Prevention (AFSP)
199 Water St.
11th Floor
New York, NY 10038   212-363-3500
                                              888-333-2377
                                         FAX: 212-363-6237
                                            info@afsp.org
                                              afsp.org

Robert Gebbia, Chief Executive Officer
Christine Yu Moutier, Chief Medical Officer
Stephanie Rogers, Executive Vice President & Chief Communications Officer
The American Foundation for Suicide Prevention is a voluntary health organization that gives those affected by suicide a nationwide community empowered by research, education, and advocacy to take action against this disease. AFSP achieves their goal by funding scientific research, educating the public about mental health and suicide prevention, and supporting survivors of suicide loss and all those affected by suicide.

618 American Herbalists Guild (AHG)
PO Box 3076
Asheville, NC 28802-3076   617-520-4372
                          office@americanherbalistsguild.com
                          www.americanherbalistsguild.com
Keren Dolan, Chair
Samuel Perry, Vice Chair
Tenby Owens, Treasurer
A nonprofit, educational organization that represents the voices of herbalists specializing in the medicinal use of plants. Their mission is to promote a high level of professionalism and education in the study and practice of therapeutic herbalism.
1989

619 American Massage Therapy Association (AMTA)
500 Davis St.
Suite 900
Evanston, IL 60201   877-905-2700
                                         info@amtamassage.org
                                          www.amtamassage.org

Christine Bailor-Goodlander, President
Kimberly Kane-Santos, President-Elect
AMTA is a nonprofit professional organization for massage therapists. AMTA works to establish massage therapy as integral to the maintenance of good health and complementary to other therapeutic processes. AMTA aims to advance the profession through ethics and standards, certification, school accreditation, continuing education, professional publications, legislative efforts, public education, and fostering the development of members.

620 American Occupational Therapy Association (AOTA)
6116 Executive Blvd.
Suite 200
North Bethesda, MD 20852-4929   301-652-6611
                                              800-729-2682
                                        customerservice@aota.org
                                             www.aota.org

Sherry Keramidas, Executive Director
Neil Harvison, Chief Officer, Knowledge Division
Matthew Clark, Chief Officer, Innovation & Engagement
A national professional association that advances the quality, availability, use, and support of occupational therapy through standard setting, advocacy, education, and research on behalf of its members.

621 American Organization for Bodywork Therapies of Asia (AOBTA)
391 Wilmington Pike
Suite 3, Box 260
Glen Mills, PA 19342   484-841-6023
                                           office@aobta.org
                                            www.aobta.org

Sarah Goldenberg, President
Gregory Casey, Vice President
Stuart Watts, Treasurer & Secretary
The American Organization for Bodywork Therapies of Asia is a professional membership organizaton that promotes Asian Bodywork Therapy and its practitioners while honoring a diversity of disciplines. AOBTA serves its community of members by supporting appropriate credentialing; defining scope of practice and educational standards; and providing resources for training, professional development, and networking. AOBTA advocates public policy to protect its members.
1989

622 American Public Health Association (APHA)
800 I St. NW
Washington, DC 20001   202-777-2742
                                         FAX: 202-777-2534
                                         TTY:202-777-2500
                                             www.apha.org

Georges C. Benjamin, Executive Director
Mighty Fine, Interim Associate Executive Director
James Carbo, Chief of Staff
The association works to protect all Americans and their communities from preventable, serious health threats. APHA represents a broad array of health officials, educators, environmentalists, policy-makers, and health providers at all levels working both within and outside governmental organizations and educational institutions.
1972

623 American Red Cross
430 17th St. NW
Washington, DC 20006   800-733-2767
                                            www.redcross.org

Bonnie McElveen-Hunter, Chair
Gail J. McGovern, President & Chief Executive Officer
Brian J. Rhoa, Chief Investment Officer

The American Red Cross is an emergency assistance organization offering services in the following areas: disaster relief and recovery; blood donations; health and safety training and education; support for military and veteran families; and international relief and development programs.

624 American Society for the Alexander Technique (AmSAT)
11 W Monument Ave.
Suite 510
Dayton, OH 45402-1233   937-586-3732
                                                800-473-0620
                                             info@amsatonline.org
                                             www.amsatonline.org

Geordie Macminn, Chair
Lisa DeAngelis, Chair Elect
Renee Schneider, Secretary
The Alexander Technique is a self-help method for improving balance and coordination and increasing movement awareness by eliminating habitual reactions of misuse in every day activities. AmSat, a professional organization of Alexander Technique teachers, aims to define, maintain, and promote the Alexander Technique at its highest standard of professional practice and conduct.
1987

625 American Society of Clinical Hypnosis (ASCH)
529 14th Street NW
Suite 1280
Washington, DC 20045   410-940-6585
                                                info@asch.net
                                                www.asch.net

Louis F. Damis, President
John Hall, Treasurer
David Alter, Secretary
The American Society of Clinical Hypnosis is an organization of health and mental health care professionals using clinical hypnosis. ASCH aims to further the knowledge, understanding, and application of hypnosis in health care; to promote the recognition and acceptance of hypnosis as an important tool in clinical health care; and to provide a professional community for clinicians and researchers using hypnosis.
1957

626 American Therapeutic Recreation Association
401 Edgewater Place
Suite 600
Wakefield, MA 01880   703-234-4140
                                             www.atra-online.com

Cliff Burnham, President
Deborah A. Tysor, Secretary
Laura Kelly, Treasurer
Represents the interests and needs of more than 10,000 recreational therapists.
1984

627 American Tinnitus Association (ATA)
PO Box 424049
Washington, DC 20042-4049   800-634-8978
                                                ata.org

Torryn P. Brazell, Executive Director
David Hadley, Chair
ATA is an organization dedicated to finding cures for tinnitus and hyperacusis. ATA's research program focuses on providing seed grants for new areas of tinnitus scientific exploration.

628 Amputee Coalition
601 Pennsylvania Ave. NW
Suite 600, South Bldg.
Washington, DC 20004   888-267-5669
                                          www.amputee-coalition.org

John Register, Executive Board Chair
David S. Sanders, Secretary
R. Carter Wood III, Treasurer
The Amputee Coalition is a nonprofit organization dedicated to assisting and empowering people affected by limb loss through education, support groups, and vocal advocacy.
1986

629 Anxiety and Depression Association of America (ADAA)
8701 Georgia Ave.
Suite 412
Silver Spring, MD 20910   240-485-1001
                                            FAX: 240-485-1035
                                            information@adaa.org
                                                adaa.org

Susan K. Gurley, Executive Director
Charles B. Nemeroff, President
Sanjay Matthew, Chief Medical Officer & Secretary
The Anxiety and Depression Association of America is an international nonprofit organization and a leader in education, training, and research for anxiety, OCD, PTSD, depression, and related disorders. ADAA encourages the advancement of scientific knowledge about the causes and treatment for mental health issues.

630 Aspies For Freedom (AFF)

                                          www.aspiesforfreedom.com
Gwen Nelson, Co-Founder
Amy Nelson, Co-Founder
Seeks to change the discourse on autism, including negative treatment in the media. Runs an online chatroom and promotes Autistic Pride Day.

631 Assistive Technology Industry Association (ATIA)
330 N Wabash Ave.
Suite 2000
Chicago, IL 60611-4267   312-321-5172
                                                877-687-2842
                                            FAX: 312-673-6659
                                                info@atia.org
                                                www.atia.org

David Dikter, Chief Executive Officer
Caroline Van Howe, Chief Operating Officer
Becky Williams, Manager, Online Education Programs
Dedicated to manufacturers, sellers and providers of assistive technology, offering education and research.

632 Association for Applied Psychophysiology and Biofeedback (AAPB)
PO Box 461797
Aurora, CO 80046-1797   800-477-8892
                                                800-477-8892
                                            FAX: 303-422-8436
                                                info@aapb.org
                                                www.aapb.org

Fredric B. Shaffer, President
Leslie Shivers, Executive Director
Jessica M. Eure, Treasurer
AAPB is a nonprofit organization that aims to advance applied psychophysiology and biofeedback through scientific research, practice, and education.
1969

633 Association of Assistive Technology Act Programs (ATAP)
655 15th Street NW
Suite 800
Washington, DC 20005   atapadmin@ataporg.org
                                                www.ataporg.org

Audrey Busch, Executive Director
Jeannie Krull, Chair
Jamie Anderson, Membership & Opertions Director
The Association of Assistive Technology Act Programs (ATAP) is a national, member-based organization consisting of state Assistive Technology Act Programs funded under the Assistive Technology Act (AT Act). It promotes, represents, and coordinates the state AT Programs at a national level.

634 Association of Children's Residential Centers (ACRC)
648 N Plankinton Ave.
Suite 245
Milwaukee, WI 53203   877-332-2272
                                          info@togetherthevoice.org
                                            togetherthevoice.org

Kari Sisson, Executive Director
Amanda Prange, Training Coordinator
Lisette Burton, Chief Policy & Practice Advisor

The Association of Children's Residential Centers advocates for quality treatment and residential interventions for youth. The organization provides support, training and resources to help members better serve children and families through residential interventions.
1956

635 Association of Educational Therapists (AET)
7044 S 13th St.
Oak Creek, WI 53154   414-908-4949
customercare@aetonline.org
www.aetonline.org

Lori Dver, President
Susan Grama, Treasurer
Pat Kimathi, Secretary
AET is a professional association for educational therapists. Educational Therapy offers children and adults with learning disabilities and other learning challenges a wide range of intensive, individualized interventions designed to remediate learning problems.
1979

636 Association of Independent Camps
American Camp Association
5000 State Rd. 67 North
Martinsville, IN 46151-7902   765-342-8456
800-428-2267
FAX: 765-342-2065
www.acacamps.org

Tom Rosenberg, President & Chief Executive Officer
The Association of Independent Camps is an affiliate of the American Camp Association. Originally founded as a committee in 1954, the AIC has served the independent camp community since 1996. They provide accreditation and public credibility, as well as camper scholarship programs.

637 Association of Medical Professionals with Hearing Losses (AMPHL)

admin@amphl.org
amphl.org

Shazia Siddiqi, President
Sarah Hein, Vice President
Jessica Williams, Secretary
The Association of Medical Professionals with Hearing Losses provides information, promotes advocacy and mentorship, and creates a network for individuals with hearing loss interested in or working in health care fields.
1999

638 Association of People Supporting Employment First (APSE)
7361 Calhoun Place
Suite 680
Rockville, MD 20855   301-279-0060
FAX: 301-279-0075
info@apse.org
www.apse.org

Erica Belois-Pacer, Director, Professional Development
Julie Christensen, Director, Policy & Advocacy
Sarah Manning, Business Operations Manager
Through advocacy and education, this nonprofit organization advances employment and self-sufficiency for all people with disabilities.
1988

639 Association of University Centers on Disabilities (AUCD)
1100 Wayne Ave.
Suite 1000
Silver Spring, MD 20910   301-588-8252
FAX: 301-588-2842
aucdinfo@aucd.org
www.aucd.org

John Tschida, Executive Director
Michele Lunsford, Director, Marketing & Communications
Dawn Rudolph, Senior Director, Technical Assistance & Network Engagement
AUCD is a membership organization consisting of University Centers for Excellence in Developmental Disabilities (UCEDD), Leadership Education in Neurodevelopmental Disabilities

(LEND) Programs, and Intellectual and Developmental Disability Research Centers (IDDRC). AUCD supports its members through advocacy, technical assistance, information dissemination, networking, and leadership.

640 Association on Higher Education & Disability (AHEAD)
16810 Kenton Drive
Suite 220
Huntersville, NC 28078   704-947-7779
FAX: 704-948-7779
www.ahead.org

Katy Washington, President
Stephan Smith, Executive Director
Oanh Huynh, Chief Financial Officer
AHEAD is a professional membership organization for individuals involved in the development of policy and in the provision of quality services to meet the needs of persons with disabilities involved in all areas of higher education, promoting full and equal participation.
4,000+ members 1977

641 BabyHearing.org
555 North 30th Street
Omaha, NE 68131   531-355-1234
www.babyhearing.org

This website provides parents/guardians of children with hearing impairments with information and resources. The website is run and funded by the Deafness and Family Communication Center based at the Children's Hospital of Philadelphia.

642 Bastyr Center for Natural Health
3670 Stone Way N
Seattle, WA 98103   206-834-4100
FAX: 206-834-4131
www.bastyrcenter.org
The Bastyr Center is the teaching clinic of Bastyr University, which provides a range of programs in science-based natural medicine. Services include naturopathic medicine, acupuncture, nutrition services, ayurvedic medicine, and counseling.

643 Beacon Tree Foundation
9201 Arboretum Pkwy.
Suite 140
N. Chesterfield, VA 23236   800-414-6427
info@beacontree.org
beacontree.org
Beacon Tree Foundation is dedicated to being an advocate for the family, providing education about treatment and financial resources to help heal children and teens struggling with mental health issues and to provide hope for the future.

644 Birth Defect Research for Children (BDRC)
976 Lake Baldwin Lane
Suite 104
Orlando, FL 32814   407-895-0802
staff@birthdefects.org
www.birthdefects.org

Betty Mekdeci, Executive Director
A nonprofit organization that provides information about birth defects of all kinds to parents and professionals. Offers a library of medical books and files of information on less common categories of birth defects and is involved in research to discover possible links between environmental exposures and birth defects.
1982

645 Bonnie Prudden Myotherapy
4330 E Havasu Rd.
Tucson, AZ 85718   520-529-3979
www.bonnieprudden.com

Enid Whittaker, Managing Director
Sandy Dirks, Treasurer
Lori Drummond, Secretary
Myotherapy is a method for relaxing muscle spasms, improving circulation, and alleviating pain. Pressure is applied using elbows, knuckles or fingers, and held for several seconds to defuse trigger points. The success of this method depends upon the use of specific corrective exercises of the freed muscles.

646 Brain & Behavior Research Foundation
747 Third Ave.
33rd Floor
New York, NY 10017   646-681-4888
                            800-829-8289
                      info@bbrfoundation.org
                           bbrfoundation.org
Jeffrey Borenstein, President & Chief Executive Officer
Miriam E. Katowitz, Vice President of the Board
Donald M. Boardman, Treasurer
The Brain & Behavior Research Foundation is a nonprofit organization committed to alleviating the suffering caused by mental illness by awarding grants in the field of mental health research.
1987

647 Brain Injury Association of America (BIAA)
3057 Nutley St.
Suite 805
Fairfax, VA 22031-1931   703-761-0750
                          FAX: 703-761-0755
                           info@biausa.org
                            www.biausa.org
Rick Willis, President & Chief Executive Officer
Page Melton Ivie, Chair
Kevin Bingham, Vice Chair
The Brain Injury Association of America is a national organization serving and representing individuals, families and professionals who are touched by a traumatic brain injury (TBI). Its mission is to improve the quality of life for people affected by brain injury through the advancement of research, treatment, education and awareness.
1980

648 Burton Blatt Institute (BBI)
Syracuse University
950 Irving Ave.
Dineen Hall, Suite 446
Syracuse, NY 13244-2130   315-443-2863
                          FAX: 315-443-9725
                               bbi.syr.edu
Peter Blanck, Chair
Michael Morris, Senior Advisor
Jonathan Martinis, Senior Director, Law & Policy
Seeks to advance the full inclusion of people with disabilities through program development, research, and public policy guidance in economic and community participation.
1905

649 CARF International
6951 East Southpoint Rd.
Tucson, AZ 85756-9407   520-325-1044
                              888-281-6531
                          FAX: 520-318-1129
                          TTY:520-495-7077
                             info@carf.org
                                 carf.org
Brian J. Boon, President & Chief Executive Officer
Leslie Ellis-Lang, Managing Director, Child & Youth Services
Darren M. Lehrfeld, Chief Accreditation Officer
An independent, nonprofit accreditor of human service providers in the areas of aging services, behavioral health, child and youth services, DMEPOS, employment and community services, medical rehabilitation, and opioid treatment programs.
1966

650 Cambia Health Foundation
100 SW Market St.
Suite E15B
Portland, OR 97201   503-225-4813
                     cambiahealthfoundation.org
Peggy Maguire, President & Chair
Rob Coppedge, Chief Executive Officer
Anjie Vannoy, Vice President, Finance & Controller
Cambia Health Foundation is the corporate foundation of Cambia Health Solutions dedicated to transforming the way people experience health care to create a more person-focused and economically sustainable health care system.
1907

651 Canadian Art Therapy Association (CATA)
PO Box 658, Stn Main
Parksville, BC, Canada V9P-2G7 admin@canadianarttherapy.org
                          canadianarttherapy.org
Amanda Gee, President
Nicole Le Bihan, Vice President
Waqas Yousafzai, Treasurer
CATA is a nonprofit organization that works in cooperation with other provincial art therapy associations to promote education and understanding of the value of art therapy, as well as provide ongoing education and professional standards for this field.
1977

652 Canine Companions for Independence (CCI)
PO Box 446
Santa Rosa, CA 95402-0446   866-224-3647
                              800-572-2275
                              www.canine.org
Paige Mazzoni, Chief Executive Officer
Keith Edwards, Chief Financial Officer
Robin Sanchez, Secretary
A nonprofit organization that enhances the lives of people with disabilities by providing highly trained assistance dogs and ongoing support to ensure quality partnerships.
1975

653 Canine Helpers for the Handicapped
Canine Helpers for the Handicapped, Inc.
5699 Ridge Rd.
Lockport, NY 14094   716-433-4035
                            chhdogs@aol.com
A nonprofit organization dedicated to training dogs in order to assist people with disabilities and promote independence.

654 Case Management Society of America (CMSA)
5034A Thoroughbred Lane
Brentwood, TN 37027   615-432-0101
                              800-216-2672
                          FAX: 615-523-1715
                            cmsa@cmsa.org
                             www.cmsa.org
Patricia Noonan, President
Nadine Carter, Treasurer
Colleen Morley, Secretary
The Case Management Society of America is an international, nonprofit organization dedicated to the support and development of the profession of case management through educational forums, networking opportunities, and legislative involvement. Case management workers play a vital role in taking care of patients' health care needs.
1990

655 Center for Creative Arts Therapy
2600 Warrenville Road
Suite 205
Downers Grove, IL 60515   847-477-8244
                   info@c4creativeartstherapy.com
                     c4creativeartstherapy.com
Azizi Marshall, Founder & Chief Executive Officer
Leslie Kane, Director, Education & Community
The Center for Creative Arts Therapy offers arts-based psychotherapy services to individuals and their families as a healthy, proactive way to achieve wellness and balance in their lives. Provides art therapy, music therapy, dance therapy and drama therapy, as well as professional counseling.

656 Center for Disability Resources
University of South Carolina School of Medicine
Department of Pediatrics
8301 Farrow Rd.
Columbia, SC 29208   803-935-5231
                          FAX: 803-935-5059
                    david.rotholz@uscmed.sc.edu
                     uscm.med.sc.edu/cdrhome
A University Affiliated Program which develops model programs designed to serve persons with disabilities and to train students in fields related to disabilities.

657 Center for Inclusive Design and Innovation
512 Means St. NW
Suite 250
Atlanta, GA 30318
404-894-8000
866-279-2964
FAX: 404-894-8323
cidi-support@design.gatech.edu
cidi.gatech.edu

Eric Trevena, Senior Director, Operations
Carolyn Phillips, Director, Services & Learning
CIDI supports individuals with disabilities of any age within the State of Georgia and beyond through expert services, research, design and technological development, information dissemination, and educational programs.

658 Center for Mind-Body Medicine
5225 Connecticut Ave. NW
Suite 414
Washington, DC 20015
202-966-7338
FAX: 202-966-2589
www.cmbm.org

James S. Gordon, Founder & Chief Executive Officer
Rosemary Lombard, Executive Director
Lynda Richtsmeier, Clinical Director
The Center for Mind-Body Medicine is a nonprofit educational organization dedicated to reviving the spirit and transforming the practice of medicine. The Center is working to create a more effective, comprehensive, and compassionate model of health care and education. The Center's model combines the precision of modern science with the best of the world's healing traditions.

659 Cerebral Palsy Foundation (CPF)
3 Columbus Circle
15th Floor
New York, NY 10019
212-520-1686
info@yourcpf.org
yourcpf.org

Rachel Byrne, Executive Director
Ila Eckhoff, Chair of the Board
James P. Volcker, Vice President & Secretary
The Cerebral Palsy Foundation is dedicated to assisting and empowering people with cerebral palsy through research in both medical breakthroughs and assistive technologies.

660 Challenged Athletes Foundation (CAF)
9591 Waples St.
San Diego, CA 92121
858-866-0959
FAX: 858-866-0958
caf@challengedathletes.org
challengedathletes.org

Kristie Entwistle, Chief Executive Officer
Virginia Tinley, Chief Legacy Officer
Kim Rohr, Operations Manager
The Challenged Athletes Foundation provides opportunities and support to physically challenged persons so they can pursue active lifestyles through physical fitness and competitive athletics.
1994

661 Change, Inc.
115 Stoner Ave.
Westminster, MD 21157
410-876-2179
info@penn-mar.org
www.changeinc.cc

Gregory T. Miller, President & Chief Executive Officer
Michael Mahon, Chief Financial Officer
Kathy Rogers, Chief Advancement Officer
A nonprofit organization that partners with families, caregivers, and advocates to provide opportunities for children with developmental disabilities. A division of Penn-Mar Human Services.

662 Child and Parent Resource Institute (CPRI)
600 Sanatorium Rd.
London, ON, Canada N6H-3W7
519-858-2774
877-494-2774
FAX: 519-858-3913
TTY: 519-858-0257
www.cpri.ca

Provides highly specialized services to children and youth from 0-18 years of age with complex mental health and/or developmental challenges on a short term inpatient and community basis.

663 Children's Alliance
420 Capitol Ave.
Frankfort, KY 40601
502-875-3399
FAX: 502-223-4200
www.childrensallianceky.org

Michelle Sanborn, President
Melissa Muse, Director, Member Services
Kathy Adams, Director, Public Policy
An association of individuals and human services organizations committed to being a voice for at-risk children and families. Interacts with the legislative and executive branches of government and assists members in developing services that most effectively meet the needs of at-risk children and families.

664 Children's Mental Health Network (CMHN)
Chapel Hill, NC 27516
information@cmhnetwork.org
www.cmhnetwork.org

Scott Bryant-Comstock, President & Chief Executive Officer
Provides neutral, independent information on children's mental health issues, while sharing ideas on ways to improve the lives of affected children and their families.

665 Children's National Medical Center
111 Michigan Ave. NW
Washington, DC 20010
202-476-5000
888-884-2327
childrensnational.org

Kurt Newman, President & Chief Executive Officer
Donna Anthony, Vice President & Chief of Staff
Denice Cora-Bramble, Chief Diversity Officer
The Children's National Medical Center provides health care services that enhance the health and well-being of children regionally, nationally, and internationally. Through leadership and innovation, the organization will create solutions to pediatric health care problems.

666 Clay Tree Society
838 Old Victoria Rd.
Nanaimo, BC, Canada V9R-6A1
250-753-5322
FAX: 250-753-2749
info@claytree.org
www.claytree.org

Dan Dube, Board Member
Alexandria Stuart, Board Member
Kellina Lang, Board Member
A nonprofit society providing day programming, assistance and support for people with developmental disabilities.
1957

667 Coalition for Health Funding
c/o Cavarocchi Ruscio Dennis Associates, LLC
600 Maryland Ave. SW
Suite 220E
Washington, DC 20024
202-271-8963
FAX: 202-484-1244
emorton@dc-crd.com
www.publichealthfunding.org

Erin Will Morton, Executive Director
Jonathan Daniels, Deputy Director
Katina Pierce, Vice President, Administration & Finance
Nonprofit alliance working to preserve and strengthen public health investments via funding for federal agencies and programs.

668 Communitas Supportive Care Society
103-2776 Bourquin Cres. W
Abbotsford, BC, Canada V2S-6A4
604-850-6608
800-622-5455
FAX: 604-850-2634
office@communitascare.com
www.communitascare.com

Kathy Doerksen, Chair
John Wiebe, Vice Chair
Jacqui Lepp, Secretary & Treasurer
Communitas Supportive Care Society is a nonprofit, faith-based organization providing care in communities across British Columbia to those living with disabilities. Services include skills-based day programs, residential care, and respite care for families.

669 **Council for Exceptional Children (CEC)**
3100 Clarendon Blvd.
Suite 600
Arlington, VA 22201-5332 888-232-7733
TTY:866-915-5000
service@exceptionalchildren.org
www.exceptionalchildren.org
Chad Rummel, Executive Director
Laurie VanderPloeg, Associate Executive Director, Professional Affairs
Craig Evans, Chief Financial Officer
The Council for Exceptional Children aims to improve the educational success of individuals with disabilities and/or gifts and talents by advocating for appropriate policies, setting professional standards, and providing resources and professional development for special educators.

670 **Council of Colleges of Acupuncture & Oriental Medicine**
9615 E. County Line Road
Suite B-584
Centennial, CO 80112 410-464-6040
FAX: 410-464-6042
support@ccaom.org
www.ccaom.org
Kris LaPointe, President
Thomas Kouo, Vice President
Jennifer Brett, Treasurer
The Council seeks to advance the standing of acupuncture and Oriental medicine (AOM) in the U.S. by promoting educational excellence within the field by deepening the knowledge, understanding and skills of the AOM practitioner.
1982

671 **Council of Parent Attorneys and Advocates (COPAA)**
PO Box 6767
Towson, MD 21285 844-426-7224
www.copaa.org
Denise Stile Marshall, Executive Director
Selene A. Almazan, Legal Director
Marcie Hipple, Director, Member Services & Events
Group of attorneys, advocates, parents and related professionals working to protect the rights of students with disabilities and their families, including promoting excellence in education.

672 **Council of State Administrators of Vocational Rehabilitation (CSAVR)**
1 Research Ct.
Suite 450
Rockville, MD 20850 301-519-8023
info@csavr.org
www.csavr.org
Stephen A. Wooderson, Chief Executive Officer
Tonia D. Ferguson, Director, Legislative Affairs
Kathy West-Evans, Director, Business Relations
The Council is made up of the chief administrators of the public rehabilitation agencies that serve people with physical and mental disabilities across the U.S.

673 **Department of Physical Medicine & Rehabilitation at Sinai Hospital**
LifeBridge Health
2401 W Belvedere Ave.
Baltimore, MD 21215-5271 443-429-0067
www.lifebridgehealth.org
Provides health-related services to the people of the Northwest Baltimore region. LifeBridge is dedicated to advancing the health of the community through a variety of health and wellness programs and services. The Department of Physical Medicine & Rehabilitation provides care to individuals with disabling conditions such as traumatic brain injury, spinal cord injury, amputees, and more.

674 **DisAbility LINK**
1901 Montreal Rd.
Suite 102
Tucker, GA 30084 404-687-8890
FAX: 404-687-8298
TTY:711
www.disabilitylink.org
Kim Gibson, Executive Director
Joseph Bryant, Financial Director
Rosemary Graham, Secretary
disABILITY LINK is an organization committed to promoting the rights of all people with disabilities in allowing them to be independent, achieve goals, have access to their community, and make decisions for themselves.

675 **Disability Funders Network (DFN)**
14241 Midlothian Turnpike
Suite 151
Midlothian, VA 23113-6500 703-795-9646
info@disabilityfunders.org
www.disabilityfunders.org
Kim Hutchinson, President & Chief Executive Officer
Kevin Webb, Chair
Susan Olivo, Treasurer
Disability Funders Network is a national membership organization dedicated to advocating for equality and rights for disabled individuals and communities.
1990

676 **Disability Research and Dissemination Center**
Arnold School of Public Health, USC
Discovery 1 Bldg.
915 Greene St.
Columbia, SC 29208 info@disabilityresearchcenter.com
www.disabilityresearchcenter.com
Suzanne McDermott, Research & Administration
Margaret A. Turk, Training & Evaluation
Roberta S. Carlin, Dissemination
The DRDC was formed in 2012 and is a partnership between the University of South Carolina (USC), the State University of New York Upstate Medical University (SUNY Upstate), and the American Association on Health and Disability (AAHD). Its five core areas are Administration, Research, Research Translation, Evaluation, and Dissemination & Policy.

677 **Disability Rights Bar Association (DBRA)**
c/o Burton Blatt Institute
950 Irving Ave.
Dineen Hall, Suite 446
Syracuse, NY 13244-2130 315-443-2863
FAX: 315-443-9725
drba-law@law.syr.edu
disabilityrights-law.org
Lydia X.Z. Brown, Co-Chair
Mehgan Sidhu, Co-Chair
Rebecca Williford, Secretary
The DRBA is an online network of attorneys who specialize in disability civil rights law.

678 **Disability Rights Florida**
2473 Care Dr.
Suite 200
Tallahassee, FL 32308 850-488-9071
800-342-0823
FAX: 850-488-8640
TTY: 800-346-4127
www.disabilityrightsflorida.org
Peter Sleasman, Executive Director
Ann Siegel, Legal Director
Cherie E. Hall, Director, Operations
A federally mandated Protection & Advocacy (P&A) organization working to ensure the safety, well-being and success of people with disabilities.
1977

679   Disability Rights International (DRI)
1825 K St. NW
Suite 600
Washington, DC 20006
202-296-0800
FAX: 202-697-5422
info@driadvocacy.org
www.driadvocacy.org

Laurie Ahern, President
Eric Rosenthal, Founder & Executive Director
Priscila Rodriguez, Associate Director, Advocacy
Promotes international oversight of disability rights by documenting human rights abuses and publishing reports on enforcement.

680   Disability Rights Louisiana
8325 Oak St.
New Orleans, LA 70118
800-960-7705
info@disabilityrightsla.org
disabilityrightsla.org

Ron Lospennato, Interim Executive Director & Director, Legal Services
Tory Rocca, Director, Public Policy and Community Engagement
Debra Weinberg, Director, Community Advocacy
Protects and advocates for the rights of seniors and individuals with disabilities in Louisiana.

681   Disability:IN
3000 Potomac Ave.
Alexandria, VA 22305
info@disabilityin.org
disabilityin.org

Jill Houghton, President & Chief Executive Officer
Brian Horn, Chief Operating Officer
Amy Naoum, Chief Financial Officer
Nonprofit specializing in disability inclusion in the workplace.

682   Disabled Athlete Sports Association (DASA)
1600 Mid Rivers Mall Circle
Suite 2272
St. Peters, MO 63376
636-477-0716
dasa@dasasports.org
www.dasasports.org

Kelly Behlmann, Founder & Executive Director
Meghan Morgan, Program Director
Jeff Franta, Director, Operations
The Disabled Athlete Sports Association is a nonprofit organization specializing in adaptive sport and fitness opportunities. DASA relies heavily upon fundraising events, grants, and individual and corporate donations to sustain its mission.
1997

683   Disabled Businesspersons Association (DBA)
6367 Alvarado Crt.
Suite 350
San Diego, CA 92120
619-594-8805
Urban Miyares, Founder
The Disabled Businesspersons Association is a nonprofit public charity and educational organization to help disabled entrepreneurs maximize their potential in the business world, and to encourage the participation and enhance the performance of disabled individuals in the work force.
1991

684   Disabled Children's Fund (DCF)
PO Box 4712
Crofton, MD 21114
240-929-4281
info@achildthrives.org
achildthrives.org

Bill Collins, Co-Founder
Erma Collins, Co-Founder
Disabled Children's Fund is a humanitarian organization serving oppressed children and families worldwide. It distributes braces, wheelchairs, crutches, walkers and rehabilitative services globally.
1997

685   Disabled Drummers Association (DDA)
www.disableddrummers.org
The Disabled Drummers Association is a nonprofit organization representing drummers with disabilities. The DDA seeks to raise public awareness and funds, advocate for the development of adaptive equipment, and provide resources and opportunities to members.
1996

686   Disabled In Action (DIA)
PO Box 30954
Port Authority Station
New York, NY 10011- 0109
646-504-4342
FAX: 646-504-4342
TTY:711
treasurer@disabledinaction.org
www.disabledinaction.org

Jean Ryan, President
Phil Beder, Treasurer
Valerie Joseph, Recording Secretary
A democratic, nonprofit, membership organization advancing civil rights and seeking to end discrimination for people with disabilities.

687   Disabled Peoples' International (DPI)
160 Elgin St.
Place Bell RPO, PO Box 70073
Ottawa, ON, Canada K2P-2M3
dpi.org
Rachel Kachaje, Chair
Jean Luc Simon, Secretary
Shoji Nakanishi, Treasurer
Aims to protect the rights of people with disabilities, while promoting their full and equal role in society.
1981

688   Disabled and Alone: Life Services for the Handicapped, Inc. (ACT for Life Services)
PO Box 340
New Hyde Park, NY 11040-0340
212-532-6740
800-995-0066
FAX: 212-532-6740
info@disabledandalone.org
www.actforlifeservices.org

Evert J. Christensen Jr., Chair
Robert Gutheil, Vice Chair
Lee A. Ackerman, Executive Director
A national nonprofit humanitarian organization whose primary concern is the well-being of disabled persons, particularly when their families can no longer care for them. The organization helps families do sensible planning for and with their disabled children; provides advocacy and oversight when the parents cannot do so; and advises families, attorneys, and financial planners about life planning for a family with a member with a disability.
1988

689   Dr. Ida Rolf Institute (DIRI)
5055 Chaparral Ct.
Suite 103
Boulder, CO 80301
303-449-5903
FAX: 303-449-5978
membership@rolf.org
www.rolf.org

Christina Howe, Executive Director & Chief Academic Officer
Mary Contreras, Director, Admissions & Recruitment
Samantha Sherwin, Director, Faculty & Student Services
The Rolf Institute is a nonprofit corporation, dedicated to educating individuals on Rolfing Structural Integration. It is recognized by the US Government as a tax-exempt educational and scientific research organization.
1971

690   Early Childhood Technical Assistance Center (ETCA)
CB 8040
Chapel Hill, NC 27599-8040
919-962-2001
FAX: 919-966-7463
ectacenter@unc.edu
ectacenter.org

Christina Kasprzak, Co-Director
Meghan Vinh, Co-Director
ECTA Center, funded by the Office of Special Education Programs, is a technical assistance center supporting Part C and Section 619 IDEA programs in building quality early intervention and preschool special education service systems, improving and sustaining state systems, and enhancing outcomes for children with disabilities and their families.

691 Easterseals
141 W Jackson Blvd.
Suite 1400A
Chicago, IL 60604   312-726-6200
                                     800-221-6827
                                  FAX: 312-726-1494
                              info@easterseals.com
                                    easterseals.com

Catherine Georges, Chair
Nicole Cooper, 1st Vice Chair
Joan Rockey, Treasurer
Easterseals provides services, education, outreach and advocacy
for people with disabilities, veterans, senior citizens and their
families. Programs include early intervention, workforce development, adult day care, autism services, mental health services,
and more.

692 Elwyn
111 Elwyn Rd.
Media, PA 19063   610-891-2000
                                   info@elwyn.org
                                       elwyn.org

Charles S. McLister, President & Chief Executive Officer
Rex Carney, Chief of Staff
Len Kirby, Chief Operating Officer
A nonprofit organization developing programs for children and
adults with disabilities and disadvantages.
Founded in 1852.

**693 Employer Assistance and Resource Network on
      Disability Inclusion (EARN)**
Cornell University, ILR School
201 Dolgen Hall
Ithaca, NY 14853   askearn@cornell.edu
                                    www.askearn.org

Susanne Bruyere, Co-Director
Wendy Strobel Gower, Co-Director
Free network for employers providing education on building in-
clusive workplace cultures.

694 Enable America, Inc.
101 E Kennedy Blvd.
Suite 3250
Tampa, FL 33602   877-362-2533
                                  FAX: 813-221-8811
                         richard.salem@enableamerica.org
                               www.enableamerica.org
Richard J. Salem, Founder & Chief Executive Officer
Sandy Moonert, Program Director
Enable America, Inc. is a nonprofit organization that is dedicated
to increasing employment among people with disabilities in the
United States.

695 Esalen Institute
55000 Highway One
Big Sur, CA 93920   831-667-3000
                                     888-837-2536
                                  info@esalen.org
                                    www.esalen.org

Gordon Wheeler, President
Dave Morin, Chairman of the Board
Michael Murphy, Co-Founder
An alternative education center devoted to East/West philoso-
phies, experiential/didactic workshops, and a steady influx of
philosophers, psychologists, artists, and religious thinkers.
1962

696 Family Resource Center on Disabilities
11 E. Adams St.
Suite 1002
Chicago, IL 60603   312-939-3513
                                   info@frcd.org
                                     www.frcd.org
A not-for-profit advocacy organization dedicated to improving
services for all children with disabilities by providing support
and services to affected families, informing parents of their
rights, and helping parents become advocates for their children.
Offers family support services, training, seminars, and information and referral services. Publishes a monthly newsletter.

**697 Family Run Executive Director Leadership Association
      (FREDLA)**
10632 Patuxent Pkwy.
Suite 234
Columbia, MD 21044   410-707-4547
                                   info@fredla.org
                                     www.fredla.org

Pat Hunt, Executive Director
Millie Sweeney, Deputy Director
Malisa Pearson, Project Coordinator
Aims to strengthen the leadership and organizational capacity of
family-run organizations.

698 Family Voices
561 Virginia Rd, Bldg. 4
Suite 300
Concord, MA 01742   781-674-7224
                                     888-835-5669
                              www.familyvoices.org

Allysa Ware, Executive Director
Cara Coleman, Director, Public Policy & Advocacy
Roseani Snchez, Director, Programs
A not-for-profit organization dedicated to ensuring that children's health issues are addressed as public and private
health-care systems undergo change in communities, states, and
the nation. They are a national grassroots clearinghouse for information and education in ways to improve health care for children
with disabilities and chronic conditions. Family Voices provides
materials including pamphlets, a newsletter, and one-page papers
on important topics.

699 Favarh ARC
225 Commerce Dr.
Canton, CT 06019-2478   860-693-6662
                                  FAX: 860-693-8662
                                favarh@favarh.org
                                    www.favarh.org

Suzanne Sinacore, President
Ernie Mack, Vice President
Tom Smith, Treasurer
Favarh ARC provides a variety of programs and services to adults
with developmental, physical, or mental disabilities and their
families throughout the Farmington Valley communities of Avon,
Burlington, and more. Favarh's programs are designed to enhance the personal, social, emotional, vocational, and living capabilities of persons with disabilities.
1958

700 Fedcap Rehabilitation Services
633 Third Ave.
6th Floor
New York, NY 10017   212-727-4200
                                  FAX: 212-727-4374
                                  TTY:646-606-5950
                                  info@fedcap.org
                                    www.fedcap.org

Steve Coons, President
George Rios, Director, Operations
Amy Reisner, Director, Contract Administration
Fedcap helps people with barriers achieve economic independence through employment. Through evaluation, vocational and
soft-skills training, job placement, job creation, and support programs, each year Fedcap helps thousands of Americans overcome
obstacles, rebuild their lives, and find and keep meaningful
employment.
1935

701 Federation for Children with Special Needs
529 Main St.
Suite 1M3
Boston, MA 02129   617-236-7210
                                     800-331-0688
                                  FAX: 617-241-0330
                                fcsninfo@fcsn.org
                                     www.fcsn.org

Pam Nourse, Executive Director
John Reichenbach, President
Matthew Trivella, Treasurer

The Federation for Children with Special Needs provides information, support, and assistance to parents of children with disabilities, their professional partners, and their communities.
1975

702 Feingold Association of the US
10955 Windjammer Dr. S
Indianapolis, IN 46256   631-369-9340
membership@feingold.org
www.feingold.org
An organization of families and professionals, the Feingold Association of the United States is dedicated to helping children and adults apply proven dietary techniques for better behavior, learning, and health.
1976

703 Feldenkrais Guild of North America (FGNA)
401 Edgewater Pl.
Suite 600
Wakefield, MA 01880   781-876-8935
FAX: 781-645-1322
www.feldenkraisguild.com
Nancy Haller, President
Fariya Doctor, Secretary
Erik LaSeur, Treasurer
This organization sets the standards for and certifies all Feldenkrais practitioners in North America. In order to practice, a practitioner must be a graduate of an FGNA accredited program (a minimum of 800 instruction hours over a three to four year period), and agree to follow both the Code of Professional Conduct and the Standards of Practice. FGNA may be contacted for further information about the Feldenkrais Method or for a list of Feldenkrais practitioners sorted by region.

704 Flying Manes Therapeutic Riding, Inc.
PO Box 508
Scarsdale, NY 10583   917-524-6648
info@flyingmanes.org
flyingmanes.org
Flying Manes is a therapeutic riding center located at Riverdale Stables in New York. Flying Manes aims to help individuals with emotional, cognitive, and physical disabilities in a safe and enjoyable environment.
Founded in 2009.

705 Freedom from Fear
308 Seaview Ave.
Staten Island, NY 10305   718-351-1717
help@freedomfromfear.org
freedomfromfear.org
Mary Guardino, Founder & Executive Director
Freedom From Fear is a national nonprofit mental health advocacy organization whose goal is to better the lives of all those affected by anxiety, depressive, and related disorders through advocacy, education, research, and community support.
1984

706 Fos Feminista

212-248-6400
online@fosfeminista.org
www.fosfeminista.org
Giselle Carino, Chief Executive Officer
Works to generate health and population policies, programs, and funding that promote and protect the rights and health of girls and women worldwide.

707 Genova Diagnostics
63 Zillicoa St.
Asheville, NC 28801   828-253-0621
800-522-4762
info@gdx.net
www.gdx.net
Jeffrey Ledford, Chief Executive Officer
Craig Thiel, Chief Financial Officer
Jeff Ellis, Chief Commercial Officer
Genova Diagnostics specializes in nutritional, metabolic, and toxicant analyses. Genova is committed to helping health care professionals identify nutritional influences on health and disease, and laboratory procedures in nutritional and biochemical testing.
1984

708 Goodwill Industries International
15810 Indianola Dr.
Rockville, MD 20855   contactus@goodwill.org
www.goodwill.org
Steven C. Preston, President & Chief Executive Officer
Goodwill strives to achieve the full participation in society of disabled persons and other individuals with special needs by expanding their opportunities and occupational capabilities through a network of autonomous, nonprofit, community-based organizations providing services throughout the world in response to local needs.
2002

709 Grand Lodge of the International Association of Machinists and Aerospace Workers
9000 Machinists Pl.
Upper Marlboro, MD 20772   301-967-4500
info@iamaw.org
www.goiam.org
Robert Martinez, Jr., International President
Brian Bryant, General Vice President, Headquarters
Monica Lee Silbas, Chief of Staff to the International President
Offers placements, programs, and resources for persons with disabilities.

710 HEATH Resource Center at the National Youth Transitions Center
George Washington University
2134 G St. NW
Washington, DC 20052-0001   askheath@gwu.edu
www.heath.gwu.edu
Christopher Nace, Principal Investigator
The HEALTH Resource Center is a national clearinghouse for information about education after high school for people with disabilities. Also serves as an information exchange about educational support services, policies, procedures, adaptations, and opportunities on American campuses, vocational-technical schools, adult education programs, independent living centers, and other training entities after high school.

711 Habilitation Benefits Coalition
c/o Powers Pyles Sutter & Verville PC
1501 M St. NW
7th Floor
Washington, DC 20005   habcoalition.wordpress.com
The HAB Coalition coordinates, sustains and promotes a unified voice for organizations who are independently active in their support for habilitative services and devices.

712 Haldimand-Norfolk Resource Education and Counseling
101A Nanticoke Creek Parkway
Townsend, ON, Canada N0A-1S0   519-587-2441
800-265-8087
FAX: 519-587-4798
info@hnreach.on.ca
www.hnreach.on.ca
Wendy Carron, Executive Director
Mark Smith, President
Stephanie Anderson, Vice President
Haldimand-Norfolk REACH is a multi-service agency, providing children's mental health services, developmental services, Autism services, youth justice services, family services, a residential program for transitional-aged youth and several early learning and care services including licensed childcare, Ontario Early Years Centre(s) and Community Action Program for Children.

713 Hanger, Inc.
10910 Domain Drive
3rd Floor
Austin, TX 78758   512-614-4612
877-442-6437
FAX: 512-614-4615
hangerclinic.com
Pete Stoy, Chief Executive Officer
Gabrielle Adams, Senior Vice President & Chief Accounting Officer
James Campbell, Senior Vice President & Chief Clinical Officer

Hanger Clinic specializes in orthotic and prosthetic services with clinic locations across the country.

714   Health Action
5276 Hollister Ave.
Suite 257
Santa Barbara, CA 93111   805-617-3390
www.healthaction.net
Roger Jahnke, Co-Founder & Chief Executive Officer
Rebecca McLean, Co-Founder
Health Action's mission is to foster innovation in health care that will increase health status, customer satisfaction, profitability, support provider efficiency, enhance clinical outcomes, and encourage consumer self-managed care.

715   Hearing Health Foundation (HHF)
PO Box 1397
New York, NY 10018   212-257-6140
866-454-3924
FAX: 212-257-6139
TTY: 888-435-6104
info@hhf.org
hearinghealthfoundation.org
Timothy Higdon, President & Chief Executive Officer
Noemi Disla, Director, Finance, Operations & Administration
Christopher Geissler, Director, Program & Research Support
Hearing Health Foundation promotes hearing health and advocates for the prevention and cure of hearing loss and tinnitus through research.
1958

716   High Technology Foundation
1000 Galliher Dr.
Suite 1000
Fairmont, WV 26554   304-363-5482
877-363-5482
info@wvhtf.org
www.wvhtf.org
Dr. Frank W. Blake, Chair
James L. Estep, President & Chief Executive Officer
High Technology Foundation is dedicated to maximizing economic development in West Virginia through the high-technology business sector.
1990

717   Hogg Foundation for Mental Health
3001 Lake Austin Blvd.
Austin, TX 78703   512-471-5041
hogg-operations@austin.utexas.edu
hogg.utexas.edu
Octavio N. Martinez, Jr., Executive Director
Vicky Coffee, Director, Programs
Crystal Viagran, Director, Finance & Operations
The Hogg Foundation for Mental Health is a nonprofit organization that is dedicated to the advancement of mental wellness for the people of Texas through outreach programs, conferences, seminars, research grants, and more.

718   Homeopathic Educational Services
812C Camelia St.
Berkeley, CA 94710   510-649-0294
800-359-9051
email@homeopathic.com
www.homeopathic.com
Dana Ullman, Owner & Director
Resource center for homeopathic products and services including books, tapes, research, medicines, medicine kits, software for the general public and health professionals, and correspondence courses.
1975

719   Hope Network Neuro Rehabilitation
3075 Orchard Vista Dr. SE
PO Box 890
Grand Rapids, MI 49546   616-301-8000
800-695-7273
FAX: 616-301-8010
RehabReferral@hopenetwork.org
www.hopenetwork.org
Bob Von Kaenel, President & Chief Executive Officer
Tim Becker, Chief Operating Officer
John McInerney, Chief Information Officer
Neuro Rehabilitation is a service line of Hope Network, helping those with brain or spinal cord injuries or other neurological conditions recover through treatment techniques and person-centered care.

720   Humanity & Inclusion (HI)
8757 Georgia Ave.
Suite 420
Silver Spring, MD 20910   301-891-2138
FAX: 301-891-9193
info.usa@hi.org
www.hi-us.org
Jeff Meer, Executive Director
Nancy A. Kelly, President
Christine Kaunch, Treasurer
International organization promoting disability rights, rehabilitation, and safety in areas of emergency and conflict.

721   Immune Deficiency Foundation
7550 Teague Road
Suite 220
Hanover, MD 21076   800-296-4433
FAX: 410-321-9165
info@primaryimmune.org
primaryimmune.org
Jorey Berry, President & Chief Executive Officer
Sarah Rose, Chief Financial Officer
Tammy C. Black, Chief Communications Officer
The Immune Deficiency Foundation is the national patient organization dedicated to improving the diagnosis, treatment, and quality of life of persons with primary immunodeficiency diseases through advocacy, education, and research.

722   Indiana Association for Home and Hospice Care (IAHHC)
6320-G Rucker Rd.
Indianapolis, IN 46220   317-775-6675
FAX: 317-775-6674
evan@iahhc.org
www.iahhc.org
Evan Reinhardt, Executive Director
Katie Ociepka, Director, Development
Tori Raderstorf, Director, Communications & Events
The Indiana Association for Home & Hospice Care represents home nursing services and inpatient hospice care services. The association offers education and resources, advocacy, and a career center to its members.

723   Institute for Educational Leadership (IEL)
4301 Connecticut Ave. NW
Suite 100
Washington, DC 20008   202-822-8405
FAX: 202-872-4050
iel@iel.org
iel.org
Eddie Koen, President
Maame Appiah, Vice President, Finance & Talent
S. Kwesi Rollins, Vice Resident, Leadership & Engagement
Assists under-funded communities by preparing children, youth, adults, and families for postsecondary education and training, leading to better career options and greater community engagement.

724 **International Academy of Independent Medical Evaluators**
3606 SE 151st Court
Vancouver, WA 98683
844-484-2463
iaime@iaime.org
www.iaime.org

Diana Kraemer, President
James Underhill, President Elect
Gary Pushkin, Secretary & Treasurer
IAIME is an organization serving physicians involved in disability management. Their courses and products cover disability management and evaluations for physicians, health care providers, attorneys, regulators, legislators, and others involved in the care of injured persons.

725 **International Association of Yoga Therapists (IAYT)**
PO Box 251563
Little Rock, AR 72225
928-541-0004
www.iayt.org

Alyssa Wostrel, Executive Director
Molly McManus, President
Susan Steiger Tebb, Vice President
IAYT supports research and education in yoga and serves yoga practitioners, teachers, therapists, health care professionals, and researchers worldwide. Its mission is to establish yoga as a recognized and respected therapy in the Western world. IAYT also serves members, the media, and the general public as a comprehensive source of information about contemporary yoga education, research, and statistics.
1989

726 **International Child Amputee Network**
PO Box 13812
Tuscon, AZ 85732
child-amputee.net
I-CAN provides information, support and education to children with traumatic and congenital limb difference and their families.

727 **International Chiropractors Association (ICA)**
6400 Arlington Blvd.
Suite 650
Falls Church, VA 22042
703-528-5000
FAX: 703-528-5023
info@chiropractic.org
www.chiropractic.org

Beth Clay, Executive Director & Chief Executive Officer
Selina Sigafoose-Jackson, President
Joseph Betz, Vice President
The Association strives to protect, promote and advance chiropractic throughout the world.
1926

728 **International Clinic of Biological Regeneration (ICBR)**
PO Box 509
Florissant, MO 63032
800-826-5366
FAX: 314-921-8485
icbr@aol.com
www.icbr.com

Judith A. Smith, Co-Founder & Director
William Johnson, Director, Medical Services
The International Clinic of Biological Regeneration is an international cell therapy center dedicated to constantly improving therapeutic results by selecting newer, safer, and more effective treatments.
1981

729 **International Expressive Arts Therapy Association (IEATA)**
PO Box 40707
San Francisco, CA 94140-0707
415-489-0698
info@ieata.org
ieata.org

The International Expressive Arts Therapy Association is a nonprofit organization dedicated to supporting expressive arts therapists, artists, educators, consultants, and others using creative processes for personal growth and community development.

730 **International League Against Epilepsy (ILAE)**
1747 Pennsylvania Ave. NW
Suite 1000
Washington, DC 20006
860-586-7547
ilae.org

Julie Hall, Executive Director
Linda Beza, Director, Finance
Priscilla Shisler, Director, Engagement & Education
ILAE is a nonprofit organization dedicated to the advancement and dissemination of knowledge about epilepsy and to promoting research, education, and training to improve service and care for patients.
Founded in 1909.

731 **International Ventilator Users Network (IVUN)**
50 Crestwood Executive Ctr.
Suite 440
St. Louis, MO 63126-1916
314-534-0475
FAX: 314-534-5070
info@ventusers.org
www.ventnews.org

Mark Mallinger, President & Chairperson
Frederick M. Maynard, Vice President
Marny K. Eulberg, Secretary
IVUN's mission is to enhance the lives and independence of individuals using ventilators by promoting education, networking and advocacy. IVUN is an affiliate of Post-Polio Health International.
1960

732 **Invisible Disabilities Association (IDA)**
PO Box 4067
Parker, CO 80134
invisibledisabilities.org
Wayne Connell, Founder, President & Chief Executive Officer
Jess Stainbrook, Executive Director & Vice President
The Invisible Disabilities Association (IDA) encourages, educates, and connects people and organizations touched by illness, pain, and disability around the globe.

733 **JDRF**
200 Vesey St.
28th Floor
New York, NY 10281
800-533-2873
FAX: 212-785-9595
info@jdrf.org
www.jdrf.org

Aaron J. Kowalski, Chief Executive Officer
Sanjoy Dutta, Chief Scientific Officer
Bala Balasubramanian, Chief Information Officer
A nonprofit, nongovernmental diabetes research organization. JDRF's mission is to find a cure for diabetes and its complications through the support of research. JDRF also sponsors international workshops and conferences for biomedical researchers, and individual chapters offer support groups and other activities for families affected by diabetes. JDRF has more than 110 chapters and affiliates worldwide. They publish a quarterly newsletter.
1970

734 **Job Accommodation Network (JAN)**
PO Box 6080
Morgantown, WV 26506-6080
304-216-8189
800-526-7234
TTY:877-781-9403
jan@askjan.org
askjan.org

JAN's mission is to facilitate the employment and retention of workers with disabilities by providing employers, employment providers, people with disabilities, their family members, and other interested parties with information on job accommodations, self-employment, and small business opportunities and related subjects.

735   Joni and Friends (JAF)
PO Box 3333
Agoura Hills, CA 91376-3333   818-707-5664
                                                          800-736-4177
                                              FAX: 818-707-2391
                                          www.joniandfriends.org
Joni Eareckson Tada, Founder & Chief Executive Officer
Laura Gardner, President & Chief Operating Officer
Arnulfo Cueva, Chief Financial Officer
A nonprofit organization seeking to accelerate Christian ministry
with people affected by disabilities. JAF provides resources and
training to churches to help create disability-welcoming environments, offers family retreats and mobility programs, and mentors
people with disabilities to lead and provide service in their
churches and communities.

736   Lambton County Developmental Services (LCDS)
339 Centre St.
Petrolia, ON, Canada N0N-1R0   519-882-0933
                                              FAX: 519-882-3386
                                        humanresources@lcds.on.ca
                                             www.lcdspetrolia.ca
Jill Cousins, President
Barb Frayne, Treasurer
John Douglas, Secretary
A network of experts and volunteers working together to provide
support services and employment services for people with devel-
opmental disabilities.

737   Laurent Clerc National Deaf Education Center
800 Florida Ave. NE
Washington, DC 20002   202-651-5855
                                              FAX: 202-651-5857
                                             TTY:202-250-2856
                                       clerc.center@gallaudet.edu
                                     www.clerccenter.gallaudet.edu
Provides resources, information, training and research on deaf
education and deaf and hard of hearing children.

738   Learning Disabilities Association of America (LDA)
4068 Mount Royal Boulevard
Suite 224B
Allison Park, PA 15101   412-341-1515
                                            info@ldaamerica.org
                                            www.ldaamerica.org
Cindy Cipoletti, Chief Executive Officer
Tracy Gregoire, Director, Healthy Children Project
Nina DelPrato, Administrative Manager
LDA aims to provide opportunities for success and support to individuals with learning disabilities, their parents, teachers, and
other professionals. It carries out its mission by supporting research on learning disabilities, advocating for early identification and best practice interventions, and protecting the rights of
all persons with learning disabilities.
1964

**739   Learning Disabilities Association of New York State
(LDANYS)**
1202 Troy-Schenectady Road
Bldg. 1
Latham, NY 12110   518-608-8992
                                              FAX: 518-608-8993
A nonprofit organization advocating for children and adults with
learning disabilities. LDA is a three-tiered organization comprised of a national organization, state affiliates and local chapters. They aim to support and empower individuals with learning
disabilities throughout their lives.

740   Learning Disabilities Worldwide
179 Bear Hill Rd.
Suite 104
Waltham, MA 02451   help@ldworldwide.org
                                            www.ldworldwide.org
Teresa Allissa Citro, Chief Executive Officer
Nicholas D. Young, Chairman
Matthias Grunke, Vice Chairman
Learning Disabilities Worldwide, Inc. is an international profes-
sional organization dedicated to improving the educational, pro-
fessional, and personal outcomes for individuals with learning
disabilities and other related disorders.
1965

741   LoSeCa Foundation
215-1 Carnegie Dr.
St. Albert, AB, Canada T8N-5B1   780-460-1400
                                              FAX: 780-459-1380
                                           chorpestad@loseca.ca
                                                www.loseca.ca
Carmen Horpestad, Executive Director & Chief Executive Officer
Jules Lefebvre, Director, Operations
Rebecca McLeod, Manager, Human Resources
A nonprofit organization that provides support services to adults
with developmental disabilities.

742   Mainstream
300 S Rodney Parham Rd.
Suite 5
Little Rock, AR 72205   501-280-0012
                                                          800-371-9026
                                              FAX: 501-280-9267
                                             TTY: 501-280-9262
                                           www.mainstreamilrc.com
A non-residential, consumer-driven independent living resource
center for persons with disabilities. Mainstream operates with the
conviction that people with disabilities have the right and responsibility to make choices, to control their lives and to participate
fully and equally in the community. Mainstream offers the following services free of charge: Advocacy, Peer Support, Training
and Education, Information and Referral, Ramp program, and
more.
1987

743   March of Dimes
1550 Crystal Dr.
Suite 1300
Arlington, VA 22202   888-663-4637
                                          www.marchofdimes.org
Karen Walker Johnson, Interim President & CEO
Alan Brogdon, SVP, Chief Operating Officer & Officer of the Board
*Adrian P. Mollo, SVP, General Counsel & Assistant Secretary of
the Board*
The mission of the March of Dimes is to improve the health of ba-
bies by preventing birth defects and infant mortality.

744   McKinnon Body Therapy Center
2940 Webster St.
Oakland, CA 94609   510-465-3488
                                          info@mckinnonbtc.com
                                              mckinnonbtc.com
The McKinnon Body Therapy Center offers certificate programs
and courses in massage therapy. They provide continuing education for massage therapists and other health professionals seeking to expand their skills.
1973

745   Mental Health America (MHA)
500 Montgomery St.
Suite 820
Alexandria, VA 22314   703-684-7722
                                                          800-969-6642
                                              FAX: 703-684-5968
                                            info@mhanational.org
                                            www.mhanational.org
Schroeder Stribling, President & Chief Executive Officer
Mary Giliberti, Chief Public Policy Officer
Jessica Kennedy, Chief of Staff & Chief Financial Officer
A nonprofit organization addressing issues related to mental
health and mental illness. MHA works to improve the mental
health of all Americans, especially individuals with mental disorders, through advocacy, education, research, and service.
1909

746   MindFreedom International (MFI)
454 Willamette, Suite 216
PO Box 11284
Eugene, OR 97440-3484   541-345-9106
                                                          877-623-7743
                                              FAX: 480-287-8833
                                         office@mindfreedom.org
                                              mindfreedom.org
Sarah Smith, Office Manager
Al Galves, Board Member
Susan Musante, Board Member

Nonprofit organization dedicated to winning human rights and alternatives for people with psychiatric disabilities.

747   Muscular Dystrophy Association USA (MDA)
161 N Clark
Suite 3550
Chicago, IL 60601   800-572-1717
resourcecenter@mdausa.org
www.mda.org
Donald S. Wood, President & Chief Executive Officer
Jeremy Kraut-Ordover, Chief Development Officer
Sharon Hesterlee, Chief Research Officer
MDA provides comprehensive medical services to people with neuromuscular diseases at hospital-affiliated clinics across the country. The Association's worldwide research program, which funds over 400 individual scientific investigations annually, represents the largest single effort to advance knowledge of neuromuscular diseases and to find cures and treatments for them. In addition, MDA conducts far-reaching educational programs for the public and professionals.
1950

748   National Association for Holistic Aromatherapy (NAHA)
6000 S. 5th Ave.
Pocatello, ID 83204   877-232-5255
FAX: 919-894-0271
info@naha.org
www.naha.org
Sharon Falsetto Chapman, Chief Journal Editor
Kelly Holland Azzaro, Assistant Journal Editor
The NAHA is an educational, nonprofit organization dedicated to enhancing public awareness of the benefits of true aromatherapy. It offers aromatherapy Tele-classes & membership benefits, and acts as a referral service.

749   National Association of Blind Merchants (NABM)
National Federation of the Blind
7450 Chapman Hwy.
Suite 319
Knoxville, TN 37920   888-687-6226
president@merchants-nfb.org
blindmerchants.org
Nicky Gacos, President
Ed Birmingham, First Vice President
Michael Colbrunn, Second Vice President
Serving as an advocacy and support group, NABM is a membership organization of blind persons employed in self-employment work or the Randolph-Sheppard Vending Program. The organization provides information on issues affecting blind merchants, including rehabilitation, social security, and tax.

750   National Association of City and County health Officials
1201 Eye St. NW
4th Floor
Washington, DC 20005   202-783-5550
FAX: 202-783-1583
info@naccho.org
naccho.org
Lori Tremmel Freeman, Chief Executive Officer
Nicole Silverman, Chief, Programs & Services
Adriane Casalotti, Chief, Government & Public Affairs
Strengthens and advocates for local health departments to improve the health of communities.

751   National Association of Councils on Developmental Disabilities (NACDD)
1825 K St. NW
Suite 600
Washington, DC 20006   202-506-5813
info@nacdd.org
www.nacdd.org
Kimberly Mercer-Schleider, President
Aaron Carruthers, Vice President
Julie Horntvedt, Secretary
NACDD is the national association for the 56 State and Territorial Councils on Developmental Disabilities (DD Councils) which receive federal funding to support programs that promote self-determination, integration, and inclusion for all Americans with developmental disabilities.

752   National Association of Disability Representatives (NADR)
1305 W 11th St.
Suite 222
Houston, TX 77008   202-822-2155
800-747-6131
FAX: 972-245-6701
admin@nadr.org
www.nadr.org
Michael Wener, President
Christopher Mazzulli, Vice President
Kelly Blad, Secretary
NADR is an organization of Professional Social Security Claimants Representatives that focus on issues involving policies to protect the interest of people with disabilities. NADR conducts annual conventions open to members and non-members with educational seminars to keep practitioners up to date on Social Security rulings, regulatory changes, and practice improvements.

753   National Association of State Directors of Developmental Disabilities Services (NASDDDS)
301 N Fairfax St.
Suite 101
Alexandria, VA 22314-2633   703-683-4202
cmcgraw@nasddds.org
www.nasddds.org
Mary P. Sowers, Executive Director
Dan Berland, Director, Federal Policy
Carrie M. McGraw, Director, Communications
NASDDDS is the representative for the nation's agencies providing services to people with intellectual and developmental disabilities. They aim to promote the development of effective, efficient service delivery systems for individuals with disabilities.

754   National Business & Disability Council (NBDC)
The Viscardi Center
201 I.U. Willets Rd.
Albertson, NY 11507   516-465-1400
info@viscardicenter.org
viscardicenter.org/services/nbdc
Dr. Chris Rosa, President & Chief Executive Officer
Sheryl P. Buchel, Executive Vice President & Chief Financial Officer
Michael Caprara, Chief Information Officer
The NBDC is a resource for employers seeking to integrate people with disabilities into the workplace and companies seeking to reach them in the consumer marketplace.

755   National Care Planning Council
PO Box 1118
Centerville, UT 84014   801-298-8676
800-989-8137
FAX: 801-295-3776
info@longtermcarelink.net
www.longtermcarelink.net
Thomas E. Day, Director
The National Care Planning Council's mission is to help families with long term care planning for seniors. Services include training, eldercare articles, books, workshops and seminars, networking and more.

756   National Center for College Students with Disabilities (NCCSD)
8015 West Kenton Circle
Suite 230
Huntersville, NC 28078   844-730-8048
TTY:651-583-7499
nccsd@ahead.org
www.nccsdonline.org
Wendy Harbour, Co-Principal Investigator & Center Director
Stephan Smith, Co-Principial Investigator & Project Director
Richard Allegra, Associate Director, Education & Outreach Services
A federally-funded project under the U.S. Department of Education, housed at the Association on Higher Education And Disability (AHEAD). It provides assistance and information to students, families, educators and more; collects information and conducts research; and reports to the Department of Education.
Founded in 2015.

757   National Center for Education in Maternal and Child Health (NCEMCH)
Georgetown University

MCHnavigator@ncemch.org
www.ncemch.org

Rochelle Mayer, Research Professor & Director
John Richards, Executive Director
Provides information on children with special health needs, child health and development, adolescent health, nutrition, violence and injury prevention, and other issues of maternal and child health for health professionals and the public.

758   National Center for Health, Physical Activity and Disability
4000 Ridgeway Dr.
Birmingham, AL 35209   800-900-8086
FAX: 205-313-7475
nchpad@uab.edu
www.nchpad.org

James Rimmer, Principal Investigator
Angela Grant, Business Manager
Jeff Underwood, Program Director
NCHPAD promotes health for people with disability through increased participation in all types of physical and social activities. These include fitness and aquatic activities, recreational and sports programs, adaptive equipment usage, and more.
1999

759   National Center on Deaf-Blindness (NCDB)
Hellen Keller National Center
141 Middle Neck Rd.
Sands Point, NY 11050   516-366-0047
support@nationaldb.org
www.nationaldb.org

Sam Morgan, Project Director
Julie Durando, Project Co-Director
Peggy Malloy, Information Services & Technology Coordinator
Funded by the federal Department of Education, the Center seeks to improve quality of life for children who are deaf-blind and their families.

760   National Center on Disability and Journalism (NCDJ)
Walter Cronkite School of Journalism, AZ State U.
555 N Central Ave.
Phoenix, AZ 85004   ncdj.org
Kristin Gilger, Director
John Kuziej, Graduate Assistant
Jake Geller, Inaugural Director
Supports journalists as they cover people with disabilities, concerned with accuracy, fairness and diversity in news coverage.
1998

761   National Certification Commission for Acupuncture and Oriental Medicine
2001 K St. NW
3rd Floor
Washington, DC 20036   202-381-1140
888-381-1140
FAX: 202-381-1141
info@thenccaom.org
www.nccaom.org

Mina Larson, Chief Executive Officer
Olga Cox, Chief Operations Officer
Irene Basore, Director, Administration & Governance
National organization that provides professional certification for entry-level practitioners of acupuncture and Oriental medicine (AOM), representing 98 percent of the states that regulate acupuncture.

762   National Collaborative Workforce on Disability (NCWD/Youth)
c/o Institute for Educational Leadership
4301 Connecticut Avenue, NW
Suite 100
Washington, DC 20008-2304   877-871-0744
www.ncwd-youth.info
Provides assistance to state and local workforce development systems to better serve youth of all types of ability.

763   National Council on Independent Living (NCIL)
P.O. Box 31260
Washington, DC 20006   202-207-0334
844-778-7961
FAX: 202-207-0341
TTY: 202-207-0340
ncil@ncil.org
www.ncil.org

Theo Braddy, Executive Director
Jenny Sichel, Director, Operations
Denise Law, Coordinator, Member Services
A national cross-disability grassroots organization, NCIL advances independent living and the rights of people with disabilities through consumer-driven advocacy.

764   National Disability Rights Network (NDRN)
820 1st St. NE
Suite 740
Washington, DC 20002   202-408-9514
FAX: 202-408-9520
TTY:202-408-9521
info@ndrn.org
www.ndrn.org

Marlene Sallo, Executive Director
Belinda Miller, Deputy Executive Director, Finance & Administration
David Card, Deputy Executive Director, External Relations
Voluntary national membership association of protection and advocacy systems and client assistance programs. Promoting and strengthening the role and performance of its members in providing quality legally based advocacy services.

765   National Federation of Families for Children's Mental Health (NFFCMH)
15800 Crabbs Branch Way
Suite 300
Rockville, MD 20855   240-403-1901
ffcmh@ffcmh.org
www.ffcmh.org

Lynda Gargan, Executive Director
A national family-run organization serving to provide advocacy at the national level for the rights of children and youth with emotional, behavioral, and mental health challenges and their families. The FFCMH provides leadership and technical assistance to a nation-wide network of family run organizations, and collaborates with organizations to transform mental and substance abuse health care in the U.S.
1989

766   National Guild of Hypnotists (NGH)
PO Box 308
Merrimack, NH 03054-0308   603-429-9438
FAX: 603-424-8066
ngh@ngh.net
www.ngh.net

Dr. Dwight Damon, President
Don Mottin, Vice President
Jereme Bachand, Executive Director
The National Guild of Hypnotists is a not-for-profit, educational corporation committed to advancing the field of hypnotism.
1950

767   National Health Council
1730 M St. NW
Suite 500
Washington, DC 20036-4561   202-785-3910
FAX: 202-785-5923
nationalhealthcouncil.org

Randall L. Rutta, Chief Executive Officer
Linda Beza, Senior Vice President, Finance & Administration
Susan Gaffney, Executive Vice President, Membership, Development & Events
Seeks to provide a unified voice for people living with chronic diseases and disabilities, and their caregivers.

768   National Institute on Disability, Independent Living, and Rehabilitation Research (NIDILRR)
Administration for Community Living
330 C St. SW
Washington, DC 20201   202-401-4634
                                        acl.gov
Anjali Forber-Pratt, Director
Alison Barkoff, Acting Administrator & Assistant Secretary, Aging
Vicki Gottlich, Deputy Administrator, Policy & Evaluation
NIDILRR, formerly the National Institute on Disability and Rehabilitation Research (NIDRR), aims to promote new research into the abilities of individuals with disabilities, and to use that research to allow those individuals to improve and use those skills within their community. NIDILRR also aims to maximize the full inclusion and integration of individuals with disabilities into society.

769   National Organization on Disability (NOD)
77 Water St.
13th Floor
New York, NY 10005   646-505-1191
                                    FAX: 646-505-1184
                                        info@nod.org
                                        www.nod.org
Carol Glazer, President
Moeena Das, Chief Operating Officer
Bernard Blake, Director, Finance & Operations
The National Organization on Disability is a private, nonprofit organization that promotes the full and equal participation of men, women, and children with disabilities in all aspects of American life.
1982

770   National Rehabilitation Association (NRA)
1520 Belle View Blvd
Suite 5142
Alexandria, VA 22307   703-836-0850
                                        888-258-4295
                                    info@nationalrehab.org
                                    nationalrehab.org
Satinder Atwal, Chief Administrator Officer
James Liin, Coordinator, Membership
NRA members work to eliminate barriers and increase employment opportunities for people with disabilities. They provide opportunities for advocacy and increase awareness of issues through professional development and access to current research topics.

771   National University of Natural Medicine (NUNM)
49 South Porter St.
Portland, OR 97201   503-552-1555
                                    reception@nunm.edu
                                        nunm.edu
Melanie Henriksen, President & CEO
Gerald Bores, Executive Vice President & Chief Financial Officer
Kathy Stanford, Vice President, Human Resources
NUNM is an accredited naturopathic medical university, and leads the research on natural medicine. They offer programs in naturopathic medicine, classical Chinese medicine, integrative mental health, global health, massage therapy, and more.
1956

772   National Vaccine Information Center (NVIC)
21525 Ridgetop Circle
Suite 100
Sterling, VA 20166   703-938-0342
                                    FAX: 571-313-1268
                                    contactus@nvic.org
                                        www.nvic.org
Barbara Loe Fisher, Co-Founder & President
Kathi Williams, Co-Founder & Vice President
Theresa Wrangham, Executive Director
Provides resources on vaccination and health.

773   National Women's Health Network (NWHN)
1413 K St. NW
4th Floor
Washington, DC 20005   202-682-2640
                                    FAX: 202-682-2648
                                        nwhn@nwhn.org
                                        www.nwhn.org
Denise Hyater-Lindenmuth, Executive Director
Erin Evans, Director, Operations
Denys Symonette Mitchell, Director, Policy & Partnerships
The National Women's Health Network seeks to improve women's health by developing and promoting a critical analysis of health issues in order to affect policy and support consumer decision-making. The Network aspires to a health care system that is guided by social justice and reflects the needs of diverse women.
1975

774   Native American Disability Law Center
905 W. Apache St.
Farmington, NM 87401   505-566-5880
                                        800-862-7271
                                    FAX: 505-566-5889
                                    info@nativedisabilitylaw.org
                                    www.nativedisabilitylaw.org
Therese Yanan, Executive Director
The Native American Disability Law Center is a private nonprofit organization that advocates for the legal rights of Native Americans with disabilities. Through advocacy and education, the center empowers Native people with disabilities to lead independent lives in their own communities.

775   North Hastings Community Integration Association
2 Alice St.
PO Box 1508
Bancroft, ON, Canada K0L-1C0   613-332-2090
                                    FAX: 613-332-4762
                                    communityliving@nhcia.ca
                                        www.nhcia.ca
Sandra Phillips, Executive Director
Lloyd Churchill, President
Brenda Locke, Vice President
NHCIA offers daily living supports, life planning, community access, dual diagnosis supports, respite services, assistance with funding and resource referral information. The association works closely with many community services, groups, schools, and businesses to offer individualized supports to children, youth and adults with an intellectual disability and their families.

776   Not Dead Yet
497 State St.
Rochester, NY 14608   708-420-0539
                                        notdeadyet.org
Diane Coleman, President & Chief Executive Officer
Anita Cameron, Director, Minority Outreach
Jules Good, Assistant Director/Policy Analyst
Disability rights group opposing the legalization of assisted suicide and euthanasia.

777   PACER Center (Parent Advocacy Coalition for Educational Rights)
8161 Normandale Blvd.
Bloomington, MN 55437   952-838-9000
                                        800-537-2237
                                    FAX: 952-838-0199
                                        pacer@pacer.org
                                        www.pacer.org
Tonia Teasley, Executive Director
Mission is to expand opportunities and enhance the quality of life of children and young adults with disabilities and their families based on the concept of parents helping parents. Offers workshops, individual assistance, and written information for children with disabilities, their parents and families, and professionals working with them. Computer Resource Center/Software Lending Library available.
1977

778   PEAK Parent Center
917 East Moreno Ave.
Suite 140
Colorado Springs, CO 80903   719-531-9400
                                    FAX: 719-531-9452
                                    info@peakparent.org
                                    www.peakparent.org

Michele Williers, Executive Director
Pam Christy, Director, Parent Training & Information
PEAK Parent Center is Colorado's federally-designated Parent
Training and Information Center (PTI). As a PTI, PEAK supports
and empowers parents, providing them with information and
strategies to use when advocating for their children with disabilities. PEAK works one-on-one with families and educators helping them realize new possibilities for children with disabilities by
expanding knowledge of special education and offering new
strategies for success.
1986

779   Pacific Institute of Aromatherapy
PO Box 6723
San Rafael, CA 94903   415-479-9120
                                   FAX: 415-479-0614
                 www.pacificinstituteofaromatherapy.com
Kurt Schnaubelt, Founder & Director
The Pacific Institute on Aromatherapy offers certification
courses, seminars, books, and products on aromatherapy treat-
ments and essential oils.
1983

780   Parent Professional Advocacy League (PPAL)
77 Rumford Ave.
Waltham, MA 02453   866-815-8122
                                   FAX: 617-542-7832
                                   info@ppal.net
                                   www.ppal.net

Pam Sager, Executive Director
Meri Viano, Associate Director
Candice Gabrey, Program Manager, Juvenile Justice
A statewide organization focusing on the interests of families
with children with mental health needs. PPAL advocates for improved and better access to mental health services for children
and their families.

781   Parents Helping Parents (PHP)
1400 Parkmoor Ave.
Suite 100
San Jose, CA 95126   408-727-5775
                                   855-727-5775
                                   FAX: 408-286-1116
                                   info@php.com
                                   www.php.com

Maria Daane, Executive Director
Janet Nunez, Director, Programs
Mark Fishler, Director, Development
Dedicated to assisting children with any type of special need:
mental, physical, emotional, or learning disability. Mission is to
help children with special needs receive love, hope, respect, and
services needed to achieve their full potential by strengthening
their families and the professionals who serve them. Develops
programs and produces educational and support materials, including information packets, brochures, and a newsletter.

782   Partnership on Employment and Acessible Technology
(PEAT)

                                   info@peatworks.org
                                   www.peatworks.org
Bill Curtis-Davidson, Co-Director
Corinne Weible, Co-Director
Lex Huth, Director, Communications
Funded by the U.S. Department of Labor's Office of Disability
Employment Policy (ODEP), PEAT fosters collaboration around
building and buying accessible technology in the workplace.

783   Partnership to Improve Patient Care
100 M St. SE
Suite 750
Washington, DC 20003   www.pipcpatients.org
Sara van Geertruyden, Executive Director
Thayer Surette Roberts, Deputy Director
Tony Coelho, Chair
Promotes a patient-centric healthcare system including compara-
tive effectiveness research, the assessment of treatment value
through shared decision-making, and alternate payment models.

784   People First of Canada
20-226 Osborne St. North
Winnipeg, MB, Canada R3C-1V4   204-784-7362
                                   FAX: 204-784-7364
                                   info@peoplefirstofcanada.ca
                                   www.peoplefirstofcanada.ca
Shelley Fletcher, Executive Director
Catherine Rodgers, Director, Communications
Monica Schroeder, National Project Coordinator
People First of Canada is the national voice for people who have
been labeled with an intellectual disability. People First is a
movement of people who want all citizens to live equally in the
country.

785   Peter and Elizabeth C. Tower Foundation
2351 North Forest Rd.
Suite 106
Getzville, NY 14068-1225   716-689-0370
                                   FAX: 716-689-3716
                                   info@thetowerfoundation.org
                                   thetowerfoundation.org

Tracy A. Sawicki, Executive Director
Donald W. Matteson, Chief Program Officer
Charles E. Colston Jr., Program Officer
The Peter and Elizabeth C. Tower Foundation supports community programming that results in children, adolescents, and young
adults affected by substance use disorders, learning disabilities,
mental illness, and intellectual disabilities achieving their full
potential.
1990

786   Post-Polio Health International
50 Crestwood Executive Ctr.
Suite 440
St. Louis, MO 63126   314-534-0475
                                   FAX: 314-534-5070
                                   info@post-polio.org
                                   www.post-polio.org

Mark Mallinger, President
Frederick M. Maynard, Vice President
Brian M. Tiburzi, Executive Director
To enhance the lives and independence of polio survivors, home
ventilator users, their caregivers and families, and health profes-
sionals through education, networking, and advocacy.

787   Postpartum Support International (PSI)
6706 SW 54th Ave.
Portland, OR 97219   503-894-9453
                                   800-944-4773
                                   FAX: 503-894-9452
                                   support@postpartum.net
                                   postpartum.net
Wendy N. Davis, Executive Director
Lianne Swanson, Executive Administrator
Birdie Gunyon Meyer, Certification Director
The mission of Postpartum Support International is to promote
awareness, prevention, and treatment of mental health issues re-
lated to childbearing in every country worldwide.
1987

788   Primary Care Collaborative
601 13th St. NW
Suite 430N
Washington, DC 20005   202-417-2076
                                   EWalrod@thepcc.org
                                   www.pcpcc.org

Ann Grenier, President & Chief Executive Officer
Larry McNeely, Director, Policy
Loren Vandegrift, Director, IT

Advocates for a health system built on patient-centered primary care. Its four aims are better care, better health, lower costs, and greater joy for clinicians and staff in delivery of care.

789 Professional Association of Therapeutic Horsemanship International (PATH Intl.)
PO Box 33150
Denver, CO 80233 303-452-1212
800-369-7433
FAX: 303-252-4610
pathintl@pathintl.org
www.pathintl.org
Kathy Alm, Chief Executive Officer
Carrie Garnett, Director, Membership & Operations
Kaye Marks, Director, Marketing & Communications
A national nonprofit equestrian organization dedicated to serving individuals with disabilities by giving disabled individuals the opportunity to ride horses. Establishes safety standards, provides continuing education, and offers networking opportunities for both its individuals and center members. Produces educational materials including fact sheets, brochures, booklets, audio-visual tapes, a directory, and PATH Intl. magazine Strides.

790 Rehabilitation International
866 United Nations Plaza
Office 422
New York, NY 10017 212-420-1500
FAX: 212-505-0871
info@riglobal.org
www.riglobal.org
Teuta Rexhepi, Secretary General
Zhang Haidi, President
RI and its members develop and promote initiatives to protect the rights of people with disabilities and improve rehabilitation and other crucial services for disabled people and their families. RI also works toward increasing international collaboration and advocates for policies and legislation recognizing the rights of people with disabilities and their families, including the establishment of a UN Convention on the Rights and Dignity of Persons with Disabilities.
1922

791 RespectAbility
43 Town & Country Drive
Suite 119-181
Fredericksburg, VA 22405 202-517-6272
info@respectability.org
www.respectability.org
Ariel Simms, President & Chief Executive Officer
Lauren Appelbaum, Vice President, Communications, Entertainment & News Media
Graciano Petersen, Senior Director, Talent, Culture & Leadership Development
Nonprofit, nonpartisan organization providing free educational tools and resources to end stigmas and advance opportunities for people with disabilities and their families.

792 Ronald McDonald House Charities (RMHC)
110 N Carpenter St.
Chicago, IL 60607 630-623-7048
info@rmhc.org
www.rmhc.org
Ginger Hardage, Chairman of the Board
Katie Fitzgerald, President & Chief Executive Officer
Stacey Bifero, Chief Financial Officer
Ronald McDonald House programs for families with sick children can be found in more than 64 countries around the world. Each house is run by a local nonprofit agency comprised of members of the medical community, McDonald's owners, businesses and civic organizations, and parent volunteers.

793 Ryan White HIV/AIDS Program
Health Resources & Services Administration
5600 Fishers Lane
Rockville, MD 20857 301-443-3376
hab.hrsa.gov/about-ryan-white-hivaids-program
Laura Cheever, Associate Administrator
Heather Hauck, Deputy Associate Administrator
The Ryan White HIV/AIDS Program provides a comprehensive system of care that includes primary medical care and essential support services for people living with HIV who are uninsured or underinsured. The Program works with cities, states, and local community-based organizations to provide HIV care and treatment services to more than half a million people each year.

794 Shirley Ryan AbilityLab
355 East Erie
Chicago, IL 60611 312-238-1000
844-355-2253
FAX: 312-238-1369
www.sralab.org
Peggy Kirk, Co-President & Chief Executive Officer
Nancy E. Paridy, Co-President & Chief Administrative Officer
Richard L. Lieber, Chief Scientific & Senior Vice President of Research
Shirley Ryan AbilityLab is a research hospital integrating medical and research experts together in real time, applying research and providing patient care in physical medicine and rehabilitation. The AbilityLab has five Innovation Centers, each focusing on an area of biomedical science: Brain; Nerve, Muscle & Bone; Cancer; Spinal Cord; and Pediatric.

795 Society for Post-Acute and Long-Term Care Medicine (AMDA)
10500 Little Patuxent Pkwy.
Suite 210
Columbia, MD 21044 410-740-9743
800-876-2632
FAX: 410-740-4572
info@paltc.org
paltc.org
Milta Little, President
Rajeev Kumar, Vice President
Swati Gaur, Treasurer
The Society for Post-Acute and Long-Term Care Medicine is a medical society representing medical directors, physicians, nurse practitioners, physician assistants, and other professionals working in post-acute and long-term care settings. The Society's mission is to advance the development of medical practitioners in all post-acute and long-term care settings through professional development, clinical guidance, and advocacy.
1977

796 Sofia University
3333 Harbor Blvd.
Costa Mesa, CA 92626 888-820-1484
student_services@sofia.edu
sofia.edu
Allan Cahoon, President
Chris Nguyen, Chief Financial Officer & Vice President, Administration
Sofia University is a private, WSCUC-accredited institution focusing on humanistic and transpersonal psychology.
1975

797 Spartan Stuttering Laboratory
Michigan State University
1026 Red Cedar Rd.
East Lansing, MI 48824 517-884-2406
jsy@msu.edu
stutteringlab.msu.edu
The Spartan Stuttering Laboratory is a nonprofit organization that provides specialized assessment and treatment for children, adolescents, and adults who stutter and their families. They also provide education, training, and support for speech-language pathologists who work with people who stutter, and conduct an active program of basic and clinical research on the nature and treatment of stuttering across age groups.

798 St. Paul Abilities Network
4637-45 Ave.
St. Paul, AB, Canada T0A-3A3 780-645-3441
866-645-3900
FAX: 780-645-1885
www.stpaulabilitiesnetwork.ca
Anthony Opden Dries, Executive Director
Len Gagne, President
Mike Proctor, Vice President
Provides support and opportunities to encourage the development of an individual's full potential through education, advocacy, and community partnerships.
1964

799   **Starbridge**
1650 South Ave.
Suite 200
Rochester, NY 14620   585-546-1700
                                          800-650-4967
                                   FAX: 585-224-7100
                                   www.starbridgeinc.org
Nikisha Ridgeway, President & Chief Executive Officer
Elissa Burke, Chief Program Officer
Terry O'Hare, Chief Financial Officer
A nonprofit organization dedicated to educating, supporting, and advocating for people who have disabilities, their families, and their circles of support.

800   **Student Disability Services (SDS)**
Wayne State University
5155 Gullen Mall
1600 Undergraduate Library
Detroit, MI 48202   313-577-1851
                                   FAX: 313-577-4898
                                   TTY:313-202-4216
                                   studentdisability@wayne.edu
                                   www.studentdisability.wayne.edu
Mission is to ensure a university experience in which individuals with disabilities have equitable access to programs and to empower students to self-advocate in order to fulfill their academic goals.

801   **TASH**
1825 K Street NW
Suite 1250
Washington, DC 20006-1202   202-817-3264
                                   FAX: 202-999-4722
                                   info@tash.org
                                   www.tash.org
Michael Brogioli, Executive Director
DeVonne Parks, Director, Membership & Meetings
Donald Taylor, Manager, Membership & Communications
Formerly The Association for Persons with Severe Handicaps, it is an international association of people with disabilities, their family members, other advocates, and professionals fighting for a society in which inclusion of all people in all aspects of society is the norm.
ther pages 1975

802   **The Advocacy Centre**
205 Hall Street
Nelson, BC, Canada V1L-4E9   250-352-5777
                                          877-352-5777
                                   FAX: 250-352-5723
                                   advocacycentre@nelsoncares.ca
                                   advocacycentre.org
The Advocacy Centre's mission is to advocate for the rights of women, children, and other oppressed groups. The Centre aims to provide one-on-one advocacy, change unfair legislation and policy, and support those working on issues such as poverty, violence against women, mental illness, and child abuse and neglect. The Centre serves communities in the West Kootenay region.
1988

803   **The Cherab Foundation**
2301 NE Savannah Rd
Suite 1771
Jensen Beach, FL 34957   772-335-5135
                                   help@cherab.org
                                   cherabfoundation.org
Lisa Geng, Founder & President
Jolie Abreu, Vice President
The Cherab Foundation is a world-wide nonprofit organization working to improve the communication skills and education of all children with speech and language delays and disorders. The Cherab Foundation is committed to assisting with the development of new therapeutic approaches, preventions, and cures to neurologically-based speech disorders.

804   **The Davis Center**
305 White Heron Circle
Fayetteville, NY 13066   862-251-4637
                                   ddavis@thedaviscenter.com
                                   www.thedaviscenter.com
Dorinne S. Davis, Director

Offers sound-based therapies supporting positive change in learning, development, and wellness. All ages/all disabilities. Uses The Davis Model of Sound Intervention, an alternative approach.

805   **The Hanen Centre**
1075 Bay St.
Suite 515
Toronto, ON, Canada M5S-2B1   416-921-1073
                                         877-426-3655
                                   FAX: 416-921-1225
                                   info@hanen.org
                                   hanen.org
Elaine Weitzman, Executive Director
The Hanen Centre's mission is to provide parents, caregivers, early childhood educators, and speech-language pathologists with the knowledge and training they need to help young children develop the best possible language, social, and literacy skills. This includes children with or at risk of language delays and those with developmental challenges such as Autism Spectrum Disorder.

806   **The Obesity Medicine Association (OMA)**
7173 S Havana St.
Suite 600-130
Centennial, CO 80112   303-770-2526
                                   FAX: 303-779-4834
                                   info@obesitymedicine.org
                                   obesitymedicine.org
Teresa Fraker, Executive Director
Joan Hablutzel, Senior Director, Education, Events & Operations
Christian DeSousa, Director, Membership & Engagement
The Obesity Medicine Association is an organization of physicians, nurse practitioners, physician assistants, and other health care providers with special interest and experience in the comprehensive treatment of obesity.

807   **The Steve Fund**
PO Box 9070
Providence, RI 02940   401-249-0044
                                   info@stevefund.org
                                   stevefund.org
Brandi Pretlow, Vice President, Programs & Services
Monica Ingkavet, Director, Programs & Partnerships
Annelle B. Primm, Senior Medical Director
The Steve Fund is dedicated to the mental health and emotional well-being of young people of color. It offers programs and services designed to assist both institutions of higher education and nonprofits in improving their capacity to support the mental health and emotional well-being of students of color. Programs and services include workshops, webinars, expert speakers, training, and technology innovations.

808   **Therapeutic Touch International Association (TTIA)**
TTIA Box 130
Delmar, NY 12054   518-325-1185
                                   FAX: 509-693-3537
                                   ttia@therapeutictouch.org
                                   therapeutictouch.org
Madonna Pence, President
Christine Easley, Treasurer/Development
Lin Bauer, Contact, Education
This international cooperative network of health care professionals is committed to excellence in healing through Therapeutic Touch. The organization serves as a resource for persons in the field of health care, laypersons, and other organizations interested in information on Therapeutic Touch, and for therapists and teachers searching for teaching and learning materials related to Therapeutic Touch.
1979

809   **Thresholds**
4101 N Ravenswood Ave.
Chicago, IL 60613   773-572-5500
                                   thresholds@thresholds.org
                                   www.thresholds.org
Mark Ishaug, Chief Executive Officer
Mark Furlong, Chief Operating Officer
Brent Peterson, Chief Development Officer
Provider of recovery services for persons with mental illnesses and substance abuse disorders in Illinois. It offers 30 programs at

more than 75 locations throughout Chicago and surrounding suburbs and counties. Services include case management, housing, employment, education, psychiatry, primary care, substance use treatment, and research.

810 United States Disabled Golf Association (USDGA)
598 Dixie Rd.
Clinton, NC 28328
910-214-5983
info@usdga.net
www.usdga.net

Jason Faircloth, Founder
The US Disabled Golf Association provides people with physical, sensory, and mental disabilities an opportunity to play golf at the highest level in the USA.
Founded in 2015.

811 United States Trager Association
550M Richie Highway
Severna Park, MD 21146
440-834-0308
FAX: 888-525-7645
exec@tragerus.org
www.tragerapproach.us

Offers sessions and courses on the Trager Approach, a gentle and effective approach to movement education and mind/body integration.

812 Universal Pediatrics
3345 106th Circle
Urbandale, IA 50322
800-383-0303
www.universalpediatrics.com

Tucker Anderson, Chief Executive Officer
Universal Pediatrics provides high-tech in-home medical care to children and young adults. Emphasis is placed on the provision of services in the rural areas, the ability to service high tech needs, and the promotion of primary nurse concept.
1985

813 Upledger Institute International (UII)
11211 Prosperity Farms Rd.
Suite D-325
Palm Beach Gardens, FL 33410
561-622-4334
800-233-5880
FAX: 561-622-4771
info@upledger.com
www.upledger.com

Kathy Woll, Chief Operating Officer
Dawn Langnes Shear, Chief Development Officer
Alex Jozefyk, Chief Financial Officer
A healthcare resource center focused on comprehensive education programs, advanced treatment options, and outreach initiatives. The Institute has trained more than 125,000 healthcare professionals throughout the globe in the therapeutic approach.

814 Viability
60 Brookdale Dr.
Springfield, MA 01104
413-781-5359
info@viability.org
viability.org

Francis Fitzgerald, Chair
Steve Dean, Vice Chair
Charlene Smolkowicz, Treasurer
Viability's mission is to help individuals with disabilities achieve their full potential. Services include day programs, employment services, and job training and placements.

815 Volunteers of America (VOA)
1660 Duke St.
Alexandria, VA 22314
703-341-5000
800-899-0089
info@voa.org
www.voa.org

Michael King, President & Chief Executive Officer
Joseph A. Budzynski, Executive Vice President & Chief Financial Officer
Jatrice Martel Gaiter, Executive Vice President, External Affairs
Volunteers of America is a nonprofit organization serving vulnerable groups, including veterans, at-risk youth, people with disabilities, homeless persons and families, and individuals recovering from addiction. Services include housing, behavioral and mental health services, and community outreach.

816 WORLD
389 30th St.
Oakland, CA 94609
510-986-0340
FAX: 510-986-0341
womenhiv.org

Ingrid Floyd, Interim Executive Director
Erica Conners, Associate Executive Director
Denise Jones, Operations Manager
Women Organized to Respond to Life-threatening Disease supports women, girls, families and communities affected by HIV through education, wellness, advocacy, and leadership development.

817 Women to Women Healthcare
170 US Route 1
Suite 110
Falmouth, ME 04105
207-846-6163
800-540-5906
FAX: 207-846-6167
support@womentowomenhealthcarecenter.com
www.womentowomenhealthcarecente r.com

Marcelle Pick, Co-Founder & Director
Aims to combine alternative and conventional medicine in women's health. Provides integrative care for women and specializes in chronic and difficult cases.

818 World Federation for Mental Health
6800 Park Ten Blvd.
Suite 220-N
San Antonio, TX 78213
info@wfmh.global
wfmh.global

Nasser Loza, President
Silvia Raggi, Corporate Secretary
Andrew Mohanraj, Treasurer
WFMH is an international membership organization that seeks to prevent mental and emotional disorders, advance the proper treatment and care of those with such disorders, and promote mental health.
1948

819 World Institute on Disability (WID)
3075 Adeline St.
Suite 155
Berkeley, CA 94703
510-225-6400
FAX: 510-225-0477
wid@wid.org
www.wid.org

Marcie Roth, Executive Director & Chief Executive Officer
Kat Zigmont, Senior Director, Operations & Deputy Director
Reggie Johnson, Senior Director, Marketing & Communications
The mission of the World Institute on Disability (WID) is to eliminate barriers to full social integration and increase employment, economic security, and health care for persons with disabilities. WID creates innovative programs and tools; conducts research, public education, training, and advocacy campaigns; and provides technical assistance.

820 YAI: National Institute for People with Disabilities
220 E 42nd St.
8th Floor
New York, NY 10017
212-273-6100
communications@yai.org
www.yai.org

Kevin Carey, Interim Chief Executive Officer
Vanda Angelillo, Acting Chief Financial Officer
Anthony Ottrando, Chief Human Resources Officer
YAI is dedicated to enhancing the lives of people with developmental disabilities and their families. The organization works with individuals, families, government, corporate partners, donors, and foundations to ensure that people with disabilities are recognized for their abilities, achieve the goals that are important to them, and are integrated in the community.

821 Youth MOVE National
PO Box 1075
Saugatuck, MI 49453
800-580-6199
info@youthmovenational.org
youthmovenational.org

Arc Telos Saint Amour, Executive Director
Victoria Eckert, Associate Director
Lydia Proulx, Director, Youth Programs

Aims to strengthen services and systems for issues such as mental health, juvenile justice, education, and child welfare.
Founded in 2007.

822   Youth as Self Advocates (YASA)
Family Voices
561 Virginia Rd, Bldg. 4
Suite 300
Concord, MA 01742   781-674-7224
                                        888-835-5669
                          www.familyvoices.org/yasa
Allysa Ware, Executive Director, Family Voices
National program created by youth with disabilities for other youth, helping them to better advocate for themselves.

Camps

Alabama

823 Camp ASCCA
Alabama's Special Camp for Children and Adults
PO Box 21
5278 Camp Ascca Dr.
Jacksons Gap, AL 36861
256-825-9226
FAX: 256-269-0714
info@campascca.org
www.campascca.org

Matt Rickman, Camp Director
John Stephenson, Administrator
Jocelyn Jones, Secretary
Camp Evoked Potential is held one week out of the year for children aged 6-18 with epilepsy at Camp ASCCA. Fully funded by The Epilepsy Foundation, persons wishing to attend the camp must apply. The camp provides a barrier free setting situated on 230 acres of wooded land at Lake Martin. The camp is staffed with medical personnel trained to care for children with all types of disabilities and provides a variety of camp activities.
1976

824 Camp Seale Harris
Southeastern Diabetes Education Services
500 Chase Park S.
Ste 104
Birmingham, AL 35244
205-402-0415
FAX: 205-402-0416
info@campsealeharris.org
www.campsealeharris.org

Rhonda McDavid, Executive Director
John Latimer, Director, Camp & Community Programs
Shelby Harrison, Manager, Communications & Events
Offering overnight, family, day and community program camps, Camp Seale Harris is a nonprofit organization that offers residential camps for children and teens with diabetes. With multiple programs in Alabama, the volunteer camp counselors are trained adults living with diabetes, to better help the camp attendees gain independence in learning to manage their diabetes. Camp programs run all year round.
1949

825 Camp Shocco for the Deaf
216 North St. E
PO Box 602
Talladega, AL 35161
800-264-1225
Camp Shocco for the Deaf is a Christian Camp for children and teens with a hearing impairment, whose parents are deaf or are siblings of a person that are deaf. The camp runs for 1 week and offers a range of camp activities.

826 Camp Smile-A-Mile
Smile-A-Mile Place
1600 2nd Ave. S.
Birmingham, AL 35233
205-323-8427
FAX: 205-323-6220
info@campsam.org
www.campsam.org

Bruce Hooper, Executive Director
Kellie Reece, Chief Operating Officer
Katie Langley, Special Events Director
Camp Smile-A-Mile offers 7 different educational camp opportunities for children and their families who have been affected by childhood cancer in Alabama. The programs run all year long, in a variety of formats.

827 Camp Smile-A-Mile: Jr./Sr. Camp
Smile-A-Mile Place
1600 2nd Ave. S.
Birmingham, AL 35233
205-323-8427
FAX: 205-323-6220
info@campsam.org
www.campsam.org

Carrie Pomeroy, Program Director
Kellie Reece, Chief Operating Officer
Camp Smile-A-Mile's Jr./Sr. Camp is for high school juniors, seniors, and new high school graduates that are both on and off therapy. The weekend camp works to instill independence and responsibility in regards to their diagnosis.

828 Camp Smile-A-Mile: Off Therapy Family Camp
Smile-A-Mile Place
1600 2nd Ave. S.
Birmingham, AL 35233
205-323-8427
FAX: 205-323-6220
info@campsam.org
www.campsam.org

Carrie Pomeroy, Program Director
Kellie Reece, Chief Operating Officer
Camp Smile-A-Mile's Off Therapy Family Camp is a specialized camp for off-therapy patients and their families. Campers up to the age of 18 who are no longer receiving therapy are eligible to attend the camp.

829 Camp Smile-A-Mile: On Therapy Family Camp
Smile-A-Mile Place
1600 2nd Ave. S.
Birmingham, AL 35233
205-323-8427
FAX: 205-323-6220
info@campsam.org
www.campsam.org

Carrie Pomeroy, Program Director
Kellie Reece, Chief Operating Officer
A program of Camp Smile-A-Mile, On Therapy Family Camp is for patients up to 18 years of age, who are currently receiving therapy. The Family Camp is designed to give patients and their immediate families the opportunity to connect outside of an hospital environment.

830 Camp Smile-A-Mile: Sibling Camp
Smile-A-Mile Place
1600 2nd Ave. S.
Birmingham, AL 35233
205-323-8427
FAX: 205-323-6220
info@campsam.org
www.campsam.org

Carrie Pomeroy, Program Director
Kellie Reece, Chief Operating Officer
Camp Smile-A-Mile's Sibling Camp is a specialized camp for the siblings of children and teens with cancer. Campers attending the Sibling Camp range in age from 6-18 and no patients or parents attend the camp.

831 Camp Smile-A-Mile: Teen Weeklong Camp
Smile-A-Mile Place
1600 2nd Ave. S.
Birmingham, AL 35233
205-323-8427
FAX: 205-323-6220
info@campsam.org
www.campsam.org

Carrie Pomeroy, Program Director
Kellie Reece, Chief Operating Officer
A weeklong summer camp session for children, 13 through to the 10th grade, who have cancer. The session is open to those who are and aren't receiving therapy, with campers participating in activities such as swimming, snorkeling, and campfires.

832 Camp Smile-A-Mile: Young Adult Retreat
Smile-A-Mile Place
1600 2nd Ave. S.
Birmingham, AL 35233
205-323-8427
FAX: 205-323-6220
info@campsam.org
www.campsam.org

Carrie Pomeroy, Program Director
Kellie Reece, Chief Operating Officer
A program of Camp Smile-A-Mile, the Young Adult Retreat is for childhood cancer survivors ages 19-30. The retreat is held over a summer weekend and offers educational and camping activities for participants. Those wanting to attend the retreat do not have to be former campers of Camp Smile-A-Mile.

833 **Camp Smile-A-Mile: Youth Weeklong Camp**
Smile-A-Mile Place
1600 2nd Ave. S.
Birmingham, AL 35233   205-323-8427
                              FAX: 205-323-6220
                              info@campsam.org
                              www.campsam.org

Carrie Pomeroy, Program Director
Kellie Reece, Chief Operating Officer
A weeklong summer camp session for children, ages 6-12, who
have cancer. The session is open to those who are and aren't receiving therapy, with campers participating in activities such as
arts and crafts, fishing, boating, archery, and canoeing.

834 **Camp WheezeAway**
YMCA Camp Chandler
880 South Lawrence Street
Montgomery, AL 36104   334-229-4362
                              jikner@ymcamontgomery.org
                              ymcamontgomery.org/camp/wheezeaway

Jennifer Ikner, Contact
For children ages 8-12 with moderate to severe asthma, Camp
WheezeAway offers week long summer camp programs that foster confidence building skills. The camp is free and managed by
medical professionals. Those with children wishing to attend
must apply to the camp and complete a selection process.

835 **Easterseals Camp ASCCA**
PO Box 21
5278 Camp Ascca Dr.
Jacksons Gap, AL 36861   256-825-9226
                                FAX: 256-269-0714
                                info@campascca.org
                                www.campascca.org

Matt Rickman, Camp Director
John Stephenson, Administrator
Jocelyn Jones, Secretary
Easterseals Camp ASCCA is Alabama's Special Camp for Children and Adults, offering therapeutic recreation for children and
adults with both physical and intellectual disabilities. The camp
is located on 260 acres of barrier free woodland on Lake Martin
and campers experience a wide variety of educational and recreational activities, including but not limited to: horseback riding,
fishing, tubing, swimming, environmental education, arts, canoeing, and zip-lining. 1 week camp fees are $750.00.
1976

836 **Happy Camp**
Merrimack Hall Performing Arts Center
3320 Triana Blvd SW.
Huntsville, AL 35805   256-534-6455
                              info@merrimackhall.com
                              www.merrimackhall.com/happy-headquarters
For ages 3-12, Happy Camp is Merrimack Hall's annual half-day
performing arts camp for children with special needs. Open to
children with a wide range of physical or intellectual disabilities
at any art level, activities include: music, theater, dance, and visual art. Happy Camp has a 1:1 staff-to-camper ratio. Camp time
is from 9am - 12pm every day of the week.

837 **Rapahope Children's Retreat Foundation**
205 Lambert Ave.
Suite A
Mobile, AL 36604   251-476-9880
                          info@rapahope.org
                          www.rapahope.org

Melissa McNichol, Executive Director
Roz Dorsett, Assistant Director
Rapahope is an organization that offers a one week long summer
camp for children who have, or who have had cancer. For children
ages 7-17, the camp offers a wide range of summer camp activities, including but not limited to, swimming, kayaking, horseback riding, and arts. The camp is offered at no cost to campers or
their families.

Alaska

838 **Adam's Camp**
56 Inverness Drive East
Suite 250
Englewood, CO 80112   303-563-8290
                             contact@adamscamp.org
                             www.adamscampcolorado.org

Brian Conly, Executive Director
Paige Heydon, Director, Finance & Development
Adam's Camp is a nonprofit organization providing therapeutic
programs and recreational camps for children and the families of
children with special needs. Programs offered include Early Start
Therapy Camp (6 months to 4 years old), Mountain Therapy
Camps (ages 5 and up), and the Overnight Adventure Camps
(ages 9 and up). Additional location offered in Northern Ireland.

839 **Camp Webber**
Alpine Alternatives
750 E. Fireweed Lane
Suite 101
Anchorage, AK 99507-1105   907-561-6655
                                  FAX: 907-563-9232
                                  admin@alpinealternatives.net
                                  alpinealternatives.net
A program of Alpine Alternatives, Camp Webber is a developmental sports camp for children ages 8-19 who are blind or visually impaired. The camp provides 1-on-1 instructional education,
with campers participating in physical activities such as swimming, goalball, beep baseball, tandem biking, tack and field
events, rock climbing, hiking, canoeing, and archery.
1984

Arizona

840 **Arizona Camp Sunrise & Sidekicks**
530 E. McDowell Road
Suite 107-295
Phoenix, AZ 85004   480-382-8564
                           info@swkcf.org
                           www.swkidscancerfoundation.org
Arizona Camp Sunrise & Sidekicks offers a variety of programs
running all year long for children and their siblings who have had
or currently have cancer. Arizona Camp Sunrise & Sidekicks, was
the first camp in the state specifically tailored for children with
cancer, and the camp is the only one in Arizona offering a camp
for siblings affected by cancer through their Sidekicks program.
Offered for children ages 8-18.

841 **Camp AZDA**
American Diabetes Association
2451 Crystal Drive
Suite 900
Phoenix, AZ 85014   800-342-2338
                           ampazda@diabetes.org
                           www.diabetes.org/node/1086
Camp AZDA is the Arizona summer camp program of the American Diabetes Association for children with diabetes. The camp is
held at Friendly Pines in Prescott, Arizona with children participating in traditional camp activities while receiving educational
information on managing their diabetes.

842 **Camp Abilities Tucson**
8987 East Tanque Verde Rd.
Suite 309-104
Tucson, AZ 85749   campabilitiestucson@gmail.com
                          www.campabilitiestucson.org

Murry Everson, Camp Director
Maria Lepore-Stevens, Camp Director
Camp Abilities is a privately funded educational sport camp for
children and young adults who are blind, deaf-blind or have multiple disabilities including visual impairment. The camp offers
sports instruction, with a 1:1 camper to coach ratio, tailored to fit
the needs of the individual. The location of camp sessions is the
Arizona School for the Deaf and Blind and costs $300.00 per
person.

843   Camp Candlelight
Epilepsy Foundation Arizona
941 S Park Lane
Tempe, AZ 85281
602-282-3515
800-332-1000
AZ@EFA.org
epilepsyaz.org/events/campcandlelight
Suzanne Matsumori, Executive Director
Min Skivington, Program Manager
Camp Candlelight provides children ages 8 to 17 a unique camp experience that mixes traditional summer camp with special sessions that teach campers about their seizures and gives them resources to manage the challenges that the seizures represent. Staff inclues a neurologist, several nurses, and a school psychologist, in addition to traditional camp staff who are given specialized training in responding appropriately to the needs of kids with epilepsy.

844   Camp Civitan
Civitan Foundation, Inc.
12635 N. 42nd Street
Phoenix, AZ 85032
602-953-2944
info@campcivitan.org
www.civitanfoundationaz.com
Dawn Trapp, Executive Director
Camp Civitan offers week long summer camp programs, and weekend programs throughout the year, to children with developmental disabilities. The camp is fully wheelchair accessible, is staffed by medical professionals and there is a 2:1 ratio of campers to staff. Camp Civitan offers campers the experience of traditional camp activities including, swimming, adaptive sports, fishing, music, arts and crafts, and talent shows.
1968

845   Camp H.U.G.
Arizona Hemophilia Association
826 North 5th Ave
Phoenix, AZ 85003
602-955-3947
info@arizonahemophilia.org
www.arizonahemophilia.org/camp-programs
Leigh Goldstein, Executive Director
Vickie Parra, Programs & Conferences Manager
Jessica Jackson, Finance Manager
Camp H.U.G (Hemophilia Uniting Generations) is a weekend camp program of the Arizona Hemophilia Association. The camp is for families who have a member with hemophilia, WWD, and/or other bleeding disorders.

846   Camp Honor
Arizona Hemophilia Association
826 North 5th Ave
Phoenix, AZ 85003
602-955-3947
info@arizonahemophilia.org
www.arizonahemophilia.org/camp-programs
Leigh Goldstein, Executive Director
Vickie Parra, Programs & Conferences Manager
Jessica Jackson, Finance Manager
Camp Honor offers a week long summer camp to children affected by an inherited bleeding disorders. Camp Honor offers children the chance to partcipate in outdoor activities and educational opportunities.

847   Camp Not-A-Wheeze
2689 E Michelle Way
Gilbert, AZ 85234
602-336-6575
FAX: 602-336-6576
info@campnotawheeze.org
campnotawheeze.org
Alan Crawford, Camp Director
Week-long summer camp for children aged 7-14 with moderate to severe asthma living in Arizona. Campers attending Camp Not-A- Wheeze, participate in a wide range of activities such as, horseback riding, hiking, canoeing, and fishing as well as an asthma education class. Those wishing to attend must fill out and send in a camper application.

848   Camp Rainbow
Phoenix Childrens Hospital
1919 E Thomas Rd
Phoenix, AZ 85016
602-933-1000
888-908-5437
camprainbow@phoenixchildrens.com
www.phoenixchildrens.org
Emilie Jarboe, Camp Director
Camp Rainbow is for children aged 7-17 who have or had cancer or a chronic blood disorder. The camp is offered for one week during the summer, held at camp Friendly Pines in Prescott, Arizona. Campers must be patients of Phoenix Children's Hospital's Center for Cancer and Blood Disorders, with the camp offering participants the opportunity to experience traditional camp activities including but not limited to, horseback riding, canoeing, fishing, swimming, and archery.

849   Lions Camp Tatiyee
5283 W White Mountain Blvd
Lakeside, AZ 85929
480-380-4254
pam@camptatiyee.org
camptatiyee.org
Richard Page, President
Lions Camp Tatiyee is the only organization in Arizona providing a week long summer camp for individuals with special needs. There is no cost for the camp and all of the programs are adaptable. Some activities that campers can participate in are, go-karting, fishing, art, games, cooking, rock wall, swimming, dances and campfires.

850   Nick & Kelly Heart Camp
Nick & Kelly Children's Fund
1321 E Bayview Dr
Tempe, AZ 85283
480-838-1529
contact@nickandkellyfund.org
www.nkheartcamp.org
Nick & Kelly's Heart Camp is a free camp for children and teens ages 7-17 with congenital heart disease. The camp is held at Friendly Pines in Prescott, Arizona with campers participating in activities such as nature walks, water sports, arts and crafts, and recreational activities.

Arkansas

851   Camp Aldersgate
2000 Aldersgate Road
Little Rock, AR 72205
501-225-1444
FAX: 501-225-2019
hello@campaldersgate.net
www.campaldersgate.net
Sonya S. Murphy, Chief Executive Officer
Shelley Myers, Chief Operating Officer & Chief Financial Officer
Brooke Wilson, Director, Communications
Camp Aldersgate is a nonprofit organization, offering summer, weekend camps, and year-round social service programs to children, teens and adults with special needs. The camp promotes outdoor recreation and socialization in a completely accessible environment.

852   Camp Quality Arkansas
PO Box 7754
Little Rock, AR 72217
870-926-3324
arkansas@campqualityusa.org
www.campqualityusa.org/ar
Nick Hankins, Executive Director
Jordan Law, Assistant Director
Audrey Wilkins, Camper Coordinator
Camp Quality is an international camping program for children with cancer. The Arkansas Camp Quality is held at Camp Powderfork in Bald Knob, Arkansas and offers children and their siblings summer camps and year round camping opportunities. Volunteer doctors and nurses are at the camp 24 hours a day, and there is a 1:1 staff to camper ratio.

853 Camp Sunshine
Burn Program at Arkansas Children's
1 Children's Way
Slot 225
Little Rock, AR 72202   501-364-1635
wilkinsonge@archildrens.org
www.archildrens.org/services/burn-program
Gretta Wilkinson, Camp Director
Camp Sunshine is a 4-day no-cost summer camp for children and
teens, 4-16, who have experienced burn injuries. Camp Sunshine
works to assist campers in the transformation from burn victim to
burn survivor. In order to attend the camp, campers must have survived a 10% or greater full thickness burn and/or may have significant scarring, disability or scarring to the hands or face.
1991

854 Kota Camp
Junior League Of Little Rock
401 South Scott Street
Little Rock, AR 72201   501-375-5557
info@jllr.org
www.jllr.org/community/kota-camp/
Maradyth McKenzie, President
Tabitha McNulty, President Elect
Jenna Martin, Treasurer
Kota Camp is offered to children aged 6-16 with disabilities or
medical conditions. Kota derived from a word used by the
Quapaw Native American Tribe indigenous to Arkansas, means
friend, and reflects the goals of the camp. Children with a disability bring a sibling or friend without a disability, to create a environment of inclusion, participate in camp activities, and promote
an understanding of those with special needs. The camp is held at
Camp Aldersgate in Little Rock.

California

855 Bearskin Meadow Camp
Diabetic Youth Families
5167 Clayton Rd
Suite F
Concord, CA 94521   925-680-4994
FAX: 925-680-4863
info@dyf.org
www.dyf.org
Davey Warner, Executive Director
Kaylor Glassman, Director, Programs
*Marissa Clarke-Howard, Director, Development & Communica-
tions*
Bearskin Meadow Camp, is a camp program offered by the Diabetes Youth Families organization to children (7-13), teens (14-17),
and families who are affected by type 1 diabetes. The camp has
traditional camp activities as well as educational opportunities
for campers.

856 Camp Beyond The Scars
Burn Institute
8825 Aero Drive
Suite 200
San Diego, CA 92123-2269   858-541-2277
FAX: 858-541-7179
ccoppenrath@burninstitute.org
www.burninstitute.org/camp-beyond-the-scar s
Susan Day, Executive Director
Tessa Haviland, Director, Marketing & Events
Benjamin Hemmings, Director, Operations
Camp Beyond the Scars, is a weeklong sleepaway summer camp
for children aged 8-17 who have survived a burn injury. Staffed
by adult burn survivors, healthcare professionals, and off-duty
firefighters, the camp provides an inclusive environment for burn
survivors to participate in activities including, swimming, basketball, volleyball, archery, golf, and arts and crafts. The camp is
free of charge, and is hosted at a camp facility in Romano,
California.
1987

857 Camp Bloomfield
Wayfinder Family Services
5300 Angeles Vista Blvd.
Los Angeles, CA 90043   323-295-4555
800-352-4555
FAX: 323-296-0424
www.wayfinderfamily.org
Miki Jordan, Chief Executive Officer
Jay Allen, President & Chief Operating Officer
Fernando Almodovar, Chief Financial Officer
Camp Bloomfield is a summer camp with week long sessions for
children and youth who are blind, visually impaired or multi-disabled. The 45 acre campground offers campers a variety of activities, specifically designed to meet the needs of the children, with
campers attending at no cost.

858 Camp Christian Berets
2508 Oakdale Rd.
Suite 10
Modesto, CA 95355   209-524-7993
FAX: 209-524-7979
www.christianberets.org
Kevin Van Donselaar, Executive Director
Mark Burns, Chairperson
Kelly Luth, Treasurer
Camp for children, students and adults with special needs.

859 Camp Conrad Chinnock
Diabetes Camping And Educational Services, Inc.
2400 E. Katella Ave.
Suite 800
Anaheim, CA 92806   844-744-2267
FAX: 909-752-5354
info@diabetescamping.org
www.diabetescamping.org
Rocky Wilson, Executive Director
Ryan Martz, Development & Program Director
Dale Lissy, Camp Manager
Camp Conrad Chinnock offers year round recreational, social,
and educational opportunities for children and families with type
1 diabetes.

860 Camp Grizzly
NorCal Services for Deaf & Hard of Hearing
4044 N Freeway Blvd.
Sacramento, CA 95843   916-349-7500
FAX: 916-349-7578
TTY:916-349-7500
campgrizzly@norcalcenter.org
www.campgrizzly.org
Molly Bowen, Program Leader
Cheryl Bella, Program Leader
A program of NorCal Services for Deaf & Hard of Hearing, Camp
Grizzly is a coed camp for children aged 7-18 who have a hearing
impairment. Camp Grizzly takes place at the Camp Lodestar
campground facilities and offers sporting activities, performing
and creative arts, hiking, swimming, playgrounds and campfires.

861 Camp Hollywood HEART
One Heartland
26001 Heinz Rd.
Willow River, MN 55795   888-216-2028
helpkids@oneheartland.org
www.oneheartland.org
Patrick Kindler, Executive Director
Katie Donlin, Operations Manager
Kadien Bartels-Merkel, Program Director
A program of One Heartland, a nonprofit organization working to
provide camping programs for children with serious illnesses or
experiencing social isolation. Camp Hollywood HEART is a
weeklong summer camp for youths, ages 15-20, who are infected
or affected by HIV/AIDS. The camp is held in Malibu, California
and is partnership camp between One Heartland and Hollywood
Heart.

862 Camp Kindle
Project Kindle
27203 Golden Willow Way
Santa Clarita, CA 91387
877-800-2267
eva@projectkindle.org
www.projectkindle.org
Eva Payne, Founder & Chief Executive Officer
Mandy Nickolite, Vice President
Camp Kindle provides year-round cost free recreational, educational and support services for children with special needs and life challenges.
1998

863 Camp Krem
Camping Unlimited
102 Brook Lane
Boulder Creek, CA 95006
831-338-3210
campkrem@campingunlimited.org
campingunlimited.org
Christina Krem DiGirolamo, Camp Director
Leon Wong, Head of Camper Services
Kristen Carter, Virtual Program Coordinator
Camp Krem - Camping Unlimited offers year-round and summer camping programs for children and adults with developmental disabilities. With a variety of different programs and many facilities on the campground such as a swimming pool, arts and crafts building, amphitheater, music pavilion, and archery range, Camp Krem provides its campers with recreation, education, and adventure opportunities.

864 Camp No Limits California
No Limits Foundation
700 S Wren Dr.
Big Bear Lake, CA 92315
207-569-6411
FAX: 877-406-5106
campnolimits@gmail.com
www.nolimitsfoundation.org
Mary Leighton, Founder & Executive Director
Kelsey Moody, Program Operations Manager
Alix Sandler, Marketing & Development Director
Camp No Limits California, a location of Camp No Limits, is a recreational and educational camp for youth who have experienced limb loss. Camp No Limits, is a program of the nonprofit organization No Limits Foundation. The California camp is held in Big Bear where campers have access to ropes courses, zip lines, and a swimming pool.

865 Camp Okizu
Okizu Foundation
83 Hamilton Dr.
Suite 200
Novato, CA 94949-5755
415-382-9083
FAX: 415-382-8384
info@okizu.org
www.okizu.org
Suzie Randall, Executive Director
Heather Ferrier, Director, Family Services
Sarah Uldricks, Director, Marketing & Special Events
Camp Okizu offers a variety of medically supervised, residential camp programs for families who have a child diagnosed with cancer. Programs are offered throughout the year free of charge.

866 Camp Okizu: Family Camp
Okizu Foundation
83 Hamilton Dr.
Suite 200
Novato, CA 94949-5755
415-382-9083
FAX: 415-382-8384
enrollment@okizu.org
www.okizu.org
Suzie Randall, Executive Director
Heather Ferrier, Director, Family Services
Sarah Uldricks, Director, Marketing & Special Events
Camp Okizu's Family Camp is no-cost camp designed for the families of children, and children who have been diagnosed with cancer. The Family Camp is offered as a weekend program, running on multiple weekends from April to September.

867 Camp Okizu: Oncology Camp
Okizu Foundation
83 Hamilton Dr.
Suite 200
Novato, CA 94949-5755
415-382-9083
FAX: 415-382-8384
enrollment@okizu.org
www.okizu.org
Suzie Randall, Executive Director
Heather Ferrier, Director, Family Services
Sarah Uldricks, Director, Marketing & Special Events
A program of Camp Okizu, the Oncology Camp is for children and teens, ages 6-17, who have or have had cancer. The camp is a residential summer camp program and is staffed by pediatric oncology departments from the participating hospitals.

868 Camp Okizu: SIBS Camp
Okizu Foundation
83 Hamilton Dr.
Suite 200
Novato, CA 94949-5755
415-382-9083
FAX: 415-382-8384
enrollment@okizu.org
www.okizu.org
Suzie Randall, Executive Director
Heather Ferrier, Director, Family Services
Sarah Uldricks, Director, Marketing & Special Events
SIBS (Special and Important Brothers and Sisters) Camp is for the sibling or siblings, ages 6-17, of a child who has, has had, or has died from cancer. The camp is a no-charge, residential summer program, that provides campers the opportunity to learn new skills and get support from others who have experienced having a sibling with cancer.

869 Camp Okizu: Teens-N-Twenties Camp
Okizu Foundation
83 Hamilton Dr.
Suite 200
Novato, CA 94949-5755
415-382-9083
FAX: 415-382-8384
enrollment@okizu.org
www.okizu.org
Suzie Randall, Executive Director
Heather Ferrier, Director, Family Services
Sarah Uldricks, Director, Marketing & Special Events
Camp Okizu: Teens-N- Twenties Camp is a weekend recreation and support program that is offered 4 times a year for pediatric oncology patients and their siblings ages 18-25.

870 Camp Pacifica
California Lions Camp
1836 K Street
Merced, CA 95340-4818
559-373-0961
deafcamppacifica@gmail.com
camp-pacifica.org
Angelica Martinez, Camp Director
John Martinez, Assistant Director
Camp Pacifica provides a summer camp experience for children, boys and girls, aged 7-15 who have a hearing impairment. The camp is located in the foothills of Sierra on 52 acres of forested woodland. Activities include, but are not limited to, archery, canoeing, ropes course, swimming, horseback riding, and riflery. The camp costs $360, plus a registration fee.
1978

871 Camp Paivika
Ability First
PO Box 3367
Crestline, CA 92325
909-338-1102
FAX: 909-338-2502
camppaivika@abilityfirst.org
www.abilityfirst.org/camp-paivika
Kelly Kunsek, Camp Director
Lauren Wilson, Program Director
Tina Ronning-Fraynd, Coordinator, Camper Services
As a program of AbilityFirst, Camp Paivika offers overnight summer programs for children, teens and adults with developmental and physical disabilities. The camp is completely accessible and the staff is trained to provide any assistance or personal care a camper needs. Located in San Bernardino National Forest, Camp

Paivika provides a traditional summer camp experience in a safe and fun environment.
1947

872   Camp ReCreation
9272 Madison Ave.
Orangeville, CA 95662   916-988-6835
camprecreation@outlook.com
www.camprecreation.org
Kathi Barber, Camp Director
Camp ReCreation offers residential summer camps and year round programs for children, teens, and adults with developmental disabilities. The summer camp is held at Camp Ronald McDonald in Lassen National Forest. With a 1:1 staff to camper ratio, Camp ReCreation offers wide variety of camp activities, and campers wishing to participate must fill out a camper application.
1983

873   Camp Reach for the Sky
The Seany Foundation
3530 Camino del Rio N
Suite 101
San Diego, CA 92108   858-551-0922
www.theseanyfoundation.org
Amy Robins, Co-Founder, The Seany Foundation
Paula Lutzky, Chief Financial Officer
Emily Brody, Director, Marketing & Media
Previously run by the American Cancer Society, Camp Reach for the Sky (CR4TS) is now run by The Seany Foundation and provides an opportunity for children with cancer and their siblings to attend a free summer camp. Camp Reach for the Sky offers a multiple programs, including a Resident Oncology Camp, a Sibling Camp and Day Camps.

874   Camp Ronald McDonald at Eagle Lake
2555 49th Street
Sacramento, CA 95817   916-734-4230
FAX: 916-734-4238
info@rmhcnc.org
www.campronald.org
Catherine Ithurburn, Chief Executive Officer
Pip Pipkins, Camp Manager
Camp Ronald McDonald at Eagle Lake collaborates with other nonprofit organizations to provide week long summer camp opportunities for children with special medical needs, financial hardship and/or emotional, developmental or physical disabilities. The camp is fully accessible.

875   Camp Ronald McDonald for Good Times
4560 Fountain Avenue
Los Angeles, CA 90029   323-666-6400
FAX: 626-744-9969
www.campronaldmcdonald.org
Erica Mangham, Executive Director
Brian Crater, Associate Executive Director
Chad Edwards, Program Director
Free year-round residential camping for children with cancer and their families.

876   Camp Sunburst
Sunburst Projects United States Headquarters
2143 Hurley Way
Suite 240
Sacramento, CA 95825   916-440-0889
FAX: 916-440-1208
admin@sunburstprojects.org
www.sunburstprojects.org
Jacob Bradley-Rowe, Executive Director
Camp Sunburst is a youth oriented leadership camp that promotes and creates an environment to help youth learn self confidence to change negative social patterns and break cycles of HIV/AIDS infections. Activities campers will participate in include, boating, swimming, art, dance, and sports.

877   Camp Sunshine Dreams
PO Box 28232
Fresno, CA 93729-8232   stephanie@campsunshinedreams.org
www.campsunshinedreams.org
Stephanie Scharbach, Contact
Pam Aiello, Contact

Camp Sunshine Dreams provides a summer camp experience to children aged 8-15 with cancer and their siblings.

878   Camp Taylor
Camp Taylor, Inc.
8224 West Grayson Rd.
Modesto, CA 95358-9094   209-545-3853
camp@kidsheartcamp.org
www.kidsheartcamp.org
Kimberlie Gamino, Founder & Executive Director
With several programs, Camp Taylor provides youth, teens, and the families of children with heart disease the opportunity to go to a free medically supervised summer sleepaway camp. Campers are able to enjoy activities such as, swimming, snorkeling, horseback riding, rock-wall, skits, archery, and heart education.
2002

879   Camp Taylor: Family Camp
Camp Taylor, Inc.
8224 West Grayson Rd.
Modesto, CA 95358-9094   209-545-3853
camp@kidsheartcamp.org
www.kidsheartcamp.org/familycampca
Kimberlie Gamino, Founder & Executive Director
A program of Camp Taylor, Family Camp is for children of all ages, with congenital heart disease and/or acquired heart disease, and their family including parents and siblings. The camp offers parental heart education and support programs for parents and siblings. Family Camp is geared towards children too young to attend Youth or Teen Camp, or those who are not ready to attend a residential camp.

880   Camp Taylor: Leadership Camp
Camp Taylor, Inc.
8224 West Grayson Rd.
Modesto, CA 95358-9094   209-545-3853
camp@kidsheartcamp.org
www.kidsheartcamp.org/leadershipcamp
Kimberlie Gamino, Founder & Executive Director
Leadership Camp is for teens and youth, ages 16-21, who have previously attended a Camp Taylor California camp program, wishing to be camp mentor for youth, teen, and family camps. Campers wishing to attend this camp should make it known to either a camp counselor or camp director.

881   Camp Taylor: Teen Camp
Camp Taylor, Inc.
8224 West Grayson Rd.
Modesto, CA 95358-9094   209-545-3853
camp@kidsheartcamp.org
www.kidsheartcamp.org/teencamp
Kimberlie Gamino, Founder & Executive Director
The Teen Camp program at Camp Taylor is for teens ages 13-17, with congenital heart disease and/or acquired heart disease. Campers participate in heart education and traditional camp activities. Campers wishing to attend the camp must apply, with campers being accepted on a first come basis.

882   Camp Taylor: Young Adult Program
Camp Taylor, Inc.
8224 West Grayson Rd.
Modesto, CA 95358-9094   209-545-3853
camp@kidsheartcamp.org
www.kidsheartcamp.org/leadershipcamp
Kimberlie Gamino, Founder & Executive Director
The Young Adult Program at Camp Taylor is designed for previous heart campers ages 18-35 with congenital heart disease. The program works to provide support, education, and the opportunities to participate in social events in order to help with the transition to adulthood.

883   Camp Taylor: Youth Camp
Camp Taylor, Inc.
8224 West Grayson Rd.
Modesto, CA 95358-9094   209-545-3853
camp@kidsheartcamp.org
www.kidsheartcamp.org/youthcamp
Kimberlie Gamino, Founder & Executive Director
A program of Camp Taylor, Youth Camp is designed for children, ages 7-12, with congenital heart disease and/or acquired heart disease. Campers participate in heart education and traditional

camp activities. Campers wishing to attend the camp must apply, with campers being accepted on a first come basis.

884 Camp Tuolumne Trails
22988 Ferretti Road
Groveland, CA 95321   209-962-7534
info@tuolumnetrails.org
www.tuolumnetrails.org
Jacqui Montero, Director of Camper Operations
Tuolumne Trails is a camp for individuals with special medical needs. With week-long summer camp options, Camp Tuolumne Trails is a completely accessible camp, with a 3:1 staff to camper ratio, that allows campers to participate in camping activities in a safe environment. Campers wishing to attend must complete the application and session assignment process.
Founded in 2002.

885 Camp del Corazon
11615 Hesby St
North Hollywood, CA 91601-3620   818-754-0312
FAX: 818-754-0377
info@campdelcorazon.org
www.campdelcorazon.org
Kevin Shannon, President & Medical Director
Chrissie Endler, Executive Director
Kristina Caberto Wallace, Director of Development & Operations
Camp del Corazon is a nonprofit corporation offering a no cost summer camp and other programs to children aged 7-17 living with heart disease. Campers or their guardians must fill out a camp application, with acceptance into the camp dependant upon a nurse review of the parent and cardiology portions of the application.
1995

886 Camp-A-Lot and Camp-A-Little
The Arc of San Diego
3030 Market Street
San Diego, CA 92102   619-685-1175
FAX: 619-234-3759
info@arc-sd.com
www.arc-sd.com
Anthony J. DeSalis, President & Chief Executive Officer
Programs of The Arc of San Diego, Camp - A - Lot (ages 18 and up) and Camp - A - Little (ages 5-17) offer recreational summer camp opportunities for individuals with physical and developmental disabilities.

887 Coelho Epilepsy Youth Summer Camp
Epilepsy Foundation Of Northern California
909 Marina Village Pkwy
Suite 239
Alameda, CA 94501   510-922-8687
800-632-3532
FAX: 510-922-8659
efnca@epilepsynorcal.org
www.epilepsynorcal.org
Carlos Quesada, Chief Executive Officer
Miriam Swanson, Programs Manager
Kimberly Bari, Programs Ambassador
Offered to children aged 9-17, Coelho Epilepsy Youth Summer Camp provides a week-long sleepaway camp for children with epilepsy. Staffed by medical professional throughout the entire week, campers participate in traditional camp activities. Parents or guardians must fill out an application for a camper.

888 Dream Street
Dream Street Foundation
324 S. Beverly Dr.
Suite 500
Beverly Hills, CA 90212   424-333-1371
FAX: 310-388-0302
www.dreamstreetfoundation.org
Patty Grubman, Founder
Run by The Dream Street Foundation, Dream Street Camps provide camping programs for children (aged 4-14) and young adults (18-24) with chronic and life threatening illnesses. The kids program runs in California, with the young adults program running in Arizona. The programs are free of charge, and campers can participate in different activities such as, swimming, arts and crafts, sports, horseback riding, and archery.

889 Easterseals Camp
Easterseals Southern California
1063 McGaw Avenue
Suite 100
Irvine, CA 92614   951-264-4855
amanda.showalter@essc.org
www.easterseals.com/southerncal
Mark Bertrand, Chair
Claudia Villamizar, First Vice Chair
Maureen Cormier, Second Vice Chair
Easterseals Camp is a week long summer camp for children and adults with disabilities. Held at Camp Oakes in the San Bernardino Mountains. Campers participate in activities including, crafts, hayrides, talent shows, dances, swimming, canoeing, archery, hiking, and rope courses. There is a 1:2 counselor to camper ratio. The cost of the camp is $1,248 per camper.

890 Easterseals Camp Harmon
16403 Highway 9
Boulder Creek, CA 95006   831-338-3383
campharmon@es-cc.org
www.campharmon.org
Jeff Terpstra, Chair
Robert Guerin, Vice Chair
Greg Jensen, Secretary
Camp Harmon, the Easterseals Central California camp, offers residential summer camps programs to individuals ages 8-65 with disabilities. Each session at Camp Harmon is designed for a specific age group and offers campers the opportunity to experience traditional summer camp activities. There is a 3:1 counsellor to camper ratio, with camp fees are based on $140.00 a day base.

891 Enchanted Hills Camp for the Blind
Lighthouse for the Blind
1155 Market St.
10th Floor
San Francisco, CA 94103   415-431-1481
FAX: 415-863-7568
info@lighthouse-sf.org
www.lighthouse-sf.org
W. Brandon Cox, Chief Operating Officer
Michelle Knapik, Chief Financial Officer
Enchanted Hills Camp for the Blind is located on 311 acres of land on Mt. Veeder, offering programs for children, teens, adults, deaf-blind, seniors, and families of the blind. The camp gives campers the experience of traditional summer camp but is adapted to meet the needs of the campers.

892 Firefighters Kids Camp
Firefighters Burn Institute
3101 Stockton Blvd.
Sacramento, CA 95820   916-739-8525
valorie@ffburn.org
www.ffburn.org
Valorie Smart, Camp Contact
Joe Pick, Executive Director
Rachel Crowell, Assistant Director
Firefighters Kids Camp is a program run by the Firefighters Burn Institute for children ages 6-17, who are survivors of burns. With activities such as rocking climbing, bicycling, hiking, kayaking, swimming, and arts and crafts, the ratio of staff to campers is 3:1, with on site 24/7 nurse and physical therapist ensuring a safe and fun environment.

893 Lions Wilderness Camp for Deaf Children, Inc.
Lions Wilderness Camp Headquarters
PO Box 8
Roseville, CA 95661-9998   lionscampfordeaf@gmail.com
www.lionswildcamp.org
David Velasquez, Camp Program Director
Lions Wilderness Camp gives deaf children aged 7-15 an outdoor camp experience helping children to learn outdoor skills and enjoy nature.

894   Little Heroes Family Burn Camp
Firefighters Burn Institute
3101 Stockton Blvd.
Sacramento, CA 95820   916-739-8525
                                        www.ffburn.org

Valorie Smart, Camp Contact
Joe Pick, Executive Director
Rachel Crowell, Assistant Director
Little Heroes Preschool Burn Camp is a burn recovery program
run by the Firefighters Burn Institute. The camp is for children
ages 1-6, who are survivors of burns, and their families. The program runs for 3 days, providing support and education for those
attending.

895   New Horizons Summer Day Camp
YMCA of Orange County
13821 Newport Ave.
Suite 150
Tustin, CA 92780   714-508-7616
                                newhorizons@ymcaoc.org
                         www.ymcaoc.org/new-horizons
Jeff McBride, Chief Executive Officer
New Horizons is a program by the YMCA offering day camps for
adults with developmental disabilities. Outings in the community
are supervised and create an environment that fosters social inter-
action, skill building, and friendship.

896   Quest Camp
907 San Ramon Valley Blvd.
Suite 202
Danville, CA 94526   925-743-2900
                                        800-313-9733
                                FAX: 925-743-1937
                                www.questcamps.com
Robert B. Field, PhD., Founder & Executive Director
Debra Forrester-Field, MA, Administrative Director
Aprilyn Artz, MA, Clinical Director
Quest Camps are designed using the Quest Camp Therapeutic
System developed specifically to help and reduce a campers psy-
chological disability. With locations in San Francisco East Bay,
California, Huntington Beach, California, and Pittsburgh, Penn-
sylvania, camps have a 6:1 camper to staff ratio, with campers re-
ceiving sport instruction and participate in physical activity, arts,
and games.
1989

897   Special Camp For Special Kids
31641 La Novia Ave
San Juan Capistrano, CA 92675   949-661-0108
                                FAX: 949-661-8637
                                lindsay.eres@smes.org
                                www.specialcamp.org
Lindsay Eres, Executive Director
Katie McCombs, Associate Program Director
Katie Schwartz, Assistant Director
For youths with disabilities, Special Camps for Special Kids, of-
fers day camps with a 1:1 volunteer counselor to camper.

898   The Painted Turtle
1300 4th Street
Suite 300
Santa Monica, CA 90401   310-451-1353
                                        866-451-5367
                                FAX: 310-451-1357
                                info@thepaintedturtle.org
                                www.thepaintedturtle.org
Page Adler, Chairman of the Board & Co-Founder
Lou Adler, Producer & Co-Founder
The Painted Turtle provides year round camp programs for chil-
dren, siblings, and families with children who have chronic and
life threatening illnesses. The camp is located in Lake Hughes,
California.

Colorado

899   Adam's Camp: Colorado
Adam's Camp
1101 County Road 53
Granby, CO 80446   303-563-8290
                                FAX: 303-563-8291
                                Contact@AdamsCamp.org
                                www.adamscampcolorado.org
Brian Conly, Executive Director
Paige Heydon, Director, Finance & Development
Adam's Camp is a nonprofit organization providing therapeutic
programs and recreational camps for children and the families of
children with special needs. The Colorado location of Adam's
Camp, offers both therapy and adventure camps. The adventure
camp is held at the YMCA - Snow Mountain Ranch in Granby,
Colorado.

900   Aspen Camp
4862 Snowmass Creek Rd.
Snowmass, CO 81654   970-315-0513
                                TTY:970-315-0513
                                hi@aspencamp.org
                                www.aspencamp.org
Karen Immerson, Vice President
Eric Kaika, Treasurer
Open to the deaf community, including family members and
friends as well as those who are deaf, deaf blind, hard of hearing,
and late deafened, Camp Aspen provides year round programs for
youth and adults.

901   Breckenridge Outdoor Education Center
PO Box 697
Breckenridge, CO 80424   970-453-6422
                                        800-383-2632
                                FAX: 970-453-4676
                                boec@boec.org
                                www.boec.org
Sonya Norris, Executive Director
Karen Skruch, Finance Director
Jeff Inouye, Ski Program Director
Breckenridge Outdoor Education Center (BOEC) provides year
round educational outdoor experiences to individuals with physical and intellectual disabilities. Some programs BOEC offer include, Adaptive Ski and Ride School, Wilderness Programs and
adaptive programs for individuals with brain injuries, multiple
sclerosis, and Parkinson's Disease.
1976

902   Camp Rocky Mountain Village
Easterseals Colorado
393 S. Harlan St.
Suite 250
Lakewood, CO 80226   303-233-1666
                                FAX: 303-569-3857
                        campinfo@eastersealscolorado.org
                                www.easterseals.com/co
Roman Krafczyk, President & Chief Executive Officer
Krasimir Koev, Chief Operating Officer
Kerry Erdahl, Chief Financial Officer
A program of Easterseals Colorado, Rocky Mountain Village in
Empire Colorado is a fully accessible camp, with summer camps
sessions for children and adults with disabilities. Activities in-
clude but are not limited to swimming, fishing, overnight camp-
ing, outdoor cooking, arts and crafts, and a zip line.

903   Camp Wapiyapi
191 University Blvd.
PO Box 294
Denver, CO 80206   303-534-0883
                                FAX: 303-534-0874
                                Wapiyapi@wapiyapi.org
                                www.campwapiyapi.org
Darla Dakin, Chief Executive Officer
Megan Blanc, Summer Camp Director
Camp Wapiyapi is a nonprofit organization that fosters friend-
ships, fun and healing outside of the hospital for families facing
childhood cancer through a camp experience. For patients ages
6-17. Full-time onsite volunteer medical staff available 24/7.

904 **Challenge Aspen**
PO Box 6639
Snowmass Village, CO 81615 970-923-0578
FAX: 970-923-7338
info@challengeaspen.org
www.challengeaspen.org

Lindsay Cagley, Chief Executive Officer
Anne Adams, Chief Operating Officer
Jenni Petersen, Chief Financial Officer
Challenge Aspen provides recreational, cultural experiences and summer camps for individuals who have cognitive or physical challenges. Programs are tailored to fit a diversity of needs and interests.
1995

905 **Children's Hospital Burn Camps Program**
13123 E 16th Ave.
PO Box 580
Aurora, CO 80045 720-777-8295
FAX: 720-777-7270
learnmore@noordinarycamps.org
www.noordinarycamps.org

Trudy Boulter, Camp Director
Tim Schuetz, Outreach Coordinator
The Children's Hospital Colorado Burn Camps Program provides rehabilitation and reintegration opportunities for children, teens, adults, and families who have been affected by burn injuries. The Camps Program has partnerships with 7 hospitals across the United States and offers year-round programs.

906 **Children's Hospital Burn Camps Program: England Exchange Program Burn Camp**
13123 E 16th Ave.
PO Box 580
Aurora, CO 80045 720-777-8295
FAX: 720-777-7270
learnmore@noordinarycamps.org
www.noordinarycamps.org

Trudy Boulter, Camp Director
Tim Schuetz, Outreach Coordinator
An international exchange program for campers, ages 13-15, between the Children's Hospital Burn Camps Program and The Manchester Children's Hospital Burns Camp in England. Campers are able to explore a new culture, food, and climate. The camp is located in the Lake District.

907 **Children's Hospital Burn Camps Program: Family Burn Camp**
13123 E 16th Ave.
PO Box 580
Aurora, CO 80045 720-777-8295
FAX: 720-777-7270
learnmore@noordinarycamps.org
www.noordinarycamps.org

Trudy Boulter, Camp Director
Tim Schuetz, Outreach Coordinator
The Family Burn Camp is for families who have been affected by a burn injury. The camp is designed to give families the opportunity to interact and connect with other families who have had a similar experiences.

908 **Children's Hospital Burn Camps Program: Summer Burn Camp**
13123 E 16th Ave.
PO Box 580
Aurora, CO 80045 720-777-8295
FAX: 720-777-7270
learnmore@noordinarycamps.org
www.noordinarycamps.org

Trudy Boulter, Camp Director
Tim Schuetz, Outreach Coordinator
The Summer Burn Camp is part of the Children's Hospital Colorado Burn Camps Program, and offers a weeklong summer camp for children and teens, ages 8-18 who have been affected by burn injuries. The camp is held in Estes Park in partnership with Cheley Colorado Camps, and activities include, hiking, mountain biking, challenge courses, horseback riding, mountain climbing, fishing, archery, crafts, riflery, and swimming.

909 **Children's Hospital Burn Camps Program: Winter Burn Camp**
13123 E 16th Ave.
PO Box 580
Aurora, CO 80045 720-777-8295
FAX: 720-777-7270
learnmore@noordinarycamps.org
www.noordinarycamps.org

Trudy Boulter, Camp Director
Tim Schuetz, Outreach Coordinator
The Winter Burn Camp is for older campers, ages 13-18, who have previously attended the Cheley Children's Hospital Colorado Summer Burn Camp. Held in Steamboat Springs, Colorado at the Steamboat Grand Lodge campers participate in a week of skiing and/or snowboarding.

910 **Children's Hospital Burn Camps Program: Young Adult Retreat**
13123 E 16th Ave.
PO Box 580
Aurora, CO 80045 720-777-8295
FAX: 720-777-7270
learnmore@noordinarycamps.org
www.noordinarycamps.org

Trudy Boulter, Camp Director
Tim Schuetz, Outreach Coordinator
A program of the Children's Hospital Colorado Burn Camps Program, the Young Adult Retreat is designed to address the specific issues facing burn survivors ages 18-25. The retreat offers a variety of recreational and workshop opportunities working to address the topics of relationships, body image, and goal setting.

911 **City of Lakewood Recreation and Inclusion Services for Everyone (R.I.S.E.)**
City Of Lakewood
480 S Allison Pkwy
Lakewood, CO 80226 303-987-4867
TTY:303-987-7057
rise@lakewood.org
www.lakewood.org/rise

The Recreation and Inclusion Services for Everyone (R.I.S.E.) of Lakewood is a therapeutic recreation program for individuals with disabilities, age 6 through senior adult. Some programs offered by R.I.S.E include field trips, social dances, sports and camping.

912 **Cochlear Implant Camp**
Listen Foundation
6950 E Belleview Ave.
Suite 203
Greenwood Village, CO 80111 303-781-9440
cochlearimplantcamp@gmail.com
www.listenfoundation.org/cicamp

Janette Cantwell, Camp Director
Held at the YMCA Rockies Estes Park Center, the camp offers a wide range of activities for children from 3-17 years old with cochlear implants. The camp is held during the summer and also offers programs for parents and families. The cost is $800 for a family of four.

913 **Colorado Lions Camp**
28541 Hwy 67 N
PO Box 9043
Woodland Park, CO 80863 719-687-2087
FAX: 719-687-7435
coloradolionscamp@msn.com
www.coloradolionscamp.org

Erin Newport, Camp Director
Brenna Bonnelycke, Executive Assistant
Colorado Lions Camp offers summer camp and weekend respite programs for individuals aged 8 and up with special needs. The camp is designed to promote independence and provide an opportunity for campers to discover their potential in a safe environment.

914   First Descents
3827 Lafayette St.
Suite 161
Denver, CO 80205   303-945-2490
                                          FAX: 866-592-6911
                                        info@firstdescents.org
                                        www.firstdescents.org

Brad Ludden, Founder
Debbie King-Ford, Chairperson
Michael Kantor, Treasurer

First Descents offers free outdoor adventure programs for young
adults ages 18-39 who have, or who have had cancer. Activities
include climbing, paddling and surfing, all offered in a safe
environment.

915   Roundup River Ranch
8333 Colorado River Rd.
Gypsum, CO 81637   970-524-2267
                                          FAX: 888-524-2477
                                     info@roundupriverranch.org
                                     www.roundupriverranch.org

Ruth B. Johnson, President & Chief Executive Officer
Sterling Nell Leija, Director of Operations
Kendra Perkins, Camp Director

Roundup River Ranch provides traditional camp experiences for
children and their families with chronic and serious illnesses. The
Ranch is located in Gypsum, Colorado, with all programs offered
free of charge.

Connecticut

916   Arthur C. Luf Children's Burn Camp
Connecticut Burns Care Foundation
601 Boston Post Rd.
Milford, CT 06460   203-878-6744
                                          FAX: 203-878-4044
                                       cbcf@ctburnsfoundation.org
                                       www.ctburnsfoundation.org

Armand J. Cantafio, President
Thomas Smith, Camp Director

The Arthur C. Luf Children's Burn Camp provides a free of
charge camp experience for children and teens, ages 8-18, who
have survived life altering burn injuries. Camp activities include
hiking, fishing, archery, boating, ropes course, and campfires.
The volunteer staff is composed of retired firefighters, medical
personnel, and burn survivors.
1978

917   Camp Discovery
American Academy of Dermatology
PO Box 1968
Des Plaines, IL 60017   847-240-1280
                                              866-503-7546
                                              888-462-3376
                                          FAX: 847-240-1859
                                        www.campdiscovery.org

A program of the American Academy of Dermatology, Camp Discovery is a camp held in 5 locations across the United States for
children with chronic skin conditions. Campers can participate in
activities such as fishing, swimming, archery and horseback riding. The Connecticut camp is held in Andover, Connecticut at
Channel 3 Kids Camp.
1993

918   Camp Harkness
The Arc Eastern Connecticut
125 Sachem St.
Norwich, CT 06360   860-889-4435
                                          FAX: 860-889-4662
                                          info@thearcect.org
                                     thearcect.org/camp-harkness

Kathleen Stauffer, Chief Executive Officer

A week-long summer camp program for individuals with intellectual and developmental disabilities. The camp is held at Camp
Harkness in Waterford, CT.

919   Camp Horizons
127 Babcock Hill Rd.
PO Box 323
South Windham, CT 06266   860-456-1032
                                          FAX: 860-456-4721
                                          www.horizonsct.org

Adam Milne, Chair
Chris McNaboe, President & CEO
Kathleen McNaboe, Vice President

Camp Horizons offers summer camp and weekend camps for children and adults with developmental disabilities.

920   Camp Isola Bella
410 Twin Lakes Rd.
Salisbury, CT 06079   860-824-5558
                                          FAX: 860-824-4276
                                          TTY:860-596-0110
                                       ibdirector@asd-1817.org
                              asd-1817.org/programs/camp-isola-bella

David Guardino, Director

Owned and operated by the American School for the Deaf, Camp
Isola Bella provides summer camp opportunities for children who
are deaf or hard of hearing. Staff is able to communicate with the
campers regardless of the mode of communication, including
sign language, oral, aural, lipreading or a mix, and activities include, but are not limited to, swimming, ropes course, canoeing,
water skiing, archery, hiking, sports, and sailing.

921   Camp No Limits Connecticut
No Limits Foundation
Quinnipiac University
305 Sherman Avenue
Hamden, CT 06518   207-569-6411
                                       campnolimits@gmail.com
                                     www.nolimitsfoundation.org

Mary Leighton, Founder & Executive Director
Kelsey Moody, Program Operations Manager
Alix Sandler, Marketing & Development Director

Camp No Limits Connecticut, a location of Camp No Limits, is a
recreational and educational camp for youth who have experienced limb loss. Camp No Limits, is a program of the nonprofit
organization No Limits Foundation. The Connecticut camp is
hosted at Quinnipiac's York Hill campus and provides campers
the opportunity to participate in a variety of different sports,
including ice and sled hockey.

922   Easterseals Camp Hemlocks
Easterseals Oak Hill
120 Holcomb St.
Hartford, CT 06112   860-286-3108
                                       barry.simon@OakHillCT.org
                                     www.easterseals.com/oakhill

Barry M. Simon, President & CEO

A summer camp program of Easterseals Oak Hill, Camp Hemlocks is a completely accessible camp for youth and adults with
physical, sensory, intellectual, and developmental disabilities.
Activities include swimming, boating, fishing, arts and crafts,
and climbing tower.

923   SeriousFun Children's Network
SeriousFun Support Center Office
230 East Ave.
Suite 107
Norwalk, CT 06855   203-562-1203
                                          FAX: 203-341-8707
                                     info@seriousfunnetwork.org
                                          www.seriousfun.org

Blake Maher, Chief Executive Officer
Justin Fusaro, Chief Financial Officer
Tara Fisher, Chief Marketing Officer

The SeriousFun Children's Network is an international organization of camps and programs for children and the families of children with serious illnesses. The Network has 30 camps and
programs worldwide.

924 The Hole in the Wall Gang Camp
565 Ashford Center Rd.
Ashford, CT 06278
860-429-3444
info@holeinthewallgang.org
www.holeinthewallgang.org
James H. Canton, Chief Executive Officer
Padraig Barry, Chief Strategy Officer
Kevin Magee, Chief Financial Officer
The Hole in the Wall Gang Camp offers summer and weekend camp experiences for children and the siblings of children with serious illnesses. Located in Ashford, Connecticut, campers are able to participate in traditional camp activities in a medically safe environment.

925 The Rainbow Club
The Barton Center for Diabetes Education, Inc.
30 Ennis Rd.
PO Box 356
North Oxford, MA 01537-0356
508-987-2056
FAX: 508-987-2002
info@bartoncenter.org
www.bartoncenter.org
Lynn Butler-Dinunno, Executive Director
Jenna Dufresne, Director, Health Services
Sarah Balko, Director, Camps & Programs
A program of The Barton Center for Diabetes Education, The Rainbow Club is a day camp held in Greenwich, Connecticut for children and teens, ages 5-15 with diabetes. Campers receive diabetes education and participate in games, crafts, and water activities. An adult program designed for parents runs in conjunction with the day camp session.

Delaware

926 Camp Manito & Camp Lenape
United Cerebral Palsy Of Delaware
700A River Rd.
Wilmington, DE 19809
302-764-2400
FAX: 302-764-8713
TTY:302-764-8708
ucpde@ucpde.org
www.ucpde.org/summer-camps
Moni Edgar, Executive Director
Kim Evans, Director, Camp Program
Camp Manito, located in New Castle County and Camp Lenape, serving Kent and Sussex Counties, are summer camps run by United Cerebral Palsy of Delaware for children and young adults, ages 3-21, with orthopedic disabilities. Both campsites are accessible and activities include swimming, arts and crafts, music, sports, computer education, and outings.

927 Children's Beach House
100 W 10 St.
Suite 411
Wilmington, DE 19801-1674
302-655-4288
FAX: 302-655-4216
www.cbhinc.org
Richard T. Garrett, Executive Director
Patrice Tosi, Vice President, Advancement
Children's Beach House (CBH) is a nonprofit organization providing support and education for children with special needs. CBH offers summer and weekend programs at the Lewes facility on Delaware Bay. Activities are modified for each camper and include, but are not limited to, swimming, sailing, kayaking, arts and crafts, sports, and campfires.

District of Columbia

928 Camp Lighthouse
Columbia Lighthouse for the Blind
1825 K St. NW
Suite 1103
Washington, DC 20006
202-454-6400
FAX: 202-955-6401
info@clb.org
www.clb.org
Tony Cancelosi, President & CEO
Jocelyn Hunter, Senior Director, Communications
Toya Horten, Director, Administrative Operations
Camp Lighthouse is a one week day camp program run by Columbia Lighthouse for the Blind. The camp is for children ages 6-12 with visual impairments.

929 Paddy Rossbach Youth Camp
Amputee Coalition
601 Pennsylvania Ave. NW
Suite 600, South Bldg.
Washington, DC 20004
888-267-5669
www.amputee-coalition.org
Cassandra Isidro, President & Chief Executive Officer
A 6-day camp for youths ages 10-17 who have limb loss or limb difference. Activities include sports, swimming, fishing, arts and crafts. Also offers a Leadership Camp for 18- and 19-year-olds transitioning from high school to college and careers.

Florida

930 Camp Amigo
Children's Burn Camp Of North Florida, Inc.
PO Box 368
Tallahassee, FL 32302
850-509-6200
www.campamigo.com
Rusty Roberts, President
Camp Amigo provides a one week summer camp experience for children ages 6-18 who live in Florida and have survived a burn injury.

931 Camp Boggy Creek
30500 Brantley Branch Rd.
Eustis, FL 32736
352-483-4200
866-462-6449
FAX: 352-483-0589
info@campboggycreek.org
www.boggycreek.org
June Clark, President & CEO
Lisa Hicks, Chief Development Officer
David Mann, Camp Director
Part of the SeriousFun Children's Network, Camp Boggy Creek provides year round camping opportunities for children with serious illnesses throughout Florida. The camp has week-long summer camp sessions and retreat weekends.

932 Camp No Limits Florida
No Limits Foundation
8411 25th Street East
Parrish, FL 34219
207-569-6411
campnolimits@gmail.com
www.nolimitsfoundation.org
Mary Leighton, Founder & Executive Director
Kelsey Moody, Program Operations Manager
Alix Sandler, Marketing & Development Director
Camp No Limits Florida, a location of Camp No Limits, is a recreational and educational camp for youth who have experienced limb loss. Camp No Limits is a program of the nonprofit organization No Limits Foundation. The Florida camp is hosted at the Clearwater Marine Aquarium in Clearwater, Florida.

933   Camp Thunderbird
Quest, Inc.
PO Box 531125
Orlando, FL 32853   407-218-4300
                                     888-807-8378
                               FAX: 407-218-4301
                               contact@questinc.org
                  www.questinc.org/quests-camp-thunderbird
John Gill, President & Chief Executive Officer
Brooke Eakins, Chief Operating Officer
Todd Thrasher, Chief Financial Officer
A program of Quest, Inc. Camp Thunderbird provides recreational programs for children and adults with developmental disabilities. The camp has six-day overnight sessions with age specific programming. Activities include sports, games, arts and performance, and nature studies.

934   Center Academy at Pinellas Park
6710 86th Ave. N
Pinellas Park, FL 33782   727-541-5716
                               FAX: 727-544-8186
                               infopp@centeracademy.com
                               www.centeracademy.com
Mack R. Hicks, Founder & Chair
Andrew P. Hicks, Chief Executive Officer & Clinical Director
Eric V. Larson, President & Chief Operating Officer
Specifically designed for the learning disabled child and other children with difficulties in concentration, strategy, social skills, impulsivity, distractibility and study strategies. Programs offered include attention training, visual-motor remediation, socialization skills training, relaxation training, and more.

935   Dr. Moises Simpser VACC Camp
Nicklaus Children's Hospital
3200 SW 62nd Ave.
Suite 203
Miami, FL 33155-4076   305-662-8222
                               FAX: 786-268-1765
                               bela.florentin@mch.com
                               www.vacccamp.com
Bela Florentin, Camp Coordinator
Tania Diaz, Camp Clinical Coordinator
VACC Camp is a week-long overnight camp program for ventilation-assisted children and their families. The program includes sailing, swimming, field trips to local attractions, campsite entertainment, structured games, free play, and more. Parents have formal and informal opportunities to network among themselves.

936   Dream Oaks Camp
Foundation For Dreams, Inc.
16110 Dream Oaks Pl.
Bradenton, FL 34212   941-746-5659
                               www.foundationfordreams.org
Elena Cassella, Executive Director
AnnaMaria Carleton, Director, Children Services
Lauralie Benge, Office Manager
Dream Oaks Camp offers weekend, summer day, summer residential, and specialty camps for children ages 7-17 with special needs and chronic illnesses. The camp is a program of the Foundation for Dreams with a 3:1 staff to camper ratio. Activities include horseback riding, nature programs, sports, games, swimming, talent shows, and arts and crafts.

937   Easterseals Camp Challenge
Easterseals Florida
2010 Crosby Way
Winter Park, FL 32792   407-629-7881
                               www.easterseals.com/florida
Susan Ventura, President & CEO
Rob Porcarco, Chief Operating Officer
Rikesha Blake, Chief Financial Officer
Located in Sorrento, Florida, Easterseals Camp Challenge provides camp opportunities for children and adults with cognitive and physical disabilities.

938   Florida Diabetes Camp
Florida Camp for Children & Youth with Diabetes
PO Box 14136
Gainesville, FL 32604-2136   352-334-1321
                               FAX: 352-334-1326
                               fccydd@floridadiabetescamp.org
                               www.floridadiabetescamp.org
Gary Cornwell, Executive Director
Chris Stakely, Assistant Director
Janet Silverstein, Medical Director
The Florida Diabetes Camp offers weekend and summer camps for children with type 1 diabetes. The camp combines traditional camp activities and diabetes related educational sessions for campers in order to provide a fun and safe environment.

939   Hand Camp
Hands to Love
3450 Hull Rd., Suite 3341
PO Box 140572
Gainesville, FL 32614-0572   352-273-7382
                               FAX: 352-273-7388
                               info@handstolove.org
                               www.handstolove.org
John Hosman, President
Sean Branch, Vice President
Brian Caslow, Treasurer
A program of Hands to Love, an organization for children and the families of children with upper limb differences, Hand Camp is an annual event held in Starke, Florida at Camp Crystal Lake. Hand Camp offers camp activities, networking and support groups, and special guests.

940   Kris' Camp
Kris' Camp/Therapy Intensive Programs, Inc.
1132 Green Hill Trace
Tallahassee, FL 32317   850-445-4821
                               kberger62@gmail.com
                               www.kriscamp.org
Kathy Berger, Director
Kris' Camp provides programs for children with autism and special needs. The camp offers therapy programs led by art, education, music, occupational, physical, and speech therapists.

941   Sertoma Camp Endeavor
1300 Camp Endeavor Blvd.
Dundee, FL 33838   352-422-3435
                               campendeavorceo@gmail.com
                               www.campendeavorfl.org
Maureen Tambasco, Camp CEO
Scott Botelho, Camp Assistant Director
Sertoma Camp Endeavor provides camp programs for deaf and hard of hearing youth. Programs are designed to promote social and personal growth, environmental awareness, and independence.

Georgia

942   Aerie Experiences
GA   404-285-0467
                               mdweneta@aerieexperiences.com
                               aerieexperiences.com
Matthew Weneta, Owner & Director
Located north of Atlanta, Georgia with summer camp expeditions taking place in Georgia, North Carolina, and Tennessee, Aerie Experiences provides programs for children, families and individuals with special needs. Aerie Experiences is focused on those affected by Aspergers, High Functioning Autism, Learning Disabilities, ADHD, and Neurobiological Disorders.

943   Camp Breathe Easy
American Lung Association
2452 Spring Rd. SE
Smyrna, GA 30080
Operated by the Georgia Chapter of American Lung Association, Camp Breathe Easy is a summer camp program for children ages 6-13 with asthma. Campers are able to participate in a wide variety of camp experiences such as swimming, fishing, archery, and canoeing, with asthma education incorporated into the program. Camp Breathe Easy is held at Camp Twin Lakes in Rutledge, GA.

944 Camp Caglewood
Caglewood, Inc.
5182 Glen Forrest Dr.
Flowery Branch, GA 30542   info@caglewood.org
                                  www.caglewood.org
Paul Freeman, Co-Founder
Jessica Freeman, Co-Founder
A special needs camping program, Camp Caglewood provides active weekend programs for children and adults with developmental disabilities.

945 Camp Dream
Camp Dream Foundation
4355 Cobb Pkwy.
Suite J117
Atlanta, GA 30339   678-367-0040
                                  info@campdreamga.org
                                  www.campdreamga.org
Gary Marshall, Executive Director
Hunter Steng, Operations Director
Amy Blankenship, Medical Director
Camp Dream provides recreational camp programs, Summer Camp and Camp Out, for children and young adults with physical and developmental disabilities.

946 Camp Firefly
The Firefly Foundation
5737 Kanan Rd.
Suite 180
Agoura Hills, CA 91301   campfirefly89@gmail.com
                                  www.campfirefly.com
Camp Firefly offers a week-long camping experience for terminally and seriously ill children and their families. Camp Firefly is held in Georgia.

947 Camp Hawkins
GA Baptist Children's Homes & Family Ministries
800 Rudeseal Rd.
Mount Airy, GA 30563   770-463-3800
                                  georgiachildren.org/camp-hawkins
Kenneth Z. Thompson, President & CEO
Camp Hawkins is a residential summer camp for youth ages 8-21 with developmental disabilities, learning disorders, traumatic brain injury or other special needs. Activities include swimming, canoeing, arts and crafts, games, and Bible study. The camp has locations in Baxley, GA and Mt. Airy, GA.

948 Camp Independence
Camp Twin Lakes
1391 Keencheefoonee Rd.
Rutledge, GA 30663   404-785-0631
                                  campindependence@choa.org
                                  www.choa.org/camps/camp-independence
Donna Hyland, President & CEO, Children's Healthcare of Atlanta
Camp Independence is an overnight, week-long summer camp for children and teens ages 8-18 who have kidney disease, are on dialysis, or have received an organ transplant.

949 Camp Juliena
Georgia Center of the Deaf and Hard of Hearing
2296 Henderson Mill Rd.
Suite 115
Atlanta, GA 30345   404-381-8447
                                  888-297-9461
                                  FAX: 404-297-9465
                                  info@gcdhh.org
                                  www.gcdhh.org/camp-juliena
Jimmy Peterson, Executive Director
Andrea Alston, Coordinator, Community Outreach
A week-long residential summer camp for deaf or hard of hearing youth. Activities help campers develop leadership, team-building, social, and communication skills.

950 Camp Kudzu
Camp Kudzu, Inc.
5885 Glenridge Dr.
Suite 160
Atlanta, GA 30328   833-995-8398
                                  info@campkudzu.org
                                  www.campkudzu.org
Robert G. Shaw, Executive Director
Danielle Holmes, Senior Development Coordinator
Carrie Claiborne, Medical Coordinator
Camp Kudzu is a nonprofit organization, offering overnight summer camp, day camp, family camps, and teen programs for individuals and the families of individuals with type 1 diabetes. Programs are held at various locations across Georgia and provide campers with traditional camp experiences and diabetes education.

951 Camp Sunshine
1850 Clairmont Rd.
Decatur, GA 30033   404-325-7979
                                  866-786-2267
                                  FAX: 404-325-7929
                                  info@mycampsunshine.com
                                  www.mycampsunshine.com
Sally Hale, Executive Director
Tenise Newberg, Program Director
Ann Baker, Program Director
Camp Sunshine provides recreational, educational, support, and camp programs for children with cancer and their families.

952 Camp Twin Lakes
1100 Spring St.
Suite 406
Atlanta, GA 30309   404-231-9887
                                  FAX: 404-577-8854
                                  camps@camptwinlakes.org
                                  www.camptwinlakes.org
Jill Morrisey, Chief Executive Officer
Daniel C. Mathews, Chief Operations Officer
Cheryl Belair, Chief Development Officer
Camp Twin Lakes provides fully accessible, year round camp programs for children with serious illnesses, disabilities, and other life challenges. Camp Twin Lakes has locations in Rutledge and Winder, Georgia.

953 Camp Twin Lakes: Rutledge
1391 Keencheefoonee Rd.
Rutledge, GA 30663   706-557-9070
                                  FAX: 706-557-9147
                                  camps@camptwinlakes.org
                                  www.camptwinlakes.org
Jill Morrisey, Chief Executive Officer
Daniel C. Mathews, Chief Operations Officer
Cheryl Belair, Chief Development Officer
A location of Camp Twin Lakes, which offers camp programs for children with serious illnesses, disabilities, and other life challenges. The Rutledge campus is fully accessible and includes a pool, ropes course, farm, and paddleboat activities.

954 Camp Twin Lakes: Will-A-Way
210 S Broad St.
Unit 5
Winder, GA 30680   770-867-6123
                                  FAX: 770-867-6130
                                  camps@camptwinlakes.org
                                  www.camptwinlakes.org
Jill Morrisey, Chief Executive Officer
Daniel C. Mathews, Chief Operations Officer
Cheryl Belair, Chief Development Officer
A location of Camp Twin Lakes, which offers camp programs for children with serious illnesses, disabilities, and other life challenges. The Will-A-Way campus is fully accessible and includes a gymnasium, ropes course, zip line, rock wall, outdoor ampitheater, beachfront, and equestrian program.

955 Squirrel Hollow Summer Camp
The Bedford School
5665 Milam Rd.
Fairburn, GA 30213   770-774-8001
                                FAX: 770-774-8005
                                info@thebedfordschool.org
                                www.thebedfordschool.org

Betsy Box, Admissions Director
Jeff James, Head of School
Allison Day, Associate Head of School

A program of The Bedford School, Squirrel Hollow Summer Camp offers summer sessions for students with academic needs due to a learning disability. Students receive academic instruction in reading, writing, and math through a variety of teaching techniques, with students grouped by age and skill level. The camp also incorporates recreational activities such as swimming, games, and a challenge course.

Hawaii

956 Camp Anuenue
Honolulu, HI   808-349-7325
                                campanuenue@gmail.com
                                www.campanuenue.com

B.K. Cannon, President & Director
Alison James, Vice President & Director
Des Medeiros, Medical Director

Camp Anuenue is a nonprofit organization that offers a week long camping experience for children ages 7-18 who have or have had cancer. The camp is held at Camp Mokule'ia on the North Shore of Oahu and accepts children from Hawaii and US territories in the Pacific including Guam, Saipan, Samoa, and Marshall Islands.

957 Camp Taylor: Family Camp
Camp Taylor, Inc.
Hilton Hawaiian Village
2005 Kalia Road
Honolulu, HI 96815   209-545-3853
                                camp@kidsheartcamp.org
                                www.kidsheartcamp.org/familycamphi
Kimberlie Gamino, Founder & Executive Director

A program of Camp Taylor, Family Camp is for children of all ages, with congenital heart disease and/or acquired heart disease, and their family including parents and siblings. The camp offers parental heart education and support programs for parents and siblings. The camp is held at the Hilton Hawaiian Village and is open to families from all of the Hawaiian Islands.

Idaho

958 Camp Hodia
Idaho Diabetes Youth Programs, Inc.
5439 W Kendall St.
Boise, ID 83706   208-891-1023
                                info@hodia.org
                                www.hodia.org
Lisa Gier, Executive Director
Morgan Coenen, Director, Programs
Ciera Miller, Director, Marketing

Camp Hodia offers a variety of educational camp programs for children and teens with type 1 diabetes.

959 Camp No Limits Idaho
No Limits Foundation
Camp Cross Marine Rt.
Coeur d'Alene, ID 83814   207-569-6411
                                campnolimits@gmail.com
                                www.nolimitsfoundation.org
Mary Leighton, Founder & Executive Director
Kelsey Moody, Program Operations Manager
Alix Sandler, Marketing & Development Director

Camp No Limits Idaho, a location of Camp No Limits, is a recreational and educational camp for youth who have experienced limb loss. Camp No Limits, is a program of the nonprofit organization No Limits Foundation. The camp is held at Camp Cross on

Lake Coeur d'Alene. Unavailable in 2022 due to COVID-19 restrictions.

960 Camp Rainbow Gold
216 W Jefferson St.
Boise, ID 83702   208-350-6435
                                info@camprainbowgold.org
                                www.camprainbowgold.org

Elizabeth Lizberg, Executive Director
Tracy Bryan, Program Director
Christl Holzl, Development Director

Camp Rainbow Gold is a independent, nonprofit organization providing year round camp programs, support groups, and scholarships for children, siblings, and the family of children who have been diagnosed with cancer. All camp programs are offered free of charge, with campers participating in activities such as fishing, hiking, campfires, and crafts. The camp is held in the Sawtooth National Forest.

961 Cristo Vive International: Idaho Camp
139 McLean Lane
Kooskia, ID 83539   208-507-1241
                                www.cristovive.net
Carol McLean, Camp Coordinator

Christian camp with programming for individuals who are blind/deaf, physically or mentally challenged, have multiple disabilities, Down Syndrome, Autism/Asperger's, ADHD/ADD, Cerebral Palsy, and their families and siblings.

Illinois

962 ADA Camp GranADA
American Diabetes Association
55 E Monroe St.
Suite 3420
Chicago, IL 60603   312-346-1805
                                illinoiscamps@diabetes.org
                                www.diabetes.org

Camp GranADA is an American Diabetes Association resident camp located in Monticello, Illinois at the 4H Memorial Campground. For children with diabetes, ages 8-16.

963 ADA Teen Adventure Camp
American Diabetes Association
55 E Monroe St.
Suite 3420
Chicago, IL 60603   312-346-1805
                                illinoiscamps@diabetes.org
                                www.diabetes.org

Paula Williams, Contact

Camping for teenagers with diabetes. Coed, ages 14 to 17. Camp dates are early in August. Located at the YMCA Camp Duncan in Ingleside, Illinois. Featured activities include archery, boating, roller skating, ropes course, and swimming.

964 ADA Triangle D Camp
American Diabetes Association
55 E Monroe St.
Suite 3420
Chicago, IL 60603   312-346-1805
                                illinoiscamps@diabetes.org
                                www.diabetes.org

Triangle D Camp is a resident camp program for children with diabetes. A coed camp for participants aged 9-13 years old, with swimming, row boating, canoeing, ropes course, camp games, archery, soccer, basketball, volleyball, and diabetes education as the camp's featured activities. The camp is held at YMCA Camp Duncan in Ingleside, Illinois.

965 Camp "I Am Me"
Illinois Fire Safety Alliance
426 W Northwest Hwy.
Mount Prospect, IL 60056   847-390-0911
                                FAX: 847-390-0920
                                ifsa@ifsa.org
                                www.ifsa.org/programs/camp

Philip Zaleski, Executive Director
Riley Anderson, Program Coordinator
Jenny Tzortzos, Community Outreach Coordinator

Camp I Am Me is a one-week summer camp for children and teens who have experienced burn injuries. The camp is held in Ingleside, Illinois at YMCA Camp Duncan. Activities include archery, games, canoes, kayaks, sailboats, campfires, fishing, ropes course, swimming, and specialized workshops related to burn injuries.

966 Camp Callahan
Camp Callahan, Inc.
PO Box 5253
Quincy, IL 62305   217-883-0137
                                          www.campcallahan.com
Peg Ratliff, Camp Director
Brandy Schlieper, Program Director
Camp Callahan is dedicated to providing a camp experience for youth with disabilities. The camp is held at Saukenauk Scout Reservation.

967 Camp Discovery
American Academy of Dermatology
PO Box 1968
Des Plaines, IL 60017   847-240-1280
                                          866-503-7546
                                          888-462-3376
                                     FAX: 847-240-1859
                                          www.campdiscovery.org
A program of the American Academy of Dermatology, Camp Discovery is a camp held in 5 locations across the United States for children with chronic skin conditions. Campers can participate in activities such as fishing, swimming, archery and horseback riding.
1993

968 Camp FRIENDship
Easterseals Chicagoland & Greater Rockford
1939 W 13th St.
Suite 300
Chicago, IL 60608-1226   312-491-4110
                                     FAX: 312-733-0247
                                          ddohoney@easterealschicago.org
                                          www.easterseals.com/chicago
Sara Ray Stoelinga, President & CEO
Sarah J. Boburka, Executive Vice President & CFO
Rebecca Clark, Vice President, Disability Services
A program of Easterseals, Camp FRIENDship is a summer camp program designed to help children ages 5-14 with autism, nonverbal learning disabilities, and intellectual disabilities. The camp promotes the acquiring of social skills in a safe and fun learning environment.

969 Camp Little Giant
Touch of Nature Environmental Center
Southern Illinois University
Mail Code 6888
Carbondale, IL 62901   618-453-3950
                                     FAX: 618-453-1188
                                          jcave@siu.edu
                                          www.ton.siu.edu
Jasmine Cave, Director
A program of the Southern Illinois University and held at the Touch of Nature Environmental Center, Camp Little Giant is a residential camp offering camping opportunities for people with physical, cognitive and developmental disabilities.

970 Camp New Hope
PO Box 764
Mattoon, IL 61938   217-895-2341
                                     FAX: 217-895-3658
                                          officemanager@campnewhopeillinois.org
                                          campnewhopeillinois.org
Paul Semple, Office Manager
Pat Crum, Site Coordinator
Camp New Hope is a year round recreational experience for individuals 8 and up with developmental and physical disabilities. The camp offers summer, weekend respite, and bowling programs. Camp New Hope is situated on 41 acres of land on Lake Mattoon.

971 Camp One Step
Children's Oncology Services Inc.
213 W Institute Pl.
Suite 410
Chicago, IL 60610   312-924-4220
                                     FAX: 312-878-7374
                                          info@camponestep.org
                                          www.camponestep.org
Jeff Infusino, President
Darryl Winston Perkins, Jr., Chief Programs Officer
Katie Weil, Vice President, Philanthropy
Camp One Step provides 11 different year round camp programs for children and teens ages 7-19 who have been diagnosed with cancer. Camp One Step is open to children and families who live in Illinois, Wisconsin, and the Midwest.

972 Camp Quality Illinois
PO Box 641
Lansing, IL 60438   708-895-8311
                                          illinois@campqualityusa.org
                                          www.campqualityusa.org/il
Mary Lockton, Executive Director
Dawn Winters, Treasurer
Camp Quality is an international camping program for children with cancer. The Illinois Camp Quality is held in Frankfort, Illinois at Camp Manitoqua & Retreat Center and offers children and their siblings summer camps and year round support programs. Volunteer doctors and nurses are at the camp 24 hours a day, and there is a 1:1 staff to camper ratio.

973 Camp Red Leaf
26710 W Nippersink Rd.
Ingleside, IL 60041   847-740-5010
                                     FAX: 847-740-5014
                                          www.campredleaf.org
Ari Strulowitz, Executive Director
Angela McNeal, Camp Director
Tyesha Smith, Business Manager
Camp Red Leaf provides camp programs for individuals ages 9 and up with developmental disabilities. Programs include youth day and overnight as well as adult overnight and travel camp sessions.

974 Illinois Wheelchair Sport Camps
University of Illinois
1207 S Oak St.
Champaign, IL 61820   217-333-1970
                                     FAX: 217-244-0014
                                          sportscamp@illinois.edu
                                          www.disability.illinois.edu/camps
Illinois Wheelchair Sport Camps is hosted at the University of Illinois and offers a variety of summer resident wheelchair sport programs such as track, basketball, and individual skills camps.

975 MDA Summer Camp
Muscular Dystrophy Association National Office
161 N Clark
Suite 3550
Chicago, IL 60601   800-572-1717
                                          resourcecenter@mdausa.org
                                          mda.org/summer-camp
Donald S. Wood, President & Chief Executive Officer
Jeremy Kraut-Ordover, Chief Development Officer
Sharon Hesterlee, Chief Research Officer
MDA Summer Camp is a program of the Muscular Dystrophy Association providing a one-week summer camp for children with muscular dystrophy and related muscle-debilitating diseases.

976 Nothern Suburban Special Recreation Association Day Camps
3105 MacArthur Blvd.
Northbrook, IL 60062   847-509-9400
                                     FAX: 847-509-1177
                                          TTY:711
                                          info@nssra.org
                                          www.nssra.org/programs/camps
Blair Hill, Recreation Manager, Camps
The Northern Suburban Special Recreation Association (NSSRA) offers year round day camps for children and youth with disabilities.

977 Rimland Services for Autistic Citizens
1265 Hartrey Ave.
Evanston, IL 60202
847-328-4090
FAX: 847-328-8364
TTY:847-328-4090
www.rimland.org

Lorraine Ganz, President
Barbara Cooper, Secretary
Services include residential living, community day services, and health and wellness programs.

978 Shady Oaks Camp
16300 Parker Rd.
Homer Glen, IL 60491
708-301-0816
FAX: 708-301-5091
soc16300@sbcglobal.net
www.shadyoakscamp.org

Scott Steele, Executive Director
Katie Clark, Camp Director
Gary Schaid, Assistant Director
Shady Oaks is a summer camp for people with disabilities. The camp provides a recreational camp experience with a 1:1 camper to staff ratio.

979 Timber Pointe Outdoor Center
Easterseals Central Illinois
Easterseals Central Illinois
Peoria, IL 61603-3201
309-686-1177
FAX: 309-686-7722
www.easterseals.com/ci

Melissa Riddle, President & CEO
Eric Glow, Vice President, Clinical Services
Timber Pointe Outdoor Center (TPOC) is a specialized outdoor recreational center for individuals with disabilities, which is owned and operated by Easterseals Central Illinois and is located on Lake Bloomington. TPOC offers year round programs, including summer and day camps, in a completely accessible environment.

Indiana

980 Anderson Woods
4630 Adyeville Rd.
Bristow, IN 47515
812-639-1079
andersonwoods@psci.net
www.andersonwoods.org

Isaac Gatwood, Executive Co-Director
Megan Gatwood, Executive Co-Director
Anderson Woods is a private, nonprofit organization providing summer camp experiences for children and adults with special needs. The camp typically runs in June and July.

981 CHAMP Camp
494 S Emerson Ave.
Suite H-1
Greenwood, IN 46143
317-679-1860
FAX: 317-245-2291
brittany@champcamp.org
www.champcamp.org

Brittany Sichting, Contact
Emily Miller, Contact
CHAMP Camp is a one week summer camp experience for children and youth ages 6-18 who have tracheostomies or require respiratory assistance. The camp is held at Bradford Woods in Martinsville, Indiana, and activities include fishing, boating, canoeing, arts, swimming, and a 50 foot alpine tower climb.

982 Camp About Face
Riley Hospital For Children, Indiana Univ. Health
705 Riley Hospital Dr.
Indianapolis, IN 46202
317-944-5000
rileychildrens.org/support-services
Camp About Face is a one week summer program designed to benefit children and youth ages 8-18 with craniofacial anomalies. Camping activities include swimming, nature projects and camp outs that are supplemented by social work, medical support and educational sessions which help to build self-esteem and self-confidence.

983 Camp Brave Eagle
Indiana Hemophilia & Thrombosis Center
8326 Naab Rd.
Indianapolis, IN 46260
317-871-0000
www.campbraveeagle.org

Jennifer Maahs, Camp Director
Camp Brave Eagle is a summer camp for children and the siblings of children with bleeding disorders living in the state of Indiana. The camp is supervised by experienced medical staff.

984 Camp John Warvel
American Diabetes Association
8604 Allisonville Rd.
Suite 140
Indianapolis, IN 46250
317-352-9226
campsupport@diabetes.org
www.diabetes.org

A program of the American Diabetes Association, Camp John Warvel is a summer camp program for children with type 1 diabetes. The camp is designed to promote independence, confidence, and a healthy lifestyle through education, nutrition, and exercise. There is a 4:1 camper to staff ratio. The camp is held at Camp Crosley in North Webster, Indiana.

985 Camp Little Red Door
Little Red Door Cancer Agency
1801 N Meridian St.
Indianapolis, IN 46202-1411
317-925-5595
FAX: 317-925-5597
camp@littlereddoor.org
www.littlereddoor.org

Fred Duncan, Director & CEO
Mandy Pietrykowski, Chief Advancement Officer
Steve Williams, Chief Financial Officer
Camp Little Red Door is a one week summer camp for children and teens who have or have had cancer. The camp is held at Bradford Woods in Martinsville, Indiana with campers participating in traditional camp activities.

986 Camp Millhouse
25600 Kelly Rd.
South Bend, IN 46614
574-233-2202
FAX: 574-233-2511
campmillhouse@gmail.com
www.campmillhouse.org

Diana Breden, Executive Director
Melissa Swank, Camp Director
Camp Millhouse is a residential summer camp for children and adults with varying disabilities. Ages of campers range from 7 to 75+. The camp offers six week-long summer sessions as well as spring and fall weekend sessions. Activities include arts and crafts, swimming, ropes course, and sports. The camp offers low camper to staff ratios and 24-hour supervision and nursing staff.

987 Camp PossAbility
Camp PossAbility, Inc.
PO Box 370
Huntertown, IN 46748
260-341-5732
info@camppossability.org
www.camppossability.org

Sam Albro, President
Lauren E. Harmison, Founder & Vice President
Camp PossAbility is a one-week summer camp for young adults ages 18-40 with a traumatic spinal cord injury. The camp is held at Bradford Woods in Martinsville, Indiana.

988 Camp Quality Kentuckiana
PO Box 35474
Louisville, KY 40232
502-507-3235
kentuckiana@campqualityusa.org
www.campqualityusa.org/ki

Eddie Bobbitt, Executive Director
Charlie Obranowicz, Camp Director
Heather Barry, Camper Coordinator
Camp Quality is an international camping program for children with cancer. Camp Quality Kentuckiana, serves Kentucky and Indiana and offers children and their siblings summer camps and year round support programs. Volunteer doctors and nurses are at the camp 24 hours a day, and there is a 1:1 staff to camper ratio.

989 Camp Red Cedar
3900 Hursh Rd.
Fort Wayne, IN 46845
                                    260-637-3608
                          FAX: 260-637-5483
                          redcedar@campredcedar.com
                          www.campredcedar.com

Carrie Perry, Director
Shelly Detcher, Assistant Director
Theresa Prentice, Facilities Manager
Camp Red Cedar is open to children and adults with or without
disabilities. The camp offers summer residental and summer day
camps along with year round theraputic and conventional horseback riding. Other activities include fishing, hiking, swimming,
and arts and crafts.

990 Camp Riley
Riley's Children Foundation
30 S Meridian St.
Suite 200
Indianapolis, IN 46204-3509   317-634-4474
                                          877-867-4539
                          FAX: 317-634-4478
                          riley@rileykids.org
                          www.rileykids.org/about/camp-riley
Elizabeth Elkas, President & CEO
Meghan Miller, Chief Operations Officer
Karen Spataro, Chief Communications Officer
Camp Riley is an annual summer camp program for children and
teens ages 8-18 with physical disabilities. The program offers
camp activities in a safe and accessible environment. The camp is
held at Bradford Woods in Martinsville, Indiana.

991 Happiness Bag
Happiness Bag, Inc.
3833 Union Rd.
Terre Haute, IN 47802   812-234-8867
                          FAX: 812-238-0728
                          info@happinessbag.org
                          www.happinessbag.org
Happiness Bag provides adaptive education and recreational services, including summer day camps and respite care programs,
for children and adults with disabilities.

992 Hillcroft Services
501 W Air Park Dr.
Muncie, IN 47303   765-284-4166
                          www.hillcroft.org

Debbie Bennett, President & CEO
Abby Halstead, Chief Financial Officer
Jessica Hammett, Chief Operations Officer
Offers a summer camp program for children with autism spectrum
disorders.

993 Hoosier Burn Camp
PO Box 233
Battle Ground, IN 47920   765-567-0115
                          FAX: 765-567-0195
                          info@hoosierburncamp.org
                          www.hoosierburncamp.org
Mark Koopman, Executive Director
Abby James, Program Manager
Valerie McCain, Administrative Assistant
Hossier Burn Camp is nonprofit organization that provides an an-
nual summer camp and monthly events for children and teens
ages 8-18 who have suffered a burn injury. The camp is held at
Camp Tecumseh in Brookston, Indiana.

994 Indiana Deaf Camp
1434 S Wausau St.
Warsaw, IN 46580   260-602-6758
                          FAX: 317-844-1034
                          TTY:574-306-4063
                          info@indeafcamps.org
                          www.indeafcamps.org

Barbara Stenacker, Executive Director
Curtis Sigafoose, Director
Indiana Deaf Camp is for children ages 4-17 who have hearing
loss or are related to individuals with hearing loss.

Iowa

995 Camp Albrecht Acres
14837 Sherrill Rd.
PO Box 50
Sherrill, IA 52073   563-552-1771
                          FAX: 563-552-2732
                          office@albrechtacres.org
                          www.albrechtacres.org

Eric Veltstra, Executive Director
Cassi Banwarth, Director, Programming
Camp Albrecht Acres is a nonprofit organization offering a residential summer camp program for children and adults with special needs.

996 Camp Courageous of Iowa
12007 190th St.
PO Box 418
Monticello, IA 52310-0418   319-465-5916
                          FAX: 319-465-5919
                          info@campcourageous.org
                          www.campcourageous.org

Charlie Becker, Chief Executive Officer
A year round residential and respite care facility for individuals
with special needs and their families. Campers range in age from
1-105 years old. Activities include traditional activities like canoeing, hiking, swimming, and crafts, plus adventure activities
like caving and rock climbing.

997 Camp Hertko Hollow
4200 University Ave.
Suite 320
Des Moines, IA 50266   515-471-8523
                                          855-502-8500
                          FAX: 515-288-2531
                          www.camphertkohollow.com
Jessica Thornton, Executive Director
Deb Holwegner, Camp Director
Camp Hertko Hollow is an educational and recreational summer
camp program for children and teens ages 6-17 with diabetes.
Campers participate in traditional camp activities and learn about
living with diabetes.

998 Camp Sunnyside
Easterseals Iowa
401 NE 66th Ave.
Des Moines, IA 50313   515-289-1933
                          FAX: 515-289-4069
                          campandrespite@eastersealsia.org
                          www.easterseals.com/ia

Sherri Nielsen, President & CEO
Margaret Ingram, Chief Financial Officer
Allison Piazza, Chief Development Officer
Open to campers age 4 and up, with or without disabilities, Camp
Sunnyside is owned and operated by Easterseals Iowa and offers
week and day summer camps.

999 Camp Tanager
Tanager Place
1614 W Mount Vernon Rd.
Mount Vernon, IA 52314   319-363-0681
                          FAX: 319-365-6411
                          campmail@tanagerplace.org
                          www.camptanager.org
Donald Pirrie, Camp Director
Camp Tanager offers a wide variety of programs, including medical camps in partnership with local Iowa hospitals. The week long
medical programs are for children and teens ages 5-17 with
chronic illnesses and disabilities such as hemophilia, diabetes
and Tourette's syndrome.

Kansas

1000 Camp Discovery Kansas
American Diabetes Association
608 W Douglas Ave.
Wichita, KS 67203   316-684-6091
                                     campsupport@diabetes.org
                                     www.diabetes.org

Lora Furstner, Contact
A program of the American Diabetes Association, Camp Discovery· Kansas is for children and teens ages 8-16 with diabetes. Campers participate in traditional camp activities while receiving educational information on diabetes. The camp is held at Rock Springs 4-H Center in Junction City, Kansas.

1001 Camp Planet D
American Diabetes Association
608 W Douglas Ave.
Wichita, KS 67203   316-684-6091
                                     campsupport@diabetes.org
                                     www.diabetes.org

Lora Furstner, Contact
A program of the American Diabetes Association, Camp Planet D is for children and teens ages 7-15 with diabetes. Campers participate in traditional camp activities while receiving educational information on diabetes. The camp is held at the Tall Oaks Conference Center in Linwood, Kansas.

1002 Camp Quality Kansas
11802 W. Pine
Wichita, KS 67278   316-304-3865
                                     kansas@campqualityusa.org
                                     www.campqualityusa.org/ks

Kandi LaMar, Executive Director
Brittney Reed, Psychosocial Coordinator & Personnel Chair
Camp Quality is an international camping program for children with cancer. Camp Quality Kansas offers children and their siblings summer camps and year round support programs. Volunteer doctors and nurses are at the camp 24 hours a day, and there is a 1:1 staff to camper ratio.

1003 Camp Sweet Betes
American Diabetes Association
608 W Douglas Ave.
Wichita, KS 67203   316-684-6091
                                     campsupport@diabetes.org
                                     www.diabetes.org

Lora Furstner, Contact
A program of the American Diabetes Association, Camp Sweet Betes is a day camp for children ages 5-8 with diabetes. Campers learn techniques for managing nutrition, exercise, and medication. The camp is held at Trinity Presbyterian Church in Wichita, Kansas.

Kentucky

1004 Camp Quality Kentuckiana
PO Box 35474
Louisville, KY 40232   502-507-3235
                                     kentuckiana@campqualityusa.org
                                     www.campqualityusa.org/ki

Eddie Bobbitt, Executive Director
Charlie Obranowicz, Camp Director
Heather Barry, Camper Coordinator
Camp Quality is an international camping program for children with cancer. Camp Quality Kentuckiana, serves Kentucky and Indiana and offers children and their siblings summer camps and year round support programs. Volunteer doctors and nurses are at the camp 24 hours a day, and there is a 1:1 staff to camper ratio.

1005 Kids Cancer Alliance
611 W Main St., Suite 300
PO Box 24337
Louisville, KY 40224   502-365-1538
                                     info@kidscanceralliance.org
                                     www.kidscanceralliance.org

Shelby Russell, Executive Director
Leah McComb, Program Director
Brandon Padgett, Program Coordinator
The Kids Cancer Alliance is a nonprofit organization that provides summer camps and support programs for children and the families of children with cancer. Camp programs include oncology and sibling camps, as well as teen and and family retreats.

1006 Lions Camp Crescendo
1480 Pine Tavern Rd.
PO Box 607
Lebanon Junction, KY 40150   502-264-0120
                                     wibblesb@aol.com
                                     www.lccky.org

Billie J. Flannery, Administrator
Organization dedicated to enhancing quality of life for youths, including those with disabilities, through the delivery of a traditional camping experience.

1007 The Center for Courageous Kids
1501 Burnley Rd.
Scottsville, KY 42164   270-618-2900
                                     FAX: 270-618-2902
                                     info@courageouskids.org
                                     www.courageouskids.org

Joanie O'Bryan, President & CEO
Clint Cobb, Chief Operations Officer
Allysa Gooden, Director, Development
The Center for Courageous Kids is a year round medical camp for children who have chronic or life-threatening illnesses. Offers week-long summer camp sessions and family retreat weekend sessions.

Louisiana

1008 Camp Bon Coeur
300 Ridge Rd.
Suite K
Lafayette, LA 70506   337-233-8437
                                     FAX: 337-233-4160
                                     info@heartcamp.com
                                     www.heartcamp.com

Susannah Craig, Executive Director
Chelsea Doyle, Summer Program Coordinator
Jessica Becnel, Family Support Group Coordinator
Camp Bon Coeur is a nonprofit organization offering summer camp sessions for children with congenital heart defects. Also offers weekend family camps, monthly support groups, and outings for individuals with heart defects and their families.

1009 Camp Challenge
PO Box 10591
New Orleans, LA 70181   504-347-2267
                                     FAX: 866-295-3803
                                     campdirector@campchallenge.org
                                     www.campchallenge.org

Cathy Allain, Camp Director
R. Tony Ricard, Assistant Camp Director
Camp Challenge is a nonprofit organization offering a week long summer camp for young hematology and oncology patients, including children who have or have had cancer or sickle cell disorders. The camp has an on-site medical team available 24 hours a day. It is held at Louisiana Lions Camp in Leesville, Louisiana.

1010 Camp Pelican
PO Box 10235
New Orleans, LA 70181   888-617-1118
                                     FAX: 866-295-3803
                                     camppelican@gmail.com
                                     www.camppelican.org

A joint venture between the Louisiana Pulmonary Disease Camp, Inc. and the Louisiana Lions League for Crippled Children, Camp Pelican is a week long overnight summer camp for children with pulmonary disorders, including severe asthma and cystic fibrosis, living in the state of Louisiana.

1011 Camp Quality Louisiana
1800 Forsythe Ave.
Suite 2, Box 307
Monroe, LA 71201   315-547-4319
                                    louisiana@campqualityusa.org
                                    www.campqualityusa.org/la

Alan Barth, Executive Director
Gay Nell Barth, Camp Director
Monica Mock, Activities Coordinator
Camp Quality is an international camping program for children with cancer. The Louisiana Camp is held at Kings Camp in Mer Rouge, Louisiana and offers children and their siblings summer camps and year round camping opportunities. Volunteer doctors and nurses are at the camp 24 hours a day, and there is a 1:1 staff to camper ratio.

1012 Louisiana Lions Camp
292 L. Beauford Dr.
Anacoco, LA 71403   337-239-6567
                                         FAX: 337-239-9975
                                         lalions@lionscamp.org
                                         www.lionscamp.org

Raymond E. Cecil, Executive Director & Camp Director
Owned and operated by the Louisiana Lions League, Inc. the Louisiana Lions Camp is a no cost residential summer camp for children with intellectual and physical disabilities. Campers are able to experience traditional summer camp activities in a medically safe and fun environment. The Camp is also host to the American Diabetes Association, Camp Victory, and Camp Pelican.

1013 MedCamps of Louisiana
102 Thomas Rd.
Suite 615
West Monroe, LA 71291   318-329-8405
                                         FAX: 318-329-8407
                                         info@medcamps.com
                                         www.medcamps.com

Caleb Seney, Executive Director
Kacie Hobson, Camp Director
MedCamps of Louisiana offers week-long residential summer camp programs for children with chronic illnesses and physical or developmental disabilities. Each week during the summer a different camp is held, specifically designed for a particular disability.

Maine

1014 Camp CaPella
PO Box 552
Holden, ME 04429   207-843-5104
                                         www.campcapella.org

Deb Breindel, Director
Camp CaPella provides recreational and educational opportunities for children and adults with disabilities. The camp is located on Phillips Lake in Dedham, Maine and offers a variety of programs including day camps, overnight camps, family vacation packages, and travel camp.

1015 Camp Lawroweld
288 West Side Rd.
Weld, ME 04285   207-585-2984
                                         bchase@nnec.org
                                         www.camplawroweld.org

Trevor Schlisner, Director
Camp Lawroweld offers several camp programs including a week-long summer camp for individuals who are blind or visually impaired.

1016 Camp No Limits Maine
No Limits Foundation
114 Pine Tree Camp Road
Rome, ME 04963   207-569-6411
                                         campnolimits@gmail.com
                                         www.nolimitsfoundation.org

Mary Leighton, Founder & Executive Director
Kelsey Moody, Program Operations Manager
Alix Sandler, Marketing & Development Director
Camp No Limits Maine, a location of Camp No Limits, is a recreational and educational camp for youth who have experienced limb loss. Camp No Limits is a program of the nonprofit organization No Limits Foundation. The camp is held at Pine Tree Camp in Rome, Maine and is supported by Maine Adaptive Sports & Recreation.

1017 Camp Sunshine
35 Acadia Rd.
Casco, ME 04015   207-655-3800
                                         FAX: 207-655-3825
                                         info@campsunshine.org
                                         www.campsunshine.org

Michael Katz, Executive Director
Maureen McAllister, Director, Operations
Michael Smith, Director, Development
Camp Sunshine is a free, year round camp for children and families of children with cancer, hematologic conditions, renal disease, systemic lupus, and solid organ transplantation. The camp also has bereavement programs for families.

1018 Camp sNOw Maine
No Limits Foundation
15 South Ridge Road
Newry, ME 04261   207-569-6411
                                         campnolimits@gmail.com
                                         www.nolimitsfoundation.org

Mary Leighton, Founder & Executive Director
Kelsey Moody, Program Operations Manager
Alix Sandler, Marketing & Development Director
Camp sNOw Maine is a location of Camp No Limits, a recreational and educational camp for youth who have experienced limb loss. Camp No Limits is a program of the nonprofit organization, No Limits Foundation. Partnered with Maine Adaptive Sports & Recreation, the camp includes winter activities including, skiing and snowboarding. The camp takes place in March. Unavailable in 2022 due to COVID-19 restrictions.

1019 Pine Tree Camp
Pine Tree Society
114 Pine Tree Camp Rd.
Rome, ME 04963   207-386-5990
                                         FAX: 207-397-5324
                                         ptcamp@pinetreesociety.org
                                         www.pinetreesociety.org

Dawn Willard-Robinson, Camp Director
Mary Schafhauser, Assistant Camp Director
Lori Chesley, Coordinator, Camp Relations
Offering day camps, overnight camps, retreats, and specialized programs, Pine Tree Camp provides children and adults with disabilities the opportunity to participate in recreational activities, such as swimming, fishing, kayak, hiking, and boating. The camp is located in North Pond in Rome, Maine.

Maryland

1020 Camp Great Rock
Brainy Camps, Children's National
1 Inventa Pl.
4th Floor West
Silver Spring, MD 20910   202-476-5142
                                brainycamps@childrensnational.org
                                www.brainycamps.com/camps/camp-great-rock
Sandra Cushner-Weinstein, Director, Brainy Camps
Camp Great Rock is a one-week overnight summer camp for children and teens ages 7-17 with epilepsy. Campers participate in a variety of activities and receive educational information regarding epilepsy.

1021 Camp Littlefoot
The Treatment and Learning Centers
2092 Gaither Rd.
Suite 100
Rockville, MD 20850
301-424-5200
FAX: 301-424-8063
info@ttlc.org
www.ttlc.org
Patricia Ritter, Executive Director
Camp Littlefoot offers a variety of programs for children requiring speech-language and/or occupational therapy.

1022 Camp No Limits Maryland
No Limits Foundation
11 Horseshoe Point Lane
North East, MD 21901
207-569-6411
campnolimits@gmail.com
www.nolimitsfoundation.org
Mary Leighton, Founder & Executive Director
Kelsey Moody, Program Operations Manager
Alix Sandler, Marketing & Development Director
Camp No Limits Maryland, a location of Camp No Limits, is a recreational and educational camp for youth who have experienced limb loss. Camp No Limits, is a program of the nonprofit organization No Limits Foundation.

1023 Camp SunSibs
Johns Hopkins Children's Center
1800 Orleans St.
Baltimore, MD 21287
www.hopkinsmedicine.org
Joe Young, Director
A weekend camp for children ages 5-16 who have siblings diagnosed with cancer.

1024 Camp Sunrise
Johns Hopkins Children's Center
1800 Orleans St.
Baltimore, MD 21287
campsunriseappliations@gmail.com
www.hopkinsmedicine.org
Ashley Richards, Camp Director
Lauren Murphy, Camper Coordinator
Camp Sunshine is a week-long summer camp open to children and teens ages 4-18 who are currently being treated for cancer or who have undergone bone marrow transplants at Johns Hopkins Hospital.

1025 Deaf Camps, Inc.
Manidokan Outdoor Ministry Center
1600 Harpers Ferry Rd.
Knoxville, MD 21758
deafcampsinc@gmail.com
deafcampsinc.org
Louise Rollins, President
Erin Krug, Vice President
David Shepard, Secretary
Deaf Camps, Inc. is a volunteer-run nonprofit organization dedicated to providing camp experiences for deaf and hard of hearing children and children learning American Sign Language.

1026 Easterseals Camp Fairlee
Easterseals Delaware & Maryland's Eastern Shore
61 Corporate Circle
New Castle, DE 19720
302-324-4444
fairlee@esdel.org
www.easterseals.com/de
Kenan J. Sklenar, President & CEO
Pamela Reuther, Chief Operating Officer
Easterseals Camp Fairlee provides year-round recreation and respite to children and adults with all types of disabilities. Best known for week long summer camp sessions June-August. Camp Fairlee was rebuilt in 2015 with new cabins, activity, center, health center and dining hall. Activities include, but are not limited to, swimming, wall climbing, zip lining, canoeing, kayaking, arts and crafts, indoor and outdoor games. Accredited by the American Camp Association.

1027 League at Camp Greentop
The League for People with Disabilities, Inc.
1111 E Cold Spring Lane
Baltimore, MD 21239
410-323-0500
info@leagueforpeople.org
www.leagueforpeople.org
David Greenberg, President & CEO
Margy Ryan, Senior Vice President, Finance
Shiketa Jenkins, Vice President, Workforce, Community & Youth Programs
A traditional sleepaway summer camp for youth and adults with disabilities. The League at Camp Greentop is located in Thurmont, Maryland, and has youth and all ages sessions, with campers participating in activities such as swimming, arts and crafts, sports, and games.

1028 Lions Camp Merrick
PO Box 56
Nanjemoy, MD 20662
301-870-5858
FAX: 301-246-9108
info@lionscampmerrick.org
www.lionscampmerrick.org
Heidi A. Fick, Executive Director
Donna Wadsworth, Office Administrator
A recreational camp for children ages 6-16 who are deaf, blind, or have type 1 diabetes. Camp activities include archery, canoeing, ropes courses, swimming, fishing, and games.

Massachusetts

1029 Camp Howe
557 East St.
PO Box 326
Goshen, MA 01032
413-268-7635
FAX: 413-268-8206
office@camphowe.com
www.camphowe.com
Terrie Campbell, Executive Director
Camp Howe provides camp programs for youth ages 7 to 17. The camp's ECHO Program offers one-week and two-week sessions for youth with physical and developmental disabilities.

1030 Camp Jabberwocky
200 Greenwood Ave. Ext.
PO Box 1357
Vineyard Haven, MA 02568
508-693-2339
info@campjabberwocky.org
www.campjabberwocky.org
Liza Gallagher, Executive Director
Kelsey Grousbeck, Director, Outreach
Camp Jabberwocky offers summer camp and family camp programs for individuals with physical and intellectual disabilities. The camp is located in Martha's Vineyard with campers usually staying between 1 and 4 weeks. Camp activities include day trips, horseback riding, barbecues, boating, biking, and spending time at the beach.

1031 Camp Starfish
636 Great Rd.
Suite 2
Stow, MA 01775
978-637-2617
FAX: 978-637-2617
info@campstarfish.org
www.campstarfish.org
Emily Golinsky, Interim Executive Director
Jamie Mahnken, Camp Director
Laura Petersen, Director, Staff Experience
Camp Starfish provides summer camps, day camps, and year round respite programs for children with emotional, behavioral, and learning disabilities. Camp Starfish has a 1:1 staff to camper ratio at all times.

1032 Eagle Hill School: Summer Program
Eagle Hill School
242 Old Petersham Rd.
PO Box 116
Hardwick, MA 01037   413-477-6000
                                   FAX: 413-477-6837
                                   www.eaglehill.school

PJ McDonald, Head of School
Michael Riendeau, Assistant Head of School, Academic Affairs
Kristyl Kelly, Assistant Head of School, Student Life
A program of Eagle Hill School, a school for students diagnosed with learning disabilities including ADHA. The Eagle Hill Summer session is a five week summer camp for students ages 10-16 with learning disabilities. The summer session incorporates education and recreation to address the specific academic and social skills of the student.

1033 Kamp for Kids at Camp Togowauk
Behavioral Health Network Inc.
417 Liberty St.
Springfield, MA 01104   413-246-9675
                                   www.bhninc.org

Steve Winn, President & CEO
Anne Benoit, Program Manager
Kamp for Kids at Camp Togowauk is an integrated summer camp for youth with or without disabilities.

1034 Open Hearts Camp
The Edward J. Madden Open Hearts Camp
250 Monument Valley Rd.
Great Barrington, MA 01230   413-528-2229
                                   hearts@openheartscamp.org
                                   www.openheartscamp.org

David Zaleon, Executive Director
The Open Hearts Camp is a summer camp program divided into four age-specific sessions for children and teens who have had open heart surgery. Campers must be in stable health and the program blends sports, recreation, arts and crafts and rest periods into a camper's day.

1035 Summer@Carroll
Carroll School
25 Baker Bridge Rd.
Lincoln, MA 01773   781-259-8342
                      summeradmissions@carrollschool.org
                                   www.carrollschool.org

Kristin Curry, Director
Donna Brown, Assistant Director
A program of the Carroll School, an independent day school for elementary and high school students diagnosed with learning disabilities, Summer@Carroll is a 5 week day camp incorporating education and recreation for children with learning disabilities. Students participate in academic classes in the morning, splitting into smaller groups during the afternoon for recreational activities. Campers attending the day camp do not have to be students of the school during the regular school year.

1036 The Barton Center
The Barton Center for Diabetes Education, Inc.
30 Ennis Rd.
PO Box 356
North Oxford, MA 01537-0356   508-987-2056
                                   FAX: 508-987-2002
                                   info@bartoncenter.org
                                   www.bartoncenter.org

Lynn Butler-Dinunno, Executive Director
Jenna Dufresne, Director, Health Services
Sarah Balko, Director, Camps & Programs
The Barton Center for Diabetes Education is a year round camp, retreat and conference center offering education, recreation, and support programs for children and teens with diabetes and their families. The center offers a variety of programs in Massachusetts, Connecticut, and New York.

1037 The Barton Center Camp Joslin
The Barton Center for Diabetes Education, Inc.
30 Ennis Rd.
PO Box 356
North Oxford, MA 01537-0356   508-987-2056
                                   FAX: 508-987-2002
                                   info@bartoncenter.org
                                   www.bartoncenter.org

Lynn Butler-Dinunno, Executive Director
Jenna Dufresne, Director, Health Services
Sarah Balko, Director, Camps & Programs
A summer camp program of The Barton Center for Diabetes Education, Camp Joslin provides boys ages 6-16 with diabetes a traditional summer camp experience combined with diabetes education. Activities include sports, swimming, kayaking, canoeing, fishing, hiking, arts and crafts, and campfires.

1038 The Barton Center Clara Barton Camp
The Barton Center for Diabetes Education, Inc.
30 Ennis Rd.
PO Box 356
North Oxford, MA 01537-0356   508-987-2056
                                   FAX: 508-987-2002
                                   info@bartoncenter.org
                                   www.bartoncenter.org

Lynn Butler-Dinunno, Executive Director
Jenna Dufresne, Director, Health Services
Sarah Balko, Director, Camps & Programs
A summer camp program of the Barton Center for Diabetes Education, Clara Barton Camp provides girls ages 6-16 with diabetes a traditional summer camp experience combined with diabetes education. Activities include sports, swimming, kayaking, canoeing, fishing, hiking, arts and crafts, and campfires.

1039 The Barton Center Danvers Day Camp
The Barton Center for Diabetes Education, Inc.
30 Ennis Rd.
PO Box 356
North Oxford, MA 01537-0356   508-987-2056
                                   FAX: 508-987-2002
                                   info@bartoncenter.org
                                   www.bartoncenter.org

Lynn Butler-Dinunno, Executive Director
Jenna Dufresne, Director, Health Services
Sarah Balko, Director, Camps & Programs
A coed day camp for children and teens, ages 5-15, with type 1 diabetes. The camp is held in Danvers, Massachusetts at the St. John's Preparatory School. Campers get the opportunity to explore the 175-acre facility, play games, and construct art pieces.

1040 The Barton Center Family Camp
The Barton Center for Diabetes Education, Inc.
30 Ennis Rd.
PO Box 356
North Oxford, MA 01537-0356   508-987-2056
                                   FAX: 508-987-2002
                                   info@bartoncenter.org
                                   www.bartoncenter.org

Lynn Butler-Dinunno, Executive Director
Jenna Dufresne, Director, Health Services
Sarah Balko, Director, Camps & Programs
The Barton Center Family Camp is offered for the families of youth with diabetes. Families participate in traditional camp activities and diabetes education sessions.

1041 The Barton Center Worcester Day Camp
The Barton Center for Diabetes Education, Inc.
30 Ennis Rd.
PO Box 356
North Oxford, MA 01537-0356   508-987-2056
                                   FAX: 508-987-2002
                                   info@bartoncenter.org
                                   www.bartoncenter.org

Lynn Butler-Dinunno, Executive Director
Jenna Dufresne, Director, Health Services
Sarah Balko, Director, Camps & Programs
A coed day camp for children and teens ages 5-15 with diabetes. The camp is held in North Oxford, Massachusetts at the Clara Barton Birthplace Museum. Campers experience boating, canoeing, arts and crafts, and camp games.

1042 The Bridge Center
470 Pine St.
Bridgewater, MA 02324   508-697-7557
info@thebridgectr.org
www.thebridgectr.org
Karen Ellis, Finance Coordinator
Abby Ross, Year Round & Summer Camp Program Coordinator
Peggy O'Neill, Coordinator, Volunteers
A therapeutic recreational facility in Bridgewater, Massachusetts offering after-school programs, special events, school vacation full-week and summer day camp programs for individuals with disabilities.

Michigan

1043 Camp Barefoot
The Fowler Center for Outdoor Learning
2315 Harmon Lake Rd.
Mayville, MI 48744   989-673-2050
FAX: 989-673-6355
info@thefowlercenter.org
www.thefowlercenter.org
Lynn M. Seeloff, Camp Director
Lillia Sheline, Program Director
Offered to adults 18 or older with traumatic brain injuries/closed head injuries. A wide variety of activities are offered. The participants in Camp Barefoot request their week's activities, allowing each participant to design their own activity schedule.

1044 Camp Catch-A-Rainbow
YMCA Storer Camps
6941 Stony Lake Rd.
Jackson, MI 49201   517-536-8607
FAX: 517-536-4922
ccar@ymcastorercamps.org
www.ymcastorercamps.org
Katie Wilson, Camp Catch-A-Rainbow Coordinator
Camp Catch-A-Rainbow is a free camp for cancer survivors ages 4-17. The camp is held at YMCA Storer Camps in Jackson, Michigan.

1045 Camp Chris Williams
MI Coalition for Deaf & Hard of Hearing People
PO Box 16234
Lansing, MI 48901-6234   586-932-6090
campchris@michdhh.org
www.michdhh.org/camp-chris-williams
Val Boyer, Camp Director
A program of the Michigan Coalition for Deaf and Hard of Hearing, Camp Chris Williams is a one week summer camp for youths ages 11-17 who are deaf or hard of hearing. Sessions are normally held the first full week of August each year. Registration is online only.

1046 Camp Grace Bentley
8250 Lakeshore Rd.
Burtchville Township, MI 48059   313-962-8242
campgracebentley@gmail.com
campgracebentley.org
Camp Grace Bentley offers day summer camp programs for children and teens ages 7-16 with physical and mental disabilities. Each camper is screened before attending the camp to ensure the camp can meet the needs of the camper. Activities include swimming, campfires, movie nights, team sports, arts and crafts, karaoke night, and dances.

1047 Camp Midicha
American Diabetes Association
20700 Civic Center Dr.
Suite 100
Southfield, MI 48076   248-433-3830
campsupport@diabetes.org
www.diabetes.org
Camp Midicha is the Michigan summer camp program of the American Diabetes Association for children with diabetes. The camp is hosted at YMCA Camp Copneconic in Fenton, Michigan.

1048 Camp Quality North Michigan
PO Box 345
Boyne City, MI 49712   231-582-2471
mioffice@campqualityusa.org
www.campqualityusa.org/MI
Jean McDonough, Executive Director
Amy Smitter, Development Director
Camp Quality is an international camping program for children with cancer. The Michigan Camp Quality is held in Lake Ann, Michigan and offers children and their siblings summer camps and year round camping opportunities. Volunteer doctors and nurses are at the camp 24 hours a day, and there is a 1:1 staff to camper ratio.

1049 Camp Quality South Michigan
PO Box 345
Boyne City, MI 49712   231-582-2471
mioffice@campqualityusa.org
www.campqualityusa.org/MI
Jean McDonough, Executive Director
Amy Smitter, Development Director
Camp Quality is an international camping program for children with cancer. The South Michigan Camp Quality is held in Fenton, Michigan and offers children and their siblings summer camps and year round camping opportunities. Volunteer doctors and nurses are at the camp 24 hours a day, and there is a 1:1 staff to camper ratio.

1050 Echo Grove Camp
Salvation Army
1101 Camp Rd.
Leonard, MI 48367   248-628-3108
FAX: 248-628-7055
shayna.stubblefield@usc.salvationarmy.org
www.echogrove.org
Shayna Stubblefield, Program Director
The Salvation Army's Echo Grove Camp offers a structured camping program for children, adults and seniors referred through Corps Community Centers. In addition to outdoor recreation, camps may include religious, musical and skill-building instruction.

1051 Indian Trails Camp
IKUS Life Enrichment Services
O-1859 Lake Michigan Dr. NW
Grand Rapids, MI 49534   616-677-5251
FAX: 616-677-2955
info@ikuslife.org
www.ikuslife.org
Scott Blakeney, Executive Director
Amy DeMott, Director, Programs & Services
Nikki Outhier, Director, Development
The Indian Trails Camp is a program of IKUS Life Enrichment Services. The camp offers summer, day, and weekend respite programs for individuals of all ages with disabilities. Campers are able to participate in adaptive recreation opportunities in a barrier-free environment.

1052 St. Francis Camp On The Lake
10120 Murrey Rd.
Jerome, MI 49249   517-688-9212
FAX: 517-688-9298
director@saintfranciscamp.org
www.saintfranciscamp.org
Victoria Petty, Camp Director
St. Francis Camp on the Lake offers residential summer camps, day camps, and respite care for children and adults with developmental and intellectual disabilities.

1053 Trail's Edge Camp
c/o Mott Respiratory Care, 8-714
1540 E Hospital Dr. SPC 4208
Ann Arbor, MI 48109-4208   director.trailsedgecamp@gmail.com
www.trailsedgecamp.org
Jeff Cain, Director
Betsy Howell, Activities Coordinator
Trail's Edge Camp is a one-week summer camp for children and teens ages 5-18 who are ventilator dependent. Campers are able to participate in camp activities such as games, horseback riding, and fishing. The camp is limited to 32 campers and campers must

be able to communicate with other children through speech or sign language.

Minnesota

1054 AuSM Summer Camp
Autism Society of Minnesota
2380 Wycliff St.
Suite 102
St. Paul, MN 55114
651-647-1083
FAX: 651-642-1230
camp@ausm.org
www.ausm.org

Ellie Wilson, Executive Director
Dawn Brasch, Senior Director, Finance & Operations
Kelly Thomalla, Senior Director, Integration & Advancement
A program of the Autism Society of Minnesota (AuSM), the Summer Camps are offered to children, teens, and adults with autism, ages 6 and up, in a variety of formats including day and residential summer camp. The camp offers the following programs: Camp Hand in Hand, for ages 9+, held at Camp Knutson in Crosslake, Minnesota; Camp Discovery, for ages 10+, held at True Friends/Courage North in Lake George, Minnesota; and Wahode Day Camps, for ages 6-12, held at Camp Butwin in Eagan, Minnesota.

1055 Camp Buckskin
PO Box 389
Ely, MN 55731
763-432-9177
info@campbuckskin.com
www.campbuckskin.com

Tom Bauer, Camp Co-Director
Mary Bauer, Camp Co-Director
Camp Buckskin is for campers ages 6-18 with underdeveloped social skills who may struggle to interact with others and make friends. The camp is also open to children who have been diagnosed with AD/HD, Aspergers, and/or a learning disability.

1056 Camp Confidence
Confidence Learning Center
1620 Mary Fawcett Memorial Dr.
East Gull Lake, MN 56401
218-828-2344
info@confidencelearningcenter.org
www.campconfidence.com

Jeff Olson, Executive Director
Bob Slaybaugh, Camp Director
Camp Confidence works to promote self-confidence and self-esteem for individuals with developmental and cognitive disabilities. Programs run year round with campers participating in hands on activities and outdoor recreation experiences.

1057 Camp Courage
True Friends
8046 83rd St. NW
Maple Lake, MN 55358
952-852-0101
800-450-8376
FAX: 952-852-0123
info@truefriends.org
www.truefriends.org

John Leblanc, President & CEO
Conor McGrath, Senior Director, Camp & Operations
Jon Salmon, Director, Programs
Camp is located in Maple Lake, Minnesota. Summer sessions for campers with a variety of disabilities. Camp Courage is owned and operated by True Friends.

1058 Camp Courage North
True Friends
37569 Courage North Dr.
Lake George, MN 56458
952-852-0101
800-450-8376
FAX: 952-852-0123
info@truefriends.org
www.truefriends.org

John Leblanc, President & CEO
Conor McGrath, Senior Director, Camp & Operations
Jon Salmon, Director, Programs
Camp is located in Lake George, Minnesota. Summer camp programs for individuals with disabilities. Camp Courage North is owned and operated by True Friends.

1059 Camp Eden Wood
True Friends
6350 Indian Chief Rd.
Eden Prairie, MN 55346
952-852-0101
800-450-8376
FAX: 952-852-0123
info@truefriends.org
www.truefriends.org

John Leblanc, President & CEO
Conor McGrath, Senior Director, Camp & Operations
Jon Salmon, Director, Programs
Offers resident camp programs for children, teenagers and adults with developmental, physical or multiple disabilities.

1060 Camp Heartland
One Heartland
26001 Heinz Rd.
Willow River, MN 55795
888-216-2028
helpkids@oneheartland.org
www.oneheartland.org

Patrick Kindler, Executive Director
Katie Donlin, Operations Manager
Kadien Bartels-Merkel, Program Director
A program of One Heartland, a nonprofit organization working to provide camping programs for children with serious illnesses or experiencing social isolation, Camp Heartland is a weeklong summer camp for children, ages 7-15, who are infected or affected by HIV/AIDS. The camp is held in Willow River, Minnesota.

1061 Camp Knutson
11148 Manhattan Pt. Blvd.
Crosslake, MN 56442
218-543-4232
camp.knutson@lssmn.org
www.lssmn.org/campknutson

Jared Griffin, Senior Camp Director
Caitlin Malin, Program Director
Camp Knutson is an accessible camp that hosts a variety of different programs for children with special needs such as skin disease, autism, down syndrome, heart disease, and children who have HIV/AIDS.

1062 Camp Odayin
Camp Odayin
3503 High Point Dr. N
Suite 250
Oakdale, MN 55128
651-351-9185
FAX: 651-351-9187
info@campodayin.org
www.campodayin.org

Sara Meslow, Executive Director
Alison Boerner, Assistant Director
Matt Olson, Finance Director
Camp Odayin provides camping experiences for youth and the families of youth with heart disease. Camp Odayin offers a variety of programs including residential, day, family, and winter camps as well as retreats.

1063 Camp Odayin Family Camp
Camp Odayin
3503 High Point Dr. N
Suite 250
Oakdale, MN 55128
651-351-9185
FAX: 651-351-9187
info@campodayin.org
www.campodayin.org

Sara Meslow, Executive Director
Alison Boerner, Assistant Director
Matt Olson, Finance Director
Camp Odayin's Family Camp is a two-night program for families with a child who has heart disease.

1064 Camp Odayin Residential Camp
Camp Odayin
3503 High Point Dr. N
Suite 250
Oakdale, MN 55128
651-351-9185
FAX: 651-351-9187
info@campodayin.org
www.campodayin.org

Sara Meslow, Executive Director
Alison Boerner, Assistant Director
Matt Olson, Finance Director
A program of Camp Odayin, the Residential Camp is for children in grades 1-11 with heart disease. Camps are hosted at Camp Lutherdale in Elkhorn, WI and Camp Knutson in Crosslake, MN.

1065 Camp Odayin Summer Camp
Camp Odayin
3503 High Point Dr. N
Suite 250
Oakdale, MN 55128
651-351-9185
FAX: 651-351-9187
info@campodayin.org
www.campodayin.org

Sara Meslow, Executive Director
Alison Boerner, Assistant Director
Matt Olson, Finance Director
Camp Odayin offers a variety of summer camp programs for children in grades 1-11 with heart disease. Camper eligibility is determined upon the recommendation of a pediatric cardiologist and the camp's medical director.

1066 Camp Odayin Winter Camp
Camp Odayin
3503 High Point Dr. N
Suite 250
Oakdale, MN 55128
651-351-9185
FAX: 651-351-9187
info@campodayin.org
www.campodayin.org

Sara Meslow, Executive Director
Alison Boerner, Assistant Director
Matt Olson, Finance Director
A winter camp program for youth in grades 1-12 with heart disease.

1067 Cristo Vive International: Minnesota Camp
Ironwood Springs Christian Ranch
7291 County 6 Rd. SW
Stewartville, MN 55976
218-910-8151
cvimncamp@gmail.com
www.cristovive.net

Kristin Munoz, Camp Coordinator
Christian camp with programming for individuals who are blind/deaf, physically or mentally challenged, have multiple disabilities, Down Syndrome, Autism/Asperger's, ADHD/ADD, Cerebral Palsy, and their families and siblings.

1068 Down Syndrome Camp
Down Syndrome Foundation
17186 Daniel Lane
Eden Prairie, MN 55346
651-321-2267
www.downsyndromefoundation.org

Angie Kniss, President & Founder
Nick Engbloom, Secretary
Ellie Wilson, Counselor Coordinator
A week-long coed summer camp for youth ages 10-21 who have Down Syndrome. The camp is held at Camp Knutson in Crosslake, Minnesota. The camp is fully accessible and activities include swimming, boating, fishing, tubing, paddleboarding, horseback riding, arts and crafts, and campfires. The camp's staff is trained to work with children and adults with special needs.

1069 True Friends
10509 108th St. NW
Annandale, MN 55302
952-852-0101
800-450-8376
FAX: 952-852-0123
info@truefriends.org
www.truefriends.org

John Leblanc, President & CEO
Conor McGrath, Senior Director, Camp & Operations
Jon Salmon, Director, Programs
True Friends provides camp experiences for children and adults with disabilities. Programs are held at five locations: Camp Courage in Maple Lake, MN; Camp Eden Wood in Eden Prairie, MN; Camp Friendship in Annandale, MN; Camp Courage North in Lake George, MN; and True Friends' office in Plymouth, MN.

Mississippi

1070 Camp Dream Street
3863 Morrison Rd.
Utica, MS 39175
601-885-3793
info@dreamstreetms.org
www.dreamstreetms.org

Aimee Adler, Director
Ashley Rubinsky, Assistant Director
Dream Street is a five-day camp program for children ages 8-14 with physical disabilities. The camp offers activities such as swimming, arts and crafts, horseback riding and more.

Missouri

1071 Camp Barnabas
PO Box 3200
Springfield, MO 65808
417-476-2565
info@campbarnabas.org
www.campbarnabas.org

John Tillack, Chief Executive Officer
Krystal Simon, Chief Operations Officer
Mike Mrosko, Camp Director
Camp Barnabas is a Christian camp for children, the siblings of children, and adults with special needs. The camp serves children and adults ages 7 and up.

1072 Camp Encourage
4025 Central St.
Kansas City, MO 64111
816-830-7171
FAX: 816-301-6228
info@campencourage.org
www.campencourage.org

Kelly Lee, Executive Director
Aimee Gorrow, Program Coordinator
Provides overnight and summer camp sessions for children and youth with autism spectrum disorders.

1073 Camp Hickory Hill
PO Box 1942
Columbia, MO 65205
573-445-9146
camphickoryhill@gmail.com
www.camphickoryhill.com

Jessica Bernhardt, Camp Director
Camp Hickory Hill is a residential summer camp for children ages 7-17 with diabetes. Campers participate in traditional summer camp activities as well as educational programs.

1074 Camp MITIOG
7615 N Platte Purchase Dr.
Suite 116
Kansas City, MO 64118
www.campmitiog.org
A week long summer camp for children with Spina Bifida. Camp MITIOG is held in Excelsior Springs, Missouri at the Lake Doniphan Conference and Retreat Center, which is a wheelchair accessible environment. Campers participate in activities such as swimming, fishing, canoeing, arts and crafts, nature classes, classes on self-help medical care and evening campfires.

1075 Camp No Limits Missouri
No Limits Foundation
13528 State Route AA
Potosi, MO 63664
207-569-6411
campnolimits@gmail.com
www.nolimitsfoundation.org
Mary Leighton, Founder & Executive Director
Kelsey Moody, Program Operations Manager
Alix Sandler, Marketing & Development Director
Camp No Limits Missouri, a location of Camp No Limits, is a recreational and educational camp for youth who have experienced limb loss. Camp No Limits is a program of the nonprofit organization No Limits Foundation. Unavailable in 2022 due to COVID-19 restrictions.

1076 Camp Quality Central Missouri
PO Box 953
Jefferson City, MO 65012
636-795-7229
cmo@campqualityusa.org
www.campqualityusa.org/cmo
Casey Bucher, Co-Director
Erin Carl, Co-Director
Camp Quality is an international camping program for children with cancer. The Central Missouri Camp is held in St.Clair, Missouri and offers children and their siblings summer camps and year round camping opportunities. Volunteer doctors and nurses are at the camp 24 hours a day, and there is a 1:1 staff to camper ratio.

1077 Camp Quality Greater Kansas City
3111 SE 3rd Terr.
Lee's Summit, MO 64063
816-244-6912
gkc@campqualityusa.org
www.campqualityusa.org/gkc
Crystal Davison, Executive Director
Rachael Slagle, Program Coordinator
Jacinda Farmer, Camp Director
Camp Quality Greater Kansas City is a local chapter of a nationwide nonprofit dedicated to serving children with cancer and their families. They host a signature week-long summer camping experience for children with cancer and their siblings in addition to programs and support throughout the year for the entire family. Their mission is to promote hope while fostering life skills. Hosted at the Lake Maurer Retreat Center, each camper is paired 1:1 with a companion volunteer during camp.

1078 Camp Quality Northwest Missouri
1325 Village Dr.
St. Joseph, MO 64506
816-232-2267
nwmo@campqualityusa.org
www.campqualityusa.org/nwmo
Niccole Marshall, Executive Director
Lynette Bingaman, Office Manager
Camp Quality is an international camping program for children with cancer. The Northwest Missouri Camp is held in Stewartsville, Missouri and offers children and their siblings summer camps and year round camping opportunities. Volunteer doctors and nurses are at the camp 24 hours a day, and there is a 1:1 staff to camper ratio.

1079 Camp Quality Ozarks
PO Box 302
Joplin, MO 64802
417-455-6196
ozarks@campqualityusa.org
www.campqualityusa.org/oz
Kristin Patterson, Executive Director
Angee Tingle, Treasurer
Denise Dieckhoff, Secretary
Camp Quality is an international camping program for children with cancer. The Missouri Ozarks Camp is held in Neosho, Missouri and offers children and their siblings summer camps and year round camping opportunities. Volunteer doctors and nurses are at the camp 24 hours a day, and there is a 1:1 staff to camper ratio.

1080 Sunnyhill Adventures
6555 Sunlit Way
Dittmer, MO 63023
636-274-9044
sunnyhilladventures.org
Rob Darroch, Director

Summer camps and year-round programs are offered for youth and adults of all abilities.

1081 Wonderland Camp
18591 Miller Circle
Rocky Mount, MO 65072
573-392-1000
info@wonderlandcamp.org
www.wonderlandcamp.org
Jill Wilke, Executive Director
Stephanie Dehner, Director, Administration
Mike Clayton, Director, Fund Development & Communication
Wonderland Camp provides residential summer camps and year round weekend camps for children, teens, and adults with disabilities.

Montana

1082 Big Sky Kids Cancer Camps
Eagle Mount Bozeman
6901 Goldenstein Lane
Bozeman, MT 59715
406-586-1781
FAX: 406-586-5794
bigskykids@eaglemount.org
www.eaglemount.org
Kevin Sylvester, Executive Director
Shannon Stober, Senior Director, Programs
Trevor Olson, Director, Operations
Provides recreational opportunities for kids and young adults ages 5-23 with cancer. Big Sky offers skiing, swimming, fishing, ice skating, golf, cycling, and other outdoor activities.

1083 Camp Mak-A-Dream
PO Box 1450
Missoula, MT 59806
406-549-5987
FAX: 406-549-5933
info@campdream.org
www.campdream.org
Kim McKearnan, Executive Director
Jennifer Benton, Program Director
Camp Mak-A-Dream provides a cost-free summer camp experience to children, teens, young adults, women and families affected by cancer. Participants experience regular camp activities such as swimming and zip lining, as well as the chance to interact with ranch staff.

1084 Charles Campbell Childrens Camp
PO Box 23342
Billings, MT 59102
406-670-2496
campbellcamp@msn.com
billingslions.org/clubnews/campbell-camp
Doug Hanson, Director
Sue Hanson, Director
Camp is open to young adults with physical disabilities that include sight or hearing impairment, spina bifida, cerebral palsy, gross motor skill impairments and other disabilities. Campers enjoy hiking, swimming, fishing, dances, campfires and much more.

Nebraska

1085 Camp Floyd Rogers
PO Box 541058
Omaha, NE 68154
402-885-9022
director@campfloydrogers.com
www.campfloydrogers.com
Dylan Helberg, Camp Director
Carrie Busing, Operations Director
A camp for children ages 8-18 with diabetes. While at the camp, campers enjoy activities, participate in special events, engage in evening programs, and meet other children their own age with diabetes.

1086 Camp Kindle
Project Kindle
PO Box 81147
Lincoln, NE 68501
877-800-2267
eva@projectkindle.org
www.campkindle.org

Eva Payne, Founder & President
Mandy Nickolite, Vice President & Camp Director
Camp Kindle provides educational and recreational camp programs for children and youth with a chronic or life-threatening illness, disability, or life challenge.

1087 Camp Quality Heartland
PO Box 24322
Omaha, NE 68124
402-450-1674
heartland@campqualityusa.org
www.campqualityusa.org/htl

Stephanie Purcell, Executive Director
Laura Peitzmeier, Camp Director
Jordan Peitzmeier, Treasurer
Camp Quality is for children with cancer and their siblings. The camp offers a stress-free environment that offers exciting activities and fosters new friendships, while helping to give the children courage, motivation and emotional strength.

1088 Easterseals Nebraska Camp
Easterseals Nebraska
12565 West Center Rd.
Omaha, NE 68144
402-930-4053
FAX: 888-611-6396
campesn@ne.easterseals.com
www.easterseals.com/ne

James C. Summerfelt, President & CEO
Lily Sughroue, Director, Respite & Recreation
Offers a variety of camp and recreational programs to help people with disabilities gain independence in a safe and adapted environment.

1089 Kamp Kaleo
46872 Willow Springs Rd.
Burwell, NE 68823
308-346-5083
kampkaleo@gmail.com
www.kampkaleo.com

David Butz, Camp Administrator
Offers an overnight summer camp for individuals with developmental disabilities. Participants can expect to experience outdoor recreational activities such as canoeing, fishing, and swimming, and there is a strong focus on religious education.

1090 National Camps for Blind Children
Christian Record Services
5900 S 58th St.
Suite M
Lincoln, NE 68516
402-488-0981
FAX: 402-488-7582
info@christianrecord.org
www.christianrecord.org

Diane Thurber, President
Lonnie Kreiter, Vice President, Finance
National Camps for Blind Children is a program of Christian Record Services offering summer camps for individuals who are considered legally blind.

Nevada

1091 Camp Buck
Nevada Diabetes Association
18 Stewart St.
Reno, NV 89501
775-856-3839
800-379-3839
FAX: 775-348-7591
camp@diabetesnv.org
www.diabetesnv.org

Sarah Gleich, Executive Director
Nate Gibson, Director, Camps
Dakota Ostrenger, Director, Marketing
Co-ed summer camp for children ages 7-17 with diabetes. Campers participate in recreational and athletic activities as well as diabetes education.

1092 Camp Lotsafun
Amplify Life
480 Galletti Way
Bldg. 2
Sparks, NV 89431
775-827-3866
FAX: 775-827-0334
info@amplifylife.org
www.amplifylife.org

Jessica Daum, Executive Director
Luis Chavez Torres, Program Coordinator
Cindy Oesterle-Prescott, Office Manager
Provides therapeutic, educational, and recreational opportunities for individuals with developmental disabilities. Camp activities include swimming, kayaking, pet therapy, arts and crafts, drama and music. The camp is held at Eagle Lake, California.

1093 CampCare
PO Box 12155
Reno, NV 89510-2155
775-323-3737
cmoore@campcarenevada.org
www.campcarenevada.org

Carol Moore, Camp Director
The camp provides programs for individuals with special needs such as ADHD, autism and cerebral palsy.

1094 Discovery Day Camp
Nevada Blind Children's Foundation
95 S Arroyo Grande Blvd.
Henderson, NV 89012
702-735-6223
info@nvblindchildren.org
nvblindchildren.org/programs/day-camp

Emily Smith, Chief Executive Officer
Maribel Garcia, Director, Programs
Paula Farrell, Director, Finances & Facilities
A summer day camp program for children in grades K-12 who are visually impaired. Discovery Day Camp provides traditional camp activities that have been adapted to meet the needs of children with visual impairments.

New Hampshire

1095 Adam's Camp: New England
26 Shaker Rd.
Concord, NH 03301
508-901-9610
NewEngland@AdamsCamp.org
www.adamscampnewengland.org

Adrienne Evans, Executive Director
Offers both therapy and adventure camps for children and the families of children with special needs and developmental delays. Camps are available in New Hampshire and Massachusetts.

1096 Camp Allen
56 Camp Allen Rd.
Bedford, NH 03110
603-622-8471
FAX: 603-626-4295
michael@campallennh.org
www.campallennh.org

Michael Constance, Executive Director
Stephen Daley, Camp Director
Debra Schulte, Office Manager
A residential summer camp for individuals with disabilities. All of the activities are conducted by individual coordinators under the supervision of the Program Director. Activities include aquatics, arts, crafts, games and nature programs. All camp events, special events, evening programs, and field trips are scheduled throughout the summer and are structured to meet the individual abilities and needs of each camper.

1097 Camp Carefree
American Diabetes Association
Lions Camp Pride
154 Camp Pride Way
New Durham, NH 03855
campsupport@diabetes.org
www.diabetes.org

Phyllis Woestemeyer, Director
The camp is located at Lions Camp Pride in New Durham, New Hampshire. Camp Carefree is a American Diabetes Association summer camp for children with diabetes.

1098 Camp Connect
Easterseals New Hampshire
555 Auburn St.
Manchester, NH 03103   603-782-2066
                                        www.easterseals.com/nh
Maureen Beauregard, President & CEO
Andrew MacWilliam, Chair
Tom Sullivan, Vice Chair
A summer day camp for children in grades K-12 with Asperger Syndrome, Autism, Nonverbal Learning Disorder, and other social communication disorders. The camp has a large focus on continuing to address academic needs of the campers, but also incorporates music, drama, and arts and crafts.

1099 Camp Inter-Actions
Inter-Actions
170 West Rd.
Suite 6-B
Portsmouth, NH 03801   603-319-6120
                                        campinfo@inter-actions.org
                                        inter-actions.org
Debbie Gross, Camp Director
Camp Inter-Actions is a summer camp for children ages 8-15 who are blind or visually impaired. The camp is located in Kingston, New Hampshire and runs one, two, and three week sessions. Activities include swimming, fishing, adapted sports/games, woodworking, pottery, and more.

1100 Camp Sno Mo
Easterseals New Hampshire
Hidden Valley Reservation
260 Griswold Ln.
Gilmanton Iron Works, NH 03837   603-364-5818
                                        cellis@eastersealsnh.org
                                        www.easterseals.com/nh
Maureen Beauregard, President & CEO
Chris Ellis, Camp Director
Camp Slo Mo is is a camp program for children with disabilities. Activities include water sports, team sports, hiking, archery, arts and crafts, and more offered in an accessible setting.

1101 Camp Wediko
Wediko Children's Services, New Hampshire Campus
11 Bobcat Blvd.
Windsor, NH 03244   603-478-5236
                                        FAX: 603-478-2049
                                        www.wediko.org
Edward Zadravec, Interim Executive Director
This program is a six-week residential program for youth ages 8-19 with social, emotional, and behavior challenges. This program serves children with disabilities such as ADHD, autism, mood disorders, and more.

1102 Camp Yavneh: Yedidut Program
Summer Office
18 Lucas Pond Rd.
Northwood, NH 03261   603-942-5593
                                        info@campyavneh.org
                                        www.campyavneh.org/yedidut
Bil Zarch, Executive Director
Miriam Loren, Director, Camper Care & Yedidut
Michelle Rosenhek Zelermyer, Director, Summer Camp
A residential Jewish summer camp program for children with disabilities. Traditional camp activities with a strong focus on Judaism and Jewish education.

New Jersey

1103 Camp Chatterbox
Children's Specialized Hospital
200 Somerset St.
New Brunswick, NJ 08901   908-301-5548
                                        campchatterbox@childrens-specialized.org
                                        csh.recdesk.com
Sara Barnhill, Clinical Coordinator
Camp Chatterbox is an overnight camp for people ages 5-22 who use augmentative communication devices. The camp offers recreational activities such as swimming, arts, and sports.

1104 Camp Deeny Riback
208 Flanders Netcong Rd.
Flanders, NJ 07836   973-929-2901
                                        FAX: 973-463-3998
                                        camps@jccmetrowest.org
                                        cdr.jccmetrowest.org
Dana Gottfried, Director
Debra Scher, Assistant Director
Todd Seideman, Assistant Director
A Jewish summer camp for children of all ages. The camp integrates children with special needs through their Camp Friends program. The camp provide traditional outdoor camp activities.

1105 Camp Dream Street
Kaplen JCC on the Palisades
411 East Clinton Ave.
Tenafly, NJ 07670   201-569-7900
                                        FAX: 201-569-7448
                                        info@jccotp.org
                                        www.jccotp.org
Jordan Shenker, Chief Executive Officer
Miriam Chilton, Chief Operating Officer
Kevin Cunningham, Chief Financial Officer
Dream Street is a camp program for children with cancer and other blood disorders. Activities include swimming, arts and crafts, horseback riding and more.

1106 Camp Jaycee
Camp Jaycee Administrative Office
985 Livingston Ave.
North Brunswick, NJ 08902   732-737-8279
                                        FAX: 732-737-8279
                                        info@campjaycee.org
                                        www.campjaycee.org
Maureen Brennan, Camp Director
Nicole Goodwin, Coordinator, Camping Services
Camp Jaycee offers residential summer camp programs for adults with developmental and intellectual disabilities. The campsite is located in Effort, PA.

1107 Camp Jotoni
51 Old Stirling Rd.
Warren, NJ 07059   908-753-4244
                                        www.campjotoni.org
Josh Burke, Director
Sponsored by the Arc of Somerset County, Camp Jotoni is a day and residential camp for children and adults with developmental disabilities. Campers are ages 5-21.

1108 Camp Merry Heart
Easterseals New Jersey
21 O'Brien Rd.
Hackettstown, NJ 07840   908-852-3896
                                        FAX: 908-852-9263
                                        recreaton@nj.easterseals.com
                                        www.easterseals.com/nj
Brian Fitzgerald, President & CEO
An organized program of swimming, arts and crafts, boating, nature study and travel offered to campers with a variety of disabilities.

1109 Camp Nejeda
Camp Nejeda Foundation
910 Saddleback Rd.
PO Box 156
Stillwater, NJ 07875   973-383-2611
                                        FAX: 973-383-9891
                                        info@campnejeda.org
                                        www.campnejeda.org
Bill Vierbuchen, Executive Director
Ginnie Ramberger, Registrar & Staff Coordinator
Jim Daschbach, Camp Director
For children with diabetes, ages 7-16. Provides an active and safe camping experience which enables the children to learn about and understand diabetes. Activities include boating, swimming, fishing, archery, and camping skills.

1110 Camp Quality New Jersey
PO Box 264
Adelphia, NJ 07710   908-556-6548
newjersey@campqualityusa.org
www.campqualityusa.org/nj
Kaitlin DeGennaro Wilson, Executive Director
Camp Quality is for children with cancer and their siblings. The
camp offers a stress-free environment that offers exciting activities and fosters new friendships, while helping to give the children courage, motivation and emotional strength.

1111 Camp Sun'N Fun
The Arc Gloucester
1555 Gateway Blvd.
West Deptford, NJ 08096   856-629-4502
camp@thearcgloucester.org
www.thearcgloucester.org
Lisa Conley, Chief Executive Officer
Camp is located in Williamstown, New Jersey. Summer sessions
for campers with developmental disabilities. Coed, ages 5+. Activities include swimming, arts and crafts, sports, games, music,
dance and drama.

1112 Explorer's Club Camp
New Behavioural Network
2 Pin Oak Lane
Suite 250
Cherry Hill, NJ 08003   856-874-1616
FAX: 856-424-7660
nbh@nbngroup.com
www.newbehavioralnetwork.com/summer-camp
Explorer's Club Camp is a summer day camp program for children ages 4-17 who have ADHD, Austism Spectrum Disorder,
and other behavior challenges. The camp's goal is to maintain
progress made during the school year while giving campers a fun
camp experience. Full and half day sessions offered.

1113 Happiness Is Camping
62 Sunset Lake Rd.
Hardwick, NJ 07825   908-362-6733
FAX: 908-362-5197
rich@happinessiscamping.org
www.happinessiscamping.org
Laura San Miguel, President
Julie McMahon, Secretary
Beth Fuchs, Treasurer
Located in Hardwick, New Jersey, Happiness is Camping is a
week-long camp for kids with cancer and their siblings, ages
6-16. The camp is free for all attendees, and campers participate
in a variety of traditional outdoor activities, including canoeing,
fishing, swimming, archery, and more.

1114 Harbor Haven Summer Program
4 Hanover Rd.
Unit C3
Florham Park, NJ 07932   908-964-5411
FAX: 908-964-0511
info@harborhaven.com
www.harborhaven.com
Robyn Tanne, Director
Kim Van Woeart, Associate Director
Ryan Cox, Assistant Director
A seven-week summer program for children ages 3-15 with mild
special needs. Harbor Haven offers traditional outdoor recreation
activities and a daily academic period which reinforces math,
reading, and language arts.

1115 Mane Stream
83 Old Turnpike Rd.
PO Box 305
Oldwick, NJ 08858   908-439-9636
FAX: 908-439-2338
info@manestreamnj.org
www.manestreamnj.org
Trish Hegeman, Executive Director
Jane Banta, Camp Director
Louisa Bartok, Manager, Marketing & Communications
A summer day camp for children with physical and cognitive
challenges, their siblings, and non-disabled children. The camp is
primarily focused on horsemanship lessons, with activities such

as riding lessons, grooming, tacking, leading, basic horse care,
and more. Eight week-long sessions available.

1116 Rising Treetops at Oakhurst
111 Monmouth Rd.
Oakhurst, NJ 07755   732-531-0215
FAX: 732-531-0292
info@risingtreetops.org
www.risingtreetops.org
Robert Pacenza, Executive Director
Charles Sutherland, Camp Director
Lori Schenck, Assistant Director, Services
A summer and day camp for adults and children with special
needs, including autism and physical and intellectual disabilities.
Campers experience traditional camp activities while gaining
skills for greater independence.

1117 Round Lake Camp
NJY Camps
21 Plymouth St.
Fairfield, NJ 07004   973-575-3333
FAX: 973-575-4188
rlc@njycamps.org
www.roundlakecamp.org
Aryn Barer, Director
Round Lake Camp is for children ages 7-17 with learning differences and social communication disorders. Campers enjoy swimming, boating, sailing, mountain biking, and arts and crafts. The
camp is located in Milford, PA.

New Mexico

1118 ADA Camp 180
American Diabetes Association
Fort Lone Tree Camp
307 Fort Lone Tree Rd.
Capitan, NM 88316   602-861-4731
campsupport@diabetes.org
www.diabetes.org
A program of the American Diabetes Association, Camp 180 provides camp experiences for children ages 8-12 and teens ages
13-16 with diabetes. The camp is held at Fort Lone Tree Camp in
Capitan, New Mexico.

1119 Camp Enchantment
Rio Grande Community Development Corporation
318 Isleta Blvd. SW
Albuquerque, NM 87105   info@campenchantment.org
www.campenchantment.org
Shayna Rosenblum, Camp Director
A summer camp for children and teens ages 7-17 who have been
diagnosed with cancer. The camp is held at Manzano Mountain
Retreat in Torreon, NM. Activities include swimming, kayaking,
dancing, archery, and more. The camping session is seven days.

1120 Camp Rising Sun
Center for Development and Disability
2300 Menaul Blvd. NE
Albuquerque, NM 87107   505-272-3000
800-270-1861
FAX: 505-272-5896
hsc.unm.edu/cdd
Paul Brouse, Camp Director
Held at the Manzano Mountain Retreat southeast of Albuquerque, Camp Rising sun is a summer camp designed specifially for
children and teens with Autism Spectrum Disorder and their
peers, ages 8-17. Activities include hiking, sports, photography,
kayaking, campouts, and other nature activities.

New York

1121 ADA Camp Aspire
American Diabetes Association
809 Five Points Rd.
Rush, NY 14543   585-458-3040
www.diabetes.org

A program of the American Diabetes Association, Camp Aspire provides camp experiences for children with diabetes. The camp is held at the Rochester Rotary Sunshine Campus in Rush, New York.

1122 Autism Summer Respite Program
Commonpoint Queens
58-20 Little Neck Pkwy.
Little Neck, NY 11362 718-225-6750
larmband@commonpointqueens.org
www.commonpointqueens.org/summercamp
Lisa Armband, Contact
An afternoon camping program for children, teens, and young adults ages 5-21 with Autism and similar disabilities. Located at Sam Field Center.

1123 AutismUp: YMCA Summer Social Skills Program
AutismUp
50 Science Pkwy.
Rochester, NY 14620 585-248-9011
FAX: 585-248-9159
contact@autismup.org
autismup.org
Sarah Milko, Executive Director
Christina Hilton, Director, Finance & Operations
Lisa Ponticello, Director, Marketing & Development
This program is a collaboration between AutismUp and the Greater Rochester YMCA. The Summer Social Skills Program is a day camp held at Camp Arrowhead for children, 4-16, with Autism Spectrum Disorders. Half day and full day sessions available, and campers are integrated into regular camp activities.

1124 Camp Abilities Brockport
The College at Brockport, State Univ of New York
350 New Campus Drive
Brockport, NY 14420 585-395-5361
llieberman@brockport.edu
www.campabilities.org
Lauren Lieberman, Camp Director
Alex Stribing, Assistant Director
Emily Gilbert, Aquatics Director
A one-week sports camp for children who are visually impaired, blind or deaf blind. Children learn to be more physically active, which in turn improves their health and well being.

1125 Camp Adventure
KiDS NEED MoRE
PO Box 305
Copiague, NY 11726 631-608-3135
FAX: 631-532-4944
info@kidsneedmore.org
kidsneedmore.org
Melissa Firmes, President
John Ray, Treasurer
Jacqueline Lorenz, Secretary
Camp Adventure is a one-week sleep away camp for children and teens ages 6-18 dealing with cancer and other life threatening illnesses. The camp takes place on Shelter Island at Quinipet Camp and Retreat Center.

1126 Camp Anne
AHRC New York City
228 Four Corners Lane
Ancramdale, NY 12503 518-329-5649
FAX: 518-329-5689
michael.rose@ahrcnyc.org
camping.ahrcnyc.org
Michael Rose, Camp Director
A day summer camp program for children and adults with intellectual and developmental disabilities. The camp offers activities such as cooking, crafts, nature, sports, swimming, and more. Camp Anne offers three 11-day sessions for adults ages 21-59, and two 11-day sessions for childres ages 5-20. Each session can accommodate 100 campers.

1127 Camp COAST
Empowering People's Independence (EPI)
2 Townline Circle
Rochester, NY 14623 585-442-4430
FAX: 585-442-6964
info@epiny.org
www.epiny.org
Michael Radell, Camp Director
Camp COAST is a summer camp for young adults ages 18+ with epilepsy and I/DD.

1128 Camp EAGR
Empowering People's Independence (EPI)
2 Townline Circle
Rochester, NY 14623 585-442-4430
FAX: 585-442-6964
info@epiny.org
www.epiny.org
Michael Radell, Camp Director
Camp EAGR is a summer sleep-away camp for children with epilepsy and their siblings. Activities include swimming, horseback riding, and rock climbing.

1129 Camp Good Days and Special Times
1332 Pitsford-Mendon Rd.
PO Box 665
Mendon, NY 14506 585-624-5555
800-785-2135
FAX: 585-624-5799
info@campgooddays.org
www.campgooddays.org
Wendy Bleier-Mervis, Executive Director
Sheri Watkins, CFO & Director, Administration
The camp is dedicated to improving the quality of life for children and adults affected by cancer or other life challenges. The camp offers week-long sessions that are free of charge.

1130 Camp High Hopes
82 Pixley Rd.
Chenango Forks, NY 13746 607-226-5474
joe@camphighhopes.org
www.camphighhopes.org
Joe Brennan, Director
Hope Woodcock-Ross, Health Director
A week-long summer camp program for boys with hemophilia. The camp has a 24-hour physician and nursing staff. Ages 7-17, boys only.

1131 Camp Huntington
56 Bruceville Rd.
High Falls, NY 12440-5100 845-687-7840
855-707-2267
FAX: 855-707-2267
www.camphuntington.com
Daniel Falk, Executive Director
Dylan Sloan, Program Director
Margaret Short, Health Director
A co-ed residential summer camp specifically designed to focus on adaptive and therapeutic recreation. Campers include those with learning and developmental disabilities, ADD/HD, Autism Spectrum Disorders, Asperger's, PDD, and other special needs. Programs focus on recreation and social skills, independence, and participation.

1132 Camp Kehilla
Henry Kaufmann Campgrounds
75 Colonial Springs Rd.
Wheatley Heights, NY 11798 516-484-1545
jwasserman@sjjcc.org
www.campkehilla.org
Joe Wasserman, Camp Director
Victoria Granatelli, Assistant Camp Director
A year-round camp for children, teens, and young adults with developmental disabilities and other neurodevelopmental conditions. Ages 5-21.

1133   Camp Little Oak
Aldersgate Camp & Retreat Center
7955 Brantingham Rd.
Greig, NY 13345   425-770-1801
                                              camplittleoak.org

Hannah Russell, Camp Director

A non-profit, week-long summer camp for girls diagnosed with a bleeding disorder. The camp is held at Aldersgate Camp in Greig, New York. Camp Little Oak runs traditional summer camp activities such as swimming, canoeing, and archery, as well as provides education about blood disorders and conducts community service projects.

1134   Camp Mark Seven
Mark Seven Deaf Foundation
144 Mohawk Hotel Rd.
Old Forge, NY 13420   315-207-5706
                                         TTY:315-357-6089
                                    registrar@campmark7.org
                                          www.campmark7.org

Dave Staehle, Camp Director

A camp program for hard-of-hearing, deaf and hearing people. Coed, open to all ages. The camp is located on the Fourth Lake in the Adirondack Mountains.

1135   Camp Pa-Qua-Tuck
2 Chet Swezey Rd.
Center Moriches, NY 11934   631-878-1070
                                    www.camppaquatuck.com

Alyssa Pecorino, Executive Director
Melissa Locrotondo, Chief of Programming
Tommy Ryan, Director, Respite Camp

Camp Pa-Qua-Tuck is a residential camp for individuals with physical and developmental disabilities. The camp also offers Respite Camp, a weekend camp program for ages 6-40.

1136   Camp Ramapo
Ramapo for Children
Rt. 52/Salisbury Turnpike
PO Box 266
Rhinebeck, NY 12572   845-876-8403
                                         FAX: 845-876-8414
                                 office@ramapoforchildren.org
                                   www.ramapoforchildren.org

Matthew McKnight, Camp Director
Lenora Sealey, Associate Camp Director

A residential summer camp for youth ages 6-16 with social, emotional, or learning challenges.

1137   Camp Reece
1782 S Johnsburg Rd.
Johnsburg, NY 12843-1909   212-289-4872
                                       info@campreece.org
                                         www.campreece.org

Duncan Lester, Executive Director
Octavia Man, Camp Director
Kiersten Twitchell, Camp Director

A sleep-away camp for children ages 10-17 with special needs. The camp is located at Skidmore College and offers activities such as photography, rafting, biking, sports, and more. The camp serves boys and girls with disabilities such as ADD/ADHD, learning disabilities, and high-functioning autism. There are two 3-week sessions or the full 6-week session available.

1138   Camp Sisol
Jewish Community Center of Greater Rochester/JCC
1200 Edgewood Ave.
Rochester, NY 14618   585-461-2000
                                         FAX: 585-461-0805
                               bettertogether@jccrochester.org
                                        www.jccrochester.org

Josh Weinstein, Chief Executive Officer

Coed, ages 5-16. Camp Sisol accommodates children with special needs.

1139   Camp Tova
92nd Street Y
1395 Lexington Ave.
New York, NY 10128   212-415-5573
                                                www.92y.org

Seth Pinsky, Chief Executive Officer
Alyse Myers, President
Lauren Wexler, Director, Camps

Camp Tova is a program for children with developmental disabilities. Campers participate in sports, arts, and outdoor activities and develop their creative, social, and physical skills.

1140   Camp Venture, Inc.
25 Smith St.
Suite 510
Nanuet, NY 10954   845-624-3860
                                        www.campventure.org

Matthew Shelley, Chief Executive Officer
Celia Solomita, Chief Financial Officer
Marie Pardi, Chief Program Officer

Camp Venture is a day camp for children ages 5-12 with and without developmental disabilities. Located in Stony Point, the camp also offers a young adult group for teens ages 13-21 with developmental disabilities. Children will experience regular camp activities while benefitting from group engagement.

1141   Camp Whitman on Seneca Lake
PO Box 24393
Rochester, NY 14624   315-201-0193
                                         FAX: 315-531-4002
                                   camp@campwhitman.org
                                       www.campwhitman.org

Lea Kone, Camp Director

Provides camp opportunities for individuals with developmental disabilities. Campers are encouraged to participate in a full range of activities including games, sports, swimming, singing, and dancing.

1142   Clover Patch Camp
Center for Disability Services
55 Helping Hand Lane
Glenville, NY 12302   518-384-3042
                                         FAX: 518-384-3001
                                  cloverpatchcamp@cfdsny.org
                                   www.cloverpatchcamp.org

Cindy Francis, Camp Director
Jackie Richards, Director, Residential Services

Clover Patch Camp is operated by the Center for Disability Services and is located in Glenville, New York. The camp is for individuals with a variety of disabilities. For ages 5+.

1143   Double H Ranch
97 Hidden Valley Rd.
Lake Luzerne, NY 12846   518-696-5676
                                         FAX: 518-696-4528
                                  myurenda@doublehranch.org
                                      www.doublehranch.org

Max Yurenda, CEO & Executive Director
Kate Walsh, Camp Director
Alex Griffen, Assistant Camp Director, Programs

Summer residential camp and winter sports programs for children and young adults ages 6-16 who have cancer and other life threatening illnesses. The programs are free of charge and some of the recreational activities include bead making, arts and crafts, tennis, soccer, and volleyball.

1144   Friendship Circle Day Camp
Friendship Circle Upper East Side
419 E 77th St.
New York, NY 10075   office@friendshipcirclenyc.org
                                   www.friendshipcirclenyc.org

Shlomo Gutnick, Executive Director
Sara Gutnick, Program Director
Dassy Chein, Program Coordinator

The Friendship Circle Day Camp allows children with special needs the opportunity to have a full camp experience. Campers participate in activities such as field trips, music, arts and crafts, and performances.

1145 Gow School Summer Programs
2491 Emery Rd.
South Wales, NY 14139   716-687-2004
                                 FAX: 716-687-2003
                                 summer@gow.org
                                 www.gow.org

Matthew Fisher, Director
Co-ed summer programs for students ages 8-16 with dyslexia or similar learning disabilities. Offers a blend of morning academics, afternoon/evening traditional camp activities and weekend overnights.

1146 Kamp Kiwanis
New York District Kiwanis Foundation
9020 Kiwanis Rd.
Taberg, NY 13471   315-336-4568
                                 FAX: 315-336-3845
                                 kamp@kampkiwanis.org
                                 www.kampkiwanis.org

Rebecca Lopez Clemence, Executive Director
Luke Clemence, Camp Director
Dori Gross, Assistant Camp Director
Kamp Kiwanis is a mainstream camp for underprivileged youth with and without special needs. Twenty campers with disabilities are integrated into weekly sessions. Programs are offered for children, teens, and adults.

1147 Katy Isaacson Elaine Gordon Lodge
AHRC New York City
653 Colgate Rd.
Box 37
East Jewett, NY 12424   518-589-6000
                                 FAX: 518-589-6583
                                 matthew.hatcher@ahrcnyc.org
                                 camping.ahrcnyc.org

Matt Hatcher, Camp Director
An alternative and traditional summer day camp for adults and teens with intellectual and developmental disabilities. The lodge offers five 11-day sessions for adults ages 18-29, and one session for teens ages 13-17. Activities include boating, swimming, pony rides, sports, and more.

1148 Lisa Beth Gerstman Camp
Lisa Beth Gerstman Foundation
439 Oak St.
Suite 1
Garden City, NY 11530   516-594-4400
                                 FAX: 516-594-7085
                                 info@lisabethgerstman.org
                                 www.lisabethgerstman.org

Harvey Gerstman, Co-Founder
Carol Gerstman, Co-Founder
Linda Gerstman, Co-Founder
A summer day camp for children with special needs. Activities include swimming, sports, and arts and crafts. Camps are located across the New York Metropolitan Area.

1149 Maplebrook School
5142 Route 22
Amenia, NY 12501   845-373-9511
                                 FAX: 845-373-7029
                                 admissions@maplebrookschool.org
                                 www.maplebrookschool.org

Donna Konkolics, Head of School
Roger Fazzone, President
Jennifer Scully, Assistant Head, Postsecondary Studies
A coeducational boarding school which offers a six week camp for children with learning differences and ADD.

1150 Marist Brothers Mid-Hudson Valley Camp
1455 Broadway
PO Box 197
Esopus, NY 12429   845-384-6620
                                 info@maristbrotherscenter.org
                                 www.maristbrotherscenter.org

Jim Sheldon, Camp Director
Timothy Hagan, Director, Operations
Donnell Neary, Assistant Director
The camp provides week-long summer sessions for children who have a variety of special needs and illnesses, including cancer and physical, developmental, and mental disabilities. Each session is specific to the special need or illness.

1151 Mosholu Day Camp
Mosholu Montefiore Community Center
3450 Dekalb Ave.
New York, NY 10467   718-882-4000
                                 frontdesk@mmcc.org
                                 www.mmcc.org/camp

Rita Santelia, Chief Executive Officer
Shakil M. Khan, Chief Financial Officer
Jackina Farshtey, Chief of Staff
A day camp program for children in grades 1-10. The day camp offers specific programs for children and teens who are developmentally disabled. Camp Sunshine is for children ages 5-12, and Camp Elan is for children ages 12-16.

1152 Southampton Fresh Air Home
36 Barkers Island Rd.
Southampton, NY 11968   631-283-1594
                                 FAX: 631-283-7596
                                 www.sfah.org

Thomas Naro, Executive Director
David Billingham, Camp Director
Nathan Unwin, Assistant Camp Director
A residential camp facility accommodating physically challenged children. The Special Needs Summer Camp is for children and teens ages 8-18. One or three week sessions available, as well as day camp. The SFAH provides adapted programs and activities that allow campers to develop physically, emotionally, and psychologically.

1153 Special Services Summer Day Camp
Commonpoint Queens
58-20 Little Neck Pkwy.
Little Neck, NY 11362   718-225-6750
                                 larmband@commonpointqueens.org
                                 www.commonpointqueens.org/summercamp
Lisa Armband, Contact
A day camp program for children and youth ages 5-21 with developmental disabilities. Activities include dancing, swimming, arts and crafts, and community-based field trips. The program is held at the Henry Kaufmann Campgrounds.

1154 Summit Camp
55 W 38th St.
4th Floor
New York, NY 10018   570-253-4381
                                 info@summitcamp.com
                                 www.summitcamp.com

Shepherd Baum, Director
Leah Love, Assistant Director
Thea Mullis, Travel Director
The camp is located in Honesdale, Pennsylvania, and is for children ages 8-19 who have a variety of developmental, social, or learning challenges. In addition to traditional camp activities, Summit Camp has a strong focus on social skills development and interpersonal growth.

1155 Sunshine Campus
809 Five Points Rd.
Rush, NY 14543   585-533-2080
                                 www.sunshinecamp.org

Tracey Dreisbach, Executive Director
Brandi Koch, Camp Director
Jarod Alexander, Facility Director
The camp is located in Rush, New York. Camping sessions for children and young adults with a variety of disabilities. Ages 7-21. Campers experience a variety of traditional summer camp activities, including climbing wall, swimming, boating, hiking, and sports.

1156 VISIONS Vacation Camp for the Blind (VCB)
VISIONS Center on Blindness
111 Summit Park Rd.
Spring Valley, NY 10977   845-354-3003
                                 888-245-8333
                                 info@visionsvcb.org
                                 www.visionsvcb.org

Krystal Findley-Jones, Director

A nonprofit agency that promotes the independence of people of all ages who are blind or visually impaired. Camp offers Braille classes, computers with large print and voice output, support groups, discussions, cooking classes, personal and home management training, and large print and Braille books.

1157   Wagon Road Camp
Children's Aid Society
117 W 124th St.
3rd Floor
New York, NY 10027   212-949-4800
                                        www.childrensaidnyc.org
Phoebe Boyer, President & CEO
Vince Canziani, Camp Director
Wagon Road Day Camp is a co-ed program for children ages 6-13 with a variety of disabilities held in Chappaqua, New York. Activities include athletics, horsemanship, theater arts, nature studies, and arts and crafts.

1158   West Hills Day Camp
21 Sweet Hollow Rd.
Huntington, NY 11743   631-427-6700
                                           FAX: 631-427-6504
                                        info@westhillscamp.com
                                           westhillsdaycamp.com
Susan Diamond, Director
Kimberly Doxey, Director
A summer day camp program for children with autism spectrum disorders an other related neurobiological disorders. Located on Long Island, activities include swimming, climbing/ropes course, photography, arts and crafts, and more.

1159   YMCA Camp Chingachgook on Lake George
Capital District YMCA
1872 Pilot Knob Rd.
Kattskill Bay, NY 12844   518-656-9462
                                           FAX: 518-656-9362
                                        chingachgook@cdymca.org
                                          www.lakegeorgecamp.org
Jine Andreozzi, Executive Director
Mike Obermayer, Director, Summer Program
Carol Lewis, Office Manager
Offers sailing programs for people with disabilities.

North Carolina

1160   Camp Carefree
275 Carefree Lane
Stokesdale, NC 27357   336-427-0966
                                        directors@campcarefree.org
                                          www.campcarefree.org
Diane Samelak, Executive Director
Tony McCallum, Program Director
JeNai Davis, Program Director
A free, one-week camp for children with chronic illnesses. The camp also offers programs for siblings of ill children and children with a sick parent.

1161   Camp Carolina Trails
American Diabetes Association
1300 Baxter St.
Suite 150
Charlotte, NC 28204   704-373-9111
                                        campsupport@diabetes.org
                                             www.diabetes.org
The camp is for children ages 7-16 years of age who have diabetes. The camp is held on the YMCA's Camp Hanes campground in King, North Carolina. Activities include swimming, hiking, and field games. The camp employs a complete medical staff consisting of registered nurses, dieticians, and pediatric endoctrinologists.

1162   Camp Dogwood
7062 Camp Dogwood Dr.
PO Box 39
Sherrills Ford, NC 28673   828-478-2135
                                          tammy@nclionsinc.org
                                        nclionscampdogwood.org
Tammy Thomas, Camp Administrator

A recreational facility on Lake Norman offering 10 week-long sessions for adults who are blind and visually impaired. Ages 18 and up. Activities include swimming, tubing, local field trips, bowling, and more. Service dogs welcome.

1163   Camp New Hope
PO Box 154
Glendale Springs, NC 28629   336-982-3797
                                           campnewhopenc.com
Randy Brown, Executive Director
Camp New Hope is a privately owned facility for children with life-threatening medical conditions and their families. Families are able to enjoy fishing, canoeing, tubing, swimming, and more at their leisure.

1164   Camp Royall
250 Bill Ash Rd.
Moncure, NC 27559   919-542-1033
                                           FAX: 919-533-5324
                                      camproyall@autismsociety-nc.org
                                   www.autismsociety-nc.org/camp-royall
Sara Gage, Director
A week-long overnight and day camp for children and adults with autism. Campers participate in traditional camp activities such as swimming, boating, hiking, and arts and crafts. Counselor-to-camper ratio is 1:1 or 1:2, depending on the campers' needs.

1165   Camp Sertoma
Millstone 4-H Center
1296 Mallard Dr.
Ellerbe, NC 28338   sertomadeafcamp@gmail.com
                                          www.campsertomaclub.org
Sandy Waterman, Contact
Keith Russell, Camp Director, Millstone 4-H Center
Camp Sertoma is a camp program for deaf and hard of hearing youth. Activities include swimming, canoeing, fishing, hiking, hayrides, campfires, and games. Coed, ages 8-16.

1166   Camp Tekoa
United Methodist Camp Tekoa
PO Box 1793
Flat Rock, NC 28731-1793   828-692-6516
                                           FAX: 828-697-3288
                                             www.camptekoa.org
John Isley, Executive Director
Dave Bollen, Assistant Director
Karen Rohrer, Business Manager
Offers special needs camp programs for individuals with developmental disabilities.

1167   SOAR Summer Adventures
226 SOAR Lane
PO Box 388
Balsam, NC 28707   828-456-3435
                                           FAX: 801-820-3050
                                          admissions@soarnc.org
                                              www.soarnc.org
John Willson, Executive Director
A nonprofit adventure program working with disadvantaged youth diagnosed with learning disabilities in an outdoor, challenge-based environment. Focuses on esteem building and social skills development through rock climbing, backpacking, whitewater rafting, mountaineering, sailing, snorkeling, and more. Offers two week, one month, and semester programs. Locations include North Carolina, Florida, Wyoming, California, New York, Belize, Costa Rica, and the Caribbean.

1168   Talisman Summer Camp
64 Gap Creek Rd.
Zirconia, NC 28790   828-697-6313
                                        info@talismancamps.com
                                          www.talismancamps.com
Linda Tatsapaugh, Operations Director & Owner
Robiyn Mims, Admissions Director & Owner
Cory Greene, Camp Director
Talisman Summer Camp is located 40 minutes south of Asheville, North Carolina. Offers a program of hiking, rafting, climbing, and caving for young people with autism, ADHD and learning disabilities. Coed, ages 6-22.

1169 Victory Junction
4500 Adam's Way
Randleman, NC 27317
336-498-9055
info@victoryjunction.org
www.victoryjunction.org
Chad Coltrane, President & CEO
Lisa Weber, Chief Financial Officer
Frances Beasley, Chief Development Officer
The camp serves children with a variety of chronic medical conditions or serious illnesses, including Autism, Cancer, Craniofacial Anomalies, Diabetes, Sickle Cell, Spina Bifida and more. Victory Junction provides traditional camp activities and also includes a NASCAR themed area.

North Dakota

1170 Camp Sioux
American Diabetes Association
106 Solid Rock Circle
Park River, ND 58270
763-593-5333
campsupport@diabetes.org
www.diabetes.org
Camp Sioux, located in Park River, ND, is a week-long residential summer camp for children ages 8-15 who are living with diabetes. Programs encourage independence and self management with appropriate medical supervision to ensure the best possible experience for every camper. Nutrition activities, blood glucose monitoring, and injections/medications are integrated into the camp program.

Ohio

1171 Camp Arye
Jewish Community Center of Greater Columbus
1125 College Ave.
Columbus, OH 43209
614-231-2731
FAX: 614-231-8222
www.columbusjcc.org
Raeann Cronebach, Director
Ariana Solomon, Inclusion Coordinator
A Jewish summer camp for children and young adults with developmental, physical, emotional, mental and learning disabilities. Camp Arye is co-ed and for children in grades 1-7.

1172 Camp Cheerful
Achievement Centers For Children
15000 Cheerful Lane
Strongsville, OH 44136-5420
440-238-6200
FAX: 440-238-1858
www.achievementcenters.org
Sally Farwell, President & CEO
Scott Peplin, Executive Vice President & CFO
Deborah Osgood, Vice President, Development & Marketing
Camp Cheerful provides a number of day and overnight camping options for children and adults who have disabilities. The camp hosts traditional camp activities as well as year-round therapeutic horseback riding sessions and an accessible high ropes challenge course during the summer. The focus of activities is to increase the quality of life while encouraging confidence and independence.

1173 Camp Christopher: SumFun Day Camp
Catholic Charities Disability Services
Camp Christopher
930 N Hametown Rd.
Akron, OH 44333
330-376-2267
800-296-2267
campchristopher@ccdocle.org
ccdocle.org/programs/sumfun-day-camp
Tess Flannery, Contact
A multi-week summer day camp for children, teens, and young adults ages 5-21 with developmental disabilities. Campers participate in regular camp activities while building confidence and social skills.

1174 Camp Echoing Hills
36272 County Rd. 79
Warsaw, OH 43844
740-327-2311
www.ehvi.org
Lauren Unger, Camp Administrator
Summer camp for children and adults with physical, intellectual and developmental disabilities. The camp focuses on religion, social interaction, and skill development.

1175 Camp Emanuel
PO Box 752343
Dayton, OH 45475
937-477-5504
crawford@campemanuel.org
www.campemanuel.weebly.com
Brian Demarke, President
Stephanie Ackner, Vice President
Mary Foreman, Secretary
Camp Emanuel is a camp for hearing impaired and hearing youth. There are day sessions for children 5-14 and overnight resident sessions for children and teens 9-17. The camp aims to promote descision making, self-esteem, and acceptance by integrating non-hearing children with hearing children.

1176 Camp Hamwi
LifeCare Alliance - Central Ohio Diabetes Assoc.
1699 West Mound St.
Columbus, OH 43223
614-278-3130
amyer@lifecarealliance.org
www.lifecarealliance.org
Anthony Myer, Director, Youth & Family Program
A summer camp for kids with diabetes, ages 7-17. Sessions are divided by age group, with a Junior Challenge Week for ages 7-12 and a Senior Challenged week for ages 13-17. Activities include horseback riding, sports, swimming, and other outdoor activities.

1177 Camp Happiness
Catholic Charities Disability Services
7911 Detroit Ave.
Cleveland, OH 44102
216-334-2900
FAX: 216-334-2905
ccdocle.org/programs/camp-happiness
Marilyn Scott, Director
Lauren Mailey, Program Administrator
Camp Happiness welcomes children and young adults ages 5-21 with intellectual and developmental disabilities. In addition to recreational services, Camp Happiness also provides educational and social services to help participants continue to practice and develop skills throughout the year.

1178 Camp Ho Mita Koda
14040 Auburn Rd.
Newbury, OH 44065
440-739-4095
info@camphomitakoda.org
www.camphomitakoda.org
Ian Roberts, Executive Director
Eric Brown, Camp Director
Camp Ho Mita Koda is a summer camp for children with type 1 diabetes. The camp aims to provide outdoor activities while also educating and building life skills for children with diabetes. Offers overnight camp, family camp, specialty camp, and leadership development programs.

1179 Camp Joy
10117 Old 3C Hwy.
PO Box 157
Clarksville, OH 45113
937-289-2031
info@camp-joy.org
camp-joy.org
Jen Eismeier, Executive Director
Casey Miller, Director, Operations
Jen Alvis, Director, Business Operations
A summer camp organization for children and teens with a variety of disabilities. Sessions for children, teens and young adults with asthma, HIV/AIDS, spina bifida, limb loss, cancer, blood diseases, and immune disorders.

1180 Camp Ko-Man-She
Diabetes Dayton
2555 S Dixie Dr.
Suite 112
Dayton, OH 45409
937-220-6611
FAX: 937-224-0240
admin@diabetesdayton.org
www.diabetesdaytoncamp.com
Susan McGovern, Executive Director
Camp Ko-Man-She is located in Bellefontaine, Ohio, and is held annually for children with diabetes. The camp's goal is for children to socialize with other children who also have diabetes and to have fun outdoors in a medically supervised setting. Co-ed, ages 8-17.

1181 Camp Korelitz
American Diabetes Association
Camp Joy
10117 Old 3C Hwy.
Clarksville, OH 45113
513-759-9330
campsupport@diabetes.org
www.diabetes.org
A week-long residential camp for children ages 9-15 with diabetes. Camp Korelitz is a program of the American Diabetes Association, and is held at Camp Joy in Clarksville, Ohio. Activities include climbing walls, archery, and canoeing, as well as discussions and education about nutrition and diabetes.

1182 Camp Nuhop
1077 Township Rd. 2916
Perrysville, OH 44864
419-938-7151
www.nuhop.org
Trevor Dunlap, Executive Director & CEO
Chris Clyde, Associate Director
Matt Poland, Director, Outdoor Education
A summer residential program for youth ages 6-18 with learning disabilities, behavioral disorders, or other neuroatypical disorders. Activities include outdoor education and team-building workshops. The staff-to-camper ratio is 3:7 or 3:8.

1183 Camp Oty'Okwa
24799 Purcell Rd.
South Bloomingville, OH 43152-9740
740-385-5279
rperkins@bbbscentralohio.org
campotyokwa.org
Rick Perkins, Camp Director
Matt Smith, Youth Camp Director
Emily Kridel, Environmental Education Director
Owned and operated by Big Brothers Big Sisters of Central Ohio, this summer camp accommodates children with disabilities such as ADD/ADHD, autism, learning disabilities, and behavioral or mood disorders.

1184 Camp Paradise
SHC, The Arc of Medina County
4283 Paradise Rd.
Seville, OH 44273
330-722-1900
shc@shc-medina.org
shc-medina.org/camp-paradise
Melanie Kasten-Krause, Executive Director
Shelly Wharton, Associate Executive Director
Michael Beh, Director, Finance
Camp Paradise is a summer camp for adults with developmental disabilities. The camp offers five weeks of themed programs. Day and residential camp available. Activities include music, art therapy, sports, swimming, bonfires, and more.

1185 Camp Quality Ohio
PO Box 358
Uniontown, OH 44685
234-738-2073
ohio@campqualityusa.org
www.campqualityusa.org/oh
Sarah Givens, Executive Director
Brian Krebs, Camp Director
Kelly Krebs, Camper Registrar
Camp Quality is for children with cancer and their siblings. The camp offers a stress-free environment that offers exciting activities and fosters new friendships, while helping to give the children courage, motivation and emotional strength.

1186 Camp Stepping Stone
Stepping Stones Inc. - Given Campus
5650 Given Rd.
Cincinnati, OH 45243
513-831-4660
FAX: 513-831-5918
steppingstonesohio.org
Chris Adams, Executive Director
Sam Allen, Director, Programs & Operations
Chris Brockman, Director, Facilities
A summer day camp program for youth with disabilities, ages 5-22. Activities include swimming, fishing, art, and music. Three separate three-week sessions are available. The camp is located at the Stepping Stones Given Campus in Cincinnati, Ohio.

1187 Camp Tiponi
Diabetes Dayton
2555 S Dixie Dr.
Suite 112
Dayton, OH 45409
937-220-6611
FAX: 937-224-0240
admin@diabetesdayton.org
www.diabetesdaytoncamp.com
Susan McGovern, Executive Director
A summer camp for youth with type 2 diabetes, prediabetes, or metabolic disorders. Campers participate in activities such as swimming, archery, hiking, and sports while gaining education and skills needed to maintain a healthy lifestyle. The camp is located at Camp Willson in Bellefontaine, Ohio.

1188 Courageous Acres
Courageous Community Services
12701 Waterville Swanton Rd.
Whitehouse, OH 43571
419-875-6828
FAX: 419-875-5598
info@ccsohio.org
www.ccsohio.org
Laura Kuhlenbeck, Executive Director
Courageous Acres is an accessible summer camp for children, teens, and adults with disabilities. Open to individuals ages 4+ in Northwest Ohio and Southeast Michigan.

1189 Flying Horse Farms
5260 State Route 95
Mt. Gilead, OH 43338
419-751-7077
FAX: 419-751-7010
info@flyinghorsefarms.org
flyinghorsefarms.org
Nichole E. Dunn, President & CEO
Rachel Escusa, Chief Advancement Officer
Stacey Kyser, Director, Development
Flying Horse Farms is a camp for children with serious illnesses, ages 7-15, and their families. The camp serves campers diagnosed with cancer, heart conditions, asthma, blood disorders, and more. Activities include swimming, fishing, and other traditional camp activities.

1190 Highbrook Lodge
Cleveland Sight Center
1909 E 101st St.
Cleveland, OH 44106
216-791-8118
FAX: 216-791-1101
TTY:216-791-8119
info@clevelandsightcenter.org
www.clevelandsightcenter.org
Larry Benders, President & CEO
Kevin Krencisz, Chief Financial & Administrative Officer
Jassen Tawil, Director, Business Development & Customer Success
Camp is located in Chardon, Ohio. Summer sessions for children, adults and families who are blind or have low vision. Sessions include a wide range of outdoor camp activities. Camp activities focus on gaining independent skills, mobility, orientation and self-confidence in an accessible and traditional camp setting.

1191 Insight Horse Camp
Marmon Valley
7754 State Route 292 S
Zanesfield, OH 43360
937-593-8000
FAX: 937-593-6900
info@marmonvalley.com
marmonvalley.com
Matt Wiley, Executive Director

A coed resident camp program for children who are blind or visually impaired. The main focus of camp is on learning basic horsemanship skills. Campers also participate in traditional camp activities and Bible study discussions.

1192 **Recreation Unlimited: Day Camp**
Recreation Unlimited Foundation
7700 Piper Rd.
Ashley, OH 43003 740-548-7006
FAX: 740-747-2640
info@recreationunlimited.org
www.recreationunlimited.org
Paul L. Huttlin, Executive Director & CEO
Sarah Kelley, Camps Director
Camping sessions for children and teens, ages 5-22, with physical or developmental disabilities and their siblings. The camp provides a full day of traditional camp activities and aims to create an inclusive experience for all participants.

1193 **Recreation Unlimited: Residential Camp**
Recreation Unlimited Foundation
7700 Piper Rd.
Ashley, OH 43003 740-548-7006
FAX: 740-747-2640
info@recreationunlimited.org
www.recreationunlimited.org
Paul L. Huttlin, Executive Director & CEO
Sarah Kelley, Camps Director
Camping sessions for children and adults with a variety of physical and developmental disabilities. Two week long sessions for ages 8-22, one week long session for ages 18-35, and four week long sessions for ages 23 and up. The camp provides traditional outdoor recreation such as fishing, archery, exploration, campfires and more. A week long winter camp is offered for ages 18 and up.

1194 **Recreation Unlimited: Respite Weekend Camp**
Recreation Unlimited Foundation
7700 Piper Rd.
Ashley, OH 43003 740-548-7006
FAX: 740-747-2640
info@recreationunlimited.org
www.recreationunlimited.org
Paul L. Huttlin, Executive Director & CEO
Sarah Kelley, Camps Director
Camping sessions for children and adults with a variety of physical and developmental disabilities. There are seven weekend camps for youth ages 8-22 and eight weekend camps for adults ages 23 and up. Traditional outdoor activities are provided, along with lodging, meals, site nursing, and more.

1195 **Recreation Unlimited: Specialty Camp**
Recreation Unlimited Foundation
7700 Piper Rd.
Ashley, OH 43003 740-548-7006
FAX: 740-747-2640
info@recreationunlimited.org
www.recreationunlimited.org
Paul L. Huttlin, Executive Director & CEO
Sarah Kelley, Camps Director
Weekend and week-long camping sessions for youth and adults. The camps are dedicated to a specific disability or health concern and designed to meet the needs of certain groups.

1196 **Rotary Camp**
Rotary Club of Akron
4460 Rex Lake Dr.
Akron, OH 44319 330-644-4512
FAX: 330-644-1013
danr@akronymca.org
www.akronrotary.org
Dan Reynolds, Camp Director
Offers camping experiences for children and adults with disabilities. Rotary Camp provides traditional camping experiences while focusing on socialization and independence.

1197 **St. Augustine Rainbow Camp**
Disability Ministries at St. Augustine Parish
2486 W 14th St.
Cleveland, OH 44113 216-781-5530
FAX: 216-781-1124
TTY:216-302-2375
augustine.rainbow.camp@gmail.com
www.staugustinecleveland.org
Rev. William O'Donnell, Administrator
Day camp for disabled and non-disabled youth ages 5-13. The camp serves youth from the deaf, hard-of-hearing, blind, and developmentally disabled communities of Greater Cleveland, as well as youth from the Tremont area.

1198 **Stepping Stones: Camp Allyn**
Stepping Stones Inc. - Allyn Campus
1414 Lake Allyn Rd.
Batavia, OH 45103 513-831-4660
FAX: 513-831-5918
steppingstonesohio.org
Chris Adams, Executive Director
Sam Allen, Director, Programs & Operations
Chris Brockman, Director, Facilities
An overnight residential camp for children and adults with disabilities. Coed, ages 16-65. Campers participate in crafts, swimming, hiking, and sports activities. The camp session lasts five days and is located at the Stepping Stones Allyn Campus in Batavia, Ohio.

1199 **YMCA Outdoor Center Campbell Gard**
4803 Augspurger Rd.
Hamilton, OH 45011 513-867-0600
FAX: 513-867-0127
campoffice@gmvymca.org
www.ccgymca.org
Pete Fasano, Executive Director
The camp is located in Hamilton, Ohio. Offers camp programs for youth with developmental disabilities. Runs overnight and day sessions for ages 7-22 and families.

Oklahoma

1200 **Camp CANOE**
Camp Fire Heart of Oklahoma
3309 E Hefner Rd.
Oklahoma City, OK 73131 405-478-5646
info@campfirehok.org
www.campfirehok.org
Penn Henthorn, Director, Programs & Camps
Camp CANOE is a summer day camp for children with autism and Down Syndrome. Camp CANOE focuses on skills such as self-reliance, confidence, communication, social skills, problem-solving, and more.

1201 **Camp ClapHans**
J.D. McCarty Center
2002 E Robinson St.
Norman, OK 73071 405-307-2865
camp@jdmc.org
www.campclaphans.com
Bobbie Hunter, Camp Director
A summer camp for children, teens, and young adults ages 8-18 with developmental disabilities. Activities include archery, arts and crafts, scavenger hunts, stargazing, and more. Sessions are four days and three nights, and are limited to 12 campers per session (6 boys and 6 girls).

1202 **Camp Endres**
Diabetes Solutions of Oklahoma, Inc.
3333 NW 63rd
Suite 100
Oklahoma City, OK 73116 405-843-4386
FAX: 888-665-2741
natalie@dsok.net
dsok.net/programs/camp-endres-day-camp
Kim Boaz-Wilson, Executive Director
Natalie Bayne, Camp Director

Camp Endres is a summer camp for individuals with diabetes. Programs include Day Camp (ages 4-10), Junior (ages 7-13), Senior (ages 14-18), Adult (ages 21+), and Family Camp sessions.

1203 **Camp Lo-Be-Gon**
American Diabetes Association
5401 S Harvard
Suite 120
Tulsa, OK 74135
918-492-3839
FAX: 918-492-4262
campsupport@diabetes.org
www.diabetes.org

A summer camp for youth ages 6-15 with diabetes. The camp is held at Camp Loughridge in Tulsa, Oklahoma.

1204 **Camp Loughridge**
4900 W 71st St.
Tulsa, OK 74131
918-446-4194
registrar@camploughridge.org
camploughridge.org

Jacob McIntosh, Executive Director
Loren Pirtle, Program Director
Camp Loughridge is a Christian summer day camp for children ages 6-10. The camp offers an Autism Inclusion program for children diagnosed with austism. Space is limited to two campers with autism per session.

1205 **Camp Perfect Wings**
Baptist General Convention of Oklahoma
3800 N May Ave.
Oklahoma City, OK 73112
405-942-3800
www.oklahomabaptists.org

Becka Johnson, Camp Director
Camp program for children and adults with special needs, ages 8 and up. Activities include canoeing, pool games, low ropes challenges, and crafts. Held in spring/early summer.

Oregon

1206 **Adventures Without Limits**
1341 Pacific Ave.
Forest Grove, OR 97116
503-359-2568
FAX: 503-359-4671
info@awloutdoors.org
awloutdoors.com

Brad Bafaro, Founder & Executive Director
Jennifer Wilde, Director, Outreach & Development
Carrie Morton, Program Director
Adventures Without Limits facilitates inclusive outdoor adventures for people of all ages and ability levels. Trip activities include hiking, rafting, caving, rock climbing, kayaking, snowshoeing, and more.

1207 **B'nai B'rith Camp: Kehila Program**
6443 SW Beaverton-Hillsdale Hwy.
Suite 234
Portland, OR 97221
503-496-7444
FAX: 503-452-0750
info@bbcamp.org
bbcamp.org

Michelle Koplan, Chief Executive Officer
Ben Charlton, Chief Program Officer
Bette Amir-Brownstein, Camp Director
The Kehila Program at B'nai B'rith Camp is a Jewish summer camp program for children with special needs. This program is run during the camp's Maccabee session.

1208 **Camp Magruder**
17450 Old Pacific Hwy.
Rockaway Beach, OR 97136
503-355-2310
FAX: 503-355-8701
troy@campmagruder.org
www.campmagruder.org

Troy Taylor, Camp Director
Hope Montgomery, Program Director
Rik Gutzke, Facilities Manager
Camp is located in Rockaway Beach, Oregon. Sessions for teens and adults with developmental disabilities through Camp Hope.

1209 **Camp Meadowood Springs**
77650 Meadowood Rd.
Weston, OR 97886
541-276-2752
FAX: 541-276-7227
camp@meadowoodsprings.org
www.meadowoodsprings.org

Michelle Nelson, Camp Director
This camp is designed to help children with communication disorders and learning differences. A full range of activities in recreational and clinical areas is available.

1210 **Camp Millennium**
2880 NW Stewart Pkwy.
Suite 200
Roseburg, OR 97471
541-677-0600
campmoregon@gmail.com
campmillennium.org

Mindy Bean, Camp Director
Steve Maine, Program Director
A week-long residential summer camp for children diagnosed with cancer, ages 5-16. The camp is free to attend, and activities include hiking, archery, horeseback riding, and more.

1211 **Camp Starlight**
PO Box 13107
Portland, OR 97213
503-964-1516
info@camp-starlight.org
camp-starlight.org

Melanie Smith-Wilusz, Camp Director
Kit Noble, Operations Director
Spike Huntington-Kline, Program Director
Camp Starlight is a week-long sleep-away summer camp for children in Oregon and Washington whose lives are affected by HIV/AIDS. There is a 1:1 staff-to-camper ratio. Activities include swimming, hiking, arts and crafts, archery, sports, and games. The camp is free to attend.

1212 **Camp Taloali**
15934 N Santiam Hwy. SE
PO Box 32
Stayton, OR 97383
503-400-6547
campadmin@taloali.org
www.taloali.org

Randall Smith, Camp Administrator
Summer sessions for children who are deaf, hard of hearing, or have a hearing impairment. Camp Taloali emphasizes communication, leadership, and social development.

1213 **Camp Ukandu**
601 SW 2nd Ave.
Suite 2300
Portland, OR 97204
503-276-2178
info@ukandu.org
www.ukandu.org

Jason Hickox, Executive Director
Ashley Light, Development Director
Kendra Gish, Program Director
Camp Ukandu is a summer camp for children and teens with cancer, ages 8-18, and their siblings. Activities include campfires, horseback riding, rock walls, and more. The camp is free to attend.

1214 **Creating Memories**
Creating Memories for Disabled Children
59895 Pollock Rd.
Joseph, OR 97846
541-398-0169
cmfdc777@yahoo.com
creatingmemoriesfordisabledchildren.com

Ken Coreson, Founder
Creating Memories for Disabled Children is a camp for children and adults with disabilities. The camp's goal is to connect individuals with disabilities to nature. The camp offers a variety of outdoor activities, including hiking and fishing. Attendance is free.

1215 Easterseals Oregon Summer Camp
Easterseals Oregon
7300 SW Hunziker St.
Suite 103
Portland, OR 97223   503-228-5108
                                      FAX: 503-228-1352
                              www.easterseals.com/oregon

Carol Salter, President & CEO
A camp program for children with disabilities. Activities include boating and fishing, swimming, horseback riding, arts and crafts, archery, sports and recreation, outdoor education, and campfires.

1216 Gales Creek Diabetes Camp
Gales Creek Camp Foundation
6950 SW Hampton St.
Suite 242
Tigard, OR 97223   503-968-2267
                                      FAX: 503-992-6785
                              office@galescreekcamp.org
                                 www.galescreekcamp.org

Robert Dailey, Executive Director
Maddie Ehl, Office & Programming Manager
Camp is located in Gales Creek, Oregon. Summer sessions for children with Type 1 diabetes. Coed and family and pre-school family camps also available. Gales Creek also helps teach campers about testing themselves, giving injections, and how to manage their own bodies.

1217 Hull Park and Retreat Center
Oral Hull Foundation for the Blind
43233 SE Oral Hull Rd.
PO Box 157
Sandy, OR 97055   503-668-6195
                                   oralhull@gmail.com
                                           oralhull.org

Kerith Vance, Executive Director
The Oral Hull Foundation for the Blind provides recreational, educational, and social activities programs designed to fit the needs of guests with vision loss. Programs include week-long summer and winter retreats and three-night getaways for adults with vision impairments.

1218 Mt Hood Kiwanis Camp
10725 SW Barbur Blvd.
Suite 50
Portland, OR 97219   503-452-7416
                                        info@mhkc.org
                                           www.mhkc.org

Dave McDonald, Executive Director
Allan Cushing, Director, Operations
Skye Burns, Director, Development & Communications
Camp is located in Government Camp, Oregon. Summer sessions for children and adults with a variety of disabilities. Coed, ages 12 and up. Family and off-site adventure programs available.

1219 Strength for the Journey
Oregon-Idaho Conference UMC - Camp Registrar
1505 SW 18th Ave.
Portland, OR 97201   503-802-9214
                            registrar@gocamping.org
                              suttlelake.gocamping.org

Daniel Petke, Co-Director, Suttle Lake Camp
Jane Petke, Co-Director, Suttle Lake Camp
Camp is located near Sisters, Oregon at Suttle Lake Camp. Strength for the Journey is a program for adults living with HIV/AIDS.

1220 Suttle Lake Camp
29551 Suttle Lake Rd.
Sisters, OR 97759   541-595-6663
                              suttlelake@gocamping.org
                              suttlelake.gocamping.org

Daniel Petke, Co-Director
Jane Petke, Co-Director
Offers a variety of camp programs, including sessions for individuals with HIV/AIDS.

1221 Upward Bound Camp
40151 Gates School Rd.
Gates, OR 97346   503-897-2447
                                      FAX: 503-897-4116
                            camp@upwardboundcamp.org
                              www.upwardboundcamp.org

Diane Turnbull, Executive Director
Upward Bound Camp is a Christian camp for children and adults with a variety of disabilities, ages 12 and up.

Pennsylvania

1222 Aces Adventure Weekend
Camp Hebron
957 Camp Hebron Rd.
Halifax, PA 17032   412-281-7244
                              www.easterseals.com/wcpenna

James G. Bennett, President & CEO
A weekend respite program for youth with high-functioning Austism, ages 11-22. Activities include canoeing, rock climbing, and cooking. The camp takes place at Camp Hebron in Halifax, Pennsylvania.

1223 Camp AIM
YMCA of Greater Pittsburgh
680 Andersen Dr.
Suite 400
Pittsburgh, PA 15220   412-227-3800
                                campaiminfo@gmail.com
                              www.ycamps.org/camp-aim

Kevin Bolding, President & CEO
Angela Schuettler, Chief Financial Officer
Carolyn Grady, Chief Development Officer
Camp AIM is a 6-week summer program for children, teens, and young adults with physical, cognitive, social/communication, and emotional/behavioral disabilities. The program combines life skills and social and recreational activities with music, art, physical education, and more. Ages 3-21.

1224 Camp Achieva
711 Bingham St.
Pittsburgh, PA 15203   412-995-5000
                                         888-272-7229
                                      FAX: 412-995-5001
                                    cscuilli@achieva.info
                                        www.achieva.info

Stephen H. Suroviec, President & CEO
Cathy Scuilli, Camp Director
Achieva provides life-long services such as early intervention therapies, in-home support, older adult protective services, and more, to individuals with disabilities. Offers summer day camp programs for youth up to age 21 with intellectual disabilities. The camp is located in Monaca, Pennsylvania.

1225 Camp Akeela
Camp Akeela Winter Address
314 Bryn Mawr Ave.
Bala Cynwyd, PA 19004   866-680-4744
                                      FAX: 866-462-2828
                                     www.campakeela.com

Eric Sasson, Camp Director
Debbie Sasson, Camp Director
Ben Jerez, Staffing Director
Camp Akeela is a co-ed, overnight camp for children and young adults ages 9-17 who have been diagnosed with Asperger's Syndrome or a non-verbal learning disability. The camp is located in Thetford Center, Vermont.

1226 Camp Amp
Easterseals Western & Central Pennsylvania, York
2550 Kingston Rd.
Suite 219
York, PA 17402   717-741-3891
                                      FAX: 717-741-5359
                              www.easterseals.com/wcpenna

James G. Bennett, President & CEO
Dane Schick, Director, Camping & Recreation

Camp Amp is an overnight summer camp for children ages 7-17 with any disability or special need. The camp offers a mini session and a full week session. Activities include talent shows, sports, swimming, ropes course, hiking, and more. Camp Amp's goal is to foster independence and encourage socialization.

1227   Camp Can Do
Administrative Office
3 Unami Trail
Chalfont, PA 18914   717-273-6525
campcandoforever.org

Tom Prader, Director, Patient Camp
Stephanie Cole, Director, Patient Camp
Caitlyn McLarnon, Director, Sibling Camp
Camp Can Do is for children ages 8-17 who have been diagnosed with cancer in the last five years. The camp also offers a session for siblings of children with cancer.

1228   Camp Courage
American Diabetes Association
YMCA Camp Soles
134 Camp Soles Ln.
Rockwood, PA 15557   412-824-1181
campsupport@diabetes.org
www.diabetes.org

A summer camp program of the American Diabetes Association. The camp is held at the YMCA Camp Soles, and is for children ages 8-16 with diabetes. The camp runs traditional outdoor activities and employs on-site medical staff and dieticians.

1229   Camp Discovery
American Academy of Dermatology
PO Box 1968
Des Plaines, IL 60017   847-240-1280
866-503-7546
888-462-3376
FAX: 847-240-1859
www.campdiscovery.org

A program of the American Academy of Dermatology, Camp Discovery is a camp held in 5 locations across the United States for children with chronic skin conditions. Campers can participate in activities such as fishing, swimming, archery and horseback riding. The Pennsylvania camp is held in Millville, Pennsylvania at Camp Victory.
1993

1230   Camp Freedom
American Diabetes Association
150 Monument Rd.
Suite 100
Bala Cynwyd, PA 19004   610-828-5003
campsupport@diabetes.org
www.diabetes.org

Camp Freedom is a resident summer camp located in Schwenksville, Pennsylvania at Camp Kweebec. Sessions for children and teens with diabetes. Coed, ages 6-16.

1231   Camp Hot-to-Clot
National Hemophilia Foundation - Western PA
20411 Route 19
Unit 14
Cranberry Township, PA 16066-7512   724-741-6160
FAX: 724-741-6167
www.hemophilia.org

Brittani Spencer, President
Kara Dornish, Executive Director
Camp Hot-to-Clot is a summer camp for children ages 7-17 with bleeding disorders and their siblings. The camp is held at Camp Kon-O-Kwee in Fombell, PA. Activities include rock climbing, arts and crafts, field games, and more.

1232   Camp Lee Mar
Winter Address
805 Redgate Rd.
Dresher, PA 19025   215-658-1708
FAX: 215-658-1710
ari@leemar.com
www.leemar.com

Ari Segal, Director
Lynsey Trohoske, Assistant Director
Laura Leibowitz, Assistant Director

Seven week summer camp for children and young adults ages 7-21 with developmental, learning, communication, and other disabilities. The camp incorporates an Academic and Speech program with traditional camp activities.

1233   Camp Lily Lehigh Valley
Easterseals Eastern Pennsylvania
1501 Lehigh St.
Suite 201
Allentown, PA 18103   610-289-0114
camp@esep.org
www.easterseals.com/esep

Nancy Knoebel, President & CEO
Janine Noel, Camp Director
Camp Lily is a week-long day camp for children and young adults with a variety of disabilities. Coed, ages 8-21. The camp offers a variety of traditional camp activities and field trips so that campers can enhance their social skills and increase their independence. The camp takes place on the campus of Cedar Crest College.

1234   Camp Orchard Hill
640 Orange Rd.
Dallas, PA 18612   570-333-4098
FAX: 570-333-4058
office@camporchardhill.com
www.camporchardhill.com

Jim Payne, Executive Director
Derek Hodne, Program Director
Matt Chase, Facilities Director
Camp Orchard Hill provides day and overnight summer camps for ages 4-17. The camp is inclusive to children with mild to moderate special needs. Special needs campers participate alongside non-disabled campers in a multitude of outdoor activities.

1235   Camp Ramah in the Poconos
2100 Arch St.
Philadelphia, PA 19103   215-885-8556
FAX: 215-885-8905
info@ramahpoconos.org
www.ramahpoconos.org

Rabbi Joel Seltzer, Executive Director
Rachel Dobbs Schwartz, Camp Director
Bruce I. Lipton, Director, Finance & Operations
Camp Ramah is a Jewish summer camp that runs three separate programs for children with various disabilities and their families. There are two residential programs and one family program, the Tikvah Family Camp.

1236   Camp STAR
2504 Atlas St.
Pittsburgh, PA 15235   412-370-5481
www.chp.edu

Cindy McCue, Camp Director
A week-long summer camp for children and teens ages 8-18 who are amputees. The camp is held at the YMCA Camp Kon-O-Kwee in Fombell, Pennsylvania. Activities include arts and crafts, zip lining, canoeing, rock climbing, and more. Campers are also able to learn about prosthetics, physical and recreational therapy, and limb care.

1237   Camp Setebaid
Setebaid Services, Inc.
PO Box 196
Winfield, PA 17889-0196   570-524-9090
FAX: 570-523-0769
info@setebaidservices.org
www.setebaidservices.org

Mark Moyer, Executive Director
Camping sessions for children with diabetes. The camp also hosts a family day for children with diabetes and their families.

1238   Camp Spencer Superstars
YMCA Camp Kon-O-Kwee
126 Nagel Rd.
Fombell, PA 16123   724-758-6238
FAX: 724-758-2705
campkon-o-kwee@ymcapgh.org
www.ycampkok.org

Charlie Deer, Camp Director
An overnight respite camp for adults, ages 18 and up, with special needs. The camp is fully inclusive and aims to encourage campers

to develop social and life skills. Campers have access to all activities and programs, such as canoeing, bonfires, swimming, and more.

1239 Camp Victory
58 Camp Victory Rd.
PO Box 810
Millville, PA 17846   570-458-6530
www.campvictory.org
Jamie Huntley, Executive Director
Kate Stepnick, Camp Director
Camp Victory provides camping opportunities for children with chronic health problems or physical or mental challenges.

1240 Camp Wesley Woods: Exceptional Persons Camp
1001 Fiddlersgreen Rd.
Grand Valley, PA 16420   814-436-7802
info@wesleywoods.com
www.wesleywoods.com
Emily Reed, Chair
The Exceptional Persons Camp is a camp program for individuals with disabilities. Activities include swimming, games, sports, crafts, and Bible study.

1241 Camp Woodlands
The Woodlands Foundation
134 Shenot Rd.
Wexford, PA 15090   724-935-6533
www.woodlandsfoundation.org
Samantha Ellwood, Executive Director
Denise Balkovec, Deputy Director, Advancement & Operations
Clarissa Amond, Program Manager
Camp Woodlands is a camp for youth, teens, and adults with varying disabilities and chronic illness. The camp runs a number of programs for children, teens, adults, and seniors.

1242 Dragonfly Forest Summer Camp
YMCA Camp Speers
143 Nichecronk Rd.
Dingmans Ferry, PA 18328   570-828-2329
FAX: 570-828-2984
campspeers@philaymca.org
www.dragonflyforest.org
Dragonfly Forest Summer Camp program provides children with autism and medical needs such as asthma, sickle cell anemia and hemophilia the opportunity to enjoy an overnight camp experience in an environment that is safe and equipped to meet a variety of physical, medical, and psychological needs.

1243 Handi Camp
Handi Vangelism Ministries International
PO Box 122
Akron, PA 17501-0122   717-859-4777
FAX: 717-721-7662
info@hvmi.org
www.hvmi.org
Tim Sheetz, Founder
Mark Amey, Assistant Director, Handi Camp
Brian Robinson, Office Manager, Handi Camp
Christian overnight camping program for people with disabilities, ages 9-50, in Eastern Pennsylvania. Sponsored by Handi Vangelism Ministries International.

1244 Innabah Camps
United Methodist Church: Eastern Pennsylvania
712 Pughtown Rd.
Spring City, PA 19475   610-469-6111
FAX: 610-469-0330
www.innabah.org
Michael Hyde, Director
Samantha Wagaman, Assistant Director
Gina James, Office Manager
Innabah Camps runs a number of sessions for children, teens, and adults with developmental disabilities. The Challenge camps are for ages 12 and up.

1245 Mainstay Life Services Summer Program
Mainstay Life Services
200 Roessler Rd.
Pittsburgh, PA 15220   412-344-3640
FAX: 412-344-5486
info@mainstaylifeservices.org
mainstaylifeservices.org
Kim Sonafelt, Chief Executive Officer
Barbara Dyer, Coordinator, Community Services
Mainstay Life Services' summer respite and recreation program offers one or two week sessions on a college campus in Pittsburgh, Pennsylvania. The program is open to adults age 18 and over who live with families and caregivers.

1246 Outside In School Of Experiential Education, Inc.
PO Box 639
Greensburg, PA 15601   724-837-1518
FAX: 724-837-0801
www.myoutsidein.org
Michael C. Henkel, Executive Director
Camp programs primarily focus on substance abuse, but some services are available for special needs related to school/work. Programs are for boys ages 13-18.

1247 Phelps School Academic Support Program
583 Sugartown Rd.
Malvern, PA 19355   610-644-1754
FAX: 610-540-0156
admis@thephelpsschool.org
www.thephelpsschool.org
Charles A. McGeorge, Head of School
The Phelps School is a college preparatory day and boarding school dedicated to the individual boy. They serve students in grades 6 through 12/PG in a supportive and structured environment. Their supplemental Academic Support Program offers small (4:1) courses in reading, writing, and mathematics, as well as introductions to history and science, for young men with diagnosed learning differences. Also features a dedicated Executive Functioning Skill resource center.

1248 Sequanota Lutheran Conference Center and Camp
PO Box 245
Jennerstown, PA 15547   814-629-6627
contact@sequanota.com
www.sequanota.com
Rev. Nathan Pile, Executive Director
Angie Pile, Director, Business Management
Ann Ferry, Director, Hospitality
Runs Camp Bethesda, a summer camp for adults with developmental and intellectual disabilities. For ages 18 and up.

1249 Variety Club Camp and Developmental Center
2950 Potshop Rd.
PO Box 609
Worcester, PA 19490   610-584-4366
FAX: 610-584-5586
www.varietyphila.org
Dominique Bernardo, Chief Executive Officer
Nicholas Larcinese, Director, Programming
Kristin Podwojski, Director, Operations
Year-round camping and recreation facility for children with special needs and their families. Includes summer camping, aquatics, weekend retreats and other specialty programs. Coed, ages 5-21.

1250 West Penn Burn Camp
Allegheny Health Network
120 Fifth Ave.
Suite 2900
Pittsburgh, PA 15222   412-578-5295
www.ahn.org
Christine Perlick, Outreach Coordinator
Founded in 1986, West Penn Burn camp is a week-long overnight camp for children and teens, ages 7-17, who have burn injuries. The camp provides traditional camp activities as well as therapeutic services through the support and guidance of camp counselors. The camp is held at the YMCA Camp Kon-O-Kwee in Fombell, Pennsylvania.

1251 YMCA Camp Fitch
12600 Abels Rd.
North Springfield, PA 16430   814-922-3219
                                            877-863-4824
                                            FAX: 814-922-7000
                                            registrar@campfitchymca.org
                                            campfitchymca.org

Tom Parker, Executive Director
Joe Wolnik, Summer Camp Director
Brandy Duda, Outdoor Education Director
Camp is located in North Springfield, Pennsylvania. Camp programs include sessions for children with diabetes or epilepsy.

Rhode Island

1252 Camp Mauchatea
Rhode Island Lions Sight Foundation, Inc.
PO Box 19671
Johnston, RI 02919-0671   www.lions4sight.org
Robert P. Andrade, President
Earle U. Schahrff III, First Vice President
Steve Krohn, Secretary
Camp serving those who are blind/visually impaired. Campers enjoy developing and maintaining friendships with fellow campers. Some of the activities include boating and other water sports, as well as hiking and nature studies.

1253 Camp Ruggles
PO Box 353
Chepachet, RI 02814   401-567-8914
                                            campruggles@gmail.com
                                            www.campruggles.org
Jim Field, Executive Director
Ethan Roe, Assistant Director
Camp Ruggles is located in Glocester, RI and is a summer day camp for children with emotional and behavioral disabilities. The camp offers 240 hours of supervised therapeutic care for children ages 6-12.

1254 Canonicus Camp & Conference Center
54 Exeter Rd.
Exeter, RI 02822   401-294-6318
                                            FAX: 401-294-7780
                                            www.canonicus.org
Kathy Black, Director, Conferencing
Amanda Hosley, Director, Camping Ministries
Matt Black, Facilities Manager
Canonicus Camp offers camp and conference programs and facilities for children, adults, and groups with special needs. The camp is owned by the American Baptist Churches of Rhode Island.

1255 Hasbro Children's Hospital Asthma Camp
593 Eddy St.
Providence, RI 02903   401-444-8340
                                            malsina@lifespan.org
                                            www.hasbrochildrenshospital.org
Miosotis Alsina, Administrative Director
Camp for children with asthma, hosted by Canonicus Camp and Conference Center. Children learn about asthma and asthma management through interactive and educational activities. The camp also offers activities such as swimming, canoeing, and arts and crafts. Coed, ages 9-13.

South Carolina

1256 Burnt Gin Camp
SC Department of Health and Environmental Control
2100 Bull St.
Columbia, SC 29201   803-898-0784
                                            FAX: 803-898-0613
                                            campburntgin@dhec.sc.gov
                                            www.scdhec.gov
Marie Aimone, Camp Director
A residential camp for youth who have physical disabilities and/or chronic illnesses. Camp Burnt Gun runs four six-day sessions for children ages 7-15; two six-day sessions for teenagers ages 16-20; and one four-day session for young adults ages 21-25. The camp is held in Wedgefield, South Carolina.

1257 Camp Adam Fisher
PO Box 2543
Columbia, SC 29202-2543   campadamfisher@gmail.com
                             www.campadamfisher.com
Scott McFarland, Camp Director
Maria McGregor Mullendore, Assistant Camp Director
Katherine Lewis, Medical Director
A week-long overnight camp for children with diabetes and their siblings, ages 6-17. Campers enjoy swimming, horseback riding, tubing, basketball, volleyball, and arts and crafts, while also learning how to manage their diabetes so they can live longer, healthier lives.

1258 Camp Courage
Prisma Health Children's Hospital
900 W Faris Rd.
2nd Floor
Greenville, SC 29605   864-455-8898
                                            FAX: 864-455-5164
                                            www.ghschildrens.org/programs
Ericka Turner, Camp Director
Camp Courage is a non-profit organization that provides a summer camp experience for children and teens with cancer or blood disorders. Programs include week-long summer camps for children, weekend camp for siblings, fall carnival for patients and families, counselor training sessions, evening and weekend retreats, and monthly support groups. The camp is held at Pleasant Ridge Camp and Retreat Center.

1259 Camp Debbie Lou
726 Lucky Run
Latta, SC 29565   843-845-2617
Dean Richardson, Camp Director
For children between the ages of 4-14 who have been diagnosed with cancer and their families.

1260 Camp Luv-A-Lung
Prisma Health Children's Hospital
900 W Faris Rd.
2nd Floor
Greenville, SC 29605   864-455-8898
                                            FAX: 864-455-5164
                                            www.ghschildrens.org/programs
Jessica Herron, Contact
A summer camp for children ages 6-12 who have respiratory problems. The camp takes place at Pleasant Ridge Camp and Retreat Center in Marietta, South Carolina. Activities include swimming, archery, campfires, arts and crafts, and more.

1261 Camp Spearhead
Greenville County Recreation District
4806 Old Spartanburg Rd.
Taylors, SC 29687   864-467-3398
                                            FAX: 864-288-6499
                                            campspearhead@greenvillecounty.org
                                            www.greenvillerec.com
Randy Murr, Therapeutic Recreation Manager
Camp for children with disabilities ages 8 and up. The camp is held at Pleasant Ridge Camp and Retreat Center in Marietta, South Carolina. Activities include canoeing, kayaking, swimming, archery, sports, and games.

South Dakota

1262 Camp Friendship
PO Box 1986
Rapid City, SD 57709-1986   www.campfriendshipsd.org
Held in the Black Hills of South Dakota, Camp Friendship is for individuals with physical and developmental disabilities. Activities include fishing, swimming, arts and crafts, campfires, and more. The camp consists of three sessions with two- and three-day overnight camps.

1263 Camp Gilbert
Camp Gilbert, Inc.
PO Box 89406
Sioux Falls, SD 57109-9406
605-610-8775
campgilbertinfo@gmail.com
www.campgilbert.com

Laura Parish, Camp Director
For children ages 8-18 with diabetes. Campers can enjoy a week of canoeing, swimming, sing-a-longs, crafts, and games, while also attending educational programs covering nutrition, exercise and lifestyle management.

1264 NeSoDak
Lutherans Outdoors in South Dakota
2001 S Summit Ave.
Sioux Falls, SD 57197
605-947-4440
800-888-1464
nesodak@losd.org
www.losd.org/nesodak

Vicki Foss, Director
Camp is located in Waubay, South Dakota. Hosts Camp Gilbert, a summer camp program for children with diabetes. Coed, ages 8-18.

Tennessee

1265 ACM Lifting Lives Music Camp
Vanderbilt Kennedy Center
110 Magnolia Circle
Nashville, TN 37203
615-322-8240
vkc.vumc.org

Jeffrey Neul, Director, IDDRC
Erik Carter, Co-Director, UCEDD
Elise McMillan, Co-Director, UCEDD
A camp for individuals with developmental disabilities where they can come to celebrate music by participating in songwriting workshops, recording sessions and live performances. For ages 18 and up. The program is specifically designed for people with Williams syndrome.

1266 All Days Are Happy Days Summer Camp
UTHSC Center on Developmental Disabilities
920 Madison Ave.
Suite 939
Memphis, TN 38103
901-448-6511
888-572-2249
FAX: 901-448-3844
TTY:901-448-4677
www.uthsc.edu/cdd

Bruce Keisling, Executive Director
Week long camp for children ages 6-11 years of age who have been diagnosed with ADHD. The goal of the camp is to provide activities specifically designed for children with ADHD and to educate children and their parents on the treatment and management of ADHD and related behaviours.

1267 Bill Rice Ranch
627 Bill Rice Ranch Rd.
Murfreesboro, TN 37128
615-893-2767
800-253-7423
FAX: 615-898-0656
info@billriceranch.org
www.billriceranch.org

Wil Rice IV, President
Troy Carlson, Vice President
Matt Downs, Camp Director
Camping for hearing impaired children and youth ages 9-19. Also runs camps and retreats for deaf or hearing impaired adults.

1268 Camp Conquest
3934 West Union Rd.
Millington, TN 38053
901-545-2267
info@campconquest.com
www.campconquest.com

Becca Bryant, Camp Director
Camp Conquest is a Christian camp that provides life-changing experiences for children and adults with special needs, chronic illnesses, and disabilities. Activities include horseback riding, canoeing, ropes course, rock climbing wall, zip line, lake slide, swimming pool, and more.

1269 Camp Discovery
Tennessee Jaycees and Tennessee Jaycee Foundation
400 Camp Discovery Lane
Gainesboro, TN 38562
931-268-0239
director@jayceecamp.org
www.jayceecamp.org

Chester Lowe, Vice President
Serves children, teens, and adults ages 7 and up with disabilities. The camp is a project of the Tennessee Jaycees and the Tennessee Jaycee Foundation.

1270 Camp Joy
Lakeshore Camp and Retreat Center
1458 Pilot Knob Rd.
Eva, TN 38333
731-584-6102
FAX: 731-584-2267
office@lakeshorecamp.org
lakeshorecamp.org/summer-camp

Rev. Gary D. Lawson, Sr., Executive Director
Allison Doyle, Program Director
Katlyn White, Director, Communications
A summer camp for adults ages 31 and up with disabilities. The camp takes place at Lakeshore Camp and Retreat Center and runs regular camp activities such as swimming, arts and crafts, and other outdoor activities.

1271 Camp Koinonia
Koinonia Foundation of Tennessee
244 N Peters Rd.
Suite 211
Knoxville, TN 37923
865-888-7365
info@kftn.org
www.kftn.org/campkoinonia

Jacqui Pearl, Executive Director
Camp program for children and young adults ages 7-21 with disabilities. The camp offers recreational activities such as canoeing, music and games. The camp is operated by the Koinonia Foundation and the University of Tennessee's Therapeutic Recreation Program.

1272 Camp Oginali
Koinonia Foundation of Tennessee
244 N Peters Rd.
Suite 211
Knoxville, TN 37923
865-888-7365
info@kftn.org
www.kftn.org/campkoinonia

Jacqui Pearl, Executive Director
A weekend retreat for individuals ages 7 and up with Down syndrome. The camp is held every fall at Camp Montvale. Activities include fishing, low ropes courses, cooking, arts and crafts, and more.

1273 Camp Okawehna
Dialysis Clinic, Inc.
1633 Church St.
Suite 500
Nashville, TN 37203
615-327-3061
FAX: 605-341-8814
campo@dciinc.org
www.dciinc.org/camps

Andy Parker, Camp Director
Week-long summer camp for children ages 6-18 with kidney disease. Children who have had kidney transplants as well as children on hemodialysis and peritoneal dialysis are welcome.

1274 Camp Sugar Falls
American Diabetes Association
220 Great Circle Rd.
Nashville, TN 37228
615-298-3066
campsupport@diabetes.org
www.diabetes.org

Camp Sugar Falls is a day camp for children ages 6-17 who have diabetes and their siblings. Activities include education sessions, athletics and exercise. The camp is held at YMCA Camp Widjiwagan in Antioch, Tennessee.

1275 Camp Wonder
Lakeshore Camp and Retreat Center
1458 Pilot Knob Rd.
Eva, TN 38333
731-584-6102
FAX: 731-584-2267
office@lakeshorecamp.org
lakeshorecamp.org/summer-camp
Rev. Gary D. Lawson, Sr., Executive Director
Allison Doyle, Program Director
Katlyn White, Director, Communications
A summer camp for children and adults ages 14-30 with disabilities. The camp takes place at Lakeshore Camp and Retreat Center. Activities include swimming, crafts, games, and more traditional camp activities.

1276 Easterseals Tennessee Camping Program
Easterseals Tennessee
500 Wilson Pike Cir.
Suite 228
Brentwood, TN 37027
615-292-6640
FAX: 615-251-0994
www.easterseals.com/tennessee
Tim Ryerson, President & CEO
Offers overnight, day, and weekend programs for youths ages 7-16 and adults ages 16 and up with disabilities or traumatic brain injuries. The camps are held at the YMCA's Camp Widjiwagan.

1277 LeBonheur Cardiac Kids Camp
LeBonheur Children's Hospital
848 Adams Ave.
Memphis, TN 38103
866-870-5570
cardiac@lebonheur.org
www.lebonheur.org
Christopher Knott-Craig, MD, Co-Director, Heart Institute
Jeffrey Towbin, MD, Co-Director, Heart Institute
Camp for LeBonheur patients ages 10-17 who are being treated for a congenital heart condition or have a pacemaker. The camp provides recreational and educational activities while promoting healthy lifestyles.

Texas

1278 Camp Ailihpomeh
Texas Bleeding Disorders Camp Foundation
20212 Champion Forest Dr.
Suite 700-312
Spring, TX 77379
info@camp-ailihpomeh.org
www.camp-ailihpomeh.org
Grant Spikes, Camp Director
Amanda Wolgamott, Camp Administrator
A six-day overnight camp for boys ages 7-17 who have a bleeding disorder. The camp takes place at Camp John Marc and provides recreational and educational activities.

1279 Camp Aranzazu
5420 Loop 1781
Rockport, TX 78382
361-727-0800
FAX: 361-727-0818
info@camparanzazu.org
www.camparanzazu.org
Virginia Calton Ballard, Executive Director, Camp Aranzazu Foundation
Amelia Halsam, Camp Director
Lillian Anfosso, Finance & Administrative Director
A summer camp program for children with a variety of special needs and chronic illnesses, such as cancer, autism, asthma, cerebral palsy, Down Syndrome, epilepsy, and more. Activities center around emphasizing spiritual awareness, environmental awareness, team building and sports, the arts, and social skills.

1280 Camp Be An Angel
2003 Aldine Bender Rd.
Houston, TX 77032
281-219-3313
angel@beanangel.org
www.beanangel.org/camp
Marti Boone, Executive Director
Margaret Adsit, Development Director
Russ Massey, Program Director

Camp Be An Angel is a summer camp program for children with special needs under the age of 22 and their immediate families.

1281 Camp Blessing
7227 Camp Blessing Lane
Brenham, TX 77833
281-259-5789
info@campblessing.org
campblessing.org
Greg Anderson, Executive Director
Rachel Landon, Programs Coordinator
Dean Forland, Facilities Manager
A Christian summer camp for children and adults with special needs and their siblings. The camp serves individuals ages 7 and up with a physical, developmental, or intellectual disability. Camp Blessing offers traditional summer camp activities for campers of all levels of ability.

1282 Camp CAMP
Children's Association for Maximum Potential
PO Box 27086
San Antonio, TX 78227
210-671-5411
FAX: 210-671-5225
campmail@campcamp.org
www.campcamp.org
Susan Osborne, Chief Executive Officer
Brandon G. Briery, Chief Program Officer & Executive Camp Director
Sarah Coulombe, Chief Administrative Officer
Camping for children, teens, and adults ages 5-50 with a variety of disabilities and their siblings. The camp is held in Center Point, Texas. Activities are modified to include each camper's physical or developmental needs.

1283 Camp CPals
5501A Balcones
Suite 160
Austin, TX 78731
866-742-7284
info@cpathtexas.com
www.cpathtexas.com
Victoria Polega, President
Marielle Deckard, Secretary
Jamie Eppele, Director, Development
Camp CPals is an overnight weekend camp for campers of all ages with cerebral palsy. The camp's goal is to allow campers to gain confidence, independence, learn new skills, and meet other people with cerebral palsy. The camp is held in Burton, Texas.

1284 Camp Can-Do
YMCA Camp Carter
6200 Sand Springs Rd.
Fort Worth, TX 76114
817-738-9241
camper@ymcafw.org
www.ymcacampcarter.org
Holly Martin, Executive Camp Director
A week-long summer camp designed specifically for blind/visually impaired children, ages 6-12. The camp is held at the YMCA Camp Carter, and activities include hiking, canoeing, skeet shooting, and more.

1285 Camp Discovery
American Academy of Dermatology
PO Box 1968
Des Plaines, IL 60017
847-240-1280
866-503-7546
888-462-3376
FAX: 847-240-1859
www.campdiscovery.org
A program of the American Academy of Dermatology, Camp Discovery is a camp held in 5 locations across the United States for children with chronic skin conditions. Campers can participate in activities such as fishing, swimming, archery and horseback riding. The Texas camp is held in Burton, Texas at Camp For All.
1993

1286 Camp John Marc
4925 Greenville Ave.
Suite 400
Dallas, TX 75206   214-360-0056
mail@campjohnmarc.org
www.campjohnmarc.org

Kevin Randles, Executive Director
Megan White, Camp Director
Bre Loveless, Operations Manager
Year-round camping for children with a variety of chronic medical and physical challenges. Campers can participate in a number of traditional camp activities.

1287 Camp Neuron
Epilepsy Foundation Texas
2401 Fountain View Dr.
Suite 900
Houston, TX 77057   713-789-6295
888-548-9716
FAX: 713-789-5628
info@eftx.org
eftx.org

Donna Stahlhut, Chief Executive Officer
Camp Neuron offers an overnight camping experience for children and teens ages 8-14 with epilepsy or a diagnosed seizure disorder. There is no cost to attend the camp, and the camp is located at the Texas Lions Camp in Kerrville, Texas.

1288 Camp New Horizons North
American Diabetes Association
4100 Alpha Rd.
Dallas, TX 75244   972-392-1181
campsupport@diabetes.org
www.diabetes.org

Sherry Hill, Contact
A week-long summer camp program of the American Diabetes Association for children ages 5-12 and teens ages 13-17 with diabetes. The camp is held at Cross Creek Ranch in Parker, Texas.

1289 Camp New Horizons South
American Diabetes Association
4100 Alpha Rd.
Dallas, TX 75244   972-392-1181
campsupport@diabetes.org
www.diabetes.org

Sherry Hill, Contact
A summer camp program of the American Diabetes Association for children ages 5-12 and teens ages 13-17 with diabetes. The camp is held at Southern Creek Ranch in Dallas, Texas.

1290 Camp No Limits Texas
No Limits Foundation
1220 Old San Antonio Rd
Buda, TX 78610   207-569-6411
campnolimits@gmail.com
www.nolimitsfoundation.org

Mary Leighton, Founder & Executive Director
Kelsey Moody, Program Operations Manager
Alix Sandler, Marketing & Development Director
Camp No Limits Texas, a location of Camp No Limits, is a recreational and educational camp for youth who have experienced limb loss. Camp No Limits is a program of the nonprofit organization No Limits Foundation. The weeklong camp is for children ages 5 and up, with campers participating in a variety of activities such as archery, kayaking, and fishing. The camp is held at Camp For All in Buda, Texas.

1291 Camp NoLoHi
American Diabetes Association
4100 Alpha Rd.
Dallas, TX 75244   972-392-1181
campsupport@diabetes.org
www.diabetes.org

Sherry Hill, Contact
A summer camp program for children ages 5-13 and teens ages 14-17 with diabetes. The camp is held in Lubbock, Texas. Activities include swimming, fishing, outdoor games, and arts and crafts.

1292 Camp Quality Texas
18035 Melissa Springs Dr.
Tomball, TX 77375   713-553-7872
texas@campqualityusa.org
www.campqualityusa.org/TX

Falyne Kirkpatrick, Executive Director
Eric Pitts, Co-Camp Director
Lyndsey Gerhart, Co-Camp Director
Camp Quality is for children with cancer and their siblings. The camp offers a stress-free environment that offers exciting activities and fosters new friendships, while helping to give the children courage, motivation and emotional strength.

1293 Camp Rainbow
American Diabetes Association
4100 Alpha Rd.
Dallas, TX 75244   972-392-1181
campsupport@diabetes.org
www.diabetes.org

A summer camp for children ages 4-17 with diabetes. A program of the American Diabetes Association, the camp is held at Victory Camp in Alvin, Texas.

1294 Camp Sandcastle
American Diabetes Association
4100 Alpha Rd.
Dallas, TX 75244   972-392-1181
campsupport@diabetes.org
www.diabetes.org

A week long day camp for children ages 5-17 with type 1 diabetes. This camp is a program of the American Diabetes Association and is held at Camp Aranzazu in Rockport, Texas.

1295 Camp Spike 'n' Wave
Epilepsy Foundation Texas
2401 Fountain View Dr.
Suite 900
Houston, TX 77057   713-789-6295
888-548-9716
FAX: 713-789-5628
info@eftx.org
eftx.org

Donna Stahlhut, Chief Executive Officer
Camp Spike 'n' Wave is a residential camp for children and teens ages 8-14 with epilepsy or a seizure disorder. The camp is located at Camp For All in Burton, Texas, and runs activities such as swimming, boating, and sports. There is no cost to attend the camp.

1296 Camp Summit
17210 Campbell Rd.
Suite 180-W
Dallas, TX 75252   972-484-8900
FAX: 972-620-1945
camp@campsummittx.org
www.campsummittx.org

Carla R. Weiland, President & CEO
Lisa Braziel, Director, Camp Operations & Strategy
Amanda Davis, Camp Director
Camp Summit offers camping for children and adults with a variety of disabilities. The program is coed, for ages 6-99.

1297 Camp Sweeney
PO Box 918
Gainesville, TX 76241   940-665-2011
FAX: 940-665-9467
info@campsweeney.org
www.campsweeney.org

Ernie Fernandez, Camp Director
Bob Cannon, Program Director
Billie Hood, Business Manager
Camp Sweeney teaches self-care and self-reliance to children ages 5-18 with type 1 diabetes. Campers participate in activities such as swimming, fishing, horseback riding and arts and crafts while learning how to self manage their diabetes.

1298 Camp for All
6301 Rehburg Rd.
Burton, TX 77835
979-289-3752
FAX: 979-289-5046
bdeans@campforall.org
www.campforall.org

Pat Prior Sorrells, President & CEO
Mary Beth Mosley, Development Director
April McIntosh, Human Resource & Finance Director
Camp For All is a fully accessible year-round camp facility located in Burton, Texas. The camp is for children and adults with a variety of disabilities. Some disabilities that the camp serves include autism, muscular dystrophy, spinal cord injuries, and more.

1299 Charis Hills Camp
498 Faulkner Rd.
Sunset, TX 76270
940-964-2145
FAX: 940-964-2147
info@charishills.org
www.charishills.org

Rand Southard, Co-Director
Colleen Southard, Co-Director
Cara Krueger, Program Director
A Christian summer camp for children with learning disabilities, such as ADD/ADHD, Autism, Asperger's, and more. Campers will participate in traditional camp activities while also learning about Christ and improving social skills, self-esteem and confidence.

1300 Cristo Vive International: Texas Camp Conroe
702 Barbara Lane
Conroe, TX 77301
832-703-3733
www.cristovive.net

Rachel Larson, Camp Coordinator
Christian camp with programming for individuals who are blind/deaf, physically or mentally challenged, have multiple disabilities, Down Syndrome, Autism/Asperger's, ADHD/ADD, Cerebral Palsy, and their families and siblings.

1301 Cristo Vive International: Texas Camp Rio Grande Valley
4300 S US Highway 281
Edinburg, TX 78539
956-532-8033
www.cristovive.net

Mayra Green, Camp Coordinator
Christian camp with programming for individuals who are blind/deaf, physically or mentally challenged, have multiple disabilities, Down Syndrome, Autism/Asperger's, ADHD/ADD, Cerebral Palsy, and their families and siblings.

1302 Dallas Academy
950 Tiffany Way
Dallas, TX 75218
214-324-1481
FAX: 214-327-8537
www.dallas-academy.com

Elizabeth Murski, Head of School
Dallas Academy is a school for children with diagnosed learning differences such as autism, ADD/ADHD, dyslexia, and more. The academy offers a number of summer camps and programs.

1303 Hill School of Fort Worth
4817 Odessa Ave.
Fort Worth, TX 76133
817-923-9482
FAX: 817-923-4894
hillschool@hillschool.org
www.hillschool.org

Roxann Breyer, Head of School
Matt Errico, Dean, Student Success
Jimmy Cessna, Registrar
Provides an alternative learning environment for students with learning differences. Hill School caters to individuals with disabilities by offering smaller class sizes and individualized learning programs. Offers an academic summer program during the month of June.

1304 Kamp Kaleidoscope
Epilepsy Foundation Texas
2401 Fountain View Dr.
Suite 900
Houston, TX 77057
713-789-6295
888-548-9716
FAX: 713-789-5628
info@eftx.org
eftx.org

Donna Stahlhut, Chief Executive Officer
Kamp Kaleidoscope is a residential camp for teens ages 15-19 with epilepsy or a seizure disorder. The camp takes place at the YMCA Collin County Adventure Camp in Anna, Texas, and is provided at no cost.

1305 Texas Lions Camp
PO Box 290247
Kerrville, TX 78029
830-896-8500
FAX: 830-896-3666
tlc@lionscamp.com
www.lionscamp.com

Stephen S. Mabry, President & CEO
Karen-Anne King, Vice President, Summer Camps
Milton Dare, Director, Development
Texas Lions Camp is a camp dedicated to serving children ages 7-16 in Texas with physical disabilities. While at camp, campers will participate in a variety of activities and be encouraged to become more independent and self-confident.

Utah

1306 Action X-Treme Camp
National Ability Center
1000 Ability Way
Park City, UT 84060
435-649-3991
FAX: 435-658-3992
info@discovernac.org
www.discovernac.org

Dan Glasser, Chief Executive Officer
Week-long overnight camp for teens with physical and visual disabilities. Activities include skiing, snowboarding, rock climbing, and more.

1307 Camp Giddy-Up
National Ability Center
1000 Ability Way
Park City, UT 84060
435-649-3991
FAX: 435-658-3992
info@discovernac.org
www.discovernac.org

Dan Glasser, Chief Executive Officer
Camp Giddy Up is a horsemanship camp, ages 8-18, for campers with and without disabilities. Campers will be participating in all activities related to horseback riding, including grooming, riding, and barn activities.

1308 Camp Hobe
PO Box 520755
Salt Lake City, UT 84152-0755
801-631-2742
www.camphobekids.org

Christina Beckwith, Executive Director
Ashley Clinger, Deputy Director
Nicole Bailey, Program Director
A summer camp for children with cancer (and similarly-treated disorders) and their siblings. The camp's goal is to allow kids to take part in a normal aspect of childhood in a safe and medically supervised environment. Camp Hob, offers a two-day session for ages 4-7, one five-day session for ages 7-12, and one five-day session for ages 12-19.

1309 Camp ICANDO
American Diabetes Association
Holladay, UT
campsupport@diabetes.org
www.diabetes.org

A summer camp program of the American Diabetes Association. Camp ICANDO is for children ages 5-12 with diabetes. The camp runs traditional camp activities and combines them with informal diabetes education.

1310 Camp Kostopulos
Kostopulos Dream Foundation
4180 E Emigration Canyon Rd.
Salt Lake City, UT 84108
801-582-0700
FAX: 801-583-5176
kdf@campk.org
www.campk.org

Mircea Divricean, President & CEO
Michael Divricean, Chief Operating Officer
Natalie Norris, Administrative Manager
Summer camping for children and adults ages 7 and up with disabilities. There are four types of summer camp programs offered: Day Camp, Residential Camp, Travel Trip Camp, and Partner Day Camps. There is also year round recreation on site and community based activities. Programs are designed to foster independence, confidence, physical fitness, and social and communication skills.

1311 Camp Nah-Nah-Mah
University of Utah Health Care Burn Camp Programs
50 N Medical Dr.
Salt Lake City, UT 84132
801-585-2847
healthcare.utah.edu/burncenter

Kristen Quinn, Camp Director
For children ages 6-13 who are burn survivors. Some of the activities include canoeing, rock climbing and archery. The camp takes place in Millcreek Canyon and is a five-day overnight camp.

1312 Discovery Camp
National Ability Center
1000 Ability Way
Park City, UT 84060
435-649-3991
FAX: 435-658-3992
info@discovernac.org
www.discovernac.org

Dan Glasser, Chief Executive Officer
Summer and winter camps for children ages 8-18 with and without physical and developmental disabilities. Also offers overnight camps for adults.

1313 FCYD Camp Utada
Foundation for Children and Youth with Diabetes
1995 W 9000 S
West Jordan, UT 84088
801-566-6913
www.fcydcamputada.org

Dave Okubo, MD, Co-Founder & Trustee
Elizabeth Elmer, Co-Founder & Trustee
Nathan Gedge, Co-Founder & Trustee
Camp Utada is a summer camp for children with diabetes. Coed, ages 1-18 and families.

1314 Kids Rock The World Day Camp
National Ability Center
1000 Ability Way
Park City, UT 84060
435-649-3991
FAX: 435-658-3992
info@discovernac.org
www.discovernac.org

Dan Glasser, Chief Executive Officer
A day camp program for children and teens ages 11-16 with diabetes. Activities include cycling, indoor climbing, arts and crafts, and more.

1315 Overnight Camps
National Ability Center
1000 Ability Way
Park City, UT 84060
435-649-3991
FAX: 435-658-3992
info@discovernac.org
www.discovernac.org

Dan Glasser, Chief Executive Officer
Overnight Camps are available for teens and young adults ages 15-24. Campers participate in traditional camp activities during the day. During the evenings, campers may attend campfires and sometimes sleep in tents.

1316 Pathfinders Camp
National Ability Center
1000 Ability Way
Park City, UT 84060
435-649-3991
FAX: 435-658-3992
info@discovernac.org
www.discovernac.org

Dan Glasser, Chief Executive Officer
Outdoor camp for children ages 8-14 with physical disabilities and their siblings and friends. Activities include adaptive cycling, rock climbing, paddle boarding, and more.

Vermont

1317 Camp Thorpe
PO Box 82
Brandon, VT 05733
802-247-6611
director@campthorpe.org
www.campthorpe.org

Heather Moore, Executive Director
Lyllie Harvey, Director, Operations
Karen Davidson, Assistant Director
Camp Thorpe is a residential summer camp for children, teens and adults with a range of social, behavioral, mental, and developmental disabilities. The camp offers two programs: Mountain Reach (ages 12-20) and Pine Haven (ages 21 and up).

1318 Silver Towers Camp
PO Box 166
Ripton, VT 05766
802-388-6446
FAX: 802-388-0219
www.vtelks.org/programs/silver-towers

Carolyn Ravenna, Camp Director
Two-week residential camp for individuals ages 6-75 with physical or mental disabilities. Activities include swimming, horseback riding, music, sing-a-longs, dancing, nature studies and more.

1319 Vermont Overnight Camp
The Barton Center for Diabetes Education, Inc.
30 Ennis Rd.
PO Box 356
North Oxford, MA 01537-0356
508-987-2056
FAX: 508-987-2002
info@bartoncenter.org
www.bartoncenter.org

Lynn Butler-Dinunno, Executive Director
Jenna Dufresne, Director, Health Services
Sarah Balko, Director, Camps & Programs
The Vermont Overnight Camp provides children and teens ages 6-16 with diabetes a traditional summer camp experience combined with diabetes education. Activities include sports, swimming, kayaking, canoeing, fishing, hiking, arts and crafts, and campfires. The camp is held at Camp Ta-Kum-Ta in South Hero, Vermont.

Virginia

1320 Camp Dickenson
Holston Conference of United Methodist Church
801 Camp Dickenson Lane
Fries, VA 24330
276-744-7241
office@campdickenson.com
www.campdickenson.com

Anthony Gomez, Camp Director
Camp Dickenson's Celebration Camp is a four-day camp for youth and adults with mild to moderate developmental disabilities. Activities include archery, hiking, swimming, and games.

1321 Camp Easterseals UCP
Easterseals UCP North Carolina & Virginia
900 Camp Easter Seals Rd.
New Castle, VA 24127
540-864-5750
camp@eastersealsucp.com
www.easterseals.com/ncva

Luanne Welch, President & CEO
Alex Barge, Camp Director
Summer camp, weekend respite, and family camp sessions for children and adults with disabilities and special needs. Therapeutic recreation activities including swimming, fishing, sports, horseback riding, rock climbing, and more.

1322 Camp Holiday Trails
400 Holiday Trails Lane
Charlottesville, VA 22903
434-977-3781
FAX: 866-342-7850
info@campholidaytrails.org
www.campholidaytrails.org

Tina LaRoche, Executive Director
McKenzie Markham, Program Director
Katrina Beitz, Director, Communications
Private, nonprofit camp for children with special health needs and various chronic illnesses. Coed, ages 7-17. Activities include canoeing, swimming, horseback riding, arts and crafts, drama, ropes course, etc. 24-hour medical supervision by doctor and nursing staff.

1323 Camp Jordan
Camp Hanover
3163 Parsleys Mill Rd.
Mechanicsville, VA 23111
804-779-2811
info@camphanover.org
www.camphanover.org

Doug Walters, Executive Director
Harry Zweckbronner, Associate Director, Programs
Lisa VanderPloeg, Office Manager
Camp Jordan is a sleepover camp session for children with diabetes in grades 6-12. The camp is a part of Camp Hanover, and activities include hiking, archery, campfires, paddle boards, and more.

1324 Camp Loud And Clear
Holiday Lake 4-H Educational Center
1267 4-H Camp Rd.
Appomattox, VA 24522
434-248-5444
FAX: 434-248-6749
info@holidaylake4h.com
holidaylake4h.com

Preston Willson, President & CEO
Heather Benninghove, Center Director
Levi Callahan, Program Director
Camp Loud And Clear is a summer camp for youth ages 9-18 who are deaf or have hearing loss. Activities include swimming, archery, Bible study, and more.

1325 Camps for Children & Teens with Diabetes
American Diabetes Association
2451 Crystal Dr.
Suite 900
Arlington, VA 22202
800-342-2383
campsupport@diabetes.org
www.diabetes.org

Tracey D. Brown, Chief Executive Officer
Charlotte Carter, Chief Financial Officer
Charles Henderson, Chief Development Officer
The American Diabetes Association sponsors day camps, family camps and resident camps for children and teens. These camps provide an opportunity for children with diabetes to go to camp, meet other children and gain a better understanding of their diabetes. Camps are located all across the country.

1326 Civitan Acres
Eggleston Services
1161 Ingleside Rd.
Suite A
Norfolk, VA 23502
757-625-2044
info@egglestonservices.org
www.egglestonservices.org

Paul J. Atkinson, President & CEO
Ron Fritch, Chief Financial Officer
Tasha Jones, Vice President, Rehabilitation Services

Offers a summer camp for adults and children with disabilities. Sessions run for one week and aim to help campers improve their emotional, intellectual, and physical dimensions of life.

1327 Loudoun County Adaptive Recreation Camps
Loudoun County Parks, Recreation & Community Svcs
PO Box 7800
Leesburg, VA 20177-7800
703-777-0343
FAX: 703-771-5354
prcs@loudoun.gov
www.loudoun.gov

Steve Torpy, Director
Loudoun County's Adaptive Recreation Camps offer and promote integration opportunities for individuals with disabilities. All camps are designed to meet the individual needs of the participants and aim to provide traditional summer camp experiences.

1328 Oakland School & Camp
128 Oakland Farm Way
Troy, VA 22974
434-293-9059
FAX: 434-296-8930
information@oaklandschool.net
www.oaklandschool.net

Carol Williams, Head of School
A highly individualized program that stresses improving reading ability. Subjects taught are reading, English composition, math and word analysis. Recreational activities include horseback riding, sports, swimming, tennis, crafts, archery and camping. For girls and boys, ages 7-13. Students who attend the summer camp often have a variety of learning disabilities, such as ADHD, dyslexia, visual/auditory processing disorders, and more.

Washington

1329 Camp Beausite NW
PO Box 1227
Port Hadlock, WA 98339
360-732-7222
campbeausitenw.org

Raina Baker, Executive Director
The camp is located in Chimacum, Washington. Campers range from 7-65 in age and includes those with developmental disabilities, cerebral palsy, autism, Down syndrome, and other physical or mental disabilities. The camp offers five week-long overnight summer camp sessions for adults and children.

1330 Camp Goodtimes
The Goodtimes Project
7400 Sand Point Way NE
Suite 101S
Seattle, WA 98115
206-556-3489
FAX: 206-877-4437
info@thegoodtimesproject.org
www.thegoodtimesproject.org

Bridget K. Dolan, Executive Director
Tanya Krohn, Director, Programming
Becky Felak, Program & Event Manager
A week-long residential summer camp for children ages 8-17 diagnosed with cancer and their siblings. The Goodtimes Project also runs Kayak Adventure Camp for childhood cancer survivors, aged 18-25.

1331 Camp Killoqua
15207 E Lake Goodwin Rd.
Stanwood, WA 98292
360-652-6250
killoqua@campfiresnoco.org
www.campkilloqua.org

Cassie Anderson, Camp Director, Outdoor Education & Operations
Pearl Verbon, Camp Director, Summer Camp, Rentals & Retreats
Camp Killoqua offers Inclusion Programs for all of its traditional camp programs. The inclusion program allows campers ages 7-21 with mild to moderate developmental disabilities the chance to participate in any Camp Killoqua session.

1332 Camp Korey
3616 Colby Ave.
PMB 247
Everett, WA 98201
425-440-0850
FAX: 425-404-2158
info@campkorey.org
campkorey.org

Chris McReynolds, Co-President
Tim Rose, Co-President
Sue Colbourne, Vice President
A summer camp for children with life-altering medical conditions and their families. The camp is free of charge and aims to allow children to experience camp in a safe environment with specialized medical support.

1333 Camp Sealth
14500 SW Camp Sealth Rd.
Vashon, WA 98070-8222
206-463-3174
FAX: 206-463-6936
info@campfireseattle.org
campfireseattle.org

Rick Taylor, Executive Director
Kristen Cook, Marketing & Development Director
Carrie Kishline, Summer Camp Director
Camp Sealth is a camp program for youth ages 5-17. The camp is open to children with a variety of abilities and special needs.

1334 Easterseals Camp Stand by Me
Easterseals Washington
17809 S Vaughn Rd. NW
PO Box 289
Vaughn, WA 98394
253-884-2722
campadmin@wa.easterseals.com
www.easterseals.com/washington

Cathy Bisaillon, President & CEO
Angela Cox, Camp Director
Camp Stand by Me is a camp program for children and adults with disabilities. Offers week-long summer sessions and weekend respite in the fall, winter, and spring.

1335 Prime Time, Inc.
6 S. 2nd St.
Suite 815
Yakima, WA 98901
509-248-2854
FAX: 509-248-5505
office@campprimetime.org
www.campprimetime.org

Bill Schorzman, Camp Manager
Merita Sletten, Office Manager
Camp Prime Time serves children with developmental disabilities or serious or terminal illnesses and their families.

1336 STIX Diabetes Programs
PO Box 8308
Spokane, WA 99203
509-484-1366
FAX: 509-955-1329
stix@stixdiabetes.org
www.stixdiabetes.org

Tonya Kobluk, Director, Administration & Camps
Cindy Schneider, Director, Community Outreach
Jill Strom, Director, Development
STIX Diabetes Programs is a non-profit organization providing camp experiences for children and teens with diabetes. STIX offers a three-day non-residential day camp for children ages 6-8; a week-long residential camp for youth ages 9-16; and an excursion-based Adventure Camp for teens ages 16-19.

West Virginia

1337 Mountaineer Spina Bifida Camp
534 New Goff Mountain Rd.
Charleston, WV 25313
info@drewsday.org
www.drewsday.org

Suzie Humphreys, Contact
A summer camp for individuals with spina bifida. Campers can participate in activities such as swimming, wheelchair hockey, baseball, and more.

Wisconsin

1338 Camp Daypoint
American Diabetes Association
375 Bishops Way
Brookfield, WI 53005
414-778-5500
campsupport@diabetes.org
www.diabetes.org

Becky Barnett, Camp Director
Camp Daypoint is a day camp for children ages 5-9 with diabetes. Activities include swimming, crafts, hikes, games, and more. The camp is held at YMCA Camp St. Croix in Hudson, Wisconsin.

1339 Camp Kee-B-Waw
Easterseals Wisconsin
1450 State Hwy. 13
Wisconsin Dells, WI 53965
608-254-8319
800-422-2324
FAX: 608-277-8333
TTY: 608-277-8031
camp@eastersealswisconsin.com
camp.eastersealswisconsin.com

Paul Leverenz, President & CEO
Carissa Peterson, Vice President, Camp & Respite Services
Stevie Thomas, Director, Camp Operations
Located at Camp Wawbeek, Camp Kee-B-Waw is a day camp for children ages 6-13 from Wisconsin Dells and surrounding communities.

1340 Camp Klotty Pine
Great Lakes Hemophilia Foundation
638 N 18th St.
Milwaukee, WI 53233
414-937-6782
888-797-4543
FAX: 414-257-1225
info@glhf.org
glhf.org

Karin Koppen, Camp Director
An overnight summer camp for children ages 7-15 who have been diagnosed with a bleeding disorder. The camp is held at Camp Lakotah in Wautoma, Wisconsin. The camp runs recreational camp activities such as archery, canoeing, and campfires, as well as education about their disorder and self-infusion instruction.

1341 Camp Needlepoint
American Diabetes Association
375 Bishops Way
Brookfield, WI 53005
414-778-5500
campsupport@diabetes.org
www.diabetes.org

Becky Barnett, Camp Director
Camp Needlepoint is a summer camp for children who have type 1 diabetes. Coed, ages 8-16. The camp takes place at the YMCA Camp St. Croix in Hudson, Wisconsin.

1342 Easter Seal Camp Wawbeek
Easterseals Wisconsin
1450 State Hwy. 13
Wisconsin Dells, WI 53965
608-254-8319
800-422-2324
FAX: 608-277-8333
TTY: 608-277-8031
camp@eastersealswisconsin.com
camp.eastersealswisconsin.com

Paul Leverenz, President & CEO
Carissa Peterson, Vice President, Camp & Respite Services
Stevie Thomas, Director, Camp Operations
Camp Wawbeek is a summer camp for children and adults with physical disabilities. Coed, ages 7 and up. During the summer, the camp runs six-day youth and teen sessions; six-day adult, young adult, and transition sessions; and weekend sessions from September to May.

1343 **Lutherdale Bible Camp**
Lutherdale Ministries
N7891 US Hwy. 12
Elkhorn, WI 53121
262-742-2352
FAX: 888-248-4551
info@lutherdale.org
www.lutherdale.org

Jeff Bluhm, Executive Director
David Box, Associate Director
Paul Degner, Operations & Facilities Manager
Lutherdale Bible Camp currently offers Team USA, a summer camp program for adults with developmental disabilities. Activities include talent show, parade, and campfires.

1344 **Phantom Lake YMCA Camp**
S110W30240 YMCA Camp Rd.
Mukwonago, WI 53149
262-363-4386
office@phantomlakeymca.org
www.phantomlakeymca.org

Karin Mulrooney, Chair
Sara Hacker, Secretary
Bill Canfield, Treasurer
Phantom Lake Camp offers day and residential camping sessions for children ages 3-17. All programs are open to individuals with disabilities.

1345 **Timbertop Camp for Youth with Learning Disabilities**
PO Box 423
Plover, WI 54467
715-869-6262
info@timbertopcamp.org
www.timbertopcamp.org

Pete Matthai, Camp Director
Timbertop Camp is a seven-day outdoor camp for children and youth with learning disabilities. Campers participate in traditional camp activities as well as activities that focus on enhancing cooperative abilities, interpersonal relationships, and self-esteem. The program includes nature exploration, canoeing, arts and crafts, archery, fishing, games, reading instruction, and campfires.

1346 **Wisconsin Badger Camp**
1250 US-151 BUS
PO Box 723
Platteville, WI 53818
608-348-9689
FAX: 608-348-9737
wiscbadgercamp@badgercamp.org
www.badgercamp.org

Brent Bowers, Executive Director
Austin Rist, Program Director
Steve Van Kooten, Camp Director
Wisconsin Badger Camp, established in 1966, is a summer camp that serves individuals with developmental disabilities. Badger Camp offers eight one-week sessions and one two-week session, with one week for children ages 3-13, one week for teens ages 14-21, and eight weeks for adults.

1347 **Wisconsin Elks/Easterseals Respite Camp**
Easterseals Wisconsin
1550 Waubeek Rd.
Wisconsin Dells, WI 53965
608-254-2502
800-422-2324
FAX: 608-277-8333
TTY: 608-277-8031
camp@eastersealswisconsin.com
camp.eastersealswisconsin.com

Paul Leverenz, President & CEO
Carissa Peterson, Vice President, Camp & Respite Services
Stevie Thomas, Director, Camp Operations
The Wisconsin Elks/Easterseals Respite Camp is a year-round camp for individuals with disabilities, including those with severe or multiple disabilities. Activities include arts and crafts, sports, games, high ropes course, and local field trips.

1348 **Wisconsin Lions Camp**
Wisconsin Lions Foundation
3834 County Rd. A
Rosholt, WI 54473
715-677-4969
877-463-6953
FAX: 715-677-4527
info@wisconsinlionscamp.com
www.wisconsinlionscamp.com

Evett Hartvig, Executive Director
Andrea Yenter, Camp Director
Phillip Potter, Assistant Camp Director
Provides camp programs for youth and adults in Wisconsin with disabilities, including autism, intellectual disabilities, diabetes, epilepsy, visual impairments, and hearing impairments. ACA accredited, located in central Wisconsin, near Stevens Point.

Wyoming

1349 **Camp Hope**
3920 W 45th St.
Casper, WY 82604
307-259-3327
FAX: 307-472-5008
camphopewyoming@gmail.com
www.camphopewy.net

Steve Johnson, Director
Nancy Johnson, Director
Camp Hope is a camp for children and young adults with diabetes. Activities include hiking, swimming, sports and games.

1350 **Eagle View Ranch**
SOAR
184 Uphill Rd.
PO Box 584
Dubois, WY 82513
307-455-3084
FAX: 801-820-3050
admissions@soarnc.org
www.soarnc.org

John Willson, Executive Director
Jeremy Neidens, Director, Eagle View Ranch
Camp for youth with ADHD and learning disabilities. Campers participate in a broad range of wilderness adventure experiences that help them to overcome challenges and develop problem-solving skills, effective communication strategies, and social skills.

Clothing

1351 Adaptations by Adrian
PO Box 7
San Marcos, CA 92079-0007   760-744-3565
888-214-8372
FAX: 760-471-7560
adrians1@sbcglobal.net
www.adaptationsbyadrian.com
Fashions for the physically challenged child. Clothing offers Velcro closures, front pockets, concealed back openings and fashions for seated posture.

1352 Basic Rear Closure Sweat Top
Buck & Buck
3111 27th Ave S
Seattle, WA 98144-6502   206-722-4196
800-458-0600
FAX: 800-317-2182
info@buckandbuck.com
www.buckandbuck.com
Julie Buck, Owner
Top opens completely down the back for ease of dressing with snaps. *$19.00*

1353 Booties with Non-Skid Soles
Buck & Buck
3111 27th Ave S
Seattle, WA 98144-6502   206-722-4196
800-458-0600
FAX: 800-317-2182
info@buckandbuck.com
www.buckandbuck.com
Julie Buck, Owner
Acrylic knit or quilted cotton/poly and shearling inner. *$17.00*

1354 Buck and Buck Clothing
3111 27th Ave S
Seattle, WA 98144-6502   206-722-4196
800-458-0600
FAX: 800-317-2182
info@buckandbuck.com
www.buckandbuck.com
Julie Buck, Owner
Clothing for the disabled and elderly.
88 pages Yearly

1355 Budget Cotton/Poly Open Back Gown
Buck & Buck
3111 27th Ave S
Seattle, WA 98144-6502   206-722-4196
800-458-0600
FAX: 800-317-2182
info@buckandbuck.com
www.buckandbuck.com
Julie Buck, Owner
Short raglan sleeves, lace at neck and bodice over lapping snapback closure. *$14.00*

1356 Budget Flannel Open Back Gown
Buck & Buck
3111 27th Ave S
Seattle, WA 98144-6502   206-722-4196
800-458-0600
FAX: 800-317-2182
info@buckandbuck.com
www.buckandbuck.com
Julie Buck, Owner
3/4 raglan sleeve, lace at neck and bodice. *$17.00*

1357 Carolyn's Low Vision Products
3938 S. Tamiami Trail
Sarasota, FL 34231-3622   941-373-9100
800-648-2266
info@carolynscatalog.com
www.carolynscatalog.com
John Colton, Owner
A trusted leader in low-vision products. Free national mail-order catalog of items for visually impaired and blind people. Well versed in a variety of eye diseases that damage vision and have an expertise in helping customers making product purchasing decisions for their needs.

1358 Cotton Full-Back Vest
Buck & Buck
3111 27th Ave S
Seattle, WA 98144-6502   206-722-4196
800-458-0600
FAX: 800-317-2182
info@buckandbuck.com
www.buckandbuck.com
Julie Buck, Owner
Wide shoulder straps that don't slide off shoulders. *$5.00*

1359 Cotton/Poly House Dress
Buck & Buck
3111 27th Ave S
Seattle, WA 98144-6502   206-722-4196
800-458-0600
info@buckandbuck.com
www.buckandbuck.com
Julie Buck, Owner
Comes in short and long sleeves, assorted florals and plaids. *$36.00*

1360 Creative Designs
3704 Carlisle Ct
Modesto, CA 95356-924   209-523-3166
800-335-4852
robes4you@aol.com
www.robes4you.com
Barbara Arnold, Owner
Designer of the original Change-A-Robe and the new Handi-Robe, which allows the wearer to put it on without having to stand up. Robes are designed especially for physically challenged, disabled individuals, and wheelchair users. *$69.95*

1361 Dusters
Buck & Buck
3111 27th Ave S
Seattle, WA 98144-6502   206-722-4196
800-458-0600
info@buckandbuck.com
www.buckandbuck.com
Julie Buck, Owner
Three types: Floral, Budget Better. Snap front styles and gathered yokes, flannel $16.00-$24.00. *$36.00*

1362 Dutch Neck T-Shirt
Buck & Buck
3111 27th Ave S
Seattle, WA 98144-6502   206-722-4196
800-458-0600
FAX: 800-317-2182
info@buckandbuck.com
www.buckandbuck.com
Julie Buck, Owner
Stretchy neck makes it easy to get over the head. *$5.50*

1363 Exquisite Egronomic Protective Wear
Plum Enterprises
P.O. Box 85
Valley Forge, PA 19481-85   610-783-7377
800-321-7586
FAX: 610-783-7577
info@plument.com
www.plument.com
Janice Carrington, President/CEO
Egronomic Protective Wear; ProtectaCap custom-fitting headgear has earned an unparalleled reputation for quality, safety, and comfort. ProtectaCap+Plus technologically-advanced protective headgear closes the gap between hard and soft helmets. Comes with optional ProtectaChin Guard and new sporty design. Protectahip protective undergarment is the intelligent, innovative solution to the problem of hip injuries for both men and women.

1364 Flannel Gowns
Buck & Buck
3111 27th Ave S
Seattle, WA 98144-6502   206-722-4196
800-458-0600
info@buckandbuck.com
www.buckandbuck.com

Julie Buck, Owner
Comes in long or short with a deep button-front opening for ease of slipping on. Shorter long length. *$21.00*

1365 Flannel Pajamas
Buck & Buck
3111 27th Ave S
Seattle, WA 98144-6502   206-722-4196
800-458-0600
FAX: 800-317-2182
info@buckandbuck.com
www.buckandbuck.com

Julie Buck, Owner
$25.00

1366 Float Dress
Buck & Buck
3111 27th Ave S
Seattle, WA 98144-6502   206-722-4196
800-458-0600
info@buckandbuck.com
www.buckandbuck.com

Julie Buck, Owner
A safe bet for everyone from a size medium to a 3X. Gathered yoke front and back and literally yards of fabric for fullness. Comes in cotton or polyester. *$32.00*

1367 Foot Snugglers
Buck & Buck
3111 27th Ave S
Seattle, WA 98144-6502   206-722-4196
800-458-0600
FAX: 800-317-2182
info@buckandbuck.com
www.buckandbuck.com

Julie Buck, Owner
Quilted poly/cotton outers lined with plush shearling pile, provide a thick, comfortable cushion which helps minimize the pressure points on tender areas. *$.30*

1368 Headliner Hats
Designs for Comfort
PO Box 671044
Marietta, GA 30066-2429   770-565-8246
800-443-9226
FAX: 770-565-8425
headliner@mindspring.com
www.headlinerhats.com

Curt Maurer, President
A patented cap and hairpiece combination, the Headliner is both a quick, stylish coverup and an upbeat wig alternative for women experiencing hair care problems or hair loss. Ideal for social gatherings and outdoor activities as well as for sleeping and hospital stays. *$25.00*

1369 His & Hers
Wishing Wells Collection
Ste 965
11684 Ventura Blvd
Studio City, CA 91604-2699   818-840-6919
FAX: 818-760-3878
www.dawnwells.com

Dawn Wells, Owner
This sleep shirt is designed for him or her. *$21.99*

1370 Knee Socks
Buck & Buck
3111 27th Ave S
Seattle, WA 98144-6502   206-722-4196
800-458-0600
FAX: 800-317-2182
info@buckandbuck.com
www.buckandbuck.com

Julie Buck, Owner

Comes in regular and large size. $3.00 - $8.00

1371 M&M Health Care Apparel Company
Fashion Collection
1541 60th St
Brooklyn, NY 11219-5023   718-871-8188
800-221-8929
FAX: 718-436-2067
info@fashionease.com
www.fashionease.com

Abraham Klein, Owner
Specialized clothing for disabled people.

1372 Muu Muu
Buck & Buck
3111 27th Ave S
Seattle, WA 98144-6502   206-722-4196
800-458-0600
info@buckandbuck.com
www.buckandbuck.com

Julie Buck, Owner
Comes in long and short styles, assorted bright floral prints. $20.00-$22.00. *$31.00*

1373 Nightshirts
Buck & Buck
3111 27th Ave S
Seattle, WA 98144-6502   206-722-4196
800-458-0600
FAX: 800-317-2182
info@buckandbuck.com
www.buckandbuck.com

Julie Buck, Owner
Come in flannel or cotton patterns and prints in sizes S/M, 4XL, 2XL/3XL *$29.00*

1374 Open Back Nightgowns
Buck & Buck
3111 27th Ave S
Seattle, WA 98144-6502   206-722-4196
800-458-0600
FAX: 800-317-2182
info@buckandbuck.com
www.buckandbuck.com

Julie Buck, Owner
Come in cotton (sizes S-4X) or flannel (sizes S-3X). *$20.00*

1375 Panties
Buck & Buck
3111 27th Ave S
Seattle, WA 98144-6502   206-722-4196
800-458-0600
FAX: 800-317-2182
info@buckandbuck.com
www.buckandbuck.com

Julie Buck, Owner
Come in nylon or cotton, band leg for comfort. *$5.00*

1376 Polyester House Dress
Buck & Buck
3111 27th Ave S
Seattle, WA 98144-6502   206-722-4196
800-458-0600
info@buckandbuck.com
www.buckandbuck.com

Julie Buck, Owner
Comes in short and long sleeves, assorted florals. *$36.00*

1377 Printed Rear Closure Sweat Top
Buck & Buck
3111 27th Ave S
Seattle, WA 98144-6502   206-722-4196
800-458-0600
FAX: 800-317-2182
info@buckandbuck.com
www.buckandbuck.com

Julie Buck, Owner
Comes in assorted colors, plain or with animal motifs and snaps all the way down the back. *$28.00*

1378 Professional Fit Clothing
Ste 1
831 N Lake St
Burbank, CA 91502-1600
818-563-1975
800-422-2348
FAX: 818-563-1834
sales@professionalfit.com
www.professionalfit.com

Kurt Rieback, Owner
Professional fit clothing caters to homes that care for people with developmental disabilities and individuals who are physically challenged. Our clothing is fashionable, affordable and can be adapted to each person's special needs.

1379 Propet Leather Walking Shoes
Buck & Buck
3111 27th Ave S
Seattle, WA 98144-6502
206-722-4196
800-458-0600
FAX: 800-317-2182
info@buckandbuck.com
www.buckandbuck.com

Julie Buck, Owner
Two velcro straps, leather upper, shock-absorbing sole. *$58.00*

1380 Rear Closure Shirts
Buck & Buck
3111 27th Ave S
Seattle, WA 98144-6502
206-722-4196
800-458-0600
FAX: 206-722-1144
info@buckandbuck.com
www.buckandbuck.com

Julie Buck, Owner
Snaps down the back on T-shirts and dress shirts. *$33.00*

1381 Rear Closure T-Shirt
Buck & Buck
3111 27th Ave S
Seattle, WA 98144-6502
206-722-4196
800-458-0600
FAX: 800-317-2182
info@buckandbuck.com
www.buckandbuck.com

Julie Buck, Owner
Closes down the back with velcro snaps. *$10.00*

1382 Seersucker Shower Robe
Buck & Buck
3111 27th Ave S
Seattle, WA 98144-6502
206-722-4196
800-458-0600
FAX: 800-317-2182
info@buckandbuck.com
www.buckandbuck.com

Julie Buck, Owner
Totally covers a man or woman being wheeled to and from the shower or bath. A crisp, light weight shower robe. *$34.00*

1383 Side Velcro Slacks
Buck & Buck
3111 27th Ave S
Seattle, WA 98144-6502
206-722-4196
800-458-0600
FAX: 800-317-2182
info@buckandbuck.com
www.buckandbuck.com

Julie Buck, Owner
Slacks open down both sides from waist to hip with snap closures at sides. *$36.00*

1384 Side-Zip Sweat Pants
Buck & Buck
3111 27th Ave S
Seattle, WA 98144-6502
206-722-4196
800-458-0600
FAX: 800-317-2182
info@buckandbuck.com
www.buckandbuck.com

Julie Buck, Owner
Out-seam zippers un-zip 22-inch zippers down both sides to enable dressing a resident with severe leg contractures. *$25.00*

1385 Spec-L Clothing Solutions
849 Performance Drive
Stockton, CA 95206
714-427-0781
800-445-1981
FAX: 800-683-6510
www.clothingsolutions.com

Jim Lechner, Owner
The nation's leading designer and manufacturer of assistive clothing for men and women. Free 56 page catalog available.

1386 Specialty Care Shoppe
16126 E 161st St S
Bixby, OK 74008-7325
918-366-2901
FAX: 918-366-9445
www.specialtycareshoppe.com

K J Marshall, Owner
Catalog of attractive, affordable clothing and accessories for adults with special needs. Includes items for edema, incontinence, alzheimers, limited mobility, and hand impairment.

1387 Super Stretch Socks
Buck & Buck
3111 27th Ave S
Seattle, WA 98144-6502
206-722-4196
800-458-0600
FAX: 800-317-2182
info@buckandbuck.com
www.buckandbuck.com

Julie Buck, Owner
This sock has been improved to stretch laterally throughout the foot area as well as at the top. *$3.75*

1388 Support Plus
5581 Hudson Industrial Parkway
PO Box 2599
Hudson, OH 44236-0099
508-359-2910
866-229-2910
FAX: 800-950-9569
www.supportplus.com

Ed Janos, President
Offers a selection of support undergarments, braces and shoes for the physically challenged and medical professionals.

1389 TRU-Mold Shoes
42 Breckenridge St
Buffalo, NY 14213-1555
716-881-4484
800-843-6653
FAX: 716-881-0406
www.trumold.com

Husain Syed, Production Manager
Custom made, fully molded shoes, relieve pressure in sensitive areas by taking all of the weight off the painful areas.

1390 Thigh-Hi Nylon Stockings
Buck & Buck
3111 27th Ave S
Seattle, WA 98144-6502
206-722-4196
800-458-0600
FAX: 800-317-2182
info@buckandbuck.com
www.buckandbuck.com

Julie Buck, Owner
A sheer, full length stocking. *$4.50*

1391 Trunks
Buck & Buck
3111 27th Ave S
Seattle, WA 98144-6502
206-722-4196
800-458-0600
FAX: 800-317-2118
info@buckandbuck.com
www.buckandbuck.com

Julie Buck, Owner
Come in cotton or nylon, flare leg, full cut. *$5.00*

1392 **Velcro Booties**
Buck & Buck
3111 27th Ave S
Seattle, WA 98144-6502   206-722-4196
                                          800-458-0600
                                     FAX: 800-317-2182
                               info@buckandbuck.com
                               www.buckandbuck.com

Julie Buck, Owner
The high-domed toe, and extra-wide, non-skid sole design accommodates virtually every foot related problem. *$20.00*

1393 **Washable Shoes**
Buck & Buck
3111 27th Ave S
Seattle, WA 98144-6502   206-722-4196
                                          800-458-0600
                                     FAX: 800-317-2182
                               info@buckandbuck.com
                               www.buckandbuck.com

Julie Buck, Owner
Vinyl upper with velcro closure, nonskid sole. *$20.00*

1394 **Waterproof Bib**
Buck & Buck
3111 27th Ave S
Seattle, WA 98144-6502   206-722-4196
                                          800-458-0600
                                     FAX: 800-317-2182
                               info@buckandbuck.com
                               www.buckandbuck.com

Julie Buck, Owner
Made with 3 layers of fabric including waterproof backing, these attractive bibs will not soak through like most others, protecting clothing from stains. *$18.00*

1395 **Wishing Wells Collection**
Ste 965
11684 Ventura Blvd
Studio City, CA 91604-2699   818-840-6919
                                     FAX: 818-760-3878
                               www.dawnwells.com

Dawn Wells, Owner
Lorraine Parker, General Manager
Features designs full of back overlap construction and all velcro closures clothing.

Computers

Assistive Devices

1396 Ability Research
PO Box 1721
Minnetonka, MN 55345-721
952-939-0121
FAX: 952-227-5809
info@abilityresearch.net
www.abilityresearch.net

Suzanne Severson, Administrator
Manufacturers and marketers of assistive technology equipment.

1397 Academic Software Inc
3504 Tates Creek Rd
Lexington, KY 40517-2601
859-552-1020
FAX: 253-799-4012
asistaff@acsw.com
www.acsw.com

Warren E Lacefield PhD, President
Penelope Ellis, Marketing Director
Sylvia P Lacefield, Graphic Artist
Employs a unique, goal-oriented approach to aid individuals in identifying adaptive devices with potential to support various physical limitations. Devices are categorized in seven databases: Existence, Travel, In-situ Motion, Environmental Adaptation, Communication, and Sports & recreation. ADLS provides its users with device descriptions, pictures and lists of sources for locating products and product information.

1398 Adaptivation
Ste 100
2225 W 50th St
Sioux Falls, SD 57105-6536
605-335-4445
800-723-2783
FAX: 605-335-4446
info@adaptivation.com
www.adaptivation.com

Jonathan Eckrich, President
Manufacturers of switches, voice output devices and enviromental controls.

1399 Analog Switch Pad
Academic Software
331 W 2nd St
Lexington, KY 40507-1113
859-233-2332
800-842-2357
FAX: 859-231-0725

Warren E Lacefield PhD, President
Penelope Ellis, Marketing Director
A touch-activated, force-adjustable, low-voltage DC, electronic switch designed to control battery-operated toys, environmental controls, and computer access interfaces. This device features a large activation area that is soft and compliant to the touch. Force sensitivity is adjusted by a small dial from approximately 1 ounce to 32 ounces activation pressure, applied over an area ranging from the size of a fingertip to the size of the entire switch surface.

1400 Arkenstone: The Benetech Initiative
480 S California Ave
Palo Alto, CA 94306-1609
650-644-3400
FAX: 650-475-1066
www.hrdag.org

Jim Fruthterman, CEO
Roberta G Brosnaha, General Manager/VP
Patrick Ball, Executive Director
Offers various models of ready-to-read personal computers for the disabled.

1401 Augmentative Communication Systems (AAC)
ZYGO-USA
48834 Kato Road
Suite 101A
Freemont, CA 94538
510-249-9660
800-234-6006
FAX: 510-770-4930
www.zygo-usa.com

Lawrence Weiss, President
Full range of AAC systems and assistive technology including computer-based systems and computer access programs and devices.

1402 Away We Ride IntelliKeys Overlay
Soft Touch Inc
12301 Central Ave NE
Ste 205
Blaine, NE 55434
763-755-1402
888-755-1402
sales@marblesoft.com
www.softtouch.com

Joyce Meyer, President
Four full color preprinted overlays to use with Away We Ride. Just put them on an IntelliKeys keyboard and you are ready to go.

1403 BIGmack Communication Aid
AbleNet, Inc.
2625 Patton Road
Roseville, MN 55113-1137
651-294-2200
800-322-0956
FAX: 651-294-2259
customerservice@ablenetinc.com
www.ablenetinc.com

Jennifer Thalhuber, President & CEO
Paul Sugden, CFO & Trustee
A single message communication aid, BIGmack has 2 minutes of memory and has a 5 inches in diameter switch surface. *$155.00*

1404 Close-Up 6.5
Norton- Lambert Corporation
PO Box 4085
Santa Barbara, CA 93140-4085
805-964-6767
www.norton-lambert.com

Jeannie Vesely, Marketing Coordinator
Remotely controls PC's via modem. Telecommute from your home or laptop PC to your office PC. Run applications, update spreadsheets, print documents remotely and access networks on remote PCs. Features: fast screen and file transfers, synchronize files, unattended transfers, multi-level security, transaction logs, automated installation. *$99.95*

1405 Concepts on the Move Advanced Overlay CD
Soft Touch Inc
12301 Central Ave NE
Ste 205
Blaine, MN 55434
763-755-1402
888-755-1402
FAX: 763-862-2920
sales@marblesoft.com
www.softtouch.com

Joyce Myer, President
Use this overlay CD with Concepts on the Move Advanced Preacademics. Overlays match the concepts and graphics in the program. Includes standard overlays with all the choices and SoftTouch's changeable format overlays. Print and laminate the blank templates. Then print and laminate the picture keys in all three sizes - small, medium and large. Includes Overlay Printer by IntelliTools for easy printing. *$115.00*

1406 Concepts on the Move Basic Overlay CD
Soft Touch Inc
12301 Central Ave NE
Ste 205
Blaine, MN 55434
763-755-1402
888-755-1403
FAX: 763-862-2920
sales@marblesoft.com
www.softtouch.com

Joyce Meyer, President
Use this Overlay CD with Concepts on the Move Basic Preacademics. Overlays match the concepts and graphics in the program. Includes standard overlays with all the choices and SoftTouch's changeable format overlays. Print and laminate the blank templates. Then print and laminate the picture keys in all three sizes - small, medium and large. It is easy and fast to place the images on the blank templates. *$115.00*

1407 Darci Too
WesTest Engineering Corporation
810 Shepard Ln
Farmington, UT 84025-3846
801-451-9191
FAX: 801-451-9393
larryk@westest.com
westest.com

Robert Lessmann, President
A universal device which allows people with physical disabilities to replace the keyboard and mouse on a personal computer with a device that matches their physical capabilities. DARCI TOO works with almost any personal computer and provides access to all computer functions. *$995.00*

1408 Eyegaze Computer System
LC Technologies Inc
10363A Democracy Lane
Fairfax, VA 22030
703-385-7133
800-393-4293
FAX: 703-385-7137
www.eyegaze.com

Nancy Cleveland, Medical Coordinator
Enables people with physical disabilities to do many things with their eyes that they would not otherwise do with their hands.

1409 Five Green & Speckled Frogs IntelliKeys Overlay
Soft Touch Inc
12301 Central Ave NE
Ste 205
Blaine, MN 55434
763-755-1402
888-755-1403
FAX: 763-862-2920
sales@marblesoft.com
www.softtouch.com

Joyce Meyer, President
Seven full color preprinted overlays to use with Five Green and Speckled Frogs. Just put them on an IntelliKeys keyboard and you are ready to go. *$49.00*

1410 GW Micro
725 Airport North Office Park
Fort Wayne, IN 46825-6707
260-489-3671
FAX: 260-489-2608
www.gwmicro.com

Dan Weirich, Sales Executive
Marty Hord, Sales Manager
Computer hardware and software products for people with disabilities.

1411 InvoTek, Inc.
1026 Riverview Dr
Alma, AR 72921
479-632-4166
FAX: 479-632-6457
invotek.org

Thomas Jakobs, President
Diane Jakobs, Vice President, Operations
John Riggins, Chief Marketing Officer
InvoTek, Inc. is a research and development company that improves the quality of life for people who find it difficult or impossible to use their hands by giving them new, efficient ways to access computers.

1412 Jelly Bean Switch
AbleNet, Inc.
2625 Patton Road
Roseville, MN 55113-1137
651-294-2200
800-322-0956
FAX: 651-294-2259
customerservice@ablenetinc.com
www.ablenetinc.com

Jennifer Thalhuber, President & CEO
Paul Sugden, CFO & Trustee
A momentary touch switch made of shatterproof plastic, small and sensitive to 2-3 ounces of pressure, this switch is provided audible feedback when activated and is a compact version of the Big Red Switch. Choice of colors: red, blue, green and yellow. *$75.00*

1413 Large Print Keyboard Labels
Hooleon Corp
P.O.Box 589
Melrose, NM 88124-589
575-253-4503
800-937-1337
FAX: 928-634-4620
sales@hooleon.com
www.hooleon.com

Shannen Aikman, Admin Manager/Sales
Joan Crozier, President/Sales
Pressure sensitive labels for computer keyboards.

1414 MessageMate
Words+ Inc
42505 10th Street W
Lancaster, CA 93534-7059
661-723-6523
800-869-8521
FAX: 661-723-2114
www.words-plus.com

Jeff Dahlan, President
Ginger Woltosz, General Manager
Lightweight, hand-held communicator providing high-quality analog recording capability using either direct select keyboards or 1 to 2 switch access. Price ranges from $549.00 to $999.00. *$1550.00*

1415 Mouthsticks
Performance Health
28100 Torch Parkway
Suite 700
Warrenville, IL 60555-3938
630-393-6000
FAX: 630-393-7600
customsupport@performancehealth.com
www.performancehealth.com

Francis Dirksmeier, Chief Executive Officer
Greg Nulty, Chief Financial Officer
Jim Plewa, Chief Sales Officer
Wide offering of mouthsticks: BK 5380, 5381, 5383, 5385, 6002, or BK 5370 series). Designed for typing and page turning. Suitable for both personal and professional use. *$48.86*

1416 Old MacDonald's Farm IntelliKeys Overlay
Soft Touch Inc
12301 Central Ave NE
Ste 205
Blaine, MN 55434
763-755-1402
888-755-1403
FAX: 763-862-2920
sales@marblesoft.com
www.softtouch.com

Joyce Meyer, President
Extend your students' learning with more than 45 pre-made overlays that support all of the skills learned at the farm. Use with the IntelliKeys keyboard. Simply print and use. Print an extra set to make off computer activities, too. Note: Requires Overlay Maker or Overlay Printer by IntelliTools.

1417 Origin Instruments Corporation
854 Greenview Dr
Grand Prairie, TX 75050
972-606-8740
FAX: 972-606-8741
support@orin.com
www.orin.com

Origin Instruments develops and delivers access solutions for people who do not have the ability to control a computer or iOS Device (iPad, iPhone or iPod touch) with their hands.

1418 Perfect Solutions
2685 Treanor Ter
Wellington, FL 33414-6460
561-790-1070
800-726-7086
FAX: 561-790-0108
perfect@gate.net
www.perfectsolutions.com

Andrew Kramer, President
A computer for every student and it speaks! Wireless laptop computers starting at $299.00 are ideal for students to carry with them all day. Text-to-speech and web browsing are available. *$299.00*

1419 Phillip Roy, Inc.
P.O. Box 130
Indian Rocks Beach, FL 33785-130

727-593-2700
800-255-9085
FAX: 877-595-2685
info@philliproy.com
www.philliproy.com

Ruth Bragman, PhD, President
Phil Padol, Consultant
Offers multimedia materials appropriate for use with individuals with disabilities. Programs range from preschool through the adult level. Many of the programs are high interest topics/low vocabulary, ideal for transition and employability skills. Materials are also available which focus on social and personal development. Lesson Plans, teacher's guides, pre/post assessment, and other support materials are provided at no additional cost.

1420 SS-Access Single Switch Interface for PC's with MS-DOS
Academic Software
3504 Tates Creek Road
Lexington, KY 40517-2601

859-552-1020
800-842-2357
FAX: 253-799-4012
asistaff@acsw.com
www.acsw.com

Warren E Lacefield PhD, President
Penelope Ellis, Marketing Director
A general purpose single switch hardware and software interface for DOS and the IBM and compatible PC family. It is designed to be easy to install, simple to use, and compatible with the widest possible range of computers and application software programs. SS-ACCESS! connects to one of the PC serial ports and provides a jack to connect an external switch. The DOS version of the software works by sending a user defined keystroke to the PC keyboard buffer whenever the switch is pressed. *$90.00*

1421 Simplicity
Words+
42505 10th Street W
Lancaster, CA 93534-7059

661-723-6523
800-869-8521
FAX: 661-723-2114
info@words-plus.com
www.words-plus.com

Jeff Dahlan, President
Ginger Wolosz, General Manager
Swing-down mount for portable computers and other devices is made from high-quality aircraft aluminum. Simplicity contains very few moving parts and installs in minutes, providing a positive, secure support for computer/device in both the stored and overlap position. *$1199.00*

1422 Songs I Sing at Preschool IntelliKeys Overlay
Soft Touch
12301 Central Ave NE
Ste 205
Blaine, MN 55434

763-755-1402
888-755-1403
FAX: 763-862-2920
sales@marblesoft.com
www.softtouch.com

Joyce Meyer, President
Pre-made overlays for use with Songs I Sing at Preschool. Simply print and use with an IntelliKeys keyboard. Print an extra set to make off computer activities, too.

1423 Switch Basics IntelliKeys Overlay
Soft Touch
12301 Central Ave NE
Ste 205
Blaine, MN 55434

763-755-1402
888-755-1403
FAX: 763-862-2920
sales@marblesoft.com
www.softtouch.com

Joyce Meyer, President
Four preprinted overlays to use with Switch Basics. Just put them on an IntelliKeys keyboard and you're ready to go.

1424 Teach Me Phonemics Blends Overlay CD
SoftTouch Inc.
12301 Central Ave NE
Ste 205
Blaine, MN 55434

763-755-1402
888-755-1403
FAX: 763-862-2920
sales@marblesoft.com
www.softtouch.com

Roxanne Butterfield, Marketing
Joyce Meyer, President
Teach Me Phonemics Blends Overlay CD contains over 40 IntelliKeys overlays for use with Teach Me Phonemics - Blends program. Choose either 4-item or 9-item layout to match the presentation you use in the program. Print extra copies of the overlays for off computer activites, too.

1425 Teach Me Phonemics Medial Overlay CD
SoftTouch Incorporated
Ste C
17117 Oak Dr
Omaha, NE 68130-2193

402-330-1301
877-763-8868
FAX: 402-334-8478
support@softtouch.com
www.softtouch.com

Kip Fisher, Manager
Roxanne Butterfield, Marketing
Teach Me Phonemics Medial Overlay CD contains over 40 IntelliKeys overlays for use with Teach Me Phonemics - Medial program. Choose either 4-item or 9-item layout to match the presentation you use in the program. Print extra copies of the overlays for off computer activites, too.

1426 Teach Me Phonemics Overlay Series Bundle
SoftTouch
Ste 401
4300 Stine Rd
Bakersfield, CA 93313-2352

661-396-8676
877-763-8868
FAX: 661-396-8760
www.softtouch.com

Roxanne Butterfield, Marketing
Joyce Meyer, President
Teach Me Phonemics Overlay Series Bundle includes one copy of each Teach Me Phonemics Overlay CD - Initial, Medial, Final and - four CD's in all.

1427 Teach Me to Talk Overlay CD
Soft Touch
12301 Central Ave NE
Ste 205
Blaine, MN 55434

763-755-1402
888-755-1403
FAX: 763-862-2920
sales@marblesoft.com
www.softtouch.com

Joyce Meyer, President
For older version of Teach Me to Talk. Mac only version with red label and PC only version with yellow label. More than 48 pre-made overlays that match the activities on Teach Me to Talk. Simply print and use with an IntelliKeys keyboard. Print an extra set to make off computer activities, too.

1428 Teach Me to Talk: USB-Overlay CD
Soft Touch
12301 Central Ave NE
Ste 205
Blaine, MN 55434

763-755-1402
888-755-1403
FAX: 763-862-2920
sales@marblesoft.com
www.softtouch.com

Joyce Meyer, President
Revised version of Teach Me to Talk Overlays for the newest version that is USB IntelliKeys compatible. This CD contains more than 48 overlays that match the activities and updated graphics of Teach Me to Talk. Includes Overlay Printer by IntelliTools for easy printing.

1429 Teen Tunes Plus IntelliKeys Overlay
Soft Touch
12301 Central Ave NE
Ste 205
Blaine, MN 55434
763-755-1402
888-755-1403
FAX: 763-862-2920
sales@marblesoft.com
www.softtouch.com

Joyce Meyer, President
Seven full color, preprinted overlays to use with Teen Tunes Plus.
Just put them on an IntelliKeys keyboard and you're ready to go.
$49.00

1430 U-Control III
Words+
42505 10th St W
Lancaster, CA 93534-7059
575-253-4503
800-869-8521
FAX: 661-723-2114
www.words-plus.com

Jeff Dahlen, President
Ginger Wolosz, General Manager
Works with the Words+ system (EX Keys, Morse WSKE, Scanning WSKE, Talking Screen) to provide wireless, portable control of items which are already infrared-controlled such as a TV, VCR, CD player, etc. *$499.00*

1431 WinSCAN: The Single Switch Interface for PC's with Windows
Academic Software
3504 Tates Creek Rd
Lexington, KY 40517-2601
859-522-1020
FAX: 253-799-4012
asistaff@acsw.com
www.acsw.com

Warren E Lacefield, President
Penelope Ellis, Marketing Director/COO
A general purpose single-switch control interface for Windows.
It provides single-switch users independent control access to educational and productivity software, multimedia programs, and recreational activities that run under Windows 3.1 and higher versions on IBM and compatible PC's. The user can navigate through Windows; choose program icons and run programs, games, and CD's; even surf the Internet with WinSCAN and his or her adaptive switch. *$349.00*

1432 Words+ IST (Infrared, Sound, Touch)
Words+
42505 10th St W
Lancaster, CA 93534-7059
575-253-4503
800-869-8521
FAX: 661-723-2114
www.words-plus.com

Jeff Dahlan, President
Ginger Wolosz, General Manager
A unique switch that is activated by slight movement or faint sound. The switch provides user control when connected to a device driven by a single switch. Individuals are currently accessing a wide variety of communication and computer systems with movement using the IST switch. *$395.00*

Braille Products

1433 Braille Keyboard Labels
Hooleon Corporation
PO Box 589
Melrose, NM 88124-589
928-634-7515
800-937-1337
FAX: 928-634-4620
sales@hooleon.com
www.hooleon.com

Barry Green, Sales Manager
Joan Crozier, President/Sales
Also large print keyboard labels and large print with Braille.

1434 Braille Paper
Maxi Aids
42 Executive Blvd.
Farmingdale, NY 11735-4710
631-752-0521
800-522-6294
FAX: 631-752-0689
TTY: 631-752-0738
sales@maxiaids.com
www.maxiaids.com

Elliot Zaretsky, Founder, President & CEO
Paper for braille embossing. Sizes include 8.5 by 11 inch and 11 by 11.5 inch.

1435 Brailon Plastic Sheets
Maxi Aids
42 Executive Blvd.
Farmingdale, NY 11735-4710
631-752-0521
800-522-6294
FAX: 631-752-0689
TTY: 631-752-0738
sales@maxiaids.com
www.maxiaids.com

Elliot Zaretsky, Founder, President & CEO
Brailon plastic sheets used with Thermoform machines to copy braille text and graphics.

1436 Brailon Thermoform Duplicator
American Thermoform Corporation
1758 Brackett St
La Verne, CA 91750-5855
909-593-6711
800-331-3676
FAX: 909-593-8001
pnunnelly@americanthermoform.com
www.americanthermoform.com

Patrick Nunnelly, VP
Gary Nunnelly, Owner
This copy machine, for producing tactile images, copies any brailled or embossed original, by a vacuum forming process. This model is for the reproduction of teaching aids and mobility maps.

1437 Duxbury Braille Translator
Duxbury Systems
Ste 6
270 Littleton Rd
Westford, MA 01886-3523
978-692-3000
FAX: 978-692-7912
info@duxsys.com
www.duxburysystems.com

Joe Sullivan, President
A complete line of easy to use word processing and Braille translation software available for Windows (including 64 bit windows. Applications for anyone wanting to produce or communicate with Braille; signs, note cards, textbooks, business communications and forms, telephone bills, etc. Simple to use, FREE technical support. Free one year upgrades. DBT is for producing Braille in English, Spanish, French, Portuguese, Italian, Latin, Greek, German and 125 other languages. *$600.00*

1438 Enabling Technologies Company
1601 NE Braille Pl
Jensen Beach, FL 34957-5345
772-225-3687
800-777-3687
FAX: 772-225-3299
info@brailler.com
www.brailler.com

Tony Schenk, President
Kate Schenk, Product Manager Western US
Greg Schenk, Sales & Marketing
Manufactures the most complete line of American made Braille embossers, including desktop or portable models capable of producing high quality single sided or interpoint Braille. Also carries a complete line of adaptive technology aids for the blind community at affordable prices.

1439   Freedom Scientific Blind/Low Vision Group
11800 31st Ct N
St Petersburg, FL 33716-1805   727-803-8000
                                      800-444-4443
                                FAX: 727-803-8001
                            info@freedomscientific.com
                            www.freedomscientific.com

Brad Davis, VP Hardware Product Management
Dr Lee Hamilton, President/CEO
Developer and manufacturer of assistive technology products for people who are blind or who have low vision. Innovative blindness products include: JAWS® screen reading software; the PAC Mate Omni™, an accessible Pocket PC; the SARA™ scanning and reading appliance; OpenBook™ scanning and reading software; FSReader™ DAISY player; FaceToFace™ deaf-blind communications solution; and PAC Mate and Focus Braille Displays. *$16.95*

1440   Hooleon Corporation
PO Box 589
Melrose, NM 88124-589   928-634-7515
                                      800-937-1337
                                FAX: 928-634-4620
                                sales@hooleon.com
                                www.hooleon.com

Kim Green, Manager
Joan Crozier, President/Sales
Large print and combination Braille adhesive keytop labels for computer keyboards. Helps visually impaired computer users access correct key strokes either by sight or by touch. Raised Braille meets ADA specifications and large print fills key top surface.

1441   Humanware
1 UPS Way
P.O. Box 800
Champlain, NY 12919   800-722-3393
                                FAX: 888-871-4828
                               info@humanware.com
                                  humanware.com

Gilles Pepin, CEO
Humanware manufactures electronics to provide solutions that empower the visually impaired.

1442   Large Print/Braille Keyboard Labels
Infogrip
Ventura, CA 93001   503-828-1221
                                      866-606-8551
                               support@infogrip.com
                                 www.infogrip.com

Liza Jacobs, President
Aaron Gaston, Vice President
Makes a standard keyboard more accessible for visually impaired individuals with large print or Braille keyboard labels. Characters on the large print labels are .5 by .25 inches, about 3 times larger than standard keyboard characters. Braille labels are available as clear labels with Braille dots or large print with Braille. Each set includes all the keys used on a standard Windows keyboard. *$29.00*

1443   Raised Dot Computing
Duxbury Systems Incorporated
270 Littleton Rd.
Unit 6
Westford, MA 01886-3523   978-692-3000
                                FAX: 978-692-7912
                               info@duxsys.com
                             www.duxburysystems.com

Joe Sullivan, President
Peter Sullivan, VP of Software Development
Genevieve Sullivan, Treasurer
Software for the visually impaired.

1444   Touchdown Keytop/Keyfront Kits
Hooleon Corporation
P.O.Box 589
304 West Denby Ave
Melrose, NM 88124   575-253-4503
                                      800-937-1337
                                FAX: 575-253-4299
                                Sales@Hooleon.com
                                www.hooleon.com

Bob Crozier, Founder
Joan Crozier, President
Barry Green, Sales Manager
These kits enlarge the key legends of a computer and include Braille for easy recognition.

Information Centers & Databases

1445   ATTAIN
Division of Disability Aging & Rehab Services
Ste 1400
32 E Washington St
Indianapolis, IN 46204-3552   317-232-1147
                                      800-528-8246
                                FAX: 317-486-8809

Gary R Hand, Executive Director
Peter Bisbecos, Manager
Nonprofit organization that creates system change by expanding the availability of community-based technology-related activities, outreach services, empowerment and advocacy activities through the development of a comprehensive, consumer-responsive, statewide program to serve individuals with disabilities, of all ages and all disabilities, their families, caregivers, educators and service providers. Provides training, information and referrals, system change and assessments for equipment needs.

1446   AbleData
103 W Broad St
Suite 400
Falls Church, VA 22046   301-608-8998
                                      800-227-0216
                                FAX: 301-608-8958
                                TTY: 301-608-8912
                             abledata@neweditions.net
                                www.abledata.com

Katherine Belknap, Director
David Johnson, Publications Director
AbleData is an electronic database containing information on assistive technology and rehabilitation equipment products for children and adults with physical, cognitive and sensory disabilities. AbleData staff can perform database searches or the database can be searched via the website, informed consumer guides or fact sheets.

1447   Aloha Special Technology Access Center
710 Green St
Honolulu, HI 96813-2119   808-523-5547
                                FAX: 808-536-3765
                                astachi@yahoo.com

Ali Silvert, President
Ms. Jacquely Brand, Founder
Computer technology center.

1448   Birmingham Alliance for Technology Access Center
Birmingham Independent Living Center
206 13th St S.
Birmingham, AL 35233-1317   205-251-2223
                                FAX: 205-251-0605
                                TTY:205-251-2223
                                www.drradvocates.org

Kathy Lovell, President
Phil Klebine, Vice President
Daniel Kessler, Executive Director
Computer technology center.

1449   Bluegrass Technology Center
409 Southland Drive
Lexington, KY 40503   859-294-4343
                                        800-209-7767
                                        FAX: 866-576-9625

Debbie Sharon, Acting Executive Director
Linnie Lee, Assistive Technology Specialist
Jean Isaacs, Assistive Technology Consultant
Provides assistive technology information, consulting and training for education, health professionals, consumers and parents of consumers. Maintains extensive lending library of assistive devices and adapted toys. Statewide training such as; AAC, how to obtain funding for assistive technology, augmentative and alternate communication, equipment implementation strategies, specific to hardware and software, etc.

1450   CITE: Lighthouse for Central Florida
215 East New Hampshire Street
Orlando, FL 32804   407-898-2483
                                        FAX: 407-898-0236
                                        csacca@lcf-fl.org
                    www.lighthousecentralflorida.org/Default.asp
Lee Nasehi, MSW, President/CEO
Donna Esbensen CPA,MBA, VP/CFO
Jeff Whitehead, MPA, MS, Director of Program Services
CITE promotes the independence of adults and children with blindness, low vision and other disabilities through technology, education, support and advocacy.

1451   Carolina Computer Access Center
P.O.Box 247
Cramerton, NC 28032   704-342-3004
                                        FAX: 704-342-1513
Linda Schilling, Executive Director
Nonprofit, community-based technology resource center for people with disabilities, providing information about and demonstration of the technology tools that enable individuals with disabilities to control and direct their own lives. Services and programs include: assessments, demonstrations, resource information, lending library, workshops and outreach.

1452   Center for Accessible Technology
3075 Adeline
Suite 220
Berkeley, CA 94703   510-841-3224
                                        FAX: 510-841-7956
                                        info@cforat.org
                                        www.cforat.org
Dmitri Belser, Executive Director
Eric Smith, Associate Director
A consumer-based technology resource and demonstration center for adults and children with disabilities, families, teachers, and professionals. The primary focus is on assistive technology for computer access. Seen by appointment only.

1453   Center for Applied Special Technology
40 Harvard Mills Square
Suite 3
Wakefield, MA 01880-3233   781-245-2212
                                        FAX: 781-245-5212
                                        cast@cast.org
                                        www.cast.org/
Anne Meyer, Founder
David H. Rose, Founder
Lisa Poller, Co-President
Expands opportunities for individuals with special needs through innovative use of computers and related technology. We pursue this mission through research and product development that further universal design for learning.

1454   Center for Assistive Technology & Inclusive Education Studies
2000 Pennington Rd.
P.O.Box 7718
Ewing, NJ 08628-0718   609-771-3016
                                        FAX: 609-637-5179
                                        caties@tcnj.edu
                                        caties.pages.tcnj.edu
Amanda Norvell, President
Matt Bender, VP
Regina Morin, Parliamentarian

Computer technology center offering resource time, workshops, technology, training and evaluations.

1455   Center on Evaluation of Assistive Technology
National Rehabilitation Hospital
102 Irving St NW
Washington, DC 20010   202-877-1000
                                        TTY:202-726-3996
                                        justin.m.carter@medstar.net
                                        www.medstarhealth.org
Kenneth A. Samet, FACHE, President, CEO
Michael J. Curran, EVP, Chief Administrative and Financial Officer
Christine Swearingen, EVP, Planning, Marketing and Community Relations
The center develops ways of collecting, producing and distributing information to help users, prescribers and third-party payers make intelligent selections of devices.

1456   Compuserve: Handicapped Users' Database
5000 Arlington Centre Blvd
Columbus, OH 43220-2913   614-326-1002
                                        800-848-8990
                                        FAX: 614-538-4023
                            webcenters.netscape.compuserve.com
This nationwide database with bulletin boards provides information for persons with disabilities and the issues and technologies that are of interest to them.

1457   Computer Access Center
P.O. Box 12464
Albuquerque, NM 87195   505-242-9588
                                        info@cac.org
                                        www.cac.org
Richard Barlow, Board of Director
Richard Rohr, Board of Director
Michael Poffenberger, Board of Director
Computer technology center.

1458   Computer Center for Visually Impaired People: Division of Continuing Studies
Baruch College
1 Bernard Baruch Way
Box H-648
New York, NY 10010   646-312-1420
                                        FAX: 646-312-5101
                                        www.baruch.cuny.edu/ccvip
Karen Gourgey, Director
Judith Gerber, Operations Manager
Lynette Tatum, Training Specialist
Offers courses, tutors, equipment and assistance.

1459   Computer Resources for People with Disabilities
Hunter House Publishers, Inc
424 Church Street
Suite 2240
Nashville, TN 37219   615-255-BOOK
                                        info@turnerpublishing.com
                                        www.hunterhouse.com
Kiran Rana, Publisher
Chris Alexander, Author
Sheila Alson, Author
Part One describes conventional and assistive technologies and gives strategies for accessing the Internet. Part Two features easy-to-use charts organized by key access concerns, and provides detailed descriptions of software, hardware, and communication aids. Part Three is a gold mine of Web resources, publications, support organizations, government programs, and technology vendors.

1460   Computer-Enabling Drafting for People with Physical Disabilities
County College of Morris
214 Center Grove Road
Randolph, NJ 07869-2086   973-328-5000
                                        888-226-8001
                                        FAX: 973-328-5067
                                        www.ccm.edu
Edward J Yaw, President
Dr. Dwight Smith, Vice President of Academic Affairs
Karen VanDerhoof, Vice President for Business and Finance

Since they opened in 1968, more than 40,000 graduates have passed through their halls. Many have become teachers, nurses, police officers, doctors and engineers. CCM has also been a community resource for those seeking to enhance their careers through additional education. They drafted a newsletter on Computer-Enabling Drafting for People with Physical Disabilities

1461 DIRLINE
National Library of Medicine
8600 Rockville Pike
Bethesda, MD 20894   301-594-5983
                                                888-346-3656
                                              FAX: 301-402-1384
                                              TTY:800-735-2258
                                               www.nlm.nih.gov/

Dr. Donald A B. Lindberg, Director
Milton Corn, Deputy Director
Betsy Humphreys, Deputy Director
18,000 listings of organizations that serve as information resources, including libraries, professional associations and government agencies.

1462 Developmental Disabilities Council
626 Main Street, Suite A
P.O.Box 3455
Baton Rouge, LA 70821-3455   225-342-6804
                                                800-450-8108
                                              FAX: 225-342-1970
                                           shawn.fleming@la.gov
                                               www.laddc.org

Sandee Winchell, Executive Director
Shawn Fleming, Deputy Director
Derek White, Program Manager
The Louisiana Developmental Disabilities Council is made up of people from every region of the state who are appointed by the governor to develop and implement a five year plan to address the needs of persons with disabilities. Membership includes persons with developmental disabilities, parents, advocates, professionals, and representatives from public and private agencies.

1463 Employment Resources Program
330 South Grand Avenue West
Springfield, IL 62704   217-523-2587
                                                800-447-4221
                                              FAX: 217-523-0427
                                              TTY: 217-523-2587
                                                scil@scil.org
                                                www.scil.org

Pete Roberts, Executive Director
Susanne Cooper, Program Director
Robin Ashton- Hale, Reintegration Coordinator
An information and referral service that encourages inquiries from professionals, individuals with disabilities, family members, organizations or anyone requesting information pertaining to disabilities. The staff at DRN uses both computer listings and in-house library files to provide the programs services. The DRN program is funded by a grant from the Illinois Department of Rehabilitation Services.

1464 Functional Skills Screening Inventory
Functional Resources
3905 Huntington Dr
Amarillo, TX 79019-4047   806-353-1114
                                              FAX: 806-353-1114
                                               www.winfssi.com

Ed Hammer, Owner
Heather Becker PhD, Owner
Assesses the individual's level of functional skills and identifies supports needed by educational, rehabilitation and residential programs serving moderately and severely disabled persons. Includes environmental assessments as well as profiles of jobs and training sites.

1465 High Tech Center
Sacramento State
6000 J Street
Sacramento, CA 95819   916-278-6011
                                                sswd@csus.edu
                                                www.csus.edu

Alexander Gonzalez, President
Judy Dean, Co-Director
Melissa Repa, Co-Director
The Center offers assessment and training in adaptive hardware/software for eligible students with disabilities at Sacramento State upon referral from the Office of Services to Students with Disabilities.

1466 Idaho Assistive Technology Project
121 W 3rd St
Moscow, ID 83843-2268   208-885-3557
                                              FAX: 208-885-3628
                                               www.idahoat.org

Ron Seiler, Project Director
Sue House, Information Specialist
A federally funded program managed by the center on disabilities and human development at the university of Idaho. The goal of the IATP is to increase the availability of assistive technology devices and services for Idahoans with disabilities. The IATP offers free trainings and technical assistance, a low-interest loan program, assistive technology assessments for children and agriculture workers, and free informational materials.

1467 Increasing Capabilities Access Network
525 W.Capitol
Little Rock, AR 72201   501-666-8868
                                                800-828-2799
                                              FAX: 501-666-5319
                                              TTY: 501-666-8868
                                                nfo@ar-ican.org
                                             www.arkansas-ican.org

Bryen Ayres, Member of Advisory Council
Billy Altom, Member of Advisory Council
Adrienne Brown, Member of Advisory Council
A consumer responsive statewide systems change program promoting assistive technology for persons of all ages with disabilities. The program provides information on new and existing technology and maintains an equipment exchange free of charge. Training on assistive technology is also provided.

1468 International Center for the Disabled
340 E 24th St
New York, NY 10010-4019   212-585-6000
                                              FAX: 212-585-6161
                                                info@icdnyc.org
                                                www.icdnyc.org

Jill Bowman, Manager
Les Halpert, CEO
The ICD is a comprehensive outpatient rehabilitation facility, providing medical rehabilitation, behavioral health and vocational services to children and adults with a broad range of physical, communication, emotional and cognitive disabilities.

1469 Kentucky Assistive Technology Service Network
200 Juneau Dr.
Suite 200
Louisville, KY 40243   502-429-4484
                                                800-327-5287
                                              FAX: 502-429-7114
                                               www.katsnet.org

Derrick Cox, Manager
Statewide network of four regional assistive technology centers with a central coordinating office in Louisville and two regional centers in eastern Kentucky. Network services include but are not limited to assistive technology of services, loan of assistive devices, funding information and referral, assessment and evaluations, consultations on appropriate technologies, training, and technical assistance.

1470 **Learning Independence Through Computers**
2301 Argonne Drive
Baltimore, MD 21218   410-554-9134
                                   FAX: 410-261-2907
                                        info@linc.org
                                        www.linc.org

Theo Pinette, Executive Director
Sandy Fishman, Office and Computer Center Coordinator
Angela Tyler, Volunteer Services Manager
V-LINC creates technological solutions to improve the independence and quality of life for individuals of all ages with disabilities in Maryland. We do this through a mix of off-the-shelf computer software and equipment, and one-of-a-kind, customized assistive technology.

1471 **MEDLINE**
Dialog Corporation
2250 Perimeter Park Drive
Suite 300
Morrisville, NC 27560   800-334-2564
                                        919-804-6400
                                   FAX: 919-804-6410
                                        www.dialog.com

Tim Wahlberg, Genral Manager
Morten Nicholaisen, VP Global Sales and Account Mana
Libby Trudell, VP Strategic Initiatives
Bibliographic citations to biomedical literature.

1472 **Maine CITE**
University of Maine at Augusta
46 University Avenue
Augusta, ME 04330   207-621-3195
                                   FAX: 207-629-5429
                                   TTY:877-475-4800
                                      iweb@mainecite.org
                                        www.mainecite.org

Robert McPhee, Member of Advisory Council
Deborah Gardner, Member of Advisory Council
Anita Dunham, Member of Advisory Council
Computer technology center.

1473 **Maryland Technology Assistance Program**
Maryland Department of Disabilities
2301 Argonne Drive
Rm T-17
Baltimore, MD 21218   410-554-9361
                                        800-832-4827
                                   FAX: 410-554-9237
                                   TTY: 866-881-7488
                                        www.mdtap.org

James McCarthy, Executive Director
Denise Schuler, Assistive Technology Specialist
Tanya Goodman, Loan Program Assistant Director
Assistive technology center. Information and referral, equipment display loans and demonstration, funding sources, alternative media, training, workshops and seminars. Rural outreach for individuals with disability in Maryland.

1474 **Minnesota STAR Program**
358 Centennial Office Building 658
Saint Paul, MN 55155- 1402   651-201-2640
                                        800-627-3529
                                        888-234-1267
                                   FAX: 651-282-6671
                                      star.program@state.mn.us

Chuck Rassbach, Program Director
Jennis Delisi, Program Staff
Jaoan Gillum, Program Staff
STAR's mission is to help all Minnesotans with disabilities gain access to and acquire the assistive technology they need to live, learn, work and lay. The Minnesota STAR program is federally funded by the Rehabilitation Services Administration.

1475 **Mississippi Project START**
2550 Peachtree Street
Jackson, MS 39216   601-987-4872
                                        800-852-8328
                                   FAX: 601-364-2349
                                     pgaltelli@mdrs.ms.gov
                                        www.msprojectstart.org

Patsy Galtelli, Executive Director
Dorothy Young, Project Director
Nekeba Simmons, Administrative Assistant
Project START is a Tech Act project established to bring about systems change in the field of assistive technology in the State of Mississippi. Activities include providing training opportunities for consumers and service providers on subjects such as state-of-the-art AT devices, their application and funding resources; referral information on AT evaluation centers; technical assistance to AT users; establishment of an AT equipment loan program and an Information and Referral Service.

1476 **National Technology Database**
American Foundation for the Blind/ AF B Press
2 Penn Plaza
Suite 1102
New York, NY 10121   212-502-7600
                                        800-232-5463
                                   FAX: 888-545-8331
                                        afbinfo@afb.net
                                        www.afb.org

Carl.R Augusto, President and CEO
Robin Vogel, Vice President, Resource Development
Kelly Bleach, Chief Administrative Officer
This database includes resources for visually impaired persons,
$99.00

1477 **New Jersey Department of Labor & Workforce Development**
Office of the Commissioner
1 John Fitch Plaza
P.O.Box 110
Trenton, NJ 08625-0110   609-292-7060
                                   FAX: 609-633-1359
                                        www.state.nj.us/labor

Harold J. Wirths, Commissioner
Aaron R. Fichtner, Ph.D., Deputy Commissioner
Frederick J. Zavaglia, Chief of Staff
Oversees various federal and state vocational rehabilitation services including sheltered workshops and independent living centers; adjudication of permanent disability claims filed with the Social Security Administration; oversees New Jersey's temporary disability program covering non-work related illnesses and injuries

1478 **New Mexico Technology Assistance Program**
625 Silver Ave SW
Suite 100 B
Albuquerque, NM 87102   505-841-4464
                                        877-696-1470
                                   FAX: 505-841-4467
                                        www.tap.gcd.state.nm.us

Tracy Agiovlasitis, Program Manager
Examines and works to eliminate barriers to obtaining assistive technology in New Mexico. Has established a statewide program for coordinating assistive technology services; is designed to assist people with disabilities to locate, secure, and maintain assistive technology.

1479 **Northern Illinois Center for Adaptive Technology**
3615 Louisiana Rd
Rockford, IL 61108   815-229-2163
Dave Grass, President
Computer technology center.

1480 OCCK
1710 W. Schilling Road
Salina, KS 67402-1160
785-827-9383
800-526-9731
FAX: 785-823-2015
TTY: 785-827-9383
occk@occk.com
www.occk.com

Shelia Nelson Stout, President, CEO
Carolee Miner, CEO
Computer technology center; training center for employment and independent living for people with disabilities; family support center. Kansas AgrAbility program coordinator, Kansas equipment exchange site.

1481 Options, Resource Center for Independent Living
318 3rd St. NW
East Grand Forks, MN 56721
218-773-6100
800-726-3692
FAX: 218-773-7119
options@myoptions.info
www.rcil.com

Burt Danovitz, Executive Director
The RCIL aggressively advocates for and defends the rights of persons with disabilities. RCIL believes in integration adn assisting people to reach their full potential, encouraging a culture of risk-taking, creativity and innovation through our programs and services. They monitor and assess the current legal climate around rights for persons with disabilities on an ongoing bases and are committed and deliberate in speaking about the problems and obstacles faced by persons with disabilities.

1482 Parents, Let's Unite for Kids
516 N 32nd St
Billings, MT 59101-6003
406-255-0540
800-222-7585
FAX: 406-255-0523
TTY: 406-657-2055
info@pluk.org

Roger Holt, Executive Director
Computer technology center. Parents, Let's Unite for Kids offers an assistive technology lab that is open to people of all ages. The lab is a computer and assistive technology demonstration site. There is no charge for services.

1483 Pennsylvania's Initiative on Assistive Technology
Temple University
1755 N. 13th St.
Student Center, Room 411 South
Philadelphia, PA 19122-6024
215-204-1356
800-204-7428
FAX: 215-204-6336
TTY: 866-268-0579
ATinfo@temple.edu
www.disabilities.temple.edu

Kim Singleton, Director
Pennsylvania's Initiative on Assistive Technology (PIAT) offers information and referral about assistive Technology (AT), device demonstrations, and awareness-level presentations. PIAT also operates Pennsylvania's AT Lending Library, a free, state-supported program that loans AT devices to Pennsylvanians of all ages.

1484 Rehabilitation Engineering and AssistiveTechnology Society of North America (RESNA)
2001 K Street NW
3rd Floor North
Washington, DC 20006
202-367-1121
FAX: 202-367-2121
info@resna.org
www.resna.org

Maureen Linden, President
Andrea Van Hook, Interim Executive Director
RESNA improves the potential of people with disabilities to achieve their goals through the use of technology. RESNA promotes research, development, education, advocacy and provision of technology; and by supporting the people engaged in these activities.

1485 SACC Assistive Technology Center
P.O.Box 1325
Simi Valley, CA 93062-1325
805-582-1881
www.semel.ucla.edu

Debi Schultze, CEO
SACC connects children, adults and seniors with special needs to computers, technologies and resources. We provide information and referral, assessments, tutoring, presentations and outreach awareness.

1486 South Dakota Department of Human Services: Computer Technology Services
Properties Plaza
500 East Capitol Avenue
Pierre, SD 57501
605-773-5990
800-265-9684
FAX: 605-773-5483
TTY: 605-773-6412
infodhs@state.sd.us
dhs.sd.gov

Dan Lusk, Division Director
Ted Williams, Director
Eric Weiss, Director
Computer technology center.

1487 Star Center
1119 Old Humboldt Rd
Jackson, TN 38305-1752
731-668-3888
888-398-5619
FAX: 731-668-1666
TTY: 731-668-9664
information@starcenter.tn.org
www.starcenter.tn.org

John Borden, CEO
Nation's largest assistive technology center dedicated to helping children and adults with disabilities achieve their goals for competitive employment, effective learning, returning to or starting school and independent living. Programs include: high-tech training, music therapy, art therapy, low vision evaluation, orientation and mobility evaluation and training, augmentative communication evaluation, vocational evaluations, assistive technology, job placement services and job skills training.

1488 Students with Disabilities Office
University of Texas at Austin
100 West Dean Keeton A5800
Austin, TX 78712-1100
512-471-5017
FAX: 512-471-7833
deanofstudents@austin.utexas.edu
deanofstudents.utexas.edu

Soncia Reagins-Lilly, Ed.D., Senior Associate VP for Student Affairs & Dean of Students
Douglas Garrard, Ed.D., Senior Associate Dean of Students
Wanda Brune, Administrative Associate

1489 TASK Team of Advocates for Special Kids
100 W Cerritos Ave
Anaheim, CA 92805
714-533-8275
866-828-8275
FAX: 714-533-2533
task@taskca.org
www.taskca.org

Marta Anchondo, Executive Director
Tom Bratkovich, Treasurer
Leana Way, Director
Computer technology center.

1490 Tech Connection
35 Haddon Avenue
Shrewsbury, NJ 07702
732-747-5310
FAX: 732-747-1896
info@frainc.org
www.frainc.org

Bill Sheeser, President
Nancy Phalanukom, Executive Director
Sue Levine, Program Administrator
Offers a noncommercial center to examine and try computers, adapted equipment, alternative input devices, and a variety of software. Program of Family Resource Associates and a member of the Alliance for Technology Access (ATA), a growing national coalition of computer resource centers, professionals, technol-

ogy developers and vendors, interacting with new technology to enrich the lives of people with disabilities. Tech Connection offers evaluations, for computer technology.

1491 Tech-Able
1451 Klondike Road, Suite D
Conyers, GA 30094   770-922-6768
                                FAX: 770-922-6769

Cassandra Baker, Executive Director
Pat Hanus, Program Assistant
Erika Ruffin-Mosley, Assistive Technology Trainer
Provide assistive technology to individuals with disabilities, toy-lending and software libraries, product demonstration, access to technology devices and fabrication of keyguards for keyboards. Low vision consultant on Thursdays; computer training for persons with disabilities.

1492 Technology Access Center of Tucson
P.O.Box 13178
Tucson, AZ 85732-3178   520-638-2733
                                FAX: 520-519-7954
                                tact1@qwestoffice.net
                                www.uacoe.arizona.edu/tact/
A resource center that provides assistive technology services for people with disabilities. Center personnel develop, provide and coordinate those services in communities throughout Middle Tennessee. Services are designed to assist people with disabilities to learn about, choose, acquire and use assistive technology devices. Services are offered to any child or adult with sensory, motor or cognitive disabilities, their family members, and professionals who serve them and employ them.

1493 Technology Assistance for Special Consumers
1856 Keats Dr NW.
Huntsville, AL 35810   256-859-8300
                                FAX: 256-859-4332
                                ucphuntsville.org/what-we-do/t-a-s-c/
Cheryl Smith, Chief Executive Officer
T.A.S.C. is a computer resource center with 10 computers, which are equipped with special adaptations for those who are blind, visually impaired, or severely physically disabled. The staff demonstrates and trains individuals on this equipment so that they can become more independent at home, school, and work. Over 2,500 pieces of educational software are available.

1494 Tidewater Center for Technology Access Special Education Annex
1415 Laskin Rd
Virginia Beach, VA 23451   757-424-2672
                                FAX: 757-263-2801
                                www.tcta.access.org
Pat Mc Gee, Manager
Myra Jessie Flint, Designee
Nonprofit organization providing persons with disabilities access, support, and knowledge—re: technology; organization contracts for consultations, workshops and training, or conventional and assistive technologies including computers, augmented communication devices and software; resources: extensive lending library of educational software; books and videotape library; yearly individual membership and corporate membership fees; working/presentation and evaluation fees available upon request.

1495 Vermont Assistive Technology Project: Department of Aging & Disabilities
Agency of Human Services
103 South Main Street
Weeks Building
Waterbury, VT 05671-2305   802-871-3353
                                800-750-6355
                                FAX: 802-871-3048
                                TTY: 802-241-1464
                                atp.vermont.gov
Amber Fulcher, Program Director
Sharon Alderman, Assistive Technology Reuse Coordinator
Emma Cobb, Assistive Technology Services Coordinator
Increase the awareness and change policies to insure assistive technology is available to all Vermonters with disabilities.

Keyboards, Mouses & Joysticks

1496 A4 Tech (USA) Corporation
5585 Brooks St
Montclair, CA 91763-4547   909-988-9633
                                www.a4tech.com
Robert C
Manufacturers of a cordless mouse, trackballs and joysticks that emulate mouse controls, flatbed scanners, modified keyboards, and other specialty mouses.

1497 Abacus
3150 Patterson Ave SE
Grand Rapids, MI 49512   616-698-0330
                                800-451-4319
                                FAX: 616-698-0325
                                www.abacuspub.com
Arnie Lee, President
Designs a mouse software program that permits programs written for one computer to be run on another computer.

1498 Ability Center of Greater Toledo
5605 Monroe St.
Sylvania, OH 43560   419-885-5733
                                FAX: 419-882-4813
                                www.abilitycenter.org
Tim Harrington, Executive Director
Ash Lemons, Associate Director
Debbie Andriette, Director, Human Resources
Manufactures keyboard wrist supports to help prevent repetitive motion disorders.

1499 Dreamer
TS Micro Tech
17109 Gale Ave
City of Industry, CA 91745-1810   626-939-8998
                                FAX: 626-839-8516
Steve Heung, Owner
An intelligent, add-on function keyboard providing single-keystroke access to multiple-keystroke functions.

1500 FlexShield Keyboard Protectors
Hooleon Corporation
P.O.Box 589
Melrose, NM 88124-589   928-634-7515
                                800-937-1337
                                FAX: 928-634-4620
Barry Green, Sales Manager
Joan Crozier, President
Transparent keyboard protectors allowing instant recognition of keytop legends. They have a matte finish to reduce glare. Also available are large print and braille keyboard labels and large print/braille combo labels.

1501 IntelliKeys
Intelli Tools
1720 Corporate Circle
Petaluma, CA 94954   707-773-2000
                                800-899-6687
                                FAX: 707-773-2001
                                info@intellitools.com
                                www.intellitools.com
Dayton Johnson, VP, Sales
Arjan Khalsa, CEO
Alternative, touch-sensitive keyboards; plugs into any Macintosh or Windows computer. *$395.00*

1502 IntelliKeys USB
Intelli Tools
1720 Corporate Circle
Petaluma, CA 94954   707-773-2000
                                800-899-6687
                                FAX: 707-773-2001
                                info@intellitools.com
                                www.intellitools.com
Dayton Johnson, VP, Sales
Arjan Khalsa, CEO
IntelliKeys alternative keyboard for USB computers and Windows 2000, Mac OSX. *$69.95*

1503 Key Tronic KB 5153 Touch Pad Keyboard
KeyTronic
N. 4424 Sullivan Road
Spokane Valley, WA 99216

509-928-8000
FAX: 509-927-5555
EMSsales@keytronicems.com
www.keytronic.com

Craig.D Gates, President/CEO
Ronald.F Klawitter, EVP of Administration and Chief Financial Officer
Douglas G. Burkhardt, Executive Vice President of Worldwide Operations
Integrates a regular full-function keyboard, a numeric keypad with a cursor key capability and a touch pad into one unit.

1504 King Keyboard
Infogrip
Ventura, CA 93001

503-828-1221
866-606-8551
support@infogrip.com
www.infogrip.com

Liza Jacobs, President
Aaron Gaston, Vice President
Giant alternative keyboard that plugs directly into a computer - no special interface is required. The keys are 1.25 inches in diameter, slightly recessed, and provide both tactile and auditory feedback. The King has a built-in keyboard so that you can rest on its surface without activating keys. This keyboard allows you to control both keyboard and mouse functions, making it great for people who have difficulty maneuvering a standard mouse. *$130.00*

1505 Large Print Keyboard
Infogrip
Ventura, CA 93001

503-828-1221
866-606-8551
support@infogrip.com
www.infogrip.com

Liza Jacobs, President
Aaron Gaston, Vice President
Standard Windows keyboard with large print keys. The keyboard and its keys are the same size as a standard keyboard; however, the print has been enhanced. The characters measure .5 by .25 inches, about 3 times larger than standard keyboard characters. *$130.00*

1506 Magic Wand Keyboard
In Touch Systems
11 Westview Road
Spring Valley, NY 10977

845-354-7431
800-332-6244
sc@magicwandkeyboard.com
www.magicwandkeyboard.com

Jerry Crouch, President
Susan Crouch, VP
The magic wand keyboard allows your child to use a keyboard and mouse easily-no light beams, microphones, or sensors to wear of position. This miniature computer keyboard has zero-force keys that work with the slightest touch of a wand (hand-held of mouthstick). No strength required.

1507 McKey Mouse
In Touch Systems
11 Westview Road
Spring Valley, NY 10977

845-354-7431
800-332-6244
sc@magicwandkeyboard.com
www.magicwandkeyboard.com

Jerry Crouch, President
Susan Crouch, VP
Microsoft compatible mouse for persons with little or no hand/arm movement; it's an option for the Magic Wand Keyboard and adds full mouse function without adding any extra devices.

1508 OnScreen
Infogrip
Ventura, CA 93001

503-828-1221
866-606-8551
support@infogrip.com
www.infogrip.com

Liza Jacobs, President
Aaron Gaston, Vice President

OnScreen features word prediction/completion (with an editable dictionary), Key Dwell Timer (a timer that selects a key under the cursor), integrated Verbal Keys Feedback, Show and Hide Keys (turns on/off keys to prevent access and minimize confusion) a Smart Window (automatically re-positions the keyboard or panels off of the area in use). OnScreen also offers edit, numeric, macro, calculator and Windows enhancement capabilities. *$200.00*

1509 PortaPower Plus
Words+
42505 10th Street West
Lancaster, CA 93534-7059

661-723-7723
800-869-8521
FAX: 661-723-5524
info@simulations-plus.com
www.simulations-plus.com

Walter S Woltosz, M.S., M.A.S., President, CEO
John A. DiBella, Vice President, Marketing & Sales
John R. Kneisel, Chief Financial Officer
Rechargeable battery pack designed to give longer life and remote usage time to laptop computers and other portable battery-operated devices and accessories. Requires a 12 volt auto adapter. *$149.00*

1510 Unicorn Keyboards
Intelli Tools
1720 Corporate Circle
Petaluma, CA 94954

707-773-2000
800-899-6687
FAX: 707-773-2001
info@intellitools.com
www.intellitools.com

Dayton Johnson, VP, Sales
Arjan Khalsa, CEO
Alternative keyboards with membrane surface and large, user-defined keys. Large and small sizes are available. *$250.00*

Scanners

1511 Scanning WSKE
Words+
42505 10th Street West
Lancaster, CA 93534-7059

661-723-7723
888-266-9294
FAX: 661-723-5524
info@simulations-plus.com
www.simulations-plus.com

Walter S Woltosz, M.S., M.A.S., President, CEO
John A. DiBella, Vice President, Marketing & Sales
John R. Kneisel, Chief Financial Officer
A software and a hardware product designed to operate on an IBM compatible PC. The software provides dual word prediction, abbreviation expansion, five different methods of voice output, and access to commercial software applications.

1512 System 2000/Versa
Words+
42505 10th Street West
Lancaster, CA 93534-7059

661-723-7723
800-869-8521
FAX: 661-723-5524
info@simulations-plus.com
www.simulations-plus.com

Walter S Woltosz, M.S., M.A.S., President, CEO
John A. DiBella, Vice President, Marketing & Sales
John R. Kneisel, Chief Financial Officer
Provides all of the strategies currently being used in AAC, from dynamic display color pictographic language, to dual-word prediction text language, in a single system.

1513 Zygo-Usa
SVC Corporation
48834 Kato Road Suite 101-A
Fremont, CA 94538

510-249-9660
800-234-6006
FAX: 510-770-4930
www.zygo-usa.com

Adam Weiss, VP, Sales & Marketing

ZYGO-USA has been involved in manufacturing and distributing assistive technologies since 1974. They specialize in augmentative and alternative computer access. They offer a wide range of technology products to our clients so they can achieve a greater independence and to enhance the quality of their lives. These soloutins improve and individual's ability to learn, work, and interact with family and friends.

Screen Enhancement

1514 Boxlight
Boxlight Corporation
151 State Highway 300, Suite A
P.O. Box 2609
Belfair, WA 98528
360-464-2119
866-972-1549
sales@boxlight.com
www.boxlight.com

Herb Myers, CEO/Founder
Sloan Myers, Founder
Hank Nance, President
BOXLIGHT is a global presentation solutions partner for trainers, educators and professional speakers. Solutions include projector sales, national rental service, technical support, repair, and presentation peripherals. For more information visit us online.

1515 FDR Series of Low Vision Reading Aids
Optelec U S
Breslau 4
Barendrecht, LT 92081-8358
886-783-444
800-826-4200
FAX: 886-783-400
info@optelec.com
in.optelec.com

Stephan Terwolbeck, President
Michiel van Schaik, VP
Janet Lennex, Director of Customer Excellence
The Low Vision Reading Aids features; high resolution, positive and negative display, a high-quality zoom lens, versatile swivel and a 12 inch or 19 inch high-resolution monitor, color or black and white, computer compatible, or portable.

1516 InFocus
AI Squared
130 Taconic Business Park Road
Manchester Center, VT 05255
802-362-3612
800-859-0270
FAX: 802-362-1670
sales@aisquared.com
www.aisquared.com

David Wu, CEO
Jost Eckhardt, VP of Engineering
Scott Moore, VP of Marketing
A memory-resident program that magnifies text and graphics - the entire screen, a single line or a portion of the screen.

1517 Portable Large Print Computer
Human Ware
1800, Michaud street
Drummondville, CA 94520-1213
819-471-4818
888-723-7273
FAX: 925-681-4630
ca.info@humanware.com
www.humanware.com/en-australia/home

Real Goulet, Chairman
Gilles Pepin, CEO
Michel Cote, Corporate Director
A portable large print computer which magnifies up to 64 times. It is linked to a PC and has a hand-held camera.

1518 ZoomText
A I Squared
130 Taconic Business Park Road
Manchester Center, VT 05255
802-362-3612
800-859-0270
FAX: 802-362-1670
sales@aisquared.com
www.aisquared.com

David Wu, CEO
Jost Eckhardt, VP of Engineering
Scott Moore, VP of Marketing
A RAM-resident program that enlarges screen characters up to eight times. It runs on IBM PC, XT, AT and PS/2.

Speech Synthesizers

1519 Artic Business Vision (for DOS) and Artic WinVision (for Windows 95)
Artic Technologies
3456 Rodchester Road
Troy, MI 48083
248-689-9883
FAX: 248-588-2650
info@ablezone.com

Dale McDaniel, Founder
Kathy Gargagliano, Founder
A speech processor for blind computer users featuring true interactive speech with spread sheets, word processors, database managers, etc. Now available with both Windows 3.1 and Windows 95 access. *$495.00*

1520 Computerized Speech Lab
Kay Elemetrics Corporation
3 Paragon Drive
Montvalle, NJ 07645
973-628-6200
800-289-5297
FAX: 201-391-2063
www.kaypentax.com

John Crump, President
Hardware/software for the acquisition, analysis/display, playback and storage of speech signals.

1521 DynaVox Technologies Speech Communication Devices
Dyna Vox Technologies
2100 Wharton St
Suite 400
Pittsburgh, PA 15203-1945
412-381-4883
866-396-2869
FAX: 412-381-5241
www.dynavoxtech.com

Ed Donnelly, CEO
Michelle Heying, President and COO
Kenneth Misch, CFO
Develops and manufactures speech communication devices that help individuals who are unable to speak due to speech, language and/or learning disabilities to communicate quickly and easily.

1522 Electronic Speech Assistance Devices
Luminaud, Inc.
8688 Tyler Blvd
Mentor, OH 44060
440-255-9082
800-255-3408
FAX: 440-255-2250
info@luminaud.com
www.luminaud.com

Thomas M. Lennox, President
Dorothy Lennox, Vice President
Offers a full line of speech aids, voice amplifiers, mini-vox amplifiers, laryngectomec products.

1523 Keywi
Hoffmann + Krippner Inc.
200 Westpark Drive
Suite 270
Peachtree City, GA 30269
770-487-1950
FAX: 770-487-1945
www.keywi-usa.com

Membrane keyboard and membrane switch technology

1524 Mega Wolf Communication Device
Wayne County Regional Educational Service Agency
33500 Van Born Rd
Wayne, MI 48184-2474 734-334-1300
FAX: 734-334-1620
www.resa.net

Lynda S. Jackson, President
Kenneth E. Berlinn, Vice President
James Petrie, Secretary
A low cost voice output communication device which is primarily intended to provide the power of speech to those individuals who are most severely challenged mentally and/or physically. The WOLF device is User programmable and uses the Texas Instruments' Touch and Tell case and touch panel; ADAMLAB electronics with synthesized (robotic) voice. For users able to point with approximately 6 ounces of pressure. *$400.00*

1525 Talking Screen
Words+
42505 10th St W
Lancaster, CA 93534-7059 661-723-7723
888-266-9294
FAX: 661-723-5524
info@simulations-plus.com
www.simulations-plus.com

Walter S Woltosz, M.S., M.A.S., Chairman, President and Chief Ex
John R. Kneisel, Chief Financial Officer
John DiBella, Vice President, Marketing and Sales
An augmentative communication program that allows the user to select graphic symbols on the display to produce speech output. Symbols can be used either singly or in sequence as picture abbreviations. *$1395.00*

1526 Turnkey Computer Systems for the Visually, Physically, and Hearing Impaired
E VA S
39 Canal St P.O. Box 371
Westerly, RI 02891-1511 401-596-3155
800-872-3827
FAX: 401-596-3979
TTY: 401-596-3500
contact@evas.com
www.evas.com

Gerald Swerdlick, Owner
Jerry Swerdlick, CEO
Offers clear speech with pleasant inflection and tonal quality as well as variable pitch, intonation and voices.

1527 Voice-It
V XI Corporation Incorporated
271 Locust Street
Denver, NH 03820 603-742-2888
800-742-8588
FAX: 603-742-5065
info@vxicorp.com
www.vxicorp.com

Michael Ferguson, President
Tom Manero, Chief Financial Officer
Phil Pane, Vice President Operations
Adds voice to popular spreadsheet and word processing applications on IBM PCs and compatibles, turning spreadsheets and word processing documents into talking documents.

1528 Window-Eyes
G W Micro
725 Airport North Office Park
Fort Wayne, IN 46825 260-489-3671
FAX: 260-489-2608
www.gwmicro.com

Dan Weirich, Owner/Vice President of Sales an
Doug Geoffray, Owner
Provides access to available software automatically reading information important to the user while ignoring the rest. A screen reader for the windows operative system.

Software: Math

1529 AIMS Multimedia
Discovery Education
8145 Holton Dr
Florence, KY 41042-3009 859-342-7200
FAX: 877-324-6830

Mike Wright, Director
Lynn Fassett, Administrative Assistant
Cindy Vogt, Human Resources Executive
AIMS Multimedia is a leader in the production and distribution of training and educational programs for the business and K-12 communities via YHS, interactive CD-ROM, DVD and Internet streaming video.

1530 Basic Math: Detecting Special Needs
Allyn & Bacon
One Liberty Square
Suite 1200
Boston, MA 02109-3988 617-261-0040
800-852-8024
FAX: 617-944-7273
samplingdept@pearson.com
www.greenellp.com

Thomas M Greene, Attorney at Law
Michael Tabb, Attorney at Law
Describes special mathematics needs of special learners.
180 pages
ISBN 0-205116-35-3

1531 Campaign Math
Mindplay
4400 E. Broadway Blvd
Suite 400
Tucson, AZ 85711-1726 520-888-1800
800-221-7911
FAX: 520-888-7904
mail@mindplay.com
www.mindplay.com

Judith Bliss, CEO
Brian Williams, Development Manager
Lisa Garcia, Director of Educational Services
A complete program on the electoral process as well as a math package which teaches ratios, fractions and percentages.

1532 Educational Activities Software
5600 W 83rd Street
Suite 300, 8200 Tower
Bloomington, MN 55437 866-243-8464
FAX: 239-225-9299
jwest@orchardlng.com
www.edmentum.com

Vin Riera, President & Chief Executive Officer
Rob Rueckl, Chief Financial Officer
Dave Adams, Chief Academic Officer
Comprehensive MATH SKILLS software tutorials teach concepts ranging from rounding and tables to measuring area. MAC/WIN compatible. *$369.00*
Per Unit

1533 Fraction Factory
Queue
80 Hathaway Drive
Stratford, CT 06615 800-232-2224
FAX: 800-775-2729
jdk@queueinc.com
qworkbooks.com

Anna Christopoulos, General Manager
Peter Uhrynowski, Comptroller
Steve Pernett, Director of Printing and Graphic
In 1980, Jonathan Kantrowitz started Queue, Inc. as an educational software company. After twenty thriving years publishing and distributing high-quality software to educators, Queue began transitioning from software to workbooks, focusing on state-specific test preparation.

1534 Information & Referral Services
Information + Referral Services
2590 N. Alvernon Way
Tucson, AZ 85712
520-323-1708
FAX: 520-325-8841
www.azinfo.org

Patti Caldwell, Executive Director
Chuck Palm, Treasurer
Ben Rensvold, Vice President
Provides information about health and human services for people in Arizona over the telephone. Information specialists help callers clarify their needs, and provide referrals to the appropriate service agency.

1535 King's Rule
WINGS for Learning
1600 Green Hills Rd
Scotts Valley, CA 95066-4981
831-426-2228
FAX: 831-464-3600

Ani Stocks, Owner
A software mathematical problem solving game. Students discover mathematical rules as they work their way through a castle and generate and test a working hypothesis by asking questions.

1536 Learning About Numbers
C&C Software
5713 Kentford Cir
Wichita, KS 67220-3131
316-683-6056
800-752-2086

Carol Clark, President
Three programs use the power of computer graphics to provide young children with a variety of experiences in working with numbers. *$50.00*

1537 Math Rabbit
Learning Company
Ste 1900
100 Pine St
San Francisco, CA 94111-5205
415-659-2000
800-825-4420
FAX: 415-659-2020
thelearningco@hmhpub.com
www.hmhco.com

Linda K. Zecher, President, Chief Executive Officer and Director
Eric Shuman, Chief Financial Officer
William Bayers, Executive Vice President and General Counsel
Teaches early math concepts by matching objects to numbers, then adding and subtracting up to 18.

1538 Math for Everyday Living
Educational Activities Software
5600 W 83rd Street
Suite 300, 8200 Tower
Bloomington, MN 55437
866-243-8464
FAX: 239-225-9299
jwest@orchardlng.com
www.edmentum.com

Vin Riera, President & Chief Executive Officer
Rob Rueckl, Chief Financial Officer
Dave Adams, Chief Academic Officer
Real life math skills are taught with this tutorial and practice software program. Examples include Paying for a Meal (addition and subtraction), Working with Sales Slips (multiplication), Unit Pricing (division), Sales Tax (percent), Earning with Overtime (fractions) plus more. Software: CD-ROM, Windows, MAC, and DOS. *$159.00*

1539 Math for Successful Living
Siboney Learning Group
5600 W 83rd Street
Suite 300, 8200 Tower
Bloomington, MN 55437
866-243-8464
FAX: 239-225-9299
jwest@orchardlng.com
www.edmentum.com

Vin Riera, President & Chief Executive Officer
Rob Rueckl, Chief Financial Officer
Dave Adams, Chief Academic Officer
These programs include managing a checking account, budgeting, shopping strategies and buying on credit.

1540 Piece of Cake Math
Queue Inc
80 Hathaway Drive
Stratford, CT 06615
800-232-2224
FAX: 800-775-2729
jdk@queueinc.com
www.qworkbooks.com

Anna Christopoulos, General Manager
Peter Uhrynowski, Comptroller
Steve Pernett, Director of Printing and Graphic
In 1980, Jonathan Kantrowitz started Queue, Inc. as an educational software company. After twenty thriving years publishing and distributing high-quality software to educators, Queue began transitioning from software to workbooks, focusing on state-specific test preparation.

1541 Puzzle Tanks
WINGS for Learning
1600 Green Hills Rd
Scotts Valley, CA 95066-4981
831-426-2228
FAX: 831-464-3600

Ani Stocks, Owner
A mathematical problem solving game that involves multi-step problems.

1542 Right Turn
WINGS for Learning
1600 Green Hills Rd
Scotts Valley, CA 95066-4981
831-426-2228
FAX: 831-464-3600

Ani Stocks, Owner
Requires students to predict, experiment and learn about the mathematical concepts of rotation and transformation.

1543 RoboMath
4400 E. Broadway Blvd
Suite 400
Tucson, AZ 85711-1726
520-888-1800
800-221-7911
FAX: 520-888-7904
mail@mindplay.com
www.mindplay.com

Judith Bliss, CEO
Brian Williams, Development Manager
Lisa Garcia, Director of Educational Services
A complete program on the electoral process as well as a math package which teaches ratios, fractions and percentages.

1544 Stickybear Math I Deluxe
Optimum Resource
1 Mathews Drive
Suite 107
Hilton Head Island, SC 29926- 3689
843-689-8000
FAX: 843-689-8008
info@stickybear.com
www.stickybear.com

Richard Hefter, President
Sharpen basic addition and subtraction skills with this captivating series of math exercises. Grades Pre-K to 2. Available in as single edition with sizing up to 30 users at a site. English/Spanish. *$59.95*

1545 Stickybear Math II Deluxe
Optimum Resource
1 Mathews Drive
Suite 107
Hilton Head Island, SC 29926- 3689
843-689-8000
FAX: 843-689-8008
info@stickybear.com
www.stickybear.com

Richard Hefter, President
Multiplication and division, beginning with the elementary problems and developing into the more complex problems with regrouping. Grades 2-4. Available for single user through the 30 user site package. English/Spanish. *$59.95*

1546 Stickybear Math Splash
Optimum Resource
1 Mathews Drive
Suite 107
Hilton Head Island, SC 29926- 3689   843-689-8000
FAX: 843-689-8008
info@stickybear.com
www.stickybear.com

Richard Hefter, President
Unique multiple activities keep the learning level high while children acquire skills in addition, subtraction, multiplication and division. K-5th grade. Available as single edition up to 30 user site package. English/Spanish. *$59.95*

1547 Stickybear Math Word Problems
Optimum Resource
1 Mathews Drive
Suite 107
Hilton Head Island, SC 29926- 3689   843-689-8000
FAX: 843-689-8008
info@stickybear.com
www.stickybear.com

Richard Hefter, President
Hundreds of different word problems make it easy for students to practice basic math skills around analyzing and solving word problems. Grades 1-5. Available as single edition up to 30 user site package. English/Spanish. *$59.95*

1548 Stickybear Money
Optimum Resource
1 Mathews Drive
Suite 107
Hilton Head Island, SC 29926- 3667   843-689-8000
FAX: 843-689-8008
info@stickybear.com
www.stickybear.com

Chris Gintz, President
Teaches children to recognize US coins and paper money and introduces simple counting. K to 3rd grade. Bilingual. *$59.95*

1549 Stickybear Numbers Deluxe
Optimum Resource
1 Mathews Drive
Suite 107
Hilton Head Island, SC 29926- 3689   843-689-8000
FAX: 843-689-8008
info@stickybear.com
www.stickybear.com

Richard Hefter, President
Counting and number recognition are as easy as 1-2-3 with this award-winning program. Teaches number recognition of numbers 0-9 and 0-30. Pre-K to 2nd grade. Available as single edition up to 30 user site package. *$59.95*

1550 Tomorrow's Promise: Mathematics
Compass Learning
203 Colorado Street
Austin, TX 78701   512-478-9600
800-678-1412
866-586-7387
www.compasslearning.com

Eric Loeffel, President
Trey Chambers, Chief Financial Officer
Arthur Vanderveen, Vice President, Business Strategy and Development
By integrating interdisciplinary content and real-world application of skills, this product emphasizes the practical value of fundamental math skills. It helps your students develop a problem-solving aptitude for ongoing mathematics achievement.

Software: Miscellaneous

1551 Adventures in Musicland
Electronic Courseware Systems
1713 S State St
Champaign, IL 61820-7258   217-359-7099
800-832-4965
FAX: 217-359-6578
support@ecsmedia.com
ecsmedia.com.np/

G Peters, President
Jodie Varner, Marketing Manager
This unique set of music games features characters from Lewis Carroll's, Alice in Wonderland. Players learn through pictures, sounds, and animation which help develop understanding of musical tones, composers, and musical symbols. Games include MusicMatch, Melody Mixup, Picture Perfect and Sound Concentration. *$49.95*

1552 Ai Squared
130 Taconic Business Park Road
Manchester Center, VT 05255-669   802-362-3612
800-859-0270
FAX: 802-362-1670
sales@aisquared.com
www.aisquared.com

David Wu, CEO
Jost Eckhardt, VP of Engineering
Scott Moore, VP of Marketing
Developers of software for the visually impaired.

1553 All About You: Appropriate Special Interactions and Self-Esteem
P CI Educational Publishing
P.O.Box 34270
San Antonio, TX 78265-4270   210-377-1999
800-594-4263
800-471-3000
FAX: 888-259-8284

Lee Wilson, President and CEO
Randy Pennington, Executive VP
Jeff McLane, Founder
This game offers parents and game players a new line of communication when discussing various issues such as learning to be thoughtful, respecting the rights and feelings of others, how to make and keep friends and more. *$49.95*

1554 All Star Review
Tom Snyder Productions
100 Talcott Ave
Watertown, MA 02472-5703   800-342-0236
www.tomsnyder.com

Rick Abrams, Manager
Tom Synder, Founder
Bridget Dalton, Ed.D., Author
This package turns group review into a baseball game for small and large groups.

1555 Attainment Company
I ET Resources
504 Commerce Parkway
P.O. Box 930160
Verona, WI 53593- 0160   608-845-7880
800-327-4269
FAX: 800-942-3865
info@attainmentcompany.com
www.attainmentcompany.com

Autumn Garza, President
Don Bastian, CEO
Augmentative and alternative communication, software, videos, print and hands-on functional life skills and basic academic materials for development.

1556 Attention Getter
Soft Touch
12301 Central Ave NE Ste 205
4300 Stine Rd
Blaine, MN 55434
763-755-1402
888-755-1402
FAX: 763-862-2920
support@marblesoft.com
www.softtouch.com

Joyce Meyer, President
The whimsical photos morph to another photo and then to a third photo in categories. Paired with interesting sounds and music, the photo animations are so engaging that the student is motivated to activate the computer to see and hear the next one. This is a perfect vehicle to achieve goals aimed at attention getting, activating a switch or intentionally. Compatible with USB IntelliKeys keyboards.

1557 Attention Teens
Soft Touch
12301 Central Ave NE Ste 205
Blaine, MN 55434
763-755-1403
888-755-1403
FAX: 763-862-2921
support@marblesoft.com
www.softtouch.com

Joyce Meyer, President
Attention Teens (formerly known as Loony Teens) is a program for teens with disabilities who need powerful input to get their attention. Attention Teens is a computer program to do just this. Paired with interesting sounds and music, the photo animations are so engaging that the student is motivated to activate the computer to see and hear the next one. Compatible with USB IntelliKeys keyboards.

1558 Away We Ride
Soft Touch
12301 Central Ave NE Ste 205
4300 Stine Rd
Blaine, MN 55434
763-755-1404
888-755-1404
FAX: 763-862-2922
support@marblesoft.com
www.softtouch.com

Joyce Meyer, President
Software for children and teens. For Macintosh and PC.

1559 Battenberg & Associates
11135 Rolling Springs Dr
Carmel, IN 46033-3629
317-843-2208
Jan Battenberg, Owner
Offers various software programs that develop the user's visual memory, sequencing skills, word recognition, hand-eye coordination and more.

1560 Behavior Skills: Learning How People Should Act
PCI Education Publishing
P.O.Box 34270
San Antonio, TX 78265-4270
210-377-1999
800-471-3000
FAX: 888-828-
www.pcieducation.com

Jeff Clain, CEO
Erin Kinard, VP Product Development/Publisher
Helps players learn what behavior is acceptable and what behavior is not acceptable in the real world. *$49.95*

1561 Blocks in Motion
Don Johnston
26799 West Commerce Drive
Volo, IL 60073
847-740-0749
800-999-4660
FAX: 847-740-7326
info@donjohnston.com
www.donjohnston.com

Don Johnston, Founder
Ruth Ziolkowski, President
Kevin Johnston, Director of Product Design
This unique art and motion program makes drawing, creating and animating fun and educational for all users. Based on the Piagetian Theory for motor-sensory development, this program promotes the concept that the process is as educational and as much fun as the end result. *$79.00*

1562 Car Builder Deluxe
Optimum Resource
1 Mathews Drive
Suite 107
Hilton Head Island, SC 29926- 3689
843-689-8000
FAX: 843-689-8008
info@stickybear.com
www.stickybear.com

Richard Hefter, President
As design engineers, users build cars on screen, specifying chassis length, wheelbase, engine type, transmission, fuel tank size, suspension, steering, tires and brakes. All functional choices are interrelated and will affect the performance of the final design. Grades 3 & up. *$59.99*

1563 Center for Best Practices in Early Childhood
Horrabin Hall 32
Macomb, IL 61455
309-298-1634
FAX: 309-298-2305
jk-johanson@wiu.edu
www.wiu.edu/thecenter/

Linda Robinson, Assistant Director
The Center, part of the College of Education and Human Services at Western Illinois University, provides products, training materials, and information related to best practices for educators and families of young children with disabilities.

1564 Clock
Compass Learning
203 Colorado Street
Austin, TX 78701-3922
512-478-9600
800-678-1412
866-586-7387
www.compasslearning.com

Eric Loeffel, President
Trey Chambers, Chief Financial Officer
Arthur Vanderveen, Vice President, Business Strategy and Development
An extremely simple, easy-to-use program for children who are learning how to read the time of day from clocks and digital displays. Apple and MS-DOS and Mac available. *$39.95*

1565 Community Skills: Learning to Function in Your Neighborhood
Programming Concepts
8700 Shoal Creek Boulevard
Austin, TX 78757-6897
210-377-1999
800-594-4263
800-471-3000
FAX: 888-259-8284
www.proedinc.com

Lee Wilson, President and CEO
Randy Pennington, Executive VP
Jeff McLane, Founder
Offers parents and educators a functional way to teach community life skills. *$49.95*

1566 Companion Activities
Soft Touch
12301 Central Ave NE Ste 205
4300 Stine Rd
Blaine, MN 55434
763-755-1404
888-755-1404
FAX: 763-862-2922
support@marblesoft.com
www.softouch.com

Joyce Meyer, President
Print your own books, worksheets, flash cards, board games, matching games, bingo games, card games and many more. This CD offers numerous companion activities to different SoftTouch software titles. Activities range from very easy to difficult. Companion activities are great tools to reinforce learning. Use the work sheets - black and white and color - in the inclusion class for students with special needs.

1567 Concepts on the Move Advanced Preacademics
Soft Touch
12301 Central Ave NE Ste 205
P.O.Box 490215
Blaine, MN 55449
763-862-2920
888-755-1402
FAX: 763-862-2922
support@marblesoft.com
www.marblesoft.com

Joyce Meyer, President
Choose from five concepts groups: categories, occupations, functions, goes with and prepositions. Use our Steps to Learning Design to choose how many concepts to present at one time and where to place each one in the scan array, on screen keyboard or IntelliKeys keyboard. Watch and listen as the concept morphs or changes and music plays. The words are also shown to reinforce emerging literacy skills. Compatible with USB IntelliKeys.

1568 Cooking Class: Learning About Food Preparation
Programming Concepts
8700 Shoal Creek Boulevard
Austin, TX 78757-6897
512-451-3246
800-897-3202
800-471-3000
FAX: 800-397-7633
general@proedinc.com
www.proedinc.com

Jeff McLane, Founder
Lee Wilson, President and CEO
Randy Pennington, Executive VP
This game offers parents and educators a new way to teach basic preparation skills. Kitchen safety and sanitation are stressed throughout the game. *$49.95*

1569 Dilemma
Educational Activities Software
5600 West 83rd Street
Suite 300, 8200 Tower
Bloomington, MN 55437
800-447-5286
FAX: 239-225-9299
info@edmentum.com
www.edmentum.com

Vin Riera, President/CEO
Dan Juckniess, SVP, Sales & Professional Services
Stacey Herteux, VP, Human Resources
Realistic stories with a choice of different gripping endings, color graphics, a built-in dictionary and a user controlled reading rate make these computer programs compelling enough to interest all students. Comprehension and vocabulary questions follow each story. *$159.00*

1570 Dino-Games
Academic Software
3504 Tates Creek Road
Lexington, KY 40517-2601
859-552-1020
859-552-1040
FAX: 253-799-4012
asistaff@acsw.com
www.acsw.com

Dr. Warren E Lacefield PhD, President
Penelope D. Ellis, COO, Sales & Marketing Director
Sylvia B. Lacefield, Graphic Artist
Dino-Games are single switch software programs for early switch practice. Dinosaur games provide practice in pattern recognition, cause and effect demonstration, directionality training, number concepts and problem solving. They are compatible with most popular switch interfaces and alternate keyboards. For Macintosh, IBM and compatibles. DINO-LINK is a matching game; DINO-MAZE is a series of maze games; DINO-FIND is a game of concentration; and DINO-DOT is a collection of dot-to-dot games.
$39.95 per game

1571 Directions: Technology in Special Education
DREAMMS for Kids
273 Ringwood Road
Freeville, NY 13068-5606
607-539-3027
FAX: 607-539-9930
janet@dreamms.org
www.dreamms.org

Janet P. Hosmer, Editor/Publisher
Chester D. Hosmer, Jr., Technical Editor
Susan Lait, Regular Contributor
A CD containing all of 'Directions' past articles and information gathered from their newsletter which lists resources for assistive and adaptive computer ethnologies in the home, school and community. *$24.95*

1572 ESI Master Resource Guide
Educational Software Institute
4213 S 94th St
Omaha, NE 68127-1223
402-592-3300
800-955-5570
FAX: 402-592-2017

Lee Myers, President
Kathy Cavanaugh, Catalog Manager
Educational Software Institute (ESI) provides a one-stop shop to purchase software titles by all of the best publishers. The ESI Master Gold Book catalog and CD-ROM represents more than 400 software publishers, with information on more than 8,000 software titles. Take the confusion out of software selection by calling ESI for all of your software needs - including competitive prices, software previews, knowledgeable assistance, and the largest selection available all in one place.
Yearly

1573 EZ Keys
Words+
42505 10th Street West
Suite 109
Lancaster, CA 93534- 7059
661-723-7723
888-266-9294
FAX: 661-723-5524
info@simulations-plus.com
www.simulations-plus.com

Walter S Woltosz, M.S., M.A.S., Chairman, President and Chief Executive Officer
John A. Dibella, VP, Marketing & Sales
Virginia E. Woltosz. M.B.A., Secretary & Treasurer
A software and hardware product designed to operate on an IBM compatible PC. The software provides dual word prediction, abbreviation expansion, five different methods of voice output and access to commercial software applications. *$1395.00*

1574 Early Games for Young Children
Queue Incorporated
80 Hathaway Drive
Stratford, CT 06615
800-232-2224
FAX: 800-775-2729
jdk@queueinc.com
www.qworkbooks.com

Anna Christopoulos, General Manager
Peter Uhrynowski, Comptroller
Steve Perrett, Director of Printing and Graphics
Software that includes nine activities that entertain preschoolers in honing basic math and language skills.

1575 Early Music Skills
Electronic Courseware Systems
1713 S State St
Champaign, IL 61820-7258
217-359-7099
800-832-4965
FAX: 217-359-6578
support@ecsmedia.com
www.ecsmedia.com

G Peters, President
Jodie Varner, Marketing Manager
A tutorial and drill program designed for the beginning music student. It covers four basic music reading skills: recognition of line and space notes; comprehension of the numbering system for the musical staff; visual and aural identification of notes moving up and down; and recognition of notes stepping and skipping up and down. *$39.95*

1576 Eating Skills: Learning Basic Table Manners
PCI Education Publishing
P.O.Box 34270
San Antonio, TX 78265-4270   210-377-1999
                                          800-594-4263
                                          FAX: 210-377-1121

Erin Kinard, VP Product Development/Publisher
Jeff Clain, CEO
Offers parents and educators a functional way to teach and reinforce basic table manners. *$49.95*

1577 Electronic Courseware Systems
1713 S State St
Champaign, IL 61820-7258   217-359-7099
                                          800-832-4965
                                          FAX: 217-359-6578
                                          support@ecsmedia.com
                                          www.ecsmedia.com

Jodie Varner, Manager
G Peters, President
Offers a complete library of instructional software for music, math, science and social studies.

1578 Fall Fun
Soft Touch
12301 Central Ave NE Ste 205
P.O.Box 490215
Blaine, MN 55449   763-862-2920
                                          888-755-1402
                                          FAX: 763-862-2922
                                          support@marblesoft.com
                                          www.marblesoft.com

Joyce Meyer, President
Your students can begin their day with the Pledge of Allegiance, Pumpkins, Owls, and Cats. Witches adorn Five Pumpkins Sitting on the Gate. Five Fat Turkeys out smart the pilgrims with song and antics. The owl and cat have songs of their own. A variety of activities reinforce concepts such as short, tall, first, second, third, same and different. Fall Fun includes cause and effect and easy to more difficult levels. Eight songs in all.

1579 Five Green & Speckled Frogs
Soft Touch
12301 Central Ave NE Ste 205
P.O.Box 490215
Blaine, MN 55449   763-862-2920
                                          888-755-1402
                                          FAX: 763-862-2922
                                          support@marblesoft.com
                                          www.marblesoft.com

Joyce Meyer, President
Laugh, learn and sing with Five Humorous Frogs. Activities start with cause and effect and progress to teach directionality and simple subtraction. This classic song makes learning numbers and number worlds easy. Selections can be set to 2, 3, 4, 5, or 6 on-screen choices. Two games are included. One teaches direction on a number line. If the child moves the frog in the correct direction, the frog gets a point. The other game teaches beginning subtraction.

1580 Free and User Supported Software for the IBM PC: A Resource Guide
McFarland & Company
960 NC Highway 88 W
P.O.Box 611
Jefferson, NC 28640-8813   336-246-4460
                                          800-253-2187
                                          FAX: 336-246-5018
                                          info@mcfarlandpub.com
                                          www.mcfarlandpub.com

Robert McFarland Franklin, Founder
Kenneth.J Ansley, Author
Victor.D Lopez, Author
A selection of word processing, database management, spreadsheets, and graphics programs are described and evaluated. Describes how the program works and its strengths and weaknesses. Rating charts cover such aspects as ease of use, ease of learning, documentation, and general utility. *$27.50*
224 pages Paperback
ISBN 0-89950 -99-0

1581 GoalView: Special Education and RTI Student Management Information System
Learning Tools International
2391 Circadian Way
Santa Rosa, CA 95407-5439   707-521-3530
                                          800-333-9954

Cathy Zier, President/CEO
Natalie Sipes, VP
Michael R. Paul, Director of IT/Senior Web Engine
A Web Based information system for students, educators and parents that enables accountability and achievement tracking; prepares IDEA compliant IEP's in minutes; provides over 250,000 education standards and special education goals and objectives in English and Spanish; generates Federal compliance reports; and creates IDEA GoalCard progress reports for students, schools and districts for every reporting period.

1582 HELP
V OR T Corporation
P.O.Box G (George)
Menlo Park, CA 94026   650-322-8282
                                          888-757-8678
                                          FAX: 650-327-0747
                                          custserv@vort.com
                                          vort.com

Tom Holt, Owner
A software version of HELP, covers over 650 skills in 6 developmental areas; cognitive, motor skills, language, gross motor, social and self-help.

1583 Handbook of Adaptive Switches and Augmentative Communication Devices
Academic Software
3504 Tates Creek Road
Lexington, KY 40517-2601   859-552-1020
                                          859-552-1040
                                          FAX: 253-799-4012
                                          asistaff@acsw.com
                                          www.acsw.com

Dr. Warren E Lacefield PhD, President
Penelope D. Ellis, COO, Sales & Marketing Director
Cindy L George, Author
This second edition contains physical descriptions and laboratory test data for a variety of commercially available pressure switches and augmentative communication devices and chapters on physical interaction, seating and positioning, and control access. It is an essential tool for assistive technology professionals and therapists who make decisions concerning physical access. *$60.00*
300 pages Hardcover

1584 HandiWARE
Microsystems Software
600 Worcester Rd
Framingham, MA 01702-5303   508-626-8511
                                          800-828-2600
                                          FAX: 508-879-1069
                                          infor@microsys.com
                                          www.handiware.com

Terri McGrath, Sales/Marketing
Bill Kilroy, Product Manager
Adapted access software, assists persons with physical, hearing and visual impairments in accessing computers running DOS and Windows. HandiWARE is a suite of 8 software programs which provide users with screen magnification, alternate keyboard access, word prediction, augmentative communication, hands free telephone access, a visual beep. $20.00-$595.00.

1585 How to Write for Everyday Living
Educational Activities Software
5600 West 83rd Street
Suite 300, 8200 Tower
Bloomington, MN 55437-585   800-447-5286
                                          FAX: 239-225-9299
                                          info@edmentum.com
                                          www.edmentum.com

Vin Riera, President/CEO
Dan Juckniess, SVP, Sales & Professional Services
Stacey Herteux, VP, Human Resources

An individualized Life Skills WRITING Software program emphasizing the reading, writing, communication and reference skills needed for real-life tasks: preparing a resume, an employment form, a business letter and envelope, a learner's permit, a social security application and banking forms. *$159.00*

1586   I KNOW American History
Soft Touch
12301 Central Ave NE Ste 205
P.O.Box 490215
Blaine, MN 55449-2352   763-862-2920
                                               888-755-1402
                                          FAX: 763-862-2922
                                   support@marblesoft.com
                                        www.marblesoft.com

Joyce Meyer, President
The new I KNOW programs is the way students practice attending, choice making and turn-taking while uncovering learning puzzles. Each press reveals more of the image while the narrator reads the text on the screen. Offers three levels of language: short phrases, short sentences and longer sentences to match the student's learning level. Choose from the five topic areas: American Symbols, Westward Movement, Early Colonial Americans, Industrial Revolution and Biographies.

1587   I KNOW American History Overlay CD
Soft Touch
12301 Central Ave NE Ste 205
P.O.Box 490215
Blaine, MN 55449-2352   763-862-2920
                                               888-755-1402
                                          FAX: 763-862-2922
                                   support@marblesoft.com
                                        www.marblesoft.com

Joyce Meyer, President
Use this Overlay CD with I KNOW American History program. Includes standard overlays and SoftTouch's changeable overlays. Includes Overlay Printer by IntelliTools. Use Overlay Maker by IntelliTools (not included) to modify the overlays or to make additional learning materials.

1588   Incite Learning Series
Don Johnston
26799 West Commerce Drive
Volo, IL 60073   847-740-0749
                                               800-999-4660
                                          FAX: 847-740-7326
                                    info@donjohnston.com
                                       www.donjohnston.com

Don Johnston, Founder
Ruth Ziolkowski, President
Kevin Johnston, Director of Product Design
A collection of original short films and a thought-provoking instruction model to engage every student in the critical thinking and feeling process. This research-based program was developed around the science of how students learn best using the theory of 'anchored instruction' and 'front-loading' standards-based curriculum. *$79.00*

1589   Innovation Management Group
179 Niblick Rd
Ste 454
Paso Robles, CA 93446   818-701-1579
                                               800-889-0987
                                          FAX: 818-936-0200
                                     cs@imgpresents.com
                                       www.imgpresents.com

Jerry Hussong, VP of Marketing
Publisher of the Assistive Technology Suite. The ultimate set of general purpose, adaptive computer access available today. Site License includes ALL computers and ALL active students and teachers at a single or multi-site location.

1590   IntelliPics Studio 3
Intelli Tools
1720 Corporate Cir
Petaluma, CA 94954-6924   707-773-2000
                                               800-547-6747
                                          FAX: 707-773-2001

Arjan Khalsa, CEO

Multimedia authoring tool for both students and teachers to create activities, games, quizzes, slide shows, reports and presentations. *$395.00*

1591   KIDS (Keyboard Introductory Development Series)
Electronic Courseware Systems
1713 S State St
Champaign, IL 61820-7258   217-359-7099
                                               800-832-4965
                                          FAX: 217-359-6578
                                     support@ecsmedia.com
                                          www.ecsmedia.com

G Peters, President
Jodie Varner, Marketing Manager
A four disk series for the very young. Zoo Puppet Theater reinforces learning correct finger numbers for piano playing; Race Car Keys teaches keyboard geography by recognizing syllables or note names; Dinosaurs Lunch teaches placement of the notes on the treble staff; and Follow Me asks the student to play notes that have been presented aurally. *$49.95*

1592   Keyboard Tutor, Music Software
Electronic Courseware Systems
1713 S State St
Champaign, IL 61820-7258   217-359-7099
                                               800-832-4965
                                          FAX: 217-359-6578
                                     support@ecsmedia.com
                                          www.ecsmedia.com

G Peters, President
Jodie Varner, Marketing Manager
Presents exercises for learning elementary keyboard skills including knowledge of names of the keys, piano keys matched to notes, notes matched to piano keys, whole steps and half steps. Each lesson allows unlimited practice of the skills. The program may be used with or without a midi keyboard attached to the computer. *$39.95*

1593   Keyboarding by Ability
Teachers Institute for Special Education
9933 NW 45th St
Sunrise, FL 33351-4744   954-235-7940
                                          FAX: 866-843-0765
                          Support@Special-Education-Soft.com
                           www.special-education-soft.com

Gary Byowitz, President
Allows the learning disabled or dyslexic student to acquire keyboarding skills through visually cued alphabetical approach designed and tested to meet the specific learning style needs of this unique population at every grade level. Package contains: IBM software, a set of lesson plans and instructional goals; supplemental graded data input exercises. *$369.00*

1594   Keyboarding for the Physically Handicapped
Teachers Institute for Special Education
9933 NW 45th Street
Sunrise, FL 33351   954-235-7940
                                          FAX: 866-843-0765
                          Support@Special-Education-Soft.com
                           www.special-education-soft.com

Jack Heller, Director/Owner
Gary Byowitz, President
Custom designed touch typing programs for any student. A person needs order by the number of usable fingers on each hand (not counting the thumb), and whether or not a one finger or a head-pointer edition is wanted. Package includes IBM software; a complete set of lesson plans and instructional goals. *$149.95*

1595   Keyboarding with One Hand
Teachers Institute for Special Education
P.O.Box 2300
Wantagh, NY 11793-140   FAX: 516-781-4070
                                         jackheller@aol.com

Jack Heller, Director
This 22 lesson tutorial developed through 25 years of research, testing and teaching allows a student with one hand to acquire employable keyboarding skills using a touch system designed for the standard IBM PC keyboard. *$79.95*

1596 LPDOS Deluxe
Optelec U S
3030 Enterprise Court
STE C
Vista, CA 92081-8358   800-826-4200
                                 FAX: 800-368-4111
                                   info@optelec.com
                                    us.optelec.com

Stephan Terwolbeck, President
Michiel van Schaik, VP
Janet Lennex, Director of Customer Excellence
Large print software programs. *$595.00*

1597 Large Print DOS
Optelec U S
3030 Enterprise Court
STE C
Vista, CA 92081-8358   800-826-4200
                                 FAX: 800-368-4111
                                   info@optelec.com
                                    us.optelec.com

Stephan Terwolbeck, President
Michiel van Schaik, VP
Janet Lennex, Director of Customer Excellence

1598 Laureate Learning Systems
110 E Spring St
Winooski, VT 05404-1898   802-655-4755
                                      800-562-6801
                                 FAX: 802-655-4757
                               www.laureatelearning.com

Mary Wilson, Owner
Kathy Hollandsworth, Office Manager
Laureate publishes award-winning talking software for children
and adults with disabilities. Programs cover cause and effect, language development, cognitive processing, and reading.
High-quality speech, colorful graphics and amusing animation
make learning fun. Accessible with touchscreen, single switch,
keyboard and mouse. No reading required. Available on a hybrid
CD-ROM for Windows and Macintosh. Visit our website for
more information or call for a free catalog.

1599 Learning Company
Ste 400
222 3rd Ave SE
Cedar Rapids, IA 52401-1542   319-395-9626
                                      888-242-6747
                                 FAX: 319-395-0217
                                   info@riverdeep.net
                                   web.riverdeep.net
Barry O'Callaghan, Executive Chairman & Chief Executive Officer
Tony Mulderry, Executive Vice President, Corporate Development
Ciara Smyth, Executive Vice President, Global Business Operations
Software for children. For Macintosh or Windows (3.1 DOS or
Windows 95, Windows 98 required). The Learning Company has
been added to Riverdeep.

1600 Little Red Hen
Compass Learning
203 Colorado Street
Austin, TX 78701   512-478-9600
                                      800-678-1412
                                      866-586-7387
                                 FAX: 619-622-7873
                             support@compasslearning.com
                               www.compasslearning.com
Eric Loeffel, President, CEO
Tammy Deal, VP, Human Resources
Eric Wasser, VP, Sales
Children learn about the rewards of hard work when they dis-
cover who the Little Red Hen's friends miss out on freshly baked
bread. Puzzles, rhymes, story writing and other interactive exer-
cises enhance the creative learning process. *$34.95*

1601 Looking Good: Learning to Improve Your Appearance
Programming Concepts
8700 Shoal Creek Boulevard
Austin, TX 78757-6897   512-451-3246
                                      800-897-3202
                                      800-471-3000
                                 FAX: 800-397-7633
                                 general@proedinc.com
                                  www.proedinc.com

Jeff McLane, Founder
Lee Wilson, President and CEO
Randy Pennington, Executive VP
This game offers a creative way to discuss all areas of grooming.
$49.95

1602 Monkeys Jumping on the Bed
Soft Touch
12301 Central Ave NE Ste 205
P.O.Box 490215
Blaine, MN 55449-2352   763-862-2920
                                      888-755-1402
                                 FAX: 763-862-2922
                                 support@marblesoft.com
                                  www.marblesoft.com

Joyce Meyer, President
This program combines a favorite preschool song with number
and color activities. Children and adults will enjoy engaging music and delightful animation. Students with cognitive delays respond to upbeat music and interesting sounds. Large graphics
help learners focus on the action. Several important concepts are
presented in enjoyable activity formats. Students learn cause and
effect in Let's Play and Just for Fun.

1603 Morse Code WSKE
Words+
42505 10th Street West
Suite 109
Lancaster, CA 93534- 7059   661-723-7723
                                      888-266-9294
                                 FAX: 661-723-5524
                               info@simulations-plus.com
                               www.simulations-plus.com
Walter S Woltosz, M.S., M.A.S., Chairman, President and Chief Ex-
ecutive Officer
John A. Dibella, VP, Marketing & Sales
Virginia E. Woltosz. M.B.A., Secretary & Treasurer
A software and hardware product designed to operate on an IBM
compatible PC.

1604 Multi-Scan Single Switch Activity Center
Academic Software
3504 Tates Creek Road
Lexington, KY 40517-2601   859-552-1020
                                      859-552-1040
                                 FAX: 253-799-4012
                                   asistaff@acsw.com
                                    www.acsw.com

Dr. Warren E Lacefield PhD, President
Penelope D. Ellis, COO, Sales & Marketing Director
Cindy L George, Author
A single switch activity center containing four educational
games: Match, Maze, Dot-to-Dot, and Concentration, along with
six graphics libraries; Dinosaurs, Sports, Animals, Independent
Living, Vocations, and Cosmetology. MULTI-SCAN allows you
to select a graphic library, choose games for each user, and adjust
the difficulty level and other settings for each game. Other features allow you to save the game setups under each user's name
and print out individual performance reports after sessions.
$154.00

1605 Muppet Learning Keys
WINGS for Learning
1600 Green Hills Rd
Scotts Valley, CA 95066-4981   831-426-2228
                                 FAX: 831-464-3600

Ani Stocks, Owner
Designed to introduce children to the world of the computer as
they become familiar with letters, numbers and colors.

1606 My Own Pain
Soft Touch
12301 Central Ave NE Ste 205
P.O.Box 490215
Blaine, MN 55449-2352
763-862-2920
888-755-1402
FAX: 763-862-2922
support@marblesoft.com
www.marblesoft.com

Joyce Meyer, President
Three activities - three levels. Press the switch and the paint brush chooses the color and paints the vehicle. Music reinforces the sounds when the picture is complete. A second activity allows the student to choose the color and paint the vehicle parts any color he or she wants. The third activity is a blueprint. Print the color that matches the one in the wire drawing. Color the drawing to complete the picture.

1607 NanoPac
4823 S Sheridan Rd
Suite 302
Tulsa, OK 74145-5717
918-665-0329
800-580-6086
FAX: 918-665-0361
TTY: 918-665-2310
www.nanopac.com

Silvio Cianfrone, President
NanoPac offers assistive technology for those with low vision, blindness and reading disabilities. Some of their products include voice recognition, environmental controls, text to speech, magnifiers and door openers.

1608 Old MacDonald's Farm Deluxe
Soft Touch
12301 Central Ave NE Ste 205
P.O.Box 490215
Blaine, MN 55449-2352
763-862-2920
888-755-1402
FAX: 763-862-2922
support@marblesoft.com
www.marblesoft.com

Joyce Meyer, President
Toddlers, preschoolers and early elementary students will be entertained and captivated by the six major activities and animations in the delightful program. Includes 18 real animation images or 9 cartoon like characters. The teacher or child can choose which animals they want to sing about. Some activities are designed for children within the normal population, others are designed for students with moderate and severe disabilities.

1609 Optimum Resource Educational Software
Optimum Resource
1 Mathews Drive
Suite 107
Hilton Head Island, SC 29926
843-689-8000
FAX: 843-689-8008
info@stickybear.com
www.stickybear.com

Richard Hefter, President
A complete topical curriculum of reading, math, keyboard skills and science programs that are age and skill specific. Programs include: Early Learning for Pre-K to 1st grade with introductions to numbers, language, shapes, and time; Language Arts from Pre-K to 12; Math for Pre-K to 12; two distinct Science programs; Tools for Educators provides Spelling and Math generators; and Bilingual programs for Pre-K through 9th grade. All are available as single user up to 30 user site packages.

1610 Optimum Resources/Stickybear Software
1 Mathews Drive
Suite 107
Hilton Head Island, SC 29926
843-689-8000
FAX: 843-689-8008
info@stickybear.com
www.stickybear.com

Richard Hefter, President
Publisher of award-winning educational software for thirty years. Programs in use by millions of students nationwide. *$59.95*

1611 Please Understand Me: Software Program and Books
Cambridge Educational
132 West 31st Street
17th Floor
New York, NY 10001
800-322-8755
FAX: 800-678-3633
custserv@films.com
www.films.com

Promotes self-understanding while helping each student understand they are different from others. *$69.00*
209 pages BiAnnual
ISBN 0-927368-56-x

1612 Pond
WINGS for Learning
1600 Green Hills Rd
Scotts Valley, CA 95066-4981
831-426-2228
FAX: 831-464-3600

Ani Stocks, Owner
Software game that teaches pattern recognition and encourages observation, trial and error and the interpretation of data.

1613 Print, Play & Learn #1 Old Mac's Farm
Soft Touch Incorporated
12301 Central Ave NE Ste 205
P.O.Box 490215
Blaine, MN 55449-2352
763-862-2920
888-755-1402
FAX: 763-862-2922
support@marblesoft.com
www.marblesoft.com

Joyce Meyer, President
Once your students have completed Old Mac's Farm, let them use the fun off-computer activities to continue learning. Over 25 activities with 250 sheets you print. Board games, dot-to-dot drawings, word puzzles, make a scene, flash cards. Concentration, sentence strips, worksheets and much more are available for teachers to expand their teaching goals. This CD is full of activities to print and use.

1614 Print, Play & Learn #7: Sampler
Soft Touch
12301 Central Ave NE Ste 205
P.O.Box 490215
Blaine, MN 55449-2352
763-862-2920
888-755-1402
FAX: 763-862-2922
support@marblesoft.com
www.marblesoft.com

Joyce Meyer, President
Print, Play and Learn Sampler gives you over 200 activities organized by training, easy, medium and hard levels so you can ready to help your student advance. Activities cover a wide range of basic knowledge, including colors, shapes, numbers, letters and much, much more. Note: Requires Overlay Maker or Overlay Printer by IntelliTools and a color printer.

1615 Puzzle Power: Sampler
Soft Touch
12301 Central Ave NE Ste 205
P.O.Box 490215
Blaine, MN 55449-2352
763-862-2920
888-755-1402
FAX: 763-862-2922
support@marblesoft.com
www.marblesoft.com

Joyce Meyer, President
Puzzle Power - Sampler offers a variety of puzzles in different themes. Each theme puzzle is followed by a puzzle of one item in this category. For example, first solve a puzzle for occupations. Then, solve a puzzle that is a baker. The pictures are large, clear and easily identifiable.

1616 Puzzle Power: Zoo & School Days
Soft Touch
12301 Central Ave NE Ste 205
P.O.Box 490215
Blaine, MN 55449-2352 763-862-2920
888-755-1402
FAX: 763-862-2922
support@marblesoft.com
www.marblesoft.com

Joyce Meyer, President

Here is a program for all of our students who need puzzle skills, but cannot access commercial puzzles. Puzzle Power puzzles start with just two pieces and progress to 16 pieces. The pictures are large, clear and easily identifiable. Four different activities enable all students to be successful. Automatic Placement: the student just presses the switch or keyboard to place the pieces. Magnet Mouse: all the student needs to do is move the mouse and it drops into place.

1617 Rodeo
Soft Touch
12301 Central Ave NE Ste 205
P.O.Box 490215
Blaine, MN 55449-2352 763-862-2920
888-755-1402
FAX: 763-862-2922
support@marblesoft.com
www.marblesoft.com

Joyce Meyer, President

Rodeo action and familiar tunes for teens and preteens. Four activities invite students to learn, laugh, and sing as they go to the rodeo with up to six age-peer friends. Age-appropriate graphics with surprising animations reinforce the learning. The graphics are large and colorful, the melodies familiar, and the words descriptive of the action on the screen.

1618 Shop Til You Drop
Soft Touch
12301 Central Ave NE Ste 205
P.O.Box 490215
Blaine, MN 55449-2352 763-862-2920
888-755-1402
FAX: 763-862-2922
support@marblesoft.com
www.marblesoft.com

Joyce Meyer, President

Designed specifically for preteens and teens with moderate and severe disabilities, this program will become a staple for the classroom. The student goes shopping and can choose which outfits to put together. They may choose to purchase the outfit - of course, with mom's credit card. Another activity is a video arcade game about money. Shop 'Til You Drop can be adjusted from a single switch cause-and-effect program to row-and-column scanning to direct choice.

1619 Songs I Sing at Preschool
Soft Touch
12301 Central Ave NE Ste 205
P.O.Box 490215
Blaine, MN 55449-2352 763-862-2920
888-755-1402
FAX: 763-862-2922
support@marblesoft.com
www.marblesoft.com

Joyce Meyer, President

Songs I Sing at Preschool offers many options for the teacher and the student. Over the years, our software has used music because our students really respond to the sounds and rhythms of songs. Teachers select which songs to present, how many to present at one time and where to place each song on the overlay, keyboard or scan array.

1620 Stickybear Early Learning Activities
Optimum Resource
1 Mathews Drive
Suite 107
Hilton Head Island, SC 29926 843-689-8000
FAX: 843-689-8008
info@stickybear.com
www.stickybear.com

Richard Hefter, President

Two modes of play allow youngsters to learn through prompted direction or by the discovery method. Lively animation and sound keep attention levels high as children learn writing, counting, shapes, opposites and colors. Stickybear Early Learning Activities is bilingual, so youngsters can build skills in both English and Spanish. Pre-K to 1st grade. *$59.95*

1621 Stickybear Kindergarden Activities
Optimum Resource
1 Mathews Drive
Suite 107
Hilton Head Island, SC 29926 843-689-8000
FAX: 843-689-8008
info@stickybear.com
www.stickybear.com

Richard Hefter, President

This dynamic new multifaceted program covers a wide range of preschool skills that go far beyond the strictly academic. At Stickybear's house, children discover the alphabet, numbers, shapes, colors, plus - social skills, important safety messages and delightful off-screen activities that foster creativity. Over three hours of original music can be composed by a child and saved for future use. *$59.95*

1622 Stickybear Science Fair Light
Optimum Resource
1 Mathews Drive
Suite 107
Hilton Head Island, SC 29926 843-689-8000
FAX: 843-689-8008
info@stickybear.com
www.stickybear.com

Richard Hefter, President

The first in the new series of science-based programs Stickybear Science Fair Light presents a content rich environment which allows students in grades 7-12 to explore, experiment with and understand light and it's properties. The program presents experiments, both structured and free-form, which allow users to work with prisms, lenses, color mixing, optical illusions and more. *$59.95*

1623 Stickybear Town Builder
Optimum Resource
1 Mathews Drive
Suite 107
Hilton Head Island, SC 29926 843-689-8000
FAX: 843-689-8008
info@stickybear.com
www.stickybear.com

Richard Hefter, President

Children learn to read maps, build towns, take trips and use a compass in this simulation program. *$59.95*

1624 Stickybear Typing
Optimum Resource
1 Mathews Drive
Suite 107
Hilton Head Island, SC 29926 843-689-8000
FAX: 843-689-8008
info@stickybear.com
www.stickybear.com

Richard Hefter, President

Sharpen typing skills with three challenging activities: Stickybear Keypress, Stickybear Thump and Stickybear Stories. Pre-K to 5th. *$59.95*

1625 Storybook Maker Deluxe
Compass Learning
203 Colorado Street
Austin, TX 78701 512-478-9600
800-678-1412
866-586-7387
FAX: 619-622-7873
support@compasslearning.com
www.compasslearning.com

Eric Loeffel, President, CEO
Tammy Deal, VP, Human Resources
Eric Wasser, VP, Sales

Using Storybook Maker Deluxe and their imaginations, students can create and publish stories filled with exciting graphics. Students can write stories and watch as the text appears in the setting they've chosen. Engaging sounds and music, plus lively animations, provide positive learning reinforcement throughout the program. *$44.95*

1626 Super Challenger
Electronic Courseware Systems
1713 S State St
Champaign, IL 61820-7258   217-359-7099
800-832-4965
FAX: 217-359-6578
www.ecsmedia.com

Jodie Varner, Manager
G Peters, President
An aural-visual musical game that increases the player's ability to remember a series of pitches as they are played by the computer. The game is based on a 12-note chromatic scale, a major scale, and a minor scale. Each pitch is reinforced visually with a color representation of a keyboard on the display screen. Computer/software. *$39.95*

1627 Switch Basics
Soft Touch
12301 Central Ave NE Ste 205
P.O.Box 490215
Blaine, MN 55449-2352   763-862-2920
888-755-1402
FAX: 763-862-2922
support@marblesoft.com
www.marblesoft.com

Joyce Meyer, President
Discover whimsical animations and real life pictures while learning switch operations. Intriguing and humorous, nine different programs offer a multitude of learning experiences for all ages. Program options include: cause and effect, scanning, step scanning, row and column activities for one or two players. Watch the clouds roll away revealing African animals; visit the beauty salon or barber shop; work two to sixteen piece puzzles; or add swimming fish to a huge aquarium.

1628 Switch Interface Pro 5.0
Don Johnston
26799 West Commerce Drive
Volo, IL 60073   847-740-0749
800-999-4660
FAX: 847-740-7326
info@donjohnston.com
www.donjohnston.com

Don Johnston, Founder
Ruth Ziolkowski, President
Kevin Johnston, Director of Product Design
Allows individuals with physical disabilities to access the computer. Five ports accommodate multiple switches and emulate everything from a single-click to a return. Consequently, individuals gain access to the widest variety of switch-accessible software available. It requires no software and can be used with both Windows and Macintosh computers. *$79.00*

1629 Teach Me Phonemics Series Bundle
SoftTouch
Ste 401
4300 Stine Rd
Bakersfield, CA 93313-2352   661-396-8676
877-763-8868
FAX: 661-396-8760
support@softtouch.com
www.funsoftware.com

Joyce Meyer, President
Roxanne Butterfield, Marketing
The Teach Me Phonemics Series Bundle includes one copy of each Teach Me Phonemics program - Initial, Medial, Final and Blends - four CD's in all.

1630 Teach Me Phonemics Super Bundle
SoftTouch
Ste 401
4300 Stine Rd
Bakersfield, CA 93313-2352   661-396-8676
877-763-8868
FAX: 661-396-8760
www.funsoftware.com

Roxanne Butterfield, Marketing
Joyce Meyer, President
Teach Me Phonemics Super Bundle includes all 4 Teach Me Phonemics programs and all 4 Teach Me Phonemics overlay CD's - eight CD's in all.

1631 Teach Me Phonemics: Blends
SoftTouch
Ste 401
4300 Stine Rd
Bakersfield, CA 93313-2352   661-396-8676
877-763-8868
FAX: 661-396-8760

Roxanne Butterfield, Marketing
Joyce Meyer, President
Teach Me Phonemics - Blends helps students explore words and hear the initial blend sounds. It features musical interludes and movement to engage the student. Teachers select the best combination options to motivate and engage the student. Options turn off and on the fly so you can quickly make changes to keep the student engaged.

1632 Teach Me Phonemics: Final
SoftTouch
Ste 401
4300 Stine Rd
Bakersfield, CA 93313-2352   661-396-8676
877-763-8868
FAX: 661-396-8760

Roxanne Butterfield
Joyce Meyer, President
Teach me Phonemics - Final helps students explore words and hear the final sounds. It features musical interludes and movement to engage the student. Options turn off and on the fly so you can quickly make changes to keep the student engaged.

1633 Teach Me Phonemics: Initial
SoftTouch
12301 Central Ave NE
Ste 205
Blaine, MN 55434   763-755-1402
888-755-1403
FAX: 763-862-2920
sales@marblesoft.com
www.softtouch.com

Roxanne Butterfield, Marketing
Joyce Meyer, President
Teach Me Phonemics - Initial helps students explore the words and hear the initial sounds. It features musical interludes and movement to engage the student. Teachers select the best combination options to motivate and engage the student. Options turn off and on the fly so you can quickly make changes to keep the student engaged.

1634 Teach Me Phonemics: Medial
SoftTouch
12301 Central Ave NE
Ste 205
Blaine, MN 55434   763-755-1402
888-755-1403
FAX: 763-862-2920
sales@marblesoft.com
www.softtouch.com

Roxanne Butterfield, Marketing
Joyce Meyer, President
Teach Me Phonemics - Medial helps students explore the words and hear the medial sounds. It features musical interludes and movement to engage the student. Teachers select the best combination options to motivate and engage the student. Options turn off and on the fly so you can quickly make changes to keep the student engaged.

1635 Teach Me to Talk
Soft Touch
12301 Central Ave NE Ste 205
P.O.Box 490215
Blaine, MN 55449-2352   763-862-2920
                                       888-755-1402
                                  FAX: 763-862-2922
                              support@marblesoft.com
                                  www.marblesoft.com

Joyce Meyer, President
The first activity Teach Me to Talk is used as a springboard for the
student to learn to speak the word. There are 150 real pictures.
When a picture is chosen, it appears on a clear background with
musical interludes, movement, written word and spoken word. It
culminates by morphing to the corresponding black and white
Mayer-Johnson symbol. The second activity Story Time, takes
some of these nouns and puts them in four line poetry. This helps
students hear the word in the midst of a sentence.

1636 Teen Tunes Plus
Soft Touch
12301 Central Ave NE Ste 205
P.O.Box 490215
Blaine, MN 55449-2352   763-862-2920
                                       888-755-1402
                                  FAX: 763-862-2922
                              support@marblesoft.com
                                  www.marblesoft.com

Joyce Meyer, President
Introduce switch use to older students with disabilities. Large interesting graphics, a variety of musical interludes, and surprising
animations are combined with calm soothing music and beautiful
pictures in the software specifically designed for preteens and
teens with severe cognitive delays and/or physical disabilities,
and older students learning to use a switch.

1637 There are Tyrannosaurs Trying on Pants in My Bedroom
Compass Learning
203 Colorado Street
Austin, TX 78701-3922   512-478-9600
                                       800-678-1412
                                       866-586-7387
                                  FAX: 619-622-7873
                           support@compasslearning.com
                               www.compasslearning.com

Eric Loeffel, President, CEO
Tammy Deal, VP, Human Resources
Eric Wasser, VP, Sales
In this popular story, Saturday chores turn into fun-filled frolick-
ing when dinosaurs come for a visit. Sounds, music and animation
make learning about phonics and vocabulary dyno-mite. *$34.95*

1638 Three Billy Goats Gruff
Compass Learning
203 Colorado Street
Austin, TX 78701-3922   512-478-9600
                                       800-678-1412
                                       866-586-7387
                                  FAX: 619-622-7873
                           support@compasslearning.com
                               www.compasslearning.com

Eric Loeffel, President, CEO
Tammy Deal, VP, Human Resources
Eric Wasser, VP, Sales
Motivating exercises and creative activities provide hours of
learning fun while young students follow the adventure of The
Three Billy Goats Gruff in this animated version of the timeless
tale. *$34.95*

1639 Three Little Pigs
Compass Learning
203 Colorado Street
Austin, TX 78701-3922   512-478-9600
                                       800-678-1412
                                       866-586-7387
                                  FAX: 619-622-7873
                           support@compasslearning.com
                               www.compasslearning.com

Eric Loeffel, President, CEO
Tammy Deal, VP, Human Resources
Eric Wasser, VP, Sales

Help young students build reading comprehension and writing
skills with this interactive version of the children's classic, The
Three Little Pigs. Animated storytelling and creative activities
inspire children to read, write and rhyme. *$34.95*

1640 TouchCorders
Soft Touch
12301 Central Ave NE Ste 205
P.O.Box 490215
Blaine, MN 55449-2352   763-862-2920
                                       888-755-1402
                                  FAX: 763-862-2922
                              support@marblesoft.com
                                  www.marblesoft.com

Joyce Meyer, President
TouchCorders are the flexible and easy-to-use communicator designed by Jo Meyer and Linda Bidabe for reach classroom use.
TouchCorders are sensitive to touch at every angle and give the
student kinesthetic feedback. With the unique Add 'n Touch system, Jo connects the puzzles bases of 2 or more TouchCorders on
the fly to present vocabulary, sequencing, story telling, social
stories, concepts and other curriculum and communication
opportunities.

1641 TouchWindow Touch Screen
Riverdeep Incorporated
100 Pine Street
Suite 1900
San Francisco, CA 94111   415-659-2000
                                       800-542-4222
                                  FAX: 415-659-2020
                                  info@riverdeep.net
                                  www.riverdeep.net
Barry O'Callaghan, Executive Chairman & Chief Executive Officer
Tony Mulderry, Executive Vice President, Corporate Development
Ciara Smyth, Executive Vice President, Global Business Operations
Software for children. *$335.00*

1642 Turtle Teasers
Soft Touch
12301 Central Ave NE Ste 205
P.O.Box 490215
Blaine, MN 55449-2352   763-862-2920
                                       888-755-1402
                                  FAX: 763-862-2922
                              support@marblesoft.com
                                  www.marblesoft.com

Joyce Meyer, President
Three Games, Three Levels from Easy, Medium to Hard. The
Shell Game - easy: Watch one of the three turtles get the tomato.
Then watch carefully as they switch positions and pop shut.
Choose incorrectly and the frog disappears until the correct one is
displayed. The Pond - medium: Watch the tomato disappear
somewhere in the pond scene. Tomato Dump - hard: Hit the shell
and it turns into the tomato, giving a score. There are different difficulty levels to equalize all students.

1643 What Was That!
Compass Learning
203 Colorado Street
Austin, TX 78701-3922   512-478-9600
                                       800-678-1412
                                       866-586-7387
                                  FAX: 619-622-7873
                           support@compasslearning.com
                               www.compasslearning.com

Eric Loeffel, President, CEO
Tammy Deal, VP, Human Resources
Eric Wasser, VP, Sales
In this bedtime story, noises in the night send three brother bears
scurrying out of bed. Thoughtful questions test young readers'
comprehension, while games, voice recording, writing practice
and other playful activities stimulate their creativity.

1644 Wivik 3
Prentke Romich Company
1022 Heyl Road
Wooster, OH 44691

330-262-1984
800-262-1984
FAX: 330-263-4829
info@prentrom.com
www.prentrom.com

Dave Hershberger, President & CEO
Barry Romich, Co-Founder
On-screen keyboard provides access to any application in the latest Windows operating systems. Selections are made by clicking, dwelling or switch scanning. Enhancements include word prediction and abbreviation expansion.

1645 WordMaker
Don Johnston
26799 West Commerce Drive
Volo, IL 60073

847-740-0749
800-999-4660
FAX: 847-740-7326
info@donjohnston.com
www.donjohnston.com

Don Johnston, Founder
Ruth Ziolkowski, President
Kevin Johnston, Director of Product Design
The computer version of Dr Patricia Cunningham's book 'Systematic Sequential Phonics They Use.' The program systematically builds spelling and word decoding skills for struggling readers and writers. *$79.00*

1646 Write: Out Loud
Don Johnston
26799 West Commerce Drive
Volo, IL 60073

847-740-0749
800-999-4660
FAX: 847-740-7326
info@donjohnston.com
www.donjohnston.com

Don Johnston, Founder
Ruth Ziolkowski, President
Kevin Johnston, Director of Product Design
Write: Out Loud is an easy-to-use talking word processor that uses text-to-speech and revision and editing supports to help students write more effectively, more often and with more enthusiasm as they share creative thoughts on paper. *$79.00*

1647 You Tell Me: Learning Basic Information
Programming Concepts
8700 Shoal Creek Boulevard
Austin, TX 78757-6897

512-451-3246
800-897-3202
800-471-3000
FAX: 800-397-7633
general@proedinc.com
www.proedinc.com

Jeff McLane, Founder
Lee Wilson, President and CEO
Randy Pennington, Executive VP
This game teaches and reinforces basic information all individuals need to know. Questions asked in this game help prepare people to communicate personal identification information important to community survival. *$49.95*

Software: Professional

1648 Acrontech International
5500 Main St
Williamsville, NY 14221-6755   FAX: 716-854-4014
This company supplies software, audio mixers, and closed-caption televisions.

1649 DPS with BCP
V OR T Corporation
P.O.Box G (George)
Menlo Park, CA 94026

650-322-8282
888-757-8678
FAX: 650-327-0747
custserv@vort.com
vort.com

Tom Holt, Owner
This program uses unique DPS branching techniques to access goals and objectives.

1650 Descriptive Language Arts Development
Educational Activities Software
5600 West 83rd Street
Suite 300, 8200 Tower
Bloomington, MN 55437

888-351-4199
800-447-5286
FAX: 239-225-9299
info@edmentum.com
www.edmentum.com

Vin Riera, President/CEO
Dan Juckniess, SVP, Sales & Professional Services
Stacey Herteux, VP, Human Resources
This multimedia language arts development program provides instruction and application of fundamental English skills and concepts. *$395.00*

1651 Diagnostic Report Writer
Parrot Software
P.O. Box 250755
West Bloomfield, MI 48325

248-788-3223
800-727-7681
FAX: 248-788-3224
support@parrotsoftware.com
www.parrotsoftware.com

Dr. Frederic Weiner, Ph. D., CCC-SP, President, Owner
Creates a three page single-spaced diagnostic report for a child with a communication disorder from a list of questions; sections of the report include developmental and background history, oral peripheral exam, speech and language analysis, summary and recommendations.

1652 Draft: Builder
Don Johnston
26799 West Commerce Drive
Volo, IL 60073

847-740-0749
800-999-4660
FAX: 847-740-7326
info@donjohnston.com
www.donjohnston.com

Don Johnston, Founder
Ruth Ziolkowski, President
Kevin Johnston, Director of Product Design
A software-based graphic organizer that breaks down the writing process into manageable chunks to structure planning, organizing, and draft-writing. *$79.00*

1653 EZ Dot
CAPCO Capability Corporation
3910 S. Union Court
Spokane Valley, WA 99206-6345

509-927-8195
800-827-2182
FAX: 800-827-2182
info@skilltran.com
www.skilltran.com

Jeff Truthan, President
A critical software tool used in vocational counseling, job restructuring, recruitment and placement, better utilization of workers, and safety issues. This software offers occupational data by title, code, industry, GEO, DPT, or OGA. *$295.00*

1654 EZ Keys for Windows
Words+
Ste 109
42505 10th St W
Lancaster, CA 93534-7059
661-723-6523
800-869-8521
FAX: 661-723-2114
info@words-plus.com
Jean Dobbs, Editorial Director
Tim Gilmer, Editor
Josie Byzek, Managing Editor
A software and hardware product designed to operate on an IBM compatible PC. The software provides dual word prediction, abbreviation expansion, five different methods of voice output and access to commercial software applications. *$1395.00*

1655 Goals and Objectives
JE Stewart Teaching Tools
P.O.Box 15308
Seattle, WA 98115-308
206-262-9538
FAX: 206-262-9538
Jeff Stewart, Owner
Goals and Objectives software helps teachers make student plans including IEP's, IPP's and IHP's. The system provides curricula for all students and programs to develop and evaluate plans, print reports and make data forms. Systems are available for Windows and Macintosh for $139.

1656 Goals and Objectives IEP Program Curriculum Associates LLC
153 Rangeway Road
P.O.Box 2001
North Billerica, MA 01862-0901
978-667-8000
800-225-0248
FAX: 800-366-1158
www.curriculumassociates.com
Frank E. Ferguson, Chairman
Renee Foster, President & Publisher
Woody Palk, Senior Vice President, Sales
BRIGANCE CIBS-R standardized scoring conversion software, is a teacher's tool that prints goal and objective pages of the IEP. In less than two minutes per student, a teacher types student data into the computer.

1657 Nasometer
Kay Elemetrics Corporation
3 Paragon Drive
Montvale, NJ 07645
973-628-6200
800-289-5297
FAX: 201-391-2063
sales@kaypentax.com
www.kaypentax.com
John Crump, President
Steve Crump, Direct Sales
Measures the ratio of acoustic energy for the nasal and real-time visual cueing during therapy. Used clinically in the areas of cleft palate, motor speech disorders, hearing impairment and palatal prosthetic fittings.

1658 PSS CogRehab Software
Psychological Software Services
3304 W 75th St
Indianapolis, IN 46268-1664
317-257-9672
FAX: 317-257-9674
www.neuroscience.cnter.com
Odie L Bracy, Executive Director
PSS CogRehab Software is a comprehensive and easy-to-use multimedia cognitive rehabilitation software available, for clinical and educational use with head injury, stroke LD/ADD and other brain compromises. The packages include 64 computerized therapy tasks which contain modifiable parameters that will accommodate most requirements. Exercises include attention and executive skills, multiple modalities of visuosatial and memory skills, simple, complex, problem-solving skills.
$260 - $2500

1659 Parrot Easy Language Simple Anaylsis
Parrot Software
P.O.Box 250755
West Bloomfield, MI 48325
248-788-3223
800-727-7681
FAX: 248-788-3224
support@parrotsoftware.com
www.parrotsoftware.com
Dr. Frederic Weiner, Ph. D., CCC-SP, President, Owner
Designed for grammatical analysis of language samples. The user types and translates language samples of up to 100 utterances.

1660 SOLO Literacy Suite
Don Johnston
26799 West Commerce Drive
Volo, IL 60073
847-740-0749
800-999-4660
FAX: 847-740-7326
info@donjohnston.com
www.donjohnston.com
Don Johnston, Founder
Ruth Ziolkowski, President
Kevin Johnston, Director of Product Design
Places all of the right tools, and a wide-range of embedded learning supports, at their fingertips. SOLO includes word prediction, a text reader, graphic organizer and talking word processor, putting students in charge of their own learning and accommodations. Students of varying ages and abilities have access to, and make progress in, the general education curriculum. *$79.00*

1661 TOVA
Universal Attention Disorders
3321 Cerritos Avenue
Los Alamitos, CA 90720
562-594-7700
800-729-2886
FAX: 800-452-6919
info@tovatest.com
www.tovatest.com
Lawrence M. Greenberg, MD
A computerized assessment which, in conjunction with classroom behavior ratings, is a highly effective screening tool for ADD. TOVA includes software, complete instructions, and supporting data including norms.

1662 Visi-Pitch III
Kayelemetrics Corporation
3 Paragon Drive
Montvale, NJ 07645
973-628-6200
800-289-5297
FAX: 201-391-2063
sales@kaypentax.com
John Crump, President
Steve Crump, Direct Sales
Assists the speech/voice clinician in assessment and treatment tasks across an expansive range of disorders.

Software: Reading & Language Arts

1663 Choices, Choices 5.0
Tom Snyder Productions
100 Talcott Avenue
Watertown, MA 02472-5703
800-342-0236
www.tomsnyder.com
Tom Snyder, Founder
Bridget Dalton, Ed.D, Author
Peggy Healy Stearns, Ph.D., Author
Teaches students to take responsibility for their behavior. Helps students develop the skills and awareness they need to make wise choices and to think through the consequences of their actions.

1664 Co: Writer
Don Johnston
26799 West Commerce Drive
Volo, IL 60073   847-740-0749
                                      800-999-4660
                                 FAX: 847-740-7326
                              info@donjohnston.com
                              www.donjohnston.com

Don Johnston, Founder
Ruth Ziolkowski, President
Kevin Johnston, Director of Product Design
A software-based writing assistant that uses word prediction to cut through writing barriers and improve written expression. It is intended for students who struggle to write because of difficulty with spelling, syntax, and translating thoughts into writing. As students type, Co: Writer learns the context of the sentence and accurately 'predicts' words even when spelled phonetically or inventively. *$79.00*

1665 Community Exploration
Compass Learning
203 Colorado Street
Austin, TX 78701-3922   512-478-9600
                                     800-678-1412
                                     866-586-7387
                                FAX: 619-622-7873
                          support@compasslearning.com
                            www.compasslearning.com

Eric Loeffel, President, CEO
Tammy Deal, VP, Human Resources
Eric Wasser, VP, Sales
An award-winning learning adventure takes students who are learning English as a second language on a field trip to the make-believe town of Cornerstone. More than 50 community locations come to life with sound and animation. While exploring places in this typical American community where people live, work and play, students also enhance important English-language skills. Offers an exciting approach for any age student who needs to improve their English language proficiency. 4-12. *$19.95*

1666 Conversations
Educational Activities Software
5600 West 83rd Street
Suite 300, 8200 Tower
Bloomington, MN 55437   888-351-4199
                                     800-447-5286
                                FAX: 239-225-9299
                                info@edmentum.com
                                  www.edmentum.com

Vin Riera, President/CEO
Dan Juckniess, SVP, Sales & Professional Services
Stacey Herteux, VP, Human Resources
Using American digitized voices, CONVERSATIONS provides 14 different dialogues in which the student can participate. The topics offer learners important information about American culture and the workplace. Available for DOS. *$195.00*

1667 Core-Reading and Vocabulary Development
Educational Activities
P.O.Box 87
Baldwin, NY 11510   516-223-4666
                                     800-797-3223
                                FAX: 516-623-9282
                                     www.edact.com

Alfred Harris, President
Carol Stern, VP
Students begin with 36 basic words and progress to more than 200. Reading and writing activities are coordinated and integrated throughout the program for more substantial permanent learning. Five units covering readability levels from pre-primer to grade three.
Full Program

1668 Friday Afternoon
203 Colorado Street
Austin, TX 78701-3922   512-478-9600
                                     800-678-1412
                                     866-586-7387
                                FAX: 619-622-7873
                          support@compasslearning.com
                            www.compasslearning.com

Eric Loeffel, President, CEO
Tammy Deal, VP, Human Resources
Eric Wasser, VP, Sales
Save hours of preparation time and dazzle your students with interesting new activities to supplement their classroom learning. With Friday afternoon, you'll produce flash cards, word puzzles, even customized bingo cards and more, all at the click of a mouse. MacIntosh diskette. *$99.95*

1669 How to Read for Everyday Living
Educational Activities Software
5600 West 83rd Street
Suite 300, 8200 Tower
Bloomington, MN 55437   888-351-4199
                                     800-447-5286
                                FAX: 239-225-9299
                                info@edmentum.com
                                  www.edmentum.com

Vin Riera, President/CEO
Dan Juckniess, SVP, Sales & Professional Services
Stacey Herteux, VP, Human Resources
Basic vocabulary and key words are taught and, when need, retaught using alternative teaching strategies. Passages that students read help put the vocabulary into context. Each lesson is followed by crossword and other puzzles check comprehension.

1670 Learning English: Primary
203 Colorado Street
Austin, TX 78701-3922   512-478-9600
                                     800-678-1412
                                     866-586-7387
                                FAX: 619-622-7873
                          support@compasslearning.com
                            www.compasslearning.com

Eric Loeffel, President, CEO
Tammy Deal, VP, Human Resources
Eric Wasser, VP, Sales
Four stories and rhymes help students familiarize themselves with essential English language concepts, recognize patterns in language and associate words with objects. *$49.95*

1671 Learning English: Rhyme Time
Compass Learning
203 Colorado Street
Austin, TX 78701-3922   512-478-9600
                                     800-678-1412
                                     866-586-7387
                                FAX: 619-622-7873
                            www.compasslearning.com

Eric Loeffel, President, CEO
Tammy Deal, VP, Human Resources
Eric Wasser, VP, Sales
Using classic children's rhymes in an animated multimedia program, students work on language skills, vocabulary and comprehension.

1672 Lexia I, II and III Reading Series
Lexia Learning Systems
200 Baker Ave Ext.
Concord, MA 01742   978-405-6200
                                     800-435-3942
                                     800-507-2772
                                FAX: 978-287-0062
                              info@lexialearning.com
                              www.lexialearning.com

Nick Gaehde, President and CEO
Paul More, Vice President, Finance
Collin Earnst, Vice President of Marketing
Lexia's software helps children and adults with learning disabilities master their core reading skills. Based on the Orton Gillingham method, Lexia Early Reading, Phonics Based Reading and SOS (Strategies for Older Students) apply phonics principles to help students learn essential sound-symbol

correspondence and decoding skills. The Quick Reading Tests generate detailed skill reports in only 5-8 minutes per student to provide data for further instruction. Price: $40-400 per workstation.

1673 Memory Castle
WINGS for Learning
1600 Green Hills Rd
Scotts Valley, CA 95066-4981   831-426-2228
                                     FAX: 831-464-3600
Ani Stocks, Owner
Introduces a strategy to increase memory skills via an adventure Q198 game. Set in a castle, the game requires memory, reading, spelling skills and more to win.

1674 On a Green Bus: A UKanDu Little Book
Don Johnston
26799 West Commerce Drive
Volo, IL 60073   847-740-0749
                                     800-999-4660
                                     FAX: 847-740-7326
                                     info@donjohnston.com
                                     www.donjohnston.com

Don Johnston, Founder
Ruth Ziolkowski, President
Kevin Johnston, Director of Product Design
This early literacy program that consists of several create-your-own 4-page animated stories that help build language experience on each page and then watch the page come alive with animation and sound. After completing the story, students can print it out to make a book which can be read over and over again. Because there are no wrong answers, all children can have a successful literacy experience. *$45.00*

1675 Open Book
Freedom Scientific
11800 31st Court North
St Petersburg, FL 33716   727-803-8000
                                     800-444-4443
                                     FAX: 727-803-8001
                                     info@freedomscientific.com
                                     www.freedomscientific.com
Lee Hamilton, President, CEO, and Chairman of
Mike Self, Sales Representative (Alabama)
Joseph McDaniel, Sales Representative (Alaska and
Software that reads scanned text allowed and includes other features that aid the vision-impaired. *$995.00*

1676 Optimum Resource Software
1 Mathews Drive
Suite 107
Hilton Head Island, SC 29926   843-689-8000
                                     FAX: 843-689-8008
                                     info@stickybear.com
                                     www.stickybear.com

Richard Hefter, President
Optimum Resource publishes over 100 K-12 education curriculum software titles under its varietal brands, StickyBear, MiddleWare, High School and Tools for Teachers. Most programs are available in Bilingual English/Spanish, and are offered with options for the single user through 30 users.

1677 Parts of Speech
Optimum Resource
1 Mathews Drive
Suite 107
Hilton Head Island, SC 29926   843-689-8000
                                     FAX: 843-689-8008
                                     info@stickybear.com
                                     www.stickybear.com

Richard Hefter, President
Designed to help students build grammar and vocabulary as they strengthen reading and writing ability. Grades 3 to 9. *$59.95*

1678 Programs for Aphasia and Cognitive Disorders
Parrot Software
P.O.Box 250755
West Bloomfield, MI 48325   248-788-3223
                                     800-727-7681
                                     FAX: 248-788-3224
                                     support@parrotsoftware.com
                                     www.parrotsoftware.com
Dr. Frederic Weiner, Ph. D., CCC-SP, President, Owner
Over 50 different computer programs that facilitate language, memory and attention training. Programs are available for MS DOS, WINDOWS and Apple II.

1679 Punctuation Rules
Optimum Resource
1 Mathews Drive
Suite 107
Hilton Head Island, SC 29926   843-689-8000
                                     FAX: 843-689-8008
                                     info@stickybear.com
                                     www.stickybear.com

Richard Hefter, President
Punctuation Rules is designed to help students improve their punctuation skills. Students work with appropriate level sentences which follow common rules of punctuation. The program covers material ranging from categories of sentences to forming possessives and allows students to gain strength in their ability to correctly use periods, commas, apostrophes, question marks, colons, hyphens, quotation marks, exclamation points and more. Grades 3-9. Bilingual. *$59.95*

1680 Quick Reading Test, Phonics Based Reading, Reading SOS (Strategies for Older Students)
Lexia Learning Systems
200 Baker Ave Ext.
Concord, MA 01742   978-405-6200
                                     800-435-3942
                                     800-507-2772
                                     FAX: 978-287-0062
                                     info@lexialearning.com
                                     www.lexialearning.com

Nick Gaehde, President and CEO
Paul More, Vice President, Finance
Collin Earnst, Vice President of Marketing
Lexia's software helps children and adults with learning disabilities master their core reading skills. Based on the Orton Gillingham method, Phonics Based Reading and S.O.S. (Strategies for the Older Student) apply phonics principles to help students learn essential sound-symbol correspondence and decoding skills. The Quick Reading Tests generate detailed phonemic skills reports in only 5-8 minutes per student to provide teachers with accurate data to focus their instruction. Price: $67-$500.

1681 Quick Talk
Educational Activities Software
5600 West 83rd Street
Suite 300, 8200 Tower
Bloomington, MN 55437   888-351-4199
                                     800-447-5286
                                     FAX: 239-225-9299
                                     info@edmentum.com
                                     www.edmentum.com

Vin Riera, President/CEO
Dan Juckniess, SVP, Sales & Professional Services
Stacey Herteux, VP, Human Resources
Students will learn and use new vocabulary immediately: high-frequency, everyday vocabulary words are introduced and used contextually using human speech, graphics and text. Voice-interactive program (MS-DOS). *$65.00*

1682 **Race the Clock**
Mindplay
4400 E. Broadway Blvd
Suite 400
Tucson, AZ 85711
520-888-1800
800-221-7911
FAX: 520-888-7904
mail@mindplay.com
www.mindplay.com

Dan Figurski, Senior Vice President of Business
Chris Coleman, VP, Business Development
Judith Bliss, CEO
A matching game, uses the animation capabilities to teach verbs.
The player chooses a matching game from a menu.

1683 **Read: Out Loud**
Don Johnston
26799 West Commerce Drive
Volo, IL 60073
847-740-0749
800-999-4660
FAX: 847-740-7326
info@donjohnston.com
www.donjohnston.com

Don Johnston, Founder
Ruth Ziolkowski, President
Kevin Johnston, Director of Product Design
An accessible text reader that provides access to the curriculum.
It features high-quality text to speech and study tools that help
students read with comprehension. *$79.00*

1684 **Reader Rabbit**
Learning Company
Ste 1900
100 Pine St
San Francisco, CA 94111-5205
415-659-2000
800-825-4420
FAX: 415-659-2020
thelearningco@hmhpub.com
www.thelearningcompany.com

Linda K. Zecher, President and CEO
Eric Shuman, Chief Financial Officer
John K. Dragoon, Executive Vice President and Chi
Supports young students in building fundamental reading readi-
ness skills in a playful, multi-sensory environment.

1685 **Reading Comprehension Series**
Optimum Resource
1 Mathews Drive
Suite 107
Hilton Head Island, SC 29926- 3765
843-689-8000
FAX: 843-689-8008
info@stickybear.com
www.stickybear.com

Richard Hefter, President
The Reading Comprehension Series, includes seven volumes
packed with intriguing multi-level stories. Each volume will capture the interest of children ages 8-14 while teaching them crucial
reading comprehension skills. These open-ended programs are
versatile and easy to use, and Bilingual. *$59.95*

1686 **Simon SIO**
Don Johnston
26799 West Commerce Drive
Volo, IL 60073
847-740-0749
800-999-4660
FAX: 847-740-7326
info@donjohnston.com
www.donjohnston.com

Don Johnston, Founder
Ruth Ziolkowski, President
Kevin Johnston, Director of Product Design
A researched and widely field-tested phonics program for begin-
ning readers, developed in collaboration with Dr. Ted
Hasselbring of Vanderbilt University. The program uses a per-
sonal tutor to deliver individualized instruction and corrective
feedback. *$79.00*

1687 **Sound Sentences**
Educational Activities Software
5600 West 83rd Street
Suite 300, 8200 Tower
Bloomington, MN 55437
888-351-4199
800-447-5286
FAX: 239-225-9299
info@edmentum.com
www.edmentum.com

Vin Riera, President/CEO
Dan Juckniess, SVP, Sales & Professional Services
Stacey Herteux, VP, Human Resources
This sound-interactive program breaks away from traditional language instruction. Instead of formal concentration on verb and
basic vocabulary, students meet everyday English with colloquialisms they will hear in real life situations. They reinforce their
knowledge of sentence structure while acquiring the ability to
communicate in daily settings. (For MAC, MS-DOS and Windows). *$65.00*

1688 **Spelling Rules**
Optimum Resource
1 Mathews Drive
Suite 107
Hilton Head Island, SC 29926- 3765
843-689-8000
FAX: 843-689-8008
info@stickybear.com
www.stickybear.com

Richard Hefter, President
A curriculum based, easy-to-use program that provides students
with the practice they need to build strong spelling skills. Concepts discussed include plurals, compounds, i-before-e, capital-
ization, and more. Grades 3 to 9. Bilingual. *$59.95*

1689 **Start-to-Finish Library**
Don Johnston
26799 West Commerce Drive
Volo, IL 60073
847-740-0749
800-999-4660
FAX: 847-740-7326
info@donjohnston.com
www.donjohnston.com

Don Johnston, Founder
Ruth Ziolkowski, President
Kevin Johnston, Director of Product Design
Offers struggling readers a wide selection of engaging narrative
chapter books written at two readability levels (2-3rd and 4-5th
grade) and delivered in three media formats. Professionally-nar-
rated audio and computer supports help scaffold reading to ensure success. *$79.00*

1690 **Start-to-Finish Literacy Starters**
Don Johnston
26799 West Commerce Drive
Volo, IL 60073
847-740-0749
800-999-4660
FAX: 847-740-7326
info@donjohnston.com
www.donjohnston.com

Don Johnston, Founder
Ruth Ziolkowski, President
Kevin Johnston, Director of Product Design
A reading series intended for students with multiple disabilities
who are in 3-12th grade, but reading at a beginning level. Dr. Karen Erickson developed this series, which combines switch-accessible software with three types of text. *$79.00*

1691 **Stickybear Reading Comprehension**
Optimum Resource
1 Mathews Drive
Suite 107
Hilton Head Island, SC 29926- 3765
843-689-8000
FAX: 843-689-8008
info@stickybear.com
www.stickybear.com

Richard Hefter, President
This multi-level reading comprehension program helps children
improve reading skills with 30 high-interest stories and question
sets created by the Weekly Reader editors. Children learn to recognize main ideas, define sequence, using context to identify
words, and more. Grades 2 to 4. Bilingual. *$59.95*

1692 Stickybear Reading Fun Park
Optimum Resource
1 Mathews Drive
Suite 107
Hilton Head Island, SC 29926- 3765   843-689-8000
FAX: 843-689-8008
info@stickybear.com
www.stickybear.com

Richard Hefter, President
Children discover and practice critical reading skills as the Stickybear family guides users through unique, action-packed activities, each with multiple levels of difficulty and skills that address both the auditory and visual needs of budding readers. Pre-K through 3rd grade. *$59.95*

1693 Stickybear Reading Room Deluxe
Optimum Resource
1 Mathews Drive
Suite 107
Hilton Head Island, SC 29926- 3765   843-689-8000
FAX: 843-689-8008
www.stickybear.com

Richard Hefter, President
Children build vocabulary and reading comprehension skills using hundreds of word/picture sets and thousands of put-together sentence parts. K-3rd grade. Bilingual, English/Spanish. *$59.95*

1694 Stickybear Spelling
Optimum Resource
1 Mathews Drive
Suite 107
Hilton Head Island, SC 29926- 3765   843-689-8000
FAX: 843-689-8008
www.stickybear.com

Richard Hefter, President
Children discover and practice critical spelling skills as they work with three unique action-packed activities, each with four graded levels of difficulty. The program is open-ended and teachers may add, change and modify the word lists for each individual. Stickybear Spelling contains more than 2000 recorded words. Levels may be set to allow students of different ages or abilities to compete effectively. Grades 2 through 4. *$59.95*

1695 Tomorrow's Promise: Language Arts
Compass Learning
13500 Evening Creek Drive North
Suite 600
San Diego, CA 92128   858-668-2586
866-475-0317
FAX: 858-408-2903
info@bridgepointeducation.com
www.bridgepointeducation.com
Andrew S. Clark, Founder, Chief Executive Officer
Diane Thompson, SVP, General Counsel
Charlene Dackerman, SVP, Human Resources
You'll strengthen students' grammar, usage and vocabulary skills and promote higher order thinking skills with this comprehensive Language Arts curriculum. It utilizes cross-curricular, thematic instruction engaging multimedia learning exercises that encourage writing, speaking and listening proficiency. Promotes higher order thinking skills. *$279.95*

1696 Tomorrow's Promise: Reading
Compass Learning
203 Colorado Street
Austin, TX 78701-3922   512-478-9600
800-678-1412
866-586-7387
FAX: 619-622-7873
www.compasslearning.com
Eric Loeffel, President, CEO
Tammy Deal, VP, Human Resources
Eric Wasser, VP, Sales
This multimedia curriculum balances thematic, interactive exploration with core skills development, increasing your students' early reading proficiency, building a solid literacy foundation and fostering a lifelong love for reading. *$279.95*

1697 Tomorrow's Promise: Spelling
Compass Learning
203 Colorado Street
Austin, TX 78701-3922   512-478-9600
800-678-1412
866-586-7387
FAX: 619-622-7873
www.compasslearning.com
Eric Loeffel, President, CEO
Tammy Deal, VP, Human Resources
Eric Wasser, VP, Sales
Lovable characters and engaging multimedia effects put young students on a fast-track to early spelling proficiency with fourteen activities and three games. A full year's instruction on each CD includes 30 world lists per grade, in story context, or create word lists to suit your needs. This program addresses students' multiple learning styles and rewards students as they progress through each stage of spelling skill acquisition. *$99.95*

1698 Vocabulary Development
Optimum Resource
1 Mathews Drive
Suite 107
Hilton Head Island, SC 29926- 3765   843-689-8000
FAX: 843-689-8008
www.stickybear.com

Richard Hefter, President
A featured program in the middle school series. Vocabulary Development is designed to help students increase vocabulary as they strengthen reading skills. Students relate their current knowledge of vocabulary to the context in which they discover an unfamiliar word. Utilizing a variety of contextual aids, this program illustrates synonyms, antonyms, prefixes, suffixes, homophones, multiple meanings and context clues, allowing students to apply experience and context. *$59.95*

1699 Whoops
Cornucopia Software
P.O.Box 6111
Albany, CA 94706   510-528-7000
supportstaff@practicemagic.com
www.practicemagic.com

Christina Morua, Manager
Checks spelling three ways. It checks words as they are typed, it checks an entire screen and highlights the errors and it reads ASCII text files from a disk and lists errors.

Software: Vocational

1700 Films Media Group
Infobase Publishing
132 W 31st St, 17th Floor
New York, NY 10001   800-322-8755
FAX: 800-678-3633
custserv@factsonfile.com
www.infobaselearning.com
Melinda Gallo, Senior Account Executive
Educational publisher of DVD programming for schools and libraries. *$64.86*
ISBN 0-927368-59-5

1701 Functional Literacy System
Conover Company
4 Brookwood Court
Appleton, WI 54914   920-231-4667
800-933-1933
FAX: 800-933-1943
support@conovercompany.com
www.conovercompany.com
Terry Schmitz, Founder and Owner
Mike , Vice President of Operations
Art Janowiak, Vice President of Sales
Assessment and skill building for basic functional literacy. This multimedia software program is adult in format and uses live action video taken in actual community settings to help learners become more capable of functioning independently. Twenty different programs are currently available. *$99.00*

1702 Learning Activity Packets
4 Brookwood Court
Appleton, WI 54914   920-231-4667
                                 800-933-1933
                            FAX: 800-933-1943
                    support@conovercompany.com
                         www.conovercompany.com
Terry Schmitz, Founder and Owner
Mike , Vice President of Operations
Art Janowiak, Vice President of Sales
Demonstrates how basic academic skills relate to 30 major career areas. LAPs provide valuable diagnostics in applied academic applications and demonstrates to users the importance of academics as they relate to the workplace. Software. *$99.00*

1703 Microcomputer Evaluation of Careers & Academics (MECA)
Conover Company
4 Brookwood Court
Appleton, WI 54914   920-231-4667
                                 800-933-1933
                            FAX: 800-933-1943
                    support@conovercompany.com
                         www.conovercompany.com
Terry Schmitz, Founder and Owner
Mike , Vice President of Operations
Art Janowiak, Vice President of Sales
A cost-effective, technology-based, career development system which provides users with opportunities to get their hands dirty. The MECA system utilizes work simulations and is built around common occupational clusters. Each cluster, or career area, consists of hands-on WORK SAMPLES which provide a variety of career exploration and assessment experiences, linked to LEARNING ACTIVITY PACKETS, which integrate basic academic skills into the career planning and placement process. $580-$1,070.

1704 OASYS
Vertek
12835 Bellevue-Redmond Road
Suite 310
Bellevue, WA 98005   425-455-9921
                                 800-220-4409
                            FAX: 425-454-7264
Debra Callahan, Sales Representative, Northern California
Tim Whitney, Sales Representative, Ohio, Michigan
Beverly Duncan, Sales Representative, Florida
A software system that matches a person's skills and abilities to occupations and employers.

1705 Reading in the Workplace
Educational Activities Software
5600 West 83rd Street
Suite 300, 8200 Tower
Bloomington, MN 55437-585   888-351-4199
                                 800-447-5286
                            FAX: 239-225-9299
                         info@edmentum.com
                         www.edmentum.com
Vin Riera, President/CEO
Dan Juckniess, SVP, Sales & Professional Services
Stacey Herteux, VP, Human Resources
A job-based, reading software program using real-life problems and solutions to capture students' attention and improve their vocabulary and comprehension skills. Units include: automotive, clerical, health care and construction. *$295.00*

1706 Stickybear Typing
Optimum Resource
1 Mathews Drive
Suite 107
Hilton Head Island, SC 29926- 3765   843-689-8000
                                FAX: 843-689-8008
                           www.stickybear.com
Richard Hefter, President
The award winning Stickybear Typing program allows users to sharpen typing skills and achieve keyboard mastery with three engaging and amusing multi-level activities. *$59.95*

1707 Work-Related Vocational Assessment Systems: Computer Based
Valpar International
P.O.Box 5767
Tucson, AZ 85703-767   262-797-0840
                                 800-633-3321
                            FAX: 262-797-8488
                         sales@valparint.com
                         www.valparint.com
Neal Gunderson, President
Criterion-referenced to Department of Labor standards. Evaluate academic levels for reading, spelling, math and language, interests, personalities, cognitive and physical aptitudes.

1708 Workplace Skills: Learning How to Function on the Job
Programming Concepts
8700 Shoal Creek Boulevard
Austin, TX 78757-6897   512-451-3246
                                 800-897-3202
                            FAX: 800-397-7633
                         general@proedinc.com
                         www.proedinc.com
Jeff McLane, Founder
Lee Wilson, President and CEO
Randy Pennington, Executive VP
Offers parents and educators a functional means by which to discuss all aspects of finding and keeping a job. *$49.95*

Word Processors

1709 Co:Writer: Talking Word Processor
Don Johnston
26799 West Commerce Drive
Volo, IL 60073   847-740-0749
                                 800-999-4660
                            FAX: 847-740-7326
                         info@donjohnston.com
                         www.donjohnston.com
Don Johnston, Founder
Ruth Ziolkowski, President
Kevin Johnston, Director of Product Design
User-friendly talking word processor provides multi-sensory learning and positive reinforcements for writers of all ages and ability levels.

1710 DARCI
Wes Test Engineering Corporation
810 Shepard Lane
Farmington, UT 84025   801-451-9191
                            FAX: 801-451-9393
                                 westest.com
Robert Lessmann, President
James Lynds
Provides transparent access to all computer functions by replacing the computer's keyboard with a smart joystick. *$975.00*

1711 Eye Relief Word Processing Software
SkiSoft Publishing Corporation
P.O.Box 364
Lexington, MA 02420-4   781-863-1876
                                 www.skisoft.com
Ken Skier, President
Cynthia Skier, CFO
Large-type word processing program for visually-impaired PC users. *$295.00*

1712 IntelliTalk
Intelli Tools
24 Prime Parkway
Natick, MA 01760   707-773-2000
                                 800-547-6747
                            FAX: 707-773-2001
                    customerservice@cambiumtech.com
Beth Davis, Director Sales Operations
Lori Castle, Supervisor
Arjan Khalsa, CEO
Talking word-processing program available for MacIntosh, Apple IIe, IBM compatible and Windows computers. *$39.95*

1713   **Large Type**
P.O.Box T
Hewitt, NJ 07421-2088   973-853-6585
                                                   800-736-2216
                                              FAX: 928-832-2894
                                               www.angelfire.com

Don Selwyn, Vice President
Rev. Tom Schwanda, President & Chairman
Robt. Fondiller, Ph.D., P.E, Vice President
Display enlargement programs for visually impaired users. Consist of a variety of programs for different needs, ranging from basic to full-featured.

1714   **Pegasus LITE**
Words+
Ste 109
42505 10th St W
Lancaster, CA 93534-7059   661-723-6523
                                                   800-869-8521
                                              FAX: 661-723-2114
                                            info@words-plus.com

Phil Lawrence, VP
Provides all of the strategies currently being used in AAC, from dynamic display color pictographic language, to dual-word prediction text language, in a single system. *$6995.00*

1715   **Up and Running**
Intelli Tools
24 Prime Parkway
Natick, MA 01760   707-773-2000
                                                   800-547-6747
                                              FAX: 707-773-2001
                              customerservice@cambiumtech.com

Beth Davis, Director Sales Operations
Lori Castle, Supervisor
Arjan Khalsa, CEO
Instantly use hundreds of popular commercial software programs with this custom collection of setups and overlays. *$69.95*

Conferences & Shows

General

1716 AACRC Annual Conference
Association of Children's Residential Centers
648 N Plankinton Ave.
Suite 245
Milwaukee, WI 53203   414-403-1565
                                                       877-332-2272
                                          info@togetherthevoice.org
                                                togetherthevoice.org
Kari Sisson, Executive Director
Amanda Prange, Training Coordinator
Lisette Burton, Chief Policy & Practice Advisor
August

1717 AADB National Conference
American Association of the Deaf-Blind
248 Rainbow Drive
Suite 14864
Livingston, TX 77399-2048   aadb-info@aadb.org
                                                       www.aadb.org
Rene Pellerin, President
A week of general meetings, workshops, tours and evening recreational activities.

1718 AAIDD Annual Meeting
American Assn on Intellecutal/Devel. Disabilities
8403 Colesville Rd.
Suite 900
Silver Spring, MD 20910   202-387-1968
                                               FAX: 202-387-2193
                                                 maria@aaidd.org
                                                        aaidd.org
Maria Alfaro, Senior Manager, Meetings & Website
This annual meeting offers workshops, symposia, multiperspective sessions, and social events over four days.
June

1719 AAO Annual Meeting
American Academy Of Opthamology
655 Beach St.
San Francisco, CA 94109-1336   415-561-8500
                                               FAX: 415-561-8533
                                        www.aao.org/annual-meeting
David W. Parke II, Chief Executive Officer
Debra Rosencrance, VP, Meetings & Events
Offers the most comprehensive program with more than 2000 scientific presentations and six subspecialty day programs.
October/November

1720 ACA Annual Conference
American Counseling Association
P.O. Vox 31110
Alexandria, VA 22310-9998   800-347-6647
                                               FAX: 800-473-2329
                                        www.counseling.org/conference
Shawn E. Boynes, Chief Executive Officer
Promotes the development of professional counselors, advances the counseling profession, and uses the profession and practice of counseling to promote respect for human dignity and diversity.
March/April

1721 ADA Annual Scientific Sessions
American Diabetes Association
2451 Crystal Dr.
Suite 900
Arlington, VA 22201   800-342-2383
                                             askada@diabetes.org
                                                 www.diabetes.org
Tracey D. Brown, Chief Executive Officer
Linda Cann, SVP, Professional Services
Brings together physicians, scientists and other health care professionals from around the world to learn about the latest advances in basic and clinical science for diabetes.

1722 AER Annual International Conference
Assoc. for Educ. & Rehab of the Blind/Vis. Imp.
5680 King Centre Dr.
Suite 600
Alexandria, VA 22315   703-671-4500
                                               FAX: 703-671-6391
                                          conference@aerbvi.org
                                                   www.aerbvi.org
Neva Fairchild, President
Dedicated to rendering support and assistance to the professionals who work in all phases of education and rehabilitation of blind and visually impaired children and adults.
July

1723 AG Bell Global Listening and Spoken Language Symposium
Alexander Graham Bell Association
3417 Volta Pl., NW
Washington, DC 20007   202-337-5220
                                               FAX: 202-337-8314
                                               TTY:202-337-5221
                                                 info@agbell.org
                                            agbellsymposium.com
Emilio Alonso-Mendoza, Chief Executive Officer
A meeting of professionals who serve those who are deaf and hard of hearing.
June/July

1724 APSE National Conference
APSE
7361 Calhoun Place
Suite 680
Rockville, MD 20855   301-279-0060
                                               FAX: 301-279-0075
                                                  info@apse.org
                                                    www.apse.org
Erica Belois-Pacer, Director, Professional Development
Julie Christensen, Director, Policy & Advocacy
Sarah Manning, Business Operations Manager
A major conference on Supported Employment. The conference includes sessions presented by nationally recognized leaders in the field. Conference attendees come from all 50 states, Canada and several foreign countries and include professionals in supported employment, occupational therapy, rehabilitation technology and other related fields.
July

1725 ASHA Convention
American Speech-Language-Hearing Association
2200 Research Blvd.
Rockville, MD 20850-3289   301-296-5700
                                                    800-638-8255
                                               FAX: 301-296-8580
                                             convention@asha.org
                                                convention.asha.org
Arlene A. Pietranton, Chief Executive Officer
Craig E. Coleman, VP, Planning
Exhibits by companies specializing in alternative and augmentative communication products, publishers, software and hardware companies, and hearing aid testing equipment manufacturers. Speech-Language Pathologists are professionals who identify, assess, and treat speech and language problems. Audiologists are hearing health care professionals who specialize in preventing, identifying and assessing hearing disorders as well as providing audiologic treatment including hearing aids and more.
November

1726 ASIA Annual Scientific Meeting
American Spinal Injury Association
9702 Gayton Rd.
Suite 306
Richmond, VA 23238   877-274-2724
                                        asia.office@asia-spinalinjury.org
                                           www.asia-spinalinjury.org
Patty Duncan, Executive Director
Carolyn Moffatt, Association Manager
Kim Ruff, Administrative Assistant

Professional association for physicians and other health professionals working in all aspects of spinal cord injury. Also holds an annual scientific that surveys the latest advancements in the field.
May

1727 ATIA Conference
Assistive Technology Industry Association
330 N Wabash Ave.
Suite 2000
Chicago, IL 60611-4267   312-321-5172
                                                877-687-2842
                                          FAX: 312-673-6659
                                                info@atia.org
                                                 www.atia.org

David Dikter, Chief Executive Officer
Caroline Van Howe, Chief Operating Officer
Becky Williams, Manager, Online Education Programs
The ATIA Conference is the largest international conference showcasing excellence in assistive technology.

1728 Abilities Expo
299 N Euclid Ave.
2nd Floor
Pasadena, CA 91101   323-363-2099
                                             info@abilities.com
                                                 abilities.com

David Korse, President & CEO
Caryn Bates, Director, Operations
Abilities Expo is a national event for people with disabilities, their families, caregivers, and healthcare professionals. Meets in Phoenix, Dallas, Chicago, Los Angeles, Miami, Houston, New York, and Toronto.

1729 American Academy for Cerebral Palsy and Developmental Medicine Annual Conference
555 East Wells
Suite 1100
Milwaukee, WI 53202   414-918-3014
                                          FAX: 414-276-2146
                                             info@aacpdm.org
                                               www.aacpdm.org

Tamara Wagester, Executive Director
Erin Trimmer, Senior Meetings Manager
The Annual Meeting is a 3-day event, held in the Fall, designed to provide targeted opportunities for dissemination of information in the basic sciences, prevention, diagnosis, treatment, and technical advances as applied to persons with cerebral palsy and development disorders.
September

1730 American Academy of Audiology Conference
American Academy of Audiology
11480 Commerce Park Dr.
Suite 220
Reston, VA 20191   703-790-8466
                                          FAX: 703-790-8631
                                        infoaud@audiology.org
                                               www.audiology.org

Patrick E. Gallagher, Executive Director
Kathryn Werner, Chief Operating Officer
Amy Miedema, VP, Communications & Membership
The American Academy of Audiology is the world's largest professional organization for audiologists. The Academy is dedicated to providing quality hearing care services through professional development, education, research, and increased public awareness of hearing and balance disorders.
March-April

1731 American Academy of Environmental Medicine Annual Conference
717 Kreutzberg Rd.
Boerne, TX 78006   316-684-5500
                                          FAX: 888-411-1206
                                              www.aaemonline.org

Diego Saporta, President
Barry Smeltzer, Executive Director
Renee Grandi, Secretary
The Academy is an association of physicians and other professionals engaged in investigating and coming up with preventive

strategies for medical care relating to environmentally triggered illnesses.
November 2nd-5th

1732 American Board of Disability Analysts Annual Conference
1483 N. Mt. Juliet Rd.
Suite 175
Nashville, TN 37122   629-255-0870
                                          FAX: 615-296-9980
                                            office@eventsm3.com
                                          www.americandisability.org
Bi-annual conference held for members to meet and discuss current events and attend seminars.

1733 Annual Conference on Dyslexia and Related Learning Disabilities
New York Branch International Dyslexia Association
1550 Deer Park Ave.
Suite C
Long Island, NY 11729   631-261-7441
                                               www.lidyslexia.org

Concetta Russo, President
Caryl Deiches, Vice President
Carolyn McIntyre, Secretary
The International Dyslexia Association (IDA) is an organization focused on the complex issues of dyslexia and related language-based learning disabilities which make it difficult to learn to read and write.
March

1734 Annual TASH Conference
TASH
1825 K Street NW
Suite 1250
Washington, DC 20006-1202   202-817-3264
                                          FAX: 202-999-4722
                                                info@tash.org
                                           www.tash.org/conferences

Michael Brogioli, Executive Director
DeVonne Parks, Director, Membership & Meetings
Donald Taylor, Manager, Membership & Communications
Each year, the TASH Conference connects attendees to information and resources, facilitates connections between stakeholders within the disability movement, and helps attendees reignite their passion for an inclusive world.
December

1735 Arc National Convention, The
The Arc
1825 K St., NW
Suite 1200
Washington, DC 20006   202-534-3700
                                                800-433-5255
                                          FAX: 202-534-3731
                                             convention.thearc.org

Peter Berns, Chief Executive Officer
Tanisha Forte, Director, Conference & Events
Experts and professionals gather from all over the world share best practices, struggles, successes and hopes for the future, and continue the conversation about protecting and promoting the human and civil rights for individuals with intellectual and developmental disabilities.
October

1736 Attention Deficit Disorders Association, Southern Region: Annual Conference
12345 Jones Rd.
Suite 287-7
Houston, TX 77070   281-897-0982
                                          FAX: 281-894-6883
                                          addaoffice@sbcglobal.net
                                                www.adda-sr.org

Carlye Read, President
Barbara Beard, Vice President
Judy German, Treasurer
The Attention Deficit Disorders Association provides a resource network, supports individuals impacted by ADHHD and related

condition and to advocate for the development of community resources.
February

1737 Blind Children's Center Annual Meeting
Blind Children's Center
4120 Marathon St.
Los Angeles, CA 90029-3584
323-664-2153
info@blindchildrenscenter.org
www.blindchildrenscenter.org
Sarah E. Orth, CEO
Fernanda Armenta-Schmitt, Director, Education & Family Services
A family-centered agency which serves children with visual impairments from birth to school-age. The center-based and home-based services help the children to acquire skills and build their independence. The Center utilizes its expertise and experience to serve families and professionals worldwide through support services, education and research.
September

1738 Blinded Veterans Association National Convention
Blinded Veterans Association
1101 King St.
Suite 300
Alexandria, VA 22314
800-669-7079
bva@bva.org
www.bva.org
Donald D. Overton, Jr., Executive Director
The convention has three functions: to serve as a platform for Association business, to educate blinded veterans about the resources available to them, and to provide a means whereby blinded veterans can support one another.
August

1739 CQL Accreditation
Council on Quality and Leadership
100 West Rd.
Suite 300
Towson, MD 21204
410-275-0488
info@thecouncil.org
www.c-q-l.org/accreditation
Mary Kay Rizzolo, President & CEO
Katherine Dunbar, VP, Accreditation
CQL Accreditation is a leader in working with human service organizations and systems to continuously define, measure and improve quality of life and quality of services.

1740 Centers of Excellence Leadership Conference
National Parkinson Foundation
200 SE 1st St.
Suite 800
Miami, FL 33131
800-473-4636
contact@parkinson.org
parkinson.org
John L. Lehr, CEO
James Beck, VP & Chief Scientific Officer
Yashnahia Cortorreal, VP & Chief Human Resources & Administration Pfficer
The mission of the National Parkinson Foundation is to make life better for people affected by Parkinson's through expert care, research, and education. The goal of the conference is to convene the medical directors, center coordinators and other leaders from the Centers of Excellence to discuss the latest research and best practices in care delivery and to highlight NPF's programs.
July/August

1741 Closing the Gap's Annual Conference
P.O. Box 68
Henderson, MN 56044
507-248-3294
FAX: 507-248-3810
www.closingthegap.com
Dolores Hagen, Co-Founder
Budd Hagen, Co-Founder
Topics cover a broad spectrum of technology as it is being applied to all disabilities and age groups in education, rehabilitation, vocation and independent living. People with disabilities, special educators, rehabilitation professionals, administrators, service/care providers, personnel managers, government officials,

and hardware/software developers share their experiences and insights at this significant networking experience.
October/November

1742 Conference of the Association on Higher Education & Disability (AHEAD)
8015 West Kenton Circle
Suite 230
Huntersville, NC 28078
704-947-7779
FAX: 704-948-7779
www.ahead.org
Katy Washington, President
Stephan Smith, Executive Director
Howard Kramer, Conference Director
An annual conference focused on aiding and meeting the needs of persons with disabilities attending higher education institutions.

1743 Council for Exceptional Children Annual Convention and Expo
3100 Clarendon Blvd.
Suite 600
Arlington, VA 22201-5332
888-232-7733
TTY:866-915-5000
service@cec.sped.org
cecconvention.org
Chad Rummel, Executive Director
Sharon Rodriguez, Governance & Executive Services Coordinator
Works to improve the educational success of children with disabilities and/or gifts and talents.
March/April

1744 Disability Matters
Springboard Consulting
4740 S Ocean Blvd.
Suite 505
Highland Beach, FL 33487
973-813-7260
FAX: 973-813-7261
info@consultspringboard.com
www.consultspringboard.com
Nadine Vogel, Chief Executive Officer
Elizabeth Ladu, Chief Financial Officer
Ivette Lopez, Chief of Staff
Features outstanding content as delivered by leading disability experts from corporations, academia, national non-profits and governments across North America. Conferences also take place in Europe and Asia-Pacific.

1745 Eye Bank Association of America Annual Meeting
Eye Bank Association of America
1101 17th St., NW
Suite 400
Washington, DC 20036
202-775-4999
FAX: 202-429-6036
www.restoresight.org
Kevin Corcoran, CAE, President & CEO
Genevieve Casaceli, Education & Programs Manager
Bernie Dellario, Director, Finance
A four day program, which includes a series of presentations in administrative, hospital development, scientific and technical fields that are relative to eye banking.
June

1746 IDF National Conference
Immune Deficiency Foundation
7550 Teague Road
Suite 220
Hanover, MD 21076
800-296-4433
FAX: 410-321-9165
info@primaryimmune.org
primaryimmune.org
Jorey Berry, President & Chief Executive Officer
Sarah Rose, Chief Financial Officer
Tammy C. Black, Chief Communications Officer
The four-day conference brings together primary immunodeficiency patients, caregivers and clinicians to participate in youth programs, panel discussions, educational sessions and networking opportunities.
June

1747 Lowe Syndrome Conference
Lowe Syndrome Association
P.O. Box 417
Chicago Ridge, IL 60415   216-630-7723
                                    www.lowesyndrome.org
Lisa Waldbaum, President
Jane Gallery, Treasurer
Tiffany Johnson, Director, Medical & Scientific Affairs
An international conference held approximately every two years
where family, friends, medical and other professionals gather to
exchange ideas and information.
June

1748 NACDD Annual Conference
1825 K St. NW
Suite 600
Washington, DC 20006   202-506-5813
                                    info@nacdd.org
                                    www.nacdd.org
Donna A. Meltzer, Chief Executive Officer
Rafael Rolon-Muñiz, Communications & Program Coordinator
Erin Prangley, Director, Public Policy
NACDD is the national association for the 56 State and Territorial
Councils on Developmental Disabilities (DD Councils) which re-
ceive federal funding to support programs that promote self-de-
termination, integration, and inclusion for all Americans with
developmental disabilities.
July

1749 NADR Conference
National Association of Disability Representatives
1305 W 11th St.
Suite 222
Houston, TX 77008   202-822-2155
                                    admin@nadr.org
                                    www.nadr.org
Michael Wener, President
Christopher Mazzulli, Vice President
Kelly Blad, Secretary
NADR is an organization of Professional Social Security Claim-
ants Representatives that focus on issues involving policies to
protect the interest of people with disabilities. NADR conducts
annual conventions open to members and non-members with edu-
cational seminars to keep practitioners up to date on Social Security rulings, regulatory changes, and practice improvements.
April

1750 NASW-NYS Chapter
NASW
188 Washington Ave.
Albany, NY 12210   518-463-4741
                                    800-724-6279
                                    FAX: 518-463-6446
                                    info.naswnys@socialworkers.org
                                    www.naswnys.org
Samantha Fletcher, Executive Director
Marcia Schwartzman Levy, President
Workshops, keynote speakers, and presentations offered at this
event will develop and enhance practice skills and knowledge in
the provision of quality mental health and community services.
March

1751 NEXT Conference & Exposition
American Physical Therapy Association
1111 North Fairfax St.
Alexandria, VA 22314-1488   703-684-2782
                                    800-999-2782
                                    FAX: 703-706-8536
                                    consumer@apta.org
                                    apta.org
Sharon L. Dunn, President
Matthew R. Hyland, Vice President
Kip Schick, Secretary
The American Physical Therapy Association is a national profes-
sional organization sponsors this annual conference. The goal is
to foster advancements in physical therapy practice, research,
and education.

**1752 National Association for the Dually Diagnosed
Conferences**
12 Hurley Ave.
Kingston, NY 12401   845-331-4336
                                    info@thenadd.org
                                    www.thenadd.org
Jeanne M. Farr, CEO
Michelle Jordan, Office Manager
Jeffrey Schmunk, Operations Manager
NADD is a non-for-profit membership organization designed to
promote awareness of, and services for, individuals who have
co-occuring intellectual disability and mental illness. NADD
provides training, consultation services, and publishes journals
and books. it also offers two conferences per year.

1753 National Council on the Aging Conference
251 18th St. S.
Suite 500
Arlington, VA 22202   571-527-3900
                                    membership@ncoa.org
                                    www.ncoa.org
James Knickman, Interim President & CEO
Donna Whitt, Senior Vice President, Chief Financial Officer
Kristin Kiefer, Chief Administrative Officer
Offers ideas and programs to increase program and administra-
tive skills through NCOA's professional development tracks and
offering of continuing education units.
May

1754 PVA Summit & Expo
Paralyzed Veterans of America
801 18th St. NW
Washington, DC 20006-3517   800-424-8200
                                    TTY:800-795-4327
                                    summit@pva.org
                                    summitpva.org
Charles Brown, National President
Marcus Murray, National Secretary
Carl Blake, Executive Director
The annual 3-day medical conference brings together leaders
from medicine, health care, policy, and government to explore
and implement holistic strategies to strengthen the continuum of
care for patients with spinal cord injuries or related diseases.

1755 PWSA (USA) Conference
Prader-Willi Alliance Of New York
244 5th Ave.
Suite D-110
New York, NY 10001   800-442-1655
                                    alliance@prader-willi.org
                                    www.prader-willi.org/conference
Amy McDougall, President
Barbara McManus, Treasurer
Brian Burgin, 1st Vice President
Through conferences, publications, electronic communication
and networking (parent-to-parent, parent-to professional, and
professional-to-professional), the Prader-Willi Alliance pro-
vides a valuable resource for individuals and families sharing the
same concerns.
July

**1756 Pacific Rim International Conference on Disability And
Diversity**
Center on Disability Studies
1410 Lower Campus Rd.
Unit 171F
Honolulu, HI 96822   808-956-8816
                                    prinfo@hawaii.edu
                                    pacrim.coe.hawaii.edu
Patricia Morrissey, Director of the Center on Disability
The Pacific Rim International Conference on Disability and Di-
versity encourages and respects voices from diverse perspective
across numerous areas including voices from persons represent-
ing all disability areas, and experiences of family members and
supporters across all disability and diversity areas.

1757   **RESNA Annual Conference**
Rehab Engineering & Assistive Tech. North America
2001 K Street NW
3rd Floor North
Washington, DC 20006   202-367-1121
                                    FAX: 202-367-2121
                                    info@resna.org
                                    www.resna.org

Maureen Linden, President
Andrea Van Hook, Interim Executive Director
Sponsored by a multidisciplinary association for the advancement of rehabilitation and assistive technologies, this annual conference brings together a large number of rehabilitation professionals, products and services from around the world and has something to offer for both professionals and consumers. The conference provides an informative and thought provoking forum for anyone with interests in rehabilitation technology.
June

1758   **Rehabilitation International World Congress**
866 United Nations Plaza
Office 422
New York, NY 10017   212-420-1500
                                    FAX: 212-505-0871
                                    info@riglobal.org
                                    www.riglobal.org

Teuta Rexhepi, Secretary General
Zhang Haidi, President
RI is a global network of people with disabilities, service providers, researchers, government agencies, and advocates protecting and promoting the rights and inclusion of people with disabilities.
Quadrennial

1759   **Southwest Conference On Disability**
University of New Mexico
2300 Menaul Blvd., NE
Albuquerque, NM 87107   505-272-3000
                                    FAX: 505-272-2014
           HSC-swdisabilityconference@salud.unm.edu
               www.cdd.unm.edu/apps/SWConf/pre sentation
The Center for Development and Disability (CDD), is New Mexico's University Center for Excellence in Developmental Disabilities Education, Research and Service that respond to the needs of individuals with developmental disabilities and their families.

1760   **Tourette Association of America National Education Conference**
42-40 Bell Blvd.
Suite 205
Bayside, NY 11361   888-486-8738
                                    support@tourette.org
                                    tourette.org

Amanda Talty, President & CEO
This is a biannual conference that includes members of the TS community and their families, educators, TS advocates, physicians, researchers, allied professionals, and TSA staff members. Attendees interact, socialize, share ideas, discuss issues of concern, and learn from experts.
1972

1761   **Young Onset Parkinson Conference**
National Parkinson Foundation & ADPF
200 SE 1st St.
Suite 800
Miami, FL 33131   800-473-4636
                                    FAX: 305-537-9901
                                    contact@parkinson.org
                                    www.parkinson.org

John L. Lehr, President and CEO
James Beck, Vice President, Chief Scientific Officer
Yasnahia Cortorreal, Vice President, Human Resources & Administration
Purpose is to find the cause and cure for Parkinson's Disease and related neurodegenerative disorders through research, education and dissemination of current information to patients, care-givers and families.
Annual

Construction & Architecture

Associations

1762 Adaptive Environments Center
200 Portland Street
Suite 1
Boston, MA 02114   617-695-1225
                              FAX: 617-482-8099
                   info@HumanCenteredDesign.org
                      www.humancentereddesign.org

Ralph Jackson, FAIA, President
Chris Pilkington, Vice President
Nancy Jenner, Treasurer
Develops educational programs and materials on universal design, Americans with Disabilities Act, home adaptation, and more. Central Adaptive Environments publication list also available.

1763 American Institute of Architects
1735 New York Ave. NW
Washington, DC 20006-5292   800-242-3837
                        memberservices@aia.org
                                 www.aia.org

Robert A. Ivy, FAIA, EVP/Chief Executive Officer
Abigail Warnecke Gorman, Chief of Staff
Sarah Dodge, SVP, Advocacy & Relationships
The organization, with 200 chapters worldwide and 95,000 members, advocates for the value of architecture and ethical standards in the profession.

1764 American Society of Landscape Architects
636 Eye St. NW
Washington, DC 20001-3736   202-898-2444
                                     888-999-2752
                              FAX: 202-898-1185
                                 info@asla.org
                                  www.asla.org

Roxanne Blackwell, Co-Interim EVP & CEO
Curt Millay, Co-Interim EVP & CEO
Susan Cahill-Aylward, Director, Information & Professional Practice
Professional organization for landscape architects in the U.S., with 15,000 members.

1765 Building Owners and Managers Association International
1101 15th St., NW
Suite 800
Washington, DC 20005   202-326-6300
                              FAX: 202-326-6377
                                info@boma.org
                                 www.boma.org

Henry Chamberlain, President & COO
Patricia Areno, Senior Vice President
Luci Vallejo, Director, Executive Services
Conducts seminars nationwide and publishes resource guidebooks for building owners and managers on ADA requirements for commercial facilities and places of public accommodation.

1766 Department of Insurance/OSFM
North Carolina Department of Insurance
325 N. Salisbury St.
Raleigh, NC 27603   919-647-0014
                              FAX: 919-715-0067
                       tara.barthelmess@ncdoi.gov
Tara Barthelmess, Chief Accessibility Code Consultant
The Chief Accessibility Code Consultant interprets building code accessibility requirements for new and existing buildings undergoing construction or alteration. The position also receives and initiates investigation of accessibility-related complaints within the State of North Carolina whenever possible.

1767 Institute for Human Centered Design
Formerly Adaptive Environments
200 Portland St
Ste 1
Boston, MA 02214   617-695-1225
                              FAX: 617-482-8099
                              TTY:617-695-1225
                   info@humancentereddesign.org
                      humancentereddesign.org

Valerie Fletcher, Executive Director
Gabriela Bonome-Sims, Director, Administration & Finance
Formerly known as Adaptive Environments, the Insititute focuses on collaborating and working with citizens to design communal places to be accessible for all, including those with disabilities.

1768 Mark Elmore Associates Architects
Ste 104
42 East St
Crystal Lake, IL 60014-4400   815-455-7260
                                     800-801-7766
                              FAX: 815-455-2238
                       www.elmore-architects.com

Mark A Elmore, Owner
Architectural designs for accessible residential and commercial buildings. ADA compliance reviews.

1769 National Conference on Building Codes and Standards
505 Huntmar Park Drive
Suite 210
Herndon, VA 20170   703-437-0100
                              FAX: 703-481-3596
                                 www.ncsbcs.org

Cynthia Wilk, President
Robert C. Wible, Executive Director
Debbie Becker, Administrative Assistant
Serves as a forum in the interchange of information and provides technical services, education and training to our members to enhance the public's social and economic well being through safe, durable, affordable, accessible and efficient buildings.

1770 National Council of Architectural Registration Boards (NCARB)
1401 H Street NW
Suite 500
Washington, DC 20006   202-879-0520
                                     ncarb.org

Michael J. Armstrong, Chief Executive Officer
Mary S. de Sousa, Chief Operating Officer
Guillermo Ortiz de Zarate, Chief Innovation & Information Officer
Research service in print and online information. Large collection of books and periodicals on the building/architectural environments.

1771 National Institute of Building Sciences
1090 Vermont Ave. NW
Suite 700
Washington, DC 20005   202-289-7800
                              FAX: 202-289-1092
                                nibs@nibs.org
                                 www.nibs.org

Lakisha Ann Woods, President & CEO
Rebecca Liko, Vice President, Finance & Controller
Sarah Swango, Senior Director, Business Development
The organization supports advances in building science and technology to improve the built environment. The U.S. Congress established it in the the Housing and Community Development Act of 1974.

1772 Overcoming Mobility Barriers International
1022 S 4st St
Omaha, NE 68105   402-342-5731
                              FAX: 402-342-5731

Kay Neil, Executive Director
Members are government officials, service consumers and providers, and other persons interested in removing mobility barriers for elderly, handicapped and disadvantaged persons. Advises and works in conjunction with other groups and government agencies to establish safety standards for special equipment used in retrofitting vehicles and works to retrain drivers in the use of nonconventional driving controls.

1773 PVA Architecture
Paralyzed Veterans of America
801 18th St. NW
Washington, DC 20006-3517
202-416-7645
800-424-8200
TTY:800-795-4327
pvaarchitecture@pva.org
www.pva.org

Charles Brown, National President
Marcus Murray, National Secretary
Carl Blake, Executive Director
Provides architectural consulting services related to accessible designs. Experience includes product design and building codes and standards.

1774 United States Access Board
Ste 1000
1331 F St NW
Washington, DC 20004-1111
202-272-0080
800-872-2253
FAX: 202-272-0081
TTY: 800-993-2822
info@access-board.gov
www.access-board.gov

Lance Robertson, Chair
Gregory S. Fehribach, Vice Chair
Offers information and technical assistance to the public on accessible design under the Americans with Disabilities Act and other laws. Guidance and publications are available free that address access to facilities, transit vehicles and information technology.

Publications & Videos

1775 Access Currents
United States Access Board
1331 F Street, NW
Suite 1000
Washington, DC 20004-1111
202-272-0080
800-872-2253
FAX: 202-272-0081
TTY: 800-993-2822
info@access-board.gov
www.access-board.gov

Lance Robertson, Chair
Gregory S. Fehribach, Vice Chair
Offers information and referrals on architectural accessibility for architects, designers, government agencies, building owners and consumers. A list of free publications is available on request.
bi-monthly

1776 Access Equals Opportunity
Council of B BB s Foundation
3033 Wilson Blvd
Suite 600
Arlington, VA 22201
703-276-0100
www.bbb.org

Beverly Baskin, Senior VP, Chief Mission Officer
Genie Barton, Vice President and Director, Onl
Rodney L. Davis, Senior VP Enterprise Programs
These six Title III compliance guides for existing small businesses offer creative cheap and easy suggestions for complying with the public accommodations section of the ADA. Each guide is industry specific for: retail stores, car sales/service, restaurants/bars, medical offices and fun/fitness centers. They include suggestions for readily achievable removal of architectural barriers; effective communication; and guidance for nondiscriminatory policies or procedures. *$2.50*

1777 Access for All
Hospital Audiences
548 Broadway
3rd Floor
New York, NY 10012
212-575-7676
FAX: 212-575-7669

David Sweeny, Executive Director
Jane Kleinsinger, Director of Operations
Jill Bernard, Marketing & Outreach Manager

Provides physical and program accessibility information for people with disabilities to New York City cultural institutions including theaters, museums, galleries, etc.

1778 Accessible Home of Your Own
Accent Special Publications
Bloomington, IL 61702-700
Raymond C Cheever, Publisher
Betty Garee, Editor
This guide includes 14 articles on the popular subject of how to make a disabled persons home more accessible. *$7.99*
52 pages Paperback 1990
ISBN 0-915708-29-9

1779 Adaptable Housing: A Technical Manual for Implementing Adaptable Dwelling
H U D U SE R
P.O.Box 23268
Washington, DC 20026-3268
202-708-3178
800-245-2691
FAX: 202-708-9981
TTY: 800-927-7589
helpdesk@huduser.org
www.huduser.org

Patrick J. Tewey, Director, Budget, Contracts, and Program Control Division
Jacqueline D Buford, Director, Management and Administrative Services Division
Jean Lin Pao, General Deputy Assistant Secretary
An illustrated manual describing methods for implementing adaptability in housing. *$3.00*

1780 Architect Magazine
Hanley Wood Media Inc.
One Thomas Circle NW
Washington, DC 20003
202-452-0800
etters@architectmagazine.com
www.architectmagazine.com

Ned Cramer, Editor-in-Chief
Grieg O'Brien, Managing Editor
Official journal of the American Institute of Architects

1781 BOMA Magazine
Building Owners & Managers Association
1101 15th St., NW
Suite 800
Washington, DC 20005
202-326-6300
FAX: 202-326-6377
info@boma.org
www.boma.org

Henry Chamberlain, President & COO
Courtney McKay, Vice President, Communications & Marketing
Official magazine of the Building Owners & Managers Association.

1782 Consumer's Guide to Home Adaptation
Institute for Human Centered Design
200 Portland Street
Suite 1
Boston, MA 02114
617-695-1225
FAX: 617-482-8099
TTY:617-695-1225
info@HumanCenteredDesign.org
www.humancentereddesign.org

Valerie Fletcher, Executive Director
Tzesika Iliovits, Project Manager, Inclusive Design Projects
A workbook that enables people with disabilities to plan the modifications necessary to adapt their homes. Describes how to widen doorways, lower countertops, etc. *$12.00*
52 pages Paperback
ISBN 0-970835-80-9

1783 **Design for Acessibility**
National Endowment for the Arts Office
400 7th Street, SW
Washington, DC 20506-0001
202-682-5400
FAX: 202-682-5715
webmgr@arts.gov
arts.gov

Jane Chu, Chairman
Joan Shigekawa, Senior Deputy Chairman
Mike Burke, Chief Information Officer
A handbook for compliance with Section 504 of the Rehabilitation Act of 1973 and the Americans with Disabilities Act of 1990 including technical assistance on making arts programs accessible to staff, performers and audience.
101 pages
ISBN 0-160042-83-6

1784 **Directory of Accessible Building Products**
N AH B Research Center
400 Prince George's Blvd
Upper Marlboro, MD 20774
301-249-4000
800-638-8556
FAX: 301-430-6180
www.homeinnovation.com

Michael Luzier, CEO & President
Michelle Desiderio, Vice President of Innovation Services
Tom Kenney, P.E, Vice President of Engineering & Research
Contains descriptions of more than 200 commercially available products designed for use by people with disabilities and age-related limitations. Paperback. *$5.00*
104 pages Yearly

1785 **Do-Able Renewable Home**
AARP Fulfillment
601 E Street NW
Washington, DC 20049
202-434-3525
888-687-2277
877-342-2277
FAX: 202-434-3443
member@aarp.org
www.aarp.org

John Wider, President, CEO, AARP Services Inc.
Lisa M. Ryerson, President, AARP Foundation
Robert R. Hagans, Jr., Executive Vice President & Chief Financial Officer
Describes how individuals with disabilities can modify their homes for independent living. Room-by-room modifications are accompanied by illustrations.

1786 **ECHO Housing: Recommended Construction and Installation Standards**
601 E Street NW
Washington, DC 20049
202-434-3525
888-687-2277
877-342-2277
FAX: 202-434-3443
member@aarp.org
www.aarp.org

John Wider, President, CEO, AARP Services Inc.
Lisa M. Ryerson, President, AARP Foundation
Robert R. Hagans, Jr., Executive Vice President & Chief Financial Officer
Illustrated design, construction, and installation standards for temporary dwelling units for elderly people on single family residential property.

1787 **Electronic House: Enhanced Lifestyles with Electronics**
Electronic House
111 Speen Street, Suite 200
P.O. Box 989
Framingham, MA 01701-2000
508-663-1500
800-375-8015
FAX: 508-663-1599
eheditorial@ehpub.com
electronichouse.com

Kenneth D. Moyes, President
Karen Bligh, Marketing Director
John Brillon, Web Creative Director
Dedicated to home automation. Featuring both extravagant and affordable smart homes that can be controlled with one touch. EH covers electronic systems that give homeowners more security, entertainment, convenience, and fun. Articles cover whole house control and subsystems like residential lighting, security, home theater, energy management and telecommunications. *$23.95*
84 pages BiMonthly
ISSN 0886-66 3

1788 **Fair Housing Design Guide for Accessibility**
National Council on Multifamily Housing Industry
1201 15th Street NW
Washington, DC 20005
202-266-8200
800-368-5242
FAX: 202-266-8400
www.nahb.com

Kevin Kelly, Chairman of the Board
Tom Woods, First Vice Chairman of the Board
Ed Brady, Second Vice Chairman of the Board
Specifically tailored to address the needs of architects and builders. The book includes a detailed technical analysis of the legislation's impact on multifamily design, highlights potential construction problems, and identifies possible solutions. *$29.95*

1789 **Ideas for Making Your Home Accessible**
Accent Books & Products
P.O.Box 700
Bloomington, IL 61702-0700
309-378-2961
800-787-8444
FAX: 309-378-4420
acmtlvng@aol.com
www.accentonliving.com

Raymond C Cheever, Publisher
Betty Garee, Editor
Offers over 100 pages of tips and ideas to help build or remodel a home. Includes many special devices and where to get them. *$7.50*
94 pages Paperback
ISBN 0-91570 -08-6

1790 **Landscape Architecture Magazine**
American Society of Landscape Architects
636 Eye St. NW
Washington, DC 20001-3736
202-898-2444
888-999-2752
FAX: 202-898-1185
landscapearchitecturemagazine.org

Bradford McKee, Editor
Michael D. O'Brien, Publisher
Official publication of the American Society of Landscape Architects.

1791 **National Institute of Building Sciences**
1090 Vermont Ave. NW
Suite 700
Washington, DC 20005
202-289-7800
FAX: 202-289-1092
nibs@nibs.org
www.nibs.org

Lakisha Ann Woods, President & CEO
Rebecca Liko, Vice President, Finance & Controller
Sarah Swango, Senior Director, Business Development
The organization supports advances in building science and technology to improve the built environment. The U.S. Congress established it in the the Housing and Community Development Act of 1974.

1792 **Removing the Barriers: Accessibility Guidelines and Specifications**
A PP A
1643 Prince Street
Alexandria, VA 22314
703-684-1446
FAX: 703-549-2772
webmaster@appa.org
www.appa.org

John F. Bernhards, Associate Vice President
E. Lander Medlin, Executive VP
Steve Glazner, Director of Knowledge Management

Offers site accessibility, building entrances, doors, interior circulation, restrooms and bathing facilities, drinking fountains and additional resources. *$45.00*
125 pages
ISBN 0-91335 -59-9

1793   Smart Kitchen/How to Design a Comfortable, Safe & Friendly Workplace
Ceres Press
P.O.Box 87
Woodstock, NY 12498-87   845-679-5573
                                   FAX: 845-679-5573
                                      cem620@aol.com
                                    healthyhighways.com

David Goldbeck, Owner
This book provides information about designing kitchens that may be helpful to people with disabilities as well as safe and energy efficient. *$16.95*
132 pages Paperback

1794   United Spinal Association
75-20 Astoria Blvd
Suite 120
East Elmhurst, NY 11370- 1177   718-803-3782
                                        800-444-0120
                                   FAX: 718-803-0414
                                 mkurtz@unitedspinal.org
                                   www.unitedspinal.org

Paul Tobin, President
Maria Kurtz, Executive Assistant
Information on spinal cord injury and laws and regulations concerning people with disabilities, including veterans.
Monthly

1795   Whole Building Design Guide
National Institute of Building Sciences
1090 Vermont Ave. NW
Suite 700
Washington, DC 20005   202-289-7800
                                   FAX: 202-289-1092
                                        nibs@nibs.org
                                       www.wbdg.org

Lakisha Ann Woods, President & CEO
Kristen Petersen, Managing Director, Marketing & Communications
Online portal with access to published materials on integrated whole-building design techniques and technologies, with an emphasis on integrated design and team efforts during planning and programming.

Education

Aids for the Classroom

1796 ACT Assessment Test Preparation Reference Manual
American College Testing Program
P.O. Box 414
Iowa City, IA 52243-0414   319-337-1270
                                  act.org

Marten Roorda, Chief Executive Officer
Suzana Delanghe, Chief Commercial Officer
Lucas Kuhlmann, Chief Technology Officer
This reference manual was developed as a resource for high school teachers and counselors in assisting students with test preparation. Offers accommodation for individuals with disabilities.

1797 AEPS Child Progress Record: For Children Ages Three to Six
Brookes Publishing
PO Box 10624
Baltimore, MD 21285-624   410-337-9580
                                 800-638-3775
                            FAX: 800-638-3775
                 custserv@brookespublishing.com
                     www.brookespublishing.com

Paul Brooks, President
Melissa Behm, Executive VP
George Stamathis, VP and Publisher
This chart helps monitor change by visually displaying current abilities, intervention targets, and child progress. In packages of 30. *$21.00*
8 pages Gate-fold
ISBN 1-557662-51-7

1798 AEPS Curriculum for Three to Six Years
Brookes Publishing
PO Box 10624
Baltimore, MD 21285-0624   410-337-9580
                                  800-638-3775
                             FAX: 410-337-8539
                webmaster@brookespublishing.com
                     www.brookespublishing.com

Paul H. Brookes, Chairman of the Board
Jeffrey D. Brookes, President
George S. Stamathis, VP/Publisher
Used after the AEPS® Test is completed and scored, this developmentally sequenced curriculum allows professionals to match the child's IFSP/IEP goals and objectives with activity-based interventions — beginning with simple skills and moving on to more advanced skills. *$65.00*
304 pages Spiral-bound
ISBN 1-557665-65-6

1799 AEPS Data Recording Forms: For Children Ages Three to Six
Brookes Publishing
PO Box 10624
Baltimore, MD 21285-624   410-337-9580
                                 800-638-3775
                            FAX: 800-638-3775
                 custserv@brookespublishing.com
                        www.readplaylearn.com

Paul Brooks, President
These forms can be used by child development professionals on four separate occasions to pinpoint and then monitor a child's strengths and needs in the six key areas of skill development measured by the AEPS Test. Packages of 10. *$24.00*
36 pages Saddle-stiched
ISBN 1-557662-49-5

1800 AEPS Family Interest Survey
Brookes Publishing
PO Box 10624
Baltimore, MD 21285-624   410-337-9580
                                 800-638-3775
                            FAX: 800-638-3775
                 custserv@brookespublishing.com
                     www.brookespublishing.com

Paul Brooks, President
Tracy Gracy, Educational Sales Manager
This is a 30-item checklist that helps families to identify interests and concerns to address in a child's IEP/IFSP. Comes in packages of 30. *$15.00*
8 pages Saddle-stiched
ISBN 1-557660-98-0

1801 Adaptivemall.com
15 South Second Street
Dolgeville, NY 13329   315-429-7112
                              800-371-2778
                         FAX: 315-429-8862
                  info@adaptivemall.com
                  www.adaptivemall.com

Katie Bergeron Peglow, Chief Operating Officer
Adaptivemall.comr help families find the best equipment to support their children at their highest functioning level.

1802 Advanced Language Tool Kit
School Specialty
625 Mt. Auburn Street, 3rd Floor
PO Box 9031
Cambridge, MA 02139-9031   617-547-6706
                                  800-225-5750
                             FAX: 888-440-2665
              Feedback.EPS@schoolspecialty.com
                      eps.schoolspecialty.com

Rick Holden, President, EPS
Jean S Osman, Co-Author
Paula D Rome, Author
Provides an overview o the structure, organization, and sound units that are needed to develop skills for advanced reading and spelling. The kit contains a teacher's manual and 3 pack of cards, with features similar to the cards in the Language Tool Kit. *$60.00*
ISBN 0-838885-48-9

1803 All Kinds of Minds
School Specialty
625 Mt. Auburn Street, 3rd Floor
PO Box 9031
Cambridge, MA 02139-9031   617-547-6706
                                  800-225-5750
                             FAX: 888-440-2665
              Feedback.EPS@schoolspecialty.com
                      eps.schoolspecialty.com

Rick Holden, President, EPS
Melvin D Levine, Author
A fictitious account of five different students who have learning disabilities. *$33.00*
296 pages
ISBN 0-838820-90-5

1804 American Sign Language Handshape Cards
T J Publishers, Distributor
Ste 206
817 Silver Spring Ave
Silver Spring, MD 20910- 4617   301-585-4440
                                       800-999-1168
                                  FAX: 301-585-5930
                              tjpubinc@aol.com

Angela K Thames, President
Jerald A Murphy, VP
Durable flashcards illustrate basic handshapes, classifiers and the American manual alphabet. An instructional booklet describes games for differing skill levels to improve vocabulary, increase hand and eye coordination, sign recognition and usage. *$16.95*

1805 Asthma Action Cards: Child Care Asthma/Allergy Action Card
Asthma and Allergy Foundation of America
8201 Corporate Drive
Suite 1000
Landover, MD 20785
202-466-7643
800-727-8462
FAX: 202-466-8940
info@aafa.org
www.aafa.org

Tom Flanigan, Chariman
William Mclin, President and CEO
Yolanda Miller, VP and CFO
Includes necessary information a provider needs to care for a young child who has asthma and allergies. The card includes a medication plan, a list of the child's specific signs and symptoms that indicate the child is having trouble breathing, and steps on how to handle an emergency situation.

1806 Asthma Action Cards: Student Asthma Action Card
Asthma and Allergy Foundation of America
1233 20th St NW
Suite 610
Washington, DC 20036-2330
202-833-1700
800-727-8462
FAX: 202-833-2351
info@aafa.org
www.swmlaw.com

Bill Mc Lin, Executive Director
Ben C Hadden, VP Finance & Treasurer
Bill Lin, Executive Director
Tool for communicating school aged children's and teen's asthma managment plan to school personnel. Includes sections for asthma triggers, daily medications, and emergency directions.

1807 Auditory-Verbal Therapy for Parents and Professionals
Alexander Graham Bell Association
3417 Volta Place, NW
Washington, DC 20007
202-337-5220
FAX: 202-337-8314
TTY:202-337-5221
info@agbell.org
www.listeningandspokenlanguage.org
Meredith K. Sugar, Esq. (OH), President
Donald M. Goldberg, Immediate Past President
Ted A. Meyer, M.D., Ph.D. (SC, President-Elect, Secretary, Treasurer
A must-have for hearing health professionals, students entering hearing health fields and parents who want to explore the theory and practices of auditory-verbal therapy. *$54.95*
313 pages Paperback

1808 Autism Community Store
7800 E. Iliff Ave.
Suite J
Denver, CO 80231
303-309-3647
866-709-4344
FAX: 303-756-2311
support@autismcommunitystore.com
www.autismcommunitystore.com
Shannon Sullivan, Co-Founder
The Autism Community Store is a parent-owned autism and special needs resource, a special little shop helping families, teachers and therapists get hard-to-find products for kids with ASD, PDD-NOS, Aspergers, SPD, ADHD and other special needs at reasonable prices.

1809 Autism-Products.com
8776 E. Shea Blvd.
Suite 106-552
Scottsdale, AZ 85260
FAX: 815-550-1819
Kelly@Autism-Products.com
www.autism-products.com
Supplies products for children dealing with Austim.

1810 Beginning Reasoning and Reading
School Specialty
625 Mt. Auburn Street, 3rd Floor
PO Box 9031
Cambridge, MA 02139-9031
617-547-6706
800-225-5750
FAX: 888-440-2665
Feedback.EPS@schoolspecialty.com
eps.schoolspecialty.com
Rick Holden, President, EPS
Joanne Carlisle, Author
This workbook develops basic language and thinking skills that build the foundation for reading comprehension. Workbook exercises reinforce reading as a critical reasoning activity. *$10.45*
ISBN 0-838830-01-3

1811 Blue Skies: A Complete Multi-Media Curriculum on the Cloud
Phillip Roy, Inc.
P.O. Box 130
Indian Rocks Beach, FL 33785
727-593-2700
800-255-9085
FAX: 877-595-2685
info@philliproy.com
www.philliproy.com
Ruth Bragman, PhD, President
Phil Roy Padol, Consultant
A complete PDF duplicatable curriculum that indlues Life Skills Curriculum, Academic Curriculum, Vocational Curriculum, Special Educational Curriculum, and Parenting/Early Learning Curriculum. This curriculum was designed for students to learn to be successful. Lesson plans, teacher's guides, pre/post assessments, and other support materials provided. *$495.00*
ISBN 1-568184-12-8

1812 Buy!
JE Stewart Teaching Tools
PO Box 15308
Seattle, WA 98115-308
206-262-9538
FAX: 206-262-9538
Jeff Stewart, Owner
Teaches 50 words as they appear in commercial and community situations such as clinic, sale, receipt, price and cleaner. These words are functional at school, on the job and shopping. *$32.50*
116 pages
ISBN 1-877866-05-9

1813 Catalog for Teaching Life Skills to Persons with Development Disability
PCI Education Publishing
PO Box 34270
San Antonio, TX 78265-4270
210-377-1999
800-594-4263
FAX: 888-259-8284
Lee Wilson, President/CEO
Erin Kinard, VP Product Development/Publisher
Randy Pennington, VP, Sales & Marketing
Over 200 educational products that help individuals learn and maintain the life skills they need to succeed in an inclusive society.

1814 Classroom GOALS: Guide for Optimizing Auditory Learning Skills
Alexander Graham Bell Association
3417 Volta Pl. NW
Washington, DC 20007
202-337-5220
FAX: 202-337-8314
TTY:202-337-5221
info@agbell.org
www.agbell.org
Emilio Alonso-Mendoza, Chief Executive Officer
This reader-friendly teacher's guide filled with tips, source materials and sample charts and plans is designed for educators who have yearned for a resource that explains how to incorporate auditory goals into academic learning for students with different degrees of hearing loss. *$34.95*
Paperback

1815 **Classroom Notetaker: How to Organize a Program Serving Students with Hearing Impairments**
Alexander Graham Bell Association
3417 Volta Pl. NW
Washington, DC 20007   202-337-5220
                                      FAX: 202-337-8314
                                      TTY:202-337-5221
                                      info@agbell.org
                                      www.agbell.org

Emilio Alonso-Mendoza, Chief Executive Officer
This detailed manual for instructors, administrators and staff notetakers promotes classroom notetaking within long-term educational programs as absolutely vital for students who are deaf and hard of hearing from elementary school to college. *$24.95*
127 pages Paperback

1816 **Community Services for the Blind and Partially Sighted Store: Sight Connection**
9709 Third Ave NE
Ste 100
Seattle, WA 98115-2027   206-525-5556
                                      800-458-4888
                                      FAX: 206-525-0422
                                      info@sightconnection.org
                                      www.sightconnection.org

Miles Otoupal, Chair
Jonathan Avedovech, Vice Chair
David McBride, Treasurer
Over 400 products specifically designed to make life easier for people with vision loss.

1817 **Community Signs**
JE Stewart Teaching Tools
P.O.Box 15308
Seattle, WA 98115-308   206-262-9538
                                      FAX: 206-262-9538

Jeff Stewart, Owner
Teaches 50 words like go, fire, rest room, men, women, danger and walk needed to successfully navigate our environment. *$32.50*

1818 **Comprehensive Assessment of Spoken Language (CASL)**
AGS
PO Box 99
Circle Pines, MN 55014-99   800-328-2560
                                      FAX: 800-471-8457
                                      agsmail@agsnet.com
                                      www.agsnet.com

Kevin Brueggeman, President
Robert Zaske, Market Manager
CASL is an individually and orally administered research-based, theory-drive oral language assessment battery for ages 3 through 21. Fifteen tests measure language processing skills - comprehension, expression, and retrieval - in four language structure categories: lexical/semantic, syntactic, supralinguistic and pragmatic. *$299.95*

1819 **Creative Arts Therapy Catalogs**
MMB Music
9051 Watson Road
Suite 161
Saint Louis, MO 63126-1019   314-531-9635
                                      800-543-3771
                                      FAX: 314-531-8384
                                      info@mmbmusic.com
                                      www.mmbmusic.com

Marcia Goldberg, President
Catalogs of books, videos, recordings for the creative arts and wellness (music, art, dance, poetry, drama, therapies, photography).

1820 **Cursive Writing Skills**
School Specialty
625 Mt. Auburn Street, 3rd Floor
PO Box 9031
Cambridge, MA 02139-9031   617-547-6706
                                      800-225-5750
                                      FAX: 888-440-2665
                                      Feedback.EPS@schoolspecialty.com
                                      eps.schoolspecialty.com

Rick Holden, President, EPS
Diana Hanbury King, Author
Boosts writing achievement through handwriting skills. Handwriting instruction helps students become fluent writers, allowing them to focus on their thoughts and ideas rather than on letter and word formation. *$12.00*

1821 **Different Roads to Learning**
37 East 18th Street
10th Floor
New York, NY 10003   212-604-9637
                                      800-853-1057
                                      FAX: 212-206-9329
                                      info@difflearn.com
                                      www.difflearn.com

Julie Azuma, Founder
Its product line supports the social, academic and communicative development of children on the autism spectrum through Applied Behavior Analysis (ABA) and Verbal Behavior interventions

1822 **Discount School Supply**
PO Box 6013
Carol Stream, IL 60197-6013   800-627-2829
                                      FAX: 800-879-3753
                                      customerservice@discountschoolsupply.com
                                      www.discountschoolsupply.com

Ron Elliott, Founder
Kelly Crampton, Chief Executive Officer
Discount School Supply offers the highest quality educational products at the lowest possible prices, supported by an extraordinary level of service.

1823 **Do2learn**
3204 Churchill Road
Raleigh, NC 27607   919-755-1809
                                      FAX: 919-420-1978
                                      www.do2learn.com

Do2learnprovides thousands of free pages with social skills and behavioral regulation activities and guidance, learning songs and games, communication cards, academic material, and transition guides for employment and life skills.

1824 **Don Johnston**
26799 West Commerce Drive
Volo, IL 60073   847-740-0749
                                      800-999-4660
                                      FAX: 847-740-7326
                                      info@donjohnston.com
                                      www.donjohnston.com

Don Johnston, Founder
Ruth Ziolkowski, President
Kevin Johnston, Director of Product Design
A provider of quality products and services that enable people with special needs to discover their potential and experience success. Products are developed for the areas of Physical Access, Augmentative Communication and for those who struggle with reading and writing.

1825 **Dyslexia Training Program**
School Specialty
625 Mt. Auburn Street, 3rd Floor
PO Box 9031
Cambridge, MA 02139-9031   617-547-6706
                                      800-225-5750
                                      FAX: 888-440-2665
                                      Feedback.EPS@schoolspecialty.com
                                      eps.schoolspecialty.com

Rick Holden, President, EPS
This 2-year, cumulative series of daily 1-hour video lessons and accompanying Student's Books and Teacher's Guides is a structured, multisensory sequence of alphabet, reading, spelling, cursive handwriting, listening, language history, and review

activities. Written by the Texas Scottish Rite Hospital for Children.

1826 ESpecial Needs
11704 Lackland Industrial Drive
St. Louis, MO 63146   314-692-2424
877-664-4565
FAX: 314-692-2428
www.especialneeds.com
eSpecial Needs is a global supplier of equipment, programs, and curricula for physical education and recreation professionals, as well as products, equipment, and programs for professionals who deal with children and adults with physical and developmental disabilities.

1827 Encyclopedia of Basic Employment and Daily Living Skills
Phillip Roy, Inc.
13064 Indian Rocks Rd.
P.O. Box 130
Indian Rocks Beach, FL 33785   727-593-2700
800-255-9085
FAX: 877-595-2685
info@philliproy.com
www.PhillipRoy.com
Ruth Bragman, PhD, President
Phil Roy Padol, Consultant
Contains developmental skills for special education students. Contains lessons in 6 curriculum areas covering 80 objects with 541 lessons. Also includes objectives, instructional strategies, and assessment tasks. Curriculum is in PDF format and unlimited duplication is allowed after purchase. *$300.00*
ISBN 1-568184-15-8

1828 Exceptional Teaching Inc
Exceptional Teaching Inc
3994 Oleander Way
PO Box 2330
Castro Valley, CA 94546   510-889-7282
800-549-6999
FAX: 510-889-7382
info@exceptionalteaching.com
www.exceptionalteaching.com
Helene Holman, Owner/manager
Providing educational products for those with special needs via catalog and online store.

1829 Explode the Code
School Specialty
625 Mt. Auburn Street, 3rd Floor
PO Box 9031
Cambridge, MA 02139-9031   617-547-6706
800-225-5750
FAX: 888-440-2665
Feedback.EPS@schoolspecialty.com
eps.schoolspecialty.com
Rick Holden, President, EPS
Nancy M Hall, Author
Helps students build the essential literacy skills needed for reading success: phonological awareness, decoding, vocabulary, comprehension, fluency and spelling. *$6.20*
Grades K-4, 1-3

1830 Food!
JE Stewart Teaching Tools
PO Box 15308
Seattle, WA 98115-308   206-262-9538
FAX: 206-262-9538
Jeff Stewart, Owner
Teaches 50 words like salt, pepper, hamburger, fruit, milk and soup, seen commonly on menus, packages and in directions used at home and at play. *$32.50*

1831 Fun for Everyone
AbleNet, Inc.
2625 Patton Road
Roseville, MN 55113-1137   651-294-2200
800-322-0956
FAX: 651-294-2259
customerservice@ablenetinc.com
www.ablenetinc.com
Jennifer Thalhuber, President & CEO
Paul Sugden, CFO & Trustee
Today, simple technology allows children and adults with disabilities to participate in leisure activities they were limited or excluded from in the past. *$20.00*

1832 Fundamentals of Autism
Slosson Educational Publications Inc.
538 Buffalo Road
East Aurora, NY 14052-280   716-652-0930
800-655-3840
888-756-7760
FAX: 716-655-3840
slossonprep@gmail.com
www.slosson.com
Steven Slosson, President
John Slosson, VP
David Slosson, VP
The Fundamentals of Autism handbook provides a quick, user friendly, effective and accurate approach to help in identifying and developing educationally related program objectives for children diagnosed as autistic. These materials have been designed to be easily and functionally used by teachers, therapists, special education/learning disability resource specialists, psychologists and others who work with children diagnosed as autistic. *$56.00*
72 pages

1833 GO-MO Articulation Cards- Second Edition
Sage Publications
2455 Teller Road
Thousand Oaks, CA 91320   805-499-9774
800-818-7243
FAX: 800-583-2665
info@sagepub.com
www.sagepub.com
Blaise R Simqu, President & CEO
Tracey Ozmina, VP and COO
Chris Hickok, Senior VP and CFO
The most popular system used for remedying defective speech articulation in children and adults. This popular card set was the first and is still the best therapy tool of its kind, as it continues to produce results and maintains the interest of students of all ages.

1834 Gillingham Manaual
School Specialty
625 Mt. Auburn Street, 3rd Floor
PO Box 9031
Cambridge, MA 02139-9031   617-547-6706
800-225-5750
FAX: 888-440-2665
Feedback.EPS@schoolspecialty.com
eps.schoolspecialty.com
Rick Holden, President, EPS
Anna Gillingham, Author
Bessie W Stillman, Co-Author
Remedial training for children with specific disability in reading, spelling, and penmanship.
352 pages 69.95
ISBN 0-83880 -00-

1835 Guide to Teaching Phonics
School Specialty
625 Mt. Auburn Street, 3rd Floor
PO Box 9031
Cambridge, MA 02139-9031   617-547-6706
800-225-5750
FAX: 888-440-2665
Feedback.EPS@schoolspecialty.com
eps.schoolspecialty.com
Rick Holden, President, EPS
June Lyday Orton, Author

Education / Aids for the Classroom section.

This flexible teacher's guide presents multisensory procedures developed in association with the late Dr. Samuel Orton. They consist of 100 phonograms for teaching phonetic elements and their sequences in words for reading, writing and spelling. Also contains coordinated Phonics Cards. *$19.25*

96 pages
ISBN 0-838802-41-9

1836 Homemade Battery-Powered Toys
Special Needs Project
324 State Street
Suite H
Santa Barbara, CA 93101-2364
818-718-9900
800-333-6867
FAX: 818-349-2027
editor@specialneeds.com
www.specialneeds.com

Hod Gray, Owner
Laraine Gray, Coordinator
Describes how to make simple switches and educational devices for severely handicapped children. *$7.50*

1837 Idaho Assistive Technology Project
University of Idaho
PO Box 444061
Moscow, ID 83844-4061
208-885-6097
800-432-8324
FAX: 208-885-6145
janicec@uidaho.edu
www.idahoat.org

Janice Carson, Project Director
Sue House, Information/Referral Specialst
A federally funded program managed by the Center on Disabilities and Human Development at the University of Idaho. The goal is to increase the availability of assistive technology devices and services for Idahoans with disabilities. *$15.00*

1838 If It Is To Be, It Is Up To Me To Do It!
AVKO Educational Research Foundation
3084 Willard Road
Birch Run, MI 48415-9404
810-686-9283
866-285-6612
FAX: 810-686-1101
webmaster@avko.org
www.avko.org

Don McCabe, President, Research Director Emeritus, Birch Run, Michigan
Linda Heck, VP, Clio, Michigan
Michael Lane, Treasurer, Clio, Michigan
A student and tutor's text, for use on dyslexics and non-dyslexics, by parents, spouses, or friends. *$29.95*
206 pages
ISBN 1-564007-42-1

1839 Inclusive Play People
Educational Equity Concepts
Fl 8
100 5th Ave
New York, NY 10011-6903
212-243-1110
FAX: 212-627-0407
TTY:212-725-1803
www.iconcapital.com

Jacqueline Johnson, Manager
Six sturdy multiracial wooden figures that provide a unique variety of nonstereotyped work and family roles and are inclusive of disabled and nondisabled people of various ages. For block building and dramatic play. *$25.00*

1840 Individualized Keyboarding
AVKO Educational Research Foundation
3084 Willard Road
Birch Run, MI 48415-9404
810-686-9283
866-285-6612
FAX: 810-686-1101
webmaster@avko.org
www.avko.org

Don McCabe, President, Research Director Emeritus, Birch Run, Michigan
Linda Heck, VP, Clio, Michigan
Michael Lane, Treasurer, Clio, Michigan

Utilizes a multi-sensory approach to teach typing skills. It not only teaches typing skills, it also reinforces the reading patterns that are necessary for typing proficiency. *$14.95*
96 pages
ISBN 1-654004-01-5

1841 Instruction of Persons with Severe Handicaps
McGraw-Hill School Publishing
PO Box 182604
Columbus, OH 43272
877-833-5524
FAX: 614-759-3749
customer.service@mcgraw-hill.com
www.mcgraw-hill.com

Harold McGraw, President and CEO
Jack Callahan, Executive VP
John Berisford, Executive VP of HR
A complete introduction to the status of education as it pertains to people with severe handicaps.

1842 Kaplan Early Learning Company
1310 Lewisville Clemmons Rd
Lewisville, NC 27023
336-766-7374
800-334-2014
FAX: 800-452-7526
info@kaplanco.com
www.kaplanco.com

Hal Kaplan, President & CEO
Kaplan Early Learning Company is a international provider of products and services that enhance children's learning.

1843 Keeping Ahead in School
Educators Publishing Service
PO Box 9031
Cambridge, MA 2139-9031
617-547-6706
800-225-5750
FAX: 888-440-2665
feedback@epsbooks.com
www.epsbooks.com

Charles H Heinle, VP
Alexandra S Bigelow, Author
Gunnar Voltz, President
This book helps students not only understand their own strengths and weaknesses but also more fully appreciate their individuality. He suggests specific ways to approach work, bypass or overcome learning disorders, and manage other struggles that may beset students in school. *$24.75*
320 pages Paperback
ISBN 0-838820-69-7

1844 KeyMath Teach and Practice
AGS
P.O.Box 99
Circle Pines, MN 55014-99
800-328-2560
FAX: 800-471-8457
agsmail@agsnet.com
www.agsnet.com

Kevin Brueggeman, President
Robert Zaske, Market Manager
This set of materials provides all the tools needed to assess students' math skills..and the strategies to deal with problem areas. Three sets are available: Basic Concepts Package; Operations Package; and Applications Package. $219.95 each or $599.95 for whole set.

1845 Lakeshore Learning Materials
2695 E. Dominguez Street
Carson, CA 90895
310-537-8600
800-421-5354
FAX: 800-537-5403
lakeshore@lakeshorelearning.com
www.lakeshorelearning.com

Bo Kaplan, President/CEO
Josh Kaplan, VP Merchandising
Mat , Vice President of Operations
Offers books, resources, testing materials, assessment information and special education materials for the professional in the field of special education.
190 pages

1846   Language Parts Catalog
School Specialty
625 Mt. Auburn Street, 3rd Floor
PO Box 9031
Cambridge, MA 02139-9031   617-547-6706
                                              800-225-5750
                                        FAX: 888-440-2665
                         Feedback.EPS@schoolspecialty.com
                                        eps.schoolspecialty.com

Rick Holden, President, EPS
Melvin D Levine, Author
Offers a humorous and informative explanation of the various aspects of language and how they operate. Laid out in the form of a catalog, the book presents various parts that can help students improve their language abilities. *$12.65*
ISBN 0-838819-80-X

1847   Language Tool Kit
School Specialty
625 Mt. Auburn Street, 3rd Floor
PO Box 9031
Cambridge, MA 02139-9031   617-547-6706
                                              800-225-5750
                                        FAX: 888-440-2665
                         Feedback.EPS@schoolspecialty.com
                                        eps.schoolspecialty.com

Rick Holden, President, EPS
Paula D Rome, Author
Jean S Osman, Co-Author
Designed for use by a teacher or parents, teaches reading and spelling to students with specific language disability. *$43.25*
32 pages English Edition
ISBN 0-838885-20-3

1848   Language, Speech and Hearing Services in School
American Speech-Language-Hearing Association
10801 Rockville Pike
Rockville, MD 20852-3226   301-296-5700
                                              800-638-8255
                                        FAX: 301-296-8580
                                        actioncenter@asha.org
                                              www.asha.org

Paul Rao, President
Robert Augustine, VP of Finance
Arlene Pietranton, Executive Director
Professional journal for clinicians, audiologists and speech-language pathologists. *$30.00*

1849   Learning American Sign Language
Harris Communications
15155 Technology Dr
Eden Prairie, MN 55344   800-825-6758
                                        FAX: 952-906-1099
                                        TTY:952-388-2152
                                        info@harriscomm.com
                                              www.harriscomm.com

Ray Harris, CEO
Offers over 700 titles on ASL including books, videotapes, CDs & DVDs. Free catalog available.
Video & Book

1850   Learning Resources
380 N. Fairway Drive
Vernon Hills, IL 60061   800-333-8281
                                        FAX: 888-892-8731
                                        info@learningresources.com
                                              www.learningresources.com
Learning Resourcesr is a global manufacturer of innovative, hands-on educational products. The Company's 1100+ high-quality products are sold in more than 80 countries, serving children and their families, preschool, kindergarten, primary, and middle-school markets.

1851   Learning to Sign in My Neighborhood
T J Publishers
2544 Tarpley Rd
Suite 108
Carrollton, TX 75006-2288   972-416-0800
                                              800-999-1168
                                        FAX: 301-585-5930
                                        tjpubinc@aol.com

Angela K Thames, President
Jerald A Murphy, VP
Beautifully illustrated coloring book lets children learn signs from kids just like themselves! Recommended for ages 4 and up, let children have fun while they learn signs for words typically used in day-to-day activities. *$3.50*
32 pages Softcover
ISBN 0-93266 -36-1

1852   Literacy Program
School Specialty
625 Mt. Auburn Street, 3rd Floor
PO Box 9031
Cambridge, MA 02139-9031   617-547-6706
                                              800-225-5750
                                        FAX: 888-440-2665
                         Feedback.EPS@schoolspecialty.com
                                        eps.schoolspecialty.com

Rick Holden, President, EPS
Paula D Rome, Author
Jean S Osman, Co-Author
Written by the Texas Scottish Rite Hospital for Children. A one-year course that consists of 160 one-hour videotaped lessons accompanied by student workbooks, designed for high school students and adults who read below sixth grade level.

1853   Literature Based Reading
Oryx Press
4041 N Central Ave
Phoenix, AZ 85012-3330   602-265-2651
                                              800-279-6799
                                        FAX: 800-279-4663
Series offering children's books and activities to enrich the K-5 curriculum.

1854   Living an Idea: Empowerment and the Evolution of an Alternative School
Brookline Books
8 Trumbull Rd, Suite B-001
Northampton, MA 1060-4533   413-584-0184
                                              800-666-2665
                                        FAX: 413-584-6184
                                        brbooks@yahoo.com
                                              www.brooklinebooks.com

William H Walters, Author
Esther Wilder, Co-Author
This book is about the creation and 14 year evolution of a public alternative inner-city high school. The school lived an idea - empowerment. Students were encouraged to participate in shaping many aspects of their education, teachers were responsible for running the school, and parents invited to help govern. *$27.95*
ISBN 0-91479 -68-9

1855   Low Tech Assistive Devices: A Handbook for the School Setting
Therapro, Inc.
225 Arlington Street
Framingham, MA 02139-8723   508-872-9494
                                              800-257-5376
                                        FAX: 508-875-2062
                                        info@therapro.com
                                              www.therapro.com

Karen Conrad Weihrauch, President & Owner
A how-to book with step by step directions and detailed illustrations for fabrication of frequently requested low-tech assistive devices. *$29.95*
320 pages Paperback

1856 MTA Readers
Educators Publishing Service
625 Mt. Auburn Street, 3rd Floor
PO Box 9031
Cambridge, MA 02139-9031   617-547-6706
                                  800-225-5750
                              FAX: 888-440-2665
                    Feedback.EPS@schoolspecialty.com
                                 www.epsbooks.com

Rick Holden, President, EPS
Illustrated readers for grades 1-3 that accompany the MTA Reading and Spelling Program (Multisensory Teaching Approach). Phonetic elements in a structured, but entertaining context.
48+ pages $4.65 - $11.65
ISBN 0-83882 -33-3

1857 Making School Inclusion Work: A Guide to Everyday Practice
Brookline Books
8 Trumbull Rd, Suite B-001
Northampton, MA 2445-4533   413-584-0184
                                   800-666-2665
                              FAX: 413-584-6184
                                brbooks@yahoo.com
                             www.brooklinebooks.com

William H Walters, Author
Esther Wilder, Co-Author
This book tells the reader how to conduct a truly inclusive program, regardless of ethnic or racial background, economic level and physical or cognitive ability. *$24.95*
254 pages
ISBN 0-914791-96-4

1858 Making the Writing Process Work: Strategies for Composition and Self-Regulation
Brookline Books
8 Trumbull Rd, Suite B-001
Northampton, MA 2445-4533   413-584-0184
                                   800-666-2665
                              FAX: 413-584-6184
                                brbooks@yahoo.com
                             www.brooklinebooks.com

William H Walters, Author
Esther Wilder, Co-Author
This book is geared toward students who have difficulty organizing their thoughts and developing their writing. The specific stategies teach students how to approach, organize, and produce a final written product. *$24.95*
240 pages Paperback
ISBN 1-571290-10-9

1859 Manual Alphabet Poster
TJ Publishers
Ste 108
2544 Tarpley Rd
Carrollton, TX 75006-2288   972-416-0800
                                   800-999-1168
                              FAX: 972-416-0944
                                TJPubinc@aol.com
                             www.TJpublishers.com

Pat O'Rourke, President
Poster presents the manual alphabet. *$4.50*

1860 Many Faces of Dyslexia
International Dyslexia Association
40 York Rd.
4th Floor
Baltimore, MD 21204-5243   410-296-0232
                              FAX: 410-321-5069
                             info@dyslexiaida.org
                                 dyslexiaida.org

Margaret Byrd Rawson, Author
Provides information on the teaching and rehabilitation techniques for people with dyslexia. *$20.00*
269 pages Paperback

1861 Match-Sort-Assemble Job Cards
Exceptional Education
PO Box 15308
Seattle, WA 98115-308   206-262-9538
Jeff Stewart, Owner
Teaches workers to use a series of symbolic cues to control their own production cycles. *$565.00*
Class Set

1862 Match-Sort-Assemble Pictures
Exceptional Education
PO Box 15308
Seattle, WA 98115-308   206-262-9538
Jeff Stewart, Owner
People with profound, severe and moderate developmental disabilities have immediate access with MSA Pictures. Students work with pictures (and if necessary a template) to match, sort, assemble and disassemble parts that vary in shape, length and diameter. *$426.00*
Class Set

1863 Match-Sort-Assemble SCHEMATICS
Exceptional Education
PO Box 15308
Seattle, WA 98115-308   206-262-9538
Jeff Stewart, Owner
Students with moderate and mild developmental disabilities and those who have completed MSA Pictures are ready for MSA Schematics. It increases abstraction and displacement of instruction from the work clearly and simply. *$495.00*
Class Set

1864 Match-Sort-Assemble TOOLS
Exceptional Education
PO Box 15308
Seattle, WA 98115-308   206-262-9538
                              FAX: 475-486-4510
Jeff Stewart, Owner
Students and clients learn to use the tools required for many jobs in light industry. Mastery of the production cycle with independence, endurance and the ability to learn new tasks through pictures and schematics and basic hand functions will help clients acquire and maintain employment in a competitive field. *$595.00*
Class Set

1865 Meeting-in-a-Box
Asthma and Allergy Foundation of America
1233 20th St NW
Suite 610
Washington, DC 20036-7322   202-833-1700
                                   800-7AS-THMA
                              FAX: 202-833-2351
                                   info@aafa.org
Bill McLin, Executive Director
A series of self-contained, comprehensive kits that contain all the necessary components for a successful asthma presentation.

1866 More Food!
JE Stewart Teaching Tools
PO Box 15308
Seattle, WA 98115-308   206-262-9538
                              FAX: 206-262-9538
Jeff Stewart, Owner
Teaches 50 more words found in restaurants, grocery stores, cookbooks such as pizza, carrot, tacos, oysters and pineapple. These words are functional at home, going shopping and during leisure. *$32.50*

1867 More Work!
J E Stewart Teaching Tools
PO Box 15308
Seattle, WA 98115-308   206-262-9538
                              FAX: 206-262-9538
Jeff Stewart, Owner
Teaches 50 words as they appear on parts, tools, job instructions, signs and labels, such as fill, grasp, release, lock, search, position and select. These words are functional in school and on-the-job. *$32.50*

1868 Multisensory Teaching Approach
Educators Publishing Service
PO Box 9031
Cambridge, MA 2139-9031

617-367-2700
800-225-5750
FAX: 617-547-0412
www.epsbooks.com

Comprehensive multisensory program in reading, writing, spelling, alphabet and dictionary skills for remedial and regular instruction. Based on Orton-Gillingham and Alphabetic Phonics. A complete program organized in kits, with additional classroom materials, supplementary materials, and handwriting programs. *$110 - $140*
ISBN 0-83888 -10-9

1869 National Autism Resources
6240 Goodyear Rd.
Benicia, CA 94510

707-745-3308
877-249-2393
FAX: 877-259-9419
customerservice@nationalautismresources.com
www.nationalautismresources. com

National Autism Resources Inc. provides cost effective, research based therapeutic tools globaly that meet the needs of people on the autism spectrum across their lifespan since 2008.

1870 Peabody Articulation Decks
AGS
PO Box 99
Circle Pines, MN 55014-99

651-287-7220
800-328-2560
FAX: 763-786-9007
agsmail@agsnet.com
www.agsnet.com

Keith Powel, Special Education Transition Coo
Robert Zaske, Marketing Manager
Complete kit of playing-card sized PAD decks let students focus on the 18 most commonly misarticulated English consonants and blends. *$115.95*
ISBN 0-88671 -75-4

1871 Phonemic Awareness in Young Children: A Classroom Curriculum
Brookes Publishing
PO Box 10624
Baltimore, MD 21285-624

410-337-9580
custserv@brookespublishing.com
www.brookespublishing.com

Clary Creighton, Exhibits Coordinator
Tracy Gray, Educational Sales Manager
Paul Brooks, Owner
This is a supplemental, whole-class curriculum for improving pre-literacy listening skills. It contains activities that are fun, easy to use, and proven to work in any kindergarten classroom - general, bilingual, inclusive, or special education. This program takes only 15-20 minutes a day. *$24.95*
208 pages Spiral-bound
ISBN 1-557663-21-1

1872 Phonics for Thought
Educators Publishing Service
PO Box 9031
Cambridge, MA 2139-9031

617-367-2700
800-225-5750
FAX: 617-547-0412
www.epsbooks.com

$8.00
Paperback

1873 Phonological Awareness Training for Reading
Sage Publications
2455 Teller Road
Thousand Oaks, CA 91320

805-499-9774
800-818-7243
FAX: 800-583-2665
info@sagepub.com
www.sagepub.com

Blaise R Simqu, President & CEO
Tracey Ozmina, Executive VP
Chris Hickok, Executive VP and CFO

Designed to increase the level of phonological awareness in young children. Can be taught individually or in small groups and takes about 12 to 14 weeks to complete if children are taught in short sessions three or four times a week. *$129.00*

1874 Play!
JE Stewart Teaching Tools
PO Box 15308
Seattle, WA 98115-308

206-262-9538
FAX: 206-262-9538

Jeff Stewart, Owner
Teaches 50 more words as they appear at recreation sites, on signs and labels and in newspapers and magazines, such as movie, visitor, ticket, gallery and zoo. These words are functional in school and at leisure. *$32.50*

1875 Power Breathing Program
Asthma and Allergy Foundation of America
8201 Corporate Drive
Suite 1000
Landover, MD 20785

202-466-7643
800-727-8462
FAX: 202-466-8940
info@aafa.org
www.aafa.org

Bill McLin, Executive Director
Devoloped the only asthma education program specifically designed for and pre-tested with teens. Teens with asthma have special challenges. This interactive program covers everything from the basics of asthma to dealing with their asthma in social situations, in college, and on the job. Includes everything you need to present this three-four session program. *$295.00*

1876 Primary Phonics
School Specialty
625 Mt. Auburn Street, 3rd Floor
PO Box 9031
Cambridge, MA 02139-9031

617-547-6706
800-225-5750
FAX: 888-440-2665
Feedback.EPS@schoolspecialty.com
eps.schoolspecialty.com

Rick Holden, President, EPS
Barbara W Makar, Author
A program of storybooks and coordinated workbooks that teaches reading for grades K-2. A structured phonetic approach. Contains 8 student workbooks, with 8 sets of 10 coordinated storybooks; consonant workbooks; initial consonant blend workbooks; picture dictionary, and coloring book.
ISSN 0838-83 0

1877 Reading for Content
School Specialty
625 Mt. Auburn Street, 3rd Floor
PO Box 9031
Cambridge, MA 02139-9031

617-547-6706
800-225-5750
FAX: 888-440-2665
Feedback.EPS@schoolspecialty.com
eps.schoolspecialty.com

Rick Holden, President, EPS
Carol Einstein, Author
A series of 4 books designed to help students improve their reading comprehension skills. Each book contains 43 reading passages followed by 4 questions. Two questions as for a recall of main ideas, and two ask the student to draw conclusions from what they have read. *$11.45*
96 pages

1878 Reading from Scratch
Educators Publishing Service
P.O.Box 9031
Cambridge, MA 2139-9031

617-367-2700
800-225-5750
FAX: 617-547-0412
www.epsbooks.com

Contains multisensory reading and spelling material and oral and written lessons and exercises in syntax, grammar, and precomposition topics. Complete set.
$6.25 - $49.30
ISBN 0-83888 -75-5

1879 Recipe for Reading
School Specialty
625 Mt. Auburn Street, 3rd Floor
PO Box 9031
Cambridge, MA 02139-9031
617-367-2700
800-225-5750
FAX: 888-440-2665
Feedback.EPS@schoolspecialty.com
eps.schoolspecialty.com

Rick Holden, President, EPS
Nina Traub, Author
Frances Bloom, Co-Author
Contains comprehensive, multisensory, phonics-based reading program presents a skill sequence and lesson structured designed for beginning, at-risk, or struggling readers.

1880 Rewarding Speech
Speech Bin
PO Box 1579
Appleton, WI 54912-1579
772-770-0007
888-388-3224
FAX: 888-388-6344
customercare@schoolspecialty.com
www.speechbin.com

Jan J Binney, Senior Editor
Reproducible reward certificates for children. *$12.95*
32 pages

1881 SAYdee Posters
Speech Bin
PO Box 1579
Appleton, WI 54912-1579
772-770-0007
888-388-3224
FAX: 888-388-6344
customercare@schoolspecialty.com
www.speechbin.com

Jan J Binney, Senior Editor
Colorful speech and language posters. *$20.00*
24 pages
ISBN 0-93785 -47-5

1882 Sensation Products
74 Cotton Mill Hill
Unit A-350
Brattleboro, VT 5301
802-254-4480
FAX: 802-254-4481
www.sensationproducts.com
Since 2000, Sensation Products has been the wholesale supplier for school supply companies that serve Special Populations.

1883 Sensory University Toy Company, The
4992 Bristol Industrial Hwy
Buford, GA 30518
888-831-4701
FAX: 770-904-6418
sales@sensoryuniversity.com
sensoryuniversity.com
Sensory University provides special needs products and toys for the children treated in their facility. Over the years, the inventory has increased to cover a full spectrum of educational items and pediatric fitness products, as well as a library of over 100 titles dedicated to improving the lives of children with many different forms of developmental delay.

1884 Sequential Spelling: 1-7 with 7 Student Response Books
AVKO Educational Research Foundation
3084 Willard Rd
Birch Run, MI 48415-9404
810-686-9283
866-285-6612
FAX: 810-686-1101
webmaster@avko.org
www.avko.org

Deborah Wolf, President
Aaron Miller, Vice President
Sequential Spelling uses immediate student self-correction. It builds from easier words of a word family such as all and then builds on them to teach; all, tall, stall, install, call, fall, ball, and their inflected forms such as: stalls, stalled, stalling, installing, installment. *$89.95*
72 pages $8.95 each
ISBN 1-56400 -11-6

1885 Signing Naturally Curriculum
Harris Communications
15155 Technology Dr
Eden Prairie, MN 55344
800-825-6758
FAX: 952-906-1099
TTY:952-388-2152
info@harriscomm.com
www.harriscomm.com

Ray Harris, CEO
A series based on the functional approach that is the most popular and widely used sign language curriculum designed for teaching American Sign Language. Book and videotape set for level 3. Teacher's curriculum is also available. *$89.95*

1886 Small Wonder
AGS
PO Box 99
Circle Pines, MN 55014-99
651-287-7220
800-328-2560
FAX: 763-786-9007
agsmail@agsnet.com
www.agsnet.com

Kevin Brueggeman, President
Robert Zaske, Marketing Manager
This infant through toddler program offers a delightful array of activities to teach babies about themselves, others, their surroundings and the world outside. Level One - zero to 18 months; Level Two 18-36 months. Discount price of $389.95 when both levels ordered. *$229.95*
ISBN 0-91347 -62-5

1887 Solving Language Difficulties
School Specialty
625 Mt. Auburn Street, 3rd Floor
PO Box 9031
Cambridge, MA 02139-9031
617-547-6706
800-225-5750
FAX: 888-440-2665
Feedback.EPS@schoolspecialty.com
eps.schoolspecialty.com

Rick Holden, President, EPS
Amey Steere, Author
Caroline Z Peck, Co-Author
This basic workbook can be used in any corrective reading program. It deals extensively with syllables, syllable division, prefixes, suffixes and accent. *$9.75*
176 pages
ISBN 0-838803-26-1

1888 Speech Bin
Abilitations
PO Box 1579
Appleton, WI 54912-1579
772-770-0007
800-513-2465
FAX: 80- 51- 246
onlinehelp@schoolspecialty.com
www.speechbin.com

Jan J Binney, Senior Editor
Activities, worksheets and games to encourage practice of speech and language skills. *$25.00*
128 pages
ISBN 0-93785 -42-4

1889 Speech-Language Delights
1965 25th Ave
Vero Beach, FL 32960-3062
772-770-0007

1890 Spell of Words
School Specialty
625 Mt. Auburn Street, 3rd Floor
PO Box 9031
Cambridge, MA 02139-9031
617-547-6706
800-225-5750
FAX: 888-440-2665
Feedback.EPS@schoolspecialty.com
eps.schoolspecialty.com

Rick Holden, President, EPS
Elsie T Rak, Author

Covers syllabication, word building along with prefixes, phonograms, word patterns, suffixes, plurals, and possessives. *$14.70*
128 pages Grades 7-Adult

1891 Spellbound
School Specialty
625 Mt. Auburn Street, 3rd Floor
PO Box 9031
Cambridge, MA 02139-9031   617-547-6706
                                            800-225-5750
                                       FAX: 888-440-2665
                     Feedback.EPS@schoolspecialty.com
                                  eps.schoolspecialty.com

Rick Holden, President, EPS
Elsie T Rak, Author
This workbook begins with teaching simple, consistent rules and then moves on to those that are more difficult. By an inductive process, students use their own observations to confirm the spelling rules they learn. Each portion of the text is followed by exercises for drill and kinesthetic reinforcement. *$12.85*
144 pages Grades 7-Adult
ISBN 0-838801-65-X

1892 Spelling Dictionary
School Specialty
625 Mt. Auburn Street, 3rd Floor
PO Box 9031
Cambridge, MA 02139-9031   617-547-6706
                                            800-225-5750
                                       FAX: 888-440-2665
                     Feedback.EPS@schoolspecialty.com
                                  eps.schoolspecialty.com

Rick Holden, President, EPS
Gregory Hurray, Author
Contains the most frequently used and misspelled words for students at these grade levels. Designed to be useable and reliable, to build research and writing skills, and to help teachers promote independent learning in a classroom setting *$6.35*
ISBN 0-838820-56-5

1893 Starting Over
School Specialty
625 Mt. Auburn Street, 3rd Floor
PO Box 9031
Cambridge, MA 02139-9031   617-547-6706
                                            800-225-5750
                                       FAX: 888-440-2665
                     Feedback.EPS@schoolspecialty.com
                                  eps.schoolspecialty.com

Rick Holden, President, EPS
Joan Knight, Author
For students who are ready to try to learn to read again, or for those who are learning English as a second language. *$38.40*
ISBN 0-838881-65-5

1894 Studio 49 Catalog
MMB Music
9051 Watson Road
Suite 161
Saint Louis, MO 63126-1019   314-531-9635
                                            800-543-3771
                                       FAX: 314-531-8384
                                        info@mmbmusic.com
                                         www.mmbmusic.com

Marcia Goldberg, President
Michelle Greenlaw, VP
Percussion instruments for school, therapy, church and family.

1895 Syracuse Community-Referenced Curriculum Guide for Students with Disabilties
Brookes Publishing
PO Box 10624
Baltimore, MD 21285-624   410-337-9580
                                            800-638-3775
                                       FAX: 410-337-8539
                      custserv@brookespublishing.com
                                  www.readplaylearn.com

Paul Brooks, President
Serving learners from kindergarten through age 21, this field-tested curriculum is a for professionals and parents devoted to directly preparing a student to function in the world. it examines the role of community living domains, functional academics, and embedded skills and includes practical implementation strategies and information for preparing students whose learning needs go beyond the scope of traditional academic programs. *$54.95*
416 pages Spiral-bound
ISBN 1-557660-27-1

1896 Teaching Individuals with Physical and Multiple Disabilities
McGraw-Hill, School Publishing
PO Box 182604
Columbus, OH 43272   877-833-5524
                                       FAX: 614-759-3749
                                         www.mcgraw-hill.com

Harold McGraw, President and CEO
Jack Callahan, Executive VP
John Berisford, Executive VP of HR
Focuses on the functional needs of the handicapped and the teaching skills of background teachers that they need to help them reach the highest possible level of self-sufficiency.
410 pages

1897 Teaching Students Ways to Remember
Brookline Books
8 Trumbull Rd, Suite B-001
Northampton, MA 1060   60- 66- 703
                                            800-666-2665
                                       FAX: 413-584-6184
                                         brbooks@yahoo.com
                                      www.brooklinebooks.com

Teaches techniques for improving or strengthening memory. *$21.95*
ISBN 0-914797-67-0

1898 Teaching Test-Taking Skills: Helping Students Show What They Know
Brookline Books
8 Trumbull Rd, Suite B-001
Northampton, MA 1060   60- 66- 703
                                            800-666-2665
                                       FAX: 414-584-6184
                                         brbooks@yahoo.com
                                      www.brooklinebooks.com

Test-taking skills that, when used effectively, contribute to test-wise performance and help students work productively with test materials. *$21.95*
ISBN 0-914797-76-X

1899 Therapy Shoppe
P.O. Box 8875
Grand Rapids, MI 49518   616-696-7441
                                            800-261-5590
                                       FAX: 616-696-7471
                                    info@therapyshoppe.com
                                      www.therapyshoppe.com

Thousand's of extraordinary fidgets, sensory products, therapy toys, weighted and deep pressure specialties for autism and other special needs, occupational therapy supplies, unique classroom resources, and other innovative products for play, learning, self-regulation, handwriting, sensory integration, and sensory-motor skills development.

1900 To Teach a Dyslexic
AVKO Educational Research Foundation
3084 Willard Rd
Birch Run, MI 48415-9404   810-686-9283
                                            866-686-9283
                                       FAX: 810-686-1101
                                        webmaster@avko.org
                                              www.avko.org

Deborah Wolf, President
Aaron Miller, Vice President
A video available in DVD or video CD that shows Don McCabe working with a dyslexic teenager. The video helps teachers learn more about dyslexia and how to go about teaching a dyslexic student using the AVKO methodology and philosophy. This is a free video.
288 pages Paperback

1901 Tools for Transition
AGS
PO Box 99
Circle Pines, MN 55014-99   651-287-7220
800-328-2560
FAX: 763-786-9007
agsmail@agsnet.com
www.agsnet.com

Kevin Brueggeman, President
Robert Zaske, Marketing Manager
This program prepares students with learning disabilities for postsecondary education. *$129.95*

1902 United Art and Education
PO Box 9219
Fort Wayne, IN 46899-9219   260-478-1121
800-322-3247
FAX: 800-858-3247
www.unitednow.com

United Art Education founded in 1960 is committed to serve schools, organizations and individuals with quality products. Their goal is to make shopping fun for every customer, whether you're an art instructor, elementary teacher, school supply buyer, fine artist or parent.

1903 VAK Tasks Workbook: Visual, Auditory and Kinesthetic
Educational Tutorial Consortium
4400 S 44th St
Lincoln, NE 68516-1109   402-489-8133
FAX: 402-489-8160

T Elli Cross, Owner
A workbook emphasizing the multisensory approach to teaching vocabulary and spelling. It is intended for middle-grade and older students working with prefixes, roots, suffixes, homonyms, and the spelling of easily confused endings. Includes spelling posters. *$7.00*
96 pages Paperback

1904 Volunteer Transcribing Services
Ste 200
205 E 3rd Ave
San Mateo, CA 94401-4028   650-357-1571
FAX: 650-632-3510

Alanah Hoffman, Coordinator
VTS is a nonprofit California corporation that produces large print school books for visually impaired students in grades K-12.

1905 Wordly Wise 3000
School Specialty
625 Mt. Auburn Street, 3rd Floor
PO Box 9031
Cambridge, MA 02139-9031   617-547-6706
800-225-5750
FAX: 888-440-2665
Feedback.EPS@schoolspecialty.com
eps.schoolspecialty.com

Rick Holden, President, EPS
Kenneth Hodkinson, Author
Sandra Adams, Co-Author
Begins with a word list of 8-12 words, followed by clear, brief definitions and sentences that illustrate the meaning of the word. Books B and C often present more than one meaning of a word. Throughout all three books, drawings illustrate the meanings.
ISSN 0838-84 8

1906 Work!
JE Stewart Teaching Tools
PO Box 15308
Seattle, WA 98115-308   206-328-7664
FAX: 206-262-9538

Jan Gleason, Executive Director
Teaches 50 words as they appear on parts, tools, job instructions, signs, labels such as: hard hat, assembly, clamp, cut, drill, package and schedule. These words are functional in school and on-the-job. *$32.50*

1907 Working Together & Taking Part
A GS
PO Box 99
Circle Pines, MN 55014-99   651-287-7220
800-328-2560
FAX: 763-786-9007
agsmail@agsnet.com
www.agsnet.com

Kevin Brueggeman, President
Robert Zaske, Market Manager
Two programs to build children's social skills in grades 3-6 through folk literature. Has 31 activity-rich lessons, teaching skills like: following rules, accepting differences, speaking assertively and helping others. Discount price of $279.00 when ordering both. *$149.95*

Associations

1908 AVKO Educational Research Foundation
3084 Willard Rd
Birch Run, MI 48415-9404   810-686-9283
FAX: 810-686-1101
webmaster@avko.org
www.avko.org

Don McCabe, President
Linda Heck, Vice President
Comprised of individuals interested in helping others learn to read and spell. Develops and sells materials for teaching dyslexics or others with learning disabilities using a method involving audio, visual, kinesthetic and oral (multi-sensory) techniques.

1909 Academy of Rehabilitative Audiology
PO Box 2323
Albany, NY 12220-0323   ara@audrehab.org
www.audrehab.org

Karen Doherty, Ph.D, President
Brittney Carlson, Au.D, Ph.D, Treasurer
Ali Marinelli, Au.D, Ph.D, Secretary
The Academy of Rehabilitative Audiology provides professional education, research and programs for hearing handicapped persons. The primary purpose of the ARA is to promote excellence in hearing care through the provision of comprehensive rehabilitative and habilitative services.

1910 Alternative Work Concepts
PO Box 11452
Eugene, OR 97440   541-345-3043
FAX: 541-345-9669
www.alternativeworkconcepts.org

Liz Fox, Executive Director
To promote individualized, integrated, and meaningful employment opportunities in the community for adults with multiple disabilities; to improve the quality of life and provide continuous opportunities for personal growth for these individuals; and to assist businesses with workforce diversification.

1911 American Migraine Foundation
19 Mantua Rd.
Mount Royal, NJ 08061   856-423-0043
FAX: 856-423-0082
amf@talley.com
www.achenet.org

Lawrence C. Newman, MD, FAHS, Chair
Christine Lay, MD, FAHS, Vice-Chair
Nim Lalvani, MPH, Executive Director
Nonprofit, patient-health, professional partnership dedicated to advancing the treatment and management of headaches and to raising the public awareness of headache as valid, biologically based illness.

1912 American School Counselor Association
American Counselling Association
1101 King St.
Suite 310
Alexandria, VA 22314-2957

703-683-2722
800-306-4722
FAX: 703-997-7572
asca@schoolcounselor.org
www.schoolcounselor.org

Richard Wong, Executive Director
Kathleen Rakestraw, Director of Communications
Jennifer Walsh, Director of Education and Training
ASCA focuses on providing professional devleopment, enhancing school counseling programs, and research effective school counseling practices. Mission is to promote excellence in professional school counseling and the development of all students.

1913 Association for Driver Rehabilitation Specialists
200 First Ave. NW
Suite 505
Hickory, NC 28601

866-672-9466
FAX: 828-855-1672
info@aded.net
www.aded.net

Elizabeth Green, Executive Director
Adrienne Segundo, Credentialing Specialist
Keith Segundo, Director, Education
The Association for Driver Rehabilitation Specialists was established to support professionals working in the field of driver education and driver training and transportation equipment modifications for persons with disabilities through education and information dissemination.

1914 Association on Higher Education & Disability (AHEAD)
8015 West Kenton Circle
Suite 230
Huntersville, NC 28078

704-947-7779
FAX: 704-948-7779
www.ahead.org

Katy Washington, President
Stephan Smith, Executive Director
Oanh Huynh, Chief Financial Officer
AHEAD is a professional membership organization for individuals involved in the development of policy and in the provision of quality services to meet the needs of persons with disabilities involved in all areas of higher education, promoting full and equal participation.
4,000+ members

1915 CARF International
6951 East Southpoint Rd.
Tucson, AZ 85756-9407

520-325-1044
888-281-6531
FAX: 520-318-1129
TTY:520-495-7077
info@carf.org
carf.org

Brian J. Boon, President & Chief Executive Officer
Leslie Ellis-Lang, Managing Director, Child & Youth Services
Darren M. Lehrfeld, Chief Accreditation Officer
An independent, nonprofit accreditor of human service providers in the areas of aging services, behavioral health, child and youth services, DMEPOS, employment and community services, medical rehabilitation, and opioid treatment programs.
1966

1916 CEC Pioneers Division (CEC-PD)
Council for Exceptional Children (CEC)
3100 Clarendon Blvd.
Suite 600
Arlington, VA 22201-5332

888-232-7733
TTY:866-915-5000
cecpioneers@gmail.com
cecpioneers.exceptionalchildren.org

Chad Rummel, Executive Director
Exists to support the programs and activities of the Council for Exceptional Children.

1917 Center for Inclusive Design and Innovation
512 Means St. NW
Suite 250
Atlanta, GA 30318

404-894-8000
866-279-2964
FAX: 404-894-8323
cidi-support@design.gatech.edu
cidi.gatech.edu

Carolyn Phillips, Director, Services & Learning
CIDI supports individuals with disabilities of any age within the State of Georgia and beyond through expert services, research, design and technological development, information dissemination, and educational programs.

1918 Council for Children with Behavioral Disorders (CCBD)
Council for Exceptional Children (CEC)
3100 Clarendon Blvd.
Suite 600
Arlington, VA 22201-5332

888-232-7733
TTY:866-915-5000
service@cec.sped.org
www.ccbd.net

Chad Rummel, Executive Director, CEC
Advocates for the education and welfare of youth with behavioral and emotional disorders.

1919 Council for Educational Diagnostic Services (CEDS)
Council for Exceptional Children (CEC)
3100 Clarendon Blvd.
Suite 600
Arlington, VA 22201-5332

888-232-7733
TTY:866-915-5000
cedscec@gmail.com
ceds.exceptionalchildren.org

Chad Rummel, Executive Director
Focused on diagnostic and prescriptive procedures involving the education of gifted persons or those with disabilities.

1920 Council for Exceptional Children (CEC)
3100 Clarendon Blvd.
Suite 600
Arlington, VA 22201-5332

888-232-7733
TTY:866-915-5000
service@exceptionalchildren.org
www.exceptionalchildren.org

Chad Rummel, Executive Director
Laurie VanderPloeg, Associate Executive Director, Professional Affairs
Craig Evans, Chief Financial Officer
The Council for Exceptional Children aims to improve the educational success of individuals with disabilities and/or gifts and talents by advocating for appropriate policies, setting professional standards, and providing resources and professional development for special educators.

1921 Council of Administrators of Special Education (CASE)
Osigian Office Center
101 Katelyn Circle
Suite E
Warner Robins, GA 31088

478-333-6892
FAX: 478-333-2453
lpurcell@casecec.org
www.casecec.org

Luann Purcell, Executive Director
Provides professional leadership and personal and professional development for special education administrators.

1922 Disability Research and Dissemination Center
Arnold School of Public Health, USC
Discovery 1 Bldg.
915 Greene St.
Columbia, SC 29208

info@disabilityresearchcenter.com
www.disabilityresearchcenter.com

Suzanne McDermott, Research & Administration
Margaret A. Turk, Training & Evaluation
Roberta S. Carlin, Dissemination
The DRDC was formed in 2012 and is a partnership between the University of South Carolina (USC), the State University of New York Upstate Medical University (SUNY Upstate), and the American Association on Health and Disability (AAHD). Its five core

areas are Administration, Research, Research Translation, Evaluation, and Dissemination & Policy.

1923 Division for Communication, Language, and Deaf/Hard of Hearing (DCD)
Council for Exceptional Children (CEC)
3100 Clarendon Blvd.
Suite 600
Arlington, VA 22201-5332
888-232-7733
TTY:866-915-5000
service@cec.sped.org
dcdcec.org

Chad Rummel, Executive Director, CEC
Dedicated to improving education for deaf/hard of hearing students, and those with communicative disabilities.

1924 Division for Culturally and Linguistically Diverse Exceptional Learners (DDEL)
Council for Exceptional Children (CEC)
3100 Clarendon Blvd.
Suite 600
Arlington, VA 22201-5332
888-232-7733
TTY:866-915-5000
ddel.exceptionalchildren@gmail.com
ddel.exceptionalchildren.org

Chad Rummel, Executive Director
Serves culturally and linguistically diverse students with disabilities.

1925 Division for Early Childhood (DEC)
PO Box 662089
Los Angeles, CA 90066
310-428-7209
FAX: 855-678-1989
dec@dec-sped.org
www.dec-sped.org

Peggy Kemp, Executive Director
Diana Stanfill, Associate Director
Brittany Clark, Operations Manager
Serves educators who work with children with special needs from birth through age 8.

1926 Division for Early Childhood of the Council for Exceptional Children
Council for Exceptional Children
3100 Clarendon Blvd.
Suite 600
Arlington, VA 22201-5332
888-232-7733
TTY:866-915-5000
service@cec.sped.org
www.dec-sped.org

Peggy Kemp, Executive Director
Diana Stanfill, Associate Director
Brittany Clark, Operations Coordinator
Promotes policies and advances evidence-based practices that support families and enhance the optimal development of young children who have or are at risk for developmental delays and disabilities.

1927 Division for Learning Disabilities (DLD)
Council for Exceptional Children (CEC)
3100 Clarendon Blvd.
Suite 600
Arlington, VA 22201-5332
888-232-7733
TTY:866-915-5000
service@cec.sped.org
www.teachingld.org

Chad Rummel, Executive Director, CEC
Seeks to enhance services, research, and legislation for persons with learning disabilities.

1928 Division for Physical, Health & Multiple Disabilities: Complex and Chronic Conditions
Council for Exceptional Children (CEC)
3100 Clarendon Blvd.
Suite 600
Arlington, VA 22201-5332
888-232-7733
TTY:866-915-5000
cecdphmd@gmail.com
ccc.exceptionalchildren.org

Chad Rummel, Executive Director

Dedicated to quality education for all individuals with physical disabilities, multiple disabilities, and special health care needs.

1929 Division for Research (CEC-DR)
Council for Exceptional Children (CEC)
3100 Clarendon Blvd.
Suite 600
Arlington, VA 22201-5332
888-232-7733
TTY:866-915-5000
service@cec.sped.org
www.cecdr.org

Chad Rummel, Executive Director, CEC
Seeks to advance research into education for the gifted and/or disabled.

1930 Division of International Special Education and Services (DISES)
Council for Exceptional Children (CEC)
3100 Clarendon Blvd.
Suite 600
Arlington, VA 22201-5332
888-232-7733
TTY:866-915-5000
info@dises-cec.org
dises-cec.org

Chad Rummel, Executive Director, CEC
Dedicated to special education programs in other countries.

1931 Division of Visual and Performing Arts Education (DARTS)
Council for Exceptional Children (CEC)
3100 Clarendon Blvd.
Suite 600
Arlington, VA 22201-5332
888-232-7733
TTY:866-915-5000
cecdartswebmaster@gmail.com
darts.exceptionalchildren.org

Chad Rummel, Executive Director
Promotes art, music, drama, and dance for students with disabilities.

1932 Division on Autism and Developmental Disabilities (DADD)
Council for Exceptional Children (CEC)
3100 Clarendon Blvd.
Suite 600
Arlington, VA 22201-5332
888-232-7733
TTY:866-915-5000
service@cec.sped.org
www.daddcec.com

Chad Rummel, Executive Director, CEC
Seeks to improve quality of life for individuals with autism and other intellectual disabilities, especially youth.

1933 Division on Career Development and Transition (DCDT)
Council for Exceptional Children (CEC)
3100 Clarendon Blvd.
Suite 600
Arlington, VA 22201-5332
888-232-7733
TTY:866-915-5000
jrazeghi@gmu.edu
www.exceptionalchildren.org

Chad Rummel, Executive Director
Dedicated to assisting disabled students with their transition from school to adult life.

1934 Division on Visual Impairments and Deafblindness (DVIDB)
Council for Exceptional Children (CEC)
3100 Clarendon Blvd.
Suite 600
Arlington, VA 22201-5332
888-232-7733
TTY:866-915-5000
dvidbwebmaster@gmail.com
dvidb.exceptionalchildren.org

Chad Rummel, Executive Director
Dedicated to assisting students with visual impairments or deafblindness.

1935 Filomen M. D'Agostino Greenberg Music School
111 E 59th St.
New York, NY 10022   315-842-4489
music@fmdgmusicschool.org
fmdgmusicschool.org

Leslie Jones, Executive Director
Dalia Sakas, Director, Music Studies
Amanda Wheeler, Director, Administration
Formerly affiliated with the Lighthouse Guild, the Filomen M. D'Agostino Greenberg Music School is the only community music school in the US for people who are blind or visually impaired, offering instruction and an accessible music technology center.

1936 HEAL: Health Education AIDS Liaison
New York, NY   347-867-4497
michaelellner2@gmail.com
www.healaids.com

Michael Ellner, President
Barnett J. Weiss, Board Member
Roberto Giraldo, Board Member
Nonprofit, community-based educational organization providing information, hope, and support to people who are HIV positive or living with AIDS. The men and women at HEAL are health professionals, people living with life threatening diseases, and volunteers.

1937 Incight
111 SW Columbia St
Suite 940
Portland, OR 97201   971-244-0305
scott@incight.org
incight.org

Scott Hatley, Executive Director
Vail Horton, Director, Results
Hannah Rankin, Director, Results
Incight in a non-profit organization that supports people with disabilities in the areas of education, employment, and independent living. Incight offers programs that address workplace descrimination, college application process and recreational needs of those they serve.

1938 Innovations in Special Education Technology Division (ISET)
Council for Exceptional Children (CEC)
3100 Clarendon Blvd.
Suite 600
Arlington, VA 22201-5332   888-232-7733
TTY:866-915-5000
service@cec.sped.org
www.isetcec.org

Chad Rummel, Executive Director, CEC
Advocates for technology and media to assist gifted persons and those with disabilities.

1939 International Childbirth Education Association
110 Horizon Dr.
Suite 210
Raleigh, NC 27615   919-674-4183
FAX: 919-459-2075
info@icea.org
www.icea.org

Katesha Phillips, Executive Director
Jenna Westheimer, Membership & Certification Coordinator
Allison Winter, Marketing Coordinator
The Association offers teaching certificates, seminars, continuing education workshops, and mail order center.

1940 International Dyslexia Association
40 York Rd.
4th Floor
Baltimore, MD 21204   410-296-0232
FAX: 410-321-5069
info@dyslexiaida.org
dyslexiaida.org

Sonja Banks, Chief Executive Officer
David Holste, Chief Financial Officer
Jason Marshall, Interim Chief Communications & Engagement Officer
Provides free information and referral services for diagnosis and tutoring for parents, educators, physicians, and individuals with dyslexia. Membership includes yearly journal and quarterly newsletter, and Pennsylvania newsletter; discounts to conferences and events.

1941 Job Accommodation Network
PO Box 6080
Morgantown, WV 26506-6080   304-216-8189
800-526-7234
FAX: 304-293-5407
TTY: 877-781-9403
jan@askjan.org
askjan.org

JAN's mission is to facilitate the employment and retention of workers with disabilities by providing employers, employment providers, people with disabilities, their family members, and other interested parties with information on job accommodations, self-employment, and small business opportunities and related subjects.

1942 LD Online
2775 S. Quincy St.
Arlington, VA 22206   FAX: 703-998-2060
ldonline@weta.org
ldonline.org

Noel Gunther, Executive Director
Christian Lindstrom, Director, Learning Media
Lydia Breiseth, Director, Colorin Colorado
LD OnLine seeks to help children and adults reach their full potential by providing accurate and up-to-date information and advice about learning disabilities and ADHD. The site features hundreds of helpful articles, multimedia, monthly columns by noted experts, first person essays, children's writing and artwork, a comprehensive resource guide, very active forums, and a Yellow Pages referral directory of professionals, schools, and products.

1943 Lighthouse Guild
250 West 64th Street
New York, NY 10023   800-284-4422
www.lighthouseguild.org

Calvin W. Roberts, President & CEO
James M. Dubin, Chairman
Lawrence E. Goldschmidt, Vice Chairman & Treasurer
Lighthouse Guild is a not-for-profit vision & healthcare organization, addressing the needs of people who are blind or visually impaired, including those with multiple disabilities or chronic medical conditions.

1944 Michigan Psychological Association
124 W Allegan St.
Suite 1900
Lansing, MI 48933   517-347-1885
FAX: 517-484-4442
www.michiganpsychologicalassociation.org

Antu Segal, President
Valencia Montgomery, Treasurer
Cynthia S. Rodriguez, Secretary
Nonprofit organization of over 1000 psychologists, working to advance psychology as a science and a profession and to promote the public welfare by encouraging the highest professional standards, offering public education and providing a public service, and by participating in the public policy process on behalf of the profession and health care consumers.

1945 National Association for Adults with Special Learning Needs
P.O. Box 716
Bryn Mawr, PA 19010   naasln.org
Richard Cooper, Co-President
Joan Hudson-Miller, Co-President
Frances A. Holthaus, Vice President
NAASLN is an association for those who serve adults with special learning needs. NAASLN members include educators, trainers, employers and human service providers.

1946 National Association of Colleges and Employers
62 Highland Ave.
Bethlehem, PA 18017   610-868-1421
admin@naceweb.org
naceweb.org

Jennifer Lasater, President
Shawn Vanderziel, Executive Director

A national association with services for career planning, placement and recruitment professionals.

1947 National Association of Parents with Children in Special Education
3642 E Sunnydale Dr.
Chandler Heights, AZ 85142   800-754-4421
                                   FAX: 800-424-0371
                                   contact@napcse.org
                                   www.napcse.org

George Giuliani, President
NAPCSEis a national membership organization dedicated to rendering all possible support and assistance to parents whose children receive special education services, both in and outside of school.

1948 National Association of State Directors of Special Education
1000 Diagonal Rd.
Suite 600
Alexandria, VA 22314   703-519-3800
                                 FAX: 703-519-3808
                                 www.nasdse.org

John Eisenberg, Executive Director
Valerie Williams, Director, Government Relations
Joanne Cashman, Member Services
NASDSE focuses on improving educational services and outcomes for children and youth with disabilities throughout the United States, the Department of Defense, the federated territories and the Freely Associated States of Palau, Micronesia and the Marshall Islands.

1949 National Center for Homeopathy
1120 Route 73
Suite 200
Mount Laurel, NJ 08054   856-437-4752
                                 FAX: 856-439-0525
                                 www.homeopathycenter.org

Deb Dupnik, Executive Director
Natascha Williams, Meeting Manager
Steve Clark, Membership Coordinator
The National Center for Homeopathy (NCH) is a non-profit organization dedicated to promoting health through homeopathy by advancing the use and practice of homeopathy.

1950 National Council on Rehabilitation Education (NCRE)
1099 E. Champlain Dr.
Suite A-137
Fresno, CA 93720   559-906-0787
                                 info@ncre.org
                                 ncre.org

David A. Rosenthal, Ph.D, CRC, President
Mona Robinson, Ph.D, CRC, First Vice President
Allison Fleming, Ph.D, CRC, Second Vice President
Members include academic institutions and organizations, professional educators, researchers, and students. Assists in the documentation of the effect of education in improving services to persons with disabilities; determines the skills and training necessary for effective rehabilitation services; develops role models, standards and uniform licensure and certification requirements for rehabilitation personnel.

1951 National Education Association of the United States
1201 16th St. NW
Washington, DC 20036-3290   202-833-4000
                                 FAX: 202-822-7974
                                 www.nea.org

Lily Eskelsen Garcia, President
Becky Pringle, Vice President
Princess R. Moss, Secretary/Treasurer
The National Education Association (NEA) is committed to advancing the cause of public education.

1952 National Society for Experiential Education
19 Mantua Rd.
Mount Royal, NJ 08061   856-423-3427
                                 FAX: 856-423-3420
                                 nsee@talley.com
                                 www.nsee.org

Haley Burst, Executive Director
Wendy Stevens, Meeting Manager
Arianna B., Program Manager
National nonprofit organization which advocates experiential learning and works with college administrators and high school and college internship programs.

1953 Servcies for Students with Disabilities (SSD)
College Board
P.O. Box 7504
London, KY 40742-7504   212-713-8333
                                 844-255-7728
                                 FAX: 866-360-0114
                                 ssd@info.collegeboard.org
                                 www.collegeboard.com

David Coleman, Chief Executive Officer
Jeremy Singer, President
Tracy MacMahon, Senior Vice President, Operations
National, nonprofit association dedicated to preparing, inspiring and connecting students to college and opportunity. Provide the accomodations students with disabilities need to complete test and other evaluations.

1954 Society for Disability Studies
P.O. Box 5570
Eureka, CA 95502   510-206-5767
                                 sds@disstudies.org
                                 www.disstudies.org

Devva Kasnitz, Ph.D, Interim Executive Director
SDS is a scholarly association of more than 400 artists, scholars and activists who promote Disability Studies, recognizing disability as a complex and valuable aspect of human experience.

1955 Teacher Education Division (TED)
Council for Exceptional Children (CEC)
3100 Clarendon Blvd.
Suite 600
Arlington, VA 22201-5332   888-232-7733
                                 TTY:866-915-5000
                                 service@cec.sped.org
                                 tedcec.org

Chad Rummel, Executive Director, CEC
Sharon Rodriguez, Governance & Executive Services Coordinator
Advocates for continual professional development of professionals in special education and related fields.

1956 The AG Academy for Listening and Spoken Language
Alexander Graham Bell Association
3417 Volta Pl. NW
Washington, DC 20007   202-337-5220
                                 FAX: 202-337-8314
                                 TTY:202-337-5221
                                 academy@agbell.org
                                 agbellacademy.org

Jenna Voss, Chair
Emilio Alonso-Mendoza, Chief Executive Officer
Listening and Spoken Language Specialists (LSLST) work with infants and children who are deaf or hard of hearing and their families seeking a listening and spoken language outcome in a variety of settings: home-based intervention, public schools, independent schools, private therapy, clinical centers for the deaf and hard of hearing, audiological and cochlear implant centers.

1957 The Association for the Gifted (TAG)
Council for Exceptional Children (CEC)
3100 Clarendon Blvd.
Suite 600
Arlington, VA 22201-5332   888-232-7733
                                 TTY:866-915-5000
                                 tag.cec@gmail.com
                                 cectag.com

Chad Rummel, Executive Director, CEC
Sharon Rodriguez, Governance & Executive Services Coordinator
Serves parents and professionals working with gifted and talented children.

1958 United Cerebral Palsy
1825 K St. NW
Suite 600
Washington, DC 20006-5638   202-776-0406
                                    www.ucp.org

Armando Contreras, President & CEO
Anita Porco, Vice President, Affiliate Network
Michael Ludgardo, Manager, Development
United Cerebral Palsy (UCP) educates, advocates and provides
support services to ensure a life without limits for people with a
spectrum of disabilities. UCP and its nearly 68+ affiliates have a
mission to advance the independence, productivity and full citizenship of people with a broad range of disabilities by providing
services and support to children and adults.

Directories

1959 ADDitude Directory
108 West 39th St.
Suite 805
New York, NY 10018   646-366-0830
                            FAX: 646-366-0842
                            customerservice@additudemag.com
                            directory.additudemag.com
The ADDitude Directory is a comprehensive directory that contains listings from some of the nation'sleading specialists in attention deficit disorder (ADD/ADHD) and learning disabilities.

**1960 BOSC: Directory of Facilities for People with Learning
Disabilities**
Books on Special Children
PO Box 3378
Amherst, MA 1004-3378   413-256-8164
                               FAX: 413-256-8896

Michael Young, President
Directory of schools, independent living programs, clinics and
centers, colleges and vocational programs, agencies and commercial products. Five sections in special post binder that can be updated annually. Hardcover. *$70.00*
300+ pages Yearly
ISSN 0961-3888

1961 Community Resource Directory
5300 Hiatus Road
Sunrise, FL 33351   954-745-9779
                           800-963-5337
                           webmaster@adrcbroward.org
                           www.adrcbroward.org
The document contains over 355 pages of updated information regarding programs and services for elder residents of Broward.

1962 Complete Learning Disabilities Resource Guide
Grey House Publishing
4919 Route 22
P.O. Box 56
Amenia, NY 12501   518-789-8700
                          800-562-2139
                          FAX: 518-789-0556
                          books@greyhouse.com
                          www.greyhouse.com

Leslie Mackenzie, Publisher
Laura Mars, Editorial Director
Jessica Moody, Vice President, Marketing
A comprehensive educational guide offering over 6,000 listings
on associations and organizations, schools, government agencies, testing materials, camps, products, books, newsletters, legal
information, classroom materials and more. Includes separate
chapters on ADD and Literacy, as well as informative articles.
$165.00
800 pages Annual

1963 Complete Mental Health Resource Guide
Sedgwick Press/Grey House Publishing
4919 Route 22
P.O. Box 56
Amenia, NY 12501   518-789-8700
                          800-562-2139
                          FAX: 518-789-0556
                          books@greyhouse.com
                          www.greyhouse.com

Leslie Mackenzie, Publisher
Laura Mars, Editorial Director
Jessica Moody, Vice President, Marketing
This directory offers comprehensive information covering the
field of behavioral health, with critical information for both the
layman and the mental health professional. It covers, in depth, 22
specific mental disorders, and includes informative descriptions
and a complete list of resources. *$165.00*
800 pages Annual

1964 Complete Resource Guide for Pediatric Disorders
Sedgwick Press/Grey House Publishing
4919 Route 22
P.O. Box 56
Amenia, NY 12501   518-789-8700
                          800-562-2139
                          FAX: 518-789-0556
                          books@greyhouse.com
                          www.greyhouse.com

Leslie Mackenzie, Publisher
Laura Mars, Editorial Director
Jessica Moody, Vice President, Marketing
An annual directory for professionals, parents and caregivers.
Provides valuable information on more than 200 pediatric conditions, disorders, diseases and disabilities, including informative
descriptions and a wide variety of resources, from associations to
publications. *$165.00*
1000 pages Annual

**1965 Complete Resource Guide for People with Chronic
Illness**
Grey House Publishing
4919 Route 22
P.O. Box 56
Amenia, NY 12501   518-789-8700
                          800-562-2139
                          FAX: 518-789-0556
                          books@greyhouse.com
                          www.greyhouse.com

Leslie Mackenzie, Publisher
Laura Mars, Editorial Director
Jessica Moody, Vice President, Marketing
This directory is structured around the 80 most prevalent chronic
illnesses. Each chronic illness chapter includes an informative
description, plus a comprehensive listing of resources and support services available for people diagnosed with chronic illness
and their network of supportive individuals. *$165.00*
1000 pages Annual

1966 Directory Of Services For People With Disabilities
117 W. Duval St.
Suite 205
Jacksonville, FL 32202-4111   904-630-4940
                                     FAX: 904-630-3476
                                     TTY:904-630-4933
                                     disabledservices@coj.net
                                     www.coj.net
The agencies listed in this guide can be of great assistance to per-
sons with disabilities and their family members.

1967 Directory for Exceptional Children
Prorter Sargent
2 LAN Drive
Suite 100
Westford, MA 01886
978-692-5092
800-342-7470
FAX: 978-692-4714
info@carnegiecomm.com
www.carnegiecomm.com

Joe Moore, President, CEO
Mark Cunningham, SVP, Enrollment Marketing
Melissa Rekos, SVP, Digital Services
Supports parents and professionals seeking the optimal educational, therapeutic or clinical environment for special-needs youth. *$75.00*
1120 pages Trienniel
ISBN 0-875581-50-1

1968 Educators Resource Guide
Grey House Publishing
4919 Route 22
PO Box 55
Amenia, NY 12501
518-789-8700
800-562-2139
FAX: 845-373-6390
books@greyhouse.com
www.greyhouse.com

Leslie Mackenzie, Publisher
Laura Mars, Editorial Director
Jessica Moody, Vice President, Marketing
Gives education professionals immediate access to Associations and Organizations, Conferences and Trade Shows, Educational Research Centers, Employment Opportunities and Teaching Abroad, School Library Services, Scholarships, Financial Resources and much more. *$145.00*
650 pages Annual

1969 Greater Milwaukee Area Health Care Guide for Older Adults
PO Box 285
Germantown, WI 53022
262-253-0901
FAX: 262-253-0903
info@seniorresourcesonline.com
www.seniorresourcesonline.com

Gary Knippen, President
This directory is designed for older adults, family members and professionals looking for health care options in Milwaukee, Ozaukee, Washington and Waukesha counties. The directory is comprehensive with all providers included at no charge.

1970 Greater Milwaukee Area Senior Housing Options
PO Box 285
Germantown, WI 53022
262-253-0901
FAX: 262-253-0903
info@seniorresourcesonline.com
www.seniorresourcesonline.com

Gary Knippen, President
This directory is designed for older adults, family members and professionals looking for senior housing options in Milwaukee, Ozaukee, Washington and Waukesha counties. The directory is comprehensive with all providers included at no charge.

1971 Indiana Directory of Disability Resources
225 S. University Street
ABE Bldg.
West Lafayette, IN 47907-2093
765-494-5013
800-825-4264
bng@ecn.purdue.edu
engineering.purdue.edu/~bng/IDDR/
The purpose of the Indiana Directory of Disability Resources (IDDR) is to provide Hoosiers with a useful guide to disability services and to increase the public's awareness of the available resources.

1972 Nevada's Care Connection
3416 Goni Road
Suite D-132
Carson City, NV 89706
702-486-3600
cpasquale@adsd.nv.gov
www.nevadaadrc.com

Cheyenne Pasquale, ADRC Project Manager

Nevada's Care Connection: Aging and Disability Resource Center (ADRC) program provides information and access to programs and services that benefit Nevada's seniors, people with disabilities and caregivers.

1973 Northeast Wisconsin Directory of Servicesfor Older Adults
PO Box 285
Germantown, WI 53022
262-253-0901
FAX: 262-253-0903
info@seniorresourcesonline.com
www.seniorresourcesonline.com

Gary Knippen, President
This directory is designed for older adults, family members and professionals looking for housing and health care options in Brown, Calumet, Door, Fond du Lac, Green Lake, Kewaunee, Manitowoc, Marinette, Marquette, Oconto, Outagamie, Shawano, Sheboygan, Waupaca, Waushara and Winnebago counties.

1974 ODHH Directory of Resources and Services
1521 N. 6th Street
Harrisburg, PA 17102
717-783-4912
TTY:717-783-4912
RA-LI-OVR-ODHH@pa.gov
ODHH is the office for the Deaf & Hard of Hearing's one-stop listing of resources and services for people who are deaf or hard of hearing.

1975 Responding to Crime Victims with Disabilities
2000 M Street NW
Suite 480
Washington, DC 20036
202-467-8700
FAX: 202-467-8701
www.victimsofcrime.org

Philip M. Gerson, Chair
G. Morris Gurley, Vice-Chair
Mai Fernandez, Executive Director
The mission of the National Center for Victims of Crime is to forge a national commitment to help victims of crime rebuild their lives. It is dedicated to serving individuals, families, and communities harmed by crime.

1976 Selective Placement Program Coordinator Directory
1900 E Street, NW
Washington, DC 20415-1000
202-606-1800
www.opm.gov
Selective Placement Program Coordinator (SPPC) who helps management recruit, hire and accommodate people with disabilities

1977 South Central Wisconsin Directory of Services for Older Adults
PO Box 285
Germantown, WI 53022
262-253-0901
www.seniorresourcesonline.com

Gary Knippen, President
This directory is designed for older adults, family members and professionals looking for housing and health care options in Columbia, Dane, Dodge, Grant, Green, Iowa, Jefferson, Juneau, Lafayette, Richland, Rock, Sauk, and Walworth counties.

1978 Southeast Wisconsin Directory of Servicesfor Older Adults
PO Box 285
Germantown, WI 53022
262-253-0901
www.seniorresourcesonline.com

Gary Knippen, President
This directory is designed for older adults, family members and professionals looking for housing and health care options in Kenosha, Racine and Walworth counties.

1979 Teaching Special Students in Mainstream
Books on Special Children
P.O.Box 305
Congers, NY 10920-305
845-638-1236
FAX: 845-638-0847
Overview of mainstream, team of professionals managing classroom behavior, tips for teachers, social acceptance and handling of specific differences. *$33.00*
515 pages Softcover

Educational Publishers

1980   AFB Press
American Foundation for the Blind / AFB Press
2 Penn Plaza
Suite 1102
New York, NY 10121   212-502-7600
                                           FAX: 888-545-8331
                                              afbinfo@afb.net
                                                  www.afb.org
Carl R. Augusto, President and CEO
Paul Schroeder, Vice President, Programs and Policy
Rick Bozeman, Chief Financial Officer
Develops, publishes, and sells a wide variety of informative
books, pamphlets, periodicals, and videos for students, professionals, and researchers in the blindness and visual impairment
fields, for people professionally involved in making the mainstream community accessible, and for blind and visually impaired people and their families; publication and video orders.

1981   Academic Therapy Publications
Academic Therapy Publications / High Noon Books
20 Leveroni Ct.
Novato, CA 94949-5746   415-883-3314
                                               800-422-7249
                                          FAX: 888-287-9975
                                    sales@academictherapy.com
                                       www.academictherapy.com
Jim Arena, President
Stacy Frauwirth, Assessment Project Manager
Holly Melton, Head Writer & Senior Project Manager
Academic Therapy Publications produces and distributes psy-
chological and educational tests used by professionals involved
in special education and learning differences in the K-12 school
system as well as adult services.

1982   AccessText Network
512 Means St. NW
Suite 250
Atlanta, GA 30318   866-271-4968
                                   membership@accesstext.org
                                           www.accesstext.org
Dawn Evans, AccessText Network Coordinator
AccessText is a conduit between the publishing world and colleges and universities across the country, with a shared mission to
ensure students with disabilities have equal access to their textbooks in an accessible format and in a timely manner.

1983   American Counseling Association (ACA)
P.O. Box 31110
Alexandria, VA 22310-9998   800-347-6647
                                          FAX: 800-473-2329
                                             www.counseling.org
Richard Yep, Chief Executive Officer
Kimberly N. Torres-Rivera, President
Edil Torres-Rivera, President-Elect
Offers tools and books for counseling professionals.

1984   Association of University Centers on Disabilities (AUCD)
AUCD
1100 Wayne Ave.
Suite 1000
Silver Spring, MD 20910   301-588-8252
                                          FAX: 301-588-2842
                                             aucdinfo@aucd.org
                                                 www.aucd.org
John Tschida, Executive Director
Michele Lunsford, Director, Marketing & Communications
*Dawn Rudolph, Senior Director, Technical Assistance & Network
Engagement*
AUCD is a membership organization consisting of University
Centers for Excellence in Developmental Disabilities (UCEDD),
Leadership Education in Neurodevelopmental Disabilities
(LEND) Programs, and Intellectual and Developmental Disabil-
ity Research Centers (IDDRC). AUCD supports its members
through advocacy, technical assistance, information
dissemination, networking, and leadership.

1985   Brookes Publishing Company
PO Box 10624
Baltimore, MD 21285-0624   410-337-9580
                                               800-638-3775
                                          FAX: 410-337-8539
                                webmaster@brookespublishing.com
                                       www.brookespublishing.com
Paul H. Brookes, Chairman of the Board
Jeffrey D. Brookes, President
George S. Stamathis, VP/Publisher
Publishes highly respected resources in early childhood, early in-
tervention, inclusive and special education, developmental dis-
abilities, learning disabilities, communication and language,
behavior and mental health.

1986   Brookline Books
8 Trumbull Rd
B-001
Northampton, MA 01060   413-584-0184
                                               800-666-2665
                                          FAX: 413-584-6184
                                          brbooks@yahoo.com
                                           www.brooklinebks.com
Offering books ranging from non-fiction to poetry that both share
vital stories about disability and education, and present strategies
and possible solutions in situations related to general education
or to specific circumstances.

1987   Brooks/Cole Publishing Company
511 Forest Lodge Rd
Pacific Grove, CA 93950-5040   831-373-0728
                                               800-354-9706
                                          FAX: 831-375-6414
Offers books in Special Education for those preparing to be special educators and for in-service professionals.

1988   BurnsBooks Publishing
680 Ridge Road
Middletown, CT 6457   860-344-0233
                                          FAX: 860-344-0233
                                        burnsbookspub@aol.com
                                       www.burnsbookspublishing.com
urnsBooks create confidence and overcome anxiety in the new
reader through the use of carefully controlled vocabulary, larger
print, and greater spaces between sentences.

1989   Charles C Thomas Publisher LTD
2600 S 1st Street
Springfield, IL 62704-4730   217-789-8980
                                               800-258-8980
                                          FAX: 217-789-9130
                                          books@ccthomas.com
                                             www.ccthomas.com
Michael P. Thomas, President
Publishes specialty titles and textbooks in medicine, dentistry,
nursing, and veterinary medicine, as well as a complete line in the
behavioral sciences, criminal justice, education, special education, and rehabilitation. Aims to accommodate the current needs
for information.

1990   DisabilityAdvisor.com
37 North Orange Ave.
Suite 500
Orlando, FL 32801   321-332-7800
                                               888-393-1010
                                          FAX: 888-985-6060
                                       www.disabilityadvisor.com
Joseph E. Ram, Publisher
Kay Derochie, Editor
Jackie Booth, Ph.D., Editor
DisabilityAdvisor.com provides free information on federal and
state disability benefits programs and other resources for readers
and their families. This includes disabled children and students,
military veterans, injured workers and disabled seniors. Readers
are encouraged to submit their questions and comments online.
The website also offers information on managing finances, education, parenting, relationships and other issues of interest to the
disabled and their friends and families.

1991 Dolphin Computer Access
231 Clarksville Road
Suite 7
Princeton Junction, NJ 8550

866-797-5921
FAX: 609-799-0475
info@dolphinusa.com
www.yourdolphin.com

Noel Duffy, Managing Director
Dolphin helps vision and print impairments

1992 Gallaudet University Press
800 Florida Avenue, NE
Washington, DC 20002-3695

202-651-5488
FAX: 202-651-5489
gupress@gallaudet.edu
gupress.gallaudet.edu

David F Armstrong, Executive Director
Publishes scholarly trade books and journals about deaf people
and their language, history, and culture for deaf people, parents of
deaf children, professionals, educators and the general public.
Produces spring and fall catalogs.

1993 Greenwood Publishing Group
88 Post Rd W
Westport, CT 06880-4208

203-226-3571
FAX: 203-222-1502
webmaster@greenwood.com
greenwood.com

Wayne Smith, President
Kirstin Olsen, Author
ABC-CLIO and Greenwood Press are recognized as indus-
try-leading providers of the highest-quality reference materials.
These imprints offer authoritative reference scholarship and innovative coverage of history and humanities topics across the
secondary and higher education curriculum.

1994 Grey House Publishing
4919 Route 22
P.O. Box 56
Amenia, NY 12501

518-789-8700
800-562-2139
FAX: 518-789-0556
books@greyhouse.com
www.greyhouse.com

Leslie Mackenzie, Publisher
Laura Mars, Editorial Director
Jessica Moody, Vice President, Marketing
Grey House Publishing publishes directories, handbooks and reference works for public, high school and academic libraries and
the business and health communities. Most titles are available as
online databases.

1995 Hammill Institute on Disabilities
8700 Shoal Creek Blvd.
Austin, TX 78757-6897

512-451-3521
FAX: 512-451-3728
info@hammill-institute.org
hammill-institute.org
The Institute was organized for charitable, scientific, and educational purposes to enhance the well-being of people with disabilities, their parents and caretakers. The Institute publishes journals
and monographs on the subject in collaboration with other
associations.

1996 Harbor House Law Press
PO Box 480
Hartfield, VA 23071

804-758-8400
FAX: 202-318-3239
webmaster@wrightslaw.com
www.harborhouselaw.com
Harbor House Law Pressdevelops user-friendly publications
about special education law and advocacy.

1997 High Noon Books
Academic Therapy Publications / High Noon Books
20 Leveroni Ct
Novato, CA 94949-5746

800-422-7249
888-287-9975
products@academictherapy.com
www.highnoonbooks.com

Jim Arena, President
Holly Melton, Head Writer & Senior Project Manager
High Noon Books produces and distributes a variety of pho-
nic-based and high-interest/low level chapter books, ebooks, and
audio for beginning, at-risk, and struggling readers.

1998 Information from HEATH Resource Center
National Clearinghouse on Postsecondary Education
2134 G Street, N.W.
Washington, DC 20052

202-939-9320
800-544-3284
FAX: 202-833-5696
www.HEATH-resource-center.org
The HEATH Resource Center operates the national clearinghouse on postsecondary education for individuals with disabilities. Support from the US Department of Education enables the
Center, a program of the America Council on Education, to serve
as an information exchange on educational support services; adaptations; and opportunities at American campuses, vocational-technical schools, adult education programs, independent
living centers, and other postsecondary training entities.

1999 Lynne Rienner Publishers
1800 30th St.
Ste. 314
Boulder, CO 80301

303-444-6684
FAX: 303-444-0824
www.rienner.com
Lynne Rienner Publishers founded in 1984 publishes in the fields
of international studies and comparative politics (all world regions), US politics, and sociology and criminology (with a US
focus).

2000 MAPCON Technologies
8191 Birchwood Court
Suite A
Johnston, IA 50131-2930

515-331-3358
800-223-4791
FAX: 515-331-3373
www.mapcon.com

Joel Tesdall, President/CEO
Diane Wiand, Client Solutions Advocate
Lora Whicker, Accounting
MAPCON is a computerized maintainance management soft-
ware.

2001 McGraw-Hill Company
PO Box 182605
Columbus, OH 43218

800-338-3987
FAX: 609-308-4480
customer.service@mheducation.com
www.mcgraw-hill.com

David Levin, President, CEO
Ellen Haley, President, CTB
Peter Cohen, President, School Education
Offers a catalog of testing resources and materials for the special
educator.

2002 National Association of School Psychologists
4340 East West Hwy.
Suite 402
Bethesda, MD 20814

301-657-0270
866-331-6277
FAX: 301-657-0275
TTY: 301-657-4155
www.nasponline.org

Kathleen Minke, Executive Director
Laura Benson, Chief Operating Officer
Represents over 25,000 school psychologists and related professionals. It serves its members and society by advancing the profession of school psychology and advocating for the rights,
welfare, education and mental health of children, youth and their
families.

2003   **National Center for Learning Disabilities**
32 Laight St
2nd Floor
New York, NY 10013

212-545-7510
888-575-7373
FAX: 212-545-9665
info@ncld.org
www.ncld.org

Frederic M Poses, Chairman
Mimi Corcoran, President & CEO
Rashonda Ambrose, Director of Strategic Partnerships
Contains features, articles, human interest news and other practical material to benefit children and adults with learning disabilities and their families, as well as educators and other helping professionals. The center also offers online forums and other resources on their website.
Quarterly

2004   **PEAK Parent Center**
917 East Moreno Ave.
Suite 140
Colorado Springs, CO 80903

719-531-9400
FAX: 719-531-9452
info@peakparent.org
www.peakparent.org

Michele Williers, Executive Director
Pam Christy, Director, Parent Training & Information
PEAK Parent Center is Colorado's federally-designated Parent Training and Information Center (PTI). As a PTI, PEAK supports and empowers parents, providing them with information and strategies to use when advocating for their children with disabilities. PEAK works one-on-one with families and educators helping them realize new possibilities for children with disabilities by expanding knowledge of special education and offering new strategies for success.
1986

2005   **PRO-ED**
8700 Shoal Creek Boulevard
Austin, TX 78757-6897

512-451-3246
800-897-3202
FAX: 512-451-8542
info@proedinc.com
www.proedinc.com

PRO-ED Inc. is a publisher of standardized tests, books, curricular resources, and therapy materials. PRO-ED Inc's products are used by professionals, parents, and students around the world.

2006   **Peytral Publications**
P.O. Box 1162
Minnetonka, MN 55345

952-949-8707
TTY:952-906-9777
www.peytral.com

An independent publisher and distributor of special education materials which promote Success for All Learners.

2007   **Prufrock Press**
PO Box 8813
Waco, TX 76714

254-756-3337
800-998-2208
FAX: 800-240-0333
jmcintosh@prufrock.com
www.prufrock.com

Joel McIntosh, Publisher
Lacy Compton, Senior Editor
Rachel Taliaferro, Editor
Publishes books, textbooks, teaching materials supporting the education of gifted, advanced, and twice-exceptional learners.

2008   **Research Press**
P.O. Box 7886
Champaign, IL 61826

217-352-3273
800-519-2707
FAX: 217-352-1221
orders@researchpress.com
www.researchpress.com

Robert W. Parkinson, Founder
Dr Richard M Foxx, Author
Jeffrey S. Allen, Author
Research Press is an independent, family-owned business founded in 1968 by Robert W. Parkinson (1920-2001). During the past 40 years, the company has earned a solid reputation for publishing practical and effective educational and mental health resources. Authors from the early years include well-known names in the field of psychology, such as B.F. Skinner, Albert Ellis, Gerald Patterson, Wesley Becker, John Guttmann, Richard Foxx, Arnold Lazarus, and Joseph Cautela.

2009   **Research Press Company**
2612 N. Mattis Ave.
Champaign, IL 61822

217-352-3273
800-519-2707
FAX: 217-352-1221
www.researchpress.com

Research Press is an independent, family-owned business founded in 1968 by Robert W. Parkinson

2010   **Sage Publications**
2455 Teller Road
Thousand Oaks, CA 91320

805-499-0721
800-818-7243
FAX: 800-583-2665
info@sagepub.com
www.sagepub.com

Sara Miller McCune, Founder, Publisher & Executive Chairman
Blaise R Simqu, President/CEO
Chris Hickok, Senior Vice President & Chief Financial Officer
Publishes books, text books, journals, reference books, and databases mainly related to psychology, special education and speech, language and hearing.

2011   **Special Needs Project**
Special Needs Project
324 State Street
Suite H
Santa Barbara, CA 93101-2364

818-718-9900
800-333-6867
FAX: 818-349-2027
editor@specialneeds.com
www.specialneeds.com

Hod Gray, Owner
Publishes child development textbooks, books about aspergers syndrome, autism, and other disabilities.

2012   **Supporting Success for Children with Hearing Loss**
15619 Premiere Drive
Suite 101
Tampa, FL 33624

850-363-9909
FAX: 480-393-4331
accounting@successforkidswithhearingloss.com
successforkidswithhearinglo ss.com

Karen Anderson, PhD, Director
Improving the Outcomes of Children with Hearing Loss

2013   **Woodbine House**
6510 Bells Mill Road
Bethesda, MD 20817

800-843-7323
info@woodbinehouse.com
www.woodbinehouse.com

Woodbine House is a publisher specializing in books about children with special needs.

State Agencies: Alabama

2014   **Alabama Department of Education: Division of Special Education Services**
50 North Ripley St
P.O. Box 302101
Montgomery, AL 36104

334-242-9700
FAX: 334-262-2677
www.alsde.edu

Crystal Richardson, Program Coordinator
Provides technical assistance to all education agencies serving Alabama's gifted children as well as children with disabilities.

State Agencies: Alaska

2015 Alaska Department of Education: Special Education
State of Alaska
801 West 10th St
Ste 200, P.O.Box 110500
Juneau, AK 99811-0500 907-465-8693
FAX: 907-465-2806
TTY:907-465-2815
sped@alaska.gov
www.education.alaska.gov/TLS/SPED
Dr. Susan McCauley, Division Director
Paul Prussing, Deputy Director
Cassidy Jones, Special Education Programs Manager
Administers special educational programs to the disabled residents of Alaska, through the Division of Teaching & Learning Support.

State Agencies: Arkansas

2016 Arkansas Department of Special Education
1401 West Capitol Ave, Victory Bldg
Suite 450
Little Rock, AR 72201 501-682-4221
FAX: 501-682-3456
TTY:501-682-4222
spedsupport@arkansas.gov
arksped.k12.ar.us

Tom Hicks, Interim Associate Director
Ella Albert, Management Project Analyst
Howie Knoff, Director
Provides oversight of all educational programs for children and youth with disabilities, ages 3 to 21. Provides technical assistance to all public agencies providing educational services to this population.

State Agencies: California

2017 California Department of Education: Special Education Division
1430 N Street
Sacramento, CA 95814-5901 916-319-0800
FAX: 916-327-3516
scheduler@cde.ca.gov
www.cde.ca.gov
Tom Torlakson, State Superintendent of Public Instruction and Director of E
Fred Balcom, Director
Gordon Jackson, Director
Information and resources to serve the unique needs of persons with disabilities so that each person will meet or exceed high standards of achievement in academic and nonacademic skills.

State Agencies: Colorado

2018 Colorado Department of Education: Special Education Service Unit
Colorado Department of Education
201 E Colfax Ave
Denver, CO 80203-1704 303-866-6600
FAX: 303-830-0793
www.cde.state.co.us
Ed Steinberg, Commissioner
Provides consultation on materials and educational services for visually handicapped children, supervises volunteer services, transcribes textbooks for visually handicapped students.

State Agencies: Connecticut

2019 Connecticut Department of Education: Bureau of Special Education
165 Capitol Avenue
Hartford, CT 06106 860-713-6543
FAX: 860-713-7014
www.sde.ct.gov

Anne Louise Thompson, Bureau Chief
Lisa Spooner, Administrative Assistant
Regina Gaunichaux, Secretary
The State Board of Education believes each student is unique and needs an educational environment that provides for, and accommodates, his or her strengths and areas of needed improvement.

2020 Department of Rehabilitation Services & Bureau of Education And Services for the Blind
State of Connecticut Agency
184 Windsor Ave
Windsor, CT 06095-4536 860-602-4000
800-842-4510
FAX: 860-602-4020
TTY: 860-602-4221
brian.sigman@ct.gov
www.ct.gov/besb
The Bureau of Education and Services for the Blind (BESB), within the Department of Rehabilitation Services provides resources, comprehensive low vision services, specialized education services, life skills training, case management, and vocational services to individuals of all ages who are legally blind and to children who are visually impaired.

State Agencies: Delaware

2021 Department of Public Instruction: Exceptional Children & Special Programs Division
Department of Education
Ste 2
401 Federal St
Dover, DE 19901-3639 302-739-5471
FAX: 302-739-2388
www.doe.k12.de.us
Martha Toomey, Executive Director

State Agencies: DC

2022 Administration for Community Living
330 C St. SW
Washington, DC 20201 202-401-4634
www.acl.gov
Anjali Forber-Pratt, Director
Alison Barkoff, Acting Administrator & Assistant Secretary, Aging
Vicki Gottlich, Deputy Administrator, Policy & Evaluation
ACL's mission is to maximize the independence and well-being of people with disabilities so that they can participate fully in society. ACL achieves its goals by funding services provided by community-based organizations and investing in research, education and innovation.

2023 District of Columbia Public Schools: Special Education Division
1200 First Street, NE
Washington, DC 20002-4210 202-442-5885
202-442-5517
FAX: 202-442-5026
www.dcps.dc.gov
Paul L Vance MD, Superintendent
Committed to providing a continuum of services that offers students with disabilities the opportunity to actively participate in the learning environment of their neighborhood school.

2024 Federal Emergency Management Agency
500 C Street S.W.
Washington, DC 20472   202-646-2500
                              800-621-3362
                              TTY:800-427-5593
                              www.fema.gov

W. Craig Fugate, Administrator
Michael Coen, Jr., Chief of Staff
Joseph Nimmich, Deputy Administrator
FEMA's mission is to support the citizens and first responders to ensure that as a nation we work together to build, sustain and improve our capability to prepare for, protect against, respond to, recover from and mitigate all hazards.

2025 Lab School of Washington
4759 Reservoir Rd NW
Washington, DC 20007-1921   202-965-6600
                              www.labschool.org

Mimi W. Dawson, Chair
Mac Bernstein, Vice Chair
Mike Tongour, Secretary
The Lab School six week summer session includes individualized reading, spelling, writing, study skills and math programs. A multisensory approach addresses the needs of bright learning disabled children. Related services such as speech/language therapy and occupational therapy are integrated into the curriculum. Elementary/Intermediate; Junior High/High School.

2026 National Clearinghouse on Family Support and Children's Mental Health
Ste 800
1 Dupont Cir NW
Washington, DC 20036-1149   202-939-9320
                              800-544-3284
                              FAX: 202-833-4760
                              ncfy.acf.hhs.gov/

State Agencies: Florida

2027 Florida Department of Education: Bureau of Exceptional Education And Student Services
325 West Gaines Street
Turlington Building, Suite 1514
Tallahassee, FL 32399   850-245-0505
                              FAX: 850-245-9667
                              Monica.Verra-Tirado@fldoe.org
                              www.fldoe.org/ese
Monica Verra-Tirado, Ed.D., Bureau Chief
Gerard Robinson, Commissioner
Randy Hanna, Chancellor
Administers programs for students with disabilities and for gifted students. Coordinates student services throughout the state and participates in multiple inter-agency efforts designed to strengthen the quality and variety of services to students with special needs.

2028 Florida State College at Jacksonville Services for Students with Disabilities
501 W State St
Jacksonville, FL 32202   904-633-8100
                              888-873-1145
                              FAX: 904-633-5955
                              info@fscj.edu
                              fscj.edu
Randle P DeFoor, Chair
Cynthia A Bioteau, President
Richard Turner, Associate Vice President of Enrollment Management
Florida State College ensures acessibility of its services, activities, facilities and academic programs to students with disabilities. Special accmmodations are provided to anyone with a physical, mental or learning disability.

State Agencies: Hawaii

2029 Hawaii Department of Education: Special Needs
Hawaii Department of Education
3430 Leahi Ave
Honolulu, HI 96815-4246   808-941-3894
                              FAX: 808-941-3894
Margaret Donovan MD, State Administrator
Provides consultation on educational services for local schools, offers psychological testing and evaluation, maintains resource rooms in district schools and more for the blind and handicapped throughout the state.

State Agencies: Illinois

2030 Illinois State Board of Education: Department of Special Education
100 N 1st St
Springfield, IL 62777   217-782-5589
                              FAX: 217-782-0372
                              www.isbe.net
Elizabeth Hanselman, Asst Superintendent Special Ed.
Mission is to advance the human and civil rights of people with disabilities in Illinois. Statewide advocacy organization providing self-advocacy assistance, legal services, education and public policy initiatives. Designated to implement the federal protection and advocacy system; has broad statutory power to enforce the rights of people with physical and mental disabilities, including developmental disabilities and mental illnesses.

State Agencies: Indiana

2031 Indiana Department of Education: Special Education Division
Indiana Department of Education
South Tower, Suite 600
115 W. Washington Street
Indianapolis, IN 46204-2731   317-23- 661
                              877-851-4106
                              FAX: 317-23- 800
                              webmaster@doe.in.gov
                              www.doe.in.gov/
Robert A Marra, Manager
Tony Bennett, Chair
Provides consultation on educational services for local schools, offers psychological testing and evaluation, maintains resource rooms in district schools and more for the blind and handicapped throughout the state.

State Agencies: Iowa

2032 Iowa Department of Public Instruction: Bureau of Special Education
400 E 14th St
Des Moines, IA 50319-9000   515-457-2000
                              FAX: 515-242-6019
                              www.educateiowa.gov/
Tom Kuehl, CEO
Jason Glass, Director
Jeff Berger, Administrative Services

State Agencies: Kansas

2033 Kansas State Board of Education: Special Education Services
900 SW Jackson Street
Topeka, KS 66612-1212
785-296-3201
800-203-9462
FAX: 785-296-7933
TTY: 785-296-6338
contact@ksde.org
www.ksde.org

Ethan Erickson, Director
Kathy Gosa, Director
Denise Kahler, Director
Provides leadership and support for exceptional learners receiving special education services throughout Kansas schools and communities.

State Agencies: Kentucky

2034 Kentucky Department of Education: Divisionof Exceptional Children's Services
500 Mero St
Capital Tower Plaza
Frankfort, KY 40601
502-564-4770
FAX: 502-564-7749
www.education.ky.gov

Darlene Jesse, Director
Provides consultation on educational services for local schools, offers psychological testing and evaluation, maintains resource rooms in district schools and more for the blind and handicapped throughout the state.

State Agencies: Louisiana

2035 Louisiana Department of Education: Office of Special Education Services
Louisiana Department of Education
1201 North Third Street
Baton Rouge, LA 70802
225-342-0090
877-453-2721
FAX: 225-342-0193
www.doe.state.la.us

David Elder, Manager
Kim Fitch, Director Human Resources
George Nelson, President

State Agencies: Massachusetts

2036 Getting Ready for the Outside World (G.R.O.W.)
Riverview School
551 Route 6A East Sandwich
Cape Cod, MA 2537-1448
508-888-0489
FAX: 508-833-7001
admissions@riverviewschool.org
www.riverviewschool.org

Janice James, Vice Chairman
Deborah Cowan, Vice Chair
James Shallcross, Treasurer
Riverview School's G.R.O.W. Program is a unique ten month transitional prgoram (1-3 years) for young adults with complex language, learning and cognitive disabilities. This post secondary program is designed to further develop academic, vocational and independent living skills, to enable students to function as independently as possible.

2037 Massachusetts Department of Education: Program Quality Assurance
Massachusetts Department of Education
75 Pleasant Street
Malden, MA 2148-4906
781-388-3300
FAX: 617-388-3476
boe@doe.mass.edu
www.doe.mass.edu/pqa/

Pamela Kaufamann, Administrator

State Agencies: Maryland

2038 Agency for Healthcare Research and Quality
540 Gaither Road
Rockville, MD 20850
301-427-1364
www.ahrq.gov

Richard G. Kronick, PhD, Director, Director
Sharon B. Arnold, PhD, Deputy Director
The Agency for Healthcare Research and Quality's (AHRQ) mission is to produce evidence to make health care safer, higher quality, more accessible, equitable, and affordable, and to work within the U.S. Department of Health and Human Services and with other partners to make sure that the evidence is understood and used.

2039 Center for Mental Health Services
5600 Fishers Lane
Rockville, MD 20857
877-726-4727
TTY:800-487-4889
samhsainfo@samhsa.hhs.gov
www.samhsa.gov

Tom Coderre, Acting Deputy Assistant Secretary
Sonia Chessen, Chief of Staff
Trina Dutta, Senior Advisor
The Center for Mental Health Services leads federal efforts to promote the prevention and treatment of mental disorders.

2040 Centers for Medicare & Medicaid Services
7500 Security Blvd.
Baltimore, MD 21244
410-786-3000
877-267-2323
TTY:866-226-1819
www.cms.gov

Chiquita Brooks-LaSure, Administrator
Jonathan Blum, Principal Deputy Administrator
Karen Jackson, Deputy Chief Operating Officer
US federal agency which administers Medicare, Medicaid, and the State Children's Health Insurance Program.

2041 Maryland State Department of Education: Division of Special Education
200 West Baltimore Street
Baltimore, MD 21201-2595
410-767-0100
888-246-0016
FAX: 410-333-8165
www.marylandpublicschools.org

Nancy S Grasmick, State Superintendent
Dr. Lillian Lowery, Superintendent of Schools
James V. Foran, Assistant State Superintendent
Collaborates with families, local early intervention systems, and local school systems to ensure that all children and youth with disabilities have access to appropriate services and educational opportunities to which they are entitled under federal and state laws.

2042 National Human Genome Research Institute
National Institutes of Health
Building 31, Room 4B09
31 Center Drive, MSC 2152
Bethesda, MD 20892-2152
301-402-0911
FAX: 301-402-2218
lbrody@mail.nih.gov
www.genome.gov

Eric D. Green, M.D., Ph.D., Director
Lawrence Brody, Ph.D., Director
Bettie Graham, Ph.D., Director
The National Human Genome Research Institute began as the National Center for Human Genome Research (NCHGR), which was

established in 1989 to carry out the role of the National Institutes of Health (NIH) in the International Human Genome Project (HGP).

2043 National Institute of General Medical Sciences
45 Center Drive MSC 6200
Bethesda, MD 20892-6200
301-496-7301
info@nigms.nih.gov
www.nigms.nih.gov

Jon R. Lorsch, Ph.D., Director
Judith H. Greenberg, Ph.D., Deputy Director
Ann Hagan, Ph.D., Associate Director
The National Institute of General Medical Sciences (NIGMS) supports basic research that increases understanding of biological processes and lays the foundation for advances in disease diagnosis, treatment and prevention.

State Agencies: Michigan

2044 Michigan Department of Education: Special Education Services
608 W. Allegan Street
PO Box 30008
Lansing, MI 48909
517-373-3324
FAX: 517-373-7504
DHS-OCS-PEP@michigan.gov
www.michigan.gov/mde

John C. Austin, President
Kathleen N. Straus, President of the State Board
Michelle Fecteau, Executive Director
Oversees the administrative funding of education and early intervention programs and services for young children and students with disabilities.

2045 Services for Students with Disabilities
University of Michigan
G-664 Haven Hall
505 South State St.
Ann Arbor, MI 48109-1045
734-763-3000
FAX: 734-936-3947
TTY:734-615-4461
ssdoffice@umich.edu
www.ssd.umich.edu

Stuart Segal, Director
Offers information to students of the University of Michigan and their parents.

State Agencies: Minnesota

2046 Community Supports for People with Disabilities (CSP)
South Central Technical College (SCTC)
1920 Lee Blvd
North Mankato, MN 56003-2504
507-389-7200
800-722-9359
online@southcentral.edu
www.southcentral.edu

Christensen Tami, Executive Director
Keith Stover, President
Human services program available as a physical or online program, designed for those wanting to earn a certificate, diploma or associate degree as a Direct Support Professional for use in the health and human services industries. The program comprises eight courses relating to professional services and support for people with disabilities.

2047 Professional Development Programs
6303 Osgood Ave. N.
Ste 104
Stillwater, MN 55082
651-439-8865
877-439-8865
FAX: 877-259-5906
www.pdppro.com

Cindy Lacosse, VP
Lori Lacrosse, President

Sponsors cutting edge and popular continuing education workshops and symposia of interest to professionals who provide services to children and adults with special needs.

State Agencies: Missouri

2048 Missouri Department of Elementary and Secondary Education: Special Education Programs
205 Jefferson St
PO Box 480
Jefferson City, MO 65102
573-751-5739
FAX: 573-526-4404
TTY:800-735-2966

Stephen Barr, Assistant Commissioner
The Office of Special Education administers state and federal funds to support services for students and adults with disabilities.

State Agencies: Mississippi

2049 Mississippi Department of Education: Office of Special Services
359 North West Street
P.O. Box 771
Jackson, MS 39201
601-359-3513
FAX: 601-987-3892

Dr Tom Burnham, Superintendent
Key priorities are: reading, early literacy, student achievement, teachers/teaching, leadership/principals, safe and orderly schools, parent relations/community involvement, and technology.

State Agencies: Montana

2050 Department of Public Health Human Services
PO Box 4210
Helena, MT 59604-4210
406-444-5622
FAX: 406-444-1970
www.dphhs.mt.gov

Anna Whitin Sorrell, Director
Bernie Jacobs, Chief Legal Counsel
Deb Sloat, Human Resources Office
Provides consultation on educational services for local schools, offers psychological testing and evaluation, maintains resource rooms in district schools and more for the blind and handicapped throughout the state.

State Agencies: North Carolina

2051 National Institute of Environmental Health Sciences
111 T.W. Alexander Drive
Research Triangle Park, NC 27709
919-541-4580
birnbaumls@niehs.nih.gov
www.niehs.nih.gov

Linda S. Birnbaum, Ph.D., Director
Richard Woychik, Ph.D., Deputy Director
Sheila A. Newton, Ph.D., Policy, Planning, and Evaluation
The mission of the NIEHS is to discover how the environment affects people in order to promote healthier lives.

2052 North Carolina Department of Public Instruction: Exceptional Children Division
301 N Wilmington St
Raleigh, NC 27601
919-807-3300
FAX: 919-715-1569
www.ncpublicschools.org

June St. Clair Atkinson, Ed.D, State Superintendent of Public Instruction
Mike McLaughlin, Senior Policy Advisor to the State Superintendent
Rachel Beaulieu, Legislative & Community Affairs Director

The mission is to assure that students with disabilities develop mentally, physically, emotionally, and vocationally through the provision of an appropriate individualized education in the least restrictive environment.

State Agencies: North Dakota

2053 North Dakota Department of Education: Special Education
600 E. Boulevard Avenue, Dept. 201
Floors 9, 10, and 11
Bismarck, ND 58505-0440
701-328-2260
866-741-3519
FAX: 701-328-2461
TTY: 701-328-4920
mdanderson@nd.gov
www.dpi.state.nd.us

Kirsten Baesler, State Superintendent
Jerry Coleman, Director, School Finance & Organization
Linda Schloer, Child Nutrition & Food Distribution, Director
Provides consultation on educational services for local schools, offers psychological testing and evaluation, maintains resource rooms in district schools and more for the blind and handicapped throughout the state.

State Agencies: Nebraska

2054 Nebraska Department of Education: Special Populations Office
1200 N Street, Suite 400
PO Box 98922
Lincoln, NE 68509
402-471-2186
877-253-2603
FAX: 402-471-2909
NDEQ.moreinfo@Nebraska.gov
deq.ne.gov

Rod Gangwish Shelton, Council Member
Douglas Anderson Aurora, Council Member
Mark Whitehead Lincoln, Council Member
Assists school districts in establishing and maintaining effective special education programs for children with disabilities (date of diagnosis through the school year when a child reaches 21). Major function: provide technical assistance to school districts and to parents of children with disabilities, assist programs in meeting state and federal special education regulations. Also responsible for assuring that the rights of children with disabilities and their parents are protected.

State Agencies: New Hampshire

2055 Institute on Disability
University of New Hampshire
10 West Edge Drive
Suite 101
Durham, NH 03824
603-862-4320
FAX: 603-862-0555
contact.iod@unh.edu
www.iod.unh.edu

Charles E. Drum, Director & Professor
Andrew Houtenville, Director of Research
Matthew Gianino, Director of Communications
Provides coherent university-based focus for the improvement of knowledge, policies, and practices related to the lives of persons with disabilities and their families.

2056 New Hampshire Department of Education: Bureau for Special Education Services
101 Pleasant Street
Concord, NH 03301-3860
603-271-3494
FAX: 603-271-1953
Lori.Temple@doe.nh.gov
www.education.nh.gov

Santina Thibedeau, Administrator
Virginia Barry, Commissioner
Linda Breden, Secretary
The mission of Special Education is to improve educational outcomes for children and youth with disabilities by providing and promoting leadership, technical assistance and collaboration statewide. Provides oversight and implementation of federal and state laws that ensure a free appropriate public education for all children and youth with disabilities in New Hampshire.

State Agencies: New Jersey

2057 New Jersey Department of Education: Office of Special Education Program
New Jersey Department of Education
PO Box 500
Trenton, NJ 8625-500
609-292-0147
FAX: 609-984-8422
www.nj.gov/education/specialed/info/

Barbara Gantwerk, Director
Alfred Murray, Executive Director

2058 New Jersey Speech-Language-Hearing Association
174 Nassau St
Suite 337
Princeton, NJ 08542
888-906-5742
FAX: 888-729-3489
info@njsha.org
njsha.org

Mary Faella, President
Robynne Kratchman, Vice President
Joan Warner, Treasurer
The New Jersey Speech-Language-Hearing Association offers services to audiologists, speech-language pathologists, and scientists studying in these fields. Services include resources, advocacy, information and programs to help foster professional development.

2059 The Arc of New Jersey
985 Livingston Ave
North Brunswick, NJ 08902
732-246-2525
FAX: 732-214-1834
info@arcnj.org
arcnj.org

Joanne Bergin, President
Thomas Baffuto, Executive Director
Celine Fortin, Associate Executive Director
The Arc of New Jersey is committed to enhancing the quality of life of children and adults with intellectual and developmental disabilities and their families, through advocacy, empowerment, education and prevention.

State Agencies: New Mexico

2060 New Mexico State Department of Education
300 Don Gaspar Ave
Santa Fe, NM 87501-2744
505-827-6508
FAX: 505-827-6696
www.sde.state.nm.us

Bill Trant, Assistant Director
Judy Parks, Assistant Director
Provides consultation on educational services for local schools, offers psychological testing and evaluation, maintains resource rooms in district schools and more for the blind and handicapped throughout the state.

State Agencies: Nevada

2061   Nevada Department of Education: Special Eduction Branch
700 E Fifth St
Carson City, NV 89701-5096   775-687-9800
                                         FAX: 775-687-9101
                                         www.doe.nv.gov

Nick Gakalatos, Manager
The Office of Special Ed and School Improvement Program of the Nevada State Department of Education is responsible for management of state and federal programs providing educational opportunities for students with diverse learning needs. Included are such programs as: special education/disabled (IDEA); disadvantaged/at-risk programs (Title I/IASA); early childhood programs (Title I/ESEA); early childhood programs; migrant education; English language learners; NRS 395 student placement program.

State Agencies: New York

2062   New York State Education Department
1606 One Commerce Plz
Albany, NY 12234   518-474-5930
                                         FAX: 518-486-6880
                                         www.nysed.gov

Bernard Margolis, Manager
Provides vocational rehabilitation and educational services for eligible individuals with disabilities throughout New York State. Services include evaluation, counseling, job placement, and referral to other agencies.

State Agencies: Ohio

2063   Ohio Department of Education: Division of Special Education
Ohio Department of Education
25 S Front St
Columbus, OH 43215-4183   614-995-1545
                                             877-644-6338
                                         FAX: 614-728-1097
                                         TTY: 888-886-0181
                                         www.ode.state.oh.us

Mike Armstrong, Manager
Provides technical assistance to educational agencies for the development and implementation of educational services to meet the needs of students with disabilities and/or those who are gifted. Provides information to parents. Administers state and federal funds allocated to educational agencies for the provision of services to students with disabilities and/or those who are gifted.

2064   The Arc of Allen County
546 S Collett St
Lima, OH 45805   419-225-6285
                                         FAX: 419-228-7770
                                         info@thearcofohio.org
                                         www.arcallencounty.org

Brad Perrott, Executive Director
Vicki Alves, Day Service Manager
Lisa Hengstler, Office Assistant
Offers services to people with intellectual and developmental disabilities. Some programs include day care, educational training, human rights advocacy, and information and referral.

State Agencies: Oklahoma

2065   Oklahoma State Department of Education
2500 N Lincoln Blvd
Oklahoma City, OK 73105-4599   405-521-3301
                                         FAX: 405-521-6205

Misty Kimbrough, Manager
Sandy Garrett, Administrator
Janet Barresi, State Superintendent
Provides consultation on educational services for local schools, offers psychological testing and evaluation, maintains resource rooms in district schools and more for the blind and handicapped throughout the state.

State Agencies: Oregon

2066   Oregon Department of Education: Office of Special Education
Oregon Department of Education:
255 Capitol St NE
Salem, OR 97310-1300   503-945-5600
                                         FAX: 503-378-2897
                                         www.dpeducation.com

Bruce Goldberg, Manager
Heidi Cockrell, Executive Assistant
Katy Coba, Executive Director
State agency ensuring provision of special education services to children with disabilities from birth to age 21.

State Agencies: Pennsylvania

2067   Pennsylvania Department of Education: Bureau of Special Education
333 Market St
Harrisburg, PA 17126-333   717-783-6788
                                         FAX: 717-783-6139
                                         TTY:717-783-8445
                                         00specialed@psupen.psu.edu
                                         www.pde.state.pa.us

Linda Rhen, Administrator
John Tommasini, Assistant Director
Provides effective and efficient administration of the Commonwealth of Pennsylvania's resources dedicated to enabling school districts to maintain high standards in the delivery of special education services and programs for all exceptional students.

State Agencies: Rhode Island

2068   Rhode Island Department of Education: Office of Special Needs
255 Westminster St
Providence, RI 2903   401-222-4600
                                         FAX: 401-784-9513
                                         www.ride.ri.gov

Al Moscola, Manager
Alfred Moscola, Manager
Provides consultation on educational services for local schools, offers psychological testing and evaluation, maintains resource rooms in district schools and more for the blind and handicapped throughout the state.

State Agencies: South Carolina

2069   South Carolina Assistive Technology Program (SCATP)
Center for Disability Resources
8301 Farrow Rd
Columbia, SC 29208-3245   803-935-5263
                                            800-915-4522
                                       FAX: 800-935-5342
                                       www.sc.edu/scatp

Carol Page, Program Director
Mary Bechter, Program Coordinator
SCATP is a federally funded project concerned with getting technology into th hands of people with disabilities so that they might live, work, learn and be a more independent part of the community.

2070   South Carolina Department of Education: Office of Exceptional Children
1429 Senate St
Suite 808
Columbia, SC 29201-3730   803-734-8224
                                       FAX: 803-734-4824
                                  sdeservicedesk@sde.ok.gov
                                       www.scschools.com

Susan Durant, State Director
Provides consultation on educational services for local schools, offers psychological testing and evaluation, maintains resource rooms in district schools and more for the blind and handicapped throughout the state.

State Agencies: South Dakota

2071   South Dakota Department of Education & Cultural Affairs: Office of Special Education
700 Governors Dr
Pierre, SD 57501-2291   605-773-3804
                                       FAX: 605-773-6041

Chelle Somsen, Manager
Dorothy Liegl, Manager

State Agencies: Tennessee

2072   Tennessee Department of Education
710 James Robertson Pkwy
Nashville, TN 37243-1219   615-741-2731
                                            888-212-3162
                                       FAX: 615-741-1791

Ruth S Letson, Manager
Kevin Huffman, Commissioner
Provides consultation on educational services for local schools, offers psychological testing and evaluation, maintains resource rooms in district schools and more for the blind and handicapped throughout the state.

State Agencies: Texas

2073   Texas Education Agency
1701 N Congress Ave
Austin, TX 78701-1494   512-463-8532
                                       FAX: 512-463-8057
                                       www.tealighthouse.org

Shirley J Neeley, Commissioner of Education
Provides consultation on educational services for local schools, offers psychological testing and evaluation, maintains resource rooms in district schools and more for the blind and handicapped throughout the state.

2074   Texas Education Agency: Special Education Unit
1701 Congress Ave
PO Box 420637
Austin, TX 77242-637   512-463-8532
                                       FAX: 512-463-8057
                                       info@tdea.org
                                       www.tdea.org

Gene Lenz, Deputy Associate Commissioner
Shirley Neeley, Administrator

2075   Texas School of the Deaf
1102 S Congress Ave
Austin, TX 78704-1791   512-462-5353
                                            800-332-3873
                                       FAX: 512-462-5424
                                       ercod@tsd.state.tx.us
                                       tsd.state.tx.us

Claire Bugen, Superintendent
Russell West, Residential Services Director
Gary Bego, Business and Operations Director
Ensures that students excel in an environment where they learn, grow and belong. Supports deaf students, families and professionals in Texas by providing resources through outreach services.

State Agencies: Utah

2076   Utah State Office of Education: At-Risk and Special Education Service Unit
Utah State Office of Education
250 East 500 South
P.O.Box 144200
Salt Lake City, UT 84114-4200   801-538-7500
                                       FAX: 801-538-7521
                                  webmaster@schools.utah.gov
                                       schools.utah.gov

Sandra Cox, Financial Analyst
Mark Peterson, Director
Glenna Gallo, State Director of Special Educat
Provides consultation on educational services for local schools, offers psychological testing and evaluation, maintains resource rooms in district schools and more for the blind and handicapped throughout the state.

State Agencies: Virginia

2077   National Science Foundation
4201 Wilson Blvd
Arlington, VA 22230   703-292-5111
                                       TTY:703-292-5090
                                       info@nsf.gov
                                       www.nsf.gov

France A. Cȩrdova, Director
Richard O. Buckius, Chief Operating Officer
Michael Van Woert, Executive Officer/Director
NSF is the only federal agency whose mission includes support for all fields of fundamental science and engineering, except for medical sciences.

2078   Virginia Department of Education: Divisionof Pre & Early Adolescent Education
Virginia Department Of Education
James Monroe Building, 101, N. 14th
P.O.Box 2120
Richmond, VA 23219   804-236-3631
                                       FAX: 804-236-3635
                                  webmaster@doe.virginia.gov
                                       www.pen.k12.va.us

Dr. Steven R Staples, Superintendent of Public Instruction
Kent Dickey, Deputy Superintendent, Finance & Operations
Chris Sorensen, Director, Budget
Provides consultation on educational services for local schools, offers psychological testing and evaluation, maintains resource rooms in district schools and more for the blind and handicapped throughout the state.

State Agencies: Washington

2079 Superintendent of Public Instruction: Special Education Section
Old Capitol Building, 600 Washingto
P.O. Box 47200
Olympia, WA 98504-7200
360-725-6000
FAX: 360-586-0247
TTY:360-664-3631
www.k12.wa.us

Randy I. Dorn, State Superintendent of Public I
Alan Burke, Deputy Superintendent
Robert Butts, Assistant Superintendent
Provides leadership, service and support for the development and implementation of research-based curriculum to assure that all learners achieve at all levels.

State Agencies: West Virginia

2080 West Virginia Department of Education: Office of Special Education
Rm 6
1900 Kanawha Blvd E
Charleston, WV 25305-0001
304-558-3660
FAX: 304-558-3741
wvde.state.wv.us

Liza Cordeiro, Executive Director
Mary Nunn, Assistant Director
Marshall Patton, Executive Director
Provides consultation on educational services for local schools, offers psychological testing and evaluation, maintains resource rooms in district schools and more for the blind and handicapped throughout the state.

State Agencies: Wyoming

2081 Wyoming Department of Education
2300 Capitol Avenue
Hathaway Building, 2nd Floor
Cheyenne, WY 82002-2060
307-777-7690
FAX: 307-777-6234
edu.wyoming.gov

Cindy Hill, WDE Superintendent
Deb Lindsey, Division Administrator, Assessment
Teri Wigert, Division Administrator, Support Systems & Resources
Mission is to lead, model, and support continuous improvement of education for everyone in Wyoming.

Magazines & Journals

2082 Adapted Physical Activity Programs
Human Kinetics
1607 N. Market Street
P.O.Box 5076
Champaign, IL 61820
800-747-4457
FAX: 217-351-1549
info@hkusa.com
www.humankinetics.com

Patty Lehn, Publicity Manager
Lori Cooper, Marketing Manager
Bill Dobrik, Sales Associate
Human Kinetics produces a variety of resources for adapted physical education practitioners, including books on activities, a research journal and higher education references. *$24.00*
Quarterly
ISSN 0736-58 9

2083 Advance for Providers of Post-Acute Care
Merion Publications
2900 Horizon Drive
King of Prussia, PA 19406
610-278-1400
800-355-5627
FAX: 610-278-1421
webmaster@advanceweb.com
advanceweb.com

Timothy Baum, MS, CRNP, Author
A free magazine for providers of post-acute care.

2084 American Journal of Occupational Therapy (AJOT)
American Occupational Therapy Association
6116 Executive Blvd.
Suite 200
North Bethesda, MD 20852-4929
301-652-6611
800-729-2682
customerservice@aota.org
ajot.aota.org

Sherry Keramidas, Executive Director
Stacey Reynolds, Editor-in-Chief
Official peer-reviewed publication of the American Occupational Therapy Association.
6 issues/year

2085 American Journal on Intellectual and Developmental Disabilities (AJIDD)
AAIDD
8403 Colesville Rd.
Suite 900
Silver Spring, MD 20910
202-387-1968
FAX: 202-387-2193
aaidd.org

Frank Symons, Editor
American Journal on Intellectual and Developmental Disabilities (AJIDD)is a scientific, scholarly, and archival multidisciplinary journal for reporting original contributions to knowledge of intellectual disability, its causes, treatment, and prevention.
Bimonthly

2086 Behavioral Disorders
Council for Exceptional Children
3100 Clarendon Blvd.
Suite 600
Arlington, VA 22201-5332
888-232-7733
TTY:866-915-5000
services@exceptionalchildren.org
www.exceptionalchildren.org

Bryan G. Cook, Editor
Daniel M. Maggin, Co-Editor
Provides professionals with a means to exchange information and share ideas related to research, empirically tested educational innovations and issues and concerns relevant to students with behavioral disorders.
Quarterly

2087 CEC Catalog
Council for Exceptional Children
3100 Clarendon Blvd.
Suite 600
Arlington, VA 22201-5332
888-232-7733
TTY:866-915-5000
service@exceptionalchildren.org
www.exceptionalchildren.org/store

Chad Rummel, Executive Director
Laurie VanderPloeg, Associate Executive Director, Professional Affairs
Craig Evans, Chief Financial Officer
Catalog from the Council for Exceptional Children offering books, guides, materials, and specialty items for special educators.

2088   **Career Development and Transition for Exceptional Individuals**
2455 Teller Road
Thousand Oaks, CA 91320
800-818-7243
FAX: 800-583-2665
journals@sagepub.com
cde.sagepub.com

Blaise R. Simqu, President/ CEO
Tracey A. Ozmina, EVP/ COO
Chris Hickok, SVP/ CFO
Career Development and Transition for Exceptional Individuals (CDTEI) specializes in the fields of secondary education, transition, and career development for persons with documented disabilities and special needs.

2089   **Case Manager Magazine**
Elsevier Health
3251 Riverport Lane
Maryland Heights, MO 63043
314-447-8070
800-222-9570
textbook@elsevier.com

Thomas Reller, Vice President Global Corporate
Harald Boersma, Senior Manager Corporate Relatio
Ylann Schemm, Corporate Relations Manager
This national magazine is for medical case managers, social workers, counselors and home health professionals who work with people with serious injury or illness. It is a membership benefit of CMSA, the national association for case managers. *$55.00*
84 pages BiMonthly

2090   **Catalyst**
The Catalyst
Ste 275
1259 El Camino Real
Menlo Park, CA 94025-4208
800-647-0314
Sue Swezey, Editor
Digest of news and information on the use of computers in special education. *$15.00*
20 pages Quarterly

2091   **Challenge Magazine**
451 Hungerford Drive
Suite 100
Rockville, MD 20850
301-217-0960
FAX: 301-217-0968
Info@dsusa.org
www.disabledsportsusa.org
Kirk Bauer, Executive Director
Claire Duffy, Program Coordinator
Orlando Gill, Field Representative
Challenge Magazine is a publication of Disabled Sports USA, providing adaptive sports information to adults and children with disabilities, including those who are visually impaired, amputees, spinal cord injured (paraplegic and quadriplegic), and those who have multiple sclerosis, head injury, cerebral palsy, autism and other related intellectual disabilities.

2092   **Clinical Connection**
American Advertising Dist of Northern Virginia
708 Pendleton St
Alexandria, VA 22314-1819
703-549-5126
FAX: 703-548-5563
Kathie Harrington, M.A., CCC, Author
Covers speech language pathology.

2093   **College and University**
AACRAO
One Dupont Circle NW
Suite 520
Washington, DC 20036
202-293-9161
FAX: 202-872-8857
reillym@aacrao.org
aacrao.org

Brad Myers, President
Dan Garcia, President Elect
Adrienne McDay, Past President
Scholarly research journal. American Association of Collegiate Registrars and Admissions Offers (AACRAO) is a nonprofit, voluntary, professional, educational association of degree-granting, postsecondary institutions, government agencies, private educa-

tional organizations and education-oriented businesses in the United States and abroad. $80 per year US; $90 per year international.
30 pages Quarterly
ISSN 0010-0889

2094   **Communication Disorders Quarterly**
2455 Teller Road
Thousand Oaks, CA 91320
800-818-7243
FAX: 800-583-2665
journals@sagepub.com
cde.sagepub.com

Blaise R. Simqu, President/ CEO
Tracey A. Ozmina, EVP/ COO
Chris Hickok, SVP/ CFO
Communication Disorders Quarterly (CDQ) presents cutting edge information on typical and atypical communication — from oral language development to literacy.

2095   **Continuing Care**
Stevens Publishing Corporation
14901 Quorum Dr,
Suite 425
Dallas, TX 75254
972-687-6700
FAX: 972-687-6750
info@1105media.com
1105media.com

Neal Vitale, President & Chief Executive Officer
Richard Vitale, Senior Vice President & Chief Financial Officer
Mike Valenti, Executive Vice President
A national magazine for case management and discharge planning professionals published monthly except for December. *$119.00*
34 pages Monthly

2096   **Counseling Psychologist**
American Psychological Association
2455 Teller Road
Thousand Oaks, CA 91320
805-499-0721
800-818-7243
FAX: 800-583-2665
info@sagepub.com
www.sagepub.com

Sara Miller McCune, Founder, Publisher & Executive Chairman
Blaise R Simqu, President/CEO
Chris Hickok, Senior Vice President & Chief Financial Officer
Thematic issues in the theory, research and practice of counseling psychology. *$78.00*
Bi-Monthly

2097   **Counseling and Values**
American Counseling Association
P.O. Box 31110
Suite 600
Alexandria, VA 22310-9998
800-347-6647
FAX: 800-473-2329
ahconley@vcu.edu
www.counseling.org

Shawn E. Boynes, Chief Executive Officer
Abigail H. Conley, Editor
Aliza Lambert, Editorial Assistant
Counseling and Values is the official journal of the Association for Spiritual, Ethical, and Religious Values in Counseling (ASERVIC), a member association of the American Counseling Association. Counseling and Values is a professional journal of theory, research, and informed opinion concerned with the relationships among psychology, philosophy, religion, social values, and counseling. *$20.00*
Bi-annual

2098   **Counselor Education & Supervision**
American Counseling Association
P.O. Box 31110
Alexandria, VA 22310
800-347-6647
FAX: 800-473-2329
acesjournal@gmail.com
www.counseling.org

Shawn E. Boynes, Chief Executive Officer
Spencer G. Niles, Editor
Amanda La Guardia, Associate Editor

Dedicated to the growth and development of the counseling profession and those who are served. *$14.00*
Quarterly

2099   Disability & Society
711 3rd Avenue
8th Floor
New York, NY 10017
212-216-7800
800-634-7064
FAX: 212-564-7854
www.routledge.com

Len Barton, Author
The study of disability has traditionally been influenced mainly by medical and psychological models. The aim of this new text, Disability and Society, is to open up the debate by introducing alternative perspectives reflecting the increasing sociological interest in this important topic.

2100   Disability Studies Quarterly
552 Park Hall
Buffalo, NY 14260-4130
marembis@buffalo.edu
dsq-sds.org

Michael Rembis, Interim Editor-in-Chief
Tanja Aho, Interim Managing Editor
Disability Studies Quarterly (DSQ) is the journal of the Society for Disability Studies (SDS). It is a multidisciplinary and international journal of interest to social scientists, scholars in the humanities, disability rights advocates, creative writers, and others concerned with the issues of people with disabilities.

2101   Disability and Health Journal
American Association on Health and Disabiity
110 N Washington St.
Suite 407
Rockville, MD 20850
301-545-6140
FAX: 301-545-6144
contact@aahd.us
www.aahd.us/disability-and-health-journal

Monika Mitra, Editor
Margaret A. Turk, Co-Editor
Roberta Carlin, Executive Director
Disability and Health Journal is a scientific, scholarly and multidisciplinary journal for reporting original contributions that advance knowledge in disability and health.

2102   Early Intervention
Early Childhood Intervention Clearinghouse
51 Gerty Drive
Room 20
Champaign, IL 61820-7469
217-333-1386
877-275-3227
FAX: 217-244-7732
Illinois-eic@illinois.edu
www.eiclearinghouse.org

Susan Fowler, Director
Features articles, conference calendar, material reviews and news concerning early childhood intervention and disability.
4 pages Quarterly

2103   Emerging Horizon
PO Box 278
Ripon, CA 95366-0278
209-599-9409
emerginghorizons.com
Travel information for wheel chair users and slow walkers.

2104   Exceptional Children (EC)
Council for Exceptional Children
3100 Clarendon Blvd.
Suite 600
Arlington, VA 22201-5332
888-232-7733
TTY:866-915-5000
service@exceptionalchildren.org
www.exceptionalchildren.org

John Wills Lloyd, Editor
William Therrien, Editor
Peer-reviewed journal with articles including research, literature surveys and position papers concerning exceptional children, special education and mainstreaming.
Quarterly

2105   Focus on Autism and Other Developmental Disabilities
Sage Publications
2455 Teller Road
Thousand Oaks, CA 91320
805-499-0721
800-818-7243
FAX: 800-583-2665
info@sagepub.com
www.sagepub.com

Sara Miller McCune, Founder, Publisher & Executive Chairman
Blaise R. Simqu, President & CEO
Chris Hickok, Senior Vice President & Chief Financial Officer
Practical management, treatment and planning strategies; a must for persons working with individuals with autism and other developmental disabilities. *$43.00*
64 pages Quarterly

2106   Focus on Exceptional Children
Love Publishing Company
9101 East Kenyon Avenue
Suite 2200
Denver, CO 80237
303-221-7333
FAX: 303-221-7444
lpc@lovepublishing.com
www.lovepublishing.com

Steve Graham, Consulting Editor
Ron Nelson, Consulting Editor
Eva Horn, Consulting Editor
Contains research and theory-based articles on special education topics, with an emphasis on application and intervention, of interest to teachers, professors and administrators. *$36.00*
Monthly

2107   HerbalGram
American Botanical Council
6200 Manor Rd.
Austin, TX 78723-4345
512-926-4900
800-373-7105
FAX: 512-926-2345
abc@herbalgram.org
herbalgram.org/resources/herbalgram/

Mark Blumenthal, Founder, Executive Director & Editor
Tyler Smith, Editor
Hannah Bauman, Associate Editor
Official quarterly journal of the American Botanical Council.

2108   HomeCare Magazine
Cahaba Media Group
1900-28th Ave S.
Ste 200
Birmingham, AL 35209
205-212-9402
cahabamedia.com

Wally Evans, Publisher
Greg Meineke, Vice President, Sales
Stephanie Gibson Lepore, Editor
The business magazine of the home medical equipment industry offering information on legislation and regulations affecting the homecare industry, monthly profiles of suppliers, operational tips, newest products in the industry, advice on sales, government regulations. *$65.00*
120 pages Monthly

2109   I Wonder Who Else Can Help
AARP
601 E Street NW
Washington, DC 20049
202-434-3525
888-687-2277
877-342-2277
FAX: 202-434-3443
member@aarp.org
www.aarp.org

John Wider, President, CEO, AARP Services Inc.
Lisa M. Ryerson, President, AARP Foundation
Robert R. Hagans, Jr., Executive Vice President & Chief Financial Officer
Contains information about crisis counseling, needs and resources, written in lay terms.

2110 Inclusion
AAIDD
8403 Colesville Rd.
Suite 900
Silver Spring, MD 20910   202-387-1968
FAX: 202-387-2193
aaidd.org

Colleen Thoma, Co-Editor
LaRon Scott, Co-Editor
Lauren Bruno, Editorial Coordinator
Inclusionis an open submission ejournal. Inclusion is published quarterly in an online-only format, enabling timely dissemination of emerging and promising research, policy, and practices.
Quarterly

2111 Intellectual and Developmental Disabilities (IDD)
AAIDD
8403 Colesville Rd.
Suite 900
Silver Spring, MD 20910   202-387-1968
FAX: 202-387-2193
aaidd.org

Amy S. Hewitt, Editor
Intellectual and Developmental Disabilities (IDD) is a peer reviewed multidisciplinary journal disseminating information on policies, practices, and concepts relating to intellectual and developmental disabilities.
Bimonthly

2112 Intervention in School and Clinic
Sage Publications
2455 Teller Road
Thousand Oaks, CA 91320   805-499-0721
800-818-7243
FAX: 800-583-2665
info@sagepub.com
www.sagepub.com

Sara Miller McCune, Founder, Publisher & Executive Chairman
Blaise R. Simqu, President & CEO
Chris Hickok, Senior Vice President & Chief Financial Officer
A hands-on, how-to resource for teachers and clinicians working with students for whom minor curriculum and environmental modifications are ineffective. *$35.00*
64 pages

2113 Journal of Addictions & Offender Counseling
American Counseling Association
P.O. Box 31110
Alexandria, VA 22310-9998   703-823-9800
800-347-6647
FAX: 800-473-2329
jaoc.iaaoc@utoledo.edu
www.counseling.org

Shawn E. Boynes, Chief Executive Officer
John M. Laux, Editor
Rochelle Cade, Associate Editor
Official journal of the International Association of Addictions and Offender Counselors, a member association of the American Counseling Association. Contains information on programs, theory, and research into addictions and offender counseling. *$25.00*
Bi-annual

2114 Journal of Applied School Psychology
Haworth Press
711 Third Avenue
New York, NY 10017   212-216-7800
800-354-1420
FAX: 212-244-1563
subscriptions@tandf.co.uk
www.haworthpress.com

This journal disseminates the latest and the highest quality information to all professionals who provide special services in the schools and related educational settings. Haworth Press are now acquired by the Taylor & Francis Journals. *$60.00*
BiAnnually

2115 Journal of Counseling & Development
American Counseling Association
P.O. Box 31110
Alexandria, VA 22310-9998   800-347-6647
FAX: 800-473-2329
jcd@unt.edu
www.counseling.org

Shawn E. Boynes, Chief Executive Officer
Matthew Lemberger-Truelove, Editor
Nick Lazzareschi, Editorial Assistant
Publishes practice, theory, and research articles across 18 different counseling and development specialty areas. Sections include research, assessment and diagnosis, theory and practice, and trends. *$35.00*
128 pages Quarterly

2116 Journal of Disability Policy Studies
2455 Teller Road
Thousand Oaks, CA 91320   800-818-7243
FAX: 800-583-2665
journals@sagepub.com
cde.sagepub.com

Blaise R. Simqu, President/ CEO
Tracey A. Ozmina, EVP/ COO
Chris Hickok, SVP/ CFO
Journal of Disability Policy Studies (DPS) addresses compelling variable issues in ethics, policy and law related to individuals with disabilities.

2117 Journal of Emotional and Behavioral Disorders
Sage Publications
2455 Teller Road
Thousand Oaks, CA 91320   805-499-0721
800-818-7243
FAX: 800-583-2665
info@sagepub.com
www.sagepub.com

Sara Miller McCune, Founder, Publisher & Executive Chairman
Blaise R. Simqu, President & CEO
Chris Hickok, Senior Vice President & Chief Financial Officer
An international, multidisciplinary journal featuring articles on research, practice and theory related to individuals with emotional and behavioral disorders and to the professionals who serve them. *$39.00*
64 pages Quarterly

2118 Journal of Learning Disabilities
Sage Publications
2455 Teller Road
Thousand Oaks, CA 91320   805-499-0721
800-818-7243
FAX: 800-583-2665
info@sagepub.com
www.sagepub.com

Sara Miller McCune, Founder, Publisher & Executive Chairman
Blaise R. Simqu, President & CEO
Chris Hickok, Senior Vice President & Chief Financial Officer
An international, multidisciplinary publication containing articles on practice, research and theory related to learning disabilities. Published bi-monthly. *$49.00*
Magazine

2119 Journal of Midwifery & Women's Health (JMWH)
American College of Nurse Midwives
8403 Colesville Rd.
Suite 1230
Silver Spring, MD 20910   240-485-1800
FAX: 240-485-1818
membership@acnm.org
midwife.org

Melissa D. Avery, Editor-in-Chief
Linda A. Hunter, Deputy Editor
Ira Kantrowitz-Gordon, Deputy Editor
Official journal of the American College of Nurse Midwives.

2120   Journal of Motor Behavior
Heldref Publications
325 Chestnut Street
Suite 800
Philadelphia, PA 19106   215-625-8900
                                              800-354-1420
                                         FAX: 215-625-2940
                        customer.service@taylorandfrancis.com
                                            www.heldref.org

Emilli Pawlowsky, Marketing Manager
Laura Rosse, Assistant Marketing Manager
Douglas Kirkpatrick, Publisher
A professional journal aimed at psychologists, therapists and educators who work in the areas of motor behavior, psychology, neurophysiology, kinesiology, and biomechanics. Offers up-to-date information on the latest techniques, theories and developments concerning motor control. Titles previously published by Heldref Publications will be joining the T&F portfolio. *$77.00*
115 pages Quarterly

2121   Journal of Musculoskeletal Pain
Haworth Press
711 Third Avenue
New York, NY 10017   212-216-7800
                                              800-354-1420
                                         FAX: 212-244-1563
                              subscriptions@tandf.co.uk
                                       www.haworthpress.com
This journal serves as a central resource for the dissemination of information about musculoskeletal pain. Haworth Press are now acquired by the Taylor & Francis Journals. *$75.00*
110 pages Quarterly

2122   Journal of Positive Behavior Interventions
2455 Teller Road
Thousand Oaks, CA 91320   800-818-7243
                                         FAX: 800-583-2665
                                   journals@sagepub.com
                                           cde.sagepub.com

Blaise R. Simqu, President/ CEO
Tracey A. Ozmina, EVP/ COO
Chris Hickok, SVP/ CFO
Journal of Positive Behavior Interventions (PBI) offers sound, research-based principles of positive behavior support for use in school, home and community settings with people with challenges in behavioral adaptation.

2123   Journal of Postsecondary Education & Disability (JPED)
AHEAD
8015 West Kenton Circle
Suite 230
Huntersville, NC 28078   704-947-7779
                                         FAX: 704-948-7779
                                        jped@ahead.org
                                            www.ahead.org

Stephan Smith, Executive Director
Ezekiel Kimball, Executive Editor
Ryan Wells, Executive Editor
An annual publication dedicated to the advancement of full participation in higher education for persons with disabilities. The journal focuses on a variety of related topics that emphasize research, issues, and trends related to the theory and practice of postsecondary disability services.
Quarterly

2124   Journal of Prosthetics and Orthotics
330 John Carlyle Street
Suite 210
Alexandria, VA 22314   703-836-7114
                                         FAX: 703-836-0838
                                       info@abcop.org
                                           www.abcop.org

Catherine Carter, Executive Director
Debbie Ayres, Director, Marketing & Public Relations
Stephen Fletcher, CPO, LPO, Director, Clinical Resources
Provides the latest research and clinical thinking in orthotics and prosthetics, including information on new devices, fitting techniques and patient management experiences. Each issue contains

research-based information and articles reviewed and approved by a highly qualified editorial board. *$60.00*
64 pages Quarterly
ISSN 1040-88 0

2125   Journal of Reading, Writing and Learning Disabled International
Hemisphere Publishing Corporation
7625 Empire Drive
Florence, KY 41042-2919   800-634-7064
                                         FAX: 800-248-4724
                                orders@taylorandfrancis.com
                                  www.taylorandfrancis.com
Articles on reading, writing and learning disabilities, including mainstreaming issues. *$9.00*

2126   Journal of Rehabilitation
National Rehabilitation Association (NRA)
1520 Belle View Blvd
Suite 5142
Alexandria, VA 22307   703-836-0850
                                              888-258-4295
                          journalofrehab@email.arizona.edu
                         nationalrehab.org/journal-of-rehabilitation
Wendy Parent-Johnson, Editor
Official journal of the National Rehabilitation Association.
Quarterly

2127   Journal of School Health Association
Suite 403
4340 East West Highway
Bethesda, MD 20814   301-652-8072
                                         FAX: 301-652-8077
                                       info@ashaweb.org
                                            ashaweb.org

Jeffrey K. Clark, President
Stephen Conley, Executive Director
Julie Greenfield, Marketing and Conferences Direct
This is a monthly journal which offers information to professionals and parents on school health. Membership dues, $95.00.

2128   Journal of Special Education
Sage Publications
2455 Teller Road
Thousand Oaks, CA 91320   805-499-0721
                                              800-818-7243
                                         FAX: 800-583-2665
                                       info@sagepub.com
                                           www.sagepub.com
Sara Miller McCune, Founder, Publisher & Executive Chairman
Blaise R. Simqu, President & CEO
Chris Hickok, Senior Vice President & Chief Financial Officer
Internationally known as the prime research journal in special education. JSE provides research articles of special education for individuals with disabilities, ranging from mild to severe. Published quarterly. *$39.00*
Magazine

2129   Journal of Vocational Behavior
Academic Press, Journals Division

The Journal of Vocational Behavior publishes empirical and theoretical articles that expand knowledge of vocational behavior and career development across the life span. Research presented in the journal encompasses the general categories of career choice, implementation, and vocational adjustment and adaptation. The articles are also valuable for applications in counseling and career development programs in colleges and universities, business and industry, government, and the military. *$7.00*

2130   Learning Disabilities: A Contemporary Journal
179 Bear Hill Rd.
Suite 104
Waltham, MA 02451   978-897-5399
                                         FAX: 978-897-5355
                                      help@ldworldwide.org
                                           www.ldw-ldcj.org

Matthias Grunke, Editor
Teresa Allissa Citro, Editor
Marco G. P. Hessels, Associate Editor

Learning Disabilities: A Contemporary Journal (LDCJ) is a peer-reviewed forum for research, practice, and opinion regarding learning disabilities (LD) and associated disorders.

2131   Learning Disabilities: A Multidisciplinary Journal
Learning Disabilities Association of America
4068 Mount Royal Boulevard
Suite 224B
Allison Park, PA 15101   412-341-1515
                                                    FAX: 412-344-0224
                                                    info@ldaamerica.org
                                                    www.ldaamerica.org

Cindy Cipoletti, Executive Director
Dr. Joe Morgan, Editor
The journal is a vehicle for disseminating the most current thinking on learning disabilities and to provide information on research, practice, theory, issues, and trends regarding learning disabilities from the perspectives of varied disciplines involved in broadening the understanding of learning disabilities.

2132   Learning Disability Quarterly
2455 Teller Road
Thousand Oaks, CA 91320   800-818-7243
                                                    FAX: 800-583-2665
                                                    journals@sagepub.com
                                                    ldq.sagepub.com

Blaise R. Simqu, President/ CEO
Tracey A. Ozmina, EVP/ COO
Chris Hickok, SVP/ CFO
Learning Disability Quarterly (LDQ) publishes high-quality research and scholarship concerning children, youth, and adults with learning disabilities.

2133   MDA/ALS Newsmagazine
Muscular Dystrophy Association
161 N Clark
Suite 3550
Chicago, IL 60601   800-572-1717
                                                    alsn.mda.org
Donald S. Wood, President & Chief Executive Officer
Presents news related to muscular dystrophy and other neuromuscular diseases including research, personal profiles, fundraising activities and patient services.

2134   Movement Disorders
555 East Wells Street
Suite 1100
Milwaukee, WI 53202- 3823   414-276-2145
                                                    FAX: 414-276-3349
                                                    info@movementdisorders.org
                                                    www.movementdisorders.org

Matthew B. Stern, President
Oscar S. Gershanik, President-Elect
Francisco Cardoso, Secretary
Movement Disorders, the official Journal of the International Parkinson and Movement Disorder Society (MDS), is a highly read and referenced journal covering all topics of the field - both clinical and basic science.

2135   People & Families
PO Box 700
Trenton, NJ 8625-700   609-292-345
                                                    800-792-8858
                                                    FAX: 609-292-7114
                                                    TTY: 609-777-3238
                                                    njcdd@njcdd.org
                                                    www.njcdd.org

Kevin T. Jonathan, Waller
Editor
People & Families, the NJCDD's nationally recognized magazine, focuses on issues of importance to the developmental disabilities community in New Jersey.

2136   Psychiatric Staffing Crisis in Community Mental Health
Nat l Council for Community Behavioral Healthcare
76 Ninth Avenue
New York, NY 10011   201-559-3882
                                                    800-THE-BOOK
                                                    amilevoj@bn.com
                                                    www.barnesandnoble.com

Andy Milevoj, Vice President, Investor Relations
Mary Ellen Keating, SVP, Corporate Communications & Public Affairs
Carolyn Brown, Director of Corporate Communications
Find out some of the simple, low-cost ways you can increase workplace satisfaction among staff psychiatrists and compete successfully for their talents. *$20.00*

2137   Quest Magazine
Muscular Dystrophy Association
161 N Clark
Suite 3550
Chicago, IL 60601   800-572-1717
                                                    ResourceCenter@mdausa.org
                                                    www.mda.org/quest
Donald S. Wood, President & Chief Executive Officer
Magazine of the Muscular Dystrophy Association.

2138   Readings: A Journal of Reviews and Commentary in Mental Health
American Orthopsychiatric Association
3524 Washington Avenue
P.O. Box 1048
Sheboygan, WI 53081-1048   920-457-5051
                                                    800-558-7687
                                                    FAX: 920-457-1485
                                                    info@americanortho.com
                                                    www.americanortho.com

Michael Bogenschuetz, President
Randy Benz, Chief Executive Officer
Charles Achter, Assistant Controller
Reviews of recent books in mental health and allied disciplines. Includes essay reviews and brief reviews. *$25.00*
32 pages Quarterly

2139   Rehab Pro
1926 Waukegan Rd
Suite 1
Glenview, IL 60025-1770   847-657-6964
                                                    FAX: 847-657-6963
                                                    carlw@tcag.com
                                                    www.rehabpro.org

Carl Wangman, Executive Director
The magazine is to promote the profession and to inform the public about the activities of the national organization, its state chapter affiliates, and the work of its special interest sections.
38 pages BiMonthly

2140   Remedial and Special Education
Sage Publications
2455 Teller Road
Thousand Oaks, CA 91320   805-499-0721
                                                    800-818-7243
                                                    FAX: 800-583-2665
                                                    info@sagepub.com
                                                    www.sagepub.com
Sara Miller McCune, Founder, Publisher & Executive Chairman
Blaise R. Simqu, President & CEO
Chris Hickok, Senior Vice President & Chief Financial Officer
A professional journal that bridges the gap between theory and practice. Emphasis is on topical reviews, syntheses of research, field evaluation studies and recommendations for the practice of remedial and special education. Published six times a year. *$39.00*
64 pages

2141 Structural Integration: The Journal of the Rolf Institute
5055 Chaparral Ct.
Suite 103
Boulder, CO 80301   303-449-5903
                              FAX: 303-449-5978
                                    www.rolf.org
Christina Howe, Executive Director & Chief Academic Officer
Mary Contreras, Director, Admissions & Recruitment
Samantha Sherwin, Director, Faculty & Student Services
Professional journal consisting of articles on research, practice
building, faculty perspectives, reviews, and other topics relating
to the field of Rolfing Structural Integration.

2142 Teaching Exceptional Children (TEC)
Council for Exceptional Children
3100 Clarendon Blvd.
Suite 600
Arlington, VA 22201-5332   888-232-7733
                               TTY:866-915-5000
                     service@exceptionalchildren.org
                         www.exceptionalchildren.org
Dawn Rowe, Academic Editor
Journal designed for teachers of gifted students and students with
disabilities, featuring practical methods and materials for class-
room use. Published six times per year.

Newsletters

2143 APA Access
750 First Street, NE
Washington, DC 20002-4242   202-336-5500
                                     800-374-2721
                              rllowman@gmail.com
                                     www.apa.org
Rodney L. Lowman, PhD, Chair
Barry Anton, PhD, President
Bonnie Markham, PhD, PsyD, Treasurer
Exclusively for APA members, APA Access provides a helpful in-
sider's view of the latest APA news. Each monthly issue high-
lights an array of current topics, such as advocacy updates,
continuing education opportunities, press releases, previews of
Monitor on Psychology articles, APA publishing news, new APA
products and a calendar of events.

2144 Alert
Association on Handicapped Student Service Program
P.O.Box 21192
Columbus, OH 43221   614-365-5216
                              FAX: 614-365-6718
Keeps members informed about Association activities, current
legislative issues, innovative programs, and more. *$30.00*

2145 Children's Mental Health and EBD E-news
PACER Center
8161 Normandale Blvd.
Bloomington, MN 55437   952-838-9000
                                     800-537-2237
                              FAX: 952-838-0199
                                  pacer@pacer.org
                                    www.pacer.org
Tonia Teasley, Executive Director
Newsletter providing resources for parents with children affected
by mental health and emotional or behavioral issues.

2146 Counseling Today
American Counseling Association
P.O. Box 31110
Alexandria, VA 22310   800-347-6647
                              FAX: 800-473-2329
                                 ct.counseling.org
Richard Yep, Chief Executive Officer
Aims to serve individuals active in professional counseling, as
well as other citizens, community leaders and policy makers who
appreciate the importance of the role of professional counselors
in today's society. The publication features news and articles on
professional counseling developments, resources, strategies,
regulations, and more.
Monthly

2147 Disability Compliance for Higher Education
LRP Publications
P.O. Box 24668
West Palm Beach, FL 33416-4668   561-622-2423
                                     800-341-7874
                              FAX: 561-622-1375
                                 custserve@lrp.com
                                        lrp.com
Kenneth F. Kahn, Owner and President
Ed Chase, Vice President
The only newsletter that is dedicated to the exclusive coverage of
disability issues that affect colleges and universities. *$195.00*
8 pages Monthly

2148 Disability Pride Newsletter
900 Rebecca Avenue
Pittsburgh, PA 15221   800-633-4588
                              FAX: 412-371-9430
                                  lgray@trcil.org
Rachel Rogan, CEO
Gregory Daigle, Chief Financial Officer
Lisa Wilson, HR Program Manager
Three Rivers Center for Independent Living (TRCIL) is a
non-residential, non-profit, community-based human service or-
ganization. There purpose is to assist people with disabilities to
lead self-directed and productive lives within the community.

2149 Disability Resources Monthly
Disability Resources
4 Glatter Ln
South Setauket, NY 11720-1032   631-585-0290
                              FAX: 631-585-0290
Avery Klauber, Executive Director
A newsletter that monitors, reviews and reports on resources for
independent living. A monthly newsletter that features short topical articles, news items and reviews of books, pamphlets, periodicals, videotapes, on-line services, organizations and other
resources for and about people with disabilities. It is intended primarily for librarians, social workers, educators, rehabilitation
specialists, disability advocates, ADA coordinators and other
health and social service professionals. *$33.00*
4 pages Monthly
ISSN 1070-72 0

2150 Early Childhood Reporter
LRP Publications
P.O. Box 24668
West Palm Beach, FL 33416-4668   561-622-2423
                                     800-341-7874
                              FAX: 561-622-1375
                                 custserve@lrp.com
                                    www.lrp.com
Kenneth F. Kahn, Owner and President
Ed Chase, Vice President
Monthly reports with information on federal, state, and local leg-
islation affecting the implementation of early intervention and
preschool programs for children with disabilities. *$145.00*
12-16 pages $10 shipping

2151 FYI
AAIDD
8403 Colesville Rd.
Suite 900
Silver Spring, MD 20910   202-387-1968
                              FAX: 202-387-2193
                                     aaidd.org
Margaret A. Nygren, Executive Director & Chief Executive Officer
Kathleen McLane, Director, Publications Program
Zach Gordon, Production Coordinator, Publications Program
A monthly newsletter that provides news about AAIDD re-
sources, educational opportunities, and activities.

2152 Family Engagement
PACER Center
8161 Normandale Blvd.
Bloomington, MN 55437   952-838-9000
                                     800-537-2237
                              FAX: 952-838-0199
                                  pacer@pacer.org
                                    www.pacer.org
Tonia Teasley, Executive Director

E-newsletter providing parents and professionals with resources for supporting family engagement with schools.

2153 Fellow Insider
AAIDD
8403 Colesville Rd.
Suite 900
Silver Spring, MD 20910 202-387-1968
FAX: 202-387-2193
aaidd.org
Margaret A. Nygren, Executive Director & Chief Executive Officer
Kathleen McLane, Director, Publications Program
Zach Gordon, Production Coordinator, Publications Program
Quarterly newsletter for Fellows of the American Association on Intellectual and Developmental Disabilities.

2154 Field Notes
AAIDD
8403 Colesville Rd.
Suite 900
Silver Spring, MD 20910 202-387-1968
FAX: 202-387-2193
aaidd.org
Margaret A. Nygren, Executive Director & Chief Executive Officer
Kathleen McLane, Director, Publications Program
Zach Gordon, Production Coordinator, Publications Program
A monthly newsletter providing summaries of studies published in peer reviewed journals, along with links to the original articles.

2155 Gram Newsletter, The
PO Box 1114
Claremont, CA 91711 909-621-1494
Arline Krieger, President
Pam Hamilton, 1st Vice-President
EunMi Cho, 3rd Vice-President
The Learning Disabilities Association of California's (LDA-CA's) quarterly newsletter, The GRAM, provides LDA-CA members with timely information.

2156 Growing Readers
LD Online
2775 S. Quincy St.
Arlington, VA FAX: 703-998-2060
ldonline@weta.org
www.ldonline.org
Noel Gunther, Executive Director
Christian Lindstrom, Director, Learning Media
Monthly tips for raising strong readers and writers, written especially for parents. Used by schools and PTAs in parent newsletters, and by libraries and community literacy organizations.

2157 Healthline
CV Mosby Company
1600 John F. Kennedy Boulevard
Suite 1800
Philadelphia, PA 19103-2822 215-239-3900
800-523-1649
FAX: 215-239-3990
www.us.elsevierhealth.com
Health and fitness information for healthcare professionals and the general public alike.
Monthly

2158 Help Newsletter
Learning Disabilities Association of Arkansas
P.O. Box 23514
Little Rock, AR 72221 501-666-8777
FAX: 501-666-8777
www.ldaarkansas.org
Nathan Green, President
Rebecca Walker, VP
Becca Green, Past President, Treasurer
Information on how to overcome obstacles and to achieve in spite of learning disabilities. *$30.00*
8 pages Quarterly

2159 HerbalEGram
American Botanical Council
6200 Manor Rd.
Austin, TX 78723-4345 512-926-4900
800-373-7105
FAX: 512-926-2345
abc@herbalgram.org
herbalgram.org
Mark Blumenthal, Founder, Executive Director & Editor
Hannah Bauman, Assistant Editor
Electronic newsletter of the American Botanical Council, with current editions available to members only.

2160 Insights
135 Parkinson Avenue
Staten Island, NY 10305 800-223-2732
FAX: 718-981-4399
apda@apdaparkinson.org
www.apdaparkinson.org
Fred Greene, Chairman
Patrick McDermott, 1st Vice Chairman
Jerry Wells, Esq., Secretary
APDA was founded in 1961 with the dual purpose to Ease the Burden - Find the Cure for Parkinson's disease.

2161 Inspiring Possibilities
PACER Center
8161 Normandale Blvd.
Bloomington, MN 55437 952-838-9000
800-537-2237
FAX: 952-838-0199
pacer@pacer.org
www.pacer.org
Tonia Teasley, Executive Director
From PACER's National Parent Center on Transition and Employment, the e-newsletter provides news and updates for youth with disabilities transitioning from school to the workforce.

2162 LD Monthly Report
LD Online
2775 S. Quincy St.
Arlington, VA FAX: 703-998-2060
ldonline@weta.org
www.ldonline.org
Noel Gunther, Executive Director
Christian Lindstrom, Director, Learning Media
LD OnLine seeks to help children and adults reach their full potential by providing accurate and up-to-date information and advice about learning disabilities and ADHD.

2163 MA Report
National Allergy and Asthma Network
Ste 200
3554 Chain Bridge Rd
Fairfax, VA 22030-2709 703-385-4403
FAX: 703-352-4354
Offers information on medical breakthroughs, patient care, public awareness, activities and events focusing on the allergy and asthma patient. This newsletter is the only Monthly Asthma Report that a patient will need to keep fully informed with medical articles written by experts in the field. .
Monthly

2164 Member Update
AAIDD
8403 Colesville Rd.
Suite 900
Silver Spring, MD 20910 202-387-1968
FAX: 202-387-2193
aaidd.org
Margaret A. Nygren, Executive Director & Chief Executive Officer
Kathleen McLane, Director, Publications Program
Zach Gordon, Production Coordinator, Publications Program
A weekly newsletter providing updates on professional development opportunities, including conferences and webinars, job postings, calls for papers, and opportunities to join advisory committees and provide comments on federal initiatives.

2165 National Bullying Prevention Center Newsletter
PACER Center
8161 Normandale Blvd.
Bloomington, MN 55437   952-838-9000
                                        800-537-2237
                                   FAX: 952-838-0199
                                     pacer@pacer.org
                                      www.pacer.org

Tonia Teasley, Executive Director
Provides resources from PACER's National Bullying Prevention Center (NBPC). Publishes information on bullying prevention as well as news on anti-bullying events. Published quarterly and during National Bullying Prevention Month in October.

2166 O&P Almanac
American Orthotic & Prosthetic Association
330 John Carlyle Street
Suite 200
Alexandria, VA 22314   571-431-0876
                                   FAX: 571-431-0899
                                     info@aopanet.org
                                      www.aopanet.org

Anita Liberman-Lampear, MA, President
Charles H. Dankmeyer, Jr, CPO, President-Elect
James Campbell, CO, Ph.D., Vice President
Offers in-depth coverage on orthotics and prosthetics to current professional, government, business and reimbursement activities affecting the orthotics and prosthetics industry. *$59.00*
80 pages Monthly

2167 Occupational Therapy in Health Care
Haworth Press
711 Third Avenue
New York, NY 10017   212-216-7800
                                        800-354-1420
                                   FAX: 212-244-1563
                              subscriptions@tandf.co.uk
                                 www.haworthpress.com
Each issue focuses on significant practices and concerns involving occupational therapy and therapists. Haworth Press are now acquired by the Taylor & Francis Journals. *$75.00*

2168 Ohio Coalition for the Education of Children with Disabilities
165 W Center St, 3rd Floor, Chase B
Suite 302
Marion, OH 43302   740-382-5452
                                        800-374-2806
                                   FAX: 740-383-6421
                                       ocecd@ocecd.org
                                        www.ocecd.org

Martha Lause, Manager
Lee Ann Derugen, Co-Director
Margaret Burley, Executive Director
Forum is a newsletter reporting on educational, legislative and other developments affecting persons with disabilities.
8 pages

2169 PACER E-News
PACER Center
8161 Normandale Blvd.
Bloomington, MN 55437   952-838-9000
                                        800-537-2237
                                   FAX: 952-838-0199
                                     pacer@pacer.org
                                      www.pacer.org

Tonia Teasley, Executive Director
E-newsletter providing information on special events and other news. Published monthly.

2170 PACER Partners
PACER Center
8161 Normandale Blvd.
Bloomington, MN 55437   952-838-9000
                                        800-537-2237
                                   FAX: 952-838-0199
                                     pacer@pacer.org
                                      www.pacer.org

Tonia Teasley, Executive Director
Published by PACER's Development Office, the newsletter connects families, friends, donors, and the staff of PACER.

2171 PACESETTER
PACER Center
8161 Normandale Blvd.
Bloomington, MN 55437   952-838-9000
                                        800-537-2237
                                   FAX: 952-838-0199
                                     pacer@pacer.org
                                      www.pacer.org

Tonia Teasley, Executive Director
Provides resources and information on special education and PACER programs. PACER's main newsletter.

2172 SAMHSA News
US Department of Health and Human Services
5600 Fishers Lane
Rockville, MD 20857   877-726-4727
                                   TTY:800-487-4889
                              samhsainfo@samhsa.hhs.gov
                                      www.samhsa.gov

Tom Coderre, Acting Assistant Secretary
Sonia Chessen, Chief of Staff
Trina Dutta, Senior Advisor
This quarterly agency newsletter reports on information on substance abuse, mental health treatment and prevention programs of the Substance Abuse and Mental Health Services Administration.
Quarterly

2173 Sibling Information Network Newsletter
AJ Pappanikou Center
270 Farmington Avenue
Suite 181
Farmington, CT 06030   860-679-1500
                                        866-623-1315
                                   FAX: 860-679-1571
                                   TTY: 860-679-1502
                               contact.us.ucedd@uchc.edu
                                    www.uconnucedd.org

Mary Beth Bruder, PhD, UCEDD/LEND Director
Gerarda Hanna, J.D., M.Ed., Associate UCEDD Director
Gabriela Freyre-Calish, MSW, Coordinator, Director, Cultural Diversity
Contains information aimed at the varying interested of our membership. Program descriptions, requests for assistance, conference announcements, literature summaries and research reports.
$8.50

2174 Sibpage
AJ Pappanikou Center
270 Farmington Avenue
Suite 181
Farmington, CT 06030   860-679-1500
                                        866-623-1315
                                   FAX: 860-679-1571
                                   TTY: 860-679-1502
                               contact.us.ucedd@uchc.edu
                                    www.uconnucedd.org

Mary Beth Bruder, PhD, UCEDD/LEND Director
Gerarda Hanna, J.D., M.Ed., Associate UCEDD Director
Gabriela Freyre-Calish, MSW, Coordinator, Director, Cultural Diversity
Developed specifically for children containing games, recipes, pen pals, and articles written by siblings relating to developmental disabilities.
4 pages

2175 Special Edge
Resources in Special Education
Fl 4
1107 9th St
Sacramento, CA 95814-3616   916-492-9999
                                        877-493-7833
                                   FAX: 916-492-4004

Virigina Reynolds, President
Provides education news, collaborative programs, amendments to the laws, tools for accommodations, resource information, a calendar of events, and more.
BiMonthly

2176 Special Education Report
LRP Publications
360 Hiatt Dr
Dept. 150F
Palm BeachGardens, FL 33418
800-341-7874
FAX: 561-622-2423
custserve@lrp.com
lrp.com

Current, pertinent information about federal legislation, regulations, programs and funding for educating children with disabilities. Covers federal and state litigation on the Individuals with Disabilities Education Act and other relevant laws. Looks at innovations and research in the field.

2177 Topics in Early Childhood Special Education
Sage Publications
2455 Teller Road
Thousand Oaks, CA 91320
805-499-0721
800-818-7243
FAX: 800-583-2665
info@sagepub.com
www.sagepub.com

Sara Miller McCune, Founder, Publisher & Executive Chairman
Blaise R. Simqu, President & CEO
Chris Hickok, Senior Vice President & Chief Financial Officer
Designed for professionals helping young children with special needs in areas such as assessment, special programs, social policies and developmental aids. *$43.00*
Quarterly

2178 Treatment Review
AIDS Treatment Data Network
57 Willoughby St.
2nd Floor
Brooklyn, NY 11201
347-473-7400
800-734-7104
TTY:212-925-9560
info@housingworks.org
www.housingworks.org

Charles King, Chair
Linney Smith, Vice Chair
Earl Ward, Vice Chair
Individual members receive treatment education, counseling, referrals and case management support. Services are available in both English and Spanish. The Treatment Review newsletter includes descriptions of approved, alternative and experimental treatments, as well as announcements of seminars and forums on treatments and clinical trials.
Quarterly

2179 VIP Newsletter
Blind Children's Fund
6761 West US 12
P.O. Box 363
Three Oaks, MI 49128
989-779-9966
FAX: 269-756-3133
www.blindchildrensfund.org

Karla B. Kwast, Executive Director
Jeremy Murphy, President
Robert R. Storrer Jr., Vice President
Provides parents and professionals with information, materials and resources that help them successfully teach and nurture blind, visually and multi-impaired infants and preschoolers. *$10.00*

Professional Texts

2180 7 Steps for Success
Council for Exceptional Children
3100 Clarendon Blvd.
Suite 600
Arlington, VA 22201-5332
888-232-7733
TTY:866-915-5000
service@exceptionalchildren.org
www.exceptionalchildren.org

Elizabeth C. Hamblet, Author
A book helping young adults with disabilities transitioning from high school to college.

2181 A Guide to Teaching Students With Autism Spectrum Disorders
Council for Exceptional Children
3100 Clarendon Blvd.
Suite 600
Arlington, VA 22201-5332
888-232-7733
TTY:866-915-5000
service@exceptionalchildren.org
www.exceptionalchildren.org

Monica E. Delano, Co-Author
Darlene E. Perner, Co-Author
This book is a resource for all special educators and general educators who work with students with autism spectrum disorders (ASD). The underlying premise is that students with ASD should be explicitly taught a full range of social, self-help, language, reading, writing and math skills, as are their typically developing classmates.

2182 A Teacher's Guide to Isovaleric Acidemia
150 North 18th Avenue
Phoenix, AZ 85007
602-542-1025
FAX: 602-542-0883
www.azdhs.gov

Will Humble, Director
Thomas Salow, Manager
Resource book for preschool teachers and school staff on isovaleric academia basics and classroom activities. *$2.50*

2183 A Teacher's Guide to Methylmalonic Acidemia
Arizona State Department of Health Services
150 North 18th Avenue
Phoenix, AZ 85007
602-542-1025
FAX: 602-542-0883
www.azdhs.gov

Will Humble, Director
Thomas Salow, Manager
Resource book for preschool teachers and school staff on methylmalonic academia basics and classroom activities. *$2.50*

2184 A Teacher's Guide to PKU
Arizona Department of Health Services
150 North 18th Avenue
Phoenix, AZ 85007
602-542-1025
FAX: 602-542-0883
www.azdhs.gov

Will Humble, Director
Thomas Salow, Manager
Resource book for preschool teachers and school staff on PKU basics, NutraSweet warning, and classroom activities. *$2.50*
13 pages

2185 AD/HD and the College Student: The Everything Guide to Your Most Urgent Questions
750 First Street, NE
Washington, DC 20002-4242
202-336-5500
800-374-2721
rllowman@gmail.com
www.apa.org

Patricia O. Quinn, MD, Author
Whether you are looking for information or facing an urgent situation,AD/HD and the College Studentprovides answers to your most pressing questions. Organized in a question-and-answer format, this guide is loaded with helpful information, practical tips, and resources.

2186 ADD Challenge: A Practical Guide for Teachers
2612 N. Mattis Ave.
P.O. Box 7886
Champaign, IL 61822
217-352-3273
800-519-2707
FAX: 217-352-1221
orders@researchpress.com
www.researchpress.com

Robert W. Parkinson, Founder
Steven B. Gordon, Author
Dr Richard M Foxx, Author
Research Press is an independent, family-owned business founded in 1968 by Robert W. Parkinson (1920-2001).

2187 ADHD Coaching: A Guide for Mental Health Professionals
750 First Street, NE
Washington, DC 20002-4242   202-336-5500
                                  800-374-2721
                                  rllowman@gmail.com
                                  www.apa.org

Frances Prevatt, PhD, Co-Author
Abigail Levrini, PhD, Co-Author
This book describes the underlying principles as well as the nuts and bolts of ADHD coaching. Step-by-step details for gathering information, conducting the intake, establishing goals and objectives, and working through all stages of coaching are included, along with helpful forms and a detailed list of additional resources.

2188 ADHD in the Classroom: Strategies for Teachers
Guilford Publication
72 Spring Street
New York, NY 10012   212-431-9800
                                  800-365-7006
                                  FAX: 212-966-6708
                                  info@guilford.com
                                  www.guilford.com

Bob Matloff, President
Seymour Weingarten, Editor-in-Chief
Russell A. Barkley, Author
Designed specifically to help teachers with their ADHD students, thereby providing a better learning environment for the entire class. *$95.00*
ISBN 0-898629-85-3

2189 ADHD in the Schools: Assessment and Intervention Strategies
72 Spring Street
New York, NY 10012   212-431-9800
                                  800-365-7006
                                  FAX: 212-966-6708
                                  info@guilford.com
                                  www.guilford.com

Bob Matloff, President
Seymour Weingarten, Editor-in-Chief
George J. DuPaul, Author
The landmark volume emphasizes the need for a team effort among parents, community-based professionals, and educators. Provides practical information for educators that is based on empirical findings. Chapters Focus on how to identify and assess students who might have ADHD, the relationship between ADHD and learning disabilities; how to develop and supplement classroom-based programs. Communication strategies to assist physicians and the need for community-based treatments *$36.00*
269 pages Paperback
ISBN 0-898622-45-X

2190 AEPS Curriculum for Birth to Three Years
Brookes Publishing
P.O.Box 10624
Baltimore, MD 21285-0624   410-337-9580
                                  800-638-3775
                                  FAX: 410-337-8539
                                  custserv@brookespublishing.com
                                  readplaylearn.com
Directly linked to IEP/IFSP goals developed for a child from the AEPS test measure, the AEPS curriculum provides a complete set of learning activities to facilitate children's acquisition of functional skills. *$59.95*
496 pages
ISBN 1-557660-96-4

2191 Access to Health Care
World Institute on Disability
3075 Adeline St.
Suite 155
Berkeley, CA 94703   510-225-6400
                                  FAX: 510-225-0477
                                  wid@wid.org
                                  www.wid.org

Marcie Roth, Executive Director & Chief Executive Officer
Kat Zigmont, Senior Director, Operations & Deputy Director
Reggie Johnson, Senior Director, Marketing & Communications

Policy bulletins focusing on the capacity of the private and public health insurance systems to respond to the health care needs of persons with disabilities or chronic illness.

2192 Activity-Based Approach to Early Intervention, 2nd Edition
Brookes Publishing
P.O.Box 10624
Baltimore, MD 21285-0624   410-337-9580
                                  800-638-3775
                                  FAX: 410-337-8539
                                  webmaster@brookespublishing.com
                                  www.brookespublishing.com

Paul H. Brookes, Chairman of the Board
Jeffrey D. Brookes, President
George S. Stamathis, VP/Publisher
Activity-based intervention shows how to use natural and relevant events to teach infants and young children, of all abilities, effectively and efficiently. *$24.00*
240 pages
ISBN 1-55766 -87-5

2193 Adapted Physical Education for Students with Autism
Charles C. Thomas
2600 S First St
Springfield, IL 62704-4730   217-789-8980
                                  800-258-8980
                                  FAX: 217-789-9130
                                  books@ccthomas.com
                                  www.ccthomas.com

Kimberly Davis, Author
Focuses on the physical education needs and curriculum for autistic children. Available in cloth, paperback and hardcover. *$27.95*
142 pages Paper
ISBN 0-398060-85-1

2194 Adapting Early Childhood Curricula for Children with Special Needs (9th Edition)
Pearson Higher Education
330 Hudson St
New York, NY 10013   212-641-2400
                                  www.pearsonhighered.com

Ruth E. Cook, Author
M. Diane Klein, Author
Deborah Chen, Author
This highly readable, well researched, and current resource uses a developmental focus, rather than a disability orientation, to discuss typical and atypical child development and curricular adaptations, and encourage the treatment of students as children first, without regard to their learning differences. *$102.67*
528 pages Loose-Leaf or Access Code Card 1915
ISBN 0-134019-41-3

2195 Adapting Instruction for the Mainstream: A Sequential Approach to Teaching
McGraw-Hill School Publishing
P.O. Box 182605
Columbus, OH 43218   800-338-3987
                                  FAX: 609-308-4480
                                  customer.service@mheducation.com
                                  mcgraw-hill.com

David Levin, President, CEO
Ellen Haley, President, CTB
Peter Cohen, President, School Education
This text gives both regular and special education teachers everything they need to help mildly handicapped students succeed in the mainstream.
226 pages

2196 Adaptive Education Strategies Building on Diversity
Brookes Publishing Company
P.O.Box 10624
Baltimore, MD 21285-0624   410-337-9580
                                       800-638-3775
                                  FAX: 410-337-8539
                        webmaster@brookespublishing.com
                           www.brookespublishing.com
Paul H. Brookes, Chairman of the Board
Jeffrey D. Brookes, President
George S. Stamathis, VP/Publisher
Based on more than two decades of systematic research, this comprehensive manual provides a road map to the effective implementation of adaptive education. *$35.00*
304 pages Paperback
ISBN 1-557880-84-0

2197 Adolescents and Adults with Learning Disabilities and ADHD
370 Seventh Avenue
Suite 1200
New York, NY 10001-1020   800-365-7006
                                  FAX: 212-966-6708
                                       info@guilford.com
                                       www.guilford.com
No%ol Gregg, PhD, Author
Most of the literature on learning disabilities and attention-deficit/hyperactivity disorder (ADHD) focuses on the needs of elementary school-age children, but older students with these conditions also require significant support.

2198 Adultspan Journal
American Counseling Association
P.O. Box 31110
Alexandria, VA 22310-9998   800-347-6647
                                  FAX: 800-473-2329
                                       www.counseling.org
Shawn E. Boynes, Chief Executive Officer
Kaprea F. Johnson, Editor
Covers issues that affect people in young, middle, and older adulthood.

2199 Advanced Sign Language Vocabulary: A Resource Text for Educators
Charles C. Thomas
2600 S First St
Springfield, IL 62704-4730   217-789-8980
                                       800-258-8980
                                  FAX: 217-789-9130
                                       books@ccthomas.com
                                       www.ccthomas.com
Elizabeth E. Wolf, Author
Janet R. Coleman, Author
This book is a collection of advanced sign language vocabulary for use by educators, interpreters, parents or anyone wishing to enlarge their sign vocabulary. *$53.95*
202 pages Spiralbound
ISBN 0-398057-22-2

2200 Advances in Cardiac and Pulmonary Rehabilitation
Haworth Press
711 Third Avenue
New York, NY 10017   212-216-7800
                                       800-354-1420
                                  FAX: 212-244-1563
                             subscriptions@tandf.co.uk
                                       www.haworthpress.com
Enhance your rehabilitation program with this authoritative volume. Haworth Press are now acquired by the Taylor & Francis Journals. *$34.95*
74 pages Hardcover
ISBN 0-866869-86-3

2201 Aging Brain
Taylor & Francis Group
Ste 800
325 Chestnut St
Philadelphia, PA 19106-2608   215-625-8900
                                       800-354-1420
                                  FAX: 215-625-2940
                          www.taylorandfrancisgroup.com
Elderly treatment.
225 pages Paperback
ISBN 0-85066 -78-0

2202 Aging and Disability: Crossing Network Lines
Springer Publishing
11 West 42nd Street
15th Floor
New York, NY 10036   212-431-4370
                                       877-687-7476
                                  FAX: 212-941-7842
                             marketing@springerpub.com
                                       springerpub.com
Theodore C. Nardin, CEO/Publisher
Jason Roth, VP/Marketing Director
Annette Imperati, Marketing/Sales Director
Michelle Putnam has set forth this volume to reflect the current research, facilitate collaboration across service networks, and encourage movement toward more effective service policies. Professional stakeholders evaluate the bridges and barriers to crossing network lines, and chapter on current websites, agencies, and coalitions provides the much needed tools to bring collaboration into practice.

2203 Aging and Rehabilitation II: The State ofthe Practice
Springer Publishing Company
11 W 42nd St
15th Fl
New York, NY 10036-8002   212-431-4370
                                       877-687-7476
                                  FAX: 212-941-7842
                                       cs@springerpub.com
                                       www.springerpub.com
Ted Nardin, chief Executive Officer
Jason Roth, Vice President, Marketing & Sales
Kathy Weiss, Senior Sales Director
Current, multidisciplinary investigations of various practice issues. Leading experts in the field use a practical perspective to provide specific comments on interventions. The scope of this work encompasses the autonomy of elderly disabled, mobility, mental health and value issues, as well as basic aspects in rehabilitation of the elderly. *$8.95*
348 pages Hardcover 1990
ISBN 0-826170-80-3

2204 Alphabetic Phonics Curriculum
Educators Publishing Service
625 Mount Auburn Street
3rd Floor
Cambridge, MA 02138- 3039   617-547-6706
                                       800-225-5750
                        Feedback.EPS@schoolspecialty.com
                                       www.epsbooks.com
Rick Holden, President, EPS
Ungraded multisensory curriculum for teaching phonics and the structure of language. Uses Orton-Gillingham approach to teach handwriting, spelling, reading, reading comprehension, and oral and written expression. program includes basic manual, workbooks, tests, teachers' guides, drill cards and all cards. *$28.15*
ISSN 8388-42

2205 **Alternative Educational Delivery Systems**
National Association of School Psychologists
4340 East West Highway
Suite 402
Bethesda, MD 20814   301-657-0270
866-331-NASP
FAX: 301-657-0275
TTY: 301-657-4155
webmaster@naspweb.org
nasponline.org

Stephen E. Brock, President
Todd A. Savage, President-Elect
Laura Benson, Chief Operating Officer
A book offering information to the professional on how to enhance educational options for all students.

2206 **Alternative Teaching Strategies**
Special Needs Project
324 State Street
Suite H
Santa Barbara, CA 93101-2364   818-718-9900
800-333-6867
FAX: 818-349-2027
editor@specialneeds.com
www.specialneeds.com

Hod Gray, Owner
Offers help for teachers who teach behaviorally troubled students.

2207 **Antecedent Control: Innovative Approaches to Behavioral Support**
Brookes Publishing
P.O.Box 10624
Baltimore, MD 21285-0624   410-337-9580
800-638-3775
FAX: 410-337-8539
webmaster@brookespublishing.com
www.brookespublishing.com

Paul H. Brookes, Chairman of the Board
Jeffrey D. Brookes, President
George S. Stamathis, VP/Publisher
This book explains the theory and methodology of antecedent control. The treatment techniques in this book are effective for both children and adults.
416 pages Paperback
ISBN 1-55766-34-3

2208 **Anxiety-Free Kids: An Interactive Guide for Parents and Children**
Prufrock Press
PO Box 8813
Waco, TX 76714-8813   800-998-2208
FAX: 800-240-0333
info@prufrock.com
www.prufrock.com

Joel McIntosh, Publisher & Marketing Director
Lacy Compton, Senior Editor
Rachel Taliaferro, Editor
Offers parents strategies that help children happy and worry-free, methods that relieve a child's excessive anxieties and phobias, and tools for fostering interaction and family-oriented solutions.
$19.95
280 pages Paperback
ISBN 1-593633-43-1

2209 **Applied Rehabilitation Counseling (Springer Series on Rehabilitation)**
Springer Publishing Company
11 W 42nd St
15th Fl
New York, NY 10036-8002   212-431-4370
877-687-7476
FAX: 212-941-7842
cs@springerpub.com
www.springerpub.com

Ted Nardin, Chief Executive Officer
Jason Roth, Vice President, Marketing & Sales
Kathy Weiss, Senior Sales Director
This comprehensive text describes current theories, techniques, and their applications to specific disabled populations. Perspec-

tives on varying counseling approaches such as psychodynamic, existential, gestalt, behavioral and psychoeducational orientations are systematically outlined in an easy-to-follow format. Practical applications for counseling are emphasized with attention given to strategies, goal-setting and on-going evaluations.
$43.95
404 pages Paperback 1986
ISBN 0-826153-71-2

2210 **Art-Centered Education and Therapy for Children with Disabilities**
Charles C. Thomas
2600 S First St
Springfield, IL 62704-4730   217-789-8980
800-258-8980
FAX: 217-789-9130
books@ccthomas.com
www.ccthomas.com

Frances E. Anderson, Author
This book has been written to help both the regular education, and art and special education teachers, both pre- and in-service, better understand some of the issues and realities of providing education and remediation to children with disabilities. The book is also offered as model concept that has govern the author's personal and professional career of over thirty years. *$41.95*
284 pages Paperback
ISBN 0-398060-06-1

2211 **Assessing the Handicaps/Needs of Children**
Books on Special Children
P.O.Box 3378
Amherst, MA 01004-3378   413-256-8164
FAX: 413-256-8896
Papers on treatment, rehab and social support in assessing the needs of developmentally disabled children. *$66.00*
260 pages Hardcover
ISBN 0-12218-02-0

2212 **Assessment & Management of Mainstreamed Hearing-Impaired Children**
Sage Publications
2455 Teller Road
Thousand Oaks, CA 91320   805-499-0721
800-818-7243
FAX: 800-583-2665
info@sagepub.com
www.sagepub.com

Sara Miller McCune, Founder, Publisher & Executive Chairman
Blaise R. Simqu, President & CEO
Chris Hickok, Senior Vice President & Chief Financial Officer
The theoretical and practical considerations of developing appropriate programming for hearing-impaired children who are being educated in mainstream educational settings are presented in this book.

2213 **Assessment Log & Developmental Progress Charts for the Carolina Curriculum**
Brookes Publishing
P.O.Box 10624
Baltimore, MD 21285-0624   410-337-9580
800-638-3775
FAX: 410-337-8539
webmaster@brookespublishing.com
www.brookespublishing.com

Paul H. Brookes, Chairman of the Board
Jeffrey D. Brookes, President
George S. Stamathis, VP/Publisher
This 28-page booklet allows the progress of children with skills in the 12-36 month development range to be easily recorded. Available in packages of 10. *$23.00*
28 pages Saddle-stiched
ISBN 1-557662-21-5

2214 Assessment and Remediation of Articulatoryand Phonological Disorders
McGraw-Hill School Publishing
PO Box 182604
Columbus, OH 43218
877-833-5524
800-338-3987
FAX: 609-308-4480
customer.service@mheducation.com
www.mcgraw-hill.com

David Levin, President/Chief Executive Officer
David Stafford, Senior Vice President/General Counsel
Maryellen Valaitis, Senior Vice President Human Resources
Offers comprehensive coverage of articulation disorders.

2215 Assessment in Mental Handicap: A Guide to Assessment Practices & Tests
Brookline Books
8 Trumbull Rd
Suite B-001
Northampton, MA 01060
413-584-0184
800-666-2665
FAX: 413-584-6184
brbooks@yahoo.com
www.brooklinebooks.com

Esther Wilder, Co-Author
Helps professionals understand the rationale and uses for assessment practices, and provides details of appropriate instruments within each type: adaptive behavior scales, assessment of behavioral disturbances, early development and Plagetian tests. *$20.00*
Hardcover
ISBN 0-91479-31-X

2216 Assessment of Children and Youth
Longman Education/Addison Wesley
1185 Avenue of the Americas
New York, NY 10036-2601
212-997-8500
866-203-6215
TTY:800-231-5469
www.hess.com

Dr. Mark R. Williams, Chairman of the Board
Gregory P. Hill, President/COO
John B. Hess, Chief Executive Officer
Introductory text for preservice and in-service special educators on assessment, based on the principle that every child is unique. Comprehensive coverage of both formal and informal assessment instruments. *$50.00*
640 pages Paperback
ISBN 0-80131-02-5

2217 Assessment of Individuals with Severe Disabilities
Brookes Publishing Company
PO Box 10624
Baltimore, MD 21285-0624
410-337-9580
800-638-3775
FAX: 410-337-8539
custserv@brookespublishing.com
www.brookespublishing.com

Paul H. Brookes, Chairman
Jeffrey D. Brookes, President
Melissa A. Behm, ExecutiveVice President
This expanded text offers instructors guidelines to design a comprehensive educational assessment for individuals with severe disabilities. *$34.00*
432 pages Paperback
ISBN 1-557660-67-0

2218 Assessment of the Technology Needs of Vending Facilitiy Managers In Tennessee
Mississippi State University
108 Herbert - South
Room 150/PO Drawer 6189
Mississippi State Univers, MS 39762-6189
662-325-2001
800-675-7782
FAX: 662-325-8989
TTY: 662-325-2694
nrtc@colled.msstate.edu
www.blind.msstate.edu

Jacqui Bybee, Research and Training Coordinato
Michele Capella McDonnall, Ph.D., Research Professor/Interim Director
Jessica Thornton, Business Manager
This report summarizes the results and recommendations of a survey conducted of vending facility managers throughout the state of Tennessee who participate in the Randolph-Sheppard program. *$15.00*
39 pages Paperback

2219 Assessment: The Special Educator's Role
Brookes Publishing Company
PO Box 10624
Baltimore, MD 21285-0624
410-337-9580
800-638-3775
FAX: 410-337-8539
custserv@brookespublishing.com
www.brookespublishing.com

Paul H. Brooks, Chairman
Jeffrey D. Brookes, President
Melissa A. Behm, ExecutiveVice President
Aimed at students with little or no classroom experience in assessment, the book focuses on the integration of dynamic, curriculum-based and norm-referenced data for diagnostic decisions and program planning.
580 pages Casebound
ISBN 0-53421-32-1

2220 Assistive Technology in the Schools: A Guide for Idaho Educators
Idaho Assistive Technology Project
University of Idaho
1187 Alturas Dr.
Moscow, ID 83843-8331
205-885-3557
800-432-8324
FAX: 208-885-6102
idahoat@uidaho.edu
www.idahoat.org

LaRhae Rhoads, Author
Ron Seiler, Author
Michelle Doty, Author
This manual is designed to provide educators, parents, students with disabilities and related service providers with assistance in identifying, selecting, and acquiring assistive technology (AT) devices and services.

2221 Asthma Management and Education
Asthma and Allergy Foundation of America
8201 Corporate Drive
Suite 1000
Landover, MD 20785
202-466-7643
800-727-8462
info@aafa.org
www.aafa.org

Lynn Hanessian, Chair
Mitchell Grayson, MD, Chair, Research
Barbara Corn, Chair, Governance
One session, two hour program developed to educate allied health professionals about up-to-date asthma care and patient education, information and materials. Includes hands on experience with peak flow meters and demonstrations of medical devices.

2222 Aston-Patterning
PO Box 3568
Incline Village, NV 89450-3568   775-831-8228
                                   FAX: 775-831-8955
                            office@astonkinetics.com
                              www.astonkinetics.com
J Aston, Owner
Angelina Calafiore, Office Manager
Integrated system of movement education, body assessment, environmental modification and fitness training.

2223 Attention Deficit Disorder in Children
Charles C. Thomas
2600 S First St
Springfield, IL 62704-4730   217-789-8980
                                    800-258-8980
                               FAX: 217-789-9130
                                books@ccthomas.com
                                 www.ccthomas.com
CC Thomas has been producing a strong list of specialty titles and textbooks in the biomedical sciences since 1927.

2224 Aural Habilitation
Alexander Graham Bell Association
3417 Volta Pl NW
Washington, DC 20007-2737   202-337-5220
                               FAX: 202-337-8314
                               TTY: 202-337-5221
                                   info@agbell.org
                  www.listeningandspokenlanguage.org
Meredith K. Sugar, Esq. (OH), President
Ted A. Meyer, M.D., Ph.D, President-Elect/Secretary-Treasurer
Emilio Alonso-Mendoza, Chief Executive Officer
This classic text for professionals, educators and parents discusses verbal learning and aural habilitation of young children with hearing losses to ensure that each child is educated in the best setting. It discusses communication, normal development of spoken language, speech audiologic assessment, hearing aids and use of residual hearing, and program designs for individualized needs, including the assessment and planning of IEPs. *$26.95*
324 pages

2225 Behavior Analysis in Education: Focus on Measurably Superior Instruction
Brookes Publishing Company
PO Box 10624
Baltimore, MD 21285-0624   410-337-9580
                                    800-638-3775
                               FAX: 410-337-8539
                          custserv@brookespublishing.com
                            www.brookespublishing.com
Paul H. Brookes, Chairman
Jeffrey D. Brookes, President
Melissa A. Behm, ExecutiveVice President
Designed to disseminate measurably superior instructional strategies to those interested in advancing sound, pedagogically effective, field-tested educational practices, this book is intended for graduate-level courses and seminars in special education and/or psychology focusing on behavior analysis and instruction.
512 pages Casebound
ISBN 0-53422-60-9

2226 Behavior Modification
Sage Publications
2455 Teller Rd
Thousand Oaks, CA 91320-2218   805-499-0721
                                         800-818-7243
                                    FAX: 800-583-2665
                                      info@sagepub.com
                                       www.sagepub.com
Sara Miller McCune, Founder, Publisher and Executive Chairman
Blaise R. Simqu, President & CEO
Chris Hickok, Senior Vice President & Chief Financial Officer
Describes in detail for replication purposes assessment and modification techniques for problems in psychiatric, clinical, educational and rehabilitation settings. *$53.00*
640 pages Quarterly

2227 Behind Special Education
Love Publishing Company
9101 E Kenyon Ave
Suite 2200
Denver, CO 80237-1854   303-221-7333
                            FAX: 303-221-7444
                            lpc@lovepublishing.com
                            www.lovepublishing.com
This new work is a critical analysis of the nature of disability, special education, school organization and reform progress. *$24.95*
ISBN 0-89108-17-4

2228 Biomedical Concerns in Persons with Down's Syndrome
Paul H Brookes Publishing Company
PO Box 10624
Baltimore, MD 21285-0624   410-337-9580
                                    800-638-3775
                               FAX: 410-337-8539
                          custserv@brookespublishing.com
                            www.brookespublishing.com
Paul H. Brookes, Chairman
Jeffrey D. Brookes, President
Melissa A. Behm, ExecutiveVice President
Written by leading authorities and spanning many disciplines and specialties, this comprehensive resource provides vital information on biomedical issues concerning individuals with Down's Syndrome. *$45.00*
336 pages Hardcover
ISBN 1-557660-89-1

2229 Breaking Barriers
AbleNet, Inc.
2625 Patton Road
Roseville, MN 55113-1137   651-294-2200
                                    800-322-0956
                               FAX: 651-294-2259
                          customerservice@ablenetinc.com
                                www.ablenetinc.com
Jennifer Thalhuber, President & CEO
Paul Sugden, CFO & Trustee
A practical resource for parents, caregivers, teachers and therapists. *$15.00*

2230 Building Skills for Independence in the Mainstream
15619 Premiere Drive
Suite 101
Tampa, FL 33624   850-363-9909
                       FAX: 480-393-4331
            accounting@successforkidswithhearingloss.com
                    successforkidswithhearinglo ss.com
Karen L. Anderson, Director/ Co-Author
Gale Wright, Co-Author
Building Skills for Independence in the Mainstream was developed as a Guide for DHH professionals to support their work with classroom teachers and with students to develop the skills needed for independence with hearing aids and self-advocacy.

2231 Building Skills for Success in the Fast-Paced Classroom
15619 Premiere Drive
Suite 101
Tampa, FL 33624   850-363-9909
                       FAX: 480-393-4331
            accounting@successforkidswithhearingloss.com
                    successforkidswithhearinglo ss.com
Karen L. Anderson, PhD, Co-Author
Kathleen A. Arnoldi, MA
The purpose of this book is to provide resources that will assist these students in optimizing their achievement through improved access and self-advocacy. The information contained in this book targets the expanded core curriculum, or those skills that must be mastered in order to benefit from the core curriculum. This book is meant to be a practical ready-to-go resource for professionals who work with school-age children with hearing loss.

2232 Building the Healing Partnership: Parents, Professionals and Children with Chronic Illnesses
Brookline Books
8 Trumbull Rd
Ste B-001
Northampton, MA 01060
413-584-0184
800-666-2665
FAX: 413-584-6184
brbooks@yahoo.com
www.brooklinebks.com

Patricia Tanner Leff, Author
Elaine H. Walizer, Author
Successful programs understand that the disabled child's needs must be considered in the context of a family. This book was specifically written for practitioner's who must work with families but who have insufficient training in family systems assessment and intervention. It is a valuable blend of theory and practice with pointers for applying the principles. *$24.95*
312 pages Paperback 1992
ISBN 0-914797-60-3

2233 CAI, Career Assessment Inventories for the Learning Disabled
Academic Therapy Publications
20 Leveroni Crt
Novato, CA 94949-5746
415-883-3314
800-422-7249
FAX: 888-287-9975
sales@academictherapy.com
www.academictherapy.com

Carol Weller, Author
Mary Buchanan, Author
Takes personality, ability and interest into account in pointing learning disabled students of all ages toward intelligent and realistic career choices. Contains binder with paperback teaching guide plus 50 interest inventories and 50 abilities inventories.
64 pages 1983
ISBN 0-878793-50-X

2234 Caring for Children with Chronic Illness
11 W 42nd St
15th Floor
New York, NY 10036-8002
212-431-4370
877-687-7476
FAX: 212-941-7842
cs@springerpub.com
www.springerpub.com

Ursula Springer, President
Theodore C. Nardin, CEO/Publisher
Jason Roth, VP/Marketing Director
A critical look at the current medical, social, and psychological framework for providing care to children with chronic illnesses. Emphasizing the need to create integrated, interdisciplinary approaches, it discusses issues such as the roles of families, professionals, and institutions in providing health care, the impact of a child's illness on various family structures, financing care, the special problems of chronically ill children as they become adolescents and more. *$36.95*
320 pages Hardcover
ISBN 0-82615-00-1

2235 Carolina Curriculum for Infants and Toddlers with Special Needs (3rd Edition)
Brookes Publishing
P.O. Box 10624
Baltimore, MD 21285-0624
410-337-9580
800-638-3775
FAX: 410-337-8539
custserv@brookespublishing.com
www.brookespublishing.com

Nancy M. Johnson-Martin, Author
Susan M. Attermeier, Author
Bonnie J. Hacker, Author
This book includes detailed assessment and intervention sequences, daily routine integration strategies, sensorimotor adaptations, and a sample 24-page assessment log that shows readers how to chart a child's individual progress.
504 pages Spiral-bound

2236 Carolina Curriculum for Preschoolers with Special Needs
Brookes Publishing
PO Box 10624
Baltimore, MD 21285-0624
410-337-9580
800-638-3775
FAX: 410-337-8539
custserv@brookespublishing.com
www.brookespublishing.com

Paul H. Brookes, Chairman
Jeffrey D. Brookes, President
Melissa A. Behm, ExecutiveVice President
This curriculum provides detailed teaching and assessment techniques, plus a sample 28-page assessment log that shows readers how to chart a child's individual progress. This guide is for children between 2 and 5 in their developmental stages who are considered at risk for developmental delay or who exhibit special needs. *$34.00*
352 pages Spiral-bound
ISBN 1-55766 -32-8

2237 Challenge of Educating Together Deaf and Hearing Youth: Making Manistreaming Work
Charles C. Thomas
2600 S First St
Springfield, IL 62704-4730
217-789-8980
800-258-8980
FAX: 217-789-9130
books@ccthomas.com
www.ccthomas.com

Those who have this challenge of education: teachers, administrators, other professionals, parents, and concerned individuals will benefit from this book. Also available in cloth. *$51.35*
198 pages Hardcover
ISBN 0-398063-91-5

2238 Challenged Scientists: Disabilities and the Triumph of Excellence
Greenwood Publishing Group
130 Cremona Drive
Santa Barbara, CA 93117
805-968-1911
800-368-6868
FAX: 866-270-3856
CustomerService@abc-clio.com
www.abc-clio.com

This volume points out how the increasing need for scientists in this country can be lessened by utilizing a long overlooked pool of scientific talent in those persons who are scientifically oriented but who happen to have physical or sensory disabilities. Hardcover. $49.95-$55.00.
208 pages
ISBN 0-275938-73-5

2239 Child Care and the ADA: A Handbook for Inclusive Programs
Brookes Publishing
PO Box 10624
Baltimore, MD 21285-0624
410-337-9580
800-638-3775
FAX: 410-337-8539
custserv@brookespublishing.com
www.brookespublishing.com

Paul H. Brookes, Chairman
Jeffrey D. Brookes, President
Melissa A. Behm, ExecutiveVice President
This book is designed for educators and administrators in child care settings. It offers a straightforward discussion of the Americans with Disabilities Act including children with disabilities in community programs. *$25.95*
240 pages Paperback
ISBN 1-55766 -85-5

2240 Child with Disabling Illness
Lippincott, Williams & Wilkins
16522 Hunters Green Pkwy
Hagerstown, MD 21740
301-223-2300
800-638-3030
FAX: 301-223-2400
orders@lww.com
www.lww.com

$108.50
700 pages

2241 Childhood Behavior Disorders: Applied Research & Educational Practice
Sage Publications
2455 Teller Road
Thousand Oaks, CA 91320-2218

805-499-0721
800-818-7243
FAX: 800-583-2665
info@sagepub.com
www.sagepub.com

Sara Miller McCune, Founder, Publisher & Chairperson
Blaise R. Simqu, President & Chief Executive Officer
Chris Hickok, Senior Vice President & Chief Financial Officer
The only comprehensive overview of childhood behavior disorders. This book gives you the how and why for helping children with behavior disorders.

2242 Childhood Disablity and Family Systems(Routledge Library Editions) (Volume 5)
Routledge (Taylor & Francis Group)
711 Third Ave
New York, NY 10017

212-216-7800
800-634-7064
FAX: 202-564-7854
enquiries@taylorandfrancis.com
www.routledge.com

Michael Ferrari, Editor
Marvin B. Sussman, Editor
Focuses on what the presence of a disabled child means to a family. Those professionals involved in teaching, research, and direct care with families having disabled children will value the coverage of such topics as the contemporary context of disability, ethical issues, family effects, and care systems. First published in 1987 by Haworth Press, the book is now published under Routledge. *$140.00*
256 pages Hardcover 1916
ISBN 1-138101-55-9

2243 Children and Youth Assisted by Medical Technology in Educational Settings, 2nd Edition
Brookes Publishing
PO Box 10624
Baltimore, MD 21285-0624

410-337-9580
800-638-3775
FAX: 410-337-8539
custserv@brookespublishing.com
www.brookespublishing.com

Paul H. Brookes, Chairman
Jeffrey D. Brookes, President
Melissa A. Behm, Executive Vice President
Contains detailed daily care guidelines and emergency-response techniques, including information on working with a range of students who have the HIV infection, that rely on ventilators, that utilize tube feeding, or require catheterization. Also covers every aspect of planning for inclusive classrooms, including information on personnel training, entrance planning and transition, legal requirements, and transportation issues. *$52.00*
432 pages Spiral-bound
ISBN 1-55766 -36-3

2244 Children's Needs Psychological Perspective
National Association of School Psychologists
4340 East West Hwy.
Suite 402
Bethesda, MD 20814

301-657-0270
866-331-6277
FAX: 301-657-0275
TTY: 301-657-4155
www.nasponline.org

Kathleen Minke, Executive Director
Laura Benson, Chief Operating Officer
This monograph was developed with the recognition that many factors beyond the classroom and the child's own personal characteristics influence school success.
637 pages

2245 Choices: A Guide to Sex Counseling with Physically Disabled Adults
Krieger Publishing Company
1725 Krieger Dr
Malabar, FL 32950

321-724-9542
800-724-0025
FAX: 321-951-3671
info@krieger-publishing.com
www.krieger-publishing.com

Maureen E. Neistadt, Author
Provides rehabilitation professionals with the basic information necessary for limited sexuality counseling of physically disabled adults. *$20.90*
132 pages
ISBN 0-898749-03-4

2246 Choosing Options and Accommodations for Children
Brookes Publishing
PO Box 10624
Baltimore, MD 21285-0624

410-337-9580
800-638-3775
FAX: 410-337-8539
custserv@brookespublishing.com
www.brookespublishing.com

Bridging the gap between the philosophy and practice of inclusive education, this important manual provides a practical assessment and planning process for the inclusion of students with disabilities in general education classrooms. *$29.00*
192 pages
ISBN 1-55766 -06-5

2247 Cirriculum Development for Students with Mild Disabilities
Charles C. Thomas
2600 S First St
Springfield, IL 62704-4730

217-789-8980
800-258-8980
FAX: 217-789-9130
books@ccthomas.com
www.ccthomas.com

Carroll J. Jones, Author
This book was designed to provide the foundation from which to write cirrocumuli that will provide academic and social skills for Individual Education Programs (IEPs). *$38.95*
258 pages Spiral-Paper
ISBN 0-398070-18-2

2248 Clinical Alzheimer Rehabilitation
Springer Publishing
11 W 42nd St
15th Floor
New York, NY 10036-8002

212-431-4370
877-687-7476
FAX: 212-941-7842
cs@springerpub.com
www.springerpub.com

Theodore C. Nardin, CEO/Publisher
Jason Roth, VP/Marketing Director
Annette Imperati, Marketing/Sales Director
This comprehensive and easy-to-read guidebook contains the latest research on dementia and AD in the elderly population, including the causes and risk factors of AD, diagnosis information, and symptoms and progressions of the disease. Significant emphasis is given to the physical, mental, and verbal rehabilitation challenges of patients with AD. The authors outline specific rehabilitation goals for the physical therapist, speech-language pathologist, and general caregiver.

2249 Clinical Management of Childhood Stuttering, 2nd Edition
Sage Publications
2455 Teller Road
Thousand Oaks, CA 91320-2218

805-499-0721
800-818-7243
FAX: 800-583-2665
info@sagepub.com
www.sagepub.com

Sara Miller McCune, Founder, Publisher, Chairperson
Blaise R. Simqu, President/CEO
Chris Hickok, Senior Vice President/CFO

Updates and integrates recent findings in childhood stuttering into a broad range of therapeutic strategies for assessing and treating the young dysfluent child. *$38.00*
336 pages

2250   Cognitive Approaches to Learning Disabilities
Sage Publications
2455 Teller Road
Thousand Oaks, CA 91320-2218   805-499-0721
                                      800-818-7243
                              FAX: 800-583-2665
                              info@sagepub.com
                              www.sagepub.com

Sara Miller McCune, Founder, Publisher, Chairperson
Blaise R. Simqu, President/CEO
Chris Hickok, Senior Vice President/CFO
The first to bridge the gap between cognitive psychology and information processing theory in understanding learning disabilities. *$39.00*
495 pages Hardcover

2251   Cognitive Strategy Instruction That Really Improves Children's Academic Skills
Brookline Books
8 Trumbull Rd
Suite B-001
Northampton, MA 01060   413-584-0184
                                      800-666-2665
                              FAX: 413-584-6184
                              brbooks@yahoo.com
                              www.brooklinebooks.com

Esther Isabe Wilder, Author
A concise and focused work that summarily presents the few procedures for teaching strategies that aid academic subject matter learning: decoding reading comprehension, vocabulary, math, spelling and writing. Learning unrelated facts and science. Completely revised in 1995. *$27.95*
Paperback
ISBN 1-571290-07-9

2252   Collaborating for Comprehensive Services for Young Children and Families
Brookes Publishing Company
PO Box 10624
Baltimore, MD 21285-0624   410-337-9580
                                     800-638-3775
                             FAX: 410-337-8539
                             custserv@brookespublishing.com
                             www.brookespublishing.com

Paul H. Brookes, Chairman
Jeffrey D. Brookes, President
Melissa A. Behm, ExecutiveVice President
Taking collaboration a step beyond basic implementation, this useful book shows agency and school leaders how to coordinate their efforts to stretch human services dollars while still providing quality programs. Provides the building blocks needed to establish a local interagency coordinating council. *$37.00*
272 pages
ISBN 1-557661-03-0

2253   Collaborative Teams for Students with Severe Disabilities
Brookes Publishing
PO Box 10624
Baltimore, MD 21285-0624   410-337-9580
                                     800-638-3775
                             FAX: 410-337-8539
                             custserv@brookespublishing.com
                             www.brookespublishing.com

Paul H. Brookes, Chairman
Jeffrey D. Brookes, President
Melissa A. Behm, ExecutiveVice President
How can educators, parents and therapists work together to ensure the best possible educational experience for students with severe disabilities? This resource describes how a collaborative team can successfully create exciting learning opportunities for students, while teaching them to participate fully at home, school, work and play. *$30.00*
304 pages
ISBN 1-55766 -88-3

2254   Communicating with Parents of Exceptional Children
Love Publishing Company
9101 E Kenyon Ave
Suite 2200
Denver, CO 80237-1854   303-221-7333
                             FAX: 303-221-7444
                             lpc@lovepublishing.com
                             www.lovepublishing.com

Roger L. Kroth, Author
Denzil Denzil Edge, Author
This book shows how teachers can facilitate parent involvement with children's education. It presents the mirror model of parent involvement, family, dynamics, how to listen actively to parents, values and perceptions, problem-solving, parent conferences and training groups. *$19.95*
ISBN 0-89108 -67-4

2255   Communication & Language Acquisition: Discoveries from Atypical Development
Brookes Publishing
PO Box 10624
Baltimore, MD 21285-0624   410-337-9580
                                     800-638-3775
                             FAX: 410-337-8539
                             custserv@brookespublishing.com
                             www.brookespublishing.com

Paul H. Brookes, Chairman
Jeffrey D. Brookes, President
Melissa A. Behm, ExecutiveVice President
This text demonstrates how the study of language acquisition in children with atypical development promotes advances in basic theory. *$44.00*
352 pages Hardcover
ISBN 1-557662-79-7

2256   Communication Skills for Working with Elders
Springer Publishing Company
11 W 42nd St
15th Floor
New York, NY 10036-8002   212-431-4370
                                    877-687-7476
                             FAX: 212-941-7842
                             cs@springerpub.com
                             www.springerpub.com

Ursula Springer, President
Theodore C. Nardin, CEO/Publisher
Jason Roth, VP/Marketing Director
How aging and illness affects communication. *$17.95*
160 pages Softcover
ISBN 0-82615 -20-7

2257   Communication Unbound
Teachers College Press
Ste 2115
14781 Memorial Dr
Houston, TX 77079-5210   415-738-4323
                             FAX: 415-738-4329
                             tcc.orders@aidcvt.com
                             www.pearsonhighered.com

Complete title is 'Communication Unbound: How Facilitated Communication is Challenging the Traditional Views of Autism and Ability/Disability'. Reveals the wonder of expression by people who have been trapped in silence and diminished by presumptions of their incompetence. *$18.95*
240 pages Paperback
ISBN 0-087737-21-4

2258   Complete Handbook of Children's Reading Disorders: You Can Prevent or Correct LDs
Gallery Bookshop
319 Kasten Street
PO Box 270
Mendocino, CA 95460-270   707-937-2215
                             FAX: 707-937-3737
                             info@gallerybookshop.com
                             www.gallerybooks.com

Tony Miksak, Owner
The complete handbook of children's reading disorders. *$34.95*
732 pages Paperback
ISBN 0-80772 -83-3

2259 Computer Access/Computer Learning
Special Needs Project
324 State Street
Suite H
Santa Barbara, CA 93101-2364

818-718-9900
800-333-6867
FAX: 818-349-2027
editor@specialneeds.com
www.specialneeds.com

Mark Darrow, Founder,The Prolotherapy Institu
A resource manual in adaptive technology and computer training.
$22.50

2260 Consulting Psychologists Press
1055 Joaquin Rd
Suite. 200
Mountain View, CA 94043-1243

650-969-8901
800-624-1765
FAX: 650-969-8608
custserv@cpp.com

Carl E. Thoresen, Chairman
Jeffrey Hayes, President and Chief Executive Officer
Andrew Bell, Vice President of International
Catalog offering job assessment software, career development reports, educational assessment information and books for the professional.

2261 Counseling Persons with Communication Disorders and Their Families
Sage Publications
2455 Teller Road
Thousand Oaks, CA 91320-2218

805-499-0721
800-818-7243
FAX: 800-583-2665
info@sagepub.com
www.sagepub.com

Sara Miller McCune, Founder, Publisher & Chairperson
Blaise R. Simqu, President & CEO
Chris Hickok, Senior Vice President & Chief Financial Officer
A learning manual for speech-language pathologists and audiologists on how to deal with the emotional issues facing them in their work with clients with communication disorders and their families. *$29.00*
187 pages

2262 Counseling in the Rehabilitation Process
Charles C. Thomas
2600 S First St
Springfield, IL 62704-4730

217-789-8980
800-258-8980
FAX: 217-789-9130
books@ccthomas.com
www.ccthomas.com

Gerald L. Gandy, Author
E. Davis Martin Jr, Author
Richard E. Hardy, Author
This text provides the reader with a comprehensive overview and introduction to the field of rehabilitation counseling and services, and also has applicability in the growing field of community counseling. *$51.95*
358 pages paper 1999
ISBN 0-398069-70-4

2263 Creating Positive Classroom Environments: Strategies for Behavior Management
Brooks/Cole Publishing Company
511 Forest Lodge Rd
Pacific Grove, CA 93950-5040

831-373-0728
800-354-9706
FAX: 831-375-6414
bc-info@brookscole.com
www.cengage.com

A hands-on text that offers an approach to classroom management that encourages situation-specific decision making. Presenting research-based information on how to establish an effective behavior management system in both regular and special education settings, the book centers on ways to help students manage their own behavior, rather than on ways their behavior can be managed by teachers, peers, parents or other adults. .
448 pages Paperbound
ISBN 0-53422 -54-4

2264 Cristine M. Trahms Program for Phenylketonuria
University of Washington
PO Box 357920
Seattle, WA 98195

206-598-1800
877-685-3015
FAX: 206-598-1915
pku@u.washington.edu
www.depts.washington.edu/pku

C. Ronald Scott, MD, Professor, Pediatrics, Division
Clinical program for children and adults with phenylketonuria.

2265 Critical Voices on Special Education: Problems & Progress Concerning the Mildly Handicapped
State University of New York Press
22 Corporate Woods Boulevard
3rd Floor
Albany, NY 12211-2504

518-472-5000
866-430-7869
FAX: 518-472-5038
info@sunypress.edu
www.sunypress.edu

James Peltz, Associate Director
Janice Vunk, Assistant to the Director
Scott B Sigmon, Editor
Problems and progress concerning the mildly handicapped. *$24.95*
265 pages Paperback 1990
ISBN 0-79140 -20-3

2266 Cultural Diversity, Families and the Special Education System
Teachers College Press
1234 Amsterdam Ave
New York, NY 10027-6602

212-678-3929
800-575-6566
FAX: 212-678-4149
tcpress@tc.columbia.edu
www.teacherscollegepress.com

Beth Harry, Author
This timely and thought-provoking book explores the quadruple disadvantage faced by the parents of poor, minority, handicapped children whose first language is not that of the school they attend. *$22.95*
296 pages Paperback
ISBN 0-807731-19-6

2267 Curriculum Decision Making for Students with Severe Handicaps
Teachers College Press
1234 Amsterdam Ave
New York, NY 10027-6602

212-678-3929
800-575-6566
FAX: 212-678-4149
www.teacherscollegepress.com

The inclusion of severely handicapped students within the scope of public education has brought about many changes for teachers in special education, this book helps the professional to distinguish which avenues are the best to take. *$17.95*
192 pages Paperback
ISBN 0-807728-61-6

2268 Deciphering the System: A Guide for Families of Young Disabled Children
Brookline Books
8 Trumbull Rd
Ste B-001
Northampton, MA 01060

413-584-0184
800-666-2665
FAX: 413-584-6184
brbooks@yahoo.com
www.brooklinebks.com

Paula Beckman, Author
This book informs parents of disabled children (0-5) of their rights and the service system, e.g., ways to manage the cumulating information, tips on IEP and IFSP meetings and the educa-

tional assessment process, and how parents can work with multiple service providers. It includes contributions from both parents and professionals who have experience with the service system. *$21.95*
208 pages Paperback 1999
ISBN 0-914797-87-5

2269 Defining Rehabilitation Agency Types
Mississippi State University
108 Herbert - South
Room 150 Industrial Education Depar
Mississippi State, MS 39762-6189   662-325-2001
                                          800-675-7782
                                          FAX: 662-325-8989
                                          TTY: 662-325-2694
                                          nrtc@colled.msstate.edu
                                          www.blind.msstate.edu
Jacqui Bybee, Research Associate II
Michele Capella McDonnall, Ph.D., Research Professor/Interim Director
Jessica Thornton, Business Manager
Relationships of participant selection and cost factors of service delivery across rehabilitation agency types. A national survey of state agencies for the blind was conducted to examine factors that define the characteristics of different agencies; similar programs were grouped together. Classification criteria were developed to distinguish agencies into logical groups based on line of authority, funding and operating procedures. *$10.00*
15 pages Paperback

2270 Designing and Using Assistive Technology: The Human Perspective
Brookes Publishing
PO Box 10624
Baltimore, MD 21285-0624   410-337-9580
                                  800-638-3775
                                  FAX: 410-337-8539
                                  custserv@brookespublishing.com
                                  www.brookespublishing.com
Paul H. Brookes, Chairman
Jeffrey D. Brookes, President
Melissa A. Behm, ExecutiveVice President
Presented here is a holistic perspective on how and why people choose and use AT. Features personal insights and the latest research on design and development. *$31.00*
352 pages Paperback
ISBN 1-55766 -14-9

2271 Developing Cross-Cultural Competence:Guideto Working with Young Children & Their Families
Brookes Publishing
PO Box 10624
Baltimore, MD 21285-0624   410-337-9580
                                  800-638-3775
                                  FAX: 410-337-8539
                                  custserv@brookespublishing.com
                                  www.brookespublishing.com
Paul H. Brookes, Chairman
Jeffrey D. Brookes, President
Melissa A. Behm, ExecutiveVice President
This enlightening book perceptively and sensitively explores cultural, ethnic, and language diversity in human services. For those who work with families whose infants and young children may have or be at risk for a disability or chronic illness. (Second Edition) *$32.00*
448 pages Paperback
ISBN 1-55766 -31-9

2272 Developing Individualized Family Support Plans: A Training Manual
Brookline Books
Suite B-001
8 Trumbull Rd
Northampton, MA 01060   413-584-0184
                               800-666-2665
                               FAX: 413-584-6184
                               brbooks@yahoo.com
                               www.brooklinebooks.com
Esther Wilder, Co-Author

This manual provides in-service training coordinators, administrators, supervisors and university personnel with a compact package of functional and practical methods to train professionals about implementing family-centered individualized family support plans (IFSP'S). Also, case studies provide concrete examples to aid in learning to write IFSP's. *$24.95*
ISBN 0-914797-69-7

2273 Developing Staff Competencies for Supporting People with Disabilities
Brookes Publishing
PO Box 10624
Baltimore, MD 21285-0624   410-337-9580
                                  800-638-3775
                                  FAX: 410-337-8539
                                  custserv@brookespublishing.com
                                  www.brookespublishing.com
Paul H. Brookes, Chairman
Jeffrey D. Brookes, President
Melissa A. Behm, ExecutiveVice President
This timely second edition, now in a new easier to read format, gives service providers helpful strategies for increasing effectiveness and maintaining well-being while working in the rewarding yet challenging field of human services. *$34.00*
480 pages Paperback
ISBN 1-55766 -07-3

2274 Development of Language
McGraw-Hill, School Publishing
220 E Danieldale Rd
Desoto, TX 75115-2490   800-648-2970
                               FAX: 800-593-4418
                               www.mhschool.com
An organizational book based on the developmental stages of language.
464 pages

2275 Developmental Disabilities of Learning
Gallery Bookshop
319 Kasten Street
PO Box 270
Mendocino, CA 95460-270   707-937-2215
                                 FAX: 707-937-3737
                                 info@gallerybookshop.com
                                 www.gallerybooks.com
Tony Miksak, Owner
Manual for professionals on developmental and learning disabilities in the growing child. *$25.00*
224 pages Illustrated

2276 Developmental Disabilities: A Handbook for Occupational Therapists
Haworth Press
711 Third Avenue
New York, NY 10017   212-216-7800
                            800-354-1420
                            FAX: 212-244-1563
                            subscriptions@tandf.co.uk
                            www.haworthpress.com
Provides broad coverage of the spectrum of problems confronted by patients with developmental disabilities and the many kinds of occupational therapy services these individuals need. Experts identify exemplary institutional and community service programs for treating patients with autism, cerebral palsy, epilepsy, and other conditions. Haworth Press are now acquired by the Taylor & Francis Journals. *$74.95*
268 pages Hardcover
ISBN 0-866569-59-6

2277 Developmental Disabilities: A Handbook for Interdisciplinary Practice
Brookline Books
8 Trumbull Rd
Suite B-001
Northampton, MA 01060   413-584-0184
                               800-666-2665
                               FAX: 413-584-6184
                               brbooks@yahoo.com
                               www.brooklinebooks.com
Esther Wilder, Co-Author

Successful interdisciplinary team practice for persons with developmental disabilities that require each team member to understand and respect the contributions of the others. This handbook explains the professions most often represented on interdisciplinary teams: their natures, concerns and roles in the interdisciplinary context. *$29.95*
256 pages
ISBN 1-571290-03-6

2278 Developmental Variation and Learning Disorders
Educators Publishing Service
PO Box 9031
Cambridge, MA 02139-9031   617-367-2700
800-225-5750
FAX: 617-547-0412
eps@schoolspecialty.com
www.epsbooks.com

Rick Holden, President
Discusses seven major areas of development and four major areas of academic proficiency and then ties this information together by examining factors that predispose a child to dysfunction and disability, offering guidelines to assessment and management, and analyzing long-range outcomes and factors that promote resiliency for parents, educators and clinicians. *$69.00*
640 pages Cloth
ISBN 0-838819-92-3

2279 Digest of Neurology and Psychiatry
Institute of Living: Hartford Hospital
80 Seymour Street
Hartford, CT 06106-3309   860-545-5000
800-673-2411
FAX: 860-545-5066
www.harthosp.org
Douglas Elliot, Chair of the Board
Stuart K. Markowitz, MD, FACR, President/SVP
Gerald J. Boisvert, HHC Regional Vice President / Chief Financial Officer,
Abstracts and reviews of selected current literature in psychiatry, neurology and related fields.

2280 Disability Funding News
8204 Fenton St
Silver Spring, MD 20910-4502   301-588-6380
800-666-6380
FAX: 301-588-6385
www.cdpublications.com
Mike Gerecht, Publisher

2281 Disability Studies and the Inclusive Classroom
711 3rd Avenue
8th Floor
New York, NY 10017   212-216-7800
800-634-7064
FAX: 212-564-7854
www.routledge.com

Susan Baglieri, Co-Author
Arthur Shapiro, Co-Author
This book's mission is to integrate knowledge and practice from the fields of disability studies and special education. Parts I & II focus on the broad, foundational topics that comprise disability studies (culture, language, and history) and Parts III & IV move into practical topics (curriculum, co-teaching, collaboration, classroom organization, disability-specific teaching strategies, etc.) associated with inclusive education.

2282 Disability and Rehabilitation
Taylor & Francis
7625 Empire Dr
Florence, KY 41042-2919   800-634-7064
FAX: 800-248-4724
orders@taylorandfrancis.com
www.taylorandfrancis.com
An international, multidisciplinary journal seeking to encourage a better understanding of all aspects of disability, and to promote the rehabilitation process. *$395.00*
Monthly
ISSN 0963-82 8

2283 Disability, Sport and Society
711 3rd Avenue
8th Floor
New York, NY 10017   212-216-7800
800-634-7064
FAX: 212-564-7854
www.routledge.com
Nigel Thomas, Co-Author
Andy Smith, Co-Author
Disability sport is a relatively recent phenomenon, yet it is also one that, particularly in the context of social inclusion, is attracting increasing political and academic interest. The purpose of this important new text - the first of its kind - is to introduce the reader to key concepts in disability and disability sport and to examine the complex relationships between modern sport, disability and other aspects of wider society.

2284 Disabled Rights: American Disability Policy and the Fight for Equality
3240 Prospect Street, NW
Suite 250
Washington, DC 20007   202-687-5889
FAX: 202-687-6340
gupress@georgetown.edu
press.georgetown.edu/
Jacqueline Vaughn Switzer, Author
Disabled Rights explains how people with disabilities have been treated from a social, legal, and political perspective in the United States.

2285 Divided Legacy: A History of the Schism in Medical Thought, The Bacteriological Era
North Atlantic Books
2526 Martin Luther King Jr. Way
Berkeley, CA 94704   510-549-4270
800-337-2665
FAX: 510-549-4276
orders@northatlanticbooks.com
www.northatlanticbooks.com
Alla Spector, Director of Finance & Office Operations
Doug Reil, Executive Director/Associate Publisher
Ed Angel, Director of Office Administration
Concluding volume of Coulter's history of medical philosophy, from ancient times to today. Covers the origins of bacteriology and immunology in world medicine; describes the clash between orthodox and alternative medicine.

2286 Early Communication Skills for Children with Down Syndrome
Woodbine House
6510 Bells Mill Rd
Bethesda, MD 20817-1636   301-897-3570
800-843-7323
FAX: 301-897-5838
info@woodbinehouse.com
www.woodbinehouse.com
Nancy Gray Paul, Acquisitions Editor
Libby Kumin, Author
An expert shares her knowledge of speech and language development in young children with Down syndrome. Intelligibility, hearing loss, apraxia and other factors that affect communications are discussed. It also covers speech-language assessments and alternative communication options and literacy. *$19.95*
368 pages
ISBN 1-890627-27-5

2287 Early Intervention: Implementing Child & Family Services for At-Risk Infants and Toddlers
PRO-ED Inc.
8700 Shoal Creek Blvd
Austin, TX 78757-6897   512-451-3246
800-897-3202
FAX: 800-397-7633
general@proedinc.com
www.proedinc.com
Marci J. Hanson, Author
Eleanor W. Lynch, Author
New directions and recent legislation have produced a need for this guide which is designed for professionals facing the chal-

lenge of program development for disabled and at-risk infants, toddlers and their families. *$68.20*
394 pages Paperback 1995
ISBN 0-890796-21-1

2288   Ecology of Troubled Children
Brookline Books Publications
8 Trumbull Rd
Suite B-001
Northampton, MA 01060   413-584-0184
                                     800-666-2665
                                FAX: 413-584-6184
                                brbooks@yahoo.com
                                www.brooklinebooks.com

Esther Isabe Wilder, Author
Designed for frontline mental health clinicians working with children with serious emotional disturbances; shows how to make children's' worlds more supportive by changing the places, activities and people in their lives. *$15.95*
256 pages
ISBN 1-571290-57-5

**2289   Educating Children with Disabilities: A
Transdisciplinary Approach**
Brookes Publishing
PO Box 10624
Baltimore, MD 21285-0624   410-337-9580
                                      800-638-3775
                                 FAX: 410-337-8539
                            custserv@brookespublishing.com
                                www.brookespublishing.com

Paul H. Brookes, Chairman
Jeffrey D. Brookes, President
Melissa A. Behm, Executive Vice President
Widely respected textbook presents you with the strategies you need for developing an inclusive curriculum, integrating health care and educational programs and addressing needs and concerns. *$38.00*
512 pages
ISBN 1-557662-46-0

**2290   Educating Children with Multiple Disabilities: A
Transdisciplinary Approach**
Brookes Publishing
PO Box 10624
Baltimore, MD 21285-0624   410-337-9580
                                      800-638-3775
                                 FAX: 410-337-8539
                            custserv@brookespublishing.com
                                www.brookespublishing.com

Paul H. Brookes, Chairman
Jeffrey D. Brookes, President
Melissa A. Behm, ExecutiveVice President
Emphasizing transdisciplinary cooperation between teachers, therapists, nurses and parents, this book describes a general model and specific techniques for effectively educating children with multiple disabilities. *$29.00*
496 pages Paperback
ISBN 1-557662-46-0

**2291   Educating Individuals with Disabilities: IDEIA 2004 and
Beyond (1st Edition)**
Springer Publishing Company
11 W 42nd St
15th Fl
New York, NY 10036-8002   212-431-4370
                                     877-687-7476
                                FAX: 212-941-7842
                                cs@springerpub.com
                                www.springerpub.com

Ted Nardin, Chief Executive Officer
Jason Roth, Vice President, Marketing & Sales
Kathy Weiss, Director, Sales
Discusses how learning-disabled students are identified and assessed today, in light of the 2004 Individuals with Disabilities Education Improvement Act. Grigorenko's interdisciplinary collection is the first to comprehensively review the IDEIA 2004 Act and distill the changes professionals working with learning-disabled students face. The text takes an overarching per-spective, first discussing the IDEIA in its historical, political, and legal context. *$100.00*
512 pages Hardcover 1908
ISBN 0-826103-56-1

**2292   Educating Students Who Have Visual Impairments with
Other Disabilities**
Brookes Publishing
PO Box 10624
Baltimore, MD 21285-0624   410-337-9580
                                      800-638-3775
                                 FAX: 410-337-8539
                            custserv@brookespublishing.com
                                www.brookespublishing.com

Paul H. Brookes, Chairman
Jeffrey D. Brookes, President
Melissa A. Behm, ExecutiveVice President
This introductory text provides techniques for facilitating functional learning in students with a wide range of visual impairments and multiple disabilities. With a concentration on educational needs and learning styles, the authors of this multidisciplinary volume demonstrate functional assessment and teaching adaptations that will improve students' inclusive learning experiences. *$49.95*
552 pages Paperback
ISBN 1-557662-80-0

2293   Educating all Students in the Mainstream
Brookes Publishing Company
PO Box 10624
Baltimore, MD 21285-0624   410-337-9580
                                      800-638-3775
                                 FAX: 410-337-8539
                            custserv@brookespublishing.com

Paul H. Brookes, Chairman
Jeff Brookes, President
Melissa A. Behm, ExecutiveVice President
Incorporating the research and viewpoints of both regular and special educators, this textbook provides an effective approach for modifying, expanding, and adjusting regular education to meet the needs of all students. *$34.00*
304 pages
ISBN 1-557660-22-0

**2294   Educational Audiology for the Limited Hearing Infant
and Preschooler**
Charles C. Thomas
2600 S First St
Springfield, IL 62704-4730   217-789-8980
                                     800-258-8980
                                FAX: 217-789-9130
                                books@ccthomas.com
                                www.ccthomas.com

Donald Goldberg, Author
Nancy Coleffe-Schenck, Author
Doreen Pollack, Author
Offers information on current concepts and practices in audio-logic screening and evaluation, development of the listening function, development of speech, development of language, the role of parents, parent education, mainstreaming of the limited-hearing child, and program modifications for the severely learning disabled child. Also includes information on auditory assessment, sensory aides, cochlear implants, acoupedics and auditory verbal programs. *$79.95*
430 pages Paperback
ISBN 0-398067-51-1

2295   Educational Care
Educators Publishing Service
625 Mount Auburn St
3rd Floor
Cambridge, MA 02138-3039   617-547-6706
                                     800-225-5750
                            Feedback.EPS@schoolspecialty.com
                                www.eps.schoolspecialty.com

Paula Fabbro, Sales Consultant
Leo Micale, Sales Consultant
Kristen Colson, Sales Consultant
This book, written for both parents and teachers, is based on the view that education should be a system of care that is able to look

after the specific needs of individual students. Using case studies, it analyzes various types of learning disorders and then suggests ways to help students with these problems. *$31.50*
325 pages
ISBN 0-838819-87-7

2296 Educational Intervention for the Student
Charles C. Thomas
2600 S First St
Springfield, IL 62704-4730

217-789-8980
800-258-8980
FAX: 217-789-9130
books@ccthomas.com
www.ccthomas.com

CC Thomas has been producing a strong list of specialty titles and textbooks in the biomedical sciences since 1927.

2297 Educational Prescriptions
Educators Publishing Service
625 Mount Auburn St
3RD Floor
Cambridge, MA 02138-3039

617-547-6706
800-225-5750
Feedback.EPS@schoolspecialty.com

Paula Fabbro, Sales Consultant
Leo Micale, Sales Consultant
Kristen Colson, Sales Consultant
This book provides specific recommendations for the classroom management of students who are experiencing subtle developmental and/or learning difficulties. Intended for regular classroom teachers, specific examples of accommodations teachers can make are provided for grades 1-3 and 4-6. *$13.50*
64 pages
ISBN 0-838819-90-7

2298 Effective Instruction for Special Education
Sage Publications
2455 Teller Road
Thousand Oaks, CA 91320-2218

805-499-0721
800-818-7243
FAX: 800-583-2665
info@sagepub.com
www.sagepub.com

Sara Miller McCune, Founder, Publisher, Chairperson
Blaise R. Simqu, President/CEO
Chris Hickok, Senior Vice President/CFO
This exciting and wide-ranging book provides special educators with effective methods for teaching students with mild and moderate learning and behavioral problems, as well as for teaching remedial students in general. *$37.00*
419 pages Paperback

2299 Effectively Educating Handicapped Students
Longman Publishing Group
9th Fl
Upper Saddle River, NJ 07458-1813

201-236-3281
800-922-0579
FAX: 201-236-3290
www.pearsoned.com

For educators and other professionals who work with deaf and hearing impaired students in preschool and elementary programs. A developmental approach provides the foundation for several intervention methods including preparation for instruction, language, speech, audition and speechreading.
468 pages Paperback
ISBN 0-801303-17-6

2300 Emotional Problems of Childhood and Adolescence
McGraw-Hill School Publishing
PO Box 182604
Columbus, OH 43218

877-833-5524
800-338-3987
FAX: 609-308-4480
customer.service@mheducation.com
www.mcgraw-hill.com

David Levin, President/Chief Ex
David Stafford, Senior Vice President/General Counsel
Maryellen Valaitis, Senior Vice President Human Resources
For future special educators, psychologists and others who work with emotionally disturbed children and adolescents.

2301 Enabling & Empowering Families: Principles & Guidelines for Practice
Brookline Books
8 Trumbull Rd
Suite B-001
Northampton, MA 01060

413-584-0184
800-666-2665
FAX: 413-584-6184
brbooks@yahoo.com
www.brooklinebooks.com

Esther Wilder, Co-Author
This book was written for practitioners who must work with families but who have insufficient training in family systems assessment and intervention. The authors' system enables professionals to help the family identify its needs, locate the formal and informal resources to meet these needs and develop the abilities to effectively access these resources. *$24.95*
220 pages
ISBN 0-914797-59-X

2302 Evaluation and Educational Programming of Students with Deafblindness & Severe Disabilities
Charles C. Thomas
2600 S First St
Springfield, IL 62704-4730

217-789-8980
800-258-8980
FAX: 217-789-9130
books@ccthomas.com
www.ccthomas.com

Carroll J. Jones, Author
Subtitle: Sensorimotor Stage. This second edition offers a very complete package of information on the special education of deaf-blind students; including detailed diagnostic information to assist the instructor in evaluating the physical, social, mental status of the student, as well as the educational progress. *$50.95*
265 pages Spiral-Paper 2001
ISBN 0-398072-16-2

2303 Evaluation and Treatment of the Psychogeriatric Patient
Haworth Press
711 Third Avenue
New York, NY 10017

212-216-7800
800-354-1420
FAX: 212-244-1563
subscriptions@tandf.co.uk
www.haworthpress.com

This pertinent book assists occupational therapists and other health care providers in developing up-to-date psychogeriatric programs and understands details of treating the cognitively impaired elderly. Haworth Press are now acquired by the Taylor & Francis Journals. *$74.95*
111 pages Hardcover
ISBN 1-560240-52-0

2304 Exceptional Children in Focus
McGraw-Hill School Publishing
PO Box 182604
Columbus, OH 43218

877-833-5524
800-338-3987
FAX: 609-308-4480
customer.service@mheducation.com
www.mcgraw-hill.com

David Levin, President/Chief Ex
David Stafford, Senior Vice President/General Counsel
Maryellen Valaitis, Senior Vice President Human Resources
Combines a light, personal look at the problems of special educators experiences with the basic facts of exceptionality.
288 pages

2305 Exceptional Lives: Special Education in Today's Schools, 4th Edition
Pearson Education
1 Lake St
Upper Saddle River, NJ 07458-1813

201-236-3281
800-922-0579
FAX: 201-236-3290
www.pearsoned.com

Comprehensive coverage is built upon six guiding principles: 1) high expectations for individuals with disabilities and their educators, 2) inclusion for all students, 3) relationships and friend-

ships as essential outcomes of collaboration, 4) positive contributions by students with disabilities, 5) the importance of choice and self-advocacy for students with disabilities, and 6) full citizenship for all students with disabilities. Emphasizes the daily lives of students and educators. *$90.00*
592 pages
ISBN 0-131126-00-8

2306   Facilitating Self-Care Practices in the Elderly
Haworth Press
711 Third Avenue
New York, NY 10017   212-216-7800
                                                      800-354-1420
                                                FAX: 212-244-1563
                                        subscriptions@tandf.co.uk
                                              www.haworthpress.com
This up-to-date book is a synthesis of current knowledge from published sources and expert consultants relating to three commonly occurring problems in home health care practice: self-administration of medications, family caregiving issues, and teaching the elderly. Haworth Press are now acquired by the Taylor & Francis Journals. *$74.95*
185 pages Hardcover
ISBN 1-560240-13-X

2307   Family-Centered Early Intervention with Infants and Toddlers
Brookes Publishing
PO Box 10624
Baltimore, MD 21285-0624   410-337-9580
                                                     800-638-3775
                                                FAX: 410-337-8539
                                   custserv@brookespublishing.com
                                         www.brookespublishing.com
Paul H. Brookes, Chairman
Jeffrey D. Brookes, President
Melissa A. Behm, ExecutiveVice President
This informative text provides professionals with insight and practical guidelines to help fulfill the federal requirements for provision of early intervention services. *$37.00*
368 pages Hardcover
ISBN 1-557661-24-3

2308   Feeding Children with Special Needs
Arizona Department of Health Services
150 North 18th Avenue
Phoenix, AZ 85007-2607   602-542-1025
                                                FAX: 602-542-0883
                                                     www.azdhs.gov
Will Humble, Director
Jeff Bloomberg, J.D., Manager
Robert Lane, Esq., Administrative Counsel
Guide designed to help develop a greater awareness of the special challenges involved in the nutrition and feeding concerns for children with special health care needs, and ways to approach the issues. *$5.00*

2309   Focal Group Psychotherapy
New Harbinger Publications
5674 Shattuck Ave
Oakland, CA 94609-1662   510-652-0215
                                                     800-748-6273
                                                FAX: 800-652-1613
                                   customerservice@newharbinger.com
                                              www.newharbinger.com
Matthew McKay, Founder
Patrick Fanning, Co-Founder/Writer
Guide to leading brief, theme-based groups. This book offers an extensive week-by-week description of the basic concepts and interventions for 14 theme or focal groups for: codependency, rape victims, shyness, survivors of incest, agoraphobia, survivors of toxic parents, depression, child molesters, anger control, domestic violence offenders, assertiveness, alcohol and drug abuse, eating disorders, and parent training. *$59.95*
544 pages Cloth
ISBN 1-879237-18-0

2310   Free Hand: Enfranchising the Education of Deaf Children
TJ Publishers

Margaret Walworth, Author
Donald F. Moores, Author
Terrence J. O'Rourke, Author
A select group of nationally prominent educators, linguists and researchers met at Hofstra University to consider the most vital and controversial question in education of the deaf: what role should ASL play in the classroom? Become part of that discussion with A Free Hand. *$16.95*
204 pages Softcover
ISBN 0-93266 -40-X

2311   Friendship 101
Council for Exceptional Children
3100 Clarendon Blvd.
Suite 600
Arlington, VA 22201-5332   888-232-7733
                                                  TTY:866-915-5000
                                     service@exceptionalchildren.org
                                          www.exceptionalchildren.org
Juliet E. Hart Barnett, Co-Author & Editor
Kelly J. Whalon, Co-Author & Editor
Book and webinar for general special educators who work with children with autism spectrum disorder (ASD). Presents evidence-based practices shown to enhance social competence in children with ASD.

2312   Functional Assessment Inventory Manual
Stout Vocational Rehab Institute
655 15th St. NW
Suite 800
Washington, DC 20005   715-232-1411
                                                     800-538-3742
                                                FAX: 715-232-2356
                                         botterbuschd@uwstout.edu
                                                    www2.epa.gov
Gina McCarthy, Administrator
Gwen Keyes Fleming, Chief of Staff
Bob Perciasepe, Deputy Administrator
The Functional Assessment is a systematic enumeration of a client's vocationally relevant strengths and limitations. *$12.00*
96 pages Paperback
ISBN 0-916671-53-4

2313   Get Ready for Jetty!: My Journal About ADHD and Me
750 First Street, NE
Washington, DC 20002-4242   202-336-5500
                                                     800-374-2721
                                                rllowman@gmail.com
                                                      www.apa.org
Jeanne Kraus, Author
Jetty writes about these things as well as her recent ADHD diagnosis in her journal.

2314   Getting Around Town
Council for Exceptional Children
3100 Clarendon Blvd.
Suite 600
Arlington, VA 22201-5332   888-232-7733
                                                  TTY:866-915-5000
                                     service@exceptionalchildren.org
                                          www.exceptionalchildren.org
M. Sherril Moon, Co-Author
Emily M. Luedtke, Co-Author
Elizabeth Halloran-Tornquist, Co-Author
This book provides examples of possible IEP goals and field-tested lesson plans for individual students or entire classes across all age and grade levels. *$34.95*

2315   Global Perspectives on Disability: A Curriculum
Mobility International USA
132 E Broadway
Suite 343
Eugene, OR 97401   541-343-1284
                                                FAX: 541-343-6812
                                                  TTY:541-343-1284
                                           clearinghouse@miusa.org
                                                    www.miusa.org
Susan Sygall, Chief Executive Officer
Cindy Lewis, Director, Programs

Designed for secondary and higher education instructors. Includes five lesson plans covering disability awareness, disability rights and international perspectives on disability. Available in alternative formats.

2316   Glossary of Terminology for Vocational Assessment/Evaluation/Work
Rehabilitation Resource University
University of Wisconsin-Stou
Menomonie, WI 54751   715-232-2236
                                              FAX: 715-232-2356
                                          gundlachj@uwstout.edu

Ronald Fry, Manager
Jennifer Gundlach Klatt, Program Assistant
This glossary contains 254 terms and their definitions. Primary focus is on the terminology related to the practice and professionals of vocational assessment, vocational evaluation and work adjustment. *$9.50*
40 pages Softcover

2317   Graduate Technological Education and the Human Experience of Disability
Haworth Press
711 Third Avenue
New York, NY 10017   212-216-7800
                                                 800-354-1420
                                            FAX: 212-244-1563
                                      subscriptions@tandf.co.uk
                                          www.haworthpress.com

This book examines graduate schools of theology and their limited familiarity with the study of disability — and the presence of people with disabilities in particular — on their campuses. This text offers critical research and illuminates new pathways for theologia and practice in the community of faith. It offers suggestions for incorporating disability studies into theological education and religious life. Haworth Press are now acquired by the Taylor & Francis Journals. *$34.95*
115 pages Hardcover
ISBN 0-789060-08-6

2318   HIV Infection and Developmental Disabilities
Brookes Publishing
PO Box 10624
Baltimore, MD 21285-0624   410-337-9580
                                                 800-638-3775
                                            FAX: 410-337-8539
                                     custserv@brookespublishing.com
                                      www.brookespublishing.com

Paul H. Brookes, Chairman
Jeffrey D. Brookes, President
Melissa A. Behm, ExecutiveVice President
A resource for service providers pinpointing the most crucial medical, legal and educational issues to control HIV infection. *$47.00*
320 pages
ISBN 1-557660-83-2

2319   Handbook for Implementing Workshops for Siblings of Special Children
Special Needs Project
324 State Street
Suite H
Santa Barbara, CA 93101-2364   818-718-9900
                                                 800-333-6867
                                            FAX: 818-349-2027
                                          editor@specialneeds.com
                                          www.specialneeds.com

Mark Darrow, Founder,The Prolotherapy Institu
Based on three years of professional experience, this handbook provides guidelines and techniques for those who wish to start and conduct workshops for siblings. *$40.00*

2320   Handbook for Speech Therapy
Psychological & Educational Publications
PO Box 520
Hydesville, CA 95547   800-523-5775
                                            FAX: 800-447-0907
                                   psych-edpublications@suddenlink.net
Basic handbook for beginning speech teachers, shows how speech sounds are made, what their individual characteristics are,

how they relate to each other, what the most common errors are, and how to correct those errors.
143 pages paperback

2321   Handbook for the Special Education Administrator
Edwin Mellen Press
PO Box 450
Lewiston, NY 14092-1205   716-754-2266
                                            FAX: 716-754-4056
                                       jrupnow@mellenpress.com
                                          www.mellenpress.com

Arthur R. Crowell, Author
Bonnie Crogan, Marketing
Irene Miller, Accounting
Organization and procedures for special education. *$49.95*
96 pages Hardcover
ISBN 0-88946 -22-9

2322   Handbook of Acoustic Accessibility
15619 Premiere Drive
Suite 101
Tampa, FL 33624   850-363-9909
                                            FAX: 480-393-4331
                              accounting@successforkidswithhearingloss.com
                                   successforkidswithhearinglo ss.com

Joseph J. Smaldino, Co-Author
Carol Flexer, Co-Author
Most students with hearing loss are educated in mainstream education classrooms the majority of each school day.Communication - between peers and with teachers - is the coin of education and upon which a wealth of knowledge is built.Unfortunately for students with hearing loss, the typical classroom environment is hazardous for listening and interferes with access to all classroom communication.

2323   Handbook of Developmental Education
Greenwood Publishing Group
130 Cremona Drive
Santa Barbara, CA 93117   805-968-1911
                                                 800-368-6868
                                            FAX: 866-270-3856
                                    CustomerService@abc-clio.com
                                             www.abc-clio.com

Wayne
This comprehensive handbook has brought together the leading practitioners and researchers in the field of developmental education to focus on the developmental learning agenda. Hardcover.
400 pages $65 - $75
ISBN 0-275932-97-4

2324   Handbook on Supported Education for Peoplewith Mental Illness
Brookes Publishing
PO Box 10624
Baltimore, MD 21285-0624   410-337-9580
                                                 800-638-3775
                                            FAX: 410-337-8539
                                     custserv@brookespublishing.com
                                      www.brookespublishing.com

Paul H. Brookes, Chairman
Jeffrey D. Brookes, President
Melissa A. Behm, ExecutiveVice President
Here you will find all necessary information that mental health professionals need in order to provide supported education services. There are specific suggestions on how to help people with mental illness return to or remain in college, trade school, or GED programs. Also addressed are funding and legal issues, accommodations, and specific interventions.
208 pages Paperback
ISBN 1-55766 -52-1

2325   Head Injury Rehabilitation: Children
Taylor & Francis
47 Runway Dr
Ste G
Levittown, PA 19057-4738   267-580-2622
                                            FAX: 215-785-5515

Rehabilitation guide for the help of children or adolescents that have suffered brain injury.
460 pages Cloth
ISBN 0-85066 -67-1

2326 Health Care Management in Physical Therapy
Charles C. Thomas
2600 S First St
Springfield, IL 62704-4730
217-789-8980
800-258-8980
FAX: 217-789-9130
books@ccthomas.com
www.ccthomas.com
CC Thomas has been producing a strong list of specialty titles and textbooks in the biomedical sciences since 1927.

2327 Health Care for Students with Disabilities
Brookes Publishing Company
PO Box 10624
Baltimore, MD 21285-0624
410-337-9580
800-638-3775
FAX: 410-337-8539
custserv@brookespublishing.com
www.brookespublishing.com
Paul H. Brookes, Chairman
Jeffrey D. Brookes, President
Melissa A. Behm, ExecutiveVice President
This practical guidebook provides detailed descriptions of the 16 health-related procedures most likely to be needed in the classroom by students with disabilities. *$25.00*
304 pages Paperback
ISBN 1-557660-37-9

2328 Helping Learning- Disabled Gifted Children Learn Through Compensatory Active Play
Charles C. Thomas
2600 S First St
Springfield, IL 62704-4730
217-789-8980
800-258-8980
FAX: 217-789-9130
books@ccthomas.com
www.ccthomas.com
James Harry Humphrey, Author
$36.95
156 pages Hardcover 1990
ISBN 0-398056-95-1

2329 Helping Students Grow
American College Testing Program
500 ACT Drive
PO Box 168
Iowa City, IA 52243-0168
319-337-1000
info@keytrain.com
www.act.org
Jon Whitmore, Chief Executive Officer
Tom J. Goedken, Chief Financial Officer/Senior Vice President
Patricia C. Steinbrech, Chief Information Officer
Designed to assist counselors in using the wealth of information generated by the ACT Assessment.

2330 Home Health Care Provider: A Guide to Essential Skills
Springer Publishing
11 W 42nd St
15th Floor
New York, NY 10036-8002
212-431-4370
877-687-7476
FAX: 212-941-7842
cs@springerpub.com
www.springerpub.com
Theodore C. Nardin, CEO/Publisher
Jason Roth, VP/Marketing Director
Annette Imperati, Marketing/Sales Director
This book is designed to foster quality care to home care recipients. Prieto provides information, tips, and techniques on personal care routines as well as additional responsibilities, including home safety and maintenance, meal planning, errand running, caring for couples, and making use of recreational time. The book focuses on the psycho-social needs of home care recipients, stressing the need to maintainthe house as a home, and sustaining the recipient's way of life throughout caregiving.

2331 How to Teach Spelling/How to Spell
Educators Publishing Service
625 Mount Auburn St
3rd Floor
Cambridge, MA 02138-3039
617-547-6706
800-225-5750
Feedback.EPS@schoolspecialty.com
Paula Fabbro, Sales Consultant
Leo Micale, Sales Consultant
Kristen Colson, Sales Consultant
This is a comprehensive resource manual based on the Orton-Gillingham approach to reading and spelling. It recommends what and how much to teach at each grade level at the beginning of each lesson or section. There are four student manuals that accompany this. *$22.50*
Teachers Manual
ISBN 0-838818-47-1

2332 Human Exceptionality: School, Community,and Family (12th Edition)
Cengage Learning
20 Channel Center St
Boston, MA 02210
617-289-7700
617-289-7844
www.cengage.com/us
Michael L. Hardman, Author
M. Winston Egan, Author
Clifford J. Drew, Author
An evidence-based testament to the critical role of cross-professional collaboration in enhancing the lives of exceptional individuals and their families. This text's unique lifespan approach combines powerful research, evidence-based practices, and inspiring stories, engendering passion and empathy and enhancing the lives of individuals with exceptionalities.
544 pages Hardcover

2333 I Can't Hear You in the Dark: How to Lean and Teach Lipreading
Charles C. Thomas
2600 S First St
Springfield, IL 62704-4730
217-789-8980
800-258-8980
FAX: 217-789-9130
books@ccthomas.com
www.ccthomas.com
Betty Woerner Carter, Author
The goal of this text is to improve communication and strengthen relationships with others. *$40.95*
226 pages Spiral-Paper 1997
ISBN 0-398067-89-2

2334 I Heard That!
3417 Volta Pl NW
Washington, DC 20007-2737
202-337-5220
FAX: 202-337-8314
TTY:202-337-5221
info@agbell.org
www.listeningandspokenlanguage.org
Meredith K. Sugar, Esq. (OH), President
Ted A. Meyer, M.D., Ph.D, President-Elect/Secretary-Treasurer
Emilio Alonso-Mendoza, Chief Executive Officer
Provides a framework for teachers, clinicians and parents when writing objectives and designing activities to develop listening skills in children with hearing loss from newborn to 3 years. *$7.95*
36 pages

2336 If It Is To Be, It Is Up To Us To Help!
AVKO Educational Research Foundation
3084 Willard Rd
Ste W
Birch Run, MI 48415-9404
810-686-9283
866-285-6612
FAX: 810-686-1101
www.avko.org
Don Mc Cabe, President
Ted A. Meyer, M.D., Ph.D, Vice-President
Michael Lane, Treasurer
A book of lesson plans for an Adult Community Education Course for Volunteer Tutors. Contains information on how to go

about establishing such a course and how to secure cooperation from local and national organizations. Free as an e-book for Foundation members. *$14.95*
ISBN 1-56400 -42-1

2337   Images of the Disabled, Disabling Images
ABC-CLIO
130 Cremona Dr
Santa Barbara, CA 93117   805-968-1911
                                         800-368-6868
                                    FAX: 866-270-3856
                            customerservice@abc-clio.com
                                       www.abc-clio.com

Alan Gartner, Author
Combines an examination of the presentation of persons with disabilities in literature, film and the media with an analysis of the ways in which these images are expressed in public policy concerning the disabled. *$84.00*
227 pages Hardcover 1986
ISBN 0-275921-78-6

2338   Implementing Family-Centered Services in Early Intervention
Brookline Books
8 Trumbull Rd
Suite B-001
Northampton, MA 01060   413-584-0184
                                         800-666-2665
                                    FAX: 413-584-6184
                                   brbooks@yahoo.com
                                www.brooklinebooks.com

This book describes a team-based decision-making workshop for implementing family-centered services in early interventions. Unlike a training curriculum, it focuses on the decisions that teams must make as they seek to become family-centered. *$19.95*
180 pages Paperback
ISBN 0-91479 -62-

2339   Including All of Us: An Early Childhood Curriculum About Disability
Educational Equity Concepts
381 Park Ave South
Suite 701
New York, NY 10016   212-243-1110
                                    FAX: 212-367-4640
                                     lcolon@fhi360.org
                                       www.fhi360.org

Frank Schneiger, President
Antonia Cottrell Martin, Founder and President
Merle Froschl, Director, Educational Equity
The first nonsexist, multicultural, mainstreamed curriculum. Step-by-step activities incorporate disability into three curriculum areas: Same/Different (hearing impairment), Body Parts (visual impairment), and Transportation (mobility impairment). *$14.95*
144 pages
ISBN 0-93162 -00-4

2340   Including Students with Severe and Multiple Disabilites in Typical Classrooms
Brookes Publishing
PO Box 10624
Baltimore, MD 21285-0624   410-337-9580
                                         800-638-3775
                                    FAX: 410-337-8539
                            custserv@brookespublishing.com
                              www.brookespublishing.com

Paul H. Brookes, Chairman
Jeffrey D. Brookes, President
Melissa A. Behm, ExecutiveVice President
This straightforward and jargon free resource gives instructors the guidance needed to educate learners who have one or more sensory impairments in addition to cognitive and physical disabilities. *$32.95*
224 pages Paperback
ISBN 1-55766 -39-8

2341   Including Students with Special Needs: A Practical Guide for Classroom Teachers
Allyn & Bacon
75 Arlington St
Suite 300
Boston, MA 02116-3988   ab_webmaster@abacon.com
                      www.pearson.com/us/higher-education.html
Focuses on educating students with special needs in inclusive settings based on substantive admisistrative backing, support for general education teachers, and an understanding that sometimes not all needs can be met in a single location.
544 pages
ISBN 0-20528 -85-4

2342   Inclusive & Heterogeneous Schooling: Assessment, Curriculum, and Instruction
Brookes Publishing
PO Box 10624
Baltimore, MD 21285-0624   410-337-9580
                                         800-638-3775
                                    FAX: 410-337-8539
                            custserv@brookespublishing.com
                              www.brookespublishing.com

Paul H. Brookes, Chairman
Jeff Brookes, President
Melissa A. Behm, ExecutiveVice President
Presents methods for successfully restructuring classrooms to enable all students, particularly those with disabilities, to flourish. Provides specific strategies for assessment, collaboration, classroom management, and age-specific instruction. *$34.95*
448 pages Paperback
ISBN 1-55766 -02-9

2343   Independent Living Approach to Disability Policy Studies
World Institute on Disability
3075 Adeline St.
Suite 155
Berkeley, CA 94703   510-225-6400
                                    FAX: 510-225-0477
                                          wid@wid.org
                                          www.wid.org

Marcie Roth, Executive Director & Chief Executive Officer
Kat Zigmont, Senior Director, Operations & Deputy Director
Reggie Johnson, Senior Director, Marketing & Communications
A collection of essays and bibliographies aiming to build a framework for understanding how the relationship between public policy, disability studies and disability policy studies will impact the future.

2344   Information & Referral Center
Mississippi State University
108 Herbert - South
Room 150/PO Drawer 6189
Mississippi State Univers, MS 39762-6189   662-325-2001
                                            800-675-7782
                                       FAX: 662-325-8989
                                       TTY: 662-325-2694
                                 nrtc@colled.msstate.edu
                                   www.blind.msstate.edu

Jacqui Bybee, Research and Training Coordinato
Michele Capella McDonnall, Ph.D., Research Professor/Interim Director
Jessica Thornton, Business Manager
A comprehensive website that includes information about client assistance programs, vocational rehabilitation agencies, low vision clinics and information about blindness and low vision. *$25.00*
150 pages

2345   Instructional Methods for Students
Allyn & Bacon
75 Arlington St
Suite 300
Boston, MA 02116-3988   ab_webmaster@abacon.com
                          www.home.pearsonhighered.com
Instructional methods for students with learning and behavior problems.
450 pages
ISBN 0-205087-35-3

2346 Interactions: Collaboration Skills for School Professionals
Longman Education/Addison Wesley
75 Arlington St
Suite 300
Boston, MA 02116-3988   ab_webmaster@abacon.com
Shows school professionals how to develop and use the skills necessary for effective collaboration among teachers, school support staff, and parents of children with special needs. *$35.00*
270 pages Paperback
ISBN 0-80131-21-2

2347 International Journal of Arts Medicine
MMB Music
9051 Watson Road
Suite 161
Saint Louis, MO 63126   314-531-9635
800-543-3771
FAX: 314-531-8384
info@mmbmusic.com
www.mmbmusic.com
Norm Goldberg, Founder/chairman
Exploration of the creative arts and healing. Presents peer-reviewed articles clearly written by educators in the creative arts, as well as internationally prominent physicians, therapists and health care professionals.

2348 Interpreting Disability: A Qualitative Reader
Teachers College Press
1234 Amsterdam Avenue
New York, NY 10027   212-678-3929
800-575-6566
FAX: 212-678-4149
tcpress@tc.columbia.edu
www.tcpress.com
Brian Ellerbeck, Executive Acquisitions Editor
Marie Ellen Larcada, Senior Acquisitions Editor
Emily Spangler, Acquisitions Editor
This book offers a collection of exemplary qualitative research affecting people with disabilities and their families. Instead of focusing upon methodological details, the chapters illustrate the variety of styles and formats that interpretive research can adopt in reporting its results. *$24.95*
328 pages Paperback
ISBN 0-807731-21-8

2349 Intervention Research in Learning Disabilities
Gallery Bookshop
319 Kasten Street
PO Box 270
Mendocino, CA 95460-270   707-937-2215
FAX: 707-937-3737
info@gallerybookshop.com
www.gallerybooks.com
Tony Miksak, Owner
Based on the Symposium on Intervention Research, this volume presents 12 papers addressing issues in intervention research, academic interventions, social and behavioral interventions, and postsecondary interventions. *$30.00*
347 pages

2350 Introduction to Learning Disabilities
Allyn & Bacon
75 Arlington St
Suite 300
Boston, MA 02116-3988   www.pearsonhighered.com
Presents the current state of research in the area of learning disabilities, as well as intervention ideas and programs. Includes updated material on the 1997 re-authorization of IDEA (Individuals with Disabilities Education Act) and expanded coverage of ADHD and its relationship to learning disabilities. Presents the latest information on the characteristics of persons with learning disabilities, causes, and educational interventions.
608 pages
ISBN 0-20529-43-4

2351 Introduction to Special Education: Teaching in an Age of Challenge, 4th Edition
Allyn & Bacon
75 Arlington St
Suite 300
Boston, MA 02116-3988   www.pearsonhighered.com
Provides an applied approach to children with disabilities through the use of specific research and suggestions to focus on how the educational practices impact the lives of children, their families, and their teachers.
640 pages cloth
ISBN 0-20526-94-4

2352 Introduction to the Profession of Counseling
McGraw-Hill School Publishing
PO Box 182604
Columbus, OH 43218   877-833-5524
800-338-3987
FAX: 609-308-4480
customer.service@mheducation.com
www.mcgraw-hill.com
David Levin, President/Chief Executive Officer
David Stafford, Senior Vice President/General Counsel
Maryellen Valaitis, Senior Vice President Human Resources
Offers information, theories and techniques for counseling numerous cases from drug addiction to special populations.
464 pages

2353 Issues and Research in Special Education
Teachers College Press
PO Box 20
Williston, VT 05495-0020   800-575-6566
FAX: 802-664-7626
tcp.orders@aidcvt.com
www.teacherscollegepress.com
Provides up-to-date research and discourse on a wide range of topics affecting professionals in the field of special education. *$38.00*
264 pages Hardcover
ISBN 0-807731-95-1

2354 Kendall Demonstration Elementary School Curriculum Guides
Gallaudet University Bookstore
800 Florida Ave NE
Washington, DC 20002-3695   202-651-5488
800-621-2736
FAX: 202-651-5489
TTY: 888-630-9347
gupress@gallaudet.edu
www.gupress.gallaudet.edu
Dr. T Alan Hurwitz, President
Edward Bosso, Vice President for Administration
Dr. Lynne Murray, Vice President for Development
KDES is a day school serving students from birth through age 15, beginning with the Parent-Infant Program and ending in grade 8. Students come from the Washington, D.C., metropolitan area.

2355 Language Arts: Detecting Special Needs
Allyn & Bacon
75 Arlington St
Suite 300
Boston, MA 02116-3988   617-848-7500
800-852-8024
FAX: 617-944-7273
www.home.pearsonhighered.com
Bill Barke, Chairman/CEO
Nancy Forfyth, President
Kevin Stone, Vice President
Describes special language arts needs of special learners.
180 pages paperback
ISBN 0-205116-36-1

2356 Language Learning Practices with Deaf Children
Sage Publications
2455 Teller Road
Thousand Oaks, CA 91320   805-499-9774
                                 800-818-7243
                            FAX: 800-583-2665
                    books.claim@sagepub.com
                            www.sagepub.com

Sara Miller McCune, Founder, Publisher, Chairperson
Stephen P. Quigley, Co-Author
Susan Rose, Co-Author
This new edition describes the variety of language-development theories and practices used with deaf children without advocating anyone. *$38.00*
321 pages Hardcover

2357 Language and Communication Disorders in Children
McGraw-Hill School Publishn
PO Box 182604
Columbus, OH 43218   877-833-5524
                                800-338-3987
                           FAX: 609-308-4480
              customer.service@mheducation.com
                           www.mcgraw-hill.com

David Levin, President/Chief Executive Officer
David Stafford, Senior Vice President/General Counsel
Maryellen Valaitis, Senior Vice President Human Resources
Comprehensive coverage encompassing all aspects of children's language disorders.
512 pages

2358 Learning Disabilities, Literacy, and Adult Education
Brookes Publishing
PO Box 10624
Baltimore, MD 21285-0624   410-337-9580
                                800-638-3775
                           FAX: 410-337-8539
             custserv@brookespublishing.com
                    www.brookespublishing.com

Paul H. Brookes, Chairman
Jeffrey D. Brookes, President
Melissa A. Behm, ExecutiveVice President
This book focuses on adults with severe learning disabilities and the educators who work with them. Described are the characteristics, demographics, and educational and employment status of adults with LD and the laws that protect them in the workplace and in educational settings.
450 pages Paperback
ISBN 1-55766 -47-5

2359 Learning Disabilities: Concepts and Characteristics
McGraw-Hill School Publishing
220 E Danieldale Rd
Desoto, TX 75115-2490   972-224-4772
                                800-442-9685
                           FAX: 972-228-1982

Harold McGraw III, Chairman/ President/ Chief Ex
Jack F. Callahan, Executive Vice President, Chief
James A. McLoughlin, Co-Author
Covers the conceptual basis of learning disabilities, identification, etiology and diagnosis.
448 pages

2360 Learning Disability: Social Class and the Cons of Inequality In American Education
Greenwood Publishing Group
130 Cremona Drive
Santa Barbara, CA 93117   805-968-1911
                                800-368-6868
                           FAX: 866-270-3856
              CustomerService@abc-clio.com
                           www.abc-clio.com

James Carrier, Author
Presents a detailed historical description of the social and educational assumptions integral to the idea of learning disability.
167 pages $43.95 - $47.95
ISBN 0-313253-96-X

2361 Learning and Individual Differences
National Association of School Psychologists
4340 East West Hwy.
Suite 402
Bethesda, MD 20814   301-657-0270
                                866-331-6277
                           FAX: 301-657-0275
                           TTY: 301-657-4155
                           www.nasponline.org

Kathleen Minke, Executive Director
Laura Benson, Chief Operating Officer

2362 Learning to Feel Good and Stay Cool: Emotional Regulation Tools for Kids With AD/HD
750 First Street, NE
Washington, DC 20002-4242   202-336-5500
                                800-374-2721
                    rllowman@gmail.com
                           www.apa.org

Judith M. Glasser, PhD, Co-Author
Kathleen G. Nadeau, PhD, Co-Author
Packed with practical advice and fun activities, this book will show you how to Understand your emotions, Practice healthy habits to stay in your Feel Good Zone, Feel better when you get upset, Know the warning signs that you are heading into your Upset Zone, Problem-solve so upsets come less often

2363 Learning to See: American Sign Language asa Second Language
Gallaudet University Press
800 Florida Ave NE
Washington, DC 20002-3695   202-651-5206
                                800-621-2736
                           FAX: 800-621-8476
                           TTY: 888-630-9347
              clerc.center@gallaudet.edu
                    www.gupress.gallaudet.edu

Dr. T Alan Hurwitz, President
Edward Bosso, Vice President for Administration
Phyliss Wilcox, Co-Author
This important book has been updated to help teachers teach American Sign Language as a second language, including information on Deaf culture, the history and structure of ASL, teaching methods and issues facing educators. *$19.95*
160 pages Softcover

2364 Let's Write Right: Teacher's Edition
AVKO Educational Research Foundation
3084 Willard Rd
Ste W
Birch Run, MI 48415-9404   810-686-9283
                                866-285-6612
                           FAX: 810-686-1101

Barry Chute, President
Julie Guyette, Vice President
Don Mc Cabe, Research Director
A manuscript and cursive writing program designed not only to teach handwriting but help with reading and spelling patterns as well. Teaches students to learn to read cursive as manuscript is being taught and ease the transition to cursive by using a D'Nealian-like script. Exercises involve phoically consistent patterns to help reinforce fluency with spelling and handwriting. *$39.95*
164 pages

2365 Library Manager's Guide to Hiring and Serving Disabled Persons
McFarland & Company
960 NC Hwy 88 W
Jefferson, NC 28640   336-246-4460
                                800-253-2187
                           FAX: 336-246-5018
              infoinso@mcfarlandpub.com
                    www.mcfarlandbooks.com

Kieth C. Wright, Author
Judith F. Davie, Author
Information for library staff on hiring and serving disabled persons. *$27.50*
171 pages Library binding 1990
ISBN 0-899505-16-3

2366 Life-Span Approach to Nursing Care for Individuals with Developmental Disabilities
Brookes Publishing
PO Box 10624
Baltimore, MD 21285-0624

410-337-9580
800-638-3775
FAX: 410-337-8539
custserv@brookespublishing.com
www.brookespublishing.com

Paul H. Brookes, Chairman
Jeffrey D. Brookes, President
Melissa A. Behm, ExecutiveVice President
This reference book was written by and for nurses. This guide addresses fundamental nursing issues such as health promotion, infection control, seizure management, adaptive and assistive technology, and sexuality. Also offered are in-depth case studies, helpful charts and tables, and problem-solving strategies. *$49.95*
464 pages Hardcover
ISBN 1-557661-51-0

2367 Mainstreaming Deaf and Hard of Hearing Students: Questions and Answers
Gallaudet University Bookstore
800 Florida Ave NE
Washington, DC 20002-3600

202-651-5000
800-451-1073
FAX: 202-651-5489
TTY: 888-630-9347
clerc.center@gallaudet.edu
www.gupress.gallaudet.edu

Dr. T Alan Hurwitz, President
Debra S. Lipkey, University Budget Director
Donald Beil, Chief of Staff
This booklet presents mainstreaming as one educational option and suggests some considerations for parents, teachers and administrators. *$6.00*
40 pages

2368 Mainstreaming Exceptional Students: A Guide for Classroom Teachers
Allyn & Bacon
75 Arlington St
Suite 300
Boston, MA 02116-3988

617-848-7500
800-852-8024
FAX: 617-944-7273
www.home.pearsonhighered.com

Nancy Forfyth, President
Bill Barke, CEO
Jane B. Schulz, Co-Author
Covers the various categories of exceptional students and discusses educational strategies and classroom management.
464 pages paperback
ISBN 0-20515-24-6

2369 Mainstreaming: A Practical Approach for Teachers
McGraw-Hill School Publishing
PO Box 182604
Columbus, OH 43218

877-833-5524
800-338-3987
FAX: 609-308-4480
customer.service@mheducation.com
www.mcgraw-hill.com

David Levin, President/Chief Executive Officer
David Stafford, Senior Vice President/General Counsel
Maryellen Valaitis, Senior Vice President Human Resources
Provides teachers, administrators and school psychologists with the background, techniques and strategies they need to offer appropriate services for mildly handicapped students in the mainstream classroom.

2370 Managing Diagnostic Tool of Visual Perception
Gallery Bookshop
319 Kasten Street
PO Box 270
Mendocino, CA 95460-270

707-937-2215
FAX: 707-937-3737
info@gallerybookshop.com
www.gallerybooks.com

Constantine Mangina, Author

For diagnosing specific perceptual learning abilities and disabilities. *$14.00*
ISBN 0-80580-83-4

2371 Medical Rehabilitation
Lippincott, Williams & Wilkins
227 S 6th St
Suite 227
Philadelphia, PA 19106-3713

215-545-5630
800-777-2295
FAX: 215-732-9988
www.lpub.com

Cheryl Murkey, Manager
Information for the professional on new techniques and treatments in the medical rehabilitation fields. *$80.50*
368 pages Illustrated
ISBN 0-88167-85-5

2372 Meeting the ADD Challenge: A Practical Guide for Teachers
Research Press
PO Box 7886
Champaign, IL 61826-9177

217-352-3273
800-519-2707
FAX: 217-352-1221
rp@researchpress.com
www.researchpress.com

Robert W. Parkinson, Founder
Dr. Michael Asher, Co-Author
Dr. Steven B Gordon, Co-Author
$24.95
ISBN 0-878223-45-9

2373 Mental & Physical Disability Law Digest
A BA Commission on Mental and Physical Disability
1050 Connecticut Ave. N.W.
Suite 400
Washington, DC 20036-1019

202-662-1000
800-285-2221
FAX: 202-442-3439
cmpdl@abanet.org
www.americanbar.org

Robert M. Carlson, Chair, House of Delegates:
James R. Silkenat, President
William C. Hubbard, President-Elect
Provides comprehensive, summary and analysis of federal and state disability and state disability laws from mental disability law and disability discrimination law perspectives. *$60.00*
376 pages
ISBN 1-590310-05-5

2374 Mental Health Concepts and Techniques for the Occupational Therapy Assistant
Lippincott, Williams & Wilkins
227 S 6th St
Suite 227
Philadelphia, PA 19106-3713

215-521-8300
800-777-2295
FAX: 301-824-7390
www.lpub.com

J Lippincott, CEO
This text offers clear and easily understood explanations of the various theoretical and practiced health models. *$36.00*
344 pages
ISBN 0-88167-53-X

2375 Mental Health and Mental Illness
Lippincott, Williams & Wilkins
227 S 6th St
Suite 227
Philadelphia, PA 19106-3713

215-592-5400
800-777-2295
FAX: 301-824-7390
www.lpub.com

Kathy Sykes, Manager
Concise, comprehensive and completely up to date, this book presents the most current theory in mental health nursing for the student and the new practitioner. *$28.95*
480 pages
ISBN 0-39755-73-7

2376 Mentally Ill Individuals
Mainstream
Ste 830
3 Bethesda Metro Ctr
Bethesda, MD 20814-6301
301-961-9299
800-247-1380
FAX: 301-654-6714

Charles Moster
Mainstreaming mentally ill individuals into the workplace. *$2.50*
12 pages

2377 Midland Treatment Furniture
Performance Health
28100 Torch Parkway
Suite 700
Warrenville, IL 60555-3938
630-393-6000
FAX: 630-393-7600
customersupport@performancehealth.com
www.performancehealth.com

Francis Dirksmeier, Chief Executive Officer
Greg Nulty, Chief Financial Officer
Jim Plewa, Chief Sales Officer
This catalog has the biggest selection of OT/PT products anywhere. Whether you deal with larger or smaller caseloads, you need treatment furniture you can count on. Midland Treatment Furniture from SPR is designed and built to stand up to the heaviest use. From tilt tables and traction packages to mat platforms and parallel bars, you'll find the complete line of Midland Treatment Furniture inside this brochure. All products are assembled from premium materials and carefully crafted.
Free

2378 Multisensory Teaching of Basic Language Skills: Theory and Practice
Brookes Publishing
PO Box 10624
Baltimore, MD 21285-0624
410-337-9580
800-638-3775
FAX: 410-337-8539
custserv@brookespublishing.com
www.brookespublishing.com

Paul H. Brookes, Chairman
Jeffrey D. Brookes, President
Melissa A. Behm, ExecutiveVice President
This book presents specific multisensory methods for helping students who are having trouble learning to read due to dyslexia or other learning disabilities. Recommended techniques are offered for teaching alphabet skills, composition, comprehension, handwriting, math, organization and study skills, phonological awareness, reading and spelling. *$59.00*
608 pages Hardcover
ISBN 1-557663-49-1

2379 Music, Disability, and Society
1852 North 10th Street
Philadelphia, PA 19122
215-926-2140
800-621-2736
www.temple.edu/tempress

Alex Lubet, Author
In Music, Disability, and Society, Alex Lubet challenges the rigid view of technical skill and writes about music in relation to disability studies. He addresses the ways in which people with disabilities are denied the opportunity to participate in music.

2380 Occupational Therapy Across Cultural Boundaries
Haworth Press
711 Third Avenue
New York, NY 10017
212-216-7800
800-354-1420
FAX: 212-244-1563
subscriptions@tandf.co.uk
www.taylorandfrancisgroup.com

Derek Mapp, Non-Executive Chairman
Roger Horton, CEO
Emma Blaney, Group HR Director - Head of Corporate Responsibility
Examines the concept of culture from a unique perspective, that of individual occupational therapists who have worked in environments very different from those in which they were educated or had worked previously. Journal publications formerly pub-

lished by Haworth Press are now listed on the Taylor & Francis Journals website. *$74.95*
107 pages Hardcover
ISBN 1-560242-23-X

2381 Occupational Therapy Approaches to Traumatic Brain Injury
Routledge (Taylor & Francis Group)
711 Third Ave
New York, NY 10017
212-216-7800
800-634-7064
FAX: 212-564-7854
enquiries@taylorandfrancis.com
www.routledge.com

Laura H. Krefting, Author
Jerry A. Johnson, Author
Focusing on the disabled individual, the family, and the societal responses to the injured, this comprehensive book covers the spectrum of available services from intensive care to transitional and community living. Formerly published by Haworth Press, titles are now listed on Routledge/Taylor Francis Group. *$140.00*
137 pages Hardcover
ISBN 1-560240-64-4

2382 Overcoming Dyslexia in Children, Adolescents and Adults
Sage Publications
2455 Teller Road
Thousand Oaks, CA 91320
805-499-9774
800-818-7243
FAX: 800-583-2665
books.claim@sagepub.com
www.sagepub.com

Sara Miller McCune, Founder, Publisher, Chairperson
Blaise R Simqu, President/CEO
Tracey A. Ozmina, Executive Vice President & Chief
This book describes some forms of dyslexia in detail and then relates those problems to the social, emotional and personal development of dyslexic individuals. *$34.00*
350 pages Paperback

2383 Oxford Textbook of Geriatric Medicine
Oxford University Press
198 Madison Ave
New York, NY 10016-4308
212-726-6000
800-445-9714
FAX: 919-677-1303
custserv.us@oup.com
global.oup.com

Rebecca Seger, Director, Institutional Sales, Americas
Lesa Moran Owen, Library Sales Operations Manager
Lenny Allen, Director, Institutional Accounts
This comprehensive text brings together extensive experience in clinical geriatrics with a strong scientific base in research. *$125.00*
784 pages

2384 Pain Centers: A Revolution in Health Care
Lippincott Williams And Wilkins
227
227 S 6th St
Philadelphia, PA 19106-3713
215-521-8300
800-777-2295
FAX: 301-824-7390
www.lpub.com

J Lippincott, CEO
$103.00
280 pages

2385 Parental Concerns in College Student Mental Health
Haworth Press
711 Third Avenue
New York, NY 10017
212-216-7800
800-354-1420
FAX: 212-244-1563
subscriptions@tandf.co.uk
www.taylorandfrancisgroup.com
Derek Mapp, Non-Executive Chairman
Roger Horton, CEO
Emma Blaney, Group HR Director - Head of Corporate Responsibility
An instructive guide for parents and mental health professionals regarding the most important issues about psychological development in college students. Journal publications formerly published by Haworth Press are now listed on the Taylor & Francis Journals website. *$74.95*
204 pages Hardcover
ISBN 0-866567-20-8

2386 Parents and Teachers
Alexander Graham Bell Association
3417 Volta Pl NW
Washington, DC 20007-2737
202-337-5220
866-337-5220
FAX: 202-337-8314
TTY: 202-337-5221
info@agbell.org
www.listeningandspokenlanguage.org
Kathleen S. Treni, M.Ed., M.A., President
Meredith K. Knueve, Esq., Secretary-Treasurer
Alexander T. Graham, Executive Director/CEO
This excellent book offers in-depth guidance to parents and teachers whose partnership can foster language in school-aged children with hearing impairments. The first section examines roles of parents, teachers, professionals and children in language acquisition, residual hearing and audiological management, language development stages and readying children for preschool. The second portion of the book presents specific objectives and teaching strategies to use at school and at home. *$27.95*
386 pages

2387 Patient and Family Education
Springer Publishing Company
11 W 42nd St
15th Floor
New York, NY 10036-8002
212-431-4370
877-687-7476
FAX: 212-941-7842
cs@springerpub.com
www.springerpub.com
Dr. Ursula Springer, President
Ted Nardin, CEO
James C. Costello, Vice President, Journal Publishi
This guide outlines the actual clinical content needed to develop, implement and maintain patient education programs. Conveniently arranged in one-hour long lesson plans, each disease or condition is organized in an easy-to-follow format. *$26.95*
272 pages Softcover
ISBN 0-82615-41-7

2388 Person to Person: Guide for Professionals Working with the Disabled
Paul H Brookes Publishing Company
PO Box 10624
Baltimore, MD 21285-0624
410-337-9580
800-638-3775
FAX: 410-337-8539
custserv@brookespublishing.com
www.brookespublishing.com
Paul H. Brookes, Chairman
Jeffrey D. Brookes, President
Melissa A. Behm, Executive Vice President
This second edition of an already-popular book helps professionals approach interactions with a people-first, disability second attitude. *$29.00*
288 pages Paperback
ISBN 1-557661-00-6

2389 Personality and Emotional Disturbance
Taylor & Francis
Ste G
47 Runway Dr
Levittown, PA 19057-4738
267-580-2622
FAX: 215-785-5515
Richard Roberts, CEO
The brain injured person has unique needs. Recent findings have highlighted that it is the personality, behavioral and emotional problems which most prohibit a return to work, create the greatest burden for the long-term care and rehabilitation of physical and cognitive functions. *$72.00*
260 pages Cloth
ISBN 0-85066 -71-3

2390 Phenomenology of Depressive Illness
Human Sciences Press
233 Spring St
New York, NY 10013-1522
212-229-2859
877-283-3229
FAX: 212-463-0742
ainy@aveda.com
www.aveda.edu
Provides the reader with a detailed knowledge of the clinical characteristics of depressive disorders that will permit judgement of the general ability of the various theoretical models of depressive disorders. *$42.95*
263 pages Cloth
ISBN 0-89885 -69-9

2391 Physical Disabilities and Health Impairments: An Introduction
McGraw-Hill School Publishing
PO Box 182604
Columbus, OH 43218
877-833-5524
800-338-3987
FAX: 609-308-4480
customer.service@mheducation.com
www.mcgraw-hill.com
David Levin, President/Chief Executive Officer
David Stafford, Senior Vice President/General Counsel
Maryellen Valaitis, Senior Vice President Human Resources
A comprehensive text which presents a wealth of up-to-date medical information for teachers.

2392 Physical Education and Sports for Exceptional Students
McGraw-Hill Company
2460 Kerper Blvd
Dubuque, IA 52001-2224
800-338-3987
FAX: 614-755-5654
www.mhhe.com/hper/physed
Michael Horvat, Author
Harold McGraw III, Chairman, President and Chief Ex
Jack F. Callahan, Executive Vice President, Chief
Physical education for exceptional students and teaching students with learning and behavior exceptionalities.
Cloth

2393 Physical Management of Multiple Handicaps: A Professional's Guide
Brookes Publishing Company
PO Box 10624
Baltimore, MD 21285-0624
410-337-9580
800-638-3775
FAX: 410-337-8539
custserv@brookespublishing.com
www.brookespublishing.com
Paul H. Brookes, Chairman
Jeffrey D. Brookes, President
Melissa A. Behm, ExecutiveVice President
Comprehensive guide, takes a transdisciplinary approach to therapeutic/technological management of persons with multiple handicaps. *$36.00*
352 pages Hardcover
ISBN 1-557660-47-6

2394 Physically Handicapped in Society
Ayer Company Publishers
Ste 322
400 Bedford St
Manchester, NH 03101-1195   603-669-9307
                                    888-267-7323
                              FAX: 603-669-7945
                                  www.ayerpub.com

Kathy Train, Office Manager
Ellie Phipps, Customer Service
A group of 39 books. Biographies that offer studies on attitudes, sociological and psychological. Please write or call for catalog. *$965.00*
Hardcover
ISBN 0-40513 -00-3

2395 Practicing Rehabilitation with Geriatric Clients
Springer Publishing Company
11 W 42nd St
15th Floor
New York, NY 10036-8002   212-431-4370
                                    877-687-7476
                              FAX: 212-941-7842
                                 cs@springerpub.com
                                 www.springerpub.com

Dr. Ursula Springer, President
Ted Nardin, CEO
James C. Costello, Vice President, Journal Publishi
Physical therapy in the geriatric client, psychological and psychiatric considerations in the rehabilitation of the elderly. *$32.95*
256 pages Hardcover
ISBN 0-82616-80-5

2396 Pragmatic Approach
Educators Publishing Service
625 Mount Auburn St
3RD Floor
Cambridge, MA 02138-3039   617-547-6706
                                    800-225-5750
                              FAX: 617-547-0285

Paula Fabbro, Sales Consultant
Leo Micale, Sales Consultant
Kristen Colson, Sales Consultant
Monograph on evaluation of children's performances on Slingerland Pre-Reading Screening Procedures to Identify First Grade Academic Needs. *$6.00*
56 pages
ISBN 0-838816-85-1

2397 Preschoolers with Special Needs: Children At-Risk, Children with Disabilities
Allyn & Bacon
75 Arlington St
Suite 300
Boston, MA 02116-3988   617-848-7500
                                 800-852-8024
                           FAX: 617-944-7273
                        www.home.pearsonhighered.com

Bill Barke, CEO
Janet W. Lerner, Co-Author
Barbara Lowenthal, Co-Author
Explores ways of providing preschool children with special needs and their families with a learning environment that will help them develop and learn. Emphasizes the needs of preschoolers age three to six and provides information to teachers and others who work with young children in all settings. Current models of curricula, which incorporate new features from research and practical expreiences with children who have special needs, are described and discussed. *$59.00*
336 pages cloth
ISBN 0-205358-79-9

2398 Preventing Academic Failure - Teachers Handbook
Educators Publishing Service
625 Mount Auburn St
3rd Fl
Cambridge, MA 02138-3039   617-547-6706
                                    800-225-5750
                              FAX: 617-547-0285
                              eps.schoolspecialty.com

The PAF Teacher Handbook is a detailed guide for using the PAF program. It includes ungraded multisensory curriculum coordinating Orton-Gillingham and Merrill Linguistic reading techniques for language disabled students. Resource offers lessons on teaching phonics, spelling and reading to reinforce the development of language skills. A separate handwriting program is available. *$67.25*
Paperback
ISBN 0-838852-71-8

2399 Preventing School Dropouts
Sage Publications
2455 Teller Road
Thousand Oaks, CA 91320   805-499-9774
                                    800-818-7243
                              FAX: 800-583-2665
                           books.claim@sagepub.com
                                  www.sagepub.com

Sara Miller McCune, Founder, Publisher, Chairperson
Blaise R Simqu, President/ CEO
Tracey A. Ozmina, Executive Vice President & Chief
For secondary teachers, special education and regular, who have difficulty teaching youth in their classes. Presented are 120 tactics, specific instructional techniques, for helping adolescents to stay in school. Each tactic is written in a format that includes five sections. *$38.00*
509 pages

2400 Prevocational Assessment
Exceptional Education
P.O.Box 15308
Seattle, WA 98115-308   206-262-9538
                          FAX: 475-486-4510

Jeff Stewart, Owner
Use the PACG to assess your students in nine areas (attendance and endurance, learning and behavior, communication skills, social skills, grooming and eating and toileting) covering 46 specific workshop experiences. *$12.00*
16 pages Complete Set
ISBN 1-87786-23-7

2401 Primary Special Needs and the National Curriculum
7625 Empire Drive
Florence, KN 41042-2919   800-634-4724
                           orders@taylorandfrancis.com

Ann Lewis, Author
This new edition of Ann Lewis's widely acclaimed text has been substantially revised and updated to take into account the recent revisions to the National Curriculum and the guidance of the Code of Practice.

2402 Progress Without Punishment: Approaches for Learners with Behavior Problems
Teachers College Press
1234 Amsterdam Ave
New York, NY 10027-6602   212-678-3929
                                    800-575-6566
                              FAX: 212-678-4149
                              tcpress@tc.columbia.edu
                           www.teacherscollegepress.com

Anne M. Donnellan, Author
In this volume, the authors argue against the use of punishment, and instead advocate the use of alternative intervention procedures. *$17.95*
184 pages Paperback
ISBN 0-807729-11-6

2403 Promoting Postsecondary Education for Students with Learning Disabilities
Sage Publications
2455 Teller Road
Thousand Oaks, CA 91320   805-499-9774
                                    800-818-7243
                              FAX: 800-583-2665
                           books.claim@sagepub.com
                                  www.sagepub.com

Sara Miller McCune, Founder, Publisher, Chairperson
Stan F. Shaw, Co-Author
Joan M. McGuire, Co-Author

Primarily designed for postsecondary service providers who are responsible for serving college students with learning disabilities. *$41.00*
440 pages

2404   Psychiatric Mental Health Nursing
Lippincott, Williams & Wilkins
227 S 6th St
Suite 227
Philadelphia, PA 19106-3713   215-521-8300
                                             800-777-2295
                                         FAX: 301-824-7390
J Lippincott, CEO
This text emphasizes and contrasts the roles of the generalist nurse and the psychiatric nurse specialist. *$52.00*
1120 pages Illustrated

2405   Psychoeducational Assessment of Visually Impaired and Blind Students
Sage Publications
2455 Teller Road
Thousand Oaks, CA 91320   805-499-9774
                                             800-818-7243
                                         FAX: 800-583-2665
                                    books.claim@sagepub.com
                                          www.sagepub.com
Sara Miller McCune, Founder, Publisher, Chairperson
Blaise R Simqu, President/CEO
Tracey A. Ozmina, Executive Vice President & Chief
Professional reference book that addresses the problems specific to assessment of visually impaired and blind children. Of particular value to the practitioner are the extensive reviews of available tests, including ways to adapt those not designed for use with the visually handicapped. *$29.00*
140 pages Paperback
ISBN 0-890791-08-2

2406   Psychological and Social Impact of Illness and Disability
Springer Publishing
11 W 42nd St
15th Floor
New York, NY 10036-8002   212-431-4370
                                             877-687-7476
                                         FAX: 212-941-7842
                                       cs@springerpub.com
                                         www.springerpub.com
Dr. Ursula Springer, President
Ted Nardin, CEO
Ph.D. Orto Arthur E. Dell, Editor
The newest edition of Psychological and Social Impact of Illness and Disability continues the tradition of presenting a realistic perspective on life with disabilities and then improves upon its predecessors with the inclusion of illness as a major influence on client care needs. Further broadening the scope of this edition is the inclusion of personal perspectives and stories from those living with illness or disabilities. These stories offer a look into what it is like to cope with these issues.

2407   Reading and Deafness
Sage Publications
2455 Teller Road
Thousand Oaks, CA 91320   805-499-9774
                                             800-818-7243
                                         FAX: 800-583-2665
                                    books.claim@sagepub.com
                                          www.sagepub.com
Sara Miller McCune, Founder, Publisher, Chairperson
Beverly J Trezek, Co-Author
Peter V. Paul, Co-Author
Three areas are looked at in this book: deaf children's prereading development of real-world knowledge, cognitive abilities and linguistic skills. *$39.00*
422 pages

2408   Readings on Research in Stuttering
Longman Publishing Group
1 Penn Plaza
Suite 2222
New York, NY 10119   646-556-8401
                                         FAX: 646-556-8415
                                         coffee@rothfos.com
                                          www.rothfos.com
Dan Dwyer, CEO
Thomas Minogue, CFO
Maria Tanpinco-Queyquep, Traffic Manager
Collection of the key journal articles published on stuttering over the past decade, addressing trends in recent research in the field.
231 pages Paperback
ISBN 0-801304-10-5

2409   Recreation Activities for the Elderly
Springer Publishing Company
11 W 42nd St
15th Floor
New York, NY 10036-8002   212-431-4370
                                             877-687-7476
                                         FAX: 212-941-7842
                                       cs@springerpub.com
                                         www.springerpub.com
Dr. Ursula Springer, President
Ted Nardin, CEO
James C. Costello, Vice President, Journal Publishi
Included in this volume are simple crafts that utilize easily obtainable, inexpensive materials, hobbies focusing on collections, nature, and the arts' and games emphasizing both mental and physical activity. *$23.95*
240 pages Softcover
ISBN 0-82616 -30-1

2410   Reference Manual for Communicative Sciences and Disorders
Pro- Ed Publications
8700 Shoal Creek Blvd
Austin, TX 78757-6897   512-451-3246
                                             800-897-3202
                                         FAX: 512-451-8542
                                          info@proedinc.com
                                           www.proedinc.com
Raymond D. Kent, Author
An indispensable guide to standards and values essential in the assessment of communication disorders. *$54.00*
393 pages

2411   Rehabilitation Interventions for the Institutionalized Elderly
Haworth Press
711 Third Avenue
Floor 8th
New York, NY 10017   212-216-7800
                                             800-354-1420
                                         FAX: 212-564-7854
                                 subscriptions@tandf.co.uk
Derek Mapp, Non-Executive Chairman
Roger Horton, CEO
Emma Blaney, Group HR Director - Head of Corporate Responsibility
Gerontology professionals offer suggestions to enrich the quality of rehabilitation services offered to the institutionalized elderly. This volume examines up to the minute ideas, some that would have been unlikely even a few years ago, that focus exclusively on rehabilitation services for the institutionalized elderly. Journal publications formerly published by Haworth Press are now listed on the Taylor & Franc *$44.95*
77 pages Hardcover
ISBN 0-866568-33-6

2412 **Rehabilitation Nursing for the Neurological Patient**
Springer Publishing Company
11 W 42nd St
15th Fl
New York, NY 10036-8002

212-431-4370
877-687-7476
FAX: 212-941-7842
cs@springerpub.com
www.springerpub.com

Ted Nardin, Chief Executive Officer
Jason Roth, Vice President, Sales & Marketing
Kathy Weiss, Director, Sales
Reviews the physiology, pathophysiology, & nursing management of problems frequently encountered in neuro-rehabilitation and reviews the pathphysiology of specific disabilities & the related nursing interventions. *$32.95*
229 pages Hardcover 1992
ISBN 0-826176-60-7

2413 **Rehabilitation Resource Manual: VISION**
Resources for Rehabilitation
22 Bonad Rd
Winchester, MA 01890-1302

781-368-9094
FAX: 781-368-9096
info@rfr.org
www.rfr.org

Marshall E. Flax, MS, Author
A desk reference that enables service providers, librarians and others to make effective referrals. Includes guidelines on establishing self-help groups, information on research and service organizations, and chapters on assistive technology, for special population groups and by eye condition. *$44.95*
Biennial

2414 **Rehabilitation Technology**
CRC Press
6000 Broken Sound Pkwy NW
Ste 300
Boca Raton, FL 33487

800-634-7064
FAX: 800-374-3401
orders@crcpress.com
www.crcpress.com

Glenn E. Hedman, Author
Learn how the use of technological devices can enhance the lives of disabled children. Informs physical therapists, occupational therapists, and rehabilitation technologists about the devices that are available today and provides important background information on these devices. CRC Press is part of the Taylor & Francis Group. *$39.95*
173 pages Hardcover 1990
ISBN 1-560240-33-4

2415 **Report Writing in Assessment and Evaluation**
Stout Vocational Rehab Institute
University of Wisconsin-Stout
712 South Broadway
Menomonie, WI 54751

715-232-1478
FAX: 715-232-2356
giffordj@uwstout.edu
www.uwstout.edu

Charles W. Sorensen, Chancellor
Judy Gifford, Director
Stephen W. Thomas, Author
This examines questions of who are you writing for and what does the referral source want. Defines characteristics of good reports, common problems, writing in different settings, types of reports, getting ready to write, and writing prescriptive recommendations. *$17.75*
188 pages Softcover

2416 **Resource Room, The**
State University of New York Press
22 Corporate Woods Boulevard
3rd Floor
Albany, NY 12210-2314

518-472-5000
866-430-7869
FAX: 518-472-5038
info@sunypress.edu
www.sunypress.edu

Barry Edwards McNamara, Author

Provides teachers and administrators with helpful, practical information and explores the role of the resource room teacher as it relates to three major functions: assessment, instruction and consultation. It will also assist supervisors and administrators in evaluating their resource programs. *$28.95*
148 pages Paperback
ISBN 0-887069-84-0

2417 **Resources for Rehabilitation**
22 Bonad Rd
Winchester, MA 01890-1302

781-368-9094
FAX: 781-368-9096
info@rfr.org
www.rfr.org

Provides training and information to professionals and the public about disabilities and resources available to help. Publishes resource guides, professional publications and patient/client educational materials. Conducts custom designed training programs and workshops.

2418 **Restructuring High Schools for All Students: Taking Inclusion to the Next Level**
Brookes Publishing
PO Box 10624
Baltimore, MD 21285-0624

410-337-9580
800-638-3775
FAX: 410-337-8539
custserv@brookespublishing.com
www.brookespublishing.com

Paul H. Brookes, Chairman
Jeffrey D. Brookes, President
Melissa A. Behm, ExecutiveVice President
Details the process of creating an inclusive, collaborate community of learners and teachers at the secondary level. *$29.95*
304 pages Paperback
ISBN 1-557663-13-0

2419 **Restructuring for Caring and Effective Education: Administrative Guide**
Brookes Publishing
PO Box 10624
Baltimore, MD 21285-0624

410-337-9580
800-638-3775
FAX: 410-337-8539
custserv@brookespublishing.com
www.brookespublishing.com

Paul H. Brookes, Chairman
Jeffrey D. Brookes, President
Melissa A. Behm, ExecutiveVice President
In this empowering book, leading general and special education schools reform experts synthesize the major school restructuring initiatives and describe the processes and rationale for changing the organizational structure and instructional practices of schools. *$29.00*
384 pages Paperback
ISBN 1-55766-91-3

2420 **Scoffolding Student Learning**
Brookline Books
8 Trumbull Rd
Suite B-001
Northampton, MA 01060

413-584-0184
800-666-2665
FAX: 413-584-6184
brbooks@yahoo.com
www.brooklinebooks.com

Paul H. Brookes, Chairman
Jeffrey D. Brookes, President
Melissa A. Behm, ExecutiveVice President
Collection of papers on the theory and practice of scoffolding—an interactive style of instructions that helps students develop more powerful thinking tools. *$21.95*
180 pages Paperback
ISBN 1-571290-36-2

2421 **Selective Nontreatment of Handicapped**
Oxford University Press
2001 Evans Rd
Cary, NC 27513-2009 919-677-0977
800-445-9714
FAX: 919-677-1303
custserv.us@oup.com
www.global.oup.com

Lesa Moran Owen, Library Sales Operations Manager
Rebecca Seger, Director, Institutional Sales, Americas
Lenny Allen, Director, Institutional Accounts
Information on selective nontreatment of handicapped newborns, moral dilemmas in neonatal medicine. *$17.95*
304 pages Paperback

2422 **Semiotics and Dis/ability: Interogating Categories of Difference**
State University of New York Press
22 Corporate Woods Boulevard
3rd Floor
Albany, NY 12210-2314 518-472-5000
866-430-7869
FAX: 518-472-5038
info@sunypress.edu
www.sunypress.edu

James Peltz, Associate Director
Linda Rogers, Editor
Examines the ways the words disability and difference and socially and culturally constructed. *$25.95*
265 pages Paperback 1990
ISBN 0-791449-06-6

2423 **Service Coordination for Early Intervention: Parents and Friends**
Brookline Books
8 Trumbull Rd
Suite B-001
Northampton, MA 01060 413-584-0184
800-666-2665
FAX: 413-584-6184
brbooks@yahoo.com
www.brooklinebooks.com

Deborah D. Hatton, Co-Author
R. A. McWilliam, Co-Author
P. J. Winton, Co-Author
This book helps administrators and professionals to structure early intervention and ongoing services so that professionals work collaboratively with parents to promote the health, well being and development of children with special needs. *$19.95*
110 pages Paperback
ISBN 0-91479 -91-3

2424 **Services for the Seriously Mentally Ill: A Survey of Mental Health Centers**
Nat'l Council for Community Behavioral Healthcare
12300 Twinbrook Pkwy
Ste 320
Rockville, MD 20852-1606 301-984-6200
FAX: 301-881-7159

Linda Rosenberg, CEO
Dale K Klatzker, Board Chair
This ground-breaking report documents what administrators and practitioners have maintained for many years: community mental health organizations devote a significant percentage of the human and financial resources to serving the seriously mentally ill. *$30.00*

2425 **Sexuality and Disability**
Springer Publishing
11 W 42nd St
15th Fl
New York, NY 10036-8002 212-431-4370
FAX: 212-460-1575
www.springer.com

Sigmund Hough, Editor-in-Chief
A journal devoted to the psychological and medical aspects of sexuality in rehabilitation and community settings. The journal features original scholarly articles that address the psychological and medical aspects of sexuality in the field of rehabilitation, case studies, clinical practice reports, and guidelines for clinical practice.
Quarterly

2426 **Shop Talk**
PO Box 7886
Champaign, IL 61826-9177 217-352-3273
800-519-2707
FAX: 217-352-1221
rp@researchpress.com
www.researchpress.com

Robert W. Parkinson, Founder
Philip Roth, Author

2427 **Signed English Schoolbook**
Gallaudet University Press
800 Florida Ave NE
Washington, DC 20002-3600 202-651-5488
800-451-1073
FAX: 202-651-5489
TTY: 888-630-9347
clerc.center@gallaudet.edu
www.gupress.gallaudet.edu

Harry Bornstein, Co-Author
Karen L. Saulnier, Co-Author
Dr. T Alan Hurwitz, President
The Signed English Schoolbook provides vocabulary for teachers and others who serve school-age children and adolescents and covers the full range of school activities. *$13.95*
184 pages Softcover

2428 **Social Skills for Students With Autism Spectrum Disorders and Other Developmental Disorders**
Council for Exceptional Children
3100 Clarendon Blvd.
Suite 600
Arlington, VA 22201-5332 888-232-7733
TTY:866-915-5000
service@exceptionalchildren.org
www.exceptionalchildren.org

Laurence R. Sargent, Co-Author
Toni Cook, Co-Author
Darlene E. Perner, Co-Author
A book teaching children to understand their own behaviours. *$24.95*

2429 **Social Studies: Detecting and Correcting Special Needs**
Allyn & Bacon
75 Arlington St
Suite 300
Boston, MA 02116-3988 617-848-7500
800-852-8024
FAX: 617-944-7273
www.home.pearsonhighered.com

Harry Bornst Barke, CEO
Nancy Forfyth, President
Lana J. Smith, Co-Author
Describes social studies and special needs for special learners.
180 pages
ISBN 0-205121-51-9

2430 **Social and Emotional Development of Exceptional Students: Handicapped**
Charles C. Thomas
2600 S First St
Springfield, IL 62704-4730 217-789-8980
800-258-8980
FAX: 217-789-9130
books@ccthomas.com
www.ccthomas.com

Michael P. Thomas, President
Carroll J. Jones, Author
Sixteen years after the passage of P.L. 94-142, the dream of special educators to educate the handicapped and nonhandicapped children and youth together resulting in increased academic gains and age-appropriate school skills for handicapped children and youth has not yet materialized. This book helps eliminate an existing void by providing teachers with understandable information regarding the social and emotional development of

exceptional students. Also in cloth at $41.95 (ISBN# 0-398-05781-8) *$29.95*
218 pages Softcover
ISBN 0-398061-94-7

2431   Special Education Today
LifeWay Christian Resources Southern Baptist Conv.
One LifeWay Plaza
Nashville, TN 37234   615-251-2000
                                               800-458-2772
                                          FAX: 615-532-9412
                                             www.lifeway.com

Thom S. Rainer, President/CEO
Brad Waggoner, Executive Vice President
Eric Geiger, Vice President, Church Resources Division
This unique quarterly publications ministers to people with special education needs and to their families, the church, and other caregivers. It offers a variety of helps and encouragement, including: What's working in churches, Suggestions for adapting teaching techniques, inspirational stories about people who have disabilities, Parenting and family issues, Ideas for reaching, witnessing, worship, and recreation. *$4.25*
36 pages Quarterly

2432   Special Education for Today
Allyn & Bacon
75 Arlington St
Suite 300
Boston, MA 02116-3988   617-848-7500
                                               800-852-8024
                                          FAX: 617-944-7273
                                  www.home.pearsonhighered.com

See search r Barke, CEO
Michael S. Rosenberg, Co-Author
David L. Westling, Co-Author
An undergraduate introduction to special education covering all major areas of exceptionality. Contains pedagogical features designed to make the book accessible to the undergraduate.
576 pages hardcover
ISBN 0-138264-53-8

2433   Speech and the Hearing-Impaired Child
Alexander Graham Bell Association
3417 Volta Pl NW
Washington, DC 20007-2737   202-337-5220
                                               866-337-5220
                                          FAX: 202-337-8314
                                          TTY: 202-337-5221
                                             info@agbell.org
                         www.listeningandspokenlanguage.org
Meredith K. Sugar, Esq. (OH), President
Ted A. Meyer, M.D., Ph.D, President-Elect/Secretary-Treasurer
Emilio Alonso-Mendoza, Chief Executive Officer
This textbook for professionals deals with basic theoretical issues in the acquisition of speech and the form of language (phonetics and phonology) in children with hearing losses. It provides a systematic framework to develop and evaluate speech target behaviors and their underlying subskills. *$29.95*
402 pages Paperback

2434   Speech-Language Pathology and Audiology: An Introduction
McGraw-Hill School Publishing
PO Box 182604
Columbus, OH 43218   877-833-5524
                                               800-338-3987
                                          FAX: 609-308-4480
                            customer.service@mheducation.com
                                          www.mcgraw-hill.com
David Levin, President/Chief Executive Officer
David Stafford, Senior Vice President/General Counsel
Maryellen Valaitis, Senior Vice President Human Resources
Offers classroom-tested coverage of clinical objectives and functioning.
301 pages

2435   Spinal Cord Dysfunction
Oxford University Press
2001 Evans Rd
Cary, NC 27513-2009   919-677-0977
                                               800-451-7556
                                          FAX: 919-677-1303
                                          humanres@oup-usa.org
Lesa Moran Owen, Library Sales Operations Manager
Rebecca Seger, Director, Institutional Sales, Americas
Lenny Allen, Director, Institutional Accounts
Offers information on restoration of function after spinal cord damage as seen from the point of view of identification of impaired or absent function in the nerve cells and processes which survive after the initial insult, intact but with impaired functions. *$95.00*
368 pages

2436   Steps to Success: Scope & Sequence for Skill Development
15619 Premiere Drive
Suite 101
Tampa, FL 33624   850-363-9909
                                          FAX: 480-393-4331
             accounting@successforkidswithhearingloss.com
                           successforkidswithhearinglo ss.com
Lynne H. Price, Author
Steps to Success is a curriculum for students who are deaf or hard of hearing in grades kindergarten through 12.

2437   Strategies for Teaching Learners with Special Needs
McGraw-Hill School Publishing
PO Box 182604
Columbus, OH 43218   877-833-5524
                                               800-338-3987
                                          FAX: 609-308-4480
                            customer.service@mheducation.com
                                          www.mcgraw-hill.com
David Levin, President/Chief Executive Officer
David Stafford, Senior Vice President/General Counsel
Maryellen Valaitis, Senior Vice President Human Resources
This is a text that helps special educators develop the full range of teaching competencies needed to be effective.
560 pages

2438   Strategies for Teaching Students with Learning and Behavior Problems
Allyn & Bacon
75 Arlington St
Suite 300
Boston, MA 02116-3988   617-848-7500
                                               800-852-8024
                                          FAX: 617-944-7273
                                  www.home.pearsonhighered.com
Bill Barke, CEO
Nancy Forfyth, President
Sharon R. Vaughn, Co-Author
Provides descriptions of methods and strategies for teaching students with learning and behvior problems, managing professional roles, and collaborating with families, professionals, and paraprofessionals.
544 pages
ISBN 0-205113-89-3

2439   Students with Acquired Brain Injury: The School's Response
Brookes Publishing
PO Box 10624
Baltimore, MD 21285-0624   410-337-9580
                                               800-638-3775
                                          FAX: 410-337-8539
                            custserv@brookespublishing.com
                                  www.brookespublishing.com
Ann Glang, Editor
Bonnie Todis, Editor
Paul H. Brooks, Chairman of the Board
This book is designed for school professionals and describes a range of issues that this population faces and presents proven means of addressing them in ways that benefit all students. Included topics are hospital-to-school transitions, effective assessment strategies, model programs in public schools, interventions

to assist classroom teachers, and ways to involve family members in the educational program. *$29.95*
424 pages Paperback
ISBN 1-55766 -85-1

2440 Students with Mild Disabilities in the Secondary School
Longman Group
75 Arlington St
Suite 300
New York, NY 10036-2601   212-782-3300
                             800-852-8024
                   www.home.pearsonhighered.com

William Hitchings, Co-Author
Michael Horvath, Co-Author
Bonnie Schmalle, Co-Author
Provides methods and strategies for curriculum delivery to students with mild disabilities at the secondary school level.
2313G pages Paperback
ISBN 0-801301-66-1

2441 Supporting and Strengthening Families
Brookline Books
8 Trumbull Rd
Suite B-001
Northampton, MA 01060   413-584-0184
                          800-666-2665
                          FAX: 413-584-6184
                          brbooks@yahoo.com
                          www.brooklinebooks.com

Carl J Dunst, Author
A collection of papers addressing the theory, methods, strategies, and practices involved in adopting an empowerment and family-centered resources approach to supporting families and strengthening individual and family functioning. *$30.00*
252 pages Paperback
ISBN 0-91479 -94-8

2442 TESTS
Slosson Educational Publications
538 Buffalo rd
PO Box 280
East Aurora, NY 14052   716-652-0930
                          888-756-7766
                          FAX: 800-665-3840
                          slossonprep@gmail.com
                          www.slosson.com

Steven W. Slosson, President
Dr. Georgina Moynihan, Office Personnel
Slosson Educational Publications, Inc. offers educators an extensive selection of testing products, along with books on autism. ADED and other special needs materials. Our catalog includes 30 pages of speech-language testing and language rehabilitation products. The behavioral conduct. Special needs section includes checklist and scales on aberrant/disruptive behavior, tapes on ADD, as well as products for dyslexia and remediation of reversals.

2443 Teacher's Guide to Including Students with Disabilities in Regular Physical Education
Brookes Publishing
PO Box 10624
Baltimore, MD 21285-0624   410-337-9580
                             800-638-3775
                             FAX: 410-337-8539
                             custserv@brookespublishing.com
                             www.brookespublishing.com

Martin E. Block, Author
Melissa A. Behm, Executive Vice President
Paul H. Brooks, Chairman of the Board
Provides simple and creative strategies for meaningfully including children with disabilities in regular physical education programs. *$39.00*
288 pages Paperback
ISBN 1-557661-56-1

2444 Teachers Working Together
Brookline Books
8 Trumbull Rd
Suite B-001
Northampton, MA 01060   413-584-0184
                          800-666-2665
                          FAX: 413-584-6184
                          brbooks@yahoo.com
                          www.brooklinebooks.com

Carol Davis, Co-Author
Alice Yang, Co-Author
This collection of papers describes collaboraborative efforts for such classroom settings as preschools, elementary, middle and high schools, for content area teaching and into the transition to work. Each chapter describes actual practice and analyzes what is required to accomplish this collaboration. *$19.95*
Paperback
ISBN 1-57139 -66-4

2445 Teachig Students with Special Needs in Inclusive Classrooms
SAGE Publications
2455 Teller Rd
Thousand Oaks, CA 91320   800-818-7243
                            FAX: 800-583-2665
                            orders@sagepub.com
                            us.sagepub.com

Diane P. Bryant, Author
Brian P. Bryant, Author
Deborah D. Smith, Author
Using the research-validated ADAPT framework, Teaching Students with Special Needs in Inclusive Classrooms helps future teachers determine how, when, and with whom to use proven academic and behavioral interventions to obtain the best outcomes for students with disabilities. This book will provide the skills and inspiration that teachers need to make a positive difference in the educational lives of struggling learners.

2446 Teaching Adults with Learning Disabilities
Krieger Publishing Company
1725 Krieger Drive
Malabar, FL 32902   321-724-9542
                      800-724-0025
                      FAX: 321-951-3671
                      info@krieger-publishing.com
                      www.krieger-publishing.com

Dale R. Jordan, Author
R Krieger, Owner
Designed to teach literacy providers and classroom instructors how to recognize specific learning disability (LD) patterns and block reading, spelling, writing and arithmetic skills in students of all ages. One of the major problems faced by literary providers is keeping low-skill adults involved in basic education programs long enough to increase their literacy skills to the level of success. Shows instructors in adult education how to modify teaching strategies. *$25.50*
160 pages
ISBN 0-894649-10-8

2447 Teaching Children With Autism in the General Classroom
Prufrock Press
PO Box 8813
Waco, TX 76714-8813   254-756-3337
                        800-998-2208
                        FAX: 254-756-3339
                        gbates@prufrock.com
                        www.prufrock.com

Joel McIntosh, Publisher & Marketing Director
Ginny Bates, Customer Service and Office Manager
Lacy Compton, Senior Editor
Provides an introduction to inclusionary practices that serve children with autism, giving teachers the practical advice they need to ensure each students receives the quality education he or she deserves. *$39.95*
350 pages Paperback
ISBN 1-593633-64-6

2448 **Teaching Disturbed and Disturbing Students: An Integrative Approach**
Sage Publications
2455 Teller Road
Thousand Oaks, CA 91320
805-499-9774
800-818-7243
FAX: 800-583-2665
books.claim@sagepub.com
www.sagepub.com

Sara Miller McCune, Founder, Publisher, Chairperson
Blaise R Simqu, President & CEO
Tracey A. Ozmina, Executive Vice President & Chief
Using an integrative approach, this text provides teachers with step-by-step details of how to implement and use the methods and theories discussed in each chapter. *$37.00*
465 pages

2449 **Teaching Every Child Every Day: Integrated Learning in Diverse Classrooms**
Brookline Books
8 Trumbull Rd
Suite B-001
Northampton, MA 01060
413-584-0184
800-666-2665
FAX: 413-584-6184
brbooks@yahoo.com
www.brooklinebooks.com

Karen R. Harris, Editor
Steve Graham, Editor
Don Deshler, Editor
Collection of articles addressing various issues in teaching to diverse classrooms—varied in need for special educational services, English proficiency, and socioeconomic and racial backgrounds. *$19.95*
224 pages Paperback
ISBN 0-57129-40-0

2450 **Teaching Infants and Preschoolers with Handicaps**
Mc Graw- Hill, School Publishing
PO Box 182604
Columbus, OH 43218
877-833-5524
800-338-3987
FAX: 609-308-4480
customer.service@mheducation.com
www.mcgraw-hill.com

David Levin, President/Chief Executive Officer
David Stafford, Senior Vice President/General Counsel
Maryellen Valaitis, Senior Vice President Human Resources
Builds a solid background in early childhood special education.
380 pages

2451 **Teaching Language-Disabled Children: A Communication/Games Intervention**
Brookline Books
8 Trumbull Rd
Ste B-001
Northampton, MA 01060
413-584-0184
800-666-2665
FAX: 413-584-6184
brbooks@yahoo.com
www.brooklinebks.com

Susan Conant, Author
Offers practitioners specific teaching methods for helping students play communication games. *$22.95*
185 pages Hardcover 1983
ISBN 0-914797-38-7

2452 **Teaching Learners with Mild Disabilities: Integrating Research and Practice**
Brooke Publishing
PO Box 10624
Baltimore, MD 21285-0624
410-337-9580
800-638-3775
FAX: 410-337-8539
custserv@brookespublishing.com
www.brookespublishing.com

Ruth Lyn Meese, Author
Melissa A. Behm, Executive Vice President
Paul H. Brooks, Chairman of the Board

The authors illustrate interactions among regular teachers, special education teachers and students with mild disabilities through the use of hypothetical case studies of students and teachers.
496 pages Paperbound
ISBN 0-53421-02-0

2453 **Teaching Mathematics to Students with Learning Disabilities**
Sage Publications
2455 Teller Road
Thousand Oaks, CA 91320
805-499-9774
800-818-7243
FAX: 800-583-2665
www.sagepub.com

Sara Miller McCune, Founder, Publisher, Chairperson
Blaise R Simqu, President & CEO
Nancy S. Bley, Co-Author
New trends in school mathematics have surfaced in the teaching world. Problem-solving, estimation and the use of computers are receiving considerably greater emphasis than in the past and these areas are included in the new text. *$38.00*
486 pages Paperback

2454 **Teaching Mildly and Moderately Handicapped Students**
Allyn & Bacon
75 Arlington St
Suite 300
Boston, MA 02116-3988
617-848-7500
800-852-8024
FAX: 617-944-7273
www.home.pearsonhighered.com

Bill Barke, CEO
Nancy Forfyth, President
B. R. Gearheart, Author
A cross-categorical text providing teaching ideas and techniques. Focuses on the theme of learning as a constructive process in which the learner interacts with the environment, constructing new systems of knowledge, Behavioral techniques and research are also presented.
hardcover
ISBN 0-138939-00-4

2455 **Teaching Reading to Children with Down Syndrome: A Guide for Parents and Teachers**
Woodbine House
6510 Bells Mill Rd
Bethesda, MD 20817-1636
301-897-3570
800-843-7323
FAX: 301-897-5838
info@woodbinehouse.com
www.woodbinehouse.com

Irvin Shapell, Publisher
Patricia Logan Oelwein, Author
Beth Binns, Special Marketing Manage
Guide includes lessons customized to meet the unique interests and learning style of each child. *$16.95*
371 pages Paperback
ISBN 0-933149-55-7

2456 **Teaching Reading to Disabled and Handicapped Learners**
Charles C. Thomas
2600 S First St
Springfield, IL 62704-4730
217-789-8980
800-258-8980
FAX: 217-789-9130
books@ccthomas.com
www.ccthomas.com

Michael P. Thomas, President
Freddie W. Litton, Author
Harold D. Love, Author
Designed as a text for undergraduate and graduate students, this resource aims to help the many children, adolescents, and adults who encounter difficulty with reading. It guides prospective and present special education teachers in assisting and teaching handicapped learners to read. The text integrates traditional methods

with newer perspectives to provide and effective reading program in special education. *$43.95*
252 pages Paperback 1996
ISBN 0-398062-48-X

2457 Teaching Reading to Handicapped Children
Love Publishing Company
9101 E Kenyon Ave
Suite 2200
Denver, CO 80237-1854   303-221-7333
                                    FAX: 303-221-7444
                                    lpc@lovepublishing.com
                                    www.lovepublishing.com

Charles H. Hargis, Author
The author covers skills teaching through letter sound association, word identification, synthetic and analytic methods and others, plus testing and assessment. *$24.95*
ISBN 0-89108 -13-5

2458 Teaching Self-Determination to Students with Disabilities
Brookes Publishing
PO Box 10624
Baltimore, MD 21285-0624   410-337-9580
                                    800-638-3775
                                    FAX: 410-337-8539
                                    custserv@brookespublishing.com
                                    www.brookespublishing.com

Michael L. Wehmeyer, Co-Author
Martin Agran, Co-Author
Paul H. Brooks, Chairman of the Board
Basic skills for successful transition. This teacher-friendly source will help educators prepare students with disabilities with the specific skills they need for a satisfactory, self-directed life once they leave school. *$34.95*
384 pages Paperback
ISBN 1-55766 -02-5

2459 Teaching Students with Learning Problems
McGraw-Hill School Publishing
PO Box 182604
Columbus, OH 43218   877-833-5524
                                    800-338-3987
                                    FAX: 609-308-4480
                                    customer.service@mheducation.com
                                    www.mcgraw-hill.com

David Levin, President/Chief Executive Officer
David Stafford, Senior Vice President/General Counsel
Maryellen Valaitis, Senior Vice President Human Resources
Expanded coverage of learning strategies, generalization training, self-monitoring techniques, and techniques for increasing the time students spend on academic tasks.
608 pages

2460 Teaching Students with Learning and Behavior Problems
Sage Publications
2455 Teller Road
Thousand Oaks, CA 91320   805-499-9774
                                    800-818-7243
                                    FAX: 800-583-2665
                                    www.sagepub.com

Sara Miller McCune, Founder, Publisher, Chairperson
Blaise R Simqu, President & CEO
Sharon R. Vaughn, Co-Author
$65.00
444 pages Paperback
ISBN 0-890799-28-4

2461 Teaching Students with Mild and Moderate Learning Problems
Allyn & Bacon Longman College Faculty
75 Arlington St
Suite 300
Boston, MA 02116-3988   617-367-0025
                                    800-852-8024
                                    FAX: 617-367-2155
                                    www.home.pearsonhighered.com

Bill Barke, CEO
John Langone, Author
Kevin Stone, Vice President

Provides teachers with skills for assisting students with mild to moderate handicaps in making successful transitions in school and community environments.
496 pages
ISBN 0-205123-62-7

2462 Teaching Students with Moderate/Severe Disabilities, Including Autism
Charles C. Thomas
2600 S First St
Springfield, IL 62704-4730   217-789-8980
                                    800-258-8980
                                    FAX: 217-789-9130
                                    books@ccthomas.com
                                    www.ccthomas.com

Michael P. Thomas, President
Elva Duran, Author
This resource and guide was written to help teachers, parents, and other caregivers provide the best educational opportunities for their students with moderate and severe disabilities. The author addresses functional language and other language intervention strategies, vocational training, community based instruction, transition and postsecondary programming, the adolescent student with autism, students with multiple disabilities, parent and family issues, and legal concerns. *$58.95*
416 pages Paperback
ISBN 0-398067-01-5

2463 Teaching Students with Special Needs in Inclusive Settings
Allyn & Bacon
75 Arlington St
Suite 300
Boston, MA 02116-3988   617-848-7500
                                    800-852-8024
                                    FAX: 617-944-7273

Tom E.C. Smith, Co-Author
Edward A. Polloway, Co-Author
James Patton, Co-Author
This text is intended to be a survey text providing practical guidance to general education teachers. It will help them to meet the diverse needs of students with disabilities.
544 pages
ISBN 0-20527 -16-6

2464 Teaching Young Children to Read
Brookline Books
8 Trumbull Rd
Suite B-001
Northampton, MA 01060   413-584-0184
                                    800-666-2665
                                    FAX: 413-584-6184
                                    brbooks@yahoo.com
                                    www.brooklinebooks.com

Dolores Durkin, Author
John P.
Detailed instructions on teaching reading to preschoolers. Gradually develops full fluency. *$16.95*
192 pages Paperback
ISBN 0-57129 -48-6

2465 Teaching the Bilingual Special Education Student
Ablex Publishing Corporation
P.O.Box 811
Stamford, CT 06904-811   FAX: 201-767-6717
This book focuses on teaching those students who are bilingual, handicapped and in need of special instruction. It responds to the complex and practical issues of teaching these students in an effective way.
ISBN 0-89391 -23-4

2466 **Teaching the Learning Disabled Adolescent: Strategies and Methods**
Love Publishing Company
9101 E Kenyon Ave
Ste 2200
Denver, CO 80237-1813
303-221-7333
FAX: 303-221-7444
lpc@lovepublishing.com
www.lovepublishing.com
Gordon R. Alley, Author
This book gives expert strategies and methods for teaching learning disabled adolescents how, rather than what, to learn. *$39.95*
360 pages Hardcover 1979
ISBN 0-891080-94-5

2467 **Technology and Handicapped People**
Springer Publishing Company
11 W 42nd St
15th Floor
New York, NY 10036-8002
212-431-4370
877-687-7476
FAX: 212-941-7842
cs@springerpub.com
www.springerpub.com
Dr. Ursula Springer, President
Ted Nardin, CEO
James C. Costello, Vice President, Journal Publishing
Important information for concerned professionals about new rehabilitation techniques and treatments for handicapped people.
$29.95
224 pages Hardcover
ISBN 0-82614-10-8

2468 **Textbooks and the Student Who Can't Read Them: A Guide for Teaching Content**
Brookline Books
8 Trumbull Rd
Suite B-001
Northampton, MA 01060
413-584-0184
800-666-2665
FAX: 413-584-6184
brbooks@yahoo.com
www.brooklinebooks.com
Based on a careful analysis of 10 textbook programs, the author concisely and sensibly indicate s the procedures that facilitate teachers' use of regular grade level textbooks with low-reading students. *$21.95*
Paperback
ISBN 0-91479-57-3

2469 **The Education of Children with Acquired Brain Injury**
David Fulton Publishers (Routledge)
711 Third Ave
New York, NY 10017
212-216-7800
FAX: 212-564-7854
orders@taylorandfrancis.com
www.routledge.com
Sue Walker, Author
Beth Wicks, Author
Teachers have to be aware of their pupils' special educational needs. Find out what an acquired brain injury is and how to maximize learning opportunities for those with the condition with this book.
128 pages

2470 **The Fundamentals of Special Education: A Practical Guide for Every Teacher**
Corwin Press Inc.
2455 Teller Rd
Thousand Oaks, CA 91320
805-499-9734
800-233-9936
FAX: 805-499-5323
order@corwin.com
us.corwin.com
Bob Algozzine, Author
Jim Ysseldyke, Author
This guide highlights major concepts in special education-from disability categories, identification issues, and IEPs to appropri-

ate learning environments and the roles general and special educators play.
104 pages

2471 **The K&W Guide to Colleges for Studentswith Learning Disablties (13th Edition)**
The Princeton Review - Penguin Random House
1745 Broadway
New York, NY 10019
212-782-9000
customerservice@penguinrandomhouse.com
www.penguinrandomhouse.com
An updated guide to the more than 900 colleges with programs for the learning disabled. *$31.99*
848 pages Paperback 1916
ISBN 1-101920-38-6

2472 **There's a Hearing Impaired Child in My Class**
Gallaudet University Bookstore
800 Florida Ave NE
Washington, DC 20002-3600
202-651-5000
800-451-1073
FAX: 202-651-5489
TTY: 888-630-9347
clerc.center@gallaudet.edu
Debra Nussbaum, Author
Dr. T Alan Hurwitz, President
Edward Bosso, Vice President for Administration
This complete package provides basic facts about deafness, practical strategies for teaching hearing impaired children, and the question-and-answer information for all students. *$16.95*
44 pages

2473 **Toward Effective Public School Program for Deaf Students**
Teachers College Press
525 W 120th St
New York, NY 10027-6605
212-678-3000
800-575-6566
FAX: 212-678-4149
webcomments@tc.columbia.edu
www.tc.columbia.edu
Susan H. Fuhrman, Ph.D., President of the College
Harvey Spector, Vice President for Finance and Administration
Suzanne M. Murphy, Vice President for Development and External Affairs
This book translates research and data into useable recommendations and possible courses of action for organizing effective public school programs for deaf students. *$22.95*
272 pages Paperback
ISBN 0-807731-59-5

2474 **Treating Adults with Physical Disabilities: Access and Communication**
World Institute on Disability
3075 Adeline St.
Suite 155
Berkeley, CA 94703
510-225-6400
FAX: 510-225-0477
wid@wid.org
www.wid.org
Marcie Roth, Executive Director & Chief Executive Officer
Kat Zigmont, Senior Director, Operations & Deputy Director
Reggie Johnson, Senior Director, Marketing & Communications
A training curriculum for medical professionals who want to improve the quality of care for people with disabilities and chronic illnesses. Also covers architectural, communication, attitudinal and economic policy barriers to quality health care and specific skills to increase good communication and rapport.

2475 **Treating Cerebral Palsy for Clinicians by Clinicians**
Sage Publications
2455 Teller Road
Thousand Oaks, CA 91320
805-499-9774
800-818-7243
FAX: 800-583-2665
www.sagepub.com
Sara Miller McCune, Founder, Publisher, Chairperson
Blaise R Simqu, President & CEO
Tracey A. Ozmina, Executive Vice President & Chief

A clinical manual for professionals beginning to work with persons who have cerebral palsy. *$31.00*
312 pages

2476 Treating Disordered Speech Motor Control
Sage Publications
2455 Teller Road
Thousand Oaks, CA 91320   805-499-9774
                                 800-818-7243
                            FAX: 800-583-2665
                            www.sagepub.com
Sara Miller McCune, Founder, Publisher, Chairperson
Blaise R Simqu, President & CEO
Deanie Vogel, Author
This book about neuromotor disturbances of speech production is aimed at practicing professionals and advanced graduate students interested in the neuropathologies of communication. *$36.00*
410 pages

2477 Treating Families of Brain Injury Survivors
Springer Publishing Company
11 W 42nd St
15th Floor
New York, NY 10036-8002   212-431-4370
                                 877-687-7476
                            FAX: 212-941-7842
                            cs@springerpub.com
                            www.springerpub.com
Dr. Ursula Springer, President
Ted Nardin, CEO
James C. Costello, Vice President, Journal Publishi
Provides the mental health practitioner with a comprehensive program for helping families of head injury survivors cope with the change in their lives. Includes background on medical aspects of head injury, family structure functioning and special needs of various family members.
220 pages
ISBN 0-82616 -20-1

2478 Understanding and Teaching Emotionally Disturbed Children & Adolescents
Sage Publications
2455 Teller Road
Thousand Oaks, CA 91320   805-499-9774
                                 800-818-7243
                            FAX: 800-583-2665
                            www.sagepub.com
Sara Miller McCune, Founder, Publisher, Chairperson
Blaise R Simqu, President & CEO
Tracey A. Ozmina, Executive Vice President & Chief
The teacher's handbook provides information that will change misconceptions about children who are frequently labeled as emotionally disturbed. It also gives information about a wide variety of intervention methods and approaches for use in educational settings. *$41.00*
620 pages Hardover

2479 Using the Dictionary of Occupational Titles in Career Decision Making
Stout Vocational Rehab Institute
University of Wisconsin Stou
Menomonie, WI 54751   715-232-2470
                            FAX: 715-232-5008
                            luij@uwstout.edu
John Lui, Contact Person
This is a self-study manual for learning how to use the 1991 U.S. Department of Labor's Dictionary of Occupational Titles. It gives the DOT user a tool to understand the DOT and then put its information to work. Shows how to quickly obtain information about the work performed in 12,741 occupations listed and described in the DOT and the worker requirements for those occupations. *$24.00*
142 pages Softcover

2480 VBS Special Education Teaching Guide
Life Way Christian Resources Southern Baptist Conv
1 Lifeway Plz
Nashville, TN 37234-1001   615-251-2000
                            www.lifeway.com
Tom Hellam, VP of Executive Communications a
Thom Rainer, President & CEO
This book contains teaching plans for five bible study sessions with reproducible handouts for learners. The plans use multisensory, experiential-based learning activities designed for adults and older youth who have developmental disabilities. Suggestions for Bible learning, crafts, recreation, snacks and theme interpretation are included. Designed primarily for Vacation Bible School, but may be used in camp/retreat settings. *$9.95*
56 pages Yearly

2481 Vermont Interdependent Services Team Approach (VISTA)
Brookes Publishing
PO Box 10624
Baltimore, MD 21285-624   410-337-9580
                                 800-638-3775
                            FAX: 410-337-8539
                            custserv@brookespublishing.com
                            www.brookespublishing.com
Paul Kelly, National Textbook Sales Manager
Tracy Gray, Educational Sales Manager
Paul Brooks, President
A guide to coordinating educational support services. This manual enables IEP team members to fulfill the related services provisions of IDEA as they make effective support services decisions using a collaborative team approach. *$27.95*
176 pages Spiral bound
ISBN 1-55766 -30-4

2482 What School Counselors Need to Know
Council for Exceptional Children
3100 Clarendon Blvd.
Suite 600
Arlington, VA 22201-5332   888-232-7733
                            TTY:866-915-5000
                            service@exceptionalchildren.org
                            www.exceptionalchildren.org
Barbara E. Baditoi, Co-Author
Pamelia E. Brott, Co-Author
This book provides counselors (and school administrators) with essential information to make the most of their participation in providing special education services. *$25.95*

2483 When You Have a Visually Impaired Student in Your Classroom: A Guide for Teachers
American Foundation for the Blind
2 Penn Plaza
Suite1102
New York, NY 10121   212-502-7600
                                 800-232-5463
                            FAX: 888-545-8331
                            afbinfo@afb.net
                            afb.org
Carl Augusto, President
This guide provides information on students' abilities and needs, resources and educational team members, federal special education requirements, and technology materials used by students. *$9.95*
84 pages
ISBN 0-891283-93-5

2484 Working Bibliography on Behavioral and Emotional Disorders
Natl. Clearinghouse for Alcohol & Drug Information
1 Choke Cherry Road
Rockville, MD 20857   301-468-2600
                                 877-SAM-SA 7
                            FAX: 301-468-6433
Lizabeth J Foster, Librarian/Info. Resource Manager
Pamela S. Hyde, Administrator
NCADI is a service of the U.S. Substance Abuse and Mental Health Services Administration. As the national focal point for information on alcohol and other drugs, NCADI collects, prepares, classifies, and distributes information about alcohol, to-

bacco and other drugs, prevention strategies and materials, research, treatment, etc.
40 pages

2485 Working Together with Children and Families: Case Studies
Brookes Publishing Company
PO Box 10624
Baltimore, MD 21285-624
410-337-9580
800-638-3775
FAX: 410-337-8539
custerv@brookespublishing.com
www.brookespublishing.com
Paul Kelly, National Textbook Sales Manager
Tracy Gray, Educational Sales Manager
Paul Brooks, Owner
Early interventionists will be able to bridge the gap between theory and practice with this edited collection of case studies. *$23.00*
336 pages
ISBN 1-557661-23-5

2486 Working with Visually Impaired Young Students: A Curriculum Guide for 3 to 5 Year Olds
Charles C. Thomas
2600 S First St
Springfield, IL 62704-4730
217-789-8980
800-258-8980
FAX: 217-789-9130
books@ccthomas.com
www.ccthomas.com
Michael P. Thomas, President
Ellen Trief, Editor
The first step in the education process of a visually impaired child is the early identification and treatment by an eye care specialist. This book is geared to the age of birth through 3-years. Available in cloth, paperback and hardcover. *$42.95*
194 pages Paperback
ISBN 0-398068-75-2

Testing Resources

2487 ADD-SOI Center, The
2007 Cedar Avenue
Manhattan Beach, CA 90266
310-546-6500
FAX: 310-546-9068
ADDSOI@aol.com
www.addsoi.com
The ADD-SOI Center provides services and assessments for ADD (Attention Deficit Disorder), ADHD, and SOI at our Manhattan Beach, California facility.

2488 AEPS Child Progress Report: For Children Ages Birth to Three
Brookes Publishing
PO Box 10624
Baltimore, MD 21285-624
410-337-9580
800-638-3775
FAX: 410-337-8539
custserv@brookespublishing.com
www.brookespublishing.com
Paul Kelly, National Textbook Sales Manager
Tracy Gray, Educational Sales Manager
Paul Brooks, Owner
This chart helps monitor change by visually displaying current abilities, intervention targets, and child progress. In packages of 30. *$18.00*
6 pages Gate-fold
ISBN 1-55766 -65-0

2489 AEPS Data Recording Forms: For Children Ages Birth to Three
Brookes Publishing
PO Box 10624
Baltimore, MD 21285-624
410-337-9580
800-638-3775
FAX: 410-337-8539
custserv@brookespublishing.com
readplaylearn.com
Paul Brooks, Owner
Melissa Behm, Executive Vice President
These forms can be used by child development professionals on four separate occasions to pinpoint and then monitor a child's strengths and needs in the six key areas of skill development measured by the AEPS Test. Packages of 10. *$23.00*
36 pages Saddle-stiched
ISBN 1-55766 -97-2

2490 AEPS Measurement for Birth to Three Years
Brookes Publishing
PO Box 10624
Baltimore, MD 21285-624
410-337-9580
800-638-3775
FAX: 410-337-8539
custserv@brookespublishing.com
www.brookespublishing.com
Paul Kelly, National Textbook Sales Manager
Tracy Gray, Educational Sales Manager
Paul Brooks, Owner
This dynamic volume explains the Assessment, Evaluation and Programming System, provides the complete AEPS Test and parallel assessment/evaluation tools for families and includes the forms and plans needed for implementation. *$39.00*
352 pages

2491 AEPS Measurement for Three to Six Years
Brookes Publishing
PO Box 10624
Baltimore, MD 21285-624
410-337-9580
800-638-3775
FAX: 410-337-8539
custserv@brookespublishing.com
www.brookespublishing.com
Paul Kelly, National Textbook Sales Manager
Tracy Gray, Educational Sales Manager
Paul Brooks, Owner
Resources in early childhood, early intervention, inclusive and special education, developmental disabilities, learning disabilities, communication and language, behavior, and mental health. *$57.00*
400 pages Spiral-bound
ISBN 1-55766 -87-1

2492 AIR: Assessment of Interpersonal Relations
Sage Publications
2455 Teller Road
Thousand Oaks, CA 91320
805-499-0721
800-818-7243
FAX: 800-583-2665
info@sagepub.com
www.sagepub.com
Sara Miller McCune, Founder, Publisher, Chairperson
Blaise R Simqu, President & CEO
A thoroughly researched and standardized clinical instrument assessing the quality of adolescents' interpersonal relationships in a hierarchical fashion, including global relationship quality and relationship quality with three domains: Family, Social and Academic. *$89.00*

2493 ALST: Adolescent Language Screening Test
Sage Publications
2455 Teller Road
Thousand Oaks, CA 91320
805-499-0721
800-818-7243
FAX: 800-583-2665
info@sagepub.com
www.sagepub.com
Sara Miller McCune, Founder, Publisher, Chairperson
Blaise R Simqu, President & CEO

Provides speech/language pathologists and other interested professionals with a rapid thorough method for screening adolescents (ages 11-17). *$119.00*

2494 Adaptive Mainstreaming: A Primer for Teachers and Principals, 3rd Edition
Longman Publishing Group
1330 Avenue of the Americas
New York, NY 10019
212-641-2400
800-745-8489
www.pearson.com

Glen Moreno, Chairman
Marjorie Scardino, Chief Executive Officer
An introduction to education for handicapped and gifted students. Presents research-based rationales for teaching exceptional students in the least restrictive environment. Provides historical perspectives, offers realistic descriptions of prevailing practices in the field, and reviews trends and new directions.
366 pages Paperback
ISBN 0-582285-04-6

2495 Ages & Stages Questionnaires
Brookes Publishing
PO Box 10624
Baltimore, MD 21285-624
410-337-9580
800-638-3775
FAX: 410-337-8539
custserv@brookespublishing.com
www.brookespublishing.com

Paul Kelly, National Textbook Sales Manager
Tracy Gray, Educational Sales Manager
Paul Brooks, Owner
ASQ is an economical and field-tested system for identifying whether infants and young children may require further developmental evaluation and offers a screening and tracking program that helps early intervention professionals, service coordinators, and administrators maximize financial resources while promoting the health and growth of the children they serve. Set includes 11 color-coded, reproducible questionnaires, 11 reproducible, age appropriate scoring sheets. *$135.00*

2496 American College Testing Program
500 Act Drive
PO Box 168
Iowa City, IA 52243-168
319-337-1000
FAX: 319-339-3021
act.org

John Whitmore, CEO
Mark D Musik, President Emeritus
An independent, nonprofit organization that provides a variety of educational services to students and their parents, to high schools and colleges, and to professional associations and government agencies.

2497 Assessing Students with Special Needs
Longman Publishing Group
10 Bank Street
9th Floor
White Plains, NY 10606-1933
914-993-5000
www.ablongman.com

Joanne Dresner, President
Step-by-step guide to informal, classroom assessment of students with special needs.
174 pages Paperback
ISBN 0-801301-77-7

2498 Assessment Log & Developmental Progress Charts for the CCPSN
Brookes Publishing
P.O.Box 10624
Baltimore, MD 21285-624
410-337-9580
800-638-3775
FAX: 410-337-8539
custserv@brookespublishing.com
www.brookespublishing.com

Paul Kelly, National Textbook Sales Manager
Tracy Gray, Educational Sales Manager
Paul Brooks, Owner

This 28-page booklet allows readers to actually chart the ongoing progress of each preschool child. Available in packages of 10. *$22.00*
28 pages Saddle-stiched
ISBN 1-55766 -39-5

2499 Assessment of Learners with Special Needs
Allyn & Bacon
75 Arlinton Street
Ste 300
Boston, MA 2116-3988
617-848-7500
800-852-8024
FAX: 617-944-7273
www.ablongman.com

Bill Barke, CEO
Thomas Longman, Founder
The central goal of this book is to help teachers become sophisticated, informed test consumers in terms of choosing, using and interpreting commercially prepared tests for their special needs students.
508 pages Casebound
ISBN 0-205227-33-3

2500 Benchmark Measures
Educators Publishing Service
PO Box 9031
Cambridge, MA 2139
617-547-6706
800-225-5750
FAX: 888-440-2665
feedback@epsbooks.com
www.epsbooks.com

Charles H Heinle, VP
Alexandra S Bigelow, Author
Gunnar Voltz, President
Ungraded test containing three sequential levels that assess alphabet and dictionary skills, reading, handwriting and spelling, and correspond to the first three schedules of the Alphabetic Phonics curriculum. The tests can be used at any level to measure a student's general knowledge of phonics. *$64.40*
Kit

2501 Brain Clinic, The
19 West 34th Street
Penthouse
New York, NY 10001
212-268-8900
nurosvcs@aol.com
thebrainclinic.com

Dr. James Lawrence Thomas, Director
The brain clinic offers diagnosis and Treatment of ADD, Learning Disabilities, Migraines, and Traumatic Brain Injury.

2502 CREVT: Comprehensive Receptive and Expressive Vocabulary Test
Sage Publications
2455 Teller Road
Thousand Oaks, CA 91320
805-499-0721
800-818-7243
FAX: 800-583-2665
info@sagepub.com
www.sagepub.com

Sara Miller McCune, Founder, Publisher, Chairperson
Blaise R Simqu, President & CEO
A new, innovative, efficient measure of both receptive and expressive oral vocabulary. The CREVT has two subtests and is based on the most current theories of vocabulary development, suitable for ages 4 through 17. *$174.00*
Complete Kit

2503 Carolina Curriculum for Preschoolers with Special Needs
Brookes Publishing
P.O.Box 10624
Baltimore, MD 21285-624
410-337-9580
800-638-3775
FAX: 410-337-8539
custserv@brookespublishing.com
www.brookespublishing.com

Paul Kelly, National Textbook Sales Manager
Tracy Gray, Educational Sales Manager
Paul Brooks, Owner

This curriculum provides detailed teaching and assessment techniques, plus a sample 28-page Assessment Log that shows readers how to chart a child's individual progress. This guide is for children between 2 and 5 in their developmental stages who are considered at risk for developmental delay or who exhibit special needs. *$35.95*
352 pages Spiral-bound
ISBN 1-557660-32-8

2504   Center For Personal Development
405 North Wabash Ave.
Suite 208 & 1114
Chicago, IL 60611

312-755-7000
FAX: 312-755-7001
info@chicagotherapist.com
www.chicagotherapist.com

Steven Nakisher, Licensed Clinical Psychologist
Cara McCanse, Licensed Clinical Psychologist
Sarah Krcmarik, Staff Psychotherapist
The Center for Personal Development was founded in 1998 to provide a diverse range of high-quality mental health services.

2505   Center for Human Potential
525 East 100 South
Suite 120
Salt Lake City, UT 84102

801-483-2447
801-486-8705
www.c4hp.com

C. Brendan Hallett Psy.D., Clinical Director
Michael DeCaria, Ph.D., Licensed Clinical Psychologist
Annice Julian, Psy.D., Licensed Clinical Psychologist
Center for Human Potentialis a human services company that helps individuals, businesses and organizations reach their potential by achieving balance in the fundamental areas of life: Emotional, Physical, Mental, Spiritual and Financial. We offer individual, couples, and family counseling to help with a number of issues.

2506   Center for Neuropsychology, Learning & Development
1955 Pauline Blvd
Suite 100A
Ann Arbor, MI 48103

734-994-9466
FAX: 734-994-9465
www.cnld.org

Roger E. Lauer, Clinical Director
Jodene Goldenring Fine, Ph.D., Licensed Psychologist
CNLD was founded over 20 years ago to serve Southeast Michigan and the greater Ann Arbor community by providing quality mental health care for children, adolescents, adults and families.

2507   Center for Student Health and Counseling
1825 SW Broadway
Portland, OR 97201

503-725-3000
800-547-8887
FAX: 503-725-4882
askadm@pdx.edu
www.pdx.edu/shac/ldadhd

Portland State University's mission is to enhance the intellectual, social, cultural and economic qualities of urban life by providing access throughout the life span to a quality liberal education for undergraduates and an appropriate array of professional and graduate programs especially relevant to metropolitan areas.

2508   Children's Assessment Center, The
2500 Bolsover St.
Houston, TX 77005

713-986-3300
FAX: 713-986-3553
info@cac.hctx.net
cachouston.org

Brady E. Crosswell, Chairman
Gail Prather, President
Elaine Stolte, Executive Director
The Children's Assessment Center (CAC)provides a safe haven to sexually abused children and their families.

2509   Cognitive Solutions Learning Center
2409 N. Clybourn Ave.
Chicago, IL 60614

773-755-1775
FAX: 773-439-5499
info@helpforld.com
www.helpforld.com/index.php/about-us/

Dr. Ari Goldstein, Founder
Jason Almodovar, M.S.Ed., Office Manager
Cognitive Solution offers a broad range of services, including learning disability and attention deficit disorder assessment and remediation, executive functions training, and the latest neurofeedback technologies.

2510   DAYS: Depression and Anxiety in Youth Scale
Sage Publications
2455 Teller Road
Thousand Oaks, CA 91320

805-499-0721
800-818-7243
FAX: 805-376-9443
info@sagepub.com
www.sagepub.com

Sara Miller McCune, Founder, Publisher, Chairperson
Blaise R Simqu, President & CEO
A unique battery of three norm-references scales useful in identifying major depressive disorder and overanxious disorders in children and adolescents. *$129.00*
Complete Kit

2511   DOCS: Developmental Observation Checklist System
Pro- Ed Publications
8700 Shoal Creek Blvd
Austin, TX 78757-6897

512-451-3246
800-897-3202
FAX: 800-397-7633
general@proedinc.com
www.proedinc.com

Donald D Hammill, Owner
Courtney King, Marketing Coordinator
A three-part system for the assessment of very young children with respect to general development, adjustment behavior and parent stress and support. *$124.00*

2512   Dennis Developmental Center
1 Children's Way
Little Rock, AR 72202-3591

501-364-1100
TTY:501-364-1184
www.archildrens.org

Arkansas Children's Hospital (ACH) is the a pediatric medical center in Arkansas.

2513   Developmental Services Center
Therapeutic Nursery Program
4525 Lee St NE
Washington, DC 20019

202-388-3216
FAX: 202-576-8799

Alice Anderson
Offers assessment information and evaluation for developmentally delayed students.

2514   Frames of Reference for the Assessment of Learning Disabilities
Brookes Publishing
P.O.Box 10624
Baltimore, MD 21285-624

410-337-9580
800-638-3775
FAX: 410-337-8539
custserv@brookespublishing.com
www.brookespublishing.com

Paul Kelly, National Textbook Sales Manager
Tracy Gray, Educational Sales Manager
Paul Brooks, Owner
New views on measurement issues. Here you'll find an in=depth look at the fundamental concerns facing those who work with children with learning disabilities - assessment and identification. *$55.00*
672 pages Hardcover
ISBN 1-55766 -38-3

2515 How to Conduct an Assessment
FSSI
3905 Huntington Dr
Amarillo, TX 79109-4047   806-353-1114
                                 FAX: 806-353-1114

Ed Hammer, Owner
The Functional Skills Screening Inventory,this behavioral checklist allows for parents and professionals to observe critical behaviors in individuals with multiple disabilities (7 years to adult years).

2516 Inclusive & Heterogeneous Schooling: Assessment, Curriculum, and Instruction
Brookes Publishing
P.O.Box 10624
Baltimore, MD 21285-624   410-337-9580
                                 800-638-3775
                                 FAX: 410-337-8539
                                 custserv@brookespublishing.com
                                 www.brookespublishing.com

Paul Kelly, National Textbook Sales Manager
Tracy Gray, Educational Sales Manager
Paul Brooks, Owner
Presents methods for successfully restructuring classrooms to enable all students, particularly those with disabilities, to flourish. Provides specific strategies for assessment, collaboration, classroom management, and age-specific instruction. *$34.95*
448 pages Paperback
ISBN 1-557662-02-9

2517 Infant & Toddler Convection of Fairfield: Falls Church
Joseph Willard Health Center
3750 Old Lee Hwy
Fairfax, VA 22030-1806   703-246-7180
                                 FAX: 703-246-7307

Susan Sigler, Program Coordinator
Allan Phillips, Director Early Intervention
Offers assessments, evaluations and educational/therapeutic infant programs for parents infants and toddlers birth to age 3.
Sliding Scale

2518 K-BIT: Kaufman Brief Intelligence Test
AGS
Ste 1000
5910 Rice Creek Pkwy
Shoreview, MN 55126-5023   651-287-7220
                                 800-328-2560
                                 FAX: 800-471-8457
                                 agsmail@agsnet.com
                                 www.agsnet.com

Kevin Brueggeman, President
Robert Zaske, Market Manager
Quick and easy-to-use, KBIT assesses verbal and non-verbal abilities through two reliable subtests - vocabulary and matricies.
$124.95
Ages 4-90

2519 K-FAST: Kaufman Functional Academic Skills Test
AGS
Ste 1000
5910 Rice Creek Pkwy
Shoreview, MN 55126-5023   651-287-7220
                                 800-328-2560
                                 FAX: 800-471-8457
                                 agsmail@agsnet.com
                                 www.agsnet.com

Robert Zaske, Market Manager
Helps assess a person's capacity to function effectively in society regarding functional reading and math skills. *$99.95*
Ages 15-85+

2520 K-SEALS: Kaufman Survey of Early Academic and Language Skills
AGS
5910 Rice Creek Pkwy
Shoreview, MN 55126-5025   651-287-7220
                                 800-328-2560
                                 FAX: 800-471-8457
                                 agsmail@agsnet.com
                                 www.agsnet.com

Kevin Brueggeman, President
Robert Zaske, Market Manager
An individually administered test of children's of both expressive and receptive skills, pre-academic skills and articulation. K-SEALS offers reliable scores usually in less than 25 minutes. *$179.95*
Ages 3-0; 6-11

2521 KLST-2: Kindergarten Language Screening Test Edition, 2nd Edition
Sage Publications
2455 Teller Road
Thousand Oaks, CA 91320   805-499-9774
                                 800-818-7243
                                 FAX: 800-583-2665
                                 info@sagepub.com
                                 www.sagepub.com

Paul Kelly, National Textbook Sales Manager
Blaise R Simqu, President & CEO
Identifies children who need further diagnostic testing to determine whether or not they have language deficits that will accelerate academic failure. *$94.00*

2522 Kaufman Test of Educational Achievement(K-TEA)
AGS
PO Box 99
Circle Pines, MN 55014-99   800-328-2560
                                 FAX: 800-471-8457
                                 agsmail@agsnet.com
                                 www.agsnet.com

Robert Zaske, Marketing Manager
Kevin Brueggeman, President
K-TEA is an individually administered diagnostic battery that measures reading, mathematics, and spelling skills. Setting the standards in achievement testing today, K-TEA Comprehensive provides the complete diagnostic information you need for educational assessment and program planning. The Brief Forum is indispensable for school and clinical psychologists, special education teachers when a quick a measure of achievement is needed. *$249.95*

2523 Learning House
264 Church Street
Guilford, CT 6437   203-453-3691
Susan Santora, Founder and Director
Learning House is a professional community committed to enhancing the lives of individuals with dyslexia and other learning disabilities in safe and supportive surroundings.

2524 LearningRx
5085 List Drive
Suite 200
Colorado Springs, CO 80919   719-264-8808
                                 www.learningrx.com

Dr. Ken Gibson, Founder
LearningRx is a brain training program.

2525 Life Centered Career Education: A Contemporary Based Approach
Council for Exceptional Children
3100 Clarendon Blvd.
Suite 600
Arlington, VA 22201-5332   888-232-7733
                                 TTY:866-915-5000
                                 service@exceptionalchildren.org
                                 www.exceptionalchildren.org

Chad Rummel, Executive Director
Laurie VanderPloeg, Associate Executive Director, Professional Affairs
Craig Evans, Chief Financial Officer

Provides a framework for building 97 functional skill competencies appropriate for preparing for adult life and special education students. *$28.00*
175 pages

2526 Measure of Cognitive-Linguistic Abilities(MCLA)
Speech Bin
PO Box 1579
Appleton, VA 54912-1579

772-770-0007
888-388-3224
FAX: 888-388-6344
onlinehelp@schoolspecialty.com
www.speechbin.com

Jan J Binney, Senior Editor
A diagnostic test of cognitive-linguistic abilities of adolescents and adults with traumatically induced brain injuries. High level. Normed. *$89.00*
100 pages
ISBN 0-93785 -72-

2527 Miriam
501 Bacon Avenue
St. Louis, MO 63119-1512

314-968-3893
FAX: 314-962-0482
athorp@miriamstl.org
www.miriamstl.org/learning-center

Andrew Thorp, Executive Director
Sarah Scott, Development Director
Carol Faust, Business Manager
Miriam improves the quality of life for children with learning disabilities and their families through innovative and comprehensive programs.

2528 Neuropsychology Assessment Center
One University Place
Chester, PA 19013

610-499-4273
www.widenernac.org

Mary F. Lazar, PsyD, Director
Wendy M. Sarkisian, PsyD, Assistant Director
Located in the Philadelphia area, the Neuropsychology Assessment Center (NAC) specializes in neuropsychological evaluations for the investigation of a variety of psychological conditions.

2529 ONLINE
West Virginia Research and Training Center
P.O.Box 1004
Institute, WV 25112-1004

304-766-9495
800-624-8284
FAX: 304-766-2689
www.icdi.wvu.edu

Clifford Lantz, President
A quarterly newsletter offering information about hardware technology, software (commercial and home grown); applications that work and bonuses such as an exchange program for copyright-free software. *$25.00*
Quarterly

2530 OWLS: Oral and Written Language Scales LC/OE & WE
AGS
P.O.Box 99
Circle Pines, MN 55014-99

800-328-2560
FAX: 800-471-8457
www.agsnet.com

Kevin Brueggeman, President
Robert Zaske, Market Manager
One kit provides an assessment of listening comprehension while the other assesses oral expression tasks: semantic, syntactic, pragmatic, and supralinguistic aspects of language. Written Expression may be administered individually or in small groups. *$249.95*

2531 PAT-3: Photo Articulation Test
Sage Publications
2455 Teller Road
Thousand Oaks, CA 91320

805-499-9774
800-818-7243
FAX: 800-583-2665
info@sagepub.com
www.sagepub.com

Paul Kelly, National Textbook Sales Manager
Blaise R Simqu, President & CEO
This test consists of 72 color photographs. The first 69 photos test consonants and all but one vowel and one diphthong. The remaining pictures test connected speech and the remaining vowel and diphthong. *$144.00*
Complete Kit

2532 Peabody Early Experiences Kit (PEEK)
AGS
P.O.Box 99
Circle Pines, MN 55014-99

800-328-2560
FAX: 800-471-8457
www.agsnet.com

Kevin Brueggeman, President
Robert Zaske, Market Manager
1,000 activities and all the materials you need to build youngsters' cognitive, social and language skills. Manuals, puppets, manipulatives, picture card deck, picture mini decks and more to teach early development concepts. *$789.95*

2533 Peabody Individual Achievement Test-Revised Normative Update (PIAT-R-NU)
AGS
P.O.Box 99
Circle Pines, MN 55014-99

800-328-2560
FAX: 800-471-8457
www.agsnet.com

Kevin Brueggeman, President
Robert Zaske, Market Manager
PIAT-R-NU is an efficient individual measure of academic achievement. Reading, mathematics, and spelling are assessed in a simple, non-threatening format that requires only a pointing response for most items. This multiple choice format makes the PIAT-R ideal for assessing individuals who hesitate to give a spoken response, or have limited expressive abilities. *$289.98*

2534 Peabody Language Development Kits (PLDK)
AGS
P.O.Box 99
Circle Pines, MN 55014-99

800-328-2560
FAX: 800-471-8457
www.agsnet.com

Kevin Brueggeman, President
Robert Zaske, Market Manager
The main goals of the Peabody Kit language program are to stimulate overall language skills in Standard English and, for each level of the program, advance children's cognitive skills about a year. *$649.95*
Level P
ISBN 0-88671 -25-1

2535 Pediatric Early Elementary (PEEX II) Examination
Educators Publishing Service
625 Mount Auburn Street
3rd Floor
Cambridge, MA 2138- 3039

617-547-6706
800-225-5750
FAX: 888-440-2665
feedback@epsbooks.com
www.epsbooks.com

Charles H Heinle, VP
Alexandra S Bigelow, Author
Gunnar Voltz, President
Assesses the second-fourth grade child's performance on thirty-two tasks in six specific areas of development: fine-motor function, language, gross-motor function, memory, visual processing, and delayed recall. At three points during the exam, the child is rated on selective attention and behavior and effect. *$15.40 - $93*
ISBN 0-83888 -80-6

2536 Pediatric Exam of Educational-PEERAMID Readiness at Middle Childhood
Educators Publishing Service
625 Mount Auburn Street
3rd Floor
Cambridge, MA 2138- 3039
617-547-6706
800-225-5750
FAX: 888-440-2665
feedback@epsbooks.com
www.epsbooks.com

Charles H Heinle, VP
Alexandra S Bigelow, Author
Gunnar Voltz, President
Assesses the 4th-10th grade child's performance on thirty-one tasks in six specific areas: minor neurological indicators, fine-motor function, language, gross-motor function, temporal-sequential organization, and visual processing. Complete set.
$15.40 - $109
ISBN 0-83888 -99-3

2537 Pediatric Examination of Educational Readiness
Educators Publishing Service
625 Mount Auburn Street
3rd Floor
Cambridge, MA 2139- 3039
617-547-6706
800-225-5750
FAX: 888-440-2665
feedback@epsbooks.com
www.epsbooks.com

Charles H Heinle, VP
Alexandra S Bigelow, Author
Gunnar Voltz, President
Assesses the Pre-1st grade child's performance on twenty-nine tasks in six specific areas of development: orientation, gross-motor, visual-fine motor, sequential, linguistic and preacademic learning. The child is rated on ten dimensions of selective attention/activity processing efficiency and adaptation. Complete set.
$12.85 - $86.40
ISBN 0-83888 -80-1

2538 Pediatric Extended Examination at-PEET Three
Educators Publishing Service
625 Mount Auburn Street
3rd Floor
Cambridge, MA 2138- 3039
617-547-6706
800-225-5750
FAX: 888-440-2665
feedback@epsbooks.com
www.epsbooks.com

Charles H Heinle, VP
Alexandra S Bigelow, Author
Gunnar Volta, President
Assesses the preschool-age child's performance on twenty-eight tasks in five basic areas of development: gross-motor, language, visual-fine motor, memory, and intersensory integration. Complete set.
$13.75 - $126
ISBN 0-83888 -79-4

2539 Pre-Reading Screening Procedures
Educators Publishing Service
625 Mount Auburn Street
3rd Floor
Cambridge, MA 2138- 3039
617-547-6706
800-225-5750
FAX: 888-440-2665
feedback@epsbooks.com
www.epsbooks.com

Charles H Heinle, VP
Alexandra S Bigelow, Author
Gunnar Voltz, President
This revised group test, for grades K-1, evaluates auditory, visual and kinesthetic strengths in order to identify children who may have some form of dyslexia or specific language disability.
$18.00
Grades K-1
ISBN 0-83885 -23-4

2540 Preparing for ACT Assessment
American College Testing Program
500 Act Drive
PO Box 168
Iowa City, IA 52243-168
319-337-1000
FAX: 319-339-3021
act.org

Richard L Ferguson, CEO
Designed to help high school students ready themselves for the ACT Assessment's subject area tests, explains the purposes of the four tests, describes their content and format, provides tips and exercises to improve student's test-taking skills and includes a complete sample text with scoring key.

2541 Psycho-Educational Assessment of Preschool Children
National Association of School Psychologists
Ste 105
4340 East West Hwy
Bethesda, MD 20814-4468
301-657-0270
866-331-NASP
FAX: 301-657-0275
ADMIN@SOELIN.COM
soelin.com

Susan Gorin, Executive Director
This is a contributed text on assessing specific skills of preschool children.
592 pages

2542 RULES: Revised
Speech Bin
PO Box 1579
Appleton, VA 54912-1579
772-770-0007
888-388-3224
FAX: 888-388-6344
customercare@schoolspecialty.com
www.speechbin.com

Jan J Binney, Senior Editor
Treatment program for young children who have phonological disorders. *$43.95*
280 pages
ISBN 0-93785 -51-3

2543 Receptive-Expressive Emergent-REEL-2 Language Test, 2nd Edition
Sage Publications
2455 Teller Road
Thousand Oaks, CA 91320
805-499-9774
800-818-7243
FAX: 800-583-2665
info@sagepub.com
www.sagepub.com

Paul Kelly, National Textbook Sales Manager
Blaise R Simqu, President & CEO
A revision of the popular scale used for the multidimensional analysis of emergent language. The REEL-2 is specifically designed for use with a broad range of at risk infants and toddlers in the new multidisciplinary programs developing under P.L. 99-457. *$79.00*

2544 Regents' Center for Learning Disorders
103 Hooper Street
Athens, GA 30602
706-542-4589
FAX: 706-583-0001
rcld@uga.edu
rcld.uga.edu

Tasha Falkingham, Office Manage
Karen Myers, Budget Analyst
Trish Foels, Staff Clinician, Psychologist
Provide assessment, training, research, andresources related to students who have learning disorders (e.g., Attention-Deficit/Hyperactivity Disorder, Autism Spectrum Disorders, Learning Disabilities, Emotional Disorders, and Traumatic Brain Injury) that impact their functioning in the academic environment.

2545 Schmieding Developmental Center
519 Latham Drive
Lowell, AR 72745
479-750-0125
FAX: 479-750-0323
www.archildrens.org

Mary Ann Scott, PhD, Program Director
Damon Lipinski, PhD, Program Director
Jerie Beth Karkos, MD, Medical Director
Arkansas Children's Hospital (ACH) is the a pediatric medical center in Arkansas.

2546 Slingerland Screening Tests
Educators Publishing Service
625 Mount Auburn Street
3rd Floor
Cambridge, MA 2138- 3039
617-547-6706
800-435-7728
FAX: 888-440-2665
feedback@epsbooks.com
www.epsbooks.com

Charles H Heinle, VP
Alexandra S Bigelow, Author
Gunnar Voltz, President
These tests, by Beth Slingerland, for individuals or groups of children, grades 1-6, identify children who show indications of having specific language disability in reading, handwriting, spelling or speaking. Form D evaluates personal orientation in time and space as well as the ability to express ideas in writing. *$14.80 - $27.45*
ISBN 0-83882 -02-2

2547 Special Needs Advocacy Resource Book
Prufrock Press
PO Box 8813
Waco, TX 76714-8813
800-998-2208
FAX: 800-240-0333
info@prufrock.com
www.prufrock.com

Joel McIntosh, Publisher & Marketing Director
Rich Weinfield, Author
Michelle Davis, Author
Subtitle: What You Can Do Now to Advocate for Your Exceptional Child's Education. This is a unique hadnbook that teaches parents how to work with schools to achieve optimal learning situations and accommodations for their child's needs. *$19.95*
328 pages
ISBN 1-593633-09-7

2548 Speech Bin
PO Box 1579
Appleton, VA 54912-1579
772-770-0007
888-388-3224
FAX: 888-388-6344
customercare@schoolspecialty.com
www.speechbin.com

Jan J Binney, Senior Editor
Catalog offering test materials, assessment information, books and special education resources for speech-language pathologists, occupational and physical therapists, audiologists, and other rehabilitation professionals in schools, hospitals, clinics and private practices.
ISSN 4773-324

2549 Stuttering Severity Instrument for Children and Adults
Psychological & Educational Publications
P.O.Box 520
Hydesville, CA 95547-520
707-768-1807
800-523-5775
FAX: 800-447-0907

Morrison Gardner, President
With this tool teachers can determine whether to schedule a child for therapy or to evaluate the effects of treatment.

2550 TLC Speech-Language/Occupational TherapyCamps
2092 Gaither Rd.
Suite 100
Rockville, MD 20850
301-424-5200
FAX: 301-424-8063
TTY:301-424-5203
info@ttlc.org
www.ttlc.org

Patricia Ritter, Executive Director
TLC provides small group summer programs for children with special needs. Offers speech-language and occupational therapy summer camps for children ages 3-7.

2551 Taking Part: Introducing Social Skills to Young Children
AGS
P.O.Box 99
Circle Pines, MN 55014-99
800-328-2560
FAX: 800-471-8457
www.agsnet.com

Kevin Brueggeman, President
Robert Zaske, Market Manager
The first social skills curriculum to be linked directly to an assessment tool. More than 30 lessons correlate with the skills assessed by the Social Skills Rating System, a multirater approach to assessing prosocial and problem behaviors. *$149.95*

2552 Teaching of Reading: A Continuum from Kindergarten through College, The
AVKO Educational Research Foundation
3084 Willard Rd
Birch Run, MI 48415-9404
810-686-9283
866-285-6612
FAX: 810-686-1101
avko.org

Don Mc Cabe, Executive Director
A textbook for teaching teachers how to teach language arts with lessons about dyslexia, phonics, learning to write, the connection between reading and spelling, and diagnostic and prescriptive tests. Free as an e-book for Foundation members. *$49.95*
364 pages

2553 Test Critiques: Volumes I-X
Sage Publications
2455 Teller Road
Thousand Oaks, CA 91320
805-499-9774
800-818-7243
FAX: 800-583-2665
info@sagepub.com
www.sagepub.com

Paul Kelly, National Textbook Sales Manager
Blaise R Simqu, President & CEO
Provides the professional and nonprofessional with in-depth, evaluative studies of more than 800 of the most widely used of these assessment instruments. *$649.00*

2554 Test of Early Reading Ability Deaf or Hard of Hearing
Pro- Ed Publications
8700 Shoal Creek Blvd
Austin, TX 78757-6816
512-451-3246
800-897-3202
FAX: 800-397-7633
general@proedinc.com
www.proedinc.com

Donald D Hammill, Owner
Courtney King, Marketing Coordinator
This adaptation of the TERA-2 for simultaneous communication of American Sign Language is the ONLY individually administered test of reading designed for children with moderate to profound sensory hearing loss. *$169.00*
Complete Kit

2555 Test of Language Development: Primary
Sage Publications
2455 Teller Road
Thousand Oaks, CA 91320
805-499-9774
800-818-7243
FAX: 800-583-2665
info@sagepub.com
www.sagepub.com

Paul Kelly, National Textbook Sales Manager
Blaise R Simqu, President & CEO

TOLD P:2 and TOLD 1:2 are the most popular tests of spoken language used by clinicians today. They are used to identify children who have language disorders and to isolate the particular types of disorders they have. Primary Edition for ages 1-4 to 8-11: Intermediate Edition for ages 8-6 to 12-11.

2556 Test of Mathematical Abilities, 2nd Edition
Sage Publications
2455 Teller Road
Thousand Oaks, CA 91320   805-499-9774
                                 800-818-7243
                            FAX: 800-583-2665
                             info@sagepub.com
                              www.sagepub.com

Paul Kelly, National Textbook Sales Manager
Blaise R Simqu, President & CEO
The latest version was developed for use in grades 3 through 12. It measures math performance on the two traditional major skill areas in math as well as attitude, vocabulary and general application of math concepts in real life. *$84.00*

2557 Test of Nonverbal Intelligence, 3rd Edition
Sage Publications
2455 Teller Road
Thousand Oaks, CA 91320   805-499-9774
                                 800-818-7243
                            FAX: 800-583-2665
                             info@sagepub.com
                              www.sagepub.com

Paul Kelly, National Textbook Sales Manager
Blaise R Simqu, President & CEO
A language-free measure of intelligence, aptitude and reasoning. The administration of the test requires no reading, writing, speaking or listening on the part of the test subject. The items included in this test are problem-solving tasks that increase in difficulty. Each item presents a set of figures in which one or more components is missing. The test items include one or more of the characteristics of shape, position, direction, rotation, contiguity, shading, size, movement or pattern. *$229.00*
Complete Kit

2558 Test of Phonological Awareness
Sage Publications
2455 Teller Road
Thousand Oaks, CA 91320   805-499-9774
                                 800-818-7243
                            FAX: 800-583-2665
                             info@sagepub.com
                              www.sagepub.com

Paul Kelly, National Textbook Sales Manager
Blaise R Simqu, President & CEO
Measures young children's awareness of the individual sounds in words. Children who are sensitive to the phonological structure of words in oral language have a much easier time learning to read than children who are not. *$143.00*

2559 Test of Written Spelling, 3rd Edition
Pro- Ed Publications
8700 Shoal Creek Blvd
Austin, TX 78757-6897   512-451-3246
                                 800-897-3202
                            FAX: 800-397-7633
                             general@proedinc.com
                              www.proedinc.com

Donald D Hammill, Owner
Courtney King, Marketing Coordinator
This revised edition assesses the student's ability to spell words whose spellings are readily predictable in sound-letter patterns, words whose spellings are less predictable and both types of words considered together. *$74.00*

2560 Texas Scottish Rite Hospital for Children
2222 Welborn Street
Dallas, TX 75219   214-559-5000
                            FAX: 800-421-1121
                             tsrhdv@tsrh.org
                              www.tsrhc.org

Robert L. Walker, President/ CEO
Mark G. Bateman, SVP, Public Relations
Leslie A. Clonch, Jr., Vice President/ CIO

TSRHC treats children with orthopedic conditions, such as scoliosis, clubfoot, hand disorders, hip disorders and limb length differences, as well as certain related neurological disorders and learning disorders, such as dyslexia.

2561 Woodcock Reading Mastery Tests
Pearson
5601 Green Valley Dr
Bloomington, MN 55437-1099   800-627-7271
                               FAX: 800-232-1223
                       pearsonassessments@pearson.com
                         www.pearsonassessments.com

Christine Carlson, Product Manager
Doug Kubach, President & CEO
The Woodcock Reading Mastery Tests - Revised provides an interpretive system and age range to help you assess reading skills of children and adults. Two forms, G and II, make it easy to test and retest, or you can combine the results of both forms for a more comprehensive assessment. Revised with recent updates. *$329.95*

2562 Young Children with Special Needs: A Developmentally Appropriate Approach
Allyn & Bacon
75 Arlington Street
Ste 300
Boston, MA 2116-3988   617-848-7500
                                    800-852-8024
                               FAX: 617-944-7273
                                www.ablongman.com

Bill Barke, CEO
Thomas Longman, Founder
This book is designed to prepare students in making curriculum decisions in order to care for and foster the development of young children with special needs in normal early childhood settings.
270 pages
ISBN 0-20518 -94-X

Treatment & Training

2563 ABLE Program MCC-Longview
3200 Broadway
Kansas City, MO 64111-2105   816-604-1000
                               FAX: 816-672-2719
                          joan.bergstrom@mcckc.edu
                                mcckc.edu/ABLE

Joan Bergstrom, Director
Kay Owens, Administrative Assistant
Intensive support services program for post secondary students with neurological disabilities. The ABLE Program can be reached at mcckc.edu/ABLE

2564 Academy for Guided Imagery
30765 Pacific Coast Hwy
Ste 355
Malibu, CA 90265-3643   800-726-2070
                               FAX: 800-727-2070
                                 info@acadgi.com
                                 www.acadgi.com

David E Bresler, President
The Academy aims to teach people to access and use the power of the mind/body connection for healing, and to further understanding of the imagery process in human life and development. They provide systematic training and guidance to health professionals who are interested in the use of Guided Imagery in their practice. The Academy's Imagery Store offers guided imagery CDs, DVDs and books for self-healing.

2565 Adventist HealthCare
820 West Diamond Avenue
Suite 600
Gaithersburg, MD 20878   301-315-3030
                               FAX: 301-315-3000
                         www.adventisthealthcare.com

David E. Weigley, M.B.A., Chairman
Robert T. Vandeman, Vice-Chair
Terry Forde, Secretary

dventist HealthCare, based in Gaithersburg, Md., is a not-for-profit organization of dedicated professionals who work together to provide excellent wellness, disease management and health-care services to the community.

2566 Asthma & Allergy Education for Worksite Clinicians
Asthma and Allergy Foundation of America
8201 Corporate Drive
Suite 1000
Landover, VA 20785
202-466-7643
800-727-8462
FAX: 202-466-8940
info@aafa.org
aafa.org

Bill Mc Lin, President & CEO
Helen Taylor, Information Specialist
Developed to teach health professionals in the worksite about asthma and allergies and ultimately improve the health of the employees who have theses de\iseases. The program gives worksite clinicians the knowledge and tools they need to give employees guidance on how to control environmental factors both in the home and in the workplace, self-manage thier asthma and/or allergies and to determaine if ti is necessary for employees to see an allergist if symptoms persist.

2567 Asthma & Allergy Essentials for Children's Care Provider
Asthma and Allergy Foundation of America
8201 Corporate Drive
Suite 1000
Landover, VA 20785
202-466-7643
800-727-8462
FAX: 202-466-8940
info@aafa.org
aafa.org

Bill Mc Lin, President & CEO
Helen Taylor, Information Specialist
Course gives child care providers the tools and knowledge they need to care for children with asthma and allergies. During the interactive, three hour program, a trained health professional teaches providers how to recognize the signs and symptoms of an asthma or allergy episode, how to institute environmental control measures to prevent these episodes, and how to properly use medication and the tools for asthma management. In areas of the country serviced by AAFA's 14 chapters.

2568 Asthma Care Training for Kids (ACT)
Asthma and Allergy Foundation of America
8201 Corporate Drive
Suite 1000
Landover, VA 20785
202-466-7643
FAX: 202-466-8940
info@aafa.org
www.aafa.org

Bill Mc Lin, President & CEO
Helen Taylor, Information Specialist
Interactive program for children ages seven to 12 and their families. Children and their families attend three group sessions seperately to learn their own unique styles and then come together at the end of each session to share their knowledge.

2569 Ayurvedic Institute
PO Box 23445
Albuquerque, NM 87292-1445
505-291-9698
800-863-7721
FAX: 505-294-7572
ayurveda.com

Wynn Werner, Administrator
Directed by Dr. Vasant Lad, trains people in Ayurveda.

2570 Brooks Rehabilitation Hospital
3599 University Blvd S
Jacksonville, FL 32216
904-345-7600
FAX: 904-345-7619
www.brookshealth.org

Gary W. Sneed, Chairman
Michael Spigel, President/ COO
Douglas M. Baer, Chief Executive Officer
Brooks Rehabilitation provides the most advanced therapy and medical care.

2571 Center for Parent Information and Resources
35 Halsey St
4th Floor
Newark, NJ 07102
973-642-8100
www.parentcenterhub.org

Debra A. Jennings, Director
Myriam Alizo, Project Assistant
Lisa K□pper, Product Development Coordinator
The Center for Parent Information and Resources (CPIR) serves as a central resource of information and products to the community of Parent Training Information (PTI) Centers and the Community Parent Resource Centers (CPRCs), so that they can focus their efforts on serving families of children with disabilities.

2572 Center for Spinal Cord Injury Recovery
261 Mack
Detroit, MI 48201
866-724-2368
FAX: 313-745-9064
krodgers@dmc.org
www.centerforscirecovery.org

Krystal Rodgers, Administrative Assistant
The Center for SCI Recoveryr (CSCIR)provides long-term, high intensity, non-traditional, activity based therapy to maximize recovery.

2573 Cottage Rehabilitation Hospital
400 W. Pueblo Street
Santa Barbara, CA 93105
805-682-7111
mzate@sbch.org
www.cottagehealth.org

Cottage Health is a not-for-profit hospital system that includes Santa Barbara Cottage Hospital, Cottage Children's Hospital, Cottage Rehabilitation Hospital, Santa Ynez Valley Cottage Hospital, and Goleta Valley Cottage Hospital.

2574 Courage Kenny Rehabilitation Institute
Allina Health
800 E 28th St.
Minneapolis, MN 55407
612-863-4495
www.allinahealth.org

Courage Kenny Rehabilitation Institute was created in 2013 by the merger of Sister Kenny Rehabilitation Institute and Courage Center. A part of Allina Health, the Institute offers rehabilitation and community services for children and adults with injuries and disabilities.

2575 Harriet & Robert Heilbrunn Guild School
JGB Audio Library for the Blind
15 W 65th St
New York, NY 10023-6601
212-769-6200
800-284-4422
FAX: 212-769-6266
www.JGB.org

Allen R Morse, JD, PhD, President & CEO
Ken Stanley, Manager
A Jewish Guild for the blind.

2576 Howard School, The
1192 Foster St NW
Atlanta, GA 30318-4329
404-377-7436
FAX: 404-377-0884
admissions@howardschool.org
howardschool.org

Marifred Cilella, Head Of School
The Howard School educates students 5 years old through 12th grade with language learning disabilities and learning differences. Small student/teacher ratios allow for instruction that is personalized to complement the individual learning styles and to help each student understand his/her learning process. Students gain the tools and strategies needed to become independent, life-long learners.

2577 Kennedy Krieger Institute
707 North Broadway
Baltimore, MD 21205
443-923-9200
800-873-3377
888-554-2080
www.kennedykrieger.org

Jennifer Accardo, M.D., Neurologist
Adrianna Amari, Ph.D., Training & Research Coordinator
Roberta L. Babbitt, Ph.D, Program Director

Kennedy Krieger Institute is an internationally recognized institution dedicated to improving the lives of children and young adults with pediatric developmental disabilities and disorders of the brain, spinal cord and musculoskeletal system, through patient care, special education, research, and professional training.

2578 Kessler Institute for Rehabilitation
1199 Pleasant Valley Way
West Orange, NJ 07052

973-731-3600
877-322-2580
FAX: 973-243-6819
www.kessler-rehab.com

Sue Kida, President
Provides physical medicine and rehabilitation through the integration of highly specialized care, treatment, technology, education, research, and advocacy.

2579 Lake Michigan Academy
West Michigan Learning Disabilities Foundation
2428 Burton St SE
Grand Rapids, MI 49546-4806

616-464-3330
FAX: 616-285-1935

Amy Barto, Executive Director
Is a private day school for children with learning disabilities.

2580 Levinson Medical Center
98 Cutter Mill Road
Suite 90
Great Neck, NY 11021

516-482-2888
800-334-7323
FAX: 516-482-2480
drlevinson@aol.com
www.dyslexiaonline.com

Dr. Harold Levinson, Psychiatrist, Neurologist
Carolyn Malman, Office Manager
Lisa Danziger, Patient Coordinator
Medical center groundbreaking medical treatment offers rapid and often dramatic help to suffering dyslexic/ADHD children and adults

2581 Mad Hatters: Theatre That Makes a World of Difference
P.O.Box 50002
Kalamazoo, MI 49005-2

FAX: 269-385-5868

Bobbe A Luce, Executive Director
A nationally-known theater which has presented effective and innovative programs to more than 175,000 people in over 1,150 performances in the past 15 years. Our presentations and training programs are a proven method of changing attitudes and behaviors. The Mad Hatters is a leader in the field of sensitivity training to build community and foster the inclusion of all people in society. Fees: $500-$4000 per program, depending on topic and audience.

2582 MedStar National Rehabilitation Network
102 Irving Street NW
Washington, DC 20010

202-877-1000
www.medstarnrh.org

At MedStar National Rehabilitation Network, they treat adults and children with disabling illness or injury.

2583 Missouri Rehabilitation Center
One Hospital Drive
Columbia, MO 65212

573-882-4141
www.muhealth.org

University of Missouri Health Care offers a full spectrum of care, ranging from primary care to highly specialized, multidisciplinary treatment for patients with the most severe illnesses and injuries.

2584 Neuroxcel
401 Northlake Blvd.
North Palm Beach, FL 33048

866-391-6247
www.neuroxcel.com

Neuroxcelr Corporation is a Palm Beach, FL-based post rehabilitation Inclusive Fitness Strength and Conditioning Training Center, committed to improving the lives of individuals with a spinal cord injury (SCI), stroke, neurological conditions and various other special populations.

2585 Ramapo Training
Ramapo for Children
Rt. 52/Salisbury Turnpike
PO Box 266
Rhinebeck, NY 12572

845-876-8403
FAX: 845-876-8414
office@ramapoforchildren.org
www.ramapoforchildren.org

Adam Weiss, Chief Executive Officer
Bruce Kuziola, Chief Financial & Administrative Officer
Adam St. Bernard Jacobs, Director, Development & Communications
Ramapo Training was established to provide staff training and program support for educational and recreational programs, especially those that serve children-at-risk and those with special needs.

2586 Sandhills School
1500 Hallbrook Dr
Columbia, SC 29209-4021

803-695-1400
FAX: 803-695-1214
info@sandhillsschool.org
www.sandhillsschool.org

Anne Vickers, Head of School
Erika Senneseth, Asst Head of School
Angela Daniel, Director of Development
Exists to provide educational programs and intellectual development for average to above average students, six to 15, who learn differently and to promote the development of self-awareness, joy in learning and a vision of themselves as life-long learners.

2587 Senior Program for Teens and Young Adults with Special Needs
Camp J CC
6125 Montrose Rd
Rockville, MD 20852-4860

301-881-0100
FAX: 301-881-6549
jcccamp@jccgw.org
www.jccgw.org

Scott Cohen, President
Mindy Burger, Vice President for Development
The senior Program is a transitional program for teens and young adults with severe learning disabilities and multiple disabilities. Socialization, recreation and independent living skills are enhanced in a fun enviroment. Activities include art, music, recreational swim and more.

2588 Spinal Cord Injury Center
132 S. 10th Street
375 Main Building
Philadelphia, PA 19107

215-955-6579
FAX: 215-955-5152

Marilyn P. Owens, RN, BSN, Project Coordinator
Brittany Hayes, Research Coordinator
Jacqueline Robinson, Administrative Assistant
SCI provides medical care for their injuries, along with emotional, social, vocational and psychological rehabilitation to cope with the changes in their bodies and in their lifestyles that often result from the injury.

2589 Stanford Health Care
300 Pasteur Drive
Stanford, CA 94304

650-498-3333
800-756-9000
stanfordhealthcare.org

Amir Dan Rubin, President and CEO
Raj Behal, MD, Chief Quality Officer
James Hereford, Chief Operating Officer
Stanford Health Care provides patients with the very best in diagnosis and treatment.

2590 Teacher of Students with Visual Impairments
3635 Coal Mountain Rd.
Cumming, GA 30028   c.willings@teachingvisuallyimpaired.com
www.teachingvisuallyimpaired.com

Teaching Students with Visual Impairments.

2591 The Glenholme School
Devereux Advanced Behavioral Health Connecticut
81 Sabbaday Ln.
Washington, CT 06793   860-868-7377
                                            FAX: 860-868-7894
                            info@theglenholmeschool.org
                            www.theglenholmeschool.org
The Glenholme School is an independent, co-educational special
needs boarding and day school for young people, ages ten to adult
in middle school, high school, postgraduate, transitional living
for career development. The positive atmosphere provides guidance for students with special needs to achieve competent social
and academic levels. The comprehensive learning environment
supports the success of students with various learning
disabilities, from Asperger's to Tourette's.

2592 UAB Spain Rehabilitation Center
1720 2nd Ave South
Birmingham, AL 35294   205-934-4011
                                          TTY:205-934-4642
                                               www.uab.edu

Ray L. Watts, M.D., President
G. Allen Bolton Jr., VP, Financial Affairs
UAB's missionis to be a research university and academic health
center that discovers, teaches and applies knowledge for the intellectual, cultural, social and economic benefit of Birmingham,
the state and beyond.

**2593 University of Maryland Rehabilitation and Orthopaedic
Institute**
Uni of MD Rehab & Ortho Institute
2200 Kernan Drive
Baltimore, MD 21207   410-448-2500
                                                  888-453-7626
                                          TTY:800-735-2258
                                      www.umrehabortho.org
Cynthia A. Kelleher, MPH, MBA, Interim President and CEO
John P. Straumanis, VP, Medical Affairs
W. Walter Augustin, III, CPA, VP of Financial Services
University of Maryland Rehabilitation & Orthopaedic Institute
(formerly Kernan Hospital), a committed provider of orthopaedic
surgery and the largest inpatient rehabilitation hospital and provider of rehabilitation services in the state of Maryland, has been
serving the Baltimore community for over 100 years.

2594 Vanguard School, The
Valley Forge Specialized Educational Services
1777 N Valley Rd
Paoli, PA 19301   610-296-6700
                                          FAX: 610-640-0132
                                  www.vanguardschool-pa.org

Tim Lanshe, Director of Education
James Kirkpatrick, CFO
Peg Osborne, Admissions Director
An Approved Private School (APS) for students aged 4-21 years
with exceptionalities including autism spectrum disorder, mild
emotional disturbances and/or neurological impairments.

2595 Worthmore Academy
3535 Kessler Boulevard East Dr
Indianapolis, IN 46220-5154   317-902-9896
                                                  877-700-6516
                                          FAX: 317-251-6516
                            bjackson@worthmoreacademy.org
                            www.worthmoreacademy.org
Brenda Jackson, Director
Alyssa Blaire Cook, Assistant Director
A place where children with learning disabilities receive individ-
ualized instruction to help remediate his or her condition. The
most common learning disabilities we work with are Dyslexic,
A.D.D, A.D.H.D, Autism Spectrum (including Asperger's Syn-
drome), and communication disorders.

Exchange Programs

General

2596 A Guide to International Educational Exchange
Mobility International USA
132 E Broadway
Suite 343
Eugene, OR 97401   541-343-1284
                                FAX: 541-343-6812
                                TTY:541-343-1284
                                clearinghouse@miusa.org
                                www.miusa.org

Susan Sygall, Chief Executive Officer
Cindy Lewis, Director, Programs
A Guide to International Educational Exchange, Community Service and Travel for People with Disabilities includes information travel and international programs, as well as personal experience stories from people with disabilities who have had successful international experiences.
600 pages

2597 American Institute for Foreign Study
River Plaza 9 W Broad St
Stamford, CT 6902-3788   203-399-5000
                                866-906-2437
                                FAX: 203-399-5590
                                info@aifs.com
                                www.aifs.com

William L Gertz, CEO
Organizes cultural exchange programs throughout the world for more than 50,000 students each year and arranges insurance coverage for our own participants as well as participants of other organizations. Also provides summer travel programs overseas and in the US ranging from one week to a full academic year.

2598 American Universities International Programs
307 S College Ave
Fort Collins, CO 80524-2801   970-495-0084
                                888-730-2847
                                FAX: 970-495-0114
                                info@auip.com
                                www.auip.com

Laurie Klith, Executive Director
Study abroad organization sending students to universities in Australia and New Zealand.

2599 American-Scandinavian Foundation
58 Park Ave
38 Street
New York, NY 10016-3007   212-779-3587
                                FAX: 212-686-1157
                                info@amscan.org
                                scandinaviahouse.org

Edward Gallagher, President
Promotes international understanding through educational and cultural exchange between the United States and Denmark, Finland, Iceland, Norway and Sweden.

2600 Antioch College
One Morgan Place
Yellow Springs, OH 45387-1635   937-319-6082
                                FAX: 937-319-6085

Mark Roosevelt, President
Thomas Brookley, CFO & COO
Gariot Louima, Chief Communications Officer
Education abroad offers numerous programs which can be included in undergraduate and graduate study programs.

2601 Army and Air Force Exchange Services
PO Box 660202
Dallas, TX 75266-202   214-312-2011
                                800-527-2345
                                FAX: 800-446-0163
                                TTY: 800-423-2011
                                www.aafes.com

James Moore, Senior VP
MG Bruce Casella, Commander/CEO

Brings a tradition of value, service, and support to its 11.5 million authorized customers at military installations in the United States, Europe and in the Pacific.

2602 Association for International Practical Training
10400 Little Patuxent Pkwy
Suite 250
Columbia, MD 21044-3519   410-997-2200
                                FAX: 410-992-3924
                                aipt@aipt.org
                                aipt.org

Elizabeth Chazottes, CEO
Nonprofit organization dedicated to encouraging and facilitating the exchange of qualified individuals between the US and other countries so they may gain practical work experience and improve international understanding.

2603 Basic Facts on Study Abroad
International Education
809 United Nations Plz
New York, NY 10017-3503   212-883-8200
                                FAX: 212-984-5452
                                publications@un.org
                                iie.org

Allen E Goodman, CEO
Peggy Blumenthal, Executive Vice President
Information book including foreign study planning, educational choices, finances and study abroad programs. *$35.00*
30 pages

2604 Beaver College
Arcadia University
450 S Easton Rd
Glenside, PA 19038-3215   215-572-2901
                                888-232-8379
                                FAX: 215-572-2174

Lorna Stern, Deputy Director
One of the largest college-based study abroad programs in the country. Prices from $8000.00 semester to $22000.00 a year.

2605 Buffalo State (SUNY)
1300 Elmwood Ave
South Wing 410
Buffalo, NY 14222-1095   716-878-4620
                                FAX: 716-878-3054
                                intleduc@buffalostate.edu

Lee Ann Grace, Asst Dean Int'l/Exchange Program
Provides international educational exchange opportunities for students of university age and older through its Office of International Education.

2606 Building Bridges: Including People with Disabilities in International Programs
Mobility International USA
132 E Broadway
Suite 343
Eugene, OR 97401   541-343-1284
                                FAX: 541-343-6812
                                TTY:541-343-1284
                                clearinghouse@miusa.org
                                www.miusa.org

Susan Sygall, Chief Executive Officer
Cindy Lewis, Director, Programs
Empowers people with disabilities around the world through international exchange and international development to achieve their human rights. The international exchange programs usually last two-four weeks and are held throughout the year in the US and abroad. Activities include living with homestay families, leadership seminars, disability rights workshops, cross cultural learning and teambuilding activities such as river rafting and challenging courses.

2607 Davidson College, Office of Study Abroad
Davidson College
PO Box 7171
Davidson, NC 28035-7171   704-894-2000
                                FAX: 704-894-2005
                                kocampbell@davidson.edu
                                www3.davidson.edu

Carol Quillen, President

Recognizes the value of study abroad for both the devlopment of worl understanding and the development of the student as a broadminded, objective and mature individual.

2608   High School Students Guide to Study, Travel, and Adventure Abroad
300 Fore Street
Portland, ME 4101

207-553-4000
FAX: 207-553-4299
contact@ciee.org
www.ciee.org

Robert E. Fallon, CEO & President
Kenton Keith, Senior Vice President for Progra
This guide provides high school students with all the information they need for a successful trip abroad. Included are sections to help students find out if they're ready for a trip abroad, make the necessary preparations and get the most from their experience. Over 200 programs are described including language study, summer camps, homestays, study tours and work camps. The program descriptions include information for people with disabilities.
ISSN 0312-11

2609   IPSL Institute of Global Learning
4110 SE Hawthorne Blvd.
Suite 200
Portland, OR 97214

503-395-4775
FAX: 503-954-1881
info@ipsl.org
ipsl.org

Thomas Morgan, President
Arianne Newton, Director, Programs
IPSL is an educational organization servicing students, colleges, universities, service agencies and related organizations around the world by fostering programs that link volunteer service and academic study. IPSL is a registered Social Benefit Corporation that is committed to its mission and dedicated to promoting an ethic of service. They invest over 83% of our revenues directly back into the communities where they serve.

2610   International Christian Youth Exchange
134 W 26th St
New York, NY 10001-6803

212-206-7307
FAX: 212-633-9085

Ed Gragert
Offers participants a unique experience to learn about another culture and make friends from different countries.

2611   International Student Exchange Programs (I SEP)
1655 N Fort Myer Drive
Suite 400
Arlington, VA 22209

703-504-9960
FAX: 703-243-8070
info@isep.org
www.isep.org

Dr. Thomas Hochstettler, Chair
Dr. Tony Atwater, President
ISEP is a network of 275 post-secondary institutions in the United States and 38 other countries cooperating to provide affordable international educational experiences for a diverse student population.

2612   International University Partnerships
University of Pennsylvania
1011 South Dr
Indiana, PA 15705-1046

724-357-2100
FAX: 724-357-6213
iup.edu

David Werner, President
Offers a variety of international educational exchange programs to students who wish to study overseas.

2613   Lake Erie College
391 W. Washington St.
Painesville, OH 44077

440-296-1856
800-533-4996
FAX: 440-375-7005
admissions@lec.edu
www.lec.edu

Michael Victor, President
Michael Keresman lll, Director

Sends students abroad for a term or longer to develop intellectual awareness and individual maturity.

2614   Lane Community College
4000 E 30th Ave
Eugene, OR 97405

541-463-3100
FAX: 541-463-5201
asklane@lanecc.edu
www.lanecc.edu

Margaret Hamilton, Ph.D, President
Lane Community College offers a wide variety of instructional programs including transfer credit programs, career and technical degree and certificate programs, continuing education noncredit courses, ESL, GED programs, and customized training for local businesses. The college offers support services for those with disabilities through their Center for Accessible Resources.

2615   Lions Clubs International
300 W 22nd St
Oak Brook, IL 60523-8842

630-571-5466
FAX: 630-571-8890
www.lionsclubs.org

Joe Preston, International President
Jitsuhiro Yamada, First Vice President
Robert E. Corlew, Second Vice President
Over 46,000 individual clubs in over 194 countries and geographical areas which provide community service and promote better international relations. Clubs work with local communities to provide needed and useful programs for sight, diabetes and hearing, and aid in study abroad.

2616   Lisle
900 County Road 269
Leander, TX 78641-1633

512-259-4404
Barbara E Bratton, Owner
Educational organization which works toward world peace and better quality of human life through increased understanding between persons of similar and different cultures.

2617   National 4-H Council
7100 Connecticut Ave
Chevy Chase, MD 20815-4934

301-961-2800
FAX: 301-961-2894
www.4-h.org

Donald Floyd, President
Jennifer Sirangelo, Executive Vice President
4-H opened the door for young people to learn leadership skills and explore ways to give back. 4-H revolutionized how youth connected to practical, hands-on learning experiences while outside of the classroom.

2618   New Directions for People with Disabilities
5276 Hollister Ave.
Suite 207
Santa Barbara, CA 93111

805-967-2841
888-967-2841
FAX: 805-964-7344
hello@newdirectionstravel.org
www.newdirectionstravel.org

Dee Duncan, Executive Director
A nonprofit organization providing local, national, and international travel vacations and holiday programs for people with mild to moderate developmental disabilities.
1985

2619   People to People International
911 Main Street
Suite 2110
Kansas City, MO 64105-2246

816-531-4701
FAX: 816-561-7502
ptpi@ptpi.org
www.ptpi.org

Mary Eisenhower, CEO
Roseanne Rosen, Senior Vice President of Operati
Brian Hueben, Senior Director, Administration
Exchanges international understanding and friendship through educational, cultural and humantarian activities involving the exchange of ideas and experiences directly among people of different countries and diverse cultures. Is also dedicated to enhancing cross cultural communication within each communityand across communities and nations.

2620   Rotary Youth Exchange
Rotary International
1560 Sherman Ave
Evanston, IL 60201-4818
                                      847-866-3000
                                      866-976-8279
                            FAX: 847-328-4101
                     youthexchange@rotary.org
                                  www.rotary.org

Kalyan Banerjee, International President
Noel A Bajat, Vice President
Kenneth R Boyd, Director
This worldwide organization of business and professional leaders provides humanitarian service, encourages high ethical standards in all vocations, and helps build goodwill and peace in the world. Approximately 1.2 million Rotarians belong to more than 31,000 Rotary clubs located in 167 countries for exchange opportunities.

2621   Scandinavian Exchange
24 Dickinson Street
Amherst, MA 1002
                                      413-253-9737
                            FAX: 413-253-5282
             howery@scandinavianseminar.org
                    www.scandinavianseminar.org

Jacqueline D Waldman, CEO
William Kaufmann, Chair
Student exchange program founded in 1949.

2622   Sister Cities International
915 15th Street, NW
4th Floor
Washington, DC 20005
                                      202-347-8630
                            FAX: 202-393-6524
                        info@sister-cities.org
                                sister-cities.org

Patrick Madden, President
Jim Doumas, Executive Vice President, & Inte
A non profit citizen diplomacy network creating and strengthening partnerships between US and international communities in an effort to increase global cooperation at the municipal level, to promote cultural understnading and to stimulate economic development. Encourages local community development and volunteer action by motivating and empowering private citizens, municipal officials and business leaders to conduct long term programs of mutual benefits including exchange situations.

2623   State University of New York
1400 Washington Ave
Albany, NY 12222-100
                                      518-442-3300
                            FAX: 518-442-5383
                     ugadmissions@albany.edu
                                 www.albany.edu

George Philip, President
Alain Kaloyeros, Senior Vice President & CEO
Susan Phillips, Provost & VP for Academic Affai
Offers over 150 international educational exchange programs in 37 different countries. Broad mission of excellence in undergraduate and graduate education, research and public service engages 17,000 diverse students in nine schools and colleges across three campuses.

2624   University of Minnesota at Crookston
2900 University Ave
Crookston, MN 56716-5000
                                      218-281-6510
                                      800-862-6466
                            FAX: 218-281-8050
                          UMCinfo@umn.edu
                                www.crk.umn.edu

Charles Casey, CEO
Eric Kaler, President
The University of Minnesota, Crookston (UMC) is a public, baccalaureate, coeducational institution and a coordinate campus of the University of Minnesota

2625   University of Oregon
5000 N Willamette Blvd
Portland, OR 97203-5798
                                      503-943-8000
                            FAX: 503-725-3067
                          webmaster@up.edu
                                          up.edu

Patricia Esley, Manager
Rev.E.Willia Beauchamp, President
James Lyons, VP University Relations
Study/cultural experience is available in Tokyo and other Japanese cities as part of the Japan Studies Program at the University.

2626   Western Washington University
516 High St
Bellingham, WA 98225-5996
                                      360-650-3000
                            FAX: 360-650-3022
                                  www.wwu.edu

Bruce Shepard, President
Paul Dunn, Senior Executive Asst. to the Pr
Barbara Stoneberg, Assistant to the President

2627   World Experience Teenage Exchange Program
2440 S Hacienda Blvd
Suite 116
Hacienda Heights, CA 91745-4763
                                      626-330-5719
                                      800-633-6653
                            FAX: 626-333-4914

Kerry Gonzales, President
Marge Archaumbault, President
Offers a quality and affordable program for over two decades and continues to provide students and host families a youth exchange program based on individual attention, with the help of an international network of overseas directors and USA coordinators.

2628   World of Options
Mobility International USA
132 E Broadway
Suite 343
Eugene, OR 97401
                                      541-343-1284
                            FAX: 541-343-6812
                            TTY:541-343-1284
                      clearinghouse@miusa.org
                                  www.miusa.org

Susan Sygall, Chief Executive Officer
Cindy Lewis, Director, Programs
Empowering people with disabilities around the world through international exchange and international development to achieve their human rights.
338 pages

2629   Youth for Understanding International Exchange
6400 Goldsboro Road
Suite 100
Bethesda, MD 20817-5841
                                      240-235-2100
                                      800-833-6243
                            FAX: 240-352-2104
                          admissions@yfu.org
                                          yfu.org

Rachel Andreson, Founder
Samantha Brizzolara, Chair
Youth for Understanding (YFU) International Exchange, an educational, nonprofit organization, prepares young people for the opportunities and responsabilities in a changing, independent world. With YFU, students can choose a year, semenster, or summer program in one or more than 35 countries worldwide. More than 200,000 young people from more than 50 nations in Asia, Europe, North and South America, Africa and the Pacific have participated in YFU exchanges.

Foundations & Funding Resources

Alabama

2630 **Alabama Power Foundation**
PO Box 2641
Birmingham, AL 35203   205-257-2508
                              powerofgood.com

Myla Calhoun, President
Hallie Bradley, Manager, Community Initiatives
Brandon Glover, Manager, Strategic Initiatives
Honoring its mission to strengthen the communities the company serves, the foundation focuses its efforts on organizations that support education, civic activities, health services, the environment and the arts. By supporting the state's educational system from pre-K to universities, the foundation is investing in Alabama's future and the well-being of its residents.

2631 **Andalusia Health Services**
700 River Falls Street
PO Box 667
Andalusia, AL 36420   334-222-2030
                         FAX: 334-222-7844
                     chrissie@andalusiachamber.com
                     www.andalusiachamber.com

Janna McGlamory, President
Debbie Marcum, Vice President
Ashley Eiland, Executive Vice President
Only offers grants to the residents of Covington County in Alabama who are pursuing a degree in a medical field.

2632 **Arc Of Alabama, The**
557 S Lawrence St
Montgomery, AL 36104-4611   334-262-7688
                                  866-243-9557
                              FAX: 334-834-9737
                        www.thearcofal.org/#!contact/c1d94

Larry Bailey, President
Sherron Culpepper, 1st Vice President
Bruce Koppenhoeffer, 2nd Vice President
The Arc of Alabama, Inc. is a volunteer-based membership organization made up of individuals with intellectual, developmental and other disabilities, their families, friends, interested citizens, and professionals in the disability field.

2633 **Rapahope Children's Retreat Foundation**
205 Lambert Ave.
Suite A
Mobile, AL 36604   251-476-9880
                     info@rapahope.org
                     www.rapahope.org

Melissa McNichol, Executive Director
Roz Dorsett, Assistant Director
Rapahope is an organization that offers a one week long summer camp for children who have, or who have had cancer. For children ages 7-17, the camp offers a wide range of summer camp activities, including but not limited to, swimming, kayaking, horseback riding, and arts. The camp is offered at no cost to campers or their families.

Alaska

2634 **Arc of Alaska**
The Arc of Anchorage
2211 Arca Dr
Anchorage, AK 99508-3462   907-277-6677
                                  800-258-2232
                              FAX: 907-272-2161
                              TTY: 907-277-0735
                          info@thearcofanchorage.org

Rod Shipley, President
Dave Falsey, Vice President
Meredith Parham, Secretary
The Arc helps Alaskans who experience developmental disabilities, behavioral health concerns or deafness achieve lives of dignity and independence as valued members of our community.

2635 **Rasmuson Foundation**
301 West Northern Lights Blvd.
Suite 400
Anchorage, AK 99503   907-297-2700
                             877-366-2700
                         FAX: 907-297-2770
                         www.rasmuson.org

Edward B. Rasmuson, Chairman
Cathryn Rasmuson, Vice Chair
Diane Kaplan, President & CEO
The Rasmuson Foundation invests both in individuals and well managed organizations dedicated to improving the quality of life for Alaskans.

Arizona

2636 **American Foundation Corporation**
4518 North 32nd Street
Phoenix, AZ 85018   602-955-4770
                       FAX: 602-955-4700
                    www.americanfoundation.org

Ben L. Schaub, Founder and CEO
The American Foundation can be your sponsor, and help your company set up a corporate foundation in a public charity or support organization format.

2637 **Arizona Autism Resources**
The Arc of Arizona
PO Box 90714
Phoenix, AZ 85066   602-234-2721
                           800-433-5255
                       FAX: 602-234-5959
                       arc@arcarizona.org
                       www.arcarizona.org

Robert Snyder, President
Michael Leyva, Vice President
Jon Meyers, Executive Director
The Arc is committed to securing for all people with developmental disabilities the opportunity to choose and realize their goals in regard to where they live, learn, work and play.

2638 **Arizona Community Foundation**
2201 E Camelback Road
Suite 405B
Phoenix, AZ 85016   602-381-1400
                           800-222-8221
                       FAX: 602-381-1575
                       info@azfoundation.org
                       www.azfoundation.org

Ron Butler, Chair
Shelly Cohn, Vice Chair
Steven G. Seleznow, President & CEO
The mission of the Arizona Community Foundation is to empower and align philanthropic interests with community needs and build a legacy of living.

2639 **Arizona Instructional Resource Center for Students who are Blind or Visually Impaired, The**
Foundation For Blind Children
1235 E. Harmont Drive
Phoenix, AZ 85020   602-678-5800
                           800-322-4870
                       FAX: 602-678-5819
                   mashton@SeeItOurWay.org
                   www.seeitourway.org

Dee Nortman, CFO
Marc Ashton, Chief Executive Officer
Barbra Smith, Chief of Staff
The Foundation for Blind Children contracts with the Arizona Department of Education to provide statewide media services for students between pre-kindergarten and 12th grade who have a visual impairment or are blind andEneed their instructional materials in a specialized medium such as braille, large print, or electronic files as well as adaptive equipment.

2640 Civitan Foundation
12635 N. 42nd Street
Phoenix, AZ 85032   602-953-2944
                                     www.civitanfoundationaz.com
Dawn Trapp, Executive Director
The foundation aims to enhance the quality of life for children and adults with developmental disabilities through programs such as camp, employment opportunities, adult learning, respite, and summer programs for teens.
1968

2641 Margaret T Morris Foundation
PO Box 592
Prescott, AZ 86302-592   928-445-6633
                                     FAX: 928-445-6633
Susan Rheem, Executive Director

Arkansas

2642 Arc of Arkansas
2004 Main St
Little Rock, AR 72206-1526   501-375-7770
                                     FAX: 501-372-4621
                                     www.arcark.org
Willie Jones, President
Steve Hitt, Chief Executive Officer
Roger Williams, Chief Financial Officer
Serving people with disabilites and their families for over forty years.

2643 Winthrop Rockefeller Foundation
225 East Markham Street
Suite 200
Little Rock, AR 72201   501-376-6854
                                     FAX: 501-374-4797
                                     webfeedback@wrfoundation.org
                                     www.wrfoundation.org
Phillip N. Baldwin, Chair
David Rainey, Ed.D., Vice chair
Sherece Y. West-Scantlebury, Ph.D, President & CEO
Mission is to improve the quality of life in Arkansas. It focuses its grantmaking efforts in three areas: education, economic development and civic affairs. Education projects funded in the past have included grants to schools that are working to involve teachers and parents in making decisions about what happens at their schools, projects that work to remove prejudice from the educational process and more. Major grants are made to support the development of new programs.

California

2644 AIDS Healthcare Foundation
6255 Sunset Blvd.
21st Floor
Los Angeles, CA 90028   323-860-5200
                                     www.aidshealth.org
Michael Weinstein, President
Peter Reis, Senior Vice President
Scott Carruthers, Chief Pharmacy Officer
The Los Angeles-based AIDS Healthcare Foundation (AHF) is a global nonprofit organization providing medicine and advocacy to people all around the world. AHF is currently the largest provider of HIV/AIDS medical care in the U.S.

2645 Ahmanson Foundation
9215 Wilshire Blvd
Beverly Hills, CA 90210   310-278-0770
                                     info@theahmansonfoundation.org
                                     www.theahmansonfoundation.org
William H. Ahmanson, President
Karen Ahmanson Hoffman, Managing Director & Secretary
Kristen K. O'Connor, CFO & Treasurer
The Foundation primarily gives in Southern California with major emphasis in Los Angeles County. The Foundation focuses on the arts and humanities, education, mental health and support for a broad range of social welfare programs.

2646 Alice Tweed Touhy Foundation
205 E Carrillo Street
Suite 219
Santa Barbara, CA 93101-7186   805-962-6430
Jeanne Mc Kay, Manager
Rehabilitation, recreation and building funds are given to organizations only within the Santa Barbara area.

2647 Alternating Hemiplegia of Childhood Foundation
2000 Town Center
Suite 1900
Southfield, MI 48075   313-663-7772
                                     FAX: 313-733-8987
                                     sharon@ahckids.org
                                     ahckids.org
Lynn Egan, President
Joshua Marszalek, Vice President
Gene M Andrasco, Treasurer
Non-profit organization dedicated to promoting professional and public awareness of Alternating Hemiplegia of Childhood (AHC) and providing current information to affected individuals and their families. The foundation also supports ongoing medical research into the cause, treatment and potential cure of AHC and maintains a registry of families, affected chidren and physicians who are familiar with AHC.

2648 Arc of California
1225 8th Street
Suite 350
Sacramento, CA 95815   916-552-6619
                                     800-698-6619
                                     FAX: 916-441-3494
                                     www.thearcca.org
Tony Anderson, Executive Director
Richard Fitzmaurice, President
Betsy Katz, Secretary
Advocates for people with intellectual and all developmental disabilities since 1953. The ARC of California is committed to securing for all people with developmental disabilities, in partnership with thier families, legal guardians or conservators the opportunity to choose and realize their goals of where and how they learn, live, work and play.

2649 Atkinson Foundation
1660 Bush Street
Suite 300
San Mateo, CA 94109   415-561-6540
                                     FAX: 650-357-1101
                                     sangeles@pfs-llc.net
                                     www.atkinsonfdn.org
Elizabeth Curtis, Administrator
Stacey Angels, Grants Manager
The Foundation focuses and awards grants to community service and civic organizations serving the residents of San Mateo County, California through programs that benefit children, youth, seniors, the disadvantaged and those in need of rehabilitation. Grants are also made to local churches and schools, and overseas for sustainable development, health education and family planning. No grants to individuals or for research, travel, special events, annual campaigns, media and publications.

2650 Baker Commodities Corporate Giving Program
4020 Bandini Blvd
Vernon, CA 90058   323-268-2801
                                     FAX: 323-268-5166
                                     info@bakercommodities.com
Jim Andreoli, President
Baker Commodities has been one of the nation's leading providers of rendering, and grease removal services. Baker Commodities, Inc. is a completely sustainable company, recycling animal by-products and kitchen waste into valuable products that can be used to feed livestock, power vehicles, and act as a base for everyday items.

2651 Bank of America Foundation
315 Montgomery St
Fl 8
San Francisco, CA 94104-1803   415-622-8248
                                      888-488-9802
                                      FAX: 704-386-6444
                                      www.bankamerica.com/foundation
Ilana Orin, Manager
The Foundation will consider grants in four categories including: Health & Human Services, which provides support to health & human service organizations primarily through grants to the United Way campaigns; Education, with the focus on preparing people to become productive employees and participating citizens; Conservation & Environment, the improvement of California communities for the benefit of their citizens; and Culture & The Arts, supporting the leading performing and visual arts groups.

2652 Blind Babies Foundation
1814 Franklin Street
Suite 300
Oakland, CA 94612   510-446-2229
                                      FAX: 510-446-2262
                                      www.blindbabies.org
Dottie Bridge, President
Sharon Sacks, PhD, 1st Vice President
Clare Friedman, PhD, 2nd Vice President
Founded in 1949, the foundation provides home-based early intervention services to families with young children with vision impairment in the Northern and Central regions of California.

2653 Bothin Foundation
1660 Bush Street
Suite 300
San Francisco, CA 94109   415-561-6540
                                     FAX: 415-561-6477
                                     ccasey@pfs-llc.net
Lyman H. Casey, President
A. Michael Casey, Vice President & Treasurer
Devon Laycox, Vice President
The Bothin Foundation makes grants for capital, building, and equipment needs to organizations providing direct services to low-income, at risk children, youth and families, the elderly, and the disabled in San Francisco, Marin, Sonoma, and San Mateo counties.

2654 Briggs Foundation
1969 Lancewood Ln
Carlsbad, CA 92009-6826   760-704-6481
                                     FAX: 760-704-6483
Blaine A Briggs, President
Private non-operating foundation.

2655 Burns-Dunphy Foundation
5 3rd Street
Suite 528
San Francisco, CA 94103-3213   415-421-6995
                                     FAX: 415-882-7774
Walter Gleason
Cressey Nakagawa
Grants are given to promote wellness for the visually impaired, physically and mentally disabled and to promote research in these areas.

2656 California Community Foundation
221 S. Figueroa Street
Suite 400
Los Angeles, CA 90012   213-413-4130
                                     FAX: 213-383-2046
                                     info@ccf-la.org
                                     www.calfund.org
Cynthia A. Telles, Chairman
Antonia Hernandez, President & CEO
John E. Kobara, EVP & COO
Areas of funding priority include grants for the disabled, child welfare, rehabilitation, developmentally disabled, employment projects, research and computer projects. Giving is limited to the greater Los Angeles area.

2657 California Endowment
1000 N Alameda St
Los Angeles, CA 90012   213-628-1001
                                     800-449-4149
                                     FAX: 213-703-4193
                                     questions@calendow.org
Zac Guevara, Vice Chair
Robert Ross, President & CEO
Martha Jimenez, EVP/ Counsel
California Endowment's mission is to expand access to affordable, quality health care for underserved individuals and communities, and to promote fundamental improvements in the health status of all Californians.

2658 Carrie Estelle Doheny Foundation
707 Wilshire Boulevard
Suite 4960
Los Angeles, CA 90017   213-488-1122
                                     FAX: 213-488-1544
                                     doheny@dohenyfoundation.org
                                     www.dohenyfoundation.org
Robert A. Smith,III, President
Nina Shepherd, CAO/ CFO
Pam Thomas, Grants Administrator
The Foundation primarily funds local, not-for-profit organizations endeavoring to advance education, medicine and religion, to improve the health and welfare of the sick, aged, incapacitated, and to aid the needy.

2659 Coeta and Donald Barker Foundation
3740 Cahuenga Blvd
Studio City, CA 91604   760-340-1162
                                     818-980-3630
                                     FAX: 818-980-2709
                                     info@scga.org
                                     www.scga.org
Nancy Harris, President
Kevin Heaney, Executive Director
Andrea Fredlin, Admin Asst., Club Services
It is an independent organization that gives its attention to organizations that are charitable or nonprofit under the laws of the state of Oregon or California.

2660 Conrad N Hilton Foundation
30440 Agoura Road
Agoura Hills, CA 91301   818-851-3700
                                     FAX: 310-694-9051
                                     cnhf@hiltonfoundation.org
                                     hiltonfoundation.org
Steven M. Hilton, Chairman, President & CEO
Barron Hilton, Chairman Emeritus
Donald H Hubbs, Director Emeritus
Our grant-making style is to initiate and develop major long-term projects and then seek out the organizations to implement them. As a consequence of this proactive approach, the Foundation does not generally consider unsolicited proposals. Our major projects currently include: blindness prevention and treatment, support the work of the Catholic Sisters, drug abuse prevention among youth, support of the Conrad N. Hilton College of Hotel and Restaurant Management, and much more.

2661 Crescent Porter Hale Foundation
1660 Bush Street
Suite 300
San Francisco, CA 94109   415-561-6540
                                     FAX: 415-561-5477
                                     evalentine@pfs-llc.net
                                     www.crescentporterhale.org
E. William Swanson, President
Sr. Estela Morales, MSW, Vice President
Eunice Valentine, Executive Director
Serves organizations in the San Francisco Bay Area who are involved in the following areas of concern: education in the fields of art and music; private elementary, high school and university education; capital funding; and other worthwhile programs which can be demonstrated as serving broad community purposes, leading toward the improvement of the quality of life.

2662 David and Lucile Packard Foundation
343 Second Street
Los Altos, CA 94022 650-917-7142
FAX: 650-948-5793
communications@packard.org
www.packard.org

Susan Packard Orr, Chairman
Julie E. Packard, Vice Chairman
Nancy Packard Burnett, Vice Chairman
This foundation provides grants to nonprofit organizations in the following areas: conservation; population; science; children, familes, and communities; arts and organizational effectiveness; and philanthropy. It provides national and international grants and also has a special focus on the Northern California Counties.

2663 Deutsch Foundation
5454 Beethoven St
Los Angeles, CA 90066 310-862-3000
877-340-7700
FAX: 310-862-3100
deutschinc.com

Linda Sawyer, Chairman
Kim Getty, President, North America
Val Difebo, CEO, Deutsch NY
Learning disabled, visually impaired, mental health, eye research, child welfare, speech and hearing impaired, physically disabled and independence projects are funded through this Foundation. Giving is limited to California.

2664 Dream Street Foundation
324 S. Beverly Dr.
Suite 500
Beverly Hills, CA 90212 424-333-1371
FAX: 310-388-0302
www.dreamstreetfoundation.org
Patty Grubman, Founder
Provides nationwide camping programs for children and young adults with cancer, chronic and life threatening illnesses.

2665 East Bay Community Foundation
De Domenico Building
200 Frank H Ogawa Plaza
Oakland, CA 94612 510-836-3223
FAX: 510-836-7418
jwhead@eastbaycf.org
www.ebcf.org

Sherry M. Hirota, Chair
Ingrid Lamirault, Vice Chair
Peter Garcia, Vice Chair
A collection of funds created by many people, organizations and businesses, the Foundation helps those people and groups to support effective nonprofit organizations to the East Bay and beyond.

2666 Evelyn and Walter Hans Jr
114 Sansome Street
Suite 600
San Francisco, CA 94104 415-856-1400
FAX: 415-856-1500
www.haasjr.org

Walter J. Haas, Chair
Ira S. Hirschfield, President & Trustee
Michael Blake, VP of Finance
A private foundation interested in programs which assist people who are hungry, homeless, or at risk of homelessness; enable older adults to maintain independent lives in the community and support Hispanic community development in San Francisco's Mission District. The Foundation also encourages proposals for corporate social responsibility efforts within the business community.

2667 Family Caregiver Alliance
785 Market St.
Suite 750
San Francisco, CA 94103 415-434-3388
800-445-8106
FAX: 415-434-3508
info@caregiver.org
www.caregiver.org

Ping Hao, MBA, President
Jacquelyn Kung, Vice President
Kathleen Kelly,MPA, Executive Director
To improve the quality of life for caregivers and those they care for through information, services, and advocacy.

2668 Financial Aid for the Disabled and Their Families
Reference Service Press
2310 Homestead Rd.
Suite C1 #219
Los Altos, CA 94024 650-861-3170
FAX: 650-861-3171
info@rspfunding.com
www.rspfunding.com

Gail Schlachter, President
R David Weber, Editor-in-Chief
Mike Fields, Database and Website Manager
This directory, which Children's Bookwatch calls invaluable describes more than 1,100 financial aid opportunities available to support persons with disabilities and members of their families. Updated ever 2 years. *$39.50*
300 pages
ISBN 1-588410-31-5

2669 Firemans Fund Foundation
Firemans Fund Insurance Companies
777 San Marin Dr
Novato, CA 94998 415-899-2000
800-227-1700
FAX: 415-899-3600

Lori Dickerson Fouche, President & CEO
Jill Paterson, Chief Financial Officer
Eleanor Barnard, Chief Distribution & Sales
Provides discretionary grants to the disabled only in Marin and Sonoma counties in the San Francisco Bay area.

2670 Fred Gellert Foundation
1038 Redwood Highway
Building B, Suite 2
Mill Valley, CA 94941 415-381-7575
FAX: 415-381-8526
foundationcenter.org/grantmaker/fredgellert/
Fred Gellert, Founder
Patty Oday, Administrator
Focuses on organizations and programs serving residents of San Mateo and San Francisco and Marin counties in California, with the exception of environmentally concerned organizations.

2671 Gallo Foundation
P.O. Box 1130
Modesto, CA 95353-1130 209-579-3204
877-687-9463
FAX: 209-341-3307
www.ejgallo.com
John Gallo, Senior VP Operations
Physically and mentally disabled, child welfare, Special Olympics, United Cerebral Palsy and Easter Seal Society are among the grants provided by this foundation.

2672 Glaucoma Research Foundation
251 Post Street
Suite 600
San Francisco, CA 94108 415-986-3162
800-826-6693
FAX: 415-986-3763
question@glaucoma.org
www.glaucoma.org

Andrew Iwach, MD, Board Chair
Robert L. Stamper, MD, Vice Chair
Thomas M. Brunner, President/CEO
A national organization dedicated to protecting the sight of people with glaucoma through research and education. The Foundation conducts and supports research that contributes to improved

patient care and a better understanding of the disease process. Provides education, advocacy and emotional support to patients and their families.

2673   Harden Foundation
1636 Ercia Street
Salinas, CA 93906   831-442-3005
                                            FAX: 831-443-1429
                                        joe@hardenfoundation.org
                                        www.hardenfoundation.org
Patricia Tynan Chapman, President
C. Bill Elliott, Vice President/Treasurer
Joseph C. Grainger, Executive Director
Founded to assist charitable organizations in the Salinas Valley.

2674   Henry J Kaiser Family Foundation
2400 Sand Hill Rd
Menlo Park, CA 94025-6941   650-854-9400
                                            FAX: 650-854-4800
                                                 www.kff.org
Drew Altman, President/CEO
Gary Claxton, Vice President
Esther Dicks, Vice President
A non-profit, private operating foundation focusing on the major health care issues facing the US, with a growing role in global health. Kaiser develops and runs its own research and communications programs, sometimes in partnership with other non-profit research organizations or major media companies.

2675   Henry W Bull Foundation
Santa Barbara Bank & Trust
P.O. Box 2340
Santa Barbara, CA 93120   202-720-7871
                                            FAX: 805-884-1404
                                        info@coreprojects.com
                                      www.activistfacts.com/about/
Janice Gibbons, VP/Senior Trust Officer
Grant given to a wide range of organizations that include those which provide services for the disabled; arts, education, services for elderly and youth grants awarded two times a year. Grant size ranges from $500 to $5,000. Proposal deadlines April 1, Sept 1.

2676   Irvine Health Foundation
18301 Von Karman Avenue
Suite 440
Irvine, CA 92612-0120   949-253-2959
                                            FAX: 949-253-2962
                                                 info@ihf.org
                                                 www.ihf.org
Timothy L. Strader, Sr., Chairman
Carol Mentor McDermott, Vice Chairman
Edward B. Kacic, President
Mission is to improve the physical, mental and emotional well-being of all Orange County residents.

2677   Joseph Drown Foundation
1999 Avenue of the Stars
Suite 2330
Los Angeles, CA 90067   310-277-4488
                                            FAX: 310-277-4573
                                             staff@jdrown.org
                                             www.jdrown.org
Norman C Obrow, President
Giving is focused primarily in California. No support for religious purposes or to individuals. Goal is to assist individuals in becoming successful, self-sustaining, contributing citizens.

2678   Kenneth T and Eileen L Norris Foundation
11 Golden Shore
Suite 450
Long Beach, CA 90802   562-435-8444
                                            FAX: 562-436-0584
                                             grants@ktn.org
                                        www.norrisfoundation.org
Lisa D Hanson, Chairman
Ronald R Barnes, Executive Director & Trustee
Walter J Zanino, Controller
The Foundation is primarily focused on medicine and education. To a lesser extent the foundation contributes to community programs including visually impaired, autism, mentally and physically disabled, deaf and mental health in the Southern California

area. Average grant size in this area is $5,000-$10,000. Grants are also given in the area of culture and youth.

2679   Koret Foundation
33 New Montgomery Street
Suite 1090
San Francisco, CA 94105-4526   415-882-7740
                                            FAX: 415-882-7775
                                          info@koretfoundation.org
                                          www.koretfoundation.org
Susan Koret, Board Chair
Anita L. Friedman, President
Michael J. Boskin, President
Koret seeks to fund outstanding examples of innovative approaches to community challenges and opportunities.

2680   LA84 Foundation
2141 W Adams Blvd
Los Angeles, CA 90018   323-730-4600
                                            FAX: 323-730-9637
                                                 info@la84.org
                                                 www.la84.org
Frank M. Sanchez, Chair
Anita L. DeFrantz, President
F. Patrick Escobar, VP, Grants & Programs
The LA84 Foundation was established to manage Southern California's share of the surplus from the highly successful 1984 Olympic Games in Los Angeles and offers sports programs, a premier sports library and meeting facilities. The foundation currently serves two million youth in eight Southern California counties.

2681   LJ Skaggs and Mary C Skaggs Foundation
1221 Broadway
21st Floor
Oakland, CA 94612-1837   510-451-3300
                                            FAX: 510-451-1527
                                             skaggs@fablaw.com
Philip M Jelley, President
Jayne C Davis, Vice President
Robert N Janopaul, Director
The Foundation presently makes grants under four program categories: performing arts, social concerns, projects of historic interest and special projects.

2682   Legler Benbough Foundation
2550 Fifth Avenue
Suite 132
San Diego, CA 92103   619-235-8099
                                            FAX: 619-235-8077
                                    peter@benboughfoundation.org
Peter K. Elsworth, President
John G. Rebelo, Jr., Treasurer
Nbob Kelly, Director
The mission of the foundation is to improve the quality of life of the people of San Diego. The foundation focuses on three target areas for funding, one in the area of providing economic opportunity, one in the area of enhancing cultural opportunity, and one that provides focus for health, education and welfare funding.

2683   Levi Strauss Foundation
1155 Battery St
San Francisco, CA 94111-1264   415-501-7208
                                                 800-872-5384
                                            FAX: 415-544-3490
                          www.levistrauss.com/levi-strauss-foundation
Chip Bergh, President & CEO
Roy Bagattini, EVP/President
Lisa Collier, EVP/President
Has a funding initiative to support organizations which provide services for people with AIDS, and/or educational programs which help prevent the further spread of the HIV virus. The Foundation will assist in the development and enhancement of such services only in those communities where Levi Strauss & Co. has plants and distribution centers.

2684 Louis R Lurie Foundation
555 California Street
Suite 5100
San Francisco, CA 94104-1707   415-392-2470
FAX: 415-421-8669
www.foundationcenter.org/grantmaker/lurie
Nancy Terry, Foundation Administrator
Visually impaired, hard-of-hearing and physically disabled in the
San Francisco Bay Area and Metropolitan Chicago areas only.

2685 Luke B Hancock Foundation
360 Bryant St
Palo Alto, CA 94301-1409   650-321-5536
FAX: 650-321-0697
Ruth Ramel, Director
Has concentrated its resources over the past year on programs
which provide job training and employment for at-risk youth.
Consortium funding with other foundations in areas where there
is unmet need; emergency and transitional funding; and selected
funding for music education. .

2686 Marin Community Foundation
5 Hamilton Landing
Suite 200
Novato, CA 94949   415-464-2500
FAX: 415-464-2555
info@marincf.org
www.marincf.org
Cleveland Justis, Chair
Thomas Peters, Ph.D., President & CEO
Sid Hartman, CFO/COO
Mission is to encourage and apply philanthropic contributions to
help improve the human condition, embrace diversity, promote a
humane and democratic society, and enhance the communities
quality of life, now and for future generations.

2687 Mary A Crocker Trust
57 Post Street
Suite 610
San Francisco, CA 94104-5023   650-576-3384
FAX: 415-982-0141
staff@mactrust.org
www.mactrust.org
Established in 1889, the Foundation is interested in Bay Area programs such as environment, education and community relations.

2688 MedicAlert Foundation International
5226 Pirrone Crt
Salida, CA 95368   800-432-5378
customer_service@medicalert.org
www.medicalert.org
Barton G. Tretheway, CAE, Chairt
David Leslie, President & CEO
Melody Howard, Vice President Of Call Center Operations
A trusted emergency support network dedicated to educating
emergency responders and medical personnel for facing everyday emergency situations, as well as providing emergency care
services for members.

**2689 National Center on Caregiving at Family Caregiver
Alliance (FCA)**
785 Market Street
Suite 750
San Francisco, CA 94103   415-434-3388
800-445-8106
FAX: 415-434-3508
info@caregiver.org
www.caregiver.org
Ping Hao, MBA, President
Jacquelyn Kung, Vice President
Kathleen Kelly, MPA, Executive Director
FCA offers programs at national, state and local levels to support
and sustain caregivers. The National Center on Caregiving
(NCC) program works to advance the development of high-quality, cost-effective policies and programs for caregivers in every
state of the country. Uniting research, public policy and services,
the NCC serves as a central source of information on caregiving
and long term care issues for policy makers, service providers,
media, funders and family caregivers.

2690 National Foundation of Wheelchair Tennis
940 Calle Amanecer
Suite B
San Clemente, CA 92673-6218   714-361-3663
FAX: 714-361-6603
www.nfwt.org
Bill Butler
Founded in January of 1980, the intention of this foundation is to
assist the newly physically disabled individual to realize his full
potential in society by enhancing his esteem, independence productivity and physical capabilities regardless of age, sex, creed or
disability extent.

2691 Parker Foundation
2604-B El Camino Real
Suite 244
Carlsbad, CA 92008   760-720-0630
FAX: 760-720-1239
mail@theparkerfoundation.org
www.theparkerfoundation.org
Judy McDonald, President
Gordon Swanson, Vice President
Ann Davies, Secretary
The assets are directed to projects which will contribute to the
betterment of any aspect of the people of San Diego County, Cali-
fornia and solely to entities which, among other things, are orga-
nized exclusively for charitable purposes and are operating in
San Diego County, California.

2692 Pasadena Foundation
301 East Colorado Boulevard
Suite 810
Pasadena, CA 91101-2824   626-796-2097
FAX: 626-583-4738
pcfstaff@pasadenacf.org
www.pasadenacf.org
David M. Davis, Chair
Judy Gain, Vice Chair
Jennifer Fleming DeVoll, Executive Director
The mission of the Pasadena Foundation is to improve the quality
of life for citizens of the Pasadena area through support of non-
profit organizations that provide services beneficial to the
community.

2693 RC Baker Foundation
P.O. Box 6150
Orange, CA 92863-6150   714-750-8987
F L Scott, Manager
Established in 1952, for general philanthropic purposes. The
bulk of assistance and support has been to religious, scientific,
educational institutions and youth organizations.

2694 Ralph M Parsons Foundation
888 West Sixth Street
Suite 700
Los Angeles, CA 90017   213-362-7600
FAX: 213-482-8878
www.rmpf.org
James A. Thomas, Chairman
Elizabeth Lowe, Vice Chairman
Wendy Garen, President & CEO
The Foundation is concerned with the encouragement and sup-
port of projects and programs deemed beneficial to mankind in
several major areas of interest such as: education; social impact;
civic and cultural; health and special products. Only funds in Los
Angeles County.

2695 Robert Ellis Simon Foundation
312 S Canyon View Drive
Los Angeles, CA 90049-3812   310-275-7335
Joan Willens
Mental health and visually impaired grants are the main concerns
of this organization.

2696 San Francisco Foundation
One Embarcadero Cente
Suite 1400
San Francisco, CA 94111   415-733-8500
                                   FAX: 415-477-2783
                                        info@sff.org
                                        www.sff.org

Sandra R Hernandez, CEO
Nick Hodges, VP for Philanthropic Services
Bobbie Chapman, Director of Business Development
The Foundation's purpose is to improve life, promote greater equality of opportunity and assist those in need or at risk in the San Francisco Bay Area. The Foundation strives to protect and enhance the unique resources of the Bay Area, committed to equality of opportunity for all and the elimination of any injustice, seeks to enhance human dignity and seeks to establish mutual trust, respect and communication among the Foundation.

2697 Santa Barbara Foundation
1111 Chapala Street
Suite 200
Santa Barbara, CA 93101   805-963-1873
                                   FAX: 805-966-2345
                                  info@sbfoundation.org
                                   www.sbfoundation.org

Eileen Sheridan, Chair
James Morouse, Vice Chair
Ronald Gallo, President & CEO
The Foundations mission is to enrich the lives of the people of Santa Barbara County through philanthropy. The Foundation awards grants to nonprofits within the County in the areas of education, health, human services, personal development, cluture, recreation, community enhancement and environment. No support is given to individuals except through student aid.

2698 Seany Foundation
3530 Camino del Rio N
Suite 101
San Diego, CA 92108   858-551-0922
                              www.theseanyfoundation.org

Paula Lutzky, Chief Financial Officer
Emily Brody, Director, Marketing & Media
Tiana LaCerva, Director, Special Events
Funds programs dedicated to bringing joy to children with cancer and their families.

2699 Sidney Stern Memorial Trust
860 Via de la Paz
PO Box 457
Pacific Palisades, CA 90272   310-459-2117
                         info@sidneysternmemorialtrust.org
                          www.sidneysternmemorialtrust.org

Betty Hoffenberg, Director
A Southern California-based foundation providing grants to nonprofit organizations for various projects. The foundation gives priority to the following areas of interest: education, health and science, community service projects, youth, services to the mentally and emotionally disabled, the arts, organizations and activities serving California. The Board prefers to make contributions to organizations that use the funds directly in the furtherance of their charitable and public purposes.

2700 Sierra Health Foundation
1321 Garden Hwy
Sacramento, CA 95833   916-922-4755
                                   FAX: 916-922-4024
                                   info@sierrahealth.org
                                    www.sierrahealth.org

Jose Hermocillo, Chair
David W. Gordon, Vice Chair
Chet P. Hewitt, President & CEO
The Foundation strives to establish a collaborative relationship with its grantees, and with other funders and foundations, through an open dialogue. The Foundation approaches each grant as a partnership, with opportunities for the grantee and grantor to work cooperatively to enhance the effectiveness of the grant project.

2701 Silicon Valley Community Foundation
2400 West El Camino Real
Suite 300
Mountain View, CA 94040-1498   650-450-5400
                                   FAX: 650-450-5401
                                 info@siliconvalleycf.org
                                  www.siliconvalleycf.org

C.S. Parker, Chair
Samuel Johnson,Jr., Vice Chair
Emmitt D. Carson, Ph.D, President & CEO
Serving all of San Mateo & Santa Clara counties, Silicon Valley Foundation has more than $1.5B in assets under management and 1500 philanthropic funds. The community provides grants through donor advised and corporate funds in addition to its own Community Endowment Fund. In addition, the community foundation serves as a regional center for philanthropy, providing donors simple and effective ways to give locally & globally.

2702 Sonora Area Foundation
362 S Stewart Street
Sonora, CA 95370   209-533-2596
                                   FAX: 209-533-2412
                                    www.sonora-area.org

Jim Johnson, President SAF
Roger Francis, Vice President
Edward B. Wyllie, Executive Director
The Sonora Area Foundation strengthens its community through assisting donors, making grants, and providing leadership.

2703 Stella B Gross Charitable Trust C/O Bank of The West Trust Department
PO Box 1121
San Jose, CA 95108-1121   408-947-5203
Gabe Padilla, Trust Admin
Organization must be federal and state tax-exempt and reside within the bounds of Santa Clara County, California to be eligible.

2704 Teichert Foundation
3500 American River Dr
Sacramento, CA 95864   916-484-3011
                                   FAX: 916-484-6506
                                    www.teichert.com

Frederick Teichert, LHD, Executive Director
Awards grants to community organizations and provides employee matching grants. Teichert Foundation expresses the companie's commitment to build and preserve a healthy and prosperous region.

2705 WM Keck Foundation
550 South Hope Street
Suite 2500
Los Angeles, CA 90071- 2617   213-680-3833
                                   FAX: 213-614-0934
                                     info@wmkeck.org
                                      www.wmkeck.org

Allison Keller, Executive Director & CFO
Maria Pellegrini, Ph.D, Executive Director of Programs
Thomas Everhart, Ph.D, Senior Scientific Advisor
Created to support accredited colleges and universities with particular emphasis on the sciences, engineering and medical research. The Foundation also maintains a Southern California Grant Program that provides support for non-profit organizations in the field of civic and community services, health care, precollegiate education and the arts.

2706 Wayfinder Family Services
5300 Angeles Vista Blvd.
Los Angeles, CA 90043   323-295-4555
                                      800-352-2290
                                   FAX: 323-296-0424
                                   www.wayfinderfamily.org

Miki Jordan, Chief Executive Officer
Jay Allen, President & Chief Operating Officer
Fernando Almodovar, Chief Financial Officer
Formerly Junior Blind of America, Wayfinder provides programs and services for children and adults who are blind or visually impaired and their families to achieve independence and self-esteem. Programs include: Camp Bloomfield, Visions: Adventures in Learning, Infant-Family Program, Early Childhood Program, Special Education School, Children's Residential Program,

Davidson Program for Independence, and Student Transition and Enrichment Program, Vision Screening and After School enrichment.

2707 Whittier Trust
Whittier Trust Company
1600 Huntington Dr
South Pasadena, CA 91030   626-441-5111
                                   FAX: 626-441-0420
                                   hrdept@whittiertrust.com
                                   www.whittiertrust.com

Michael J Casey, Chairman
David A Dahl, President & CEO
Brian H Flynn, Senior Vice President, Business Development

Whittier Trust offers financial services and expertise in the area of family wealth management. Some of their other areas of consultation include philanthropic advising, investment management, legal services and real estate.

2708 Willam G Gilmore Foundation
1660 Bush Street
Suite 300
San Francisco, CA 94109   415-561-0650
                                   FAX: 415-561-5477

William N Hancock, Owner

Colorado

2709 AV Hunter Trust
650 South Cherry Street
Suite 535
Glendale, CO 80246- 1897   303-399-5450
                                   FAX: 303-399-5499
                                   afreeman@pfs-llc.net
                                   www.avhuntertrust.org

Mary K. Anstine, President
George C. Gibson, Vice President
Barbara L. Howie, Executive Director

Donated nearly $50 million to nonprofit organizations serving those who captured Mr. Hunter's attention and sparked his compassion. Trust gives aid, comfort, support, or assistance to children or aged people or indigent adults.

2710 Adolph Coors Foundation
215 St. Paul Street
Suite 300
Denver, CO 80206   303-388-1636
                                   FAX: 303-388-1684
                                   www.coorsfoundation.org

John W. Jackson, Executive Director
Jeanne L. Bistranin, Senior Program Officer
Carrie C. Tynan, Program Officer

Applicant organizations must be classified as 501 and must operate within the United States. The areas covered by the Foundation are health, education, youth, community services, civic and cultural and public affairs.

2711 Arc of Colorado
1580 Logan Street
Suite 730
Denver, CO 80203   303-864-9334
                                   800-333-7690
                                   FAX: 303-864-9330
                                   mrymer@thearcofco.org
                                   www.thearcofco.org

Randy Patrick, President
Tonna Kelly, Vice President
Marijo Rymer, Executive Director

A private not-for-profit, membership-based, grassroots association. The Arc of Colorado is the state office whith local units located in various areas throughout the state.

2712 Bonfils-Stanton Foundation
Daniels and Fisher Tower
1601 Arapahoe St.
Suite 500
Denver, CO 80202   303-825-3774
                                   FAX: 303-825-0802
                                   webinfo@bonfils-stanton.org
                                   bonfils-stantonfoundation.org

Gary P. Steuer, President/CEO
Gina A. Ferrari, Director, Grants Program
Ann M. Hovland, CFO/Treasurer

Grants limited to Colorado 501 (c)(3) organizations and are evaluatied based on alignment with these Foundation objectives: 1) The Bonfils-Stanton Foundation supports cultural organizations that consistently demonstrate artistic excellence, visionary leadership, and adaptive capacity; and 2) They idenitfy and nurture grassroots innovative organizations and initiative that enhance the values, spirit, and diversity of Denver's cultural community.

2713 Comprecare Foundation
PO Box 740610
Arvada, CO 80006   303-432-2808
                                   FAX: 303-432-2808
                                   www.comprecarefoundation.org

Milton W. Bollman, Chairman of the Board
Dr. Ellen Mangione, MD, MPH, Vice Chairman
James R. Gilsdorf, Executive Director

The purpose of the Comprecare Foundation is to encourage, aid or assist specific health related programs and to make grants to support the activities of organizations which are designed to advance and promote health care education, the delivery of health care services, and the improvement of community health and welfare.

2714 Denver Foundation
55 Madison Street
8th Floor
Denver, CO 80206   303-300-1790
                                   FAX: 303-300-6547
                                   information@denverfoundation.org
                                   www.denverfoundation.org

Sandra Shreve, Chair
Ginny Bayless, Vice Chair and Chair-Elect
David M Miller, President & CEO

Neighbors helping neighbors, that's what the foundation is for. As Denver's only community foundation we've been accepting charitable donations since 1925. Those funds have been given back to the community in ongoing grants to nonprofit organizations - organizations that touch nearly every meaningful artistic, cultural, civic, health and human services interest of metro Denver's citizens.

2715 El Pomar Foundation
10 Lake Circle
Colorado Springs, CO 80906   719-633-7733
                                   800-554-7711
                                   FAX: 719-577-5702
                                   grants@elpomar.org
                                   www.elpomar.org

William J. Hybl, Chairman/CEO
William Ward, Vice Chair
R. Thayer Tutt, Jr., President/CIO

Mission of El Pomar is to enhance, encourage and promote the current and future well being of the people of Colorado through grantmaking and community stewardship.

2716 Helen K and Arthur E Johnson Foundation
1700 Broadway
Suite 1100
Denver, CO 80290-1718   303-861-4127
                                  800-232-9931
                                  FAX: 303-861-0607
                                  www.johnsonfoundation.org

Ms. Lynn H. Campion, Chairman
Ms. Berit K. Campion, Vice Chair
John H Alexander Jr, President

A nonprofit, grantmaking private foundation incorporated under the laws of the State of Colorado in 1948. The Foundation is a general purpose foundation whose grant program consists of a wide variety of creative efforts to solve problems and to enrich the quality of life. The areas of interest are: education, youth, health, community services, civic and culture and senior citizens. Grants limited to the state of Colorado.

2717 Listen Foundation
6950 E Belleview Ave.
Suite 203
Greenwood Village, CO 80111   303-781-9440
                                            info@listenfoundation.org
                                            www.listenfoundation.org

Allison Biever, President
David Kelsall, MD, Medical Director
The Listen Foundation provides access to Listening and Spoken Language Therapy (LSL) for children are deaf and hard of hearing.

Connecticut

2718 Aetna Foundation
151 Farmington Ave
Hartford, CT 06156   860-273-0123
                                            800-872-3862
                                            www.aetnahealthinsurance.com

Mark T Bertolini, Chairman/CEO
Karen S. Rohan, President
William J. Casazza, EVP & General Counsel
The Aetna Foundation is the independent charitable and philanthropic arm of Aetna Inc. The Foundation helps build healthy communities by promoting volunteerism, forming partnerships and funding initiatives that improve the quality of life where our employees and customers live and work.

2719 Arc of Connecticut
43 Woodland Street
Suite 260
Hartford, CT 6105-2300   860-246-6400
                                            FAX: 860-246-6406
                                            arcct@aol.com
                                            www.arcct.com

Leslie Simoes, Interim Executive Director
The Arc of Connecticut is an advocacy organization committed to protecting the rights of people with intellectual, cognitive, and developmental disabilities and to promoting opportunities for their full inclusion in the life of thier communities.

2720 Community Foundation of Southeastern Connecticut
68 FederalStreet
PO Box 769
New London, CT 06320   860-442-3572
                                            877-442-3572
                                            FAX: 860-442-0584
                                            maryam@cfect.org
                                            www.cfect.org

Susan Pochal, Chair
Dianne E. Williams, Vice Chair
Maryam Elahi, President & CEO
Provides donors with an easy and convenient way to give back to our community with joy and impact. We make grants to nonprofit organizations and support their efforts to strengthen our community.

2721 Connecticut Mutual Life Foundation
140 Garden St
Hartford, CT 6154   860-727-3000
Astrida Olds, Executive Director
Distinguished throughout its long history by unusual commitment to high principles of corporate purpose and business ethics. That commitment has been reflected not only in the firm belief that normal business functions must be carried out with a sense of responsibility beyond that required by the marketplace. Maintains an ongoing program of corporate contributions, a nationwide matching gifts plan for all employees on behalf of private and public education, skills training programs, and more.

2722 Cornelia de Lange Syndrome Foundation
302 West Main Street
#100
Avon, CT 06001   860-676-8166
                                            800-753-2357
                                            FAX: 860-676-8337
                                            info@cdlsusa.org
                                            www.cdlsusa.org

Robert Boneberg, Esq., President
Richard Haaland, Ph.D., Vice President
David Harvey, Vice President
Provides information about birth defects caused by Cornelia de Lange Syndrome.

2723 Fidelco Guide Dog Foundation
103 Vision Way
Bloomfield, CT 06002   860-243-5200
                                            FAX: 860-769-0567
                                            admissions@fidelco.org
                                            www.fidelco.org

Karen C. Tripp, Chair
G. Kenneth Bernhard, Esq., Vice Chair
Gregg Barratt, Chief of Staff
The Fidelco Guide Dog Foundation creates increased freedom and independence for men and women who are blind by providing them with guide dogs.

2724 GE Foundation
General Electric Company
3135 Easton Tpke
Fairfield, CT 6828   203-373-3216
                                            FAX: 203-373-3029
                                            gefoundation@ge.com
                                            www.ge.com

Jeffrey R. Immelt, Chairman/ CEO
Daniel C. Heintzelman, Vice Chair
Jeffrey S. Bornstein, SVP & CFO, GE
Believes that our greatest national resource is the work force. If we are to successfully compete in the global arena, then we become involved in improving the education of all of our citizens. The Foundation sets examples for others to emulate helping people with their international grant program to higher education and to health care for children in developing countries.

2725 Hartford Foundation for Public Giving
10 Columbus Blvd
8th Floor
Hartford, CT 06106   860-548-1888
                                            FAX: 860-524-8346
                                            lindakelly@hfpg.org
                                            www.hfpg.org

Yvette Melendez, Chair
Bonnie J. Malley, Vice Chair
Linda J. Kelly, President
Developmentally disabled, housing, deaf, recreation and education grants.

2726 Hartford Insurance Group
1 Hartford Plz
Hartford, CT 6155-1708   860-547-5000
                                            www.thehartford.com

Christopher Swift, Chairman/ CEO
Doug Elliot, President
Beth Bombara, Chief Financial Officer
Giving is primarily in the Hartford, CT area and in communities where the company has a regional office. No support is available for political or religious purposes. Grants are given in the areas of education, health and United Way organizations.

2727 Henry Nias Foundation
20 Carmen Rd
Milford, CT 6460-7508   203-874-2787
Charles D Fleischman, President
Giving limited to NY metropolitan area. Arts, cultural programs, medical school/education, and children and youth.

2728 **Jane Coffin Childs Memorial Fund for Medical Research**
333 Cedar St, SHM
L300
New Haven, CT 6510-3206
203-785-4612
FAX: 203-785-3301
www.jccfund.org

Dr Randy Schekman, Director
The Fund awards fellowships to suitably qualified individuals for full time postdoctoral studies in the medical and related sciences bearing on cancer.

2729 **John H and Ethel G Nobel Charitable Trust**
Bankers Trust Company
1 Fawcett Pl
PO Box 1297
New York, NY 1008-1297
203-629-7120
FAX: 203-629-7170

Paul J Bisset, VP

2730 **Scheuer Associates Foundation**
960 Lake Ave
Greenwich, CT 6831-3032
203-622-5002
FAX: 203-622-5002

Thomas Scheuer, President

2731 **Swindells Charitable Foundation Trust**
Shawmut Bank
1221SW YamhillStreet
Suite 100
Portland, OR 97205-2303
503-222-0689
FAX: 503-222-0726
dwecker@swindellstrust.org
www.swindellstrust.org

Maggie Willard, President
Grants made to charitable organizations or societies incorporated for the relief of sick and suffering poor children and/or the relief of sick suffering and indigent aged men and women and/or the support of public charitable hospitals. Geographic area includes Hartford, CT area primarily. Application is required, deadlines are Feb. 1 and Aug. 1.

Delaware

2732 **Arc of Delaware**
2 S Augustine Street
Suite B
Wilmington, DE 19804-2504
302-996-9400
FAX: 302-996-0683
TTY:800-232-5460
eraign@arcde.org
www.thearcofdelaware.org

Bill Seufert, President
Becky Hill, Vice President
Merry Jones, Vice President
The Arc of Delaware is a non-profit organization of volunteers and staff who work together to improve the quality of life for people with disabilitiesand their families. We strive to include all children and adults with cognitive, intellectual and developmental disabilities in every community.

2733 **Longwood Foundation**
100 W 10th St
Suite 1109
Wilmington, DE 19801-1694
302-683-8200
FAX: 302-654-2323
www.longwoodfoundation.com

There du Pont, President
Peter Morrow, Executive Director
Offers grants to the mentally and physically disabled - capital, program, education and housing grants in the state of Delaware.

District of Columbia

2734 **Alexander and Margaret Stewart Trust**
Brawner Building
888 17th Street NW
Suite 1250
Washington, DC 20006-3321
202-333-1277
FAX: 202-333-3128
aplatt@projectsinternational.com
www.projectsinternational.com

Chas W. Freeman, Chairman
Peter J.C, Young, President
Imtiaz T. Ladak, Chief Financial Officer
Grants are given only to the Washington, DC area organizations providing care or treatment to cancer patients or those with childhood afflictions.

2735 **American Hotel and Lodging Association Foundation**
1201 Eye St. NW.
Suite 1100
Washington, DC 20005
202-289-3100
FAX: 202-289-3199
ahleffoundation@ahla.com
www.ahlafoundation.org

Rosanna Maietta, President
Shelly Weir, Senior VP, Career Development
Kara Filer, VP, Donor Relations & Development
Programs include apprenticeship, community-based initiatives for youth, hospitality certification, funding for employee education, and a career center.

2736 **Arc of the District of Columbia**
415 Michigan Avenue, NE
Suite 150
Washington, DC 20017- 2144
202-636-2950
FAX: 202-635-7086
www.arcdc.net

Robert A. Anderson, President
Mary Lou Meccariello, Executive Director
Michael Gonzales, Chief Operating Officer
Advocating for and providing services to persons with developmental disabilities.

2737 **Eugene and Agnes E Meyer Foundation**
The Meyer Foundation
1250 Connecticut Ave NW
Suite 800
Washington, DC 20036- 2620
202-483-8294
FAX: 202-328-6850
meyer@meyerfdn.org
www.meyerfoundation.org

Joshua Bernstein, Chair
Deborah Ratner Salzberg, Vice Chair
Nicky Goren, President & CEO
Awards grants to projects dealing with the learning disabled, blind, mental health and vocational training in the Washington metropolitan area.

2738 **Federal Student Aid Information Center**
US Department of Education
400 Maryland Ave SW
Washington, DC 20202
202-275-5446
800-872-5327
www.ed.gov

Arne Duncan, Secretary of Education
Tony Miller, Deputy Secretary
Martha Kanter, Under Secretary
Answers questions about Federal student aid from students, parents and Members of Congress, as well as financial aid administrators.

2739 **GEICO Philanthropic Foundation**
1 Geico Plz
Washington, DC 20076
301-986-3000
800-841-3000
FAX: 301-986-2851
www.geico.com

Tony M Nicely, CEO
Hospitals, physically disabled and Special Olympics.

2740 Jacob and Charlotte Lehrman Foundation
1836 Columbia Rd NW
Washington, DC 20009-2002   202-328-8400
FAX: 202-338-8405
www.lehrmanfoundation.org

Elizabeth Berry, Director
Robert Lehrman, Trustee
Samuel Lehrman, Trustee
The Jacob & Charlotte Lehrman Foundation supports and seeks to enrich Jewish life in Washington DC, Israel and around the world. It is committed to making Washington a better place for all people and supports the arts, education and undeserved children, the environment, and healthcare.

2741 John Edward Fowler Memorial Foundation
79 Fifth Avenue
16th Street
New York, NY 10003-3076   212-620-4230
800-424-9836
FAX: 212-807-3677
www.foundationcenter.org

Bradforth K. Smith, President
Lisa Philp, Vice President
Lawrence T. McGill, Vice President
Although not a program priority, the foundation does offer grants to the physically disabled in the Washington, DC area only.

2742 Joseph P Kennedy Jr Foundation
1133 19th Street NW
12th Floor
Washington, DC 20036-3604   202-393-1250
FAX: 202-824-0351

Rebecca Salon, President
Steven Eidelman, Executive Director
Has two firm objectives: to seek the prevention of developmental disabilities, and to improve the way society deals with its citizens who are already affected. The Foundation uses its funds in areas where a multiplier effect can be achieved through development of innovative models for the prevention and amelioration, through provision of seed money that encourages new researchers, and thorough use of the Foundation's influence to promote public awareness.

2743 Kiplinger Foundation
1100 13th Street, NW
Suite 750
Washington, DC 20005-3938   202-887-6400
800-544-0155
FAX: 202-778-8976
www.kiplinger.com

Knight Kiplinger, VP
Limited to the greater Washington, DC area, the grants focus primarily on education, social welfare, cultural activities and community programs. Matching grants to eligible secondary or higher education institutions are provided on behalf of employees and retirees of Kiplinger Washington Editors, Inc. The Foundation does not fund scholarships.

2744 Morris and Gwendolyn Cafritz Foundation
1825 K St NW
Ste 1400
Washington, DC 20006-1271   202-223-3100
800-544-0155
FAX: 202-296-7567
info@cafritzfoundation.org
www.cafritzfoundation.org

Calvin Cafritz, Chairman/President/ CEO
John E. Chapoton, Vice Chairman and Treasurer
Ed McGeogh, Vice President - Asset Managemen
Grants are awarded to only 501(c)(3) organizations that are in the DC area. Grants are not awarded for capitol purposes, special events, endowments, or to individuals.

2745 Paul and Annetta Himmelfarb Foundation
4545 42nd St NW
Ste 203
Washington, DC 20016-4623   202-966-3796
M Preston, Executive Director
Primary areas of interest include health, children, human need, and Israel.

2746 Public Welfare Foundation
1200 U St NW
Washington, DC 20009-4443   202-965-1800
info@publicwelfare.org
www.publicwelfare.org

Lydia M. Marshall, Chair
Mary E. McClymont, President
Phillipa Taylor, Chief Financial and Administrati
The foundation's funding is specifically targeted to economically disadvantaged populations. Proposals must fall within one of the following categories: criminal justice, disadvantaged elderly, disadvantaged youth, environment, health and population and reproductive health, human rights and global security, and community economic developmental and participation. Proposals should be addressed to the Review Committee.

Florida

2747 Able Trust
3320 Thomasville Road
Suite 200
Tallahassee, FL 32308   850-224-4493
FAX: 850-224-4496
TTY:850-224-4493
info@abletrust.org
www.abletrust.org

Susanne Homant, President
Guenevere Crum, Senior Vice President
Kathryn McManus, MA, Chief Development Director
The Able Trust is a non-profit, public/private partnership that supports non-profit vocational rehabilitation programs throughout Florida with fundraising, grant making and public awareness of disability issues.

2748 American Academy of Pain Medicine Foundation
American Academy of Pain Medicine
4380-B Montgomery Road
Suite 1025
Ellicott City, MD 20143   800-917-1619
FAX: 407-749-0714
painmed.org/aapm-foundation

Farshad M. Ahadian, President
The Foundation supports AAPM's core purpose to optimize the health of patients in pain and eliminate the major health problem of pain by advancing the practice and the specialty of pain medicine.
1911

2749 Arc of Florida
2898 Mahan Dr
Ste 1
Tallahassee, FL 32308-5462   850-921-0460
800-226-1155
info@arcflorida.org
www.arcflorida.org

Pat Young, President
Dick Bradley, Vice President Administration
Linda Bloom, Vice President Advocacy
Advocates for all people with developmental disablilities, through education, awareness, research, advocacy and the support of families, friends and community.

2750 Bank of America Client Foundation
50 Central Avenue
Suite 750
Sarasota, FL 34236-5900   941-951-4103
maryann.l.smith@ustrust.com
www.fdnweb.org/boacf/

Maryann L. Smith, Vice President, Senior Trust Off
Committed to creating meaningful change in the communities we serve through our philanthropic efforts, associate volunteerism, community development activities and investing, support of arts and culture programming and environmental initiatives.

2751 Barron Collier Jr Foundation
2600 Golden Gate Pkwy
Naples, FL 34105-3227   239-262-2600
                                FAX: 239-262-1840
ContactUs@BarronCollier.com
www.barroncollier.com
Karen V. Triplett, Director of Property Management
Jose Medina, Facilities Manager
Barron Collier Companies - dedicated to the responsible development, management and stewardship of its extensive land holdings
and other assets in the businesses of agriculture, real estate, and
mineral management.

2752 Camiccia-Arnautou Charitable Foundation
Ste 402
980 N Federal Hwy
Boca Raton, FL 33432-2712   561-368-5757
                                FAX: 561-368-8505

Ronda Gluck, President

2753 Chatlos Foundation
PO Box 915048
Longwood, FL 32791-5048   407-862-5077
info@chatlos.org
www.chatlos.org

Bill Chatlos, Trustee
Funds nonprofit organizations in the USA and around the globe.
Funding is provided in the following areas of giving: Bible Col-
leges/Seminaries, Religious Causes, Medical Concerns, Liberal
Arts Colleges and Social Concerns. Category of placement is determined by the organizations overall mission rather than the project under consideration. The Foundation does not make
scholarship grants directly to individuals but rather to educational institutions which in turn select recipients.

2754 Edyth Bush Charitable Foundation
199 E Welbourne Ave
Ste 100
Winter Park, FL 32789-4365   407-647-4322
                                     888-647-4322
                                FAX: 407-647-7716
dodahowski@edythbush.org
www.edythbush.org
Gerald F. Hilbrich, Chairman
Herbert W. Holm, Vice Chairman
David A. Odahowski, President/CEO
Funding is resrticted to 501c3 nonprofit organizations located
and operating in Orange, Osceola, Seminole and Lake Counties,
Florida. Visit www.edythbush.org for a list of funding policies.

2755 FPL Group Foundation
700 Universe Blvd
Juno Beach, FL 33408-2657   561-694-4000
                                     888-488-7703
                                FAX: 561-694-4620
PoweringFlorida@FPL.com
www.fpl.com
Maria V. Fogarty, Senior Vice President, Internal
James L. Robo, President and Chief Operating Of
Joseph T. Kelliher, Executive Vice President, Federa
The company consistently outperforms national averages for ser-
vice reliability while customer bills are below the national aver-
age. A clean energy leader, FPL has one of the lowest emissions
profiles and one of the leading energy efficiency programs among
utilities nationwide. FPL is a subsidiary of Juno Beach,
Fla.-based NextEra Energy, Inc.

2756 Jefferson Lee Ford III Memorial Foundation
9600 Collins Ave
Bal Harbour, FL 33154-2202   305-868-2609
                                FAX: 305-868-2640
Sanford L King, Director
Yvonne Quatrale, President
Disabled children, hearing and speech center. Grants are only
given to tax exempt organizations, no individual grants are
offered.

2757 Jessie Ball duPont Fund
40 East Adams Street
Ste 300
Jacksonville, FL 32202-3302   904-353-0890
                                     800-252-3452
                                FAX: 904-353-3870
contactus@dupontfund.org
www.dupontfund.org
Sherry P. Magill, President
Mark D. Constantine, Vice President for Strategy
Barbara Roole, Senior Program Officer
Established under the terms of the will of the late Jessie Ball
duPont. The fund is a national foundation having a special though
not exclusive interest in issues affecting the South. The Fund
works with the approximately 325 individual institutions to
which Mrs. duPont personally contributed during the five-year
period, 1960 through 1964.

2758 Lost Tree Village Charitable Foundation
8 Church Lane
North Palm Beach, FL 33408-2908   561-622-3780
                                FAX: 561-841-6773
info@losttreefoundation.org
www.losttreefoundation.org
Pam Rue, Executive Director
Teresa Elu, Executive Assistant
Bob Heon, Controller
The Lost Tree Village Charitable Foundation is dedicated to
building a stronger community and improving the quality of life
for all local residents. Grants are awarded annually to local
non-profit health and human service organizations providing information, expertise and assistance to those in need. Applications
are only accepted from organizations located in Palm Beach and
Southern Martin Counties. Visit the website for guidelines and
further information.

2759 Miami Foundation, The
40 NW 3rd Street
Suite 405
Miami, FL 33128   305-371-2711
                                FAX: 305-371-5342
info@miamifoundation.org
www.miamifoundation.com
Javier Alberto Soto, President and CEO
Rebecca Mandelman, VP for Strategy and Engagement
The Foundation approaches all of its program activities with a focus on building the community. We conduct acticvities and support efforts that build community assets and relationships among
individuals, organizations, and communities that connect people
with resources and opportunities to improve their quality of life.

2760 Mount Sinai Medical Center
4300 Alton Road
Miami Beach, FL 33140-6574   305-674-2121
                                     305-674-2777
www.msmc.com/foundation
Wayne Chaplin, Chairman
Steven D. Sonenreich, President & CEO
Jason Loeb, Foundation President
Autism Research

2761 National Parkinson Foundation
200 SE 1st Street
Suite 800
Miami, FL 33131-1494   800-473-4636
contact@parkinson.org
www.parkinson.org
John L. Lehr, President & CEO
James Beck, SVP & Chief Scientific Officer
*Yasnahia Cortorreal, VP & chief Human Resources & Administra-
tion Officer*
The mission of the NPF is to improve the quality of care for people with Parkinson's disease through research, education, and
outreach.

2762 **Publix Super Markets Charities**
Publix Super Market Corporation Office
PO Box 407
Lakeland, FL 33802-0407   800-242-1227
www.publix.com

Gino DiGrazia, Vice President of Finance
Maria Brous, Director of Media & Community R
Kimberly Reynolds, Media & Community Relations
In addition to giving to thousands of local projects, Publix annually supports five organizations in companywide campaigns: Special Olympics, March of Dimes, Children's Miracle Network, United Way and Food for All

2763 **The Cherab Foundation**
2301 NE Savannah Rd
Suite 1771
Jensen Beach, FL 34957   772-335-5135
help@cherab.org
cherabfoundation.org

Lisa Geng, Founder & President
Jolie Abreu, Vice President
The Cherab Foundation is a world-wide nonprofit organization working to improve the communication skills and education of all children with speech and language delays and disorders. The Cherab Foundation is committed to assisting with the development of new therapeutic approaches, preventions, and cures to neurologically-based speech disorders.

Georgia

2764 **Arc Of Georgia**
100 Edgewood Ave NE
Ste 1675
Atlanta, GA 30303-3068   678-733-8969
888-401-1581
FAX: 678-733-8970
info@thearcofgeorgia.org
www.thearcofgeorgia.org

Torin Togut, President
David Glass, Vice President
Julie Lee, Secretary
The Arc of Georgia advocates for the rights and full participation of all children and adults with intellectual and developmental disabilities. Together with our network of members and other local Chapters, we improve systems of supports and services, connect families, inspire communities, and influence public policy.

2765 **Community Foundation for Greater Atlanta**
50 Hurt Plz SE
Ste 449
Atlanta, GA 30303-2915   404-688-5525
FAX: 404-688-3060
info@cfgreateratlanta.org
www.cfgreateratlanta.org

Suzanne Boas, Board Chair
Alicia Philipp, President
Robert Smulian, Vice President of Philanthropic
The Community Foundation for Greater Atlanta is a creative, cost-effective and tax-efficient way for people to invest in our community. We help donors and their families meet their charitable goals by educating them or critical issues and by matching them with organizations that serve their interests. By working with donors and the community, we improve the quality of life for residents in our region.

2766 **Florence C and Harry L English Memorial Fund**
Sun Trust Bank Atlanta
PO Box 4418
Mail Code 041
Atlanta, GA 30302   404-588-8250
FAX: 404-724-3082

Anil T. Cheriyan, Chief Information Officer
Kenneth J. Carrig, Chief Human Resources Officer
Rilla S. Delorier, Chief Marketing and Client Exper
Grants only made to Metro Atlanta non-profit organizations; no grants to churches or individuals.

2767 **Georgia Power**
96 Annex
Atlanta, GA 30308-3374   404-506-6526
888-655-5888
www.georgiapower.com

W. Paul Bowers, Chairman/ President/ CEO
John L. Pemberton, Senior VP/SPO
Georgia Power is an investor-owned, tax-paying utility that serves 2.25 million customers in all but four of Georgia's 159 counties.

2768 **Grayson Foundation**
1701 Willa Place Drive
Kernersville, NC 2728   336-650-9914
graysonfoundation@gmail.com
www.graysonfoundation.net

Donna Sherrell, Finance- Public Relations
Tricia Gladstone, Behavior Analyst-Finance Public
Roger Sherrell, Information Technology-Web Manag
Grayson Foundation enhances the quality of public educationfor the students of the Grayson cluster of schools by providing funds which enrich and extend educational oppurtunities.

2769 **Harriet McDaniel Marshall Trust in Memory of Sanders McDaniel**
Sun Trust Bank Atlanta
96 Annex
PO Box 4418
Atlanta, GA 30396   404-588-8250
888-891-0938
FAX: 404-724-3082

Anil T. Cheriyan, Chief Information Officer
Kenneth J. Carrig, Chief Human Resources Officer
Rilla S. Delorier, Chief Marketing and Client Exper
Grants only made to Metro Atlanta non-profit organizations, no grants to churches or individuals.

2770 **IBM Corporation**
1 New Orchard Rd
Armonk, NY 10504-1772   914-499-1900
800-425-3333
TTY:804-068-4225
response@in.ibm.com
www.ibm.com

Samuel J Palmisano, Chairman
Virginia M. Rometty, President and Chief Executive Of
Rodney C. Adkins, Senior Vice President
Manages disability programs (which leverage IBM resources through partnerships) designed to train persons with disabilities and assist them in gaining employment. Also, disseminates information regarding products and resources for persons with disabilities with those of other companies and organizations.

2771 **John H and Wilhelmina D Harland Charitable Foundation**
3565 Piedmont Road, NE
Two Piedmont Center, Suite 710
Atlanta, GA 30305-1502   404-264-9912
FAX: 404-266-8834
info@harlandfoundation.org
www.harlandfoundation.org

Margaret C. Reiser, President
Winifred S. Davis, Vice President/Treasurer
Robert E. Reiser, Secretary
The Harland Charitable Foundation was established in 1972 by John H. and Wilhelmina D. Harland to support worthy local causes in Atlanta, with a particular interest in improving the welfare of children and youth as well as support of community services and arts and culture.

2772 **Lettie Pate Whitehead Foundation**
191 Peachtree Street NE
Suite 3540
Atlanta, GA 30303- 2951   404-522-6755
FAX: 404-522-7026
fdns@woodruff.org
www.woodruff.org

James B. Williams, Chairman
James M. Sibley, Vice Chairman
Lawrence L. Gellerstedt, President /CEO

Non-profit organization dedicated to the support of needy women in nine southeastern states.

2773 Rich Foundation
222 Summer Street
Stamford, CT 06901
203-359-2900
FAX: 203-328-7980
info@fdrich.com
www.fdrich.com

A private foundation under section 509(a) of the Internal Revenue Code designed primariliy for the benefit of the residents and charitable organizations of lower Fairfield County.

2774 SunTrust Bank, Atlanta Foundation
Sun Trust Bank Atlanta
PO Box 4418
Mail Code 041
Atlanta, GA 30302
404-588-8250
FAX: 404-724-3082
www.suntrust.com

Anil T. Cheriyan, Chief Information Officer
Kenneth J. Carrig, Chief Human Resources Officer
Rilla S. Delorier, Chief Marketing and Client Exper

Hawaii

2775 Arc of Hawaii
3989 Diamond Head Rd
Honolulu, HI 96816-4413
808-737-7995
FAX: 808-732-9531
info@thearcinhawaii.org
www.thearcinhawaii.org

Thomas Huber, President
Lee Moriwaki, Vice President
Duane Bartholomew, Secretary

The Arc is a national, grassroots organization of and for people with intellectual and related developmental disabilities. With more then 140,000 members in 1000 local and state chapters. The Arc is the largest volunteer organization devoted soley to working on behalf of people with intellectual disabilities.

2776 Atherton Family Foundation
827 Fort Street Mall
Honolulu, HI 96813-2817
808-566-5524
888-731-3863
FAX: 808-521-6286
foundations@hcf-hawaii.org

Patricia R. Giles, Vice President
Judith M. Dawson, President
Frank C. Atherton, Vice President and Treasurer

Supports educational projects, programs and institutions as the highest priority, with the enterprises of a religious nature and those concerned with health and social services given careful attention. The Foundation is one of the largest private resources in the State devoted exclusively to the support of activities of a charitable nature.

2777 GN Wilcox Trust
Bank of Hawaii
PO Box 3170
Honolulu, HI 96802-3170
808-649-8580
800-272-7262
FAX: 808-538-4006
stafford.kiguchi@boh.com
www.boh.com

Paul Boyce, AVP and Grants Administrator
Elaine Moniz, Trust Specialist
William L. Carpenter, Senior Vice President

Benefits the people of Hawaii by funding programs that support social services, education, culture, the arts, youth services, religion, health and rehabilitation.

2778 Hawaii Community Foundation
827 Fort Street Mall
Honolulu, HI 96813-2817
808-537-6333
888-731-3863
FAX: 808-521-6286
info@hcf-hawaii.org
www.hawaiicommunityfoundation.org

Kelvin Taketa, President/CEO
Chris van Bergeijk, Vice President/Chief Operating Officer
Joseph Martyak, Vice President of Communications

The Hawaii Community Foundation is a public, statewide, charitable services and grantmaking organization supported by donor contributions for the benefit of Hawaii's people.

2779 McInerny Foundation Bank Of Hawaii, Corporate Trustee
PO Box 3170
Honolulu, HI 96802-3170
808-649-8580
800-272-7262
FAX: 808-538-4006
stafford.kiguchi@boh.com
www.boh.com

Paula Boyce, Avp And Grants Administrator
Elaine Moniz, Trust Specialist
William L. Carpenter, Senior Vice President

Although the Trust is broad-purposed, it does not make grants to churches or individuals, nor for endowments, reserve purposes, deficit financing, or for the purchase of real estate.

2780 Sophie Russell Testamentary Trust Bank Of Hawaii
PO Box 3170
Honolulu, HI 96802-3170
808-649-8580
800-272-7262
FAX: 808-538-4006
stafford.kiguchi@boh.com
www.boh.com

Paula Boyce, Asst. Vice President
Elaine Moniz, Trust Specialist
William L. Carpenter, Senior Vice President

Supports qualified tax-exempt charitable organizations, in the State of Hawaii only. Offers grants to the Humane Society and institutions giving nursing care and serving the physically and mentally handicapped.

Illinois

2781 Alzheimer's Association
225 N Michigan Ave
Fl 17
Chicago, IL 60601-7633
312-335-8700
800-272-3900
FAX: 866-699-1246
TTY: 312-335-5886
info@alz.org
www.alz.org

Stewart Putnam, Chair
Christopher Binkley, Vice Chair
Harry Johns, President/CEO

Mission is to eliminate Alzheimer's disease through the advancement of research, to provide and enhance care and support for all affected, and to reduce the risk of dementia through the promotion of brain health.

2782 American National Bank and Trust Company
33 N La Salle St
PO Box 191
Danville, VA 24543-0191
312-661-6000
800-240-8190
FAX: 815-961-7745
www.amnb.com

Charles H. Majors, Chairman/ CEO
Jeffrey V. Haley, President
Charles T. Canaday, Jr., Senior Vice President

Supports the endeavors of organizations working to meet the critical needs of the city and its surrounding communities. Success is greatly affected by the well-being of the communities the company serves, thus the foundation seeks to fulfill the social obligations both through financial funding and human resources. The

Foundation funding categories include organizations and programs involved in economic development, education, community and social services, healthcare and culture and the arts.

2783   Amerock Corporation
P.O.Box 7018
Rockford, IL 61125-7018   815-963-9631
                                                          800-435-6959
                                                    FAX: 800-618-6733
                                                       www.amerock.com

Robert Bailey, President
Grants are given to organizations promoting wellness, health and rehabilitation of the visually impaired and physically disabled.

2784   Arc of Illinois
The Illinois Life Span Project
20901 S La Grange Rd
Ste 209
Frankfort, IL 60423-3213   815-464-1832
                                                          800-588-7002
                                                    FAX: 815-464-5292
                                                      www.thearcofil.org

Brain Rubin, President
Therese Devine, Vice President
Tony Paulauski, Executive Director
The Arc of Illinois is committed to empowering persons with disabilities to achieve full participation in community life thru informed choices.

2785   Benjamin Benedict Green-Field Foundation
18313 Greenleaf Ct
Tinley Park, IL 60487-2176   708-444-4241
                                                    FAX: 708-614-0496
                                               www.greenfieldfoundation.org
Colin Fisher, Chairman of the Board
Kathryn Groenendal, President
Dan Jarke, Vice President
A privately endowed grantmaking organization trying to improve the qaulity of life for children and the elderly in the city of chicago.

2786   Blowitz-Ridgeway Foundation
1701 E Woodfield Rd
Suite 201
Schaumburg, IL 60173-5127   847-330-1020
                                                    FAX: 847-330-1028
                                               laura@blowitzridgeway.org
                                                 www.blowitzridgeway.org
Daniel L Kline, President
Pierre R. LeBreton, Ph.D., Vice-President
Thomas P. Fitzgibbon, Treasurer
Provides limited program, capital and research grants to organizations aiding the physically and mentally disabled, and agencies serving children and youth. Grants generally limited to Illinois.

2787   Chaddick Institute for Metropolitan Development
2352 N. Clifton Ave.
Suite 130
Chicago, IL 60614-2302   773-325-7310
                                                    FAX: 312-362-5506
                                               lasadvising@depaul.edu
                                                       las.depaul.edu
Joseph P Scwieterman PhD, Director
Marisa Schulz, LEED AP, Assistant Director
Justin Kohls, Program Manager
Advances the principals of effective land use, transportation, and community planning. Offers planners, attorneys, developers, and entrepreneurs a forum to share expertise on difficult land-use issues through workshops, conferences, and policy studies.

2788   Chicago Community Trust
225 North Michigan Avenue
Suite 2200
Chicago, IL 60601- 4501   312-616-8000
                                                    FAX: 312-616-7955
                                                          www.cct.org
Frank M. Clark, Chairman
Terry Mazany, President /CEO
Jamie Phillippe, Vice President-Development and D
A community foundation established in 1915, which receives gifts and bequests from individuals, families or organizations in-

terested in providing through the community foundation, financial support for the charitable agencies or institutions which serve the residents of metropolitan Chicago.

2789   Chicago Community Trust and Affiliates
225 North Michigan Avenue
Suite 2200
Chicago, IL 60601- 4501   312-616-8000
                                                    FAX: 312-616-7955
                                                    TTY:312-853-0394
                                                          www.cct.org
Frank M. Clark, Chairman
Terry Mazany, President /CEO
Jamie Phillippe, Vice President-Development and D
Provides critical charitable resources in the arts, community and economic development, education, health and wellness, hunger and homeless alleviation, legal services, programs for youth, the elderly, and people with disabilities, and services to assure that basic human needs are met for all members of our community.

2790   Community Foundation of Champaign County
307 W University Ave
Champaign, IL 61820-3411   217-359-0125
                                                    FAX: 217-352-6494
                                                          www.cfeci.org
Brooke Didier Starks, Chair
Tom Costello, Vice-Chair
Joan M. Dixon, President /CEO
A network of cultural resource providers and educational organizations who collaborate in the creation, coordination, and promotion of cultural resource programs for Champaign County Schools.

2791   Dr Scholl Foundation
1033 Skokie Blvd
Ste 230
Northbrook, IL 60062-4109   847-559-7430
                                               www.drschollfoundation.com
Pamela Scholl, President
The Foundation is dedicated to providing financial assistance to organizations committed to improving our world. Grants are made annually after an executive review by the staff and all the directors.

2792   Duchossois Foundation
Chamberlain Group
845 N Larch Ave
Elmhurst, IL 60126-1114   630-279-3600
                                                    FAX: 630-530-6091
                                                 employment@duch.com
                                                          www.duch.com
Richard L. Duchossois, Chairman
Robert L. Fealy, President /COO
Craig J. Duchossois, Chief Executive Officer
Established in 1984, the foundation returns dollars to the communities supporting its facilities and employees. Within these following areas, organizations are carefully selected on the basis of community needs and the organization's value and performance. Areas aimed at include: medical research, children/youth programs and cultural institutions.

2793   Evenston Community Foundation
1560 Sherman Ave
Suite 535
Evanston, IL 60201-5910   847-492-0990
                                                    FAX: 847-492-0904
                                                 info@evanstonforever.org
                                                 www.evanstonforever.org
Sara Schastok, Phd., President and CEO
Gwen Jessen, Vice President for Philanthropy
Marybeth Schroeder, Vice President for Programs
The Foundation is a publicly supported philanthropic organization dedicated to enriching Evanston and the lives of its people, now and in the future. The Foundation builds and manages its own and other community endowments, addresses Evanston's changing needs through grant making, and provides leadership on important community needs.

2794   Field Foundation of Illinois
200 S Wacker Dr
Ste 3860
Chicago, IL 60606-5848   312-831-0910
                                     FAX: 312-831-0961
                                     byoung@fieldfoundation.org
                                     www.fieldfoundation.org

Lyle Logan, Board Chair
Aurie A. Pennick, Executive Director and Treasurer
Sarah M. Linsley, Secretary
The Field Foundation seeks to provide support for community,
civic and cultural organizations in the Chicago area, enabling
both new and established programs to test innovations, to expand
proven strengths or to address specific, time-limited operational
needs.

2795   Francis Beidler Charitable Trust
53 W Jackson Blvd
Ste 530
Chicago, IL 60604-3422   312-922-3792
                                     FAX: 312-922-3799

Francis Beidler, Owner
Children/youth, services. Community development, business
promotion, crime and violence prevention. Federated giving programs, higher education, human services and family planning.

2796   Fred J Brunner Foundation
9300 King St
Franklin Park, IL 60131-2114   847-678-3232
                                     FAX: 847-678-0642

Fred J Brunner, CEO
General disability grants.

2797   George M Eisenberg Foundation for Charities
Ste 480
2340 S Arlington Heights Rd
Arlington Heights, IL 60005-4507   847-981-0545
                                     FAX: 847-941-0548

James Marousis, Manager

2798   Grover Hermann Foundation
233 S Wacker Dr
Suite 6600
Chicago, IL 60606-6473   312-258-5500
                                     FAX: 312-258-5600
                                     rsafer@schiffhardin.com
                                     www.schiffhardin.com

Ronald S. Safer, Managing Partner, Executive Comm
Provides funds for educational, health, public policy, community
and religious organizations throughout the United States. Its major interests are in higher education and health.

2799   John D and Catherine T MacArthur Foundation
Office of Grants Management
140 S Dearborn St
Chicago, IL 60603-5285   312-726-8000
                                     FAX: 312-920-6258
                                     TTY:312-920-6285
                                     4answers@macfound.org
                                     www.macfound.org

Marjorie M. Scardino, Chair
Julia Stasch, Interim President
Cecilia A. Conrad, Vice President-MacArthur Fellows
The Foundation supports creative people and effective institutions committed to building a more just, verdant, and peaceful
world. In addition, we work to defend human rights, advance
global conservation, & security, make cities better places, and understand how technology is affecting children and society.

2800   Les Turne Amyotrophic Laterial Sclerosis Foundation
5550 Touhy Ave
Ste 302
Skokie, IL 60077-3254   847-679-3311
                                     888-257-1107
                                     FAX: 847-679-9109
                                     info@lesturnerals.org
                                     www.lesturnerals.org

Ken Hoffman, President
Andrea Paul Backman, Executive Director
Shari Diamond, RN, BSN, Director of Patient Services

Voluntary health organization dedicated to raising funds for ALS
research, patient services and public awareness. Provides educational materials for affected individuals and family members,
health care professionals, and the general public. Program services include referrals and counseling; audio-visual aids and periodic newsletters. Offers support groups and patient networking
to affected individuals, family members, and caregivers.

2801   Little City Foundation
1760 W Algonquin Rd
Palatine, IL 60067-4799   847-358-5510
                                     FAX: 847-358-3291
                                     info@littlecity.org
                                     www.littlecity.org

Matthew B. Schubert, President
B. Timothy Desmond, Executive Vice President
David Rose, Vice President
Offers innovative and personalized programs to fully assist and
empower children & adults with autism and other intellectual and
developmental disabilities. With a commitment to attaining a
greater quality of life for Illinois most vulnerable citizens, they
actively promote choice, person-centered planning and a holistic
approach to health and wellness. 'ChildBridge' services include
in-home personal & family supports, clinical behavior intervention, 24/7 residential services and much more.

2802   MAGIC Foundation for Children's Growth
6645 North Ave
Oak Park, IL 60302-1057   708-383-0808
                                     800-362-4423
                                     FAX: 708-383-0899
                                     ContactUs@magicfoundation.org
                                     www.magicfoundation.org

Rich Buckley, Chairman
Ken Dickard, Vice Chairman
Mary Andrews, CEO and Co-Founder
This is a national nonprofit organization providing support and
education regarding growth disorders in children and related
adult disorders, including adult GHD. Dedicated to helping children whose physical growth is affected by a medical problem by
assisting families of afflicted children through local support
groups, public education/awareness, newsletters, specialty
divisions and programs for the children.

2803   McDonald's Corporation Contributions Program
2111 McDonalds Dr
Oak Brook, IL 60523-5500   630-623-3000
                                     800-244-6227
                                     FAX: 630-623-5700
                                     www.mcdonalds.com

Don Thompson, President and Chief Executive Of
Tim Fenton, Chief Operating Officer
Peter J. Bensen, Executive Vice President and Chi

2804   Michael Reese Health Trust
150 N Wacker Dr
Ste 2320
Chicago, IL 60606-1608   312-726-1008
                                     FAX: 312-726-2797
                                     www.healthtrust.net

Herbert S. Wander, Chairman
The Hon. How Carroll, Vice Chairman
Walter R. Nathan, Secretary
The trust seeks to improve the health of people in Chicago's met-
ropolitan communities through effective grantmaking in health
care, health education, and health research.

2805   National Eye Research Foundation
910 Skokie Blvd
Ste 207a
Northbrook, IL 60062-4033   847-564-9400
                                     800-621-2258
                                     FAX: 847-564-0807
                                     info@nerf.org
                                     www.subway.com

Joel Tenner, Manager
Dedicated to improving eye care for the public and meeting the
professional needs of eye care practitioners; sponsors eye research projects on contact lens applications and eye care problems. Special study sections in such fields as orthokertology,
primary eyecare, pediatrics, and through continuing education

programs. Provides eye care information for the public and professionals. Educational materials including pamphlets. Program activities include education and referrals.

2806 National Foundation for Ectodermal Dysplasias
6 Executive Dr
Suite 2
Fairview Heights, IL 62208-1360   618-566-2020
                                           FAX: 618-566-4718
                                           info@nfed.org
                                           www.nfed.org

Anil Vora, President
George Barbar, Vice President
Mary Fete, Executive Director
To empower and connect people touched by ectodermal dysplasias through education, support, and research.

2807 National Headache Foundation
820 N Orleans St
Ste 411
Chicago, IL 60610-3131   312-274-2650
                                                888-643-5552
                                           FAX: 312-640-9049
                                           info@headaches.org
                                           www.headaches.org

Seymour Diamond, M.D., Executive Chairman
Roger K. Cady, M.D., Associate Executive Chairman
Arthur H. Elkind, M.D., President
Foundation exists to enhance the healthcare of headache sufferers. It is a source of help to sufferers' families, physicians who treat headache sufferers, allied healthcare professionals and to the public.

2808 OMRON Foundation OMRON Electronics
1 Commerce Dr
Schaumburg, IL 60173-5330   847-843-7900
                                                800-556-6766
                                           FAX: 847-884-1866
                                           aoisales@omron.com
                                           www.omron247.com

Tastu Goto, CEO
Supports local community projects through direct donations and matching employee-directed contributions.

2809 Parkinson's Disease Foundation
1359 Broadway
Suite 1509
New York, NY 10018-2331   212-923-4700
                                                800-457-667
                                           FAX: 212-923-4778
                                           info@pdf.org
                                           www.pdf.org

Howard D. Morgan, Chair
Constance Woodruff Atwell, Ph.D., Vice Chair
Robin Anthony Elliott, President
International voluntary not-for-profit organization dedicated to patient services; education of affected individuals, family members, and healthcare professionals; and promotion and support of research for Parkinson's Disease and related disorders. Offers an extensive referral service to guide affected individuals to proper diagnosis and clinical care. Provides referrals to genetic counseling and support groups; promotes patient advocacy; and offers a variety of educational and support materials

Quarterly

2810 Peoria Area Community Foundation
331 Fulton St
Ste 310
Peoria, IL 61602-1449   309-674-8730
                                           FAX: 309-674-8754
                                           jim@communityfoundationci.org
                                           www.communityfoundationci.org

Donna Maracci, Chair
David Wynn, Vice Chair
Mark Roberts, CEO
Established to meet a wide variety of social, cultural, educational and other charitable needs throughout Central Illinois.

2811 Polk Brothers Foundation
20 W Kinzie St
Ste 1110
Chicago, IL 60654-5815   312-527-4684
                                           FAX: 312-527-4681
                                           questions@polkbrosfdn.org
                                           www.polkbrosfdn.org

Sandra P. Guthman, Chair
Raymond F. Simon, Vice Chair
Gordon S. Prussian, Secretary
The Polk Brothers Foundation seeks to improve the quality of life for the people of Chicago. We partner with local nonprofit organizations that work to reduce the impact of poverty and provide area residents with better access to quality education, preventive health care and basic human services.

2812 Retirement Research Foundation
8765 W Higgins Rd
Ste 430
Chicago, IL 60631-4170   773-714-8080
                                           FAX: 773-714-8089
                                           info@rrf.org
                                           www.rrf.org

Nathaniel P. McParland, M.D., Chairman
Ruth Ann Watkins, Secretary
Downey R. Varey, Treasurer
A private philanthropy with primary interest in improving the quality of life of older persons in the United States.

2813 Sears-Roebuck Foundation
3333 Beverly Rd
Hoffman Estates, IL 60179   847-286-2500
                                                800-932-3188
                                           FAX: 800-326-0485
                                           www.sears.com

W Bruce Johnson, CEO
Has a special interest in projects that address women, families, and diversity, but awards most of its funding to disease-specific charities and United Way in the Chicago area.

2814 Siragusa Foundation
1 E Wacker Dr
Ste 2910
Chicago, IL 60601-1912   312-755-0064
                                           FAX: 312-755-0069
                                           www.siragusa.org

John E. Hicks, Chair & President
Ross D. Siragusa, Vice Chair
John R. Siragusa, Treasurer
The Siragusa Foundation, is a private family foundation that is committed to honoring its founder by sustaining and developing Chicago's extraordinary nonprofit resources.

2815 Square D Foundation
1415 S Roselle Rd
Palatine, IL 60067-7337   847-397-2600
                                           FAX: 847-925-7500
                                           www.schneider-electric.com

Makes donations for operating support, capital development needs, and special projects to nonprofit organizations that have been granted exemption from the Federal Income Tax. The Foundation has a strong commitment to the following areas: health and welfare, education, civic and community affairs, and culture and the arts. Support of higher education is also made for scholarships, endowments for facility and acquisition or expansion of equipment or facilities, through Matching Gift Program.

2816 WP and HB White Foundation
540 W Frontage Rd
Ste 3240
Northfield, IL 60093-1232   847-446-1441
Margaret Blandford, Executive Director
The Foundation's funds are allocated on a continuing basis within the metropolitan area of Chicago where our founder's business prospered. The Foundation helps organizations specializing in the visually impaired, mental health, youth and recreation.

2817 Washington Square Health Foundation
875 N Michigan Ave
Ste 3516
Chicago, IL 60611-1957
312-664-6488
FAX: 312-664-7787
washington@wshf.org
www.wshf.org

William N. Werner, MD, MPH, Board Chair
Howard Nochumson, Executive Director/President
William B. Friedeman, Secretary
Grants funds in order to promote and maintain access to adequate healthcare for all people in the Chicagoland area regardless of race, sex, creed or financial need.

2818 Wheat Ridge Ministries
1 Pierce Pl
Ste 250 E
Itasca, IL 60143-2634
630-766-9066
800-762-6748
FAX: 630-766-9622
www.wheatridge.org

Kevin Boettcher, Chair
Richard Herman, President
Brain Becker, Senior Vice President
Weat Ridge supports more then 100 new health-related ministries each year through a variety of grant programs

Indiana

2819 Arc of Indiana
107 N Pennsylvania St
Suite 800
Indianapolis, IN 46204- 2423
317-977-2375
800-382-9100
FAX: 317-977-2385
thearc@arcind.org
www.arcind.org

Kerry Fletcher, President
Marlene Lu, Vice President
Mike Foddrill, Treasurer
Arc of Indiana is commited to people with cognitive and developmental disabilities realizing their goals of learning, living, working, and playing in the community.

2820 Ball Brothers Foundation
222 S Mulberry St
Muncie, IN 47305-2802
765-741-5500
FAX: 765-741-5518
info@ballfdn.org
www.ballfdn.org

James A. Fisher, Chairman/CEO
Jud Fisher, President/Chief Operating Office
Frank B. Petty, Vice Chairman
The Ball Brothers Foundation is dedicated to the stewardship legacy of the Ball brothers and to the pursuit of improving the quality of the Muncie, Delaware County, east Central Indiana and Indiana, through philanthropy and leadership.

2821 Community Foundation of Boone County
102 N. Lebanon
Suite 200
Lebanon, IN 46052
317-873-0210
FAX: 317-873-0219
info@communityfoundationbc.org
www.communityfoundationbc.org

Marc Applegate, Chairman of the Board
Ray Ingham, Vice Chair
Mike Harlos, Treasurer
The Community Foundation of Boone County provides pathways for connecting people who care with causes that matter for now and in the future.

2822 John W Anderson Foundation
402 Wall St
Valparaiso, IN 46383-2562
219-462-4611
FAX: 219-531-8954
andersonfnd@aol.com

Bruce Wargo, Manager

Physically and mentally disabled, recreation and youth agencies in Northwest Indiana area.

Iowa

2823 Arc of Iowa
114 S. 11th Street
Ste 302
West Des Moines, IA 50265- 3259
515-402-1618
800-362-2927
FAX: 515-330-2195
casey@thearcofiowa.org
www.thearcofiowa.org

Casey Westhoff, Executive Director
The Arc of Iowa exists to ensure that people with intellectual disabilities and developmental disabilities receive the services, supports and opportunities necessary to fully realize their right to live, work and enjoy life in the community without discrimination.

2824 Hall-Perrine Foundation
115 3rd St SE
Ste 803
Cedar Rapids, IA 52401-1222
319-362-9079
FAX: 319-362-7220
www.hallperrine.org

William Whipple, Chairman
Jack Evans, President
Darrel Morf, Vice President
This foundation is dedicated tio improving the quality of life for peole in Linn County, IA by responding to the changing social, economic, and cultural needs of the community.

2825 Mid-Iowa Health Foundation
3900 Ingersoll Ave
Ste 104
Des Moines, IA 50312-3535
515-277-6411
FAX: 515-271-7579
info@midiowahealth.org
www.midiowahealth.org

Becky Miles-Polka, Chairman
Rob Hayes, Vice Chair
Suzanne Mineck, President
Mission is to serve as a partner and catalyst for improving the health of vulnerable people in greater Des Moines.

2826 Principal Financial Group Foundation
711 High St
Des Moines, IA 50392
515-247-5111
800-986-3343
FAX: 515-235-5724

Larry Zimpleman, Chairman/ President/ CEO
Daniel J. Houston, President - Retirement, Insuranc
James P. McCaughan, President - Principal Global Inv
The Principal Financial Group is a leading global financial company offering businesses, individuals and industrial clients a wide range of financial products and services.

2827 Siouxland Community Foundation
505 5th St
Suite 412
Sioux City, IA 51101-1507
712-293-3303
FAX: 712-293-3303
office@siouxlandcommunityfoundation.org
www.siouxlandcommunityfoundation .org

Richard J. Dehner, President
Robert F. Meis, Vice President
Marilyn J. Hagberg, Secretary
The Siouxland Community Foundation strives to enhance the quality of life in the greater Siouxland tri-state area by seeking charitable gifts to build permanent endowments as charitable capital for the community, providing a flexable vehicle to receive and distribute gifts of any size, making grants in response to community needs, and providing services that will help shape the well-being of Siouxland.

Kansas

2828 Arc of Kansas
2701 SW Randolph Ave
Topeka, KS 66611-1536
785-232-0597
FAX: 785-232-3770
info@tarcinc.org
www.tarcinc.org

Barbara Duncan, President
Matthew Bergman, Vice President
Travis Stryker, Secretary
Organzation works to ensure that the estimated 7.2 million Americans with intellectual and developmental disabilities have the services and supports they need to grow, develop, and live in communities across the nation.

2829 Hutchinson Community Foundation
1 North Main, Suite 501
PO Box 298
Hutchinson, KS 67504-0298
620-663-5293
FAX: 620-663-9277
info@hutchcf.org
www.hutchcf.org

Aubrey Abbot Patterson, President and Executive Director
Terri L. Eisiminger, Vice President of Administration
Janet Hamilton, Community Investment Officer
Connects donors to community needs and opportunities, increases philanthropy and provides community leadership.

2830 Richard W Higgins Charitable Foundation
Marshall & Ilsley Trust of Florida
2520 South Iowa
Ste 100
Lawrence, KS 66046-2713
877-202-9234
www.applebees.com

Ken Krei, President
Jessica James, Executive Chef
Patrick Humphrey, Executive Chef
Gives primarily for medical research with geographical focus on New York and Florida.

Kentucky

2831 Arc of Kentucky
706 E. Main Street
Suite A
Frankfort, KY 40601-2408
502-875-5225
800-281-1272
FAX: 502-875-5226
arcofky@aol.com
arcofky.org

James Cheely, President
Patty Dempsey, Executive Director
Ellen Nicholson, Secretary
The Arc of Kentucky works to ensure a quality of life for children and adults with intellectual and developmental disabilities to help in securing a positive future. The Arc values services and supports that enhance the quality of life through independence, friendship, choice and respect for individuals with intellectual and developmental disabilities.

Louisiana

2832 Arc of Louisiana
606 Colonial Dr
Ste G
Baton Rouge, LA 70714-6535
225-383-1033
866-966-6260
FAX: 225-383-1092
info@thearcla.org
www.thearcla.org

Larry Pete, President
Henry Friloux, Vice President
Kelly Serrett, Executive Director

The Arc of Louisiana advocates for and with individuals with intellectual and developmental disabilities and their families that they shall live to their fullest potential.

2833 Baton Rouge Area Foundation
402 N 4th St
Baton Rouge, LA 70802-5506
225-387-6126
877-387-6126
FAX: 225-387-6153
mverma@braf.org
www.braf.org

C. Kris Kirkpatrick, Chair
S. Dennis Blunt, Vice Chair
John G. Davies, President/CEO
The Foundation provides grants to nonprofits to make lives better in the region. It also takes on projects, often with parters, to remake Baton Rouge.

2834 Community Foundation of Shreveport-Bossier
401 Edwards St
Ste 105
Shreveport, LA 71101-5551
318-221-0582
FAX: 318-221-7463
info@cfnla.org
www.cfnla.org

Janie D. Richardson, Chairman
Thomas H. Murphy, Vice Chairman
Terry C. Davis, Ph.D, Secretary
Provides a variety of charitable funds and gift options to help our partners achieve their vision for a stronger, more vibrant community. By bringing together fund donors, their financial advisors and non profit agencies, the Foundation is a powerful catalyst for building charitable giving and effecting positive change in our area

Maine

2835 BCR Foundation
83 Mussey Rd.
Scarborough, ME 04074
207-883-8000
800-227-6111
FAX: 207-883-0100
solutions@bcr.net

Specializes on the delivery of a variety of telecommunications products and services to include digital and VoIP telephone systems, voicemail systems, computer-telephone applications, and the installation of data, voice and video cabling.

2836 No Limits Foundation
265 Centre Dr.
Wales, ME 04280
207-569-6411
info@nolimitsfoundation.org
www.nolimitsfoundation.org

Mary Leighton, Founder & Executive Director
Kelsey Moody, Program Operations Manager
Alix Sandler, Marketing & Development Director
Non-profit organization offering camps for children with limb loss and differences.

2837 UNUM Charitable Foundation
Maine Association of Non Profits
565 Congress St
Ste 301
Portland, ME 04101-3308
207-871-1885
FAX: 207-780-0346
Manp@NonprofitMaine.org
www.nonprofitmaine.org

Doug Woodbury, Board President
Ted Scontras, Board Vice President
Joan Smith, Board Treasurer
The Foundation encourages projects that: stimulate others in the private or public sector to participate in problem solving; advance innovative and cost-effective approaches for addressing defined, recognized needs; and demonstrate ability to obtain future project funding, if needed. The foundation generally limits its consideration of capital campaign requests to the Greater Portland, Maine area.

Maryland

2838   American Health Assistance Foundation
22512 Gateway Center Dr
Clarksburg, MD 20871-2005   301-948-3244
                                         800-437-2423
                                    FAX: 301-258-9454
                                    info@brightfocus.org
                                    www.brightfocus.org

Stacy Pagos Haller, President/CEO
Donna Callison, Vice President of Development
Michael Buckley, Vice President of Public Affairs
The American Health Assistance Foundation (AHAF) is a registered non-profit organization that funds research into cures for Alzheimer's disease, macular degeneration and glaucoma, and provides the public with informantion about risk factors, preventative lifestyles, availiable treatments and coping strategies.

2839   American Occupational Therapy Foundation
4720 Montgomery Lane
Suite 202
Bethesda, MD 20814-3449   240-292-1079
                                    FAX: 240-396-6188
                                         aotf@aotf.org
                                         aotf.org

Diana L. Ramsay, Chair
Wendy J. Coster, Vice Chair
Scott Campbell, CEO
AOFT provides advanced research, education and public awareness for occupational therapy, so that all people may participate fully in life regardless of their physical, social, mental or developmental circumstances.

2840   Arc of Maryland
121 Cathedral St, 2B
PO Box 1747
Annapolis, MD 21401- 1747   410-571-9320
                                         888-272-3449
                                    FAX: 410-974-6021
                                    info@thearcmd.org
                                    www.thearcmd.org

Richard Dean, President
Aileen O'Hare, Vice President
Annette Hinkle, Treasurer
The Arc of Maryland works to create a world where children and adults with cognitive and developmental disabilities have and enjoy equal rights and opportunities.

2841   Baltimore Community Foundation
2 E Read Street
Floor 9
Baltimore, MD 21202-6903   410-332-4171
                                    FAX: 410-837-4701
                                    questions@bcf.org
                                    www.bcf.org

Raymond L. Bank, Chair
Tedd Alexander, Vice Chair
Laura L. Gamble, Vice Chair
Makes grants in Baltimore City and Baltimore County; see website for how to apply. BCF is governed by a 30-member board of trustees, made up of a cross section of Baltimore.

2842   Candlelighters Childhood Cancer Foundation
10920 Connecticut Ave.
PO Box 498
Kensington, MD 20895- 0498   301-962-3520
                                         855-858-2226
                                    FAX: 301-962-3521
                                         staff@acco.org
                                         www.acco.org

Naomi Bartley, President
Janine Lynne, Vice President
Ken Phillips, Treasurer
An international organization providing information and support, and advocacy to parents of children with cancer and survivors of childhood cancer.Health and Education professionals also welcome as members.Network of local support groups. Information on disabilities related to treatment of childhood cancer. Publications.

2843   Children's Fresh Air Society Fund
Baltimore Community Foundation
2 E Read St
Baltimore, MD 21202-2470   410-332-4171
                                    FAX: 410-837-4701
                                         grants@bcf.org
                                         bcf.org

Tom E. Wilcox, President
Danista Hunte, Vice President, Community Invest
Ralph M. Serpe, CFRE, Vice President, Development
Makes grants to nonprofit camps to provide tuition for disadvantaged and disabled Maryland children to attend summer camp. See website for how to apply.

2844   Clark-Winchcole Foundation
3 Bethesda Metro Ctr
Suite 550
Bethesda, MD 20814-5358   301-654-3607
Laura Phillips, President
Supported tax-exempt charitable organizations operating in the metropolitan area of Washington, DC in the following areas: deaf, higher education and physically disabled.

2845   Columbia Foundation
10630 Little Patuxent Parkway
Century Plaza, Suite 315
Columbia, MD 21044   410-730-7840
                                    FAX: 410-997-6021
                                    www.cfhoco.org

Bruce Harvey, Chair
Joseph Maranto, Vice Chair
Barb Van Winkle, Secretary
The Columbia Foundation serves as a catalyst for building a more caring, creative and effective community in Howard County by promoting and creating opportunities for personal and corporate philanthropy, managing endowments, anticipating and responding to community needs, and strategically granting funds.

2846   Corporate Giving Program
Ryland Group
11000 Broken Land Pkwy
Columbia, MD 21044   410-715-7022
                                         800-267-0998
                                    FAX: 410-715-7909

Bruce N Haas, President
Contributions of equipment, volunteers and financial support to organizations working to meet the challenges and needs of modern society.

2847   Cystic Fibrosis Foundation
6931 Arlington Rd
2nd floor
Bethesda, MD 20814-5200   301-951-4422
                                         800-344-4823
                                    FAX: 301-951-6378
                                         info@cff.org
                                         www.cff.org

Catherine C. McLoud, Board Chair
Robert J. Beall, Ph.D., President/Chief Executive Office
C. Richard Mattingly, Executive Vice President
The mission of the Cystic Fibrosis Foundation, a nonprofit donor-supported organization is to assure the development of the means to cure and control cystic fibrosis and to improve the quality of life for those with the disease.

2848   Foundation Fighting Blindness
7168 Columbia Gateway Dr.
Suite 100
Columbia, MD 21046   410-423-0600
                                         800-683-5555
                                    TTY:410363713951
                                    info@FightBlindness.org
                                    www.blindness.org

William T. Schmidt, Chief Executive Officer
Valerie Navy-Daniels, Chief Development Officer
Stephen M. Rose, PhD, Chief Research Officer
The Foundation Fighting Blindness (FFB) works to promote research in order to prevent, treat and restore vision. FFB is currently the world's leading private funder of retinal disease research, funding over 100 research grants and 150 researchers.

2849   George Wasserman Family Foundation
Grossberg Company
6707 Democracy Blvd
Suite 300
Bethesda, MD 20817-1176   301-571-4977
                                          FAX: 301-571-6250

Helen Salud, Manager
Anthony Cpa, Partner

2850   Giant Food Foundation
8301 Professional Pl
Ste 115
Landover, MD 20785-2351   301-341-4100
                                               888-469-4426
                                      jmiller@giantfood.com
                                         www.giantfood.com

Anthony Hucker, President
Brian Beatty, Director of Marketing
Stefanie Cain, District Director
Offers grants in the areas of mental health, recreation, community
and cultural programs, art, and educational programs for the
health and prosperity of the greater Washington area.

2851   Harry and Jeanette Weinberg Foundation
7 Park Center Ct
Owings Mills, MD 21117-4200   410-654-8500
                                          FAX: 410-654-4900
                                   cdemchak@hjweinberg.org
                                     hjweinbergfoundation.org

Ellen M. Heller, Chair
Barry I. Schloss, Treasurer
Alvin Awaya, Vice-President
The Harry & Jeanette Weinberg Foundation, Inc. is dedicated to
assisting the poor, primarily through operating and capital grants
to direct service organizations located in Baltimore, Hawaii,
Northeastern Pennsylvania, New York, Israel and the Former So-
viet Union. These grants are focused on meeting basic needs such
as shelter, nutrition, health & socialization & on enhancing an individual's ability to meet those needs. Within that focus, emphasis is placed on the elderly & Jewish community.

2852   Immune Deficiency Foundation
7550 Teague Road
Suite 220
Hanover, MD 21076   800-296-4433
                                          FAX: 410-321-9165
                                   info@primaryimmune.org
                                         primaryimmune.org
Jorey Berry, President & Chief Executive Officer
Sarah Rose, Chief Financial Officer
Tammy C. Black, Chief Communications Officer
The Immune Deficiency Foundation is the national patient orga-
nization dedicated to improving the diagnosis, treatment, and
quality of life of persons with primary immunodeficiency dis-
eases through advocacy, education, and research.

2853   Kennedy Krieger Institute
707 North Broadway
Baltimore, MD 21205   443-923-9200
                                               800-873-3377
                                               888-554-9400
                                         TTY:443-923-2645
                           findaspecialist@kennedykrieger.org
                                     www.kennedykrieger.org

Gary W. Goldstein, MD
Internationally recognized for improving the lives of children
and adolescents with disorders and injuries of the brain, spinal
cord and musculoskeletal system, the Kennedy Krieger Institute
serves more than 20,000 individuals each year through inpatient
and outpatient clincs, home and community services and
school-based programs. Kennedy Krieger provides a wide range
of services for children and young adults with developmental
concerns mid to severe, and is home to a team of investigators.

2854   Miracle-Ear Children's Foundation
5000 Cheshire Ln N
Minneapolis, MN 55446-3706   763-268-4000
                                               800-464-8002
                                          FAX: 763-268-4365
                                   www.miracle-ear.com/en-us/

Nonprofit organization that provides hearing aids to children
whose families to not qualify for public assistance. Provides
hearing aid fittings and follow-up care and services free of charge
through Miracle-Ear Hearing Centers. Provides information on
alternative communication. Offers educational materials and
brochures.

2855   National Federation of the Blind
200 E. Wells St.
at Jernigan Place
Baltimore, MD 21230   410-659-9314
                                          FAX: 410-685-5653
                                               nfb@nfb.org
                                                 nfb.org

Mark A. Riccobono, President
John Berggren, Executive Director, Operations
Anil Lewis, Executive Director, Blindness Initiatives
The National Federation of the Blind (NFB) works to help blind
people achieve self-confidence, self-respect and self-determination and to achieve complete integration into society on a basis of
equality. The Federation provides public educations, information
and referral services, scholarships, literature and publications,
adaptive equipment, advocacy services, legal services,
employment assistance and more.

2856   Optometric Extension Program Foundation
2300 York Road
Suite 113
Timonium, MD 21093   410-561-3791
                                          FAX: 949-250-8157
                                     Kelin.Kushin@oep.org
                                            www.oepf.org

Paul A. Harris, OD, President
Robin Lewis, OD, Vice President
Kelin Kushin, Executive Director
Vision care for learning disabilities and head trauma patients.

2857   Sjogren's Syndrome Foundation
6707 Democracy Blvd
Suite 325
Bethesda, MD 20817-1164   301-530-4420
                                               800-475-6473
                                          FAX: 301-530-4415
                                       tms@sjogrens.org
                                         www.sjogrens.org

Kenneth Economou, Chairman of the Board
Stephen Cohen, OD, Chairman-Elect
Vidya Sankar, DMD, MHS, Treasurer
Provides patients practical information and coping strategies that
minimize the effects of Sjogren's syndrome. In addition, the
Foundation is the clearinghouse for medical information and is
the recognized national advocate for Sjogren's syndrome. *$25.00
Monthly*

2858   The ACNM Foundation, Inc.
American College of Nurse Midwives
PO Box 380272
Cambridge, MA 02238-0272   240-485-1800
                                          FAX: 617-876-5822
                                    membership@acnm.org
                                          fdn@acnm.org

Holly Powell Kennedy, President
Mary K. Collins, Vice President
Susan DeJoy, Treasurer
Charitable foundation of the American College of Nurse Mid-
wives.

Massachusetts

2859   Abbot and Dorothy H Stevens Foundation
P.O. Box 111
North Andover, MA 01845   978-688-7211
                                          FAX: 978-686-1620

Josh Miner, Executive Director
Established in 1953, Purpose is giving primarily to the arts, education, conservation, and health and human services.

2860   Arc of Massachusetts, The
217 South St
Waltham, MA 02453-2710   781-891-6270
                                       FAX: 781-891-6271
                                       arcmass@arcmass.org
                                       www.arcmass.org

Leo Sarkissian, Executive Director
Joshua Komyerox, Government Affairs Director
Brenda Asis, Development Director
Quarterly newsletter for The Arc of Massachusetts is Advocate.

2861   Arc of Northern Bristol County
141 Park St
Attleboro, MA 02703-3020   508-226-1445
                                              888-343-3301
                                       FAX: 508-226-1476
                                       info@arcnbc.org
                                       arcnbc.org

Richard Harwood, Chairperson
Valerie Zagami, Vice Chairperson
Paul Oliveira, Treasurer
Mission is to strive for the right of all people with developmental
disabilities to be valued as individuals, to experience choice, and
to be fully included in all aspects of community life

2862   Boston Foundation
75 Arlington St
10th Fl
Boston, MA 02116-3992   617-338-1700
                                       FAX: 617-338-1604
                                       tbf.org

Michael Keating, Esq., Chair
Catherine D'Amato, Vice Chair
Paul S. Grogan, President & CEO
The Foundation's grantmaking, special initiatives and civic leadership promote innovation across a broad range of compelling
community issues, from educational excellence to affordable
housing to workforce development and the arts.

2863   Boston Globe Foundation
P.O. Box 55819
Boston, MA 02205-5819   617-929-2000
                                       bostonglobe.com

Mary Jacobus, President
The mission of the Boston Globe Foundation is to empower community-based organizations to effect real change in the ares of
greatest need, where the Globe is uniquely postioned to add the
most value. Priority focus areas: strengthen the reading, writing
and critical thinking of young people, while fostering their inherent love of learning. Strengthen the roads that link people to culture. Strengthen the civic fabric of the city. Be responsive to the
needs of our immediate community.

2864   Bushrod H Campbell and Ada F Hall Charity Fund
Palmer & Dodge
111 Huntington Ave
Boston, MA 02199-7610   617-239-0540
                                       FAX: 617-227-4420

Brenda Taylor, Foundation Administrator
The fund's areas of interest include organizations and/or their
projects supporting aid to the elderly, healthcare and population
control. Medical research grants are administered through the
Medical Foundation. No grants are awarded to individuals and
the geographical area of support is limited to organizations located in Massachusetts within the area of Boston and Route 128.

2865   Clipper Ship Foundation
77 Summer St
8th Floor
Boston, MA 02110-1006   617-391-3088
                                       FAX: 617-426-7087
                                       hblaisdell@gmafoundations.com
                                       clippershipfoundation.org

Ron Ancrum, President
Makes grants to federally tax-qualified non-profit organizations
offering human services to individuals living in Greater Boston
and the cities of Lawrence and Brockton.

2866   Community Foundation of Western Massachusetts
1500 Main Street, Suite 2300
P.O. Box 15769
Springfield, MA 01115-5769   413-732-2858
                                       FAX: 413-733-8565
                                       wmass@communityfoundation.org
                                       www.communityfoundation.org

Katie Allan Zobel, President and CEO
Nancy Reiche, M.S.W., Vice President for Programs
Donna Roseman David, Chief Financial Officer/Chief Ad
Provides a simple way to achieve the charitable objectives of donors most effectively; supports nonprofit organizations that offer
programs in the arts, education, human services, healthcare,
housing, and the environment; and works to improve the quality
of life in our region.

2867   Frank R and Elizabeth Simoni Foundation
1401 Boston Providence Tpke
Norwood, MA 02062-5053   781-762-3449
                                       FAX: 781-769-6166

Matthew Mac Donald, President
Ann Mac Donald, Secretary
Robert Mac Donald, Clerk

2868   Friendly Ice Cream Corp Contributions Program
1855 Boston Rd
Wilbraham, MA 01095-1002   413-543-3544
                                              800-966-9970
                                       FAX: 413-731-4467
                                       friendlys.com

John Maguire, Chief Financial Officer
Steve Weigel, EVP, Chief Operating Officer
Pat Hickey, EVP, Chief Financial Officer

2869   Greater Worcester Community Foundation
370 Main St
Ste 650
Worcester, MA 01608-1738   508-755-0980
                                       FAX: 508-755-3406
                                       info@greaterworcester.org
                                       greaterworcester.org

Gerald Gaudette III, Chair
Warner S. Fletcher, Vice Chair
Thomas J. Bartholomew, Treasurer
By focusing on the entire community rather then on any specific
issue, the community foundation is able to address matters of
greater importance to the people of the region. The Foundation
has built a permanent, flexable endowment and has distributed
grants and awards to a broad range of organizations and people
throughout the region.

2870   Hyams Foundation
50 Federal St
9th Floor
Boston, MA 02110   617-426-5600
                                       FAX: 617-426-5696
                                       info@hyamsfoundation.org
                                       hyamsfoundation.org

Martella Wilson-Taylor, Chair
Angela Brown, Director of Programs
Mike Givens, Communications Manager
The mission of the foundation is to increase economic and social
stregnth within low-income communities in Boston and Chelsea,
Massachusetts. Some areas they provide funding to include com-
munity identified issues, racial justice and transitional funding.

2871   Raytheon Company Contributions Program
870 Winter St
Waltham, MA 02451-1449   781-522-3000
                                       FAX: 781-860-2172
                                       raytheon.com

Thomas A. Kennedy, Chief Financial Officer
David C. Wajsgras, Senior Vice President
Keith J. Peden, Senior Vice President
Industry leader in defense and government electronics, space, in-
formation technology, technical services, and business aviation
and special mission aircraft.

2872 TJX Foundation
TJX Companies
770 Cochituate Rd
Framingham, MA 01701-4666
508-390-1000
FAX: 508-390-2091
www.tjx.com

Carol Meyrowitz, CEO
The purpose of the TJX Foundation's Giving Program is to support qualified, tax-exempt nonprofit organizations that provide services which promote and improve the quality of life for children, women and families in need.

2873 The Beveridge Family Foundation, Inc.
3 Upland Ln.
West Newbury, MA 01985
800-229-9667
administrator@beveridge.org
www.beveridge.org

Ward Slocum Caswell, President
Philip Caswell, Chairman and Vice President
Ruth S. DuPont, Treasurer
The mission of The Frank Stanley Beveridge Foundation, Inc. is to preserve and enhance the quality of life by embracing and perpetuating Frank Stanley Beveridge's philanthropic vision through grantmaking initiatives in support of The Stanley Park of Westfield, Inc. and programs in youth development, health, education, religion, art, and environment primarily in Hampden and Hampshire Counties, Massachusetts.

2874 Vision Foundation
8901 Strafford Cir
Knoxville, TN 37923-1500
865-357-4603
FAX: 865-690-9322

Gordon Adams, President
Offers counseling, support groups, seminars and transportation for the blind providing 600 members.

Michigan

2875 Ann Arbor Area Community Foundation
301 N Main St
Ste 300
Ann Arbor, MI 48104-1296
734-663-0401
FAX: 734-663-3514
info@aaacf.org
aaacf.org

Michelle Crumm, Chair
Tim Wadhams, Vice Chair
Neel Hajra, President & CEO
Interested in funding projects which will improve the quality of life for citizens of the Ann Arbor area. Eligible projects generally fall within these categories: education, culture, social service, community development, environmental awareness and health and wellness. The Foundation aims to support creative approaches to community needs and problems by making grants which will benefit the widest possible range of people.

2876 Arc of Michigan
State of Michigan
1325 S Washington Ave
Lansing, MI 48910-1652
517-487-5426
800-292-7851
FAX: 517-487-0303
dhoyle@arcmi.org
arcmi.org

Shari Fitzpatrick, President
Kim Brown, Vice President
Bob Altizer, Secretary
The Arc Michigan empowers local chapters to assure that citizens with disabilities are valued and that they and their families participate fully in and contribute to the life of their community.

2877 Berrien Community Foundation
2900 S State St
Ste 2e
Saint Joseph, MI 49085-2467
269-983-3304
FAX: 269-983-4939
bcf@BerrienCommunity.org
berriencommunity.org

Hillary Bubb, Chair
Mabel Mayfield, Vice Chair
Lisa Cripps-Downey, President
The Foundation is a union of numerous gifts, bequests and other contributions that form permanent endowments and other funds.

2878 Blind Children's Fund
P.O. Box 187
Grand Ledge, MI 48837
517-488-4887
www.blindchildrensfund.org

Carrie L Owens, Board President
Diana Popp, Executive Director
Provides parents and professionals information materials and resources to help them teach and nurture blind and visually impaired children so they may reach their potential.

2879 Community Foundation of Monroe County
P.O. Box 627
28 S. Macomb St.
Monroe, MI 48161-627
734-242-1976
FAX: 734-242-1234
info@cfmonroe.org
cfmonroe.org

Kathleen Russeau, MBA, Executive Director
Michele Sandiefer, Office Manager
Julie Rhinehart, YAC Coordinator
The mission of the Community Foundation of Monroe County is to encourage and facilitate philanthropy in Monroe County.

2880 Cowan Slavin Foundation
7881 Dell Rd
Saline, MI 48176-9744
734-944-1439
FAX: 734-944-3529

David Bovee, Owner

2881 Daimler Chrysler
Automobility Program
P.O. Box 5080
Troy, MI 48007-5080
800-255-9877
FAX: 855-409-0475
rebates@chrysler.com

Provides a cash reimbursement to assist in reducing the cost of adaptive driving equipment and conversion aids installed on new model Daimler Chrysler LLC vehicles. Up to a maximum of $1000 on Dodge Caravan, Grand Caravan, and Chrysler Town and Country vans and up to $750 on all other vehicles.

2882 Frank & Mollie S VanDervoort Memorial Foundation
4646 Okemos Rd
Okemos, MI 48864-1795
517-349-7232
Ann L Gessert, Secretary

2883 Fremont Area Community Foundation
4424 W. 48th Street
PO Box B
Fremont, MI 49412-176
231-924-5350
FAX: 231-924-5351
tfacf.org

Robert Zeldenrust, Chair
William Johnson, Vice Chair
Carla Roberts, President & CEO
A local nonprofit organization serving the residence of Newaygo County. We connect the needs of the community with those who have the conviction to make a lasting impact. Our mission is to improve the quality of life for the people of Newaygo County.Zeldenrust

2884 Grand Rapids Foundation
185 Oakes St SW
Grand Rapids, MI 49503-4008 616-454-1751
FAX: 616-454-6455
grfound@grfoundation.org
grfoundation.org

Paul M. Keep, Chair
Laurie Finney Beard, Vice Chair
Diana R. Sieger, President
Grand Rapids Community Foundation leads the community in making positive, sustainable change. Through our grantmaking and leadership initiatives we help foster academic achievement, build economic prosperity, achieve healthy ecosystems, encourage healthy people, support social enrichment, and create vibrant neighborhoods.

2885 Granger Foundation
6267 Aurelius Rd
Lansing, MI 48911-2187 517-393-1670
FAX: 517-393-1382
grangerconstruction.com

Alton Granger, Chairman
Glenn D. Granger, President & CEO
The primary purpose of the Granger Foundation is to enhance the quality of life within the Greater Lansing, Michigan Area. Our mission is to support Christ-centered activities. We also support efforts that enhance the lives of youth in our community.

2886 Harvey Randall Wickes Foundation
4800 Fashion Square Blvd
Suite 472
Saginaw, MI 48604- 2677 989-799-1850
FAX: 989-799-3327
www.tgci.com

James Finkbeiner
Grants for rehabilitation.

2887 Havirmill Foundation
3505 Greenleaf Blvd
Ste 203
Kalamazoo, MI 49008-2580 269-375-1193
millenniumrestaurants.com

Ken Miller, CEO, Principal Partner
Matthew Burian, President
Bob Lewis, Operating Partner

2888 Kelly Services Foundation
999 W Big Beaver Rd
Troy, MI 48084-4782 248-362-4444
FAX: 248-244-4588
kfirst@kellyservices.com
kellyservices.com

George S. Corona, Chief Operating Officer
Carl T. Camden, President & CEO
Terence E. Adderley, Executive Chairman

2889 Kent County Arc
2922 Fuller Ave. NE
Ste 201
Grand Rapids, MI 49505 616-459-3339
FAX: 401-737-8907
info@arckent.org
www.arckent.org

Pam Cross, President
Tim Lundgren, Vice-President
Tammy Finn, Executive Director
Providing individuals with disabilties meaningful opportunities throughout their communities.

2890 Kresge Foundation
3215 W Big Beaver Rd
Troy, MI 48084-2818 248-643-9630
FAX: 248-643-0588
info@kresge.org
kresge.org

Rip Rapson, President & CEO
Amy B. Coleman, VP & CFO
Ariel H. Simon, Vice President, Chief Program
This foundation offers challenge grants for capital projects, most often for construction or renovation of buildings, but also for the purchase of major equipment and real estate. As challenge grants, they are intended to stimulate new, private gifts in the midst of an organized fund raising effort. Offers special opportunities to build capacity, both in providing enhanced facilities in which to present programs and in generating private support. Only charitable organizations may apply.

2891 Lanting Foundation
1575 S Shore Dr
Holland, MI 49423-4436 616-335-2033
Arlyn Lanting, Partner

2892 Rollin M Gerstacker Foundation
PO Box 1945
Midland, MI 48641-1945 989-631-6097
www.gerstackerfoundation.org

Gail E. Lanphear, Chairperson
Lisa J. Gerstacker, President
E. N. Brandt, Vice President /Secretary
The Rollin M. Gerstacker Foundation was founded by Mrs. Eda U. Gerstacker in 1957, in memory of her husband. Its primary purpose is to carry on, indefinitely, financial aid to charities of all types supported by Mr. and Mrs. R.M. Gerstacker during their lifetimes. These charities are concentrated in the states of Michigan and Ohio.

2893 Steelcase Foundation
PO Box 1967
GH-4E
Grand Rapids, MI 49501-1967 616-246-4695
FAX: 616-475-2200
foundation@Steelcase.com
steelcase.com

Julie Ridenour, President
The Foundation focuses on the areas of human service, health, education, community development, the arts and the environment; giving particular concern to people who are disadvantaged, disabled, young and elderly as they attempt to improve the quality of their lives.
1951

Minnesota

2894 Arc of Minnesota
800 Transfer Road
Suite 7A
St. Paul, MN 55114 651-523-0823
800-582-5256
FAX: 651-523-0829
mail@arcmn.org
www.arcmn.org

John Rentschler, President
Lisa Schoneman, Vice President
Amy Hewitt, Secretary
Your membership in The Arc of Minnesotta benefits persons with developmental disabilities and their families as they live, learn, work and play. Please join today!

2895 Burnett Foundation
P.O. Box 633
Northfield, MN 55057-6881 817-877-3344
tomburnettfamilyfoundation@msn.com
www.tomburnettfoundation.org

V. Neils Agather, Executive Director

2896 Deluxe Corporation Foundation
Deluxe Corporation
3680 Victoria St N
Shoreview, MN 55126-2966 651-483-7111
800-328-0304
FAX: 651-483-7270
feedback@deluxe.com
ww.deluxe.com

Lee J Schram, CEO
Terry D. Peterson, CFO /Senior VP
Malcolm J. McRoberts, Senior Vice President, Small Bus
Funds programs such as schools, museums, programs for the disadvantaged. We believe programs and services like these represent the heart and soul of our communities.

2897 General Mills Foundation
P.O. Box 9452
Minneapolis, MN 55440-9452
800-248-7310
FAX: 763-764-8330
corporate.response@genmills.com
generalmills.com

Kendall J. Powell, Chairman/CEO
Ann W.H. Simonds, Senior Vice President
Keith A Woodward, Vice President/Treasurer

2898 Hugh J Andersen Foundation
342 5th Ave N
Suite 200
Bayport, MN 55003-4502
651-439-1557
888-439-9508
FAX: 651-439-9480
contact@srinc.biz
www.srinc.biz

Brad Kruse, Program Director
Established in 1962, this fund is a nonprofit charitable corporation classified as a private foundation. The Foundation was established as a general charitable fund, but now identifies projects that build individual and community capacity to be a priority. Giving is focused primarily in the counties of Washington, Minnesota, & St, Croix, Polk and Pierce of Wl. Grants are given in the areas of human services, health, education, arts and culture, community services and the environment.

2899 James R Thorpe Foundation
5866 Oakland Avenue
Minneapolis, MN 55417-5418
763-250-9304
info@jamesrthorpefoundation.org
www.jamesrthorpefoundation.org

Tim Thorpe, President
Robert C. Cote, Treasurer
Kerrie Blevins, Foundation Manager
Foundation based on values of respect and compassion, and is dedicated to making the greater Minneapolis area better for all its citizens.

2900 Jay and Rose Phillips Family Foundation
615 First Ave. NE
Ste. 330
Minneapolis, MN 55413
612-623-1654
FAX: 612-623-1653
info@phillipsfamilyfoundationmn.org

Patrick Troska, Executive Director
Joel Luedtke, Senior Program Officer
Tracy Lamparty, Grants and Operations Manager

2901 Minneapolis Foundation
80 S 8th St
800 IDS Center
Minneapolis, MN 55402-2100
612-672-3878
866-305-0543
FAX: 612-672-3846
email@mplsfoundation.org
www.mplsfoundation.org

Sandra L. Vargus, President & CEO
Jean M. Adams, Chief Operating Officer & CFO
Teresa Morrow, Vice President, External Relations
Provides a variety of charitable fund and gift options to help Minnesotans make a difference.

2902 Ordean Foundation
424 W Superior St
Duluth, MN 55802-1591
218-726-4785
Steve Mangan, Executive Director
Grants are given for a variety of purposes including: treatment and rehabilitation for persons who are chronically or temporarily mentally ill, persons whose physical capacity is impaired by injury or illness, promotes mental and physical health of the elderly, provides for youth guidance programs designed to avoid delinquency, and provides relief, aid and charity to people with no or low incomes. Grants are only offered to certain cities and townships near and around St. Louis County/Duluth.

2903 Otto Bremer Foundation
445 Minnesota St
Ste 2250
Saint Paul, MN 55101-2161
651-227-8036
888-291-1123
FAX: 651-312-3665
obf@ottobremer.org
www.ottobremer.org

Kari Suzuki, Director of Operations
Diane Benjamin, Executive Director
Danielle Cheslog, Grants Manager
Mission is to assist people in achieving full economic, civic and social participation in and for the betterment of their communities.

2904 Rochester Area Foundation
400 South Broadway
Suite 300
Rochester, MN 55904
507-282-0203
FAX: 507-282-4938
info@rochesterarea.org
rochesterarea.org

JoAnn Stormer, President
Max Evans, Administration/Communications
Ann Fahy-Gust, Grants and Impact Officer
The mission of the Rochester Area Foundation is to strengthen community philanthropy by promoting responsible and informed giving and to assist donors in meeting their charitable objectives.

Mississippi

2905 Arc of Mississippi
704 North President Street
Jackson, MS 39202
601-355-0220
800-717-1180
FAX: 601-355-0221
info@arcms.org
www.arcms.org

Kim Duffy, President
Ronnie Raggio, Senior Vice-President
Shirley Miller, Secretary
The Arc is Committed to securing for all people with developmental disabilities the opportunity to choose and realize their goals of where and how they learn live work and play.

Missouri

2906 Allen P & Josephine B Green Foundation
1055 Broadway
Suite 130
Kansas City, MO 64105
816-627-3420
FAX: 816-268-3420
greenfoundation@gkccf.org
www.greenfdn.org

Matthew Fuller, Manager of Community Investment
While the Foundation makes grants in a variety of fields, in the past its major support was in the field of medical research. During a 20-year period, 1951-71, it contributed over $900,000 to research in Parkinson's and related diseases of the nervous system; $600,000 for research in pediatric neurology and lesser amounts in other areas of medical research, but the board is now trending in other directions. Grants are limited to Missouri and none are offered to individuals.

2907 Anheuser-Busch
1 Busch Pl
Saint Louis, MO 63118-1852
314-577-2000
800-342-5283
FAX: 314-577-2900
anheuser-busch.com

August A Busch Iv, President
Supports education, helped fund health and human services organizations, provided disaster relief, and worked to preserve the environment.

2908 Arc of the US Missouri Chapter
PO Box 7823
Columbia, MO 65205
573-552-7648
www.arcofmissouri.org

2909 Greater Kansas City Community Foundation & Affiliated Trusts
1055 Broadway Blvd
Suite 130
Kansas City, MO 64105-1595
816-842-0944
866-719-7886
FAX: 816-842-8079
info@gkccf.org
www.growyourgiving.org
William S. Berkley, Past Chair
Dr. Jim Hinson, Vice Chair
William H. Coughlin, President
Mission is to improve the quality of life in Greater Kansas City by increasing charitable giving, connecting donors to community needs they care about, and providing leadership on critical community issues.

2910 Greater St Louis Community Foundation
319 N 4th St
Ste 300
Saint Louis, MO 63102-1906
314-588-8200
FAX: 314-588-8088
Stephen J. Rafferty, Chair
Thomas R. Collins, Vice Chair & Secretary
Amelia A.J. Bond, President & CEO
To improve the quality of life across the region by helping individuals, families and businesses make a difference through charitable giving.

2911 H&R Block Foundation
1 H and R Block Way
Kansas City, MO 64105-1905
816-854-4363
FAX: 816-854-8025
foundation@hrblock.com
www.blockfoundation.org
Henry W. Bloch, Chairman/ Treasurer/ Director
Thomas M. Bloch, Vice Chairman & Director
David P. Miles, President
A charitable organization under the not-for-profit corporation law of the state of Missouri. Grants are made only to organizations which are tax exempt from Federal Income taxation and which are not classified as private foundations. Major emphasis is placed in the metropolitan areas of Kansas City, Missouri: and Columbus, Ohio. The goal is to provide proportionately significant support of relatively few activities, as opposed to minor support for a great many.

2912 James S McDonnell Foundation
1034 S Brentwood Blvd
Suite 1850
Saint Louis, MO 63117- 1284
314-721-1532
FAX: 314-721-7421
info@jsmf.org
jsmf.org
Susan M Fitzpatrick, President
John T. Bruer, President Emeritus
Cheryl A. Washington, Grants Manager
The Foundation supports scientific, educational, and charitable causes locally, nationally and internationally.

2913 Lutheran Charities Foundation of St Louis
8860 Ladue Road
Suite 200
Saint Louis, MO 63124
314-231-2244
FAX: 314-727-7688
info@lutheranfoundation.org
www.lutheranfoundation.org
Karl A. Dunajcik, Chairperson of the Board
Ann L. Vazquez, President/CEO
Melinda K. McAliney, Program Director
Seeks the improved care of people in the greater St. Louis metropolitan region. Lutheran Foundation of St. Louis manages the endowment established upon the sale of the Lutheran Medical Center and provides grant awards for health, human care, Lutheran congregations' community service programs, and Lutheran education.

2914 RA Bloch Cancer Foundation
1 H and R Block Way
Kansas City, MO 64105-1905
816-854-5050
800-433-0464
FAX: 816-854-8024
hotline@blochcancer.org
www.blochcancer.org
Vangie Rich, Executive Director
Rosanne Wickman, Hotline Director
Provides a hotline that matches newly diagnosed cancer patients with someone who has survived the same kind of cancer. Offers free infomration, resources and support groups, and distributes lists of multidisciplinary second opinion centers. Also supplies three books at no charge: Fighting Cancer; Cancer.. There's Hope; and A Guide for Cancer Supporters. All services and books are free of charge.

2915 Victor E Speas Foundation
10434 Indiana Ave
Kansas City, MO 64137-1532
816-868-9300
mo.grantmaking@ustrust.com
www.bankofamerica.com
Latricia Scott Adams, President
VCC is a membership-based organization that brings together area volunteer managers and others interested in volunteerism for mutual support, exchange of ideas and information, and educational programs of timely interest.

Nebraska

2916 Arc of Nebraska
215 Centennial Mall South
Suite 508
Lincoln, NE 68508
402-475-4407
888-519-6524
FAX: 402-475-0214
info@arc-nebraska.org
www.arc-nebraska.org
Debbie Salomon, President
David Rowe, 1st Vice President
Kadi Holmberg, 2nd Vice President
Arc of Nebraska is commited to helping children and adults with disabilities secure the oppurtunity to choose and realize their goals of where and how they learn, live, work, and play.

2917 Cooper Foundation
1248 O St
Suite 870
Lincoln, NE 68508-1493
402-476-7571
FAX: 402-476-2356
info@cooperfoundation.org
cooperfoundation.org
Jack Campbell, Chair
Brad Korell, VP Business Development
Art Thompson, President
Serves only Nebraska with the primary interest in education, arts and humanities and the human services area.

2918 Mosaic
4980 S 118th St
Omaha, NE 68137-2200
402-896-9988
877-366-7242
FAX: 402-896-1511
info@mosaicinfo.org
www.mosaicinfo.org
Linda Timmons, President/CEO
Cindy Schroeder, Chief Financial Officer
Raul Saldivar, Chief Operating Officer
Headquarters for the faith-based organization providing services to people with disabilities in communities nationwide, and in conjunction with international partners. Mosaic was born of a merger of these two Lutheran organizations: Bethpage and Martin Luther Homes Society.

2919 Slosburg Family Charitable Trust
10040 Regency Cir
Ste 200
Omaha, NE 68114-3734 402-391-7900
FAX: 402-391-2991
richdale.com

David Slosburg, Owner

2920 Union Pacific Foundation
1400 Douglas Street
Omaha, NE 68179 , 402-544-5000
888-870-8777
888-877-7267
FAX: 402-501-0021
www.up.com

John J. Koraleski, Executive Chairman
Lance M. Fritz, President & COO of Union Pacific
Eric L. Butler, EVP, Marketing and Sales
The Union Pacific Foundation is the philanthropic arm of the Union Pacific Corporation and Union Pacific Railroad. Union Pacific believes that the quality of life in the communities in which its employees live and work is an integral part of its own success.

Nevada

2921 EL Wiegand Foundation
165 W Liberty St
Suite 200
Reno, NV 89501-1955 775-333-0310
FAX: 775-333-0314
www.thewiegandfoundationinc.com
Kristen A Avansino, President/Executive Director

2922 Nell J Redfield Foundation
PO Box 61
Reno, NV 89504-0061 775-323-1373
FAX: 775-323-4476
redfieldfoundation@yahoo.com

Jerry Smith, Manager
Gerald C. Smith, V.P. and Secy

2923 William N Pennington Foundation
441 W Plumb Ln
Reno, NV 89509-3766 775-333-9100
FAX: 775-333-9111

William Pennington, Owner

New Hampshire

2924 Agnes M Lindsay Trust
660 Chestnut St
Manchester, NH 03104-3550 603-669-1366
866-669-1366
FAX: 603-665-8114
admin@lindsaytrust.org
lindsaytrust.org

Susan E. Bouchard, Administrative Director
Ernest E. Dion, CPA, Trustee
Alan G. Lampert, Esq., Trustee
Funding for health and wefare organizations, special needs, mental health, blind, deaf and cultural programs to organizations, specifically for capital needs, not operating funds, located in the New England states of Maine, Massachusetts, New Hampshire and Vermont. We highly recommend you visit our web site.

2925 Foundation for Seacoast Health
100 Campus Dr
Ste 1
Portsmouth, NH 03801-5892 603-422-8200
FAX: 603-422-8206
ffsh@communitycampus.org
ffsh.org

Debra S. Grabowski, Executive Director
Kathleen Taylor, Finance Director
Eligio Santana, Facility Manager
Giving limited to Portsmouth, Rye, New Castle, Greenland, Newington, North Hampton, NH; and Kittery, Eliot, and York, ME.

New Jersey

2926 American Migraine Foundation
19 Mantua Rd.
Mount Royal, NJ 08061 856-423-0043
FAX: 856-423-0082
amf@talley.com
www.achenet.org

Lawrence C. Newman, MD, FAHS, Chair
Christine Lay, MD, FAHS, Vice-Chair
Nim Lalvani, MPH, Executive Director
Nonprofit, patient-health, professional partnership dedicated to advancing the treatment and management of headaches and to raising the public awareness of headache as valid, biologically based illness.

2927 Arc of New Jersey
985 Livingston Ave
N Brunswick, NJ 08902-1843 732-246-2525
FAX: 732-214-1834
arcnj.org

Robert Hage, President
Joanne Bergin, First Vice President
Kevin Sturges, Second Vice President
The Arc of New Jersey is committed to enhancing the quality of life of children and adults with intellectual and developmental disabilities and their families, through advocacy, empowerment, education and prevention.

2928 Arnold A Schwartz Foundation
15 Mountain Blvd
Warren, NJ 7059-5611 908-757-7800
FAX: 908-757-8039

Steven A Kunzman, President

2929 Campbell Soup Foundation
1 Campbell Pl
Camden, NJ 08103-1701 800-257-8443
media@campbellsoup.com
campbellsoup.com

Denise M. Morrison, President/CEO
Anthony P. DiSilvestro, Senior Vice President
Mark Alexander, President
Goal of this foundation is to match the company's assets with community needs in order to help forge solutions to community challenges. The Foundation believes that involvement at the community level can play a catalytic role in improving the quality of life. Giving is located in the areas of education, nutrition and health, cultural and youth related programs. The major focus of the foundation is on nutrition and health related matters, and places a high priority on Camden, New Jersey areas.

2930 Children's Hopes & Dreams Wish Fulfillment Foundation
280 US Highway 46
Dover, NJ 07801-2084 706-482-2248
FAX: 706-482-2289

Provides continual support for children and their families through the International Pen-Pal Program and the Kid's Kare Packages program. All services are free. Fulfills the last dreams of children with life threatening illnesses.

2931 Community Foundation of New Jersey
35 Knox Hill Road Morristown
PO Box 338
Morristown, NJ 07963-0388 973-267-5533
800-659-5533
FAX: 973-267-2903
info@cfnj.org
www.cfnj.org

Hans Dekker, President
Madeline Rivera, Program Officer
Susan I. Soldivieri, Chief Financial Officer
The Community Foundation of New Jersey is an alliance of families, businesses, and foundations that work together to create lasting differences in lives and communities today and tomorrow.

2932 FM Kirby Foundation
17 DeHart Street
PO Box 151
Morristown, NJ 07963-0151   973-538-4800
www.fdncenter.org/grantmaker/kirby
S. Dillard Kirby, President and Director
Jefferson W Kirby, Vice President and Director
Alice Kirby Horton, Assistant Secretary and Director
Family foundation, grants made to a wide range of nonprofit organizations in education, health and medicine, the arts and humanities, civic and public affairs, as well as religious, welfare and youth organizations.

2933 Fannie E Rippel Foundation
14 Maple Avenue
Suite 200
Morristown, NJ 07960   973-540-0101
FAX: 973-540-0404
info@rippelfoundation.org
www.rippelfoundation.org
Laura K Landy, President/ CEO
Chana Fitton, Chief Operating Officer
John D. Campbell, Chairman
Core purposes: research and treatment related to cancer and heart disease, the health of women and the elderly, and the quality of our nation's hospitals.

2934 Fund for New Jersey
One Palmer Square East
Suite 303
Princeton, NJ 08542   609-356-0421
fundfornj.org
Kiki Jamieson, President
Lucy Vandenberg, Senior Program Officer
Laura Mandell, Office Manager
Our grants promote projects that share a high purpose of furthering effective democracy through a range of methods encompassing education, advocacy, public policy analysis, and community problem-solving.

2935 Merck Company Foundation
2000 Galloping Hill Road
Kenilworth, NJ 07033   908-740-4000
merck.com
Kenneth C. Frazier, Chairman
Robert M. Davis, Executive Vice President and Chi
Willie A. Deese, EVP and President, Merck Manufac
Mission of the foundation is to support organizations and innovative programs in alignment with four strategic profiles: Improving access to quality health care and the appropriate use of medicines and vaccines,building capacity in the biomedical and health sciences, promoting environments that support innovation, economic growth and development in and ethical and fair context, and supporting communities where Merck employees work and live.

2936 Nabisco Foundation
7 Campus Dr
Parsippany, NJ 07054-4413   973-682-7096
FAX: 973-503-3018
Henry Sandbach, Director

2937 Ostberg Foundation
PO Box 1098
Alpine, NJ 07620-1098   201-569-6800
FAX: 201-767-8006

2938 Prudential Foundation
Prudential Financial
751 Broad St
15th Floor
Newark, NJ 07102-3714   973-802-6000
FAX: 973-802-7486
community.resources@prudential.com
prudential.com
John R Strangfeld, Chairman and CEO
Mark B. Grier, Vice Chairman
Charles Lowrey, Executive Vice President, Chief
Gives priority to national programs that further our objectives and programs serving areas where The Prudential has a substan-

tial employee presence. Places special emphasis on the home state of New Jersey and the headquarters city, Newark.

2939 Robert Wood Johnson Foundation
Route 1 and College Road East
P.O. Box 2316
Princeton, NJ 08543-2316   609-452-8701
877-843-7953
FAX: 888-727-1966
mail@rwjf.org
rwjf.org
Roger S. Fine, Chairman
Risa Lavizzo-Mourey, President and CEO
Robin E. Mockenhaupt, Chief of Staff
Our mission is to assure that all Americans have access to basic health care at reasonable cost, improve care and support for people with chronic health conditions, promote healthy communities and lifestyles and also, reduce the personal, social and economic harm caused by substance abuse.

2940 Victoria Foundation
31 Mulberry Street
5th Floor
Newark, NJ 07102-1397   973-792-9200
FAX: 973-792-1300
info@victoriafoundation.org
www.victoriafoundation.org
Frank Alvarez, President
Margaret H. Parker, Vice President
Gary M. Wingens, Treasurer
Desire is to help individuals in need reach their potential remains. Provides emergency coal for needy families and treated rheumatic fever in children.

New Mexico

2941 Arc of New Mexico
3655 Carlisle NE
Albuquerque, NM 87110-1644   505-883-4630
800-358-6493
FAX: 505-883-5564
rcostales@arcnm.org
arcnm.org
John Hall, President
Dolores Harden, Senior Vice President
Elaine Palma, Secretary
Mission is to improve the quality of life for individuals with developmental disabilities of all ages by advocating for equal opportunities and choices in where and how they learn, live, work, play and socialize. The Arc of New Mexico promotes self-determination, healthy families, effective community support systems and partnerships.

2942 Frost Foundation
511 Armijo St
Suite A
Santa Fe, NM 87501-2899   505-986-0208
info@frostfound.org
frostfound.org
Mary Amelia Whited-Howell, President
Philip B. Howell, Executive Vice President
Taylor F. Moore, Secretary/Treasurer
The Frost Foundation was created to be operated excusively for educational, charitable, and religious purposes.

2943 McCune Charitable Foundation
345 E Alameda St
Santa Fe, NM 87501-2229   505-983-8300
FAX: 505-983-7887
mccune@nmmccune.org
nmmccune.org
Sarah McCune Losinger, Chair
Wendy Lewis, Executive Director
Henry Rael, Program Officer
Dedicated to enriching the health, education, environment, and cultural and spiritual life of New Mexicans.

2944 Santa Fe Community Foundation
501 Halona Street
Santa Fe, NM 87505
505-988-9715
FAX: 505-988-1829
foundation@santafecf.org
www.santafecf.org

Suzanne Ortega Cisneros, Chair
Barry Herskowitz, Vice Chair
Kenneth Romero, Secretary

New York

2945 AFB Center on Vision Loss
American Foundation for the Blind
2 Penn Plaza
Suite 1102
New York, NY 10121-4524
212-502-7600
FAX: 888-545-8331
afbinfo@afb.net
afb.org

Carl R Augusto, President & CEO
Kelly Bleach, Chief Administrative Officer
Rick Bozeman, Chief Financial Officer
National nonprofit organization that expands possibilities for people with vision loss.

2946 Altman Foundation
521 5th Ave
Fl 35
New York, NY 10175-3500
212-682-0970
FAX: 212-682-1648
info@altman.org
altmanfoundation.org

Karen L. Rosa, President
Jeremy Tennenbaum, Chief Financial Officer
Ann E. Maldonado, Office Manager
For the benefit of such charitable and educational institutions in the City of New York as said directors shall approve. Foundation grants support programs and institutions that enrich the quality of life in the city, with a particular focus on initiatives that help individuals, families and communities benefit from the services and opportunities that will enable them to achieve their full potential.

2947 Ambrose Monell Foundation
1 Rockefeller Plz
Suite 301
New York, NY 10020-2002
212-586-0700
FAX: 212-245-1863
www.monellvetlesen.org

Ambrose K. Monell, President and Treasurer
Eugene P. Grisanti, Vice-President
George Rowe, Vice-President
Voluntary aiding and contributing to religious, charitable, scientific, literary, and educational uses and purposes, in New York, elsewhere in the US and throughout the world.

2948 American Chai Trust
41 Madison Ave
Suite 400
New York, NY 10010-2202
212-889-0575
FAX: 212-743-8120
info@perlmanandperlman.com
www.perlmanandperlman.com

2949 American Foundation for Suicide Prevention (AFSP)
199 Water St.
11th Floor
New York, NY 10038
212-363-3500
888-333-2377
FAX: 212-363-6237
info@afsp.org
afsp.org

Robert Gebbia, Chief Executive Officer
Christine Yu Moutier, Chief Medical Officer
Stephanie Rogers, Executive Vice President & Chief Communications Officer
The American Foundation for Suicide Prevention is a voluntary health organization that gives those affected by suicide a nationwide community empowered by research, education, and advocacy to take action against this disease. AFSP achieves their goal by funding scientific research, educating the public about mental health and suicide prevention, and supporting survivors of suicide loss and all those affected by suicide.

2950 American Foundation for the Blind
2 Penn Plaza
Suite 1102
New York, NY 10121
800-232-5463
www.afb.org

Kirk Adams, President & CEO
Darren M. Davis, Executive Administrator Executive Office
The American Foundation for the Blind (AFB) is a national nonprofit that is dedicated to removing barriers, creating solutions, and expanding possibilities for the blind and visually impaired. The AFB is focused on spreading access to technology, elevating the quality of information and tools for professional who serve people with vision loss, and the promotion of independent living for those with vision loss.

2951 Arthur Ross Foundation
20 E 74th St
Ste 4c
New York, NY 10021-2654
212-737-7311
FAX: 212-650-0332

Arthur Ross, President

2952 Artists Fellowship
47 5th Ave
New York, NY 10003-4303
212-255-7740
info@artistsfellowship.org
www.artistsfellowship.org

Babette Bloch, President
Private, charitable foundation that assists professional fine arts and their families in times of emergency, disability, or bereavement.

2953 Bodman Foundation
767 3rd Ave
4th Floor
New York, NY 10017-2023
212-644-0322
FAX: 212-759-6510

John N. Irwin III, Chairman
Russell P. Pennoyer, President
Peter Frelinghuysen, Vice President
Foundation concentrates their grant programs in New York City, but foundation also makes some grants in Northern New Jersey. Funding is concentrated in six program areas: Arts & Culture, Education, Employment, Health, Public Policy and Youth and Families.

2954 Brain & Behavior Research Foundation
747 Third Ave.
33rd Floor
New York, NY 10017
646-681-4888
800-829-8289
info@bbrfoundation.org
bbrfoundation.org

Jeffrey Borenstein, President & Chief Executive Officer
Miriam E. Katowitz, Vice President of the Board
Donald M. Boardman, Treasurer
The Brain & Behavior Research Foundation is a nonprofit organization committed to alleviating the suffering caused by mental illness by awarding grants in the field of mental health research.
1987

2955 Brooklyn Home for Aged Men
P.O.Box 280062
Brooklyn, NY 11228
718-745-1638
FAX: 718-745-0813
www.brooklynhome.org

Catherine M. Birdseye, Co-President
William E. Spaulding, Co-President
Andelusia Wheeler, Co-President
The Brooklyn Home For Aged Men has served the community for more than one hundred years. Although originally set up as a residence for men, it later accepted women and couples as well.

2956 Cancer Care
275 7th Avenue
22nd Floor
New York, NY 10001-6754 212-712-8400
800-813-4673
FAX: 212-712-8495
info@cancercare.org
www.cancercare.org

Patricia J. Goldsmith, Chief Executive Officer
John Rutigliano, Chief Operating Officer
Sue Lee, Senior Director of Development
A national non-profit organization that provides free, professional support services to anyone affected by cancer: people with cancer, caregivers, children, loved ones, and the bereaved.

2957 Children's Tumor Foundation
120 Wall Street
16th Floor
New York, NY 10005-3904 212-344-6633
800-323-7938
FAX: 212-747-0004
info@ctf.org
ctf.org

Linda Halliday Martin, Chairperson
Colin Bryar, Vice Chairperson
Annette Bakker, PhD, President and Chief Scientific Officer
A nonprofit 501 (c)(3) medical foundation, dedicated to improving the health and well-being of individuals and families affected by neurofibromatosis. The Foundation sponsors medical research, clinical services, public education programs and patient support services. It is the central source for up-to-date and accurate information about NF. It also assists patients and families with referrals to NF clinics and healthcare professionals specializing in NF. The goal is to find a cure for NF.

2958 Commonwealth Fund
1 E 75th St
New York, NY 10021-2692 212-606-3800
FAX: 212-606-3500
info@cmwf.org
www.commonwealthfund.org

Benjamin K. Chu, Chairman
Cristine Russell, Vice Chairman
Donald Moulds, Executive Vice President for Pro
A private foundation with the broad charge to enhance the common good. Carries out this mandate by supporting efforts that help people live healthy and productive lives, and by assisting certain groups with serious and neglected problems. Supports independent research on health and social issues and makes grants to improve heathcare practice and policy.

2959 Community Foundation for Greater Buffalo
726 Exchange Street,
Suite 525
Buffalo, NY 14210 716-852-2857
FAX: 716-852-2861
mail@cfgb.org
cfgb.org

Marsha Joy Sullivan, Chair
William Joyce, Vice Chair
Gary L. Mucci, Secretary
Mission is connecting people, ideas, and resources to improve lives in Western New York

2960 Community Foundation of Herkimer & Oneida Counties
2608 Genesee Street
Utica, NY 13502-4728 315-735-8212
FAX: 315-735-9363
info@foundationhoc.org
foundationhoc.org

Alicia Dicks, President/CEO
Gilles Lauzon, Director of Finance
Elayne Johnson, Director of Fund Administration
Mission of the foundation is to improve the lives of the residents of Herkimer and Oneida Counties.

2961 Community Foundation of the Capitol Region
Six Tower Place
Albany, NY 12203-3749 518-446-9638
FAX: 518-446-9708
info@cfgcr.org
www.cfgcr.org

Karen Bilowith, President/CEO
Mindy Derosia, Development Officer
Shelly Connolly, Program Assistant
Mission is to strengthen our community by attracting charitable endowments both large and small, maximizing benefits to donors, making effective gtants, and providing leadership to address community needs.

2962 Comsearch: Broad Topics
Foundation Center
79 5th Ave
New York, NY 10003-3034 212-620-4230
800-424-9836
FAX: 212-807-3677
communications@foundationcenter.org
www.fdncenter.org

Bradford K. Smith, President
Lisa Philip, Vice President for Strategic Phi
Jen Bokoff, Director of GrantCraft
Subset publications of The Foundation Grants Index, are printouts of actual foundation grants, covering 26 key areas of grantmaking. This tool is designed for fundraisers who wish to examine grantmaking activities in a broad field of interest.
$55.00

2963 DE French Foundation
Ste 503
120 Genesee St
Auburn, NY 13021-3672 315-252-3634
Walter Lowe, Owner

2964 Dana Foundation
Dana Alliance for Brain Initiatives
505 Fifth Avenue
6th floor
New York, NY 10017 212-223-4040
FAX: 212-317-8721
danainfo@dana.org
www.dana.org

Edward F Rover, President/Chairman
Burton M. Mirsky, Executive Vice President, Finance
Barbara Rich, Ed.D., Executive Vice President, Communications
A private philanthropy with principal interests in brain science, immunology, and arts education.

2965 David J Green Foundation
Ste 12
599 Lexington Ave
New York, NY 10022-6030 212-317-8820
FAX: 212-371-5099

Valerie Ventolora, Manager
Michael Greene, Manager

2966 Easterseals New York
633 3rd Ave.
New York, NY 10017 212-943-4364
www.easterseals.com/newyork

Shawn McCurley, Interim Executive Director
Mary Moran, Executive Director, Early Childhood Development Programs
Lora Winghart, Regional Director, Western Region
Offers resources and expertise that allow children and adults with disabilities to live with dignity and independence. Provides programs and solutions that enhance the lives of people with disabilities, while heightening community awareness and acceptance.

2967 Edna McConnel Clark Foundation
415 Madison Ave
Tenth Floor
New York, NY 10017-7949
212-551-9100
FAX: 212-421-9325
info@emcf.org
emcf.org

Nancy Roob, President
Woodrow C. McCutchen, Vice President, Senior Portfolio
Kelly Fitzsimmons, Vice President, Chief Program an
Helps young people, ages 9-24, from low-income backgrounds become independent, productive adults.

2968 Edward John Noble Foundation
Fl 19
32 E 57th St
New York, NY 10022-8562
212-759-4212
FAX: 212-888-4531

June Noble Larkin, Owner
June Larkin, Owner

2969 Epilepsy Foundation of Long Island
1500 Hempstead Turnpike
East Meadow, NY 11554
516-739-7733
888-672-7154
FAX: 516-739-1860
efli.org

Thomas Hopkins, President & CEO
Paul Giotis, Chief Operating Officer
Lawrence Boord, Chief Financial Officer
Provides education, counseling and residential care to Long Island residents with epilepsy and related conditions.

2970 Episcopal Charities
1047 Amsterdam Avenue
New York, NY 10025-1747
212-316-7575
episcopalcharities@dioceseny.org
episcopalcharities-newyork.org

John Talty, President
Lorraine A. LaHuta, Vice President
Evan A. Davis, Secretary
Provides funding and support to a broad range of community-based human service programs throughout the Diocese of New York. These programs, sponsored by Episcopal congregations, serve disadvantaged individuals, youth and families on a non-sectarian basis.

2971 Esther A & Joseph Klingenstein Fund
125 Park Ave.
Suite 1700
New York, NY 10017
212-492-6181
www.klingfund.org
Supports, in the early stages of their careers, young investigators engaged in basic or clinical research that may lead to a better understanding of neurological and psychiatric disorders.

2972 Fay J Lindner Foundation
189 Wheatley Road
Brookville, NY 11545
516-686-4440
www.fayjlindnercenter.org

Terrence Ullrich, President
Dr. Robert Steinberger, Vice President
Thomas F. Moore, Treasurer

2973 Ford Foundation
320 E 43rd St
New York, NY 10017-4890
212-573-5000
FAX: 212-351-3677
office-of-communications@fordfoundation.org
www.fordfound.org

Darren Walker, President
Kenneth T Monterio, Vice President, Secretary and Ge
Alfred Ironside, Vice President/Communications
A resource for innovative people and institutions worldwide. Goals are to: strenghthen democratic values; reduce poverty and injustice; promote international cooperation; and advance human achievement. While not specific to disabilities, the Ford Foundation operates on several levels that indirectly assist and support those with disabilities through human and civil rights issues, social justice support, economic fairness and opportunity, and access to education involvements.

2974 Fortis Foundation
28 Liberty Street
New York, NY 10005-1401
212-859-7197
FAX: 212-859-7010
ir.assurant.com

Elaine D. Rosen, Chair
Howard L. Carver, Director
Melissa Kivett, Senior Vice President, Investor

2975 Foundation Center
79 5th Ave
16th Street
New York, NY 10003-3076
212-620-4230
800-424-9836
FAX: 212-807-3677
communications@foundationcenter.org
foundationcenter.org

Bradford K Smith, President
Lisa Philip, VP, Strategic Philanthropy
Jen Bokoff, Director of GrantCraft
The Foundation Center publishes Foundation Directory Online, with key facts on the US grantmakers and their grants.

2976 Foundation Center Library Services
Foundation Center
79 5th Ave
16th Street
New York, NY 10003-3076
212-620-4230
800-424-9836
FAX: 212-807-3677
communications@foundationcenter.org
foundationcenter.org

Bradford K Smith, President
Lisa Philip, VP, Strategic Philanthropy
Jen Bokoff, Director of GrantCraft
The Center disseminates current information on foundation and corporate giving through our national collections in New York City and Washington D.C., our field offices in San Francisco and our network of over 180 cooperating libraries in all 50 states and abroad.

2977 Foundation for Advancement in Cancer Therapy
PO Box 1242
Old Chelsea Station
New York, NY 10113-1242
212-675-6349
info@rethinkingcancer.org
www.rethinkingcancer.org

Ruth Sackman, Founder
A clearinghouse for information regarding alternative cancer therapies, emphasizing nutritional and metabolic approaches.

2978 Gebbie Foundation
215 Cherry St
Jamestown, NY 14701-5207
716-487-1062
FAX: 716-484-6401
info@gebbie.org
www.gebbie.org

Gregory J Edwards, CEO
Daniel Kathman, President
Jonathan Taber, Vice President
Giving in Chautauqua County, and secondly, in neighboring areas of western New York. Giving is offered in other areas only when the project is consonant with program objectives that cannot be developed locally.

2979 Gladys Brooks Foundation
1055 Franklin Avenue
Suite 208
Garden City, NY 11530
www.gladysbrooksfoundation.org
Jessica L Rutledge, Director
The purpose of this Foundation is to provide for the intellectual, moral and physical welfare of the people of this country by establishing and supporting nonprofit libraries, educational institutions, hospitals and clinics. The Foundation will make grants only to private, publicly supported, nonprofit, tax-exempt organizations.

2980 Glickenhaus Foundation
546 5th Ave
New York, NY 10036-5000
212-953-7800
info@glickenhaus.com
Seth M. Glickenhaus, Senior Partner and Chief Investm

2981 Guide Dog Foundation for the Blind
371 East Jericho Turnpike
Smithtown, NY 11787-2976
631-930-9000
800-548-4337
FAX: 631-930-9009
info@guidedog.org
www.guidedog.org

James C. Bingham, Chair
Alphonce J. Brown, Vice Chair
Barbara J. Kelly, Secretary
Providing mobility through the use of trained guide or service dogs to individuals who are blind or with other special needs.

2982 Hearing Health Foundation (HHF)
PO Box 1397
New York, NY 10018
212-257-6140
866-454-3924
FAX: 212-257-6139
TTY: 888-435-6104
info@hhf.org
hearinghealthfoundation.org
Timothy Higdon, President & Chief Executive Officer
Noemi Disla, Director, Finance, Operations & Administration
Christopher Geissler, Director, Program & Research Support
Hearing Health Foundation promotes hearing health and advocates for the prevention and cure of hearing loss and tinnitus through research.
1958

2983 Hearst Foundations
300 W 57th St
Fl 26
New York, NY 10019-3741
212-649-2000
FAX: 212-887-6855
hearst.com
Steven R. Swartz, President and Chief Executive Of
National philanthropic resources for organziations and institutions working in the fields of education, health, culture and social services. Goal is to ensure that people of all backgrounds have the opportunity to build healthy, productive and inspiring lives.

2984 Henry and Lucy Moses Fund
405 Lexington Ave
New York, NY 10174-1299
212-554-7800
FAX: 212-554-7700
www.mosessinger.com
Irving Sitnick, President
Provides legal services to many prominent industries, individuals and families in the New York City area.

2985 Herman Goldman Foundation
Fl 18
61 Broadway
New York, NY 10006-2708
212-797-9090
Alan Nisselson, President
A private nonoperating foundation.

2986 Kenneth & Evelyn Lipper Foundation
Fl 6
101 Park Ave
New York, NY 10178
212-883-6333
Kenneth Lipper, Director

2987 Long Island Alzheimer's Foundation
5 Channel Drive
Port Washington, NY 11050-2216
516-767-6856
FAX: 516-767-6864
www.liaf.org
Paul Eibeler, Chairman
Fred Jenny, Executive Director
Sean Phillips, Director of Development

2988 Louis and Anne Abrons Foundation
First Manhattan Company
399 Park Avenue
New York, NY 10022-7001
212-756-3300
FAX: 212-223-4175
firstmanhattan.com

David Manischewitz, CEO
Sam Colin, Senior Managing Director
Allan Glick, Senior Managing Director

2989 Margaret L Wendt Foundation
Ste 277
40 Fountain Plz
Buffalo, NY 14202-2200
716-855-2146
FAX: 716-855-2149

Robert J Kresse, Manager

2990 Merrill Lynch & Company Foundation
250 Vesey St
New York, NY 10080
212-449-1000
800-637-7455
FAX: 212-449-7969
ml.com

Brian T Moynihan, CEO
John Theil, Head
Andy M Sieg, Managing Director
Ongoing support for the arts, health, human services, and civic issues. Merrill Lynch's philanthropic priority is a sustained investment in education. Q992

2991 Metzger-Price Fund
Ste 2300
230 Park Ave
New York, NY 10169
212-867-9500
FAX: 212-599-1759

Isaac A Saufer, Secretary/Treasurer

2992 Milbank Foundation for Rehabilitation
116 Village Boulevard
Suite 200
New York, NY 08540
609-951-2283
FAX: 609-951-2281
fdnweb.org/milbank

Jeremiah M. Bogert, Chairman & Secretary
Jeremiah Milbank III, President and Treasurer
Carl Helstrom, Executive Director
Awarding grants from trust funds based on a competitive selection process or the preferences of the foundation managers and granters. The foundations mission is to integrate people with disabilities into all aspects of american life. Current priorities include, but are not limited to: consumer-focused initiatives that enable people with disablties to lead fulfilling,independent lives; innovative policy research and education on market-based approaches to health care and rehabilitation..

2993 Morgan Stanley Foundation
1585 Broadway
New York, NY 10036-8293
212-761-4000
FAX: 212-761-0086
mediainquiries@morganstanley.com
morganstanley.com
James P. Gorman, Chairman and Chief Executive Off
Thomas Nides, Vice Chairman
Jeff Brodsky, Chief Human Resources Officer
The Foundation's overachieving mission is threefold: build the potential of individuals and families, encourage and support employees' charitable efforts, and strengthen relationships with our communities.

2994 National Foundation for Facial Reconstruction
333 East 30th St.
Lobby Office
New York, NY 10016-4974
212-263-6656
FAX: 212-263-7534
info@myface.org
myface.org

Barbara H. Zuckerberg, President
John R. Gordon, Chairman
Sondra Neuschotz, Secretary
A nonprofit organization whose major purposes are to provide facilities for the treatment and assistance of individuals who are un-

able to afford private reconstructive surgical care, to train and educate professionals in this surgery, to encourage research in the field and to carry on public education.

2995 National Hemophilia Foundation
7 Penn Plaza
Suite 1204
New York, NY 10001
212-328-3700
888-463-6643
FAX: 212-328-3777
info@hemophilia.org
www.hemophilia.org

Leonard Valentino, President & CEO
Dawn Rotellini, Chief Operating Officer
Kevin Mills, Chief Scientific Officer
Dedicated to finding better treatments and cures for bleeding and clotting disorders and to preventing the complications of these disorders through education, advocacy and research.

2996 Neisloss Family Foundation
Ste 7
1737 Veterans Hwy
Central Islip, NY 11749-1533
631-234-1600
FAX: 631-234-1066

Stanley Neisloss, President/Owner

2997 New York Community Trust
909 3rd Ave
22nd Floor
New York, NY 10022-4752
212-686-0010
FAX: 212-532-8528
aw@nyct-cfi.org
nycommunitytrust.org

Lorie A Slutsky, President
Carolyn M Weiss, CFO
Mary Z. Greenebaum, Chief Investment Officer
The organization's goal is to out charitable money to work, making grants to the city's nonprofit community and building an endowment to tackle future problems.

2998 New York Foundation
10 E 34th St
10th Floor
New York, NY 10016-4327
212-594-8009
info@nyf.org
nyf.org

Marlene Provizer, Chair
Roger Schwed, Vice Chair
Sue A Kaplan, Secretary
Grants are given that involve New York City or a particular neighborhood of the city. Emphasize advocacy and community organizing. Address a critical need or disadvantaged population, particularly youth or the elderly. Are strongly identified with a particular community. Require an amount of funding to which a Foundation grant would make a substantial contribution. And can show a clear role for the Foundation's funds.

2999 Northern New York Community Foundation
120 Washington St
Suite 400
Watertown, NY 13601-3376
315-782-7110
FAX: 315-782-0047
info@nnycf.org
www.nnycf.org

Joseph W. Russell, President
Linda S. Merrell, Vice President
Jacquelyn A. Schell, Secretary
Raises, manages and administers an endowment and collection of funds for the benefit of the community

3000 Parkinson's Disease Foundation
1359 Broadway
Room 1509
New York, NY 10018-7867
212-923-4700
800-457-6676
FAX: 212-923-4778
info@pdf.org
www.pdf.org

Howard D Morgan, Chair
Constance Atwell, Vice Chair
Isobel Konecky, Secretary

The Parkinson's Disease Foundation is a leading national presence in Parkinson's disease research, education and public advocacy. We are working for the nearly one million people in the US who live with Parkinson's by funding promising scientific research to find the causes of and a cure for Parkinson's while supporting people with Parkinson's, their families and caregivers through educational programs and support services.

3001 Peter and Elizabeth C. Tower Foundation
2351 North Forest Rd.
Suite 106
Getzville, NY 14068-1225
716-689-0370
FAX: 716-689-3716
info@thetowerfoundation.org
thetowerfoundation.org

Tracy A. Sawicki, Executive Director
Donald W. Matteson, Chief Program Officer
Charles E. Colston Jr., Program Officer
The Peter and Elizabeth C. Tower Foundation supports community programming that results in children, adolescents, and young adults affected by substance use disorders, learning disabilities, mental illness, and intellectual disabilities achieving their full potential.
1990

3002 Reader's Digest Foundation
Readers Digest Association
Readers Digest Rd
Pleasantville, NY 10570
914-238-1000
FAX: 914-238-4559
letters@rd.com
rd.com

Mary G Berner, CEO
Dedicated to creating opportunities and promoting efforts that encourage individuals to make a positive difference in their communities, and to supporting programs designed to help young people learn, grow and enrich their lives.

3003 Research to Prevent Blindness
645 Madison Ave
Floor 21
New York, NY 10022-1010
212-752-4333
800-621-0026
FAX: 212-688-6231
www.rpbusa.org

Diane S. Swift, Chair
Brian F. Hofland PhD, President
David H Brenner, Vice President and Secretary
National voluntary health foundation supported by foundations, corporations and voluntary gifts and bequests from individuals. Established to stimulate basic and applied research into the causes, prevention and treatment of blinding eye diseases.

3004 Rita J and Stanley H Kaplan Foundation
Rm 306
866 United Nations Plz
New York, NY 10017-1822
212-688-1047
FAX: 212-688-6907
www.kaplanfoundation.org

Nancy Kaplan Belsky, President
Susan B. Kaplan, Vice President
Scott Kaplan Belsky, Secretary & Treasurer

3005 Robert Sterling Clark Foundation
135 E 64th St
New York, NY 10065-7045
212-288-8900
FAX: 212-288-1033
rscf@rsclark.org
rsclark.org

James Allen Smith, Chairman
Vincent McGee, President
Clara Miller, Treasurer
Giving primarily in New York with emphasis on advocacy, research, and public education aimed at informing New York City of state policies.

3006 Skadden Fellowship Foundation
4 Times Sq
New York, NY 10036-6518   212-735-3000
                                FAX: 212-735-2000
                                info@skadden.com
                                www.skadden.com

Alan C. Myers, Director
William Schumann, Legal Assistant
The aim of the Foundation is to give Fellows the freedom to pursue public intrest work, thus the Fellows create their own projects at public interest organizations with at least 2 lawyers on staff before they apply.

3007 St George's Society of New York
216 E 45th St
Suite 901
New York, NY 10017-3304   212-682-6110
                                FAX: 212-682-3465
                                info@stgeorgessociety.org
                                stgeorgessociety.org

John Shannon, Almoner
Anna Titley, Director of Operations and Commu
Samantha Hamilton, Director of Development and Memb
St George's Society provides monthly stipends to the elderly and the handicapped.

3008 Stanley W. Metcalf Foundation
Ste 503
120 Genesee St
Auburn, NY 13021-3672   315-252-3634
Walter Lowe, Owner

3009 Stonewall Community Foundation
446 West 33rd Street
New York, NY 10001-1913   212-367-1155
                                FAX: 212-367-1157
                                stonewall@stonewallfoundation.org
                                www.stonewallfoundation.org

Dante Mastri, President
Neill Coleman, Vice President
Chris Davis, Secretary
Mission is to promote the well being of lesbian, gay, bisexual, and transgender (LGBT) individuals and strengthen the LGBT community. They do this by increasing resources; targeting those resources strategically to areas of greatest need; and by serving as a catalyst and clearinghouse for ideas and solutions. Through grant-making donor-advised funds, endowment funds and charitable education, Stonewall supports LGBT organizations and helps donors realize their philanthropic goals.

3010 Surdna Foundation
330 Madison Ave
30th Floor
New York, NY 10017-5016   212-557-0010
                                grants@surdna.org
                                surdna.org

Jocelyn Downie, Chairperson
Peter B Benedict, Vice Chairperson
Lawrence S.C Griffth, Secretary & Treasurer
The Foundation makes grants in the areas of environment, community revitalization, effective citizenry, the arts and the non-profit sector.

3011 The Adaptive Sports Foundation
100 Silverman Way
PO Box 266
Windham, NY 12496   518-734-5070
                                FAX: 518-734-6740
                                info@adaptivesportsfoundation.org
                                www.adaptivesportsfoundation.org

Robert W Stubbs, Chair
Todd Munn, Executive Director
Pam Greene, Program Director
The Adaptive Sports Foundation is a non-profit organization providing programs for children and adults with physical and cognitive disabilities. Programs center around outdoor physical activities and sports, including skiing and snowboarding, canoeing and cycling.

3012 Tisch Foundation
Fl 19
655 Madison Ave
New York, NY 10065-8043   212-521-2930
                                FAX: 212-521-2983

Mark J Krinsky, VP

3013 Van Ameringen Foundation
509 Madison Avenue
New York, NY 10022-5501   212-758-6221
                                FAX: 212-688-2105
                                info@vanamfound.org
                                www.vanamfound.org

Kenneth A. Kind, President / Treasurer
Steadman Westergaard, Vice President and Secretary
Eleanor Sypher, Executive Director
From its beginning the Foundation has sought to stimulate prevention, education, and direct care in the mental health field with an emphasis on those individuals and populations having an impoverished background and few opportunities, for whom appropriate intervention would produce positive change.

3014 Verizon Foundation
1 Verizon Way
Basking Ridge, NJ 07920-1097   866-247-2687
                                FAX: 908-630-2660
                                www.verizon.com

Lowell C McAdam, Chairman & CEO
Roy H Chestnutt, Executive Vice President
James J Gerace, Chief Communications Officer
Mission is to improve education, literacy, family safety and healthcare by supporting Verizon's commitment to deliver technology that touches life. We focus our philanthropic efforts on 3 areas: Education, Safety and Health. & Volunteerism.

3015 Western New York Foundation
11 Summer St
Third Floor
Buffalo, NY 14209-2256   716-839-4225
                                FAX: 716-883-1107
                                bgosch@wnyfoundation.org
                                www.wnyfoundation.org

Jennifer S. Johnson, Chairman
James A. W. McLeod, President
John N. W. Walsh III, Vice President
The Western New York Foundation makes grants in the seven counties of Western New York State: Erie, Niagra, Genesee, Wyoming, Allegany, Cattaraugus and Chautauqua

3016 William T Grant Foundation
570 Lexington Avenue
18th Floor
New York, NY 10022-6837   212-752-0071
                                FAX: 212-752-1398
                                info@wtgrantfdn.org
                                wtgrantfoundation.org

Adam Gamoran, President
Vivian Tseng, Vice President, Program
Deborah McGinn, Vice President, Finance and Admi
Purpose is to further the understanding of human behavior through research. The mission focuses on improving the lives of youth ages 8 to 25 in the United States.

North Carolina

3017 Arc of North Carolina
343 East Six Forks Rd.
Suite 320
Raleigh, NC 27609   919-782-4632
                                800-662-8706
                                FAX: 919-782-4634
                                info@arcnc.org
                                www.arcnc.org

Adonis Brown, President
Robert Rusty Bradstock, Senior Vice President
Rhonda Schandevel, Secretary
Committed to securing for all people with developmental disabilities the opportunity to choose and realize their goals of where and how they learn, live, work, and play.

3018 Bob & Kay Timberlake Foundation
1660 E Center Street Ext
Lexington, NC 27292-1309
336-243-7777
800-776-0822
FAX: 336-249-2469
bobtimberlake.com

Daniel Timberlake, President

3019 Duke Endowment
800 East Morehead Street
Charlotte, NC 28202-4012
704-376-0291
FAX: 704-376-9336
dukeendowment.org

Eugene W. Cochrane Jr., President
Arthur E. Morehead IV, Vice President/General Counsel
Susan L. McConnell, Director of Higher Education
Mission is to serve the people of North Carolina and South Carolina by supporting selected programs of higher education, health care, children's welfare, and spiritual life.

3020 First Union Foundation
301 S College St
Charlotte, NC 28288
704-383-0525
FAX: 704-374-2484

Judy Allison, Director

3021 Foundation for the Carolinas
220 N. Tryon Street
Charlotte, NC 28202
704-973-4500
800-973-7244
FAX: 704-973-4599
mmarsicano@fftc.org
fftc.org

Michael Marsicano, Ph.D., President & CEO
Brian Collier, Executive Vice President
Debra S. Watt, SVP, Information Technology
Giving primarily to organizations serving the citizens of North and South Carolina.

3022 Kate B Reynolds Charitable Trust
128 Reynolda Village
Winston Salem, NC 27106-5123
336-397-5500
800-485-9080
FAX: 336-723-7765
kbr.org

Karen McNeil-Miller, President
Lori Fuller, Director, Evaluation and Learnin
Joel Beeson, Director, Operations
Mission is to improve the quality of life and quality of health for the financially needy of North Carolina. Grants resricted to the state of North Carolina only.

3023 Mary Reynolds Babcock Foundation
2920 Reynolda Rd
Winston Salem, NC 27106-3016
336-748-9222
FAX: 336-777-0095
info@mrbf.org
mrbf.org

Jennifer Barksdale, Finance Officer
Toshawia Bruner, Office Assistant
Lavastian Glenn, Network Officer
For 1994, this foundation is committed to an extensive educational and planning process to better understand the Southeast and to articulate the role the foundation seeks to play in the region into the twenty-first century.

3024 Triangle Community Foundation
324 Blackwell St
Suite 1220
Durham, NC 27701-3690
919-474-8370
FAX: 919-941-9208
info@trianglecf.org
trianglecf.org

Lacy M. Presnell, Chair
Pat Nathan, Secretary
C. Perry Colwell, Assistant Secretary
Triangle Community Foundation connects philanthropic resources with community needs, creates opportunity for enlightned change and encourages philanthropy as a way of life.

North Dakota

3025 Alex Stern Family Foundation
4141 28th South Avenue
Suite 102
Fargo, ND 58104-8403
701-271-0263
FAX: 701-271-0408
alexsternfamilyfoundation.org

Don Scott, Executive Director
Rondi McGovern, Trustee
Dan Carey, Trustee
The Foundation supports the arts, social welfare/human services, education, youth recreation, civic projects and health issues for the benefit of the greater Fargo-Moorhead area.

3026 Arc of North Dakota
2500 DeMers Avenue
Grand Forks, ND 58201-2420
701-772-6191
877-250-2022
FAX: 701-772-2195
thearc@arcuv.com
www.thearcuppervalley.com

Peggy Johnson, President
Joan Karpenko, First Vice President
Ruth Jenny, Secretary
Mission is to work in partnership with our constituents, members and affiliated chapters to ensure that children and adults with intellectual and developmental disabilities have the supports, benefits, and services they need, and are accepted, respected and fully included in their communities.

3027 North Dakota Community Foundation
309 N Mandan Street
309 N Mandan Street, Suite 2
P.O.Box 387
Bismarck, ND 58502-0387
701-222-8349
kdvorak@ndcf.net
www.ndcf.net

Kevin J Dvorak, CFP, President & CEO
Amy N. Warnke, CFRE, Development Director East
Kara L. Geiger, Development Director West
The mission of the North Dakota Community Foundation is to improve the quality of life for North Dakota's citizens through charitable giving and promoting philanthropy.

Ohio

3028 Akron Community Foundation
345 W Cedar St
Akron, OH 44307-2407
330-376-8522
FAX: 330-376-0202
jpetures@akroncf.org

Mark Alio, Chair
Steven Cox, Vice Chair
Dr. Sandra Selby, Secretary
Mission is to improve the quality of life in the Greater Akron area by building permanent endowments, and providing philanthropic leadership that enables donors to make lasting investments in the community.

3029 Albert G and Olive H Schlink Foundation
49 Benedict Avenue, Suite C
Norwalk, OH 44857
curtis@hwak.com
www.schlinkfoundation.org

3030 Arc of Ohio
1335 Dublin Rd
Suite 100-A
Columbus, OH 43215-7037
614-487-4720
800-875-2723
FAX: 614-487-4725
info@thearcofohio.org
thearcofohio.org

Gary Tonks, Executive Director
John Hannah, President
Connie Calhoun, Vice President
The mission of The Arc of Ohio is to advocate for human rights, personal dignity and community participation of individuals with

developmental disabilities, through legislative and social action, information and education, local chapter support and family involvement.

3031   Bahmann Foundation
8041 Hosbrook Rd
Suite 210
Cincinnati, OH 45236-2909   513-891-3799
FAX: 513-891-3722
info@bahmann.org
www.bahmann.org

John Gatch, Executive Director
The mission of the Bahmann Foundation is to reduce isolation of low-income older adults through technology.

3032   Cleveland Foundation
1422 Euclid Ave
Suite 1300
Cleveland, OH 44115-2063   216-861-3810
FAX: 216-861-1729
Hello@CleveFdn.org
clevelandfoundation.org

James A. Ratner, Chairman
Paul J. Dolan, Vice Chairman
Ronald B. Richard, President and CEO
In general, grants are made in (but not restriced to) the areas of arts and culture, community development, economic development, education, environment, health and human services.

3033   Columbus Foundation and Affiliated Organizations
1234 E Broad St
Columbus, OH 43205-1453   614-251-4000
FAX: 614-251-4009
info@columbusfoundation.org
columbusfoundation.org

Doug F. Kridler, President & CEO
Raymond J. Biddiscombe, CPA, Senior Vice President - Finance
Lisa Schweitzer Courtice, P, EVP - Community Research and Gra
The Columbus Foundation offers a range of charitable fund types that can be used for individuals, families and businesses.

3034   Eleanora CU Alms Trust
Fifth Third Bank
Department 00864
9990 Montgomery Rd
Cincinnati, OH 45263   513-793-2200
Robert W Laclair, President
Giving is limited to Cincinnati, OH.

3035   Eva L And Joseph M Bruening Foundation
Foundation Management Services
1422 Euclid Ave
Suite 966
Cleveland, OH 44115-1952   216-621-2901
FAX: 216-621-8198
www.fmscleveland.com

Janet E. Narten, Founder
Cristin N. Slesh, President
Valerie Schramm, Operations Assistant
Charitable foundation providing grants to nonprofit organizations located inCuyahoga county Ohio. No grant are awarded to inviduals.

3036   Fred & Lillian Deeks Memorial Foundation
P.O.Box 1118
Cincinnati, OH 45201-1118   937-339-2329
FAX: 937-339-1861

3037   GAR Foundation
277 East Mill Street
Akron, OH 44308   330-576-2926
FAX: 330-294-5315
info@garfdn.org

Christine Amer Mayer, President
Kirstin S. Toth, Senior Vice President
Candace Campbell Jackson, Consulting Program Officer
The mission of the Foundation is to strengthen communities in our region through discerning and creative support of worthy organizations.

3038   George Gund Foundation
1845 Guildhall Building
45 Prospect Avenue, West
Cleveland, OH 44115-1008   216-241-3114
FAX: 216-241-6560
info@gundfdn.org
gundfoundation.org

Geoffrey Gund, President & Treasurer
Ann L. Gund, Vice President
David T. Abbott, Executive Director
The George Gund Foundation was established in 1952 as a private, nonprofit institution with the sole purpose of contributing to human well-being and the progress of society.

3039   Greater Cincinnati Foundation
200 West Fourth St.
Cincinnati, OH 45202-2775   513-241-2880
FAX: 513-852-6886
info@gcfdn.org
www.gcfdn.org

Kathryn e. Merchant, President/CEO
Terri Masur, Executive Assistant
Elizabeth Reiter Benson, APR, Vice President for Communic
Offers a wide variety of giving tools to help people achieve their charitable goals and create lasting good work in their communities.

3040   HCR Manor Care Foundation
333 N. Summit St.
P.O.Box 10086
Toledo, OH 43699-0086   419-252-5500
FAX: 419-252-6404
foundation@hcr-manorcare.com
hcr-manorcare.com

Paul A Ormond, Chairman, President and CEO
An independent, not-for-profit corporation that provides funding for organizations and programs that address the needs of the elderly and individuals requiring post-acute care services.

3041   HWH Foundation
Canton, OH   330-818-1300
contacthwh@hwhfoundation.org
www.hwhfoundation.org

Elizabeth Lacey Hoover, Chairman
Colton Hoover Chase, Vice Chairman
Mark Butterworth, Executive Director
The Herbert W Hoover Foundation funds unique opportunities that provide solutions to issues related to the Community, Education and the Environment.

3042   Harry C Moores Foundation
100 South Third Street
Columbus, OH 43215-4291   614-227-2300
FAX: 614-227-2390
info@bricker.com
bricker.com

Kurtis A Tunnell, Managing Partner
Ahmad Sino, Chief Information Officer
Steve P Odum, Chief Financial Officer

3043   Helen Steiner Rice Foundation
1301 Western Ave.
Cincinnati, OH 45203   513-287-7022
800-877-2665
helensteinerrice.com

Virginia J. Ruehlmann, Creative Consultant
Dorothy C. Lingg, Office Manager
Willis D. Gradison, Jr., Board of Trustee
Non-profit corporation whose purpose is to award grants to worthy charitable programs that aid the poor, the needy, and the elderly.

3044   Nationwide Foundation
One Nationwide Plaza
Columbus, OH 43215-2220   614-249-7111
800-882-2822
FAX: 614-249-5721
www.nationwide.com

Kirt A. Walker, President & COO
Stephen S. Rasmussen, Chief Executive Officer

The Nationwide Foundation is an independent corporation funded by Nationwide Companies to help positively impact the quality of life in communities where our associates, agents and their families live and work.

3045 Nordson Corporate Giving Program
28601 Clemens Rd
Westlake, OH 44145-1148
440-892-1580
FAX: 440-892-9507
kladiner@nordson.com
nordson.com

Michael F. Hilton, President & Chief Executive Officer
Gregory A. Thaxton, Senior Vice President & CFO
John J. Keane, Senior Vice President
Nordson Corporation encourages individual financial support of nonprofit organizations, colleges, and universities

3046 Parker-Hannifin Foundation
6035 Parkland Blvd
Cleveland, OH 44124-4141
216-896-3000
800-272-7537
FAX: 216-896-4000
parker.com

Donald E. Washkewicz, Chairman & CEO
Lee C. Banks, Executive Vice President
Robert P. Barker, Executive Vice President
To be a leading worldwide manufacturer of components and systems for the builders and users of durable goods.

3047 Reinberger Foundation
30000 Chagrin Blvd.
Suite 300
Cleveland, OH 44124-4439
216-292-2790
FAX: 216-292-4466
info@reinbergerfoundation.org
www.reinbergerfoundation.org

Karen R. Hooser, President
Sally R. Dyer, Trustee
Richard H. Oman, Trustee
Committed to enhancing the quality of life for individuals from all walks of life. To achieve this goal, proposals in the areas of the arts, education, healthcare, and social service are favored.

3048 Robert Campeau Family Foundation
7 West Seventh Street
Cincinnati, OH 45202-2424
513-579-7000
FAX: 513-579-7555
Terry J Lundgren, Chairman and Chief Executive Officer

3049 Sisler McFawn Foundation
P.O.Box 149
Akron, OH 44309
330-849-8887
FAX: 330-996-6215
Charlotte M Stanley, Grants Manager
Trust restricts give to certain programs and types of organizations. You can see recent giving has been by referring to the list of grants approved and paid during the past year. Call foundation office to request a guidelines brochure and list.

3050 Stark Community Foundation
400 Market Ave North
Suite 200
Canton, OH 44702-1557
330-454-3426
FAX: 330-454-5855
info@starkcf.org
www.starkcommunityfoundation.org

Mark Samolczyk, President
Patricia Quick, VP & CFO
Chris Decker, Finance & Systems Officer
Stark Community Foundation is dedicated to promoting the betterment of Stark County and enhancing the quality of life of all its citizens.

3051 Stocker Foundation
201 Burns Road
Elyria, OH 44035
440-366-4884
FAX: 440-366-4656
contact@stockerfoundation.org
stockerfoundation.org

Brenda Norton, President
Dawn Dobras, Treasurer
Patricia O'Brien, Executive Director

The Stocker Foundation seeks creative ideas and projects that are catalysts for constructive change in the community through arts and culture, community needs, education, health social services and women's issues.

3052 Toledo Community Foundation
300 Madison Avenue
Suite 1300
Toledo, OH 43604-1583
419-241-5049
FAX: 419-242-5549
toledocf@toledocf.org
www.toledocf.org

David F. Waterman, Chair
Dr. Anthony Armstrong, Vice Chair
Rita N.A. Mansour, Secretary
The Toledo Community Foundation is a public, charitable foundation which exists to improve the quality of life in the region.

3053 William J and Dorothy K O'Neill Foundation
7575 Northcliff Ave.
Suite 205
Cleveland, OH 44144
216-831-4134
FAX: 216-378-0594
info@oneill-foundation.org
www.oneillfdn.org

Leah S Gary, President & CEO
Symone R McClain, Manager of Grants
Timothy M. McCue, MPH, Senior Program Officer

3054 Youngstown Foundation
100 Federal Plaza East, Suite 101
P.O.Box 1162
Youngstown, OH 44503-1162
330-744-0320
FAX: 330-744-0344
Jan@youngstownfoundation.org
www.youngstownfoundation.org

Jan Strasfeld, Executive Director
Crissi Jenkins, Program Coordinator
Rena Colarossi, Admin. Assistant
Funds proposals that provide direct services to children with medically diagnosed disabilities. Grants are awarded to Ohio non-profit agencies that are qualified under the Internal Revenue Service Code 501 (c) (3) for the care of such children in the greater Youngstown Area.

Oklahoma

3055 Anne and Henry Zarrow Foundation
401 S Boston Ave
Suite 900
Tulsa, OK 74103-4012
918-295-8004
FAX: 918-295-8049
bmajor@zarrow.com
www.zarrow.com

A broad-based funding foundation. However, ares of emphasis include Jewish causes, the indignant, the disenfranchised and the homeless. The Foundation meets on a quarterly basis, in the months of February, April, September and November. Proposals are due on the first day of the following months:January, April, August and October. Any proposals recieved after the due date will be held until the next quarter's meeting.

3056 Sarkeys Foundation
530 East Main St
Norman, OK 73071-5823
405-364-3703
FAX: 405-364-8191
angela@sarkeys.org
sarkeys.org

Kim Henry, Executive Director
Lori Sutton, Facilities Manager
Angella Holladay, Director of Grants Management
Improves the quality of life in Oklahoma. Offers contributions in the areas of social services, arts and cultural programs, educational funding and health care and medical research. Funding only in agencies in the state of Oklahoma.

Oregon

3057 Arc of Oregon
2405 Front Street NE
Suite 120
Salem, OR 97301-4342   503-581-2726
877-581-2726
FAX: 503-363-7168
www.thearcoregon.org

Marcie Ingledue, Executive Director
Tiffany Tombleson, Administrative Assistant
Paula Boga, OSNT Program Director
Guardianship, Advocacy and Planning Services. Oregon special needs trust; information and referral.

3058 Cambia Health Foundation
100 SW Market St.
Suite E15B
Portland, OR 97201   503-225-4813
cambiahealthfoundation.org

Peggy Maguire, President & Chair
Rob Coppedge, Chief Executive Officer
Anjie Vannoy, Vice President, Finance & Controller
Cambia Health Foundation is the corporate foundation of Cambia Health Solutions dedicated to transforming the way people experience health care to create a more person-focused and economically sustainable health care system.
1907

3059 Chiles Foundation
1614 Mahan Center Boulevard
Suite 104
Tallahassee, Fl 32308   805-385-7800
FAX: 805-385-7808
kchiles@lawtonchiles.org
chilesfoundation.org

Kitty Chiles, Executive Director
Bud Chiles, President
Dr. Wil J. Blechman, Board Member
Giving in Oregon, with emphasis on Portland, and the Pacific Northwest.

3060 Jackson Foundation
P.O.Box 3168
Portland, OR 97208-3168   503-275-4414
march.voyles@usbank.com
www.thejacksonfoundation.com

Robert H Depew, Vice President & Senior Trust Of
Libby Voyles, Trust Relationship Associate
Purpose is to respond to the requests deemed appropriate to promote the welfare of the public of the city of Portland or the State of Oregon or both.

3061 Leslie G Ehmann Trust
P.O.Box 3168
Portland, OR 97208-3168   503-275-5929
800-522-9100
FAX: 503-275-4117

William Dolan, Trustee

Pennsylvania

3062 Air Products Foundation
7201 Hamilton Blvd
Allentown, PA 18195-9642   610-481-4911
FAX: 610-481-5900
gigmrktg@airproducts.com
www.airproducts.com

Seifi Ghasemi, Chairman & CEO
M. Scott Crocco, Senior Vice President
Guillermo Novo, Senior Vice President
Giving primarily in areas of company operations throughout the US.

3063 Arc of Pennsylvania
301 Chestnut Street
Suite 403
Harrisburg, PA 17101-2535   717-234-2621
800-692-7258
FAX: 717-234-2622
info@thearcpa.org
thearcpa.org

Maureen Cronin, Executive Director
Pam Klipa, Government Relations Director
Gwen Adams, Operations Director
The Arc's mission is to work to include all children and adults with cognitive, intellectual, and developmental disabilities in every community. We promote active citizenship and inclusion in every community.

3064 Arcadia Foundation
105 E Logan St
Norristown, PA 19401-3058   202-747-0876
Marilyn L Steinbright, President
Robert Carmona-Borjas, Founder

3065 Brachial Plexus Palsy Foundation
210 Springhaven Cir
Royersford, PA 19468-1178   brachialplexuspalsyfoundation.org
Nonprofit organization dedicated to raising funds for support of families who hae children with brachial plexus injuries. Supports medical facilities that research and treat such injuries, holds fund-raising events to support further research, has support groups, and produces educational materials including a newsletter, Outreach, and brochures.

3066 Columbia Gas of Pennsylvania Corporate Giving
650 Washington Rd
Pittsburgh, PA 15228-2702   412-572-7104
FAX: 412-572-7140
www.columbiagaspamd.com/html/
Rosemary Martinelli, Manager Corporation

3067 Connelly Foundation
100 Front Street,
Suite 1450
West Conshohocken, PA 19428-2873   610-834-3222
FAX: 610-834-0866
info@connellyfdn.org
connellyfdn.org

Josephine C. Mandeville, Chair & President
Emily C Riley, Executive Vice President
Lewis W Bluemle, Senior Vice President
Seeks to foster learning and to improve the quality of life in the Greater Philadelphia area. The Foundation supports local non-profit organizations in the fields of education, health and human services, arts and culture and civic enterprise.

3068 Dolfinger-McMahon Foundation
30 South 17th Street
Philadelphia, PA 19103-4196   215-979-1768
www.dolfingermcmahonfoundation.org
Sheldon M. Bonovitz, Trustee
David E. Loder, Trustee
Frank G. Cooper, Counsel

3069 Heinz Endowments
Howard Heinz Endowment
625 Liberty Ave
30 Dominion Tower
Pittsburgh, PA 15222- 3115   412-281-5777
FAX: 412-281-5788
bobbyvagt@heinz.org
heinz.org

Grant Oliphant, President
Edward Kolano, Vice President Finance and Admin
Ann C. Plunkett, Director, Human Resources
Mission is to help our region thrive as a whole community-economically, ecologically, educationaly, and culturally while advancing the state of knowledge and practice in the fields in which we work.

3070 Henry L Hillman Foundation
310 Grant Street
Suite 2000
Pittsburgh, PA 15219   412-338-3466
foundation@hillmanfo.com
hillmanfamilyfoundations.org

David K Roger, President
Lisa R Johns, Treasurer & Senior Program Officer
Lauri K. Fink, Senior Program Officer
Established with a broad purpose to improve the quality of life in Pittsburgh and southwestern Pennsylvania.

3071 Jewish Healthcare Foundation of Pittsburgh
650 Smithfield Street
Suite 2400
Pittsburgh, PA 15222- 3915   412-594-2550
FAX: 412-232-6240
info@jhf.org
jhf.org

Karen Wolk Feinstein, PhD, President and Chief Executive Of
Carla Barricella, Communications Director
Lindsey Kirstatter Hartle, Accounting Manager
The mission of the JHF is to support and foster the provision of healthcare services, healthcare education, and, when appropriate, medical and scientific research, and to respond to the health-related needs of elderly, underprivileged, indigent, and undeserved persons in both the Jewish and general community throughout Western Pennsylvania. .

3072 Juliet L Hillman Simonds Foundation
310 Grant Street
Suite 2000
Pittsburgh, PA 15219   412-338-3466
FAX: 412-338-3520
foundation@hillmanfo.com
hillmanfamilyfoundations.org

David K. Roger, President
Lisa R. Johns, Treasurer and Senior Program Off
Lauri K. Fink, Senior Program Officer

3073 Oberkotter Foundation
1600 Market St
Suite 3600
Philadelphia, PA 19103-7212   215-751-2601
FAX: 215-751-2678
info@oberkotterfoundation.org
oberkotterfoundation.org

George H Nofer, Executive Director
Mildred L. Oberkotter, M.S.W., Trustee
Bruce A. Rosenfield, J.D., Trustee
The Oberkotter Foundation focuses its efforts on supporting families who have chosen listening and spoken language for their child and on opportunities for children learning listening and spoken language to develop their social, emotional, language and educational skills.

3074 PECO Energy Company Contributions Program
Fl 7toorh
2301 Market St
Philadelphia, PA 19103-1338   215-841-4000
800-494-4000
FAX: 215-841-6830
www.peco.com

Denis P O'Brien, SVP/CEO
Michael A. Innocenzo, SVP/COO
Phillip S. Barnett, SVP/CFO/Treasurer

3075 PNC Bank Foundation
249 5th Ave
Pittsburgh, PA 15222-2707   412-762-2000
FAX: 412-762-7829
marianna.hallett@pnc.com
www.pncbank.com

Samuel R Patterson, Senior VP
The PNC Foundation's priority is to form partnerships with community-based nonprofit organizations within the markets PNC serves in order to enhance educational opportunities for children, particularly underserved pre-K children though our signature, PNC Grow Uo Great Program, and to promote the growth of targeted communities through economic development initiatives.

3076 Philadelphia Foundation
1234 Market St
Suite 1800
Philadelphia, PA 19107-3704   215-563-6417
FAX: 215-563-6882
philafound.org

R Andrew Swinney, President
Pat Meller, Vice President for Finance & Adm
Andrea Congo, Executive Assistant
The Philadelphia Foundation improves our community by advancing change, leading on issues of importance, forging meaningful relationships and providing knowledge, resources and stewardship.

3077 Pittsburgh Foundation
Five PPG Place
Suite 250
Pittsburgh, PA 15222-5405   412-391-5122
FAX: 412-391-7259
oliphantg@pghfdn.org
pittsburghfoundation.org

Maxwell King, President and CEO
Jonathan Brelsford, Vice President of Investments
Jay Donato, Senior Investment Analyst
The Pittsburgh Foundation works to improve the quality of life in the Pittsburgh region by evaluating and addressing community issues, promoting responsible philanthropy, and connecting donors to the critical needs of the community.

3078 Shenango Valley Foundation
7 West State Street
Suite 301
Sharon, PA 16146-2713   724-981-5882
866-901-7204
FAX: 724-983-9044
comm-foundation.org

Lawrence E. Haynes, Executive Director
Amy Atkinson, Associate Director
Shelly Mason, Chief Financial Officer
Mission is to promote the betterment of our region and enhancement of the quality of life for all of its citizens.

3079 Staunton Farm Foundation
650 Smithfield Street
Suite 210
Pittsburgh, PA 15222- 3907   412-281-8020
FAX: 844-281-8020
office@stauntonfarm.org
stauntonfarm.org

Joni S. Schwager, Executive Director
Bethany Hemingway, Program Officer
Jason Fate, Office Manager
Dedicated to improving the lives of people who live with mental illness.

3080 Stewart Huston Charitable Trust
50 South First Avenue
Coatesville, PA 19320-3418   610-384-2666
FAX: 610-384-3396
admin@stewarthuston.org
stewarthuston.org

Scott G. Huston, Executive Director
Charles L. Huston III, Trustee
Shelton P Sanford, Trustee
The purpose of the Trust is to provide funds, technical assistance and collaboration on behalf of non-profit organizations engaged exclusively in religious, charitable or educational work; to extend opportunities to deserving needs persons and, in general, to promote any of the above causes.

3081 Teleflex Foundation
155 S Limerick Rd
Limerick, PA 19468-1603   610-948-5100
FAX: 610-948-5101
teleflex.com

Jeffrey P Black, CEO
The Teleflex Foundation strives to create an impact on the quality of life in Teleflex communities and build supportive relationships among our stakeholders. The Foundation places a priority on progrmas that have the commitmenet and volunteer involvement of Teleflex communities.

3082 USX Foundation
600 Grant St
Pittsburgh, PA 15219-2702
412-433-1121
FAX: 412-433-6847
www.ussteel.com

CD Mallick, General Manager
Patricia Funaro, Program Manager
Giving primarily in areas of company operations located within
the United States.

3083 William B Dietrich Foundation
Duane Morrs Llt
30 S 17th St
Philadelphia, PA 19103-4001
215-979-1000
FAX: 215-979-1020
www.duanemorris.com

William B Dietrich, President

3084 William Talbott Hillman Foundation
310 Grant Street
Suite 2000
Pittsburgh, PA 15219
412-338-3466
FAX: 212-792-2677
foundation@hillmanfo.com
hillmanfamilyfoundations.org

David K. Roger, President
Lisa R. Johns, Treasurer and Senior Program Off
Lauri K. Fink, Senior Program Officer

**3085 William V and Catherine A McKinney Charitable
Foundation**
20 Stanwix St
Pittsburgh, PA 15222-4802
412-644-8332
FAX: 412-644-6058
verizon.com

William M Schmidt, Senior Vice President

Rhode Island

3086 Arc South County Chapter
2 Barber Avenue
Warwick, RI 02886-3549
401-480-9355
paul@pence.com
www.riroads.com

Developmentally disabled center/service assistance to individuals with developmental disabilities.

3087 Arc of Blackstone Valley
500 Prospect St.
Wing B, Suite 203
Pawtucket, RI 02860- 4332
401-727-0150
800-257-6092
FAX: 401-727-1545
contact@bvcriarc.org
www.bvcriarc.org

Kathleen O'Neill, President
Thomas E. Hodge, Vice President
John J. Padien III, Chief Executive Officer
A private nonprofit organization providing residential, developmental, employment and recreational programs and services to
more then 400 individuals with intellectual and related
disabilities

3088 Arc of Northern Rhode Island
The Homestead Group Administrative Offices
68 Cumberland St
Suite 200
Woonsocket, RI 02895-3323
401-765-3700
FAX: 401-765-1124
arcofnri.org

The mission of the Homestead Group is to help the people we support lead the lives they want and deserve

3089 Champlin Foundations
2000 Chapel View Boulevard
Suite 350
Cranston, RI 02920
401-944-9200
FAX: 401-944-9299

Jonathan K. Farnum, Distribution Committee
John Gorham, Distribution Committee
Dione D. Kenyon, Distribution Committee
Giving in the Rhode Island area. Champlin does not give grants to
individuals, only to RI tax-exempt organizations.

3090 CranstonArc
The Keystone Group
PO Box 20130
Cranston, RI 02920-942
401-941-1112
FAX: 401-383-8751
info@accesspointri.org
www.accesspointri.org

Thomas Kane, President & CEO
Kevin McHale, Chief Operating Officer
Maureen Russo, Director of Human Resources
Mission is to empower persons with differing abilities to claim
and enjoy their right to dignity and respect through their lives.

3091 Down Syndrome Society of Rhode Island
4635 Post Road
Warwick, RI 02818
401-463-5751
FAX: 401-463-5337
TTY:800-745-5555
coordinatordssri@verizon.net
www.dssri.org

Claudia M. Lowe, Coordinator
Marilyn Blanche
Jeff DiMillio
The Down Syndrome Society of Rhode Island (DSSRI) is dedicated to promoting the rights, dignity and potential of all individuals with Down syndrome through advocacy, education, public
awareness, and support.

3092 Frank Olean Center
93 Airport Rd
Westerly, RI 02891-3420
401-596-2091
FAX: 401-596-3945
info@oleancenter.org
oleancenter.org

Joan Gradilone, President
Tony Vellucci, Executive Director
Rick Harley, Vice President
A non-profit organization representing and providing services
and supports to persons with developmental disabilities and their
families throughout Southern Rhode Island and Southeastern
Connecticut.

3093 Horace A Kimball and S Ella Kimball Foundation
23 Broad Street
Westerly, RI 02891-1879
401-348-1238
FAX: 401-364-3565
www.hkimballfoundation.org

Thomas F Black III, President
Norman D. Baker, Jr., Secretary and Treasurer
Edward C. Marth, Foundation Trustees
Makes grants almost exclusively to Rhode Island operatives
(charities) or those benefitting Rhode Island residents and
causes.

3094 James L. Maher Center
120 Hillside Avenue
Newport, RI 02840
401-846-0340
FAX: 401-849-4267
www.mahercenter.org

Jack Casey, President
William Maraziti, Executive Director
Barbara Burns, President
The mission is to advance independence and opportunity for chil-
dren and adults with developmental disabilities and their
families.

3095 Rhode Island Arc
99 Bald Hill Rd
Cranston, RI 02920-2647
401-463-9191
FAX: 401-463-9244
riarc@compuserve.com

Mary Lou Mc Caffray, Executive Director

3096 Rhode Island Foundation
One Union Station
Providence, RI 02903-1758
401-274-4564
FAX: 401-331-8085
info@rifoundation.org
rifoundation.org

Neil Steinberg, President & CEO
Wendi DeClercq, Executive Assistant
James S. Sanzi, Esq., Vice President of Development
The Rhode Island Foundation works to build a better Rhode Island as a philanthropic resource, for people, communities, organizations, and programs.

South Carolina

3097 Arc of South Carolina
1202 12th Street
Cayce, SC 29033
803-748-5020
FAX: 803-445-1026
TheArc@ArcSC.org
www.arcsc.org

Margie Williamson, Executive Director
Caroline Kistler, Project Director
Carly Prince, Case Manager
The Arc of South Carolina advocates for and alongside people with cognitive, intellectual and developmental disabilities and their families.

3098 Center for Disability Resources
University of South Carolina School of Medicine
Department of Pediatrics
8301 Farrow Rd.
Columbia, SC 29208
803-935-5231
FAX: 803-935-5059
david.rotholz@uscmed.sc.edu
uscm.med.sc.edu/cdrhome

A University Affiliated Program which develops model programs designed to serve persons with disabilities and to train students in fields related to disabilities.

3099 Colonial Life and Accident Insurance Company Contributions Program
1200 Colonial Life Blvd W
Columbia, SC 29210-7670
803-798-7000
FAX: 803-731-2618

Randy Horn, President & CEO
Bill Deeham, Senior Vice President of Sales
Tim Arnold, Senior Vice President of Sales

Tennessee

3100 Arc of Anderson County
728 Emory Valley Road, Suite 42
P.O.Box 4823
Oak Ridge, TN 37831-4823
865-481-0550
arc@arcaid.org
www.thearcandersoncounty.com

Sally Browning, President
Dargie Arwood, Executive Director
Ginny Miceli, President
The Arc of Anderson County provides support and advocacy to people with cognitive, intellectual and developmental disabilities. The Arc provides support, information and training for families and caregivers of adults and children with these disabilities.

3101 Arc of Davidson County
111 N Wilson Blvd
Nashville, TN 37205-2411
615-248-4112
FAX: 615-322-9184
arcdc.org

Kate Deitzer, President
Cynthia Gardner, Vice President
Thom Druffel, Treasurer
Provides services to adults and children with intellectual and developmental disabilities.

3102 Arc of Hamilton County
4613 Brainerd Rd
Chattanooga, TN 37411-3826
423-624-6887
800-624-6887
FAX: 423-624-3974
arcofhamilton@aol.com
thearchc.org

Shawn Ellis, Executive Director
Provides assistance to individuals and families with developmental disabilities, in the form of advocacy, information, and support coordination

3103 Arc of Tennessee
151 Athens Way
Suite 100
Nashville, TN 37228-1367
615-248-5878
800-835-7077
FAX: 615-248-5879
info@thearctn.org
thearctn.org

John Lewis, President
John Shouse, Vice President
Donna Lankford, Secretary
Advocacy, information, referral and support for people with intellectual and developmental disabilities and their families.

3104 Arc of Washington County
110 East Mountcastle Drive
Johnson City, TN 37601-7557
423-928-9362
FAX: 423-928-7431
kim@arcwc.org
www.arcwc.org

Malessa Fleenor, Executive Director
Kim Reid, Human Resources, Quality Assuran
Kim Wheeler, Respite Coordinator
Is a non-profit organization that serves individuals with disabilities and their families. They have an independent support coordination service, as well as, early intervention, family support and respite services.

3105 Arc of Williamson County
129 W Fowlkes St
Suite 151
Franklin, TN 37064-3562
615-790-5815
FAX: 615-790-5891
sbbarc@thearcwc.org
thearcwc.org

Donna Isbell, President
Steve Cassidy, Vice President
Ashley Coulter, Secretary
The Arc is a family-based organization committed to securing for all people with intellectual, developmental, or other disabilities the opportunity to choose and realize their goals of where and how they live, learn, work, and play.

3106 Arc-Diversified
453 Gould Dr
Cookeville, TN 38506
931-432-5981
800-239-9029
FAX: 931-432-5987

3107 Benwood Foundation
736 Market St
Suite 1600
Chattanooga, TN 37402-4812
423-267-4311
FAX: 423-267-9049
info@benwood.org
benwood.org

Sarah Morgan, President
Kristy Huntley, Program & Financial Officer
Connie Perrin, Accounting & Grants Manager
Benwood Foundation seeks to stimulate creative and innovative efforts to build and strengthen the Chattanooga community.

3108 Community Foundation of Greater Chattanooga
1270 Market St
Chattanooga, TN 37402-2713
423-265-0586
FAX: 423-265-0587
info2@cfgc.org
cfgc.org

Peter T. Cooper, President
Rebecca Underwood, Vice President, Finance & Admini
Marty Robinson, Vice President, Donor Relations
A non-profit organization which receives, holds, invests and distributes assets contributed by individuals and organizations for the benefit of Chattanooga, its citizens and its institutions.

3109 Education and Auditory Research Foundation
PO Box 330867
Nashville, TN 37203-7506
615-627-2724
800-545-4327
FAX: 615-627-2728
www.earfoundation.org

Michael Glasscock, President
Provides the general public support services promoting the integration of the hearing and balance impaired into mainstream society; to provide practicing ear specialists continuing medical education courses and related programs specifically regarding rehabilitation and hearing preservation; to educate young people and adults about hearing preservation and early detection of hearing loss, enabling them to prevent at an early age hearing and balance disorders.

3110 International Paper Company Foundation
6400 Poplar Ave
Memphis, TN 38197
901-419-9000
800-207-4003
FAX: 901-419-4439
internationalpaper.comm@ipaper.com
internationalpaper.com

Mark S Sutton, Chairman & CEO
David J Bronczek, President & CEO
C. Cato Ealy, Senior Vice President, Corporate
The Foundation's primary focus is education-specifically environmental education, iliteracy programs for young children and minority career development opportunities for college bound youth.

3111 Montgomery County Arc
1825 K Street
NW, Suite 1200
Washington, DC 20006-2145
202-534-3700
800-433-5255
FAX: 202-534-3731
info@thearc.org
www.thearc.org

Ronald Brown, President
Elise McMillan, Vice President
Peter V Berns, Chief Executive Officer
Organization works to ensure that the estimated 7.2 million Americans with intellectual and developmental disabilities have the services and supports they need to grow, develop and live in communities across the nation.

Texas

3112 Abell-Hangar Foundation
P.O.Box 430
Midland, TX 79702-0430
432-684-6655
FAX: 432-684-4474
abell-hanger.org

David L Smith, Executive Director
The Foundation makes grants to nonprofit organizations, which are involved in such undertakings for public welfare, including but not limited to, education, health services, human services, arts and cultural activities and community or social benefit.

3113 Albert & Bessie Mae Kronkosky Charitable Foundation
112 East Pecan
Suite 830
San Antonio, TX 78205-1574
210-475-9000
888-309-9001
FAX: 210-354-2204
kronkosky.org

Palmer Moe, Managing Director
Mission is to produce profound good that is tangible and measurable in Bandera, Bexar, Comal, and Kendall counties in Texas by implimenting the Kronkosky's charitable purposes.

3114 American Express Foundation
P.O. Box 981540
El Paso, TX 79998-1540
800-528-4800
TTY:800-221-9950
americanexpress.com

Kenneth I Chenault, Chairman & Chief Executive Officer
L. Kevin Cox, Chief Human Resources Officer
Marc D. Gordon, Executive Vice President
Grants are awarded in the three program areas: Community Service, Cultural Heritage, and Economic Independence. Most grants are made for projects operating where the company has a major employee or market presence.

3115 Arc of Texas, The
8001 Centre Park Dr
Suite 100
Austin, TX 78754-5118
512-454-6694
800-252-9729
FAX: 512-454-4956
www.thearcoftexas.org

Charlie Huber, President
John Schneider, Vice President
Amy Mizcles, Executive Director
The Arc of Texas creates opportunities for all people with intellectual and developmental disabilities to actively participate in their communities and make the choices that affect their lives in a positive manner.

3116 BA and Elinor Steinhagen Benevolent Trust
Chase Bank of Texas
700 North St.
Suite D
Beaumont, TX 77701-3928
409-832-6565
FAX: 409-832-7532
www.setxnonprofit.org

Jean Moncla, CTFA, President
Ivy Pate, Treasurer
Chester Jourdan, Executive Director

3117 Brown Foundation
P.O.Box 130646
Houston, TX 77219-0646
713-523-6867
FAX: 713-523-2917
bfi@brownfoundation.org
brownfoundation.org

Nancy Pittman, Executive Director
The purpose of the Brown Foundation is to distribute funds for public charitable purposes, principally for support, encouragement and assistance to education, the arts and community service.

3118 **CH Foundation**
P.O.Box 94038
Lubbock, TX 79493-4038   806-792-0448
                                FAX: 806-792-7824
                                ksanford@chfoundation.com
                                www.chfoundationlubbock.com
Kay Sanford, Executive Director
Heather Hocker, Grants Administrator
Cheryl Sanford, Administrative Assistant
Mission of the CH foundation is to significantly improve human services and cultural and educational opportunities for the residents of the South Plain of Texas.

3119 **Cockrell Foundation**
1000 Main St
Suite 3250
Houston, TX 77002-6338   713-209-7500
Ernest H. Cockrell, President
Nancy Williams, Executive Vice President
Purpose is for giving for higher education at the University of Texas at Austin; support also for cultural programs, social services, youth services and health care. Limitations are giving in Houston, Texas and no grants are awarded to individuals.

3120 **Communities Foundation of Texas**
5500 Caruth Haven Ln
Dallas, TX 75225-8146   214-750-4222
                                FAX: 214-750-4210
                                jsmith@cftexas.org
                                cftexas.org
Brent E. Chrisopher, President & CEO
Elizabeth W. Bull, Senior Vice President
Jeverley R. Cook, Ph.D., Executive Director
Mission is to improve lives, we serve the community by investing wisely and making effective charitable grants.

3121 **Community Foundation of North Texas**
306 West 7th
Suite 1045
Fort Worth, TX 76102-4906   817-877-0702
                                FAX: 817-632-8711
                                cfntx.org
Nancy E. Jones, President
Rob Miller, Director of Finance
Vicki Andrews, Director of Operations
Community Foundation is a tax exempt organization that provides stewardship for many individual charitable funds. With its specialized services, Community Foundation of North Texas gives donors efficient charitable fund administration.

3122 **Cullen Foundation**
601 Jefferson St
40th Floor
Houston, TX 77002-7900   713-651-8837
                                FAX: 713-651-2374
                                cullenfdn.org
Isaac Arnold, Jr, President
Wilhelmina E Robertson, Vice President and Secretary
Meredith T Cullen, Assistant Secretary
Grants are restricted to Texas-based organizations for programs in Texas, primarily in the Houston area.

3123 **Curtis & Doris K Hankamer Foundation**
Ste 530
9039 Katy Fwy
Houston, TX 77024-1656   713-461-8140
Gregory A Herbst, Manager

3124 **Dallas Foundation**
3963 Maple Avenue
Ste. 390
Dallas, TX 75219-4447   214-741-9898
                                FAX: 214-741-9848
                                info@dallasfoundation.org
                                dallasfoundation.org
Mary M. Jalonick, President & CEO
Gary W. Garcia, Senior Director of Development
Dawn Townsend, Director of Marketing & Communications
Serves as a leader, catalyst and resource for philanthropy by providing donors with a flexible means of making gifts to charitable causes that enhance our community.

3125 **David D & Nona S Payne Foundation**
P.O.Box 174
Pampa, TX 79066-174   806-665-0063
Vanessa G Buzzard, Director
The David & Nona S Payne Foundation was established in August 1980. Mrs Payne established the foundation and did much of her charitable giving in honor of her late husband.

3126 **El Paso Natural Gas Foundation**
P.O.Box 2511
Houston, TX 77252-2511   713-420-2600
                                FAX: 713-420-5312
                                foundation@elpaso.com
                                www.kindermorgan.com
Douglas Foshee, CEO
Focuses on the areas in locations where we have significant facilities or concentrated employees. Primary area of focus is Civic and Community, Education and Health and Human Services. Secondary area of focus is Arts and Culture and Environment.

3127 **Epilepsy Foundation of Southeast Texas**
2401 Fountain View Dr
Suite 900
Houston, TX 77057-4821   713-789-6295
                                888-548-9716
                                info@eftx.org
                                www.epilepsy.com/texas
Donna Stahlhut, CEO
Rebecca Moreau, Program Director
Amanda Walker Rockwell, Senior Development Coordinator
The Epilepsy Foundation of Southeast Texas is a non-profit organization devoted to improving the lives of people with epilepsy in Texas. Services offered by the foundation include public education programs, medical care, therapy and recreation programs.

3128 **Epilepsy Foundation: Central and South Texas**
10615 Perrin Beitel Rd
Suite 602
San Antonio, TX 78217   210-653-5353
                                888-606-5353
                                FAX: 210-653-5355
                                staff@efcst.org
                                www.efcst.org
Ariel Robbins, Program Manager
The Epilepsy Foundation of Central & South Texas is a voluntary health organization serving people with epilepsy. Services offered include youth programs, seizure clinics, support groups, referrals and more.

3129 **Harris and Eliza Kempner Fund**
2201 Market St
12th Floor
Galveston, TX 77553-1529   409-765-6671
                                FAX: 409-765-9098
                                kempnercapital.com
Diana L. Bartula, Vice President, Chief Compliance Officer
V. Delynn Greene, Vice President, Head Trader
Mission is to further the vision and heritage of the Kemper Family's commitment to philanthropy and sense of responsibility to society.

3130 **Hillcrest Foundation**
Bank of America
P.O.Box 830241
Dallas, TX 75283   214-209-1965
Daniel Kelly, VP

3131 **Hoblitzelle Foundation**
5556 Caruth Haven Lane
Suite 200
Dallas, TX 75225-8020   214-373-0462
                                kstone@hoblitzelle.org
                                www.hoblitzelle.org
William T Solomon, Chairman
Caren H. Prothro, Vice Chairman
J. McDonald Williams, Treasurer
Grants made by the directors are usually focused on specific, non-recurring needs of the educational, social service, medical, cultural, and civic organizations in Texas, particularly in the Dallas area.

3132 Hogg Foundation for Mental Health
3001 Lake Austin Blvd.
Austin, TX 78703
512-471-5041
hogg-operations@austin.utexas.edu
hogg.utexas.edu

Octavio N. Martinez, Jr., Executive Director
Vicky Coffee, Director, Programs
Crystal Viagran, Director, Finance & Operations
The Hogg Foundation for Mental Health is a nonprofit organization that is dedicated to the advancement of mental wellness for the people of Texas through outreach programs, conferences, seminars, research grants, and more.

3133 Houston Endowment
600 Travis St
Suite 6400
Houston, TX 77002-3003
713-238-8100
FAX: 713-238-8101
houstonendowment.org

Ann B. Stern, President
Sheryl L. Johns, Vice President for Admin.
F. Xavier Pena, Vice President for Finance
A private philanthropic foundation that improves life for people of the greater Houston area through its contributions to charitable organizations and educational institutions.

3134 John G & Marie Stella Kennedy Memorial Foundation
555 N Carancahua
Suite 1700, Tower II
Corpus Christi, TX 78401-0851
361-887-6565
FAX: 361-887-6582

Judge J. A. Garcia, President and Director
Marc A. Cisneros, Chief Executive Officer
Sylvia Whitmore, Chief Operating Officer
To advance and nurture activities that contribute to the foundation's core, Catholic values.

3135 John S Dunn Research Foundation
3355 West Alabama
Suite 990
Houston, TX 77098-1722
713-626-0368
FAX: 713-626-3866
jsdrf@swbell.net
johnsdunnfoundation.org

J. Dickson Rogers, President
Dan S. Wilford, Vice President
John R. Wallace, Secretary and Treasurer

3136 Lola Wright Foundation
515 Congress Avenue
10th Floor
Austin, TX 78701
512-397-2001
amber.carden@ustrust.com
fdnweb.org/lolawright

Wilford Flowers, President and Director
Paul Hilgers, Vice-President and Director
Ron Oliveira, Secretary and Director

3137 Meadows Foundation
3003 Swiss Ave
Dallas, TX 75204-6049
214-826-9431
800-826-9431
FAX: 214-827-7042
www.mfi.org

Linda P Evans, President and CEO
Tom Gale, Vice President and Chief Investment Officer
Paula Herring, Vice President and Treasurer
The Meadows Foundation exists to assist people and institutions of Texas improve the quality and circumstances of life for themselves and future generations.

3138 Moody Foundation
2302 Post Office St
Suite 704
Galveston, TX 77550-1994
409-797-1500
colleent@moodyf.org
moodyf.org

Frances Moody-Dahlderg, Chairman & Executive Director
Jamie G. Williams, Human Resources Director
Garrik Addison, Chief Financial Officer

Created for the perpetual benefit of present and future generations.

3139 Pearle Vision Foundation
2534 Royal Ln
Dallas, TX 75229-3884
214-821-7770
www.pearlevision.com

Leo Priolo Jr, Owner
Organization dedicated to sight preservation through vision research and education.

3140 San Antonio Area Foundation
303 Pearl Parkway
Suite 114
San Antonio, TX 78215
210-225-2243
FAX: 210-225-1980
info@saafdn.org
saafdn.org

Marie Smith, Chair
G.P. Singh, Vice Chair
Michelle R. Scarver, Secretary
The San Antonio Area Foundation aspires to significantly enhance the quality of life in our community by providing outstanding service to donors, producing significant asset growth, strengthning community collaboration and managing an exemplary grants program.

3141 Shell Oil Company Foundation
40 Bank Street
London, TX 77252-2463
281-544-7171
FAX: 713-241-3329
info@shellfoundation.org
www.shellfoundation.org

Malcolm Brinded, Chairman
Ben van Beurden, Trustee
William Kalema, Trustee
A not-for-profit foundation funded by donations from Shell Oil Company and other participating Shell companies and subsidiaries.

3142 South Texas Charitable Foundation
P.O.Box 2459
Victoria, TX 77902
512-573-4383
Rayford L Keller, Secretary

3143 Sterling-Turner Foundation
5850 San Felipe Street
Suite 125
Houston, TX 77057-3292
713-237-1117
FAX: 713-223-4638
jeannie.arnold@stfdn.org
www.sterlingturnerfoundation.org

T. R. Reckling, President
Isla C. Reckling, Treasurer
Patricia Stilley, Executive Director
Sterling Turner Foundation is a private trust which can assist any Section 501 (c) (3) organization in the state of Texas. The Foundation is not permitted to assist any individuals

3144 TLL Temple Foundation
109 Temple Blvd
Lufkin, TX 75901-7321
936-639-5197
Wayne Corley, Executive Director

3145 William Stamps Farish Fund
Ste 1250
1100 Louisiana St
Houston, TX 77002-5232
713-757-7313
Terry Ward, Manager

Utah

3146 Arc of Utah
18585 Coastal Hwy # 19
Rehoboth Beach, DE 19971
801-364-5060
800-371-3060
FAX: 801-364-6030
gacosta@dunndunn.com
www.bewitchedtattoos.com

Kathy Scott, Executive Director

The Arc of Utah advocates for and with cognitive, intellectual and developmental disabilities and their families through awareness, outreach, education, support and public policy.

3147 Marriner S Eccles Foundation
79 S Main St
Salt Lake City, UT 84111-1929   801-532-0934
Shannon K Toronto

3148 Questar Corporation Contributions Program
333 South State Street
P.O. Box 45433
Salt Lake City, UT 84145-0433   801-324-5000
Ronald W Jibson, President & CEO
Craig C Wagstaff, Executive vice president
Micheal Dunn, Executive vice president
Focuses on promoting a healthy environment by investing in and fulfilling its corporate responsibility to support the well-being of communitites where Questar and its subsidiaries conduct business.

Vermont

3149 Vermont Community Foundation
3 Court Street
Middlebury, VT 05753   802-388-3355
                              FAX: 802-388-3398
                              info@vermontcf.org
                              www.vermontcf.org
Stuart Comstock-Gay, President
Nina McDonnell, Grants Administrator
Janet McLaughlin, Special Projects Director
Helps build and manage charitable funds created by individuals, families, groups, organizations, and institutions to improve the quality of life in Vermont.

Virginia

3150 Arc of Virginia
2147 Staples Mill Road
Richmond, VA 23230   804-649-8481
                            FAX: 804-649-3585
                            info@thearcofva.org
                            www.thearcofva.org
Howard Cullum, President
Shareen Young-Chavez, President-Elect
Marisa Laios, Vice President
The Arc of Virginia advocactes for individuals with developmental disabilities and their families, so they may all lead productive and fulfilling lives.

3151 Beacon Tree Foundation
9201 Arboretum Pkwy.
Suite 140
N. Chesterfield, VA 23236   800-414-6427
                                   info@beacontree.org
                                   beacontree.org
Beacon Tree Foundation is dedicated to being an advocate for the family, providing education about treatment and financial resources to help heal children and teens struggling with mental health issues and to provide hope for the future.

3152 Camp Foundation
P.O.Box 813
Franklin, VA 23851   757-562-3439
Bobby B Worrell, CEO

3153 Community Foundation of Richmond & Central Virginia
7501 Boulder View Drive
Suite 110
Richmond, VA 23225- 4047   804-330-7400
                                  FAX: 804-330-5992
                                  info@tcfrichmond.org
                                  tcfrichmond.org
Darcy Oman, President
Bobby Thalhimer, Senior Advisor
Molly Dean Bittner, Vice President
The Community Foundation provides effective stewardship of philanthropic assets entrusted to its care by donors who wish to enhance the quality of community life.

3154 John Randolph Foundation
112 North Main Street
P.O.Box 1606
Hopewell, VA 23860- 1161   804-458-2239
                                  FAX: 804-458-3754
                                  lsharpe@johnrandolphfoundation.org
                                  www.johnrandolphfoundation.org
Lisa H. Sharpe, Executive Director
M. Stephen Cates, Director of Finance and Accounti
Kiffy Werkheiser, Development Program Officer
The John Randolph Foundation is a community-based Foundation working to improve the health and quality of life for residents of Hopewell and surrounding areas through Grants and Scholarships.

3155 National Right to Work Legal Defense Foundation
8001 Braddock Rd.
Springfield, VA 22160   703-321-8510
                               800-336-3600
                               FAX: 703-321-9319
                               nrtw.org
Raymond LaJeunesse, Vice President & Legal Director
Byron S. Andrus, Staff Attorney
Matthew B. Gilliam, Staff Attorney
The National Right to Work Legal Defense Foundation is a nonprofit, charitable organization. Its mission is to eliminate coercive union power and compulsory unionism abuses through strategic litigation, public information, and education programs.
1968

3156 Norfolk Foundation
101 W. Main Street,
Suite 4500
Norfolk, VA 23510-2103   757-622-7951
                                FAX: 757-622-1751
                                mbrunson@hamptonroadscf.org
                                www.hamptonroadscf.org
Deborah M DiCroce, Ed.D., President and CEO
Tim McCarthy, Chief Financial Officer
Kay A. Stine, CFRE, Vice President for Development
The mission of the Norfolk Foundation is to inspire philanthropy and transform the quality of life in southeastern Virginia.

3157 Robey W Estes Family Foundation
Robey W Estes Jr
3901 West Broad Street
P.O. Box 25612
Richmond, VA 23230-5612   866-378-3748
                                 estes-express.com
Robey W Estes Jr, President and CEO

3158 Virginia Beach Foundation
Suite 4500
101 W. Main Street,
Virginia Beach, VA 23454   757-422-5249
                                  FAX: 757-422-1849
                                  mbrunson@hamptonroadscf.org
                                  www.hamptonroadscf.org
Deborah M DiCroce, President
Tim McCarthy, Chief Financial Officer
Mission is to stimulate the establishment of endowments to serve the people of Virgina Beach now and in the future. Respond to changing, emerging, community needs. Provide a vehicle and a service for donors with varied interests. Serve as a resource, broker, catalyst and leader in the community.

Washington

3159 **Arc of Washington State**
2638 State Avenue NE
Olympia, WA 98506-4880   360-357-5596
                                888-754-8798
                          FAX: 360-357-3279
                          info@arcwa.org
                          arcwa.org

Cindy O'Neill, Board President
Sue Elliott, Executive Director
Angie Ziska, Secretary
Mission is to advocate for the rights and full participation of all people with intellectual and developmental disabilities.

3160 **Ben B Cheney Foundation**
3110 Ruston Way
Suite A
Tacoma, WA 98402-5308   253-572-2442
                        Info@benbcheneyfoundation.org
                        benbcheneyfoundation.org

Bradbury F. Cheney, President
Piper Cheney, Vice President
Carolyn J. Cheney, Secretary Treasurer
The Foundation makes grants in communities where the Cheney Lumber Company was active. The Foundation's goal is to improve the quality of life in those communities by making grants to a wide range of activities.

3161 **Community Foundation of North Central Washington**
9 South Wenatchee Ave
Wenatchee, WA 98801-3332   509-663-7716
                          FAX: 888-317-8314
                          info@cfncw.org
                          www.cfncw.org

Beth Stipe, Executive Director
Kristy Harris, Chief Financial Officer
Lila R. Edlund, Director of Administration
Assists donors by helping identify their specific charitable and goals and provide grants and scholarships that help groups and people address critical issues in North Central Washington

3162 **Glaser Progress Foundation**
1601 Second Avenue
Suite 1080
Seattle, WA 98101-9223   206-728-1050
                          FAX: 206-728-1123

Martin Collier, Executive Director
Mitchell Fox, Program Officer
Melessa Rogers, Operations Manager
The Glaser Progress Foundation focuses on four program areas: measuring progress, animal advocacy, independent media and global HIV/AIDS.

3163 **Greater Tacoma Community Foundation**
950 Pacific Avenue
Suite 1100
Tacoma, WA 98402-4423   253-383-5622
                          FAX: 253-272-8099
                          info@gtcf.org
                          www.gtcf.org

Rose Lincoln Hamilton, President and CEO
Shirley Brockmann, CPA, Vice President Finance & Adminis
Elyse Rowe, Chief of Strategy and Community
Mission is fostering generosity by connecting people who care with causes that matter, forever enriching our community.

3164 **Inland Northwest Community Foundation**
421 West Riverside Avenue
Suite 606
Spokane, WA 99201-0405   509-624-2606
                                888-267-5606
                          FAX: 509-624-2608
                          admin@inwcf.org
                          www.inwcf.org

Mark Hurtubise, Ph.D., J.D., President and CEO
Troy Braga, CPA, Controller
P J Watters, Director of Gift Planning

Serving 20 counties throughout Eastern Washington and Northern Idaho, mission is to foster vibrant and sustainable communities in the Inland Northwest.

3165 **Medina Foundation**
801 2nd Ave
Suite 1300
Seattle, WA 98104-1517   206-652-8783
                          FAX: 206-652-8791
                          info@medinafoundation.org
                          www.medinafoundation.org

Jennifer Teunon, Executive Director
Jessica Case, Program Officer
Aana Lauckhart, Program Officer
A family foundation that works to foster positive change in the Greater Puget Sound area. The Foundation strives to improve the human condition by supporting organizations that provide critical services to those in need.

3166 **Norcliffe Foundation**
999 3rd Ave
Suite 1006
Seattle, WA 98104-4001   206-682-4820
                          FAX: 206-682-4821
                          arline@thenorcliffefoundation.com
                          www.thenorcliffefoundation.com

Arline Hefferline, Foundation Manager
Nora P. Kenway, President
Geographic area of funding limited to the Puget Sound Region in and around Seattle, Washington.

3167 **Stewardship Foundation**
1145 Broadway
Suite 1500
Tacoma, WA 98402-1278   253-620-1340
                          FAX: 253-572-2721
                          info@stewardshipfdn.org
                          www.stewardshipfdn.org

William T. Weyerhaeuser, Chair
Gail T. Weyerhaeuser, Vice Chair and Treasurer
Chi-Dooh, Director
Christian, evangelical organizations - national or international impact.

3168 **Weyerhaeuser Company Foundation**
33663 Weyerhaeuser Way South
Federal Way, WA 98003   253-924-2345
                                800-525-5440
                          www.weyerhaeuser.com

Daniel S Fulton, President & CEO
Patricia M Bedient, EVP & CFO
Sandy D McDade, SVP & General Counsel
Although the foundation does fund programs for disabled persons from time to time, it is not a specific priority for the foundation. Since it was formed in 1948, the foundation has given more than $81.1 million to nonprofit organizations and is one of the oldest funds for corporate philanthropy in the country. Nearly all of its contributions have been made within the communities where Weyerhaeuser employees live and work and awards approximately 600 grants annually.

West Virginia

3169 **Arc Of West Virginia, The**
912 Market Street
Parkersburg, WV 26101-4737   304-422-3151

3170 **Bernard McDonough Foundation**
311 Fourth Street
Parkersburg, WV 26101-5315   304-424-6280
                          FAX: 304-424-6281
                          www.mcdonoughfoundation.org

Robert W Stephens, Ed.D., President
Mary Riccobene, Vice President
Francis C. McCusker, Treasurer
Directors and officers continue the legacy of the McDonoughs by providing grants that create a healthier, more educated and culturally appreciative citizenry.

3171 High Technology Foundation
1000 Galliher Dr.
Suite 1000
Fairmont, WV 26554
304-363-5482
877-363-5482
info@wvhtf.org
www.wvhtf.org

Dr. Frank W. Blake, Chair
James L. Estep, President & Chief Executive Officer
High Technology Foundation is dedicated to maximizing economic development in West Virginia through the high-technology business sector.
1990

Wisconsin

3172 Arc of Dunn County
2602 Hils Court
Menomonie, WI 54751-4160
715-235-7373
FAX: 715-233-3565
www.arcofdunncounty.org

Rebecca Cooper, Executive Director
Kathy Lausted, Guardianship Director
Advocating for the rights of citizens with disabilities.

3173 Arc of Eau Claire
4800 Golf Road
Suite 450
Eau Claire, WI 54701-6130
715-833-1735
FAX: 715-833-1215
frcec@frcec.org
www.frcec.org

Brook Steele, President
Melanie Koehler, Vice President
Dr. Jennifer Eddy, Secretary
Mission is to provide programs and services that build on family strengths through prevention, education, support and networking in collaboration with other resources in the community.

3174 Arc of Fox Cities
211 E. Franklin St.
Suite A
Appleton, WI 54911
920-735-0943
FAX: 920-725-1531
info@arcfoxcities.com
arcfoxcities.com

Laura McCormick, President
Todd Klauer, Vice President
Bryan Mueller, Secretary
Mission statement is to utilize advocacy, respect and concern to empower all people with disabilities to have the opportunity to choose and realize their goal of a full life and a secure future.

3175 Arc of Racine County
6214 Washington Ave
Suite C-6
Racine, WI 53404-3350
262-634-6303
info@thearcofracine.org
www.thearcofracine.org

Peggy Foreman, Executive Director
Alison Henry, Program Manager
Ross Gietzel, Program Assistant
The Arc of Racine's mission is to advocate for and provide information and services to improve lives.

3176 Arc of Wisconsin Disability Association
2800 Royal Ave
Suite 202
Monona, WI 53713-1518
608-222-8907
877-272-8400
FAX: 608-222-8908
arcw@att.net

John Beisbier, President
Donna Auchue, Vice President
Tina Beauprey, Secretary
The Arc-Wisconsin strives to be a major force in advocating and promoting self-determined quality of life opportunities for poeple with developmental and related disabilities and their families.

3177 Arc-Dane County
6602 Grand Teton Plz
Madison, WI 53719-1091
608-833-1199
FAX: 608-833-1307
arcdanecounty@gmail.com
arcdanecounty.org

Ken Hobbs, President
John Leemkuil, Vice President
Mark Lederer, Secretary
The Arc-Dane County is a non-profit organization whose primary objective is to support children and adults with developmental disabilities and their families through advocacy to assure these individuals are offered the same opportunities and have the rights due all people. The Arc-Dane County provides numerous services through education, overall support, and legislation that assists those individuals with developmental disabilities be it within their homes, communities, or at work.

3178 Faye McBeath Foundation
101 W. Pleasant Street
Suite 210
Milwaukee, WI 53212- 3157
414-272-2626
FAX: 414-272-6235

P. Michael Mahoney, Chair
Mary T. Kellner, Vice Chair
Gregory M. Wesley, Secretary
A private independent foundation providing grants to tax exempt nonprofit organizations principally the metropolitan Milwaukee area.

3179 Helen Bader Foundation
233 North Water Street
4th Floor
Milwaukee, WI 53202- 5761
414-224-6464
FAX: 414-224-1441
info@hbf.org
www.hbf.org

Daniel J. Bader, President/CEO
Lisa G. Hiller, VP, Administration
Maria Lopez Vento, VP, Programs and Partnerships
Strives to be a philanthropic leader in improving the quality of life of the diverse communities in which it works. The Foundation makes grants, convenes partners, and shares knowledge to affect emerging issues in key areas.

3180 Johnson Controls Foundation
5757 N Green Bay Ave
P.O. Box 591
Milwaukee, WI 53201- 4408
414-524-1200
800-333-2222
FAX: 414-524-2077
johnsoncontrols.com

Stephen A Molinaroli, Chairman, President and CEO
Dr. Breda Bolzenius, Vice President, Vice Chairman
Kim Metcalf-Kupres, Vice President and Chief Marketing Officer
Organized and directed to be operated for charitable purposes which include the distribution and application of financial support to soundly managed and operated organizations or causes which are fundamentally philanthropic.

3181 Lynde and Harry Bradley Foundation
1241 N Franklin Pl
Milwaukee, WI 53202-2901
414-291-9915
FAX: 414-291-9991
www.bradleyfdn.org

Dennis J. Kuester, Chairman
David V. Uihlein, Vice Chairman
Michael W. Grebbe, President and CEO
The Foundation's programs support limited, competent government; a dynamic marketplace for economic, intellectual and cultural activity; a vigorus defense at home and abroad, of American ideas and institutions; and scholarly studies and academic achievement.

3182 Milwaukee Foundation
101 W Pleasant St
Suite 210
Milwaukee, WI 53212-3963   414-272-5805
                            FAX: 414-272-6235
info@greatermilwaukeefoundation.org
www.greatermilwaukeefoundation.org
Ellen M Gilligan, President and CEO
Marcus White, Vice President
Kathryn J. Dunn, Vice President
Guided by three tenets- helping donors create personal legacies of giving that last beyond their lifetimes, investing donor funds for maximum return with minimal risk, and playing a leadership role tackling the communities most challenging needs.

3183 Northwestern Mutual Life Foundation
720 E Wisconsin Ave
Milwaukee, WI 53202-4703   414-271-1444
www.northwesternmutual.com
John E Schlifske, Chairman and CEO
Gregory C. Oberland, President
Michael G. Carter, Executive Vice President and CFO

3184 Patrick and Anna M Cudahy Fund
70 E. Lake St.,
Suite 1120
Chicago, Il 60601   312-422-1442
                      FAX: 312-641-5736
laurenkrieg@cudahyfund.org
cudahyfund.org
Janet S Cudahy MD, President
Lauren Krieg, Executive Director
A general purpose foundation which primarily supports organizations in Wisconsin and the metropolitan Chicago area. Interests are social service, youth, and education with some giving for the arts, and other areas.

3185 SB Waterman & E Blade Charitable Foundation
Marshall & Ilsley Trust Company
111 E. Kilbourn Ave.,
Milwaukee, WI 53202-2980   414-287-8700
                            FAX: 414-765-8200
Thomas C Boettcher, Director
Giving primarily to health associations. Geographical focus is Wisconsin.

Wyoming

3186 Arc of Natrona County
314 W. Midwest Ave
P.O. Box 393
Casper, WY 82601   307-577-4913
                      800-433-5255
                    FAX: 307-577-4014
info@thearc.org
arcofnatronacounty.org
Beau Covert, President
Dr. Nathan Edwards, Vice President
Kelley Reimer, Treasurer
Organization works to ensure that the estimated 7.2 million Americans with intellectual and developmental disabilities have the services and supports they need to grow, develop and live in communities across the nation.

Funding Directories

3187 Chronicle Guide to Grants
318 S. Lee Street
Alexandria, DC 20037-1146   202-466-1200
                            800-287-6072
                          FAX: 202-452-1033
help@philanthropy.com
heideninc.com
Phil Semas, Manager
Edward J. Heiden, President

A computerized research tool, on floppy disks or a CD-ROM, for immediate use on any IBM compatible personal computer. Offers electronic listings of 10,000 grants from hundreds of foundations, with a subscription that offers 1,000 plus new listings every two months. Each listing offers grant information as well as names, addresses and phone numbers of the grant-making organizations. *$295.00*

3188 College Student's Guide to Merit and Other No-Need Funding
Reference Service Press
5000 Windplay Dr
Suite 4
El Dorado Hills, CA 95762-9319   916-939-9620
                                  FAX: 916-939-9626
info@rspfunding.com
www.rspfunding.com
Gail Schlachter, Founder
R. David Weber, Editor
Sandy Hirsh, Editor
More than 1,200 funding opportunities for currently-enrolled or returning college students are described in this directory. *$32.50*
450 pages
ISBN 1-588410-41-2

3189 Community Health Funding Report
CD Publications
8204 Fenton St
Silver Spring, MD 20910-4502   301-588-6380
                                  800-666-6380
                                FAX: 301-588-6385
www.cdpublications.com
Michael Gerecht, President
The once twice-monthly report is now web-based to allow for breaking news updates and up the the minute information about funding, including: public and private grant announcements; reports on successful health programs nationwide; interviews with grant officials; plus national news on health policy topics affecting various organizations. *$439.00*
Web-based

3190 Directory of Financial Aids for Women
Reference Service Press
2310 Homestead Rd
Suite C1 #219
Los Altos, CA 94024   650-861-3170
                        FAX: 650-861-3171
info@rspfunding.com
www.rspfunding.com
Gail Schlachter, Founder
R. David Weber, Editor
Sandy Hirsh, Editor
Funding programs listed support study, research, travel, training, career development, or innovative effort at any level; descriptions of more than 1,700 funding programs - representing billions of dollars in financial aid set aside for women; also an annotated bibliography of 60 key directories that identify even more financial aid opportunities and a set of indexes that let you search the directory by title, sponsor, researching, tenability, subject, and deadline. *$45.00*
578 pages Biennial
ISBN 1-588410-00-5

3191 Disability Funding News
8204 Fenton St
Silver Spring, MD 20910-4502   301-588-6380
                                  800-666-6380
                                FAX: 301-588-6385
www.cdpublications.com
Michael Gerecht, President

3192 FC Search
Foundation Center
79 fifth Avenue
New York, NY 10003-3034 · · · · · · · · · 212-620-4230
800-424-9836
FAX: 212-807-3677
order@foundationcenter.org
foundationcenter.org
Bradford K Smith, President
Lisa Philip, Vice President for Strategic Phi
Jen Bokoff, Director of GrantCraft
Provides access to the Foundation Center's comprehensive database of funders in a convenient CD-ROM format. *$1845.00*

3193 Federal Grants & Contracts Weekly
LRP Publications
360 Hiatt Drive
Palm Beach Gardens, FL 33418-1718 · · · · 800-341-7874
FAX: 561-622-2423
custserve@lrp.com
www.lrp.com
Kelly Sullivan, Editor
Kenneth F. Kahn, President
The latest funding announcements of federal grants for project opportunities in research, training and services. Provides profiles of key programs, tips on seeking grants, updates on legislation and regulations, budget developments and early alerts to upcoming funding opportunities. *$340.00*
Weekly

3194 Financial Aid for Asian Americans
Reference Service Press
2310 Homestead Rd
Suite C1 #219
Los Altos, CA 94024 · · · · · · · · · · · · 650-861-3170
FAX: 650-861-3171
info@rspfunding.com
www.rspfunding.com
Gail Schlachter, Founder
R. David Weber, Editor
Sandy Hirsh, Editor
This is the source to use if you are looking for financial aid for Asian Americans; nearly 1,000 funding opportunities are described. *$35.00*
336 pages
ISBN 1-588410-02-1

3195 Financial Aid for Hispanic Americans
Reference Service Press
2310 Homestead Rd
Suite C1 #219
Los Altos, CA 94024 · · · · · · · · · · · · 650-861-3170
FAX: 650-861-3171
info@rspfunding.com
www.rspfunding.com
Gail Schlachter, Founder
R. David Weber, Editor
Sandy Hirsh, Editor
Nearly 1,300 funding programs open to Americans of Mexican, Puerto Rican, Central American, or other Latin American heritage are described here. *$37.50*
472 pages
ISBN 1-588410-03-X

3196 Financial Aid for Native Americans
Reference Service Press
2310 Homestead Rd
Suite C1 #219
Los Altos, CA 94024 · · · · · · · · · · · · 650-861-3170
FAX: 650-861-3171
info@rspfunding.com
www.rspfunding.com
Gail Schlachter, Founder
R. David Weber, Editor
Sandy Hirsh, Editor
Detailed information is provided on 1,500 funding opportunities open to American Indians, Native Alaskans, and Native Pacific Islanders. *$37.50*
562 pages
ISBN 1-588410-04-8

3197 Financial Aid for Research and Creative Activities Abroad
Reference Service Press
2310 Homestead Rd
Suite C1 #219
Los Altos, CA 94024 · · · · · · · · · · · · 650-861-3170
FAX: 650-861-3171
info@rspfunding.com
www.rspfunding.com
Gail Schlachter, Founder
R. David Weber, Editor
Sandy Hirsh, Editor
Described here are 1,200 funding programs (scholarships, fellowships, grants, etc.) available to support research, professional, or creative activities abroad. *$45.00*
378 pages
ISBN 1-588410-82-5

3198 Financial Aid for Veterans, Military Personnel and their Dependents
Reference Service Press
2310 Homestead Rd
Suite C1 #219
Los Altos, CA 94024 · · · · · · · · · · · · 650-861-3170
FAX: 650-861-3171
info@rspfunding.com
www.rspfunding.com
Gail Schlachter, Founder
R. David Weber, Editor
Sandy Hirsh, Editor
According to Reference Book Review, this directory (with its 1,100 entries) is the most comprehensive guide available on the subject. *$40.00*
392 pages
ISBN 1-588410-43-9

3199 Financial Aid for the Disabled and Their Families
Reference Service Press
2310 Homestead Rd
Suite C1 #219
Los Altos, CA 94024 · · · · · · · · · · · · 650-861-3170
FAX: 650-861-3171
info@rspfunding.com
www.rspfunding.com
Gail Schlachter, Founder
R. David Weber, Editor
This directory, which Children's Bookwatch calls invaluable describes more than 1,100 financial aid opportunities available to support persons with disabilities and members of their families. Updated every 2 years. *$37.50*
508 pages Every other yr.
ISBN 1-588410-01-3

3200 Foundation & Corporate Grants Alert
LRP Publications
360 Hiatt Drive
Palm Beach Gardens, FL 33418-1718 · · · · 800-341-7874
FAX: 561-622-2423
custserve@lrp.com
www.lrp.com
Kelly Sullivan, Editor
Kenneth F. Kahn, President
A complete guide to foundation and corporate grant opportunities for nonprofit organizations. Tracks developments and trends in funding and provides notification of changes in foundations' funding priorities. *$245.00*
Monthly
ISSN 1062-46 6

3201 Foundation 1000
Foundation Center
79 fifth Avenue
New York, NY 10003-3076 · · · · · · · · · 212-620-4230
800-424-9836
FAX: 212-807-3691
order@foundationcenter.org
www.foundationcenter.org
Bradford K Smith, President
Lisa Philip, Vice President for Strategic Phi
Jen Bokoff, Director of GrantCraft

Offers comprehensive information on the 1000 largest foundations in the US. *$195.00*

3202 Foundation Directories
Foundation Center
79 fifth Avenue
New York, NY 10003-3034

212-620-4230
800-424-9836
FAX: 212-807-3677
order@foundationcenter.org
foundationcenter.org

Bradford K Smith, President
Lisa Philip, Vice President for Strategic Phi
Jen Bokoff, Director of GrantCraft
Lists key facts on the top 20,000 US foundations. *$125.00*
ISBN 0-87954 -36-1

3203 Foundation Grants to Individuals
Foundation Center
79 fifth Avenue
New York, NY 10003-3034

212-620-4230
800-424-9836
FAX: 212-807-3677
order@foundationcenter.org
foundationcenter.org

Bradford K Smith, President
Lisa Philip, Vice President
Jen Bokoff, Director of GrantCraft
The only publication that provides extensive coverage of foundation funding prospects for individual grantseekers. *$40.00*
Biennially

3204 From the State Capitals: Public Health
Wakeman/Walworth
P.O.Box 7376
Alexandria, VA 22307-376

703-768-9600
FAX: 703-768-9690

Mark Willen, Editor
Digest of state and municipal health care financing and cost containment measures, includes medical legislation, disease control, etc. *$245.00*
6 pages

3205 Grant Guides
Foundation Center
79 fifth Avenue
New York, NY 10003-3034

212-620-4230
800-424-9836
FAX: 212-807-3677
order@foundationcenter.org
foundationcenter.org

Bradford K Smith, President
Lisa Philip, Vice President
Jen Bokoff, Director of GrantCraft
Provides descriptions of actual foundation grants awarded in various subject fields. *$35.00*
ISBN 0-87954 -90-6

3206 Guide to Funding for International and Foreign Programs
79 fifth Avenue
New York, NY 10003-3034

212-620-4230
800-424-9836
FAX: 212-807-3677
order@foundationcenter.org
foundationcenter.org

Bradford K Smith, President
Lisa Philip, Vice President
Jen Bokoff, Director of GrantCraft
Grantmakers featured in this guide provide funding for international relief, disaster assistance, human rights, civil liberties, community development, conferences, and education. *$190.00*

3207 Guide to US Foundations their Trustees, Officers and Donors
Foundation Center
79 fifth Avenue
New York, NY 10003-3034

212-620-4230
800-424-9836
FAX: 212-807-3677
order@foundationcenter.org
foundationcenter.org

Bradford K Smith, President
Lisa Philip, Vice President for Strategic Phi
Jen Bokoff, Director of GrantCraft
Provides crucial facts on grantmaking. Each entry includes contact information, current assets, annual contributions, officers, donors and more. *$135.00*

3208 High School Senior's Guide to Merit and Other No-Need Funding
Reference Service Press
2310 Homestead Rd
Suite C1 #219
Los Altos, CA 94024

650-861-3170
FAX: 650-861-3171
info@rspfunding.com
www.rspfunding.com

Gail Schlachter, Founder
R. David Weber, Editor
Sandy Hirsh, Editor
Here's your guide to 1,100 funding programs that never look at income level when making awards to college bound high school seniors. *$29.95*
400 pages
ISBN 1-588410-44-X

3209 How to Pay for Your Degree in Business & Related Fields
Reference Service Press
2310 Homestead Rd
Suite C1 #219
Los Altos, CA 94024

650-861-3170
FAX: 650-861-3171
info@rspfunding.com
www.rspfunding.com

Gail Schlachter, Founder
R. David Weber, Editor
Sandy Hirsh, Editor
If you need funding for an undergraduate or graduate degree in business or related fields, this is the directory to use (500+ funding programs described). *$30.00*
290 pages
ISBN 1-588411-45-1

3210 How to Pay for Your Degree in Education& Related Fields
Reference Service Press
2310 Homestead Rd
Suite C1 #219
Los Altos, CA 94024

650-861-3170
FAX: 650-861-3171
www.rspfunding.com

Gail Schlachter, Founder
R. David Weber, Editor
Sandy Hirsh, Editor
Here's hundreds of funding opportunities available to support undergraduate and graduate students preparing for a career in education, guidance etc. *$30.00*
250 pages
ISBN 1-588411-46-x

3211 National Directory of Corporate Giving
Foundation Center
79 fifth Avenue
New York, NY 10003-3034

212-620-4230
800-424-9836
FAX: 212-807-3677
order@foundationcenter.org
foundationcenter.org

Bradford K Smith, President
Lisa Philip, Vice President for Strategic Phi
Jen Bokoff, Director of GrantCraft

Offers over 2,000 corporate funders, current giving reviews and profiles of sponsoring companies. *$195.00*

3212   Older Americans Report
Business Publishers
2222 Sedwick Drive
Durham, NC 27713-1995

240-514-0600
800-223-8720
FAX: 800-508-2592
custserv@bpinews.com
www.bpinews.com

Leonard Eiser, Publisher

Follows all programs and funding sources in education, housing, job training, therapy, Social Security Supplemental Security Income, Medicare, Medicaid and more of importance to persons with disabilities. Also covers the latest on the Americans with Disabilities Act. Publishes a newsletter. *$327.00*

3213   Student Guide
US Department of Education
400 Maryland Avenue SW
Washington, DC 20202

202-401-2000
800-872-5327
FAX: 202-401-0689
TTY: 800-437-0833
customerservice@inet.ed.gov
ed.gov

Arne Duncan, Secretary of Education
Jim Shelton, Deputy Secretary
Ted Mitchell, Under Secretary

Describes the major student aid programs the US Department of Education administers and gives detailed information about program procedures.
74 pages

Government Agencies

Federal

3214 Administration on Aging
Administration for Community Living
330 C St. SW
Washington, DC 20201 202-401-4634
acl.gov/about-acl/administration-aging
Alison Barkoff, Acting Administrator & Assistant Secretary, Aging
Administers the Older Americans Act of 1965 to assist states and
local communities in developing programs and services for older
persons.

3215 Administration on Children, Youth and Families
330 C St. SW
Washington, DC 20201 202-401-4634
www.acf.hhs.gov/acyf
Elizabeth Darling, Acting Commissioner
Responsible for federal programs that support social services for
children, youth, and families; protective services for at-risk
youth; and adoption services for children with special needs.

3216 Administration on Disabilities
Administration for Community Living
330 C St. SW
Washington, DC 20201 202-401-4634
acl.gov
Anjali Forber-Pratt, Director
Alison Barkoff, Acting Administrator & Assistant Secretary, Aging
Vicki Gottlich, Deputy Administrator, Policy & Evaluation
Ensures that individuals with disabilities and their families participate in the design of and have access to culturally competent
services, supports, and other assistance and opportunities that
promote independence, productivity, and integration and
inclusion into the community.

**3217 Americans with Disabilities Act Information and
Technical Assistance**
US Department of Justice
950 Pennsylvania Ave. NW
9th Floor
Washington, DC 20530 202-307-0663
800-514-0301
FAX: 202-307-1197
TTY: 800-514-0383
www.ada.gov
Rebecca B. Bond, Chief
Anne Raish, Principal Deputy Chief
Christina Galindo-Walsh, Deputy Chief
The ADA assures that Americans with disabilities have the same
opportunities as all Americans. To this end, the Justice Depart-
ment produces publications and conducts programs to increase
compliance of the ADA nationwide.

3218 Centers for Medicare & Medicaid Services
7500 Security Blvd.
Baltimore, MD 21244 410-786-3000
877-267-2323
TTY:866-226-1819
www.cms.gov
Chiquita Brooks-LaSure, Administrator
Jonathan Blum, Principal Deputy Administrator
Karen Jackson, Deputy Chief Operating Officer
Responsible for administering Medicare, Medicaid, and the Chil-
dren's Health Insurance Program. Formerly the Health Care Fi-
nancing Administration.

3219 Civil Rights Division/Disability Rights Section
US Department of Justice
950 Pennsylvania Ave. NW
9th Floor
Washington, DC 20530 202-307-0663
800-514-0301
FAX: 202-307-1197
TTY: 800-514-0383
www.ada.gov
Rebecca B. Bond, Chief
Anne Raish, Principal Deputy Chief
Christina Galindo-Walsh, Deputy Chief
The US Department of Justice answers questions about the Amer-
icans with Disabilities Act (ADA) and provides free materials by
mail and fax through the ADA Information Line.

**3220 Committee for Purchase from People Who Are Blind or
Severely Disabled**
1401 S. Clark St.
Suite 715
Arlington, VA 22202-3259 703-603-2100
800-999-5963
FAX: 703-328-2909
info@abilityone.gov
www.abilityone.gov
*Kimberly Zeich, Acting Executive Director & Chief Executive Offi-
cer*
*Irene Glaeser, Acting Deputy Executive Director & Chief Operating
Officer*
Kelvin Wood, Chief of Staff
A federal agency that administers the Javits-Wagner-O'Day Program, directing federal agencies to purchase products and services from nonprofit agencies that employ people who are blind
or have other severe disabilities. Provides a wide range of vocational options to individuals with severe disabilities.

3221 Equal Opportunity Employment Commission
131 M St. NE
Washington, DC 20507 800-669-4000
TTY:800-669-6820
info@eeoc.gov
www.eeoc.gov
Charlotte A. Burrows, Chair
Janet Dhillon, Commissioner
Keith E. Sonderling, Commissioner
This agency is responsible for enforcing workplace anti-discrim-
ination laws, including the Americans with Disabilities Act
(ADA) and the Rehabilitation Act.

3222 Federal Communications Commission
45 L St. NE
Washington, DC 20554 202-418-0500
888-225-5322
FAX: 866-418-0232
fccinfo@fcc.gov
fcc.gov
Jessica Rosenworcel, Chairwoman
Brendan Carr, Commissioner
Geoffrey Starks, Commissioner
Enforces ADA telecommunications provisions which require
that companies offering telephone service to the general public
must offer telephone relay services to individuals who use text
telephones or similar devices. Also enforces closed captioning
rules, hearing compatibility and access to equipment and services
for people with disabilities.

3223 Health Resources and Services Administration (HRSA)
US Department of Health and Human Services
5600 Fishers Lane
Rockville, MD 20857 301-443-3376
877-464-4772
TTY:877-897-9910
www.hrsa.gov
Diana Espinosa, Deputy Administrator
Jordan Grossman, Chief of Staff
Carole Johnson, Administrator
The Health Resources and Services Administration provides pro-
grams for people with HIV/AIDS, pregnant women, mothers, and
other individuals in need of high quality primary health care.

3224 National Cancer Institute
9609 Medical Center Dr.
Rockville, MD 20850
800-422-6237
TTY:800-332-8615
nciinfo@nih.gov
www.cancer.gov

Norman E. Sharpless, Director
Douglas R. Lowy, Principal Deputy Director
James Doroshow, Deputy Director, Clinical & Translational Research
The National Cancer Institute conducts and supports research, training, health information dissemination, and programs related to cancer, cancer rehabilitation, and the care of cancer patients.
1975

3225 National Coalition of Federal Aviation Employees with Disabilities
Federal Aviation Administration
6500 South MacArthur, AML-4023
RRF Building-185
Oklahoma City, OK 73169
405-954-6877
greg.brooks@faa.gov
www.ncfaed.org

Gregory A. Brooks, National President
NCFAED works on improving work conditions for employees; expanding National Coalition to serve all FAA employees; promoting equal opportunity for people with disabilities in the FAA workplace; assisting the FAA in its commitment to remove physical and attudinal barriers which inhibit opportunities for people with disabilities; and aligning with internal and external organizations to attract future generations of people with disabilities to the FAA as employees.

3226 National Council on Disability
1331 F St. NW
Suite 850
Washington, DC 20004
202-272-2004
FAX: 202-272-2022
TTY:202-272-2074
www.ncd.gov

Anne Sommers McIntosh, Executive Director
Joan M. Durocher, General Counsel & Director, Policy
Lisa Grubb, Director, Administration, Finance & Operations
Federal agency led by members appointed by the President of the United States and confirmed by the United States Senate. The overall purpose of the National Council is to promote policies, programs, practices and procedures that guarantee equal opportunities to persons with disabilities.

3227 National Eye Institute
National Institutes of Health
31 Center Dr.
MSC 2510
Bethesda, MD 20892-2510
301-496-5248
2020@nei.nih.gov
www.nei.nih.gov

Michael F. Chiang, Director
Santa Tumminia, Deputy Director
Melanie Reagan, Acting Executive Officer
As part of the federal government's National Institutes of Health (NIH), the National Eye Institute finances intramural and extramural research on eye diseases and visual disorders.

3228 National Institute of Arthritis and Musculoskeletal and Skin Diseases
National Institutes of Health
31 Center Dr., MSC 2350
Building 31, Room 4C02
Bethesda, MD 20892-2350
301-496-8190
877-226-4267
FAX: 301-480-2814
TTY: 301-565-2966
www.naims.nih.gov

Lindsey A. Criswell, Director
Robert H. Carter, Deputy Director
Rick Phillips, Acting Associate Director, Management & Operations
The mission of the National Institute of Arthritis and Musculoskeletal and Skin Diseases is to advance understanding and treatment of diseases of the bones, joints, muscles, and skin

by supporting research, training scientists, and disseminating information on such diseases.

3229 National Institute of Diabetes and Digestive and Kidney Diseases
National Institutes of Health
31 Center Dr.
Bethesda, MD 20892
800-860-8747
TTY:866-569-1162
healthinfo@niddk.nih.gov
www.niddk.nih.gov

Griffin P. Rodgers, Director
Gregory G. Germino, Deputy Director
Camille Hoover, Executive Officer
The National Institute of Diabetes and Digestive and Kidney Diseases conducts and supports research, training, and science-based information dissemination on diabetes, digestive diseases, and kidney, urologic, and hematologic diseases.

3230 National Institute of Mental Health
National Institutes of Health
6001 Executive Blvd.
Room 6200, MSC 9663
Bethesda, MD 20892-9663
866-615-6464
TTY:866-415-8051
nimhinfo@nih.gov
www.nimh.nih.gov

Joshua A. Gordon, Director
Shelli Avenevoli, Deputy Director
The mission of the National Institute of Mental Health is to advance the prevention, recovery, and cure of mental illnesses through basic and clinical research.

3231 National Institute of Neurological Disorders and Stroke
National Institutes of Health
PO Box 5801
Bethesda, MD 20824
800-352-9424
www.ninds.nih.gov

Nina Schor, Deputy Director
The mission of the National Institute of Neurological Disorders and Stroke is to reduce the burden of neurological disease by supporting neuroscience research, funding and conducting training and career development programs, and disseminating scientific information on neurological health.

3232 National Institute on Aging
31 Center Dr., MSC 2292
Building 31, Room 5C27
Bethesda, MD 20892
800-222-2225
TTY:800-222-4225
niaic@nia.nih.gov
www.nia.nih.gov

Richard J. Hodes, Director
Lisa Mascone, Deputy Director, Management
Luigi Ferrucci, Scientific Director
The National Institute on Aging (NIA) is the primary federal agency engaged in researching Alzheimer's disease, providing resources to scientists and educating the public on the results of studies.

3233 National Institute on Deafness and Other Communication Disorders
National Institutes of Health
31 Center Dr.
MSC 2320
Bethesda, MD 20892-2320
301-827-8183
800-241-1044
TTY:800-241-1055
nidcdinfo@nidcd.nih.gov
www.nidcd.nih.gov

Debara L. Tucci, Director
Judith A. Cooper, Deputy Director
Timothy J. Wheeles, Executive Officer
The National Institute on Deafness and Other Communication Disorders supports and conducts research to help prevent, detect and diagnose disabilities that affect hearing, balance, taste, smell, voice, speech, and communication.
1988

3234 **National Institute on Disability, Independent Living, and Rehabilitation Research (NIDILRR)**
Administration for Community Living
330 C St. SW
Washington, DC 20201   202-401-4634
                                                        acl.gov

Anjali Forber-Pratt, Director
Alison Barkoff, Acting Administrator & Assistant Secretary, Aging
Vicki Gottlich, Deputy Administrator, Policy & Evaluation
Serving as the federal government's disability research agency, NIDILRR provides research, training, and technical assistance to maximize the full inclusion of individuals with disabilities into society; promotes the use of rehabilitation technology for individuals with disabilities; and ensures the distribution of practical scientific and technological information in usable formats.

3235 **Office of Disability Employment Policy**
US Department of Labor
200 Constitution Ave. NW
Washington, DC 20210   202-693-7880
                                                        866-633-7365
                                                        odep@dol.gov
                                        www.dol.gov/agencies/odep

Melissa Turner, Executive Officer
Taryn M. Williams, Assistant Secretary
Jennifer Sheehy, Deputy Assistant Secretary
Non-regulatory federal agency that promotes and develops policies that increase employment opportunities for people with disabilities.

3236 **Office of Fair Housing and Equal Opportunity**
US Department of Housing & Urban Development
451 7th St. SW
Washington, DC 20410   202-708-1112
                                            TTY:202-708-1455
                                        www.hud.gov/program_offices

Marcia L. Fudge, Secretary
Adrianne Todman, Deputy Secretary
Jenn Jones, Chief of Staff
The Office of Fair Housing and Equal Opportunity (FHEO) enforces and develops laws and policies that eliminate housing discrimination and ensure that all Americans have equal access to housing. The laws enforced by FHEO include Titles II and III of the Americans with Disabilities Act and Section 504 of the Rehabilitation Act.

3237 **Office of Retirement and Disability Policy (ORDP)**
Social Security Administration

                                        800-772-1213
                                        TTY:800-325-0778
                                        www.ssa.gov/policy
Stephen G. Evangelista, Acting Deputy Commissioner
Dawn S. Wiggins, Associate Commissioner
Natalie T. Lu, Associate Commissioner
Serves as the principal advisor to the Commissioner of Social Security on major policy issues, including those relating to disability policy.

3238 **Office of Special Education Programs**
US Department of Education
400 Maryland Ave. SW
Washington, DC 20202   202-401-2000
                                                        800-872-5327
                                            TTY:800-730-8913
                                www.ed.gov/about/offices/list/osers/osep
Valerie C. Williams, Director
David Cantrell, Deputy Director
Assists infants, toddlers, children and youth with disabilities by providing leadership and financial support to states and local districts.

3239 **President's Committee on People with Intellectual Disabilities**
Administration for Community Living
330 C St. SW
Washington, DC 20201   202-401-4634
                                                        acl.gov

Anjali Forber-Pratt, Director
Alison Barkoff, Acting Administrator & Assistant Secretary, Aging
Vicki Gottlich, Deputy Administrator, Policy & Evaluation

Established by the presidential executive order to advise the President of the United States and the Secretary of Health and Human Services on issues concerning citizens with intellectual disabilities. PCPID is overseen and supported by the Administration for Community Living (ACL).

3240 **Rehabilitation Services Administration**
US Department of Education
400 Maryland Ave. SW
Washington, DC 20202   202-401-2000
                                                        800-872-5327
                                            TTY:800-730-8913
                                                        www2.ed.gov

The Rehabilitation Services Administration (RSA) oversees formula and discretionary grant programs that help individuals with physical or mental disabilities obtain employment and live more independently through the provision of such supports as counseling, medical and psychological services, job training and other individualized services.

3241 **Social Security Administration**

                                        800-772-1213
                                        TTY:800-325-0778
                                        www.ssa.gov

Stephen G. Evangelista, Acting Deputy Commissioner
Dawn S. Wiggins, Associate Commissioner
Natalie T. Lu, Associate Commissioner
Administers old age, survivors, and disability insurance programs under Title II of the Social Security Act. Also administers the federal income maintenance program under Title XVI of the Social Security Act. Maintains network of local/regional offices nationwide.

3242 **Substance Abuse and Mental Health Services Administration (SAMHSA)**
US Department of Health and Human Services
5600 Fishers Lane
Rockville, MD 20857   877-726-4727
                                            TTY:800-487-4889
                                        samhsainfo@samhsa.hhs.gov
                                                        www.samhsa.gov

Tom Coderre, Acting Deputy Assistant Secretary
Sonia Chessen, Chief of Staff
Trina Dutta, Senior Advisor
SAMHSA aims to advance substance use and mental health services and improve the lives of people living with mental and substance use disorders.

3243 **US Department of Education: Office for Civil Rights**
400 Maryland Ave. SW
Washington, DC 20202-1100   800-421-3481
                                                        800-872-5327
                                            TTY:800-730-8913
                                                        ocr@ed.gov
                                www2.ed.gov/about/offices/list/ocr
Prohibits discrimination in programs and activities funded by the Department of Education. Investigates complaints and provides technical assistance to individuals and entities with rights and responsibilities under Section 504.

3244 **US Department of Labor: Office of Federal Contract Compliance Programs**
200 Constitution Ave. NW
Washington, DC 20210   866-487-2365
                                            TTY:877-889-5627
                                        webmaster@dol.gov
                                        www.dol.gov/agencies/ofccp

Jenny R. Yang, Director
Dariely Rodriguez, Chief of Staff
Michele Hodge, Deputy Director
Prohibits contractors and subcontractors from discriminating against applicants or employees.

3245 US Department of Transportation
1200 New Jersey Ave. SE
Washington, DC 20590
202-366-4000
855-368-4200
TTY:711
www.dot.gov

Pete Buttigieg, Secretary
Polly Trottenberg, Deputy Secretary
Laura Schiller, Chief of Staff
Enforces ADA provisions that require nondiscrimination in public and private mass transportation systems and services.

3246 US Department of Veterans Affairs
800-698-2411
TTY:711
www.va.gov

Denis McDonough, Secretary
Tanya J. Bradsher, Chief of Staff
The Department of Veterans Affairs provides programs for veterans and their families. Programs include health care, rehabilitation services, compensation for disabilities, veterans benefits, and more.

3247 US Office of Personnel Management
1900 E St. NW
Washington, DC 20415-1000
202-606-1800
TTY:800-877-8339
opm.gov

Kiran Ahuja, Director
Provides human resources leadership and support to federal agencies. Administers a merit system for federal employment that includes recruiting, examining, training, and promoting people on the basis of knowledge and skills, regardless of sex, race, religion or other factors.

Alabama

3248 Alabama Council For Developmental Disabilities
RSA Union Building
RSA Union Building
PO Box 301410
Montgomery, AL 36130- 1410
334-242-3973
800-232-2158
FAX: 334-242-0797
Myra.Jones@mh.alabama.gov
www.acdd.org

Stefan Eisen, Jr., Chair, Parent Advocate
Sophia Whitted, Fiscal Manager
Elmyra Jones-Banks, Executive Director
Serves as an advocate for Alabama's citizens with developmental disabilities and their families; to empower them with the knowledge and opportunity to make informed choices and exercise control over their own lives; and to create a climate for positive socialchange to enable them to be respected, independent and productive integrated members of society.

3249 Alabama Department of Public Health
The RSA Tower, 201 Monroe Street
PO Box 303017
Montgomery, AL 36130-3017
334-206-5300
800-ALA-1818
www.adph.org

Kathy Vincent, Staff Assistant
Donald E Williamson, Administrator
Provides professional services for the improvement and protection of the public's health through disease prevention and the assurance of public health services to resident and transient populations of the state regardless of social circumstances or the ability to pay.

3250 Alabama Department of Rehabilitation Services
602 S. Lawrence St.
Montgomery, AL 36104
334-293-7500
800-441-7607
FAX: 334-293-7383
TTY: 800-499-1816
www.rehab.alabama.gov

Michelle K. Glaze, District 1, Mobile
Jimmy Varnado, District 2, Montgomery
Eddie Williams, District 5, Hunstville
To enable Alabama's children and adults with disabilities to achieve their maximum potential.

3251 Alabama Department of Senior Services
201 Monroe Street
RSA Tower Suite 350
Montgomery, AL 36140
334-242-5743
877-425-2243
FAX: 334-242-5594
Ageline@adss.alabama.gov

Irene Collins, Executive Director
Thomas Ray Edwards, Board Chairman
Dr. Horace Patterson, Vice-Chair
The mission of the Alabama Department of Senior Services is to promote the independence and dignity of those we serve through a comprehensive and coordinated system of quality services

3252 Alabama Disabilities Advocacy Program
University of Alabama
P.O.Box 870395
Tuscaloosa, AL 35487-0395
205-348-4928
800-826-1675
FAX: 205-348-3909
adap@adap.ua.edu

Anita Davidson, Legal Assistant
Janet Owens, Accounting Specialist
James Tucker, Director
The federally mandate statewide protection and advocacy system serving eligible individuals with disabilities in Alabama. ADAP has five program components: Protection and Advocacy for persons with developmental disabilities (PADD), Protection and Advocacy for Individuals with Mental Illness (PAIMT), Protection and Advocacy of Individual Rights (PAIR), Protection and Advocacy for Assistive Technology (PAAT) and Protection & Advocacy For Beneficiaries of Social Security (PABSS).

3253 Alabama Division of Rehabilitation and Crippled Children
602 S Lawrence Street
Montgomery, AL 36104
334-293-7500
800-441-7607
FAX: 334-293-7383
www.rehab.state.al.us

Cary F Boswell, Commissioner
Steven Kayes, Board Member
Jimmie Varnado, Board Member

3254 Alabama Governor's Committee on Employment of Persons with Disabilities
602 S. Lawrence St.
Montgomery, AL 36104
334-293-7500
800-441-7609
FAX: 334-293-7383
TTY: 800-499-1816
www.rehab.alabama.gov

Jane E. Burdeshaw, Commissioner
The Alabama Governor's Committee on Employment of People with Disabilities (AGCEPD) is a program of the Alabama Department of Rehabilitation Services (ADRS).

3255 Alabama State Department of Human Resources
Childcare Services Division
50 North Ripley Street
Montgomery, AL 36130
334-242-1310
FAX: 334-353-1115
barry.spear@dhr.alabama.gov
www.dhr.state.al.us

Nancy T. Buckner, Commissioner
Nancy Jinright, Chief of Staff/Ethics Officer
John Hardy, Communications

Partners with communities to promtoe family stability and provide for the safety and self-sufficiency of vulnerable Alabamians.

3256 Client Assistance Program: Alabama
400 South Union Street
Suite 465
Montgomery, AL 36104   334-263-2749
800-288-3231
FAX: 334-230-9765
rachel.hughes@rehab.alabama.gov
www.sacap.alabama.gov

Rachel Hughes, Director/Advocate

3257 Disability Determination Service: Birmingham
P.O.Box 830300
Birmingham, AL 35283-0300   205-989-2100
800-292-8106
FAX: 205-989-2295
ssa.gov

Tommy Warren, Executive Director
Janet Cox, Owner

3258 Social Security: Mobile Disability Determination Services
PO Box 2371
Mobile, AL 36652-2371   251-433-2820
800-292-6743
FAX: 251-436-0599
www.ssa.gov

Tommy Warren, Executive Director
Jack Miller, Office Manager

3259 South Central Alabama Mental Health (SCAMHC)
19815 Bay Branch Rd.
Andalusia, AL 36420   334-222-2523
877-530-0002
www.scamhc.org

Quasi-governmental organization established by local government entities, providing a range of services to approximately 4,500 mentally ill, substance abuse, and developmentally disabled individuals in Butler, Coffee, Covington and Crenshaw Counties.

3260 Workers Compensation Board Alabama
649 Monroe Street
Montgomery, AL 36131   334-242-2868
800-528-5166
FAX: 334-353-8262
webmaster@labor.alabama.gov
labor.alabama.gov/wc

Charles DeLamar, Director
Al Pelham, Supervisor
Sandy Hallmark, Supervisor
The Workers' Compensation Division is responsible for the administration of the Alabama Workers' Compensation Law to ensure proper payment of benefits to employees injured on the job and encourage safety in the work place

Alaska

3261 ATLA
2217 E Tudor Rd
Ste 4
Anchorage, AK 99507-1068   907-563-2599
800-723-2852
FAX: 907-563-0699
www.atla.biz

Kathy Privratsky, Executive Director
Mystie Rail, Commissioner
Margaret Cisco, AT Specialist
Assistive Technology sales and services. ATLA is Alaska's only assistive technology resource center.

3262 Alaska Commission on Aging
150 Third Street #103
PO Box 110693
Juneau, AK 99811- 0693   907-465-3250
FAX: 907-465-1398
dhss.alaska.gov/acoa

Mary Shields, Chair
Rolf Numme, Vice Chair
Denise Daniello, Executive Director
Works to promote and protect the health and well-being of Alaskans.

3263 Alaska Department of Handicapped Children
Ste 314
1231 Gambell St
Anchorage, AK 99501-4664   907-346-1995
Gregory Lee, CEO

3264 Alaska Division of Vocational Rehabilitation:
801 W. 10th Street,
Suite A
Juneau, AK 99801-1878   907-465-2814
800-478-2815
FAX: 907-465-2856
dawn.duval@alaska.gov
labor.alaska.gov

Dianne Blummer, Commissioner
David G Stone, Deputy commissioner
John Cannon, Director
Provides comprehensive services to people with disabilities to assist in achieving an employment outcome.

3265 Client Assistance Program: Alaska
2900 Boniface Pkwy
Ste 100
Anchorage, AK 99504-3195   907-333-2211
800-478-0047
FAX: 907-333-1186
www.icdri.org/legal/AlaskaCAP.htm

Pam Stratton, Executive Director
We provide informatory referral to other programs in Alaska that are funded under the Rehabilitation Act of 1973 as amended; Individual assistance or advocacy, if an individual with disability has applied for or received services from an agency funded under the Rehabilitation Act and has concerns or questions we will work with them to help resolve their concerns with the agency.

3266 Department Of Health & Social Services - Division Of Behaviorial Health
350 Main Street
Suite 214
Juneau, AK 99801-1149   907-465-3370
800-465-4828
FAX: 907-465-2668
www.alaska.gov

Albert E. Wall, Director
Stacy Toner, Division Operations Manager
Liz Clement, Program Coordinator
The division plans for and provides appropriate prevention, treatment and support for families impacted by mental disorders or developmental disabilities while maximizing self-determination. Community based services are provided by grantees. Inpatient services are provided in two division operated facilities.

3267 Governor's Committee on Employment and Rehabilitation of People with Disabilities
Division of Vocational Rehabilitation (DVR)
801 W 10th Street
Suite A
Juneau, AK 99801-1878   907-465-2814
800-478-2815
FAX: 907-465-2815
dawn.duval@alaska.gov
www.labor.state.ak.us/dvr

Cheryl Walsh, Executive Director
Carries on a continuing program to promote the employment and rehabilitation of citizens with disabilities in the State of Alaska. Advocates for a comprehensive statewide system for access to assistive technology. Obtains and maintains cooperation with public and private groups and individuals in this field.

3268 Governor's Council on Disabilities and Special Education
3601 C Street
Suite 740
Anchorage, AK 99524-0249   907-269-8990
                                  888-269-8990
                             FAX: 907-269-8995
                             GCDSE@alaska.gov
                             www.hss.state.ak.us/gcdse/
Patrick Reinhart, Executive Director
Rich Sanders, Planner III
Britteny M Howell, M.A., ABD, Research Analyst III
The Governor's Council on Disabilities & Special Education was created to meet Alaska's diverse needs.

3269 Protection & Advocacy System: Alaska
Disability Law Center of Alaska
3330 Arctic Blvd
Ste 103
Anchorage, AK 99503-4580   907-565-1002
                                  800-478-1234
                             FAX: 907-565-1000
                             akpa@dlcak.org
Deborah Smith, President
James M Shine Sr
Deals with rights of the disabled. Works in conjunction with agencies, law offices and family members.

3270 Protection & Advocacy for Persons with Developmental Disabilities: Alaska
Advocacy Services of Alaska
Ste 101
615 E 82nd Ave
Anchorage, AK 99518-3100   907-222-2652
                                  866-275-7273
                             FAX: 907-677-8777
                             TTY: 866-232-4525
Greg Schomaker, Manager

3271 Workers Compensation Division
Department of Labor & Workforce Development
PO Box 115512
Juneau, AK 99811-5512   907-465-2790
                             FAX: 907-465-2797
                             workerscomp@alaska.gov
                             www.labor.state.ak.us/wc
Clark Bishop, Commissioner
Trena Heikes, Division Director
Michael Monagle, Director
The Division of Workers' Compensation is the agency charged with the administration of the Alaska Workers' Compensation Act (Act). The Act provides for the payment by employers or their insurance carriers of medical, disability and reemployment benefits to injured workers

Arizona

3272 Arizona Department of Economic Security
1717 W Jefferson
Phoenix, AZ 85007   602-542-4791
                             www.azdes.gov
Michael Trailor, Director
The Department of Economic Security is a human service agency providing services in six areas: Aging and Community Services, Benefits and Medical Eligibility, Child Support Enforcement, Children and Family Services, Developmental Disabilities and Employment and Rehabilitation Services.

3273 Arizona Department of Health Services
150 North 18th Avenue
Ste 330
Phoenix, AZ 85007-3243   602-542-1025
                             FAX: 602-542-0883
                             www.azdhs.gov
Will Humble, Director
Neal Young, Director
Lynne Smith, Chief Exeuctive Officer

The mission of Children's Rehabilitative Services is to improve the quality of life for children by providing family-centered medical treatment, rehabilitation, and related support services to enrolled individuals who have certain medical, handicapping, or potentially handicapping conditions.

3274 Arizona Division of Aging and Adult Services
1789 West Jefferson Street
Site Code 950A
Phoenix, AZ 85007-3202   602-542-4446
                             FAX: 602-542-6655
                             www.azdes.gov
Rex Critchfield, Manager
Neal Young, Director
Lynne Smith, Chief Executive Officer
The Division supports at-risk Arizonans to meet their basic needs and to live safely, with dignity and independence.

3275 Arizona Rehabilitation State Services for the Blind and Visually Impaired
4620 N 16th St, B-106
Ste 100
Phoenix, AZ 85016-5121   602-266-9579
                             FAX: 602-264-7819
                             www.azdes.gov
Paul Howell, Vocational Rehab Supervisor
Suzanne Sayre f, Rehab Counselor for Blind
Offers clients a conservation program, eye examinations, treatments, counseling, social work, psychological testing and evaluation, professional training, computer training and more for the visually impaired. The staff includes 56 full time employees.

3276 Developmental Disability Council: Arizona
2828 N Country Club Rd
Ste 100
Tucson, AZ 85716-3202   602-542-4049
                                  800-889-5893
                             FAX: 602-542-5320
                             www.cpes.com
David A Berns, Manager
Nebal Chavez, Executive Director
Susan Madison, Manager
The mission of the GovernorOs Council on Developmental Disabilities is to bring together persons with disabilities representing Arizona cultural diversity and their families and other community members, to protect rights, eliminate barriers, and jointly promote equal opportunities

3277 Governor's Council on Developmental Disabilities
1700 West Wasington Street
Suite 420
Phoenix, AZ 85007   520-325-9688
                                  877-665-3176
                             FAX: 520-325-3561
                             lclausen@azdes.gov
                             azgovernor.gov/DDPC/
Larry Clausen, Executive Director
Shelly Adams, Executive Secretary
The purpose of the council is to advocate for and assure that individuals with developmental disabilities and their families participate in the design of and have access to culturally competent services, supports and provides opportunities to become integrated and included in the community.

3278 International Dyslexia Association: Arizona Branch
Meredith Puls AZ-IDA
985 W. Silver Spring Place
Oro Valley, AZ 85755-6548   480-941-0308
                             arizona.ida@gmail.com
Meredith Puls, President
Rebekah Dyer, Vice President
Melissa A. L. Pallister, Treasurer
Provides free information and referral services for diagnosis and tutoring for parents, educators, physicians, and individuals with dyslexia. Membership includes yearly journal and quarterly newsletter, and Pennsylvania newsletter; discounts to conferences and events.

3279 Protection & Advocacy for Persons with Disabilities: Arizona

Arizona Center for Disability Law
5025 E Washington St
Suite 202
Phoenix, AZ 85034

602-274-6287
800-927-2260
FAX: 602-274-6779
TTY: 602-274-6287
center@azdisabilitylaw.org
www.azdisabilitylaw.org

Anthony DiRienzi, President
Art Gode, Vice President
J. J. Rico, Executive Director

The Center provides disability-related legal information and advice to individuals who need their services and assistance. In addition to limited legal representation, their goal is to provide efficient, streamlined services to educate people with disabilities and their support on how to enforce their legal rights through self-advocacy. Guides and documents are available online by selecting Self-Advocacy Materials button on the homepage.

3280 Social Security: Phoenix Disability Determination Services

Social Security Admission
4000 North Central Avenue
Suite 1800
Phoenix, AZ 85714

520-638-2000
800-772-1213
TTY:800-325-0778
www.ssa.gov

The Social Security Administration functions as the principal agency of the United States federal government that administers Social Security, or more specifically, the federal Old-Age, Survivors, and Disability Insurance (OASDI) program. The OASDI pays retirement, disability, and survivorsO benefits to qualifying individuals.

3281 Social Security: Tucson Disability Determination Services

4710 South Palo Verde Road
Tucson, AZ 85714-2030

520-638-2000
800-772-1213
TTY:800-325-0778
www.ssa.gov

The Social Security Administration functions as the principal agency of the United States federal government that administers Social Security, or more specifically, the federal Old-Age, Survivors, and Disability Insurance (OASDI) program. The OASDI pays retirement, disability, and survivorsO benefits to qualifying individuals.

Arkansas

3282 Arkansas Assistive Technology Projects

Increasing Capabilities Access
900 W.7th Street
Little Rock, AR 72201-4538

501-666-8868
800-828-2799
FAX: 501-666-5319
info@ar-ican.org

Eddie Schmeckenbecher, Supervisor
Essie Hardin, Secretary
Bryan Ayres, Advisory Counsel

A consumer responsive, statewide program promoting assistive technology devices and sources for persons of all ages with all disabilities. Referral and information services provide information about devices, where to obtain them and their cost.

3283 Arkansas Division of Aging & Adult Services

Department of Human Services
PO Box 1437
Slot-S-530
Little Rock, AR 72203-1437

501-682-2441
FAX: 501-682-8155
aging.services@arkansas.gov
www.state.ar.us/dhs/aging

Craig Cloud, Director
Stephenie Blocker, Assistant Director
Brad Nye, Assistant Director

The division provides services geared for adults and the elderly including supervised living, home delivered meals, adult day care, senior centers, personal care, household chores, and adult protective services.

3284 Arkansas Division of Developmental Disabilities Services

Donaghey Plaza
PO Box 1437
Little Rock, AR 72203-1437

501-682-1001
FAX: 501-682-8820

Charlie Green, Manager

State agency to assist persons with developmental disabilities and their family in obtaining appropriate assistance and services.

3285 Arkansas Division of Services for the Blind

Department Of Health and Human Services
700 Main St
Little Rock, AR 72203-4608

501-682-5463
800-960-9270
FAX: 501-682-0366
TTY: 800-285-1131
humanservices.arkansas.gov/dsb

Terry Sheeler, Chairman
Dickie Walker, Vice Chairman
Sandy Edwards, Secretary

State program which offers services in the areas of health, counseling, social work, self help and education for the visually and multihandicapped. The staff includes 4 full time and 13 part time members including mobility specialists and rehabilitation teachers.

3286 Arkansas Governor's Developmental Disabilities Council

5800 West 10th Street
Suite 805
Little Rock, AR 72204- 1763

501-661-2589
855-627-7580
FAX: 501-661-2399
ddcouncil.org

Regina Wilson, Executive Director
Teresa Sandar, Family Services Coordinator
Lee Russell, Information Oficer

A federally-funded state agency established to bring the perspective of individuals with developmental disabilities and his or her family or natural support system to policy makers and make improvements to the service system.

3287 Baptist Health Rehabilitation Institute

Baptist Heath
9601 Baptist Health Dr.
Little Rock, AR 72205-7299

501-202-1839
888-BAP-TIST
FAX: 501-202-7352
www.baptist-health.com

Ellen Callaway, Director, Rehabilition Therapy

Acute rehab facility serving patients with ortho, spinal cord injury, brain injury, CVA, arthritis, cardiac and generalized weakness; JCAHO and CARF accredited; 17 outpatient therapy centers throughout central Arkansas.

3288 Children's Medical Services

P.O.Box 1437
Little Rock, AR 72203-1437

501-682-8207
800-482-5850
FAX: 501-682-8247
www.cms-kids.com

Nancy Holder, Program Director
Iris Fehr, Nursing Director

A collection of programs for eligible children with special needs. Each one of our programs and services are family-centered and designed to help children with a variety of conditions and needs.

3289 President's Committee on People with Disabilities: Arkansas
7th & Main St
Little Rock, AR 72203

3290 Social Security: Arkansas Disability Determination Services
701 Pulaski Street
Little Rock, AR 72201-3990

501-682-3030
800-772-1213
FAX: 501-682-7553
www.socialsecurity.gov

Arthur Boutiette, COO

California

3291 California Department of Aging
1300 National Drive
Suite 200
Sacramento, CA 95834-1992

916-419-7500
FAX: 916-928-2267
TTY:800-735-2929
webmaster@aging.ca.gov
aging.ca.gov

Lora Connoly, Director
Diane Paulsen, Chief Deputy Director
Anna Esparza, Executive Assistant
The Department contracts with the network of Area Agencies on Aging, who directly manage a wide array of federal and state-funded services that help older adults find employment; support older and disabled individuals to live as independently as possible in the community; promote healthy aging and community involvement; and assist family members in their vital care giving role

3292 California Department of Handicapped Children
714 P Street
Rm 323
Sacramento, CA 95814-6401
916-445-4171
Maridee Gregory
Diana Bonta, Chief Executive Officer

3293 California Department of Rehabilitation
721 Capitol Mall
Sacramento, CA 95814-3510

916-324-1313
800-952-5544
TTY:916-558-5807
externalaffairs@dor.ca.gov

Joe Xavier, Director
David Supkofl, Manager
Assists people with disabilities, particularly those with severe disabilities, in obtaining and retaining meaningful employment and living independently in their communities. The department develops, purchases, provides and advocates for programs and services in vocational rehabilitation, habilitation and independent living with a priority on serving persons with all disabilities, especially those with the most severe disabilities.

3294 California Governor's Committee on Employment of People with Disabilities
Employment Development Department
800 Capitol Mall
PO Box 826880
Sacramento, CA 94280-0001

916-654-8055
800-695-0350
FAX: 916-654-9821
TTY: 916-654-9820
www.edd.ca.gov

Charlie Kaplan, Staff Director
GCEPD works to eliminate the barriers that preclude equal consideration for employment opportunities for people with disabilities. The Governor's Committee is responsible for providing leadership to increase the numbers of people with disabilities in the California workforce.

3295 California Protection & Advocacy: (PAI) A Nonprofit Organization
Protection and Advocacy (PA I)
1831 K Street
Sacramento, CA 95811-4114

916-504-5800
800-776-5746
FAX: 916-504-5802
SERVICES@DISABILITYRIGHTSCA.ORG
www.disabilityrightsca.org

Catherine Blakemore, Executive Director
Andrew Mudryk, Deputy Director
Alan Gildestein, Managing Attorney
Advancing the human and legal rights of people with disabilities.

3296 California State Council on Developmental Disabilities
1507 21st Street
Suite 210
Sacramento, CA 95811-5297

916-322-8481
866-802-0514
FAX: 916-443-4957
council@scdd.ca.gov
www.scdd.ca.gov

April Lopez, Chairperson
Jenny Ning Yang, Interim Vice-Chairperson
Tammy Eudy, Office Assistant
The State Council on Developmental Disabilities (SCDD) is established by state and federal law as an independent state agency to ensure that people with developmental disabilities and their families receive the services and supports they need.

3297 Client Assistance Program: California
CA Health and Human Services Agency Dept of Rehab
721 Capitol Mall
PO Box 944222
Sacramento, CA 95814

916-324-1313
800-952-5544
FAX: 916-558-5391
TTY:916- 558-580
capinfo@dor.ca.gov
www.dor.ca.gov

Tony P Sauer, Director
We have a three-pronged mission to provide services and advocacy that assist people with disabilities to live independently, become employed and have equality in the communities in which they live and work.

3298 International Dyslexia Association: Central California Branch
4594 E Michigan Ave
Fresno, CA 93703-1556

559-251-9385
800-222-3123
FAX: 599-252-1216
info@dyslexiaida.org
dyslexiaida.org

Joy Moody, President
Provides free information and referral services for diagnosis and tutoring for parents, educators, physicians, and individuals with dyslexia. Membership includes yearly journal and quarterly newsletter, and Pennsylvania newsletter; discounts to conferences and events.

3299 Long Beach Department of Health and Human Services
2525 Grand Avenue
Long Beach, CA 90815-1765

562-570-4000
FAX: 562-570-4049
www.longbeach.gov/health/

Ron Arias, Executive Director
Michael Johnson, Manager
The Long Beach Department of Health and Human Services (Health Department) has been improving the health of the Long Beach community for over a century.

3300 Los Angeles County Department of Health Services
313 N Figueroa Street
Los Angeles, CA 90012-2602

213-240-8101
800-427-8700
FAX: 213-250-4013

Mitchell H Katz, MD, Director
Hal F. Yee, Jr., M.D., Ph.D., Chief Medical Officer
Allan Wecker, Chief Financial Officer

Los Angeles County Department of Health Services is one of the US's largest publicly supported health systems. The system is the main provider of health care for the area's poor and uninsured. It provides general medical and surgical care and is affiliated with the medical school at USC. The system also manages the Emergency Medical Services (EMS) Agency and the Community Health Plan HMO, a low-cost managed care plan for members of Medicaid and other state-funded programs.

3301 Social Security: California Disability Determination Services
3164 Garrity Way
Richmond, CA 94806-1983   800-772-1213
TTY:800-325-0778
www.ssa.gov
Sally Keen, San Francisco Regional PDF Coord

3302 Social Security: Fresno Disability Determination Services
Social Security
1052 C St
Fresno, CA 93706-3245   559-487-5391
800-772-1213
FAX: 510-970-2947
TTY: 800-325-0778
www.ssa.gov
Sally Keen, Regional PDF Coordinator

3303 Social Security: Oakland Disability Determination Services
P.O. Box 24225
Oakland, CA 94623-1225   510-622-3506
800-772-1213
TTY:800-325-0778
www.ssa.gov

3304 Social Security: Sacramento Disability Determination Services
P.O. Box 997121
Suite A
Sacramento, CA 95899-7121   916-515-4400
800-772-1213
FAX: 916-263-5310
TTY: 916-381-9445
ssa.gov

3305 Social Security: San Diego Disability Determination Services
P.O. Box 85326
San Diego, CA 92186-5326   619-278-4300
800-772-1213
FAX: 619-278-4303
TTY: 800-325-0778
www.ssa.gov

Colorado

3306 Colorado Department of Aging & Adult Services
1575 Sherman St
10th Floor
Denver, CO 80203-1702   303-866-5700
FAX: 303-620-2696
cdhs.communications@state.co.us
Reggie Bicha, Executive Director
A department providing services to the elderly.

3307 Colorado Developmental Disabilities Council
1120 Lincoln
Suite 706
Denver, CO 80203   720-941-0176
FAX: 720-941-8490
cddpc.email@state.co.us
coddc.org
Katherine Carol, Chairperson
Irene Aguilar, Colorado Senate
Marcia Tewell, Executive Director
The mission is to advocate in collaboration with and on behalf of people with developmental disabilities for the establishment and

implementation of public policy which will further their independence, productivity and integration.

3308 Colorado Division of Mental Health
3824 W. Princeton Circle
Denver, CO 80236-3111   303-866-7400
FAX: 303-866-7428
colorado.gov
Patrick K. Fox, Director
Administration of public health program

3309 Colorado Health Care Program for Children with Special Needs
4300 Cherry Creek Drive south
Denver, CO 80246-1530   303-692-2370
800-886-7689
FAX: 303-753-9249
cdphe.psdrequests@state.co.us
www.colorado.gov/cdphe/hcp
Christopher Stanley, Board member
Angie Goodger, HCP Consultant
Kelsey Minor, HCP Consultant
Provides information and state aid to children with disabilities.

3310 Division of Workers' Compensation Dapartment of Labor & Employment
633 17th Street
Suite 201
Denver, CO 80202-3660   303-318-8700
800-388-5515
888-390-7936
FAX: 303-575-8882
cdle_workers_compensation@state.co.us
www.colorado.gov/cdle
Ellen Golombek, Executive Director
Infomation regarding Division Rules and procedures for Claimants, Employers, Adjusters, and parties to claim.

3311 Eastern Colorado Services for the Disabled
P. O. Box 1682
617 South 10th Avenue
Sterling, CO 80751-3168   970-522-7121
FAX: 970-522-1173
rhonda@ecsdd.org
www.easterncoloradoservices.org
Rhonda Roth, Executive Director
Traci Schrade, Finance Director
Melissa Dassaro, Case Management Director
Case coordination, infant stimulation, family support, residential and vocational programs.

3312 International Dyslexia Association: Rocky Mountain Branch
740 Yale Rd.
Boulder, CO 80305-5010   303-721-9425
855-5ID- RMB
FAX: 303-721-9425
ida_rmb@yahoo.com
www.dyslexia-rmbida.org
Karen Leopold, President
Lynn Kuhn, Secretary
Yona Sammartino, Administrative Director
Provides free information and referral services for diagnosis and tutoring for parents, educators, physicians, and individuals with dyslexia. Membership includes yearly journal and quarterly newsletter, and Pennsylvania newsletter; discounts to conferences and events.

3313 Legal Center for People with Disabilities & Older People
455 Sherman St
Ste 130
Denver, CO 80203-4403   303-722-0300
800-288-1376
FAX: 303-722-0720
TTY: 303-722-3619
John R. Posthumus, President
Stephen P. Rickles, Vice President
Nancy Tucker, Secretary
Uses the legal system to protect and promote the rights of people with disabilities and older people in Colorado through direct legal representation, advocacy, education and legislative analysis.

The Legal Center is Colorado's Protection and Advocacy System. Call for a free publications and products list.

Connecticut

3314 Connecticut Board of Education and Servicefor the Blind
184 Windsor Avenue
Windsor, CT 06095-4536

860-602-4000
800-842-4510
FAX: 860-602-4020
TTY: 860-602-4221
brian.sigman@CT.GOV
www.ct.gov/besb/site/default.asp

Amy Porter, Commissioner
Offers rehabilitative services and information for persons with legal blindness and childrenwhonare visually impaired that are residents of Connecticut.

3315 Connecticut Commission on Aging
210 Capitol Avenue
Hartford, CT 06106

860-240-5200
FAX: 860-240-5204

Julia Evans Starr, Executive Director
Deborah Migneault, Senior Policy Analyst
Alyssa Norwood, Project Manager
Advocates on beha;f of elderly persons in Connecticut by regularly monitoring their status, assessing the impact of current and propsed initiatives, and conducting activities which promote the interests of these individuals and report to the Governor and the Legislature.

3316 Connecticut Department of Children and Youth Services
505 Hudson Street
Hartford, CT 06106

860-550-6300
FAX: 860-724-2001
Commissioner.dcf@ct.gov
www.ct.gov

Gary Scappini, Manager
Bruce Douglas, Executive Director

3317 Connecticut Developmental Disabilities Council
263 Farmington Avenue
Farmington, CT 6030

860-679-1561
800-653-1134
FAX: 860-679-1571
TTY: 860-679-1502
ctkasa.org

Ed Preneta, Executive Director
Kids As Self Advocates (KASA) is a national grassroots network that helps youth with special needs and their friends become self-advocates, helps other people in the community understand what it's like to live with special health care needs.

3318 Connecticut Office of Protection and Advocacy for Persons with Disabilities
60B Weston Street
Suite B
Hartford, CT 06120-1551

860-297-4300
800-842-7303
FAX: 860-566-8714
TTY: 860-297-4320
www.ct.gov/opapd

Craig B Henrici, Executive Director
Alexandria Bode, Board Member
Thomas Behrendt, Board Member
Provides information, referrals, advocacy assistance & limited legal services to people with disabilities in the state of Connecticut whose civil rights have been violated or who are experiencing the difficulty securing relevant support services. P & A supports the development of community advocacy groups by providing training & technical assistance. P & A is responsible for investigating abuse & neglect of all individuals with intellectual disability ages 18-59.

3319 Social Security: Hartford Area Office
960 Main Street
2nd Floor
Hartford, CT 06103-1228

877-619-2851
800-772-1213
FAX: 860-566-1795
TTY: 860-525-4967
www.ssa.gov

Jan Gilbert, Professional Relations Coord.

Delaware

3320 Delaware Assistive Technology Initiative(DATI)
461 Wyoming Road
Newark, DE 19716-0269

302-831-0354
FAX: 302-831-4690
TTY:800-870-3284
dati@asel.udel.edu
www.dati.org

Beth Mineo, Project Director
Joann McCafferty, Staff Assistant
The Delaware Assistive Technology Initiative (DATI) connects Delawareans who have disabilities with the tools they need in order to learn, work, play and participate in community life safely and independently. DATI services include: Equipment demonstration centers in each county; no-cost, short-term equipment loans that let you try before you buy; Equipment Exchange Program; AT workshops and other training sessions; advocacy for improved AT access policies and funing and several more.

3321 Delaware Client Assistance Program
United Cerebral Palsy Association
254 E Camden Wyoming Ave
Camden, DE 19934-1303

302-698-9336
800-640-9336
FAX: 302-698-9338
icdri.org/legal/DelawareCAP.htm

Melissa Shahan, Executive Director
Provides advocacy services for persons involved with programs covered under the Rehabilitation Act of 1973 as amended, information and referrals on ADA, Title I.

3322 Delaware Department of Health and Social Services
Administration Building D HS S Campus
1901 N Du pont Highway
Main Building
New Castle, DE 19720-1160

302-255-9040
800-464-4357
FAX: 302-255-4429
TTY: 302-744-4556
dhssinfo@state.de.us
www.dhss.delaware.gov

Rita Landgraf, Cabinet Secretary
Henry Smith III, Deputy secretary
Provides most of the human services available through Delaware State Government, including Medicaid, the Children's Health Insurance Program, food stamps, welfare-to-work, vaccines for children, child support enforcement, public health programs, and general services for the aging. Also for individuals with developmental and physical disabilities, visual impairments, mental illness and other vulnerable populations.

3323 Delaware Department of Public Instructing
Townsend Building
401 Federal Street
Dover, DE 19901- 1402

302-735-4000
800-433-5292
FAX: 302-739-4654
deeds@doe.k12.de.us
www.doe.k12.de.us

Mark T. Murphy, Secretary of Education
David J. Blowman, Deputy Secretary
Mary Kate McLaughlin, Chief of Staff
A publicly funded, state agency that gives information about local facilities and administers supplemental funds for visually handicapped students in local schools. It also maintains special teachers of sight conservation and braille programs for both children and adults.

3324 Delaware Developmental Disability Council
410 Federal Street 2nd Floor
Suite 2
Dover, DE 19901- 3640 302-739-3333
800-464-4357
FAX: 302-739-2015
pat.maichle@state.de.us
Barbara Monaghan, Council Chair
Patricia L. Maichle, Senior Administrator
Kristin Cosden, Social Service Administrator
Working to ensure that people with developmental disabilities enjoy the same quality of life as the rest of society.

3325 Delaware Division for the Visually Impaired
1901 North Dupont Highway
New Castle, DE 19720-1160 302-255-9800
FAX: 302-255-4441
dhssinfo@state.de.us
www.dhss.delaware.gov/dvi/
Rita Landgraf, Secretary
Henry Smith, Deputy Secretary
Betsy Deldeo, Office Manager
State agency serving the visually impaired persons from birth, with or without other handicaps. Services offered include vocational rehabilitation, independent living, orientation and mobility, technology assessment, transition from school to work.

3326 Delaware Protection & Advocacy for Persons with Disabilities
Arc of Delaware
144 E Market St
Georgetown, DE 19947-1411 302-856-6019
FAX: 302-856-6133
Becky Allen, Executive Director

3327 Delaware Workers Compensation Board
Industrial Accident Board de dept
4425 North Market Street
Wilmington, DE 19802-1307 302-761-8085
FAX: 302-761-6601
www.delawareworks.com
James Cagle, Manager
The Office of Workers' Compensation administers and enforces state laws, rules and regulations regarding industrial accidents and illnesses.

3328 Social Security: Wilmington Disability Determination
U S Department of Health and Human Services
1528 S 16th Street
Wilmington, NC 28401-3908 866-964-6227
800-772-1213
FAX: 910-254-3444
TTY: 910-815-4695
www.socialsecurity.gov
J Allen Murphy, Founder
Vickie O'Brien, Manager

3329 The Division for the Visually Impaired
Herman M. Holloway, Sr. Campus
1901 N Dupont Hwy
New Castle, DE 19720 302-255-9800
FAX: 302-255-4441
dhssinfo@state.de.us
dhss.delaware.gov
Alan Wingrove, General Manager
Romy Mikhail, Customer Service, Quality & ISO Manager
The Division for the Visually Impaired provides educational, vocational and technical support to people with visual impairments. Some programs offered include education, employment support, guidance for living independently and using assistive devices, business enterprise programs, volunteer opporunities and more.

District of Columbia

3330 District of Columbia Department of Handicapped Children
D C General Hospital
Bldg 10
1900 Massachusetts Ave SE
Washington, DC 20003- 2542 202-541-6337
FAX: 202-675-7694
Jacqueline Mcmorris, Acting Chief
Nayab Ali, MD

3331 District of Columbia Office on Aging
500 K Street NE
Washington, DC 20002-2714 202-724-5622
FAX: 202-724-4979
TTY:202-724-8925
dcoa@dc.gov
dcoa.dc.gov
John M Thompson, Executive Director
Deborah Royster, General Counsel
Tanya Reid, Executive Assistant
Serves the District of Columbia residents 60 years of age and older. Contact the Information and Assistance Unit for more information about innovative programs and services offered by the Office.

3332 Information, Protection & Advocacy for Persons with Disabilities
IPACHI
220 I Street, N.E.
Suite 130
Washington, DC 20002 202-547-0198
FAX: 202-547-2083
jbrown@uls-dc.org
www.acf.hhs.gov/programs/add/states/pas.html
Jane Brown, Executive Director
Ronald Tyson, Information/Referral
Offers services and support for persons with disabilities in the Washington, DC area.

3333 Information, Protection and Advocacy Center for Handicapped Individuals
220 I Street, N.E.
Suite 130
Washington, DC 20002-2340 202-547-0198
FAX: 202-547-2083
jbrown@uls-dc.org
www.acf.hhs.gov/programs/add/states/pas.html
Jane Brown, Executive Director
Serves all persons with disabilities in the DC, Maryland and Virginia areas offering them legal representation and advocacy, information and referrals and several publications.

3334 International Dyslexia Association of DC
40 York Rd., 4th Floor
Baltimore, MD 21204-1016 410-296-0232
800-222-3123
FAX: 410-321-5069
info@dyslexiaida.org
dyslexiaida.org
Ruth R Tifford LCSW, President
Provides free information and referral services for diagnosis and tutoring for parents, educators, physicians, and individuals with dyslexia. Membership includes yearly journal and quarterly newsletter, and Pennsylvania newsletter; discounts to conferences and events.

3335 Public Technology Institute
660 North Capitol St. NW
Suite 400
Washington, DC 20001 202-626-2400
info@pti.org
www.pti.org
Alan R. Shark, Executive Director
Leonard Scott, Director, Public Safety Technology Programs
Susan Cable, Program Manager, Citizen-Engaged Communities
Supports local government executives and elected officials through research, education, consulting services, and recogni-

tion programs. Research includes how technology can better benefit people with disabilities.
28 pages

3336   Wage and Hour Division of the Employment Standards Administration
US Department of Labor
200 Constitution Ave NW
Washington, DC 20210-1   202-693-5000
                                      866-487-2365
                                      FAX: 202-219-8822
                                      TTY: 877-889-5627
                                      webmaster@dol.gov
                                      www.dol.gov

Hilda Solis, Secretary of Labor
Seth Harris, Deputy Secretary
Elizabeth Kim, Executive Secretariat Director
Administers regulations governing the employment of individuals with disabilities in sheltered workshops and the disabled workers industries.

3337   Washington Hearing and Speech Society
2150 N 107th St, Suite 205
Seattle, WA 98133-2633   206-209-5271
                                      FAX: 206-367-8777
                                      office@wslha.org
                                      www.wslha.org

Paul Diez, President
Judith Bernier, Secretary
Julie Leonardo, Treasurer
Offers individuals with hearing or speech impairments, in the DC area, speech, reading classes, audiological services and new aids.

3338   Well Mind Association of Greater Washington
18606 New Hampshire Ave
Ashton, MD 20861-9789   301-774-6617
                                      FAX: 301-946-1402
Holistic mental health information and publications, public lectures in the Washington D.C. area, and nationwide referrals.

3339   Workers Compensation Board: District of Columbia
4058 Minnesota Avenue, NE,
Washington, DC 20019-5626   202-724-7000
                                      202-698-4817
                                      FAX: 202-673-6993
                                      does@dc.gov

Deborah A Carroll, Director
The Workers' Compensation Program processes claims and monitors the payment of benefits to injured private-sector employees in the District of Columbia

---

Florida

3340   ARC Gateway
3932 North 10th Avenue
Pensacola, FL 32503-2807   850-434-2638
                                      FAX: 850-438-2180
                                      info@arc-gateway.org
                                      www.arc-gateway.org

Peter Mougey, President
Patricia Young, Vice President
Lynn Erickson, Secretary
ARC Gateway is a non-profit organization that serves children who have or are at risk of developmental disabilities as well as adults with developmental disabilitie

3341   Assistive Technology Educational Network of Florida
1207 S Mellonville Avenue
Sanford, FL 32771-2240   800-558-6580
                                      FAX: 407-320-2379
                                      Diane_Penn@scps.k12.fl.us
                          www.icdri.org/Assistive%20Technology/aten.htm
Dee Wright, Executive Secretary
Diane Penn, MA, Technology Specialist
Provides state-wide information, awareness and training for students, family members, teachers and other professionals in the area of assisted technology; a quarterly newsletter and a network of specialists (Local Assistive Technology Specialists) trained by ATEN to provide support at the district level.

3342   Bureau Of Exceptional Education And Student Services
325 West Gaines Street Suite 614
Tallahassee, FL 32399   850-245-0475
                                      FAX: 850-245-0953
                                      Monica.Verra-Tirado@fldoe.org
                                      www.fldoe.org

Pam Stewart, Education Commissioner
Monica Verra Tirado, Bureau Chief
Chatherine Aponte Gray, Administrative Assistant
Provides consultative services for the establishment and operation of school programs for visually impaired students. Provides assistance for in-service teacher training through state or regional workshops or technical assistance to individual programs.

3343   Department of Health & Rehabilitative Services
1317 Winewood Blvd
Building 1
Tallahassee, FL 32399-700   850-487-1111
                                     FAX: 850-922-2993
                                     www.dcf.state.fl.us

David Wilkins, Secretary
Ramin Kouzehkanani, Deputy Secretary
John Bryant, Manager
The Florida Department of Children and Families has adopted an integrated approach to programs and services as we work to help improve the lives of individuals and families.

3344   Disability Rights Florida
2473 Care Dr.
Suite 200
Tallahassee, FL 32308   850-488-9071
                                     800-342-0823
                                     FAX: 850-488-8640
                                     TTY: 800-346-4127
                                     www.disabilityrightsflorida.org

Peter Sleasman, Executive Director
Ann Siegel, Legal Director
Cherie E. Hall, Director, Operations
A federally mandated Protection & Advocacy (P&A) organization working to ensure the safety, well-being and success of people with disabilities.
1977

3345   Division of Workers Compensation
200 East Gaines Street
Tallahassee, FL 32399-0318   850-413-3089
                                     877-693-5236
                                     FAX: 850-413-2950
                                     Tanner.Holloman@myfloridacfo.com

Tanner Holloman, Division Director
Andrew Sabolic, Assistant Director
Terry Kester, Chief Information Officer
To actively ensure the self-execution of the workers' compensation system through education and informing all stakeholders of their rights and responsibilities, leveraging data to deliver exceptional value to our customers and stakeholders, and holding parties accountable for meeting their obligations.

3346   Florida Adult Services
1317 Winewood Boulevard
Building 1, Room 202
Tallahassee, FL 32399-700   850-488-2881
                                     800-962-2873
                                     800-273-8255
                                     FAX: 850-922-4193
                                     www.myflfamilies.com

Robert Anderson, State Director
Jan Chaney, Administrative Assistant
Roy Car, Data/Systems
The Florida Department of Children and Families has adopted an integrated approach to programs and services as we work to help improve the lives of individuals and families.

3347 **Florida Department of Handicapped Children**
4030 Esplanade Way
Suite 380
Tallahassee, FL 32399-7016
850-488-4257
866-273-2273
FAX: 850-245-1075
www.apd.myflorida.com

Mike Gresham, Executive Director
John Bryant, Manager
The APD works in partnership with local communities and private providers to assist people who have developmental disabilities and their families.

3348 **Florida Department of Mental Health and Rehabilitative Services**
1317 Winewood Blvd
Building 1
Tallahassee, FL 32399-700
850-487-1111
FAX: 850-922-2993
www.dcf.state.fl.us

David Wilkins, Secretary
Ramin Kouzehkanani, Deputy Secretary

3349 **Florida Developmental Disabilities Council**
124 Marriott Drive
Suite 203
Tallahassee, FL 32301-2981
850-488-4180
800-580-7801
FAX: 850-922-6702
TTY: 888-488-863
fddc@fddc.org
fddc.org

Sylvia James Miller, Council Chair & Parent Advocate
Tricia Riccardi, Council Vice-Chair
Debra Dowds, Executive Director
To advocate and promote meaningful participation in all aspects of life for Floridians with developmental disabilities.

3350 **Florida Division of Vocational Rehabilitation**
4070 Esplanade Way
Building 1
Tallahassee, FL 32399- 7016
850-245-3399
800-451-4327
FAX: 850-245-3316
TTY: 850-488-2867
rehabworks.org

Bill Palmer, Manager
Linda Parnell, Manager
Aleisa Mckinlay, Director
State agency serving individuals with physical or mental disabilities that interfere with them keeping or maintaining employment.

3351 **International Dyslexia Association: Florida Branch**
40 York Rd., 4th Floor
Baltimore, MD 21204-3896
410-296-0232
800-222-3123
FAX: 410-321-5069
ear228@aol.com
dyslexiaida.org

Kristen Penczek, Executive Director
David Holste, Director Of Operations
Stacy Friedman, Manager of Operation
Provides free information and referral services for diagnosis and tutoring for parents, educators, physicians, and individuals with dyslexia. Membership includes yearly journal and quarterly newsletter, and Pennsylvania newsletter; discounts to conferences and events.

3352 **Social Security Administration**
2002 Old Saint Augustine Rd
Suite B12
Tallahassee, FL 32301-4861
850-942-8978
800-772-1213
FAX: 850-942-8980
ssa.gov

Carrie Tucker, Operations Supervisor
Sheila Lee, Management Support Specialist
Administers the Title II and Title XVII disability programs. To be insured for Title II benefits, applicants must have worked in covered employment for at least five of the last ten years prior to be-

coming disabled. To be eligible for Title XVII disability benefits, applicants must meet an income and resource test.

3353 **Social Security: Miami Disability Determination**
Social Security
11401 W Flagler St
Miami, FL 33174-1023
305-226-0449
800-772-1213
TTY:800-325-0778
www.ssa.gov

Robert L Meekins, Deputy General for Executive Ope

3354 **Social Security: Orlando Disability Determination**
Social Security
P.O. Box 144040
Orlando, FL 32814-2231
407-648-6673
800-342-2065
TTY:407-245-7057
www.ssa.gov

John C Massolio Jr, Founder
Neil Bush, President

3355 **Social Security: Tampa Disability Determination**
Social Security Administration
PO Box 340572
Tampa, FL 33694-572
813-878-2906
800-772-1213
www.dbsatampabay.org

John Balcomb, President
Carol Yaros, 1st Vice President
Cheryl McGhan , 2nd Vice President
The Depression and Bipolar Support Alliance Tampa Bay , is a nonprofit and all volunteer organization for individuals, family and friends of those who have been diagnosed with bipolar disorder, depression and other affective disorders.

Georgia

3356 **ADA Technical Assistance Program**
Southeast Disability & Business Technical Assist.
1419 Mayson Street NE
Atlanta, GA 30324
404-541-9001
800-949-4232
FAX: 404-541-9002
ADAsoutheast@law.syr.edu
www.sedbtac.org

Pamela Williamson, Project Director
Cheri Hofmann, Information Specialist
Cyndi Smith, Office Assistant
One of ten regional centers funded by NIDRR, to provide information and technical assistance to assist in voluntary compliance with the Americans with Disabilities Act, and accessible education-based information technology.

3357 **Division of Birth Defects and Developmental Disabilities**
1600 Clifton Road
Atlanta, GA 30333-4027
404-498-3800
800-232-4636
TTY:888-232-6348
cdcinfo@cdc.gov
www.cdc.gov

Coleen A Boyle, Director
The mission of CDC's National Center on Birth Defects and Developmental Disabilities (NCBDDD) is to promote the health of babies, children and adults and to enhance the potential for full, productive living.

3358 **Georgia Advocacy Office**
One West Court Square
Suite 625
Decatur, GA 30030
404-885-1234
800-537-2329
FAX: 404-378-0031
info@thegao.org
thegao.org

Ruby Moore, Executive Director
Crystal Rasa, Program Manager
Mona Givens, Director of Investigation

Protection and advocacy services for Georgians with disabilities.

3359 Georgia Client Assistance Program
Division of Rehabilitation Services
2 Peachtree Street NW
Suite 29-250
Atlanta, GA 30303- 3141   404-656-4507
                                 800-822-9727
                                 FAX: 404-651-6880
                                 dhs.georgia.gov/

Mark Trail, Manager
Robertiena Fletcher, Chair
Franklin G Auman, Vice Chair
Helps eligible persons with complaints, appeals and understanding available benefits under the 1992 Rehabilitation Act Amendments and Title I of the Americans with Disabilities Act. CAP investigates complaints, mediates conflict, represents complainants in appeals, provides legal services if warranted, advocates for due process, identifies and recommends solutions to system problems, advises of benefits available under the 1992 Rehab Act Amendments and Americans with Disabilities Act.

3360 Georgia Council On Developmental Disabilities
2 Peachtree St N.W.
26th Floor, Suite 246
Atlanta, GA 30303-3141   404-657-2126
                                 888-275-4233
                                 FAX: 404-657-2132
                                 TTY:404-657-2133
                                 eric.jacobson@gcdd.ga.gov
                                 www.gcdd.org

Eric E. Jacobson, Executive Director
Caitlin Childs, Organizing Director
Dottie Adams, Family/Individual Support Dir.
The Georgia Council on Developmental Disabilities collaborates with Georgia's citizens, public and private advocacy organizations and policymakers to positively influence public policies that enhance the quality of life for people with disabilities and their families. GCDD provides this through education and advocacy activities, program implementation, funding and public policy analysis and research.
Quartlery

3361 Georgia Department of Aging
2 Peachtree Street NW
33rd Floor
Atlanta, GA 30303-3142   404-657-5258
                                 866-552-4464
                                 FAX: 404-657-5285
                                 dhs.georgia.gov/

Stephen Dolinger, President
Andrea Fuller-Ruffin, Administrator
The Division of Aging Services (DAS) works to continuously improve the effectiveness and efficiency of services.

3362 Georgia Department of Handicapped Children
2600 Skyland Dr NE
Atlanta, GA 30319-3640   404-679-1625
                                 FAX: 404-679-1630

Ron Jackson, Manager
Frank Koues, Auditor

3363 Georgia Division of Mental Health, Developmental Disabilities & Addictive Diseases
Two Peachtree Drive NW
24th Floor
Atlanta, GA 30303-3142   404-657-2252
                                 800-715-4225
                                 FAX: 404-657-2310
                                 mhddad.dhr.georgia.gov

Kimberly Ryan, Board Member
David Glass, Board member
Ellice P. Martin, Board Member
MHDDAD provides treatment and support services to people with mental illnesses and addictive diseases, and support to people with developmental disabilities. MHDDAD serves people of all ages with the most severe and likely to be long-term conditions.

3364 Georgia State Board of Workers' Compensation
270 Peachtree St NW
Atlanta, GA 30303-1299   404-656-3875
                                 800-533-0682
                                 FAX: 404-657-1767
                                 sbwc.georgia.gov

Frank McKay, Chairman
Elizabeth Gobeil, Director
Delece A. Brooks, Executive Director
To provide superior access to the Georgia Workers' Compensation program for injured workers and employers in a manner that is sensitive, responsive, and effective and to insure efficient processing and swift, fair resolution of claims, while encouraging workplace safety and return to work.

3365 International Dyslexia Association: Georgia Branch
1951 Greystone Rd.
Atlanta, GA 30318   404-256-1232
                               info@idaga.org
                               www.idaga.org

Jennifer Kopp, President
jennings Miller, Vice-President
Robert Moore, Treasurer
Provides free information and referral services for diagnosis and tutoring for parents, educators, physicians, and individuals with dyslexia. Membership includes yearly journal and quarterly newsletter, and Pennsylvania newsletter; discounts to conferences and events.

3366 Social Security: Atlanta Disability Determination
401 W Peachtree St NW
Suite 2860 Flr 28
Atlanta, GA 30308-3538   800-772-1213
                                 TTY:800-325-0778
                                 www.socialsecurity.gov

3367 Social Security: Decatur Disability Determination
2853 Candler Rd
Suite 8
Decatur, GA 30034-1421   800-772-1213
                                 TTY:800-325-0778
                                 ssa.gov

Hawaii

3368 Assistive Technology Resource Centers of Hawaii
200 North Vineyard Boulevard
Suite 430
Honolulu, HI 96817-5362   808-532-7110
                                 800-645-3007
                                 FAX: 808-532-7120
                                 TTY: 808-532-7113
                                 atrc-info@atrc.org
                                 www.atrc.org

Barbara Fischlowitz-Leong, Executive Director
Jodi Asato, Deputy Director
Edna Kaahaaina, Office Manager
Provides information and referral to anyone interested in assistive technology devices and services. Operates equipment loan. Bank Provides training to consumer and professional groups including self-advocacy skills for consumers and family members. Works to ensure that schools, vocational rehabilitation agencies and health insurers provide assessments, funding and training in the use of assistive technology devices and services for their clients. Low-interest loan programs available.

3369 Diabetes Network of East Hawaii
1221 Kilauea Ave
Suite 70
Hilo, HI 96720-4264   808-935-1673
                                 FAX: 808-935-6760

Steve Fukunada, Manager

3370 Disability and Communication Access Board
1010 Richards St
Suite 118
Honolulu, HI 96813   808-586-8121
FAX: 808-586-8129
dcab@doh.hawaii.gov
hawaii.gov/health/dcab

Francine Wai, Executive Director
Bill-Wayne Nakamatsu, Parking Program Specialist
Provides ADA coordination for state & county government; reviews state & county construction documents to appropriate federal & state accessibility guidelines; credentials American sign language interpreters; coordinates parking for persons with disabilites; coordinates information & referral for consumers, parents and others seeking disability related information.

3371 Hawaii Assistive Technology Training and
200 North Vineyard Boulevard
Suite 430
Honolulu, HI 96817-5362   808-532-7110
800-645-3007
FAX: 808-532-7120
atrc-info@atrc.org
www.atrc.org

Barbara Fischlowitz-Leong, Executive Director

3372 Hawaii Department for Children With Special Needs
Department of Health
741 Sunset Avenue
Honolulu, HI 96816-2343   808-733-9070
FAX: 808-733-9068
patricia.heu@doh.hawaii.gov
health.hawaii.gov

Patricia Heu, Manager
Karen Mak, Manager
Children with Special Health Needs Branch(CSHNB) is working to assure that all children and youth with special health care needs (CSHCN) will reach optimal health, growth, and development, by improving access to a coordinated system of family-centered health care services and improving outcomes, through systems development, assessment, assurance, education, collaborative partnerships, and family support.

3373 Hawaii Department of Health, Adult Mental Health Division
P.O.Box 3378
Honolulu, HI 96801-3378   808-586-4686
FAX: 808-586-4745
The Adult Mental Health Division is one part of theHawaii State Department of Health,State of Hawaii. The Mission of the Department of Health is to protect and improve health and the environment for all people in Hawaii.

3374 Hawaii Department of Human Services
Hawaii Department of Human Serv
P.O. Box 339
Honolulu, HI 96813   808-586-4892
FAX: 808-586-4890
dhs@dhs.hawaii.gov
humanservices.hawaii.gov

Rachael Wong, Director
Pankaj Bhanot, Deputy Director
Lisa Nakao, Admin Assis. & Legislative Coor.
To provide timely, efficient and effective programs, services and benefits for the purpose of achieving the outcome of empowering Hawaii's most vulnerable people; and to expand their capacity for self-sufficiency, self-determination, independence, healthy choices, quality of life, and personal dignity.

3375 Hawaii Disability Compensation Division Department of Labor and Industrial Relations
830 Punchbowl Street
Room 209
Honolulu, HI 96813-5095   808-586-9200
FAX: 808-586-9219
dlir.director@hawaii.gov
hawaii.gov/labor

Walter Kawamura, Administrator
Clyde Imada, Workers Comp Chief
The Disability Compensation Division (DCD) administers the Workers' Compensation (WC) law, the Temporary Disability Insurance (TDI) law, and the Prepaid Health Care (PHC) law. All employers with one or more employees, whether working full-time or part-time, are directly affected.

3376 Hawaii Disability Rights Center
1132 Bishop Street
Suite 2102
Honolulu, HI 96813-3701   808-949-2922
800-882-1057
FAX: 808-949-2928
info@hawaiidisabilityrights.org
hawaiidisabilityrights.org

John Dellera, Executive Director
Ann Collins, Director Of Operations
IT IS THE POLICY OF HDRCto advocate for as many people with disabilities in the State of Hawaii, on as wide a range of disability rights issues, as our resources allow; and to resolve rights violations with the lowest feasible level of intervention; but, if necessary, to also provide full legal representation to protect the rights of people with disabilities, consistent with authorizing statutes and Center priorities.

3377 Hawaii Executive Office on Aging
250 South Hotel Street
Suite 406
Honolulu, HI 96813-2831   808-586-0100
800-468-4644
FAX: 808-586-0185
hawaii.gov/health/eoa

Noemi Pendleton, Manager
Virginia Pressler, Director
Keith Y. Yamamoto, Deputy Director
State unit on aging responsible for policy formulation, program development, planning, information dissemination, advocacy and other activities, for persons age 60 and over.

3378 Hawaii State Council on Developmental Disabilities
919 Ala Moana Blvd
Suite113
Honolulu, HI 96814-4920   808-586-8100
FAX: 808-586-7543

Waynette K Y Cabral, Executive Administrator
Joe Shacter, Planner
Debbie Miyasaka Gushiken, Community & Legislative Liaison
The mission of the council is to support people with developmental disabilities to control their own destiny and determine the quality of life they desire. The Council: engages in analysis and policy development; provides training in legislative advocacy and leadership development for individuals with disabilities and their families; demonstrates new approaches to services and supports; informs policymakers about developmental disability issues; and fosters interagency collaboration.

3379 International Dyslexia Association: Hawaii Branch
913 Alewa Dr.
Honolulu, HI 96817-1610   808-538-7007
hida@dyslexia-hawaii.org

Charles Bering, President
Deborah Knight, Vice President
Laurie Moore, Treasurer
Provides free information and referral services for diagnosis and tutoring for parents, educators, physicians, and individuals with dyslexia. Membership includes yearly journal and quarterly newsletter. Call for conference dates.

3380 Social Security: Honolulu Disability Determination
Social Security
300 Ala Moana Blvd
Honolulu, HI 96850-1   808-541-3600
800-772-1213
TTY:800-825-0778
hivrsbd@kestrok.com
www.ssa.gov

Neil Shim, Administrator

3381 State Planning Council on Developmental Disabilities
919 Ala Moana Blvd
Room 101
Honolulu, HI 96814-4920
808-586-8121
FAX: 808-586-8129
TTY:808-586-8121
dcab@doh.hawaii.gov
hawaii.gov/health/dcab

Michael Okamoto, Chairperson
Peter Fritz, Vice Chairperson
Francine Wai, Executive Director
Consists of 25 Hawaii residents appointed by the governor. The council addresses the needs of the people with developmental disabilities: specifically, develops a state plan that sets the priorities for persons with developmental disabilities.

Idaho

3382 Idaho Commission on Aging
341 W Washington
Boise, ID 83702-1
208-334-3833
800-926-2588
FAX: 208-334-3033
ICOA@aging.idaho.gov
www.idahoaging.com

Sam Haws, Administrator
Cathy Hart, State Ombudsman
Jeff Weller, Deputy Administrator
There number one priority is to provide the best possible service through this single point of entry website where people of all incomes and ages can obtain information on a full range of long-term care support programs and services.

3383 Idaho Council on Developmental Disabilities
Health and Wellfare
700 W. State Street
Suite 119
Boise, ID 83702-5868
208-334-2178
800-544-2433
FAX: 208-334-3417
info@icdd.idaho.gov
icdd.idaho.gov

Jim Baugh, Council Member
Christine Pisani, Executive Director
Tracy Warren, Program Specialist/Planner
The mission of the Idaho Council on Developmental Disabilities is to promote the capacity of people with developmental disabilities and their families to determine, access, and direct the services and/or support they need to live the lives they choose, and to build the communities ability to support their choices.

3384 Idaho Department of Handicapped Children
Statehouse
Boise, ID 83720-1
208-334-8000
Thomas Bruck, Chief
Sandy Frazier, Manager

3385 Idaho Disability Determinations Service
PO Box 21
Boise, ID 83707-0021
208-327-7333
800-626-2681
FAX: 208-327-7331
TTY: 800-377-3529
labor.idaho.gov

Roger B Madsen, Director
Rogelio Valdez, Executive Director
Under contract with the Social Security Administration, makes determinations of medical eligibility for disability benefits.

3386 Idaho Industrial Commission
P.O. Box 83720
Boise, ID 83720-0041
208-334-6000
800-950-2110
FAX: 208-334-2321
mholbrook@iic.idaho.gov
www.iic.idaho.gov

Mindy Montgomery, Manager
Beth Kilian, Commission Secretary

Free rehabilitation services to workers' who have suffered on the job injuries in Idaho. Field offices throughout the state.

3387 Idaho Mental Health Center
1720 Westgate Dr
Boise, ID 83704-7164
208-334-0808
800-926-2588
FAX: 208-334-0828

Richard Armstrong, Director
Darrell Kerby, Chairperson
Tom Stroschein, Vice Chair
The State of Idaho provides state funded and operated community based mental health care services through Regional Behavioral Health Centers (RBHC) located in each of the seven geographical regions of the state. Each RBHC provides mental health services through a system of care that is both community-based and consumer-guided.

Illinois

3388 Attorney General's Office: Disability Rights Bureau & Health Care Bureau
100 W Randolph Street
Chicago, IL 60601-3218
312-814-3000
877-305-5145
FAX: 312-793-0802
TTY: 800-964-3013
illinoisattorneygeneral.gov

Lisa Madigan, Manager
Raymond Throlkeld, Chief Health Care Bureau
Information on Illinois' Comprehensive Health Insurance Plan and architectural accessibility. Enforcement of Illinois' access law and standards and other disability rights laws. Information on initiatives such as: Opening the Courthouse Doors to People with Disabilities; the abuse, neglect or financial exploitation of people with disabilities and voter accessibility. Other information and referrals.

3389 Client Assistance Program (CAP)
Illinois State Board of Education
100 South Grand Ave. E.
Springfield, IL 62794
217-524-0695
800-641-3929
888-460-5111
FAX: 217-524-1184
dhs.cap@illinois.gov
www.dhs.state.il.us

James T. Dimas, Secretary
Francisco Alvarado, Manager
Quinetta L. Wade, Rehabilitation Services
The Client Assistance Program (CAP) helps people with disabilities receive quality Vocational Rehabilitation services by advocating for their interests and helping them identify resources, understand procedures, resolve problems, and protect their rights in the rehabilitation process, and employment.

3390 Equip for Equality
20 North Michigan Avenue
Suite 300
Chicago, IL 60602- 4861
312-341-0022
800-537-2632
FAX: 312-541-7544
TTY: 800-610-2779
contactus@equipforequality.org
equipforequality.org

Zena Naiditch, President/CEO
Barry C Taylor, Vice President
Lia Burkey, Administrative Assistant
Equip for equality is an independent, private, not-for-profit organization designated by the Governor in 1985 to implement the federally mandated Protection and Advocacy (P&A) System in Illinois. The mission of Equip for Equality is to advance the human and civil rights of children and adults with disabilities in Illinois.

3391 Equip for Equality - Carbondale Office
300 East Main St
Suite 18
Carbondale, IL 62901 618-457-7930
 800-758-0559
 FAX: 618-457-7985
 TTY: 800-610-2779
 contactus@equipforequality.org
 equipforequality.org

Zena Naiditch, President/CEO
Barry C Taylor, Vice President
Lia Burkey, Administrative Assistant
Equip for equality is an independent, private, not-for-profit organization designated by the Governor in 1985 to implement the federally mandated Protection and Advocacy (P&A) System in Illinois. The mission of Equip for Equality is to advance the human and civil rights of children and adults with disabilities in Illinois.

3392 Equip for Equality - Moline Office
1515 Fifth Ave
Suite 420
Moline, IL 61265 309-786-6868
 800-758-6869
 FAX: 309-797-8710
 TTY: 800-610-2779
 contactus@equipforequality.org
 equipforequality.org

Zena Naiditch, President/CEO
Barry C Taylor, Vice President
Lia Burkey, Administrative Assistant
Equip for equality is an independent, private, not-for-profit organization designated by the Governor in 1985 to implement the federally mandated Protection and Advocacy (P&A) System in Illinois. The mission of Equip for Equality is to advance the human and civil rights of children and adults with disabilities in Illinois.

3393 Equip for Equality - Springfield Office
1 West Old State Capitol Plaza
Suite 816
Springfield, IL 62701 217-544-0464
 800-758-0464
 FAX: 217-523-0720
 TTY: 800-610-2779
 contactus@equipforequality.org
 equipforequality.org

Zena Naiditch, President/CEO
Barry C Taylor, Vice President
Lia Burkey, Administrative Assistant
Equip for equality is an independent, private, not-for-profit organization designated by the Governor in 1985 to implement the federally mandated Protection and Advocacy (P&A) System in Illinois. The mission of Equip for Equality is to advance the human and civil rights of children and adults with disabilities in Illinois.

3394 Illinois Assistive Technology Project
1 West Old State Capitol Plaza
Suite 100
Springfield, IL 62701-1200 217-522-7985
 800-852-5110
 FAX: 217-522-8067
 TTY: 217-522-9966
 iatp@iltech.org
 iltech.org

Wilhelmina Gunther, Executive Director
Shelly Lowe, Finance/Personnel Manager
Yvonne Miller, Administrative Assistant
Directed by and for people with disabilities and their family members. As a federally mandated program, IATP strives to break down barriers and change policies that make getting and using technology difficult. IATP offers solutions to help people find what is available in products and services that will best meet their needs, where to find it, and how to get it.

3395 Illinois Council on Developmental Disability
State of Illinois Center
100 W Randolph St
16-100
Chicago, IL 60601-3218 312-814-2121
 800-843-6154
 FAX: 312-814-7441
 www2.illinois.gov

Sheila T. Romano, Executive Director
Dennis Sienko, Manager
The Illinois Council on Developmental Disabilities (ICDD) is dedicated to leading change in Illinois so that all people with developmental disabilities are able to exercise their rights to freedom and equal opportunity.

3396 Illinois Department of Mental Health and Developmental Disabilities
Suite 3b
314 E Madison
Springfield, IL 62701 217-782-6680
 FAX: 217-524-3834

Karen Perrin, Manager
Lori Stone, Director

3397 Illinois Department of Rehabilitation
100 South Grand Avenue East
Springfield, IL 62762-1304 217-782-6680
 800-843-6154
 FAX: 217-524-3834
 TTY: 800-447-6404
 DHS.WEBBITS@ILLINOIS.GOV
 www.dhs.state.il.us/page.aspx?item=29736

Robert Kilbury, Director
Timothy Martin, Manager
DHS's Division of Rehabilitation Services is the state's lead agency serving individuals with disabilities. DRS works in partnership with people with disabilities and their families to assist them in making informed choices to achieve full community participation through employment, education, and independent living opportunities.

3398 Illinois Department on Aging
One Natural Resources Way
Suite 100
Springfield, IL 62702-1271 217-785-2870
 800-252-8966
 FAX: 217-785-4477
 TTY: 888-206-1327
 www2.illinois.gov

John K. Holton, Director
Jennifer Reif, Deputy Director
Matthew Ryan, Chief of Staff
The MISSION of the Illinois Department on Aging is to serve and advocate for older Illinoisans and their caregivers by administering quality and culturally appropriate programs that promote partnerships and encourage independence, dignity, and quality of life.

3399 International Dyslexia Association: Illinois Branch
751 Roosevelt Rd.
Suite 116
Glen Ellyn, IL 60137 630-469-6900
 FAX: 630-469-6810
 www.readibida.org

Jo Ann Paldo, President
Foley Burckardt, Vice President
Joan Budovec, Treasurer
Provides free information and referral services for diagnosis and tutoring for parents, educators, physicians, and individuals with dyslexia in Illinois. Membership includes yearly journal and quarterly newsletter.

3400 Social Security: Springfield Disability Determination
3112 CONSTITUTION DR
Springfield, IL 62704-1323 877-279-9504
 800-772-1213
 TTY:800-325-0778
 ssa.gov

3401 Workers Compensation Board Illinois
100 W Randolph St
Ste 8-200
Chicago, IL 60601-3227   312-814-6611
                                        866-352-3033
                                   FAX: 312-814-6523
                          infoquestions.wcc@illinois.gov
                                     www2.illinois.gov

Joann Fratianni, Chairman
The Illinois Workers' Compensation Commission resolves disputes between employees and employers regarding work-related injuries and illnesses.

Indiana

3402 Indiana Client Assistance Program
4701 N. Keystone Avenue
Suite 222
Indianapolis, IN 46204-1191   317-722-5555
                                       800-622-4845
                                  FAX: 317-722-5564
                                  TTY: 317-722-5555
                        www.icdri.org/legal/IndianaCAP.htm

Michael Burks, Chairman
Wen Lu, Secretary and Treasurer

3403 Indiana Developmental Disability Council
402 West Washington Street
Room E145
Indianapolis, IN 46204-2801   317-232-7770
                                  FAX: 317-233-3712
                                       www.in.gov

Katrina Gossett, Chair
Dawn Adams JD, Agency representative
Suellen Jackson-Boner, Executive Director
The Indiana Governor's Council is an independent state agency that facilitates change. Our mission is to promote public policy which leads to the independence, productivity and inclusion of people with disabilities in all aspects of society

3404 Indiana Protection & Advocacy Services Commission
4701 N. Keystone Avenue
Suite 222
Indianapolis, IN 46205-1561   317-722-5555
                                       800-622-4845
                                  FAX: 317-722-5564
                          ExecutiveDirector@ipas.in.gov
                                     www.in.gov/ipas

Dawn Adams, Executive Director
Milo Gray, Client & Legal Services Director
Gary Richter, Support Services Director
An independent state agency established to protect and promote the rights of individuals with disabilities through empowerment and advocacy.

3405 Indiana State Commission for the Handicapped
P.O.Box 1964
Indianapolis, IN 46206   317-233-1292

3406 International Dyslexia Association: Indiana Branch
Fisher, IN 46038   317-926-1450
                                     www.ida-indiana.org

Kim Haughee, President
Sara Silvey, Vice President
Ginger Lentz, Secretary
The Indiana Branch was formed to help the members of the learning disabilities community in Indiana. Promotes understanding and facilitate treatment of the Specific Language Disability (Dyslexia) in children and adults, promotes teacher training and educational intervention strategies for dyslexic students and to foster effective teaching, supports research in the field and early identification of dyslexia, serves as a clearinghouse for information and to actively disseminate knowledge.

Iowa

3407 Governor's Developmental Disability Council
617 East Second Street
Des Moines, IA 50309-1831   515-281-9082
                                       800-452-1936
                                  FAX: 515-281-9087
                                       idaction.com/

Becky Harker, Executive Director
Rik Shannon, Public Policy Manager
Janet Shoeman, Program Planner/Contract Manager
The Council identifies, develops and promotes public policy and support practices through capacity building, advocacy, and systems change activities. The purpose is to ensure that people with developmental disabilities and their families are included in planning, decision making, and development of policy related to services and supports that affect their quality of life and full participation in communities of their choice.

3408 International Dyslexia Association: Iowa Branch
P.O. Box 11188
Cedar Rapids, IA 52410-1188   765-507-9432
                                     info@iowaida.org
                                     ia.dyslexiaida.org

Denise Little, President
Tricia Krsek, Vice President
Genevieve Monthie, Secretary
The purpose of the Iowa Branch of IDA is to increase awareness of dyslexia and promote services that address the importance of diagnosis and remediation for those not meeting their reading potential. Providese services and assistance in a way that promotes unity, support, and cooperation among those who work with these individuals so that all communities in Iowa benefit from the skills and talents of its citizens.

3409 Iowa Child Health Specialty Clinics
100 Hawkins Drive
Room 247 CDD
Iowa City, IA 52242-1016   319-356-1117
                                       866-219-9119
                                  FAX: 319-356-3715
                          kathy-colbert@uiowa.edu
                                     www.chsciowa.org

Jeffrey Lobas, Director
Brian Wilkes, Director Of Operations
Child Health Specialty Clinics has a mission to improve the health, development, and well-being of Iowa's children and youth with special health care needs in partnership with families, service providers, and communities.

3410 Iowa Commission of Persons with Disabilities
Department of Human Rights
Lucas State Office Bldg, 2nd Floor
Des Moines, IA 50319- 2006   515-242-6171
                                       888-219-0471
                                  FAX: 515-242-6119
                                  TTY: 888-219-0471
                                     www.state.ia.us/dhr/pd

Jill Fulitano-Avery, Administrator
To equalize opportunities for full participation in employment and other areas of the state's economic, educational, social and political life for Iowans with disabilities.

3411 Iowa Compass
Center for Disabilities & Development
100 Hawkins Dr
Suite S295
Iowa City, IA 52242-1011   800-779-2001
                                  TTY:877-686-0032
                          iowa-compass@uiowa.edu
                                     www.iowacompass.org

Michael Lightbody, Project Director
Carolyn Petitgout, CRS, Admin Services Coordinator & Database Editor
Iowa Compass offers free information and program referrals to thousands of unique local, state and national organizations serving people with complex health related conditions and disabilities.
BiMonthly

3412 **Iowa Department for the Blind**
State Of Iowa
524 4th Street
Des Moines, IA 50309-2364   515-281-1333
                                         800-362-2587
                                    FAX: 515-281-1263
                                    TTY: 515-281-1355
                            information@blind.state.ia.us
                                         www.IDBonline.org

Richard Sorey, Director
Jodi Aldini, Library Support Staff
Julie Aufdenkamp, Transition Specialist, Transitio
Mission is to be the means for persons who are blind to obtain
univeral access and full participation as citizens in whatever roles
they may choose.

3413 **Iowa Department of Human Services**
1305 E Walnut St
Des Moines, IA 50319-114   515-242-6510
                                         800-972-2017
                                    FAX: 515-281-4597

Terry E Branstad, Governor
Charles M Palmer, Director
Sally Titus, Deputy Director
Help individuals and families to achieve stable and healthy lives.

3414 **Iowa Department on Aging**
510 E 12th Street
Suite 2
Des Moines, IA 50319-9025   515-725-3333
                                        800-532-3213
                                   FAX: 866-236-1430
                                        www.aging.iowa.gov

Donna K. Harvey, Director
Danika Welch, Executive Secretary
Joel Wulf, Administrator

3415 **Iowa Protection & Advocacy for the Disabled**
400 East Court Avenue
Suite 300
Des Moines, IA 50309   515-278-2502
                                        800-779-2502
                                   FAX: 515-278-0539
                                        info@DRIowa.org
                                   disabilityrightsiowa.org

Christine Glosser, President
Todd Lantz, Vice President
Jane Hudson, Executive Director
Disability Rights IOWA aims to defend and promote the human
and legal rights of Iowans who have disabilities and mental
illness.

3416 **Social Security: Des Moines Disability Determination**
Social Security Administration
Riverpoint Office Complex
455 SW 5TH ST STE F
Des Moines, IA 50309-2115   515-284-4260
                                        800-772-1213
                                   FAX: 515-284-4394
                                   TTY: 800-325-0778
                                        ssa.gov

Leroy Brown, Manager

3417 **Workers Compensation Board Iowa**
1000 East Grand Avenue
Des Moines, IA 50319-0209   515-281-5387
                                   FAX: 515-281-6501
                                        www.iowaworkforce.org

Joseph S Cortese II, Commissioner
Janna E. Martin, Commissioner
Sandy Breckenridge, Administrative Secretary
The Workers' Compensation Act is a part of the Iowa Code designed to provide certain benefits to employees who receive injury (85), occupational disease (85A) or occupational hearing
loss (85B) arising out of and during the course of their
employment.

Kansas

3418 **Beach Center on Families and Disability**
University of Kansas
1200 Sunnyside Ave.
Room 3134
Lawrence, KS 66045-7534   785-864-7600
                                        866-783-3378
                                        beachcenter@ku.edu
                                        www.beachcenter.org

Michael Wehmeyer, Director
A federally funded center that conducts research and training in
the factors that contribute to the successful functioning of families with members who have disabilities.

3419 **International Dyslexia Association: Kansas/Missouri
Branch**
16628 Bond St.
Overland Park, KS 66221   816-945-2665
                                        ksmoida@gmail.com
                                        ksmo.dyslexiaida.org

Cathy Denesia, President
Holly Aranda, Vice President
Nora Wolf, Treasurer
Provides free information and referral services for diagnosis and
tutoring for parents, educators, physicians, and individuals with
dyslexia in Illinois. Membership includes yearly journal and
quarterly newsletter.

3420 **Kansas Advocacy and Protective Services**
214 SW 6th Ave.,
Ste 100
Topeka, KS 66603-3726   785-273-9661
                                        877-776-1541
                                   FAX: 785-273-9414
                                   TTY: 877-335-3725
                                        www.drckansas.org/

Rocky Nichols, Executive Director
Debbie White, Deputy Director
Lane Williams, Deputy Director
Protection and advocacy for persons with disabilities.

3421 **Kansas Client Assistance Program**
635 SW Harrison
Suite 100
Topeka, KS 66603   785-273-9661
                                        877-776-1541
                                   FAX: 785-273-9414
                                   TTY: 877-335-3725
                                        rocky@drckansas.org
                                   www.icdri.org/legal/KansasCAP.htm

3422 **Kansas Commission on Disability Concerns**
900 SW Jackson
Suite 100
Topeka, KS 66612-1246   785-296-1722
                                        800-295-5232
                                   FAX: 785-296-1795
                                        KCDCoffice@ks.gov
                                        kcdcinfo.ks.gov

Martha Gabehart, Executive Director
Kerrie Bacon, Employment Liaison
The Kansas Commission on Disability Concerns provides dis-
ability-related supports and information to the people of Kansas.
The commission offers legislative advocacy, education and re-
source networking to ensure full and equal citizenship for all
Kansans with disabilities.

3423 **Kansas Department on Aging**
503 S Kansas Ave
New England Building
Topeka, KS 66603- 3404   785-296-4986
                                        800-432-3535
                                   FAX: 785-296-0256
                                   TTY: 785-291-3167
                                   wwwmail@kdads.ks.gov
                                        www.kdads.ks.gov

Kathy Greenlee, Manager
Barbara Conant, Public Information Officer
Kari Bruffett, Secretary

Services and information for Kansas seniors, over age 60.

3424 Kansas Developmental Disability Council
Disability Rights Center of Kansas
915 SW Harrison
DSOB Rm 141
Topeka, KS 66612-3726
785-296-2608
877-431-4604
FAX: 785-296-2861
TTY: 877-335-3725
sgieber@kcdd.org
www.kcdd.org/

Steve Gieber, Executive Director
Craig Knutson, Public Policy Coordinator
Charline Cobbs, Senior Administrative Assistant
The purpose of the Kansas Council on Developmental Disabilities (KCDD) is to support people of all ages with developmental disabilities so they have the opportunity to make choices regarding both their participation in society, and their quality of life.

Kentucky

3425 Kentucky Cabinet for Health and Family Services
275 E Main St.
Frankfort, KY 40621
502-564-5497
800-372-2973
FAX: 502-564-9523
chfs.ky.gov

Jeffrey D. Howard, Commissioner
Oversees program areas relating to aging, behavioral/developmental health, children with special needs, family resources, medicaid, public health, and more.

3426 Kentucky Council on Developmental Disability
1151 So. Fourth Street
Louisville, KY 40203
502-584-1239
800-372-2973
FAX: 502-584-1261
info@councilondd.org
councilondd.org

Richard Bush, President
Dave Fowler, Treasurer
Missy Kinnaird, Secretary
Implementation of Developmental Disabilities Planning Council responsible under P.L. 101-496.

3427 Kentucky Office for the Blind
275 E Main St
Frankfort, KY 40621
502-564-4754
800-321-6668
FAX: 502-564-2951
TTY: 502-564-2929
blind.ky.gov

Cora McNabb, Executive Director
Deanna Doll, Vocational Rehabilitation Counselor
Tonisha Everhart, Vocational Rehabilitation Counselor
Provides career services and assistance to adults with severe visual handicaps who want to become productive in the home or work force. The office also runs a Client Assistance Program established to provide advice, assistance and information available from rehabilitation programs to persons with handicaps.

3428 Kentucky Office of Aging Services
Cabinet for Health Services
275 East Main Street
Suite 1E-B
Frankfort, KY 40621
502-564-6930
FAX: 502-564-4595
TTY:888-642-1137
David.Boswell@ky.gov

Deborah Anderson, Commissioner
Chris Harbeck, Executive Secretary
Marnie Mountjoy, Staff Assistant
The Kentucky Office of Aging Services is the state agency directly responsible for programs and services for people with disabilities. Efforts are made to fully integrate the service response information that considers broad farmiliar implications.

3429 Kentucky Protection & Advocacy
100 Fair Oaks Ln 3rd Fl
Frankfort, KY 40601-1108
502-564-2967
800-372-2988
FAX: 502-564-0848
kypa.net

Marsha Hockensmith, Executive Director
Protection and advocacy, Kentucky's federally-mandated protection and advocacy system, protects & promotes the disability rights of individuals through free legally-based advocacy, technical assistance, and education.

3430 Social Security: Frankfort Disability Determination
Social Security
140 Flynn Avenue
Frankfort, KY 40601
866-964-1724
800-772-1213
FAX: 502-226-4519
TTY: 502-226-4519
www.ssa.gov

Stephen Jones, Director
Burton Sisk, Manager

3431 Social Security: Louisville Disability Determination
Social Security
601 W Broadway
Room 101
Louisville, KY 40202-2227
866-716-9671
800-772-1213
TTY:502-582-5238
ssa.gov

Louisiana

3432 Louisiana Assistive Technology Access Network
3042 Old Forge Dr.
P O Box 14115
Baton Rouge, LA 70898
225-925-9500
800-270-6185
FAX: 225-925-9560
www.latan.org/

Jim Parks, President & CEO
Sandee Winchell, Executive Director
An information and training resource on Assistive Technology for the State of Louisiana. LATAN operates three regional centers to provide better access for consumers.

3433 Louisiana Center for Dyslexia and Related Learning Disorders
PO Box 2050
Thibodaux, LA 70310-1
985-448-4214
FAX: 985-448-4423
karen.chauvin@nicholls.edu
www.nicholls.edu

Karen Chauvin, Director
Jason Talbot, Assessment & Research Coor
Ashley D Munson, Senior Program Coordinator
Provides free information and referral services for diagnosis and tutoring for parents, educators, physicians and individuals with dyslexia. The voice of our membership is heard in 48 countries. Membership includes yearly journal and quarterly newsletter. Call for conference dates.

3434 Louisiana Department of Aging
Office of Elderly Affairs
PO Box 629
Baton Rouge, LA 70821-0629
225-342-9500
FAX: 225-342-5568
robin.wagner@la.gov
new.dhh.louisiana.gov/

Tara LeBlanc, Assistant Secretary
Robin Wagner, Deputy Assistant Secretary
Kirsten Clebart, Director
Serves as a focal point for Louisiana's senior citizens and administers a broad range of home and community based services through a network of 37 Area Agencies on Aging. Serve as the focal point for the development, implementation, and administration of the public policy for the state of Louisiana, and address the needs of the state's elderly citizens.

Government Agencies / Maine

3435 Louisiana Department of Health - Mental Health Services
PO Box 629
Baton Rouge, LA 70821-0629
225-342-9500
888-342-6207
FAX: 225-342-5568
ldhinfo@la.gov
new.dhh.louisiana.gov

Rebekah Gee, Ph.D, Secretary
Michelle Alletto, Deputy Secretary
Jimmy Guidry, Ph.D, State Health Officer
The Office of Behavioral Health's mental health services provide a variety of treatments for people who have different types of mental illnesses. Also offered are treatment clinics and family support services.

3436 Louisiana Developmental Disability Council
PO Box 3455
626 Main Street, Suite A
Baton Rouge, LA 70821-3455
225-342-6804
800-450-8108
FAX: 225-342-1970
shawn.fleming@la.gov
www.laddc.org

Sandra Sam Beech, Chairperson
Brenda Cosse, Vice Chairperson
Sandee Winchell, Executive Director
The Council's mission is to lead and promote advocacy, capacity building, and systemic change to improve the quality of life for individuals with developmental disabilities and their families.

3437 Louisiana Learning Resources System
2525 Wyandotte St
Baton Rouge, LA 70805-6464
225-355-6197
FAX: 225-357-3508

Bobbie Robertson, Administrator
Provides consultation on educational seOrvices for local schools, offers psychological testing and evaluation, maintains resource rooms in district schools and more for the blind and handicapped throughout the state.

3438 Social Security: Baton Rouge Disability Determination
Department of Social Services
5455 Bankers Ave
Baton Rouge, LA 70808
866-613-3070
800-772-1213
FAX: 225-219-9399
TTY: 225-382-2090
adren.wilson@dss.state.la.us
www.ssa.gov

Shirley Williams, Director
Ann Williamson, Manager

3439 Workers Compensation Board Louisiana
1001 North 23rd Street
Post Office Box 94094
Baton Rouge, LA 70804-9094
225-342-3111
800-259-5154
FAX: 225-342-7960
owd@lwc.la.gov
www.laworks.net

Curt Eysink, Executive Director
Carey Foy, Deputy Executive Director
Renee Ellender Roberie, Chief Financial Officer
The Louisiana Workforce Commission's vision is to make Louisiana the best place in the country to get a job or grow a business, and our goal is to be the country's best workforce agency.

Maine

3440 Maine Assistive Technology Projects
University of Maine at Augusta
Georgia Institute of Technology
490 Tenth Street
Atlanta, GA 30332-0156
404-894-4960
FAX: 404-894-9320
catea@coa.gatech.edu
assistivetech.net

A statewide program promoting assistive technology devices and services for persons of all ages with all disabilities.

3441 Maine Bureau of Elder and Adult Services
11 State House Station
41 Anthony Avenue
Augusta, ME 04333
207-287-9200
800-262-2232
FAX: 207-287-9229
www.maine.gov

Ricker Hamilton, Director
AnnMarie Stevens, Administrative Assistant
Lois Emerson, Office Specialist I
Adult Protective Services (APS), is responsible for providing or arranging for services to protect incapacitated and/or dependent adults in danger.

3442 Maine Department of Health and Human Services
221 State Street
Augusta, ME 04333-0040
207-287-3707
FAX: 207-287-3005
www.maine.gov/dhhs

Mary C. Mayhew, Commissioner
Sam Adolphsen, Chief Operating Officer
Ricker Hamilton, Deputy Commissioner of Programs
Provision of an array of services to people with nental illness, substance abuse issues, children with special needs and people with developmental disabilities.

3443 Maine Developmental Disabilities Council
225 Western Avenue
Suite 4
Augusta, ME 04330
207-287-4213
800-244-3990
FAX: 207-287-8001
nancy.e.cronin@maine.gov
www.maineddc.org

Nancy Cronin, Executive Director
Rachel Dyer, Associate Director
Erin Howes, Office Manager
The MDDC is a partnership of people with disabilities, their families, and agencies which identifies barriers to community inclusion, self-determination, and independence, and acts to effect positive change.

3444 Maine Division for the Blind and Visually Impaired
21 Enterprise Dr
Suite 2
Augusta, ME 04333-0073
207-624-5120
800-760-1573
FAX: 207-624-5133
TTY: 800-633-0770
mdol@maine.gov
www.maine.gov/rehab/dbvi

Harold Lewis, Director
Sandra Cavanaugh, Executive Director
Works to bring about full access to employment, independence and community integration for people with disabilities in Maine.

3445 Maine Office of Elder Services
State of Maine
11 State House Station
41 Anthony Avenue
Augusta, ME 04333
207-287-9200
800-262-2232
FAX: 207-287-9229
TTY: 800-606-0215
mdol@maine.gov

James Martin, Director
Gary Wolcott, Associate Director
Romaine Turyn, Aging Service Manager
The Office of Elder Services (OES), an Office within the Maine Department of Health and Human Services, promotes programs and services for older adults, their families and for people with disabilities.

320

3446 Maine Workers' Compensation Board
27 State House Station
Augusta, ME 04333
207-287-3751
888-801-9087
FAX: 207-287-7198
TTY:877-832-5525
www.maine.gov/wcb

Paul H Sighinolfi, Executive Director
Lindsay Lizzotte, Secretary Specialist
Gary Koocher, Management Representative
The general mission of the Maine Workers' Compensation Board is to serve the employees and employers of the State fairly and expeditiously by ensuring compliance with the workers' compensation laws, ensuring the prompt delivery of benefits legally due, promoting the prevention of disputes, utilizing dispute resolution to reduce litigation and facilitating labor-management cooperation.

3447 Social Security: Maine Disability Determination
330 Civic Center Dr
Suite 4
Augusta, ME 04330-6325
866-882-5422
800-772-1213
TTY:207-623-4190
ssa.gov

Louis Tepin, Manager
This office makes the medical determination about whether a consumer is disabled and, therefore, medically eligible for Social Security benefits. Legally, an individual is considered disabled if he or she is unable to do any substantial gainful work activity because of a medical condition (or conditions), that has lasted, or can be expected to last for at least 12 months, or that is expected to result in death.

Maryland

3448 Health Resources & Services Administration: State Bureau of Health
5600 Fishers Lane
Rockville, MD 20857
301-443-3376
877-464-4772
TTY:877-897-9910
www.hrsa.gov

Diana Espinosa, Deputy Administrator
Jordan Grossman, Chief of Staff
Carole Johnson, Administrator
Through appropriated funds, supports education programs, credentialing analysis, and development of human resources needed to staff the U.S. health care system.

3449 International Dyslexia Association: Maryland Branch
International Dyslexia Association
P.O. Box 233
Brookland, MD 21022-0233
800-509-4980
md.dyslexiaida.org

Annette Fallon, President
Karen Fallon, Vice President
Timothy Yearick, Secretary
Nonprofit organization providing free information and referral services for diagnosis and tutoring for parents, educators, physicians, and individuals with dyslexia. Membership includes yearly journal and quarterly newsletter. Call for conference dates.

3450 Maryland Client Assistance Program Division of Rehabilitation Services
2301 Argonne Drive
Baltimore, MD 21218-1628
410-554-9442
888-554-0334
FAX: 410-554-9362
TTY: 443-798-2840
dors@maryland.gov
dors.maryland.gov

Suzanne R. Page, DORS Director
Helps individuals with disabilities understand the rehabilitation process and receives appropriate and quality services from the Division of Rehabilitation Services and other programs and facilities providing services under the Rehabilitation Act of 1973.

3451 Maryland Department of Aging
State Office Building
301 West Preston Street
Suite 1007
Baltimore, MD 21201- 2393
410-767-1100
800-243-3425
FAX: 410-333-7943
www.mdoa.state.md.us/

Stuart Rosenthal, Chair
Sharonlee J. Vogel, Vice-Chair
Rona E. Kramer, Secretary
The Department of Aging protects the rights and quality of life of older persons in Maryland. To meet the needs of senior citizens, the Department administers programs throughout the State, primarily through local area agencies on aging.

3452 Maryland Department of Handicapped Children
201 W Preston St
Unit 50
Baltimore, MD 21201-2301
410-335-6470
www.msa.md.gov

Judson Force, Director
Children's Medical Services is a joint federal/state/local program which assists in obtaining specialized medical, surgical and related habilitative/rehabilitative evaluation and treatment services for children with special health care needs and their families. To be eligible for the program's services, an individual must be a resident of Maryland, younger than 22 years, have or be suspected of having an eligible medical condition and meet both medical and financial criteria.

3453 Maryland Developmental Disabilities Council
217 E Redwood Street
Suite 1300
Baltimore, MD 21202-3313
410-767-3670
800-305-6441
FAX: 410-333-3686
www.md-council.org

Brian Cox, Executive Director
Catherine Lyle, Deputy Director
Rachel London, Director, Children & Family Poli
A public policy organization comprised of people with disabilities and family members who are joined by state officials, service providers and other designated partners. The Council is an independent, self-governing organization that represents the interests of people with developmental disabilities and their families.

3454 Maryland Division of Mental Health
201 W. Preston Street
Baltimore, MD 21201
410-767-6500
877-463-3464
dhmh.healthmd@maryland.gov

Norma Pinette, Executive Director
Van T. Mitchell, Secretary
Our Public Health Services Division oversees vital public services to Maryland residents including infectious disease and environmental health concerns, family health services and emergency preparedness and response activities.

3455 Maternal and Child Health Bureau - Health Resources and Services Administration
5600 Fishers Lane
Rockville, MD 20857
301-443-3376
877-464-4772
TTY:877-897-9910
www.hrsa.gov

Diana Espinosa, Deputy Administrator
Jordan Grossman, Chief of Staff
Carole Johnson, Administrator
Offers information, books and pamphlets to professionals, parents and children facing health issues or disabilities.

3456 Social Security: Baltimore Disability Determination
711 West 40th Street
Ste 415 Rotunda Mall
Baltimore, MD 21211-2120
800-772-1213
TTY:800-325-0778
ssa.gov

This office makes the medical determination about whether a consumer is disabled and, therefore, medically eligible for Social Security benefits. Legally, an individual is considered disabled if he or she is unable to do any substantial gainful work activity because of a medical condition (or conditions), that has lasted, or can be expected to last for at least 12 months, or that is expected to result in death.

3457 Workers Compensation Board Maryland
10 East Baltimore Street
Baltimore, MD 21202-1641
410-864-5100
800-492-0479
FAX: 410-333-8122
info@wcc.state.md.us
www.wcc.state.md.us

R. Karl Aumann, Chairperson
Mary K. Ahearn, Chief Executive Officer
David E. Jones, Chief Financial Officer

Massachusetts

3458 Center for Public Representation
22 Green Street
Northampton, MA 01060-3708
413-586-6024
FAX: 413-586-5711
info@cpr-ma.org
centerforpublicrep.org

Bob Agoglia, President
Nickie Chandler, Clerk/Treasurer
Bob Riedel, Director
The Center seeks to improve the quality of lives of people with mental illness and other disabilities through the systemic enforcement of their legal rights while promoting improvements in services for citizens with disabilities

3459 Massachusetts Assistive Technology Partnership
Children s Hospital Boston
1295 Boylston St
Suite 310
Boston, MA 02215-3407
617-355-7820
800-848-8867
FAX: 617-355-6345

Marylyn Howe, Project Director
Pat Hill, Training Coordinator
A statewide program promoting assistive technology devices and services for persons with all disabilities.

3460 Massachusetts Client Assistance Program
Massachusetts Office on Disability
1 Ashburton Pl
Suite 1305
Boston, MA 02108-1518
617-727-7440
800-322-2020
www.mass.gov/anf/employment-equal-access-disa
Barbara Lybarger, Assistant Director
Myra Berloff, Director
Michael Dumont, Assistant Director
Provides advocacy and information services.

3461 Massachusetts Department of Mental Health
25 Staniford St.
Boston, MA 02114-2503
617-626-8000
TTY:617-727-9842
dmhinfo@massmail.state.ma.us
www.mass.gov/dmh
Joan Mikula, Commissioner
The Massachusetts Department of Mental Health, as the State Mental Health Authority, assures and provides access to services and supports to meet the mental health needs of individuals of all ages, enabling them to live, work and participate in their communities. The Department establishes standards to ensure effective and culturally competent care to promote recovery. The Department sets policy, promotes self-determination, protects human rights and supports mental health training and research.

3462 Massachusetts Developmental Disabilities Council
100 Hancock Street
Second Floor, Suite 201
Quincy, MA 02169-4398
617-770-7676
FAX: 617-770-1987
TTY:617-770-9499
www.state.ma.us/mddc/

Daniel Shannon, Executive Director
Faith Behum, Disability Policy Specialist
Kristin Britton, Director of Public Policy
Group of citizens which analyzes needs of people with severe, lifelong disabilities and works to improve public policy. MDDC produces several publications and has committees and a grants program to study and advocate for changes in the service system.

3463 Social Security: Boston Disability Determination
110 Chauncy Street
Boston, MA 02111
617-727-7600
800-772-1213
TTY:800-882-2040
www.socialsecurity.gov

Michael F. Bertrand, Commissioner

3464 Workers Compensation Board Massachusetts
Rm 211
1 Ashburton Pl
Boston, MA 02108-1518
617-626-7122
FAX: 617-727-1090
www.state.ma.us/dia

Russell Gilfus, Manager
The Massachusetts Workers' Compensation system is in place to make sure that workers are protected by insurance if they are injured on the job or contract a work-related illness. Under this system, employers are required by Massachusetts General Laws c. 152, 25A to provide workers' compensation (WC) insurance coverage to all their employees.

Michigan

3465 Department of Blind Rehabilitation
Western Michigan University
1903 W Michigan Ave
Kalamazoo, MI 49008-5218
269-387-3455
FAX: 269-387-3567
g.dennis@wmich.edu
www.wmich.edu/visionstudies

James Leja, Chair
Charles Adams, Faculty Specialist I
Gayla Dennis, Office Coordinator
The Department of Blindness and Low Vision Studies at Western Michigan University is recognized internationally as the oldest, largest and best program of its kind. It originated in 1961 with a graduate degree in Orientation and Mobility, responding to the need for professionals to rehabilitate the many military personnel blinded during World War Two and the Korean War.

3466 Michigan Association for Deaf and Hard of Hearing
5236 Dumond Court
Suite C
Lansing, MI 48917-6001
517-487-0066
800-968-7327
FAX: 517-487-0202
TTY: 517-487-2586
info@madhh.org
www.madhh.org

Nancy Asher, Executive Director
Pat Walton, Office Manager
MADHH is a statewide collaboration agency dedicated to improving the lives of people who are deaf and hard of hearing through leadership in education, advocacy & services. Interpreter IC print-out, assistive devices available.

3467 Michigan Association for Deaf, and Hard of Hearing
5236 Dumond Court
Suite C
Lansing, MI 48917-6001   517-487-0066
                                800-968-7327
                          FAX: 517-487-2586
                          www.madhh.org

Nancy Asher, Executive Director
Pat Walton, Office Manager
MADHH is a statewide collaboration agency dedicated to improving the lives of people who are deaf and hard of hearing through leadership in education, advocacy and services.

3468 Michigan Client Assistance Program
4095 Legacy Pkwy
Ste 500
Lansing, MI 48911-4264   517-487-1755
                                800-288-5923
                          FAX: 517-487-0827
                          TTY: 800-288-5923
                          molson@mpas.org
                          www.mpas.org

Kate Pew Wolters, President
Thomas Landry, 1st Vice President
John McCulloch, 2nd Vice President
The Client Assistance Program (CAP) assists people who are seeking or receiving services from Michigan Rehabilitation Services, Consumer Choice Programs, Michigan Commission for the Blind, Centers for Independent Living, and Supported Employment and Transition Programs. The CAP program is part of Michigan Protection and Advocacy Service, Inc.

3469 Michigan Coalition for Staff Development and School Improvement
12236 6 1/2 Mile Road
MCES
Battle Creek, MI 49014-1062   269-967-2086
                                800-444-2014
                          FAX: 517-371-1170
TheMichigan Coalition of Essential Schools(MCES) has serviced over 60 public and private schools in the state over the past 14 years. Our experienced staff, consisting of K-12 educators in the classroom and building and district leadership, is poised and ready to help schools build and sustain capacity for whole school change and increased student achievement.

3470 Michigan Commission for the Blind - Gaylord
Ste 102
209 W 1st St
Gaylord, MI 49735-1386   989-732-2448
                                800-292-4200
                          FAX: 989-731-3587
                          www.michigan.gov

Judy Terwilliger, Manager
The mission of the Michigan Commission for the Blind (MCB) is to provide opportunity to individuals who are blind or visually impaired to achieve employability and/or function independently in society. The MCB vision is that someday it will be said that Michigan is a great place for blind people to live, learn, work, raise a family, and enjoy life

3471 Michigan Commission for the Blind
Michigan Dept Of Energy, Labor & Economic Growth
PO Box 30652
Lansing, MI 48909-8152   517-373-2062
                                800-292-4200
                          FAX: 517-335-5140
                          TTY: 517-373-4025
                          turneys@michigan.gov
                          www.michigan.gov/mcb

Patrick Cannon, State Director
The Michigan Commision for the blind is a state government agency that provides state and federally funded training and other services to individuals who are legally blind (blind and visually impaired). Services are provided to people of all ages throughout the state of Michigan toward the goal of employment and/or independence.

3472 Michigan Commission for the Blind Training Center
PO Box 30652
Lansing, MI 48909   517-373-2062
                              800-292-4200
                        FAX: 517-335-5140
                        TTY: 517-373-4025
                        mossc@michigan.gov
                        www.michigan.gov/mcb

Cheryl L Heibeck, Director
Bruce Schultz, Assistant Director
Residential facility that provides instruction to legally blind adults in braille, computer operation and assistive technology, handwriting, cane travel, cooking, personal management, industrial arts and also crafts. During training students will develop career plans which may include work experience, internships, volunteer opprtunities and even part-time paid employment.

3473 Michigan Commission for the Blind: Escanaba
305 Ludington St
State Office Bldg., 1st Floor
Escanaba, MI 49829-4029   906-786-8602
                                800-323-2535
                          FAX: 906-786-4638
                          michigan.gov/mcb

Bernie Kramer, Manager
The mission of the Michigan Commission for the Blind (MCB) is to provide opportunity to individuals who are blind or visually impaired to achieve employability and/or function independently in society. The MCB vision is that someday it will be said that Michigan is a great place for blind people to live, learn, work, raise a family, and enjoy life

3474 Michigan Commission for the Blind: Flint
125 E Union St
Seventh Floor
Flint, MI 48502-2041   810-760-2030
                                800-292-4200
                          FAX: 810-760-2032

Debbie Wilson, Manager
Vocational and Independent living skills training for individuals who are legally blind.

3475 Michigan Commission for the Blind: Grand Rapids
250 Ottawa Avenue
Grand Rapids, MI 49503-4029   906-786-8602
                                800-323-2535
                          FAX: 906-786-4638
                          michigan.gov/mcb

Bernie Kramer, Manager
The mission of the Michigan Commission for the Blind (MCB) is to provide opportunity to individuals who are blind or visually impaired to achieve employability and/or function independently in society. The MCB vision is that someday it will be said that Michigan is a great place for blind people to live, learn, work, raise a family, and enjoy life

3476 Michigan Council of the Blind and Visually Impaired (MCBVI)
Neal Freeling
350 Ottawa Ave NW
Grand Rapids, MI 49503-2316   616-356-0180
                                800-292-4200
                          FAX: 616-356-0199
                          michigan.gov/mcb

Bernie Kramer, Manager
MCBVI is a diverse group of very friendly people from around the state working together to improve the lives of all citizens who are blind or visually impaired.

3477 Michigan Department of Handicapped Children
3423 N Martin Luther King Jr Blvd
Lansing, MI 48906-2934   517-484-9312
                          FAX: 517-484-9836

Alan Curtiss, President
Bobbie Butler, Manager

3478 Michigan Developmental Disabilies Council
201 Townsend Street
Suite 120
Lansing, MI 48910-1646   517-335-3158
                                      FAX: 517-335-2751
                                      TTY:517-335-3171
                          mdch-dd-council@michigan.gov
                          www.michigan.gov/ddcouncil

Nick Lyon, Director
Nancy Grijalva, Assistant
Tim Becker, Chief Deputy Director
The Michigan DD Council is a group of citizens from across the state. Its membership is made up of: people with developmental disabilities; people from families who have, among their members, people with developmental disabilities; and professionals from state and local agencies charged with assisting people with developmental disabilities.

3479 Michigan Office of Services to the Aging
P.O.Box 30676
Lansing, MI 48909-8176   517-373-8230
                                    FAX: 517-373-4092
                           OSAInfo@michigan.gov
                           www.michigan.gov/osa

Wendi Middleton, Division Director
Kari Sederburg, Director
Carol Dye, Senior Executive Assistant
State unit on aging; allocates and monitors state and federal funds for the Older American Act services: nutrition, community services, administers home and community based waiver, develops programs through Area Agencies on Aging, advocates on behalf of seniors with legislature, governor, state departments, federal government, responsible for state planning of aging services, develops formula for distribution of state and federal funds.

3480 Michigan Protection & Advocacy Service
4095 Legacy Pkwy
Ste 500
Lansing, MI 48911-4264   517-487-1755
                                    800-288-5923
                                    FAX: 517-487-0827
                           molson@mpas.org
                           www.mpas.org

Kate Pew Wolters, President
Thomas Landry, 1st Vice President
John McCulloch, 2nd Vice President
People with disabilities have to deal with a wide variety of issues. TThey try to answer any questions you may have relating to disability. They have experience in the following areas: discrimination in education, employment, housing, and public places; abuse and neglect; Social Security benefits; Medicaid, Medicare and other insurance; housing; Vocational Rehabilitation; HIV/AIDS issues; and many other disability-related topics

3481 Michigan Rehabilitation Services
300 N. Washington Sq.
Lansing, MI 48913   517-335-4590
                                    888-784-7328
                                    FAX: 517-373-0059
                                    TTY: 517-373-4035
                           zimmermanng@michigan.org
                           www.michigan.org

George Zimmermann, Vice President
Michelle Begnoche, Communications Specialist
Bonnie Fink, Travel Consultant Coordinator
A state and federally funded program that helps persons with disabilities prepare for and fund a job that matches their interests and abilities. Assistance is also available to workers with disabilities who are having difficulty keeping a job. A person is eligible for MRS services if he or she has a disability, is unemployed and needs vocational rehabilitation services to prepare for and find a job or independent living services.

3482 Social Security Administration
1100 West High Rise
6401 Security Blvd.
Baltimore, MD 21235-3878   517-393-3876
                                    800-772-1213
                                    FAX: 517-393-4686
                                    TTY: 800-325-0778
                           jennifer.bower@ssa.gov
                                    ssa.gov

Tiffany L. Flick, Executive Secretary
Michael J. Astrue, Commissioner
Carolyn W. Colvin, Deputy Commissioner
We deliver services through a nationwide network of over 1,400 offices that include regional offices, field offices, card centers, teleservice centers, processing centers, hearing offices, the Appeals Council, and our State and territorial partners, the Disability Determination Services. We also have a presence in U.S. embassies around the globe. For the public, we are the face of the government. The rich diversity of our employees mirrors the public we serve.

3483 State of Michigan Workers' Compensation Agency
PO Box 30016
Lansing, MI 48909-7516   888-396-5041
                                    FAX: 517-322-1808
                           wcinfo@michigan.gov
                           www.michigan.gov/wca/

Mark C. Long, Director
Jack A. Nolish, Deputy Director
Julie Lenneman, Administrative Assistant
Michigan's injured workers and their employers are governed by the Workers' Disability Compensation Act. This Act was first adopted in 1912 and provides compensation to workers who suffer an injury on the job and protects employers' liability. The mission of the Workers' Compensation Agency is to efficiently administer the Act and provide prompt, courteous and impartial service to all customers.

Minnesota

3484 International Dyslexia Association: Upper Midwest Branch
International Dyslexia Association
5021 Vernon Ave. S
Suite 159
Minneapolis, MN 55436-2102   612-486-4242
                           info.umw@dyslexiaida.org
                           umw.dyslexiaida.org

Tom Strewler, President
Donna Burns, Member at Large
Jennifer Bennett, Secretary
The Upper Midwest Branch of the International Dyslexia Association serves the residents of Minnesota, North Dakota, South Dakota, and Winnipeg, Canada. They offer local educational conferences about dyslexia and related subjects, Orton-Gillingham training for teachers, tutors, and parents, quarterly speaker series, member discounts on conferences, information line, and tutor referral.

3485 Minnesota Assistive Technology Project
STAR
358 Centennial Office Building
658 Cedar Street
Saint Paul, MN 55155-1402   651-201-2640
                                    888-234-1267
                                    800-627-3529
                                    FAX: 651-282-6671
                           star.program@state.mn.us

Chuck Rassbach, Program Director
Kim Moccia, Program Coordinator
Jennie Delisi, Resource Specialist
A statewide program promoting assistive technology devices and services for persons of all ages with all disabilities.

3486   **Minnesota Board on Aging**
P.O. Box 64976
Saint Paul, MN 55164-0976   651-431-2500
                                    800-882-6262
                                    800-333-2433
                                    FAX: 651-431-7453
                                    TTY:800-627-3529
                                    www.mnaging.org

Don Samuelson, Chair
Jean Wood, Executive Director
Leonard Axelrod, Board Member
A state unit on aging for the state of Minnesota. Funds 14 area agencies on aging throughout the state that provide services at the local level. The mission is to keep older people in the homes or places of residence for as long as possible.

3487   **Minnesota Children with Special Needs, Minnesota Department of Health**
P.O.Box 64882
Saint Paul, MN 55164-0882   651-201-3650
                                    800-728-5420
                                    FAX: 651-201-3655
                                    TTY: 651-201-5797
                                    health.cyshn@state.mn.us

Dr. Edward Ehlinger, Commissioner
Daniel L. Pollock, Deputy Commissioner
Jeanne F. Ayers, Assistant Commissioner
Minnesota Children with Special Health Needs (MCSHN) provides leadership through partnerships with families and other key stakeholders to improve the access and quality of all systems impacting children and youth with special health care needs and their families.

3488   **Minnesota Department of Human Services: Behavioral Health Division**
P.O. Box 64981
Saint Paul, MN 55164   651-431-2225
                                    800-366-5411
                                    FAX: 651-431-7418
                                    dhs.info@state.mn.us
                                    mn.gov/dhs/adult-mental-health

Emily Piper, Commissioner
Charles E. Johnson, Deputy Commissioner
Amy Dellwo, Acting Chief of Staff
Oversees the provision of services to people with mental illness in the state of Minnesota. Services are provided on the local level through a network of 87 county social service departments.

3489   **Minnesota Department of Labor & Industry Workers Compensation Division**
443 Lafayette Rd N
Saint Paul, MN 55155-4301   651-284-5005
                                    800-342-5354
                                    TTY:651-297-4198
                                    dli.communications@state.mn.us
                                    doli.state.mn.us

Ken Petersom, Commissioner
Jessica Looman, Deputy Commissioner
James Honerman, Communications
To reduce the impact of work related injuries for employees and employers. Advice is given and questions answered on the toll-free number.

3490   **Minnesota Disability Law Center**
430 1st Avenue North
Suite 300
Minneapolis, MN 55401- 1780   612-334-5970
                                    800-292-4150
                                    FAX: 612-334-5755
                                    TTY: 612-332-4668
                                    website@mylegalaid.org
                                    mylegalaid.org/about/our-work/disability-law

Mary L. Knoblauch, Chair
Cathy Haukedahl, Executive Director
Andrea Kaufman, Director of Development
Provides free, civil, legal assistance to Minnesotans with disabilities on issues related to their disability.

3491   **Minnesota Governor's Council on Developmental Disabilities**
370 Centennial Office Building
658 Cedar St.
Saint Paul, MN 55155   651-296-4018
                                    877-348-0505
                                    FAX: 651-297-7200
                                    TTY: 800-627-3529
                                    admin.dd@state.mn.us
                                    mn.gov/mnddc

John Hoffman, Chair
Colleen Wieck, PhD, Executive Director
Andrei Hahn, Planner
The mission of the Minnesota Governor's Council on Developmental Disabilities is to provide information, education, and training that will lead to increased independence, productivity, integration and inclusion for people with developmental disabilities and their families.

3492   **Minnesota Protection & Advocacy for Persons with Disabilities**
Minnesota Disability Law Center
2324 University Avenue West
Suite 101B
Saint Paul, MN 55114-1742   651-228-9105
                                    800-292-4150
                                    FAX: 651-222-0745
                                    statesupport@mnlegalservices.org

Mary Kaczorek, Supervising Attorney
Ann Conroy, Office Manager
Elsa Marshall, Education for Justice Coordinato
Provide public legal information on legal issues impacting the rights of low-income Minnesotans

3493   **Minnesota State Council on Disability(MSCOD)**
121 E 7th Place
Suite 107
Saint Paul, MN 55101-2114   651-361-7800
                                    800-945-8913
                                    FAX: 651-296-5935
                                    council.disability@state.mn.us
                                    www.disability.state.mn.us

Joan Willshire, Executive Director
Linda Gremillion, Business Operations Manager
Margot Imdieke Cross, Accessibility Specialist
The MSCOD collaborates, advocates, advises and provide technical information to expand opportunities, increase the quality of life and empower all persons with disabilities. This mission is accomplished by: providing information, referral and technical assistance to thousands of individuals every year via email, letter or telephone; through trainings on a variety of disability related topics; through publications and its web site; and through its advocacy and advisory work.

3494   **Minnesota State Services for the Blind**
2200 University Avenue West
Suite 240
Saint Paul, MN 55114-1840   651-539-2300
                                    800-652-9000
                                    FAX: 651-649-5927
                                    TTY: 651-642-0506
                                    star.program@state.mn.us
                                    mn.gov/deed/job-seekers/blind-visual-i

Richard Strong, Executive Director
Kenneth Trebelhorn, Council Member
Jan Bailey, Chair
State agency serving blind and visually impaired persons with rehabilitation, information access, assistive technology, training and job placement services. Extensive older blind program.

3495   **Social Security: St. Paul Disability Determination**
5210 Perry Robinson
Lansing, MI 48911-3878   877-512-5944
                                    800-772-1213
                                    FAX: 517-393-4686
                                    TTY: 800-325-0778
                                    jennifer.bower@ssa.gov
                                    www.ssa.gov

Karena L. Kilgore, Executive Secretary
Carolyn W. Colvin, Commissioner
Carolyn W. Colvin, Deputy Commissioner

We deliver services through a nationwide network of over 1,400 offices that include regional offices, field offices, card centers, teleservice centers, processing centers, hearing offices, the Appeals Council, and our State and territorial partners, the Disability Determination Services. We also have a presence in U.S. embassies around the globe. For the public, we are the face of the government. The rich diversity of our employees mirrors the public we serve.

Mississippi

3496 International Dyslexia Association: Louisiana Branch
1217 N. 32nd Ave.
Hattiesburg, MS 39401   601-467-1662
carla.carlos4dys@gmail.com
la.dyslexiaida.org

Carla Carlos, President
Lisa Best, Treasurer
Gale Pick, Secretary
Provides free information and referral services for diagnosis and tutoring for parents, educators, physicians, and individuals with dyslexia in Illinois. Membership includes yearly journal and quarterly newsletter.

3497 Mississippi Assistive Technology Division
1281 Highway 51
PO Box 1698
Jackson, MS 39215-1698   601-853-5160
800-443-1000
FAX: 601-853-5158
www.mdrs.ms.gov

Jean Massey, Superintendent of Education
Carey Wright, Superintendent of Education
Jack Virden, Chairman
A statewide program promoting assistive technology devices and services for persons of all ages with all disabilities.

3498 Mississippi Client Assistance Program
Mississippi Department of Rehabilitation Services
500-G East Woodrow Wilson Drive
P.O. Box 4958
Jackson, MS 39296   601-982-7051
FAX: 601-982-1951
www.msdisabilities.com

Dr. Ken Cleveland, President
Presley Posey, Executive Director
Dr. Michael Ogburn, Executive Director
Advocacy program for clients/client applicants for state of MS vocational services.

3499 Mississippi Department of Mental Health
1101 Robert E Lee Bldg
239 North Lamar Street
Jackson, MS 39201   601-359-1288
877-240-8513
FAX: 601-359-6295
TTY: 601-359-6230
www.dmh.ms.gov

Sampat Shivengi, M.D., Chair
George N. Harrison, Vice Chair
Edwin C. Legrand, Executive Director
Administers Mississippi's public programs of serving persons with mental illness, developmental disabilities, alcohol and substance abuse problems, and alzheimer's disease and related dementia.

3500 Mississippi Division of Aging and Adult Services
Mississippi Department Of Human Services
750 North State Street
Jackson, MS 39202-3033   601-355-5536
800-345-6347
877-882-4916
FAX: 601-359-3664
www.mdhs.state.ms.us/

Donald R. Taylor, Executive Director
Julia M. Todd, Director
Judy Collins, Director
Protects the rights of older citizens while expanding their opportunities and access to quality services.

3501 Mississippi State Department of Health
Children s Medical Program
570 East Woodrow Wilson Drive
Post Office Box 1700
Jackson, MS 39216-1700   601-576-7400
866-458-4948
FAX: 601-364-7447
web@HealthyMS.com
www.msdh.state.ms.us

Larry Clark, Director
Vickey Berryman, Director, Bureau of Licensure
Jim Craig, Director, Office of Health Pro
Financial assistance to families of children with physical handicaps. Rehabilitative in nature and has as its goal the correction or reduction of physical handicaps. Eligibility determined by diagnosis and provided to children from birth to age twenty-one. Financial eligibility is determined by factors of family income, family size, estimated cost of treatment and family liabilities. Categories include, but are not limited to: orthopedic, congenital heart defects, cerebral palsy, etc.

3502 Mississippi: Workers Compensation Commission
1428 Lakeland Dr
P.O. Box 5300, 39296-5300
Jackson, MS 39216-4718   601-987-4200
866-473-6922
FAX: 601-987-4220
www.mwcc.state.ms.us

Liles Williams, Chairman
John Junkin, Commissioner
Debra Gibbs, Commissioner
Our goal is to provide the public with useful information regarding Workers' Compensation in the state of Mississippi.

Missouri

3503 Institute for Human Development
University of Missouri-Kansas City
215 W. Pershing Road
6th floor
Kansas City, MO 64108- 2639   816-235-1770
800-444-0821
FAX: 888-503-3107
TTY: 800-452-1185
beckmanncc@umkc.edu
www.ihd.umkc.edu

Carl F. Calkins, Ph.D., Director
Kay Conklin, Training Director
Cindy Beckmann, Assistant to the Director
A statewide program promoting person-centered planning and services for persons of all ages with all disabilities.

3504 Missouri Division Of Developmental Disabilities
Missouri Department Of Mental Health
1706 E. Elm St.
P.O.Box 687
Jefferson City, MO 65102   573-751-4122
800-364-9687
FAX: 573-751-8224
ddmail@dmh.mo.gov
www.dmh.mo.gov

Jay Nixon, Governor
Keith Schafer, Ed.D., Director
Bob Bax, Deputy Director
The Missouri Department of Mental Health was first established as a cabinet-level state agency by the Omnibus State Government Reorganization Act, effective July 1, 1974. State law provides three principal missions for the department: (1) the prevention of mental disorders, developmental disabilities, substance abuse, and compulsive gambling; (2) the treatment, habilitation, and rehabilitation of Missourians who have those conditions; and (3) the improvement of public understanding and attitudes

3505 **Missouri Protection & Advocacy Services**
925 S Country Club Dr
Jefferson City, MO 65109-4510   573-893-3333
                                        866-777-7199
                                    FAX: 573-893-4231
                                    TTY: 800-735-2966
                                        moadvocacy.org

Joe Wrinkle, Chair
Barbara H. French, Vice Chair
Shawn De Loyola, Executive Director
MO P&A potects the rights of individuals with disabilities by
providing advocacy and legal services for disability related issues. As Missouri's Protection and Advocacy system, Mo P&A
investigates allegations of abuse, neglect, death, and violations
of rights against individuals with disabilities. Those who contact
Mo P&A can receive information, referrals, advocacy services or
legal counsel provided through one of nine federally-funded
programs.

3506 **Missouri Rehabilitation Services for the Blind**
615 Howerton Court
PO Box 2320
Jefferson City, MO 65102-2320   573-751-3221
                                        800-592-6004
                                    FAX: 573-751-3091
                                        askrsb@dss.mo.gov
                                        www.dss.mo.gov/fsd/rsb/

Mark Laird, Executive Director
Ronald J. Levy, Director
Brian Kinkade, Deputy Director
Offers services for the totally blind, legally blind, visually im-
paired, including counseling, educational, recreational, rehabili-
tation, computer training and professional training services.

3507 **Social Security: Jefferson City Disability Determination**
129 SCOTT STATION ROAD
Jefferson City, MO 65101-4421   877-405-9803
                                        800-772-1213
                                    FAX: 517-393-4686
                                    TTY: 800-325-0778
                                        jennifer.bower@ssa.gov
                                        www.ssa.gov

Karena L. Kilgore, Executive Secretary
Carolyn W. Colvin, Commissioner
Carolyn W. Colvin, Deputy Commissioner
We deliver services through a nationwide network of over 1,400
offices that include regional offices, field offices, card centers,
teleservice centers, processing centers, hearing offices, the Appeals Council, and our State and territorial partners, the Disability Determination Services. We also have a presence in U.S.
embassies around the globe. For the public, we are the face of the
government. The rich diversity of our employees mirrors the
public we serve.

3508 **Workers Compensation Board Missouri**
Department of Labor and Industrial Realtions
421 East Dunkin Street
P.O. Box 58
Jefferson City, MO 65102-0058   573-751-4231
                                        800-775-2667
                                        800-320-2519
                                    FAX: 573-751-4945
                                        workerscomp@labor.mo.gov
                                        labor.mo.gov/DWC/

Butch Albert, Chairman
James Avery, Commissioner
Curtis E. Chick, Commissioner
The Missouri Division of Workers' Compensation administers
the programs providing services to all stake holders including
workers who have been injured on the job or been exposed to occupational disease arising out of and in the course of employment. The Division makes sure that an injured worker receives
benefits that he/she is entitled to under the Missouri Workers'
Compensation law. The Division's Administrative Law Judges
have the authority to approve settlements or issue awards after a
hear

3509 **Addictive & Mental Disorders Division**
555 Fuller Ave
PO Box 202905
Helena, MT 59620-2905   406-444-3964
                                    FAX: 406-444-4435
                                        www.dphhs.mt.gov/amdd/

Lou Thompson, Administrator
Joan Cassidy, Chemical Dependency Bureau Chief
E. Lee Simes, Medical Director
The mission of the Addictive and Mental Disorders Division
(AMDD) of the Montana Department of Public Health and Hu-
man Services is to implement and improve an appropriate state-
wide system of prevention, treatment, care, and rehabilitation for
Montanans with mental disorders or addictions to drugs or
alcohol.

3510 **Disability Rights Montana**
1022 Chestnut Street
Helena, MT 59601-890   406-449-2344
                                        800-245-4743
                                    FAX: 406-449-2418
                                    TTY: 406-449-2344
                                        advocate@disabilityrightsmt.org
                                        www.disabilityrightsmt.org/janda3/

Bernadette Franks-Ongoy, Executive Director
Kelli Kaufman, Director of Finance & Administra
Steve Heaverlo, Director of Programs/Advocacy Sp
Protects and advocates the human and legal rights of Montanans
with mental and physical disabilities while advancing dignity,
equality, and self-determination. Designated federal P&A, with
AT, CAP, PADD, PAIMI and PAIR programs. Advocacy and legal
services for abuse, neglect, rights violations, access, discrimination in employment, accommodations and housing, and assistance with vocational rehabilitation/visual services.

3511 **MonTECH**
029 McGill Hall
University of Montana
Missoula, MT 59803   406-243-5751
                                        877-243-5511
                                    FAX: 406-243-4730
                                        montech@ruralinstitute.umt.edu
                                        montech.ruralinstitute.umt.edu

Anna Goldman, Program Director
Chris Clasby, Program Coordinator
Leslie Mullette
Specializing in Assistive Technology and oversee a variety of AT
related grants and contracts. The overall goal is to develop a comprehensive, statewide system of assistive technology related assistance. Striving to ensure that all people in Montana with
disabilities have equitable access to assistive technology devices
and services in order to enhance their independence, productivity
and quality of life.

3512 **Montana Blind & Low Vision Services**
111 N Last Chance Gulch, Suite 4C
PO Box 4210
Helena, MT 59604-4210   406-444-2590
                                        877-296-1197
                                    FAX: 406-444-3632
                                        dphhs.mt.gov

Lou Thompson, Administrator
Joan Cassidy, Chemical Dependency Bureau Chief
E. Lee Simes, Medical Director
Mission: promoting work and independence for Montanans with
disabilities.

3513 **Montana Council on Developmental Disabilities**
2714 Billings Ave
Helena, MT 59601-9767   406-443-4332
                                        866-443-4332
                                    FAX: 406-443-4192
                                        www.mtcdd.org

Deborah Swingley, CEO/Executive Director
Dee Burrell, Contract Manager
The Council is made up of Montanans both with and without de-
velopmental disabilities, who believe in improving the lives of
Montana's citizens who have a disability. We concentrate on is-

sues related to self-determination, education, employment, transportation, housing, recreation, health care, community inclusion and the overall quality of life of people with developmental disabilities. As a Council we are committed to both question, and action as we work to discover and promote creative ways t

3514   Montana Department of Aging
Room 210
111 Sanders
Helena, MT 59604   406-444-7734
                                           FAX: 406-444-3465
                                           www.agingcare.com

Keith Messmer, Manager
Jeff Sturm, President

3515   Montana Department of Handicapped Children
111 North Sanders Street
Helena, MT 59620   406-444-7734
                                           FAX: 406-444-3465
                                           dphhs.mt.gov

Keith Messmer, Manager

**3516   Montana Protection & Advocacy for Persons with
          Disabilities**
1022 Chestnut Street
Helena, MT 59601-820   406-449-2344
                                                 800-245-4743
                                           FAX: 406-449-2418
                                           TTY: 406-449-2344
                                advocate@disabilityrightsmt.org
                           www.disabilityrightsmt.org/janda3/
Susie McIntyre, President
Will Warberg, Sales and Marketing Manager
Bernadette Franks-Ongoy, Executive Director
Disability Rights Montana is the federally-mandated civil rights protection and advocacy system for Montana. We have the legal authority to represent almost any person with a disability.

3517   Montana State Fund
P.O.Box 4759
Helena, MT 59604-4759   406-495-5000
                                                 800-332-6102
                                           FAX: 406-495-5020
                                           TTY: 406-495-5030
                                    www.montanastatefund.com
Elizabeth Best, Chairman
Montana State Fund is committed to the health and economic prosperity of Montana through superior service, leadership and caring individuals, working in an environment of teamwork, creativity and trust.

3518   Social Security: Helena Disability Determination
10 W 15th St
Ste 1600
Helena, MT 59626-9704   406-441-1270
                                                 800-772-1213
                                           TTY:406-441-1278
                                    www.socialsecurity.gov
Karena L. Kilgore, Executive Secretary
Carolyn W. Colvin, Commissioner
Carolyn W. Colvin, Deputy Commissioner
Social Security offers online information and services to third parties who do business with them.

Nebraska

3519   Nebraska Advocacy Services
134 S 13th St
Suite 600
Lincoln, NE 68508-1930   402-474-3183
                                                 800-422-6691
                                           FAX: 402-474-3274
                             info@disabilityrightsnebraska.org
                             www.disabilityrightsnebraska.org
Jill Flagel, Chairperson
Mary Angus, Vice-Chairperson
Timothy F. Shaw, Chief Executive Officer
Offers protection and advocacy services to people with developmental disabilities or mental illness. Direct assistance provided if

issue within broad case priorities. Sliding scale fee. Information and referral at no cost.

3520   Nebraska Client Assistance Program
301 Centennial Mall South
P. O. Box 94987
Lincoln, NE 68509-4987   402-471-3656
                                                 800-742-7594
                                           FAX: 402-471-3656
                                victoria.rasmussen@nebraska.gov
                                           www.cap.state.ne.us/
The Nebraska Client Assistance Program (CAP) is a free service to help you find solutions if you are having problems with Vocational Rehabilitation, Nebraska Commission for the Blind and Visually Impaired or Centers for Independent Living.

3521   Nebraska Commission for the Blind & Visually Impaired
4600 Valley Rd
Suite 100
Lincoln, NE 68510-4844   402-471-2891
                                                 877-809-2419
                                           FAX: 402-471-3009
                                kathy.stephens@nebraska.gov
                                           ncbvi.state.ne.us
Pearl Van zandt, Executive Director
Carlos Servan, Deputy Director
Bob Deaton, Deputy Director
Offers services for the totally blind, legally blind, visually impaired, and more with health, counseling, educational, recreational, rehabilitation, computer training and professional training services.

**3522   Nebraska Department of Health & Human Services of
          Medically Handicapped Children's Prgm**
301 Centennial Mall S
5TH Floor
Lincoln, NE 68508-2529   402-471-3121
                                                 800-383-4278
                                           FAX: 402-471-3577
                                           dhhs.ne.gov

Kerry Winterer, Chief Executive Officer
Amy Borer, Admininstrative Assistant,Divisi
Dan Howell, CEO,Beatrice State Developmental
Maternal and child health, Title V, children with special health care needs; community based, statewide programs to facilitate diagnoses and care of children with disabilities and chronic medical conditions.

**3523   Nebraska Department of Health and Human Services,
          Division of Aging Services**
P.O.Box 95026
301 Centennial Mall South
Lincoln, NE 68509-5026   402-471-2115
                                                 800-942-7830
                                           FAX: 402-471-3577
                                           dhhs.ne.gov

Kerry Winterer, Chief Executive Officer
Amy Borer, Admininstrative Assistant,Divisi
Dan Howell, CEO,Beatrice State Developmental
The Council focuses on persons who experience a severe disability that occurs before the individual attains the age of 22, which includes persons with physical disabilities, mental/behavioral health conditions and persons that are served by the current state developmental disabilities system.

3524   Nebraska Department of Mental Health
4545 South 86th Street
Lincoln, NE 68526-2529   402-483-6990
                                                 888-210-8064
                                           FAX: 402-483-7045
                                           www.nmhc-clinics.com
Jill Zlomke McPherson, Executive Director
Thomas I. McPherson, Technical Coordinator
Lee Zlomke, Clinical Director
Nebraska Mental Health Centers is a family mental health clinic for people from all walks of life. Among the many services we provide are psychological evaluations, individual and group counseling, substance abuse care, neuropsychological services, domestic violence group intervention and help for victims of domestic violence, treatment for eating disorders, an ADHD clinic, Women's Counseling and much more.

3525 Nebraska Planning Council on Developmental Disabilities
Department of Health and Human Services
P.O.Box 95026
Lincoln, NE 68509-5026
402-471-2115
FAX: 402-471-3577
TTY:402-471-9570
dhhs.ne.gov/developmental_disabilities/Pages/
Mary Gordon, Executive Director
Kerry Winterer, Chief Executive Officer
Amy Borer, Admininstrative Assistant,Divisi
The Council focuses on persons who experience a severe disability that occurs before the individual attains the age of 22, which includes persons with physical disabilities, mental/behavioral health conditions and persons that are served by the current state developmental disabilities system.

3526 Nebraska Workers' Compensation Court
State of Nebraska
P.O.Box 98908
Lincoln, NE 68509-8908
402-471-6468
800-599-5155
FAX: 402-471-8231
www.wcc.ne.gov/
Glenn W. Morton, Administrator
Susan K. Davis, Public Information Manager
Jacqueline J Boesen, General Counsel
It is the web site of the Nebraska Workers' Compensation Court. The court maintains this web site to enhance public access and provide general information regarding workers' compensation in Nebraska.

3527 Social Security: Lincoln Disability Determination
Department of Education
P.O.Box 94987
Lincoln, NE 68509-4987
402-471-2295
800-772-1213
TTY:402-471-3659
www.socialsecurity.gov
Karena L. Kilgore, Executive Secretary
Carolyn W. Colvin, Commissioner
Carolyn W. Colvin, Deputy Commissioner
Social Security offers online information and services to third parties who do business with them.

Nevada

3528 Aging and Disability Services Division
3416 Goni Rd
Suite D 132
Carson City, NV 89706-8008
775-687-4210
800-992-0900
FAX: 775-687-0574
adsd@adsd.nv.gov
adsd.nv.gov
Jane Gruner, Administrator
Tina Gerber-Winn, Deputy Administrator
Michele Ferral, Deputy Administrator
Provides services for seniors in Nevada including community based care. advocacy and volunteer programs. Call write or e-mail for more information.

3529 Nevada Assistive Technology Project
Ste 32
3656 Research Way
Carson City, NV 89706-7932
775-687-4452
888-337-3839
FAX: 775-687-3292
Todd Butterworth, Manager
Serves all ages and all disabilities through partnerships with community organizations. The NATP provides training, advocacy, funding, information and referral services, a newsletter and weekly television show.

3530 Nevada Bureau of Vocational Rehabilitation
500 East Third Street
Carson City, NV 89713
775-684-0400
FAX: 775-684-4184
TTY:775-684-0360
detr.state.nv.us
Maureen Cole, Administrator
Melaine Mason, Deputy Administrator, Operations
Janice John, Deputy Administrator, Programs
Bureau of Vocational Rehabilitation is a state and federally funded program designed to help people with disabilities become employed and to help those already employed perform more successfully through training, counseling and other support methods.

3531 Nevada Community Enrichment Program (NCEP)
2550 University Avenue
Suite 330N
Saint Paul, MN 55114
651-645-7271
800-466-7722
FAX: 651-645-0541
TTY: 800-627-352
info@accessiblespace.org
Mark E. Hamel, Esq., Chair
Kay Knutson, Vice Chair
John W. Adams, MBA, Secretary
Comprehensive neurological rehabilitation and life skills training.

3532 Nevada Developmental Disability Council
896 W. Nye Ln.
Suite 202
Carson City, NV 89703
775-687-8619
FAX: 775-684-8626
www.nevadaddcouncil.org
Jodi Thornley, Chairman
Santa Perez, Vice Chairman
Sherry Manning, Executive Director
The mission of the Nevada Developmental Disabilities Council is to provide resources at the community level which promote equal opportunity and life choices for people with disabilities through which they may positively contribute to Nevada society.

3533 Nevada Disability Advocacy and Law Center -Sparks/Reno Office
2820 West Charleston
Boulevard #11
Las Vegas, NV 89102
702-257-8150
888-349-3843
FAX: 702-257-8170
lasvegas@ndalc.org
www.ndalc.org
Reggie Bennettr, Secretary/Treasurer
Jana Spoor, President
John Miller, Vice President
Nevada's protection and advocacy system for the human legal and service rights of individuals with disabilities. NDALC has offices in Reno/Sparks and Las Vegas, with services provided statewide.

3534 Nevada Division for Aging: Las Vegas
175 Berkeley Street
Boston, MA 02116
888-398-8924
libertymutual.com
Michael J. Babcockrs, Director
Marian L. Heard, Director
Martn P. Slark, Director
Develops, coordinates and delivers a comprehensive support service system in order for Nevada' senior citizens to lead independent, meaningful and dignified lives.

3535 Nevada Division of Mental Health and Developmental Services
5865 Lakeshore Road
Buford, GA 30518
770-945-4441
FAX: 678-482-1965
Keith Mixon, CEO/President
Offers treatment, prevention, education, habitation and rehabilitation for mental disorders. Works with advocacy groups, families, agencies and the community.

3536 Social Security: Carson City Disability Determination
1170 Harvard Way
Reno, NV 89502-2107
775-784-5221
800-772-1213
FAX: 775-784-5501
TTY: 800-325-0778
www.socialsecurity.gov

Karena L. Kilgore, Executive Secretary
Carolyn W. Colvin, Commissioner
Carolyn W. Colvin, Deputy Commissioner
Social Security offers online information and services to third parties who do business with them.

3537 State of Nevada Client Assistance Program
1631 W. Craig Rd.
Suite # 9-162
North Las Vegas, NV 89032-3767
702-635-4020
800-633-9879
800-633-9879
FAX: 702-642-7020
TTY: 800-633-9879

To provide information to and safegaurd rights of applicants and clients or individuals who seek services such as vocational rehabilitation or independent living from agencies which provide those services under the Rehabilitation Act, and to provide information to individuals about the employment discrimination title of the Americans with Disabilities Act.

3538 Workers Compensation Board Nevada
1301 North Green Valley Parkway
Suite 200
Henderson, NV 89074
702-486-9000
FAX: 775-687-6305
dirweb.state.nv.us

New Hampshire

3539 New Hampshire Workers Compensation Board
46 Donovan St
Concord, NH 03301-2624
603-225-2841
800-698-2364
FAX: 603-226-6903
www.nhprimex.org

Ty Gagne, CEO
Jonathan Kipp, Operations Manager
Julie Converse, Director of Finance
Primex3 stands ready to provide our school, municipal, and county government members with the most comprehensive coverages and services available to New Hampshire local government.

3540 New Hampshire Assistive Technology Partnership Project
Department of Education
10 West Edge Drive
Suite 101
Durham, NH 03824
603-862-4320
FAX: 603-862-0555
atinnh.org

Jan Nisbet, Director
Mary Schuh, Associate Director
Eve Fralick, Associate Director
The goal of the New Hampshire Assistive Technology Partnership Project is to increase access to assistive technology through the creation and support of consumer driven systems for the provision of state-of-the-art assistive technology products and services for citizens with disabilities in the state of New Hampshire.

3541 New Hampshire Bureau of Developmental Services
Department of Health and Human Services
129 Pleasant St
Concord, NH 03301-3852
603-271-5034
FAX: 603-271-5166
www.dhhs.nh.gov

Matthew Ertas, Director
Peggy Sue Greenwood, Administrative Assistant
Developmental Services promotes opportunities for normal life experiences for persons with developmental disabilities and aquired brain disorders in all areas of community life: employ-

ment, housing, recreation, social relationships and community association. Services and supports are organized throught a central state office and ten private nonprofit community area agencies. Family support is provided to families of children with chronic health conditions or are developmentally disabled.

3542 New Hampshire Client Assistance Program
121 South Fruit Street
Suite 101
Concord, NH 03301-8518
603-271-2773
800-852-3405
FAX: 603-271-2837
Disability@nh.gov
www.state.nh.us/disability/caphomepage.html

Bill Hagy, Ombudsman
John Richards, Executive Director
Jillian Shedd, Accessibility Coordinator
The Commission's goal is to remove the barriers, architectural, attitudinal or programmatic, that bar persons with disabilities from participating in the mainstream of society.

3543 New Hampshire Commission for Human Rights
64 South Street
Concord, NH 03301-8501
603-225-3431
800-735-2964
FAX: 603-224-3766
webmaster@nh.gov
www.nh.gov

Peggy Mc Allister, Executive Director
Enforces New Hampshire law against discrimination in housing, employment or public accomodations. Disability discrimination is prohibited under New Hampshire law. Takes formal charges and investigates them.

3544 New Hampshire Department of Mental Health
129 Pleasant Street
Concord, NH 03301-3852
603-226-0111
FAX: 603-271-5058
www.dhhs.nh.gov

Donald Shumway, Director
Paul Garmon
Tim Rourke, Religious Leader

3545 New Hampshire Developmental Disabilities Council
2 1/2 Beacon Street
21 Fruit Street
Concord, NH 03301- 4447
603-271-3236
800-852-3345
800-852-3236
FAX: 603-271-1156
TTY: 800-735-2964
nhddc.org

Kristen McGraw, Chairman
Katherine Epstein, Vice-Chair
Carol Stamatakis, Executive Director
Offers information, referral and support services to disabled persons. A federally funded state agency.

3546 New Hampshire Division of Elderly and Adult Services
Bureau of Elderly & Adult Services
129 Pleasant St
Concord, NH 03301-3852
603-271-4680
800-351-1888
FAX: 603-271-4643
pio@dhhs.state.nh.us
www.dhhs.state.nh.us

Nicholas A. Toumpas, Comissioner
Mary Maggioncaida, Administrator
Marilee Nihan, Deputy Commissioner
The Bureau of Elderly and Adult Services provides a variety of social and long-term supports to adults age 60 and older and to adults between the ages of 18 and 60 who have a chronic illness or disability. These services range from home care, meals on wheels, care management, transportation assistance and assisted living to nursing home care.

3547 New Hampshire Governor's Commission on Disability
121 South Fruit Street
Suite 101
Concord, NH 03301-8518
603-271-2773
800-852-3405
FAX: 603-271-2837
Disability@nh.gov
www.nh.gov/disability

Paul Van Blarigan, Chairman
Charles J. Saia, Executive Director
Michael Coe, Accessibility Coordinator
The Commission's goal is to remove the barriers, architectural, attitudinal or programmatic, that bar persons with disabilities from participating in the mainstream of socie

3548 New Hampshire Protection & Advocacy for Persons with Disabilities
Disabilities Rights Center, Inc
64 North Main Street
Suite 2, 3rd Floor
Concord, NH 03301-4913
603-228-0432
800-834-1721
FAX: 603-225-2077
TTY: 800-834-1721
advocacy@drcnh.org
drcnh.org

Paul Levy, President
Joanne Malloy, Vice President
Richard Cohen, Executive Director
Legal services for individuals with disabilities; I & R.

3549 Social Security: Concord Disability Determination
Ste 100
70 Commercial St
Concord, NH 03301-5005
603-224-1939
800-772-1213
TTY:800-325-0778
www.ssa.gov

Karena L. Kilgore, Executive Secretary
Carolyn W. Colvin, Commissioner
Carolyn W. Colvin, Deputy Commissioner
Social Security offers online information and services to third parties who do business with them.

3550 Workers Compensation Board New Hampshire
PO Box 2076
95 Pleasant Street
Concord, NH 03301
603-271-3176
800-272-4353
FAX: 603-271-2668
workerscomp@labor.state.nh.us
www.nh.gov/labor

Kathryn J. Barger, Director, Workers' Compensation
George N. Copadis, Commissioner of Labor
David M. Wihby, Deputy Commissioner
The Department of Labor monitors Employers, Workers Compensation, and Insurance Carriers to insure that they are in compliance with NH Labor laws. These laws range from minimum wage, overtime, safety issues and workers compensation.

New Jersey

3551 Division of Developmental Disabilities
210 South Broad Street
3rd Floor
Trenton, NJ 08608
609-292-9742
800-922-7233
FAX: 609-777-0187
TTY: 609-633-7106
advocate@drnj.org
www.njpanda.org

James W Smith Jr, Executive Director
New Jersey's designated protection and advocacy system for poeple with disabilities and provides legal, nonlegal individual and systems advocacy.

3552 International Dyslexia Association: New Jersey Branch
P.O. Box 32
Long Valley, NJ 07853
908-876-1179
FAX: 908-876-3621
njida@msn.com
nj.dyslexiaida.org

Patricia Barden, President
Provides free information and referral services for diagnosis and tutoring for parents, educators, physicians, and individuals with dyslexia in Illinois. Membership includes yearly journal and quarterly newsletter.

3553 New Jersey Commission for the Blind and Visually Impaired
153 Halsey St, Fl 6
PO Box 47017
Newark, NJ 7101-4701
973-648-3333
877-685-8878
FAX: 973-693-5046
www.state.nj.us/humanservices/cbvi

Daniel B. Frye, J.D., Executive Director
Bernice Davis, Executive Assistant
Edward Szajdecki, Manager
The mission of the New Jersey Commission for the Blind and Visually Impaired is to promote and provide services in the areas of education, employment, independence and eye health through informed choice and partnership with persons who are blind or visually impaired, their families and the community. Serves Bergen, Essex, Hudson, Morris, Passaic, Sussex and Warren Counties.

3554 New Jersey Department of Aging
210 South Broad Street
3rd Floor
Trenton, NJ 08608
609-292-9742
800-922-7233
FAX: 609-777-0187
TTY: 609-633-7106
advocate@drnj.org
www.drnj.org

Walter Anthony Woodberry, Chairman
Andrew McGeady, Vice Chairman
Linda K. Soley, Treasurer

3555 New Jersey Department of Health/Special Child Health Services
New Jersey Department of Health and Senior Service
P.O.Box 360
Trenton, NJ 08625-0360
609-777-7778
FAX: 609-292-3580
www.nj.gov/health/fhs/sch/

Jennifer Velez, ESQ, Commissioner
Provides services for New Jersey children that will prevent or reduce the effects of a developmental delay, chronic illness or behavioral disorder.

3556 New Jersey Division of Mental Health Services
Department Human Services
222 South Warren Street
P.O. Box 700
Trenton, NJ 8625- 700
609-292-3717
800-382-6717
FAX: 609-341-3333
www.state.nj.us/humanservices

Jennifer Velez, ESQ, Commissioner
Lynn A. Kovich, Assistant Commissioner
Oversees the public mental health system for the state of New Jersey. Operates six regional and specialty psychiatric hospitals, and contracts with over 125 not-for-profit agencies to provide a comprehensive system of community mental health services throughout all counties in the state.

3557 **New Jersey Governor's Liaison to the Office of Disability Employment Policy**
1 John Fitch Plaza
P. O.Box 110
Trenton, NJ 08625-110
609-659-9045
FAX: 609-633-9271
Constituent.Relations@dol.state.nj.us
lwd.state.nj.us/labor
Harold J. Wriths, Commissioner
Frederick J. Zavaglia, Chief of Staff
Aaron R. Fichtner, Ph.D., Deputy Commissioner

The Division of Vocational Rehabilitation Services provides vocational rehabilitation services to prepare and place in employment eligilbe individuals with disabilities who, because of their disabling conditions, would otherwise be unable to secure and/or mantain employment

3558 **New Jersey Protection & Advocacy for Persons with Disabilities**
210 South Broad Street
3rd Floor
Trenton, NJ 08608
609-292-9742
800-922-7233
FAX: 609-777-0187
TTY: 609-633-7106
advocate@drnj.org
www.drnj.org
Walter Anthony Woodberry, Chairman
Andrew McGeady, Vice Chairman
Linda K. Soley, Treasurer

3559 **Regional ADA Technical Assistance Center**
United Cerebral Palsy Associations of New Jersey
201 Dolgen Hall
Ithaca, NY 14853
607-255-6686
800-949-4232
FAX: 607-255-2763
northeastada@cornell.edu
www.northeastada.org
LaWanda H. Cook, Ph.D., Extension Associate/Training Spe
Hannah Rudstam, Ph.D., Director of Training
Erin Sember-Chase, Project Coordinator and Technic

3560 **Social Security Administration**
1100 West High Rise
6401 Security Blvd.
Baltimore, MD 21235
800-772-1213
TTY:800-325-0778
www.ssa.gov
Karena L. Kilgore, Executive Secretary
Carolyn W. Colvin, Commissioner

Social Security disability is a social insurance program that workers and employers pay for with their Social Security taxes. Eligibility is based on your work history, and the amount of your benefit is based on your earnings. Social Security also has a disability program for people with limited income and resources- the Supplemental Security Income (SSI) program. For more information on these federal programs, please call our nationwide toll-free number.

New Mexico

3561 **New Mexico Aging and Long-Term Services Department**
2550 Cerrillos Rd
P.O. Box 27118
Santa Fe, NM 87505-3260
505-476-4799
866-451-2901
FAX: 505-476-4836
www.nmaging.state.nm.us
Miles Copeland, Deputy Secretary
Retta Ward, Secretary
Jason Sanchez, Administrative Services Division
Information and services for seniors, people with disabilities and their families.

3562 **New Mexico Client Assistance Program**
1720 Louisiana Blvd NE
Site 204
Albuquerque, NM 87110- 7070
505-256-3100
800-432-4682
FAX: 505-256-3184
info@drnm.org
www.drnm.org
Katie Toledo, Chairperson
Cyndy Costanza, Vice Chairperson
Jeanne A. Hamrick, President
The mission of Disability Rights New Mexico (DRNM) is to protect, promote and expand the legal and civil rights of persons with disabilities. DRNM is an independent, private nonprofit agency operating federally mandated and other advocacy programs in pursuit of this mission.

3563 **New Mexico Commission for the Blind (NMCFTB)**
2905 Rodeo Park Dr E
Bldg 4, Suite 100
Santa Fe, NM 87505
505-476-4479
888-513-7968
www.cfb.state.nm.us
Arthur A. Schreiber, Chairman
Shirley Lansing, Commissioner
Robert Reidy, Commissioner
Offers services for the totally blind, legally blind, visually impaired, and more with health, counseling, educational, recreational, rehabilitation, computer training and professional training services.

3564 **New Mexico Department of Health: Children's Medical Services**
1190 S Saint Francis Dr
Santa Fe, NM 87505-4173
505-841-6100
800-797-3260
FAX: 505-827-2530
Gloria Bonner, Program Manager
Susan Baum, Medical Director
Freida Adams, Nurse Coordinator
Title V MCH Program for children with special health care needs from birth to age 21 years. Services provided include: diagnosis, medical intervention, clinics and service coordination.

3565 **New Mexico Governor's Committee on Concerns of the Handicapped**
491 Old Santa Fe Trl
Santa Fe, NM 87501-2753
505-476-0412
877-696-1470
FAX: 505-827-6328
gcd@state.nm.us
www.gcd.state.nm.us/
Susan Gray, Chair
Curtiss Wilson, Vice Chair
Jim Parker, Director

3566 **New Mexico Protection & Advocacy for Persons with Disabilities**
1720 Louisiana Blvd NE
Site 204
Albuquerque, NM 87110- 7070
505-256-3100
800-432-4682
FAX: 505-256-3184
info@drnm.org
www.drnm.org
Katie Toledo, Chairperson
Cyndy Costanza, Vice Chairperson
Jeanne A. Hamrick, President
The mission of Disability Rights New Mexico (DRNM) is to protect, promote and expand the legal and civil rights of persons with disabilities. DRNM is an independent, private nonprofit agency operating federally mandated and other advocacy programs in pursuit of this mission.

3567 New Mexico Technology Assistance Program
625 Silver Ave SW
Suite 100 B
Albuquerque, NM 87102   505-841-4464
                                      877-696-1470
                                 FAX: 505-841-4467
                              www.tap.gcd.state.nm.us

Tracy Agiovlasitis, Program Manager
Examines and works to eliminate barriers to obtaining assistive
technology in New Mexico. Has established a statewide program
for coordinating assistive technology services; is designed to assist people with disabilities to locate, secure, and maintain
assistive technology.

3568 New Mexico Workers Compensation Administration
2410 Centre Avenue SE
P.O.Box 27198
Albuquerque, NM 87125-7198   505-841-6000
                                      800-255-7965
                                 FAX: 505-841-6009
                              www.workerscomp.state.nm.us/

Ned S. Fuller, Director
Robert E. Doucette, Executive Deputy Director
Darin A. Childers, General Counsel
Regulates workers' compensation in New Mexico.

3569 Social Security: Santa Fe Disability Determination
6401 Security Blvd.
Baltimore, MD 21235   800-772-1213
                                 TTY:800-325-0778
                                www.socialsecurity.gov

Karena L. Kilgore, Executive Secretary
Carolyn W. Colvin, Commissioner
Carolyn W. Colvin, Deputy Commissioner

**3570 Southwest Branch of the International Dyslexia
Association**
International Dyslexia Association
3915 Carlisle Blvd. NE
Albuquerque, NM 87107   505-255-8234
                                      800-222-3123
                                 FAX: 505-262-8547
                              swida@southwestida.org

Carolee Dean, President
Claudia Gutierrez, Vice President
Michelle Wick, Recording Secretary
Provides free information and referral services for diagnosis and
tutoring for parents, educators, physicians, and individuals with
dyslexia. The voice of our membership is heard in 48 countries.
Membership includes yearly journal and quarterly newsletter.
Call for conference dates.

3571 Workers Compensation Board New Mexico
2410 Centre Avenue SE
P.O.Box 27198
Albuquerque, NM 87125-7198   505-841-6000
                                      800-255-7965
                                 FAX: 505-841-6009
                              www.workerscomp.state.nm.us/

Ned S. Fuller, Director
Robert E. Doucette, Executive Deputy Director
Darin A. Childers, General Counsel
Regulates workers' compensation in New Mexico.

New York

**3572 Albany County Department for Aging and Albany Social
Services**
112 State Street
Room 900
Albany, NY 12207-2304   518-447-7000
                                 FAX: 518-447-7188
                              aging@albanycounty.com
                                    albanycounty.com

George Brown, Commissioner
Judy L. Coyne, Commissioner
Kathleen M. Dalton, Ph.D., Commissioner

The Point of Entry access line provides information and assistance and comprehensive referrals, and or assessments for the elderly, adults and children with disabilities, their family, or
service providers.

3573 Jawonio
260 N Little Tor Road
New City, NY 10956-2627   845-708-2000
                                 FAX: 845-634-7731
                                 TTY:845-639-3521
                                    www.jawonio.org

Jill A. Warner, Executive Director & CEO
Matthew Shelly, Chief Program Officer
Diana Hess, Chief Communications Officer
A dedicated community resource providing services to more than
500 children and adults annually. Provide early intervention, day
care and pre-school special ed to our children. Job training, day
habilitation, recreation, medical and service coordination for
adults.

3574 Jawonio Vocational Center
260 N Little Tor Rd
New City, NY 10956-2627   845-708-2000
                                 FAX: 845-634-7731
                                 TTY:845-639-3521
                                        jawonio.org

Jill A. Warner, Executive Director & CEO
Matthew Shelly, Chief Program Officer
Diana Hess, Chief Communications Officer
A dedicated community resource providing services to more than
500 children and adults annually. Provide early intervention, day
care and pre-school special ed to our children. Job training, day
habilitation, recreation, medical and service coordination for
adults.

**3575 NYS Commission on Quality of Care & Advocacy for
Persons with Disabilities**
401 State St
Schenectady, NY 12305-2300   518-388-2892
                                 FAX: 518-388-2890

Andrew M. Cuomo, Governor
Roger Bearden, Chair
Bruce Blower, Member

3576 NYSARC
393 Delaware Ave
Delmar, NY 12054-3094   518-439-8311
                                      800-724-2094
                                 FAX: 518-439-1893
                                     info@nysarc.org
                                        nysarc.org

Laura J. Kennedy, President
Patricia Campanella, Senior Vice President
Joseph M. Bognanno, Vice President

3577 National Alliance on Mental Illness of New York State
99 Pine Street
Suite 302
Albany, NY 12207-1336   518-462-2000
                                      800-950-3228
                                 FAX: 518-462-3811
                                    info@naminys.org
                                    www.naminys.org

Sherry Grenz, President
Wend Burch, Executive Director
Sharon Clairmont, Finance & Business Office Dir.

3578 New State Office of Mental Health Agency
Office of Mental Health
44 Holland Ave
Albany, NY 12229   518-474-4403
                                      800-597-8481
                                 FAX: 518-474-2149
                                    www.omh.ny.gov

Mike Hogan, Commissioner
Promoting the mental health of all New Yorkers with a particular
focus on providing hope and recovery for adults with serious
mental illness and children with serious emotional disturbances.

3579 New York Client Assistance Program
855 Central Avenue
Suite 110
Albany, NY 12206
518-459-6422
FAX: 518-459-7847
TTY:518-459-6422
www.nls.org

3580 New York Department of Handicapped Children
Department of Heath Education
Corning Tower
Empire State Plaza
Albany, NY 12237
518-456-0665
866-881-2809
FAX: 518-456-1126
www.health.ny.gov

Andrew M. Cuomo, Governor
Dr James B. Crucetti, MD, MPH, Commissioner
Howard Zucker, Acting Commissioner

3581 New York State Commission for the Blind
52 Washington St
Rensselaer, NY 12144-2796
518-473-7793
866-871-3000
FAX: 518-486-7550
www.ocfs.state.ny.us

Madeline Raciti, Manager
Offers services for the totally blind, legally blind, visually impaired, and more with health, counseling, educational, recreational, rehabilitation, computer training and professional training services.

3582 New York State Commission on Quality of Care
401 State St
Schenectady, NY 12305-2300
518-388-2892
FAX: 518-388-2890

Andrew M. Cuomo, Governor
Roger Bearden, Chair
Bruce Blower, Member

3583 New York State Congress of Parents and Teachers
1 Wembley Ct
Albany, NY 12205-6258
518-452-8808
877-569-7782
FAX: 518-452-8105
pta.office@nyspta.org
nyspta.org

Bonnie Russell, President
Gracemarie Rozea, First Vice President
Judy Van Harren, Secretary
Parent Teacher Association and PTA are registered service marks of the National Congress of Parents and Teachers (National PTA). Only those groups chartered by the New York State PTA are entitled to use the name PTA. Any other use constitutes trademark infringement.

3584 New York State Office of Advocates for Persons with Disabilities
Ste 1001
1 Empire State Plz
Albany, NY 12223-1100
518-449-7860
800-522-4369
FAX: 518-473-6005

Gary O'Brien, Chair Commissioner
Provides information and referral services; administers NYS Tech Art Project; promotes implementation of disability-related laws.

3585 New York State Office of Mental Health
44 Holland Ave
Albany, NY 12229-1
518-474-4403
800-597-8481
FAX: 518-474-2149
www.omh.state.ny.gov in

Michael Hogan, Ph.D.
Promoting the mental health of all New Yorkers with a particular focus on providing hope and recovery for adults with serious mental illness and children with serious emotional disturbances.

3586 New York State TRAID Project
New York State Commisionon Qualityof Careand Advoc
Ste 1001
1 Empire State Plz
Albany, NY 12223-1100
518-449-7860
800-522-4369
FAX: 518-473-6005

Cliff Sigfride, Manager

3587 Parent to Parent of New York State
500 Balltown Rd
Schenectady, NY 12304-2247
518-381-4350
800-305-8817
FAX: 518-393-9607
mjuda@ptopnys.org
parenttoparentnys.org

Louise Nitto, President
Jim Costello, Vice President
Elizabeth Smithmeyer, Secretary
Parent to Parent of NYS, which began in 1994, is a statewide not for profit organization established to support and connect families of individuals with special needs. The 13 offices, located throughout NYS, are staffed by Regional Coordinators, who are parents or close relatives of individuals with special needs.

3588 Protection and Advocacy Agency of NY
401 State St
Schenectady, NY 12305-2303
518-388-2892
FAX: 518-388-2890

Andrew M. Cuomo, Governor
Roger Bearden, Chair
Bruce Blower, Member

3589 Regional Early Childhood Director Center
89 Washington Ave.
Room 580 EBA
Albany, NY 12234
518-474-2925
800-222-5627
accesadm@mail.nysed.gov
www.acces.nysed.gov
Provides information, support and referral assistance to parents and professionals who are concerned with chilren with special needs or handicapping condition between the ages of birth to five.

3590 Schools And Services For Children With Autism Spectrum Disorders.
116 E 16th St
5th Floor
New York, NY 10003-2164
212-677-4650
FAX: 212-254-4070

Ellen Miller-Wachtel, Chairman
Shon E. Glusky, President
Owen P. J. King, Treasurer
This publication fun resource for children provides extreme coverage of services for children with autism, asbergez syndrome, and/or PDD.

3591 Singeria/Metropolitan Parent Center
2082 Lexington Ave.
4th Floor
New York, NY 10035
212-643-2840
866-867-9665
FAX: 212-496-5608
intake@sinergiany.org
sinergiany.org

Len Torres, President
Johnny C. Rivera, Vice President
Paola Jordan, Treasurer

3592 Social Security: Albany Disability Determination
1 Clinton Ave
Albany, NY 12207
518-431-4051
800-772-1213
TTY:518-431-4050
www.ssa.gov

Karena L. Kilgore, Executive Secretary
Carolyn W. Colvin, Commissioner
Carolyn W. Colvin, Deputy Commissioner

3593 State Agency for the Blind and Visually Impaired
52 Washington St
Rensselaer, NY 12144-2834
518-473-7793
866-871-3000
FAX: 518-486-7550
info@ocfs.state.ny.us
www.ocfs.state.ny.us

3594 State Education Agency Rural Representative
89 Washington Avenue
Albany, NY 12234
518-474-3852
FAX: 518-473-2860
RegentsOffice@mail.nysed.gov
www.nysed.gov

Merryl H. Tisch, Chancellor
Anthony S. Bottar, Vice Chancellor

3595 State Mental Health Representative for Children and Youth
44 Holland Ave
Albany, NY 12229
518-473-6328
www.rcybc.ca

David Woodlock, Deputy Commissioner

3596 United We Stand of New York
98 Moore St
Brooklyn, NY 11206-3326
718-302-4313
FAX: 718-302-4315
uwsofny@aol.com

Lourdes Rivera-Putz, Executive Director
Lourdes Figueroa, Intake/Receptionist
Carmen Soltero, Outreach/Trainer
Assists families with improving the quality of life for all individuals with disabilities.

3597 University Afiliated Program/Rose F Kennedy Center
1971
1300 Morris Park Avenue
Bronx, NY 10461
718-430-2000
www.einstein.yu.edu

Maris D. Rosenberg, Interim Director
Christine M. Baric, Assistant Director
John J. Foxe, Director

3598 University of Rochester Medical Center
601 Elmwood Ave
Rochester, NY 14642
585-275-8762
FAX: 585-275-3366
phil_davidson@urmc.rochester.edu
www.rochester.edu

Brad Berk, MD, PhD, CEO

3599 VESID
New York State Education Department
89 Washington Ave.
Room 580 EBA
Albany, NY 12234
800-222-5627
FAX: 518-474-8802
accesadm@mail.nysed.gov
www.acces.nysed.gov/vr/

Dr Rebecca Cort, Deputy Commissioner
Vocational and educational services for individuals with disabilities.

3600 VSA Arts of New York City
2700 F Street, NW
Washington, DC 20566
202-467-4600
800-444-1324
FAX: 717-225-6305
bbvsanyc@msn.com

David M. Rubenstein, Chairman
Deborah F. Rutter, President
Christoph Eschenbach, Music Director
Provides art, educational and creative expression experiences to thousands of children, youth, and adults with disabilities who reside in the five boroughs of New York City. It provides opportunities for people with disabilities to demonstrate their accomplishments in the arts and foster increased understanding and acceptance.

3601 Westchester Institute for Human Development
Cedarwood Hall
Valhalla, NY 10595
914-493-8150
info@WIHD.org
www.wihd.org

William H. Bave, Chairman
Pamela Thornton, Vice Chairman
Ansley Bacon PhD, President/CEO
WIHD advances policies and practices that foster the healthy development and ensure the safety of all children, strengthen families and communities, and promote health and well-being among people of all ages with disabilities and special health care needs.

3602 Workers Compensation Board New York
PO Box 5205
328 State Street
Schenectady, NY 12305-2318
518-462-8880
877-632-4996
FAX: 518-473-1415
www.wcb.ny.gov

Andrew M. Cuomo, Governor
Robert E. Beloten, Chairman
Richard A. Bell, Commissioner

North Carolina

3603 Developmental Disability Services Section
Building 325n
Albemarle
Raleigh, NC 27699
919-420-7901
FAX: 919-420-7917
www.dhhs.state.nc.us/mhddsas/

Diana Simmons, Human Resources Manager
Ureh N. Lekwauwa, Chief, Clinical Policy
Courtney Cantrell, Acting Director
Makes policies and monitors public services and supports to people with mental illness, developmental disabilities and substance abuse throughout North Carolina.

3604 International Dyslexia Association: North Carolina Branch
NC
nc.dyslexiaida.org
Kris Cox, President
Provides free information and referral services for diagnosis and tutoring for parents, educators, physicians, and individuals with dyslexia in Illinois. Membership includes yearly journal and quarterly newsletter.

3605 North Carolina Workers Compensation Board
4340 Mail Service Center
Raleigh, NC 27699-4340
919-807-2501
800-688-8349
FAX: 919-508-8210
infospec@ic.nc.gov
www.ic.nc.gov

Julian Bunn, Owner

3606 North Carolina Assistive Technology Project
1110 Navaho Dr
Suite 101
Raleigh, NC 27609-7322
919-872-2298
FAX: 919-850-2792

Ricki Cook, Project Director
Annette Lauber, Funding Specialist
Jacquelyne Gordon, Consumer Resource Specialist
The North Carolina Assistive Technology Project exists to create a statewide, consumer-responsive system of assistive technology services for all North Carolinians with disabilities. The project's activities impact children and adults with disabilities across all aspects of their lives.

3607 North Carolina Children & Youth Branch
North Carolina Publc of Health
1928 Mail Service Ctr
Raleigh, NC 27699-1900
919-839-6262
FAX: 919-733-8034

Lawrence J Wheeler, Manager
Cathy Kluttz, Unit Manager Special Service
Dianne Tyson, Help Line Manager

3608 North Carolina Client Assistance Program
2806 Mail Service Ctr
Raleigh, NC 27699-2806
919-855-3600
800-215-7227
FAX: 919-715-2456
nccap@dhhs.nc.gov
cap.state.nc.us

John Marens, Director
Diane Rawdarowicz, Client Advocate
Sharon Wisner, Client Advocate
A federally funded program designed to assist individuals with disabilities in understanding and using rehabilitation services. CAP serves as an integral part of the rehabilitation system by advising and informing individuals of all services and benefits available to them through programs authorized under both the Rehabilitation Act and Title 1 of the Americans with Disabilities Act.

3609 North Carolina Developmental Disabilities
3125 Poplarwood Court
Suite 200
Raleigh, NC 27604-7368
919-850-2901
800-357-6916
FAX: 919-850-2915
Info@nccdd.org
www.nc-ddc.org

Caroline Valand, Executive Director
A planning council established to assure that individuals with developmental disabilities and their families participate in the planning of and have access to culturally competent services, supports, and other assistance and opportunities that promote independence, productivity, and integration and inclusion into the community; and to promote, through systemic change, capacity building and advocacy activities, a consumer and family-centered comprehensive system.

3610 North Carolina Division of Aging
2101 Mail Service Ctr
Raleigh, NC 27699-2001
919-855-4800
FAX: 919-733-0443
ncdhhs.gov

Dennis Streets, Manager
Jim Slate, Director
Laketha Miller, Controller

3611 North Carolina Industrial Commission
4340 Mail Service Center
Raleigh, NC 27699-4340
919-807-2501
800-688-8349
FAX: 919-508-8210
infospec@ic.nc.gov
www.ic.nc.gov

J Howard Bunn Jr, Chairman
Peg Dorer, Executive Director

3612 Social Security Administration
4701 Old Wake Forest Rd
Raleigh, NC 27609-4919
877-803-6311
800-772-1213
800-325-0778
FAX: 919-790-2860
TTY:919-790-2773
www.socialsecurity.gov

Karena L. Kilgore, Executive Secretary
Carolyn W. Colvin, Commissioner
Provides information on how to obtain social security through a disability.

North Dakota

3613 Division of Mental Health and Substance Abuse
600 East Boulevard Avenue
Dept 325
Bismarck, ND 58505- 0250
701-328-2310
800-472-2622
FAX: 701-328-2359
dhseo@nd.gov
www.nd.gov/humanservices

Dennis Goetz, Executive Director
Kerry Wicks, Executive Director
Andrew J. McLean, Medical Director
The Department of Human Services' Mental Health and Substance Abuse Services Division provides leadership for the planning, development, and oversight of a system of care for children, adults, and families with severe emotional disorders, mental illness, and/or substance abuse issues.

3614 North Dakota Workers Compensation Board
50 E Front Ave
Bismarck, ND 58504
701-328-3800
800-777-5033
FAX: 701-329-9911
TTY: 701-328-3786

Brent Edison, Director

3615 North Dakota Client Assistance Program
400 East Broadway
Suite 409
Bismarck, ND 58501-4071
701-328-2950
800-472-2670
FAX: 701-328-3934
panda@nd.gov
www.ndpanda.org/cap

Dennis Lyon, CEO
Janelle Olson, Advocate
Paula Rustad, Office Assistant
CAP assists clients and client applicants of North Dakota Vocational Rehabilitation services, Tribal Vocational Rehabilitation, or Independent Living services.

3616 North Dakota Department of Human Resources
1237 W Divide Ave
Suite 6
Bismarck, ND 58501-1208
701-328-5300
800-451-8693
FAX: 701-328-5320
dhsaging@nd.gov
www.nd.gov

Shane Goettle, Manager

3617 North Dakota Department of Human Services
600 E Boulevard Ave
Dept 325
Bismarck, ND 58505-0250
701-328-2310
800-472-2622
FAX: 701-328-2359
dhseo@nd.gov
www.nd.gov/dhs

Carol K Olson, Executive Director
Dennis Goetz, Executive Director
Kerry Wicks, Executive Director
Provides services that help vulnerable North Dakotans of all ages to maintain or enhance their quality of life, which may be threatened by lack of financial resources, emotional crises, disabling conditions, or an inability to protect themselves.

3618 Protection & Advocacy Project
1984
400 East Broadway
Suite 409
Bismarck, ND 58501-4071
701-328-2950
800-472-2670
FAX: 701-328-3934
panda@nd.gov
ndpanda.org

Teresa Larsen, Executive Director
Janelle Olson, Advocate
Paula Rustad, Office Assistant

The Protection and Advocacy is a state agency whose purpose is to advocate for and protect the rights of people with disabilities. The Protection and Advocacy Project has programs to serve people with developmental disabilities, mental illnesses and other types of disabilities. The projects programs and services are free to eligible individuals.

3619 Social Security: Bismarck Disability Determination
1680 E Capitol Ave
Bismarck, ND 58501-5603

701-250-4200
800-772-1213
TTY:701-250-4620
ssa.gov

Karena L. Kilgore, Executive Secretary
Carolyn W. Colvin, Commissioner
Carolyn W. Colvin, Deputy Commissioner

3620 Workers Compensation Board North Dakota
1600EastCenturyAvenue
Suite1
Bismarck, ND 58503-649

701-328-3800
800-777-5033
FAX: 701-328-3820
www.workforcesafety.com

Sandy Blunt, CEO

Ohio

3621 Epilepsy Council of Greater Cincinnati
Ste 550
895 Central Ave
Cincinnati, OH 45202-5700

513-721-2905
877-804-2241
FAX: 513-721-0799
ecgc@fuse.net

Kathy Stewart, Executive Director

3622 International Dyslexia Association: Central Ohio Branch
P.O. Box 1601
Westerville, OH 43086

614-899-5711
coh.dyslexiaida.org

Mike McGovern, President
Blythe Wood, Vice President
Chris Lowe, Secretary
Provides free information and referral services for diagnosis and tutoring for parents, educators, physicians, and individuals with dyslexia. Membership includes yearly journal and quarterly newsletter.

3623 Ohio Bureau for Children with Medical Handicaps
Ohio Department of Health
246 N. High St
P.O.Box 1603
Columbus, OH 43215-1603

614-466-3543
800-755-4769
FAX: 614-728-3616
bcmh@odh.ohio.gov
www.odh.ohio.gov

John R. Kasich, Governor
James Bryant Md, Bureau Chief
Alvin Jackson, MD, Director
Provides funding for the diagnosis, treatment and coordination of services for eligible Ohio children, under age 21, with medical handicaps; conducts quality assurance activities to establish standards of care and determine unmet needs of children with handicaps and their families; collaborates with public health nurses to increase access to care; and assists families to access and use third party resources. Conducts a separate program for adults with cystic fibrosis.

3624 Ohio Bureau of Worker's Compensation
30 W Spring St
Columbus, OH 43215-2256

800-335-0996
FAX: 877-321-9481
TTY:800-292-4833
ombudsperson@bwc.state.oh.us
www.bwc.ohio.gov

Stephen Buehrer, Administrator/CEO
Dale Hamilton, Chief Operating Officer (COO)
Kevin Abrams, Chief of Employers Services
To provide a quality, customer-focused workers' compensation insurance system for Ohio's employers and employees.

3625 Ohio Client Assistance Program
50 W. Broad St.
Suite 1400
Columbus, OH 43215-5923

614-466-7264
800-282-9181
FAX: 614-752-4197
TTY: 614-728-2553
www.olrs.ohio.gov

Donald Bishop, Executive Director

3626 Ohio Department of Aging
1982
50 W Broad St
Fl 9
Columbus, OH 43215-3363

614-466-5500
866-243-5678
888-243-5678
FAX: 614-466-5741
TTY:614-466-6191
www.aging.ohio.gov

Bonnie Kantor-Burman, Director
John Ratliff, Public Information Officer
The department serves and represents about 2 million Ohioans age 60 & older. They advocate for the needs of all older citizens with emphasis on improving the quality of life, helping senior citizens live active, healthy, & independent lives, & promoting positive attitudes toward aging & older people. Committed to helping the frail elderly who choose to remain at home by providing home & community based services, their goal is to promote the level of choice, independence & self-care.

3627 Ohio Department of Mental Health
30 E Broad St
8th Floor
Columbus, OH 43215-3414

614-466-4775
877-275-6364
FAX: 614-752-8410

Michael Hogan, Director
Christine Vincenty, Manager

3628 Ohio Developmental Disabilities Council
899 E Broad St, Ste 203
Columbus, OH 43205

614-466-5205
800-766-7426
FAX: 614-466-0298
www.ddc.ohio.gov

Carolyn Knight, Executive Director
Mark Seifarth, Chair
Robert Shuemak, Vice Chair
The Ohio Developmental Disabilities Council is one of 55 councils found in all states and territories which provides funding for systems change grant projects. The DD Council is a planning and advocacy agency that seeks to improve the lives of Ohioans with disabilities.

3629 Ohio Developmental Disability Council (ODDC)
899 E Broad St, Ste 203
Columbus, OH 43205

614-466-5205
800-766-7426
FAX: 614-466-0298
www.ddc.ohio.gov

Carolyn Knight, Executive Director
Mark Seifarth, Chair
Robert Shuemak, Vice Chair

3630 Ohio Governor's Council on People with Disabilities
400 E Campus View Blvd
Columbus, OH 43235-4685
614-438-1200
800-282-4536
gcpd.ohio.gov

Jacqueline Romer-Sensky, Chairman
Jack Licate, Vice Chairman
Kevin Miller, Executive Director

The Governor's Council on People with Disabilities exists to: Advise the Governor and General Assembly on statewide disability issues, promote the value of diversity, dignity and the quality of life for people with disabilities, be a catalyst to create systemic change promoting awareness of disability-related issues that will ultimately benefit all citizens of Ohio, Educate and advocate for: partnerships at the local, state and national level, promotion of equality, access and independence.

3631 Ohio Rehabilitation Services Commission
400 E Campus View Blvd
Columbus, OH 43235-4604
614-438-1200
800-282-4536
ohio.gov

Kevin Miller, Executive Director

RSC is Ohio's state agency that provides vocational rehabilitation (VR) services to help people with disabilities become employed and independent. We also offer a variety of services to Ohio businesses, resulting in quality jobs for individuals who have disabilities.

3632 Ohio Women, Infants, & Children Program - Ohio Department of Health
246 N High St
Columbus, OH 43215-2406
614-644-8006
FAX: 614-564-2470

Michele Frizzell, Chief, Bureau of Nutrition Svcs.

3633 Social Security: Columbus Disability Determination
90 E Washington Bridge Rd
Suite 140
Worthington, OH 43085
614-888-5339
800-772-1213
TTY:614-288-0226
www.socialsecurity.gov

Karena L. Kilgore, Executive Secretary
Carolyn W. Colvin, Commissioner
Carolyn W. Colvin, Deputy Commissioner

Oklahoma

3634 Oklahoma Workers Compensation Board
Department of Labor
3017 N. Stiles, Suite 100
Oklahoma City, OK 73105
405-521-6100
888-269-5353
FAX: 405-521-6018
labor.info@labor.ok.gov
www.ok.gov/odol

Jim Marshall, Chief of Staff
Mark Costello, Commissioner of Labor
Lizzette McNeill, Communications Director

3635 Oklahoma Client Assistance Program/Office of Disability Concerns
2401 NW 23rd Street
Suite 90
Oklahoma City, OK 73107- 2431
405-521-3756
800-522-8224
FAX: 405-522-6695
www.ok.gov

Todd Lamb, Governor
Gary Jones, Auditor and Inspector
E. Scott Pruitt, Attorney General

CAP informs and advises applicants and consumers about the vocational rehabilitation process and services available under the Federal Rehabilitation Act, including services provided by DVR and DVS. CAP staff can help you communicate concerns to the DVR/DVS and assist you with administrative, mediation, fair hearing, legal and other solutions

3636 Oklahoma Department of Human Services Aging Services Division
25 Sigourney Street, 10th Floor
Hartford, CT 06106
405-521-3646
866-218-6621
800-522-7233
FAX: 860-424-5301

Margaret Ger Murkette, MSW, Director
Ed Lake, Director

3637 Oklahoma Department of Labor
3017 N. Stiles
Suite 100
Oklahoma City, OK 73105-5206
405-521-6100
888-269-5353
FAX: 405-521-6018
www.labor.ok.gov

Mark Castello, Commissioner
Jim Marshall, Chief of Staff
Stacy Bonner, Deputy Commissioner

3638 Oklahoma Department of Mental Health & Substance Abuse Services
1200 NE 13th Street
P.O.Box 53277
Oklahoma City, OK 73152-3277
405-522-3908
800-522-9054
FAX: 405-522-3650
TTY: 405-522-3851
www.odmhsas.org

J. Andy Sullivan, Chairperson
Gail Henderson, Vice-Chair
Terri White, Commissioner

State agency providing mental helath , substance abuse and domestic violence services.

3639 Oklahoma Department of Rehabilitation Services
3535 NW 58th St.
Suite 500
Oklahoma City, OK 73112-4824
405-951-3400
800-845-8476
FAX: 405-951-3529
www.oklahoma.gov/okdrs.html

Melinda Fruendt, Executive Director

The Oklahoma Department of Rehabilitation Services (DRS) provides assistance to Oklahomans with disabilities through vocational rehabilitation, employment, independent living, residential and outreach programs, and the determination of medical eligibility for disability benefits.

3640 Workers Compensation Board Oklahoma
1915 N Stiles Ave
Oklahoma City, OK 73105-4918
405-522-8600
800-522-8210

Leroy E Young, D.O., Chairman
Joyce Sanders, Supervisor
Michael J. Harkey, Vice Presiding Judge

Oregon

3641 International Dyslexia Association: Oregon Branch
International Dyslexia Association
P.P. Box 2609
Portland, OR 97208-2609
503-228-4455
info@orbida.org
or.dyslexiaida.org

Jane Cooper, President
Danielle Thompson, Vice President
Anne Mauboussin, Treasurer

Provides free information and referral services for diagnosis and tutoring for parents, educators, physicians, and individuals with dyslexia. Membership includes yearly journal and quarterly newsletter.

3642 Office of Vocational Rehabilitation Services (OVRS)
500 Summer St NE
Salem, OR 97301-1063   503-945-5944
                                FAX: 503-378-2897
                                TTY:503-945-6214
                                www.oregon.gov/dhs

Erinn Kelley-Siel, Director
Gene Evans, Communication Director
Eric Moore, Chief Financial Officer
The mission of OVRS to assist Oregonians with disabilities to achieve and maintain employment and independence.

3643 Oregon Advocacy Center
620 SW 5th Ave
5th Floor
Portland, OR 97204-1428   503-243-2081
                                800-452-6094
                                FAX: 503-243-1738
                                TTY: 800-556-5351

Robert Joondeph, Executive Director
Barbara Herget, Operations Director
The protection and advocacy system for Oregon.

3644 Oregon Client Assistance Program
620 SW 5th Ave
5th Floor
Portland, OR 97204-1420   503-243-2081
                                FAX: 503-243-1738
                                TTY:800-556-5351

Robert Joondeph, Executive Director

3645 Oregon Department of Mental Health
500 Summer St NE
Salem, OR 97301-1063   503-945-5944
                                FAX: 503-378-2897
                                TTY:503-945-6214
                                www.oregon.gov/DHS

Erinn Kelley-Siel, Director
Gene Evans, Communication Director
Eric Moore, Chief Financial Officer
Sets out the purpose and guides the activities of our large, complex organization. Vision is for better outcomes for clients and communities through collaboration, integration and shared responsibility.

3646 Oregon Technology Access for Life
2225 Lancaster Drive NE
Salem, OR 97305-1396   503-361-1201
                                800-677-7512
                                FAX: 503-370-4530
                                TTY: 503-361-1201
                                www.accesstechnologiesinc.org

Laurie Brooks, President
A statewide program promoting assistive technology devices and services for persons of all ages with all disabilities.

3647 Social Security: Salem Disability Determination
90 E Washington Bridge Rd
Suite 140
Worthington, OH 43085-3772   614-888-5339
                                800-722-1213
                                TTY:614-288-0226
                                www.socialsecurity.gov

Karena L. Kilgore, Executive Secretary
Carolyn W. Colvin, Commissioner
Carolyn W. Colvin, Deputy Commissioner

3648 Vocational Rehabilitation Agency: Oregon Commission for the Blind
535 SE 12th Avenue
Portland, OR 97214-2408   971-673-1588
                                888-202-5463
                                FAX: 503-234-7468
                                ocb.mail@state.or.us
                                www.oregon.gov/blind

Dacia Johnson, Executive Director
A resource for visually impaired Oregonians, as well as their families, friends, and employers. Nationally recognized programs and staff that make a difference in people's lives every day.

3649 Washington County Disability, Aging and Veteran Services
Ste 208
180 E Main St
Hillsboro, OR 97123-4054   503-640-3489
                                FAX: 503-693-6124

Jeff Hill, Director
Janet Long, Support Staff
Provides services to individuals through the Older Americans Act, state in home care services and represent, veterans in benefit claims process with Federal VA.

Pennsylvania

3650 Disability Rights of Pennsylvania (DRP)
Harrisburg Office
301 Chestnut St
Suite 300
Harrisburg, PA 17101   717-839-5235
                                800-692-7443
                                FAX: 717-236-0192
                                TTY: 877-375-7139
                                ldo@disabilityrightspa.org
                                www.disabilityrightspa.org

Jeneice Davis, Chairman
Peri Jude Radecic, CEO
Kelly Darr, Legal Director
The Disability Rights of Pennsylvania is a statewide, non-profit corporation dedicated to advancing and protecting the civil rights of adults and children with disabilities by ensuring access to community services, a full and inclusive education and the freedom to live free of discrimination, abuse and neglect.

3651 International Dyslexia Association: Pennsylvania Branch
1062 E. Lancaster Ave.
Suite 15A
Rosemont, PA 19010   610-527-1548
                                855-220-8885
                                www.pbida.org

Lisa Goldstein, President
Tracy Bowes, Office Manager
Provides free information and referral services for diagnosis and tutoring for parents, educators, physicians, and individuals with dyslexia. Membership includes yearly journal and quarterly newsletter, and Pennsylvania newsletter.

3652 Mental Health Association in Pennysylvania
1414 N Cameron St
1st Floor
Harrisburg, PA 17103-1049   717-346-0549
                                855-220-8885
                                FAX: 717-236-0192
                                www.mhapa.org

Julia Walker, Esq., President
Michael Brody, President & CEO
Marge Dailey, Director of Human Resources
The Mental Health Association in Pennysylvania is a non-profit providing services to those struggling with mental health issues. Services include advocacy, education and public policy.

3653 Pennsylvania Workers Compensation Board
651 Boas Street
Room 1700
Harrisburg, PA 17121-2510   717-787-5279
                                FAX: 717-772-0342
                                dli.state.pa.us

Joseph Brimmeier, CEO

3654 Pennsylvania Bureau of Blindness & Visual Services
Department of Pennsylvania
1521 N 6th St
Harrisburg, PA 17102   717-787-3201
                                800-622-2842
                                FAX: 717-787-3210
                                www.dli.state.pa.us

David Denotaris, Director
Jennifer Cave, Clerk Typist 3
Offers services for the totally blind, legally blind, visually impaired, and more with health, counseling, educational, recre-

ational, rehabilitation, computer training and professional training services.

3655 Pennsylvania Client Assistance Program
1515 Market Street
Suite 1300
Philadelphia, PA 19102- 1819   215-557-7112
                                      888-745-2357
                                 FAX: 215-557-7602
                              www.equalemployment.org

Stephen S. Pennington, Executive Director
Jamie C Ray, Assistant Director
Margaret Passio-McKenna, Senior Advocate

The Pennsylvania Client Assistance Program is dedicated to ensuring that the rehabilitation system in Pennsylvania is open and responsive to your needs. CAP help is provided to you at no charge, regardless of income. CAP helps people who are seeking services from the Office of Vocational Rehabilitation, Blindness and Visual Services, Centers for Independent Living and other programs funded under federal law.

3656 Pennsylvania Department of Aging
555 Walnut St
5th Floor
Harrisburg, PA 17101-1919   717-783-1550
                                FAX: 717-783-6842
                                    aging@pa.gov
                               www.aging.state.pa.us

Nora Eisenhower, Manager

3657 Pennsylvania Department of Children with Disabilities
P.O. Box 2675
Harrisburg, PA 17105-2675   717-787-2600
                                FAX: 717-772-0323
                             www.pachildren.state.pa.US

Tom Corbett, Governor
Shelly Yanoff, Commission Chair

3658 Pennsylvania Developmental Disabilities Council
605 South Drive
Room 561
Harrisburg, PA 17120   717-789-6057
                                     877-685-4452
                                 TTY:717-705-0819
                                     www.paddc.org

Amy High, Vice Chairperson
Graham Mulholland, Executive Director
Sandra Amador Dusek, Deputy Director

3659 Public Interest Law Center of Philadelphia
United Way Building, 2nd Floor
1709 Benjamin Franklin Parkway
Philadelphia, PA 19103-5153   215-627-7100
                                FAX: 215-627-3183
                                      pilcop.org

Eric J. Rothschild, Chair
Brian T. Feeney, Vice Chair
Jennifer R. Clarke, Executive Director

A non-profit, public interest law firm with a Disabilities Project specializing in class action suits brought by individuals and organizations.

3660 Social Security: Harrisburg Disability Determination
Suite 160
90 E Washington Bridge Rd
Worthington, OH 17101-1925   614-888-5339
                                     800-722-1213
                                 TTY:614-288-0226
                                        ssa.gov

Karena L. Kilgore, Executive Secretary
Carolyn W. Colvin, Commissioner
Carolyn W. Colvin, Deputy Commissioner

3661 Workers Compensation Board Pennsylvania
651 Boas Street
Room 1700
Harrisburg, PA 17121-2510   717-787-5279
                                FAX: 717-772-0342
                                 www.dli.state.pa.us

Tom Corbett, Governor
Julia K. Hearthway, Secretary
Joseph Brimmeier, CEO

Rhode Island

3662 Department of Behavioral Healthcare, Developmental Disabilities and Hospitals
The Hazard Building
41 West Rd.
Cranston, RI 02920   401-462-3201
                                   www.bhddh.ri.gov

Rebecca Boss, Director
Michelle Place, Assistant to the Director

State department responsible for creating and administering systems of care for individuals with disabilities, specifically focused on mental health and mental illness, developmental disabilities, substance abuse and long term hospital care.

3663 Rhode Island Department Health
3 Capitol Hl
Providence, RI 02908-5097   401-222-3855
                                FAX: 401-222-6548

Mary Salerno, Manager
Patricia Nolan, Executive Director
Pamela Corcoran, Disability Health Program

3664 Rhode Island Department of Elderly Affairs
74 West Road
Hazard Bldg, 2nd Floor
Cranston, RI 02920- 3001   401-462-3000
                                FAX: 401-462-0740

Corrine Russo, Manager

3665 Rhode Island Department of Mental Health
Cottage 405 Court B
Cranston, RI 02920   401-462-2003
                                FAX: 401-462-2008
                                    www.butler.org

George W. Shuster, Chairman
Dennis D. Keefe, President & CEO
Reed Cosper, Manager

3666 Rhode Island Developmental Disabilities Council
400 Bald Hill Rd
Suite 515
Warwick, RI 02886-1692   401-737-1238
                                FAX: 401-737-3395
                                TTY:401-737-1238
                                    riddc@riddc.org
                                     www.riddc.org

Charles Zawacki, Chairperson, Individual & Family
John Susa, Chairperson, Executive Committee
Anne Frank, Chairperson, Individual & Family

The Rhode Island Developmental Disabilities Council works to make Rhode Island a better place for people with developmental disabilities to live, work, go to school, and be part of their community.

3667 Rhode Island Disability Law Center
275 Westminster St
Suite 401
Providence, RI 02903-3434   401-831-3150
                                     800-733-5332
                                FAX: 401-274-5568
                                TTY: 401-831-5335
                                    info@ridlc.org
                                     www.ridlc.org

Raymond A Marcaccio, Esq., Chair
Raymond L Bandusky, Executive Director
Darby Castigliego, Director of Finance & Administration

The Rhode Island Disability Law Center (RIDLC) provides free legal assistance to persons with disabilities. Services include individual representation to protect rights or to secure benefits and services, self-help information, educational programs and administrative and legislative advocacy.

3668   Rhode Island Governor's Commission on Disabilities
John O Pastore Center
Warwick City Hall
3275 Post Road
Warwick, RI 02920-3049   401-738-2000
                                                            FAX: 401-462-0106
                                                            www.warwickri.gov

Bob Cooper, Executive Secretary
The Commision is responsible for: coordinating compliance by
state agencies with federal and state disablity right laws; approv-
ing or modifying state and local goverment agency's open meeting accessibility for persons with disabilities transition plans;
assisting local boards of canvassers to ensure accessible polling
places locations; aproving or rejecting requests to waive the state
building code's standards for accessibility at facilities to be
leased by state agencies..

3669   Rhode Island Parent Information Network
1210 Pontiac Avenue
Cranston, RI 02920   401-270-0101
                                                            800-464-3399
                                                            FAX: 401-270-7049
                                                            info@ripin.org
                                                            ripin.org

Kathleen DiChiara, Chairman
Ammala Douangsavanh, Vice Chairman
Stephen Brunero, Executive Director
A nonprofit organization established by parents and concerned
professionals providing culturally appropriate information,
training and support for families and professionals designed to
improve educational and life outcomes for all children. Serving
the State of Rhode Island.

**3670   Rhode Island Services for the Blind and Visually
Impaired**
40 Fountain St
Providence, RI 02903-1830   401-421-7005
                                                            800-752-8088
                                                            FAX: 401-421-9259
                                                            TTY: 401-421-7016
                                                            www.ors.ri.gov

Kathleen Grygiel, Administrator
Ronald Racine, Associate Director
Laurie DiOrio, Acting Associate Director
Offers services for the totally blind, legally blind, visually impaired, and more with health, counseling, educational, recreational, rehabilitation, computer training and professional
training services.

3671   Services for the Blind and Visually Impaired
40 Fountain St
Providence, RI 02903-1830   401-421-7005
                                                            FAX: 401-222-1328
                                                            TTY:401-421-7016
                                                            www.ors.ri.gov

Kathleen Grygiel, Administrator
Ronald Racine, Associate Director
Laurie DiOrio, Acting Associate Director
Offers services for the blind and visually impaired.

3672   Social Security: Providence Disability Determination
Social Security
40 Fountain Street
6th Floor
Providence, RI 02903-3246   401-222-3182
                                                            800-772-1213
                                                            FAX: 401-222-3868
                                                            TTY: 401-273-6648
                                                            Deborah.A.Cannon@ssa.gov
                                                            www.ssa.gov

Karena L. Kilgore, Executive Secretary
Carolyn W. Colvin, Commissioner
Delivers services through a nationwide network of over 1,400 offices that include regional offices, field offices, card centers,
teleservice centers, processing centers, hearing offices, the Appeals Council, and our State and territorial partners, the Disability Determination Services. We also have a presence in U.S.
embassies around the globe. For the public, we are the face of the
government. The rich diversity of our employees mirrors the
public we serve.

3673   Workers Compensation Board Rhode Island
1 Dorrance Plz
Providence, RI 02903-3973   401-458-5000
                                                            FAX: 401-222-3121

George E Healy Jr, Manager
George Healy Jr, Manager

South Carolina

3674   Protection & Advocacy for People with Disabilities
Ste 208
3710 Landmark Dr
Columbia, SC 29204-4034   803-782-0639
                                                            866-275-7273
                                                            FAX: 803-790-1946
                                                            TTY: 866-232-4525
                                                            info@pandasc.org
                                                            protectionandadvocacy-sc.org

Gloria Prevost, Executive Director
Anne Trice, Director of Administration
J. Ashley Twombley, Chair
An independent, nonprofit organization responsible for safe
guarding rights of South Carolinians with disabilities and other
handicapped individuals without regard to age, income, severity
of disability, sex, race, or religion.

3675   Social Security: West Columbia Disability Determination
P.O. Box 60
Columbia, SC 29171-0060   803-896-6400
                                                            800-772-1213
                                                            FAX: 803-822-4318
                                                            TTY: 800-325-0078
                                                            www.socialsecurity.gov

Karena L. Kilgore, Executive Secretary
Carolyn W. Colvin, Commissioner
Carolyn W. Colvin, Deputy Commissioner
We deliver services through a nationwide network of over 1,400
offices that include regional offices, field offices, card centers,
teleservice centers, processing centers, hearing offices, the Appeals Council, and our State and territorial partners, the Disability Determination Services. We also have a presence in U.S.
embassies around the globe. For the public, we are the face of the
government. The rich diversity of our employees mirrors the
public we serve.

3676   South Carolina Assistive Technology Project
Midlands Center
8301 Farrow Road
Columbia, SC 29203   803-935-5263
                                                            800-915-4522
                                                            FAX: 803-935-5342
                                                            TTY: 803-935-5263
                                                            jjendron@usit.net
                                                            www.sc.edu/scatp/

Carol Page, Ph.D, CCC-SLP, A, Program Director
Janet Jendron, Program Coordinator
Mary Alice Bechtler, Program Coordinator
A statewide program promoting assistive technology devices and
services for persons of all ages with all disabilities. Recently a
statewide AT resource, demonstrations and equipment loan center and lab annual expo and training and workshops on a variety
of disabilities and technology topics.

3677   South Carolina Client Assistance Program
Governor's Office oe Executive Policy & Programs
1205 Pendleton St
Columbia, SC 29201-3756   803-734-0285
                                                            800-868-0040
                                                            FAX: 803-734-0546
                                                            TTY: 803-734-1147
                                                            cap@oepp.sc.gov

Denise Riley Pensmith, MSW, Executive Director
Cindy Popenhagen, Administrative Assistant
The Client Assistance Program (CAP) helps citizens of the State
by acting as advocates regarding services provided by the Vocational Rehabilitation Department (VR), Commission for the
Blind, and all Independent Living programs and projects funded
under the Rehabilitation Act of 1973. As advocates, CAP staff

can investigate, negotiate, mediate, and pursue administrative, and other remedies to ensure that clients' rights are protected.

3678   South Carolina Commission for the Blind (SCCB)
1430 Confederate Ave.
Columbia, SC 29201-79   803-898-8731
publicinfo@sccb.sc.gov
www.sccb.state.sc.us
Goal is to help individuals with visual impairments prepare for and obtain appropriate employment.

3679   South Carolina Department of Children with Disabilities
2600 Bull St
Columbia, SC 29201-1708   803-434-4260
Miroslav Cuturic, Director
Peter Getz, Administrator

3680   South Carolina Department of Mental Health
Office of Administration
PO Box 485
Columbia, SC 29202   803-898-8581
800-273-8255
TTY:800-647-2066
webmaster@scdmh.org
scdmh.net
Mark W. Binkley, Interim State Director
The S.C. Department of Mental Health gives priority to adults, children, and their families affected by serious mental illnesses and significant emotional disorders. We are committed to eliminating stigma and promoting the philosophy of recovery, to achieving our goals in collaboration with all stakeholders, and to assuring the highest quality of culturally competent services possible.

3681   South Carolina Developmental Disabilities Council
Office of the Governor
1205 Pendleton St
Suite 461
Columbia, SC 29201-3756   803-734-0465
FAX: 803-734-1409
TTY:803-734-1147
jvancleave@oepp.sc.gov
www.scddc.state.sc.us
Valarie Bishop, Executive Director
Cheryl English, Program Information Coordinator
Kimberly Johnson Fontanez, Grants Administrator
The mission of the South Carolina Developmental Disabilities Council is to provide leadership in advocating, funding and implementing initiatives which recognize the inherent dignity of each individual, and promote independence, productivity, respect and inclusion for all persons with disabilities and their families.

3682   Workers Compensation Board: South Carolina
PO Box 1715
Columbia, SC 29202-1715   803-737-5700
FAX: 803-737-5768
www.state.sc.us/wcc
Gary Cannon, Executive Director
Kim Balleutine, Admin. Assistant

South Dakota

3683   Children's Special Health Services Program
600 E Capitol Ave
Pierre, SD 57501-2536   605-773-3361
800-738-2301
FAX: 605-773-5683
DOH.info@state.sd.us
www.doh.sd.gov
Dianne Weyer, Manager
Barb Hemmelman, Program Manager
Health KiCC is a program, funded through federal and state monies, that provides financial assistance for medical appointments, procedures, treatments, medications and travel reimbursement for children with certain chronic health conditions.

3684   Division of Labor and Management
South Dakota Department of Labor
700 Governors Dr
Pierre, SD 57501-2291   605-773-3101
FAX: 605-773-6184
dlr.sd.gov
Sara Minton, Executive Director
Pamela S Roberts, Secretary
Marcia Hultman, Deputy Secretary of Labor and D
Our mission is to promote economic opportunity and financial security for individuals and businesses through quality, responsive and expert services; fair and equitable employment solutions; and safe and sound business practices.

3685   Health KiCC
South Dakota Department of Health
600 E Capitol Ave
Pierre, SD 57501-2536   605-773-3361
800-738-2301
FAX: 605-773-5683
DOH.info@state.sd.us
www.doh.sd.gov
Dianne Weyer, Manager
Health KiCC is a program, funded through federal and state monies, that provides financial assistance for medical appointments, procedures, treatments, medications and travel reimbursement for children with certain chronic health conditions.

3686   South Dakota Advocacy Services
221 S Central Ave
Ste. 38
Pierre, SD 57501-2479   605-224-8294
800-658-4782
FAX: 605-224-5125
sdas@sdadvocacy.com
sdadvocacy.com
Sandy Stocklin Hook, Partners Coordinator
Designated protection and advocacy progam for South Dakota providing legal, administrative, mediation and other services to elgible persons with disabilities in the state.

3687   South Dakota Department of Aging
700 Governors Dr
Pierre, SD 57501-2291   605-773-3656
866-854-5465
FAX: 605-773-4085
Marilyn Kinsman, Division Director
Lynne Valenti, Deputy Secretary
Amy Iversen-Pollreisz, Deputy Secretary
The Division of Adult Services and Aging (ASA) provides home and community service options to individuals 60 years of age and older and 18 years of age and older with physical disabilities, regardless of income.

3688   South Dakota Department of Human Services
Hillsview Plaza
3800 E Hwy 34
Pierre, SD 57501   605-773-5990
FAX: 605-773-5483
infodhs@state.sd.us
dhs.sd.gov
Shawnie Rechtenbaugh, Secretary
Provides resources for individuals with developmental disabilities, including rehabilitation services, services for the blind and visually impaired, and long-term services and supports.

3689   South Dakota Department of Social Services Division of Behavioral Health
700 Governors Dr.
Pierre, SD 57501   605-367-5236
855-878-6057
FAX: 605-773-7076
DSSbh@state.sd.us
dss.sd.gov/behavioralhealth
Laurie Gill, Secretary
Brenda Tidbull-Zeltinger, Deputy Secretary
Tiffany Wolfgang, Division Director
South Dakota's state mental health authority.

3690 South Dakota Division of Rehabilitation
700 Governors Dr
Pierre, SD 57501-2291   605-773-3101
                                      FAX: 605-773-6184
                                          www.sdjobs.org

Sara Minton, Executive Director
Pamela S Roberts, Secretary
Marcia Hultman, Deputy Secretary of Labor and D
Offers diagnosis, evaluation and physical restoration services,
counseling, social work, educational and professional training,
employment and rehabilitation services for the disabled.

3691 Workers Compensation Board: South Dakota
700 Governors Dr
Pierre, SD 57501-2291   605-773-3101
                                      FAX: 605-773-6184
                                          www.sdjobs.org

Sara Minton, Executive Director
Marcia Hultman, Secretary
Lyle Harter, Director of Administrative Services
Our mission is to promote economic opportunity and financial security for individuals and businesses through quality, responsive
and expert services; fair and equitable employment solutions;
and safe and sound business practices.

Tennessee

3692 Disability Determination Services
400 Deaderick St
Nashville, TN 37243-1403   800-342-1117
                              DHS.CustomerService@tn.gov
                                      www.tennessee.gov

Thea Smith, Human Resources Program Specialist
Wendy Davis, Finance & Administration
Cherrell Campbell-Street, Assistant Commissioner
The Disability Determination Services is a branch of the Division
of Rehabilitation Services in the Department of Human Services.
Its main responsibility is to process Social Security and Supple-
mental Security Income disability claims.

3693 International Dyslexia Association: Tennessee Branch
Knoxville, TN   865-207-4918
                              msamwood@bellsouth.net
                                          www.tnida.org

Emily Dempster, President
Erin Alexander, Senior Vice President
Nikki Davis, Secretary
The Tennessee Branch of the International Dyslexia Association
(TN-IDA) was formed to increase awareness about Dyslexia in
the state of Tennessee. TN-IDA supports efforts to provide information regarding appropriate language arts instruction to those
involved with language-based learning differences and to encourage the identity of these individuals at-risk for such
disorders as soon as possible.

3694 Tennessee Assistive Technology Projects
Citizens Plaza State Office Buildin
511 Union St.
Nashville, TN 37219-1403   615-313-5183
                                          800-732-5059
                                      TTY:615-313-5695
                                          TN.TTAP@tn.gov
                                              www.tn.gov

Bill Haslam, Governor
Raquel Hatter, Commissioner
Beth White, Manager
A statewide program promoting assistive technology devices and
services for persons of all ages with all disabilities.

3695 Tennessee Client Assistance Program
Tennessee Protection and Advocacy
P.O.Box 121257
Nashville, TN 37212-1257   615-298-1080
                                          800-342-1660
                                      FAX: 615-298-2046

Shirley Shea, Executive Director
Doris Lopez, Assistant Executive Director

3696 Tennessee Commission on Aging and Disability
502 Deaderick Street
9th Floor
Nashville, TN 37243-860   615-741-2056
                                      FAX: 615-741-3309
                                      www.tn.gov/aging.html

Richard M. Honn, Executive Director
Ryan Ellis, Aging Info. & Data Director
Kathy Zamata, Aging Program Director

3697 Tennessee Council on Developmental Disabilities
500 James Robertson Pkwy
1st Floor
Nashville, TN 37243   615-532-6615
                                      FAX: 615-532-6964
                                          tnddc@tn.gov
                                              tn.gov/cdd

Wanda Willis, Executive Director
Lynette Porter, Deputy Director
Alicia Cone, Director of Grant Program
The council is a state agency that leads initiatives to improve disability policies by educating policymakers and the public about
best practices in disability services, facilitating collaboration
across organizations, and producing educational publications on
the subject.

3698 Tennessee Department of Children with Disabilities
511 Union St.
Nashville, TN 37219-9004   615-741-9701
                                          800-861-1935
                                      FAX: 615-253-5216
                                              www.tn.gov

Ruth S Letson, Manager
Haticile Buchanan, Manager
Mary Beth Franklyn, CS Program Director
Tennessee's children thrive in safe, healthy and stable families.
Families thrive in healthy, safe and strong communities. Tennes-
see's citizens benefit from the best child welfare and juvenile jus-
tice agency in the country.

3699 Tennessee Department of Mental Health
500 Deaderick Street
Nashville, TN 37243-3400   615-532-6597
                                          800-560-5767
                                      FAX: 615-532-6514

Doug Varney, Commissioner
Grant Lawrence, Director Office of Communication
Bob Grunow, Deputy Commissioner
TDMH is the state's mental health and substance abuse authority.
Its mission is to plan for and promote the availability of a comprehensive array of quality prevention, early intervention, treatment, habilitation, and rehabilitation services and supports based
on the needs and choices of individuals and families served. Responsible for policy, and oversight, and for advocacy of the
consumer within the state.

3700 Tennessee Division of Rehabilitation
400 Deaderick St
Nashville, TN 37243-1403   615-313-4700
                                          800-270-1349
                                      TTY:615-313-5695
                                              www.tn.gov

Patsy Matthews, Commissioner
Randall Beasley, Manager
Raquel Hatter, Commissioner
Offers rehabilitation, medical and therapeutic information and
referrals to the disabled.

3701 Workers Compensation Division Tennessee
Dept of Labor & Workforce Development
220 French Landing Drive
1st Floor
Nashville, TN 37243- 1002   615-741-6642
                                          800-332-2667
                                      FAX: 615-532-1468
                                          wc.info@tn.gov
                              www.tn.gov/labor-wfd/wcomp.html

Karla Davis, Commissioner
Alisa Malone, Deputy Commissioner
Stephanie Mitchell, General Counsel

Administers the workers' compensation system and promote a better understanding of the program's benefits by informing employees and employers of their rights and responsibilities. Workers' Compenstation administers a mediation program for disputed claims, encourage workplace safety, participate in a public awareness campaign concerning fraud, and oversee an information awareness program for educating the public on laws and regulations which define workers' compensation requirements.

Texas

3702 Disability Policy Consortium
2222 West Braker Lane
Austin, TX 78758-1024
512-454-4816
800-252-9108
FAX: 512-323-0902
disabilitytx.org

Mary Faithful, Executive Director
Roberta Rosenberg-Roque, Manager
An independent group of statewide advocacy organizations that strives to achieve the development and full implementation of public policy that promotes and supports the rights, inclusion, integration and independence of Texans with disabilities.

3703 Disability Rights Texas
2222 West Braker Lane
Austin, TX 78758-1024
512-454-4816
866-362-2851
www.disabilityrightstx.org

Mary Faithfull, Executive Director
Patty Anderson, Deputy Director
A federally designated legal protection and advocacy agency (P&A) for people with disabilities in Texas. Helps people with disabilities understand and exercise their rights under the law, ensuring their full and equal participation in society.

3704 Division of Special Education
1701 Congress Ave.
Austin, TX 78701-1402
512-463-9414
FAX: 512-463-9838
teainfo@tea.state.tx.us
www.tea.state.tx.us

Cory Green, Federal & State Education Policy
Donna Bahorich, Chair
Ruban Cortez Jr., Secretary
The Texas Education Agency is the state agency that oversees primary and secondary public education. It is headed by the commissioner of education. The mission of TEA is to provide leadership, guidance and resources to help schools meet the educational needs of all students

3705 Easterseals Central Texas
2324 Ridepoint Dr.
Suite F1
Austin, TX 78754
512-615-6800
FAX: 512-615-7121
www.easterseals.com/centraltx

Tod Marvin, President
Easterseals provides a wealth of programs and services to help promote independence and create opportunities for people with disabilities.

3706 Easterseals North Texas
1424 Hemphill St.
Fort Worth, TX 76104
888-617-7171
www.easterseals.com/northtexas

Tod Marvin, President
Jennifer Friesen, Vice President, Programs & Services
Easterseals provides a wealth of programs and services to help promote independence and create opportunities for people with disabilities.

3707 El Valle Community Parent Resource Center
Ste J
530 S Texas Blvd
Weslaco, TX 78596-6262
956-969-0215
800-680-0255
FAX: 956-968-7102

Robert Garza, Owner

3708 Grassroots Consortium
Greenroots Consortium
6202 Belmark St
Houston, TX 77087-6324
713-643-9576
FAX: 713-643-6291
Speckids@aol.com

Agnes A Johnson, Director

3709 International Dyslexia Association: Austin Branch
Austin, TX
512-452-7658
aus.dyslexiaida.org

Mary Bach, President
Karen Monteith, Vice President
Herman H. Klare, Treasurer
Provides free information and referral services for diagnosis and tutoring for parents, educators, physicians, and individuals with dyslexia in Illinois. Membership includes yearly journal and quarterly newsletter.

3710 National Alliance on Mental Illness (Texas)
P.O. Box 300817
Austin, TX 78703
512-693-2000
FAX: 512-693-8000
officemanager@namitexas.org
namitexas.org

John Dornheim, President
Holly Doggett, Executive Director
Greg Hansch, Public Policy Director
NAMI Texas is the state headquarters of the National Alliance on Mental Illness, a national nonprofit that aims to improve the lives of all persons affected by mental illness. NAMI Texas oversees over 25 local affiliates throughout the state. NAMI Texas raises awareness about mental illness through the dissemination of information, and seeks to address the mental health needs of Texans through education and support programs for persons with mental illness, families, friends, and professionals.

3711 Parent Connection
1020 Riverwood Ct
Conroe, TX 77304-2811
936-756-8321
800-839-8876
parentCNCT@aol.com
www.parentingaspergerscommunity.com/pu

Dave Angel, Founder
Includes parenting help and Aspergers advice, including parenting tips, tricks and techniques to help your child with Aspergers. Worldwide membership base is helping parents to understand their child with Aspergers better and make their home & family life a better place to be.

3712 Parents Supporting Parents Network
8001 Centre Park Drive
Suite 100
Austin, TX 78754
512-454-6694
800-252-9729
FAX: 512-454-4956
secretary@thearcoftexas.org
www.thearcoftexas.org

Charlie Huber, President
John Schneider, Vice-President
Nancy Lepley, Treasurer
Since our founding in 1950 by a group of parents of children with intellectual and developmental disabilities, The Arc at the local, state and national level has been instrumental in the creation of virtually every program, service, right, and benefit that is now available to more than half a million Texans with intellectual and developmental disabilities. Today, The Arc continues to advocate for including people with intellectual and developmental disabilities in all aspects of society.

3713   Partners Resource Network
Ste B
1090 Longfellow Dr
Beaumont, TX 77706-4819   409-898-4684
                                           800-866-4726
                                      FAX: 409-898-4869
                            partnersresource@sbcglobal.net
                                           partnerstx.org

Janice Meyer, Executive Director
Statewide network of three parent training and information centers.

3714   Social Security: Austin Disability Determination
P.O. Box 149198
Austin, TX 78714-9198   512-437-8311
                                           800-772-1213
                                           800-252-9627
                                      FAX: 512-437-8595
                                      TTY:512-916-5958
                                        dan.tippit@ssa.gov
                                           www.ssa.gov

Karena L. Kilgore, Executive Secretary
Carolyn W. Colvin, Commissioner
Carolyn W. Colvin, Deputy Commissioner
Delivers services through a nationwide network of over 1,400 offices that include regional offices, field offices, card centers, teleservice centers, processing centers, hearing offices, the Appeals Council, and State and territorial partners, the Disability Determination Services.

3715   Statewide Information at Texas School for the Deaf
1102 S Congress Ave
Austin, TX 78704-1728   512-462-5353
                                      FAX: 512-462-5353
                                    webmaster@tsd.state.tx.us
                                       www.tsd.state.tx.us

Sonia Karimi Bridges, Video Communication Specialist
Avonne Brooker-Rutowski, Program Specialist
David Coco, Program Specialist
Welcome to Texas School for the Deaf, a place where students who are deaf or hard of hearing including those with additional disabilities, have the opportunity to learn, grow and belong in a culture that optimizes individual potential and provides accessible language and communication across the curriculum. Our educational philosophy is grounded in the belief that all children who are deaf and hard of hearing deserve a quality language and communication-driven program that provides education tog

3716   Texas Advocates Supporting Kids with Disabilities
P.O.Box 162685
Austin, TX 78716-2685   512-310-2102
                                      FAX: 512-310-2102
                                       ASKTASK@aol.com

3717   Texas Commission for the Blind
P.O. Box 149198
Austin, TX 78714-9198   512-459-8575
                                           800-252-5204
                                      FAX: 512-424-4730
                                       www.dars.state.tx.us

Canzata Crowder, Manager
Offers services for the totally blind, legally blind, and visually impaired, with counseling, educational, recreational, rehabilitation, computer training and professional training services.

3718   Texas Commission for the Deaf and Hard of Hearing
D A R S
P.O. Box 149198
Austin, TX 78714-9198   512-407-3250
                                           800-628-5115
                                      FAX: 512-424-4730
                                      TTY: 512-407-3251
                                       www.dars.state.tx.us

Veronda L. Durden, Commissioner
Glenn Neal, Deputy Commissioner
David Myers, Executive Director

3719   Texas Council for Developmental Disabilities
6201 E Oltorf St
Suite 600
Austin, TX 78741-7509   512-437-5432
                                           800-262-0334
                                      FAX: 512-437-5434
                                      TTY: 512-437-5431
                                        tcdd@tcdd.texas.gov
                                       txddc.state.tx.us

Mary Durheim, Chairman
Andrew D. Crim, Vice Chairman
Roger Webb, Executive Director
The Texas Council for Developmental Disabilities is a 27-member board dedicated to ensuring that all Texans with developmental disabilities, about 411,479 individuals, have the opportunity to be independent, productive and valued members of their communities. The mission of the Texas Council for Developmental Disabilities is to create change so that all people with disabilities are fully included in their communities and exercise control over their own lives.

3720   Texas Department of Human Services
701 W 51st St
P.O. Box 149030
Austin, TX 78751-2312   512-438-3011
                                           888-834-7406
                                      FAX: 512-472-0603
                                      TTY: 888-425-6889
                                        mail@dads.state.tx.us
                                       www.dads.state.tx.us

Jon Weizenbaum, Commissioner
Kristi Jordan, Associate Commissioner
Chris Adams, Deputy Commissioner

3721   Texas Department on Aging
701 W 51st St
P.O. Box 149030
Austin, TX 78751-2312   512-438-3011
                                           800-252-9240
                                       www.dads.state.tx.us

Jon Weizenbaum, Commissioner
Kristi Jordan, Associate Commissioner
Chris Adams, Deputy Commissioner

3722   Texas Federation of Families for Children's Mental Health
Ste 505
7701 N Lamar Blvd
Austin, TX 78752-1000   512-407-8844
                                           866-893-3264
                                      FAX: 512-407-8266
                                           www.txffcmh.org

Patti Derr, Executive Director
Pat Calley, Chairperson
S Barron, Operations Director

3723   Texas Governor's Committee on People with Disabilities
1100 San Jacinto Blvd
P.O. Box 12428
Austin, TX 78701- 1935   512-463-2000
                                      FAX: 513-463-5745
                              www.governor.state.tx.us/disabilities
Angela English, LPC, LMFT, Executive Director
Erin Lawler, JD, MS, Accessibility and Disability Rig
Nancy Van Loan, Executive Assistant
The Governor's Committee on People with Disabilities is within the office of the Governor. The committee's mission is to further opportunities for persons with disabilities to enjoy full and equal access to lives of independence, productivity, and self-determination. The committee is composed of 12 members appointed by the governor and of nonvoting ex officio members.

3724 Texas Health and Human Services (HHS)
Brown-Heatly Building
4900 N Lamar Blvd.
Austin, TX 78751-3247   512-424-6500
                                     TTY:512-424-6597
                                         hhs.texas.gov

Courtney N. Phillips, Executive Commissioner
Cecile Young, Chief Deputy Executive Commissioner
John Hellerstedt, Commissioner, Department of State Health
Services
Responsible for health services in the state of texas, including
mental health and substance abuse treatment.

3725 Texas Respite Resource Network
P.O. Box 149030
710 West 51st Street
Austin, TX 78714- 9030   512-438-5555
                                     FAX: 512-438-4374
                                        archrespite.org

Jill Kagan, Program Director
Liz Newhouse, Assistant Director
Mike Mathers, Executive Director
A state clearinghouse and technical assistance network for respite in Texas. TRRN identifies, initiates and improves respite
options for families caring for individuals with disabilities on the
local, state and national levels. TRRN provides training/techni-
cal assistance to programs/groups wanting to establish respite
services.

3726 Texas Technology Access Project
Center for Disabilities Studies
10100 Burnet Rd
Austin, TX 78758-4445   512-232-0740
                                         800-828-7839
                                     FAX: 512-232-0761
                                     TTY: 512-232-0762
                            rogerlevy@austin.utexas.edu
                            techaccess.edb.utexas.edu

Roger Levy, Program Director
Darlene West, Assistive Technology Coordinator
Steve Thomas, Operations and External Relation
Their mission is to increase access for people with disabilities to
assistive technology that provides them more control over their
immediate environments and an enhanced ability to function
independently.

3727 Texas UAP for Developmental Disabilities
University of Texas
1 University Station
Austin, TX 78712   512-471-3434
                                         800-828-7839
                                         www.utexas.edu

Gregory L. Fences, President
Judith H. Langlois, Executive Vice President
Gregory J. Vincent, Vice President
Welcome to The University of Texas at Austin. Founded in 1883,
UT is one of the largest and most respected universities in the nation. Ours is a diverse learning community, with students from every state and more than 100 countries. We're a university with
world talent and Texas traditions. Discover more about us online
and come visit our beautiful campus in person.

3728 Texas Workers Compensation Commission
333 Guadalupe
P.O. Box 149104
Austin, TX 78701-1645   512-676-6000
                                         800-578-4677
                                         800-252-3439
                                     FAX: 512-804-4401
                                     TTY:512-322-4238
                            WebStaff@tdi.state.tx.us
                                        www.tdi.texas.gov

Robert Shipe, Executive Director
Rod Bordelon, Commissioner
Workers' compensation is a state-regulated insurance program
that pays medical bills and replaces some lost wages for employees who are injured at work or who have work-related diseases or
illnesses.

3729 United Cerebral Palsy of Texas
National Cerebral Palsy of American
Ste 145
1016 La Posada Dr
Austin, TX 78752-3828   512-472-8696
                                         800-798-1492
                                     FAX: 512-472-8026

Jean Langendorf, Executive Director
Offers a unique array of programs and services designed for one
specific purpose: to ensure that people with cerebral palsy and
similar disabilities have the opportunity to participate fully and
equally in every aspect of our society.

Utah

3730 Access Utah Network
Ste 100
155 S 300 W
Salt Lake City, UT 84101-1288   801-533-4636
                                         800-333-8824
                                     FAX: 801-533-3968

Mark L. Smith, Information Specialist
Access Utah Network is Utah's prime source for information and
referral for individuals with disabilities and their caregivers
since 1990. Our operators can provide you with the information
you need to find accessible housing, assistive technology and financial and social supports needed to live independently with a
disability. Call us or explore our web site today to see how Access
Utah Network can help you become more independent.

3731 Social Security: Salt Lake City Disability Determination
Social Security
P.O. Box 144032
Salt Lake City, UT 84111-4032   801-321-6500
                                         800-772-1213
                                         800-221-3493
                                     FAX: 801-321-6599
                                     TTY:801-524-5047
                               Dave.Carlson@ssa.gov
                                         www.ssa.gov

Karena L. Kilgore, Executive Secretary
Carolyn W. Colvin, Commissioner
Carolyn W. Colvin, Deputy Commissioner
We deliver services through a nationwide network of over 1,400
offices that include regional offices, field offices, card centers,
teleservice centers, processing centers, hearing offices, the Appeals Council, and our State and territorial partners, the Disability Determination Services. We also have a presence in U.S.
embassies around the globe. The rich diversity of our employees
mirrors the public we serve.

3732 Utah Assistive Technology Projects
Utah State University
6855 Old Main Hl
Logan, UT 84322-6855   435-797-3824
                                         800-524-5152
                                     TTY:435-797-2355
                                         www.uatpat.org

Sachin Pavithran, Program Director
Alma Burgess, UATP Data Collection Coordinator
Clay Christensen, Lab Coordinator
A statewide program promoting assistive technology devices and
services for persons of all ages with all disabilities.

3733 Utah Client Assistance Program
205 N 400 W
Salt Lake City, UT 84103-1125   801-363-1347
                                         800-662-9080
                                     FAX: 801-363-1437
                            www.disabilitylawcenter.org

Bryce Fifield Ph.D, President
Jared Fields, Vice President
Barbara M. Campbell, Treasurer
Since 1979, the Disability Law Center (DLC) has helped thousands of Utahns with disabilities and their families. The DLC has
broad statutory powers to safeguard the human and civil rights of
persons with disabilities. We provide self-advocacy assistance,
legal services, disability rights education, and public policy ad-

vocacy on behalf of the more than 400,000 Utah residents with disabilities. Our services are available statewide and without regard for ability to pay.

3734 Utah Department of Aging and Adult Services
195 North 1950 West
Salt Lake City, UT 84116

801-538-3910
877-424-4640
FAX: 801-538-4395
debooth@utah.gov

Nels Holmgren, Director
Michael S. Styles, Assistant Director
Michelle Benson, Director
The department administers a wide variety of home and community-based services for Utah residents who are 60 or older. Programs and services are primarily delivered by a network of 12 Area Agencies on Aging which reach all geographic areas of the state. Their goal is to provide services that allow people to remain independent.

3735 Utah Department of Human Services: Division of Services for People with Disabilities
195 North 1950 West
Salt Lake City, UT 84116

801-538-4171
844-275-3773
dhsinfo@utah.gov
dspd.utah.gov

Information and referral services for people with disabilities, including DD/MR, brain injury and physical disabilities throughout the state of Utah.

3736 Utah Division Of Substance Abuse & Mental Health
Utah Department of Human Services
195 No. 1950 West
Salt Lake City, UT 84116-1550

801-538-4171
FAX: 801-538-4016
WWW.DHS.UTAH.GOV

Lana Stohl, Executive Director

3737 Utah Division of Services for the Disabled
195 North 1950 West
Salt Lake City, UT 84116

801-538-3910
877-424-4640
FAX: 801-538-4395

Paul T. Smith, Division Director
Clay Hiatt, Fiscal Management
Offers services for the totally blind, legally blind, visually impaired, and more with health, counseling, educational, recreational, rehabilitation, computer training and professional training services.

3738 Utah Governor's Council for People with Disabilities
155 S 300 W
Suite 100
Salt Lake City, UT 84101-1288

801-533-4636
FAX: 801-533-3968
www.gcpd.org/

Mark Smith, Manager
Angela Allen, Administrative Secretary

3739 Utah Labor Commission
160 E 300 S
3rd Floor
Salt Lake City, UT 84114-6600

801-530-6800
800-222-1238
FAX: 801-530-6390
laborcom@utah.gov
laborcommission.utah.gov

Jaceson R Maughan, Commissioner
Alison Adams-Perlac, Director
Britton Beims, Employment Discrimination Investigation
The Utah Labor Commission is a regulatory agency that works to ensure safety in the workplace. The commission also offers services related to workplace injuries, wage issues, descrimination and industrial accidents.

3740 Utah Protection & Advocacy Services for Persons with Disabilities
Disability Law Center
205 N 400 W
Salt Lake City, UT 84103-1125

801-363-1347
800-662-9080
FAX: 801-363-1437
www.disabilitylawcenter.org

Bryce Fifield Ph.D, President
Jared Fields, Vice President
Barbara M. Campbell, Treasurer
Since 1979, the Disability Law Center (DLC) has helped thousands of Utahns with disabilities and their families. The DLC has broad statutory powers to safeguard the human and civil rights of persons with disabilities. We provide self-advocacy assistance, legal services, disability rights education, and public policy advocacy on behalf of the more than 400,000 Utah residents with disabilities. Our services are available statewide and without regard for ability to pay.

Vermont

3741 Disability Law Project
57 N Main St
Rutland, VT 05701-3246

800-889-2047
FAX: 802-775-0022
nbreiden@vtlegalaid.org
vtlegalaid.org

Nanci Smith, President
Jessica Porter, Vice President/Secretary
John Holme, Treasurer
Legal services (protection and advocacy) for people with disabilities on legal issues arising from disability. Statewide. Adults and children. Employment, education, discrimination, housing, public benefits, health care.

3742 Disability Rights Vermont
141 Main Street
Suite 7
Montpelier, VT 05602-2916

802-229-1355
800-834-7890
FAX: 802-229-1359
TTY: 800-889-2047
info@disabilityrightsvt.org
www.disabilityrightsvt.org

Sarah Wendell-Launderville, President
David Gallagher, Vice president
Crocker Paquin, Treasurer
Advocacy and legal services for people with mental illness on legal issues arising, out of disabilities. Children and adults.

3743 Social Security: Vermont Disability Determination Services
Ste 6
93 Pilgrim Park Rd
Waterbury, VT 05676-1729

802-241-2463
800-734-2463
800-772-1213
FAX: 802-241-2492
www.ssa.gov

Karena L. Kilgore, Executive Secretary
Carolyn W. Colvin, Commissioner
Carolyn W. Colvin, Deputy Commissioner
We deliver services through a nationwide network of over 1,400 offices that include regional offices, field offices, card centers, teleservice centers, processing centers, hearing offices, the Appeals Council, and our State and territorial partners, the Disability Determination Services. We also have a presence in U.S. embassies around the globe. The rich diversity of our employees mirrors the public we serve.

3744 Vermont Assistive Technology Projects
103 S Main St
Weeks Building
Waterbury, VT 05671-2305   800-750-6355
                                         800-750-6355
                                    FAX: 802-871-3048
                                    TTY: 802-241-1464
                                         atp.vermont.gov

Amber Fulcher, Program Director
Sharon Alderman, Assistive Technology Reuse Coord
Emma Cobb, Assistive Technology Services Co
Increase awareness and change policies to insure assistive technology (AT) is available to all Vermonters with disabilities. Our Commitment is to enable Vermonters with disabilities to have greater independence, productivity, and confidence. To provide them with a clear and direct avenue toward integration and inclusion within the work force and community.

3745 Vermont Client Assistance Program
57 N Main St
Rutland, VT 05701-3246   802-775-0021
                                         800-769-7459
               www.vocrehabvermont.org/html/clientassistance
Patrick Flood, Commissioner
The Client Assistance Program (CAP) is an independent advocacy program to help if you are applying for or receiving services from one of the following sources: Division of Vocational Rehabilitation (VR); Vermont Center for Independent Living (VCIL); Division for the Blind and Visually Impaired (DBVI); Vermont Association of Business, Industry & Rehabilitation (VABIR); Vermont Association for the Blind and Visually Impaired (VABVI); Supported Employment Programs; Transition Programs.

3746 Vermont Department of Aging
103 S Main St
Weeks Building
Waterbury, VT 05671-1601   802-241-2401
                                    FAX: 802-871-3281
                                    TTY: 802-241-3557
                                         dail.vermont.gov

Susan Wehry, Commissioner
Marybeth McCaffrey, Director
Linda Henzel, Executive Staff Assistant

3747 Vermont Department of Developmental and
103 S Main St
Weeks Building
Waterbury, VT 05671-1601   802-241-2401
                                    FAX: 802-871-3281
                                    TTY: 802-241-3557
                                         dail.vermont.gov

Jonathan Wood, Manager

3748 Vermont Department of Disabilities, Aging and Independent Living
Aging and Disabilities
103 S Main St
Waterbury, VT 05671-1601   802-241-2401
                                    FAX: 802-241-2325
                                         dail.vermont.gov

Susan Wehry, Commissioner
Camille George, Deputy Commissioner

3749 Vermont Department of Health: Children with Special Health Needs
Vermont Department Of Health
108 Cherry Street
Burlington, VT 05402-70   802-863-7200
                                         800-464-4343
                                    FAX: 802-865-7754
                                         healthvermont.gov

Harry Chen, M.D., Commissioner
Barbara Cimaglio, Deputy Commissioner for Alcohol
Tracy Dolan, Deputy Commissioner for Public H
Multidisciplinary clinics and family support for children with chronic conditions, birth to age 21 years.

3750 Vermont Developmental Disabilities Council
103 S Main St
Waterbury, VT 05671-9800   082-241-2220
Cynthia D LaWare, Secretary
The mission of VTDDC is to facilitate connections and to promote supports that bring people with developmental disabilities into the heart of Vermont Communities.

3751 Vermont Division for the Blind & Visually Impaired
Agency of Human Svcs Dept Disabilities, Aging & IL
103 S Main St
Weeks Building
Waterbury, VT 5671-2304   802-871-3038
                                         800-405-5005
                                         888-405-5005
                                    FAX: 802-871-3048
                                         www.dbvi.vermont.gov

Fred Jones, Director
Scott Langley, Counselor
Heather Allen, Administrative Assistant
Offers services for the totally blind, legally blind, visually impaired, and more with health, counseling, educational, recreational, rehabilitation, computer training and professional training services.

3752 Vermont Division of Disability & Aging Services
103 S Main St
Weeks Building
Waterbury, VT 05671-1601   802-241-2401
                                    FAX: 802-871-3281
                                    TTY: 802-241-3557
                                         www.dail.vermont.gov

Susan Wehry, Commissioner
Marybeth McCaffrey, Director
Linda Henzel, Executive Staff Assistant
Provides services to adults and children with developmental disabilities all to the aging.

3753 Workers Compensation Board Vermont
Department of Labor
5 Green Mountain Drive
PO Box 488
Montpelier, VT 05601- 0488   802-828-2286
                                    FAX: 802-828-2195
                                         labor.vermont.gov

J. Stephen Monahan, Director of Workers' Compensation & Safety
Welcome to the Vermont Department of Labor's website. VDOL's primary focus is to provide services that assist businesses, workers, and job seekers.

Virginia

3754 Aging and Disability Services
2100 Washington Blvd
4th Floor
Arlington, VA 22204   703-228-1700
                                    TTY: 703-228-1788
                                         arlaaa@arlingtonva.us
                                         aging-disability.arlingtonva.us
Anita Friedman, Director, Department of Human Services
The Aging and Disability Services Division offers care coordination, home care, and supportive services to the aging residents of Arlington. Services are provided to adults over 60, adults with developmental disabilities and their caregivers.

3755 International Dyslexia Association: Virginia Branch
3126 West Cary St.
Suite 102
Richmond, VA 23221   866-893-0583
                                         va.dyslexiaida.org

Lisa Snidery, President
Lisa Harrah, Vice President
Robin Hegner, Secretary
Provides free information and referral services for diagnosis and tutoring for parents, educators, physicians, and individuals with dyslexia in Illinois. Membership includes yearly journal and quarterly newsletter.

3756 Virginia Department for the Blind and Vision Impaired (DBVI)
397 Azalea Ave.
Richmond, VA 23227
804-371-3140
800-622-2155
www.vdbvi.org

Raymond E. Hopkins, Commissioner
Rick L. Mitchell, Deputy Commissioner, Services
Matt Koch, Deputy Commissioner, Enterprises
Offers services for the totally blind, legally blind, visually impaired, and more with health, counseling, educational, recreational, rehabilitation, computer training and professional training services.

3757 Virginia Department of Mental Health
P.O.Box 1797
Richmond, VA 23218-1797
804-786-3921
FAX: 804-371-6638
TTY:804-371-8977
www.dbhds.virginia.gov

Debra Ferguson, Commissioner
John Pezzoli, Deputy Commissioner
Daniel Herr, Assistant Commissioner of Behavi
Available to citizens statewide, Virginia's public mental health, intellectual disability and substance abuse services system is comprised of 16 state facilities and 40 locally-run community services boards (CSBs) The CSBs and facilities serve children and adults who have or who are at risk of mental illness, serious emotional disturbance, intellectual disabilities, or substance abuse disorders.

3758 Virginia Developmental Disability Council
103 S Main St
Waterbury, VT 05671-9800
082-241-2220
Cynthia D LaWare, Secretary
The mission of VTDDC is to facilitate connections and to promote supports that bring people with developmental disabilities into the heart of Vermont Communities.

3759 Virginia Office Protection and Advocacy for People with Disabilities
1512 Willow Lawn
Suite 100
Richmond, VA 23230-3034
804-225-2042
800-552-3962
FAX: 804-662-7057
info@dLCV.org
disabilitylawva.org

Coleen Miller, Executive Director
LaToya Blizzard, Deputy Director
Mickie Chapman, IT Specialist
Through zealous and effective advocacy and legal representation to: protect and advance legal, human, and civil rights of persons with disabilities; combat and prevent abuse, neglect, and discrimination; and promote independence, choice, and self-determination by persons with disabilities.

3760 Virginia Office for Protection & Advocacy
5005 Mitchelldale
Suite #100
Houston, TX 77092-3034
713-574-5287
866-964-2867
FAX: 281-476-7800
info@dLCV.org

V Coleen Miller, Executive Director
Rusty Hill, Administrative Assistant
LaToya Blizzard, Deputy Director for Fiscal and O
An independent state agency that helps ensure that the rights of persons with disabiltiies in the Commonwealth are protected. The mission of DRVD is to provide zealous and effective advocacy and legal representation to protect and advance legal, human and civil rights of persons with disabilities, combat and prevent abuse, neglect and discrimination, and promote independence, choice and self-determination by persons with disabilities.

3761 Virginia Office for Protection and Advocacy
5005 Mitchelldale
Suite #100
Houston, TX 77092-3034
713-574-5287
866-964-2867
FAX: 281-476-7800
info@dLCV.org

V Coleen Miller, Executive Director
Rusty Hill, Administrative Assistant
LaToya Blizzard, Deputy Director for Fiscal and O
An independent state agency that helps ensure that the rights of persons with disabiltiies in the Commonwealth are protected. The mission of DRVD is to provide zealous and effective advocacy and legal representation to protect and advance legal, human and civil rights of persons with disabilities, combat and prevent abuse, neglect and discrimination, and promote independence, choice and self-determination by persons with disabilities.

3762 Virginia's Developmental Disabilities Planning Council
Stae Agency
1100 Bank Street
7th Floor
Richmond, VA 23219-3426
804-786-0016
800-846-4464
FAX: 804-662-7662
TTY: 800-811-7893
info@vbpd.virginia.gov
www.vaboard.org

Korinda Rusinyak, Chairman
Charles Meacham, Vice Chairman
Dennis Manning, Secretary
To create a Commonwealth that advances opportunities for independence, personal decision-making and full participation in community life for individuals with developmental disabilities.

Washington

3763 DSHS/Aging & Adult Disability Services Administration
P.O.Box 45130
Olympia, WA 98504-5130
360-902-7797
800-737-0617
FAX: 360-902-7848
TTY: 800-737-7931

Dan Murphy, Director
Bea Rector, Project Director
Tamarra Paradee, Executive Secretary
The Aging and Disability Services Administration assists children and adults with developmental delays or disabilities, cognitive impairment, chronic illness and related functional disabilities to gain access to needed services and supports by managing a system of long-term care and supportive services that are high quality, cost effective, and responsive to individual needs and preferences.

3764 Disability Rights: Washington
315 5th Avenue South
Suite 850
Seattle, WA 98104-2691
206-324-1521
800-562-2702
FAX: 206-957-0729
TTY: 206-957-0728
info@dr-wa.org
www.disabilityrightswa.org

Mark Stroh, Executive Director
David Carison, Director of Legal Advocacy
Emily Cooper, Staff Attorney
WPAS is a private, non-profit right protection agency for persons with disabilities residin in Washington state. Our advocacy services include information referral, technical assistance, training, publications and systemic advocacy.

3765 International Dyslexia Association: Washington State Branch
P.O. Box 27435
Seattle, WA 98165 info@wabida.org
wabida.org

Kristie English, President
Jessica Ruger, Vice President
Beverly Wolf, Treasurer
Provides free information and referral services for diagnosis and tutoring for parents, educators, physicians, and individuals with dyslexia in Arkansas, Idaho, Montana and Washington state. Membership includes yearly journal and quarterly newsletter.

3766 Social Security: Olympia Disability Determination
Social Security
P.O. Box 9303-MS-45550
Olympia, WA 98507 360-664-7356
800-772-1213
800-562-6074
FAX: 360-586-0851
TTY:800-325-0778
Jennifer.Elsen@ssa.gov
www.ssa.gov

Karena L. Kilgore, Executive Secretary
Carolyn W. Colvin, Commissioner
Carolyn W. Colvin, Deputy Commissioner
We deliver services through a nationwide network of over 1,400 offices that include regional offices, field offices, card centers, teleservice centers, processing centers, hearing offices, the Appeals Council, and our State and territorial partners, the Disability Determination Services. We also have a presence in U.S. embassies around the globe. The rich diversity of our employees mirrors the public we serve.

3767 WA Department of Services for the Blind
4565 7th Avenue SE
PO Box 40959
Lacey, WA 98504-0959 206-906-5500
800-552-7103
info@dsb.wa.gov
www.dsb.wa.gov

Michael MacKillop, Acting Executive Director
Vocational rehabilitation for the blind.

3768 Washington Client Assistance Program
2531 Rainier Ave S
Seattle, WA 98144-5328 206-721-5999
800-544-2121
888-721-6072
FAX: 206-721-4537
TTY:206-721-6072
www.washingtoncap.org

Jerry Johnson, Executive Director
Bob Huven, rehabilitation coordinator
Advocacy and information assistance for persons of disability seeking services through vocational rehabilitation or other program under the 1973 Rehabilitation Act as commented. We provide counseling.

3769 Washington Developmental Disability
2600 Martin Way E
Suite F
Olympia, WA 98506-4974 360-586-3560
800-634-4473
FAX: 360-586-2424
Ed.Holen@ddc.wa.gov
www.ddc.wa.gov

Diana Zottman, Chairman
Ed Holen, Executive Director
Brain Dahl, Support Coordinator
Developmental Disabilities Council members are appointed by the Governor to plan comprehensive services for the State of Washington's citizens with developmental disabilities.

3770 Washington Governor's Committee on Disability Issues & Employment
605 Woodland Square Loop SE
Lacey, WA 98503 360-438-3168
FAX: 928-447-6579
gcdetz@gmail.com
www.gcde.org

Martin Haule, Director
Toby Olson, Manager

3771 Washington Office of Superintendent of Public Instruction
600 Washington St. S.E.
P. O. Box 47200
Olympia, WA 98504-7200 360-725-6000
TTY:360-644-3631
www.k12.wa.us

Randy Dorn, State Superintendent
Gil Mendoza, Deputy Superintendent
JoLynn Berge, Assistant Superintendent
The Office of Superintendent of Public Instruction (OSPI) is the primary agency charged with overseeing K-12 education in Washington state. OSPI works with the state's 296 school districts to administer basic education programs and implement education reform on behalf of more than one million public school students.

3772 Washington State Developmental Disabilities Council
2600 Martin Way E
Suite F
Olympia, WA 98506-4974 360-586-3560
800-634-4473
FAX: 360-586-2424
Ed.Holen@ddc.wa.gov
www.ddc.wa.gov

Diana Zottman, Chairman
Ed Holen, Executive Director
Brain Dahl, Support Coordinator
Developmental Disabilities Council members are appointed by the Governor to plan comprehensive services for the State of Washington's citizens with developmental disabilities.

3773 Workers Compensation Board Washington
State of Washington
7273 Linderson Way SW
Tumwater, WA 98501-5414 360-902-5800
800-547-8367
FAX: 360-902-5798
TTY: 360-902-5797
www.lni.wa.gov

Judy Schurke, Director
Lisa Rodriguez, Executive Assistant
Vickie Kennedy, Special Assistant
&I is a diverse state agency dedicated to the safety, health and security of Washington's 3.2 million workers. We help employers meet safety and health standards and we inspect workplaces when alerted to hazards. As administrators of the state's workers' compensation system, we are similar to a large insurance company, providing medical and limited wage-replacement coverage to workers who suffer job-related injuries and illness. Our rules and enforcement programs also help ensure workers are pai

West Virginia

3774 Bureau of Employment Programs Division of Workers' Compensation
State of West Virginia
407 Virginia Street East
Charleston, WV 25301-2531 304-357-0101
800-628-4265
FAX: 304-357-0788
helpdesk@kanawha.us
kanawha.us

Patricia Starkey, Manager
Vern Cormick, Manager
Michael ' Campbell, Director of IT

Kanawha County today is an exciting technology center that is earning recognition in information technology, medical research, chemical synthesis research, and telecommunications.

3775 Disability Determination Section
Ste 500
500 Quarrier St
Charleston, WV 25301-2913

304-343-5055
800-772-1213
800-344-5033
FAX: 304-353-4212
www.ssa.gov

Karena L. Kilgore, Executive Secretary
Carolyn W. Colvin, Commissioner
Delivers services through a nationwide network of over 1,400 offices that include regional offices, field offices, card centers, teleservice centers, processing centers, hearing offices, the Appeals Council, and our State and territorial partners, the Disability Determination Services. We also have a presence in U.S. embassies around the globe. The rich diversity of our employees mirrors the public we serve.

3776 Social Security: Charleston Disability Determination
Social Security
500 Quarrier Street
Suite 500
Charleston, WV 25301-2913

304-343-5055
800-772-1213
800-344-5033
FAX: 304-353-4212
www.ssa.gov

Karena L. Kilgore, Executive Secretary
Carolyn W. Colvin, Commissioner
Carolyn W. Colvin, Deputy Commissioner
We deliver services through a nationwide network of over 1,400 offices that include regional offices, field offices, card centers, teleservice centers, processing centers, hearing offices, the Appeals Council, and our State and territorial partners, the Disability Determination Services. We also have a presence in U.S. embassies around the globe. The rich diversity of our employees mirrors the public we serve.

3777 West Virginia Advocates
1207 Quarrier St
Suite 400
Charleston, WV 25301-1826

304-346-0847
800-950-5250
FAX: 304-346-0867
kellie.l.aikman@wv.gov
wvadvocates.org

Terry Dilcher, President
John Galloway, Treasurer
Don Neurman, Secretary
West Virginia Advocates, Inc. (WVA) is the federally mandated protection and advocacy system for people with disabilities in West Virginia. WVA is a private, nonprofit agency. Our services are confidential and free of charge.

3778 West Virginia Client Assistance Program
West Virginia Advocates
1900 Kanawha Blvd E
Room 9
Charleston, WV 25305-1

304-558-3780
FAX: 304-558-4092

Clarice Hausch, Executive Director

3779 West Virginia Department of Aging
1900 Kanawha Blvd. East
Charleston, WV 25305

304-558-3317
877-987-3646
FAX: 304-558-5609
www.wvseniorservices.gov

Robert E. Roswall, Commissioner
Nel Kimble
The information we offer is tailored to those who are seeking to locate programs and services for themselves or their loved ones and also for professionals who may be looking for up-to-date information relating to the field of aging.

3780 West Virginia Department of Children with Disabilities
Children with Special Health Care Needs
One Davis Square
Suite 100 East
Charleston, WV 25301-1757

304-558-0684
FAX: 304-558-1130
DHHRSecretary@wv.gov
www.dhhr.wv.gov

Douglas M. Robinson, Deputy Commissioner
Virginia Mahan, Executive Secretary
Karen Villanueva-Matkovich, General Counsel
The Bureau for Public Health directs public health activities at all levels within the state to fulfill the core functions of public health: the assessment of community health status and available resources; policy development resulting in proposals to support and encourage better health; and assurance that needed services are available, accessible, and of acceptable quality.

3781 West Virginia Department of Health
One Davis Square
Suite 100 East
Charleston, WV 25301

304-558-0684
FAX: 304-558-1130
DHHRSecretary@wv.gov
www.dhhr.wv.gov

Douglas M. Robinson, Deputy Commissioner
Virginia Mahan, Executive Secretary
Karen Villanueva-Matkovich, General Counsel
The Bureau for Public Health directs public health activities at all levels within the state to fulfill the core functions of public health: the assessment of community health status and available resources; policy development resulting in proposals to support and encourage better health; and assurance that needed services are available, accessible, and of acceptable quality.

3782 West Virginia Developmental Disabilities Council
110 Stockton St
Charleston, WV 25387

304-558-0416
FAX: 304-558-0941
TTY:304-558-2376
dhhrwvddc@wv.gov
www.ddc.wv.gov

Diana Zottman, Chairman
Ed Holen, Executive Director
Brain Dahl, Support Coordinator
Working to assure that West Virginians with developmental disabilities receive the services, supports, and other forms of assistance they need to exercise self-determination and achieve independence, productivity, integration, and inclusion in the community.
6-8 pages Quarterly Newsl

3783 West Virginia Division of Rehabilitation Services
107 Capitol Street
Charleston, WV 25301-2609

304-356-2060
800-642-8207
www.wvdrs.org

Donna L. Ashworth, Acting Director
Kay Goodwin, Cabinet Secretary
DRS' mission is to enable and empower individuals with disabilities to work and to live independently.

Wisconsin

3784 Disability Rights Wisconsin: Milwaukee Office
Ste 3230
6737 W Washington St
Milwaukee, WI 53214-5651

414-773-4646
800-708-3034
FAX: 414-773-4647
TTY: 888-758-6049
info@drwi.org
disabilityrightswi.org

Ted Skemp, President
Beth Moss, Vice President
Susan Gramling, Secretary
The protection and advocacy agency for people with disabilities in Wisconsin. DRW provides guidance, advice, investigation, ne-

gotiation and in some cases legal representation to people with disabilities and their families. Local and state level systems advocacy and training are also provided.

3785 International Dyslexia Association: Wisconsin Branch
1616 Graham Ave.
Eau Claire, WI 54701   608-355-0911
wi.dyslexiaida.org

Tammy Tillotson, President
Kimberly Chan, Treasurer
Pattie Huse, Secretary
Provides free information and referral services for diagnosis and tutoring for parents, educators, physicians, and individuals with dyslexia in Illinois. Membership includes yearly journal and quarterly newsletter.

3786 Social Security: Madison Field Office
6011 Odana Rd
Madison, WI 53719-1101   866-770-2262
800-772-1213
FAX: 608-270-1021
TTY: 800-325-0778
wi.fo.madison@ssa.gov
www.ssa.gov

3787 West Virginia Department of Health
One Davis Square
Suite 100 East
Charleston, WV 25301   304-558-0684
800-441-4576
FAX: 304-558-1130
DHHRSecretary@wv.gov
www.dhhr.wv.gov

Rocco S. Fucillo, Cabinet Secretary
Susan Shelton Perry, Deputy Secretary for Legal Servi
Ellen Cannon, Privacy Officer
The Department of Health and Family Services operates the federal Title V Maternal and Child Health Block Grant Program for Children with Special Health Care Needs. The program provides program monitoring, consultation and technical assistance to five regional CSHCN centers throughout Wisconsin; a Birth Defects Monitoring and Surveillance Program and a Universal Newborn Hearing Screening Program.

3788 Wisconsin Board for People with Developmental Disabilities (WBPDD)
201 W Washington Ave
Suite 111
Madison, WI 53703-2796   608-266-7826
888-332-1677
FAX: 608-267-3906
TTY: 608-266-6660
wcdd.org

Jennifer Ondrejka, Manager
Joshua Ryf, Office Manager
Statewide systems advocacy group for people with developmental disabilities in Wisconsin.

3789 Wisconsin Bureau of Aging
State Office of Wisconsin
1 West Wilson Street
Madison, WI 53703   608-266-1865
FAX: 608-267-3203
TTY: 888-701-1251
DHSwebmaster@wisconsin.gov

Donna Mc Dowell, Executive Director
Gail Schwersenska, Section Chief
Dennis G. Smith, Secretary
Keeps and updates information and printed materials on senior housing directories, nursing home listings, and home care agencies.

3790 Wisconsin Coalition for Advocacy: Madison Office
16 N Carroll St
Suite 400
Madison, WI 53703-2762   608-267-0214
800-928-8778
FAX: 608-267-0368

Kim Hogan, Intake Specialist
Mr Lynn Breedlove, Executive Director

The protection and advocacy agency for people with disabilities in Wisconsin. WCA provides guidance, advice, investigation, negotiation and in some cases legal representation to people with disabilities and their families. Local and state level systems advocacy and training are also provided.

3791 Wisconsin Governor's Committee for People with Disabilities
1 West Wilson Street
Madison, WI 53703   608-266-1865
877-865-3432
FAX: 608-266-3386
TTY: 888-701-1251
DHSwebmaster@wisconsin.gov

Donna Mc Dowell, Executive Director
Gail Schwersenska, Section Chief
Dennis G. Smith, Secretary
To advise the Governor and state agencies on problems faced by people with disabilities; to review legislation affecting people with disabilities; to promote effective operation of publicly-administered or supported programs serving people with disabilities; to promote the collection, dissemination and incorporation of adequate information about persons with disabilities for purposes of public planning at all levels of government.

3792 Workers Compensation Board Wisconsin
Room C100, 201 E. Washington Avenue
P. O. Box 7901
Madison, WI 53707-7901   608-266-1340
FAX: 608-267-0394
dwd.wisconsin.gov/wc

Reggie Newson, Secretary
Jonathan Barry, Deputy Secretary
John Metcalf, Division Administrator
The Worker's Compensation Division administers programs designed to ensure that injured workers receive required benefits from insurers or self-insured employers; encourage rehabilitation and reemployment for injured workers; and promote the reduction of work-related injuries, illnesses, and deaths.

Wyoming

3793 Social Security: Cheyenne Disability Determination
Social Security
821 W Pershing Blvd
Cheyenne, WY 82002-1   307-777-7341
800-438-5788
FAX: 307-637-0247
Jeff.Graham@ssa.gov
ssa.gov

Karena L. Kilgore, Executive Secretary
Carolyn W. Colvin, Commissioner
Carolyn W. Colvin, Deputy Commissioner
We deliver services through a nationwide network of over 1,400 offices that include regional offices, field offices, card centers, teleservice centers, processing centers, hearing offices, the Appeals Council, and our State and territorial partners, the Disability Determination Services. We also have a presence in U.S. embassies around the globe. The rich diversity of our employees mirrors the public we serve.

3794 WY Department of Health: Mental Health and Substance Abuse Service Division
401 Hathaway Building
Cheyenne, WY 82002-1   307-777-7656
800-535-4006
FAX: 307-777-7439
TTY: 307-777-5581
www.health.wyo.gov

Thomas O. Forslund, Director
Lee Clabots, Deputy Director
Bob Peck, Chief Financial Officer
State office responsible for purchase of service and program development policy.

3795 **Workers Compensation Board Wyoming**
350 South Washington Street
PO Box 1068
Afton, WY 83110-3004   307-886-9260
                                        FAX: 307-886-9269

3796 **Wyoming Client Assistance Program**
Protection and Advocacy System
2nd Fl
320 W 25th St
Cheyenne, WY 82001-3069   307-632-2682
                                        877-854-5041
                                        FAX: 307-638-0815
                                        wypanda@vcn.com
                                        ap.org

Jeanne Thobro, Manager
Jeanne A Thobro, Executive Director

3797 **Wyoming Department of Aging**
State Department of Wyoming
401 Hathaway Building
Cheyenne, WY 82002-1   307-777-7656
                                        800-442-2766
                                        FAX: 307-777-7439
                                        wyaging@wyo.gov
                                        health.wyo.gov

Thomas O. Forslund, Director
Lee Clabots, Deputy Director
Bob Peck, Chief Financial Officer
The Wyoming Department of Health's Aging Division is committed to providing care, ensuring safety and and promoting independent choices for Wyoming's older adults

3798 **Wyoming Developmental Disability Council**
122 W 25th St
1st. Fl. West, Herschler Building,
Cheyenne, WY 82002   307-777-7230
                                        800-438-5791
                                        FAX: 307-777-5690
                                        wgcdd@wyo.gov

Shannon Buller, Executive Director
Von Maul, Administrative Assistant
Sam Janney, Public Information Officer
Our purpose is to assure that individuals with developmental disabilities and their families participate in and have access to needed community services, individualized supports and other forms of assistance that promote independence, productivity, integration and inclusion in all facets of community life.

3799 **Wyoming Protection & Advocacy for Persons with Disabilities**
7344 Stockman Street
Cheyenne, WY 82009   307-632-3496
                                        FAX: 307-638-0815
                                        wypanda@wypanda.com
                                        wypanda.com

Tori Rosenthal, President
Jeanne A Thobro, Executive Director
Wyoming Protection & Advocacy System, Inc. (P&A), established in 1977, is the official non-profit corporation authorized to implement certain mandates of several federal laws. Enacted by Congress, these laws provide various protection and advocacy services.

Independent Living Centers

Alabama

3800 Birdie Thornton Center
2350 Hine Street
Athens, AL 35611
256-232-0366
FAX: 256-230-9398

Kristy Allen King, Program Director
Heather Mereidth, Program Professional, QMRP
Rabieb Clem, Senior Aid
The Birdie Thornton Center is devoted to providing care, education, and training to adults with developmental delays and disabilities.

3801 Independent Living Center of Mobile
5301 Moffett Rd
Suite 110
Mobile, AL 36618-2926
251-460-0301
FAX: 251-341-1267
TTY:251-460-2872
Michaeld@ilcmobile.org
ilcmobile.org

Michael Davis, Executive Director
Darmita Flood, Administrative Assistant
Barbara Hattier, ILS/Transportation Coordinator
Helping people with disabilities become independent.

3802 Independent Living Resources Of Greater Birmingham: Alabaster
120 Plaza Cir, Suite C
P. O. Box 2048
Alabaster, AL 35007-7034
205-685-0570
FAX: 205-251-0605
TTY:205-685-0570
www.ilrgb.org

Kathy Lovell, President
Phil Klebine, Vice President
Susan Parker, Secretary
The mission of this Independent Living Center is to empower people with disabilities to fully participate in the community.

3803 Independent Living Resources of Greater Birmingham: Jasper
300 Birmingham Ave
PO Box 434
Jasper, AL 35502-3811
205-387-0159
FAX: 205-387-0162
TTY:205-387-0159
www.ilrgb.org

Kathy Lovell, President
Phil Klebine, Vice President
Susan Parker, Secretary
The purpose of this Independent Living Center is to empower people with disabilities to fully participate in the community.

3804 Independent Living Resources of Greater Birmingham
1418 6th Avenue North
Birmingham, AL 35203-1317
205-251-2223
FAX: 205-251-0605
TTY:205-251-2223

Kathy Lovell, President
Phil Klebine, Vice President
Susan Parker, Secretary
The mission of this Independent Living Center is to empower people with disabilities to fully participate in the community.

3805 Montgomery Center for Independent Living
600 S Court St
Montgomery, AL 36104-4106
334-240-2520
FAX: 334-240-6869
TTY:334-240-2520
mcil@bellsouth.net
www.cilmontgomery.org

Scott Renner, Executive Director
Barbara F. Crozier, President
Kenneth Marshall, Vice President

Encourgaes people with disabilities to support one another in reaching their own independent living goals.

3806 State of Alabama Independent Living/Homebound Service (SAIL)
Alabama Department of Rehabilitation Services
602 S. Lawrence St.
Montgomery, AL 36104
www.rehab.alabama.gov
The following services are provided to Alabamians with significant disabilities: specialized in-home education and counseling; attendant care; training; and medical services.

Alaska

3807 Access Alaska: ADA Partners Project
1217 East 10th Ave
Suite 105
Anchorage, AK 99501-2044
907-248-4777
800-770-4488
888-462-1444
FAX: 907-263-1942
TTY:907-248-8799
info@accessalaska.org
accessalaska.org

Lorali Simon, President
Mike O'Neill, Vice President
Jim Duffield, Treasurer
Assisting Alaskans with disabilities to live independently in the community of their choice.

3808 Access Alaska: Fairbanks
526 Gaffney Rd
Suite 100
Fairbanks, AK 99701-4914
907-479-7940
800-770-7940
FAX: 907-474-4052
TTY: 907-474-8619
info@accessalaska.org
accessalaska.org

Lorali Simon, President
Mike O'Neill, Vice President
Jim Duffield, Treasurer
A local non profit agency using its resources to actively promote a society where persons with disabilities can live and work independently in the community of their choice.

3809 Access Alaska: Mat-Su
1075 Check St,
Suite 109
Wasilla, AK 99654-6937
907-357-2588
800-770-0228
FAX: 907-357-5585
info@accessalaska.org
accessalaska.org

Lorali Simon, President
Mike O'Neill, Vice President
Jim Duffield, Treasurer
Provides independent living services to persons with significant disabilities. Mission is to encourage and promote the total integration of persons with disabilities into the community of their choice. Services include independent living skills training, information and referral, advocacy, peer support, and at home modifications.

3810 Alaska SILC
Ste 206
1217 East 10th Ave
Anchorage, AK 99501-1760
907-248-4777
800-770-4488
888-294-7452
FAX: 907-263-1942
info@accessalaska.org
www.alaskasilc.org

Jim Beck, Executive Director
Lorali Simon, President
Mike O'Neill, Vice President
The Alaska Statewide Independent Living is committed to promoting a philosophy of consumer control, peer support, self help, self determination, equal access, and individual and systems ad-

vocacy, in order to maximize leadership, empowerment, independence, productivity, and to support full inclusion and integration of individuals with disabilities into the mainstream of American society.

3811 Arctic Access
P.O.Box 930
Kotzebue, AK 99752-930   907-412-0695
                                       877-442-2393
                                   TTY:907-442-2393

Roger Wright Jr, Executive Director
Russell Williams, Jr, Elder & Disability Resource Coor
Audrey Aanes
The Arctic Access Independent Living Center provides services and opportunities for elders and others with disabilities so they may remain in their village and be as active as possible with their families and commuties in the North West Arctic and Bering Straits Regions of Alaska.

3812 Hope Community Resources
540 W Intl Airport Rd
Anchorage, AK 99518-1105   907-561-5335
                                     800-478-0078
                                FAX: 907-564-7429
                                 info@hopealaska.org
                                      hopealaska.org

Robert Owens, President
John Dittrich, Vice President
Eugene 'Gene' Bates, Treasurer
Provider of services to individuals who experience a disability.

3813 Kenai Peninsula Independent Living Center
265 E. Pioneer Suite 201
P.O.Box 2474
Homer, AK 99603- 2474   907-235-7911
                                     800-770-7911
                                FAX: 907-235-6236
                                      peninsulailc.org

Candy Norman, President
Mike Harmer, Vice President
Offers peer counseling, disability education and awareness, attendant care registry and information on accessible housing.

3814 Kenai Peninsula Independent Living Center: Seward
201 Third Avenue, Suite 101Bs
P. O. Box 3523
Seward, AK 99664-3523   907-224-8711
                                FAX: 907-224-7793
                                 www.peninsulailc.org

Candy Norman, President
Mike Harmer, Vice President
Offers peer counseling, disability, education and awareness, attendant care registry and information on accessible housing.

3815 Keni Peninsula Independent Living Center: Central Peninsula
47255 Princeton Avenue
Suite 8
Soldotna, AK 99669   907-262-6333
                                FAX: 907-260-4495
                                 www.peninsulailc.org

Candy Norman, President
Mike Harmer, Vice President
Offers peer counseling, disability education and awareness, attendant care registry and information on accessible housing.

3816 Southeast Alaska Independent Living
3225 Hospital Drive
Suite 300
Juneau, AK 99801-7863   907-586-4920
                                     800-478-7245
                                FAX: 907-586-4980
                                TTY: 907-523-5285
                                 info@sailinc.org
                                      sailinc.org

Robert Purvis, President
Jeff Irwin, Vice President
Suzanne Williams, Secretary
To empower consumers with disabilities by providing services and information to support them in making choices that will positively affect their independence and productivity in society.

3817 Southeast Alaska Independent Living: Ketchikan
602 Dock St
Suite 107
Ketchikan, AK 99901-6574   907-225-4735
                                     888-452-7245
                                FAX: 907-247-4735
                                 ketchikan@sailinc.org
                                      www.sailinc.org

Robert Purvis, President
Jeff Irwin, Vice President
Suzanne Williams, Secretary
To empower consumers with disabilities by providing services and information to support them in making choices that will positively affect their independence and productivity in society.

3818 Southeast Alaska Independent Living: Sitka
514 Lake St
Suite C
Sitka, AK 99835-7405   907-747-6859
                                     888-500-7245
                                FAX: 907-747-6783
                                 sitka@sailinc.org
                                      www.sailinc.org

Robert Purvis, President
Jeff Irwin, Vice President
Suzanne Williams, Secretary
To empower consumers with disabilities by providing services and information to support them in making choices that will positively affect their independence and productivity in society.

Arizona

3819 ASSIST! to Independence
P.O.Box 4133
Tuba City, AZ 86045-4133   928-283-6261
                                     888-848-1449
                                FAX: 928-283-6284
                                TTY: 928-283-6672
                               assist01@frontiernet.net
                             www.assisttoindependence.org

Michael Blatchford, Executive Director
Priscilla Lane, IL Services Coordinator/Dep Dir
A community based, American Indian owned and operated non-profit agency that was established by and for people with disabilities and chronic health conditions to help fill some of the gaps in service delivery.

3820 Arizona Bridge to Independent Living
5025 E Washington St
Suite 200
Phoenix, AZ 85034-7439   602-256-2245
                                     800-280-2245
                                FAX: 602-254-6407
                                      www.abil.org

Mary Slaughter, Chairman
Brad Wemhaner, Vice Chairman
Michael Somsan, Secretary
ABIL offers and promotes programs designed to empower people with disabilities to take personal responsibility so they may achieve or continue independent lifestyles within the community.

3821 Arizona Bridge to Independent Living: Phoenix
1229 E.Washington St.
Suite D405
Phoenix, AZ 85034   602-296-0551
                                     800-280-2245
                                FAX: 602-256-0184
                                TTY: 602-296-0591
                                      www.abil.org

Mary Slaughter, Chairman
Brad Wemhaner, Vice Chairman
Michael Somsan, Secretary
ABIL offers and promotes programs designed to empower people with disabilities to take personal responsibility so they may achieve or continue independent lifestyles within the community.

3822 Arizona Bridge to Independent Living: Mesa
2150 S Country Club Dr
Suite 10
Mesa, AZ 85210-6879   480-655-9750
                                       800-280-2245
                                  FAX: 480-655-9751
                                  TTY: 480-655-9750
                                       www.abil.org

Mary Slaughter, Chairman
Brad Wemhaner, Vice Chairman
Michael Somsan, Secretary
ABIL offers and promotes programs designed to empower people with disabilities to take personal responsibility so they may achieve or continue independent lifestyles within the community.

3823 Community Outreach Program for the Deaf
268 W Adams St
Tucson, AZ 85705-6534   520-792-1906
                                  FAX: 520-770-8554
                                  TTY: 520-792-1906
                                       request@copdaz.org
                                       copdaz.org

Anne Levy, Executive Director
A non-profit organization, which has been serving the needs of people in Southern Arizona who are deaf or hard of hearing.

3824 DIRECT Center for Independence
1001 N Alvernon Way
Tucson, AZ 85711   520-624-6452
                                       800-342-1853
                                  FAX: 520-792-1438
                                       direct@directilc.org
                                       www.directilc.org

Vicki Cuscino, President
A non-consumer directed, community-based advocacy organization, that promotes independent living and offers a variety of programs for all people with disabilities which encourage them to achieve their full potential and to participate in the community.

3825 New Horizons Independent Living Center: Prescott Valley
8085 E Manley Dr
Prescott Valley, AZ 86314-6154   928-772-1266
                                       800-406-2377
                                  FAX: 928-772-3808
                                  TTY: 928-772-1266

Deborah Henderson, Office Manager
Liz Toone, Executive Director
Nick Perry, President
To provide services and advocacy which empower and enable people with disabilities to self-determine the goals and activities of their lives.

3826 Services Maximizing Independent Living and Empowerment (SMILE)
1931 South Arizona Ave
Suite 4
Yuma, AZ 85364-5721   928-329-6681
                                       855-209-8363
                                  FAX: 928-329-6715
                                  TTY: 928-782-7458
                                       info@smile-az.org
                                       www.smile-az.org

Laura Duval, Executive Director
Brenda Howard, Finance Manager/ Admin Assistant
Shawnnita Miranda, Advocate/ Home modification Mana
SMILE continually advocates for the Independent Living Philosophy, both individually and system wide. The Board and staff constantly strives to improve the system by writing letters, training staff, providing services, and creating public awareness as to the services and opportunities open to people who have disabilities.

3827 Sterling Ranch: Residence for Special Women
Sterling Ranch
P.O.Box 36
Skull Valley, AZ 86338-36   928-442-3289
                                  FAX: 928-442-9272
                                       www.sterlingranch.info

Russell Dryer, Executive Director
Trent Nichel, Manager

A nonprofit residence for women with developmental disabilities which has been in operation since 1947. As a small facility (19 residents) the orientation is personal and family-like. Offers activities that range from gardening, quilting, academics, sign-language, crafts and a myriad of field trips and excursions. Private rooms and spacious living on 4 1/2 acres.

Arkansas

3828 Arkansas Independent Living Council
11324 Arcade Drive
Suite 7
Little Rock, AR 72212   501-372-0607
                                       800-772-0607
                                  FAX: 501-372-0598
                                       arkansasilc@att.net
                                       www.ar-silc.org

Sha Stephens, Executive Director
Cheryl , Director
Brenda Stinebuck, Chair
A non-profit organization promoting independent living for people with disabilities.

3829 Delta Resource Center for Independent Living
11324 Arcade Drive
Little Rock, AR 72212-6249   501-372-0607
                                       800-772-0607
                                  FAX: 501-372-0598
                                       drcilar@yahoo.com
                                       www.ar-silc.org

Sha Stephens, Executive Director
Katy Morris, Director
Cheryl , Director
Provides services, support, and advocacy which enables people with severe disabilities to live as independently as possible within their family and community.

3830 Mainstream
300 S Rodney Parham Rd.
Suite 5
Little Rock, AR 72205   501-280-0012
                                       800-371-9026
                                  FAX: 501-280-9267
                                  TTY: 501-280-9262
                                       www.mainstreamilrc.com

A non-residential, consumer-driven independent living resource center for persons with disabilities. Mainstream operates with the conviction that people with disabilities have the right and responsibility to make choices, to control their lives and to participate fully and equally in the community. Mainstream offers the following services free of charge: Advocacy, Peer Support, Training and Education, Information and Referral, Ramp program, and more.
1987

3831 Our Way: The Cottage Apt Homes
9175 Greenback Lane
Orangevale, CA 95662-6616   501-225-5030
                                       888-879-9584
                                  FAX: 501-225-5190
                                       rentthecottages.com

Katrina Williams, Manager
Crystal Brown, Assistant Manager
Advocacy and information services. One bedroom apartments for mobility impaired and elderly 62 years or older persons.
Based on income

3832 Sources for Community IL Services
1918 N Birch Ave
Fayetteville, AR 72703-2408   479-442-5600
                                       888-284-7521
                                  FAX: 479-442-5192
                                  TTY: 479-251-1378
                                       jmather@arsources.org
                                       www.arsources.org

Brent Williams, PhD, President
Elise Burt, Treasurer
Burke Fanari, Secretary

Provides services, support, and advocacy for individuals with disabilities, their families and the community.

3833 Spa Area Independent Living Services
621 Albert Pike
Hot Springs, AR 71913   501-624-7710
                                       800-255-7549
                                  FAX: 501-624-7003

Dejan S. Vojnovic, President
Joseph E. Anderson, Vice President - Real Estate
Bryan S. Cox, Vice President - Technology
Provides services and advocacy by and for persons with all types of disabilities. The goal is to assist individuals with disabilities to achieve thier maximum potential within their families and communities.

California

3834 Access Center of San Diego
8885 Rio San Diego Dr
Suite 131
San Diego, CA 92108-1625   619-293-3500
                                       800-300-4326
                                  FAX: 619-293-3508
                                  TTY: 619-293-7757
                                  info@a2isd.org
                                  www.a2isd.org

Louis Frick, Executive Director
Derek Parker, Chair
Jacquelyn E. Nash, Vice Chair
Access to Independence is an independent living center (ILC), a nonresidential, cross-disability, non-profit corporations that provide services to people with disabilities to help maximize their independence and fully integrate into their communities. Access to Independence is one of 391 ILCs across the country and one of 29 serving Californians. Like all ILCs, Access to Independence offers required federal and state programs and services to people of all disability types and ages at no charge.

3835 Access to Independence
8885 Rio San Diego Drive
Suite 131
San Diego, CA 92108- 1625   619-293-3500
                                      800-300-4326
                                 FAX: 619-293-3508
                                 TTY: 619-293-7757
                                 info@a2isd.org
                                 www.a2isd.org

Louis Frick, Executive Director
Derek Parker, Chair
Jacquelyn E. Nash, Vice Chair
A community resource for people with disabilities to lead independent lives.

3836 Access to Independence of Imperial Valley
101 Hacienda Drive
Suite 13
Calexico, CA 92231-2875   760-768-2044
                                      866-976-3515
                                 FAX: 760-768-4977
                                 TTY: 619-293-7757
                                 info@a2isd.org

Louis Frick, Executive Director
Derek Parker, Chair
Jacquelyn E. Nash, Vice Chair
A community resource for people with disabilities to lead independent lives.

3837 Access to Independence of North County
209 E Broadway
Vista, CA 92084-6005   760-643-0447
                                 FAX: 760-435-9206
                                 info@a2isd.org

Louis Frick, Executive Director
Derek Parker, Chair
Jacquelyn E. Nash, Vice Chair
A community resource for people with disabilities to lead independent lives.

3838 Beaumont Senior Center: Community Access Center
1310 Oak Valley Parkway
Beaumont, CA 92223-2218   951-769-8524
                                 FAX: 951-769-8519
                                 TTY:909-769-2794

Laurie Hoirup, Director
A non profit organization; one of 29 similar programs throughout the state of California CAC is a community resource, advocate, and educator for Riverside County residents with disabilities.

3839 California Foundation For Independent Living Centers
1234 H Street
Suite 100
Sacramento, CA 95814-1912   916-325-1690
                                 FAX: 916-325-1699
                                 TTY:916-325-1695
                                 cfilc@cfilc.org
                                 www.cfilc.org

Robert Hand, Chairperson
Ana Acton, Vice Chairperson
Tink Miller, Executive Director
Community Rehabilitation Services, Inc. (CRS) is a private, non-profit agency established in 1974 to assist persons with disabilities within the East/North East areas of Los Angeles County to enhance their options for living independently. Any person who is 18 yrs of age or more with physical, sensory, mental/emotional or developmental disabilities can work with us to become more self-sufficient. Our intake procedures provide an orientation to the staff, facilities and services at CRS.

3840 California Foundation for Independent Living Centers
1235 H Street
Suite 100
Sacramento, CA 95814-1913   916-325-1690
                                 FAX: 916-325-1699
                                 TTY:916-325-1695
                                 cfilc@cfilc.org
                                 www.cfilc.org

Robert Hand, Chairperson
Ana Acton, Vice Chairperson
Tink Miller, Executive Director
CFILC's mission is to support independent living centers in their local communities through advocating for systems change and promoting access and integration for people with disabilities.

3841 California State Independent Living Council (SILC)
1235 H Street
Suite 100
Sacramento, CA 95814-4010   916-325-1690
                                      866-866-7452
                                 FAX: 916-325-1699
                                 TTY: 866-745-2889
                                 www.calsilc.org

Susan M. Madison, Chairman
Eli Gelardin, Vice Chairman
Liz Pazdral, Executive Director
To maximize options for independence for persons with disabilities

3842 Center for Independence of the Disabled
Suite 103
2001 Winward Way
San Mateo, CA 94404-3062   650-645-1780
                                 FAX: 650-645-1785
                                 TTY:650-522-9313
                                 www.cidsanmateo.org

Brad Friedman, Co-President
Laura Whitsitt Hillyard, Co-President
Thomas J. Devine, Vice President
Increase the social, educational, and economic participation of persons with disabilities in San Mateo County, and to encourage, support, and provide options for self determination, equal access and freedom of choice.

3843 Center for Independence of the Disabled- Daly City
Ste 256
355 Gellert Blvd
Daly City, CA 94015-2675 650-991-5124
FAX: 650-757-2075
TTY:650-991-5182
dalycity5@aol.com
www.cidbelmont.org

Kent Mickelson, Director
The Daly City Branch office fulfills its mission by serving disabled consumers in Brisbane, Colma, Daly City, El Granada, Half Moon Bay, Montara, Moss Beach, Pacifica, Pescadero, Princeton and South San Francisco. Our mission is to increase the social, educational, economic, social and political participants of persons with disabilities in San Mateo county, California.

3844 Center for Independent Living
Suite 103
2001 Winward Way
San Mateo, CA 94404 650-645-1780
FAX: 650-645-1785
TTY:510-522-9313
bburgess@cilberkeley.org
www.cidsanmateo.org

Beatrice Burgess, Interim Executive Director
Jody Yarborough, President
Michael Levinson, Vice President
The Center for Independent Living, Inc (CIL) is a national leader in helping people with disabilities live independently and become productive members of society. Advocates for greater accessibility in communities, designing techniques in independent living and providing direct services to people with disabilities.
1972

3845 Center for Independent Living: East Oakland
Suite 100
3075 Adeline Street
Berkeley, CA 94703-2403 510-841-4776
FAX: 510-841-6168
info@cilberkeley.org
www.cilberkeley.org

Melissa Male, Chair
Bea Worthen, Vice-Chair
Paul Hippolitus, Secretary
A national leader in helping people with disabilities live independently and become productive, fully participating members of society.

3846 Center for Independent Living: Oakland
Suite 100
3075 Adeline Street
Berkeley, CA 94703-1285 510-841-4776
FAX: 510-841-6168
TTY:510-444-1837
info@cilberkeley.org
cilberkeley.org

Melissa Male, Chair
Bea Worthen, Vice-Chair
Paul Hippolitus, Secretary
A national leader in supporting disabled people in their efforts to lead independent lives.

3847 Center for Independent Living: Tri-County
2822 Harris Street
Eureka, CA 95503 707-445-8404
877-576-5000
FAX: 707-445-9751
TTY: 707-445-8405
aa@tilinet.org
www.tilinet.org

Gail Pascoe, President
Linda Arnold, Vice President
Kevin O'Brien, Treasurer

3848 Center for Independent Living:Fresno
3475 Wesy Shaw Ave
Suite 101
Fresno, CA 93711 559-276-6777
FAX: 559-276-6778
TTY:559-276-6779

Bob Hand, Manager

3849 Center for Independent Living; Oakland
1904 Franklin Street
Suite 320
Oakland, CA 94612-2324 510-763-9990
FAX: 510-763-4910
TTY:510-536-2271
info@cilberkeley.org
cilberkeley.org

Melissa Male, Chair
Bea Worthen, Vice-Chair
Hank Stratford, Treasurer
Independent living center to maximise the options for independence for persons with disabilities.

3850 Center of Independent Living: Visalia
121 E Main
Suite 101
Visalia, CA 93291-6262 559-622-9276
FAX: 559-622-9638

Fran Phillips, Executive Directorram Manager
Renee Ezelle, Manager

3851 Central Coast Center for IL: San Benito
1234 H Street
Suite 100
Sacramento, CA 95814-1914 916-325-1690
FAX: 916-325-1699
TTY:916-325-1695
www.cfilc.org

Ana Acton, Chairperson
Larry Grable, Vice Chairperson
Nayana Shah, Treasurer
To advocate for barrier-free access and equal opportunity for people with disabilities to participate in the community life by increasing the capacity of Independent Living Centers to achieve their missions.

3852 Central Coast Center for Independent Living
318 Cayuga St.
Suite 208
Salinas, CA 93901-2600 831-757-2968
FAX: 831-757-5549
TTY:831-757-3949
cccil.org

Jennifer L. Williams, President
Elsa Quezada, Executive Director
Brenda Cardoza, Information and Referral Special
CCCIL promotes the independence of people with disabilities by supporting their equal and full participation in community life. CCCIL provides advocacy, education and support to all people with disabilities, their families and the community.

3853 Central Coast Center: Independent Living - Santa Cruz Office
1350 - 41st Avenue
Suite 101
Capitola, CA 95010-3930 831-462-8720
FAX: 831-462-8727
TTY:831-462-8729
www.cccil.org

Jennifer L. Williams, President
Elsa Quezada, Executive Director
Brenda Cardoza, Information and Referral Special
CCCIL promotes the independence of people with disabilities by supporting their equal and full participation in community life. CCCIL provides advocacy, education and support to all people with disabilities, their families and the community.

3854 Central Coast for Independent Living
1111 San Felipe Rd
Suite 107
Hollister, CA 95023-2814 831-636-5196
FAX: 831-637-0478
TTY:831-637-6235
www.cccil.org

Jennifer L. Williams, President
Elsa Quezada, Executive Director
Brenda Cardoza, Information and Referral Special
CCCIL promotes the independence of people with disabilities by supporting their equal and full particpation in community life.

CCCIL provides advocacy, education and support to all people with disabilities, their families and the community.

3855 Central Coast for Independent Living: Watsonville
18 W. Beach St.
Suite Y
Watsonville, CA 95076-4371
831-724-2997
FAX: 831-724-2915
TTY:831-786-0915
www.cccil.org

Jennifer L. Williams, President
Elsa Quezada, Executive Director
Brenda Cardoza, Information and Referral Special
An advocacy and information center organized by and for people with disabilities that strives to make our communities more accessible and to empower people with disabilities with information and skills to live fulfilling lives in our communities.

3856 Communities Actively Living Independent and Free
634 S Spring St
2nd Floor
Los Angeles, CA 90014-3921
213-627-0477
FAX: 213-627-0535
TTY:213-623-9502
info@calif-ilc.org

Lillibeth Navarro, Founder & Executive Director
Alex San Martin, Temporary Chair
Fernando Roldan, Board Secretary
Envisions a culturally diverse independent living center designed to empower the Disability Community.

3857 Community Access Center
6848 Magnolia Ave
Suite 150
Riverside, CA 92506-2858
951-274-0358
FAX: 951-274-0833
TTY:951-274-0834
execdir@ilcac.org
www.ilcac.org

Mark Dyer, President
Janet Newcomer, Vice President
Perry Halteman, Secretary
A non-profit organization; one of 29 similar programs throughout the state of California. CAC is a community resource, advocate, and educator for Riverside County residents with disabilities.

3858 Community Access Center: Indio Branch
83233 Indio Blvd
Indio, CA 92201-4748
760-347-4888
FAX: 760-347-0722
TTY:760-347-6802
pmgr3@ilcac.org
www.ilcac.org

Mark Dyer, President
Janet Newcomer, Vice President
Perry Halteman, Secretary
To empower persons with disabilities to control their own lives, create an accessible community and advocate to achieve complete social, economic, and political integration. We implement this vision by providing information, supportive services and independent living skills training.

3859 Community Access Center: Perris
371 Wilkerson Ave
Perris, CA 92570-2241
951-443-1158
FAX: 951-443-2608
TTY:951-443-1158
www.ilcac.org

Mark Dyer, President
Janet Newcomer, Vice President
Perry Halteman, Secretary
Community Access Center empowers persons with disabilities to control their own lives, create an accessible community and advocate to achieve complete social, economic, and political integration. CAC also implements this vision by providing information, suportive services and independent living skills training.

3860 Community Rehabilitation Services
844 E. Mission Road
Suite A & B
San Gabriel, CA 91776- 2759
323-266-0453
FAX: 626-614-1590
TTY:323-266-3016

Frances Garcia, Executive Director
CRS is an independent living center that provides free services to persons with disabilities in the areas of advocacy, housing and independent living skills; assistive technology, employment, personal assistant services, peer counseling and information and referral.

3861 Community Resources for Independence: Mendocino/Lake Branch
Ste B
415 Talmage Rd
Ukiah, CA 95482-7486
707-463-8875
FAX: 707-463-8878
TTY:707-463-4498

Tanner Silva, Manager
A non-profit corporation established by a group of disabled and non-disabled individuals to advance the rights of persons with disabilities to equal justice, access, opportunity and participation in the communities.

3862 Community Resources for Independence: Napa
Ste 208
1040 Main St
Napa, CA 94559-2605
707-258-0270
FAX: 707-258-0275
TTY:707-257-0274

Tyler Stanley, Manager
Matthew Shultz, Independent Living Advocate
A non-profit corporation established by a group of disabled and non-disabled individuals to advance the rights of persons with disabilities to equal justice, access, opportunity and participation in the communities.

3863 Community Resources for Independent Living: Hayward
3311 Pacific Ave
Livermore, CA 94550-5013
925-371-1531
FAX: 925-373-5034
TTY:925-371-1533
info@cril-online.org
crilhayward.org

Sheri Burns, Executive Director
Michael Galvan, PhD., Program Director
April Monroe, Finance Director
CRIL offers independent living services at no charge to persons with disabilities living in southern and eastern Alameda county. CRIL is also a resource for disability awareness education and training, advocacy and technical advice.

3864 Community Resources for Independent Living
39155 Liberty St
Suite A100
Fremont, CA 94538-1503
510-794-5735
crilhayward.org

Sheri Burns, Executive Director
Michael Galvan, PhD., Program Director
April Monroe, Finance Director
Community Resources for Independent Living is a peer-based disability organization that advocates and provides resources for people with disabilities to improve lives and make communities fully accessible.

3865 DRAIL (Disability Resource Agency for Independent Living)
501 W Weber Ave
Ste 200-A
Stockton, CA 95203-6239
209-477-8143
FAX: 209-477-7730
TTY:209-465-5643
barry@drail.org
www.drail.org

Terry Gray, President
Michael Kim Cornelius, Treasurer
Adeline Bagwell, Secretary

A non-profit corporation that is community based, consumer controlled, consumer choice, cross disability center for independent living.

3866 Dayle McIntosh Center: Laguna Niguel
24031 El Toro Road
Suite 300
Laguna Hills, CA 92653-3632   949-460-7784
  800-422-7444
  FAX: 949-334-2302
  TTY: 800-735-2929
  www.daylemc.org

Libby Partain, President
Cindy McLeroy, Vice President
Eva Casas-Sarmiento, Secretary
DMC advances empowerment and inclusion of all persons with disabilities. DMC is the largest Independent Living Center in California, and was named in memory of a young woman with a severe physical disability who worked to found the center.

3867 Disability Resource Agency for Independent Living: Modesto
920-12th Street
Modesto, CA 95354-543   209-521-7260
  FAX: 209-521-4763
  TTY:209-576-2409
  larry@drail.org
  www.drail.org

Terry Gray, President
Michael Kim Cornelius, Treasurer
Adeline Bagwell, Secretary
A non-profit corporation that is community based, consumer controlled, consumer choice, cross disability center for independent living.

3868 Disability Services & Legal Center
521 Mendocino Ave.
Santa Rosa, CA 95401-1649   707-528-2745
  FAX: 707-528-9477
  TTY:707-528-2151
  www.disabilityserviceandlegal.org

Adam Brown, Chairman
Shirley Johnson-Foell, Board President
Jack Geary, Board Member
A non-profit corporation established by a group of disabled and non-disabled individuals to advance the rights of persons with disabilities to equal justice, access, opportunity and participation in the communities.

3869 Disabled Resources Center
2750 E Spring St
Suite 100
Long Beach, CA 90806-2263   562-427-1000
  FAX: 562-427-2027
  TTY:562-427-1366
  info@drcinc.org
  drcinc.org

C. Timothy Lashlee, President
Dora Hogan, Vice President
Finola Campbell, Treasurer
To empower people with disabilities to live independently in the community, to make their own decisions about their lives and to advocate on their own behalf.

3870 FREED Center for Independent Living
2059 Nevada City Hwy
Suite 102
Grass Valley, CA 95945- 3227   530-477-3333
  800-655-7732
  FAX: 530-477-8184
  TTY: 530-477-8194
  freed.org

Ana Acton, Executive Director
To eliminate barriers to full equality for people with disabilities through programs which promote independent living.

3871 FREED Center for Independent Living: Marysville
508 J St
Marysville, CA 95901-5636   530-742-4476
  TTY:530-742-4474
  freed.org

Claudia Hallis, Manager
To eliminate barriers to full equality for people with disabilities through programs which promote independent living.

3872 First Step Independent Living
1174 Nevada St
Redlands, CA 92374-2893   800-362-0312
Independent living center, empowers people with disabilities to become active, productive, members of the community.

3873 Independent Living Center of Kern County
5251 Office Park Dr
Suite 200
Bakersfield, CA 93309   661-325-1063
  877-688-2079
  800-529-9541
  FAX: 661-325-6702
  TTY:661-325-6702
  info@ilcofkerncounty.org
  www.ilcofkerncounty.org

Jimmie Soto, Executive Director
Tammy Hartsch, Finance Manager
Harvey Clowers, Special Projects and AT Coordina
A consumer-based consumer-directed non-profit agency assisting persons with disabilities to live independently in their community. The ILCKC presently offers a wide range of services to a growing population of persons with disabilities.

3874 Independent Living Center of Lancaster
606 East Avenue K4
Lancaster, CA 93535-2844   661-942-9726
  FAX: 661-945-5690
  TTY:661-723-2509
  www.ilcsc.org

Taura Jacob, Manager
Marcy Hernandez
Niyanta Dave
ILCSC is a non-profit, consumer based, non-residential agency providing a wide range of services to a growing population of people with disabilities. ILCSC is dedicated to empowering persons with disabilities to exercise indpendence-pofessionally, personally and creatively-while striving to educate the community on their needs.

3875 Independent Living Resource Center
7425 El Camino Real
Suite R
Atascadero, CA 93422-4656   805-464-3203
  FAX: 805-462-1166
  TTY:805-462-1162
  info@ilrc-trico.org
  www.ilrc-trico.org

Kit McMillion, President
Larry Laborde, Vice President
Dani Anderson, Executive Director
To assist and encourage individuals to achieve their optimal level of self-sufficiency while eliminating the architectural, communication and attitudinal barriers which prevent them from full participation in the community.

3876 Independent Living Resource Center: Santa Barbara
423 W Victoria St
Santa Barbara, CA 93101-3619   805-284-9051
  FAX: 805-963-1350
  TTY:805-963-0595
  info@ilrc-trico.org
  www.ilrc-trico.org

Kit McMillion, President
Larry Laborde, Vice President
Dani Anderson, Executive Director
To assist and encourage individuals to achieve their optimal level of self-sufficiency while eliminating the architectural, communication and attitudinal barriers which prevent them from full participation in the community.

3877 Independent Living Resource Center: San Francisco
825 Howard Street
San Francisco, CA 94103-4128
415-543-6222
FAX: 415-543-6318
TTY:415-543-6698
info@ilrcsf.org
ilrcsf.org

Juma Byrd, President
Kolya Kirienko, Vice President
Ben MacMullan, Treasurer
To ensure that people with disabilities are full social and economic partners, both within their families and in a fully accessible community.

3878 Independent Living Resource Center: Santa Maria Office
327 East Plaza Dr
Suite 3A
Santa Maria, CA 93454-6930
805-354-5948
FAX: 805-349-2416
TTY:805-925-0015
info@ilrc-trico.org
www.ilrc-trico.org

Kit McMillion, President
Larry Laborde, Vice President
Dani Anderson, Executive Director
To assist and encourage individuals to achieve their optimal level of self-sufficiency while eliminating the architectural, communication and attitudinal barriers which prevent them from full participation in the community.

3879 Independent Living Resource Center: Ventura
1802 Eastman Ave
Suite 112
Ventura, CA 93003-5759
805-256-1036
FAX: 805-650-9278
TTY:805-650-5993
info@ilrc-trico.org
www.ilrc-trico.org

Kit McMillion, President
Larry Laborde, Vice President
Dani Anderson, Executive Director
An organization of, by and for persons with disabilities who reside or work in the service area. Purpose is to assist and encourage individuals to achieve their optimal level of self-sufficiency while eliminating the architectural, communication and attitudinal barriers which prevent them from full participation in the community.

3880 Independent Living Resource of Contra Coast
1850 Gateway Blvd
Suite 120
Concord, CA 94520-3293
925-363-7293
FAX: 925-363-7296
www.ilrscc.org

Sarah BirdwelL, Board President
Kathy Mitsopoulos, Board Vice President
Teri Ruggiero, Board Secretary
Offers workshops, services are accessible to individuals with cognitive disabilities, physical disabilities, deaf and hard of hearing, emotional disabilities, visual impairments, learing disabilities and seniors.

3881 Independent Living Resource of Fairfield
470 Chadbourn Rd
Ste. B
Fairfield, CA 94534
707-435-8174
FAX: 707-435-8177
www.ilrscc.org

Sarah BirdwelL, Board President
Kathy Mitsopoulos, Board Vice President
Teri Ruggiero, Board Secretary
To empower people with disabilities to: control their own lives, provide advocacy and support for individuals with disabilities to live independently, create an accessible community free of physical and attitudinal barriers.

3882 Independent Living Resource: Antioch
3727 Sunset Lane
#103
Antioch, CA 94509-1761
925-754-0539
TTY:925-755-0934
www.ilrscc.org

Sarah BirdwelL, Board President
Kathy Mitsopoulos, Board Vice President
Teri Ruggiero, Board Secretary
Non-profit organizations run and controlled by persons with disabilities. They are non-residential, community-based centers where people with disabilities can receive assistance with a variety of daily living issues and learn the skills they need to take controll of their lives from people who have had similar experiences living with a disability.

3883 Independent Living Resource: Concord
1850 Gateway Blvd
Suite 120
Concord, CA 94520-3293
925-363-7293
FAX: 925-363-7296
gilc@ilrccc.org
www.ilrscc.org

Sarah BirdwelL, Board President
Kathy Mitsopoulos, Board Vice President
Teri Ruggiero, Board Secretary
To empower people with disabilities to: control their own lives, provide advocacy and support for individuals with disabilities to live independently, create an accessible community free of physical and attitudinized barriers.

3884 Independent Living Resources (ILR)
Bldg 2a
101 Broadway
Richmond, CA 94804-1945
510-233-7400
info@ilrccc.org

Marvin Dyson, Manager
Provides services to meet the diverse needs of people who have a variety of disabilities in all age groups.

3885 Independent Living Service Northern California: Redding Office
169 Hartnell Ave
Suite 128
Redding, CA 96002-1849
530-242-8550
800-464-8527
FAX: 530-241-1454
TTY: 530-242-8550
actionctr.org

Lauri Evans, President
Frank Smith, Vice President
Evan Levang, Executive Director
Independent Living Services of Northern California is a private non profit organization that provides support services to help empower community members with disabilities.

3886 Independent Living Services of Northern California
Jennifer Roberts Building
1161 East Ave
Chico, CA 95926-1018
530-893-8527
800-464-8527
FAX: 530-893-8574
TTY: 530-893-8527
actionctr.org

Lauri Evans, President
Frank Smith, Vice President
Evan Levang, Executive Director
Independent Living Services of Northern California is a private, non profit organization that provides support services to help empower community members with disabilities.

3887 Marin Center for Independent Living
710 4th St
San Rafael, CA 94901-3213
415-459-6245
FAX: 415-459-7047
TTY:415-459-7027
marincil.org

Chris Schultz, President
Joe Brnnett, Vice President
Eli Gelardin, Executive Director

A non-profit organization that provides advocacy and services for seniors and persons with disabilities.

3888 Mother Lode Independent Living Center(DRAIL: Disability Resource Agency for Independent
Living)
67 Linoberg St
Suite A.
Sonora, CA 95370-4646 209-532-0963
FAX: 209-532-1591
TTY:209-288-3309
barry@drail.org
www.drail.org

Terry Gray, President
Michael Kim Cornelius, Treasurer
Adeline Bagwell, Secretary
DRAIL is a non-profit, community based, consumer controlled, cross disability center for independent living.

3889 Placer Independent Resource Services
11768 Atwood Rd
Suite 29
Auburn, CA 95603 530-885-6100
800-833-3453
FAX: 530-885-3032
TTY: 530-885-0326
lbrewer@pirs.org
pirs.org

Eldon Luce, President
Michael Cummings, Vice President
Dan Roye, Director
A non profit independent living center whose mission is to advocate, empower, educate and provide services for people with disabilities that would enable them to live more independently.

3890 Resources for Independent Living
420 i St, Level B.
Suite 3
Sacramento, CA 95814-2319 916-446-3074
FAX: 916-446-2443
leonc@ril-sacramento.org
www.ril-sacramento.org

Ramona Garcia, Board Chairperson
Francisco Godoy, Vice Chairperson
Joanne Bodine, Treasurer
Promoting the socio-economic independence of persons with disabilities by providing peer-supported, consumer-directed independent living services and advocacy.

3891 Rolling Start
570 W 4th St
Suite 107
San Bernardino, CA 92401-1438 909-884-2129
FAX: 909-386-7446
TTY:909-884-7396

John Anaya, Chairperson
Kathi Pryor, Treasurer
Francis Bates, Executive Director
Empowers and educates people with disabilities to achieve the independent life of their choice.

3892 Rolling Start: Victorville
17330 Bear Valley Road
Suite A102
Victorville, CA 92395 760-843-7959
FAX: 760-843-7977
TTY:760-951-8175

John Anaya, Chairperson
Kathi Pryor, Treasurer
Francis Bates, Executive Director
Empowers and educates people with disabilities to achieve the independent life of their choice.

3893 Services Center For Independent Living
107 S Spring Street
Claremont, CA 91711-549 909-621-6722
800-491-6722
FAX: 909-445-0727
TTY: 949-445-0726
www.scil-ilc.org

Larry Grable, Executive Director
Janice Ornelas, Independent Living Specialist
Angela Nwokike, System Change Advocate
Dedicated to expanding access, information and resources to help increase independence and enhance the quality of life for the East San Gabriel Valley residents with disabilities.

3894 Silicon Valley Independent Living Center
25 N. 14th St.
Suite 1000, 10th floor
San Jose, CA 95112 408-894-9041
FAX: 669-231-4795
info@svilc.org
svilc.org

Patricia Kokes, President
Richard A. Wentz, Vice President
Gabe Lopez, Treasurer
A private, consumer-driven, nonprofit corporation that offers quality services to individuals with disabilities in Silicon Valley.

3895 Silicon Valley Independent Living Center: South County Branch
7881 Church Street
Suite C
Gilroy, CA 95020-7346 408-843-9100
FAX: 408-842-4791
TTY:408-842-2591
info@svilc.org
svilc.org

Patricia Kokes, President
Richard A. Wentz, Vice President
Gabe Lopez, Treasurer
A private, consumer-driven, non-profit corporation that offers quality services to individuals with disabilities in Silicon Valley.

3896 Southern California Rehabilitation Services
7830 Quill Dr
Suite D
Downey, CA 90242-3440 562-862-6531
FAX: 562-923-5274
TTY:562-869-0931
scrs-ilc.org

Lisa Hayes, President
Michael Strong, Vice President
Carol Trees, Secretary/Treasurer
Empowers persons with disabilities to achieve their personalized goals through community education and individualized services that provide the knowledge, skills, and confidence building to maximize their quality of life.

3897 Through the Looking Glass
3075 Adeline St.
Ste. 120
Berkeley, CA 94703 510-848-1112
800-644-2666
FAX: 510-848-4445
TTY: 510-848-1005
tlg@lookingglass.org
www.lookingglass.org

Maureen Block, J.D., Board President
Thomas Spalding, Board Treasurer
Alice Nemon, D.S.W., Board Secretary
To create, demonstrate and encourage non-pathological and empowering reesources and model early intervention services for families with disability issues in parent or child which integrate expertise derived from personal disability experience and disability culture.

3898 Tri-County Independent Living Center
2822 Harris Street
Eureka, CA 95503
707-445-8404
877-576-5000
FAX: 707-445-9751
TTY: 707-445-8405
aa@tilinet.org
www.tilinet.org

Gail Pascoe, President
Linda Arnold, Vice President
Kevin O'Brien, Treasurer
Promotes the philosophy of independent living, to connect individuals to services, and to create and accessible community, so that people with disabilities can have control over their lives and full access to the communities in which they live.

3899 Westside Center for Independent Living
12901 Venice Blvd
Los Angeles, CA 90066-3509
310-390-3611
888-851-9245
FAX: 310-390-4906
TTY: 310-398-9204
www.wcil.org

David Geffen, President
Chris Knauf, 1st Vice President
Brenda Green, Secretary
The Westside Center for Independent Living (WCIL) helps people living with disabilities maintain self-sufficient and productive lives through non-residential peer support services and training programs. Independent Living promotes self-determination, community living, full participation in community life and access to the same opportunities and resources available to people without disabilities.

Colorado

3900 Atlantis Community
201 S Cherokee St
Denver, CO 80223-1836
303-733-9324
FAX: 303-733-6211
TTY:303-733-0047
info@atlantiscommunity.org

David Hays, Manager
Provide direct services, and to empower people with disabilities integrating, with full and equal rights, into all parts of society including employment, affordable, accessible, housing, transportation, recreation, communication, education, and public places while exercising and exerting choice and self determination.

3901 Center for Independence
740 Gunnison Ave
Grand Junction, CO 81501-3222
708-588-0833
FAX: 708-588-0406
center-for-independence.org

Linda Taylor, Executive Director
The Center for Independence works to promote community solutions and to empower individuals with disabilities to live independently.

3902 Center for People with Disabilities
615 Main St
Longmont, CO 80501-4983
303-772-3250
FAX: 303-772-5125
TTY:303-772-3250
info@cpwd.org
www.cpwd-ilc.org

Dale Gaar, Board President
Deborah.A Conley, Board Vice President
Nancy Phares-Zook, Board Secretary
Provides resources, information, and advocacy to assist people with disabilities in overcoming barriers to independent living.

3903 Center for People with Disabilities: Pueblo
1304 Berkley Ave
Pueblo, CO 81004-3002
719-546-1271
800-659-3656
FAX: 719-546-1374
ivaleneamidei@yahoo.com
www.ilcpueblo.org

Larry Williams, Executive Director
One of the 10 centers for independent living in Colorado founded under Title VII of the Rehabilitation Act of 1973 as amended in 1978. All new centers under this Independent Living (CIL) Title of the Act received initial and ongoing grants through this new Federal Program created by the Act.

3904 Center for People with Disabilities: Boulder
1675 Range St
Boulder, CO 80301-2722
303-442-8662
888-929-5519
FAX: 303-442-0502
info@cpwd.org
www.cpwd-ilc.org

Dale Gaar, Board President
Deborah.A Conley, Board Vice President
Nancy Phares-Zook, Board Secretary
Providing resources, information and advocacy to people with disabilities. Assist people with disabilities in transitioning from nursing homes to independent living in the community. Also provide personal assistance services.

3905 Colorado Springs Independence Center
729 South Tejon Street
Colorado Springs, CO 80903
719-471-8181
FAX: 719-471-7829
TTY:719-471-2076
www.theindependencecenter.org

Owen S. , Board Chair
Billy A. , Chair Elect
Billy B. , Secretary
To empower persons with disabilities to maximize their independence within the community and to remove barriers which impact their quality of life, while encouraging them to live independently in their community.

3906 Connections for Independent Living
1331 8th Avenue
Greeley, CO 80631-4027
970-352-8682
800-887-5828
FAX: 970-353-8058
TTY: 970-352-8682
pattid4z@yahoo.com
www.connectionsforindependentliving.org

Beth Danielson, Executive Director
Michael Stevens, Director of Services
Alicia Garza, Director
Certified IL Center, I and R advocacy, peer support, skills training, sign language interpretations, reader services, housing. Cross-disability, all ages.

3907 Denver CIL
Ste 100
777 Grant St
Denver, CO 80203-3501
303-837-1020
FAX: 303-837-0859
www.denverhousing.org

Greg Beran, Owner
Ismael Guerrero, Executive Director
Joshua Crawley, Agency Counsel
Provides resources, information, and advocacy to assist people with disabilities in overcoming barriers to independent living.

3908 Disability Center for Independent Living
4821 East 38th Avenue
Denver, CO 80207-1232
303-320-1345
FAX: 303-320-1345
TTY:303-322-2330
avillasenor.dcil@gmil.com
www.accil.net

Larry Williams, Executive Director
John Wooster, Consultant
Anthony Gonzales, Housing Coordinator

Independent living center providing quality services for people with disabilities.

3909 Disabled Resource Services
1017 Robertson Street
Unit B
Fort Collins, CO 80524-3915
970-482-2700
FAX: 970-449-6972
TTY:970-407-7060
disabledresourceservices.org

George Tremblay, Chairman
John Weins, Vice Chairman
Nancy Jackson, Executive Director
To empower individuals with disabilities to achieve their maximum level of independence and to gain personal dignity within society. Disabled Resource Services, as a private non-profit state certified center for independent living, is dedicated to working with individuals with all types of disabilities in Larimer County to promote their independence and equality through services which support advocacy, awareness and access to their community.

3910 Disbled Resource Services
640 E Eisenhower Blvd
Loveland, CO 80537-3954
970-667-0816
FAX: 970-593-6582
disabledresourceservices.org

George Tremblay, Chairman
John Weins, Vice Chairman
Nancy Jackson, Executive Director
To empower individuals with disabilities to achieve their maximum level of independence and to gain personal dignity within society.

3911 Greeley Center for Independence
2780 28th Ave
Greeley, CO 80634-7803
970-339-2444
800-748-1012
FAX: 970-339-0033
gciinc@gciinc.org
www.gciinc.org

Chari Armagost, Chief Financial Officer
Sarita Reddy, PH. D, Executive Director
Rob Rabe, Director of Outpatient Service
Provides places of growth, transition and encouragement, where people with temporary and permanent disabilities can reach toward their maximum potential of personal independence and wellness.

3912 Independent Life Center
P.O.Box 612
Craig, CO 81626-612
970-826-0833
888-526-0833
FAX: 970-826-0832
TTY: 970-826-0833

Larry Williams, Executive Director
John Wooster, Consultant
Anthony Gonzales, Housing Coordinator
Provides resources, information, and advocacy to assist people with disabilities in overcoming barriers to independent living.

3913 Southwest Center for Independence
3473 Main Avenue
#23
Durango, CO 81301-5474
970-259-1672
866-962-2158
FAX: 970-259-0947
TTY: 970-259-1672
swindependence.org/

Martha Mason, Executive Director
Mariellen Walz, Chair
Patricia Ziegler, Assistant Director
Empowering individuals with disabilities and their families to achieve their maximum level of independence in work, play and other areas of life.

3914 Southwest Center for Independence: Cortez
2409 East Empire Street
PO Box 640
Cortez, CO 81321-9164
970-570-8001
866-962-2158
FAX: 970-565-7169
director@swilc.org
swindependence.org/

Mariellen Walz, Chair
Johnny Bulson, Vice Chair
Jason Armstrong, Treasurer
Empowers indiviudals with disabilities and their families to achieve their maximum level of independence in work, play and other areas of life.

Connecticut

3915 Center for Disability Rights
764-B Campbell Ave
764 Campbell Ave
W Haven, CT 06516- 3786
203-934-7077
FAX: 203-934-7078
TTY:203-934-7079
info@cdr-ct.org
cdr-ct.org

Marc Gallucci, Executive Director
Chris Zurcher, Consumer Relations
Dana Canevari, I&R Specialist
Resources, information, and advocacy to assist people with disabilities in overcoming barriers to independent living.

3916 Center for Independent Living SC
26 Palmers Hill Rd
Stamford, CT 06902-2113
203-353-8550
FAX: 203-353-1423
TTY:203-353-8550

Dana Canevari, Director
Provides resources, information, and advocacy to assist people with disabilities in overcoming barriers to independent living.

3917 Chapel Haven
1040 Whalley Ave
New Haven, CT 06515-1740
203-397-1714
FAX: 203-937-2466
admissions@chapelhaven.org
chapelhaven.org

Michael Storz, President
The only combined state-accredited special education facility and independent living facility for adults with cognitive disabilities.

3918 Connecticut State Independent Living Council
151 New Park Ave
Hartford, CT 06106
860-523-0126
FAX: 860-523-5603
info@ctsilc.org
ctsilc.org

Katherine Pellerin, President
Keith Mullinar, Vice President
Alexia Bouckoms, Treasurer
The mission of the council is to promote equal access, opportunities, and social inclusion for people with disabilities in all spheres of society.

3919 Disabilities Network of Eastern Connecticut
19 Ohio Avenue
Suite 2
Norwich, CT 06360-2111
860-823-1898
FAX: 860-886-2316
CFerry@dnec.org
dnec.org

Katherine Pellerin, President
Robert Davidson, Vice President
Jane O'Friel, Secretary/Treasurer
Dedicated to supporting and advancing the rights of individuals with disabilities. The goal is to creat a completely inclusive society where people live together in communities regardless of their abilities.

3920 Disability Resource Center of Fairfield County
80 Ferry Blvd
Suite 205
Stratford, CT 06615-6079   203-378-6977
                                            FAX: 203-375-2748
                                            TTY:203-378-3248
                                            www.accessinct.org

Ethel M R, President
Thomas D, Vice-President
Anthony Lacava, Executive Director
A crosss-disability resource and advocacy organization for people with disabilities that has provided unique, consumer-directed services both for individuals and for the communities of Fairfield County.

3921 Independence Northwest Center for Independent Living
1183 New Haven Rd
Suite 200
Naugatuck, CT 06770-5033   203-729-3299
                                            FAX: 203-729-2839
                                            TTY:203-729-1281
                                        info@independencenorthwest.org
                                        www.independencenorthwest.org

Maureen Mayo, President
Tom Ford, Vice President
Charles Marino, Treasurer
Provides services in such areas as peer counseling, advocacy, independent living skills training and information and referral.

3922 New Horizons Village
37 Bliss Rd
Unionville, CT 06085   860-673-8893
                                            FAX: 860-675-4369
                            Michael.Shaw@NewHorizonsVillage.com
                                        newhorizonsvillage.com

Carolyn Fields, Administrator
A 68 unit apartment complex designed for people who have severe physical disabilities.

Delaware

3923 Freedom Center for Independent Living
400 N Broad St
Middletown, DE 19709-1089   302-376-4399
                                                866-687-3245
                                            FAX: 302-376-4395
                                            TTY: 302-376-4397
                                            info@fcilde.org
                                            fcilde.org

Hersernest Cole, Executive Director
Lillian Evans, Independent Living Specialist
Protects the Civil Rights and promote the empowerment of persons with disabilities and their families through our independent living philosophy.

3924 Independent Living
Apt 210
1800 N Broom St
Wilmington, DE 19802-3854   302-429-6693
                                            FAX: 302-429-8031
                                            TTY:302-429-8034

Susan Cycyk, Executive Director
Providing skilled support and caring guidance to adults with disabilities. Our case management services include: daily living skills training, medical coordination, transportation assistance, financial management, housing assistance, and vocational/educational planning.

3925 Independent Resource Georgetown
Ste 37
410 S Bedford St
Georgetown, DE 19947-1850   302-854-9330
                                            FAX: 302-854-9408
                                            TTY:302-854-9340

Larry Henderson, Director
Pat Boyd, Manager
Provides independent living services to persons who experience a significant disability. Offers skills training, individually and in small groups, peer support/peer counseling and information and referral services. Strives to remove the architectural and attitudnal barriers through individual and systems advocacy.

3926 Independent Resources: Dover
154 South Governor's Avenue
Dover, DE 19904-7311   302-735-4599
                                            FAX: 302-735-5623
                                            TTY:302-735-5629
                            lhenderson@independentresources.org
                                            www.iri-de.org

Tes DelTufo, Office Director
Carolyn Miller, IL Specialist
Debbie Justice, IL Specialist
Private, non-profit, consumer-controlled, community based organization providing services and advocacy by and for persons with all types of disabilities. Their goal is to assist individuals with disabilities to achieve their maximum potential within their families and communities.

3927 Independent Resources: Wilmington
6 Denny Rd
Suite 101
Wilmington, DE 19809-3444   302-765-0191
                                            FAX: 302-765-0195
                                            TTY:302-765-0194
                                            www.iri-de.org

Larry D Henderson, Executive Director
Phyllis Farrare, Director of Operations
Private, non-profit, consumer-controlled, community based organization providing services and advocacy by and for persons with all types of disabilities. Their goal is to assist individuals with disabilities to achieve their maximum potential within their families and communities.

3928 Mosaic Of De
4980 S. 118TH ST
Omaha, NE 68137   302-456-5995
                                                877-366-7242
                                            FAX: 402-896-1511
                                            info@mosaicinfo.org
                                            mosaicinfo.org

Terry Olson, Executive Director
Linda Timmons, President and CEO
Raul Saldivar, Chief Operating Officer
Provides services to adults with developmental disabilities who reside in homes and apartments. Services are designed to provide them with opportunities for choices and participation in the life of their communities. Supports are geared to assist each individual in becoming more independent in activities of daily living, vocational skills, community mobility and transportation, and recreation and leisure activities.

District of Columbia

3929 District of Columbia Center for Independent Living
1400 Florida Ave NE
Washington, DC 20002-5032   202-388-0033
                                            FAX: 202-398-3018
                                            info@dccil.org
                                            dccil.org

Rev. Patric Hailes Fears, President
Dr. John Thompson, Vice President
Carl Bartels, Treasurer
Mission is to maximize the leadership, empowerment, independence, and productivity of individuals with disabilities, and to integrate these individuals into the mainstream of American society.

3930 National Council on Independent Living (NCIL)
P.O. Box 31260
Washington, DC 20006   202-207-0334
                                                844-778-7961
                                            FAX: 202-207-0341
                                            TTY: 202-207-0340
                                            ncil@ncil.org
                                            www.ncil.org

Theo Braddy, Executive Director
Jenny Sichel, Director, Operations
Denise Law, Coordinator, Member Services

A national cross-disability grassroots organization, NCIL advances independent living and the rights of people with disabilities through consumer-driven advocacy.

Florida

3931 Ability 1st
1300 E. Green Street
Pasadena, CA 91106   626-396-1010
                                           877-768-4600
                                      FAX: 626-396-1021
                                   info@abilityfirst.org
                                        abilityfirst.org
Steve Brockmeyer, Chairman
John Kelly, Vice Chairman
Lori.E Gangemi, President
To empower persons with disabilities to live independently and participate actively in their community.

3932 Adult Day Training
Goodwill Industries - Suncoast
10596 Gandy Blvd N
St Petersburg, FL 33702-1422   727-523-1512
                                           888-279-1988
                                      FAX: 727-563-9300
                                      TTY:727-579-1068
                       gw.marketing@goodwill-suncoast.com
                                www.goodwill-suncoast.org
Deborah A. Passerini, President & Chief Executive Officer
Tracey Boucher, Corporate Treasurer & Chief Financial Officer
Kris Rawson, Vice President for Mission Services & Chief Mission Officer
An innovative program which uses job skills to teach self-help, daily living, communication, mobility, travel, decision-making, behavioral and social skills. This focus provides concrete, transferable experiences to help prepare individuals for greater community inclusion by achieving the highest possible degree of independence in their daily life, increasing their confidence and supporting their successful transitions to less structured, self-sufficient environments.

3933 CIL of Central Florida
720 N Denning Dr
Winter Park, FL 32789-3020   407-623-1070
                                      FAX: 407-623-1390
                                   info@cilorlando.org
                                        cilorlando.org
Jason Vennings, Development Director
Kim Byerly, Chair
Cheryl Stone, Secretary
A private, non-profit organization dedicated to helping people with disabilities achieve their self-determined goals for independent living.

3934 Caring and Sharing Center for Independent Living
12552 Belcher Rd S
Largo, FL 33773-3014   727-539-7550
                                           866-539-7550
                                      FAX: 727-539-7588
                       www.disabilityachievementcenter.org
Barbara Dandro, Treasurer
Mary Bucca, Secretary
Patricia Bell, Director
Empowering people with disabilities.

3935 Caring and Sharing Center: Pasco County
12552 Belcher Rd S
Largo, FL 33773-3014   727-539-7550
                                           866-539-7550
                                      FAX: 727-539-7588
                       www.disabilityachievementcenter.org
Barbara Dandro, Treasurer
Mary Bucca, Secretary
Patricia Bell, Director
Empowering people with disabilities.

3936 Center for Independent Living in Central Florida
720 N Denning Dr
Winter Park, FL 32789-3095   407-623-1070
                                      FAX: 407-623-1390
                                   info@cilorlando.org
                                        cilorlando.org
Jason Vennings, Development Director
Kim Byerly, Chair
Cheryl Stone, Secretary
In partnership with the community, promotes personal right snad responsiblities among people with all disabilities.

3937 Center for Independent Living of Broward
4800 N State Road 7
Suite 102
Lauderdale Lakes, FL 33319-5811   954-722-6400
                                           888-722-6400
                                      FAX: 954-735-1958
                                   cilb@cilbroward.org
                                   www.cilbroward.org
Craig Lilienthal, President
Christopher Sharp, VP
Shea Smith, Treasurer
Offers assistance to people with disabilities in fulfilling the goals of independence and self-sufficiency.

3938 Center for Independent Living of Florida Keys
103400 Overseas Hwy
Suite 243
Key Largo, FL 33037-2849   305-453-3491
                                           877-335-0187
                                      FAX: 305-453-3488
                                      TTY: 305-453-3491
                                   cilkeys@cilkeys.org
                                   www.cilofthekeys.org
Brenda K Pierce, Executive Director
Offers assistance to persons with disabilities in acquiring independent living and self-advocacy skills in order to obtain and maintain independence and self-sufficiency.

3939 Center for Independent Living of N Florida
1823 Buford Ct
Tallahassee, FL 32308-4465   850-575-9621
                                      FAX: 850-575-5740
                                      TTY:850-575-5245
                                   cilnf@nettally.com
                                   www.ability1st.info
Judith Barrett, Executive Director
Offers assistance to persons with disabilities in acquiring independent living and self-advocacy skills in order to obtain and maintain independence and self-sufficiency

3940 Center for Independent Living of NW Florida
3600 N Pace Blvd
Pensacola, FL 32505-4240   850-595-5566
                                           877-245-2457
                                      FAX: 850-595-5560
                                   cil-drc@cil-drc.org
                                        cil-drc.org
James Hicks, President
Kathleen Wilks, Secretary
John Bouchard, Treasurer
Provides services such as information and referral, peer counseling, housing, advocacy, training, independent living skills training, free wheelchairs, loan locker, assistive technology.

3941 Center for Independent Living of North Central Florida
3445 NE 24th Street
Ocala, FL 34470-9214   352-368-3788
                                           877-232-8261
                                      FAX: 352-629-0098
                                        www.cilncf.org
Joe Dyke, President
Robert Miller, Vice President
David Christie, Treasurer
Empowers people with disabilities to exert their individual rights to live as independently as possible, make personal life choices and achieve full community inclusion.

3942 Center for Independent Living of North Central Florida
222 SW 36th Ter
Gainesville, FL 32607-2863
352-378-7474
800-265-5724
FAX: 352-378-5582
TTY: 352-372-3443
www.cilncf.org

Joe Dyke, President
Robert Miller, Vice President
David Christie, Treasurer
Empowering people with disabilities to exert their individual rights to live as independently as possible, make personal life choices and achieve full community inclusion.

3943 Center for Independent Living of S Florida
6660 Biscayne Blvd
Miami, FL 33138-6285
305-751-8025
FAX: 305-751-8944
TTY: 305-751-8891
soflacil.org

Alvin W. Roberts, President
Gregg Goldfarb, Vice President
Timothy Werner, Ph.D, Secretary
A community based non for profit, independent living center serving people of all ages with any type of disability. Services: Basic education, GED preperation, American sign language advocacy, peer support, information and referral, independent living skills training, housing assistance, transportation assistance, home modiifications, transition from nursing facility to the community assisatnace filing ADA complaints, accessibility surveys, diability awareness traing.

3944 Center for Independent Living of SW Florida
2321 Bruner Ln
Fort Myers, FL 33912-1904
239-277-1447
800-435-7352
FAX: 239-277-1647

Ronald J Muschong, Interim Executive Director
Helping people with disabilities achieve independence and self-determination in their lives.

3945 Coalition for Independent Living Options: Okeechobee
1680 SW Bayshore Boulevard
Suite 231
Port St. Lucie, FL 34984
772-878-3500
FAX: 772-878-3344
www.cilo.org

Scott Shoemaker, President
Sharon D'Eusanio, Vice President
Joseph Fields Jr., Esquire, Secretary
Private non-profit promoting independences for people with disabilities in Palm Beach, Martin, St. Lucie & Okeechobee Counties. Services include advocacy, independent living skills & training, peer support, after school & summer programs for teens, crime victim support services, and verterans transition services.

3946 Coalition for Independent Living Options: Fort Pierce
6800 Forest HIll Boulevard
West Palm Beach, FL 33413
561-966-4288
FAX: 561-966-0441
www.cilo.org

Scott Shoemaker, President
Sharon D'Eusanio, Vice President
Joseph Fields Jr., Esquire, Secretary
Private non-profit promoting independences for people with disabilities in Palm Beach, Martin, St. Lucie & Okeechobee Counties. Services include advocacy, independent living skills & training, peer support, after school & summer programs for teens, crime victim support services, and verterans transition services.

3947 Coalition for Independent Living Options
6800 Forest HIll Boulevard
West Palm Beach, FL 33413-3310
561-966-4288
FAX: 561-966-0441
www.cilo.org

Scott Shoemaker, President
Sharon D'Eusanio, Vice President
Joseph Fields Jr., Esquire, Secretary
Private non-profit promoting independences for people with disabilities in Palm Beach, Martin, St. Lucie & Okeechobee Counties. Services include advocacy, independent living skills & training, peer support, after school & summer programs for teens, crime victim support services, and verterans transition services.

3948 Coalition for Independent Living Options: Stuart
1680 SW Bayshore Boulevard
Suite 231
Port St. Lucie, FL 34984
772-878-3500
FAX: 772-878-3344
www.cilo.org

Scott Shoemaker, President
Sharon D'Eusanio, Vice President
Joseph Fields Jr., Esquire, Secretary
Private non-profit promoting independences for people with disabilities in Palm Beach, Martin, St. Lucie & Okeechobee Counties. Services include advocacy, independent living skills & training, peer support, after school & summer programs for teens, crime victim support services, and verterans transition services.

3949 Disability Resource Center
300 W. 5th St.
Panama City, FL 32401-4704
850-769-6890
FAX: 850-769-6891
outreach@drcpc.org
www.drcpc.org

Robert Cox, Executive Director
Becky Cadwell, Independent Living Specialist
They are commiteed to collaborating with other disability/consumer-focused organizations in their community

3950 Lakeland Adult Day Training
3033 Drane Field Rd
Suite 5
Lakeland, FL 33811-3305
863-701-1351
TTY: 863-701-1356
gw.marketing@goodwill-suncoast.com
www.goodwill-suncoast.org

Oscar J. Horton, Chairman
Martin W. Gladysz, Vice Chairman
Heather Ceresoli, Vice Chairman
An innovative program which uses job skills to teach self-help, daily living, communication, mobility, travel, decision-making, behavioral and social skills. This focus provides concrete, transferable experiences to help prepare individuals for greater community inclusion by achieving the highest possible degree of independence in their daily life, increasing their confidence and supporting their successful transitions to less structured, self-sufficient environments.

3951 Lighthouse Central Florida
215 E New Hampshire St
Orlando, FL 32804-6403
407-898-2483
FAX: 407-895-5255
lvaneepoel@lcf-fl.org
www.lighthousecentralflorida.com

Alex B. Hull, Chair
David Stahl, Vice Chair
Paul Prewitt, Secretary
Promote the independence and success of people living with vision impairment.

3952 Miami-Dade County Disability Services and Independent Living (DSAIL)
701 NW 1st Court
Miami, FL 33136-1647
786-469-4600
FAX: 305-547-7355
www.miamidade.gov

Michael Moxam, Manager
Lucia Davis-Raiford, Director
Offers information and referral services serving all types of disabilities with the goal of assisting the disabled acquiring independence and control over their lives. Teaches independent living skills, job readiness and placement, home health care, sensitivity training, training in ASL and Braille, counsel people with disabilities or wide range of problems.

3953 Ocala Adult Day Training
2920 W Silver Springs Blvd
Ocala, FL 34475-5654
352-629-0456
TTY:352-629-0874
gw.marketing@goodwill-suncoast.com
www.goodwill-suncoast.org

Oscar J. Horton, Chairman
Martin W. Gladysz, Vice Chairman
Heather Ceresoli, Vice Chairman
An innovative program which uses job skills to teach self-help, daily living, communication, mobility, travel, decision-making, behavioral and social skills. This focus provides concrete, transferable experiences to help prepare individuals for greater community inclusion by achieving the highest possible degree of independence in their daily life, increasing their confidence and supporting their successful transitions to less structured, self-sufficient environments.

3954 Pinellas Park Adult Day Training
7601 Park Blvd
Pinellas Park, FL 33781-3704
727-541-6205
TTY:727-544-5835
gw.marketing@goodwill-suncoast.com
www.goodwill-suncoast.org

Oscar J. Horton, Chairman
Martin W. Gladysz, Vice Chairman
Heather Ceresoli, Vice Chairman
An innovative program which uses job skills to teach self-help, daily living, communication, mobility, travel, decision-making, behavioral and social skills. This focus provides concrete, transferable experiences to help prepare individuals for greater community inclusion by achieving the highest possible degree of independence in their daily life, increasing their confidence and supporting their successful transitions to less structured, self-sufficient environments.

3955 SCCIL at Titusville
571-W Haverty Court
Rockledge, FL 32955
321-633-6011
FAX: 321-633-6472
TTY:706-724-6324
jilldunham9@gmail.com
www.virtualcil.net

Jill Dunham-Schuller, Executive Director
Directory of Independent Living Centers throughout the United States.

3956 Self Reliance
8901 N Armenia Ave
Tampa, FL 33604-1041
813-375-3965
FAX: 813-375-3970
TTY:813-375-3972
bruehl@self-reliance.org
www.self-reliance.org

Finn Kavanagh, Executive Director
Michele Pineda, Director of Finance & Operations
Gary Martoccio, Programs Director
A cross disability agency providing services to both children and adults with disabilities to identify and overcome barriers to independence in their lives. Self Reliance also promotes independence through empowering persons with disabilities and improving the communities in which they live.

3957 Space Coast Center for Independent Living
571 Haverty Court, Suite W.
Rockledge, FL 32955
321-633-6011
FAX: 321-633-6472
spacecoastcil.org

Michael Lavoie, President
Howard Fetes, VP
Jason Miller, Treasurer/Secretary
Provides overall services for individuals with al types of disabilities. Offers peer support, advocacy, skills training, accessibility surveys, support groups, transportation, specialized equipment and sign language interpreter referral services and home modifications.

3958 Suncoast Center for Independent Living, Inc.
3281 17th Street
Sarasota, FL 34235
941-351-9545
FAX: 941-316-9320
Info@scil4u.org
www.scil4u.org

Kevin Sanderson, Chair
Michael Fluker, Executive Director
Vicke Mack, Treasurer
Helping people with disabilities live independently.

3959 disAbility Solutions for Independent Living
119 S Palmetto Ave
Suite 180
Daytona Beach, FL 32114- 4369
386-255-1812
866-310-1039
FAX: 386-255-1814
TTY: 386-252-6222
info@dsil.org
www.dsil.org

Julie M Shaw, Executive Director
To maximize the leadership, empowerment, independence and productivity of individuals with disabilities, to promote and attain integration and full inclusion of individuals with disabilities in all aspects of our society; accomplished through consumer control, peer support, education, self-determination, equal access and individual and systems advocacy

Georgia

3960 Arms Wide Open
5036 Snapfinger Woods Dr.
Suite 205
Decatur, GA 30035- 1677
678-404-7696
FAX: 770-498-2778
kenmorris@armswideopen.org
www.armswideopen.org

Ken Morris, Director
Arms Wide Open operates a durable medical equipment loan program and a life care program. The mission of Arms Wide Open is to provide support services to the aged, disabled and chronically ill for the purpose of helping them to avoid institutional placement.

3961 Bain, Inc. Center For Independent Living
316 W Shotwell St.
Bainbridge, GA 39819-3906
229-246-0150
888-830-1530
FAX: 229-246-1715
TTY: 888-830-1530
www.baincil.org

Virginia Harris, Executive Director
Malissa Thompson, Program Manager
Tomonia Becon, Nursing Home Transition Coordina
A non-residential Center for Independent Living serving eleven counties throughout Southwest. BAIN is a non-profit, community based resource and advocacy center run by and for individuals with disabilities.

3962 DisAbility LINK
1901 Montreal Rd.
Suite 102
Tucker, GA 30084
404-687-8890
FAX: 404-687-8298
TTY:711
www.disabilitylink.org

Kim Gibson, Executive Director
Joseph Bryant, Financial Director
Rosemary Graham, Secretary
Committed to promoting the rights of all people with disabilities.

3963 Disability Connections
170 College St
Macon, GA 31201-1656
478-741-1425
800-743-2117
FAX: 478-755-1571
disabilityconnections.com

Jerilyn Leverett, Executive Director

A private non-profit organization that looks to enable all people with disabilities to attain and have access to all opportunities in life.

3964 Division of Rehabilitation Services
Georgia Department of Labor
410 Mall Blvd
Suite B
Savannah, GA 31406-4869
912-356-2226
FAX: 912-356-2875
TTY:912-356-2940
dol.state.ga.us

Mark Bultler, Commissioner
Jody Lane, Manager
George Foley, Manager
Vocational rehabilitation services.

3965 Living Independence for Everyone (LIFE)
5105 Paulsen Street
Suite 143-B
Savannah, GA 31405
912-920-2414
800-948-4824
FAX: 912-920-0007
www.lifecil.com

Mark Schreiber, President
Stuart Klugler, Vice President
John Paul Berlon, Secretary
The Southeast's Regional disability resource center that offers a wide range of resources, education, and advocacy to the community to help level the playing field for people with disabilities to create a world in which everyone can fully participate.

3966 Multiple Choices Center for Independent Living
145 Barrington Dr.
Athens, GA 30605-3133
706-850-4025
www.multiplechoices.us

Doug Hatch, President
Donald Veater, VP
Elllen Des Jardines, Secretary
To break down all barriers to inclusion by enhancing the equality of life and empowering people with disabilities through advocacy, education and training.

3967 North District Independent Living Program
Ste 209
311 Green St NW
Gainesville, GA 30501-3364
770-535-5930
Sharon McCurry, Coordinator
Cindy Hanna, Executive Director
Information and referral, advocacy, peer counseling, service coordination and ADA consultation.

3968 Southwest District Independent Living Program
P.O.Box 1606
Albany, GA 31702-1606
229-430-4170
FAX: 229-430-4466

Bill Layton, Director
Diane Davis, Executive Director
Offers peer counseling, disability education and awareness, attendant care registry, and information on accessible home for the disabled.

3969 Statewide Independent Living Council of Georgia
315 West Ponce de Leon Avenue
Suite 600
Decatur, GA 30030-2617
770-270-6860
888-288-9780
FAX: 770-270-5957
shellys5@hotmail.com
silcga.org

Steve Oldaker, President
Angela Denise Davis, Vice President
Mark Schreiber, Treasurer
Founded to ensure that people with disabilities have opportunities to live as independently as possible.

3970 Walton Options for Independent Living
948 Walton Way
Augusta, GA 30901-519
706-724-6262
877-821-8400
FAX: 706-724-6729
TTY: 706-724-6262
tjohnston@waltonoptions.org
www.waltonoptions.org

Tiffany Cilford, Executive Director
Ann Campbell-Kelly, Special Projects Coordinator
Alyson Schwartz, Special Projects Coordinator
Services include individual and systems advocacy, peer support, skills training (including basic computer and return to work skills), information and referral services and transition from institutions back to the community.

Hawaii

3971 Center For Independent Living- Kauai
State Office Building 3060 Eiwa Str
Lihue, HI 96766-6529
808-274-3484
FAX: 808-245-3485
kauaiddc@pixi.com

Humberto Blanco, Administrator
Teri Yamashiro, IL Specialist
Offers peer counseling, disability education, attendant care registry, outreach services and advocacy.

3972 Hawaii Center For Independent Living
1055 Kinoole Street
Suite 105le St
Hilo, HI 96720-3872
808-935-3777
800-420-6928
TTY:808-935-7888
www.cil-hawaii.org

Gordon Fuller, Executive Director
Provides an array of support services for people with all types of disabilities of any age.

3973 Hawaii Center for Independent Living-Maui
220 Imi Kala Street
Suite 103
Wailuku, HI 96793-1209
808-242-4966
866-303-4245
800-420-6928
FAX: 808-244-6978
TTY:808-242-4968
www.cil-hawaii.org

Clytie Nishihara, Manager
T Lay , Administrative Assistant
Offers disability education and awareness, advocacy and counseling.

3974 Hawaii Centers for Independent Living
200 N. Vineyard Blvd Bldg. A501
Honolulu, HI 96817-3950
808-522-5400
800-420-6928
FAX: 808-522-5427
www.cil-hawaii.org

Cheryl Mizusaawa, Executive Director
M.J. (Kimo) Keawe, COO & Executive Director
Our staff and Board of directors are excellent advocates with the disabled community. We will connect you with resources to make your own choices for housing, employment, and personal care and to find assistive devices and technology to improve quality of life. On both the islands of Oahu and Hawaii, we have an independent living specialist who is fluent in American sign language and is well known in the deaf community.

3975 Kauai Center for Independent Living
4340 Nawiliwili Rd.
Lihue, HI 96766-6529
808-246-4800
800-420-6928
FAX: 808-245-7218
www.cil-hawaii.org

Laurao Tobosa, Program Coordinator
Provides a variety of support services for people with all types of disabilities.

Idaho

3976 American Falls Office: Living Independently for Everyone (LIFE)
250 S. Skyline
Idaho Falls, ID 83402-4508
208-529-8610
FAX: 208-529-6804
diane@idlife.org
www.idlife.org

Dean Nilson, Executive Director
Tina Noreen, Programs Coordinator
Mickey Palmer, Fiscal Intermediary Manager
Enables people with disabilities to manage their own lives, make their own choices, and give information and knowledge to assist in living with dignity and bravado.

3977 Dawn Enterprises
280 Cedar Street P.O.Box 388
Blackfoot, ID 83221-388
208-785-5890
FAX: 208-785-3095
dawnent.org

Donna Butler, Executive Director
Teresa Oakes, Assistant Director/Fiscal Coordi
To assist individuals of Southeastern Idaho with mental, physical or social disabilities in achieving independence through employment training, skill training, social development, or living enhancements up to each individual's maximum capability.

3978 Disability Action Center NW
505 N Main St
Moscow, ID 83843-2615
208-883-0523
800-475-0070
FAX: 208-883-0524
www.dacnw.org

Larry Topp, President
Jean Coil, Vice President
Mark Leeper, CEO
A non-profit community partnership working to promote the independence and equality of all individuals with disabilities in all aspects of society. $45.00

3979 Disability Action Center NW: Coeur D'Alene
7560 N Government Way
Suite 1
Coeur D Alene, ID 83815- 4069
208-664-9896
800-854-9500
FAX: 208-666-1362
www.dacnw.org

Larry Topp, President
Jean Coil, Vice President
Mark Leeper, CEO
A non-profit community partnership working to promote the independence and equality of all individuals with disabilities in all aspects of society.

3980 Disability Action Center NW: Lewiston
330 5th Street
Suite A1
Lewiston, ID 83501-2086
208-746-9033
800-746-9033
FAX: 208-746-1004
www.dacnw.org

Larry Topp, President
Jean Coil, Vice President
Mark Leeper, CEO
A non-profit community partnership working to promote the independence and equality of all individuals with disabilities in all aspects of society.

3981 Idaho Falls Office: Living Independently for Everyone (LIFE)
250 S. Skyline
Idaho Falls, ID 83402-3702
208-529-8610
800-631-2747
FAX: 208-232-2753
www.idlife.org

Dean Nielson, Executive Director
Tina Noreen, Programs Coordinator
Mickey Palmer, Fiscal Intermediary Manager

Enables people with disabilities to manage their own lives, make their own choices, and give information and knowledge to assist in living with dignity and bravado.

3982 LIFE: Fort Hall
1333 Moursund
Houston, TX 77019
713-520-0232
FAX: 713-520-5785
TTY:713-520-0232
www.ilru.org

Lex Frieden, Director
Enables people with disabilities to manage their own lives, make thier own choices, and give information and knowledge to assist in living with dignity and bravado.

3983 Living Independence Network Corporation
1878 W Overland Rd
Boise, ID 83705-3142
208-336-3335
FAX: 208-384-5037
info@lincidaho.org
lincidaho.org

Roger Howard, Executive Director
A non-profit organization empowering people with disabilities to achieve their desired level of independence.

3984 Living Independence Network Corporation: Twin Falls
1182 Eastland Dr North
Suite C
Twin Falls, ID 83301-8972
208-733-1712
FAX: 208-733-7711
info@lincidaho.org
www.lincidaho.org

Melva Heinrich, Executive Director
A non-profit organization empowering people with disabilities to achieve their desired level of independence.

3985 Living Independence Network Corporation: Caldwell
1609 Kimball Ave
Ste. 201
Caldwell, ID 83605-6965
208-454-5511
FAX: 208-454-5515
TTY:208-454-5511
info@lincidaho.org
www.lincidaho.org

Heidi Caldwell, Executive Director
A non-profit organization empowering people with disabilities to achieve their desired level of independence.

3986 Living Independent for Everyone (LIFE): Pocatello Office
640 Pershing Ave
PO Box 4185
Pocatello, ID 83201-3702
208-232-2747
800-631-2747
FAX: 208-232-2753
TTY: 208-232-2747
tracy@idlife.org
www.idlife.org

Dean Nielson, Executive Director
Mickey Palmer, Fiscal Intermediary Manager
Tina Noreen, Programs Coordinator
Enables people with disabilities to manage thier own lives, make their own choices, and give information and knowledge to assist in living with dignity and bravado.

3987 Living Independently for Everyone (LIFE): Blackfoot Office
Living Independently for Everyone (LIFE): Pocate
570 W. Pacific
P.O.Box 86
Blackfoot, ID 83221-86
208-785-9648
FAX: 208-785-2398
lori@idlife.org
www.idlife.org

Dean Nielson, Executive Director
Tina Noreen, Programs Coordinator
Mickey Palmer, Fiscal Intermediary Manager
Enable people with disabilities to manage their own lives, make their own choices, and give information and knowledge to assist in living with dignity and bravado.

3988 Living Independently for Everyone: Burley
2311 Park Ave
Suite 7
Burley, ID 83318-2170
208-678-7705
FAX: 208-678-7771
www.idlife.org

Dean Nielson, Executive Director
Mickey Palmer, Fiscal Intermediary Manager
Tina Noreen, Programs Coordinator
Enables people with disabilities to manage their own lives, make their own choices, and give information and knowledge to assist in living with dignity and bravado.

3989 Southwestern Idaho Housing Authority
1108 W Finch Dr
Nampa, ID 83651-1732
208-467-7461
FAX: 208-463-1772

David W Patten, Manager

Illinois

3990 Access Living of Metropolitan Chicago
115 W Chicago Ave
Chicago, IL 60654-3209
312-640-2100
800-613-8549
FAX: 312-640-2101
TTY: 312-640-2102
accessliving.org

Marca Bristo, CEO
Bhuttu Mathews, Disability Resources Coordinator
Gary Arnold, Public Relations Coordinator
Established in 1980, access living is a change agent commited to fostering an incusive society that enables Chicagoans with disabilities to live fully engaged and self-directed lives. Nationally recognized as a leading force in the disability community. Access Living challenges stereotypes, protects civil rights, and champions social reform.

3991 Center on Deafness
3444 Dundee Rd
Northbrook, IL 60062-2258
847-559-0110
FAX: 847-559-8199
TTY: 847-559-9493
www.centerondeafness.org

Bonnie Simon, Executive Director
Donna Gomez, Residential Services/ Adult Plac
Brandi Buie, School Intake
COD is dedicated to providing quality services for persons who are deaf or hard of hearing and their families, through educational, vocational, and residential services in a therapuetic, community-based environment

3992 Community Residential Alternative
Coleman Tri- County Services
22 Veterans Drive, ST. A
P.O. Box 869
Harrisburg, IL 62946-2017
618-252-0275
FAX: 618-252-2389
TTY: 618-269-4211
cts.62946@frontier.com
colemantricounty.tripod.com

Samantha Austin, Executive Director
Six bed group home that provides a residential alternative for the developmentally disabled adult. This program is designed to promote independence in daily living skills, economic self-sufficiency, and integration into the community.

3993 Division of Rehabilitation Services
Department of Human Services
100 South Grand Avenue East
Springfield, IL 62762-2625
217-782-2093
800-843-6154
FAX: 217-524-2471
DHS.WebBits@illinois.gov
www.dhs.state.il.us

Carol Adams, President
Provides medical, therapeutic and counseling services for the disabled, as well as employment services.

3994 DuPage Center for Independent Living
3130 Finley Rd.
Ste. 500
Downers Grove, IL 60515-5877
630-469-2300
FAX: 630-469-2606
TTY: 630-469-2300
www.dupagecil.org

Charles Stack, Board President
Bette Lawrence Water, Vice President
John Lausas, Treasurer
A non residential, community based, not for profit agency wich provides advocacy and services to persons with disabilities in DuPage County.

3995 Fite Center for Independent Living
1230 Larkin Ave
Elgin, IL 60123-6200
847-695-5818
FAX: 847-695-5892

Linda Bradford-Foster, Chairman, Board Treasurer
Gracia Bittner, Board Secretary
Provides services to people with disabilities in Kane, Kendall and McHenry counties. Our non-residential agency provides independent living skills training, advocacy, systemic + individual peer counseling, information and referral and housing services. Also provides technical assistance to businesses and agencies to work with people with disabilities. Locations in Elgin and Aurora. Please call for further details.

3996 Illinois Department of Rehab Services
Department of Human Services
100 South Grand Avenue East
Springfield, IL 62762-1
217-782-2093
800-843-6154
FAX: 217-524-2471
DHS.WebBits@illinois.gov
www.dhs.state.il.us

Carol Adams, President
Karen Perrin, Manager
The state's lead agency serving individuals with disabilities. DRS works in partnership with people with disabilities and their families to assist them in making informed choices to achieve full community participation through employment, education, and independent living opportunities.

3997 Illinois Valley Center for Independent Living
18 Gunia Dr
La Salle, IL 61301-9780
815-224-3126
800-822-3246
FAX: 815-224-3576
ivcil@ivcil.com
ivcil.com

John Hurst, President
Gary Rydleski, Vice President
Sue Faber, Secretary
A nonprofit service and advocacy organization that assists persons with disabilities in opening doors to their independence.

3998 Illinois and Iowa Center for Independent Living
501 11th St.
PO Box 6156
Rock Island, IL 61231-6156
309-793-0090
877-541-2505
855-744-8918
FAX: 309-793-5198
www.iicil.com

Liz Sherwin, Executive Director
Alfonso Ayew-Ew, Blind Independent Living Skill S
Eddie Williams, CommunityReintegration Advocate
To create and maintain independence options for people with disabilities by advocating for civil rights, providing services, and promoting full participation of disabled individuals in all aspects of the community.

3999   Impact Center for Independent Living
2735 E Broadway
Alton, IL 62002-1859   618-462-1411
                                           888-616-4261
                                   FAX: 618-474-5309
                                   staff@impactcil.org
                                   impactcil.org

Susy Woods, President
Judy O'Malley, Vice President
Bishop Samuel White, Treasurer
Promotes pride and respect for people with disabilities by sharing
the tools that are necessary to take control of one's own life.

4000   Jacksonville Area CIL: Havana
220 W Main St
Havana, IL 62644-1138   309-543-6680
                                           877-759-2187
                                   FAX: 309-543-6711
                                   info@jacil.org
                                   www.jacil.org

Phil Foxworth, President
Mark Arnold, Vice President
Ruth Lanier, Secretary
Committed to enabling persons with disabilities to gain effective
control and director of their own lives in the home, in the work-
place and in the community.

4001   Jacksonville Area Center for Independent Living
15 Permac Road
Jacksonville, IL 62650-2071   217-245-8371
                                   FAX: 217-245-1872
                                   TTY:217-245-8371
                                   info@jacil.org
                                   www.jacil.org

Phil Foxworth, President
Mark Arnold, Vice President
Ruth Lanier, Secretary
Committed to enabling persons with disabilities to gain effective
control and direction of their own lives in the home, in the work-
place and in the community.

4002   LIFE Center for Independent Living
2201 Eastland Dr
Suite 1
Bloomington, IL 61704   309-663-5433
                                           888-543-3245
                                   FAX: 309-663-7024
                                   TTY:309-663-5433
                                   rickielee@lifecil.org
                                   www.lifecil.org

Rickielee Benecke, Executive Director
Jill Doran, Associate Director
Brianne Anderson, Office Manager
A community-based, not-for-profit, non-residential organization
that promotes disability rights, equal access, and full community
participation for persons with disabilities.

4003   LINC-Monroe Randolph Center
Ste 4
1514 S Main St
Red Bud, IL 62278-1382   618-282-3700
                                   FAX: 618-282-2740
                                   TTY:618-282-3700

Violete Nast, Manager

4004   Lake County Center for Independent Living
377 N Seymour Ave
Mundelein, IL 60060-2322   847-949-4440
                                   FAX: 847-949-4445
                                   TTY:847-949-0641
                                   lindsey@lccil.org
                                   www.lccil.org

Kelli Brooks, Executive Director
Andy Balint, Director of Finance
Lety Cruz, Bilingual Program Assistant
Lake County Center for Indepdendent Living is a disability rights
organization governed and staffed by a majority of people with
disabilities. LCCIL offers services and advocacy that promote a
fully accessible society, which expects participation by persons
with disabilities.

4005   Life Center for Independent Living: Pontiac
318 West Madison Street
Pontiac, IL 61764-1785   815-844-1132
                                   FAX: 815-844-1148
                                   lifecil@lifecil.org
                                   lifecil.org

Gail Kear, Executive Director
Jill Doran, Associate Director
Brianne Anderson, Office Manager
A community-based, not-for-profit, non-residential organization
that promotes disability rights, equal access, and full community
participation for persons with disabilities.

4006   Living Independently Now Center (LINC)
120 E a St
Belleville, IL 62220-1401   618-235-9988
                                   FAX: 618-233-3729
                                   TTY:618-235-9988
                                   info@lincinc.org
                                   www.lincinc.org

Linda Conley, President
Ron Tialdo, Vice-President
Lynn Jarman, Executive Director
Empowers persons with disabilities to live independently and to
promote accessibility and inclusion in all areas.

4007   Living Independently Now Center: Sparta
Western Egyptian Building
207 West 4th Street
Waterloo, IL 62298   618-317-4028
                                   info@lincinc.org
                                   www.lincinc.org

Linda Conley, President
Ron Tialdo, Vice-President
Lynn Jarman, Executive Director
Empowers persons with disabilities to live independently and to
promote accessibility and inclusion in all areas.

4008   Living Independently Now Center: Waterloo
Western Egyptian Building
207 West 4th Street
Waterloo, IL 62298-1336   618-317-4028
                                   info@lincinc.org
                                   www.lincinc.org

Linda Conley, President
Ron Tialdo, Vice-President
Lynn Jarman, Executive Director
Empowers persons with disabilities to live independently and to
promote accessibility and inclusion in all areas.

4009   Mosaic: Pontiac
4980 S. 118th St.
Omaha, NE 68137   877-366-7242
                                   FAX: 402-896-1511
                                   www.mosaicinfo.org

Max Miller, Chairperson
James Zils, Vice Chairperson
Lisa Negstad, 2nd Vice Chairperson
A faith-based organization serving people with developmental
disabilities.

**4010   Opportunities for Access: A Center for Independent
Living**
4206 Williamson Pl
Suite 3
Mount Vernon, IL 62864-6705   618-244-9212
                                   FAX: 618-244-9310
                                   TTY:618-244-9575
                                   ofacil.org

Michael Egbert, Executive Director
Serves, trains and provides information to persons with disabilities, family members and significant others and service providers. Services include: advocacy, information and referral, peer
support, skills training, volunteer programs and other related services. Services are free. A cross disability community based, non-
residential, nonprofit organization serving Clay, Clinton,
Edwards, Effingham, Fayette, Hamilton, Jasper, Jefferson,
Marion, Wabash, Washington, Wayne and White Counties.

4011 Options Center for Independent Living: Bourbonnais
22 Heritage Dr
Suite 107
Bourbonnais, IL 60914-2510
815-936-0100
FAX: 815-936-0117
TTY:815-936-0132
www.optionscil.org

Mark Mantarian, President
Ronald D. Smith, Vice President
Dina Raymond, Co-Secretary
A non-residential, not-for-profit, community-based organization
that promotes independent living for people with disabilities.

4012 Options Center for Independent Living: Watseka
103 Laird Ln
Suite 103
Watseka, IL 60970
815-432-1332
FAX: 815-432-1360
TTY:815-432-1361

Mark Mountain, President
Ronald D. Smith, Vice President
Dina Raymond, Co-Secretary
A non-residential, not-for-profit, community-based organization
that promotes independent living for people with disabilities.

4013 PACE Center for Independent Living
1317 E Florida Ave
Urbana, IL 61801-6007
217-344-5433
FAX: 217-344-2414
TTY:217-344-5024
info@pacecil.org
pacecil.org

Evelyn Brown, President
Fred Neubert, Vice President
Nancy McClellan-Hickey, Executive Director
Promotes the full participation of people with disabilities in the
rights and responsibilities of society. Provides services, which
assist people with disabilities in achieving or maintaining
independence.

4014 Progress Center for Independent Living
7521 Madison St
Forest Park, IL 60130-1407
708-209-1500
FAX: 708-209-1735
TTY:708-209-1826
info@progresscil.org
www.progresscil.org

Anne Gunter, Independent Living Advocate
Kim Liddell, Independent Living Advocate
Horacio Esparza, Executive Director
A community-based, non-profit, non-residential, service and ad-
vocacy organization operated for people with disabilities, by
people with disabilities.

4015 Progress Center for Independent Living: Blue Island
12940 Western Ave
Blue Island, IL 60406-3766
708-388-5011
FAX: 708-388-5016
TTY:708-389-8250
info@progresscil.org
www.progresscil.org

Horacio Esparza, Executive Director
Anne Gunter, Independent Living Advocate
Kim Liddell, Independent Living Advocate
A community-based, non-profit, non residential, service and ad-
vocacy organization operated for people with disabilities, by
people with disabilities.

4016 Regional Access & Mobilization Project
202 Market St
Rockford, IL 61107-3954
815-968-7467
FAX: 815-968-7612
TTY:815-968-2401
rampcil.org

Shari Snyder, President
Tina Kaatz, Vice President
Craig Fetty, Secretary
To promote an accessible society that allows and expects full par-
ticipation by people with disabilities.

4017 Regional Access & Mobilization Project: Belvidere
530 S State St
Suite 103
Belvidere, IL 61008-3711
815-544-8404
FAX: 815-544-1896
TTY:815-544-8404
rampcil.org

Shari Snyder, President
Tina Kaatz, Vice President
Craig Fetty, Secretary
Promote an accessible society that allows and expects full partici-
pation by people with disabilities.

4018 Regional Access & Mobilization Project: De Kalb
115 N First Street
Dekalb, IL 60115-3055
815-756-3202
FAX: 815-756-3556
TTY:815-756-4263
rampcil.org

Shari Snyder, President
Tina Kaatz, Vice President
Craig Fetty, Secretary
Promotes an accessible society that allows and expects full
partiipation by persons with disabilities.

4019 Regional Access & Mobilization Project: Freeport
2155 W Galena Ave
Freeport, IL 61032-3013
815-233-1128
FAX: 815-233-0743
TTY:815-233-1128
rampcil.org

Shari Snyder, President
Tina Kaatz, Vice President
Craig Fetty, Secretary
Promotes an accessible society that allows and expects full
partiipation by persons with disabilities.

4020 Soyland Access to Independent Living(SAIL)
2449 E Federal Dr
Decatur, IL 62526-2160
217-876-8888
800-358-8080
FAX: 217-876-7245
TTY: 217-876-8888
jwooters@decatursail.com
www.decatursail.com

Jeri J Wooters, Executive Director
Betty Watkins, Rural Outreach Coordinator
A community-based, non-residential Center for Independent Living whose purpose is to promote and practice independent living
for all people with disabilities.

4021 Soyland Access to Independent Living: Charleston
757 Windsor Rd
Charleston, IL 61920-7474
217-345-7245
FAX: 217-345-7226
TTY:217-345-7245
triplec@consolidated.net
www.decatursail.com

Betty Watkins, Rural Outreach Coordinator
Jeri J Wooters, Executive Director
A community-based, non-residential Center for Independent Living whose purpose is to promote and practice independent living
for all people iwth disabilities.

4022 Soyland Access to Independent Living: Shelbyville
1810 W.S. 3rd ST P.O.Box 650
Shelbyville, IL 62565-650
217-774-4322
FAX: 217-774-4368
TTY:217-774-4322
sailsel@consolidated.net
www.decatursail.com

Jeri J Wooters, Executive Director
Betty Watkins, Rural Outreach Coordinator
A community-based, non-residential Center for Independent Living whose purpose is to promote and practice independent living
for all people with disabilities.

4023 Soyland Access to Independent Living: Sullivan
1102 W Jackson St
Sullivan, IL 61951-1067
217-728-3186
FAX: 217-728-2299
TTY: 217-728-3186
sulsail@wireless111.com
www.decatursail.com

Betty Watkins, Rural Outreach Coordinator
Jeri J Wooters, Executive Director
A community-based, non-residential Center for Independent Living whose purpose is to promote and practice independent living for all people with disabilities.

4024 Springfield Center for Independent Living
330 South Grand Ave W
Springfield, IL 62704-3716
217-523-4032
800-447-4221
FAX: 217-523-0427
TTY: 217-523-4032
scil@scil.org
scil.org

Pete Roberts, Executive Director
Susan Coopers, Program Director
Denise Groesch, Reintegration Coordinator
To increase opportunities for equality, integration and independence for all persons with disabilities through advocacy, services, and public education.

4025 Stone-Hayes Center for Independent Living
39 N Prairie St
Galesburg, IL 61401-4613
309-344-1306
888-347-4245
FAX: 309-344-1305
TTY: 309-344-1306

Vanya Peterson, Executive Director
Michael Bohnenkamp, Associate Director
John Hunigan, Office Manager
The purpose of INCIL is to facilitate the collaboration of all Centers for Independent Living in Illinois for promoting, through the Independent Living Movement, equal opportunities and civil rights for all persons with disaibilities.

4026 West Central Illinois Center for Independent Living
639 York St.
Suite 204
Quincy, IL 62301-1065
217-223-0400
FAX: 217-223-0479
TTY: 217-223-0475
info@wcicil.org
www.wcicil.org

Glenda Hackemack, Executive Director
Dale Winner, Information & Referral Coordinat
Dustin Gorde Director of Community, Jenny
A not-for-profit advocacy center funded by state and federal grants to provide services to people with disabilities.

4027 West Central Illinois Center for Independent Living: Macomb
440 N Lafayette St
Macomb, IL 61455-1512
309-833-5766
FAX: 309-833-4690
TTY: 217-223-0475
info@wcicil.org
www.wcicil.org

Glenda Hackemack, Executive Director
Dale Winner, Information & Referral Coordinat
Dustin Gorde Director of Community, Jenny
A not-for-profit advocacy center funded by state and federal grants to provide services to people with disabilities.

4028 Will Grundy Center for Independent Living
2415 W Jefferson St
Suite A
Joliet, IL 60435-6464
815-729-0162
FAX: 815-729-3697
TTY: 815-729-2085
will-grundycil.org

Elaine Sommer, President
Chris Boyk, Vice President
Dianne Mundle, Treasurer

A cross-disability, community based organization that strives for equalityand empowerment of persons with disabilities in the Will and Grundy County areas.

Indiana

4029 Assistive Technology Training and Information Center (ATTIC)
1721 Washington Ave
Vincennes, IN 47591-4823
812-886-0575
877-96A-8842
FAX: 812-886-1128
inbox@atticindiana.org
www.atticindiana.org

Patricia Stewart, Executive Director
Rebecca Anderson, Assistant Director
Mark Schmitt, Fiscal Controller
ATTIC provides support, information and education for individuals with disabilities and for families of children with special needs, and the professionals who assist these families. All disabilities, all ages.

4030 DAMAR Services
6067 Decatur Blvd.
Indianapolis, IN 46241
317-856-5201
FAX: 317-856-2333
info@damar.org
damar.org

Gail Shiel, Chairman
Rick Torbeck, Vice Chairman
Jim Dalton, Psy.D., HSPP, President and CEO
Builds better futures for children and adults facing life's greatest developmental and behavioral challenges.

4031 Everybody Counts Center for Independent Living
3616 Elm St
Room 3
East Chicago, IN 46410-7097
219-229-5055
888-769-3636
FAX: 219-769-5326
TTY: 219-756-3323
info@everybodycounts.org
everybodycounts.org

Teresa Torres, Executive Director
Emma Lewis Sullivan, On Loan Consultant
Mark Torres, Systems Manager
A nonprofit corporation dedicated to the achievement of maximum independence and enhanced quality of life for persons with disabilities.

4032 Four Rivers Resource Services
Hwy. 59 South
P.O. Box 249
Linton, IN 47441-249
812-847-2231
FAX: 812-847-8836
fourrivers@frrs.org
frrs.org

Stephen Sacksteder, Executive Director
Robin Duncan, Chief Financial Officer
Dean Dorrell, Information Systems Director
FRRS is established to enable individuals with disabilities and other challenges to attain self independence and natural interdependence, inclusion in normal life experiences and opportunities, and general life enrichment, by working in partnership with them, their families and the communities in and around Greene, Sullivan, Daviess, and Martin Counties.

4033 Future Choices Independent Living Center
309 N High St
Muncie, IN 47305-1618
765-741-8332
866-741-3444
FAX: 765-741-8333
futurechoices.org

Beth Y. Quarles, President
Provides unlimited options for minorities, youth, and Hoosiers with disabilities.

4034 Independent Living Center of Eastern Indiana (ILCEIN)
1818 W Main St
Richmond, IN 47374-3822
765-939-9226
877-939-9226
FAX: 765-935-2215
www.ilcein.org

Jim McCormick, Executive Director
Dean Turner, Administrative Director
Ann Barnhart, Compliance Manager
Serving Fayette, Franklin, Henry, Decatur, Rush, Union and Wayne Counties.

4035 Indianapolis Resource Center for Independent Living
5302 East Washington Street
Indianapolis, IN 46219
317-926-1660
866-794-7245
FAX: 317-926-1687
info@abilityindiana.org
www.abilityindiana.org

Judy Townsend, President
Dave Trulock, Vice President
Jacqueline Troy, Treasurer
Provides services, support and information to people with disabilities to help insure equal access to all aspects of community life.

4036 League for the Blind and Disabled
5821 S Anthony Blvd
Fort Wayne, IN 46816-3701
260-441-0551
800-889-3443
FAX: 260-441-7760
TTY: 800-889-3443
the-league@the-league.org
the-league.org

David A. Nelson, CEO/President
Catherine Collins, Chair
Anne Palmer, Administrative Assistant
To provide and promote opportunities that empower people with disabilities to achieve their potential.

4037 Martin Luther Homes of Indiana
Mosaic
26 N Brown Ave
Terre Haute, IN 47803-1523
812-235-3399
FAX: 812-235-1590

Providing a wide array of services to assist individuals and families in achieving positive life goals. Services to persons with disabilities and other special needs include community living options, training and employment options, spiritual growth and development options, training and counseling support.

4038 Ruben Center for Independent Living
5302 East Washington Street
Indianapolis, IN 46219-3227
317-926-1660
FAX: 317-926-1687
TTY:219-397-6496
info@abilityindiana.org
www.abilityindiana.org

Judy Townsend, President
Dave Trulock, Vice President
Jacqueline Troy, Treasurer
An independent living center providing support, information and education.

4039 SILC, Indiana Council on Independent Living (ICOIL)
P.O.Box 7083
Indianapolis, IN 46207-7083
317-232-1303
800-545-7763
FAX: 317-232-6478

Nancy Young, Program Director
Richard Simers, SILC Chairperson

4040 Southern Indiana Center for Independent Living
1494 W. Main Street
PO Box 308
Mitchell, IN 47446-1943
812-277-9626
800-845-6914
FAX: 812-277-9628
sicilindiana.org

Al Tolbert, Executive Director
Darlene Webster, Independent Living Center Direct

SICIL is a consumer controlled, community based, cross-disability, non-residential and not for profit organization that promotes and practices the philosophy of independent living: consumer control, peer support, self-help, self-determination, equal access, and individual and community advocacy. SICIL also promotes accesible and affordable housing, recreation and transportation.

4041 Wabash Independent Living Center & Learning Center (WILL)
1 Dreiser Square
Terre Haute, IN 47807
812-298-9455
877-915-9455
FAX: 812-299-9061
TTY: 877-915-9455
info@thewillcenter.org
www.thewillcenter.org

Don Rogers, Chairman
Jody Pomfret, Vice Chairman
Kevin Burke, Treasurer
To empower people with disabilities to ensure that they have full and complete access to community resources to promote their independence

Iowa

4042 Black Hawk Center for Independent Living
2800 Falls Ave.
P.O. Box 2275
Waterloo, IA 50701-2275
319-291-7755
888-291-7754
FAX: 319-291-7781
TTY:800-735-2942
To create and maintain independence options by working with people with disabilities.

4043 Central Iowa Center for Independent Living
655 Walnut St
Suite 131
Des Moines, IA 50309-3930
515-243-1742
888-503-2287
FAX: 515-243-5385

Bob Jeppesen, Executive Director
Frank Strong, Associate Director
Crystal Toman, Office Coordinator
CICIL is a community based, non-profit, non-residential program serving persons with disabilities. CICIL assists all persons, regardless of disability in making choices about their own lives and in experiencing success in achieving independence.

4044 Evert Conner Rights & Resources CIL
730 S Dubuque St
Iowa City, IA 52240-4202
319-338-3870
800-982-0272
FAX: 319-354-1799

Scott Gill, Executive Director
Provides community services like disability awareness training and classroom presentations. Individual services include independent living skills training and peer counseling. All services are custom designed to support the independence of people with disabilities in their own community.

4045 Hope Haven
1800 19th St
PO Box 70
Rock Valley, IA 51247-1098
712-476-2737
FAX: 712-476-3110
hopehaven.org

Dr. Kent Eric Eknes, President
Ron Boote, Vice President
David Vanningen, Executive Director
Unleashes the potential in people through work and life skills so that they may enjoy a productive life in their community.

4046   League of Human Dignity, Center for Independent Living
1520 Avenue M
Council Bluffs, IA 51501-1185   712-323-6863
                                    FAX: 712-323-6811
                              Cinfo@leagueofhumandignity.com
                                www.leagueofhumandignity.com

Carrie England, Director
League of Human Dignity actively promotes the full integration of individuals with disabilities into society. To this end, the League will advocate their needs and rights, and provide quality services to involve these persons in becoming and remaining independent citizens.

4047   Martin Luther Homes of Iowa
P.O. Box 2316
Princeton, NJ 08543-2316   877-843-7953
                                    FAX: 563-568-3992
                                          www.rwjf.org

Mary Lynn ReVoir, Project Director
Fred Naumann III, Communications
Richard Wicks, Executive Director

4048   South Central Iowa Center for Independent Living
117 1st Ave W
Oskaloosa, IA 52577-3243   641-672-1867
                                       800-651-7911
                                    FAX: 641-672-1867
                                   brookie43@gmail.com
                              www.iowasilc.org/cilinfo.html
Deb Philpot, Executive Director
Provides services, support, information and referral to people with disabilities to help insure equal access to all aspects of community life.

4049   Three Rivers Center for Independent Living
900 Rebecca Avenue
Pittsburgh, PA 15221-2938   412-371-7700
                                       800-633-4588
                                    FAX: 412-371-9430
                                    TTY: 412-371-6230
                                        lgray@trcil.org
Stanley A. Holbrook, President & Executive Director
Lisa Wilson, HR Program Manager
Rachel Rogan, Director of Waiver Services
Providing a wide array of services to assist individuals and families in achieving positive life goals.

Kansas

4050   Advocates for Better Living For Everyone(A.B.L.E.)
Ste C
521 Commercial St
Atchison, KS 66002   913-367-1830
                                       888-845-2879
                                    FAX: 913-367-1830
Ken Gifford, President & CEO
A not for profit agency providing services within the State of Kansas. ABLE looks to assist people with disabilities as well as any other member of the community to live an integrated, quality life with dignity, respect, and independence.

4051   Center for Independent Living SW Kansas: Liberal
1023 N Kansas Ave
Suite 2
Liberal, KS 67901-2655   620-624-5500
                                       800-327-4048
                                    FAX: 620-624-6576
                                    TTY: 620-624-5500
                                        www.cilswks.org
Victor Otero, Manager
Crystal Tharp, Independent Living Advocate
Dedicated to helping people achieve full participation in society.

4052   Center for Independent Living Southwest Kansas
P.O.Box 2090
Garden City, KS 67846-2090   620-276-1900
                                       800-736-9443
                                    FAX: 620-271-0200
Troy Horton, Executive Director
Dedicated to helping people achieve full participation in society.

4053   Center for Independent Living Southwest Kansas: Dodge City
2601 Central Ave
Dodge City, KS 67801-6200   620-227-6660
                                       800-326-1366
                                    FAX: 620-227-8185
                                    TTY: 620-227-6660
Mary Jane Sandoval, Independent Living Advocate
Dedicated to helping people achieve full participation in society

4054   Coalition for Independence
4911 State Ave
Kansas City, KS 66102-1749   913-321-5140
                                       866-201-3829
                                    FAX: 913-321-5182
                                    TTY: 913-321-5216
                                          cfi-kc.org
Clarence Smith, Executive Director
Laarni Sison, Executive Assistant
Claire Marr, Lead Independent Living Speciali
Facilitates positive and responsible independence for all people with disabilities by acting as an advocate for individuals with disabilities, providing services, and promoting accessibility and acceptance.

4055   Cowley County Developmental Services
P.O.Box 618
Arkansas City, KS 67005-618   620-442-5270
                                       866-442-5270
                                    FAX: 620-442-5623
Bill Brooks, Executive Director
Provides services for persons with developmental disabilities in Cowley County.

4056   Independence
2001 Haskell Ave
Lawrence, KS 66046-3249   785-841-0333
                                       888-824-7277
                                    FAX: 785-841-1094
                              comment@independenceinc.org
                                    independenceinc.org
Karen McGrath, President
Bruce Passman, Vice President
Sandra London, Lieb
Provides advocacy, services, and education for people with disabilities and our communities.

4057   Independent Connection
1710 W. Schilling Road
P.O.Box 1160
Salina, KS 67402- 1160   785-827-9383
                                       800-526-9731
                                    FAX: 785-823-2015
                                    TTY: 785-827-9383
                                          www.occk.com
Shelia Nelson-Stout, President/CEO
Deanna L. Lamer, Senior Director,Human Resources
Tasha Suppes, Human Resources Coordinator
Dedicated to helping people with physical or mental disabilities remove barriers to employment, independent living, and full participation in their communities.

4058   Independent Connection: Abilene
Suite 221
300 N. Cedar St.
Abilene, KS 67410   785-263-2208
                                    FAX: 785-263-3795
                                    TTY:785-263-2208
                                          www.occk.com
Shelia Nelson-Stout, President/CEO
Deanna L. Lamer, Senior Director,Human Resources
Tasha Suppes, Human Resources Coordinator

Dedicated to helping people with physical or mental disabilities remove barriers to employment, independent living, and full participation in their communities.

4059   Independent Connection: Beloit
501 W 7th St
Beloit, KS 67420-2107

785-738-5423
FAX: 785-738-3320
TTY:785-738-5423
www.occk.com

Shelia Nelson-Stout, President/CEO
Deanna L. Lamer, Senior Director,Human Resources
Tasha Suppes, Human Resources Coordinator
Dedicated to helping people with physical or mental disabilities remove barriers to employment, independent living, and full participation in their communities.

4060   Independent Connection: Concordia
1502 Lincoln St
Concordia, KS 66901-4830

785-243-1977
FAX: 785-243-4524
TTY:785-243-1977
www.occk.com

Shelia Nelson-Stout, President/CEO
Dedicated to helping people with physical or mental disabilities remove barriers to employment, independent living, and full participation in their communities.

4061   Independent Living Resource Center
3033 W 2nd St N
Wichita, KS 67203-5357

316-942-6300
800-479-6861
FAX: 316-942-2078
ilrcks.org

Jean Shuler, President
Angie Schmidt, Vice Chairman
Derrick Prichard, Secretary/Treasurer
Empower people with disabilities to lead independent lives by providing advocacy, education and direct services. Serve people with all types of disabilities; permanent or temporary, physical disabilities, mental disabilities, and developmental disabilities.

4062   Kansas Services for the Blind & Visually Impaired
2601 SW East Circle Dr N
Topeka, KS 66606-2445

785-296-3738
800-547-5789
FAX: 785-291-3138
srskansas.org

Dennis Ford, Manager
Michael Donnelly, Director
Helps persons who are blind or visually to improve their quality of life. KSBVI provides people with an array of services and experiences aimed at overcoming not only the physical difficulties brought on by the loss of vision, but also the fear of change associated with vision loss. KSBVI can also help with job search and retention activities; life skills training; access to medical services; and technical assistance.

4063   LINK: Colby
505 N Franklin Ave
Suite G
Colby, KS 67701-2342

785-462-7600
800-736-9418
TTY:785-462-7600
brianatwell@linkinc.org
www.linkinc.org

Brian Atwell, Executive Director
Promotes and supports the civil rights of people with disabilities and empowers them to achieve a life of independence and equality.

4064   Living Independently in Northwest Kansas: Hays
2401 E 13th St
Hays, KS 67601-2663

785-625-6942
800-596-5926
FAX: 785-625-2334
TTY: 785-625-6942
brianatwell@linkinc.org
www.linkinc.org

Brian Atwell, Executive Director

Promotes and supports the civil rights of people with disabilities and empowers them to achieve a life of independence and equality.

4065   Prairie IL Resource Center
103 W 2nd St
Pratt, KS 67124-2644

620-672-9600
FAX: 620-672-9601
info@pilr.org
www.pilr.org

Dave Mullins, President
Stephanie Guthrie, Vice President
Chris Owens, Executive Director
To achieve the full inclusion and acceptance of people with disabilities through education and advocacy

4066   Prairie Independent Living Resource Center
17th S Main St
Hutchinson, KS 67501

620-663-3989
888-715-6818
FAX: 620-663-4711
TTY:620-663-9920
info@pilr.org
www.pilr.org

Dave Mullins, President
Stephanie Guthrie, Vice President
Chris Owens, Executive Director
To achieve the full conclusion and acceptance of people with disabilities through education and advocacy

4067   Resource Center for Independent Living
104 S. Washington Ave.
Iola, KS 66749-8805

620-365-8144
877-944-8144
FAX: 620-365-7726
rcilinc.org

Chad Wilkins, Executive Director
Committed to working with individuals, families, and communities to promote independent living and individual choice to persons with disabilities.

4068   Resource Center for Independent Living, Inc. (RCIL)
409 Columbia St.
Utica, NY 13503-210

315-797-4642
800-580-7245
FAX: 315-797-4747
TTY: 315-797-5837
rcilinc.org

Chad Wilkins, Executive Director
Committed to working with individuals, families, and communities to promote independent living and individual choice to persons with disabilities. As a center for independent living in Kansas, we provide advocacy, peer counseling, information and referral, independent living skills training and deinstitutionalization. In addition to these services, we also provide HOBS payroll services and a variety of programs benefiting individuals with disabilities.

4069   Resource Center for Independent Living: Emporia
215 West Sixth Avenue
Suite 202
Emporia, KS 66801-2886

620-342-1648
888-261-4024
FAX: 620-342-1821
info@rcilinc.org
rcilinc.org

Deone Wilson, Executive Director
Beth Combes, Information & Outreach Coordinat
Amy Richardson, Targeted Case Manager
Committed to working with individuals, families, and communities to promote independent living and individual choice to persons with disabilities.

4070 **Resource Center for Independent Living: Arkansas City**
P.O. Box 257
1137 Laing
Osage City, KS 66523
785-528-3105
800-580-7245
FAX: 785-528-3665
TTY: 785-528-3106
info@rcilinc.org
rcilinc.org

Deone Wilson, Executive Director
Tania Harrington, Director of Quality Assurance
Adam Burnett, Director of Core Services
Committed to working with individuals, families, and communities to promote independent living and individual choice to persons with disabilities.

4071 **Resource Center for Independent Living: Burlington**
P.O. Box 257
1137 Laing
Osage City, KS 66523
785-528-3105
800-580-7245
FAX: 785-528-3665
TTY: 785-528-3106
info@rcilinc.org
rcilinc.org

Deone Wilson, Executive Director
Tania Harrington, Director of Quality Assurance
Adam Burnett, Director of Core Services
Committed to working with individuals, families, and communities to promote independent living and individual choice to persons with disabilities.

4072 **Resource Center for Independent Living: Coffeyville**
P.O. Box 257
1137 Laing
Osage City, KS 66523
785-528-3105
800-580-7245
FAX: 785-528-3665
TTY: 785-528-3106
info@rcilinc.org
rcilinc.org

Deone Wilson, Executive Director
Tania Harrington, Director of Quality Assurance
Adam Burnett, Director of Core Services
Committed to working with individuals, families, and communities to promote independent living and individual choice to persons with disabilities.

4073 **Resource Center for Independent Living: El Dorado**
615 1/2 N Main St
El Dorado, KS 67042-2027
316-322-7853
800-960-7853
FAX: 316-322-7888
info@rcilinc.org
rcilinc.org

Macy Gaines, Independent Living Specialist
Doris Hammons, Targeted Case Manager
Shirley Mullin, Targeted Case Manager
Committed to working with individuals, families, and communities to promote independent living and individual choice to persons with disabilities.

4074 **Resource Center for Independent Living: Ft Scott**
P.O. Box 257
1137 Laing
Osage City, KS 66523
785-528-3105
800-580-7245
FAX: 785-528-3665
TTY: 785-528-3106
info@rcilinc.org
rcilinc.org

Deone Wilson, Executive Director
Tania Harrington, Director of Quality Assurance
Adam Burnett, Director of Core Services
Committed to working with individuals, families, and communities to promote independent living and individual choice to persons with disabilities.

4075 **Resource Center for Independent Living: Ottawa**
233 W 23rd Street
Ottawa, KS 66067-3533
785-242-1805
800-995-1805
FAX: 785-242-1448
rcilinc.org

Chad Wilkins, Executive Director
Committed to working with individuals, families, and communities to promote independent living and individual choice to persons with disabilities.

4076 **Resource Center for Independent Living: Overland Park**
Ste 100
10200 W 75th St
Shawnee Mission, KS 66204-2242
913-362-6618
877-439-2847
FAX: 913-677-2742
rcilinc.org

Chad Wilkins, Executive Director
RCIL is committed to working with individuals, families, and communities to promote independent living and individual choice to persons with disabilities.

4077 **Resource Center for Independent Living: Topeka**
1507 S.W. 21stStreet
Suite 203
Topeka, KS 66604-2356
785-267-1717
877-719-1717
FAX: 785-267-1711
info@rcilinc.org
rcilinc.org

Rosie Cooper, Director of Independent Living S
Stuart Jones, Assistive Technology Specialist
Mikel McCary, Assistive Technology Specialist
Committed to working with individuals, families, and communities to promote independent living and individual choice to persons with disabilities.

4078 **Southeast Kansas Independent Living (SKIL)**
1801 Main
P.O. Box 957
Parsons, KS 67357-957
620-421-5502
800-688-5616
FAX: 620-421-3705
TTY: 620-421-0983
skil@skilonline.com
www.skilonline.com

Nancy Varner, Chairman
Janet Spillman, Vice Chairman
Shari Coatney, CEO/President
To empower, integrate and maximize independence for all persons with disabilities.

4079 **Southeast Kansas Independent Living: Independence**
107 East Main
P.O.Box 944
Independence, KS 67301-944
620-331-1006
866-927-1006
FAX: 620-331-1257
TTY: 620-331-1006
skilindy@skilonline.com
www.skilonline.com

Nancy Varner, Chairman
Janet Spillman, Vice Chairman
Shari Coatney, CEO/President
To empower, integrate and maximize independence for all persons with disabilities.

4080 **Southeast Kansas Independent Living: Chanute**
2 W. Main
P.O.Box 645
Chanute, KS 66720-645
620-431-0757
866-927-0757
FAX: 620-431-7274
TTY: 620-431-0757
skilchanute@skilonline.com
www.skilonline.com

Nancy Varner, Chairman
Janet Spillman, Vice Chairman
Shari Coatney, CEO/President

To empower, integrate and maximize independence for all persons with disabilities.

4081 Southeast Kansas Independent Living: Columbus
123 N. Kansas
P.O. Box 478
Columbus, KS 66725-1801   620-429-3600
                                            866-927-3600
                                       FAX: 620-429-1027
                          skilcolumbus@skilonline.com
                                       www.skilonline.com

Nancy Varner, Chairman
Janet Spillman, Vice Chairman
Shari Coatney, CEO/President
To empower, integrate and maximize independence for all persons with disabilities.

4082 Southeast Kansas Independent Living: Fredonia
623 Monroe
P.O.Box 448
Fredonia, KS 66736-448   620-378-4881
                                            866-927-4881
                                       FAX: 620-378-4851
                                       TTY: 620-378-4881
                            skilfredonia@skilonline.com
                                       www.skilonline.com

Nancy Varner, Chairman
Janet Spillman, Vice Chairman
Shari Coatney, CEO/President
To empower, integrate and maximize independence for all persons with disabilities.

4083 Southeast Kansas Independent Living: Hays
510 W. 29thStreet, Suite A
PO Box 366
Hays, KS 67601-366   785-628-8019
                                            800-316-8019
                                       FAX: 785-628-3116
                                       TTY: 785-628-3128
                               skilhays@skilonline.com
                                       www.skilonline.com

Nancy Varner, Chairman
Janet Spillman, Vice Chairman
Shari Coatney, CEO/President
To empower, integrate and maximize independence for all persons with disabilities.

4084 Southeast Kansas Independent Living: Pittsburg
1403 N. Broadway
P.O.Box 1706
Pittsburg, KS 66762-1706   620-231-6780
                                            866-927-6780
                                       FAX: 620-232-9915
                                       TTY: 620-231-6780
                            skilpittsburg@skilonline.com
                                       www.skilonline.com

Nancy Varner, Chairman
Janet Spillman, Vice Chairman
Shari Coatney, CEO/President
To empower, integrate and maximize independence for all persons with disabilities.

4085 Southeast Kansas Independent Living: Sedan
113 West Main
P.O.Box 340
Sedan, KS 67361-340   620-725-3990
                                            866-906-3990
                                       FAX: 620-725-3942
                                       TTY: 620-725-3990
                               skilsedan@skilonline.com
                                       www.skilonline.com

Nancy Varner, Chairman
Janet Spillman, Vice Chairman
Shari Coatney, CEO/President
To empower, integrate and maximize independence for all persons with disabilities.

4086 Southeast Kansas Independent Living: Yates Center
119 W. Butler
P.O.Box 129
Yates Center, KS 66783-129   620-625-2818
                                            866-927-2818
                                       FAX: 620-625-2585
                                       www.skilonline.com

Nancy Varner, Chairman
Janet Spillman, Vice Chairman
Shari Coatney, CEO/President
To empower, integrate and maximize independence for all persons with disabilities.

4087 Three Rivers Independent Living Center
504 Miller Drive
P.O.Box 408
Wamego, KS 66547-0408   785-456-9915
                                            800-555-3994
                                       FAX: 785-456-9923
                                       TTY: 785-456-9915
                             reception@threeriversinc.org
                                       www.threeriversinc.org

Audrey Schremmer-Philips, Executive Director
Keyna Steinbrock, IL Specialist
Erica Christie, Director of Supports & Services
A nonprofit organization promoting the self reliance of individuals with disabilities through education, advocacy, training and support.

4088 Three Rivers Independent Living Center: Clay
719 5th Street
P.O.Box 33
Clay Center, KS 67432-0033   785-632-6117
                                       FAX: 785-632-6117
                                       TTY:785-632-6117
                             reception@threeriversinc.org
                                       www.threeriversinc.org

Audrey Schremmer-Philips, Executive Director
Keyna Steinbrock, IL Specialist
Erica Christie, Director of Supports & Services
A non-profit organization promoting the self reliance of individuals with disabilities through, education, advocacy, training and support.

4089 Three Rivers Independent Living Center: Manhattan
401 Houston St.
Manhattan, KS 66502   785-776-9294
                                            800-432-2703
                                       FAX: 785-776-9479
                             reception@threeriversinc.org
                                       www.threeriversinc.org

Audrey Schremmer-Philips, Executive Director
Keyna Steinbrock, IL Specialist
Erica Christie, Director of Supports & Services
A non profit organization promoting the self reliance of individuals with disabilities through education, advocacy, training and support.

4090 Three Rivers Independent Living Center: Seneca
416 Main St
Seneca, KS 66538-1926   785-336-0222
                                       FAX: 785-336-0288
                             reception@threeriversinc.org
                                       www.threeriversinc.org

Audrey Schremmer-Philips, Executive Director
Keyna Steinbrock, IL Specialist
Erica Christie, Director of Supports & Services
A non profit organization promoting the self reliance of individuals with disabilities through education, advocacy, training and support.

4091 Three Rivers Independent Living Center: Topeka
P.O.Box 4152
Topeka, KS 66604-4152   785-273-0249
                                       FAX: 785-273-0249
                             reception@threeriversinc.org
                                       www.threeriversinc.org

Audrey Schremmer-Philips, Executive Director
Keyna Steinbrock, IL Specialist
Erica Christie, Director of Supports & Services

A non profit organization promoting the self reliance of individuals with disabilities through education, advocacy, training and support.

4092 Topeka Independent Living Resource Center
501 SW Jackson St
Suite 100
Topeka, KS 66603-3300
785-233-4572
FAX: 785-233-1561
TTY:785-233-4572
tilrcweb@tilrc.org
tilrc.org

Mike Oxford, Executive Director
Evan Korynta, Operations Manager
Angie Harter, Independent Living Advocacy Staf
A civil and human rights organization that advocates for justice, equality and essential services for a fully integrated and accessible society for all people with disabilities.

4093 Whole Person: Nortonville
7301 Mission Road
Suite 135
Prairie Village, KS 66208- 3006
913-262-1294
877-767-8896
FAX: 913-262-2392
info@thewholeperson.org
www.thewholeperson.org

Rick O'Neal, President
Jim Atwater, Vice President
MIchelle Ford, Secretary
Assists people with disabilities to live independently and encourages change within the community to expand opportunities for independent living.

4094 Whole Person: Nortonville, The
7301 Mission Road
Suite 135
Prairie Village, KS 66208- 3006
913-262-1294
877-767-8896
FAX: 913-262-2392
info@thewholeperson.org
www.thewholeperson.org

Rick O'Neal, President
Jim Atwater, Vice President
MIchelle Ford, Secretary
Assists people with disabilities to live independently and encourages change within the community to expand opportunities for independent living.

4095 Whole Person: Prairie Village
7301 Mission Rd
Prairie Village, KS 66208-3006
913-262-1294
FAX: 913-262-2392
info@thewholeperson.org
www.thewholeperson.org

Rick O'Neal, President
Jim Atwater, Vice President
MIchelle Ford, Secretary
Assists people with disabilities to live independently and encourages change within the community to expand opportunities for independent living.

4096 Whole Person: Prairie Village, The
7301 Mission Road
Suite 135
Prairie Village, KS 66208- 3006
913-262-1294
877-767-8896
FAX: 913-262-2392
info@thewholeperson.org
www.thewholeperson.org

Rick O'Neal, President
Jim Atwater, Vice President
MIchelle Ford, Secretary
Assists people with disabilities to live independently and encourages change within the community to expand opportunities for independent living.

4097 Whole Person: Tonganoxie
7301 Mission Road
Suite 135
Prairie Village, KS 66208- 3006
913-262-1294
877-767-8896
FAX: 913-262-2392
info@thewholeperson.org
www.thewholeperson.org

Rick O'Neal, President
Jim Atwater, Vice President
MIchelle Ford, Secretary
Assists people with disabilities to live independently and encourages change within the community to expand opportunities for independent living.

Kentucky

4098 Center for Accessible Living
501 S. 2nd Street
Ste 200
Louisville, KY 40202-2121
502-589-6620
888-813-8497
FAX: 502-589-3980
TTY:502-589-6690
www.calky.org

Jan Day, CEO
Michael Markiewicz, Chief Financial Officer
Jeanne M. Gallimore, Branch Director
To assist the individuals with disabilities who seek to live independently.

4099 Center for Accessible Living: Murray
1051 N 16th St
Suite C
Murray, KY 42071-8511
270-753-7676
888-261-6194
FAX: 270-753-7729
TTY:270-767-0549
www.calky.org

Jeanne M. Gallimore, Branch Director
Susan Tharpe, Coordinator of Services
Jan Day, CEO
To assist the individuals with disabilities who seek to live independently.

4100 Center for Independent Living: Kentucky Department for the Blind
Independent Living Office
Rear
409 N Miles St
Elizabethtown, KY 42701-1834
270-766-5126
Buel E Stalls Jr, Office Manager and IL Specialist
Nancy Bachuss, Manager
Offers peer counseling, attendant care registry and other services to the community as they relate to the blind community. The Murray office is an independent living regional office which covers 20 far western counties of Kentucky.

4101 Disability Coalition of Northern Kentucky
Ste 219
525 W 5th St
Covington, KY 41011-1293
859-431-7668
FAX: 859-431-7688
TTY:800-648-6057

Kitt Heeg, Executive Director
Empowering people with disabilities through education, networking, and positive attitudes.

4102 Disability Resource Initiative
624 Eastwood St
Bowling Green, KY 42103-1602
270-796-5992
877-437-5045
FAX: 270-796-6630

Marilyn Mitchell, Executive Director
Tracy Cole, Independent Living Specialist
Steve Burchett, IT Specialist
One of the most important premises in Independent Living is that people with disabilities are the most knowledgable about their

own needs. Because of this all of their services are designed to be consumer-driven. Within each service, Center Staff work with both participant and provider to achieve and maintain an Independent Lifestyle.

4103 Independence Place
1093 S. Broadway
Suite 1218
Lexington, KY 40504-1787
859-266-2807
877-266-2807
FAX: 859-335-0627
TTY: 800-648-6056
info@independenceplaceky.org
www.independenceplaceky.org

Michael Fein, Chairman
Carla Webster, Vice Chairwoman
Pamela Roark-Glisson, Executive Director
To assist people with disabilities to achieve their full potential for community inclusion through improving access, choice and equal opportunity.

4104 Pathfinders for Independent Living
105 E Mound St
Harlan, KY 40831-2355
606-573-5777
877-340-PATH
FAX: 606-573-5739
TTY: 606-573-5777

Sandra Goodwyn, Executive Director
Andrew Saylor, Director of IT (Internal) and Fi
Stacy Marple, Director of IT (External)
They publish a newsletter called LifeLine 4-5 times a year. Most articles are written by Sandra Goodwyn. Editor is Andrew Saylor. Serves people with disabilities to maintain as much independence as they desire

4105 SILC Department of Vocational Rehabilitation
209 Saint Clair St
Frankfort, KY 40601-1817
502-564-4440
800-372-7172
FAX: 502-564-6745
sarahf.richardson@ky.gov

Sarah Richardson, SILC Liaison
We recognize and respect the contributions of all individuals as a necessary and vital part of a productive society.

Louisiana

4106 New Horizons: Central Louisiana
Ste 18
2406 Ferrand St
Monroe, LA 71201-3236
318-323-4374
800-428-5505
FAX: 318-323-5445
nhilc@nhilc.org
www.nhilc.org

Alan Loosley, President
Sharon Geddes, Vice-President
Clint Snell, Vice-President for Finance
A private, non-profit, non-residential, consumer-controlled, community-based organization that enables people with disabilities to live independently.

4107 New Horizons: Northeast Louisiana
3717 Government Street
Suite 7
Alexandria, LA 71301-4037
318-484-3596
888-361-3596
FAX: 318-484-3640
nhilc@nhilc.org
www.nhilc.org

Alan Loosley, President
Sharon Geddes, Vice-President
Clint Snell, Vice-President for Finance
A private, non-profit, non-residential, consumer controlled, community based organization that enables people with disabilities to live independently.

4108 New Horizons: Northwest Louisiana
1111A Hawn Avenue
Shreveport, LA 71106-6144
318-671-8131
877-219-7327
FAX: 318-688-7823
www.nhilc.org

Alan Loosley, President
Sharon Geddes, Vice-President
Clint Snell, Vice-President for Finance
A private, non-profit, non-residential, consumer-controlled, community based organization that enables people with disabilities to live independently.

4109 Resources for Independent Living: Baton Rouge
New Orleans Resources for Independent Living
3233 South Sherwood Forest Blvd.
Suite 101A
Baton Rouge, LA 70816
225-753-4772
877-505-2260
FAX: 225-753-4831
www.noril.org

Yavonka G. Archaga, Executive Director
Alisha S. Hammond, Assistant Director
Rosie Calvin, Program Manager
RIL provides quality services to individuals with disabilities to assist with living independent. RIL also offers services to inculde information and referral, advocacy, peer support and independent living skills training.

4110 Resources for Independent Living: Metairie
2001 21st Street Kenner
Kenner, LA 70062
504-522-1955
877-505-2260
FAX: 504-522-1954

Yavonka G. Archaga, Executive Director
Alisha S. Hammond, Assistant Director
Rosie Calvin, Program Manager
RIL provides quality services to individuals with disabilities to assist with living independently. RIL also offers an array of services to include information and referral, advocacy, peer support and independent living skills training.

4111 Southwest Louisiana Independence Center: Lake Charles
2016 Oak Park Boulevard
Lake Charles, LA 70601-5391
337-477-7198
888-403-1062
FAX: 337-477-7198
TTY: 337-477-7198
www.slic-la.org

SILC provides Information and Referral, Advocacy, Peer Counseling and other Independent Living Services, to develop community options for persons with significant disabilities in Southwest and Central Louisiana, and to assist them in achieving and maintaining self-sufficient, productive lives.

4112 Southwest Louisians Independence Center: Lafayette
850 Kaliste Saloom Rd
Suite 118
Lafayette, LA 70508-4230
337-269-0027
888-516-5009
FAX: 337-233-7660
www.slic-la.org

SLIC provides Information and Referral, Advocacy, Peer Counseling and other Independent Living Services, to develop community options for persons with significant disabilities in Southwest and South Central Louisiana, and to assist them in achieving and maintaining self-sufficient, productive lives. PCA provider services

4113 Volunteers of America of Greater New Orleans
4152 Canal St.
New Orleans, LA 70119
504-482-2130
FAX: 504-482-1922
voagno.org

Robert C. Rhoden, Chair
Wayne M. Baquet, Chair Elect
James M. Le Blanc, President/CEO
Volunteers of America Greater New Orleans offers many services that aim to improve the lives of children, youth, and families.

4114 **W Troy Cole Independent Living Specialist**
Ste H
1900 Lamy Ln
Monroe, LA 71201-9200   318-323-4374
Katherine Carnell, Manager

.

Maine

4115 **Alpha One: Bangar**
3300 Ponce de Leon Blvd.
Coral Gables, FL 33134   305-567-9888
                                               877-228-7321
                                          FAX: 305-567-1317
                                       info@alpha-1foundation.org
                                             www.alpha1.org

John W. Walsh, President & CEO, Co-founder
Marcia F. Ritchie, Vice President/ COO
Marsha A. Carnes, Director of Program Evaluation
Committed to being a leading enterprise providing the community with information, services and products that create opportunities for people with disabilities to live independently. Provides many services including adaptive and mobility equipment selection, peer support, advocacy, information and referral services, adapted drive evaluation and training, and consumer directed personal assistance.

4116 **Alpha One: South Portland**
127 Main St
South Portland, ME 04106-2647   207-767-2189
                                               800-640-7200
                                          FAX: 207-799-8346
                                          TTY: 207-767-5387
                                           www.alphaonenow.com

Dennis Stubbs, Chairman
Bob McPhee, Vice-Chairman
Darlene Stewart, Independent Living Specialist
Committed to being a leading enterprise providing the community with information, services and products that create opportunities for people with disabilities to live independently. Offers adaptive equipment loan program, independent living skills instruction, adapted driver evaluation and training, information and referral services, peer support, advocacy, access design consultation, and more.

4117 **Motivational Services**
71 Hospital Street
P.O.Box 229
Augusta, ME 04332-0229   207-626-3465
                                          FAX: 207-626-3469
                                          TTY:207-621-2542
                                           www.mocomaine.com

Connie Dunn, President
Grace Leonard, Vice President/Secretary
Faith Madore, Treasurer
Improving the lives of people with disabilities through housing, employment and community support.

4118 **Shalom House**
106 Gilman St
Portland, ME 04102-3034   207-874-1080
                                          FAX: 207-874-1077
                                          TTY:207-842-6888
                                    generalmail@shalomhouseinc.org
                                          shalomhouseinc.org

Megan Lewis, Human Resources Manager
Mary Haynes-Rodgers, Executive Director
Kristine Lausier, Quality Assurance Administrator
Offers hope for adults living with severe mental illness by providing a choice of quality housing and support services that help people lead stable and fulfilling lives in the community.

Maryland

4119 **Broadmead**
13801 York Rd
Cockeysville, MD 21030-1899   410-527-1900
                                               877-STA-HOME
                                             www.broadmead.org

Ann H. Heaton, Chair
John E. Howl, Chief Executive Officer
Patricia Gordon, Chief Financial Officer/Treasure
To provide continuing care services to a diverse group of seniors in a warm, congenial community founded and operated in the spirit of the Religious Society of Friends.

4120 **Eastern Shore Center for Independent Living**
309 Sunburst Highway
Suite 13
Cambridge, MD 21613-2050   410-221-7701
                                               800-705-7944
                                          FAX: 410-221-7714
                                          TTY: 410-221-4150
                                           www.autismspeaks.org

Liz Feld, President
Alec M. Elbert, Chief Strategy & Dev Officer
Jamitha Fields, VP, Community Affairs
ESCIL provides services to people with all disabilities regardless of age, religion, gender, ethnicity, race or national origin. In addition to the core services of information and referral, skills training, peer support and advocacy, ESCIL also offers assistance with accessibility modifications, Americans with Disabilities Act education and training, housing referrals and counseling, transportation referral and information, Brailling capabilities, Personal Attendent Services referral, and more.

4121 **Freedom Center**
14 W. Patrick Street
Suite 10
Frederick, MD 21701   301-846-7811
                                          FAX: 301-846-9070
                                    advocate@thefreedomcenter-md.org
                                          thefreedomcenter-md.org

Jamey George, Executive Director
Russell Holt, President
Patrick Mcmurtray, Vice-President
A walk in center for independent living, provides services and supports to empower individuals with disabilities to lead self-directed, independent, and productive lives in a barrier-free community.

4122 **Housing Unlimited**
Ste G1
1398 Lamberton Dr
Silver Spring, MD 20902-3435   301-592-9314
                                          FAX: 301-592-9318
                                    information@housingunlimited.org
                                          www.housingunlimited.org

Nancy Cohen, President Emerita
Russell Phillips, President
Robyn S. Raysor, Vice President
To address the housing crisis for adults with psychiatric disabilities who reside in Montgomery County, Maryland.

4123 **Independence Now**
12301 Old Columbia Pike
Suite 101
Silver Spring, MD 20904-1656   301-277-2839
                                          FAX: 301-625-9777
                                             info@innow.org
                                                innow.org

Robert Watson, President
Sarah Sorensen, Executive Director
Todd Thorpe, Director of Operations
A nonprofit organization created by people with disabilities and provides services that promote independence and the inclusion of people with disabilities in their communities.

4124 Independence Now: The Center for Independent Living
12301 Old Columbia Pike
Suite 101
Silver Spring, MD 20904
301-277-2839
FAX: 301-625-9777
info@innow.org
innow.org

Robert Watson, President
Sarah Sorensen, Executive Director
Todd Thorpe, Director of Operations
A nonprofit organization created by people with disabilities to provide services that promote independence and the inclusion of people with disabilities within their communities.

4125 Making Choices for Independent Living
Ste 202
1118 Light St
Baltimore, MD 21230-4152
410-234-8195
888-560-2221

Jimmie Joku Cooper, Owner
Provides services to help empower people with disabilities to lead self-directed, independent and productive lives in the community and protect their civil rights.OUTOF ORDER.

4126 Resources for Independence
30 N. Mechanic Street
Unit B
Cumberland, MD 21502-2705
301-784-1774
800-371-1986
FAX: 301-784-1776
www.rficil.org

Lori Magruder, Executive Director
John Michaels, Assistant Director
Robert Cannon, Benefits Counselor
Private, non-profit, consumer-controlled, community-based organization providing services and advocacy by and for persons with all type of disabilities. Their goal is to create opportunities for independence, and to assist individuals with disabilities to achieve their maximum level of independent functioning within their families and communities.

4127 Southern Maryland Center for LIFE
P.O.Box 657
Charlotte Hall, MD 20622-657
301-884-4498
FAX: 301-884-6099
www.somd.com

Marie Robinson, Executive Director
Carrie Lanthier, Administrative Assistant
A non-profit community based organization which provides services to disabled people who live or work in the tri-county area. Our mission is to empower people with disabilities to lead self-directed, independent, and productive lives in their community.

Massachusetts

4128 Adlib
215 North St
Pittsfield, MA 01201-4644
413-442-7047
800-232-7047
FAX: 413-443-4338
adlib@adlibcil.org
adlibcil.org

Linda Febles, President
Michael Hinkley, Vice President
Allison Bedard, Treasurer
Offers information and referral services, independent living skills training, peer counseling, individual and group advocacy services available to all people with disabilities. Access consultation provided to businesses, agencies and institutions in accordance to the Americans with Disabilities Act.

4129 Arc of Cape Cod
P.O.Box 428
171 Main Street
Hyannis, MA 02601-428
508-790-3667
FAX: 508-775-5233
info@arcofcapecod.org
www.arcofcapecod.org

Provides adults with developmental disabilities a full range of individual supports to assist them in becoming valued members of their community.

4130 Boston Center for Independent Living
5th Floor
60 Temple Place
Boston, MA 02111-1324
617-338-6665
FAX: 617-338-6661
TTY:617-338-6662
www.bostoncil.org

Sergio Goncalves, Chairman
Linda Landry, Vice Chairman
Stacey Zelbow, Treasurer
A frontline civil rights organization led by people with disabilities that advocates to eliminate discrimination, isolation and segregation by providing advocacy, information and referral, peer support, skills training, and PCA services in order to enhance the independence of people with disabilities.

4131 Cape Organization for Rights of the Disabled (CORD)
106 Bassett Ln.
Hyannis, MA 02601
508-775-8300
800-541-0282
FAX: 508-775-7022
TTY: 508-775-8300
cordinfo@cilcapecod.org
www.cilcapecod.org

Coreen Brinckerhoff, CEO & Chair
Mike Magnant, President & COO
Gretchen Arvanitopoulos, Vice President
The Cape Organization for the Rights of the Disabled is dedicated to advancing independence, productivity, and integration of people with disabilities into mainstream society. CORD is the Center for Independent Living (CIL) and is a member of the Aging and Disability Resources Consortium (ADRC) serving Cape Cod and the Islands.

4132 Center for Living & Working: Fitchburg
76 Summer Street
Suite 110
Fitchburg, MA 01420-5785
978-345-1568
TTY:978-345-1568
centerlwA@centerlw.org
www.centerlw.org

Cindy Purcell, Board President
Mary Ann Donovan, Treasurer
Ed Roth, Secretary
The Center for Living and Working is a non-profit Independent Living Center which takes its direction from persons with disabilities. The Center advocates to empower persons with disabilities to take active roles in their lives and in their community in which they live. Also provides comprehensive and innovative programs and services in order to maximize individual independence and opportunities.

4133 Center for Living & Working: Framingham
484 Main St
Suite 345
Worcester, MA 01608-1824
508-798-0350
FAX: 508-797-4015
TTY:508-755-1003
opsearch@centerlw.org
www.centerlw.org

Cindy Purcell, Board President
Mary Ann Donovan, Treasurer
Ed Roth, Secretary
The Center for Living and Working is a non-profit Independent Living Center which takes its direction from persons with disabilities. The Center advocates to empower persons with disabilities to take active roles in their lives and in their community in which they live. Also provides comprehensive and innovative programs and services in order to maximize individual independence and opportunities.

4134 **Center for Living & Working: Worcester**
484 Main St
Suite 345
Worcester, MA 01608-1824   508-798-0350
                                   FAX: 508-797-4015
                                   TTY:508-755-1003
                                   opsearch@centerlw.org
                                   www.centerlw.org

Cindy Purcell, Board President
Mary Ann Donovan, Treasurer
Ed Roth, Clerk/Secretary
The Center for Living and Working is a non-profit Independent Living Center which takes its direction from persons with disabilities. The Center advocates to empower persons with disabilities to take active roles in their lives and in their community in which they live. Also provides comprehensive and innovative programs and services in order to maximize individual independence and opportunities.

4135 **Developmental Evaluation and Adjustment Facilities**
215 Brighton Ave
Allston, MA 02134-2013   617-254-4041
                                 800-886-5195
                                 FAX: 617-254-7091
                                 info@deafinconline.org
                                 deafinconline.org

Sharon L. Applegate, Executive Director
Kelly Kim, President
John Sullivan, Treasurer
Encourages and empowers deaf, hard of hearing, deafblind and late-deafened individuals to lead independent and productive lives.

4136 **Independence Associates**
100 Laurel Street
1st Suite 122
East Bridgewater, MA 02301-4012   508-583-2166
                                          800-649-5568
                                          FAX: 508-583-2165
                                          info@iacil.org
                                          iacil.org

Mark Lewis, President
James Clark, Treasurer
Anita Ashdon, Secretary
Provides comprehensive services which will enhance the range of acceptable options available to the consumer and improve the quality of life of persons with disabilities; to work on behalf of the objective of the disablility rights and independent living movement.

4137 **Independent Living Center of Stavros: Greenfield**
55 Federal St
Greenfield, MA 01301-2546   413-774-3001
                                    www.stavros.org

Glenn Hartmann, President
Nancy Bazanchuk, Vice President
Donna M. Bliznak, Treasurer
Promoting independence and access in the communities for persons with disabilities and deaf people.

4138 **Independent Living Center of Stavros: Springfield**
210 Old Farm Road
Amherst, MA 01002-2704   413-256-0473
                                 800-804-1899
                                 FAX: 413-256-0190
                                 www.stavros.org

Glenn Hartmann, President
Nancy Bazanchuk, Vice President
Donna M. Bliznak, Treasurer
Promoting independence and access in the communities for persons with disabilities and deaf people.

4139 **Independent Living Center of the North Shore & Cape Ann**
27 Congress St
Suite 107
Salem, MA 01970-5577   978-741-0077
                               888-751-0077
                               FAX: 978-741-1133
                               ilcnsca.org

Mary Margaret Moore, Executive Director
Marion A Dawicki, President
Patricia Cox, Vice President
A service and advocacy center run by and for people with disabilities that supports the struggle of people who have all types of disabilities to live independently and participate fully in community life.

4140 **MetroWest Center for Independent Living**
280 Irving Street
Framingham, MA 01702-7306   508-875-7853
                                    FAX: 508-875-8359
                                    TTY:508-875-7853
                                    info@mwcil.org
                                    mwcil.org

Youcef J. Bellil, President
Michael Kennedy, Vice President
Edward J. Carr, Treasurer
To help individuals with disabilities become productive and contributing members of the community and to eliminate barriers within the community that impede this process.

4141 **Multi-Cultural Independent Living Center of Boston**
329 Centre Street
Jamaica Plain, MA 02130-1232   617-942-8060
                                       FAX: 617-942-8630
                                       TTY:617-288-2707
                                       info@milcb.org
                                       milcb.org

Derrick Dominique, Executive Director
Ana Ortiz, Director of Services
Eleanor Slaughter, Senior IL Advocate
Seeks to create opportunities for people with disabilities and their families in unserved/under-served populations and cultures who reside in Boston's inner city.

4142 **Northeast Independent Living Program**
20 Ballard Rd
Lawrence, MA 01843-1018   978-687-4288
                                  FAX: 978-689-4488
                                  TTY:978-687-4288
                                  help@nilp.org
                                  nilp.org

June Cowen, Executive Director
Nanette Goodwin, Assistant Director
Lisa DiGiuseppe, Director of Finance
A consumer controlled Independent Living Center providing Advocacy and Services to people with all disabilities in the greater Merrimack Valley who wish to live as independently as possible in the commuity.

4143 **Renaissance Clubhouse**
176 Walker St
2nd Floor
Lowell, MA 01854-3126   978-454-7944
                                FAX: 978-937-7867
                                renclub1@gmail.com

Elaine Walker, Executive Director
Pammy Sadoie, Assistant Director
Offers daily structure, assistance wtih jobs, retirement, and housing.

4144 **Southeast Center for Independent Living**
66 Troy Street
Suite 3
Fall River, MA 02720-3023   508-679-9210
                                    FAX: 508-677-2377
                                    TTY:508-679-9210
                                    scil@secil.org
                                    secil.org

Lisa M Pitta, Executive Director
Damase Cote, President
Paul Remy, Vice President

The Philosophy of Independent Living, maintains that individuals with disabilities have the right to choose services and make decisions for themselves. This belief is the foundation and guiding principle of all of SCIL's policies and operations. SCIL provides training, information and support to help consumers achieve individual goals, experience personal growth and participate fully in community life.

4145 **Student Independent Living Experience Massachusetts Hospital School**
560 Harrison Avenue
Suite 600
Boston, MA 02118-2447
617-338-6409
800-843-5879
TTY:800-328-3202
www.mass.gov

Offers young adults with disabilities an opportunity to participate in a group learning situation, where they will develop independent and transitional living skills through a residential or non-residential model.

Michigan

4146 **Ann Arbor Center for Independent Living**
3941 Research Park Drive
Ann Arbor, MI 48108-6852
734-971-0277
FAX: 734-971-0826
www.annarborcil.org

Carolyn Grawi, Executive Director
Chris Baty, Theater Coordinator
Bryan Wilkinson, Director of Operations and Sales
AACIL assists people with disabilities and their families in living full and productive lives. AACIL assures the equality of opportunity, full participation, independent living and economic self-sufficiency of people with disabilities in the community.

4147 **Arc Michigan**
1325 S Washington Ave
Lansing, MI 48910-1652
517-487-5426
800-292-7851
FAX: 517-487-0303
dhoyle@arcmi.org
arcmi.org

Donald Teegarden, President
Laurel Robb, Vice President
Dohn Hoyle, Executive Director
Exists to empower local chapters of The ARC to assure that citizens with developmental disabilities are valued and that they and their families can participate fully in and contribute to the life of their community.

4148 **Arc/Muskegon**
601 Terrace Street
Suite 101
Muskegon, MI 49440-2197
231-777-2006
FAX: 231-777-3507
info@arcmuskegon.org
www.arcmuskegon.org

Tim Michalski, President
Brenda McCarthy Wiener, Vice President
Margaret O'Toole, Executive Director
Offers information and referral, advocacy services and peer counseling.

4149 **Bad Axe: Blue Water Center for Independent Living**
614 N Port Crescent Street
P.O. Box 29
Bad Axe, MI 48413-1207
989-269-5421
810-987-9337
FAX: 989-269-5422
info@bwcil.org
www.bwcil.org

Karen Massaro-Mundt, President
Chuck Wanninger, Treasurer
Jim Whalen, Executive Director
A non-profit, consumer-based organization that advocates, informs and supports persons with disabilities in the community.

4150 **Bay Area Coalition for Independent Living**
Ste 17
701 S Elmwood Ave
Traverse City, MI 49684-3185
231-929-4865
FAX: 231-929-4896
steve@bacil.org

Steve Wade, Director

4151 **Capital Area Center for Independent Living**
2812 N. Martin Luther King Jr. Blvd
Lansing, MI 48906
517-999-2760
877-652-3777
FAX: 517-999-2767
TTY: 800-649-3777
www.cacil.org

Mark Pierce, Executive Director
Jeffrey Gass, Financial Manager
Justine Bond, Independent Living Specialist
CACIL provide training, mentoring, and referrals to help people with disabilities and their families live productive lives.

4152 **Caro: Blue Water Center for Independent Living**
1184 Cleaver Rd
Caro, MI 48723-1143
989-673-3678
810-987-9337
FAX: 989-673-3656
info@bwcil.org
www.bwcil.org

Karen Massaro-Mundt, President
Chuck Wanninger, Treasurer
Jim Whalen, Executive Director
A non-profit, consumer-based organization that advocates, informs and supports persons with disabilities in the community.

4153 **Center for Independent Living of Mid-Michigan**
3941 Research Park Drive
Ann Arbor, MI 48108-6832
734-971-0277
FAX: 734-971-0826
www.annarborcil.org

Carolyn Grawi, Executive Director
Chris Baty, Theater Coordinator
Bryan Wilkinson, Director of Operations and Sales
Comprised of over 51 percent of people with disabilities, and advocates for the rights of people with disabilities in the Mid-Michigan area. Call for information on disability issues or for assistance in obtaining services, within your community.

4154 **Community Connections of Southwest Michigan**
5671 N. Skeel Ave.
Suite 8
Oscoda, MI 48750
989-569-6001
800-578-4245
FAX: 269-925-7141

Kathy Ellis, Director
An advocacy organization that teaches and empowers people with disabilities to make choices about living life to the fullest, controlling and directing their own lives and asserting their rights and responsibilites within their Berrien County communities.

4155 **Cristo Rey Handicappers Program**
1717 N High St
Lansing, MI 48906-4529
517-372-4700
FAX: 517-372-8499
www.cristo-rey.org

Marlene M Berens, Manager
To care for the spiritual and social needs of individuals and families by offering services that encourage self-sufficiency and recognize the dignity of the human person.

4156 **Detroit Center for Independent Living**
1042 Griswold
Suite 2
Port Huron, MI 48060
810-987-9337
810-987-9337
FAX: 810-987-9548
info@bwcil.org
www.bwcil.org

Karen Massaro-Mundt, President
Chuck Wanninger, Treasurer
Jim Whalen, Executive Director

BWCIL is a consumer-based organization designed to serve persons with disabilities who have physical, psychiatric, sendory, cognitive, and multiple disabilities through the provision of advocacy, information and referral, service provision, and the promotion of needed services so to maximize the individual's optimal level of independence.

4157   Disability Advocates of Kent County
3600 Camelot Drive SE
Grand Rapids, MI 49546-8103   616-949-1100
                                        FAX: 616-949-7865
                                        contact@dakc.us
                                        disabilityadvocates.us

David Bulkowski, JD, Executive Director
Denise Borges, Employment Specialist
Jackson Botsford, Accessibility Specialist
Exists to advocate, assist, educate and inform on independent living options for persons with disabilities and to create a barrier-free society for all.

4158   Disability Connection
27 E. Clay Avenue
Muskegon, MI 49442   231-722-0088
                                        866-322-4501
                                    FAX: 231-722-0066
                                        dcilmi.org

John Wahlberg, President
Michael Hamm, Vice President
Tamera Collier, Executive Director
To advocate, educate, empower, and provide resources for persons with disabilities and promote accessible communities.

4159   Disability Network Southwest Michigan
517 E Crosstown Pkwy
Kalamazoo, MI 49001-2867   269-345-1516
                                    FAX: 269-345-0229
                                        info@dnswm.org
                                        www.dnswm.org

Cameron J. Lambe, Chair
Cheri Stoltzner, Vice Chair
Joel W Cooper, President
To educate and empower people with disabilities to create change intheir own lives, and to advocate for social change to create inclusive communities. As a center for independent living, they are part of the disability rights movement.

4160   Disability Network of Mid-Michigan
1705 S. Saginaw Road
Midland, MI 48640-6825   989-835-4041
                                        800-782-4160
                                    FAX: 989-835-8121
                                        dnmm.org

Tom Provoast, President
Dr. Barbara Gibson, Vice President
David Emmel, Executive Director
To promote and encourage independence for all people with disabilities.

4161   Disability Network of Oakland & Macomb
16645 15 Mile Rd
Clinton Township, MI 48035-2206   586-268-4160
                                        800-284-2457
                                    FAX: 586-285-9942
                                        info@dnom.org
                                        dnom.org

Andrew Maurer, Chairperson
Randy Charon, Vice Chairperson
Kellie Boyd, Executive Director
Commited to advancing personal choice, independence, and positive social change for persons with disabilities through advocacy, education and outreach.

4162   Disability Network/Lakeshore
426 Century Lane
Holland, MI 49423-2200   616-396-5326
                                        800-656-5245
                                    FAX: 616-396-3220
                                    TTY: 616-396-5326
                                        info@dnlakeshore.org
                                        dnlakeshore.org

Michelle Chaney, President
Amber Marcy, Vice President
Brian Dykhuis, Treasurer
A cross-disability, community-based organization providing advocacy, education, and information and referral to persons with disabilities in Ottawa and Allegan counties.

4163   Grand Traverse Area Community Living Management Corporation
935 Barlow St
Traverse City, MI 49686-4250   231-932-9030
                                        www.gtaclmc.org

Mary Jean Brick, Administrative Director
We are a training home for individuals with developmental disabilities over the age of 18

4164   Great Lakes/Macomb Rehabilitation Group
Apt 104
4 E Alexandrine St
Detroit, MI 48201-2032   313-832-3371
                                    FAX: 313-832-3850

Jeannie Meece-Brooks, Contact
Independent living center. .

4165   JARC
30301 Northwestern Hwy
Suite 100
Farmington Hills, MI 48334-3277   248-538-6611
                                        877-767-7781
                                    FAX: 248-538-6615
                                        jarc@jarc.org
                                        jarc.org

Ronald Applebaum, President
Richard A. Loewenstein, Chief Executive Officer
Randy P. Baxter, Chief Financial Officer
A nonprofit, nonsecretarian agency dedicated to enabling people with disabilities to live full, dignified lives in the community, and to providing support and advocacy for their families.

4166   Lapeer: Blue Water Center for Independent Living
392 West Nepessing Street
Lapeer, MI 48446-2192   810-664-9098
                                        810-987-9337
                                    FAX: 810-664-0937
                                        info@bwcil.org
                                        www.bwcil.org

Karen Massaro-Mundt, President
Chuck Wanninger, Treasurer
Jim Whalen, Executive Director
A non-profit, consumer-based organization that advocates, informs and supports persons with disabilities in the community.

4167   Livingston Center for Independent Living
3075 E Grand River Ave
Suite 108
Howell, MI 48843-6585   517-545-1741
                                    FAX: 517-548-1751
                                        www.virtualcil.net

Dan Durci, Director
Independent living skills training and empowerment training for persons with disabilities.

4168   Michigan Commission for the Blind: Independent Living Rehabilitation Program
235 S. Grand Ave.
P.O. Box 30037
Lansing, MI 48909-1254   989-758-1765
                                        800-292-4200
                                    FAX: 989-758-1405
                                        www.michigan.gov

Debbie Wilson, Manager
Patrick Cannon, Agency Director

Rehabilitation teaching, independent living skills for persons over 55 with severe vision loss.

4169 Michigan Commission for the Blind: Detroit
Ste 4-450
3038 W Grand Blvd
Detroit, MI 48202-6012

313-456-1646
FAX: 313-456-1645
mcnealg@michigan.gov

Gwen McNeal, Supervisor
Shawnese Laury-Johnson, Assistant East Region Manager
Promotes the inclusion of people with legal blindness into our communities on a full and equal basis through empowerment, education, participation, and choice.

4170 Monroe Center for Independent Living
1285 N Telegraph Rd
Monroe, MI 48162-3368

734-242-5919
mrawlings@aacil.org
monroecil.tripod.com

Linda Maier, Manager
To act as a catalyst for personal and social change through the empowerment of people with disabilities; and, to replace the perception of disability as tragic with a disability culture promoting pride, power and personal style.

4171 Port Huron: Blue Water Center for Independent Living
1042 Griswold St
Suite 2
Port Huron, MI 48060-5431

810-987-9337
810-987-9337
FAX: 810-987-9548
info@bwcil.org

Karen Massaro-Mundt, President
Chuck Wanninger, Treasurer
Jim Whalen, Executive Director
A non-profit, consumer-based organization that advocates, informs and supports persons with disabilities in the community.

4172 Sandusky: Blue Water Center for Independent Living
103 East Sanilac Road
Suite 3
Sandusky, MI 48471-1615

810-648-2555
810-987-9337
FAX: 810-648-2583
info@bwcil.org

Karen Massaro-Mundt, President
Chuck Wanninger, Treasurer
Jim Whalen, Executive Director
A non-profit, consumer-based organization that advocates, informs and supports persons with disabilities in the community.

4173 Southeastern Michigan Commission for the Blind
4450 Grandy St
Detroit, MI 48207

313-456-0334
877-932-6424
FAX: 313-456-1645
www.michigan.gov

Patrick Cannon, Executive Director
Pat Bragg, Manager
Vocational rehabilitation agency. Personal adjustment vocational assessment and training, job placement and follow-up services. .

4174 Superior Alliance for Independent Living(SAIL)
1200 Wright Street
Suite A
Marquette, MI 49855

906-228-5744
800-379-7245
FAX: 906-228-5573
TTY: 906-228-5744
www.upsail.com

Elgie Dow, President
Aaron Andres, Vice President
Amy Maes, Executive Director
Promotes the inclusion of people with disabilities into our communities on a full and equal basis through empowerment, education, participation and choice.

4175 disAbility Connections
409 Linden Ave
Jackson, MI 49203-4065

517-782-6054
FAX: 517-782-3118
www.disabilityconnect.org

Michael Jackson, President
James Gorse, Vice President
Lesia Pikaart, Executive Director
Supporting Jackson County residents in their efforts to lead independent, fulfilling, productive lives.

Minnesota

4176 Access North Center for Independent Living of Northeastern MN
1309 East 40th Street
Hibbing, MN 55746

218-262-6675
800-390-3681
FAX: 218-262-6677
info@accessnorth.net
www.accessnorth.net

Donald Brunette, Executive Director
Patty Baratto, Administrative Assistant
Assists individuals to live independently, pursue meaningful goals, and have equal opportunities and choices. Other offices are located in Duluth, Brainerd, Walker & Aitkin.

4177 Accessible Space, Inc.
2550 University Avenue West
Suite 330N
Saint Paul, MN 55114-1085

651-645-7271
800-466-7722
FAX: 651-645-0541
TTY: 800-627-3529
info@accessiblespace.org
www.accessiblespace.org

Mark E. Hamel, Esq., Chairman
Kay Knutson, Vice Chairman
Steve Schugel, Treasurer
Accessible, rent-subsidized apartments for very low-income adults with qualifying physical disabilities as well as seniors. Accessible Space, Inc., sponsors, develops and manages housing & ASI apartments are rent based on income and are located across the country.

4178 Courage Center
800 E. 28th St.
Minneapolis, MN 55407-4298

612-863-4200
866-880-3550
FAX: 763-520-0577
TTY: 763-520-0245
couragekenny@allina.com
www.allinahealth.org

Jan Malcolm, CEO
Alice Johnson, Chief Financial Officer
Stephen Bariteau, Chief Development Officer
A nonprofit rehabilitation and resource center that advances the lives of children and adults experiencing barriers to health and independence. Specialize in treating brain injury, spinal cord injury, stroke, chronic pain, autism and disabilities experienced since birth.

4179 Freedom Resource Center for Independent Living: Fergus Falls
125 W Lincoln Avenue
Suite 7
Fergus Falls, MN 56537-2152

218-998-1799
800-450-0459
FAX: 218-998-1798
freedom@freedomrc.org
www.freedomrc.org

Nate Aalgaard, Executive Director
Angie Bosch, Office Coordinator
Mark Mark Bourdon Bourdon, Program Director
Freedom Resource Center assists people in working towards goals they establish for themselves.

4180 Metropolitan Center for Independent Living
Ste 16
1600 University Ave W
Saint Paul, MN 55104-3825   651-646-8342
                                     FAX: 651-603-2006
                                     TTY:651-603-2001
                                homeramps@gmail.com
MCIL is dedicated to the full promotion of independent living
philosophy by supporting individuals with disabilities in their
personal efforts to pursue self-directed lives.

4181 Minnesota Association of Centers for Independent Living
215 North Benton Drive
Sauk Rapids, MN 56379   320-529-9000
                                          888-529-0743
                                     FAX: 320-529-0747
                            ilicil@independentlifestyles.org
                                 independentlifestyles.org

Cara Ruff, Executive Director
Jay Keller, Board Chairman
Pamela Kotzenmacher, Treasurer
A non-profit organization whose purpose is to advocate for the in-
dependent living needs of people with disabilities who are citi-
zens of the State of Minnesota

4182 OPTIONS
Ste B
123 S Main St
Crookston, MN 56716-1970   218-281-5722
                                     FAX: 218-281-5722
                                     TTY:218-281-5722
Gordie Haug, Manager
Provides people with disabilities advocacy, information, skills
training and peer mentoring relationships to help them achieve
their personal goals of how and where they live their lives.

4183 Options Interstate Resource Center for Independent Living
2200 2nd Street SW
Rochester, MN 55902-1887   507-285-1815
                                          800-726-3692
                                     FAX: 218-773-7119
                                     TTY: 218-773-6100
                                 options@myoptions.info
                                        www.macil.org
Vicki Dalle Molle, President
Randy Sorensen, Executive Director
Located in Minnesota, but also serves North Dakota.

4184 Perry River Home Care
330 High Way Pen S
Saint Cloud, MN 56304   320-255-1882
                                     FAX: 320-255-5137
Berna Florentine, CEO
Ken Figge, President
Courtney Salzi, Administrator
Offers skilled nursing services RN, LPN, TV Therapy, Pediatrics,
Rehabilitation Services, PT, OT, ST, Paraprofessional staff,
Home Health Aides, Homemakers, Personal Care Attendents,
Companions, Live-ins, Sleep overs, Respite care, Extended
hours.

4185 SMILES
820 Winnebago Ave
Suite 1
Fairmont, MN 56031-3619   507-345-7139
                                          888-676-6498
                                     FAX: 507-235-3488
                                        www.smilescil.org
Brain Koch, President
Doug Robinson, Vice President
Alan Augustin, Executive Director
A nonprofit organization committed to providing a wide array of
services that assist individuals with disabilities that live inde-
pendently, pursue meaningful goals, and enjoy the same opportu-
nities and choices as all persons.

4186 SMILES: Mankato
709 S. Front Street
Suite 7
Mankato, MN 56001-3887   507-345-7139
                                          888-676-6498
                                     FAX: 507-345-8429
                                smiles@smilescil.org
                                        smilescil.org
Brain Koch, President
Doug Robinson, Vice President
Alan Augustin, Executive Director
A nonprofit organization committed to providing a wide array of
services that assist individuals with disabilities that live inde-
pendently, pursue meaningful goals, and enjoy the same
oportunities and choices as all persons.

4187 Southeastern Minnesota Center for Independent Living: Red Wing
2200 2nd Street SW
Rochester, MN 55902   507-285-1815
                                          888-460-1815
                                     FAX: 507-288-8070
                                semcil@semcil.org
                                        www.semcil.org
Brian Koch, President
Doug Robinson, Vice President
Alan Augustin, Executive Director
Non profit organization that assists people with disabilities to be-
come independent and productive community members.

4188 Southeastern Minnesota Center for Independent Living: Rochester
2200 Second Street SW
Rochester, MN 55902-3980   507-285-1815
                                          888-460-1815
                                     FAX: 507-288-8070
                                semcil@semcil.org
                                        www.semcil.org
Brain Koch, President
Doug Robinson, Vice President
Alan Augustin, Executive Director
A non profit organization that assists people with disabilities to
become independent and productive community members.

4189 Southwestern Center for Independent Living
2864 S Nettleton Ave
Suite 700
Springfield, MO 65807   417-886-1188
                                          800-676-7245
                                     FAX: 417-886-3619
                                     TTY: 417-886-1188
                                scil@swcil.org
                                        www.swcil.org
Randy Custer, Board President
Emilio Vela, CEO
Shannon Porter, Deputy Director
SWCIL is a private, non-profit community-based organization
providing independent living services to assist people with disabilities in obtaining and maintaining the greatest control over
their lives. Services are available in southwestern Minnesota to
persons of all ages, with any disability. Services include community access, education & outreach, mental health counseling,
youth services, transition services and more.

4190 Vinland Center Lake Independence
3675 Ihduhapi Road
Loretto, MN 55357-308   763-479-3555
                                          866-956-7612
                                     FAX: 763-479-2605
                                vinland@vinlandcenter.org
                                        www.vinlandcenter.org
Gerald Seck, President
Mary Roehl, Executive Director
Colleen Larson, Operations Manager
A Minnesota based rehabilitation center which offers services in
three distinct service areas: vocational rehabilitation; inclusive
community programs; and for people with cognitive disabilities,
specially adapted chemical dependency treatment.

Mississippi

4191   **Alpha Home Royal Maid Association for the Blind**
PO Drawer 30
Hazlehurst, MS 39083-30   601-894-1771
FAX: 601-894-2993

Howard Becker, Director
Offers attendant care registry, information on accessible housing and referrals.

4192   **Gulf Coast Independent Living Center**
18 JM Tatum Industrial Drive
Hattiesburg, MS 39401-8341   601-544-4860
FAX: 601-582-2544

Albert Holifield, Executive Director
Independent living center.

4193   **Jackson Independent Living Center**
1981 Hollywood Dr
Jackson, TN 38305-2131   731-668-2211
800-848-0298
FAX: 731-668-0406
TTY: 601-351-1585
information@jcil.tn.org
www.j-cil.com/contact-us.html

Denea Smith, Director
Timothy Jackson
Provides services to consumers with severe disabilities.

4194   **LIFE of Mississippi**
1304 Vine St
Jackson, MS 39202-3429   601-969-4009
800-748-9398
FAX: 601-969-1662
TTY: 800-748-9398
www.lifeofms.com

Augusta Smith, Executive Director
Margie Moore, Project Coordinator
Densie Smith, Assistant
To empower people wit significant disabilities to be as independent and as fully involved in their communities as they can and want to be.

4195   **LIFE of Mississippi: Biloxi**
2030 Pass Road
Suite C
Biloxi, MS 39531   228-388-2401
FAX: 228-338-2413
www.lifeofms.com

Augusta Smith, Executive Director
Ruby Jackson, I.L. Specialist
Kim Allison, IL Specialist/ B2I
To empower people with significant disabilities to be as independent and as fully involved in their communities as they can and want to be.

4196   **LIFE of Mississippi: Greenwood**
502a W Park Ave
Greenwood, MS 38930-2906   662-453-9940
FAX: 662-453-9934
www.lifeofms.com

Augusta Smith, Executive Director
Pam Wraggs, I.L. Specialist
Ruth Elliott, IL Specialist Assistant
To empower people with significant disabilities to be as independent and as fully involved in their communities as they can and want to be.

4197   **LIFE of Mississippi: Hattiesburg**
710 Katie Ave
Hattiesburg, MS 39401-4377   601-583-2108
www.lifeofms.com

Augusta Smith, Executive Director
Margie Moore, Project Coordinator
Densie Smith, Assistant
To empower people with significant disabilities to be as independent and as fully involved in their communities as they can and want to be.

4198   **LIFE of Mississippi: McComb**
915-A S. Locust Street
McComb, MS 39648-4817   601-684-3079
www.lifeofms.com

Augusta Smith, Executive Director
Margie Moore, Project Coordinator
Densie Smith, Assistant
To empower people with significant disabilities to be as independent and as fully involved in their communities as they can and want to be.

4199   **LIFE of Mississippi: Meridian**
Ste 103a
2440 N Hills St
Meridian, MS 39305-2653   601-485-7999
www.lifeofms.com

Augusta Smith, Executive Director
Margie Moore, Project Coordinator
Densie Smith, Assistant
To empower people with significant disabilities to be as independent and as fully involved in their communities as they can and want to be.

4200   **LIFE of Mississippi: Oxford**
Ste 5
404 Galleria Dr
Oxford, MS 38655-4383   662-234-7010
www.lifeofms.com

Augusta Smith, Executive Director
Margie Moore, Project Coordinator
Densie Smith, Assistant
To empower people with significant disabilities to be as independent and as fully involved in their communities as they can and want to be.

4201   **LIFE of Mississippi: Tupelo**
1051 Cliff Gookin Blvd
Tupelo, MS 38801-6739   662-844-6633
FAX: 662-844-6803
www.lifeofms.com

Emily Word, Regional Coordinator
Ronnie Jernigan, I.L. Specialist/HOT
Wayne Lauderdale, I.L. Specialist
To empower people with significant disabilities to be as independent and as fully involved in their communities as they can and want to be.

Missouri

4202   **Access II Independent Living Center**
101 Industrial Parkway
Gallatin, MO 64640-1280   660-663-2423
888-663-2423
FAX: 660-663-2517
access@accessii.org
www.accessii.org

Heather Swymeler, Executive Director
Brandy Gannan, Program Manager
Amber Wells, Financial Director
The mission of Access II is to remove architectural and attitudinal barriers that limit the independence of persons with disabilities, promote a positive change in attitudes about disability and persons with disabilities, and encourage greater independence for persons with disabilities within our communities. As a Center for Independent Living, Access II is comitted to the provision of a full range of independent living services.

4203   **Bootheel Area Independent Living Services**
PO Box 326
Kennett, MO 63857-326   573-888-0002
888-449-0949
FAX: 573-888-0708
TTY:573-888-0002
tshaw@bails.org
www.bails.org

Tim Shaw, Executive Director
BAILS goal is to foster an open, barrier free society flor all people regardless of their disability. BAILS service area is predomi-

nantly rural and includes the Southeast Missouri counties of: Dunklin, New Madrid, Pemiscot and Stoddard.

4204 Coalition for Independence: Missouri Branch Office
6724 Troost Ave
Ste. 408
Kansas City, MO 66131   816-822-7432
                                    FAX: 816-363-3469
                                    TTY:913-321-5126
Clarenece Smith, Executive Director
Coalition For Independence (CFI) is to facilitate positive and responsible independence for all people with disabilities by acting as an advocate for individuals with disabilities, providing services, and promoting accessibility and acceptance.

4205 Delta Center for Independent Living
PO Box 550
Suite #107
St. Peters, MO 63376-5608   636-926-8761
                                    866-727-3245
                                    FAX: 636-447-0341
                                    info@dcil.org
                                    www.dcil.org
Jennifer Mueller-Sparrow, President
Don Whalen, Vice President
Otis Pitts, Secretary
A non profit corporation which assists people with significant disabilities who want to live more independently.

4206 Disability Resource Association
130 Brandon Wallace Way
Festus, MO 63028-1726   636-931-7696
                                    FAX: 636-931-4863
                                    TTY:636-937-9016
                        dra@disabilityresourceassociation.org
                        www.disabilityresourceassociation. org
Craig Henning, Executive Director
Nancy Pope, Assistant Director
Suzan Weller, Director/Resource Developer
Independent Living Cener.

4207 Easterseals Midwest
11933 Westline Industrial Dr.
St. Louis, MO 63146   800-200-2119
                                    info@esmw.org
                        www.easterseals.com/midwest
Wendy Sullivan, Chief Executive Officer
Jeff Arledge, Chief Financial Officer
Tom Barry, Chief Development Officer
Easterseals Midwest helps people with disabilities live and work with dignity in their communities. Programs include community living and independent supported living arrangement services, with support in the following areas: housing, health and safety, money management, nutrition, transportation, and more.

4208 Independent Living Center of Southeast Missouri
511 Cedar St
Poplar Bluff, MO 63901-7301   573-686-2333
                                    888-890-2333
                                    FAX: 573-686-0733
                                    TTY:573-776-1178
                                    info@ilcsemo.org
                                    www.ilcsemo.org
Bruce Lynch, Executive Director
Debbie Hardin, Independent Living Director
To make Southeast Missouri barrier free for all persons with disabilities, enabling them to live more independently, extending their rights to control and direct their own lives and empowering them to live more producitve lives.

4209 Midland Empire Resources for Independent Living (MERIL)
4420 South 40th St
Saint Joseph, MO 64503-2157   816-279-8558
                                    800-637-4548
                                    FAX: 816-279-1550
                                    TTY: 816-279-4943
                                    www.meril.org
Dr. Robert Bush, Chair
Jaren Pippitt, Vice Chair
Wayne Crawford, Secretary

Designed to promote independent living and to enhance the quality of life for persons with disabilities by empowering them to control and direct their lives.

4210 Northeast Independent Living Services
909 Broadway
Suite 350
Hannibal, MO 63401   573-221-8282
                                    877-713-7900
                                    FAX: 573-221-9445
                                    www.neilscenter.org
Rose McNally, President
Dawn Davis, Vice President
Brooke Kendrick, Executive Director
To empower persons with disabilities to live as full and productive members of society.

4211 On My Own
428 E Highland Ave
Nevada, MO 64772-2609   417-667-7007
                                    800-362-8852
                                    FAX: 417-667-6262
                                    www.omoinc.org
Jennifer Gundy, Executive Director
A non profit independent living center.

4212 Ozark Independent Living
109 Aid Ave
West Plains, MO 65775-3529   417-257-0038
                                    888-440-7500
                                    FAX: 417-257-2380
                                    TTY: 888-440-7500
                                    info@ozarkcil.com
                                    ozarkcil.com
Michael Conner, Vice Chair
Scott Schneider, Secretary/Treasurer
Cindy Moore, Executive Director
OIL was created to provide independent living services to persons with disabilities who reside in the following counties in Missouri: Oregon Ozark, Shannon, Wright, Howell, Texas, and Douglas. OIL is non-profit, on-residential supported by grants, donations, and volunteers

4213 Paraquad
5240 Oakland Ave
Saint Louis, MO 63110-1436   314-289-4200
                                    FAX: 314-289-4201
                                    TTY:314-289-4252
                                    contactus@paraquad.org
                                    www.paraquad.org
Robert Funk, Executive Director
Paraquad works to empower people with disabilities to increase their independence through choice and opportunity.

4214 Places for People
4130 Lindell Blvd
Saint Louis, MO 63108-2914   314-535-5600
                                    FAX: 314-535-6037
                                    www.placesforpeople.org
Kevin Kissling, President
Robin Kolker Adkins, Vice President
Joe Yancey, Executive Director
Places for People provides individualized, high quality and effective services to adults with serious and persistent mental disorders to assist them in living, working and socializing responsibility to serve those individuals who rely on public funding.

4215 RAIL
3024 Dupont Circle
Jefferson City, MO 65109   573-526-7039
                                    877-222-8963
                                    888-667-2117
                                    FAX: 573-751-1441
                                    mo.silc@vr.dese.mo.gov
                                    www.mosilc.org
Chris Camene, Chairperson
Jessica Hatfield, Vice-Chairperson
Barrnie Cooper, Secretary/Treasurer
RAIL is an Independent Living Center, one of twenty-two in the State of Missouri, RAIL's Mission is to assist persons with dis-

abilities to live as independently as they choose within the communities of their choice. RAIL offers four core services which are: Advocacy, Peer Support, Information & Referral, and Independent Living Skills Training. RAIL is a Consumer Services Directed Program vendor

4216   SEMO Alliance for Disability Independence
1913 Rusmar St
Cape Girardeau, MO 63701-7623   573-651-6464
                                      800-898-7234
                                      FAX: 573-651-6565
                                      TTY: 573-651-6464
                                      www.sadi.org

Timothy D. Woodard, President
Michelle Spooler, Vice-President
Leemon Priest, Secretary
A community based, non-profit, nonresidential center for independent living that is committed to providing services to persons with disabilities to enable them to remain in their own home and community, not an institution.

4217   Services for Independent Living
1401 Hathman Place
Columbia, MO 65201-5552   573-874-1646
                                      800-766-1968
                                      FAX: 573-874-3564
                                      TTY: 573-874-4121
                                      www.silcolumbia.org

Dan Dunham, President
Bonnie Gregg, Vice President
Amy Henderson, Treasurer
A non-residential, community-based center for independent living. Provides individualized and group services to persons with severe disabilities in the Mid-Missouri area; works to help people with disabilities achieve their highest potential in independent living and community life.

4218   Southwest Center for Independent Living (S CIL)
2864 S Nettleton Ave
Springfield, MO 65807-5970   417-886-3619
                                      800-676-7245
                                      FAX: 417-886-3619
                                      TTY: 417-886-1188
                                      scil@swcil.org
                                      www.swcil.org

Amy C. Lewis, President
Mark Grantham, Vice President
Gary Maddox, Chief Executive Officer
Provides services, advocacy, and resources for people with any disability in Christian, Dallas, Greene, Lawrence, Polk, Stone, Taney and Webster Counties of Southwest Missouri.

4219   Sunnyhill, Inc.
11140 So. Towne Square
Ste. 100
Saint Louis, MO 63123   314-845-3900
                                      www.sunnyhillinc.org
Donny Mitchell, Chief Operating Officer
Amy Wheeler, Vice President, Program Services
Luke Mraz, Director, Development & Community Partnerships
Services are provided to adults and children with developmental disabilities. Supported living arrangements are located in St. Louis city, St. Louis county and St. Charles County. Group home and camp services are located in Dittmer, MO. Travel program also available.

4220   Tri-County Center for Independent Living
1420 HWY 72 East
Rolla, MO 65401   573-368-5933
                                      FAX: 573-368-5991
                                      TTY:573-368-5933
                                      www.tricountycenter.com
Victoria Evans, Executive Director
Mission is to eliminate physical and attitudinal barriers through the power of advocacy, enlightenment, and reformation.

4221   West Central Independent Living Solutions
610 N Ridgeview Dr
Suite B
Warrensburg, MO 64093-9323   660-422-7883
                                      800-236-5175
                                      FAX: 660-422-7895
                                      TTY: 660-422-7894
                                      info@w-ils.org
                                      www.w-ils.org

David De Frain, President
James Piatt, Vice President
Kathy Kay, Executive Director
Works to empower people with disabilities to become more independent by providing independent living skills training, peer support, information and referral and advocacy. West Central Independent Living Solutions now has satellite offices in Sedalia, MO and Lexington.

4222   Whole Person, The
3710 Main Street
Kansas City, MO 64111-7501   816-225-0301
                                      800-878-3037
                                      FAX: 816-931-0529
                                      TTY: 816-561-0304
                                      info@thewholeperson.org
                                      www.thewholeperson.org

Rick O'Neal, President
Jim Atwater, Vice President
Julie Dejean, CEO
The Whole Person, assists people with disabilities to live independently and encourages change within the community to expand opportunities for independent living.

4223   Whole Person: Kansas City
3710 Main Street
Kansas City, MO 64111-7501   816-561-0304
                                      800-878-3037
                                      FAX: 816-931-0529
                                      TTY: 816-627-2202
                                      info@thewholeperson.org
                                      www.thewholeperson.org

Rick O'Neal, President
Jim Atwater, Vice President
Julie Dejean, CEO
Assists people with disabilities to live independently and encourages change within the community to expand opportunities for independent living.

Montana

4224   Living Independently for Today and Tomorrow
1201 Grand Avenue
Suite 1
Billings, MT 59102-2033   406-259-5181
                                      800-669-6319
                                      FAX: 406-259-5259
                                      TTY: 406-245-1225
                                      www.lifft.org

Bobbie Becker, Executive Director
Martha Carstensen, Program Director
LIFFT's Independent living program works with people with disabilities so they can live independently and have access to the community. LIFFT staff, most of whom have disabilities, serve as mentors to people as they work to achieve the goals they have set for themselves.

4225   Montana Independent Living Project, Inc.
825 Great Northern Blvd
Suite 105
Helena, MT 59601-4715   406-442-5755
                                      800-735-6457
                                      FAX: 406-442-1612
                                      TTY: 406-442-5755
                                      bmaffit@milp.us
                                      www.milp.us

Bob Maffit, Executive Director
Les Clark, Independent Living Specialist
Charlene White, Financial Manager

A not-for-profit agency that provides services that promote independence for people with disabilities.

4226 North Central Independent Living Services
1120 25th Ave
Black Eagle, MT 59414-1037
406-452-9834
800-823-6245
FAX: 406-453-3940

Tom Osborn, Executive Director
North Central Independent Living Services is located in Great Falls and provides services from Glacier County across the Hi-Line to the North Dakota border. A satellite office is set up in Glasgow.

4227 Summit Independent Living Center: Kalipsell
1203 Highway 2 W.
Suite #35
Kalispell, MT 59901-6020
406-257-0048
800-995-0029
FAX: 406-257-0634
TTY: 406-257-0048
webmaster@bils.org
www.summitilc.org

Steve Hackler, President
Larry Riley, Vice President
Jenny Montgomery, Secretary
To promote community awareness, equal access, and the independence of people with disabilities through advocacy, education, and the advancement of civil rights.

4228 Summit Independent Living Center: Hamilton
316 North 3rd St
Suite #113
Hamilton, MT 59840-2479
406-363-5242
800-398-9013
FAX: 406-375-9035
webmaster@bils.org
www.summitilc.org

Steve Hackler, President
Larry Riley, Vice President
Jenny Montgomery, Secretary
To promote community awareness, equal access, and the independence of people with disabilities through advocacy, education, and the advancement of civil rights.

4229 Summit Independent Living Center: Missoula
700 SW Higgins Ave
Suite #101
Missoula, MT 59803-1489
406-728-1630
800-398-9002
FAX: 406-829-3309
missoula@summitilc.org
www.summitilc.org

Steve Hackler, President
Larry Riley, Vice President
Jenny Montgomery, Secretary
To promote community awareness, equal access, and the independence of people with disabilities through advocacy, education, and the advancement of civil rights.

4230 Summit Independent Living Center: Ronan
124 Main St.
Ronan, MT 59864-2718
406-215-1604
866-230-6936
FAX: 406-552-1028
ronan@summitilc.org
www.summitilc.org

Steve Hackler, President
Larry Riley, Vice President
Jenny Montgomery, Secretary
To promote community awareness, equal access, and the independence of people with disabilities through advocacy, education, and the advancement of civil rights.

Nebraska

4231 Center for Independent Living of Central Nebraska
3335 West Capital Street
Grand Island, NE 68803-1730
308-382-9255
877-400-1004
FAX: 308-384-7832
TTY: 308-382-9255
jthomas@cilne.org
www.cilne.org

Joni Thomas, Executive Director
Irene Britt, Western Program Manager
Lesia Gracia, Independent Living Specialist
Offers independent living skills training, peer sharing, information and referral, housing counseling and referral, accessibility and barrier removal consultation including ADA training and technical assistance, driver education and training, assistive technology services including demonstration and equipment loan, and a free lending library of adapted toys and ability switches for children with severe disabilities. Serves all diabilities and all ages.

4232 League of Human Dignity: Lincoln
1701 P St
Lincoln, NE 68508-1799
402-441-7871
888-508-4758
FAX: 402-441-7650
TTY:402-441-7871
info@leagueofhumandignity.com
www.leagueofhumandignity.com

Mike Schafer, CEO
The mission of the League of Human Dignity is to actively promote the full integration of individuals with disabilities into society. To this end, we will advocate their needs and rights, and provide quality services to involve these persons in becoming and remaining independent citizens.

4233 League of Human Dignity: Norfolk
400 Elm Ave
Norfolk, NE 68701-4033
402-371-4475
800-843-5785
FAX: 402-371-4625
TTY: 402-371-4475
ninfo@leagueofhumandignity.com
leagueofhumandignity.com

Mike Shafer, CEO
Jean M. Kloppenborg, Norfolk CIL Director
The mission of the League of Human Dignity is to actively promote the full integration of individuals with disabilities into society. To this end, we will advocate their needs and rights, and provide quality services to involve these persons in becoming and remaining independent citizens.

4234 League of Human Dignity: Omaha
5513 Center St
Omaha, NE 68106-3001
402-595-1256
800-843-5784
FAX: 402-595-1410
oinfo@leagueofhumandignity.com
www.leagueofhumandignity.com

Mike Schafer, CEO
Bob Gomez, Executive Director
The mission of the League of Human Dignity is to actively promote the full integration of individuals with disabilities into society. To this end, we will advocate their needs and rights, and provide quality services to involve these persons in becoming and remaining independent citizens.

4235 Mosaic of Axtell Bethpage Village
1044 23rd Rd.
PO Box 67
Axtell, NE 68924
308-743-2401
FAX: 308-743-2659
www.mosaicinfo.org/axtell

Max Miller, Chairperson
James Zils, Vice Chairperson
Linda Timmons, President/ CEO
Provides services that respect the human dignity and rights of each person. An interdisciplinary team of family, staffmembers and professional consultatns support individuals served in devel-

oping personal goals and programs, helping them to fully partici-pate in Axtell's community life. Mosaic at Axtell offers residential and community services.

4236 Mosaic of Beatrice
722 S. 12th St.
PO Box 607
Beatrice, NE 68310-607   402-223-4066
                                     FAX: 402-223-4951
                                www.mosaicinfo.org/beatrice

Max Miller, Chairperson
James Zils, Vice Chairperson
Linda Timmons, President/ CEO
Provides individualized services, living options, work choices, spiritual nurture and advocacy to people with disabilities in more than 250 communities across 14 states and Great Britain through the work of 4,800 employees.

4237 Mosiac: York
220 W South 21st St
York, NE 68467-9316   402-362-2180
                                     FAX: 402-362-2961
                                       www.mosaicinfo.org

Max Miller, Chairperson
James Zils, Vice Chairperson
Linda Timmons, President/ CEO
Providing a wide array of services to assist individuals and fami-lies in achieving positive life goals. Services to persons with dis-abilities and other special needs include community living options, training and employment options, spiritual growth and development options, training and counseling support.

Nevada

4238 Carson City Center for Independent Living
900 Mallory Way
Carson City, NV 89701   775-841-2580
Sandra Coyle, Owner
Helps consumers continue to live independently in the commu-nity through a variety of individual and community services.

4239 Northern Nevada Center for Independent Living: Fallon
1919 Grimes St
Suite B
Fallon, NV 89406-3100   775-423-4900
                                           800-885-3712
                                     FAX: 775-423-1399
                                     TTY: 775-423-4900
                                    nncilf@cccomm.net
                                          www.nncil.org

Lisa Bonie, Executive Director
Hilda Velasco, Operations Manager
Joni Inglis, Independent Living Advocate
Independent Living Center.

4240 Rural Center for Independent Living
1895 E Long St
Carson City, NV 89706-3214   775-841-2580
                                     FAX: 775-841-2580
                                      ruralcil@yahoo.com

Dee Dee Foremaster, Executive Director
Advocacy, Benefit Assistance, social security assistance, peer support, housing information and home-less day drop-in center for individuals with disabilities.

4241 Southern Nevada Center for Independent Living: North Las Vegas
3100 E Lake Mead Blvd
North Las Vegas, NV 89030-7380   702-649-3822
                                           800-398-0760
                                     FAX: 702-649-5022
                                     TTY: 702-649-3822
                                     sncilnv@aol.com
                                          www.sncil.org

Connie Kratky, President
Elliot Yug, Vice - President
Pamela Rake, Secretary

SNCIL is committed to removing barriers preventing indpendent living by providing services designed to empower people with disabilities.

4242 Southern Nevada Center for Independent Living: Las Vegas
2950 S. Rainbow Blvd.
Suite 220
Las Vegas, NV 89146-5611   702-889-4216
                                           800-870-7003
                                     FAX: 702-889-4574
                                     TTY: 702-889-4216
                                     sncil2@aol.com
                                          www.sncil.org

Connie Kratky, President
Elliot Yug, Vice - President
Pamela Rake, Secretary
SNCIL is committed to removing barriers preventing Independ-ent Living by providing services designed to empower people with disabilities.

New Hampshire

4243 Granite State Independent Living Foundation
21 Chenell Drive
Concord, NH 3301-4079   603-228-9680
                                           800-826-3700
                                     FAX: 603-444-3128
                                     TTY: 603-228-9680
                                        info@gsil.org
                                           www.gsil.org

Ken Traum, Chair
Lorna D. Greer, Vice Chair
Clyde E. Terry, CEO
GSIL is a statewide non-profit that recognizes the fact that all of us will need some type of support in the course of the lives. GSIL offers tools and resources so that individuals can participate as fully as the choose in their lives, families and communities. Con-tact the Independent Living Foundation for referrals to living situations.

New Jersey

4244 Alliance Center for Independance
Alliance for Disabled in Action
629 Amboy Ave, First Floor
Edison, NJ 08837-3579   732-738-4388
                                     FAX: 732-738-4416
                                     TTY:732-738-9644
                                     adacil@adacil.org
                                          www.adacil.org

Colleen Roche, Chair
Bernard Zuckerman, Treasurer
Carole Tonks, Executive Director
Alliance for Disabled in Action is a private, not-for-profit center for independent living serving people in Middlesex, Somerset and Union Counties of New Jersey. ADA's mission is to support and promote choice, self-direction and independent living in the lives of people with disabilities, with the right of individuals to inclusion in the community as the primary goal.

4245 Camden City Independent Living Center
2600 Mount Ephraim Ave
Camden, NJ 8104-3236   856-966-0800
                                     FAX: 856-966-0832
                                     TTY:856-966-0830
                                     vedasmithccilc@aol.com
                                       www.camdencityilc.org

Bruce Smith, Chairperson
John Quann, Vice Chairperson
Tanya Brown, Treasurer
Provides services designed to empower people with disabilities. To provide services to individuals with significant disabilities. Services include information referral, advocacy, peer support, and independent living skills training. CCILC services individuals in Camden City

4246   Center for Independent Living: Long Branch
279 Broadway
Suite #201
Long Branch, NJ 7740-6940   732-571-4884
                                        FAX: 732-571-4003
                                        TTY:732-571-4878
                                        www.moceanscil.org

Jennifer Sterner, Vice Chair
Maureen Poling, Secretary
Stan Soden, Director IL Services
Offers peer support, disability education and personal assistant
services. Serving Monmouth and Ocean Counties with information and referrals, advocacy, peer support and independent living
instructions.

4247   Center for Independent Living: South Jersey
1150 Delsea Drive
Suite #1
Westville, NJ 8093-2251   856-853-6490
                                             800-413-3791
                                        FAX: 856-853-1466
                                        TTY: 856-853-7602

Hazel Lee-Briggs, Executive Director
Danuta Debicki, Program Manager
Terryama Davis, Independent Living Specialist
Dedicated to providing people with disabilities in Gloucester and
Camden counties the opportunity to actively participate in society, to provide freedom of choice, to work, to own a home, raise a
family and in general, to participate to the fullest extent in
day-to-day activities. The center provides information and referrals, advocacy, peer support, and independent living skills
training.

4248   DAWN Center for Independent Living
66 Ford Road
Suite 121
Denville, NJ 7834-1235   973-625-1940
                                             888-383-3296
                                        FAX: 973-625-1942
                                        TTY: 973-625-1932
                                        info@dawncil.org
                                        www.dawncil.org

Elizabeth Lehmann, President
Gabrielle Waldman, Vice President
Carmela Slivinski, Executive Director
DAWN is the Center for Independent Living serving Morris, Sussex and Warren counties. DAWN empowers people with disabilities to strive for equality and to take control of their own lives by
providing the tools that encourage independence and self-advocacy, promoting public awareness of the needs, desires and rights
to individuals living with disabilities, and offering community
activities that create new experiences and opportunities.

4249   Dial: Disabled Information Awareness & Living
2 Prospect Village Plaza
Floor 1
Clifton, NJ 7013-1918   973-470-8090
                                             866-277-1733
                                        FAX: 973-470-8171
                                        TTY: 973-470-2521
                                        info@dial-cil.org
                                        www.dial-cil.org

Cynthia DeSouza, President
Anthony Gianduso, Vice President
John Petix, Executive Director
Promotes the full inclusion of all people living with disabilities
into society and encourage the consumers and the community at
large to seek involvement in this self-governing organization to
the fullest extent.

4250   Disability Rights New Jersey
New Jersey Protection and Advocacy
210 S. Broad Street
Floor 3
Trenton, NJ 08608-2407   609-292-9742
                                             800-922-7233
                                        FAX: 609-777-0187
                                        TTY: 609-633-7106
                                        advocate@drnj.org
                                        www.drnj.org

Walter Anthony Woodberry, Chair
Andrew McGeady, Vice Chair
Linda K. Soley, Treasurer
Assistive Technology Advocacy Center provides assistance to
personswith disabilities in helping them to obtain assistive tech-
nology devices and/or services.

4251   Family Resource Associates
35 Haddon Ave
Shrewsbury, NJ 7702-4007   732-747-5310
                                        FAX: 732-747-1896
                                        info@frainc.org
                                        www.frainc.org

Allan Proske, President
Bill Sheeser, Vice President
John Feeney, Treasurer
FRA is dedicated to helping children, adolescents and people of
all ages with disabilities to reach their fullest potential. FRA also
connects individuals to independence through modern therapies
and advanced technology. FRA provides direct services to those
in the greater Nonmouth/Ocean County area.

4252   Heightened Independence and Progress: Hackensack
131 Main St
Suite #120
Hackensack, NJ 7601-7182   201-996-9100
                                        FAX: 201-996-9422
                                        TTY:201-966-9424
                                        www.hipcil.org

Eileen Goff, President/CEO
Trish Carney, Finance and Development Director
Empowers people with disabilities to achieve independent living
through outreach, advocacy and education.

4253   Heightened Independence and Progress: Jersey City
35 Journal Square
Suite #703
Jersey City, NJ 7306-4105   201-533-4407
                                        FAX: 201-533-4421
                                        TTY:201-533-4409
                                        www.hipcil.org

Jean Csaposs, Board Chair
Lottie Esteban, First Vice Chair
Eileen Goff, President/CEO
Empowering People with Disabilities to Achieve Independent
Living through Outreach, Advocacy, and Education.

4254   Progressive Center for Independent Living
3525Quakerbridge Rd.
Suite 904
Hamilton, NJ 8619-3710   609-581-4500
                                             877-917-4500
                                        FAX: 609-581-4555
                                        TTY: 609-581-4550
                                        info@pcil.org
                                        www.pcil.org

Norman Smith, President
John Witman, Vice President
Scott Elliott, Executive Director
Advocates for the rights of people with disabilities to achieve and
maintain independent lifestyles. The Center has programs to assist with employment, transition from school to adult life, and
emergency preparedness.

4255 Progressive Center for Independent Living: Flemington
4 Walter E Foran Blvd
Suite 410
Flemington, NJ 8822-4669   908-782-1055
                                 877-376-9174
                                 FAX: 908-782-6025
                                 TTY: 908-782-1081
                                 info@pcil.org
                                 pcil.org

Norman Smith, President
John Witman, Vice President
Scott Elliott, Executive Director
Advocates for the rights of people with disabilities to achieve and
maintain independent lifestyles.

4256 Project Freedom
223 Hutchinson Rd
Robbinsville, NJ 8691-3457   609-448-2998
                                 FAX: 609-448-7293
                                 ProjectFreedom1@aol.com
                                 www.projectfreedom.org

Tim Doherty, Executive Director
Norman A. Smith, Assoc Ex Director
Elizabeth Maxwell, Office Manager
Dedicated to developing, supporting, and advocating opportuni-
ties for independent living persons with disabilities.

4257 Project Freedom: Hamilton
715 Kuser Rd
Hamilton, NJ 8619-3924   609-588-9919
                                 FAX: 609-588-8831
                                 cfunk@projectfreedom.org
                                 www.projectfreedom.org

Cecilia Funk, Social Service Coordinator
Judy Wilkinson, Office Manager
Paul Campanella, Property Manager
Dedicated to developing, supporting, and advocating opportuni-
ties for independent living persons with disabilities.

4258 Project Freedom: Lawrence
1 Freedom Blvd
Lawrence, NJ 8648-4531   609-278-0075
                                 FAX: 609-278-1250
                                 jelsowiny@projectfreedom.org
                                 www.projectfreedom.org

Jacklene Elsowiny, Social Serv Coordinator
Tim Doherty, Executive Director
Stephen Schaefer, CFO
Dedicated to developing, supporting, and advocating opportuni-
ties for independent living persons with disabilities.

4259 Total Living Center
6712 Washington Ave
Egg Harbor Township, NJ 8234-1999   609-645-9547
                                     FAX: 609-813-2318
                                     TTY:609-645-9593

Jo Hudson, President
Cliff Anderson, Vice President
Cathy Shaner, Secretary
Total Living Center is a non-profit organization whose mission is
to empower individuals with significant disabilities to maximize
their potential for independence and productivity, to live as fully
as possible within the community, taking responsibility for themselves, and sharing this commitment with others.

New Mexico

4260 Ability Center
715 E Idaho Ave.
Suite 3E
Las Cruces, NM 88001   575-526-5016
                                 800-376-4372
                                 FAX: 575-526-1202
                                 TTY: 575-210-5272
                                 freedom@theabilitycenter.org
                                 www.theabilitycenter.org
The Ability Center is a private, nonresidential, nonprofit, New
Mexico corporation. As a center for independent living (CIL)

TACIL provides a variety of support services for individuals with
disabilities.

4261 CASA Inc.
116 West Baltimore Street
Hagerstown, MD 21740   301-739-4990
                                 FAX: 301-790-0064
                                 casa4@myactv.net
                                 www.casaabq.com

Sherry Donovan, President
Linda Davis, Vice-President
Melinda Marsden, Treasurer
Offers peer counseling and information and referral services.

4262 CHOICES Center for Independent Living
200 E 4th St.
Suite #200
Roswell, NM 88201-6237   575-627-6727
                                 800-387-4572
                                 FAX: 575-627-6754
                                 TTY: 505-627-6727

Julia Calvert, Executive Director
Offers many core services including independent living skills
training, peer support, information and referral, advocacy and
transition.

4263 New Mexico Technology Assistance Program
625 Silver Ave SW
Ste. 100 B
Albuquerque, NM 87102   505-841-4464
                                 877-696-1470
                                 FAX: 505-841-4467
                                 Tracy.Agiovlasitis@state.nm.us
                                 www.tap.gcd.state.nm.us

Tracy Agiovlasitis, Program Manager
Examines and works to eliminate barriers to obtaining assistive
technology in New Mexico. Has established a statewide program
for coordinating assistive technology services; is designed to assist people with disabilities to locate, secure, and maintain
assistive technology.

4264 New Vistas
1205 Parkway Dr.
Suite A
Santa Fe, NM 87501-2483   505-471-1001
                                 FAX: 505-471-4427
                                 info@newvistas.org
                                 www.newvistas.org

Victor Ortega, President
Libby Gonzales, Vice-President
Gay Romero, Secretary/Treasurer
Partners with and supports people with disabilities and families
of children with special needs to enrich their quality of life in
New Mexico.

4265 San Juan Center for Independence
1204 San Juan Blvd
Farmington, NM 87401   505-566-5827
                                 877-484-4500
                                 FAX: 505-566-5842
                                 TTY: 505-566-5827
                                 sjci@sjci.org
                                 www.sjci.org

Patricia Ziegler, Executive Director
Tim Carver, CFO
SJCI is a New Mexico private non residential, nonprofit corporation that serves people with disabilities. The purpose of SJCI is to
provide a variety of community based, consumer driven service
to people with disablities to promote independence, self-resi-
dence and intergration into the community.

New York

4266   AIM Independent Living Center: Corning
271 E 1st St
Corning, NY 14830-2924
607-962-8225
FAX: 607-937-5125
TTY:607-962-8225
troche@aimcil.com
www.aimcil.com

Rene Snyder, Executive Director
Sabrina Mineo-O'Connell, President
George Spisack, Vice President
AIM is a non-profit organization dedicated to people with disabilities, their families, friends, the businesses that serve them and those with an interest in disabilities. The mission of AIM is to support the individuals ability to make independent, self-directing choices through education, advocacy, information and referral.

4267   AIM Independent Living Center: Elmira
650 Baldwin St.
Elmira, NY 14901-2216
607-733-3718
FAX: 607-733-0180
TTY:607-733-7764
troche@aimcil.com
www.aimcil.com

Rene Snyder, Executive Director
Sabrina Mineo-O'Connell, President
George Spisack, Vice President
AIM's goal is to enable the consumer to live an independent and comfortable lifestyle in the security of their home environment so they may feel dignity and pride in their achievements while controling their own care.

4268   ARISE
635 James St
Syracuse, NY 13203-2661
315-472-3171
FAX: 315-472-9252
TTY:315-479-6363
info@ariseinc.org
www.ariseinc.org

Tania Anderson, President
Sue Judge, Vice President
Michael Cook, Treasurer
Founded in 1979, ARISE's mission is to work with people of all abilities to create a fair and just community in which everyone can fully participate. As a center for independent living, ARISE is a non-profit organization run by and for individuals with disabilities. ARISE serves over 3,000 children and adults with disabilities each year through our programs and services in several broad areas including advocacy, employment, independent living/integrated recreation programs, and much more.

4269   ARISE: Oneida
131 Main St
Suite #107
Oneida, NY 13421-1644
315-363-4672
FAX: 315-363-4675
TTY:315-363-2364
info@ariseinc.org
www.ariseinc.org

Tania Anderson, President
Sue Judge, Vice President
Michael Cook, Treasurer
A consumer controlled, non-profit Independent Living Center that promotes the full inclusion of people with disabilities in the community.

4270   ARISE: Oswego
9 Fourth Avenue
Oswego, NY 13126-1803
315-342-4088
FAX: 315-342-4107
TTY:315-342-8696
info@ariseinc.org
www.ariseinc.org

Tania Anderson, President
Sue Judge, Vice President
Michael Cook, Treasurer

A consumer controlled, non-profit Independent Living Center that promotes the full inclusion of people with disabilities in the community.

4271   ARISE: Pulaski
2 Broad St
Pulaski, NY 13142-4446
315-298-5726
FAX: 315-298-5729
info@ariseinc.org
www.ariseinc.org

Tania Anderson, President
Sue Judge, Vice President
Michael Cook, Treasurer
A consumer controlled, non-profit Independent Living Center that promotes the full inclusion of people with disabilities in the community.

4272   Access to Independence of Cortland County, Inc.
26 N Main St
Cortland, NY 13045-2198
607-753-7363
FAX: 607-756-4884
info@aticortland.org
www.aticortland.org

Judy Bentley, Chair
Peter Morse-Ackley, Vice Chair
Chad W. Underwood, CEO
Access to Independence is Cortland County's foremost disability resource. It empowers people to lead independent lives in their community and strives to open doors to full participation and access for all.

4273   Action Toward Independence: Middletown
130 Dolson Avenue
Suite 35
Middletown, NY 10940-6563
845-343-4284
FAX: 845-342-5269

Stephen McLaughlin, Executive Director
Joann Hargabus, Services Director, Orange Cnty.
Gilles Malkine, Services Director, Sullivan Cnty
Independent living center that serves Orange & Sullivan counties. Provides programs and services to individuals who have disabilities and to their families. These services include peer counseling, individual & systems advocacy, independent living, skills training, information and referral, benefits advisement, recreation and a drop in center. We are designed to enable people with disabilities to achieve independence, inclusion and participation in their communities.

4274   Action Toward Independence: Monticello
309 E Broadway
Suite A
Monticello, NY 12701-8810
845-794-4228
FAX: 845-794-4475
TTY:845-794-4228
www.atitoday.org

Steve McLaughlin, Executive Director
Joann Hargabus, Director of Services
A not-for-profit, non residential, peer run, referral and advocacy agency for persons with disaiblities in Orange and Sullivan counties. Our services are aimed at promoting accessibility, community integration, and equal opportunity in all aspects of society for persons with all types of disabilities.

4275   BRiDGES
873 Route 45
Suite 108
New City, NY 10956
845-624-1366
FAX: 845-624-1369
info@bridgesrc.org
www.bridgesrc.org

Patricia Ranieri, President
David Jacobsen, Ph.D, Psy.D, Executive Director
Michael Coleman, Director of Finance & Controller
BRiDGES is a community-based non-profit organization that serves people with disabilities. Services provided by them include personal assistance self-employers, independent living services, volunteer opportunities, advocacy and more.

4276 Bronx Independent Living Services
4419 Thrid Avenue
Suite 2C
Bronx, NY 10457

718-515-2800
FAX: 718-515-2844
TTY:718-515-2803
webmaster@bils.org
www.bils.org

Barbara Linn, President
Anita Richichi, Vice President
Sheldon Mann, Treasurer
BILS is a not-for-profit community agency serving people with all kinds of disabilities. The mission is to empower people with disabilities toward living independent lives. BILS assists individuals by providing advocacy, peer counseling, housing information, and independent living training/counseling.

4277 Brooklyn Center for Independence of the Disabled
27 Smith Street
Suite #200
Brooklyn, NY 11201

718-998-3000
FAX: 718-998-3743
TTY:718-998-7406
advocate@bcid.org
www.bcid.org

Joan Peters, Executive Director
Sandrina Kingston, Program Director
Princess Davis, Office Manager
Operated by a majority of people with disabilities, BCID is dedicated to guaranteeing the civil rights of people with disabilities. BCID exists to improve the quality of life of brooklyn residents with disabilities thgouh programs that empower them to gain greater control of their lives and achieve full and equal integration into society.

4278 Capital District Center for Independence
845 Central Ave
South 3
Albany, NY 12206-1342

518-459-6422
FAX: 518-459-7847
TTY:518-459-6422
info@cdciweb.com
www.cdciweb.com

Laurel Kelley, Executive Director
Dawn Werner, Deputy Director
Judy Zuchero, Program Director
One of 37 Independent Living Centers in New York State, the Center is a non-residential, community based organization, which primarily serves Albany and Schenetady Counties. The Center's mission is to assist people with disabilities to acquire self-advocacy skills and by teaching through example, consumers achieve greater control over the direction of their lives.

4279 Catskill Center for Independence
6104 State Highway 23
Oneonta, NY 13820

607-432-8000
FAX: 607-432-6907
TTY:607-432-8000
ccfi@ccfi.us
www.ccfi.us

Chris Zachmeyer, Executive Director
Christine Worden, Assistant Director
One of 37 community-based independent living centers located throughout the state of New York. As an advocacy agency, we provide a vareity of services to people with disabilities, their friends and family members. In addition, we provide advocacy, training, and technical assistance to our community members, organizations, businesses and state and local governments in a variety of disability related areas. Serves Otsego, Delaware and Schoharie counties.

4280 Center for Community Alternatives
115 E Jefferson St
Suite #300
Syracuse, NY 13202-2018

315-422-5638
FAX: 315-471-4924
cca@communityalternatives.org
www.communityalternatives.org

Kwame Johnson, President
Susan R. Horn, Esq., Vice-President
Carole A. Eady, Secretary
Promotes reintegrative justice and a reduced reliance on incarceration through advocacy, services and public policy development in pursuit of civil and human rights.

4281 Center for Independence of the Disabled of New York
841 Broadway
Suite 301
New York, NY 10003-4708

212-674-2300
FAX: 212-254-5953
TTY:212-674-5619
info@cidny.org
www.cidny.org

Martin Eichel, President
Anne M. Davis, Vice President
John O'Neill, Vice President
To ensure full integration, independence and equal opportunity for all people with disabilities by removing barriers to the social, economic, cultural and civic life of the community.

4282 Center for Independence of the Disabled of New York
841 Broadway
Suite 301
New York, NY 10003-4708

212-674-2300
FAX: 212-254-5953
TTY:212-674-5619
info@cidny.org
www.cidny.org

Martin Eichel, President
Anne M. Davis, Vice President
John O'Neill, Vice President
To ensure full integration, independence and equal opportunity for all people with disabilities by removing barriers to the social, economic, cultural and civic life of the community.

4283 DD Center/St Lukes: Roosevelt Hospital Center
St Lukes Roosevelt
1000 10th Ave
New York, NY 10019-1192

212-473-2045
FAX: 212-473-0501

Charles Raimondo, VP
Farooq Chaudry, MD
Independent living center that advocates for people with disabilities by assisting with the application process of housing, benefits, etc.

4284 Finger Lakes Independence Center
215 5th St
Ithaca, NY 14850-3403

607-272-2433
FAX: 607-272-0902
TTY:607-272-2433
flic@clarityconnect.com
www.fliconline.org

Lenore Schwager, Executive Director
FLIC assists all people with disabilities, their families and friends to promote independence and make informed decisions in pursuit of their goals. The servides provided are free of charge, and services are primarily served to residents of Tompkins, Schyler counties.

4285 Harlem Independent Living Center
289 St. Nicholas Avenue
Suite #21
New York, NY 10027- 4805

212-222-7122
800-673-2371
FAX: 212-222-7199
harlemilc@aol.com
www.hilc.org

Christina Curry, Executive Director
Edward Randolph, Resource Specialist
Dr. Herbert Thornhill, Emeritus
A non-profit agency that advocates for people with disabilities by assisting with the application process of housing, benefits, etc. Our services are free of charge.
Monthly

4286 Independent Living
5 Washington Terrace
Newburgh, NY 12550
845-565-1162
FAX: 845-565-0567
TTY: 845-565-0337
info@myindependentliving.org
www.myindependentliving.org

Doug J Hovey, President & CEO
Shannon Zawiski, Chief Operating Officer
Emily Robisch, Chief Financial Officer
A non-profit agency run by people with disabilities for others
with disabilities. The agency offers programs and services to enhance quality of life, including benefits advising, personal assistance services, advocacy, employment and mental health
services, recovery center, supportive housing and more.

4287 Long Island Center for Independent Living
3601 Hempstead Tpke
Suites 208 & 500
Levittown, NY 11756-1331
516-796-0144
FAX: 516-520-1247
TTY: 516-796-0135
licil@aol.com
www.licil.net

Joan Lynch, Executive Director
LICIL is committed to the empowerment of consumers with disabilities. LICIL staff functions as ambassadors to the belief that
individuals with disabilities have a responsibility to take an active role in their own lives and self determined view of their
futures.

4288 Massena Independent Living Center
156 Center St.
Massena, NY 13662-1495
315-764-9442
877-397-9613
FAX: 315-764-9464
mindepli@twcny.rr.com
www.milcinc.org

Jeff Reifensnyder, Executive Director
Provides a variety of non-residential direct services as well as educating the public through community awareness campaigns.
Also seeks to address the current appropriate unmet needs of persons experiencing a disability.

4289 NYS Independent Living Council
111 Washington Ave
Suite #101
Albany, NY 12210-2280
518-427-1060
877-397-4126
FAX: 518-427-1139
bradw@nysilc.org
www.nysilc.org

Brad Williams, Executive Director
Patty Black, Administrative Assistant
Provides support and technical assistance to 37 independent living centers-community-based organizations directed by and for
people with disabilities.

4290 Nassau County Office for the Physically Challenged
60 Charles Lindberg Blvd
Uniondale, NY 11553-4812
516-227-7399
www.nassaucountyny.gov

Edward P. Mangano, County Executive
This agency serves as the ADA compliance coordinating office
for all Nassau County governmental facilities, programs and services. It also serves in an advisory capacity to local, regional and
national policy-making organizations, planning committees and
legislative bodies and conducts advocacy as well as direct programs and services to enhance inclusion by people with disabilities to employment, consumerism and transportation.

4291 North Country Center for Independent Living
80 Sharron Avenue
Plattsburgh, NY 12901-3827
518-563-9058
FAX: 518-563-0292
TTY: 518-563-9058
andrew@ncci-online.com
www.ncci-online.com

Ted Graser, President
Kathy Latinville, Vice President
Robert Poulin, Executive Director

To empower people with disabilities to live more independent
and productive lives, and to promote beneficial policies and community understanding of disability issues.

4292 Northern Regional Center for Independent Living: Watertown
210 Court St
Suite #107
Watertown, NY 13601-4546
315-785-8703
800-585-8703
FAX: 315-785-8612
TTY: 315-785-8704
nrcil@nrcil.net
www.nrcil.net

Ronald Griffin, Chair
Michael Simmons, Vice Chair
Melanie Adkins, Secretary
A disability rights and resource center that promotes community
efforts to end discrimination, segregation, and prejudice against
people with disabilities.

4293 Northern Regional Center for Independent Living: Lowville
7632 N State St
Lowville, NY 13367-1318
315-376-8696
FAX: 315-376-3404
TTY: 315-376-8696
karenb@nrcil.net
www.nrcil.net

Ronald Griffin, Chair
Michael Simmons, Vice Chair
Melanie Adkins, Secretary
A disability rights and resource center that promotes community
efforts to end discrimination, segregation, and prejudice against
people with disabilities.

4294 Options for Independence: Auburn
75 Genesee St
Auburn, NY 13021-3667
315-255-3447
FAX: 315-255-0836
www.ariseinc.org

Tania Anderson, President
Sue Judge, Vice President
Michael Cook, Treasurer
Options for Independence is an Independent Living Center which
assists people with disabilities to gain opportunities, make their
own decisions, pursue activities and become part of comunity
life. Options provides a variety of services to all people with disabilities, their families, friends, and service providers in Cayuga
and Seneca Counties.

4295 Putnam Independent Living Services
1961 Route 6
2nd Floor
Carmel, NY 10512-2324
845-228-7457
FAX: 845-228-7460
TTY: 866-933-5390
info@wilc.org
www.putnamils.org

Joe Bravo, Executive Director
Mildred Caballero-Ho, Deputy Executive Director
Margaret Valenzuela, Program Director, IL Services
A non-profit, community-based advocacy and resource center
that serves people with all types of disabilities.

4296 Regional Center for Independent Living
497 State St
Rochester, NY 14608-1642
585-442-6470
FAX: 585-271-8558
TTY: 585-442-6470
bdarling@rcil.org
www.rcil.org

Shelly Perrin, Chairperson
Bobbi Wallach, Vice Chairperson
Bruce E Darling, Executive Director
To empower people with disabilities to self-advocate, to live in-
dependently and to enhance the quality of community life.

4297 **Resource Center for Accessible Living**
727 Ulster Ave
Kingston, NY 12401-1709   845-331-0541
        FAX: 845-331-2076
        TTY:845-331-4527
        office@rcal.org
        www.rcal.org

Paul Scarpati, President
Paula Kindos-Carberry, Co-Vice President
Bernadette Mueller, Co-Vice President
RCAL is a non-profit, community based service and advocacy run by and for people with any type of disability. RCAL is dedicated to assisting and empowering individuals, of all ages, to live independently and participate in all aspects of community life.

4298 **Resource Center for Independent Living**
347 W Main St
Amsterdam, NY 12010-2225   518-842-3561
        FAX: 518-842-0905
        TTY:518-842-3593

Shelly Perrin, Chairperson
Bobbi Wallach, Vice Chairperson
Bruce E Darling, Executive Director
Peer counseling, advocacy, independent living skills training, information and referral services, self-advocacy training, ADA consultation, home and community based services, community education, benefits advisement and more. All programs and services are available in English and Spanish.

4299 **Southern Adirondack Independent Living**
418 Geyser Rd
Country Club Plaza
Ballston Spa, NY 12020-6002   518-584-8202
        FAX: 518-584-1195
        www.sail-center.org

Karen Thayer, Executive Director
Anna Livingston, Assistant Director
Barbara Potvin, Executive Assistant
To assist individuals with disabilities to become independent empowered self-advocates.

4300 **Southern Adirondack Independent Living Center**
71 Glenwood Ave
Queensbury, NY 12804-1728   518-792-3537
        FAX: 518-792-0979
        TTY:518-792-0505

Karen Thayer, Executive Director
Anna Livingston, Assistant Director
Shirley Dumont, Director of Advocacy
To assist individuals with disabilities to become independent empowered self-advocates.

4301 **Southern Tier Independence Center**
135 E Frederick St
Binghamton, NY 13904-1224   607-724-2111
        FAX: 607-772-3600
        TTY:607-724-2111
        stic@stic-cil.org
        www.stic-cil.org

Maria Dibble, Executive Director
Frank Pennisi, Accessibility Services
STIC provides assistance and services to all people with disabilities of all ages to increase their independence in all aspects of integrated community life. STIC also serves their families and friends, and businesses, agencies, and goverments to enable them to better meet the needs of people with disabilities, and finally STIC educates and influences the community in pursuit of full inclusion of people with disabilities.

4302 **Southwestern Independent Living Center**
843 N Main St
Jamestown, NY 14701-3546   716-661-3010
        FAX: 716-661-3011
        TTY:716-661-3012
        info@ilc-jamestown-ny.org

Marie T Carrubba, Executive Director
Linda Rumbaugh, Independent Living Specialist
Christine Ahlstrom, Independent Living Specialist
A non-residential, private, nonprofit agency established to provide services throughout Chautauqua County that will assist individuals with disabilities in reaching maximum independence and an enriched quality of life.

4303 **Staten Island Center for Independent Living, Inc.**
470 Castleton Ave
Staten Island, NY 10301   718-720-9016
        FAX: 718-720-9664
        TTY:718-720-9870
        ldesantis@siciliving.org
        www.siciliving.org

Lorraine DeSantis, Executive Director
Claudia J. Stanton, Office Manager
Michelle Sabatino, Independent Living Specialist
Mission is to provide all individuals with disabilities the information, life skills training, and facilitative assistance which contributes to independence, individuality, and integration in the community and provides the skills and knowledge necessary to function in the least restrictive, personally fulfilling, most self reliant and productive manner.

4304 **Suffolk Independent Living Organization(SILO)**
2111 Lakeland Ave.
Suite A
Ronkonkoma, NY 11779   631-880-7929
        FAX: 631-946-6377
        TTY:631-946-6585
        www.siloinc.org/?

Edward Ahern, Manager
Glenn Campbell, Co-Executive Director
A not-for-profit organization that helps the disabled become more independent and more involved in the community by providing them with information on referrals on Housing, Education, Employment and Benefits.

4305 **Taconic Resources for Independence**
82 Washington St
Suite #214
Poughkeepsie, NY 12601-2305   845-452-3913
        866-948-1094
        FAX: 845-485-3196
        tri@taconicresources.org
        www.taconicresources.org

Cynthia L. Fiore, Executive Director
Patrick Muller, Program Director
Diane Barkstrom, Program Director/Staff Interpret
A center for independent living, benefits advisement information, and referral, advocacy, independent living skills, peer counseling, parent advocacy, sign language interpreters.

4306 **Westchester Disabled on the Move**
984 N. Broadway
Suite LL-10
Yonkers, NY 10701-1320   914-968-4717
        FAX: 914-968-6137
        info@wdom.org
        www.wdom.org

Gail Cartenuto Cohn, President
Mattie Trupia, Vice President
Sandra Dolman, Secretary
WDOM empowers people with disabilities to control their own lives; advocates for civil rights and a barrier free society; encourages people with disabilities to participate in the political process; educates government, business, other entities, and a society as a whole to understand, accept, and accommodate people with disabilities; creates an environment that inspires self-respect

4307 **Westchester Independent Living Center**
200 Hamilton Avenue
2nd Floor
White Plains, NY 10601- 1809   914-682-3926
        FAX: 914-682-8518
        TTY:866-933-5390
        Contact@wilc.org
        www.wilc.org

Joseph Bravo, Executive Director
A not-for-profit, community-based advocacy and resource center that serves people with all types of disabilities.

North Carolina

4308 Disability Awareness Network
609 Country Club Dr.
Suite C
Greenville, NC 27834-6210   252-353-5522
FAX: 252-353-5160
DAWNpittco@aol.com

Jackie Hansley, Owner
Information and referral for diabled persons; peer counseling for diabled persons; advocacy on ADA issues; independent living skills and training.

4309 Disability Rights & Resources
5801 Executive Center Dr.
Suite #101
Charlotte, NC 28212-8870   704-537-0550
800-755-5749
FAX: 704-566-0507
TTY: 704-537-0550
mailto@disability-rights.org
www.disability-rights.org

Maura Chavez, President
Marta Fales, Vice President
Holly Howell, Secretary
To guard the civil rights of people wtih disabilities by empowering ourselves and others to live as we choose.

4310 Joy: A Shabazz Center for Independent Living
235 N Greene St
Greensboro, NC 27401-2410   336-272-0501
FAX: 336-272-0575
TTY:336-272-0501

Aaron Shabazz, Executive Director
James Wells, President
Stephen Simpson, Vice-President
A non-profit, consumer oriented, Center for Independent Living (CIL) providing advocacy, peer counseling and peer support, independent living skills, training, information and referrals, with other related services for persons with disabilites.

4311 Live Independently Networking Center
P.O.Box 1135
Newton, NC 28658-1135   828-464-0331
FAX: 828-464-7375
TTY:828-464-2838

Donavon Kirby, Deputy Director
Private, nonprofit, federally funded center for independent living located in Western North Carolina.

4312 Live Independently Networking Center: Hickory
2830 16th St NE
Apt. 17
Hickory, NC 28601-8606   828-464-0331
FAX: 828-464-7375
Private, non-profit, federally funded center for independent living

4313 Pathways for the Future Center for Independent Living
525 Mineral Springs Dr
Sylva, NC 28779-9077   828-631-1167
FAX: 828-631-1169
TTY:828-631-1167

Barbara Davis, Executive Director
Dedicated to increasing independence, changing attitudes, promoting equal access and building a peer support network in western North Carolina through the use of community education, independent living services and advocacy.

4314 Western Alliance Center for Independent Living
30b London Rd
Asheville, NC 28803-2706   828-274-0444
FAX: 828-274-4461
westernalliance.org

Katy Hollingsworth, Manager
Jerry Brewton, Independent Living Specialist

4315 Western Alliance for Independent Living
108 New Leicester Highway
Asheville, NC 28806   828-298-1977
FAX: 828-298-0875
khollingsworth@disabilitypartners.org
www.disabilitypartners.org

Kathy Hollingsworth, Associate Director
Rosemary Weaver, Independent Living Specialist
Mechelle Holt, Volunteer/Program Coordinator

North Dakota

4316 Dakota Center for Independent Living: Dickinson
26-1st street East
Suite 103
Dickinson, ND 58601-5103   701- 48- 436
800-489-5013
FAX: 701- 48- 436
TTY: 800489501363
dcil@ndsupernet.com
www.dakotacil.org

Robin Were, President
Claudia Ziegler, Vice president
Carol Mihulka, Secretary/Treasurer
Believes in self-determination for people with disabilities and creates the environment in which it is achieved.

4317 Dakota Center for Independent Living: Bismarck
3111 E Broadway Ave
Bismarck, ND 58501-5085   701-222-3636
800-489-5013
FAX: 701-222-0511
TTY: 701-222-3636
maryr@dakotacil.org
www.dakotacil.org

Robin Were, President
Claudia Ziegler, Vice president
Carol Mihulka, Secretary/Treasurer
Believes in self-determination for people with disabilities and creates the environment in which it is achieved.

4318 Fraser
2902 University Drive South
Fargo, ND 58103-6053   701-232-3301
FAX: 701-237-5775
fraser@fraserltd.org
fraserltd.org

Sandra Leyland, Executive Director
Mark Brodshaug, President
Michael Kirk, Vice President
Private non-profit, federally funded center for independent living

4319 Freedom Resource Center for Independent Living: Fargo
2701 9th Ave S
Suite H
Fargo, ND 58103-8712   701-478-0459
800-450-0459
FAX: 701-478-0510
TTY: 701-478-0459
freedom@freedomrc.org
www.freedomrc.org

Nate Aalgaard, Executive Director
Angie Bosch, Office Coordinator
Mark Mark Bourdon Bourdon, Program Director
To work toward equality and inclusion for people with disabilities through programs of empowerment, community education, and systems change.

4320   Resource Center for Independent Living: Minot
300 3rd Ave SW
Suite F
Minot, ND 58701-4346   701-839-4724
                                                   800-377-5114
                                              FAX: 701-838-1677
                                              TTY: 701-839-4724
                        independencecil@independencecil.org
                                     www.independencecil.org/?

Susan Ogurek, Chair
Scott Burlingame, Executive Director
Dee Tischer, Senior Independent Living Specia
A resource center for independent living. Mission is to advocate
for the freedom of choice for individuals with disabilities to live
independently through the removal of all barriers.

Ohio

4321   Ability Center of Greater Toledo
5605 Monroe St.
Sylvania, OH 43560   419-885-5733
                                              FAX: 419-882-4813
                                              www.abilitycenter.org

Tim Harrington, Executive Director
Ash Lemons, Associate Director
Debbie Andriette, Director, Human Resources
To assist people with disabilities to live, work and socialize
within a fully accessible community.

4322   Ability Center of Greater Toledo: Bryan
1425 East High St.
Suite 108
Bryan, OH 43506   419-633-1400
                                                   855-633-1400
                                              FAX: 419-633-1410
                                              www.abilitycenter.org

Tim Harrington, Executive Director
Angie Burton, Manager, Youth Programs
To assist people with disabilities to live, work and socialize
within a fully accessible community. The Bryan office serves residents in Defiance, Fulton, Henry, and Williams Counties.

4323   Access Center for Independent Living
901 S Ludlow St
Dayton, OH 45402-2614   937-341-5202
                                              FAX: 937-341-5217
                                              TTY:937-341-5218
                                                   info@acils.com
                                                   www.acils.com/?

Darrell Price, IL Team Co-Leader
Tonya Banther, IL Team Co-Leader
Melody Burba, Information & Referral Specialis
Offers peer counseling, disability education and other services to
the community.

4324   Center for Independent Living Options
2031 Auburn Avenue
Cincinnati, OH 45219-2436   513-241-2600
                                              FAX: 513-241-1707
                                              TTY:513-241-7170
                                                   cilo.net

Lin Laing, Executive Director
Justin Bifro, President
Brian Frazier, Vice-President
The oldest center for independent living in Ohio serving individ-
uals with disabilities in the Greater Cincinnati/Northern Ken-
tucky region.

4325   Fairfield Center for Disabilities and Cerebral Palsy
681 E 6th Ave
Lancaster, OH 43130-2602   740-653-5501
                                              FAX: 740-653-6046
                                              fcdcp@sbcglobal.net
                                                   www.fcdcp.org

David Macioci, President
David Welsh, Vice-President
Mary Snider, Treasurer
Adult Day Program and Transportation. The mission of the
Fairfield Center for disabilities and Cerebral Palsy, Inc, is to cre-

ate a better future for people with a disability by increasing and
enhancing their lifestyle opportunities.

4326   Linking Employment, Abilities and Potential
2545 Lorain Ave.
Cleveland, OH 44113-3102   216-696-2716
                                              FAX: 216-687-1453
                                                   www.leapinfo.org

Charles Heindrichs, President
Brian Roof, Vice President
Vincent Shemo, Treasurer
Consumer-directed to ensure a society of equal opportunity for
all persons, regardless of disability.

**4327   Mid-Ohio Board for an Independent Living
         Environment (MOBILE)**
690 S High St
Columbus, OH 43206-1016   614-443-5936
                                              FAX: 614-443-5954
                                              TTY:614-443-5957
                                                   info@mobileonline.org
                                                   www.mobileonline.org

Darry Moore, President
Thomas Shapaka, Vice-President
Mark Morton, Treasurer
A non-profit Center for Independent Living directed by persons
with disabilities. MOBILE was founded on principles that affirm
the right of persons with disabilities to live their lives with a full
measure of liberty and human dignity.

4328   Ohio Statewide Independent Living Council
670 Morrison Road
Suite 200
Gahanna, OH 43230-5324   614-892-0390
                                                   800-566-7788
                                              FAX: 614-861-0392
                                                   www.ohiosilc.org

Kay Grier, Executive Director
Eugene Iacovetta, Special Projects Coordinator
Mary Butler, Systems Change Coordinator
Committed to promoting a philosophy of consumer control, peer
support, self-help, self-determination, equal acess, and individual and systems advocacy, in order to maximize leadership, empowerment, independence, productivity and to support full
inclusion and integration of individuals with disabilities into the
mainstream of American society.

4329   Rehabilitation Service of North Central Ohio
270 Sterkel Blvd
Mansfield, OH 44907-1508   419-756-1133
                                                   800-589-1133
                                              FAX: 419-756-6544
                                                   info@therehabcenter.org
                                                   www.therehabcenter.org

Veronica L. Groff, President/CEO
Susan Baker, Chairman
Dan Wiegand, Vice-Chairman
Private nonprofit organization providing coordinated, team-ori-
ented comprehensive outpatient rehabilitation services to children and adults of all ages. Serves 8 counties in N/C Ohio. Four
umbrella areas of service include medical rehabilitation services,
vocational rehabilitation services, behavioral health service and
drug and alcohol addiction services. Medical rehabilitation services include physical therapy, occupational therapy, speech
therapy and audiology.

4330   Samuel W Bell Home for Sightless
3775 Muddy Creek Rd
Cincinnati, OH 45238-2055   513-241-0720
                                              FAX: 513-241-1481
                                                   swbellhome@fuse.net
                                                   www.samuelbell.org

Timothy Lighthal, President
Kevin Kappa, Vice-President
Miles L.Hoff, Treasurer
Offers a residential, independent living environment for blind
and legally blind adults.

4331 **Services for Independent Living**
25100 Euclid Ave
Suite #105
Cleveland, OH 44117-2663   216-731-1529
                                  FAX: 216-731-3083
                                  TTY:216-731-1529
                                  www.sil-oh.org

Lynn Hildebrand, Executive Director
Offers support ADA, consultation and education, advocacy, transitional education services, independent living skills training, information and referrals.

4332 **Society for Equal Access: Independent Living Center**
1458 5th St NW
New Philadelphia, OH 44663-1224   330-343-9292
                                    888-213-4452
                                    FAX: 330-602-7425
                                    TTY:330-602-2557
                                    www.seailc.org

Scott Huston, President
Edna Fillinger, Vice-President
Victoria Eichel, Secretary
The Society works with individuals to become more independent. Our agency assists with peer support, advocacy, information and referral, independent living skills and transportation. Our goal is to move those with challenges in the direction ofn independence.

Oklahoma

4333 **Ability Resources**
823 S Detroit Ave
Suite #110
Tulsa, OK 74120-4223   918-592-1235
                                   800-722-0886
                                   FAX: 918-592-5651
                                   www.ability-resources.org
Carla Lawson, Executive Director
To assist people with disabilities in attaining and maintaining their personal independence.

4334 **Green County Independent Living Resource Center**
4100 S.E. Adams Rd
Suite C-106
Bartlesville, OK 74006- 8409   918-335-1314
                                   800-559-0567
                                   FAX: 918-333-1814
                                   TTY: 918-335-1314
Vicki Haws, Executive Director
Independent living skills training, information and referrals, advocacy, a loan library of adaptive equipment and books. Services available to all individuals with disabilities and their family members who reside in Northeastern Oklahoma.

4335 **Oklahomans for Independent Living**
601 East Carl Albert Parkway
McAlester, OK 74501-5410   918-426-6220
                                   800-568-6821
                                   FAX: 918-426-3245
                                   TTY: 918-426-6263
                                   www.oilok.org
Pam Pulchny, Executive Director/ADAspecialist
Terry Yates, Administrative Assistant/Bookke
Leanna Amos, Service Management Specialist
OIL encourages individuals of all ages, with all types of disabilities to increase: personal dependence; empowerment and self determiation; and ful integration and participation in their work, community, school and home activities.

4336 **Progressive Independence**
121 N Porter Avenue
Norman, OK 73071-5834   405-321-3203
                                   800-801-3203
                                   FAX: 405-321-7601
                                   TTY: 405-321-2942
                                   www.progind.org

Scott Spray, Chairperson
Teresa Tisdell, Vice Chair
Mark Newman, Treasurer

Preovides four cores services of Information & Referral, Individaul& Systems Advocacy, Peer Counseling, and Skills Training; in addition, offers accessible computer lab, short term DME loans, ande benefits counseling for SSI/SSDI.

Oregon

4337 **Abilitree**
2680 NE Twin Knolls Dr.
Suite 3
Bend, OR 97701   541-388-8103
                                   FAX: 541-389-2337
                                   TTY:541-388-8103
                                   www.abilitree.org
Tim Johnson, Executive Director
Greg Sublett, Director of Operations
April O'Meara, Marketing Director
CORIL empowers people with disabilities to maximize their independence, productivity and inclusio in community life. CORIL envisions a society where all people have the opportunity to develop their full capabilities with independence, productivity and more meaningful involvment in local community events and activities.

4338 **Eastern Oregon Center for Independent Living**
1021 SW 5th Ave
Ontario, OR 97914-3301   541-889-3119
                                   866-248-8369
                                   FAX: 541-889-4647
                                   eocil@eocil.org
                                   www.eocil.org
Kirt Toombs, Executive Director
EOCIL is a nonprofit community based resource and advocacy center that promotes independent living and equal access for all persons with disabilities. EOCIL serves consumers in the counties of: Baker, Gilliam, Grant, harney, Malheur, Morrow, Umatilla, Union, Wallowa and Wheeler.

4339 **HASL Independent Abilities Center**
305 NE 'E' Street
Grants Pass, OR 97526   541-479-4275
                                   800-758-4275
                                   FAX: 541-479-7261
                                   TTY: 541-479-3588
                                   haslstaff@yahoo.com
                                   www.haslonline.org
Randy Samuelson, Executive Director
To promote public awareness of the special needs and legal rights of individuals with cross-disabilities; to facilitate their integration into society and provide support through advocacy, peer counseling, skills training and information and referral to encourage independence.

4340 **Independent Living Resources**
1839 NE Couch St.
Portland, OR 97232   503-232-7411
                                   FAX: 503-232-7480
                                   TTY:503-232-8404
                                   info@ilr.org
                                   www.ilr.org/?
Barry Fox-Quamme, Executive Director
May Altman, LCSW, Associate Director
Barbara Norris, Office Manager/Executive Assistant
ILR looks to promote the philosophy of Independent Living by creating opportunities, encouraging choices, advancing equal access, and furthering the level of independence for all people with disabilities

4341 **Laurel Hill Center**
2145 Centennial Plaza
Eugene, OR 97401-2474   541-485-6340
                                   FAX: 541-984-3124
                                   TTY:541-684-6822
                                   info@laurel.org
                                   www.laurel.org
Tom Fauria, President
DAVE Burtner, Vice-President
EDUARDO Sifuentez, Secretary

Provides natoinall-recognized, recovery-focused rehabilitation services in Lane County, Oregon, for people with severe and persistent mental illnesses

4342 Progressive Options
611 S.W. Hurbert Street
Suite A
Newport, OR 97365-9678
541-265-4674
FAX: 541-574-4313
TTY:541-574-1927
progop541@yahoo.com
www.progressive-options.org

Rhonda Walker, Executive Director
Progressive Options seeks to provide free services and support to people with disabilities of all kinds to help them achieve and maintain maximum independence and self-sufficiency in Lincoln County and surrounding areas in Oregon.

4343 SPOKES Unlimited
1006 Main St
Klamath Falls, OR 97601-6029
541-883-7547
FAX: 541-885-2469
TTY:541-883-7547
www.spokesunlimited.org

Wendy Howard, Executive Director
Mission is to enhance the ability of people with disabilities to live more independently.

4344 Umpqua Valley Disabilities Network
736 SE Jackson Street
Roseburg, OR 97470-110
541-672-6336
FAX: 541-672-8606
TTY:541-440-2882
uvdn@uvdn.org
www.uvdn.org

David Fricke, Executive Director
Heather Vialpando, Executive Assistant
UVDN's mission is to promote independent living and community inclusion for people with disabilities.

Pennsylvania

4345 Abilities in Motion
210 N 5th St
Reading, PA 19601-3304
610-376-0010
888-376-0120
FAX: 610-376-0021
TTY: 610-228-2301
www.abilitiesinmotion.org

Terry Graul, Board President
David Lerch, Vice-President
Bonnie Milke, Treasurer
Dedicated to advancing the rights of persons with disabilities in orer to promote a full life in the community through the prevention and elimination of physical, psychological, social and attitudinal barriers which serve to deny them the rights and privileges common to the general public.

4346 Anthracite Region Center for Independent Living
Pennsylvania Council on Independent Living
8 West Broad St
Suite 228
Hazleton, PA 18201-6418
570-455-9800
800-777-9906
FAX: 570-455-1731
TTY: 570-455-9800
dcorcoran@anthracitecil.org

Irene Mordosky, President
Margo Madden, Vice-President
Rand Martin, Treasurer
Enables individuals with disabilities to attain their highest possible level of independence.

4347 Brian's House
757 Springdale Dr.
Exton, PA 19341-8531
610-399-1175
ekihara@brianshouse.org
brianshouse.org

Diana L. Ramsay, MPP, OTR, FAOT, Resident and Chief Executive Off
Peter M. Shubiak, MA, Executive Vice President and Chi
Lori Plunkettt, Executive Director
A non-profit organization that provides residential, vocational and recreational/respite programs for children and adults with intellectual and developmental disabilities.

4348 Community Resources for Independence
3410 W 12th St
Erie, PA 16505-3649
814-838-7222
800-530-5541
FAX: 814-838-8491
TTY: 814-838-8115
www.crinet.org

Timothy Finegan, Executive Director
William Essigmann, Administrative Program Manager
Carl Berry, Human Resources Director
A community based, nonprofit, nonresidential organization that offers services and assistance to enable people with disabilities to expand their options, pursue their goals, and achieve and maintain self-sufficient and producitve lives in the community.

4349 Community Resources for Independence, Inc., Bradford
3410 West 12th Street
Erie, PA 16505
814-838-7222
800-530-5541
FAX: 814-838-8491
TTY: 814-838-8115
crinet.org

Timothy J. Finegan, Executive Director
William Essigmann, Administrative Program Manager
Carl Berry, Human Resources Director
Community Resources for Independence, Inc is committed to preserve, enhance and enrich the quality of life for all people with disabilities.

4350 Community Resources for Independence: Lewistown
33 East Hale Street
Suite L
Lewistown, PA 17044-2160
717-248-8011
800-309-0989
FAX: 717-248-8029
www.crinet.org

Timothy Finegan, Executive Director
William Essigmann, Administrative Program Manager
Carl Berry, Human Resources Director
A community based, nonprofit, nonresidential organization that offers services and assistance to enable people with disabilities to expand their options, pursue their goals, and achieve and maintain self-sufficient and producitve lives in the community.

4351 Community Resources for Independence: Altoona
1331 Twelth Ave
Suite #103
Altoona, PA 16601
814-994-2645
866-944-2645
FAX: 814-944-2683
www.crinet.org

Timothy Finegan, Executive Director
William Essigmann, Administrative Program Manager
Carl Berry, Human Resources Director
A community based, nonprofit, nonresidential organization that offers services and assistance to enable people with disabilities to expand their options, pursue their goals, and achieve and maintain self-sufficient and producitve lives in the community.

4352 Community Resources for Independence: Clarion
1200 Eastwood Drive
Suite #1
Clarion, PA 16214-8824 814-297-7141
800-372-0140
FAX: 814-297-7161
www.crinet.org

Timothy J. Finegan, Executive Director
William Essigmann, Administrative Program Manager
Carl Berry, Human Resources Director
A community based, nonprofit, nonresidential organization that offers services and assistance to enable people with disabilities to expand their options, pursue their goals, and achieve and maintain self-sufficient and producitve lives in the community.

4353 Community Resources for Independence: Clearfield
209 E Locust St
Clearfield, PA 16830-2422 814-765-6405
866-619-6405
FAX: 814-765-1269
www.crinet.org

Timothy Finegan, Executive Director
William Essigmann, Administrative Program Manager
Carl Berry, Human Resources Director
A community based, nonprofit, nonresidential organization that offers services and assistance to enable people with disabilities to expand their options, pursue their goals, and achieve and maintain self-sufficient and producitve lives in the community.

4354 Community Resources for Independence: Hermitage
3875 East State St
Suite B
Hermitage, PA 16148-3415 724-347-4121
FAX: 724-347-5966
www.crinet.org

Timothy J. Finegan, Executive Director
William Essigmann, Administrative Program Manager
Carl Berry, Human Resources Director
A community based, nonprofit, nonresidential organization that offers services and assistance to enable people with disabilities to expand their options, pursue their goals, and achieve and maintain self-sufficient and producitve lives in the community.

4355 Community Resources for Independence: Lewisburg
11 Reitz Blvd
Suite #105
Lewisburg, PA 17837-1493 570-524-4314
800-332-4135
FAX: 570-524-9236
www.crinet.org

Timothy J. Finegan, Executive Director
William Essigmann, Administrative Program Manager
Carl Berry, Human Resources Director
A community based, nonprofit, nonresidential organization that offers services and assistance to enable people with disabilities to expand their options, pursue their goals, and achieve and maintain self-sufficient and producitve lives in the community.

4356 Community Resources for Independence: Oil City
250 Elm St
Oil City, PA 16301-1413 814-677-4655
866-209-3882
FAX: 814-677-4915
www.crinet.org

Tim Finegan, Executive Director
William Essigmann, Administrative Program Manager
Carl Berry, Human Resources Director
A community based, nonprofit, nonresidential organization that offers services and assistance to enable people with disabilities to expand their options, pursue their goals, and achieve and maintain self-sufficient and producitve lives in the community.

4357 Community Resources for Independence: Warren
1003 Pennsylvania Ave W
Warren, PA 16365-1837 814-726-3404
866-579-3404
FAX: 814-726-3428
www.crinet.org

Timothy Finegan, Executive Director
William Essigmann, Administrative Program Manager
Carl Berry, Human Resources Director

A community based, nonprofit, nonresidential organization that offers services and assistance to enable people with disabilities to expand their options, pursue their goals, and achieve and maintain self-sufficient and producitve lives in the community.

4358 Community Resources for Independence: Wellsboro
38 Plaza Ln
Wellsboro, PA 16901-1766 570-724-5852
866-401-7911
FAX: 570-724-3945
www.crinet.org

Timothy Finegan, Executive Director
William Essigmann, Administrative Program Manager
Carl Berry, Human Resources Director
A community based, nonprofit, nonresidential organization that offers services and assistance to enable people with disabilities to expand their options, pursue their goals, and achieve and maintain self-sufficient and producitve lives in the community.

4359 Freedom Valley Disability Center
3607 Chapel Road
Suite B
Newtown Square, PA 19073-3602 610-353-6640
800-427-4754
FAX: 610-353-6753
TTY: 610-353-8900

Ann Cope, Executive Director
Assists persons with disabilities in the achievement of independent living goals. Also promotes individual and community options to maximize independence for persons with disabilities. Serves people with disabilities in Chester, Delaware, and Montgomery Counties.

4360 Institute on Disabilities At Temple Univ.
Temple University
1755 N. 13th St
Student Center, Rm. 4115
Philadelphia, PA 19122-6099 215-204-1356
FAX: 215-204-6336
iod@temple.edu
www.disabilities.temple.edu

James Earl Davis, Phd, Interim Executive Director
Celia Feinstein, Co-Executive- Director
Amy Goldman, Co-Executive- Director
Leads by example, creating connections and promoting networks within and among communitites so that people with disabilities are recognized as integral to the fabric of community life.

4361 Lehigh Valley Center for Independent Living
713 North 13th Street
Allentown, PA 18102-9121 610-770-9781
800-495-8245
FAX: 610-770-9801
TTY: 610-770-9789
info@lvcil.org
www.lvcil.org

Scott Berman, President
Michelle Mitchell, Vice President
Amy Beck, Executive Director
Serves persons in Lehigh and Northampton Counties with any type of disability and/or his/her family.

4362 Liberty Resources
714 Market St
Suite #100
Philadelphia, PA 19106-2337 215-634-2000
888-634-2155
FAX: 215-634-6628
TTY:215-634-6630
lrinc@libertyresources.org
www.libertyresources.org

Edwin Bomba, Chairman
Mary Ellen Caffrey, Chairman
Estelle B. Richman, Vice-Chairman
A non-profit, consumer driven organization that advocates and promotes Independent Living for persons with disabilities.

4363   Life and Independence for Today
503 E Arch St
Saint Marys, PA 15857-1779

814-781-3050
800-341-5438
FAX: 814-781-1917
TTY: 814-781-3050
lift@liftcil.org
www.liftcil.org

Stephen DePrater, President
Linda McKinstry, Vice-President
Larry Caggeso, Treasurer
Offers services to enable people with disabilities to achieve new goals and broaden their horizons. It enables them to achieve and maintain self-sufficient and productive lives.

4364   Northeastern Pennsylvania Center for Independent Living
1142 Sanderson Ave
Suite #1
Scranton, PA 18509

570-344-7211
800-344-7211
FAX: 570-344-7218
TTY: 570-344-5275
nepacilinfo@nepacil.org

Robert Treptow, President
Michael Sporer, Secretary
Chris Armone,Esq, Treasurer
Established to assist in removing barriers and expanding independent living options available to people with disabilities.

4365   South Central Pennsylvania Center for Independence Living
1019 Logan Blvd
Altoona, PA 16602-2434

814-949-1905
800-237-9009
FAX: 814-949-1909
TTY: 814-949-1912
www.cilscpa.org

Susan Estep, Executive Director
The missio of the Center for Independent Living of South Central PA is to empower people with disabilities to lead independent lives in their commnuitites. The Center covers Bedford, Blair, cambria, Fulton, Huntingdon, Indiana and Somerset counties.

4366   Three Rivers Center for Independent Living: New Castle
900 Rebecca Ave
Pittsburgh, PA 15221-9383

412-371-7700
800-633-4588
FAX: 412-371-9430
TTY: 412-371-6230
www.trcil.myfastsite.net/

Kourtney T. Diaz, Chairperson
Shanicka Kennedy, Esq, Vice-Chairperson
Stanley A Holbrook, President
To empower people with disabilities to enjoy self-directed, personally meaningful lives by providing outstanding consumer controlled services and by advocating for effective community college.

4367   Three Rivers Center for Independent Livi ng: Washington
900 Rebecca Ave
Pittsburgh, PA 15221-4425

412-371-7700
800-633-4588
FAX: 412-371-9430
TTY: 412-371-6230
www.trcil.myfastsite.net/

Stanley A Holbrook, President
Kourtney T. Diaz, Chairperson
Shanicka Kennedy, Esq, Vice-Chairperson
To empower people with disabilities to enjoy self-directed, personally meaningful lives by providing outstanding consumer controlled services and by advocating for effective community college.

4368   Three Rivers Center for Independent Living
900 Rebecca Ave
Pittsburgh, PA 15221-2938

412-371-7700
800-633-4588
FAX: 412-371-9430
TTY: 412-371-6230
www.trcil.myfastsite.net/

Stanley A Holbrook, President
Kourtney T. Diaz, Chairperson
Shanicka Kennedy, Esq, Vice-Chairperson
To empower people with disabilities to enjoy self-directed, personally meaningful lives by providing outstanding consumer controlled services and by advocating for effective community college.

4369   Tri-County Patriots for Independent Living
69 East Beau St
Washington, PA 15301-4711

724-223-5115
877-889-0965
FAX: 724-223-5119
TTY: 724-228-4028
www.tripil.com

Kathleen Kleinmann, Chief Executive Officer
Maxine Berton, Administrative Assistant
Jeffry D. Woods, Chief Information Officer
Brings together individuals who share common problems in equal access, education, housing, employment, attendant care, transportation, and access to technology.

4370   Voices for Independence
1107 Payne Ave
Erie, PA 16503-1741

814-874-0064
866-407-0064
FAX: 814-874-3497
TTY: 814-874-0064
web@vficil.org
www.vficil.org

Shona Eakin, Executive Director
Edna Anabui, Executive Administrative Assista
Doug McClintock, Director of Finances
To empower people with disabilities and promote independent living.

Rhode Island

4371   Arc of Blackstone
500 Prospect St.
Wing B, Suite 203
Pawtucket, RI 2860- 4396

401-727-0150
800-257-6092
FAX: 401-727-1545
contact@bvcriarc.org
www.bvcriarc.org

Kathleen O'Neill, President
Thomas E. Hodge, Vice-President
Joseph F. McEnness, Treasurer
Committed to supporting people with developmental disabilities secure the opportunity to choose and realize their goals of where and how they live, learn, work and play

4372   Franklin Court Assisted Living
180 Franklin St
Bristol, RI 2809-3352

401-253-3679
FAX: 401-253-5855

Michelle Belmore Cabana, Chief Financial Officer
Brenda Marshall, Administrator
Lynn A. Marshall, Property Manager
Offers local seniors an affordable assisted living option with first-rate services and gracious accommodations.

4373   IN-SIGHT Independent Living
43 Jefferson Blvd
Warwick, RI 2888-1078

401-941-3322
FAX: 401-941-3356
cbutler@in-sight.org
www.in-sight.org

Jean Saylor, Chairman
Robert Tyler, Vice-Chairman
James Hahn, Treasurer

Creating opportunities and choices for people who are blind and visually impaired

4374 Ocean State Center for Independent Living
1944 Warwick Avenue
Warwick, RI 2889-2448
401-738-1013
866-857-1161
FAX: 401-738-1083
TTY: 401-738-1015
info@oscil.org
www.oscil.org

Lorna Ricci, Executive Director
OSCIL is a consumer controlled, community based, nonprofit organization established to provide a range of independent living services to enhance, through self direction, the quality of life of Rhode Islander with significant disability and to promote integration into the community.

4375 Office of Rehabilitation Services
40 Fountain Street
Providence, RI 02903-1898
401-421-7005
TTY:401-421-7016
www.ors.ri.gov

Ron Racine, Associate Director
Beth Rioles, Administrator, DDS
Laurie DiOrio, Administrator, SBVI
Goal is to help individuals with physical and mental disabilities prepare for and obtain appropriate employment.

4376 PARI Independent Living Center
500 Prospect St
Pawtucket, RI 2860-6259
401-725-1966
FAX: 401-725-2104
TTY:401-725-1966
www.pari-ilc.org

Leo Canuel, Executive Director
Sue Bilodau, Program Director
Offers information and referral services, personal care attendant services, home modifications, advocacy services and peer counseling, independent living skills training, and recycled equipment.

South Carolina

4377 Columbia Disability Action Center
136 Stonemark Lane
Suite #100
Columbia, SC 29210
800-681-6805
FAX: 803-779-5114
TTY:803-779-0949
www.able-sc.org/

David Dawson, President
Rochelle Gadson, Vice President
Joe Butler, Treasurer
A non-profit consumer governed Center for Independent Living. Programs and services support persons with disabilities in taking full advantage of community resources, enhancing personal opportunities, and determining the direction of their lives.

4378 Disability Action Center
330B Pelham Rd
Suite 100 A
Greenville, SC 29615-3116
864-235-1421
800-681-7715
FAX: 864-235-2056
TTY: 864-235-8798
amayne@dacsc.org
www.able-sc.org/

David Dawson, President
Rochelle Gadson, Vice President
Joe Butler, Treasurer
Empowering people with disabilities to reach their highest level of independence.

4379 Graham Street Community Resources
306 Graham St
Florence, SC 29501-4735
843-665-6674
FAX: 843-665-6674

Faye Thompson, Manager

Promotes independent living and empowers people with disabilities to reach their highest level of independence.

4380 South Carolina Independent Living Council
136 Stonemark Lane
Suite #100
Columbia, SC 29210-7318
803-217-3209
800-994-4322
FAX: 803-731-1439
TTY: 803-217-3209
scilc@scilconline.org
www.scsilc.com

Mike Le Fever, President
Committed to equal opportunity, equal access, self determination, independence, and choice for all people with disabilities and pursues these goals by the means available.

4381 Walton Options for Independent Living: North Augusta
325 Georgia Ave
North Augusta, SC 29841-3848
803-279-9611
FAX: 803-279-9135
tjohnston@waltonoptions.org
www.waltonoptions.org

Cynthia Anzek, Executive Director
Empowers persons of all ages with all types of disabilities to reach their highest level of independence, community inclusion and employment.

South Dakota

4382 Adjustment Training Center
607 N 4th St
Aberdeen, SD 57401-2733
605-229-0263
FAX: 605-225-3455
www.aspiresd.org

Jennifer Gray, Executive Director
Arlette Keller, Director of Service Coordination
Angela Huffman, Director of Nursing
Offers peer counseling, attendant care registry and referrals.

4383 Black Hills Workshop & Training Center
Black Hills Workshop
3650 Range Road
PO Box 2104
Rapid City, SD 57709-2104
605-343-4550
FAX: 605-343-0879
TTY:800-877-1113
drosby@bhws.com
www.blackhillsworks.org

Brad Saathoff, Chief Executive Officer
Janet Niehaus, VP of Finance
Michelle Aman, VP of Residential Services
Offers job placement, housing options, case coordination, supported employment and supported living for all disability groups, as well as specialized services for brian injury victims.

4384 Communication Service for the Deaf: Rapid City
200 W Cesar Chavez St
Suite 650
Austin, TX 78701-694
844-222-0002
800-642-6410
FAX: 605-394-6609
TTY: 866-273-3323
csd@csd.org
www.c-s-d.org

Dr. Benjamin Soukup, Founder, Chairman & CEO
Christopher Soukup, President
Brad Hermes, Chief Financial Officer
A private, nonprofit organization dedicated to providing broad-based services, ensuring public accessibility and increasing public awareness of issues affecting deaf and hard of hearing inividuals.

4385 **Native American Advocacy Program for Persons with Disabilities**
P.O.Box 527
Winner, SD 57580-527

605-842-3977
800-303-3975
FAX: 605-842-3983
TTY: 605-842-3977

Marla Bull Bear, Executive Director
Charles Bull Bear, Specialist
Betty Farr, Il Specialist
The mission is to encourage a healthy organization that assists Native Americans with disabilities, by providing prevention, education and training, advocacy, support, independent living skills and referrals.

4386 **Prairie Freedom Center for Independent Living: Sioux Falls**
4107 S Carnegie Cr
Suite #9
Sioux Falls, SD 57106-3100

605-362-3550
FAX: 605-367-5639
i-l-c@ilcchoices.org
www.ilcchoices.org

Steve Tripp, President
Cheri Raymond, Vice President
Matt Cain, Executive Director
Established to provide basic skills so many of us take for granted: to take care of our own needs and to make our own decisions to be independent.

4387 **Prairie Freedom Center for Independent Living: Madison**
4107 S Carnegie Cr
411 SE 10th St
Sioux Falls, SD 57106-3570

605-362-3550
FAX: 605-256-5071
i-l-c@ilcchoices.org
www.ilcchoices.org

Steve Tripp, President
Cheri Raymond, Vice President
Matt Cain, Executive Director
Established to provide basic skills so many of us take for granted: to take care of our own needs and to make our own decisions to be independent.

4388 **Prairie Freedom Center for Independent Living: Yankton**
4107 S Carnegie Cr
Suite #107
Sioux Falls, SD 57106-2800

605-362-3550
FAX: 605-668-3060
TTY:605-668-3060
www.ilcchoices.org

Steve Tripp, President
Cheri Raymond, Vice President
Matt Cain, Executive Director
Established to provide basic skills so many of us take for granted: to take care of our own needs and to make our own decisions to be independent.

4389 **South Dakota Assistive Technology Project: DakotaLink**
1161 Deadwood Ave N
Suite #5
Rapid City, SD 57702-382

605-394-6742
800-645-0673
FAX: 605-394-6744
TTY: 605-394-6742
atinfo@dakotalink.net

Pat Czerny, Manager
Patrick Czerny, Technical Services Coordinator
David Scherer, Program Coordinator
DakotaLink, the South Dakota Assistive Technology Program, provides resources and supports to individuals of all ages to ensure greater access to and acquisition of assistive technology devices and services.

4390 **Western Resources for dis-ABLED Independence**
405 East Omaha St
Suite D
Rapid City, SD 57701-2974

605-718-1930
888-434-4943
FAX: 605-718-1933
TTY: 605-718-1930
chad@wril.org
www.wril.org

Jeff Wangen, President
Dennis Coull, Vice-President
Linda Lockner, Secretary
WRDI advocates for the rights of equal inclusion of people with disabilities in all aspects of community life. WRDI also strives to identify and promote access to existing resources and to advocate for the development of new resources, which may enable people with disabilities to live more independently.

Tennessee

4391 **Center for Independent Living of Middle Tennessee**
955 Woodland St
Nashville, TN 37206-3753

615-292-5803
866-992-4568
FAX: 615-383-1176
TTY: 615-292-7790

Tom Hopton, Executive Director
Tria Bridgeman, Benefits Analyst-Jackson
Dylan Brown, Benefits Analyst-Nashville
CILMT provides persons with disabilities opportunities to be self advocates and make their own decisions regarding living arrangements, means of transportation, employment, social and recreational activities, as well as other aspects of everyday life. Serves Davidson, Cheatham, Wilson, Robertson, Rutherford, Sumner and Williamson Counties.

4392 **DisAbility Resource Center: Knoxville**
900 E Hill Ave
Suite 205
Knoxville, TN 37915-2567

865-637-3666
FAX: 865-637-5616
TTY:865-637-6976

Lillian Burch, Executive Director
Nicole Craig, Programme Director
Katherine Moore, Independent Living Specialist
DRCTN mission is to empower people with disabilities to fully integrate and participate in the community. DRC is a community-based non-residential program of services designed to assist people with disabilities to gain independence and to assist the community in eliminating barriers of independence.

4393 **Jackson Center for Independent Living**
1981 Hollywood Drive
Jackson, TN 38305-4388

731-668-2211
FAX: 731-668-0406
TTY:731-664-3970
www.j-cil.com

Glen Barr, Executive Director
JCIL works with people with significant disabilities and the Deaf Community in achieving their Independent Living Goals while assisting the community in eliminating barriers to Independent Living.

4394 **Memphis Center for Independent Living**
1633 Madison Ave
Memphis, TN 38104-2506

901-726-6404
800-848-0298
FAX: 901-726-6521
TTY: 901-726-6404
info@mcil.org
www.mcil.org

Kevin Lofton, Chairman
Marvin Glenn Bailey, Vice-Chairman
Charles M. Weirich, Jr., Board Counsel
MCIL is a community based non-profit organization whose primary mission is to facilitate the full integration of persons with disabilities into all aspects of community life.

4395 Tennessee Technology Access Program (TTAP)
400 Deaderick St
14th Fl
Nashville, TN 37243-1403

615-313-5183
800-732-5059
FAX: 615-532-4685
TTY: 615-313-5695

Kevin Wright, Director
TTAP's mission is to maintain a statewide program of technology-rated assistance that is timely, comprehensive and consumer driven to ensure that all Tennesseans with disabilities have the information, services and deices that they need to make choices about where and how they spend their time as independently as possible.

4396 Tri-State Resource and Advocacy Corporation
6925 Shallowford Rd
#300
Chattanooga, TN 37421

423-892-4774
800-868-8724
FAX: 423-892-9866
TTY: 423-892-4774
www.1trac.org

Mark Woofall, Executive Director
Pam Jackson, Independent Living Facilitator
TRAC is dedicated to improving opportunities for individuals wuth disabilities.

Texas

4397 ABLE Center for Independent Living
1931 E 37th
St # 1
Odessa, TX 79762-6906

432-580-3439
info@ablecenterpb.org

Marilyn Hancock, Executive Director
Kathleen Story MA, Independent Living Specialist
Britni Veretto, HR Manager
To promote independent living for people with disabilities.

4398 Austin Resource Center for Independent Living
825 E. Rundberg Ln
Suite E6
Austin, TX 78753-4813

512-832-6349
800-414-6327
FAX: 512-832-1869
arcil@arcil.com
www.arcil.com

Ross Davis, Chair
Linda Loach, Vice-Chair
Sylvia Davis, Secretary/Treasurer
Serving people with disabilities, their families and communities throughout Travis and surrounding counties.

4399 Austin Resource Center: Round Rock
525 Round Rock West
Suite A120
Round Rock, TX 78681-5020

512-828-4624
FAX: 512-828-4625
sally@arcil.com
www.arcil.com

Ross Davis, Chair
Linda Loach, Vice-Chair
Sylvia Davis, Secretary/Treasurer
Serving peole with disabilities, their families and communities throughout Travis and surrounding counties.

4400 Austin Resource Center: San Marcos
618 South Guadalupe St
Suite #103
San Marcos, TX 78666- 6977

512-396-5790
800-572-2973
FAX: 512-396-5794
sanmarcos@arcil.com
www.arcil.com

Ross Davis, Chair
Linda Loach, Vice-Chair
Sylvia Davis, Secretary/Treasurer

Serving people with disabilities, their families and communities throughout Travis and surounding counties.

4401 Brazoria County Center For Independent Living
1104D East Mullberry Street
Suite D
Angleton, TX 77515- 3952

979-849-7060
888-872-7957
FAX: 979-849-8465
TTY: 979-849-7060
bccil@neosoft.com
www.hcil.cc

Chamane Barrow, Manager
To promote the full inclusion, equal opportunity and participation of persons with disabilities in every aspect of community life. We believe that people with disabilities have the right to make choices affecting their lives, a right to take risks, a right to fail, and a right to succeed.

4402 Centre, The
3550 West Dallas Rd
Houston, TX 77019

713-525-8400
FAX: 713-525-8444
thecenterhouston.org

Bill Coorsh, President
Richard Rosenberg, Vice-President
Lisa F. Schott, Secretary
Provides services for more than 600 children and adults with mental developmental disabilities. The Center also offers a wide array of programs including education, vocational training and job placement services, three different residential options representing both urban and rural living environments, special programs designed to meet the needs of older adults, and a variety of therapeutic support services.

4403 Crockett Resource Center for Independent Living
1020 Loop 304 East
Crockett, TX 75835-1806

936-544-2811
FAX: 936-544-7315
TTY:936-544-2811
crcil@windstream.net
www.crockettresourcecenter.org

Sara Minton, Executive Director
Mary Killough, Chief Financial Officer
Cathy Newsome, Information/Outreach Coordinator
Provides independent living services to cross-disability groups to increase their personal self-determination and minimize dependence on others. Maintain comprehensive information on availability of resources and provides referrals to such resources. Provides instruction to assist people with disabilities to gain skills that would empower them to live independently. Peer counseling, advocacy - both individual and community by assisting to obtain support services to make changes in society.

4404 Houston Center for Independent Living (HCIL)
6201 Bonhomme Rd.
Suite 150-South
Houston, TX 77036

713-974-4621
FAX: 713-974-6927
hcil@neosoft.com

Sandra Bookman, Executive Director
Advocacy organization created by and for people with disabilities (PWD) to empower and protect their rights. Services include but not limited to: peer to peer support, individual and systems advocacy, independent living skills training, information and referral, disability cultural awareness, ASL and Braille classes, ADA technical assistance, Relocation/Transition to Community Services, computer technology training, SSA Work Incentives Technical Assistance, equipment loan program.

4405 Independent Life Styles
215 North Benton Drive
Sauk Rapids, MN 56379-1874

320-529-9000
888-529-0743
FAX: 320-529-0747
ilicil@independentlifestyles.org
www.independentlifestyles.org

Karen Ahles, Chair
Jay Keller, Educator
Cara Ruff, Executive Director

Offers peer counseling, advocacy and other services to the community.

4406 Independent Living Research Utilization Project
Institute For Rehabilitation & Research
1333 Moursund
Houston, TX 77030

713-520-0232
FAX: 713-520-5785
TTY:713-520-0232
ilru@ilru.org
www.ilru.org

Lex Frieden, Director
ILRU is a national center for information, training, research and technical assistance in independent living. Its goal is to expand the body of knowledge in independent living and to improve utilization of results of research programs and demonstration projects in this field. ILRU is a program of The Institute for Rehabilitation and Research, a nationally recognized medical rehabilitation facility for persons with disabilities. TTY phone number: (713) 520-5136.

4407 LIFE/ Run Centers for Independent Living
8240 Boston Avenue
Lubbock, TX 79423-2342

806-795-5433
FAX: 806-795-5607
TTY:806-795-5433
wilmacrain@yahoo.com
www.liferun.org

Michelle Crain, Executive Director
Committed to providing individuals with disabilities the information and skills necessary to become independent and to achieve full inclusion in every aspect of their life.

4408 Office for Students with Disabilities, University of Texas at Arlington
701 South Nedderman Drive
Arlington, TX 76019-1

817-272-3364
800-735-2989
FAX: 817-272-1447
TTY: 800-735-2989
helpdesk@uta.edu
www.uta.edu/disability

Penny Acrey, Director
Demarice Ferguson, MS, CRC, Associate Director
Scott Holmes, Assistant Director for Testing
Offers disability counseling and academic accomodation to UT Arlington community.

4409 Palestine Resource Center for Independent Living
421 Avenue a St
Palestine, TX 75801-2903

903-729-7505
888-326-5166
FAX: 903-729-7540
TTY:903-729-7505
prcil@embarqmail.com
www.palestineresourcecenter.org/?

Sara Minton, Executive Director
Mary Killough, Chief Financial Officer
Cathy Newsome, Information/Outreach Coordinator
Provides independent living services to cross-disability groups to increase their personal self-determination and minimize dependence on others. Maintain comprehensive information on availability of resources and provides referrals to such resources. Provides instruction to assist people with disabilities to gain skills that would empower them to live independently. Peer counseling, advocacy - both individual and community by assisting to obtain support services to make changes in society.

4410 Panhandle Action Center for Independent Living Skills
417 W. 10th Avenue
Amarillo, TX 79101-4316

806-374-1400
FAX: 806-374-4550
TTY:806-374-2774
www.panhandleilc.org

Joe Rogers, Executive Director
Alma Benavides, Employment Director
Chris White, Development Director
PILC is a non profit organization dedicated to the advancement of full participation in all aspects of life. PILC services are developed, directed, delivered, and governed primarily by individuals with disabilities.

4411 REACH of Dallas Resource Center on Independent Living
8625 King George
Suite 210
Dallas, TX 75235-2286

214-630-4796
FAX: 214-630-6390
TTY:214-630-5995
reachdallas@reachcils.org
www.reachcils.org

Charlotte A. Stewart, Executive Director
Information and referral, peer support/peer counseling, independent living skills training and advocacy assistance.

4412 REACH of Denton Resource Center on Independent Living
405 S. Elm St
Suite 202
Denton, TX 76201-6068

940-383-1062
FAX: 940-383-2742
reachden@reachcils.org
www.reachcils.org

Charlotte A. Stewart, Executive Director
To provide for people with disabilities so that they are enabled to lead self-directed lives and to educate the general public about disability-related topics in order to promote a barrier free community.

4413 REACH of Fort Worth Resource Center on Independent Living
1000 Macon Street
Suite 200
Fort Worth, TX 76102-4527

817-870-9082
FAX: 817-877-1622
reachftw@reachcils.org
www.reachcils.org

Charlotte A. Stewart, Executive Director
To provide services for people with disabilities so that they are enabled to lead self-directed lives and to educate the general public about disability-related topics in order to promote a barrier free community.

4414 RISE-Resource: Information, Support and Empowerment
755 11th Street
Suite 101
Beaumont, TX 77701-3723

409-832-2599
FAX: 409-838-4499
TTY:409-832-2599
www.risecil.org

Jim Brocato, Executive Director
Amanda Powe, Relocation Services Specialist
Cheryl Bass, Program Director
A non-profit center for independent living.

4415 SAILS
1028 S Alamo St
San Antonio, TX 78210-1170

210-281-1878
800-474-0295
FAX: 210-281-1759
TTY: 210-281-1878
kbrietzke@sailstx.org
www.sailstx.org

Patricia Byrd, Chair
Dennis Wolf, Vice Chair
Jerry D. King, Treasurer
SAILS advocates for the rights and empowerment of people with disabilities in San Antonio; as well as surrounding areas. Services are provided to people with disabilities in the following counties: Atacosa, Bandera, Bexar, Calhoun, Comal, DeWitt, Dimmit, Edwards, Frio, Gillespie, Goliad, Gonzalez, Guadalupe, Jackson, Karnes, La Salle, Kendall, Kerr, Kinney, Lavaca, Maverick, Medina, Real, Uvalde, Val Verde, Victoria, Wilson and Zavala.

4416 Texas Department of Assistive and Rehabilitative Services
4800 N. Lamar Blvd
Austin, TX 78756
512-472-4138
800-628-5115
FAX: 512-472-0603
TTY: 866-581-9328
dars.inquiries@dars.state.tx.us
www.dars.state.tx.us

Bill West, Manager
Daniel Bravo, Chief Operating Officer
Rebecca Trevino, Chief Financial Officer
Provides technical assistance and other support services to the state's Independent Living Council, Independent Living Centers and Independent Living Counseling programs.

4417 VOLAR Center for Independent Living
1220 Golden Key Circle
El Paso, TX 79925-5825
915-591-0800
800-591-0800
FAX: 915-591-3506
TTY: 915-591-0800
volar@volarcil.org
www.volarcil.org

Luis Chew, Executive Director
Danny Monroe, Chief Financial Officer
Nena Garcia, Records Manager/Bookkeeper
VOLAR is committed to providing independent living ervices and information and referral, and to developing community options for persons with cross disabilities to empower them to live the kind of lives they choose. VOLAR is an organization of and for people with disabilities, advocating human and civil rights, community options and empowering people to live the lives they choose. Newsletter available.

4418 Valley Association for Independent Living (VAIL)
3012 N McColl Road
McAllen, TX 78501
956-668-8245
866-400-8245
FAX: 956-878-1601
info@vailrgv.org
vailrgv.org

Woodie Johnston, Executive Director
Offers information and referral, peer couseling, MS supprt group, independent living skills training, and advocacy, work incentives planning and assistance, transitioning people with disabilities from the nursing home into the community.

4419 Valley Association for Independent Living: Harlingen
1824 W. Jefferson Ave
Suite B
Harlingen, TX 78550-5247
956-428-1126
866-400-8245
FAX: 956-428-4339

Soledad Myers, Manager
Provides information and referral, peer counseling, support groups, independent living skills training, community rehab program and advocacy

Utah

4420 Active Re-Entry
10 S Fairgrounds Rd
Price, UT 84501
435-637-4950
FAX: 435-637-4952
TTY:435-637-4950
active@arecil.org
www.arecil.org

Nancy Bentley, Executive Director
Active Re-Entry is a community based program which assists individuals with disabilities to acheive or maintain self-sufficient and productive live in their own communities. Active Re-Entry is committed to promoting the rights, dignity, and quality of life for all persons with disabilities.

4421 Active Re-Entry: Vernal
10 S Fairgrounds Rd
Price, UT 84501-9727
435-637-4950
FAX: 435-789-6090
TTY:435-789-4021
active@arecil.org
www.arecil.org

Heather Moore, President
Active Re-Entry is a community based program which assists individuals with disabilities to achieve or maintain self-sufficient and productive lives in their own communities. We are committed to promoting the rights, dignity, and quality of life for all persons with disabilities.

4422 Central Utah Independent Living Center
3445 S Main St
Salt Lake City, UT 84115-2824
801-466-5565
877-421-4500
FAX: 801-466-2363
TTY: 801-373-5044
uilc@uilc.org
www.uilc.org

Debra Mair, Executive Director
Kim Meichle, Assistant Director
Patty Trent, Fiscal Manager
Empowers people with disabilities to reach their full potential in community settings through peer support, advocacy, and education.

4423 OPTIONS for Independence
Northern Utah Center for Independent Living
106 East 1120 N
Logan, UT 84341-2215
435-753-5353
FAX: 435-753-5390
TTY:435-753-5353
www.optionsind.org

Cheryl Atwood, Executive Director
OPTIONS for Independence, the Northern Utah Center for Independent Living serves people of all ages with all types of disabilities. OPTIONS is a nonresidential Center that provides services to individuals with disabilities to facilitate their full participation in the community and raise the understanding of disability issues and access to the community. The Independent Living philosophy is strictly adhered to: consumer control and choice being the focus.

4424 OPTIONS for Independence: Brigham Satellite
106 East 1120 N
Logan, UT 84341-3379
435-753-5353
FAX: 435-753-5390
TTY:435-723-2171
dcrockett@qwestoffice.net
www.optionsind.org

Cheryl Atwood, Executive Director
Deanna Crockett, Manager
OPTIONS is a nonresidential Independent Living Center where people with disabilities can learn skills to gain more control and independence over their lives. OPTIONS raises the vision and capability of the community at large to the point where people of all abilities will have equal access.

4425 Red Rock Center for Independence
515 W 300 N
Suite A
Saint George, UT 84770-4578
435-673-7501
800-649-2340
FAX: 435-673-8808
rrci@rrci.org
www.rrci.org

Barbara Lefler, Executive Director
Jerry Salkowe, President
Celeste Sorensen, Secretary
Red Rock Center for Independence assists people with disabilities to live and participate independently.

4426 Tri-County Independent Living Center
P.O.Box 428
Ogden, UT 84402-428   801-612-3215
                                         866-734-5678
                                    FAX: 801-612-3732
                                    TTY: 801-612-3215
                                         www.uilc.org

Richard Fox, Chairperson
Kim Price, Vice-Chairperson
Greg Killpack, Secretary/Treasurer
The mission of the Tri-County ILC is to enhance independence
for all people with disabilities. Serves Davis, Weber and Morgan
Counties.

**4427 Utah Assistive Technology Program (UTAP) Utah State
University**
6855 Old Main Hill
Logan, UT 84322-6855   435-797-3811
                                         800-524-5152
                                    FAX: 435-797-2355
                                         www.uatpat.org

Sachin Pavithran, UATP Program Director
Marilyn Hammond, Utah Assistive Technology Founda
Lois Summers, UATP Staff Assistant/UATF Busine
Provides expertise, resources, and a structure to enhance and ex-
pand AT services provided by private and public agencies in
Utah. Occcurs through monitoring, coordination, information
dissemination, empowering individuals, the identification and
removal of barriers, and expanding state resources.

4428 Utah Independent Living Center
3445 S Main St
Salt Lake City, UT 84115-4453   801-466-5565
                                         800-355-2195
                                    FAX: 801-466-2363
                                    TTY: 801-466-5565
                                         uilc@uilc.org
                                         www.uilc.org

Debra Mair, Executive Director
Kim Meichle, Assistant Director
Julie Beckstead, Program Coordinator
Offers information and referral services. To assist persons with
disabilities achieve independence by providing services and activities which enhance independent living skillspromote the public's understanding, accomodation, and acceptance of their
rights, needs and abilities.

4429 Utah Independent Living Center: Minersville
P.O.Box 168
Minersville, UT 84752-168   435-691-7724
                                         rrci@rrci.org
                                         www.rrci.org

Barbara Lefler, Executive Director
Jerry Salkowe, President
Celeste Sorensen, Secretary
To enhance independence for all people with disaibilities.

4430 Utah Independent Living Center: Tooele
42 S Main St
Tooele, UT 84074-2132   435-843-7353
                                    FAX: 435-843-7359
                                    TTY:435-843-7353
                                         www.uilc.org

Debra Mair, Executive Director
Kim Meichle, Assistant Director
Julie Beckstead, Program Coordinator
Mission is to assist persons with disabilities achieve greater independence by providing services and activities which enhance independent living skills and promote the public's understanding,
accomodation, and acceptance of their rights, needs and abilities.

Vermont

4431 Vermont Assistive Technology Program
Department of Aging and Independent Living
100 State Street
Montpelier, VT 05602-2305   802-871-3353
                                         800-750-6355
                                    FAX: 802-871-3048
                                    TTY: 802-241-1464
                              www.atp.vermont.gov/tryout-centers

Julie Tucker, Program Director
David Punia ATP, Information/Education Specialist
Encompasses a state coordinating council for assistive technology issues, regional centers for demonstration, trial and technical
support with computer and augmentative communication equipment and regional seating and positioning centers.

4432 Vermont Center for Independent Living: Bennington
601 Main St
Bennington, VT 5201-2875   802-447-0574
                                         800-639-1522
                                         info@vcil.org
                                         www.vcil.org

Colleen Arcodia, Peer Advocate Counselor
Michelle Grubb, Finance & Operations Officer
Sarah Launderville, Executive Director
Believes that individuals with disabilities have the right to live
with dignity and with appropriate support in their own homes,
fully participate in their communities, and to control and make
decisions about their lives.

4433 Vermont Center for Independent Living: Chittenden
11 East State Street
Montpelier, VT 05602   802-229-0501
                                         800-639-1522
                                    FAX: 802-229-0503
                                    TTY: 802-229-0501
                                         info@vcil.org
                                         www.vcil.org

Colleen Arcodia, Peer Advocate Counselor
Nathan Besio, Peer Advocate Counselor
Chanda Beun, Receptionist/Admin Specialist
Believes that individuals with disabilities have the right to live
with dignity and with appropriate support in their own homes,
fully participate in their communities, and to control and make
decisions about their lives.

4434 Vermont Center for Independent Living: Montpelier
11 E State St
Montpelier, VT 05602-3008   802-229-0501
                                         800-639-1522
                                    FAX: 802-229-0503
                                         info@vcil.org
                                         vcil.org

Colleen Arcodia, Peer Advocate Counselor
Denise Bailey, Direct Services Coordinator
Dhiresha Blose, Development Officer
Believes that individuals with disabilities have the right to live
with dignity and with appropriate support in their own homes,
fully participate in their communities, and to control and make
decisions about their lives.

Virginia

4435 Access Independence
324 Hope Dr
Winchester, VA 22601-6800   540-662-4452
                                    FAX: 540-662-4474
                                    TTY:540-662-5556
                              askai@accessindependence.org
                              www.accessindependence.org

Donald Price, Executive Director
Brenda Ernst, Independent Living Specialist
Joan Davis, Manager Operations/Rep Payee
Offers support services to persons with disabilities to assist in
maintaining or increasing their independence and self-determi-
nation. Includes housing assistance, independent living skills

training, information, referral services, assistance and representative payee and advocacy.

4436 Appalachian Independence Center
230 Charwood Dr
Abingdon, VA 24210-2566   276-628-2979
FAX: 276-628-4931
TTY:276-676-0920
aicadmin@ntelos.net
aicadvocates.org

Greg Morrell, Executive Director
Donna Buckland, Development Director
Scarlett Cox, Operations Director
Mission is to advocate for and with people with disabilities to promote full participation in society

4437 Blue Ridge Independent Living Center
Ste B
1502 Williamson Rd NE
Roanoke, VA 24012-5100   540-342-1231
FAX: 540-342-9505
TTY:540-342-1231
brilc@brilc.org
brilc.org

Karen Michalski-Karn, Executive Director
Dana Jackson, Program Services Director
Lottie Diomedi, Independent Living Coordinator
BRILC assists people with disabilities to live independently. The Center also serves the community at large by helping to create and environment that is accessible to all. BRILC offers a variety of services ranging from referrals to community resources, support services, and direct services. These include peer counseling, support groups, training and seminars, advocacy, education, support services, awareness, aid in obtaining specialized equipment, and much more.

4438 Blue Ridge Independent Living Center: Christianburg
210 Pepper Street S
Christiansburg, VA 24073-3571   540-381-8829
FAX: 540-381-8833
TTY:540-381-9149
brilc@brilc.org
brilc.org

Karen Michalski-Karney, Executive Director
Dana Jackson, Program Services Director
Lottie Diomedi, Independent Living Coordinator
Assists people with disabilities to live independently. The center also serves the community at large by helping to create an environment that is accessible to all.

4439 Blue Ridge Independent Living Center: Low Moor
P.O.Box 7
Low Moor, VA 24457-7   540-862-0252
FAX: 540-862-0252
TTY:540-862-0252
brilc.org

Karen Michalski-Karney, Executive Director
Dana Jackson, Program Services Director
Lottie Diomedi, Independent Living Coordinator
Assists to help people with disabilities to live independently. The center also serves the community at large by helping to create an environment that is accessible to all.

4440 Clinch Independent Living Services
1139C Plaza Drive
Grundy, VA 24614-6780   276-935-6088
800-597-2322
FAX: 276-935-6342
TTY: 276-935-6088

Betty Bevins, Executive Director
Nonprofit organization providing information and referral, peer counseling, advocacy and independent living skills training to persons with disabilities.

4441 Disability Resource Center
409 Progress St
Fredericksburg, VA 22401-3337   540-373-2559
800-648-6324
FAX: 540-373-8126
TTY: 540-373-5890
drc@cildrc.org

Debe Fults, Executive Director
Eric Barnes, Equipment Connection Assistant
Grace Marshall, Community Integration Coor.
Mission is to assist people with disabilities, those who support them, and the community, through information, education and resources, to achieve the highest potential and benefit of independent living.

4442 ENDependence Center of Northern Virginia
2300 Claredon Blvd.
Suite 3305
Arlington, VA 22201-3367   703-525-3268
866-849-3852
FAX: 703-525-3585
TTY: 703-525-3553
info@ecnv.org
www.ecnv.org

Cynthia Evans, Director of Community Services
Layo Oyewole, Director of Medicaid Programs
Doris Ray, Director of Advocacy and Outreach
ECNV is a community-based resource and advocacy enter which is managed by and for people with disabilities. ENCV promotes independent living philosophy and equal access for all persons with disabilities and, like the nearly 400 centers for independent living across the country, ECNV grew from local disability rights and self-help movements.

4443 Equal Access Center for Independence
4031 University Drive
Suite #301
Fairfax, VA 22030-3409   703-934-2020
TTY:703-277-7730

David Sharp, Executive Director
Provides information and referral, peer counseling, advocacy and independent living skills training to persons with disabilities.

4444 Independence Empowerment Center
8409 Dorsey Circle
Suite 101
Manassas, VA 20110-4414   703-257-5400
FAX: 703-257-5043
TTY:703-257-5400
info@ieccil.org
www.ieccil.org

Mary D Lopez, Executive Director
Roberta McEachern, Program Director
Sheree Thomas, Grants Coordinator
A non-profit Center for Independent Living. One of over 500 centers in the United States with roots in civil rights models of the 1960's.

4445 Independence Resource Center
815 Cherry Ave
Charlottesville, VA 22903-3448   434-971-9629
FAX: 434-971-8242
TTY:434-971-9629
tvandever@ntelos.net
www.charlottesvilleirc.org

Tom Vandever, Executive Director
Brenda Gianniny, Administrator
Carolyn Berry, Participant Services Coordinator
Information and referral services.

4446 Independent Living Center Network: Department of the Visually Handicapped
Ste 300
1809 Staples Mill Rd
Richmond, VA 23230-3515   FAX: 804-355-9297
Robert W Partin, Director
Robert Kastenbaum, Partner
Information and referral services.

4447 Junction Center for Independent Living
P.O.Box 1210
Norton, VA 24273-913

276-679-5988
FAX: 276-679-6569
TTY:276-679-5988
jcil1@junctioncenter.org
junctioncenter.org

Dennis Horton, Executive Director
Cindy Mefford, Assistant to the Executive Direc
Joe Brady, Deaf and Hard of Hearing Coordin
To assist those who have significant disabilities so that they migh
live independently in the least restrictive and most integrated environment possible.

4448 Junction Center for Independent Living: Duffield
P.O.Box 408
Duffield, VA 24244-408

276-431-1195
FAX: 276-431-1196
TTY:276-431-1195
jcil1@junctioncenter.org

Dennis Horton, Executive Director
Cindy Mefford, Assistant to the Executive Direc
Joe Brady, Deaf and Hard of Hearing Coordin
To assist those who have significant disabilities so that they might live independently in the least restrictive and most integrated environment possbile.

4449 Lynchburg Area Center for Independent Living
500 Alleghany Ave
Suite #520
Lynchburg, VA 24501-2610

434-528-4971
FAX: 434-528-4976
TTY:434-528-4972
www.lacil.org

Phil Theisen, Executive Director
LACIL is a private non-profit, non-residential consumer driven organization that promotes the efforts of persons with disabilities to live independently in the community and supports the efforts of the community to be open and accessible to all citizens.

4450 Peidmont Independent Living Center
Piedmont Living Center
601 S. Belvidere Street
Richmond, VA 23220

804-782-1986
800-828-1140
FAX: 877-VHD- 123
www.vhda.com

Kit Hale, Chairman
Timothy M. Chapman, Vice Chairman
Susan Dewey, Executive Director
Empowering indiviuals with disabilities to become self-sufficient and independent within their communities.

4451 Peninsula Center for Independent Living
2021-A Cunningham Drive
Suite #2
Hampton, VA 23666-3320

757-827-0275
FAX: 757-827-0655
TTY:757-827-8800
iepcil@hvacil.org
www.hvacil.org

Ralph Shelman, Executive Director
IEPCIL is a private non-profit non-residential Agency established to provide services to people with disabilities. The Centers Philosophy is that people with a disability should play a major role in deciding their future.The center provides services to people with disabilities in the cities of Hampton, Newport News, Poquoson, Williamsburg, and counties of James City, York, and Gloucester.

4452 Piedmont Independent Living Center
1045 Main Street
Suite #2
Danville, VA 24541-1800

434-797-2530
FAX: 434-797-2568
TTY:434-797-2530

Clarence Dickerson, Executive Director
Jeanette King, ILS Coordinator/BPAD
Lori Penn, Office Manager
Empowering indiviuals with disabilities to become self-sufficient and independent within their communities.

4453 Resources for Independent Living
4009 Fitzhugh Ave
Richmond, VA 23230-3953

804-353-6503
FAX: 804-358-5606
TTY:804-353-6583
info@ril-va.org
www.ril-va.org

Gerald O'Neill, Executive Director
Marcia Guardino, Program Manager
Kelly Hickok, Community Services Manager
Assisting persons who are severly disabled to live independently in the community and to encourage necessary change within the community so independent living is a possibility.

4454 Valley Associates for Independent Living (VAIL)
Shenandoah Valley Workforce Investment Board
3210 Peoples Drive
Suite 220
Harrisonburg, VA 22801-869

540-433-6513
888-242-8245
FAX: 540-433-6313
vail@govail.org
www.govail.org

Marcia Du Bois, Executive Director
Bob Satterwhite, Executive Director
VAIL is a not-for-profit, private Center for Independent Living providing advocacy, information and referral, independent living skills training, supported employment, and peer counseling to individuals with disabilities in our planning district.

4455 Valley Associates for Independent Living: Lexington
205-B South Liberty St
Harrisonburg, VA 22801-3638

540-433-6513
888-242-8245
FAX: 540-433-6313
TTY:540-438-9265
vail@govail.org
www.govail.org

Marcia Du Bois, Executive Director
Promoting self-direction among people with disabilities and removing barriers to independence in the community.

4456 Woodrow Wilson Rehabilitation Center Training Program
243 Woodrow Wilson Avenue
Fishersville, VA 22939-1500

540-332-7000
800-345-9972
FAX: 540-332-7132
TTY: 800-811-7893
www.wwrc.net

Rick Sizemore, Executive Director
Information & referral services. Six week Virginia residential programs and evaluation services.

Washington

4457 Alliance for People with Disabilities: Seattle
1120 E. Terrace St
Suite 100
Seattle, WA 98122

206-545-7055
866-545-7055
FAX: 206-545-7059
TTY: 206-632-3456
info@disabilitypride.org
www.disabilitypride.org

Kimberly Heymann, Executive Director
Elizabeth Kennedy, Executive Assistant
Bhelle Ollero, IL Specialist
The Alliance promotes equality and choice for people with disabilities. They provide advocacy, peer support, idependent living skills training, information and referral, transition assistance for youth, civil rights legal aid, assistive technology, training and nursing home transition back into the community.

4458 Alliance of People with Disabilities: Redmond
East King County Office
1150 140th Ave NE
Suite 101
Bellevue, WA 98005-3537
425-558-0993
800-216-3335
FAX: 425-558-4773
TTY: 425-861-4773
info@disabilitypride.org
www.disabilitypride.org

Kimberly Heymann, Executive Director
Elizabeth Kennedy, Executive Assistant
Bhelle Ollero, IL Specialist
Services include: information and referral, independent living skills training, peer groups, disAbility law project (DLP), access reviews, health insurance advising, and systems advocacy.

4459 Community Services for the Blind and Partially Sighted Store: Sight Connection
9709 Third Ave NE
Suite #100
Seattle, WA 98115-2027
206-525-5556
800-458-4888
FAX: 206-525-0422
www.sightconnection.org

Mary Lewis, Secretary
Shannon Grady Martsolf, President/CEO
Miles Otoupal, Chair
Over 300 practical products for living with vision loss selected by certified vision rehabilitation specialists from Community Services for the Blind and Partially Sighted. Easy-to-use online store features large print, large photos, secure transactions, and links to other vision-related resources.

4460 DisAbility Resource Connection: Everett
607 SE Everett Mall Way
Suite 6C
Everett, WA 98208-3210
425-347-5768
800-315-3583
FAX: 425-710-0767
TTY: 425-347-5768

Charley Lane, Executive Director
disAbility Resource Connection is all about living your life as you choose. The staff is committed to assisting every individual to connect to resources, connect to skills, connect to life.

4461 Kitsap Community Resources
845 8th St
Bremerton, WA 98337-1517
360-478-2301
FAX: 360-415-2706
info@kcr.org
www.kcr.org

Larry Eyer, Executive Director
Irmgard Davis, Fiscal Officer
Rudy Taylor, Board President
Kitsap Community Resources is a local, non-profit organization dedicated to helping people in need. KCR creates hope and opportunity for low-income Kitsap County Residents by providing resources that promote self-sufficiency.

4462 Spokane Center for Independent Living
8817 E. Mission Ave.
Suite 106
Spokane Valley, WA 99212
509-326-6355
FAX: 509-327-2420
info@scilwa.org

William Kane, Executive Director
To improve the self-determination and self-reliance of people with disabilities through systems and individual advocacy, education and independent living services.

4463 Tacoma Area Coalition of Individuals with Disabilities
6315 S 19th St
Tacoma, WA 98466-6217
253-565-9000
877-538-2243
FAX: 253-565-5578
TTY: 253-565-3486
www.tacid.org

Ken Gibson, Executive Director
Steve Pierce, CFO
Jo Ann Maxwell, Deputy Executive Director - Phil

Promotes the independence of individuals with disabilities.

West Virginia

4464 Appalachian Center for Independent Living
4710 Chimney Drive
Suite # C
Charleston, WV 25302-4841
304-965-0376
800-642-3003
FAX: 304-965-0377
TTY: 800-642-3003
acil@yahoo.com
www.mtstcil.org

Ann Weeks, President and CEO
Adam Elmer, Chief Financial Officer
Georgetta Stevens, VP, Corporate Operations
A resource center for persons with disabilities and their communities. Serves Kanawha, Clay, Boone and Putnam counties.

4465 Appalachian Center for Independent Living: Spencer
811 Madison Avenue
Suite #106
Spencer, WV 25276-1900
304-927-4080
FAX: 304-927-4330
TTY: 800-642-3003
susanacil@yahoo.com
www.mtstcil.org

Ann Weeks, President and CEO
Adam Elmer, Chief Financial Officer
Georgetta Stevens, VP, Corporate Operations
A resource center for persons with disabilities and their communities. Serves Jackson, Roane, and Calhoun counties.

4466 Mountain State Center for Independent Living
329 Prince St
Beckley, WV 25801-4515
304-255-0122
FAX: 304-255-0157
TTY: 304-255-0122
aoweeks@mtstcil.org
www.mtstcil.org

Ann Weeks, President and CEO
Adam Elmer, Chief Financial Officer
Georgetta Stevens, VP, Corporate Operations
This office provides individual and systems advocacy, independent living skills development, information and referral, peer support, personal assistance services, housing referral and training, transportation. Serves Raleigh counties.

4467 Mountain State Center for Independent Living
821 Fourth Avenue
Huntington, WV 25701-1406
304-525-3324
866-687-8245
FAX: 304-525-3360
TTY: 304-525-3324
aoweeks@mtstcil.org
www.mtstcil.org

Ann Weeks, President and CEO
Adam Elmer, Chief Financial Officer
Georgetta Stevens, VP, Corporate Operations
Services provided are: individual and systems advocacy, independent living skills development, information and referral, peer support, personal assistance services, supported employment, community integration program, housing referral and training, transportation. Serves Cabell and Wayne counties.

4468 Northern West Virginia Center for Independent Living
601-603 East Brockway
Suite A & B
Morgantown, WV 26501
304-296-6091
800-834-6408
FAX: 304-292-5217
TTY: 304-296-6091
nwvcil@nwvcil.org
www.mtstcil.org

Ann Weeks, President and CEO
Adam Elmer, Chief Financial Officer
Georgetta Stevens, VP, Corporate Operations
NWVCIL is committed to the philosophy that all persons have equal access and unconditional value, that all individuals shall be

respected for their uniqueness and shall have the right to live within the community of their choice, having equal access to participate in and contribute to that community.

Wisconsin

4469 **Center for Independent Living of Western Wisconsin**
2920 Schneider Avenue East
Menomonie, WI 54751-2331
715-233-1070
800-228-3287
FAX: 715-233-1083
TTY: 800-228-3287
www.cilww.com

Tim Sheehan, Executive Director
Kay Sommerfeld, Assistant Director
Tammy Grage, Fiscal & HR Manager
Advocates for the full participation in society of all persons with disabilities. Our goal is empwowering individuals to exercise choices to maintain or increase their indpendence. Our strategy is providing consumer-driven services at no cost to persons with disiabilities in Western Wisconsin

4470 **Independence First**
540 South 1st Street
Milwaukee, WI 53204-1516
414-291-7520
FAX: 414-291-7525
TTY:414-297-7520
lschulz@independencefirst.org
www.independencefirst.org

Lee Schulz, President and CEO
John Schmid, Chair
Judy Murphy, Vice Chair
A non-profit agency directed by, and for the benefit of, persons with disabilities, primarily serving the four county metropolitan Milwaukee area.

4471 **Independence First: West Bend**
735 S Main St
West Bend, WI 53095-3965
262-306-6717
lschulz@independencefirst.org
www.independencefirst.org

Lee Schulz, President and CEO
John Schmid, Chair
Judy Murphy, Vice Chair
A non-profit agency directed by, and for the benefit of, persons with disabilities, primarily serving the four county Metropolitan Milwaukee area.

4472 **Inspiration Ministries**
N2270 State Road 67
Walworth, WI 53184-948
262-275-6131
FAX: 262-275-3355
inspirationministries.org

Robin Knoll, President
Richard Hall, Executive Vice President
Craig Pape, VP Ministry Services
Formerly known as Christian League for the Handicapped, Inspiration Ministries is a vibrant community of adults with disabilities engaged in living, working, leisure and faith activities designed to provide a complete living experience. The campus consists of a modern residential facility offering a range of living accomodations; a work center and resale shop; and Inspiration Center, a retreat/camping center designed to be 100% wheelchair accessible.

4473 **Mid-State Independent Living Consultants: Wausau**
3262 Church Street
Suite #1
Stevens Point, WI 54481-5321
715-344-4210
800-382-8484
FAX: 715-344-4414
TTY: 800-382-8484
milc@milc-inc.org
www.milc-inc.org

Tom Vandehey, President
Becky Paulson, Independent Living Consultant
Working for persons with disabilities towards empowerment to make informed choices.

4474 **Mid-state Independent Living Consultants: Stevens Point**
3262 Church Street
Suite #1
Stevens Point, WI 54481-5321
715-344-4210
800-382-8484
FAX: 715-344-4414
TTY: 800-382-8484
milc@milc-inc.org
www.milc-inc.org

Jenny Fasula, Executive Director
Karalyn Peterson, Resource Director
Committed to enhancing personal and community relationships, providing opportunities for growth, and helping people with varying abilities achieve their personal goals.

4475 **North Country Independent Living**
69 N 28th St.
Suite 28
Superior, WI 54880-5138
715-392-9118
800-924-1220
FAX: 715-392-4636
northcountryil.com

John Nousaine, Executive Director
Gloria Hakkila-Johnson, Assistant Director
Jim Glaeser, Accountant
Empowers people with disabilities.

4476 **North Country Independent Living: Ashland**
422 3rd St. W.
Suite #114
Ashland, WI 54806-1553
715-682-5676
800-499-5676
FAX: 715-682-3144
TTY: 715-682-5676
northcountryil.com

John Nousaine, Director
Empowers people with disabilities.

4477 **Options for Independent Living**
555 Country Club Road
Green Bay, WI 54307-1967
920-490-0500
888-465-1515
FAX: 920-490-0700
TTY:920-490-0600
www.optionsil.com

Thomas Diedrick, Executive Director
Kathryn C. Barry, Assistant Director
Sandra L. Popp, Independent Living Coordinator
A non-profit organization committed to empowering people with disabilities to lead independent and productive lives in their community through advocacy, the provision of information, education, technology and related services.

4478 **Options for Independent Living: Fox Valley**
820 West College Ave
Suite #5
Appleton, WI 54914
920-997-9999
888-465-1515
FAX: 920-997-9381
TTY:920-490-0600
www.optionsil.com

Thomas Diedrick, Executive Director
Kathryn C. Barry, Assistant Director
Sandra L. Popp, Independent Living Coordinator
A non-profit organization committed to empowering people with disabilities to lead independent and productive lives in their community through advocacy, the provision of information, education, technology and related services.

4479 **Society's Assets: Elkhorn**
615 E Geneva St
Elkhorn, WI 53121-2301
262-723-8181
800-261-8181
FAX: 262-723-8184
TTY: 866-840-9763
info@societysassets.org
www.societysassets.org

Bruce Nelson, Director
Jill Vigueres, Manager
To ensure the rights of all persons with disabilities to live and function as independently as possible in the community of their

choice, through supporting individual's efforts to achieve control over their lives and become integrated into community life.

4480   Society's Assets: Kenosha
5455 Sheridan Road
Suite 101
Kenosha, WI 53140-4103   262-657-3999
                          800-317-3999
                          FAX: 262-657-1672
                          TTY: 866-840-9762
                          info@societysassets.org
                          www.societysassets.org

Sue Liu, Manager
Bruce Nelsen, Executive Director
To ensure the rights of all persons with disabilities to live and function as independently as possible in the community of their choice, through supporting individuals efforts to achieve controll over their lives and become integrated into community life. Offers home care and independent living services.

4481   Society's Assets: Racine
5200 Washinton Ave
Suite #225
Racine, WI 53406-4238   262-637-9128
                         800-378-9128
                         FAX: 262-637-8646
                         TTY: 886-840-9761
                         info@societysassets.org
                         www.societysassets.org

Deb Pitsch, Administrator
Karen Olufs, Director Independent Living
Jean Rumachik, Director Home Care Services
Society's Assets assists people with disabilities to live as independently as possible. A non-profit human services agency, Society's Assets provides information and referal, independent living skills training, peer support, advocacy, and supportive home care. Home health care is provided by SAI Home Health Care. The agency serves 5 counties in southeastern Wisconsin and also provides information about interpreters, employment, benefits, home modifications, assistive equipment and accessibility.
Fees vary

Wyoming

4482   RENEW: Gillette
35 Fairgrounds Road
Newcastle, WY 82701   307-746-4733
                       888-253-4653
                       FAX: 307-746-9701
                       www.renew-wyo.com

Donna Bombeck, Chairwoman
Carolyn Holso, Vice Chairwoman
Renee Nack, Secretary
Empowering persons with disabilities to enrich their lives.

4483   RENEW: Rehabilitation Enterprises of North Eastern Wyoming
1969 S Sheridan Ave
Sheridan, WY 82801-6108   307-672-7481
                           888-309-2020
                           FAX: 307-674-5117
                           pr@renew-wyo.com
                           www.renew-wyo.com

Donna Bombeck, Chairwoman
Carolyn Holso, Vice Chairwoman
Renee Nack, Secretary
Multi-disciplinary organization dedicated to the highest possible economic and social independence for persons with disabilities. Extensive referral service, specialized employment placement, occupational therapy, psychological services, evaluation services, and coordination of external services as needed to meet client plans and objectives.

4484   Rehabilitation Enterprises of North Eastern Wyoming: Newcastle
35 Fairgrounds Rd
Newcastle, WY 82701-2625   307-746-4733
                            888-693-9245
                            FAX: 307-746-9701
                            www.renew-wyo.com

Donna Bombeck, Chairwoman
Carolyn Holso, Vice Chairwoman
Renee Nack, Secretary
Empowering persons with disabilities to enrich their lives.

4485   Wyoming Services for Independent Living
1156 South 2nd
Lander, WY 82520-3905   307-332-4889
                         800-266-3061
                         FAX: 307-332-2491
                         TTY: 307-332-7582
                         www.wysil.org

Susan Hoesel, Business Manager
Donna Langelier, Program Manager
Marcia Henthorn, Program Manager
Committed to enhancing personal and community relationships, providing opportunities for growth, and helping people with varying abilities achieve thier personal goals.

Law

Associations & Referral Agencies

4486 Center for Disability and Elder Law, Inc.
205 W. Randolph
Suite 1610
Chicago, IL 60606 312-376-1880
FAX: 312-376-1885
info@cdelaw.org
www.cdelaw.org

Caroline Manley, Executive Director
Stephanie Ridella Vittands, Staff Attorney
A not-for-profit legal services organization which provids legal services to low income persons residing in Chicago and Cook County, Il., who are either elderly and/or persons with disabilities. CDEL provides legal services by matching qualified candidates with volunteer attorneys who represent them, pro-bono, in a wide range of civil legal matters; and through special initiatives including the Senior Center Initiative (SCI) and the Senior Tax Opportunity program.

4487 Center for Workplace Compliance
1501 M Street NW
Suite 400
Washington, DC 20005 202-629-5650
FAX: 202-629-5651
info@cwc.org
cwc.org

Joseph S. Lakis, President
Michael Eastman, Senior Vice President, Policy
Danny Patrella, Vice President, Compliance
Formerly known as the Equal Employment Advisory Council, it is a nonprofit employer association providing guidance to its member companies on understanding and complying with their affirmative action obligations.
1976

4488 Chicago Lawyers' Committee for Civil Rights Under Law
100 N LaSalle Street
Suite 600
Chicago, IL 60602-2400 312-630-9744
FAX: 312-630-1127
info@clccrul.org
www.clccrul.org

Bonnie Allen, Executive Director
Timna Axel, Director, Communications
Aneel Chablani, Chief Counsel
Promotes and protects civil rights of low-income, minority and disadvantaged people in the social, economic, and political systems of the nation.

4489 CrescentCare Legal Services
1631 Elysian Fields Ave.
New Orleans, LA 70117 504-323-2642
www.aidslaw.org

J. Lind, Attorney
J. Johnson, Attorney
J. Holmes, Attorney
The mission of CrescentCare Legal Services (formerly AIDSLAW Louisiana) is to provide excellent, specialized legal services for people living with HIV/AIDS in Louisiana, to improve their quality of life and access to health care, related to their HIV/AIDS status.

4490 DNA People's Legal Services
PO Box 306
Window Rock, AZ 86515 928-871-4151
FAX: 928-871-5036
www.dnalegalservices.org

Kathy Gallagher, Development Director
A nonprofit legal aid organization working to protect civil rights, promote tribal sovereignty and alleviate civil legal problems for people who live in poverty in the Southwestern United States.
1967

4491 Disability Law Colorado
455 Sherman St.
Suite 130
Denver, CO 80203 303-722-3619
800-288-1376
FAX: 303-722-0720
disabilitylawco.org

Mary Anne Harvey, Executive Director
Alison L. Butler, Esq., Director, Legal Services
Mark Ivandick, Managing Attorney/Program Coordinator
Protects and promotes the rights of people with disabilities and older people in Colorado through direct legal representation, advocacy, education and legislative analysis.

4492 Disability Rights Advocates
2001 Center St
4th Floor
Berkeley, CA 94704-1204 510-665-8644
FAX: 510-665-8511
frontdesk@dralegal.org
dralegal.org

Michelle Caiola, Managing Director, Litigation
Kate Hamilton, Managing Director, Development & Operations
Stuart Seaborn, Managing Director, Litigation
Disability Rights Advocates is a non-profit legal center representing people with disabilities, advocating for them when their civil rights have been violated. Their clients include those with mobility, sensory, cognitive, and psychiatric disabilities.

4493 Disability Rights Education and Defense Fund
3075 Adeline Street
Suite 210
Berkeley, CA 94703 510-644-2555
FAX: 510-841-8645
info@dredf.org
dredf.org

Susan Henderson, Executive Director
Claudia Center, Legal Director
Silvia Yee, Senior Staff Attorney
Nonprofit organization dedicated to advancing the civil rights of individuals with disabilities through legislation, litigation, informal and formal advocacy and education and training of lawyers, advocates and clients with respect to disability issues. DREDF also provides training, advocacy, technical assistance and referrals for parents of disabled children.

4494 Disability Rights Texas
2222 West Braker Lane
Austin, TX 78758-1024 512-454-4816
866-362-2851
www.disabilityrightstx.org

Mary Faithfull, Executive Director
Patty Anderson, Deputy Director
A federally designated legal protection and advocacy agency (P&A) for people with disabilities in Texas. Helps people with disabilities understand and exercise their rights under the law, ensuring their full and equal participation in society.

4495 Guardianship Services Associates
41A South Blvd
Oak Park, IL 60302-2777 708-386-5398
FAX: 708-386-5970

Robert R. Wohlgemuth, Executive Director
Information and counseling on guardianship and its alternatives. Can provide direct assistance in obtaining guardianship for disabled adults in Cook County. Also provides information and direct assistance on durable powers of attorney.

4496 Independence Economic Development
210 W Truman Road
Independence, MO 64050 816-252-5777
FAX: 816-254-1641
info@inedc.biz
www.iced.org

J.D. Kehrman, President
Jodi Krantz, Vice President
Xander Winkel, Executive Director, Ennovation Center
A non-profit, public/private partnership established for the purpose of supporting and enhancing the economic growth of independence.

4497 Independent Living Research Utilization
1333 Moursund
Houston, TX 77030-7031
713-520-0232
FAX: 713-520-5785
TTY:713-520-0232
ilru@ilru.org
ilru.org

Lex Frieden, Director
Richard Petty, Co-Director
Brooke Curtis, Program Coordinator

The ILRU is a national center for information, training, research, and technical assistance in independent living. Its goal is to expand the body of knowledge in independent living and to improve utilization of results of research programs and demonstration projects in this field.

4498 Judge David L Bazelon Center for Mental Health Law
1090 Vermont Avenue NW
Suite 220
Washington, DC 20005
202-467-5730
communications@bazelon.org
www.bazelon.org

Holly O'Donnell, CEO
Ira Burnim, Director, Legal
Jennifer Mathis, Director, Policy & Legal Advocacy

A nonprofit organization devoted to improving the lives of people with mental illnesses through changes in policy and law.

4499 Legal Action Center
810 1st Street
Suite 200
Washington, DC 20002
202-544-5478
FAX: 202-544-5712
lacinfo@lac.org
www.lac.org

Paul N. Samuels, Director & President
Anita R. Marton, Senior Vice President
Ellen Weber, Vice President, Health Initiatives

The only non-profit law and policy organization in the United States whose sole mission is to fight discrimination against people with histories of addiction, HIV/AIDS, or criminal records, and to advocate for sound public policies in these areas.

4500 Legal Counsel for Health Jusice
17 North State Street
Suite 900
Chicago, IL 60602
312-427-8990
FAX: 312-427-8419
legalcouncil.org

Tom Yates, Executive Director
Ellyce Anapolsky, Senior Staff Attorney
Julie Brennan, Program Director

Formerly known as the AIDS Legal Council of Chicago, the group provides legal assistance for people with illness and/or disability.

4501 National Health Law Program (NHeLP)
3701 Wilshire Blvd
Suite 750
Los Angeles, CA 90010
310-204-6010
www.healthlaw.org

Amy Chen, Senior Attorney
Abigail Coursolle, Senior Attorney
Elizabeth G. Taylor, Executive Director

A national public interest law firm that seeks to improve health care for America's working and unemployed poor, minorities, the elderly and people with disabilities. NHeLP serves legal services programs, community-based organizations, the private bar, providers and individuals who work to preserve a health care safety net for the millions of uninsured or underinsured low-income people.
1970

4502 National Right to Work Legal Defense Foundation
8001 Braddock Rd.
Springfield, VA 22160
703-321-8510
800-336-3600
FAX: 703-321-9319
nrtw.org

Raymond LaJeunesse, Vice President & Legal Director
Byron S. Andrus, Staff Attorney
Matthew B. Gilliam, Staff Attorney

The National Right to Work Legal Defense Foundation is a nonprofit, charitable organization. Its mission is to eliminate coercive union power and compulsory unionism abuses through strategic litigation, public information, and education programs.
1968

4503 Ohio Civil Rights Commission (OCRC)
Rhodes State Office Tower
30 East Broad Street, 5th Floor
Columbus, OH 43215
614-466-2785
888-278-7101
FAX: 614-644-8776
crc.ohio.gov

G. Michael Payton, Executive Director
Darlene Sweeney-Newbern, Director, Regional Operations
Stephanie Bostos-Demers, Chief Legal Counsel

Primary function is to enforce state laws against discrimination.

4504 REACH/Resource Centers on Independent Living
8625 King George
Suite 210
Dallas, TX 75235-2286
214-630-4796
FAX: 214-630-6390
TTY:214-630-5995
reachdallas@reachcils.org
www.reachcils.org

Sylvia Hodgins, President
Charlotte A. Stewart, Executive Director
Penny Acrey, Secretary

Providing services for people with disabilities so that they are empowered to lead self-directed lives and educating the general public on disability-related topics in order to promote a barrier-free community.

Resources for the Disabled

4505 ADA In Details: Interpreting the 2010 Americans with Disabilities Act Stands
Wiley Publishing
111 River St
Hoboken, NJ 07030-5774
201-748-6000
FAX: 201-748-6088
info@wiley.com
www.wiley.com

Matthe S. Kissner, Chief Executive Officer
Christopher Caridi, Senior Vice President

Helps readers understand the facilities requirements of the Americans with Disabilities Act Accessibility Guidelines. Presents the technical requirements for accessible elements and spaces in new construction, alterations and additions. $40.00
304 pages Paperback 1917
ISBN 9-781119-27-7

4506 Americans With Disabilities Act Annotated: Legislative History, Regulations & Commentary
Disability Rights Education and Defense Fund
3075 Adeline Street
Suite 210
Berkeley, CA 94703
510-644-2555
FAX: 510-841-8645
info@dredf.org
dredf.org

Arlene B. Mayerson, Author

Also known as the Blue Book, written in narrative form for both professionals and lay people, this work offers detailed, thorough analysis of all of the law's provisions, encompassing ADA legislative history, the statute and regulations. Available in alternative formats.

4507 **Americans with Disabilities Act Manual**
US Department of Justice
950 Pennsylvania Ave. NW
9th Floor
Washington, DC 20530
202-307-0663
800-514-0301
FAX: 202-307-1197
TTY: 800-514-0383
www.ada.gov

Rebecca B. Bond, Chief
Anne Raish, Principal Deputy Chief
Christina Galindo-Walsh, Deputy Chief
An in-depth analysis of the legal and practical implications of the
ADA using non-technical language. *$20.00*

4508 **Americans with Disabilities Act: Selected Resources for Deaf**
Gallaudet University Bookstore
800 Florida Avenue NE
Washington, DC 20002-3695
202-651-5000
800-621-2736
FAX: 202-651-5508
clerc.center@gallaudet.edu
www.gallaudet.edu

Priscilla O'Donnell, Bookstore Manager
Iva Williams, Bookstore Secretary
Elaine Vance, Human Resources Director
This resource identifies programs and publications specific to the
ADA and deafness and also lists ADA materials and programs for
people with any disability.

4509 **Approaching Equality**
T J Publishers
Ste 108
2544 Tarpley Rd
Carrollton, TX 75006-2288
972-416-0800
800-999-1168
FAX: 301-585-5930
TJPubinc@aol.com

Frank Bowe, Author
Public education laws guarantee special education for all deaf
children, but may find the special education system confusing, or
are unsure of their rights under current laws. For anyone with an
interest in education, advocacy and the deaf community, this
book reviews dramatic developments in education of deaf children, youth and adults since COED's 1988 report, Toward Equality. *$12.95*
112 pages
ISBN 0-93266-39-6

4510 **Assessment of the Feasibility of Contracting with a Nominee Agency**
Mississippi State University
PO Drawer 6189
Mississippi State, MS 39762
662-325-2001
FAX: 662-325-8989
rrtc@colled.msstate.edu
www.blind.msstate.edu

Michelle Capella McDonnall, Interim Director
Stephanie Hall, Business Manager
Douglas Bedsaul, Research and Training Coordinator
Only five State Licensing Agencies currently utilize nominee
agreements. This study compared the Pennsylvania BE program
with four states that utilize nominee agencies and four states that
do not. *$20.00*
152 pages Paperback

4511 **Can America Afford to Grow Old?**
Brookings Institution
1775 Massachusetts Ave NW
Washington, DC 20036-2103
202-797-6000
FAX: 202-797-6004
www.brookings.edu

William Antholis, Managing Director
Steven Bennett, Vice President and Chief Operating Officer
Kimberly Churches, Vice President for Development
Social security laws and regulations. *$8.95*
144 pages Paperback
ISBN 0-815700-43-1

4512 **Childcare and the ADA**
Eastern Washington University
Rm 223
705 W 1st Ave
Spokane, WA 99201-3909
509-623-4200
FAX: 509-623-4230
susan.vanmeter@mail.ewu.edu

Nancy Ashworth, Director Child Development
Allen Barrom, Manager
Provides information on how childcare providers must comply
with the ADA. Eight videotapes plus an instructional manual
with examples of situations and problems. *$85.00*
Set

4513 **Common ADA Errors and Omissions in New Construction and Alterations**
US Department of Justice
950 Pennsylvania Ave. NW
9th Floor
Washington, DC 20530
202-307-0663
800-514-0301
FAX: 202-307-1197
TTY: 800-514-0383
www.ada.gov

Rebecca B. Bond, Chief
Anne Raish, Principal Deputy Chief
Christina Galindo-Walsh, Deputy Chief
Lists a sampling of common accessibility errors or omissions that
have been identified through the Department of Justice's ongoing
enforcement efforts.
13 pages

4514 **Commonly Asked Questions About Child Care Centers and the Americans with Disabilities Act**
US Department of Justice
950 Pennsylvania Ave. NW
9th Floor
Washington, DC 20530
202-307-0663
800-514-0301
FAX: 202-307-1197
TTY: 800-514-0383
www.ada.gov

Rebecca B. Bond, Chief
Anne Raish, Principal Deputy Chief
Christina Galindo-Walsh, Deputy Chief
Explains how the requirements of the ADA apply to Child Care
Centers. Also describes some of the Department of justice's on-
going enformcement efforts in the child care area and it provides
a resource list on sources of information on the ADA.
13 pages

4515 **Commonly Asked Questions About Title III of the ADA**
US Department of Justice
950 Pennsylvania Ave. NW
9th Floor
Washington, DC 20530
202-307-0663
800-514-0301
FAX: 202-307-1197
TTY: 800-514-0383
www.ada.gov

Rebecca B. Bond, Chief
Anne Raish, Principal Deputy Chief
Christina Galindo-Walsh, Deputy Chief
A 6-page publication providing information for state and local
governments about ADA requirements for ensuring that people
with disabilities receive the same services and benefits as
provided to others.
on-line

4516   Commonly Asked Questions About the ADA and Law Enforcement
US Department of Justice
950 Pennsylvania Ave. NW
9th Floor
Washington, DC 20530   202-307-0663
                                                  800-514-0301
                                             FAX: 202-307-1197
                                             TTY: 800-514-0383
                                                  www.ada.gov

Rebecca B. Bond, Chief
Anne Raish, Principal Deputy Chief
Christina Galindo-Walsh, Deputy Chief
A publication explaining ADA requirements for ensuring that people with disabilities receive the same law enforcement services and protections as provided to others.
13 pages on-line

4517   Complying with the Americans with Disabilis Act
Greenwood Publishing Group
130 Cremona Drive
Santa Barbara, CA 93117   805-968-1911
                                                  800-368-6868
                                             FAX: 866-270-3856
                                     CustomerService@abc-clio.com
                                                  www.greenwood.com

Don Fresh, Author
Peter W Thomas, Co-Author
John Gosden, Library Resource Consultants
A guidebook for management and people with disabilities. This unique guidebook presents a comprehensive analysis of the new Americans with Disabilities Act (ADA), the most significant federal civil rights law in almost 30 years, and its impact on over four million American businesses, state and local governments, non-profit associations, 87 percent of American's private sector jobs, and 22.7 million working-age people with disabilities. *$117.95*
280 pages Hardcover
ISBN 0-899307-14-0

4518   Court-Related Needs of the Elderly and Persons with Disabilities
Mental Health Commission
2700 Martin Luther King Jr Ave SE
Washington, DC 20032- 2601   202-282-0027
                                             FAX: 202-373-7982
This book features the ground-breaking recommendations from the national Conference on the Court-Related Needs of the Elderly and Persons with Disabilities, funded by the States Justice Institute and co-sponsored by the American Bar Association and National Judicial College. Accompanying the recommendations are detailed commentaries and extensive background research papers organized around issues. *$20.00*
276 pages

4519   Criminal Law Handbook on Psychiatric & Psychological Evidence & Testimony
New York City Bar
42 West 44th Street
New York, NY 10036-6604   212-382-6600
                                             FAX: 212-768-8116
                                                  phynes@nycbar.org
                                                  www.nycbar.org

Bret Parker, Executive Director
Debra Raskin, President
Alan Rothstein, General Counsel
The Criminal Law Handbook provides lawyers, judges and forensic experts with comprehensive, in-depth treatment of admissibility (and limitations on admissibility) of psychiatric and psychological evidence and testimony pertaining to key criminal mental health law standards. *$47.00*

4520   Department of Justice ADA Mediation Program
US Department of Justice
950 Pennsylvania Ave. NW
9th Floor
Washington, DC 20530   202-307-0663
                                                  800-514-0301
                                             FAX: 202-307-1197
                                             TTY: 800-514-0383
                                                  www.ada.gov

Rebecca B. Bond, Chief
Anne Raish, Principal Deputy Chief
Christina Galindo-Walsh, Deputy Chief
Provides an overview of the Department's Mediation Program and examples of successfully mediated cases.
6 pages

4521   Dimensions of State Mental Health Policy
Greenwood Publishing Group
130 Cremona Drive
Santa Barbara, CA 93117   805-968-1911
                                                  800-368-6868
                                             FAX: 866-270-3856
                                     CustomerService@abc-clio.com
                                                  www.greenwood.com

Christopher Hudson, Author
Arthur J Cox, Co-Author
John Gosden, Library Resource Consultants
Introduces students to the emerging field of state mental health policy, its history, current policies, organizational models and required programming knowledge. *$86.95*
320 pages Hardcover
ISBN 0-275932-52-7

4522   Disability Compliance for Higher Education
LRP Publications
360 Hiatt Dr
Palm Beach Gardens, FL 33418   561-622-6520
                                                  800-341-7874
                                             FAX: 561-622-0757
                                                  lrpitvp@lrp.com
                                                  www.lrp.com
Kenneth Kahn, CEO
Gives guidance on the most difficult issues faced, such as supporting students with psychological disabilities, ensuring accessibility, understanding OCR rulings, and more. *$57.29*
300 pages

4523   Disability Discrimination Law, Evidence and Testimony
ABA Commission on Mental & Physical Disability Law
1050 Connecticut Ave. N.W.
Suite 400
Washington, DC 20036   202-662-1000
                                                  800-285-2221
                                             FAX: 202-442-3439
                                                  cmpdl@americanbar.org
                                                  www.americanbar.org

John W Parry JD, Author
Explains and analyzes key aspects of disability discriminiation law from several different perspectives to guide you through the myriad federal and state statutes, court cases, and regulations. *$105.00*
694 pages Paperback
ISBN 1-604420-12-8

4524   Disability Law in the United States
William Hein & Company
2350 North Forest Rd.
Getzville, NY 14068-1296   716-882-2600
                                                  800-828-7571
                                             FAX: 716-883-8100
                                                  mail@wshein.com
                                                  www.wshein.com

Dr Bernard D Reams Jr, Author
Peter J McGovern, Co-Author
Jon S Schultz, Co-Author
Offers thousands of pages of information on the laws and legislation affecting the disabled in the United States. Its purpose is to provide a clear and comprehensive mandate to end discrimination against individuals with disabilities and to bring disabled persons

into the economic and social midstream of American Life.
$675.00
5750 pages
ISBN 0-899417-97-3

4525 Disability Under the Fair Employment & Housing Act: What You Should Know About the Law
California Department of Fair Employment & Housing
2218 Kausen Drive
Suite 100
Elk Grove, CA 95758   916-478-7251
                                        800-884-1684
                                 FAX: 916-227-2870
                          contact.center@dfeh.ca.gov
                                    www.dfeh.ca.gov

Phyllis W Cheng, Director
Intended to highlight and summarize workplace disability laws enforced by the California Department of Fair Employment and Housing. It will familiarize people with the content of these laws, including recent changes and amendments to state statutes and attendent accommodation responsibilities.

4526 Discrimination is Against the Law
California Department of Fair Employment & Housing
2218 Kausen Drive
Suite 100
Elk Grove, CA 95758   916-478-7251
                                        800-884-1684
                                 FAX: 916-227-2870
                          contact.center@dfeh.ca.gov
                                    www.dfeh.ca.gov

Phyllis Cheng, Director
Enforces California state laws that prohibit harassment and discrimination in employment, housing, and public accomodations and that provide for pregnancy leave and family and personal leave.

4527 Education of the Handicapped: Laws, Legislative Histories and Administrative Document
William S Hein & Co Inc
2350 North Forest Rd.
Getzville, NY 14068-1296   716-882-2600
                                        800-828-7571
                                 FAX: 716-883-8100
                                    mail@wshein.com
                                    www.wshein.com

Bernard D Reams Jr, Editor
Focuses upon Elementary and Secondary Education Act of 1965 and its amendment, Education For All Handicapped Children Act of 1975 and its amendments and acts providing services for the blind, deaf, developmentally disabled, etc. *$2950.00*
55 volumes
ISBN 0-899411-57-6

4528 ElderLawAnswers.com
150 Chestnut Street
4th Floor, Box 15
Providence, RI 02903   617-267-9700
                                        866-267-0947
                          support@elderlawanswers.com
                                www.elderlawanswers.com

Harry S Margolis, Founder/President
Mark Miller, Director of Product and Business Development
Ken Coughlin, Managing Editor
Supports seniors, their families and their attorneys in achieving their goals by providing

4529 Employment Discrimination Based on Disability
California Department of Fair Employment & Housing
2218 Kausen Drive
Suite 100
Elk Grove, CA 95758   916-478-7251
                                        800-884-1684
                                 FAX: 916-227-2870
                          contact.center@dfeh.ca.gov
                                    www.dfeh.ca.gov

Phyllis W Cheng, Director
Prohibits employment discrimination and harassment based on a person's disability or perceived disability. Also requires employers to reasonably accommodate individuals with mental or physi-

cal disabilities unless the employer can show that to do so would cause an undue hardship.

4530 Employment Standards Administration Department of Labor (ESA)
200 Constitution Ave NW
Washington, DC 20210-1   800-321-6742
                                   TTY:877-889-5627
                                          osha.gov

David Michaels, Assistant Secretary
Jordan Barab, Deputy Assistant Secretary
Richard Fairfax, Deputy Assistant Secretary
Monitors compliance with sub-minimum wage requirements for handicapped workers in sheltered workshops, competitive industry and hospitals and institutions under Section 14 of the Fair Labor Standards Act of 1938.

4531 Enforcing the ADA: A Status Report from the Department of Justice
US Department of Justice
950 Pennsylvania Ave. NW
9th Floor
Washington, DC 20530   202-307-0663
                                        800-514-0301
                                 FAX: 202-307-1197
                                 TTY: 800-514-0383
                                        www.ada.gov

Rebecca B. Bond, Chief
Anne Raish, Principal Deputy Chief
Christina Galindo-Walsh, Deputy Chief
A brief report issued by the Justice Department each quarter providing timely information about ADA cases and settlements, building codes that meet ADA accessibility standards, and ADA technical assistance activities.

4532 Federal Laws of the Mentally Handicapped: Laws, Legislative Histories and Admin. Documents
William Hein & Company
2350 North Forest Rd.
Getzville, NY 14068-1296   716-882-2600
                                        800-828-7571
                                 FAX: 716-883-8100
                                    mail@wshein.com
                                    www.wshein.com

Bernard D Reams Jr, Editor
Chronological compilation of all relevant federal laws dealing with the mentally handicapped along with supporting documentation necessary to create a complete legislative history.
$3500.00
42 Volume/Set
ISBN 0-899411-06-1

4533 Formed Families: Adoption of Children with Handicaps
Haworth Press
711 Third Avenue
New York, NY 10017   212-216-7800
                                        800-354-1420
                                 FAX: 212-244-1563
                          subscriptions@tandf.co.uk
                                www.haworthpress.com

William Cohen, Owner
Provides broad coverage of the issues relating to the adoption of children with handicaps. Concerned professionals can find here all the answers about clinical programs, legal issues, estimates of frequency, and important factors related to positive and negative outcomes of these adoptions. *$74.95*
242 pages Hardcover
ISBN 0-866569-14-6

4534 Free Appropriate Public Education: The Law and Children with Disabilities
Love Publishing Company
9101 E Kenyon Avenue
Suite 2200
Denver, CO 80237
303-221-7333
FAX: 303-221-7444
lpc@lovepublishing.com
www.lovepublishing.com

H Rutherford Turnbull III, Author
Matthew J Stowe, Co-Author
Nancy E Huerta, Co-Author
Includes the 2004 IDEA reauthorization and the proposed regulations. This up-to-the-minute resource brings you the most recent developments in legislation, case law techniques, due process, parent participation and much, much more. *$78.00*
448 pages Hardcover
ISBN 0-891083-25-2

4535 Health Care Quality Improvement Act of 1986
William Hein & Company
2350 North Forest Rd.
Getzville, NY 14068-1296
716-882-2600
800-828-7571
FAX: 716-883-8100
mail@wshein.com
www.wshein.com

Bernard D Reams Jr, Editor
In order to encourage more stringent peer review by doctors and hospitals, and to protect reporting physicians and institutions from retaliatory lawsuits, Congress enacted The Health Care Quality Improvement Act. The Act was also intended to address the increasing incidence of medical malpractice and to prevent the ease with which incompetent practitioners moved from state to state. Hardcover. *$125.00*
721 pages
ISBN 0-899416-93-4

4536 Housing and Transportation of the Handicapped
William Hein & Company
2350 North Forest Rd.
Getzville, NY 14068-1296
716-882-2600
800-828-7571
FAX: 716-883-8100
mail@wshein.com
www.wshein.com

Bernard D Reams Jr, Editor
National laws, recognizing the problems encountered by the handicapped in the areas of Housing and Transportation and providing assistance in an effort to surmount those problems, span more than half a century. *$1552.50*
30000 pages 250 documents
ISBN 0-899412-47-5

4537 Human Resource Management and the Americans with Disabilities Act
Greenwood Publishing Group
130 Cremona Drive
Santa Barbara, CA 93117
805-968-1911
800-368-6868
FAX: 866-270-3856
CustomerService@abc-clio.com
www.greenwood.com

John G Veres, Author
Ronald R Sims, Co-Author
John Gosden, Library Resource Consultants
Concrete advice for human resource professionals on how to cope with the vague, often obscure provisions of the Americans with Disabilities Act. *$107.95*
232 pages Hardcover
ISBN 0-899308-57-9

4538 International Handbook on Mental Health Policy
Greenwood Publishing Group
130 Cremona Drive
Santa Barbara, CA 93117
805-968-1911
800-368-6868
FAX: 866-270-3856
CustomerService@abc-clio.com
www.greenwood.com

John Gosden, Library Resource Consultants
Lina Gosden, Library Resource Consultants
Steve Pearson, Library Resource Consultants
The first major reference book for academics and practitioners that provides a systematic survey and analysis of mental health policies in twenty representative countries. *$179.95*
512 pages Hardcover
ISBN 0-313275-67-8

4539 Knowing Your Rights
A AR P Fulfillment
601 E St NW
Washington, DC 20049-1
202-434-3525
800-687-2277
FAX: 202-434-3443
TTY: 877-434-7598
member@aarp.org
www.aarp.org

William D. Novelli, CEO
Lynn Smith, Director of Human Resources
Describes how changes in Medicare's reimbursement policies are designed to reduce health care costs and suggests steps that Medicare beneficiaries, their families and friends can take to assure that they continue to receive quality care under the Prospective Payment System.
19 pages

4540 Law Center Newsletter
Public Interest Law Center of Philadelphia
1709 Benjamin Franklin Parkway
United Way Building
Philadelphia, PA 19103
215-627-7100
FAX: 215-627-3183
www.pilcop.org

Eric J Rothschild, Chair
Brian T Feeney, Vice Chair
Jennifer R. Clarke, Executive Director
Information on mental health, foster care and public education. Provides all updates concerning the law in these areas.

4541 Legal Center for People with Disabilities& Older People
455 Sherman St
Suite 130
Denver, CO 80203
303-722-0300
800-288-1376
FAX: 303-722-0720
TTY: 303-722-3619

Mary Anne Harvey, Executive Director
John R. Posthumus, President
Stephen P. Rickles, Vice President
Uses the legal system to protect and promote the rights of people with disabilities and older people in Colorado through direct legal representation, advocacy, education and legislative analysis. The Legal Center is Colorado's Protection and Advocacy System. We are also the State Ombudsman for nursing homes and assisted living facilities. Call for a free publications and products list.

4542 Legal Right: The Guide for Deaf and Hard of Hearing People
National Association of the Deaf
8630 Fenton Street
Suite 820
Silver Spring, MD 20910- 3819
301-587-1789
FAX: 301-587-1791
TTY:301-587-1789
www.nad.org

Christopher Wagner, Board Chair
Howard A. Rosenblum, Chief Executive Officer
Marc P. Charmatz, Staff Attorney
This revised fifth edition is in easy-to-understand language, offering the latest state and federal statues and administrative pro-

cedures that prohibit discrimination against the deaf, hard of hearing and other physically challenged people. *$32.50*
264 pages Paperback
ISBN 1-563680-00-9

4543 Legal Rights of Persons with Disabilities
LRP Publications
360 Hiatt Dr
Palm Beach Gardens, FL 33418-7106   561-622-6520
                                             800-341-7874
                                        FAX: 561-622-0757
                                          lrpitvp@lrp.com
                                              www.lrp.com

Kenneth Kahn, CEO
Shows what is required, permitted and guaranteed by federal disability laws-including the ADA, Section 504 of the Rehabilitation Act and the IDEA. Explores the boundaries of accceptable behavior under disability laws and provides guidelines to help clients fulfill their legal obligations. *$365.00*
2722 pages

4544 Legislative Handbook for Parents
NAPVI
250 W 64th St
New York, NY 10023   800-284-4422
                                      napvi@lighthouseguild.org
                                             www.napvi.org

Alan R. Morse, President/CEO
Mark G. Ackermann, Executive Vice President
James M. Dubin, Chairman
A publication for parents who make direct contact with public officials on behalf of their children. Sample letters, do's-and-dont's, and a glossary of legislative terms are some of the topics that are contained in this manual. *$5.50*
24 pages Paperback

4545 Legislative Network for Nurses
Business Publishers
2222 Sedwick Drive
Durham, NC 27713   800-223-8720
                                        FAX: 800-508-2592
                                          www.bpinews.com

Provides up-to-date information on the nursing shortage, nurse training programs, AIDS and Hepatitis B, unionization, registered care technologies, compensation, child care, home health care staffing and much more. *$286.00*
8 pages Newsl./BiMonthly

4546 Loving Justice
Exceptional Parent Library
P.O.Box 1807
Englewood Cliffs, NJ 7632-1207   201-947-6000
                                             800-535-1910
                                        FAX: 201-947-9376
                                          eplibrary@aol.com
                                            www.eplibrary.com

How the Americans with Disabilities Act affects religious institutions, including congregations, hospitals, nursing homes, seminaries, universities and more. *$10.95*

4547 Making News: How to Get News Coverage of Disability Rights Issues
Advocado Press
PO Box 406781
Louisville, KY 40204   888-739-1920
                                        FAX: 502-899-9562
                                        www.advocadopress.org

Tari Susan Hartman, Author
Mary Johnson, Co-Author
This book gives examples and tips on how to fight back and get on the front pages, lead the newscasts and influence public debate. *$10.95*
165 pages Paperback
ISBN 0-962706-43-4

4548 Medicare and Medicaid Patient and Program Protection Act of 1987
William Hein & Company
2350 North Forest Rd.
Getzville, NY 14068-1296   716-882-2600
                                             800-828-7571
                                        FAX: 716-883-8100
                                          mail@wshein.com
                                            www.wshein.com

Bernard D Reams Jr, Editor
Enables the HHS to protect patients and federal health care programs from censured practitioners. The Act broadens the authority of HHS to exclude practitioners from Medicare and Medicaid programs; strengthens the monetary penalities HHS may impose on violators; provides for criminal penalties in certain cases; and requires states to inform HHS regarding sanctions against health care providers. *$195.00*
3 Volumes
ISBN 0-899416-95-0

4549 Mental & Physical Disability Law Reporter
American Bar Association
1050 Connecticut Ave. N.W.
Suite 400
Washington, DC 20036-1019   202-662-1570
                                             800-285-2221
                                        FAX: 202-442-3439
                                          cmpdl@abanet.org
                                             www.abanet.org

Robert M Carlson, Chair
James R Silkenat, President
Jack L Rives, Executive Director
Contains over 2,000 summanes per year of federal and state court decisions and legislation that affect persons with mental and physical disabilities. Includes bylined articles by experts in the field regarding disability law developments and trends. *$384.00*
350+ pages BiMonthly

4550 Mental Disabilities and the Americans with Disabilities Act
Greenwood Publishing Group
130 Cremona Drive
Santa Barbara, CA 93117   805-968-1911
                                             800-368-6868
                                        FAX: 866-270-3856
                                   CustomerService@abc-clio.com
                                           www.greenwood.com

John Gosden, Library Resource Consultants
Lina Gosden, Library Resource Consultants
Steve Pearson, Library Resource Consultants
A clear, practical compliance guide, written by a psychologist, to help organizations conform to provisions on mental disabilities in the Americans with Disabilities Act. Hardcover. *$91.95*
216 pages Hardcover
ISBN 0-899308-26-5

4551 Mental Disability Law, Evidence and Testimony
ABA Commission on Mental & Physical Disability Law
1050 Connecticut Ave. N.W.
Suite 400
Washington, DC 20036-1019   202-662-1000
                                             800-285-2221
                                             www.abanet.org

Robert M Carlson, Chair
James R Silkenat, President
Jack L Rives, Executive Director
Provides a comprehensive analysis of federal and state statues and case law with a disability discrimination focus. *$95.00*
491 pages Paperback
ISBN 1-590318-32-3

4552 Mental Health Law Reporter
Business Publishers
2222 Sedwick Drive
Durham, NC 27713   240-514-0600
                                             800-223-8720
                                        FAX: 800-508-2592

Leonard A Eiserer, Publisher
Jeremy Bond, Editor MHLR
Bob Grupe, Editor MHLR

MHLR brings you the most timely, focused and thorough information on the legal issues that concern mental health practitioners in mental health litigation. Topics include: malpractice litigation, patient-therapist confidentiality, sexual victimization of patients, the insanity defense, social security administrative case law and much more. *$286.00*
8 pages Monthly

4553 Mental and Physical Disability Law Reporter
American Bar Association
1050 Connecticut Ave. N.W.
Suite 400
Washington, DC 20036-1019   202-662-1000
                                    800-285-2221
                           service@americanbar.org
                           www.americanbar.org

Wm T Robinson III, President
The only periodical that comprehensively covers civil and criminal mental disability law and disability discrimination law. *$324.00*
150+ pages Bimonthly

4554 Mentally Disabled and the Law
William S Hein & Company
2350 North Forest Rd.
Getzville, NY 14068-1296   716-882-2600
                                    800-828-7571
                           FAX: 716-883-8100
                           mail@wshein.com
                           www.wshein.com

Samuel Brakel, Author
John Parry, Co-Author
Barbara A Weiner, Co-Author
Chapters retained from 1961 and 1971 editions have been substantially rewritten. Two subjects-sterilization and sexual psychopathy-have been integrated into chapters on family law. Three new chapters on treatment rights, provider-patient relationship and rights of mentally disabled persons in the community. Sixteen new tables supplement the existing revised 41. *$92.00*
845 pages
ISBN 0-910059-05-5

4555 Myths and Facts
US Department of Justice
950 Pennsylvania Ave. NW
9th Floor
Washington, DC 20530   202-307-0663
                               800-514-0301
                        FAX: 202-307-1197
                        TTY: 800-514-0383
                        www.ada.gov

Rebecca B. Bond, Chief
Anne Raish, Principal Deputy Chief
Christina Galindo-Walsh, Deputy Chief
A 3-page publication dispelling some common misconceptions about the ADA's requirements and implementation.

4556 NAD Broadcaster
National Association of the Deaf
8630 Fenton Street
Suite 820
Silver Spring, MD 20910- 3819   301-587-1789
                                  FAX: 301-587-1791
                                  TTY:301-587-1789
                                  nad.info@nad.org
                                  www.nad.org

Christopher Wagner, Board Chair
Howard A. Rosenblum, Chief Executive Officer
Marc P. Charmatz, Staff Attorney
National newspaper published 11 times a year by the nation's largest organization safeguarding the accessbility and civil rights of 28 million deaf and hard of hearing Americans in education, employment, health care, and telecommunications. Membership: individual $30 per year. *$7.00*

4557 No Longer Disabled: the Federal Courts & the Politics of Social Security Disability
Greenwood Publishing Group
130 Cremona Drive
Santa Barbara, CA 93117   805-968-1911
                                  800-368-6868
                           FAX: 866-270-3856
                           CustomerService@abc-clio.com
                           www.greenwood.com

John Gosden, Library Resource Consultants
Lina Gosden, Library Resource Consultants
Steve Pearson, Library Resource Consultants
This book is a case study of judicial policy making. It focuses on the role of adjudication in the making and refining of federal policy. *$107.95*
208 pages Hardcover
ISBN 0-313254-24-9

4558 Nolo's Guide to Social Security Disability Getting and Keeping Your Benefits
NOLO
950 Parker St
Berkeley, CA 94710-2524   800-955-4775
                           FAX: 800-645-0895
                           www.nolo.com

David Morton, Author
This guide demystifies the program and tells you everything you need to know about qualifying and applying for benefits, maintaining your benefits, and appealing the denial of a claim. *$25.49*
512 pages paperback
ISBN 1-413311-04-4

4559 Opening the Courthouse Door: An ADA Access Guide for State Courts
American Bar Association
1050 Connecticut Ave. N.W.
Suite 400
Washington, DC 20036-1019   202-662-1000
                                    800-285-2221
                           service@americanbar.org
                           www.americanbar.org

Wm T Robinson III, President
Practical step-by-step guide walks the reader through the courthouse and court process, presenting a menu of straightforawrd access ideas to enhance communications in court, make the facility more accessbile, and nodify rules and procedures. *$12.00*
78 pages

4560 PPAL In Print
Parent Professional Advocacy League
77 Rumford Ave.
Waltham, MA 02453   866-815-8122
                     FAX: 617-542-7832
                     info@ppal.net
                     www.ppal.net

Pam Sager, Executive Director
Meri Viano, Associate Director
Candice Gabrey, Program Manager, Juvenile Justice
The Parent Professional Advocacy League (PPAL) is a statewide organization focusing on the interests of families with children with mental health needs. PPAL advocates for improved and better access to mental health services for children and their families.

4561 Power of Attorney for Health Care
Center for Public Representation
P.O.Box 260049
Madison, WI 53726-49   608-251-4008
                               800-369-0388
                        FAX: 606-251-1263

Discusses Wisconsin law regarding medical decisions, the Cruzan case and ethical considerations in addition to legal implications and advantages of this document. Book tells how to create a personalized Power of Attorney document, including language for the special provisions portion. *$49.95*
132 pages
ISBN 0-93262 -38-0

4562   **Special EDitions**
Disability Rights Education and Defense Fund
3075 Adeline Street
Suite 210
Berkeley, CA 94703   510-644-2555
                                      FAX: 510-841-8645
                                         info@dredf.org
                                              dredf.org

Susan Henderson, Executive Director
Special news releases by the Disability Rights Education and Defense Fund, available electronically online.
Quarterly

4563   **Summaries of Legal Precedents & Law Review**
Through the Looking Glass
3075 Adeline St
Suite 120
Berkeley, CA 94703   510-848-1112
                                            800-644-2666
                                      FAX: 510-848-4445
                                   TLG@lookingglass.org
                                   www.lookingglass.org

Megan Kirshbaum, Executive Director
Summarizes legal precedents and law review articles relevant to marital custody and child protection situations of parents with diverse disabilities. *$25.00*
24 pages

4564   **TASH Connections**
TASH
1825 K Street NW
Suite 1250
Washington, DC 20006-1202   202-817-3264
                                      FAX: 202-999-4722
                                           info@tash.org
                                             www.tash.org

Connections is the online magazine written exclusively for, and by, TASH members, containing articles on new developments in the disability field, while challenging readers to consider issues affecting people with disabilities, their families and advocates.
Quarterly

4565   **Title II & III Regulation Amendment Regarding Detectable Warnings**
US Department of Justice
950 Pennsylvania Ave. NW
9th Floor
Washington, DC 20530   202-307-0663
                                            800-514-0301
                                      FAX: 202-307-1197
                                      TTY: 800-514-0383
                                              www.ada.gov

Rebecca B. Bond, Chief
Anne Raish, Principal Deputy Chief
Christina Galindo-Walsh, Deputy Chief
This document suspends the requirements for detectable warnings at curb ramps, hazardous vehicular areas, and reflecting pools.

4566   **Title II Complaint Form**
US Department of Justice
950 Pennsylvania Ave. NW
9th Floor
Washington, DC 20530   202-307-0663
                                            800-514-0301
                                      FAX: 202-307-1197
                                      TTY: 800-514-0383
                                              www.ada.gov

Rebecca B. Bond, Chief
Anne Raish, Principal Deputy Chief
Christina Galindo-Walsh, Deputy Chief
Standard form for filing a complaint under title II of the ADA or section 504 of the Rehabilitation Act of 1973, which prohibit discrimination on the basis of disability by State and local governments and by recipients of federal financial assistance.

4567   **Title II Highlights**
US Department of Justice
950 Pennsylvania Ave. NW
9th Floor
Washington, DC 20530   202-307-0663
                                            800-514-0301
                                      FAX: 202-307-1197
                                      TTY: 800-514-0383
                                              www.ada.gov

Rebecca B. Bond, Chief
Anne Raish, Principal Deputy Chief
Christina Galindo-Walsh, Deputy Chief
Outline of the key requirements of the ADA for State and local governments. Provides detailed information in bullet format for quick reference.
8 pages

4568   **Title III Technical Assistance Manual and Supplement**
US Department of Justice
950 Pennsylvania Ave. NW
9th Floor
Washington, DC 20530   202-307-0663
                                            800-514-0301
                                      FAX: 202-307-1197
                                      TTY: 800-514-0383
                                              www.ada.gov

Rebecca B. Bond, Chief
Anne Raish, Principal Deputy Chief
Christina Galindo-Walsh, Deputy Chief
Explains in lay terms what businesses and non-profit agencies must do to ensure access to their goods, services, and facilities.
83 pages

4569   **Toward Independence**
National Council on Disability
81 E. Main Street
Xenia, OH 45385   937-376-3996
                                      FAX: 937-376-2046
                                           info@ti-inc.org

Mary Rose Zink, Chair
Paul Osterfeld, Vice Chair
Mark Schlater, Executive Director
A 1986 report to the U.S. Congress on the federal laws and programs serving people with disabilities, and recommendations for legislation.

4570   **UCP Washington Wire**
United Cerebral Palsy
1825 K Street NW
Suite 600
Washington, DC 20006-1601   202-776-0406
                                            800-872-5827
                                      FAX: 202-776-0414
                                            info@ucp.org
                                              www.ucp.org

Stephen Bennett, President/CEO
Publication that provides a comprehensive source of information on federal legislation, agency regulations, court decisions and other issues of interest to the disability community.
weekly

4571   **US Department of Health and Human Services Office for Civil Rights**
200 Independence Ave SW
Room 509F, HHH Building
Washington, DC 20201   202-619-0403
                                            800-368-1019
                                      TTY:800-537-7697
                                         ocrmail@hhs.gov
                                              www.hhs.gov

Georgina Verdugo, Director
The Department's civil rights and health privacy law enforcement agency, OCR investigates complaints, enforces rights, and promulgates regulations, develops policy and provides technical assistance and public education to ensure understanding of and compliance with non-discrimination and health information privacy laws.

4572 US Department of Labor
200 Constitution Ave NW
Washington, DC 20210   866-487-2365
                                              www.dol.gov

Hilda L Solis, Secretary of Labor
Seth D Harris, Deputy Secretary
To foster, promote, and develop the welfare of the wage earners,
job seekers, and retirees of the United States; improve working
conditions, advance opportunities for profitable employment;
and assure work-related benefits and rights.

**4573 US Department of Labor Office of Federal Contract
Compliance Programs**
200 Constitution Ave NW
Washington, DC 20210   312-596-7010
                                              866-487-2365
                                        FAX: 312-596-7044
                         OFCCP-MW-PreAward@dol.gov
                                              www.dol.gov

Melissa L Speer, Interim Regional Director
To enforce, for the benefit of job seekers and wage earners, the
contractual promise of affirmative action and equal employment
opportunity required of those who do business with the Federal
government.

4574 University Legal Services AT Program
Ste 130
220 i St NE
Washington, DC 20002-4364   202-547-4747
                                              877-221-4638
                                        FAX: 202-547-2083
                                        TTY: 202-547-2657
                                        atpdc@uls-dc.org

Jane Brown, Executive Director
Designed to empower individuals with disabilities; to promote
consumer involvement and advocacy, and provide information,
referral and training as they relate to accessing assistive technology services and devices; and to identify and improve access to
funding resources.

4575 William S Hein & Company
2350 North Forest Rd.
Getzville, NY 14068-1296   716-882-2600
                                              800-828-7571
                                        FAX: 716-883-8100
                                        mail@wshein.com
                                              www.wshein.com

Kevin Marmion, President
Offers a catalog of periodicals, publications and reprints, micro-
forms and government publications on medical, handicapped and
health law.

Libraries & Research Centers

Alabama

4576 Alabama Institute for Deaf and Blind Library and Resource Center
205 E South Street
P.O. Box 698
Talladega, AL 35160
256-761-3206
FAX: 256-761-3352
aidb.org

Dr. John Mascia, President
Teresa Lacy, Director, Library & Resource Center
Book collection includes discs, cassettes, braille and large print. Also closed-circuit TV and magnifiers. Offers braille production and binding.

4577 Alabama Radio Reading Service Network(ARRS)
Public Radio WBHM 90.3 FM
650 11th St S
Birmingham, AL 35233-1
205-934-2606
800-444-9246
FAX: 205-934-5075
wbhm.org

Audrey Atkins, Marketing Manager
Scott E Hanley, General Manager
Theresa Kidd, Office Manager
Services and readings are broadcast over a subcarrier service of public radio WBHM. This is a statewide service devoted to Alabama's blind and handicapped community.

4578 Alabama Regional Library for the Blind and Physically Handicapped
Alabama Public Library Service
6030 Monticello Dr
Montgomery, AL 36130-1
334-213-3906
800-392-5671
FAX: 334-213-3993
revans@apls.state.al.us

Mike Coleman, Blind & Physically Handicapped Division
Tim Emmons, Blind & Physically Handicapped Division
Nancy Pack, Director
Recreational reading in special format for persons unable to use standard print. Reference materials offered include materials on blindness and other handicaps, films, local subjects and authors.

4579 Dothan Houston County Library System
Formerly Houston-Love Memorial Library
445 N Oates St
Dothan, AL 36303
334-793-9767
dhcls@dhcls.org
www.dhcls.org

Jason DeLuc, Library Director
Charlotte Mitchell, Main Library Manager
Offers magnifiers, summer reading programs and more for the blind and physically handicapped. Scanner, software, jaws for Windows.

4580 Huntsville Subregional Library for the Blind & Physically Handicapped
Huntsville-Madison County Public Library
915 Monroe St SW
Huntsville, AL 35804-0000
256-532-5980
FAX: 256-532-5994
bphdept@hmcpl.org
www.hmcpl.org

Laurel Best, Executive Director
Talking books for people who are blind or disabled offering reference materials on the blind and other disabilities, large-print photocopier, thermaform duplicator and more.

4581 Public Library Of Anniston-Calhoun County
108 E 10th St
Anniston, AL 36201
256-237-8501
library@publiclibrary.cc
publiclibrary.cc

Reference materials on blindness, cassettes, large print books and discs.

4582 Technology Assistance for Special Consumers
UCP Huntsville
1856 Keats Drive
Huntsville, AL 35810
256-859-8300
FAX: 256-859-4332
ucphuntsville.org

Cheryl Smith, Chief Executive Officer
Provide individuals with disabilities, their families and/or advocates, and associated professionals access to assistive technology devices and services to increase independence at home, school, and work.

Alaska

4583 Alaska State Library Talking Book Center
State of Alaska
344 W 3rd Ave
Ste 125
Anchorage, AK 99501-2338
907-465-1304
888-820-4525
FAX: 907-269-6580
tbc@alaska.gov
talkingbooks.alaska.gov

Patience Frederiksen, Director, Division of Libraries, Archives & Museums
Freya Anderson, Requisitions Librarian
Ginny Jacobs, Library Assistant
The Alaska State Library Talking Book Center is a cooperative effort between the Library of Congress National Library Service for the Blind and Physically Handicapped and the Alaska State Library to provide print handicapped Alaskans with talking book and Braille service. The Talking Book Center has 55,000 audiobooks that can be checked out to eligible Alaskans whose visual or physical handicap prevents them from reading standard print materials.

Arizona

4584 Arizona Braille and Talking Book Library
Arizona State Library
1030 N 32nd St
Phoenix, AZ 85008-5108
602-255-5578
800-255-5578
FAX: 602-286-0444
www.azlibrary.gov

Linda Montgomery, Director
Audio and braille books and magazines, summer reading program, volunteer-produced audio books, audo described, films and more.

4585 Books for the Blind of Arizona
Unit A107
6120 E 5th St
Tucson, AZ 85711-2536
602-792-9153
FAX: 520-886-9839

Betty Evans, Chairperson
Offers large print photocopier, textbooks, recreational, career, vocational, braille books, talking books, cassettes, large print books and more for the visually impaired K-12, college students and adults.

4586 Children's Center for Neurodevelopmental Studies
5430 W Glenn Dr
Glendale, AZ 85301-2628
623-915-0345
FAX: 623-937-5425
admin@ccnsaz.org
www.thechildrenscenteraz.org

Kent Rideout, Executive Director
Dawna Sterner, Preschool & Education Informatio
Catherine Orsak, Therapy Information
The Center is a non-profit school and therapy center for children with autism and other developmental delays specializing in the use of sensory integration.

4587   Flagstaff City-Coconino County Public Library
300 W Aspen Ave
Flagstaff, AZ 86001-5304   928-779-7670
                                                  TTY:928-214-2417
                                                  www.flagstaffpubliclibrary.org
Reference materials on blindness and other handicaps, braille
writer, magnifiers and large-print photocopier. Large-type
books, closed captioned videos, adapters and books on tape.

4588   Fountain Hills Lioness Braille Service
P.O.Box 18332
Fountain Hills, AZ 85269-8332   480-837-3961
Jean Hauck, Chairperson
Braille and large print books on the subjects of recreation, career
and vocations, religion, novels and cookbooks for the visually
impaired.

4589   Prescott Public Library
215 E Goodwin St
Prescott, AZ 86303-3911   928-777-1500
                                                  FAX: 928-771-5829
                                                  prescottlibrary.info
Roger Saft, Director
Martha Baden, Public Services Manager
Teresa Vonk, Support Services Manager
Large print, braille and audio books; magnifiers; text to voice
scanner; talking book machine application; toy library for chil-
dren with special needs; special needs product catalogs; home
book delivery; descriptive videos; 43 point PC monitor.

4590   Special Needs Center/Phoenix Public Library
1221 N Central Ave
Phoenix, AZ 85004-1867   602-262-4636
                                                  TTY:602-254-8205
                                                  www.phoenixpubliclibrary.org
Offers large print books and magazines, print/braille books, amd
braille magazines, Descriptive video services videotapes, several
video print enlargers and computer workplace for persons with
disabilities.

4591   World Research Foundation
P.O. Box 20828
Sedona, AZ 86341-8804   928-284-3300
                                                  FAX: 928-284-3530
                                                  info@wrf.org
                                                  wrf.org
Steven A Ross, President
LaVerne Boeckmann, Co-Founder
Large research library of alternative medicine; offers a computer
search and printout of specific health issues for a nominal fee.

Arkansas

**4592   Arkansas Regional Library for the Blind and Physically
Handicapped**
900 West Capitol Avenue
Suite 100
Little Rock, AR 72201-3108   501-682-2053
                                                  www.library.arkansas.gov
J D Hall, Manager of BPH Services
Dwain Gordon, Deputy Director
Danny Koonce, Public Information Specialist
Public library books in recorded or braille format. Popular fiction
and nonfiction books for all ages, books and players are on free
loan, sent to patrons by mail and may be returned postage free.
Anyone who cannot see well enough to read regular print with
glasses on or who has a disability that makes it difficult to hold a
book or turn the pages is eligible.

4593   Arkansas School for the Blind
P.O.Box 668
Little Rock, AR 72203-668   501-296-1810
                                                  800-362-4451
                                                  FAX: 501-296-1831
                                                  www.arkansasschoolfortheblind.org
Khayyam Eddings, Chairperson
Jennifer Benedetti, Elementary Principal
Teresa Doan, Special Education Supervisor

Students at the ASB receive a quality education from specially
trained instructors of the Visually Impaired in all academic areas.
ASB features a comprehensive Music and Art program, as well as
extensive extra-curricular activities. ASB is a proud member of
the Arkansas Activities Association and The North Central
Association of Schools for the Blind.

4594   Educational Services for the Visually Impaired
2402 Wildwood Avenue
Suite 112
Sherwood, AR 72120-5085   501-835-5448
                                                  FAX: 501-835-6840
                                                  Angyln.Young@arkansas.gov
                                                  www.esvi.org
Angyln Young, State Coordinator
Cindy Lester, Data Management Specialist
Cynthia Kelly, ESVI Office Manager
Offers textbooks, braille books and more to the visually impaired
grades K-12 in the Arizona area.

**4595   Library for the Blind and Physically Handicapped SW
Region of Arkansas**
P.O.Box 668
2057 North Jackson St
Magnolia, AR 71754-668   870-234-1991
                                                  FAX: 870-234-5077
                                                  library@cocolib.org
Rhonda Rolen, Director
Dana Thornton, Assistant Director
Becky Verschage, Processing Clerk
A free library service that serves adults and children who meet the
eligiblity requirements, offers free loan of cassette machine and
recorded books, which meet the reading preferences of a highly
diverse clientele.

**4596   Northwest Ozarks Regional Library for the Blind and
Handicapped**
Fayetteville, AR 72701   479-575-2000
                                                  www.uark.edu
Offers a summer reading program, closed-circuit TV, magnifiers,
braille writers and large print books.

California

4597   Braille Institute Library
741 N Vermont Ave
Los Angeles, CA 90029-3594   323-663-1111
                                                  800-808-2555
                                                  FAX: 323-663-0867
                                                  la@brailleinstitute.org
                                                  brailleinstitute.org
Leslie E. Stocker, President
Sally H. Jameson, Vice President of Programs and S
Peter A. Mindnich, Executive Vice President
Braille Institute provides an environment of hope and encourage-
ment for people who are blind and visually impaired through inte-
grated educational, social and recreational programs and
services.

4598   Braille Institute Santa Barbara Center
2031 De La Vina St
Santa Barbara, CA 93105-3895   805-682-6222
                                                  800-272-4553
                                                  FAX: 805-687-6141
                                                  sb@brailleinstitute.org
                                                  brailleinstitute.org
Leslie E. Stocker, President
Sally H. Jameson, Vice President of Programs and S
Peter A. Mindnich, Executive Vice President
Offers programs, services and information for persons with vi-
sual impairments.

4599 Braille Institute Sight Center
741 N Vermont Ave
Los Angeles, CA 90029-3594   323-663-1111
                                              800-808-2555
                                         FAX: 323-663-0867
                                         la@brailleinstitute.org
                                            brailleinstitute.org
Sally H. Jameson, Vice President of Programs and S
Leslie E Stocker, President
Peter A. Mindnich, Executive Vice President
Offers help, programs, services and information to the blind and
visually impaired children and adults.

4600 Braille and Talking Book Library: California
P.O. Box 942837
Sacramento, CA 94237-0001   916-654-0640
                                              800-952-5666
                             www.library.ca.gov/services/btbl.html
Stacey A. Aldrich, State Librarian
Debbie Newton, Bureau Chief, Administrative Ser
Phyllis Smith, Manager, Human Resources and Bus
Free service for eligible Northern California residents.

**4601 California State Library Braille and Talking Book
Library**
PO Box 942837
Sacramento, CA 94237-0001   916-654-0640
                                              800-952-5666
                                         btbl@library.ca.gov
                                            www.btbl.ca.gov
A division of the California State Library, the Braille and Talking
Book Library (BTBL) is a free service offering braille and
audiobook to readers in Northern California who cannot read due
to a visual or physical disability. The BTBL is an affiliate of the
National Service for the Blind and Physically Handicapped.

4602 Clearinghouse for Specialized Media and Translations
1430 N St
Ste 3207
Sacramento, CA 95814-5901   916-319-0800
                                         FAX: 916-323-9732
                                         www.cde.ca.gov/re/pn/sm
Jonn Paris-Salb, Manager
Provides materials in accessible formats; aural media, braille,
large print, digital talking books and electronic media access
technology.

4603 Dental Amalgam Syndrome (DAMS) Newsletter
725-9 Tramway Ln NE
Albuquerque, NM 87122-1672   505-291-8239
                                         FAX: 505-294-3339
Dedicated to informing the public about the potential risks of
mercury in dental amalgam fillings.

**4604 Fresno County Free Library Blind and Handicapped
Services**
2420 Mariposa Street
Fresno, CA 93721-3640   559-600-7323
                                              800-742-1011
                             wendy.eisenberg@fresnolibrary.org
                                    www.fresnolibrary.org/tblb
Wendy Eisenberg, Manager
Laurel Prysiazny, County Librarian
Magnifiers, home visits, volunteer-produced cassette books,
discs and cassettes.

4605 Glaucoma Research Foundation
251 Post St
Ste 600
San Francisco, CA 94108-5017   415-986-3162
                                              800-826-6693
                                         FAX: 415-986-3763
                                         question@glaucoma.org
                                            glaucoma.org
Tom Brunner, President and CEO
Nancy Graydon, Executive Director of Development
Andrew L. Jackson, Director of Communications
Clinical and laboratory studies of glaucoma. We work to prevent
vision loss from glaucoma by investing in innovative research,
education and support with the ultimate goal of finding a cure.

4606 Herrick Health Sciences Library
Alta Bates Medical Center
2001 Dwight Way
Berkeley, CA 94704-2608   510-869-6777
                                         FAX: 510-204-4091
                                         www.altabatessummit.org
Laurie Bagley, Librarian
Carol Hirsch-Butler, Administrator
Carolyn Kemp, Regional Manager of Public Relations
Information on rehabilitation, psychiatry and psychoanalysis.

4607 Kuzell Institute for Arthritis and Infectious Diseases
Medical Research Institute Of San Francisco
2200 Webster St.
San Francisco, CA 94115-1821   415-561-1734
Edward Byrd, Owner
One of seven units comprising the Medical Research Institute of
San Francisco that offers basic and applied research in arthritis
and related diseases.

4608 New Beginnings: The Blind Children's Center
4120 Marathon St
Los Angeles, CA 90029-3584   323-664-2153
                                         info@blindchildrenscenter.org
                         blindchildrenscenter.org/document-library
Sarah E. Orth, CEO
Fernanda Armenta-Schmitt, Director, Education & Family Services
The purpose of the Center is to turn initial fears into hope. Helps
children and their families become independent by creating a climate of safety and trust. Children learn to develop self confidence
and to master a wide range of skills. Services include an infant
stimulation program, educational preschool, interdisciplinary assessment services, family services, correspondence program, toll
free national hotline and a publication and research service.

**4609 Research & Training Center on Mental Health for Hard
of Hearing Persons**
California School of Professional Psychology
Ste 140
6215 Ferris Sq
San Diego, CA 92121-3279   619-282-4443
                                              800-HEA-R619
                                         FAX: 800-642-0266
Raymond J Trybus, Director
Thomas J Goulder, Associate Director
Funded by the National Institute on Disability and Rehabilitation
Research, this training center aims to address issues of psycho-
logical relevance to persons who are hard of hearing or late deaf-
ened (as distinct from prelingually, culturally deaf persons). Also
serves as information clearinghouse on this topic.

4610 Rosalind Russell Medical Research Center for Arthritis
Suite 600
350 Parnassus Ave
San Francisco, CA 94117   415-476-1141
                                         FAX: 415-476-3526
                                         rrac@medicine.ucsf.edu
Ephraim P Engleman, MD, Center Director
David Wofsy, MD, Associate Director
Paula R. Gambs, Chair
Arthritis research and its probable causes.

**4611 San Francisco Public Library for the Blindand Print
Handicapped**
100 Larkin St
San Francisco, CA 94102-4705   415-557-4400
                                         FAX: 415-557-4252
                                         TTY:415-557-4433
                                         webmail@sfpl.org
                                            www.sfpl.org
Toni Cordova, Chief of Communications, Program
Toni Bernardi, Special Projects Manager
Laura Lent, Chief of Collections & Technical
Foreign-language books on cassette, children's books on cas-
settes and more.

4612 San Jose State University Library
150 E San Fernando St
San Jose, CA 95112-3580

408-808-2000
FAX: 408-924-1118
www.sjlibrary.org

Don W Kassing, President
Jane Light, Library/Executive Director
Jeff Barber, Security Officer
Information on physical disabilities, accessibility and learning disabilities.

Colorado

4613 AMC Cancer Research Center
3401 Quebec Street
Suite 3200
Denver, CO 80207

303-233-6501
800-321-1557
FAX: 303-239-3400
amc.org

Gary Kortz, Chairman
Steven D. Toltz, Treasurer
Cheryl Kisling, Secretary
Provides trained counselors who provide understanding and support for cancer patients; information and referral services; and screening programs.

4614 Boulder Public Library
1001 Arapahoe Ave
Boulder, CO 80302-6015

303-441-3100
www.boulderlibrary.org

Melinda Mattling, Manager
Priscilla Hudson, Manager
Offers braille books, cassettes, talking books, large print photocopier, large print books and more for the visually impaired.

4615 Colorado Talking Book Library
180 Sheridan Blvd
Denver, CO 80226-8101

303-727-9277
800-685-2136
FAX: 303-727-9281
ctbl.info@cde.state.co.us

Debbie Macleod, Executive Director
Provides free library service to Coloradans of all ages who are unable to read standard print due to visual, physical or learning disabilities whether permanent or temporary. Provides audio, braille and large-print books and magazines.

4616 National Jewish Medical & Research Center
1400 Jackson St
Denver, CO 80206-2762

303-388-4461
877-225-5654
www.nationaljewish.org

Michael Salem, MD, President and CEO
Richard A. Schierburg, Chair
Robin Chotin, Vice Chair
The only medical center in the country whose research and patient care resources are dedicated to respiratory and immunologic diseases.

Connecticut

4617 Connecticut Braille Association
107 Vanderbilt Ave
West Hartford, CT 6110-1514

860-953-4445
FAX: 860-378-0205

Nick Martino, Owner
Offers textbooks, cassettes, large print books, braille books and more.

4618 Connecticut Library for the Blind and Physically Handicapped
231 Capitol Avenue
Hartford, CT 06106-1569

860-757-6500
860-866-4478
FAX: 860-721-2056
ctaylor@cslib.org

Kendall Wiggin, State Librarian
Ursula Hunt, Administrative Assistant
Shelley Delisle, IT Manager
Network library of the National Library Service for the Blind and Physically Handicapped, Library of Congress. Lends books and magazines in Braille or recorded formats along with the necessary playback equipment, free, for any Connecticut adult or child who is unable to read regular print due to a visual or physical disability. All materials are mailed to and from library patrons by postage-free mail

4619 Connecticut State Library
Connecticut State Government
231 Capitol Ave
Hartford, CT 06106-1569

860-757-6500
866-866-4478
FAX: 860-721-2056
isref@cslib.org

Kendall Wiggin, State Librarian
Ursula Hunt, Administrative Assistant
Shelley Delisle, IT Manager
Discs, cassettes, braille, reference materials on blindness and other handicaps, closed-circuit TV and large-print photocopier.

4620 Connecticut Tech Act Project: Connecticut Department of Social Services
Bureau of Rehabilitations Services
25 Sigourney St
11th Floor
Hartford, CT 06106-5041

860-424-4881
800-537-2549
FAX: 860-424-4850
TTY: 860-424-4839
arlene.lugo@ct.gov
www.cttechact.com

Arlene Lugo, Program Director
Single point of entry, advocacy, information and referral, peer counseling, and access to objective expert advice and consultation for people with disabilities.

4621 Prevent Blindness Connecticut
101 Whitney Avenue
New Haven, CT 06510

203-722-4653
800-850-2020
FAX: 203-722-4691

Kathryn Garre-Ayars, President and CEO
Tahesha Bryan, Administrative Assistant
Naomi Hayner, Connecticut Program Manager
The mission of Prevent Blindness Connecticut is to save sight and prevent blindness through eye screenings, education, safety activities and research.

4622 Yale University: Vision Research Center
310 Cedar St, LH 108
PO Box 208023
New Haven, CT 06520- 8023

203-785-2759
800-395-7949
FAX: 203-785-7303
pamela.berkheiser@yale.edu
medicine.yale.edu/pathology

George Shafranov, Chairman
Pam Burkheiser, Manager
Robert J. Alpern, Dean
Vision including studies on growth and development.

Delaware

4623 Delaware Assistive Technology Initiative (DATI)
Alfred I. duPont Hospital for Children
461 Wyoming Road
Newark, DE 19716-0269

302-831-0354
800-870-3284
FAX: 302-831-4690
TTY: 302-651-6794
dati@asel.udel.edu
www.dati.org

Beth Mineo Mollica, Director
Sonja Rathel, Project Coordinator
The Delaware Assistive Technology Initiative (DATI) connects Delawareans who have disabilities with the tools they need in order to learn, work, play and participate in community life safely and independently. DATI services include: Equipment demonstration centers in eah county; no-cost, short-term equipment loans that let you try before you buy; Equipment Exchange Program; AT workshops and other training sessions; advocacy for improved AT access policies and funding and several more.

4624 Delaware Library for the Blind and Physically Handicapped
Government
121 Duke of York Street
Dover, DE 19901-7430

302-739-4748
800-282-8676
FAX: 302-739-6787
debph@lib.de.us
libraries.delaware.gov

Dr. Annie E. Norman, Director
Sonja Brown, Administrative Specialist
Beth-Ann Ryan, Deputy Director
Books on cassette and playback equipment are provided to patrons who are unable to read regular printed books.

4625 Elwyn Delaware
321 E 11th St.
Wilmington, DE 19801-3417

302-658-8860
info@elwyn.org
elwyn.org

Charles S. McLister, President & CEO, Elwyn
Provides work training, job placement and supported employment, and elder care services.

District of Columbia

4626 District of Columbia Public Library: Services for the Deaf Community
District of Columbia Public Library
901 G St NW, Room 215
Washington, DC 20001-4531

202-727-0321
FAX: 202-727-0321
TTY:202-559-5368
library_deaf_dc@yahoo.com
dclibrary.org

Venetia Demson, Chief Adaptive Services
Janice Roseu, Library for the Deaf Community
Offers reference services through videophone, signers for library programs, sign language classes, information about deafness, print and non-print materials for persons who have hearing disabilities. Book talks on deaf culture and American Sign Language story hours for kids, and Saturday sessions on employment-related skills are offered. Videophones for public use are available at the MLK Library.

4627 District of Columbia Regional Library for the Blind and Physically Handicapped
901 G St NW
Washington, DC 20001-4531

202-727-0321
FAX: 202-727-1129
TTY:202-727-2145
lbphb_2000@yahoo.com
www.dclibrary.org

Richard Reyes-Gavilan, Executive Director
Jonathan Butler, Director of Business Services
Barbara Kirven, Director of Human Resources
Regional library/RPH is network library in the Library of Congress, National Library Services for the Blind and Physically Handicapped.

4628 Georgetown University Center for Child and Human Development
P.O. Box 571485
Washington, DC 20057

202-687-5000
FAX: 202-687-8899
TTY:202-687-5000
gucdc@georgetown.edu
gucchd.georgetown.edu

Phyllis R. Magrab, PhD, Director
John J. DeGioia, President
The Georgetown University Center for Child and Human Development (GUCCHD) was established over 50 years ago to improve the quality of life for all children and youth and their families, especially those with special health care needs, behavioral health challenges, or disabilities. Located in the nation's capital, this center both directly serves vulnerable children and their families, as well as influences local, state, national, and international programs and policy.

4629 National Institute on Disability, Independent Living, and Rehabilitation Research (NIDILRR)
Administration for Community Living
330 C St. SW
Washington, DC 20201

202-401-4634
acl.gov

Anjali Forber-Pratt, Director
Alison Barkoff, Acting Administrator & Assistant Secretary, Aging
Vicki Gottlich, Deputy Administrator, Policy & Evaluation
NIDILRR is the US government's primary disability research agency.

Florida

4630 Brevard County Talking Books Library
Brevard County Libraries
2725 Judge Fran Jamieson Way
Viera, FL 32940

321-633-2000
FAX: 321-633-1964
TTY:321-633-1838
kbriley@brev.org
www.brevardcounty.us/PublicLibraries

Camille Johnson, Manager
Catherine J Schweinsburg, Library Services Director
Subregional library for the blind and physically handicapped, assistive reading devices collection, reference materials on blindness and other handicaps, descriptive videos, CCTV, phonic ear, reading edge and LOUD-R assistive listening devices available.

4631 Broward County Talking Book Library
100 S Andrews Ave
Fort Lauderdale, FL 33301-1830

954-357-7444
FAX: 954-357-5548
www.broward.org

Robert E. Cannon, Director
Carolyn Kayne, Manager
Reference materials on blindness and other handicaps, films, closed-circuit TV, discs, cassettes and a book discussion group is offered.

4632   **Dade County Talking Book Library**
Miami Dade Public Library System
101 West Flagler Street
Miami, FL 33130   305-375-2665
           800-451-9544
           FAX: 305-757-8401
           talkingbooks@mdpls.org
           www.mdpls.org

Raymond Sanpiago, Executive Director
Lainey Brooks, Development Officer
Sylvia Mora Oria, Assistant Director
A free Outreach Service of the Miami-Dade Public Library System. A network library, or subregional, of the National Library Service for the Blind and Physically Handicapped, Library of Congress, and of the Florida Bureau of Braille and Talking Books Library Service.

4633   **Florida Division of Blind Services**
Regional Library
325 West Gaines Street
Turlington Building, Suite 1114
Tallahassee, FL 32399-0400   850-245-0300
           800-342-1828
           FAX: 850-245-0363
           dbs.myflorida.com

Mike Gunde, Manager
Susan Roberts, Bureau Chief
Robert Doyle, Director
Discs, cassettes, closed-circuit TV, large-print photocopier, films, children's books on cassettes and more.

4634   **Florida Instructional Materials Center forthe Visually Impaired (FIMC-VI)**
4210 W Bay Villa Ave
Tampa, FL 33611-1206   813-837-7826
           800-282-9193
           FAX: 813-837-7979
           FloridaBrailleChallenge@gmail.com
           www.fimcvi.org

Mary Stoltz, Database Manager
Jeffrey Fitterman, Technology Specialist
Teresa Gutierrez, Administrative Secretary
Operates a clearinghouse depository and production center for braille, large print and digital texts. Provides assistance in assessment of materials and specialized apparatus, organizes and trains volunteers for material production for the visually impaired, and provides professional development for teachers of the visually impaired. Provides electronic texts to NIMAS-eligible students in Florida.

4635   **Hillsborough County Talking Book Library**
Tampa-Hillsborough County Public Library
900 N Ashley Dr
Tampa, FL 33602-3704   813-273-3652
           FAX: 813-273-3707
           TTY:813-273-3610
           www.hcplc.org

Joe Stines, Director of Libraries
Marcee Challener, Assitant Director
David Wullschleger, Chief of Operations
Serves as the reference hub and resource center for all citzens of Hillsborough County and as the flagship library of the Tampa-Hillsborough County Public Library System.

4636   **Jacksonville Public Library: Talking Books/Special Needs**
303 N Laura St
Jacksonville, FL 32202-3505   904-630-2665
           FAX: 904-630-0604
           www.jpl.coj.net/lib/talkingbooks.html
Barbara Gubbin, Executive Director
Offers cassettes and digital books, reference materials on blindness and ADA issues, newsline, descriptive videos, and some assistive devices.

4637   **Lee County Library System: Talking Books Library**
2001 N. Tamiami Trail N.E.
North Fort Myers, FL 33903-4855   239-533-4320
           800-854-8195
           FAX: 239-485-1146
           TTY: 239-995-2665
           talkingbooks@leegov.com
           www.lee-county.com/library

Cynthia N Cobb, Director
Terri Crawford, Deputy Director
Debbie Parrott, Manager
Provides free books and magazines to Lee County residents of all ages who have any disability that prevents them from reading printed material. Books are played on special players provided free by the National Library Service. Circulates low tech assistive aids and devices for temporary loan to Lee County Library card holders. Directs people to assistive technology and disability related resources.

4638   **Louis de la Parte Florida Mental Health Institute Research Library**
University of South Florida
4202 E. Fowler Ave. LIB122
Tampa, FL 33620   813-974-2729
           FAX: 813-974-7242
           lib.usf.edu/fmhi

William A. Garrison, Dean
Florence Jandreau, CAP, Senior Assistant to the Dean
Claudia Dold, Assistant University Librarian
Information offered on mental illness, autism and pervasive developmental disabilities mental health research and archives management.

4639   **Orange County Library System: Audio-Visual Department**
101 E Central Blvd
Orlando, FL 32801-2429   407-835-7323
           FAX: 407-835-7649
           TTY:407-835-7641
           comments@ocls.info
           www.ocls.info

Ted Maines, President
Lisa Franchina, Vice President
Bob Tessier, Comptroller
Serves the residents of the Orange County Library District, with headquarters in downtown Orlando.

4640   **Pearlman Biomedical Research Institute**
Mt Sinai Medical Center
1600 NW 10th Ave
Miami Beach, FL 33140   305-674-2121
           FAX: 305-674-2198
           william-abraham@msmc.com

William Abraham, Director
A 32,000 square feet facility located on the main campus of Mount Sinai. The institute consists of laboratory space, research and administrative offices. The studies conducted within the facility are primarily pre-clinical research.

4641   **Pinellas Talking Book Library for the Blind and Physically Handicapped**
1330 Cleveland St
Clearwater, FL 33755-5103   727-441-8408
           FAX: 727-441-8398
           TTY:727-441-3168
           contactus@pplc.us
           www.pplc.us

William Horne, Chair
Cheryl Morales, Executive Director
David Saari, Facilities Manager
The Pinellas Public Library Cooperative serves Pinellas County residents in member cities and the unincorporated county. The Cooperative Office provides cooridination of activities and funding as well as marketing services for the the member counties. The Talking Book Library servces Pinellas, Manatee, and Sarasota counties.

4642 Talking Book Service: Mantatee County Central Library
1112 Manatee Avenue West
Bradenton, FL 34206-1000
941-748-4501
FAX: 941-751-7098
www.mymanatee.org

Patricia Schubert, Manager
Offers children's books on disc and cassette and more reference materials for the blind and physically handicapped.

4643 Talking Books Library for the Blind and Physically Handicapped
Palm Beach County Library
3650 Summit Blvd
West Palm Beach, FL 33406-4114
561-233-2600
888-780-4962
FAX: 561-233-2627
webmaster@pbclibrary.org
www.pbclibrary.org

John Callahan, Executive Director
Bill Rautenberg, Chair
Harriet Helfman, Vice Chair
Established in 1967, today the County Library system serves Palm Beach County through the Main Library, 2 Regional Libraries, 11 Branch Libraries, a Bookmobile and a library annex. It continues to expand through our involvement with library networks, the Internet, and the World Wide Web.

4644 Talking Books/Homebound Services
Brevard County Library System
2725 Judge Fran Jamieson Way
Viera, FL 32940
321-633-2000
FAX: 321-633-1838
kbriley@brev.org
www.brevardcounty.us/PublicLibraries

Kay Briley, Librarian
Camille Johnson, Executive Director
Offers reference materials on blindness and other handicaps. Subregional library for the blind and physically handicapped, assistive reading devices collection, reference materials on blindness and other handicaps; CCTV, phonic ear, reading edge and LOUD-R assistive listening devices available.

4645 University of Miami: Bascom Palmer Eye Institute
Department Of Ophthalmalogy
900 NW 17th St
Miami, FL 33136-1119
305-243-2020
888-845-0002
FAX: 305-326-7000
www.bascompalmer.org

Michael Gittelman, CEO
Teresa Spaulding, Manager
Eduardo C. Alfonso, M.D., Professor and Chairman
Clinical and basic research into blindness and visual impairments.

4646 University of Miami: Mailman Center for Child Development
1601 NW 12th Ave
Miami, FL 33136-1005
305-243-6395
FAX: 305-326-7594
pedsinformation@med.miami.edu
pediatrics.med.miami.edu

William Donelan, Vice President for Medical Admin
William W. O'Neill, M.D., Executive Dean, Chief Medical Of
Pascal J. Goldschmidt, M.D., SVP, Dean, CEO
Focuses on birth defects and children's illnesses.

4647 West Florida Regional Library
200 W Gregory St
Pensacola, FL 32502-4822
850-436-5060
FAX: 850-436-5039
TTY:850-436-5063
hhudson@ci.pensacola.fl.us

Eugene Fischer, Executive Director
Helen Hudson, Outreach Librarian
Offers children's print/braille books.

Georgia

4648 Athens Talking Book Center-Athens-Clarke County Regional Library
2025 Baxter St
Athens, GA 30606-6331
706-613-3655
800-531-2063
FAX: 706-613-3660

Stacey Chandler, Manager
Discs, cassettes, large print books, reference materials on blindness, descriptive videos, films, closed-circuit TV, magnifiers, braille writer, summer reading programs, cassette books and magazines and more.

4649 Augusta Talking Book Center
823 Telfair Street
Augusta, GA 30901-2232
706-821-2600
FAX: 706-724-6762
TTY:706-722-1639
www.ecgrl.org

Lillie Hamilton, Board Of Trustee
Audrey Bell, Manager
Loran Gray, Board Of Trustee
Discs, cassettes, braille writer, films, large print books, summer reading program, magnifiers and reference materials on blindness and other handicaps.

4650 Bainbridge Subregional Library for the Blind & Physically Handicapped
S W Georgia Regional Library
301 S Monroe St
Bainbridge, GA 39819-4029
229-248-2665
800-795-2680
FAX: 229-248-2670
lbph@swgrl.org
www.swgrl.org

Susans Wittle, Manager
Kathy Hutchins, Supervisor
The library houses a large collection of recorded materials as well as reference materials. For recorded and Braille materials that are provided by the National Library Service (NLS) but not currently in stock at the Bainbridge Library, the Regional Library in Atlanta can be contacted to Interlibrary Loan the requested materials.

4651 Columbus Subregional Library For The Blind And Physically Handicapped
1120 Bradley Dr
Columbus, GA 31906-2813
706-649-0780
800-652-0782
FAX: 706-649-1914
TTY: 706-649-0974

Dorothy Bowen, Librarian
Braille writer, magnifiers, closed-circuit TV, large-print photocopier, cassette books and magazines, children's books on cassette, home visits and other reference materials on blindness and other handicaps.

4652 Emory Autism Resource Center
Emory University
1551 Shoup Ct
Decatur, GA 30033
404-727-8350
FAX: 404-727-3969
tohannon@emory.edu
www.emory.edu/HOUSING/CLAIRMONT/autism.html

James W. Wagner, President
Larry Hagan, IT Manager
Paul B. Pruett, MD, Director of Residency Education
Offers on-line bulletin boards which are relevant to autism.

4653 Emory University Laboratory for Ophthalmic Research
1365b Clifton Rd NE
Atlanta, GA 30322-1013
404-778-4530
FAX: 404-778-4002
pbennet@emory.edu
www.eyecenter.emory.edu

James W. Wagner, President
Larry Hagan, IT Manager
Paul B. Pruett, MD, Director of Residency Education

Various studies into the aspects of blindness.

4654 Georgia Library for the Blind and Physically Handicapped
Georgia Public Library
1800 Century Place
Suite 150
Atlanta, GA 30345-4304

404-235-7200
800-248-6701
FAX: 404-756-4618
georgialibraries.org

Stella Cone, Director
Deborah Scott, Business Manager
Dr. Lamar Veatch, Librarian
Discs, cassettes, braille, films, closed-circuit TV, braille writer, large-print photocopier, cassette books and magazines.

4655 Hall County Library: East Hall Branch and Special Needs Library
127 Main St NW
Gainesville, GA 30501-3614

770-532-3311
FAX: 770-532-4305
TTY:770-531-2520
info@hallcountylibrary.org
www.hallcountylibrary.org

Adrian Mixson, Manager
Summer reading programs, braille writer, magnifiers, scanners and readers, audio described videos, closed captioned videos, closed-circuit TV, large-print photocopier, cassette books and magazines, large print books, children's books on cassette, home visits and other reference materials on blindness and other handicaps.

4656 Macon Library for the Blind and Physically Handicapped
Washington Memorial Library
1180 Washington Ave
Macon, GA 31201-1762

478-744-0800
FAX: 478-742-3161
www.co.bibb.ga.us/library

Thomas Jones, Director
Leila Brittain, Finance Officer
Hannah Warren, Office Manager
Summer reading programs, braille writer, magnifiers, closed-circuit TV, large-print photocopier, cassette books and magazines, children's books on cassette, home visits and other reference materials on blindness and other handicaps.

4657 National Center on Birth Defects and Developmental Disabilities
Centers for Disease Control and Prevention
1600 Clifton Rd NE
MS E-87
Atlanta, GA 30333

404-639-3311
800-232-4636
FAX: 404-498-3070
TTY: 888-232-6348
cdcinfo@cdc.gov
www.cdc.gov/ncbddd/

Coleen A. Boyle, PhD, MSHyg, Director
Stephanie Dulin, MBA, Deputy Director
Vicki Kipreos, PMP, Management Officer
Promotes child development, prevents birth defects and developmental disabilities.

4658 North Georgia Talking Book Center
LaFayette-Walker Public Library
305 S Duke St
La Fayette, GA 30728-2936

706-638-8312
888-506-0509
888-506-0509
FAX: 706-638-4028
www.chrl.org

Tim York, Manager
June DeLong, Library Assistant
Martha McKeehan, Library Assistant
We offer books on cassette for the visual and physically disabled induvidual, books in braille, magazines on cassette, zoom text screen magnifier, computer voice program, large-print photocopier, summer reading program, home visits na dother reference materials on blindness and other disabilities.

4659 Oconee Regional Library
801 Bellevue Ave
Dublin, GA 31021-4847

478-272-5710
FAX: 478-275-5381
georgialibraries.org

Stella Cone, Director
Deborah Scott, Business Manager
Dr. Lamar Veatch, Librarian
Summer reading programs, braille writer, magnifiers, closed-circuit TV, large-print photocopier, cassette books and magazines, children's books on cassette, home visits and other reference materials on blindness and other handicaps.

4660 Rome Subregional Library for the Blind and Physically Handicapped
205 Riverside Pkwy
Rome, GA 30161-2922

706-236-4611
888-263-0769
FAX: 706-236-4631
TTY: 706-236-4618

Diana Mills, Librarian
Delana Hickman, Manager
The regional library system serves Floyd and Polk counties. System headquarters are located in Rome, Georgia, within the Rome/Floyd County Library Branch.

4661 South Georgia Regional Library-Valdosta Talking Book Center
300 Woodrow Wilson Dr
Valdosta, GA 31602-2532

229-333-0086
FAX: 229-333-0364
commissioner@lowndescounty.com
sgrl.org

Chuck Gibson, Manager
Summer reading programs, Braille writer, magnifiers, closed-circuit TV, large print photocopier, cassette books and magazines, children's books on cassette, home visits and other reference materials on blindness and other handicaps.

4662 Talking Book Center Brunswick-Glynn County Regional Library
208 Gloucester St
Brunswick, GA 31520-7007

912-267-1212
FAX: 912-267-9597
www.trrl.org

Betty Ransom, Librarian
Joe Shinnick, Executive Director
The Three Rivers Regional Library system is named for 3 rivers that flow through all 7 counties of the library system. The Three Rivers Regional Library system serves patrons in Brantley, Camden, Charlton, Glynn, Long, McIntosh, and Wayne counties in southeast Georgia.

Hawaii

4663 Assistive Technology Resource Centers of Hawaii (ATRC)
200 North Vineyard Boulevard
Suite 430
Honolulu, HI 96817-5362

808-532-7110
800-645-3007
FAX: 808-532-7120
TTY: 808-532-7110
atrc-info@atrc.org
www.atrc.org

Barbara Fischlowitz-Leong, Executive Director
Jeff Ah Sam, Technical Assisstant
Jodi Asato, Deputy Director
Provides information and training on assistive technology devices, services, and funding resources. Conducts presentations and demonstrations in the community to increase AT awareness and promote self-advocacy among people with disabilities.

4664   Hawaii State Library for the Blind and Physically Handicapped
874 Dillingham Blvd
Honolulu, HI 96817-4505

808-845-9221
800-559-4096
FAX: 808-733-8449
honcclib@hawaii.edu
www2.honolulu.hawaii.edu/library

Fusako Miyashiro, Manager
Supported by the Hawaii State Public Library System and the National Library Service for the Blind and Physically Handicapped, Library of Congress. Staff with knowledge of sign language; Special interest periodicals; Books on deafness and sign language; captioned media; Special Services: Radio Reading Service, Talking Books Reader's Club, educational and cultural programs, machine lending agency. Braille, cassette and large type. Regional and National service, quarterly newsletter.

Idaho

4665   Idaho Assistive Technology Project
University of Idaho
121 West Sweet Ave
Moscow, ID 83843-2268

208-885-3557
800-432-8324
FAX: 208-885-6145
idahoat@uidaho.edu
www.idahoat.org

Janice Carson, Project Director
Irene Lunsford, Loan Program Manager
Julie Magelky, Loan Program Coordinator
A federally funded program managed by the Center on Disbailities and Human Development at the University of Idaho. The goal of the IATP is to increase the availability of assistive technology devices and services for Idahoans with disabilities. The IATP offers free trainings and technical assistance, a low-interest loan program, assistive technology assessments for children and agriculture workers, and free informational materials.

4666   Idaho Commission for Libraries: Talking Book Service
325 W State St
Boise, ID 83702-6055

208-334-2150
800-458-3271
FAX: 208-334-4016
talkingbooks@libraries.idaho.gov
www.libraries.idaho.gov/tbs

Ann Joslin, Manager
Irene Lunsford, Library Consultant
David Harrell, IT & Telecommunications Resources Manager
Offers audio and braille books and magazines, equipment, and accessories. All materials are mailed free to users' homes. Service is available free to all Idaho residents with a disability which limits their ability to use print materials.

Illinois

4667   Chicago Public Library Talking Book Center
400 S State St
Chicago, IL 60605-1216

312-747-4300
800-757-4654
FAX: 312-747-4962
www.chipublib.org

Linda Johnson Rice, President
Christopher Valenti, Vice President
Cristina Benitez, Secretary
Summer reading programs, braille writer, closed-circuit TV, large print photocopier, cassette books and magazines, children's books on cassette, home visits and other reference materials on blindness and other handicaps. Three assistive technology centers designed and equipped for the blind and visually impaired, funded by the National Library Service for the Blind and Handicapped, a division of the Library of Congress. All services FREE!

4668   Department of Ophthalmology and Visual Science
1855 W Taylor St
Chicago, IL 60612-7242

312-996-7000
800-625-2013
FAX: 312-996-7770
TTY: 312-413-0123
www.uic.edu

Paula Allen-Meares, Chancellor
Lon S. Kaufman, Vice Chancellor for Academic Aff
Mitra Dutta, Vice Chancellor for Research
Offers help, support, information and research for persons with vision problems, including Retinitis Pigmentosa.

4669   Guild for the Blind
65 E. Wacker Place
Suite 1010
Chicago, IL 60601-7463

312-236-8569
FAX: 312-236-8128
www.second-sense.org

Brett Christenson, President
Laura Rounce, Vice President
Michael P. Wagner, Treasurer
provides worship on vision rehabilitation, training on computers and other adaptive technology, career counseling, and professional development workshops and offers assistive devices for sale.

4670   Horizons for the Blind
125 Erick St.
A103
Crystal Lake, IL 60014

815-444-8800
800-318-2000
FAX: 815-444-8830
mail@horizons-blind.org
www.horizons-blind.org

Camille Caffarelli, Executive Director
Jeff T. Thorsen, First Vice President & Treasurer
Keith Myers, Second Vice President
Horizons for the Blind is a nonprofit organization working to improve the quality of life for people who are blind or visually impaired by increasing access to consumer products, services, culture, arts, education, and recreation.

4671   Illinois Early Childhood Intervention Clearinghouse
51 Gerty Drive
Champaign, IL 61820-7469

217-333-1386
877-275-3227
FAX: 217-244-7732
Illinois-eic@illinois.edu
www.eiclearinghouse.org

Charlton Brandt, Manager
Patricia Traylor, Project Associate
Free lending library of materials related to early childhood and disability. Books, audiovisuals and articles available. Computerized database with more than 31,000 items available to Illinois residents.

4672   Illinois Machine Sub-Lending Agency
607 S Greenbriar Rd
Carterville, IL 62918-1602

618-985-8375
800-455-2665
FAX: 618-985-4211
imsastaff@imsa.lib.il.us

Loretta Broomfield, Director
The Illinois Machine Sublending Agency (IMSA) is a division of the Illinois Network of Talking Book and Braille Libraries. The primary responsibility of IMSA is to maintain Talking Book equipment and accessories and to issue Talking Book equipment and accessories to Illinois residents who are registered for the service. IMSA is also the support center for patrons in need of assistance with the Braille and Audio Reading Download (BARD) service.

4673   Illinois Regional Library for the Blind and Physically Handicapped
1055 W Roosevelt Rd
Chicago, IL 60608-1559

312-746-9210
800-331-2351
FAX: 312-746-9192

Shawn Thomas, Reference Librarian
Barbara Perkins, Acting Director

Summer reading programs, braille writer, magnifiers, closed-circuit TV, large-print photocopier, cassette books and magazines, descriptive videos, children's books on cassette, home visits and other reference materials on blindness and other handicaps.

4674 Mid-Illinois Talking Book Center
600 High Point Ln
East Peoria, IL 61611-9396   309-694-9200
                                    800-426-0709

Rose Chenoweth, Director
Michelle Moran, Assistant
Rebecca Rollings, Assistant
Providing a free library service to anyone unable to read regular print because of a visual or physical disability. There are books and magazines on tape and playback equipment; and also in Braille. Books and magazines are mailed free to and from library patrons, wherever they reside.

4675 National Eye Research Foundation (NERF)
Ste 207a
910 Skokie Blvd
Northbrook, IL 60062-4033   847-564-4652
                                   800-621-2258
                              FAX: 847-564-0807
                                   info@nerf.org
                                   www.nerf.org

Joel Tenner, Manager
Dedicated to improving eye care for the public and meeting the professional nees of eye care practitioners; sponsors eye research projects on contact lens applications and eye care problems. Special study sections in such fields as orthokertology, primary eyecare, pediatrics, and through continuing education programs. Provides eye care information for the public and professionals. Educational materials including pamphlets. Program activities include education and referrals.

4676 National Lekotek Center
2001 N. Clybourn
Chicago, IL 60614   773-528-5766
                                   800-366-7529
                              FAX: 773-537-2992
                                   www.lekotek.org

Elaine D. Cottey, Chair
Joanna Horsnail, Chair Elect
Eric Gastevich, Treasurer
Toy library and play-centered programs for children with special needs and their families with branches in 17 states. Sliding fee scale. Lekotek also has a Toy Resource Helpline that provides individualized assistances in the selection of toys and play materials and general resources for families with children with disabilities.

4677 Northwestern University Multipurpose Arthritis & Musculoskeletal Center
420 East Superior Street
Chicago, IL 60611-4296   312-503-8194
                              FAX: 312-503-1204
                      www.feinberg.northwestern.edu
Cynthia Barnard, MBA, Director, Quality Strategies
John Vozenilek, MD, Assistant Professor
Eric G. Neilson, MD, Vice President for Medical Affairs
Conducts biomedical, educational and health services research into musculoskeletal diseases.

4678 Skokie Accessible Library Services
Skokie Public Library
5215 Oakton St
Skokie, IL 60077-3680   847-673-7774
                              FAX: 847-673-7797
                              TTY:847-673-8926
                                   www.skokie.lib.il.us
Carolyn A. Anthony, Director
John J. Graham, President
Diana Hunter, Vice President/President Emerita
Library services for people with disabilities, including electronic aids, materials in special formats, programs and special services.

4679 University of Illinois at Chicago: Lions of Illinois Eye Research Institute
University of Illinois at Chicago
1855 West Taylor Street, m/c 648
Room 3.138
Chicago, IL 60612   312-996-6591
                              FAX: 312-996-7770
                                   eyeweb@uic.edu
                                   www.uic.edu

Rolanda Geddis, Manager
Paula Alen Meares, Chancellor
Jerry Bauman, Vice President for Health Affairs
Visual impairments and blindness research, including glaucoma studies.

4680 Voices of Vision Talking Book Center at DuPage Library System
125 Tower Drive
Burr Ridge, IL 60527-2771   630-734-5055
                                   800-426-0709
                              FAX: 630-208-0399
                      info@illinoistalkingbooks.org
                      www.illinoistalkingbooks.org

Karen L. Odean, Director
Provides library service to persons who are unable to use standard printed material because of visual or physical disabilities. Part of the Illinois network of Talking Book Libraries. The service is free to those who are eligable. Provides books and magazines on audio-cassettes. Special playback equipment needed to use the books is also loaned. Braille books and magazines are also available. The collection includes popular books, classics and children's literature.

Indiana

4681 Allen County Public Library
900 Library Plaza
Fort Wayne, IN 46802-3699   260-421-1200
                              FAX: 260-421-1386
                              TTY:260-421-1302
                           Genealogy@ACPL.Info
                                   www.acpl.lib.in.us

Jeffrey R. Krull, Director
Martin E. Seifert, President
Alan McMahan, Vice President
Summer reading programs, braille writer, magnifiers, closed-circuit TV, large-print photocopier, cassette books and magazines, children's books on cassette, home visits and other reference materials on blindness and other handicaps.

4682 Bartholomew County Public Library
536 5th St
Columbus, IN 47201-6225   812-379-1255
                              FAX: 812-379-1275
                           library@barth.lib.in.us
                                   barth.lib.in.us

Beth Poor, Executive Director
Summer reading programs, braille writer, magnifiers, closed-circuit TV, large-print photocopier, cassette books and magazines, children's books on cassette, home visits and other reference materials on blindness and other handicaps.

4683 Elkhart Public Library for the Blind and Physically Handicapped
300 S 2nd St
Elkhart, IN 46516-3109   574-522-2223
                                   800-622-4970
                              FAX: 574-522-2174
                                   www.myepl.org/epl

Connie Jo Ozinga, Executive Director
Barbara G. Anderson, President
Janice E. Dean, Vice-President
Summer reading programs, braille writer, magnifiers, closed-circuit TV, large-print photocopier, cassette books and magazines, children's books on cassette, home visits and other reference materials on blindness and other handicaps.

4684 Indiana Resource Center for Autism
2853 E 10th St
Bloomington, IN 47408-2696
812-855-6508
800-825-4733
FAX: 812-855-9630
TTY: 812-855-9396
iidc@indiana.edu
www.iidc.indiana.edu/irca

Dr Cathy Pratt Ph.D., BCBA, Director
Donna Beasley, Administrative Program Secretary
Pamela Anderson, Outreach/Resource Specialist
The Indiana Resource Center for Autism staff conduct outreach training and consultations, engage in research and develop and disseminate information focused on building the capicity of local communities, organizations, agencies and families to support children and adults across the autism spectrum in typical work, school, home and community settings. Please check our website for a complete list of publications.

4685 Indiana University: Multipurpose Arthritis Center
School Of Medicine, Rheumatology Division
509 E. 3rd Street
Bloomington, IN 47401-3654
812-855-0516
FAX: 812-855-9943
research.iu.edu

Dr. Kenneth Brandt MD, Director
Carmichael Center, Vice President for Research
Steven A Martin, Associate Vice President for Research
The mission of the center is to pursue major biomedical research interests relevant to the rheumatic diseases. Current areas of emphasis include; articular cartilage biology, pathogenesis of articular cartilage breakdown in osteoarthritis, causes of pain and disability in QA, the pathogenesis and treatment of various forms of amyloidosis, the pathogenesis of dermatomyositis, and immunologic and biochemical markers of cartilage breakdown and repair.

4686 Lake County Public Library Talking Books Service
1919 W 81st Ave
Merrillville, IN 46410-5488
219-769-3541
FAX: 219-769-0690
www.lcplin.org

Larry Acheff, Manager
Large-print books, descriptive videos, braille writer, magnifiers, closed-circuit TV, large-print photocopier, cassette books and magazines, children's books on cassette, and other reference materials on blindness and other handicaps.

4687 Special Services Division: Indiana State Library
140 N Senate Ave
Indianapolis, IN 46204-2207
317-232-3675
800-622-4970
FAX: 317-253-3209
TTY: 317-232-7763
www.in.gov/isloutage

Roberta Brooker, Manager
Barbara Maxwell, State Librarian
C Ewick, Manager
Circulates a collection of braille, recorded, and large print books and magazines and the special equipment needed to play the recorded materials to anyone in Indiana who cannot read regular print due to a visual or physical disability.

4688 St. Joseph Hospital Rehabilitation Center
700 Broadway
Fort Wayne, IN 46802-1402
260-425-3000
FAX: 260-425-3741
www.stjoehospital.com

Kirk Ray, CEO
Bob Hailes, Vice President
Information offered on rehabilitation.

4689 Talking Books Service Evansville Vanderburgh County Public Library
200 SE Martin Luther King Jr Blvd
Evansville, IN 47713- 1802
812-428-8200
866-645-2536
FAX: 812-428-8397
tbs@evpl.org
www.evpl.org

Marcia Learned Au, COO
Connie Davis, Vice President
Marcia Au, Executive Director
The Talking Book Service of the Evansville Vanderburgh Public Library is part of a nationwide network of cooperating libraries headed by the National Library Service & a division of the Library of Congress. This free program provides library services and materials in alternative formats to person who are unable to use standard print material due to a visual or physical handicap.

Iowa

4690 Iowa Department for the Blind Library
State Of Iowa
524 4th Street
Des Moines, IA 50309-2364
515-281-1333
800-362-2587
FAX: 515-281-1263
TTY: 515-281-1355
contact@blind.state.ia.us
www.IDBonline.org

Richard Sorey, Director
Mike Hoenig, Chair
Steve Hagemoser, Commision Board Member
Summer reading programs, large print, disc, Braille and cassette books and magazines, descriptive videos and reference materials on blindness and other handicaps.

4691 Iowa Registry for Congenital and Inherited Disorders
University of Iowa
Department of Epidemiology, Univers
100 BVC, Room W260
Iowa City, IA 52242-5000
319-335-4107
866-274-4237
FAX: 319-335-4030
ircid@uiowa.edu
www.public-health.uiowa.edu/ircid/

Paul Romitti, Ph.D, Director
Kim Keppler-Noreuil, M.D, Clinical Director for Birth Defects
Katherine. Mathews, M.D, Clinical Director for Neuromuscular Disorders
The mission of the Iowa Registry for Congenital and Inherited Disorders is; maintain statewide surveillance for collecting information on selected congenital and inherited disorders in Iowa, monitor annual trends in occurrence and mortality of these disorders, provide data for research studies and educational activities for the prevention and treatment of these disorders.

4692 Library Commission for the Blind
State Of Iowa
524 4th Street
Des Moines, IA 50309-2364
515-281-1333
800-362-2587
FAX: 515-281-1263
TTY: 515-281-1355
contact@blind.state.ia.us

Karen A Keninger, Director
Aldini Jodi, Library Support Staff
Barber Kim, Independent Living Supervisor
Summer reading programs, Braille writer, magnifiers, closed-circuit TV, large print photocopier, cassette books and magazines, children's books on cassette and other reference materials on blindness and other handicaps.

Kansas

4693 **Center for the Improvement of Human Functioning**
3100 N Hillside St
Wichita, KS 67219-3904
316-682-3100
FAX: 316-682-5054
information@riordanclinic.org
www.riordanclinic.org

Hugh D Riordan, President
Ron Hunninghake MD, Chief Medical Officer
Brian Riordan, Chief Executive Officer
Medical, research, and educational facility specializing in the treatment of chronic illness.

4694 **Central Kansas Library Systems Headquarters (CSLS)**
1409 Williams St
Great Bend, KS 67530-4020
620-792-4865
800-362-2642
FAX: 620-793-7270
www.ckls.org

Harry Williams, Administrator
Vickie Herl, Adminstrative Manager
Marquita Boehnke, Department Head
Summer reading programs, braille writer, magnifiers, closed-circuit TV, large-print photocopier, cassette books and magazines, children's books on cassette, home visits and other reference materials on blindness and other handicaps. Assistive technology available. Serving 17 counties in Central Kansas.

4695 **Manhattan Public Library**
629 Poyntz Ave
Manhattan, KS 66502-6131
785-776-4741
800-432-2796
FAX: 785-776-1545
refstaff@mhklibrary.org
manhattan.lib.ks.us

Linda Knupp, Director
John Pecoraro, Assistant Director
Brice Hobrock, President
Summer reading programs, Braille writer, magnifiers, closed-circuit TV, large-print photocopier, cassette books and magazines, children's books on cassette, home visits and other reference materials on blindness and other disabilities.

4696 **Northwest Kansas Library System Talking Books**
2 Washington Square
Norton, KS 67654-1615
785-877-5148
800-432-2858
FAX: 785-877-5697
www.nwkls.org

George Seamon, Director
Alice Evans, Business Manager & Acquisitions
David Fischer, Technology Consultant
Offers books on disc and cassette. Library of Congress talking book and program for qualified individuals. Also offers descriptive videos to eligible persons.

4697 **South Central Kansas Library System**
321 North Main Street
South Hutchinson, KS 67505-1145
620-663-3211
800-234-0529
FAX: 620-663-9797
sckls.info

Paul Hawkins, Director
Sharon Barnes, Technology Consultant
Larry Papenfuss, Director of Information Technology
Serving public, school, academic and special libraries in 12 counties since 1968, the South Central Kansas Library System (SCKLS) is the "go to" resource for innovative services, quality member awareness and assistance.

4698 **State Library of Kansas**
Esu Memorial Union
300 SW 10th Ave.
Room 312-N
Topeka, KS 66612-1593
620-341-6280
800-362-0699
KTB@ks.gov
kslib.info/talking-books

Cindy Roupe, State Librarian
Michael Lang, Director
Kansas Talking Books provides personalized library support and materials in a specialized format to eligible Kansas residents to ensure that all may read. Features: Audiobooks, magazines and audio equipment mailed directly to your house and returned postage free; special equipment lent to you at no charge; downloadable books from the Braille and Audio Reading Download (BARD) website or by using the new BARD app.

4699 **Topeka & Shawnee County Public Library Talking Books Service**
1515 SW 10th Ave
Topeka, KS 66604-1374
785-580-4400
800-432-2925
FAX: 785-580-4496
TTY: 785-580-4544
www.tscpl.org

Stephanie Hall, Manager
Gina Millsap, Chief Executive Officer
Robert Banks, Chief Operating Officer
Talking books is a free service that provides cassette and digital books and equipment to people who are unable to read or use standard print materials because of a visual or physical impairment. There are no fees. To apply for Talking Books you must fill out and submit an application, have it certified by the appropriate authority and return it to the library. You can find an application on our website or have one mailed out to you by contacting our office.

4700 **Wichita Public Library/Talking Book Service**
Wichita Public Library
223 S Main St
Wichita, KS 67202-3795
316-261-8500
FAX: 316-262-4540
TTY:316-262-3972
admin@wichita.lib.ks.us

Cynthia Berner-Harris, Executive Director
Eric J. Larson, Member of the Board
Furnish recorded reading material (books and magazines) for visually and physically challenged citizens.

4701 **Wichita Public Library/Talking Book Service**
223 S Main St
Wichita, KS 67202-3795
316-261-8500
FAX: 316-262-4540
TTY:316-262-3972
admin@wichita.lib.ks.us

Cynthia Berner-Harris, Executive Director
Eric J. Larson, Member of the Board
Furnish recorded reading material (books and magazines) for visually and physically challenged citizens.

Kentucky

4702 **EnTech: Enabling Technologies of Kentuckiana**
Spaulding University
851 South 3rd Street
Louisville, KY 40203-2115
502-585-9911
800-896-8941
FAX: 502-585-7103
www.spalding.edu

Laura Strickland, Manager
Mary Kaye Steinmietz, Outreach Coordinator
Tori Murden McClure, President
Assistive technology resource and demonstration center, serving persons of all ages and disabilities in Kentucky and Southern Indiana. Services include: assistive technology information, demonstration, evaluation, training, technical support and short-term loan of equipment.

4703 Kentucky Talking Book Library - Kentucky Dept. for Libraries and Archives
300 Coffee Tree Road
PO Box 537
Frankfort, KY 40602-0537
502-564-8300
800-372-2968
FAX: 502-564-5773
ktbl.mail@ky.gov
www.kdla.ky.gov

Barbara Penegor, Regional Librarian
Lauren Abner, Field Services
Katherine K. Adelberg, E-Rate Coordinator
Provides library service to those who are physically unable to read print. Audio and braille books and magazines are available via mail or download.

4704 Louisville Free Public Library
301 York Street
Louisville, KY 40203-2257
502-574-1611
FAX: 502-574-1666
lfpl.org

Craig Buthod, Manager
Summer reading programs, braille writer, magnifiers, closed-circuit TV, large-print photocopier, cassette books and magazines, children's books on cassette, home visits and other reference materials on blindness and other handicaps.

Louisiana

4705 Central Louisiana State Hospital Medical and Professional Library
P.O.Box 5031
Pineville, LA 71361-5031
318-484-6200
FAX: 318-484-6501
www.doa.la.gov

Patrick Kelly, CEO
Carol Gee, Manager
Information offered on psychiatry, psychology and mental health.

4706 Louisiana State Library
701 North 4th St
Baton Rouge, LA 70802-5345
225-342-4913
800-543-4702
FAX: 225-219-4804
admin@state.lib.la.us
www.state.lib.la.us

Rebecca Hamilton, Assistant Secretary, State Libra
Diane Brown, Deputy State Librarian
Beverly Dugas, Business Manager
Summer reading programs, braille writer, magnifiers, closed-circuit TV, large-print photocopier, cassette books and magazines, children's books on cassette. Descriptive videos and other reference materials on blindness and other handicaps.

4707 Louisiana State University Genetics Section of Pediatrics
533 Bolivar St
New Orleans, LA 70112-1349
504-568-6151
FAX: 504-568-8500
postmaster@lsuhsc.edu
www.medschool.lsuhsc.edu

Steve Nelson, MD, Dean
Janis Letourneau, MD, Associate Dean for Faculty & Ins
Cathi Fontenot, MD, Associate Dean for Alumni Affair
Our goal is to continue building a strong department in which all of the faculty are successful in attracting funding, and committed to establishing productive programs that bring credit to the Department and to the Health Sciences Center as a whole.

4708 State Library of Louisiana: Services for the Blind and Physically Handicapped
701 North 4th St
Baton Rouge, LA 70802-5345
225-342-4913
800-543-4702
FAX: 225-219-4804
www.state.lib.la.us

Rebecca Hamilton, Assistant Secretary, State Libra
Diane Brown, Deputy State Librarian
Beverly Dugas, Business Manager
Summer reading programs, braille publications, cassette books and magazines, children's books on cassette and other reference materials on blindness and other handicaps. Louisiana Hotlines - quarterly newsletter. Affiliated with National Library Service for the Blind and Physically Handicapped, Washington, DC. Louisiana Voices recording program uses volunteers to record books for the blind.

Maine

4709 Bangor Public Library
145 Harlow St
Bangor, ME 04401-4900
207-947-8336
FAX: 207-945-6694
www.bpl.lib.me.us

Barbara Mc Dade, Executive Director
Norman Minsky, President
Franklin E. Bragg II, MD, Vice President
Summer reading programs, braille writer, magnifiers, closed-circuit TV, large-print photocopier, cassette books and magazines, children's books on cassette, home visits and other reference materials on blindness and other handicaps.

4710 Cary Library
107 Main Street
Houlton, ME 04730-2196
207-532-1302
FAX: 207-532-4350
www.cary.lib.me.us

Iva Sussman, Chair
Forrest Barnes, Treasurer
Gary Hagan, Secretary
Summer reading programs, braille writer, magnifiers, closed-circuit TV, large-print photocopier, cassette books and magazines, children's books on cassette, home visits and other reference materials on blindness and other handicaps.

4711 Lewiston Public Library
200 Lisbon St
Lewiston, ME 04240-7234
207-513-3004
FAX: 207-784-3011
TTY:207-200-1511
LPLReference@LewistonMaine.gov
lplonline.org

Rick Speer, Library Director
Marcela Peres, Adult Services Librarian
David Moorhead, Children's Librarian
Summer reading programs, braille writer, magnifiers, closed-circuit T.V., large-print photocopier, cassette books and magazines, children's books on cassette, home visits and other reference materials on blindness and other handicaps.

4712 Maine State Library
Maine State
64 State House Sta
Augusta, ME 04333-64
207-287-5650
800-762-7106
FAX: 207-287-5624
TTY: 888-577-6690
benitad@ursus3.ursus.maine.edu
maine.gov

Chris Boynton, Manager
J Gary Nichols, State Librarian
Melora Norman, Manager
Summer reading programs, cassette books and magazines, children's books on cassette, home visits and other reference materials on blindness and other handicaps.
Newsl./BiAnnual

4713 **New England Regional Genetics Group**
P.O.Box 920288
Needham, MA 02492-4   781-444-0126
                                  FAX: 781-444-0127
                                  mfgnergg@verizon.net
                                  www.nergg.org

Marinell Newtown, President
Jennifer Walsh, Secretary
Merrill Henderson, Treasurer
New Englands primary network for collaborative exchange of genetic health information and education.

4714 **Portland Public Library**
5 Monument Sq
Portland, ME 04101-4072   207-871-1700
                                  FAX: 207-871-1703
                                  reference@portland.lib.me.us
                                  portlandlibrary.com

Stephen J. Podgajny, Executive Director
Clare E. Hannan, Head of Finance and Operations
Linda Albert, Head of Human Resources
Summer reading programs, magnifiers, closed-circuit T.V., large-print photocopier, cassette books and magazines, children's books on cassette, home visits and other reference materials on blindness and other handicaps.

4715 **Waterville Public Library**
73 Elm Street
Waterville, ME 04901-6078   207-872-5433
                                  FAX: 207-873-4779
                                  wplhelpdesk@waterville.lib.me.us
                                  www.watervillelibrary.org
Sarah Sugden, Executive Director
Marnie Terhune, President
William Grant, Treasurer
Summer reading programs, braille writer, magnifiers, closed-circuit T.V., large-print photocopier, cassette books and magazines, children's books on cassette, home visits and other reference materials on blindness and other handicaps.

Maryland

4716 **Johns Hopkins University Dana Center for Preventive Ophthalmology**
Wilmer Ophthalmology Institute
600 N Wolfe St
Wilmer Suite 122
Baltimore, MD 21287-9019   410-955-2777
                                  FAX: 410-955-2542
                                  boland@jhu.edu
Harry Quigley, Director
Emily W. . Gower, Ph.D, Director
Joanne . Katz, Sc.D, Director/Professor and Associate Chair
Established in 1979, the Dana Center for Preventive Ophthalmology is dedicated to improving knowlege of risk factors for ocular disease and public health approaches to the prevention of these diseases and their ensuing visual impairment and blindness worldwide.

4717 **Johns Hopkins University: Asthma and Allergy Center**
5501 Hopkins Bayview Cir
Baltimore, MD 21224-6821   410-550-0545
                                  FAX: 410-550-1733
                                  jhuallergy@jhmi.edu
                                  hopkins-arthritis.org
Lawrence Lichtenstein, Director
Studies of allergic diseases and individuals with allergic disease, pulmonary diseases and diseases involving inflammation and immunological processes.

4718 **Maryland State Library for the Blind and Physically Handicapped**
Maryland State Department of Education
415 Park Avenue
Baltimore, MD 21201-3603   410-230-2424
                                  800-964-9209
                                  FAX: 410-333-2095
                                  TTY: 800-934-2541
                                  referenc@lbph.lib.md.us
Jill Lewis, Manager
Diana Jarvis, Administrative Specialist
LaTarsha Wilson, Secretary
Provide comprehensive library services to the eligible blind and physically handicapped residents of the State of Maryland. The vision is to provide innovative and quality services to meet the needs and expectations of the patrons of Maryland.

4719 **Montgomery County Department of Public Libraries/Special Needs Library**
6400 Democracy Blvd
Bethesda, MD 20817-1638   240-777-0922
                                  TTY:301-897-2203
                                  montgomerycountymd.gov
Susan F Cohen, Assistant Head Librarian
James Montgomery, Owner
Joseph Eagan, Branch Manager
Serves the library information and reading needs of people with disabilities, family members, students and service providers. Some of its services include books, periodicals, and videos on disability issues, adaptive technology, community information; the National Library for the Blind and Physically Handicapped Talking Book program; large print books; and computer room with adaptive technology.

4720 **National Epilepsy Library (NEL)**
Epilepsy Foundation
8301 Professional Pl
Landover, MD 20785-7223   866-330-2718
                                  800-332-1000
                                  FAX: 877-687-4878
                                  ContactUs@efa.org
                                  www.epilepsyfoundation.org
Marl A Finucane, Executive Vice President
Patty Dukes, Vice President Operations/Human
Mimi Browne, Director, HRSA programs
Contains information about epilepsy and seizure disorders and serves physicians and other health professionals. Provides in-house bibliographic database (ESDI), searches and documents delivery and interlibrary loans. Maintains the Albert and Ellen Grass Archives.

4721 **National Federation of the Blind Jernigan Institute**
200 E. Wells St.
at Jernigan Place
Baltimore, MD 21230   410-659-9314
                                  FAX: 410-685-5653
                                  nfb@nfb.org
                                  nfb.org/programs-services
Anil Lewis, Executive Director, Blindness Initiatives
Cutting-edge research and training is conducted through the NFB Jernigan Institute to address the real problems of blindness, such as model education and rehabilitation methods to empower the blind or improved instruction in Braille. The Jacobus tenBroek Library is also hosted at the NFB headquarters.

4722 **National Institute on Aging**
31 Center Dr., MSC 2292
Building 31, Room 5C27
Bethesda, MD 20892   800-222-2225
                                  TTY:800-222-4225
                                  niaic@nia.nih.gov
                                  www.nia.nih.gov
Richard J. Hodes, Director
Lisa Mascone, Deputy Director, Management
Luigi Ferrucci, Scientific Director
The National Institute on Aging (NIA) is the primary Federal agency engaged in researching Alzheimer's disease.

4723 **National Rehabilitation Information Center (NARIC)**
8400 Corporate Drive
Suite 500
Landover, MD 20785-2245   301-459-5984
800-346-2742
FAX: 301-459-4263
TTY: 301-459-5984
naricinfo@heitechservices.com
www.naric.com

Mark X. Odum, Project Director
Natalie J. Collier, Library & Acquisitions Manager
Tamara J. Pyle, Library & Information Services Coordinator
NARIC is a federally-funded library and information center that focuses on disability and rehabilitation information.

4724 **Red Notebook**
Friends of Libraries for Deaf Action
2930 Craiglawn Rd
Silver Spring, MD 20904-1816   301-572-5168
FAX: 301-572-5168
TTY:301-572-5168
folda86@aol.com

Alice L Hagemeyer, MLS, Founder/President
Merrie A. Davidson, Associate
Ricardo Lopez, MS, Associate
A binder containing fact sheets, library reprints, announcements and other printed informational materials that are related to both deaf and library issues. It is designed to help build communication among individuals and groups within the deaf community. The focus is on assisting libraries in providing cost-effective and efficient library and information services to these consumers in a unbiased fashion.

4725 **Social Security Library**
U S Social Security Administration
6401 Security Blvd
Baltimore, MD 21235-6401   800-772-1213
TTY:800-325-0778
www.socialsecurity.gov

Bill Vitek, Manager
Jo B Barnhart, Chief Executive Officer
Information on social security and disability insurance.

4726 **Trace Research and Development Center**
Univ. of Maryland, College of Information Studies
4130 Campus Dr.
College Park, MD 20742   301-405-2043
trace-info@umd.edu
trace.umd.edu

Kate Vanderheiden, Program Manager
Research focused on how standard information and communication technology products may be designed so that more people with disabilities can use them.

4727 **Warren Grant Magnuson Clinical Center**
National Institue Health
9000 Rockville Pike
Bethesda, MD 20892-1   301-496-2563
800-411-1222
FAX: 301-480-2984
TTY: 866-411-1010
prpl@mail.cc.nih.gov
www.cc.nih.gov

John I Gallin, MD, Clinical Center Director
Clare Hastings, PhD, RN, FAA, Chief Nurse Officer
Maureen E. Gormley, MPH, MA, RN, Chief Operating Officer
Established in 1953 as the research hospital of the National Institutes of Health. Designed so that patient care facilities are close to research laboratories so new findings of basic and clinical scientists can be quickly applied to the treatment of patients. Upon referral by physicians, patients are admitted to NIH clinical studies.

Massachusetts

4728 **Boston University Arthritis Center**
Boston University
715 Albany St
Boston, MA 02118-2526   617-638-4640
FAX: 617-638-5226
www.bumc.bu.edu

Karen Antman, Dean & Provost, Medical School
Meg Aranow, Director
Barbara A. Cole, Associate VP for Research Admin
The Arthritis Center focuses its educational, research and patient care efforts on the diagnosis and treatment of rheumatic diseases. These include the many forms of arthritis; the auto-immune diseases such as Scleroderma, Systemic Lupus, Erythematosus, Rheumatoid Arthritis; localized pain syndromes such as tendonitis, bursitis, and carpal tunnel syndrome; and metabolic bone disorders such as osteoporosis.

4729 **Boston University Center for Human Genetics**
840 Memorial Drive
Suite 101
Cambridge, MA 02139   617-638-7083
FAX: 617-638-7092
amilunsk@bu.edu
www.chginc.org

Aubrey Milunsky, Co-Director
Jeff Milunsky, M.D., F.A.C., Director of Clinical Genetics
Research and molecular diagnosis.

4730 **Boston University Robert Dawson Evans Memorial Dept. of Clinical Research**
75 East Newton St
Boston, MA 02118-2657   617-247-5019
FAX: 617-638-8728

Norman G Levinsky, Director
Jack Ansel, MD
Integral unit of the University Hospital specializing in arthritis and connective tissue studies.

4731 **Braille and Talking Book Library, Perkins School for the Blind**
175 North Beacon Street
Watertown, MA 02472-2751   617-972-3434
800-852-3133
FAX: 617-926-2027
Info@Perkins.org
www.perkins.org

Frederic M. Clifford, Chairman
Philip L. Ladd, Vice Chairman
Dave Power, CEO & President
The Braille and Talking Book Library loans braille and recorded reading materials and the playback equipment necessary to use them. You are eligible for services if you are unable to read print due to a disability.

4732 **Brigham and Women's Hospital: Asthma and Allergic Disease Research Center**
75 Francis St
Boston, MA 02115-6110   617-732-5500
855-278-8010
FAX: 617-730-2858
arc@partners.org

Matthew H Liang, Director
Elizabeth G Nabel, President
Arthur Mombourquette, Vice President of Support Servic
Integral unit of the hospital focusing research attention on asthma and allergy related disorders.

4733 Brigham and Women's Hospital: Robert B Brigham Multipurpose Arthritis Center
Brigham and Women s Hospital
75 Francis St
Boston, MA 02115-6110　　　　　617-732-5500
855-278-8010
FAX: 617-432-0979
www.brighamandwomens.org

Matthew H Liang, Director
Elizabeth G Nabel, President
Arthur Mombourquette, Vice President of Support Servic
Research studies into arthritis and rheumatic diseases.

4734 Caption Center
Media Access Group at WGBH
One Guest St.
Boston, MA 02135　　　　　　　617-300-3600
FAX: 617-300-1020
access@wgbh.org
www.wgbh.org/caption

Pat McDonald, Director
The Caption Center was the world's first captioning agency providing access to television for viewers who are visually impaired and/or hard of hearing. The Center develops new solutions and uses closed captioning and descriptive video to promote access to technology .

4735 Center for Interdisciplinary Research on Immunologic Diseases
Childrens Hospital Medical Center
300 Longwood Avenue
Boston, MA 02115-5724　　　　　617-355-6000
800-355-7944
FAX: 617-355-0443
TTY: 617-730-0152
webteam@tch.harvard.edu
www.childrenshospital.org

Sandra L. Fenwick, President and Chief Executive Officer
Kevin Churchwell, MD, Executive Vice President
Dick Argys, Senior Vice President and Chief Administrative Officer
Organizational research unit of the Children's Hospital that focuses on the causes, prevention and treatments of asthma, infections and allergies.

4736 Harvard University Howe Laboratory of Ophthalmology
Massachusetts Eye & Ear Infirmary
243 Charles Street
Boston, MA 02114-3002　　　　　617-523-7900
FAX: 617-573-4380
TTY: 617-573-5498
richard.godfrey@schepens.harvard.edu
www.masseyeandear.org/

Wycliffe Grousbeck, Chairman
John Fernandez, President and CEO
Jonathan Uhrig, Treasurer
Development ophthalmology and eye research.

4737 Laboure College Library
303 Adams Street
Dorchester Center, MA 02124-5698　　617-296-8300
FAX: 617-296-7947
admissions@laboure.edu
laboure.edu

Andrew Callo, Manager
Maureen A. Smith, President
Offers information on physical disabilities, independent living, peer counseling and advocacy.

4738 Massachusetts Rehabilitation Commission
600 Washington Street
Boston, MA 02111　　　　　　　617-204-3603
800-245-6543
FAX: 617-727-1354
TTY: 800-245-6543
www.mass.gov/mrc

Elmer C Bartels, Commissioner
Deval L. Patrick, Governor
Timothy P. Murray, Lieutenant Governor
Vacational Rehabilitation and Independent Living for people with disabilities.

4739 Schepens Eye Research Institute
20 Staniford Street
Boston, MA 02114-2508　　　　　617-912-0100
FAX: 617-912-0118
geninfo@vision.eri.harvard.edu

John Fernandez, President and CEO
Debra Rogers, Vice President for Ophthalmology
Alan A Ryan, Director Research Finance
Prominent center for research on eye, vision, and blinding diseases; dedicated to research that improves the understanding, management, and prevention of eye diseases and visual deficiencies; fosters collaboration among its faculty members; trains young scientists and clinicians from around the world; promotes communication with scientists in allied fields; leader in the worldwide dispersion of basic scientific knowledge of vision.

4740 Talking Book Library at Worcester Public Library
3 Salem Sq
Worcester, MA 01608-2015　　　　508-799-1730
800-762-0085
FAX: 508-799-1676
www.worcpublib.org

James Izatt, Dept Head
Braille embosser, magnifiers, closed-circuit TV, adapted computers, cassette books and magazines, children's books on cassette, reference materials on blindness and other disabilities.

Michigan

4741 Artificial Language Laboratory
Michigan State University
220 Trowbridge Rd
East Lansing, MI 48824-1042　　　517-353-5940
FAX: 517-353-4766
finaid@msu.edu
www.msu.edu

Dr. John B Eulenberg, Phd, Director
Stephen R. Blosser, BSME, Technical Director
Shawn A. Miller, Laboratory Manager
Multidisciplinary research center in the Audiology & Speech Science department, Michigan State University. Its basic research program includes speech analysis and synthesis. Applied research is carried out on computer-based systems for persons who are blind and for persons with cerebral palsy and head injury. The laboratory develops physical, cognitive and linguistic assessment technology.

4742 Burger School for the Autistic
31735 Maplewood St.
Garden City, MI 48135-1993　　　734-793-1830
FAX: 734-762-8533
garden-city.lib.mi.us

James B Lenze, Library Director
Dan Lodge, Adult Librarian
Lindsay Fricke, Youth Librarian
Burger school for students with autism is the largest public school in the United States that specializes in the education of students with autism.

4743 Chi Medical Library
Ingham Regional Medical Center
401 West Greenlawn
Lansing, MI 48910-2819　　　　517-975-6000
irmc.org

Judy Barnes, Manager
Consumer health and patient education collection in books, videotapes, pamphlets. Open to the public.

4744 Glaucoma Laser Trial
Sinai Hospital of Detroit: Dept. of Opthalmology
31 Center Drive
Bethesda, MI 20892-2510　　　　301-496-5248
kcl@nei.nih.gov
www.nei.nih.gov

Paul A. Sieving, M.D., Ph.D., Director
The purpose of the trial is to compare the safety and long-term efficacy of argon laser treatment of the trabecular meshwork with standard medical treatment for primary open-angle glaucoma.

4745   Grand Traverse Area Library for the Blind and Physically Handicapped
610 Woodmere Ave
Traverse City, MI 49686-3103

231-932-8500
877-931-8558
FAX: 231-932-8578
webmaster@tadl.tcnet.org
www.tadl.org

Metta Lansdale, Library Director
Thomas Kachadurian, President
Jason Gillman, Vice President
The LBPH was established as a sub-regional library in 1972 and currently provides services for 783 registered individuals in 16 counties, 171 of these registrants are Grand Traverse County residents. Anyone unable to read regular printed materials because of visual or physical limitations may be eligible.

4746   Kent District Library for the Blind and Physically Handicapped
814 West River Center Dr. NE
Comstock Park, MI 49321-3420

616-784-2007
877-243-2466
FAX: 616-336-3256
WyomingYouthStaff@kdl.org
www.kdl.org

Charles R Myers, Chair
Vickie Hoekstra, Vice Chair
Carol Simpson, Secretary
Summer reading programs, braille writer, magnifiers, large-print photocopier, cassette books and magazines, children's books on cassette, and other reference materials on blindness and other handicaps.

4747   Macomb Library for the Blind & Physically Handicapped
40900 Romeo Plank
Clinton Township, MI 48038-1132

586-226-5020
800-203-5274
FAX: 586-286-0634
mlbph@cmpl.org
www.cmpl.org

Larry Neal, Library Director
Fred L. Gibson, Jr., President
Peter M. Ruggirello, Vice Chairman
Braille writer, closed-circuit T.V., large-print books, cassette books and magazines, children's books on cassette, other reference materials on blindness and other handicaps, descriptive videos and bifokal kits. Assistive technology including JAWS, Zoomtext, OpenBook, and Duxbury.

4748   Michigan Braille and Talking Book Library
P.O.Box 30007
702 W. Kalamazoo St
Lansing, MI 48909-7507

517-373-5614
800-992-9012
FAX: 517-373-5865
btbl@michigan.gov
www.michigan.gov/btbl

Sue Chinault, Manager
Provides library service to people with visual or physical disabilities that are unable to utilize standard print materials. Digital book cartridges (audio books) and/or braille books are sent directly to the patron's home, completely free of charge. This program is available to all Michigan residents.

4749   Michigan Library for the Blind and Physically Handicapped
Genesee District Library
G-4195 Pasadena Rd.
Flint, MI 48504

810-732-1120
866-732-1120
fun@thegdl.org
www.thegdl.org/services/talking-book-center

William Delaney, Chair
David Conklin, Director
Amy Goldyn, Finance Manager
Offers Genesee County residents with visual or physical impairments a service allowing them to borrow talking books application through the Talking Book Center.

4750   Michigan's Assistive Technology Resource
Physically Impaired Association of Michigan
1023 S Us Highway 27
Saint Johns, MI 48879-2423

989-224-0333
800-274-7426
FAX: 989-224-0330
www.cenmi.org

Jeff Diedrich, Manager
Maryann Jones, Coordinator
Barbara Warren, Information Specialist
Provides information services, support materials, technical assistance, and training to local and intermediate school districts in michigan to increase their capacity to address the needs of students with disabilities for assistive technology.

4751   Mideastern Michigan Library Co-op
503 S Saginaw St
Suite 711
Flint, MI 48502

810-232-7119
800-641-6639
FAX: 810-232-6639
dhooks@mmlc.info
www.mmlc.info

Denise Hooks, Director
Irene Bancroft, Administrative Specialist
Provides resources and supports for member libraries in the areas of funding, advocacy, educational opportunities for librarians and networking with other libraries. Its members include Library for the Blind and Physically Handicapped, and Braille and Talking Book Library.

4752   Muskegon Area District Library for the Blind and Physically Handicapped
4845 Airline Rd
Unit 5
Muskegon, MI 49444-4503

231-737-6248
877-569-4801
FAX: 231-737-6307
TTY: 231-722-4103
madl.org

Stephen Dix, Director
Richard Schneider, Assistant Director
Brenda Hall, Business Manager
Braille typewriter, magnifiers, closed-circuit TV, large-print photocopier, cassette books and magazines, children's books on cassette, home visits and other reference materials on blindness and other handicaps, The Reading Edge, and large print books.

4753   Northland Library Cooperative
Library Cooperative/ Library for the blind
220 W. Clinton St.
Charlevoix, MI 49720

231-855-2206
www.nlc.lib.mi.us

Jennifer Dean, Director
Christine Johnston, Executive Director
Roger Mendel, Director
Summer reading programs, Braille writer, magnifiers, closed-circuit TV, large-print photocopier, cassette books and magazines, children's books on cassette and other reference materials on blindness and other handicaps.

4754   Oakland County Library for the Visually & Physically Impaired
1200 N Telegraph Rd
Pontiac, MI 48341-1032

248-858-5050
800-774-4542
FAX: 248-858-1153
TTY: 248-452-2247
www.oakgov.com/lvpi

Dave Conklin, Manager
The Oakland County Library for the Visually and Physically Impaired was established in 1974 to provide access to free library service for County residents who are unable to read standard printed material because of a visual impairment or physical limitation.

4755 St. Clair County Library Special Technologies Alternative Resources (S.T.A.R.)
210 McMorran Blvd
Port Huron, MI 48060-4014 810-982-3600
800-272-8570
FAX: 810-982-3600
TTY: 810-455-0200
www.sccl.lib.mi.us/LBPH.aspx

Arnold H. Larson, Chairperson
Arlene M. Marcetti, Trustee
Kathleen J. Wheelihan, Trustee
Offers library services to the blind, deaf and blind, visually disabled, phsyically disabled, and reading disabled.

4756 University of Michigan: Orthopaedic Research Laboratories
1500 E. Medical Center Drive
Ann Arbor, MI 48109 734-936-6641
800-211-8181
FAX: 734-647-0003
www.med.umich.edu

Steve Goldstein, Lab Director
Paul Castillo, C.P.A., Chief Financial Officer
Michael ME Johns, M.D., Interim Executive Vice President for Medical Affairs
Develops and studies the causes and treatments for arthritis including new devices and assistive aids.

4757 Upper Peninsula Library for the Blind
1615 Presque Isle Ave
Marquette, MI 49855-2811 906-228-7697
800-562-8985
FAX: 906-228-5627
TTY: 906-228-7697
webmaster@uproc.lib.mi.us
www.uplibraries.org

Suzanne Dees, Executive Director
Summer reading programs, braille writer, magnifiers, closed-circuit T.V., large-print photocopier, cassette books and magazines, children's books on cassette, home visits and other reference materials on blindness and other handicaps.

4758 Washtenaw County Library for the Blind & Physically Handicapped
P.O.Box 8645
Ann Arbor, MI 48107-8645 734-222-6860
FAX: 734-222-6803
ewashtenaw.org

Mary Udoji, Manager
Michigan Subregional Library, Library of Congress National Library Service network. General library service for persons unable to use standard print materials for various physical reasons. Lends audio books and listening equipment, large type books, descriptive videos. Provides reference information and programs. Kurzweil scanner with components which convert standard print to Braille, large type or audio and closed circuit TV magnifier on site.

4759 Wayne County Regional Library for the Blind
30555 Michigan Ave
Westland, MI 48186-5310 734-727-7300
888-968-2737
FAX: 734-727-7333
TTY: 734-727-7330

Vanessa Morris, Regional Librarian
Sue Steiger, Librarian
Rebecca Farmer, Student Intern
Summer reading programs, braille writer, magnifiers, closed-circuit T.V., large-print photocopier, cassette books and magazines, children's books on cassette, and other reference materials on blindness and other handicaps.

4760 Wayne State University: CS Mott Center for Human Genetics and Development
42. W. Warren Avenue
Detroit, MI 48202-1405 313-577-1485
FAX: 313-577-8554
rsokol@med.wayne.edu
www.media.wayne.edu

Robert Sokol, Director
Matthew Lockwood, Director of Communications
Tom Reynolds, Associate Director of Public Relations
Human growth and development disorders.

Minnesota

4761 Century College
3300 Century Ave North
White Bear Lake, MN 55110-1252 651-779-3300
800-228-1978
FAX: 651-779-3417
TTY: 651-773-1715
century.edu

Dr. Ron Anderson, President
Steven Ritt, Vice President
Harold M. Johnson, Treasurer
Programs of study - Orthotic Practitioner, Orthotic Technician, Prosethetic Practitioner, Prosthetic Technician. In addition, Century College offers more than 50 other programs in liberal arts, career and occupational programs.

4762 Communication Center/Minnesota State Services for the Blind
Services for the Blind
332 Minnesota Street
Suite 200
Saint Paul, MN 55101-1351 651-642-0500
800-652-9000
FAX: 651-649-5927
DEED.CustomerService@state.mn.us
www.mnssb.org

Katie Clark Sieben, Commissioner
Brian Allie, Chief Information Officer
Kim Babine, Director Government Affairs
Special library service for the blind and physically handicapped providing tape and Braille transcription of textbooks and vocational materials; Minnesota Radio Talking Book providing current newspaper, magazines and best selling books; Dial-in-News, a touch tone phone accessed newspaper service; Library of Congress cassette and phonograph talking book equipment; repair services for special audio reading equipment, with most services free to Minnesota Residents.

4763 Duluth Public Library
520 W Superior St
Duluth, MN 55802-1578 218-730-4200
FAX: 218-723-3822
www.duluth.lib.mn.us

Carla Powers, Library Manager
Renee Zurn, Digital & Outreach Manager
Davis Ouse, Public Services Manager
Main library computer lab contains one Sorenson Relay and accessibility computer with zoom text JAWS software.

4764 Minnesota Library for the Blind and Physically Handicapped
Department of Education
1500 Highway 36 West
Roseville, MN 55113 651-582-8200
800-722-0550
FAX: 507-333-4832
charlene.briner@state.mn.us
education.state.mn.us

Catherine A. Durivage, Manager
Rene Perrance, Librarian
Charlene Briner, Chief of Staff
Provides books and magazines in Braille, large print, records, and cassettes to qualified residents of Minnesota who have a visual or physical impairment, including reading disabilities due to an organic cause certified by a medical doctor, that prevents residents

from reading standard print or physically handling a book. Equipment for in-house use include magnifiers, braillers, listening equipment, and CCTV. Reference collection for in-house use only on visual impairment topics.

4765 Special U
University of Minnesota
P.O.Box 721-Umhc
Minneapolis, MN 55455

612-625-3846
800-276-8642
FAX: 612-624-0997
kdwb-var@umn.edu

Brings together comprehensive sources of information related to youth with chronic or disabling conditions and their families. Topics include psychosocial issues, disability awareness, developmental processes, family, sexuality, education, employment, independent living, cultural issues, gender issues, service delivery, professional issues, advocacy and legal issues, and health issues. Special focus on transition from childhood to adolesecence to adulthood.

Mississippi

4766 Blind and Physically Handicapped Library Services
Mississippi Library Commission
3881 Eastwood Dr
Jackson, MS 39211-6473

601-432-4492
877-594-5733
FAX: 601-432-4478
mlcref@mlc.lib.ms.us
www.mlc.lib.ms.us

Shellie Zeigler, BPHLS Director
Christy Williams, Director of Administrative Services Bureau
Gloria Washington, Public Relations Director
BPHLS serves as the MS Regional Library for the Library of Congress, NLS for the Blind and Physically Handicapped. Book collections include audio cassette, CDs, digital books, Braille, large print, children's 18-20 point large print, and standard print reference collection. Descriptive videos, magazines in Braille or on cassette are available, as well as equipment: adaptive workstation, Braille embosser, closed-circuit TV, magnifier, speech input/output, and more. Check for eligibility.

4767 Mississippi Library Commission
3881 Eastwood Dr
Jackson, MS 39211-6473

601-432-4111
800-647-7542
FAX: 601-354-4181
TTY: 601-354-6411
mslib@mlc.lib.ms.us
www.mlc.lib.ms.us/index.html

Susan Cassagne, Executive Director
Katherine Buntin, Senior Library Consultant
Tracy Carr, Library Services Bureau Director
Summer reading programs, braille writer, magnifiers, closed-circuit T.V., large-print photocopier, cassette books and magazines, children's books on cassette, home visits and other reference materials on blindness and other handicaps.

4768 Mississippi Library Commission\Talking Book and Braille Services
3881 Eastwood Dr
Jackson, MS 39211-6473

601-432-4111
800-446-0892
FAX: 601-354-4181
mslib@mlc.lib.ms.us

Susan Cassagne, Executive Director
Katherine Buntin, Senior Library Consultant
Tracy Carr, Library Services Bureau Director
Library service for the print handicapped braille, cassette and disc materials (books & periodicals) for children and adults. Large print RG production (copier & printer), braille embosser and other handicaps.

Missouri

4769 Assemblies of God Center for the Blind
1445 N Boonville Ave
Springfield, MO 65802-1894

417-862-2781
855-642-2011
FAX: 417-863-6614
www.blind.ag.org

Paul Weingartner, Director
Caryl Weingartner, Office Administrator
Sarah Sykes, Certified Braille Transcriber
Offers braille and electronic text lending library, Sunday School materials for all ages, braille and audio periodicals, resource assistance, and resources for blind children and children of blind parents. Children's braille books with tactile graphics are also avaiable for purchase or loan, as well as books in digital media for adaptive reading services.

4770 Church of the Nazarene
Nazarene Publishing House
P.O. Box 843116
Kansas City, MO 64184-3116

816-333-7000
800-877-0700
FAX: 800-849-9827
it@nazarene.org
www.nazarene.org

Dr.Eugenio R Duarte, Board of General Superintendents
Dr.Jerry D. Porter, Board of General Superintendents
Dr. David A Busic, Board of General Superintendents
Offers braille and large print books. Also offers a lending library and cassettes for the blind.

4771 Judevine Center for Autism
1333 W Lockwood Avenue
Saint Louis, MO 63132-3252

314-432-6200
800-780-6545
FAX: 888-507-4453
judevine@judevine.org
www.judevine.org

Becky Blackwell, President
Evaluations and assessments, parent and professional training programs, consultations, workshops, seminars, family support, clinical therapies, adult programs and support, residential services.

4772 Lutheran Blind Mission
7550 Watson Rd
Saint Louis, MO 63119-4409

314-918-0415
888-215-2455
FAX: 314-963-0738
blind.mission@blindmission.org

Sherry Lambing, Manager
Dave Andrus, Executive Director
Nancy Crawford, Manager
Offers Christian books in braille and large print books and cassettes for the blind and visually impaired, on loan, as well as Christian periodicals in braille, large print and cassette tape.

4773 University of Missouri: Columbia Arthritis Center
University of Missouri
1 Hospital Dr
Columbia, MO 65212-1

573-882-4141
FAX: 573-884-3996
www.muhealth.org

James Ross, Chief Executive Officer
Mitch Wasden, Chief Operating Officer
Anita Larsen, Chief Nurse Executive
Research into arthritis and rheumatic diseases. One of the most comprehensive health-care networks in Missouri, our 5 hospitals and numerous clinics, all staffed by University Physicians, offer the finest primary, secondary, and tertiary health-care services. We also provide education for future health-care providers and participate in important research.

4774 Wolfner Talking Book & Braille Library
Secretary State Office
600 West Main Street
PO Box 387
Jefferson City, MO 65101-387   573-751-4936
                                      800-392-2614
                                FAX: 573-526-2985
                                TTY: 800-347-1379
                                wolfner@sos.mo.gov
                                www.sos.mo.gov/wolfner/

Richard J Smith, Division Director
Paul Mathews, Reader Advisor, A-CO
Brandon Kempf, Reader Advisor, CP-G & Wi-Z
Wolfner Library provides reading material for Missouri State residents unable to read standard print due to a visual or physical disability. Book formats are recorded books on digital cartridge and cassette, braille and some childrens books in large print. Wolfner Library also lends out descriptive videos, playback equipment for the cartridges and cassettes are also on loan.

Montana

4775 MonTECH
029 McGill Hall
University of Montana
Missoula, MT 59803   406-243-5751
                                      877-243-5511
                          montech@ruralinstitute.umt.edu
                          montech.ruralinstitute.umt.edu

Kathy Laurin PhD, Project Director
Chris Clasby MSW MATP, Project Coordinator
James Poelstra MA, Info Technology Specialist
Specializing in Assistive Technology and oversee a variety of AT related grants and contracts. The overall goal is to develop a comprehensive, statewide system of assistive technology related assistance. Striving to ensure that all people in Montana with disabilities have equitable access to assistive technology devices and services in order to enhance their independence, productivity and quality of life.

4776 Montana State Library-Talking Book Library
1515 East 6th Ave
P.O. Box 201800
Helena, MT 59620-1800   406-444-2064
                                      800-332-5087
                                FAX: 406-444-0266
                                TTY: 406-444-4799
                                      mtbl@mt.gov
                          msl.mt.gov/talking_book_library
Christie Briggs, Regional Librarian/Supervisor
Erin Harris, Director Recording and Volunteer Programs
Carolyn Meier, Library Clerk/Circulation
The Library offers FREE alternative audio and Braille reading materials for Montana citizens who cannot read standard print materials because of a visual, physical or reading handicap. Over 50,000 titles on 4-track cassette, WebBraille, Web0pac, WebBlud, summer reading programs, braille writer, magnifiers, closed-circuit T.V., large-print photocopier, cassette books and magazines, children's books on cassette, home visits and other reference materials on blindness and other handicaps.

Nebraska

4777 Nebraska Assistive Technology Partnership Nebraska Department of Education
Ste C
5143 S 48th St
Lincoln, NE 68516-2261   402-471-0734
                                      888-806-6287
                                      888-806-6287
                                FAX: 402-471-6052
                                TTY: 402-471-0734
                                nlc.nebraska.gov/tbbs/

Steve Miller, Manager
Lilly Blase, Program Coordinator

Provides statewide assistive technology and home modification services for Nebraskans of all ages and disabilities.

4778 Nebraska Library Commission: Talking Book and Braille Service (TBBS)
Talking Book and Braille Service
1200 N St
Suite 120
Lincoln, NE 68508-2023   402-471-4038
                                      800-742-7691
                                FAX: 402-471-6244
                                nlc.readadv@nebraska.gov
                                      nlc.nebraska.gov/tbbs

David Oertli, Executive Director
Kay Goehring, Reader Services Coordinator
Bill Ainsley, Audio Production Studio Manager
Provides eligible users with free audio books, audio magazines and Braille via the mail. Also features in-house studios for audiobook production.

Nevada

4779 Las Vegas-Clark County Library District
7060 W. Windmill Lane
Las Vegas, NV 89113   702-734-7323
                                FAX: 702-507-6187
                                      www.lvccld.org

Keiba Crear, Chair
Michael Saunders, Vice Chair
Randy Ence, Secretary
Summer reading programs, braille writer, magnifiers, closed-circuit T.V., large-print photocopier, cassette books and magazines, children's books on cassette, home visits and other reference materials on blindness and other handicaps.

4780 Nevada State Library and Archives
100 North Stewart Street
Carson City, NV 89701-4285   775-684-3313
                                      800-922-2880
                                FAX: 775-684-3330

Michael Fischer, Director
Ann Brinkmeyer, Head of Government Publications
Kathy Edwards, Government Publications Libraria
Summer reading programs, braille writer, magnifiers, closed-circuit T.V., large-print photocopier, cassette books and magazines, children's books on cassette, home visits and other reference materials on blindness and other handicaps.

New Hampshire

4781 New Hampshire State Library: Talking Book Services
117 Pleasant St
Concord, NH 03301-3852   603-271-3429
                                      800-491-4200
                                FAX: 603-271-8370
                                TTY: 800-735-2964
                                michael.york@dcr.nh.gov
                                www.nh.gov/nhsl/talking_books
Michael York, State Librarian
Janet Eklund, Administrator of Library Operations
Donna Gilbreth, Supervisor
Regional Library for National Library Service for the Blind & Physically Handicapped offers digital and cassette books, magazines on cassette, children's books on digital and on cassette, descriptive videos, playaways, and downloadable digital audio books, and Braille services.

New Jersey

4782 **Autism New Jersey**
500 Horizon Dr.
Suite 530
Robbinsville, NJ 08691   609-588-8200
800-4AU-TISM
FAX: 609-588-8858
information@autismnj.org
www.autismnj.org

Suzanne Buchanan, Executive Director
Ellen Schisler, Associate Executive Director
Elena Graziosi, Manager of Information Services
Autism New Jersey is the largest statewide network of parents and professionals dedicated to improving lives of individuals with autism spectrum disorders. Self-advocates, families, the professionals who work with them, government officials, the media, and concerned state residents all turn to Autism New Jersey for information, compassionate support, and training.

4783 **Children's Specialized Hospital Medical Library - Parent Resource Center**
200 Somerset St.
New Brunswick, NJ 08901   888-244-5373
www.childrens-specialized.org

Warren E. Moore, President & CEO
Charles Chianese, Vice President & Chief Operating Officer
Joseph J. Dobosh Jr., Vice President & Chief Financial Officer
Contains some 3,000 books, and journals specializing in nursing, pediatrics, child neurology, and rehabilitation. Also provides a Parent Resource Center, a special collection of books, videos and pamphlets designed to meet the information needs of parents and families, as well as the local community.

4784 **Christopher & Dana Reeve Foundation**
636 Morris Turnpike
Suite 3A
Short Hills, NJ 07078   973-379-2690
800-225-0292
FAX: 973-912-9433
infospecialist@christopherreeve.org
www.christopherreeve.org

John M Hughes, Chairman
John E McConnell, Vice Chairman
Peter Wilderotter, President & CEO
A national clearinghouse for information, referral and educational materials on paralysis. The foundation also offers a free book titled 'Paralysis Resource Guide' in English or Spanish, as well as a free library.

4785 **Eye Institute of New Jersey**
New Jersey Medical School
Suite 6100
PO Box 1709
Newark, NJ 07101-1709   973-972-2065
FAX: 973-972-2068

Jacinta Ogbonna, Administrative director
Department A
Ophthamology, including research into cornea, retina and neuro-ophthamalogy.

4786 **Mycoclonus Research Foundation**
Apt 17d
200 Old Palisade Rd
Fort Lee, NJ 7024-7060   201-585-0770
FAX: 201-585-0770
www.pspinformation.com/index.html

Mark Seiden, VP
Supports clinical and basic research into the cause and treatment of myoclonus; four international workshops facilitated the sharing of information by physicians, scientists, and investigators active in the field, resulted in three publications; supports promising research projects, clinical neurological fellows, with special emphasis on posthypoxic myoclonus and encourages all who are interested in futhering the understanding, treatment, and cure of myoclonus.

4787 **New Jersey Library for the Blind and Handicapped**
2300 Stuyvesant Ave
Trenton, NJ 8618-3226   609-530-4000
800-792-8322
FAX: 609-406-7181
TTY: 609-530-4000
tbbc@njstatelib.org
njlbh.org

Adam Szczepaniak, Director
Maria Baratta, Assistant Director
Summer reading programs, braille writer, magnifiers, closed-circuit T.V., large-print, cassette, braille books and magazines, children's books on cassette, and other reference materials on blindness and other handicaps. Provides reading material on audio, cassette, large print and braille to eligible NJ residents.

New Mexico

4788 **New Mexico State Library for the Blind and Physically Handicapped**
1209 Camino Carlos Rey
Santa Fe, NM 87507-4400   505-476-9700
1 -0 -6 5
FAX: 505-476-9776
TTY: 800-659-4915
lbph@state.nm.us
www.nmstatelibrary.org

David L. Caffey, Chairperson
Norice Lee, Vice Chairperson
Eugene Gant, Public Education Department Appointee
Summer reading programs, braille writer, magnifiers, closed-circuit T.V., large-print photocopier, cassette books and magazines, children's books on cassette, home visits and other reference materials on blindness and other handicaps.

New York

4789 **Andrew Heiskell Braille and Talking Book Library**
New York Public Library
40 W 20th St
New York, NY 10011-4211   212-206-5400
FAX: 212-206-5418
TTY:212-206-5458
ahlbph@nypl.org
www.nypl.org/locations/heiskell

Tony Marx, President and CEO
Mary Lee Kennedy, Chief Library Officer
Anne L. Coriston, Vice President for Public Service
The library provides talking books and talking book players to the five boroughs of New York City, and braille books to New York City and Long Island. These items may be circulated in person or through the mail without charge to the borrower. Deposit collections may be arranged with agencies that provide service to people with visual impairments. The library also circulates large print books and materials in other formats.

4790 **Center on Human Policy: School of Education**
Syracuse University
302 Huntington Hall
Syracuse, NY 13244   315-443-3851
800-894-0826
FAX: 315-443-4338
thechp@syr.edu
thechp.syr.edu

Alan Foley, Director
The Center on Human Policy is an organization that works to ensure the rights of people with disabilities. This is accomplished through research, teaching, and advocacy in policy.

4791 **DREAMMS for Kids**
190 Whispering Oaks Dr
Longs, SC 29568-6973   607-539-3027
FAX: 607-539-9930
janet@dreamms.org
www.dreamms.org

Janet Hosmer, Executive Director

DREAMMS is committed to increasing the use of computers, high quality instructional technology, and assistive technologies for students with special needs in schools, homes and the workplace.

4792 Ehrman Medical Library
New York University Medical Center
577 First Avenue
Room 117
New York, NY 10016-6402
212-263-5394
FAX: 212-263-6534
HSL_admin@nyumc.org
hsl.med.nyu.edu

N. Rambo, Chair/Director
D. Peters, Executive Assistant
N. Romanosky, Department Administrator
Our mission of the Fredrick L. Ehrman Library is to enhance learning, research and patient care and New York University Medical Center by effectively managing knowledge-based resources, providing client-centered information services and education, and extending access through new initiatives in information technology.

4793 Finger Lakes Developmental Disabilities Service Office
44 Holland Avenue
Albany, NY 12229-0001
518-474-3625
866-946-9733
FAX: 585-461-8764
opwdd.ny.gov/

Mike Feeney, Director
Carolyn Bassett, Manager
Andrew M Cuomo, Governor
Information on developmental disabilities.

4794 Helen Keller International
Fl 12
352 Park Ave S
New York, NY 10010-1723
212-532-0544
877-535-5374
FAX: 212-532-6014
info@hki.org
hki.org

Henry C. Barkhorn III, Chairman
Desmond G. FitzGerald, Vice Chairman
Mary Crawford, Secretary
Nonprofit international organization whose mission is to combat the causes and consequences of blindness and malnutrition.

4795 Helen Keller National Center for Deaf - Blind Youths And Adults
141 Middle Neck Rd
Sands Point, NY 11050-1218
516-944-8900
FAX: 516-944-7302
TTY:516-944-8637
hkncinfo@hknc.org
www.hknc.org

Joseph McNulty, Executive Director
HKNC is the only national vocational and rehabilitation program providing services exclusively to youth and adults who are deaf-blind.

4796 Institute for Basic Research in Developmental Disabilities
1050 Forest Hill Rd
Staten Island, NY 10314-6399
718-494-0600
FAX: 718-698-3803
ibr@opwdd.ny.gov
opwdd.ny.gov

Khalid Iqbal, Department Chairman
Joseph J Maturi, Acting Director
Wojciech Kaczmarski, Research Scientist
The Institute for Basic Research in Developmental Disabilities offers services to New Yorkers with developmental disabilities. Services include research, clinical studies, education, publications, employment supports and more.

4797 Institute for Visual Sciences
221 E 71st St
New York, NY 10021-4139
212-517-0400
FAX: 212-472-0295
www.mmm.edu/

Judson R. Shaver, Ph.D., President
Paul Ciraulo, Executive Vice President for Administration and Finance
Carol L Jackson, Vice President for Student Affairs and Dean of Students
Ophthalmology with emphasis on the development of care for the eye.

4798 JGB Cassette Library International
15 W 65th St
New York, NY 10023-6601
212-769-6200
800-284-4422
FAX: 212-769-6266
www.guildhealth.org

Jerry Bechhofer, President
Summer reading programs, braille writer, magnifiers, closed-circuit T.V., large-print photocopier, cassette books and magazines, children's books on cassette, home visits and other reference materials on blindness and other handicaps.

4799 Nassau Library System
900 Jerusalem Ave
Uniondale, NY 11553-3097
516-292-8920
FAX: 516-565-0950
outreach@nassaulibrary.org
nassaulibrary.org

Ken Ulric, President
Barbara Behrens, Vice President
Kathy Seyfried, Treasurer
Information about public library services in Nassau County, including services for people with disabilities and the Senior Connections volunteer project (information and referral for seniors and their families).

4800 National Braille Association
95 Allens Creek Road
95 Allens creek road
Suite 202
Rochester, NY 14618
585-427-8260
FAX: 585-427-0263
nbaoffice@nationalbraille.org
www.nationalbraille.org

David Shaffer, Executive Director
Jan Carroll, President
Cindi Laurent, Vice President
Only national organization dedicated to the professional development of individuals who prepare and produce braille materials.

4801 New York State Talking Book & Braille Library
New York State Library and Education
Cultural Education Center
222 Madison Avenue
Albany, NY 12230-1
518-474-5930
800-342-3688
FAX: 518-474-5786
tbbl@mail.nysed.gov

Loretta Ebert, Research library director
Lends audio and braille books and specialized playback equipment to eligible borrowers with print disabilities. Service is completely free. Serves 55 counties of upstate NY (Westchester and above). Also provides service to schools, nursing homes, and other facilities.

4802 Postgraduate Center for Mental Health
124 E 28th St
New York, NY 10016-8402
212-576-4150
FAX: 212-696-1679
www.dvguide.com/newyork/postgrad.html

Marge Slobetz, Assistant Director
Marie Serrano, Manager
Evaluations and psychotherapy by social workers psychologists for children, adolescents, families and couples. Neuropsychological testing and remedation for learning disabilities.

4803 Rehabilitation Research Library
Human Resources Center
Albertson, NY 11507
516-741-2010
FAX: 516-746-3298

Amnon Tishler, Research Librarian
Susan Feifer, Manager
Information on rehabilitation and occupational rehabilitation.

4804 State University of New York Health Sciences Center
450 Clarkson Avenue
Brooklyn, NY 11203-2098
718-270-1000
FAX: 718-778-5397
www.downstate.edu

Meg O'Sullivan, Assistant Vice President
Jennifer Hayes, Staff Assistant
Child psychiatry research programs.

4805 Suffolk Cooperative Library System: Long Island Talking Book Library
Long Island Talking Book Library System
2 Penn Plaza
Suite 1102
New York, NY 10121
212-502-7600
888-545-8331
FAX: 631-286-1647
TTY: 631-286-4546
communications@afb.net
www.afb.org

Carl R Augusto, President & CEO
Kelly Bleach, Chief Administrative Officer
Rick Bozeman, Chief Financial Officer
Offers a variety of support services to its 55 member libraries and other patrons including, an extensive talking book program, assistive technology and other services for people with disabilities.

4806 United Spinal Association
75-20 Astoria Blvd
Suite 120
East Elmhurst, NY 11370
718-803-3782
800-444-0120
FAX: 718-803-0414
mkurtz@unitedspinal.org
www.unitedspinal.org

James Weisman, President & CEO
Abby Ross, COO
Information on spinal cord injury and laws and regulations concerning people with disabilities, including veterans.

4807 Wallace Memorial Library
Rochester Institute Of Technology
90 Lomb Memorial Dr
Rochester, NY 14623-5603
585-475-2551
FAX: 585-475-7220
TTY: 585-475-2760
twc@rit.edu
wallacecenter.rit.edu

Lynn Wild, Associate Provost for Faculty Development
Shirley Bower, Director RIT Libraries
Julia Lisuzzo, Director of TWC Administration
Information on physical disabilities and deafness.

4808 Xavier Society for the Blind
Two Penn Plaza,
Suite 1102
New York, NY 10121-4595
212-473-7800
800-637-9193
FAX: 212-473-7801
info@xaviersocietyfortheblind.org
www.xaviersocietyfortheblind.org

Fr. John Sheehan, SJ, Chairman of the Board / CEO
Fr. Claudio Burgaleta, SJ, Vice-President
Mr. Victor Gainor, Secretary
Provides spiritual and inspirational reading material to visually impaired persons in suitable format: braille, large print and cassette, throughout U.S. and Canada. Services are provided both by way of regular periodical publications sent through the mail and non-returnable; and by means of a lending library where books are returned. All services are provided free.

North Carolina

4809 Genova Diagnostics
63 Zillicoa St.
Asheville, NC 28801
828-253-0621
800-522-4762
info@gdx.net
www.gdx.net

Jeffrey Ledford, Chief Executive Officer
Ceco Ivanov, Chief Information Officer
Jeff Ellis, Chief Commercial Officer
Genova Diagnostics specializes in nutritional, metabolic, and toxicant analyses. Genova is committed to helping health care professionals identify nutritional influences on health and disease, and laboratory procedures in nutritional and biochemical testing.
1987

4810 North Carolina Library for the Blind and Physically Handicapped
109 East Jones Street
Raleigh, NC 27635-1
919-807-7450
888-388-2460
FAX: 919-733-6910
TTY: 919-733-1462
nclbph@ncdcr.gov

Francine Martin, Manager
Carl Ginger Rush, Secretary
James Benton, President
Free loan of large print, braille, and cassette tape books and magazines and specialized playback equipment to registered eligible North Carolinians. Call for an application form. Collection contains general fiction and nonfiction titles. Registered borrowers may subscribe to receive descriptive videos for a one time fee.

4811 Pediatric Rheumatology Clinic
Duke Medical Center
P.O. Box 3212
Durham, NC 27708-3212
919-684-8111
FAX: 919-684-6616
rabin001@mc.duke.edu
www.duke.edu

Rebecca H. Buckley, Medical Director
Michael Duke, Owner
Clinical and laboratory pediatric rheumatoid studies.

4812 University of North Carolina at Chapel Hill: Neuroscience Research Building
115 Mason Farm Road
Chapel Hill, NC 27599-7250
919-843-8536
FAX: 919-966-9605
www.med.unc.edu/ophth/

Ricky D. Bass, MBA, MHA, Associate Chair for Administration
Sandy Scarlett, Development Director
Cassandra J. Barnhart, MPH, Manager of Research Administration
An interdepartmental research center on the campus of the UNC-Chapel Hill School of Medicine. Mission is to promote neuroscience research with specific emphasis on developmental , cellular, and disease-related processes.

North Dakota

4813 North Dakota State Library Talking Book Services
604 E Boulevard Ave
Bismarck, ND 58505-0800
701-328-4622
800-472-2104
FAX: 701-328-2040
TTY: 800-892-8622
ndsl.lib.state.nd.us

Doris Ott, Manager
Hullen E. Bivins, State Lbirarian
Susan Hammer-Schneider, Head Disability Serves
The Talking Books Program provides patrons with free access to cassette books and magazines. The Talking Books Program is administered by the National Library Service for the Blind and Physically Handicapped.

Ohio

4814 Case Western Reserve University
10900 Euclid Ave
Cleveland, OH 44106-4901
216-368-2000
president@case.edu
www.case.edu

Barbara R. Snyder, President
Stanton L. Gerson, MD
W.A. Bud Baeslack, Provost and Executive Vice President
Programs which encompass the arts and sciences, engineering, health sciences, law, management, and social work.

4815 Case Western Reserve University Northeast Ohio Multipurpose Arthritis Center
11100 Euclid Ave
Cleveland, OH 44106-1716
216-844-3969
888-844-8447

Fred Rothstein, Executive Director
Basic and clinical research into the causes, diagnosis and treatment of arthritis.

4816 Cincinnati Children's Hospital Medical Center
University Of Cincinnati Uap
3333 Burnet Ave
Cincinnati, OH 45229-3026
513-636-4200
800-344-2462
FAX: 513-636-2837
TTY: 513-636-4900
www.cincinnatichildrens.org

James Anderson, CEO
James M Anderson, Chief Executive Officer
David Schonfeld, Executive Director
Dedicated to providing the highest level of pediatric care. As Greater Cincinnati's only pediatric hospital, Cincinnati Children's is committed to bringing the very best medical care to children in our community.

4817 Cleveland FES Center
11000 Cedar Ave
Suite 230
Cleveland, OH 44106-3056
216-231-3257
FAX: 216-231-3258
TTY:216-231-3257
fescenter.case.edu

Robert Kirsch, Executive Director
Peckham P Hunter, Director
Research and development center on functional electrical stimulation. Houses the FES Information Center, a resource center with a library. Publications, newsletters and videotapes for persons with disabilities and others interested in electrical stimulation are offered.

4818 Cleveland Public Library
325 Superior Ave E
Cleveland, OH 44114-1271
216-623-2800
FAX: 216-623-2800
cpl.org

Felton Thomas, Executive Director
Thomas D. Corrigan, President
Maritza Rodriguez, Vice President
Summer reading programs, braille writer, magnifiers, closed-circuit T.V., large-print photocopier, cassette books and magazines, children's books on cassette, and other reference materials on blindness and other handicaps.

4819 Ohio Regional Library for the Blind and Physically Handicapped
National Library Office
800 Vine St
Cincinnati, OH 45202-2009
513-369-6900
800-582-0335
FAX: 513-369-3111
TTY: 516-665-3384
www.cincinnatilibrary.org

Kimber L. Fender, Director
Ross A Wright, President
Paul G Sittenfeld, Vice President
Summer reading programs, braille writer, magnifiers, closed-circuit T.V., large-print photocopier, cassette books and magazines,

children's books on cassette, and other reference materials on blindness and other handicaps.

4820 State Library of Ohio: Talking Book Program
National Library Service in Washington
Ste 100
274 E 1st Ave
Columbus, OH 43201-3692
614-644-7061
800-686-1531
FAX: 614-466-3584
library.ohio.gov

Jo Budler, Manager
Jim Buchman, Dir Patron & Catalog Services
Peter Bates, Deputy Director
A machine-lending agency for the visually impaired. Provides free recorded books, and magazines to approximately 26,000 eligible blind, visually impaired, physically handicapped, and reading disabled Ohio residents.

Oklahoma

4821 Oklahoma Library for the Blind & Physically Handicapped
300 NE 18th St
Oklahoma City, OK 73105-3296
405-521-3514
800-523-0288
FAX: 405-521-4582
TTY: 405-521-4672
library@drs.state.ok.us
www.library.state.ok.us

Paul Adams, Library Director
Vicky Golightly, Public Information Officer
Braille writer, magnifiers, closed-circuit T.V., large-print photocopier, cassette books and magazines, children's books on cassette, home visits and other reference materials on blindness and other handicaps.

4822 Oklahoma Medical Research Foundation
825 NE 13th St
Oklahoma City, OK 73104-5097
405-271-6673
800-522-0211
FAX: 405-271-7510
contact@omrf.org
www.omrf.org

Dr. Stephen Prescott, President
Mike D. 'Chip' Morgan, Executive VP and COO
Adam Cohen, Senior VP and General Counsel
Focuses on arthritis and muscoloskeletal disease research.

4823 Tulsa City-County Library System: Outreach Services
Tulsa City: County Library System
400 Civic Centre
Tulsa, OK 74103-3857
918-549-7323
os@tulsalibrary.org
www.tulsalibrary.org

Tracy Warren, Director
Tulsa City-County Library's Outreach Services Department provides library services to individuals that are unable to regularly visit a library, including monthly bookmobile visits and deliveries to residents of senior sites, along with mailing materials to homebound individuals/caretakers residing in their own homes.

Oregon

4824 Oregon Health Sciences University, Elks' Children's Eye Clinic
Casey Eye Institute
3181 S.W. Sam Jackson Park Rd.
Portland, OR 97239-3098
503-494-3000
888-222-8311
FAX: 503-494-4286
www.ohsucasey.com

Earl A Palmer, Director
Eleen Reyster, Clinic Manager
James Rosenbaum, Manager

The elks children's eye clinic is the major charitable project of the Oregon State Elks association. The clinic would not be possible without the organization's dedication and commitment to providing eye care for babies and children.

4825 Oregon Talking Book & Braille Services
250 Winter St NE
Salem, OR 97301-3950

503-378-5389
800-452-0292
FAX: 503-585-8059
TTY: 503-378-4334
www.oregon.gov/OSL/TBABS/Pages/index.aspx

Mary Kay Dahlgreen, Interim State Librarian
Robin Speer, Fund Development Officer
Susan Westin, Program Manager
We serve the blind and physically disabled. Cassette books and magazines, Braille books-magazines, for children and adults. Descriptive videos. Audiocassette machines are provided free of charge. Call us for an application.

4826 Talking Book & Braille Services Oregon State Library
250 Winter St NE
Salem, OR 97301-3950

503-378-5389
800-452-0292
FAX: 503-585-8059
TTY: 503-378-4334
www.oregon.gov/OSL/TBABS/Pages/index.aspx

Mary Kay Dahlgreen, Interim State Librarian
Robin Speer, Fund Development Officer
Susan Westin, Program Manager
Braille writer, magnifiers, large-print photocopier, cassette books and magazines, children's books on cassette and braille books.

Pennsylvania

4827 Associated Services for the Blind and Visually Impaired
ASB
919 Walnut Street
Philadelphia, PA 19107-5237

215-627-0600
FAX: 215-922-0692
asbinfo@asb.org
www.asb.org

Karla S. McCaney, President & CEO
Beth Deering, Chief Program Officer
Sylvia Purnell, Director of Learning & Development
Associated Services for the Blind and Visually Impaired (ASB), is a private, nonprofit organization working to provide services, education, training, and resources to promote self-esteem, independence, and self determination in people who are blind or visually impaired. In addition, ASB advocates for the rights of blind and visually impaired persons through community actions and public education.

4828 Carnegie Library of Pittsburgh Library for the Blind & Physically Handicapped
4400 Forbes Ave
Pittsburgh, PA 15213-4007

412-622-3114
800-242-0586
FAX: 412-687-2442
info@carnegielibrary.org
carnegielibrary.org

Cathy Chaparro, Manager
Sue Murdock, Manager
Jane Dayton, Assistant Director
Loans recorded books/magazines and playback equipment, large print books and described videos to western PA residents unable to use standard printed materials due to a visual, physical, or physically-based reading disability.

4829 Free Library of Philadelphia: Library for the Blind and Physically Handicapped
1901 Vine Street
Philadelphia, PA 19103

215-686-5322
reardons@freelibrary.org
www.library.phila.gov

Tobey Gordon Dichter, Chair
Richard A. Greenawalt, First Vice Chair
Miriam Spector, Vice Chair

Summer reading programs for children and teens. Closed-circuit T.V.for enlarging print for low vision; computers with screen readers and large print; cassette books and magazines; braille books and magazines; and descriptive videos for the blind and visually impaired. Unique and acclaimed adult education program for all disabilities. State of the art book recording facilities.

4830 Pennsylvania College of Optometry Eye Institute
8360 Old York Rd
Elkins Park, PA 19027-1598

215-780-1400
FAX: 215-780-1336

Since 1919 the college has led the field in education, in research, and in new approaches to vision diagnosis and correction.

4831 Reading Rehabilitation Hospital
Box 250
Rr 1
Reading, PA 19607

610-796-6297
FAX: 610-796-6353

Richard Kruczek, CEO
Doug Mehrkam, Owner
Information on physical disabilities, stroke, head injuries, aging and spinal cord injuries.

Rhode Island

4832 Office Of Library & Information Services for the Blind and Physically Handicapped
1 Capitol Hill
4th Floor
Providence, RI 02908-5803

401-574-9300
FAX: 401-574-9320
olis.webmaster@olis.ri.gov
www.olis.ri.gov

Howard Boksenbaum, Chief Library Officer
Chaichin Chen, Library Program Specialist: LORI
Debbie Cullerton, Information Services Technician:
Offers information and services for the visually impaired including reference materials, braille printers, braille writers, large-print books and more.

4833 Talking Books Plus
Library for the Blind & Physically Handicapped
1 Capitol Hill
4th Floor
Providence, RI 02908-5803

401-574-9300
FAX: 401-574-9320
olis.webmaster@olis.ri.gov
www.olis.ri.gov

Howard Boksenbaum, Chief Library Officer
Chaichin Chen, Library Program Specialist: LORI
Debbie Cullerton, Information Services Technician:
Offers talking book services for the blind and physically handicapped. Collection includes reference materials, braille printer, braille writer, large-print books, adaptive computer workstations and referrals to appropriate agencies/programs for other services.

South Carolina

4834 Medical University of South Carolina Arthritis Clinical/Research Center
171 Ashley Avenue
Charleston, SC 29425-100

843-792-1414
800-424-MUSC
FAX: 843-792-7121
academicdepartments.musc.edu/musc/

Jennie Ariail, Director
Tom Gasque Smith, Associate Director
Dr. David Cole, President
Offers patient care services and basic and clinical research on various types of arthritis and connective tissue diseases.

4835   **South Carolina State Library**
1500 Senate Street
P.O.Box 11469
Columbia, SC 29211-1469   803-734-8026
                                  FAX: 803-734-4757
                          reference@statelibrary.sc.gov
                                     statelibrary.sc.gov

Debbie Anderson, Administrative Coordinator
Flora A. DuBose, Administrative Specialist
Leesa Benggio, Acting Director
Summer reading programs, braille writer, magnifiers, closed-circuit T.V., large-print photocopier, cassette books and magazines,
children's books on cassette, home visits and other reference materials on blindness and other handicaps.

South Dakota

4836   **South Dakota State Library**
800 Governors Dr
Pierre, SD 57501-2294   605-773-3131
                                        800-423-6665
                                  FAX: 605-773-6962
                                  TTY: 605-773-4950
                               library@state.sd.us
                                     library.sd.gov

Dr. Lesta V. Turchen, President
Monte Loos, Vice President
Sarah Easter, Secretary
Summer reading programs, braille writer, magnifiers, closed-circuit T.V., large-print photocopier, cassette books and magazines,
children's books on cassette, home visits and other reference materials on blindness and other handicaps.

Tennessee

4837   **Tennessee Library for the Blind and Physically
Handicapped**
Tennessee State Library Archives
403 7th Ave N
Nashville, TN 37243-1409   615-741-3915
                                        800-342-3308
                                  FAX: 615-532-8856
                                  tlbph.tsla@tn.gov
                          www.tennessee.gov/tsla/lbph/
Ruth Hemphill, Director
Ed Byrne, Assistant Director
Blake Fontenay, Communications Director
Provides free public library service to residents of Tennessee who
are unable to read standard print due to a physical disability. Co-
operating library with national network of libraries serving peo-
ple with print disabilities, operating under the auspices

Texas

4838   **Baylor College of Medicine Birth Defects Center**
One Baylor Plaza
Houston, TX 77030-2348   713-798-4951
                                  FAX: 832-825-3141
                                  www.bcm.edu/obgyn/tcfs
Frank Greenberg, Director
Dr. Paul Klotman, President
One of the few centers in the world that performs fetal surgery.
Provides integrated, multidisciplinary care for mothers, carrying
babies with genetic or anatomic birth defects requiring therapy
before or immediately after birth. This collaboration enable.

4839   **Baylor College of Medicine: Cullen Eye Institute**
Baylor College of Medicine
One Baylor Plaza
Houston, TX 77030-2743   713-798-4951
                                        888-562-3937
                                  FAX: 713-798-1521
                          www.bcm.edu/eye/index.cfm?pmid=0
Dan B. Jones, Professor and Chair
Al Vaughan, Manager
Michael Cassidy, Plant Manager
Research activities focus on restoring vision and preventing
blindness through a better understanding of the disease.

4840   **Brown-Heatly Library**
4800 N Lamar Blvd
P O Box 149198
Austin, TX 78756-2316   800-252-5204
                                        800-628-5115
                                     www.dars.state.tx.us
Veronda L. Durden, Commissioner
Glenn Neal, Deputy Commissioner
Daniel Bravo, Chief Operating Officer
Houses a collection of books, audio and video tapes and periodi-
cals focusing on rehabilitation, disabilities, employment skills
and practices and management for the Texas Rehabilitation Com-
mission. Houses materials on developmental and other
disabilities.

4841   **Center for Research on Women with Disabilities**
Baylor College of Medicine
One Baylor Plaza
Houston, TX 77030-3411   713-798-5782
                                        800-443-7693
                                  FAX: 713-798-4688
                                  crowd@bcm.tmc.edu
                                     www.bcm.edu/crowd
Kathy Fire, Administrator
Margaret A. Nosek, Executive Director
Martha Mendez, Secretary
Research organization dedicated to conducting research and pro-
moting, developeing, and disseminating information to expand
the life choices of women with disabilities. Conducts research
and training activities on issues related to the health,
independence

4842   **Christian Education for the Blind**
Suite 702
4200 S Freeway Dr
Fort Worth, TX 76115   817-920-0044
                                  FAX: 817-920-0777
                                  bceb@evl.net
Rodger Dyer, Executive Director
Offers braille and large print books and cassettes for the visually
impaired.

4843   **Houston Public Library: Access Center**
500 McKinney St
Houston, TX 77002-5000   832-393-1313
                                  FAX: 832-393-1474
                                  TTY:832-393-1539
                               website@hpl.lib.tx.us
                                     houstonlibrary.org
Rhea Brown Lawson, Director
Roosevelt Weeks, Deputy Director
Greg Simpson, Assistant Director
Offers full library services to the visually and hearing impaired in
Houston, TX at no charge. Houses unique and critical services for
its users including online access to the Internet in a private and
secure area.

4844   **Talking Book Program/Texas State Library**
Talking Book Program
1201 Brazos St.
PO Box 12927
Austin, TX 78711-2927   512-463-5458
                                        800-252-9605
                                  FAX: 512-936-0685
                               tbp.services@tsl.state.tx.us
                                     www.texastalkingbooks.org
Ava M Smith, Director

Providing free library service to Texans of all ages who are unable to read standard print material due to visual, physical, or reading disabilities-whether permanent or temporary. The program offers more than 80,000 titles in fiction and nonfiction, plus 80 national magazines for adults and children.

4845 University of Texas Southwestern Medical Center/Allergy & Immunology
5323 Harry Hines Blvd
Dallas, TX 75390-7208   214-648-3111
                                    www.utsouthwestern.edu

Diane Jeffries, Director
Priscilla Alderman, Executive Assistant
Daniel K Podolsky, President
Mission is to improve the health care in our community, Texas, our nation, and the world through innovation and education. To educate the next generation of leaders in patient care, biomedical science and disease prevention. To conduct high-impact, intern

4846 University of Texas at Austin Library
101 E 21st St
Austin, TX 78712-900   512-495-4350
                                      FAX: 512-495-4347
                                    webform@lib.utexas.edu
                                        www.lib.utexas.edu

Douglas Dempster, Manager
Sheldon Ekland-Olson, Chief Executive Officer
Dr. Fred Heath, Vice Provost and Director
Provides access to information for all users, including those with disabilities, in accordance with the overall mission of the General Libraries of the University of Texas at Austin.

Utah

4847 Utah State Library Division: Program for the Blind and Disabled
250 North 1950 West
Suite A
Salt Lake City, UT 84116- 7901   801-715-6789
                                          800-662-5540
                                      FAX: 801-715-6767
                                      TTY: 801-715-6721
                                          blind@utah.gov
                                      www.blindlibrary.utah.gov

Donna Morris, Director
Lisa Nelson, Program Manager
Michael Sweeney, Readers Advisor Librarian
The Program for the Blind and Disabled provides the kinds of materials found in public libraries in formats accessible to the blind and disabled. Books and magazines are available in braille, in large print, on audio cassettes, and on audio digital books. Services are provided by the Utah State Library Division in cooperation with the Library of Congress, National Library Service for the Blind and Physically Handicapped. Services are provided free of charge to eligible readers.

Vermont

4848 National Center for PTSD
VA Medical Center (116D)
215 N Main St
White River Junction, VT 05009   802-296-5132
                                          802-296-6300
                                      FAX: 802-296-5135
                                          ncptsd@va.gov
                                        www.ptsd.va.gov

Paula P Schnurr, PhD, Executive Director
Cybele Merrick, MA, MS, Associate Director for Education
Nancy Bernardy, PhD, Associate Director of Clinical Networking
The National Center for PTSD works to improve care for America's Veterans and others who suffer from trauma or PTSD. The center engages in researchand provides education and training for diagnosis and treatment of the disorder.

4849 Vermont Department of Libraries - Special Services Unit
578 Paine Tpke N
Berlin, VT 05602   802-828-3273
                                          800-479-1711
                                      FAX: 802-828-3109
                          libraries.vermont.gov/library_for_the_blind
Teresa Faust, Special Services Librarian
Sara Blow, Library Assistant
Jennifer Hart, Librarian
Regional network library pf the National Library Service for the Blind & Physically Handicapped. The SSU makes available reading material in large print and NLS talking book formats, including these special collections: children's print braille books, audio described videos and DVDs.

4850 Vermont Department of Libraries -Special Services Unit
578 Paine Tpke N
Berlin, VT 05602-9139   802-828-3273
                                          800-479-1711
                                      FAX: 802-828-3109
                                    www.libraries.vermont.gov/ssu
Teresa Faust, Special Services Librarian
Sara Blow, Library Assistant
Jennifer Hart, Librarian

Virginia

4851 Access Services
Fairfax County Public Library
12000 Government Center Pkwy
Suite 123
Fairfax, VA 22035-1   703-324-7329
                                      FAX: 703-222-3193
                                      TTY:703-324-8365
                                    access@fairfaxcounty.gov
                                        fairfaxcounty.gov

Janice Kuch, Branch Manager
Beena Pandey, Volunteer Coordinator
Ken Plummer, Outreach Manager
Offers talking books, TDD access, assistive devices such as decoders for three-week loans, support groups for people who are visually impaired, adapted computer work station with braille printer and assistive listening devices.

4852 Alexandria Library Talking Book Service
5005 Duke St
Alexandria, VA 22304-2903   703-746-1702
                                      FAX: 703-519-5917
                                      TTY:703-519-5911
                                    www.alexandria.lib.va.us

Rose T. Dawson, Director
Renee DiPilato, Deputy Director
Linda Wesson, Communications Officer
Summer reading programs, braille writer, magnifiers, closed-circuit T.V., large-print photocopier, cassette books and magazines, children's books on cassette, home visits and other reference materials on blindness and other handicaps.

4853 Arlington County Department of Libraries
Arlington County Library
1015 N Quincy St
Arlington, VA 22201-4603   703-228-5990
                                      FAX: 703-228-7720
                                      TTY:703-228-6320
                                    libraries@arlingtonva.us
                                        arlingtonva.us

Diane Kresh, Director
Margaret Brown, Chief
Anne Gable, Administrative Services/Technology Division Chief
Summer reading programs, braille writer, magnifiers, closed-circuit T.V., large-print photocopier, cassette books and magazines, children's books on cassette, home visits and other reference materials on blindness and other handicaps.

4854 Braille Circulating Library for the Blind
2700 Stuart Ave
Richmond, VA 23220-3305
804-359-3743
FAX: 804-359-4777
bclministries.org

Rev. Brian J Barton, Sr., Executive Director
Offers library materials for the blind and visually impaired on a free-loan basis. Serves the entire USA and 41 foreign countries with cassette tapes, reel to reel tapes, braille books, large print books along with talking book records.

4855 Central Rappahannock Regional Library
1201 Caroline St
Fredericksburg, VA 22401-3701
540-372-1144
FAX: 540-899-9867
TTY:540-371-9165
webmaster@crrl.org
www.librarypoint.org

Donna Cote, Executive Director
Alison Heartwell, Librarian
Offers reference materials on blindness and other disabilities.

4856 Council for Exceptional Children (CEC)
Council for Exceptional Children
3100 Clarendon Blvd.
Suite 600
Arlington, VA 22201-5332
888-232-7733
TTY:866-915-5000
service@exceptionalchildren.org
www.exceptionalchildren.org

Chad Rummel, Executive Director
Laurie VanderPloeg, Associate Executive Director, Professional Affairs
Craig Evans, Chief Financial Officer
The Council for Exceptional Children aims to improve the educational success of individuals with disabilities and/or gifts and talents by advocating for appropriate policies, setting professional standards, and providing resources and professional development for special educators.

4857 James Branch Cabell Library
Virginia Commonwealth University
901 Park Avenue
PO Box 842033
Richmond, VA 23284-2033
804-828-1110
866-828-2665
866-828-2665
FAX: 804-828-0151
library@vcu.edu
www.library.vcu.edu

John Birch, Media Specialist II
Wesley Chenault, Head
Yuki Hibben, Assistant Head
Provides individualized orientations and assistance with library research and equipment.

4858 Newport News Public Library System
2400 Washington Ave
3rd Floor
Newport News, VA 23607- 4301
757-926-8000
FAX: 757-926-1365
icieszyn@ci.newport-news.va.us
newportnewsva.com

Thomas P. Herbert, P.E., Chair
Wendy C. Drucker, Vice Chair
Sam Workman, Assistant Director of Development
Summer reading programs, braille writer, magnifiers, closed-circuit T.V., large-print photocopier, cassette books and magazines, children's books on cassette, home visits and other reference materials on blindness and other handicaps.

4859 Northern Virginia Resource Center for Deafand Hard of Hearing Persons
3951 Pender Dr
Suite 130
Fairfax, VA 22030-6035
703-352-9056
FAX: 703-352-9058
TTY:703-352-9056
info@nvrc.org
nvrc.org

William Boyd, Chair
Jim Faughnan, Vice Chair
Steve Williams, Treasurer
Empowering deaf and hard of hearing individuals and their families through education, advocacy and community involvement.

4860 Roanoke City Public Library System
706 S Jefferson St
Roanoke, VA 24016-5191
540-853-2473
FAX: 540-853-1781
main.library@roanokeva.gov
www.roanokegov.com/library

Michael L. Ramsey, President
Barbara Lemon, Vice President
Summer reading programs, braille writer, magnifiers, closed-circuit T.V., large-print photocopier, cassette books and magazines, children's books on cassette, home visits and other reference materials on blindness and other handicaps.

4861 Staunton Public Library Talking Book Center
1 Churchville Ave
Staunton, VA 24401-3229
540-885-6215
800-995-6215
FAX: 540-332-3906
www.talkingbookcenter.org

Lisa Eye, Reader Advisor
Lynn Harris, President
Daniel Swift, Treasurer
Offers free library service by circulating recorded books, magazines, and playback equipment to individuals unable to use standard print materials because of visual or physical impairment.

4862 University of Virginia Health System General Clinical Research Group
P.O.Box 800787
Charlottesville, VA 22908-0787
434-924-2394
FAX: 434-924-9960
gcrc.med.virginia.edu

Pamela Sprouse, Administrator
Eugene J. Barrett, Program Director
Mary Lee Vance, Associate Director
Provides investigators with the specialized resources necessary to conduct advanced clinical research. The facility includes ten inpatient beds, skilled research nurses, a core assay laboratory, a metabolic kitchen, outpatient facilities, computing and st

4863 Virginia Autism Resource Center
4100 Price Club Blvd
PO Box 842020
Richmond, Virginia, VA 23284-2020
804-674-8888
877-667-7771
877- -
FAX: 804-276-3970
www.varc.org

Carol Schall, Ph.D., Director
Florence McLeod, Administrative Assistant
Dawn Hendricks, Ph.D., Faculty/instructor
VARC promotes and facilitates best practices for those diagnosed within the autism spectrum. Information, resources, and education and training help parents, educators, service providers and medical professionals provide effective support from early childhood through adulthood.

4864 Virginia Beach Public Library Special Services Library
936 Independence Blvd
Virginia Beach, VA 23455-6006
757-385-2680
FAX: 757-464-6741
spaddock@vbgov.com
www.vbgov.com/dept/library

Marcy Sims, Library Director
David Palmer, Public Services Manager
Susan Paddock, Library Manager

A public library for people with visual and physical disabilities, braille writer, magnifiers, closed-circuit T.V., large-print photocopier, cassette books and magazines, children's books on cassette, and other reference materials on blindness and other d

4865 Virginia Chapter of the Arthtitis Foundation
2201 W. Broad St
Suite 100
Richmond, VA 23220-3937
800-365-3811
800-456-4687
FAX: 804-359-4900
cmogel@arthritis.org
www.arthritis.org/virginia

Gail Norman, Interim President/CEO
Terri Harris, Chief Financial Officer
Nick Turvas, Senior VP of Health/Wellness
Provides free information, services and counseling to the public. Services include assistance in locating and accessing government and other health care programs for persons with arthritis, referral to doctors specializing in the treatment of arthritis,

4866 Virginia State Library for the Visually and Physically Handicapped
395 Azalea Ave
Richmond, VA 23227-3623
804-266-2477
800-552-7015
FAX: 804-266-2478
virginiavoice.org

Paula I. Otto, President
Susan C. Rucker, Secretary/Treasurer
Nicholas B Morgan, Executive Director
Summer reading programs, braille writer, magnifiers, closed-circuit T.V., large-print photocopier, cassette books and magazines, children's books on cassette, home visits and other reference materials on blindness and other handicaps.

Washington

4867 Meridian Valley Clinical Laboratory
801 SW 16th St
Suite 126
Renton, WA 98057-2632
425-271-8689
855-405-8378
FAX: 425-271-8674
meridian@meridianvalleylab.com
www.meridianvalleylab.com

Dr. Jonathan Wright, Medical Director
A clinical test facility dedicated to providing the most accurate and informative data for patient diagnosis and therapeutic monitoring. With our current research and up-to-date information and various aspects of clinical nutritional medicine, our methodo

4868 Ophthalmic Research Laboratory Eye Institute/First Hill Campus
747 Broadway
Seattle, WA 98122-4307
206-386-6000
800-833-8879
TTY:206-386-2022
www.swedish.org

Bryan Mueller, CEO
Dan Harris, CFO
Heidi Aylsworth, Chief Strategy Officer
Color vision physiology, vision disorders and blindness research.

4869 Washington Talking Book and Braille Library
2021 9th Ave
Seattle, WA 98121-2783
206-615-0400
800-542-0866
FAX: 206-615-0437
TTY: 206-615-0418
wtbbl@sos.wa.gov
wtbbl.org

Danielle Miller, Director and Regional Librarian
Amy Ravenholt, Assistant Program Manager
Mandy Gonnsen, Youth Services Librarian
Summer reading programs, braille writer, magnifiers, closed-circuit T.V., large-print photocopier, cassette books and magazines,

children's books, and other reference materials on blindness and other handicaps, online catalog, reference station with assis

West Virginia

4870 Cabell County Public Library/Talking Book Department/Subregional Library for the Blind
455 9th St
Huntington, WV 25701-1417
304-528-5700
FAX: 304-528-5739
cabell.lib.wv.us

Judy K. Rule, Director
Angela Straight, Assistant Director
Mary Lou Pratt, Adult Services Coordinator
Summer reading programs, Braille writer, magnifiers, closed-circuit TV, cassette books and magazines, children's books on cassette reference materials on blindness and other handicaps, enlargers and Arkenstone Reader.

4871 Division of Rehabilitation Services: Staff Library
107 Capitol St
Charleston, WV 25301-2609
304-356-2060
800-642-8207
FAX: 304-766-4913
wvdrs.org

Carol Johnson, Manager
Specialized library with information on disabilities and the rehabilitation there of special collections: deaf and hard of hearing, visually impaired/blind, wellness center, literacy and career. The library has assistive devices such as CCTV, scanner and

4872 Kanawha County Public Library
123 Capitol St
Charleston, WV 25301-2686
304-343-4646
FAX: 304-348-6530
kanawha.lib.wv.us

Cheryl Morgan, President
Jennifer Pauer, First Vice President
Elizabeth O. Lord, Second Vice President
Summer reading programs, large print PC option, magnifiers, large type books, cassette books, and magazines, children's books on cassette, home visits and other reference materials on blindness and other handicaps

4873 Ohio County Public Library Services for the Blind and Physically Handicapped
52 16th St
Wheeling, WV 26003-3671
304-232-0244
FAX: 304-232-6848
wheeling.weirton.lib.wv.us

Jimmie McCamic, Chairman
Michael Baker, Secretary-Treasurer
Greg Marquart, Trustee
The Ohio Public Library exists to provide books and related materials that will assist the residents of the community in the pursuit of knowledge, information, education, research, and recreation in order to promote an enlightned citizenry and to enrich t

4874 Talking Book Department, Parkersburg and Wood County Public Library
3100 Emerson Ave
Parkersburg, WV 26104-2414
304-420-4587
FAX: 304-420-4589

Lindsay Place, Talking Books Dept. Coordinator
Brian Raitz, Director
Free program loaning recorded books and magazines, braille books and magazines to people who are unable to read or use standard print due to a visual or physical impairment.

4875 West Virginia Autism Training Center
Marshall University College Of Educational & Human
Old Main 316
1 John Marshall Drive
Huntington, WV 25755-1   304-696-2332
800-344-5115
FAX: 304-696-2846
www.marshall.edu/atc/

Amanda Plumley, Executive Office Manager
Ginny Painter, Communications Director
Joe Ciccarello, Associate Executive Director

Provides education, training, and treatment programs for W Virginians who have autism, pervasive devolopmental disorders or Asperger's disease and have formally been registered with the center.

4876 West Virginia Library Commission
1900 Kanawha Blvd E
Charleston, WV 25305-9   304-558-2041
800-642-9021
FAX: 304-558-2044
www.librarycommission.wv.gov

Karen Goff, Secretary
Deborah McNeal, Personnel Officer
Steve Tyler, Supervisor

Summer reading programs, braille writer, magnifiers, closed-circuit T.V., large-print photocopier, cassette books and magazines, children's books on cassette, home visits and other reference materials on blindness and other handicaps.

4877 West Virginia School for the Blind Library
301 E Main St
Romney, WV 26757-1828   304-822-4840
FAX: 304-822-3370
cjohn@access.mountain.net
wvde.state.wv.us

Patsy Shank, Administrator
Cynthia Johnson, Librarian

Summer reading programs, braille writer, magnifiers, closed-circuit T.V., large-print photocopier, cassette books and magazines, children's books on cassette, home visits and other reference materials on blindness and other handicaps.

Wisconsin

4878 Brown County Library
Central Library Downtown
515 Pine Street
Green Bay, WI 54301-3743   920-448-4400
FAX: 920-448-4376
TTY:920-448-4400
bc_library@co.brown.wi.us
www.co.brown.wi.us/library

Terry Watermelon, President
Kathy Pletcher, Vice President
Carla Buboltz, Secretary

Summer reading programs, braille writer, magnifiers, closed-circuit TV, large-print photocopier, cassette books and magazines, children's books on cassette, home visits and other reference materials on blindness and other handicaps.

4879 Eye Institute of the Medical College of Wisconsin and Froedtert Clinic
925 N 87th St
Milwaukee, WI 53226-4812   414-456-2020
FAX: 414-456-6300
eyecare@mcw.edu
doctor.mcw.edu

Jane D Kivlin, Director
Richard Schultz, MD, Director

A national leader as a full-service academic opthalmology program. Dedicated to the highest quality patient care, education, and vision research, the faculty and staff strive to provide state-of-the-art clinical and surgical patient care in a compassionat

4880 Wisconsin Regional Library for the Blind& Physically Handicapped
813 W Wells St
Milwaukee, WI 53233-1436   414-286-3045
800-242-8822
FAX: 414-286-3102
TTY: 414-286-3548
lbph@mpl.org

Marsha J Valance, Manager
Meredith Wittmann, Regional Librarian

Circulates recorded materials, playback equipment and braille materials to print-handicapped Wisconsin residents.

Wyoming

4881 Wyoming Services for the Visually Impaired
Wyoming Department of Education
2300 Capitol Ave
Cheyenne, WY 82002-0050   307-777-7690
FAX: 307-777-6234
jackie.miller@wyo.gov
edu.wyoming.gov/in-the-classroom/special-prog

Ron Micheli, Chairman
Scotty Ratliff, Vice-Chair
Pete Ratliff, Treasurer

Services for the Visually Impaired assists people of all ages who have low vision or are blind. The goal is to provide information, education, and support to individuals with low vision in order that they may lead enjoyable and productive lives with maxim

4882 Wyoming's New Options in Technology(WYNOT) - University of Wyoming
1000 E University Ave
Laramie, WY 82071-2000   307-766-2761
888-989-9463
FAX: 307-766-2763
TTY: 800-908-7011
wind.uw@uwyo.edu
wind.uwyo.edu/wynot

William MacLean Jr., Ph.D., Executive Director
Designed to develop and implement a consumer oriented statewide system of technology-related assistance for people with disabilities of all ages.

Media, Print

Children & Young Adults

4883 Assistive Technology for Infants and Toddlers with Disabilities Handbook
Idaho Assistive Technology Project
University of Idaho
1187 Alturas Dr.
Moscow, ID 83843- 2268
800-432-8324
FAX: 208-885-6102
idahoat@uidaho.edu
www.idahoat.org

LaRae Rhoads, Author
Ron Seiler, Author
This handbook is designed as a guide for parents and families in Idaho who have infants and toddlers with developmental delays or disabilities.

4884 Assistive Technology for School-Age Children with Disabilities - Handbook
Idaho Assistive Technology Project
University of Idaho
1187 Alturas Dr.
Moscow, ID 83843- 2268
208-885-3557
800-432-8324
FAX: 208-885-6102
idahoat@uidaho.edu
www.idahoat.org

LaRae Rhoads, Author
Ron Seiler, Author
Michelle Doty, Author
A handbook designed to provide guidance and information for parents who have school-aged children with disabilities, focusing on resources for assistive technologies available for their children.

4885 Children's Understanding of Disability
Routledge (Taylor & Francis Group)
711 Third Ave.
New York, NY 10017
212-216-7800
800-634-7064
FAX: 202-564-7854
enquiries@taylorandfrancis.com
www.routledge.com

Ann Lewis, Author
Children's Understanding of Disability is a valuable addition to the debate surrounding the integration of children with special needs into ordinary schools. Taking the viewpoint of the children themselves, it explores how pupils with severe learning difficulties and their non-disabled classmates interact. Ann Lewis examines what happens when non-disabled children and pupils with severe learning difficulties work together regularly over the course of a year.
Hardcover

4886 Complete IEP Guide: How to Advocate for Your Special Ed Child (8th Edition)
NOLO (Internet Brands)
909 N. Sepulveda Blvd
11th Fl.
El Segundo, CA 90245
310-280-4000
www.nolo.com

Lawrence Siegel, Attorney/Author
This all-in-one guide will help you understand special education law, identify your child's needs, prepare for meetings, develop the IEP and resolve disputes.
384 pages

4887 Don't Call Me Special: A First Look at Disability
Barron's Educational Series
250 Wireless Blvd
Hauppauge, NY 11788
800-645-3476
FAX: 631-494-3723
barrons@barronseduc.com
www.barronseduc.com

Pat Thomas, Author
This picture book explores questions and concerns about physical disabilities in a simple and reassuring way. Youger children can find out about individual disabilities, special equipment that is available to help the disabled, and how people of all ages can deal with disabilities and live happy and full lives.
Paperback

4888 Everything Parent's Guide to Special Education
Adams Media
4868 Innovation Dr
Bldg 2
Fort Collins, CO 80525
855-278-0402
www.adamsmediastore.com

Amanda Morin, Author
This handbook offers parents assistance, advice, and aid on navigating special education for their child, with information on assessment, evaluation, specific needs for specific disabilities, current law, and dealing with parent-school conflict. It includes worksheets, forms, and sample documents to help parents be effective advocates for their child's learning.

4889 It isn't Fair!: Siblings of Children with Disabilities
Praeger - ABC-CLIO
130 Cremona Dr
Santa Barbara, CA 93117
805-968-1911
800-368-6868
FAX: 866-270-3856
CustomerService@abc-clio.com
www.abc-clio.com/praeger

Stanley D. Klein, Editor
Maxwell J. Schleifer, Editor
This book presents a wide range of perspectives on the relationship of siblings to children with disabilities. These perspectives are written in the first person by parents, young adult siblings, younger siblings, and professionals.
200 pages

4890 Life Beyond the Classroom: Transition Strategies for Young People with Disabilities
Brookes Publishing
P.O.Box 10624
Baltimore, MD 21285-0624
410-337-9580
800-638-3775
FAX: 410-337-8539
custserv@brookespublishing.com
www.brookespublishing.com

Paul Wehman, Author
This textbook is an essential guide to planning, designing, and implementing successful transition programs for students with disabilities.
616 pages

4891 Mayor of the West Side
Fanlight Productions
32 Court St
21st Fl.
Brooklyn, NY 11201
718-488-8900
800-876-1710
FAX: 718-488-8642
info@fanlight.com
www.fanlight.com

Judd Ehrlich, Director
What happens when love gets in the way of letting go? As a teenager with multiple disabilities prepares for his Bar Mitzvah, his family and community consider what Mark's life will be like when they are no longer able to protect him.

4892 New Horizons Independent Living Center
8085 E Manley Dr
Prescott Valley, AZ 86314-6154
928-772-1266
800-406-2377
FAX: 928-772-3808
TTY: 928-772-1266
www.nhilc.org

Gale Dean, Executive Director
Alan Loosley, President
Sharon Geddes, Vice President
The mission of New Horizons Independent Living Center is to provide programs and services in Northern Arizona which encourage and empower people with disabilities to self-determine the goals and activities of their lives.

4893 Rolling Along with Goldilocks and the Three Bears
Woodbine House
6510 Bells Mill Rd
Bethesda, MD 20817   800-843-7323
info@woodbinehouse.com
www.woodbinehouse.com

Cindy Meyers, Author
Carol Morgan, Illustrator
The familiar fairytale with a special needs twist. Ages 3-7.
28 pages

4894 Shriner's Hospitals for Children Newsletter
3101 SW Sam Jackson Park Rd
Portland, OR 97201   503-241-5090
FAX: 503-221-3498
www.shrinershospitalforchildren.org
Bi-annual publication from the Shriners Hospital for Children in
Portland, Oregon. Free. Produced by the medical staff.

4895 Sibling Forum: A FRA Newsletter
Family Resource Associates
35 Haddon Ave
Shrewsbury, NJ 07702-4007   732-747-5310
FAX: 732-747-1896
info@frainc.org
www.frainc.org
A newsletter for brothers and sisters, aged 10 through teen, whose
sibling has a disablilty. Includes input from readers, library resources and discussion of feelings. $12/year for families,
$20/year for professionals.
Quarterly

**4896 Sibshops: Workshops for Siblings of Children with
Special Needs**
Sibling Supporting Project
322-6512 23rd Ave NW
Seattle, WA 98117   206-297-6368
info@siblingsupport.org
www.siblingsupport.org

Don Meyer, Author
Patricia Vadasy, Author
Sibshops is a program that brings together 8-to 13-year-old brothers and sisters of children with special needs. The siblings receive
support and information in a recreational setting, so they have fun
while they learn.
264 pages

4897 Special Education Report
LRP Publications
360 Hiatt Dr
Dept. 150F
Palm Beach Gardens, FL 33418   800-341-7874
FAX: 561-622-2423
custserv@lrp.com
www.lrp.com
Published monthly, Special Education Report is the independent
news service on law, policy and funding of programs for disabled
children.
Monthly Newsletter

4898 Special Format Books for Children and Youth Ages 3-19
New York State Talking Book and Braille Library
Cultural Education Center
222 Madison Ave
Albany, NY 12230-0001   518-474-5935
800-342-3688
FAX: 518-474-7041
tbbl@nysed.gov
www.nysl.nysed.gov/tbbl/index.html
The New York State Talking Book and Braille Library (TBBL)
lends audio and braille books and magazines to eligible residents
of upstate New York who have a qualifying print disability.

**4899 The Sibling Slam Book: What It's Really Like To Have a
Brother or Sister with Special Needs**
Sibling Support Project
6512 23rd Ave NW
Ste 322
Seattle, WA 98117   206-297-6368
info@siblingsupport.org
www.siblingsupport.org

Don Meyer, Author
A brutally honest, non-PC look at the lives, experiences, and
opinions of siblings without disabilities who have siblings with
disabilities. Formatted like the slam books passed around in many
junior high and high schools, this one poses a series of 50 personal questions, with responses drawn from the author's interviews with over 80 teens from across the United States. It reflects
experiences that range from positive to negative.

4900 The Sibling Survival Guide
Sibling Support Project
6512 23rd Ave. NW
Ste 322
Seattle, WA 98117   206-297-6368
info@siblingsupport.org
www.siblingsupport.org

Don Meyer, Author
Emily Holl, Author
Edited by experts in the field of disabilities and sibling relationships, The Sibling Survival Guide focuses on the topmost concerns identified in a survey of hundreds of siblings.

4901 Views from Our Shoes
Sibling Support Project
6512 23rd Ave NW
Ste 322
Seattle, WA 98117   206-297-6368
www.siblingsupport.org

Don Meyer, Author
Siblings share what it is like to have a brother or sister with a disability. Age 9 and up.
106 pages Paperback

**4902 What About Me? Growing Up with a Developmentally
Disabled Sibling**
Da Capo Press/ Perseus Books Group
Order Department
210 American Dr
Jackson, TN 38301   800-343-4499
FAX: 800-351-5073
www.perseusbooksgroup.com

Bryna Siegel, Author
Stuart Silverstein, Author
A compassionate and accessible guide on living with and caring
for a developmentally disabled sibling.
316 pages Paperback

4903 What It's Like to be Me
Friendship Press
P.O.Box 37844
Cincinnati, OH 45222-844   513-948-8733
FAX: 513-761-3722
This was written and illustrated entirely by children with handi-
capped conditions. These contributions invite the reader to set
aside any pity or prejudices and listen. Black and white, and color
drawings and photographs make this book visually appealing, en-
joyable for all ages.

Community

4904   'Cultural Life,' Disability, Inclusion, and Citizenship: Moving Beyond Leisure in Isolation
Routledge (Taylor & Francis Group)
711 Third Ave
New York, NY 10017   212-216-7800
                                     800-634-7064
                          FAX: 202-564-7854
                  enquiries@taylorandfrancis.com
                             www.routledge.com

Simon Darcy, Editor
Jerome Singleton, Editor
This book concentrates on disability citizenship in leisure.
90 pages Hardback

4905   Active Citizenship and Disability: Implementing the Personalization of Support
Cambridge University Press
Shaftesbury Rd
Cambridge, UK CB2-8BS   information@cambridge.org
                              www.cambridge.org

Andrew Power, Author
Janet E. Lord, Author
Allison S. DeFranco, Author
This book provides an international comparative study of the implementation of disability rights law and policy focused on the emerging principles of self-determination and personalisation. The case studies examine how different jurisdictions have reformed disability law and policy and reconfigured how support is administered and funded to ensure maximum choice and independence is accorded to people with disabilities.
518 pages Paperback; Hardcover

4906   California Community Care News
Community Residential Care Association of CA
1924 Alhambra Blvd
P.O. Box 163270
Sacramento, CA 95816-9270   916-455-0723
                          FAX: 916-455-7201
                             www.crcac.com

Charles W Skoien Jr, Director/Lobbyist
Denise Johnson, Consultant
Forum for the exchange of ideas, information and opinions among clients, families and service providers. Information regarding services and assisted living programs for the elderly, mentally ill and disabled.
Monthly

4907   Community Disability Services: An Evidence-Based Approach to Practice
Purdue University Press
Stewart Center 190
504 W State St
West Lafayette, IN 47907-2058   265-494-2038
                          pupress@purdue.edu
                       www.thepress.purdue.edu

Ian Dempsey, Editor
Karen Nankervis, Editor
Articles by an array of international experts provide as an excellent resource for professionals and students involved in the area of disability studies. The book is divided into three parts: (1) disability and modern society; (2) working with people who are challenged; and (3) working within a disability-services environment. This approach mirrors the contemporary debate within a practice framework reflecting how individuals, organizations, and communities deal with the problem and solutions.
304 pages Paperback

4908   Comprehensive Care Coordination for Chronically Ill Adults
Wiley-Blackwell
111 River St
Hoboken, NJ 07030-5774   201-748-6000
                                     877-762-2974
                          FAX: 201-748-6088
                             info@wiley.com
                               www.wiley.com

Cheryl Schraeder, Editor
Paul S. Shelton, Editor
A combination of theory and case studies, this book presents the growing demographic of chronically ill adults in the U.S., offering models for change and improvement in quality of care; recommendations on relevant and current literature; and descriptions of successful care outcomes.
440 pages Paperback

4909   Hallmarks and Features of High-Quality Community-Based Services
Independent Living Research Utilization (ILRU)
1333 Moursund
Houston, TX 77030   713-520-0232
                          FAX: 713-520-5785
                               ilru@ilru.org
                                   ilru.org

This brief paper describes and expands on five hallmarks that are felt to greatly impact the quality of community-based services. While this list of qualities is neither exhaustive nor comprehensive, it does draw from the findings and insights of professionals in community building, and aims to inform readers of those areas that are considered to be of vital importance to high-quality experience of community services.

4910   Human Exceptionality: School, Community, and Family (12th Edition)
Cengage Learning
20 Channel Center St
Boston, MA 02210   617-289-7700
                          FAX: 617-289-7844
                           www.cengage.com/us

Michael L. Hardman, Author
M. Winston Egan, Author
Clifford J. Drew, Author
An evidence-based testament to the critical role of cross-professional collaboration in enhancing the lives of exceptional individuals and their families. This text's unique lifespan approach combines powerful research, evidence-based practices, and inspiring stories, engendering passion and empathy and enhancing the lives of individuals with exceptionalities.
544 pages Hardcover

4911   Inclusive Leisure Services (3rd Edition)
Venture Publishing Inc.
1999 Cato Ave
State College, PA 16801   814-234-4561
                          FAX: 814-234-1651
                         www.venturepublish.com

John Dattilo, Author
This text will educate future and current leisure services professionals about attitude development and actions that promote positive attitudes about people who have experienced discrimination and segregation. It provides strategies that will facilitate meaningful leisure participation by all participants, while respecting their rights.
560 pages Hardcover

4912   Independent Living for Persons with Disabilities and Elderly People
IOS Press
6751 Tepper Dr
Clifton, VA 20124   703-830-6300
                          FAX: 703-830-2300
                          sales@iospress.com
                             www.iospress.nl

Mounir Mokhtari, Editor
Discusses the need for assistive technology in making homes more accessible for the elderly and people with disabilities. Goes on to suggest the application of these technologies in other areas of the community, such as hospitals and schools, which allow

those with disabilities and the elderly to live their lives with some independence and autonomy.
216 pages Softcover

4913   Independent Living for Physically Disabled People
People With Disabilities Press (iUniverse)
1663 Liberty Dr
Bloomington, IN 47403   812-330-2909
                                                 800-288-4677
                                            FAX: 812-355-4085
                                            media@iuniverse.com
                                            www.iuniverse.com

Nancy M. Crewe, Author
Irving Kenneth Zola, Author
This book describes the philosophy of independent living, from legislative strides to community centres, as well as future trends.
436 pages

4914   Pathways To Inclusion (2nd Edition)
Captus Press
1600 Steeles Ave W
Concord, ON, Canada L4K-4M2   416-736-5537
                                            FAX: 416-736-5793
                                            info@captus.com
                                            www.captus.com

John Lord, Author
Peggy Hutchison, Author
Pathways to Inclusion 2nd edition addresses the organizational strategies that have been used in the past and highlights areas for change. Human service organizations are examined, pinpointing common characteristics that have led to improved quality of life for people with disabilities and other vulnerable citizens.
328 pages Paperback

Employment

4915   A Supported Employment Workbook: Individual Profiling and Job Matching
Jessica Kingsley Publishers
73 Collier St
London, UK N19BE   hello@jkp.com
                                                 www.jkp.com

Steve Leach, Author
Created with the goal of helping job developers, this guide offers practical tools and strategies to help job development professionals assist their clients. The workbook includes vocational forms, job analysis forms, and support review charts, and offers aid to professionals in assisting disabled persons to find and secure stable jobs in their communities.
224 pages Paperback

4916   Career Success for Disabled High-Flyers
Jessica Kingsley Publishers
73 Collier St
London, UK N19BE   hello@jkp.com
                                                 www.jkp.com

Sonali Shah, Author
Drawing on case studies of 31 disabled adults, this book suggests that individual traits and patterns of behaviour are key factors in career success, and shows that it is often society rather than impairment that hinders professional progression. It will provide role models and valuable insights for young career-minded disabled people.
208 pages Paperback

4917   Job Success for Persons with Developmental Disabilities
Jessica Kingsley Publishers
73 Collier St
London, UK N19BE   hello@jkp.com
                                                 www.jkp.com

David B. Wiegan, Author
This book provides a comprehensive approach to developing a successful jobs program for persons with developmental disabilities, drawn from the author's extensive experience and real success.
160 pages Paperback

4918   Making News: How to Get News Coverage of Disability Rights Issues
The Advocado Press

                                     contact145@advocadopress.org
                                            www.advocadopress.org
Book gives how-to information on influencing media coverage of disability issues.
165 pages

4919   Making Self-Employment Work for People with Disabilities
Brookes Publishing
P.O.Box 10624
Baltimore, MD 21285-0624   410-337-9580
                                                 800-638-3775
                                            FAX: 410-337-8539
                                     custserv@brookespublishing.com
                                     www.brookespublishing.com

Cary Griffin, Author
David Hammis, Author
Beth Keeton, Author
Practical support for individuals with significant disabilities in starting and maintaining a small business. Covers building a business plan; pinpointing interests, strengths, and goals; and finding helpful information and support
288 pages

4920   Road Ahead: Transition to Adult Life for Persons with Disabilities (3rd Edition)
IOS Press
6751 Tepper Dr
Clifton, VA 20124   703-830-6300
                                            FAX: 703-830-2300
                                            sales@iospress.com
                                            www.iospress.nl

Keith Storey, Editor
Dawn Hunter, Editor
Explores transition planning, assessment, instructional strategies, career development and support, social life, quality of life, supported living, and post-secondary education for people with disabilities.
318 pages

4921   The Job Developer's Handbook: Practical Tactics for Customized Employment
Brookes Publishing
P.O. Box 10624
Baltimore, MD 21285-0624   410-337-9580
                                                 800-638-3775
                                            FAX: 410-337-8539
                                     custserv@brookespublishing.com
                                     www.brookespublishing.com

Cary Griffin, Author
David Hammis, Author
Tammara Geary, Author
One of the most practical employment books available, this forward-thinking guide walks employment specialists step by step through customized job development for people with disabilities, revealing the best ways to build a satisfying, meaningful job around a person's preferences, skills, and goals.
264 pages

General Disabilities

4923   A Guide to Disability Rights Laws
US Department of Justice
950 Pennsylvania Ave. NW
9th Floor
Washington, DC 20530   202-307-0663
                                                 800-514-0301
                                            FAX: 202-307-1197
                                            TTY: 800-514-0383
                                            www.ada.gov

Rebecca B. Bond, Chief
Anne Raish, Principal Deputy Chief
Christina Galindo-Walsh, Deputy Chief

A 21-page booklet providing a brief description of the ADA, the Telecommunications Act, Fair Housing Act, Air Carrier Access Act, Voting Accessibility for the Elderly and Handicapped Act, National Voter Registration Act, Civil Rights of Institutionalized Persons Act, Individuals with Disabilities in Education Act, Rehabilitation Act, Architectural Barriers Act, and the federal agencies to contact for more information.
Available in Large Print & Braille

4924   A Practical Guide to Art Therapy Groups
Routledge (Taylor & Francis Group)
711 Third Ave
New York, NY 10017   212-216-7800
                                      800-634-7064
                                 FAX: 202-564-7854
                         enquiries@taylorandfrancis.com
                                    www.routledge.com

Diane Fausek, Author
Unique approaches, materials, and device will inspire you to tap into your own well of creativity to design your own treatment plans. It lays out the ingredients and the skills to get the results you want. Includes strategies that have been used for people with Alzheimer's, geri-psychiatric conditions and developmental disabilities.
124 pages Hardcover; Paperback

4925   A World Awaits You
Mobility International USA
132 E Broadway
Suite 343
Eugene, OR 97401   541-343-1284
                                 FAX: 541-343-6812
                                 TTY:541-343-1284
                            clearinghouse@miusa.org
                                  www.miusa.org/away

Susan Sygall, Chief Executive Officer
Cindy Lewis, Director, Programs
Publication from Mobility International USA featuring stories from people with disabilities who have participated in international exchange experiences.
Annually

4926   ADA Guide for Small Businesses
US Department of Justice, Civil Rights Division
950 Pennsylvania Ave. NW
9th Floor
Washington, DC 20530   202-307-0663
                                      800-514-0301
                                 FAX: 202-307-1197
                                 TTY: 800-514-0383
                                       www.ada.gov

Rebecca B. Bond, Chief
Anne Raish, Principal Deputy Chief
Christina Galindo-Walsh, Deputy Chief
A 15-page booklet for businesses that provide goods and services to the public. This publication explains basic ADA requirements, illustrates ways to make facilities accessible, and provides information about tax credits and deductions.

4927   ADA Information Services
US Department of Justice, Civil Rights Division
950 Pennsylvania Ave. NW
9th Floor
Washington, DC 20530   202-307-0663
                                      800-514-0301
                                 FAX: 202-307-1197
                                 TTY: 800-514-0383
                                       www.ada.gov

Rebecca B. Bond, Chief
Anne Raish, Principal Deputy Chief
Christina Galindo-Walsh, Deputy Chief
A 2-page list with the telephone numbers and internet addresses of federal agencies and other organizations that provide information and technical assistance to the public about the ADA.

4928   ADA Pipeline
DRTAC: Southeast ADA Center
1419 Mayson Street NE
Atlanta, GA 30324   404-385-0636
                                      800-949-4232
                                 FAX: 404-385-0641
                                     www.sedbtac.org

Cyndi Smith, B.S., Office Assistant
Mary Morder, Information Technology Support
Sally Z. Weiss, B.A., Director
16 pages Quarterly

4929   ADA Questions and Answers
US Department of Justice, Civil Rights Division
950 Pennsylvania Ave. NW
9th Floor
Washington, DC 20530   202-307-0663
                                      800-514-0301
                                 FAX: 202-307-1197
                                 TTY: 800-514-0383
                                       www.ada.gov

Rebecca B. Bond, Chief
Anne Raish, Principal Deputy Chief
Christina Galindo-Walsh, Deputy Chief
A 31-page booklet giving an overview of the ADA's requirements affecting employers, businesses, nonprofit service agencies, and state and local governments programs, including public transportation.

4930   ADA Tax Incentive Packet for Business
US Department of Justice
950 Pennsylvania Ave. NW
9th Floor
Washington, DC 20530   202-307-0663
                                      800-514-0301
                                 FAX: 202-307-1197
                                 TTY: 800-514-0383
                                       www.ada.gov

Rebecca B. Bond, Chief
Anne Raish, Principal Deputy Chief
Christina Galindo-Walsh, Deputy Chief
A 13-page packet of information to help businesses understand and take advantage of the tax credit and deduction available for complying with the ADA.

4931   ADA and City Governments: Common Problems
US Department of Justice
950 Pennsylvania Ave. NW
9th Floor
Washington, DC 20530   202-307-0663
                                      800-514-0301
                                 FAX: 202-307-1197
                                 TTY: 800-514-0383
                                       www.ada.gov

Rebecca B. Bond, Chief
Anne Raish, Principal Deputy Chief
Christina Galindo-Walsh, Deputy Chief
A 9-page document that contains a sampling of common problems shared by city governments of all sizes, provides examples of common deficiencies and explains how these problems affect persons with disabilities.

4932   ADA-TA: A Technical Assistance Update from the Department of Justice
US Department of Justice
950 Pennsylvania Ave. NW
9th Floor
Washington, DC 20530   202-307-0663
                                      800-514-0301
                                 FAX: 202-307-1197
                                 TTY: 800-514-0383
                                       www.ada.gov

Rebecca B. Bond, Chief
Anne Raish, Principal Deputy Chief
Christina Galindo-Walsh, Deputy Chief
A serial publication that answers Common Questions about ADA requirements and provides Design Details illustrating particular design requirements. The first edition addresses Readily Achievable Barrier Removal and Van Accessible Packing Spaces.

4933   AEPS Family Report: For Children Ages Birth to Three
Brookes Publishing
P.O.Box 10624
Baltimore, MD 21285-0624   410-337-9580
                                     800-638-3775
                              FAX: 410-337-8539
                     custserv@brookespublishing.com
                         www.brookespublishing.com

Diane Bricker, Author
Betty Capt, Author
JoAnn Johnson, Author
This is a 64-item questionnaire that asks parents to rank their child's abilities on specific skills. In packages of 10.
28 pages Saddle-stiched

4934   ARC's Government Report
Arc of the District of Columbia
817 Varnum St NE
Washington, DC 20017-2144   202-636-2950
                              FAX: 202-636-2996
                                     www.arcdc.net

Mary Lou Meccariello, Executive Director
Ed Cabatic, Director of Finance
Randy Shingler, Chief Operating Officer
Reports on government activities related to individuals with disabilities with a focus on persons with developmental disabilities.
$50.00

4935   ARCA Newsletter
ARCA - Dakota County Technical College
1300 145th St E
Rosemount, MN 55068-2932   651-423-8301
                                     877-937-3282
                              FAX: 651-423-7028
                                     dctc.edu

Ron Thomas, President
Offers information on support groups, conventions, books, manuscripts and programs for the rehabilitation professional and the disabled.
Monthly

4936   Accent on Living Magazine
Cheever Publishing
P.O.Box 700
Bloomington, IL 61702-700   309-378-2961
                                     800-787-8444
                              FAX: 309-378-4420

Julie Cheever, Marketing Manager
A magazine published for forty four years, serves physically disabled people, with general interest, travel, and home modification features. *$12.00*
112 pages Quarterly

4937   Access Design Services: CILs as Experts
Independent Living Research Utilization ILRU
1333 Moursund
Houston, TX 77030   713-520-0232
                              FAX: 713-520-5785
                                     ilru@ilru.org
                                     ilru.org

Lex Frieden, Director, ILRU
Richard Petty, Co-Director
Featuring the Access Design Services of Alpha One in Maine, this month's Readings is another of the winners of the recent competition for innovative CIL programs.
10 pages

4938   Access To Independence Inc.
Access to Independence
3810 Milwaukee Street
Madison, WI 53714   608-242-8484
                                     800-362-9877
                              FAX: 608-242-0383
                              TTY: 608-242-8485
                         info@accesstoind.org
                         www.accesstoind.org

Dee Truhn, Executive Director
Jason Belaungy, Assistant Director
Geri , Finances/HR

Independent Living Center serving people of any age and all types of disabilities in south-central Wisconsin. Empower people with disabilities, through advocacy, education, and support.
24 pages Semi-Annual

4939   Access for 911 and Telephone Emergency Services
US Department of Justice
950 Pennsylvania Ave. NW
9th Floor
Washington, DC 20530   202-307-0663
                                     800-514-0301
                              FAX: 202-307-1197
                              TTY: 800-514-0383
                                     www.ada.gov

Rebecca B. Bond, Chief
Anne Raish, Principal Deputy Chief
Christina Galindo-Walsh, Deputy Chief
A 10-page publication explaining the requirements for direct, equal access to 911 for persons who use teletypewritters (TTYs).

4940   Achieving Diversity and Independence
Independent Living Research Utilization ILRU
1333 Moursund
Houston, TX 77030   713-520-0232
                              FAX: 713-520-5785
                                     ilru@ilru.org
                                     ilru.org

Lex Frieden, Director, ILRU
Richard Petty, Co-Director
10 pages

4941   Activity-Based Intervention: 2nd Edition
Brookes Publishing
P.O.Box 10624
Baltimore, MD 21285-0624   410-337-9580
                                     800-638-3775
                              FAX: 410-337-8539
                     custserv@brookespublishing.com
                              readplaylearn.com

Paul H. Brooks, Chairman
Jeffrey D. Brookes, President
Melissa A. Behm, Executive Vice President
This 14 minute video illustrates how activity-based intervention can be used to turn everyday events and natural interactions into opportunities to promote learning in young children who are considered at risk for developmental delays or who have mild to significant disabilities. *$39.00*
ISBN 1-55766 -86-3

4942   Ad Lib Drop-In Center: Consumer Management, Ownership and Empowerment
Independent Living Research Utilization ILRU
1333 Moursund
Houston, TX 77030   713-520-0232
                              FAX: 713-520-5785
                                     ilru@ilru.org
                                     ilru.org

Lex Frieden, Director, ILRU
Richard Petty, Co-Director
Joe describes how Ad Lib ensured consumer control in their Drop-In Center: the DIC came about because of consumer input, and consumers are involved in planning the program; members can choose to become volunteers or paid staff members. All of the staff at the DIC are consumers; and active consumer advisory board helps develop policies and programs and provides input to the Ad Lib board.
10 pages

4943   Adobe News
Santa Barbara Foundation
15 E Carrillo St
Santa Barbara, CA 93101-2706   805-963-1873
                                     805-966-2345
                              FAX: 805-966-2345

Ron Gallo, CEO
8 pages Bi-Annually

4944 Advocate
Arc Massachusetts
217 South St
Waltham, MA 02453-2710
781-891-6270
FAX: 781-891-6271
arcmass@arcmass.org
www.arcmass.org

Leo V. Sarkissian, Executive Director
Judy Zacek, Associate Editor
Beth Rutledge, Production Coordinator
Advocate is The Arc of Massachusetts' quarterly newsletter. This is one of the ways in which we inform and educate people about current topics in the field of developmental disabilities. *$20.00*
8-12 pages Quarterly

4945 American Herb Association Newsletter
P.O.Box 353
Nevada City, CA 95959-353
530-265-9552
FAX: 530-274-3140
www.ahaherb.com

Information on many different herbs and herb usues. *$20.00*

4946 Americans with Disabilities Act Checklist for New Lodging Facilities
US Department of Justice
950 Pennsylvania Ave. NW
9th Floor
Washington, DC 20530
202-307-0663
800-514-0301
FAX: 202-307-1197
TTY: 800-514-0383
www.ada.gov

Rebecca B. Bond, Chief
Anne Raish, Principal Deputy Chief
Christina Galindo-Walsh, Deputy Chief
This 34-page checklist is a self-help survey that owners, franchisors, and managers of lodging facilities can use to identify ADA mistakes at their facilities.

4947 Americans with Disabilities Act Handbook
Aspen Publishers
76 9th Ave
7th Floor
New York, NY 10011-4962
212-790-2000
FAX: 212-771-0885
www.aspenpublishers.com

Henry H Perritt Jr Esq, Author
Bob Lemmond, President and CEO
Gustavo Dobles, Vice President & Chief Content Officer
The Americans With Disabilities Act (ADA) Handbook provides comprehensive coverage of the ADA's employment, commercial facilities, and public accommodations provisions as well as coverage of the transportation, communication, and federal, local, and state government requirements. *$599.00*
1671 pages 2X per year
ISBN 0-735531-48-X

4948 An Interdisciplinary Journal for the Social Study of Health, Illness and Medicine
Sage Publications
2455 Teller Rd
Thousand Oaks, CA 91320-2218
805-499-0721
800-818-7243
FAX: 805-499-0871
hea.sagepub.com

Alan Radley, Editor
Blaise Simqu, Chief Executive Officer
Quarterly

4949 Annual Report Sarkeys Foundation
530 E Main St
Norman, OK 73071-5823
405-364-3703
FAX: 405-364-8191
susan@sarkeys.org
sarkeys.org

Kim Henry, Executive Director
Lorri Sutton, Executive Assistant
Susan C. Frantz, Senior Program Officer
Yearly

4950 Applied Kinesiology: Muscle Response in Diagnosis, Therapy and Preventive Medicine
Inner Traditions
P.O.Box 388
Rochester, VT 05767-388
802-767-3174
800-246-8648
FAX: 802-767-3726
orders@innertraditions.com
www.InnerTraditions.com

Jessica Arsenault, Sales Associate
Rob Meadows, VP Sales & Marketing
$12.95
144 pages
ISBN 0-892813-28-8

4951 Arc Connection Newsletter
Arc of Tennessee
151 Athens Way
Suite 100
Nashville, TN 37228-1367
615-248-5878
800-835-7077
FAX: 615-248-5879
pcooper@thearctn.org
thearctn.org

Carrie Hobbs Guiden, Executive Director
Peggy Cooper, Membership, Chapter and Communications Manager
Nicole Davidson, Business Manager
The Arc of Tennessee is a nonprofit organization that offers advocacy, information, referral and support to people with intellectual or developmental disabilities and their families. This is their publication. It is free to members. *$10.00*
12 pages Quarterly

4952 Aromatherapy Book: Applications and Inhalations
2526 Martin Luther King Jr. Way
Berkeley, CA 94704
510-549-4270
FAX: 510-549-4276
info@northatlanticbooks.com
www.northatlanticbooks.com

Minda Armstrong, Print Production Manager
Richard Grossinger, Founding Publisher
Janet Levin, Director of Sales & Distribution
A book of practical and researched information about aromatherapy. *$18.95*
400 pages
ISBN 1-556430-73-6

4953 Aromatherapy for Common Ailments
Simon & Schuster
100 Front St
Delran, NJ 8075-1181
856-461-6500
800-323-7445
FAX: 856-824-2402
www.simonsays.com

David Schaeffer, VP
Explains aromatherapy with emphasis on medicinal uses.
96 pages
ISBN 0-671731-34-3

4954 As I Am
Fanlight Productions
32 Court Street
21st Floor
Brooklyn, NY 11201
718-488-8900
800-876-1710
FAX: 718-488-8642
info@fanlight.com
www.fanlight.com

Ben Achtenberg, Owner
Anthony Sweeney, Marketing Director
Three young people with developmental disabilities speak for themselves about their lives, the problems they face and their hopes and expectations for the future. *$99.00*
ISBN 1-572950-58-7

4955 Attitudes Toward Persons with Disabilities
Springer Publishing Company
11 West 42nd Street
15th Floor
New York, NY 10036

212-431-4370
877-687-7476
FAX: 212-941-7842
marketing@springerpub.com
www.springerpub.com

James C. Costello, Vice President, Journal Publishing
Diana Osborne, Production Manager
Megan Larkin, Managing Editor, Journals
This volume examines what is known of people's complex and multifaceted attitudes toward persons with disabilities. Divided into five areas of concern: theory, origin of attitudes, attitude measurement, attitudes of specific groups and attitude change. *$38.95*
352 pages Hardcover
ISBN 0-82616-90-1

4956 Authoritative Guide to Self- Help Resourcein Mental Health
Guilford Press
72 Spring St
New York, NY 10012-4019

212-431-9800
800-365-7006
FAX: 212-966-6708
info@guilford.com
www.guilford.com

Linda F Campbell PhD, Author
Thomas P Smith PsyD, Author
Robert Sommer PhD, Author
Reviews and rates 600+ self-help books, autobiographies, and popular films, and evaluates hundreds of Internet sites. Addresses 28 of the most prevalent clinical disorders and life challenges- from ADHD, Alzheimer's, and anxiety disorders, to marital problems, mood disorders and weight management. Also in cloth at $45.00 (ISBN# 1-57230-506-1) *$25.00*
377 pages Paperback
ISBN 1-572305-80-0

4957 AwareNews
Services for Independent Living
26250 Euclid Ave
Suite 801
Euclid, OH 44132

216-731-1529
FAX: 216-731-3083
sil@stratos.net
www.sil-oh.org

Molly Foos, Executive Director
Katherine Foley, Director of Advocacy
Lisa Marn, Assistant Director
12 pages Quarterly

4958 Bach Flower Therapy: Theory and Practice
Inner Traditions
1 Park St
Rochester, VT 05767

802-767-3174
FAX: 802-767-3726
customerservice@InnerTraditions.com
www.innertraditions.com

Ehud Sperling, Owner
Contemporary study of Bach's techniques, intended for practitioners and lay readers alike. Includes lists of symptoms to facilitate diagnosis, ans aims to provide an understanding of psychosomatic elements in relation to physical complaints.
ISBN 0-892812-39-7

4959 Barrier Free Travel: A Nuts and Bolts Guide for Wheelers and Slow Walkers (3rd Edition)
Demos Health Publishing
11 W 42nd St
15th Fl
New York, NY 10036

212-683-0072
barrierfreetravel.net

Candy Harrington, Author

Billed as the definitive guide to accessible travel, this indispensable resource contains detailed information about the logistics of planning accessible travel by plane, train, bus and ship. *$19.95*
200 pages Paperback
ISBN 1-932603-83-2

4960 Beliefs, Values, and Principles of Self Advocacy
Brookline Books
34 University Rd
Brookline, MA 02445-4533

800-666-2665
FAX: 617-734-3952
brbooks@yahoo.com
www.brooklinebooks.com

Written by self-advocates around the world, they tell about the beliefs, values, and principles important to them, and the empowerment and personal growth they experience through self-advocacy. *$7.00*
48 pages Paperback
ISBN 0-57129-22-2

4961 Beliefs: Pathways to Health and Well Being
Metamorphous Press
P.O.Box 10616
Portland, OR 97296-616

503-228-4972
FAX: 503-223-9117

David Balding, Publisher
Explores behavioral technologies and belief change strategies that can alter beliefs that support unhealthy habbits such as smoking, overeating, and drug use. Also covers the changing of thinking processes that create phobias and unreasonable fears, retraining the immune system to eliminate allergies and to deal optinally with cancer, AIDS, and other diseases. Includes strategies to transform unhealthy beliefs into lifelong constructs of wellness.

4962 Bench Marks
Governor's Council on Developmental Disabilities
1717 W Jefferson St
Phoenix, AZ 85007-3202

602-542-4049
800-889-5893
FAX: 602-542-5320

Micheal Ward, Executive Director
Susan Madison, Manager
Quarterly

4963 Bodie, Dolina, Smith & Hobbs, P.C.
21 W Susquehanna Ave
Suite 110
Towson, MD 21204-5218

410-823-1250
877-739-1013
FAX: 443-901-0802
chobbs@bodie-law.com
www.bodie-law.com

Chester Hobbs, Esquire
Thomas G. Bodie, Lawyer
Wallace Dann, Lawyer
Law firm; provides estates, trusts and guardianship administration, estate planning, elder law, tax issues, bankruptcy, foreclosures, and real estate issues. *$25.00*
Quarterly

4964 Body Reflexology: Healing at Your Fingertips
Parker Publishing Company
Ste 2605
1501 Broadway
New York, NY 10036-5600

212-869-6350

Hy Dubin, President
Features step-by-step instructions of how to send healing flows of energy through the body to relieve back pain, headaches, arthritis, and other afflictions. Illustrated.
343 pages Hardcover
ISBN 0-132997-36-3

4965   Body Silent: The Different World of the Disabled
WW Norton & Company
324 State Street
Suite H
Santa Barbara, CA 93101-2364   818-718-9900
                                     800-333-6867
                                FAX: 818-349-2027
                        editor@specialneeds.com
                            www.specialneeds.com

The author's personal account of his progressive and terminal loss of muscle function caused by a spinal tumor, resulting in quadripilegia. Includes society's fears, myths, and misunderstandings about disability and the damage they inflict. *$9.95*
256 pages
ISBN 0-393320-42-1

4966   Body of Knowledge/Hellerwork
406 Berry St
Mount Shasta, CA 96067-2548   530-926-2500
                                    theheller@aol.com
                                    www.josephheller.com

Joseph Heller, Owner
Information, referral directory, training and certification.

4967   Bridge Newsletter
Arizona Bridge to Independent Living
1229 E Washington St
Phoenix, AZ 85034-1101   602-256-2245
                               800-280-2245
                          FAX: 602-254-6407
                                    abil.org

Phil Pangrazio, President & CEO
Regina Mitzel, V. P. & Chief Administrative Officer
Amina Kruck, V.P. of Advocacy
12 pages Monthly

4968   Bridging the Gap: A National Directory of Services for Women & Girls with Disabilities
Educational Equity Concepts
71 Fifth Avenue
New York, NY 10016-5506   212-725-1803
                          FAX: 212-725-0947
                          TTY: 212-725-1803
                               www.edequity.org

Ellen Rubin, Coordinator Disability Programs
Merle Froschl, Editor
Contains a resource section of publications and videos geared specifically to women and girls with disabilities. Available in print, on cassette, and also in braille. *$24.95*
ISBN 0-931629-16-0

4969   Bulletin of the Association on the Handicapped
Assoc. on Handicapped Student Service Program
P.O.Box 21192
Columbus, OH 43221-0192   614-365-5216
                          FAX: 614-365-6718

Membership journal including Association news, articles and sections such as Literature in Review and Speak Out. *$16.00*

4970   CDR Reports
Council for Disability Rights
Ste 1540
20 N Wacker Dr
Chicago, IL 60606-2903   312-201-4800
                          FAX: 312-444-1977
                               www.disabilityrights.org

Jo Holzer, Executive Director/Editor
Bruce Moore, Employment Specialist
$15.00
8 pages Monthly

4971   California Financial Power of Attorney
NOLO
950 Parker St
Berkeley, CA 94710-2524   510-549-1976
                               800-955-4775
                          FAX: 510-548-5902
                               www.nolo.com

Maira Dizgalvis, Trade Customer Service Manager
Susan McConnell, Director Sales
Natasha Kaluza, Sales Assistant

A plain-English book packed with forms and instructions to give a trusted person the legal authority to handle your financial affairs.
Paperback

4972   Caring for America's Heroes
Oklahoma City VA Medical Center
921 NE 13th St
Oklahoma City, OK 73104-5007   405-270-0501
                                FAX: 405-270-1560
                                     www.oklahoma.va.gov

Steven Gentlin, Director
Kathleen Fogarty, Associate Director
D Robert McCaffree MD, Chief of Staff

4973   Center for Health Research: Eastern Washington University
Showalter 209a
Cheney, WA 99004   509-359-2279
                         800-221-9369
                    FAX: 509-359-2778
                    sharon.wilson@mail.ewu.edu

Produces eight videotapes, accompanying printed materials, and a videotaped public services announcement to serve as training and resource materials for use by daycare centers.

4974   Center for Libraries and Educational Improvement
400 Maryland Ave SW
Washington, DC 20202-1   202-260-2226
                               800-872-5327
                          FAX: 202-401-0689
                          TTY: 800-437-0833
                               www.ed.gov

Administers the Library Services Construction Act, which authorizes grants to the states for library services to the physically handicapped.

4975   Centering Corporation Grief Resources
7230 Maple Street
Omaha, NE 68134   402-553-1200
                        866-218-0101
                   FAX: 402-533-0507
                        j1200@aol.com
                        www.centering.org

Joy Johnson, Founder
Dr. Marvin Johnson, Founder
Janet Roberts, Executive Director
A full catalog of all our available bereavement resources. We are a small, non-profit organization providing help to families in crisis situations.
32 pages BiAnnually

4976   Centers for Disease Control and Prevention
US Department of Health and Human Services
1600 Clifton Rd NE
Atlanta, GA 30329-4018   404-639-3311
                               800-232-4636
                          FAX: 404-498-1177
                               www.cdc.gov

Robert Delaney, Plant Manager
Publishes an annually updated list of infectious and communicable diseases transmitted through the handling of food in accordance with Section 103 of Title I.

4977   Child With Special Needs: Encouraging Intellectual and Emotional Growth
Addison-Wesley Publishing Company
Ste 300
75 Arlington St
Boston, MA 02116-3988   617-848-7500
                              800-238-9682
                         FAX: 617-944-7273
                              www.awprofessional.com

Bill Barke, CEO
Covering all kinds of disabilities — including cerebral palsy, autism, developmental, ADD, and language problems — this guide offers parents specific ways of helping all special needs chidren reach their full intellectual and emotional potential. *$32.00*
496 pages
ISBN 0-201407-26-4

4978 Chinese Herbal Medicine
Shambhala Publications
300 Massachusetts Avenue
Boston, MA 02115   617-424-0030
                                FAX: 617-236-1563
                                editors@shambhala.com
                                shambhala.com

Richard Reoch, President
Gives an in-depth look into herbal medicine.
176 pages
ISBN 0-877733-98-8

**4979 Christian Approach to Overcoming Disability: A
Doctor's Story**
Haworth Press
10 Alice St
Binghamton, NY 13904-1503   607-722-5857
                                    800-429-6784
                                FAX: 607-722-6362
                                orders@haworthpress.com
                                www.haworthpress.com

William Cohen, Owner
$29.95
128 pages
ISBN 0-789022-57-5

4980 Closing the Gap
P.O. Box 68
Henderson, MN 56044   507-248-3294
                                FAX: 507-248-3810
                                www.closingthegap.com

Dolores Hagen, Co-Founder
Budd Hagen, Co-Founder
Explores use of microcomputers as personal and educational
tools for persons with disabilities.
36+ pages BiMonthly

**4981 Conference of the Association on Higher Education &
Disability (AHEAD)**
8015 West Kenton Circle
Suite 230
Huntersville, NC 28078   704-947-7779
                                FAX: 704-948-7779
                                www.ahead.org

Katy Washington, President
Stephan Smith, Executive Director
Howard Kramer, Conference Director
An annual conference focused on aiding and meeting the needs of
persons with disabilities attending higher education institutions.

4982 Constellations
Minnesota STAR Program
Ste 309
50 Sherburne Ave
Saint Paul, MN 55155-1402   651-296-2771
                                    800-657-3862
                                FAX: 651-282-6671
                                star.program@state.mn.us

Chuck Rassbach, Executive Director
Free quarterly publication from the Minnesota STAR Program.
8 pages Quarterly

4983 Coping+Plus: Dimensions of Disability
Greenwood Publishing Group
130 Cremona Drive
Santa Barbara, CA 93117   805-968-1911
                                    800-368-6868
                                FAX: 866-270-3856
                                CustomerService@abc-clio.com
                                www.abc-clio.com

Matt Laddin, Vice President of Marketing
Mike Saltzman, Director-Eastern Territories & National Accounts
James Lingle, International Sales & Marketing
Everyone can learn new or more effective coping skills and strat-
egies to deal with times of loss, crisis and disability. $55-$59.95
280 pages Hardcover
ISBN 0-275945-44-8

4984 Council News
Northern Nevada Center for Independent Living
999 Pyramid Way
Sparks, NV 89431-4471   775-353-3599
                                FAX: 775-353-3588
                                www.nncil.org

Lisa Bonie, Executive Director
Hilda Velasco, Operations Manager
Joni Inglis, Independent Living Advocate
NNCIL was founded in 1982 by a small group of people with disabilities, who believe that each person, regardless of the severity
of his or her disability, has the potential to grow, develop and
share fully the joys and responsibilities of our society.
12 pages Quarterly

4985 Counseling in Terminal Care & Bereavement
Brookes Publishing
P.O.Box 10624
Baltimore, MD 21285-0624   410-337-9580
                                    800-638-3775
                                FAX: 410-337-8539
                                custserv@brookespublishing.com
                                readplaylearn.com

Paul H. Brooks, Chairman
Jeffrey D. Brookes, President
Melissa A. Behm, Executive Vice President
Provides practical suggestions for addressing the needs of patients and family members who are anticipating or currently dealing with grief and bereavement, such as hospice care, hospitals,
or at home care. *$34.00*
210 pages Paperback
ISBN 1-85433 -78-7

**4986 Creating Wholeness: Self-Healing Workbook Using
Dynamic Relaxation, Images and Thoughts**
Plenum Publishing Corporation
233 Spring St
7th Floor
New York, NY 10013-1522   212-620-8000
                                    800-644-4831
                                FAX: 212-460-1575
                                ainy@aveda.com
                                www.aveda.edu

232 pages
ISBN 0-306441-72-1

4987 DRS Connection
Disabled Resource Services
Ste 101
424 Pine St
Fort Collins, CO 80524-2421   970-482-2700
                                FAX: 970-407-7072

Nancy Jackson, Executive Director
4 pages Quarterly

4988 Demand Response Transportation Through a Rural ILC
Independent Living Research Utilization ILRU
1333 Moursund
Houston, TX 77030   713-520-0232
                                FAX: 713-520-5785
                                ilru@ilru.org
                                ilru.org

Lex Frieden, Director, ILRU
Richard Petty, Co-Director
Oklahomans for Independent Living's transportation program
was selected as exemplary becuase they marketed it by emphasizing people with disabilities as economic constituency.
10 pages

4989 Developing Organized Coalitions and Strategic Plans
Independent Living Research Utilization ILRU
1333 Moursund
Houston, TX 77030   713-520-0232
                                FAX: 713-520-5785
                                ilru@ilru.org
                                ilru.org

Lex Frieden, Director, ILRU
Richard Petty, Co-Director
10 pages

4990   Dictionary of Congenital Malformations& Disorders
Informa Healthcare
Fl 16
52 Vanderbilt Ave
New York, NY 10017-3846   212-520-2777
                                        FAX: 212-661-5052
                                     orders@crcpress.com
                                      www.tandfonline.com

$55.00
193 pages
ISBN 0-850705-77-1

4991   Dictionary of Developmental Disabilities Terminology
Brookes Publishing
P.O.Box 10624
Baltimore, MD 21285-0624   410-337-9580
                                              800-638-3775
                                        FAX: 410-337-8539
                                custserv@brookespublishing.com
                                    www.brookespublishing.com

Paul H. Brooks, Chairman
Jeffrey D. Brookes, President
Melissa A. Behm, Executive Vice President
With more than 3,000 easy-to-understand entries, this dictionary
provides thorough explanations of terms associated with devel-
opmental disabilities and disorders. *$55.95*
368 pages Hardcover
ISBN 1-557662-45-2

4992   Directory of Members
American Network of Community Options & Resources
1101 King St
Suite 380
Alexandria, VA 22314-2962   703-535-7850
                                        FAX: 703-535-7860
                                          ancor@ancor.org
                                               ancor.org

Dave Toeniskoetter, President
Chris Sparks, Vice President
Julie Manworren, Secretary/Treasurer
The Directory lists over 600 agencies that provide residential services and supports in 48 states and the District of Columbia. The
listings include the name of the Executive Directors, the name,
address, and phone number of the agency, describe the types of
services that are provided and how many individuals receive services from that agency. *$25.00*
189 pages

4993   Disability Awareness Guide
Central Iowa Center for Independent Living
655 Walnut St
Suite 131
Des Moines, IA 50309-3930   515-243-1742
                                        FAX: 515-243-5385

Bob Jeppesen, Executive Director
Frank Strong, Assistant Director Programs
Bob Jepson, Manager
The Disability Awareness Guide contains information about our
center; who we are and what we do. It also contains the telephone
numbers of local and national agencies and resources available
for people with disabilities.

4994   Disability Rights Movement
Children's Press
Sherman Tpke
Danbury, CT 6813   800-621-1115
                                        FAX: 800-374-4329

Elena Rockman, Marketing Manager
Author Deborah Kent illuminates both the history of the National
Disability Rights Movement and the inspiring personal stories of
individuals with various disabilities. *$18.00*
32 pages Hardcover
ISBN 0-53106 -32-3

**4995   Disabled People's International Fifth World Assembly as
Reported by Two US Participants**
Independent Living Research Utilization ILRU
1333 Moursund
Houston, TX 77030   713-520-0232
                                        FAX: 713-520-5785
                                             ilru@ilru.org
                                                 ilru.org

Lex Frieden, Director, ILRU
Richard Petty, Co-Director
This report describes the international conference on independent living held in Mexico City in December 1998 as experienced
by staff members from two U.S. centers. Kaye Beneke interviewed Luis Chew and Marco Antonio Coronado for this edition
of Readings in Independent Living.
10 pages

4996   Disabled We Stand
Brookline Books
34 University Rd
Brookline, MA 02445-4533   800-666-2665
                                        FAX: 617-734-3952
                                       brbooks@yahoo.com
                                     www.brooklinebooks.com

This book is impassioned, often angry, but also hopeful and practical, suggesting a series of actions that will lead to constructive
change. It is imbued with spirit and energy of disabled people
who are determined to take their lives into their own hands.
$10.95
Paperback
ISBN 0-25331 -80-0

4997   Disabled, the Media, and the Information Age
Greenwood Publishing Group
130 Cremona Drive
Santa Barbara, CA 93117   805-968-1911
                                              800-368-6868
                                        FAX: 866-270-3856
                                 CustomerService@abc-clio.com
                                        www.abc-clio.com

Matt Laddin, Vice President of Marketing
Mike Saltzman, Director-Eastern Territories & National Accounts
James Lingle, International Sales & Marketing
A short and easy-to-read overview of how disabled Americans
have been portrayed by the media and how images and the role of
the handicapped are changing. *$55.00*
264 pages Hardcover
ISBN 0-313284-72-5

4998   Discovery Newsletter
North Dakota State Library Talking Book Services
Dept 250
604 E Boulevard Ave
Bismarck, ND 58505-605   701-328-2000
                                              800-843-9948
                                        FAX: 701-328-2040
                                       sbschneider@nd.gov
                           ndsl.lib.state.nd.us/DisabilityServices.html

Doris Ott, Manager
The North Dakota State Library Disability Services produces the
Doscovery Newsletter containing information on services,
books, catalogs and of interest to the patron.
6 pages Bi-Annually

4999   EP Resource Guide
Exceptional Parent Library
P.O.Box 1807
Englewood Cliffs, NJ 7632-1207   201-947-6000
                                              800-535-1910
                                        FAX: 201-947-9376
                                        eplibrary@aol.com
                                         www.eplibrary.com

Lists directories of national organizations, associations, products and services. *$9.95*

5000 ESCIL Update Newsletter
Eastern Shore Center for Independent Living
9 Sunburst Ctr
Cambridge, MD 21613-2057   410-221-7701
                                            800-705-7944
                                       FAX: 410-221-7714

Shirley Tarbox, Executive Director
Jean Reed, Administrative Assistant
Lisa Morgan, Director IL Services
6 pages Quarterly

5001 Easy Things to Make Things Simple: Do It Yourself Modifications for Disabled Persons
Brookline Books
34 University Rd
Brookline, MA 02445-4533   800-666-2665
                                       FAX: 617-734-3952
                                       brbooks@yahoo.com
                                       www.brooklinebooks.com

This book aims at older adults and others with physical limitations who require adaptations for safer and easier living in the kitchen, bathroom, bedroom, yard, and garden. The adaptations can be done inexpensively, from common materials. Large print format and detailed diagrams, plus special sections with advice caregivers . *$15.95*
160 pages Paperback
ISBN 1-571290-24-9

5002 Enabling Romance: A Guide to Love, Sex & Relationships for the Disabled

Ken Kroll, Author
Erica Levy Klein, Author
An uncensored, illustrated guide to intimacy and sexual expression for persons with physical disabilities.

5003 Encyclopedia of Disability
Sage Publications
2455 Teller Rd
Thousand Oaks, CA 91320-2218   805-499-0721
                                       info@sagepub.com
                                       www.sagepub.com

Gary L Albrecht, Editor
Blaise Simqu, Chief Executive Officer
A five volume set that covers disabilities A-Z *$850.00*
2500 pages
ISBN 0-761925-65-1

5004 EveryBody's Different: Understanding and Changing Our Reactions to Disabilities
Brookes Publishing
P.O.Box 10624
Baltimore, MD 21285-0624   410-337-9580
                                            800-638-3775
                                       FAX: 410-337-8539
                                       custserv@brookespublishing.com
                                       readplaylearn.com

Paul H. Brooks, Chairman
Jeffrey D. Brookes, President
Melissa A. Behm, Executive Vice President
This book discusses the emotions, questions, fears, and stereotypes that people without disabilities sometimes experience when they interact with people who do have disabilities. The author teaches readers to become more at ease with the concept of disability and to communicate more effectively with each other. Features activities and exercises that encourage self-examination, helping people to create more enriching personal relationships and work toward a fully inclusive society.
Paperback
ISBN 1-55766 -59-9

5005 Everybody's Guide to Homeopathic Medicines
Jeremy P Tarcher
375 Hudson St
New York, NY 10014-3658   212-366-2000
                                       academic@penguin.com
                                       www.us.penguingroup.com

John Makinson, Chairman and CEO
Coram Williams, CFO

Covers alternative treatments in homeopathic medicines.
375 pages
ISBN 0-874778-43-3

5006 Everyday Social Interaction: A Program for People with Disabilities
Brookes Publishing
P.O.Box 10624
Baltimore, MD 21285-0624   410-337-9580
                                            800-638-3775
                                       FAX: 410-337-8539
                                       custserv@brookespublishing.com
                                       readplaylearn.com

Paul H. Brooks, Chairman
Jeffrey D. Brookes, President
Melissa A. Behm, Executive Vice President
This source guides teachers and human services professionals in helping people with disabilities acquire social interaction skills and develop satisfying relationships. Included is a checklist and task analyses that shows how complex skills can be broken down into major components for easy performance monitoring accompanied by tips on social courtesies, rewards, praise, and criticism. *$41.95*
342 pages Paperback
ISBN 1-55766 -58-4

5007 Family Challenges: Parenting with a Disability
Aquarius Health Care Videos
P.O.Box 1159
Sherborn, MA 01770-7159   508-650-1616
                                            888-440-2963
                                       FAX: 508-650-4216
                                       aqvideos@tiac.net
                                       www.aquariusproductions.com

Lesile Kussmann, Owner
When a parent has a disability, everyone in the family is affected. For children, these experiences may profoundly influence their lives and views of the world. In this sensitive film, you will hear about different roles that all the family members take on at varying times. *$195.00*

5008 Force A Miracle
Writer's Showcase Press

A testament to the inner human strength to overcome extreme adversity, to triumph and continue a worthwhile and self-rewarding life. *$14.95*
244 pages
ISBN 0-595226-88-4

5009 Forum
Coalition for the Education of Disabled Children
165 W Center St
Marion, OH 43302-3742   740-382-7362
                                            800-374-2806
                                       FAX: 740-382-3428

Tracie Wilson, Manager
Leeann Derugen, Manager
Forum is a newsletter reporting on legislative and other developments affecting persons with disabilities.
Quarterly

5010 Foundation Fundamentals for Nonprofit Organizations
Foundation Center
Department Ze
79 5th Ave
New York, NY 10003-3034   212-620-4230
                                            800-424-9836
                                       FAX: 212-807-3677
                                       order@foundationcenter.org
                                       www.fdncenter.org

Bradford K. Smith, President
Lisa Philip, Vice President for Strategic Philanthropy
Lawrence T. McGill, Vice President for Research
This video is designed to give fundraisers a general overview of the foundation funding process and to introduce them to the many resources available through our libraries and cooperating collec-

tions. The video gives clear, step-by-step instructions on how to build a fundraising program. *$24.00*
Video

5011   Four-Ingredient Cookbook
Laurel Designs
Apt A
1805 Mar West St
Belvedere Tiburon, CA 94920-1962   FAX: 415-435-1451
Janet Sawyer, Owner
Lynn Montoya, Owner
Simple, easy to follow recipes, each containing four ingredients. Particularly suited to persons with limited physical ability. Includes 400 recipes, appetizers to desserts. *$9.00*

5012   Frequently Asked Questions About Multiple Chemical Sensitivity
Independent Living Research Utilization ILRU
1333 Moursund
Houston, TX 77030   713-520-0232
                                       FAX: 713-520-5785
                                          ilru@ilru.org
                                              ilru.org
Lex Frieden, Director, ILRU
Richard Petty, Co-Director
This FAQ covers important information about multiple chemical sensitivity and environmental illness. The FAQ describes the conditions, recommends strategies for improving access, and lists resources for CILs and other organizations. As the fact sheet states, centers must set an example in assuring that all people can enter their offices.
10 pages

5013   Genetic Disorders Sourcebook
Omnigraphics
615 Griswold Street
Suite 520
Detroit, MI 48226   610-461-3548
                                          800-234-1340
                                       FAX: 800-875-1340
                                  contact@omnigraphics.com
                                  www.omnigraphics.com
Peter Ruffner, Co-Founder
Fred Ruffner, Co-Founder
Provides information on hereditary diseases and disorders. *$7800.00*
650 pages
ISBN 0-789892-41-1

5014   Genetic Nutritioneering
McGraw-Hill Company
2460 Kerper Blvd
Dubuque, IA 52001-2224   563-588-1451
                                          800-338-3987
                                       FAX: 614-755-5654
Kurt Strand, VP
Describes how to modify the expression of genetic traits, potentially preventing heart disease, cancer, arthritis, and hormone-related problems. Features how to slow biological aging and reduce the risk of age-related diseases. *$16.95*
288 pages
ISBN 0-879839-21-X

5015   Going to School with Facilitated Communication
Syracuse University, School of Education
230 Huntington Hall
Syracuse, NY 13244-1   315-443-4752
                                       FAX: 315-443-2258
                                          jhrusso@syr.edu
                                          www.soe.syr.edu
Shirley Adamczyk, Administrative Assistant
Rachael Gazdick, Executive Director
Isabelle M. Glod, Administrative Assistant
A video in which students with autism and/or severe disabilities illustrate the use of facilitated communication focusing on basic principles fostering facilitated communication.
Video

5016   Grief: What it is and What You Can Do
Centering Corporation
7230 Maple Street
Omaha, NE 68134   402-553-1200
                                          866-218-0101
                                       FAX: 402-533-0507
                                          j1200@aol.com
                                          www.centering.org
Joy Johnson, Founder
Dr. Marvin Johnson, Founder
Janet Roberts, Executive Director
General grief information for all grief issues. *$3.50*
32 pages Paperback

5017   Guidelines on Disability
US Department of Housing & Urban Development
451 7th St SW
Washington, DC 20410-1   202-708-1112
                                       TTY:202-708-1455
                                  portal.hud.gov/hudportal/HUD
Shaun Donovan, Secretary
Helen R. Kanovsky, Acting Deputy Secretary
Jennifer Ho, Senior Advisor to the Secretary
Contains information on housing and accessibility for persons with disabilities.

5018   Handbook of Services for the Handicapped
Greenwood Publishing Group
130 Cremona Drive
Santa Barbara, CA 93117   805-968-1911
                                          800-368-6868
                                       FAX: 866-270-3856
                                  CustomerService@abc-clio.com
                                  www.abc-clio.com
Matt Laddin, Vice President of Marketing
Mike Saltzman, Director-Eastern Territories & National Accounts
James Lingle, International Sales & Marketing
A handy reference book offering information and services for disabled individuals. $59.95-$65.00.
291 pages Hardcover
ISBN 0-313213-85-2

5019   Healing Herbs
Rodale Press
33 E Minor St
Emmaus, PA 18098-1   610-967-5171
                                       FAX: 610-967-8963
Maria Rodale, Chairman/Chief Executive Officer
Scott D. Schulman, President
Heather Rodale, Board Member/Vice President/ Leadership Development
Covers everything from growing the herbs to home remedies.

5020   Helen Keller National Center for Deaf- Blind Youths And Adults
141 Middle Neck Rd
Sands Point, NY 11050-1218   516-944-8900
                                       FAX: 516-944-7302
                                          hkncinfo@hknc.org
                                          www.hknc.org
Joseph McNulty, Executive Director
HKNC is the only national vacational and rehabilitation program providing services exclusively to youth and adults who are deaf-blind.

5021   Hospice Alternative
Harper Collins Publishers/Basic Books
10 E 53rd St
New York, NY 10022-5244   212-207-7000
                                          800-242-7737
                                       FAX: 212-207-7203
Jane Friedman, CEO
An account of the hospice experience. An innovative and humane way of caring for the terminally ill. *$8.95*
256 pages
ISBN 0-46503 -61-0

5022 How to File a Title III Complaint
US Department of Justice
950 Pennsylvania Ave. NW
9th Floor
Washington, DC 20530
202-307-0663
800-514-0301
FAX: 202-307-1197
TTY: 800-514-0383
www.ada.gov

Rebecca B. Bond, Chief
Anne Raish, Principal Deputy Chief
Christina Galindo-Walsh, Deputy Chief
This publication details the procedure for filing a complaint under Title III of the ADA.

5023 How to Live Longer with a Disability
Accent Books & Products
PO Box 700
Bloomington, IL 61702-700
309-378-2961
800-787-8444
FAX: 309-378-4420
acmtlvng@aol.com

Raymond C Cheever, Publisher
Betty Garee, Editor
Eleven chapters to help you enjoy every aspect of your life, and live easier and happier. Includes sexuality and disability, getting more from the medical community and benefit programs. Co-authored by Robert Mauro, sociologist and Elle Becker, counselor and psychologist, both disabled. *$11.50*
266 pages Paperback
ISBN 0-19570 -38-8

5024 Ideas for Kids on the Go
Accent Books & Products
PO Box 700
Bloomington, IL 61702-700
309-378-2961
800-787-8444
FAX: 309-378-4420
acmtlvng@aol.com

Raymond C Cheever, Publisher
Betty Garee, Editor
This guide shows kids with physical disabilities how to go for it! Lists products and where to get them, and includes tips from others for having fun and getting ahead. Ages 1-18. *$6.95*
69 pages Paperback
ISBN 0-91570 -17-5

5025 If I Only Knew What to Say or Do
AARP Fulfillment
601 E St NW
Washington, DC 20049-1
202-434-2277
800-424-3410
FAX: 202-434-3443
TTY: 877-434-7598
member@aarp.org
www.aarp.org

Carol Raphael, Chair
Ronald E. Daly, Sr., Board Vice Chair
Jeannine English, President
Provides a concise discussion of how to help a friend in crisis. Learn what to say and what not to say.

5026 If it Weren't for the Honor: I'd Rather Have Walked
Accent Books & Products
PO Box 700
Bloomington, IL 61702-700
309-378-2961
800-787-8444
FAX: 309-378-4420
acmtlvng@aol.com

Raymond C Cheever, Publisher
Betty Garee, Editor
Revealing, often humorous, highly interesting and important reading. This book offers an account told by the author who was on the scene and actually saw and participated in many events that paved the way for progress for all those with disabilities. *$14.50*
262 pages Paperback
ISBN 0-91570 -41-8

5027 Imagery in Healing Shamanism and Modern Medicine
Shambhala Publications
300 Massachusetts Avenue
Horticultural Hall
Boston, MA 02115
617-424-0030
888-424-2329
FAX: 617-236-1563
editors@shambhala.com
www.shambhala.com

Richard Reoch, President
Patients use self imagery to fight sickness and pain throughout their lives. *$15.95*
272 pages
ISBN 1-570629-34-x

5028 Independence
Easterseals
1219 Dunn Ave
Daytona Beach, FL 32114-2405
386-255-4568
877-255-4568
FAX: 386-258-7677

Jeff Blass, Chairman
Austin Brownlee, Chair-Elect
Becky Rutland, Vice Chair
4-6 pages Quarterly

5029 Independent Living Centers and Managed Care: Results of an ILRU Study on Involvement
Independent Living Research Utilization ILRU
1333 Moursund
TIRR Memorial Hermann Research Cent
Houston, TX 77030-7031
713-520-0232
FAX: 713-520-5785
ilru@ilru.org
www.ilru.org

Lex Frieden, Director, ILRU
Richard Petty, Co-Director
Vinh Nguyen, Program Director
This month's Readings presents findings from an ILRU study of roles centers are taking vis-a-vis managed care. Initiated in spring 1998, we asked Drew Batavia to take the lead in conducting this study for us. We were interested in collecting data on frequency with which centers are contacted by consumers with managed care problems. This is a study that will need to be repeated periodically as our experiences with managed care evolves. Meanwhile, here are the initial findings.
10 pages

5030 Independent Living Challenges the Blues
Independent Living Research Utilization ILRU
1333 Moursund
TIRR Memorial Hermann Research Cent
Houston, TX 77030-7031
713-520-0232
FAX: 713-520-5785
ilru@ilru.org
www.ilru.org

Lex Frieden, Director, ILRU
Richard Petty, Co-Director
Vinh Nguyen, Program Director
Patricia's article highlights the Georgia SILC's health care advocacy efforts: the Georgia legislature passed a bill enabling Georgia Bleu to convert to for-profit status without a distribution of assets to similar nonprofit corporations; the Georgia SILC joined other health care advocates in filing a class action law suit to challenge the legality of the conversion; the Georgia SILC continues advocacy efforts to involve people with disabilities in developing and monitoring health care policy.
10 pages

5031 Independent Living Office
Department of Housing & Urban Development (HUD)
451 7th St SW
Washington, DC 20410-1
202-863-2800
Ted Tozer, President
Rafael Diaz, Chief Information Officer/Chief Information Officer
Mike Anderson, Chief Human Capital Officer
This office within HUD is charged with encouraging the construction of housing that is accessible to handicapped persons. The Office of Independent Living encourages modifications of

apartments and other dwellings so that handicapped persons can enter without assistance.

5032 **Information Services for People with Developmental Disabilities**
Greenwood Publishing Group
130 Cremona Drive
Santa Barbara, CA 93117

805-968-1911
800-368-6868
FAX: 866-270-3856
CustomerService@abc-clio.com
www.abc-clio.com

Matt Laddin, Vice President of Marketing
Mike Saltzman, Director - Eastern Territories
James Lingle, International Sales & Marketing
Overviews the information needs of people with developmental disabilities and tells librarians how to meet them. $65.oo-$75.00.
368 pages Hardcover
ISBN 0-313287-80-5

5033 **Innovative Programs: An Example of How CILs Can Put Their Work in Context**
Culture
1333 Moursund
TIRR Memorial Hermann Research Cent
Houston, TX 77030-7031

713-520-0232
FAX: 713-520-5785
ilru@ilru.org
www.ilru.org

Lex Frieden, Director, ILRU
Richard Petty, Co-Director
Vinh Nguyen, Program Director
Another winner in the innovative CIL competition- Steve Brown describes the Talking Books Program of Southeast Alaska Independent Living, discussing their efforts to record the oral history and life experiences of people with disabilities in the larger context of disability culture.
10 pages

5034 **Insurance Solutions: Plan Well, Live Better**
Demos Medical Publishing
11 West 42nd Street
15th Floor
New York, NY 10036

212-683-0072
800-532-8663
FAX: 212-683-0118
support@demosmedical.com
www.demosmedpub.com

Paul Choi, Vice-President of Finance and Operations
Matt Conmy, Sr. Director of Sales
Thomas Hastings, Marketing Manager
Learn how to look at various insurance options from a new perspective — including life, disability, health, and long-term care. Concrete information for dealing with potential problems in your coverage, to secure your financial future. *$24.95*
192 pages 2002
ISBN 1-888799-55-2

5035 **International Directory of Libraries for the Disabled**
KG Saur/Division of RR Bowker
121 Chanlon Rd
New Providence, NJ 7974-1541

908-286-1090
800-521-8110

Michael Cairns, CEO
An essential resource for improving the quality and quantity of materials available to the print-handicapped audience. Featuring talking books, braille books, large print books as well as production centers for these materials. *$46.00*
257 pages
ISBN 3-59821 -81-1

5036 **Issues in Independent Living**
Independent Living Research Utilization
1333 Moursund
TIRR Memorial Hermann Research Cent
Houston, TX 77030-7031

713-520-0232
FAX: 713-520-5785
ilru@ilru.org
www.ilru.org

Lex Frieden, Executive Director
Vinh Nguyen, Program Director
This booklet is a report of the National Study Group on the Implications of Health Care Reform for Americans with Disabilities and Chronic Health Conditions.
30 pages

5037 **JAMA: The Journal of the American Medical Association**
American Medical Association
PO Box 10946
Chicago, IL 60654-4820

312-670-7827
800-262-2350
FAX: 312-464-5909
subscriptions@jamanetwork.com
jama.jamanetwork.com

Howard Bauchner, MD, Editor-in-Chief
Articles cover all aspects of medical research and clinical medicine. *$66.00*

5038 **JCIL Advocate Times**
Jackson Center for Independent Living
409 Linden Ave
Jackson, MI 49203-4065

517-782-6054
FAX: 517-782-3118

Lesia Pikaart, Executive Director
JoAnn Lucas, Associate Director
Quarterly

5039 **Jason & Nordic Publishers, Inc.**
PO Box 441
Hollidaysburg, PA 16648-441

814-696-2929
FAX: 814-696-4250

Norma Mc Phee, Owner/CEO
Norma Phee
Turtle Books for children with disabilities present heroes who look like them, have problems like theirs, have similar doubts and feelings in non-threatening, fun stories. They are motivational, bridge the gap and promote understanding among peers and siblings. 22 children's books (grades preK-3) plus Sensitivity and Awareness Guide containing lesson plans, activities, background information keyed to the series. Disabilities include: Down syndrome, cerebral palsy, blindness, deafness and more.

5040 **Journal of Social Work in Disabilty & Rehabilitation**
Haworth Press
10 Alice St
Binghamton, NY 13904-1503

607-722-5857
800-429-6784
FAX: 607-722-6362
orders@haworthpress.com
www.haworthpress.com

William Cohen, Owner
John T Oardeck PhD, Editor
S Harrington-Miller, Advertising
Presents and explores issues related to disabilities and social policy, practice, research, and theory. Reflecting the broad scope of social work in disabilty practice, this interdisciplinary journal examines vital issues aspects of the field — from innovative practice methods, legal issues, and literature reviews to program descriptions and cuttinf-edge practice research.
Quarterly

5041 Just Like Everyone Else
World Institute on Disability
3075 Adeline St.
Suite 155
Berkeley, CA 94703   510-225-6400
FAX: 510-225-0477
wid@wid.org
www.wid.org

Marcie Roth, Executive Director & Chief Executive Officer
Kat Zigmont, Senior Director, Operations & Deputy Director
Reggie Johnson, Senior Director, Marketing & Communications
Intended for general audiences, the publication provides perspective, inspiration and information about the Independent Living Movement and the Americans with Disabilities Act.

5042 Keep the Promise: Managed Care and People with Disabilities
American Network of Community Options & Resource
1101 King St
Ste 380
Alexandria, VA 22314-2962   703-535-7850
FAX: 703-535-7860
ancor@ancor.org
www.ancor.org

Dave Toeniskoetter, President
Chris Sparks, Vice President
Julie Manworren, Secretary/Treasurer
This publication presents a detailed review of the process and the lessons learned. Details a way for all stake holders to work together for a state or local system.
119 pages $18 - $22

5043 Keeping Our Families Together
Through the Looking Glass
3075 Adeline St.
Ste. 120
Berkeley, CA 94703-2212   510-848-1112
800-644-2666
FAX: 510-848-4445
TTY: 510-848-1005
tlg@lookingglass.org
www.lookingglass.org

Maureen Block, J.D., Board President
Thomas Spalding, Board Treasurer
Alice Nemon, D.S.W., Board Secretary
Report of the National Task Force on parents with disabilities and their families. Available in braille, large print or cassette. *$2.00*
12 pages

5044 Learn About the ADA in Your Local Library
US Department of Justice
950 Pennsylvania Ave. NW
9th Floor
Washington, DC 20530   202-307-0663
800-514-0301
FAX: 202-307-1197
TTY: 800-514-0383
www.ada.gov

Rebecca B. Bond, Chief
Anne Raish, Principal Deputy Chief
Christina Galindo-Walsh, Deputy Chief
A 10-page annotated list of 95 ADA publications and one videotape that are available in 15,000 public libraries throughout the country.

5045 LifeLines
Disabled & Alone/Life Services for the Handicapped
1441 Broadway
23rd Floor
New York, NY 10018-2326   212-532-6740
800-995-0066
FAX: 212-532-6740
info@disabledandalone.org
www.disabledandalone.org/lifelines.html

Leslie D. Park, Chair
Rex L. Davidson, Vice President
Lee Alan Ackerman, Executive Director

Newsletter providing current and valuable information about lifetime care and planning for persons with disabilities and their families and the organizations serving them. Free upon request.
4-10 pages Biannual

5046 Lifelong Leisure Skills and Lifestyles for Persons with Developmental Disabilities
Brookes Publishing
PO Box 10624
Baltimore, MD 21285-0624   410-337-9580
800-638-3775
FAX: 410-337-8539
custserv@brookespublishing.com
www.readplaylearn.com

Paul H. Brooks, Chairman
Jeffrey D. Brookes, President
Melissa A. Behm, Executive Vice President
This instructional manual offers ideas and detailed examples that describe how to guide individuals of all ages through popular activities using adaptations that foster skill acquisition and inclusion. Some of the concepts explored are home-school-community collaboration, choice making and the dignity of risk, and leisure skill acquisition for the life span. *$35.00*
352 pages Paperback
ISBN 1-55766 -47-2

5047 Livin'
Lehigh Valley Center for Independent Living
435 Allentown Dr
Allentown, PA 18109-9121   610-770-9781
FAX: 610-770-9801
info@lvcil.org
www.lvcil.org

Amy Beck, Executive Director
Cara Steidel, Director of Finance
Greg Bott, Director of Development
4 pages Quarterly

5048 Living in a State of Stuck
Brookline Books
8 Trumbull Rd
Suite B-001
Northampton, MA 01060   413-584-0184
800-666-2665
FAX: 413-584-6184
brbooks@yahoo.com
www.brooklinebooks.com
Offers explanations on how adaptive technologies affect the lives of people with disabilities. *$24.95*
3rd ed., paper
ISBN 1-571290-27-3

5049 Living in the Community
Independent Living Research Utilization ILRU
1333 Moursund
TIRR Memorial Hermann Research Cent
Houston, TX 77030-7031   713-520-0232
FAX: 713-520-5785
ilru@ilru.org
www.ilru.org

Lex Frieden, Director, ILRU
Richard Petty, Co-Director
Vinh Nguyen, Program Director
James, Lori, and Jamey describe the elements of their successful program to move people out of nursing homes and into the community: providing funding for deposits, first month's rent and other neccessities, including assistive technology; providing training and the other core services before and after consumers leave the nursing home; developing relationships with housing and other service providers.
10 pages

5050 **Loud, Proud and Passionate**
Mobility International USA
132 E Broadway
Suite 343
Eugene, OR 97401
541-343-1284
FAX: 541-343-6812
TTY:541-343-1284
clearinghouse@miusa.org
www.miusa.org

Susan Sygall, Chief Executive Officer
Cindy Lewis, Director, Programs
A resource book for international development and women's organization about including women with disabilities in projects in the community. Informs women with disabilities about the efforts and successes of their peers worldwide.

5051 **Love: Where to Find It, How to Keep It**
Accent Books & Products
PO Box 700
Bloomington, IL 61702-700
309-378-2961
800-787-8444
FAX: 309-378-4420
acmtlvng@aol.com

Raymond C Cheever, Publisher
Betty Garee, Editor
Offers ideas such as how to meet other single people, avoid the wrong type; communications skills and much more for the disabled person wanting to date. *$6.95*
104 pages Paperback
ISBN 0-91570-31-0

5052 **MOOSE: A Very Special Person**
Brookline Books
8 Trumbull Rd
Suite B-001
Northampton, MA 01060
413-584-0184
800-666-2665
FAX: 413-584-6184
brbooks@yahoo.com
www.brooklinebooks.com
Moose, which in very human terms, teaches us that each of us is different and that we have our own unique capacity for loving, sharing, enjoying and learning. *$10.95*
Paperback
ISBN 0-91479-73-5

5053 **Mainstream Magazine**
2973 Beech St
San Diego, CA 92102-1529
619-232-2727
FAX: 619-234-3155
www.mainstream-mag.com

Cyndi Jones, Executive Director
The authoritative, national voice of people with disabilities, publishes in-depth reports on employment, education, new products and technology, legislation and disability rights advocacy, recreation and travel, disability arts and culture, plus personality profiles and challenging commentary. *$24.00*
Monthly

5054 **Making Changes: Family Voices on Living Disabilities**
Brookline Books
8 Trumbull Rd
Suite B-001
Northampton, MA 01060
413-584-0184
800-666-2665
FAX: 413-584-6184
brbooks@yahoo.com
www.brooklinebooks.com
What are the day to day impacts on the family when a disabled child is born? Or when a child who grows up without a disability becomes disabled through accident or disease? This provocative set of reports illuminates the conditions of those peoples lives, and the way they and those around them adjust to the disabilities. *$16.95*
216 pages Paperback
ISBN 0-91479-93-

5055 **Making Informed Medical Decisions: Where to Look and How to Use What You Find**
Patient-Centered Guides
1005 Gravenstein Highway North
Sebastopol, CA 95472
707-827-7000
FAX: 707-829-0104
support@oreilly.com
www.oreilly.com

Nancy Oster, Author
Making Informed Medical Decisions acts like a friendly reference librarian, explaining: tips for researching for someone else; medical journal articles; statistics and risk; standard treatment options; clinical trial; making an ally of your doctor; and determining your own best course. *$17.95*
381 pages Paperback
ISBN 1-565924-59-2

5056 **Making Wise Decisions for Long-Term Care**
AARP Fulfillment
601 E St NW
Washington, DC 20049-1
202-434-2277
800-424-3410
FAX: 202-434-3443
TTY: 877-434-7598
member@aarp.org
www.aarp.org

Carol Raphael, Chair
Ronald E. Daly, Sr., Board Vice Chair
Jeannine English, President
Here's a comprehensive consumer education effort in the area of long-term care.
28 pages

5057 **Making a Difference**
Georgia Council On Developmental Disabilities
2 Peachtree St N.W.
Suite 26-246
Atlanta, GA 30303-3141
404-657-2126
888-275-4233
FAX: 404-657-2132
TTY: 404-657-2133
eejacobson@dhr.state.ga.us
www.gcdd.org

Eric E Jacobson, Executive Director
Pat Nobbie, Deputy Director
Dottie Adams, Family/Individual Support Dir.
The Georgia Council on Developmental Disabilities collaborates with Georgia's citizens, public and private advocacy organizations and policymakers to positively influence public policies that enhance the quality of life for people with disabilities and their families. GCDD provides this through education and advocacy activities, program implementation, funding and public policy analysis and research.

5058 **Making a Difference: A Wise Approach**
Easterseals
141 W Jackson Blvd.
Suite 1400A
Chicago, IL 60604
312-726-6200
800-221-6827
FAX: 312-726-1494
info@easterseals.com
www.easterseals.com

Angela F. Williams, President & CEO
Glenda Oakley, Chief Financial Officer
Marcy Traxler, Senior Vice President, Network Advancement
The town of Wise, Virginia, and its leading citizen, Virgil Craft, personify what Making a Difference is all about when a community supports implementing the provisions of the Americans with Disabilities Act. Craft, a person with a disability, has spent his life giving back to the community. The community, in turn, has supported Craft's efforts to improve the environment, education, healthcare and access for disabled persons. A 16-minute video.

5059   Managing Your Activities
Arthritis Foundation
PO Box 78423
Atlanta, GA 30357-0669   404-237-8771
                                          800-933-7023
                                     FAX: 404-872-0457
                                      help@arthritis.org
                                       www.arthritis.org

John H Klippel, CEO/ President

5060   Managing Your Health Care
Arthritis Foundation
PO Box 78423
Atlanta, GA 30357-0669   404-237-8771
                                          800-933-7023
                                     FAX: 404-872-0457
                                      help@arthritis.org
                                       www.arthritis.org

John H Klippel, CEO/ President

**5061   Medical Aspects of Disability: A Handbook For The
          Rehabilitation Professional**
Springer Publishing Company
11 West 42nd Street
15th Floor
New York, NY 10036   212-431-4370
                                          877-687-7476
                                     FAX: 212-941-7842
                                     cs@springerpub.com
                                      www.springerpub.com

Ursula Springer, President
Theodore C. Nardin, CEO/Publisher
Jason Roth, VP/Marketing Director
$62.92
744 pages
ISBN 0-826179-71-1

5062   Meeting the Needs of Employees with Disabilities
Resources for Rehabilitation
22 Bonad Road
Ste 19a
Winchester, MA 01890-4330   781-368-9080
                                     FAX: 781-368-9096
                                        orders@rfr.org
                                          www.rfr.org

Susan Greenblatt, Editor
Provides information to help people with disabilities retain or obtain employment. Information on government programs and laws, supported employment, training programs, environmental adaptations and the transition from school to work are included. Chapters on mobility impairment, vision impairment and hearing and speech impairments. *$47.95*
167 pages Biennial
ISBN 0-92971 -13-5

5063   NCD Bulletin
National Council on Disability
1331 F Street Northwest
Suite 850
Washington, DC 20004- 1138   202-272-2004
                                     FAX: 202-272-2022
                                         ncd@ncd.gov
                                          www.ncd.gov

Jeff Rosen, Chairperson
Kamilah Oni Martin-Proctor, Co-Vice Chair
Lynnae Ruttledge, Co-Vice Chair
Reports on the latest issues and news affecting people with disabilities.
2 pages Monthly

**5064   NCDE Survival Strategies for Overseas Living for People
          with Disabilities**
Mobility International USA
132 E Broadway
Suite 343
Eugene, OR 97401   541-343-1284
                                     FAX: 541-343-6812
                                     TTY:541-343-1284
                                  clearinghouse@miusa.org
                                        www.miusa.org

Susan Sygall, Chief Executive Officer
Cindy Lewis, Director, Programs
This book will provide individuals with disabilities information, resources and guidance on pursuing international exchange opportunities. It addresses disability-related aspects of the international exchange process such as choosing a program, applying, preparing for the trip, adjusting to a new country and returning home.

5065   National Hookup
ISC
16 Liberty St
Larkspur, CA 94939-1520   415-924-3549
                                     FAX: 415-927-9556

Russ Bohlke, Manager
Newsletter published by ISC, a national organization of people with physical disabilities. *$6.00*
12-16 pages Quarterly

5066   New Horizons in Sexuality
Accent Books & Products
PO Box 700
Bloomington, IL 61702-700   309-378-2961
                                          800-787-8444
                                     FAX: 309-378-4420
                                       acmtlvng@aol.com

Raymond C Cheever, Publisher
Betty Garee, Editor
This manual helps both males and females progress toward a satisfying post-injury relationship. *$7.95*
50 pages Paperback
ISBN 0-91570 -42-6

5067   New Voices: Self Advocacy By People with Disabilities
Brookline Books
8 Trumbull Rd
Suite B-001
Northampton, MA 01060   413-584-0184
                                          800-666-2665
                                     FAX: 413-584-6184
                                      brbooks@yahoo.com
                                     www.brooklinebooks.com

A collection of original papers, many by self advocates, that vividly illustrate the dynamic, ever-growing self-advocacy movement — persons with disabilities speaking out and seeking better non-institutional living situations, social and political equality and decent jobs at reasonable pay. *$29.95*
274 pages Paperback
ISBN 1-57129 -04-4

5068   North Star Community Services
3420 University Ave
Waterloo, IA 50701-2050   319-236-0901
                                          888-879-1365
                                     FAX: 319-236-3701
                                    jmuller@northstarcs.org
                                      www.northstarcs.org

Mark Witmer, Executive Director
Matt Hinders, Director of Operations & Safety
Bridget Hartmann, Director of Human Resources
North Star Community Services is a rehabilitative services organization with home office in Waterloo, IA and several branch offices in Northeast, Northern and Central Iowa. North Star helps indiviuals with disabilities live and work in their communities. Services include: adult day services, supported community living services, employment services, and case management/service coordination.

5069 Nothing is Impossible: Reflections on a New Life
Ballantine Books
1745 Broadway
10th Floor
New York, NY 10019   212-782-9000
rhkidspublicity@randomhouse.com
www.atrandom.com
Edward Warren, Owner
Reeve offers a uniquely powerful message of hope on topics ranging from the controversial stem cell debate to the mind-body connection he credits with his recent physical improvements. *$6.99*
224 pages
ISBN 0-345470-73-7

5070 Nutritional Desk Reference
Keats Publishing
P.O.Box 876
New Canaan, CT 06840   203-966-8721
800-323-4900

5071 Nutritional Influences on Illness:
Third Line Press
4751 Viviana Dr
Tarzana, CA 91356-5038   818-996-0076
third-line.com
Melvyn R Werbach, Owner
A comprehensive summary of the world's knowledge concerning the relationship between dietary and nutrtional factors and illness. This book does not try to promote any particular school of thought. Instead of the author telling readers his opinion as to what research says, he makes it easy for them to see data for themselves and then form their own opinions.
504 pages
ISBN 0-879835-31-1

5072 Oregon Perspectives
Oregon Council on Developmental Disabilities
540 24th Pl NE
Salem, OR 97301-4517   503-945-9941
800-292-4154
FAX: 503-945-9947
www.ocdd.org
Laura Bronson, Office Manager
Beth Kessler, Planning & Communications Coordi
A quarterly publication from the Oregon Council on Developmental Disabilities.

5073 Organ Transplants: Making the Most of Your Gift of Life
Patient-Centered Guides
1005 Gravenstein Highway North
Sebastopol, CA 95472   707-827-7000
FAX: 707-829-0104
support@oreilly.com
www.oreilly.com
Robert Finn, Author
Over 64,000 people in the US are awaiting an organ transplant. Although transplant surgeries are now fairly routine and can give their recipients the gift of new life, the road to getting a transplant can be long and harrowing. Living with immunosuppressive drugs and strong emotional responses can also be more challenging than families imagine. Medical journalist Robert Finn answers the concerns of these families, with the latest facts about transplantation - as well as the stories behind them. *$5.99*
326 pages Paperback
ISBN 1-565926-34-X

5074 PEAK Parent Center
917 East Moreno Ave.
Suite 140
Colorado Springs, CO 80903   719-531-9400
FAX: 719-531-9452
info@peakparent.org
www.peakparent.org
Michele Williers, Executive Director
Pam Christy, Director, Parent Training & Information
PEAK Parent Center is Colorado's federally-designated Parent Training and Information Center (PTI). As a PTI, PEAK supports and empowers parents, providing them with information and strategies to use when advocating for their children with disabili-

ties. PEAK works one-on-one with families and educators helping them realize new possibilities for children with disabilities by expanding knowledge of special education and offering new strategies for success.
1986

5075 Parallels in Time
MN Governor's Council on Development Disabilities
658 Cedar St
Saint Paul, MN 55155-1603   651-296-4018
877-348-0505
FAX: 651-297-7200
admin.dd@state.mn.us
www.mncdd.org
Colleen Wieck PhD, Executive Director
Parallels in Time traces present attitudes and the treatment of people with disabilities, and supplements the first weekend seesion of Partners in Policymaking. This CD-ROM includes the History of the Parent Movement and the History of the Independent Living Movement, as well as personal stories of self advocates, leaders in the self advocacy movement.

5076 Part of the Team
Easterseals
Ste 1800
230 W Monroe St
Chicago, IL 60606-4851   312-726-6800
FAX: 312-726-1494
Janet D Jamieson, Communications Manager
James Williams Jr, Chief Executive Officer
Designed for employers of all sizes, rehabilitation organizations and all others concerned with the employment of people with disabilities. It addresses managers' concerns and questions about supervising persons with disabilities and can be used as a discussion/team-building tool for employees with and without disabilities. The video recognizes people with disabilities as strong contenders for almost any job. *$15.00*

5077 Partnering with Public Health: Funding& Advocacy Opportunities for CILs and SILCs
Independent Living Research Utilization ILRU
1333 Moursund
Houston, TX 77030-7031   713-520-0232
FAX: 713-520-5785
ilru@ilru.org
ilru.org
Lex Frieden, Director, ILRU
Richard Petty, Co-Director
Laura Rauscher discusses how CILs and SCILs can use funding from the Centers for Disease Control and partnerships with public health agencies to provide innovative programs promoting the health of people with disabilities.
10 pages

5078 Peer Counseling: Roles, Functions, Boundaries
Independent Living Research Utilization ILRU
1333 Moursund
Houston, TX 77030-7031   713-520-0232
FAX: 713-520-5785
ilru@ilru.org
ilru.org
Lex Frieden, Director, ILRU
Richard Petty, Co-Cirector
In this article, the following points were discussed: describing peer support as counseling suggests safeguards and expectations which cannot be provided by nonprofessionals; the purpose of peer counseling is to promote the independent living philosophy and encourage consumers to embrace it; peer counseling cannot and is not intended to help individuals deal with intense emotional stress, whether it is related to their disability or to something else.
10 pages

5079 Peer Mentor Volunteers: Empowering People for Change
Independent Living Research Utilization ILRU
1333 Moursund
Houston, TX 77030-7031   713-520-0232
                                   FAX: 713-520-5785
                                      ilru@ilru.org
                                         ilru.org

Lex Frieden, Director, ILRU
Richard Petty, Co-Director
Arizona Bridge to Independent Living (ABIL) in Phoenix, featured in this issue, is another winner in the innovative CIL program competition.
10 pages

5080 People and Families
New Jersey Council on Developmental Disabilities
20 West State Street, 6th Floor
P.O.Box 700
Trenton, NJ 08625-0700   609-292-3745
                                        800-792-8858
                                   FAX: 609-292-7114
                                   TTY: 609-777-3238
                                      njcdd@njcdd.org
                                        www.njcdd.org

Elaine Buchsbaum, Chairman
Christopher Miller, Vice Chair
Alison M. Lozano, Ph.D, Executive Director
A free magazine for people with disabilities, their families and the public about disability topics such as personal assistance, deinstitutionalization, health care and community living. Published by the New Jersey council on Developmental Disabilities, a federally funded advocacy and policy advisory body. The council has 25 members - 15 consumer/product volunteers and 10 professionals.
48 pages Quarterly

5081 People with Disabilities & Abuse: Implications for Center for Independent Living
Independent Living Research Utilization ILRU
1333 Moursund
P.O.Box 700
Houston, TX 77030-7031   713-520-0232
                                   FAX: 713-520-5785
                                      ilru@ilru.org
                                         ilru.org

Lex Frieden, Director, ILRU
Richard Petty, Co-Director
10 pages

5082 People with Disabilities Who Challenge the System
Brookes Publishing
P.O.Box 10624
Baltimore, MD 21285-0624   410-337-9580
                                        800-638-3775
                                   FAX: 410-337-8539
                             custserv@brookespublishing.com
                                      readplaylearn.com

Paul H. Brooks, Chairman
Jeffrey D. Brookes, President
Melissa A. Behm, Executive Vice President
Helpful forms, tables, and case studies plus an emphasis on self-determination point the way to the development of supports so that people who are deaf-blind, have severe to profound physical and cognitive disabilities, or have serious behavior problems can be fully included in the classroom, workplace, and community. *$34.00*
464 pages Paperback
ISBN 1-55766-29-0

5083 People's Voice
Independence CIL
300 3rd Ave SW
Suite F
Minot, ND 58701-4346   701-839-4724
                                        800-377-5114
                                   FAX: 701-838-1677
                        independencecil@independencecil.org
                                   independencecil.org

Susan Ogurek, Chair
Heather Wittliff, Vice Chair
Scott Burlingame, Executive Director
8 pages Quarterly

5084 Personal Perspectives on Personal Assistance Services
World Institute on Disability
3075 Adeline St.
Suite 155
Berkeley, CA 94703   510-225-6400
                                   FAX: 510-225-0477
                                        wid@wid.org
                                        www.wid.org

Marcie Roth, Executive Director & Chief Executive Officer
Kat Zigmont, Senior Director, Operations & Deputy Director
Reggie Johnson, Senior Director, Marketing & Communications
A collection of personal essays that explores a range of perspectives on Personal Assistance Services. Family issues and PAS concerns for people with various different disabilities, of different ages and as members of minority groups are addressed.

5085 Perspectives
National Assoc of State Directors of DD Services
113 Oronoco St
Alexandria, VA 22314-2015   703-683-4202
                                   FAX: 703-684-1395
                                   dberland@nasddds.org

Nancy Thaler, Executive Director
Provides a concise summary of national policy developments and initiatives affecting persons with devlopmental disabilities and the programs that serve them. From bills pending before Congress, to the growth in Medicaid-funded services, to changes in federal-state Medicaid policies and the shift of responsibility from Washington to the states, keeps readers in tune with the latest national issues shaping publically funded disability services. *$95.00*
Monthly

5086 Place to Live
Accent Books & Products
P.O.Box 700
Bloomington, IL 61702-700   309-378-2961
                                       800-787-8444
                                   FAX: 309-378-4420
                                   acmtlvng@aol.com

Raymond C Cheever, Publisher
Betty Garee, Editor
Many disabled people have found that group housing or accessible apartments are the best alternative to living in a nursing home. These articles tell about some of the alternatives people have found so they can live independently. Just one idea might be the answer for better living for you. *$4.95*
64 pages Paperback
ISBN 0-91570-30-2

5087 Psychological & Social Impact of Disability
Springer Publishing Company
11 West 42nd Street
15th Floor
New York, NY 10036   212-431-4370
                                        877-687-7476
                                   FAX: 212-941-7842
                                      cs@springerpub.com
                                      www.springerpub.com

James C. Costello, Vice President, Journal Publishing
Diana Osborne, Production Manager
Megan Larkin, Managing Editor, Journals
$49.95
488 pages
ISBN 0-826122-13-2

5088 Psychology and Health
Springer Publishing Company
11 West 42nd Street
15th Floor
New York, NY 10036
212-431-4370
877-687-7476
FAX: 212-941-7842
cs@springerpub.com
www.springerpub.com
James C. Costello, Vice President, Journal Publishing
Diana Osborne, Production Manager
Megan Larkin, Managing Editor, Journals
Content of this book spans a wide range of clinical conditions, including somatization disorders, chronic pain, migraine, anxiety and cancer. *$29.95*
256 pages

5089 Psychology of Disability
Springer Publishing Company
11 West 42nd Street,
15th Floor
New York, NY 10036-3915
212-431-4370
877-687-7476
FAX: 212-941-7842
cs@springerpub.com
www.springerpub.com
James C. Costello, Vice President, Journal Publishing
Diana Osborne, Production Manager
Megan Larkin, Managing Editor, Journals
Reactions to the disabled. *$27.95*
288 pages
ISBN 0-82613-40-1

5090 Quality of Life for Persons with Disabilities
Brookline Books
8 Trumbull Road
Suite B-001
Northampton, MA 01060
413-584-0184
800-666-2665
FAX: 413-584-6184
brbooks@yahoo.com
www.brooklinebooks.com
James C. Costello, Vice President, Journal Publishing
Quality of life generally refers to a person's subjective experience of his or her life and focuses attention on how the individual with a disabling condition experiences the world. This book presents a comprehensive and international view of this concept as applied to a broad range of settings in which persons with disabilities live, work and play. *$35.00*
Paperback
ISBN 0-91479-92-1

5091 REACHing Out Newsletter
REACH of Dallas Resource on Independent Living
8625 King George
Suite 210
Dallas, TX 75235-2286
214-630-4796
FAX: 214-630-6390
TTY: 214-630-5995
reachdallas@reachcils.org
reachcils.org
Charlotte A. Stewart, Executive Director
Quarterly newsletter from REACH of Dallas Resource Center on Independent Living.
16 pages Quarterly

5092 RTC Connection
Research and Training Center
University of Wisconsin Stou
Menomonie, WI 54751
715-232-2236
FAX: 715-232-2251
menz@uwstout.edu
Julie Larson, Program Assistant
Bi-annual reports on disability and rehabilitation research and policy topics.
Newsletter

5093 Relaxation: A Comprehensive Manual for Adults and Children with Special Needs
Research Press
2612 N. Mattis Ave.
P.O.Box 7886
Champaign, IL 61822-9177
217-352-3273
800-519-2707
FAX: 217-352-1221
orders@researchpress.com
www.researchpress.com
This unique contribution to the field of relaxation training presents: self relaxation techniques designed for adults, methods for teaching relaxation to adults and older children, and procedures for teaching relaxation to young children and children with developmental disabilities. The clear, concise text is supplemented by over 100 helpful illustrations. *$19.95*
Paperback
ISBN 0-878221-86-8

5094 Resources for People with Disabilities and Chronic Conditions
Resources for Rehabilitation
Ste 19a
33 Bedford St
Lexington, MA 02420-4330
781-890-6371
FAX: 781-861-7517
Susan Greenblatt
A comprehensive resource directory that helps people with disabilities and chronic conditions achieve their maximum level of independence. Chapters on spinal cord injuries, low back pain, diabetes, hearing and speech impairments, epilepsy, multiple sclerosis. Describes organizations, products and publications. *$49.95*
215 pages Biennial
ISBN 0-92971-12-7

5095 Role Portrayal and Stereotyping on Television
Greenwood Publishing Group
130 Cremona Drive
P O Box 1911
Santa Barbara, CA 93117-4208
203-226-3571
800-368-6868
805-968-1911
FAX: 866-270-3856
customerservice@abc-clio.com
www.abc-clio.com
An annotated bibliography of studies relating to women, minorities, aging, health and handicaps.
214 pages $55 - $59.95
ISBN 0-313248-55-9

5096 Screening in Chronic Disease
Oxford University Press
2001 Evans Rd
Cary, NC 27513-2009
800-445-9714
877-773-4325
FAX: 919-677-1303
custserv.us@oup.com
global.oup.com
Thomas Carty, Senior Vice President
Early detection, or screening, is a common strategy for controlling chronic disease, but little information has been available to help determine which screening procedures are worthwhile, until this textbook. *$42.50*
256 pages

5097 Sexual Adjustment
Accent Books & Products
P.O.Box 700
Bloomington, IL 61702-700
309-378-2961
800-787-8444
FAX: 309-378-4420
acmtlvng@aol.com
Raymond C Cheever, Publisher
Betty Garee, Editor
Essential information concerning sexual adjustment for the paraplegic male. *$4.95*
73 pages Paperback
ISBN 0-19570-00-0

5098 Sexuality and Disabilities: A Guide for Human Service Practitioners
Haworth Press
2&4 Park Square
Abingdon, FL 33487-1503 561-994-0555
FAX: 561-241-7856
orders@taylorandfrancis.com
This book addresses persons with physical, sensory, intellectual and cognitive disabilities and their concerns in the areas of intimacy, family issues, sexuality and sexual functioning. *$74.95*
159 pages Hardcover
ISBN 1-560243-75-9

5099 Sickened: The Memoir of a Muchausen by Proxy Childhood
Bantam Books
1745 Broadway
10th Floor
New York, NY 10019-4039 212-782-9000
FAX: 212-572-6066
crownpublicity@randomhouse.com
www.randomhouse.com
From early childhood, Julie Gregory was continually X-rayed, medicated, and operated on — in the vain pursuit of an illness that was created in her mother's mind. Munchausen by proxy (MBP) in which the caretaker — almost always the mother — invents or induces symptoms in her child because she craves the attention of medical professionals. *$24.95*
256 pages Hardcover
ISBN 0-553803-07-7

5100 Socialization Games for Persons with Disabilities
Charles C. Thomas
2600 S First St
Springfield, IL 62704-4730 217-789-8980
800-258-8980
FAX: 217-789-9130
books@ccthomas.com
www.ccthomas.com

Michael P. Thomas, President
This text will assist those who want to teach severely multiple disabled students by providing information on: general principles of intervention and classroom organization; managing the behavior of students; physically managing students and using adaptive equipment; teaching eating skills; teaching toileting, dressing, and hygiene skills; teaching cognition, communication, and socialization skills; teaching independent living skills; and teaching infants and preschool students. *$38.95*
176 pages Paperback
ISBN 0-398067-46-5

5101 Sometimes You Just Want to Feel Like a Human Being
Brookes Publishing
P.O.Box 10624
Baltimore, MD 21285-0624 410-337-9580
800-638-3775
FAX: 410-337-8539
custserv@brookespublishing.com
readplaylearn.com
Paul Brooks, Owner
Case studies of empowering psychotherapy with people with disabilities. This text reveals how counseling can be beneficial to individuals with disabilities of all kinds, including autism, developmental disabilities, sensory impairment, cerebral palsy, or HIV infection. *$26.95*
272 pages Paperback
ISBN 1-55766 -96-0

5102 South Carolina Assistive Technology Program
8301 Farrow Road
University Center for Excellence
Columbia, SC 29203-2920 803-935-5263
800-915-4522
FAX: 803-935-5342
carol.page@uscmed.sc.edu
www.sc.edu/scatp/

Carol Page, Ph.D, Program Director
Mary r Alice Bechtle, Program Coordinator
Janet Jendron, Program Coordinator

The South Carolina Assistive Technology Program (SCATP) is a federally funded program concerned with getting technology into the hands of people with disabilities so that they might live, work, learn and be a more independent part of the community. We provide an equipment loan and demonstration program, an on-line equipment exchange program, training, technical assistance, publications, an interactive CDROM (SC Curriculum Access through AT), an information listserv and work with various state com
7-8 pages Bi-annually

5103 Space Coast CIL News
Space Coast Center for Independent Living
571 Haverty Court,
Suite W
Rockledge, FL 32955-2566 321-633-6011
FAX: 321-633-6472
TTY:321-784-9008
www.sccil.net
Michael Lavoie, President
Howard Fetes, Vice-President
Non-profit organization that provides services which enable people with disabilities to live as independently as possible.
12 pages Quarterly

5104 Special Needs Trust Handbook
Aspen Publishers
7th Fl
76 9th Ave
New York, NY 10011-4962 301-644-3599
800-638-8437
www.aspenpublishers.com
Bob Lemmond, President and CEO
Gustavo Dobles, Vice President and Chief Content Officer
Susan Pikitch, Vice President and Chief Financial Officer
The Special Needs Trusts Handbook is the single-volume, comprehensive resource that provides information on how to handle the complex requirements of drafting and administering trusts for clients who are mentally or physically disabled, or who wish to provide for others with disabilities. *$245.00*
900 pages
ISBN 0-735572-88-7

5105 Special Siblings: Growing Up With Someone with A Disability
Brookes Publishing
P.O.Box 10624
Baltimore, MD 21285-0624 410-337-9580
800-638-3775
FAX: 410-337-8539
custserv@brookespublishing.com
readplaylearn.com
Paul Brooks, Owner
The author reveals what she experienced as the sister of a man with cerebral palsy and developmental disability — and shares what others have learned about being and having a special sibling. Weaving a lifetime of memories and reflections with relevant research and interviews with more than 100 other siblings and experts, McHugh explores a spectrum of feelings — from anger and guilt to love and pride — and helps readers understand the issues siblings may encounter. *$21.95*
256 pages Paperback
ISBN 1-557666-07-5

5106 TERI
251 Airport Rd
Oceanside, CA 92058-1321 760-721-1706
teriinc.org
Cheryl Kilmer, CEO & Founder
William E. Mara, Chief Operating Officer
Krysti DeZonia, Ed.D, Director of Education & Research
A private, nonprofit corporation which has been developing and operating programs for individuals with developmental disabilities since 1980. Offers staff training videos, staff training tools and technique manuals.

5107   **That All May Worship: An Interfaith Welcome to People with Disabilities**
American Association of People with Disabilities
2020 Pennsylvania Ave.
Mailbox 263
Washington, DC 20006   202-521-4316
800-840-8844
communications@aapd.com
www.aapd.com/publications
Maria Town, President & Chief Executive Officer
Jasmin Bailey, Operations Director
Christine Liao, Programs Director
An interfaith handbook to assist congregations in welcoming people with disabilities to promote acceptance and full participation.

5108   **The Ultimate Guide to Sex and Disability**
Read How You Want Large Print Books

800-797-9277
support@readhowyouwant.com
www.readhowyouwant.com
Miriam Kaufman, Author
For everyone, men and women of all ages and sexual identities, The Ultimate Guide to Sex and Disability covers the span of disabilities - from chronic fatigue and back pain to spinal cord injury, multiple sclerosis, cystic fibrosis, cerebral palsy, and many others.

5109   **To Live with Grace and Dignity**
LRP Publications

Lydia Gans, Author
This book combines photographs and essays to allow the reader to enter some of the real day to day relationships that develop between individuals with disabilities and their personal assistants. The individuals included in this book represent a wide range of ages, disabilities and cultural backgrounds.
72 pages Paperback
ISBN 0-934753-85-7

5110   **Touch/Ability Connects People with Disabilities & Alternative Health Care Pract.**
Independent Living Research Utilization ILRU
1333 Moursund
Houston, TX 77030-7031   713-520-0232
FAX: 713-520-5785
ilru@ilru.org
ilru.org
Lex Frieden, Director, ILRU
Richard Petty, Co-Director
The people at DIRECT center for Independence and Touch/Ability in Tuscon, Arizona, have collaborated to develop a wellness program that makes alternative health care choices available to people with disabilities. The Touch/Ability Wellness program was selected as one of last year's winners in the Innovative CILs competition because of this outcome of increased options open to people with disabilities.
10 pages

5111   **US Role in International Disability Activities: A History**
World Institute on Disability
3075 Adeline St.
Suite 155
Berkeley, CA 94703   510-225-6400
FAX: 510-225-0477
wid@wid.org
www.wid.org
Marcie Roth, Executive Director & Chief Executive Officer
Kat Zigmont, Senior Director, Operations & Deputy Director
Reggie Johnson, Senior Director, Marketing & Communications
This study serves as an introduction to US involvement in the field of international rehabilitation and disability.

5112   **Understanding and Accommodating Physical Disabilities: Desk Reference**
Greenwood Publishing Group
130 Cremona Drive
P O Box 1911
Santa Barbara, CA 93117- 4208   203-226-3571
800-368-6868
805-968-1911
FAX: 866-270-3856
customerservice@abc-clio.com
www.abc-clio.com
Medical conditions that qualify as disabilities under the American's with Disabilities Act are explained in non-medical terminology. Hardcover.
200 pages $52.95 - $55
ISBN 0-899308-14-7

5113   **Vestibular Disorders Association**
Vestibular Disorders Association
5018 NE 15th Ave.
P.O. Box 13305
Portland, OR 97211   503-229-7705
800-837-8428
FAX: 503-229-8064
info@vestibular.org
www.vestibular.org
Cynthia Ryan, MBA, Executive Director
Tony Staser, Development Director
Kerrie Denner, Outreach Coordinator
The mission of the Vestibular Disorders Association is to serve people with vestibular disorders by providing access to information, offering a support network, and elevating awareness of the challenges associated with these disorders. They also aim to support and empower vestibular patients on their journey back to balance. *$15.00*
ISBN 0-963261-15-0

5114   **Visions & Values**
Idaho Council on Developmental Disabilities
650 W. State St., Room 100
P. O. Box 83720
Boise, ID 83720-5840   208-332-1824
800-544-2433
FAX: 208-334-2307
C. L. Butch Otter, Governor
A quarterly publication from the Idaho Council on Developmental Disabilities.

5115   **Weiner's Herbal**
Quantum Books
355 Middlesex Avenue
Wilmington, MA 01887-1406   978-988-2470
FAX: 617-577-7282
www.quantumbooks.com
William Szabo, Owner
A-Z index covering all aspects of herbs.
Paperback
ISBN 0-812825-86-1

5116   **When the Brain Goes Wrong**
Fanlight Productions
32 Court Street,
21st Floor
Brooklyn, NY 11201-1731   718-488-8900
800-876-1710
FAX: 718-488-8642
info@fanlight.com
www.fanlight.com
Ben Achtenberg, Owner
Nicole Johnson, Publicity Coordinator
Anthony Sweeney, Marketing Director
An extraordinary and provocative series of seven short films which profile individuals with a range of brian dysfunctions. The seven brief segments focus on schizophrenia, manic depression, epilepsy, head injury, headaches and addiction. In addition to the personal stories, the segments include interviews with physicians who speak briefly about what is known about the disorders and treatment. #131 *$245.00*
ISBN 1-572951-31-1

5117 Women with Physical Disabilities: Achieving & Maintaining Health & Well-Being
Spina Bifida Association of America
1600 Wilson Blvd.
Suite 800
Arlington, VA 22209-4226　　　　　202-944-3285
800-621-3141
FAX: 202-944-3295
sbaa@sbaa.org
www.spinabifidaassociation.org

Ana Ximenes, Chair
Sara Struwe, President & CEO
Cindy Brownstein, CEO
Introduces the critical concept of womens health in the context of physical disabilities. *$42.00*

5118 Work in the Context of Disability Culture
Independent Living Research Utilization ILRU
1333 Moursund
Houston, TX 77030-7031　　　　　713-520-0232
FAX: 713-520-5785
ilru@ilru.org
ilru.org

Lex Frieden, Director, ILRU
Richard Petty, Co-Director
Another winner in the innovative CIL competition-Steve Brown describes the Talking Books Program of Southeast Alaska Independent Living, discussing their efforts to record the oral history and life experiences of people with disabilities in the larger context of the disability culture.
10 pages

5119 Your Role in Inclusion Theatre
Houston, TX　　　　　713-202-8840
Inclusiontheater@gmail.com

Deborah E. Nowinski, Author/Inclusion Specialist
A guidebook for educators who wish to create a successful theatre environment for individuals of all abilities. The book also includes stories, tips, and games. *$19.95*
192 pages
ISBN 1-517357-49-8

Parenting: General

5120 AEPS Family Report: Birth to Three Years
Brookes Publishing
P.O. Box 10624
Baltimore, MD 21285-0624　　　　　410-337-9580
800-638-3775
FAX: 410-337-8539
custserv@brookespublishing.com
www.brookespublishing.com

Diane Bricker, Author
Betty Capt, Author
JoAnn Johnson, Author
This Family Report was developed for use in conjunction with the AEPSr for children birth to 3 years to obtain information from parents and other caregivers about their children's skills and abilities across major areas of development. Available in packages of 10.
28 pages Saddle-stitched

5121 AEPS Family Report: For Children Ages Three to Six
Brookes Publishing
P.O.Box 10624
Baltimore, MD 21285-0624　　　　　410-337-9580
800-638-3775
FAX: 410-337-8539
custserv@brookespublishing.com
www.brookespublishing.com

Diane Bricker, Author
Betty Capt, Author
JoAnn Johnson, Author
This is a 64-item questionnaire that asks parents to rank their child's abilities on specific skills. In packages of 10 paperback.
28 pages Saddle-stiched

5122 Adapted Physical Activity
Human Kinetics
1607 N Market St
P.O.Box 5076
Champaign, IL 61820-5076　　　　　800-747-4457
FAX: 217-351-1549
info@hkusa.com
www.humankinetics.com
Human Kinetics produces a variety of resources for adapted physical education practitioners, including books on activities, a research journal and higher education references.

5123 Assistive Technology for Parents with Disabilities Handbook
Idaho Assistive Technology Project
University of Idaho
1187 Alturas Dr.
Moscow, ID 83843- 2268　　　　　208-885-3557
800-432-8324
FAX: 208-885-6102
idahoat@uidaho.edu
www.idahoat.org
handbook providing resources and information on assistive technology for parents with disabilities.

5124 Babyface: A Story of Heart and Bones
Penguin Books USA
375 Hudson St
New York, NY 10014　　　　　212-366-2000
consumerservices@penguinrandomhouse.com
www.penguin.com

Jeanne McDermott, Author
A must read for families that seek insight into coping with a chronic condition. Many useful resources provided.
288 pages Paperback

5125 Backyards and Butterflies: Ways to Include Children with Disabilities in Outdoor Activities
Brookline Books
8 Trumbull Rd
Ste B-001
Northampton, MA 01060　　　　　413-584-0184
800-666-2665
FAX: 413-584-6184
brbooks@yahoo.com
www.brooklinebks.com

Doreen Greenstein, Author
Suzanne Bloom, Author
An illustrated book with dozens of imaginative ways parents can include children with physical disabilities in outdoor activities. Offers clear concise, how-to directions for constructing homemade toys, utensils, and other items that can be enjoyed outside safely and comfortably.
72 pages Paperback

5126 Beyond Tears: Living After Losing a Child
St. Martin's Griffin (Macmillan Publishers)
75 Varick St
New York, NY 10013　　　　　212-226-7521
press.inquiries@macmillan.com
us.macmillan.com/smp

Ellen Mitchell, Author
Meant to comfort and give direction to bereaved parents, Beyond Tears is written by nine mothers who have each lost a child. This revised edition includes a new chapter written from the perspective of surviving siblings. The death of a child is that unimaginable loss no parent ever expects to face. In this book, nine mothers share their individual stories of how to survive in the darkest hour.

5127 Broken Dolls: Gathering the Pieces: Caringfor Chronically Ill Children
St. Paul Press

Jennifer Travis Cox, Author
Told from the point of view of the author, this book tracks the challenges faced by parents and caregivers of chronically ill-children - both in terms of medical care and emotional impact. It offers advice based on the author's own experiences caring for her

child, as well as insights from other families who have gone through the same experience.
164 pages Paperback

5128 **Building the Healing Partnership: Parents, Professionals and Children**
Brookline Books
8 Trumbull Road
Suite B-001
Northampton, MA 01060
413-584-0184
800-666-2665
FAX: 413-584-6184
brbooks@yahoo.com
www.brooklinebooks.com
Successful programs understand that the disabled child's needs must be considered in the context of a family. This book was specifically written for practitioner's who must work with families but who have insufficient training in family systems assessment and intervention. It is a valuable blend of theory and practice with pointers for applying the principles. *$24.95*
Paperback
ISBN 0-91479-63-8

5129 **Children with Disabilities**
Brookes Publishing
P.O.Box 10624
Baltimore, MD 21285-0624
410-337-9580
800-638-3775
FAX: 410-337-8539
custserv@brookespublishing.com
www.brookespublishing.com
Mark L Batshaw MD, Editor
Paul Brooks, Owner
Lauren Rohe, Regional Sales Consultant
Extensive coverage of genetics, heredity, pre- and postnatal development, specific disabilities, family roles, and intervention. Features chapters on substance abuse, HIV and AIDS, Down syndrome, fragile X syndrome, behavior management, transitions to adulthood, and health care in the 21st century. Also reveals the causes of many conditions that can lead to developmental disabilities. *$69.95*
912 pages Hardcover
ISBN 1-557665-81-8

5130 **Conditional Love: Parents' Attitudes Toward Handicapped Children**
Greenwood Publishing Group
130 Cremona Drive
P O Box 1911
Santa Barbara, CA 93117- 4208
203-226-3571
800-368-6868
805-968-1911
FAX: 866-270-3856
customerservice@abc-clio.com
www.abc-clio.com
Offers parents information on understanding disabled children and mainstreaming them into their normal family life. *$49.95*
312 pages
ISBN 0-89789-24-7

5131 **Coordinacion De Servicios Centrado En La Familia**
Brookline Books
8 Trumbull Road
Suite B-001
Northampton, MA 01060
413-584-0184
800-666-2665
FAX: 413-584-6184
brbooks@yahoo.com
www.brooklinebooks.com
This book, translated into Spanish from the English original, is designed to orient and educate parents about issues of service coordination, to assist families in caring for an infant or toddler with developmental delays or disabilities. *$7.00*
34 pages Paperback
ISBN 0-91479-90-5

5132 **Developing Personal Safety Skills in Children with Disabilities**
Brookes Publishing
P.O.Box 10624
Baltimore, MD 21285-0624
410-337-9580
800-638-3775
FAX: 410-337-8539
custserv@brookespublishing.com
readplaylearn.com
Paul Brooks, Owner
A guide for teachers, parents, and caregivers, this volume explores the issue of personal safety for children with disabilities and offers strategies for empowering and protecting them at home and in school. Recognizing that children with disabilities are vulnerable to abuse, this work explores why children with disabilities need personal safety skills, offers, curriculum ideas and exercises, and advocates the development of self-esteem and assertiveness so that children can protect themselves. *$34.00*
220 pages Paperback
ISBN 1-557661-84-7

5133 **Developmental Disabilities in Infancy and Childhood**
Brookes Publishing
P.O.Box 10624
Baltimore, MD 21285-0624
410-767-6100
800-638-3775
FAX: 410-767-5850
custserv@brookespublishing.com
readplaylearn.com
Paul Brooks, Owner
This two volume set explores advances in assessment and treatment, retains a clinical focus, and incorporates recent developments in research and theory. Can be purchased individually or as a set (Vol. 1: Neurodevelopmental Diagnosis and Treatment Vol. 2: The Spectrum of Developmental Disabilities). *$210.00*
Hardcover
ISBN 1-55766O-CA-P

5134 **Dictionary of Developmental Disabilities Terminology**
Brookes Publishing
P.O.Box 10624
Baltimore, MD 21285-0624
410-337-9580
800-638-3775
FAX: 410-337-8539
custserv@brookespublishing.com
readplaylearn.com
Paul Brooks, Owner
Answers thousands of questions for medical or human services professionals, parents or advocates of children with disabilities, or students preparing for their careers. Provides thorough explanations of the most common terms associated with disabilities. *$55.95*
368 pages Hardcover
ISBN 1-557662-45-2

5135 **Encyclopedia of Genetic Disorders & Birth Defects**
Facts on File
132 W 31st St
17th Floor
New York, NY 10001-3406
800-322-8755
FAX: 800-678-3633
custserv@factsonfile.com
www.infobasepublishing.com/
Mark Donnell, President
Layperson-accessible entries on genetic terminology and genetically-influenced conditions. *$71.50*
474 pages
ISBN 0-816038-09-0

5136 **Exceptional Parent Magazine**
Psy-Ed Corporation
416 Main Street
Johnstown, PA 15901-2032
814-361-3860
877-372-7368
FAX: 814-361-3861
www.eparent.com
Vanessa B Ira, Contributing Writer / Editor
Joseph M. Valenzano, Jr., President, CEO & Publisher
Rick Rader, MD, Editor-in-Chief

Magazine that provides information, support, ideas, encouragement, and outreach for parents and families of children with disabilities and the professionals who work with them. *$39.95*
85 pages Monthly

5137   Face of Inclusion
Special Needs Project
Ste H
324 State St
Santa Barbara, CA 93101-2364   805-962-8087
                                                 800-333-6867
                                        FAX: 805-962-5087
                                        eplibrary@aol.com
                                        www.eplibrary.com

Hod Gray, Owner
A unique and moving parents' perspective of inclusion for administrators, teachers, and parents of children with disabilities. *$99.00*

5138   Families Magazine
New Jersey Developmental Disabilities Council
20 West State Street, 6th Floor
P.O.Box 700
Trenton, NJ 08625-0700   609-292-3745
                                                 800-792-8858
                                        FAX: 609-292-7114
                                        TTY: 609-777-3238
                                        njcdd@njcdd.org
                                        www.njddc.org

Elaine Buchsbaum, Chairman
Christopher Miller, Vice Chair
Alison M. Lozano, Ph.D, Executive Director
Quarterly magazine for people with disabilities, their families and the public, features family profiles, news, columns and the New Jersey Family support councils newsletter.
Quarterly

5139   Families, Illness & Disability
Through the Looking Glass
3075 Adeline St
Ste. 120
Berkeley, CA 94703-2212   510-848-1112
                                                 800-644-2666
                                        FAX: 510-848-4445
                                        TTY: 510-848-1005
                                        tlg@lookingglass.org
                                        www.lookingglass.org

Maureen Block, J.D., Co-Founder
Karen Fessel, Ph.D., Executive Director
$35.00
320 pages

5140   Family Interventions Throughout Disability
Springer Publishing Company
11 West 42nd Street,
15th Floor
New York, NY 10036-3915   212-431-4370
                                                 877-687-7476
                                        FAX: 212-941-7842
                                        cs@springerpub.com
                                        www.springerpub.com

Theodore C Nardin, Chief Executive Officer
James C. Costello, Vice President, Journal Publishing
Diana Osborne, Production Manager
Family attitudes throughout chronic illness and disability. *$31.95*
320 pages
ISBN 0-82615-80-4

5141   Family-Centered Service Coordination: A Manual for Parents
Brookline Books
8 Trumbull Road
Suite B-001
Northampton, MA 01060   413-584-0184
                                                 800-666-2665
                                        FAX: 413-584-6184
                                        brbooks@yahoo.com
                                        www.brooklinebooks.com

A manual designed to orient and educate parents about issues of service coordination, to assist families in caring for an infant or toddler with developmental delays or disabilities. *$7.00*
34 pages Paperback
ISBN 0-91479-90-5

5142   Handbook About Care in the Home
AARP Fulfillment
601 E St NW
Washington, DC 20049-1   202-434-2277
                                                 888-687-2277
                                        TTY: 877-434-7598
                                        member@aarp.org
                                        www.aarp.org

Offers valuable information for the disabled.
24 pages

5143   LifeLines
Disabled & Alone/Life Services for the Handicapped
1441 Broadway
23rd Floor
New York, NY 10018-2326   212-532-6740
                                                 800-995-0066
                                        FAX: 212-532-6740
                                        info@disabledandalone.org
                            www.disabledandalone.org/lifelines.html

Leslie D. Park, Chair
Rex L. Davidson, Vice President
Lee Alan Ackerman, Executive Director
Newsletter providing current and valuable information about lifetime care and planning for persons with disabilities and their families and the organizations serving them. Free upon request.
4-10 pages Biannual

5144   Living with a Brother or Sister with Special Needs: A Book for Sibs
Sibling Support Project
6512 23rd Ave NW
Ste 322
Seattle, WA 98117   206-297-6368
                                        info@siblingsupport.org
                                        www.siblingsupport.org

Don Meyer, Author
Patricia Vadasy, Author
Living with a Brother or Sister with Special Needs focuses on the intensity of emotions that brothers and sisters experience when they have a sibling with special needs, and the hard questions they ask. It talks about the good and not-so-good parts of having a brother or sister who has special needs, and offers suggestions for how to make life easier for everyone in the family.
144 pages Paperback

5145   Loving & Letting Go
Centering Corporation
7230 Maple Street
Omaha, NE 68134-5064   402-553-1200
                                                 866-218-0101
                                        FAX: 402-533-0507
                                        j1200@aol.com
                                        www.centering.org

Joy Johnson, Founder
Dr. Marvin Johnson, co-Founder
For parents who decide to turn away from aggressive medical intervention for their critically ill newborn. *$5.95*
48 pages Paperback

5146   Mobility Training for People with Disabilities
Charles C. Thomas
2600 S First St
Springfield, IL 62704-4730   217-789-8980
                                                 800-258-8980
                                        FAX: 217-789-9130
                                        books@ccthomas.com
                                        www.ccthomas.com

Michael P. Thomas, President

5147 Mother to Be
Through the Looking Glass
3075 Adeline St
Ste. 120
Berkeley, CA 94703-2212

510-848-1112
800-644-2666
FAX: 510-848-4445
TTY: 510-848-1005
tlg@lookingglass.org
www.lookingglass.org

Maureen Block, J.D., Co-Founder
Karen Fessel, Ph.D., Executive Director
Guide to pregnancy and birth for women with disabilities. *$34.00*
410 pages

5148 New Language of Toys: Teaching Communication Skills to Children with Special Needs
Spina Bifida Association of America
1600 Wilson Blvd.
Suite 800
Arlington, VA 22209-4226

202-944-3285
800-621-3141
FAX: 202-944-3295
sbaa@sbaa.org
www.spinabifidaassociation.org

Ana Ximenes, Chair
Sara Struwe, President & CEO
Cindy Brownstein, CEO
A guide for parents and teachers and a reader-friendly resource guide that provides a wealth of information on how play activities affect a child's language development and where to get the toys and materials to use in these activities. *$19.00*

5149 Newsline
Federation for Children with Special Needs
529 Main St.
Suite 1M3
Boston, MA 02129

617-236-7210
800-331-0688
FAX: 617-241-0330
fcsninfo@fcsn.org
www.fcsn.org

Pam Nourse, Executive Director
Offers information and resources for families of children with disabilities, as well as event announcements, project updates, news and more.
Quarterly

5150 On the Road to Autonomy: Promoting Self-Competence in Children & Youth with Disabilities
Brookes Publishing
P.O.Box 10624
Baltimore, MD 21285-0624

410-337-9580
800-638-3775
FAX: 410-337-8539
custserv@brookespublishing.com
readplaylearn.com

Paul Brooks, Owner
This book provides detailed conceptual, practical, and personal information regarding the promotion of self-esteem, self-determination, and coping skills among children and youth with and without disabilities. *$48.00*
432 pages Paperback
ISBN 1-55766-35-5

5151 Pain Erasure
M Evans and Company
216 E 49th St
New York, NY 10017-1546

212-979-0880
FAX: 212-486-4544

Mary Evans, Owner
This book explains Bonnie Prudden's method for pain relief using myotherapy, a method hailed by doctors and patients.
ISBN 0-345331-02-8

5152 Parent Centers and Independent Living Centers: Collectively We're Stronger
Independent Living Research Utilization ILRU
1333 Moursund
Houston, TX 77030-7031

713-520-0232
FAX: 713-520-5785
ilru@ilru.org
ilru.org

Lex Frieden, Director, ILRU
Richard Petty, Co-Director
This article describes several examples of effective working relationships of PTIs and CILs. The examples highlight how parent and consumer organizations have identified complimentary strengths and formed partnerships to better support children with disabilities and their families. These partnerships can also be a very important way of involving youth in the disability movement so they may become leaders of tomorrow.
10 pages

5153 Parent-Child Interaction and Developmental Disabilities
Greenwood Publishing Group
130 Cremona Drive
P O Box 1911
Santa Barbara, CA 93117

800-368-6868
805-968-1911
FAX: 866-270-3856
customerservice@abc-clio.com
www.abc-clio.com

This volume brings together the original papers by international scholars and practitioners on the question of the effects of parent interaction with developmentally disabled children. *$65.00-$69.50.*
395 pages Hardcover
ISBN 0-275928-35-7

5154 Parenting
Accent Books & Products
P.O.Box 700
Bloomington, IL 61702-700

309-378-2961
800-787-8444
FAX: 309-378-4420
acmtlvng@aol.com

Raymond C Cheever, Publisher
Betty Garee, Editor
Experienced parents (who are disabled) discuss: raising children from infant to teens, balancing career and motherhood, discipline methods and more when both parents are disabled. *$7.95*
83 pages
ISBN 0-91570-26-4

5155 Parenting with a Disability
Through the Looking Glass
3075 Adeline St
Ste. 120
Berkeley, CA 94703-2212

510-848-1112
800-644-2666
FAX: 510-848-4445
TTY: 510-848-1005
tlg@lookingglass.org
www.lookingglass.org

Maureen Block, J.D., Board President
Rusty Hendlin, M.A., LMFT, Director of Medi-Cal Services
Thomas Spalding, Board Treasurer
International newsletter. Available in braille, large print or cassette.
3 per year

5156 Perspectives on a Parent Movement
Brookline Books
8 Trumbull Rd
Suite B-001
Northampton, MA 1060-4533

413-584-0184
800-666-2665
FAX: 413-584-6184
brbooks@yahoo.com
www.brooklinebooks.com

This book captures Rosemary Dybwad's truly innovative wisdom and pioneering for people with intellectual limitations in these previously unpublished essays and speeches. *$17.95*
Paperback
ISBN 0-91479 -74-3

5157   Sexuality and the Developmentally Handicapped
Edwin Mellen Press
P.O.Box 450
Lewiston, NY 14092-450   716-754-2266
                                    FAX: 716-754-4056
                                    jrupnow@mellenpress.com
                                    mellenpress.com

Herbert Richardson, Owner
Presents the knowledge, attitudes, and skills pertinent to responding to the sexual problems of developmentally handicapped persons, their families and communities. Details fully documented cases, issues concerning the law, and resource materials available. *$89.95*
245 pages Hardcover
ISBN 0-88946 -32-5

5158   Shattered Dreams-Lonely Choices: Birth Parents of Babies with Disabilities
Greenwood Publishing Group
130 Cremona Drive
Santa Barbara, CA 93117-4208   203-226-3571
                                    800-368-6868
                                    805-968-1911
                                    FAX: 866-270-3856
                                    customerservice@abc-clio.com
                                    www.abc-clio.com
Written by a mother who, without warning, gave birth to a boy with Down Syndrome, this book is meant to help parents through the initial shock and the realization that they are not able to care for their child. $29.95-$35.00. *$29.95*
208 pages Hardcover
ISBN 0-897892-86-0

5159   Since Owen, A Parent-to-Parent Guide for Care of the Disabled Child
Special Needs Project
324 State Street
Suite H
Santa Barbara, CA 93101-2364   818-718-9900
                                    800-333-6867
                                    FAX: 818-349-2027
                                    editor@specialneeds.com
                                    www.specialneeds.com

Hod Gray, Owner
Against the background of his experience as the parent of a severely disabled young man, Callahan writes conscientiously to other parents. *$16.95*
486 pages

5160   Sleep Better! A Guide to Improving Sleep for Children with Special Needs
Brookes Publishing
P.O.Box 10624
Baltimore, MD 21285-624   410-337-9580
                                    800-638-3775
                                    FAX: 410-337-8539
                                    custserv@brookespublishing.com
                                    readplaylearn.com

Paul Brooks, Owner
This book offers step-by-step, how to instructions for helping children with disabilities get the rest they need. For problems ranging from bedtime tantrums to night waking, parents and caregivers will find a variety of widely tested and easy-to-implement techniques that have already helped hundreds of children with special needs. *$21.95*
288 pages Paperback
ISBN 1-55766 -15-7

5161   Something's Wrong with My Child!
Charles C. Thomas
2600 S First St
Springfield, IL 62704-4730   217-789-8980
                                    800-258-8980
                                    FAX: 217-789-9130
                                    books@ccthomas.com
                                    www.ccthomas.com

Michael P. Thomas, President
This text provides professionals and parents with the opportunity to gain insights into a family that has benefited positively and constructively from the presence of a member with a disability. The author presents a compilation of easy-to-read material that's based on real-life experiences. *$39.95*
234 pages Paperback 1998
ISBN 0-398068-99-8

5162   Sometimes I Get All Scribbly
Exceptional Parent Library
P.O.Box 1807
Englewood Cliffs, NJ 7632-1207   201-947-6000
                                    800-535-1910
                                    FAX: 201-947-9376
                                    eplibrary@aol.com
                                    www.eplibrary.com
Clinical, educational and emotional information from the point of view of a parent. *$16.00*

5163   Son-Rise: The Miracle Continues
2080 South Undermountain Road
Sheffield, MA 01257-9643   413-229-2100
                                    877-766-7473
                                    FAX: 413-229-3202
                                    sonrise@option.org
                                    www.son-rise.org

Barry Neil Kaufman, Co-Founder/ Co-Originator/Senior Teacher/Trainer
Samahria Lyte Kaufman, Co-Founder/ Co-Originator/Senior Teacher/Trainer
Bryn Hogan, ATCA Senior Staff
Documents Raun Kaufman's astonishing development from a lifeless, autistic child into a highly verbal, lovable youngster with no traces of his former condition. Details Raun's extraordinary progress from the age of four into young adulthood, also shares moving accounts of five families that successfully used the Son-Rise Program to reach their own special children.
372 pages
ISBN 0-915811-53-7

5164   Special Kids Need Special Parents: A Resource for Parents of Children With Special Needs
Berkley Publishing Group
375 Hudson Street
New York, NY 10014-3657   212-366-2372
                                    FAX: 212-366-2933
                                    ecommerce@us.penguingroup.com
                                    www.us.penguingroup.com
The author, herself the parent of a child with special needs, draws on interviews with health care professionals, nationally recognized authorities, and other partens to give readers the answers, advice, and comfort they crave. *$13.95*
319 pages Paperback
ISBN 0-425176-62-2

5165   Special Parent, Special Child
Exceptional Parent Library
P.O.Box 1807
Englewood Cliffs, NJ 7632-1207   201-947-6000
                                    800-535-1910
                                    FAX: 201-947-9376
                                    eplibrary@aol.com
                                    www.eplibrary.com
Offers information for facing the challenges of being a special parent. *$21.95*
Hardcover

5166 **Strategies for Working with Families of Young Children with Disabilities**
Brookes Publishing
P.O.Box 10624
Baltimore, MD 21285-624   410-337-9580
                                                 800-638-3775
                                            FAX: 410-337-8539
                            custserv@brookespublishing.com
                                            readplaylearn.com

Paul Brooks, Owner
This text offers useful techniques for collaborating with and supporting families whose youngest members either have a disability or are at risk for developing a disability. The authors address specific issues such as cultural diversity, transitions to new programs, and disagreements between families and professionals. *$33.00*
272 pages Paperback
ISBN 1-55766 -57-6

5167 **That's My Child**
Exceptional Parent Library
P.O.Box 1807
Englewood Cliffs, NJ 7632-1207   201-947-6000
                                                 800-535-1910
                                            FAX: 201-947-9376
                                            eplibrary@aol.com
                                            www.eplibrary.com

Offers information to help parent successfully navigate the maze of resources and services available for children with special needs. *$12.95*

5168 **The Complete Guide to Creating a Special Needs Life Plan**
Jessica Kingsley Publishers
73 Collier St
London, UK N19BE   hello@jkp.com
                                                 www.jkp.com

Hal Wright, Author
The purpose of special needs planning is to create the best possible life for an adult with a disability. This book provides comprehensive guidance on creating a life plan to transition a special needs child to independence or to ensure they are well cared for in the future.
360 pages

5169 **They Don't Come with Manuals**
Fanlight Productions
32 Court Street, 21st Floor
Brooklyn, NY 11201-1731   718-488-8900
                                                 800-876-1710
                                            FAX: 718-488-8642
                                            orders@fanlight.com
                                            www.fanlight.com

Ben Achtenberg, Owner
Anthony Sweeney, Marketing Director
Nicole Johnson, Publicity Coordinator
The parents and adoptive parents in this video speak candidly of their day to day experiences caring for children with physical and mental disabilities. *$145.00*

5170 **They're Just Kids**
Aquarius Health Care Videos
30 Forest Road
P.O. Box 249
Millis, MA 02054-7159   508-376-1244
                                            FAX: 508-376-1245
                                            aqvideos@tiac.net
                                            www.aquariusproductions.com

Lesile Kussmann, President
Joyce Farmer, Assistant Director
The importance and value of inclusion, excellent for anyone working with kids with disabilities. The documentary explores the advantages of the inclusion of disabled children in the classroom, cub scouts and other extracurricular activities. *$99.00*
Video

5171 **To a Different Drumbeat**
Alliance for Parental Involvement in Education
P.O.Box 59
East Chatham, NY 12060-59   518-392-6900
                                            FAX: 518-392-6900

Parents of special needs children contributed to this book. *$16.95*

5172 **Uncommon Fathers**
Woodbine House
6510 Bells Mill Rd
Bethesda, MD 20817-1636   301-897-3570
                                                 800-843-7323
                                            info@woodbinehouse.com
                                            woodbinehouse.com

Irv Shapell, Owner
Nineteen fathers talk about the life-altering experience of having a child with special needs and offer a welcome, seldom-heard perspective on raising kids with disabilities, including autism, cerebral palsy, and Down syndrome. Uncommon Fathers is the first book for fathers by fathers, but it is also helpful to partners, family, friends, and service providers. *$14.95*
206 pages Paperback
ISBN 0-933149-68-9

5173 **We Can Speak for Ourselves: Self Advocacy by Mentally Handicapped People**
Brookline Books
8 Trumbull Rd
Suite B-001
Northampton, MA 1060-4533   413-584-0184
                                                 800-666-2665
                                            FAX: 413-584-6184
                                            brbooks@yahoo.com
                                            www.brooklinebooks.com

Practical advice and support for parents, group resident workers, and others interested in fostering self-advocacy for people with developmental disabilities. *$10.00*
246 pages Paperback
ISBN 0-25336 -65-9

5174 **You May Be Able to Adopt**
Through the Looking Glass
3075 Adeline St
Ste. 120
Berkeley, CA 94703-2212   510-848-1112
                                                 800-644-2666
                                            FAX: 510-848-4445
                                            TTY: 510-848-1005
                                            tlg@lookingglass.org
                                            www.lookingglass.org

Maureen Block, J.D., Board President
Rusty Hendlin, M.A., LMFT, Director of Medi-Cal Services
Thomas Spalding, Board Treasurer
A guide to the adoption process for prospective mothers with disabilities and their partners. Available in braille, large print or cassette. *$10.00*
112 pages

5175 **You Will Dream New Dreams**
Kensington Publishing
119 West 40th Street
New York, NY 10018   800-221-2647
                                            www.kensingtonbooks.com

Steven Zacharius, Chairman, President & CEO
A parent's support group in print. The shared narratives come from those with newly diagnosed children, adult disabled children, and everything in between. *$13.00*
278 pages Paperback
ISBN 1-575665-60-3

5176 **Your Child Has a Disability: A Complete Sourcebook of Daily and Medical Care**
Brookes Publishing
P.O.Box 10624
Baltimore, MD 21285-624   410-337-9580
                                                 800-638-3775
                                            FAX: 410-337-8539
                            custserv@brookespublishing.com
                                            readplaylearn.com

Paul Brooks, Owner

Offers expert advice on a wide range of issues-from finding the right doctor and investigating the medical aspects of a child's condition to learning care techniques and fulfilling education requirements. *$24.95*
368 pages Paperback
ISBN 1-557663-74-2

Parenting: Specific Disabilities

5177 Cancer Clinical Trials: A Commonsense Guide to Experimental Cancer Therapies and Trials
DiaMedica Inc.
2 Carlson Pkwy N
Ste 165
Minneapolis, MN 55447
763-270-0603
FAX: 763-710-4456
www.diamedica.com

Tomasz M. Beer, Author
Larry W. Axmaker, Author
Cancer Clinical Trials is a comprehensive, no-nonsense, and readable guide for anyone who is considering therapeutic options in addition to standard cancer therapy. The book seeks to share knowledge about cancer clinical trials with people living with cancer, their families and loved ones. It will help readers decide if a clinical trial is a good option for them, to choose an appropriate trial, and to navigate through the clinical trial process.
192 pages

5178 Different Dream Parenting: A Practical Guide to Raising a Child with Special Needs
Discovery House Publishers
3000 Kraft Ave SE
P.O. Box 3566
Grand Rapids, MI 49512
800-653-8333
support@dhp.org
dhp.org

Jolene Philo, Author
In Different Dream Parenting, author Jolene Philo offers guidance and encouragement through biblical insights and her own personal experiences. Find spiritual wisdom, practical resources, and tools that can help you become an extraordinary advocate for your child. Discover how you can move beyond the challenges and experience the joy of being your childs biggest and best supporter.
336 pages

5179 Essential First Steps for Parents of Children with Autism
Woodbine House
6510 Bells Mill Rd
Bethesda, MD 20817
301-897-3570
800-843-7323
info@woodbinehouse.com
www.woodbinehouse.com

Lara Delmolino, Author
Sandra L. Harris, Author
When autism is diagnosed or suspected in young children, overwhelmed parents wonder where to turn and how to begin helping their child. Drs. Delmolino and Harris, experienced clinicians and ABA therapists, eliminate the confusion and guesswork by outlining the pivotal steps parents can take now to optimize learning and functioning for children ages 5 and younger.
154 pages Paperback

5180 Final Report: Challenges and Strategies of Disabled Parents: Findings from a Survey (1997)
Through the Looking Glass
3075 Adeline St
Ste. 120
Berkeley, CA 94703-2212
510-848-1112
800-644-2666
FAX: 510-848-4445
TTY: 510-848-1005
tlg@lookingglass.org
www.lookingglass.org

Linda Toms Barker, Author
Vida Maralani, Author

This milestone TLG-directed report presents findings from the first national survey of parents with disabilities. The report includes a description of parents with disabilities, barriers to parenting among adults with disabilities, transportation issues, personal assistance, adaptive parenting equipment, housing, as well as recommendations for legal and service system changes.

5181 Pervasive Developmental Disorders: Findinga Diagnosis and Getting Help
Patient-Centered Guides/O'Reilly Media
1005 Gravenstein Highway North
Sebastopol, CA 95472
707-827-7000
FAX: 707-829-0104
support@oreilly.com
www.oreilly.com

Mitzi Waltz, Author
This book encompassess both the practical aspects and the personal stories and emotional facets of living with PDD-NOS, the most common pervasive developmental disorder. Parents of an undiagnosed child may suspect many things, from autism to servere allergies. Pervasive Developmental Disorders is for parents (or newly diagnosed adults) who struggle with this neurological condition that profoundly impacts the life of child and family.
580 pages Paperback 1999

5182 Teaching Children with Down Syndrome about Their Bodies, Boundaries, and Sexuality
Woodbine House
6510 Bell Mills Rd
Bethesda, MD 20817
800-843-7323
info@woodbinehouse.com
www.woodbinehouse.com

Terri Couwenhoven, Author
Drawing on her unique background as both a sexual educator and mother of a child with Down syndrome, the author blends factual information and practical ideas for teaching children with Down syndrome about their bodies, puberty, and sexuality. This book gives parents the confidence to speak comfortably about these sometimes difficult subjects.
332 pages Paperback

5183 Thinking Differently: An Inspiring Guidefor Parents of Children with Learning Disabilities
William Morrow Paperbacks (HarperCollins)
195 Broadway
New York, NY 10007
212-207-7000
orders@harpercollins.com
www.harpercollins.com

David Flink, Author
An innovative, comprehensive guide—the first of its kind—to help parents understand and accept learning disabilities in their children, offering tips and strategies for successfully advocating on their behalf and helping them become their own best advocates.

5184 Your Child in the Hospital: A Practical Guide for Parents (3rd Edition)
Childhood Cancer Guides/O'Reilly Media
1005 Gravenstein Hwy N
Sebastopol, CA 95472
707-827-7019
800-889-8969
FAX: 707-824-8268
orders@oreilly.com
shop.oreilly.com

Nancy Keene, Author
This book offers advice from dozens of veteran parents on how to cope with a child's hospitalization, relieving anxious parents so they can help dispel their child's fears and concerns. Parents will find easy-to-read tips on preparing their child, handling procedures without trauma, and preventing insurance snafus. The second edition features a journal to help open communication and give the child a measure of control over the experience.
176 pages Paperback

Parenting: School

5185 Allergy & Asthma Today
Allergy & Asthma Network
8229 Boone Blvd
Ste 260
Vienna, VA 22182
800-878-4403
FAX: 703-288-5271
canderson@allergyasthmanetwork.org
www.allergyasthmanetwork.org

Tonya Winders, President
Charmayne Anderson, Director, Advocacy
Gary Fitzgerald, Managing Editor
Practical, medical,information for school patients, physicians, caregivers and families.

5186 Carolina Curriculum for Infants and Toddlers with Special Needs (3rd Edition)
Brookes Publishing
P.O.Box 10624
Baltimore, MD 21285-0624
410-337-9580
800-638-3775
FAX: 410-337-8539
custserv@brookespublishing.com
www.brookespublishing.com

Nancy M. Johnson-Martin, Author
Susan M. Attermeier, Author
Bonnie J. Hacker, Author
This book includes detailed assessment and intervention sequences, daily routine integration strategies, sensorimotor adaptations, and a sample 24-page Assessment Log that shows readers how to chart a child's individual progress.
504 pages Spiral-bound

5187 Choosing Outcomes and Accommodations for Children (COACH) (2nd Edition)
Brookes Publishing
P.O.Box 10624
Baltimore, MD 21285-0624
410-337-9580
800-638-3775
FAX: 410-337-8539
custserv@brookespublishing.com
www.brookespublishing.com

Michael F. Giangreco, Author
Chigee J. Cloninger, Author
Virginia Salce Iverson, Author
A guide to educational planning for students with disabilities, second edition. Focuses on life outcomes such as social relationships and participation in typical home, school, and community activities.
232 pages Spiral bound

5188 Complete IEP Guide: How to Advocate for Your Special Ed Child (8th Edition)
NOLO (Internet Brands)
909 N. Sepulveda Blvd
11th Fl.
El Segundo, CA 90245
310-280-4000
www.nolo.com

Lawrence Siegel, Author/Attorney
This all-in-one guide will help you understand special education law, identify your child's needs, prepare for meetings, develop the IEP and resolve disputes.
384 pages

5189 Exceptional Student in the Regular Classroom (6th Edition)
Pearson
330 Hudson St
New York, NY 10013
212-641-2400
www.pearsoned.com

Bill R. Gearheart, Author
Mel W. Weishan, Author
Carol J. Gearheart, Author
Offers good, solid information through a practical understandable presentation unencumbered by specialized jargon. Covers topics associated with special learners.
517 pages

5190 Study Power Workbook: Exercises in Study - Skills to Improve Your Learning and Your Grades
Brookline Books
8 Trumbull Rd
Ste B-001
Northampton, MA 1060-4533
413-584-0184
800-666-2665
FAX: 413-584-6184
brbooks@yahoo.com
www.brooklinebks.com

Sara Beth Huntley, Author
William Luckie, Author
Wood Smethurst, Author
The techniques in the easy-to-use, self-teaching manual have yielded remarkable success for students from elementary to medical school, at all levels of intelligence and achievement. Key skills covered include: listening, note taking, concentration, summarizing, reading comprehension, memorization, test taking, preparing papers and reports, time management, and more. These abilities are vital to success throughout every stage of learning; the benefits will last a lifetime.

Parenting: Spiritual

5191 A Good and Perfect Gift: Faith, Expectations, and a Little Girl Named Penny
Bethany House Publishers (Baker Publishing Group)
6030 E Fulton Rd
Ada, MI 49301
616-676-9185
800-877-2665
FAX: 616-676-9573
bakerpublishinggroup.com

Amy Julia Becker, Author
When her first baby, Penny, is given a frightening diagnosis, Amy Julia's world comes crashing down. Could she continue to trust God's goodness through what felt like personal tragedy? But challenging surprises often lead to unforeseen joy, and disappointments can turn into blessings. This wise and beautiful book is more than a courageous story of raising a child against the odds—it is a journey through the unexpected ups and downs of life and the discoveries that come along the way.
240 pages

5192 Before and After Zachariah
Chicago Review Press
814 N Franklin St
Chicago, IL 60610
312-337-0747
800-888-4741
FAX: 312-337-5110
www.chicagoreviewpress.com

Fern Kupfer, Author
This intimate chronicle of one family's life with a severely brain damaged child is recently back in print.
247 pages 1982

5193 Bethy and the Mouse: A Father Remembers His Children with Disabilities
Brookline Books
8 Trumbull Rd
Ste B-001
Northampton, MA 1060-4533
413-584-0184
800-666-2665
FAX: 413-584-6184
brbooks@yahoo.com
www.brooklinebks.com

Donald C. Bakely, Author
A moving collection of poetry, photographs, and prose following a father's experiences with two disabled children—one with Down Syndrome and one with an underdeveloped brain.
184 pages Paperback 1999

5194 Disabled God: Toward a Liberatory Theology of Disability
Abingdon Press
2222 Rosa L. Parks Blvd
Nashville, TN 37288
615-749-6615
800-251-3320
orders@abingdonpress.com
www.abingdonpress.com

Nancy L. Eisland, Author
Draws on themes of the disability rights movement to identify people with disabilities as members of a socially disadvantaged minority group rather than as individuals who need to adjust. Highlights the history of people with disabilities in the church and society.
139 pages Paperback 1994

5195 Farewell, My Forever Child
CreateSpace, an Amazon Company
4900 Lacross Rd
North Charleston, SC 29406
843-760-8000
www.createspace.com

Kalila Smith, Author
Based on her own experiences following the loss of her 29-year-old daughter, Kalila Smith discusses the complex grief felt by parents who have lost a developmentally disabled child, and offers strategies to help families achieve peace and deal with the loss.
134 pages

5196 In Time and with Love: Caring for the Special Needs Infant and Toddler
William Morrow Paperbacks (HarperCollins)
195 Broadway
New York, NY 10007
212-207-7000
orders@harpercollins.com
www.harpercollins.com

Marilyn Segal, Author
Roni Leiderman, Author
Wendy S. Masi, Author
For families and caregivers of preteen and handicapped children in their first three years - more than one hundred tips for adjusting and coping. Part of the Your Child At Play series.
240 pages

5197 Journal of Disability & Religion
Routledge (Taylor & Francis Group)
711 Third Ave
New York, NY 10017
212-216-7800
800-354-1420
FAX: 202-564-7854
orders@taylorandfrancis.com
www.tandfonline.com

This journal aims to inform religious professionals about developments in the field of disability and rehabilitation in order to facilitate greater contributions on the part of pastors, religious educators and pastoral counselors.
Quarterly

5198 Spiritually Able: A Parents Guide to Teaching Faith To Children with Special Needs
Loyola Press
3441 N Ashland Ave
Chicago, IL 60657
800-621-1008
FAX: 773-281-0555
customerservice@loyolapress.com
www.loyolapress.com

David Rizzo, Author
Both memoir and manual, Spiritually Able: A Parent's Guide to Teaching the Faith to Children with Special Needs is a life-preserver to parents who are seeking ways to grow and nourish a deeper relationship to God and their faith for their child with special needs. Full of tips, advice, and personal accounts, Spiritually Able helps bridge the gap and invites all into the welcoming embrace of the Church.
140 pages

5199 The Spiritual Art of Raising Children with Disabilities
Judson Press
P.O. Box 851
Valley Forge, PA 19482
800-458-3766
www.judsonpress.com

Kathleen Deyer Bolduc, Author
In The Spiritual Art of Raising Children with Disabilities, Bolduc uses the metaphor of the mosaic to life as parents of children with disabilities. Readers are walked through the process using the spiritual disciplines to help you recognize God's presence in your life and regain the balance we all need. this book offers readers the unique perspective of a parent raising a child with disabilities and dealing with it through faith and spiritual direction.
192 pages Paperback

5200 Worst Loss: How Families Heal from the Death of a Child
Holt Paperbacks (Macmillan Publishers)
75 Varick St
New York, NY 10013
212-226-7521
press.inquiries@macmillan.com
us.macmillan.com/henryholt

Barbara D. Rosof, Author
Combines anecdotal case histories and the latest research to help bereaved parents cope with the loss of a child, offering practical and comforting advice on how to overcome the disabling symptoms of grief.
304 pages 1995

Professional

5201 American Journal of Physical Medicine & Rehabilitation
Lippincott, Williams & Wilkins
2001 Market St
Ste 5
Philadelphia, PA 19103-1551
215-521-8300
800-638-3030
FAX: 215-521-8902
orders@lww.com
www.lww.com

Walter R. Frontera, MD, PHD, Editor-in-Chief
Journal of the Association of Academic Psychiatrists. Articles covering research and clinical studies and applications of new equipment, procedures and therapeutic advances.
Monthly

5202 American Journal of Psychiatry
American Psychiatric Association
1000 Wilson Blvd
Ste 1825
Arlington, VA 22209-3924
703-907-7322
800-368-5777
FAX: 703-907-1091
ajp@psych.org
ajp.psychiatryonline.org

Robert Freedman, Editor
Peer-reviewed articles focus on developments in biological psychiatry as well as on treatment innovations and forensic, ethical, economic, and social topics.
Monthly

5203 American Journal of Public Health (AJPH)
American Public Health Association
800 I St. NW
Washington, DC 20001
202-777-2742
FAX: 202-777-2534
TTY:202-777-2500
www.apha.org

Georges C. Benjamin, Executive Director
Alfredo Morabia, Editor-in-Chief
Michael C. Costanza, Senior Deputy Editor
Association journal containing editorials, commentary, and analyses on public health.
Monthly

5204 Art Therapy
American Art Therapy Association
4875 Eisenhower Ave.
Suite 240
Alexandria, VA 22304

703-548-5860
888-290-0878
FAX: 703-548-5860
info@arttherapy.org
arttherapy.org

Jordan Potash, Editor-in-Chief
Publishes articles on news, developments, ideas and research relating to the field of art therapy.
Quarterly

5205 CAREERS & the disABLED Magazine
Equal Opportunity Publications
445 Broad Hollow Rd
Ste 425
Melville, NY 11747-3615

631-421-9421
FAX: 631-421-1352
info@eop.com
www.eop.com

Barbara Capella Loehr, Editor
A career magazine for professional career seekers who have disabilities. Profiles disabled people who have achieved successful careers. Features a career section in Braille, career guide.

**5206 Clinician's Practical Guide to
Attention-Deficit/Hyperactivity Disorder**
Brookes Publishing
P.O.Box 10624
Baltimore, MD 21285-0624

410-337-9580
800-638-3775
FAX: 410-337-8539
custserv@brookespublishing.com
www.brookespublishing.com

Marianne Mercugliano, Author
Quick reference volume with comprehensive data on psychoeducational and neuropsychological assessment, related symptoms, drug and counseling therapies and critical issues.
368 pages

**5207 Counseling Parents of Children with Chronic Illness or
Disability**
Wiley
111 River St
Hoboken, NJ 07030-5774

201-748-6000
877-762-2974
FAX: 201-748-6088
info@wiley.com
www.wiley.com

Hilton Davis, Author
This book aims to help medical staff and carers relate to parents in ways that facilitate their adaptation to their child's illness. The key to this is in effective communication.
148 pages Paperback

**5208 Creating Options for Family Recovery: A Provider's
Guide to Promoting Parental Mental Health**
Employment Options Inc.
82 Brigham St
Marlboro, MA 01752-3137

508-485-5051
FAX: 508-485-8807
options@employmentoptions.org
www.employmentoptions.com

Joanne Nicholson, Author
Toni Wolf, Author
Chip Wilder, Author
This book seeks to advise professionals and providers on strategies to use when working with families who are dealing with mental illness, assisting them with the promotion of a healthy recovery. The resources in this guide are drawn from over 20 years of research and practice, and the lived experiences of parents, children and family members.
120 pages Paperback

5209 Cystic Fibrosis: Medical Care
Lippincott, Williams & Wilkins
16522 Hunters Green Pkwy
Hagerstown, MD 21740

301-223-2300
800-638-3030
FAX: 301-223-2400
orders@lww.com
www.lww.com

David M. Orenstein, Author
Beryl J. Rosenstein, Author
Robert C. Stern, Author
A guide to the medical community to the principles and practices of cystic fibrosis care. After chapters on the molecular and cellular bases of CF and its diagnosis, they cover the major organ systems affected by CF and deal with surgery for CF patients, transplantation (lung and liver), hospitalization, and terminal care. Also included are chapters on special populations, exercise, and laboratory testing.
365 pages

5210 Disability & Rehabilitation Journal
Taylor & Francis Online
6000 Broken Sound Pkwy NW
Ste 300
Boca Raton, FL 33487

212-216-7800
800-634-7064
FAX: 212-564-7854
enquiries@taylorandfrancis.com
www.taylorandfrancis.com

Dave Muller, Editor-in-Chief
Peer-reviewed journal offering the latest news, research, and insights on disability and rehabilitation medicine.
Bi-weekly

**5211 Disability Analysis Handbook: Tools for Independent
Practice**
American Board of Disability Analysts
1483 N. Mt. Juliet Rd.
Suite 175
Nashville, TN 37122

629-255-0870
FAX: 615-296-9980
office@eventsm3.com
www.americandisability.org

Handbook providing information on physical and mental disabilities, including diabetes, substance abuse, aging, nonverbal learning, chronic pain, etc.
396 pages

**5212 Enhancing Everyday Communication for Children with
Disabilities**
Brookes Publishing
P.O.Box 10624
Baltimore, MD 21285-0624

410-337-9580
800-638-3775
FAX: 410-337-8539
custserv@brookespublishing.com
www.brookespublishing.com

Jeff Sigafoos, Author & Editor
Michael Arthur-Kelly, Author
Nancy Butterfield, Author
Practical and concise, this introductory guide is filled with real-world tips and strategies for anyone working to improve the communication of children with moderate, severe, and multiple disabilities. Emphasizing the link between behavior and communication, three respected researchers transform up-to-date research and proven best practices into instructional procedures and interventions ready for use at home or in school.
176 pages Paperback

5213 Ethical Issues In Home Health Care (2nd Edition)
Charles C. Thomas
2600 S First St
Springfield, IL 62704-4730

217-789-8980
800-258-8980
FAX: 217-789-9130
books@ccthomas.com
www.ccthomas.com

Sheri Smith, Author
Rosalind Ekman Ladd, Author
Lynn Pasquerella, Author

This book will help to answer some of the growing number of ethical questions and more complex issues that home health care nurses face. The cases presented in each chapter of the book are fictionalized situations based on interviews conducted with home health care nurses in both hospital-sponsored and private agencies, in hospices, and in urban and rural settings. Each chapter of the book is devoted to one of the main areas of concern for home health care nurses.
258 pages

5214   Journal of Public Health
Oxford Journals, Oxford University Press
2001 Evans Rd
Cary, NC 27513   919-677-0977
                                             800-852-7323
                                        FAX: 919-677-1714
                                      www.oxfordjournals.org

Eugene Milne, Editor
Ted Schrecker, Editor
Scholarly articles on issues that relate to public health and the healthcare system.

5215   PM&R Journal
American Academy of Physical Medicine & Rehab
9700 W Bryn Mawr Ave
Ste 200
Rosemont, IL 60018-5701   847-737-6000
                                             877-227-6799
                                        FAX: 847-737-6001
                                        TTY: 800-437-0833
                                          info@aapmr.org
                                        www.pmrjournal.org

Stuart M. Weinstein, Editor-in-Chief
Cathy Mendelsohn, Managing Editor
Covers medical, social and employment aspects of vocational rehabilitation. The content of PM&R includes articles that are contemporary and important to both research and clinical practice. The various sections of the journal include original research such as clinical trials, outcomes studies, and clinically relevant translational science; reviews (narrative and analytical); case presentations; point/counterpoint debates; ethical/legal topics; practice management updates; and statistical themes.
Monthly

5216   Provider Magazine
American Health Care Association
1201 L St NW
Washington, DC 20005-4024   202-842-4444
                                             888-656-6669
                                        FAX: 202-842-3860
                                          sales@ahca.org

Joanne Erickson, Editor-in-Chief
Amy Mendoza, Managing Editor
Magazine for long-term healthcare professionals.
Monthly

5217   Public Health Reports
Association of Schools & Programs of Public Health
1900 M St NW
Ste 710
Washington, DC 20036   202-296-1099
                                        FAX: 202-296-1252
                                      www.publichealthreports.org

Frederic E. Shaw, Editorn-in-Chief
Sasha M. Ruiz, Acting Managing Editor
PHR is a peer-reviewed journal published on a bi-monthly basis. Each issue offers recurring guest columns such as Local Acts, Global Health Matters, ASPPH From the Schools and Programs of Public Health, Law and the Public's Health, Public Health Chronicles, NCHS Dataline, and the Surgeon General's Perspectives.
Bi-monthly

5218   Sociopolitical Aspects of Disabilities(2nd Edition)
Charles C. Thomas
2600 S First St
Springfield, IL 62704-4730   217-789-8980
                                             800-258-8980
                                        FAX: 217-789-9130
                                         books@ccthomas.com
                                          www.ccthomas.com

Willie V. Bryan, Author
Provides understanding of the social and political histories of people with disabilities in the United States. This understanding is pivotal in working with persons with disabilities, to provide background and perspective on current policies and attitudes.
284 pages

5219   Starting and Sustaining Genetic Support Groups
Johns Hopkins University Press
2715 N Charles St
Baltimore, MD 21218-4363   410-516-6900
                                        FAX: 410-516-6968
                                      webmaster@jhupress.jhu.edu
                                          www.press.jhu.edu

Joan O. Weiss, Author
Jayne S. Mackta, Author
Guide to the establishment and maintenance of genetic support groups for individuals with genetic disorders and their families. For therapists and group leaders. Discusses practical matters including finding a leader, fund-raising, organizing peer support training programs.
152 pages

5220   The Essential Brain Injury Guide (5th Edition)
Brain Injury Association of America
3057 Nutley St.
Suite 805
Fairfax, VA 22031-1931   703-761-0750
                                        FAX: 703-761-0755
                                          info@biausa.org
                                          shop.biausa.org

Rick Willis, President & Chief Executive Officer
Page Melton Ivie, Chair
Kevin Bingham, Vice Chair
The expanded and updated Essential Brain Injury Guide 5.0 is a hard cover, 25 chapter, 500-page text that provides information about brain injury, as well as brain injury treatment and rehabilitation. *$135.00*

5221   What Psychotherapists Should Know about Disabilty
Guilford Press
370 Seventh Ave
Ste 1200
New York, NY 10001-1020   800-365-7006
                                        FAX: 212-966-6708
                                          info@guilford.com
                                          www.guilford.com

Rhoda Olkin, Author
This comprehensive volume provides the knowledge and skills that mental health professionals need for more effective, informed work with clients with disabilities. Topics addressed include etiquette with clients with disabilities; special concerns in assessment, evaluation, and diagnosis. Filled with clinical examples and observations, the volume also discusses strategies for enhancing teaching, training, and research.
368 pages

5222   Women with Visible & Invisible Disabilitiees: Multiple Intersections, Issues, Therapies
Routledge (Taylor & Francis Group)
711 Third Ave
New York, NY 10017   212-216-7800
                                             800-634-7064
                                        FAX: 202-564-7854
                                      enquiries@taylorandfrancis.com
                                          www.routledge.com

Martha E. Banks, Editor
Ellyn Kaschak, Editor
Addresses the issues faced by women with disabilities, examines the social construction of disability, and makes suggestions for

the development and modification of culturally relevant therapy to meet the needs of disabled women.
414 pages Hardcover; Paperback

Specific Disabilities

5223 **inMotion Magazine**
Amputee Coalition
601 Pennsylvania Ave. NW
Suite 600, South Bldg.
Washington, DC 20004   888-267-5669
                    www.amputee-coalition.org
Cassandra Isidro, President & Chief Executive Officer
inMotion Magazine is published bimonthly for amputees, caregivers and health care professionals, offering timely and comprehensive information. Offered both in print and online, free subscription.
1991

Vocations

5224 **Ability Magazine**
P.O. Box 10878
Costa Mesa, CA 92627   www.abilitymagazine.com
Features articles on living, working, playing and entertainment for the disabled.
Bi-monthly

5225 **Chemists with Disabilities Committee - American Chemical Society**
American Chemical Society
1155 16th St NW
Washington, DC 20036   202-872-4600
                    800-227-5558
                 FAX: 202-872-4574
                    cwd@acs.org
                    www.acs.org

John Johnston, Ph.D, MBA, Chair
James Schiller, Chair Elect
Paula Christopher, Staff Liaison
Promotes the full involvement of individuals with physical and learning disabilities in educational and career opportunities in the chemical and allied sciences. CWD members help individuals with disabilities to connect with employers and educators of persons with disabilities.

5226 **Demystifying Job Development: Field-Based Approaches to Job Development for the Disabled**
Training Resource Network
266 Roaring Dr.
St. Augustine, FL 32084   FAX: 904-823-3554
                    www.trn-store.com

David Hoff, Author
Cecilia Gandolfo, Author
Marty Gold, Author
A guide to successful placement of individuals with severe disabilities in quality jobs in the community.
105 pages

5227 **Hiring Idahoans with Disabilities**
Idaho Assistive Technology Project
University of Idaho
1187 Alturas Dr.
Moscow, ID 83843- 8331   208-885-3557
                    800-432-8324
                 FAX: 208-885-6102
                    idahoat@uidaho.edu

Jane Frederickson, Author
Kristen Hagen, Author
The purpose of this handbook is to inform employers in Idaho business and industry about the promise of hiring Idahoans with disabilities.

5228 **Life Beyond the Classroom: Transition Strategies for Young People with Disabilities**
Brookes Publishing
P.O.Box 10624
Baltimore, MD 21285-0624   410-337-9580
                    800-638-3775
                 FAX: 410-337-8539
                    www.brookespublishing.com

Paul Wehman, Author
Specialists in a variety of disciplines use creative and practical techniques to ensure careful transition planning, to build young people's confidence and competence in work skills, and to foster support from businesses and community organizations for training and employment programs.
616 pages

5229 **More Than a Job: Securing Satisfying Careers for People with Disabilities**
Brookes Publishing
P.O. Box 10624
Baltimore, MD 21285-0624   800-638-3775
                 FAX: 410-337-8539
             custserv@brookespublishing.com
                    www.brookespublishing.com

Paul Wehman, Editor
John Kregel, Editor
This book transforms job placement into career counseling for people with physical and developmental disabilities. It presents step-by-step guidelines for helping people with disabilities to identify their own interests.
384 pages 1998

5230 **OT Practice Magazine**
American Occupational Therapy Association
6116 Executive Blvd.
Suite 200
North Bethesda, MD 20852-4929   301-652-6611
                    800-729-2682
                 otpractice@aota.org
             www.aota.org/Publications-News/otp.aspx
Sherry Keramidas, Executive Director
OT Practice covers professional information on all aspects of occupational therapy practice today. Features include hands-on techniques, continuing education, legislative issues, career advice, job opportunities, and the latest professional news. Also available online.

5231 **Occupational Therapy and Vocational Rehabilitation**
Wiley
111 River St
Hoboken, NJ 07030-5774   201-748-6000
                    877-762-2974
                 FAX: 201-748-6088
                    info@wiley.com
                    www.wiley.com

Joanne Ross
This book introduces the occupational therapist to the practice of vocational rehabilitation. As rehabilitation specialists, Occupational Therapists work in a range of diverse settings with clients who have a variety of physical, emotional and psychological conditions. This book highlights the contribution, which can be made by occupational therapists in assisting disabled, ill or injured workers to access, remain in and return to work.
280 pages Paperback

5232 **Work and Disability: Contexts, Issues & Strategies for Enhancing Employment Outcomes**
PRO-ED Inc.
8700 Shoal Creek Blvd
Austin, TX 78757-6897   512-451-3246
                    800-897-3202
                 FAX: 800-397-7633
                    general@proedinc.com
                    www.proedinc.com

Edna Mora Szymanski, Editor
Randall M. Parker, Editor
492 pages

Media, Electronic

Audio/Visual

5234 A Place for Me
Educational Productions
9000 SW Gemini Dr
Beaverton, OR 97008-7151

503-644-7000
800-950-4949
FAX: 503-350-7000
custserve@edpro.com
www.teachingstrategies.com

Diane Trister Dodge, Founder/President/Lead Author
Arnitra Duckett, VP, Sales & Strategic Marketing
In this video, parents discuss the issues they face in planning for their child's future. This program is designed to stimulate discussion of these issues and help increase awareness of the options available in your local community.

5235 Able to Laugh
Fanlight Productions
32 Court St.
21st Floor
Brooklyn, NY 11201-4421

718-488-8900
800-876-1710
FAX: 718-488-8642
info@fanlight.com
www.fanlight.com

Jonathan Miller, President
Patricio Guzman, Director
Meredith Miller, Sales Manager
An exploration of the world of disability as interpreted by six professional comedians who happen to be disabled. It is also about the awkward ways disabled and able-bodied people relate to one another. *$199.00*
ISBN 1-572951-05-2

5236 Acting Blind
Fanlight Productions
32 Court St.
21st Floor
Brooklyn, NY 11201-4421

718-488-8900
800-876-1710
FAX: 718-488-8642
info@fanlight.com
www.fanlight.com

Jonathan Miller, President
Patricio Guzman, Director
Meredith Miller, Sales Manager
Takes audiences behind the scenes as a company of non-professional actors rehearse a play about life without sight. The performers have no problem imagining themselves in these roles: they are blind themselves. *$229.00*

5237 Adaptive Baby Care
Through the Looking Glass
3075 Adeline St
Suite 120
Berkeley, CA 94703-2577

510-848-1112
800-644-2666
FAX: 510-848-4445
TTY: 510-848-1005
tlg@lookingglass.org
www.lookingglass.org

Megan Kirshbaum, Executive Director
Paul Preston, Assoc. Dir
This publication is presented as a catalyst for problem-solving regarding the development of adaptive baby care equipment. This newest publication is designed for parents, family members and professionals. It includes: guidelines for problem-solving baby care barriers; photographs and descriptions of prototypes and resources for adaptive baby care equipment; adaptive baby care techniques; adaptive baby care equipment checklist; commercial product safety commission guidelines; and local and natio
$250.00

5238 Adaptive Baby Care Equipment Video and Book
Through the Looking Glass
Through the Looking Glass
3075 Adeline St
Suite 120
Berkeley, CA 94703-2577

510-848-1112
800-644-2666
FAX: 510-848-4445
TTY: 510-848-1005
tlg@lookingglass.org
www.lookingglass.org

Stephanie Miyashiro, Board President
Thomas Spalding, Board Treasurer
Alice Nemon, D.S.W., Board Secretary
Includes Adaptive Baby care Equipment: Guide Lines; Prototypes and Resources, plus a twelve minute video. Available in braille, large print or cassette. *$79.00*

5239 All About Attention Deficit Disorders, Revised
Parent Magic
800 Roosevelt Rd
B-309
Glen Ellyn, IL 60137-5839

630-208-0031
800-442-4453
FAX: 630-208-7366
www.parentmagic.com

Nancy Roe, Administrator/Exec Admin
Thomas Phelan, Owner/President/CEO
A psychologist and expert on ADD outlines the symptoms, diagnosis and treatment of this neurological disorder. Video ($49.95 - 2 parts) and audio cassette ($24.95). Also in DVD format (1 disk-$39.93).

5240 Autism
Aquarius Health Care Media
30 Forest Rd
PO Box 249
Millis, MA 2054-1511

508-376-1244
FAX: 508-376-1245
www.nmm.net

Lesile Kussmann, Owner/President/Producer
Kathy Newkirk, Director
Jane Hutchinson, Assoc. Director
This video takes you into the lives of autistic people and their families to understand more about autism. What defines autism and how can we help those living with the disability? Children, teens, and adults are also profiled and we begin to see the varying levels of development and new technology to help these people communicate. Preview Available. *$149.00*
Video

5241 Basic Course in American Sign Language(B100) Harris Communications, Inc.
Harris Communications
15155 Technology Dr
Eden Prairie, MN 55344

800-825-6758
FAX: 952-906-1099
TTY:952-388-2152
info@harriscomm.com
www.harriscomm.com

Ray Harris, CEO
This series of four one-hour tapes is designed to illustrate the various exercises and dialogues in the text. *$39.95*
Video

5242 Beginning ASL Video Course
Harris Communications
15155 Technology Dr
Eden Prairie, MN 55344

800-825-6758
FAX: 952-906-1099
TTY:952-388-2152
info@harriscomm.com
www.harriscomm.com

Ray Harris, CEO
You'll watch a family teach you to learn American Sign Language during funny and touching family situations. A total of 15 tapes in the course.
Video

5243 Blindness
Landmark Media
3450 Slade Run Dr
Falls Church, VA 22042-3940
703-241-2030
800-342-4336
FAX: 703-536-9540
info@landmarkmedia.com

Michael Hartogs, President/Owner
Joan Hartogs, Owner/Vice President
Peter Hartogs, Vice President
Landmark Media is an independent family-owned company currently celebrating our 28th anniversary. We have been fortunate to be able to offer the finest quality educational DVDs available.
$250.00
Video

5244 Boy Inside, The
Fanlight Productions
32 Court St.
21st Floor
Brooklyn, NY 11201-4421
718-488-8900
800-876-1710
FAX: 718-488-8642
info@fanlight.com
www.fanlight.com

Jonathan Miller, President
Patricio Guzman, Director
Meredith Miller, Sales Manager
Filmmaker Marianne Kaplan tells the personal and often distressing story of her son Adam, a 12-year-old with Asperger Syndrome, during a tumultuous year in the life of their family.

5245 Braille Documents
Metrolina Association for the Blind
704 Louise Ave
Charlotte, NC 28204-2128
704-887-5118
800-926-5466
FAX: 704-372-3872
bschmiel@mabnc.org
www.mabnc.org

Robert Scheffel, President
Richard Hartness, Vice President, Product Design & Development
Barbara Schmiel, Vice President, Accessible Braille Services
This production shop creates Braille and large-print documents. We work with our clients to find the most cost effective solutions for their needs. Unlike other modified statement service providers, we accept your existing style of statement or allow you to design your own statement.Documents may be received in electronic data files as encrypted data sent over public networks, data sent to a file transfer protocol drop box, or data sent over a dedicated data line. ABS also accepts paper hardcopi

5246 Bringing Out the Best
PO Box 9177
Dept. 11W
Champaign, IL 61826-9177
217-352-3273
800-519-2707
FAX: 217-352-1221
orders@researchpress.com
www.researchpress.com

David Parkinson, Chairman
Russell Pence, President
Gail Salyards, Dir. Of Marketing/President

5247 Business as Usual
Fanlight Productions
32 Court St.
21st Floor
Brooklyn, NY 11201-4421
718-488-8900
800-876-1710
FAX: 718-488-8642
info@fanlight.com
www.fanlight.com

Jonathan Miller, President
Patricio Guzman, Director
Meredith Miller, Sales Manager
An enlightening documentary, brings a unique international perspective to this struggle. This film examines five innovative programs which create opportunities for people with mental and physical disabilities to own and operate their own businesses.
$145.00

5248 Buying Time: The Media Role in Health Care
Fanlight Productions
32 Court St.
21st Floor
Brooklyn, NY 11201-4421
718-488-8900
800-876-1710
FAX: 718-488-8642
info@fanlight.com
www.fanlight.com

Jonathan Miller, President
Patricio Guzman, Director
Meredith Miller, Sales Manager
This video program is a thoughtful and disturbing examination in the role of the media in determining the allocation of health care resources. This program is a powerful tool on ethics, policy, journalism, sociology, medicine and nursing as well as for professional workshops, and continuing education programs. *$99.00*

5249 Caring for Persons with Developmental Disabilities
PO Box 9177
Dept. 11W
Champaign, IL 61826-9177
217-352-3273
800-519-2707
FAX: 217-352-1221
www.researchpress.com

David Parkinson, Chairman
Russell Pence, President
Gail Salyards, Dir. Of Marketing/President

5250 Clockworks
Learning Corporation of America
6493 Kaiser Dr
Fremont, CA 94555-3610
510-490-7311
Oonchia Chia, Owner
Scotty, who has Down Syndrome, is fascinated by clocks. This film follows him on his adventures of employment in the clock shop.
Film

5251 Close Encounters of the Disabling Kind
Mainstream
6930 Carroll Ave
Suite 204
Takoma Park, MD 20912-4468
301-891-8777
FAX: 301-891-8778

Lillie Harrison, Information Programs Clerk
Fritz Rumpel, Editor
A training video that provides a hiring manager with information on how to learn the basics of disability etiquette and, by the end of the video, seems much better prepared and willing to interview qualified individuals with disabilities. Includes trainer and trainee guides. *$99.95*
Video

5252 Deaf Children Signers
Harris Communications
15155 Technology Dr
Eden Prairie, MN 55344
800-825-6758
FAX: 952-906-1099
TTY:952-388-2152
info@harriscomm.com
www.harriscomm.com

Ray Harris, CEO
Graduate to voicing for Deaf children ages 5-11. This unique tape lets eleven young children demonstrate their abilities by signing about what is important to them. *$49.95*
Video

5253 Deaf Culture Series
Harris Communications
15155 Technology Dr
Eden Prairie, MN 55344
800-825-6758
FAX: 952-906-1099
TTY:952-388-2152
info@harriscomm.com
www.harriscomm.com

Ray Harris, CEO
Each video in this five-part series features a topic dealing with the unique culture of deaf people. It is an excellent resource for deaf

studies programs, Interpreter Preparation programs and Sign Language programs. *$49.95*
Video

5254   Do You Hear That?
Alexander Graham Bell Association
3417 Volta Pl. NW
Washington, DC 20007   202-337-5220
                                   FAX: 202-337-8314
                                   TTY:202-337-5221
                                       info@agbell.org
                                       www.agbell.org
Emilio Alonso-Mendoza, Chief Executive Officer
This video shows auditory-verbal therapy sessions of a therapist working individually with 11 children who range in age from 7 months to 7 years old and have hearing aids or cochlear implants.
Video

5255   Doing Things Together
Britannica Film Company
345 4th St
San Francisco, CA 94107-1206   415-928-8466
                                   FAX: 415-928-5027
Dave Bekowich, Owner
Steve went with his parents to an amusement park. He met another boy named Martin who at first was shocked by Steve's prosthetic hand.
Film

5256   Emerging Leaders
Mobility International USA
132 E Broadway
Suite 343
Eugene, OR 97401   541-343-1284
                                   FAX: 541-343-6812
                                   TTY:541-343-1284
                                clearinghouse@miusa.org
                                       www.miusa.org
Susan Sygall, Chief Executive Officer
Cindy Lewis, Director, Programs
Pioneering short-term international disability leadership programs in the U.S. and abroad with 2,000 youth, young adults and professionals from over 100 countries.
Video

5257   Face First
Fanlight Productions
32 Court St.
21st Floor
Brooklyn, NY 11201-4421   718-488-8900
                                        800-876-1710
                                   FAX: 718-488-8642
                                       info@fanlight.com
                                       www.fanlight.com

Jonathan Miller, President
Patricio Guzman, Director
Meredith Miller, Sales Manager
In this documentary, the stories told reflect the reality faced by all those who are seen as different. Despite their difficult experiences, the survival of the profiled individuals affords comic relief &, by adulthood, they possess unusual strengths that shape their careers in pediatrics, disability care, public speaking, and journalism. *$195.00*

5258   Family-Guided Activity-Based Intervention for Toddlers & Infants
Brookes Publishing
PO Box 10624
Baltimore, MD 21285-0624   410-337-9580
                                        800-638-3775
                                   FAX: 410-337-8539
                             custserv@brookespublishing.com
Paul Brooks, Owner
This 20-minute video was created to assist early childhood professionals to incorporate therapeutic intervention into daily living. It includes a discussion and demonstration of how intervention professionals actively may involve caregivers in the

planning and implementation of activities aimed at encouraging development of a child's target skills *$37.00*
20 Minutes
ISBN 1-55766 -19-3

5259   Filmakers Library
124 E 40th St
Suite 901
New York, NY 10016-1798   212-808-4980
                                   FAX: 212-808-4983
                                       www.filmakers.com
Sue Oscar, Co-President
Linda Gottesman, Co-President
Andrea Traubner, Dir., Broadcast Sales
Filmakers Library has been a leading source of outstanding films for the education, library, and non-theatrical markets. Now, as an imprint of award-winning online publisher Alexander Street Press, Filmakers Library is able to offer online streaming access to most of our titles, ensuring that our films receive the greatest possible exposure and accessibility through the most flexible delivery platforms. We market and promote our films throughout the world by direct mail, print advertising, exhib

5260   Filmakers Library: An Imprint Of Alexander Street Press
124 E 40th St
Suite 901
New York, NY 10016-1798   212-808-4980
                                   FAX: 212-808-4983
                                       www.filmakers.com
Sue Oscar, Co-President
Linda Gottesman, Co-President
Andrea Traubner, Dir., Broadcast Sales
Filmakers Library has been a leading source of outstanding films for the education, library, and non-theatrical markets. Now, as an imprint of award-winning online publisher Alexander Street Press, Filmakers Library is able to offer online streaming access to most of our titles, ensuring that our films receive the greatest possible exposure and accessibility through the most flexible delivery platforms. We market and promote our films throughout the world by direct mail, print advertising, exhib
$100 - $300

5261   Films & Videos on Aging and Sensory Change
Lighthouse International
111 E 59th St
New York, NY 10022-1202   212-821-9200
                                        800-829-0500
                                   FAX: 212-821-9706
                                       info@lighthouse.org
Joanna Mellor, VP Information Services
Tara Cortes, President
An annotated list of over 80 films and videos dealing with age-related sensory change, divided into sections on vision impairment, hearing impairment, and multiple sensory impairments. *$5.00*

5262   Heart to Heart
Blind Children's Center
4120 Marathon St
Los Angeles, CA 90029-3584   323-664-2153
                             info@blindchildrenscenter.org
                                 www.blindchildrenscenter.org
Nancy Chernus-Mansfield, Co-Author
Dori Hayashi, Co-Author
Parents of blind and partially sighted children talk about their feelings. *$35.00*
VHS/DVD

5263   Helping Hands
Fanlight Productions
32 Court St.
21st Floor
Brooklyn, NY 11201-4421   718-488-8900
                                        800-876-1710
                                   FAX: 718-488-8642
                                       info@fanlight.com
                                       www.fanlight.com

Jonathan Miller, President
Patricio Guzman, Director
Meredith Miller, Sales Manager

The ADA mandates equal access and opportunity for the 43 million people with disabilities in the United States. These individuals may have limited speech, sight or mobility; a developmental disability; or a medical condition which limits some life activities. Many, however, are ready, willing and very able to join the workforce. This video demonstrates that many modifications or adaptations can be made simply by using ingenuity or common sense — such as keeping the aisles clear, etc. *$145.00*
37 Minutes

5264 Home is in the Heart: Accommodating Peoplewith Disabilities in the Homestay Experience
Mobility International USA
132 E Broadway
Suite 343
Eugene, OR 97401   541-343-1284
               FAX: 541-343-6812
               TTY:541-343-1284
               clearinghouse@miusa.org
               www.miusa.org

Susan Sygall, Chief Executive Officer
Cindy Lewis, Director, Programs
Provides information and ideas for exchange organizations. Discusses how to recruit homestay families, meet accessibility needs and accommodate international participants with disabilities.
Video

5265 How Difficult Can This Be ? (Fat City) - Rick Lavoie
CACLD
PO Box 210
Barnstable, MA 02630-210   508-362-1052
               scheduling@ricklavoie.com
               www.ricklavoie.com

Rick Lavoie, Film Maker
This unique program allows viewers to experience the same frustration, anxiety and tension that children with learning disabilities face in their daily lives. Teachers, social workers, psychologists, parents and friends who have participated in Richard Lavoie's workshop reflect upon their experience and the way it changed their approach to L.D. children. 1989.

5266 How We Play
Fanlight Productions
32 Court St.
21st Floor
Brooklyn, NY 11201-4421   718-488-8900
               800-876-1710
               FAX: 718-488-8642
               info@fanlight.com
               www.fanlight.com

Jonathan Miller, President
Patricio Guzman, Director
Meredith Miller, Sales Manager
Though most of the people in this new, short documentary are in wheelchairs, and one is blind, they are anything but handicapped. Playing tennis, snorkeling, whitewater canoeing, practicing karate - they are living proof that a disability can be a challenge, not an obstacle. *$99.00*

5267 I'm Not Disabled
Landmark Media
3450 Slade Run Dr
Falls Church, VA 22042-3940   703-241-2030
               800-342-4336
               FAX: 703-536-9540
               info@landmarkmedia.com

Michael Hartogs, President
Joan Hartogs, Vice President
Peter Hartogs, Vice President
Young people talk about their disabilities and the importance of sports in their lives. The afflictions range from blindness and missing limbs to paralysis. Through physical education and therapy they enjoy freedom of movement and participate in sports such as tennis, basketball, kayaking, skiing, and swimming. *$195.00*
Video

5268 Imagery Procedures for People with Special Needs
Research Press
PO Box 9177
Dept. 11W
Champaign, IL 61826-9177   217-352-3273
               800-519-2707
               FAX: 217-352-1221
               rp@researchpress.com
               www.researchpress.com

David Parkinson, Chairman
Russell Pence, President
Gail Salyards, Dir. Of Marketing/President
This video was developed at the Groden Center and illustrates imagery based procedures including the use of positive reinforcement, covert modeling, and a self-control triad to assists individuals to self-regulate their behaviors in stressful situations or under conditions that may evoke extreme fear. Recommended for professionals and family members interested in teaching self-control strategies that individuals with autism spectrum disorders can use in community settings. *$195.00*
32 Minutes

5269 In the Middle
Fanlight Productions
c/o Icarus Films
32 Court Street, 21st Floor
Brooklyn, NY 11201   718-488-8900
               800-876-1710
               FAX: 718-488-8642
               info@fanlight.com
               www.fanlight.com

Ben Achtenberg, Founder, Owner
Documents the problems and joys shared by Ryanna, who has Spina Bifida, and her parents, teachers and classmates during her first year of being mainstreamed in a Head Start Program. *$99.00*

5270 Include Us
Exceptional Parent Library
PO Box 1807
Englewood Cliffs, NJ 7632-1207   201-947-6000
               800-535-1910
               FAX: 201-947-9376
               eplibrary@aol.com

First children's video to feature a proportionate number of children with disabilities. Inclusion works via eight songs. *$19.95*

5271 Intensive Early Intervention and Beyond
PO Box 9177
Dept. 11W
Champaign, IL 61826-9177   217-352-3273
               800-519-2707
               FAX: 217-352-1221
               www.researchpress.com

David Parkinson, Chairman
Russell Pence, President
Gail Salyards, Dir. Of Marketing/President

5272 Invisible Children
Learning Corporation of America
6493 Kaiser Dr
Fremont, CA 94555-3610   510-490-7311
Oonchia Chia, Owner
Renaldo was blind, Mandy was deaf, and Mark had Cerebral Palsy and used a wheelchair. These child-size puppet characters interacted with non-handicapped puppets.
Film

5273 Let's Eat Video
Blind Children's Center
4120 Marathon Street
Los Angeles, CA 90029-3584   323-664-2153
               info@blindchildrenscenter.org
               blindchildrenscenter.org

Jill Brody, Co-Author
Lynne Webber, Co-Author
Babies and toddlers with visual impairments lack one major avenue of exploration, and this significantly infulences their awareness, perceptions, and anticipation of the food which is presented to them. *$35.00*
VHS/DVD

5274 Look Who's Laughing
Aquarius Health Care Videos
30 Forest Rd
PO Box 249
Millis, MA 2054-1511   508-376-1244
                                   FAX: 508-376-1245
                                    aqvideos@tiac.net
                            www.aquariusproductions.com
Lesile Kussmann, Owner/President/Producer
Kathy Newkirk, Director
Jane Hutchinson, Assoc. Director
This video is packed with laugh-out-loud comedic moments, but
is also full of intelligent and inspiring messages. Look Who's
Laughing introduces viewers to some of today's funniest comedians - who just happen to be physically disabled. We hear them talk
openly and honestly about their limitations as well as their abilities and talents. Helpful for those who work with the disabled and
motivational to both the disabled and able-bodied. Preview option available. *$95.00*
Video

5275 My Body is Not Who I Am
Aquarius Health Care Videos
30 Forest Rd
PO Box 249
Millis, MA 2054-1511   508-376-1244
                                   FAX: 508-376-1245
                                    aqvideos@tiac.net
                            www.aquariusproductions.com
Lesile Kussmann, Owner/President/Producer
Kathy Newkirk, Director
Jane Hutchinson, Assoc. Director
This thought-provoking video introduces viewers to people who
openly discuss the struggles and triumphs they have experienced
living in a body that is physically disabled. They talk honestly
about the social stigma of their disability and the problems they
face in terms of mobility, health care and family relationships, as
well as the challenges of emotional and sexual intimacy. Preview
option available. *$195.00*
Video

5276 My Country
Aquarius Health Care Videos
30 Forest Rd
PO Box 249
Millis, MA 2054-1511   508-376-1244
                                   FAX: 508-376-1245
                                    aqvideos@tiac.net
                            www.aquariusproductions.com
Lesile Kussmann, Owner/President/Producer
Kathy Newkirk, Director
Jane Hutchinson, Assoc. Director
By telling the stories of three people with disabilities and their
struggle for equal rights under the law, this film draws a powerful
parallel between the efforts of disability rights activists and the
civil rights struggle of the 1960s. Great for disability awareness
programs, and for discussions of disability rights issues. Should
be part of every college curriculum on disabilities. Awarded Best
of Show Superfest 98. Preview option available. *$195.00*
Video

5277 Narcolepsy
Fanlight Productions
c/o Icarus Films
32 Court Street, 21st Floor
Brooklyn, NY 11201   718-488-8900
                                        800-876-1710
                                   FAX: 718-488-8642
                                    info@fanlight.com
                                     www.fanlight.com
Ben Achtenberg, Founder, Owner
Jason Margolis, Producer
Presents the experiences of three individuals who lives and rela-
tionships have been disrupted by narcolepsy. Rental $50/day.
$199.00
VHS/25 Minutes

5278 No Barriers
Aquarius Health Care Videos
30 Forest Rd
PO Box 249
Millis, MA 2054-1511   508-376-1244
                                   FAX: 508-376-1245
                                    aqvideos@tiac.net
                            www.aquariusproductions.com
Lesile Kussmann, Owner/President/Producer
Kathy Newkirk, Director
Jane Hutchinson, Assoc. Director
Everyone faces the world with different abilities and disabilities.
But everyone has at least one goal in common..to break through
their own barriers says Mark Wellman. Mark, a paraplegic, knows
this well. No Barriers takes us into Mark's world where he defies
the odds for most able bodied individuals by climbing Yosemite's
Half Dome and El Capitan. This video is more than inspiring and
fun to watch..it helps one make that paradigm shift from can't do
to can do! Preview option available *$90.00*
Video

5279 On The Spectrum
Fanlight Productions
32 Court St.
21st Floor
Brooklyn, NY 11201-4421   718-488-8900
                                        800-876-1710
                                   FAX: 718-488-8642
                                    info@fanlight.com
                                     www.fanlight.com
Jonathan Miller, President
Patricio Guzman, Director
Meredith Miller, Sales Manager
Adults living with Asperger syndrome describe the ways AS has
affected their lives, their work and their relationships. They dis-
cuss learning to cope with the disorder and the comfort and rein-
forcement of participating with others 'like them' in an
Asperger's support group. 53 min. *$199.00*

5280 Open for Business
Disability Rights Education and Defense Fund
3075 Adeline Street
Suite 210
Berkeley, CA 94703-2219   510-644-2555
                                        800-841-8645
                                   FAX: 510-841-8645
                                      info@dredf.org
                                       www.dredf.org
Sue Henderson, Executive Director
Jenny . Kern, Esq, President/Chair
Claudia Center, Esq, Treasurer
Documentary video captures the drama and emotions of the his-
toric civil rights demonstration of people with disabilities in
1977, resulting in the signing of the 504 Regulations, the first
Federal Civil Rights Law protecting people with disabilities. In-
cludes contemporary news footage and news interviews with par-
ticipants and demonstration leaders. *$179.00*

5281 Open to the Public
Aquarius Health Care Videos
30 Forest Rd
PO Box 249
Millis, MA 2054-1511   508-376-1244
                                   FAX: 508-376-1245
                                    aqvideos@tiac.net
                            www.aquariusproductions.com
Lesile Kussmann, Owner/President/Producer
Kathy Newkirk, Director
Jane Hutchinson, Assoc. Director
Provides an overview of the Americans with Disabilities Act as it
applies to state and local governments. The ADA doesn't provide
recommendations for solving common problems, but this film
could provide enough information for governments to solve some
common problems without turning to high-priced consultants.
Preview option available. *$125.00*
Video

5282 **Our Own Road**
Aquarius Health Care Videos
30 Forest Rd
PO Box 249
Millis, MA 2054-1511
508-376-1244
FAX: 508-376-1245
aqvideos@tiac.net
www.aquariusproductions.com

Lesile Kussmann, Owner/President/Producer
Kathy Newkirk, Director
Jane Hutchinson, Assoc. Director
This video shows the disabled helping other people who are disabled and portrays the sense of pride they get from helping others. This multicultural program features many different healing techniques, and teaches the importance of helping those who are disabled become independent and productive. *$99.00*

5283 **Outsider: The Life and Art of Judith Scott**
Fanlight Productions
32 Court St.
21st Floor
Brooklyn, NY 11201-4421
718-488-8900
800-876-1710
FAX: 718-488-8642
info@fanlight.com
www.fanlight.com

Jonathan Miller, President
Patricio Guzman, Director
Meredith Miller, Sales Manager
Judith Scoot has Down Syndrome, is deaf, and does not speak. Yet after 35 years of institutionalization, with the help of a sister who never gave up on her, she emerged to create a series of sculptures that have fascinated and mystified art experts and collectors around the world. 26 minutes. *$199.00*

5284 **Passion for Justice**
Fanlight Productions
32 Court St.
21st Floor
Brooklyn, NY 11201-4421
718-488-8900
800-876-1710
FAX: 718-488-8642
info@fanlight.com
www.fanlight.com

Jonathan Miller, President
Patricio Guzman, Director
Meredith Miller, Sales Manager
An unusually penetrating examination of the question of inclusion, this is an engaging portrait of Bob Perske, the author of Unequal Justice, and a crusader for the legal rights of people with developmental disabilities. A Passion for Justice asks challenging questions about society's responsibility to this population, and about ways to protect everyone's rights to equality and justice. *$99.00*
29 Minutes

5285 **Phoenix Dance**
Fanlight Productions
32 Court St.
21st Floor
Brooklyn, NY 11201-4421
718-488-8900
800-876-1710
FAX: 718-488-8642
info@fanlight.com
www.fanlight.com

Jonathan Miller, President
Patricio Guzman, Director
Meredith Miller, Sales Manager
A heroic journey of transformation and healing, Phoenix Dance challenges our expectations of what it means to be disabled. In March, 2001, renowned dancer Homer Avila discovered that the pain in his hip was cancer. A month later, his right leg and most of his hip were amputated. *$199.00*

5286 **Pool Exercise Program - Arthritis Water Exercise / Arthritis Foundation**
Arthritis Foundation Distribution Center
PO Box 932915
Atlanta, GA 31193-2915
440-872-7100
800-283-7800
FAX: 404-872-0457
aforders@arthritis.org
www.arthritis.org

John Klippel, President/CEO
This video features water exercises that will help you increase and maintain joint flexibility, strengthen and tone muscles, and increase endurance. All exercises are performed in water at chest level. No swimming skills are necessary. *$19.50*

5287 **Potty Learning for Children who Experience Delay**
Exceptional Parent Library
PO Box 1807
Englewood Cliffs, NJ 7632-1207
201-947-6000
800-535-1910
FAX: 201-947-9376
eplibrary@aol.com

This video presents a unique developmental approach to supporting the child in learning independence in the management of bathroom skills. *$39.95*

5288 **Pushin' Forward**
Fanlight Productions
32 Court St.
21st Floor
Brooklyn, NY 11201-4421
718-488-8900
800-876-1710
FAX: 718-488-8642
info@fanlight.com
www.fanlight.com

Jonathan Miller, President
Patricio Guzman, Director
Meredith Miller, Sales Manager
Growing up poor and Latino, James Lilly was a gang member and drug dealer until, at fifteen, he was shot in the back and paralyzed. Today, he shares his story with inner city kids, and tells them about one thing that helped him move on; wheelchair racing. In Pushin' Forward he takes on the world's longest wheelchair race, from Fairbanks to Anchorage, Alaska, in six days! 39 minutes. *$229.00*

5289 **Recognizing Children with Special Needs**
Films Media Group
132 W. 31st St
16th Fl.
New York, NY 10001
800-322-8755
FAX: 800-678-3633
custserv@films.com
www.films.com

A great overview for caregivers of children on how to recognize special needs. Often-times it is the little things children do everyday to compensate for, or express, a disability that can be observed by their caregiver. All types of disabilities are addressed: emotional, physical, psychological, and chronic illness. A wonderful tool for teachers, childcare staff, and students on how to play a vital role in our children's development. Preview option available.
DVD/Video

5290 **Relaxation Techniques for People with Special Needs**
Research Press
PO Box 9177
Dept. 11W
Champaign, IL 61826-9177
217-352-3273
800-519-2707
FAX: 217-352-1221
rp@researchpress.com
www.researchpress.com

David Parkinson, Chairman
Russell Pence, President
Gail Salyards, Dir. Of Marketing/President
The developers discuss and demonstrate how to use special relaxation procedures with children and adolescents who have developmental disabilities. They emphasize the need for students to learn relaxation as a means of coping with stress and developing

self-control. During the scenes of Dr June Groden conducting relaxation training, viewers will see how to correctly use the training procedures, how to use reinforcement during training and how to use guided imagery. 23 minutes. Includes book. *$195.00*
Video

5291   Right at Home
Aquarius Health Care Videos
30 Forest Rd
PO Box 249
Millis, MA 2054
508-376-1244
FAX: 508-376-1245
aqvideos@tiac.net
www.aquariusproductions.com

Lesile Kussmann, Owner/President/Producer
Kathy Newkirk, Director
Jane Hutchinson, Assoc. Director

Shows simple solutions for complying with the Fair Hoiusing Act amendments. Emphasizes low-cost, practical solutions, and working with people with disabilities to find the best applicable solution. Ideal for people with disabilities and their families, as well as housing providers, university courses, and disability awareness organizations. Preview option is available. *$99.00*
Video

5292   Seat-A-Robics
PO Box 630064
Little Neck, NY 11363-64
718-631-4007
Daria Alinovi, President

Offers a variety of safe, affordable and medically approved video exercise programs that are listed in our video chapter. In addition the company offers two resources. The first Healthy Eating & Facts For Kids is geared specifically to health professionals and educators that work with disabled children ($39.95). The second is a recreational resource guide that stimulates children to be creative and get involved. It keeps them actively engaged while having fun and getting fit ($29.95).

5293   Shining Bright: Head Start Inclusion
Brookes Publishing
PO Box 10624
Baltimore, MD 21285-624
410-337-9580
800-638-3775
FAX: 410-337-8539
custserv@brookespublishing.com

Paul Brooks, Owner

This documentary depicts the collaborative efforts of a Head Start and a local education agency to include children with severe disabilities in a Head Start program. This video addresses issues such as support for children with severe health impairments, benefits of participating in Head Start, ability of teachers with a general education background to serve children with severe disabilities, and staff relations. Includes a 28-page saddle-stitched booklet. *$45.00*

23 Minutes
ISBN 1-55766 -95-9

5294   Small Differences
Aquarius Health Care Videos
30 Forest Rd
PO Box 249
Millis, MA 2054-1511
508-376-1244
FAX: 508-376-1245
aqvideos@tiac.net
www.aquariusproductions.com

Lesile Kussmann, Owner/President/Producer
Kathy Newkirk, Director
Jane Hutchinson, Assoc. Director

What happens when you give children with and without disabilities a camera and ask them to produce a video about disabilities? The result is an uplifting, award-winning disability video that both children and adults can relate to. The kids interviewed adults and children with physical and sensory disabilities. A top-quality production that increases understanding and awareness. Winner, Columbus International Film & Video Festival. Winner, National Education Media Network. Preview option availabe *$110.00*
Video

5295   Someday's Child
Educational Productions
9000 SW Gemini Dr
Beaverton, OR 97008-7151
503-644-7000
800-950-4949
FAX: 503-350-7000
custserv@edpro.com
www.edpro.com

Diane Trister Dodge, Founder/President/Lead Author
Arnitra Duckett, VP, Sales & Strategic Marketing

This video focuses on three families' search for help and information for their children with disabilities.

5296   Sound & Fury
Aquarius Health Care Videos
30 Forest Rd
PO Box 249
Millis, MA 2054-1511
508-376-1244
FAX: 508-376-1245
aqvideos@tiac.net
www.aquariusproductions.com

Lesile Kussmann, Owner/President/Producer
Kathy Newkirk, Director
Jane Hutchinson, Assoc. Director

This film takes viewers inside the seldom seen world of the deaf to witness a painful family struggle over a controversial medical technology called the cochlear implant. Some of the family members celebrate the implant as a long overdue cure for deafness while others fear it will destroy their language and way of life. This documentary explores this seemingly irreconcilable conflict as it illuminates the ongoing struggle for identity among deaf people today. *$195.00*
Video

5297   Special Children/Special Solutions
Option Indigo Press
2080 S Undermountain Rd
Sheffield, MA 1257-9643
413-229-8727
800-714-2779
FAX: 413-229-8727
indigo@option.org

Barry Kaufmans, Owner/Founder/Author
Samahria Kaufmans, Owner/Founder

This four-tape audio series presents concrete, down-to-earth, no-nonsense alternatives which are full of love and acceptance for the special child while being wholly supportive of parents, professionals and helpers who want to reach out. The accepting (nonjudgmental) attitude presented is the basis of all Samahria's work and is the foundation for the nurturing teaching process that has encouraged and helped parents, children and others to accomplish more than most would have believed. *$55.00*
Audio

5298   Technology for the Disabled
Landmark Media
3450 Slade Run Dr
Falls Church, VA 22042-3940
703-241-2030
800-342-4336
FAX: 703-536-9540
info@landmarkmedia.com
landmarkmedia.com

Michael Hartogs, President
Joan Hartogs, Vice President
Peter Hartogs, Vice President

Physically disabled people cope with the frustrations of a body they cannot control. The computer age has made many disabled more self-reliant; armless feed themselves, the blind read newspapers and the voiceless speak through marvelous technological breakthroughs. *$195.00*
Video

5299 Three R's for Special Education: Rights, Resources, Results
Brookes Publishing
PO Box 10624
Baltimore
MD, 21 0624-624   410-337-9580
                                               800-638-3775
                                               FAX: 410-337-8539
                                    custserv@brookespublishing.com
Paul Brooks, Owner
This is a guide for parents, and a tool for educators. Through this video parents learn how to work through the steps of the special education system and work toward securing the best education and services for their children. Reviews the laws to protect children with disabilities in easy to understand language. Also provides a list of national organizations that can offer resources, information and advice to parents. *$49.95*
50 Minutes
ISBN 0-96461 -80-7

5300 Tools for Students
Aquarius Health Care Videos
30 Forest Rd
PO Box 249
Millis, MA 2054-1511   508-376-1244
                                               FAX: 508-376-1245
                                               aqvideos@tiac.net
                                    www.aquariusproductions.com
Lesile Kussmann, Owner/President/Producer
Kathy Newkirk, Director
Jane Hutchinson, Assoc. Director
Provides a series of 26 fun occupational therapy sensory processing activities. Designed as an in-home, in-workshop, and in-class exercise leader with students. Activities include: Strenghten the muscles necessary for normal activities, provide the muscles necessary to enhance alertness and concentration, increase the ability to use good posture, help social skills and fitting in and increase coordination; concludes with emphasis on team collaboration between the student, teacher, and parents. *$99.00*
Video

5301 Twitch and Shout
Fanlight Productions
c/o Icarus Films
32 Court Street, 21st Floor
Brooklyn, NY 11201   718-488-8900
                                               800-876-1710
                                               FAX: 718-488-8642
                                               info@fanlight.com
                                               www.fanlight.com
Ben Achtenberg, Founder, Owner
Laurel Chitden, Producer
This documentary provides an intimate journey into the startling world of Tourette Syndrome (TS), a genetic disorder that can cause a bizarre range of involuntary movements, vocalizations, and compulsions. Through the eyes of a photojournalist with TS, the film introduces viewers to others who have this puzzling disorder. This is an emotionally absorbing, sometimes, unsettling, and finally uplifting program about people who must contend with a society that often sees them as crazy or bad. *$225.00*

5302 Video Guide to Disability Awareness
Aquarius Health Care Videos
30 Forest Rd
PO Box 249
Millis, MA 2054-1511   508-376-1244
                                               FAX: 508-376-1245
                                               aqvideos@tiac.net
                                    www.aquariusproductions.com
Lesile Kussmann, Owner/President/Producer
Kathy Newkirk, Director
Jane Hutchinson, Assoc. Director
President Clinton opens and concludes this informative video about disability awareness. A series of candid interviews with people who have a wide range of disabilities provide personal insights into the issues surrounding visual, hearing, physical and mental disabilities. Video comes with written reference guide and is also available with open or closed captioning. Preview option available. *$195.00*
Video

5303 Video Intensive Parenting
Systems Unlimited/LIFE Skills
1556 S 1st Ave
Iowa City, IA 52240-6007   319-356-5412
Geoffrey Lauer, Program Director
Bill Gorman, President
Ginny Kirschling, Public Information Specialist
Parents who have children with special needs share their reactions to their child's diagnosis and how they have learned to cope with their feelings. *$69.95*

5304 Vital Signs: Crip Culture Talks Back
Fanlight Productions
32 Court St.
21st Floor
Brooklyn, NY 11201-4421   718-488-8900
                                               800-876-1710
                                               FAX: 718-488-8642
                                               info@fanlight.com
                                               www.fanlight.com
Jonathan Miller, President
Patricio Guzman, Director
Meredith Miller, Sales Manager
This edgy, raw video documentary explores the politics of disability through the performances, debates and late-night conversations of artists at a recent national conference of disabilities and the art's. Vital Signs conveys the intensity, variety and vitality of disability culture today. *$225.00*
Video

5305 What About Me?
Educational Productions
9000 SW Gemini Dr
Beaverton, OR 97008-7151   503-644-7000
                                               800-950-4949
                                               FAX: 503-350-7000
                                               custserve@edpro.com
                                    www.teachingstrategies.com
Diane Trister Dodge, Founder/President/Lead Author
Arnitra Duckett, VP, Sales & Strategic Marketing
This video focuses on two siblings of children with disabilities. The siblings (Brian and Julie) share their perspectives, their worries, concerns and victories about living with a sibling with a disability.

5306 When Billy Broke His Head..and Other
Fanlight Productions
32 Court St.
21st Floor
Brooklyn, NY 11201-4421   718-488-8900
                                               800-876-1710
                                               FAX: 718-488-8642
                                               info@fanlight.com
                                               www.fanlight.com
Jonathan Miller, President
Patricio Guzman, Director
Meredith Miller, Sales Manager
When Billy Golfus, an award-winning journalist, became brain damaged as the result of a motor scooter accident, he joined the ranks of the 43 million Americans with disabilities, this country's largest and most invisible minority. He helped create this video, which blends humor with politics and individual experience with a chorus of voices, to explain what it is really like to live with a disability in America. #136 *$195.00*
ISBN 1-57295 -36-2

5307 When I Grow Up
Britannica Film Company
345 4th St
San Francisco, CA 94107-1206   415-928-8466
                                               FAX: 415-928-5027
Dave Bekowich, Owner
At a costume party each child was to come as what they wanted to be when they grew up. Some of the children had handicaps, and they talked about why their handicaps would not prevent them from fulfilling their desires.
Film

5308 **When Parents Can't Fix It**
Fanlight Productions
32 Court St.
21st Floor
Brooklyn, NY 11201-4421   718-488-8900
                                 800-876-1710
                            FAX: 718-488-8642
                                 info@fanlight.com
                                 www.fanlight.com

Jonathan Miller, President
Patricio Guzman, Director
Meredith Miller, Sales Manager
This documentary looks at the lives of five families who are raising children with disabilities - the problems they face, how they have learned to cope, and the rewards and stresses of adapting to their child's condition. It explores the medical complexities and financial pressures families encounter, the emotional and physical toll on parents and siblings, and the dangers of child abuse in this population. It offers a very realistic look at different family strengths and coping styles.
58 Min. DVD/VHS
ISBN 1-572958-76-6

5309 **White Cane and Wheels**
Fanlight Productions
32 Court St.
21st Floor
Brooklyn, NY 11201-4421   718-488-8900
                                 800-876-1710
                            FAX: 718-488-8642
                                 info@fanlight.com
                                 www.fanlight.com

Jonathan Miller, President
Patricio Guzman, Director
Meredith Miller, Sales Manager
Carmen and Steve once dreamed of lives on stage and screen, but their plans were cut short by her blindness and his muscular dystrophy. This program is a funny and touching exploration of a relationship filled with frustration, but held together with patience, stubborness, forgiveness, and love. 26 minutes. *$169.00*

Web Sites

5310 **ADA Questions and Answers**
US Department of Justice, Civil Rights Division
950 Pennsylvania Ave. NW
9th Floor
Washington, DC 20530   202-307-0663
                                 800-514-0301
                            FAX: 202-307-1197
                            TTY: 800-514-0383
                                 www.ada.gov

Rebecca B. Bond, Chief
Anne Raish, Principal Deputy Chief
Christina Galindo-Walsh, Deputy Chief
A 31-page booklet giving an overview of the ADA's requirements affecting employers, businesses, nonprofit service agencies, and state and local governments programs, including public transportation. Available in electronic format only.

5311 **Ability Jobs**
Ability Magazine
P.O. Box 10878
Costa Mesa, CA 92627   www.abilityjobs.com
Provides an electronic classified system which allows employers to recruit qualified individuals with disabilities, and people with disabilities to locate employment opportunities.

5312 **AbleApparel - Affordable Adaptive Clothing and Accessories**
2121 Hillside Ave
New Hyde Park, NY 11040-2712   516-873-6552
                            FAX: 516-248-7308
                                 www.ableapparel.com

Mary Ann Tenaglia, Partner
Marie Harmon, Partner
Donna Lo Monica, Partner/Designer

AbleApparel is always designing and creating new products that will make Matty's life and others with disabilities a little easier. Most of the people spoken to regardless of age want to be able to wear clothes that are functional, affordable and, above all, fashionable.

5313 **AbleData**
103 W Broad St
Suite 400
Falls Church, VA 22046   301-608-8998
                                 800-227-0216
                            FAX: 301-608-8958
                            TTY: 301-608-8912
                                 www.abledata.com

Katherine Belknap, Director
David Johnson, Publications Director
AbleData provides objective information on assistive technology and rehabilitation equipment available from domestic and international sources to consumers, organizations, professionals, and caregivers within the United States. AbleData serves the nation's disability, rehabilitation and senior communities.

5314 **Access Unlimited**
570 Hance Rd
Binghamton, NY 13903-5700   607-669-4822
                                 800-849-2143
                            FAX: 607-669-4595
                                 www.accessunlimited.com

Thomas Egan, President/Owner
Tom 'TC' Cole, National Sales Manager
Adaptive transportation and mobility equipment for people with disabilities. ccess Unlimited products empower people with disabilities to regain control of their mobility.

5315 **Ai Squared**
130 Taconic Business Park
Manchester Center, VT 05255-9752   802-362-3612
                                    800-859-0270
                               FAX: 802-362-1670
                                    sales@aisquared.com
                                    www.aisquared.com

David Wu, CEO
Jost Eckhardt, VP of Engineering
Doug Hacker, VP of Business Development
Ai Squared has been a leader in the assistive technology field for over 20 years. Our flagship product, ZoomText, is the world's best magnification and reading software for the vision impaired. We pride ourselves on delivering the highest quality software products and superior technical support.

5316 **Alternatives in Education for the Hearing Impaired (AEHI)**
9300 Capitol Drive
Wheeling, IL 60090-7207   847-850-5490
                            FAX: 847-850-5493
                                 info@agbms.org
                                 www.agbms.org

Sandra L. Mosetick, Board President Emeritus
Bridget Chevez, Board President
Daniel Konopacki, Treasurer
AEHI is a program of the Alexander Graham Bell Montessori School in Mt. Prospect, IL, that fosters literacy and empowers people with hearing impairments to achieve their full potential through unique educational options. AEHI provides Cued Speech workshops, individualized parental training and support, educational consulting, professional development opportunities, and access to a wide variety of information on Cued Speech and its benefits.

5317 **American Academy of Audiology (AAA)**
11480 Commerce Park Dr.
Suite 220
Reston, VA 20191   703-790-8466
                            FAX: 703-790-8631
                                 infoaud@audiology.org
                                 www.audiology.org

Patrick E. Gallagher, Executive Director
Kathryn Werner, Chief Operating Officer
Amy Miedema, VP, Communications & Membership
The American Academy of Audiology is the world's largest professional organization for audiologists. The Academy is dedi-

cated to providing quality hearing care services through professional development, education, research, and increased public awareness of hearing and balance disorders.

5318 American Association of People with Disabilities (AAPD)
2020 Pennsylvania Ave.
Mailbox 263
Washington, DC 20006   202-521-4316
                                               800-840-8844
                                        communications@aapd.com
                                               www.aapd.com
Maria Town, President & Chief Executive Officer
Jasmin Bailey, Operations Director
Christine Liao, Programs Director
Nonprofit cross-disability member organization dedicated to ensuring economic self-sufficiency and political empowerment for Americans with disabilities. AAPD works in coalition with other disability organizations for the full implementation and enforcement of disability nondiscrimination laws, particularly the Americans With Disabilities Act (ADA) of 1990 and the Rehabilitation Act of 1973.

5319 American College of Rheumatology, Researchand Education Foundation
2200 Lake Boulevard NE
Atlanta, GA 30319-5310   404-633-3777
                                          FAX: 404-633-1870
                                        acr@rheumatology.org
                                          www.rheumatology.org
Audrey B. Uknis, MD, President
David I. Daikh, MD, PhD, Foundation President
Jan K. Richardson, PT, PhD, O, ARHP President
The American College of Rheumatology's mission is advancing rheumatology. The organization represents over 8,500 rheumatologists and rheumatology health professionals around the world. The ACR offers its members the support they need to ensure that they are able to continue their innovative work by providing programs of education, research, advocacy , and practice support.

5320 American Liver Foundation
39 Broadway
Suite 2700
New York, NY 10006-3054   212-668-1000
                                          FAX: 212-483-8179
                                        www.liverfoundation.org
Ryan Reczek, National Director, Field Development
Rolf Taylor, National Director, Corporate Relations
Pritha Kuchaculla, National Director, Programs
Is the only national voluntary health organization dedicated to preventing, treating, and curing hepatitis and other liver and gall bladder diseases through research and education.

5321 American Mobility: Personal Mobility Solutions
60 Island St
Lawrence, MA 1840-1835   978-794-3030
                                        www.americanmobility.com
David Lacroix, President
Source of Pride Scooters, Jazzy Power Chairs, personal mobility vehicles, and lift and recline chairs.

5322 American Speech-Language and Hearing Association
2200 Research Blvd
Rockville, MD 20850-3289   301-296-5700
                                               800-638-8255
                                          FAX: 301-296-8580
                                          TTY: 301-296-5650
                                        actioncenter@asha.org
                                               www.asha.org
Wayne A. Foster, PhD, CCC-SLP/A, Chair, Audiology Advisory Council
Patricia A. Prelock, PhD, CCC-SLP, President
Carolyn W. Higdon, EdD, CCC-SLP, Vice President for Finance
Exhibits by companies specializing in alternative and augmentative communications products, publishers, software and hardware compinies, and hearing aid testing equipment manufacturers.

5323 Americans with Disabilities Act: ADA Home Page
                                               800-514-0301
                                          TTY:800-514-0383
                                        webmaster@usdoj.gov
                                               www.ada.gov
Provides facts on the Americans with Disabilities Act and other information relating to disability rights.

5324 Aspies For Freedom (AFF)
                                        www.aspiesforfreedom.com
Gwen Nelson, Co-Founder
Amy Nelson, Co-Founder
Seeks to change the discourse on autism, including negative treatment in the media. Runs an online chatroom and promotes Autistic Pride Day.

5325 Association for the Cure of Cancer of the Prostate (CaP CURE)-Prostate Cancer Foundation
1250 Fourth St
Suite 360
Santa Monica, CA 90401-1444   310-570-4700
                                               800-757-2873
                                          FAX: 310-570-4701
                                               info@pcf.org
                                               www.pcf.org
Mike Milken, Founder/Chairman
Jonathon Simons, MD, President/CEO
Ralph Finerman, Chief Financial Officer/Treasurer/Secretary
CURE is a nonprofit public charity that is dedicated to supporting prostate cancer research and hastening the conversion of research into cures or controls.

5326 Asthma and Allergy Foundation of America
8201 Corporate Drive
Suite 1000
Landover, MD 20785-2266   800-727-8462
                                               info@aafa.org
                                               www.aafa.org
Lynn Hanessian, Chair
Michele Abu Carrick, LICSW, Co-Chair, Governance
Judi McAuliffe, RN, Co-Chair, Programs & Services
AAFA is dedicated to improving the quality of life for people with asthma and allergic diseases through education, advocacy and research.

5327 AudiologyOnline
12333 Sowden Rd.
Ste. B. #79931
Houston, TX 77080-2059   800-753-2160
                                          FAX: 210-579-7010
                                        www.audiologyonline.com
Ted A. Meyer, Chair
Catharine McNally, Chair-Elect
Susan Lenihan, Secretary
Online continuing education resources for audiology professionals.

5328 BDRC Newsletter
Birth Defect Research for Children
976 Lake Baldwin Lane
Suite 104
Orlando, FL 32814   407-895-0802
                                        staff@birthdefects.org
                                        www.birthdefects.org
Betty Mekdeci, Executive Director
A monthly electronic newsletter offering the latest news, research, and updates on birth defects.
Monthly

5329 Braille and Audio Reading Download (BARD)
National Library Service
1291 Taylor St NW
Washington, DC 20542   202-707-5100
                                               800-424-8567
                                               888-657-7323
                                          FAX: 202-707-0712
                                        NLSDownload@loc.gov
                                               nlsbard.loc.gov

501

A program of the National Library Service, where eligible users may download Braille and audiobooks.

5330 Cancer Research Institute
29 Broadway
4th Floor
New York, NY 10006
212-688-7515
800-992-2623
FAX: 212-832-9376
info@cancerresearch.org
www.cancerresearch.org
Jill O'Donnell-Tormey, CEO & Director of Scientific Affairs
Lynne Harmer, Director of Grants Administration and Special Events
Alfred R. Massidas, Chief Financial Officer and Director of Human Resources
Nonprofit organization dedicated to cancer immunotherapy.

5331 Center on the Social & Emotional Foundations for Early Learning (CSEFEL)
Vanderbilt University 110 Magnolia
Box 328 GPC
Nashville, TN 37203
615-322-8150
FAX: 615-343-1570
ml.hemmeter@vanderbilt.edu
csefel.vanderbilt.edu
Mary-Louise Hemmeter, Principal Investigator
Rob Corso, Project Coordinator
Tweety Yates, Project Coordinator
The center will: focus on promoting the social and emotional developmental of children as a means of preventing challenging behaviors; collaborate with existing T/TA providers for the purpose of ensuring the implementation and sustainability of practices at the local level; provide ongoing identification of training needs and preferred delivery formats of local programs and T/TA providers; disseminate evidence-based practices.

5332 Damon Runyon Cancer Research Foundation
Walter Winchell Foundation
One Exchange Plaza, 55 Broadway
Suite 302
New York, NY 10006-3720
212-455-0500
877-722-6237
info@damonrunyon.org
www.damonrunyon.org
Lorraine Egan, President/Chief Executive Officer
Elizabeth Portland, Director of Development
Marialice C. Pagnotta, Director of the Damon Runyon Broadway Tickets Service
The Damon Runyon Cancer Research Foundation funds early career cancer researchers who have the energy, drive and creativity to become leading innovators in their fields. We identify the best young scientists in the nation and support them through four award programs: our Fellowship, Pediatric Cancer Fellowship, Clinical Investigator and Innovation Awards.

5333 DisAbility Information and Resources
jlubin@eskimo.com
www.makoa.org
Jim Lubin, Creator/Owner
Offers dozens of links to sites with information, services and products for the disabled.

5334 Disability Rights Activist
www.disrights.org
Provides information to enable anyone intersted in the rights of disabled people to work for those rights.

5335 DisabilityAdvisor.com
37 North Orange Ave.
Suite 500
Orlando, FL 32801
321-332-7800
888-393-1010
FAX: 888-985-6060
www.disabilityadvisor.com
Joseph E. Ram, Publisher
Kay Derochie, Editor
Jackie Booth, Ph.D., Editor

DisabilityAdvisor.com provides free information on federal and state disability benefits programs and other resources for readers and their families. This includes disabled children and students, military veterans, injured workers and disabled seniors. Readers are encouraged to submit their questions and comments online. The website also offers information on managing finances, education, parenting, relationships and other issues of interest to the disabled and their friends and families.

5336 DisabilityResources.org
Four Glatter Lane
Dept. IN
Centereach, NY 11720-1032
631-585-0290
FAX: 631-585-0290
Julie Klauber, Co-founder/Managing Editor
Avery Klauber, Co-Founder/Executive Director
Sally Rosenthal, Contributing Editor
Disability Resources, inc. is a nonprofit 501(c)(3) organization established to promote and improve awareness, availability and accessibility of information that can help people with disabilities live, learn, love, work and play independently.

5337 Discover Technology
Houston, TX
713-885-1519
dtinc8888@hotmail.com
www.discovertechnology.com
Amantha Cole, Founder
The primary mission of Discover Technology, Inc.is to create and administer computer labs for persons with disabilities, to encourage communication between persons with and without disabilities and to educate the general population about the disabled population.

5338 Dynamic Living
125 Old Iron Ore Road
Bloomfield, CT 06002-1315
860-683-4442
888-940-0605
FAX: 860-243-1910
www.dynamic-living.com
Andrea Tannenbaum, Owner
Kitchen products, bathroom helpers, and unique daily living products that provide a convienient, comfortable, and safe environment for people with disabilities.

5339 ERIC Clearinghouse on Disabilities and Gifted Education
www.hoagiesgifted.org/eric
The ERIC Clearinghouse was disbanded by the government in 2003. This website acts as an archive of ERIC material.

5340 ElderLawAnswers.com
150 Chesnut St
4th Floor, Box #15
Providence, RI 02903
866-267-0947
support@elderlawanswers.com
www.elderlawanswers.com
Harry S. Margolis, Founder/President
Ken Coughlin, Editor
Mark Miller, Director of Product and Business Development
Provides information about legal issues facing senior citizens and a searchable directory of attorneys.

5341 Exploring Autism: A Look at the Genetics of Autism
Box 3445 DUMC
Durham, NC 27710
FAX: 919-684-0952
Chantelle Wolpert, Project Director
Dedicated to helping families who are living with the challenges of autism stay informed about the exciting breakthroughs involving the genetics of autism. Report and explain new genetic research findings. Explain genetic principles as they relate to autism, provide the latest research news, and seek your imput.

5342 FHI 360
1825 Connecticut Ave., NW
Suite 800
Washington, DC 20009-5721   202-884-8000
                                   FAX: 202-884-8400
                         CareerCenterSupport@fhi360.org
                                         www.fhi360.org
Willard Cates Jr, MD, MPH, President Emeritus
Albert J. Siemens, PhD, Chief Executive Officer
Patrick C. Fine, MS, Chief Operating Officer
FHI 360 is a nonprofit human development organization dedicated to improving lives in lasting ways by advancing integrated, locally driven solutions.

5343 Foundation Fighting Blindness
7168 Columbia Gateway Dr.
Suite 100
Columbia, MD 21046   410-423-0600
                                          800-683-5555
                                      TTY:410363713951
                                   info@FightBlindness.org
                                         www.blindness.org
William T. Schmidt, Chief Executive Officer
Valerie Navy-Daniels, Chief Development Officer
Stephen M. Rose, PhD, Chief Research Officer
The Foundation Fighting Blindness (FFB) works to promote research in order to prevent, treat and restore vision. FFB is currently the world's leading private funder of retinal disease research, funding over 100 research grants and 150 researchers.

5344 Freedom Scientific
11830 31st Court North
St. Petersburg, FL 33716-1805   727-803-8000
                                          800-444-4443
                                     FAX: 727-803-8001
                                 info@freedomscientific.com
                                 www.freedomscientific.com
Lee Hamilton, President/CEO/Chairman
Mike Self, Sales Representative
Joseph McDaniel, Sales Representative
Assistive technology for blind and visually impaired computer users.

5345 Gallaudet University Press
800 Florida Ave, NE
Washington, DC 20002-3695   202-651-5488
                                     FAX: 202-651-5489
                                   gupress@gallaudet.edu
                                   www.gupress.gallaudet.edu
Gallaudet University Press is a vital, self-supporting member of the Gallaudet educational and scholarly community. The mission of the Press is to disseminate knowledge about deaf and hard of hearing people, their languages, their communities, their history, and their education through print and electronic media.

5346 Glaucoma Research Foundation
251 Post Street
Suite 600
San Francisco, CA 94108-5017   415-986-3162
                                          800-826-6693
                                   question@glaucoma.org
                                         www.glaucoma.org
Andrew Iwach, MD, Board Chair/Executive Director
Thomas r M. Brunne, President/CEO
H. Allen Bouch, Vice Chair
Our mission is to prevent vision loss from glaucoma by investing in innovative research, education, and support with the ultimate goal of finding a cure.

5347 HealthyWomen
P.O. Box 430
Red Bank, NJ 07701   732-530-3425
                                          877-986-9472
                                     FAX: 732-865-7225
                                   info@healthywomen.org
                                   www.healthywomen.org
Oxana K Pickeral, Ph.D, MBA, Chair
Beth Battaglino, CEO
Phyllis E Greenberger, MSW, Senior Vice President, Science &
Health Policy

Website providing information for women with disabilities, health professionals, researchers, and caretakers.

5348 Herb Research Foundation
5589 Arapahoe Ave
Suite 205
Boulder, CO 80303-8115   303-449-2265
                                           www.herbs.org
Rob McCaleb, President
John Lowe, Director of Research
Research and public education on the health benefits of medicinal plants. Dedicated to world health through the informed use of herbs.

5349 Hypokalemic Periodic Paralysis Resource Page
155 West 68th St
Suite 1732
New York, NY 10023-5830   407-339-9499
                                         lfeld@cfl.rr.com
                                   www.periodicparalysis.org
Jacob Levitt, President/Medical Director
Linda Feld, Vice President
Provides understandable information on HKPP, dynamia linkage to several additional sources of helpful information on the Internet, and offers several online networking opportunities.

5350 INCLUDEnyc
Formerly Resources for Children with Special Needs
116 E. 16th St.
5th Fl.
New York, NY 10003   212-677-4650
                                     FAX: 202-254-4070
                                    info@includenyc.org
                                       www.includenyc.org
Barbara Glassman, Executive Director
Todd Dorman, Senior Director of Communications and Outreach
Mariko Sakita, Director of Parent & Family Services
Provides free services and resources for youth and families with disabilities in all five state boroughs. Organizational services include: Parenting & Advocacy; School and Community Activities; Parent counseling and Training for students with Autism; Medicaid Waiver services; Transition and Adult Services; and Social skills and building relationships.

5351 Innovation Management Group
179 Niblick Road
Suite 454
Paso Robles, CA 93446-4845   818-701-1579
                                          800-889-0987
                                     FAX: 818-936-0200
                                   sales@imgpresents.com
                                     www.imgpresents.com
US and international onscreen keyboards, Word Prediction, Switch Scanning, Hover and Dwell, Joystick emulation, and Magnification software programs.

5352 Interstitial Cystitis Association
1760 Old Meadow Road
Suite 500
McLean, VA 22102-2651   703-442-2070
                                          800-435-7422
                                     FAX: 703-506-3266
                                      icamail@ichelp.org
                                          www.ichelp.org
Barbara Gordon, Co-Chair/Executive Director
Eric Zarnikow, MBA, Co-Chair
Marilynn Schreibstein, CFO
The Interstitial Cystitis Association (ICA) advocates for interstitial cystitis (IC) research dedicated to discovery of a cure and better treatments, raises awareness, and serves as a central hub for the healthcare providers, researchers and millions of patients who suffer with constant urinary urgency and frequency and extreme bladder pain called IC. (IC is also referred to as painful bladder syndrome, bladder pain syndrome, and chronic pelvic pain.)

5353 JoanBorysenko.Com
PO Box 1300
Tesuque, NM 87574   www.joanborysenko.com
Joan Borysenko, Founder

503

Publishes resources for credible information about the intersection of mind-body health, positive psychology, and spiritual exploration.

5354   LD OnLine - WETA Public Television
2775 S. Quincy Street
Arlington, VA 22206-2269   FAX: 703-998-2060
ldonline@weta.org
www.ldonline.org

Noel Gunther, Executive Director
Christian Lindstrom, Director, Learning Media
Tina Chovanec, Director, Reading Rockets
LD OnLine seeks to help children and adults reach their full potential by providing accurate and up-to-date information and advice about learning disabilities and ADHD. The site features hundreds of helpful articles, multimedia, monthly columns by noted experts, first person essays, children's writing and artwork, a comprehensive resource guide, very active forums, and a Yellow Pages referral directory of professionals, schools, and products.

5355   Lighthouse Guild
250 West 64th Street
New York, NY 10023   800-284-4422
www.lighthouseguild.org

Calvin W. Roberts, President & CEO
James M. Dubin, Chairman
Lawrence E. Goldschmidt, Vice Chairman & Treasurer
Lighthouse Guild is a not-for-profit vision & healthcare organization, addressing the needs of people who are blind or visually impaired, including those with multiple disabilities or chronic medical conditions.

5356   Lyme Disease Foundation
PO Box 332
Tolland, CT 6084-332   860-870-0070
FAX: 860-870-0080
www.lyme.org

Karen Forschuer, Chairman
Thomas Forschuer, Executive Director
Provides critical information about tick-borne disease prevention, improves healthcare and funds research for solutions. 500,000 children, adults, and professionals assisted 25 countries.

5357   Mainstream Living
333 SW 9th St
Des Moines, IA 50309   515-243-8115
FAX: 515-243-5017
www.mainstreamliving.org
Provides a full range of community-based residential and non-residential supports to people with disabilities, including community housing, therapy, and employment services.

5358   Mainstream Online Magazine of the Able-Disabled

www.mainstream-mag.com

Cyndi Jones, Publisher
William G. Stothers, Editor
The leading news, advocacy and lifestyle magazine for people with disabilities.

5359   Microsoft Accessibility Technology for Everyone
One Microsoft Way
Redmond, WA 98052-6399   425-882-8080
800-642-7676
FAX: 425-936-7329
TTY: 800-892-5234
www.microsoft.com/enable

William Gates III, Chairman
Steven Ballmer, CEO/Director
Information about accessibility features and options included in Microsoft products.

5360   MossRehab ResourceNet
1200 West Tabor Road
Philadelphia, PA 19141-3099   215-456-9900
800-225-5567
www.mossresourcenet.org

John Whyte, Owner
Ruth Lefton, COO
Anthony Allonardo, Director of Technology

MossRehab, a modern, 147-bed facility, offers comprehensive care to people with a broad range of conditions—including stroke, brain injury, orthopaedic and musculoskeletal disabilities, spinal cord dysfunction, pulmonary disorders, amputations, and other forms of disability.

5361   Multiple Sclerosis National Research Institute
11350 SW Village Parkway
Port St. Lucie, FL 34987-2352   858-597-3872
866-676-7400
FAX: 858-597-3804
www.ms-research.org

Robin Offord, Chairman
Richard Houghten, President/CEO
Donald B. Cooper, C.F.O
Multiple Sclerosis National Research Institute is a division of Torrey Pines Institute for Molecular Studies, a not-for-profit basic research center dedicated to the discovery and development of innovative research methods that lead to treatments for major medical conditions, including multiple sclerosis, AIDS, Alzheimer's disease, pain, heart disease, many types of cancer, and more.

5362   National Alliance of the Disabled(NAOTD)

Walton Dutcher, Executive Director/Operations
Fred Temple, Director
Spike Spikberg, Director
The National Alliance OF The DisAbled is an online informational and advocacy organization dedicated to working towards gaining equal rights for the disAbled in all areas of life.

5363   National Birth Defect Registry
Birth Defect Research for Children
976 Lake Baldwin Lane
Suite 104
Orlando, FL 32814   407-895-0802
staff@birthdefects.org
www.birthdefects.org

Betty Mekdeci, Executive Director
Data collection project by Birth Defect Research for Children to answer parents' questions about birth defects.

5364   National Brain Tumor Foundation - National Brain Tumor Society
55 Chapel Street
Suite 200
Newton, MA 02458-2599   617-924-9997
800-770-8287
FAX: 617-928-9998
info@braintumor.org
www.braintumor.org

Jeffrey Kolodin, Chair
Michael Nathanson, Vice Chair
N. Paul TonThat, Executive Director
An organization serving people whose lives are affected by brain tumors. The organization is dedicated to promoting a cure for brain tumors, improving the quality of life and giving hope to the brain tumor community by funding meaningful research and providing patient resources, timely information and education.

5365   National Business & Disability Council
201 I.U. Willets Road
Albertson, NY 11507-1516   516-465-1516
lfrancis@viscardicenter.org
www.business-disability.com

Michael C. Pascucci, Executive Leadership Team Chairman
Laura Francis, Executive Director
John D. Kemp, President
The NBDC is the leading resource for employers seeking to integrate people with disabilities into the workplace and companies seeking to reach them in the consumer marketplace.

5366 National Organization on Disability (NOD)
77 Water St.
13th Floor
New York, NY 10005

646-505-1191
FAX: 646-505-1184
info@nod.org
www.nod.org

Carol Glazer, President
Moeena Das, Chief Operating Officer
Bernard Blake, Director, Finance & Operations
The National Organization on Disability is a private, nonprofit organization that promotes the full and equal participation of men, women, and children with disabilities in all aspects of American life.
1982

5367 National Rehabilitation Information Center (NARIC)
8400 Corporate Drive
Suite 500
Landover, MD 20785-2266

301-459-5984
800-346-2742
FAX: 301-459-4263
TTY: 301-459-5984
www.naric.com

Mark X. Odum, Project Director
Serves both professionals and the general public intersted in disability and rehabilitation.

5368 National Youth Leadership Network Youth Leader Blog (NYLN)

nyln.org
Articles and documentaries about youth leadership, including overcoming disabilities.

5369 Nebraska Library Commission: Talking Book and Braille Service (TBBS)
Talking Book and Braille Service
1200 N St
Suite 120
Lincoln, NE 68508-2023

402-471-4038
800-742-7691
FAX: 402-471-6244
nlc.readadv@nebraska.gov
nlc.nebraska.gov/tbbs

David Oertli, Executive Director
Kay Goehring, Reader Services Coordinator
Bill Ainsley, Audio Production Studio Manager
Provides eligible users with free audio books, audio magazines and Braille via the mail. Also features in-house studios for audiobook production.

5370 NeuroControl Corporation
8333 Rockside Rd
Valley View, OH 44125-6134

216-912-0101
800-378-6955
FAX: 216-912-0129

Helps people with spinal cord injuries lead more independent lives.

5371 Newsletter of PA's AT Lending Library
Temple University Institute on Disabilities
1755 N 13th Street
Student Center, Room 411S
Philadelphia, PA 19122-6024

215-204-1356
800-204-PIAT
FAX: 215-204-6336
TTY: 215-204-1805
iod@temple.edu
www.disabilities.temple.edu/atlend

Celia Feinstein, Co-Executive Director of the Institute on Disabilities
Amy Goldman, Co-Executive Director of the Institute on Disabilities
Ann Marie, Deputy Director
Newsletter from the Assistive Technology Lending Library in Pennsylvania. It is produced quarterly, is free of charge, and is available online only.
4-8 pages Quarterly

5372 Office of Juvenile Justice and Delinquency Prevention
810 Seventh St NW
Washington, DC 20531-3718

202-307-5911
800-851-3420
FAX: 301-519-5600
www.ojjdp.gov

Kathi Grasso, Director, Concentration of Federal Efforts Program
Robert Listenbee, Jr., Administrator
Melodee Hanes, Principal Deputy Administrator
The Office of Juvenile Justice and Delinquency Prevention (OJJDP) provides national leadership, coordination, and resources to prevent and respond to juvenile delinquency and victimization. OJJDP supports states and communities in their efforts to develop and implement effective and coordinated prevention and intervention programs and to improve the juvenile justice system so that it protects public safety, holds offenders accountable, and provides treatment and rehabilitative services tailored

5373 Osteogenesis Imperfecta Foundation
804 W. Diamond Ave.
Suite 210
Gaithersburg, MD 20878- 1414

301-947-0083
800-981-2663
FAX: 301-947-0456
bonelink@oif.org
www.oif.org

Mary Beth Huber, Director of Program Services
Tom Costanzo, Director of Finance & Administration
Erika Ruebensaal Carte, Director of Communications & Development
Strives to improve the quality of life for indivduals with this brittle bone disorder through research, education, awareness, and mutual support.

5374 Quantum Technologies
25242 Arctic Ocean Drive
Lake Forest, CA 92630-6217

949-930-3400
FAX: 949-399-4600
www.qtww.com

Dale Rasmussen, Chairman
Alan Niedzwieck, President/Director
W. Brian Olson, Chief Executive Officer
Provides access to information and tools for independence to serve the visually impaired and those with a learning disability.

5375 Regional Resource Centers Program
1 Quality Street
Suite 721
Lexington, KY 40507

859-257-4921
FAX: 859-257-4353
TTY:859-257-2903
mike.abell@uky.edu
www.rrcprogram.org

Shauna Crane, RRCP Coordinator
Perry Williams, OSEP, Team Member
Mike Abell, Team Member
The Regional Resource Centers Program provides service to all states as well as the Pacific jurisdictions, the Virgin Islands, and Puerto Rico. The six regional program centers are funded by the federal Office of Special Education Programs (OSEP) to assist state education agencies in the systemic improvement of education programs, practices, and policies that affect children and youth with disabilities.

5376 Research!America
1101 King Street
Suite 520
Alexandria, VA 22314-2960

703-739-2577
800-366-2873
FAX: 703-739-2372
info@researchamerica.org
www.researchamerica.org

Hon. John Edward Porter, Chair
Hon. Michael Castle, Vice Chair
Mary Woolley, President/CEO
Builds active public support for more government and private-industry research to find treatments and cures for both physical and mental disorders.

5377   Social Security Online
5 Park Centre Court
Suite 100
Owings Mills, MD 21117-1   800-772-1213
                                     TTY:800-325-0778
                                     www.ssa.gov
Carolyn W. Colvin, Commissioner
James A. Kissko, Chief of Staff
Katherine A. Thornton, Deputy Chief of Staff
Official website of the Social Security Administration.

5378   Special Clothes for Children
PO Box 333
E. Harwich, MA 02645-333   508-430-2410
                                     FAX: 508-430-2410
                                     TTY:508-430-2410
                                     lou@lnrmusic.com
Judi
A catalog of adaptive clothing for children with disabilities -
helping boys and girls with special needs meet the world with
pride and confidence since 1987.

5379   The Arc of the United States
1825 K St NW
Suite 1200
Washington, DC 20006   202-534-3700
                                     800-433-5255
                                     FAX: 202-534-3731
                                     info@thearc.org
                                     www.thearc.org
Peter Berns, Chief Executive Officer
Ruben Rodriguez, Chief Operating Officer
Julie Ward, Senior Executive Officer, Public Policy
The Arc promotes and protects the rights of people with intellectual and developmental disabilities and actively supports their inclusion and participation in the community throughout their
lifetimes. The Arc's clients include people with autism, Down
syndrome, Fragile X syndrome, and various other developmental
disabilities. Some services offered by The Arc include public policy advocacy, education and vocational services.

5380   V Foundation for Cancer Research
106 Towerview Court
Cary, NC 27513-3595   919-380-9505
                                     800-454-6698
                                     info@jimmyv.org
                                     www.jimmyv.org
Sherrie Mazur, Director of Marketing & Communication
Danielle Smith, Director of Corporate and Market Development
Mark Steudel, Associate Director of Development for Prospect
Research
Named after basketball coach and broadcaster, Jim Valvano. The
V Foundation funds critical stage research conducted by young
researchers at NCI approved cancer research facilities.

5381   ValueOptions
240 Corporate Blvd.
Norfolk, VA 23502-4900   757-459-5100
                                     FAX: 501-707-0940
                                     TTY:877-334-0077
                                     www.valueoptions.com
Heyward R. Donigan, President/CEO
Scott Tabakin, Chief Financial Officer
Kyle A. Raffaniello, Executive Vice President and Chief Strategy
Officer
Serves over 22 million people in behavioral healthcare through
publicaly funded, federal, and commercial contracts.

5382   Wardrobe Wagon: The Special Needs Clothing Store
258B Route 46 E
Fairfield, NJ 7004-2324   973-244-2414
                                     800-992-2737
                                     wardrobew@aol.com
                                     www.wardrobewagon.com
E Oppenberg, President
Bonnie Oppenberg
Jerome Oppenberg, Owner
Wearing apparel for individuals with special clothing needs.

5383   We Magazine
130 William St
New York, NY 10038   646-769-2722
                                     FAX: 212-375-6266
                                     TTY:212-375-6235
                                     sales@wemedia.com
Lifestyle magazine for people with disabilities.

5384   We Media
1801 Reston Parkway
Suite 300
Reston, VA 20190-4303   703-880-2659
                                     help@wemedia.com
                                     www.wemedia.com
Andrew Nachison, Founder
Dale Peskin, Founder
Online network for people with disabilities.

5385   WebABLE
                          www.hisoftware.com/press/webable.html
Provides disability-related internet resources.

5386   WheelchairNet
6425 Penn Ave
Suite 401 BAKSQ, Department of Reha
Philadelphia, PA 15206   412-624-6279
                                     ruffing@pitt.edu
                                     www.wheelchairnet.org
Joseph Ruffing, Communications Specialist
A virtual community of people who care about wheelchairs.

5387   World Association of Persons with Disabilities
2441 N Sterling Ave
302W
Oklahoma, OK 73127-2009   405-672-4440
                                     www.wapd.org
Byron R. Kerford, Founder/Leader
Thomas J. Mecke, Executive Director
Sierra Hebron, Director of Human Resources
Dedicated to improving the quality of life for those with disabili-
ties.

Toys & Games

General

5389 Age Appropriate Puzzles
7756 Winding Way
Fair Oaks, CA 95628-5735   916-961-3507
                                       FAX: 916-961-0765

Cheryl Meyers, President
These unique puzzles teach numerous concepts: picture, name, color and shape recognition. Each of the two themes (holidays, and clothing) comes with self-adhesive stickers that name each picture in English, Hmong, Russian, Spanish and Vietnamese. A notch at each puzzle piece makes grasping and lifting the pieces easy to use. They are designed for children from 18 months and up. Special needs children, preschool through high school would also benefit. *$9.95*

5390 All-Turn-It Spinner
AbleNet, Inc.
2625 Patton Road
Roseville, MN 55113-1137   651-294-2200
                                            800-322-0956
                                       FAX: 651-294-2259
                          customerservice@ablenetinc.com
                                    www.ablenetinc.com

Jennifer Thalhuber, President & CEO
Paul Sugden, CFO & Trustee
The All-Turn-It Spinner is a random spinner that comes with a dice overlay allowing users to participate in any commercially-available game that require dice. Activate the spinner with its built-in switch or connect an external switch. Overlays are interchangeable with AbleNet designed spinner games or users can create their own overlay. *$145.00*

5391 Anthony Brothers Manufacturing
Convert-O-Bike
9 Capper Drive
Dailey Industrial Park,
Pacific, MO 63069-5196   636-257-0533
                                            800-346-6313
                                       FAX: 636-257-5473
                                        www.angelesstore.com

Tim Lynch, Director of Sales
David Curry, General Manager
Michelle Vondera, Customer Service Manager
Manufacture wheeled toys and goods for disabled children.

5392 Automatic Card Shuffler
Maxi Aids
42 Executive Blvd.
Farmingdale, NY 11735-4710   631-752-0521
                                            800-522-6294
                                       FAX: 631-752-0689
                                       TTY: 631-752-0738
                                    sales@maxiaids.com
                                       www.maxiaids.com

Elliot Zaretsky, Founder, President & CEO
Allows for hands-free card shuffling. Holds up to two decks at a time. Designed for those with limited hand dexterity. *$13.95*

5393 Backgammon Set: Deluxe
Maxi Aids
42 Executive Blvd.
Farmingdale, NY 11735-4710   631-752-0521
                                            800-522-6294
                                       FAX: 631-752-0689
                                       TTY: 631-752-0738
                                    sales@maxiaids.com
                                       www.maxiaids.com

Elliot Zaretsky, Founder, President & CEO
Backgammon game board set featuring raised white dividers and color contrast for players with low vision. *$59.95*

5394 Board Games: Peg Solitaire
Maxi Aids
42 Executive Blvd.
Farmingdale, NY 11735-4710   631-752-0521
                                            800-522-6294
                                       FAX: 631-752-0689
                                       TTY: 631-752-0738
                                    sales@maxiaids.com
                                       www.maxiaids.com

Elliot Zaretsky, Founder, President & CEO
This version of the solo board game uses wood marbles and a wood game board with 33 indentations. *$12.95*

5395 Board Games: Snakes and Ladders
Maxi Aids
42 Executive Blvd.
Farmingdale, NY 11735-4710   631-752-0521
                                            800-522-6294
                                       FAX: 631-752-0689
                                       TTY: 631-752-0738
                                    sales@maxiaids.com
                                       www.maxiaids.com

Elliot Zaretsky, Founder, President & CEO
A board game for two to four players. Comes with a raised board and wood die braille spinner. *$72.59*

5396 Braille Playing Cards
Maxi Aids
42 Executive Blvd.
Farmingdale, NY 11735-4710   631-752-0521
                                            800-522-6294
                                       FAX: 631-752-0689
                                       TTY: 631-752-0738
                                    sales@maxiaids.com
                                       www.maxiaids.com

Elliot Zaretsky, Founder, President & CEO
Playing cards that offer regular print and braille on plastic cards for the blind or visually impaired player.

5397 Braille: Bingo Cards, Boards and Call Numbers
Maxi Aids
42 Executive Blvd.
Farmingdale, NY 11735-4710   631-752-0521
                                            800-522-6294
                                       FAX: 631-752-0689
                                       TTY: 631-752-0738
                                    sales@maxiaids.com
                                       www.maxiaids.com

Elliot Zaretsky, Founder, President & CEO
Bingo products for the visually impaired. Cards, boards and call numbers in regular print and braille.

5398 Braille: Rook Cards
Maxi Aids
42 Executive Blvd.
Farmingdale, NY 11735-4710   631-752-0521
                                            800-522-6294
                                       FAX: 631-752-0689
                                       TTY: 631-752-0738
                                    sales@maxiaids.com
                                       www.maxiaids.com

Elliot Zaretsky, Founder, President & CEO
This set of cards for Rook, the popular bidding card game with 23 variations, has regular size print and braille print for the blind/visually impaired player. *$18.95*

5399 Cards: Musical
ASB
919 Walnut Street
Philadelphia, PA 19107-5237   215-627-0600
                                       FAX: 215-922-0692
                                        asbinfo@asb.org
                                          www.asb.org

Karla S. McCaney, President & CEO
Beth Deering, Chief Program Officer
Sylvia Purnell, Director of Learning & Development
These cards, for all occasions, play music when they are opened for the visually impaired and blind persons. *$2.50*

5400 Cards: UNO
Maxi Aids
42 Executive Blvd.
Farmingdale, NY 11735-4710

631-752-0521
800-522-6294
FAX: 631-752-0689
TTY: 631-752-0738
sales@maxiaids.com
www.maxiaids.com

Elliot Zaretsky, Founder, President & CEO
Traditional card game in braille for blind or visually impaired players. *$14.50*

5401 Chess Set: Deluxe
Maxi Aids
42 Executive Blvd.
Farmingdale, NY 11735-4710

631-752-0521
800-522-6294
FAX: 631-752-0689
TTY: 631-752-0738
sales@maxiaids.com
www.maxiaids.com

Elliot Zaretsky, Founder, President & CEO
Wooden board contains holes for inserting pieces. Black pieces contain a metal tip to distinguish them from white pieces. *$46.95*

5402 Dice: Jumbo Size
ASB
919 Walnut Street
Philadelphia, PA 19107-5237

215-627-0600
FAX: 215-922-0692
asbinfo@asb.org
www.asb.org

Karla S. McCaney, President & CEO
Beth Deering, Chief Program Officer
Sylvia Purnell, Director of Learning & Development
The large white and black dice are over-sized and have grooved dots to indicate the numbers, for easy reading for the visually handicapped. *$4.95*

5403 Dominoes with Raised Dots
Maxi Aids
42 Executive Blvd.
Farmingdale, NY 11735-4710

631-752-0521
800-522-6294
FAX: 631-752-0689
TTY: 631-752-0738
sales@maxiaids.com
www.maxiaids.com

Elliot Zaretsky, Founder, President & CEO
Standard set with tactile pieces for easier identification. *$14.95*

5404 Dual Switch Latch and Timer
AbleNet, Inc.
2625 Patton Road
Roseville, MN 55113-1137

651-294-2200
800-322-0956
FAX: 651-294-2259
customerservice@ablenetinc.com
www.ablenetinc.com

Jennifer Thalhuber, President & CEO
Paul Sugden, CFO & Trustee
Dual Switch Latch and Timer allows a user to activate a battery-operated toy or appliance in the latch, timed seconds and timed minutes modes of control. Choose for one user and one device at a time. *$235.00*

5405 Early Learning 1
MarbleSoft
12301 Central Ave NE
Suite 205
Blaine, MN 55434-4902

763-755-1402
888-755-1402
FAX: 763-862-2920
sales@marblesoft.com
www.marblesoft.com

Vicki Larson, Manager
Early learning 2.1 includes four activities that teach prereading skills. Single and dual-switch scanning are built in and special prompts allow blind students to use all levels of difficulty. Includes Matching Colors, Learning Shapes, Counting Numbers and Letter Match. Runs on Windows 98 or later and MAC OS 9 or OSX (classic not required). *$70.00*

5406 Enabling Devices
50 Broadway
Hawthorne, NY 10532

914-747-3070
800-832-8697
FAX: 914-747-3480
sales@enablingdevices.com
www.enablingdevices.com

Seth Kanor, President & CEO
Enabling Devices is a company dedicated to developing affordable learning and assistive devices to help people of all ages with disabling conditions. Founded by Steven E. Kanor, Ph.D. and orginally known as Toys for Special Children, the company has been creating innovative communicators, adapted toys and switches for the physically challenged for more than 35 years.

5407 Four in a Row Game: Tactile
Maxi Aids
42 Executive Blvd.
Farmingdale, NY 11735-4710

631-752-0521
800-522-6294
FAX: 631-752-0689
TTY: 631-752-0738
sales@maxiaids.com
www.maxiaids.com

Elliot Zaretsky, Founder, President & CEO
Comes with game console, 23 red disks, and 23 yellow disks. Red disks are drilled for tactile identification. *$22.95*

5408 Hands-Free Controller
Nintendo
PO Box 957
Redmond, WA 98073-957

800-255-3700
www.nintendo.com

Yoshio Tsuboike, Editor-in-Chief
Nintendo controller for the physically disabled.

5409 National Lekotek Center
2001 N. Clybourn Av.
1st Floor
Chicago, IL 60614-3716

773-528-5766
800-366-PLAY
FAX: 773-537-2992
TTY: 773-973-2180
www.lekotek.org

Elaine D. Cottey, Chair
Joanna Horsnail, Chair
Eric Gastevich, Treasurer
Maximizes the development of children with special needs through play. Supports families through nationwide family play centers, toy lending libraries and computer play programs. Publishes six-page newsletter three times per year.

5410 New Language of Toys: Teaching Communication Skills to Children with Special Needs
Spina Bifida Association of America
4590 MacArthur Blvd,NW,
Suite 250
Washington, DC 20007- 4226

202-944-3285
800-621-314
FAX: 202-944-3295
sbaa@sbaa.org
www.spinabifidaassociation.org

Lisa Raman, Director-National Resource Center
Mary Nethercutt, National Walk Director
Christopher Vance, Director of Development
A guide for parents and teachers and a reader-friendly resource guide that provides a wealth of information on how play activities affect a child's language development and where to get the toys and materials to use in these activities. *$19.00*

5411 **Playing Card Holders**
Maxi Aids
42 Executive Blvd.
Farmingdale, NY 11735-4710

631-752-0521
800-522-6294
FAX: 631-752-0689
TTY: 631-752-0738
sales@maxiaids.com
www.maxiaids.com

Elliot Zaretsky, Founder, President & CEO
A playing card holder for those with arthritis, dexterity issues or visual impairments. Holds up to 15 cards. *$8.95*

5412 **Puzzle Games: Cooking, Eating, Community and Grooming**
PCI
PO Box 34270
San Antonio, TX 78265-4270

210-670-3866
800-594-4263
FAX: 218-210-3771

Janie Haugen, Program Director
Jeff McLane, President/CEO
Rebecca Phillips, Executive Director
Each game has 63 pieces which are 2 inches in size. The completed full color puzzle is 19 inch x 15 inch. Step 1 - Work the puzzle. Step 2 - Match picture or word cards to the correct space on the puzzle. These puzzles teach basic life skills. *$19.95*

5413 **Single Switch Games**
MarbleSoft
12301 Central Ave NE
Suite 205
Blaine, MN 55434-4902

763-755-1402
888-755-1402
888-755-1402
FAX: 763-862-2920
sales@marblesoft.com
www.marblesoft.com

Vicki Larson, Manager
Mark Larson
Theres alot of educational software for single switch users, but how about something that's just fun? We've taken some games similar to the ones you enjoyed as a kid and made them work just right for single switch users. Includes Single Switch Maze, A Frog's Life, Switching Lanes, Switch Invaders, Slingshot Gallery and Scurry. Runs on Windows 98 or later and MAC OS9 or OSX (classic not required) *$60.00*

5414 **Socialization Games for Persons with Disabilities**
Charles C. Thomas
2600 S First St
Springfield, IL 62704-4730

217-789-8980
800-258-8980
FAX: 217-789-9130
books@ccthomas.com
www.ccthomas.com

Michael P. Thomas, President
Nevalyn Nevil, Author
Marna Beatty, Author
This text will assist those who want to teach severely multiple disabled students by providing information on: general principles of intervention and classroom organization; managing the behavior of students; physically managing students and using adaptive equipment; teaching eating skills; teaching toileting, dressing, and hygiene skills; teaching cognition, communication, and socialization skills; teaching independent living skills; and teaching infants and preschool students. *$38.95*
176 pages Paperback
ISBN 0-398067-46-5

5415 **Tactile Checkers Set**
Maxi Aids
42 Executive Blvd.
Farmingdale, NY 11735-4710

631-752-0521
800-522-6294
FAX: 631-752-0689
TTY: 631-752-0738
sales@maxiaids.com
www.maxiaids.com

Elliot Zaretsky, Founder, President & CEO

A wooden board with peg holes and high-contrast tactile squares. Game pieces are tactile wooden discs with pegs. *$33.92*

5416 **Take a Chance**
Speech Bin
1965 25th Ave
Vero Beach, FL 32960-3062

772-770-0007
800-477-3324
FAX: 772-770-0006
info@speechbin.com

Jan J Binney, Senior Editor
Card game for practice of commonly misarticulated speech sounds. *$18.75*
16 pages Book & Cards
ISBN 0-93785 -46-7

5417 **Tic Tac Toe**
Maxi Aids
42 Executive Blvd.
Farmingdale, NY 11735-4710

631-752-0521
800-522-6294
FAX: 631-752-0689
TTY: 631-752-0738
sales@maxiaids.com
www.maxiaids.com

Elliot Zaretsky, Founder, President & CEO
Comes with wooden board with peg holes/grooves and three-dimensional tactile game pieces. *$8.95*

Travel & Transportation

Newsletters & Books

5418   A World Awaits You
Mobility International USA
132 E Broadway
Suite 343
Eugene, OR 97401   541-343-1284
                                   FAX: 541-343-6812
                                   TTY:541-343-1284
                                   clearinghouse@miusa.org
                                   www.miusa.org/away

Susan Sygall, Chief Executive Officer
Cindy Lewis, Director, Programs
A journal of success stories and tips of people with disabilities participating in international exchange programs.
Annually

5419   Hostelling North America
Hostelling International
8455 Colesville Rd.
Suite 1225
Silver Spring, MD 20910   240-650-2100
                                   FAX: 240-650-2094
                                   www.hiusa.org

Charles Hokanson, Chair
Violet Apple, Vice Chair
Eric Oetjen, Vice Chair
HI-USA has hostels in major cities, in national and state parks, near beaches, and in the mountains. Hostelling North America is a directory of hostels in U.S. and Canada, including hostels that are accessible.
400 pages

5420   Sports 'N Spokes Magazine
Paralyzed Veterans of America
801 18th St. NW
Washington, DC 20006-3517   800-424-8200
                                   888-888-2201
                                   TTY:800-795-4327
                                   info@pva.org
                                   www.sportsnspokes.com

Tom Fjerstad, Editor
Andy Nemann, Assistant Editor
John Groth, Editorial Coordinator
Publication of the PVA, a congressionally chartered veterans service organization. Sports 'N Spokes serves as a source for wheelchair sports and recreation.

5421   United States Department of the Interior National Park Service
1849 C St. NW
Washington, DC 20240   202-208-6843
                                   www.nps.gov

Shawn Benge, Deputy Director, Operations
Lena McDowall, Deputy Director, Management & Administration
Susan Farinelli, Acting Chief of Staff
Offers an informational packet containing books, guides and tours for the disabled and elderly.

5422   Wheelin Around e-Guide
Wheelers Accessible Van Rentals
6614 W Sweetwater Ave.
Glendale, AZ 85304   623-776-8830
                                   800-456-1371
                                   FAX: 623-900-2708
                                   corporate@wheelersavr.com
                                   www.wheelersvanrentals.com

Wheelers' objective is to make the world more accessible by providing solutions to transportation challenges. The Wheelin Around e-Guide provides information on the accessible transportation options offered by Wheelers.
1987

Associations & Programs

5423   American Airlines
                                   800-433-7300
                                   www.aa.com

Robert Isom, Chief Executive Officer
Derek Kerr, Vice Chair & Chief Financial Officer
Maya Leibman, Executive Vice President & Chief Information Officer
This airline trains employees to make sure that passengers with disabilities enjoy convenient, safe, and comfortable travel.

5424   American Hotel and Lodging Association
1250 Eye St. NW
Suite 1100
Washington, DC 20005   202-289-3100
                                   FAX: 202-289-3199
                                   membership@ahla.com
                                   www.ahla.com

Chip Rogers, President & Chief Executive Officer
Kevin Carey, Executive Vice President & Chief Operating Officer
Brian Crawford, Executive Vice President, Government Affairs
Disseminates information, develops and conducts a series of seminars for the hotel and motel industry at state-level association conferences, and develops and distributes an ADA Compliance handbook for use by the lodging industry.

5425   Amtrak
1 Massachusetts Ave. NW
Washington, DC 20001   215-856-7924
                                   800-872-7245
                                   TTY:800-523-6590
                                   www.amtrak.com

Stephen J. Gardner, President & Chief Executive Officer
Eleanor D. Acheson, Executive Vice President & General Counsel
Roger Harris, Executive Vice President, Marketing & Revenue
Amtrak provides services for passengers with disabilities and works to make facilities more accessible. Contact Amtrak's Special Services Desk at 1-800-USA-RAIL at least 24 hours in advance to arrange for special assistance. The type of equipment and accessibility vary from train to train and station to station.

5426   Easterseals Project Action Consulting
1101 Vermont Ave. NW
Suite 510
Washington, DC 20005   202-347-3066
                                   844-227-3772
                                   TTY:202-347-7385
                                   espaconsulting@easterseals.com
                                   www.projectaction.com

Carol Wright Kenderdine, Assistant Vice President, Mobility & Transportation
Grozda Tisma, Procurement & Special Project Coordinator
Kristi McLaughlin, Consultant
A national technical assistance program designed to improve access to transportation services for people with disabilities and assist transit providers in implementing the Americans with Disabilities Act.

5427   General Motors Mobility Program for Persons with Disabilities
GM Mobility Program
PO Box 33170
Detroit, MI 48232   800-323-9935
                                   FAX: 866-234-3036
                                   TTY:800-833-9935
                                   mobility@gm.com
                                   www.gmmobility.com

GM Mobility Program provides up to $1000 reimbursement toward mobility adaptations for drivers or passengers and/or vehicle alerting devices for drivers who are deaf or hard of hearing. Provided on eligible new Chevrolet, Buick, Cadillac and GMC vehicles. Complete GMC financing available. GM Mobility also offers free resource information, including list of area adaptive equipment installers, plus free resource video.

5428 Marriott International
10400 Fernwood Rd.
Bethesda, MA 20817
301-380-3000
800-228-9290
www.marriott.com

J.W. Marriott Jr., Executive Chairman
Anthony Capuano, Chief Executive Officer
Stephanie Linnartz, President
Marriott International operates 30 brands and 7000+ properties across 131 countries and territories, with an emphasis on diversity, inclusion, sustainability and social impact.

5429 MedEscort International
PO Box 8766
Allentown, PA 18105
800-255-7182
service@medescort.com
www.medescort.com

Craig Poliner, President
MedEscort International serves the health care community throughout the world. They specialize in the long-distance transportation of patients by air ambulance, commercial airline, or other forms of transportation. Other services include pre-trip preparations, bedside to bedside service, ground transportation service, and worldwide travel coordination.

5430 MossRehab Travel Resources
Moss Rehabilitation Hospital
60 Township Line Rd.
Elkins Park, PA 19027
215-663-6000
800-225-5667
FAX: 215-663-8891
www.mossrehab.com

Thomas Smith, Chief Operating Officer
Alberto Esquenazi, Chief Medical Officer
Eileen Hartranft, Program Director
Offers information and resources for persons with special traveling/accessibility needs.

5431 Nantahala Outdoor Center
13077 Hwy. 19 W
Bryson City, NC 28713
828-785-4851
reservations@noc.com
www.noc.com

Colin McBeath, President
Nantahala Outdoor Center offers whitewater rafting adventures on six rivers in the Southeast for all skill levels, as well as kayak and canoe adaptive instruction. NOC can tailor whitewater programs to a variety of skills and ability levels, modify gear, and pace instruction.

5432 Paralyzed Veterans of America
801 18th St. NW
Washington, DC 20006-3517
800-424-8200
TTY:800-795-4327
info@pva.org
www.pva.org

Charles Brown, National President
Marcus Murray, National Secretary
Carl Blake, Executive Director
A national organization serving veterans and individuals with spinal cord injury/disorder (SCI/D), as well as their family members and caregivers.

5433 Rehabiliation Engineering Research Center on Accessible Public Transportation
SUNY Buffalo, School of Architecture & Planning
3435 Main St.
Buffalo, NY 14214-3087
716-829-5899
www.rercapt.org

Aaron Steinfeld, Co-Director
Jordana Maisel, Co-Director
A partnership between the Robotics Institute at Carnegie Mellon University and the Center for Inclusive Design and Environmental Access at University at Buffalo, the RERC on Accessible Public Transportation conducts research and develops methods to further advance accessible transportation systems and equipment.

5434 Shilo Inns & Resorts
11707 NE Airport Way
Portland, OR 97220
503-641-6565
800-222-2244
guestservices@shiloinns.com
www.shiloinns.com

Mark S. Hemstreet, Founder & Owner
Shilo Inns offers special assist rooms at many locations throughout the Western United States. These rooms include larger sized bathrooms equipped with assistance railings and wheelchair access. Special assist dogs are welcome at most Shilo Inns.

5435 Travelers Aid International
110 Maryland Ave. NE
Suite 508
Washington, DC 20002
202-546-1127
www.travelersaid.org

Kathleen Baldwin, President & Chief Executive Officer
Edward Powers, Membership Director
Ellen Horton, Communications Director
Provides crisis intervention and casework services, limited financial assistance, protective travel assistance and information and referrals for travelers, transients, and newcomers.

5436 US Servas
PO Box 3419
Berkeley, CA 94703-0419
800-509-1450
info@usservas.org
www.usservas.org

Marguerite Hills, Chair
Joanne Ferguson Cavanaugh, Secretary
Steve Kanters, Treasurer
International network that links travelers with hosts in 120+ countries with the hope of building world peace through understanding and friendship.

5437 Wheelers Accessible Van Rentals
6614 W Sweetwater Ave.
Glendale, AZ 85304
623-776-8830
800-456-1371
FAX: 623-900-2708
corporate@wheelersavr.com
www.wheelersvanrentals.com

Rental wheelchairs and scooter accessible vans. Technically advanced engineering features bring a world of independence to the user. Locations throughout the U.S.
1987

5438 Wilderness Inquiry
1611 County Rd. B West
Suite 315
St. Paul, MN 55113
612-676-9400
FAX: 612-676-9401
info@wildernessinquiry.org
www.wildernessinquiry.org

Kim Keprios, Executive Director
Julie K. Edmiston, Associate Executive Director
Jeff Hanson, Operations Manager
Allows people of all ages and abilities to share the adventure of wilderness travel.
1978

Tours

5439 Able Trek Tours
510 K St.
PO Box 384
Reedsburg, WI 53959
608-524-3021
800-205-6713
FAX: 608-524-8302
staff@abletrektours.com
abletrektours.com

Don Douglas, Owner & President
Able Trek Tours offers vacation programs and charter bus services for individuals with special needs.

5440 Access Pass
National Park Service
1849 C St. NW
Washington, DC 20240   202-208-6843
                              www.nps.gov
Shawn Benge, Deputy Director, Operations
Lena McDowall, Deputy Director, Management & Administration
Susan Farinelli, Acting Chief of Staff
A free passport to federally operated parks, monuments, historic sites, recreation areas, and wildlife refuges for persons who are permanently disabled.

5441 Accessible Journeys
35 W Sellers Ave.
Ridley Park, PA 19078   610-521-0339
                              800-846-4537
                              FAX: 610-521-6959
Howard McCoy, President & Chief Executive Officer
Accessible Journeys is a vacation planner and tour operator for wheelchair travelers and people with disabilities.

5442 Anglo California Travel Service
10620 Creston Dr.
Los Altos, CA 94024   408-257-2257
                              800-339-4484
                              FAX: 408-257-2664
                              anglocalifornia@yahoo.com
                              www.anglocalifornia.com
Audrey Cooper, Contact
Tony Cooper, Contact
Provides plans for one and two week accessible tours.
1968

5443 Courier Travel
532 Duane St.
Glen Ellyn, IL 60137   630-469-0511
                              info@couriertravelinc.com
                              www.couriertravelinc.com
Fred Mueller, Owner
Offers specialized assistance for independent travel or tours for persons with disabilities. Vacations include cruises and travel in the USA and abroad.

5444 Cunard Line
24303 Town Center Dr.
Suite 200
Valencia, CA 91355   800-728-6273
                              www.cunard.com
Simon Palethorpe, President
The Cunard Line is a British cruise line providing luxury cruise vacations and ocean travel experiences. The fleet consists of Queen Elizabeth, the Queen Mary 2, and the Queen Victoria. The Cunard Line accommodates guests with disabilities and reduced mobility.

5445 Dialysis at Sea Cruises
5230 Land O' Lakes Blvd.
PO Box 1158
Land O' Lakes, FL 34639-9998   813-775-4040
                              800-544-7604
                              FAX: 727-372-7490
                              info@dialysisatsea.com
                              www.dialysisatsea.com
Steve Debroux, Owner
Provides travel opportunities for persons on hemodialysis and CAPD. Handles all aspects of their travel and medical requirements. Not sold through travel agents. Makes all reservations and coordinates the total set-up and operation of an onboard ship mobile dialysis clinic. Cruises run from seven days to three weeks and have departures from cities around the world on a variety of cruise lines.
1977

5446 Dvorak Raft Kayak & Fishing Expeditions
17921 US Hwy. 285
Nathrop, CO 81236   719-539-6851
                              800-824-3795
                              info@dvorakexpeditions.com
                              www.dvorakexpeditions.com
Bill Dvorak, Co-Owner
Jaci Dvorak, Co-Owner

Dvorak offers a wide range of whitewater rafting trips on the Arkansas, Colorado, Dolores, Gunnison, Green, North Platte, Rio Grande, and San Miguel rivers ranging from half-day to multi-day excursions. Provides river trips for people who are deaf, visually impaired, and physically or mentally disabled. Colorado's first Licensed Outfitter.
1969

5447 Easy Access Travel
1716 Morning Glory
Carrollton, TX 75007   951-202-2208
                              debra@easyaccesstravel.com
                              www.easyaccesstravel.com
Debra Kerper, Owner
Specializes in accessible cruise vacations and land tours for individuals with disabilities.

5448 Environmental Traveling Companions
Fort Mason Center
2 Marina Blvd.
Suite C385
San Francisco, CA 94123   415-474-7662
                              FAX: 415-474-3919
                              info@etctrips.org
                              www.etctrips.org
Diane Poslosky, Executive Director
Magen Kuzma, Administrative Director
Jenny Jedeikin, Communications Manager
Provides accessible outdoor experiences for people with disabilities and under-resourced youth.

5449 Guide Service of Washington
1400 Eye St. NW
Washington, DC 20005-2259   202-628-2842
                              FAX: 202-638-2812
                              sales@dctourguides.com
                              www.dctourguides.com
A guide service offering tours of Washington DC and vicinity.
1964

5450 New Directions For People With Disabilities
5276 Hollister Ave.
Suite 207
Santa Barbara, CA 93111   805-967-2841
                              888-967-2841
                              FAX: 805-964-7344
                              hello@newdirectionstravel.org
                              www.newdirectionstravel.org
Dee Duncan, Executive Director
A nonprofit organization providing local, national, and international travel vacations and holiday programs for people with mild to moderate developmental disabilities.
1985

5451 Norwegian Cruise Line
7665 Corporate Center Dr.
Miami, FL 33126   866-234-7350
                              www.ncl.com
Harry Sommer, President & Chief Executive Officer
Christine Da Silva, Senior Vice President, Branding & Communications
Todd Hamilton, Senior Vice President, Sales
Accommodates guests with disabilities and special needs, but advance notice is required. Cruise fares vary.

5452 ROW Adventures
PO Box 579
Coeur d'Alene, ID 83816   208-765-0841
                              800-451-6034
                              FAX: 208-667-6506
                              info@rowadventures.com
                              www.rowadventures.com
Peter Grubb, Co-Founder
Betsy Bowen, Co-Founder
Jonah Grubb, Operations Manager
Offers one to six day rafting trips to physically disadvantaged people. Designs custom itineraries, or trips with a special focus for small groups. For those with special dietary needs, they prepare special meals. They also offer canoe trips along the trail of Lewis and Clark on Montana's upper Missouri River.
1979

5453 **Sundial Special Vacations**
750 Marine Dr.
Suite 100
Astoria, OR 97103

503-325-4484
800-547-9198
FAX: 503-325-4536
info@sundial-travel.com
www.sundialtour.com

Bruce Conner, Owner
Provides special vacations for developmentally disabled persons. Tour ratio is 1 to 4 depending on capabilities.
1968

5454 **The Guided Tour, Inc.**
7900 Old York Rd.
Suite 111-B
Elkins Park, PA 19027

215-782-1370
FAX: 215-635-2637
director@guidedtour.com
www.guidedtour.com

Ari Segal, Director
Jon Fash, Administrator
Lynsey Trohoske, Administrator
The Guided Tour is a program that offers supervised vacations for adults with developmental disabilities.
1965

5455 **Trips Inc.**
PO Box 10885
Eugene, OR 97440

541-686-1013
trips@tripsinc.com
www.tripsinc.com

Jim Peterson, Founder & President
Leslie Peterson, Executive Director
Rhonda Reed, Accounting & Travel Manager
Trips Inc. Special Adventures provides travel outings to adults with intellectual and developmental disabilities.

5456 **Ventures Travel**
3600 Holly Lane N
Suite 95
Plymouth, MN 55447
952-852-0107
Jayleen Pfitzer, Manager
Seeks to enhance independence and self-esteem and provide necessary support to facilitate safe and memorable travel experiences for people with developmental disabilities.

5457 **Wilderness Inquiry**
1611 County Rd. B West
Suite 315
St. Paul, MN 55113

612-676-9400
FAX: 612-676-9401
info@wildernessinquiry.org
www.wildernessinquiry.org

Kim Keprios, Executive Director
Julie K. Edmiston, Associate Executive Director
Jeff Hanson, Operations Manager
Allows people of all ages and abilities to share the adventure of wilderness travel.

Vehicle Rentals

5458 **Accessible Vans of America**

866-224-1750
www.accessiblevans.com

David Adams, Executive Director
Accessible Vans of America (AVA) is dedicated to providing wheelchair accessible vehicles to people with disabilities.

5459 **Avis Rent A Car System, LLC**
6 Sylvan Way
Parsippany, NJ 07054

973-496-3500
800-352-7900
TTY:800-331-2323
www.avis.com

Joe Ferraro, President & Chief Executive Officer
Brian Choi, Chief Financial Officer
Izzy Martins, Executive Vice President, Americas

Avis Access is a program of Avis Rent A Car that provides a full range of complementary products and services to drivers and passengers with physical disabilities. Products or services include transfer boards, hand controls, swivel seats, and more.

5460 **National Car Rental System**
600 Corporate Park Dr.
St. Louis, MO 63105

844-393-9989
888-273-5262
www.nationalcar.com

Chrissy Taylor, President & Chief Executive Officer
Andrew C. Taylor, Executive Chairman
Accommodates special requests subject to availability. Offers hand controls, bench seats, extra mirrors and vans with lifts at many major locations.
1947

5461 **Northwest Limousine Service**
Yonkers, NY 10710

914-294-0777
northwestlimony@gmail.com
northwestlimoinc.com

Offers wheelchair accessible transportation.

5462 **The Creative Mobility Group, LLC**
32217 Stephenson Hwy.
Madison Heights, MI 48071

248-577-5430
888-940-8337
FAX: 248-577-5450
info@creativemobilitygroup.com
www.creativemobilitygroup.com

Christina Duggan, Contact
Provides wheelchair accessible van rentals, as well as mobility scooter rentals, stairlift rentals, ramp rentals, and wheelchair rentals. Locations in Madison Heights, Michigan; Wayne, Michigan; and Byron Center, Michigan.
Founded in 2009.

5463 **Wheelchair Getaways**
PO Box 1098
Mukilteo, WA 98275

425-353-8213
866-224-1750
888-433-6970
FAX: 425-355-6159
www.wheelchairgetaways.com

Wheelchair Getaways is a wheelchair/scooter accessible van rental company with over 30 franchise locations serving major cities and airports throughout the continental US and Hawaii. Rentals by the day, week, month or longer. Delivery/pickup available. Now owned by Accessible Vans of America.
1988

5464 **Wheelers Accessible Van Rentals**
6614 W Sweetwater Ave.
Glendale, AZ 85304

623-776-8830
800-456-1371
FAX: 623-900-2708
corporate@wheelersavr.com
www.wheelersvanrentals.com

Wheelers provides accessible rental services through many locations across the United States.
1987

Veteran Services

National Administrations

5465 Department of Medicine and Surgery Veterans Administration
810 Vermont Ave NW
Washington, DC 20420
202-273-8504
800-827-1000
www.va.gov

David J. Shulkin, Secretary
Vivieca Wright, Chief of Staff
Provides hospital and outpatient treatment as well as nursing home care for eligible veterans in Veterans Administration facilities. Services elsewhere provided on a contract basis in the United States and its territories. Provides non-vocational inpatient residential rehabilitation services to eligible legally blinded veterans of the armed forces of the United States.

5466 Department of Veterans Affairs Regional Office - Vocational Rehab Division
810 Vermont Ave NW
Washington, DC 20420
202-273-8504
800-827-1000
www.va.gov

David J. Shulkin, Secretary
Vivieca Wright, Chief of Staff
Vocational rehabilitation is a program of services administered by the Department of Veterans Affairs for service members and veterans with service-connected physical or mental disabilities. If persons are compensibly disabled and are found in need of rehabilitation services because they have an employment handicap, this program can prepare them for a suitable job; get and keep that job; assist persons to become fully productive and independent.

5467 Department of Veterans Benefits
810 Vermont Ave NW
Washington, DC 20420
202-461-6913
800-827-1000
www.va.gov

David J. Shulkin, Secretary
Vivieca Wright, Chief of Staff
Furnishes compensation and pensions for disability and death to veterans and their dependents. Provides vocational rehabilitation services, including counseling, training, assistance and more towards employment, to blinded veterans disabled as a result of service in the armed forces during World War II, Korea and the Vietnam era; also provides rehabilitation services to certain peace-time veterans.

5468 Disabled American Veterans Headquarters
3725 Alexandria Pike
Cold Spring, KY 41076
877-426-2838
feedback@davmail.org
www.dav.org

David W Riley, Chairman
Barry Jesinoski, Executive Director
James Killen, Associate National Communications Director
Serves America's disabled veterans and their families. Direct services include legislative advocacy; professional counseling about compensation, pension, educational and job training programs and VA health care; and assistance in applying for those entitlements.

5469 Federal Benefits for Veterans and Dependents
810 Vermont Ave NW
Washington, DC 20420
202-273-6763
800-827-1000
www.benefits.va.gov

David J. Shulkin, Secretary
Viveca Wright, Chief of Staff
Offers information on benefits for veterans and their families.
93 pages
ISBN 0-16048 -58-

5470 US Department of Veterans Affairs National Headquarters
810 Vermont Ave NW
Washington, DC 20420
202-273-5400
800-827-1000
www.va.gov

David J. Shulkin, Secretary
Vivieca Wright, Chief of Staff
A federal agency that provides healthcare services to military veterans at VA medical centers and outpatient clinics located throughout the country; several non-healthcare benefits including disability compensation, vocational rehabilitation, education assistance, home loans, and life insurance; and provides burial and memorial benefits to veterans and family members at 135 national cemeteries.
80 pages

5471 Veteran's Voices Writing Project
406 W 34th St
Suite 103
Kansas City, MO 64111-3043
816-701-6844
veteransvoices@sbcglobal.net
www.veteransvoices.com

Deann Mitchell, President
Sheryl Liddle, Vice President
Marianne Watson, Treasurer
Individuals and organizations united to encourage veterans to write for pleasure and rehabilitation. The organization also maintains speakers' bureau and audio tape versions for the blind. Also offered are numerous monetary awards, articles, book reviews, cartoons and drawings, light verse, poetry and short stories.
$15.00
64 pages Magazine
ISSN 0504-07 9

Alabama

5472 Alabama VA Benefits Regional Office - Montgomery
U.S. Department of Veteran Affairs
345 Perry Hill Rd
Montgomery, AL 36109
800-827-1000
FAX: 334-213-3565
montgomery.query@vba.va.gov
www.va.gov

Cory A. Hawthorne, Director
Erica P. Worthington, Assistant Director
Jamie Bozeman, Vocational Rehabilitation & Employment Officer
The Veterans Benefits Administration (VBA) provides a variety of benefits and services to Servicemembers, Veterans, and their families.

5473 Alabama VA Medical Center - Birmingham
Veterans Health Administration U.S. Dept. of VA
700 S. 19th St
Birmingham, AL 35233
205-933-8101
www.birmingham.va.gov

Thomas Smith, Director
Veterans medical clinic offering disabled veterans medical treatments.

5474 Central Alabama Veterans Healthcare System
Veterans Health Administration, U.S. Dept. of VA
215 Perry Hill Rd
Montgomery, AL 36109-3798
334-272-4670
800-214-8387
www.centralalabama.va.gov

Paul Bockelman, Interim Director
Thomas Huettemann, Associate Director for Resources
Linda Townsend-Green, Acting Associate Director, Operations
CAVHCS exists to provide excellent services to veterans across the continuum of healthcare. We take pride in providing delivery of timely quality care by staff who demonstrate outstanding customer service, the advancement of health care through research, and the education of tomorrow's health care providers.

5475 Tuscaloosa VA Medical Center
Veterans Health Administration, US Dept. of VA
3701 Loop Rd E
Tuscaloosa, AL 35404-5015
205-554-2000
888-269-3045
FAX: 205-554-2845
www.tuscaloosa.va.gov

John F. Merkle, Medical Center Director
David L. Carden, Associate Director, Nursing & Patient Care Services
Carlos Berry, Chief of Staff
To serve America's Heroes by improving their health and well-being through Veteran and Family Centered Care.

Alaska

5476 Alaska VA Healthcare System - Anchorage
1201 North Muldoon Road
Ste 115
Anchorage, AK 99504-5914
907-257-4700
888-353-7574
FAX: 907-561-7183
www.alaska.va.gov

Linda L. Boyle, Interim Director
Shawn Bransky, Associate Director
Veterans medical clinic offering disabled veterans medical treatments.

5477 DAV Department of Alaska
2925 Debarr Rd
Room 3101
Anchorage, AK 99508-2983
907-257-4803
FAX: 907-258-9828
www.davmembersportal.org

Pamela F. Beale, Alaska Commander
Robert W. Bingham, Membership Chairman

5478 Veteran Benefits Administration - Anchorage Regional Office
U.S. Department of Veteran Affairs
1201 Muldoon Rd
Anchorage, AK 99504
907-257-4803
800-827-1000
anchorage.query@vba.va.gov
www.benefits.va.gov/anchorage

Robert A. McDonald, Secretary of Veterans
Robert D. Snyder, Chief of Staff
The Anchorage Regional Office is remotely managed by the Salt Lake City Regional Office. The VBA operation includes a one-stop Veterans Service Center made up of the merged Adjudication and Veterans Service Divisions. There is also a one person Loan Guaranty Division and a Vocational Rehabilitation and Employment Division.

Arizona

5479 Carl T Hayden VA Medical Center
Veterans Health Administration, US Dept. of VA
650 E Indian School Rd
Phoenix, AZ 85012-1839
602-277-5551
800-554-7174
FAX: 602-222-6472
g.vhacss@forum.va.gov
www.phoenix.va.gov

D Gregg Gordon, President
Marva Greene, Vice President
John Fears, CEO

5480 Northern Arizona VA Health Care System
Veterans Health Administration, US Dept. of VA
500 Hwy 89N
Prescott, AZ 86313-5001
928-445-4860
800-949-1005
FAX: 928-768-6076
g.vhacss@forum.va.gov
www.prescott.va.gov

Deborah Thompson, Manager

5481 Southern Arizona VA Healthcare System
Veterans Health Administration, US Dept. of VA
3601 S 6th Ave
Tucson, AZ 85723
520-792-1450
800-470-8262
FAX: 520-629-1818
g.vhacss@forum.va.gov
www.tucson.va.gov

Jonathan H. Gardner, MPA, FACHE, Director
Jennifer S Gutowski, MHA, FACHE, Associate Director
Katie A. Landwehr, MBA, Assistant Director
The Southern Arizona VA Health Care System (SAVAHCS) located in Tucson AZ serves over 170,000 Veterans located in eight counties in Southern Arizona and one county in Western New Mexico.

Arkansas

5482 Eugene J Towbin Healthcare Center
Veterans Health Administration, US Dept. of VA
2200 Fort Roots Dr
North Little Rock, AR 72114-1706
501-257-1000
800-827-1000
FAX: 501-257-1779
g.vhacss@forum.va.gov
www.littlerock.va.gov

Michael R. Winn, Director
Toby T. Mathew, MHA/MBA, Deputy Director
Cyril O. Ekeh, MHA, Associate Director
CAVHS is reaching out to veterans through its community-based outpatient clinics in Mountain Home, El Dorado, Hot Springs, Mena, Pine Bluff, Searcy, Conway, Russellville, its Home Health Care Service Center in Hot Springs, and a VA Drop-In Day Treatment Center for homeless veterans in downtown Little Rock.

5483 Fayetteville VA Medical Center
Veterans Health Administration, US Dept. of VA
1100 N College Ave
Fayetteville, AR 72703-1944
479-443-4301
800-691-8387
g.vhacss@forum.va.gov
www.fayettevillear.va.gov

W. Todd Grams, Chief Financial Officer
Glenn D. Haggstrom, Principal Executive Director
Stephen W. Warren, Principal Deputy Assistant Secretary
Honor America's Veterans by providing exceptional health care that improves their health and well-being.

5484 John L McClellan Memorial Hospital
Veterans Health Administration, US Dept. of VA
4300 W 7th St
Little Rock, AR 72205-5446
501-257-1000
800-827-1000
g.vhacss@forum.va.gov
www.littlerock.va.gov

Michael R. Winn, Director
Toby T. Mathew, MHA/MBA, Deputy Director
Cyril O. Ekeh, MHA, Associate Director
CAVHS is reaching out to veterans through its community-based outpatient clinics in Mountain Home, El Dorado, Hot Springs, Mena, Pine Bluff, Searcy, Conway, Russellville, its Home Health Care Service Center in Hot Springs, and a VA Drop-In Day Treatment Center for homeless veterans in downtown Little Rock. Throughout its rich 90 year history, CAVHS has been widely recognized for excellence in education, research, and emergency preparedness, and -first and foremost -for a tradition of quality an

5485 North Little Rock Regional Office
Veterans Benefits Administration, US Dept. of VA
2200 Fort Roots Drive
Building 65
N Little Rock, AR 72114-1756   501-370-3820
                                      800-827-1000
                        FAX: 501-370-3829
                        littlerock.query@vba.va.gov
                                      www.va.gov

Eric K. Shinseki, Secretary
Stephen W. Warren, Principal Deputy Assistant Secretary
W. Todd Grams, Chief Financial Officer
The Little Rock VA Regional Office offers services to veterans in the State of Arkansas and the city of Texarkana in Bowie County, Texas. Based on 2004 information provided by the Office of Policy, Planning, and Preparedness, the veteran population of Arkansas is 268,000 and the city of Texarkana, Texas, has a veteran population of 3,545. With a staff of approximately 124 employees, the Regional Office determines entitlement to disability compensation and pension, survivors' benefits, vocational

California

5486 Jerry L Pettis Memorial VA Medical Center
Veterans Health Administration, US Dept. of VA
11201 Benton St
Loma Linda, CA 92357-1000   909-825-7084
                                      800-741-8387
                        g.vhacss@forum.va.gov
                                      www.lomalinda.va.gov
Barbara Fallen, RD, MPA, FACHE, Acting Director
Prachi V. Asher, FACHE, Assistant Director
Dwight C. Evans, M.D., Chief of Staff
Since 1977, VA Loma Linda Healthcare System has been improving the health of the men and women who have so proudly served our nation. We consider it our privilege to serve your health care needs in any way we can.

5487 Long Beach VA Medical Center
Veterans Health Administration, US Dept. of VA
5901 E 7th St
Long Beach, CA 90822-5201   562-826-8000
                                      800-827-1000
                                      888-769-8387
                        g.vhacss@forum.va.gov
                                      www.longbeach.va.gov
Isabel Duff, Medical Center Director
John M. Tryboski, MSN, Associate Director
Anthony DeFrancesco, FACHE, Associate Director

5488 Los Angeles Regional Office
Veterans Benefits Administration, US Dept. of VA
11000 Wilshire Blvd
Los Angeles, CA 90024-3602   800-827-1000
                        losangeles.query@vba.va.gov
                                      www.va.gov
Eric K. Shinseki, Secretary
Stephen W. Warren, Principal Deputy Assistant Secretary
W. Todd Grams, Chief Financial Officer
The Los Angeles Regional Office (RO) provides benefits and services to approximately 706,000 veterans residing in the Southern California counties of Los Angeles, San Bernardino, Riverside, Ventura, Santa Barbara, San Luis Obispo, and Kern. VA benefits expenditures for veterans residing within the jurisdiction of the RO exceed $800 million annually. All Loan Guaranty activities for the six counties are under jurisdiction of the Phoenix Regional Office.

5489 Martinez Outpatient Clinic
Veterans Health Administration, US Dept. of VA
150 Muir Rd
Martinez, CA 94553-4668   925-372-2000
                                      800-382-8387
                        g.vhacss@forum.va.gov
                                      www.va.gov
John H Simms, Director
Brian E. Schuman, Chief of Police

The Martinez Outpatient Clinic offers a full range of medical, surgical, mental health, and diagnostic outpatient services, including nuclear medicine, ultrasound, CT and MRI. The Center for Rehabilitation and Extended Care is located adjacent to the outpatient clinic.

5490 Oakland VA Regional Office
Veterans Benefits Administration US Dept. of VA
1301 Clay Street
12th Floor
Oakland, CA 94612-5217   800-827-1000
                        oakland.query@vba.va.gov
                                      www.benefits.va.gov/oakland
Geri Spearman, Director
The jurisdiction includes all Northern California, except for Modoc, Lassen, Alpine and Mono counties, which are assigned to the Reno Regional Office. All Loan Guaranty activities are under the jurisdiction of the Phoenix Regional Office. Seven service organizations are collocated on the eleventh floor of the Federal Office building occupied by the regional office.

5491 Rehabilitation Research and Development Center
Department of Veteran s Affairs
810 Vermont Avenue, NW
Washington, DC 94304-1207   202-443-0575
                        FAX: 202-495-6153
                        tiffany.asqueri@va.gov
Patricia A. Dorn, Ph.D., Acting Director, Rehab R&D Service
Ricardo Gonzalez, Administrative Officer
Gloria Winford, Staff Assistant
The VA Center of Excellence on Mobility in Palo Alto, CA is dedicated to developing innovative clinical treatments and assistive devices for veterans with physical disabilities to increase their independence and improve their quality of life. The clinical emphasis of the center is to improve mobility, either ambulation or manipulation, in individuals with neurologic impairments or orthopaedic impairments. We do not publish any printed books, journals or periodicals.

5492 Sacramento Medical Center
Veterans Health Administration U S Department of V
10535 Hospital Way
Mather, CA 95655-4200   916-843-7000
                                      800-382-8387
                        g.vhacss@forum.va.gov
                                      www.northerncalifornia.va.gov
David G. Mastalski, Interim Director
Donna Iatarola, RN, MSN, Associate Director
William T. Cahill, MD, Chief of Staff
It is an integrated health care delivery system, offering a comprehensive array of medical, surgical, rehabilitative, mental health and extended care to veterans in Northern California. The health system is comprised of a medical center in Sacramento; a rehabilitation and extended care facility in Martinez, and seven outpatient clinics.

5493 San Diego VA Regional Office
Veterans Benefits Administration, US Dept. of VA
8810 Rio San Diego Dr
San Diego, CA 92108-1698   858-552-8585
                                      800-827-1000
                        FAX: 858-552-7436
                        oakland.query@vba.va.gov
                                      www.benefits.va.gov/sandiego
Janet M Peyton, Administrative Officer
The San Diego VA Regional Office provides benefit services for over 600,000 Veterans and their dependents in the Southern California Counties of Imperial, Orange, Riverside and San Diego. Since the Regional Office shares occupancy of the building with a VA Outpatient Clinic and the Employment Development Department of the State of California, it truly offers a one stop Service Center.

5494 **VA Central California Health Care System**
Veterans Health Administration, US Dept. of VA
2615 E Clinton Ave
Fresno, CA 93703-2223

559-225-6100
888-826-2838
FAX: 559-268-6911
g.vhacss@forum.va.gov
www.fresno.va.gov

Joanne Krumberger, Director
Susan Shyshka, Associate Director
Patricia Richardson Ed.D, RN, N, Nursing Executive
VA Central California Health Care System (VACCHCS) has been improving the health of the men and women who have so proudly served our nation. We consider it our privilege to serve your health care needs in any way we can.

5495 **VA Greater Los Angeles Healthcare System**
Veterans Health Administration US Dept. of VA
11301 Wilshire Blvd
Los Angeles, CA 90073-1003

310-478-3711
800-827-1000
FAX: 310-268-4848
g.vhacss@forum.va.gov
www.losangeles.va.gov

Donna M. Beiter, RN, MSN, Director
Christopher Sandles, Assistant Director
Marlene Brewster, RN, MSN, Acting Associate Director, Nursing and Patient Care Services
The VA Greater Los Angeles Healthcare System is the largest, most complex healthcare system within the Department of Veterans Affairs.GLA consists of three ambulatory care centers, a tertiary care facility and 10 community based outpatient clinics. GLA serves veterans residing throughout five counties: Los Angeles, Ventura, Kern, Santa Barbara, and San Luis Obispo. There are 1.4 million veterans in the GLA service area. GLA is affiliated with both UCLA School of Medicine and USC School of Medici

5496 **VA Northern California Healthcare System**
Veterans Health Administration, US Dept. of VA
150 Muir Rd
Martinez, CA 94553-4668

925-372-2000
800-382-8387
g.vhacss@forum.va.gov
www.northerncalifornia.va.gov

David G. Mastalski, Interim Director
Donna Iatarola, RN, MSN, Associate Director
William T. Cahill, MD, Chief of Staff
VA Northern California Health Care System (VANCHCS) is an integrated health care delivery system, offering a comprehensive array of medical, surgical, rehabilitative, mental health and extended care to veterans in Northern California. The health system is comprised of a medical center in Sacramento; a rehabilitation and extended care facility in Martinez, and seven outpatient clinics.

5497 **VA San Diego Healthcare System**
Veterans Health Administration, US Dept. of VA
3350 La Jolla Village Dr
San Diego, CA 92161

858-552-8585
800-331-8387
g.vhacss@forum.va.gov
www.sandiego.va.gov

Jeffrey T. Gering, FACHE, Director
Cynthia Abair, MHA, Associate Director
Robert M. Smith, MD, Chief of Staff/Medical Director
We provide medical, surgical, mental health, geriatric, spinal cord injury, and advanced rehabilitation services. VASDHS has 296 authorized beds, including skilled nursing beds and operates several regional referral programs including cardiovascular surgery and spinal cord injury. The facility also supports three Vet Centers at the following locations: Chula Vista, San Diego, and San Marcos.

Colorado

5498 **Boulder Vet Center**
4999 Pearl East Circle
Suite 106
Boulder, CO 80301

303-440-7306
877-927-8387
FAX: 303-449-3907
www.va.gov

Gail N Bennett, Office Manager
Michael J Pantaleo, Team Leader
Annette Matlock, Counselor
Offers trauma and readjustment from military and civilian life counseling and assistance with disability claims, military benefits and employment are provided.

5499 **Colorado/Wyoming VA Medical Center**
Veterans Benefits Administration US Dept. of VA
155 Van Gordon St
Suite 395
Lakewood, CO 80225

303-914-2680
800-827-1000
denver.query@vba.va.gov
www.denver.va.gov

Forest Farley Jr, Medical Center Director
Thomas E Bowen, Chief of Staff

5500 **Denver VA Medical Center**
Veterans Health Administration, US Dept. of VA
1055 Clermont St
Suite 6A138
Denver, CO 80220-3808

303-393-2869
888-336-8262
www.denver.va.gov

Lynnette Roth, Executive Director
Peggy Kearns MS, RD, FACHE, Associate Director
Judith Burke RN, MS, NEA-BC, Associate Director, Patient Care Services
Construction of our 1.1m sq foot, $800m replacement facility is well under way! Concrete is being poured, steel is being put in, and we're working hard to open in 2015.

5501 **Grand Junction VA Medical Center**
Veterans Health Administration
2121 North Ave
Grand Junction, CO 81501-6428

970-242-0731
866-206-6415
FAX: 970-244-1300
g.vhacss@forum.va.gov
www.grandjunction.va.gov

Patricia A. Hitt, MS, Acting Director
Michael Murphy, Manager
Randal France, M.D., Chief Psychiatry Service/ Int. Chf. of Staff
The VAMC operates 53 beds comprised of 23 acute care and 30 Transitional Care Unit beds. The VAMC provides primary and secondary care including acute medical, surgical, and psychiatric inpatient services, as well as a full range of outpatient services.

Connecticut

5502 **Hartford Regional Office**
Veterans Benefits Administration
555 Willard Ave
Building 2E
Newington, CT 6111-2631

860-666-6951
800-827-1000
hartford.query@vba.va.gov

Jeanette A Chirico Post, Network Director
The Hartford Regional Office now provides one-stop service to veterans and their families seeking assistance in compensation, pension, and vocational rehabilitation and employment in an accessible campus environment.

5503   Hartford Vet Center
25 Elm St
Suite A
Rocky Hill, CT 06067-2305   860-563-8800
                                             877-927-8387
                                        FAX: 860-563-8805
                                             www.va.gov

Donna Hryb LCSW, Team Leader
Pedro Ortiz, Counselor
Amy Otzel, Counselor
A U.S. Department of Veterans Affairs counseling center offering counseling to Vietnam era and combat veterans. Sexual trauma/harassment counseling, medical screening and benefit referral is available to all veterans.

5504   VA Connecticut Healthcare System: Newington Division
Veterans Health Administration U S Department. of
555 Willard Ave
Newington, CT 6111-2631   860-666-6951
                                             800-827-1000
                                        FAX: 860-667-6764
                                        g.vhacss@forum.va.gov
                                        www.connecticut.va.gov

Janice M. Boss, MS, Director
Margaret Veazey, RN, MSN, Associate Director for Patient Care Services
John Callahan, Associate Director
The mission of VA Connecticut Healthcare Systems is to fulfill a nation's commitment to its veterans by providing quality healthcare, promoting health through prevention and maintaining excellence in teaching and research. Provides primary, secondary and tertiary care in medicine, geriatrics, neurology, psychiatry and surgery with an operating capacity of 211 hospital beds.

5505   VA Connecticut Healthcare System: West Haven
Veterans Health Administration, US Dept. of VA
950 Campbell Ave
West Haven, CT 06516-2770   203-932-5711
                                             800-827-1000
                                        FAX: 203-937-3868
                                        g.vhacss@forum.va.gov
                                        www.connecticut.va.gov

Janice M. Boss, MS, Director
Margaret Veazey, RN, MSN, Associate Director for Patient Care Services
John Callahan, Associate Director
The mission of VA Connecticut Healthcare Systems is to fulfill a nation's commitment to its veterans by providing quality healthcare, promoting health through prevention and maintaining excellence in teaching and research. Provides primary, secondary and tertiary care in medicine, geriatrics, neurology, psychiatry and surgery with an operating capacity of 211 hospital beds.

Delaware

5506   Delaware VA Regional Office
Veterans Benefits Administration US Dept. of VA
1601 Kirkwood Hwy
Wilmington, DE 19805-4917   302-994-2511
                                             800-461-8262
                                        FAX: 302-633-5516
                                        wilmington.query@vba.va.gov
                                        www.wilmington.va.gov

Daniel D. Hendee, FACHE, MHA, Director
Mary Alice Johnson, MS, RN, Associate Director for Patient Care Services
William E. England, Associate Director for Finance and Operations
We offer comprehensive services ranging from preventive screenings to long-term care. Wilmington VAMC proudly serves Veterans in multiple locations for convenient access to the services we provide.

5507   Wilmington VA Medical Center
Veterans Health Administration, US Dept. of VA
1601 Kirkwood Hwy
Wilmington, DE 19805-4917   302-994-2511
                                             800-461-8262
                                        FAX: 302-633-5516
                                        g.vhacss@forum.va.gov
                                        www.wilmington.va.gov

Daniel D. Hendee, FACHE, MHA, Director
Mary Alice Johnson, MS, RN, Associate Director for Patient Care Services
William E. England, Associate Director for Finance and Operations
We offer comprehensive services ranging from preventive screenings to long-term care. Wilmington VAMC proudly serves Veterans in multiple locations for convenient access to the services we provide.

5508   Wilmington Vet Center
2710 Centerville Road
Suite 103
Wilmington, DE 19808- 4917   302-994-1660
                                             877-927-8387
                                        FAX: 302-994-8361
                                             www.va.gov

Joan Spencer, Team Leader
Patricia Elwood, Office Manager
Valerie Feeley, Counselor
Veterans counseling program offering individual counseling services, advocacy services and group counseling. The focus is the counseling of all veterans coping with the aftermath of war, sexual abuse/harassment in the military and all veterans of the Vietnam era. The center also has an active outreach program to seek veterans needing services. Hours of operation are between 8:00 AM - 4:30 PM, Monday - Friday and other times by appointment only. Services are free.

District of Columbia

5509   Disabled American Veterans
Legislative HQ
807 Maine Ave SW
Washington, DC 20024   202-554-3501
                                        FAX: 202-554-3581
                                        feedback@davmail.org
                                             www.dav.org

David W Riley, Chairman
Delphine Metcalf-Foster, National Commander
J. Marc Burgess, National Adjutant
Serves America's disabled veterans and their families. Direct services include legislative advocacy; professional counseling about compensation, pension, educational and job training programs and VA health care; and assistance in applying for those entitlements.

5510   PVA Adaptive Sports
Paralyzed Veterans of America
801 18th St. NW
Washington, DC 20006-3517   800-424-8200
                                        TTY:800-795-4327
                                        info@pva.org
                                        www.pva.org/adaptive-sports

Charles Brown, National President
Marcus Murray, National Secretary
Carl Blake, Executive Director
Sports include air guns, bass fishing, billiards, boccia, bowling, golf, handcycling, quad rugby, and trapshooting.

5511   VA Medical Center, Washington DC
50 Irving St NW
Washington, DC 20422-1   202-745-8000
                                             800-827-1000
                                             877-328-2621
                                        g.vhacss@forum.va.gov
                                        www.washingtondc.va.gov

Brian A. Hawkins, MHA, Medical Center Director
Bryan C. Matthews, MBA, Associate Medical Center Director
Natalie Merckens, Assistant Medical Center Director

Acute general and specialized services in medicine, surgery, neurology, and psychiatry.

5512   Washington DC VA Medical Center
Veterans Health Administration, US Dept. of VA
50 Irving St NW
Washington, DC 20422-1   202-745-8000
                                                          800-827-1000
                                                          877-328-2621
                                                     FAX: 202-754-8530
                                                g.vhacss@forum.va.gov
                                               www.washingtondc.va.gov
Brian A. Hawkins, MHA, Medical Center Director
Bryan C. Matthews, MBA, Associate Medical Center Director
Natalie Merckens, Assistant Medical Center Director
Acute general and specialized services in medicine, surgery, neurology, and psychiatry.

Florida

5513   Bay Pines VA Medical Center
Veterans Health Administration, US Dept. of VA
10000 Bay Pines Blvd
PO Box 5005
Bay Pines, FL 33744   727-398-6661
                                                         800-827-1000
                                                         888-820-0230
                                                 g.vhacss@forum.va.gov
                                                    www.baypines.va.gov
Suzanne M. Klinker, Medical Center Director
Kristine Brown, MPH, Associate Director
Teresa Kumar, RN, MSN, CPHQ, Associate Director for Patient / Nursing Services
Since 1933, Bay Pines VA Healthcare System has been improving the health of the men and women who have so proudly served our nation. We consider it our privilege to serve your health care needs in any way we can. Our services are available to Veterans living in a ten county catchment area in west central Florida.

5514   Gainesville Division, North Florida/South Georgia Veterans Healthcare System
Veterans Health Administration, US Dept. of VA
1601 SW Archer Rd
Gainesville, FL 32608-1611   352-376-1611
                                                         800-324-8387
                                                    FAX: 352-379-7445
                                                 g.vhacss@forum.va.gov
                                       www.northflorida.va.gov/northflorida
Thomas Wisnieski, MPA, FACHE, Director
Nancy Reissener, Deputy Director
Maureen Wilkes, Associate Director
In addition to our medical centers in Gainesville and Lake City, we offer services in three satellite outpatient clinics and several community-based outpatient clinics across North Florida and South Georgia.

5515   James A Haley VA Medical Center
Veterans Health Administration, US Dept. of VA
13000 Bruce B Downs Blvd
Suite T72
Tampa, FL 33612-4745   813-972-2000
                                                         800-827-1000
                                                         888-811-0107
                                                 g.vhacss@forum.va.gov
                                                     www.tampa.va.gov
Kathleen R. Fogarty, Director
Roy L. Hawkins Jr., Deputy Director
David J. VanMeter, Associate Director
Comprehensive health care is provided through primary care, tertiary care, and long-term care in areas of medicine, surgery, psychiatry, physical medicine and rehabilitation, spinal cord injury, neurology, oncology, dentistry, geriatrics, and extended care.

5516   Miami VA Medical Center
Veterans Health Administration, US Dept. of VA
1201 NW 16th St
Suite B822
Miami, FL 33125-1693   305-575-7000
                                                         800-827-1000
                                                         888-276-1785
                                                    FAX: 305-575-3266
                                                 g.vhacss@forum.va.gov
                                                     www.miami.va.gov
Paul M. Russo, Director
Mark E. Morgan, Associate Director
Marcia Lysaght, Associate Director, Patient Care Services
The Miami VA is an accredited comprehensive medical provider, providing general medical, surgical, inpatient and outpatient mental health services, the Miami VA Healthcare System includes an AIDS/HIV center, a prosthetic treatment center, spinal cord injury rehabilitative center, and Geriatric Research, Education, and Clinical Center (GRECC).

5517   St. Petersburg Regional Office
Veterans Benefits Administration, US Dept. of VA
9500 Bay Pines Blvd
St Petersburg, FL 33708   727-319-7492
                                                         800-827-1000
                                                stpete.query@vba.va.gov
                                                          www.va.gov
Warren McPherson, Executive Director

5518   West Palm Beach VA Medical Center
Veterans Health Administration, US Dept. of VA
7305 N Military Trl
West Palm Beach, FL 33410-7417   561-422-8262
                                                         800-972-8262
                                                    FAX: 561-882-6707
                                                 g.vhacss@forum.va.gov
                                               www.westpalmbeach.va.gov
Charleen R. Szabo, FACHE, Medical Center Director
Cristy McKillop, FACHE, MHA, Medical Center Associate Director
Gloria A. Bays, MSN, ARNP, NE-BC, Associate Director for Patient Care Services
The medical center is a general medical, psychiatric and surgical facility. It is a teaching hospital, providing a full range of patient care services, with state-of-the-art technology as well as education and limited research. Comprehensive healthcare is provided through primary care and long-term care in the areas of dentistry, extended care, medicine, neurology, oncology, pharmacy, physical medicine, psychiatry, rehabilitation and surgery. The West Palm Beach VA Medical Center operates a Blin

Georgia

5519   Atlanta Regional Office
Veterans Benefits Administration, US Dept. of VA
1700 Clairmont Road
Decatur, GA 30033-1210   404-463-3100
                                                         800-827-1000
                                                    FAX: 404-929-5819
                                                atlanta.query@vba.va.gov
                                                          www.va.gov
Chick Krautler, Executive Director
The Atlanta VA Regional Office is responsible for delivering non-medical VA benefits and services to Georgia Veterans and their dependent family members. This is accomplished through the administration of comprehensive and diverse benefit programs established by Congress.

5520   Atlanta VA Medical Center
Veterans Health Administration, US Dept. of VA
1670 Clairmont Rd
Decatur, GA 30033-4004   404-321-6111
                                                         800-827-1000
                                                    FAX: 404-728-7734
                                                 g.vhacss@forum.va.gov
                                                     www.atlanta.va.gov
Leslie B. Wiggins, Director
Tom Grace, MBA/MHA, Associate Director
Sheila Meuse, PhD, Assistant Director

The Atlanta VA Medical Center (VAMC), located on 26 acres in Decatur, is one of eight medical centers in the VA Southeast Network. It is a teaching hospital, providing a full range of patient care services complete with state-of-the-art technology, education, and research.

5521   Augusta VA Medical Center
Veterans Health Administration, US Dept. of VA
950 15th Street Downtown/1 Freedom
Augusta, GA 30904-6258   706-733-0188
                                                        800-827-1000
                                              FAX: 706-731-7227
                                        g.vhacss@forum.va.gov

Robert U. Hamilton, MHA, FACHE, Medical Center Director
Richard Rose, Associate Director
Michelle Cox-Henley, MS, RN, Associate Director for Nursing/Patient Services

The Charlie Norwood VA Medical Center is a two-division Medical Center that provides tertiary care in medicine, surgery, neurology, psychiatry, rehabilitation medicine, and spinal cord injury. The Downtown Division is authorized 155 beds (58 medicine, 37 surgery, and 60 spinal cord injury). The Uptown Division, located approximately three miles away, is authorized 315 beds (68 psychiatry, 15 blind rehabilitation and 40 medical rehabilitation. In addition, a 132-bed Restorative/Nursing Home C

5522   Carl Vinson VA Medical Center
Veterans Health Administration, US Dept. of VA
1826 Veterans Blvd
Dublin, GA 31021-3699   478-272-1210
                                              FAX: 478-277-2717
                                              www.dublin.va.gov

John S. Goldman, Director
Gerald M. DeWorth, Associate Director
Sue Preston, RN, Associate Director for Patient and Nursing Services

Since 1948, Carl Vinson VA Medical Center has been improving the health of the men and women who have so proudly served our nation. We consider it our privilege to serve your health care needs in any way we can. Services are available to veterans living in the Middle Georgia area.

5523   Southeastern Paralyzed Veterans of America
4010 Deans Bridge Rd.
Hephzibah, GA 30815   706-796-6301
                                                        800-292-9335
                                              FAX: 706-796-0363
                                           paravet@comcast.net
                                        www.southeasternpva.org

Carl Morgan, President
Kurt Glass, Vice President
Lonnie Burnett, Treasurer

Works to maximize the quality of life for its members and all people with SCI/D as a leading adovocate for healthcare, SCI/D research and education, veteran's benefits, and rights, accessibility and the removal of architectural barriers, sports programs, and disability rights.
1946

Hawaii

5524   Hilo Vet Center
70 Lanihuli St
Suite 102
Hilo, HI 96720-2067   808-969-3833
                                                        877-927-8387
                                              FAX: 808-969-2025
                                                         www.va.gov

Felipe Sales, Team Leader
Samuelito Labasan, Office Manager
Peter Ehlich, Counselor

Veterans medical clinic offering disabled veterans medical treatments, readjustment and PTSD counseling to combat veterans

5525   Honolulu VBA Regional Office
Veterans Benefits Administration, US Dept. of VA
459 Patterson Road, E-Wing
Honolulu, HI 96819-1522   808-566-1412
                                                        800-827-1000
                                              FAX: 808-433-0478
                                     honolulu.query@vba.va.gov
                                     www.vba.va.gov/ro/honolulu

Claude M Kicklighter, Chief of Staff
Alan Furuno, Manager
Alvin Kalawe, Elderly Program Coordinator

The Honolulu Regional Office is responsible for administering VA's benefit programs under the leadership and direction of the Under Secretary for Benefits for the Veterans Benefits Administration. Formerly part of the Honolulu VA Medical & Regional Office Center (VAMROC), the Honolulu Regional Office (RO) was renamed as a stand alone RO on June 2, 2003. The office is co-located with the Spark M. Matsunaga Pacific Islands Health Care System medical center, on the grounds of the Tripler Army Medic

5526   Pacific Islands Health Care System
Veterans Health Administration, US Dept. of VA
459 Patterson Rd
Honolulu, HI 96819-1522   808-433-0600
                                                        800-214-1306
                                              FAX: 808-433-0390
                                           g.vhacss@forum.va.gov
                                              www.hawaii.va.gov

William F. Dubbs, M.D., Acting Director
Brandon K. Yamamoto, Acting Associate Director
Jane Wellman, APRN, Associate Director of Patient Care Services

The VA Pacific Islands Health Care System (VAPIHCS) Honolulu provides a broad range of medical care services, serving an estimated 127,600 veterans throughout Hawaii and the Pacific Islands. The VAPIHCS provides outpatient medical and mental health care through a main Ambulatory Care Clinic on Oahu (Honolulu) and through five Community Based Outpatient Clinics (CBOCs) on the neighboring islands including: Hawaii (Hilo and Kona), Maui, Kauai, and Guam.

Idaho

5527   Boise Regional Office
Veterans Benefits Administration, US Dept. of VA
444 W. Fort Street
Boise, ID 83702-4531   800-827-1000
                                        boise.query@vba.va.gov
                                                         www.va.gov

Jim Vance, Director
Pat Teague, Service Officer
Tom Ressler, Manager

The Boise Regional Office administers monetary benefits to 17,283 veterans in Idaho, Utah, and Oregon. The Regional Office issued monthly disability and death benefit payments of over $15 million in January 2007. VBA's annual compensation and pension benefits for veterans residing within the RO's jurisdiction now exceed $185 million

5528   Boise VA Medical Center
Veterans Health Administration, US Dept. of VA
500 W Fort St
Boise, ID 83702-4531   208-422-1000
                                                        800-827-1000
                                              FAX: 208-422-1326
                                           g.vhacss@forum.va.gov
                                              www.boise.va.gov

Jennifer T Shalz, Chief of Staff

We truly hope to improve your health and well-being and will make your visit or stay as pleasant as possible. We are committed to veterans and the nation and strive to continually enhance the care we provide. We also train future healthcare professionals, conduct research and support our nation in times of emergency. In all of these activities, our employees will respect and support your rights as a patient.

Illinois

5529 Edward Hines Jr Hospital
Veterans Health Administration, US Dept. of VA
5000 South 5th Avenue
Hines, IL 60141
708-202-8387
800-827-1000
FAX: 708-202-2684
g.vhacss@forum.va.gov
www.hines.va.gov

Joan Ricard, FACHE, Hospital Director
Dr. Daniel Zomchek, Associate Director
Carol A. Gouty, RN, MSN, PhD, Associate Director of Patient Care
Specialized clinical programs include Blind Rehabilitation, Spinal Cord Injury, Neurosurgery, Radiation Therapy and Cardiovascular Surgery. The hospital also serves as the VISN 12 southern tier hub for pathology, radiology, radiation therapy, human resource management and fiscal services. Hines VAH currently operates 471 beds and six community based outpatient clinics in Elgin, Kankakee, Oak Lawn, Aurora, LaSalle, and Joliet.

5530 Marion VA Medical Center
Veterans Health Administration U S Department of V
2401 W Main St
Marion, IL 62959-1188
618-997-5311
800-827-1000
www.marion.va.gov

Paul Bockelman, Medical Center Director
Frank Kehus, Associate Director
The VA Medical Center in Marion, Illinois, is a general medical and surgical facility that operates 55 acute care beds and a 60 bed Community Living Center. Ten Outpatient Clinics that provide primary care and behavioral medicine services are located in Harrisburg; Carbondale; Effingham; and Mt. Vernon, IL; Paducah; Hanson; Owensboro; and Mayfield, Kentucky; Vincennes and Evansville, IN.

5531 North Chicago VA Medical Center
Veterans Health Administration, US Dept. of VA
3001 North Green Bay Rd
North Chicago, IL 60064-3048
847-688-1900
800-393-0865
g.vhacss@forum.va.gov
www.lovell.fhcc.va.gov

Patrick L. Sullivan, Director
Captain Jos, A. Acosta, MC, US, Commanding Officer/Deputy Director
Captain Jami Kersten, Associate Director
The arrangement incorporates facilities, services and resources from the North Chicago VA Medical Center (VAMC) and the Naval Health Clinic Great Lakes (NHCGL). A combined mission of the health care center means active duty military, their family members, military retirees and veterans are all cared for at the facility.

5532 VA Illiana Health Care System
Veterans Health Administration, US Dept. of VA
1900 E Main St
Danville, IL 61832-5198
217-554-3000
800-320-8387
FAX: 217-554-4552
g.vhacss@forum.va.gov
www.danville.va.gov

Emma Metcalf, MSN, RN, Director
Diana Carranza, Associate Director
Alesia Coe, MSN, RN, Associate Director for Patient Care Services
Since 1898, our buildings, facilities, patients, and missions have changed, but remaining constant is VA Illiana Health Care System's endeavor in improving the health of the men and women who have so proudly served our nation. Being the 8th oldest VA facility, we consider it our privilege to serve your health care needs in any way we can.

Indiana

5533 Indianapolis Regional Office
Veterans Benefits Administration
575 N Pennsylvania St
Indianapolis, IN 46204-1563
317-226-7860
800-827-1000
TTY:800-829-4833
indianapolis.query@vba.va.gov
www.benefits.va.gov/indianapolis
The Department of Veterans Affairs provides a variety of services and benefits to honorably discharged veterans of the U. S. Military and their dependents. The purpose of this Web page is to assist Indiana's veterans, their dependents and survivors, in contacting the nearest VA facility to inquire about their veterans benefits or health care services. The State of Indiana maintains a Web page for veterans that explains many of the programs that are available to them.

5534 Richard L Roudebush VA Medical Center
Veterans Health Administration, US Dept. of VA
1481 W 10th St
Indianapolis, IN 46202-2803
317-554-0000
800-827-1000
FAX: 317-554-0127
g.vhacss@forum.va.gov
www.indianapolis.va.gov

Thomas Mattice, Director
Jeff Nechanicky, Associate Director
Kimberly Radant, Associate Director for Patient Care Services
Since 1932, Richard L. Roudebush VA Medical Center has been improving the health of the men and women who have so proudly served our nation. We consider it our privilege to serve your health care needs in any way we can. Services are available to more than 196,000 veterans living in a 45-county area of Indiana and Illinois.

5535 VA North Indiana Health Care System: Fort Wayne Campus
Veterans Health Administration, US Dept. of VA
2121 Lake Ave
Fort Wayne, IN 46805-5100
260-426-5431
800-360-8387
g.vhacss@forum.va.gov
www.northernindiana.va.gov

Denise M. Deitzen, Medical Center Director
Audrey L. Frison, MHA, RN, Associate Director
Helen Rhodes MPA, RN, Associate Director for Operations
The Fort Wayne Campus offers primary and secondary medical and surgical services. Primary care clinics are available at both medical center campuses and at Community Based Outpatient Clinics (CBOCs) located in South Bend, Goshen, Peru and Muncie Indiana. Recently completed renovations and construction, and continuous maintenance, ensure an attractive, state-of-the-art healthcare environment.

5536 VA Northern Indiana Health Care System: Marion Campus
Veterans Health Administration, US Dept. of VA
1700 E 38th St
Marion, IN 46953-4568
765-674-3321
800-360-8387
g.vhacss@forum.va.gov
www.northernindiana.va.gov

Denise M. Deitzen, Medical Center Director
Audrey L. Frison, MHA, RN, Associate Director
Helen Rhodes MPA, RN, Associate Director for Operations
The Marion Campus offers a full range of mental health, nursing home care, and extended care services. Primary care clinics are available at both medical center campuses and at Community Based Outpatient Clinics (CBOCs) located in South Bend, Goshen, Peru and Muncie Indiana.

Iowa

5537 Des Moines VA Medical Center
Veterans Health Administration, US Dept. of VA
3600 30th St
Des Moines, IA 50310-5753

515-699-5999
800-294-8387
FAX: 515-699-5862
g.vhacss@forum.va.gov
www.centraliowa.va.gov

Donald Cooper, Director
Susan Martin, Associate Director for Resources and Operations
Tammy Neff, RN, MBA, MSN, M, Acting Associate Director for Patient Services/Nurse Executi
The VA Central Iowa Health Care System (VACIHCS) operates a Veterans Health Administration (VHA) medical facility in Des Moines, with Community Based Outpatient Clinics (CBOCs) in Mason City, Fort Dodge, Knoxville, Marshalltown and Carroll. The medical center provides acute and specialized medical and surgical services, residential outpatient treatment programs in substance abuse and post-traumatic stress and a full range of mental health and long-term care services.

5538 Des Moines VA Regional Office
Veterans Benefits Administration, US Dept. of VA
210 Walnut Street
Des Moines, IA 50309-2115

515-323-7580
800-827-1000
FAX: 515-323-7580
leander@vba.va.gov
www.va.gov

Rich Anderson, Service Director
The Des Moines VA Regional Office provides Compensation, Pension and Vocational Rehabilitation and Counseling services for all military veterans in the State of Iowa. The Des Moines VA Regional Office currently provides approximately $260 million in benefits to the approximately 270,000 veterans in Iowa.

5539 Iowa City VA Medical Center
Veterans Health Administration, US Dept. of VA
601 Highway 6 West
Iowa City, IA 52240-2202

319-338-0581
800-637-0128
866-687-7382
FAX: 319-339-7171
g.vhacss@forum.va.gov
www.iowacity.va.gov

Barry Sharp, Director
Timothy McMurry, Associate Director for Operations
Dawn Oxley, RN, Associate Director Patient Care Services/Nurse Executive
Tertiary care facility, affiliated teaching hospital, and research center seving an aging veteran populatiaon in eastern Iowa and western Illinois. Satellite clinics are located in Bettendord, Dubuque, and Waterloo, Iowa and in Quincy and Galesburg, Illinois.

5540 Knoxville VA Medical Center
Veterans Health Administration, US Dept. of VA
1515 W Pleasant St
Knoxville, IA 50138-3399

641-842-3101
800-816-8878
FAX: 641-828-5124
g.vhacss@forum.va.gov
www.centraliowa.va.gov

Claudia M Kicklighter

5541 VA Central Iowa Health Care System
3600 30th St
Des Moines, IA 50310-5753

515-699-5999
800-294-8387
FAX: 515-699-5862
www.centraliowa.va.gov

Donald Cooper, Director
Susan Martin, Associate Director for Resources and Operations
Tammy Neff, RN, MBA, MSN, M, Acting Associate Director for Patient Services/Nurse Executi
The VA Central Iowa Health Care System (VACIHCS) operates a Veterans Health Administration (VHA) medical facility in Des Moines, with Community Based Outpatient Clinics (CBOCs) in Mason City, Fort Dodge, Knoxville, Marshalltown and Carroll. The medical center provides acute and specialized medical and surgical services, residential outpatient treatment programs in substance abuse and post-traumatic stress and a full range of mental health and long-term care services, as well as sub-acute and r

Kansas

5542 Colmery-O'Neil VA Medical Center
Veterans Health Administration, US Dept. of VA
2200 SW Gage Blvd
Topeka, KS 66622

785-350-3111
800-574-8387
g.vhacss@forum.va.gov
www.topeka.va.gov

A. Rudy Klopfer, FACHE, Director
John Moon, Associate Director
Nelson L. Dean, RN, BSN, MA, Associate Director for Patient Care Services
Since 1946, the staff of the Colmery-O'Neil VA Medical Center has been serving veterans. Today, we proudly serve our nation's veterans with excellent health care as part of the VA Eastern Kansas Health Care System (VAEKHCS). We consider it our privilege to serve your health care needs in any way we can.

5543 Dwight D Eisenhower VA Medical Center
Veterans Health Administration, US Dept. of VA
4101 4th Street Trafficway
Leavenworth, KS 66048-5014

913-682-2000
800-952-8387
g.vhacss@forum.va.gov
www.leavenworth.va.gov

A. Rudy Klopfer, FACHE, Director
John Moon, Associate Director
Nelson L. Dean, RN, BSN, MA, Associate Director for Patient Care Services
Since 1886, the staff of the Dwight D. Eisenhower VA Medical Center has been serving veterans. Today, we proudly serve our nation's veterans with excellent health care as part of the VA Eastern Kansas Health Care System (VAEKHCS). We consider it our privilege to serve your health care needs in any way we can.

5544 Kansas VA Regional Office
Veterans Benefits Administration, US Dept. of VA
5500 E Kellogg Dr
Wichita, KS 67218-1607

800-827-1000
wichita.query@vba.va.gov
www.benefits.va.gov/wichita

Edgar L Tucker, Medical Center Director

5545 Robert J Dole VA Medical Center
Veterans Health Administration, US Dept. of VA
5500 E Kellogg Dr
Wichita, KS 67218-1607

316-685-2221
800-827-1000
888-827-6881
FAX: 316-651-3666
g.vhacss@forum.va.gov
www.wichita.va.gov

Kevin Inkley, MA, Director
Vicki Bondie, MBA, Associate Director
Carol A. Kaster, MA, RN, Associate Director of Patient Care/Nurse Executive
For over 70 years, the Dole VA Medical and Regional office center has been honored to serve Kansas area veterans. The center provides a full range of primary and specialty acute and extended care services to veterans in 59 counties of Kansas. Special emphasis programs include substance abuse, post traumatic stress disorder (PTSD), women's health, spinal cord injury, visual impairment, prosthetic and sensory aids, and homeless services.

Kentucky

5546 Lexington VA Medical Center
Veterans Health Administration, US Dept. of VA
1101 Veterans Dr
Lexington, KY 40502-2235   859-281-4900
                                            800-352-4000
                                            g.vhacss@forum.va.gov
                                            www.lexington.va.gov

Martin J. Traxler, Acting Medical Center Director
Patricia Breeden, MD, Acting Chief of Staff
Laura Faulkner, Acting Associate Medical Center Director
The Lexington Veterans Affairs Medical Center is a fully accredited, two-division, tertiary care medical center with an operating bed complement of 199 hospital beds. Acute medical, neurological, surgical and psychiatric inpatient services are provided at the Cooper Division, located adjacent to the University of Kentucky Medical Center. Other available services include: emergency care, medical-surgical units, acute psychiatry, ICU, progressive care unit, (includes Cardiac Cath Lab) ambulatory s

5547 Louisville VA Medical Center
Veterans Health Administration, US Dept. of VA
800 Zorn Ave
Louisville, KY 40206-1433   502-287-4000
                                            800-376-8387
                                            g.vhacss@forum.va.gov
                                            www.louisville.va.gov

Wayne L. Pfeffer, MHSA, FACHE, Medical Center Director
Douglas V Paxton, Sr, Associate Director / Operations
Pamala Thompson, RN, MSA, MSN, Associate Director for Patient Care Services
Since 1952, Robley Rex VAMC has been improving the health of the men and women who have so proudly served our nation. We consider it our privilege to serve your health care needs in any way we can. Services are available to more than 166,000 veterans living in a 35-county area of the Kentuckiana area.

5548 Louisville VA Regional Office
Veterans Benefits Administration, US Dept. of VA
800 Zorn Avenue
Louisville, KY 40206-1433   502-287-4000
                                            800-376-8387
                                            louisville.query@vba.va.gov
                                            www.louisville.va.gov

Wayne L. Pfeffer, MHSA, FACHE, Medical Center Director
Douglas V Paxton, Sr, Associate Director / Operations
Pamala Thompson, RN, MSA, MSN, Associate Director for Patient Care Services
Since 1952, Robley Rex VAMC has been improving the health of the men and women who have so proudly served our nation. We consider it our privilege to serve your health care needs in any way we can. Services are available to more than 166,000 veterans living in a 35-county area of the Kentuckiana area.

Louisiana

5549 Alexandria VA Medical Center
Department of Veterans Affairs
2495 Shreveport Highway
Pineville, LA 71360-9004   318-466-4000
                                             800-375-8387
                                             FAX: 318-483-5029
                                             richard.wright2@va.gov
                                             www.alexandria.va.gov

Martin J. Traxler, Medical Center Director
Yolanda Sanders-Jackson, Associate Director
Jose N Rivera, MD, Acting Chief of Staff
The VAMC Alexandria is categorized as a primary and secondary care facility. It is a teaching hospital, providing a full range of primary care services with state-of-the-art technology and education. Comprehensive acute and extended health care is provided on a primary and secondary basis in areas of medicine, surgery, psychiatry, physical medicine and rehabilitation, neurology, oncology, dentistry, geriatrics, and extended care. The Medical Center serves a potential veteran population of over 1

5550 New Orleans VA Medical Center
Veterans Health Administration, US Dept. of VA
1601 Perdido St
New Orleans, LA 70112-1262   504-412-3700
                                            800-935-8387
                                            FAX: 504-589-5210
                                            Stacie.Rivera@med.va.gov
                                            www.neworleans.va.gov

John D Church Jr, Medical Director/President
Fernando Rivera, Association Medical Center Direc
Sam Lucero, Special Assistant to Director
A teaching hospital, providing a full range of patient care services, with state-of-the-art technology as well as education and research. Comprehensive health care is provided through primary care, tetiary care, and long-term care in areas of medicine, surgery, psychiatry, physical medicine and rehabilitation, neurology, oncology, dentistry, geriatrics, and extended care.

5551 Shreveport VA Medical Center
Veterans Health Administration, US Dept. of VA
510 E Stoner Ave
Shreveport, LA 71101-4295   318-221-8411
                                            800-827-1000
                                            www.shreveport.va.gov

Shirley M. Bealer, Medical Center Director
Todd M. Moore, Assistant Medical Center Director
Erik J. Glover, Associate Medical Center Director

Maine

5552 Maine VA Regional Office
Veterans Benefits Administration, US Dept. of VA
1 VA Center
Augusta, ME 4330-6719   207-623-8411
                                            877-421-8263
                                            togus.query@vba.va.gov
                                            www.va.gov

Dale Demers, Director
Scott Karczewski, Manager

5553 Togus VA Medical Center
Veterans Health Administration, US Dept. of VA
1 VA Center
Augusta, ME 04330-6795   207-623-8411
                                            877-421-8263
                                            FAX: 207-623-5792
                                            g.vhacss@forum.va.gov

Scott Karczewski, Regional Office Director
Denise Benson, Veterans Sevice Center Manager
Gregg Morin, Assistant Veterans Service Center Manager

Maryland

5554 Baltimore Regional Office
Veterans Benefits Administration, US Dept. of VA
31 Hopkins Plz
Baltimore, MD 21201-2825   800-827-1000
                                            baltimore.query@vba.va.gov
                                            www.va.gov

Jerry L Calhoun
The Baltimore Regional Office serves 484,013 veterans living in the State of Maryland, 2% of the national veteran population. The Regional Office's jurisdiction includes all counties in the State of Maryland. The Baltimore Regional Office has an assigned staffing of 218. We provide services at the VA Medical Center in Baltimore and Transition Assistance throughout the State. We actively participate in a homeless veterans outreach program based at the Maryland Center for the Veterans Educatio

5555 Baltimore VA Medical Center
Veterans Health Administration, US Dept. of VA
10 N Greene St
Baltimore, MD 21201-1524   410-605-7000
                                  800-463-6295
                             FAX: 410-605-7901
                             g.vhacss@forum.va.gov
                             www.maryland.va.gov

Dennis H. Smith, Director
Nancy Quailey-Giannopoulis, Associate Director for Operations
Frederick P. Soetje, Associate Director for Finance
The Baltimore Medical Center is nationally recognized for its outstanding patient safety and state-of-the-art technology, the VA Maryland Health Care System is proud of its reputation as a leader in veterans' health care, research and education.

5556 Fort Howard VA Medical Center
Veterans Health Administration, US Dept. of VA
9600 N Point Rd
Fort Howard, MD 21052-3050   410-477-1800
                                  800-351-8387
                             FAX: 410-477-7177
                             www.mdva.state.md.us

Thomas Hutchins, Secretary

5557 Maryland Veterans Centers
10 N Greene St
Baltimore, MD 21201-1524   410-605-7000
                                  800-463-6295
                             FAX: 410-605-7901
                             www.maryland.va.gov

J Y Jacks, Manager
Dennis H Smith, Executive Director
Veterans medical clinic offering disabled veterans medical treatments.

5558 Perry Point VA Medical Center
Veterans Health Administration, US Dept. of VA
Circle Drive
Perry Point, MD 21902   410-642-2411
                                  800-949-1003
                             FAX: 410-642-1165
                             g.vhacss@forum.va.gov
                             www.maryland.va.gov

Dennis H. Smith, Director
Nancy Quailey-Giannopoulis, Associate Director for Operations
Frederick P. Soetje, Associate Director for Finance
It is nationally recognized for its outstanding patient safety and state-of-the-art technology, the VA Maryland Health Care System is proud of its reputation as a leader in veterans' health care, research and education.

5559 VA Maryland Health Care System
10 N Greene St
Baltimore, MD 21201-1524   410-605-7000
                                  800-463-6295
                             FAX: 410-605-7900
                             www.maryland.va.gov

Dennis H. Smith, Director
Nancy Quailey-Giannopoulis, Associate Director for Operations
Frederick P. Soetje, Associate Director for Finance
A dynamic and exciting health care organization that is dedicated to providing quality, compassionate and accessible care and service to Maryland's veterans. As a part of one of the largest health care systems in the United States, the VAMHCS has a reputation as a leader in veterans' health care, reserch and education. Provides comprehensive service to veterans including medical, surgical, rehabilitative, nurological and mental health care on both an inpatient and outpatient basis.

Massachusetts

5560 Boston VA Regional Office
Veterans Benefits Administration, US Dept. of VA
15 New Sudbury Street
JFK Bldg
Boston, MA 2203-9928   617-232-9500
                                  800-827-1000
                             boston.query@vba.va.gov
                             www.boston.va.gov

Liza Catucci, Administrative Officer
Michael Lawson, President

5561 Edith Nourse Rogers Memorial Veterans Hospital
Veterans Health Administration US Dept. of VA
200 Springs Rd Bldg #23
Bedford, MA 1730-1114   781-687-2000
                                  800-827-1000
                             FAX: 781-687-3536
                             g.vhacss@forum.va.gov
                             www.bedford.va.gov

Michael Mayo-Smith, Manager

5562 Northampton VA Medical Center
Veterans Health Administration, US Dept. of VA
421 N Main St
Leeds, MA 1062   413-584-4040
                                  800-827-1000
                             g.vhacss@forum.va.gov

Richard Woloss, Manager

5563 VA Boston Healthcare System: Brockton Division
Veterans Health Administration, US Dept. of VA
940 Belmont St
Brockton, MA 02301-5596   508-583-4500
                                  800-865-3384
                             FAX: 617-323-7700
                             g.vhacss@forum.va.gov
                             www.boston.va.gov

Vincent Ng, Acting Director
Susan A. MacKenzie, PhD, Associate Director
Cecilia McVey, BSN, MHA, CAN, Associate Director Nursing & Patient Care Services
VA Boston Healthcare System's consolidated facility consists of the Jamaica Plain campus, located in the heart of Boston's Longwood Medical Community; the West Roxbury campus, located on the Dedham line; and the Brockton campus, located 20 miles south of Boston in the City of Brockton.

5564 VA Boston Healthcare System: Jamaica Plain Campus
Veterans Health Administration, US Dept. of VA
150 S Huntington Ave
Boston, MA 2130-4817   617-232-9500
                                  800-865-3384
                             FAX: 617-278-4549
                             g.vhacss@forum.va.gov
                             www.boston.va.gov

Vincent Ng, Acting Director
Susan A. MacKenzie, PhD, Associate Director
Cecilia McVey, BSN, MHA, CAN, Associate Director Nursing & Patient Care Services
VA Boston Healthcare System's consolidated facility consists of the Jamaica Plain campus, located in the heart of Boston's Longwood Medical Community; the West Roxbury campus, located on the Dedham line; and the Brockton campus, located 20 miles south of Boston in the City of Brockton.

5565 VA Boston Healthcare System: West Roxbury Division
Veterans Health Administration, US Dept. of VA
1400 VFW Pkwy
West Roxbury, MA 2132-4927   617-323-7700
                                  800-865-3384
                             g.vhacss@forum.va.gov
                             www.boston.va.gov

Susan A Mac Kenzie, Associate Director
VA Boston Healthcare System's consolidated facility consists of the Jamaica Plain campus, located in the heart of Boston's Longwood Medical Community; the West Roxbury campus, located on the Dedham line; and the Brockton campus, located 20 miles south of Boston in the City of Brockton.

Michigan

5566 **Aleda E Lutz VA Medical Center**
Veterans Health Administration, US Dept. of VA
1500 Weiss St
Saginaw, MI 48602-5251   989-497-2500
                                             800-827-1000
                                       FAX: 989-791-2428
                                    g.vhacss@forum.va.gov
                                       www.saginaw.va.gov

Jeff Nechanicky, Acting Medical Center Director
Stephanie Young, Associate Director
Penny Holland, R.N., MSN, Associate Director for Patient Care
Svcs
Since 1950, the Aleda E. Lutz VA Medical Center has been improving the health of the men and women who have so proudly served our nation. We consider it our privilege to serve your health care needs in any way we can. Services are available to more than 31,000 veterans living in the Central and Northern 35 counties of Michigan's Lower Peninsula.

5567 **Battle Creek VA Medical Center**
Veterans Health Administration, US Dept. of VA
5500 Armstrong Rd
Battle Creek, MI 49037-7314   269-966-5600
                                             888-214-1247
                                             888-214-1247
                                       FAX: 269-966-5483
                                    g.vhacss@forum.va.gov
                                    www.battlecreek.va.gov

Mary Beth Skupien, Director
Edward Dornoff, Associate Director
Kay Bower, Associate Director for Patient Care Services
Since 1924, the Battle Creek, Michigan VA Medical Center has been improving the health of the men and women who have so proudly served our nation. The Battle Creek VA Medical Center consists of 104 medical and psychiatric beds, 32 residential rehabilitation beds, and 103 nursing home care unit beds. In addition, specialized services offered include a Palliative Care Unit, a Substance Abuse Clinic, a Post Traumatic Stress Disorder Program and a Domicilliary.

5568 **Iron Mountain VA Medical Center**
Veterans Health Administration, US Dept. of VA
325 East H Street
Iron Mountain, MI 49801-4760   906-774-3300
                                             800-827-1000
                                       FAX: 906-779-3114
                                    g.vhacss@forum.va.gov
                                    www.ironmountain.va.gov

James W. Rice, Medical Center Director
William Caron, FACHE, Associate Medical Center Director
Andrea Collins, RN, MSN, Associate Director for Nursing and Patient Care Service
OGJVAMC is a primary and secondary level care facility with 17 acute care beds, 13 in the medical/surgical ward and 4 in the intensive care unit (ICU). The main facility provides limited emergency and acute inpatient care, and collaborates with larger VA Medical Centers in Milwaukee and Madison, WI, to provide higher-level emergency and specialty care services. OGJVAMC also provides rehabilitation and extended care, including palliative and hospice care, in its 40-bed Community Living Center.

5569 **John D Dingell VA Medical Center**
Veterans Health Administration, US Dept. of VA
4646 John R St
Detroit, MI 48201-1916   313-576-1000
                                             800-827-1000
                                       FAX: 313-576-1112
                                    g.vhacss@forum.va.gov
                                       www.detroit.va.gov

Pamela J. Reeves, M.D., Director
Annette Walker, M.S.H.A., B.S., Associate Director
Ann M. Herm, R.N., B.S.N., M., Associate Director, Patient Care Services
Our mission is to provide timely, compassionate and high quality care to those we serve by encouraging teamwork, education, research, innovation, and continuous improvement.

5570 **Michigan VA Regional Office**
Veterans Benefits Administration, US Dept. of VA
477 Michigan Ave
Patrick V McNamara Federal Building
Detroit, MI 48226-1217   800-827-1000
                                    detroit.query@vba.va.gov
                                 www.benefits.va.gov/detroit

David Leonard, Director
Dennis W Paradowski, Assistant Director
The Regional Office Staff are dedicated to providing responsive and timely service to the veterans of Michigan and their families. Their duties include processing and making decisions on claims for disability compensation, and assisting with applications for a wide range of VA benefits.

5571 **VA Ann Arbor Healthcare System**
Veterans Health Administration, US Dept. of VA
2215 Fuller Rd
Ann Arbor, MI 48105-2303   734-769-7100
                                             800-361-8387
                                       FAX: 734-761-7870
                                    g.vhacss@forum.va.gov
                                       www.annarbor.va.gov

Robert P. McDivitt, FACHE, Director
Randall E. Ritter, Associate Director
Stacey Breedveld, R.N., Associate Director Patient Care
Since 1953, the VA Ann Arbor Healthcare System (VAAAHS) has provided state-of-the-art healthcare services to the men and women who have so proudly served our nation. We consider it our privilege to serve your healthcare needs in any way we can.

5572 **Vet Center Readjustment Counseling Service**
1940 Eastern Ave SE
Grand Rapids, MI 49507-2771   616-285-5795
                                             800-905-4675
                                       FAX: 616-285-5898
                                             www.va.gov

William Busby, Executive Director
Branden K Lyon, Counselor
Lynn Hall, Clinical Coordinator
Providing a broad range of counseling outreach and referral services to eligible veterans in order to help make readjustments to cilvilian life.

Minnesota

5573 **Minneapolis VA Medical Center**
Veterans Health Administration, US Dept. of VA
1 Veterans Dr
Minneapolis, MN 55417-2399   612-725-2000
                                             866-414-5058
                                       FAX: 612-725-2049
                                    g.vhacss@forum.va.gov
                                     www.minneapolis.va.gov

Judy Johnson-Mekota, Director
Erik J. Stalhandske, Associate Director
Kent Crossley, Chief of Staff
Minneapolis VA Health Care System (VAHCS) is a teaching hospital providing a full range of patient care services with state-of-the-art technology, as well as education and research. Comprehensive health care is provided through primary care, tertiary care and long-term care in areas of medicine, surgery, psychiatry, physical medicine and rehabilitation, neurology, oncology, dentistry, geriatrics and extended care.

5574 **St. Cloud VA Medical Center**
Veterans Health Administration, US Dept. of VA
4801 Veterans Dr
Saint Cloud, MN 56303-2015   320-252-1670
                                             800-247-1739
                                       FAX: 320-255-6472
                                    g.vhacss@forum.va.gov
                                       www.stcloud.va.gov

Barry I. Bahl, Director
Cheryl Thieschafer, Associate Director
Meri Hauge, BSN, MSN Nurse, Executive/Associate Director for Patient Care Services

Specialty care services include audiology, cardiology, dentistry, hematology, oncology, optometry, orthopedics, podiatry, pulmonology, urology and rheumatology. A new Ambulatory Surgery (same-day) Center opened in the fall of 2011 and will provide access to additional outpatient surgical procedures. The medical center offers extensive mental health programming, including acute psychiatric care, Residential Rehabilitation Treatment programs and an outpatient mental health clinic. The programs u

5575   St. Paul Regional Office
Veterans Benefits Administration, US Dept. of VA
1 Federal Dr
Fort Snelling, MN 55111-4080   800-827-1000
                                           stpaul.query@vba.va.gov
                                           www.benefits.va.gov/stpaul

Vincent Crawford, Director

5576   Vet Center
405 E Superior St
Ste 160
Duluth, MN 55802-2240   218-722-8654
                                           877-927-8387
                                           FAX: 218-723-8212
                                           www.vetcenter.va.gov

Cynthia Macaulay MEd, Counselor
Rob Evanson, Counselor
Debbie Burt, Office Manager
Counseling, social services and benefits assistance for combat veterans and those sexually traumatized in the military.

Mississippi

5577   Biloxi/Gulfport VA Medical Center
Veterans Health Administration, US Dept. of VA
400 Veterans Ave
Biloxi, MS 39531-2410   228-523-5000
                                           800-296-8872
                                           FAX: 228-563-2898
                                           g.vhacss@forum.va.gov
                                           www.biloxi.va.gov

Anthony L. Dawson, Director
Nancy Weaver, Associate Director
Kenneth Shimon, Chief of Staff

5578   Jackson Regional Office
Veterans Benefits Administration, US Dept. of VA
1600 E Woodrow Wilson Ave
Jackson, MS 39216-5100   601-364-7000
                                           800-827-1000
                                           FAX: 601-364-7007
                                           jackson.query@vba.va.gov
                                           www.benefits.va.gov/jackson

Neil Anthony Mcphie, Chairman
Barbara Sapin, Vice Chairman

Missouri

5579   Harry S Truman Memorial Veterans' Hospital
Veterans Health Administration, US Dept. of VA
800 Hospital Dr
Columbia, MO 65201-5275   573-814-6000
                                           800-827-1000
                                           FAX: 573-814-6551
                                           g.vhacss@forum.va.gov
                                           www.columbiamo.va.gov

Sallie Houser-Hanfelder, Director
Robert Ritter, Associate Director
Lana Zerrer, Chief of Staff

5580   John J Pershing VA Medical Center
Veterans Health Administration, US Dept. of VA
1500 N Westwood Blvd
Poplar Bluff, MO 63901-3318   573-686-4151
                                           888-557-8262
                                           FAX: 573-778-4156
                                           g.vhacss@forum.va.gov
                                           www.poplarbluff.va.gov

Merk Hedstrom, Medical Center Director
Linda Haga, Research Contact

5581   Kansas City VA Medical Center
Veterans Health Administration, US Dept. of VA
4801 E Linwood Blvd
Kansas City, MO 64128-2226   816-861-4700
                                           800-827-1000
                                           g.vhacss@forum.va.gov
                                           www.kansascity.va.gov

Kenneth Grasing, Research/Development
Ram Sharma, Administrative Officer
Kent Hill, Executive Director
The Kansas City VA Medical Center is a modern, well-equipped teriary care inpatient and outpatient center. As the third largest teaching hospital in the metropolitan area, it maintains educational affiliations with the University of Kansas School of Medicine.

5582   St. Louis Regional Office
Veterans Benefits Administration, US Dept. of VA
400 S 18th St
Saint Louis, MO 63103-2265   800-827-1000
                                           stlouis.query@vba.va.gov
                                           www.stlouis.va.gov

5583   St. Louis VA Medical Center
Veterans Health Administration, US Dept. of VA
915 N Grand Blvd
Saint Louis, MO 63106-1621   314-652-4100
                                           800-228-5459
                                           FAX: 314-289-7009
                                           g.vhacss@forum.va.gov
                                           www.stlouis.va.gov

Dolores Minor, Administrative Officer

Montana

5584   Montana VA Regional Office
3633 Veterans Drive
Fort Harrison, MT 59636-188   406-442-7310
                                           800-827-1000
                                           www.va.gov

5585   V.A. Montana Healthcare System
US Dept. of VA
3687 Veterans Drive
PO Box 1500
Fort Harrison, MT 59636-1500   406-442-6410
                                           877-468-8387
                                           FAX: 406-447-7916
                                           ftharrison.query@vba.va.gov
                                           www.montana.va.gov

Christine Gregory, Director
Vicki Thennis, Interim Associate Director
Trena Bonde, Chief of Staff
This is a complete, medically reliable dictionary of congenital malformations and disorders. As the authors explain, 'Down syndrome is the only common congenital disorder, the other defects and disorders are rare or very rare, some having been reported fewer than 20 times worlwide.' This dictionary covers them all. Examples: Aagenaes syndrome, Acrocallosal syndrome, and Acrodysostosis

5586 VA Montana Healthcare System
Veterans Health Administration, US Dept. of VA
1892 William St
Fort Harrison, MT 59636   406-447-7945
                                 800-827-1000
                                 FAX: 406-447-7965
                                 g.vhacss@forum.va.gov
                                 www.montana.va.gov

Joseph Underkofel, Executive Director
Gregory Johnson, MD

5587 Vet Center
Readjusment Counciling Service Western Mountain Re
2795 Enterprise Ave.
Suite 1
Billings, MT 59102-3238   406-657-6071
                                 FAX: 406-657-6603
                                 www.va.gov

Bob Phillips, Manager
Luanne Anderson, Office Manager
Barry Osgard MS, Counselor
Readjustment counseling service for counseling veterans who
are having difficulty adjusting from military service especially
those diagnosed with PTSD.

Nebraska

5588 Grand Island VA Medical System
Veterans Health Administration, US Dept. of VA
2201 N Broadwell Ave
Grand Island, NE 68803-2153   308-382-3660
                                 866-580-1810
                                 g.vhacss@forum.va.gov

John Hilbert, Executive Director
Daniel L Parker, Deputy Director

5589 Lincoln Regional Office
Veterans Benefits Administration, US Dept. of VA
3800 Village Dr.
Lincoln, NE 68501-4103   402-471-4444
                                 800-827-1000
                                 FAX: 402-479-5124
                                 lincoln.query@vba.va.gov
                                 www.veteranprograms.com

Bill Gibson, CEO
Daniel Parker, Deputy Director

5590 Lincoln VA Medical Center
Veterans Health Administration, US Dept. of VA
600 S 70th St
Lincoln, NE 68510-2451   402-489-3802
                                 800-827-1000
                                 FAX: 402-486-7860
                                 g.vhacss@forum.va.gov
Ryon L Adams, Research/Development Coordinator

5591 VA Nebraska-Western Iowa Health Care System
Veterans Health Administration, US Dept. of VA
4101 Woolworth Ave
Omaha, NE 68105-1850   402-449-0610
                                 800-451-5796
                                 FAX: 402-449-0684
                                 www.nebraska.va.gov

Marci Mylan, Director
Rowen Zetterman, Chief of Staff

Nevada

5592 Las Vegas Veterans Center
1919 S. Jones, Suite A
Las Vegas, NV 89146-905   702-251-7873
                                 FAX: 702-388-6664
                                 www.lasvegas.va.gov

Daryl Harding, Resident Counselor LCSW
Matt Watson, Team Leader MSW
Veterans clinical counseling center for veterans and their dependent individual and group counseling, marital and family counseling, alcohol and drug assessment referral or treatment. Community education and consultation, employment counseling.

5593 Reno Regional Office
Veterans Benefits Administration
1000 Locust St
Reno, NV 89502-2597   775-328-1486
                                 800-827-1000
                                 FAX: 775-328-1447
                                 reno.query@vba.va.gov
                                 www.reno.va.gov

Joseph E Dardillo, Administrative Officer

5594 VA Sierra Nevada Healthcare System
Veterans Health Administration, US Dept. of VA
957 Kirman Ave
Reno, NV 89502-2597   775-786-7200
                                 888-838-6256
                                 FAX: 775-328-1816
                                 www.reno.va.gov

Kurt W. Schlegelmich, Director
Michael C. Tadych, Associate Director
Rachel Crossley, Associate Director

5595 VA Southern Nevada Healthcare System
Veterans Health Administration, US Dept. of VA
6900 North Pecos Rd
Las Vegas, NV 89086   702-791-9000
                                 800-827-1000
                                 FAX: 707-636-3027
                                 g.vhacss@forum.va.gov
                                 www.lasvegas.va.gov

Isabel M. Duff, Acting Director
Ramu Komanduri, Chief of Staff
Sandra L. Solem, Acting Nurse Executive

New Hampshire

5596 Manchester Regional Office
Veterans Benefits Administration, US Dept. of VA
275 Chestnut St
Manchester, NH 3101-2411   800-827-1000
                                 manchester.query@vba.va.gov
                                 www.va.gov

Jerry Beale, Director

5597 Manchester VA Medical Center
Veterans Health Administration, US Dept. of VA
718 Smyth Rd
Manchester, NH 03104-7007   603-624-4366
                                 800-892-8384
                                 g.vhacss@forum.va.gov
                                 www.manchester.va.gov

Susan MacKenzie, Acting Med Center Director
Tammy A. Krueger, Associate Director
Andrew J. Breuder, Chief of Staff

5598 New Hampshire Veterans Centers
103 Liberty St
Manchester, NH 3104-3118   603-668-7060
                                 800-562-3127
                                 FAX: 603-666-7404
                                 www.va.gov

Caryl Ahern, Manager
Paulette Landry, Office Manager
Veterans clinic offering combat veterans outpatient counseling

New Jersey

5599 Disabled American Veterans: Ocean County
P.O.Box 1806
Toms River, NJ 8754-1806   732-929-0907
Mary Bencivenga, Contact

5600 East Orange Campus of the VA New Jersey Healthcare System
385 Tremont Ave
East Orange, NJ 07018-1023
973-676-1000
FAX: 973-676-4226
www.newjersey.va.gov

Kenneth Mizrach, Director
Glen Giaquinto, Associate Director
John A. Griffith, Associate Director

5601 Lyons Campus of the VA New Jersey Healthcare System
Veterans Health Administration, US Dept. of VA
151 Knollcroft Rd
Lyons, NJ 7939-5001
908-647-0180
800-827-1000
FAX: 908-647-3452
g.vhacss@forum.va.gov
www.newjersey.va.gov

James J Farsetta, Director
Donna Henderson, Coordinator

5602 Newark Regional Office
Veterans Benefits Administration, US Dept. of VA
20 Washington Pl
Newark, NJ 07102-3174
973-645-1441
800-827-1000
newark.query@vba.va.gov
www.newjersey.va.gov

Stephen G Abel, Deputy Commissioner for Veterans

New Mexico

5603 New Mexico State Veterans' Home
992 South Broadway
Truth or Consequences, NM 87901-927
575-894-4200
800-964-3976
FAX: 575-894-4270

Lori S Montgomery, Administrator
Carol B Wilson, Admission Coordinator
Veterans medical clinic offering disabled veterans medical treatments.

5604 New Mexico VA Healthcare System
Veterans Health Administration, US Dept. of VA
1501 San Pedro Dr SE
Albuquerque, NM 87108-5154
505-265-1711
800-465-8262
FAX: 505-256-2855
g.vhacss@forum.va.gov
www.albuquerque.va.gov

George Marnell, Executive Director
Pamela Crowell, Acting Associate Director
Peter Woodbridge, Chief of Staff

New York

5605 Albany VA Medical Center: Samuel S Stratton
Veterans Health Administration, US Dept. of VA
113 Holland Ave
Albany, NY 12208-3410
518-626-5000
800-233-4810
888-838-7890
FAX: 518-626-5500
g.vhacss@forum.va.gov
www.albany.va.gov

Donald W Stuart, Associate Director (Interim)
Linda W Weiss, Director
Laurdes Irzarry, Chief of Staff

5606 Albany Vet Center
Ste 2
17 Computer Dr W
Albany, NY 12205-1618
518-458-7998
FAX: 518-458-8613

Lloyd Mc Omber, Owner
Melodie Krahula, Team Leader

Provides readjustment counseling for combat veterans and also provides benefits and job counseling for all veterans.

5607 Bath VA Medical Center
Veterans Health Administration US Dept. of VA
76 Veterans Avenue
Bath, NY 14810
607-664-4000
877-845-3247
888-823-9659
FAX: 607-664-4000
g.vhacss@forum.va.gov
www.bath.va.gov

Michael Swartz, Medical Center Director
David B. Krueger, Associate Director
Felipe Diaz, Chief of Staff

5608 Bronx VA Medical Center
Veterans Health Administration, US Dept. of VA
130 W Kingsbridge Rd
Bronx, NY 10468-9938
718-584-9000
800-877-6976
FAX: 718-733-1223
g.vhacss@forum.va.gov
www.bronx.va.gov

Eric Langhoff, Director
Vincent F Immiti, Associate Director
Kathleen M. Capitulo, Chief of Staff

5609 Brooklyn Campus of the VA NY Harbor Healthcare System
Veterans Health Administration, US Dept. of VA
800 Poly Place
Brooklyn, NY 11209-7104
718-836-6600
800-827-1000
g.vhacss@forum.va.gov
www.nyharbor.va.gov

Martina A Parauda, Director
Veronica J Foy, Associate Director, Facilities &
Michael S Simberkoff, Executive Chief of Staff

5610 Buffalo Regional Office - Department of Veterans Affairs
Veterans Benefits Administration
130 South Elmwood Avenue
Buffalo, NY 14202-2465
716-852-3028
800-827-1000
www.va.gov

5611 Canandiagua VA Medical Center
Veterans Health Administration, US Dept. of VA
400 Fort Hill Ave
Canandaigua, NY 14424-1159
585-394-2000
800-204-9917
g.vhacss@forum.va.gov
www.canandaigua.va.gov

Craig S Howard, Medical Center Director
Margaret Owens, Associate Director
Dr. Robert B Babcock, Chief of Staff

5612 Castle Point Campus of the VA Hudson Valley Healthcare System
Veterans Health Administration, US Dept. of VA
Route 9D
Castle Point, NY 12511
845-831-2000
800-827-1000
FAX: 845-838-5193
g.vhacss@forum.va.gov
www.hudsonvalley.va.gov

Gerald F Culliton, Director
John M. Gary, Associate Director
Patricia A. Burke, Associate Director

5613 New York City Campus of the VA NY Harbor Healthcare System
Veterans Health Administration, US Dept. of VA
423 E 23rd St
New York, NY 10010-5011
212-686-7500
800-827-1000
FAX: 718-567-4082
g.vhacss@forum.va.gov
www.nyharbor.va.gov

Camille R Varacchi, Administrative Officer

5614 **New York Regional Office**
Veterans Benefits Administration, US Dept. of VA
245 W Houston St
New York, NY 10014-4805

212-714-0699
800-827-1000
FAX: 212-807-4042
newyork.query@vba.va.gov
www.va.gov

Ronna Brown, President

5615 **Northport VA Medical Center**
Veterans Health Administration, US Dept. of VA
79 Middleville Rd
Northport, NY 11768-2296

631-261-4400
800-827-1000
FAX: 631-266-6710
g.vhacss@forum.va.gov
www.northport.va.gov

Philip C Moschitta, Medical Center Director
Rosie A Chatman, Associate Director for Patient &
Maria Favale, Associate Director

5616 **Syracuse VA Medical Center**
Veterans Health Administration, US Dept. of VA
800 Irving Ave
Syracuse, NY 13210-2716

315-425-4400
800-792-4334
888-838-7890
g.vhacss@forum.va.gov
www.syracuse.va.gov

James Cody, VA Medical Center Director
Judy Hayman, Associate Medical Center Director
William H Marx, Chief of Staff

5617 **Torah Alliance of Families of Kids with Disabilities**
T AF KI D
1433 Coney Island Ave
Brooklyn, NY 11230-4119

718-252-2236
FAX: 718-252-2216

Juby Shapiro, Manager
Serves over 1k families whose children have a variety of disabilities and special needs. Many of these families are large families in the low socioeconomic level. Offers monthly meetings, guest lectures, parent matching, information of new developments in software, technology and techniques, sibling support groups, pen pal lists, audio and video library, alternative medicine and nutrition information and education on legal awareness and rights of disabled citizens.

5618 **VA Hudson Valley Health Care System**
Veterans Health Administration, U S Department of
2094 Albany Post Road
Montrose, NY 10548-1454

914-737-4400
FAX: 845-788-4244
www.hudsonvalley.va.gov

James J Farsette, Network Director
Michael Sabo, Executive Director

5619 **VA Western NY Healthcare System, Batavia**
Veterans Health Administration, US Dept. of VA
222 Richmond Ave
Batavia, NY 14020-1227

585-297-1000
800-827-1000
FAX: 585-786-1258
g.vhacss@forum.va.gov
www.va.gov

William F Feeley, Medical Center Director
Miguel Rainstein, Chief of Staff
Jason C Petti, Associate Medical Center Directo

5620 **VA Western NY Healthcare System, Buffalo**
Veterans Health Administration, US Dept. of VA
3495 Bailey Ave
Buffalo, NY 14215-1129

716-834-9200
800-532-8387
www.buffalo.va.gov

Brian Stiller, Medical Center Director
Jason C. Petti, Chief of Staff
Royce Calhoun, Associate Medical Center Directo

North Carolina

5621 **Asheville VA Medical Center**
Veterans Health Administration, US Dept. of VA
1100 Tunnel Rd
Asheville, NC 28805-2043

828-298-7911
800-932-6408
FAX: 828-299-2502
g.vhacss@forum.va.gov
www.asheville.va.gov

Cynthia Beyfogle, Executive Director
David A. Pattillo, Assistant Medical Director
James Wells, Chief of Staff

5622 **Charlotte Vet Center**
2114 Ben Craig Drive
Charlotte, NC 28262-2350

704-549-8025
FAX: 704-549-8261
www.va.gov

Loretta Deaton, Team Leader
Cynthia Algra, Office Manager
Billy Moore, Counselor
Preadjustment Counseling for Combat Veterans with Post Traumatic Stress Disorder (PTSD).

5623 **Durham VA Medical Center**
Veterans Health Administration, US Dept. of VA
508 Fulton St
Durham, NC 27705-3875

919-286-0411
800-827-1000
888-878-6890
FAX: 919-286-5944
www.durham.va.gov

Deanne M Seekins, Director
Rudy A Klopfer, Associate Director
John D Shelburne, Chief of Staff
Since 1953, Durham Veterans Affairs Medical Cetner has been improving the health of the men and women who have so proudly served our nation. We consider it our privilege to serve your health care needs in any way we can. Services are available to more than 200,000 veterans living in a 26-county area of central and eastern North Carolina.

5624 **Fayetteville VA Medical Center**
Veterans Health Administration, US Dept. of VA
2300 Ramsey St
Fayetteville, NC 28301-3856

910-488-2120
800-771-6106
FAX: 910-822-7926
g.vhacss@forum.va.gov
www.va.gov

Elizabeth Goolsby, Director
James Galkowski, Associate Director, Operations
Jesse Howard III, Acting Chief of Staff
Since 1940,the Fayetteville VA Medical Center (VAMC) hasimproved the health of the men and women who have so proudly served our nation. We consider it our privilege to serve your health care needs in any way we can. Medical, mental health, women's health careand specialty servicesare available to more than 157,000 veterans living in a 21-county area of North Carolina and South Carolina.

5625 **WG Hefner VA Medical Center - Salisbury**
Vet Health Administration U S Department of VA
1601 Brenner Ave
Salisbury, NC 28144-2515

704-638-9000
800-469-8252
FAX: 704-638-3395
g.vhacss@forum.va.gov
www.salisbury.va.gov

Kaye Green, Director
Linette Barker, Associate Medical Center Directo
Subbarao Pemmaraju, Chief of Staff (Interim)
Since 1953, Hefner VAMC has been improving the health of the men and women who have so proudly served our nation. We consider it our privilege to serve your health care needs in any way we can. Primary and secondary inpatient health care are available to more than 287,000 veterans living in a 24-county area of the Central Piedmont Region of North Carolina. This includes the Char-

lotte area with over 100,000 veterans, and the Winston-Salem area with 65,000 veterans.

5626 Winston-Salem Regional Office
Veterans Benefits Administration, US Dept. of VA
251 N Main St
Winston-Salem, NC 27155-2 336-768-5560
800-827-1000
FAX: 336-768-7295
TTY: 800-829-4833
winsalem.query@vba.va.gov
www.va.gov

Glenn Cobb, Executive VP

North Dakota

5627 Fargo VA Medical Center
Veterans Health Administration, US Dept. of VA
2101 North Elm
Fargo, ND 58102-2417 701-232-3241
800-410-9723
FAX: 701-239-7166
g.vhacss@forum.va.gov
www.va.gov

Michael J Murphy, Healthcare Center Director
Dale DeKrey, Associate Director for Operation
J Brian Hancock, Chief of Staff

5628 North Dakota VA Regional Office - Fargo Regional Office
Veterans Benefits Administration, US Dept. of VA
2101 Elm St N
Fargo, ND 58102-2417 701-451-4690
800-410-9723
FAX: 701-451-4690
fargo.query@vba.va.gov
www.fargo.va.gov

Thomas Santoro, Director Research Department

Ohio

5629 Chillicothe VA Medical Center
Veterans Health Administration, US Dept. of VA
17273 State Route 104
Chillicothe, OH 45601-9718 740-773-1141
800-358-8262
888-838-6446
FAX: 740-772-7023
g.vhacss@forum.va.gov
www.chillicothe.va.gov

Wendy J. Hepker, Medical Center Director
Keith Sullivan, Associate Medical Center Directo
Deborah M Meesig, Chief of Staff

The Chillicothe VA Medical Center provides acute and chronic mental health services, primary and secondary medical services, a wide range of nursing home care services, specialty medical services as well as specialized women Veterans health clinics. The facility is an active ambulatory care setting and serves as a chronic mental health referral center for VA Medical Center in southern Ohio and parts of West Virginia and Kentucky

5630 Cincinnati VA Medical Center
Veterans Health Administration, US Dept. of VA
3200 Vine St
Cincinnati, OH 45220-2213 513-861-3100
800-827-1000
888-267-7873
FAX: 513-475-6500
g.vhacss@forum.va.gov
www.cincinnati.va.gov

Linda Smith, Director
David Ninneman, Associate Director
Robert Falcone, Chief of Staff

5631 Cleveland Regional Office
Veterans Benefits Administration, US Dept. of VA
1240 E 9th St
Cleveland, OH 44199-2068 800-827-1000
FAX: 216-522-8262
cleveland.query@vba.va.gov
www.va.gov

P Hunter Peckham, Director
Robert Ruff, Assistant Director
William Bunkley, Minority Veterans Program Coordi

5632 Dayton VA Medical Center
Veterans Health Administration U S Department of V
4100 W 3rd St
Dayton, OH 45428-9000 937-268-6511
800-368-8262
888-838-6446
FAX: 937-262-2170
g.vhacss@forum.va.gov
www.dayton.va.gov

Glenn Costie, Acting Director
Mark Murdock, Associate Director
James T. Hardy, Chief of Staff

The Dayton VAMC is a state of the art teaching facility that has been serving Veterans for 146 years, having accepted its first patient in 1867. The Dayton VA Medical Center provides a full range of health care through medical, surgical, mental health (inpatient and outpatient), home and community health programs, geriatric (nursing home), physical medicine and therapy services, neurology, oncology, dentistry, and hospice.

5633 Louis Stokes VA Medical Center - Wade Park Campus
Veterans Health Administration, US Dept. of VA
10701 East Blvd
Cleveland, OH 44106-1702 216-791-3800
877-838-8262
888-838-6446
FAX: 440-838-6017
g.vhacss@forum.va.gov
www.cleveland.va.gov

Susan M Fuehrer, Medical Center Director
Darwin Goodspeed, Associate Medical Center Director
Murray D. Altose, Chief of Staff

Oklahoma

5634 Jack C. Montgomery VA Medical Center
Veterans Benefits Administration, US Dept. of VA
1011 Honor Heights Dr
Muskogee, OK 74401-1318 918-577-3000
800-827-1000
muskogee.query@vba.va.gov
www.muskogee.va.gov

Alef Nancy Graham, Manager

5635 Jack C. Montomery VA Medical Center
1011 Honor Heights Dr
Muskogee, OK 74401-1318 918-577-3000
800-827-1000
muskogee.query@vba.va.gov
www.muskogee.va.gov

James R. Floyd, Medical Director
Inez Reitz, Acting Associate Director
Thomas D. Schneider, Chief of Staff

5636 Oklahoma City VA Medical Center
Veterans Health Administration, US Dept. of VA
921 NE 13th St
Oklahoma City, OK 73104-5007 405-456-1000
800-827-1000
FAX: 405-270-1560
www.oklahoma.va.gov

Jimmy A. Murphy, Director
Debra A. Colombe, Associate Director
Mark Huycke, Chief of Staff

5637 Oklahoma Veterans Centers Vet Center
3033 N Walnut Ave
Ste W101
Oklahoma City, OK 73105-2833   405-270-5184
                                      FAX: 405-270-5125

Peter Sharp, Manager
Steve Kenzie, Owner
PTSP counseling for all combat Veterans and victims of sexual
trauma/sexual harassment.

Oregon

5638 Oregon Health Sciences University
3181 SW Sam Jackson Park Rd
Portland, OR 97239-3098   503-494-8311
                                 ohsu.edu

Joe Robertson, President
James Morgan, Executive Director

5639 Portland Regional Office
Veterans Benefits Administration, US Dept. of VA
100 SW Main St, Floor 2
Portland, OR 97204-2802   503-373-2388
                                 800-827-1000
                                 portland.query@vba.va.gov
                                 www.va.gov

5640 Portland VA Medical Center
Veterans Health Administration, US Dept. of VA
3710 SW U.S. Veterans Hospital Rd.
Portland, OR 97239-2964   503-220-8262
                                 800-949-1004
                                 FAX: 503-273-5319
                                 g.vhacss@forum.va.gov
                                 www.portland.va.gov

John E Patrick, Director
David Stockwell, Deputy Director of Administration
Tom Anderson, Chief of Staff
The Portland VA Medical Center (PVAMC) is a 303-bed consolidated facility with two main divisions. The medical center serves
as the quaternary referral center for Oregon, Southern Washington, and parts of Idaho for the U.S. Department of Veterans Affairs. The Portland VAMC is located atop Marquam Hill on 28.5
acres overlooking the city of Portland. In addition to comprehensive medical and mental health services, the Portland VAMC supports ongoing research and medical education, including nati

5641 Roseburg VA Medical Center
Veterans Health Administration, US Dept. of VA
913 NW Garden Valley Blvd
Roseburg, OR 97471-6523   541-440-1000
                                 800-549-8387
                                 FAX: 541-440-1225
                                 g.vhacss@forum.va.gov
                                 www.roseburg.va.gov

Jim Willis, Director
Mark Traines, MD

5642 Southern Oregon Rehabilitation Center & Clinics
Veterans Health Administration, US Dept. of VA
8495 Crater Lake Hwy
White City, OR 97503   541-826-2111
                              800-809-8725
                              FAX: 541-830-3500
                              g.vhacss@forum.va.gov
                              www.southernoregon.va.gov

George Andries, Executive Director

Pennsylvania

5643 Butler VA Medical Center
Veterans Health Administration, US Dept. of VA
325 New Castle Rd
Butler, PA 16001-2418   724-282-7171
                               800-362-8262
                               FAX: 724-282-7640
                               g.vhacss@forum.va.gov
                               www.butler.va.gov

John Gennaro, Director
Rebecca Hubscher, Associate Director
Sharon Parson, Nurse Executive
VA Butler Healthcare is located in the heart of Butler County, on
the bus line, and convenient to community support services for
Western Pennsylvania and Eastern Ohio-area Veterans. We have
been attending to Veterans' total care since 1947 and are the
health care choice for over 18,000 Veterans - providing comprehensive Veteran care including primary, specialty, and mental
health care - as well as health maintenance plans, management of
chronic conditions and preventative medicine needs.

5644 Coatesville VA Medical Center
Veterans Health Administration, US Dept. of VA
1400 Blackhorse Hill Rd
Coatesville, PA 19320-2040   610-384-7711
                                    800-290-6172
                                    888-558-3812
                                    g.vhacss@forum.va.gov
                                    www.coatesville.va.gov

Gary Devansky, Director
Sheila Chelleppa, Chief of Staff
Nancy Schmid, Associate Director Patient Care

5645 Erie VA Medical Center
Veterans Health Administration, US Dept. of VA
135 E 38th Street Blvd
Erie, PA 16504-1559   814-868-8661
                             800-274-8387
                             888-860-2124
                             FAX: 814-860-2425
                             g.vhacss@forum.va.gov
                             www.erie.va.gov

Michael Adelman, Medical Center Director
Melissa Sundin, Associate Medical Center Directo
Dr. Anthony Behm, Chief of Staff

5646 James E Van Zandt VA Medical Center
Veterans Health Administration, US Dept. of VA
2907 Pleasant Valley Blvd
Altoona, PA 16602-4377   814-943-8164
                                800-827-1000
                                FAX: 814-940-7898
                                g.vhacss@forum.va.gov
                                www.va.gov

Cecil B Hengeveld, Director
Gerald Williams, Executive Director

5647 Lebanon VA Medical Center
Veterans Health Administration, US Dept. of VA
1700 S Lincoln Ave
Lebanon, PA 17042-7597   717-272-6621
                                800-409-8771
                                FAX: 717-228-5907
                                g.vhacss@forum.va.gov
                                www.lebanon.va.gov

Robert (Bob) Callahan Jr., Director
Robin C. Aube-Warren, Associate Director
Kanan Chatterjee, Chief of Staff

5648 Pennsylvania Veterans Centers
Veterans Health Administration, U S Department of
135 E 38th St
Erie, PA 16504   814-868-8661
                        800-274-8387
                        FAX: 717-861-8589
                        www.erie.va.gov

Michael Aldeman, medical Center Director
Melissa Sundin, Associate Director
Anthony Behm, Chief of Staff

Veterans medical clinic offering disabled veterans medical treatments.

5649 Philadelphia Regional Office and Insurance Center
Veterans Benefits Administration, US Dept. of VA
5000 Wissahickon Ave
Philadelphia, PA 19144-4867
215-336-3003
800-827-1000
FAX: 215-336-5542
phillyro.query@vba.va.gov
www.va.gov

Sonny Dicrecchio, Executive Director

5650 Philadelphia VA Medical Center
Veterans Health Administration, US Dept. of VA
3900 Woodland Avenue
Philadelphia, PA 19104
215-823-5800
800-949-1001
g.vhacss@forum.va.gov
www.philadelphia.va.gov

Joseph M Dalpiaz, Director
Ralph Schapira, Chief of Staff
Margaret O'Shea Caplan, Associate Director for Finance

5651 Pittsburgh Regional Office
Veterans Benefits Administration
1000 Liberty Avenue
Pittsburgh, PA 15222
412-688-6100
800-827-1000
FAX: 412-688-6121
pittsburgh.query@vba.va.gov
www.pittsburgh.va.gov

Micahel E Moreland

5652 VA Pittsburgh Healthcare System, University Drive Division
Veterans Health Administration, US Dept. of VA
University Dr
Pittsburgh, PA 15240-2400
412-688-6000
866-482-7488
FAX: 412-688-6901
g.vhacss@forum.va.gov
www.pittsburgh.va.gov

Timothy Mar Carlos, CEO

5653 VA Pittsburgh Healthcare System, Highland Drive Division
Veterans Health Administration, US Dept. of VA
7180 Highland Dr
Pittsburgh, PA 15206-1206
412-688-6000
800-827-1000
FAX: 412-365-4213
g.vhacss@forum.va.gov
www.pittsburgh.va.gov

Kristin Best, Deputy Adjutant General
Roger Sutton, MD

5654 Wilkes-Barre VA Medical Center
Veterans Health Administration, US Dept. of VA
1111 E End Blvd
Wilkes Barre, PA 18711-30
570-824-3521
877-928-2621
FAX: 570-821-7278
g.vhacss@forum.va.gov
www.wilkes-barre.va.gov

William H Mills, Director (Interim)
Douglas V Paxton Sr., Associate Director
Mirza Z Ali, Chief of Staff

Rhode Island

5655 Providence Regional Office
Veterans Benefits Administration, US Dept. of VA
380 Westminster St
Providence, RI 2903-3246
401-462-0324
800-827-1000
FAX: 401-254-2320
providence.query@vba.va.gov
www.va.gov

Daniel Evangelista, Acting Associate Director

5656 Providence VA Medical Center
Veterans Health Administration, US Dept. of VA
830 Chalkstone Ave
Providence, RI 02908-4799
401-273-7100
866-363-4486
FAX: 401-457-3360
g.vhacss@forum.va.gov
www.providence.va.gov

Vincent W Ng, Medical Center Director
William J Burney, Medical Center Associate Directo
Gregory M Gillette, Medical Center Chief of Staff
To fulfill President Lincoln's promise To care for him who shall have borne the battle, and for his widow, and his orphan by serving and honoring the men and women who are America's veterans.

South Carolina

5657 Columbia Regional Office
Veterans Benefits Administration, US Dept. of VA
6437 Garners Ferry Rd
Columbia, SC 29209-2401
803-401-1094
800-827-1000
columbia.query@vba.va.gov
www.va.gov

Jimmie Ruff, Executive Director

5658 Ralph H Johnson VA Medical Center
Veterans Health Administration, US Dept. of VA
109 Bee St
Charleston, SC 29401-5703
843-577-5011
800-827-1000
888-878-6884
FAX: 843-876-5384
g.vhacss@forum.va.gov
www.charleston.va.gov

Carolyn L Adams, Director
Scott Isaacks, Associate Director
Florence N Hutchinson, Chief of Staff

5659 William Jennings Bryan Dorn VA Medical Center
Veterans Health Administration U S Department of V
6439 Garners Ferry Rd
Columbia, SC 29209-1638
803-776-4000
800-293-8262
FAX: 803-695-6739
www.columbiasc.va.gov

Carolyn L Adams, Director
Barbara Temeck, Chief of Staff
David L. Omura, Chief of Staff

South Dakota

5660 Royal C Johnson Veterans Memorial Medical Center
Veterans Health Administration, US Dept. of VA
2501 W. 22nd St
Sioux Falls, SD 57105-5046
605-336-3230
800-316-8387
FAX: 605-333-6878
g.vhacss@forum.va.gov
www.siouxfalls.va.gov

Patrick J Kelly, Director
Sara Ackert, Associate Director
Victor Waters, Chief of Staff

5661 Sioux Falls Regional Office
Veterans Benefits Administration, US Dept. of VA
2501 W. 22nd St
Sioux Falls, SD 57105-5046
605-336-3230
800-827-1000
FAX: 605-333-5316
siouxfalls.query@vba.va.gov
www.siouxfalls.va.gov

Tennessee

5662 Alvin C York VA Medical Center
Veterans Health Administration, US Dept. of VA
3400 Lebanon Pike
Murfreesboro, TN 37129-1237
615-867-6000
800-876-7093
FAX: 615-867-5768
g.vhacss@forum.va.gov
www.tennesseevalley.va.gov

Juan Morales, Medical System Director
Janice Cobb, Associate Director, Nursing Serv
Emma Metcalf, Chief Operating Officer

5663 Memphis VA Medical Center
Veterans Health Administration, US Dept. of VA
1030 Jefferson Ave
Memphis, TN 38104-2127
901-523-8990
800-636-8262
g.vhacss@forum.va.gov
www.memphis.va.gov

Jay Robinson III, Associate Medical Center Directo
Douglas D Southall, Assistant Medical Center Directo
Margarethe Hagemann, Chief of Staff

5664 Mountain Home VA Medical Center - James H Quillen VA Medical Center
Veterans Health Administration, US Dept. of VA
Corner of Lamont & Veterans Way
Mountain Home, TN 37684
423-926-1171
877-573-3529
g.vhacss@forum.va.gov
www.mountainhome.va.gov

Charlene S Ehret, Medical Center Director
Jimmy H McGlawn, Associate Director
David R Reagan, Chief of Staff

5665 Nashville Regional Office
Veterans Benefits Administration, US Dept. of VA
110 9th Ave S
Nashville, TN 37203-3817
800-827-1000
nashville.query@vba.va.gov
www.va.gov

Michael R Walsh, Administrative Officer
Donald H Rubin, Research/Development Coordinator

5666 Nashville VA Medical Center
Veterans Health Administration, US Dept. of VA
1310 24th Ave S
Nashville, TN 37212-2637
615-327-4751
800-228-4973
FAX: 615-321-6350
g.vhacss@forum.va.gov
www.tennesseevalley.va.gov

Juan Morales, Medical System Director
Michael A Doukas, Chief of Staff
Gary D Trende, Associate Director, Nursing Serv

Texas

5667 Amarillo VA Healthcare System
Veterans Health Administration, US Dept. of VA
6010 Amarillo Blvd West
Amarillo, TX 79106-1991
806-355-9703
800-687-8262
FAX: 806-354-7869
g.vhacss@forum.va.gov
www.amarillo.va.gov

David Welch, Director
Lance Robinson, Associate Director
Grace Stringfelow, Chief of Staff

5668 Amarillo Vet Center
Department of Veterans Affairs
3414 Olsen Blvd
Suite E
Amarillo, TX 79109-3072
806-351-1104
FAX: 806-351-1104
www.va.gov

Pedro Garcia Jr., Team Leader
Simon Camarillo, Counsilor
William C Santer, Family Therapist
Provides individual, group and family counseling to veterans who served in combat theaters of World War II and Korea, veterans of the Vietnam Era, and veterans of conflicts zones in Lebanon, Grenada, Panama, the Persian Guld and Somalia.

5669 El Paso VA Healthcare Center
Veterans Health Administration, US Dept. of VA
5001 N Piedras
El Paso, TX 79930-4210
915-564-6100
800-672-3782
FAX: 915-564-7920
g.vhacss@forum.va.gov
www.elpaso.va.gov

John A. Mendoza, Director
Elizabeth Lowery, Associate Director
Homer LeMar, Interim Chief of Staff

5670 Houston Regional Office
Veterans Benefits Administration, US Dept. of VA
6900 Almeda Rd
Houston, TX 77030-4200
713-791-1414
800-827-1000
houston.query@vba.va.gov
www.va.gov

Cecil Aultman, Executive Director
Edgar Tucker, Chief Executive Officer

5671 Michael E. Debakey VA Medical Center
Veterans Health Administration, US Dept. of VA
2002 Holcombe Blvd
Houston, TX 77030-4211
713-791-1414
800-553-2278
g.vhacss@forum.va.gov
www.houston.va.gov

Adam C Walmus, Director
J Kalavar, Chief of Staff
Francisco Vazquez, Associate Director

5672 South Texas Veterans Healthcare System
Veterans Health Administration, US Dept. of VA
7400 Merton Minter
San Antonio, TX 78229-4404
210-617-5300
877-469-5300
888-686-6350
g.vhacss@forum.va.gov
www.southtexas.va.gov

Marie L. Wedon, Director
Wade Vlosich, Associate Director
Joe A. Perez, Assistant Director

5673 VA North Texas Health Veterans Affairs Care System: Dallas VA Medical Center
Veterans Health Administration, US Dept. of VA
4500 S Lancaster Rd
Dallas, TX 75216-7167
214-742-8387
800-849-3597
FAX: 214-857-1171
www.northtexas.va.gov/index.asp

Jeffrey Milligan, Director
Peter Dancy, Associate Director
Clark R. Gregg, Chief of Staff
Health care system which serves veterans with medical care and rehabilitation services including spinal cord injury center. For VA benefit inquiries contact 1-800-827-1000. This system has locations in Bonham, Dallas, and Fort Worth.

5674   Waco Regional Office
Veterans Benefits Administration, US Dept. of VA
4800 Memorial Dr
Waco, TX 76711-1   254-752-6581
                                      800-423-1111
                                      TTY:800-829-4833
                                      waco.query@vba.va.gov
                                      www.centraltexas.va.gov

William F. Harper, Chief of Staff
Russell E. Lloyd, Associate Director of Resources
Karen Spada, Associate Director for Patients
Mission is to honor America's Veterans by providing exceptional health care that improves their health and well being.

5675   West Texas VA Healthcare System
Veterans Health Administration, US Dept. of VA
300 Veterans Blvd
Big Spring, TX 79720-5566   432-263-7361
                                      800-472-1365
                                      FAX: 915-264-4834
                                      g.vhacss@forum.va.gov
                                      www.bigspring.va.gov

Andrew M. Welch, Interim Director
Kenneth Allensworth, Associate Director
Raul Zambrano, Chief of Staff
The West Texas VA Health Care System (WTVAHCS) proudly serves Veterans in 33 counties across 53,000 square miles of rural geography in West Texas and Eastern New Mexico. The George H. O'Brien, Jr. VA Medical Center is located in Big Spring, Texas and the six Community Based Outpatient Clinics (CBOC's) that comprise the remainder of the health care system are located in Abilene, TX, Stamford, TX, San Angelo, TX, Odessa, TX, Fort Stockton, TX, and Hobbs, NM.

Utah

5676   Utah Division of Veterans Affairs
Utah Division of Veterans Affairs
550 Foothill Blvd
Ste 202
Salt Lake City, UT 84113-1106   801-582-1565
                                      800-894-9497
                                      FAX: 801-326-2369
                                      www.saltlakecity.va.gov

David J Peifer, Director
Todd Andrews, Assistant to the Director
Karen H. Gribbin, Manager
Our mission is to serve the veteran who served us. The VA Salt Lake City Health Care System is committed to providing our patients with the highest Quality of Care in an environment that is safe. We do this by focusing on Continuous Process Improvement and by supporting a Culture of Safety

5677   VA Salt Lake City Healthcare System
Veterans Health Administration, US Dept. of VA
500 Foothill Drive
Salt Lake City, UT 84148-1   801-582-1565
                                      800-613-4012
                                      FAX: 801-584-1289
                                      www.saltlakecity.va.gov

Steven W Young, Director
Warren E Hill, Associate Director
Karen H. Gribbin, Chief of Staff
Our mission is to serve the veteran who served us. The VA Salt Lake City Health Care System is committed to providing our patients with the highest Quality of Care in an environment that is safe. We do this by focusing on Continuous Process Improvement and by supporting a Culture of Safety

Vermont

5678   Vermont VA Regional Office Center
Veterans Benefits Administration
215 N Main St
White River Junction, VT 05009-1   802-295-9363
                                      866-687-8387
                                      FAX: 802-290-6354
                                      whiteriver.query@vba.va.gov
                                      www.whiteriver.va.gov

Deborah Amdur, Executive Director
Danielle S. Ocker, Associate Director
Melanie Thompson, Acting Chief of Staff
The White River Junction VA Medical Center (WRJ VAMC) is responsible for the delivery of health care services to eligible Veterans in Vermont and the 4 contiguous counties of New Hampshire. These services are delivered at the Medical Center's main campus located in White River Junction, Vermont, and at its seven Outpatient Clinics (Bennington, Brattleboro, Colchester, Newport, and Rutland, Vermont; Keene and Littleton, New Hampshire). The White River Junction VA is closely affiliated with the Ge

5679   Vermont Veterans Centers
359 Dorset St
South Burlington, VT 05403-6210   802-862-1806
                                      877-927-8387
                                      FAX: 802-865-3319
                                      www.va.gov

Fred Forehand, Team Leader
William Newkirk, Counsilor
George Troutman, Counsilor
Veterans medical clinic offering disabled veterans medical treatments.

Virginia

5680   Hampton VA Medical Center
Veterans Health Administration, US Dept. of VA
100 Emancipation Dr
Hampton, VA 23667-1   757-722-9961
                                      800-827-1000
                                      FAX: 757-728-3135
                                      mike.eisenberg@med.va.gov
                                      www.hampton.va.gov

Deanne M Seekins, Medical Center Director
Benita K Stoddard, Associate Director for Operation
G. Arul, Chief of Staff

5681   Hunter Holmes McGuire VA Medical Center
Veterans Health Administration, US Dept. of VA
1201 Broad Rock Blvd
Richmond, VA 23249-1   804-675-5000
                                      800-784-8381
                                      FAX: 804-675-5236
                                      g.vhacss@forum.va.gov
                                      www.richmond.va.gov

Charles E Sepich, Director
David P Budinger, Associate Director
Julie Beales, Interim Chief of Staff

5682   Roanoke Regional Office
Veterans Benefits Administration, US Dept. of VA
116 North Jefferson St
Roanoke, VA 24016-1906   540-362-1999
                                      800-827-1000
                                      FAX: 540-563-4838
                                      www.va.gov

Roger Bohm, Executive
Bert Boyd, COO/Executive Director

5683 Salem VA Medical Center
Veterans Health Administration, US Dept. of VA
1970 Roanoke Blvd
Salem, VA 24153-6478   540-982-2463
                                    800-827-1000
                                    888-982-2463
                              FAX: 540-983-1096
                              g.vhacss@forum.va.gov
                                    www.salem.va.gov

Miguel H LaPuz, Director
Carol S Bogedain, Associate Director
Maureen McCarthy, Chief of Staff

5684 Virginia Department of Veterans Services
270 Franklin Rd SW
Roanoke, VA 24011-2204   540-857-7102
                              FAX: 540-857-6437

Colbert Boyd, Manager

Washington

5685 Jonathan M Wainwright Memorial VA Medical Center
Veterans Health Administration, US Dept. of VA
77 Wainwright Dr
Walla Walla, WA 99362-3975   509-525-5200
                                    888-687-8863
                              FAX: 509-946-3062
                                    www.va.gov

Michael W Parnicky, R and D Coordinator

5686 Seattle Regional Office
Veterans Benefits Administration
915 2nd Ave
Seattle, WA 98174-1060   206-762-1010
                                    800-827-1000
                              seattle.query@vba.va.gov
                                    www.va.gov

Va Ad Harabanim, Executive Director
Timothy Williams, Chief Executive Officer

5687 Spokane VA Medical Center
Veterans Health Administration, US Dept. of VA
4815 N Assembly St
Spokane, WA 99205-6185   509-434-7000
                                    800-325-7940
                              FAX: 509-434-7119
                              g.vhacss@forum.va.gov
                                    www.spokane.va.gov

Alan Prentiss, Chief of Staff
Dirk Minatre, Coordinator
Joseph Manley, Executive Director

5688 VA Puget Sound Health Care System
Veterans Health Administration, US Dept. of VA
1660 S Columbian Way
Seattle, WA 98108-1532   206-762-1010
                                    800-329-8387
                              g.vhacss@forum.va.gov
                                    www.pugetsound.va.gov

Michael Fisher, Director
Michael Tadych, Deputy Director
Walt Dannenberg, Assistant Director

West Virginia

5689 Huntington Regional Office
Veterans Benefits Administration, US Dept. of VA
640 4th Ave
Huntington, WV 25701-1340   304-525-5131
                                    800-827-1000
                              FAX: 304-399-9344
                              huntington.query@vba.va.gov
                                    www.va.gov

Mark Bugher, President

5690 Huntington VA Medical Center
Veterans Health Administration, US Dept. of VA
1540 Spring Valley Dr
Huntington, WV 25704-9300   304-429-6741
                                    800-827-8244
                              FAX: 304-429-6713
                                    www.huntington.va.gov

Edward H Seiler, Director
Suzanne Jene, Associate Director
Jeffery B Breaux, Chief of Staff

5691 Louis A Johnson VA Medical Center
Veterans Health Administration, US Dept. of VA
1 Medical Center Drive
Clarksburg, WV 26301-4155   304-623-3461
                                    800-733-0512
                              FAX: 304-626-7048
                              g.vhacss@forum.va.gov
                                    www.clarksburg.va.gov

William E Cox, Director
Jeffrey A Beiler II, Associate Director
Glenn R Snider, Chief of Staff

5692 Martinsburg VA Medical Center
Veterans Health Administration, US Dept. of VA
510 Butler Avenue
Martinsburg, WV 25405-9990   304-263-0811
                                    800-817-3807
                              FAX: 304-262-7433
                                    www.martinsburg.va.gov

Ann R Brown, Director
Timothy J Cooke, Associate Medical Center Directo
Jonathan E Fierer, Chief of Staff

5693 US Department Veterans Affairs Beckley Vet Center
200 Veterans Ave
Beckley, WV 25801-4301   304-255-2121
                                    877-902-5142
                              FAX: 304-254-8711
                                    www.beckley.va.gov

Karin L. McGraw, Director
Vet Center services includes individual and group readjustment
counseling, referral for benefits assistance, liason with community agencies, marital and family counseling, substance abuse
counseling, job counseling and referral, sexual trauma counseling, and community education.

Wisconsin

5694 Clement J Zablocki VA Medical Center
Veterans Health Administration U S Department of V
5000 W National Ave
Milwaukee, WI 53295-1   414-384-2000
                                    888-827-1000
                                    888-469-6614
                              FAX: 414-382-5319
                                    www.milwaukee.va.gov

Robert H Beller, Director
Michael D Erdmann, Chief of Staff
Judith A Murphy, Associate Director for Patient/N
In an effort to improve access to veterans in Milwaukee County,
the VAMC has deployed a mobile clinic that provides primary
care four days a week to veterans. The Medical Center also assists
the Vet Center located in the City of Milwaukee. In addition, this
Medical Center participates in a four-way partnership with the
WDVA, the Center for Veterans Issues, Ltd., and the Social Development Commission, to operate Vets Place Central, a 72-bed
transitional housing program.

5695 Tomah VA Medical Center
Veterans Health Administration, US Dept. of VA
500 E Veterans St
Tomah, WI 54660-3105   608-372-3971
                                    800-872-8662
                              FAX: 608-372-1224
                                    www.tomah.va.gov

Mario V. DeSanctis, Medical Center Director
David Huffman, Associate Director
David J. Houlihan, Chief of Staff

VAMCTomah has been improving the health of the men and women who have so proudly served our nation. We consider it our privelege to serve your health care needs in any way we can. Services are available to veterans living in a Western/Central area of Wisconsin.

5696   William S Middleton Memorial VA Hospital Center
Veterans Health Administration, US Dept. of VA
2500 Overlook Ter
Madison, WI 53705-2254   608-256-1901
                                         888-478-8321
                                         888-256-1901
                                         FAX: 608-280-7244
                                         www.madison.va.gov

Judy McKee, Director
John Rohrer, Associate Director
Alan J. Bridges, Chief of Staff

5697   Wisconsin VA Regional Office
Veterans Benefits Administration, US Dept. of VA
5000 W National Ave
Milwaukee, WI 53295-1   414-384-2000
                                         800-827-1000
                                         FAX: 414-382-5374
                                         milwaukee.query@vba.va.gov
                                         www.milwaukee.va.gov

Philip L Cook, Executive Director
Neil S Mandel, Research/Development Coordinator
Glen Grippen, CEO
In an effort to improve access to veterans in Milwaukee County, the VAMC has deployed a mobile clinic that provides primary care four days a week to veterans. The Medical Center also assists the Vet Center located in the City of Milwaukee. In addition, this Medical Center participates in a four-way partnership with the WDVA, the Center for Veterans Issues, Ltd., and the Social Development Commission, to operate Vets Place Central, a 72-bed transitional housing program.

Wyoming

5698   Casper Vet Center
1030 N. Poplar Suite B
Casper, WY 82601-2665   307-261-5355
                                         FAX: 307-261-5439
                                         www.vetcenter.va.gov

James Whipps, Office Manager
Vet Center offering re-adjustment counseling for combat veterans.

5699   Cheyenne VA Medical Center
Veterans Health Administration, US Dept. of VA
2360 E Pershing Blvd
Cheyenne, WY 82001-5356   307-778-7370
                                         877-927-8387
                                         888-483-9127
                                         FAX: 307-638-8923
                                         www.va.gov

Cynthia McCormack, Medical Center Director
Elizabeth Lowery, Associate Director
Jerry Zang, Chief of Staff

5700   Sheridan VA Medical Center
Veterans Health Administration, US Dept. of VA
1898 Fort Rd
Sheridan, WY 82801-8320   307-672-3473
                                         800-827-1000
                                         866-822-6714
                                         FAX: 307-672-1639
                                         www.sheridan.va.gov/index.asp

Debra L Hirschman, Director
Michele Beach, Director
Wendell Robison, Chief of Staff

5701   Wyoming/Colorado VA Regional Office
Veterans Benefits Administration, US Dept. of VA
155 Van Gordon St
Lakewood, CO 80228-1709   303-894-7474
                                         800-827-1000
                                         FAX: 303-894-7442
                                         denver.query@vba.va.gov
                                         www.va.gov

E William Belz, Director

Vocational & Employment

Employment

4922 **www.workability.one**
1017 NE Marion Place
Bend, OR 97701   541-638-8528
jobsacrossthespectrum@gmail.com
workability.one
Sheila S. Jordan, MMGT, CHCP, Founder & Managing Director
An online recruitment advertising platform that connects employers with neurodiverse, autistic and disabled job seekers.

Vocations

5233 **www.workability.one**
1017 NE Marion Place
Bend, OR 97701   541-638-8528
jobsacrossthespectrum@gmail.com
workability.one
Sheila S. Jordan, MMGT, CHCP, Founder & Managing Director
An online recruitment advertising platform that connects employers with neurodiverse, autistic and disabled job seekers.

Web Sites

5388 **www.workability.one**
1017 NE Marion Place
Bend, OR 97701   541-638-8528
jobsacrossthespectrum@gmail.com
workability.one
Sheila S. Jordan, MMGT, CHCP, Founder & Managing Director
An online recruitment advertising platform that connects employers with neurodiverse, autistic and disabled job seekers.

Alabama

5702 **ADRS Lakeshore**
Alabama Department Of Rehabilitation Services
602 S. Lawrence St.
Montgomery, AL 36104   334-293-7500
800-441-7609
FAX: 334-293-7383
TTY: 800-499-1816
www.rehab.alabama.gov
Michelle K. Glaze, District 1, Mobile
Jimmy Varnado, District 2, Montgomery
Eddie Williams, District 5, Huntsville
Rehabilitation offering employment services to severely disabled persons. Programs include Adaptive Driving Training, Assistive Technology; Employability Development, and Vocational Evaluation.

5703 **Alabama Goodwill Industries**
2350 Green Springs Highway S
Birmingham, AL 35205   205-323-6331
info@alabamagoodwill.org
www.alabamagoodwill.org
David Wells, President & Chief Executive Officer
Sophia Jones, Vice President, Organizational Development
Doug Prescott, Vice President, Operations
The mission of Goodwill is to provide rehabilitation services, training, employment, and opportunities for personal growth to the disabled/disadvantaged.

5704 **Arc of Central Alabama**
6001 Crestwood Blvd
Birmingham, AL 35212   205-323-6383
FAX: 205-323-0085
www.arcofcentralalabama.org
Chris B. Stewart, President & Chief Executive Officer
Mike Mitchell, Chief Operating Officer
N. Brooks Greene, Chief Financial Officer
The Arc of Central Alabama provides the following services to people with intellectual and developmental disabilities: day programs; residential services; employment services; early intervention; and advocacy.

5705 **Butler Adult Training Center**
South Central Alabama Mental Health
680 Hardscramble Rd.
Greenville, AL 36037   334-382-2353
FAX: 334-382-9518
www.scamhc.org
Clients receive training in Independent Living Skills, Self-Care, Language Skills, Learning, Self Direction and Economic Self-Sufficiency. The clients also participate in Special Olympics activities.

5706 **Coffee County Training Center**
South Central Alabama Mental Health
801 Aviation Blvd.
Enterprise, AL 36330   334-393-1732
FAX: 334-347-0252
www.scamhc.org
Clients 21 years and up receive training in Independent Living Skills, Self-Care, Language Skills, Learning, Self-Direction and Economic Self-Sufficiency. Transportation is also provided to clients of the center.

5707 **Easterseals: Achievement Center**
Easterseals of Alabama
510 W Thomason Circle
Opelika, AL 36801-5499   334-745-3501
866-239-2237
FAX: 334-749-5808
info@achievement-center.org
www.achievement-center.org
Star Wray, Executive Director
Randy Burke, Director, Industrial Operations
Joni House, Director, Business & Finance
Provides vocational development and extended employment programs for physically, mentally, and developmentally disabled individuals and to non-disabled persons who are culturally, socially, or economically disadvantaged.
1961

5708 **Easterseals: Opportunity Center**
6300 McClellan Blvd
Anniston, AL 36206   256-820-9960
FAX: 256-820-9592
smiles@opportunity-center.com
www.opportunity-center.com
A nationally accredited non-profit organization providing vocational evaluation/assessment, paid work training, and employment services for people with disabilities in Calhoun, Cleburne, Clay, Talladega, Coosa and Randolph counties.

5709 **Montgomery Comprehensive Career Center**
1060 East South Blvd.
Montgomery, AL 36116   334-286-1746
FAX: 334-288-7286
montgomery@alcc.alabama.gov
joblink.alabama.gov

5710 **Vocational Rehabilitation Service (VRS)**
Alabama Department Of Rehabilitation Services
602 S. Lawrence St.
Montgomery, AL 36104   334-293-7500
800-441-7609
FAX: 334-293-7383
TTY: 800-499-1816
www.rehab.alabama.gov
Availiable through any of the 20 VRS offices statewide, services can include educational services, vocational assesment, evalua-

tion and counseling, job training, assistive technology, orientation and mobility training and job placement.

5711 Vocational Rehabilitation Service - Opelika
Alabama Department Of Rehabilitation Services
520 W Thomason Circle
Opelika, AL 36801
334-749-1259
800-671-6835
FAX: 334-749-8753
TTY: 800-499-1816
www.rehab.alabama.gov

5712 Vocational Rehabilitation Service - Dothan
Alabama Department Of Rehabilitation Services
795 Ross Clark Circle NE
Ste 2
Dothan, AL 36303
334-699-8600
800-275-0132
FAX: 334-792-1783
TTY: 800-499-1816
www.rehab.alabama.gov

5713 Vocational Rehabilitation Service - Gadsden
Alabama Department of Rehabilitation Services
1100 George Wallace Dr.
Gadsden, AL 35903-6501
256-547-6974
800-671-6839
FAX: 256-543-1784
TTY: 800-499-1816
www.rehab.alabama.gov

5714 Vocational Rehabilitation Service - Homewood
Alabama Department Of Rehabilitation Services
236 Goodwin Crest Dr.
Birmingham, AL 35209
205-290-4400
800-671-6837
FAX: 205-290-0486
TTY: 800-499-1816
www.rehab.alabama.gov

5715 Vocational Rehabilitation Service - Huntsville
Alabama Department Of Rehabilitation Services
3000 Johnson Rd. SW
Huntsville, AL 35805-5847
256-650-1700
800-671-6840
FAX: 256-650-1795
TTY: 800-499-1816
www.rehab.alabama.gov

Eddie C. Williams, Manager

5716 Vocational Rehabilitation Service - Jackson
Alabama Department Of Rehabilitation Services
1401 Forest Ave.
PO Box 1005
Jackson, AL 36545
251-246-5708
800-671-6836
FAX: 251-246-5224
TTY: 800-499-1816
www.rehab.alabama.gov

5717 Vocational Rehabilitation Service - Jasper
Alabama Department Of Rehabilitation Services
4505 Hwy 78 E
Suite 300
Jasper, AL 35501
205-221-7840
800-671-6841
FAX: 205-221-1062
TTY: 800-499-1816
www.rehab.alabama.gov

5718 Vocational Rehabilitation Service - Mobile
Alabama Department Of Rehabilitation Services
3101 International Drive
Bldg. 7
Mobile, AL 36606
251-479-8611
800-671-6842
FAX: 251-478-2197
TTY: 800-499-1816
www.rehab.alabama.gov

Stephen G. Kayes, Manger

5719 Vocational Rehabilitation Service - Muscle Shoals
Alabama Department Of Rehabilitation Services
1615 Trojan Dr
Suite 2
Muscle Shoals, AL 35661
256-381-3184
800-275-0166
FAX: 256-389-3149
TTY: 800-499-1816
www.rehab.alabama.gov

5720 Vocational Rehabilitation Service - Selma
Alabama Department Of Rehabilitation Services
722 Alabama Ave.
Selma, AL 36701
334-877-2927
888-761-5995
FAX: 334-877-3796
TTY: 800-499-1816
www.rehab.alabama.gov

5721 Vocational Rehabilitation Service - Talladega
Alabama Department Of Rehabilitation Services
31 Arnold St.
Talladega, AL 35160
256-362-1300
800-441-7592
FAX: 256-362-6387
TTY: 800-499-1816
www.rehab.alabama.gov

5722 Vocational Rehabilitation Service - Troy
Alabama Department of Rehabilitation Services
1109 Troy Plaza St.
Troy, AL 36081
334-566-2491
800-441-7608
FAX: 334-566-9415
TTY: 800-499-1816
www.rehab.alabama.gov

5723 Vocational Rehabilitation Service - Tuscaloosa
Alabama Department of Rehabilitation Services
1400 James I Harrison Jr Parkway E
Suite 300
Tuscaloosa, AL 35405
205-554-1300
800-331-5562
FAX: 205-554-1369
TTY: 800-499-1816
www.rehab.alabama.gov

William Strickland, Manager

5724 Vocational Rehabilitation Services - Andalusia
Alabama Department of Rehabilitation Services
1082 Village Square Dr.
Suite 1
Andalusia, AL 36420
334-222-4114
800-671-6833
FAX: 334-427-1216
TTY: 800-499-1816
www.rehab.alabama.gov

5725 Vocational Rehabilitation Services - Anniston
Alabama Department of Rehabilitation Services
1910 Coleman Rd.
Anniston, AL 36207
256-240-8800
800-671-6834
FAX: 256-240-6580
TTY: 800-499-1816
www.rehab.alabama.gov

5726 Vocational and Rehabilitation Service - Decatur
Alabama Department of Rehabilitation Services
621 Cherry St. NE
Decatur, AL 35602
256-353-2754
800-671-6838
FAX: 256-351-2476
TTY: 800-499-1816
www.rehab.alabama.gov

5727 Wiregrass Rehabilitation Center, Inc.
795 Ross Clark Circle
Suitr 1
Dothan, AL 36303 334-792-0022
FAX: 334-712-7632
www.wrcjobs.com

John Brown, Chair
Tom West, Vice-Chairman
Ryan Hendrix, Treasurer
Trains individuals to become employable and assists them in finding jobs withing their communities. Also assists individuals who have difficulty maintaining employment, those who are on forms of public assistance such as welfare and those who are employable and underemployed.
1958

5728 Workshops Empowerment, Inc.
4244 3rd Ave. S
Birmingham, AL 35222 205-592-9683
800-368-5688
info@weincal.org
www.weincal.org

Susan Crow, Executive Director
Nathalie Brasher, Director, Programs
Kathy Dunn, Director, Operations
Provides vocational training, sheltered employment and other support services to people with disabilities in central Alabama.

Alaska

5729 Alaska Division of Vocational Rehabilitation
Department of Labor & Workforce Development
P.O. Box 115516
Juneau, AK 99811-5516 907-465-2814
800-478-2815
FAX: 907-465-2856
dol.dvr.info@alaska.gov
www.labor.state.ak.us/dvr
Duane Mayes, Director
Assists individuals with disabilities to obtain and maintain employment.

5730 Alaska Job Center Network
Alaska Department of Labor & Workforce Development
P.O. Box 115514
Juneau, AK 99811-5514 907-465-4562
FAX: 907-465-2984
TTY:907-465-4562
juneau.jobcenter@alaska.gov
www.jobs.alaska.gov

5731 Alaska State Commission for Human Rights
800 A St
Suite 204
Anchorage, AK 99501-3669 907-274-4692
800-478-4692
FAX: 907-278-8588
hrc@alaska.gov
humanrights.alaska.gov

Arizona

5732 Arizona Developmental Disabilities Planning Council (ADDPC)
3839 North 3rd St.
Suite 306
Phoenix, AZ 85012 602-542-8970
877-665-3176
FAX: 602-542-8978
addpc@azdes.gov
addpc.az.gov

Jon Meyers, Executive Director
Marcella Crane, Grants Manager
Lani St. Cyr, Fiscal Manager
A successor of the Governor's Council on Developmental Disabilities, the ADDPC serves Arizona residents with developmental disabilities and their families through research, education, advocacy, and financial support. The council aims to improve employment, self-advocacy, and community inclusion.

5733 Beacon Group
308 W Glenn St.
Tucson, AZ 85705 520-622-4874
FAX: 520-620-6620
www.beacongroup.org
Provides employment and rehabilitation opportunities for people with disabilities.

5734 Business Enterprise Program (BEP)
Arizona Department of Economic Security
3425 East Van Buren
Suite 102
Phoenix, AZ 85008 602-774-9100
FAX: 602-250-8548
des.az.gov

Michael Wisehart, Director
Provides employment opportunities for legally blind individuals to own merchandising businesses.

5735 Division of Developmental Disabilities
Arizona Department of Economic Security
1789 West Jefferson St.
Phoenix, AZ 85007 844-770-9500
FAX: 602-542-6870
DDDCustomerServiceCenter@azdes.gov
des.az.gov
Michael Wisehart, Director
Provides supports and serivces that help empower individuals with developmental disabilities to exercise their rights, lead independent lives, and be involved in their communities.

5736 Fair Employment Practice Agency: Arizona
Arizona Civil Rights Division
2005 N Central Ave.
Phoenix, AZ 85004-2926 602-542-5025
FAX: 602-542-8885
TTY:877-624-8090
www.azag.gov

Joseph Sciarrotta, Division Chief
Provides legal advice to most state agencies. The office also investigates and prosecutes consumer fraud, white collar crime, organized crime, public corruption, and civil rights.

5737 Temporary Assistance for Needy Families (TANF)
1717 W Jefferson St.
Phoenix, AZ 85007 602-542-9935
www.tanf.us/arizona.html
Assist applicants and recipients of temporary assistance to needy families to obtain job training and employment that will lead to economic independence.

5738 Vocational Rehabilitation
Department of Economic Security
1789 W. Jefferson St.
Phoenix, AZ 85007 844-770-9500
FAX: 602-542-6870
des.az.gov

Michael Wisehart, Director
This program serves individuals with disabilities seeking jobs and job training by providing them with services that prepare them for entry or rentry into the workforce.

5739 Yavapai Regional Medical Center-West
1003 Willow Creek Rd.
Prescott, AZ 86301 928-445-2700
877-843-9762
yrmc.org

Mike Beatty, Chair
Tony Ferrulli, Vice Chair
Daniel Storvick, Secretary
Widely recognized for the quality and success of the physical, occupational, and speech therapy programs it offers. Provides a wide range of programs and services that enable patients to reach their maximum level of function and independence and enjoy the highest possible quality of life.

Arkansas

5740 Arkansas Department of Workforce Services
P.O. Box 2981
Little Rock, AR 72203
501-682-2121
844-908-2178
FAX: 501-682-8845
ADWS.Info@arkansas.gov
www.dws.arkansas.gov

Charisse Childers, Director
Jay Bassett, Deputy Director
Courtney Traylor, Deputy Director

Provides a wide range of services, including unemployment insurance, employment assistance, and Temporary Assistance for Needy Families.

5741 Arkansas Rehabilitation Services (ARS)
1 Commerce Way
Little Rock, AR 72202
501-296-1600
FAX: 501-296-1141
ACECommunications@arkansas.gov
arcareereducation.org

Charisse Childers, Director
Joseph Baxter, Commissioner
Trenia Miles, Director, Adult Education

The Arkansas Rehabilitation Services prepares people with disabilities to work and lead productive, independent lives.

5742 Easterseals Arkansas
3920 Woodland Heights Rd.
Little Rock, AR 72212
501-227-3600
info@eastersealsar.com
www.easterseals.com/arkansas

Ron Ekstrand, President & Chief Executive Officer
Stephanie Smith, Executive Vice President & Chief Operating Officer
Mac Bell, Vice President, Development & Communication

Mission is to provide exceptional services to ensure that all people with disabilities or special needs have equal opportunities to live, learn, work, and play in their communities.
1944

5743 Vocational Rehabilitation Services
Arkansas Division of Services for the Blind
P.O. Box 1437
Little Rock, AR 72203
501-682-1001
TTY:501-682-8820
humanservices.arkansas.gov/about-dhs/dsb

Cindy Gillespie, Secretary
Keesa M. Smith, Deputy Director, Youth & Families
Dawn Stehle, Deputy Director, Health & State Medicaid Director

A comprehensive state program designed to assess the needs of blind or visually impaired individuals, and to plan, develop, and provide them with employment services.

California

5744 ABLE Industries, Inc.
8929 W. Goshen Ave.
Visalia, CA 93291
559-651-8150
kstump@ableindustries.org
www.ableindustries.org

Keith R. Stump, Executive Director
Tracy Hart, President
Michael Stafford, Vice President

Committed to improving the lives of people with disabilities by creating opportunities to maximize their independence through job training, employment, life skills education, and community support services.
1962

5745 AbilityFirst
626-396-1010
877-768-4600
info@abilityfirst.org
www.abilityfirst.org

Lori Gangemi, President & Chief Executive Officer
Kashif Khan, Chief Financial Officer
Keri Castaneda, Chief Program Officer

Provides programs and services to help children and adults with physical and developmental disabilities reach their full potential throughout their lives. Offers a broad range of employment, recreational, and socialization programs.

5746 Achievement House & NCI Affiliates
3003 Cuesta College Rd.
San Luis Obispo, CA 93405
805-543-9383
info@achievementhouse.org
www.achievementhouse.org

Provides vocational opportunities for individuals with special needs that respect personal choice and diversity, and reflect individualized goals that support enhanced independence, personal responsibility, and self-esteem.

5747 Anthesis
1063 W. 6th Street
Ontario, CA 91762
909-624-3555
anthesis.us

Mitch Gariador, Executive Director
Kitty DuBois, Director of Human Resources
Terri Perkins, Director of Employment Programs

Anthesis seeks to assist adults with disabilities to reach their full potential through services such as vocational training, employment preparation, and placement services.

5748 Bakersfield ARC
4500 California Ave
Bakersfield, CA 93309
661-834-2272
www.barc-inc.org

A nonprofit organization that provides essential job training, employment, and support services for the developmentally disabled and their families.
1949

5749 California Department of Fair Employment& Housing
2218 Kausen Dr.
Suite 100
Elk Grove, CA 95758
800-884-1684
TTY:800-700-2320
contact.center@dfeh.ca.gov
www.dfeh.ca.gov

Kevin Kish, Director
Mary Wheat, Chief Deputy Director
Jannette Wipper, Chief Counsel

The Department of Fair Employment and Housing protects Californians from employment, housing, and public accomodation discrimination, as well as hate violence.

5750 Colton-Redlands-Yucaipa Regional Occupational Program (CRY-ROP)
1214 Indiana Ct.
Redlands, CA 92374
909-793-3115
FAX: 909-793-6901
www.cryrop.org

Provides hands-on training programs in over 40 high-demand career fields to assist high school students and adults in acquiring marketable job skills. Works in cooperation with local high schools, adult education colleges, and employers to ensure a coordinated integration of academic and career preparation. Support services, career guidance, and services are provided to disabled people.

5751 Community Employment Services
Hope Services
30 Las Colinas Ln.
San Jose, CA 95119-1212
408-284-2850
www.hopeservices.org

Charles "Chip" Huggins, President & Chief Executive Officer
Clayton Ng, Chief Financial Officer
Sujan Vatturi, Chief Information Officer

Hope Services provides a comprehensive and integrated employment service that provides job training, job placement, and on-the-job training for individuals with developmental disabilities.

5752 Continuing Education & Employment Development Program
The Arc San Francisco
1500 Howard St.
San Francisco, CA 94103   415-255-7200
                                   FAX: 415-255-9488
                                   info@thearcsf.org
                                   www.thearcsf.org

Kristen Pedersen, Director
Jennifer Dresen, Senior Director, Programs
Nina Asay, Senior Director, Administration & Operations
Preparing individuals with disabilities for employment through real-world experiences, trainings, and internships.

5753 Desert Haven Enterprises
43437 Copeland Circle
P.O. Box 2110
Lancaster, CA 93535   661-948-8402
                                   FAX: 661-948-1080
                                   www.deserthaven.org
A private, nonprofit organization dedicated to developing, enhancing, and promoting the capabilities of persons with developmental disabilities.

5754 Employment Development Department
P.O. Box 826880
MIC 83
Sacramento, CA 94280-0001   916-654-7799
                                      800-758-0398
                                   www.edd.ca.gov
Nancy Farias, Director
Provides job and unemployment listings, disability insurance, and other information for job seekers and employers.

5755 Fresno City College: Disabled Students Programs and Services
Fresno City College
1101 E. University Ave.
Fresno, CA 93741   559-442-8237
                                   FAX: 559-499-6038
                                   TTY:559-442-8237
                        susan.arriola@fresnocitycollege.edu
                              www.fresnocitycollege.edu
Susan Arriola, Director
The Disabled Students Programs & Services (DSPS) at Fresno City College provides services for students with physical, learning and/or psychological disabilities to successfully pursue their individual educational, vocational, and personal goals. Some programs offered include basic computer training, adaptive software training, independent living and consumer skills training, note-taking assistance, special classes, and more.

5756 Heartland Opportunity Center
323 N.E. St.
Madera, CA 93638   559-674-8828
                                   FAX: 559-674-8857
Provides employment, job placement, vocational, and life skills training to adults with mental, physical and/or emotional disabilities in order to help them reach their personal and vocational goals.

5757 INALLIANCE Inc.
6950 21st Ave.
Sacramento, CA 95820   916-381-1300
                                   FAX: 916-381-9026
                                   acroom@inallianceinc.com
                                   inallianceinc.com
Andrea Croom, Executive Director
Auriel Taurone, Intake Coordinator
Committed to providing services that contribute to the independence of adults with developmental disabilities and acquired brain injury. Services focus on job placement, employment training, and the facilitation of supports necessary for integrated employment and community living.

5758 Kings Rehabilitation Center
490 E. Hanford Armona Rd.
Hanford, CA 93230   559-582-9234
                                   www.kingsrehab.com
Steve Mendoza, Executive Director
Kings Rehabilitation Center provides day program services, vocational training, and employment opportunities for individuals with disabilities.

5759 Mother Lode Rehabilitation Enterprises, Inc. (MORE)
399 Placerville Dr.
Placerville, CA 95667   530-622-4848
                                   www.morerehab.org
Susie Davies, Chief Executive Officer
Nancy Cramer, Chair
Steve Shortes, Vice Chair
A private, nonprofit organization dedicated to supporting persons with disabilities. Established by parents, educators, rehabilitation professionals, and concerned citizens in 1973, MORE now offers training for social, living, and vocational skills.
1973

5760 Napa Valley PSI Inc.
651 Trabajo Ln.
P.O. Box 600
Napa, CA 94559-600   707-255-0177
                                   lea@napavalleypsi.org
                                   www.napavalleypsi.org
Carol Gonsalves, President
Raymond Ingersoll , Vice President
Eleanor Cullum, Secretary
Provides work training, work opportunities, and job placement services for developmentally disabled adults. Emphasis is on manufacture of quality wood products, primarily wooden office furniture.

5761 PRIDE Industries
10030 Foothills Blvd.
Roseville, CA 95747-7102   916-788-2100
                                      800-550-6005
                                   FAX: 800-888-0447
                                   info@prideindustries.com
                                   www.prideindustries.com
Jeff Dern, President & Chief Executive Officer
Casey Blake, Chief Operating Officer
Everett Crane, Chief Financial Officer
Provides vocational and employment services that create jobs for people with disabilites; services include career counseling, vocational assessment, work adjustment, work services, job seeking skills, job development, job placement, on-the-job support (coaching), mentoring, independent living skills, transition services, and case management.

5762 Parents and Friends, Inc
306 E. Redwood Ave.
P.O. Box 656
Fort Bragg, CA 95437   707-964-4940
                                   FAX: 707-964-8536
                                   rmoon@parentsandfriends.org
                                   www.parentsandfriends.org
Rick Moon, Chief Executive Director
Sage Statham, President
Jacqueline Bazor, Vice President
Serves people with developmental disabilities by providing them with oppotunities to participate in their community.

5763 PathPoint
315 W. Haley St.
Suite 202
Santa Barbara, CA 93101   805-966-3310
                                   FAX: 805-966-5582
                                   jeannie.barbieri-low@pathpoint.org
                                   www.pathpoint.org
Henry Bruell, President & Chief Executive Officer
Mark Maynard, Chief People Officer
Stephanie Eubanks, Treasurer
Dedicated to providing comprehensive training and support services that empower people with disabilities or disadvantages to live and work as valued members of the community.

5764 People Services, Inc
4195 Lakeshore Blvd.
Lakeport, CA 95453
707-263-3810
FAX: 707-263-0552
info@peopleservices.org
www.peopleservices.org

Dana Lewis, Executive Director
Cindy Ustrud, President
Kathy Windrem, Vice President
Dedicated to serving as the local community agency, providing the delivery of quality services for people with disabilities.

5765 Porterville Sheltered Workshop
194 W. Poplar Ave.
Porterville, CA 93257
559-784-1399
pswcares.org

Don Sowers, Executive Director
Carol Ledbetter, Director of Program Services
Elizabeth Tellez, Director of Finance
Provides work adjustment and remunerative work programs. Their mission is to assist disabled individuals achieve a more independent and productive life.
1956

5766 Project Independence
3505 Cadillac Ave.
Suite O-103
Costa Mesa, CA 92626
714-549-3464
877-444-0144
FAX: 714-549-3559
www.proindependence.org
Robert Watson, President & Chief Executive Officer
Dorothy M. Blubaugh, Chief Operations Officer
Meka Green, Director of Human Resources
Promotes civil rights for people with developmental disabilities through services which expand independence and choice.

5767 Projects with Industry (PWI) Program
Whittier Union High School District
9401 S. Painter Ave.
Whittier, CA 90605
562-698-8121
www.wuhsd.org
The Transitional and Vocational Services Department runs the PWI program, which focuses on career planning, employment preparation, job placement, and career advancement for individuals with mild to significant disabilities.

5768 Shasta County Opportunity Center
1265 Redwood Blvd.
Redding, CA 96003
530-225-5781
FAX: 530-225-5751
oppcenter_info@co.shasta.ca.us
www.co.shasta.ca.us
Donnell Ewert, Director, Health and Human Services Agency
An employment training program for people with disabilities in Shasta County. These individuals perform paid work in a number of different work environments and at the same time learn the skills necessary to obtain competetive employment in the local community.

5769 Social Vocational Services
3555 Torrance Blvd.
Torrance, CA 90503
310-944-3303
FAX: 310-944-3304
www.socialvocationalservices.org
The leading provider of services for people with developmental disabilities in the state of California. Social Vocational Services provides a paid work program for adults with developmental disabilities.

5770 South Bay Vocational Center
20706 Main St.
Carson, CA 90745
310-817-5116
Info@SBVC1.com
www.sbvc1.com
A not-for-profit organization that has been providing excellent vocational programs and services for individuals with disabilities.

5771 The Arc Los Angeles and Orange Counties
12049 Woodruff Ave.
Downey, CA 90241
562-803-4606
FAX: 562-803-6550
www.thearclaoc.org
Dedicated to improving the lives of children and adults with intellectual and developmental disabilities and their families through educational and employment opportunities.
1956

5772 Tri-County Independent Living Center
139 5th St.
Eureka, CA 95501
707-445-8404
833-866-8444
aa@tilinet.org
www.tilinet.org
Eddie Morgan, Executive Director
Kevin O'Brien, President
Devva Kasnitz, Vice President
Aims to provide programs, services, and information for people with disabilities living in Humboldt, Del Norte, and Trinity Counties in northern California in an effort to allow choices for individuals to optimize their independence.

5773 Unyeway
11657 Riverside Dr.
Suite 165
Lakside, CA 92040
619-334-6502
FAX: 619-334-6504
www.unyeway.com
Kimberly Kelley, Executive Director
A California nonprofit that provides employment opportunities for adults with developmental disabilities such as job placement programs, remunerative work services, and work adjustment training programs.

5774 Valley Light Industries
5360 N. Irwindale Ave.
Baldwin Park, CA 91706
626-337-6200
admin@valleylightind.org
www.valleylightctr.org
Sage Newman, Chief Executive Officer
Ivan Campos, Director of Operations
Aims to recognize the unique capacities of individuals with disabilities, and provide them with the same opportunities of employment.

5775 Work Training Center
80 Independence Circle
Chico, CA 95973
530-343-7994
info@ewtc.org
www.wtcinc.org
Brett Barker, Chief Executive Director
Laura Carter, Chief Financial Officer
Julie Ellen, Director, Facilities & Maintenance
A nonprofit organization providing work and leisure services to people with disabilities.

Colorado

5776 Blue Peaks Developmental Services
703 Fourth St.
Alamosa, CO 81101-2638
719-589-5135
FAX: 719-589-0680
www.bluepeaks.org

Cindy Espinoza, Executive Director
Loren Velasquez, Operations Diretor
Brock Gallegos, Finance Director
Provides remunerative work for persons with intellectual and developmental disabilities in the San Luis Valley.

5777 Cheyenne Village
6275 Lehman Dr.
Colorado Springs, CO 80918
719-592-0200
FAX: 719-548-9947
TTY:719-592-0224
www.cheyennevillage.org

Tim Cunningham, Chief Executive Officer
Mary Dice, Chief Financial Officer
Travers Hyde, Director of Operations
Serves adults with developmental disabilities and intellectual disabilities in El Paso, Teller, and Park Counties.

5778 Colorado Civil Rights Divsion
1560 Broadway
Suite 110
Denver, CO 80202
303-894-2997
800-262-4845
TTY:711
dora_ccrd@state.co.us
www.ccrd.colorado.gov

Aubrey Elenis, Director
Embraces the Department's mission of consumer protection and works to protect individuals from discrimination in employment, housing, and at places of public accommodation through enforcement and outreach consistent with the Colorado Civil Rights Laws.

5779 Developmental Disabilities Resource Center (DDRC)
11177 West 8th Ave.
Lakewood, CO 80215
303-233-3363
contact@ddrcco.com
ddrcco.com

C. David Pemberton, President
Joanne Elliott, Vice President
Susan Hartley, Treasurer
Residental and employment programs for adults with developmental and intellectual disabilities.

5780 Division of Vocational Rehabilitation
Department of Labor and Employment
633 17th St.
Suite 1501
Denver, CO 80202
303-318-8571
CDLE_voc.rehab@state.co.us
www.colorado.gov/dvr
Assists people with disabilities to succeed at work and living independently.

5781 Dynamic Dimensions
567 18th St.
Burlington, CO 80807
719-346-5367
FAX: 719-346-6010
exdir@dynamicdimensions.org
dynamicdimensions.org

Ginny Hallagin, Executive Director
Shawn Calhoon, Finance Manager
Debbie Lamm, Assistant Executive Director & Program Manager
An organization that provides training, advocacy, job placement, and community involvement for individuals with disabilities.

5782 Eastern Colorado Services for the Developmentally Disabled (ECSDD)
617 S. 10th Ave.
Sterling, CO 80751
970-522-7121
FAX: 970-522-1173
www.ecsdd.org

Rhonda Roth, Executive Director
Kasha Sheets, Finance Director
Lori Araujo, Case Management Director
Assists developmentally disabled individuals by providing vocational opportunities within their communities.

5783 Hope Center
3400 Elizabeth St.
Denver, CO 80205-4801
303-388-4801
FAX: 303-388-0249
gghope@comcast.net
www.hopecenterinc.org

Gerie Grimes, President & Chief Executive Officer
Janell Lindsey, Acting Chair
Mary A. Davis, Secretary & Treasurer
Provides educational and vocational opportunities for special-needs and at-risk children and adults from 2-1/2 to adulthood.

5784 Imagine!
1400 Dixon Ave.
Lafayette, CO 80026-2790
303-665-7789
www.imaginecolorado.org

Rebecca Novinger, Executive Director
Jeff Tucker, Director of Human Resources
Jenna Corder, Director of Client Relations
Provides support services to people of all ages with developmental delays and cognitive disabilities including Autism Spectrum Disorder, Cerebral Palsy, and Down Syndrome.

5785 Las Animas County Rehabilitation Center
1205 Congress Dr.
P.O. Box 781
Trinidad, CO 81082-781
719-846-3388
FAX: 719-846-4543
info@scdds.com
www.scdds.com

Duane Roy, Executive Director
Mari Mason, Case Management Director
David Moore, Chief Financial Officer
Provides job placement programs, remunerative work services, and work adjustment training programs.

Connecticut

5786 Abilities Without Boundaries
615 W. Johnson Ave.
Cheshire, CT 06410
203-272-5607
FAX: 203-272-4284
www.abilitieswithoutboundaries.org

Amanda Barnes, Executive Director
Lloyd R. Saberksi, President
Clay Yalof, Vice President
Formerly known as Cheshire Occupational & Career Opportunities (COCO), Abilities Without Boundaries provides opportunities in the community through employment and social experiences for people with developmental disabilities.

5787 Allied Community Services
3 Pearson Way
Enfield, CT 06082
860-741-3701
FAX: 860-741-6870
www.alliedgroup.org

Carol Bohnet, President & Chief Executive Officer
Provides individuals with disabilities or other challenges the opportunity to live and enjoy a productive, independent, and fulfilling life.

5788 Area Cooperative Educational Services(ACES)
350 State St.
North Haven, CT 06473
203-498-6800
FAX: 203-498-6890
www.aces.org

Thomas M. Danehy, Executive Director
Timothy Howes, Deputy Executive Director
Steve Cook, Director, Human Resources
Offers adult and vocational programs for persons with disabilities.

5789 Bureau of Rehabilitation Services
Department of Rehabilitation Services
55 Farmington Ave.
12th Fl.
Hartford, CT 06105
860-424-5055
FAX: 860-424-4850
TTY:860-247-0775
kathleen.sullivan@ct.gov
www.ct.gov/brs

A program which aids disabled persons with preparing for, finding, and keeping employment.

5790 CCARC, Inc.
950 Slater Rd.
New Britain, CT 06053-1658   860-229-6665
ccarc@ccarc.com
www.ccarc.com

Lind Iovanna, Chief Executive Officer
Stacey Vonrichthofen, Chief Operating Officer
Julie Erickson, Senior Vice President
Provides support to people with a variety of disabilities by offering day, residential, recreational, and advocacy services.

5791 CW Resources
200 Myrtle St.
New Britain, CT 06053   860-229-7700
FAX: 860-229-6847
info@cwresources.org
www.cwresources.org
Offers integrated vocational training and employment opportunities for individuals with a variety of different disabilities.

5792 Connecticut Governor's Committee on Employment of People with Disabilities
Connecticut Department of Labor
200 Folly Brook Blvd.
Wethersfield, CT 06109   860-263-6007
dol.webhelp@ct.gov
www.ctdol.state.ct.us
The Committee promotes the employment of people with disabilities by developing programs and initiatives to increase statewide employment opportunities for disabled individuals.

5793 Fotheringhay Farms
The Caring Community of CT
84 Waterhole Rd.
Colchester, CT 06415   860-267-4463
FAX: 860-267-7628
info@caringcommunityct.org
caringcommunityct.org
The Caring Community offers an agri-based vocational skill development through Fotheringhay Farms in green house, barnyard, and garden settings.
1984

5794 George Hegyi Industrial Training Center
5 Coon Hollow Rd.
Derby, CT 06418   203-735-8727
A private, nonprofit agency that offers work programs to individuals with special needs.

5795 Goodwill of Southern New England
432 Washington Ave.
North Haven, CT 06473   203-777-2000
888-909-8188
www.goodwillsne.org

H. Richard Borer, President
Robert Burns, Chief Operations Officer
Marcus O. Notz, Chief Information Officer & Marketing/Public Relations
Provides training, education and other services which result in employment and expanded opportunities for people with disabilities and other barriers to employment in order to enhance their capacity for independent living, increased quality of life and work.

5796 Kennedy Center
2440 Reservoir Ave.
Trumbull, CT 06611   203-365-8522
FAX: 203-365-8533
info@kennedyctr.org
www.thekennedycenterinc.org
Richard E. Sebastian, Jr., President & Chief Executive Officer
Stuart Gordon, Vice President of Finance
Greg Pierson, Facilities Manager
Provides vocational rehabilitation, job training, and job placement services to adults with disabilities.

Delaware

5797 Delaware Division of Vocational Rehabilitation
Delaware Department of Labor
4425 North Market St.
Wilmington, DE 19802   302-761-8275
TTY:302-761-8275
www.delawareworks.com
The state's public program that helps people with physical and mental disabilities obtain or retain employment. DVR's commitment is to help people with disabilities increase independence through employment.

5798 Service Source
13 Reads Way
Suite 101
New Castle, DE 19802   302-762-0300
DRIVE@servicesource.org
www.servicesource.org

Mark Hall, President
Bruce Patterson, Chief Executive Officer
Nate Hoover, Chief Financial Officer
ServiceSource is a leading nonprofit disability resource organization with regional offices and programs located in eight states and the District of Columbia. They offer a range of innovative employment, training, habilitation, housing, and other support services. ServiceSource directly employs more than 1,500 individuals on government and commercial affirmative employment contracts.

District of Columbia

5799 District of Columbia Department of Employment Services
4058 Minnesota Ave. NE
Washington, DC 20019   202-724-7000
FAX: 202-673-6993
TTY:202-698-4817
does@dc.gov
does.dc.gov

Unique Morris-Hughes, Director
Jason Washington, Chief of Staff
Ramon Perez-Goizueta, Chief Compliance Officer
Their mission is to foster economic development and growth in the District of Columbia by providing workforce training, bringing together job seekers and employers, compensating unemployed and injured workers, and promoting safe and healthy workplaces.

5800 Goodwill of Greater Washington
1140 3rd Street NE
Suite 350
Washington, DC 20022   202-636-4225
888-817-4323
FAX: 202-526-3994
info@dcgoodwill.org
dcgoodwill.org

Catherine Meloy, President & Chief Executive Officer
Colleen Paletta, Chief Integration Officer
Jeff Rostand, Chief Financial Officer
Offers vocational training, job training, sheltered employment, and work experience.

5801 Palladium
1331 Pennsylvania Ave. NW
Suite 600
Washington, DC 20004   202-775-9680
thepalladiumgroup.com

Kim Bredhauer, Chairman
Christopher Hirst, Managing Director & Chief Executive Officer
Residential and employment programs for adults with developmental disabilities.

5802 Rehabilitation Services Administration
400 Maryland Ave. SW
Washington, DC 20202
202-401-2000
800-872-5327
TTY:800-730-8913
www2.ed.gov
State Rehabilitation Agency providing services to eligible persons with disabilities.

5803 The District of Columbia Office of Human Rights (OHR)
441 4th St. NW
Suite 570 North
Washington, DC 20001
202-727-4559
FAX: 202-727-9589
TTY:711
ohr@dc.gov
ohr.dc.gov

Hnin Khaing, Interim Director
Upholds local and federal human rights laws, and aims to eradicate discrimination and increase equal opportunity for residents of the District of Columbia.

Florida

5804 Abilities of Florida: An Affiliate of Service Source
2735 Whitney Rd.
Clearwater, FL 33760
727-538-7370
servicesource.org/florida
Provides a full range of employment services including work evaulation, training, job coaching, job placement, advocacy, and education. Also provides housing assistance and specialized to adults with cystic fibrosis.

5805 Able Trust, The
3320 Thomasville Rd.
Suite 200
Tallahassee, FL 32308
850-224-4493
FAX: 850-224-4496
info@abletrust.org
www.abletrust.org

Allison Chase, President & Chief Executive Officer
Joey D'Souza, Vice President, External Engagement
Donna Wright, Vice President, Development & Marketing
Provides grant funds for employment-related programs for nonprofit agencies in Florida. Assists families, individuals, and agencies through educational conferences and youth training programs. Provides businesses free resources for hiring people with disabilities.

5806 Florida Division of Blind Services
325 West Gaines St.
Turlington Building, Suite 1114
Tallahassee, FL 32399-0400
850-245-0300
800-342-1828
FAX: 850-245-0363
dbs.myflorida.com

Robert Doyle, Director
An organization that aims to help blind and visually impaired individuals have access to tools, support, and oppotunities in order to live independent lives. Offers a Vocational Rehabilitation program for adults, and a Transition Services program for young adults.

5807 Florida Division of Vocational Rehabilitation
4070 Esplanade Way
Tallahassee, FL 32399-7016
800-451-4327
FAX: 850-245-3399
rehabworks.org
A federal-state program that helps people with physical or mental disabilities get a job.

5808 Florida Fair Employment Practice Agency
Florida Commission on Human Relations
4075 Esplanade Way
Room 110
Tallahassee, FL 32399
850-488-7082
800-342-8170
FAX: 850-487-1007
fchrinfo@fchr.myflorida.com
fchr.state.fl.us

Michelle Wilson, Executive Director
The Commission is the state agency charged with enforcing the state's civil rights laws and serves as a resource on human relations for the people of Florida.

5809 Goodwill Life Skills Development Program
Goodwill Industries-Suncoast, Inc.
10596 Gandy Blvd.
St. Petersburg, FL 33702
727-523-1512
888-279-1988
FAX: 727-579-0850
TTY:727-579-1068
goodwill-suncoast.org

Deborah A. Passerini, President & Chief Executive Officer
Tracey Boucher, Corporate Treasurer & Chief Financial Officer
Kris Rawson, Vice President for Mission Services & Chief Mission Officer
A training program that enables people with developmental disabilities to gain independence by practicing job skills.

5810 Goodwill Temporary Staffing
Goodwill Industries-Suncoast, Inc.
10596 Gandy Blvd.
St. Petersburg, FL 33702
727-523-1512
888-279-1988
FAX: 727-579-0850
TTY:727-579-1068
goodwill-suncoast.org

Deborah A. Passerini, President & Chief Executive Officer
Tracey Boucher, Corporate Treasurer & Chief Financial Officer
Kris Rawson, Vice President for Mission Services & Chief Mission Officer
Provides employment links from potential employees, both disabled and non-disabled alike to employers with immediate employment opportunities seeking qualified candidates. Pre-screening on all applicants includes employment history, personal references, law enforcement background checks, and substance screening.

5811 Goodwill's Community Employment Services
Goodwill Industries-Suncoast, Inc.
10596 Gandy Blvd.
St. Petersburg, FL 33702
727-523-1512
888-279-1988
FAX: 727-579-0850
TTY:727-579-1068
goodwill-suncoast.org

Deborah A. Passerini, President & Chief Executive Officer
Tracey Boucher, Corporate Treasurer & Chief Financial Officer
Kris Rawson, Vice President for Mission Services & Chief Mission Officer
Provides employment opportunities for people with developmental disabilities. Community Employment Services offer on-the-job training and check ups from a support facilitator.

5812 Goodwill's Job Connection Center
Goodwill Industries-Suncoast, Inc.
10596 Gandy Blvd.
St. Petersburg, FL 33702
727-523-1512
888-279-1988
FAX: 727-579-0850
TTY:727-579-1068
www.goodwill-suncoast.org

Deborah A. Passerini, President & Chief Executive Officer
Tracey Boucher, Corporate Treasurer & Chief Financial Officer
Kris Rawson, Vice President for Mission Services & Chief Mission Officer
A local, community-based space where people can search for employment. The center offers carrer planning and exploration, employability workshops, and training.

5813 Goodwill's JobWorks
Goodwill Industries-Suncoast, Inc.
10596 Gandy Blvd.
St. Petersburg, FL 33702   727-523-1512
                                   888-279-1988
                           FAX: 727-579-0850
                           TTY:727-579-1068
                           www.goodwill-suncoast.org
Deborah A. Passerini, President & Chief Executive Officer
Tracey Boucher, Corporate Treasurer & Chief Financial Officer
Kris Rawson, Vice President for Mission Services & Chief Mission
Officer
A program that provides employment for people with disabilities
at MacDill Air Force Base in dining or postal services.

5814 Lighthouse Central Florida
215 East New Hampshire St.
Orlando, FL 32804   407-898-2483
                    FAX: 407-898-0236
                    lighthousecentralflorida.com
Kyle Johnson, President & Chief Executive Officer
Kaleb Stunkard, Executive Vice President & Chief Operations Offi-
cer
Ryan Brown, Vice President, Operations
Lighthouse Central Florida (LCF) is the only nonprofit organization offering comprehensive, professional, vision rehabilitation
services to Central Floridians of all ages with low vision or
blindness.

5815 One-Stop Service Center
Goodwill Industries-Suncoast, Inc.
10596 Gandy Blvd.
St. Petersburg, FL 33702   727-523-1512
                                   888-279-1988
                           FAX: 727-579-0850
                           TTY:727-579-1068
                           goodwill-suncoast.org
Deborah A. Passerini, President & Chief Executive Officer
Tracey Boucher, Corporate Treasurer & Chief Financial Officer
Kris Rawson, Vice President for Mission Services & Chief Mission
Officer
Provides universal job search and placement related services to
any person entering the service center. Each One-Stop Services
Center provides on-site representation from a variety of employ-
ment-related service providers. All Centers host and/or facilitate
local employment fairs and provides access to computerized job
postings.

5816 Palm Beach Habilitation Center
4522 South Congress Ave.
Palm Springs, FL 33461   561-965-8500
                         FAX: 561-433-2073
                         pbhab.com
Patty Isola, Interim Chief Executive Officer
Cara Webster, Controller
Danielle Hanson, Chief Development Officer
Providing work evaluation, work adjustment, job placement, em-
ployment, residential, and retirement services for mentally, emo-
tionally, and physically disabled adults.

5817 Primrose Center
2733 South Ferncreek Ave.
Orlando, FL 32806   407-898-7201
                    www.primrosecenter.org
Bill McCormac, Chief Executive Officer
Karen Schlachter, Chief Financial Officer
Leslie North, President & Chair
A nonprofit organization that aims to transform the lives of peo-
ple with developmental disabilities by providing opportunities to
achieve their fullest potential. Primrose Center offers an Adult
Day Program and an Employment Services Program, which pro-
vide opportunities for individuals with intellectual and develop-
mental disabilities to gain employment.

5818 Project SEARCH
Goodwill Industries-Suncoast, Inc.
10596 Gandy Blvd.
St. Petersburg, FL 33702   727-523-1512
                                   888-279-1988
                           FAX: 727-579-0850
                           TTY:727-579-1068
                           www.goodwill-suncoast.org
Deborah A. Passerini, President & Chief Executive Officer
Tracey Boucher, Corporate Treasurer & Chief Financial Officer
Kris Rawson, Vice President for Mission Services & Chief Mission
Officer
A program for students with disabilities that provides work expe-
rience.

5819 Quest, Inc.
PO Box 531125
Orlando, FL 32853   407-218-4300
                           888-807-8378
                    FAX: 407-218-4301
                    contact@questinc.org
                    www.questinc.org
John Gill, President & Chief Executive Officer
Brooke Eakins, Chief Operating Officer
Todd Thrasher, Chief Financial Officer
Quest helps individuals with developmental disabilities in Cen-
tral Florida achieve their goals by providing services that in-
crease their capabilities and quality of life. Quest serves more
than 1,000 individuals each day in the Orlando and Tampa areas.

5820 Quest, Inc. - Tampa Area
3910 US Hwy. 301 N
Tampa, FL 33619   813-423-7700
                         888-807-8378
                    FAX: 813-423-7701
                    contact@questinc.org
                    www.questinc.org
John Gill, President & Chief Executive Officer
Brooke Eakins, Chief Operating Officer
Todd Thrasher, Chief Financial Officer
Quest helps individuals with developmental disabilities in Cen-
tral Florida achieve their goals by providing services that in-
crease their capabilities and quality of life. Quest serves more
than 1,000 individuals each day in the Orlando and Tampa areas.

5821 SCARC, Inc.
                                   973-383-7442
A nonprofit organization that provides a training and employment program for adults with disabilities. SCARC offers vocational evaluation, training, work services, transportation,
supported independent living, and community based training.

5822 Seagull Industries for the Disabled
3879 Byron Dr.
West Palm Beach, FL 33404   561-842-5814
                           Info@Seagull.org
                           www.seagull.org
Laura Fowler, Chair
Judy Dynia, Vice Chair
Jim Weber, Secretary
Dedicated to improving the quality of life of mentally, physically,
and emotionally challenged adults in Palm Beach County, Florida
through advocacy and the provision of a variety of social service,
vocational training, and residential programs designed to encourage self reliance and independence.

Georgia

5823   Fair Housing and Equal Employment
Georgia Commission on Equal Opportunity
205 Jesse Hill Jr. Dr. SE
14th Floor-1470B East Tower
Atlanta, GA 30334   404-656-1736
                                               800-473-6736
                                          FAX: 404-656-4399
                                        gceo@gceo.state.ga.us
                                        www.gceo.state.ga.us
Allona Lane Cross, Executive Director & Administrator
Jonathan Paul Harris, Deputy Director
Caprisa T. Clowney, Equal Employment Division Director
The mission of the Commission on Equal Opportunity is to investigate housing and employment discrimination in the state of Georgia.

5824   Goodwill Career Centers
Goodwill of North Georgia
2201 Lawrenceville Hwy.
Suite 300
Decatur, GA 30033   404-420-9900
                                               goodwillng.org
Keith T. Parker, President & Chief Executive Officer
Jenny Taylor, Vice President of Career Services
Employment training, assessment, and job placement for people who have disabilities and/or are disadvantaged. The center also provides access to computers and phones to aid in acquiring employment.

5825   Griffin Area Resource Center
931 Hamilton Blvd.
Griffin, GA 30224   770-228-9919
                                          FAX: 770-228-9920
                                  griffinarearesourcecenter.com
Lisa Sassaman, Executive Director
Connie Moody, Director of Support Services
Kim Byrom, Day Support Supervisor
A CARF (The Rehabilitation Accreditation Commission) accredited Employment and Community Support organization providing daily services to participants with disabilities from 16 years of age and up in a 5 county area.
1955

5826   New Ventures
306 Fort Dr.
LaGrange, GA 30240   706-882-7723
                                        dhigh@newventures.org
                                               newventures.org
J.M. Rawlinson, Chair
David Kegel, Vice Chair
Kathleen Ernest, Secretary
A rehabilitation and work training facility for individuals with barriers to employability. The program utilizes community based industrial work of varying levels of difficulty. A return to work conditioning program for the industrially injured is offered which features first-day contact, workers compensation rehabilitation team management, and light-duty work conditioning. A training stipend is paid to defray costs associated with training.

5827   Vocational and Rehabilitation Agency
1718 Peachtree St. NW
Suite 376 S.
Atlanta, GA 30309   844-367-4872
                                               gvs.georgia.gov
Chris Wells, Executive Director
Thomas W. Wilson, Chair
Faye Perdue, Vice Chair
Purpose is to assist eligible individuals with disabilities to become productive members of the Georgia workforce and to live independently.

Hawaii

5828   Assets School
One Ohana Nui Way
Honolulu, HI 96818   808-423-1356
                                          FAX: 808-422-1920
                                        info@assets-school.net
                                            assets-school.net
Kitty Yannone, Chair
Assets School serves gifted and capable students, specializing in those with dyslexia and other language-based learning differences. They provide a strength-based program, complemented by outreach and training, that empowers students to become effective learners and confident self-advocates.

5829   Hawaii Fair Employment Practice Agency
Hawaii Civil Rights Commission
830 Punchbowl St.
Room 411
Honolulu, HI 96813   808-586-8636
                                          FAX: 808-586-8655
                                          TTY:808-586-8692
                                DLIR.HCRC.INFOR@hawaii.gov
                                          labor.hawaii.gov/hcrc
William Hoshijo, Executive Director
HCRC enforces state laws prohibiting discrimination in employment.

5830   Hawaii Vocational Rehabilitation Division
P.O. Box 339
Honolulu, HI 96809-0339   808-586-9741
                                          FAX: 808-586-9755
                                           dhs@dhs.hawaii.gov
                        humanservices.hawaii.gov/vocationalrehab/
Cathy Betts, Director
Joseph Campos, Deputy Director
Amanda Stevens, Public Information & Communications Officer
Provides services to Hawaiian residents who experience barriers to employment due to physical or cognitive disabilities.

5831   Lanakila Rehabilitation Center
1809 Bachelot St.
Honolulu, HI 96817   808-531-0555
                                          TTY:808-531-0555
                                        hello@lanakilapacific.org
                                        www.lanakilapacific.org
Rona Yagi Fukumoto, President & Chief Executive Officer
Karen Wong, Vice President of Administration
Dwayne Masutani, Director of Finance
Lanakila is a private nonprofit organization whose mission is to provide services and supports that assist individuals with physical, mental, or age-related challenges to live as independently as possible within their community. A broad range of services are offered which include meal/senior services, community based adult day programming for individuals with disabilities, work training opportunities, and extended/supported employment for individuals with special needs.

5832   Services for the Blind Branch
Division of Vocational Rehabilitation
1390 Miller Street
Room 209
Honolulu, HI 96813   808-586-5679
                                          FAX: 808-586-5700
                                           dhs@dhs.hawaii.gov
                        humanservices.hawaii.gov/vocationalrehab/
Daisy Hartsfield, Administrator
Provides employment services to Hawaiian residents who are blind or have visual impairments.

Idaho

5833   Idaho Commission for the Blind & Visually Impaired
341 W. Washington St.
P.O. Box 83720
Boise, ID 83720- 0012   208-334-3220
                                           800-542-8688
                                     FAX: 208-334-2963
                              bcunningham@icbvi.state.id.us
                                       www.icbvi.state.id.us

Beth Cunningham, Administrator
Steve Achabal, Independent Living Coordinator
Mike Walsh, Rehabilitation Services Chief
A state agency that provides vocational rehabilitation, independent living training, medical intervention, adaptive technology and devices, and employer advocacy.

5834   Idaho Department of Labor
317 W. Main St.
Boise, ID 83735   208-332-8942
                                     FAX: 208-639-3256
                                     www@labor.idaho.gov
                                          labor.idaho.gov
Jani Revier, Director
Provides workforce services and connects job seekers with employers.

5835   Idaho Division of Vocational Rehabilitation
650 W. State St.
Room 150
Boise, ID 83720   208-334-3390
                                     FAX: 208-334-5305
                                            vr.idaho.gov
Jane Donnellan, Administrator
Vocational Rehabilitation assists many individuals with disabilities to go to work. With VR assistance, these individuals have overcome numerous obstacles and disability related barriers to achieve employment.

5836   Idaho Governor's Committee on Employment of People with Disabilities
317 W. Main St.
Boise, ID 83735   208-332-3750
                                     FAX: 208-327-7331
                                             www.dol.gov
Purpose is to promote greater independece for people with disabilities through employment.

5837   Idaho Human Rights Commission
317 W. Main St.
Boise, ID 83735-0660   208-334-2873
                                           888-249-7025
                                     FAX: 208-334-2664
                              HRC.inquiry@labor.idaho.gov
                                       humanrights.idaho.gov
Jani Revier, Director
Administers state and federal anti-discrimination laws in Idaho in a manner that is fair, accurate, and timely. Works towards ensuring that all people within the state are treated with dignity and respect in their places of employment, housing, education, and public accomodations.

Illinois

5838   Ada S. McKinley Community Services, Inc.
1359 W. Washington Blvd.
Chicago, IL 60607   312-554-0600
                                     FAX: 312-554-0292
                                    info@adasmckinley.org
                                        adasmckinley.org
Jamal Malone, Chief Executive Officer
Peter Greetis, Director of Information Technology
Valerie R. Mercer, Senior Director of Human Resources
Mission is to serve those who, because of disabilities or other limiting conditions, need help in finding and pursuing paths leading to healthy, productive, and fulfilling lives.

5839   Anixter Center
6610 N. Clark St.
Chicago, IL 60626   773-973-7900
                                    AskAnixter@anixter.org
                                              anixter.org
Rebecca Clark , President & Chief Executive Officer
Jonathan Linas, Chair
Tanya Curtis, Secretary
A Chicago-based human services agency that assists people with disabilities to live and work successfully in the community. Anixter Center provides vocational training, employment services, residences, special education, prevention programs, community services, and health care. In addition, Anixter Center offers Illinois' only substance abuse treatment programs specifically for people with disabilities including Addiction Recovery of the Deaf.

5840   C-4 Work Center
4740 North Clark St.
Chicago, IL 60640   773-769-0205
                                           888-968-7282
                                     infoc4@c4chicago.org
                                        www.c4chicago.org
Kerri Brown, Chief Executive Officer
Doug Myers, Interim Chief Financial Officer
Patrick Dombrowski, Chief Clinical Officer
A social service provider that offers aftercare, case finding, information and referrals, vocational training, and work activities offered to mentally ill persons.

5841   Clearbrook
1835 W. Central Rd.
Arlington Heights, IL 60005   847-870-7711
                                     FAX: 847-870-7741
                                      TTY:847-870-2239
                                    info@clearbrook.org
                                       www.clearbrook.org
Anthony Di Vittorio, President
Kevin Anderko, Vice President of Human Resources
Don Frick, Vice President of Operations
A nonprofit organization that offers educational, employment, and residential services to the developmentally disabled children and adults.

5842   Cornerstone Services
777 Joyce Rd.
Joliet, IL 60436   815-741-7600
                                           877-444-0304
                                     FAX: 815-723-1177
                                     cornerstoneservices.org
Ben Stortz, President & Chief Executive Officer
Kim Hudgens, Vice President & Chief Operating Officer
Ken Mihelich, Vice President & Chief Financial Officer
Cornerstone Services provides progressive, comprehensive services for people with disabilities, promoting choice, dignity, and the opportunity to live and work in the community. Established in 1969, the agency provides developmental, vocational, employment, residential, and behavioral health services at various community-based locations. The nonprofit social service agency helps approximately 750 people each day.
1969

5843   Fulton County Rehab Center
500 N. Main St.
Canton, IL 61520   309-647-6510
Residential rehab center with health care incidental. Manufactures wood pallets and skids and offers job training and vocational rehabilitation services.

5844   Glenkirk
3504 Commercial Ave.
Northbrook, IL 60062   847-272-5111
                                               glenkirk.org
                                               glenkirk.org
Nicole Zanon, Director, Community & Family Supports
A nonprofit organization serving people in north and northwest Chicago that helps infants, children, and adults with developmental disabilities reach higher levels of independence. Glenkirk's residential, vocational, educational, and support programs include services which provide individual evaluation, therapeutic treatment, and training.

5845 Illinois Life Span Program
The Arc of Illinois
20901 LaGrange Rd.
Suite 209
Frankfort, IL 60423   800-588-7002
                                   www.illinoislifespan.org
Amie Lulinski, Executive Director
Becca Schroeder, Director of Development
Deb Fornoff, Life Span Director
A program of The Arc of Illinois that provides resources, advocacy, and services to individuals of all ages with developmental or intellectual disabilities. The program aims to help individuals with disabilities participate fully in their community.

5846 Jewish Vocational Services
216 West Jackson Blvd.
Suite 700
Chicago, IL 60606   855-275-5237
                                       ask@jcfs.org
                                   www.jvschicago.org
Stacey Shor, President & Chief Executive Officer
Karen Corken, Vice President & Chief Operating Officer
Vincent Everson, Vice President & Chief Financial Officer
Occupational training and job placement for handicapped persons of all religions.

5847 Kennedy Job Training Center
St. Coletta's of Illinois, Inc.
18350 Crossing Dr.
Tinley Park, IL 60487   708-342-5200
                                   FAX: 708-342-2579
                              information@stcolettail.org
                                       www.stcil.org

Michael Kahne, Board Chair
William A. Brennan, Secretary & Treasurer
St. Coletta's of Illinois offers vocational evaluation, vocational training work adjustment training, and job placement services for developmentally disabled and hearing impaired persons.

5848 Knox County Board of Developmental Disabilities
11700 Upper Gilchrist Rd.
Mount Vernon, OH 43050   740-397-4656
                                         kccdd.com

Robert Drews, President
Tonya Boucher, Vice President
Korey Kidwell, Recording Secretary
Offers developmental training, vocational evaluation, work adjustment training, extended training, placement, and supported employment.

5849 Kreider Services
500 Anchor Rd.
Dixon, IL 61021-0366   815-288-6691
                                   FAX: 815-288-1636
                                   TTY:815-288-5931
                                   kreiderservices.org

Mike Hickey, President
Dr. Richard L. Piller, Vice President
Don Vock, Secretary & Treasurer
A private nonprofit organization that offers day service programs, vocational training programs, job placement, supported employment, respite care, residential and family support for children ages 0-3.

5850 Lambs Farm
14245 W. Rockland Rd.
Libertyville, IL 60048   847-362-4636
                                   info@lambsfarm.org
                                      lambsfarm.org
Person-centered, comprehensive program of residential, vocational, and social support service for adults with developmental disabilities.

5851 Land of Lincoln Goodwill Industries
1220 Outer Park Dr.
Springfield, IL 62704   217-789-0400
                                       info@llgi.org
                                       www.llgi.org

Ron Culves, President & Chief Executive Officer
Jason Goodman, Vice President of Finance
Wally Proenza, Vice President of Retail Operations

Empowers people with special needs to become self-sufficient through the power of work.

5852 Orchard Village
7660 Gross Point Rd.
Skokie, IL 60077   847-967-1800
                                   FAX: 847-967-1801
                                   ov@orchardvillage.org
                                   www.orchardvillage.org
Susan Kaufman, President & Chief Executive Officer
Marlene Hodges, Executive Vice President & Chief Financial Officer
Vocational program and counseling, respite services and community living group homes for the disabled and cognitively impaired. Orchard village also operates a private school especially devoted to teaching young adults independent living and skills necessary to flourish in the community.

5853 Sertoma Centre
4343 W. 123rd St.
Alsip, IL 60803   708-371-9700
                                   FAX: 708-371-9747
                                   sertomacentre.org

Gus van den Brink, Executive Director
Sarah Wiemeyer, Assistant Executive Director
Debra Marillo, Director of Advancement & Communications
A nationally accredited, not-for-profit agency that provides services to students and adults with developmental disabilities and mental illness. MIssion is to provide opportunities that empower individuals with disabilities to achieve success.

5854 Shore Training Center
Shore Community Services
8350 Laramie Ave.
Skokie, IL 60077   847-982-2030
                                   info@shoreservices.org
                                   shoreservices.org

Alexis India Alm, Chief Executive Officer
Mission is to improve the quality of life for citizens with developmental disabilities through community based services providing education/training.

5855 The Workshop
706 West St.
P.O. Box 6087
Galena, IL 61036   815-777-2211
                                   FAX: 815-777-3386
                       theworkshopgalena@theworkshopgalena.org
                                   theworkshopgalena.org

Alyssa Havens, Executive Director
Courtney Busch, Program Director
Laura Moyer, Creative Director
An organization that provides services to individuals with disabilities in Jo Daviess County such as intake and referral, early intervention for children, vocational evaluation, and work adjustment training services.

5856 Thresholds
4101 N Ravenswood Ave.
Chicago, IL 60613   773-572-5500
                                   thresholds@thresholds.org
                                   www.thresholds.org

Mark Ishaug, Chief Executive Officer
Mark Furlong, Chief Operating Officer
Brent Peterson, Chief Development Officer
Provider of recovery services for persons with mental illnesses and substance abuse disorders in Illinois. It offers 30 programs at more than 75 locations throughout Chicago and surrounding suburbs and counties. Services include case management, housing, employment, education, psychiatry, primary care, substance use treatment, and research.

5857 Vocational Rehabilitation Services
Illinois Department of Human Services
100 South Grand Ave. East
Springfield, IL 62762   800-843-6154
                                   TTY:866-324-5553
                                   www.dhs.state.il.us

Provides support for individuals who are looking for employment. Specialized services for individuals who are blind, visually impaired, deaf, or hard of hearing.

5858 **Washington County Vocational Workshop**
781 E. Holzhauer Dr.
Nashville, IL 62263   618-327-3348
Provides job training and related services and vocational rehabilitation services.

Indiana

5859 **ADEC Resources for Independence**
19670 State Rd. 120
P.O. Box 398
Bristol, IN 46507   574-848-7451
                                 FAX: 574-848-5917
                                   info@adecinc.com
                                       adecinc.com
Donna Belusar, President & Chief Executive Officer
Timothy Donlin, Chief Financial Officer
Lisa Kendall, Vice President, Human Resources
Serves individuals of all ages with developmental disabilities and delays, as well as visual or physical impairments.

5860 **Arc Northwest Indiana**
4315 E. Michigan Blvd.
Michigan City, IN 46360   219-510-3888
                             btrowbridge@ArcNWI.com
                thearc.org/chapter/the-arc-northwest-indiana/
Peter Berns, Chief Executive Officer
Ruben Rodriguez, Chief Operating Officer
The Arc Northwest Indiana serves people with intellectual and developmental disabilities and their families by providing programs that aren't adressed by governmental agencies or local providers.

5861 **BI-County Services**
425 East Harrison St.
Bluffton, IN 46714   260-824-1253
                                 FAX: 260-824-1892
                                 bi-countyservices.com
A nonprofit organization that serves individuals with disabilities in Wells and Adam Counties. Provides infant services, Medicaid waivers, music therapy, ICF, MR, group homes, sheltered employment, pay program, and supported employment services.

5862 **Carey Services**
2724 S. Carey St.
Marion, IN 46953   765-668-8961
                                 FAX: 765-664-6747
                               info@careyservices.com
                               www.careyservices.com
James Allbaugh, President & Chief Executive Officer
Yolanda Kincaid, Chief Operations Officer
David Smith, Director of Finance
The mission of Carey Services is to create pathways towards self-sufficiency with personal satisfaction. Carey Services offers employment training and job coaching services.

5863 **Evansville Association for the Blind**
500 North 2nd Ave.
Evansville, IN 47710   812-422-1181
                               www.evansvilleblind.org
Karla L. Horrell, Executive Director
Prince Samuel, President
Fred Dormeier, Vice President
A nonprofit ogranization that offers employment services to people who are visually impaired.

5864 **Four Rivers Resource Services**
P.O. Box 249
Hwy. 59 South
Linton, IN 47441   812-847-2231
                                    fourrivers@frrs.org
                                          frrs.org
Shane Burton, Chief Executive Officer
Mel Fields, Chief Operating Officer
Employment; community living; connections; follow-along; early intervention; preschool; healthy families; child care resource, referral, and child care voucher program; impact; and transpotation services.

5865 **Gateway Services/JCARC**
3500 North Morton St.
P.O. Box 216
Franklin, IN 46131   317-738-5500
                                  www.gatewayarc.com
A nonprofit organization that offers employment services to individduals with disabilities. Economic advisors aid disabled individuals throughout the entire process of finding a job, and continue to check in on them after employment.

5866 **Goodwill of Central & Southern Indiana**
1635 W. Michigan St.
Indianapolis, IN 46222   317-524-4313
                             goodwill@goodwillindy.org
                                 www.goodwillindy.org
Kent A. Kramer, President & Chief Executive Officer
Daniel J. Riley, Senior Vice President & Chief Financial Officer
Eric Schlegel, Senior Vice President & Chief Operating Officer
Offers employment services such as vocational rehabilitation, employer support, and job coaches for individuals with disabilities.

5867 **Indiana Civil Rights Commission**
100 North Senate Ave.
Room N300
Indianapolis, IN 46204   317-232-2600
                                      800-628-2909
                                 FAX: 317-232-6580
                                 TTY: 800-743-3333
                                    info@icrc.in.gov
                                  www.in.gov/icrc
Gregory L. Wilson, Sr., Executive Director
Doneisha Posey, Deputy Director & General Counsel
Pamella Cook, Chief Financial Officer
Works to develop public policies that ensure equal opportunity in education to all and enforces the civil rights laws of the State of Indiana.

5868 **Indiana Disability Employment Initiative**
Indiana Department of Workforce Development
10 North Senate Ave.
Indianapolis, IN 46204   800-891-6499
                               www.in.gov/dwd/2416.htm
Jointly funded by the US Department of Labor's Employment and Training Administration, DEI aims to improve education, training, and employment opportunities for adults with disabilities.

5869 **New Hope Services**
725 Wall St.
Jeffersonville, IN 47130   812-288-8248
                             info@newhopeservices.org
                                newhopeservices.org
James A. Bosley, Chief Executive Officer
Jody Reschar Heazlitt, President
John Broady, Senior Vice President & Chief Financial Officer
Mission is to provide hope through services which are responsive to individual needs. New Hope Services offers a vocational training program for individuals with intellectual or physical disabilities.

5870 **New Horizons Rehabilitation**
237 Six Pine Ranch Rd.
Batesville, IN 47006   812-934-4528
                                   contact@nhrinc.org
                                     www.nhrinc.org
Provides training and services to children and adults with mental/physical disabilities. The Community Employment services helps individuals ages 14 and up acquire employment.

5871 **Noble of Indiana**
Noble, Inc.
7701 East 21st St.
Indianapolis, IN 46219   317-375-2700
                                 FAX: 317-375-2719
                                 www.mynoblelife.org
Julia Huffman, President & Chief Executive Officer
Judy Tidwell, Chief Financial Officer
Erin Hardwick, Director of Pre-Vocational Services
Since 1953, Noble of Indiana has been dedicated to its mission: to create opportunities for people with developmental disabilities to live meaningful lives.

5872 Paladin
4315 East Michigan Blvd.
Michigan City, IN 46360
219-874-4288
FAX: 219-874-2689
Paladin@paladin.care
www.paladin.care

Steve Hobby, President & Chief Executive Officer
Evelyn Marvel, Chief Financial & Operations Officer
Alanna Konieczka, Human Resources Manager
A nonprofit organization that offers pre-vocational and employment services to individuals with disabilities.

5873 Putnam County Comprehensive Services
630 Tennessee St.
Greencastle, IN 46135
765-653-9763
FAX: 765-653-3646
aranck_pccs@yahoo.com
www.pccsinc.org

Andrew Ranck, Executive Director
Ken Heeke, President
Sue McCune, Treasurer
A not-for-profit organization serving individuals with disabilities and similar characteristics in Indiana. Their mission is to provide services to individuals with disabilities in order for them to reach their optimum potential in attitudes, habits, and skills through training and integration, making them contributing members of their community, and to promote community awareness and acceptance of people with different abilities.
1968

5874 Southern Indiana Resource Solutions
1579 S. Folsomville Rd.
Boonville, IN 47601
812-897-4840
FAX: 812-897-0123
www.sirs.org

Cheryl Mullis, President & Chief Executive Officer
Adult services including jobs, community connections, and residential and childrens services, including service coordination and all therapies.

5875 Sycamore Rehabilitation Services
1001 Sycamore Ln.
P.O. Box 369
Danville, IN 46122-1474
317-745-4715
866-573-0817
FAX: 317-745-8271
info@sycamoreservices.com
sycamoreservices.com

Terry Kessinger, President
Steve Patterson, Vice President
Carol Thralls, Treasurer
Provides training and services for persons with disabilities that enhance independence in all areas of life.

Iowa

5876 Access, Inc.
20 5th St. NW
Hampton, IA 50441
641-456-2532
info@accessincorporated.org
www.accessincorporated.org

Dale Schirmer, Executive Director
A nonprofit organization providing residential and vocational services in Franklin, Butler, and Hardin counties in the state of Iowa. Residential Services include RCF/MR services, Supported Community Living Services, and Community Supervised Apartment Living Arrangement Services. Vocational Services include Work Services and Supported Employment Services. Accredited by the Commission on Accreditation of Rehabilitation Facilities since 1984, and serves individuals with a wide range of needs.

5877 Iowa Career Connection
3408 Woodland Ave.
Suite 201
West Des Moines, IA 50266
515-282-5823
contact@iowacareerconnection.com
www.iowacareerconnection.com

Specializes in accounting and human resources talent acquisition in the Upper-Midwest.

5878 Iowa Civil Rights Commission
400 E. 14th St.
Des Moines, IA 50319-0201
515-281-4121
800-457-4416
FAX: 515-242-5840
www.state.ia.us/government/crc

Stan Thompson, Executive Director
A neutral, fact-finding administrative agency that enforces the 'Iowa Civi Rights Act of 1965,' Iowa's anti-discrimination law. The commission doesn not provide legal representation. The commission's vision is a state free of discrimination.

5879 Iowa Economic Development Authority
1963 Bell Avenue
Suite 200
Des Moines, IA 50315
515-348-6200
info@iowaeda.com
www.iowaeconomicdevelopment.com

Debi Durham, Director
To engender and promote economic development policies and practices which stimulate and sustain Iowa's economic growth and climate and that integrate efforts across public and private sectors.

5880 Iowa Valley Community College
3702 S. Center St.
Marshalltown, IA 50158
641-752-4643
800-284-4823
FAX: 641-752-5909
ivinfo@iavalley.edu
www.iavalley.edu

Kristie Fisher, Chancellor
Julie Eastridge, Director of Marketing
Mike Mosher, Chief Information Officer
Offers two levels of specialized vocational preparatory programming for adults with disabilities. The Career Development Center serves dependent adults. The goal of the program is to maintain or improve skills to enable persons served to enter sheltered or supported employment. The IRP/CBVT programs are non-credit specialized vocational programs for independent adults served by Vocational Rehabilitation and our programs. The goals are for competitive placements in jobs. CARF accredited.

5881 Iowa Vocational Rehabilitation Services
510 East 12th St.
Jessie Parker Building
Des Moines, IA 50319-0240
800-532-1486
www.ivrs.iowa.gov/index.html

Iowa Vocational Rehabilitation Services aims to help individuals with disabilities achieve their employment, independence, and economic goals.

5882 New Focus
102 W. Washington St.
Centerville, IA 52544
641-437-1722
Provides vocational services for adults with disabilities. Includes work activity, supported employment, and supported community living.

Kansas

5883 Kansas Human Rights Commission
900 SW Jackson St.
Suite 568-S
Topeka, KS 66612-1258
785-296-3206
FAX: 785-296-0589
khrc@ks.gov
www.khrc.net

Ruth Glover, Executive Director
Mission is to assure equal opportunities in employment, public accommodations, and housing, as well as to prevent discrimination.

5884 **Kansas Vocational Rehabilitation Agency**
Department for Children & Families
555 S. Kansas
3rd Fl.
Topeka, KS 66603   785-368-7471
                                         www.dcf.ks.gov

Helps people with disabilities achieve employment and self-sufficiency. Also links employers with qualified and productive individuals to meet thier work force needs.

Kentucky

5885 **Kentucky Commission on Human Rights**
332 West Broadway
Suite 1400
Louisville, KY 40202   502-595-4024
                                    FAX: 502-696-5230
                                       kchr.mail@ky.gov
                               kchr.ky.gov/Pages/default.aspx
Terrance A. Sullivan, Executive Director
Samar Syeda, Executive Administrator
The state government authority that enforces the Kentucky Civil
Rights Act, making it unlawful to discriminate in the areas of em-
ployment, financial transactions, housing, and public
accommodations.

5886 **Kentucky Office for the Blind**
500 Mero Street 4th Floor NE
Frankfort, KY 40601   502-564-4440
                                          800-372-7172
                                      TTY:800-372-7172
                                      cora.mcnabb@ky.gov
                                          blind.ky.gov
Cora McNabb, Acting Executive Director
Tiffany Smither, Fiscal Administrator
The Office for the Blind offers a wide variety of employment ser-
vices aimed at providing the skills and opportunities for inde-
pendence to individuals with visual disabilities.

5887 **Kentucky Vocational Rehabilitation Agency**
500 Mero Street
4th Floor NE
Frankfort, KY 40621   502-564-4440
                                          800-372-7172
                                      TTY:800-372-7172
                                   WFD.VOCREHAB@ky.gov
                              kcc.ky.gov/Vocational-Rehabilitation/
Assists eligible individuals with disabilities achieve their employment goals.

5888 **Pioneer Vocational/Industrial Services**
150 Corporate Dr.
P.O. Box 1396
Danville, KY 40422   859-236-8413
                                          800-527-4198
                                     FAX: 859-238-7115
                                     TTY: 859-236-1251
                                pioneer@pioneerservices.org
                                   www.pioneerservices.org
Mike Pittman, Executive Director
Steve Lovell, Director of Marketing and Production
Mission is to provide vocational development and extended em-
ployment programs to people who are disabled and/or disadvantaged, and to assist them in maximizing independent living skills.
1967

Louisiana

5889 **Blind Services**
Louisiana Rehabilitation Services
1001 North 23rd St.
P.O. Box 94094
Baton Rouge, LA 70804-9094   225-342-3111
                                    FAX: 225-342-7960
                                       owd@lwc.la.gov
                                       www.laworks.net
Ava Cates, Secretary
A section of the Louisiana Rehabilitation Services, Blind Ser-
vices offers employment opportunities to individuals who are
blind or visually impaired.

5890 **COEA The Arc of East Ascension**
1122 E. Ascension Complex Blvd.
Gonzales, LA 70737-4265   225-621-2000
                                    FAX: 225-621-2022
                                   opportunities@eatel.net
                       thearc.org/chapter/the-arc-of-east-ascension/
Peter Berns, Executive Director
Ruben Rodriguez, Chief Operating Officer
Committed to affording individuals the opportunities that reflect
and support their choices, dignity, individuality, self-determina-
tion, community, coherency, and common sense. The Arc of East
Ascension offers educational, employment, community, housing,
and recreational services.

5891 **Louisiana Rehabilitation Services**
Office of Workforce Development
1001 North 23rd St.
P.O. Box 94094
Baton Rouge, LA 70804-9094   225-342-3111
                                    FAX: 225-342-7960
                                       owd@lwc.la.gov
                          www.laworks.net/WorkforceDev/LRS/LRS_Main.asp
Melissa Bayham, Director
Provides services for job seekers and job training programs for
individuals with disabilities. Programs include Blind Services
and Vocational Rehabilitation.

5892 **The Arc Westbank**
401 Gretna Blvd.
Gretna, LA 70053   504-361-1131
                                jennifer@westbankarc.org
                                       westbankarc.org
Provides day and employment services to individuals with disabilities.
1956

5893 **Vocational Rehabilitation Program**
Office of Workforce Development
1001 North 23rd St.
P.O. Box 94094
Baton Rouge, LA 70802-9094   225-342-3111
                                    FAX: 225-342-7960
                                       owd@lwc.la.gov
                                       www.laworks.net

Offers individuals with disabilities a wide range of services designed to provide them with the skills and resources needed to
compete in the interview process, get the job, keep the job, and
develop a lifetime career.

Maine

5894 **Bangor Veteran Center: Veterans Outreach Center**
615 Odlin Rd.
Suite 3
Bangor, ME 04401   207-947-3391
                                    FAX: 207-941-8195
                                       www.maine.va.gov
Denis McDonough, Secretary of Veterans Affairs
Donald M. Remy, Deputy Secretart of Veterans Affairs
Tanya J. Brasher, Chief of Staff of Veterans Affairs
Readjustment counseling services for veterans of Vietnam, Viet-
nam Era, Persian Gulf, Panama, Grenada, Lebanon, Somalia,

WWII and Korean conflicts, as well as Iraq, Afganistan, and military sexual trauma.

5895 Creative Work Systems
10 Speirs St.
Westbrook, ME 04092   207-879-1140
                                  FAX: 207-879-1146
                                  creativeworksystems.com

Heidi Howard, Executive Director
Jim Harrison, President
Carolyn Faulkner, Vice President
Provides residential, day habilitation, and supported employment services in Central and Southern Maine.

5896 Division for the Blind and Visually Impaired
Bureau of Rehabilitation Services
150 State House Station
Augusta, ME 04333-0150   207-623-7948
                        www.maine.gov/rehab/dbvi/index.shtml
The Division provides services to persons with severe visual impairments, including counseling and vocational assessment, job training and placement, and orientation and mobility instruction.

5897 Maine Commission on Disability & Employment
State Workforce Board
45 Commerce Dr.
Augusta, ME 04330   207-621-5087
                                  SWB.DOL@maine.gov
                                  www.maine.gov

Jennifer Kimble, Chair
Established in 1997, the Commission aims to influence policy related to employment for people with disabilities.

5898 Maine Department of Labor
54 State House Station
Augusta, ME 04333-0054   207-623-7900
                                  mdol@maine.gov
                                  www.state.me.us/labor
Laura Fortman, Commissioner
Provides a wide range of services such as employment, labor market information, rehabilitation/disability, and others.

5899 Maine Human Rights Commission
Maine Human Rights Commission
51 State House Station
Augusta, ME 04333   207-624-6290
                                  FAX: 207-624-8729
                                  TTY:711
                                  www.maine.gov/mhrc
Amy Sneirson, Executive Director
Barbara Archer Hirsch, Commission Counsel
Melody Piper, Operations Director
The State agency with the responsibility of enforcing Maine's anti-discrimination laws. The Commission investigates complaints of unlawful discrimination in employment, housing, education, access to public accommodations, extension of credit, and offensive names.

5900 Northeast Occupational Exchange
29 Franklin St.
Bangor, ME 04401   800-857-0500
                                  FAX: 207-561-4725
                                  TTY:207-992-2298
                                  www.noemaine.org
Charles O. Tingley, Executive Director
Sharon Greenleaf, Assistant Director
A fully licensed, comprehensive mental health and substance abuse treatment and rehabilitation facility.
1975

Maryland

5901 Ardmore Developmental Center
4300 Forbes Boulevard
Suite 110
Lanham, MD 20706   301-577-2575
                                  FAX: 301-259-3634
                                  grow@ArdmoreEnterprises.org
                                  www.ardmoreenterprises.org
Lori Sedlezky, Chief Executive Officer
David Schey, Chief Financial Officer
Melissa Scholfield, Director of People & Culture
Offers supported employment programs and vocational education for persons with intellectual and developmental disabilities, as well as residential services and a Day Support program.
1963

5902 Maryland Commission on Civil Rights (FEPA)
6 Saint Paul St.
Suite 900
Baltimore, MD 21202-1631   410-767-8600
                                  800-637-6247
                                  FAX: 410-333-1841
                                  mccr@maryland.gov
                                  www.mccr.maryland.gov
Alvin O. Gillard, Executive Director
Cleveland L. Horton II, Deputy Director
Glendora Hughes, General Counsel
The Maryland Commission on Civil Rights represents the interests of the State of Maryland in ensuring equal opportunity for all individuals in the areas of housing, public accommodations, employment, and state contracts.

5903 Maryland Department of Disabilities
217 E. Redwood St.
Suite 1300
Baltimore, MD 21202   410-767-3660
                                  800-637-4113
                                  FAX: 410-333-6674
                                  info.mdod@maryland.gov
                                  mdod.maryland.gov
Carol Beatty, Secretary
Christian Miele, Deputy Secretary
John Brennan, Assistant Deputy Secretary
The Maryland Department of Disabilities is charged with improving services for individuals with disabilities in the areas of housing, employment, community living, technology assistance, transportation, and more.

5904 Maryland Employment Network
Bel Air, MB   410-803-7184
                                  855-384-2844
                                  FAX: 410-803-8732
                                  www.ticket2workmd.org
Keirstyn Silver, Director, Self-Sufficiency & Education
Molly Hall, Program Administrator
A state-wide network of 9 partner agencies that aim to help individuals with disabilities gain quality employment.

5905 Maryland State Department of Education
Division of Rehabilitation Services (DORS)
2301 Argonne Dr.
Baltimore, MD 21218   410-554-9442
                                  888-554-0334
                                  TTY:443-798-2840
                                  dors@maryland.gov
                                  dors.maryland.gov
Scott Dennis, Assistant State Superintendent
Sandy Bowser, Executive Associate
Kimberlee Schultz, Director, Office of Public Affairs
The Division of Rehabilitation Services provides opportunities for individuals with physical and/or mental disabilities that help them gain employment. The Division is composed of the public vocational rehabilitation program, and the Disability Determination Services.

5906 Melwood
5606 Dower House Rd.
Upper Marlboro, MD 20772   301-599-8000
FAX: 301-599-0180
services@melwood.org
www.melwood.org

Larysa Kautz, President & CEO
Scott Gibson, Chief Strategy Officer
Rebecca Cheraquit, Chief Program Officer
Melwood is a dynamic nonprofit that creates jobs and opportunities to improve the lives of people with disabilities. Melwood serves more than 2000 people with disabilities each year.

5907 NFB Career Mentoring
National Federation of the Blind
200 E. Wells St.
at Jernigan Place
Baltimore, MD 21230   410-659-9314
FAX: 410-685-5653
nfb@nfb.org
www.nfb.org

Mark A. Riccobono, President
A primary initiative of the NFB Jernigan Institute, the Career Mentoring program aims to increase the employment of visually impaired adults. The National Federation of the Blind also offers an employment resource page.

5908 Office of Fair Practices
Department of Labor, Licensing & Regulation
1100 North Eutaw St.
Room 613
Baltimore, MD 21202   410-230-6319
FAX: 410-225-3282
dlofp-dllr@maryland.gov
www.dllr.state.md.us/oeope/
Yvette Dickens, Director & ADA/504 Officer
Andrea Somerville, EEO Specialist
Aims to ensure qual opportunities for all individuals by enforcing the Equal Employment Opportunity (EEO) Program, the Americans with Disabilities Act, and other equal opportunity programs.

5909 TLC Speech-Language/Occupational TherapyCamps
2092 Gaither Rd.
Suite 100
Rockville, MD 20850   301-424-5200
FAX: 301-424-8063
info@ttlc.org
www.ttlc.org
Patricia Ritter, Executive Director
TLC provides small group summer programs for children with special needs. Offers speech-language and occupational therapy summer camps for children ages 3-7.

Massachusetts

5910 Executive Office of Labor & Workforce Development
State of Massachusetts
One Ashburton Pl.
Suite 2112
Boston, MA 02108   617-626-7122
FAX: 617-727-1090
www.mass.gov

Charlie Baker, Governor
Karyn Polito, Lt. Governor
Manages the Commonwealth's workforce development and labor departments.

5911 Gateway Arts Center: Studio, Craft Store & Gallery
Vinsen Corporation
60-62 Harvard St.
Brookline, MA 02445   617-734-1577
gatewayarts@vinfen.org
www.gatewayarts.org
Rae Edelson, Director
Stephanie Schmidt-Ellis, Clinical Program Director
Ted Lampe, Program Director
Award-winning, nationally recognized arts-based rehabilitation service with over 100 talented adults with disabilities.

5912 Life-Skills, Inc.
44 Morris St.
Webster, MA 01570   508-943-0700
FAX: 508-949-6129
info@life-skillsinc.org
life-skillsinc.org

J. Thomas Amick, Chief Executive Officer
Kathy Nolan, Chief Financial Officer
Lisa Morgan, Director of Compliance
Accredited through the Commission on Accreditation of Rehabilitation Facilities; offers day, residential, and employment services for individuals with intellectual, developmental, physical, and emotional disabilities.

5913 Massachusetts Commission Against Discrimination (FEPA)
1 Ashburton Pl.
Suite 601
Boston, MA 02108   617-994-6000
FAX: 617-994-6024
TTY:617-994-6196
mcad@mass.gov
www.mass.gov

Sunila Thomas-George, Chairwoman
The commission works to eliminate discrimination on a variety of bases and areas, and strives to advance the civil rights of the people of commonwealth through law enforcement, outreach, and training.

5914 Massachusetts Commission for the Blind
600 Washington St.
Boston, MA 02111   617-727-5550
800-392-6450
FAX: 617-626-7512
www.mass.gov/eohhs/gov/departments/mcb/
David D'Arcangelo, Commissioner
Provides vocational and social rehabilitation for individuals with visual impairments.

5915 Massachusetts Governor's Commission on Employment of People with Disabilities
Department of Employment & Training
19 Standford St.
3rd Fl.
Boston, MA 02114   617-262-5239
FAX: 617-727-0315
www.dol.gov/odep/contact/

Charlie Baker, Governor
State vocational rehabilitation agency.

5916 Massachusetts Rehabilitation Commission
600 Washington St.
Boston, MA 02111   617-204-3600
FAX: 617-727-1354
TTY:800-245-6543
MRC.generalinformation@Massmail.State.MA.US
www.mass.gov
Toni Wolf, Commissioner
Helps individuals with disabilities work and live independently. The Commission runs the Vocational Rehabilitation and Community Living programs.

5917 Viability
60 Brookdale Dr.
Springfield, MA 01104   413-781-5359
info@viability.org
viability.org

Francis Fitzgerald, Chair
Steve Dean, Vice Chair
Charlene Smolkowicz, Treasurer
Viability's mission is to help individuals with disabilities achieve their full potential. Services include day programs, employment services, and job training and placements.

5918 Work Inc.
25 Beach St.
Dorchester, MA 02122

617-691-1500
info@workinc.org
workinc.org

James Cassetta, President
Sharon Smith, Chief Executive Officer
Paul Lemieux, Chief Financial Officer
A nationally recognized organization that provides supportive services need to help people with disabilities reach their career goals.

Michigan

5919 Department of Health & Human Services
333 S. Grand Ave.
P.O. Box 30195
Lansing, MI 48909

517-373-3740
TTY:800-649-3777
www.michigan.gov/mdhhs/

Elizabeth Hertel, Director
Farah Hanley, Chief Deputy for Health
David Knezek, Chief Deputy Director for Administration
The DHHS is Michigan's public assistance, child, and family welfare agency. DHS directs the operations of public assistance and service programs through a network of over 100 county department of human service offices around the state.

5920 Division on Deaf, DeafBlind & Hard of Hearing
3054 W. Grand Blvd.
Suite 3-600
Detroit, MI 48202

313-437-7035
877-499-6232
FAX: 319-456-3721
TTY: 877-499-6232
DODDBHH@Michigan.gov
www.michigan.gov/mdcr/divisions/doddbhh

Annie Urasky, Division Director
Alayna Lail, Executive Secretary
A state office with the mission of helping to improve the lives of Michigan citizens who are deaf, deafblind and hard of hearing.

5921 Michigan Department of Civil Rights
3054 W. Grand Blvd.
Suite 3-600
Detroit, MI 48202

313-456-3700
800-482-3604
FAX: 313-456-3791
TTY: 877-878-8464
MDCR-INFO@michigan.gov
www.michigan.gov/mdcr

John E. Johnson, Jr., Executive Director
Investigates and resolves discrimination complaints and works to prevent discrimination through educational programs that promote voluntary compliance with civil rights laws.

5922 Michigan Rehabilitation Services
Department of Health & Human Services
320 S. Walnut St.
Lansing, MI 48933

800-854-9090
FAX: 517-335-0135
www.michigan.gov/mrs

Jenny Piatt, Bureau Division Director
State vocational rehabilitation agency that provides specialized employment and educational services to teens and adults with disabilities in order to help them find and retain employment.

5923 Michigan Workforce Development Agency
Department of Labor and Economic Opportunity (LEO)
201 N. Washington Square
Lansing, MI 48913

517-335-5858
FAX: 517-241-8217
TTY:888-605-6722
www.michigan.gov/mdcd

Offers job development and placement services to dislocated workers with disabilities.

5924 Straits Area Services, Inc. (SAS)
1320 W. State St.
P.O. Box 6042
Cheboygan, MI 49721

231-627-4319
www.sastogether.org

Cyril Drier, President
David Johnson, Vice President
Theresa Sorenson, Treasurer
Provides community integration, supported employment, skill building, rehabilitative training, business support, work enclaves, and more to individuals with developmental disabilities.
1976

Minnesota

5925 Jewish Vocational Service of Jewish Familyand Children's Services
5905 Golden Valley Rd.
Golden Valley, MN 55422

952-546-0616
FAX: 952-593-1778
jfcs@jfcsmpls.org
www.jfcsmpls.org

Judy Halper, Chief Executive Officer
Lee Friedman, Chief Operating Officer
John Maloy, Chief Financial Officer
The mission of JVS is to be a recognized leader in delivering employment, training, and career development services that positively impact individuals of all backgrounds, businesses, and society. JVS offers a vocational rehabilitation program that includes job placement, work adjustment training, and extended employment.

5926 Minnesota Department of Employment & Economic Development: State Services for the Blind
2200 University Ave. W.
Suite 240
St. Paul, MN 55114

651-539-2300
800-722-0550
FAX: 651-649-5927
ssb.info@state.mn.us
mn.gov/deed/ssb/

Ed Lecher, Program Director
Offers tools, services, and training for individuals who are blind, DeafBlind, or have a visual impairment and are seeking employment or to live more indepedently.

5927 Minnesota Department of Employment and Economic Development: Vocational Rehab Services
332 Minnesota St.
1st National Bank Bldg., Suite E200
St. Paul, MN 55101

651-259-7114
800-657-3858
DEED.CustomerService@state.mn.us
mn.gov/deed/

Steve Grove, Commissioner
Elizabeth Frosch, Chief of Staff
Marc Majors, Deputy Commissioner of Workforce Development
Service for people with disabilities who need skills to prepare for work, or to find and keep a job.

5928 Minnesota Department of Human Rights (FEPA)
Griggs Midway Building
540 Fairview Ave North, Suite 201
St. Paul, MN 55104

651-539-1100
800-657-3704
TTY:800-627-3529
Info.MDHR@state.mn.us
mn.gov/mdhr/

Rebecca Lucero, Commissioner
Irina Vaynerman, Deputy Commissioner
Nick Pladson, General Counsel
Mission and vision is to make Minnesota discrimination free. The Minnesota Department of Human Rights investigates charges of discrimination, and ensures that businesses comply with equal opportunity requirements.

Mississippi

5929   AbilityWorks
P.O. Box 1698
Jackson, MS 39215   601-898-7076
www.mdrs.ms.gov
Vocational evaluation, work adjustment, and job placement of
disabled persons in a rehabilitation workshop. AbilityWorks is a
division of the Mississippi Department of Rehabilitation.

5930   Mississippi Department of Rehabilitation Services
1281 Highway 51
Madison, MS 39110   800-443-1000
TTY:800-443-1000
www.mdrs.ms.gov/

Anita Naik, Office Director, Special Disability Programs
Billy Taylor, Chief of Staff
*Dorothy Young, Office Director, Vocational Rehabilitation for the
Blind*
Offers low vision aids and appliances, counseling, social work,
educational and professional training, residential services, recre-
ational services, computer training and employment opportuni-
ties for Mississippians with disabilities.

5931   Mississippi Employment Security Commission
1235 Echelon Prkwy.
P.O. Box 1699
Jackson, MS 39215-1699   601-321-6000
comments@mdes.ms.gov
www.mdes.ms.gov

Jackie Turner, Executive Director
A federally funded state agency. The programs of MDES, under
direction of the governor of Mississippi, report to the federal government. The goal of the department is to help citizens of Mississippi get jobs.

**5932   National Research and Training Center on Blindness and
Low Vision**
Mississippi State University
108 Herbert-South, Room 150
PO Drawer 6189
Mississippi State, MS 39762-6189   662-325-2001
FAX: 662-325-8989
nrtc@colled.msstate.edu
www.blind.msstate.edu

Michele McDonnall, Research Professor & Director
Kendra Farrow, Program Director
Lisa Gooden-Hunley, Program Coordinator
The NRTC focuses on enhancing the employment and independ-
ence of individuals who are blind and visually impaired.

Missouri

5933   Missouri Commission on Human Rights
421 E. Dunklin
P.O. Box 1129
Jefferson City, MO 65102- 1129   573-751-3325
877-781-4236
FAX: 573-751-2905
TTY: 800-735-2966
mchr@labor.mo.gov
labor.mo.gov/MOHUMANRIGHTS

Anna S. Hui, Director
The Missouri Commission on Human Rights enforces the state's
anti-discrimination law that prohibits discrimination in housing,
employment, and places of public accommodations. It prohibits
discrimination due to race, color, religion, national origin, ances-
try, sex, disability, age, and familial status. Complaints must be
filed within 180 days of the alleged discrimination. If discrimination is found after investigation, the Commission can hold
hearings to enforce the law.

5934   Missouri Governor's Council on Disability
301 West High St., Room 620
P.O. Box 1668
Jefferson City, MO 65102   800-877-8249
FAX: 573-526-4109
TTY:573-751-2600
gcd@oa.mo.gov
disability.mo.gov/gcd/

Claudia Browner, Executive Director
The Council promotes the full participation of Missouri citizens
with disabilities, and provides information about the American
with Disabilities Act. They aim to protect persons with disabilities through equal access to services and employment
opportunities.

5935   Missouri Vocational Rehabilitation Agency
Department of Elementary & Secondary Education
205 Jefferson St.
Jefferson City, MO 65101   573-751-3251
info@vr.dese.mo.gov
dese.mo.gov

Margie Vandeven, Commissioner
A team of dedicated individuals working for the continuous improvement of education and services for all citizens. Vocational
Rehabilitation offers specialized employment and training services for individuals with a physical or mental impairment.

5936   Vocational Rehabilitation Services for the Blind
Missouri Department of Social Services
615 Howerton Court
P.O. Box 2320
Jefferson City, MO 65102-2320   573-751-4249
FAX: 573-751-4984
TTY:800-735-2966
askrsb@dss.mo.gov
dss.mo.gov/fsd/rsb/vr.htm

Robert J. Knodell, Acting Director
A state organization that aims to create employment opportunities for blind and visually impaired persons.

Montana

5937   Disability Employment & Transitions
Department of Public Health & Human Services
111 North Last Chance Gulch
P.O. Box 4210
Helena, MT 59604   406-444-5622
dphhs.mt.gov/detd

Adam Meier, Director
Provides services for individuals with disabilities who want to
become employed. Focuses on transitions from high school to
post-secondary education and work.

5938   Montana Human Rights Bureau (FEPA)
P.O. Box 1728
Helena, MT 59624-1728   406-444-2884
800-542-0807
FAX: 406-443-3234
www.erd.dli.mt.gov/human-rights
Enforces state and federal laws prohibiting unlawful discrimination based on age, marital status, disability, race/nationality,
color, religion, sex, etc., in the areas of employment, housing, education, and public accommodations.

Nebraska

5939   Nebraska Department of Labor
1111 O Street
Suite 222
Lincoln, NE 68508   402-471-4474
800-833-7352
TTY:402-471-0016
ndol.lincolnwfd@nebraska.gov
dol.nebraska.gov

John Albin, Commissioner

Services for individuals with disabilities who want to become employed.

5940 Nebraska Equal Opportunity Commission (FEPA)
1526 K Street
Suite 310
Lincoln, NE 68508-2709

402-471-2024
800-642-6112
FAX: 402-471-4059
www.neoc.ne.gov

Patrick Borchers, Chairperson
John Arnold, Vice-Chairperson
Paula Gardner, Executive Director
The Nebraska Equal Opportunity Commission is a neutral administrative agency that enforces state policy against discrimination in the areas of employment, housing, and public accommodations.

5941 Nebraska VR
Department of Education
PO Box 94987
Lincoln, NE 68509

402-471-3644
877-637-3422
FAX: 402-471-0788
marketingteam.vr@nebraska.gov
www.vr.nebraska.gov

Lindy Foley, Director
An employment program for citizens of Nebraska who experience a disability and are seeking employment.

Nevada

5942 Bureau of Vocational Rehabilitation
Rehabilitation Division
500 E. Third Street
Carson City, NV 89713

702-486-5230
TTY:702-486-1018
detr.state.nv.us

Shelley Hendren, Rehabilitation Administrator
A state and federally funded program that helps people with disabilities find employment, and helps advance the skills of disabled individuals who are already employed.

5943 Nevada Equal Rights Commission
1820 East Sahara Ave.
Suite 314
Las Vegas, NV 89104

702-486-7161
800-326-6868
FAX: 702-486-7054
detr.state.nv.us/nerc.htm

Connye Harper, Commissioner
Stewart Chang, Commissioner
Tiffany Young, Commissioner
Oversees the state's Equal Employment Opportunity program in order to make sure that all citizens of Nebraska recieve the same employment opportunities.

5944 Nevada Governor's Council on Developmental Disabilities
808 W. Nye Ln.
Carson City, NV 89703

775-684-8619
FAX: 775-684-8626
elmarquez@dhhs.nv.gov
www.nevadaddcouncil.org

Catherine Nielsen, Executive Director
The Council provides advocacy for individuals with intellectual or developmental disabilities, so that they may live more independent lives and be involved in the community.

New Hampshire

5945 New Hampshire Bureau of Vocational Rehabilitation
New Hampshire Department of Education
101 Pleasant St.
Concord, NH 03301

603-271-3494
FAX: 603-271-1953
info@doe.nh.gov
www.education.nh.gov

Lisa Hinson-Hatz, State Director
The Bureau of Vocational Rehabilitation assists citizens of New Hampshire with disabilities secure employment.

5946 New Hampshire Commission for Human Rights (FEPA)
2 Industrial Park Dr.
Building 1
Concord, NH 03301

603-271-2767
FAX: 603-271-6339
humanrights@nh.gov
www.nh.gov/hrc

Ahni Malachi, Executive Director
Sarah Burke Cohen, Assistant Director
Established for the purpose of eliminating discrimination in employment, public accomodations, and the sale or rental of housing or commercial property.

5947 New Hampshire Employment Security
45 South Fruit St.
Concord, NH 03301

603-224-3311
800-852-3400
TTY:800-735-2964
webmaster@nhes.nh.gov
www.nhes.nh.gov

George N. Copadis, Commissioner
Operates a free public employment service and provides assisted and self-directed employment and career-related services and labor market information for employers and the general public.

New Jersey

5948 ARC of Hunterdon County, The
53 Frontage Road
Suite 150
Hampton, NJ 08827

908-730-7827
www.archunterdon.org

Jeff Mattison, Executive Director
Kathy Walsh, President
Jessica Lui, Vice President
Mission is to provide support, training, and opportunities to individuals with intellectual and developmental disabilities so that they can achieve the greatest degree of independence and productivity, and become contributing, responsible, and proud members of society.

5949 ARC of Mercer County
180 Ewingville Rd.
Ewing, NJ 08638

609-406-0181
FAX: 609-406-9258
familysupports@arcmercer.org
www.arcmercer.org

Steve Cook, Executive Director
Committed to securing for all people with developmental disabilities the opportunity to choose and realize their goals.

5950 ARC of Monmouth
1158 Wayside Rd.
Tinton Falls, NJ 07712

732-493-1919
FAX: 732-493-3604
info@arcofmonmouth.org
www.arcofmonmouth.org

Lauren Zalepka, President
Joyce Nunziata, First Vice President
Robert Angel, Executive Director
A nonprofit organization providing services and supports for individuals who have cognitive and developmental disabilities and their families.

5951 Abilities Center of New Jersey
1208 Delsea Dr.
Westville, NJ 08093 856-848-1025
FAX: 856-848-8429
info@abilities4work.com
abilities4work.com

Susan Perron, President & CEO
Stephanie Berridge, Secretary & Treasurer
Jack Sheppard, Chairman
A nonprofit organization dedicated to developing employment opportunities for people with disabilities or other disadvantages through education, training, and job placement.

5952 Abilities of Northwest New Jersey Inc.
264 Rt 31 North
Washington, NJ 07882 908-689-1118
info@abilitiesnw.com
abilities-nw.com

Cynthia B. Wildermuth, Chief Executive Officer
Sue Zukoski, Chief Operating Officer
Michelle Savino, Director of Training & Quality Improvement
Private not-for-profit community rehabilitation program providing vocational training and employment services since 1974 to the disabled and disadvantaged population.

5953 Alliance Center for Independence (ACI)
629 Amboy Ave.
First Floor
Edison, NJ 08837 732-738-4388
FAX: 732-738-4416
TTY:732-738-9644
ctonks@adacil.org
www.adacil.org

Carole Tonks, Executive Director
Luke Koppisch, Deputy Director
ACI is a nonprofit Center for Independent Living that provides information and referral services and develops and implements educational programs and innovative activities that promote activism, peer support, health, wellness, employment, and independent living skills for people with disabilities.

5954 Arc of Bergen and Passaic Counties
223 Moore St.
Hackensack, NJ 07601 201-343-0322
FAX: 201-343-0401
arc@arcbp.com
arcbergenpassaic.org

Kathy Walsh, President & CEO
Catherine Pescatore, Vice President & CFO
Alice Siegel, Senior Vice President
A membership organization serving persons with disabilities and their families in Bergen and Passaic Counties, NJ.

5955 Career Opportunity Development of New Jersey
901 Atlantic Ave.
Egg Harbor City, NJ 08215-1810 609-965-6871
FAX: 609-965-3099
njcodi.org

Linda Carney, President & CEO
Karen Gardner, Chief Financial Officer
Mary Pat Braudis, Board Chairperson
A nonprofit organization that provides services to individuals with varying forms of physical, mental, and economic disabilities and disadvantages. Provides services to more than 1,500 unduplicated consumers annually.

5956 Center for Educational Advancement New Jersey
11 Minneakoning Rd.
Flemington, NJ 08822 908-782-1480
cea-nj.org

Michael Skoczek, President & CEO
Philip Ferri, Chair
Michael Collins, Treasurer
A CARF-accredited, nonprofit organization that provides opportunities for disbaled individuals to lead productive lives. Programs offered throughout Central New Jersey.

5957 Easterseals New Jersey
241 Forsgate Dr.
Jamesburg, NJ 08831 732-257-6662
www.easterseals.com/nj

Brian Fitzgerald, President & CEO
Anysa Holder, Chief Advancement Officer & Corporate Secretary
Michael Owen, Chief Human Resources Officer & General Counsel
A nonprofit organization that provides opportunities for disabled citizens of New Jersey to be independent and participate in their communities. Easterseals New Jersey serves over 9,000 individuals.

5958 Eden Autism
2 Merwick Rd.
Princeton, NJ 08540 609-987-0099
edenautism.org

Michael K. Decker, President & CEO
Jennifer Bizub, Chief Operating Officer
Melinda Gorny McAleer, Chief Development Officer
A nonprofit organization that provides a variety of services for chidlren and adults with autism. Services include individualized education, employment training/placement, group residences, and early intervention.

5959 Edison Sheltered Workshop
48 Ethel Road
Edison, NJ 08817 732-985-8834
FAX: 732-985-2216
info@eswnj.org
www.eswnj.org

Brij Chawla, Executive Director
Rick Parker, President
Mark Viggiano, Vice President
An organization that provides vocational training and job placement services for disabled individuals who are 16 years old and living in Middlesex County.

5960 Goodwill Industries of Southern New Jersey
2835 Route 73
Maple Shade, NJ 08052 856-439-0200
FAX: 856-439-0843
juli.lundberg@goodwillnj.org
goodwillnj.org

Mark Boyd, President & CEO
Michael Shaw, Chief Operating Officer
Stephen Castro, Chief Financial Officer
A nonprofit, community-based organization that empowers individuals with special needs by providing them with the opportunity to develop marketable job skills.

5961 Hudson Community Enterprises
68-70 Tuers Ave.
Jersey City, NJ 07306 201-434-3303
FAX: 201-434-3660
info@hce.works
hce.works

Joseph F. Brown, President
Vocational rehab, transition services and training programs are offered.

5962 Inroads to Opportunities
301 Cox St.
Roselle, NJ 07203 908-241-7200
FAX: 908-241-2025
ocuc@inroadsto.com
www.occupationalcenter.org

Michele Ford, President & CEO
Ken Rowinsky, Board Treasurer
Lynn Boyko, Recording Secretary
Formerly known as the Occupational Center of Union County, the organization offers vocational preparation, transition from school to work, job placement and mental health services to over 500 individuals annually.

5963 Jersey Cape
152 Crest Haven Road
Cape May Court House, NJ 08210-1651 609-465-4117
www.jerseycape.org

Joe Sittineri, Executive Director
Offers a range of employment programs and services for people with disabilities.

5964 Jewish Vocational Service (JVS) - East Orange
7 Glenwood Ave.
Lower Level
East Orange, NJ 07017
973-674-6330
info@jvsnj.org
jvsnj.org

Michael Andreas, Executive Director
Rebecca Shulman, Senior Program Director
Hetal Narciso, Chief Operating Officer
Offers vocational rehabilitation services, as well as education and literacy.

5965 Jewish Vocational Service (JVS) - Livingston
354 Eisenhower Parkway
Plaza 1, Suite 2150
Livingston, NJ 07039
973-674-6330
info@jvsnj.org
jvsnj.org

Michael Andreas, Executive Director
Rebecca Shulman, Senior Program Director
Hetal Narciso, Chief Operating Officer
Houses JVS administration, as well as providing career counseling, job placement and corporate training services.

5966 Jewish Vocational Service (JVS) - Montclair
83 Walnut St.
Montclair, NJ 07042
973-674-6330
info@jvsnj.org
jvsnj.org

Michael Andreas, Executive Director
Rebecca Shulman, Senior Program Director
Hetal Narciso, Chief Operating Officer
Provides vocational rehabilitation services.

5967 New Jersey Commission for the Blind and Visually Impaired (CBVI)
Department of Human Services
153 Halsey St
6th Floor, PO Box 47017
Newark, NJ 07101
973-648-3333
877-685-8878
askcbvi@dhs.state.nj.us
www.state.nj.us/humanservices/cbvi

Bernice Davis, Executive Director
Edward Szajdecki, Chief, Fiscal Services
Eva Scott, Director of Blindness Education
The Commission for the Blind and Visually Impaired (CBVI) promotes and provides services in the areas of education, employment, independence and eye health for persons who are blind or visually impaired, their families and the community. It seeks to provide or ensure access to services that will enable consumers to obtain their fullest measure of self-reliance and quality of life and fully integrated into their community.

5968 New Jersey Division of Vocational Rehabilitation Services (DVRS)
Department of Labor and Workforce Development
1 John Fitch Plaza
Trenton, NJ 08611
www.nj.gov/labor/career-services/
Robert Asaro-Angelo, Commissioner
Julie Diaz, Chief of Staff
Caroline M. Stout, Director, Disability Determination Services
Services for individuals with disabilities who want to become employed.

5969 New Jersey Institute for Disabilities (NJID)
10A Oak Dr.
Edison, NJ 08837
732-549-6187
www.njid.org

Robert J. Ferrara, Acting President
Robert J. Gross, Controller
Frank A. Ursino, Director of Security
Dedicated to the provision of comprehensive, superior, multi-faceted programs of service to individuals with developmental and related disabilities.

5970 Occupational Training Center of Burlington County (OTCBC)
2 Manhattan Drive
Burlington, NJ 08016
609-267-6677
FAX: 609-265-8418
info@otcbc.org
otcbc.org

Isaac Manning, Executive Director
Mission is to assist individuals with disabilities in reaching their maximum potential.

5971 Occupational Training Center (OTC)
The Arc of Camden County
520 Market Street
Camden, NJ 08102
856-768-0845
FAX: 856-767-1378
commissioners@camdencounty.com
www.camdencounty.com

Loret McClain, Contact
Provides the following to residents of Camden County: job placement; supported employment; extended employment; vocational evaluation and assessment; work adjustment training; and contract work.

5972 Pathways to Independence, Inc.
60 Kingsland Ave.
Kearny, NJ 07032
201-997-6155
www.pathwaysnj.org

Alvin Cox, Executive Director
Tessa Farrell, Program Director
Marie Yakobofski, Finance Director
Pre-vocational and vocational programming for people with disabilities. Specializing in developmental disabilities, learning disabilities and mental health issues. Serving over 100 people in Hudson, Bergen and Essex Counties. CARF accredited.

5973 Somerset Community Action Program, Inc.
155 Pierce St.
Suite F
Somerset, NJ 08873
732-846-8888
FAX: 732-214-9754
info@somersetcap.org
www.somersetcap.org

Steven Nagel, Executive Director
Sabah Hussein, Finance Director
Abdul Jackson, Program Coordinator
Provides services for low-income individuals and those with disabilities who want to become employed.

5974 St. John of God Community Services Vocational Rehabilitation
1145 Delsea Dr.
Westville Grove, NJ 08093
856-848-4700
Communications@sjogcs.org
www.sjogcs.org

Thomas Osorio, Executive Director
Serves Gloucester and Camden Counties providing special education, vocational and habilitative services to residents of southern New Jersey since 1967.

5975 The Arc Gloucester
1555 Gateway Blvd.
West Deptford, NJ 08096
856-848-8648
www.thearcgloucester.org

Lisa Conley, Chief Executive Officer
A nonprofit organization serving people with intellectual and related developmental disabilities and their families through education, advocacy, and direct services.

5976 United Cerebral Palsy Associations of New Jersey
1005 Whitehead Rd. Extension
Suite 1
Ewing, NJ 08638
609-882-4182
888-322-1918
FAX: 609-882-4054
info@advopps.org
advopps.org

Paul Ronollo, Acting Chief Executive Officer
Charlie Morin, Acting Chief Financial Officer
Scott Kutcher, Controller

Dedicated to changing lives and bringing independence to people with all types of disabilities.

New Mexico

5977 Adelante Development Center
3900 Osuna Rd. NE
Albuquerque, NM 87109
505-341-2000
FAX: 505-341-2001
info@GoAdelante.org
www.goadelante.org

Rebecca Sanford, President & CEO
Ryan Baca, Chair
Merritt Allen, Secretary
Serves Albuquerque and Belen.

5978 Goodwill Industries of New Mexico
5000 San Mateo Blvd. NE
Albuquerque, NM 87109
505-881-6401
866-376-0182
FAX: 505-884-3157
media@goodwillnm.org
goodwillnm.org

Shauna Kastle, President & CEO
Tom Downey, Chief Financial Officer
Sara Penn, Chief Services Officer
Serves Albuquerque, Santa Fe and Rio Rancho.

5979 LifeROOTS
1111 Menaul Blvd. NE
Albuquerque, NM 87107
505-255-5501
StephanieH@LifeROOTSNM.org
www.liferootsnm.org

Matthew Molina, President & CEO
Michelle Hayden, Finance Director
Angela Ortega, Community Services Director
Albuquerque, Rio Rancho and the surrounding area. Mission is to improve the abilities, interests, and choices of children and adults with physical, developmental or behavioral challenges with the goal of achieving their highest levels of self-sufficiency.

5980 New Mexico Commission for the Blind (NMCFTB)
2905 Rodeo Park Dr E
Bldg 4, Suite 100
Santa Fe, NM 87505
505-476-4479
888-513-7968
www.cfb.state.nm.us

Arthur A. Schreiber, Chairman
Shirley Lansing, Commissioner
Robert Reidy, Commissioner
Offers services for the totally blind, legally blind, visually impaired, and more with health, counseling, educational, recreational, rehabilitation, computer training and professional training services.

5981 New Mexico Division of Vocational Rehabilitation
505-954-8500
800-224-7005
www.dvr.state.nm.us

Casey Stone-Romero, Director
Robert Alirez, Chief Information Officer
Therese "Terry" Trujillo, Admin. Services Deputy Director & Chief Financial Officer
Purpose is to help people with disabilities achieve a suitable employment outcome.

5982 New Mexico Workforce Connection
New Mexico Department of Workforce Solutions
501 Mountain Rd NE
Albuquerque, NM 87102
505-843-1900
www.dws.state.nm.us

Assists with job searches, referrals and placement. Partner of the American Job Center Network.

5983 Tohatchi Area of Opportunity & Services
PO Box 49
Tohatchi, NM 87325
505-722-9287
FAX: 505-722-9189
taos-inc.org

Kimber Crowe, Chief Executive Officer
Gerald Morris, Manager, Program Service
Provides a range of programs for Native Americans with developmental disabilities.

New York

5984 Adult Career and Continuing Ed Services - Vocational Rehabilitation (ACCESS-VR)
New York State Education Department
89 Washington Ave.
Albany, NY 12234
518-474-3852
800-222-5627
www.acces.nysed.gov/vr

MaryEllen Elia, Commissioner
Aims to assist people with disabilities attain and maintain employment.

5985 National Business & Disability Council
The Viscardi Center
201 I.U. Willets Rd.
Albertson, NY 11507
516-465-1400
info@viscardicenter.org
viscardicenter.org/services/nbdc

Dr. Chris Rosa, President & Chief Executive Officer
Sheryl P. Buchel, Executive Vice President & Chief Financial Officer
Michael Caprara, Chief Information Officer
The NBDC is a resource for employers seeking to integrate people with disabilities into the workplace and companies seeking to reach them in the consumer marketplace.

5986 New York State Department of Labor
Building 12
State Office Campus
Albany, NY 12240
518-457-9000
888-469-7365
www.labor.ny.gov

Scott Melvin, Executive Deputy Commissioner
The mission of the New York State Department of Labor is to help New York work by preparing individuals for jobs. Provides direct job search and counseling services to job seekers, and can refer people who have disabilities for training opportunities. Provides unemployment insurance for those out of work through no fault of their own.

North Carolina

5987 Division of Vocational Rehabilitation Services (DVRS)
Western Regional Office
2801 Mail Service Center
Raleigh, NC 27699-2801
919-579-5100
800-689-9090
TTY:919-855-3579
www.ncdhhs.gov

Kody Kinsley, Secretary of Health & Human Services
Services include vocational evaluation, work adjustment, job placement, and an on-site work services program.

5988 Division of Vocational Rehabilitation Services (DVRS)
NC Department of Health and Human Services
2801 Mail Service Center
Raleigh, NC 27699-2801
919-579-5100
800-689-9090
TTY:919-855-3579
www.ncdhhs.gov/divisions/dvrs

Kody Kinsley, Secretary of Health & Human Services
Seeks to promote employment and independence for people with disabilities through customer partnership and community leadership.

5989 Division of Workforce Solutions
NC Department of Commerce
301 North Wilmington St.
Raleigh, NC 27601-1058   919-814-4600
info@nccommerce.com
www.nccommerce.com/jobs-training
Machelle Baker Sanders, Secretary of Commerce
Jordan Whichard, Chief Deputy Secretary
Marqueta Welton, Chief of Staff
Offers vocational assessment, training, and adult developmental activities.

5990 LIFESPAN Incorporated
1511 Shopton Rd.
Suite A
Charlotte, NC 28217   704-944-5100
www.lifespanservices.org
Ken D. Fuquay, President & Chief Ambassador, Empowerment
Christopher White, Chief Operating Officer
Robin Devore, Chief Compliance Officer
Aims to transform the lives of children and adults with developmental disabilities by providing education, employment, and enrichment programs that promote inclusion, choice, family supports, and other best practices.

5991 NCWorks Commission
NC Department of Commerce
301 North Wilmington St.
Raleigh, NC 27601-1058   919-814-4600
NCWorksCommission@nccommerce.com
www.nccommerce.com
Machelle Baker Sanders, Secretary of Commerce
Jordan Whichard, Chief Deputy Secretary
Marqueta Welton, Chief of Staff
North Carolina's workforce development board. Seeks to prepare workers in the state for the future by increasing access to education and skills training, among other initiatives.

5992 North Carolina Division of Services for the Blind
Department of Health and Human Services
2601 Mail Service Center
Raleigh, NC 27699-2601   919-527-6700
800-222-1546
www.ncdhhs.gov/divisions/dsb
Kody Kinsley, Secretary of Health & Human Services
Since 1935, the mission of the North Carolina Division of Services for the Blind has been to enable people who are blind or visually impaired to reach their goals of independence and employment.

5993 Rowan Vocational Opportunities, Inc. (RVO)
2728 Old Concord Rd.
Salisbury, NC 28146   704-633-6223
www.rowanvocopp.org
Gary Yelton, Executive Director
Skip Kraft, Director, Operations
Glenn McDonald, Director, Sales & Marketing
Offers vocational assessment, training, and adult developmental activities.

5994 Rutherford Vocational Workshop
230 Fairground Rd.
Spindale, NC 28160   828-286-4352
rutherfordlifeservices@gmail.com
rutherfordlifeservices.com
Amanda Freeman, Executive Director
T.J. Francis, Director, Finance
John Jarrett, Director, Human Resources
Offers vocational assessment, training, and adult developmental activities.

5995 Transylvania Vocational Services (TVS)
11 Mountain Industrial Drive
PO Box 1115
Brevard, NC 28712   828-884-3195
info@tvsinc.org
www.tvsinc.org
Jamie Brandenburg, Chief Executive Officer
A private nonprofit corporation with the mission to provide skills development, career opportunities and related services in a supportive environment for people with barriers to employment.

5996 WestBridge Vocational
140 Little Savannah Rd.
Sylvia, NC 28779   828-586-8981
jrigdon@westbridgevoc.org
www.westbridgevoc.org
Joe Rigdon, Product Information
A community-based employment and training program for people with disabilities. Their full-service program includes a transitional youth program for life beyond high school, job coaching, vocational assessment and job placement.

North Dakota

5997 Job Service North Dakota
Job Service North Dakota
P.O. Box 5507
Bismarck, ND 58506-5507   701-328-2825
FAX: 701-328-4000
TTY:800-366-6888
www.jobsnd.com
Doug Burgum, Executive Director
Offers vocational assessment, training, and adult developmental activities.

5998 North Dakota Department of Labor, and Human Rights
Dept 406
600 East Boulevard Avenue
Bismarck, ND 58505- 0340   701-328-2660
800-582-8032
800-366-6888
FAX: 701-328-2031
TTY:800-366-6888
labor@nd.gov
www.nd.gov/labor
Erica Thunder, Labor Commissioner
Through a work-sharing agreement with the Equal Employment Opportunity Commission (EEOC), the North Dakota Department of Labor's Human Rights Division enforces the Americans with Disabilities Act (ADA) as related to employment discrimination.

5999 North Dakota Vocational Rehabilitation Agency
100 E Divide Avenue
Bismarck, ND 58501   701-328-8950
800-755-2745
FAX: 701-328-8969
dhsvr@nd.gov
www.nd.gov/dhs/dvr/
Damian Schlinger, State Director
Alicia Halle, Assistant Director
Patty Wanner, Operations Administrator
The North Dakota Vocational Rehabilitation Agency offers services for blind and visually impaired people such as health, counseling, educational, recreational, rehabilitation, computer training and professional training services.

Ohio

6000 Bureau of Vocational Rehabilitation (BVR)
400 East Campus View Blvd.
Columbus, OH 43235   614-438-1200
800-282-4536
susan.pugh@ood.ohio.gov
ood.ohio.gov
Susan Pugh, Deputy Director
State agency that provides vocational rehabilitation services to help people with disabilities become employed and independent.

6001 Greater Cincinnati Behavioral Health Services - Employment Services
1501 Madison Rd.
Cincinnati, OH 45206   513-354-5200
gcbhs.com
Jeff O'Neil, President & CEO
Jeff Kirschner, Chief Operations Officer
Tracey Skale, Chief Medical Officer

Offers the following services: job exploration; job development; job coaching and employment supports; and specialized programs.

Oklahoma

6002   Office of Disability Concerns
1112 N May Ave.
Suite 103A
Oklahoma City, OK 73103   405-521-3756
odc@odc.ok.gov
www.odc.ok.gov
Doug MacMillan, Director
William Ginn, Disability Program Specialist, Client Assistance Program
Mission is to promote the employment of people with disabilities. The vision of the committee is to facilitate partnerships with commitment to full, high-quality employment of people with disabilities.

6003   Oklahoma Department of Rehabilitation Services
3535 NW 58th St.
Suite 500
Oklahoma City, OK 73112-4824   405-951-3400
800-845-8476
FAX: 405-951-3529
www.oklahoma.gov/okdrs.html
Melinda Fruendt, Executive Director
The Oklahoma Department of Rehabilitation Services (DRS) provides assistance to Oklahomans with disabilities through vocational rehabilitation, employment, independent living, residential and outreach programs, and the determination of medical eligibility for disability benefits.

6004   Oklahoma Employment Security Commission (OESC)
PO Box 52003
Oklahoma City, OK 73152-2003   405-557-7100
888-980-9675
TTY:800-722-0353
OESCHelps@oesc.state.ok.us
www.ok.gov/oesc
Shelley Zumwalt, Executive Director
Michelle Britten, Chief Operations Officer
Taylor Adams, Director of Communications
Connects Ohioans with work, as well as enhancing skills and providing unemployment compensation.

Oregon

6005   Bureau of Labor and Industries (BOLI)
800 NE Oregon St
Suite 1045
Portland, OR 97232   971-673-0761
BOLI_help@boli.oregon.gov
www.oregon.gov/boli
Val Hoyle, Commissioner
Protects Oregonians from unlawful discrimination, defends workers' rights, and provides training to employees and employers.

6006   Opportunities Foundation of Central Oregon
P.O. Box 430
835 E. Hwy 126
Redmond, OR 97756   541-548-2611
FAX: 541-548-9573
info@opportunityfound.org
www.opportunityfound.org
Margee O'Brien, President
Shelly Hudspeth, Vice President
Marci Campbell, Secretary
Offers supported employment, residential support and behavior consultation services, including employment at three thirft stores.

6007   Oregon Commission for the Blind
535 SE 12th Avenue
Portland, OR 97214   971-673-1588
888-202-5463
FAX: 503-234-7468
ocb.mail@state.or.us
www.oregon.gov/Blind
Dacia Johnson, Executive Director
Angel Hale, Director, Rehabilitation Services
Malinda Carlson, Director, Independent Living Services
A resource for visually impaired Oregonians, as well as their families, friends, and employers. Nationally recognized programs and staff that make a difference in people's lives every day.

6008   Oregon Department of Human Services Vocational Rehabilitation (DHS VR)
500 Summer St. NE
Suite E-15
Salem, OR 97301   503-945-5600
FAX: 503-581-6198
TTY:503-945-6214
odhs.directorsoffice@dhsoha.state.or.us
www.oregon.gov/dhs/employment/VR
Fariborz Pakseresht, Director
Ashley Carson Cottingham, Director, Aging & People With Disabilities
Lilia Teninty, Director, Office of Developmental Disabilities Services
Offers vocational assessments and training, adult developmental activities, and helps remove disability related barriers to employment.

Pennsylvania

6009   Office of Vocational Rehabilitation (OVR)
Pennsylvania Department of Labor & Industry
1521 North Sixth St.
Harrisburg, PA 17102   dli.pa.gov/Individuals/Disability-Services
Helps individuals with disabilities prepare for, obtain, and manage employment, with services provided both directly and through a network of vendors.

6010   Pennsylvania Department of Labor and Industry (DLI)
1700 Labor & Industry Building
Harrisburg, PA 17102   717-787-5729
www.dli.state.pa.us
Administers benefits to unemployed individuals, oversees the administration of worker's compensation benefits to individuals with job related injuries, and provides vocational rehabilitation to individuals with disabilities.

6011   Pennsylvania Governor's Cabinet Committee for People With Disabilities
Department of Human Services
234 Health and Welfare Bldg.
Harrisburg, PA 17105-2675   717-787-3422
800-692-7462
FAX: 717-772-2490
www.dhs.pa.gov
Teresa Miller, Chair
Mission is to assist with disabilities to secure and maintain employment and independence.

6012   Pennsylvania Human Relations Commission Agency
Executive Offices
333 Market St.
8th Fl.
Harrisburg, PA 17101-2210   717-787-4410
TTY:717-787-7279
phrc@pa.gov
phrc.state.pa.us
Jennifer Berrier, Secretary of Labor & Industry
Mission is to administer and enforce the PHRAct and the PFEOA of the Commonwealth of Pennsylvania for the identification and elimination of discrimination and the providing of equal opportunity for all persons.

Rhode Island

6013 Groden Network
610 Manton Ave.
Providence, RI 02909
401-274-6310
grodennetwork.org

Michael Pearis, Chief Executive Officer
Grace Toe, Chief Financial Officer
Cooper Woodard, Chief Clinical Officer
The Groden Network aims to support children & adults with autism, as well as other developmental disailities, by providing educational, therapeutic and other services. The Network also engages in research, and educates families as well. The Network consists of The Groden Center, The Cover Center, and The Halcyon Center.

6014 Office of Rehabilitation Services
40 Fountain Street
Providence, RI 02903-1898
401-421-7005
TTY:401-421-7016
www.ors.ri.gov

Joseph Murphy, Associate Director
Beth Rioles, Administrator, DDS
Laurie DiOrio, Administrator, SBVI
Goal is to help individuals with physical and mental disabilities prepare for and obtain appropriate employment.

6015 Rhode Island Services for the Blind and Visually Impaired
40 Fountain Street
Providence, RI 02903-1898
401-421-7005
TTY:401-421-7016
www.ors.ri.gov/SBVI.html

Ron Racine, Associate Director
Beth Rioles, Administrator, DDS
Laurie DiOrio, Administrator, SBVI
Provides qualifying people with visual impairments opportunities to become self-sustaining members of the community.

South Carolina

6016 South Carolina Commission for the Blind (SCCB)
1430 Confederate Ave.
Columbia, SC 29201-79
803-898-8731
publicinfo@sccb.sc.gov
www.sccb.state.sc.us

Goal is to help individuals with visual impairments prepare for and obtain appropriate employment.

6017 South Carolina Department of Employment and Workforce (DEW)
1550 Gadsden St.
P.O. Box 995
Columbia, SC 29202
803-737-2400
866-831-1724

D. Ellzey, Executive Director
T. Timmons, Chief Legal Officer
J. Michaelson, Chief Financial Officer
Public agency that offers job search assistance, unemployment benefits and a WIA program. Also offered are services for individuals with disabilities.

6018 South Carolina Governor's Committee on Employment of the Handicapped
S.C. Vocational Rehabilitation Department
1410 Boston Ave.
West Columbia, SC 29171
803-896-6500
800-832-7526
TTY:806-896-6553
communications@scvrd.net
www.scvrd.net

Felicia W. Johnson, Commissioner
Goal is to help individuals with physical and mental disabilities prepare for and obtain appropriate employment.

6019 South Carolina Vocational Rehabilitation Department (SCVRD)
1410 Boston Ave.
West Columbia, SC 29171
803-896-6500
800-832-7526
TTY:806-896-6553
communications@scvrd.net
www.scvrd.net

Felicia W. Johnson, Commissioner
The SCVRD's mission is to enable eligible South Carolinians with disabilities to prepare for, achieve and maintain competitive employment.

South Dakota

6020 South Dakota Department of Human Services
Hillsview Plaza
3800 E Hwy 34
Pierre, SD 57501
605-773-5990
FAX: 605-773-5483
infodhs@state.sd.us
dhs.sd.gov

Shawnie Rechtenbaugh, Secretary
Provides resources for individuals with developmental disabilities, including rehabilitation services, services for the blind and visually impaired, and long-term services and supports.

6021 South Dakota Department of Human Services: Div. of Service to the Blind & Visually Impaired
Hillview Plaza
3800 E Highway 34
Pierre, SD 57501
605-773-3195
FAX: 605-773-5483
dhs.sd.gov/servicetotheblind

Shawnie Rechtenbaugh, Secretary
To provide individualized rehabilitation services that result in optimal employment and independent living outcomes for people with visual impairments.

6022 South Dakota State Vocational Rehabilitation
Department of Human Services
3800 E Hwy 34
Hillview Plaza
Pierre, SD 57501
605-773-3195
FAX: 605-773-5483
dhs.sd.gov/rehabservices/vr.aspx

Shawnie Rechtenbaugh, Secretary
Provides employment services to people with significant disabilities.

6023 South Dakota Workforce Investment Act Training Programs
123 W Missouri Ave.
Pierre, SD 57501-0405
605-773-3101
FAX: 605-773-6184
dlr.sd.gov/workforce_services/wioa

Marcia Hultman, Department Secretary
Dawn Dovre, Deputy Secretary
Andrew Szilvasi, Technology Development
Mission is to enhance the South Dakota workforce by providing business with employment-related solutions and helping people with job placement and career transition services

Tennessee

6024 Tennessee Department Human Services: Vocational Rehabilitation Services
505 Deaderick St.
Nashville, TN 37243-1403
615-313-4891
FAX: 615-741-6508
TTY:800-270-1349
www.tn.gov/humanservices

Clarence H. Carter, Commissioner, Human Services
Determines eligibility and nature/scope of required VR services, and provides those employment-focused rehabilitation services for individuals with disabilities.

6025 Tennessee Department of Labor and Workforce Development
220 French Landing Dr.
Nashville, TN 37243   844-224-5818
www.tn.gov/workforce

Jeff McCord, Commissioner
Dewayne Scott, Deputy Commissioner
Deniece Thomas, Deputy Commissioner
Offers services to employees and employers, including job training and adult education.

6026 Tennessee Human Rights Commission
312 Rosa L Parks Ave.
23rd Fl.
Nashville, TN 37243   615-741-5825
800-251-3589
FAX: 615-253-1886
ask.thrc@tn.gov
www.tn.gov/humanrights

Muriel Malone, Interim Executive Director
Tanya Webster, Title VI Compliance Director
Dawn Cummings, General Counsel
An independent state agency charged with preventing and eradicating discrimination in employment, public accomodations, and housing.

Texas

6027 Ability Connection
8802 Harry Hines Blvd.
Dallas, TX 75235   214-351-2500
info@abilityconnection.org
abilityconnection.org

Jim Hanophy, President & CEO
Laura Mahaley, Chief Financial Officer
Brian Petty, Chief Operating Officer
Provides training and support services to children and adults with both physical and intellectual disabilities.

6028 Concentra
5080 Spectrum Dr.
Suite 1200W
Addison, TX 75001   866-944-6046
www.concentra.com

Keith Newton, President & CEO
John Anderson, Executive VP & Chief Medical Officer
John deLorimier, Executive VP, Customer Growth & Experience
Offers employers comprehensive occupational health services and state-of-the-art physical and occupational therapy. Staff works as a team to produce the best possible patient care while delivering cost savings through workers compensation disability management programs.

6029 Texas Workforce Commission (TWC)
101 E 15th St.
Austin, TX 78778-0001   800-628-5115
customers@twc.state.tx.us
www.twc.state.tx.us

Ed Serna, Interim Executive Director
Courtney Arbour, Division Director, Workforce Development
Cheryl Fuller, Division Director, Vocational Rehabilitation Services
State government agency charged with overseeing and providing workforce development services to employers and job seekers of Texas. Offers career development information, job search resources, training programs, and, as appropriate, unemployment benefits.

6030 Texas Workforce Commission: Vocational Rehabilitation Services
101 E 15th St.
Austin, TX 78778-0001   800-628-5115
customers@twc.state.tx.us
twc.texas.gov

Ed Serna, Interim Executive Director
Cheryl Fuller, Division Director, Vocational Rehabilitation Services

Helps people with disabilities prepare for, find and keep jobs. Work related services are individualized and may include counseling, training, medical treatment, assistive devices, job placement assistance and other services.

Utah

6031 Utah Department of Human Services: Division of Services for People with Disabilities
195 North 1950 West
Salt Lake City, UT 84116   801-538-4171
844-275-3773
dhsinfo@utah.gov
dspd.utah.gov

Information and referral services for people with disabilities, including DD/MR, brain injury and physical disabilities throughout the state of Utah.

6032 Utah Employment Services
2292 South Redwood Rd.
Salt Lake City, UT 84119   801-978-0378
info@utahemploy.com
www.utahemploy.com

To help individuals prepare and obtain appropriate employment.

6033 Utah Governor's Committee on Employment for People with Disabilities (GCEPD)
Utah State Office of Rehabilitation
P.O. Box 45249
Salt Lake City, UT 84145-0249   801-526-9675
dwscontactus@utah.gov
jobs.utah.gov/usor

Casey Cameron, Executive Director
Greg Paras, Deputy Director
Nate McDonald, Deputy Director
Promotes opportunities and provide support for persons with disabilities to lead self-determined lives.

6034 Utah State Office for Rehabilitation (USOR)
P.O. Box 45249
Salt Lake City, UT 84145-0249   801-526-9675
dwscontactus@utah.gov
jobs.utah.gov/usor

Casey Cameron, Executive Director
Greg Paras, Deputy Director
Nate McDonald, Deputy Director
Provides services for individuals who are blind or visually impaired, deaf or hard of hearing, and those with other disabilities, including vocational rehabilitation.

6035 Utah State Office of Rehabilitation: Vocational Rehabilitation
P.O. Box 45249
Salt Lake City, UT 84145-0249   801-526-9675
jobs.utah.gov/usor/vr

Casey Cameron, Executive Director
Greg Paras, Deputy Director
Nate McDonald, Deputy Director
Vocational Rehabilitation Services for individuals with disabilities. To assist individuals with disabilities to prepare for and obtain employment and increase their independence.

6036 Utah State Office of Rehabilitation: Services for the Blind and Visually Impaired
P.O. Box 45249
Salt Lake City, UT 84145-0249   801-526-9675
dwscontactus@utah.gov
jobs.utah.gov/usor/vr

Casey Cameron, Executive Director
Greg Paras, Deputy Director
Nate McDonald, Deputy Director
Individuals who are blind or visually impaired receive training, adjustment services, and other assistive aids.

6037 Veterans Support Center (VSC)
Union Building
Room 418
Salt Lake City, UT 84112

801-587-7722
vetcenter@sa.utah.edu
veteranscenter.utah.edu

Paul Morgan, Director
Matt Root, Veterans Program Coordinator
Angela Brink, Office Manager
Readjustment counseling services to veterans.

Vermont

6038 Vermont Department of Disabilities, Aging and Independent Living (DAIL)
280 State Dr.
HC2 South
Waterbury, VT 05671-2020

802-241-2401
FAX: 802-241-0386
dail.vermont.gov

Monica White, Interim Commissioner
Provides programs and services for people with physical and developmental disabilities, as well as those with visual impairments, and those over 60 years of age. Employment services for people with disabilities are also provided.

6039 Vermont Department of Labor
5 Green Mountain Dr.
PO Box 488
Montpelier, VT 05601- 0488

802-828-4000
labor.commissioner@vermont.gov
labor.vermont.gov

Michael A. Harrington, Commissioner
Dustin Degree, Deputy Commissioner
The primary focus is to help support the efforts to make Vermont a more competitive place to do business and create good jobs.

6040 Vermont Division of Vocational Rehabilitation
280 State Dr.
HC2 South
Waterbury, VT 05671-2040

866-879-6757
FAX: 803-241-0341
vocrehab.vermont.gov

Diane Dalmasse, Division Director
Provides employment services to individuals with physical or developmental disabilities.

Virginia

6041 Campagna Center
418 S Washington St.
Alexandria, VA 22314

703-549-0111
FAX: 703-549-2097
www.campagnacenter.org

Janice Abraham, Board Chair, President & CEO
Don Lubreski, Chief Financial Officer
Edith Hawkins, Chief Program Officer
Offers social services, on-the-job-training for parents, play therapy, physical therapy, speech therapy and other specialized services.

6042 Didlake
8641 Breeden Ave.
Manassas, VA 20110-8431

703-361-4195
866-361-4195
FAX: 703-369-7141
ask@didlake.org
www.didlake.com

Donna Hollis, Chief Executive Officer
Den,e Fortune McKnight, Vice President, Finance & Administration/CFO
Offers situational assessments, work training, employment and job placement services to people with disabilities.

6043 Richmond Research Training Center (RRTC)
PO Box 842011
1314 West Main St.
Richmond, VA 23284-2011

804-828-1851
FAX: 804-828-2193
TTY:804-828-2494
RRTC@vcu.edu
vcurrtc.org

Paul Wehman, Professor & Director
John Kregel, Associate Director
Katherine Inge, Director, Employment
Research and training center report on the supported employment of persons with developmental and other disabilities.

6044 ServiceSource Disability Resource Center
10467 White Granite Dr.
Oakton, VA 22124

703-461-6000
www.servicesource.org

Bruce Patterson, Chief Executive Officer
Mark Hall, President
Nate Hoover, Chief Financial Officer
Provides training, job placement and employment services in private sector and government contract employment.

6045 SourceAmerica
8401 Old Courthouse Rd.
Vienna, VA 22182

888-411-8424
www.sourceamerica.org

Richard Belden, President & CEO
Jeffrey McCaw, Chief Financial Officer
Wes Tyler, Executive Vice President & Chief Operating Officer
SourceAmerica facilitates the Federal AbilityOne Program, which provides employment opportunities for people with disabilities. Provides products and services to government, corporate and nonprofit clients, as well as advocating on behalf of the disabled.

6046 Virginia Department for the Blind and Vision Impaired (DBVI)
397 Azalea Ave.
Richmond, VA 23227

804-371-3140
800-622-2155
www.vdbvi.org

Raymond E. Hopkins, Commissioner
Rick L. Mitchell, Deputy Commissioner, Services
Matt Koch, Deputy Commissioner, Enterprises
Offers services for the totally blind, legally blind, visually impaired, and more with health, counseling, educational, recreational, rehabilitation, computer training and professional training services.

Washington

6047 Business Enterprise Program (BEP)
Department of Services for the Blind
PO Box 40959
4565 7th Ave. SE
Olympia, WA 98504-0959

206-906-5500
800-552-7103
info@dsb.wa.gov
dsb.wa.gov

Michael MacKillop, Acting Executive Director
The Program allows qualified legally-blind individuals to operate food service businesses in government buildings.

6048 Department of Services for the Blind (DSB)
PO Box 40959
4565 7th Ave. SE
Olympia, WA 98504-0959

206-906-5500
800-552-7103
info@dsb.wa.gov
dsb.wa.gov

Michael MacKillop, Acting Executive Director
Offers a range of services for citizens with viosual impairments, including employment services.

6049 Department of Social & Health Services: Division of Vocational Rehabilitation
Customer Service Center
P.O. Box 11699
Tacoma, WA 98411-6699

877-501-2233
TTY:800-833-6384
www1.dshs.wa.gov/dvr

Jilma Meneses, Secretary
Lisa Yanagida, Chief of Staff
Terry Redmon, Director
Mission is to empower individuals with disabilities to achieve a greater quality of life by obtaining and maintaining employment.

6050 Department of Social & Health Services: Developmental Disabilities Administration (DDA)
Customer Service Center
P.O. Box 11699
Tacoma, WA 98411-6699

877-501-2233
TTY:800-833-6384
askdshs@dshs.wa.gov
www.dshs.wa.gov/dda

Jilma Meneses, Secretary
Lisa Yanagida, Chief of Staff
Terry Redmon, Director
Offers persons with developmental disabilities quality supports and services that are individual/family driven, stable and flexible, satisfying to the person and their family, and able to meet individual needs.

6051 SL Start Washington
909 SE Everett Mall Way
Everett, WA 98208

206-365-0809
www.lsrserviceswa.com

Kendra Ellis, Executive Director
LaceyJay Switzer, Area Director Snohomish & King County
Enola Stark, Program Manager
A diversified and innovative human and health services company focused on a wide range of social, employment and long-term services.

West Virginia

6052 West Virginia Division of Rehabilitation Services (DRS)
P.O. Box 50890
Charleston, WV 25305-0890

304-356-2060
800-642-8207
TTY:304-766-4809
www.wvdrs.org

DRS specializes in helping people with disabilities who want to find a job or maintain current employment. Rehabilitation counselors at more than 30 field offices help with applications. Once eligibility is determined, counselors & clients work as a team to develop a plan to meet the individuals employment goal. Services may include work-related counseling/guidance, evaluation/assessment, job development & placement assistance, vocational training, college assistance & assistive technology.

6053 WorkForce West Virginia
P.O. Box 2753
1321 Plaza East Shopping Ctr.
Charleston, WV 25330-2753

800-252-5627
FAX: 304-558-1979
workforcelmi@wv.gov
workforcewv.org

Workforce West Virginia is funded through the U.S. Department of Labor, and oversees the state unemployment insurance program as well as workforce development services across the state.

Wisconsin

6054 Department of Workforce Development: Vocational Rehabilitation
P.O. Box 7852
201 East Washington Avenue
Madison, WI 53707

608-261-0050
800-442-3477
FAX: 608-266-1133
dvr@dwd.wisconsin.gov
dwd.wisconsin.gov/dvr

Delora Newton, Administrator
Meredith Dressel, Deputy Administrator
Assists eligible individuals with disabilities with finding employment.

Wyoming

6055 Department of Workforce Services: Vocational Rehabilitation
Disability Determination Services
5221 Yellowstone Road
Cheyenne, WY 82002

307-777-8650
FAX: 307-777-5857
wyomingworkforce.org/workers/vr

Robin Sessions Cooley, Director
Provides services to disabled individuals to enable them to reach vocational goals.

6056 Wyoming Department of Workforce Services: Unemployment Insurance Division
5221 Yellowstone Road
Cheyenne, WY 82002

307-777-8650
FAX: 307-777-5857
wyomingworkforce.org/workers/ui

Robin Sessions Cooley, Director
The Department is responsible for unemployment claims and payments, unemployment adjudication, employer protests and charging, and benefit payment control.

6057 Wyoming State Rehabilitation Council (SRC)
Disability Determination Services
5221 Yellowstone Road
Cheyenne, WY 82002

307-777-8650
FAX: 307-777-5307
wyomingworkforce.org/workers/vr/src

Robin Sessions Cooley, Director
Assists, empowers and supports people with disabilities to achieve employment, independence and intergration in the workplace and community.

Rehabilitation Facilities, Acute

Alabama

6058 **HealthSouth Lakeshore Rehabilitation Hospital**
3800 Ridgeway Dr
Birmingham, AL 35209-5599   205-868-2000
                                   FAX: 205-868-2029
                                   www.healthsouthlakeshorerehab.com
Vickie Demers, Chief Executive Officer
April Cobb, Chief Nursing Officer
Al Rayburn, Director, Therapy Operations
A 100 bed facility whos key services is physical rehabilitation.
Also specialized services (inpatient) infection isolation room. In
addition, also has outpatient physical rehabilitation and sports
medicine. Patient family support services include patient repre-
sentative, transportation for elderly/handicapped and patient
support groups. Imaging services(diagnostic & theraputic) include ct scanner, diagnostic diagnostic radioisotope facility,
MRI, and ultrasound.

6059 **HealthSouth Rehabilitation Hospital of North Alabama**
107 Governors Dr
Huntsville, AL 35801   256-535-2300
                             FAX: 256-428-2608
                             www.healthsouthhuntsville.com
Douglas H. Beverly, Chief Executive Officer
Susan Creekmore, Director, Therapy Operations
Risha Hoover, Director, Marketing Operations
A comprehensive 50-bed rehabilitation hospital serving the need
of patients in the North Alabama area. Guides patients with physically disabling conditions along an individualized treatment
pathway so they can reach their highest level of physical, social
and emotional well-being. A wide range of medical and
theraputic services are delivered by qualified and experienced
professionals.

6060 **J.L. Bedsole/Rotary Rehabilitation Hospital**
Infirmary Health
5 Mobile Infirmary Circle
Mobile, AL 36607-3513   251-435-3417
                               www.infirmaryhealth.org
D. Mark Nix, President & CEO
Kenneth C. Brewington, Chief Medical Office, Mobile Infirmary
Jennifer Eslinger, President, Mobile Infirmary
Provides rehabilitation for patients affected by stroke, spinal
cord injury, brain injury or other neurological illnesses.

6061 **More Than Just a Job**
Institute On Disability/UCED
60 5th Avenue
Suite 101
New York, NY 10011   212-366-8900
                            FAX: 603-862-0555
                            www.forbes.com
Narrative case studies and interviews with persons with disabili-
ties, their employers, families and experts in the field. *$20.00*

6062 **Rocky Mountain Resource & Training Institute**
3630 Sinton Road
Suite 103
Colorado Springs, CO 80907- 5072   719-444-0268
                                           800-949-4262
                                           FAX: 719-444-0269
                                           TTY: 800-949-4232
                                           www.adainformation.org
Jana Copeland, Principal Investigator
Patrick Going, Senior Advisor
Serves people with disabilities and provides training to the agencies that assist them. Facilitates disabled individuals' transition
from school to adult life; provides information and resources concerning assistive technology, devices, and services; promotes
and ensures compliance with the federal Americans with Disabilities Act (ADA) and other legislation promoting the rights and inclusion of people with disabilities; promotes supported
employment, strategic planning and development.

Arkansas

6063 **Central Arkansas Rehab Hospital**
2201 Wildwood Ave
Sherwood, AR 72120-5074   501-834-1800
                                 FAX: 501-834-2227
                                 www.stvincentrehabhospital.com
Lee Frazier, MPH, Dr, CEO
Dr. Sean Foley, Medical Director
Debbie Taylor, Director of Marketing Operations
A nonprofit hospital licensed for 69 acute care beds with all private rooms. Opened in 1999the hospital offers a full range of outpatient diagnostic services, including MRI,CT,PET along with
surgical procedures, cardiology, neurology, neurosurgery,
othopedic, rehab and a 24 hour emergency department staffed
with board certified emergency room physicians. Includes an outpatient surgery center, rehabilitation hospital, senior health program, diabetic program and physician offices.

6064 **HealthSouth Rehabilitation Hospital**
1401 South J St
Fort Smith, AR 72901-5158   479-785-3300
                                    FAX: 479-785-8599
                                    www.healthsouth.com
Juli Stec, CEO
Provides physical rehabilitation as its key services. Also provides other services such as end-of-life services, pain management and an infection isolation room.

6065 **Northwest Arkansas Rehabilitation Hospital**
153 E Monte Painter Dr
Fayetteville, AR 72703-4002   479-444-2233
                                      FAX: 479-444-2390
                                      www.healthsouthfayetteville.com
Marty Hurlbut, Medical Director
Denise Wilson, Director Of Clinical Services
A 60-bed acute medical rehabilitation hospital that offers com-
prehensive inpatient and outpatient rehabilitation services.

6066 **Rebsamen Rehabilitation Center**
P.O.Box 159
Jacksonville, AR 72078-159   501-985-7000
                                     FAX: 501-985-7384
                                     www.rebsamenmedicalcenter.com
Mack McAlister, Chairperson
Murice Green, Vice Chairman
Tommy Swaim, Secretary
Mission is to provide personal healthcare for your family. Vision
is to develop a family of caregivers to become your community
hospital. A 113 bed acute care facility operated by a volunteer
Board of Directors made up of community leaders. Rebsamen
Medical Center is accredited by the Joint Commission on
Accreditation of Healthcare Organizations as well as the Arkan-
sas Department of Health. Through JCAHO we voluntary sumbit
to evaluations of our compliance with nationwide hospital
standards.

Arizona

6067 **Barrow Neurological Institute Rehab Center**
350 W Thomas Rd
Phoenix, AZ 85013-4409   602-406-3000
                                FAX: 602-406-4104
                                www.stjosephs-phx.org
Jackie Aragon, VP Care Management
Linda Hunt, President
Dedicated resources to delivering compassionate, high-quality,
affordable health services; serving and advocating for our sisters
and brothers who are poor and disenfranchised; and partnering
with others in the community to improve the quality of life. Our
vision:a growing and diversified health care ministry distinguished by excellent quality and committed to expanding access
to those in need.

567

6068 HealthSouth Sports Medicine Center
5111 N Scottsdale Rd
Ste 100
Scottsdale, AZ 85250-7076   480-990-1379
FAX: 480-423-8458
www.healthsouth.com

Troy Meiners, Manager
An out patient facility specialising in sports medicine and treatment of sports injuries.

6069 Healthsouth Rehab Institute of Tucson
2650 N Wyatt Dr
Tucson, AZ 85712-6108   520-325-1300
800-333-8628
FAX: 520-327-4045
www.rehabinstituteoftucson.com

Lee Sanford, Plant Manager
Jon Larson, Medical Director
An accredited member of the Joint Commission On Accreditation of Health Care Organizaions (JCAHO) An 80 bed facility specializing in rehabilitation

6070 Scottsdale Healthcare
9630 E Shea Blvd
Scottsdale, AZ 85260-6285   480-551-5400
FAX: 480-551-5401
preiley@shc.org

Thomas Sadvary, CEO
Pegg Reiley, Chief Nursing Officer
Kathy Zarubi, Associate VP of Nursing Practice
A 343 bed full-service hospital providing medical/surgical, critical care, obstetrics, pediatrics, surgery, cardiovascular, and oncology services, as well as the Sleep Disorder Center. All patient rooms are private. Emergency department is a level II Trauma Center. The Radiology Department offers state-of-the-art diagnostic equipment, including MRI, PET/CT scanning, nuclear medicine and ultrasound. Also located are the Piper Surgery Center, Cancer Center, and several medical office plazas.

6071 St. Joseph Hospital and Medical Center
350 W Thomas Rd
Phoenix, AZ 85013-4496   602-406-3000
FAX: 602-406-4190
hospitals.dignityhealth.org/stjosephs/
Linda Hunt, President
Rehabilitation programs offered by the clinic assists clients with rehabilitation health needs in the comfort of their own home. The home care rehabilitation team of professionals focuses on correcting deficiencies in self-care, mobility skills and communication. Services offered include physical therapy, occupational therapy, speech pathology, rehabilitative nursing and restorative nursing assistants.

California

6072 Bakersfield Regional Rehabilitation Hospital
5001 Commerce Dr
Bakersfield, CA 93309-648   661-323-5500
800-288-9829
FAX: 661-633-5254
www.healthsouthbakersfield.com

Chris Yoon, Medical Director
Sandra Hegland, Chief Executive Officer
A specialty hospital that treats an array of physical disabilities. It has 60 beds and offers physical rehabilitation services including support groups and education classes on illnesses such as arthritis, asthma and strokes. No surgery facilities on site.

6073 Brotman Medical Center: RehabCare Unit
3828 Delmas Ter
Culver City, CA 90232-6806   310-836-7001
FAX: 310-202-4141

Howard Levine, CEO
The mission of Brotman Medical Center is to deliver innovative, quality health care to our patients and their families in an environment of compassion, respect, patient saftey, education, and fiscal responsibility.

6074 Casa Colinas Centers for Rehabilitation
255 E Bonita Ave
Pomona, CA 91767-1923   909-596-7733
866-724-4127
FAX: 909-593-0153
TTY: 909-596-3646
rehab@casacolina.org
www.casacolina.org

Felice Loverso, CEO/President
Steve Norin, Chairman
Stephen W. Graeber, Vice Chairman
Casa Colina will provide individuals the opportunity to maximize their medical recovery and rehabilitation potential efficiently in an environment that recognizes their uniqueness, dignity and self esteem. The vision is to strategically reposition themselves at the forefront of the post-acute continuum by becoming the center of excellence in the provision of services to persons who can benefit from rehabilitation care.

6075 Community Hospital of Los Gatos Rehabilitation Services
815 Pollard Rd
Los Gatos, CA 95032-1400   408-378-6131
FAX: 408-866-4003

Ned Borgstrom, CEO
Rehabilitation Services provide individualized treatment programs for inpatient/outpatient care. The team is supervised by a Physiatrist and may include Nurses, Physical Therapists, Occupational Therapists, Speech/Language Therapists, Psychologists, Case Managers, Dietitians, Respiratory Therapists, Recreation Therapists and/or Prosthetists/Orthotists.

6076 Garfield Medical Center
525 N Garfield Ave
Monterey Park, CA 91754-1205   626-573-2222
FAX: 626-571-8972
www.garfieldmedicalcenter.com
Philip Cohen, CEO
Provides quality care to all citizens of all ages. We are foreward looking to meet the changing health care needs of Forsyth and the surrounding area. At the same time, we are a stable organization that is financially sound. We involve all of our medical staff through good communication. We support them by trying to meet their professional needs in training, equipment and services. We emphasize good communication with all county citizens who support us financially and through the use of services

6077 Grossmont Hospital Rehabilition Center
5555 Grossmont Center
La Mesa, CA 91942   619-740-6000
800-827-4277
FAX: 619-644-4159
www.sharp.com

Michael Murphy, President/CEO
Daniel Gross, EVP
It is our mission to improve the health of those we serve with a commitment to excellence in all that we do. Our goal is to offer quality care and programs that set community standards, exceed patients' expectations and are provided in a caring, convenient, cost-effective and accessible manner.

6078 Health South Tustin Rehabilitation Hospita
14851 Yorba St
Tustin, CA 92780-2925   714-832-9200
FAX: 714-508-4550
www.healthsouth.com
Sandra Yule, CEO

6079 Holy Cross Comprehensive Rehabilitation Center
15031 Rinaldi St
Mission Hills, CA 91345-1207   818-365-8051
888-432-5464
FAX: 818-898-4472
www.providence.org
Larry Bowe, CEO
Derek Berz, COO
Known for providing exceptional treatment through its Cancer Centers, Heart Center, Orthopedics, Neurosciences and Rehabilitation Services, as well as Woman's and Children's Services. As a 254-bed, not-for-profit facility, Providence offers a full continuum of health services, from outpatient to inpatient to home

health care. Providence operates one of the only round-the-clock trauma centers in the San Fernando Valley and surrounding communities.

6080   Job Hunting Tips for the So-Called Handicapped
Special Needs Project
324 State Street
Suite H
Santa Barbara, CA 93101-2364

818-718-9900
800-333-6867
FAX: 818-349-2027
editor@specialneeds.com
www.specialneeds.com

Hod Gray, Owner
This nifty booklet from the guru of job hunting himself is sincere, useful and brief. *$4.95*

6081   Kentfield Rehabilitation Hospital & Outpatient Center
1125 Sir Francis Drake Blvd
Kentfield, CA 94904-1418

415-456-9680
FAX: 415-485-3563
info@kentfieldrehab.com
www.kentfieldrehab.com

Deborah Doherty, MD
Provides specialized inpatient and outpatient programs. We provide quality services that are patient centered and family-oriented. Under the medical direction of board-certified hospitalists and other physician specialists, our dedicated interdisciplinary teams provide a coordinated, comprehensive treatment approach to a wide range of neurological, orthopedic, pulmonary and complex medical problems.

6082   Laurel Grove Hospital: Rehab Care Unit
20103 Lake Chabot Rd
Castro Valley, CA 94546-4093

510-537-1234
FAX: 510-727-2778
nissims@sutterhealth.org
www.edenmedcenter.org

George Bischalaney, CEO & President
Kent Myers, Treasurer
Jeffrey Randall, Secretary
The mission of Eden Medical Center is carried out by our Board of Directors, employees, physicians and volunteers who are committed to providing our patients and their families with the highest quality medical care and customer service. Creating standards of excellence to ensure quality and value for our patients. Maintaining a financially sound organization through effective clinical and administrative support. Encouraging a culture that supports employees and physicians in development.

6083   Lodi Memorial Hospital West
Lodi Memorial Hospital
975 S Fairmont Ave
Lodi, CA 95240

209-334-3411
800-323-3360
FAX: 209-333-7131

Joseph Harrington, President
Ron Kreutner, Vice President And CFO
Judy Begley RN, MSN, Chief Nursing Officer
Our vision is to provide a system of health-care services which is clinically effective, quality driven and community focused in an environment that supports and encourages excellence. In partnership with our medical staff, we will assume accountability for the health of our community, be responsible for illness and injury prevention and provide care for the ill and injured. We will measure our success on quality outcomes and customer satisfaction.

6084   Long Beach Memorial Medical Center Memorial Rehabilitation Hospital
2801 Atlantic Ave
Long Beach, CA 90806-1701

562-933-2000
FAX: 562-933-9018
www.memorialcare.org

Nissar Syed, Administrator
Barry Arbuckle, President
The hospital offers rehabilitation after catastrophic injury of disabling disease to give patients the opportunity for maximum recovery. The Hospital offers many of the area's finest rehabilitation specialists and most advanced technology, making it one of Southern California's most respected rehabilitation centers.

6085   North Coast Rehabilitation Center
1165 Montgomery Drive
Santa Rosa, CA 95405-4869

707-546-3210
FAX: 707-525-8413

Joyce Cavagnaro, Admissions
Combines state-of-the-art medicine, compassionate care, and the widest array of resources to enhance your health and promote healthy communities. Dedicated to continually introducing new programs and services that help you live life to the fullest.

6086   Northridge Hospital Medical Center
18300 Roscoe Blvd
Northridge, CA 91328

818-885-8500
FAX: 818-885-5435
www.northridgehospital.org

Mike Wall, CEO
dedicating resources to delivering compassionate, high-quality, affordable health services; serving and advocating for our sisters and brothers who are poor and disinfranchised; and partnering with others in the community to improve the quality of life.

6087   PEERS Program
8912 W Olympic Blvd
Beverly Hills, CA 90211-3514

310-553-4833
FAX: 310-553-4833

Paul Berns, Medical Director
Offers a new approach for wheelchair users. PEERS uses a combination of modern physical therapy, the DOUGLAS Reciprocating Gait System and when necessary, functional electrical stimulation to assist selected individuals to walk with recently patented specially made lightweight braces.

6088   PIRS Hotsheet
Placer Independent Resource Services
11768 Atwood Rd
Ste 29
Auburn, CA 95603

530-885-6100
800-833-8453
FAX: 530-885-3032
TTY: 530-885-0326
lbrewer@pirs.org
pirs.org

Susan Miller, Executive Director
Harry Powell, President
Paul Opper, Vice President
Monthly newletter to customers and other constituents.
6 pages Monthly

6089   Providence Holy Cross Medical Center
Providence Health System
15031 Rinaldi St
Mission Hills, CA 91345-1285

818-365-8051
818-898-4603
FAX: 818-365-4472
www.providence.org

Kerry Carmody, CEO
Physicains and nurses are among the best and are recognized nationally for clinical excellence. We are committed to improving your health and wellness as you journey through life. Our services span beyond the latest advancements in medical procedures, equipment and medication to also include education and wellness services-all provided with compassion and respect. We help our patients understand and use some of the healthiest tools at their disposal, including nutrition & excercise.

6090   Queen of Angels/Hollywood Presbyterian Medical Center
1300 N Vermont Ave
Los Angeles, CA 90027-6005

213-413-3000
FAX: 213-413-3500
www.hollywoodpresbyterian.com

Kathy Wong, Manager
A 434 bed acute-care facility that has been caring for the Hollywood community and surrounding areas since 1924. The hospital is committed to serving local multicultural communities with quality medical and nursing care. With more then 500 physicians representing virtually every speciality. Ready to serve your medical needs and those of your loved ones and strive to distinguish itself as a leading healthcare provider, recognized for providing quality, innovative care in a compassionate manner.

6091   Queen of the Valley Hospital
1000 Trancas St
Napa, CA 94558-2941   707-252-4411
                                              FAX: 707-257-4032
                                                www.thequeen.org

Walt Mickens, President
Vincent Morgese, Vice President
For more then 40 years, Queen of the Valley Hospital has been the premiere medical facility in the Napa Valley. Our long history of providing high quality and caring service is founded on 4 core values:Dignity, Service, Excellence and Justice. These central principals inspire us to reach out to those in need and to help heal the whole person-mind, body and spirit.They are the driving force behind our mission to improve the health and quality of life of people in the community we serve.

6092   Rancho Los Amigos National Rehabilitation Center
7601 E Imperial Hwy
Downey, CA 90242-3496   562-401-7111
                                                 877-726-2461
                                                888-RAN-CHO1
                                             FAX: 562-401-6690
                                             TTY:562-401-8450
                         dhs.lacounty.gov/wps/portal/dhs/rancho

Jorge Orozco, CEO
Mindy Lipson Aisen, Chief Medical Officer
Michelle Sterling, Interim Chief Nursing Officer
Internationally renowned in the field of medical rehabilitation, consistently ranked in the top Rehabilitation Hospitals in the United States by U.S. News and World Report. It is one of the largest comprehensive rehabilitaion centers in the United States. Licensed for 395 beds, providing service through over 20 centers of excellence.

6093   San Joaquin Valley Rehabilitation Hospital
7173 N Sharon Ave
Fresno, CA 93720-3329   559-436-3600
                                             FAX: 559-436-3606
                                                 sjvrehab.com

Edward Palacios, CEO
Complete comprehensive rehabilitation services from acute rehab, outpatient and community fitness services.

6094   Santa Clara Valley Medical Center
County of Santa Clara
751 S Bascom Ave
San Jose, CA 95128-2699   408-885-5000
                                                 www.scvmed.org

Paul E. Lorenz, CEO
Jeffrey Arnold, Medical Officer
Trudy Johnson, Director of Patient Care Services & Nursing
The mission of the medical center is to provide high-quality, cost-effective medical care to all residence of Santa Clara County regardless of their ability to pay. Make availiable a wide range of inpatient, outpatient, emergency services within resource constraints. Maintain an environment within which the needs of our patients are paramount and where patients, their families and all our visitors are treated in a compassionate, supportive, friendly, and dignified manner.

6095   Scripps Memorial Hospital at La Jolla
9888 Genesee Ave
La Jolla, CA 92037-1205   858-626-4123
                                                 800-727-4777
                                             FAX: 858-626-6122
                                                 www.scripps.org

Sean A Deitch, President/CEO
Gary Fybel, Executive Director/Administrator
One of the county's 6 designated trauma centers, offers a wide range of clinical and surgical services including 24-hour emergency services; intensive care; interventional cardiology and radiology; radiation oncology; cardiothoracic and orthopedic services; neurology; ophthalmology; and mental health and psychology services.

6096   South Coast Medical Center
12 Mason
Ste A
Irvine, CA 92618-2733   714-669-4446
                                             FAX: 714-669-4448
                                 info@southcoastmedcenter.com

Leigh Erin Connealy, Manager
Bruce Christian, President
A 208 bed acute care hospital. Services include maternity, surgical, subacute care, psychiatric program, eating disorder treatment, chemical dependency treatment, radiology, ICU/CCU, comprehensive rehabilitation services, bariatric surgery and movement disorders program.

6097   St. Joseph Rehabilitation Center
St. Joseph Health System
2200 Harrison Ave
Eureka, CA 95501-3215   707-441-4414
                                             FAX: 707-441-4429
                                           www.stjosepheureka.org

Mission is to provide physical rehabilitation services in a positive patient-centered environment. This promotes restoration of maximum functional abilities and allows for a dignified quality of life experience. As a staff we are guided by our core values of Dignity, Excellence, Service, and Justice.

6098   St. Jude Brain Injury Network
St. Jude Hospital
130 W Bastanchury Rd
Fullerton, CA 92835-1058   714-446-5626
                                                 866-785-8332
                                             FAX: 714-446-5979
                                             ocrcuser@stjoe.org
                                                 www.tbioc.org

Jana Gable, Program Coordinator
David Bogdan, Service Coordinator
Lina Marroquin, Servicer Coordinator
Provides comprehensive planning, program referral, assists with funding possibilities, and interagency coordination of services. Areas of emphasis include day treatment, vocational and housing options, and the requirements are adults who have suffered a brain injury from an external force.

6099   St. Jude Medical Center
101 E Valencia Mesa Dr
Fullerton, CA 92835-3809   714-871-3280
                                                 800-627-8106
                                             FAX: 714-992-3029
                                           stjudemedicalcenter.org

Robert Fraschetti, President
We are one of Southern California's most respected and technologically advanced hospitals, and our four core values: dignity, excellence, service and justice are the guiding principles for everything we do. St. Jude is synonymous with exceptional care that extends beyond good medicine to a commitment to caring for you - mind, body and spirit.

6100   St. Mary Medical Center
1050 Linden Ave
Long Beach, CA 90813-3393   562-491-9000
                                             FAX: 562-491-9053
                                         www.stmarymedicalcenter.org

Chris Desicco, CEO

6101   Sunnyside Nursing Center
22617 S Vermont Ave
Torrance, CA 90502-2595   310-320-4130
                                             FAX: 310-212-3232
                                           www.sunnysidenursing.com

Shane Dahl, Administrator
Manny Cordero, Director of Nursing
El Sayad, Medical Director
Skilled nursing care facility; residential care facility; intermediate care facility; specialty hospital.

6102 UCLA Medical Center: Department of Anesthesiology, Acute Pain Services
U CL A Medical Center
1245 16th Street Medical Plz
Ste 225
Santa Monica, CA 90404   310-794-1841
                                     FAX: 310-794-1511
                                  access@mednet.ucla.edu

Michael Ferrante, Clinical Director
A 337-bed acute-care medical center, has been serving the healthcare needs of West Los Angeles and Santa Monica since 1926. Highly regarded for its primary and specialty care, the medical center features many outstanding clinical programs, including its women's and children's services, emergency services, and family medicine programs.

Colorado

6103 Children's Hospital Rehabilitation Center
University of Colorado Health Sciences Center
1056 E 19th Ave
Denver, CO 80218-1007   303-861-8888
                                         800-624-6553
                                         chipteam.org

Lou Blankenship, CEO
Michael J Farrell, Chief Operating Officer
Helen Martinez, Manager
Private not-for-profit pediatric healthcare network, the hospital is 100 percent dedicated to caring for kids of all ages and stages of growth. That dedication is evident in more then 1000 pediatric specialists and more then 2400 employees. It is also our continual dedication that has placed us at the forefront of research in childhood disease with several nationally and internationally recognized medical programs.

6104 Craig Hospital
3425 S Clarkson St
Englewood, CO 80113-2899   303-789-8000
                                     FAX: 303-789-8214
                                 khosack@craighospital.org
                                    www.craighospital.org

Michael Fordyce, President
Thomas Balazy, Medical Director
Julie Keegan, VP of Finance
A 93-bed, private, not-for-profit, free-standing, acute care and rehabilitation hospital that provides a comprehensive system of inpatient and outpatient medical care, rehabilitation, neurosurgical rehabilitative care, an equipment company, and long-term follow up services.

6105 HealthSouth Rehabilitation Hospital of Colorado Springs
HealthSouth Corporation
325 S Parkside Dr
Colorado Springs, CO 80910-3134   719-630-8000
                                     FAX: 719-520-0387
                          www.healthsouthcoloradosprings.com

Steve Schaefer, CEO
A 56 bed rehabilitation hospital, its key services are: cardiology department, physical rehabilitation, and orthopedics department. Accredidted to the Joint Commission on Accreditation of Health Care Organizations (JCAHO)

6106 Mapleton Center
North Broadway & Balsam
Boulder, CO 80301-9130   303-440-2273
                                     FAX: 303-441-0536
                                          pr@bch.org
                                          www.bch.org

David Gehant, President/CEO
Comprehensive inpatient and outpatient rehabilitation services for all age groups. Treatment provided by interdisciplinary teams and staff physicians. CARF accredited in brain injury rehabilitation, pediatric rehabilitation, pain management, work hardening and inpatient rehabilitation.

6107 Mediplex Rehab: Denver
Vibra Health Care
8451 Pearl St
Thornton, CO 80229-4804   303-288-3000
                                     FAX: 303-496-1120
                                     info@vhdenver.com
                                   www.northvalleyrehab.com

Walter Sacckett, CEO
Encompasses the broadest mix of professional talent, the finest technology and a total commitment by our people to deliver the highest quality care today, and well into the future. The services can be divided into 4 main categories: long term Acute Care and rehab. Skilled nursing facility and residential ventilator program. Outpatient services and pain management. Adult and Geriatric inpatient psychiatric services.

Connecticut

6108 Mariner Health Care: Connecticut
23 Liberty Way
Niantic, CT 06357   860-739-4007
                                     FAX: 860-701-2202

District of Columbia

6109 National Rehabilitation Hospital
102 Irving St NW
Washington, DC 20010-2949   202-877-1760
                                     FAX: 202-829-2789
                                      www.nrhrehab.org

Edward Healton, Medical Director
Robert Bunning, Associate Medical Director
A private facility dedicated solely to medical rehabilitation. The hospital offers intensive inpatient programs and full-service outpatient programs.

Florida

6110 Florida Hospital Rehabilitation Center
601 E Rollins St
Orlando, FL 32803-1248   407-303-1527
                                          855-303-3627
                                     FAX: 407-303-7566
                                     fh.web@flhosp.org

Rex Alleyne, President
Florida Hospital Orlando uses the latest technology to treat over 32,000 inpatients and 53,600 outpatients annually. This 881-bed, acute-carecommunity hospital also serves as a major tertiary facility for much of the Southeast, the Caribbean and South America

6111 HealthSouth Regional Rehab Center/Florida
20601 Old Cutler Rd
Miami, FL 33189-2441   305-251-3800
                                     FAX: 305-259-0498
                                      www.healthsouth.com

Murray Rolnick, Medical Director
Elizabeth Izquierdo, Chief Executive Officer
HealthSouth Rehabilitation Hospital of Miami is a member of the HealthSouth Corporation, the nation's largest healthcare services provider. The hospital is accredited by the Joint Commission on Accreditation of Healthcare Organizations (JCAHO) and Commission on Accreditaion of Rehabilitation Facilities (CARF). Services offered include dietary services, occupational therapy, and respitory care.

6112 HealthSouth Rehab Hospital: Largo
901 Clearwater Largo Rd N
Largo, FL 33770-4121   727-586-2999
                                     FAX: 727-588-3404
                                   www.healthsouthlargo.com

Elaine Ebaugh, CEO
Linda Russo, Director, Therapies

A specialty hospital devoted to providing comprehensive medical rehabilitation services. The hospital is licensed as a Comprehensive Medical Rehabilitation Hospital by the state of Florida, and accredited by the Joint Commission on Accreditation of Healthcare Organizations (JCAHO). HealthSouth of Largo is the only free standing Rehabilitation Hospital in the Tampa Bay region, and serves patients of all ages. Provides inpatient medical rehabilitation services as well as outpatient programs.

6113   HealthSouth Sports Medicine & Rehabilitation Center
3280 Ponce De Leon Blvd
Coral Gables, FL 33134-7252   305-444-0909
                                        FAX: 305-444-5760
                                        www.healthsouth.com

Jay Greeney, President
Ray Jaffet, Administrator
Provides specialized medical and therapeutic services designated to help physically disabled individuals reach their optimum level of independence and function by providing inpatient and outpatient comprehensive medical rehabilitation services.

6114   HealthSouth Sports Medicine and Rehabilitation Center
2141 South Highway A1A Alt
Jupiter, FL 33477   561-743-8890
                                        FAX: 561-743-8795

Diane Reiley, Manager
Outpatient orthopedic and sports medicine/physical therapy.

6115   HealthSouth Treasure Coast Rehabilitation Hospital
Health South Corporation of Alabama
1600 37th St
Vero Beach, FL 32960-4863   772-778-2100
                                        FAX: 772-567-7041
                                www.healthsouthtreasurecoast.com

Jimmy Lockhart, Medical Director
HealthSouth Treasure Coast Rehabilitation Hospital is a 90-bed inpatient comprehensive rehabilitation hospital serving Indian River, St. Lucie, Martin and Okeechobee counties. Outpatient services are available at the hospital and at four other clinics. Therapies include physical, occupational, speech and psychology services.

6116   Manatee Springs Care & Rehabilitation Center
5627 9th St E
Bradenton, FL 34203-6105   941-753-8941
                                        FAX: 941-739-4409
                                www.manateespringsrehab.com

Donna Steiermann, Administrator
Skilled rehabilitation facility specializing in PT, OT, speech therapy, aquatic therapy and an indoor pool. Piped oxygen bed for specialized respiratory care. Compassionate end of life care. Some Medicare, private insurance, and Medicaid.

6117   Perry Health Facility
207 Marshall Dr
Perry, FL 32347-1897   850-584-6334
                                        FAX: 850-838-1801

Rebkah Hatch, Administrator
Full rehabilitation team available, Physiatrist, DOR, Psychiatrist, Psychologist, RD, Geriatric Nursing, PT/OT/ST/RT, Orthotiet/Prosthetist. Provider for PPO's & HMO's as well as medicare, private insurance and medicare/medicaid.

6118   Pinecrest Rehabilitation Hospital and Outpatient Centers
Tenet South Florida
5352 Linton Blvd
Delray Beach, FL 33484-6514   561-498-4440
                                             800-283-8326
                                        FAX: 561-495-3103
                                        www.pinecrestrehab.com

Mark Bryan, CEO
Pinecrest Rehabilitation Hospital is a 90 bed, accredited hospital and is comprised of a Specialty Unit, a Neuro Trauma Unit and Joint Replacement Unit. Additional services at Pincrest include six outpatient rehab centers throughout Palm Beach County. The Outpatient Centers each focus on various specialties such as orthopedic and neurological rehab, pain management, cardiac and pulmonary rehab, occupational medicine, Hearing Institute, dizziness and balance and wellness.

6119   Rehabilitation Institute of Sarasota
3251 Proctor Rd
Sarasota, FL 34231-8538   941-921-8796
                                        FAX: 941-922-6228

Stacy Shepherd, Director Clinical Services
a 75-bed hospital that offers individualized medical and theraputic services tailored to patients and clinics for those affected with stroke, multiple sclerosis, Parkinson's, muscular dystrophy and Lou Gehrig's disease (ALS)

6120   Sea Pines Rehabilitation Hospital
101 E Florida Ave
Melbourne, FL 32901-8398   321-984-4600
                                        FAX: 321-727-7440
                                ellen.lyons-olski@healthsouth.com
                                www.healthsouthseapines.com

Stuart Miller, Medical Director
Donna Bohdal, Director of Therapy Operations
Denise McGrath, Administrator
A 90-bed facility specializing in rehabilitation of brain and spinal injuries.

6121   Shriners Hospitals for Children: Tampa
12502 USF Pine Dr
Tampa, FL 33612-9411   813-972-2250
                                             813-281-0300
                                        FAX: 813-975-7125
                                aargiz-lyons@shrinenet.org
                                www.shrinershq.org/hospitals/tampa

David Ferrell, FACHE
Maureen Maciel, Chief of Staff
Alicia Argis-Lyons, Develpoment Officer
Recognizing that the family plays a vital role in a child's ability to overcome an illness or injury, Shriners Hospitals helps the family provide the support the child needs by involving the family in all aspects of the child's care and recovery. The purpose of all Shriners Hospitals for Children is to provide care to children with orthopedic problems and burn injuries to help them lead fuller, more productive lives.

6122   South Miami Hospital
6200 SW 73rd St
South Miami, FL 33143-4679   786-662-4000
                                        FAX: 786-662-5302
                                        www.baptisthealth.net

Brian E. Keely, CEO
The mission is to improve the health and well-being of individuals, and to promote the sanctity and preservation of life, in the communities we serve. We are committed to maintaining the highest standards of clinical and service excellence, rooted in utmost integrity and moral practice.

6123   St. Anne's Nursing Center
11855 Quail Roost Dr
Miami, FL 33177-3956   305-252-4000
                                        FAX: 305-969-6752
                                www.catholichealthservices.org

Tony Farinella, Executive Director
Francisco Cruz, Medical Director
Julia Shillingford, Director of Nursing
Provides spacious, comfortable accommodations with ample recreational areas in a beautifully landscaped setting.

6124   St. Anthony's Hospital
1200 7th Ave N
St Petersburg, FL 33705-1388   727-825-1100
                                        www.stanthonys.com

William Ulbricht, President
James McClint, VP
Ron Colaguori, VP Operations
A not-for-profit, 395-bed hospital established in 1931. St. Anthony's is dedicated to improving the health of the community through community-owned health care that sets the standard for high-quality, compassionate care.

6125 St. Anthony's Rehabilitation Hospital
3487 NW 35th Ave
Lauderdale Lakes, FL 33311-1107
954-485-4023
954-739-6233
www.catholichealthservices.org
Linda Motte, Hospital Administrator
Kathy Torbertsonn, Dir. Rehab.
Provides spacious, comfortable accommodations with ample recreational areas in a beautifully landscaped setting.

6126 St. Catherine's Rehabilitation Hospital and Villa Maria Nursing Center
1050 NE 125th St
North Miami, FL 33161-5805
305-357-1735
305-891-3361
www.catholichealthservices.org
Virginia Irving, Hospital Administrator
Jim Reiss, Executive Director
Greg Hartley, Director Rehab
St. Catherine's Rehabilitation Hospital is a CARF accredited, 60 bed facility offering inpatient and outpatient rehabilitation and medical clinics; including physical, occupational, and speech therapy, neurology, neurodiagnostics, wound care, and hyperbaric medicine. Villa Maria Nursing center is a JCAHO accredited, 212 bed skilled nursing center providing short term nursing and rehabilitation , as well as long term care.

6127 St. John's Nursing Center
3075 NW 35th Ave
Lauderdale Lakes, FL 33311-1107
954-739-6233
FAX: 954-733-9579
www.catholichealthservices.org
Ralph E. Lawson, Chairman
Elizabeth Worley, Vice Chairman
Thomas Marin, Assistant Secretary
Provides spacious, comfortable accommodations with ample recreational areas in a beautifully landscaped setting.

6128 Successful Job Accommodation Strategies
LRP Publications
36- Hiatt Dr
Palm Beach Gardens, FL 33418
561-622-6520
800-341-7874
FAX: 561-622-0757
webmaster@lrp.com
www.lrp.com
Honora McDowell, Product Group Manager
Kenneth Kahn, Chief Executive Officer
This monthly newsletter provides you with quick tips, new accommodation ideas and innovative workplace solutions. You learn the outcomes of the latest cases involving workplace accommodations. *$140.00*
12 pages Monthly

6129 Tampa General Rehabilitation Center
1 Tampa General Circle
Tampa, FL 33601-1289
813-844-7000
FAX: 813-844-1477
tgh.org
Ron Hytoff, President/CEO
Devanand Mangar MD, Vice Chief of Staff
Thomas L. Bernasek MD, Chief of Staff
Offers a full range of inpatient and outpatient programs all aimed at helping patients achieve their full potentials. JCAHO and CARF accredited and V.R. designated center. A wide range of inpatient and outpatient programs are available such as Brain and Spinal Cord Injury Programs, Comprehensive Medical Rehabilitation, Pain Management, Cardiac Rehab, Pediatric Therapy Service, Sleep Disorders, Epilepsy, and Wheelchair Seating.Hosts the Florida Alliance for Assistive Services and Technolgy.

6130 University of Miami: Jackson Memorial Rehabilitation Center
University of Miami
1611 NW 12th Ave
Miami, FL 33136-1005
305-585-6970
FAX: 305-585-6092
info@jhsmiami.org
www.jhsmiami.org
Michael Butler, Chief Medical Officer

An accredited, non-profit, tertiary care hospital and the major teaching facility for the University of Miami School of Medicine. With more then 1,550 beds, Jackson Memorial is a referral center, a magnet for medical research, and home to the Ryder Trauma Center- the only adult and pediatric level 1 trauma center in Miami-Dade County.

6131 Winter Park Memorial Hospital
Florida Hospital
200 N Lakemont Ave
Winter Park, FL 32792-3273
407-646-7000
FAX: 407-646-7639
healthcare@winterparkhospital.com
www.winterparkhospital.com
Ken Bradley, CEO
Offers Acute Rehabilitation.

Georgia

6132 Candler General Hospital: Rehabilitation Unit
5353 Reynolds St
Savannah, GA 31405-6015
912-819-6000
FAX: 912-819-8829
www.sjchs.org/body.cfm?id=383
Paul Hinchey, President/CEO
Special Physical Therapy Services at Candler Outpatient Center: Aquatic therapy, pediatric services, outpaitient neurological rehabilitation program, woman's health therapy, orthotics, and spine specialty

6133 Children's Healthcare of Atlanta at Egleston
1405 Clifton Rd. NE
Atlanta, GA 30322
www.choa.org
Donna Hyland, President & CEO
Ruth Fowler, Chief Financial Officer
Stephanie M. Jernigan, Campus Director, Egleston
Rehabilitation Center at Egleston accepts children from birth to age 18 with acute or chronic problems. The length of rehab stay varies for each child according to the determined program of care. The center offers inpatient, outpatient and day rehab programs for comprehensive evaluation and treatment.

6134 Cobb Hospital and Medical Center: Rehab Care Center
3950 Austell Rd
Austell, GA 30106-1121
770-732-5126
www.wellstar.org
David Anderson, Executive VP
Michael Andrews, Chief Cancer Network Officer
Avril Beckford, Chief Pediatrics Officer
To deliver world class healthcare we equip our healthcare facilities and employees with the best technology, resources and education availiable. To deliver world class healthcare we keep seeking ways to improve the way we deliver care knowing each day holds more miracles, more life, more chances, more compassion, and more opportunities.

6135 HealthSouth Central Georgia Rehabilitation Hospital
3351 Northside Dr
Macon, GA 31210-2587
478-201-6500
FAX: 478-471-6536
www.centralgarehab.com
HealthSouth Central Georgia rehabilitation hospital is a 55 bed comprehensive medical rehabilitation hospital meeting the medical patients and famloity members in Central Georgia.

6136 Specialty Hospital
Floyd Healthcare Resources
304 Turner McCall Blvd SW
Rome, GA 30165-5621
706-509-5000
FAX: 706-802-4175
contactus@floyd.org
www.floyd.org
Kurt Stuenkel, CEO
Dee Russell, Chief Medical Officer
Our mission is to be responsive to the communities we serve with a comprehensive and technologically advanced heal care system commited to the delivery of care that is characterized by continually improving quality, accessability, affordability and personal dignity.

Hawaii

6137 **Shriners Hospital for Children: Honolulu**
1310 Punahou St
Honolulu, HI 96826-1099
808-941-4466
888-888-6314
FAX: 808-942-8573
jburda@shrinenet.org
www.shrinershospitalsforchildren.org
Kenneth Guidera, Chief Medical Officer
Eugene D'Amore, Vice President
Kathy A. Dean, Vice President Human Resources
One of 22 hospitals across North America that provide excellent, no-cost medical care to children with orthopedic problems and burn industries.

Idaho

6138 **Pocatello Regional Medical Center**
777 Hospital Way
Pocatello, ID 83201-2797
208-234-6154
FAX: 208-239-3719
robbieo@portmed.org
www.portmed.org

Mark Bukalew, Chairman
John Abreu, VP Finance
Stephen Weeg, Vice-Chairman
Pocatello Regional Medical Center offers 24-hour emergency care, specialized heart services, a dialysis center, a full service rehabilitation unit including transition care, and the Woman's Center For Health including obstetrics.

Illinois

6139 **Builders of Skills**
515 Busse Hwy
Park Ridge, IL 60068-3154
847-318-0870
FAX: 847-292-0873
www.avenuestoindependence.org
Jacqueline Kinmel, Chair
Peg O'herron, Vice Chair
Eric Johnson, Treasurer
Residential setting for hearing-impaired, developmentally disabled adults who are assisted with daily living skills.

6140 **Center for Learning**
National-Louis University
2840 Sheridan Rd
Evanston, IL 60201-1730
847-256-5150
FAX: 845-256-1057
Jerry Dachs, Manager
Psycho-educational evaluations for children, adolescents, and adults. Individualized remedial academic programs, individual counseling

6141 **DBTAC-Great Lakes ADA Center**
1640 W Roosevelt Road
Room 405
Chicago, IL 60608-1316
312-413-1407
800-949-4232
FAX: 312-413-1856
www.adagreatlakes.org
Robin Jones, Project Director
Glenn Fujiura, PhD, Director of Research and Co-Inve
Claudia Diaz, Associate Project Director
Provides training, technical assistance and consultation on the rights and resposibilities of indiviualsand entities covered by the ADA. Toll free number for technical assistance and materials provided electronically or via mail at no cost.

6142 **Institute of Physical Medicine and Rehabilitation**
6501 N Sheridan Rd
Peoria, IL 61614-2932
309-692-8110
800-957-4767
FAX: 309-692-8673

Lisa Snyder, Medical Director
Comprehensive CARF accredited programs in outpatient medical rehabilitation services. Eight outpatient locations, specialty programs include adult day services, driving evaluations, balance and visual rehabilitation board certified physiatrists.

6143 **LaRabida Children's Hospital and Research Center**
E 65th At Lake Michigan
Chicago, IL 60649
773-363-6700
FAX: 773-363-9554
pr@larabida.org
www.larabida.org

Brenda Wolf, President/CEO
Dedicated to excellence in caring for children with chronic illness, disabilitiesm or who have been abused, allowing them to achieve their fullest potential through expertise and innovation within the health care and academic communities.

6144 **Marianjoy Rehabilitation Hospital and Clinics**
26W171 Roosevelt Rd
Wheaton, IL 60187-6078
630-909-8000
800-462-2366
FAX: 630-909-8001
www.marianjoy.org

Maureen Beal, Chairperson
John Oliverio, Vice Chairman
Kathleen Dvorakk, Treasurer
Goal at Marianjoy Rehabilitation Hospital is to help you and your family return to the lifestyle you enjoyed before your illness or injury. To meet this goal, we provide you with a dedicated team of experienced professionals to assist you every step of the way.

6145 **Rush Copley Medical Center-Rehab Neuro Physical Unit**
2040 Ogden Ave
Ste 303
Aurora, IL 60504-7222
630-898-3700
866-426-7539
FAX: 630-898-3681
clord@rsh.net
www.rushcopley.com

Barry Finn, CEO
Mary Shilkaitis, VP, Patient Care Services
The mission of the medical center and the medical staff is to work together to serve your healthcare needs through excellence in education, technology and a caring touch. Rush-Copley Medical Center will be the leading healthcare provider of the greater Fox Valley area. At Rush-Copley we pride ourselves on providing everyone with extrodinary service.

Indiana

6146 **ATTAIN**
U S Department of Education/ NI DR R
32 E Washington St
Ste 1400
Indianapolis, IN 46204-3552
317-534-0236
800-528-8246
Gary Hand, Executive Director
The mission of Attain is to create solutions that enable people with functional limitations to live, learn, work and play in the community of their choice. All will have access to assistive devices. We will do this in partnership with people with functional limitations, families and members of the community through training, system change, services and support, research, dissemination and consumer advocacy.

6147 About Special Kids
7172 Graham Rd
Suite 100
Indianapolis, IN 46250-2879
317-257-8683
800-964-4746
FAX: 317-251-7488
FamilyNetw@aboutspecialkids.org
www.aboutspecialkids.org

Joe Brubaker, Executive Director
Jane Scott, Director Of Information
Nancy Stone, Project Director

A Parent to Parent organization that works throughout the state of Indiana to answer questions and provide support, information and resources. We are parents and family members of children with special needs and we help other families and professionals understand the various systems that are encountered related to special needs. Our central office is where parents from the entire state can access information, resources and support.

6148 ArtMix
1505 N. Delaware St.
Indianapolis, IN 46202
317-974-4123
FAX: 317-974-4124
info@artmixindiana.org
www.artmixindiana.org

Gayle Holtman, President/CEO
Linda Wisler, Vice President of Programs
Kathy Pataluch, Vice President of Development

Since 1982, ArtMix has been a statewide leader in its mission to transform the lives of people with disabilities through the creation of art. ArtMix programs serve over 6,000 people of all abilities each year, creating opportunities for learning, self-expression, and socialization, as well as increasing community understanding of people with disabilities. ArtMix strives to create a welcoming environment that breaks down barriers, providing an inclusive space for people of all ages and abilities.

6149 Clark Memorial Hospital: RehabCare Unit
1220 Missouri Ave
Jeffersonville, IN 47130-3743
812-282-6631
FAX: 812-283-2656
clarkmemorial.org

Martin Padgett, CEO

The mission of Clark Memorial Hospital is to provide superior health services to the people and communities we serve. The vision of Clark Memorial Hospital is to be the best community healh care provider in the United States. We value each individual and work together to explore new ways to improve the quality of life of all. We persue excellence in all we do. We treat all individuals with the same compassion, dignity, and privacy that we want in ourselves.

6150 Developmental Disabilities Planning Council
402 W Washington St
Indianapolis, IN 46204-2855
317-232-7770
FAX: 317-233-3712
www.state.in.us/gpcpd

Suellen Jackson-Boner, Executive Director
Christine Dahlberg, Associate Director
Jim Geswein, CFO

The mission of the Indiana Governor's Council is to promote public policy which leads to the independence, productivity and inclusion of people with disabilities in all aspects of society. This mission is accomplished through planning, evaluation, collaboration, education, research and advocacy. The Council is consumer-driven and is charged with determining how the service delivery system in both the public and private sectors can be most responsible to the people with disabilities.

6151 Easterseals Crossroads
4740 Kingsway Dr.
Indianapolis, IN 46205
317-466-1000
FAX: 317-466-2000
www.easterselscrossroads.org

Harold Tenbarge, Chair
Darlisa E. Davis, Treasurer
John Seever, Secretary

Provides services for people with disabilities in central Indiana.

6152 IN-SOURCE
Indiana Resource Center for Families with Special
1703 S Ironwood Dr
South Bend, IN 46613-3414
574-234-7101
800-332-4433
FAX: 574-234-7279
insource@insource.org
insource.org

Richard Burden, Executive Director
Scott Carson, Assistant Director
Dory Lawrence, Project Director

The mission of IN*SOURCE is to provide parents, families and service providers in Indiana the information and training necessary to assure effective educational programs and appropriate services for children and young adults with disabilities.

6153 Indiana Congress of Parent and Teachers
2525 N Shadeland Ave
Ste D4
Indianapolis, IN 46219-1770
317-357-5881
FAX: 317-357-3751
www.indianapta.org

Sharon Wise, President
Theresa Distelrath, VP
Job Wise, Secretary

The mission of the Indiana PTA is three-fold: to support and speak on behalf of children and youth in the schools, community and before governmental agencies and other organizations that make decisions affecting children; to assist parents in developing the skills they need to raise and protect their children; and, to encorage parent and community involvement in the public schools of this state and nation.

6154 Indiana Protection and Advocacy Services Commission
4701 N Keystone Ave
Ste 222
Indianapolis, IN 46205-1561
317-722-5555
800-838-1131
FAX: 317-722-5564
dward@ipas.IN.gov
www.in.gov/ipas

Karen Pedevilla, Education and Training Director

IPAS was created in 1977 by state law to protect and advocate the rights of people with disabilities and its Indiana's federally designated Protection (P&A) system and client assist program. It is an independent state agency, with receives no state funding and is independent from all service providers, as required by federal and state law.

6155 Kokomo Rehabilitation Hospital
829 N Dixon Rd
Kokomo, IN 46901-7709
765-452-6700
FAX: 765-452-7470

Brenda Harry, Admissions Director

a 60 bed facility specializing in rehabilitation services to the people of Indiana.

6156 Memorial Regional Rehabilitation Center
615 N Michigan St
South Bend, IN 46601-1033
574-647-1000

20-bed CARF accredited inpatient rehabilitation, outpatient orthopedic clinic and work performance program, head injury clinic. Outpatient neuro rehab and a driver education and training program are provided.

6157 Methodist Hospital Rehabilitation Institute
8701 Broadway
Merrillville, IN 46410-7035
219-738-5500
FAX: 219-755-0448
methodisthospitals.org

Ian McFadden, President/CEO
Matthew Doyle, VP & CFO
Wright Alcorn, VP Operations

Methodist Hospitals, of all the hospitals in Northwest Indiana, attracts the most complex cases across a range of specialties, including stroke, brain tumor, cancer, trauma and high-risk pregnancy. This is the result of our commitment to providing the expertise and technology needed to offer the most advanced clinical care.

6158 **NAMI Indiana**
P.O.Box 22697
Indianapolis, IN 46222-697

317-925-9399
800-677-6442
FAX: 317-925-9398
info@namiindiana.org
www.namiindiana.org

Marilynn Walker, President
Joshua Sprunger, Executive Director
Linda Williams, Program Coooridnator
NAMI Indiana is a non-profit grassroots organization dedicated to improving the lives of people afflicted by serious and persistant mental illness. We are dedicated to helping families through a network of support, education, advocacy, and promotion of research. NAMI's goal is to help establish a system of care that provides community based services for persons with serious mental illness, as well as support for them and their families.

6159 **Parkview Regional Rehabilitation Center**
2200 Randallia Dr
Fort Wayne, IN 46805-4638

260-373-4000
888-480-5151
FAX: 260-373-4288
www.parkview.com

Mike Packnett, President & CEO
Mike Browning, CFO
Rick Henvey, Chief Administrative Officer
Provides a full range of inpatient, theraputic services and programs for patients as young as 3 years of age to the very elderly. Our accute care rehabilitation center, is well equipped to care for patients with neurological and orthopedic injuries and diseases.

6160 **Programs for Children with Disabilities: Ages 3 through 5**
Indiana Department of Education
151 W Ohio St
Indianapolis, IN 46204-1905

317-232-0570
877-851-4106
FAX: 317-232-0589
specialed@doe.in.gov
www.doe.in.gov

Heather Neal, Chief of Staff
The division provides leadership and state-level support for public school gifted and talented (grades K-12) programs and for students with disabilities from ages 3-21. The division ensures that Indiana, in its compliance with the federal Individuals With Disabilities Education Act, through monitoring of special education programs, oversight of community and residential programs, provision of mediation and due process rights, and sound fiscal management.

6161 **Programs for Children with Special Health Care Needs**
Indiana State Department of Health
2 N Meridian St
Indianapolis, IN 46204-3021

317-233-1325
www.in.gov/isdh/

Sean Keefer, Chief of Staff
The Children's Special Health Care Services (CSHCS) program provides financial assistance for needed medical treatment to children with serious and chronic medical conditions to reduce complications and promote maximum quality of life.

6162 **Programs for Infants and Toddlers with Disabilities: Ages Birth through 2**
402 W Washington St
Indianapolis, IN 46204-2773

317-232-1144
800-441-7837

A family-centered, locally-based, coordinated system that provides early intervention services to infants and young children with disabilities or who are developmentally vulnerable. First Steps brings together families and professionals from education, health and social service agencies. By coordinating locally availiable services, First Steps is working to give Indiana's children and their families the widest possible array of early intervention resources.

6163 **Riley Child Development Center**
705 Riley Hospital Drive
Rm 5837
Indianapolis, IN 46202-5128

317-274-7819
FAX: 317-944-9760
info@child-dev.com

Cristy James, Communication Coordinator
Riley Hospital for Children is Indiana's only comprehensive children's hospital, with pediatric specialists in evry field of medicine and surgery. Riley is committed to providing the highest quality health care to children in a compassionate, family-centered environment. Riley is a national leader in cutting edge research and medical education, ensuring health care excellence for children for generations to come. Riley provides medical care to all children, regardless of family's ability to pay.

6164 **St. Anthony Memorial Hospital: Rehab Unit**
301 W Homer St
Michigan City, IN 46360-4358

219-879-8511
FAX: 219-877-1409
www.saintanthonymemorial.org

Joseph Allegreti, Board of Directors
Calvin Bellamy, Board of Directors
Saint Anthony Memorial is an acute care hospital located in Michigan City, primary serving La Porte and Porter Counties in Indiana as well as Berrien County Michigan.

6165 **State Division of Vocational Rehabilitation**
402 W Washington St
P O Box 7083
Indianapolis, IN 46207-7083

317-233-4475
800-545-7763
FAX: 317-232-6478
vrcommission@fssa.in.gov
www.state.in.us/fssa

Megan Ornellas, Chief of Staff
Susie Howard, Deputy Chief of Staff

Iowa

6166 **Younker Rehabilitation Center of Iowa Methodist Medical Center**
1776 W Lakes Pkwy
Des Moines, IA 50266

515-241-6161
888-584-6311
FAX: 515-241-5137
www.ihs.org

Bill Leaver, President
Kevin Vermeer, EVP
Danny Drake, VP
Iowa Health System is the state's first and largest integrated healthcare system. We are physicians, hospitals, civic leaders and local volunteers committed to providing the highest possible quality and the lowest possible cost. We serve over 70 communities in Iowa, Western Illinois, and Eastern Nebraska.

Kansas

6167 **Kansas Rehabilitation Hospital**
1504 SW 8th Ave
Topeka, KS 66606-2714

785-235-6600
FAX: 785-232-8545
www.kansasrehabhospital.com

Mark LeNeave, CEO
Mindy Mitchell, Chief Nursing Officer
A free standing physical rehabilitation hospital located in Topeka Kansas. Designated to provide a barrier-free access to all treatment and patient service areas. This 79-bed facility offers a total rehabilitation environment in a warm, caring setting that encourages patient, family and staff interaction.

6168 Mid-America Rehabilitation Hospital HealthSouth
Health South Corporation
5701 W 110th St
Overland Park, KS 66211-2503   913-491-2400
                                  FAX: 913-491-1097
                          tiffany.kiehl@healthsouth.com
                          www.midamericarehabhospital.com
Kristen De Hart, CEO
Tiffany Kiehl, Director Marketing/Operations
Paul Matlack, Director Therapy Operations
97 bed Acute Rehab hospital offering full continuum from in-patient, day treatment and outpatient services for individuals with physical limitations due to CVA, TBI, SCI, other traumas, joint replacement, etc.

Kentucky

6169 Cardinal Hill Rehabilitation Hospital
2050 Versailles Rd
Lexington, KY 40504-1499   859-254-5701
                                  800-233-3260
                              FAX: 859-231-1365
                          webmaster@cardinalhill.org
                          www.cardinalhill.org
Kerry Gillihan, CEO
William J. Lester, Medical Director
Russell Travis, Assistant Medical Director
CARF-accredited rehab center provides comprehensive inpatient and outpatient services in two locations to people with physical and cognitive disabilities. We provide diagnosis-specific programs to 100 inpatients, outpatient clinics, outpatient therapies, pain management and therapeutic pool services. The Pediatric Center serves children from birth to age 18 years of age.

6170 HealthSouth Rehabilitation of Louisville
1227 Goss Ave
Louisville, KY 40217-1287   270-769-3100
                              FAX: 502-636-0351
                          www.healthsouth.com
Tim Nichol, Manager
Regina Durbin, Administrator
HealthSouth Rehabilitation Hospitals lead the way, consistently outperforming peers with a unique, intensive approach to rehabilitative care, partnering with every patient to find a treatment plan that works for them. We offer a wide range of comprehensive rehabilitation programsfor a wide variety of diagnoses. At HealthSouth, we provide access to independent private practice physicians, specializing in physical medicine and rehabilitation, who work in conjunction with HealthSouth's highly qual

6171 Lakeview Rehabilitation Hospital
134 Heartland Dr
Elizabethtown, KY 42701-2778   270-769-3100
                              FAX: 270-769-6870
                          www.healthsouthlakeview.com
Lori Jarboes, CEO
Chris Koford, Medical Director
HealthSouth Rehabilitation Hospitals lead the way, consistently outperforming peers with a unique, intensive approach to rehabilitative care, partnering with every patient to find a treatment plan that works for them. We offer a wide range of comprehensive rehabilitation programsfor a wide variety of diagnoses. At HealthSouth, we provide access to independent private practice physicians, specializing in physical medicine and rehabilitation, who work in conjunction with HealthSouth's highly qual

6172 Shriners Hospitals for Children, Lexington
1900 Richmond Rd
Lexington, KY 40502-1204   859-266-2101
                                  800-444-8314
                              FAX: 859-268-5636
                          Dwallenius@shrinenet.org
                          www.shrinershq.org/hospitals/lexington
Warren E. Hopkins, Chairman
Kirk E. Carter, Vice Chairman
Ken R. Dougherty, Treasurer
Shriners Hospitals for Childrenr - Lexington, is a 50-bed pediatric orthopaedic hospital. Our family-centered approach to care is

designed to support the whole family during the acute and reconstructive phases of a child's injury. Located in Lexington, Ky., our hospital treats children from all over the country and around the world, and has unique relationships with some of the top hospitals and universities in the world.

Louisiana

6173 HealthSouth Specialty Hospital Of North Louisiana
1401 Ezelle St
Ruston, LA 71270-7218   318-251-3126
                                  800-548-9157
                              FAX: 318-251-1594
                          mark.rice@lifecare-hospitals.com
                          www.healthsouth.com
Mark Rice, CEO
A 90-bed specialty hospital offering both inpatient and outpatient services. Acute long term care.

6174 Our Lady of Lourdes Rehabilitation Center
4801 Ambassador Caffery Pkwy
Lafayette, LA 70508   337-470-2000
                          FAX: 318-289-2681
                          info@lourdesrmc.com
                          www.lourdesrmc.com
William Barrow, CEO
Gerald R. Boudreaux, Chairman of the Board
D. Wayne Elmore, Secretary
Our Lady of Lourdes outpatient physical medicine and rehabilitation department is comprrised of a multi-disciplinary team of physical therapists, oppcuptational therapists and speech languare pathologists.

6175 Rehabilitation Center of Lake Charles Memorial Hospital
1701 Oak Park Boulevard
Lake Charles, LA 70601-8911   337-494-3000
                              FAX: 337-494-2656
                          webmaster@lcmh.com
                          www.lcmh.com
Dale Shearer, Director
Larry Graham, President/CEO
Ben F. Thompson, MD, Medical Staff President
Rehabilitation center offering intensive physical, occupational, speech, neuropsychology, recreational therapies along with rehabilitation nursing.

6176 Shriners Hospital for Children-Shreveport
3100 Samford Ave
Shreveport, LA 71103-4239   318-222-5704
                              FAX: 318-424-7610
                          jburda@shrinenet.org
                          www.shrinershospitalsforchildren.org
Richard McCall, Chief of Staff
Phillip Gates, Assistant Chief
An interdisciplinary approach is used in patient care programs to ensure comprehensive care for each patient. The staff includes orthopaedists, pediatricians, nurses, therapists, social workers, child life specialists, and more. The Shreveport Hospital is equipped and staffed to provide care for virtually all pediatric orthopaedic problems, with the exception of acute trauma.

6177 South Louisiana Rehabilitation Hospital
715 W Worthy Rd
Gonzales, LA 70737-3844   225-647-8277
                              FAX: 225-647-2446
                          sober@powerhouseprograms.com
                          www.powerhouseprograms.com
Cody Gautreux, Executive Director
Tonja Randolph, President
Power House Programs is a male only facility for the treatment of Chemical Dependency/Dual Diagnosis, located in Gonzales, Louisiana. Applicants must have participated in a primary treatment program for substance abuse prior to acceptance. Our program is divided into 3 phases and is staffed by Board Certified Social Workers and Board Certified Substance Abuse Counselors. We provide individual, group and family therapy; plus 12 step meetings in a community setting.

6178 St. Frances Cabrini Hospital: Rehab Unit
St Frances Cabrini Hospital
3330 Masonic Dr
Alexandria, LA 71301-3899   318-487-1122
                                   FAX: 318-448-6822
                                   www.christusstfrancescabrini.org

Curman Gaines, Chairperson
Dallas Hixson, Vice Chairperson
CHRISTUS St. Frances Cabrini Hospital is a 265-bed facility located in Alexandria, Louisiana. Employing approximately 1,400 Associates and with a staff of neary 320 physicians, CHRISTUS St. Frances Cabrini Hospital offers a comprehensive array of services providing the highest quality patient care in a compassionate setting.

6179 St. Patrick Hospital: Rehab Unit
524 Doctor Michael Debakey Dr
Lake Charles, LA 70601-5725   337-491-7577
                                    888-722-9355
                                    FAX: 337-430-4284
                                    www.christusstpatrick.org

Ellen Jones, CEO
Committed to providing care and service of the highest quality for children and adults, and to ensuring that the basic human rights of expression, decision making and personal dignity are preseved. We are also committed to treating our patients with respect, understanding and Christian love. We realize that this committment involves much more then attending to your medical needs.

6180 Thibodaux Regional Medical Center
602 N Acadia Rd
PO Box 1118
Thibodaux, LA 70301-4847   985-447-5500
                                   800-822-8442
                                   FAX: 985-449-4600
                                   info@thibodaux.com
                                   www.thibodaux.com

Greg Stock, CEO
Jacob Giardina, Chairman
Andrew Hoffman, Chief of Staff
Mission is to provide the highest quality, most cost effective health care services possible to the people of Thibodaux and surrounding areas. The vision is to be the regional medical center of choice for health care services in the southeast Louisiana by recognizing the value of physicians and employees, committing to quality improvement, partnering with other health care providers, and remaining financially viable in a competitive environment.

Maine

6181 Brewer Rehab and Living Center
74 Parkway S
Brewer, ME 04412-1628   207-989-7300
                                   800-359-7412
                                   FAX: 207-989-4240

Janet Hope, Executive Director
Brewer Rehab and Living Center accomodates 106 residents. We are located in Brewer, Maine. We have a 24-hour nursing staff and experienced dedicated on-site physical therapists, occupational therapists and speech language pathologists. We have a specialized inpatient program for individuals with brain injury resulting from a traumatic injury or neurological event such as a stroke. We also have a specialized care unit for individuals with Alzheimer's disease and other dementias.

6182 New England Rehabilitation Hospital of Portland
335 Brighton Ave
Portland, ME 04102-2363   207-662-8000
                                   FAX: 207-879-8168
                                   www.nerhp.org

Elissa Charbonneau, Medical Director
Amy Morse, CEO
Mission is to provide individuals with guidance, education, support, and motivation while helping them achieve maximum independence and function. Our professionals work with the patient and family through a team approach, to establish and implement an individualized rehabilitation plan designed to meet specific patient goals.

Maryland

6183 Mt. Washington Pediatric Hospital
1708 W Rogers Ave
Baltimore, MD 21209-4596   410-578-8600
                                   FAX: 410-466-1715
                                   www.mwph.org

Sheldon Stein, President
Richard Katz, VP, Medical Affairs
Provides inpatient, outpatient and day programs for infants and children with rehabilitation and/or complex medical needs. We are dedicated to maximizing the rehabilitation and development of our patients through the delivery of interdisciplinary services and programs and providing every resource availiable to enable our patients to attain the highest quality of life within their families and their communities.

Massachusetts

6184 New Bedford Rehabilitation Hospital
4499 Acushnet Ave
New Bedford, MA 02745-4707   508-995-6900
                                   FAX: 508-998-8131
New Bedford Rehabilitation Hospital provides safe, high-quality, cost-effective medical and rehabilitation care to our patients and their families with the goal of improving quality of life and maximizing function.

6185 New England Rehabilitation Hospital: Massachusetts
2 Rehabilitation Way
Woburn, MA 01801-6098   781-939-5050
                                  FAX: 781-933-9257
                                  www.newenglandrehab.com

Deniz Ozel, Medical Director
A 168-bed comprehensive inpatient rehabilitation hospital, which includes 2 off-campus satellite units. Offers an array of area outpatient rehabilitation centers. New England Rehabilitation Hospital remains committed to a personal caring approach. The vision is to provide the communities with a complete continuum of acute rehabilitative programs and services.

6186 Shriners Burns Hospital: Boston
51 Blossom St
Boston, MA 02114-2623   617-722-3000
                                  800-255-1916
                                  FAX: 617-523-1684
                                  www.shrinershospitalsforchildren.org

Thomas D'Esmond, Administrator
Matthias Donelan, Chief of Staff
Provides treatment for children to their 18th birthday with acute, fresh burns, plastic reconstructive surgery for patients with healed burns, severe scarring and facial deformity. Some non-burn conditions such as Scalded Skin Syndrome, Cleft Lip, Cleft Palate and purpura fulminians are also treated. Call the Hospital for information. All medical treatment is without cost to the patient, parents, or any third party.

6187 Shriners Hospital Springfield Unit Springfield Unit for Crippled Children
516 Carew St
Springfield, MA 01104-2330   413-787-2000
                                  800-237-5055
                                  FAX: 413-787-2009
                                  www.shrinershospitalsforchildren.org

Kenneth Guidera, Chief Medical Officer
Eugene D'Amore, Vice President
Kathy A. Dean, Vice President Human Resources
Shriners Hospital for Children is fully equipped and staffed to provide care for pediatric orthopaedic conditions and disorders.

Michigan

6188   Covenant Healthcare Rehabilitation Program
1447 N Harrison
Saginaw, MI 48602-4316
989-583-2930
FAX: 989-583-0000
www.covenanthealthcare.com

Spence Maidlow, President
Juli Martin, Program Director
Offers a broad spectrum of programs and services ranging from obstetrics, neonatal and pediatric care, to acute care including cardiology, oncology, surgery and many other services on the leading edge of medicine. All our programs and services exemplify our commitment to providing quality, compassionate care. As a medical facility with more then 700 beds, and a complete range of medical services, Covenant stands ready to meet the healthcare needs of the 15 counties in Michigan we serve.

6189   Farmington Health Care Center
34225 Grand River Ave
Farmington, MI 48335-3440
248-477-7373
FAX: 248-477-2888

Brian Garavaglia, Administrator
Skilled nursing facility specializing in ventilator dependent residents.

6190   Flint Osteopathic Hospital: RehabCare Unit
3921 Beecher Rd
Flint, MI 48532-3602
810-606-5000
FAX: 810-762-2153
TTY: 888-633-2368
www.genesys.org

Susan Malone, Program Manager
Joy Finkenbiner, Executive Director
Genesys Health System takes great pride in the fact that we strive to deliver the highest quality health care, in a model healing environment, for the entire continuum of care needed throughout one's life. From birth to the twilight years, and everywhere in between, Genesys is there to get you back to the things you love to do.

6191   Integrated Health Services of Michigan at Clarkston
4800 Clintonville Rd
Clarkston, MI 48346-4297
248-674-0903
FAX: 248-674-3359
donna.cook@fundltc.com

Carol Doll, Admissions Director
Margaret Canny, Administrator
At Clarkston Specialty Healthcare Center, our mission is to deliver personalized care to the members of our community at a time when our support is most needed. We strive to maximize and enhance the quality of life in a compassionate and professional environment.

6192   St. John Hospital: North Shore
Ascension Health
26755 Ballard St
Harrison Township, MI 48045-2419
586-465-5501
866-501-3627
FAX: 586-466-5352
webcenter@stjohn.org
www.stjohnprovidence.org

David Sessions, CEO
A 96-bed specialty hospital that provides comprehensive physical medicine and rehabilitation, along with a wide range of medical and surgical services. St. John North Shores Hospital also provides emergency and urgent care, extensive outpatient rehabilitation services, and most ancillary diagnostic services.

Minnesota

6193   Alinna Health
800 E 28th St
Minneapolis, MN 55407-3798
612-863-4200
866-880-3550
FAX: 612-863-5698
sisterkenny@allina.com
www.allinahealth.org/ahs/ski.nsf/

Helen Kettner, Nurse-Liaison
Courage Kenny Rehabilitation Institute provides a continuum of rehabilitation services for people with short- and long-term conditions and disabilities in communities throughout Minnesota and western Wisconsin. Our goal is to improve health outcomes, make it easier for clients and families to get the right services for their needs, and reduce costs by preventing complications.

Missouri

6194   Columbia Regional Hospital: RehabCare Unit
404 N Keene St
Columbia, MO 65201-6698
573-882-2501
FAX: 573-449-7588
www.muhealth.org

James Ross, CEO
Anita Larsen, COO
A medical and physical rehabilitation program serving patients throughout Mid-Missouri with functional deficits due to neurologic, orthopaedic or other medical conditions.

6195   Jewish Hospital of St. Louis: Department of Rehabilitation
1 Barnes Jewish Hospital Plz
Saint Louis, MO 63110-1003
314-747-3000
855-925-0631
FAX: 314-454-5277
www.barnesjewish.org

Richard Liedweg, President
Mark Krieger, VP/CFO
John Lynch, Chief Medical Officer
We take exceptional care of people by providing world-class healthcare, delivering care in a compassionate, respectful and responsive way. By advancing medical knowledge and continously improving our practices. By educating current and future generations of healthcare professionals.

6196   St. Mary's Regional Rehabilitation Center
201 NW R D Mize Rd
Blue Springs, MO 64014-2513
816-228-5900
FAX: 816-655-5348

Fleury Yelvington, President/CEO
Amy McKay, Executive Director of Nursing
A 143-bed inpatient physical rehabilitation unit offering PT, OT, ST, recreational therapy, psychiatry and all other ancillary services of a full-service hospital. Specialize in orthopedic and neurologic disabilities.

6197   Three Rivers Health Care
2620 N Westwood Blvd
Poplar Bluff, MO 63901-3396
573-785-7721
800-582-9533
FAX: 573-686-5388
info@pbrmc.hma-corp.com
www.poplarbluffregional.com

Charles Stewart, Market CEO
Gerald Faircloth, Administrator
Melissa Samuelson, Chief Nursing Officer
Poplar Bluff Regional Medical Center is a regional medical center with 2 hospital campuses and more then 100 active physicians. The 423-bed facility is the largest medical center in Southeast Missouri and is located in ButlerCounty. With outreach clinics in Bloomfield, Dexter, Malden, Piedmont, and Puxico, Poplar Bluff Regional Medical Center is committed to serving its 6 county region.

Montana

6198 **St. Vincent Hospital and Health Center**
1233 N 30th St
Billings, MT 59101-165
406-657-7000
FAX: 406-657-8817
www.svhhc.org

Jason Barker, CEO
Steve Loveless, COO
Joan Thullberry, Chief Nursing Officer
Vision is to be recognized for our vitality, best in class performance and providing easy access to compassionate and trust-worthy healthcare. The healthcare we offer is based on community need. We strive to improve the health status of the community, with a special concern for the poor and those who have limited access to healthcare.

Nebraska

6199 **Madonna Rehabilitation Hospital**
5401 South St
Lincoln, NE 68506-2150
402-489-7102
800-676-5448
FAX: 402-483-9406
info@madonna.org
www.madonna.org

Marsha Lommel, CEO
Provides a complete range of inpatient and outpatient rehabilitation for patients of all ages and abilities. Through highly specialized programs and services, Madona offers individualized treatment and support to help every patient.

Nevada

6200 **University Medical Center**
1800 W Charleston Blvd
Las Vegas, NV 89102-2386
702-383-2000
FAX: 702-383-2536
feedback@umcsn.com
www.umcsn.com

Brian Brannman, CEO
Lawrence Barnard, Chief Operating Officer
Joan Brookhyser, Chief Medical Officer
University Medical Center is dedicated to providing the highest level of health care possible by maintaining its ongoing commitment to personal, individualized care for each patient.Through the latest treatment techniques, comfortable surroundings and a dedicated staff, that commitment is expressed every day, in every area of the hospital.

New Hampshire

6201 **Head Injury Treatment Program at Dover**
307 Plaza Dr
Dover, NH 03820-2455
603-742-2676
FAX: 603-749-5375
www.doverrehab.com

Sue Mills, Program Rep
Jill Bosa, Administrator
A provider of postacute services in the greater New Hampshire Seacost area. We accomodate 112 residents and are licensed by the state of New Hampshire. We employ nearly 150 licensed nurses, therapists, and other healthcare professionals, who strive to provide quality care. The goal of our patient service model is to bridge the gap between hospitalization and home so that recovery and physical functioning are maximized and hospital re-admission is minimized.

6202 **Lakeview NeuroRehabilitation Center**
244 Highwatch Road
Effingham, NH 03882
603-539-7451
800-473-4221
FAX: 603-539-8815
www.lakeviewsystem.com

Anton Merka, Chairman
Carolyn McDermott, President
Christopher Slover, Chief Executive Officer
Residential treatment center serving individuals with neurologic/behavioral disorders. Lakeview serves both children and adults in functionally based program environment. Transistional programs in various group homes also available to clients as they progress in their treatment.

6203 **Northeast Rehabilitation Hospital**
70 Butler St
Salem, NH 03079-3974
603-893-2900
800-825-7292
FAX: 603-893-1638
TTY: 800-439-2370
www.northeastrehab.com

John Prochilo, CEO
NRHN is an organization characterized by the positive and proactive commitment to the delivery of customer centered care. Our employees exemplify our organizational commitment to providing quality rehabilitation services throughout the continuum. NRHN will be prudent with all resources and will take individual and collective responsibility for fiscal health. NRHN will remain a model by which other rehabilitation and post acute networks seek to emulate.

6204 **St. Joseph Hospital Rehabilitation**
172 Kinsley St
Nashua, NH 03060-3688
603-595-3076
800-210-9000
FAX: 603-595-3635
www.stjosephhospital.com

Judy Grilli, Medical Staff Officer
A comprehensive healthcare system that serves the Greater Nashua area, western New Hampshire and Northern Massachusetts. Our hospital is licensed for 208 beds and includes a Level 2 Trauma Center. In addition to the hospital, St. Joseph Healthcare system also includes a satellite emergency center in Milford, 5 family medical centers, a large network of primary care and specialty physician practices.

New Jersey

6205 **Betty Bacharach Rehabilitation Hospital**
61 W Jimmie Leeds Rd
Pomona, NJ 08240-9102
609-652-7000
FAX: 609-652-7487
www.bacharach.org

Philip J. Perskie, Esq., Chairman
Roy Goldberg, Vice Chairman
Craig Anmuth, Medical Director
Therapists, nurses and other specialists, led by physiatrists - doctors specially trained in the medical practice of physical medicine and rehabilitation.

6206 **Children's Specialized Hospital**
200 Somerset St.
New Brunswick, NJ 08901
888-244-5373
www.childrens-specialized.org

Warren E. Moore, President & CEO
Charles Chianese, Vice President & Chief Operating Officer
Joseph J. Dobosh Jr., Vice President & Chief Financial Officer
New Jersey's largest comprehensive pediatric rehabilitation hospital, treats children and adolescents from birth through 21 years of age. Programs include spinal dysfunction, brain injury, respiratory, burn, Day Hospital, early intervention, preschool, and cognitive rehabilitation.

6207 HealthSouth Rehabilitation Hospital
14 Hospital Dr
Toms River, NJ 08755-6402
732-244-3100
FAX: 732-244-7790
www.rehabnj.com/tomsriver/

Patty Ostaszewski, CEO
Joseph Stillo, Medical Director
A comprehensive 131-bed medical rehabilitation hospital dedicated to treating individuals with a variety of physical disabilities resulting from injury and illness. We serve all of New Jersey, Manhattan, and Philiadelphia. Accredited by the Joint Commission on Accreditation of Healthcare Organizations (JCAHO). The mission of the hospital is to get people back to work, to play, to living.

6208 JFK Johnson Rehab Institute
65 James St
Edison, NJ 08820-3947
732-321-7070
FAX: 732-321-0994
www.njrehab.org

Krishna Urs, Physician
David Brown, Physician
JRI has developed programs in such specialties as stroke rehabilitation, orthopedic programs, fitness, cardiac rehabilitation, women's health, pediatrics and brain injury rehabilitation. We also offer the most sophisticated diagnostic services available.

6209 Kessler Institute for Rehabilitation
1199 Pleasant Valley Way
West Orange, NJ 07052
973-731-3600
877-322-2580
FAX: 973-243-6819
www.kessler-rehab.com

Sue Kida, President
Provides physical medicine and rehabilitation through the integration of highly specialized care, treatment, technology, education, research, and advocacy.

6210 Mediplex Rehab: Camden
1 Cooper Plz
Camden, NJ 08103-1461
856-342-2300
FAX: 856-342-7979
www.cooperhealth.org

John P. Sheridan, Jr. President/CEO
Adrienne Kirby, Phd, President/CEO
Raymond L. Baraldi, Interim Chief Medical Officer
Cooper University Hospital is the leading provider of comprehensive health services, medical education and clinical research in Southern New Jersey and the Delaware Valley. With over 550 physicians in over 75 specialties, Cooper is uniquely equipped to provide an almost unlimited number of medical services. The hospital is committed to excellence in medical education, patient care, and research. Offers training programs to medical students, residents, and nurses in a variety of specialties.

6211 Universal Institute Rehabilitation & Fitness Center
15 Microlab Rd
Ste 101
Livingston, NJ 07039
973-992-8181
800-468-5440
FAX: 973-992-7178
www.uirehab.com

Adam Steinberg, President
Lisa Lasso, Vice President, Chief Financial Officer
Universal institute is a 15,000 square foot, state of the art rehabilitation facility that specializes in neurological disorders such as brain injuries, spinal cord injury, strokes, etc. Services include PT, OT, speech patholgy, cognitive remediation, aqua therapy and EMG biofeedback.

New Mexico

6212 HealthSouth Rehabilitation Center: New Mexico
7000 Jefferson St NE
Albuquerque, NM 87109-4357
505-344-9478
800-293-7226
FAX: 505-345-6722
www.healthsouthnewmexico.com

Sylvia Kelly, CEO
Rocky BigCrane, Director of Plant Operations
Lisa Brower, Director of Therapy Operations
Our hospital offers highly specialized inpatient rehabilitation services. From hip fractures to joint replacements and stroke to Parkinson's disease - our hospital has the experts, technology and experience to meet your rehabilitation needs.

6213 St. Joseph Rehabilitation Hospital and Outpatient Center
Ardence
505 Elm St NE
Albuquerque, NM 87102-2500
505-727-4700
FAX: 505-727-4793

Janelle Raborn, Administrator/CEO
Sherrie Peterson, Director
A member of the four hospital, St. Joseph healthcare system, this facility provides inpatient and outpatient care for those requiring physical medicine and rehabilitation. Specialty programs include brain injury, stroke, spinal cord, orthopedics, occupational and physical therapies, clinical psychology, speech/language pathology, hand clinic and functional capacity evaluations. The only facility in New Mexico accredited in four areas by the commission on accreditation of rehab facilities.

New York

6214 Burke Rehabilitation Hospital
785 Mamaroneck Ave
White Plains, NY 10605-2523
914-597-2500
888-99 -URKE
FAX: 914-946-0866
web@burke.org
www.burke.org

John Ryan, Executive Director
Mary Beth Walsh, M.D., Executive Medical Director/CEO
Brett Langley, Physician .
We provide inpatient and outpatient care for a broad range of neurological, musculoskeletal, cardiac, and pulmonary disabilities caused by disease or injury. Burke treats patients who have suffered a stroke, spinal cord injury, brain injury, amputation, joint replacement, complicated fracture, arthritis, cardiac and pulmonary disease, and neurological disorders. Patients are most frequently transferred to Burke from acute care hospitals once their condition is stable and they are able to partici

6215 Occupational Therapy Strategies and Adaptations for Independent Daily Living
Haworth Press
10 Alice St
Binghamton, NY 13904-1503
607-722-5857
800-429-6784
FAX: 607-722-6362
orders@haworthpress.com
www.tandf.co.uk

This contains clinical expertise of some fourteen authors or author teams addressing the issue of occupational therapy to assist in independent daily living. Also available as hardcover. *$74.95*
186 pages Softcover
ISBN 0-866563-50-4

6216 Rusk Institute of Rehabilitation Medicine
301 East 17th Street
Second Avenue (in the Hospital for
New York, NY 10016-4901
212-263-6034
FAX: 212-263-8510
DevelopmentOffice@nyumc.org
www.med.nyu.edu/rusk

Steven Flanagan, Chairman

Operates under the auspices of the Dept. Of Rehabilitation Medicine of New York University School of Medicine, one of the nations foremost medical schools. The relationship between Rusk and other clinical and research units within the medical center contributes to an environment which provides the optimal rehabilitation setting for patients. Rusk provides patients with access to treatment across a continuum of care depending on their individual medical needs.

6217   Silvercrest Center for Nursing & Rehabilitation
144-45 87th Ave
Briarwood, NY 11435-3109   718-480-4000
                                800-645-9806
                          FAX: 718-658-2367
                    admissions@silvercrest.org
                         www.silvercrest.org
Andrea Gibbon, Clinical Care Coordinator
Penny Blakely, Unit Manager
The Silvercrest Center for Nursing and Rehabilitation has earned a wide-spread reputatiopn for combing the best in clinical care with the best in nursing care and for making available to its communities the broadest menu of services to ease a patients' path to recovery from hospital to home. The Center is for the treatment of medically complex patients beginning their recovery, for the rehabilitation of patients who need restorative therapy before going home and much more.

6218   Vocational Rehabilitation and Employment
Books on Special Children
PO Box 305
Congers, NY 10920-305   845-638-1236
                       FAX: 845-638-0847
                    www.vba.va.gov/bln/vre/
Defines kinds of work, expectations, goals and programs. Contributions in general issues of supported employment, training and management and community based programs. *$47.00*
372 pages Hardcover

North Carolina

6219   Horizon Rehabilitation Center
Trans Health Incorporated
3100 Erwin Rd
Durham, NC 27705-4505   919-383-1546
                              800-541-7750
                        FAX: 919-383-0862
A 125-bed rehabilitation, subacute and long term care facility. HRC is JCAHO and CARF accredited with a physician-directed rehabilitation program, internal case management and a therapy department composed of physical, occupational, speech, recreational and respiratory therapists - pulmonary rehabilitation/ventilator unit.

6220   Integrated Health Services of Durham
Duke University Medical Center
3100 Erwin Rd
Durham, NC 27705-4505   919-383-1546
                        FAX: 919-383-0862
Aaron Lony, Administrator

6221   Learning Services Corporation
Corporate Office
10 Speen St
Ste 4
Framingham, MA 01701-4661   508-626-3671
                                  888-419-9955
                            FAX: 866-491-7396
                       www.learningservices.com
Susan Snow, Director of Admissions
Deb. Braunling-McMorrow, Ph, President and CEO
A licensed postacute rehabilitation program for adults who have an acquired brain injury. Individuals who are enrolled in the program participate in active, intensive rehabilitation carried out by a team of neuropsychology, speech/language therapy, physical therapy, occupational therapy, vocational services, family services and life skills training. Services include residential rehabilitation, home based treatment, day treatment, subacute rehabilitation and supported living.

Ohio

6222   Columbus Rehab & Subacute
44 S Souder Ave
Columbus, OH 43222-1539   614-228-5900
                          FAX: 614-228-3989
                www.columbusrehabskillednursing.com
Kelly Fligor, Administrator
Columbus Rehabilitation and Subacute Institute is a leading provider of long-term skilled nursing care and short-term rehabilitation solutions. Our 120 bed facility offers a full continuum of services and care focused around each individual in today's ever-changing healthcare environment.

6223   Great Lakes Regional Rehabilitation Center
3700 Kolbe Rd
Lorain, OH 44053-1611   440-960-3470
                        FAX: 440-960-4636
Julie Jones, Manager
Provides excellent, innovative and comprehensive rehabilitation programs to people in our community. Committed to a better quality of life for all individuals, the Rehabilitation Center has grown to become a regional resource for individuals needing all types of rehabilitation services.

6224   HCR Health Care Services
1 Seagate
Toledo, OH 43604-1541   419-321-5470
                              800-736-4427
                        FAX: 419-252-5543
Specialty transitional care and intensive rehabilitation services. Specialized services are focused on patients with catastrophic conditions or whose length of stay at an acute care or rehabilitation hospital can be dramatically reduced by transferring to a subacute level of care.

6225   Heather Hill Rehabilitation Hospital
Heather Hill
12340 Bass Lake Rd
Chardon, OH 44024-8327   440-285-4040
                               800-423-2972
                         FAX: 440-285-0946
                      info@heatherhill.org
Ed Davis, Operations
Donald Goddard, Chief Medical Officer
Individualized treatment programs for adults and adolescents can participate in and benefit from three-plus hours a day of active therapy.

6226   Parma Community General Hospital Acute Rehabilitation Center
7007 Powers Blvd
Parma, OH 44129-5437   440-743-3000
                       FAX: 440-843-4387
                    www.parmahospital.org
David Nedrich, Chairman
Thomas P. O'Donnell, First Vice Chairman
Nancy E. Hatgas, Second Assistant Treasurer
Parma Hospital offers acute and subacute inpatient care including specialty centers for heart, cancer, robotic surgery, orthopedics, pain management, acute rehabilitation and bariatric care.

6227   Rehabilitation Institute of Ohio at Miami Valley Hospital
1 Wyoming St
Dayton, OH 45409-2793   937-208-8000
                        TTY:937-208-2006
                    www.miamivalleyhospital.com
Vanessa Sandarusi, Executive Director
Anita Marie Greer, Program Manager, Acute Therapy Services
Jessica Hallum, Nurse Manager of the Inpatient Rehabilitation Unit
The Miami Valley Hospital Rehabilitation Institute of Ohio (RIO) is one of the largest and most comprehensive rehabilitation services providers in the United States. RIO offers a full spectrum of specialized rehabilitation programs delivered by the region's most experienced rehabilitation experts.

6228 Shriners Burn Institute: Cincinnati Unit
Shriners Hospitals for Children Cincinnati
3229 Burnet Ave
Cincinnati, OH 45229-3095   513-872-6000
                                             800-875-8580
                                         FAX: 513-872-6999
                        www.shrinershospitalsforchildren.org

Richard Kagan, Chief of Staff
Petra Warner, Assistant Chief of Staff
Tony Lewgood, Interim Administrator
All the attention and resources are focused on just one kind of patient-the burn-injured child. Shriners combine excellent clinical skill, compassionate care, and innovative research, providing comprehensive pediatric burn care and reconstructive rehabilitation to achieve the best possible outcome for a child that has suffered a burn injury. There is never a charge to the patient or family for any of the medical care or services provided by the Shriners Hospitals throughout North America.

6229 St. Francis Health Care Centre
401 N Broadway St
Green Springs, OH 44836-9653   419-639-2626
                                             800-248-2552
                                         FAX: 419-639-6225

Kim Eicher, CEO
Jane Holmer, Admissions Coordinator
Provides compassionate care for the elderly and physically challenged. We are a healthcare ministry under the sponsorship of the Franciscan Sisters of Our Lady of Perpetual Help. As a Catholic facility. we respectfully offer those we serve, care hope and dignity in a joyful and compassionate manner.

6230 St. Rita's Medical Center Rehabilitation Services
730 W Market St
Lima, OH 45801-4602   419-227-3361
                                             800-232-7762
                                         FAX: 419-226-9750

James Reber, CEO
The St. Rita's Inpatient Acute Care Rehabilitation service provides individualized service to you or your family member 7 days a week, wherever you might stay in the hospital. Acute rehabilitation care includes physical, occupational, and speech therapy services. Our goal is to make you as independent as possible before your discarge to home or, when necessary to extended services in other parts of the hospital.

6231 University of Cincinnati Hospital
Health Alliance
234 Goodman St
Cincinnati, OH 45219-2316   513-584-1000
                                         FAX: 513-584-7712
                             universityhospital.uchealth.com/

James Kingsbury, President/CEO
University Hospital has an international reputation, bringing thousands of people, from the region and around the world to Cincinnati to receive care from world renowned physicians in state-of-the-art medical facilities.

6232 Upper Valley Medical/Rehab Services
3130 N County Road
25-A
Troy, OH 45373-1309   937-440-4000
                                         FAX: 937-440-7337
                                             info@uvmc.com
                                             www.uvmc.com

Rafay Atiq, Director Rehab Services
A not-for-profit health care system serving the health care needs of Miami County and the surrounding area. The health care system features a state-of-the-art acute care hospital which opened in 1998. Comprehensive inpatient and outpatient services are provided with a full compliment of diagnostic and treatment services and behavioral health care programs.

Oklahoma

6233 Hilcrest Medical Center: Kaiser Rehab Center
1125 S Trenton Ave
Tulsa, OK 74120-5498   918-579-7100
                                         FAX: 918-579-7110
                                             www.hillcrest.com

Perri Craven, Medical Director
Kaiser Rehabilitation Center offers a wide range of services to help people regain functionality and independence after a debilitating injury or illness. Our approach to rehabilitation is a team approach, bringing the expertise of physicians, therapists, nurses and other health professionals together with patient family to achieve the best possible outcome. Each patient is given an individualized treatment plan that stimulates and challenges them to achieve their maximum potential.

6234 Jane Phillips Medical Center
Jane Phillips Medical Center
3500 E Frank Phillips Blvd
Bartlesville, OK 74006-2464   918-333-7200
                                         FAX: 918-331-1360
                                             www.jpmc.org

David Stire, CEO
Mike Moore, CFO
Jane Phillips Health System is sponsored by St. John Health System. This partnership helps our patients by ensuing access to the most sophisticated levels of care availiable in this area. It offers a wide range of services, including general medicine, surgery, cardiopulmonary care, maternal and infant care, cancer treatment, geriatric care, orthopedics, and physical medicine.

6235 Jim Thorpe Rehabilitation Center at Southwest Medical Center
Southwest Medical Center
4100 S. Douglas Ave.
Oklahoma City, OK 73109   405-644-5445
                                             800-677-1238
                                         FAX: 405-644-5384

Al Moorad, Medical Director
Provides inpatient rehabilitation for people with head injuries, spinal cord injuries, orthopedic conditions, pain management, neurological diseases, strokes and a variety of diagnoses that stop individuals from being able to take care of themselves independently. Services available include medical direction, physical therapy, social work, occupational therapy, speech therapy, recreational therapy, and aftercare follow-up.

6236 Mercy Memorial Health Center-Rehab Center
1011 14th Ave NW
Ardmore, OK 73401-1828   580-223-5400
                                             800-572-1182
                                         FAX: 580-220-6463
                                             www.mercy.net

Jan Shores, Manager
Lynn Britton Britton, President/CEO
Randy Combs, Executive Vice President Strategic Growth
A full service tertiary hospital with 176 licensed beds, 913 co-workers and 100 physicians. Four primary care clinics

6237 St. Anthony Hospital: Rehabilitation Unit
St. Anthony Hospital
1000 N Lee Ave
Oklahoma City, OK 73102-1036   405-272-7000
                                             800-851-0888
                                         FAX: 405-272-7075
                                         st_anthony@ssmhc.com
                                             www.saintsok.com

S Beaver, President
18 spacious private rooms, each with bathroom, and furnishings designed with patient safety in mind. Horticulture room where patients can work with plants and flowers as part of their rehabilitation. And a residential-style training apartment with fully equipped kitchen, bathroom, and bedroom to make the patient feel more at home.

6238 Valir Health
700 NW 7th St
Oklahoma City, OK 73102-1212   405-609-3600
888-898-2080
FAX: 405-605-8638
info@valir.com
www.valir.com

Dirk O'Hara, Principal
Tonya Purvine, Corporate Compliance Officer
Inpatient Rehab Facility including all therapy services serving people who have been injured and had an illness resulting in a decreased level of independence.

Oregon

6239 Shriners Hospitals for Children: Portland
3101 SW Sam Jackson Park Rd
Portland, OR 97239-3095   503-241-5090
800-237-5055
FAX: 503-221-3701
www.shrinershospitalsforchildren.org
Michael Aiona, Chief of Staff
Craig Patchin, Administrator
Mark Thoreson, Development Officer
Pediatric orthopedic and plastic surgery; inpatient and outpatient services. No charge for any services provided at the Hospital. Diagnosis, rehabilitation, surgery, sports and recreation for ages 0-18 for people with physical disabilities involving bones, muscles or joints or in need of plastic surgery for burn scars or cleft lip/palate.

Pennsylvania

6240 Allied Services John Heinz Institute of Rehabilitation Medicine
150 Mundy St
MAC III Building, 1st Floor
Wilkes Barre, PA 18702-6830   570-826-3900
FAX: 570-830-2027
www.allied-services.org
Gerald Franceski, Chairman
Thomas Speicher, Vice-Chairman
William Conaboy, CEO
John Heinz Rehab is one of the foremost providers of rehabilitation in the country. Under the supervision of board-certified psychiatrists, a team of highly qualified professionals provides a broad range of specialized services and therapies for inpatients, with speacialized programs in the areas of brain injury, injured worker recovery and pediatrics. John Heinz Rehab is the only CARF accredited program in northeastern Pennsylvania for treatment of brain injury rehabilitation.

6241 Allied Services Rehabilitation Hospital
475 Morgan Hwy
Scranton, PA 18508-2656   570-348-1359
FAX: 570-341-4548
www.allied-services.org
Gerald Franceski, Chairman
Thomas Speicher, Vice-Chairman
William Conaboy, CEO
Committed to help people overcome challenges and reach their greatest potential by providing quality care, people-oriented services and comfort.

6242 Brighten Place
131 North Main St
Chalfont, PA 18914-245   215-997-7746
FAX: 215-997-2517
brightenplace@enter.net
William Koffros, CEO
A residential brain injury program with the mission to encourage growth and foster independence on an individual level for each resident. We are CARF accredited and provide additional services which include a day program and respite care.

6243 Chestnut Hill Rehabilitation Hospital
8601 Stenton Ave
Wyndmoor, PA 19038-8312   215-233-6200
FAX: 215-233-6879
www.extendedcare.com
Cammi Lubking, Administrator
Chestnut Hill Rehab Hospital is dedicated to meeting patients' physical, emotional, social, and vocational goals. Through innovative programs, sophisticated equipment, and support by specially trained staff members committed to the progress of every patient, Chestnut Hill achieves results.

6244 Doylestown Hospital Rehabilitation Center
595 W State St
Doylestown, PA 18901-2597   215-345-2200
FAX: 215-345-2512
www.dh.org
James Brexler, President and Chief Executive Officer
Eleanor Wilson, RN, MSN, MHA, Vice President, Patient Services/Chief Operating Officer
Dan Upton, Vice President, Chief Financial Officer
The mission of Doylestown Hospital is to provide a responsive healing environment for patients and their families, and to improve the quality of life for all members of our community. We combine the creative energies of Medical Staff, Board, Associates and Volunteers to make Doylestown Hospital a place where each patient and family feels healed and whole, even when disease cannot be cured.

6245 Health Care Solutions
500 Abbott Dr
Ste B
Broomall, PA 19008-4301   610-544-6023
800-451-1671
FAX: 610-544-6035
www.lincare.com
John Byrnes, CEO
Shawn Schabel, President/COO
Develops unique containment programs, offers equipment set-up, patient instruction, patient assessment and equipment usage. Offers clinical services that include oxygen systems, ventilators, aerosol therapy, suction equipment, T.E.N.S. programs, compression pumps, custom orthotics, enteral feeding.

6246 HealthSouth Harmarville Rehabilitation Hospital
P.O.Box 11460
320 Guys Run Road
Pittsburgh, PA 15238-460   412-828-1300
877-937-7342
FAX: 412-828-7705
www.healthsouthharmarville.com
Ken Anthony, Chief Executive Officer
Thomas Franz, M.D., Medical Director
Catherine M. Birk, M.D., Staff Physiatrist
A 202-bed facility providing inpatient and outpatient physical medicine and rehabilitation to adults and adolescents in Pennsylvania, West Virginia, Ohio and Maryland.

6247 HealthSouth Nittany Valley Rehabilitation Hospital
Health South of Nittany Valley
550 W College Ave
Pleasant Gap, PA 16823-7401   814-359-3421
800-842-6026
FAX: 814-359-5898
www.nittanyvalleyrehab.com
Richard Allatt, Medical Director
Susan Hartman, CEO
Sara Godwin, CNO
Comprehensive inpatient and outpatient facilities. Treatment for symptoms relating to: stroke, head injury, pulmonary disease, orthopedic conditions, neurological disorders, cardiac illnesses and spinal cord injuries. Healthsouth Nittany Valley Rehabilitation Hospital is a part of Healthsouth's national network of more than 2,000 facilities in 50 states.

6248   HealthSouth Rehab Hospital Of Erie
143 E 2nd St
Erie, PA 16507-1501
814-878-1200
800-234-4574
FAX: 814-878-1399
www.healthsoutherie.com

Douglas Grisier, Medical Director
Shelly Mayes, Director of Therapy Operations
An acute inpatient rehabilitation hospital that was founded in 1986. HealthSouth Erie is one of the only rehabilitation hospitals in the country to hold a triple-certification by the Joint Commission in the areas of Brain Injury, Stroke and Parkinson's disease Rehabilitation.

6249   HealthSouth Rehabilitation Hospital of Altoona
2005 Valley View Blvd
Altoona, PA 16602-4548
814-944-3535
800-873-4220
FAX: 814-944-6160
www.healthsouthaltoona.com

Scott Filler, Chief Executive Officer
Paul Sutton, Director Of Clinical Services
Rakesh Patel, D.O., Medical Director
Inpatient and outpatient physical rehabilitation programs and services.

6250   Healthsouth Rehabilitation Hospital of Greater Pittsburgh
2380 McGinley Rd
Monroeville, PA 15146-4400
412-856-2400
FAX: 412-856-9320
www.lifecare-hospitals.com

Mary Lee Dadey, Administrator
Rehabilitation and long-term acute care hospital that treats brain injury, stroke, multiple sclerosis, Parkinson's disease, back and spinal cord injuries, cancer, pulmonary disease, cardiac disease, traumatic and work injuries.

6251   Healthsouth Rehabilitation Hospital of Mechanicsburg
175 Lancaster Blvd
Mechanicsburg, PA 17055-3562
717-691-3700
800-933-3831
FAX: 717-697-6524
www.healthsouthpa.com

Mark Freeburn, CEO
Annette Bates, Director of Marketing Operations
Jeff Brandenburg, MPT, Director of Therapy Operations
HealthSouth provides comprehensive rehabilitation and recovery services to patients with stroke, brain injury, hip fracture, medically complex, pulmonary, wound, spinal cord injury, amputation, and other neuro-muscular, and orthopedic impairments. Our primary goal is to provide individualized treatment programs to people requiring physical rehabilitation and medical recovery in order to help patients get back to work, to play, to living.

6252   Healthsouth Rehabilitation Hospital of York
1850 Normandie Dr
York, PA 17408-1552
717-767-6941
FAX: 717-767-8776
www.healthsouthyork.com

Sally Arthur, Director of Human Resources
Bruce Sicilia, Medical Director
Elaine Charest, Director of Therapy Operations
A 120-bed rehabilitation hospital dedicated to providing advanced, comprehensive services to patients who have suffered head injury, spinal cord injury, stroke, burns, amputation, chronic pain and other neurological and musculoskeletal disorders. HRH of York provides outpatient services in seven locations. Healthsouth is located in York, Pennsylvania, approximately 50 miles north of Baltimore and 25 miles south of Harrisburg.

6253   Magee Rehabilitation Hospital
1513 Race St
Philadelphia, PA 19102-1177
215-587-3000
800-966-2433
FAX: 215-568-3736
www.mageerehab.org

Jack Carroll, CEO
A not-for-profit health organization which is the home to the nation's first brain injury rehabilitation program to be accredited by the Commission on the Accreditation of Rehabilitation Facilities

(CARF) and is one of 14 federally designated Regional Spinal Cord Injury Centers. Our staff and management are committed to restoring the highest level of independence possible to individuals with disabilities.

6254   Moss Rehabilitation Hospital
1200 W Tabor Rd.
Philadelphia, PA 19141
215-456-9800
FAX: 215-456-9381
www.mossrehab.com

Thomas Smith, Chief Operating Officer
Alberto Esquenazi, Chief Medical Officer
Eileen Hartranft, Program Director
An outpatient services center providing rehabilitation services. This 152 bed facility offers comprehensive care to people with broad ranges of conditions, diagnostic laboratories and a multidisciplinary team of rehabilitation professionals.

6255   Shriners Hospitals for Children, Philadelphia
Shrinners Hospitals for Children
3551 N Broad St
Philadelphia, PA 19140-4131
215-430-4000
800-281-4051
FAX: 215-430-4126
www.shrinershq.org

Alan W. Madsen, Chairman of the Board
John A. Cinotto, 1st Vice President
Dale W. Stauss, 2nd Vice President
At Shriners Hospitals for Childrenr - Philadelphia, we provide state-of-the-art medical care for children with spinal cord injuries, as well as a host of orthopaedic and neuromusculoskeletal disorders and diseases

6256   Shriners Hospitals for Children, Erie
1645 W 8th St
Erie, PA 16505-5007
814-875-8700
FAX: 814-875-8756
www.shrinershq.org

John Lubahn, Chief of Staff
Charles Walczak, Administrator
The Shriners Hospitals for Children, Erie, is a 30-bed pediatric orthopaedic hospital providing comprehensive orthopaedic care to children at no charge. The hospital is one of 22 Shriners Hospitals throughout North America. The Erie Hospital accepts and treats children with routine and complex orthopaedic and neuromuscular problems, utilizing the latest treatments and technology available in pediatric orthopaedics, resulting in early ambulation and reduced length of stay.

6257   Shriners Hospitals, Philadelphia Unit, for Crippled Children
3551 N Broad St
Philadelphia, PA 19140-4105
215-430-4000
FAX: 215-430-4079
www.shrinershq.org/hospitals/philadelphia

Randal Betz, Chief of Staff
Ernest Perilli, Administrator
Provides comprehensive medical, surgical and rehabilitative care for children with orthopaedic conditions and spinal cord injuries. All services are provided at no charge. The hospital is one of 22 located throughout North America. In addition to treating children with routine and complex orthopaedic problems, the Philadelphia hospital provides a comprehensive and individualized rehabilitation program for children and adolescents who have sustained a traumatic injury to their spine.

South Carolina

6258   Colleton Regional Hospital: RehabCare Unit
501 Robertson Blvd
Walterboro, SC 29488-5714
843-782-2000
FAX: 843-549-7562
www.colletonmedical.com

Mitchell Mongel, CEO
Colleton Medical Center's 8-bed physical and mental rehabilitation department is the oldest in the Lowcountry and has been serving the community for nearly 20 years. Strives to provide patient-centered care in a family atmosphere. The team includes nurses, physical therapists, occupational therapists, speech ther-

apists, and nutritionists. The typical patient requires rehabilitation following a stroke, spinal injury, close head injury, and orthopedic rehabilitation.

6259   HealthSouth Rehab Hospital: South Carolina
2935 Colonial Dr
Columbia, SC 29203-6811   803-254-7777
                                    FAX: 803-414-1414
                               www.healthsouthcolumbia.com

W. Anthony Jackson, CEO
Lydia Carpenter, Director of Therapy Operations
Devin Troyer, M.D., Medical Director
Offers a wide range of specialized medical and therapeutic services designed to help physically disabled individuals reach their optimum level of function and independence.

6260   Shriners Hospitals for Children, Greenville
950 W Faris Rd
Greenville, SC 29605-4255   864-271-3444
                                          866-459-0013
                                    FAX: 864-271-4471
                          www.shrinershq.org/hospitals/greenville
Randall Romberger, Administrator
Peter Stasikelis, Chief of Staff
Tracy McReynolds, Development Officer
A 50-bed pediatric orthopaedic hospital providing comprehensive orthopaedic care to children at no charge to their families. The hospital is one of 22 Shriners Hospitals throughout North America. The hospital accepts and treats children with routine and complex orthopaedic problems, utilizing the latest tretments and technology avaiilable in pediatric orthopaedics, resulting in early ambulatory and reduced length of stay.

Tennessee

6261   Health South Cane Creek Rehabilitation Center
Health South Corporation
180 Mount Pelia Rd
Martin, TN 38237-3812   731-587-4231
                                    FAX: 731-588-1454
                            dayle.unger@healthsouth.com
                              www.healthsouthcanecreek.com
Eric Garrard, CEO
William Eason, Medical Director
Lindsey Box-Rotger, BSN, RN, C, Director of Quality and Risk Management
Offers a wide variety of programs and services for patients in need of acute rehabilitation. Programs and services are avaiilable through inpatient and outpaitent. Thereapy services avaiilable are physical, occupational, speech, and respiratory.

6262   HealthSouth Chattanooga Rehabilitation Hospital
2412 McCallie Ave
Chattanooga, TN 37404-3398   423-697-9129
                                          800-763-5189
                                    FAX: 423-697-9124
                            www.healthsouthchattanooga.com
Scott Rowe, CEO
Amjad Munir, Medical Director
Karen Jonakin, Director Clinical Services
Offers orthopaedic rehabilitation, stroke rehabilitation, amputee rehabilitation, brain injury program, pain management, ventilator weaning, carpal tunnel screening, low intensity program, oncology program, aquatic therapy, day treatment, burn program and outpatient services.

6263   HealthSouth Rehabilitation Cntr/Tennessee
1282 Union Ave
Memphis, TN 38104-3414   901-722-2000
                                    FAX: 901-729-5171
                                  healthsouthmemphis.com
Tracy Willis, CEO
Toni Wackerfuss, Director of Therapy Operation
An 80-bed acute medical rehabilitation hospital that offers comprehensive inpatient and outpatient rehabilitation services.

6264   James H And Cecile C Quillen Rehabilitation Hospital
2511 Wesley St
Johnson City, TN 37601-1723   423-952-1700
                                          800-235-1994
                                    FAX: 423-283-0906
                                        www.msha.com
Tammy Bishop, Manager
A 60-bed, freestanding comprehensive medical rehabilitation hospital. Full range of outpatient and day treatment, 14-bed traumatic brain injury unit, in ground therapeutic pool, transitional living apartment, outdoor ambulation course. All inpatient and outpatient programs utilize an interdisciplinary team approach designed to improve a patient's physical and cognitive functioning.

6265   Nashville Rehabilitation Hospital
610 Gallatin Ave
Nashville, TN 37206-3225   615-650-2600
                                          800-227-3108
                                    FAX: 615-650-2562
Alan Miller, CEO
Marc Miller, President
A free-standing physical rehabilitation facility offering services to patients on an inpatient and outpatient basis. Programs include CVA, orthopedic, neuromuscular, traumatic brain injury, spinal cord injury, general rehabilitation and Bridges - geriatric psychiatric unit. Intra-disciplinary team approach is utilized to assist patients in obtaining their maximum fuctional level.

6266   Patricia Neal Rehab Center : Ft. Sanders Regional Medical Center
Covenant Health
1901 W Clinch Ave
Knoxville, TN 37916-2307   865-541-1111
                                          800-728-6325
                                    FAX: 865-541-2247
                                      www.patneal.org
J.E. Henry, Co-Chair
David Kugley, Co-Chair
Mary Dillon, M.D., Medical Director, Patricia Neal Rehabilitation Center
A CARF accredited 73-bed facility, it offers a comprehensive team approach to care. Physical, occupational, recreational, behavioral medicine and speech language therapists work with physiatrists to develop individual plans of care designed to return patients to a normal lifestyle as quickly as possible. In addition, rehabilitation nurses collaborate with specialists to teach self-care techniques and provide education to help patients reach optimal functionality.

6267   Rehabilitation Center Baptist Hospital
137 E Blount Ave
Suite 6-B
Knoxville, TN 37920-1643   865-632-5520
Primary focus: Mix of mental health and substance abuse services.

6268   Rehabilitation Center at McFarland Hospital
University Medical Center
500 Park Ave
Lebanon, TN 37087-3721   615-449-0500
                                    FAX: 615-453-7405
                              www.universitymedicalcenter.com
Saad Ehtisham, CEO
Matt Caldwell, Chief Executive Officer
Michael Cherry, Chief Financial Officer
An Acute Inpatient Rehab, located on the hospital's second floor. The center has 26 patient rooms, three therapy treatment rooms, a patient dining area, and an 'activities of daily living' area which includes a kitchen/laundry area and a patient apartment, for those individuals who will be returning home.

6269   St. Mary's Medical Center: RehabCare Center
900 E Oak Hill Ave
Knoxville, TN 37917-4505   865-545-7962
                                    FAX: 865-545-8133
                                      www.tennova.com
Jeffrey Ashin, President
Committed to providing individualized and flexable treatment programs designed for individuals who have been disabled by an injury or illness. The primary mission of the RehabCare Center is

to help patients achieve basic skills that may allow independent living and working.

6270 Sumner Regional Medical Center
555 Hartsville Pike
Gallatin, TN 37066-2400
615-328-8888
FAX: 615-328-3903
www.mysumnermedical.com

Susan Peach, BSN, MBA, CEO
Kevin Rinks, Chief Financial Officer
Michael S. Herman, Chief Operating Officer
SRMC operates as a 155-bed healthcare facility and provides quality Gallatin hospital and medical care services in numerous areas, including cancer treatment, cardiac care, same- day surgery, orthopaedics, diagnostics, women's health and rehabilitation services. As the community grows, SRMC strives to continually improve its services and programs to meet the changing needs of its service area.

Texas

6271 Bayshore Medical Center: Rehab
4000 Spencer Hwy
Pasadena, TX 77504-1202
713-359-2000
FAX: 713-359-1283
www.bayshoremedical.com

Dr. Charles Bessire, Board
Jeanna Barnard, FACHE, CEO
Alice Hopkins Adams, Board
A 345-bed facility, providing the award-winning care for which we have been nationally recoginzed. Members are here to care for the physical and emotional well-being of those who arrive at Bayshore Medical Center often frightned, in pain and perhaps even alone. We offer patients solace and security through constant communication and compassionate listening in the midst of their medical emergencies and surgical or diagnostic procedures. Kindness, empathy & quality are triats that patients trust.

6272 Cecil R Bomhr Rehabilitation Center of Nacogdoches Memorial Hospital
1204 N Mound St
Nacogdoches, TX 75961-4027
936-564-4611
FAX: 936-564-4616
info@nacmem.org
www.nacmem.org

Jerry Whitaker, Chairperson
Larry Walker, M.D., Vice-Chairperson
Lisa King, Secretary
The goal of Nacogdoches Memorial Hospital's rehabilitation services is to assist patients in attaining their highest potential activity level for independent daily living, thereby reducing the number of necessary hospitalizations. Keeping folks healthy and in their homes lowers healthcare costs for all of us.

6273 Covenant Health Systems Owens White Outpatient Rehab Center
9812 Slide Rd
Lubbock, TX 79424-1116
806-725-5627
FAX: 806-723-6009
www.covenanthealth.org

Walt Cathey, Manager
A comprehensive rehabilitation program designed to help patients attain their maximum level of independence following a debilitating stroke, illness or injury. Our fully accredited program features outpatient physical, occupational and speech language therapies, as well as certified athletic trainers and a certified strength and conditioning specialist.

6274 Gonzales Warm Springs Rehabilitation Hospital
200 Memorial Dr
Luling, TX 78648-3213
830-875-8400
FAX: 830-875-5029
www.warmsprings.org

Anthony Misitano, President/CEO
Vonnie Cromwell, Operations Manager
Statewide not-for-profit system of inpatient and outpatient rehabilitation speciality centers. Throughout the communities we serve, the Warm Springs Rehabilitation System offers hope and

acts as a catalyst for achieving an optimal quality of life by providing comprehensive physical and/or cogenitive care. Investing resources in educational and recreational programs. Supporting research efforts.

6275 Harris Methodist Fort Worth Hospital Mabee Rehabilitation Center
1301 Pennsylvania Ave
Fort Worth, TX 76104-2122
817-250-2760
866-847-7342
FAX: 814-250-6846
www.texashealth.org

Lillie Biggins, B.S.N., M.S.N, CEO/President
Elaine Nelson, R.N., M.S.N., Chief Nursing Officer
Joseph Prosser, M.D., M.B.A., Chief Medical Officer
Professionals at the Harris Methodist Fort Worth Hospital's Mabee Rehabilitation Center work closely with each patient to develop a specialzed treatment plan for personal achievement. The center offers highly trained clinical staff members and spacious facilities An incredibly wide range of treatment programs and educational services are provided for both inpatient and outpatient needs.

6276 HealthSouth Plano Rehabilitation Hospital
6701 Oakmont Blvd.
Fort Worth, TX 76132-7526
817-370-4700
FAX: 972-423-4293
www.healthsouth.com

Jon F. Hanson, Chairman
John W. Chidsey, Board of director
Donald L. Correll, Board of director
A 62-bed medical reahabilitation facility serving inpatient and out patient needs in the Northern Dallas area. The team coordinate all aspects of the patient's rehabilitation to maximize results. The overall effort is directed by board-certified physical medicine and rehabilitation physicians who specialize in medical rehabilitation. Whatever the cause of the disability, our services can benefit patients who have functional limitations in such areas as mobility, communication and self care.

6277 HealthSouth Rehab Hospital Of Arlington
3200 Matlock Rd
Arlington, TX 76015-2911
817-468-4000
FAX: 817-468-3055
www.healthsouth.com

Jon F. Hanson, Chairman
John W. Chidsey, Board of director
Donald L. Correll, Board of director
A modern 65-bed hospital dedicated to providng inpatient programs in a general rehabilitation setting for persons recovering for a disabling injury or illness. As part of our continuum of care, we also offer outpatient therapy, a day program, and individual therapy services. Our goal is to help our patients resume a productive and more meaningful life through appropriate rehabilitative care and restorative nursing in a wellness-oriented environment that promotes healing and functional recovery.

6278 HealthSouth Rehab Hospital Of Austin
1215 Red River St
Austin, TX 78701-1921
512-474-5700
FAX: 512-479-3765
www.healthsouthaustin.com

Duke Saldiver, CEO
Corey Helm Swartz, Director of Therapy Operations
Maria Arizmendez, M.D., Medical Director
A comprehensive 83 bed medical rehabilitation hospital serving the needs of patients in the Central Texas area. The mission is to promote recovery for persons with disabling conditions by providing individualized treatment so they can reach the highest level of physical, social and emotional well-being.

6279 HealthSouth Rehabilitation Center of Humble Texas
19002 McKay Blvd
Humble, TX 77338
281-446-6148
FAX: 281-446-5616
www.healthsouthhumble.com

Angie Simmons, CEO
Mikael Simpson, Director of Therapy Operations
Emile Mathurin, Jr., M.D., Medical Director
Offers comprehensive rehabilitation services for patients with diverse diagnoses. Rehabilitation can be defined as

multidisciplinary therapy designed to increase patient's overall functioning to a level that meets or exceeds where the patient was prior to illness or injury or to maximize current level of ability. The benefits of these services to patients and their families is invaluable.

6280 HealthSouth Rehabilitation Hospital
6701 Oakmont Blvd
Fort Worth, TX 76132-2957   817-370-4700
                                  FAX: 817-370-4977
                                  www.healthsouthcityview.com

Deborah Hopps, CEO
Mark Bussell, Medical Director
Mark Bussell, M.D., Medical Director
A 62-bed acute medical rehabilitation hospital that offers comprehensive inpatient and outpatient rehabilitation services.

6281 HealthSouth Rehabilitation Hospital of Beaumont
3340 Plaza 10 Dr
Beaumont, TX 77707-2551   409-835-0835
                                 FAX: 409-835-0898

Sam Coco, Director of Therapy Operations
HJ Gaspard, CEO
Linda Smith, M.D., Medical Director
A state of the art freestanding 61-bed comprehensive physical rehabilitation hospital. The hospital is specifically designed to meet the needs of individuals and their families who have experienced a disabling injury or illness or are recovering from a surgery. An experienced team of physicians, nurses, therapists, treat conditions and other disorders.

6282 HealthSouth Rehabilitation Institute Of San Antonio (RIOSA)
9119 Cinnamon Hill
San Antonio, TX 78240-5401   210-691-0737
                                    FAX: 210-558-1297
                                    www.hsriosa.com

Scott Butcher, CEO
Richard Senelick, Medical Director
Christine Chesnut, OTR, MPH, Director of Therapy Operations
HealthSouth Rehabilitation Institute of San Antonio is the largest free-standing physical rehabilitation hospital in San Antonio and is proud to enter our 11th year of delivering quality, comprehensive medical rehabilitation in a pristine environment. HealthSouth annually serves over 1,500 inpatients and more then 20,000 outpatient visits from throughout San Antonio and Mexico. 108-bed hospital has more then 300 personell on staff providing extensive experience.

6283 Hillcrest Baptist Medical Center: Rehab Care Unit
100 Hillcrest Medical Blvd
Waco, TX 76712-3239   254-202-2000
                             FAX: 254-202-8975
Fred Walters, President
Jon Ellis, Secretary
A fully accredited 393-bed acute care facility in Waco including a Level II Trauma Center, Hillcrest Family Health Center, a network of family medicine clinics; and many key services. Hillcrest is a ministry of Texas Baptists and is one of 7 health care institutions affiliated with the Baptist General Convention of Texas.

6284 Institute for Rehabilitation & Research
1333 Moursund St
Houston, TX 77030-3405   713-942-6159
                                800-447-3422
                                FAX: 713-942-5289
                                tirr.referrals@memorialhermann.org
                                www.memorialhermann.org

Jeffrey Berliner, Physician
Michelle Pu, Physician
A national center for information, training, research, and technical assistance in independent living. The goal is to extend the body of knowledge in independent living and to improve the utilization of results of research programs and demonstration projects in this field. It has developed a variety of strategies for collecting, synthesizing, and disseminating information related to the field of independent living.

6285 Midland Memorial Hospital & Medical Center
400 Rosalind Redfern Grover Parkway
Midland, TX 79701-9980   432-685-1111
                                800-833-2916
                                russell.meyers@midland-memorial.com
                                www.midland-memorial.com

J.T. Lent Jr., President
Russell Meyers, CEO
Greg Wright, Board of Directors
The Occupational and Physical Therapy Center is a specialized outpatient clinic. The clinic provides a wide variety of rehabilitation services designed to adequately assist you in returning back to your normal duties. Our highly trained professionals are here to help you with all your rehabilitation needs.

6286 Navarro Regional Hospital: RehabCare Unit
Navarro Hospital
3201 W State Highway 22
Corsicana, TX 75110-2469   903-654-6800
                                  FAX: 903-654-6955
                                  www.navarrohospital.com

Xavier Villarreal, CEO
Glenda Teri, Chief Nursing Officer
The rehab unit is located on the 4th floor and is designed for individuals who require intense rehab for an injury or disease process where the goal would be to return home. Our team is committed to helping individuals return to the highest level of functioning. Our team consists of physicians, nurses, physical therapist, occupational therapist, speech therapist, social workers, dieticians and other professionals as needed.

6287 Rebound: Northeast Methodist Hospital
12412 Judson Rd
Live Oak, TX 78233-3255   210-757-7000
                                 FAX: 210-757-5072

Joe Hernandez, Manager
Methodist Healthcare provides quality, comprehensive rehabilitation services for children and adults. Working as a team, rehabilitation professionals help patients define and achieve individual goals in restoring function and productivity.

6288 Rio Vista Rehabilitation Hospital
1740 Curie Dr
El Paso, TX 79902-2900   915-544-8336
                                800-999-8392
                                FAX: 915-544-4838

Gene Miller, Administrator

6289 San Antonio Warm Springs Rehabilitation Hospital
5101 Medical Dr
San Antonio, TX 78229-4801   210-595-2380
                                    FAX: 210-614-0649
                                    www.warmsprings.org

Kurt Meyer, SVP Operations
Rick Marek, VP Post Acute Medical
A statewide not-for-profit system of inpatient and outpatient rehabilitation specialty centers. Warm Springs Rehabilitation System offers hope and acts as a catalyst for achieving an optimal quality of life by providing comprehensive physical and/or cognitive rehabilitative care. Invensting resources in educational and recreational programs. Supporting research efforts.

6290 Shannon Medical Center: RehabCare Unit
120 E Harris Ave
San Angelo, TX 76903-5904   325-653-6741
                                   FAX: 325-657-5706
                                   www.shannonhealth.com

Bryan Horner, CEO
Irv Zeitler, VP Medical Affairs
Shane Plymell, Chief financial officer
Committed to improving the health of our community, using the latest technologies available in the spirit of caring and integrity. Strives to create an environment committed to the values of accountability, service, pride, integrity, respect and excellence. We foster growth toward the highest quality care and customer service and strive for excellent financial performance. We hire and develop the best people to accomplish these tasks.

6291   Shriners Burn Institute: Galveston Unit
815 Market St
Galveston, TX 77550-2725   409-770-6600
                                        FAX: 409-770-6919
                                        www.totalburncare.com

David Herndon, Chief Of Staff
David Ferrell, F.A.C.H.E., Administrator
Providing expert, orthopaedic and burn care to children under 18
regardless of ability to pay.

6292   Shriners Hospitals for Children, Houston
6977 Main St
Houston, TX 77030-3701   713-797-1616
                                            800-853-1240
                                        FAX: 713-797-1029
                                        www.shrinershq.org

David Ferrell, Administrator
Douglas Barnes, Chief of Staff
Melanie Lux, M.D., Director
Shriners Hospitals provides at no charge quality pediatric orthopedic serivces to children ages newborn to 18 years old. These
services include both outpatient and inpatient needs. Specialties
include cerebrel palsy, spina bifida, scoliosis, hand, hip and feet
problems. An application is required and may be completed by
phone.

6293   South Arlington Medical Center: Rehab Care Unit
3301 Matlock Rd
Arlington, TX 76015-2908   817-472-4849
                                        FAX: 817-472-4946
                                        mca@hcahealthcare.com
                                        www.medicalcenterarlington.com
Patrice Oliver, Manaager
Above all else, we are committed to the care and improvement of
human life. In recognition of this committment, we strive to deliver high-quality, cost-effective healthcare in the communities
we serve.

6294   South Texas Rehabilitation Hospital
Ernest Health
425 E Alton Gloor Blvd
Brownsville, TX 78526-3361   956-554-6000
                                        FAX: 956-350-6150
                                        www.strh.ernesthealth.com
Christopher Wilson, Medical Director
Jessie Eason, CEO
Mary Valdez, Director of Marketing
STRH was designed for the provision of specialized rehabilita-
tive care, in the only freestanding acute rehabilitation hospital
serving Brownsville and the Rio Grande Valley. The hospital provides rehabilitative services for patients with functional deficits
as a result of debilitating illnesses or injuries.

6295   St. David's Rehabilitation Center
St. David s Medical Center
621 Radam Lane
Suite 200
Austin, TX 78745-4237   512-447-1083
                                        FAX: 512-447-1338
                                        www.stdavids.com
Anisa Godinez, Medical Director
Everett Heinze, MD Neurology, Medical Director
Tom Hill, MD, Medical Director
Mission is to provide exceptional care to every patient every day
with a spirit of warmth, friendliness and personal pride. Values
are integrity, compassion, accountability, respect and excellence.

6296   Texas NeuroRehab Center
1106 W Dittmar Rd
Austin, TX 78745-6328   512-444-4835
                                            800-252-5151
                                        FAX: 512-462-6749
Alison Crawford Sinsky, Inpatient and Outpatient Manager
Ed Varando, Occupational Therapy Manager
Internationally recognized provider in brain in-
jury/neurobehavioral treatment for children, adolescents, and
adults with complex medical, physical and/or behavioral issues.
Medical rehabilitation, neurobehavioral, and neuropsychiatric
programs combine traditional therapies with education, vocational, substance abuse, and sensory integration services.

6297   Texas Specialty Hospital at Dallas
7955 Harry Hines Blvd
Dallas, TX 75235-3305   214-637-0000
Robin Burns, CEO
66 beds offering active/acute rehabilitation, brain injury day
treatment, cognitive rehabilitation, complex care, extended rehabilitation and short term evaluation.

6298   Touchstone Neurorecovery Center
Nexus Health Systems
9297 Wahrenberger Rd
Conroe, TX 77304-2441   936-788-7770
                                            800-414-4824
                                        FAX: 936-788-7785
                                        tncinfo@nhsltd.com
John W. Cassidy, MD, Executive Medical Director
Jude Theriot, MD, Medical Director
Ron Tintner, MD, Associate Clinical Director
Touchstone provides treatment and rehabilitation in a residential
environment on a tranquil, wooded 26-acre site just north of
Houston in Conroe, TX. Touchstone offers customized treatment
programs designed to help individuals with known or suspected
brain injury or neurological deficits progress to their highest
functional level possible. Touchstone offers both on-campus and
off-campus housing in home-like settings for residents based on
their needs.

6299   Valley Regional Medical Center: RehabCare Unit
100A E Alton Gloor Blvd
Brownsville, TX 78526-3328   956-350-7000
                                        FAX: 956-350-7111
                                        www.valleyregionalmedicalcenter.com
Billy Bradford Jr., Chair
Francisco Javier Del Castillo, M, Vice Chair
Subramaniam Anandasivam, MD, Board
Our mission is to treat our community as family by providing
quality compassionate care.

Utah

6300   HealthSouth Rehab Hospital Of Utah
8074 S 1300 E
Sandy, UT 84094-743   801-561-3400
                                            801-565-6666
                                        FAX: 801-565-6576
                                        www.healthsouthutah.com
Phil Eaton, CEO
William McNutt, Director of Therapy Operations
Mark Rada, M.D., Interim Medical Director
A full spectrum of services, including inpatient, outpatient, day
hospital and home health. Holistic patient care, education and
community assimilation are the hallmarks of our programs, and
evidence of our leadership in the field of rehabilitation. Working
together as a team, we are able to tailor the needs of our patients
and provide the highest quality services. We believe that education and involvement of family and friends, will assist them in
maintaining independence after discharge.

6301   LDS Hospital Rehabilitation Center
8th Ave & C Street
Salt Lake City, UT 84143-0001   801-408-1100
                                            800-527-1118
                                        FAX: 801-408-5610
                                        www.intermountainhealthcare.org
Lizz Daley, Administrator
Jim Sheets, Administrator
Located within a Trauma I Center, this facility provides comprehensive inpatient and outpatient rehabilitation to people with
physical disabilities. CARF/JCAHO accredited. Low cost family
housing is available and Medicaid/Medicare is accepted.

6302   Primary Children's Medical Center
100 Mario Capecchi Dr
Salt Lake City, UT 84113-1100   801-662-1000
                                        FAX: 801-588-2318
                                        www.intermountainhealthcare.org
Scott Parker, President
Kevin Jones, Manager
Ore-Ofe O. Adesina, MD, Ophthalmology

Primary Children's Medical Center is the pediatric center serving 5 states in the Intermountain West Utah, Idaho, Wyoming, Nevada and Montana. The 289-bed facility is equipped and staffed to treat children with complex illness and injury. PCMC is owned by Intermountain Healthcare, a non-profit health care system. In addition, it is affiliated with the Dept. of Pediatrics, University of Utah, integrating pediatric programs. The hospital is designed to meet the needs of children & their families.

6303   Shriners Hospitals for Children: Intermountain
Fairfax Road at Virginia St
Salt Lake City, UT 84103   801-536-3500
                                             800-313-3745
                                        FAX: 801-536-3782
                                        www.shrinershq.org
Kevin Martin, Administrator
Jacques D'Astous, Chief of Staff
One of nineteen hospitals in North America specializing in pediatric orthopedics (plus four hospitals providing pediatric burn treatment). This hospital serves the Intermountain region. All services provided in the hospital are at no cost to family, insurance company, nor state/federal agency regardless of ability to pay.

6304   Stewart Rehabilitation Center: McKay Dee Hospital
4401 Harrison Blvd
Ogden, UT 84403-3195   801-387-2080
                                        FAX: 801-387-7720
                                www.intermountainhealthcare.org
Corey Anden, Nurse Coordinator
Judy Grover, Manager
With 10 affiliated clinics, McKay-Dee serves northern Utah, and portions of southeast Idaho and western Wyoming. A part of Intermountain Healthcare's system of 21 hospitals, McKay-Dee Hospital Center offers nationally ranked programs such as the Heart & Vascular Institute, the Newborn ICU and a new Cancer Treatment Center.

6305   University Healthcare-Rehabilitation Center
50 N Medical Dr
Salt Lake City, UT 84132-1   801-587-3422
                                             801-58 -EHAB
                                        FAX: 801-581-2111
                                www.healthcare.utah.edu/rehab/
David Entwistle, Administrator
Trish Jensen, Program Coordinator
Provides quality, comprehensive, rehabilitation services to persons with complex rehabilitation needs, including spinal cord injuries, head trauma, stroke, and other disabling conditions. Rehabilitation Services has been serving physicians, their patients, and the community since 1965. Rehabilitation Services has been an established leader in comprehensive inpatient, outpatient and home/community rehabilitation programs. Accredited by CARF and JCAHO.

Vermont

6306   Vermont Achievement Center
88 Park St
Rutland, VT 05701-4715   802-775-2395
                                        FAX: 802-773-9656
                                        www.vac-rutland.com
Kiki Mc Shane, CEO
Rebecca Wisell, Administrator
Vermont Achievement Center is recognized as a catalyst in building a community where all people are capable of change. Individuals flourish because they are nutured, valued and treated with respect. Education is empowering. The family is the primary influence in a person's life. Children belong in a family. Families are enhanced by support of the community. Children and family services are flexible and responsive to changing needs.

Virginia

6307   Inova Mount Vernon Hospital Rehabilitation Program
Inova Rehabilitation Center
2501 Parkers Ln
Alexandria, VA 22306-3209   703-664-7000
                                             800-554-7342
                                        FAX: 703-664-7423
                                             www.inova.com
Barbara Doyle, CEO
Inova Mount Vernon Hospital is a 237-bed hospital offering patients convenience and state-of-the-art care in a community environment. Our hospital sits on 26 acres of beautifully landscaped open space, where patients can find moments of serenity in our specially designed gardens.

6308   Kluge Children's Rehabilitation Center
University of Virginia
2270 Ivy Rd
Charlottesville, VA 22903-4977   434-924-5161
                                             800-627-8596
                                        FAX: 434-924-5559
                                www.healthsystem.virginia.edu
Janet Allaire, Administrator
Richard Stevenson, Research Director
The Kluge Childrens's Rehabilitation Center (KCRC) is a place dedicated to serving children with special needs. Children between the ages of birth and 21 come to the KCRC from all over Virginia, the United States, and even overseas for many reasons. Some need specific therapy or rehabilitation after injuries, accidents, or surgery. Others have chronic illness such as diabetes, and cystic fibrosis. Many families come to find out why their child is experiencing behavior problems.

Washington

6309   Good Samaritan Healthcare Physical Medicine and Rehabilitation
Good Samaritan Hospital
407 14th Ave SE
Puyallup, WA 98372-3770   253-697-4000
                                        FAX: 253-697-5157
                                        info@goodsamhealth.org
                                        www.multicare.org
Glenn Kassman, President
Vince Schmitz, CFO
Good Samaritan is part of the Multi-Care Health System, a non-for-profit medical system serving the growing populations of Pierce and King Counties in the greater Puget Sound region of Washington. Our medical staff includes 1,600 of the regions most respected primary care physicians and specialists.

6310   Northwest Hospital Center for Medical Rehabilitation
1550 N 115th St
Seattle, WA 98133-9733   206-364-0500
                                        FAX: 206-364-0500
                                        TTY:877-694-4677
                                        www.nwhospital.org
Peter Evans, Chairman
Scott L. Hardman, Vice Chairman
James K. Anderson, Board
Provides complete medical and surgical services in both inpatient and outpatient settings. Services across multiple specialties include: 24hr emergency services, critical care, cardiac care, stroke program, cancer care, childbirth center, rehabilitation center, diagnostic imaging and education and wellness services. Mission is to raise the long-term health status of our community by providing personalized, quality care with compassion dignity, and respect.

6311   Providence Medical Center
500 17th Ave
Seattle, WA 98122-5711   206-000-1111
                                        FAX: 206-320-3387
                                        www.providence.org
Swedish offers a complete continuum of rehabilitation services, from acute inpatient care to extensive outpatient therapies, to

meet virtually every rehabilitative need for patients of all ages. Nearly 7,000 patients turn to Swedish for these services every year. Through our multidisciplinary team of physical and occupational therapists and speech-language pathologists, Swedish provides the reassurance of a high level of clinical expertise in comfortable, state-of-the-art facilities.

6312 Providence Rehabilitation Services
Providence Rehabilitation Services
1321 Colby Ave
Everett, WA 98201-1665 425-261-3825
FAX: 425-261-3823
www.providence.org

Jim Phillips, Manager
Leslie Baumgarten, Manager
Continuum of care available: Acute Care, Inpatient Rehabilitation Unit, Transitional Care, Outpatient therapies, and In-home services.

6313 Shriners Hospitals for Children: Spokane
Shriners Hospitals
911 W 5th Ave
Spokane, WA 99204-2901 509-455-7844
FAX: 509-744-1223
www.shrinershq.org/hospitals/spokane
Kristin Monasmith, Public Relations Director
Craig Patchin, Administrator
Paul M. Caskey, M.D., Chief of Staff
Provides pediatric orthopedic services plus burn scar revision to children birth to 18. All services at no charge to the family.

West Virginia

6314 HealthSouth Mountain View Regional Rehab Hospital
1160 Van Voorhis Rd
Morgantown, WV 26505-3437 304-598-1100
800-388-2451
FAX: 304-598-1103
www.healthsouthmountainview.com/
Vicki Demers, Chief Executive Officer
Govind Patel, M.D., Medical Director
Robbin Butler, OTR/L, Director of Therapy Operations
A 96-bed inpatient accute rehabilitation hospital. Outpatient services, physical, occupational and speech therapy, and interior therapy pool. Programs include neuro/stroke, brain injury, spinal cord injury and pediatric.

6315 HealthSouth Western Hills Regional Rehab Hospital
3 Western Hills Dr
Parkersburg, WV 26105-8122 304-420-1392
FAX: 304-420-1374
www.healthsouthwesternhills.com
Kalapala Rao, Medical Director
Candace Ross, Director of Human Resources
Greg Holland, Director of Marketing Operations
A 40-bed medical rehabilitation hospital serving inpatient and outpatient needs in the western West Virginia area. Our hospital is accredited by the Joint Commission on Accreditation of Healthcare Organizations (JCAHO) Our mission is to guide patients whtih physically disabling conditions along an individualized treatment pathway so they can reach the highest level of physical, social and emotional well-being. We strive to provide the highest quality care for you and your family.

Wisconsin

6316 Extendicare Health Services, Inc.
3540 South 43rd Street
Milwaukee, WI 53220-2903 414-541-1000
800-395-5000
FAX: 414-541-1942
www.extendicare.com
Timothy Lukenda, CEO
Douglas Harris, SVP
David Pearce, Vice President, General Counsel

Sunrise Care Center is a leading provider of long-term skilled nursing care and short-term rehabilitation solutions. Our 99 bed facility offers a full continuum of services and care focused around each individual in today's ever-changing healthcare environment. Our facility is Medicare and Medicaid certified.

6317 St. Catherine's Hospital
9555 76th St
Pleasant Prairie, WI 53158 262-577-8000
FAX: 262-653-5795
www.uhsi.org
Vicki Lewis, Manager
Committed to living out the healing ministries of the Judeo-Christian faiths by providing exceptional and compassionate healthcare service that promotes the dignity and well-being of the people we serve.

6318 St. Joseph Hospital
611 Saint Joseph Ave
Marshfield, WI 54449-1898 715-387-1713
FAX: 715-389-3939
www.ministryhealth.org
Michael Schmidt, CEO
Catherine Olson, Director
A values-driven healthcare delivery network of aligned hospitals, clinics, long-term care facilities, home care agencies, dialysis centers and many other programs and services in Wisconsin and Minnesota.

Wyoming

6319 Spalding Rehabilitation Hospital at Memorial Hospital of Laramie
2301 House Ave
Suite 300
Cheyenne, WY 82001-3748 307-635-4141
800-374-7687
FAX: 307-638-2656
www.imgwy.com
Mitchell Schwarzbach, Executive Director
Tanya Boerkircher, Wyoming Endoscopy Center Manager
Andrea Bailey, Charge Entry Supervisor
We are a professional corporation of physicians trained in various medical specialties and subspecialties including Internal Medicine, Gastroenterology and Chest Diseases.It is our mission to provide the highest quality, cost-effective primary and subspecialty medical care, and education to the people of southern Wyoming, western Nebraska, and northern Colorado.

Rehabilitation Facilities, Post-Acute

Alabama

6320   Alabama Department of Rehabilitation Services
602 S. Lawrence St.
Montgomery, AL 36104   334-293-7500
                                         800-441-7609
                                         FAX: 334-293-7383
                                         TTY: 800-499-1816
                                         www.rehab.alabama.gov
Jane E. Burdeshaw, Commissioner
State agency which provides services and assistance to Alabama's children and adults with disabilities.

6321   Briarcliff Nursing Home & Rehab Facility
3201 North Ware Road
McAllen, TX 78501   956-631-5542
                                         FAX: 956-631-5777
                                         www.briarcliffnursingcenter.com
Postacute rehabilitation program.

6322   Centers for The Developmentally Disabled - North Central Alabama
1602 Church St SE
P.O. Box 2091
Decatur, AL 35602   256-350-1458
                                         FAX: 256-350-1485
                                         info@cddnca.org
                                         www.cddnca.org
Earl Brightwell, Executive Director
CDD NCA provides services and programs for individuals who are mentally and/or physically challenged, or developmentally delayed. These services range from early intervention services for infants and toddlers to residential and employment programs for adults. All services are typically provided at no cost to the individual or their family, regardless of income. Funding sources for the CDD NCA include DMH, United Way, and ADRS.

6323   Cheaha Regional Mental Health Center
351 W 3rd St
Sylacauga, AL 35150   256-245-1340
                                         FAX: 256-245-1343
Cynthia L. Atkinson, Executive Director
Dr. Shakil Khan, Medical Director
Karen McKinney, Clinical Director, Mental Health Services
CRMHC provides a continuum of services for persons with intellectual disabilities, serious mental illness and substance abuse in a four county area in east Alabama, which includes Clay, Coosa, Randolph, and Talladega Counties.

6324   Children's Rehabilitation Service
Alabama Department of Rehabilitation Services
602 S. Lawrence St.
Montgomery, AL 36104   334-293-7500
                                         800-441-7609
                                         FAX: 334-293-7383
                                         TTY: 800-499-1816
                                         www.rehab.alabama.gov
Jane E. Burdeshaw, Commissioner
CRS provides individualized services to children with special health care needs from birth to age 21 and their families at home, school, and in the community. In addition, CRS provides disability services, expertise, and adaptive technology to and for local school systems, assisting teachers, school nurses and other staff in the education of children with disabilities. The CRS Hemophilia Program serves Alabama's children and adults with this life-threatening blood disorder.

6325   Chilton-Shelby Mental Health Center
110 Medical Center Dr
Calera, AL 35045   205-755-8800
                                         FAX: 205-668-4957
                                         chiltonshelby.org
Melodie D. Crawford, Chief Executive Officer
Vicki M. Potts, Chief Financial Officer
Kathryn T. Crouthers, Chief Operations Officer
Mental health rehabilitation services and more for the recovery of mentally disabled adults. Serves Chilton and Shelby counties.
Business Office Location

6326   Darden Rehabilitation Center
1001 E Broad Street
Ste C
Gadsden, AL 35903-2400   256-547-5751
                                         FAX: 256-547-5761
                                         darden@dardenrehab.org
                                         dardenrehab.org
Lynn Curry, Executive Director
Derek Coburn, Operations Manager
Dana Johnson, Program Coordinator
Work adjustment and job placement programs. Serves the counties of Etawah, Marshall, Dekalb, Clair and Cherokee.

6327   Easterseals Central Alabama
2185 Normandie Dr.
Montgomery, AL 36111   334-288-0240
                                         FAX: 334-288-7171
                                         info@eastersealsca.org
                                         www.eastersealscentralalabama.org
Lynne Stokley, Chief Executive Officer
Debbie Lynn, Administrator
Serves people with disabilities and their families by providing programs and services.

6328   Easterseals Northwest Alabama
1615 Trojan Dr.
Suite 1
Muscle Shoals, AL 35661   256-381-1110
                                         info@eastersealsnwal.org
                                         www.eastersealsnwal.org
Lynne Stokley, Chief Executive Officer
Danny Prince, Administrator
Easterseals provides services for people with disabilities and their families. Services include occupational therapy, physical therapy, speech therapy, and vocational services.

6329   Easterseals West Alabama
1110 Dr. Edward Hillard Drive
Tuscaloosa, AL 35401-7446   205-759-1211
                                         800-726-1216
                                         FAX: 205-349-1162
                                         eswa@eswaweb.org
                                         eswaweb.org
Ronny Johnston, Executive Director
Dusty Beam, Administrative Coordinator
Holly Hillard, Director, Development
Leading organization in helping children and adults with disabilities to live with equality, dignity and independence. Rehabilitation services are provided in two divisions: outpatient rehabilitation division (physical therapy, occupational therapy, speech therapy, hearing evaluation, sell and service hearind aids) and vocational division (vocational evaulation and vocational development). Services are rendered regardless of age, race, sex, color, creed, national origin, veteran's status.

6330   Easterseals West Central Alabama Rehabilitation Center
2906 Citizens Pkwy
P.O. Box 750
Selma, AL 36702-0750   334-872-8421
                                         800-801-4776
                                         FAX: 334-872-3907
                                         www.eswcarc.us
Vocational evaluation, job development, employment development, job coaching, counseling, medical services, audiology, pre-school development programs.

6331   Geer Adult Training Center
P.O.Box 419
83 South Canaan Road
Canaan, CT 06018-419   860-824-7067
                                         FAX: 205-367-8032
                                         geercares.org/content/about-geer
Yvonne Williams, Program Coordinator

6332 Goodwill Easterseals of the Gulf Coast
2440 Gordon Smith Dr.
Mobile, AL 36617-2319
251-471-1581
info@al.easterseals.com
www.gesgc.org

Peter D'Olive, Chairman
Frank Harkins, President & CEO
Bill Dillman, Vice President, Marketing & Development
Vocational, medical, pre-school education, day care, recreation and other support services.

6333 HealthSouth Corporation
3660 Grandview Parkway
Ste 200
Birmingham, AL 35243-3332
205-967-7116
800-765-4772
FAX: 225-928-0317
healthsouth.com

Jacque Shadle, CEO
Derrick Landreneau, Director of Nursing services
Dedicated to one field of medicine - physical rehabilitation medicine - and are committed to one goal, helping patients achieve the highest level of functioning possible after a debilitating injury or illness.

6334 Indian Rivers Mental Health Center - Bibb
2439 Main St
Brent, AL 35034
205-926-4681
FAX: 205-296-6016
www.irmhc.org

6335 Indian Rivers Mental Health Center - Pickens
890 Reform St.
Carrollton, AL 35447
205-367-8032
FAX: 205-367-9291
www.irmhc.org

6336 Indian Rivers Mental Health Center - Tuscaloosa
2209 - 9th St
Tuscaloosa, AL 35401
205-391-3131
FAX: 205-391-3135
www.irmhc.org

Barbara Friedman, President
Elizabeth Rice, First Vice President
Services are available to adults who have serious mental illness resulting in personal, family or work-related problems. Counseling may take place in either individual or group settings, identification, evaluation and treatment services are available to persons who experience problems related to alcohol and drug abuse and counseling services are available for children and adolescents who have a severe emotional disturbance causing discipline problems at home and school.

6337 Mobile ARC
2424 Gordon Smith Dr
Mobile, AL 36617-2397
251-479-7409
FAX: 251-473-7649
jzoghby@mobilearc.org
mobilearc.org

Jeff Zoghby, Executive Director
Amy Odom, Public Relations and Development Director
Mobile Arc, Inc. (MARC) offers a wide range of services for persons with intellectual and developmental disabilities.

6338 Southeastern Blind Rehabilitation Center
U.S. Department of Veteran Affairs
700 S 19th St
Birmingham, AL 35233-1927
205-558-4706
FAX: 205-933-4484
www.rehab.va.gov/blindrehab/
The Center is a 32-bed inpatient blind rehabilitation program which serves the southeastern region. The majority of client services are for basic adjustment and management to sight loss. Basic services include: low vision, orientation and mobility, manual skills, ADL and communications. Training on electronic mobility aids and adapted computers is also available on a restricted basis. The program maintains graduate education affiliations and an active applied research program.

6339 UAB Eye Care
University Of Alabama at Birmingham
1716 University Blvd
Birmingham, AL 35233
205-975-2020
FAX: 205-934-6755
www.uab.edu/optometry/home/eyecare

Rodney W. Nowakowski, Dean
Dr. Marsha Snow, Chief, Low Vision Patient Care
Brittney Bolen, Optometric Technician
Complete eye services, including low vision services and materials.

6340 Vaughn-Blumberg Services
2715 Flynn Rd
P.O. Box 8646
Dothan, AL 36304
334-793-3102
FAX: 334-793-7740
www.vaughnblumbergservices.com

Ed Dorsey, Executive Director
Linda Cunningham, Director of Human Resources
Billy McCarthy, Director of Finance
Provides comprehensive services for people with intellectual disabilities that reside in Houston County as well as assist in facilitating their participation in society to the fullest extent of their individual capabilities. Offers early intervention services for the mentally handicapped adult including diagnosis and evaluation and physical, speech, and occupational therapies. They also offer counseling, day training, employment assistance and residental homes.

Alaska

6341 Alaska Center for the Blind and Visually Impaired
3903 Taft Drive
Anchorage, AK 99517-3069
907-248-7770
800-770-7517
FAX: 907-248-7517
info@alaskabvi.org
www.alaskabvi.org

Regan Mattingly, Executive Director
Robert Tasso, Program Manager
Caren Ailleo, Development & Communications Director
Services to help the adult residential or community-based student become independent and self-sufficient by offering independent travel, Braille reading and writing, use of assiative technology such as talking computers, manual skills and personal, as well as home management. There is a special program for those 55 years of age and older who are experiencing a vision loss and another program for rural Alaska Native youth who are visually impaired.

Arizona

6342 Arizona Center for the Blind and Visually Impaired
3100 E Roosevelt St
Phoenix, AZ 85008-5036
602-273-7411
FAX: 602-273-7410
jlamay@acbvi.org
acbvi.org

James La May, CEO
Frank Vance, Director
Christine Boisen, Chair
A private, nonprofit organization that provides comprehensive rehabilitation services and more for the blind and visually handicapped. The staff includes 20 instructional and adminstrative professionals.

6343 Arizona Industries for the Blind
Suite 130
515 N 51st Avenue
Phoenix, AZ 85043-2711
602-771-9100
FAX: 602-353-5701
DanielMartinez@azdes.gov
www.azdes.gov/aib

Richard Monaco, General Manager
Daniel Martinez, Community Services Liaison

Offers rehabilitation services, vocational/pre-vocational evaluation and training, work adjustment, job development and employment and training opportunties for individuals who are blind.

6344   Banner Good Samaritan Medical Center
1111 E McDowell Road
Phoenix, AZ 85006-2666
602-839-2000
FAX: 602-239-5868
www.bannerhealth.com

Steve Narang, MD, Chief Executive Officer
Lorraine Hudspeth, Controller
Letty Cerpa, Senior Accountant
Nearly 1,700 physicians representing more than 50 specialties work with Banner Good Samaritan staff to care for more then 36,000 inpatients a year. Houses more then 650 licensed patient care beds. A teaching hospital that trains more then 220 physicians annually and a premier medical center in Arizona and the Southwest. Provides a comprehensive foundation of major programs and an equally impressive offering of highly specialized programs not availiable in most hospitals.

6345   Beacon Group
308 W Glenn St.
Tucson, AZ 85705
520-622-4874
FAX: 520-620-6620
www.beacongroup.org
Committed to effectively assisting adults with disabilities to maximize their personal, social, vocational and educational skills in order to attain a successful and meaningful independence within the Tucson community.

6346   Carondelet Brain Injury Programs and Services (Bridges Now)
2202 N. Forbes Blvd.
Tucson, AZ 85745-2602
520-872-7324
FAX: 520-873-3743
comments@carondelet.org
carondelet.org

Daisy M Jenkins, Executive VP, Chief HR/Administr
James K Beckmann, President/Chief Executive Officer
Alan Strauss, Executive VP, Finance and Chief Financial Officer
Comprehensive outpatient rehabilitation program. PT, OT, ST, Psychology and Rehab Counseling Services.

6347   Desert Life Rehabilitation & Care Center
1919 W Medical St
Tucson, AZ 85704-1133
520-369-9620
FAX: 520-867-6612
Amad Nazifi, Executive Director
Accomodates 240 residents. Provides skilled and intermediate nursing with occupational, physical, speech and respiratory therapy services. Offers special programs including an Alzheimer's Unit and a Young Adult program

6348   Devereux Advanced Behavioral Health Arizona - Scottsdale
Scottsdale Administrative Office
2025 N 3rd St
Suite 250
Phoenix, AZ 85004
602-283-1573
FAX: 480-443-5587
azadmissions@devereux.org
www.devereuxaz.org

Lane Barker, Executive Director
Yvette Jackson, Director of Operations
Donovan S Carman, MBA, Director of Finance
Engages in the treatment of behavioral health issues through services such as residential treatment centers, day school, outpatient services, prevention programs, adult foster care, and foster care for children. Also offered are evidence-based interventions to improve lives.

6349   Devereux Arizona - Tucson
Tuscon Administrative Office
6141 E Grant Rd
Tucson, AZ 85712
520-296-5551
FAX: 520-296-8244
azadmissions@devereux.org
www.devereuxaz.org

Lane Barker, Executive Director
Yvette Jackson, Director of Operations
Donovan S Carman, MBA, Director of Finance
Organization offering culturally competent care for individuals with emotional and behavioral health disorders. Some of the programs offered include Adult Foster Care, kinship program, Therapeutic Foster Care Program, Parent Aide and more.

6350   Freestone Rehabilitation Center
10617 E Oasis Drive
Mesa, AZ 85208
480-986-1531
FAX: 480-986-1538

Randy Gray, Executive Director
Cherie Vance, Manager

6351   HealthSouth Valley Of The Sun Rehabilitation Hospital
13460 N 67th Ave
Glendale, AZ 85304-1000
623-878-8800
FAX: 623-878-5254
healthsouth.com

Beth Bacher, Manager
A 60-bed free-standing hospital that offers acute physical rehabilitation, outpatient therapy services and day hospital treatment. Works in cooperation with local, regional and national managed care organizations and other sources to maximise patient recovery while conserving financial resources.

6352   Institute for Human Development
Northern Arizona University
912 Riordan Rd. P.O.Box 5630
Flagstaff, AZ 86011-5630
928-523-4791
FAX: 928-523-9127
TTY:928-523-1695
ihd@nau.edu
www.nau.edu/ihd

Levi Esguerra, Director
Lisa Andrew, Advisory Commitee
Lynn Black, Advisory Commitee
The Institute values and supports the independence, productivity and inclusion of Arizona's citizens with disabilities. Based on the values and beliefs, the Institute conducts training, research and services that further these goals.

6353   John C Lincoln Hospital North Mountain
250 E Dunlap Ave
Phoenix, AZ 85020-2871
602-943-2381
FAX: 602-944-8062
webmaster@jcl.com
www.jcl.com/content/northmountain/default.htm
Rhonda Forsyth, President
Bruce Pearson, FACHE, Senior Vice President
Maggi Griffin, RN, MS, Vice President & Chief Executive Officer
Mission is to assist each person entrusted to our care to enjoy the fullest gift of health possible, and work with others to build a community where a helping hand is available for our most vulnerable members.

6354   La Frontera Center
504 W 29th St
Tucson, AZ 85713-3394
520-884-9920
FAX: 520-792-0654
www.lafronteraaz.org

Kevin Heath, Board Chair
Frank Valenzuela, Vice Chair
Celestino Fernandez, Treasurer
A nonprofit community-based behavioral health agency that has been helping southern Arizona children, adults, and families since 1968.

6355 Manor Care Nursing and Rehab Center: Tucson
3705 N Swan Rd
Tucson, AZ 85718-6939
520-299-7088
FAX: 520-529-0038
www.hcr-manorcare.com

Clifton J. Porter II, Vice President, Government Relations
Martin Allen, Vice President

A leading provider of short-term post-acute medical care and re-habilitation and long-term skilled nursing care. High quality medical care is provided through registered (RN) and licensed practical (LPN) nurses and certified nursing assistants (CNA) in concert with physical , occupational and speech rehabilitation therapists. Our more then 275 skilled nursing centers are Medicare-and Medicaid-certified.

6356 Nova Care
Second Floor
680 American Avenue
King of Prussia, PA 19406-2607
800-331-8840
FAX: 602-256-7292
novacare.com

Scott Lusted, General Manager
Brian Beal, Market Manager

NovaCare Rehabilitation's highly respected clinical team provides preventative and rehabilitative services that maximize functionality and promote well-being. NovaCare Rehabilitation also provides physical therapy and athletic training services to more then 20 professional sports teams and 300 universities, colleges, and highschools thoughout the nation.

6357 Perry Rehabilitation Center
3146 E Windsor Avenue
Phoenix, AZ 85008-1199
602-956-0400
FAX: 602-957-7610
perrycenter@qwest.net
www.azafh.com

Diana Casillas, Human Resources Director
Jim Musick, President

Provides services for people with disabilities, cognitive disabilities including residential services, day treatment, job training and job placement.

6358 Phoenix Veterans Center
Ste 100
1544 W. Grant St.
Phoenix, AZ 85004-1554
602-358-8494
FAX: 602-379-4130
www.azcremationcenter.com/?

Ken Benckwitz, Manager

Veterans medical clinic offering disabled veterans medical treatments.

6359 Progress Valley: Phoenix
10505 North 69th Street
Suite 1100
Paradise Valley, AZ 85253-6106
480-922-9427
FAX: 602-274-5473
recovery@progressvalley.org
alcoholism.about.com

Susanne Lambert, Executive Director
Jennifer White, Director of Programs
Cathie Scott, Sober Housing Manager

Residential aftercare for alcoholism and chemical dependency. Certified chemical dependency counselors provide individual treatment.

6360 Rehabilitation Services Administration
Suite 102
3425 East Van Buren
Phoenix, AZ 85008-3202
602-771-9100
800-563-1221
FAX: 602-250-8584
TTY: 855-475-8194
azrsa@azdes.gov

Katharine Levandowsky, Administrator

Provides a variety of specialized services to assist in removing barriers to employment and/or independent living for individuals with physical or mental disabilities. RSA offers 3 major service programs and several specialized programs/services.

6361 Southern Arizona Association For The Visually Impaired
3767 East Grant Rd
Tucson, AZ 85716-2935
520-795-1331
FAX: 520-795-1336
reception@saavi.us
www.saavi.us

Michael Gordon, Executive Director
Amy Murillo, Associate Director
Carol Lopez, Finance Director

Offers health services, counseling, social work, home and personal management, computer training, low vision aids and more for the visually handicapped 18 years or older.

6362 Toyei Industries
Hc 58 Box 55
Ganado, AZ 86505-55
928-736-2417
888-45T-OYEI
FAX: 928-736-2495

Anthony Lincoln, CEO

Serves the needs of developmentally disabled and the severely mentally impaired adult citizens of the Navajo Nation and other Indian Nations. Staff of 60+ serves the needs of all the Navajo adults. Services include day treatment programs, and residential and group home services.

6363 Yuma Center for the Visually Impaired
328 W. Spears Street
Yuma, AZ 85365-6580
928-247-8890
FAX: 928-344-1863
https://www.azdes.gov

Calvin Roberts, Executive Director
Kathy Lucero, Store Manager
Dana Clayton, Human Resources Specialist

A private nonprofit agency offering services for totally blind and legally blind children and adults in the Arizona area.

Arkansas

6364 Arkansas Lighthouse for the Blind
P.O.Box 192666
6818 Murray St.
Little Rock, AR 72209- 2666
501-562-2222
FAX: 501-568-5275
info@arkansaslighthouse.org
arkansaslighthouse.org

Bill Johnson, Chief Executive Officer
Danny Novielli, COO
John McAtee, Chief Financial Officer

Manufacturer of textiles, apparel and paper products and employs blind and legally blind individuals.

6365 Beverly Enterprises Network
1 Thousand Beverly
Fort Smith, AR 72901-2629
479-201-2000
800-666-9996
FAX: 479-452-5131

Randy Churchey, CEO

Offers a progressive approach to subacute care. The goal of this organization is to assist injured and disabled individuals regain the level of independence to which they have been accustomed. Provides support and training programs, patient and family services and specialty programs for patients.

6366 Easterseals: Arkansas
3920 Woodland Heights Rd
Little Rock, AR 72212-2495
501-227-3600
877-533-3700
FAX: 501-227-4021
TTY: 501-227-3686
lrogers@ar.easterseals.com

Sharon Moone-Jochums, President/ CEO
Linda Rogers, VP Programs
Michael E. Stock, Treasurer

Their mission is to provide exceptional services to ensure that all people with disabilities or special needs have equal opportunities to live, learn, work and play in their communitites.

6367 HealthSouth Rehabilitation Hospital Of Fort Smith
1401 South J. Street
Fort Smith, AR 72901-5158
479-785-3300
FAX: 479-785-8599
healthsouth.com

Ryan Cassedy, CEO
Cygnet Schroeder, M.D., Medical Director
Donna Beallis, D.O., Director of Medical Management
A free-standing 80-bed comprehensive physical medicine and rehabilitation hospital offering inpatient and outpatient services. Provides specialized medical and therapy services, designed to assist physically challenged persons to reach their highest level of independent function.

6368 Lions World Services for the Blind
2811 Fair Park Blvd
Little Rock, AR 72204-5044
501-664-7100
800-248-0734
FAX: 501-664-2743
training@lwsb.org
www.wsblind.org/

Larry Dickerson, President/ CEO
Tony Woodell, President & Chief Executive Officer
Bill Smith, Director of Development
Offers services in the areas of health education, recreation, rehabilitation, counseling, employment, computer training and more for all legally blind residents of the U.S. The staff includes 56 full time employees.

6369 Little Rock Vet Center #0713
Department of Veterans Affairs of Washington DC
Suite A
201 W Broadway St
North Little Rock, AR 72114- 5505
501-324-6395
877-927-8387
FAX: 501-324-6928

Elizabeth N Ruggiero, Team Leader
Ida L Fogle, Counselor
Van A Hall, Counselor
Vet Center provides PTSD counseling to veterans of a combat zone. No medical care provided.

6370 Timber Ridge Ranch NeuroRestorative Services
4500 W Commerce Dr
North Little Rock, AR 72116
501-758-8799
800-743-6802
FAX: 501-758-8778
neuroinfo@thementornetwork.com
www.neurorestorative.com

Bill Duffy, Chief Operating Officer
Michael E. Hofmeister, MS, MBA, Vice President of Operations
Sean Byrne, MBA, Chief Financial Officer
Comprehensive, individualized services from a transdisciplinary team of licensed professionals assist clients along a course to greater independence. A separate team is dedicated to the needs of children, adolescents, and their families. A clinical team may include professionals from the disciplines of: behavior analysis, neuropsychology, physiatry, psychology, speech-language pathology, occupational therapy, physical therapy, social work, couseling, education, nursing, and case management.

California

6371 ARC Fresno-Kelso Activity Center
4567 N Marty Ave
Fresno, CA 93722-7810
559-226-6268
FAX: 559-226-6269
arcfresno@arcfresno.org
arcfresno.org

Lori Ramirez, Executive Director
Catherine Wooliever, Director of Human Resources
Jamie Marrash, Director of Program Services
The Arc Fresno is a private, non-profit 501(c)(3) organization who was founded in 1953. They provide services and supports for over 550 individuals with developmental disabilities throughout Fresno County. They currently offer eight (8) programs, and do so with the help of 145 employees.

6372 ARC Of San Diego-ARROW Center
3030 Market Street
San Diego, CA 92102-3297
619-685-1175
FAX: 619-234-3759
arc-sd.com

Anthony J. DeSalis, President & CEO
The ARC of San Diego is a provider of services to persons with disabilities.

6373 ARC Of San Diego-Rex Industries, The
9575 Aero Dr
San Diego, CA 92123-1803
858-571-4369
800-748-5575
FAX: 858-715-3788
arc-sd.com

Dwight Stratton, Chair
Jerry Wechsler, 1st Vice Chairman
David W. Schneider, President & CEO
Offers many different programs including: North County Parent/Infant Program which is an educational program for children, birth to three years who are showing delays in development or who are at risk for developmental delays. The Adult Development Center is a program for adults, eighteen and over, with a developmental disability in the severe to profound range. The program focuses on self-help, communication, daily living and pre-vocational skills. Other programs are available.

6374 ARC Of San-Diego-South Bay
1280 Nolan Avenue
Chula Vista, CA 91911-3738
619-427-7524
FAX: 619-427-4657
info@arc-sd.com
www.arc-sd.com/locations

Becky Thaller, Director
Steve Hojsan, Arc Enterprises Director
Michael Bruce, Workshop Manager
Provides remunerative work.

6375 ARC Of Southeast Los Angeles-Southeast Industries
9501 Washburn Rd
Downey, CA 90242-2913
562-803-1556
FAX: 562-803-4080
www.arcselac.org/

Provides an offsite extension of your production and warehouse facility. We have reliable and highly trained personnel to meet your needs, including pick-up and delivery service with prompt turn-around times. We offer assembly and packaging at competitive rates while maintaining the highest standards.

6376 ARC: VC Community Connections West
5103 Walker Street
Ventura, CA 93003-7358
805-650-8611
FAX: 805-644-7308
www.arcvc.org

Robert Hogan, President
Gene West, First Vice President
Eve Liebman, Recording Secretary
Caring and experienced staff is dedicated to serving participants with a variety of physical, mental and social disabilities who require a higher level of support and supervision. Using a person-centered planning approach, Arc Ventura County promotes self-directed services for all clients and families served. Adult development centers serve individuals with physical and mental disabilities, as well as people with challenging behaviors, who require assistance with basic skills such as self care.

6377 ARC: VC Ventura
5103 Walker Street
Ventura, CA 93003-7358
806-650-8611
FAX: 806-644-7308
www.arcvc.org

Robert Hogan, President
Gene West, First Vice President
Eve Liebman, Recording Secretary
Arc Ventura County is a private, nonprofit organization that provides educational, vocational and residential services for people with developmental disabilities. Informed decisions, positive changes, and integration in the community are fundamental principals in all programs. As evidence of our programming excellence, Arc Ventura County has been accredited by CARF (The Rehabilitation Accreditation Commission.

6378 AbilityFirst

626-396-1010
877-768-4600
info@abilityfirst.org
www.abilityfirst.org

Lori Gangemi, President & Chief Executive Officer
Kashif Khan, Chief Financial Officer
Keri Castaneda, Chief Program Officer
AbilityFirst serves children and adults with special needs through 24 locations in Southern California.

6379 Accentcare
17855 North Dallas Pkwy
Dallas, TX 75287-2468

972-201-3800
800-834-3059
info@accentcare.com
accentcare.com

Mark Pacala, Chairman of the Board and CEO
Vincent E. Cook, EVP and Chief Financial Officer
Melvin Warriner, SVP and Chief Culture Officer
Postacute rehabilitation program: home care aides follow through with rehabilitation instructions given by physical, occupational and speech therapists. Other home care services are available, serving special needs for Alzheimer's, blind, brain injury, MS, ostomies, parkinsonism, spinal injury and stroke.

6380 Anaheim Veterans Center
859, South Harbor Blvd
Anaheim, CA 92805-4680

714-776-0161
800-225-8387
FAX: 714-776-8904
anaheimvetcenter@yahoo.com
www.longbeach.va.gov/visitors/vet_center.asp
Veterans medical clinic offering disabled veterans medical treatments.

6381 Azure Acres Recovery Center
5777 Madison Avenue
Suite 1210
Sacramento, CA 95841-9034

877-977-3755
877-762-3735
FAX: 707-823-8972
info@azureacres.com
azureacres.com

Joe Tinervin, MSW, Executive Director
Michael Roeske, Psy.D., Clinical Director
Christie Splitstone, MA, Counselor/Case Manager
Offers rehabilitation services and residential care for the person with an alcohol or drug abuse related problems.

6382 Back in the Saddle
2 BITS Trail
P.O. Box 3336
Chelmsford, MA 01824-0936

800-865-2478
877-756-5068
FAX: 800-866-3235
help@BackInTheSaddle.com
www.thesaddle.com

Richard Smith PhD, Owner
Erika Reed, Co-Director
A long term community residential facility for head injured adults. House parents live on-site; and oversee a variety of programs which are individually designed and might include classes in community college, placement in a workshop or on a workstation, volunteer positions and home skills assignments. Recreational outing range from horseback riding to weekend camping. Apartment programs available as set-up. Price: $2800-$3000 per month.

6383 Ballard Rehabilitation Hospital
1760 W 16th St
San Bernardino, CA 92411-1150

909-473-1200
800-761-1226
FAX: 909-473-1276
www.ballardrehab.com

Edward C. Palacios, RN,MPH, Administrator
Mary Hunt, Chief Operating Officer
Patty Meinhardt, Director Marketing/Admissions
Ballard Rehab Hospital is a free standing specialty hospital and provides the complete continuum of acute rehabilitation and out-patient rehabilitation, dedicated to providing rehab care to adults and children. The following inpatient and outpatient programs are available: CNA (Stroke) Rehab; Spinal Cord Injury Rehab; Brain Injury Rehab; Pain Management Rehab; Bariatric program, pulmonary program, injured Worker Programs; and Post Amputation Rehab.

6384 Bayview Nursing and Rehabilitation
516 Willow Street
Alameda, CA 94501-6132

510-521-5600
FAX: 510-865-6441
TTY:800-735-2922
www.bayviewnursing.com/

Richard S Espinoza, Administrator
Offers a full range of medical services to meet the individual needs of our residents, including short-term rehabilitative services and long termed skilled care. Working with the resident's physician, our staff-including medical specialists, nurses, nutritionists, dietitians, and social workers-establishes a comprehensive treatment plan intended to restore you or your loved one to the highest practicable potential.

6385 Belden Center
606 Humboldt St
Santa Rosa, CA 95404-4219

707-579-2735
FAX: 707-579-4145

Casey Harding, Owner
Pamela Fadden, Owner
Postacute rehabilitation program.

6386 Blind Babies Foundation
Suite 300
1814 Franklin St
Oakland, CA 94612-3487

510-446-2229
FAX: 510-446-2262
blindbabies.org

Dottie Bridge, President
Aben Hill, 1st Vice President
Clare Friedman, PhD, 2nd Vice President
Mission: when an infant or pre school child is identified as blind or visually impaired, provides family-centered services to support the child's optimal development and access to the world.

6387 Brotman Medical Center: RehabCare Unit
Brotman Medical Center
3828 Delmas Terrace
Culver City, CA 90232-2713

310-836-7000
800-677-1238
FAX: 310-202-4105
phvc.com

Jennifer Cortez, Program Manager
Kevin O'Connor, CEO
Scott Leonard, CTO
Culver City is centrally located within the city of Los Angeles. These are two programs offering inpatient rehabilitation. The acute rehab program is designed for patients who need physical rehabilitation due to injury or medical disability. This program requires patients to participate in 3 hours therapy per day. The sub-acute program is designed especially for patients who need rehab but cannot tolerate the intensity of the acute rehab program.

6388 Build Rehabilitation Industries
12432 Foothill Blvd
Sylmar, CA 91342

818-898-0020
FAX: 818-898-1949
buildindustries.com

Comprehensive C.A.R.F. Accredited vocational rehabilitation services for adults with disabilities or other barriers to employment. Programs include: Sheltered Workshops, Work Evaluation, Work Hardening and Adjustment, Supported Employment, Job Placement, Independent Living Skills, Behavior Management, Adult Development Center, On-the-Job Training, and One-Stop Workforce Development Career Center.

6389 California Elwyn
18325 Mt. Baldy Circle
Fountain Valley, CA 92708-6115

714-557-6313
FAX: 714-963-2961
info@elwyn.org
elwyn.org

Charles S. McLister, President & CEO, Elwyn

Provides opportunities for people with disabilities who are 18 or older. Offers Individual Rehabilitation Plans and Supported Employment Services.

6390   California Eye Institute
1360 E Herndon Ave
Fresno, CA 93720-3326   559-449-5000
                                                   www.samc.com

Nancy Hollingsworth, President and CEO
Michael W. Martinez, EVP/Chief Operating and Financial Officer
Stephen Soldo, Chief Medical Officer
A private, nonprofit agency offering services such as health, educational, recreational, rehabilitation and employment counseling to the totally blind, legally blind and visually impaired. The staff includes two full time workers.

6391   Camp Recovery Center
3192 Glen Canyon Rd
Scotts Valley, CA 95066-4916   877-557-6237
                                              FAX: 831-438-2789
                                                   camprecovery.com

Michael Johnson, Ph.D, Executive Director
Tim Sinnott, Clinical Director
Zoe R., Case Manager
A free-standing social model recovery center for chemical dependency located on 25 wooded acres in the Santa Cruz Mountains. The services include: medical detoxification, complete medical evaluation, psychiatric evaluation and counseling, psychological testing, individual counseling and more. Helps the recovery from chemical dependency in a easier, warm and caring environment.

6392   Campobello Chemical Dependency Recovery Center
2448 Guerneville Road
Suite 400
Santa Rosa, CA 95402- 4030   707-546-1547
                                                   800-805-1833
                                              FAX: 707-579-1603
                                                   campobello.org
Our mission is to provide primary treatment, education, ongoing support and family services for clients seeking a more rewarding, chemically free lifestyle. Our primary goals are: to improve understanding/acceptance of the disease model of addiction. To improve self esteem. To reduce family, job and legal problems. To improve physical/emotional health. To enhance coping and problem solving strategies for recovery.

6393   Casa Colina Centers for Rehabilitation
P.O.Box 6001
255 East Bonita Avenue
Pomona, CA 91767- 6001   909-596-7733
                                                   866-724-4127
                                              FAX: 909-593-0153
                                              TTY: 909-596-3646
                                                   casacolina.org

Steve Norin, Chairman
Felice L Loverso, President
Chandrahas Agarwal, Medical Director
Casa Colina, has pioneered effective programs to create opportunity for health, productivity and self-esteem for persons with disability since 1936. Through medical rehabilitation, transitional living, residential, community, and prevention and wellness programs. Casa Colina serves more than 7,000 persons annually. Casa Colina, a non-profit organization, offers a unique spectrum of opportunities, achievement and results to patients and their families.

6394   Casa Colina Padua Village
P.O.Box 6001
255 East Bonita Avenue
Pomona, CA 91767- 6001   909-596-7733
                                                   866-724-4127
                                              FAX: 909-593-0153
                                              TTY: 909-596-3646
                                                   casacolina.org

Steve Norin, Chairman
Chandrahas Agarwal, Medical Director
Felice L Loverso, President
Long term residential services for adults with developmental disability. Residences include Malmquist House, Woodbend House, and Hillsdale House, all located in Claremont, California.

6395   Casa Colina Residential Services: Rancho Pino Verde
Casa Colina Center for Rehabilitation
P.O.Box 6001
255 East Bonita Avenue
Pomona, CA 91767- 7517   909-596-7733
                                                   866-724-4127
                                              FAX: 909-593-0153
                                              TTY: 909-596-3646
                                                   www.casacolina.org

Steve Norin, Chairman
Randy Blackman, Vice Chairman
Felice L. Loverso, President
Long term residential services in rural environment for adults with brain injury.

6396   Casa Colina Transitional Living Center
255 East Bonita Avenue
P.O.Box 6001
Pomona, CA 91767- 1923   909-596-7733
                                                   866-724-4127
                                              FAX: 909-593-0153
                                              TTY: 909-596-3646
                                                   casacolina.org

Steve Norin, Chairman
Felice L Loverso, President
Chandrahas Agarwal, Medical Director
Postacute rehabilitation program.

6397   Casa Colina Transitional Living Center: Pomona
P.O.Box 6001
255 East Bonita Avenue
Pomona, CA 91767- 6001   909-596-7733
                                                   866-724-4127
                                              FAX: 909-593-0153
                                              TTY: 909-596-3646
                                                   casacolina.org

Steve Norin, Chairman
Felice L Loverso, President
Chandrahas Agarwal, Medical Director
Post acute short term residential program for persons with brain injury. In a home-like setting, therapy promotes successful re-entry to home and community living.

6398   Cedars of Marin
PO Box 947
Ross, CA 94957-947   415-454-5310
                                              FAX: 415-454-0573
                                                   thecedarsofmarin.org

Jefferson Rice, Board Chair
James Brentano, Board Vice President
Andrew Hinkelman, Board Treasurer
The Cedars of Marin has provided residential and day programs for adults with developmental disabilities for over 91 years. Our award-winning programs help our clients to live creative, productive, joyous lives.

6399   Center for Neuro Skills
5215 Ashe Rd.
Bakersfield, CA 93313-2988   661-872-3408
                                                   800-922-4994
                                              FAX: 661-872-5150
                                              skatomski@neuroskills.com
                                                   neuroskills.com

Mark J Ashley, President/CEO and Co-Founder
A comprehensive, post-acute, community based head-injury rehabilitation program serving over 100 clients per year. Since 1980, CNS has effectively treated the entire spectrum of head-injured clients, including those with severe behavioral disorders, cognitive/perceptual impairments, speech/language problems, physical disabilities and post-concussion syndrome.

6400   Center for the Partially Sighted
Suite 150
6101 W. Centinela Ave.
Culver City, CA 90230   310-988-1970
                                              FAX: 310-988-1980
                                                   low-vision.org

La Donna S. Ringering, Ph.D, President/CEO
Pam Thompson, Director of Psychological Servic
Phyllis Amaral, Clinical Director

Services for partially sighted and legally blind people include low vision evaluations, the design and prescription of low vision devices and adaptive technology, as well as counseling and rehabilitation training (independent living skills and orientation/mobility training). Special programs include children's program, diabetes and vision loss program, Technology demonstrations. Store carries low vision aids. Catalog available.

6401   Central Coast Neurobehavioral Center OPTIONS
P.O.Box 877
800 Quintana Road Suite 2C
Morro Bay, CA 93442-877   805-772-6066
                                 FAX: 805-772-6067

Michael Mamot, CEO
Ole von Frausing-Borch, COO
Serves adults with developmental disabilities, traumatic head injuries, or other neurological impairments. OPTIONS operates two transitional living centers, eight licensed residential facilities, two licensed community integration day programs and a licensed short term stabilization center. Services offered include: supported and independent living services, group and individual vocational services, neuropsychological assessment, occupational therapy, cognitive therapy, speech therapy and more.

6402   Cerebral Palsy: North County Center
#209
8525 Gibbs Drive
San Diego, CA 92123-1758   858-571-7803
                                 FAX: 858-571-0919
                                 info@ucpsd.org
                                 www.ucpsd.org

David Carucci, Executive Director
Mary Krieger, Associate Executive Director
Bruce Neufeld, Chief Financial Officer
The mission of UCP San Diego County is to advance the independence, productivity and full citizenship of people affected by cerebral palsy and other disabilities. By making solid steps, UCP can build a better community for all in the process.

6403   Children's Hospital Central California Rehabilitation Center
9300 Valley Childrens Place
Madera, CA 93636-8762   559-353-3000
                                 www.valleychildrens.org
Todd Suntrapak, President & Chief Executive Officer
David Christensen, MD, SVP Medical Affairs & Chief Medical Officer
Beverly Hayden-Pugh, Vice President & Chief Nursing Officer
A 297-bed pediatric medical center on a 50-acre campus. We now have more then 500 doctors practicing in over 40 pediatric subspecialties with clinics and services throughout the state.

6404   Children's Hospital Los Angeles Rehabilitation Program
4650 W Sunset Blvd
Los Angeles, CA 90027-6062   323-361-4155
                                 888-631-2452
                                 FAX: 323-361-8101
                                 webmaster@chla.usc.edu
                                 www.childrenshospitalla.org
Richard D. Cordova, President & CEO
Rodney B. Hanners, Senior Vice President and Chief
Henri R. Ford, M.D.
Designated as a Level I Pediatric Trauma Canter by the Los Angeles County EMS Agency, the hospital treats more then 1,500 pediatric trauma patients per year. Performs more then 13,900 pediatric surgeries a year, including more complex surgical procedures then any other hospital in Southern California

6405   Children's Therapy Center
Ste 120
770 Paseo Camarillo
Camarillo, CA 93010-6092   805-383-1501
                                 FAX: 805-383-1504
Beth Maulhardt, Owner
Provides individual occupational therapy, speech/language therapy, family/child consulting, education services and physical therapy consultation for children. Evaluations and treatment are on an individual basis and special emphasis is placed on a multidisciplinary approach with information sharing, and often team treatment.

6406   Clausen House
88 Vernon Street
Oakland, CA 94610-4217   510-839-0050
                                 clausenhouse.org
Deborah Levy, Interim Executive Director
Michael A. Scott, Director of Development
Stan Nicholson, Director of Human Resources
Residential, supported employment, independent and supported living, adult education, and social recreation activities. Serving the developmentally disabled since 1967.

6407   Community Gatepath
350 Twin Dolphin Dr
Suite 123
Redwood City, CA 94065   650-259-8500
                                 FAX: 650-697-5010
                                 info@gatepath.org
                                 gatepath.org
Bryan Neider, CEO
Steve D'Eredita, Chief Financial Officer
Tracey Fecher, Vice President of Programs
Gatepath is a non-profit organization serving children, youth and adults with special needs and developmental disabilities and their families in the greater San Francisco Bay Area. The organization partners with various local non-profits, businesses, government agencies and third party providers to better serve this community.

6408   Community Hospital and Rehabilitation Center of Los Gatos-Saratoga
815 Pollard Rd
Los Gatos, CA 95032-1438   408-378-6131
                                 FAX: 408-866-4003
Gary Honts, CEO
Offers rehabilitation services, inpatient and outpatient care, physical therapy, occupational therapy and more for the physically challenged adult. We have a commitment to health care excellence. It is in this commitment that we have dedicated ourselves to provide personal and professional service to our patients. Our goal is to work closely with staff, physicians and the community to attain shared goals and positive changes, now and in the future.

6409   Contra Costa ARC
1340 Arnold Drive
Suite 127
Martinez, CA 94553-4189   925-370-1818
                                 FAX: 925-370-2048
                                 www.ContraCostaARC.com
Barbara Maizie, Executive Director
Diana Jorgensen, Program Coordinator
Andrey George, Administrative Coordinator
A private nonprofit membership-based organization dedicated to enhancing the quality of life of individuals with developmental disabilities.

6410   Corona Regional Medical Center- Rehabiltation Center
800 S. Main St.
Corona, CA 92882-3117   951-737-4343
                                 FAX: 951-736-7276
                                 www.coronaregional.com
Diane Mc Donald, Manager
Mark Uffer, Chief Executive Officer
Doreen Dann, Chief Nursing Officer
Offers inpatient and outpatient rehabilitation services. The Center consists of an acute rehab unit, a subacute rehab unit containing modules for long-term ventilator care, respiratory rehab, coma intervention and orthopedics. In addition to inpatient therapies, the Center's outpatient programs include sports and industrial medicine.

6411   Critical Air Medicine
Montgomery Field
8775 Aero Drive
Suite 235
San Diego, CA 92123-1705   858-300-0224
                                 800-247-8326
                                 FAX: 858-300-0228
                                 www.aircharterguide.com
Frank Craven, Publisher of the Air Charter Guide
Offers emergency medical care by air medical transport carriers. These carriers are fully equipped with medical equipment and

supplies for cardiovascular emergencies, respiratory supplies, orthopedic supplies and medications.

6412 Crutcher's Serenity House
P.O.Box D
50 Hillcrest Drive
Deer Park, CA 94576-504   707-963-3192
                                 FAX: 707-963-2309

Robert Crutcher, Owner/CEO
Lu Crutcher, Executive Director
A privately owned and operated facility that introduces to residents a new lifestyle free of all chemicals, and a new awareness of their total being. The length of the program is four weeks and is within five minutes of an acute care hospital. The Center is licensed for 19 beds, male and female located in a home-like setting with an emphasis on maintaining a family atmosphere.

6413 Daniel Freeman Rehabilitation Centers
333 N Prairie Ave
PO Box 28990
Santa Ana, CA 92799-4501   714-230-3150
                                 FAX: 714-850-0153
                                 advertising@acupuncturetoday.com
                                 www.acupuncturetoday.com
H Arndt, Associate Administrator
Gabrielle Lindsley, Business Development Manager
Evelyn Petersen, Human Resources / Payroll Manager
Comprehensive rehabilitation services which address needs and issues of the physically diabled and their families. We offer accute input rehabilitation, outpatient and short term skilled nursing rehabilitaion. Specialty areas include: brain injury, stroke, spinal chord injury, chronic pain, arthritis.

6414 Delano Regional Medical Center
1401 Garces Highway
Delano, CA 93215-3690   661-725-4800
                               drmc.com
Bahram Ghaffari, President
Jeremy Klemm, HealthStream Regional Director
Robert A. Frist, HealthStream CEO
Delano Regional Medical Center (DRMC) is proud to be known throughout California & beyond as an innovative regional hospital, deeply rooted in the local communities and committed to providing an exceptional patient experience. A non-profit acute-care facility serving a region of 10 rural central Californiatowns. With over 100 physicians on our active medical staff and additional courtesy or consulting physicians, patients are assured of receiving high-quality care in multiple specialties.

6415 Desert Regional Medical Center
1150 N Indian Canyon Dr
Palm Springs, CA 92262   760-323-6511
                                800-491-4990
                                www.desertmedctr.com
Carolyn Caldwell, Chief Executive Officer
Tracey Cowles, Physician Relations Manager
Jeanne Stanton, RN, Chair
Our dedicated physicians and caregivers provide a broad array of quality programs and services, including comprehensive cancer care, women's health services, heart care, surgical weight loss reduction and orthopedics.

6416 Devereux Advanced Behavioral Health California
P.O. Box 6784
Santa Barbara, CA 93160   805-968-2525
                                 FAX: 805-968-3247
                                 rpopke@devereux.org
                                 www.devereuxca.org
Amy Evans, Executive Director
Rebecca Popke, Marketing & Admissions Manager
Wendy Cooper, Manager of External Affairs
Serves adults age 18 through 85 who have intellectual and developmental disabilities such as emotional disturbances, neurological impairments, autism, dementia and more. Devereux California currently provides a continuum of services, including on-campus residential, day programs, behavior management and supported living services in the community.

6417 Division of Physical Medicine and Rehabilitation
San Joaquin General Hospital
500 W Hospital Rd
French Camp, CA 95231-9693   209-468-6000
                                    FAX: 209-468-6501
Offers rehabilitation services, inpatient and outpatient care, speech therapy, physical therapy, occupational therapy and more for the physically challenged individual.

6418 Dr. Karen H Chao Developmental Optometry Karen H. Chao. O.D.
Suite A
121 S Del Mar Ave
San Gabriel, CA 91776-1345   626-287-0401
                                    FAX: 626-287-1457
                                    drkhchao@yahoo.com
                                    www.healthgrades.com
Karen Chao, Owner
Karen Chao OD, Owner
Roger C. Holstein, Chief Executive Officer
Developmental optometrist specializing in the testing and treatment of vision problems and the enhancement of visual performance. Performs visual perceptual testing and training for children and adults. Undetected vision problems interfere with the ability to achieve and are highly correlated with learning difficulties and developmental problems. Provides the opportunity to overcome vision and visual-perceptual dysfunctions.

6419 Early Childhood Services
Desert Area Resources and Training
201 E Ridgecrest Blvd
Ridgecrest, CA 93555-3919   760-375-9787
                                   FAX: 760-375-1288
                                   www.dartontarget.org/
Peter V. Berns, Chief Executive Officer
Cris Bridges, Chief of Client Services
Bob Beecroft, Chief Operations Officer
Provides early intervention services to children who have disabilities or are experiencing delays in development. Provides developmental activities to promote the attainment of developmental milestones so that each child may reach his/her maximum potential. The program also provides therapeutic and educational intervention and offers support and guidance to families.

6420 East Los Angeles Doctors Hospital
4060 Whittier Boulevard
Los Angeles, CA 90023-2526   323-268-5514
                                    www.elalax.com
Hector Hernandez, Chief Executive Officer
Kamlesh Dhawan, Chief Of Staff
Michael Austerlitz, Vice-Chief Of Staff
Postacute rehabilitation program.

6421 Easterseals Northern California
2730 Shadelands Dr.
Walnut Creek, CA 94598   925-266-8400
                                customerservice@esnorcal.org
                                www.esnorcal.org
Jim Kelleher, Chief Executive Officer
Andrea Pettiford, Vice President, Operations
Creates solutions that change the lives of children and adults with disabilities and special needs, and provides support to family members.

6422 Easterseals Superior California
9812 Old Winery Place
Suite 21
Sacramento, CA 95827   916-485-6711
                              info@myeasterseals.org
                              www.easterseals.com/superior-ca
Julie Hagan-Belka, Chair
Greg Re, First Vice Chair
Lisa Avis, Treasurer
Dedicated to empowering people with disabilities by providing services, including medical rehabilitation and employment and training services, and promoting independence.

6423   Exceed: A Division of Valley Resource Center
P.O.Box 1773
1285 N. Santa Fe
Hemet, CA 92543-1773   951-766-8659
                                        800-423-1227
                                        FAX: 951-929-9758
                                        vrctwohip@aol.com

Pattie Robert, Business Development Specialist
Mary Morse, Marketing Director
Kathy Cooke, Manager
Our vision is an environment where each client is valued as an individual and is provided the opportunity to reach his/her maximum potential. Our mission is to provide service and advocacy, which creates choices and opportunities, for adults with disabilities to reach their maximum potential.

6424   Eye Medical Center of Fresno
Eye Medical Center
1360 E. Herndon Avenue
Suite 301 & 210
Fresno, CA 93720-1498   559-486-5000
                                        emcfresno.com
A private, nonprofit agency offering services such as health, educational, recreational, rehabilitation, employment and counseling to the totally blind, legally blind and visually impaired. The staff includes hundreds of full time workers.

6425   Fontana Rehabilitation Workshop
Industrial Support Systems
8333 Almeria Ave
Fontana, CA 92335-3283   909-428-3883
                                        800-755-4755
                                        FAX: 909-428-3835
                                        www.industrial-support.org

Silvia Anderson, Executive Director
U. Jones, CFO
C.Steven Bowen Plant, Operations manager
The Fontana Rehabilitation Workshop, Inc., through its business divisions is committed to maintaining a stable environment wherein people with disabilities are provided with those services and supports that enable them to overcome barriers to employment and empower them to maximize their employment potential.

6426   Foothill Vocational Opportunities
789 North Fair Oaks Avenue
Pasadena, CA 91103-3045   626-449-0218
                                        FAX: 626-449-0218
                                        info@foothillvoc.org
                                        foothillvoc.org
Foothill Vocational Opportunities maximizes the personal and economic potential of disabled individuals by creating meaningful employment opportunities. Foothill provides our clients and their families with the tools they need to live fuller, richer lives, bringing a sense of inclusion and dignity to a chronically marginalized and underdeserved group of people.

6427   Fred Finch Youth Center
3800 Coolidge Ave
Oakland, CA 94602-3399   510-482-2244
                                        FAX: 510-488-1960
                                        receptionist@fredfinch.org
                                        fredfinch.org

Thomas N. Alexander, President/CEO
FFYC seeks to provide a continuum of high quality programs for the care and treatment of children, youth, young adults, and their families, whose changing needs can best be met by a variety of mental health and support services. The goal is for the program participants to receive the most effective services in the least restrictive environment appropriate to their needs so that they may function at their highest potential.

6428   Gateway Center of Monterey County
850 Congress Ave
Pacific Grove, CA 93950-4898   831-372-8002
                                        FAX: 831-372-2411
                                        info@gatewaycenter.org
                                        gatewaycenter.org

Stephanie Lyon, Executive Director
Mike Price, Chief Financial Officer
Desiree Boller, Accounting Assistant

Our mission is to be a caring and stimulating environment for the Developmentally Disabled where all people can achieve their individual goals safely and with dignity. Our goal is to continue our programs and to find new and innovative ways of assisting the developmentally disabled to live in our community in surroundings compatable with their ability to live and work at the highest level possible.

6429   Gateway Industries: Castroville
7055 Veterans Blvd
Unit A
Burr Ridge, IL 60527   630-321-1333
                                        888-473-3744
                                        FAX: 630-321-1321
                                        www.redshift.com

Located in the Sand City Industrial Park, it provides vocational training and employment to developmentally disabled adults so they can achieve their vocational potential while also providing quality services to bussiness along the Central Coast. The sheltered work environment assists the employees by increasing their income, improving their work skills and habits, and enabling them to participate in the community.

6430   Gilroy Workshop
7471 Monterey Street
Gilroy, CA 95020-3629   408-430-2810
                                        FAX: 408-842-6770
                                        info@leadershipgilroy.org
                                        www.leadershipgilroy.org/

Kristi Alarid, Manager
Sally French, Manager
Denise Martin, Executive Director
Work adjustment and remunerative work programs.

6431   Glendale Adventist Medical Center
1509 Wilson Ter
Glendale, CA 91206-4098   818-409-8000
                                        FAX: 818-546-5609

Kevin Roberts, President/CEO
Warren Tetz, Sr. Vice President and COO
Kelly Turner, Sr. Vice President and CFO
Rehabilitative team is made up of physician specialists, as well as professional and certified staff nurses, thereapists and others who meet regularly to ensure tht each patients progress is carefully planned and closely monitored.

6432   Glendale Memorial Hospital and Health Center Rehabilitation Unit
Glendale Memorial Hospital and Health Center
1420 South Central Ave
Glendale, CA 91204-2508   818-502-1900
                                        FAX: 818-409-7688
                                        www.glendalememorialhospital.org

Catherine M. Pelley, President
Offers rehabilitation services, occupational therapy, physical therapy, residential services and more for the disabled.

6433   Goleta Valley Cottage Hospital
Cottage Health System
351 S Patterson Ave
Santa Barbara, CA 93111-2496   805-967-3411
                                        FAX: 805-681-6437
                                        cverkiak@cottagehealthsystem.org
                                        www.sbch.org

Ronald C. Wreft, President & CEO
Rosemary Bray, Clinical Manager
Diana Gray Miller, Administrator
A 122-bed acute care hospital was founded in 1966 to serve the growing community of Goleta Valley. Today, we admit more then 2,000 patients a year, see more then 17,000 emergency visits, and welcome nearly 400 newborns to our designated 'Baby Friendly' Birth Center each year. We are also recognized for our Level IV trauma designation. We take great pride in fulfilling our goal of providing each patient with comfortable, personalized care.

6434 HealthSouth Tustin Rehabilitation Hospital
Health South Corporation
14851 Yorba St
Tustin, CA 92780-2925   714-832-9200
                                    www.tustinrehab.com/

Diana Hanyak, Chief Executive Officer
Rodric Bell, Medical Director
Lindsey Barrett, Director of Case Management
HealthSouth Tustin Rehabilitation Hospital is part of the
HealthSouth Corportation, the nation's largest provider of reha-
bilitative healthcare services, we are the only facility of its
kind in Orange County. Fully accredited by the Joint Commission on
Accreditation of Healthcare Organizations (JACHO) we provide
inpatient and outpatient care designed to meed individual needs
of patients and their families.

6435 Hi-Desert Medical Center
6601 White Feather Road
Joshua Tree, CA 92252-760   760-366-3711
                                           hdmc.org

Lionel Chadwick, Chief Executive Officer
Tom Duda, Chief Financial Officer
Judy Austin, Chief Operating Officer & Chief
Postacute rehabilitation program.

6436 Home of the Guiding Hands
Suite 200
1825 Gillespie Way
El Cajon, CA 92020-0501   619-938-2850
                                    FAX: 619-938-3055
                                    info@guidinghands.org
                                        guidinghands.org

Mary Miller, President
Debby McNeil, Vice President
Michael Harris, Treasurer
The mission of Home og the Guiding Hands is to provide quality
services, training and advocacy for people with developmental
disabilities, their families, and others who will benefit.

**6437 Hospital of the Good Samaritan Acute Rehabilitation
Unit**
1225 Wilshire Blvd
Los Angeles, CA 90017-1901   213-977-2121
                                       800-366-8338
                                    FAX: 213-482-2770
                                    info@goodsam.org
                                          goodsam.org

Andrew B Leeka, President and CEO
Charles T. Munger, Chairman
Physicians, researchers and staff are united by a common mission: to foster growth into one of the most comprehensive medical centers in the West. Services offered include: cardiology and
cardiovascular services, neurosciences, movement disorders and
Parkinsons disorder, wound care center and transfusion-
medicine and surgery center.

6438 Innovative Rehabilitation Services
Hacienda La Puente Unified School District
15959 E. Gale Ave
City Of Industry, CA 91745   626-933-1000
                                    FAX: 626-934-2900
                                    info@hlpusd.k12.ca.us
                                    www.hlpusd.k12.ca.us

Matthew Smith, Site Administrator
George Stransky, Counselor
Crystal Ontiveros, Counselor
Provides innovative student-centered learning opportunities and
support services to a diverse population that enable individuals to
achieve thier goals as lifelong learners, productive workers and
effective communicators.

6439 Janus of Santa Cruz
Suite 150
200 7th Ave
Santa Cruz, CA 95062-4669   831-462-1060
                                       866-526-8772
                                           janussc.org

Rod Libbey, Executive Director
Bill Morris, Medical Director
Margie Storms, Clinical Director

A private not-for-profit corporation, licensed by the state of California. The Janus Clinic has a 3 year accreditation by the Council
on Accreditation for Health Care Facilities.

**6440 John Muir Medical Center Rehabilitation Services,
Therapy Center**
1601 Ygnacio Valley Rd
Walnut Creek, CA 94598-3122   925-939-3000
                                    FAX: 925-308-8944
                                    www.johnmuirhealth.com

Calvin Knight, President and CEO
Helen Doughty, Librarian
A 324-bed acute care facility that is designated as the only trauma
center for Contra Costa County and portions of Solano County.
Recognized as one of the region's premier healthcare providers,
areas of specialty include high-and low-risk obstetrics, orthopedics, neurosciences, cardiac care and cancer care. The campus is
accredited by the Joint Commission on Accreditation of
Healthcare Organizations (JCAHO), a national surveyor of
quality patient care.

6441 Kindred Hospital-La Mirada
14900 E. Imperial Hwy
La Mirada, CA 90638-2172   562-944-1900
                                    FAX: 562-906-3455
                                    TTY:800-735-2922
                                    www.kindredlamirada.com

April Myers, Administrator
Adam Darvish, Executive Director
Committed to the delivery of high quality care in a cost-effective
manner to enable us to become 'a model of excellence' in
Long-Term Acute Care. Committed to treat our patients and families with dignity and respect, in the same manner we would want
to be treated.

6442 King's View Work Experience Center- Atwater
559 East Bardsley Avenue
P. O. Box 688
Tulare, CA 93275-0688   559-688-7531
                                    FAX: 559-688-3509
                                    info@kingsview.org
                                    www.kingsview.org

Leon Hoover, Chief Executive Officer
Vida Jalali, Chief Financial Officer Interim
Sue Essman, Director of Human Resources
The primary mission of the Kings View Work Experience Center
(KVWEC) is to serve people who have developmental disabilities. We believe in the dignity and worth of each person and in
their right to rehabilitation, education and community integration. It is Kings View's aim to provide quality services to people
who need assistance in the development of social, vocational and
independent living skills.

6443 LaPalma Intercommunity Hospital
7901 Walker St
La Palma, CA 90623-1764   714-670-7400
                                    LPIHInfo@primehealthcare.com
                                    www.lapalmaintercommunityhospital.com

Virg Narbutas, Regional CEO
Sami Shoukair, Chief Medical Officer
Linda Gonzaba, Medical Staff Office Director
Lapalma Intercommunity Hospital endeavors to provide comprehensive, quality healthcare in a convenient, compassionate and
cost effective manner. Lapalma is consistently at the forefront of
evolving national healthcare reform. Our organization provides
an innovative and integrated healthcare delivery system. We remain ever cognizant of our patient's needs and desires for high
quality affordable healthcare.

6444 Learning Services of Northern California
131 Langley Drive
Suite B
Lawrenceville, GA 30046-9315   408-848-4379
                                       888-419-9955
                                    FAX: 866-491-7396
                                    www.learningservices.com

Dr. Debra Braunling-McMorrow, President and CEO
*Jeanne Mack, Chief Financial Officer and Vice President of Opera-
tions*
Michael Weaver, Chief Development Officer

Located on 10 acres of ranchland in rural Santa Clara Valley, our Gilroy Program offers treatment, structure, and support in a spacious, campus-based living environment. Sharing living residences are complimented by a treatment and recreation facility for individuals who require intensive support.

6445 Learning Services: Morgan Hill
131 Langley Drive
Suite B
Lawrenceville, GA 30046-9315   408-848-4379
888-419-9955
FAX: 866-491-7396
www.learningservices.com
Dr. Debra Braunling-McMorrow, President and CEO
Jeanne Mack, Chief Financial Officer and Vice President of Operations
Michael Weaver, Chief Development Officer
Located in the quaint rural town within walking distance from the old main street of Morgan Hill. Our Morgan Hill program offers the convenience and amenities of small-town living within the supportive community of Morgan Hill.

6446 Learning Services: Supported Living Programs
131 Langley Drive
Suite B
Lawrenceville, GA 30046-9315   408-848-4379
888-419-9955
FAX: 866-491-7396
www.learningservices.com
Dr. Debra Braunling-McMorrow, President and CEO
Jeanne Mack, Chief Financial Officer and Vice President of Operations
Michael Weaver, Chief Development Officer
We offer a variety of diverse and stimulating environments for people with different needs, capabilities and personal goals. Within comfortable, homelike, age-appropriate settings we provide the structure and support necessary to ensure the richest possible quality of life. Program offered in both Northern and Southern facilities of California

6447 Leon S Peters Rehabilitation Center
2823 Fresno St
Fresno, CA 93721-1324   559-459-6000
www.communitymedical.org
Florence Dunn, Chairwoman
John McGregor, Esquire, Secretary
Tim A. Joslin, President, Chief Executive Officer
Community's flagship hospital that offers world class specialized critical care with the area's only stroke unit with 24-hour vascular neurology and neurosurgery coverage and a team of specially trained stroke nurses. The world's first G4 CyberKnife. The table Mountain Rancheraia Level 1 Trauma Center. The Leon S. Peters burn center. The region's only perinatology program for high rish pregnancies and deliveries. The Da-Vinci robotic surgical system, and 3 helicopeter landing pads.

6448 Lion's Blind Center of Diablo Valley, Inc. Lions Center For The Visually Impaired
175 Alvarado Ave
Pittsburg, CA 94565-4862   925-432-3013
800-750-3937
FAX: 925-432-7014
www.seniorvision.org
Edward Schroth, Executive Director
Barbara Cronin, President
Charles Dunham, First Vice President
A private, nonprofit agency offering services such as health, educational, recreational, rehabilitation, employment and counseling to the totally blind, legally blind and visually impaired. The staff includes two full time workers.

6449 Lion's Blind Center of Oakland
2115 Broadway
Oakland, CA 94612-2698   510-450-1580
FAX: 510-654-3603
Michelle Taylor Lagunas, Executive Director/ CEO
Christina Easiley, Administrative Manager
Scott Blanks, Director of Rehabilitation Servi
A private, nonprofit organization offering services for the totally blind, legally blind, deaf-blind and multihandicapped blind. Services include: professional training, rehabilitation, education,

counseling, social work, self help and more. The staff includes 12 full time and 1 part time worker.

6450 Living Skills Center for the Visually Impaired
2430 Road 20
#B112
San Pablo, CA 94806-5005   510-234-4984
FAX: 510-234-4986
info@hcblind.org
www.hcblind.org
Patricia Williams, Executive Director
Patricia Maffei, Program Director
Ronald Hideshima, Adaptive Technology Instructor
A private, nonprofit agency offering services such as independent living skills training, recreational, employment and accessible technology training to the totally blind, legally blind and visually impaired. The staff includes six full time teachers.

6451 Loma Linda University Orthopedic and Rehabilitation Institute
25333 Barton Rd
Loma Linda, CA 92354-3123   909-558-1000
FAX: 909-558-0308
www.llu.edu
Richard H. Hart, MD, DrPH, President & Chief Executive Officer
Ronald L. Carter, PhD, Senior Vice President, Educational Affairs
Cari Dominguez, DHS, Senior Vice President, Human Resources
Offers a full range of clinical programs for both inpatients and outpatient. The specific diagnosis leading to patient admission includes stroke, spinal cord injury, traumatic or anoxic brain damage, amputation, post neurosurgery, chronic neurological disease, Guillain-Barre syndrome, arthritis, multiple trauma or other complex orthopedic problems. The facilities and professional services are comprehensive and ensure that the best care is provided to pediatric and adult patients.

6452 Manor Care Health Services- Citrus Heights
7807 Uplands Way
Citrus Heights, CA 95610-7500   916-967-2929
FAX: 916-965-8439
hcr-manorcare.com
Steven M. Cavanaugh, Chief Financial Officer
Paul A. Ormond, Chairman, President and Chief Ex
The nations leader in skilled nursing and rehabilitation care. Our facility has been serving the Sacramento area for more then 12 years. We are known for our beautiful decor, outstanding rehabilitation staff and loving nursing care. We offer short term rehabilitation, long term skilled nursing care, respite care and post hospital surgical care.

6453 Manor Care Health Services- Palm Desert
74-350 Country Club Dr
Palm Desert, CA 92260-1608   760-341-0261
FAX: 760-779-1563
hcr-manorcare.com
Steven M. Cavanaugh, Chief Financial Officer
Paul A. Ormond, Chairman, President and Chief Ex
Centrally located in the Coachella Valley, specializing in skilled nursing whith an emphasis on rehabilitation, post surgery recovery, hospice, alzheimer's care and long term care. In addition, we offer 2 unique service options for the discriminating consumer. Our Arcadia unit offers a specialized Alzheimer's care program in a dedicated secure wing. ManorCare offers rehabilitation services including physical, occupational and speech therapies for those recovering from illness injury or surgery.

6454 Manor Care Health Services-Fountain Valley
11680 Warner Ave
Fountain Valley, CA 92708-2513   714-241-9800
FAX: 714-966-1654
hcr-manorcare.com
Steven M. Cavanaugh, Chief Financial Officer
Paul A. Ormond, Chairman, President and Chief Ex
Provides 24-hour skilled nursing, rehabilitative therapies and specialized Alzheimer's care. Our in-house therapists provide physical, occupational and speech therapies in our rehabilitation area. Our team is goal oriented and focuses on producing positive outcomes for those recovering from illness, injury or surgery. Our respite care program provides a full range of services for a few days, a week or even a season.

6455 Manor Care Health Services-Hemet
1717 W Stetson Ave
Hemet, CA 92545-6882
951-925-9171
FAX: 951-925-8186
hcr-manorcare.com

Steven M. Cavanaugh, Chief Financial Officer
Paul A. Ormond, Chairman, President and Chief Ex
Provides skilled nursing, Rehabilitation services, and specialized Alzheimer's care. In addition we offer short term respite stays for family caregivers that simply need a break from the stress of daily care. Our Arcadia unit staff is specially trained in the care of residents with Alzheimer's disease. The secured unit is designed to provide a soothing and homelike environment while enhancing each resident's remaining abilities.

6456 Manor Care Health Services-Sunnyvale
1150 Tilton Dr
Sunnyvale, CA 94087-2440
408-735-7200
FAX: 408-736-8629
hcr-manorcare.com

Steven M. Cavanaugh, Chief Financial Officer
Paul A. Ormond, Chairman, President and Chief Ex
Our in-house therapists provide physical, occupational and speech therapies in our rehabilitation area. Our team is goal oriented and focuses on producing positive outcomes for those recovering from illness, injury or surgery. Our skilled nursing staff works with our therapy department and dietary department to provide positive wound care programs for patients requiring skin management care.

6457 Manor Care Health Services-Walnut Creek
1226 Rossmoor Pkwy
Walnut Creek, CA 94595-2538
925-975-5000
FAX: 925-937-1132
hcr-manorcare.com

Steven M. Cavanaugh, Chief Financial Officer
Paul A. Ormond, Chairman, President and Chief Ex
Provides luxurious long term care and rehabilitation services. In house therapists provide, physical, occupational and speech therapies in our rehabilitation area. Our team is goal oriented and focuses on producing positive outcomes for those recovering from illness, injury or surgery. Our years of combined management experience add value to our resident's quality of life.

6458 Maynord's Chemical Dependency Recovery Centers
19325 Cherokee Road
Tuolumne, CA 95379-1657
209-928-3737
800-228-8208
FAX: 209-928-1152
maynords.com

James Berry, Director
Maynord's Recovery Centers has always been dedicated to the recovery of good people whose lives are being destroyed by alcohol and drugs. Since 1978, Maynord's residential program has helped thousands of people put their lives back together after addiction has taken its toll. Today, Maynord's offers a treatment system over much of the San Joaquin Valley and the San Francisco Bay Area.

6459 Maynord's Ranch for Men
19325 Cherokee Road
Tuolumne, CA 95379-1657
209-928-3737
800-228-8208
FAX: 209-928-1152
maynords.com

James Berry, Director
Provides treatment for chemical dependency problems to men. The treatment addresses their recovery through a comprehensive plan created for their individual needs. Also offers a program for women called the Meadows.

6460 Meadowbrook Manor
431 West Remington Boulevard
Bolingbrook, IL 60440
630-759-1112
FAX: 630-759-6925
www.meadowbrookmanor.com
Postacute rehabilitation program.

6461 Meadowview Manor
41 Crestview Terrace
Bridgeport, WV 26330
304-842-7101
FAX: 304-842-7104
Provides treatment designed for women that is directed at every important facet of their lives - mentally, physically and spiritually. Clients receive a variety of treatment approaches to facilitate their recovery and a comprehensive treatment plan is created for their individual needs. Issues relating to the cause of addictions are addressed in lectures, one-on-one counseling sessions, group therapy and re entry groups. Also offers a male treatment programs called Maynord's Ranch.

6462 Memorial Hospital of Gardenia
1145 West Redondo Beach Blvd
Gardena, CA 90247-3528
310-532-4200
800-782-2288
www.avantihospitals.com

Edward Mirzabegian, Corporate Chief Executive Officer
Postacute rehabilitation program.

6463 Mercy Medical Group
Mercy Hospital
3000 Q Street
Sacramento, CA 95816
916-733-3333
www.mymercymedicalgroup.org
Located near the Old Rosevill Hospital. There are several primary care physicians, including Family Practice, Internal Medicine and Pediatrics at this location. Specialty services include Diagnostic Imaging, Laboratory and Mental Health Services.

6464 Napa County Mental Health Department
2344 Old Sonoma Road
Bldg. D
Napa, CA 94559-3708
707-259-8151
800-648-8650
www.countyofnapa.org/MentalHealth/
Work hardening and disciplinary programs.

6465 Napa Valley Support Systems
1700 Second Street Suite 212
Napa, CA 94559-1344
707-253-7490
FAX: 707-253-0115
napavalleysupportservices.org

Beth Kahiga, Executive Director
Heather Jump, Administrative Manager
Katy Vanzant, Program Director
Work hardening and disciplinary programs.

6466 North Valley Services
1040 Washington
Red Bluff, CA 96080-4509
530-527-0407
FAX: 530-527-7091
www.northvalleyservices.org

Joe Brown, President
Larry Donnelley, Vice President
Lynn DeFreece, CEO
Provides vocational rehabilitation services, such as job counseling, job training, and work experience, to unemployed and underemployed persons, persons with disabilities.

6467 Northridge Hospital Medical Center Rehabiltation Medicine
18300 Roscoe Blvd
Northridge, CA 91328-4167
818-885-8500
FAX: 818-701-7367
www.northridgehospital.org/index.htm

Mike L. Wall, President
Thomas L. Hedge, Medical Director
Joel S. Rosen, Associate Medical Director
A full service, comprehensive rehabilitation program suited to treat patients of all ages who have suffered catastrophic or debilitating injury or illness. The goal of the program is to deliver exceptional patient care to maximise each individual's skills and independence.

6468 Northridge Hospital Medical Center: Centerfor Rehabilitation Medicine
18300 Roscoe Blvd
Northridge, CA 91328-4167
818-885-8500
FAX: 818-701-7367
www.northridgehospital.com

Mike L. Wall, President
Thomas L. Hedge, Medical Director
Joel S. Rosen, Associate Medical Director
Committed to serving the health needs of our communities with particular attention to the needs of the poor, the disadvantaged, and vulneralbe, and the comfort of the suffering and dying. Catholic Healthcare West has a commitment to quality-quality healthcare services and the promotion of optimal quality of life for all of life.

6469 Old Adobe Developmental Services
1301A Rand Street
Suite A
Petaluma, CA 94954-5697
707-763-9807
FAX: 707-763-7708
www.oadsinc.org

Elizabeth Clary, Executive Director
Marie Padgett, Controller
The mission of Old Adobe to provide opportunities for individuals with developmental challenges to reach thier fullest potentials. Our job at OADS is to find ways for these individuals to find full expression in all parts of their lives. We have a partnership with the Adult Education Department of the Petaluma School District in providing services to persons with developmental challenges. We are funded by the Dept. of Rehabilitation and the Dept. Of Developmental services.

6470 Old Adobe Developmental Services-Rohnert Park Services (Behavioral)
5401 Snyder Ln.
Rohnert Park, CA 94928-3124
707-584-5859
FAX: 707-664-8057

Elizabeth Clary, Executive Director
Helen Gunderson, Administrative Assistant
The program services are designed to assist individuals who demonstrate basic work skills, to develop social skills and work habits necessary to succeed in supported or competitive employment. Most often individual program services involve working with the client to replace those behavioral excesses that have been a barrier to vocational placement.

6471 PRIDE Industries
10030 Foothills Blvd
Roseville, CA 95747-7102
916-788-2100
800-550-6005
FAX: 800-888-0447
info@prideindustries.com
prideindustries.com

Michael Ziegler, President & CEO
Bob Selvester, Vice Chair
Mike Snegg, Treasurer
To provide opportunities through employment, training, evaluation and placement maximizing community access, independence and quality of life for people with barriers to employment.

6472 Pacific Hospital Of Long Beach-Neuro Care Unit
2776 Pacific Ave
Long Beach, CA 90806-2613
562-997-2000
webmaster@phlb.org

Michael D. Drobot, CEO
Clark Todd, President
Teri Plemmons, Administrative Assistant
Our mission is to heal with compassion and to perform with distinction. Our vision: to improve the hospital's orthopedic and Spine Center of Excellence. Achieve exceptional financial performance to enhance hospital services. Improve the vertically integrated ancillary, outpatient and inpatient surgery system. Develop a professionally challenging work environment that reflects an agile, peak performance culture.

6473 Paradise Vally Hospital-South Bay Rehabilitation Center
2400 East 4th St
National City, CA 91950-2026
619-470-4321
paradisevalleyhospital.net

Prem Reddy, Chairman
Neerav Jadeja, Administrator
Luis Leon, President
South Bay Rehabilitation Center, offers a complete range of treatment for patients with physical disabilities. Our specialized inpatient and outpatient programs are designed to meet each person's individual needs or injuries, with the goal of restoring as much independence as possible and significantly improving their lives.

6474 Parents and Friends
350 South Main Street
Fort Bragg, CA 95437-5408
707-964-4940
parentsandfriends.org

Rick Moon, Executive Director
Jessica Dickey, Administrative Assistant
Kristy Tanguay, Manager
Parents and Friends provides opportunities for persons with developmental challenges and similar needs to participate fully in our community.

6475 People Services
4195 Lakeshore Blvd
Lakeport, CA 95453-6411
707-263-3810
peopleservices.org

Ilene Dumont, Executive Director
Martin Diesman, Director
Vicki Cole, Director
Providing an array of services for adults with developmental disabilities and other people with disabilities. Services include supported employment, work services, supported living, personal, social and community training, transportation, specialized individual services and much more.

6476 Petaluma Recycling Center
Old Adobe Developmental Services
315 2nd St
Petaluma, CA 94952-4230
707-763-4761
FAX: 707-763-4921

Elizabeth Clary, Executive Director
Began in 1974; has been one of the major employers of persons with developmental challenges for 26 years; is the primary recycling facility in the growing city of 52,000; accepts over 20 different kinds of recyclables; employs 20-25 persons a day.

6477 Pomerado Rehabilitation Outpatient Service
15615 Pomerado Rd
Poway, CA 92064-2405
858-485-6511
FAX: 858-613-4248

Bob Blake, Director Rehab Services
Jonathan Pee, Manager
A 107-bed acute care hospital. In addition to a round-the-clock Emergency Department, Pomerado offers the area's finest outpaitent surgery center and general medical/surgical services. Pomerado Hospital also is home to a world-class Birth Center and a Level II NICU. Fully JCAHO-accredidted, Pomerado is well-known for offering only private rooms, each with a scenic view of the North Countryside, which enhances the healing atmosphere.

6478 Pride Industries: Grass Valley
12451 Loma Rica Dr
Grass Valley, CA 95945-9059
530-477-1832
800-550-6005
FAX: 530-477-8038
info@prideindustries.com
www.prideindustries.com

Bob Olsen, Chairman
Bob Selvester, Vice Chairman
Walt Payne, President/CEO
Work adjustment and remunerative work programs. We offer an adult day program as well.

6479 Rancho Adult Day Care Center
Rancho Los Amigos Medical Center
7601 Imperial Hwy
Downey, CA 90242-3456
562-401-7111
FAX: 562-401-7991
TTY:562-401-8450
dhs.lacounty.gov/wps/portal/dhs/rancho

Valerie Orange, CEO
Margaret L Campbell, Research Director
Provides personal care, social services and a therapeutic program to older adults in order to improve their quality of life. Offers a Clinical Gerontology Service, an Alzheimer's Disease Diagnostic and Treatment Center and a Geriatric Assessment and Rehabilitation Unit.

6480 Regional Center for Rehabilitation
2288 Auburn Blvd
Sacramento, CA 95821-1618
916-421-4167
FAX: 916-925-1586

Postacute rehabilitation program.

6481 Rehabilitation Institute of Santa Barbara
2415 De La Vina St
Santa Barbara, CA 93105-3819
805-569-8999
FAX: 805-687-3707

Ralph Pollock, President
Scott Silic MBA, Vice President Of Operations
Cheryl Ellis MD, MHA, VP Medical Services
A regional rehabilitation system with an acute care hospital at the center, the Institute provides specialized inpatient and outpatient programs for brain injury, spinal cord injury, stroke, work-related injury, chronic pain, orthopedic problems and more. Offers a 46-bed acute-care rehabilitation hospital, a free-standing outpatient center, the brain injury continuum, chronic pain program.

6482 Rehabilitation Institute of Southern California
1800 E La Veta Ave
Orange, CA 92866-2902
714-633-7400
FAX: 714-633-4586
riorehab.org

Praim S. Singh, Executive Director
Carol Reese, Executive Assistant
Grace Lee, Administrative Assistant
Outpatient rehabilitation serving physically and disabled children and adults. Child development programs, adult day care for disabled seniors, child care for disabled and non-disabled children, outpatient therapy, aquatics, adult day healthcare, independent living, vocational services, social services, and housing.

6483 Rubicon Programs
2500 Bissell Avenue
Richmond, CA 94804-1815
510-235-1516
FAX: 510-235-2025
www.rubiconprograms.org

Rob Hope, Chief Program Officer
Jane Fischberg, President and Executive Director
Roger Contreras, CFO
Rubicon Programs Inc. helps people and communities build assets to achieve greater independence. Since 1973, Rubicon has built and operated affordable housing and provided employment, job training, mental health, and other supportive services to individuals who have disabilities, are homeless, or are otherwise economically disadvantaged.

6484 San Bernardino Valley Lighthouse for the Blind
762 North Sierra Way
San Bernardino, CA 92410-4438
909-884-3121
FAX: 909-884-2964
www.afb.org

Robert Mc Bay, Executive Director
Sandra Wood, Administrative Assistant
Provides training in independent living skills - cooking, mobility and orientation, sewing, Braille and typing. Also, we have classes in macrame, ceramics and basket weaving. Weekly support group and Bible study.

6485 Santa Clara Valley Blind Center, Inc.
101 N Bascom Ave
San Jose, CA 95128-1805
408-295-4016
FAX: 408-295-1398
info@visionbeyondsight.org
visionbeyondsight.org

Arnold Chew, President
John Glass, Vice President
Arlene Holmes, Secretary
SCVBC's mission is to increase the confidence, independence, and quality of life of the blind and visually impaired through educational, recreational, and rehabilitative programs.

6486 Scripps Memorial Hospital: Pain Center
4275 Campus Point Ct.
San Diego, CA 92121-1205
858-626-4123
800-727-4777
clinicalresearch@scrippshealth.com
www.scripps.org

Chris Van Gorder, President and CEO
Richard K Rothberger, Vice President, Chief Financial Officer
Robin B Brown, Chief Executive
Offers both inpatient and outpatient programs including: physical activity management, individual pain management, group therapy, medication adjustment, pain control classes, occupational therapy, biofeedback training, family counseling, vocational and leisure counseling and recreational therapy.

6487 Sharp Coronado Hospital
250 Prospect Place
Coronado, CA 92118-1999
619-522-3600
erica.carlson@sharp.com
sharp.com

Marcia Hall, CEO
Mark Tamsen, Chairman
Tom Smisek, Vice Chairman
Providing medical and surgical care, intensive care, sub-acute and long-term care, rehabilitation therapies and emergency services in a peaceful setting is part of our live+heal+grow philosophy. We are one of the county's few community-owned hospitals and are proud of our history of providing convenient , award-winning heath care to Coronado and San Diego.

6488 Shriners Hospitals For Children-Northern California
2425 Stockton Blvd.
Sacramento, CA 95817
916-453-2000
patientreferrals@shrinenet.org
www.shrinershospitalsforchildren.org

John McCabe, Executive Vice President
Dale W Stauss, Chairman
Jerry G Gantt, 1st Vice President
The only hospital in the Shriners system that houses facilities for treatment of all 3 Shriner specialties -spinal cord injuries, orthopaedic, and burns. The hospital features 80 patient beds, 9 parent apartments, 5 state-of-the-art operating rooms, a high-tech Motion Analysis lab, and an entire floor devoted to research.

6489 Shriners Hospitals for Children: Los Angeles
3160 Geneva Street
Los Angeles, CA 90020-1199
213-388-3151
patientreferrals@shrinenet.org
www.shrinershospitalsforchildren.org

John McCabe, Executive Vice President
Dale W Stauss, Chairman
Jerry G Gantt, 1st Vice President
Shriners Hospitals for Children: Los Angeles, treats children under age 18 with burn scars, orthopedic conditions, cleft lip and palate and limb deficiencies at no cost to the patient or their families.

6490 Society for the Blind
1238 S St.
Sacramento, CA 95811-3256
916-452-8271
FAX: 916-492-2483
info@societyfortheblind.org
societyfortheblind.org

Shari Roesler, Executive Director
Shane Snyder, Director of Programs
A private, local nonprofit organization providing blind and visually impaired people with the training supplies and support they need to live independent, productive and fulfilled lives with lim-

ited vision. Services include the Low Vision Clinic, Braille classes, computer training, support groups, living skills instruction, mobility training and the Products for Independence Store.

6491 Solutions at Santa Barbara: Transitional Living Center
1135 N Patterson Ave
Santa Barbara, CA 93111-1113   805-683-1995
FAX: 805-683-4793
sol1135@aol.com
solutionsatsantabarbara.com

Sue Hannigan, Director
Postacute rehabilitation program. Short-term transitional living program for individuals with traumatic brain injury, stroke, aneurysm and other neurological disorders.

6492 St. John's Pleasant Valley Hospital Neuro Care Unit
2309 Antonio Ave
Camarillo, CA 93010-1414   805-389-5800
Jerry Conway, President
Maureen M. Malone, Administrator
Raye Burkhardt, Vice President and Chief Nursing
Houses 82 acute-care beds, a 99-bed extended care unit, and the only hyperbaric medicine unit in Ventura County. Employ's 1,800 people and count 250 active medical staff.

6493 St. John's Regional Medica Center- Industrial Therapy Center
1600 North Rose Ave
Oxnard, CA 93030-3723   805-988-2500
www.stjohnshealth.org
Gudrun Moll, Vice President and Chief Nursing
Laurie Harting, President & CEO
Kim Wilson, Vice President
A non-profit health care facility offering multi-disciplinary programs for pain management and work hardening, as well as physical and occupational therapy.

6494 Sub-Acute Saratoga Hospital
13425 Sousa Lane
Saratoga, CA 95070-4663   408-378-8875
FAX: 408-378-7419
subacutesaratoga.com

Jack Stephens, President & CEO
Paul Quintana, Medical Director
Gary Vernon, NHA Administrator
Dedicated to the fulfillment of human needs, desires, and wishes in illness and in health. The cohesiveness of caring in a family community of staff, patients, and their loved ones. The celebration of each unique life through their therapeutic journey, while preserving their individual spirit. The achievement of advanced medical expertise, knowledge, and skill given with the human touch of caring toward the ultimate goal: enhancing the healing process from acute illness to the joy of going home.

6495 Synergos Neurological Center: Hayward
27200 Calaroga Avenue
Hayward, CA 94545-4383   510-264-4000
FAX: 510-264-4007
strosehospital.org

Richard C. Hardwig, Chair
Alan McIntosh, Vice Chair
Lex Reddy, President and CEO
Postacute rehabilitation program.

6496 Synergos Neurological Center: Mission Hills
27200 Calaroga Avenue
Hayward, CA 94545-4383   510-264-4000
FAX: 510-264-4007
www.strosehospital.org

Richard C. Hardwig, Chair
Alan McIntosh, Vice Chair
Lex Reddy, President and CEO
For over 30 years, St. Rose Hospital Rehabilitation Services Department has helped thousands of patients recover from illness and injury through the help of our specially trained therapists. These therapists have been trained in specific rehabilitative areas such as physical, occupational, and speech therapies.

6497 Temple Community Hospital
235 N Hoover St
Los Angeles, CA 90004-3672   213-382-7252
FAX: 213-382-1874
templecommunityhospital.com
The mission of Temple Community Hospital is to improve the quality of health in our community and to provide necessary hospital services for those individuals requiring such care.

6498 The Arc of the East Bay
1101 Walpert St
Hayward, CA 94541-3721   510-582-8151
arcalameda.org

Son Luter, President & CEO
Offers a variety of services and programs for adults and children with intellectual and developmental disabilities.

6499 Tunnell Center for Rehab
680 South Fourth Street
Louisville, CA 40202-4807   502-596-7300
FAX: 800-545-0749
web_administrator@kindred.com
kindredhealthcare.com

Mary R., Activities Assistant
Kristen W., Health and Rehabilitation Center
The Tunnell Center for Rehabilitation and Healthcare accomodates 178 residents. We are dedicated to short-term complex medical and rehabilitative care. Using a holistic care management approach we work with residents who have suffered debilitating injury or illness, and who need comprehensive nursing and rehabilitation services to achieve their highest practicable level of functional ability and independence.

6500 Ukiah Valley Association for Habilitation
Ukiah, CA 95482-689   707-468-8824
FAX: 707-468-9149
TTY:800-735-2929
www.uvah.org

Pamela Jensen, Executive Director
Kris Vipond, Business Manager
Sharrae Elston, Director
Work adjustment and suppoted employment and social and community services.

6501 Valley Center for the Blind
2491 W Shaw Avenue
Suite 124
Fresno, CA 93711-3331   559-222-4088
FAX: 559-222-4844

Bud Breslin, Executive Director
Millie Marshall, Marriage Family Therapist
Saramarie Katich, Office Mngr/Program Director
A private, nonprofit organization that offers educational, health, recreational and professional training services to the totally blind, legally blind or severely visually impaired.

6502 Villa Esperanza Services
2060 East Villa Street
Pasadena, CA 91107   626-449-2919
FAX: 626-449-2850
info@villaesperanzaservices.org
www.villaesperanzaservices.org

Candice Rogers, Chairman
Richard Hubinger, President
Vicky Castillo, CFO
Serving disabled infants to seniors in a school, adult day program, adult work program and residences and adult day health care program and care management program.

6503 Village Square Nursing And Rehabilitation Center
Kindred Healthcare, Inc.
1586 West San Marcos Blvd
San Marcos, CA 92078-4019   760-471-2986
Accomodates 118 residents offering spacious private and semi-private rooms. We are Medicare and Medi-Cal certified and contracted with most managed care insurance groups.

6504 Vista Center for the Blind & Visually Impaired
2500 El Camino Real,
Suite 100
Palo Alto, CA 94306   650-858-0202
                                   800-660-2009
                            FAX: 650-858-0214
                             info@vistacenter.org
                             www.vistacenter.org

Pam Brandin, Executive Director
Nacole Barth-Ellis, Co-Director of Development
Terry Kurfess, Co-Director of Development
Private nonprofit agency that serves the visually impaired in the San Mateo, Santa Clara, San Benito and Santa Cruz Counties with offices in Palo Alto and Santa Cruz. Offers Low Vision Evaluations, mobility training, daily living skills training, social services, counseling, support groups, computer training, other rehabilitation services, and a store.

6505 Winways at Orange County
7732 E Santiago Canyon Rd
Orange, CA 92869-1829   714-771-5276
                            FAX: 714-771-1452
                             winwaysrehab.com

Pamela Kauss, Director
The program offers clients highly personalized, comprehensive programs to meet the needs of individuals with traumatic brain injury, stroke, tumors, aneurysm, post concussive syndrome or other neurological disorders. Winways also has a special program that provides services to Spanish speaking clients, called Contigo Adelante with materials in Spanish, and Spanish speaking interpreters to assist in the therapy process.

Colorado

6506 Capron Rehabilitation Center
Penrose Hospital/ St. Francis Healthcare System
2222 N Nevada Ave
Colorado Springs, CO 80907-6819   719-776-5000
                             penrosestfrancis.org
Margaret Sabin, President & CEO
Nate Olson, Chief Executive Officer
Jameson Smith, Senior VP & Chief Admnistrative Officer
Southern Colorado's most complete inpatient and outpatient rehabilitation center.

6507 Cerebral Palsy of Colorado
801 Yosemite Street
Denver, CO 80230   303-691-9339
                            FAX: 303-691-0846
                         abilityconnectioncolorado.org
Judith I Ham, CEO
James Reuter, Chairman of the Board
Penfield Tate, Vice Chairman
Provides services for children birth-5 years, employment services for adults, information and referral, donation pickup and cell phone/ink cartridge recycling services.

6508 Cherry Hills Health Care Center
Kindred
3575 S Washington St
Englewood, CO 80110-3807   303-789-2265
Accomodates 92 residents. We serve Medicare, Medicaid, managed-care and private pay clients. Our 2 story facility has a home-like environment with a dining room and a day room one each floor. Our short-term rehab unit was designed for patients who have been in the hospital and need continued intensive nursing care or rehabilitation before returning home.

6509 Community Hospital Back and Conditioning Clinic
1060 Orchard Ave
Grand Junction, CO 81501-2997   970-243-3400
                                   800-621-0926
                            FAX: 970-856-6510
Amy Hibberd, Executive Director
David Scherman, Manager
Post-accute rehabilitation program.

6510 Devereux Advanced Behavioral Health Colorado
8405 Church Ranch Blvd.
Westminster, CO 80021   303-466-7391
                                   800-456-2536
                             www.devereuxco.org
Lisa Gaudia, Interim Clinical Director
A non-profit partner for individuals, families, schools and communities, serving people in the areas of autism, intellectual and developmental disabilities, mental health issues, and child welfare. Programs offered include residential services, community based services, educational programs, employment supports and more.

6511 Laradon Hall Society for Exceptional Children and Adults
5100 Lincoln St
Denver, CO 80216-2056   303-296-2400
                                   866-381-2163
                            FAX: 303-296-4012
                                   laradon.org

William Mitchell, Chair
Suzanne Bradeen, Vice Chair
Jason Adams, Treasurer
Laradon provides educational, vocational and residential services to children and adults with developmental disabilities and other special needs. Laradon was founded in 1948. It is among the largest and most comprehensive service providers in Colorado.

6512 Learning Services: Bear Creek
7201 W Hampden Ave
Lakewood, CO 80227-5305   303-989-6660
                                   888-419-9955
                            FAX: 866-491-7396
                             learningservices.com
Susan Snow, Director of Admissions
Dr. Debra Braunling-McMorrow, President and CEO
Jeanne Mack, Chief Financial Officer
Supported living program for persons with acquired brain injury.

6513 MOSAIC In Colorado Springs
888 W. Garden of the Gods Road
Ste 100
Colorado Springs, CO 80907-6251 719-380-0451
                            FAX: 719-380-7055
                   mosaic_cosprings@mosaicinfo.org
                   www.mosaicincoloradosprings.org
Tom Maltais, Executive Director
Mosaic in Colorado Springs provides a variety of services to assist adults and families in achieving positive goals. Services to persons with intellectual disabilities include community living options, vocational training and supported employment, spiritual growth and personal development options, and day programs habilitation and community participation.

6514 Manor Care Nursing and Rehabilitation Center: Boulder
Manor Care Ohio
2800 Palo Pkwy
Boulder, CO 80301-1540   303-440-9100
                            FAX: 303-440-9251
                             www.hcr-manorcare.com
Steven M. Cavanaugh, Chief Financial Officer
Paul A. Ormond, Chairman, President and Chief Ex
150 bed center offers a full spectrum of nursing care and rehabilitation. This includes our Arcadia Special Care Unit for Alzheimer's patients. Specialized unit for post acute skilled nursing care. Physical and massage therapies. And a 48 bed upscale Heritage unit offering additional amenities and furnishings.

6515 Manor Care Nursing: Denver
290 S Monaco Pkwy
Denver, CO 80224-1105   303-355-2525
                            FAX: 303-333-6960
                             www.hcr-manorcare.com
Steven M. Cavanaugh, Chief Financial Officer
Paul A. Ormond, Chairman, President and Chief Ex
Our center has delveloped a reputation for its luxurious environment, comprehensive rehabilitation service and focus on quality care. A wide range of individual and group activities and many gracious amenities create the finest combination of elegance and professional skilled nursing care. Arcadia, our special care unit for persons with Alzheimer's disease and related memory impair-

ments, promotes independence and preserves dignity within a safe and secure environment.

6516 Mediplex of Colorado
8451 Pearl St
Thornton, CO 80229-4804
303-288-3000
FAX: 303-286-5136
info@vhdenver.com

Jan Eyer, Chief Executive Officer

Our programs and services help each patient along the road to recovery toward our ultimate aim; the greatest possible restoration of the individual's self-esteem, ability to set goals, and self-sufficiency. Also offer specialized acute inpatient rehabilitative services, including special programs in Trauma Rehabilitation.

6517 Platte River Industries
490 Bryant St
Denver, CO 80204-4808
303-825-0041
FAX: 303-825-0564

Bob Smith, Executive Director

Postacute rehabilitation facility and program.

6518 Pueblo Diversified Industries
2828 Granada Blvd
Pueblo, CO 81005-3198
800-466-8393
FAX: 719-564-3407
info@pdipueblo.org
www.pdipueblo.net

Karen K Lillie, President & CEO
Robin Forbes, Director Human Services
Tom Drolshagen, Chief Operating Officer

A place where people can turn limitations into opportunities. People can experience the independence, pride and self worth of securing and maintaining a job.

6519 SHALOM Denver
2498 W 2nd Ave
Denver, CO 80223-1007
303-623-0251
FAX: 303-620-9584
shalomdenver.com

Arnie Kover, Disability and Employment Servic
Sara Leeper, Coordinator of Client Services
Vicky Brittain, Mailing Business Manager

SHALOM Denver provides employment, training, and job placement opportunities to people with disabilities, resettled immigrants, and people moving from welfare to work.

6520 SPIN Early Childhood Care & Education Cntr
1333 Elm Ave
Canon City, CO 81212-4431
719-275-0550
www.starpointco.com/spin

Diane Trujillo, Manager

SPIN center is a fully inclusive non-discriminating community early childhood program, offering a variety of schedule choices for families. The philosophy of the SPIN program is to promote each child's growth and development. Special attention is given to cognitive, physical, speech language and social-emotional growth. Staff is specifically trained to facilitate and prepare environments that promote exploration, key experiences, creativity and self-expression.

6521 Schaefer Enterprises
500 26th Street
P.O. Box 200009
Greeley, CO 80631-8427
970-353-0662
FAX: 970-353-2779
www.schaeferenterprises.com

Valorie Randall, Executive Director
Alex Witt, Executive Assistant
Veronica Griego, Production Director

Schaefer Enterprises, Inc., located in Greely, Colorado, is a vaulable community resource that has been fulfilling the outsourcing needs of businesses in Weld County and outlying areas since 1952.

6522 Spalding Rehab Hospital West Unit
150 Spring St
Morrison, CO 80465
303-697-4334
FAX: 303-697-0570

Postacute rehabilitation program.

Connecticut

6523 ACES/ACCESS Inclusion Program
350 State Street
North Haven, CT 06473-3218
203-498-6800
FAX: 203-234-1369
acesinfo@aces.org
www.aces.org

Thomas M Danehy, Executive Director
Erika Forte, Assistant Executive Director
Evelyn Rossetti, Manager

Provides a person centered planning approach for integrated employment, volunteer community based opportunities for adults who have developmental disabilities.

6524 Apria Healthcare
Apria Healthcare Group, Inc.
1975 Wehrle Dr
Buffalo, NY 14221
716-631-8726

Provides a broad range of high-quality and cost-effective specialty infusion therapies and related services to patients in their homes throughout the Northeastern United States. Offer home infusion antibiotic therapy, quality pharmacy services, skilled nursing services and related support services.

6525 Arc Of Meriden-Wallingford, Inc.
200 Research Parkway
Meriden, CT 06450
203-237-9975
FAX: 203-639-0946
www.arcmw.org

Pamela Fields, Executive Director
Joseph Palfini, Board President
Becky Blazejowski, Financial Director

A membership agency that provides comprehensive, full-service, community-based opportunities for people with disabilities. Guided by over 120 community members and an active Board of Directors, the Arc always has its focus on improving the lives of people with disabilities. The Arc of Meriden-Wallingford offers advocacy and assistance to our members along with advocating for the rights and choices of people with disabilities in our community.

6526 Connecticut Subacute Corporation
19 Tuttle Pl
Middletown, CT 06457-1881
860-347-6300
FAX: 860-347-2446

Evan K Lyle, Managed Care Director
Cheri Kauset, Corporate Rep.

Specializes in subacute medical and rehabilitation programming. The strength of our system is in its' ability to service a broad range of clinical and psychosocial needs which enable each individual to attain his/her optimal potential. Programming includes neurological and orthopedic rehabilitation, post-surgical and wound care management, intravenous therapy, pulmonary rehabilitation including ventilator services, and long term care.

6527 Datahr Rehabilitation Institute
4 Berkshire Blvd
Bethel, CT 06801-1001
203-775-4700
888-8DA-TAHR
FAX: 203-775-4688

Thomas Fanning, CEO

Providers of comprehensive rehabilitation services with a history of nearly 5 decades of service. This institute is recognized as a leading resource in meeting the needs of those disabled by illness, injury or developmental disorders in Connecticut and New York. A team of rehabilitation and health care professionals offering career development, residential services, supported employment, volunteer services, occupational therapy, day activities and more.

6528 Eastern Blind Rehabilitation Center
810 Vermont Avenue
Washington, DC 20420
202-461-7600
800-273-8255

Eric K. Shinseki, Secretary of Veterans Affairs
W. Scott Gould, Deputy Secretary of Veterans Affairs
Jose D Riojas, Chief of Staff

Provides residential rehabilitation services to eligible legally blind veterans in the Northeast and Middle Atlantic portions of the country. Referral applications by Veterans Administration Medical Centers and Outpatient Clinics in the geographical area served by the Blind Rehabilitation Center.

6529 FAVRAH Senior Adult Enrichment Program
23 W Avon Rd
Avon, CT 06001   860-674-8839
                                           FAX: 860-676-0275

Nancy Ralston, Manager
Provides remunerative work. Post acute rehabilitation programs and facility.

6530 Gaylord Hospital
Gaylord Farm Road
P.O.Box 400
Wallingford, CT 06492-7048   203-284-2800
                                                866-429-5673
                                           FAX: 203-284-2894
                                           TTY: 203-284-2700
                                         lcrispino@gaylord.org
                                              www.gaylord.org

James Cullen, President
Works to restore ability and build courage. Offers rehabilitation care with one goal in mind: to help patients return to their homes, communities and jobs.

6531 Hockanum Greenhouse
Hockanum Industry
290 Middle Tpke
Storrs Mansfield, CT 06268-2908   860-429-6697
                                           FAX: 860-429-7496

Christopher Campbell, Manager
Beth Chaty, Director
Betsy Treiber, Director
A non profit agency that strives to provide gainful employment, training, support and retirement services for developmentally disabled individuals through the dignity of work, community interaction and structured activities.

6532 Kuhn Employment Oppurtunities
1630 North Colony Road
P.O.Box 941
Meriden, CT 06450   203-235-2583
                                                860-347-5843
                                             www.kuhngroup.org

Paul O'Sullivan, Chairperson
Mark DuPuis, Vice Chairperson
John J. Ausanka III, Treasurer
Kuhn is committed to developing quality skill enhancement programs which provide meaningful employment for persons with disabilities so that they will become independentm gain self-esteem, and be accepted by the community. Our vision is that all individuals have the ability to fully participate in the community through work. Kuhn believes that all participants have a right to integrated community employment.

6533 Norwalk Hospital Section Of Physical Medicine And Rehabilitation
34 Maple Street
Norwalk, CT 06856   203-852-2000
                                           FAX: 800-789-4584

Diane M. Allison, Chair
Edward A. Kangas, Vice Chair
Andrew J. Whittingham, Treasurer
A 25 bed inpatient Rehabilitation Unit. This CARF and JCAHO accredidted rehab unit is located on the 8th floor of Norwalk Hospital. The focus of the rehab unit is to restore lost function and assist patients in returning to the community. Who have recently experienced a life changing medical event. The progam is tailored to meet individual therapy needs and address activities of daily living. Family and caregiver participation in the program is welcomed and encouraged.

6534 Rehabilitation Associates, Inc.
1931 Black Rock Tpke
Fairfield, CT 06825-3506   203-384-8681
                                           FAX: 203-384-0956
                                         info@rehabassocinc.com
                                 www.rehabilitationassociatesinc.com

Carol Landsman, Director

A comprehensive outpatient rehabilitation facility offering physical therapy, occupational therapy, speech-language pathology, clinical social work services and nutritional services to all age groups. Facility locations in Fairfield, Stratford, Milford, Shelton and Westport.

6535 Reliance House
40 Broadway
Norwich, CT 06360-5702   860-887-6536
                                           FAX: 860-885-1970
                                              reliancehouse.org

Jack Malone, President
Jackie Falman, Vice President
Sam Bliven, Secretary
A residential vocational and recreational support network. An active and productive clubhouse where people with mental illness can gain skills, strength and self-esteem.

6536 Yale New Haven Health System-Bridgeport Hospital
789 Howard Avenue
New Haven, CT 06519   203-384-3000
                                      www.yalenewhavenhealth.org

Marna P. Borgstrom, President and CEO
Richard D'Aquila, Executive Vice President
Peter N. Herbert, MD, Senior VP, Medical Affairs
Medical services are provided by physicians who are specialists in physical medicine and rehabilitation. The physical therapy department provides a variety of services and utilizes sophisticated modalities to restore and reinforce physical abilities.

Delaware

6537 Alfred I DuPont Hospital for Children
Division of Rehabilitation
1600 Rockland Road,
PO Box 269
Wilmington, DE 19803-269   302-651-4000
                                                888-533-3543
                                           FAX: 302-651-4055
                                         infodupont@nemours.org
                                              www.nemours.org

William G. Mackenzie, MD, Chair
David J. Bailey, President and Chief Executive Officer
Robert D. Bridges, Executive Vice President, Enterprise Services/Chief Financia
The hospital is a division of Nemours, which operates one of the nations largest subspecialty group practices devoted to pediatric patient care, teaching, and research. A 180-bed hospital that offers all the specialties of pediatric medicine, surgery, and dentistry in a spacious, comfortable, and family focused facility.

6538 Community Systems Inc.
2 Penns Way
Suite 301
New Castle, DE 19720   302-325-1500
                                           FAX: 302-325-1505
                                            communitysystems.org

David Paige, Executive Director
Amy Yento, Chair
A 4 state family of non-profit, tax exempt corporations whose mission is helping persons with disabilities to find happiness in their own homes, in their personal relationships, and as contributing members of their community.

6539 DDDS/Georgetown Center
5 Academy St
Georgetown, DE 19947-1915   302-856-5366
                                           FAX: 302-856-5305
                                          dhss.delaware.gov/dhss

Mission is to improve the quality of life for Delaware's citizens by promoting health and well-being, fostering self-sufficiency, and protecting vulnerable operations. The vision statement is that together we provide quality services as we create a better future for the people of Delaware.

6540 Delaware Association for the Blind
2915 Newport Gap Pike
Landis Lodge Building
Wilmington, DE 19808
302-998-5913
888-777-3925
FAX: 302-691-5810
dabdel.org

Janet L. Berry, Executive Director
Ken Rolph, President
Jennifer Smith, Secretary
A private, nonprofit organization that offers adjustment to blindness counseling, recreation activities, summer camps and financial assistance for the legally blind. The staff includes five full time, nine part time and twelve seasonal. Operates a store selling items for the blind.

6541 Delaware Veterans Center
810 Vermont Avenue
Washington, DC 20420
302-994-2511
800-273-8255
FAX: 302-633-5591

Slaon D Gibson, Acting Secretary of Veterans Affairs
Jose D Riojas, Chief of Staff
Richard J Griffin, Acting Inspector General
A 60-bed hospital and 60-bed NHCU, both accredited by the Joint Commission on Accreditation of Healthcare Organizations with a VBA Regional Office and 2 Vet Centers (one on campus) offering veterans the unique opportunity to obtain heathcare, benefits services, and Readjustment Counseling at one location. The center provides a wide spectrum of primary and tertiary acute and extended care inpatient and outpatient activities an an academic setting.

6542 Easterseals Delaware & Maryland's Eastern Shore
61 Corporate Cir.
New Castle, DE 19720
302-324-4444
FAX: 302-324-4441
www.easterseals.com/de

Kenan J. Sklenar, President & CEO
Pamela Reuther, Chief Operating Officer
Pamela Patone, Chief Financial Officer
Provides services to ensure that all people with disabilities or special needs and their families have equal opportunities to live, learn, work and play in their communities.

6543 Edgemoor Day Program
500 Duncan Rd
Wilmington, DE 19809-2369
302-762-9077
FAX: 302-762-1652
www.dhss.delaware.gov/dhss/main/maps/other/ed

Scott Borino, Executive Director
Carol Koyste, Manager, Finance & Administratio
Brandon Furrowh, Director, Recreation & Youth Pro
Our mission is providing affordable and accessible services which help improve the quality of life for community members of all ages through a broad range of educational, recreational, self-enrichment, and family support services. ECC is a not-for-profit, community-based, multi-service agency located just north of Wilmington. We provide a broad range of educational, recreational, self-enrichment, and family support services.

6544 Elwyn Delaware
321 E 11th St.
Wilmington, DE 19801-3417
302-658-8860
info@elwyn.org
elwyn.org

Charles S. McLister, President & CEO, Elwyn
Provides work training, job placement and supported employment, and elder care services.

6545 First State Senior Center
291a N Rehoboth Blvd
Milford, DE 19963-1303
302-422-1510
dhss.delaware.gov/dhss/main/maps/other/dddssr
Improves the quality of life for Delaware's citizens by promoting health and well-being, fostering self-sufficiency, and protecting vulnerable populations.

6546 Woodside Day Program
941 Walnut Shade Rd
Dover, DE 19901-7765
302-739-4494
FAX: 302-697-4490

Connie Grace, Supervisor
Joyce Oliver, Manager

District of Columbia

6547 Barbara Chambers Children's Center
1470 Irving St NW
Washington, DC 20010-2804
202-387-6755
FAX: 202-319-9066
barbarachambers.org

Barbara Chambers, Founder
Mission is to provide comprehensive, quality child care services to the community at large, by offering a variety of opportunities for childrens's intellectual, emotional, social and physical development in a clean, safe, and nurturing environment. Our philosophy is to provide a supportive environment in which children can be children.allowing each child to learn at his/her pace and most of all allowing the child to learn through his/her daily play.

6548 District of Columbia General Hospital Physical Medicine & Rehab Services
Room 1358
19th and Mass Ave
Washington, DC 20003
202-727-6055
FAX: 202-675-7819

Dr. Maribel Bieberach, Chairperson PM&R
Dr. Raman Kapur, Staff Physiatrist
Offers comprehensive physical medicine and rehabilitation services including in and outpatient consultations and electrodiagnostic testing; in and outpatient physical and occupational therapy; inpatient recreational therapy, and a multidisciplinary prosthetic clinic which meets once a month.

6549 George Washington University Medical Center
George Washington University Medical Center
2150 Pennsylvania Ave NW
Washington, DC 20037-3201
202-741-3000
FAX: 202-741-3183
www.gwdocs.com
Offers an Ambulatory Physical Therapy/Sports Medicine Center, a Medical Center Prosthetics/Orthotics Clinic and a Speech and Hearing Center to persons in the District of Columbia, Virginia and Maryland.

6550 HSC Pediatric Center, The
1731 Bunker Hill Rd NE
Washington, DC 20017-3026
202-832-4400
800-226-4444
FAX: 202-467-0978

Debbie Zients, CEO
Dr Murry M Pollack, VP, Medical Affairs
Eva Fowler, Media Contact
Provides the highest quality rehabilitative and transitional care for infants, children, adolescents, and young adults with special health care needs and their families in a supportive environment that respects their needs, strengths, vslues and priorities.

6551 Howard University Child Development Center
1911 5th St NW
Washington, DC 20001-2314
202-797-8134
FAX: 202-986-6580

Connie Siler, Manager
Offers children with developmental problems diagnosis, treatment, evaluation and follow along visits.

6552 Psychiatric Institute of Washington
4228 Wisconsin Ave NW
Washington, DC 20016-2138
202-885-5600
800-369-2273
FAX: 202-885-5614

Ken Courage, Chairman
Carol Desjuns, Chief Operations Officer
Howard Hoffman, Executive Medical Director

Psychiatric intensive care, crisis intervention, adult day treatment, drug treatment and other services to children and adults who have psychiatric and chemical dependency problems.

6553 Spina Bifida Program of Children's National Medical Center
Children's National Medical Center
111 Michigan Ave. NW
Washington, DC 20010
202-476-7762
888-884-2327
childrensnational.org

Christina Ho, Co-Director
Briony Varda, Co-Director
Hans Pohl, Co-Director
Provides care and treatment for infants, children and youth with spina bifida of all forms, including spina bifida occulta, meningocele, and myelomeningocele.

Florida

6554 Bayfront Rehabilitation Center
Bayfront Medical Center
701 6th St S
St Petersburg, FL 33701-4814
727-823-1234
www.bayfrontstpete.com

Kathryn Gillette, President and CEO
Eric Smith, Chief Financial Officer
Lavah Lowe, Chief Operating Officer
Bayfront Medical Center has an Inpatient Rehabilitation Hospital and two outpatient rehabilitation clinics that each provide progressive, comprehensive, individualized treatment. Specialized care in Physiatry (physical medicine), rehab nursing, occupational therapy, speech language pathology, recreational therapy, patient/family services and psychology is tailored to each patient from admission to community and/or school reintegration.

6555 Brain Injury Rehabilitation Center Dr. P. Phillips Hospital
Brain Injury Rehabilitation Center Dr. P. Phillips
9400 Turkey Lake Rd
Orlando, FL 32819-8001
407-351-8580
Shannon Elswick, President
Linda Chapin, Chairman
Mark Swanson, Chief Quality Officer
Dedicated to restoring brain injured patients with rehabilitation potential to their highest level of functioning. This is accomplished through an interdisciplinary team demonstrating personal responsibility to the patient, their family and each other.

6556 Brooks Memorial Hospital Rehabilitation Center
3599 University Blvd. South
Jacksonville, FL 32207-6215
904-858-7600
FAX: 904-858-7619
louise.spierre@brookshealth.org
www.brookshealth.org

Douglas Baer, Chief Executive Officer/President
Holly Morris, Director, Brooks Rehabilitation
Louise Spierre, Medical Director
An entire care facility featuring five day inpatient evaluation, pre-operative evaluation programs, five week pain management program, referral criteria and treatment goals, therapy services, psychological services and more to the physically challenged.

6557 Center for Pain Control and Rehabilitation
Ste 607
2780 Cleveland Ave
Fort Myers, FL 33901-5858
239-337-4332
Mary Bonnette, Owner

6558 Comprehensive Rehabilitation Center at Lee Memorial Hospital
2776 Cleveland Ave
Fort Myers, FL 33901-5864
239-343-2000
leememorial.org

James R. Nathan, Chief Executive Officer
Larry Antonucci, Chief Operating Officer
Jon Cecil, Chief Human Resources Officer

Lee Memorial hospital has achieved national recognition as one of the top 100 hospitals for stroke, orthopedics, and Intensive Care Unit (ICU) It is a 367 bed hospital that provides 24-hour emergency and trauma care, inpatient rehabilitation, orthopedics, neuroscience, trauma, cancer, diabetes, digestive, general surgery, urology, endocrinology, gastroenterology, opthamology, and many others.

6559 Comprehensive Rehabilitation Center of Naples Community Hospital
350 7th Street North
Naples, FL 34102
239-436-5000
FAX: 239-436-5250
www.nchmd.org

Allen S. Weiss, CEO
Mariann MacDonald, Chairman
Thomas Gazdic, Chairman/Treasurer
Offers rehabilitation services, inpatient and outpatient care at 5 locations in the county and more for the benefit of the disabled.

6560 Conklin Center for the Blind
405 White St
Daytona Beach, FL 32114-2999
386-258-3441
FAX: 386-258-1155
info@conklincenter.org
www.conklincenter.org

Robert T Kelly, Executive Director
The Conklin Center's mission is to empower children and adults who are blind and have one or more additional disabilities to develop their potential to be able to obtain competitive employment, live independently and fully participate in community life.

6561 Davis Center for Rehabilitation Baptist Hospital of Miami
8900 N Kendall Dr
Miami, FL 33176-2118
786-596-1960
corporatepr@baptisthealth.net
www.baptisthealth.net/bhs

Brian E. Keeley, President and Chief Executive Of
Calvin Babcock, Chairman
A full-service, nonprofit community hospital providing a full range of inpatient and outpatient rehabilitation services. The overall commitment to excellence has extended to this specialized field. Access to medical expertise and services ensures that the best in medical resources are available should an unforeseen medical problem arise.

6562 Devereux Advanced Behavioral Health Florida - Titusville Campus
1850 S. Deleon Ave.
Titusville, FL 32780
407-473-5238
800-338-3738
referral@devereux.org
www.devereuxfl.org

Gwendolyn B Skinner, Vice President of Operations
Dave Detro, Human Resource Director
Carlos F Pozzi-Montero, Psy.D, Clinical Director
The Devereux Florida Titusville Campus offers a variety of residential, foster care and community support services for youth with behavioral and intellectual/developmental disabilities. Services include a residential group home with private rooms and a therapeutic group home.

6563 Devereux Advanced Behavioral Health - Florida
Devereux Florida Corporate Office
5850 T.G. Lee Blvd.
Suite 400
Orlando, FL 32822
407-362-9210
800-338-3738
referral@devereux.org
www.devereuxfl.org

Gwendolyn B Skinner, Vice President of Operations
Dave Detro, Human Resource Director
Carlos F Pozzi-Montero, Psy.D, Clinical Director
Offering care for children with mental health, behavioral, intellectual and developmental disabilities and challenges. Some services offered include a psychiatric program, community based group homes, foster care, counseling centers, case management, abuse and neglect prevention services, community-based care and outreach programs.

6564 Devereux Florida - Orlando Campus
Devereux Orlando Campus
6147 Christian Way
Orlando, FL 32808
407-296-5300
800-338-3738
referral@devereux.org
www.devereuxfl.org

Gwendolyn B Skinner, Vice President of Operations
Dave Detro, Human Resource Director
Carlos F Pozzi-Montero, Psy.D, Clinical Director
The Orlando Campus provides intensive residential services for children and adolescents who suffer from emotional, behavioral and psychological problems. Programs offered include Devereux's Statewide Inpatient Psychiatric Program (SIPP), Residential Group Care and the Residential Treatment Center.

6565 Devereux Florida - Viera Campus
Devereux Viera Campus
8000 Devereux Dr.
Viera, FL 32940
321-242-9100
800-338-3738
FAX: 321-259-0786
vischool@devereux.org
www.devereuxfl.org

Gwendolyn B Skinner, Vice President of Operations
Dave Detro, Human Resource Director
Carlos F Pozzi-Montero, Psy.D, Clinical Director
The campus offers two residential programs for youth with developmental or behavioral challenges: the Intensive Residential Treatment Center (IRTC) and the Intellectual/Developmental Disabilities (I/DD) Program. The Viera Campus also offers six residential units and the Devereux School.

6566 Devereux Threshold Center for Autism
Threshold Center For Autism
3550 N Goldenrod Rd
Winter Park, FL 32792
407-671-7060
800-338-3738
FAX: 407-671-6005
referral@devereux.org
www.devereuxfl.org

Gwendolyn B Skinner, Vice President of Operations
Dave Detro, Human Resource Director
Carlos F Pozzi-Montero, Psy.D., Clinical Director
The Devereux Threshold Center for Autism includes a therapeutic residential program and an adult day treatment program for people with intellectual/developmental disabilities.

6567 Division of Blind Services
325 West Gaines Street
Suite 1114
Turlington Building, FL 32399-0400
850-245-0300
800-342-1828
FAX: 850-245-0386
ana.saint-ford@dbs.fldoe.org
dbs.myflorida.com

Aleisa McKinlay, Interim Director
Phyllis Vaughn, Bureau Chief, Administrative Services
William Findley, Bureau Chief, Business Enterprise Program
Serves the totally blind, legally blind, visually impaired, deaf-blind, learning disabled, and more by offering health, counseling, educational, recreational and computer training services.

6568 Easterseals Northeast Central Florida
1219 Dunn Ave.
Daytona Beach, FL 32114
386-255-4568
877-255-4568
FAX: 386-258-7677
TTY: 386-310-1157
www.easterseals.com/necfl

Steve Sevigny, Chair
Paul Schandel, Vice Chair
Ed Dimayuga, Vice Chair
Provides services for individuals with physical, intellectual, and other disabilities.

6569 Easterseals South Florida
1475 NW 14th Ave.
Miami, FL 33125
305-325-0470
FAX: 305-325-0578
www.easterseals.com/southflorida

Maurice Woods, President & CEO
Barry R. Vogel, Chief Administrative Officer
Pietro Bonacossa, Vice President, Development
The mission of Easterseals South Florida is to provide services to ensure that all children and adults with disabilities or special needs and their families have equal opportunities to live, learn, work and play in their communities.

6570 Easterseals Southwest Flordia
Sarasota, FL 34243-2001
941-355-7637
themeadowscup.com

Easterseals Sothwest Florida creates solutions that change lives for children, adults and their families through high quality therapeutic, educational and supportive services.

6571 Easterseals Southwest Florida
350 Braden Ave.
Sarasota, FL 34243
941-355-7637
FAX: 941-358-3069
www.easterseals-swfl.org

Tom Waters, President & CEO
Patrick Ryan, Chief Operating Officer
George Pfeiffer, Vice President, Government Relations
Provides services to children and adults with physical, neurological and communications disabilities and their families.

6572 Florida CORF
Columbia Medical Center: Peninsula

John Feore, Executive VP
Sandra Trovato, Executive Director
Offers Medicare authorized therapy programs for seniors, disabled and others who need rehabilitation. CORF can provide coordinated and extended services in the home after a hospital stay, or when physical status changes. Patients who are treated at CORF, include amputations, arthritis, chronic/acute pain, depression/anxiety, nerve injury, sports injury, stroke and swallowing problems.

6573 Florida Institute Of Rehabilitation Education (FIRE)
3071 Highland Oaks Terrace
Tallahassee, FL 32301-4876
850-942-3658
888-827-6033
FAX: 850-942-4518
info@lighthousebigbend.org

Barbara Ross, Executive Director
Evelyn Worley, Assistant Director
Wayne Warner, Vocational Program Director
Provides independent living and vocational rehabilitation services to Florida residents who are legally blind. Services include instruction in orientation and mobility, accessible technology, daily living skills and employability skills. Information, referral and counseling services are also offered. All services are provided without charge.

6574 Florida Institute for Neurologic Rehabilitation, Inc
1962 Vandolah Road
P O Box 1348
Wauchula, FL 33873-1348
863-773-2857
800-697-5390
FAX: 863-773-0867
finr.net

John Richards, Administrator
Stephanie Ortiz, RN, Director of Nursing
Kevin E. O'Keefe, Program Director
A residential rehabilitation facility providing a therapeutic environment in which children, adolescents and adults who have survived head-injury can develop the independence and skills necessary to re-enter the community.

6575 Fort Lauderdale Veterans Medical Center
713 NE 3rd Ave
Fort Lauderdale, FL 33304-2619   954-356-7926
FAX: 954-356-7609
www.va.gov/directory/guide/

Robert White, Executive Director
Sloan D Gibson, Acting Secretary
Jose D Riojas, Chief of Staff
Veterans medical clinic offering disabled veterans medical treatments.

6576 Halifax Hospital Medical Center Eye Clinic Professional Center
308 Farmington Avenue
Farmington, CT 06032   860-658-4388
888-444-3598
webmaster@evariant.com
www.evariant.com

Bill Moschella, CEO
Rob Grant, Executive Vice President
Michael Clark, Chief Operating Officer
Offers services for the totally blind, legally blind, visually impaired, and more with health, counseling, educational, recreational, rehabilitation, computer training and professional training services.

6577 HealthQuest Subacute and Rehabilitation Programs
Regenta Park
8700 a C Skinner Pkwy
Jacksonville, FL 32256-836   FAX: 904-641-7896
HealthQuest offers four centers within the state of Florida offering exceptional staff, comfortable surroundings and individually designed, closely monitored programs dedicated to enabling patients to achieve their goals. Each location offers a progressive and cost effective alternative to in-hospital subacute and rehabilitative care. Centers are offered in Jacksonville, Winter Park, Sarasota and Sunrise.

6578 HealthSouth Emeral Coast Sports & Rehabilitation Center
1847 Florida Avenue
Panama City, FL 32405-3730   850-784-4878
FAX: 850-769-7566
www.healthsouthpanamacity.com

Tony Bennett, CEO
Michelle Miller, Manager
Outpatient sports medicine and rehabilitation center providing physical therapy, occupational therapy, industrial rehab, work hardening/work simulation, worksite and ergonomic analysis, FCE's, work assessment and pre-employment goals of returning the clients back to work, and returning to all recreational, sports and functional activities safely.

6579 HealthSouth Rehabilitation Hospital of Tallahassee
Healthsouth Corporation
1675 Riggins Rd
Tallahassee, FL 32308-5315   850-656-4800
www.healthsouthtallahassee.com
Heath Phillips, Chief Executive Officer
Robert Robert Rowland, Medical Director
Tom Abbruscato, Controller
North Florida's sole acute rehabilitation hospital between Jacksonville, Panama City, and Gainesville. With 250 employees providing a full continuum of care form its 70 bed facility, the hospital is accredited by JCAHO, CARF and state designated and certified by Vocational Rehabilitation for traumatic brain injury, as well as a wide variety of other diagnoses. With the addition of our outpatients, the facility has served the greater community by touching the lives of over 50,000 patients.

6580 HealthSouth Rehabilitation Hospital Of Miami
20601 Old Cutler Rd
Miami, FL 33189-2441   305-251-3800
www.healthsouthmiami.com
Elizabeth Izquierdo, Chief Executive Officer
Angelo Appio, Director of Marketing Operations
Reyna M. Hernandez, Chief Financial Officer
A comprehensive source of medical rehabilitation services for Pinellas County, Florida area residents, their families and their physicians. Offers the people of Florida all the clinical, technical and professional resources of the nation's leading provider of comprehensive rehabilitation care.

6581 HealthSouth Rehabilitation Hospital of Sarasota
Health South Corporation in Burmingham Alabama
6400 Edgelake Drive
Sarasota, FL 34240-8813   941-921-8600
866-330-5822
www.healthsouthsarasota.com
Marcus Braz, Chief Executive Officer
Alexander DeJesus, Medical Director
Nancy Arnold, Director of Marketing Operations
HealthSouth Rehabilitation Hospital of Sarasota is a 96-bed inpatient rehabilitation hospital that offers comprehensive inpatient rehabilitation services designed to return patients to leading active and independent lives.

6582 HealthSouth Sea Pines Rehabilitation Hospital
Sea Pines Rehabilitation Hospital
101 E Florida Ave
Melbourne, FL 32901-8398   321-984-4600
FAX: 321-952-6532
www.healthsouthseapines.com
Stuart Miller, Medical Director
Denise McGrath, Chief Executive Officer
Donna Anderson, Director of Human Resources
Designed to return patients to leading active, independent lives, HealthSouth Sea Pines Rehabilitation Hospital is a 90-bed rehabilitation hospital that provides a higher level of comprehensive rehabilitation services.

6583 Holy Cross Hospital
Catholic Southwest
4725 North Federal Hwy
Fort Lauderdale, FL 33308-4668   954-771-8000
www.holy-cross.com
Patrick Taylor, President & CEO
Luisa Gutman, Senior Vice President
Linda Wilford, Senior Vice President
Holy Cross Hospital in Fort Lauderdale is a full-service, non-profit Catholic hospital, sponsored by the Sisters of Mercy. Holy Cross is a US News & World Report 'Best Hospital' and HealthGrades Distinguished Hospital for Clinical Excellence, 2004 and 2005

6584 Lee Memorial Hospital
2776 Cleveland Ave
Fort Myers, FL 33901-5855   239-343-2000
www.leememorial.org
Sanford Cohen, Chairman
Chris Hansen, Vice Chairman
David Collins, Treasurer
Offers a complete inpatient program of intensive rehabilitation designed to restore a patient to a more independent level of functioning. The comprehensive care includes medical rehabilitation and training for spinal cord injury, brain injury, stroke and neurological disorders.

6585 Lighthouse for the Blind of Palm Beach
1710 Tiffany Drive East
West Palm Beach, FL 33407-3224   561-586-5600
FAX: 561-84- 80
lighthousepalmbeaches.org
Marvin A. Tanck, President and CEO
Dont, Mickens, Chair
John R. Banister, Vice Chairman
A private, non-profit rehabilitation and education agency in its 55th year of service. Offers programs to assist persons who areblind or visually impaired, an on-site Industrial Center, a technology training center, an Aids and appliances Store, special equipment grant programs, outreach services for children and adults, Early Intervention and Preschool Services, and a variety of support groups. These programs provide services and education for blind children and their parents.

6586 Lighthouse for the Visually Impaired and Blind
8610 Galen Wilson Blvd
Port Richey, FL 34668-5974

727-815-0303
866-962-5254
FAX: 727-815-0203
lighthouse@lvib.org
www.lvib.org

Sylvia Stinson-Perez, Executive Director
Dr. John Mann, President
Melissa M. Suess, Orientation and Mobility Instructor
The Lighthouse offers services for visually impaired or blind
adults and children ages 0-5 years old. Counseling, educational
services, recreational services, rehabilitation, computer training
and support groups.

6587 MacDonald Training Center
5420 W Cypress Street
Tampa, FL 33607-1706

813-870-1300
866-948-6184
FAX: 813-872-6010
TTY: 813-873-7631
macdonaldcenter.org

Jim Freyvogel, President/CEO
Judith DeStasio, CFO
Debi Hamilton, Director of Services
A private, non-profit, community-based human services organization serving adults with disabilities (since 1953). Persons are
provided the opportunity to achieve their highest potential
through the Center's various programs that include day training,
employment, community living and various support services.

6588 Medicenter of Tampa
4411 North Habana Avenue
Tampa, FL 33614-7211

813-872-2771
FAX: 813-871-2831
rehabilitationandhealthcarecenteroftampa.com

Dan Davis, President
Mariluz G, Social Services Director
Brenda Pace, Secretary
Postacute rehabilitation program. A 174 bed non-profit facility
with postacute reahbilitation programs.

6589 Miami Heart Institute Adams Building
4300 Alton Rd
Miami Beach, FL 33140-2997

305-674-2121
www.msmc.com

Steven D. Sonenreich, President/CEO
The mission is to provide high quality health care to our diverse
community enhanced through teaching, research, charity care
and financial responsibility.

6590 Miami Lighthouse for the Blind
601 SW 8th Ave
Miami, FL 33130-3200

305-856-2288
FAX: 305-285-6967
info@miamilighthouse.com
miamilighthouse.org

Virginia A. Jacko, President & Chief Executive Officer
Sharon Caughill, Special Projects Manager
Jeannie Reinoso, Executive Assistant
Offers services for the legally blind and severely visually impaired (including those who are developmentally delayed) of all
ages in the areas of counseling and educational, recreational, rehabilitation, computer and vocational training services.

6591 Mount Sinai Medical Center Rehabilitation Unit
4300 Alton Rd
Miami Beach, FL 33140-2997

305-674-2121
www.msmc.com

Steven D. Sonenreich, President/CEO
A comprehensive inpatient and outpatient rehabilitation programs have been helping patients recover for more then 20 years.
Fully customized treatment plans based on the needs of each patient is 1 reason why our services are among the best in South
Florida. Our team approach takes into account the medical, physical, psychological, social, spiritual, cultural and economic needs
of patients and their families.

6592 Neurobehavioral Medicine Center
Ste 1
4821 Us Highway 19
New Port Richey, FL 34652-4259

727-849-2005
FAX: 727-849-2087

Otsenre Matos, Medical Director
Gerard Taylor PhD, Counseling/Stress Management
Donna Taylor RN, Manager
A multidisciplinary outpatient program for the evaluation and
treatment of chronic pain. Consultation services for hospitalized
patients are also provided upon request. Comprehensive treatment of individuals with closed traumatic brain injuries.

6593 North Broward Rehab Unit
North Broward Medical Center
201 E Sample Rd
Deerfield Beach, FL 33064-3596

954-941-8300
www.browardhealth.org

Douglas Ford, Chiefs of Staff
Pauline Grant, Chief Executive Officer
CARF accredited, 30-bed inpatient rehabilitation unit treating
adults with brain injuries, spinal cord injuries, stroke, orthopedic
and neurologic injuries.

6594 Northwest Medical Center
Health Care Corporation of America
2801 North State Road 7
Margate, FL 33063-5727

954-974-0400
866-256-7720
northwestmed.com

Mark Rader, CEO
Above all else, we are committed to the care and improvement of
human life. In recognition of this commitment, we strive to deliver high quality, cost effective healthcare in the communities
we serve. We recognize and affirm the unique and intrinsic work
of each individual. We treat all those we serve with compassion
and kindness. We act with absolute honesty, integrity, and fairness in the way we conduct our business and the way we live our
lives.

6595 Pain Institute of Tampa
4178 N Armenia Ave
Tampa, FL 33607-6429

813-875-5913

John E Barsa, Founder & MD
Offers a comprehensive and multidisciplinary approach to pain
controll and management. Most services are provided on-site but
other services may require you to be referred elswhere. We will
monitor and coordinate your care in a manner to provide optimal
recovery potential.

6596 Pain Treatment Center, Baptist Hospital of Miami
8900 N Kendall Dr
Miami, FL 33176-2118

786-596-1960
corporatepr@baptisthealth.net
www.baptisthealth.net

Calvin Babcock, Chairman
Brian E. Keeley, President and Chief Executive Of
Since 1960, Baptist Hospital of Miami has been one of the most
respected medical centers in South Florida. The hospitals full
range of medical and technological services is the natural choice
for a growing number of people throughout the world.

6597 Pine Castle
4911 Spring Park Rd
Jacksonville, FL 32207-7496

904-733-2650
FAX: 904-733-2681
info@pinecastle.org
pinecastle.org

Jonathan May, Executive Director
Randall Duncan, Associate Executive Director
Leigh Griffin, Director of Finance
Provides remunerative work, training, community employment
and community living options for adults with developmental
disabilities.

6598 Polk County Association for Handicapped Citizens
1038 Sunshine Dr E
Lakeland, FL 33801-6338   863-858-2252
                                            FAX: 863-665-2330

Kecia Howell, Owner
Anthony J. Senzamici Jr., 1st Vice Chairman
Carol N. Asbill, 2nd Vice Chairman
A private non-profit organization that provides an adult day
training program to people with developmental disabilities and is
under the direction of a volunteer board of directors. The primary
goal for our services is to provide people with knowledge and
practical experience to be independent adults so they can become
contributing members of their community.

6599 Quest, Inc.
PO Box 531125
Orlando, FL 32853   407-218-4300
                                                 888-807-8378
                                            FAX: 407-218-4301
                                            contact@questinc.org
                                               www.questinc.org

John Gill, President & Chief Executive Officer
Brooke Eakins, Chief Operating Officer
Todd Thrasher, Chief Financial Officer
Quest helps individuals with developmental disabilities in Central Florida achieve their goals by providing services that increase their capabilities and quality of life. Quest serves more
than 1,000 individuals each day in the Orlando and Tampa areas.

6600 Quest, Inc. - Tampa Area
3910 US Hwy. 301 N
Tampa, FL 33619   813-423-7700
                                                 888-807-8378
                                            FAX: 813-423-7701
                                            contact@questinc.org
                                               www.questinc.org
John Gill, President & Chief Executive Officer
Brooke Eakins, Chief Operating Officer
Todd Thrasher, Chief Financial Officer
Quest helps individuals with developmental disabilities in Cen-
tral Florida achieve their goals by providing services that in-
crease their capabilities and quality of life. Quest serves more
than 1,000 individuals each day in the Orlando and Tampa areas.

6601 Rehabilitation Center for Children and Adults
300 Royal Palm Way
Palm Beach, FL 33480-4305   561-655-7266
                                            FAX: 561-655-3269
                                                 info@rcca.org
                                                    rcca.org

John C. Whelton, Chairman
Jacob L. Lochner, Co-Chairman
Christopher Adams, MD
A private, nonprofit organization whose purpose is to improve
physical function, independence and communication of people
with physical disabilities. Any child or adult with a physical or
speech disability is eligible for services.

6602 Renaissance Center
3599 University Blvd
Suite 604
Jacksonville, FL 32216- 9249   904-399-0905
                                            FAX: 904-743-5109
                               www.obiplasticsurgery.com/index.php

Lewis Obi, MD

6603 Rosomoff Comprehensive Pain Center, The
5200 NE 2nd Avenue
Miami, FL 33137-2706   305-532-7246
                                            FAX: 305-534-3974

Elsayed Abdel-Moty, Director
Hubert Rossomoff, Owner
A state-of-the-art Center of Excellence offering inpatient, outpa-
tient, outpatient rehabilitation services and seniors programs.
The Center became an internationally renowned model for the
evalutation and treatment of all persons seeking pain relief.

**6604 Sarasota Memorial Hospital/Comprehensive
Rehabilitation Unit**
1700 S Tamiami Trail
Sarasota, FL 34239-3509   941-917-9000
                                            FAX: 941-917-2211
                                                  www.smh.com

Marguerite G Malone, Chair
Gregory Carter, First Vice Chair
Alex Miller, Second Vice Chair
The goal of the 34-bed Comprehensive Rehabilitation Unit
(CRU) is to increase patient functional independence, adjust to
illness or disability and successfully return to the community.
The unit is dedicated to patients who have experienced
conditions such

6605 Strive Physical Therapy Centers
2620 SE Maricamp RD
Ocala, FL 34471-4517   352-732-8868
                                            FAX: 352-732-8890
                                              www.striverehab.com

R W Shutes, Owner
Johanna Solbato, Administrator
R.W. Shutes, President and CEO
Certified as an Outpatient Rehabilitation Agency, providing a
comprehensive approach to patient evaluation and treatment. Our
objective is to return our patients back to a productive life as
quickly as possible and safely as possible.

6606 Sunbridge Care and Rehabilitation
101 East State Street,
Kennett Square, FL 19348-6105   610-444-6350
                                            FAX: 610-925-4000
                                            info@genesishcc.com
                                             www.genesishcc.com

Dan Hirschfeld, President
George V Hager, Chief Executive Officer
Robert A Reitz, Executive Vice President & Chief Operating Officer
A comprehensive medical rehabilitation facility that is committed to helping individuals with disabilities improve their quality
of life. This is a 120-bed facility offering a full range of acute and
sub-acute inpatient programs as well as community-based

6607 Tampa Bay Academy
12012 Boyette Rd
Riverview, FL 33569-5631   813-677-6700
                                                 800-678-3838
                                            FAX: 813-671-3145
                                            tlamb@tampahope.org
                                              www.tampahope.org

Renee Scott, Chair
Amy McClure, Vice-Chair
Titania Lamb, Executive Director
A psychiatric residential treatment center and partial hospitaliza-
tion program for ages 7 to 17.

6608 Tampa General Rehabilitation Center
1 Tampa General Circle
P.O.Box 1289
Tampa, FL 33606-3571   813-844-7700
                                                 866-844-1411
                                            FAX: 813-844-1477
                                                     tgh.org

James R. Burkhart, President & CEO
Bruce Zwiebel, Chief Of Staff
Deana L. Nelson, Chief Operating Officer
Offers a full range of programs all aimed at helping patients
achieve their full potentials. It is one of three centers in the state
that provides Driver Training and Evaluation Programs for persons with disabilities, and also an Assisted Reproduction Pro

6609 Tampa Lighthouse for the Blind
1106 West Platt Street
Tampa, FL 33606-2142   813-251-2407
                                            FAX: 813-254-4305
                                              tampalighthouse.org

Sheryl Brown, Executive Director
Offers services for the totally blind, legally blind, visually impaired, and more with health, counseling, educational, recreational, rehabilitation, computer training and professional
training services.

6610   The Arc Tampa Bay
1501 N Belcher Rd.
Suite 249
Clearwater, FL 33765   727-799-3330
                                         FAX: 727-799-4632
                                              thearctb.org
Seeks to support and empower people with intellectual and developmental disabilities through services such as adult day training
programs, employment programs, residential programs, and
more.

6611   Visually Impaired Persons of Southwest Florida
35 W Mariana Ave
North Fort Myers, FL 33903-5515   239-997-7797
                                         FAX: 239-997-8462

Doug Fowler, Executive Director
Margaret Ruhe Lincoln, Director of operations
Provides training in independent living skills, orientation and
mobility, counseling, computer and other communication skills,
family support groups, peer counseling, socialization and a low
vision clinic. Second location in Charlotte County. Phone: 941-6

6612   West Florida Hospital: The Rehabilitation Institute
8383 North Davis Hwy
Pensacola, FL 32514-6039   850-494-4000
                                             800-342-1123
                                         FAX: 850-494-4881
                                      www.westfloridahospital.com
Roman S Bautista, President/CEO
Carol Saxton, Senior VP Patient Care Services
A 58-bed comprehensive rehabilitation facility offering inpatient
and outpatient services. JCAHO and CARF accredited and a State
designed head and spinal cord injury center. CARF accredited
programs include: comprehensive inpatient rehab, spinal cord
inju

6613   West Gables Health Care Center
2525 SW 75th Ave
Miami, FL 33155-2800   305-262-6800
                                         FAX: 888-453-1928
                                      www.westgablesrehabhospital.com
Jose Vargas, Medical Director
Walter Concepcion, Chief Executive Officer
Cesar Sepulveda, Materials Manager
Services provide by West Gables Health Center: activities services are provided onsite to residents. Clinical laboratory services are provided, dental, dietary, housekeeping, mental health
services, nursing services, occupational therapy, pharmacy,
physic

6614   Willough at Naples
9001 Tamiami Trail East
Naples, FL 34113-3397   239-775-4500
                                             800-722-0100
                                         FAX: 239-793-0534
                                      info@thewilloughatnaples.com
                                      thewilloughatnaples.com
James O'Shea, President
A licensed psychiatric hospital in Southwest Florida which provides quality management and treatment for eating disorders and
chemical dependency in adults.

Georgia

6615   Annandale Village
3500 Annandale Ln
Suwanee, GA 30024-2150   770-945-8381
                                         FAX: 770-945-8693
                                              annandale.org
Adam Pomeranz, Chief Executive Officer
Melissa Burton, Chief Financial Officer
Keith Fenton, Chief Development & Marketing Officer
Private nonprofit residential facility for adults with developmen-
tal disabilities. Located on 124 acres just north of Atlanta.
Annandale provides full program and 24 hour residential ser-
vices, pay program services, respite care and skilled nursing
services.

6616   Atlanta Institute of Medicine and Rehabilitation
Ste E
2911 Piedmont Rd NE
Atlanta, GA 30305-2782   404-365-0160
                                         FAX: 404-365-0751

Lawrence E Eppelbaum, Founder
Galina Vayner, MD
One of the most famous medical centers in the state of Georgia.
The Institute employs more then 40 highly qualified medical pro-
fessionals and fully equipped with the latest medical equipment.
It has gathered recognition and respect from the people of Atla

6617   Bobby Dodd Institute (BDI)
2120 Marietta Blvd NW
Atlanta, GA 30318-2122   678-365-0071
                                         FAX: 678-365-0098
                                         TTY:678-365-0099
                                              bobbydodd.org
Rodney Hall, Chair
Christopher Rosselli, Vice Chair
Wayne McMillan, President & CEO
BDI annually serves approximately 400 clients in Atlanta, GA.
BDI works primarily with people with developmental disabilities
such as autism and down syndrome, but includes clients with
physical or acquired disabilities.

6618   Cave Spring Rehabilitation Center
Georgia Department of Labor
7 Georgia Ave
P.O.Box 303
Cave Spring, GA 30124-2718   706-777-2341
                                         FAX: 706-777-2366
                              gvra.georgia.gov/cave-spring-center-contacts-
Russell Fleming, Director
Karen Hulsey, Administrative Operations Coordinator
Renee Lambert, Rehabilitation Assistant

6619   Center for the Visually Impaired
739 West Peachtree St NW
Atlanta, GA 30308-1137   404-875-9011
                                         FAX: 404-607-0062
                                              cviga.org
Susan Hoy, Chair
Fontaine M. Huey, President
Doreen Zaksheske, Vice President of Finance & Operations
Offers services to people of all ages who are blind or visually impaired with training in orientation and mobility, computer technology, activities of daily living, communication skills and
employment readiness. Aso offers two children's programs, a
comm

6620   Devereux Advanced Behavioral Health Georgia
Devereux Georgia Treatment Network
1291 Stanley Rd.
Kennesaw, GA 30152   770-427-0147
                                             800-342-3357
                                         FAX: 770-427-4030
                                              info@devereux.org
                                         www.devereuxga.org
Gwendolyn B Skinner, Vice President of Operations
Dave Detro, Human Resource Director
Carlos F Pozzi-Montero, Psy.D, Clinical Director
Facility offering services to youth with emotional and behavioral
health challenges. Services include Intensive Residential Treat-
ment, Foster Care Program, Group Homes, and educational
programs.

6621   Easterseals East Georgia
1500 Wrightsboro Rd.
Augusta, GA 30904   706-667-9695
                                         FAX: 706-667-8831
                                      www.easterseals.com/eastgeorgia
Easterseals East Georgia assists people with disabilities and
other special needs to maximize opportunities for employment,
independence and full inclusion into society.

6622 **Georgia Industries for the Blind**
700 Faceville Highway
Bainbridge, GA 39819-218   229-248-2666
FAX: 229-248-2669
gvra.georgia.gov/gib/about-us

James Hughes, Executive Director
Offers services for the totally blind, legally blind, visually impaired, and more with health, counseling, educational, recreational, rehabilitation, computer training and professional training services.

6623 **Hillhaven Rehabilitation**
26 Tower Rd NE
Marietta, GA 30060-6947   770-422-8913
800-526-5782
FAX: 770-425-2085

Leslie Ann Marie Parrish, Case Manager
Valerie Hamilton, Administrator
Routine skilled and subacute medical and rehabilitation care including physical therapy, occupational therapy, speech pathology and therapeutic recreation. Programs include stroke and head injury rehab; orthopedic rehab; complex IV therapy; woundcare; can.

6624 **In-Home Medical Care**
Care Master Medical Services
240 Odell Rd
P.O.Box 278
Griffin, GA 30223-4787   770-227-1264
800-542-8889
FAX: 770-412-0014
caremastermedical.com

Nancy Frederick, VP
Eddie Grogan, Chief Executive Officer
Offers the devoted attention of a professional nurse, the use of I.V. therapies, pain management and provision of medical equipment and supplies right where the patient wants to be.

6625 **Learning Services: Harris House Program**
131 Langley Drive
Suite B
Lawrenceville, GA 30046-4446   404-298-0144
888-419-9955
FAX: 866-491-7396
learningservices.com

Dr. Debra Braunling-McMorrow, President and CEO
Susan Snow, Director of Admissions
Michael Weaver, Chief Development Officer
Situated in the small, historic district of Stone Mountain, just outside of Atlanta, this 6 bed program is designed to encourage independence while providing appropriate support for each individuals needs. Community-based productive activities are customi

6626 **Pain Control & Rehabilitation Institute of Georgia**
Ste 120
2784 N Decatur Rd
Decatur, GA 30033-5993   404-297-1400
FAX: 404-297-1427

Shulim Spektor, CEO
Anna Britman, Office Manager
Provides pain management for chronic and acute pain resulted from injuries, diseases of muscles and nerve, Reflex Sympathetic Dystrophy, perform disabilities and impairment ratings.

6627 **Savannah Association for the Blind**
214 Drayton Street
Savannah, GA 31401-4021   912-236-4473
FAX: 912-234-9286

Gregory Hodges, President
Robert Falligant, Vice-president
Gary Sadowski, Treasurer
Offers services for the totally blind, legally blind, visually impaired, and more with health, counseling, educational, recreational, rehabilitation, computer training and professional training services.

6628 **Shepherd Center for Treatment of Spinal Injuries**
2020 Peachtree Rd NW
Atlanta, GA 30309-1465   404-352-2020
FAX: 404-350-7479
admissions@shepherd.org
www.shepherd.org

Gary R. Ulicny, President & CEO
David F. Apple, Jr., M.D., Medical Director
Angela Beninga, D.O., Staff Physiatrist
Dedicated exclusively to the care of patients with spinal cord injuries and other paralyzing spinal disorders. It serves predominately residents of Georgia and neighboring states as one of the only 14 hospitals designated by the U.S. Department of Educati

6629 **Transitional Hospitals Corporation**
Ste 1000
7000 Central Pkwy NE
Atlanta, GA 30328-4592   770-821-5328
800-683-6868
FAX: 770-913-0015
csins.com

Dean Kozee, Owner
Carolyn Norton, Special Projects Consultant/Broker
Amaury Rentas, Event Insurance/Broker
A national network of intensive care hospitals providing care for patients who suffer from a chronic illness and/or catastrophic accident. The mission is founded on providing quality health care to patients who require highly skilled nursing care and acce.

6630 **Walton Rehabilitation Health System**
1355 Independence Dr
Augusta, GA 30901-1037   706-823-8584
866-492-5866
FAX: 706-724-5752
www.waltonfoundation.net

Robert Taylor, Chair
Dennis Skelley, President/CEO
David Dugan, Treasurer
A 58-bed comprehensive physical rehabilitation hospital offering inpatient and outpatient services. Services offered include: stroke recovery, orthopedic injury, pediatrics, head injury, pain management for chronic pain syndrome, TMJ/Craniofacial pain and

Hawaii

6631 **Rehabilitation Hospital of the Pacific**
226 N Kuakini St
Honolulu, HI 96817-2498   808-531-3511
FAX: 808-566-3411
rehabfoundation@rehabhospital.org
www.rehabhospital.org

John Komeiji, Chair
Glenn O. Sexton, Vice Chair
E. Lynne Madden, Secretary/Treasurer
The only acute care medical rehabilitation organization serving both Hawaii and the Pacific. For over 52 years, the hospital and its 7 outpatient clinics on Oahu, and Maui and Hawaii have been dedicated to providing comprehensive, cost effective rehabilit

Idaho

6632 **Ashton Memorial Nursing Home and Chemical Dependency Center**
700 N 2nd
Ashton, ID 83420   208-652-7461
FAX: 208-652-7595
ashtonmemorial.com

Sheila Kellogg, Administrator

6633 Idaho Elks Rehabilitation Hospital
600 N Robbins Rd
Boise, ID 83702   208-489-4444
                                                FAX: 208-344-8883
                                                info@elksrehab.org
                                                www.elksrehab.org

Joseph P. Caroselli, CEO
Doug Lewis, Chief Financial Officer
Mellisa Honsinger, Chief Operating Officer
A nonprofit hospital serving Idaho and the Pacific Northwest. All
inpatient and outpatient programs and services are supervised by
the hospital's full-time medical directors whose specialty is physical rehabilitative medicine. Services include: occupation

6634 Portneuf Medical Center Rehabilitation
777 Hospital Way
Pocatello, ID 83201-4004   208-239-1000
                                                charlesa@portmed.org
                                                www.portmed.org

Mark Buckalew, Chairman
Michael Nosacka, MD
Dan Ordyna, CEO
Provides compassionate, quality health care services needed by
the people of eastern Idaho in collaboration with other providers
and community resources.

Illinois

6635 Advocate Christ Hospital and Medical Center
4440 W 95th St
Oak Lawn, IL 60453-2600   708-684-8000
                                                FAX: 708-684-4440
                                                advocatehealth.com

Jim Skogsbergh, CEO
Bill Santulli, COO
Kate K, Director
A 665-bed, not-for-profit teaching, research and referral medical
center in Oak Lawn, Illinois. It also is home to the Advocate Hope
Childrens's Hospital, one of the most comprehensive providers
of pediatric care in the state. The medical center is a lead

**6636 Advocate Christ Medical Center & Advocate Hope
Children's Hospital**
4440 W 95th St
Oak Lawn, IL 60453-2600   708-684-8000
                                                FAX: 708-684-4440
                                                advocatehealth.com

Kenneth Lukhard, CEO
Darcie Brazel, Market Chief Nurse Executive
Jan McCrea, Rehab Services Director
The largest fully integrated not-for-profit health care delivery
system in metropolitan Chicago and is recognized as one of the
top 10 systems in the country. The mission of Advocate Health
Care is to serve the health needs of individuals, families and co

6637 Advocate Illinois Masonic Medical Center
836 W Wellington Ave
Chicago, IL 60657-5147   773-975-1600
                                                www.advocatehealth.com/immc

Jim Skogsbergh, CEO
Ajay V. Maker, MD
Consultation, education, family counseling, parent training in
behavior modification techniques offered to developmentally
disabled adults.

6638 Alexian Brothers Medical Center
800 Biesterfield Rd
Elk Grove Village, IL 60007-3396   847-437-5500
                                                www.alexian.org

Mark Frey, President/CEO
Tracy Rogers, Senior Vice President and Chief Operating Officer
Paul Belter, Senior Vice President and Chief Financial Officer
A threefold mission: Works toward maximizing physical function, enhance independent social skills and optimize communication skills consistent with an individual's ability. The Center
helps those disabled by accident or illness achieve a new personal
best

6639 Back in the Saddle Hippotherapy Program
Corcoran Physical Therapy
4200 W Peterson Ave
Chicago, IL 60646-6074   312-286-2266
                                                847-604-4145
                                                FAX: 847-673-8895

Julie Naughton, Program Coordinator
Maureen Corcoran, Physical Therapist
Tom Corcoran, Owner
A direct medical treatment used by licensed physical therapists
who have a strong treatment background in posture and movement, neuromotor function and sensory processing. The benefits
of Hippotherapy are available to individuals with just about any
disab

6640 Barbara Olson Center of Hope
3206 N Central Ave
Rockford, IL 61101-1797   815-964-9275
                                                FAX: 815-964-9607
                                                info@b-olsoncenterofhope.org
                                                b-olsoncenterofhope.org

Carm Herman, Executive Director
Pam Sondell, Director of Programs and Services
Pam Carey, Director of Human Resources
We provide vocational employment, educational and social op-
portunities for adults with developmental disabilities.

6641 Bartolucci Center, The- ILC Enterprises
6415 Stanley Ave
Berwyn, IL 60402-3130   708-745-5277
                                                FAX: 708-698-5090
                                                www.pillarscommunity.org

Zada Clarke, Chairman
Ann Schreiner, President & CEO
Jennifer Hogberg, Vice Chair
A nonprofit tax exempt private social service agency serving suburban Chicago offering day treatment and vocational counseling
to individuals who encountered a pattern of job loss due to
emotional problems.

6642 Baxter Healthcare Corporation
1 Baxter Pkwy
Deerfield, IL 60015-4625   224-948-2000
                                                800-422-9837
                                                224-948-1812
                                                FAX: 800-568-5020

*Phillip L. Batchelor, Corporate Vice President - Quality and Regu-
latory Affairs*
Jean-Luc Butel, Corporate Vice President - President, International
*Robert M. Davis, Corporate Vice President - President, Medical
Products*
Baxter International Inc. is a global healthcare company that,
through its subsidiaries assists healthcare professionals and their
patients with treatment of complex medical conditions including
hemophilia, immune disorders, kidney disease, cancer, trauma
and other conditions. Baxter applies its expertise in medical devices, pharmaceuticals, and biotechnology to make a meaningful
difference in patient's lives.

6643 Beacon Therapeutic Diagnostic and Treatment Center
10650 S Longwood Dr
Chicago, IL 60643-2617   773-881-1005
                                                FAX: 773-881-1164

Susan Reyha-Guerrero, President & CEO
Cheryl Thompson, Deputy CEO
Paul Morley, Chief Operating Officer
Offers community day treatment, education, diagnostic services,
family counseling, learning disabled, speech and hearing and
psychiatric services.

6644 Blind Service Association
17 N State St
Ste 1050
Chicago, IL 60602-3510   312-236-0808
                                                blindserviceassociation.org

Ann Lousin, President
Linda Schwartz, Executive Vice President
Arthur M. Shapiro, Secretary
Offers services for the totally blind, legally blind and visually im-
paired with reading and recording low vision network, social ser-
vices, referrals and support groups.

6645   Brentwood Subacute Healthcare Center
T HI Brentwood
5400 W 87th St
Burbank, IL 60459-2913   866-300-3257
                                       www.savaseniorcare.com
Audrey Protrowski, Director Business Development
Jill Sattersield, Administrator
John Walton, CEO
Seeks to help patients and their families through what can be a
very emotional decision-making process. We provide guidance
and consultation on everything from how to properly choose the
facility to providing resources that help you cope with the nature
of the decision itself.

6646   Caremark Healthcare Services
2211 Sanders Rd
Northbrook, IL 60062-6128   847-559-4700
                                                800-423-1411
                                            FAX: 847-559-3905
                                             www.caremark.com
Larry J. Merlo, President & CEO
Mark Cosby, Executive Vice President
An 80-service-center network providing services anywhere in
the U.S. Offers 24 hour access to nursing and pharmacy services,
case management resource centers, HIV/AIDS services,
women's health services, transplant care services, nutrition
support services

6647   Centegra Northern Illinois Medical Center
4209 West Shamrock Lane
Suite B
McHenry, IL 60050-8499   815-759-8017
                                                877-236-8347
                                            FAX: 815-759-8062
                                              www.centegra.org
Michael S. Eesley, CEO
Jason Sciarro, President
David L. Tomlinson, Executive Vice President
Providing rehabilitation services in Lake and McHenry Counties,
the Rehabilitation Unit is a complete living environment for up to
15 patients after a debilitating illness of trauma. Various loca-
tions offering a multitude of services: PT, OT, speech, HT,

6648   Center for Comprehensive Services
Mentor Network
P.O.Box 2825
Carbondale, IL 62902-2825   618-457-4008
                                                800-582-4227
                                            FAX: 618-457-5372
                               dayna.foreman@thementornetwork.com
                                                mentorabi.com
Bill Duffy, Chief Operating Officer
Michael E. Hofmeister, Vice President
Sean Byrne, Chief Financial Officer
Post-acute rehabilitation services for adults and adolescents with
acquired brain injuries. Residential, day-treatment and out-pa-
tient services tailored to individual needs.

6649   Center for Rehabilitation at Rush Presbyterian:
Johnston R Bowman Health Center
1653 W Congress Parkway
Chicago, IL 60612-3833   312-942-5000
                                            FAX: 312-942-3601
                                            TTY:312-942-2207
                                     teri_sommerfeld@rush.edu
                                                 www.rush.edu
Larry J. Goodman, CEO
A 613-bed hospital serving adults and children, the John R. Bowman Health Center and Rush University is home to one of the first
medical colleges in the Midwest and one of the nation's
top-ranked nursing colleges, as well as graduate programs in
allied he

6650   Center for Spine, Sports & Occupational Rehabilitation
345 E Superior St
Chicago, IL 60611-2654   312-238-7767
                                                800-354-7342
                                            FAX: 312-238-7709
                                             webmaster@ric.org
                                           www.rehabchicago.org
Joanne C. Smith, President & CEO
Edward B. Case, Executive Vice President
M. Jude Reyes, Chair
Offers evaluation and treatment of patients with acute and sub-
acute musculoskeletal and sports injuries. RIC offers different
levels of care, including inpatient, day rehabilitation, and outpa-
tients services, according to the special needs of each patient

6651   Children's Home and Aid Society of Illinois
125 South Wacker Drive
14th Floor
Chicago, IL 60606-4448   312-424-0200
                                      www.childrenshomeandaid.org
Beverley Sibblies, Chairman
Chris Leahy, Vice-Chairman
Mark Tresnowski, Secretary
Private state-wide. Multi-service, racially integrated staff and
client populations. Provides educational, placement and community services for children-at-risk and their families. Advocacy,
consultation and follow-up services provided according to our ph

6652   Clinton County Rehabilitation Center
1665 North Fourth Street
P O Box 157
Breese, IL 62230- 1791   618-526-8800
                                            FAX: 618-526-2021
                                            info@commlink.org
                                                commlink.org
Wesley A. Gozia, President
Judge Joseph L. Heimann, Vice President
John L. Lengerman, Treasurer
Provides Adult Day Programs (developmental training, work
training, job readiness and job placements); Residentail Pro-
grams (CILA Intermittent Care, CILA 24 hour care); Infant Pro-
grams (early interventions, early head start); Community
Services.

6653   Continucare, A Service of the Rehab Institute of Chicago
West Suburban Hospital Medical Center
3 Erie Ct
Oak Park, IL 60302-2519   708-383-6200
                                                800-354-7342
                                            FAX: 312-908-1369
Heidi Asbury MD
We respond to the needs of the whole person: body, mind and
spirit. We foster a climate of care, hospitality and a spirit of community. We develop systems and structures that attend to the
needs of those at risk of discrimination because of age, gender,
lifestyle, ethnic background, religious beliefs or socioeconomic
status.

6654   Delta Center
1400 Commercial Ave
Cairo, IL 62914-1978   618-734-2665
                                                800-471-7213
                                            FAX: 618-734-1999
                                               deltacenter.org
Lisa Tolbert, Executive Director
Lisa Tholbert, Assistant Executive Director
The Delta Center is a non-profit mental health center, substance
abuse counseling facility, and also provides various community
services to Alexander and Pulaski County, Illinois. The purpose
and mission is to promote, encourage, foster and engage exclusi

6655   Division of Rehabilitation-Education Services, University
of Illinois
Beckwith Hall
201 E. John Street
Champaign, IL 61820- 6901   217-333-4603
                                            FAX: 217-333-0248
                                          disability@uiuc.edu
Ann Fredricksen, Disability Specialist
Jon Gunderson, Coordinator
Pat Malik, Director

6656 Easterseals DuPage and Fox Valley
830 S Addison Ave.
Villa Park, IL 60181-1153   630-620-4433
                              FAX: 630-620-1148
                              info@eastersealsdfvr.org
                              www.easterseals.com/dfv

Theresa Forthofer, President & CEO
Dave Gardner, Chief Financial Officer
Kelly Moreland, Vice President, Development
The mission of Easterseals DuPage and Fox Valley is to enable infants, children and adults with disabilities to achieve maximum independence and to provide support to their families. Key services provided include physical, occupational, speech-language, nutrition and assistive technology therapies and audiology services for all ages.

6657 Easterseals Gilchrist Marchman Child Development Center
1312 S Racine Ave.
Chicago, IL 60608   312-492-7402
                       FAX: 312-492-9014
                       www.easterseals.com

Sara Ray Stoelinga, Chief Executive Officer
Ann O'Malley, Contact
An early childhood and education program for children ages 6 weeks to 5 years. Focuses on social and intellectual development through family-centered education.

6658 Easterseals Jayne Shover Center
799 S McLean Blvd.
Elgin, IL 60123   847-742-3264
                     FAX: 847-742-9436
                     www.easterseals.com/dfv

Theresa Forthofer, President & CEO
Kimberly Garcia, Contact
A free-standing, comprehensive outpatient rehabilitation center serving children and adults with physical and developmental disabilities.

6659 Easterseals Joliet Region
212 Barney Dr.
Joliet, IL 60435   815-725-2194
                      FAX: 815-725-5150
                      www.easterseals.com/joliet

Deb Condotti, President & CEO
David Gardner, Chief Financial Officer
Vanessa Hunter, Director, Residential & Social Services
Services for children and adults with disabilities and their families. Pediatric therapy, residential programs, special home placement, inclusive child care, and early intervention.

6660 El Valor
Main Office & Developmental Training Center
1850 W 21st St
Chicago, IL 60608   312-666-4511
                       FAX: 312-666-6677
                       TTY:312-666-3361
                       info@elvalor.net
                       elvalor.org

Rafael Malpica, Chairman
Rey B Gonzalez, President & CEO
Carmen Ziegler, Chief Financial Officer
El Valor's mission is to serve people with disabilities and their families, by offering programs in the areas of early childhood education, adult services and parental and community engagement.

6661 Elgin Training Center
Association For Individual Development Elgin Area
1135 Bowes Road
Elgin, IL 60123-1321   847-931-6200
                          FAX: 847-888-6079
                          www.the-association.org

Chuck Miles, Chairmen
Patrick Flaherty, Vice Chairmen
Walter Dwyer, Treasurer
Day training services to develop work habits and attitudes while providing training in small product assembly, sorting, packaging, collating, & material handling. Instruction also offered in job related knowledge & in personal, social and independent living skills. There is also an on-site specialized Autism Program. Addi-

tionally, residential programs (group homes & apartments) are also available for people with developmental disabilities.

6662 Family Counseling Center
PO Box 759
Golconda, IL 62938   618-683-2461
                        FAX: 618-683-2066
                        fccinconline.org

Larry Mizell, Executive Director
Connie Duncan, Director
Nora Beth Hacker, Financial Director
Provides counseling, developmental training, evaluations, assisted living services, referrals, psychosocial rehabilitation, and a variety of work services.

6663 Family Matters
A RC Community Support Systems
1901 S. 4th St
Ste 209
Effingham, IL 62401-4123   217-347-5428
                              866-436-7842
                              FAX: 217-347-5119
                              deinhorn@arc-css.org
                              www.fmptic.org

Debbie Einhorn, Executive Director
Nancy Mader, Project Coordinator
Parent Training and Information Center and family support programs for families of children who have disabilities from the ages of birth through 21. Services include: Parent support and training, school advocacy, home visits, information and referral, pa

6664 Five Star Industries
1308 Wells Street Road
P O Box 60
Du Quoin, IL 62832-60   618-542-5421
                           FAX: 618-542-5556
                           5starind.com

Susan Engelhardt, Executive Director
Incorporated as a private, non-profit corporation under the laws of the State of Illinois, is an equal opportunity employer and provides equal opportunity in compliance with the Civil Rights Act of 1964 and all other appropriate laws, rules and regulation

6665 HSI Austin Center For Development
1819 S Kedzie Ave
Chicago, IL 60623-2623   773-854-1676
                            FAX: 773-854-8300

Provides an educational program designed to enhance academic, behavioral and social performance of children 4-14 years of age experiencing emotional disorders that result in exclusion from the public school setting.

6666 Hyde Park-Woodlawn
950 E 61st St
Chicago, IL 60637-2623   773-324-0280
                            FAX: 773-324-0285

Clarissa Williams, Manager

6667 Illinois Center for Autism
548 South Ruby Lane
Fairview Heights, IL 62208-2614   618-398-7500
                                     FAX: 618-394-9869
                                     info@illinoiscenterforautism.org
                                     illinoiscenterforautism.org

Hardy Ware, Chairperson
Thomas E. Berry, Vice Chairperson
Gary Guthrie, Secretary
A community-based mental health/educational treatment center dedicated to serving autistic clients.

6668 Julius and Betty Levinson Center
1825 K Street NW
Suite 600
Washington, DC 60304-1557   202-776-0406
                               800-872-5827
                               FAX: 708-383-9025
                               www.ucp.org

Woody Connette, Chair
Ian Ridlon, Vice Chair
Mark Boles, Treasurer
Houses one of its three adult developmental training programs for substantially physically disabled men and women.

6669   Lake County Health Department
18 N. County Street
Waukegan, IL 60085
847-377-2000
FAX: 847-336-1517
www.lakecountyil.gov

Aaron Lawlor, Chairman
Stevenson Mountsier, Vice Chairman
Barry Burton, Administrator
Includes counseling, crisis intervention, emergency management, psychotherapy and chemotherapy management for individuals and families.

6670   Little Friends, Inc.
140 N Wright Street
Naperville, IL 60540-4799
630-355-6533
FAX: 630-355-3176
info@lilfriends.com
www.littlefriendsinc.com

Dan Casey, Chairman
Matt Johanson, Vice Chairman
Michele Calbi, Treasurer
Little Friends has been serving children and adults with autism and other developmental disabilities for over 40 years. Based in Naperville, Little Friends operates three schools, vocational training programs, community-based residential services and the

6671   MAP Training Center
7th and Mc Kinley St
Karnak, IL 62956
618-634-9401
FAX: 618-634-9090

Larry Earnhart, President
Cindy Earnhart, Community Liaison
Training, employment, residential and support services, targeted for adults with developmental disabilities.

6672   Macon Resources
2121 Hubbard Ave.
P O Box 2760
Decatur, IL 62524-2760
217-875-1910
FAX: 217-875-8899
TTY:217-875-8898
maconresources.org

Tom Hill, President
Michael Breheny, Vice President
Barb Nadler, Secretary
The purpose is to provide a comprehensive array of habilitative/rehabilitative training programs and support services to assist individuals and/or family units of an individual with a developmental disability, mental illness, or other handicapping conditi

6673   Mary Bryant Home for the Blind
2960 Stanton
Springfield, IL 62703-4385
217-529-1611
888-529-1611
FAX: 217-529-6975
mbha@marybryanthome.org
marybryanthome.org

Jerry Curry, Executive Director
Robert E. Maxey, President
Allan J. Rupel, Vice President
Supportive living facility for blind or visually impaired adults over the age of 22. A supportive living facility remodeled to foster the move to increased independence for residents. The new apartment style housing combined with personal care and other a

6674   Northern Illinois Special Recreation Association (NISRA)
285 Memorial Drive
Crystal Lake, IL 60014-3650
815-459-0737
FAX: 815-459-0388
info@nisra.org
www.nisra.org

Brian Shahinian, Executive Director
Carol Amoroso, Manager of Finance and Personnel
Kerri Ruddy, Manager of Office Services
Leisure and recreation services to those with disabilities who are unable to participate successfully in park district and city recreation programs.

6675   Oak Forest Hospital of Cook County
15900 Cicero Ave
Oak Forest, IL 60452
708-687-7200
FAX: 708-687-7979
TTY:708-687-4794
www.cchil.org

Robert Weinstein, Department Chair
Suja Mathew, Associate Chair
A 654 bed health care center devoted to the diagnosis, rehabilitation and long-term care of adults suffering from chronic illnesses, diseases and physical impairments.

6676   PARC
1913 W. Townline Road
P.O.Box 3418
Peoria, IL 61615-3418
309-691-3800
FAX: 309-689-3613
parcway.org

Pat Kawczynski, Chair
Heyl Royster, Vice Chair
Terry Waters, Treasurer
Serves all ages that are diagnosed with developmental and physical disabilities. Programs include early intervention, family support, respite care, vocational training, supported employment, adult day programs and residential.

6677   Peoria Area Blind People's Center
2905 W Garden St
Peoria, IL 61605-1316
309-637-3693
FAX: 309-637-3693
info@cicbvi.org
cicbvi.org

Carol Warren, President
Cora Quinn, Vice President
Prasad Parupalli, Treasurer
Offers services for the totally blind, legally blind, visually impaired, and more with health, counseling, educational, recreational, rehabilitation, computer training and professional training services.

6678   Pioneer Center for Human Services
4031 W Dayton St
McHenry, IL 60050
815-344-1230
FAX: 815-344-3815
TTY:815-344-6243
gethelp@pioneercenter.org

Dan McCaleb, Chairman
Sam Tenuto, Co-CEO
Frank Samuel, Co-CEO
Pioneer Center is a non-profit agency in McHenry County delivering services to more than 4,000 people annually. Pioneer Center provides developmental disability services, youth and family behavioral health services and homeless services (McHenry County PADS).

6679   Prosthetics and Orthotics Center in Blue Island
2310 York St
Blue Island, IL 60406-2411
708-597-2611
800-354-7342
FAX: 800-908-1932
www.rehabchicago.org/about/blue_island.php
Provides orthotic and prosthetic fittings and follow-up services to adults and children in the south suburbs of Chicago.

6680   RB King Counseling Center
2300 N Edward St
Decatur, IL 62526-4163
217-877-8121
FAX: 217-875-0966

Gordon Cross MD
Offers outpatient, individual, group, divorce and meditation, family and re-adjustment counseling.

6681   REHAB Products and Services
3715 N Vermilion St
Danville, IL 61832-1130
217-446-1146
FAX: 217-446-1191
workse.org

Frank L. Brunacci, President/CEO
Crystal Meece, Vice President Production
Todd Seabaugh, VP Programs
janitorial, lawn care, distribution services.

6682   RIC Northshore
Rehabilitation Institute of Chicago
345 E Superior St
Chicago, IL 60611-2654

312-238-1000
800-354-7342
webmaster@ric.org
www.rehabchicago.org

Joanne C. Smith, President/CEO
Edward B. Case, Vice President
Provides rehabilitation for sports-related injuries, musculoskeletal conditions, neurological conditions, stroke, arthritis, amputation, burns, and general deconditioning.

6683   RIC Prosthetics and Orthotics Center
Rehabilitation Institute of Chicago
345 E. Superior Street
Suite 101
Chicago, IL 60611-4615

312-238-1000
800-345-7342
FAX: 708-957-8353
webmaster@rehabchicago.org
ric.org

Martin Buckner, CPO, Inpatient Coordinator
Nicole T. Soltys, CP, Clinical Coordinator
Robert D. Lipschutz, CP, Director of Prosthetic and Orthotic Education
Offers almost all the prosthetics and orthotics services provided at RIC's main hospital in downtown Chicago, including consultations, fittings and training.

6684   RIC Windermere House
5548 S Hyde Park Blvd
Chicago, IL 60637-1909

773-256-5050
800-354-7342
FAX: 773-256-5060
www.rehabchicago.org

Meghan Scalise, Manager
Evaluation, therapeutic services and patient education are offered in the areas of arthritis, multiple sclerosis, musculoskeletal conditions, orthopedics, stroke, spinal cord injury, brain injury and sports medicine.

6685   Ray Graham Association for People with Disabilities
901 Warrenville Road
Suite 500
Lisle, IL 60532-1038

630-620-2222
FAX: 630-628-2350
TTY:630-628-2352
cathyfickerterill@yahoo.com
ray-graham.org

Michael Komoll, Chairperson
Neville Bilimoria, Vice Chairperson
Kim zoeller, President & CEO
Provides developmental services at 15 sites to infants, children and adults with disabilities. Services range from 1 hr/wk respite to full-time residential.

6686   Reach Rehabilitation Program: Americana Healthcare
9401 S Kostner Ave
Oak Lawn, IL 60453-2697

708-423-1505
FAX: 708-423-3822

Jean M Roche, Owner
Postacute rehabilitation program.

6687   Rehabilitation Achievement Center
345 E Superior St
Chicago, IL 60611-4805

312-238-1000
800-354-7342
www.ric.org

M. Jude Reyes, Chair
Mike P. Krasny, Vice Chair
Joanne C. Smith, President & CEO
Rehabilitation Institute of Chicago (RIC) has aquired the assets of the Rehabilitation Achievement Center (RAC).

6688   Rehabilitation Institute of Chicago: Alexian Brothers Medical Center
800 Biesterfield Rd
Elk Grove Village, IL 60007-3361

847-437-5500
866-253-9426
FAX: 847-631-5663
TTY: 847-956-5116
www.alexianbrothershealth.org

Mark Frey, President and Chief Executive Officer
Tracy Rogers, Senior Vice President and Chief Operating Officer
Paul Belter, Senior Vice President and Chief Financial Officer
A 32-bed rehabilitation unit under the medical direction and supervision of the Rehabilitation Institute of Chicago.

6689   Riverside Medical Center
Mental Health Unit
350 N Wall St
Kankakee, IL 60901-2991

815-933-1671
FAX: 815-935-8160
rhuber@rsh.net
riversidehealthcare.org

Phillip Kambic, CEO
Bill W. Douglas, Vice President
Offers recreation, parenting therapy, emergency services, psychological testing and inpatient treatment programs. Riverside is nationally recognized for its specialty programs in heart care, obstetrics, trauma, oncology, rehabilitation, geriatrics, occupa

6690   Robert Young Mental Health Center Division of Trinity Regional Haelth System
Trinity Health Foundation
2701 17th St
Rock Island, IL 61201-5351

309-779-2800
800-322-1431
FAX: 309-779-2027
www.unitypoint.org

Rick Seidler, President & CEO
Jim Hayes, CFO
Tamara Byram, VP, Legal/Compliance
Services include comprehensive inpatient rehabilitation, chronic pain management programs, outpatient medical rehabilitation, work hardening programs, vocational evaluation, alcohol and other drug dependency rehabilitation programs, Burn Center, and menta

6691   Sampson-Katz Center
216 West Jackson Blvd
Suite 700
Chicago, IL 60606-2104

312-673-3400
FAX: 312-553-5544
TTY:773-761-6672
jvsskc@jvschicago.org
www.jvschicago.org

Andrew M. Glick, Chair
John L. Daniels, Vice Chair
H. Debra Levin, President

6692   Shelby County Community Services
160 North Main Street
Memphis, TN 38103-650

901-222-2300
FAX: 912-222-2090
www.shelbycountytn.gov

Dottie Jones, Director
Primary focus is substance abuse treatment.

6693   Streator Unlimited
305 N Sterling St
P O Box 706
Streator, IL 61364-2369

815-673-5574
FAX: 815-673-1714
contact@streatorunlimited.org
www.streatorunlimited.org

Jeffrey Dean, Executive Director
Lynn Fukar, Director of Day Services
Julie Caestens, Director Residential Services
Vocational and personal skills training, residential services, client and family support, supported and computerized employment. Serves adults with intellectual disabilities with the goal of enabling them to reach their fullest potential, live as independ

6694 **Swedish Covenant Hospital Rehabilitation Services**
5145 N California Ave
Chicago, IL 60625-3661   773-878-8200
                                    FAX: 773-561-0490
Mark Newton, President & CEO
Provides acute rehabilitation services, subacute care and outpatient services for many types of disabling injuries and conditions, including amputation, arthritis, brain injury, general deconditioning, multiple sclerosis, musculoskeletal injuries, stroke,

6695 **TCRC Sight Center**
21310 Route 9
Tremont, IL 61568-2558   309-347-7148
                                    FAX: 309-925-4241
                                    info@tcrcorg.com
                                    www.tcrcorg.com
Jamie Durdel, President & CEO
Molly Anderson, Vice President
Offers services for persons who are totally blind, legally blind, partially sighted or visually impaired along with other disabilities. Have support group, rehabilitation classes, orientation and mobility services, counseling services, low vision clinic,

6696 **Tazewell County Resource Center**
Box 12
Rr 1
Tremont, IL 61568   309-347-7148
                                    FAX: 309-925-4241
                                    info@tcrcorg.com
                                    www.tcrcorg.com
Jamie Durdel, President & CEO
Molly Anderson, Vice President
A private, nonprofit agency providing programs for the special needs of infants, adults, children and their families residing in Tazewell County. Services offered include: birth-three infant/parent program, adult day care services, family support, residen

6697 **Trumbull Park**
10530 S Oglesby Ave
Chicago, IL 60617-6140   773-375-7022
                                    FAX: 773-375-5528
Gregory Terry, Director
Diana Moore, Site Supervisor
Ada McKinley, Manager
Offers consultation, education, general counseling, recreation, self-help and social services for children and adults.

6698 **University of Illinois Medical Center**
1740 West Taylor Street
Chicago, IL 60612-7232   312-355-4000
                                    866-600-2273
                                    FAX: 312-996-7770
                                    hospital.uillinois.edu
Rajiv Pai, Chief
Marilyn Plomann, Manager
Offers services for the totally blind, legally blind, visually impaired, and more with health, counseling, educational, recreational, rehabilitation, computer training and professional training services.

6699 **VanMatre Rehabilitation Center**
950 S Mulford Rd
Rockford, IL 61108-4274   815-381-8500
                                    866-754-3347
                                    FAX: 815-484-9953
                                    webcontentcoordinator@rhsnet.org
                                    www.vanmatrerehab.com
Gary E. Kaatz, President and Chief Executive Officer
Scott Craig, Medical Director
A CARF-accredited comprehensive rehabilitation center based within the Rockford Memorial Hospital providing inpatient and outpatient services for physically and cognitively challenged persons with debilitating illness and injuries.

6700 **Warren Achievement Center**
1220 E 2nd Ave
Monmouth, IL 61546-2404   309-734-3131
                                    FAX: 309-734-7114
                                    info@warrenachievement.com
                                    warrenachievement.com
Rick Barnhill, President
Jim Kesse, Vice President
Sherry Waite, Chief Operations Officer
For developmentally disabled children and adults. Parent-infant education programs are for parents of infants with disabilities or developmental delays; Children's Group Homes which serve children on a fulltime basis and can serve additional children on a

Indiana

6701 **Ball Memorial Hospital**
2401 W University Ave
Muncie, IN 47303-3499   765-747-3111
                                    FAX: 765-747-3313
                                    iuhealth.org/ball-memorial
Mike Haley, CEO
Offers rehabilitation services, occupational therapy, physical therapy and more for the physically challenged child or adult.

6702 **Community Health Network**
1500 N Ritter Ave
Indianapolis, IN 46219-3027   317-355-4275
                                    800-775-7775
                                    FAX: 317-351-7723
                                    www.ecommunity.com
Keith Thompson, Manager
Anita Harden, President
A leading not-for-profit health system offering convenient access to expert physicians, advanced treatments and leading edge technology, all focused on getting patients well and back to their lives. With caring compassion, Community's 5 hospitals and 70 + sites of care continually strive to improve the health and well-being of those individuals in central Indiana who entrust care to us.

6703 **Crossroads Industrial Services**
8302 E 33rd Street
Indianapolis, IN 46226   317-897-7320
                                    FAX: 317-897-9763
                                    info@crossroadsindustrialservices.com
                                    www.crossroadsindustrialservices.c om
Anne Shupe, Finance Executive
Curtiss Quirin, CEO
Assisting customers with short-term, seasonal, and long-term outsourcing needs. Many consider Crossroads an extension of their company

6704 **Department of Veterans Affairs Vet Center #418**
302 W. Washington St
Room E120
Indianapolis, IN 46204- 2738   317-232-3910
                                    800-490-4520
                                    FAX: 317-232-7721
                                    www.in.gov/veteran/sso/fac
Charles T. Applegate, Director
Provides readjustment counseling to combat veterans. Onsite assistance for employment problems, vocational rehabilitation and sexual trauma counsel.

6705 **Easterseals Rehabilitation Center**
3701 Bellemeade Ave.
Evansville, IN 47714   812-479-1411
                                    www.easterseals.com/in-sw
Kelly Schneider, President
Rea Tecson, Vice President, Administration & CFO
Laura Terhune, Vice President, Philanthropic Partnerships
Services include therapy and medical rehabilitation, assistive technology, early intervention, early care and education, and community employment.

6706 Frasier Rehabilitation Center Division of Clark Memorial Hospital
2201 Greentree N
Clarksville, IN 47129-8957
812-218-6590
FAX: 812-218-6597
www.jhsmh.org/Frazier-Rehab-Institute-
Catherine Lucas Spalding, Administrator
Designed to help patients in their adjustment to a physically limiting condition, both psychologically and physically, by helping to maximize each patient's abilities so he or she can function as independently as possible. The program treats patients whos

6707 HealthSouth Deaconess Rehabilitation Hospital
4100 Covert Ave
Evansville, IN 47714-5559
812-476-9983
800-677-3422
FAX: 812-476-4270
www.healthsouthdeaconess.com
Barbara Butler, Chief Executive Officer
Ashok . Dhingra, M.D, Medical Director
Brett Hirt, Director, Therapy Operations
AHealthSouth Deaconess Rehabilitation Hospital is a joint venture partner with Deaconess Health System. Our hospital is an 80-bed inpatient rehabilitation hospital that offers comprehensive inpatient and outpatient rehabilitation services designed to return patients to leading active and independent lives.

6708 Healthwin Specialized Care
20531 Darden Rd
South Bend, IN 46637-2999
574-272-0100
FAX: 574-277-3233
info@healthwin.org
healthwin.org
Connie McCahill, President
Lauren Davis, Vice President
John Cergnul, Treasurer
No other facility in the area has a homelike environment like ours. Its simply part of our culture. Rehabilitation therapy that includes physical, occupational, speech, respiratory and a full time in-house therapist. Other services include a wound special

6709 Memorial Regional Rehabilitation Center
615 N Michigan St
South Bend, IN 46601-1033
574-647-1000
877-282-0964
Johan Kuitse, MSA, PT, Outpatient Clinical Manager
Anne Clifford, DPT, Physical Therapists
Shanti Shrestha Dalson, DPT, Physical Therapists
20-bed CARF accredited inpatient rehabilitation, outpatient orthopedic clinic and work performance program, head injury clinic. Outpatient neuro rehab and a driver education and training program are provided.

6710 Saint Joseph Regional Medical Center- South Bend
5215 Holy Cross Parkway
Mishawaka, IN 46545-2814
574-335-5000
FAX: 574-237-7312
thefoundation@sjrmc.com
sjmed.com
Albert Gutierrez, President & CEO
Steven Gable, Vice President
Janice Dunn, CFO
Continuum of rehabilitation services offered. Included are: acute rehabilitation, a 26 bed CARF accredited comprehensive inpatient unit, a CARF certified inpatient brain injury program, a CARF outpatient day treatment brain injury program, comprehensive o

Iowa

6711 Crossroads of Western Iowa
1 Crossroads Pl
Missouri Valley, IA 51555-6069
712-642-4114
FAX: 712-642-4115
info@cwiowa.org
explorecrossroads.com
Brent Dillinger, CEO
Pat Kocour, President
Steven Van Riper, Vice President
CWI provides services in Missouri Valley, Onawa and Council Bluffs, Iowa. An array of services for people with mental illness, developmental disabilities and brain injury are provided in each location.

6712 Des Moines Division-VA Central Iowa Health Care System
3600 30th St
Des Moines, IA 50310-5753
515-699-5999
800-294-8387
FAX: 515-699-5862
www.centraliowa.va.gov
Judith Johnson-Mekota, Director
Fredrick Bahls, Chief Of Staff
Susan A. Martin, Associate Director
VA Cental Iowa Health Care System is the result of the 1997 merger of the Des Moines and Knoxville, Iowa, VA Medical Centers. This integrated healthcare system brings 2 previously separate organizational structures, located 40 miles apart, into one cohesi

6713 Easterseals Iowa
401 NE 66th Ave.
Des Moines, IA 50313
515-289-1933
FAX: 515-289-1281
TTY:515-289-4069
www.easterseals.com/ia
Sherri Nielsen, President & CEO
Margaret Ingram, Chief Financial Officer
Allison Piazza, Chief Development Officer
Provides services to Iowans with disabilities. Services include vocational and employment training, camping recreation and respite services, craft training and sales, home and farm adaptations, and transportation.

6714 Genesis Regional Rehabilitation Center
Genesis Health System
1227 E.Rusholme Street
Davenport, IA 52803-3396
563-421-1000
FAX: 563-421-3499
genesishealth.com
Doug Cropper, President & CEO
Kenneth Croken, Vice President
Joseph Lohmuller, Chief Medical Officer
Serves persons of all ages experiencing a disability, whether acquired at birth or following a serious interdisciplinary service. Rehabilitation programs include acute rehabilitation; adult rehabilitation, pediatric rehabilitation, outpatient orthopaedics

6715 Homelink
Van G Miller & Associates
1101 W S Marnan Drive
Waterloo, IA 50701-2817
319-235-7173
866-575-8483
FAX: 319-235-7822
homelinkprivacyofficer@vgm.com
www.vgmhomelink.com
Dave Kazynski, President
Rick Hibben, Coordinator
A national network of home medical equipment, respiratory therapy, rehabilitation and infusion therapy service providers with over 2,500 locations serving all fifty states.

6716 Iowa Central Industries
127 Avenue M
Fort Dodge, IA 50501-5797
515-576-2126
FAX: 515-576-2251
Tom Eckman, Executive Director

Services include evaluation and training in pre-vocational and vocational skills, personal behavior management, cognitive skills, communication skills, self-care skills and social skills. Services arranged include: independent living training, medical ser

6717 Life Skills Laundry Division
1510 Industrial Rd SW
Le Mars, IA 51031-3009   712-546-4785
                                                   FAX: 712-546-4985

Don Nore, Executive Director

6718 MIW
909 S 14th Ave
Marshalltown, IA 50158-3610   641-752-3697
                                                   FAX: 641-752-1614

Rich Byers, President/CEO
Vocational services for adults with disabilities. Includes organizational employment services, supported employment, job placement.

6719 Mercy Dubuque Physical Rehabilitation Unit
250 Mercy Drive
Dubuque, IA 52001-7320   563-589-8000
                                                   FAX: 563-589-8162
                                                   www.mercydubuque.com
Russel M. Knight, CEO
Provides services which open the door to improved communication, offering the opportunity to enrich the quality of life. Mercy offers many other branches of services including, rehabilitation services for children and a pulmonary rehabilitation program.

6720 Mercy Medical Center-Pain Services
1111 6th Ave
Des Moines, IA 50314-2611   515-247-3121
                                                   FAX: 515-248-8867
                                          webmaster@mercydesmoines.org
Dana L. Simon, MD
Dave Vellinga, President & CEO
Laurie Conner, Vice President
An outpatient program dedicated to helping people with chronic pain live more productive, satisfying lives. The program is not designed for conditions that are surgically curable, but rather approaches the problem using a comprehensive, holistic treatment.

6721 Nishna Productions-Shenandoah Work Center
902 Day Street
Shenandoah, IA 51601-70   712-246-1242
                                                   FAX: 712-246-1243

Mary Rolf, President
Sherri Clark, Executive Director
Melissa Mueller, Program Manager
Shelter, workshop and job training for the disabled. Some of the services we provide are Work Activity, Adult Day Activity Program, Personal & Social Adjustment, Residential Services, Home & Community Based Services & Employment Resources.

6722 Northstar Community Services
3420 University Avenue
Waterloo, IA 50701-2050   319-236-0901
                                                   888-879-1365
                                                   FAX: 319-236-3701
                                                   www.northstarcs.org
Mark Witmar, Executive Director
Jeff Conrey, President
Kathy Folkerts, Vice President
Provides adult day services, employment services and supported community living so people with disabilities can live and work in the community.

6723 Options of Linn County
935 2nd street
SW
Cedar Rapids, IA 52404-3100   319-892-5000
                                                   FAX: 319-892-5849
                                                   linncounty.org
Joel D. Miller, Auditor
Sharon Gonzalez, Treasurer
Options of Linn County works with community businesses in providing employment services to adults with disabilities. Options is a publicly operated service provider within the Linn County Community Services department.

6724 RISE
106 Rainbow Dr
Elkader, IA 52043-9075   563-245-1868
                                                   FAX: 563-245-2859
Ed Josten, Manager

6725 Ragtime Industries
116 N 2nd St
Albia, IA 52531-1624   641-932-7813
                                                   FAX: 641-932-7814
Lisa Glenn, Executive Director
A work-oriented rehabilitation organization which provides training for mentally and physically disabled adults in Monroe County. A variety of programs which help to develop each person's individual potential are offered.

6726 Sunshine Services
1106 East 9th St
Spencer, IA 51301-225   712-262-7805
                                                   FAX: 712-262-8369
Ann Vandehar, Executive Director

6727 Tenco Industries
710 Gateway Dr
Ottumwa, IA 52501-2204   641-682-8114
                                                   FAX: 641-684-4223
                                                   www.tenco.org
Ben Wright, Executive Director
Dixie Merritt, Vocational Director
Brenda Miller, Marketing and Development DirectoR
To advocate and provide opportunities for people with disabilities, or conditions that limit their abilities, to develop and maintain the skills necessary for personal dignity and independence in all areas of life. Provide a wide array of services to individuals with disabilities. By looking at each person as individuals, we are able to work with them to maximize their skills. Residentials services, including HCBS and CSALA are also provided in all communities.

Kansas

6728 Arrowhead West
1100 E Wyatt Earp Blvd
Dodge City, KS 67801-5337   620-227-8803
                                                   FAX: 620-227-8812
                                                   web@arrowheadwest.org
                                                   www.arrowheadwest.org
Kelly Mason, Chairperson
Michael Stein, Vice Chairperson
Lori Pendergast, President
Services and programs offered include: developmental and therapy services for children birth to age 3; adult center-based work services and community integrated employment options; adult life skills and retirement programs; and adult residential services.

6729 Big Lakes Developmental Center
1416 Hayes Dr
Manhattan, KS 66502-5066   785-776-9201
                                                   FAX: 785-776-9830
                                                   biglakes@biglakes.org
                                                   biglakes.org
Lori Feldkamp, President
Shawn Funk, Community Education Director
A private nonprofit Community Developmental Disability Organization (CDDO) serving individuals with developmental disabilities in Riley, Geary, Clay and Pottawatome counties in Kansas. Big lakes is supported by county mill levy and federal and state fundi

6730 Developmental Services of Northwest Kansas
2703 Hall St
Suite 10
Hays, KS 67601-1964   785-625-5678
                                                   800-637-2229
                                                   FAX: 785-625-8204
Jerry Michaud, President
Ruth Lang, Administrative Assistant
A private nonprofit organization serving both children and adults with disabilities. Offers services to children ages birth to three

years, youth and adults through a network of community-based and outreach programs and inter-agency agreements with other

6731 ENVISION
2301 S Water St
Wichita, KS 67213-4819
316-267-2244
FAX: 316-267-4312
Info@envisionus.com
www.envisionus.com

Sam Williams, Chair
Jon Rosell, PhD, Vice-Chair
Michael Monteferrante, President and CEO
Provides jobs, job training and vision rehabilitation services to people who are blind or low vision. A private not-for-profit agency uniquely combining employment opportunitites with rehabilitation services and public education.

6732 Heartspring
8700 E 29th St N
Wichita, KS 67226-2169
316-634-8700
800-835-1043
FAX: 316-634-0555
kgrover@heartspring.org
www.heartspring.org

Gary W. Singleton, President and CEO
Paul Faber, Executive Vice President, Operations
Katie Grover, Director Of Marketing
Heartspring provides outpatient therapies, evaluations and consultations for children with special needs through Heartspring Pediatric Services. The Heartspring School is a residential and day school for children ages 5-21 with multiple disabilities. Children with autism and their families receive resources through the Heartspring CARE program. The Heartspring Hearing Center provides services to individuals of all ages.

6733 Indian Creek Nursing Center
6515 W 103rd St
Overland Park, KS 66212-1798
913-633-7000
FAX: 913-642-3982
www.savaseniorcare.com

Randy Sutterfield, Administrator
Postacute rehabilitation program. A 120-bed nursing home facility.

6734 Johnson County Developmental Supports
111 South Cherry Street
Olathe, KS 66061-1223
913-715-5000
FAX: 913-715-0800
info@jocogov.org
www.jocogov.org

Ed Eilert, Chairman
Michael Lally, Vice Chair
Scott Tschudy, Treasurer
JCDS is the community Developmental Disability Organization for Johnson County, Kansas. Provides supports in the form of direct services to people on a daily basis.

6735 Ketch Industries
1006 E Waterman St
Wichita, KS 67211-1525
316-383-8700
800-766-3777
FAX: 316-383-8715
webmaster@ketch.org
ketch.org

Fred Badders, Chairman
Carla Bienhoff, Chairman
Loren Anthony, Secretary
The mission of Ketch is to promote independence for persons with disabilities through innovative learning experiences that support individuals choices for working, living and playing in their community.

6736 Lakemary Center
100 Lakemary Dr
Paola, KS 66071-1855
913-557-4000
FAX: 913-557-4910
lakemaryctr.org

William Craig, President
Paul Sokoloff, Chair
Gayle Richardson, Vice Chair

A private, not-for-profit day and residential training facility which provides for the assessment, education, training, therapy and social development of children and adults, moderate and severe developmental disabilities.

6737 Northview Developmental Services
700 E 14th St
Newton, KS 67117-5702
316-283-5170
FAX: 316-283-5196
northviewdev.mennonite.net/

Mary Holloway, CEO
The mission is to provide quality supportive and coordinating services to persons with developmental disabilities, assisting them to grow as they integrate into the community. Further, our mission is to improve the quality of their lives by providing acce

Kentucky

6738 Cardinal Hill Rehabilitation Hospital
Cadinal Hill Medical Center
2050 Versailles Rd
Lexington, KY 40504-1499
859-254-5701
800-233-3260
FAX: 859-231-1365
www.cardinalhill.org

Gary R. Payne, CEO
Provides occupational health services, therapy services and urgent medical treatment of injured workers.

6739 Frazier Rehab Institute
220 Abraham Flexner Way
Louisville, KY 40202-1887
502-582-7400
FAX: 502-582-7477

Jamie Ochsner, Manager
Steve Ahr, VP Frazier Rehab/Neurscience
Frazier Rehab Institute is a regional healthcare system dedicated entirely to rehabilitation. Through an expansive network of inpatient and outpatient facilites in Kentucky and southern Indiana, Frazier offers a wide array of services based on one common

6740 HealthSouth Northern Kentucky Rehabilitation Hospital
201 Medical Village Dr
Edgewood, KY 41017-3407
859-341-2044
800-860-6004
FAX: 859-341-2813
www.healthsouthkentucky.com

Richard Evans, CEO
Mary Pfeffer, Director Therapy Operations
Neal Moser, M.D., Medical Director
Offers all types of inpatient and outpatient rehabilitation services such as occupational therapy, physical therapy, speech therapy. Respiratory therpay, Psychology, Aquatics, Case Managemenet/Social Work and Nutritional Services.

6741 King's Daughter's Medical Center's Rehab Unit/Work Hardening Program
2201 Lexington Ave
Ashland, KY 41101-2843
606-408-4000
888-377-5362
FAX: 606-327-7542
info@kdmc.net
www.kdmc.com

Kristie Whitlatch, President & CEO
Matt Ebaugh, VP / Chief Strategy and Information Officer
Philip Fioret, M.D., VP / Chief Medical Officer
Offers a 27-bed, inpatient rehabilitation services unit treating physical disabilities related to accident or illness. The program provides an interdisciplinary inpatient program designed to restore the individual to the highest level of independence. It

6742 LifeSkills Industries
380 Suwannee Trail St
Bowling Green, KY 42103-6499
270-901-5000
800-223-8913
FAX: 270-782-0058
sbell@lifeskills.com
lifeskills.com

Alice Simpson, CEO

LifeSkills will be the reliable advocate, dependable safety net and provider of choice, for high quality, accessible services and supports for the citizens of south-central Kentucky whos lives are affected by mental illness, developmental disabilities or

6743   Low Vision Services of Kentucky
120 N. Eagle Creek Drive
Suite 500
Lexington, KY 40509- 1827

859-263-3900
800-627-2020
FAX: 859-977-1136
jvanarsdall@retinaky.com
www.lowvisionky.com

Regina Callihan-May, O.D.
Jeanne Van Arsdall, Co-ordinator
Maryanne Inman, Practice Administrator
Offers educational, recreational and rehabilitational services and devices for the visually impaired, legally blind, totally blind.

6744   Muhlenberg County Opportunity Center
PO Box 511
Greenville, KY 42345-1416

270-754-5590
FAX: 270-338-5977
muhlon.com

Chuck Hammonds, Manager
Charles Hamonds, Director
Post-acute rehabilitation facility with programs including a workshop with hand packaging of manufactured goods.

6745   New Vision Enterprises
1900 Brownsboro Rd
Louisville, KY 40206-2102

502-893-0211
800-405-9135
FAX: 502-893-3885

Larry Sherman, Plant Manager
Offers employment training and services for the blind and legally blind.

6746   Park DuValle Community Health Center, Inc.
3015 Wilson Ave
Louisville, KY 40211-1969

502-774-4401
FAX: 502-775-6195
www.pdchc.org

Richard K Jones, President
John Howard MD, Medical Director
Dave Gerwig, CFO
Offers services for the totally blind, legally blind, visually impaired, and more with health, counseling, educational, recreational, rehabilitation, computer training and professional training services.

Louisiana

6747   Alliance House
427 S Foster Drive
Baton Rouge, LA 70806-2723

225-987-0013
FAX: 225-346-0857

A non-residential facility serving male and female chronically mentally ill. Services include: social service, vocational evaluation, pre-vocational training and job placement.

6748   Assumption Activity Center
4201 Highway 1
Napoleonville, LA 70390-8628

985-369-2907
FAX: 985-369-2657

Warren Gonzales, Manager
A community work center providing prevocational training and extended employment for adults with disabilities. Services include: social services, work activities, specialized training and supported employment.

6749   Bancroft Rehabilitation Living Centers
425 Kings Highway East
P.O. Box 20
Haddonfield, NJ 08033-0018

504-482-3075
800-774-5516
FAX: 504-483-2135
lynn.tomaio@bancroft.org
www.bancroft.org

Dr. Robert Voogt, Owner
Toni Pergolin, President & CEO
Cynthia Boyer, Executive Director
Mission is to nurture abilities and independence of people with neurological challenges by providing a broad spectrum of advanced therapeutic and educational programs and by fostering the development of best practices in the field through research and pro

6750   Deaf Action Center Of Greater New Orleans
Catholic Charities
1000 Howard Ave
Suite 200
New Orleans, LA 70113-1903

504-523-3755
866-891-2210
FAX: 504-523-2789
TTY: 504-615-4944
www.ccano.org

Tommie A. Vassel, Chairman
Sr.Marjorie Hebert, MSC, President & CEO
This community service and resource center serves deaf, deaf-blind, hard of hearing and speech-impaired persons in the greater New Orleans area regardless of age, religion, race or secondary disability. DAC provides interpreting services, equipment distri

6751   Donaldsville Area Arc
1030 Clay St
Donaldsonville, LA 70346-3518

225-473-4516
daarc@eatel.net

Provides a range of services for developmentally disabled adults and children.

6752   East Jefferson General Hospital Rehab Center
4200 Houma Blvd
Metairie, LA 70006-2996

504-454-4000
www.ejgh.org

Newell D. Normand, Chairman
Ashton J. Ryan, Jr., Vice Chairman
Mark J, Peters, President & CEO
Provides the highest quality, compassionate healthcare to the people we serve. East Jefferson General Hospital will be the region's healthcare leader providing the highest quality care through innovation and collaboration with our team members, medical st

6753   Family Service Society
2515 Canal Street
Suite 201
New Orleans, LA 70119-6489

504-822-0800
FAX: 504-822-0831
family@fsgno.org
www.fsgno.org

L. Blake Jones, Chair
Jackie Sullivan, 1st Vice Chair
Kathleen Vogt, 2nd Vice Chair
Offers services for the totally blind, legally blind, visually impaired, and more with health, counseling, educational, recreational, rehabilitation, computer training and professional training services.

6754   Foundation Industries
9995 Highway 64
Zachary, LA 70791

225-654-6288
FAX: 225-654-3988

Jim Lambert-Oswald, President
Jim Oswald, General Manager
A private, nonprofit sheltered workshop providing extended employment and work activities for the developmentally disabled. Objectives are to build work skills through supervision and develop social interaction.

6755   **Handi-Works Productions**
2700 Lee St
Alexandria, LA 71301-4358   318-442-3377
FAX: 318-473-0858
This is a nonprofit workshop for male and female clients who have vocational handicapping conditions. All types of handicapped persons are served in this non-residential workshop.

6756   **Lighthouse for the Blind in New Orleans**
123 State St
New Orleans, LA 70118-5793   504-899-4501
888-792-0163
FAX: 504-895-4162
lighthouselouisiana.org

Curtis Eustis, Chair
Paul Masinter, Chair Elect
Tabatha George, Secretary
Offers services for the totally blind, legally blind, visually impaired, and more with health, counseling, educational, recreational, rehabilitation, computer training and professional training services.

6757   **Louisiana Center for the Blind**
101 South Trenton Street
Ruston, LA 71270-4431   318-251-2891
800-234-4166
FAX: 318-251-0109
www.louisianacenter.org

Pam Allen, Executive Director
Neita Ghrigsby, Office Manager
Janette Woodard, Residential Manager
A new kind of orientation and training center for blind persons. The center is privately operated and provides quality instruction in the skills of blindness. Offers employment assistance, computer literacy training, summer training and employment project

6758   **Louisiana State University Eye Center**
Lousiana State University
433 Bolivar Street
New Orleans, LA 70112-2272   504-568-4808
FAX: 504-412-1315
www.lsuhsc.edu

Jayne S. Weiss, Director
Kelli McMichael, Manager
The LSU Eye Center is part of the LSU Medical Center complex in downtown New Orleans. It is in the LSU-Lions Building at 2020 Gravier Street between South Bolivar and South Prieur streets.

6759   **New Orleans Speech and Hearing Center**
1636 Toledano St
New Orleans, LA 70115-4598   504-897-2606
FAX: 504-891-6048

Mary Beth Green, President
Jessica Vinturella, Treasurer
Kindall James, Secretary
This non-residential facility serves male and female clients for purposes of evaluating speech and hearing problems and providing speech therapy, hearing aids and other assistive technology for speech and hearing.

6760   **Port City Enterprises**
836 North Seventh Street
Port Allen, LA 70767-113   225-344-1142
877-344-1142
FAX: 225-344-1192
www.portcityenterprises.org

William Kleinpeter, President
Mark Graffeo, Vice President
L.J. Treuil Jr, Secretary
Offers supported employment, sheltered work and supervised programs for the developmentally disabled, ages 22 and over.

6761   **Rehabilitation Center at Thibodeaux Regional**
Rehab Care
602 N Acadia Rd
Thibodaux, LA 70301-4847   985-493-4731
800-822-8442
FAX: 985-449-4600
www.thibodaux.com/centers-services

Jan Torres, Program Manager
Rose Pipes, Clinical Coordinator
Designed to help patients in their adjustment to a physically limiting condition, both physically and psychologically, by helping to maximize each patients abilities so he or she can function as independently as possible.

6762   **St. Patrick RehabCare Unit**
RehabCare
524 Doctor Michael Debakey Dr
Lake Charles, LA 70601-5725   337-491-7590
888-722-9355
FAX: 337-491-7157

Larry A Hauskins, Manager
Ruth Thornton, Admissions
A comprehensive physical and cognitive rehabilitation program designed to help individuals who have experienced a disabling injury or illness.

6763   **The Arc - Iberville**
PO Box 264
Plaquemine, LA 70765-0264   225-687-4062
arciberville@bellsouth.net
Provides a range of services for adults and children with developmental disabilities.

6764   **The Arc Caddo-Bossier**
351 Jordan St.
Shreveport, LA 71101   318-221-8392
Janet Parker, Executive Director
Chris Hackler, COO, Program & Services
Nonprofit agency providing services to adults and children with developmental disabilities

6765   **Touro Rehabilitation Center - LCMC (Louisiana Children's Medical Center)**
1401 Foucher St
New Orleans, LA 70115-3515   504-897-8565
FAX: 504-897-8393
www.touro.com/rehab

Jeanette Ray, VP of Rehab and Post Acute Srv
Janet Clark, Director of Inpatient Rehabilitation Programs
Marylee Pontillas, Director of Outpatient Rehab Srv
Located in New Orleans' Garden District, Touro Rehabilitation is a comprehensive rehabilitation facility dedicated to the restoration of function and independence for individuals with disabilities. The scope of rehabilitation services is broad, with 3 CARF accreditations for Brain Injury, Spinal Cord Injury and General Rehabilitation. TRC opened in 1984 and offers 69 rehab beds. TRC is part of Touro Infirmary which has a proud 150 year history as a nonprofit teaching hospital.

6766   **Training, Resource & Assistive-Technology**
2000 Lakeshore Drive
New Orleans, LA 70148-1   504-280-6000
888-514-4275
FAX: 504-280-5707
ggaglian@uno.edu
www.uno.edu

Ken Zangla, Director
Naomi Moore, Assistant Director
Connie Lanier, Coordinator
Provides quality services to persons with disabilities, rehabilitation professionals, educators and employers. Built a solid reputation for its innovative training programs and community outreach efforts. The Center is recognized as a valuable resource st

Maine

6767 **Charlotte White Center**
572 Bangor Rd
Dover Foxcroft, ME 04426-3373
207-564-2426
888-440-4158
FAX: 207-564-2404
charlottewhitecenter.com

Richard M. Brown, CEO
Charles G. Clemons, COO
Dale Shaw, CFO
A nonprofit agency, devoted to assisting adults and children with developmental disabilities, mental health, physical handicaps, and elder age related issues. With headquarters in Dover-Foxcroft Maine, the agency provides multiple levels of social services.

6768 **Iris Network for the Blind**
189 Park Avenue
Portland, ME 04102-2909
207-774-6273
FAX: 207-774-0679
ashah@theiris.org
theiris.org

Leonard Cole, Chairman
Katharine Ray, 1st Vice Chairman
Bruce Roullard, 2nd Vice Chairman
A statewide resource and catalyst for people who are visually impaired or blind so they can attain their determined level of independence and integration into the community.

6769 **Roger Randall Center**
45 School St
Houlton, ME 04730-2010
207-532-4068
FAX: 207-532-7334

Rob Moran, Executive Director
Tom Moakler, President
Vicki Moody, Vice President
The Roger Randall Cneter is one of five Day Habilitation Programs adminsitered by Community Living Association, a private, non-profit agency. These programs may provide a supportive environment that allows the individual to achieve their maximum growth po

6770 **Sebasticook Farms-Great Bay Foundation**
P.O.Box 65
Saint Albans, ME 04971
207-487-4399
FAX: 207-938-5670

Tom Davis, Executive Director
Pam Erskin, Program Coordinator
Provides residential, educational and vocational services to adults who are developmentally disabled in order to maximize independent living and to provide assistance in obtaining an earned income.

6771 **Social Learning Center**
10 Shelton McMurphey Blvd
Eugene, OR 97401-3363
541-485-2711
877-208-6134
FAX: 541-485-7087
www.oslc.org

Sam Vuchinich, Ph.D, Chair
Gordon Naga Hall, Ph.D., Vice President
Susan Miller, J.D., Secretary/Treasurer
Post accute rehabilitation program.

Maryland

6772 **Blind Industries and Services of Maryland**
3345 Washington Blvd
Baltimore, MD 21227-1602
410-737-2600
888-322-4567
FAX: 410-737-2665
info@bism.org
bism.org

Donald J. Morris, Chairperson
Walter A. Brown, Vice Chairperson
Fredrick J. Puente, President

Offers a comprehensive residential rehabilitation training program for people who are blind. Areas of instruction: braille, cane travel, independent living, computer, adjustment and blindness seminars.

6773 **Center for Neuro-Rehabilitation**
2340238 N Cary St
Annapolis, MD 21223
410-263-1704
410-462-4711

Jeanne Fryer
Laurent Pierre-Philippe
Provide community-based inpatient and outpatient acute rehabilitation, vocational services and long-term care. Specializing in treating complex neurological conditions including spinal cord injuries, multiple sclerosis, strokes, and other brain injuries resulting from trauma, anoxia, tumors, genetic malformations and other related conditions. Locations in Annapolis, Bethesda, Frederick, Towson, MD and Fairfax, Va. CNR is licensed, a Medicare provider and CARF accredited.

6774 **Child Find/Early Childhood Disabilities Unit**
Montgomery County Public Schools
Ste A4
10731 Saint Margarets Way
Kensington, MD 20895- 2831
301-929-2224
FAX: 301-929-2223

Julie Bader, Supervisor
Offers free developmental screening for children ages 3 years until eligible for kindergarten, evaluation and placement services.

6775 **Greater Baltimore Medical Center**
6701 N Charles St
Baltimore, MD 21204-6881
443-849-2000
800-597-9142
FAX: 443-849-2631
www.gbmc.org

John B. Chessare MD, President & CEO
Harold J. Tucker MD, Chief Of Staff
Eric L. Melchoir, Vice President & CFO
Offers services for the visually impaired and blind with low vision exams. Rehabilitation teaching and orientation and mobility in the home or workplace. Also offers a bimonthly newsletter for $12/yr for Hoover patients and monthly share group.

6776 **James Lawrence Kernan Hospital**
2200 Kernan Drive
Baltimore, MD 21207-6697
410-285-6566
888-453-7626
FAX: 410-448-6854
www.umrehabortho.org

Michael Jablonover MD,MBA, President & CEO
John P. Straumanis MD, FAAP, Vice President
W. Walter x Augustin, III, CPA, Vice President of Financial Services
Kernan reigns as Maryland's origional orthopaedic hospital with a staff which consists of a support team of orthopaedic physician assistants and dedicated nurses in the Post Anesthesia Care Unit and on the Medical/Surgical Unit, guaranteeing the highest q

6777 **Levindale Hebrew Geriatric Center**
2401 W Belvedere Ave.
Baltimore, MD 21215-5271
410-601-9355
www.lifebridgehealth.org/Levindale
A 330-licensed bed facility providing post-acute services for patients affected by life-altering illness or injury.

6778 **Meridan Medical Center For Subacute Care**
770 York Rd
Towson, MD 21204
410-821-5500
FAX: 410-821-6735

Yvette Caldwell, Administrator
Patients receive around-the-clock professional nursing care; physical and occupational, speech and respiratory therapists also assist patients. Each patient's individualized plan of care is reviewed and updated as patient needs change. Careful discharge p

6779 Rehabilitation Opportunities
5100 Philadelphia Way
Lanham, MD 20706-4412   301-731-4242
FAX: 301-731-4191
roiworks.org

Tom Purcell, President
Bruce Shapiro, Vice President
David Fierst, Secretary
Organization offering day programs, evaluation, work adjustments and sheltered workshops for persons who are developmentally disabled.

6780 Rosewood Center

410-951-5000
888-300-7071
FAX: 410-581-6157
www.dhmh.state.md.us/dda/rosewood
Leslie Smith, Program Director
James Anzalone, Director
Rosewood Center is a State residential Center that supports adults with developmental disabilities from the central Maryland region.

6781 TLC Speech-Language/Occupational TherapyCamps
2092 Gaither Rd.
Suite 100
Rockville, MD 20850   301-424-5200
FAX: 301-424-8063
info@ttlc.org
www.ttlc.org

Patricia Ritter, Executive Director
TLC provides small group summer programs for children with special needs. Offers speech-language and occupational therapy summer camps for children ages 3-7.

6782 Workforce and Technology Center
Division of Rehabilitation Services
2301 Argonne Drive
Baltimore, MD 21218-1628   410-554-9442
888-554-0334
FAX: 410-554-9112
www.dors.state.md.us

Dan Frye, Chairperson
Josie Thomas, Vice Chairperson
Is one of nine state operated comprehensive rehabilitation facilities in the country providing a wide range of services to individuals with disabilities. The Maryland Division of Rehabilitation Services operates the Workforce and Technology Program. Avail

Massachusetts

6783 Baroco Corporation
136 West Street
Northampton, MA 01060-2711   413-534-9978
FAX: 413-585-9019
www.baroco.com

Rick Barnard, President/Owner
Suzanne Darby, Executive Administrator
Julia McLaughlin, Executive Administrator
Provides training and therapeutic support for its recipients with developmental disabilities in order to aid them in securing and maintaining placement in a less-restrictive setting.

6784 Berkshire Meadows
160 Gould Street
Suite 300
Needham, MA 02494-2300   781-559-4900
FAX: 413-528-0293
lkelly@jri.org
berkshiremeadows.org

Andy Pond, President
Gregory Canfield, Vice President
Deborah Reuman, CFO
Private, non profit school for children, adolescents, young adults who are severely, developmentally disabled. Approved special education learning center, work site program and foster care. Physical therapy, speech and language development, behavioral pro $8200.00

6785 Blueberry Hill Healthcare
75 Brimbal Ave
Beverly, MA 01915-6009   978-927-2020
FAX: 978-922-5213
admissions@BlueberryHillRehab.com
www.blueberryhillrehab.com
Ralph Epstein, Medical Director
Accomodates 146 residents. We are centrally located close to Route 128 and Route 1A in Beverly Massachusetts. We offer short-term rehab care, long term care and Alzheimer's Special Care Programs. Our interdisciplinary team designs individual care plans fo

6786 Boston University Hospital Vision Rehabilitation Services
One Boston Medical Center Place
Boston, MA 02118-2371   617-638-8000
FAX: 617-638-7769
www.bmc.org/rehab.htm

Simona Manasian, Medical Director
Karen Mattie, Director
Jenn Blake, Clinical Outpatient Supervisor
Offers services for the totally blind, legally blind, visually impaired, and more with health, counseling, educational, recreational, rehabilitation, computer training and professional training services.

6787 Burbank Rehabilitation Center
275 Nichols Rd
Fitchburg, MA 01420-1919   978-343-5000
888-840-3627
FAX: 978-343-5342
www.umassmemorialhealthcare.org

David Bennett, Chair
Eric Dickson, President & CEO
The largest community hospital and regional referral center in the area. Offers the most extensive high quality, cost-effective healthcare services in the region. The hospital provides outstanding hospital-based services such as case management of high ri

6788 Carl and Ruth Shapiro Family National Center for Accessible Media
WGBH Educational Foundation
1 Guest St.
Boston, MA 02135-2016   617-300-3400
FAX: 617-300-1035
TTY:617-300-2489
ncam@wgbh.org
ncam.wgbh.org

Donna Danielewski, Director
Madeleine Rothberg, Senior Subject Matter Expert
Geoff Freed, Director of Technology
The Carl and Ruth Shapiro Family National Center for Accessible Media (NCAM) is a research and development facility dedicated to addressing barriers to media and emerging technologies for people with disabilities in their homes, schools, workplaces, and communities.

6789 Carroll Center for the Blind
770 Centre St
Newton, MA 02458-2597   617-969-6200
800-852-3131
FAX: 617-969-6204
www.carroll.org

Josepth Abely, President
Arthur O'Neill, Vice President
Brian Charlson, Director of Computer Training Services
Offers services for the totally blind, legally blind, visually impaired, and more with health, counseling, educational, in dependent living, tronell skills, computer traing, recreational, rehabilitation, computer training and professional training services.

6790 Center for Psychiatric Rehabilitation
Boston University
940 Commonwealth Ave
West
Boston, MA 02215-1203
617-353-3549
FAX: 617-353-7700
psyrehab@bu.edu
cpr.bu.edu

Kim T. Mueser, Executive Director
Deborah Dolan, Director of operations
Larry Kohn, Director of Development
The mission of the Center is to increase knowledge, to train treatment personnel, to develop effective rehabilitation programs and to assist in organizing both personnel and programs into efficient and coordinated service delivery systems for people with

6791 Clark House Nursing Center At Foxhill Village
Kindred Healthcare
30 Longwood Dr
Westwood, MA 02090-1132
781-326-5652
800-359-7412
FAX: 781-326-4034
www.clarkhousefhv.com

Chris Wasel, Administrator
Clark House At Fox Hill Village accomodates 70 residents. We are part of the Fox Hill Village Assisted Living and Retirement Center campus. Clark House Nursing center has been named a recipient of a 2005 step II quality Award from the American Health Care

6792 College Internship Program at the Berkshire Center
18 Park St
Lee, MA 01238-1702
413-243-2576
FAX: 413-243-3351

Lucy Gosselin, Program Director
Laina Hubbard, Admissions Coordinator
Charles D. Houff, Head Therapist
A highly individualized postsecondary program for learning disabled young adults 18-30. Provides job placement services and follow-ups; college support; money management and social skills. Residential students share an apartment and have their own room.

6793 Devereux Advanced Behavioral Health Massachusetts & Rhode Island
Devereux School
60 Miles Rd.
P.O. Box 219
Rutland, MA 01543
508-886-4746
800-338-3738
FAX: 508-886-4773
tbeauvai@devereux.org
www.devereuxma.org

Stephen Yerdon, Executive Director
Bonnie Byer, Business Development Director
Evans Chiyombwe, Quality Management Director
Serving children and youth with emotional, behavioral, intellectual and developmental disorders. Services include residential treatment, community-based group homes, therapeutic foster care, special needs day school, substance abuse and autism spectrum programs, diagnostic services and in-home services.

6794 Eagle Pond Rehabilitation and Living Center
1 Love Lane
P.O.Box 208
South Dennis, MA 02660-3445
508-385-6034
FAX: 508-385-7064
www.eaglepond.com

Paul Marchwat, Executive Director
Ellen Reil, Marketing Director
Eagle Pond accomodates 142 residents. Medicare and Medicaid certified as well as being accredited by the Joint Comission (formerly (JCAHO) which enables us to contract with many insurance companies.

6795 FOR Community Services
75 Litwin Ln
Chicopee, MA 01020-4817
413-592-6142
FAX: 413-598-0478
ggolash1@aol.com

Gina Golash, Executive Director

Providing a world of meaning for individuals with developmental disabilities throughout Western Massachusetts since 1967.

6796 Fairlawn Rehabilitation Hospital
189 May Street
Worcester, MA 01602-4399
508-791-6351
FAX: 508-831-1277
www.fairlawnrehab.org

Dave Richer, CEO
Peter Bagley MD, Medical Director
Matthew Akulonis, Director Of Support Operations
Offers comprehensive rehabilitation on both an inpatient and outpatient basis. Specialty programs include: head injury, spinal cord injury, young/senior stroke, oncology, geriatrics and orthopedics.

6797 Greenery Extended Care Center: Worcester
59 Acton Street
Worcester, MA 01604-4899
508-791-3147
800-633-0887
FAX: 508-753-6267
worcester@wingatehealthcare.com
wingatehealthcare.com

Scott Schuster, Founder & President
Brian Callahan, CFO
Michael Benjamin, Vice President
173 beds offering complex care, extended rehabilitation and neurobehavioral intervention. Offering life care homes and Nursing home services. Specialties include life events and physical care, long term and home health care, and nursing homes and nursing

6798 Greenery Rehabilitation & Skilled Nursing Center
P.O.Box 1330
Middleboro, MA 02346-4330
508-947-9295
FAX: 508-947-7974

201 beds offering programs of active/acute rehabilitation, cognitive rehabilitation, respiratory care and short-term evaluations. .

6799 Harrington House Nursing And Rehabilitation Center
160 Main Street
Walpole, MA 02081-4037
508-660-3080
FAX: 508-660-1634
www.harringtonrehab.com

Joseph Haron, Medical Director
Accomodates 90 residents. Our state-of-the-art center offers post-accute services including rehabilitation and medical management. Our center also provides a long term care program including hospice services.

6800 HealthSouth Rehabilitation Hospital Of Western Massachusetts
222 State Street
Ludlow, MA 01056-3478
413-308-3300
FAX: 413-547-2738
www.healthsouthrehab.org

Victoria Healy, CEO
Adnan Dahdul, M.D., Medical Director
Deborah Cabanas, Chief Nursing Officer
A 53-bed acute Rehabilitation Hospital. The facility has been operating for 14 years and has provided rehabilitative care to patients and families in the greater Springfield area with an outstanding reputation for attention to detail and compassion. Becau

6801 Holiday Inn Boxborough Woods
242 Adams Pl
Boxborough, MA 01719-1735
978-263-8701
800-465-4329
FAX: 978-263-0518
box_sales@fine-hotels.com
www.ihg.com/holidayinn

Kevin Murray, Manager
Marcel Girard, Manager
Nancy Ellen Hurley, Chief Marketing Officer
Located on 35 acres of wooded countryside just off I-495 at exit #28. Minutes from the Mass Turnpike, Route 2, 290 and 9. Conference center located on main level with 30,000 square feet of meeting space. Guest rooms feature two-line telephones, voice mail
$129 - $159

6802 Lifeworks Employment Services
1400 Providence Highway
Suite 2300
Norwood, MA 02062- 4551
781-769-3298
FAX: 781-551-0045
www.lifeworksma.org

Dan Burke, President & CEO
Chris Page, Vice President
Brenda Calder, CFO
Providing homes, jobs, education and supportive living for people with developmental disabilities.

6803 Massachusetts Eye and Ear Infirmary & Vision Rehabilitation Center
243 Charles Street
Boston, MA 02114-3002
617-523-7900
FAX: 617-573-4178
TTY:617-523-5498
www.masseyeandear.org

Wycliffe Grousbeck, Chairman
John Fernandaz, President & CEO
Lily H. Bentas, Secretary
Visual rehabilitation encompasses a low vision rehabilitation evaluation, occupational therapy evaluation (with home visit if necessary), and social service evaluation.

6804 New England Center for Children
260 Tremont Street
Boston, MA 02116-2108
617-636-4600
FAX: 617-636-4866
cwelch@necc.org
necc.org

Lisel Macenka, Chair
James C. Burling, Vice Chair
L.Vincent Strully, President
A comprehensive year-round program for students with autism and PDD who require a highly specialized educational and behavior management program. Students are from all over the country and receive intensive, positive, behavioral counseling and social skil

6805 New England Eye Center - Tufts Medical Center
Tufts Medical Center
260 Tremont St
Boston, MA 02116
617-636-4600
800-231-3316
FAX: 617-636-4866
eli_peli@meei.harvard.edu
www.neec.com

Jeannette Spillane, Executive Director
Shana Bellus, Director, Admitting Operations
Linnea Olsson, Special Projects Consultant
The New England Eye Center offers services for the legally blind and visually impaired, as well as for health care providers. Services include health care, counseling, education, vision research and professional training. Emphasis is on mobility related vision enhancement, including devices for driving and safe walking.

6806 New Medico Rehabilitation and Skilled Nursing Center at Lewis Bay
89 Lewis Bay Rd
Hyannis, MA 02601-5207
508-775-7601
FAX: 508-790-4239

Edmund Steinle, Executive Director
Post acute rehabilitation services.

6807 Protestant Guild Learning Center
411 Waverley Oaks Rd
Suite 104
Waltham, MA 02452-8449
781-893-6000
FAX: 781-893-1171
www.theguildschool.org

Eric H. Rosenberger, President
Thomas P. Corcoran, Vice President & Treasurer
Thomas Belski, Chief Executive Officer
Offers services for the diagnostically disabled children and adolescents with ages 6-22 years with health, counseling, educational, recreational, rehabilitation, computer training and professional training services.

6808 Shaughnessy-Kaplan Rehabilitation Hospital
1 Dove Ave
Salem, MA 01970
978-745-9000
FAX: 978-740-4730
skrhinfo@partners.org
spauldingrehab.org

Anthony Sciola, CEO
Maureen Banks, RN, MS, MBA, CN, President
Mary Beth DiFilippo, Vice President
A 160-bed private, non-profit hospital. We have been providing care for residents of greater North Shore communities since 1975. Shaughnessy has 120 long-term care hospital beds and a 40-bed transitional care unit sometimes referred to as a skilled nursin

6809 Son-Rise Program
2080 South Undermountain Road
Sheffield, MA 01257-9643
413-229-2100
877-766-7473
FAX: 413-229-3202
correspondence@option.org
www.autismtreatmentcenter.org

Barry Neil Kaufman, Co Founder
Samahria Lyte Kaufman, Co Founder
THe Son-Rise Program is a powerful, effective and totally unique treatment for children and adults challengedby Autism, Autuism Spectrum Disorders, Pervasive Developmental Disorder (PDD), Asperger's Syndrome and other developmental difficulties.

6810 Southern Worcester County Rehabilitation Inc. D/B/A Life-Skills, Inc.
44 Morris St
Webster, MA 01570-1812
508-943-0700
FAX: 508-949-6129
www.life-skillsinc.org

J Thomas Amick, Executive Director
Kristin Nelson, Board President
Barbara Butrym, Board Vice President
Life-Skills, Inc. assists mentally and developmentally challenged adults with meeting their individual needs, and empowering them to take full advantage of meaningful opportunities in their communities. We provide residential, employment, transportation, behavior, and theraputic day habilitation services to 350 adults in MA. We operate thrift & consignment stores, a small cafe, an ice cream shop, mini golf & arcade center, vending and greenhouse businesses, bank courier service, and others.

6811 Vinfen Corporation
950 Cambridge Street
Cambridge, MA 02141-1001
617-441-1800
877-284-6336
FAX: 617-441-1858
TTY: 617-225-2000
info@vinfen.org
www.vinfen.org

Philip A. Mason, Ph.D., Chairperson
Bruce L. Bird, Ph.D., CEO/ President
Elizabeth K. Glaser, Chief Operations Officer
A private, nonprofit company, Vinfen Corporation is the largest human services provider in Massachusetts. Vinfen offers clinical, educational, residential and support services to individuals of all ages with mental illness and or developmental disabilities, who also may have another disability (e.g. substance abuse, homelessness, AIDS). The company also trains professionals in the mental health field and helps consumers to learn to live in community-based settings at the highest levels.

6812 Visiting Nurse Association of North Shore
5 Federal St
Danvers, MA 01923-3687
508-751-6926
800-728-1862
FAX: 978-777-0308
www.vnacarenetwork.org

Mary Ann O'Connor, CEO/ President
Stephanie Jackman-Havey, Chief Operating Officer/Chief Financial Officer
David Rose, Vice President of Human Resources
Home health services including nurses, physical, occupational and speech therapy, home health aides and more. Special programs include nutrition counseling, IV care, pediatric therapy, HIV/AIDS services and wound management. Provides services 7

days a week, 365 days a year and we accept Medicare, Medicaid and most HMO's and health insurers.

6813 Weldon Center for Rehabilitation
233 Carew St
Springfield, MA 01104-2377
413-748-6800
FAX: 413-748-6806
mercycares.com

Barbara Haswell, Manager
One of the most vital, necessary health resources in the region by helping thousands of people toward restored health and independence. A comprehensive, integrated, non-profit facility offering inpatient, outpatient, day rehabilitation and pediatric services on one site.

6814 Youville Hospital & Rehab Center
1575 Cambridge St
Cambridge, MA 02138-4398
617-876-4344
FAX: 617-547-5501

Meets the long and short term health care and rehabilitation needs of patients who are physically disabled and chronically ill. Strives to develop and maintain health as a human right on physical, social, vocational and spiritual levels. The ultimate goal of the hospital is to treat and assist each individual patient in reaching his or her optimal level of living. Services include: stroke, brain injury, spinal cord trauma, orthopedic disabilities and more.

Michigan

6815 Botsford Center For Rehabilitation & Health Improvement-Redford
28050 Grand River Ave.
Farmington Hills, MI 48336-5919
248-471-8000
877-442-7900
FAX: 313-387-3838
www.botsford.org

John Darin, Manager
A 20 bed inpatient physical rehabilitation unit, servicing individuals who have experienced a stroke, amputation, orthopedic fracture, or other neurological impairment.

6816 Bureau of Services for Blind Persons Training Center
1541 Oakland Dr
Kalamazoo, MI 49008
269-337-3848
800-292-4200
FAX: 269-337-3872
mossc@michigan.gov

Cheryl Heibeck, Director
Bruce Schultz, Assistant Director
Residential facility that provides instruction to legally blind adults in braille, computer operation and assistive technology, handwriting, cane travel, cooking, personal management, industrial arts and also crafts. During training students will develop career plans which may include work experience, internships, volunteer opprtunities and even part-time paid employment.

6817 Chelsea Community Hospital Rehabilitation Unit
775 South Main Street
Chelsea, MI 48118-1383
734-593-6000
800-231-2211
FAX: 734-475-4191
www.stjoeschelsea.org

Nancy K. Graebner, CEO/ President
Kathy Brubaker, RN, Vice President and Chief Nursing Officer
Randall Forsch, MD, Chief Medical Officer
A private, non-profit, acute care facility that combines the best of small town values with national standards of healthcare excellence. The hospital has a 19-bed acute care inpatient rehabilitation unit with comprehensive outpatient programs, including a coordinated brain injury program.

6818 Clare Branch
790 Industrial Dr
Clare, MI 48617-9224
989-386-7707
888-773-7664
FAX: 989-386-2199
mail@mmionline.com
www.mmionline.org

Cris Zeigler, Executive Director

MMI will strive to be the premier provider of person-centered services to people with barriers to employment. We will connect individuals with community resources that provide mutual benefit to them and to the community. MMI will be known for excellence in service provision, ethical business practices, a quality work environment, and for providing services that enhance the dignity and value of the people we serve.

6819 Clarkston Spec Healthcare Center
4800 Clintonville Rd
Clarkston, MI 48346-4297
800-454-5909
Margaret Canny, Administrator
120 beds offering active/acute rehabilitation, complex care, day treatment, extended rehabilitation, neurobehavioral intervention and short-term evaluation.

6820 DMC Health Care Center-Novi
42005 W 12 Mile Rd
Novi, MI 48377-3113
248-305-7575
FAX: 425-201-1450
novi@patch.com
novi.patch.com

Bud Rosenthal, CEO
Leigh Zareli Lewis, COO
Andreas Turanski, CTO
The Detroit Medical Center's record of service has provided medical excellence throughout the history of the Metropolitan Detroit area. From the founding of the Children's Hospital in 1886, to the creation of the first mechanical heart at Harpers Hospital 50 years ago, to our compassion for the underdeserved, our legacy of caring is unmatched.

6821 Eight CAP, Inc. Head Start
904 Oak Drive
Greenville, MI 48838-9277
616-754-9315
FAX: 616-754-9310
laurelm@8cap.org
www.8cap.org

Ralph Loeschner, Executive Director
Nancy Secor, Contact
Post accute rehabilitation programs.

6822 Greater Detroit Agency for the Blind and Visually Impaired
16625 Grand River Ave
Detroit, MI 48227-1419
313-272-3900
FAX: 313-272-6893
gdabvi.org

Frederick J Simpson, Board Chairman
Charles L. Cone, Vice Chairman
Leonard W Robinson, Board Secretary
Offers services for seniors 60 and over who are legally blind. Also provides eye health information, counseling, education and rehabilitation services.

6823 Hope Network Neuro Rehabilitation
3075 Orchard Vista Dr. SE
PO Box 890
Grand Rapids, MI 49546
616-301-8000
800-695-7273
FAX: 616-301-8010
RehabReferral@hopenetwork.org
www.hopenetwork.org

Bob Von Kaenel, President & Chief Executive Officer
Tim Becker, Chief Operating Officer
John McInerney, Chief Information Officer
Neuro Rehabilitation is a service line of Hope Network, helping those with brain or spinal cord injuries or other neurological conditions recover through treatment techniques and person-centered care.

6824 Lakeland Center
26900 Franklin Rd
Southfield, MI 48033-5312
248-350-8070
FAX: 248-350-8078
peggys@thelakelandcenter.net
thelakelandcenter.net

Irving Shapiro, CEO
Santhosh Madhavan, Director Physical Medicine
Gary Yashinsky, Associate Medical Director

Subacute rehabilitation program directed toward those with severe neurologic diagnoses, ie: TBI, cerebral aneurysm, anoxic encephalopathy, CVA and cerebral hemorrhage, orthopedic injuries, and spinal cord injury. Subacute rehabilitation is provided for those who recover slowly and require individualized treatment plans. Residential program available as well.

6825 Mary Free Bed Rehabilitation Hospital
235 Wealthy St SE
Grand Rapids, MI 49503-5247

616-493-9657
800-528-8989
FAX: 616-454-3939
info@maryfreebed.com
maryfreebed.com

Kent Riddle, CEO
John Butzer, MD, Medical Director
Randy DeNeff, Vice President of Finance
Founded more than 100 years ago, Mary Free Bed Rehabilitation Hospital is and 80-bed, not-for-profit, acute rehabilitation center. Its mission is to restore hope and freedom through rehabilitation to people with disabilities. Mary Free Bed offers comprehensive inpatient and outpatient rehabilitationfor children and adults using an interdisciplinary approach. Also available are numerous specialty programs designed to increase the quality of life and independence of people with disabilities.

6826 Michigan Career And Technical Institute
11611 Pine Lake Rd
Plainwell, MI 49080-9225

269-664-4461
877-901-7360
FAX: 269-664-5850

Dennis Hart, Executive Director
A residential vocational training center for adults with physical, mental or emotional disabilities.

6827 Mid-Michigan Industries
2426 Parkway Dr
Mt Pleasant, MI 48858-4723

989-773-6918
888-773-7664
888-773-7664
FAX: 989-773-1317
mmionline.com

Alan Schilling, President
Andrea Christopher, Director Admissions
Linda Wagner, Branch Director
Providing jobs and training for persons with barriers to employment. Services include vocational evaluation, job placement, supported employment, work services, prevocational training and case management

6828 New Medico Community Re-Entry Service
216 St Marys Lake Rd
Battle Creek, MI 49017-9710

FAX: 269-962-2241
James Rekshan, Executive Director

6829 Sanilac County Community Mental Health
171 Dawson St
Sandusky, MI 48471-1062

810-648-0330
888-225-4447
888-225-4447
FAX: 810-648-0319

Roger Dean, Executive Director
Post-acute rehabilitation facility and programs.

6830 Special Tree Rehabilitation System
600 Stephenson Highway
Troy, MI 48083-1110

248-616-0950
800-648-6885
FAX: 248-616-0957
info@specialtree.com
www.specialtree.com

Joseph Richart, CEO
Special Tree exists to provide hope, encouragement, and expertise for people who have experienced life-altering changes. Our team approach to rehabilitation, custom designed for each person's needs and goals, offers these individuals the best opportunity for healing and recovery.

6831 Thumb Industries
1263 Sand Beach Rd
Bad Axe, MI 48413-8817

989-269-9229
FAX: 989-269-2587
thumbindustries@hotmail.com
www.thumbindustries.com

Rhonda Wisenbaugh, Executive Director
Provides job training and employment for disabled persons. Vocational rehabilitation agency, manufactures household furnishings, direct mail advertising service.

6832 Visually Impaired Center
1422 W Court St
Flint, MI 48503-5008

810-767-4014
FAX: 810-767-0020
www.vicflint.org

Committed to developing resources and collaborative programs as well as providing services that enable independent life for people with vision loss. Services include: Information and referals, assessments of needs, peer support groups, training by a Rehabilitation teacher of the blind and visually impaired, independent living skills, computer skills, training by an Orientation and Mobility Specialist, safe traveling skills, Diabetes management/education.

6833 Welcome Homes Retirement Community for the Visually Impaired
1953 Monroe Ave NW
Grand Rapids, MI 49505-6242

616-447-7837
888-939-9292
888-939-9292
FAX: 616-447-9891

Beth Lucksted, Manager
Offers services for the totally blind, legally blind, visually impaired, and more with health, counseling, educational, recreational, rehabilitation, computer training and professional training services.

6834 William H Honor Rehabilitation Center Henry Ford Wyanclotte Hospital
Henry Ford Health System
2333 Biddle Ave
Wyandotte, MI 48192-4668

734-246-6000
FAX: 734-246-6926
www.henryfordwyandotte.com

Denise Dailing, Administration Leader
James Sexton, Chief Executive Officer
Henry Ford, Owner
Henry Ford Wyandotte Hospital offers an array of educational programs, health screenings, and support groups. The hospital is CARF accredited and has a CARF certified stroke specialty unit.

Minnesota

6835 Industries: Cambridge
601 Cleveland St S
Cambridge, MN 55008-1752

763-689-5434
FAX: 763-552-1281
jspicer@industriesinc.org
www.industriesinc.org

Daryl Peterson, Board Chair
Bruce Montgomery, Vice Chair
Marilyn Bachman, Secretary
Nonprofit organization that does vocational assessment and training for people with disabilities.

6836 Industries: Mora
500 Walnut St S
Mora, MN 55051-1936

320-679-2354
FAX: 320-679-2355
jspicer@industriesinc.org
www.industriesinc.org

Daryl Peterson, Board Chair
Bruce Montgomery, Vice Chair
Marilyn Bachman, Secretary
Nonprofit organization that does vocational assessment and training for people with disabilities.

6837 Shriners Hospitals for Children: Twin Cities
2025 E River Pkwy
Minneapolis, MN 55414-3696   612-596-6100
                                    888-293-2832
                                    888-293-2832
                               FAX: 612-339-5954
www.shrinershospitalsforchildren.org
Charles C. Lobeck, Administrator
Cary Mielke, M.D, Interim Chief of Staff
Don Engel, Development Officer
Shriners Hospital for Children-Twin Cities offers quality orthopedic medical care regardless of the patients' ability to pay.
Shriners Hospitals provide inpatient and outpatient services, surgery, casts, braces, artificial limbs, x-rays and physical and occupational therapy to any child under the age of 18 who may benefit
from treatment.

6838 Vision Loss Resources
1936 Lyndale Ave S
Minneapolis, MN 55403-3101   612-871-2222
                               FAX: 612-872-0189
                               TTY:612-382-8422
                                    info@vlrw.org
www.visionlossresources.org
Barry Shear, Chair
Lisa David, Vice Chair
Mary McDougall, Secretary
Offers services for the totally blind, legally blind, visually impaired, and more with health, counseling, educational, recreational, rehabilitation, computer training and professional
training services.

Mississippi

6839 Addie McBryde Rehabilitation Center for the Blind
PO Box 5314
Jackson, MS 39296-5314   601-364-2700
                                800-443-1000
                           FAX: 601-364-2677
H. S. McMillan, Executive Director
Shelia Browning, Deputy Director Non-Vocational P
Offers services for the totally blind, legally blind, visually im-
paired, blind and more with health, counseling, educational, rec-
reational, rehabilitation, computer training services and
orientation and mobility.

6840 Mississippi Methodist Rehabilitation Center
1350 E Woodrow Wilson Ave
Jackson, MS 39216-5198   601-981-2611
                                800-223-6672
                           FAX: 601-364-3571
www.methodistonline.org
Mark A. Adams, President/CEO
Matthew L. Holleman, III, Chair
Mike P. Sturdivant Jr, Vice Chairman
Rebuild lives that have been broken by disabilities and impairments from serious illness or severe injury. The challenge is to
help patients regain abilities, restore function and movement, and
renew emotionally. It features personal rehabilitation treatment
plans administered by specialized teams of health care professionals through a variety of outpatient programs, treatments and
other services.

Missouri

6841 Alpine North Nursing and Rehabilitation Center
4700 NW Cliff View Dr
Kansas City, MO 64150-1237   816-741-5105
                               FAX: 816-746-1301
Mike Stacks, Executive Director
Bob Richard, Administrator
Postacute rehabilitation program.

6842 Christian Hospital Northeast
11133 Dunn Rd
Saint Louis, MO 63136-6119   314-653-5000
                                    877-747-9355
                               FAX: 314-653-4130
                                    christianhospital.org
Ron McMullen, President
Bryan Hartwick, Vice President Human Resources
Sebastian Rueckert, MD, Vice President and Chief Medical Officer
A non-profit organization, a 493 bed acute care facility on 28
acres. Christian Hospital has more then 600 physicians on staff
and a diverse workforce of more then 2,5000 health-care professionals who are dedicated to providing the absolute best care with
the latest technology and medical advances.

6843 Easterseals Midwest
11933 Westline Industrial Dr.
St. Louis, MO 63146   800-200-2119
                        FAX: 314-394-4007
                             info@esmw.org
www.easterseals.com/midwest
Wendy Sullivan, Chief Executive Officer
Jeff Arledge, Chief Financial Officer
Tom Barry, Chief Development Officer
Enhances the independence and quality of life of people with dis-
abilities through services, education, outreach and advocacy.

6844 Integrated Health Services of St. Louis at Gravois
10954 Kennerly Rd
Saint Louis, MO 63128-2018   314-843-4242
                               FAX: 314-843-4031
Lisa Niehaus, Administrator
Subacute, skilled and intermediate care; ventilator/tracheostomy
management program; wound management program and complex
rehabilitation program.

6845 Metropolitan Employment & Rehabilitation Service
MERS Missouri Goodwill Industries

www.mersgoodwill.org
Mark Arens, President & Chief Executive Officer
Dawayne Barnett, Chief Financial Officer
DeAnn Briggs, Vice President, Program Services
Vocational rehabilitation, primarily with the disabled, skills
training and placement services.

6846 Poplar Bluff RehabCare Program
Lucy Lee Hospital
2620 N Westwood Blvd
Poplar Bluff, MO 63901-3396   573-785-7721
                               FAX: 573-686-5987
Jim Martin, Program Manager
Chris Murray, Care Coordinator
Darlene Hill, Care Admissions Coordinator
Provides physical medicine and rehabilitation to individuals with
a physically limiting condition. The program is designed to help
individuals function as independently as possible by maximizing
their strength and abilities.

6847 Shriners Hospitals for Children St. Louis
2001 S Lindbergh Blvd
Saint Louis, MO 63131-3597   314-432-3600
                                    800-850-2960
                               FAX: 314-432-2930
www.shrinershq.org/hospitals/st.louis
John McCabe, Executive Vice President
Kenneth Guidera, M.D., Chief Medical Officer
Eugene R. D'Amore, Vice President, Hospital Operations
Medical care is provided free of charge for children 18 and under
with orthopaedic conditions.

6848 St. Louis Society for the Blind and Visually Impaired
8770 Manchester Rd
Saint Louis, MO 63144-2724   314-960-9000
                               FAX: 314-968-9003
                                    www.slsbvi.org
David Ekin, President
Chris Pickel, Chair
Ann Shapiro, Vice Chair
Offers vision rehabilitation services for the totally blind, legally
blind, visually impaired, including counseling, educational, rec-

reational, rehabilitation, computer training and professional training services. Low vision aids and appliance available through low vision clinic by appointment.

6849 Truman Medical Center Low Vision Rehabilitation Program
Eye Foundation of Kansas City
2300 Holmes St.
Kansas City, MO 64108   816-404-1780
FAX: 816-404-1786

Nelson R. Sabates, M.D., Chairman
Monika Malecha, MD, Residency Program Director
Abraham Poulose, MD, Director of Clinics
Our program is designed to maximize daily tasks for a person with low vision. We are able to evaluate a person's home and provide recommendations as needed.

6850 Truman Neurological Center
12404 E. US 40 Highway
Independence, MO 64055-1354   816-373-5060
FAX: 816-373-5787
tnccommunity.com

James Landrum, Executive Director
Ann Johnson, Finance Director
Terri Boyce, Office Assistant
A licensed habilitation center established for the purpose of assisting persons with developmental disabilities. The minimum age is 18. Residential care is provided in four group homes in the community licensed by the DMH and CARF accredited.

Montana

6851 Benefis Healthcare
1101 26th St S
Great Falls, MT 59405-5104   406-455-5000
FAX: 406-455-2110
benefis@benefis.org
www.benefis.org

John Goodnow, CEO
Laura Goldhahn-Konen, President
Forrest Ehlinger, Chief Financial & Treasury Officer
Benefis Healthcare is a not-for-profit community asses governed by a 15-member local board of directors. Benefis is locally owned and controlled. Benefis is a Level II trauma center- one of only 4 in the state and 107 in the country.

6852 Disability Services Division of Montana
Department of Public Health
Helena, MT 59604   406-444-7734
FAX: 406-444-3465

Keith Messmer, Manager
Sandi Gory, Administrative Assistant
Janice Frisch, Chief Management Operations
Responsible for coordinating, developing and implementing comprehensive programs to assist Montanans with disabilities with activities of daily living, community base services and coordinated programs of habilitation, rehabilitation and independent living.

6853 Easterseals-Goodwill Northern Rocky Mountain
Easterseals National
425 1st Ave. N
Great Falls, MT 59401-2507   406-761-3680
www.esgw.org

Michelle Belknap, President & CEO
Provides services for children and adults with disabilities and other special needs, and support to their families.

Nebraska

6854 Las Vegas Healthcare And Rehabilitation Center
680 South Fourth Street
Louisville, KY 40202   502-596-7300
TTY:800-545-0749
web_administrator@kindredhealthcare.com
kindredhealthcare.com

Paul J. Diaz, President/ CEO

Accomodates 79 residents. Serving the community for approximately 40 years. Located in close proximity to local hospitals and surrounded by medical complexes, out center offers both short-term rehabilitation and long term.care.

6855 Sierra Pain Institute
265 Golden Ln
Reno, NV 89502-1205   775-323-7092
FAX: 775-323-5259

Lyle Smith, Owner
The program consists of a medically supervised outpatient program managed by an interdisciplinary team with input from specialties of Pain Medicine, Physical Therapy and Occupational Science. The format insures that each patient receives the full range of behavioral techniques in a well-integrated, individually tailored therapeutic regimen.

New Hampshire

6856 Department of Physical Medicine and Rehabilitation
Exeter Hospital
5 Alumni Dr
Exeter, NH 03833-2128   603-778-7311
FAX: 603-580-6592
www.exeterhospital.com

Kevin Calahan, President
Offers patient treatment, committed to enhancing the lives of individuals with short and long term physically disabling conditions.

6857 Farnum Rehabilitation Center
580 Court St
Keene, NH 03431-1718   603-354-6630
FAX: 603-355-2078

Susan Loughrey, Program Director
Judy Bell, Manager
Offers rehabilitation services, occupational therapy, physical therapy and more for the physically challenged individual.

6858 Hackett Hill Nursing Center and Integrated Care
191 Hackett Hill Rd
Manchester, NH 03102-8993   603-668-8161
FAX: 603-622-2584

Daniele Peckham, Administrator
Brett Lennerton, Administrator
A 68-bed certified nursing home.Postacute rehabilitation program.

6859 Mental Health Center: Riverside Courtyard, The
3 Twelfth St
Berlin, NH 03570-3860   603-752-7404
FAX: 603-752-5194

Eileen Theriault, Manager
A center to help people that have mental disabilities.

6860 New Hampshire Rehabilitation and Sports Medicine
Catholic Medical Center
Ste 201
769 S Main St
Manchester, NH 03102-5166   603-647-1899
800-437-9666
FAX: 603-668-5348

Stuart Draper, Owner
Victor Carbone, Manager
A specialized facility for comprehensive rehabilitation for individuals who have been injured or have a disability.

6861 New Medico, Highwatch Rehabilitation Center
Highwatch Rd
Center Ossipee, NH 03814   FAX: 603-539-8888
William Burke, Executive Director
Post-acute rehabilitation service.

6862 **Northern New Hampshire Mental Health and Developmental Services**
87 Washington St
Conway, NH 03818-6044
603-447-3347
FAX: 603-447-8893
www.northernhs.org

Dennis Mackay, CEO
Provides mental health and developmental services to northern New Hampshire, including early intervention, elderly services, residential program, outpatient services, employee assistance programs, inpatient services, etc.

New Jersey

6863 **All Garden State Physical Therapy**
44 Ridge Road
North Arlington, NJ 07031
201-998-6300
FAX: 201-998-6344

Post-acute rehabilitation program.

6864 **Bancroft**
425 Kings Highway East
PO Box 20
Haddonfield, NJ 08033- 1284
856-429-0010
800-774-5516
FAX: 856-429-1613
TTY: 856-428-2697
inquiry@bancroft.org
www.bancroft.org

Cynthia Boyer, PhD, Executive Director, Brain Injury Services
Toni Pergolin, President and Chief Executive
Clair Rohrer, Med, Executive Director, Programs for Adults
Private, not-for-profit organization serving people with disabilities since 1883. Based in Haddonfield, New Jersey, help more than 1000 children and adults with autism, developmental disabilities, brain injuries, and other neurological impairments. Operates more than 140 sites throughout the U.S. and abroad.

6865 **Daughters of Miriam Center/The Gallen Institute**
155 Hazel St
Clifton, NJ 07011-3423
973-772-3700
FAX: 973-253-5389
administration@daughtersofmiriamcenter.org
www.daughtersofmiriamcenter.o rg
Fred Feinstein, Executive Director
Dedicated to providing the highest quality care, the Center has far exceeded a stereotypical nursing home by offering a continuum of care environment, making us a leader in Jewish eldercare.

6866 **Devereux Advanced Behavioral Health New Jersey**
Devereux New Jersey
286 Mantua Grove Rd.
Building 4
West Deptford, NJ 08066
856-599-6400
FAX: 856-423-8916
drenner@devereux.org
www.devereuxnj.org

Brian Hancock, Executive Director
Christine DiGiampaolo, Human Resources Department
Kelly McGhee, Quality Improvement Department
Serves people of all ages who have special needs. Individuals with emotional, behavioral, and developmental disabilities are offered services such as community-based homes and apartments, vocational training programs, family care homes, and consulting services. Devereux New Jersey also has a residential/educational center for individuals with autism.

6867 **Ladacain Network**
Schroth School & Technical Education Center
1701 Kneeley Blvd
Wanamassa, NJ 07712-7622
732-493-5900
FAX: 732-493-5980
ladacin.org

Patricia Carlesimo, Executive Director
Provides an array of services and programs specifically for children and adults with developmental and physical disabilities. Services include approved Department of Education school programs; adult education and training; vocational training, personal care assistance services, in-home and Saturday respite; child care programs, housing opportunities, and more.

6868 **Lourdes Regional Rehabilitation Center**
Our Lady of Lourdes Medical Center
1600 Haddon Ave
Camden, NJ 08103-3101
856-757-3864
856-757-3500
FAX: 856-968-2511
www.lourdesnet.org

Alexander J. Hatala, President
Kimberly D. Barnes, Vice President, Planning and Development
Michael Hammond, Chief Financial Officer
The only comprehensive rehabilitation facility located within an acute care hospital in Southern New Jersey. Patients benefit from the proximity to the full range of state of the art medical and surgical services should the need arise.

6869 **Mt. Carmel Guild**
1160 Raymond Blvd
Newark, NJ 07102-4168
973-596-4100
FAX: 973-639-6583

Anita Holland, Manager
Offers services for the totally blind, legally blind, visually impaired, and more with health, counseling, educational, recreational, rehabilitation, computer training and professional training services.

6870 **Pediatric Rehabilitation Department, JFK Medical Center**
65 James St
Edison, NJ 08818-3947
732-321-7362
732-321-7000
FAX: 732-548-7751
www.jfkmc.org

Michael A. Kleiman, DMD, Chair
Douglas A. Nordstrom, Vice Chair
John L. Kolaya, PE, Secretary
Comprehensive interdisciplinary, family focused outpatient pediatric rehabilitation services including evaluation and individual and group treatment programs for children birth-21.

6871 **REACH Rehabilitation Program: Leader Nursing and Rehabilitation Center**
550 Jessup Rd
West Deptford, NJ 08066-1921
856-848-9551
Karen Fattore, Case Manager
Anthony Stenson, Administrator
Postacute rehabilitation program.

6872 **REACH Rehabilitation and Catastrophic Long-Term Care**
1180 Us Highway 22
Mountainside, NJ 07092-2810
908-654-0020
FAX: 908-654-8661

Allen Swanson, Manager
Archie Ordana, Manager
Postacute rehabilitation program.

6873 **Rehabilitation Specialists**
18-01 Pollitt Drive
Ste 1A
Fair Lawn, NJ 07410-2815
201-478-4200
800-441-7488
FAX: 201-478-4201
www.rehab-specialists.com

Virgilio Caraballo, President/CEO
Dustin Gordon, Director of Neuropsychological and Clinical Services
Dr. Brian Greenwald, Medical Director
Rehabilitation Specialists, founded in 1983, is a quality, cost effective community re-entry center treating individuals with acquired brain injury. A non clinical environment based in the community is utilized that offers professional services enabling participants to learn skills they need to return to a productive life. Both our Day and Residential programming emphases focus on Functional Life Skills, Work Skills and Learning Skills. Each participant's program is tailored to meet their needs.

6874 Somerset Valley Rehabilitation and Nursing Center
Care-One
11300 Cornell Park Drive
Suite 360
Cincinnati, OH 45242
513-469-7222
FAX: 513-469-7230
info@healthbridge.org
Trudi Matthews, Director of Policy and Public Relations
Subacute rehabilitation program, long term care, respite care.

6875 Summit Ridge Center
101 East State Street
Kennett Square, PA 19348
973-736-2000
FAX: 973-736-2764
genesishcc.com
Offers rehabilitation services, occupational therapy, physical therapy and more for the physically challenged. A 152-bed nursing home.

New Mexico

6876 SJR Rehabilitation Hospital
525 S Schwartz Ave
Farmington, NM 87401-5955
505-609-2625
FAX: 505-327-6562
eniemand@sjrmc.net
www.sjrrh.com
Ena M Niemand, Executive Director
Sue Clay, Program Director
Jill Morgan, Nursing Director
Uses a team of professionals to provide a comprehensive rehabilitation program. Accomplishing the best possible physical and cognitive improvement is the aim of the following treatment members: nurses, physical therapists, physicians, speech and occupational therapists, therapeutic recreation specialist. Providing inpatient and out patient services.

6877 Southwest Communication Resource
P.O.Box 788
Bernalillo, NM 87004-788
505-867-3396
FAX: 505-867-3398
info@abrazosnm.org
swcr.org
Services for infants, children and adults with developmental disabilities in Sandoval County New Mexico.

New York

6878 Aspire of Western New York
2356 N Forest Rd
Getzville, NY 14068-1224
716-838-0047
FAX: 716-894-8257
info@aspirewny.org
aspirewny.org
Thomas A. Sy, Executive Director
Janet Hansen, Chief Operating Officer
Mary Anne Coombe, V.P. of Service Coordination & Fiscal Management Services
Provides comprehensive services to individuals with disabilities from infancy through adulthood. Also serves people with all types of developmental disabilities as well as providing clinical services to persons with other types of disabilities such as: spinal cord injury, head trauma and others. Aspire employs 1500 people.

6879 Bronx Continuing Treatment Day Program
1527 Southern Blvd
Bronx, NY 10460-5619
718-893-1414
FAX: 718-893-0707
Mary Jane Purcell, Manager
Post-acute rehabilitation program.

6880 Brooklyn Bureau of Community Service
285 Schermerhorn St
Brooklyn, NY 11217-1098
718-310-5600
FAX: 718-855-1517
info@WeAreBCS.org
www.wearebcs.org
Marla Simpson, Executive Director
Anthony B. Edwards, MBA, CCF, MFM, CFO
Janelle Farris, Chief Operating Officer
Offers independent living skills, counseling, work readiness, vocational trianing, job placement and job follow-up services to individuals with disabilities (to include individuals with psychiatric, physical, and developmental disabilities). Special programs to move disabled welfare recipients from welfare to work. Publishes a bi-annual newsletter.

6881 Buffalo Hearing and Speech Center
50 E North St
Buffalo, NY 14203-1002
716-885-8318
FAX: 716-885-4229
askbhsc.org
Frank J. Polino, Chairman
Dennis J. Szefel, First Vice Chairman
Kenneth J. Wilson, Treasurer
Assists individuals with speech, language and/or hearing impairments to achieve maximum communication potential.

6882 Cora Hoffman Center Day Program
2324 Forest Ave
Staten Island, NY 10303-1506
718-447-8205
FAX: 718-815-2182
Kevin Kenney, Manager
Post-acute rehabilitation program specializing in Cerebral Palsy. Part of the Cerebral Palsey Association of New York State.

6883 Devereux Advanced Behavioral Health New York
Devereux New York
40 Devereux Way
Red Hook, NY 12571
845-758-1899
FAX: 845-758-1817
www.devereuxny.org
John Lopez, Executive Director
Arthur Roberts, Director of Human Resources
Jeffrey Obiekwe, Program Supervisor
Devereux New York provides a wide range of educational, clinical, residential, and community-based programs and services to people of all ages with intellectual disabilities, Autism Spectrum Disorder, and dual diagnoses. Some services include psychotherapy, life skills development, physical therapies, residential programs, case management, self advocacy and more.

6884 Elmhurst Hospital Center
7901 Broadway
Elmhurst, NY 11373-1368
718-334-4000
www.nyc.gov/html/hhc/ehc/html/home/home.shtml
Chris D Constantino, Executive Director
Hospital is comprised of 525 beds and is a Level I Trauma Center, and Emergency Heart Care Stattion and a 911 recieving hospital. It is the premiere health care organization for key areas such as Surgery, Cardiology, Women's health, Pediatrics, Rehabilitation Medicine, Renal and Mental Health Services.

6885 Federation Employment And Guidance Service(F-E-G-S)
315 Hudson St
New York, NY 10013-1086
212-366-8400
FAX: 212-366-8441
info@fegs.org
www.fegs.org
Gail Magaliff, CEO
Ira Machowsky, Executive Vice President
Thomas M. Higgins, CFO
The largest and most diversified private, not-for-profit health related and human service organization in the United States. With operations in over 258 facilities, residences, and off-site locations, F-E-G-S has served more then 2 million people since its inception.

6886 **Flushing Hospital**
4500 Parsons Blvd
Flushing, NY 11355-2205 718-670-5000
FAX: 718-670-3082
flushinghospital.org

Robert V. Levine, Executive Vice President/COO
Bruce J. Flanz, President/CEO
Mounir Doss, Executive Vice President/CFO
Offers services for the totally blind, legally blind, visually impaired, and more with health, counseling, educational, recreational, rehabilitation, computer training and professional training services.

6887 **Gateway Community Industries Inc.,**
1 Amy Kay Pkwy
Kingston, NY 12401-6444 845-331-1261
800-454-9395
FAX: 845-331-4920
info@gatewayindustries.org
gatewayindustries.org

Francoise C. Gunefsky, President/CEO
Eva Graham, CFO
Ralph Smith, Chief Information Officer
Gateway Community Industries, Inc., founded in 1957, is one of the leading independent not-for-profit vocational rehabilitation and training centers for people with mental and/or physical disabilities. The agency provides comprehensive services in vocational evaluation, job training, job placement, vocational work center employment, supported employment, psychiatric rehabilitation, continuing day treatment, and residential habilitation/rehabilitation.

6888 **Henkind Eye Institute Division of Montefiore Hospital**
111 East 210th Street
Bronx, NY 10467-2404 718-920-4321
www.montefiore.org
Philip O. Ozuah, MD, PhD, Executive Vice President/ COO
Steven M. Safyer, MD, President/ CEO
Joel A. Perlman, Executive Vice President, Chief Financial Officer
Offers services for the totally blind, legally blind, visually impaired, and more with health, counseling, educational, recreational, rehabilitation, computer training and professional training services. Low vision services offered.

6889 **Industries for the Blind of New York State**
194 Washington Ave
Ste 300
Albany, NY 12210-6314 518-456-8671
800-421-9010
FAX: 518-456-3587
customercare@nyspsp.org
www.abilityone.com

Richard Healey, CEO
Offers services for the totally blind, legally blind, visually impaired, and more with health, counseling, educational, recreational, rehabilitation, computer training and professional training services.

6890 **Inpatient Pain Rehabilitation Program**
550 First Avenue
New York, NY 10016 212-263-7300
FAX: 212-598-6468
www.med.nyu.edu

William Pinter Phd, Administrative Director
The Inpatient Rehabilitation Program, established in 1983 specializes in the treatment of chronic pain. Our inpatient program is one of the oldest and well established pain programs in the country. It is the only interdisciplinary inpatient pain program in the tri-state area and one of only 20 pain programs in the entire US to have CARF accreditation. Upon completion of an extensive evaluation, patients are admitted for an 18-day inpatient stay.

6891 **Koicheff Health Care Center**
2324 Forest Ave
Staten Island, NY 10303-1506 718-447-0200
FAX: 718-981-1431

Paul Castello, Clinic Director
Post-accute rehabilitation programs.

6892 **New York-Presbyterian Hospital**
622 W 168th St
New York, NY 10032-3796 212-305-4600
FAX: 212-305-1017
www.nyp.org

Steven J. Corwin, MD, CEO
Robert E. Kelly, MD, President
New York Presbyterian Hospital is internationally recognized for its outstanding comprehensive services. Its medical, surgical, and emergency care services provide each patient with the highest possible level of care. In addition, as part of the Hospital's commitment to the total well-being of each patient, it offers a range of specialized services, as well as special healthcare programs for neighboring communities.

6893 **Norman Marcus Pain Institute**
30 E 40th St
Ste 1100
New York, NY 10016 212-532-7999
FAX: 212-532-5957
support@nmpi.com
backpainusa.com

Norman J Marcus, Medical Director
We focus on muscles as the cause of most common pains, i.e. back, neck, shoulders, and headaches. We make specific muscle diagnoses and have specific treatments that in many cases will eliminate the need for surgery or relieve the pain. Patients diagnosed with herniated disc, spinal stenosis, rotator cuff tear, impingement syndrome, sciatica, fibromyalgia and headache will generally find relief.

6894 **Pain Alleviation Center**
Comprehensive Pain Management Associates
125 S Service Rd
Jericho, NY 11753-1038 516-997-7246
FAX: 516-997-7281
www.paincenter.com

Alex Weingarten, Director
Phillip Fyman, Director
Marisa French, Manager
One of the first pain clinics to gain national accreditation from the Commission on Accreditation of Rehabilitation Facilities. This is due largely to a patient-centered program based on the latest research.

6895 **Pathfinder Village**
3 Chenango Rd
Edmeston, NY 13335-2314 607-965-8377
FAX: 607-965-8655
info@pathfindervillage.org
www.pathfindervillage.org

Paul Landers, CEO
Caprice S. Eckert, Chief Financial Officer
Kelly A. Meyers, Director of Admissions
Pathfinder Village is a warm, friendly community in the rolling hills of Central New York. Here children and adults with Down Syndrome gain independence, build lasting friendships, become partners in the world and take in all that life has to offer.

6896 **Pilot Industries: Ellenville**
845-331-4300
48 Canal St
Ellenville, NY 12428-1327 845-647-7711
FAX: 845-647-7711

Peter Pierri, Executive Director
Betty Marks, Plant Manager
Post-accute rehabilitation services.

6897 **Skills Unlimited**
405 Locust Ave
Oakdale, NY 11769-1695 631-567-3320
FAX: 631-567-3285
info@skillsunlimited.org
skillsunlimited.org

Richard Kassnove, Executive Director
Our basic goals is to offer persons with disabilities the opportunity to explore and develop their full vocational potential. Our programs are unique in that by offering comprehensive services, individuals are able to deal with many different issues that could potentially affect their vocational success. Any individual that

has an impairment that interferes with their ability to work is entitles to the services that we offer.

North Carolina

6898 Center for Vision Rehabilitation
Academy Eye Associates
3115 Academy Rd
Durham, NC 27707-2652

919-493-7456
800-942-1499
FAX: 919-493-1718
henry.greene@academyeye.com
academyeye.com

Henry A Greene, Owner
Vision rehabilitation and low-vision care for the visually impaired, post-stroke, head trauma and for neuro-oncology vision complications.

6899 Diversified Opportunities
1010 Herring Ave E
Wilson, NC 27893-3311

252-291-0378
FAX: 252-291-1402
www.diversifiedopportunitiesinc.com

Cindy Dixon, Executive Director
Carlton Goff, Business Manager
Ericka Simmons, QP Program Manager
Vocational rehabilitation agency, better outcomes, lower cost, guaranteed performance standards.

6900 Forsyth Medical Center
3333 Silas Creek Pkwy
Winston Salem, NC 27103-3090

336-718-5000
FAX: 336-718-9250
www.novanthealth.org

Jeffrey T. Lindsay, President
Denise Mihal, Chief Operating Officer
Stephen J. Motew, MD, Senior Vice President
Provides care that is state-of-the-art and second to none, both because of advanced treatments availiable through our clinical research and technology to the academic excellence-and caring nature-of our doctors and nurses.

6901 Industries of the Blind
914-920 W Lee St
Greensboro, NC 27403-2803

336-274-1591
800-909-7086
FAX: 336-544-3739
customerservice@iob-gso.com
industriesoftheblind.com

David Thompson, Chairperson
Scott Thornhill, 1st Vice Chairperson
Ashley S. James, Jr., 2nd Vice Chairperson
Offers services for the totally blind, legally blind, visually impaired, and more with health, counseling, educational, recreational, rehabilitation, computer training and professional training services.

6902 Johnston County Industries
1100 East Preston Street
Selma, NC 27576-3162

919-743-8700
FAX: 919-965-8023
jcindustries.com

John Shallcross, Jr., President
Durwood Woodall, Vice President
Lina Sanders-Johnson, Secretary/Treasurer
JCI is an entrepreneurial not-for-profit corporation dedicated to empowering people with disabilities or disadvantages to succeed through training and employment

6903 Learning Services: Carolina
707 Morehead Ave
Durham, NC 27707-1319

919-688-4444
888-419-9955
FAX: 919-419-9966
learningservices.com

Debra Braunling-McMorrow, President and CEO
Jeanne Mack, Chief Financial Officer and Vice President of Operations
Michael Weaver, Chief Development Officer

Located in an historic neighborhood in the heart of Durham, this campus-style setting offers easy access to resources at 3 outstanding facilities: Duke University, The University of North Carolina at Chapel Hill, and Research Triangle Park. This program provides a range of services and activities that draw upon the many resources availiable in the community.

6904 Lions Club Industries for the Blind
4500 Emperor Blvd.
Durham, NC 27703

919-596-8277
800-526-1562
FAX: 919-598-1179
inquire@buylci.com

Bill Hudson, President
Offers services for the totally blind, legally blind, visually impaired, and more with health, counseling, educational, recreational, rehabilitation, computer training and professional training services.

6905 Lions Services Inc.
5 Penn Plaza
New York, NY 10001

21 -62 -210
lsisale@aol.com

Jimmy R Cranford, President
Jimmy Cranford, President
Offers services for the totally blind, legally blind, visually impaired, and more with health, counseling, educational, recreational, rehabilitation, computer training and professional training services.

6906 Regional Rehabilitation Center Pitt County Memorial Hospital
2100 Stantonsburg Rd
Greenville, NC 27834-2818

252-847-4448
FAX: 252-816-7552

Martha M Dixon, VP General Services
An accredited, comprehensive rehabilitation center-part of a statewide network- and we're the largest such facility in eastern North Carolina. Our service area covers 29 counties, and we offer a complete array of rehabilitation services for patients of all ages. Because the Regional Rehabilitation Center is associated with both Pitt County Memorial Hospital And the Brody School of Medicine at East Carolina University, patients have access to a full range of state of the art medical services.

6907 Rehab Home Care
2660 Yonkers Rd
Raleigh, NC 27604-3384

800-447-8692
FAX: 919-831-2211

Alan Silver, CEO
Janis Hansen, Chief Operating Officer
A Medicare/Medicaid certified, state-licensed home health agency with emphasis on rehabilitation.

6908 Thoms Rehabilitation Hospital
Thoms Rehabilitation Hospital
68 Sweeten Creek Rd
Asheville, NC 28803-2318

828-277-4800
FAX: 828-277-4812
TTY:800-735-2962
www.carepartners.org

Tracy Buchanan, President & CEO
Gary Bowers, COO
Freestanding physical rehabilitation hospital, founded 1938 - 100 beds, including 90 acute and 10 transitional - JCAHO accredited.

6909 Winston-Salem Industries for the Blind
7730 N Point Blvd
Winston Salem, NC 27106-3310

336-759-0551
800-242-7726
FAX: 336-759-0990
info@wsifb.com
www.wsifb.com

Mike Faircloth, Chairman
Karen Carey, Vice Chairman, Secretary
W. Robert Newell, Treasurer
Offers services for the totally blind, legally blind, visually impaired, and more with health, counseling, educational, recreational, rehabilitation, computer training and professional training services.

Ohio

6910   Bellefaire Jewish Children's Bureau
22001 Fairmount Blvd
Cleveland, OH 44118-4819   216-932-2800
                                           800-879-2522
                                           FAX: 216-932-6704
                                           www.bellefairejcb.org

Adam Jacobs, CEO
Adam G. Jacobs PhD, Executive Vice President
Residential treatment for ages 12 to 17 1/2 at time of admission
offering individualized psychotherapy, special education, and
group living for severaly emotionally disturbed children and adolescents. Also offers a variety of other programs including specialized and therapuetic foster care, partial hospitilization,
outpatient counseling, home-based intensive counseling and
adoption services.

6911   Christ Hospital Rehabilitation Unit
2139 Auburn Ave
Cincinnati, OH 45219-2906   513-585-2737
                                            FAX: 513-585-4353
                                            www.thechristhospital.com

Mike Keating, President and CEO
Chris Bergman, Vice President and Chief Financial Officer
Berc Gawne, MD, Vice President and Chief Medical Officer
Patients of this 555-bed, not-for-profit acute care facility receive
personalized health care provided by trained specialists using the
most sophisticated medical technology available, including
state-of-the-art intensive care units, surgical facilities, cardiac
catheterization labs, three new electrophysiology labs, and the
tristates first positron emission tomography (PET) scanning
capabilities.

6912   Cleveland Sight Center
1909 E 101st St.
Cleveland, OH 44106   216-791-8118
                                            FAX: 216-791-1101
                                            TTY:216-791-8119
                                            info@clevelandsightcenter.org
                                            www.clevelandsightcenter.org
Larry Benders, President & CEO
Kevin Krencisz, Chief Financial & Administrative Officer
Jassen Tawil, Director, Business Development & Customer Success
Social, rehabilitation, education and support services for blind
and visually impaired children and adults, early intervention program for children birth to age 6, low vision clinic, aid and appliance shop, Braille and taping transcription, training for
rehabilitation, orientation, mobility and computer access, employment services and job placement, recreation program, resident camping, talking books, radio reading services. Free
screening.

6913   Columbus Speech and Hearing Center
510 E North Broadway St
Columbus, OH 43214-4114   614-263-5151
                                            FAX: 614-263-5365
                                            columbusspeech.org

Dawn Gleason, Au.D., President/ CEO
Karen Deeter, Director of Operations
Serves persons who have speech-language and hearing challenges. Provides vocational rehabilitation services for individuals who are deaf, hard-of-hearing or deaf-blind.

**6914   CommuniCare of Clifton Nursing and Rehabilitation
Center**
Communi Care Health Services
4700 Ashwood Drive
Cincinnati, OH 45241   513-489-7100
                                            FAX: 513-281-2559
                                            communicarehealth.com
Stephen L. Rosedale, Founder/ CEO
A long term care facility which specializes in rehabilitation. Of-
fers a full range of rehabilitative services including physical ther-
apy, occupational therapy and speech therapy.

6915   Doctors Hospital
5100 W Broad St
Columbus, OH 43228-1672   614-544-1000
                                            800-837-7555
                                            FAX: 614-544-1844
                                            www.ohiohealth.com/homedoctors

David Blom, President/ CEO
Michael Bernstein, Senior Vice President and Chief
We believe our first responsibility is to the patients we serve. We
respect the physical, emotional and spiritual needs of our patients
and find that compassion is essential to fostering healing and
wholeness.

6916   Dodd Hall at the Ohio State University Hospitals
410 W 10th Ave
Columbus, OH 43210-1240   614-293-3300
                                            800-293-5123
                                            OSUCareConnection@osumc.edu
                                            www.medicalcenter.osu.edu
Steven G. Gabbe, MD, Senior Vice President / CEO
Larry Anstine, CEO
Gail Marsh, Chief Strategy Officer
Dodd Hall is a full service medical rehabilitation hospital offer-
ing comprehensive inpatient and outpatient rehabilitation.

**6917   Easterseals of Mahoning, Trumbull and Columbiana
Counties**
299 Edwards St.
Youngstown, OH 44502-1599   330-743-1168
                                            www.easterseals.com/mtc

Jody Klase, Chief Executive Officer
Michael Green, Chief Financial Officer
Outpatient medical rehabilitation, skill development, vocational
support, and transportation services.

6918   Four Oaks Center
245 N. Valley Road
Xenia, OH 45385-2605   937-562-6500
                                            FAX: 937-562-6520
                                            www.greenedd.org

Todd McManus, President
Jill A. LaRock, Director
Dr. Vijay Gupta, Vice President
Starts children on the road to discovery by providing a learning
environment rich in opportunities and encouragement. The program was designed to give children with delays or disabilities, or
those at-risk the extra help needed to develop fully. Any child under the age of six who exhibits developmental delays, handicapping conditions, or is considered at risk may qualify to
participate.

6919   Genesis Healthcare System
Rehabilitation Services
800 Forest Ave
Zanesville, OH 43701-2881   740-454-5000
                                            800-322-4762
                                            FAX: 740-455-7527
                                            llynn@genesishcs.org
                                            www.genesishcs.org

Matt Perry, President/CEO
Paul Masterson, CFO
Richard Helsper, COO
A CARF and JACHO accredited 19-bed rehabilitation facility located within Genesis Healthcare System, a 732 bed, non-profit
hospital system, located in Zanesville, Ohio. Freestanding outpatient services, including work hardening, pain management, vocational services, audiology, lymphedema, vestibular rehab,
off-the-road driving evals, aquatic therpay, womens health and
sports enhancement.

6920   George A Martin Center
3603 Washington Ave
Cincinnati, OH 45229-2009   513-221-1017
                                            FAX: 513-221-3817

Karen Doggett, Executive Director
Offers services for the totally blind, legally blind, visually impaired, and more with health, counseling, educational, recreational, rehabilitation, computer training and professional
training services.

6921 Grady Memorial Hospital
561 W Central Ave
Delaware, OH 43015-1489
740-615-1000
800-487-1115
FAX: 740-368-5114
ohiohealth.com

Bruce Hagen, Regional Executive and President

As a progressive healthcare leader, Grady Memorial Hospital is committed to excellence while providing the Deleware community with comprehensive quality service delivered with compassionate, personal care. Our membership in Ohio's largest healthcare system, Ohio Health, enables us to improve access to a broader range of healthcare services, enhance development of new programs and services, and provide a complete continuum of care for patients in the deleware area.

6922 Hamilton Adult Center
3400 Symmes Rd
Hamilton, OH 45015-1359
513-867-5970
FAX: 513-874-2977

Donald Musnuff, Executive Director

6923 Holzer Clinic
100 Jackson Pike
Gallipolis, OH 45631-1560
740-446-5000
FAX: 740-446-5532
info@holzer.org
www.holzer.org

T. Wayne Munro, MD, CEO
Brent A. Saunders, Chair
Christopher Meyer, Chief Medical Officer

Serves medical needs of patients in an 8 county area, including counties in Ohio and West Virginia.

6924 Holzer Clinic Sycamore
Holzer Medical Center
4th Avenue & Sycamore St
Gallipolis, OH 45631-1560
740-446-5244
FAX: 740-446-5448
info@holzer.org
www.holzer.org

T. Wayne Munro, MD, CEO
Brent A. Saunders, Chair
Christopher Meyer, Chief Medical Officer

Offers an individualized quality comprehensive rehabilitation program for people with disabilities by an interdisciplinary team including physical therapy, occupational, speech, nursing and social services to restore the patient to the highest degree of rehab outcomes attainable.

6925 IKRON Institute for Rehabilitative and Psychological Services
2347 Vine St
Cincinnati, OH 45213-1745
513-621-1117
FAX: 513-621-2350
ikron@ikron.org
ikron.org

Randy Strunk, MA, LPCC-S, Executive Director
Ken Carbonell, BBA, Fiscal Director
Melissa Harmeling, MA, PCC-S, Program Director

An accredited mental health facility and a certified rehabilitation center. Through a variety of creative treatment and rehabilitation services, IKRON assists adults with mental health and/or substance abuse problems to attain greater independence, to lead lives of sobriety, to obtain competitive work and live more satisfying lives. IKRON places a strong emphasis on respect and support for persons with problems of adjustment. Special contracts to persons desiring job placement.

6926 Integrated Health Services at Waterford Commons
955 Garden Lake Pkwy
Toledo, OH 43614-2777
419-382-2200
FAX: 419-381-8508

Nicole Giesige, Executive Director

A subacute and rehabilitation program specializing in ventilator weaning and management, I.V. therapeutics and pain management, wound management and subacute rehabilitation.

6927 Lester H Higgins Adult Center
3041 Cleveland Ave SW
Canton, OH 44707-3625
330-484-4814
FAX: 330-484-9416
www.theworkshopsinc.com/

Margalie Belazaire, Manager
Ed Allar, Manager
Post-accute rehabilitation service

6928 Live Oaks Career Development Campus
5936 Buckwheat Rd
Milford, OH 45150
513-575-1906
FAX: 513-575-0805

Harold Carr MD, Superintendent
Robin White, President/CEO
Jim Dixon, Principal
Post-accute rehabilitation facility and services.

6929 Metro Health: St. Luke's Medical Center Pain Management Program
2500 Metrohealth Dr
Cleveland, OH 44109-1900
216-778-7800
www.metrohealth.org

Mark Moran, President
CARF accredited comprehensive multidisciplinary pain management program.

6930 MetroHealth Medical Center
2500 Metrohealth Dr
Cleveland, OH 44109-1900
216-778-7800
www.metrohealth.org

Mark Moran, President
Located on the near west side of Cleveland, is a leader in trauma, emergency, and critical care; women's and childrens's services, including high risk obstetrical care and neonatal intensive care; comprehensive medical and surgical subspecialties.

6931 Middletown Regional Hospital: Inpatient Rehabilitation Unit
105 McKnight Dr
Middletown, OH 45044-4838
513-422-1401
800-338-4057
FAX: 513-422-1520
www.middletownhospital.org

C N Reddy, Owner
Douglas McNeill, Chief Executive Officer
Our mission is to serve and help people, improving the status of their health and the quality of thier lives. Our vision is to be the premier integrated delivery system in Southwest Ohio. Our Values are quality, respect, service and teamwork

6932 Newark Healthcare Center
680 South Fourth Street
Louisville, KY 40202
502-596-7300
TTY:800-545-0749
web_administrator@kindred.com
kindredhealthcare.com

Paul J. Diaz, President/ CEO
Accomodates 300 residents. We are located in the heart of Newark, Ohio. Newark Healthcare is a 2004 recipient of the American Health Care Association's Quality Award.

6933 Parma Community General Hospital Acute Rehabilitation Center
7007 Powers Blvd
Parma, OH 44129-5495
440-743-3000
FAX: 440-843-4387
www.parmahospital.org

David Nedrich, Chairman
Thomas P. O'Donnell, First Vice Chairman
Alex I. Koler, First Assistant Treasurer
The mission of this CARF accredited unit is to provide the most comprehensive, cost-effective, acute rehabilitation program possible in order for every patient and family to adjust to his/her disability and to achieve the maximum potential of independent functioning when returning to community living.

6934 **Peter A Towne Physical Therapy Center**
Ste 10
447 Nilles Rd
Fairfield, OH 45014-2626   513-829-7726
                                  FAX: 513-829-7726
Debbie Wilkerson, Office Manager
Outpatient, private practice physical and occupational therapy.
Three other offices in Hamilton, Monroe and West Chester.

6935 **Philomatheon Society of the Blind**
2701 Tuscarawas St W
Canton, OH 44708-4638   330-453-9157
                               www.philomatheon.com
David Miller, President
Denise Dessecker, Vice President
Angela Randall, Secretary
Offers services for the totally blind, legally blind, visually impaired, and more with health, counseling, educational, recreational, rehabilitation, computer training and professional training services.

6936 **Providence Hospital Work**
2270 Banning Rd
Cincinnati, OH 45239-6621   513-591-5600
                                   FAX: 513-591-5604
Kay Brogle, Executive Director
Post-acute rehabilitation services.

6937 **Six County, Inc.**
2845 Bell St
Zanesville, OH 43701-1794   740-454-9766
                                   800-344-5818
                                   FAX: 740-588-6452
                                   www.sixcounty.org
John A Creek, President
Tim Llewellyn, Senior VP/Community Intervention
Robert Santos, Ex Vp & Coo
Six County, Inc., is a private, not-for-profit corporation under contract with the Mental Health and Recovery Services Board. Six County, Inc., provides comprehensive community mental health services to people of all ages in each of the six Southeastern Ohio counties served: Coshocton, Guernsey, Morgan, Muskingum, Noble, and Perry. SCI's counseling centers provide a full range of services including outpatient counseling; diagnostic assessment, referrals, and psychological testing.

6938 **Society for Rehabilitation**
9290 Lake Shore Blvd
Mentor, OH 44060-1664   440-352-8993
                               800-344-3159
                               FAX: 440-352-6632
Richard Kessler, Executive Director
Vision is to provide individuals with comprehensive services to improve their quality of life. Our mission is to meet the needs of individuals and their families by delivering a wide range of affordable accessible and personalized services, providing treatment by a team of highly qualified, caring professionals. Collaborating with other agencies to meet community needs.

6939 **Southeast Ohio Sight Center**
425 E. Alvarado Street
Suite E
Fallbrook, CA 92028   800-677-4180
                             www.charityadvantage.com
Offers services for the blind and visually impaired to include functional low vision evaluations, community rehabilitation trading, counseling, educational, recreational, rehabilitation and vocational services.

6940 **St. Francis Rehabilitation Hospital**
401 N Broadway St
Green Springs, OH 44836-9638   419-639-2626
                                      800-248-2552
                                      FAX: 419-639-6225
Kim Eicher, CEO
Dan Schwanke, Chief Executive Officer
Program offers specialized treatment for patients who have suffered a head injury, spinal cord injury, or stroke, or who have an orthopedic injury. The Head Injury Program provides a continuum of care from coma stimulation through transitional living. Their physicians, nurses, counselors and therapists are dedicated

to helping our patients develop the motivation, strength and skills needed to overcome or adapt to their disability.

6941 **TAC Enterprises**
2160 Old Selma Rd
Springfield, OH 45505-4600   937-525-7400
                                    FAX: 937-525-7401
                                    info@tacind.com
                                    www.tacind.com
Clifford Meyer, CEO
TAC Enterprises provides employment opportunities for individuals to develop marketable skills by completing contract work in partnership with other industries. Work and self-help skills, social adjustment, and a variety of daily living experiences are offered to the workers by our specialized staff.

Oklahoma

6942 **Dean A McGee Eye Institute**
608 Stanton L Young Blvd
Oklahoma City, OK 73104-5065   405-271-6060
                                      800-787-9012
                                      FAX: 405-271-4442
                                      www.mei.org
Gregory L. Skuta, M.D., President/CEO
Matthew D. Brown, Executive Vice President
Lana G. Ivy, Vice President of Development
Offers services for the totally blind, legally blind, visually impaired, and more with health, counseling, educational, recreational, rehabilitation, computer training and professional training services.

6943 **Jane Phillips Medical Center**
Rehab Care
3500 E Frank Phillips Blvd
Bartlesville, OK 74006-2464   918-333-7200
                                     FAX: 918-333-7801
                                     webmaster@jpmc.org
                                     jpmc.org
David Stire, President/ COO
Mike Moore, Chief Financial Officer/Vice President Fiscal Services
Susan Herron, RN, Vice President Nursing Services
Comprehensive inpatient rehabilitation services are provided to patients with orthopedic, neurologic, and other medical conditions of recent onset or regression, who have experienced a loss of function in activities of daily living, mobility, cognition and communication.

6944 **McAlester Regional Health Center RehabCare Unit**
1 E Clark Bass Blvd
McAlester, OK 74501-4255   918-426-1800
                                  FAX: 918-421-6832
                                  nbrinlee@mrhcok.com
                                  www.mrhcok.com
David Keith, President/ CEO
Cara Bland, Chairman
Evans McBride, Vice-Chairman
A 19-bed inpatient physical rehabilitation unit serving the Southeast Oklahoma area. Offers physical therapy, occupational therapy, social work, speech and psychological services in an interdisciplinary framework.

6945 **Oklahoma League for the Blind**
501 N Douglas Ave
Oklahoma City, OK 73106-5085   405-232-4644
                                      888-522-4644
                                      FAX: 405-236-5438
                                      info@newviewoklahoma.org
                                      www.newviewoklahoma.org
Lauren White, President/CEO
Carol Campbell, Executive Assistant
John Wilson, Chief Financial Officer
Offers services for the blind and visually impaired, counseling, educational, recreational, rehabilitation, computer training and professional training services.

6946 Valley View Regional Hospital-RehabCare Unit
430 N Monte Vista St
Ada, OK 74820-4657
580-332-2323
FAX: 580-421-1395

W. Kent Rogers, President/ CEO
Comprehensive physical medicine and rehabilitation services designed to help patients in their adjustment to a physically limiting condition.

Oregon

6947 Garten Services
PO Box 13970
Salem, OR 97309
503-581-1984
FAX: 503-581-4497
garten@garten.org
garten.org

Tim Rocak, CEO
Pamela Best, CFO
Steve Babcock, Mail Services Manager
Garten's mission is to support people with disabilities in their effort to contribute to the community through employment, career, and retirement opportunities. Our actions increase society's awareness of human potential. Garten's vision is to be recognized as an organization positively demonstrating to the community that people with disabilities can be contributing and valued employees of a thriving business.

6948 Legacy Emanuel Rehabilitation Center
2801 N. Gantenbein
Portland, OR 97227-1542
503-413-2200
FAX: 503-413-1501
www.legacyhealth.org

Gary Guidetta, Executive Director
Gail Weisgerber, Manager
A non-profit tax-exempt corporation that includes 5 full-service hospitals and a children's hospital. The Legacy system provides an integrated network of healthcare services, including acute and critical care, inpatient and outpatient treatment, community health education and a variety of specialty services.

6949 Oakcrest Care Center
2933 Center St NE
Salem, OR 97301-4527
503-585-5850
FAX: 503-585-8781

Postacute rehabilitation program.

6950 Oakhill-Senior Program
1190 Oakhill Ave SE
Salem, OR 97302-3496
503-364-9086
FAX: 503-365-2879

Jan Dillon, Senior Services Manager
Garten Senior Services provides an adult day service program to seniors with and without developmental disabilities. The program will provide community opportunities, college classes and a wide variety of leisure activities in group and individual settings.

6951 Pacific Spine and Pain Center
1801 Highway 99 N
Ashland, OR 97520-9152
541-488-2255
866-482-5515
FAX: 541-482-2433

Janel R Guyette, Manager

6952 Vision Northwest
9225 SW Hall Blvd
Portland, OR 97223-6794
503-684-8389
800-448-2232
FAX: 503-684-9359
visionnw.com

Evelyn Maizels, Executive Director
Offers services for the totally blind, legally blind, visually impaired, and more with health, counseling, educational, recreational, rehabilitation, computer training and professional training services.

6953 Willamette Valley Rehabilitation Center
1853 W Airway Rd
Lebanon, OR 97355-1233
541-258-8121
FAX: 541-451-1762
wvrc.org

Martin Baughman, Executive Director
Provides the best professional vocational services to those adults in the community who, by virtue of their physical or mental limitations, are negatively impacted by their ability to attain or maintain employment.

Pennsylvania

6954 Alpine Nursing and Rehabilitation Center of Hershey
Pennstate
405 Martin Ter
State College, PA 16803-3426
814-865-1710
FAX: 814-863-9423

Melissa A Hardy, Director
Anna Shuey, Administrative Assistant
Postacute rehabilitation program.

6955 Beechwood Rehabilitation Services A Community Integrated Brain Injury Program
469 E Maple Ave
Langhorne, PA 19047-1600
215-750-4299
800-782-3299
FAX: 215-750-4327
beechwoodrehab.com

Thomas Felicetti, President
Services include residential, day treatment and community based support services. Individuals with brain injury are served. The facility is Care Accredited.

6956 Blind & Vision Rehabilitation Services Of Pittsburgh
1800 West St
Homestead, PA 15120-2578
412-368-4400
800-706-5050
FAX: 412-368-4090
www.bvrspittsburgh.org

Erika M. Arbogast, President
Brian Glass, Director of Information Services and Facilities
Leslie Montgomery, Director of Development and Public Relations
Offers services for the totally blind, legally blind, visually impaired, and more with health, counseling, educational, recreational, rehabilitation, computer training and professional training services.

6957 Bradford Regional Medical Center
116 Interstate Pkwy
Bradford, PA 16701-1036
814-368-4143
FAX: 814-368-4130
www.brmc.com

Marek Dzionara, Owner
Andrew Lehman, Executive Director
Timothy J. Finan, President and CEO
Offers rehabilitation services to individuals with an alcohol or drug related problem.

6958 Bryn Mawr Rehabilitation Hospital
414 Paoli Pike
Malvern, PA 19355-3311
610-251-5400
888-734-2241
888-734-2241
FAX: 610-647-3648

Donna M. Phillips, President
We are dedicated to serving individuals and their families whose lives can be enhanced through physical or cognitive rehabilitation. We continually strive for excellence by providing care and services which are valued by those we serve and by contributing to the community through education, research and prevention of disability.

6959 Devereux Advanced Behavioral Health - National Office
National Headquarters
444 Devereux Dr
Villanova, PA 19085   800-345-1292
                               devereuxhr@devereux.org
                                      www.devereux.org

Samuel G Coppersmith, Esq, Chairman
Robert Q Kreider, President & CEO
Marilyn B Benoit, MD, Senior Vice President, Chief Clinical &
Medical Officer
Devereux is a behavioral health organization supporting people
with autism, intellectual and developmental disabilities, and spe-
cialty mental health needs. Some of the services offered by
Devereux include diagnostics, special education, professional
training, research and advocacy.

6960 Devereux Pennsylvania
444 Devereux Dr
Villanova, PA 19085   610-788-6565
                                        800-345-1292
                                  FAX: 610-430-0567
                                     www.devereuxpa.org

Carol Oliver, MS, State Director & Vice President of Operations
Melanie Beidler, MS, Executive Director, Intellectual/Developmen-
tal Disabilities
Stephen Bruce, M.Ed, BCBA, Executive Director, Adult Services
Devereux Pennsylvania provides educational and residential programs, therapeutic foster care, case management, customized employment and community-based behavioral health programs to
children and adults with intellectual and behavioral challenges.

6961 Fox Subacute Center
2644 Bristol Rd
Warrington, PA 18976-1404   800-782-2288
James Foulke, CEO
Vic Costenko, COO
Walter Dunsmore, CFO
Fox subacute recognizes the great need for alternative programs
for today's medically compromised patients. Fox has developed
Models of Care and offers subacute programs fore the management of ventilator-dependent patients. We recognize that the best
road to recovery for these patients is an environment with special
care in an alternative setting. We believe that setting should be
outside the hospital, in facilities where the focus is on the
management of individual patients.

6962 Fox Subacute at Clara Burke
251 Stenton Ave
Plymouth Meeting, PA 19462-1220   610-828-2272
                                        800-424-7201
                                  FAX: 610-828-7939
                               admissions@foxsubacute.com
                                    www.foxsubacute.com

Terri Herd, Director of Marketing
Amy Swartley, RN, Director of Admissions
Kathy Palladino, Director of Human Resources
Fox Subacute at Clara Burke in Plymouth Meeting, PA offers at-
tentive, nurturing management of ventilator dependent, medically compromised patients in the PA, NJ, DE, Tri-State area.
This sixty-bed facility, with its picturesque setting on 16 acres in
historic Plymouth Meeting, is ideal for the specialized services
and programs offered by Fox. With a team of highly motivated
professionals, we offer the discharge alternative to prolonged
lengths of stay in more costly acute care settings.

6963 Good Samaritan Health System
4th & Walnut Sts
P.O.Box 1281
Lebanon, PA 17042-1281   717-270-7500
                                       www.gshleb.org

Robin Weiler, Manager
Frederick Davis, VP Clinical Services
Offers services for the totally blind, legally blind, visually impaired, and more with health, counseling, educational, recreational, rehabilitation, computer training and professional
training services.

6964 Good Samaritan Hospital-Health System Center
Good Samaritan Hospital
4th & Walnut Sts
P.O.Box 1281
Lebanon, PA 17042-1281   717-270-7500
                                       www.gshleb.org

June Nafziger-Eberl, Manager
Stuart Hartman, Medical Director
Comprehensive inpatient rehab unit for adults regarding general
physical rehabilitation. Specific programs include orthopedic,
neurological, stroke, amputee, etc.

**6965 Pediatric Center at Plymouth Meeting Integrated Health
Services**
491 Allendale Rd
King of Prussia, PA 19406-1426   610-265-9290
                                        800-220-7337

Fran Currick, Manager
Subacute programs such as intensive respiratory care, stressing
ventilator dependent children, pre and post transplant care, total
parenteral nutrition, IV therapy, intensive/behavioral oral feeding programs. Provides extensive discharge planning including
teaching or review for all the above programs with an emphasis
on development and accessing community resources.

**6966 Penn State Milton S. Hershey Medical Center College Of
Medicine**
500 University Dr
Hershey, PA 17033-2360   717-531-8521
                                        800-243-1455
                                  FAX: 717-531-4558
                                  www.pennstatehershey.org

Harold L Paz, CEO
Alan L. Brechbill, Executive Director
Wayne Zolko, Associate Vice President for Finance and Business
a non-sectarian, not-for-profit community hospital whose purpose is to provide high quality acute, rehabilitative and preventive health services for the entire community, regardless of creed,
race, nationality, or ability to pay.

6967 Pennsylvania Pain Rehabilitation Center
Ste 2
252 W Swamp Rd
Doylestown, PA 18901-2465   215-230-9707
                                  FAX: 215-348-5106

Kenneth Lefkowitz, Manager
Post acute rehabilitation facility and programs.

**6968 Rehabilitation & Nursing Center at Greater Pittsburgh,
The**
890 Weatherwood Ln
Greensburg, PA 15601-5777   724-837-8076
                                  FAX: 724-837-7456

Nancy Flenner, Administrator
Marsha Echard, Admissions Coordinator
Subacute care, ventilator and pulmonary managment, compre-
hensive rehabilitation.

Rhode Island

6969 In-Sight
43 Jefferson Blvd
Warwick, RI 02888-6400   401-941-3322
                                  FAX: 401-941-3356
                               cbutler@in-sight.org
                                      in-sight.org

Chris Butler, Executive Director
Lucille Gaboriault, Director of Community Resources
Paul Hopkins, Director of First Impressions
Offers services for the totally blind, legally blind, visually impaired, and more with health, counseling, educational, recreational, rehabilitation, computer training and professional
training services.

6970   Vanderbilt Rehabilitation Center
Newport Hospital
167 Point Street
Providence, RI 02903   401-444-3500
                                              www.lifespan.org

Timothy J. Babineau, President/CEO
Kenneth E. Arnold, SVP, General Counsel
Carole M. Cotter, SVP, Chief Information Officer
The Vanderbilt Rehabilitation Center at Newport Hospital has
been providing comprehensive rehabilitation sercices for more
than 40 years and is known throughout the region for its unique
programs and high-quality, patient focused care.

South Carolina

6971   Association for the Blind
One Carriage Lane
Building A
Charleston, SC 29407   843-723-6915
                                         FAX: 843-577-4312
                                              www.abvisc.org

J. Douglas Hazelton, President
Capers A. Grimball, Vice President
Lea B. Kerrison, Secretary
Offers services for people who are blind, or are visually impaired
with health, counseling, educational, recreational, rehabilitation,
computer training and professional training services.

6972   Hitchcock Rehabilitation Center
690 Medical Park Dr
Aiken, SC 29801-6348   803-648-8344
                                              800-207-6924
                                         FAX: 803-648-1631

Karen Bowlen, Administrator
Dan Hillman, Case Manager
Carrie Morgan, Finance Director
Comprehensive outpatient rehabilitation for adults, children, ge-
riatrics, pediatric therapy, special needs preschool, sports medi-
cine, home health and hospice.

6973   Mentor Network, The
3600 Forest Drive
Suite 100
Columbia, SC 29204-1891   803-799-9025
                                              800-297-8043
                                         FAX: 803-931-8959
                                         thementornetwork.com

Edward Murphy, Executive Chairman
Bruce Nardella, President and CEO
Denis Holler, Chief Financial Officer
Mentor provides a full network of individually tailored services
for people with development disabilities and their families. Individuals may be served in their homes, shared living home, or in a
host home.

Tennessee

6974   Humana Hospital: Morristown RehabCare
726 McFarland St
Morristown, TN 37814-3989   423-522-6000
                                         www.lakewayregionalhospital.com
James Perry, Program Director
Designed to help patients in their adjustment to a physically limiting condition by helping to maximize each patient's abilities so
he or she can function as independently as possible.

6975   Opportunity East Rehabilitation Services for the Blind
758 W Morris Blvd
Morristown, TN 37813-2136   423-586-3922
                                              800-278-6274
                                         FAX: 423-586-1479
                                              volblind.org

Fred Overbay, CEO
Vic Mende, Director Rehabilitation Services
Offers services for the totally blind, legally blind, visually im-
paired, and more with health, counseling, educational, recre-

ational, rehabilitation, computer training and professional
training services.

6976   Patrick Rehab Wellness Center
Lincoln County Health System
106 Medical Center Blvd
Fayetteville, TN 37334-2684   931-433-0273
                                         FAX: 931-433-0378

Gloria Meadows, Administrator
Jim Stewart, Principal
Provides rehabilitation services of physical, occupational, and
speech therapy. Also, wellness memberships are available to the
public.

6977   PharmaThera
1785 Nonconnah Blvd
Memphis, TN 38132-2104   901-348-8100
                                              800-767-6714
                                         FAX: 901-348-8270
Offers 10 locations serving patients throughout the southern
United States, each with an in-house, expertly trained staff. All
locations use the latest technologies and techniques in infusion
care to provide a broad range of individualized home infusion
therapies.

6978   Siskin Hospital For Physical Rehabilitation
1 Siskin Plz
Chattanooga, TN 37403-1306   423-634-1200
                                         info@siskinrehab.org
                                              siskinrehab.org

Bob Main, CEO
Robert P. Main, President
Dedicated exclusively to physical rehabilitation and offers specialized treatment programs in brain injury, amputation, stroke,
spinal cord injury, orthopedics, and major multiple trauma. The
hospital also provides treatment for neurological disorders and
loss of muscle strength and controll following illness or surgery.

6979   St. Mary's RehabCare Center
900 E Oak Hill Ave
Knoxville, TN 37917-4556   865-545-7962
                                         FAX: 865-545-8133

Debbie Keeton, Director
Beth Greco, Executive Director
Provides comprehensive rehabilitation services for patients experiencing CVA, head trauma, orthopedic conditions, spinal cord
injury or neurological impairment.

Texas

6980   Alpine Ridge and Brandywood
444 Devereux Drive
Victoria, TX 19085-2666   361-575-8271
                                              800-345-1292
                                         FAX: 361-575-6520
                                              devereux.org

Robert Q. Kreider, President and CEO
Margaret McGill, SVP, Chief Operations Officer
Robert C. Dunne, SVP & Chief Financial Officer, Treasurer

6981   Amity Lodge
Devereux Foundation
444 Devereux Drive
Victoria, TX 19085-2666   361-575-8271
                                              800-345-1292
                                         FAX: 361-575-6520
                                              devereux.org

Robert Q. Kreider, President and CEO
Margaret McGill, SVP, Chief Operations Officer
Robert C. Dunne, SVP & Chief Financial Officer, Treasurer
Offers residents a continuum of services ranging from minimal
care and supervision to total physical and medical care.

6982 Baylor Institute for Rehabilitation
3500 Gaston Avenue
Dallas, TX 75246-2017   214-820-9300
                                         800-4BA-YLOR
                                    FAX: 214-841-2679
                                    www.baylorhealth.com

Joel T. Allison, Chief Executive Officer
Gary Brock, President and Chief Operating Officer
LaVone Arthur, Vice President of Business Development
A 92-bed specialty hospital offering comprehensive rehabilitation services for persons with spinal cord injury, traumatic brain injury, stroke, amputation, and other orthopedic and neurological disorders.

6983 Beneto Center
Devereux Foundation
444 Devereux Drive
Victoria, TX 19085-2666   361-575-8271
                                         800-345-1292
                                    FAX: 361-575-6520
                                         devereux.org

Robert Q. Kreider, President and CEO
Margaret McGill, SVP, Chief Operations Officer
Robert C. Dunne, SVP & Chief Financial Officer, Treasurer
Offers a continuum of services for residents requiring services ranging from minimal care and supervision to total physical and medical care.

6984 CORE Health Care
E&J Health Care
400 Highway 290
Bldg B, Suite. 205,
Dripping Springs, TX 78620   512-894-0801
                                         866-683-1007
                                    FAX: 512-858-4627

Eric Makowski, CEO
Kristi Jones, Marketing/Admissions Director
Erika Mountz, MBA, OTR/L, Director of Rehabilitation
Post acute and transitional rehabilitation, long-term care, community re-entry, for brain injury and complex psychiatric disorders.

6985 Center for Neuro Skills
1320 W Walnut Hill Ln
Irving, TX 75038-3007   972-580-8500
                                         800-544-5448
                                    FAX: 972-255-3162
                              srobinson@neuroskills.com
                                         neuroskills.com

John Schultz, Administrator
Mark J. Ashley, President
Centre for Neuro Skills (CNS) seeks to provide medical rehabilitation programs, lifecare programs, advocacy, and research for people with brain injury in order to achieve a maximum quality of life.

6986 Dallas Services
4242 Office Pkwy
Dallas, TX 75204-3629   214-828-9900
                                    FAX: 214-828-9901
                                    www.dallasservices.org

Thomas . Turnage, Ph.D, Executive Director
Clark Thomas, Ph.D., Chair
Melissa Malonson, Vice-Chair
Offers four programs: An early education for children(6weeks-6yrs)with and without special needs; low-vision clinic-provides low-cost eye exams and glasses to low-income families as well as assistance to individuals who vision problems which cannot be corrected with glasses/surgery; mesquite day school-an early head start program for infants and toddlers of low-income families; and special needs advocacy and inclusion program that offers families of special need children guidance and education.

6987 Daman Villa
Devereux Foundation
444 Devereux Drive
Victoria, TX 19085-2666   361-575-8271
                                         800-345-1292
                                    FAX: 361-575-6520
                                         devereux.org

Robert Q. Kreider, President and CEO
Margaret McGill, SVP, Chief Operations Officer
Robert C. Dunne, SVP & Chief Financial Officer, Treasurer
Offers residents a continuum of services ranging from minimal care and supervision to total physical and medical care.

6988 Devereux Advanced Behavioral Health - Texas Victoria Campus
Texas Victoria Campus
120 David Wade Dr.
P.O. Box 2666
Victoria, TX 77902   361-574-7208
                                         800-383-5000
                                    FAX: 361-575-6250
                                    www.devereuxtx.org

Pam Reed, Executive Director
Offering residential services for people of all ages with emotional, behavioral, developmental, and psychiatric disorders. Services include community based living and vocational programs, residential programs and foster care.

6989 Devereux Advanced Behavioral Health Texas - League City Campus
Texas League City Campus
1150 Devereux Dr
League City, TX 77573   281-335-1000
                                         800-373-0011
                                    FAX: 281-554-6290
                                    www.devereuxtx.org

Gail Atkinson, Vice President of Operations & Marketing
Offering long-term hospitalization and intensive residential services for adolescents and young adults with emotional, behavioral, developmental and psychiatric disorders.

6990 El Paso Lighthouse for the Blind
200 Washington St
El Paso, TX 79905-3897   915-532-4495
                                    FAX: 915-532-6338
                                    www.lighthouse-elpaso.com

Craig Hays, President
Lea Cochran, Vice President
Lola Dawkins, Secretary
Enables people of all ages to embody blindness and vision impairment through training, rehabilitation, employment opportunity, advocacy and research. Provides access to opportunities and quality of life so that the blind and visually impaired can reach their fullest potential for self-sufficiency and independence.

6991 Harris Methodist Fort Worth/Mabee Rehabilitation Center
612 E. Lamar Boulevard
Arlington, TX 76011-2122   877-847-9355
                                    FAX: 817-882-2753
                                    www.texashealth.org

Louise Baldwin, President
Peggyo Ehrlich, Rehab Manager
Karen Mallett, Executive Director
A hospital based inpatient rehab program and outpatient day programs in chronic pain management, work hardening and brain injury transitional services.

6992 HealthSouth Hospital of Cypress
13031 Wortham Center Dr
Houston, TX 77065   832-280-2500
                                    feedback@healthsouth.com
                                    healthsouthcypress.com

Jerome Lengel, Executive Officer
Dewitt Hilton, Owner
Offers an individualized approach to the process of rehabilitation for severely injured or disabled individuals. The process begins with a pre-admissions assessment of each referred patient. The Center combines state-of-the-art technology and equipment with

multi-disciplinary therapy and education in a cheerful, secure environment.

6993 Heights Hospital Rehab Unit
1917 Ashland St
Houston, TX 77008-3994 713-861-6161
FAX: 713-802-8660
www.selectmedical.com
Theresa Davis, CEO
Robert A. Ortenzio, Executive Chairman and Co-Founder
Rocco A. Ortenzio, Vice Chairman and Co-Founder
This program is designed to assist patients with physical disabilities achieve their maximum functional abilities.

6994 Hillcrest Baptist Medical Center
100 Hillcrest Medical Blvd
Waco, TX 76712 254-202-2000
FAX: 254-202-5105
www.sw.org
Anne Hott Kimberly, Program Director
Ann Gammel, Nurse Manager
Debbie Meurer, Manager
Designed to assist patients in adjustment to a physically limiting condition, utilizing interdisciplinary strategies to maximize each patient's ability and capability.

6995 Institute for Rehabilitation & Research
1333 Moursund St
Houston, TX 77030-3405 713-799-5000
800-447-3422
FAX: 713-797-5289
tirr.memorialhermann.org
Carl Josehart, CEO
Jean Herzog, President
Gerard E. Francisco, M.D., Chief Medical Officer
A national center for information, training, research, and technical assistance in independent living. The goal is to extend the body of knowledge in independent living and to improve the utilization of results of research programs and demonstration projects in this field. It has developed a variety of strategies for collecting, synthesizing, and disseminating information related to the field of independent living.

6996 Integrated Health Services of Amarillo
6141 Amarillo Blvd. West
Amarillo, TX 79106 806-356-0488
FAX: 806-356-8074
Mary Bearden, Chairman
Jay L. Barrett, President
Marvin Franz, Executive Director & CEO
Provides acute, post acute, residential and outpatient health care services. IHS of Amarillo is a 153-bed facility with 120 beds licensed by The Texas Department of Health and Human Services, and is accredited by JCAHO. We serve urban and rural populations of over 500,000, drawing from a 5-state region.

6997 Kanner Center
Devereax Foundation
444 Devereux Drive
Victoria, TX 19085-2666 361-575-8271
800-345-1292
FAX: 361-575-6520
devereux.org
Robert Q. Kreider, President and CEO
Margaret McGill, SVP, Chief Operations Officer
Robert C. Dunne, SVP & Chief Financial Officer, Treasurer
A private nonprofit nationwide network of treatment services for individuals of all ages with emotional and/or developmental disabilities.

6998 Lighthouse of Houston
3602 W Dallas St
Houston, TX 77019-1704 713-527-9561
FAX: 713-284-8451
custserv@houstonlighthouse.org
houstonlighthouse.org
Gibson DuTerroil, President
Shelagh Moran, VP/COO
Serves the blind, visually impaired, deaf-blind and multihandicapped blind. Provides workshops, vocational training and placement, low vision clinic, orientation and mobility,

housing, Braille, volunteer services, senior center, visual aid sales, counseling and support, diabetic education and day health activity services and day summer camp, Summer Transition for Youth.

6999 Mainland Center Hospital RehabCare Unit
6801 Emmett F Lowry Expy
Texas City, TX 77591-2500 409-938-5000
FAX: 409-938-5501
www.mainlandmedical.com
Michael Ehrat, CEO
The RehabCare program is designed and staffed to assist functionally impaired patients improve to their maximum potential. The opportunities for improvement and adjustments are provided in a pleasant, supportive inpatient environment by therapists from the occupational, physical, recreational and speech therapy disciplines.

7000 North Texas Rehabilitation Center
1005 Midwestern Pkwy
Wichita Falls, TX 76302-2211 940-322-0771
FAX: 940-766-4943
ntrehab.org
Mike Castles, President/ CEO
Provides outpatient rehabilitation services to maximize independence or promote development to children and adults with disabilities. Programs include: physical, occupational, speech therapy, closed head injury, infant/child development, support groups, aquatics and wellness program and a child achievement program.

7001 South Texas Lighthouse for the Blind
PO BOX 9697
Corpus Christi, TX 78469-3321 361-883-6553
888-255-8011
FAX: 361-883-1041
Customer.service@stlb.net
www.stlb.net
Regis Barber, President
Nicky Ooi, Chief Operations Officer
Alana Manrow, Public Affairs Director
Their mission is to Employ, Educate and Empower their neighbors who are blind and visually impaired. They offer job opportunities in manufacturing, retail and administration, as well as orientation and mobility and adaptive technology training.

7002 Texas Specialty Hospital at Dallas
7955 Harry Hines Blvd
Dallas, TX 75235-3305 214-637-0000
FAX: 214-637-6512
Mary.Alexander@fundltc.com
Mary Alexander, CEO
Cathy Campbell, Chief Executive Officer
66 beds offering active/acute rehabilitation, brain injury day treatment, cognitive rehabilitation, complex care, extended rehabilitation and short term evaluation.

7003 Transitional Learning Center at Gavelston and Lubbock
1528 Post Office St
Galveston, TX 77550 409-762-6661
FAX: 409-763-3930
www.tlcrehab.org
Brent Masel, MD, President and Medical Director
Gary Seale, Ph.D., VP Clinical Programs
Jim Lovelace, MBA, VP of Operations
Specializes solely in post-acute brain injury. A nationally known pioneer in the field and a not for profit with a three fold mission: treatment, research and education. Offers 6 hours of therapy a day from licensed/certified staff, on site physician and nursing services and long-term living for brian injured adults at Tideway on Gavelston Island. Accredited by CARF.
1982

7004 Treemont Nursing And Rehabilitation Center
5550 Harvest Hill Rd
Dallas, TX 75230-1684 972-661-1862
FAX: 972-788-1543
Bob Barker, Administrator
Postacute rehabilitation program.

7005 **West Texas Lighthouse for the Blind**
2001 Austin St
San Angelo, TX 76903-8796 325-653-4231
FAX: 325-657-9367
customerservice@lighthousefortheblind.org
www.lighthousefortheblind.org

David Wells, Executive Director
Stephen Horton, Operations Manager
Fonda V. Galindo, Finance & Human Resources Manager
Offers services for the totally blind, legally blind, visually impaired, and more with health, counseling, educational, recreational, rehabilitation, computer training and professional training services.

Utah

7006 **Quincy Rehabilitation Institute of Holy Cross Hospital**
1050 E South Temple
Salt Lake City, UT 84102-1507 801-350-8140
FAX: 801-350-4791

Dave Jenson, President
Postacute rehabilitation program.

7007 **Wasatch Vision Clinic**
849 E 400 S
Salt Lake City, UT 84102-2928 801-328-2020
FAX: 801-363-2201
email@wasatchvision.com
eyeappointment.com

Craig Cutler, Owner
Camron Bateman OD, Doctor
Postacute rehabilitation program.

Vermont

7008 **Rutland Mental Health Services**
78 S Main St
Rutland, VT 05701-4594 802-775-2381
FAX: 802-775-4020
rmhsccn.org

Dan Quinn, President/ CEO
Scott Dikeman, Vice Chairman
Ron Holm, Secretary
A private, non-profit comprehensive community mental health center. It provides services to individuals and families for mental health and substance abuse related problems and also to persons who are developmentally disabled.

Virginia

7009 **Bay Pine-Virginia Beach**
680 South Fourth Street
Louisville, KY 40202 502-596-7300
TTY:800-545-0749
web_administrator@kindred.com
kindredhealthcare.com

Paul J. Diaz, President/ CEO
Postacute rehabilitation program.

7010 **Carilion Rehabilitation: New River Valley**
2013 S Jefferson Street
Roanoke, VA 24014 540-981-7377
FAX: 540-981-8233
www.carilionclinic.org

Nancy Howell Agee, President/CEO
James A. Hartley, Chair
Briggs W. Andrews, Corporate Secretary
CARF-accredited pain management program, work hardening program and comprehensive outpatient therapy clinic, massage therapy, outpatient programs and more. Program emphasis is on interdisiplinary behavioral rehab based pain management and functional restoration in conjunction with medical treatment. Work hardening is a transdisciplinary work simulation program

taylored to the individual. Comprehensive outpatient program is multi-disciplinary with emphasis on manual treatment.

7011 **Faith Mission Home**
3540 Mission Home Ln
Free Union, VA 22940-1505 434-985-2294
FAX: 434-985-7633
www.beachyam.org

Paul Beiler, Manager
Reuben Yoder, Director
A Christian residential center that serves 60 developmentally disabled children, including individuals with Down Syndrome, Cerebral palsy and other similar conditions. Children may be admitted from the time they are ambulatory until they reach 15 years of age. He or she may stay as long as it is in the child's best interests. The training program stresses the following areas: self-care, social, academic, vocational, crafts, speech and physical development.

7012 **ManorCare Health Services-Arlington**
333 N. Summit St.
Toledo, OH 43604 800-366-1232
CareLine@hcr-manorcare.com
hcr-manorcare.com

Marcia K Jarrell, Administrator
Ric Birch, Marketing Director
ManorCare-Arlington offers residents a full Continuum of Care in a caring environment. ManorCare's wide range of services includes subacute medical and rehabilitation programs for short term patients transitioning from hospital to home and Skilled Nursing Care.

7013 **Pines Residential Treatment Center**
825 Crawford Pkwy
Portsmouth, VA 23704-2301 757-393-0061
FAX: 757-393-1029

Lenard J Lexier, Medical Director
Judy Kemp, Admissions Director
A 310-bed residential treatment center in Portsmouth Virginia, providing a therapeutic environment for severely emotionally disturbed children and youth. Five unique programs meet behavioral, educational and emotional needs of males and females, five to twenty-two years of age. Multi-disciplinary teams devise individual service plans to enhance strengths and reverse self-defeating behavior. A highly effective positive reinforcement program with a proven track record.

7014 **Roanoke Memorial Hospital**
Carilion Health System
2013 S Jefferson Street
Roanoke, VA 24014 540-981-7377
FAX: 540-981-8233
www.carilionclinic.org

Nancy Howell Agee, President/ CEO
James A. Hartley, Chair
Briggs W. Andrews, Corporate Secretary
Carilion Health System exists to improve the health of the communities it serves. The vision is to assure accessible, affordable, high quality healthcare that meets the needs of the community. Motivate and educate individuals to improve their health. Champion community initiatives to reduce health risk

7015 **Southside Virginia Training Center**
P.O.Box 4030
Petersburg, VA 23803-30 804-524-7000
FAX: 804-524-7228
www.svtc.dbhds.virginia.gov
Bob Kaufman, Director, Administrative Service
Offers residential, vocational, occupational, physical, and speech therapies.

7016 **Woodrow Wilson Rehabilitation Center**
P.O.Box 1500
Fishersville, VA 22939-1500 540-332-7000
800-345-9972
FAX: 540-332-7132
www.wwrc.net

Rick Sizemore, Executive Director
Amy Blalock, Admissions and Marketing Director
Comprehensive residential rehabilitation center offering complete medical and vocational rehabilitation services including:

vocation evaluation, vocational training, transition from school to work, occupational therapy, physical therapy, speech, language and audiology, assistive technology, rehabilitation engineering, counseling/case management, behavioral health services, nursing and physician services, etc.

Washington

7017   Arden Rehabilitation And Healthcare Center
680 South Fourth Street
Louisville, KY 40202
502-596-7300
TTY:800-545-0749
web_administrator@kindred.com
kindredhealthcare.com

Paul J. Diaz, President/ CEO
Arden can accomodate 90 residents- post-acute/rehabilitation patients as well as long term residents. Medicare certified, the center also takes most managed healthcare insurance plans, as well as VA, respite and hospice patients.

7018   Bellingham Care Center
680 South Fourth Street
Louisville, KY 40202
502-596-7300
TTY:800-545-0749
web_administrator@kindred.com
kindredhealthcare.com

Paul J. Diaz, President/ CEO
Postacute rehabilitation program.

7019   Division of Vocational Rehabilitation Department of Social and Health Services
P.O.Box 45130
Olympia, WA 98504-5130
360-704-3560
800-737-0617
FAX: 360-570-6941
krulik@dshs.wa.gov
www1.dshs.wa.gov/dvr

Patrick Raines, Manager
Lynnea Ruttledge, Manager
Information on computers, supported employment, marketing rehabilitation facilities and transition.

7020   First Hill Care Center
1334 Terry Ave
Seattle, WA 98101
206-682-2661
FAX: 206-624-0188
www.khseattlefirsthill.com
Postacute rehabilitation program.

7021   Harborview Medical Center, Low Vision Aid Clinic
Harborview Medical Center
325 9th Ave
Seattle, WA 98104-2499
206-744-3300
TTY:206-744-3246
comment@u.washington.edu
www.uwmedicine.org

Eileen Whalen, Executive director
J. Richard Goss, M.D., Medical director
Darcy Jaffe, Chief nursing officer and senior associate for patient care
Harborview Medical Center is the only designated Level 1 adult and pediatric trauma and burn center in the state of Washington and serves as the regional trauma and burn referral center for Alaska, Montana and Idaho. UW Medicine physicians and staff based at Harborview provide highly specialized services for vascular, orthopedics, neurosciences, ophthalmology, behavioral health, HIV/AIDS and complex critical care.

7022   Integrated Health Services of Seattle
820 NW 95th St
Seattle, WA 98117-2207
206-783-7649
FAX: 206-781-1448

Jerry Harvey, Administrator
Marlette Basada, Director Nursing
Flavia Lagrange, Director Admissions
Postacute rehabilitation program. IHS provides 24 hour subacute and long-term care. We can handle vent/trach/hemo andritoneal dialysis and provide a full scope of rehabilitation services.

7023   Lakeside Milam Recovery Centers (LMRC)
3315 S. 23rd Street
Ste 102
Tacoma, WA 98405
253-272-2242
800-231-4303
FAX: 253-272-0171
help@lakesidemilam.com
www.lakesidemilam.com

Michael Kinder, Administrator
LMRC was established in 1983 with a single mission, to help victims and families recover from the pain of drug/alcohol addiction. Enlightned by the work of Dr. James Milam in the 1960's and 70's, the founders of LMRC created a treatment system based on a bedrock set of principals.

7024   Lakewood Health Care Center
11411 Bridgeport Way SW
Lakewood, WA 98499-3047
253-581-9002
800-359-7412
FAX: 253-581-7016
www.lakewoodhc.com

Gwynn Rucker, Executive Director
Patty Wood, Administrator
Linda Doll, Social Services
Accomodates 80 residents. We offer 24 hour skilled nursing services, long-term care and rehab services which include Physical, Occupational and Speech Therapy.

7025   Manor Care Health Services-Tacoma
5601 S Orchard St
Tacoma, WA 98409-1371
253-474-8421
FAX: 253-471-8857
www.hcr-manorcare.com

Tina Irwin, Administrator
124-bed skilled nursing and rehabilitation center provides services for those seeking long term Skilled Nursing Care, short term subacute care, hospice services, Alzheimer's and respite care. Our Acadia Wing, a specialized Alzheimer's care unit, provides specialized programming and trained staff that truly makes us the leader in Alzheimers Services.

7026   ManorCare Health Services-Lynnwood
3701 188th St SW
Lynnwood, WA 98037-7626
425-775-9222
FAX: 425-712-3685
www.hcr-manorcare.com

Liza Loyet, Administrator
Our in-house therapists provide physical, occupational and speech therapies in our state-of-the-art therapy gym. Our team is goal oriented and focuses on producing positive outcomes for those recovering from illness, injury or surgery.

7027   ManorCare Health Services-Spokane
6025 N Assembly St
Spokane, WA 99205-7674
509-326-8282
FAX: 509-326-4790
www.hcrmanorcare.com

Cheri Kubu, Administrator
Sandra Hayes, Administrator
Provides skilled nursing and respite stays for those needing a break from care giving. We specialize in Rehabilitation Services provided by our in-house occupational, physical and speech therapists.

7028   Northwest Continuum Care Center
Kindred Health Care
128 Old Beacon Hill Dr
Longview, WA 98632-5859
360-423-4060
FAX: 360-636-0958

Steve M. Ross, Executive Director
Tami Wilson, Director of Nursing
Mary R., Activities Assistant
Accomodates 69 residents. Employs the Angel Care Program designed to address any special needs that may arise during a resident's stay in our facility. The program focuses extra attention on residents and, in some cases, family members. The goal is to meet the special needs of the people we provide care to every day.

7029 Park Manor Convalescent Center
1710 Plaza Way
Walla Walla, WA 99362-4362   509-529-4218
                                   FAX: 509-522-1729
                                   egines@ensigngroup.net
                                   www.parkmanorcare.com

Jed Gines, Administrator
Krista Maiuri, Directr Of Nursing
Sonya Taylor, Director of Rehabilitation
Residents of Park Manor enjoy a range of activities, developed to meet their needs, including excercise programs, social and recreational activities, arts and crafts, shopping trips and other excursions. We also offer religious services.

7030 Queen Anne Health Care
Queen Anne Health Care
2717 Dexter Ave N
Seattle, WA 98109-1914   206-284-7012
                                FAX: 206-283-3936
                                www.queenannehealthcare.com

Heather Eacker, Executive Director
Mary R., Activities Assistant
Kristen W., Health and Rehabilitation Center
Our goal is to provide quality, compassionate care. Our cozy building accomodates 120 residents. We offer semi private rooms with space to add items from home for a special personalized touch

7031 Rainier Vista Care Center
920 12th Ave SE
Puyallup, WA 98372-4920   253-841-3422
                                 FAX: 253-848-3937

Linda Larson, Administrator
Nancy L. Erckenbrack, Executive Director
Kristen W., Health and Rehabilitation Center
Accomodates 120 residents. We are certified for Medicare and Medicaid and we offer a continuum of healthcare services from short-term or outpatient rehabilitation to long-term care. We offer semi-private and private rooms as well as rehabilitation and hospice suites. Rainier Vista Care Center is a recipient of the American Health Care Association Quality Award.

7032 Rehabilitation Enterprises of Washington
430 E Lauridsen Blvd
Port Angeles, WA 98362-7978   360-452-9789
                                     FAX: 360-452-9700

Brett White, President
REW is the professional trade association representing community rehabilitation programs before government and other publics. These organizations provide a wide array of employment and training services for people with disabilities. The goal is to assist member organizations to provide the highest quality rehabilitative and employment services to their customers.

7033 Seattle Medical and Rehabilitation Center
Evergreen Healthcare
12040 NE 128th St
Kirkland, WA 98034-3013   425-899-3000
                                 877-601-2271
                                 TTY:425-899-2007
                                 evergreenhealthcare.org

Al DeYoung, Chair
Robert H. Malte, Chief Executive Officer
Neil Johnson, RN, MSA, Senior Vice President & Chief Operating Officer
103 beds offering subacute rehabilitation, complex care, subacute treatment and short-term evaluation. Pulmonary unit offering long and short term care for ventilator dependent patients.

7034 Slingerland Institute for Literacy
Educators Publishing Service
12729 Northup Way
Suite 1
Bellevue, WA 98005   425-453-1190
                            FAX: 425-635-7762
                            mail@slingerland.org
                            www.slingerland.org

Bonnie Meyer, Executive Director
Elyce Newton, Program Support
A nonprofit public corporation founded in 1977 to carry on the work of Beth H. Slingerland in providing classroom teachers with the techniques, knowledge and understanding necessary for identifying and teaching children with Specific Language Disability. The main objective is to educate teachers in successful methods of identifying, diagnosing and instructing children and adults with SLD and to promote literacy through reading, writing and oral expression.

7035 Timberland Opportunities Association
400 W Curtis St
Aberdeen, WA 98520-7698   360-533-5823
                                 FAX: 360-533-5848

Jim Eddy, Executive Director
Provides training and employment for disabled people.

7036 Vancouver Health and Rehabilitation Center
400 E 33rd St
Vancouver, WA 98663-2238   360-696-2561
                                  FAX: 360-696-9275
                                  www.vancouverhealthcare.com

Jody Wigen, Human Resources
Joe Joy, Executive Director
Kristen W., Health and Rehabilitation Center
Postacute rehabilitation program.

Wisconsin

7037 Colonial Manor Medical And Rehabilitation Center
1010 E Wausau Ave
Wausau, WI 54403-3101   715-842-2028
                               FAX: 715-848-0510
                               www.colonialmanormrc.com

Ericca Ylitalo, Administrator
Shelley Solberg, Executive Director
Colonial Manor Medical and Rehabilitation Center is part of the Kindred Community and is located in Wausau, Wisconsin. The corporate headquarters are based in Louisville Kentucky. Our facility accomodates 150 residents.

7038 Waushers Industries
210 E Chicago Rd
Wautoma, WI 54982-6932   920-787-4696
                                FAX: 920-787-4698

Richard King, Human Resources
Provides various programming for individuals with disabilities in waushara county.

7039 Woodstock Health and Rehabilitation Center
3415 Sheridan Rd
Kenosha, WI 53140-1924   262-657-6175
                                FAX: 262-657-5756

Debra Lamb, Administrator
Darlene Einerson, Executive Director
Kristen W., Health and Rehabilitation Center
Offers a full range of medical services to meet the individual needs of our residents, including short term rehabilitative services and long-tern skilled care.

Rehabilitation Facilities, Sub-Acute

Alabama

7040 UAB Spain Rehabilitation Center
1717 6th Ave S
Birmingham, AL 35233-7330   205-934-3450
www.uab.edu/medicine/physicalmedicine/
Tracy L Brewer, Administrative Manager
A 49-bed rehabilitation hospital featuring advanced, individualized care for adolescents and adult patients recovering from a broad variety of health problems. Patient care teams include physiatrists (doctors who specialized in rehabilitation medicine), nurses, nurse practitioners, physical therapists, occupational therapists, speech/language pathologists, psychologists, social workers, rehabilitation professionals and other health care professionals from all areas of the UAB Health System.

Alaska

7041 Fairbanks Memorial Hospital & Denali Center
1650 Cowles St
Fairbanks, AK 99701-5998   907-452-8181
FAX: 907-458-5324
www.fmhdc.com
Sheldon Stadnyk, MD, Interim Chief Executive Officer
The Denali Center offers the following rehabilitation services: Physical Therapy, Occupational Therapy, Speech Therapy, Sub-Acute Rehab.

Arizona

7042 Desert Life Rehabilitation & Care Center
Kindred Healthcare
1919 W Medical St
Tucson, AZ 85704-1133   520-297-8311
FAX: 520-544-0930
Amad Nazifi, Executive Director
Jane Olmstead, Director of Nursing
Accomodates 240 residents. We provide skilled and intermediate nursing with occupational, physical, speech and respiratory therapy services. We offer special programs including an Alzheimer's Unit and a Young Adult Program, and are located in beautiful Southern Arizona where there is plenty of sunshine, mountains and desert views. Desert Life is a 2005 recipient of the American Health Care Association Quality Award.

7043 Hacienda Rehabilitation and Care Center
660 S Coronado Dr
Sierra Vista, AZ 85635-3386   520-459-4900
FAX: 520-458-4082
www.haciendarcc.com
Monica Vandivort, Medical Director
Kristen W., Health and Rehabilitation Center Executive Director
Becky D., Activity Director
Accomodates 100 residents. We are located in Sierra Vista, near Kartchner Caverns, Fort Huachuca, Coronado National Forest and historic Tombstone. Serving the medical needs of the community since 1983, we strive to provide care with quality, compassion and integrity.

7044 Kachina Point Health Care & Rehabilitation Center
505 Jacks Canyon Rd
Sedona, AZ 86351-7856   928-284-1000
FAX: 928-284-0626
Michael Amadei, Medical Director
Accomodates 120 residents. We have met the healthcare needs of the community since 1984. Kachina Point is a 2004 recipient of the American Health Care Association's Quality Award.

7045 Mayo Clinic Scottsdale
13400 E Shea Blvd
Scottsdale, AZ 85259-5499   480-301-8000
800-446-2279
FAX: 480-301-9310
www.mayoclinic.org/arizona
Neena S. Abraham, Gastroenterology/ Hepatology
Roberta H. Adams, Hematology/Oncology
Charles H. Adler, Parkinson's Disease and Movement Disorders Center
Mayo clinic is a not-for-profit medical practice dedicated to the diagnosis and treatment of virtually every type of complex illness. Mayo clinic staff members work together to meet your needs. You will see as many doctors, specialists, and other health care professionals as needed to provide comprehensive diagnosis, understandable answers and effective treatment.

7046 Sonoran Rehabilitation and Care Center
Kindred
4202 N 20th Ave
Phoenix, AZ 85015-5101   602-264-3824
FAX: 602-279-6234
Jeffrey Barrett, Executive Director
Offers the following rehabilitation services: Respiratory Therapy, Physical Therapy, Speech Therapy, Occupational Therapy, Restorative Therapy, Sub-Acute Rehabilitation, Wound Care.

7047 Valley Health Care and Rehabilitation Center
Kindred Health Care Center
5545 E Lee St
Tucson, AZ 85712-4205   520-296-2306
FAX: 520-296-4072
Dale Pelton, Executive Director
Sandra Lewis, Administrator
Offers the following rehabilitation services: Physical Therapy, Occupational Therapy, Speech Therapy, Sub-Acute Rehab.

California

7048 Alamitos-Belmont Rehab Hospital
3901 E 4th St
Long Beach, CA 90814-1699   562-434-8421
FAX: 562-433-6732
www.alamitosbelmont.com
John L. Sorensen, Chairman of the Board of Directors.
Jonathan Sloey, Administrator
Offers the following rehabilitation services: Speech Therapy, Occupational Therapy, Physical Therapy, Sub-Acute Rehab.

7049 Bay View Nursing and Rehabilitation Center
Kindred Health Care
516 Willow St
Alameda, CA 94501-6132   510-521-5600
FAX: 510-865-9035
www.kindredhealthcare.com
Richard S Espinoza, Administrator
Say Silva, Assistant Executive Director
Accomodates 180 residents. Bay View is a 2004 recipient of the American Health Care Association's Quality Award. We provide short-term rehabilitative care, traditional long-term skilled care and Alzheimer's/dementia special care. Our combination of clinical skill and comprehensive rehabilitation services enables us to care for a variety of complex medical conditions.

7050 Foothill Nursing and Rehab Center
401 W Ada Ave
Glendora, CA 91741-4241   626-335-9810
FAX: 626-963-0720
www.foothillnursing.com
Arnie Shafer, Executive Director
Marianne Schultz, Administrator
Offers the following rehabilitation services: Physical Therapy, Occupational Therapy, Speech Therapy, In and Out Patient Rehab.

7051 Long Beach Memorial Medical Center Memorial Rehabilitation Hospital
2801 Atlantic Ave
Ground Floor
Long Beach, CA 90806-1701   562-933-9001
FAX: 562-933-9019
www.memorialcare.org/long_beach
Barry Arbuckle, President/CEO
The goal of the MemorialCare Rehabilitation Institute is to help persons with disabilities regain independence and rebuild their lives in an environment where loved ones are involved in the rehabilitation process. We are dedicated to the pursuit of our mission, vision and values.

7052 Mercy Medical Center Mt. Shasta
914 Pine St
Mount Shasta, CA 96067-2143   530-926-6111
FAX: 530-926-0517
www.mercymtshasta.org
Greg Lippert, Senior Director of Support and Information Services
Scott Foster, Director of Hospital Finance
Sister Anne Chester, Director of Mission Integration
Mercy Medical Center is committed to furthering the healing ministry of Jesus, and to provide high-quality, affordable healthcare to the communities we serve.

7053 Northridge Hospital Medical Center
18300 Roscoe Blvd
Northridge, CA 91328-4167   818-885-8500
www.northridgehospital.org
Michael Wall, CEO
Offers the following rehabilitation services: Physical Therapy, Occupational Therapy, Speech Therapy, Sub-Acute Rehab. As a member of the Catholic Heathcare West Northridge Hospital Medical Center is committed to serving the health needs of our communities with particular attention to the needs of the poor, the disadvantaged and vulnerable, and the comfort of the suffering and dying.

7054 Riverside Community Hospital
4445 Magnolia Ave
Riverside, CA 92501   951-788-3000
FAX: 630-792-5636
complaint@jointcommission.org
www.riversidecommunityhospital.com
Jaime Wesolowski, President/CEO
Patrick Brilliant, CEO
At Riverside Community Hospital, we are able to provide the healthcare services that you and your family will need through the many stages of your life. Services like Emergency/Trauma, Labor and Delivery, Cardiac Care, Orthopedics and Transplant are among our many Centers of Excellence.

7055 Saint Jude Medical Center
101 E Valencia Mesa Dr
Fullerton, CA 92835-3809   714-871-3280
800-870-7537
FAX: 714-992-3029
www.stjudemedicalcenter.org
April De Cou, Wellness Educator
Jane Wang, Wellness Programs Supervisor
Offers the following rehabilitation services: Out-patient Rehab, Sub-Acute Rehab, Occupational Therapy, Physical Therapy, Speech and Audiology Therapy, Pain Management Program.

7056 South Coast Medical Center
12 Mason
Suite A
Irvine, CA 92618-2733   714-669-4446
FAX: 714-669-4448
info@southcoastmedcenter.com
www.mission4health.com
Leigh Erin Connealy, Manager
Bruce Christian, President
Offers the following services: physical therapy, occupational therapy, speech therapy, cardica rehabilitation, incontinence program, sub-acute rehabilitation.

7057 Valley Garden Health Care and Rehabilitation Center
1517 Knickerbocker Dr
Stockton, CA 95210-3119   209-957-4539
FAX: 209-957-5831
www.valleygardenshealth.com
Dr. Alexande Chan, Medical Director
Accomodates 120 residents. Our center provides short-term nursing and rehabilitative care as well as traditional long-term skilled care. Our combination of clinical skill and comprehensive rehabilitation services enables us to care for a variety of complex medical conditions. Rehabilitative therapies are provided as needed by physical, occupational and speech therapists.

Colorado

7058 Boulder Community Hospital Mapleton Center
1100 Balsam
PO Box 9019
Boulder, CO 80301-9019   303-440-2273
info@bch.org
www.bch.org
Lou DellaCava, Chairman
Ric Porreca, Vice Chairman
Jean Dubofsky, Secretary
159-bed acute care hospital and 24-hour emergency department.

7059 Fairacres Manor
1700 18th Ave
Greeley, CO 80631-5152   970-353-3370
FAX: 970-353-9347
Kathy Gardner, Admissions/Marketing Director
Marla Trujillo, Director of Nursing
Ben Gonzales, Admissions/Marketing Assistant Director
Offers the following rehabilitation services: Physical Therapy, Occupational Therapy, Speech Therapy, Restorative Therapy, Skilled Nursing, and Sub-Acute Rehabilitation.

7060 Rowan Community
4601 E Asbury Cir
Denver, CO 80222-4722   303-757-1228
FAX: 303-759-3390
Tammy Gleisner, Director/Admissions/Marketing Director
Jeff Jerebker, President/CEO
Bruce Odenthal, VP Operations
Rowan is a 70-bed community, small enough to support personal relationships between residents and caregivers. Our residents vary in age, reflecting the diversity of a much larger community. Rowan's focus is on a psycho-social model of care with a dynamic activities and social service program. Our staff is specially trained in behavior management and many are certified Eden AlternativeT associates and certifid Elder Care Specialists.

Connecticut

7061 Hamilton Rehabilitation and Healthcare Center
89 Viets St
New London, CT 6320-3355   860-447-1471
FAX: 860-439-0107
Steve Roizen, Executive Director
Offers the following rehabilitation services: Sub-Acute, Occupational Therapy, Speech Therapy, Physical Therapy.

7062 Hospital For Special Care (HSC)
2150 Corbin Ave
New Britain, CT 06053-2298   860-223-2761
FAX: 860-827-4849
www.hfsc.org
John J. Votto, President/CEO
Paul J. Scalise, M.D., F.C.C.P, Senior Vice President
HSC is a private, not-for-profit 200-bed rehabilitation long-term acute and chronic care hospital, widely-known and respected for its expertise in physical rehabilitation, respiratory care, and medically-complex pediatrics. Special programs for spinal cord injuries, pulmonary rehabilitation, acquired brain injuries, stroke, ventilator management and geriatrics, make HSC an important regional resource for patients with special healthcare needs.

7063   Masonic Healthcare Center
MasoniCare Corporation
22 Masonic Ave
PO Box 70
Wallingford, CT 06492-3048

203-679-5900
877-424-3537
FAX: 203-679-6459
info@masonicare.org
www.masonicare.org

Stephen B. McPherson, President
Arthur Santilli, President
The states leading provider of healthcare and retirement living
communities for seniors. We are not-for-profit and have more
then 100 years of experience behind us. We're recognized for the
quality, compassionate care and steadfast support we provide to
our residents and patients.

7064   Stamford Hospital
30 Shelburne Rd
Stamford, CT 06904-3628

203-276-1000
FAX: 203-325-7905
info@stamhealth.org
www.stamfordhospital.org

Brian Grissler, President/CEO
Kathleen Silard, EVP/Chief Operating Officer
Kevin Gage, Senior Vice President, Finance/Chief Financial Officer
A not-for-profit, community teaching hospital that has been serving Stamford and surrounding communities for more than 100
years. We have 305 inpatient beds in medicine, surgery, obstet-
rics/gynecology, psychiatry, and medical and surgical critical
care units and maintain an educational partnership with Columbia University College of Physicians and Surgeons for its teaching program in the internal medicine, family practice,
obstetrics/gynecology and surgery

7065   Windsor Rehabilitation and Healthcare Center
581 Poquonock Ave
Windsor, CT 06095-2202

860-688-7211
FAX: 860-688-6715
www.windsorrehab.com

Jeffrey Robbins, Medical Director
Accomodates 116 residents. We offer private and semi-private
rooms with access to private telephones and cable television. Our
goal is to be a comprehensive, leading care center viewed by our
community as an excellent resource for patients, families, and
professionals.

Delaware

7066   Arbors at New Castle
32 Buena Vista Dr
New Castle, DE 19720-4660

302-328-2580
FAX: 302-326-4132
www.extendicareus.com/newcastle

Annette Moore, Administrator
A subacute and rehabilitation center offering skilled medical services, infusion therapies, cardiac recovery services, renal disease
services, cancer services and digestive disease services. Skilled
rehabilitation services include physical therapy, occupational
therapy and speech therapy. Also provides case management and
discharge planning, general nursing and restorative care and
respite care.

Florida

7067   Avon Oaks Skilled Care Nursing Facility
37800 French Creek Rd
Avon, OH 44011-1763

440-934-5204
800-589-5204
jreidy@avonoaks.net
www.avonoaks.net

Natalie McIntyre, Human Resources Director
Stephanie Auvil, RN, BC, Director of Nursing
Joan Reidy, Administrator

Oaks at Avon provides a full range of skilled nursing services including infusion therapy, enteral therapy, wound care, tracheotomy care, and portable diagnostics.

7068   Boca Raton Rehabilitation Center
755 Meadows Rd
Boca Raton, FL 33486-2384

561-391-5200
FAX: 561-391-0685

Stanley Mucinic, Administrator
Tracey Dougherty, Administrator
Offers the following rehabilitation services: Occupational Ther-
apy, Speech Therapy, Physical Therapy, Sub-Acute
Rehabilitation

7069   Cape Coral Hospital
636 Del Prado Blvd
Cape Coral, FL 33990

239-424-2000
FAX: 239-574-1935
www.leememorial.org

Richard Akin, Chairman
Sanford Cohen, MD, Vice Chairman
Marilyn Stout, Treasurer
A 291-bed acute care facility, Cape Coral Hospital features all
private rooms. The hospital currently is undergoing a complete
renovation, expansion and modernization of the Weigner-Taeni
Center for Emergency Services, which will make the emergency
department the largest in Lee County.

7070   Evergreen Woods Health and Rehabilitation Center
7045 Evergreen Woods Trl
Spring Hill, FL 34608-1306

352-596-8371
FAX: 352-596-8032

Janet Hanciles, Administrator
Offers the following rehabilitation services: Sub-Acute rehabilitation, Occupational therapy, Speech pathology therapy, Physical
therapy.

7071   Healthcare and Rehabilitation Center of Sanford
950 Mellonville Avenue
Sanford, FL 32771-2237

407-322-8566
FAX: 407-322-0121
www.healthcareandrehabofsanford.com

Dr. S. Joshi, Medical Director
Kate Hilgar, Administrator
Vicky Smith, Director Admissions
We provide post-acute services, rehabilitative services, skilled
nursing, short and long term care through Physical, Occupational, and Speech Therapists; Registered and Licensed Practical
Nurses; and Certified Nursing Assistants. This is complemented
by Social Services, Activities, Nutritional Services, Housekeeping and Laundry Services. With over 224 years of combined experience, our staff of professionals is here to meet the needs of each
and every patient and resident.

7072   Highland Pines Rehabilitation Center
1111 S Highland Ave
Clearwater, FL 33756-4432

727-446-0581
FAX: 727-442-9425

Paula Anthony, Administrator
Offers the following rehabilitation services: Sub-Acute rehabili-
tation, Occupational Therapy, Speech Therapy, Physical
Therapy.

7073   Jupiter Medical Center-Pavilion
1210 S Old Dixie Hwy
Jupiter, FL 33458-7205

561-747-2234
FAX: 561-744-4467
JCouris@jupitermed.com
www.jupitermed.com

John D. Couris, President/Chief Executive Officer
Dale Hocking, Vice President, Finance/Chief Financial Officer
*Mike Fehr, Vice President, Information Services/Chief Information
Offic*
Offers the following rehabilitation services: Sub-Acute Rehabil-
itation, Occupational Therapy, Speech Therapy, Physical
Therapy.

7074 North Broward Medical Center
201 E Sample Rd
Deerfield Beach, FL 33064-4441   954-941-8300
                                        FAX: 954-941-4233
                                        www.browardhealth.org
Pauline Grant, CEO
Douglas Ford, Chief of Staff
Offers the following rehabilitation services: Sub-Acute rehabilitation, Physical Therapy, Occupational Therapy, Speech Therapy, Respiratory Therapy.

7075 Pompano Rehabilitation and Nursing Center
Senior Health Care Management
51 W Sample Rd
Pompano Beach, FL 33064-3542   954-942-5530
                                      FAX: 954-942-0941
Jeff Nusbusn, Administrator
Offers the following rehabilitation services: Sub-Acute Rehabilitation, Physical Therapy, Occupational Therapy, Speech Therapy

7076 Rehabilitation Center of Palm Beach
300 Royal Palm Way
Palm Beach, FL 33480-4385   561-655-7266
                                   FAX: 561-655-3269
                                   info@rcca.org
                                   www.rcca.org
Ellen O'Bannon, Manager
Pamela Henderson, Executive Director
Our mission is to improve the physical function, communication & independence of people with disabilities.

7077 Rehabilitation and Healthcare Center of Tampa
4411 N Habana Ave
Tampa, FL 33614-7211   813-872-2771
                              FAX: 813-871-2831
Dr. Gustavo Barrazuetta, Medical Director
We provide post-acute services, rehabilitative services, skilled nursing, short and long term care through Physical, Occupational, and Speech Therapists; Registered and Licensed Practical Nurses; and Certified Nursing Assistants. This is complemented by Social Services, Activities, Nutritional Services, Housekeeping and Laundry Services. With over 60 years of combined experience, our staff of professionals is here to meet the needs of each and every patient and resident.

7078 Shands Rehab Hospital
4101 NW 89th Blvd
Gainesville, FL 32606-3813   352-265-8938
                                    FAX: 352-265-5420
                                    www.ufhealth.org/shands-rehab-hospital
Tim Goldfarb,M.S., Chief Executive Officer
David S. Guzick, M.D., Ph.D., Senior Vice President
Ed . Jimenez, M.B.A, Senior Vice President/Chief Operating Officer
UF Health Shands Rehab Hospital is a 40-bed acute rehab hospital for patients who have suffered strokes, traumatic brain and spinal cord injuries, amputations, burns or major joint replacements.

7079 St. Anthony's Hospital
1200 7th Ave N
St Petersburg, FL 33705-1388   727-825-1100
                                      www.stanthonys.com
William Ulbricht, President
Ron Colaguori, VP Operations
James McClintic, M.D., Vice President, Medical Affairs
We offer outstanding diagnostic and treatment options of all types of cancer. Our Susan Sheppard McGillicuddy Breast Center is unmatched in the community in diagnostic services and helping patients navigate their treatment options should they find a cancer diagnosis.

7080 Winkler Court
3250 Winkler Avenue Ext
Fort Myers, FL 33916-9414   239-939-4993
                                   FAX: 239-939-1743
                                   www.winklercourt.com
Michael Collier, Medical Director
Michael Stens, Medical Director
We provide post-acute services, rehabilitative services, skilled nursing, short and long term care through Physical, Occupa-

tional, and Speech Therapists; Registered and Licensed Practical Nurses; and Certified Nursing Assistants. This is complemented by Social Services, Activities, Nutritional Services, Housekeeping and Laundry Services. With over 100 years of combined experience, our staff of professionals is here to meet the needs of each and every patient and resident.

7081 Winter Park Memorial Hospital
Florida Hospital
200 N Lakemont Ave
Winter Park, FL 32792-3273   407-646-7000
                                    FAX: 407-646-7639
                                    healthcare@winterparkhospital.com
                                    www.winterparkhospital.com
Ken Bradley, CEO
Nestled among the oak-shaded, brick-paved streets of one of the most picturesque hometowns in the country, Winter Park Memorial Hospital has continuously served the residents of Winter Park and its surrounding communities for more than 50 years.

Georgia

7082 Athena Rehab of Clayton
2055 Rex Rd
Lake City, GA 30260-3944   404-361-5144
                                  FAX: 404-363-6366
Reginald Washington, Administrator
Offers the following rehabilitation services: Sub-Acute rehabilitation, Occupational therapy, Speech therapy, Physical therapy, Restorative care.

7083 Lafayette Nursing and Rehabilitation Center
110 Brandywine Blvd
Fayetteville, GA 30214-1500   770-461-2928
                                     FAX: 770-461-8507
                                     www.lafayetterehab.com
Wendy Goza, Medical Director
Lafayette Nursing and Rehab Center accomodates 179 residents. We are Medicare certified and our center also features a 25-bed postacute rehab unit and a 24-bed dementia unit. We have RN's LPN's and CNA's 24 hours a day. We also have physician services availiable seven days a week.

7084 Savannah Rehabilitation and Nursing Center
815 E 63rd St
Savannah, GA 31405-4499   912-352-8615
                                 FAX: 912-355-4642
Sandra Casper, Executive Director
At our facility, we provide quality care with modern rehabilitation and restorative nursing techniques. We aim to provide an atmosphere which encourages family involvement in the care-planning process, with the right mix of activities addressing the social, spiritual and intellectual needs of our residents.

7085 Specialty Hospital
PO Box 1566
Rome, GA 30162-1566   706-509-4100
                             FAX: 706-509-4159
A 34-bed acute long-term care hospital located in Rome, Georgia, designed for those patients who require treatment for extended periods of time. The patients of The Specialty Hospital are those who do not need the medical resources of a general hospital but whose conditions are too severe for a lower level of care. Patients are admitted to TSH through physician and case manager referrals.

7086 Walton Rehabilitation Health System
523 13th St.
Augusta, GA 30901-1037   706-823-8505
                                866-492-5866
                                FAX: 706-724-5752
Dennis Skelley, President/CEO
Has Centers of Excellence in Stroke Brain Injury, Complex Orthopedics, Spinal Cord Injury and Pain Management. 58-bed nonprofit facility.

7087 Warner Robins Rehabilitation and Nursing Center
1601 Elberta Rd
Warner Robins, GA 31093-1393   478-922-2241
                                         FAX: 478-328-1984
                            www.warnerrobinsrehabilitation.com
Laura Fergason, Administrator
Offers the following rehabilitation services: Sub-Acute rehabilitation, Physical Therapy, Occupational Therapy, Speech Therapy.

Hawaii

7088 Aloha Nursing and Rehab Center
45-545 Kamehameha Hwy
Kaneohe, HI 96744-1943   808-247-2220
                                         FAX: 808-235-3676
                                      info@alohanursing.com
                                          alohanursing.com
Charles Harris, Executive Director
Amy Lee, Administrator
Our unique nursing care facility is nestled in the picturesque town of Kaneohe, Oahu, amid the towering Koolau Mountains and the panoramic vistas of Kaneohe Bay. In this tranquil setting, our 141-bed facility offers both long and short term care to residents who meet intermediate or skilled level of care criteria.

Idaho

7089 Boise Health And Rehabilitation Center
1001 S Hilton St
Boise, ID 83705-1925   208-345-4464
                                         FAX: 208-345-2998
Jason Ludwig, Medical Director
Aaron Moorhouse, Medical Director
Debbie Mills, Executive Director
Offers the following rehabilitation services: Sub-acute rehabilitation, occupational therapy, speech therapy, physical therapy.

7090 Eastern Idaho Regional Medical Center
3100 Channing Way
Idaho Falls, ID 83404-7533   208-529-6111
                                         FAX: 208-529-7021
                                          www.eirmc.com
Cindy Smith-Putnam, Executive Director of Business Development, Marketing & Comm
Lou Fatkin, Executive Director of Risk Management, Physician Relations,
Matt Campbell, Director of Human Resources
The largest medical facility in the region, Eastern Idaho Regional Medical Center (EIRMC) is a modern, JCAHO-accredidted, full-service hospital. EIRMC serves as the region's healthcare hub, offering specialty services including open-heart surgery, leading-edge cancer treatment, trauma, neurosurgery, intensive care for adults and infants, and a helicopeter service.

7091 Kindred Transitional Care and Rehabilitation
3315 8th St
Lewiston, ID 83501-4966   208-743-9543
                                         FAX: 208-746-8662
                                      www.lewistonrehab.com
Debbie Freeze, Administrator
Lewiston Rehabilitation and Care Center has years of experience providing diversified healthcare services. We have our own staff of physical, occupational and speech therapists. Our therapy gym and rehab kitchen are a lovely atmosphere in which to work toward your therapy goals. We are an Eden Alternative Certified facility.

7092 Mountain Valley Care and Rehabilitation Center
601 West Cameron Avenue
PO Box 689
Kellogg, ID 83837- 2004   208-784-1283
                                         FAX: 208-784-0151
                                    www.mountainvalleycare.com
Maryruth Butler, Executive Director

Mountain Valley Care and Rehabilitation Center accomodates 68 residents. We are conveniently located in the heart of Kellogg Idaho. We strive to offer quality care and superior customer service in a home-like environment. Upon admission, you or your loved one is looked after by an assigned staff member. We call this our 'Angel Care' program. Our rehabilitation program focuses on meething the individual needs of the resident so you or your loved one can see how they are going to progress.

7093 River's Edge Rehabilitation and Healthcare
Kindred Healthcare
714 N Butte Ave
Emmett, ID 83617-2799   208-365-4425
                                         FAX: 208-365-6989
                                     GDecker@ensigngroup.net
                                     www.riversedgerehab.com
Janis Shields, Executive Director
Steve Balle, MPT, Director of Rehabilitation
Margaret Williams RN, BSN, Director of Nursing
Emmett Rehab & healthcare accomodates 95 residents. We are located in Emmett, Idaho, a rural community located an easy 30 minute drive from Boise. Emmett Rehab &'healthcare has served the area for more then 40 years by providing healthcare for residents of Gem County.

Illinois

7094 Chevy Chase Nursing and Rehabilitation Center
3400 S Indiana Ave
Chicago, IL 60616-3841   312-842-5000
                                         FAX: 312-842-3790
Tony Prather, Administrator
Our approach to care is multidisciplinary; our medical staff members work together as a team in a proactive fashion, challenging residents each and every day, in order to motivate them to rehabilitate and achieve their ultimate potential.

7095 Glenview Terrace Nursing Center
1511 Greenwood Rd
Glenview, IL 60026-1513   847-729-9090
                                         FAX: 847-729-9135
                                      www.glenviewterrace.com
Ian Crook, Administrator
We're best known as the industry leader in post-hospital rehabilitation, including orthopedic rehabilitation and stroke recovery. Our highly effective rehabilitation services feature one-on-one physical, occupational, speech and respiratory therapies up to seven days a week.

7096 Halsted Terrace Nursing Center
10935 S Halsted St
Chicago, IL 60628-3189   773-928-2000
                                         FAX: 773-928-9154
Ted O'Brien, Administrator
Offers the following rehabilitation services: Sub-acute rehabilitation, physical therapy, occupational therapy, speech therapy, cardiac rehabilitation.

7097 Harmony Nursing and Rehabilitation Center
3919 W Foster Ave
Chicago, IL 60625-6056   773-588-9500
                                         FAX: 773-588-9533
                                      www.harmonychicago.com
John Sianghio, Administrator
Offers a friendly healthcare experience. You'll find compassionate experts who provide short-term rehabilitation and therapy, wound care, Alzheimer's and memory loss care, long-term nursing care and more.

7098 Imperial
1366 W Fullerton Ave
Chicago, IL 60614-2199   773-248-9300
                                         FAX: 773-935-0036
                                     www.imperialpavilion.com
David Hartman, Administrator
Mary Bangayan, M.D., Pulmonary Care Programme
Sanjay Gill, M.D., Cardiac Management Program
We offer a comprehensive approach to post acute care. One that takes into consideration our guests' unique needs, and utilizes a

7099 Jackson Square Nursing and Rehabilitation Center
5130 W Jackson Blvd
Chicago, IL 60644-4332   773-921-8000
                                      FAX: 773-287-9302
                                      www.jacksonsquarecare.com

Rick Walworth, Administrator
At Jackson Square, there is one primary goal: to help guests regain maximum independence and functioning so that they can safely, comfortably, and happily get their life back. Our physicians, therapists, and nurses use their experience, compassion, and skill-combined with the latest and best technology-to provide comprehensive rehabilitation for a wide range of physical disabilities and medical conditions.

7100 Renaissance at 87th Street
2940 W 87th St
Chicago, IL 60652-3832   773-434-8787
                                      FAX: 773-434-8717
                                      www.renaissanceat87.com

Juli Foy, Administrator
At Renaissance at 87th, there is one primary goal: to help guests regain maximum independence and functioning so that they can safely, comfortably, and happily get their life back. Our physicians, therapists, and nurses use their experience, compassion, and skill-combined with the latest and best technology-to provide comprehensive rehabilitation for a wide range of physical disabilities and medical conditions.

7101 Renaissance at Hillside
4600 N. Frontage Rd.
Hillside, IL 60162-1761   708-544-9933
                                      FAX: 708-544-9966
                                      www.ariapostacute.com

John Stare, Administrator
Utilizing a progressive healthcare model that takes into account each patient's individual needs, Aria Post Acute Care designs a personalized rehabilitation program offering guests the best chance at the fullest possible recovery.

7102 Renaissance at Midway
4437 S Cicero Ave
Chicago, IL 60632-4333   773-884-0484
                                      FAX: 773-884-0485
                                      www.renaissanceatmidway.com

Jeff Baker, Executive Director
At Renaissance at Midway, there is one primary goal: to help guests regain maximum independence and functioning so that they can safely, comfortably, and happily get their life back. Our physicians, therapists, and nurses use their experience, compassion, and skill-combined with the latest and best technology-to provide comprehensive rehabilitation for a wide range of physical disabilities and medical conditions.

7103 Renaissance at South Shore
2425 E 71st St
Chicago, IL 60649-2612   773-721-5000
                                      FAX: 773-721-6850
                                      www.rensouthshore.com

Dave Schechter, Administrator
The Renaissance at South Shore is a 248 bed skilled nursing facility with multiple services that include short-term rehabilitation, specialized dementia care and long-term care and hospice care. Our highly trained nursing professionals provide loving care in a home-like atmosphere.

7104 Schwab Rehabilitation Hospital
Mt. Sinai
1401 S California Ave
Chicago, IL 60608-1858   773-522-2010
                                      www.schwabrehab.org

Suzan Rayner, Medical Director
Lisa Thornton, Medical Staff President
Alan Channing, President/ Chief Executive Officer
Schwab Rehabilitation Hospital is a freestanding, not-for-profit, 102-bed rehabilitation hospital located on Chicago's west side. It offers a therapeutic environment of comprehensive inpatient and outpatient rehabilitation, both for adults and children.

Indiana

7105 Angel River Health and Rehabilitation
5233 Rosebud Ln
Newburgh, IN 47630-9283   812-473-4761
                                      FAX: 812-473-5190

Kay Congleton, Executive Director
Our wide array of services enables our patients and residents to receive the medical care they need, the restorative therapy they require, and the support they and their families deserve. We serve many types of patient and resident needs - from short-term rehabilitation to traditional long-term care. Our resident council meets regularly to ensure that our residents' needs are being met to their satisfaction.

7106 Chalet Village Health and Rehabilitation Center
Magnolia Health Systems
1065 Parkway St
Berne, IN 46711-2366   260-589-2127
                                      FAX: 260-589-3521
                                      www.chalet-village.net

Vicki Shepherd, Administrator
We provide dedicated, community-centered healthcare which was founded in Indiana, operates in Indiana, for people who live in Indiana.

7107 Columbus Health and Rehabilitation Center
2100 Midway St
Columbus, IN 47201-3722   812-372-8447
                                      FAX: 812-375-5117
                                      www.columbushrc.com

Sherry Harrison, Executive Director
William Lustig, Medical Director
Accomodates 235 residents. We offer a continuum of healthcare services. Our center also provides a Special Care Alzheimer's Unit. We are licensed by the Stat of Indiana and are Medicare and Medicaid approved provider. We are proud to offer a friendly home-like atmosphere while providing comprehensive healthcare services. These services include short-term medical and rehabilitation treatment, which is designed to address the individual needs of our residents and patients.

7108 Harrison Health and Rehabilitation Centre
150 Beechmont Drive
Corydon, IN 47112-1717   812-738-0550
                                      FAX: 812-738-6273
                                      www.harrisonrehab.com

Sheila Bieker, Executive Director
Bruce Burton, Medical Director
We serve many types of patient and resident needs - from short-term rehabilitation to traditional long-term care. Working with your physician, our staff - including medical specialists, nurses, nutritionists, therapists, dietians and social workers - establishes a comprehensive treatment plan intended to restore you or your loved one to the fullest practicable potential.

7109 Indian Creek Health and Rehabilitation Center
240 Beechmont Dr
Corydon, IN 47112-1718   812-738-8127
                                      877-380-7211
                                      FAX: 812-738-2917
                                      www.indiancreekhrc.com

Bonnie Fallin, Executive Director
Bruce Burton, Medical Director
140 bed facility offering the following rehabilitation services: Sub-Acute rehabilitation, Physical therapy, Occupational Therapy, Speech Therapy, pain management, Wound rehabilitation. Short and long term skilled nursing care certified for Medicare, Medicaid, Private Pay and Private Insurance. Hospice and respite care rated #1 in clinical care in southern Indiana district for 2002.

7110 Meadowvale Health and Rehabilitation Center
Kindred Health Care
1529 Lancaster St
Bluffton, IN 46714-1507   260-824-4320
                                      800-743-3333
                                      FAX: 260-824-4689

Todd Beaulieu, Executive Director
Yadagiri Jonna, Medical Director

Working with your physician, our staff - including medical specialists, nurses, nutritionists, therapists, dietitians and social workers - establishes a comprehensive treatment plan intended to restore you or your loved one to the fullest practicable potential.

7111 Muncie Health Care and Rehabilitation
680 South Fourth Street
Louisville, KY 40202
502-596-7300
800-545-0749
web_administrator@kindred.com
www.kindredhealthcare.com

Dee Harrold, Executive Director
Dr. Jeffery Hiltz, Medical Director
Offers the following rehabilitation services: Sub-Acute rehabilitation, physical therapy, occupational therapy, speech therapy.

7112 Rehabilitation Hospital of Indiana
4141 Shore Dr
Indianapolis, IN 46254-2607
317-329-2000
FAX: 317-329-2104
www.rhin.com

Ian Worden, MHA, MBA, CPA, RHI Board Chair
James G. Terwilliger, MPH, Vice Chair/Secretary
Kyle Netter, MBA, PT, Executive Director of Corporate and Affiliate Relations
We approach every patient understanding that every diagnosis, every illness, and every injury are different. It's the collective effort of trained and compassionate team members who value the quality of life of every patient and their caregivers. It's the right kind of treatment- inpatient, outpatient, and follow-up services-provided under the same roof. It's one step closer to home. It's a continuum of care

7113 Sellersburg Health and Rehabilitation Centre
7823 Old State Road 60
Sellersburg, IN 47172-1858
812-246-4272
FAX: 812-246-8160
www.sellersburgrehab.com

Dave Powell, Administrator
Chris Hansen, Executive Director
Sellersburg is a modern healthcare center conveniently located on the edge of the community. Our center accomodates 110 residents and includes a rehabilitative program with a goal of returning residents home as quickly as possible. Sellersburg is a 2006 recipient of the American Health Care Association Quality Award.

7114 Westpark Rehabilitation Center
1316 N Tibbs Ave
Indianapolis, IN 46222-3024
317-634-8330
FAX: 317-263-9442
www.westparkhealthcare.com

Dave Mc Carroll, Owner
Offers the following rehabilitation services: Sub-acute rehabilitation, occupational therapy, physical therapy, speech therapy, respiratory therapy.

7115 Westview Nursing and Rehabilitation Center
1510 Clinic Dr
Bedford, IN 47421-3530
812-279-4494
FAX: 812-275-8313
www.ascseniorcare.com/westview-nursing—rehab
Sholin Montgomery, Executive Director
Mike Spencer, Executive Director
Offers the following rehabilitation services: Sub-acute rehabilitation, physical therapy, occupational therapy, speech therapy.

7116 Windsor Estates Health and Rehab Center
429 W Lincoln Rd
Kokomo, IN 46902-3508
765-453-5600
FAX: 765-455-0110
www.kindredkokomo.com

Brenda Alfrey, Administrator
Monica Martin, Executive Director
Our wide array of services enables our patients and residents to receive the medical care they need, the restorative therapy they require, and the support they and their families deserve. We serve many types of patient and resident needs - from short-term rehabilitation to traditional long-term care.

Iowa

7117 Madison County Rehab Services
Madison County Hospital
300 W Hutchings St
Winterset, IA 50273-2109
515-462-2373
FAX: 515-462-4492

Marcia Harris, CEO
Panndee Stebbins, Director
Offers the following rehabilitation services: Sub-acute rehabilitation, occupational therapy, physical therapy, speech therapy, home health rehab, wellness programs.

7118 Mercy Subacute Care
603 E 12th St
Des Moines, IA 50309-5515
515-247-4400
FAX: 515-643-0945

Bonnie Mc Coy, Manager
Pam Nelson, Intake Coordinator
Offers the following rehabilitation services: Sub-acute rehabilitation, physical therapy, speech therapy, occupational therapy.

Kentucky

7119 Danville Centre for Health and Rehabilitation
642 N 3rd St
Danville, KY 40422-1125
859-236-3972
FAX: 859-236-0703
www.danvillecentre.com

Debbie Gibson, Executive Director
We offer short-term rehabilitative care as well as long-term care. Our emphasis is on service excellence - providing quality care in a home-like environment to allow for independence and to enable our patients and residents to receive the medical care they need, the restorative therapy they require, and the support they and their families deserve.

7120 Fountain Circle Health & Rehabilitation
Kindred Healthcare
200 Glenway Rd
Winchester, KY 40391
859-744-1800
FAX: 859-744-0285

William Whited, Executive Director
Kathryn Jones, Medical Director
Offers the following rehabilitation services: Sub-acute rehabilitation, speech therapy, physical therapy, occupational therapy.

7121 Lexington Center for Health and Rehabilitation
353 Waller Ave
Lexington, KY 40504-2974
859-252-3558
FAX: 859-233-0192

Karole Ward, Administrator
Offers the following rehabilitation services: Sub-acute rehabilitation, speech therapy, occupational therapy, physical therapy.

7122 Paducah Centre For Health and Rehabilitation
Wellsouth Health Systems
501 N 3rd St
Paducah, KY 42001-0749
270-444-9661
FAX: 270-443-9407

Jean Glisson, RN, Director of Nursing
Elizabeth Kay Chilton, Admissions Director
Tracy Summers, Rehab/Specialty Program Director
Paducah Center is an 86-bed skilled and long-term care facility with a 28-bed Alzheimer's secure unit. This unit has a private courtyard and structured activities throughout the day, and is the only true Alzheimer's secure unit in the area.

7123 Pathways Brain Injury Program
4200 Browns Ln
Louisville, KY 40220-1523
502-459-8900
FAX: 502-459-5026
www.hcr-manorcare.com

Pam Pearson, Manager
Offers the following rehabilitation services: Sub-acute rehabilitation, speech therapy, occupational therapy, physical therapy, recreational therapy.

Louisiana

7124 Guest House of Slidell Sub-Acute and Rehab Center
1051 Robert Blvd
Slidell, LA 70458-2011
985-643-5630
800-303-9872
FAX: 985-649-6065

Brandy Wheat, Administrator
116 bed healthcare center offering the following subacute services within the skilled nursing setting: physical, occupational, and speech therapies, infusion therapy, respiratory care, wound care, neurological rehabilitation, cardiac reconditioning, pain management, post surgical recovery, orthopedic rehabilitation.

7125 Irving Place Rehabilitation and Nursing Center
1736 Irving Pl
Shreveport, LA 71101-4606
318-631-9121
FAX: 318-222-2095

Webster Johnson, Administrator
Offers the following rehabilitation services: sub-acute rehabilitation, speech therapy, occupational therapy, physical therapy

Maine

7126 Augusta Rehabilitation Center
188 Eastern Ave
Augusta, ME 04330-5928
207-622-3121
800-457-1220
FAX: 207-623-7666
www.augustarehabcenter.com

Malcolm Dean, Executive Director
Cathleen O'Connor
From intensive short term rehabilitation therapy to longer-term restorative care, our Nursing and Rehabilitation Centers provide a full range of nursing care and social services to treat and support each of our patients and residents. Our clinical capabilities allow us to accept patients with greater medical complexity than a traditional nursing home. This is increasingly important as many patients require transitional care before they are ready to return home.

7127 Brentwood Rehabilitation and Nursing Center
370 Portland St
Yarmouth, ME 04096-8101
207-846-9021
800-457-1220
FAX: 207-846-1497

Malcolm Dean, Executive Director
Daniel M. Pierce, Medical Director
Brentwood accomodates 82 residents. We are located at 370 Portland Street in Yarmouth, Maine. We strive to meet the healthcare needs of the greater Yarmouth community, including Portland and Brunswick, which are located within 10 miles of the center. In addition to Brentwood's rehabilitation and skilled nursing services, we also offer Alzheimer's specialty care in a comfortable setting.

7128 Den-Mar Rehabilitation and Nursing Center
44 South St
Rockport, MA 01966-1800
978-546-6311
800-439-2370
FAX: 978-546-9185

Christine Marek, Executive Director
Den-Mar nursing and Rehab center accomodates 80 residents. We provide skilled nursing and rehabilitation services as well as long term care. We are certified for Medicare and Medicaid as well as many insurance carriers. We offer semi-private and private rooms, with many common areas for socializing.

7129 Eastside Rehabilitation and Living Center
516 Mount Hope Ave
Bangor, ME 04401-4215
207-947-6131
800-457-1220
FAX: 207-942-0884
www.eastsiderehab.com

Ryan Kelley, Executive Director
From intensive short term rehabilitation therapy to longer-term restorative care, our Nursing and Rehabilitation Centers provide a full range of nursing care and social services to treat and support each of our patients and residents. Our clinical capabilities allow us to accept patients with greater medical complexity than a traditional nursing home. This is increasingly important as many patients require transitional care before they are ready to return home.

7130 Kennebunk Nursing & Rehabilitation Center
158 Ross Rd
Kennebunk, ME 04043-6532
207-985-7141
800-457-1220
FAX: 207-985-0961

Stephen Alaimo, Executive Director
We treat a variety of conditions and provide an array of services including, but not limited to:Respiratory conditions such as pneumonia and post-acute COPD episodes Cardiac conditions and post surgical care (grafts, valves, stints) Wound Stroke Orthopedic Neurological illnesses Diabetes

7131 Norway Rehabilitation and Living Center
29 Marion Ave
Norway, ME 04268-5601
207-743-7075
800-457-1220
FAX: 207-743-9269

Carolyn Farley, Administrator
Norway Rehabilitation and Living Center has been a fixture in the Norway community since 1976. We are a 70-bed facility offering short-term rehabilitation, skilled nursing services, long term care and residential care services. Utilizing an interdisciplinary team led by a physician and consisting of qualified health care specialists, we develop individualized plans of care for each patient that are designed to restore maximum health and optimize functional abilities and independence

7132 Shore Village Rehabilitation & Nursing Center
201 Camden St
\, ME 04841-2534
207-596-6423
800-457-1220
FAX: 207-596-7235

Phyllis Nickerson, Administrator
Shore Village accomodates 60 residents and is located in the mid-coast region of the state of Maine. We have a cozy size and a primary goal for the staff is to ensure a home-like atmosphere for all the residents. Shore Village provides skilled nursing and rehabilitation, respite care, and long term care. The facility is dually certified for Medicare and Medicaid and accepts many commercial insurance plans.

Maryland

7133 Greater Baltimore Medical Center
6701 N Charles St
Baltimore, MD 21204-6881
443-849-2000
FAX: 443-849-3024
TTY:800-735-2258
www.gbmc.org

John B. Chessare, M.D., President/Chief Executive Officer
Eric L. Melchior, Executive Vice President/Chief Financial Officer
Keith Poisson, Executive Vice President/Chief Operating Officer
The 281-bed medical center (acute and sub-acute care) is located on a beautiful suburban campus and handles more than 26,700 inpatient cases and approximately 60,000 emergency room visits annually.

Massachusetts

7134 Bolton Manor Nursing Home
400 Bolton St
Marlborough, MA 01752-3912
508-481-6123
800-439-2370
FAX: 508-481-6130

Michele Ricard, Medical Director
Thomas Sullivan, Executive Director
Bolton Manor accomodates 157 residents. We are located in Marlboro, Massachusetts. We provide medical management and long-term care through comprehensive skilled and post-acute

nursing services. We also provide physical, occupational, and speech therapy services from an onsite dedicated staff of therapists. The facility is Joint Commission (formerly JCAHO) accredited and has an excellent survey history with the State Department of Public Health.

7135 Brigham Manor Nursing and Rehabilitation Center
77 High St
Newburyport, MA 01950-3071

978-462-4221
800-439-2370
FAX: 978-463-3297

Stephen Cynewski, Executive Director
Brigham Manor accomodates 64 residents. We are a Medicare-certified facility offering private, semi-private and multi-bed suites. Our bright, formal dining room, with French doors that open to a shaded courtyard, provides a warm atmosphere for entertaining family and friends. Each resident's personal tastes and medical needs are considered in the planning of our weekly menus.

7136 Country Gardens Skilled Nursing and Rehabilitation Center
2045 Grand Army Hwy
Swansea, MA 02777-3932

508-379-9700
800-439-2370
FAX: 508-379-0723

Sandy Sarza, Executive Director
Country Gardens Skilled Nursing and Rehabilitation Center accomodates 86 residents. We are located in a beautiful rural setting conveniently located about 15 minutes east of Providence and 10 minutes west of Fall River. We have provided healthcare service to the greater Swansea area for over 34 years.

7137 Country Manor Rehabilitation and Nursing Center
180 Low St
Newburyport, MA 01950-3519

978-465-5361
800-439-2370
FAX: 978-463-9366
www.countryrehab.com

Stephen Doyle, Executive Director
Country Rehabilitation and Nursing Center accomodates 123 residents. We are located in the quaint seaport town of Newburyport, Massachusetts. We provide medical management and long-term care through comprehensive skilled and intermediate nursing services. We also provide physical, occupational, and speech therapy services from an onsite dedicated staff of therapists. The center offers an Alzheimer's special care unit with staff trained in dimentia care and dementia specific programs.

7138 Franklin Skilled Nursing and Rehabilitation Center
130 Chestnut St
Franklin, MA 02038-3903

508-528-4600
800-439-2370
FAX: 508-528-7976

Paula Topijan, Executive Director
We treat a variety of conditions and provide an array of services including, but not limited to :Respiratory conditions such as pneumonia and post-acute COPD episodes,Cardiac conditions and post surgical care (grafts, valves, stints),Wound,Stroke,Orthopedic,Neurological illnesses,Diabetes

7139 Great Barrington Rehabilitation and Nursing Center
148 Maple Ave
Great Barrington, MA 01230-1906

413-528-3320
800-439-2370
FAX: 413-528-2302
www.greatbarringtonrnc.com

William Kittler, Executive Director
Andrew Potler, Medical Director
Great Barrington Rehabilitation and Nursing Center accomodates 106 residents. As part of a national network of long-term healthcare centers, we have the expertise and resources to provide care appropriate to the individual needs of each and every one of our residents. We provide personal care with minimal daily living assistance to the most skilled treatment for medically complex patients.

7140 Ledgewood Rehabilitation and Skilled Nursing Center
87 Herrick St
Beverly, MA 01915-2773

978-921-1392
800-439-2370
FAX: 978-927-8627
www.ledgewoodrehab.com

Frank Silvia, Executive Director
Ledgewood Rehabilitation and Skilled Nursing Center is a unique provider of healthcare services. We are part of a continuum of services that includes acute care services at Beverly Hospital, subacute care at Ledgewood, and care after discharge through Northeast Homecare. We believe this partnership offers the highest quality post-acute services north of Boston.

7141 Leo P La Chance Center for Rehabilitation and Nursing
59 Eastwood Cir
Gardner, MA 01440-3901

978-632-8776
FAX: 978-632-5048

Mark Alinger, Administrator
Leo P. LaChance, Founder
A privately owned facility, combines the best of medical technology with the ultimate in healing, compassionate rehabilitation and nursing care. Our goal is to help each client reach that ultimate goal of living life to the fullest.

7142 Oakwood Rehabilitation and Nursing Center
11 Pontiac Ave
Webster, MA 01570-1629

508-943-3889
800-439-2370
FAX: 508-949-6125
www.oakwoodrehab.com

Thomas Sullivan, Executive Director
Oakwood Rehabilitation and Nursing Center accomodates 81 residents. We offer 24-hour skilled nursing, inpatient rehabilitation, respite care, and hospice services. Our center has been successfully serving the greater Webster, Massachusetts, community for 35 years. We have a dedicated and caring staff and our common goal is to promote recovery and enhance quality of live whether your needs are short or long term.

7143 Walden Rehabilitation and Nursing Center
785 Main St
Concord, MA 01742-3310

978-369-6889
800-439-2370
FAX: 978-369-8392

Ladan Azarm, Executive Director
Walden Rehabilitation and Nursing Center accomodates 123 residents. We are located in the quaint town of Concord, Massachusetts, across the street from Emerson Hospital and a short drive from the town center. Walden provides medical management and long-term care through comprehensive skilled and intermediate nursing services. We also provide physical, occupational, and speech therapy services from an onsite dedicated staff of therapists.

Michigan

7144 Boulder Park Terrace
14676 W Upright St
Charlevoix, MI 49720-1201

231-547-1005
FAX: 231-547-1039

Reezie DeVet, President/CEO
Mary-Anne Ponti, COO
A partnership formed with Charlevoix Area Hospital, Boulder Park Terrace is a long-term care facility and Sub-acute Rehabilitation Center located in Chalrevoix near the shores of Lake Michigan. The Sub-acute Rehabilitation Center was created as a transition between an acute care hospital and home. Patients enter into the program to increase their strength, endurance and over-all functioning before returning home.

Minnesota

7145 Park Health And Rehabilitation Center
4415 W 36 1/2 St
St Louis Park, MN 55416-4890
952-927-9717
FAX: 952-927-7687
www.extendicare.com

Jennifer Kuhn, Administrator
Park Health & Rehabilitation Center is a leading provider of long-term skilled nursing care and short-term rehabilitation solutions. Our 93 bed facility offers a full continuum of services and care focused around each individual in today's ever-changing healthcare environment.

Missouri

7146 Barnes-Jewish Hospital Washington University Medical Center
1 Barnes Jewish Hospital Plz
Saint Louis, MO 63110-1003
314-747-3000
866-867-3627
FAX: 314-362-8877
www.barnesjewish.org

Richard Liekweg, President
John Beatty, Vice President of Human Resources
John Lynch, MD, Chief Medical Officer
Barnes-Jewish Hospital at Washington University Medical Center is the largest hospital in Missouri and the largest private employer in the St. Louis region. An affiliated teaching hospital of Washington University School of Medicine, Barnes-Jewish Hospital has a 1,700 member medical staff with many who are recognized in the 'Best Doctors in America.'

Montana

7147 Parkview Acres Care and Rehabilitation Center
200 N Oregon St
Dillon, MT 59725-3624
406-683-5105
866-253-4090
FAX: 406-683-6388

Claire Miller, Executive Director
We are Medicare and Medicaid certified skilled nursing facility which accomodates 108 residents serving scenic Dillon and surrounding Montana communities.

Nebraska

7148 Homestead Healthcare and Rehabilitation Center
4735 S 54th St
Lincoln, NE 68516-1335
402-488-0977
800-833-0920
FAX: 402-488-4507
www.homesteadrehab.com

Matt Romshek, Executive Director
Gay Bate, RN, Director of Nursing
James Murray, Administrator
Homestead Healthcare and Rehabilitation Center is one of the area's oldest providers of skilled nursing and rehabilitation services. We are a 163-bed skilled nursing and rehabilitation center nestled in a lovely, quiet established neighborhood in South Lincoln.

7149 Madonna Rehabilitation Hospital
5401 South St
Lincoln, NE 68506-2150
402-413-3000
800-676-5448
FAX: 402-486-5448
info@madonna.org
www.madonna.org

Marsha Lommel, CEO
Tom Stalder, VP Medical Affairs

Madonna provides intensive rehabilitation and expertise for a wide variety of conditions, such as: orthopedic injuries, work injuries, arthritis, amputation, neuromuscular diseases, cardiac conditions, pulmonary disease and conditions including those dependent upon a ventilator, cancer, lymphedema, osteoporosis, wounds, renal disorders, burns, fibromyalgia, multiple sclerosis, parkinson's disease and degenerative diseases.

7150 Mary Lanning Memorial Hospital
715 N Saint Joseph Ave
Hastings, NE 68901-4497
402-463-4521
866-460-5884
tanderson@mlmh.org
www.mlmh.org

Beth Schlichtman, Compensation/Benefit Services - Director
Lisa Brandt, Public Relations & Marketing Services - Director
Carrie Edwards, Home Care Services - Director
Mary Lanning Healthcare is in its 95th year of providing quality healthcare for residents of the central Nebraska area. We continue to grow and expand, working to provide patient-centered care in a positive environment, while implementing some of the newest technologies available.

Nevada

7151 Las Vegas Healthcare and Rehabilitation Center
2832 S Maryland Pkwy
Las Vegas, NV 89109-1502
702-735-5848
800-326-6888
FAX: 702-735-6218
www.lasvegaskindred.com

Randall Fuller, Executive Director
Las Vegas Healthcare accomodates 79 residents. We have been serving the community for approximately 40 years. Located in close proximity to local hospitals and surrounded by medical complexes, our center offers both short-term rehabilitation and long-term care.

New Hampshire

7152 Dover Rehabilitation and Living Center
307 Plaza Dr
Dover, NH 03820-2455
603-742-2676
800-735-2964
FAX: 603-749-5375
www.doverrehab.com

Daniel Estee, Executive Director
Dover Rehab is a provider of postacute services in the greater New Hampshire Seacost area. We accomodate 112 residents and are licensed by the state of New Hampshire. We employ nearly 150 licensed nurses, therapists and other healthcare professionals, who strive to provide quality care. The goal of our patient service model is to bridge the gap between hospitalization and home so that recovery and physical functioning are maximized and hospital readmission is minimized.

7153 Northeast Rehabilitation Clinic
70 Butler St
Salem, NH 03079-3925
603-893-2900
800-825-7292
FAX: 603-893-1638
TTY: 800-439-2370
www.northeastrehab.com

John Prochilo, CEO/Administrator
Subacute rehabilitation at NRH was designed for people who have experienced an acutely disabling orthopedic, medical, or neurologic condition but who either do not require or are unable to participate in a full acute inpatient program. Impairment groups pertinent to this level of care include brain injury, spinal cord injury (traumatic/non-traumatic), stroke, orthopedic injury, amputation, and neurologic disorder.

New Jersey

7154 Atlantic Coast Rehabilitation & Healthcare Center
485 River Ave
Lakewood, NJ 08701-4720
732-364-7100
FAX: 732-364-2442
abby@atlanticcoastrehab.com
www.atlanticcoastrehab.com

Simon Shain, Administrator
Sharon Sckbower, Director of Nursing
Atlantic Coast is family owned and operated. It's a warm, friendly place where caregivers and patients know each other by first name. But it's also an innovative and energetic place, where the most advanced therapies and cutting edge techniques are offered. It's a comprehensive health care center that provides three distinct areas of care:Rehabilitative Therapy & Sub Acute Care, Long Term Care ,Alzheimer's/Memory Impaired Care.

7155 Crestwood Nursing & Rehabilitation Center
101 Whippany Rd
Whippany, NJ 7981-1407
973-887-0311
FAX: 973-887-8355

Carol Shepard, Administrator
Sub-acute rehabilitation facility.

7156 Lakeview Subacute Care Center
130 Terhune Dr
Wayne, NJ 7470-7104
973-839-4500
87 -UBA-UTE
FAX: 973-839-2729
www.lakeviewsubacute.com

Richard Grosso, Jr, Director
Sue Ahlers, Director of Admission
Kerry Iamurri, Director of Rehab
Our comprehensive medical, nursing and rehabilitation services cater to a diverse patient population. In addition to long-term care, we offer exceptional inpatient subacute programs. We're proud to report that our average length of stay for subacute patients is a brief 14 days.

7157 Merwick Rehabilitation and Sub-Acute Care
79 Bayard Ln
Princeton, NJ 8540-3045
609-497-3000
FAX: 609-497-3024

Ryan Wismer, Administrator
76-bed skilled nursing and residential center as well as a separate 17-bed comprehensive rehabilitation center. Offers rehabilitation, physiatry, occupational therapy, respite care, speech/hearing therapy, sub-acute care.

7158 Seacrest Village Nursing Center
1001 Center St
Little Egg Harbor Twp, NJ 8087-1364
609-296-9292
FAX: 609-296-0508
info@seacrestvillagenj.com
seacrestvillagenj.com

Brian T Holloway, Administrator
Seacrest Village Nursing and Rehabilitation Center has specialized in quality rehabilitation, transitional and restorative care for more then a decade and is a perfect alternative for bridging the gap between hospital and home.

7159 St. Lawrence Rehabilitation Center
2381 Lawrenceville Rd
Lawrenceville, NJ 08648-2098
609-896-9500
FAX: 609-895-0242
epiechota@slrc.org
www.slrc.org

Kevin McGuigan, MD, Medical Director
Robyn F. Agri, MD, Doctor
Dr. Madhu Jain, Doctor
St. Lawrence Rehabilitation Center, a non-profit facility sponsored by the Roman Catholic Diocese of Trenton, is committed to maximizing the quality of human life by providing comprehensive physical rehabilitation and related programs to meet the healthcare needs of our communities.

7160 Summit Ridge Center Genesis Eldercare
20 Summit St
West Orange, NJ 07052-1501
973-736-2000
800-699-1520
FAX: 973-736-2764
info@genesishcc.com
www.genesishcc.com

Michele Cartagena, Director of Admissions
Elizabeth Orlando, Rehabilitation Program Director
Tsega Asefaha, LNHA, BS, MHA, Administrator
Summit Ridge Center provides skilled nursing, medical and rehabilitative care for patients requiring post-hospital, short stay rehabilitation and for longer term residents. Our Clinical Care Teams are focused on implementing your personalized care program to facilitate your recovery and improve your well-being.

New York

7161 Beth Abraham Health Services
612 Allerton Ave
Bronx, NY 10467-7495
718-519-4037
888-238-4223
FAX: 718-547-1366
info@bethabe.org
www.bethabrahamhealthservices.org

Maria Provenzano, Program Director
Yolanda Lester, Director of Admissions
Rosalie Bernard, Director of Nursing Services
Offers the following rehabilitation services: Sub-Acute rehabilitation, brain injury rehabilitation, pain management, post-operative recovery. Home visits and a network of community-based programs help patients and their families with a successful transition home.

7162 Central Island Healthcare
825 Old Country Rd
Plainview, NY 11803-4913
516-433-0600
FAX: 516-868-7251

Michael Ostreicher, Administrator
Serving the community for over 33 years, Central Island Healthcare is Long Island's largest and most active sub-acute care provider. We offer comprehensive programs focused on restoring our patients to their maximum potential and returning home. Central Island's 202-bed facility provides top notch professionals and the latest in rehabilitation and therapeutic equipment in a beautiful and comfortable setting.

7163 Clove Lakes Health Care and Rehabilitation Center
25 Fanning St
Staten Island, NY 10314-5307
718-289-7900
FAX: 718-761-8701
info@clovelakes.com
www.clovelakes.com

Helene Demisay, CEO
Clove Lakes seeks to rehabilitate those who have sustained injury or illness to the highest level of independence possible and support those with disabling conditions to live meaningful and productive lives.

7164 Dr. William O Benenson Rehabilitation Pavilion
36-17 Parsons Blvd
Flushing, NY 11354-5931
718-961-4300
FAX: 718-939-5032

Esther Benenson, Executive Director
Liza Marie Dowd, Director of Nursing
Erika Rossi, Director of Social Services
The Dr. William O Benson Reahibilitation Pavilion is a subacute short-term rehabilitation center committed to the excellence of elevated health care for our patients. Through the use of the most comprehensive and specialized services available, our staff of dedicated professionals are devoted to putting patients back to the road to full recovery 24 hours a day.

7165   Flushing Manor Nursing and Rehab
35-15 Parsons Blvd
Flushing, NY 11354-4297   718-961-3500
FAX: 718-461-1784

Esther Benenson, Executive Director
Dr. Ion Oltean, Medical Director
Myung Chung, Director of Nursing
At the Flusing Manor Nursing and Rehabilitation, we stress the importance of family involvement because it is the true source of strength and stability in ones life..a tie that brings us all together as a team, enhancing the quality of life of the patients in our care.

7166   Glengariff Health Care Center
141 Dosoris Ln
Glen Cove, NY 11542   516-676-1100
FAX: 516-759-0216
www.glenhaven.org

Jean Campo, Director Admissions
Michael Miness, President
Licensed skilled nursing and subacute medical and rehabilitation facility.

7167   Haym Salomon Home for The Aged
2340 Cropsey Ave
Brooklyn, NY 11214-5706   718-266-4063
FAX: 718-372-4781

Chain Lipschitz, Administrator
Religious nonmedical health care institution.

7168   Kings Harbor Multicare Center
2000 E Gun Hill Rd
Bronx, NY 10469-6016   718-320-0400
FAX: 718-671-5022
info@kingsharbor.com
www.kingsharbor.com

Morris Tenenbaum, Owner
Octavio Marin, Vice President
Kings Harbor Multicare Center provides long-term and short-term skilled nursing care for more then 700 residents. Kings Harbor is located in the Pelham Gardens neighborhood of Northeast Bronx, easily accessible to major highways and near public transportation. A 3 building campus facility with surrounding gardens ensures that residents with similar capabilities are grouped together.

7169   Northwoods of Cortland
28 Kellogg Rd
Cortland, NY 13045-3155   607-753-9631
FAX: 607-756-2968

Lawrence Mennig, Administrator
Subacute rehabilitation facility.

7170   Port Jefferson Health Care Facility
141 Dosoris Lane
Glen Cove, NY 11542   631-676-1100
FAX: 631-759-0216
www.glengariffcare.com

Ellen Harte, Administrator
Subacute medical and rehabilitative care and long term residential skilled nursing care.

7171   Rehab Institute at Florence Nightingale Health Center
1760 3rd Ave
New York, NY 10029-6810   212-410-8760
800-786-8968
FAX: 212-410-8792
Sub-acute rehabilitation facility.

7172   Schnurmacher Center for Rehabilitation and Nursing
Beth Abraham of Family Health Services
12 Tibbits Ave
White Plains, NY 10606-2438   914-287-7200
888-238-4223
FAX: 914-428-1824
info@schnurmacher.org
www.schnurmacher.org

Linda Murray, Executive Director
Thomas Camisa, Medical Director
Iryn Obaldo Fontanosa, Director of Rehabilitation
The environment at Schnurmacher is tailored to the needs of patients who require medical and nursing services but who do not need the complexity of services associated with an acute-care hospital. And Schnurmacher Subacute Medical patients are out of bed more quickly and as often as possible, which helps them maintain functional status while recovery progresses.

7173   South Shore Healthcare
275 W Merrick Rd
Freeport, NY 11520-3346   516-623-4000
FAX: 516-223-4599

Winnie Mack, RN, BSN, MPA, Regional Executive Director
Gene Tangney, Senior Vice President/ Regional Executive Director
Michael J. Dowling, President/ CEO
North Shore-LIJ Health System includes 16 award-winning hospitals and nearly 400 physician practice locations throughout New York, including Long Island, Manhattan, Queens and Staten Island. Proudly serving an area of seven million people, North Shore-LIJ delivers world-class services designed for every step of your health and wellness journey.

7174   St. Camillus Health and Rehabilitation Center
813 Fay Rd
Syracuse, NY 13219-3009   315-488-2951
FAX: 315-488-3255
info@st-camillus.org
www.st-camillus.org

Aileen Balitz, President
Patrick VanBeveren, PT, DPT, M, Supervisor of Physical Therapy
Nancy , Pirro, RN, Case Manager
Since our founding in 1969, St. Camillus' mission has been to provide high-quality services and facilities emphasizing the rehabilitation of individuals to their maximum potential. The importance of the human spirit drives all we do. We are dedicated to caring for life and helping individuals achieve their highest possible level of independence.

North Carolina

7175   Chapel Hill Rehabilitation and Healthcare Center
1602 E Franklin St
Chapel Hill, NC 27514-2892   919-967-1418
800-735-8262
FAX: 919-918-3811

Turner Prichett, Executive Director
Chapel Hill Rehabilitation and Healthcare Center accomodates 120 residents. We are located in downtown Chapel Hill on Franklin Street and we provide roud the clock nursing care 365 days a year. Intensive rehabilitation services are administered by our licensed speech, occupational and physical therapists. Our staff is trained to care for medically complex patients such as those requiring intensive wound care, dialysis, and artificial nutrition.

7176   Cypress Pointe Rehabilitation and Healthcare Center
2006 S 16th St
Wilmington, NC 28401-6613   910-763-6271
800-735-8262
FAX: 910-251-9803

Sara Deiter, Executive Director
Dr. Jose Gonzalez, Medical Director
Cypress Pointe offers comprehensive physical, occupational, speech and respiratory therapy services. Following a physician's referral, patients are evaluated to determine their needs. Recommendations are then made for the appropriate interventions and rehabilitation. If therapy is required, a personalized care plan is developed.

7177   Pettigrew Rehabilitation and Healthcare Center
1551 W Pettigrew St
Durham, NC 27705-4821   919-286-0751
800-735-8262
FAX: 919-286-5992

La'Ticia Beatty, Executive Director
Pettigrew Rehabilitation and Healthcare Center accomodates 107 residents. Our healthcare center is certified by Medicare and Medicaid. We have experienced staff members who care for our residents. We strive to improve the quality of life our residents experience as a result of the services they receive from our nursing and therapy departments.

7178 Raleigh Rehabilitation and Healthcare Center
616 Wade Ave
Raleigh, NC 27605-1237

919-828-6251
800-735-8262
FAX: 919-828-3294
www.raleighrehabhc.com

Steven Jones, Executive Director
Raleigh Rehabilitation and Healthcare Center accomodates 172 residents. We provide short-term rehabilitation-including, physical, occupational, and speech therapies-as well as long-term nursing services. We specialize in neurological disorders, complex diabetes treatment, amputation recovery and pain management. We welcome short stays (respite care). Transportation services are availiable for physician appointments and dialysis treatments.

7179 Rehabilitation and Healthcare Center of Monroe
1212 E Sunset Dr
Monroe, NC 28112-4318

704-283-8548
800-735-8262
FAX: 704-283-4664

Judy Olson, Executive Director
We accomodate 159 residents and are certified for Medicare and Medicaid. We specialize in short-term rehabilitation as well as long-term care. Our therapists, wound nurse and dietician work closely to administer wound care. We hav 2 dialysis centers within a 10-block radius and gladly accpet their patients. We have an on-staff medical director as well as a psychiatrist.

7180 Winston-Salem Rehabilitation and Healthcare Center
1900 W 1st St
Winston Salem, NC 27104-4220

336-724-2821
800-735-8262
FAX: 336-725-8314

Tom Bauer, Administrator
We accommodate 230 residents and we have approximately 250 employees. Our staffing ratio averages 1 licensed nurse for every 20 residents and 1 Certified Nursing Assistant for every 10 residents. We offer a wide range of services including but not limited to respiratory care, tracheotomy care and gastric tube feeding and we also feature an in house licensed therapy program.

Ohio

7181 Arbors East Subacute and Rehabilitation Center
5500 E Broad St
Columbus, OH 43213-1476

614-575-9003
FAX: 614-575-9101

Arbors East is a leading provider of long-term skilled nursing care and short-term rehabilitation solutions. Our 100 bed facility offers a full continuum of services and care focused around each individual in today's ever-changing healthcare environment.

7182 Arbors at Canton Subacute And Rehabilitation Center
2714 13th St NW
Canton, OH 44708-3121

330-456-2842
FAX: 330-456-5343
www.laurelsofcanton.com

Amy McDermand, Director of Marketing
Beth Jones, PT, DPT, Rehabilitation Services Director
Cindy Shingler, RN, Director of Nursing
We provide individualized, quality care to guests staying short-term for rehabilitation services or long-term for extended care services. The highest level of independence for our guests is the creed of The Laurels of Canton.

7183 Arbors at Dayton
320 Albany St
Dayton, OH 45408-1402

937-496-6200
FAX: 937-496-1990
www.extendicareus.com/dayton

Dave Maxwell, Administrator
Carlisa Pedalino, Administrator
Arbors at Dayton is a leading provider of long-term skilled nursing care and short-term rehabilitation solutions. Our 106 bed facility offers a full continuum of services and care focused around each individual in today's ever-changing healthcare environment.

7184 Arbors at Marietta
400 N 7th St
Marietta, OH 45750-2024

740-373-3597
FAX: 740-376-0004
www.extendicareus.com/marietta

Joan Florence, Director of Nursing
Kenneth Leopold, Medical Director
Arbors at Marietta is a leading provider of long-term skilled nursing care and short-term rehabilitation solutions. Our 150 bed facility offers a full continuum of services and care focused around each individual in today's ever-changing healthcare environment.

7185 Arbors at Milford
5900 Meadow Creek Dr
Milford, OH 45150-5641

513-248-1655
FAX: 513-248-7340
www.extendicareus.com/milford

Bruce Yarwood, President/CEO
Mark Ostendorf, Administrator
Arbors at Milford is a leading provider of long-term skilled nursing care and short-term rehabilitation solutions. Our 139 bed facility offers a full continuum of services and care focused around each individual in today's ever-changing healthcare environment.

7186 Arbors at Sylvania
7120 Port Sylvania Dr
Toledo, OH 43617-1158

419-841-2200
FAX: 419-841-2822
www.extendicareus.com/sylvania

Sheril Flowers, Administrator
Graig Hopple, Medical Director
Arbors at Sylvania is a leading provider of long-term skilled nursing care and short-term rehabilitation solutions. Our 79 bed facility offers a full continuum of services and care focused around each individual in today's ever-changing healthcare environment.

7187 Arbors at Toledo Subacute and Rehab Centre
2920 Cherry St
Toledo, OH 43608-1716

419-242-7458
FAX: 419-242-6514
www.extendicare.com

Jill Schlievert, Administrator
Subacute rehabilitation services and facility.

7188 Bridgepark Center for Rehabilitation and Nursing Services
145 Olive St
Akron, OH 44310-3236

330-762-0901
800-750-0750
FAX: 330-762-0905

Joseph Burick, Medical Director
A skilled nursing and rehabilitation center located in Akron, Ohio, across the street from St. Thomas Hospital with a beautiful view of the Akron skyline. Access to Interstate 77 and State Route 8 is just minutes away. Our entire staff is committed to providing caring, customer-focused skilled nursing and rehabilitation. For your convenience, we accept Medicare, Medicaid and most managed care and private insurance.

7189 Broadview Multi-Care Center
5520 Broadview Rd
Parma, OH 44134-1605

216-749-4010
FAX: 216-749-0141
www.broadviewmulticare.com

Harold Shachter, Owner
Mike Flank, VP
Broadview Multi-Care Center is a family run business with more than 40 years of experience providing quality care to the community. We are committed to meeting your needs and providing you with a warm, home-like environment. Our family is on-site and our doors are always open for your suggestions or to drop in and say hello. We always try to take and honor requests, whether it's a favorite food, an exciting activity or a particular room.

7190   Caprice Care Center
9184 Market St
North Lima, OH 44452-9558   330-965-9200
                                    FAX: 330-726-6097
                                    www.chcccompanies.com
Lori Crowl, Owner
Becky Berger, Director of Nursing
Stacey Howell, Administrator
A 106-bed skilled nursing, subacute and rehabilitation facility.
Our goal is to provide comfortable living to all who are in our
care. Caprice Health Care Center is a contemporary Medicare and
Medicaid approved facility specializing in short-term rehabilita-
tion services. The inpatient/outpatient rehab department includes
physical, occupational, speech therapies, indoor aquatic therapy
pool, as well as complimentary van transportation for outpatient
services.

7191   Cleveland Clinic
9500 Euclid Ave
Cleveland, OH 44195-2   216-444-2200
                                    800-801-2273
                                    FAX: 216-444-7021
                                    my.clevelandclinic.org/default.aspx
Gene Altus, Executive Director
Delos M. Cosgrove, MD, Chief Executive Officer, Preside
Joseph F. Hahn, MD, Chief of Staff, Vice Chairman of
A not-for-profit, multispecialty academic medical center that in-
tegrates clinical and hospital care with research and education.
Cleveland clinic was founded in 1921 by 4 renowned physicians
with a vision of providing outstanding patient care based upon
the principals of cooperation, compassion and innovation. Today,
Cleveland Clinic is one of the largest and most respected
hospitals in the country.

7192   Columbus Rehabilitation And Subacute Institute
111 West Michigan Street
Milwaukee, WI 53203-2903   800-395-5000
                                    kschaewe@extendicare.com
                                    www.extendicareus.com
Kelly Fligor, Administrator
Jillian Fountain, Secretary
Subacute rehabilitation programs and facility.

7193   LakeMed Nursing and Rehabilitation Center
70 Normandy Dr
Painesville, OH 44077-1616   440-357-1311
                                    800-750-0750
                                    FAX: 440-352-9977
                                    www.lakemednursing.com
Connie Eyman, Administrator
Vesta Jones, Executive Director
Our goal is to provide you with quality care and we are known for
our successful short-term rehab and care of the clinically complex. We also offer respite services to give caregivers a rest, and
hospice services through our local hospice care provider. Our interdisciplinary team works together as they strive to deliver quality care and responsive service to our residents.

7194   Oregon Nursing And Rehabilitation Center
904 Isaac Streets Dr
Oregon, OH 43616-3204   419-691-2483
                                    FAX: 419-697-5401
                                    www.extendicareus.com/oregon
Mark Rogers, Administrator
Subacute rehabilitation facility and services.

**7195   Sunset View Castle Nursing Homes Castle Nursing
          Homes**
434 N Washington St
Millersburg, OH 44654-1188   330-674-0015
                                    FAX: 330-763-2238
Becky Snyder, Admissions Coordinator
Kathy Edwards, Admissions And Marketing
310 licensed, certified beds. Subacute rehabilitation facility and
programs.

Oregon

7196   Care Center East Health & Specialty Care Center
Expendicare
11325 NE Weidler St
Portland, OR 97220-1950   503-253-1181
                                    FAX: 503-253-1871
                                    www.extendicareus.com
Glydon Kimbrough, Administrator
Subacute rehabilitation facility and programs

7197   Medford Rehabilitation and Healthcare Center
Kindred Healthcare
625 Stevens St
Medford, OR 97504-6719   541-779-3551
                                    800-735-1232
                                    FAX: 541-779-3658
Grant Gloor, Administrator
Dane Reeves, Executive Director
Kristen W., Health and Rehabilitation Center
We strive to provide quality, compassionate care. Our cozy build-
ing accomodates 110 residents. Our smaller size creates an invit-
ing and homelike environment. We offer semi-private rooms with
space to add items from home for a special personalized touch.

Pennsylvania

7198   Dresher Hill Health and Rehabilitation Center
1390 Camp Hill Rd
Dresher, PA 19034-2805   215-643-0600
                                    FAX: 215-641-0628
Earl Kimble, Administrator
Subacute rehabilitation facility and programs: physical/speech.

7199   Good Shepherd Rehabilitation
850 S 5th St
Allentown, PA 18103-3295   610-776-3586
                                    888-447-3422
                                    FAX: 610-776-8336
                                    goodshepherdrehab.org
John Kristel, MBA, MPT, President & CEO
Mike Bonner, MBA, Vice President, Neurosciences
*Ronald J. Petula, CPA, Senior Vice President, Finance and Chief
Financial Officer*
A world class rehabilitation network, Good Shepherd provides
comprehensive inpatient and outpatient services throughout
Pennsylvania's Lehigh Valley. Founded in 1908, Good Shepherd
has steadily expanded over last 95 years. Good Shepherd is one of
the most comprehensive rehabilitation institutes in the world.

7200   Statesman Health and Rehabilitation Center
2629 Trenton Rd
Levittown, PA 19056-1428   215-943-7777
                                    FAX: 215-943-1240
                                    www.statesmanskillednursing.com
Jamie Tanner, Administrator
Subacute rehabilitation facility and programs.

7201   UPMC Braddock
200 Lothrop St.
Pittsburgh, PA 15213-2582   412-647-8762
                                    800-533-8762
                                    FAX: 412-636-5398
                                    hospitalbill@upmc.edu
                                    upmc.com
Mark Sevco, Administrator
Rodney Jones, Vice President
With a team of more then 43,000 employees, UPMC serves the
health needs of more then 4 million people each year, improving
lives in western Pennsylvania-and beyond-through redefined
models of health care delivery and superb clinical outcomes.

7202 UPMC McKeesport
Presby
1500 5th Ave
McKeesport, PA 15132-2422   412-664-2000
                                   FAX: 412-664-2309
                                   fisherpj@upmc.edu
                                   upmc.com
Ronald H Ott, CEO
Offers 56 beds for patients who need skilled nursing care. Offers ongoing rehabilitation and educational programs to patients with cardiac, neurologic, and orthopaedic diagnosis.

7203 UPMC Passavant
9100 Babcock Blvd
Pittsburgh, PA 15237-5842   412-367-6700
                                   800-533-8762
                                   gloordc@ph.upmc.edu
                                   upmc.com
William Kristan, Dir Inpatient Physical Therapy
Teresa Petrick, Chief Executive Officer
Patients who have had an acute illness, injury, or exacerbation of a disease and no longer need the intensity of services in the acute care setting, but still require some complex medical care or supervision and rehabilitation services, may be appropriate to be transferred into the Subacute Unit.

Rhode Island

7204 Kindred Heights Nursing & Rehabilitation Center
Kindred Healthcare
680 South Fourth Street
Louisville, KY 40202   502-596-7300
                                   800-545-0749
                                   web_administrator@kindred.com
                                   www.kindredheights.com
Sandra Sarza, Manager
Jean Aubin, Director
Kindred Heights Nursing and Rehabilitation Center accomodates 58 residents and serves the needs of elders in the greater East Bay and Providence area. We are conveniently located on Wampanoag Trail in East Providence. Kindred Heights provides skilled nursing, short-term rehab and long-term care in a family environment, but we are large enough to manage the complex nursing and rehab care needs our residents may have.

7205 Oak Hill Nursing and Rehabilitation Center
Kindered Health Care
544 Pleasant St
Pawtucket, RI 02860-5776   401-725-8888
                                   800-745-6575
                                   FAX: 401-723-5720
                                   www.oakhillrehab.com
Scott M. Sandborn, Executive Director
Heidi Capela, Director Nursing
Amybeth Almeida, Director Admissions
Accomodates 143 residents. Throughout our 40 year history, Oak Hill has developed a reputation as one of the finest healthcare centers in Rhode Island. Our center consists of 3 separate units. A 34-bed post-acute unit provides care to the medically complex and those in need of extensive rehabilitative services. A 20-bed Alzheimer's Special Care Unit provides a unique style of care utilizing habilitative therapy in comfortable, home-like surroundings.

7206 Southern New England Rehab Center
200 High Service Avenue
North Providence, RI 02904   401-456-3801
                                   888-456-4501
                                   FAX: 401-456-3784
                                   www.snerc.com
Vivian Hagstrom, Manager
The Center's skilled staff of over 100 professionals provides a full range of coordinated rehabilitative care. Our clinical expertise and compassion make a big difference as we develop first-rate plans of care for the unique needs of each patient. Our medical staff is comprised of physicians board-certified in rehabilitation medicine and internal medicine.

South Carolina

7207 Tuomey Healthcare System
129 N Washington St
Sumter, SC 29150-4949   803-774-9000
                                   FAX: 803-774-8737
                                   www.tuomey.com
R Jay Cox, CEO
Here to anticipte the needs of the communities we serve, responding with proactive healthcare initiatives, providing expert rehabilitative services and delivering life-saving acute care.

Tennessee

7208 Camden Healthcare and Rehabilitation Center
680 South Fourth Street
Louisville, KY 40202   502-596-7300
                                   800-545-0749
                                   web_administrator@kindred.com
                                   kindredhealthcare.com
Mark Walker, Administrator
Subacute rehabilitation products and services, nursing and life care homes.

7209 Centennial Medical Center Tri Star Health System
2300 Patterson St
Nashville, TN 37203-1538   615-342-1000
                                   800-242-5662
                                   FAX: 615-342-1045
                                   Laurel.Haskamp@HCAHealthcare.com
                                   tristarcentennial.com
Thomas L Herron, President/Chief Executive Office
Above all else we are committed to the care and improvement of human life by caring for those we serve with integrity, compassion, a positive attitude, respect and exceptional quality.

7210 Cordova Rehabilitation and Nursing Center
955 N Germantown Pkwy
Cordova, TN 38018-6215   901-754-1393
                                   800-848-0299
                                   FAX: 901-754-3332
                                   cdadmi@gracehc.com
                                   www.gracehccordova.com
John Palmer, Administrator
Renee Tutor, Executive Director
Our professional staff can help you make an informed decision. Upon admission, our interdisciplinary team develops a comprehensive care plan to meet not only physical and rehabilitative goals, but also social and emotional needs. We understand the importance of family and resident involvement and encourage participation in the development of a personalized plan of care.

7211 Erlanger Medical Center Baronness Campus
975 E 3rd St
Chattanooga, TN 37403-2147   423-778-7000
                                   FAX: 423-778-7615
                                   guestrelations@erlanger.org
                                   www.erlanger.org
Kevin M. Spiegel, FACHE, President and CEO
James Creel, MD, Chief Medical Officer
Gregg T. Gentry, Chief Administrative Officer
Our mission is to improve the health of the people we touch. Our vision is to be recognized locally, regionally, and and nationally, as a premiere healthcare system.

7212 Huntington Health and Rehabilitation Center
635 High St
Huntingdon, TN 38344-1703   731-986-8943
                                   FAX: 731-986-3188
                                   huntingdonhealth.com
Heidi Hawkins, Administrator
Windi Summers, Admissions Director
Subacute rehabilitation facility and programs.

7213 Madison Healthcare and Rehabilitation Center
431 Larkin Springs Rd
Madison, TN 37115-5005   615-865-8520
                                800-848-0299
                          FAX: 615-868-4455

Phyllis Cherry, Executive Director
At our facility, we provide quality care with modern rehabilitation and restorative nursing techniques. We aim to provide an atmosphere which encourages family involvement in the care-planning process, with the right mix of activities addressing the social, spiritual and intellectual needs of our residents.

7214 Mariner Health of Nashville
3939 Hillsboro Cir
Nashville, TN 37215-2708   615-297-2100
                          FAX: 615-297-2197

David Reeves, Administrator
Amy Artrip, Director of Nursing
Religious nonmedical health care institution. 150-bed subacute rehabilitation facility.

7215 Pine Meadows Healthcare and Rehabilitation Center
700 Nuckolls Rd
Bolivar, TN 38008-1531   731-658-4707
                          FAX: 731-658-4769
                          www.pinemeadowshc.com

Larry Shrader, Administrator
Sharon McKeen, Admissions Director
Our goal is to take care of your loved ones. Our professional team works with skilled hands, is directed by creative minds and is guided by compassionate hearts. Upon your admission, our interdisciplinary team develops a comprehensive care plan designed with a goal of meeting not only physical and rehabilitative objectives, but also social and emotional needs. We understand the importance of family and resident involvement and encourage participation in the development of a plan of care.

7216 Primacy Healthcare and Rehabilitation Center
Kindred Health Care
6025 Primacy Pkwy
Memphis, TN 38119-5763   901-767-1040
                                800-848-0299
                          FAX: 901-685-7362

Donnie Dubert, Executive Director
Dr. Mark Hammond, Medical Director
Kristen W., Health and Rehabilitation Center
Upon a resident's admission, our interdisciplinary team develops a comprehensive care plan with a goal of meeting not only physical and rehabilitative objectives but also social and emotional needs. We understand the importance of family and resident involvement and encourage participation in the development of a personalized plan of care.

7217 Ripley Healthcare and Rehabilitation Center
118 Halliburton St
Ripley, TN 38063-2011   731-635-5180
                          FAX: 731-635-0663
                          www.ripleyhc.com

Johnny Rea, Executive Director
Brandon Whiteside, Executive Director
Jan Hodge, Admissions Directo
Upon admission, our interdisciplinary team develops a comprehensive care plan to meet not only physical and rehabilitative goals, but also social and emotional needs. We understand the importance of family and resident involvement and encourage participation in the development of a personalized care plan. Our goal is to take care of your loved ones.

7218 Shelby Pines Rehabilitation and Healthcare Center
3909 Covington Pike
Memphis, TN 38135-2281   901-377-1011
                          FAX: 901-377-0032

Rene Tutor, Executive Director
Subacute rehabiltation facility and programs.

7219 Siskin Hospital for Physical Rehabilitation
1 Siskin Plz
Chattanooga, TN 37403-1306   423-634-1200
                          FAX: 423-634-4538
                          TTY:423-634-1201
                          info@siskinrehab.org
                          siskinrehab.org

Robert Main, CEO
Lindsay Wyatt, Media Coordinator, Marketing Co
Dedicated exclusively to physical rehabilitation and offers specialized treatment programs in brain injury, amputation, stroke, spinal cord injury, orthopeadics, and major multiple trauma.

Texas

7220 North Hills Hospital
4401 Booth Calloway Rd
North Richland Hills, TX 76180-7399   817-255-1000
                          FAX: 817-255-1991
                          northhillshospital.com
Randy Moresi, CEO
North Hills Hospital's services include a wide range of cardiovascular services, surgical services, emergency services, radiology, a rehabilitation unit, a senior health center, therapy services, and women's services.

7221 Valley Regional Medical Center
100 E Alton Gloor Blvd
Brownsville, TX 78526-3328   956-350-7000
                          FAX: 956-350-7111
                          valleyregionalmedicalcenter.com

Susan Andrews, CEO
Francisco Javier Del Castillo, MD
Subramaniam Anandasivam, MD
Above all else, we are committed to the care and improvement of human life. In recognition of this committment, we strive to deliver high quality, cost effective healthcare in the communities we serve. In persuit of our mission, we recognize and affirm the unique and intrinsic worth of each individual. We treat all those we serve with compassion and kindness. We act with absolute honesty and integrity and fairness in the way we conduct our business and the way we live our lives.

Utah

7222 Crosslands Rehabilitation and Healthcare Center
680 South Fourth Street
Louisville, KY 40202   502-596-7300
                                800-545-0749
                          web_administrator@kindred.com
                          www.kindredhealthcare.com

John Williams, Executive Director
Lyle Black, Manager
Crossroads Rehabilitation and Healthcare accomodates 120 residents. We are fully Medicare and Medicaid certified. We are proud of our reputation for providing quality, compassionate care. Services availiable include in-house physical, occupational and speech therapies, as well as 24-hour licensed nursing staff coverage. We offer therapeutic recreation, in-house social services and registered dietician services, among many other professional services.

7223 Federal Heights Rehabilitation and Nursing Center
Kindred Health Care
680 South Fourth Street
Louisville, KY 40202   502-596-7300
                                800-545-0749
                          web_administrator@kindred.com
                          www.kindredhealthcare.com

Pete Zeigler, Executive Director
Dr. Charles Canfield, Medical Director
Federal Heights accomodates 120 residents. We are located near three major hospitals in the Salt Lake Valley. We specialize in providing nursing services for complex medical and rehabilitation conditions. Our discharge planning works jointly with the

family and resident in determining the future needs and goals upon discharge.

7224   St. George Care and Rehabilitation Center
Kindred Health Care Publications
1032 E 100 S
Saint George, UT 84770-3005   435-628-0488
                                        800-346-4128
                                    FAX: 435-628-7362
                                    www.stgeorgecare.com

John Larson, Plant Manager
Erin Hammon, Director of Nursing
Derrick Glum, Executive Director
St. George Care and Rehabilitation accomodates 95 residents. We offer a 4,000 square foot rehabilitation gym with an indoor therapy pool for inpatient and outpatient services. Therapy is provided to meet specific needs seven days a week. There is a dietitian on staff for individualized nutritional needs. We offer an Alzheimer's unit with specialized staff. We provide compassionate health services including physicians, nurses, physical therapists, and occupational therapist and licensed aides.

7225   St. Mark's Hospital
1200 E 3900 S
Salt Lake City, UT 84124-1390   801-268-7111
                                    FAX: 801-270-3489
                                    www.stmarkshospital.com

Steve B. Bateman, CEO
Above all else we are committed to the care and improvement of human life. In recognition of this commitment, we strive to deliver high quality, cost effective healthcare in the communities we serve. We define quality as 'caring people with the commitment to a continuous process of improvement in the services provided, that will better enable the hospital to meet or exceed our customer's needs and expectations.

7226   Wasatch Valley Rehabilitation
Kindred Healthcare
680 South Fourth Street
Louisville, KY 40202   502-596-7300
                                        800-545-0749
                                web_administrator@kindred.com
                                    www.kindredhealthcare.com

Alex Stevenson, Executive Director
Ric Toomer, Executive Director
Wasatch Valley accomodates 110 residents. We are licensed for Medicare and Medicaid and we are conveniently located in the heart of Salt Lake City with easy access from I-15 and I-215. We are known by the area hospitals as a specialist in wound care and for the care we provide to those with complex medical conditions.

Virginia

7227   Nansemond Pointe Rehabilitation and Healthcare Center
200 Constance Rd
Suffolk, VA 23434-4960   757-539-8744
                                        800-828-1140
                                    FAX: 757-539-6128
                                    www.nansemondhc.com

Mel Epelle, Executive Director
Mary R, Activities Assistant
Kristen W., Health and Rehabilitation Center
Nansemond Pointe Rehabilitation and Healthcare Center accomodates 160 residents in private and semi-private rooms. We have been serving the needs of Suffolk, Virginia and the surrounding areas for over 38 years. We offer an entire continuum of care from assisted living apartments to skilled nursing to long-term care. Our licensed therapists, working with our dedicated nursing staff, share a common goal- to help our residents improve their level of recovery and independence.

7228   Rehabilitation and Research Center Virginia Commonwealth University
1250 East Marshall Street
Richmond, VA 23298   804-828-9000
                                    FAX: 804-828-5074
                                    www.vcuhealth.org

Michael Rao, Ph.D., VCU President & VCUHS President,
Sheldon M. Retchin, M.D., VP Health Sciences & CEO, VCUHS
John Duval, Chief Executive Officer MCV Hosp
The Rehabilitation and Research Center is a collaborative effort between the Department of Physical Medicine and Rehabilitation and the Medical College of Virginia Hospitals. The goals of the Rehabilitation and Research Center at the Medical College of Virginia Hospitals (MCVH) are to provide highly-skilled, interdisciplinary, inpatient rehabilitative care to adults with complex needs; to be an advocate and educator for patients and people with disabilities.

7229   Warren Memorial Hospital
1000 N Shenandoah Ave
Front Royal, VA 22630-3598   540-636-0300
                                        800-994-6610
                                    FAX: 540-636-0258
                                complaint@jointcommission.org
                                    www.valleyhealthlink.com

Mark H. Merrill, President & Chief Executive Officer
Tonya Smith, Vice President of Operations
Pete Gallagher, Senior Vice President & CFO
A nonprofit organization of health care providers, Valley Health offers a full spectrum of services in acute care, rehabilitation and extended care facilities, and outpatient and community settings to help the people of the region manage their health and enjoy a high quality of life. Valley Health has the resources to diagnose, treat and help patients manage virtually any medical problem that may be encountered.

7230   Winchester Rehabilitation Center
333 W Cork St
Suite 230
Winchester, VA 22601-3870   540-536-5114
                                        800-994-6610
                                    FAX: 540-536-1122
                                complaint@jointcommission.org
                                    www.valleyhealthlink.com

Mark H. Merrill, President & Chief Executive Officer
Tonya Smith, Vice President of Operations
Pete Gallagher, Senior Vice President & CFO
Offers the following rehabilitation services: Sub-Acute inpatient rehabilitation, Speech therapy, Physical therapy, Occupational therapy, Disability evaluations. 30-bed inpatient center.

Washington

7231   Aldercrest Health and Rehabilitation Center
21400 72nd Ave W
Edmonds, WA 98026-7702   425-775-1961
                                    FAX: 425-771-0116
                                www.aldercrestskillednursing.com

Rick Milsow, Administrator
Aldercrest Health & Rehabilitation Center is a leading provider of long-term skilled nursing care and short-term rehabilitation solutions. Our 124 bed facility offers a full continuum of services and care focused around each individual in today's ever-changing healthcare environment.

7232   Arden Rehabilitation and Healthcare Center
16357 Aurora Ave N
Seattle, WA 98133-5651   206-542-3103
                                        800-833-6384
                                    FAX: 206-542-7192
                                    www.ardenrehab.com

Matthew Preston, Administrator
Ann Zell, Executive Director
Kristen W., Health and Rehabilitation Center
Arden Rehabilitation has been an integral part of the Shoreline community since 1953. It is a one-level building set on mature grounds with several beautiful courtyards for the residents to enjoy. Arden can accomodate 90 residents-post acute/rehabilitation

patients as well as long-term residents. Medicare certified, the center also takes most managed healthcare insurance plans, as well as VA, respite and hospice patients.

7233 Bellingham Health Care and Rehabilitation Services
1200 Birchwood Ave
Bellingham, WA 98225-1302
360-734-9295
800-833-6384
FAX: 360-671-4368
www.avamererehabofbellingham.com
Melissa Nelson, Executive Director
Dr. Richard McClenahan, Medical Director
Kristen W., Health and Rehabilitation Center
At Bellingham Health Care and Rehab, we strive to provide quality, compassionate care. Our cozy building accomodates 84 residents. Our smaller size creates an inviting and homelike environment for your loved one. We offer semi-private rooms with space to add items from home for a special personalized touch. Provides meals served restaurant style in our dinning room overlooking our beautiful grounds.

7234 Bremerton Convalescent and Rehabilitation Center
2701 Clare Ave
Bremerton, WA 98310-3313
360-377-3951
FAX: 360-377-5443
bremertonskillednursing.com
Stephanie Bonanzino, Administrator
Subacute rehabilitation facility and programs.

7235 Edmonds Rehabilitation & Healthcare Centerer
Kindred Healthcare
21008 76th Ave W
Edmonds, WA 98026-7104
425-778-0107
800-833-6384
FAX: 425-776-9532
Jane Davis, Executive Director
At Edmonds Rehabilitation and Healthcare, we strive to provide quality, compassionate care. Our center accomodates 91 residents. Our smaller size creates an inviting and homelike environment. We offer semi-private rooms with space to add items from home for a special personalized touch. Edmonds Rehabilitation and Healthcare provides delicious meals served restaurant style in our dinning room.

7236 Heritage Health and Rehabilitation Center
Kindred Health Care
3605 Y St
Vancouver, WA 98663-2647
360-693-5839
800-833-6384
FAX: 360-693-3991
www.heritagerehab.com
Michael Moses, Executive Director
Su Patchett, Director of Nursing
Heritage Health & Rehabilitation Center is the smallest free-standing healthcare center in southwest Washington with accomodations of 49, enabling more personal care and a more home-like environment. Heritage has licensed nursing staff, restorative aides, and certified nurses assistants, trained and experienced in providing Alzheimer's care, end of life/hospice care, psychiatric care, rehabilitative care, and respite care.

7237 North Auburn Rehabilitation And Health Center
111 West Michigan Street
Milwaukee, WI 53203-2903
800-395-5000
extendicare.com
Allyson Jenkins, Administrator
Subacute rehabilitation facility and programs.

7238 Northwoods Lodge
2321 NW Schold Pl
Silverdale, WA 98383-9504
360-698-3930
FAX: 360-692-2169
www.encorecommunities.com
Leslie Krueger, Owner
Debbie Griffin, Director of Rehab Services
Silverdale Campus, Executive Director
Provides you with a full-range of services from weekly housekeeping and laudry services, to grounds keeping and maintenance. Our monthy fee inculdes utilities and hot, delicious, nutritious meals served table side every day. We offer transporta-

tion services, full-time activities directors, and numerous amenities to add to your comfort and enjoyment.

7239 Pacific Specialty & Rehabilitation Center r
1015 N Garrison Rd
Vancouver, WA 98664-1313
360-694-7501
FAX: 360-694-8148
Rebecca Pruett, Administrator
Subacute rehabilitation facility and programs.

7240 Puget Sound Healthcare Center
4001 Capitol Mall Dr SW
Olympia, WA 98502-8657
360-754-9792
FAX: 360-754-2455
www.pugetsoundskillednursing.com
Sheila Oberg, Administrator
Our goal is to provide excellence in patient care, veteran's benefits and customer satisfaction. We have reformed our department internally and are striving for high quality, prompt and seamless service to veterans. Our department employees continue to offer their dedication and commitment to help veterans get the services they have earned.

7241 Vancouver Health & Rhabilitation Center
400 E 33rd St
Vancouver, WA 98663-2238
360-696-2561
800-833-6384
FAX: 360-696-9275
www.vancouverhealthcare.com
Jody Wigen, Human Resources
Joe Joy, Executive Director
Kristen W., Health and Rehabilitation Center
At Vancouver Health and Rehab Center we strive to provide quality, compassionate care. Our cozy building accomodates 98 residents. Our smaller size creates an inviting and homelike environment. We offer semi-private rooms with space to add items from home for a special personalized touch. Provides delicious meals served restaurant style in our dining room.

West Virginia

7242 War Memorial Hospital
1 Healthy Way
Berkeley Springs, WV 25411-1743
304-258-1234
FAX: 304-258-5618
complaint@jointcommission.org
www.valleyhealthlink.com
Mark H. Merrill, President & Chief Executive Officer
Tonya Smith, Vice President of Operations
Pete Gallagher, Senior Vice President & Chief Financial Officer
Offers physical therapy, occupational therapy, speech therapy, social services, and patient/family education for individuals who have experienced a recent physical disability due to disease, dysfunction, or general debilitation. Helps patients to maximize their abilities through activities of daily living, mobility, self-medication, and self-care and restore their ability to return to their previous lifestyle.

Wisconsin

7243 Cedar Spring Health and Rehabilitation Center
N27w5707 Lincoln Blvd
Cedarburg, WI 53012-2852
262-376-7676
FAX: 262-376-7808
Mary Wirth, Executive Director
Subacute rehabilitation facility and programs.

7244 Clearview-Brain Injury Center
198 Home Rd
Juneau, WI 53039-1401
920-386-3400
877-386-3400
FAX: 920-386-3800
Jane E. Hooper, Administrator
Jacqueline Kuhl, Household Coordinator
Laura Bertagnoli
A 30-bed, state certified, subacute neuro-rehabilitation program in Juneau, WI. We are located just 45 minutes northeast of Madi-

son WI and 10 minutes east of Beaver Dam, WI. We are the first and longest standing of only 2 community re-entry programs in the state of Wisconsin providing subacute neuro-rehabilitation to teens and adults who have experienced a brain injury.

7245   Colonial Manor Medical and Rehabilitation Center
1010 E Wausau Ave
Wausau, WI 54403-3101   715-842-2028
                                                  800-947-6644
                                        FAX: 715-848-0510

Ericca Ylitalo, Administrator
Shelley Solberg, Executive Director
Kristen W., Health and Rehabilitation Center
Colonial Manor Medical and Rehabilitation Center is part of the Kindred Community and is located in Wausau, Wisconsin. The corporate headquarters are based in Louisville Kentucky. Our facility accomodates 150 residents.

7246   Eastview Medical and Rehabilitation Center
729 Park St
Antigo, WI 54409-2745   715-623-2356
                                                  800-947-6644
                                        FAX: 715-623-6345

Wanda Hose, Administrator
Wanda Hose, Executive Director
Kristen W., Health and Rehabilitation Center
Eastview Medical Center and Rehabilitation Center accomodates 165 residents. We are Medicare and Medicaid certified, as well as being Joint Commission accredited. Our 'TEAM' approach means specially trained staff work around the clock to assist in meeting rehabilitative goals established by our team of professionals. We encourage family involvement in our rehabilitative process. The support of loved ones is a major key to a speedy recovery.

7247   Hospitality Nursing Rehabilitation Center
8633 32nd Ave
Kenosha, WI 53142-5187   262-694-8300
                                        FAX: 262-694-3622

Marla Benson, Administrator
LaRae Nelson, President
Lisa Behling, Secretary
Subacute rehabilitation facility and programs.

7248   Kennedy Park Medical Rehabilitation Center
Kindred Healthcare
6001 Alderson St
Schofield, WI 54476-3614   715-359-4257
                                                  800-947-6644
                                        FAX: 715-355-4867

Judy Kowalski, Manager
Jim Torgerson, Executive Director
Kristen W., Health and Rehabilitation Center
Kennedy Park Medical & Rehabilitation Center accomodates 154 residents. We are located in Schofield, WI. At Kennedy Park, we specialize in dementia care, with our Reflections and Passages Units. Short-term rehabilitation and sub-acute care are provided in a setting conducive to meeting the individual needs of our residents and patients. We also provide general nursing care for persons with long-term care needs.

7249   Middleton Village Nursing & Rehabilitation
Kindred
6201 Elmwood Ave
Middleton, WI 53562-3319   608-831-8300
                                                  800-947-6644
                                        FAX: 608-831-4253
                                     www.middletonvillage.com

Nicholas Stamatas, Manager
Ashley Ostrowski, Executive Director
Kristen W., Health and Rehabilitation Center
Middleton Village accomodates 97 residents. We specialize in post-surgical and post-acute rehabilitation and long-term care services.

7250   Mount Carmel Health & Rehabilitation Center
5700 W Layton Ave
Milwaukee, WI 53220-4099   414-281-7200
                                        FAX: 414-281-4620

Mike Berry, Administrator
Darrin Hull, Executive Director
Kristen W., Health and Rehabilitation Center
Subacute rehabilitation facility and programs.

7251   Mount Carmel Medical and Rehabilitation Center
680 South Fourth Street
Louisville, KY 40202   502-596-7300
                                                  800-545-0749
                              web_administrator@kindred.com
                                         kindredhealthcare.com

Randy Nitschke, Administrator
Jeanne Piccioni, Executive Director
Mount Carmel Medical and Rehabilitation Center accomodates 155 residents. We are located in Burlington Wisconsin. Mount Carmel Medical and Rehabilitation center is a recipient of the American Health Care Association Quality Award.

7252   North Ridge Medical and Rehabilitation Center
1445 N 7th St
Manitowoc, WI 54220-2011   920-682-0314
                                                  800-947-6644
                                        FAX: 920-682-0553

Jane Conway, Interim ED
Mary Ann Hamer, Executive Director
North Ridge Medical and Rehabiliation Center accomodates 110 residents. We have been serving the Manitowoc, Wisconsin area for over 25 years. Our goal is to provide services in a warm, homey environment. Many of our staff in all departments have a long history with North Ridge and have worked here for more then 20 years. We also take pride in the fact that we have all in-house staff. Our therapy team is availiable to provide physical, occupational and speech therapy 7 days a week.

7253   Oshkosh Medical and Rehabilitation Center
1580 Bowen St
Oshkosh, WI 54901   920-233-4011
                                        FAX: 920-233-5177

Tom Wagner, President
Subacute rehabilitation facility and programs.

7254   San Luis Medical and Rehabilitation Center
680 South Fourth Street
Louisville, KY 40202   502-596-7300
                                                  800-545-0749
                              web_administrator@kindred.com
                                      www.kindredhealthcare.com

Heather Dreier, Administrator
Tim Dietzen, Executive Director
Dr. John T. Warren, Medical Director
San Luis Medical and Rehabilitation Center accomodates 126 residents. We are located in Green bay, WI. At San Luis, we strive to meet the needs of our residents and we specialize in dementia care, with our Reflections Unit. Our goal is to provide short-term rehabilitation and sub-acute care in a setting conducive to assisting the needs of our residents.

7255   Strawberry Lane Nursing & Rehabilitation Center
130 Strawberry Lane
Wisconsin Rapids, WI 54494-2156   715-424-1600
                                        FAX: 715-424-4817

Cyndi Glodoski, Admissions Director
Carrie Russert, Administrator
Skilled nursing facility that provides both long term and short term care. Offer Alzheimer's and Dementia care units, as well as Hospice Care. Medicare and Medicaid certified.

Wyoming

7256 Mountain Towers Healthcare & Rehabilitation Center
3128 Boxelder Dr
Cheyenne, WY 82001-5808   307-634-7901
                                           800-877-9975
                                       FAX: 307-634-7910

Dan Stackis, Administrator
Toni Wyenn, Director of Nursing
Daniel G. Stackis, Executive Director
Mountain Towers Healthcare and Rehabilitation Center
accomodates 170 residents, including a 16-bed acute secure unit.
We offer a full range of nursing and medical care to meet individ-
ual needs. We have a full staff to meet the needs of our residents.

7257 South Central Wyoming Healthcare and Rehabilitation
Kindred Healthcare
542 16th St
Rawlins, WY 82301-5241   307-324-2759
                                           800-877-9975
                                       FAX: 307-324-7579

Chris Tanner, Executive Director
Anthony Janusz, Administrator
Kristen W., Health and Rehabilitation Center
South Central Wyoming Healthcare and Rehabilitation
accomodates 52 residents. We are located in Rawlings, in south
central Wyoming. We are Medicare and Medicaid certified by the
State of Wyoming. We strive to provide quality personal services,
long-term care or short-term rehabilitation to our residents in a
comfortable home-like environment.

7258 Wind River Healthcare and Rehabilitation Center
Kindred Health Care
1002 Forest Dr
Riverton, WY 82501-2918   307-856-9471
                                           800-877-9975
                                       FAX: 307-856-1665

Jo Ann Aldrich, Executive Director
Amelia Asay, Business Office Manager
Kristen W., Health and Rehabilitation Center
Offers a full range of medical services to meet the individual
needs of our residents, including short-term rehabilitative services and long-term skilled care. Working with the residents physician, our staff-including medical specialists, nurses,
nutritionists, dietitians and social workers-establishes a comprehensive treatment plan intended to restore you or your loved one
to the highest practicable potential.

Aging

Associations

7259 AARP
601 E Street NW
Washington, DC 20049
202-434-3525
888-687-2277
member@aarp.org
www.aarp.org

Jo Ann Jenkins, CEO
Formerly the American Association of Retired Persons. AARP is a collection of diverse individuals and ideas working as one to influence positive change and improve the lives of those 50 and over. AARP reflects a wide range of attitudes, cultures, lifestyles, and beliefs.
1919

7260 AARP Alabama
400 South Union Street
Suite 100
Montgomery, AL 36104
866-542-8167
alaarp@aarp.org
states.aarp.org/region/alabama

Candi Williams, State Director
Lisa Billingsley, Senior Operations Administrator
Provides information, events, news, and resources to Alabamians over 50 years of age, and to a membership of over 430,000.
1920

7261 AARP Alaska
3601 C Street
Suite 1420
Anchorage, AK 99503
866-227-7447
FAX: 907-341-2270
ak@aarp.org
states.aarp.org/region/alaska

Ken Helander, Advocacy Director
Ann Secrest, Media Contact
Serves 95,000 members in Alaska, providing information, resources, news, and advocacy on matters relevant to individuals aged 50 years and older.

7262 AARP Arizona
7250 N 16th Street
Suite 302
Phoenix, AZ 85020
866-389-5649
aarpaz@aarp.org
states.aarp.org/region/arizona

David Parra, Director, Community Outreach
Alex Suarez, Communications Contact
The chapter seeks to enhance the quality of life for all Arizonans, with an emphasis on individuals 50 years and older.

7263 AARP Arkansas
1701 Centerview Drive
Suite 205
Little Rock, AR 72211
866-544-5379
FAX: 501-227-7710
araarp@aarp.org
states.aarp.org/region/arkansas

Charlie Wagener, State President
Seeks to redefine and improve life for Arkansans over the age of 50.

7264 AARP California: Pasadena
200 S Los Robles Avenue
Suite 400
Pasadena, CA 91101- 2422
866-448-3614
FAX: 626-583-8500
caaarp@aarp.org
states.aarp.org/region/california

Nancy McPherson, State Director
Joy Hepp, Media Contact, Southern California
Provides news, tools, resources, and research to Californians 50 years and older.

7265 AARP California: Sacramento
1415 L Street
Suite 960
Sacramento, CA 95814
866-448-3614
FAX: 916-446-2223
caaarp@aarp.org
states.aarp.org/region/california

Nancy McPherson, State President
Mark Beach, Media Contact, Northern California
Provides news, tools, resources, and research to Californians 50 years and older.

7266 AARP Colorado
303 E 17th Avenue
Denver, CO 80203-5012
866-554-5376
FAX: 303-764-5999
coaarp@aarp.org
states.aarp.org/region/colorado

Bob Murphy, State Director
Angela Cortez, Media Contact
The Colorado chapter seeks to keep Coloradans 50 years and older informed, engaged, and active.

7267 AARP Connecticut
21 Oak Street
Suite 104
Hartford, CT 06106
866-295-7279
ctaarp@aarp.org
states.aarp.org/region/connecticut

Nora Duncan, State Director
Anna Doroghazi, Assoc. State Dir., Advocacy & Outreach
With nearly 600,000 members, the chapter provides recent news, information, and events for residents of Connecticut who are 50 years and older, as well as advocating for positive social change.

7268 AARP Delaware
222 Delaware Avenue
Suite 1630
Wilmington, DE 19801
866-227-7441
kiapalucci@aarp.org
states.aarp.org/region/delaware

Lucretia Young, State Director
Kimberly Iapalucci, Media Contact
Provides news, advocacy, education, and lifestyle information for residents of Delaware who are 50 years and older.

7269 AARP Florida: Doral
3750 Nw 87th Avenue
Suite 650
Doral, FL 33178
866-595-7678
FAX: 786-804-4544
flaarp@aarp.org
states.aarp.org/region/florida

Donna L. Ginn, State President
Jeff Johnson, State Director
The chapter provides information, research, and events to 2.7 million members, and Floridians 50 years and older.

7270 AARP Florida: St. Petersburg
360 Central Avenue
Suite 1750
St. Petersburg, FL 33701
866-595-7678
FAX: 727-369-5191
flaarp@aarp.org
states.aarp.org/region/florida

Donna L. Ginn, State President
Jeff Johnson, State Director
The chapter provides information, research, and events to 2.7 million members, and Floridians 50 years and older.

7271 AARP Florida: Tallahassee
200 West College Avenue
Suite 304
Tallahassee, FL 32301
866-595-7678
FAX: 850-222-8968
flaarp@aarp.org
states.aarp.org/region/florida

Donna L. Ginn, State President
Jeff Johnson, State Director
The chapter provides information, research, and events to 2.7 million members, and Floridians 50 years and older.

7272 AARP Georgia
999 Peachtree Street NE
Suite 1110
Atlanta, GA 30309   866-295-7281
                                           FAX: 404-815-7940
                                           gaaarp@aarp.org
                              states.aarp.org/region/georgia

Debra Tyler-Horton, State Director
Alisa Jackson, Media Contact
The chapter strives to help Georgians 50 years and older.

7273 AARP Hawaii
1132 Bishop Street
Suite 1920
Honolulu, HI 96813   866-295-7282
                                           FAX: 808-537-2288
                                             hiaarp@aarp.org
                               states.aarp.org/region/hawaii

Jessica Wooley, Director, Advocacy
With 150,000 members, the chapter advocates at the state level,
and provides information, resources, and volunteer opportunities.

7274 AARP Idaho
250 S 5th Street
Suite 800
Boise, ID 83702   866-295-7284
                                           FAX: 208-288-4424
                                             aarpid@aarp.org
                                states.aarp.org/region/idaho

Lupe Wissel, Idaho AARP State Media Relations
Randy Simon, Media Contact
The chapter advocates for and seeks to improve the lives of resi-
dents aged 50 years and older.

7275 AARP Illinois: Chicago
222 N LaSalle Street
Suite 710
Chicago, IL 60601   866-448-3613
                                           FAX: 312-372-2204
                                             aarpil@aarp.org
                              states.aarp.org/region/illinois

Bob Gallo, State Director
Dina Anderson, Media Contact
Advocates for and provides recent news, events, and lifestyle tips
to Illinois residents aged 50 years and older.

7276 AARP Illinois: Springfield
300 W Edwards Street
3rd Floor
Springfield, IL 62704   866-448-3613
                                           FAX: 217-522-7803
                                             aarpil@aarp.org
                              states.aarp.org/region/illinois

Bob Gallo, State Director
Dina Anderson, Media Contact
Legislative office of the Illinois chapter.

7277 AARP Indiana
One N Capitol Avenue
Suite 1275
Indianapolis, IN 46204- 2025   866-448-3618
                                           FAX: 317-423-2211
                                            inaarp@aarp.org
                              states.aarp.org/region/indiana

Sarah Waddle, State Director
Jason Tomcsi, Media Contact
The chapter seeks to improve life for residents of Indiana aged 50
years and older.

7278 AARP Iowa
600 E Court Avenue
Suite 100
Des Moines, IA 50309   866-554-5378
                                           FAX: 515-244-7767
                                                ia@aarp.org
                                  states.aarp.org/region/iowa

Brad Anderson, State Director
Jeremy Barewin, Media Contact
Provides news, information, and resources to Iowans aged 50
years and older.

7279 AARP Kansas
6220 SW 29th Street
Suite 300
Topeka, KS 66614   866-448-3619
                                           FAX: 785-232-1465
                                            ksaarp@aarp.org
                               states.aarp.org/region/kansas

Maren Turner, Kansas AARP State Media Relations
Mary Tritsch, Media Contact
The chapter provides news, events, and more to Kansans aged 50
years and older.

7280 AARP Kentucky
10401 Linn Station Road
Suite 121
Louisville, KY 40223   866-295-7275
                                            kyaarp@aarp.org
                             states.aarp.org/region/kentucky

Scott Wagenast, Associate State Director
Provides news and resources for Kentuckians over the age of 50.

7281 AARP Louisiana: Baton Rouge
301 Main Street
Suite 1012
Baton Rouge, LA 70825   866-448-3620
                                                la@aarp.org
                            states.aarp.org/region/louisiana

Denise Bottcher, State Director
Andrew Muhl, Director, Advocacy
The office seeks to advocate for and provide resources to resi-
dents of Louisiana aged 50 and over.

7282 AARP Louisiana: New Orleans
3502 S Carrollton Avenue
Suite C
New Orleans, LA 70118   866-448-3620
                                                la@aarp.org
                            states.aarp.org/region/louisiana

Denise Bottcher, State Director
Andrew Muhl, Director, Advocacy
AARP Louisiana's Community Resource Center.

7283 AARP Maine
53 Baxter Boulevard
Suite 202
Portland, ME 04101   866-554-5380
                                                me@aarp.org
                                states.aarp.org/region/maine

Lori Parham, State Director
Amy Gallant, Director, Advocacy and Outreach
Seeks to enhance the lives of Mainers aged 50 years and over
through advocacy, information sharing, volunteer opportunities,
and service. The chapter counts 230,000 members.

7284 AARP Maryland
200 St. Paul Place
Suite 2510
Baltimore, MD 21202   866-542-8163
                                           FAX: 410-837-0269
                                                md@aarp.org
                             states.aarp.org/region/maryland

Jim Campbell, State President
Nancy Carr, Assoc. State Director, Communications
The chapter seeks to enhance the lives of Maryland residents aged
50 and over, as well as caregivers, through resources and a variety
of social opportunities.

7285 AARP Massachusetts
1 Beacon Street
Suite 2301
Boston, MA 02108   866-448-3621
                                           FAX: 617-723-4224
                                                ma@aarp.org
                        states.aarp.org/region/massachusetts

Mike Festa, State Director
Cindy Campbell, Director, Communications
Provides news, events, and resources to Massachusetts residents
aged 50 and over.

7286   AARP Michigan
309 N Washington Square
Suite 110
Lansing, MI 48933   866-227-7448
                                         FAX: 517-482-2794
                                           miaarp@aarp.org
                              states.aarp.org/region/michigan
Paula D. Cunningham, State Director
The chapter seeks to enhance the quality of life for aging residents of Michigan through information, advocacy, and services.

7287   AARP Minnesota
1919 University Avenue
Suite 500
St. Paul, MN 55104   866-554-5381
                                           aarpmn@aarp.org
                              states.aarp.org/region/minnesota
Will Phillips, State Director
Maro Jo George, Associate State Director, Advocacy
Aims to connect aging residents of Minnesota with financial and other resources to enhance quality of life.

7288   AARP Mississippi
141 Township Avenue
Suite 302
Ridgeland, MS 39157   866-554-5382
                                         FAX: 601-898-5429
                                           msaarp@aarp.org
                              states.aarp.org/region/mississippi
John McDonald, AARP Missouri State Director
Ronda Gooden, Media Contact
Seeks to improve the lives of Mississippians, particularly those over 50 years of age, through events, news, resources, and advocacy.

7289   AARP Missouri
9200 Ward Parkway
Suite 350
Kansas City, MO 64114   866-389-5627
                                         FAX: 816-561-3107
                                           aarpmo@aarp.org
                              states.aarp.org/region/missouri
Craig Eichelman, State Director
Jamayla Long, Media Contact
Provides information to Missourians aged 50 and over on health, finances, and lifestyle, as well as providing advocacy.

7290   AARP Montana
30 W 14th Street
Suite 301
Helena, MT 59601   866-295-7278
                                           mtaarp@aarp.org
                              states.aarp.org/region/montana
Tim Summers, State Director
Stacia Dahl, Media Contact
With 150,000 members, the chapter provides advocacy, education, information, resources, and collaborative projects for Montana residents aged 50 and over.

7291   AARP Nebraska: Lincoln
301 S 13th Street
Suite 201
Lincoln, NE 68508   866-389-5651
                                         FAX: 402-323-6908
                                           neaarp@aarp.org
                              states.aarp.org/region/nebraska
Connie Benjamin, AARP Nebraska State President
Devorah Lanner, Media Contact
Works on behalf of over 200,000 members and their families to provide news, services, information, resources, and advocacy for individuals 50 years and older.

7292   AARP Nebraska: Omaha
1941 S 42nd Street
Suite 220
Omaha, NE 68105   402-398-9568
                                        omnebraska@aol.com
                              states.aarp.org/region/nebraska
Connie Benjamin, AARP Nebraska State President
Devorah Lanner, Media Contact
AARP Nebraska's Information Center.

7293   AARP Nevada
5820 S Eastern Avenue
Suite 190
Las Vegas, NV 89119   866-389-5652
                                           aarpnv@aarp.org
                              states.aarp.org/region/nevada
Maria Dent, State Director
Scott Gulbransen, Media Contact
Provides news, information, and resources to 320,000 members, on matters affecting the lives of individuals aged 50 and over.

7294   AARP New Hampshire
45 South Main Street
Suite 202
Concord, NH 03301   866-542-8168
                                         FAX: 603-224-6211
                                              nh@aarp.org
                         states.aarp.org/region/new-hampshire
Todd Fahey, State Director
Doug McNutt, Associate State Director, Advocacy
Provides information, resources, and advocacy services to 228,000 members, on matters relevant to individuals aged 50 years and older.

7295   AARP New Jersey
303 George Street
Suite 505
New Brunswick, NJ 08901   866-542-8165
                                         FAX: 609-987-4634
                                           aarpnJ@aarp.org
                            states.aarp.org/region/new-jersey
Stephanie Hunsinger, State Director
Jeff Abramo, Media Contact
The chapter seeks to educate and advocate for New Jersey residents aged 50 and over, and their families.

7296   AARP New Mexico
535 Cerrillos Road
Suite A
Santa Fe, NM 87501   866-389-5636
                                         FAX: 505-820-2889
                                           aarpnm@aarp.org
                           states.aarp.org/region/new-mexico
Jennifer Baier, Interim State Director
DeAnza Valencia, Associate State Director, Advocacy
The chapter advocates on behalf of individuals 50 years and older, monitoring seniors' services, utility rates, transportation services, as well as providing financial planning services to members.

7297   AARP New York: Albany
1 Commerce Plaza
Suite 706
Albany, NY 12260   866-227-7442
                                           nyaarp@aarp.org
                              states.aarp.org/region/new-york
Beth Finkel, State President
Erik Kriss, Media Contact
Provides information, resources, news, and advocacy services to residents of New York who are 50 years and older.

7298   AARP New York: New York City
750 Third Avenue
31st Floor
New York, NY 10017   866-227-7442
                                           nyaarp@aarp.org
                              states.aarp.org/region/new-york
Beth Finkel, State President
Erik Kriss, Media Contact
Provides information, resources, news, and advocacy services to residents of New York who are 50 years and older.

7299   AARP New York: Rochester
435 E Henrietta Road
Rochester, NY 14620   866-227-7442
                                           nyaarp@aarp.org
                              states.aarp.org/region/new-york
Beth Finkel, State President
Erik Kriss, Media Contact
Provides information, resources, news, and advocacy services to residents of New York who are 50 years and older.

7300 **AARP North Carolina**
5511 Capital Center Drive
Suite 400
Raleigh, NC 27606   866-389-5650
                                    ddickerson@aarp.org
                    states.aarp.org/region/north-carolina
Doug Dickerson, State Director
Michael Oldender, Manager, Outreach and Advocacy
Advocates for community issues such as health care, employment/income security, retirement planning, utilities, and protection from financial abuse, on behalf of a membership 1.1 million strong.

7301 **AARP North Dakota**
107 W Main Avenue
Suite 125
Bismarck, ND 58501   866-554-5383
                            FAX: 701-255-2242
                                   aarpnd@aarp.org
                    states.aarp.org/region/north-dakota
Josh Askvig, State Director
Doreen Redman, Assoc. State Dir., Community Outreach
Provides news, information, resources, events, advocacy, and more to North Dakotans aged 50 and over.

7302 **AARP Ohio**
17 S High Street
Suite 800
Columbus, OH 43215   866-389-5653
                            FAX: 614-224-9801
                                    ohaarp@aarp.org
                        states.aarp.org/region/ohio
Barbara Sykes, State Director
The chapter shares information, advocates, and performs community services for 1.5 million members, 50 years and older, across the state.

7303 **AARP Oklahoma**
126 N Bryant Avenue
Edmond, OK 73034   866-295-7277
                            FAX: 405-844-7772
                                       ok@aarp.org
                    states.aarp.org/region/oklahoma
Sean Voskuhl, State Director
Chad Mullen, Associate State Director, Advocacy
Assists individuals aged 50 and over through advocacy, news, information, resources, and more.

7304 **AARP Oregon**
9200 SE Sunnybrook Boulevard
Suite 410
Clackamas, OR 97015   866-554-5360
                                   oraarp@aarp.org
                      states.aarp.org/region/oregon
Ruby Haughton-Pitts, State Director
Joyce DeMonnin, Media Contact
Strives for social change for its 500,000 members, and all individuals 50 years and over, through advocacy and community services.

7305 **AARP Pennsylvania: Harrisburg**
30 N 3rd Street
Suite 750
Harrisburg, PA 17101   866-389-5654
                            FAX: 717-236-4078
                                    aarpa@aarp.org
                  states.aarp.org/region/pennsylvania
Bill Johnston-Walsh, State Director
Steve Gardner, Media Contact
Seeks to enhance the quality of life for 1.8 million members across the state.
1919

7306 **AARP Pennsylvania: Philadelphia**
1650 Market Street
Suite 675
Philadelphia, PA 19103   866-389-5654
                            FAX: 215-665-8529
                                    aarpa@aarp.org
                  states.aarp.org/region/pennsylvania
Bill Johnston-Walsh, State Director
Steve Gardner, Media Contact
Seeks to enhance the quality of life for 1.8 million members across the state.

7307 **AARP Rhode Island**
10 Orms Street
Suite 200
Providence, RI 02904   866-542-8170
                            FAX: 401-272-0596
                                        ri@aarp.org
                   states.aarp.org/region/rhode-island
Kathleen Connell, State Director
John Martin, Director, Communications
Provides news, information, resources, advocacy, and community services to those aged 50 and older in the state.

7308 **AARP South Carolina**
1201 Main Street
Suite 1720
Columbia, SC 29201   803-765-7381
                                     866-389-5655
                                    scaarp@aarp.org
                  states.aarp.org/region/south-carolina
Teresa Arnold, State Director
Nikki Hutchison, Associate State Director, Advocacy
Seeks to enhance the quality of life for members and individuals aged 50 and older, through information, resources, education, advocacy, and more.

7309 **AARP South Dakota**
5101 S Nevada Avenue
Suite 150
Sioux Falls, SD 57108   866-542-8172
                                   sdaarp@aarp.org
                   states.aarp.org/region/south-dakota
Erik Gaikowski, State Director
Provides news, information, resources, advocacy, and community services to 110,000 members and those aged 50 and older in the state.

7310 **AARP Tennessee**
150 4th Avenue N
Suite 1350
Nashville, TN 37219   866-295-7274
                                   tnaarp@aarp.org
                     states.aarp.org/region/tennessee
Rebecca Kelly, State Director
Rob Naylor, Director, Communications
Strives for positive social change for 660,000 members and individuals aged 50 and over.

7311 **AARP Texas: Austin**
1905 Aldrich Street
Suite 210
Austin, TX 78723   866-227-7443
                        states.aarp.org/region/texas
Bob Jackson, State Director
Junita Jiminez-Soto, Associate State Director, Communications
The chapter offers news, information, research, and events for individuals aged 50 and over, as well as conducting advocacy on their behalf.

7312 **AARP Texas: Dallas**
8140 Walnut Hill Lane
Suite 108
Dallas, TX 75231   866-227-7443
                        states.aarp.org/region/texas
Bob Jackson, State Director
Junita Jiminez-Soto, Associate State Director, Communications
The chapter offers news, information, research, and events for individuals aged 50 and over, as well as conducting advocacy on their behalf.

7313 AARP Texas: Houston
2323 S Shepherd Drive
Suite 1100
Houston, TX 77019   866-227-7443
                        states.aarp.org/region/texas
Bob Jackson, State Director
Junita Jiminez-Soto, Associate State Director, Communications
The chapter offers news, information, research, and events for individuals aged 50 and over, as well as conducting advocacy on their behalf.

7314 AARP Texas: San Antonio
1314 Guadalupe Street
Suite 209
San Antonio, TX 78207   866-227-7443
                        states.aarp.org/region/texas
Bob Jackson, State Director
Junita Jiminez-Soto, Associate State Director, Communications
The chapter offers news, information, research, and events for individuals aged 50 and over, as well as conducting advocacy on their behalf.

7315 AARP Utah
6975 Union Park Center
Suite 320
Midvale, UT 84047   866-448-3616
                        FAX: 801-561-2209
                        utaarp@aarp.org
                        states.aarp.org/region/utah
Alan Ormsby, State Director
Danny Harris, Director, Advocacy
Serves 211,000 members in 10 regions across the state, with advocacy, communications, programming, and outreach.

7316 AARP Vermont
199 Main Street
Suite 225
Burlington, VT 05401   866-227-7451
                        FAX: 802-651-9805
                        vtaarp@aarp.org
                        states.aarp.org/region/vermont
Greg Marchildon, State Director
Seeks to represent the concerns and interests of Vermonters aged 50 and over.

7317 AARP Virginia
707 E Main Street
Suite 910
Richmond, VA 23219   866-542-8164
                        FAX: 804-819-1923
                        vaaarp@aarp.org
                        states.aarp.org/region/virginia
Jim Dau, State Director
Serves Virginians aged 50 and older, and their families, through advocacy, information, resources, and outreach.

7318 AARP Washington
18000 International Blvd.
Suite 1020
SeaTac, WA 98188   866-227-7457
                        FAX: 206-517-9350
                        waaarp@aarp.org
                        states.aarp.org/region/washington
Doug Shadel, State Director
Serves 950,000 members through information, advocacy, and a variety of services.

7319 AARP Washington DC
100 M Street SE
Suite 650
Washington, DC 20003   866-554-5384
                        FAX: 202-434-7946
                        dcaarp@aarp.org
                        states.aarp.org/region/washington-dc
Louis Davis, Jr., State Director
Peter Rankin, Associate State Director, Advocacy
Provides information, advocacy, and a variety of services to 87,000 members aged 50 and over.

7320 AARP West Virginia
300 Summers Street
Suite 400
Charleston, WV 25301   866-227-7458
                        FAX: 304-344-4633
                        wvaarp@aarp.org
                        states.aarp.org/region/west-virginia
Gaylene Miller, State Director
Tom Hunter, Associate State Director, Communications
Provides information, resources, advocacy, and more to individuals aged 50 and over in West Virginia.

7321 AARP Wisconsin
222 W Washington Avenue
Suite 600
Madison, WI 53703   866-448-3611
                        FAX: 608-251-7612
                        wistate@aarp.org
                        states.aarp.org/region/wisconsin
Sam Wilson, State Director
Jim Flaherty, Media Contact
The chapter advocates for, and provides a variety of services to, its 840,000 members, aged 50 years and over.

7322 AARP Wyoming
2020 Carey Avenue
Mezzanine
Cheyenne, WY 82009   866-663-3290
                        wyaarp@aarp.org
                        states.aarp.org/region/wyoming
Sam Shumway, State Director
Tom Lacock, Assoc. State Dir., Advocacy & Comm.
Provides resources, information, and advocates for indviduals in Wyoming aged 50 and older, with an emphasis on health care, retirement, and utility issues.

7323 ABA Commission on Law and Aging
1050 Connecticut Avenue
Suite 400
Washington, DC 20003   202-662-8690
                        FAX: 202-662-8698
                        aging@americanbar.org
                        www.americanbar.org/aging
Charles P. Sabatino, JD, Director
Erica F. Wood, JD, Assistant Director
The Commission examines the issues that affect the elderly as victims of abuse, dispute resolution, international rights, medicare, voting, health care decision-making and other issues arising from the aging prisons populations.

7324 ACL Regional Support Center: Region I
Administration for Community Living
John F. Kennedy Building
Room 2075
Boston, MA 02203   617-565-1158
                        FAX: 617-565-4511
                        www.acl.gov
Jennifer Throwe, Regional Administrator
Region I includes CT, MA, ME, NH, RI, and VT.

7325 ACL Regional Support Center: Region II
Administration for Community Living
26 Federal Plaza
Room 38-102
New York, NY 10278   212-264-2976
                        FAX: 212-264-0114
                        www.acl.gov
Rhonda Schwartz, Regional Administrator
Region II includes NY, NJ, PR, and VI.

7326 ACL Regional Support Center: Region III
Administration for Community Living
801 Market St.
Philadelphia, PA 19107   267-831-2329
                        www.acl.gov
Laura House, Regional Administrator
Region III includes DC, DE, MD, PA, VA, and WV.

7327 ACL Regional Support Center: Region IV
Administration for Community Living
Atlanta Federal Center
61 Forsyth St. SW, Suite 5M69
Atlanta, GA 30303-8909　　　　　404-562-7600
　　　　　　　　　　　　　FAX: 404-562-7598
　　　　　　　　　　　　　www.acl.gov
Costas Miskis, Regional Administrator
Region IV includes AL, FL, GA, KY, MS, NC, SC, and TN.

7328 ACL Regional Support Center: Region IX
Administration for Community Living
90 7th St.
T-1800
San Francisco, CA 94103　　　　415-437-8780
　　　　　　　　　　　　　FAX: 415-437-8782
　　　　　　　　　　　　　www.acl.gov
Fay Gordon, Regional Administrator
Region IX includes CA, NV, AZ, HI, GU, CNMI, and AS.

7329 ACL Regional Support Center: Region V
Administration for Community Living
233 N Michigan Ave.
Suite 790
Chicago, IL 60601-5527　　　　312-938-9858
　　　　　　　　　　　　　FAX: 312-886-8533
　　　　　　　　　　　　　www.acl.gov
Lacey Boven, Regional Administrator
Region V includes IL, IN, MI, MN, OH, and WI.

7330 ACL Regional Support Center: Region VI
Administration for Community Living
1301 Young St.
Suite 106-850
Dallas, TX 75201　　　　　　214-767-1865
　　　　　　　　　　　　　FAX: 214-767-2951
　　　　　　　　　　　　　www.acl.gov
Derek Lee, Regional Administrator
Region VI includes AR, LA, OK, NM, and TX.

7331 ACL Regional Support Center: Region VII
Administration for Community Living
601 E 12th St.
Suite S-1801
Kansas City, MO 64106　　　　816-702-4180
　　　　　　　　　　　　　www.acl.gov
Lacey Boven, Regional Administrator
Region VII includes IA, KS, MO, and NE.

7332 ACL Regional Support Center: Region VIII
Administration for Community Living
1961 Stout St.
Denver, CO 80294-3638　　　　303-844-2951
　　　　　　　　　　　　　FAX: 303-844-2943
　　　　　　　　　　　　　www.acl.gov
Percy Devine, Regional Administrator
Region VIII includes CO, MT, UT, WY, ND, and SD.

7333 ACL Regional Support Center: Region X
Administration for Community Living
701 Fifth Ave., M/S RX-33
Suite 1600
Seattle, WA 98104　　　　　　206-615-2299
　　　　　　　　　　　　　FAX: 206-615-2305
　　　　　　　　　　　　　www.acl.gov
Louise Ryan, Regional Administrator
Region X includes AK, ID, OR, and WA.

7334 AMDA - The Society for Post-Acute andLong-Term Care Medicine
10500 Little Patuxent Parkway
Suite 210
Columbia, MD 21044　　　　　410-740-9743
　　　　　　　　　　　　　800-876-2632
　　　　　　　　　　　　　FAX: 410-740-4572
　　　　　　　　　　　　　info@paltc.org
Arif Nazir, MD, FACP, CMD, President
Karl Steinberg, MD, HMCD, Vice President
The only medical specialty society representing the community of over 50,000 medical directors, physicians, nurse practitioners, physician assistants, and other practitioners working in the various post-acute and long-term care (PA/LTC) settings.
1919

7335 Academy for Gerontology in HigherEducation
1220 L Street NW
Suite 901
Washington, DC 20005　　　　202-289-9806
　　　　　　　　　　　　　membership@geron.org
　　　　　　　　　　　　　www.aghe.org
Judith L. Howe, President
Lisa Hollis-Sawyer, Treasurer
Membership organization comprised of more than 130 colleges and universities that offer education and research program in the field of aging. Affiliated with the Gerontological Society of America.
1919

7336 Aging Life Care Association
3275 W Ina Road
Suite 130
Tucson, AZ 85741-2198　　　　520-881-8008
　　　　　　　　　　　　　FAX: 520-325-7925
　　　　　　　　　　　　　info@aginglifecare.org
　　　　　　　　　　　　　www.aginglifecare.org
Julie Wagner, Interim CEO
Amanda Mizell, Member Relations
Julie Wagner, Director of Administration
A nonprofit association providing geriatric care for aging individuals through sharing of knowledge in 8 areas: health and disability, financial matters, housing, planning, local resources, advocacy, legal and crisis intervention.

7337 Aging Services of Michigan
201 North Washington Square
Suite 920
Lansing, MI 48933　　　　　517-323-3687
　　　　　　　　　　　　　FAX: 517-323-4569
　　　　　　　　　　　　　www.leadingagemi.org
David Herbel, President & CEO
Deanna Mitchell, Senior Vice President for Performance & Education
Aging Services of Michigan represents and supports organizations that provide services to the elderly and disabled adults. Types of supports offered by Aging Services include advocacy, education and other programs that enhance an organization's ability to serve their constituencies.

7338 Aging Services of South Carolina
2711 Middleburg Dr
Suite 309-A
Columbia, SC 29204　　　　　803-988-0005
　　　　　　　　　　　　　FAX: 803-988-1017
　　　　　　　　　　　　　www.leadingagesc.org
Frazier Jackson, Chair
Vickie Moody, President
Aging Services of South Carolina represents non-profit organizations dedicated to providing high-quality health care, housing and services to the seniors of South Carolina. Supports include public policy initiatives and education.

7339 Aging Services of Washington
1102 Broadway
Suite 201
Tacoma, WA 98402　　　　　253-964-8870
　　　　　　　　　　　　　FAX: 253-964-8876
　　　　　　　　　　　　　info@leadingagewa.org
　　　　　　　　　　　　　leadingagewa.org
Jay Woolford, Chair
Deb Murphy, CEO
Laura Hofmann, Director, Clinical & Nursing Facility Services
LeadingAge Washington is a state association supporting non-profit organizations that specialize in housing and long term care for the elderly. Supports offered include advocacy, education and more.

7340 Aging and Disability Services
2100 Washington Blvd
4th Floor
Arlington, VA 22204   703-228-1700
                                   TTY:703-228-1788
                              arlaaa@arlingtonva.us
                          aging-disability.arlingtonva.us
Anita Friedman, Director, Department of Human Services
The Aging and Disability Services Division offers care coordination, home care, and supportive services to the aging residents of Arlington. Services are provided to adults over 60, adults with developmental disabilities and their caregivers.

7341 Aging in America
2975 Westchester Ave
Suite 301
Purchase, NY 10577   914-205-5030
                                   FAX: 718-824-4242
                              contact@aginginamerica.org
                                   aginginamerica.org
Katharine Weiss, Chair
William T Smith, President & CEO
Dina Nejman, Service Coordinator
Non-profit organization providing services for individuals and caregivers to assist them with the challenges of aging. One strategy employed towards this goal is collaboration with other organizations with experience in senior housing and community based services.

7342 AgingCare
                                   www.agingcare.com
An online resource for aiding family caregivers. AgingCare.com covers questions on assisted living, long-term and home care, veterans benefits, Alzheimer's disease, financial aid, funeral planning, and more.

7343 Alliance for Aging Research
1700 K Street NW
Suite 740
Washington, DC 20006   202-293-2856
                              info@agingresearch.org
                                   www.agingresearch.org
Sue Peschin, President & CEO
Sue Peschin, President & CEO
Non-profit organization dedicated to supporting and accelerating the pace of medical discoveries to vastly improve the universal human experience of aging and health.

7344 Alliance for Retired Americans
815 16th Street NW
4th Floor
Washington, DC 20006   202-637-5399
                                   retiredamericans.org
Robert Roach, Jr., President
Joseph Peters, Jr., Secretary & Treasurer
Joe Etta Brown, Executive Vice President
National grassroots organization advocates for a progressive political and social agenda that improves the lives of retirees and older Americans.
1920

7345 American Aging Association
2885 Sanford Ave SW
Suite 39542
Grandville, MI 49418   contact@americanagingassociation.org
                            www.americanagingassociation.org
Janko Nikolich-Zugich, Chair & CEO
Christian Sell, President
Dudley Lamming, Secretary
A group of experts dedicated to understanding the basic mechanisms of aging and the development of interventions in age-related diseases to increase human lifespans. This is accomplished through biomedical aging studies and public education.

7346 American Association for GeriatricPsychiatry
6728 Old McLean Village Drive
McLean, VA 22101   703-556-9222
                                   FAX: 703-556-8729
                              main@aagponline.org
                                   www.aagponline.org
Christopher Wood, Executive Director
Information and resources for physician members and affiliates on improving quality of life for older persons with mental disorders. Provides news, facts, tools and expert information for adults coping with mental health issues and aging.
1919

7347 American Association of Retired Persons
601 E Street NW
Washington, DC 20049   202-434-3525
                                   888-687-2277
                                   888-687-2277
                              member@aarp.org
                                   www.aarp.org
Jo Ann Jenkins, Chief Executive Officer
Scott Frisch, Executive Vice-President and COO
Cindy Lewin, Executive Vice President & General Counsel
AARP is the nation's leading organization for people age 50 and older. It serves their needs and interests through information and education, advocacy and community services provided by a network of local chapters and experienced volunteers.

7348 American Disabled for Attendant Programs Today (ADAPT)
                                   adapt.org
National organization fighting for the rights of disabled people through non-violent activism tactics and advocacy.

7349 American Geriatrics Society
40 Fulton Street
18th Floor
New York, NY 10038   212-308-1414
                                   FAX: 212-832-8646
                              info.amger@americangeriatrics.org
                                   www.americangeriatrics.org
Nancy E. Lundebjerg, CEO
Elvy Ickowicz, Senior Vice President of Operations
The premier professional organization of healthcare providers dedicated to improving the health and well-being of older adults. With an active membership of over 6,000 health care professionals, the AGS has a long history of affecting change in the provision of healthcare in older adults. The AGS Foundation for Health in Aging (FHA) aims to build a bridge between the research and practice of geriatrics health care professionals and the public.
1919

7350 American Planning Association
205 N Michigan Ave
Suite 1200
Chicago, IL 60601   312-431-9100
                                   FAX: 312-786-6700
                              foundation@planning.org
                              www.planning.org/ontheradar/aging/
Mary Kay Peck, FAICP, Chair
James Drinan, CEO
Ann Simms, Chief Operating Officer
An association supporting planners to develop communities that would be more livable for aging people. The association offers membership, a knowledge center, publications, conferences and meetings, certification, policy and advocacy services, community outreach and more.

7351 American Public Health Association
800 I St. NW
Washington, DC 20001   202-777-2742
                                   FAX: 202-777-2534
                                   TTY:202-777-2500
                                   www.apha.org
Georges C. Benjamin, Executive Director
Mighty Fine, Interim Associate Executive Director
Regina Davis Moss, Associate Executive Director
The association works to protect all Americans and their communities from preventable, serious health threats.

7352 American Society for Neurochemistry
9037 Ron Den Lane
Windermere, FL 34786 407-909-9064
FAX: 407-876-0750
asnmanager@asneurochem.org
asneurochem.org

Sheilah Jewart, Executive Director
Karen Gottlieb, Conference Coordinator
The Society aims to advance and promote cellular and molecular neuroscience knowledge, and to facilitate communication and the dissemination of information within the field and with related disciplines.

7353 American Society on Aging
575 Market Street
Suite 2100
San Francisco, CA 94105 415-974-9600
800-537-9728
FAX: 415-974-0300
info@asaging.org
www.asaging.org

Peter Kaldes, President & CEO
Robert R. Lowe, COO
Robert R Lowe, Chief Operating Officer
Health care and social service professionals, educators, researchers, administrators, businesspersons, students, and senior citizens. Works to enhance the well-being of older individuals and to foster unity among those working with and for the elderly. Offers 25 continuing education programs for professionals in aging-related fields. Publishes 'Aging Today,' a bi-monthly newspaper, and 'Generations, a quarterly journal.
1919

7354 American Urogynecologic Society
1100 Wayne Avenue
Suite 825
Silver Spring, MD 20910 301-273-0570
FAX: 301-273-0778
info@augs.org
www.augs.org

Michelle Zinnert, CEO
Colleen Hughes, COO
The leader in female pelvic medicine and reconstructive surgery.
1919

7355 Argentum
1650 King Street
Suite 602
Alexandria, VA 22314 703-894-1805
www.alfa.org

James Balda, President & CEO
Maribeth Bersani, COO
Argentum is the leading national association exclusively dedicated to supporting companies operating professionally managed, resident-centered senior living communities and the older adults and families they serve.
1919

7356 Arizona Center on Aging
1501 N Campbell
PO Box 245027
Tucson, AZ 85724 520-626-5800
FAX: 520-626-5801
info@aging.arizona.edu
www.aging.arizona.edu

Mindy Fain, MD, Co-Director
Janko Nikolich-Zugish, MD, Co-Director
The mission at Arizona Center of Aging (ACOA) is to promote healthy and functional lives for older adults through comprehensive programs in research, education and training, and clinical care.

7357 Association for Adult Development andAging
5999 Stevenson Avenue
Alexandria, VA 22304 www.aadaweb.org
Amber Randolph, President
A division of the American Counseling Association. Individuals holding a master's degree or its equivalent in adult counseling or a related field. Seeks to: improve the competence and skills of ACA and AADA members; expand professional work opportuni-

ties in adult development and aging counseling; promote the development of guidelines for professional preparation of counselors. Provides leadership and information to families, legislators, and communities.
1919

7358 Association for Gerontology in Higher Education
1220 L St NW
Suite 901
Washington, DC 20005 202-289-9806
FAX: 202-289-9824
geron@geron.org
www.aghe.org

Nina M Silverstein, President
Judith L Howe, President-Elect
Dana B Bradley, Treasurer
Membership association of colleges and universities offering gerontology education, training, and research programs on the subject of aging. The association seeks to enhance the knowledge and skills of those who work with older adults and their families.

7359 Association of Jewish Aging Services
2519 Connecticut Ave NW
Washington, DC 20008 202-543-7500
FAX: 202-543-4090
info@ajas.org
www.ajas.org

Daniel Reingold, Chair
Don Shulman, President & CEO
Rachel Stevens, Director of Operations
The Association of Jewish Aging Services is a non-profit community-based organization offering support services for the aging population. Inspired by Jewish values, the organization offers resources, conferences, education, professional development and advocacy to its members so they could better serve their communities.

7360 Association on Aging with Developmental Disabilities
2385 Hampton Ave.
St. Louis, MO 63139 314-647-8100
FAX: 314-647-8105
agingwithdd@msn.com
agingwithdd.org

Pamela Merkle, Executive Director
Michelle Darden, Program Development Coordinator
Erika Donaldson, Department Director
The organization offers services to accommodate the complex needs of older adults with developmental disabilities such as cerebral palsy, epilepsy, autism, severe learning disabilities and head injuries.

7361 BrightFocus Foundation
22512 Gateway Center Drive
Clarksburg, MD 20871 800-437-2423
FAX: 301-258-9454
info@brightfocus.org
www.brightfocus.org

Stacy Pagos Haller, President & CEO
Offers updated and trustworthy information on research, treatments, and resources. Free publications and newsletters.
1919

7362 Brookdale Center for Healthy Aging
2180 Third Avenue
8th Floor
New York, NY 10035 212-396-7835
FAX: 212-396-7852
info@brookdale.org
www.brookdale.org

Ruth K. Finkelstein, Executive Director
Jerry Antonatos, Director, Finance/Administration
Brookdale Center for Healthy Aging is one of the country's first university-based gerontology centers. The Center is dedicated to improving the lives of older adults through research, professional development, and advancements in policy and practice. Brookdale works to ensure that aging is framed not as a disease, but as another stage in the life course.
1919

7363 CARF International
6951 East Southpoint Rd.
Tucson, AZ 85756-9407
520-325-1044
888-281-6531
FAX: 520-318-1129
TTY:520-495-7077
info@carf.org
carf.org

Brian J. Boon, President & Chief Executive Officer
Leslie Ellis-Lang, Managing Director, Child & Youth Services
Darren M. Lehrfeld, Chief Accreditation Officer
An independent, nonprofit accreditor of human service providers in the areas of aging services, behavioral health, child and youth services, DMEPOS, employment and community services, medical rehabilitation, and opioid treatment programs.
1966

7364 Center for Benefits Access
National Council on Aging
251 18th Street S
Suite 500
Arlington, VA 22202
571-527-3900
centerforbenefits@ncoa.org
www.ncoa.org/centerforbenefits

Leslie Fried, Director
Benefits outreach and enrollment for seniors and younger adults with disabilities.
1919

7365 Center for Healthy Aging
National Council on Aging
251 18th Street S
Suite 500
Arlington, VA 22202
571-527-3900
cha@ncoa.org
www.ncoa.org

Binod Suwal, Senior Program Manager
Helping older adults live longer and healthier lives through evidence-based health promotion and disease prevention programs.
1919

7366 Center for Medicare Advocacy
PO Box 350
Willimantic, CT 06226
860-456-7790
FAX: 860-456-2614
mshepard@medicareadvocacy.org
www.medicareadvocacy.org

Judith A. Stein, Executive Director
Matthew Shepard, Media Contact
Offers consultation, training, presentation, and materials on an array of topics pertaining to aging.
1919

7367 Center for Positive Aging
1440 Dutch Valley Place NE
Suite 120
Atlanta, GA 30324
404-872-9191
FAX: 404-872-1737
www.centerforpositiveaging.org

Ginny Helms, President & CEO
Jacque Thornton, SVP
Jacque Thornton, Sr. Vice President
The Center for Positive Aging is a partnership of individuals, community organizations and congregations working together to provide health, educational and recreational opportunities for older persons and their families. Through our programs, services, and affiliations, we educate people of all ages and walks of life about living independent and creative lives.
1919

7368 Children of Aging Parents
PO Box 167
Richboro, PA 18954-0167
800-227-7294
FAX: 215-945-8720

Louise Fradkin, Co-Founder
Mirca Liberti, Co-Founder
A non-profit clearinghouse for caregivers of the elderly, providing information, referral, educational programs and materials to caregivers.

7369 Colorado Association of Homes and Services for the Aging
1888 Sherman St
Suite 610
Denver, CO 80203
303-837-8834
FAX: 303-837-8836
Karen@CAHSA.org
www.cahsa.org

Maureen Hewitt, President
Lynn O'Connor, President-Elect
Laura Landwirth, Executive Director
The association represents nonprofit organizations dedicated to providing health care and housing services to Colorado's elderly. Some services provided by the association include information and education to assist in developing programs for long term care.

7370 Easter Seals
40 Holly St.
Suite 401
Toronto, ON, Canada M4S-3C3
416-932-8382
877-376-6362
FAX: 416-932-9844
info@easterseals.ca
www.easterseals.ca

Dave Starrett, President & CEO
Frank Williamson, Director, Finance
Casey Sabawi, Senior Manager, National Corporate Partnerships
Provides services to those with disabilities to help them achieve greater independence, accessibility, and integration.
1919

7371 Experience Works
4401 Wilson Boulevard
Suite 220
Arlington, VA 22203
703-522-7272
866-397-9757
www.experienceworks.org

Sally A. Boofer, President & CEO
Rosemary Schmidt, CFO
Helps low income seniors with multiple barriers to employment, get the training they need to find good jobs in their local community.
1919

7372 Family Caregiver Alliance/National Centeron Caregiving
101 Montgomery Street
Suite 2150
San Francisco, CA 94104
415-434-3388
800-445-8106
www.caregiver.org

Jacquelyn Kung, PhD, Chief Executive Officer
Wyatt Ritchie, MBA, Managing Director
Caregiver information and assistance via phone or e-mail; fact sheets and publications describing and documenting caregiver needs and services.

7373 Gerontological Society of America
1220 L Street NW
Suite 901
Washington, DC 20005
202-842-1275
FAX: 202-842-1150
geron@geron.org
www.geron.org

James Appleby, Chief Executive Officer
Karen Tracy, VP, Strategic Alliances & Communications
Nonprofit professional organization with more than 5,500 members in the field of aging. Provides researchers, educators, practitioners and policy makers with opportunities to understand, advance, integrate and use basic and applied research on aging populations. Also runs the National Adult Vaccination Program (www.navp.org).

7374 Goodwill Industries International, Inc.
15810 Indianola Dr.
Rockville, MD 20855
contactus@goodwill.org
www.goodwill.org

Steven C. Preston, President & Chief Executive Officer
Goodwill strives to achieve the full participation in society of disabled persons and other individuals with special needs by expanding their opportunities and occupational capabilities

through a network of autonomous, nonprofit, community-based organizations providing services throughout the world in response to local needs.

7375   Goodwill Industries-Suncoast
10596 Gandy Boulevard
St. Petersburg, FL 33702   727-523-1512
                                           888-279-1988
                                    FAX: 727-579-0850
                                    TTY:727-579-1068
                              www.goodwill-suncoast.org
Deborah A. Passerini, President & Chief Executive Officer
Tracey Boucher, Corporate Treasurer & Chief Financial Officer
Kris Rawson, Vice President for Mission Services & Chief Mission Officer
A nonprofit, community-based organization whose mission is to help people achieve self-sufficiency through the dignity and power of work, serving people who are disadvantaged, disabled or elderly. The mission is accomplished through providing independent living skills, affordable housing, and training and placement in community employment.
1919

7376   Harvey A. Friedman Center for Aging
Washington University
St. Louis, Campus Box 8217
660 S Euclid
St. Louis, MO 63110   314-747-9212
                              centerforaging@wustl.edu
                              publichealth.wustl.edu/aging
Nancy Morrow-Howell, PhD, Director
Natalie Galucia, Center Manager
The Center promotes research, education, policy and service initiatives that enable older adults to remain healthy, active, empowered, contributing and independent for as long as possible.
1919

7377   Healthy Aging Association
3500 Coffee Rd
Suite 19
Modesto, CA 95355   209-523-2800
                                    FAX: 209-523-2800
                              healthy.aging2000@gmail.com
                              www.healthyagingassociation.org
Mike Mallory, Board President
Dianna L Olsen, Executive Director
Samantha Borba, MA, Fitness Program Manager
A non-profit organization whose mission is to help older Americans live longer, healthier, more independent lives by promoting increased physical activity through fitness programs.

7378   Heart Touch Project™
3400 Airport Avenue
Suite 42
Santa Monica, CA 90405   310-391-2558
                                    FAX: 310-391-2168
                                    www.hearttouch.org
Shawnee Isaac Smith, Co-Founder
Rene Russo, Co-Founder
Non-profit, educational and service organization devoted to the delivery of compassionate and healing touch to home or hospital-bound men, women, and children.
1919

7379   Institute for Life Course and Aging
246 Bloor Street W.
Room 238
Toronto, Ontario, Canada M5S-1V4   416-978-0377
                                    FAX: 416-978-4771
                                    aging@utoronto.ca
                              www.grandparentfamily.com
Esme Fuller-Thomson, Director
Susan Murphy, Administration
The Institute is a research center under the auspices of the Faculty of Social Work at the University of Toronto.

7380   International Federation on Aging
1 Bridgepoint Drive
Toronto, Ontario, Canada M4M-2B5   416-342-1655
                                    FAX: 416-639-2165
                                    jbarratt@ifa-fiv.org
                                    www.ifa-fiv.org
Greg Shaw, Director, Int'l & Corporate Relations
Dr. Jane Barratt, Secretary General
The IFA seeks to inform, educate and promote policies and practice to improve the quality of life of older persons around the world.
1919

7381   International Network for the Preventionof Elder Abuse
The Somers Law Firm
PO Box 368
Nassau, NY 12123   518-281-2777
                                    contactus@inpea.net
                                    www.inpea.net
Susan B. Somers, President
Amanda Phelan, Secretary
Organization for the prevention of elder abuse.
1919

7382   Jewish Council for the Aging
12320 Parklawn Drive
Rockville, MD 20852   301-255-4200
                              senior.helpline@accessjca.org
                                    www.accessjca.org
Norman Goldstein, President
Seeks to assist the elderly of all faiths lead independent lives. Provides transportation, job search assistance, fitness training, computer training and information and referrals. Conducts educational programs and presents an annual productive aging award. Maintains speakers' bureau.
1919

7383   Jewish Council for the Aging of Greater Washington
12320 Parklawn Drive
Rockville, MD 20852   301-255-4200
                              senior.helpline@accessjca.org
                                    www.accessjca.org
Norman Goldstein, President
Seeks to assist the elderly of all faiths lead independent lives. Provides transportation, job search assistance, fitness training, computer training and information and referrals. Conducts educational programs and presents an annual productive aging award. Maintains speakers' bureau.
1919

7384   Justice in Aging
1444 Eye St NW
Suite 1100
Washington, DC 20005   202-289-6976
                                    FAX: 202-289-7224
                                    info@justiceinaging.org
                                    www.justiceinaging.org
Phyllis J Holmen, Esq., Chair
Kevin Prindiville, Executive Director
Jennifer Goldberg, Directing Attorney
Justice in Aging is a non-profit legal organization whose principal mission is to protect the rights of low-income older adults and vulnerable groups in society. Through advocacy, litigation, and training of local advocates, Justice in Aging seeks to ensure the health and economic security of those they serve.

7385   Leadership Council of Aging Organizations

                                    lcao@aarp.org
                                    www.lcao.org
Coalition of national non-profit organizations concerned with the well-being of older Americans.

7386   Leading Age
2519 Connecticut Avenue NW
Washington, DC 20008-1520   202-783-2242
                                    info@LeadingAge.org
                                    www.leadingage.org
Katie Smith Sloan, President & CEO
Nicole Fallon, Vice President, Health Policy

National association of more than 6,000 nonprofit nursing homes, continuing care retirement communities, independent living centers and community service providers serving more than 60,000 older Americans each year.

7387 LeadingAge
2519 Connecticut Avenue NW
Washington, DC 20008
202-783-2242
info@leadingage.org
www.leadingage.org

Lea Chambers-Johnson, Executive Team Administrator
Robyn I Stone, Senior Vice President, Research

The work of LeadingAge is focused on advocacy, leadership development, and applied research and promotion of effective services, home health, hospice, community services, senior housing, continuing care communities, nursing homes, as well as technology solutions to seniors and thers with special needs.
1919

7388 LeadingAge Arizona
3877 N 7th St
Suite 240
Phoenix, AZ 85014
602-230-0026
FAX: 602-230-0563
pkoester@leadingageaz.org
www.arizonaleadingage.org

Steven Kolnacki, President
Pam Koester, CEO
Donald G Isaacson, Lobbyist

LeadingAge Arizona is a non-profit association representing organizations that provide health care, housing and services to the elderly citizens of Arizona. The association supports these organizations by offering them leadership, education and advocacy services.

7389 LeadingAge California
1315 I Street
Suite 100
Sacramento, CA 95814
916-392-5111
FAX: 916-428-4250
info@leadingageca.org

Kathryn Roberts, Chair
Jeannee Parker Martin, President & CEO
Jan Guiliano, Vice President of Education

LeadingAge California advocates for non-profit organizations that provide health care, housing and community services to older adults. Services offered by LeadingAge include advocacy, public education and advertising.

7390 LeadingAge Connecticut
110 Barnes Rd
Wallingford, CT 06492
203-678-4477
FAX: 203-678-4650
leadingagect@leadingagect.org
www.leadingagect.org

William Fiocchetta, Chair
Mag Morelli, President
Nurka Carrero, Office Manager

LeadingAge Connecticut is a provider of support services to non-profit organizations serving elderly and chronically ill individuals. Supports include advocacy and information provided to members of skilled nursing facilities, intermediate care facilities, residential care homes, chronic disease hospitals, adult day centers, senior housing communities and more.

7391 LeadingAge Gulf States
P.O. Box 1748
Marrero, LA 70073
504-442-0483
FAX: 504-689-3982
kcontrenchis@leadingagegulfstates.org
www.leadingagegulfstates.org

Dennis Adams, Chair
Karen Contrenchis, NFA, CASP, President
Scott Crabtree, Vice Chair

Organization offering educational and advocacy supports to long term care organizations working in the areas of senior housing, nursing homes, adult day care, assisted living, retirement communities, Alzheimer programs and home and community based services.

7392 LeadingAge Illinois
1001 Warrenville Rd
Suite 150
Lisle, IL 60532
630-325-6170
FAX: 630-325-0749
info@leadingageil.org

Deb Reardanz, Chair
Karen Messer, President & CEO
Angela Schnepf, Executive Vice President

LeadingAge Illinois represents organizations specializing in the field of senior care services, offering them advocacy, networking, public policy and employment resources to help them thrive in their missions.

7393 LeadingAge Indiana
PO Box 68829
Indianapolis, IN 46268-0829
317-733-2380
FAX: 317-733-2385
mrinebold@leadingageindiana.org
www.leadingageindiana.org

Mike Rinebold, President
Susan Darwent, Vice President of Operations
Kathy Johnson, RN, WCC, Vice President of Clinical & Regulatory Services

LeadingAge Indiana is an association representing non-profit organizations that provide health care, services and housing for seniors throughout Indiana. LeadingAge offers education, advocacy and networking opportunities to their members.

7394 LeadingAge Iowa
4200 University Ave
Suite 305
West Des Moines, IA 50266
515-440-4630
888-440-4630
FAX: 515-440-4631
info@leadingageiowa.org
www.leadingageiowa.org

Bert Vigen, Chair
Shannon Strickler, President & CEO
Matt Blake, Director, Government Relations & Member Services

LeadingAge Iowa serves non-profit and missiondriven organizations dedicated to providing quality housing, health, community, and related services to Iowa's seniors. Supports provided include advocacy, education and collaboration.

7395 LeadingAge Kentucky
2501 Nelson Miller Pkwy
Suite 101
Louisville, KY 40223
502-992-4380
FAX: 502-992-4390
info@leadingageky.org
leadingageky.org

Timothy Veno, President & CEO

LeadingAge Kentucky represents non-profit organizations that offer services for the elderly and the disabled. LeadingAge offers advocacy and educational services and resources to their members.

7396 LeadingAge Maine & New Hampshire
55 Main St
Suite 316
Newmarket, NH 03857
603-292-6441
lhenderson@leadingagemenh.org
www.leadingagemenh.org

Rebecca Smith, Chair
Deb Riddell, Vice Chair
Lisa Henderson, Executive Director

LeadingAge Maine & New Hampshire aims to promote the interests of its non-profit members which provide healthy, affordable and ethical long-term care to the older citizens of Maine and New Hampshire. LeadingAge offers this support through education, advocacy, representation and collaboration.

7397   LeadingAge Massachusetts
246 Walnut St
Suite 203
Newton, MA 02460   617-244-2999
                                    FAX: 617-244-2995
                                    www.leadingagema.org

Jered Stewart, Chairperson
Elissa Sherman, President
Lynn Monaghan, Events & Education Manager
LeadingAge Massachusetts represents non-profit providers of
health care, housing, and services for seniors in Massachusetts.
Some services offered by LeadingAge include education and
events, webinars, networking opportunities, technology re-
sources, advocacy and consumer resources.

7398   LeadingAge Missouri
3412 Knipp Dr
Suite 102
Jefferson City, MO 65109   573-635-6244
                                    FAX: 573-635-6618
                          debbiecheshire@leadingagemissouri.org
                                    www.leadingagemissouri.org

Chris Crouch, Chair
Bill Bates, CEO
Nancie McAnaugh, Chief Operating Officer
LeadingAge Missouri's work is dedicated to assisting its members to be leaders in the delivery of quality long-term health care,
housing, and services for older adults in Missouri. Some services
provided by LeadingAge include advocacy, public education,
consumer resources and more.

7399   LeadingAge Nebraska
900 N 90th St
Suite 940
Omaha, NE 68114   402-326-2790
                                    www.leadingagene.org

Julie Sebastian, Board Chair
Jeremy Hohlen, CEO
Cheryl Wichman, Director of Professional Development
LeadingAge Nebraska represents the full continuum of mis-
sion-driven, non-profit providers of health care, housing and ser-
vices for older adults in Nebraska. Some supports offered by
LeadingAge include educational conferences, webinars, work-
shops and advocacy.

7400   LeadingAge New Jersey
3705 Quakerbridge Rd
Suite 102
Hamilton, NJ 08619   609-452-1161
                                    FAX: 609-452-2907
                                    www.leadingagenj.org

Toni Lynn Davis, Chairperson
Michele M Kent, President & CEO
Diane Borgstrom, Finance Coordinator
LeadingAge New Jersey represents non-profit nursing homes, assisted living residences, residential health care centers, independent senior housing, and continuing care retirement
communities throughout New Jersey. Members are supported
through advocacy, education, and fellowship.

7401   LeadingAge New York
13 British American Blvd
Suite 2
Latham, NY 12110-1431   518-867-8383
                                    FAX: 518-867-8384
                                    info@leadingageny.org
                                    www.leadingageny.org

James W Clyne, President & CEO
Daniel J Heim, Executive Vice President
Ellen Quinn, SPHR, Vice President of Human Resources
LeadingAge New York represents non-profit, mission-driven and
public continuing care providers, including nursing homes, senior housing, adult care facilities, continuing care retirement
communities, assisted living and community service providers.
LeadingAge provides its members with education, publications,
conferences and consultation services to help them better serve
their communities.

7402   LeadingAge North Carolina
222 N Person St
Raleigh, NC 27601   919-571-8333
                                    FAX: 919-571-1297
                                    info@leadingagenc.org
                                    www.leadingagenc.org

Robert Wernet, Chair
Tom Akins, President & CEO
Leslie Roseboro, Vice President
LeadingAge North Carolina represents non-profit providers of
care, housing, health, community and related services to the elderly. One of its primary goals is to advance policies, practices
and research to empower the aging population.

7403   LeadingAge Ohio
2233 N Bank Dr
Columbus, OH 43220   614-444-2882
                                    FAX: 614-444-2974
                                    info@leadingageohio.org
                                    www.leadingageohio.org

Judy Budi, Chair
Kenneth Daniel, Vice Chair
Kathryn Brod, President & CEO
LeadingAge Ohio represents long-term care organizations. Service providers supported include those working in the fields of
senior housing, adult day care, home- and community-based services, assisted living and nursing. Some supports offered by
LeadingAge Ohio include policy advocacy, education, employment support and resources for families.

7404   LeadingAge Oklahoma
P.O. Box 1383
El Reno, OK 73036   405-640-8040
                                    inquiry@leadingageok.org
                                    leadingageok.org

Lindsay Fick, President
Mary Brinkley, Executive Director
Mark Gray, Public Policy Congress
LeadingAge Oklahoma represents non-profit organizations that
serve the aging people of Oklahoma. LeadingAge assists these organizations through advocacy, consumer services, directories,
education, a job bank and more.

7405   LeadingAge Oregon
7340 SW Hunziker
Suite 104
Tigard, OR 97223   503-684-3788
                                    FAX: 503-624-0870
                                    info@leadingageoregon.org
                                    www.leadingageoregon.org

Greg Franks, President
Ruth Gulyas, MHA, CEO
Margaret Cervenka, Deputy Director
LeadingAge Oregon represents non-profits that provide housing,
health care, community and related services to the elderly and
disabled of Oregon. LeadingAge offers its members advocacy,
networking events and education to help them succeed in their
missions.

7406   LeadingAge PA
1100 Bent Creek Blvd
Mechanicsburg, PA 17050   717-763-5724
                                        800-545-2270
                                    FAX: 717-763-1057
                                    info@leadingagepa.org
                                    www.leadingagepa.org

Susan Drabic, Chair
Ronald Barth, President & CEO
Heidie Dolan, Office Manager & Executive Assistant
LeadingAge PA's mission is to promote the interests of its members through education, advocacy, community forums and
events. Member organizations include adult day care services, assisted living residences, home care services, skilled nursing facilities and other non-profits that serve the aging population of
Pennsylvania.

7407 LeadingAge RI
1 Virginia Ave
Providence, RI 02905   401-490-7612
                                    FAX: 401-490-7614
                                    TTY:401-383-6578
                                    info@leadingageri.org
                                    www.leadingageri.org
Sandra Cullen, President
Stephanie Igoe, Vice President
James Nyberg, MPA, Director
LeadingAge RI seeks to advance excellence in the field of aging services by fostering innovation, collaboration, and ethical leadership through advocacy for public policy, education and professional development.

7408 LeadingAge Texas
2205 Hancock Dr
Austin, TX 78756   512-467-2242
                                    FAX: 512-467-2275
                                    info@leadingagetexas.org
                                    www.leadingagetexas.org
Roque Christensen, Chair
George Linial, President & CEO
Melanie Harrison, Director of Education
LeadingAge Texas provides leadership, advocacy, and education for non-profit retirement housing and nursing home communities that serve the needs of Texas retirees.

7409 LeadingAge Wisconsin
204 S Hamilton St
Madison, WI 53703   608-255-7060
                                    FAX: 608-255-7064
                                    info@leadingagewi.org
                                    www.leadingagewi.org
Fran Petrick, Chair
John Sauer, President & CEO
Jim Williams, Director of Member Enrichment
LeadingAge Wisconsin is committed to advancing the fields of long-term care, assisted living and retirement living. Towards this purpose, LeadingAge offers advocacy, education and collaborative strategies to its members so they could better serve aging people.

7410 LeadingAge Wyoming
2005 Warren Ave
Cheyenne, WY 82001   307-632-9344
                                    FAX: 307-632-9347
                                    eric@wyohospitals.com
                                    www.leadingagewyoming.org
LeadingAge Wyoming represents non-profit organizations dedicated to providing long-term care and assisted living services to Wyoming's elderly. LeadingAge works to develop policies and practices and offer education so their members can thrive in their missions.

7411 Legal Council for Health Justice
17 N State Street
Suite 900
Chicago, IL 60602   312-427-8990
                                    FAX: 312-427-8419
                                    legalcouncil.org
Tom Yates, Executive Director
Ruth Edwards, Senior Director, Program Services
Provides legal advice and services for persons who are HIV positive or have AIDS, as well as their families. Also serves individuals with disabilities and chronic illnesses, senior citizens, and the homeless.
1919

7412 LifeSpan Network
10280 Old Columbia Rd
Suite 220
Columbia, MD 21044   410-381-1176
                                    FAX: 410-381-0240
                                    www.lifespan-network.org
Dennis Hunter, Chair
Kevin Heffner, President
Danna Kauffman, Public Policy Consultant
Senior care provider representing more than 330 senior care provider organizations in Maryland and the District of Columbia. Lifespan members include non-profit and proprietary independ-

ent living, assisted living, continuing care retirement communities, nursing facilities, subsidized senior housing and community and hospital based services. LifeSpan provides education, advocacy, products and services to its members.

7413 Medicare Rights Center: New York
266 W 37th Street
3rd Floor
New York, NY 10018   212-869-3850
                                    FAX: 212-869-3532
                                    info@medicarerights.org
                                    www.medicarerights.org
Frederic Riccardi, President
Seeks to ensure the rights of senior citizens and people with disabilities to quality, affordable health care. Provides counseling services to Medicare beneficiaries with health insurance problems and questions; compiles information on inquiries to detect issues and systemic problems in Medicare claims administration. Educates beneficiaries, advocates, providers, and social workers about developments in Medicare law and how to handle problems.
1919

7414 Medicare Rights Center: Washington, DC
1444 I Street NW
Suite 1105
Washington, DC 20005   202-637-0961
                                    FAX: 202-637-0962
                                    info@medicarerights.org
                                    www.medicarerights.org
Frederic Riccardi, President
A consumer service organization that works to ensure access to affordable health care for older adults and peoplw tih disabilities through counseling and advocacy, educational programs, and public policy intiatives.
1919

7415 National Adult Day Services Association
11350 Random Hills Road
Suite 800
Fairfax, VA 22030   877-745-1440
                                    info@nadsa.org
                                    www.nadsa.org
Donna Hale, Executive Director
Lance Roberts, Associate Director, Membership
Aims to be the leading voice of the Adult Day Services industry, representing providers, associations of providers, corporations, educators, students, and retired workers.

7416 National Alliance for Caregiving
1730 Rhode Island Avenue NW
Suite 812
Washington, DC 20036   202-918-1013
                                    FAX: 202-918-1014
                                    info@caregiving.org
                                    www.caregiving.org
C. Grace Whiting, President & CEO
Coalition of organizations focused on improving the lives of family caregivers.
1919

7417 National Asian Pacific Center on Aging
1511 3rd Avenue
Suite 914
Seattle, WA 98101   206-624-1221
                                    FAX: 206-624-1023
                                    napca.org
Joon Bang, President & CEO
Tina Masuda-Draughon, CFO
Advocating for the specific needs of aging Asian Americans and Pacific Islanders.
1919

7418 National Association for Home Care and Hospice
228 Seventh St, SE
Washington, DC 20003   202-547-7424
                                    FAX: 202-547-3540
                                    www.nahc.org
Denise Schrader, Chair
Val J Halamandaris, President
Lucy Andrews, Vice Chair

Professional association representing the interests of chronically ill, disabled, and dying Americans and their caregivers. The association offers advocacy services on policy, resources related to hospice and home care, research sponsorships, education for the public on hospice services and more.

7419   National Association of Area Agencies on Aging
1730 Rhode Island Ave, NW
Suite 1200
Washington, DC 20036   202-872-0888
                                   FAX: 202-872-0057
                                        info@n4a.org
                                        www.n4a.org

Kathryn Boles, President
Doug McKenzie, Chief, Finance & Administration
Martin Kleffner, Director of Operations
The National Association of Area Agencies on Aging (n4a) is the leading voice on aging issues for Area Agencies on Aging and a champion for Title VI Native American aging programs. n4a provides advocacy, training and technical assistance, employment support and information resources to these agencies.

7420   National Association of Counties
660 N Capitol St NW
Suite 400
Washington, DC 20001   202-393-6226
                                        888-407-6226
                                   FAX: 202-393-2630
                                 nacomeetings@naco.org
                                        www.naco.org

Bryan Desloge, President
Matthew Chase, Executive Director
Deborah Stoutamire, Director of Operations
NACO brings together elected officials and aging administrators who are interested in providing quality programs and beter policies for their older constituents. NACO members work with Congress, the Administration on Aging, and other federal agencies to ensure that the nation maintains an effective and efficient safety net of services for the elderly and their families.

7421   National Association of Nutrition and Aging Services Programs (NANASP)
1612 K St NW
Suite 200
Washington, DC 20006   202-682-6899
                                   FAX: 202-223-2099
                                   pcarlson@nanasp.org
                                      www.nanasp.org

Tony Sarmiento, Chair
Robert Blancato, Executive Director
Pam Carlson, Membership & Education
A national membership organization supporting those working to provide older adults with healthy food and nutrition through community-based services. NANASP engages in advocacy on issues such as nutrition, Medicare and Medicaid, elder justice, social security and other retirement security, transportation, and older workers' issues.

7422   National Association of States United for Aging and Disabilities
1201 15th St NW
Suite 350
Washington, DC 20005   202-898-2578
                                   FAX: 202-898-2583
                                       info@nasuad.org
                                      www.nasuad.org

Gary Jessee, President
Martha Roherty, Executive Director
Camille Dobson, Deputy Executive Director
The National Association of States United for Aging and Disabilities (NASUAD) represents the nation's agencies serving in the areas of aging and disabilitie. NASUAD supports state leadership as well as national policies that support home and community based services for seniors and individuals with disabilities.

7423   National Center on Elder Abuse
Administration for Community Living
c/o USC Keck School of Medicine
1000 South Fremont Ave., Unit 22
Alhambra, CA 91803   855-500-3537
                                   FAX: 626-470-9978
                                  ncea-info@aoa.hhs.gov
                                       www.ncea.acl.gov
The NCEA is a national resource center providing up-to-date information on elder abuse, neglect and exploitation to policy makers and the public.
1919

7424   National Clearinghouse on Abuse in Later Life
1400 E Washington Avenue
Suite 227
Madison, WI 53703   608-255-0539
                                   FAX: 608-255-3560
                                      ncall@wcadv.org
                                        www.ncall.us

Bonnie Brandl, Director
Working to end abuse in later life.
1919

7425   National Committee to Preserve SocialSecurity & Medicare
111 K Street NE
Suite 700
Washington, DC 20002   202-216-0420
                                        800-966-1935
                                   FAX: 202-216-0446
                                  webmaster@ncpssm.org
                                       www.ncpssm.org

Max Richtman, President & CEO
An advocacy and education membership organization, works to protect and enhance Federal programs vital to senior's health and economic well-being.
1919

7426   National Council for Aging Care
1200 G Street NW
Washington, DC 20005   877-664-6140
                                        www.aging.com
Seeks to provide older adults with information and resources on health & well-being, caregiving, money and financial planning, and lifestyle, through their Aging.com website.

7427   National Council on Aging
251 18th Street S
Suite 500
Arlington, VA 22202   571-527-3900
                                  membership@ncoa.org
                                        www.ncoa.org
James Knickman, Interim President & CEO
Kristin Kiefer, Cheif Administrative Officer
Donna Whitt, Senior Vice President & Chief Financial Officer
Emphasizes the needs for in-home and community-based health care and social services designed to help older persons remain in or return to their homes and live independently, works to educate and assist voluntary organizations to help develop such services.
1919

7428   National Falls Prevention Resource Center
Center for Healthy Aging
251 18th Street S
Suite 500
Arlington, VA 22202   571-527-3900
                                        www.ncoa.org
Supporting the implementation and dissemination of evidence-based falls prevention programs and strategies across the nation.

7429   National Gerontological Nursing Association
121 W State St
Geneva, IL 60134   630-748-4616
                              ngna@affinity-strategies.com
                                        www.ngna.org

Joanne Alderman, President
Sandra Kuebler, Treasurer
Elizabeth Tanner, Secretary

An association providing clinical care for older adults. Their member organizations include clinicians, educators, and researchers specializing in different areas of senior care services.

7430 National Hispanic Council on Aging
734 15th St NW
Suite 1050
Washington, DC 20005
202-347-9733
FAX: 202-347-9735
nhcoa@nhcoa.org
www.nhcoa.org

Octavio Martinez, Ph.D, Chair
Yanira Cruz, Ph.D, President & CEO
Maria Eugenia Hernandez-Lane, Vice President
The National Hispanic Council on Aging (NHCOA) works to improve quality of life for Hispanic seniors. With a Hispanic Aging Network of community-based organizations across the U.S., the District of Columbia and Puerto Rico, NHCOA aims to provide public education and adovocacy in areas such as economic security, health, and housing.

7431 National Hospice & Palliative CareOrganization (NHPCO)
1731 King Street
Suite 100
Alexandria, VA 22314
703-837-1500
800-646-6460
FAX: 703-837-1233
www.nhpco.org

Edo Banach, JD, President & CEO
Hannah Yang Moore, MPH, Chief Advocacy Officer
The organization seeks to improve end-of-life care, widen access to hospice care, and improve quality of life for the dying and their loved ones.
1919

7432 National Indian Council on Aging, Inc.
8500 Menaul Blvd. NE
Suite B470
Albuquerque, NM 87112
505-292-2001
FAX: 505-292-1922
info@nicoa.org
www.nicoa.org

Randella Bluehoose, Executive Director
A non-profit organization was founded by members of the National Tribal Chairmen's Association that called for a national organization to advocate for improved, comprehensive health and social services to American Indian and Alaska Native Elders.

7433 National Institute of Senior Centers
National Council on Aging
251 18th Street S
Suite 500
Arlington, VA 22202
571-527-3900
www.ncoa.org

Supporting the nation's senior centers.
1919

7434 National Institute on Aging
31 Center Dr., MSC 2292
Building 31, Room 5C27
Bethesda, MD 20892
800-222-2225
TTY:800-222-4225
niaic@nia.nih.gov
www.nia.nih.gov

Richard J. Hodes, Director
Lisa Mascone, Deputy Director, Management
Luigi Ferrucci, Scientific Director
Seeks to understand the nature of aging, and to extend healthy, active years of life. Free resources are available on topics such as Alzheimer's & dementia, caregiving, cognitive heath, end of life care, and more.

7435 National Institutes of Health
9000 Rockville Pike
Bethesda, MD 20892
301-496-4000
nihinfo@od.nih.gov
www.nih.gov

Francis S. Collins, Director
The nation's medical research agency.
1918

7436 National Older Worker Career Center
3811 N Fairfax Drive
Suite 900
Arlington, VA 22203
703-558-4200
www.nowcc.org

Cito Vanegas, President & CEO
National non-profit promoting experienced workers as staffing options to government agencies.
1919

7437 National Resource Center on Nutrition & Aging
Meals on Wheels America
1550 Crystal Drive
Suite 1004
Arlington, VA 22202
703-548-5558
FAX: 703-548-8024
nutritionandaging.org

Ucheoma Akobundu, Director, Nutrition Strategy
Sharron Corle, Director, Learning & Development
Promoting better nutrition and active healthy aging.
1920

7438 National Senior Citizens Law Center: Oakland
1330 Broadway
Suite 525
Oakland, CA 94612
510-663-1055
www.justiceinaging.org

Kevin Prindiville, Executive Director
Advocates nationwide to promote the independence and well-being of low-income elderly individuals, as well as persons with disabilities, with particular emphais on women and racial and ethnic minorities. Advocates through litigation and agency representation and assistance to attotneys and paralegals in field programs.

7439 National Senior Citizens Law Center: Los Angeles
3660 Wilshire Boulevard
Suite 718
Los Angeles, CA 90010
213-639-0930
www.justiceinaging.org

Kevin Prindiville, Executive Director
Legal services support center specializing in the legal problems of the elderly poor. Acts as advocate on behalf of elderly, poor clients in litigation and administrative affairs. Sponsors conferences and workshops on areas of the law affecting the elderly. See Legal Resources chapter for specific state resorces.

7440 National Senior Corps Association
PO Box 360
Farmington, UT 84025
928-523-6585
sgrove@jfsmetrowest.org
www.nscatogether.org

Erin Kruse, President
Stephanie Grove, Membership Director
Provides service for aging adults.
1919

7441 National Seniors Council
1100 North Glebe Road
Suite 1010
Arlington, VA 22201
571-425-4153
nationalseniorscouncil.org

Carole Rhodes, National Director
The council seeks to serve the needs of the new generation of retirees, as an alternative to organizations such as the AARP.

7442 Office for American Indian, Alaskan Native and Native Hawaiian Elders
Administration for Community Living
330 C St. SW
Washington, DC 20201
202-401-4634
800-677-1116
olderindians@acl.hhs.gov
olderindians.acl.gov/about

Cynthia LaCounte, Director
Cecelia Aldridge, Aging Services Program Specialist, Program Officer
Administers the Title VI program by overseeing Title VI funding to programs that provide nutrition, support, and caregiver support services for Native Americans. The Office operates a website that provides technical assistance resources to Title VI

directors and serves as a forum for communication between Title VI programs.

7443 Points of Light: Atlanta
600 Means Street
Suite 210
Atlanta, GA 30318   404-979-2900
                                      FAX: 404-979-2901
                                   info@pointsoflight.org
                                   www.pointsoflight.org

Natalye Paquin, President & CEO
Robert E. Herrera, CFO
Mobilizing people to take action on the causes they care about.

7444 Points of Light: Washington, DC
1400 G Street NW
Washington, DC 20005   404-979-2900
                                      FAX: 404-979-2901
                                   info@pointsoflight.org
                                   www.pointsoflight.org

Natalye Paquin, President & CEO
Robert E. Herrera, CFO
Mobilizing people to take action on the causes they care about.

7445 Quality Improvement Organizations

                                         qioprogram.org
Coalition of 28 organizations working to make nursing homes better places to live, work and visit.
1920

7446 Senior Resource LLC

                               questions@seniorresource.com
                                   www.seniorresource.com
The company operates Seniorresource.com, which provides information to older adults on needed facilities and services, including through internet directories and an archive of E-zines.
1995 pages

7447 Senior Service America
8403 Colesville Rd
Suite 200
Silver Spring, MD 20910   301-578-8900
                                      FAX: 301-578-8947
                                      contact@ssa-i.org
                                   www.seniorserviceamerica.org

Spence Limbocker, Chair
Gary A Officer, Executive Director
Donna Satterthwaite, Director, Workforce Development
Senior Service America offers employment programs for seniors in America.

7448 Society for Neuroscience
1121 14th Street NW
Suite 1010
Washginton, DC 20005   202-962-4000
                                         marty@sfn.org
                                             sfn.org

Marty Saggese, Executive Director
Melissa Garcia, Associate Executive Director
Large international organization of scientists and physicians devoted to the study of the brain and the nervous system.
1919

7449 Tennessee Hospital Association
5201 Virginia Way
Brentwood, TN 37027   615-256-8240
                                      FAX: 615-242-4803
                                       yjames@tha.com
                                            tha.com

Alan Watson, Chairman
Craig Becker, President & CEO
Mary Layne Van Cleave, Executive Vice President & Chief Operating Officer
The Tennessee Hospital Association provides education and information to its members in the health care field so that organizations may serve their constituencies more effectively. The association also offers professional development programs in the areas of insurance, administration and operations, project management, financial services and human resources.

7450 The Gerontological Society of America
1220 L St NW
Suite 901
Washington, DC 20005   202-842-1275
                                        geron@geron.org
                                         www.geron.org

Barbara Resnick, PhD, CRNP, President
James Appleby, Executive Director & CEO
Patricia M D'Antonio, Senior Director, Professional Affairs & Membership
The organization seeks to advance the study of aging by supporting gerontology research. This is accomplished through encouraging communication among professionals, promoting research publications, expanding gerontology education programs and more.

7451 US Administration on Aging
330 C St. SW
Washington, DC 20201   202-401-4634
                                      aclinfo@acl.hhs.gov
                               acl.gov/about-acl/administration-aging
Edwin Walker, Deputy Assistant Secretary for Aging
The Administration on Aging, an agency in the US Department of Health and Human Services, and under the Administration for Community Living, provides home and community-based care for older persons and their caregivers.

7452 Unbound
1 Elmwood Avenue
Kansas City, KS 66103   913-384-6500
                                           800-875-6564
                                       mail@unbound.org
                                      www.unbound.org

Scott Wasserman, President & CEO
Seeks to advance the physical, mental, spiritual, and social welfare of the economically disadvantaged, especially children and aging persons in developing countries. US sponsors provide financial support and correspond with individuals in need; volunteers help provide social services, including medical, educational, and nutritional programs.
1919

7453 Virginia Center on Aging
Virginia Commonwealth University
Box 980229
Richmond, VA 23298   804-828-1525
                                          vcoa@vcu.edu
                                       vcoa.chp.vcu.edu

Edward F. Ansello, PhD, Director
Leland Waters, PhD, Associate Director
The Virginia Center on Aging is a statewide agency created by the Virginia General Assembly, with our home at Virginia Commonwealth University. Since 1978, VCoA has worked diligently to protect and improve the quality of life of older Virginians, so that they may remain independent and contributing members in their communities. Our four program areas include: abuse in later life, dementia research, geriatrics education, and lifelong learning.

Books

7454 Activities in Action
Routledge (Taylor & Francis Group)
270 Madison Ave
Fl 4 #4
New York, NY 10016-0601   212-695-6599
                                           800-634-7064
                                      FAX: 212-563-2269
                                   www.routledgementalhealth.com

Jeffrey Lim, Director
Francis Chua, Manager
Tamaryn Anderson, Marketing Manager
An invaluable resource which serves as a catalyst for professional and personal growth and provides a national forum on geriatric and activity issues. *$30.00*
116 pages Hardcover
ISBN 1-560241-32-4

7455 Activities with Developmentally Disabled Elderly and Older Adults
Routledge (Taylor & Francis Group)
270 Madison Ave
Fl 4 #4
New York, NY 10016-601   212-695-6599
800-637-7064
FAX: 212-563-2269
www.routledgementalhealth.com
Jeffrey Lim, Director
Francis Chua, Manager
Tamaryn Anderson, Marketing Manager
Learn how to effectively plan and deliver activities for a growing number of older people with developmental disabilities. It aims to stimulate interest and continued support for recreation program development and implementation among developmental disability and aging service systems. *$42.00*
164 pages Hardcover
ISBN 1-560241-74-4

7456 Aging and Developmental Disability: Current Research, Programming, and Practice
Routledge (Taylor & Francis Group)
270 Madison Ave
Fl 4 #4
New York, NY 10016-601   212-695-6599
800-634-7064
FAX: 212-563-2269
www.routledgementalhealth.com
Joy Hammel, Author
Susan Nochajski, Co-Author
Explores research findings and their implications for practice in relation to normative and disability-related aging experiences and issues. It discusses the effectiveness of specific intervention targeted toward aging adults with developmental disabilities such as Down's Syndrome, cerebral palsy, autism, and epilepsy, and offers suggestions for practice and future research in this area. *$48.00*
112 pages Hardcover
ISBN 0-789010-39-1

7457 Aging and Family Therapy: Practitioner Perspectives on Golden Pond
Routledge (Taylor & Francis Group)
270 Madison Ave
Fl 4 #4
New York, NY 10016-601   212-695-6599
800-634-7064
FAX: 212-563-2269
www.routledgementalhealth.com
George Hughston, Author
Victor Christopherson, Co-Author
Marilyn Bojean, Co-Author
Here are creative strategies for use in therapy with older adults and their families. This significant new book provides practitioners with information, insight, reference tools, and other sources that will contribute to more effective intervention with the elderly and their families. *$48.00*
260 pages Hardcover
ISBN 0-866567-78-7

7458 Aging in Stride
IlluminAge Communications Partners
2200 1st Ave South
Suite 400
Seattle, WA 98134-1408   206-269-6363
888-620-8816
FAX: 206-269-6350
Dennis Kenny, Owner
Elizabeth N Oettinger, Co-Author
Dennis E Kenny JD, Co-Author
Guide to aging, the special needs of older adults, and the demands of providing care and support. Experts explain potential conflicts, planning opportunities and strategies for success. Six guides. *$24.95*
Paperback

7459 Aging in the Designed Environment
Routledge (Taylor & Francis Group)
270 Madison Ave
Fl 4 #4
New York, NY 10016-601   212-216-7800
800-634-7064
FAX: 212-563-2269
www.routledgementalhealth.com
Margaret Christenson, Author
Ellen D Taira, Co-Author
The key sourcebook for physical and occupational therapists developing and implementing environmental designs for the aging. *$30.00*
146 pages Hardcover
ISBN 1-560240-31-0

7460 Aging with a Disability
Special Needs Project
324 State Street
Suite H
Santa Barbara, CA 93101-2364   818-718-9900
800-333-6867
FAX: 818-349-2027
editor@specialneeds.com
www.specialneeds.com
Hod Gray, Owner
Laura Mosqueda, Co-Author
Aging with a Disability provides clinicians with a complete guide to the care and treatment of persons aging with a disability. Divided into five parts, this book first addresses the perspective of the person with a disability and his or her family. *$24.95*
328 pages Paperback

7461 Assistive Technology for Older Persons: A Handbook
Idaho Assistive Technology Project
University of Idaho
1187 Altiras Dr.
Moscow, ID 83843   208-885-3557
800-432-8324
FAX: 208-885-6102
idahoat@uidaho.edu
www.idahoat.org
Ron Seiler, Project Director
This handbook is designed as a guide for Idaho's older citizens who, as they age, wish to preserve their independence, autonomy, productivity, and dignity. It is intended to provide information about assistive technology, home modifications, and the many service options available to older people in the mcomunities across the state.

7462 Caring for Those You Love: A Guide to Compassionate Care for the Aged
Horizon Publishers & Distributors
191 N 650 E
Bountiful, UT 84010-3628   801-295-9451
866-818-6277
FAX: 801-298-1305
www.duanescrowther.com
Duane S. Crowther, Author/President
Jean Crowther, Vice President/Sec
David Crowther, Vice President
This book is a practical guide to coping with special problems of the aged and infirm, and examines the many challenges of caring for the elderly on a personal and family level. *$12.98*
108 pages
ISBN 0-882902-70-9

7463 Chronically Disabled Elderly in Society
Greenwood Publishing Group
88 Post Rd W
Westport, CT 06880-4208   203-226-3571
800-225-5800
FAX: 877-231-6980
www.greenwood.com
Merna J Alpert, Author
Lisa Scott, President
Herman Bruggink, CEO
This timely work increases awareness of and knowledge about problems of societal living among the chronically disabled el-

derly, with implications for policy makers, educational institutions, advocacy groups, families and individuals. *$76.95*
160 pages Hardcover
ISBN 0-313291-09-8

7464 Coping and Caring: Living with Alzheimer's Disease
AARP Fulfillment
601 E St NW
Washington, DC 20049
800-687-2277
TTY:877-434-7589
member@aarp.org
www.aarp.org

Charles Leroux, Author
Steve Cone, Executive Vice President of Inte
Addresses the questions: What is Alzheimer's? How does the disease progress? How long does it last? How can families cope?
24 pages

7465 Elder Abuse and Mistreatment
Routledge (Taylor & Francis Group)
270 Madison Ave
Fl 4 #4
New York, NY 10016-601
212-695-6599
800-634-7064
FAX: 212-563-2269
www.routledgementalhealth.com

Joanna Mellor, Author
Patricia Brownell, Co-Author
Elder Abuse and Mistreatment is a comprehensive overview of current policy issues, new practice models, and up-to-date research on elder abuse and neglect. Experts in the field provide insight into elder abuse with newly examined populations to create an understanding of how to design service plans for victims of abuse and family mistreatment. The book addresses all forms of abuse and neglect, examining the value issues and ethical dilemmas that social workers face in providing service to elderl
$120.00
284 pages Paperback
ISBN 0-789030-22-1

7466 Explore Your Options
Kansas Department on Aging
503 S Kansas Ave
New England Building
Topeka, KS 66603- 3404
785-296-4986
800-432-3535
FAX: 785-296-0256
TTY: 785-291-3167
wwwmail@kdads.ks.gov
www.agingKansas.org

Maria Russo, President
This book will help you through the maze of services available to Kansas seniors. It is designed to help you take an active role in making decisions that affect your health care and living situation.

7467 Falling in Old Age
Springer Publishing Company
11 W 42nd St
Fl 15 #15
New York, NY 10036-8002
212-431-4370
877-687-7476
FAX: 212-941-7842
cs@springerpub.com
www.springerjournals.com

Ursula Springer, President
Ted Nardin, CEO
Edie Lambiase, CFO
Presented are practical techniques for the prevention of falls and for determining and correcting the causes. *$60.00*
412 pages Hardcover
ISBN 0-826152-91-6

7468 Family Intervention Guide to Mental Illness
New Harbinger Publications
5674 Shattuck Ave
Oakland, CA 94609-1662
510-652-0215
800-748-6273
FAX: 800-652-1613
customerservice@newharbinger.com
www.newharbinger.com

Matthew McKay, Owner
Kim T Mueser, Co-Author
Kirk Johnson, CFO
The Family Intervention Guide to Mental Illness outlines the nine fundamental steps to recognizing, managing, and recovering from mental illness. It provides both diagnostic information and details about therapy options and useful medications. With the right advice, determined effort, and a lot of love, you can make a difference. *$17.95*
240 pages
ISBN 1-572245-06-8

7469 Handbook of Assistive Devices for the Handicapped Elderly
Routledge (Taylor & Francis Group)
270 Madison Ave
Fl 4 #4
New York, NY 10016-601
212-695-6599
800-634-7064
FAX: 212-563-2269
www.routledgementalhealth.com

Joseph A Breuer, Author
Jeffrey Lin, Director
Francis Chua, Manager
Concise yet comprehensive reference of assistive devices for handicapped elders. *$42.00*
77 pages Hardcover
ISBN 0-866561-52-5

7470 Handbook on Ethnicity, Aging and Mental Health
Greenwood Publishing Group
88 Post Rd W
Westport, CT 6880-4208
203-226-3571
800-225-5800
FAX: 877-231-6980
www.greenwood.com

Deborah K Padgett, Author
Lisa Scott, President
Herman Bruggink, CEO
State-of-the-art reference by leading experts and first book-length appraisal of research, practices and policies concerning mental health needs of the ethnic elderly in America. *$141.95*
376 pages Hardcover
ISBN 0-313282-04-8

7471 Health Care of the Aged: Needs, Policies, and Services
Routledge (Taylor & Francis Group)
270 Madison Ave
Fl 4 #4
New York, NY 10016-601
212-695-6599
800-634-7064
FAX: 212-563-2269
www.routledgementalhealth.com

Abraham Monk, Author
Jeffrey Lim, Director
Francis Chua, Manager
Focusing on the need for developing new service delivery models for the aged, this book examines fiscal, political, and social criteria influencing this challenge of the 1990's. The aged are caught in the sweeping changes currently occurring in the financing, organizing and delivery of human health care services. *$36.00*
800 pages Hardcover
ISBN 1-560240-65-5

7472 **Health Promotion and Disease Prevention in Clinical Practice**
Lippincott, Williams & Wilkins
2001 Market Street
Two Commerce Square
Philadelphia, PA 19103-3603   215-521-8300
                                     800-638-3030
                                FAX: 215-521-8902
                          customerservice@lww.com
                                     www.lww.com

Steven H Woolf MD, Co-Author
Steven Jonas MD, Co-Author
Evonne Kaplan-Liss, Co-Author
Incorporating the latest guidelines from major organizations, including the U.S. Preventive Services Task Force, this book offers the clinician a complete overview of how to help patients adopt healthy behaviors and to deliver recommended screening tests and immunizations. *$52.95*
218 pages Softcover
ISBN 0-781775-99-1

7473 **Life Planning for Adults with Developmental Disabilities**
New Harbinger Publications
5674 Shattuck Ave
Oakland, CA 94609-1662   510-652-0215
                                800-748-6273
                           FAX: 800-652-1613
                 customerservice@newharbinger.com
                            www.newharbinger.com

Matthew McKay, Publisher
Kirk Johnson, CFO
Judith Greenbaum PhD, Author
The book begins by assessing the quality of life of the adult with a disability. It offers a wealth of suggestions for making that person's life even better. The book then focuses on long-term planning for the individual with a disability and helps answer the question, Who will take care of my child after I'm gone? *$19.95*
208 pages
ISBN 1-572244-51-1

7474 **Long-Term Care: How to Plan and Pay for It**
NOLO
950 Parker St
Berkeley, CA 94710-2524   510-549-1976
                                800-728-3555
                           FAX: 800-645-0895
                                www.nolo.com

Joseph L Matthews, Author
Ralph Warner, Chariman/CEO
Ann Heron, COO
This book helps you choose a nursing home, or find a viable alternative. Covers how to get the most out of Medicare and other benefit programs.
384 pages Paperback
ISBN 1-413305-21-0

7475 **Mentally Impaired Elderly: Strategies and Interventions to Maintain Function**
Routledge (Taylor & Francis Group)
270 Madison Ave
Fl 4 #4
New York, NY 10016-601   212-695-6599
                                800-634-7064
                           FAX: 212-653-2269
                  www.routledgementalhealth.com

Ellen D Taira, Author
Jeffrey Lim, Director
Francis Chua, Manager
Provides effective support and sensitive care for the most vulnerable segment of the elderly population, those with mental impairment. *$34.00*
171 pages Hardcover
ISBN 1-560241-68-3

7476 **Mirrored Lives: Aging Children and Elderly Parents**
Praeger Publishers
88 Post Rd W
Westport, CT 06880-4208   203-226-3571
                                800-225-5800
                           FAX: 877-231-6980
                            www.greenwood.com

Tom Koch, Author
Lisa Scott, President
Herman Bruggink, CEO
Discusses geriatric decline connected to nonterminal illness in old age. Koch takes a sensitive but thorough look at the declining years of his father. *$117.95*
240 pages Hardcover
ISBN 0-275936-71-6

7477 **Physical & Mental Issues in Aging Sourcebook**
Omnigraphics
615 Griswold Street
Suite 520
Detroit, MI 48226-3261   610-461-3548
                                800-234-1340
                           FAX: 800-875-1340
                       contact@omnigraphics.com
                          www.omnigraphics.com

Peter Ruffner, Co-Founder
Fred Ruffner, Co-Founder
Basic information about maintaining health through the post-reproductive years. Includes stats, recommendations for lifestyle modifications, a glossary and resrouce information *$84.00*
660 pages Hard cover
ISBN 0-780802-33-9

7478 **Prescriptions for Independence: Working with Older People Who are Visually Impaired**
American Foundation for the Blind/AFB Press
11 Penn Plz
Suite 300
New York, NY 10001-2006   212-502-7600
                                800-232-3044
                           FAX: 212-502-7777
                                www.afb.org

Carl Augusto, President
Gerda Groff, Co-Author
Richard Obnen, Chairman of the Board
Easy-to-read manual on how older visually impaired persons can pursue their interests and activities in community residences, senior centers, long-term care facilities and other community settings. Paperback.
99 pages Paperback
ISBN 0-891282-44-0

7479 **Sharing the Burden**
Brookings Institution
1775 Massachusetts Ave NW
Washington, DC 20036-2188   202-797-6000
                              FAX: 202-797-6004
                              www.brookings.edu

Joshua N Weiner, Author
Laurel Hixon Illston, Co-Author
Raymond J Hanley, Co-Author
The authors examine the cost of public and private initiatives and who would pay for them. Their answers emerge from a large computer simulation model that the authors developed. *$42.95*
342 pages Cloth
ISBN 0-815793-78-2

7480 **Social Security, Medicare, and Government Pensions**
NOLO
950 Parker St
Berkeley, CA 94710-2524   510-549-1976
                                800-728-3555
                           FAX: 800-645-0895
                                www.nolo.com

Joseph L Matthews, Author
Dorothy Matthews Berman, Co-Author
Ralph Warner, Chairman/CEO

Social Security, Medicare, SSI and more explained in this all-in-one resource that gets you the most out of your retirement benefits. *$24.95*
480 pages Paperback
ISBN 1-413307-53-5

7481 Successful Models of Community Long Term Care Services for the Elderly
Routledge (Taylor & Francis Group)
270 Madison Ave
Fl 4 #4
New York, NY 10016-601
212-695-6599
800-637-7064
FAX: 212-563-2269
www.routledgementalhealth.com

Eloise Killeffer, Author
Ruth Bennett, Co-Author
Jeffrey Lim, Director
Experienced practitioners provide examples of successful community-based long term care service programs for the elderly. *$72.00*
174 pages Hardcover
ISBN 0-866569-87-3

7482 Therapeutic Activities with Persons Disabled by Alzheimer's Disease
Sage Publications
804 Anacapa Stree
Sanat Barbara, CA 93101-2212
805-899-8620
info@sagepub.com
www.sagepub.com

Sara Miller McCune, Founder, Publisher, Chairperson
Blaise Simqu, CEO
Tracey Ozmina, COO
A program of functional skills for activities of daily living. Hardcover. *$86.00*
432 pages
ISBN 0-834211-62-9

7483 Visually Impaired Seniors as Senior Companions: A Reference Guide
American Foundation for the Blind/AFB Press
11 Penn Plz
Suite 300
New York, NY 10001-2006
212-502-7600
800-232-3044
FAX: 212-502-7777
www.afb.org

Carl Augusto, President
Alan Lindroth, Principal
Richard Obnen, Chairman of the Board
This useful guide describes the Senior Companion Program that is intended to broaden opportunities for older persons with disabilities. Appendix includes training materials, evaluation forms, recruitment and public relations information. *$15.00*
108 pages Paperback
ISBN 0-891282-38-6

7484 Work, Health and Income Among the Elderly
Brookings Institution
1775 Massachusetts Ave NW
Washington, DC 20036-2188
202-797-6000
FAX: 202-797-6004
www.brookings.edu

Gary Burtless, Author
Strobe Talbott, President
Steven Bennett, Vice President/COO
Employment, health and financial information for the elderly. *$26.95*
276 pages Cloth
ISBN 0-815711-76-6

Journals

7485 ATS Journals
25 Broadway
New York, NY 10004
212-315-8600
atsjournals.org

Marc Moss, President
Polly E. Parsons, President Elect
Juan C. Celedon, Secretary/Treasurer
The American Thoracic Society publishes medical research journals with a focus on respiratory issues. Publications include: Respiratory and Critical Care Medicine, Respiratory Cell and Molecular Biology, and Annals of the American Thoracic Society.

7486 Gerontology: Abstracts in Social Gerontology
National Council on the Aging
1901 L St NW
4th Floor
Washington, DC 20036-3506
202-479-1200
FAX: 202-479-0735
TTY:202-479-6674
info@ncoa.org
www.ncoa.org

James Knickman, Interim President & CEO
Detailed abstracts are provided for recent major journal articles, books, reports and other materials on many facets of aging, including: adult education, demography, family relations, institutional care and work attitudes. Item No. AB100; Journals $114.00; Member Discount: $94.00.
Quarterly

7487 Inclusive Practices
TASH
1825 K Street NW
Suite 1250
Washington, DC 20006-1202
202-817-3264
FAX: 202-999-4722
info@tash.org
www.tash.org

Andrea Ruppar, Co-Editor-in-Chief
Jennifer Kurth, Co-Editor-in-Chief
Quarterly online journal featuring articles on special topics in the disability field.
Quarterly

7488 Journal of the American Academy of Audiology (JAAA)
American Academy of Audiology
11480 Commerce Park Dr.
Suite 220
Reston, VA 20191
703-790-8466
FAX: 703-790-8631
infoaud@audiology.org
www.audiology.org

Gary P. Jacobson, Editor-in-Chief
Devin McCaslin, Deputy Editor-in-Chief
James Jerger, Emeritus Editor-in-Chief
The scholarly peer-reviewed journal of the American Academy of Audiology. Publishes articles and clinical reports in all areas of audiology.

7489 Physical & Occupational Therapy in Geriatrics
Taylor & Francis Group, LLC
325 Chestnut Street
Suite 800 #800
Philadelphia, PA 19106-2608
215-625-8900
800-354-1420
FAX: 215-625-2940
haworthpress@taylorandfrancis.com
www.tandf.co.uk

Ellen Dunleavey Taira, Editor
Barbara Pucher, CFO
Focuses on current practices and emerging issues in the care of the older client, including long-term care in institutional and community settings, crisis intervention, and innovative programming; the entire range of problems experienced by the elderly; and the current skills needed for working with older clients. *$99.00*
Quarterly

7490 Research, Advocacy, and Practice for Complex and Chronic Conditions
Council for Exceptional Children
3100 Clarendon Blvd.
Suite 600
Arlington, VA 22201-5332
888-232-7733
TTY:866-915-5000
service@exceptionalchildren.org
www.exceptionalchildren.org

Dusty Columbia Embury, Editor
Peer-reviewed journal covering research, issues, and programs relating to the needs of people with physical, health, or multiple disabilities.

Magazines

7491 A Better Tomorrow
Thomas Nelson
5301 Wisconsin Avenue NW
Suite 620
Washington, DC 20015
202-364-8000
FAX: 202-364-8910
www.thomasnelson.com/

Bruce Barbour, Publisher
Dale Hanson, Editor
Magazine focusing on issues and concerns of senior citizens.

7492 AARP Bulletin
AARP
601 E Street NW
Washington, DC 20049
888-687-2277
www.aarp.org
Resources for online classes, training and more. Topics include Computers/Technology, Health/Wellbeing, Personal Finance. AARP Membership open to individuals age 50+, benefits include access to insurance services, travel discounts, advice on healthy living, financial planning, consumer protection. AARP represents members on issues like Medicare, Social Security, and consumer safety. Publications include the AARP Magazine and AARP Bulletin.

7493 AARP Magazine
American Association of Retired Persons
601 East Street NW
Washington, DC 20049
202-434-3525
888-687-2277
member@aarp.org
www.aarp.org

A Barry Rand, CEO
Steve Cone, Executive Vice President of Integrated Value
Celebrity interviews. Features on health and finance. Movie reviews and more. All with an eye toward the topics and issues you care about most.

7494 ACE Fitness Matters
American Council on Exercise (ACE)
4851 Paramount Drive
San Diego, CA 92123
858-576-6500
888-825-3636
FAX: 858-576-6564
support@acefitness.org
www.acefitness.org/

Herb Flentye, Chair
Scott Murdoch, PhD., RD, Vice Chair
Consumer magazine covering health and fitness news. *$25.00*

7495 AER Report
Association for Education & Rehabilitation
5680 King Centre Dr.
Suite 600
Alexandria, VA 22315
703-671-4500
FAX: 703-671-6391
www.aerbvi.org

Neva Fairchild, President
Contains organizational news, conference dates and information concerning services to visually impaired people.

7496 ASN NEURO
Sage Journals
2455 Teller Road
Thousand Oaks, CA 91320
805-499-9774
journals@sagepub.com
journals.sagepub.com/home/asn

Douglas L. Feinstein, Editor-in-Chief
Sandra J. Hewitt, Deputy Editor-in-Chief
Peer-reviewed open access journal focusing on recent advances in the cellular and molecular neurosciences. It is the official publication of the American Society for Neurochemistry.

7497 Abstracts in Social Gerontology
National Council on Aging
1901 L Street NW
4th Floor
Washington, DC 20036
202-479-1200
800-677-1116
FAX: 202-479-0735
TTY: 202-479-6674
info@ncoa.org
www.ncoa.org

James Knickman, Interim President & CEO
Detailed abstracts are provided for recent major journal articles, books, reports and other materials on many facets of aging, including adult education, demography, family relations, institutional care and work attitudes. *$114.00*

7498 Adapted Physical Activity Quarterly
Human Kinetics
PO Box 5076
1607 N Market Street
Champaign, IL 61820
217-351-5076
800-747-4457
FAX: 217-351-1549
info@hkusa.com
www.humankinetics.com

Brian Holding, CEO
Rainer Martens, Founder
Journal on the study of physical activity for special populations.

7499 Aging International
Transaction Publishers
35 Berrue
New Brunswick, NJ 08901
732-445-1245
888-999-6778
FAX: 732-445-3138
orders@transactionpub.com
www.transactionpub.com/

Mary E. Curtis, Chair
Irving Louis Horowitz, Co-Founder
Journal dedicated to the well-being of older persons worldwide. Explores productive aging, empowerment, life-long learning, health promotion, and services for the elderly, with an emphasis on sharing both common concerns and practical applications. Focuses on social and economic issues, public policies, and use of resources. Published in cooperation with the International Federation on Aging.

7500 Aging News Alert
CD Publications
2222 Sedwick Drive
Durham, NC 27713
301-588-6380
855-237-1396
FAX: 800-508-2592
www.cdpublications.com

Michael Gerecht, President
Twice-monthly newsletter reporting on senior programs, funding opportunities and federal actions affecting the elderly.

7501 Aging Research & Training News
Business Publishers, Inc.
2222 Sedwick Drive
Durham, NC 27713
800-223-8720
FAX: 800-508-2592
www.bpinews.com

Kimberly Gilbert, Managing Editor
Alexa Chew, Contributing Editor

Compilation of studies of aging populations; reports on innovative programs with aging community; federal funding and laws. *$267.00*
8 pages

7502 Aging and Society
Cambridge University Press
32 Avenue of the Americas
New York, NY 10013
212-924-3900
800-221-4512
FAX: 212-691-3239
www.cambridge.org/us/information/contact
Ken Blakemore, Editor
Bill Bythwway, Editor
International journal publishing on topics which further the understanding of human aging. The journal of the Centre for policy on aging and the British Socie for Gerontology.

7503 American Journal of Geriatric Psychiatry
Elsevier
1600 John F Kennedy Boulevard
Philadelphia, PA 19103   www.journals.elsevier.com
Charles F. Reynolds III, MD, Editor-in-Chief
Peer-reviewed articles on the rapidly developing field of geriatric psychiatry, including areas such as the diagnosis and classification of psychiatric disorders, epidemiological and biological correlates of mental health of older adults, and psychopharmacology and other somatic treatments. *$582.00*

7504 American Journal of Speech-Language Pathology
American Speech-Language-Hearing Association (ASHA
2200 Research Boulevard
Rockville, MD 20850
301-296-5700
800-638-8255
FAX: 301-296-8580
www.asha.org/
Elizabeth S. McCrea, PhD, CCC-SLP, President
Barbara K. Cone, PhD, CCC-A, Vice President for Academic Affa

7505 American Legion Magazine
American Legion National Headquarters
PO Box 1055
700 N. Pennsylvania St.
Indianapolis, IN 46206
317-630-1200
800-433-3318
FAX: 317-630-1223
www.legion.org/
Daniel S. Wheeler, National Adjutant
Philip B. Onderdonk Jr., National Judge Advocate
General interest magazine for veterans. *$152.50*

7506 American Rehabilitation ServicesAdministration (RSA)
American Rehabilitation Services Administration (R
400 Maryland Avenue, SW
Washington, DC 20202
202-205-8296
800-USA-LEAR
FAX: 202-205-9874
www2.ed.gov/about/offices/list/osers/rsa
Arne Duncan, Secretary of Education
Jim Shelton, Acting Deputy Secretary
Magazine on rehabilitation of the handicapped. *$9.50*

7507 Assistive Technology
RESNA
2001 K Street NW
3rd Floor North
Washington, DC 20006
202-367-1121
FAX: 202-367-2121
info@resna.org
www.resna.org
Maureen Linden, President
Andrea Van Hook, Interim Executive Director
Journal focusing on assistive technology for persons with disabilities. *$35.00*

7508 Audecibel
International Hearing Society
16880 Middlebelt Road
Suite 4
Livonia, MI 48154
734-522-7200
800-521-5247
FAX: 734-522-0200
www.ihsinfo.org/
Kathleen Mennillo, Executive Director
Magazine publishing technical articles and product announcements on hearing aids and hearing. *$25.00*

7509 Buena Vida
Casiano Communications
1700 Fern ndez Juncos Avenue
San Juan, PR 00909
787-728-3000
800-468-8167
FAX: 787-268-1001
www.casiano.com/
Manuel A. Casiano, Chairman & CEO
Carlos Rom, Executive Vice President
Health and fitness magazine. *$23.95*

7510 Challenge Magazine
Disabled Sports, USA
451 Hungerford Drive
Suite 100
Rockville, MD 20850
301-217-0960
FAX: 301-217-0968
dsusa@dsusa.org
www.disabledsportsusa.org/
Robert Meserve, President
Steven Goodwin, Vice President
Magazine providing information on sports for people with physical disabilities.

7511 Closing the Gap
P.O. Box 68
Henderson, MN 56044
507-248-3294
FAX: 507-248-3810
www.closingthegap.com
Dolores Hagen, Co-Founder
Budd Hagen, Co-Founder
Online membership that includes access to the Solutions on-line magazine and archives, archived webinars and the Resource Directory, a guide to over 2,000 products for children and adults with disabilities

7512 Communication Outlook: Artificial LanguageLaboratory
Artificial Language Laboratory
405 Computer Center
Michigan State University
Lansing, MI 48824
517-353-0870
FAX: 517-353-4766
www.msu.edu/~artlang/CommOut.html
Dr. John B. Eulenberg, Ph.D., Director
Stephen R. Blosser, B.S.M.E., Technical Director
Magazine reporting on the newest developments in the application of technology for neurologically impaired persons. *$18.00*

7513 Conscious Choice
Conscious Communications
920 N Franklin Street
Suite 202
Chicago, IL 60610
312-440-4373
FAX: 312-751-3973
www.consciouscomms.com/
Ross Thompson, Managing Editor
Jim Slama, Publisher
Consumer magazine covering health, nutrition and environmental issues. *$184.00*

7514 Contemporary Gerontology
Springer Publishing Company
11 West 42nd Street
15th Floor
New York, NY 10036 212-431-4370
877-687-7476
FAX: 212-941-7842
cs@springerpub.com, journals@springerpub
www.springerpub.com
James C. Costello, Vice President, Journal Publishi
Theodore C. Nardin, Chief Executive Officer & Publis
Scholarly journal covering gerontology.

7515 Dementia and Geriatric Cognitive Disorders
S. Karger Publishers, Inc.
26 W Avon Road
P.O. Box 529
Unionville, CT 06085 860-675-7834
800-828-5479
FAX: 860-675-7302
www.karger.com/DEM
Victoria Chan-Pilay, Editor-in-Chief
Open-access journal devoted to the study of cognitive dysfunction in preclinical and clinical studies, concentrating on Alzheimer's and Parkinson's disease, Huntington's chorea and other neurodegenerative diseases.

7516 Disability Rag's Ragged Edge Magazine
Advocado Press
PO Box 145
Louisville, KY 40201 502-894-9492
FAX: 502-899-9562
www.advocadopress.org/
Mary Johnson, Mailing Contact/Editor
Magazine of debate on disability rights issues. ISSN# 1095-3949
$17.50
35 pages

7517 Disability Rights Now
Disability Rights Education and Defense Fund
3075 Adeline Street
Suite 210
Berkeley, CA 94703 510-644-2555
800-466-4232
FAX: 510-841-8645
info@dredf.org
dredf.org/
Claudia Center, President and Chair
Susan Henderson, Executive Director
Free quarterly publication describing the activities of the Disability Rights Education and Defense Fund, available in alternative formats.

7518 Disability Statistics Report
Institute for Health & Aging
2 Koret Way, #N-319X
UCSF Box 0602
San Francisco, CA 94143 415-476-1435
FAX: 415-476-9707
info@nursing.ucsf.edu
nursing.ucsf.edu/iha
David Vlahov, RN, PhD, Dean and Professor
Yolanda Abrea, Fiscal Analyst
Magazine providing statistical data on disability in the US as collected by the Disability Statistics Program.

7519 Disability Studies Quarterly
University of Hawaii at Manoa •
2500 Campus Road
Honolulu, HI 96822 808-956-8111
FAX: 808-956-3162
manoa.hawaii.edu/
M.R.C. Greenwood, President
Tom Apple, Chief Executive Officer
Scholarly journal containing articles on all aspects of disability.
$3545.00

7520 Disabled American Veterans Magazines
Disabled American Veterans National Headquarters
PO Box 14301
Cincinnati, OH 45250 859-441-7300
FAX: 859-441-8056
www.dav.org/
Thomas K Keller, Editor
James Chaney, Mailing Contact
Veterans magazine on disability issues. *$15.00*

7521 Disabled People as Second Class Citizens
Springer Publishing Company
11 West 42nd Street
15th Floor
New York, NY 10036 212-431-4370
877-687-7476
FAX: 212-941-7842
cs@springerpub.com, journals@springerpub
www.springerpub.com
James C. Costello, Vice President, Publisher
Theodore C. Nardin, Chief Executive Officer
Disability and legal practice. *$26.95*
320 pages

7522 Domestic Mistreatment of the Elderly:Towards Prevention
AARP
601 E Street NW
Washington, DC 20049 202-434-3525
888-687-2277
FAX: 202-434-3443
member@aarp.org
www.aarp.org
Gail E. Aldrich, Board Chair
Robert G. Romasco, President
This comprehensive publication addresses the problem of mistreatment or neglect in the home.
39 pages

7523 Duplex Planet
Duplex Planet
PO Box 1230
Saratoga Springs, NY 12866 518-692-7410
FAX: 518-692-8208
www.duplexplanet.com/
David Greenberger, Editor/ Founder
Consumer journal covering issues of aging and popular culture.
$122.50

7524 Eating Well Magazine
Eating Well
6221 Shelburne Road
Suite 100
Charlotte, VT 05482 802-985-4500
800-344-3350
FAX: 802-425-3675
www.eatingwell.com
Thomas Witschi, President
Brierley Wright, Managing Editor
Food magazine with emphasis on delicious low-fat cooking and sensible nutrition. *$19.94*

7525 Educational Gerontology
Taylor & Francis
711 3rd Avenue
8th Floor
New York, NY 10017 212-216-7800
800-634-7064
FAX: 212-564-7854
www.taylorandfrancis.com/
D Barry Lumsden, Editor
Kevin Bradley, CEO
Journal publishing original research in the fields of gerontology, adult education, and the social and behavioral sciences.

7526 Elderly Health Services Letter
Health Resources Online
P.O. Box 456
Allenwood, NJ 08720 800-516-4343
FAX: 732-292-1111
Robert K Jenkins, Publisher

An essential tool for senior services professionals. Stays on top of the most current challenges facing senior services professionals, including financing and funding senior services, marketing, positioning senior services for managed care, getting administrative support and more.

7527 Experimental Aging Research
Taylor & Francis
711 3rd Avenue
8th Floor
New York, NY 10017

212-216-7800
800-634-7064
FAX: 212-564-7854
www.taylorandfrancis.com/

Jeffrey Elias, Editor
Kevin Bradley, CEO
International journal devoted to the scientific study of the aging process.

7528 Fitness Diet and Exercise Guide
Family Circle
110 5th Avenue
New York, NY 10011

212-463-1673
800-627-4444
FAX: 212-463-1906
fcfeedback@familycircle.com
www.familycircle.com/

Darcy Jacobs, Executive Editor
Linda Fears, Vice President/Editor in Chief
Magazine suggesting ways to eat healthier and exercise better.

7529 Focus on Geriatric Care and Rehabilitation
Aspen Publishers
7201 McKinney Circle
Frederick, MD 21704

301-644-3599
800-234-1660
FAX: 800-901-9075
www.aspenpublishers.com/

Bob Lemmond, President & CEO
Gustavo Dobles, Vice President & CCO
Monthly journal written for nurses, occupational therapists and administrators in geriatric settings. *$95.00*

7530 Generations
American Society on Aging
575 Market Street
Suite 2100
San Francisco, CA 94105

415-974-9600
800-537-9728
FAX: 415-974-0300
info@asaging.org
www.asaging.org

Peter Kaldest, President & CEO
Robert R. Lowe, COO
Peer-review quarterly journal featuring guest editor. *$30.00*

7531 Geriatrics
ModernMedicine
7500 Old Oak Boulevard
Cleveland, OH 44130

440-891-2769
FAX: 440-891-2635

Don Berman, Director, Business Development
Terry Tetzlaff, Digital Traffic Coordinator
Peer-reviewed, clinical journal for physicians and laypersons relating to medical care of middle-aged and older adults.

7532 Gerontologist
Gerontological Society of America
1220 L Street North West
Washington, DC 20005

202-842-1275
FAX: 202-842-1150
geron@geron.org
www.geron.org

James Appleby, Executive Director and CEO
Linda Krogh Harootyan, Deputy Executive Director
Multidisciplinary peer-reviewed journal presenting new concepts, clinical ideas, and applied research in gerontology. Includes book and audiovisual reviews.

7533 Gerontology
S. Karger Publishers, Inc.
PO Box 529
26 West Avon Road
Unionville, CT 06085

860-675-7834
800-828-5479
FAX: 860-675-7302
karger@snet.net
www.karger.com/

W Meier-Rage, Managing Editor
Monica Brendel, President
Medical journal. *$276.00*

7534 Get Up and Go
Liberty Media Corporation
11551 Forest Central Drive
Suite 305
Dallas, TX 75243

214-341-9429
877-772-1518
FAX: 214-341-9779
www.libertymedia.com/

John C. Malone, Chairman
Gregory B. Maffei, President & CEO
Magazine (tabloid) for people age 50 and over.

7535 Independent Living Provider
Equal Opportunity Publications
1160 E Jericho Turnpike
Suite 200
Huntington, NY 11743

516-421-9421
FAX: 516-421-0359
info@eop.com
www.eop.com/

Tamara Flaum-Dreyfuss, President and Publisher
Maureen Gladstone, Account Executive
Business magazine for home health care.

7536 Informer
The Simon Foundation for Continence
PO Box 815
Wilmette, IL 60091

847-864-3913
800-23S-mon
FAX: 847-864-9758
info@simonfoundation.org
www.simonfoundation.org

Cheryle Gartley, President and Founder
Elizabeth Tr LaGro, Vice President, Communications a
Magazine for persons with bladder or bowel incontinence.

7537 Innovations
National Council on Aging
1901 L Street NW
4th Floor
Washington, DC 20036

202-479-1200
800-677-1116
FAX: 202-479-0735
TTY: 2024796674
info@ncoa.org
www.ncoa.org

James Knickman, Interim President & CEO
Explores significant developments in the field of aging through opinion articles, profiles and research summaries. Features articles on social trends, articles on specific aging programs and information on NCOA's activities. *$50.00*

7538 Inside MS
National Multiple Sclerosis Society
733 3rd Avenue
3rd Floor
New York, NY 10017

212-986-3240
800-FIG-HTMS
FAX: 212-986-7981
editor@nmss.org
www.nationalmssociety.org/

Eli Rubenstein, Chairman of the Board
Cynthia Zagieboylo, President & CEO
Magazine for people with multiple sclerosis, their families, attending professionals, and interested donors. Provides information on coping, research, legislation, medical advances and disability rights advocacy. *$2027.00*
80 pages

7539 International Journal of Aging and Human Development
Baywood Publishing Company, Inc.
PO Box 337
26 Austin Avenue
Amityville, NY 11701　　　　631-691-1270
　　　　　　　　　　　　　800-638-7819
　　　　　　　　　　　FAX: 631-691-1770
　　　　　　　　　　　www.baywood.com/
Adult development and aging featuring original research theory, critial reviews.

7540 International Journal of Technology andAging
Human Sciences Press
233 Spring Street
New York, NY 10013-1522　　212-620-8000
　　　　　　　　　　　　　800-221-9369
　　　　　　　　　　　FAX: 212-463-0742
　　　　　　　　　　　www.springer.com
Designed to serve health-care professionals, researchers, academicians and industries concerned with the convergence of two recent trends, the dramatic advances in technology and the rapidly growing elderly population. $60.00

7541 International Psychogeriatrics
Springer Publishing Company
11 West 42nd Street
15th Floor
New York, NY 10036　　　　212-431-4370
　　　　　　　　　　　　　877-687-7476
　　　　　　　　　　　FAX: 212-941-7842
　　cs@springerpub.com, journals@springerpub
　　　　　　　　　　　www.springerpub.com

James C. Costello, Vice President
Theodore C. Nardin, Chief Executive Officer
Scholarly journal covering psychogeriatric practice, research, and education worldwide.

7542 International Rehabilitation Review
Rehabilitation International
866 United Nations Plaza
Office 422
New York, NY 10017　　　　212-420-1500
　　　　　　　　　　　FAX: 212-505-0871
　　　　　　　　　　　info@riglobal.org
　　　　　　　　　　　www.riglobal.org

Teuta Rexhepi, Secretary General
Zhang Haidi, President

7543 JNeurosci
Society for Neuroscience
1121 14th Street NW
Suite 1010
Washginton, DC 20005　　　202-962-4000
　　　　　　　　　　　　　jn@sfn.org
　　　　　　　　　　　www.jneurosci.org

Marina R. Picciotto, Editor-in-Chief
Teresa Esch, Features Editor
Official peer-reviewed journal of the Society for Neuroscience, publishing research on a broad range of topics of interest to those working on the nervous system.

7544 Journal of Aging and Ethnicity
Springer Publishing Company
11 West 42nd Street
15th Floor
New York, NY 10036　　　　212-431-4370
　　　　　　　　　　　　　877-687-7476
　　　　　　　　　　　FAX: 212-941-7842
　　　　　　　　　　　www.springerpub.com

James C. Costello, Vice President
Theodore C. Nardin, Chief Executive Officer
Scholarly journal for researchers and professionals in gerontology and geriatrics, emphasizing the ethnic population of North America.

7545 Journal of Aging and Health
Sage Publications
2455 Teller Road
Thousand Oaks, CA 91320　　805-499-0721
　　　　　　　　　　　FAX: 805-499-0871
　　　　　　　　　　　www.sagepub.in/

Kyriakos S Markides, Editor
C Anderson, Circulation Manager
Journal presenting research relative to the social and behavioral factors related to aging and health.

7546 Journal of Aging and Physical Activity
Human Kinetics
PO Box 5076
1607 N Market Street
Champaign, IL 61820　　　　217-351-5076
　　　　　　　　　　　　　800-747-4457
　　　　　　　　　　　FAX: 217-351-1549
　　　　　　　　　　　info@hkusa.com
　　　　　　　　　　　www.humankinetics.com

Brian Holding, CEO
Rainer Martens, Founder
Journal examining the relationship between physical activity and the aging process.

7547 Journal of American Aging Association
American Aging Association
52373 Tyndall Falls Drive
Olmstead Falls, OH 44138　　440-793-6565
　　　　　　　　　　　FAX: 440-793-6598
　　　　　　　　　　　ameraging@gmail.com
　　　　　　　　　　　www.americanaging.org

Mitch Harman, Chairperson
LaDora Thompson, President

7548 Journal of Developmental and Physical Disabilities
Kluwer Academic Publishers
101 Philip Drive
Norwell, MA 02061　　　　212-620-8000
　　　　　　　　　　　FAX: 212-463-0742
　　　　　　　　　　　vlib.ustu.ru/storon/kluwer/

Vincent B Hassett, Editor
V Hersen, Advertising Manager
Professional journal.

7549 Journal of Ethics, Law, and Aging
Springer Publishing Company
11 West 42nd Street
15th Floor
New York, NY 10036　　　　212-431-4370
　　　　　　　　　　　　　877-687-7476
　　　　　　　　　　　FAX: 212-941-7842
　　　　　　　　　　　www.springerpub.com

James C. Costello, Vice President, Journal Publishing
Theodore C. Nardin, Chief Executive Officer & Publisher
Scholarly journal covering ethical and legal issues regarding aging for professionals who plan, administer, and provide and finance services to the elderly.

7550 Journal of Mental Health and Aging
Springer Publishing Company
11 West 42nd Street
15th Floor
New York, NY 10036　　　　212-431-4370
　　　　　　　　　　　　　877-687-7476
　　　　　　　　　　　FAX: 212-941-7842
　　　　　　　　　　　www.springerpub.com

James C. Costello, Vice President
Theodore C. Nardin, Chief Executive Officer
Scholarly journal covering aging population for mental health professionals.

7551   Journal of Nuclear Medicine
Society of Nuclear Medicine and Molecular Imaging
1850 Samuel Morse Drive
Reston, VA 20190   703-708-9000
                                          800-513-6853
                                  FAX: 703-708-9015
                                  subscriptions@snm.org
                                  jnm.snmjournals.org
Johannes Czernin, MD, Editor-in-Chief
Susan Alexander, Associate Director, Publications
Peer-reviewed journal with clinical investigations, science reports, articles benefitting continuing education, book reviews, employment opportunities, and updates on practice and research. *$58.00*

7552   Journal of Nuclear Medicine Technology
Society of Nuclear Medicine and Molecular Imaging
1850 Samuel Morse Drive
Reston, VA 20190   703-708-9000
                                          800-513-6853
                                  FAX: 703-708-9015
                                  subscriptions@snm.org
                                  tech.snmjournals.org
Kathy S. Thomas, MHA, CNMT, PET, Editor-in-Chief
Susan Alexander, Associate Director, Publications
Peer-reviewed journal dedicated to nuclear medicine technology, with information on credentialing, continuing education and licensure requirements, as well as current news and updates on the field. *$58.00*

7553   Journal of Rehabilitation
National Rehabilitation Association (NRA)
1520 Belle View Blvd
Suite 5142
Alexandria, VA 22307   703-836-0850
                                          888-258-4295
                                  journalofrehab@email.arizona.edu
                                  nationalrehab.org/journal-of-rehabilitation
Wendy Parent-Johnson, Editor
Official journal of the National Rehabilitation Association.
Quarterly

7554   Journal of Religion, Spirituality & Aging

                                  www.tandfonline.com
James W. Ellor, Editor
Features articles, research reports and reviews of new books and audiovisual resources on religion and aging.

7555   Journal of Therapeutic Horticulture
American Horticultural Therapy Association
610 Freedom Business Center
Suite 110
King of Prussia, PA 19406   610-992-0020
                                  FAX: 301-869-2397
                                  ahta.org/
MaryAnne Millan, HTR, President
Leigh Anne Starling, MS, CRC, HTR, Vice President
Journal containing articles on the therapeutic aspects of gardening and agriculture for persons with disabilities. *$15.00*

7556   Kaleidoscope: Exploring the Expirence of Disability through Literature/Fine Arts
United Disability Services
701 S Main Street
Akron, OH 44311   330-762-9755
                                  FAX: 330-762-0912
                                  www.udsakron.org
Karen A. Bozzelli, Chairperson
Bill Choler, Vice Chairperson
Magazine featuring articles on literature and the arts. Disabilitiy related. *$9.00*
64 pages

7557   Macrobiotics Today
George Ohsawa Macrobiotic Foundation
PO Box 3998
Chico, CA 95927   530-566-9765
                                          800-232-2372
                                  FAX: 530-566-9768
                                  www.ohsawamacrobiotics.com/
Carl Ferr,, President
Peter Milbury, Director
Magazine covering macrobiotics, health, and nutrition. *$20.00*

7558   Magazines in Special Media for theHandicapped
National Library Service for the Blind and Physic
1291 Taylor Street NW
Washington, DC 20011   202-707-5100
                                          800-424-8567
                                  FAX: 202-707-0712
                                  TTY: 202-707-0744
                                  www.loc.gov/nls
Karen Keninger, Director
Isabella Marques de Castilla, Deputy Director
Publication includes: List of over 100 public and private organizations that publish magazines in Braille, on cassette, on disc and computer diskette, or in large print or moon type for visually impaired and physically disabled individuals. Entries include: Name of publisher, address, price. Principal content is a bibliography of periodicals, with brief description, frequency, format, and price of each.

7559   Massage Therapy Journal
American Massage Therapy Association
500 Davis St.
Suite 900
Evanston, IL 60201   877-905-2700
                                  info@amtamassage.org
                                  www.amtamassage.org
Christine Bailor-Goodlander, President
Publication focusing on massage therapy research, techniques, and practices. *$20.00*

7560   Mature Health
New York - Haymarket
114 West 26th Street
4th Floor
New York, NY 10001   646-638-6000
Michael Heseltine, Chairman
Kevin Costello, Chief Group Executive
Magazine featuring articles on health aspects of aging, as well as articles on recreation and leisure. *$7.00*

7561   Mature Years
United Methodist Publishing House
201 8th Avenue S
PO Box 801
Nashville, TN 37202   615-749-6000
                                  FAX: 615-749-6079
                                  umph.org/
Neil Alexander, President/Publisher
Jeff Barnes, Executive Director
Magazine promoting the physical and spiritual well-being of older adults.

7562   Men's Health
Rodale Inc
400 South 10th Street
Emmaus, PA 18098   610-967-5171
                                          800-848-4735
                                  FAX: 610-967-7725
                                  RodaleBooks@cdsfulfillment.com
Maria Rodale, CEO and Chairman
Scott D. Schulman, President
Magazine offering health advice for men.

7563 Mental Health Report
Business Publishers, Inc.
2222 Sedwick Drive
Durham, NC 27713
301-495-5570
800-223-8720
FAX: 800-508-2592
www.bpinews.com

Kimberly Gilbert, Managing Editor
Alexa Chew, Contributing Editor
Magazine reporting on legislation affecting the mentally ill and their families. *$325.00*

7564 Modern Maturity
AARP
601 E Street NW
Washington, DC 20049-0003
202-434-2277
202-434-3525
FAX: 888-687-2277
member@aarp.org
www.aarp.org

Gail E. Aldrich, Board Chair
Robert G. Romasco, President
Offers news and information of concern to those 50 and older. Features articles on current events, health, recreation, housing, family life, legislation and other issues.

7565 Molecular Imaging
Sage Journals
2455 Teller Road
Thousand Oaks, CA 91320
805-499-9774
journals@sagepub.com
journals.sagepub.com/home/mix

Henry F. VanBrocklin, PhD, Editor-in-Chief
Peer-reviewed open access journal focusing on molecular imaging research, including basic science, preclinical studies and human applications. Published in association with the Society of Nuclear Medicine and Molecular Imaging.

7566 New Living
New Living Magazine
PO Box 1001
Patchogue, NY 11772
631-751-8819
800-NEW-LIVI
FAX: 631-751-8910
www.newliving.com

Christine Ly Harvey, Publisher and Editor-in-Chief
Features and articles about holistic health and fitness;herbal remedies, preventive medicine, nutrition, mind/body health, spirituality, fitness, recipes, book reviews and more!

7567 PN
PVA Publications
2111 E Highland Avenue
Suite 180
Phoenix, AZ 85016
602-224-0500
888-888-2201
FAX: 602-224-0507
www.pn-magazine.com

Richard Hoover, Editor
Sherri Shea, Marketing & Circulation Director
Magazine spotlighting independent living for paraplegics and quadriplegics. *$23.00*

7568 Prevention
Rodale Inc
400 South 10th Street
Emmaus, PA 18098
610-967-5171
800-848-4735
FAX: 910-967-8963
RodaleBooks@cdsfulfillment.com
rodaleinc.com/

Maria Rodale, CEO and Chairman
Scott D. Schulman, President
Magazine containing articles on wellness, preventive medicine, self-care, and fitness. *$21.97*

7569 Remedy
Rx Remedies
500 Highway 51 North
Suite Q
Ridgeland, MS 39157
601-981-0070
800-826-1197
FAX: 800-729-0167
www.rxremediesms.com/

Joan Montgomery, Publisher
Consumer magazine covering health and wellness for individuals over 50 years in the US. *$183.00*

7570 Research on Aging
Sage Publications
2455 Teller Road
Thousand Oaks, CA 91320
805-499-0721
FAX: 805-499-0871
info@sagepub.com
www.sagepub.in/

Angela M O'Rand, Editor
Blaise R Simqu, CEO
Social gerontology journal.

7571 SELF Magazine
Cond, Nast
4 Times Square
New York, NY 10036
212-286-2860
800-223-0780
FAX: 212-880-8248
communications@condenast.com
www.condenast.com/

Rochelle Udell, Editor-in-Chief
Larry Burstein, Publisher
Magazine serving as a health sourcebook for contemporary women.

7572 Secure Retirement, The Newsmagazine for Mature Americans
The National Committee to Preserve Social Security
111 K Street NE
Suite 700
Washington, DC 20002
202-216-0420
800-966-1935
FAX: 202-216-0446
webmaster@ncpssm.org
www.ncpssm.org

Max Richtman, President & CEO
Magazine for senior citizens and others interested in politics and government and how they affect senior concerns and issues.

7573 Senior Times Magazine
Senior Times Magazine
4400 NW 36th Avenue
Gainesville, FL 32601
352-372-5468
FAX: 352-373-9178
www.seniortimesmagazine.com/

Charlie Delatorre, Publisher
Albert Issac, Editor-in-Chief
Magazine devoted to educating senior citizens on recreational, political, health and financial issues. *$15.00*

7574 Serenity
Little Sisters of The Poor
601 Maiden Choice Lane
Baltimore, MD 21228
410-744-9367
FAX: 410-788-5614
serenitys@littlesistersofthepoor.org
www.littlesistersofthepoor.org/

S R Marguerite, Publications Coordinator
Saint Jeanne Jugan, Founder
Magazine making known the apostolate of Little Sisters of the Poor and providing a positive view of the elderly and the respect due them.
32 pages

7575 **Society of Nuclear Medicine and Molecular Imaging**
1850 Samuel Morse Drive
Reston, VA 20190
703-708-9000
FAX: 703-708-9015
feedback@snmmi.org
www.snmmi.org

Virginia Pappas, CEO
Rebecca Maxey, Director, Communications
The mission of this nonprofit scientific and professional organization is to promote the science, technology and application of nuclear medicine and molecular imaging. Molecular imaging techniques are used to diagnose and manage the treatment of brain disorders such as Alzheimer's and Parkinson's disease, among other conditions.

7576 **Spirit of Change Magazine**
Spirit of Change Magazine
PO Box 405
Uxbridge, MA 01569
508-278-9640
FAX: 508-278-9641
info@spiritofchange.org
www.spiritofchange.org/

Carol Bedrosian, Publisher/Editor
Michella Bedrosian, Advertising Director
Consumer magazine covering holistic health and New Age issues. *$255.00*

7577 **The American Wanderer**
American Volkssport Association (AVA)
1001 Pat Booker Road
Suite 101
Universal City, TX 78148
210-659-2112
FAX: 210-659-1212
AVAHQ@ava.org
www.ava.org

Henry Rosales, Executive Director, AVA
Consumer magazine covering sports and health news. *$20.00*

7578 **Ultrasonic Imaging**
Sage Journals
2455 Teller Road
Thousand Oaks, CA 91320
805-499-9774
journals@sagepub.com
journals.sagepub.com/home/uix

Ernest J. Feleppa, Editor-in-Chief
Roslyn Raskin, Managing Editor
The journal focuses on the rapid publication of original papers on the development and application of ultrasonic techniques, with emphasis on medical diagnosis. Also published are research notes, comments on papers appearing in the journal, book reviews, and occasional review articles.

7579 **VANTAGE**
Signature Group Inc.
15-598 Falconbridge Rd.
Sudbury, ON P3A 5
877-688-1989
FAX: 877-688-0808
www.signaturegroupinc.com/

Paul Misniak, Publisher
Joanie Davies, Mailing Contact
Magazine for active consumers over 55 years of age.

7580 **VFW Auxiliary**
Ladies Auxiliary to the VFW
406 W 34th Street
10th Floor
Kansas City, MO 64111
816-561-8655
FAX: 816-931-4753
info@ladiesauxvfw.org
www.ladiesauxvfw.org

Armithea Borel, National President
Marilyn Ebersole, Mailing Contact/Editor
VFW auxiliary patriotic services magazine.

7581 **Vegetarian Voice**
North American Vegetarian Society
PO Box 72
Dolgeville, NY 13329
518-568-7970
FAX: 518-568-7979
navs@telenet.net
www.navs-online.org

Maribeth Abrams, Managing Editor
Brian Graff, Executive Manager
Consumer magazine covering vegetarianism, health, cooking, environmental and animal protection issues. *$203.00*
40 pages

7582 **Veggie Life**
EGW.com
4075 Papazian Way
208
Fremont, CA 94538
925-671-9852
FAX: 925-671-0692
www.egw.com/

Shanna Masters, Editor
Rickie Wilson, Advertising Manager
Consumer magazine covering health, nutrition, and vegetarian cooking. *$23.70*
68 pages

7583 **Vim & Vigor Magazine**
McMurry
1010 E. Missouri Ave.
Phoenix, AZ 85014
602-395-5850
800-282-5850
FAX: 602-395-5853
mcmurrytmg.com/

Matthew Peterson, CEO
Fred Petrovsky, COO
Magazine offering articles on health, fitness, and medical research. *$7.00*

7584 **WebMD Magazine**
WebMD, LLC
395 Hudson Street
New York, NY 10014
www.webmd.com/magazine
Vanessa Cognard, Publisher
Kristy Hammam, Editor in Chief

7585 **eNeuro**
Society for Neuroscience
1121 14th Street NW
Suite 1010
Washginton, DC 20005
202-312-7305
eNeuro@sfn.org
www.eneuro.org

Christophe Bernard, Editor-in-Chief
Kelly Newton, Director, Scientific Publications
Open-access journal of the Society for Neuroscience.

Newsletters

7586 **AGRAM**
Assoc of Ohio Philanthropic Homes, Housing/Service
855 S Wall St
Columbus, OH 43206-1921
614-444-2882
FAX: 614-444-2974
www.aopha.org

John Alfano, CEO
Tim White, Executive Director
Weekly

7587 **Aging & Vision News**
Lighthouse International
111 E 59th St
New York, NY 10022-1202
212-821-9216
800-829-0500
FAX: 212-821-9707
info@lighthouse.org
www.lightfair.com

Laurie A Silbersweig, Editorial Director

Intended for professionals engaged in research, education or service delivery in the field of vision and aging.
6-12 pages Newsletter

7588 Aging News Alert
C D Publications
8204 Fenton St
Silver Spring, MD 20910-4502

301-588-6380
800-666-6380
FAX: 301-588-6385

Michael Gerecht, President
Ash Gerecht, Co-Owner
Reports on successful senior programs, funding opportunities, and federal actions that effect the elderly. Available in 6, 12 or 24 month subscriptions online and online/print combinations.
$192.00
8 pages Monthly

7589 CAHSA Connecting
Colorado Assoc of Homes and Services for the Aging
1888 Sherman St
Suite 610
Denver, CO 80203-1160

303-837-8834
FAX: 303-837-8836
info@cahsa.org
www.leadingagecolorado.org

Laura Landwirth, Executive Director
Elisabeth Borden, Director
Maureen Hewitt, President
CAHSA Connecting is published monthly by the Colorado Association of Homes and Services for the Aging (CAHSA)

7590 CANPFA-Line
CT Assoc of Not-for-Profit Providers of the Aging
1340 Wilmington Rdg
Berlin, CT 6037

860-828-2903
FAX: 860-828-8694
leadingagect@leadingagect.org
www.leadingagect.org

Mag Morelli, President
Nurka Carrero, Office Manager
Andrea Bellofiore, Director of Member Programs
LeadingAge Connecticut promotes and advocates for a vision of the world in which every community offers an integrated and coordinated continuum of high quality, affordable health care, housing and community based services.
Bi-Monthly

7591 Capitol Focus
Colorado Assoc of Homes and Services for the Aging
1888 Sherman St
Suite 610
Denver, CO 80203-1160

303-837-8834
FAX: 303-837-8836
info@cahsa.org
www.leadingagecolorado.org

Laura Landwirth, Executive Director
Elisabeth Borden, Director
Maureen Hewitt, President
Capitol Focus is a weekly activities summary of the Colorado Legislature for CAHSA members, provided by staff of the Colorado Association of Homes and Services for the Aging.

7592 Capsule
Children of Aging Parents
P.O.Box 167
Richboro, PA 18954-167

215-945-6900
800-227-7294
FAX: 215-945-8720
www.caps4caregivers.org

Karen Rosenberg, Director
An informative newsletter for caregivers.
Quarterly

7593 Elder Visions Newsletter
National Indian Council on Aging
8500 Menaul Blvd. NE
Suite B470
Albuquerque, NM 87112

505-292-2001
FAX: 505-292-1922
info@nicoa.org
www.nicoa.org

Randella Bluehouse, Executive Director
Provides information on issues affecting American Indian and Alaska Native Elders.
Quarterly

7594 Enabling News
Access II Independent Living Centers
101 Industrial Parkway
Gallatin, MO 64640-1280

660-663-2423
888-663-2423
FAX: 660-663-2517
TTY: 660-663-2663
access@accessii.org
www.accessii.org

Debra Hawman, Executive Director
Gary Matticks, Owner
Debra Hawman, Executive Director
It is a newsletter published by Access II.
8 pages Quarterly

7595 Independence
Easterseals
141 W Jackson Blvd.
Suite 1400A
Chicago, IL 60604

312-726-6200
800-221-6827
FAX: 312-726-1494
info@easterseals.com
www.easterseals.com

Angela F. Williams, President & CEO
Glenda Oakley, Chief Financial Officer
Marcy Traxler, Senior Vice President, Network Advancement
Newsletter featuring information on Easterseals services, stories and news from the Office of Public Affairs.
Quarterly

7596 Innovations
National Council on Aging
1901 L Street NW
4th Floor
Washington, DC 20036-3506

202-479-1200
FAX: 202-479-0735
TTY:202-479-6674
info@ncoa.org
www.ncoa.org

James Knickman, Interim President & CEO
Explores significant developments in the field of aging, keeping individuals informed on a broad range of topics.
Quarterly

7597 Legacy
Easterseals
141 W Jackson Blvd.
Suite 1400A
Chicago, IL 60604

312-726-6200
800-221-6827
FAX: 312-726-1494
info@easterseals.com
www.easterseals.com

Angela F. Williams, President & CEO
Glenda Oakley, Chief Financial Officer
Marcy Traxler, Senior Vice President, Network Advancement
Newsletter focusing on planned giving and charitable gift annuities for Easterseals.

7598 NASUA News
National Association of State Units on Aging
1201 15th Street NW
Suite 350
Washington, DC 20005-2842   202-898-2578
                                   FAX: 202-898-2583
                                   www.nasuad.org

Martha Roherty, Executive Director
Peggie Rice, Director of Policy and Legislative Affairs
Eric Risteen, Chief Operating Officer
It is the newsletter of the National Association of State Units on
Aging
Monthly

7599 NCOA Week
National Council on Aging
1901 L Street NW
4th Floor
Washington, DC 20036-3540   202-479-1200
                                   FAX: 202-479-0735
                                   TTY:202-479-6674
                                   info@ncoa.org
                                   www.ncoa.org

James Knickman, Interim President/CEO
Donna Whitt, SVP/CFO
A concise e-newsletters focused on the issues you care about, in-
cluding policies that affect funding, grants and awards you can
apply for, and best practices you can adapt for your center.
Weekly

7600 NNEAHSA
Northn New England Assoc of Homes & Svcs for Aging
PO Box 1428
Standish, ME 04084-1428   207-773-4822
                                  FAX: 207-773-0101
                                  www.agingservicesmenh.org

Sheila Deringis, Editor
Providing healthy, affordable and ethical long-term care to older
citizens throughout Maine, New Hampshire and Vermont.

7601 NSCLC Washington Weekly
National Senior Citizens Law Center
1444 Eye St NW
Suite 1100
Washington, DC 20005-6547   202-289-6976
                                  FAX: 202-289-7224
                                  www.nsclc.org

Paul Nathanson, Executive Director
Edward King, Executive Director
Edward Spurgeon, Executive Director
Provides the latest case information, administration and congres-
sional developments of importance for the elderly.

7602 Part B News
DecisionHealth
9737 Washingtonian Blvd
Two Washingtonian Center, Suite. 20
Gaithersburg, MD 20878-7364   301-287-2682
                                  855-225-5341
                                  FAX: 301-287-2535
                                  customer@decisionhealth.com
                                  www.decisionhealth.com

Scott Kraft, Editor
Scott Kraft, Director, Content Management
Steve Greenberg, President
Each week Part B News brings you comprehensive Medicare Part
B regulatory coverage, plain-English interpretive guidance, Fee
Schedule updates, claims filing strategies, coding, documenta-
tion and payment best practices, and the latest on Congressional
health care deliberations and how they affect your practice.
$519.00
Yearly

7603 Post-Polio Health
Post-Polio Health International
50 Crestwood Executive Ctr.
Suite 440
St. Louis, MO 63126   314-534-0475
                                  FAX: 314-534-5070
                                  editor@post-polio.org
                                  www.post-polio.org

Brian M. Tiburzi, Editor
Post-Polio Health supports Post-Polio Health International's educational, research, and advocacy efforts. Offers information
about relevant events. Published in February, May, August and
November.
12 pages Quarterly

7604 Quality First
American Assoc of Homes and Services for the Aging
2519 Connecticut Ave NW
Washington, DC 20008-1520   202-783-2242
                                  FAX: 202-783-2255
                                  www.leadingage.org

William L Minnix Jr, President
Features helpful tips for marketing services and earning the pub-
lic's trust through the web site.
Quarterly

7605 Senior Focus
National Council on Aging
1901 L Street
4th Floor
Washington, DC 20036-3540   202-479-1200
                                  FAX: 202-479-0735
                                  TTY:202-479-6674
                                  info@ncoa.org
                                  www.ncoa.org

James Knickman, Interim President & CEO
Contains health, financial, lifestyle tips written for seniors
Quarterly

7606 Social Security Bulletin
US Social Security Administration

                                  800-772-1213
                                  TTY:800-325-0778
                                  www.ssa.gov/policy

Stephen G. Evangelista, Acting Deputy Commissioner
Dawn S. Wiggins, Associate Commissioner
Natalie T. Lu, Associate Commissioner
Reports on results of research and analysis pertinent to the Social
Security and SSI programs. *$16.00*
Monthly

Support Groups

7607 Area Agency on Aging of Southwest Arkansas
600 Columbia Road 11 East
PO Box 1863
Magnolia, AR 71753   870-234-7410
                                  800-272-2127
                                  FAX: 870-234-6804
                                  www.agewithdignity.com

Janet Morrison, Executive Director
The Area Agency on Aging of Southwest Arkansas, Inc. is a non-
profit organization serving adults age 60 or older, family caregivers, agencies and organizations working with seniors. It is part
of a national network of more than 650 Area Agencies on Aging
throughout the United States.

7608 Area Agency on Aging: Region One
1366 E Thomas Rd
Suite 108
Phoenix, AZ 85014-5739   602-264-2255
                                  888-783-7500
                                  FAX: 602-230-9132
                                  www.aaaphx.org

Mary Lynn Kasunic, President
Jeannine Berg, Vice Chairman
Bobbie Garland, Vice Chairman

We have a vast variety of programs and services to enhance the quality of life for residents of Maricopa County, Arizona. If you would like more information about services mentioned within the website please call.

7609 High Country Council of Governments Area Agency on Aging
468 New Market Blvd
Boone, NC 28607-1820
828-265-5434
FAX: 828-265-5439
breece@regiond.org
www.regiond.org

Robert L. Johnson, Chairman
Gary D. Blevins, Vice Chair
Brenda Lyerly, Secretary
High Country Council of Governments is the multi-county planning and development agency for the seven northwestern North Carolina counties of Alleghany, Ashe, Avery, Mitchell, Watauga, Wilkes, and Yancey. The High Country region is a voluntary association of towns and counties located in the northern mountains of North Carolina.

7610 Institute on Aging
3575 Geary Blvd
San Francisco, CA 94118-3212
415-750-4111
877-750-4111
FAX: 415-750-5337
info@ioaging.org
www.ioaging.org

J. Thomas Briody, MHSc, President
Dustin Harper, Vice President, Community Living Services
Cindy Kauffman, MS, COO
Support Services for Elders (SSE) provides care coordination, household management, personal support, bookkeeping, and other assistance to help protect your financial affairs.

7611 Land-of-Sky Regional Council Area Agency on Aging
339 New Leicester Hwy
Suite 140
Asheville, NC 28806-2087
828-251-6622
FAX: 828-251-6353
info@landofsky.org
www.landofsky.org

LeeAnne Tucker, Aging & Volunteer Services Director
Terry Albrecht, Program Director
Joan Tuttle, Director
Is the designated regional organization to meet the needs of persons over 60 in Buncombe, Henderson, Madison, and Transylvania counties, by the North Carolina Division of Aging and Adult Services.

7612 Lumber River Council of Governments Area Agency on Aging
30 Cj Walker Rd
COMtech Park
Pembroke, NC 28372-7340
910-618-5533
FAX: 910-521-7556
lrcog@mail.lrcog.dst.nc.us
www.lumberrivercog.org

Michelle Gaitley, Nutrition Program Director
Renee Cooper, Nutrition Program Assistant
Kristen Elk Maynor, Aging Program Coordinator
The Family Caregiver Support Program was created to assist family members, neighbors, and friends who help care for a person over the age of 60, or minor grandchildren being reared by a grandparent over 60.

7613 Mid-America Regional Council - Aging and Adult Services
600 Broadway
Suite 200
Kansas City, MO 64105-1659
816-474-4240
FAX: 816-421-7758
marcinfo@marc.org
www.marc.org/Community/Aging/

James Stowe, Director of Aging & Adult Services
Bob Hogan, Manager of Aging Administrative Services
Shannon Halvorsen, Information & Referral Coordinator
The Department of Aging and Adult Services offers community-based services to aging people in the Cass, Clay, Jackson, Platte and Ray counties. Services include home care, transportation, legal aid, breaks for caregivers and meal delivery.

7614 Mid-Carolina Area Agency on Aging
130 Gillespie Street
3rd Floor, Post Office Drawer 1510
Fayetteville, NC 28301-1510
910-323-4191
FAX: 910-323-9330
gdye@mccog.org
www.mccog.org

James Caldwell, COG Executive Director
Glenda Dye, Aging Director
Lynda Barnett, Aging Care Manager
The Mid-Carolina Area Agency on Aging is designated for planning, administration, and advocacy of services for persons aged 60 and older and their spouses who need assistance in order to remain as independent as possible.

7615 Piedmont Triad Council of Governments Area Agency on Aging
2216 W Meadowview Rd
Suite 201
Greensboro, NC 27407-3480
336-294-4950
FAX: 336-632-0457
www.ptcog.org

Blair Barton-Percival, Director
Adrienne Calhoun, Assistant Director
Bob Cleveland, Aging Program Planner
Responsible for planning, developing, implementing, and coordinating aging services for seven counties in the Piedmont Triad (Alamance, Caswell, Davidson, Guilford, Montgomery, Randolph, and Rockingham) and their 185,00 residents age 60 and older.

7616 Southwestern Commission Area Agency on Aging
125 Bonnie Ln
Sylva, NC 28779-8552
828-586-1962
FAX: 828-586-1968
www.regiona.org

Ryan Sherby, Executive Director
Beth Cook, Workforce Development Director
Janne Mathews, Aging Program Coordinator
The Area Agency on Aging (AAA) works on behalf of older adults and their caregivers in the seven southwestern counties of North Carolina. The Southwestern Commission Area Agency on Aging was established in 1980 as mandated by the 1977 Amendments of the Older Americans Act in order for a Planning and Service Area (PSA) to receive funds from the Act.

7617 Tompkins County Office for the Aging
214 W. Martin Luther King Jr./State
Ithaca, NY 14850-4299
607-274-5482
FAX: 607-274-5495
lholmes@tompkins-co.org

Lisa Holmes, Director
Lisa Lunas, Aging Services Planner
Katrina Schickel, Aging Services Specialist
We provide objective and unbiased information regarding the array of services available for older adults and their caregivers. Established in 1975, our mission is to assist the senior population of Tompkins County to remain independent in their homes as long as is possible and appropriate, and with a decent quality of life and human dignity.

7618 Triangle J Council of Governments Area Agency on Aging
4307 Emperor Blvd
Suite 110
Durham, NC 27703
919-549-0551
FAX: 919-549-9390
ejones@tjcog.org
www.tjaaa.org

Kristen Jackson, Aging Program Coordinator
Mary Warren, Director
Ashley Price, Program Specialist
The Triangle J Council of Governments serves to facilitate and support the development of programs addressing the needs of older adults and to support investment in their talents and interests.

7619   **University of California Memory and Aging Center**
675 Nelson Rising Lane
Suite 190
San Francisco, CA 94143-1207
415-353-2057
FAX: 415-476-5591

Bruce L Miller, Director
Mary Koestler, Project Administrator
Carrie Cheung, Clinic Coordinator
Provides support for patients and families affected by
neurodegenerative diseases. In addition to our established sup-
port groups, we continue to develop new support groups.

7620   **Upper Coastal Plain Council of Governments Area**
Agency on Aging
PO Box 9
Wilson, NC 27894-9
252-234-5952
FAX: 252-234-5971
www.ucpcog.org

Greg Godard, Executive Director
Jody Riddle, AAA Program Director
Helen Page, Aging Programs Specialist
The Upper Coastal Plain Area Agency On Aging is one of 16 Area
Agencies on Aging across the state of NC, serving Region L.
Counties include Edgecombe, Halifax, Nash, Northampton, and
Wilson. The mission of the Area Agency on Aging is to empower
senior adults, family caregivers, and individuals with disabilities
residing in Edgecombe, Halifax, Nash, Northampton, and Wilson
Counties to live independent, meaningful, healthy, and dignified
lives.

Blind & Deaf

Associations

7621 American Association of the Deaf-Blind
248 Rainbow Drive
Suite 14864
Livingston, TX 77399-2048

aadb-info@aadb.org
www.aadb.org

Rene Pellerin, President
Mindy Dill, Vice President
Tara Invidiato, Secretary

The American Association of the Deaf-Blind (AADB) is a non-profit national consumer organization run by and for deaf-blind Americans and their supporters. Deaf-Blind includes all types and degrees of dual vision and hearing loss. The association offers an information clearinghouse, service provider summit, deaf-blind technology summit, research projects, interpretation services, conferences and more.

7622 American Society for Deaf Children
PO Box 23
Woodbine, MD 21797

800-942-2732
info@deafchildren.org
deafchildren.org

Alisha Joslyn-Swob, President
Mark Drolsbaugh, Vice President
Rachel Berman, Secretary

The American Society for Deaf Children provides information for the caretakers of deaf children so children can have full communication access in their home, school and community. The society covers areas such as visual language, audiologists, healthcare providers, assistive technology and more.

7623 Arena Stage
The Mead Center for American Theater
1101 Sixth St. SW
Washington, DC 20024

202-554-9066
FAX: 202-488-4056
TTY:202-484-0247
info@arenastage.org
arenastage.org

Edgar Dobie, Executive Director
Molly Smith, Artistic Director
Joseph Berardelli, CFO

Arena Stage has played a pioneering role in providing access to all productions for people with disabilities. Access services and programs include wheelchair accessible seating; infrared assistive listening devices; Braille, large print, audio description and sign interpretation at designated performances.

7624 Association of Late-Deafened Adults
8038 Macintosh Ln
Suite 2
Rockford, IL 61107-5336

815-332-1515
TTY:815-332-1515
www.alda.org

Rick Brown, President
Cynthia Moynihan, Vice President
Matt Ferrara, Treasurer

The Association of Late-Deafened Adults supports the empowerment of late-deafened people by offering programs and information resources on a variety of topics: technology, disability laws, airline travel and more.

7625 Canadian Deafblind Association
1860 Appleby Line
Unit 14
Burlington, ON, Canada L7L-7H7

905-331-6279
866-229-5832
FAX: 905-319-2027
info@cdbanational.com
www.cdbanational.com

Carolyn Monaco, President
Tom McFadden, National Executive Director

The mission of the Canadian Deafblind Association is to promote and enhance the well-being of people who are deafblind by offering them advocacy, developing and dissemination information, and supporting members and community partners who also serve deafblind people.

7626 Foundation Fighting Blindness
7168 Columbia Gateway Dr.
Suite 100
Columbia, MD 21046

410-423-0600
800-683-5555
TTY:410-363-7139
info@FightBlindness.org
www.blindness.org

Benjamin R. Yerxa, Chief Executive Officer
Jason Menzo, Chief Operating Officer
Todd Durham, VP, Clinical & Outcomes Research

The Foundation Fighting Blindness (FFB) works to promote research in order to prevent, treat and restore vision. FFB is currently the world's leading private funder of retinal disease research, funding over 100 research grants and 150 researchers.

7627 Future Reflections
Deaf-Blind Division of the Ntn'l Fed of the Blind
200 E. Wells St.
at Jernigan Place
Baltimore, MD 21230

410-659-9314
FAX: 410-685-5653
nfbpublications@nfb.org
www.nfb.org

Deborah Kent Stein, Editor

A quarterly magazine for parents and teachers of blind children.

7628 Hearing Loss Association of America
7910 Woodmont Ave
Suite 1200
Bethesda, MD 20814

301-657-2248
FAX: 301-913-9413
inquiry@hearingloss.org
www.hearingloss.org

Barbara Kelley, Executive Director
Lise Hamlin, Director of Public Policy
Carla Beyer-Smolin, National Chapter & Membership Coordinator

The mission of the Hearing Loss Association of America is to open the world of communication to people with hearing loss by offering information, education, resources, advocacy and training.

7629 Helen Keller National Center for Deaf- Blind Youths and Adults
141 Middle Neck Rd
Sands Point, NY 11050

516-944-8900
TTY:516-570-3246
hkncinfo@hknc.org
www.helenkeller.org

Kim Zimmer, President & CEO
Marc Feldman, CPA, Chief Financial Officer
Mary Fu, Chief Development Officer

The center serves deafblind people by offering them assistive technology, vocational services, education, case management, interpretation, medical and mental health services, professional training and other supports that would empower them to work and live independently within their communities.

7630 Idaho Commission for the Blind and Visually Impaired
341 W. Washington St
PO Box 83720
Boise, ID 83720-0012

208-334-3220
800-542-8688
FAX: 208-334-2963
bcunningham@icbvi.idaho.gov
www.icbvi.state.id.us

Britt Raubenheimer, Chair
Beth Cunningham, Administrator
Bailie Welton, Management Assistant

The Idaho Commission for the Blind and Visually Impaired works to empower persons who are blind or visually impaired by providing vocational rehabilitation training, skills training and educational opportunities to achieve self fulfillment ang gain employment. The Commission also strives to serve as a resource to families and employers and to expand public awareness regarding the potential of all persons who are blind or visually impaired.

7631   International Hearing Society
16880 Middlebelt Rd
Suite 4
Livonia, MI 48154   734-522-7200
                                      FAX: 734-522-0200
                                      interact@ihsinfo.org
                                              ihsinfo.org

Annette Cross, BC-HIS, President
Kathleen Mennillo, MBA, Executive Director
Fran Vincent, Director, Membership & Marketing
The International Hearing Society (IHS) represents hearing
healthcare professionals worldwide. Members include professionals engaged in the practice of testing human hearing and selecting, fitting and dispensing hearing instruments. IHS offers
accreditation programs, advocacy, education and training in
support of these services.

7632   Lilac Services for the Blind
1212 N Howard St
Spokane, WA 99201   509-328-9116
                                           800-422-7893
                                      FAX: 509-328-8965
                                      contact@lilacblind.org
                                              lilacblind.org

Eddie Eugenio, President
Cheryl L Martin, Executive Director
Robin Waller, Development Director
Lilac Services for the Blind provides independent living instruction, adaptive aids, counseling, low-vision evaluations, support
groups, Braille transcription services and more for 14 counties in
the inland Northwest.

7633   National Center on Deaf-Blindness (NCDB)
Hellen Keller National Center
141 Middle Neck Rd.
Sands Point, NY 11050   516-366-0047
                                      support@nationaldb.org
                                      www.nationaldb.org

Sam Morgan, Project Director
Julie Durando, Project Co-Director
Peggy Malloy, Information Services & Technology Coordinator
Funded by the federal Department of Education, the Center seeks
to improve quality of life for children who are deaf-blind and
their families.

7634   National Family Association for Deaf-Blind
PO Box 1667
Sands Point, NY 11050   800-255-0411
                                      FAX: 516-883-9060
                                              nfadb.org

Patti McGowan, President
Diana Griffen, Vice President
Jacqueline Izaguirre, Treasurer
The National Family Association for Deaf-Blind (NFADB) is a
nonprofit, volunteer-based family association. The association
offers advocacy, education and family supports to help create empowerment opportunities for deaf-blind people.

7635   National Federation of the Blind
200 E. Wells St.
at Jernigan Place
Baltimore, MD 21230   410-659-9314
                                      FAX: 410-685-5653
                                              nfb@nfb.org
                                              www.nfb.org

Mark A. Riccobono, President
John Berggren, Executive Director, Operations
Anil Lewis, Executive Director, Blindness Initiatives
The National Federation of the Blind (NFB) works to help blind
people achieve self-confidence, self-respect and self-determination and to achieve complete integration into society on a basis of
equality. The Federation provides public educations, information
and referral services, scholarships, literature and publications,
adaptive equipment, advocacy services, legal services,
employment assistance and more.

Camps

7636   Florida Lions Camp
Lions of Multiple District 35
2819 Tiger Lake Road
Lake Wales, FL 33898-9582   863-696-1948
                                      FAX: 863-696-2398
                                      bjcage@hotmail.com
                                      www.lionscampfl.org

Barbara Cage, Executive Director
Liz Cage, Program Director
Carissa Moen, Bookkeeping/Registrar
One-week sessions June-August for youths and adults with visual impairments and other challenging disabilities. Coed, ages 5
and up. A variety of traditional summer camp activities which include: swimming, canoeing, fishing, hiking, camping out and
cooking over a fire, games, arts & crafts, singing & dancing,
hay-wagon rides, challenge course and much more. Activities are
adapted to the age and ability of each camper to ensure maximum
participation, safety and fun.

7637   Florida School for the Deaf and Blind
207 San Marco Ave
St Augustine, FL 32084-2799   904-827-2200
                                           800-344-3732
                                      FAX: 904-827-2325
                                      www.fsdb.k12.fl.us

Dr. Jeanne Glidden Prickett, EdD, Shelter Administrator
Debbie Schuler, Administrator of Instructional S
Cindy Day, Executive Director of Parent Ser
Statewide public boarding school for eligible students who are
deaf/hard-of-hearing or blind/visually impaired. FSDB serves
children who are pre-k through high school.

Books

**7638   A Handbook for Writing Effective Psychoeducational
Reports (2nd Edition)**
PRO-ED Inc.
8700 Shoal Creek Blvd.
Austin, TX 78757-6897   512-451-3246
                                           800-897-3202
                                      FAX: 800-397-7633
                                      general@proedinc.com
                                      www.proedinc.com

Sharon Bradley-Johnson, Author
C. Merle Johnson, Author
This comprehensive book shows how to write useful reports once
assessment information has been attained. It is a valuable resource for professionals working in school systems, as well as for
those graduate students who are just learning to write reports.
$32.00
134 pages Paperback
ISBN 1-416401-40-7

**7639   Communicating with People Who Have Trouble Hearing
& Seeing: A Primer**
National Association for Visually Handicapped
22 W 21st St
Fl 6
New York, NY 10010-6943   212-255-2804
                                      FAX: 212-727-2931
                                      info@lighthouse.org
                                      www.lighthouse.org

Roger O. Goldman, Chairman
Line drawings that depict problems for those with both deficiencies. *$2.00*

7640   Helen and Teacher: The Story of Helen & Anne Sullivan Macy
American Foundation for the Blind/AFB Press
11 Penn Plz
Suite 300
New York, NY 10001-2006   212-502-7600
                                           800-232-5463
                              FAX: 212-502-7777
                                           afbinf@afb.net
                                           www.afb.org

Carl Augusto, President
Richard Obnen, Chairman Of The Board
Michael Gilliam, Vice Chairman
A pictorial biography emphasizing Hellen Keller's accomplishments in public life over a period of more than 60 years. Traces Anne Sullivan's early years and her meeting with Helen Keller, and goes on to recount the joint events of their lives. A definitive biography. $29.95.
Paperback
ISBN 0-891282-89-0

7641   Independence Without Sight and Sound: Suggestions for Practitioners
American Foundation for the Blind/AFB Press
11 Penn Plz
Suite 300
New York, NY 10001-2006   212-502-7600
                                           800-232-8463
                              FAX: 212-502-7777
                                           afbinfo@afb.net
                                           www.afb.org

Carl Augusto, President
Richard Obnen, Chairman Of The Board
Michael Gilliam, Vice Chairman
This practical guidebook covers the essential aspects of communicating and working with deaf-blind persons. Includes useful information on how to talk with deaf-blind people, and adapt orientation and mobility techniques for deaf-blind travelers. $39.95
193 pages Paperback
ISBN 0-891282-46-7

7642   Reclaiming Independence: Staying in the Drivers Seat When You Are no Longer Drive.
American Printing House for the Blind
1839 Frankfort Ave
Louisville, KY 40206-3148   502-895-2405
                                            800-223-1839
                               FAX: 502-899-2274
                                            info@aph.org
                                            www.aph.org

Tuck Tinsley, President
Joseph Paradis, Chairman
Kathleen Huebner, Vice Chairman
Useful for both individuals and professionals, this video/resource guide will help you successfuly use rehabilitation and transportation resources. $60.00

7643   Verbal View of the Web & Net
American Printing House for the Blind
1839 Frankfort Ave
Louisville, KY 40206-3148   502-895-2405
                                            800-223-1839
                               FAX: 502-899-2274
                                            info@aph.org
                                            www.aph.org

Tuck Tinsley, President
Joseph Paradis, Chairman
Kathleen Huebner, Vice Chairman
One of a series of Verbal View titles, Verbal View of the Net & Web explains how to access information on the internet and teaches accessability features of Internet Explorer. $50.00

Magazines

7644   Braille Montior
National Federation of the Blind
200 E. Wells St.
at Jernigan Place
Baltimore, MD 21230   410-659-9314
                               FAX: 410-685-5653
                                           nfbpublications@nfb.org
                                           www.nfb.org
Gary Wunder, Editor
The Braille Monitor is the leading publication of the National Federation of the Blind. It covers the events and activities of the NFB and addresses the many issues and concerns of the blind. $40.00
11 times a year

7645   Deaf-Blind American
American Association of the Deaf-Blind
248 Rainbow Drive
Suite 14864
Livingston, TX 77399-2048   aadb-info@aadb.org
                                            www.aadb.org
Rene Pellerin, President
The official magazine of the American Association of the Deaf-Blind (AADB).
Quartlery

7646   Hearing Life Magazine
Hearing Loss Association of America
7910 Woodmont Ave
Ste 1200
Bethesda, MD 20814-7022   301-657-2248
                               FAX: 301-913-9413
                                            inquiry@hearingloss.org
                                            www.hearingloss.org
Barbara Kelley, Executive Director
Formerly known as Hearing Loss Magazine, this official publication of the Hearing Loss Association of America helps individuals with hearing loss live a better life.
Bi-Monthly

7647   Hearing Professional Magazine
International Hearing Society
Ste 4
16880 Middlebelt Rd
Livonia, MI 48154-3374   734-522-7200
                               FAX: 734-522-0200
                                            knacarato@ihsinfo.org
                                            www.ihsinfo.org
Kathleen Mennillo, Executive Director
The Hearing Professional magazine is the official publication of the International Hearing Society. This quarterly publication includes industry news, membership highlights and best practices, hearing healthcare legislation, and other information and tools for hearing healthcare professionals.

Newsletters

7648   AADB E-News
American Association of the Deaf-Blind
248 Rainbow Drive
Suite 14864
Livingston, TX 77399-2048   aadb-info@aadb.org
                                            www.aadb.org
Rene Pellerin, President
Contains information about the latest events occurring within AADB and in the deaf-blind community.

7649   ALDA Newsletter
ALDA
8038 Macintosh Ln
Suite 2
Rockford, IL 61107-5336   815-332-1515
                               TTY:815-332-1515
                                            www.alda.org
Rick Brown, President

Articles, stories and poems by and about late-deafened adults.

7650 **Beam**
1850 W Roosevelt Rd
Chicago, IL 60608-1298
312-666-1331
FAX: 312-243-8539
TTY:312-666-8874
www.chicagolighthouse.org

James Kesteloot, President
Terrence Longo, Assistant Director
Quarterly newsletter of the organization offering progressive programs for the blind, visually impaired, deaf-blind and multi-disabled children and adults, including vocational programs, computer and office skills training, job placement, independent living skills, orientation and mobility training, counseling and a low vision clinic.

7651 **Deaf-Blind Perspective**
National Consortium on Deaf-Blindness
345 Monmouth Ave
Monmouth, OR 97361
503-838-8391
800-438-9376
FAX: 503-838-8150
TTY: 800-854-7013
dbp@wou.edu

John Reiman PhD, Director
Peggy Malloy, Managing Editor
A free publication with articles, essays, and announcements about topics related to people who are deaf-blind. The primary focus is on the education of children and youth with deaf-blindness. Published two times a year (Spring and Fall) by the national consortium on Deaf-blindness at the Teaching Research Institute at Western Oregon University.

7652 **Endeavor Magazine**
American Society for Deaf Children
PO Box 23
Woodbine, MD 21797
800-942-2732
info@deafchildren.org
www.deafchildren.org

Tami Dominguez, Editor
ASDC's qurterly publication featuring committee reports, stories, and fun.
Quarterly

7653 **HKNC Newsletter**
Helen Keller National Center
141 Middle Neck Rd
Sands Point, NY 11050-1218
516-944-8900
FAX: 516-944-7302
TTY:516-944-8637
hkncinfo@hknc.org
www.hknc.org

Joseph McNulty, Executive Director
Highlights recent activities at the national center.

7654 **InFocus**
7168 Columbia Gateway Dr.
Suite 100
Columbia, MD 21046
410-423-0600
800-683-5555
TTY:410-363-7139
info@FightBlindness.org
www.blindness.org

Benjamin R. Yerxa, Chief Executive Officer
Presents articles on coping, research updates, and Foundation news.
3x/year

7655 **NAT-CENT**
Helen Keller National Center
141 Middle Neck Rd
Sands Point, NY 11050-1218
516-944-8900
FAX: 516-944-7302
TTY:516-944-8637
hkncinfo@hknc.org
www.hknc.org

Joseph McNulty, Executive Director
Contains articles on legislation, services, aids and devices, human interest and issues related to deaf-blindness.

7656 **News from Advocates for Deaf-Blind**
National Family Association for Deaf-Blind
PO Box 1667
Sands Point, NY 11050
800-225-0411
FAX: 516-883-9060
www.NFADB.org

Patti McGowan, President
A membership organization which provide resources, education, advocacy, referrals and support for families with children who are deaf-blind; professionals in the field; and individuals who are deaf-blind.
20 pages TriAnnual

Software

7657 **Braille + Mobile Manager**
American Printing House for the Blind
1839 Frankfort Ave
Louisville, KY 40206-0085
502-895-2405
800-223-1839
FAX: 502-899-2284
info@aph.org
aph.org

Tuck Tinsley, President
Joseph Paradis, Chairman
Kathleen Huebner, Vice Chairman
Use it like a hand-held PDA or like a laptop. *$1395.00*

7658 **MaximEyes**
American Printing House for the Blind
1839 Frankfort Ave
Louisville, KY 40206-0085
502-895-2405
800-223-1839
FAX: 502-899-2284
info@aph.org
aph.org

Tuck Tinsley, President
Joseph Paradis, Chairman
Kathleen Huebner, Vice Chairman
MaximEyes is a plug-in for Internet Explorer that adds a toolbar that allows you to controll the size of website text and images. *$59.95*

Sports

7659 **ASD Athletics**
Alabama Institute for Deaf and Blind
205 South St E
Talladega, AL 35160-2411
256-761-3222
FAX: 256-761-3278
Ripley.Walter@aidb.state.al.us
John Jernigan, Director, Student Development (ASD)
Walter Ripley, Director, Athletics & After-School Programs
Offers students opportunities to participate in a number of organizzed sports including basketball, volleyball, baseball, football, and cheerleading. Student athletes compete at national and international levels.

Support Groups

7660 **Aurora of Central New York**
518 James Street
Suite 100
Syracuse, NY 13203-2282
315-422-7263
FAX: 315-422-4792
TTY:315-422-9746
auroraofcny.org

John Scala, President
John McCormick, President
Ryan Emery, Treasurer
Professional counseling services to assist individuals and their families deal with the trauma of hearing or vision loss.

7661 **Wendell Johnson Speech And Hearing Clinic**
University Of Iowa
250 Hawkins Dr
Iowa City, IA 52242-1025   319-335-8736
                        FAX: 319-335-8851
                        kathy-miller@uiowa.edu
        www.clas.uiowa.edu/comsci/clinical-services
Linda Souke, Clinic Director
Kathy Miller, Clinic Assistant
The clinic offers assessment and remediation for communication disorders in adults and children. The clinic also offers services during the Summer for school age children needing intervention services because of speech, language, hearing and/or reading problems.

Cognitive

Associations

7662 Academy of Cognitive Therapy
245 N. 15th St
Suite 403
Philadelphia, PA 19102   FAX: 215-537-1789
                                      info@academyofct.org
                                      www.academyofct.org

Lata K McGinn, Ph.D, President
Troy Thompson, Executive Director
Allen Miller, Ph.D, MBA, Treasurer
The Academy of Cognitive Therapy is a non-profit organization that supports continuing education and research in cognitive therapy, provides resources for professionals and the public, and offers certification for those skilled in the field.

7663 Adults & Children with Learning & Developmental Disabilities (ACLD)
807 S Oyster Bay Rd.
Bethpage, NY 11714   516-822-0028
                                      www.acld.org

Robert C. Goldsmith, Executive Director
Robert Ciatto, Chief Operating Officer
Aimee C. Keegan, Director, Development & Community Relations
Nonprofit serving Long Island by supporting individuals with developmental disabilities and their families.

7664 Albert Ellis Institute
145 East 32nd St.
9th Fl.
New York, NY 10016   212-535-0822
                                      FAX: 212-249-3582
                                      info@albertellis.org
                                      albertellis.org

Kristene A. Doyle, Director
Psychotherapy training Institute focused on the teachings of Albert Ellis, primarily the therapeutic approach known as Rational Emotive Behavior Therapy (REBT).

7665 American Academy of Child & Adolescent Psychiatry
3615 Wisconsin Ave NW
Washington, DC 20016-3007   202-966-7300
                                      FAX: 202-464-0131
                                      communications@aacap.org
                                      www.aacap.org

Gregory K Fritz, MD, President
Heidi B Fordi, CAE, Executive Director
Karen Ferguson, Deputy Director of Clinical Practice
The American Academy of Child & Adolescent Psychiatry is a non-profit organization engaged in research, education and advocacy specific to child and adolescent psychiatry. The academy's mission is to provide resources and knowledge beneficial to patients, their families and psychiatric professionals.

7666 American Delirium Society
1183 University Dr
Suite 105 - 106
Burlington, NC 27215   410-955-2343
                                      info@americandeliriumsociety.org
                                      www.americandeliriumsociety.org
Rakesh C Arora MD, Ph.D, Director
Noll Campbell, PharmD, MS, Director
John W Devlin, PharmD, Director
The American Delirium Society fosters research, education, quality improvement, advocacy and science to minimize the impact of delirium on short- and long-term health and well being and the effects of delirium on the health care system as a whole. The organization offers educational resources including videos and publications on the subject.

7667 American Psychiatric Association
1000 Wilson Blvd
Suite 1825
Arlington, VA 22209-3901   703-907-7300
                                      703-907-7300
                                      888-357-7924
                                      FAX: 703-907-1085
                                      apa@psych.org
                                      www.psychiatry.org

Anita Everett, MD, President
Saul M Levin, MD, MPA, CEO & Medical Director
Mark Myers, Director, Administrative Services
The American Psychiatric Association is a medical specialty society with over 37,000 member physicians engaged in the field of psychiatric practice, research, and academia. The association's mission is to ensure humane care and effective treatment of all persons with mental disorders, including substance use disorders. Services offered by them include collegial support, advocacy, publications and more.

7668 Anxiety and Depression Association of America (ADAA)
8701 Georgia Ave.
Suite 412
Silver Spring, MD 20910   240-485-1001
                                     FAX: 240-485-1035
                                     information@adaa.org
                                     adaa.org

Susan K. Gurley, Executive Director
Charles B. Nemeroff, President
Sanjay Matthew, Chief Medical Officer & Secretary
The Anxiety and Depression Association of America is an international nonprofit organization and a leader in education, training, and research for anxiety, OCD, PTSD, depression, and related disorders. ADAA encourages the advancement of scientific knowledge about the causes and treatment for mental health issues.

7669 Association for Behavioral and Cognitive Therapies (ABCT)
305 7th Ave
16th Floor
New York, NY 10001   212-647-1890
                                     FAX: 212-647-1865
                                     www.abct.org

Gail Steketee, Ph.D, President
Barbara Kamholz, Ph.D, Convention & Continuing Education Issues
Shireen Rizvi, Ph.D, Academic & Professional Issues
The ABCT is an organization committed to the advancement of scientific approaches to address the issues of soldiers with PTSD. The association offeres information in a number of areas: combat related stress, military posttraumatic stress disorder, military suicide and veterans' health.

7670 Association for Contextual Behavioral Science
1880 Pinegrove Dr
P.O. Box 655
Jenison, MI 49429   225-302-8688
                                     staff@contextualscience.org
                                     contextualscience.org

Emily Rodrigues, Executive Director
Courtney Zirkle, CMP, Administrative & Social Media Manager
The Association for Contextual Behavioral Science specializes in helping people through research and practice based in contextual behavioral science (including RFT and CBS). The association offers learning resources, training, internships, events, consultations, conferences, continuing education opportunities and more.

7671 Autism National Committee (AUTCOM)
3 Bedford Green
South Burlington, VT 05403   info@autcom.org
                                     www.autcom.org

Anne Bakeman, Membership Coordinator
Seeks to protect and advnce the rights of all individuals with autism, Pervasive Developmental Disorder, and related conditions.

7672 Autism Network International (ANI)
PO Box 35448
Syracuse, NY 13235-5448   www.autismnetworkinternational.org
Jim Sinclair, Coordinator

Autistic-run organization offering advocacy and self-help services for autistic people.

7673 Autism Research Institute
4182 Adams Ave.
San Diego, CA 92116-2599
866-366-3361
www.autism.com

Stephen Edelson, Ph.D, Executive Director
Anthony Morgali, Producer, ARI Media
Denise Fulton, Administrative Director
Conducts research on the causes, diagnosis and treatment of autism. The institute also offers a quarterly newsletter that reviews worldwide research, referrals to health care professionals and clinics serving autistic people, advocacy, continuing education and more.

7674 Autism Services Center
929 4th Ave.
P.O. Box 507
Huntington, WV 25701-0507
304-525-8014
FAX: 304-525-8026
www.autismservicescenter.org

Ralph N Bentley, President
Jimmie Beirne, Ph.D, CEO
The Autism Services Center assists families and agencies to meet the needs of individuals with autism and other developmental disabilities by offering services such as technical assistance in designing treatment programs, a hotline providing informational packets to callers, supported employment, day programs, residential services and more.

7675 Autism Society of Minnesota
Autism Society of Minnesota
2380 Wycliff St.
Suite 102
St. Paul, MN 55114
651-647-1083
FAX: 651-642-1230
info@ausm.org
www.ausm.org

Ellie Wilson, Executive Director
Dawn Brasch, Senior Director, Finance & Operations
Kelly Thomalla, Senior Director, Integration & Advancement
The Autism Society of Minnesota (AuSM) is a nonprofit membership organization dedicated to the education, advocacy, and support of individuals and families who have been affected by autism.

7676 Autism Treatment Center of America
2080 S Undermountain Rd
Sheffield, MA 01257-9643
413-229-2100
877-766-7473
FAX: 413-229-8931
correspondence@option.org
www.autismtreatmentcenter.org

Barry Neil Kaufman, Founder & CEO
Clyde Haberman, Senior Teacher & Director of Development
Blair Borgeson, Developmental Therapist
The Autism Treatment Center of America provides innovative training programs for parents and professionals caring for children challenged by Autism, Autism Spectrum Disorders, Pervasive Developmental Disorders (PDD) and other development difficulties. The center's Son-Rise Program teaches a comprehensive system of treatment and education designed to help families and caregivers enable their children to improve in all areas of learning.

7677 Autistic Self Advocacy Network (ASAN)
PO Box 66122
Washington, DC 20035
info@autisticadvocacy.org
autisticadvocacy.org

Julia Bascom, Executive Director
Zoe Gross, Director, Operations
Samantha Crane, Legal Directory & Director, Public Policy
Promotes a world in which equal access, rights and opportunities are available to autistic people, through advocacy and empowerment.

7678 Beck Institute for Cognitive Behavior Therapy
1 Belmont Ave
Suite 700
Bala Cynwyd, PA 19004
610-664-3020
FAX: 610-709-5336
info@beckinstitute.org
www.beckinstitute.org

Aaron T Beck, Ph.D, President Emeritus
Judith S Beck, Ph.D, President
Lisa Pote, Executive Director
The Beck Institute for Cognitive Behavior Therapy serves as a training ground for cognitive therapists and cognitive behavior therapists. The institute provides online resources, training workshops and CBT therapy for the public and mental health professionals.

7679 Best Buddies
907-1243 Islington Ave
Toronto, ON, Canada M8X-1Y9
416-531-0003
888-779-0061
FAX: 416-531-0325
info@bestbuddies.ca
bestbuddies.ca

Daniel J Greenglass, Co-Chair
Sarah McCarthy, Program Coordinator
Kimberly Janohan, Program Support
Best Buddies offers programs for people with intellectual or developmental disabilities including those with Down syndrome, autism, cerebral palsy, traumatic brain injury and other undiagnosed disabilities. Programs include schooling, transition programs, sports, scholarships and more.

7680 Biologically Inspired Cognitive Architectures Society
4450 Rivanna River Way
Suite 3707
Fairfax, VA 22030-4441
703-910-3014
FAX: 877-532-0197
info@bicasociety.org
bicasociety.org

Alexei V Samsonovich, President-Treasurer
Antonio Chella, Chair
Kamilla R Johannsdottir, Secretary
The Biologically Inspired Cognitive Architectures Society brings together researchers from disjointed fields and communities in order to combine their knowledge into forming a larger, unifying framework for the study of cognitive architectures.

7681 Brain Injury Alliance of Texas
9050 N Capital of Texas Hwy
Building 3, Suite 130
Austin, TX 78759
512-326-1212
800-392-0040
FAX: 512-478-3370
www.texasbia.org

Kelly Ramsey, President
Greg Walton, Vice President
Mendi West, Secretary-Treasurer
The Brain Injury Alliance of Texas is a community of people with brain injuries, their families and the professionals that serve them. The alliance offers information, support groups, prevention strategies, educational opportunities, public policy advocacy, a resource library and more.

7682 Brain Injury Association of America (BIAA)
3057 Nutley St.
Suite 805
Fairfax, VA 22031-1931
703-761-0750
FAX: 703-761-0755
info@biausa.org
www.biausa.org

Rick Willis, President & Chief Executive Officer
Page Melton Ivie, Chair
Kevin Bingham, Vice Chair
The Brain Injury Association of America is a national organization serving and representing individuals, families and professionals who are touched by a traumatic brain injury (TBI). Its mission is to improve the quality of life for people affected by brain injury through the advancement of research, treatment, education and awareness.
1980

711

7683 Brain Injury Association of New York State
4 Pine W Plaza
Suite 402
Albany, NY 12205
518-459-7911
800-444-6443
FAX: 518-482-5285
info@bianys.org
bianys.org

Barry Dain, President
Eileen Reardon, Executive Director
Debbie Berenda-Chilandese, Director of Finance & Administration
The Brain Injury Association of New York State is a statewide non-profit membership organization that provides education, advocacy and community support services leading to improved outcomes for children and adults with brain injuries and their families. The association also offers chapters and support groups throughout the state, prevention programs, mentoring programs, speakers bureau and publications library.

7684 BroadFutures
National Youth Transitions Center
2013 H St, NW
5th Floor
Washington, DC 20006
202-521-4304
info@broadfutures.org
broadfutures.org

Bradley P Holmes, Chairman
Carolyn K Jeppsen, CEO & President
Diana Eisenstat, Secretary
BroadFutures offers transitional programs for youth with learning disabilities. The mission of the organization is to assit these youth in overcoming barriers to employment.

7685 Center Academy
6710 86th Ave. N
Pinellas Park, FL 33782
727-541-5716
FAX: 727-544-8186
infopp@centeracademy.com
www.centeracademy.com

Mack R. Hicks, Founder & Chair
Andrew P. Hicks, Chief Executive Officer & Clinical Director
Eric V. Larson, President & Chief Operating Officer
Center Academy assists children with learning disabilities, difficulties in concentration and underdeveloped social skills. Programs offered include high impact learning, community involvement opportunities, ADHD schools, autism and asperger's schools, dyslexia treatment, special education schools and more.

7686 Cerebral Palsy Associations of New York State
Central Office & Metropolitan Services
330 W 34th St
15th Floor
New York, NY 10001-2488
212-947-5770
information@cpofnys.org
www.cpofnys.org

Stephen C Lipinski, Chairman
Susan Constantino, President & CEO
Michael A Alvaro, Executive Vice President
The Cerebral Palsy Associations of New York is a multi-service organization that provides services and programs for individuals with cerebral palsy and developmental disabilities, as well as resources for families.

7687 Child Neurology Society
1000 W County Rd E
Suite 290
Saint Paul, MN 55126
651-486-9447
FAX: 651-486-9436
nationaloffice@childneurologysociety.org
www.childneurologysociety.org

Kenneth Mack, President
Roger Larson, Executive Director
Sue Hussman, Associate Director
The Child Neurology Society is designed for patiens, parents, and professionals alike, with the aim of promoting continued research, providing support, and offering informational resources and guidance on the subject of child neurology. Members include child neurologists and related medical professionals.

7688 Children and Adults with Attention-Deficit Hyperactivity Disorder
CHADD
4601 Presidents Dr
Suite 300
Lanham, MD 20706
301-306-7070
FAX: 301-306-7090
affiliate-services@chadd.org
www.chadd.org

Michael MacKay, President
Leslie Kain, MBA, Executive Director
Robyn Maggio, MSW, Education & Training Coordinator
The Children and Adults with Attention-Deficit/Hyperactivity Disorder (CHADD) is a non-profit organization providing supports to people with ADHD. Some services offered include advocacy, education, employment, a resource directory, training programs, publications on research and more.

7689 Cognitive Neuroscience Society
267 Cousteau Place
Davis, CA 95618
916-850-0837
cnsinfo@cogneurosociety.org
www.cogneurosociety.org

Roberto Cabeza, Ph.D, Board Member
Marta Kutas, Ph.D, Board Member
Kate Tretheway, Executive Director
The Cognitive Neuroscience Society is committed to investigating the psychological, computational, and neuroscientific bases of cognition through research.

7690 Cognitive Science Society
108 E Dean Keeton
Stop A8000
Austin, TX 78712-1043
512-471-2030
FAX: 512-471-3053
cogsci@austin.utexas.edu
www.cognitivesciencesociety.org

Susan Gelman, Chair
Terry Regier, Chair Elect
Anna Drummey, Executive Officer
The Cognitive Science Society brings together researchers from around the world who desire to understand the workings of the human mind. The society's mission is to promote the study of cognitive science and build connections between researchers in various areas of study (including Artificial Intelligence, Linguistics, Anthropology, Psychology, Neuroscience, Philosophy, and Education).

7691 Cognitive Science Student Association
University of California
Berkeley, CA
cssa.berkeley@gmail.com
cssa.berkeley.edu

Timothy Guan, President
Harshali Wadge, Internal Vice President
Connor Brown, Outreach Coordinator
The Cognitive Science Student Association supports and enriches the academic life of anyone interested in the interdisciplinary field of cognitive science. Some programs offered by the association include guest lectures and information sessions, professor-student dinners, academic outreach program and California Cognitive Science Conference.

7692 Dementia Society of America
PO Box 600
Doylestown, PA 18901
800-336-3684
knowdementia@dementiasociety.org
www.dementiasociety.org

Kevin Jameson, President & Founder
The Dementia Society of America (DSA) is a nonprofit volunteer-run organization providing resources and information about dementia to individuals, corporations and organizations.

7693 **Depression and Bipolar Support Alliance**
55 E Jackson Blvd
Suite 490
Chicago, IL 60604

800-826-3632
FAX: 312-642-7243
dbsasocial@gmail.com
www.dbsalliance.org

William Gilmer, MD, Chair
Allen Doederlein, President
Cindy Specht, Executive Vice President
The Depression and Bipolar Support Alliance is a peer-directed national organization dedicated to offering supports to those living with depression or bipolar disorder. Some services they offer include peer support, education, advocacy and research.

7694 **Epilepsy Foundation**
8301 Professional Place E
Suite 200
Landover, MD 20785- 2353

800-332-1000
FAX: 301-459-1569
ContactUs@efa.org
www.epilepsy.com

Robert W Smith, Chair
Phillip M. Gattone, M.Ed, President & CEO
M. Vaneeda Bennett, Chief Development Officer
The Epilepsy Foundation is the national voluntary health agency dedicated to the welfare of people with epilepsy in the U.S. and their families. The organization works to ensure that people with seizures are able to participate in all life experiences; to improve how people with epilepsy are perceived, accepted and valued in society; and to promote research for a cure.

7695 **FOCUS Center for Autism**
126 Dowd Ave.
PO Box 452
Canton, CT 06019

860-693-8809
FAX: 860-693-0141
info@focuscenterforautism.org
www.focuscenterforautism.org

Patricia A. Cables, President
Timothy Grady, Secretary
Donna Swanson, Executive Director
FOCUS Center for Autism is a nonprofit center to help children and young adults with autism spectrum disorder, and other related disorders, achieve their full potential.

7696 **Geneva Centre for Autism**
112 Merton St.
Toronto, ON, Canada M4S-2Z8

416-322-7877
FAX: 416-322-5894
info@autism.net
www.autism.net

Abe Evreniadis, Chief Executive Officer
Kathy Shaw, Chief Financial Officer
Renita Paranjape, Senior Director, Programs & Services
The Geneva Centre for Autism's mission is to empower individuals with Autism Spectrum Disorder, and their families, to fully participate in their communities.

7697 **International OCD Foundation**
18 Tremont St
Suite 308
Boston, MA 02108

617-973-5801
FAX: 617-973-5803
info@iocdf.org
iocdf.org

Shannon A Shy, Esq, President
Jeff Szymanski, PhD, Executive Director
Pamela Layne, Director of Operations
The International OCD Foundation aims to provide resources for those living with OCD and their families. The foundation offers a research grant program, public education and a forum for professional networking.

7698 **Lewy Body Dementia Association**
912 Killian Hill Rd, SW
Lilburn, GA 30047

404-975-2322
FAX: 480-422-5434
lbda@lbda.org
www.lbda.org

Christina M Christie, President
Mike Koehler, CEO
Mark Wall, Vice President
The Lewy Body Dementia Association is a non-profit organization dedicated to raising awareness of the Lewy body dementias (LBD). The association offers services and information to people with LBD, their families and caregivers and works to promote research in the area.

7699 **Life Development Institute**
18001 N 79th Ave
Suite B-42
Glendale, AZ 85308

866-736-7811
FAX: 623-773-2788
info@life-development-inst.org
discoverldi.com

Robert Crawford, M.Ed, CEO
Veronica Lieb (Crawford), MA, President
Justin Coller, BS, Director of Operations
The Life Development Institute serves older adolescents and adults with learning disabilities, ADD and related disorders. The Institute's mission is to help program participants pursue responsible independent living, enhance academic/workplace literacy skills and facilitate employment or educational placements.

7700 **Life Unlimited**
Life Unlimited, Inc.
2135 Manor Way
Liberty, MO 64068

816-781-4332
www.lifeunlimitedinc.org

Erin Lankford, President
Scott Wingerson, Vice President
Jessie Smith, Secretary
Life Unlimited is a nonprofit working to provide support and services to individuals with developmental disabilities in the Kansas City Northland. Services include community living, day services, employment services, and recreation programs.

7701 **Mental Health America (MHA)**
500 Montgomery St.
Suite 820
Alexandria, VA 22314

703-684-7722
800-969-6642
FAX: 703-684-5968
info@mhanational.org
www.mhanational.org

Schroeder Stribling, President & Chief Executive Officer
Mary Giliberti, Chief Public Policy Officer
Jessica Kennedy, Chief of Staff & Chief Financial Officer
A nonprofit organization addressing issues related to mental health and mental illness. MHA works to improve the mental health of all Americans, especially individuals with mental disorders, through advocacy, education, research, and service.
Founded in 1909.

7702 **Multiple Sclerosis Association of America**
375 Kings Hwy N
Cherry Hill, NJ 08034

800-532-7667
FAX: 856-661-9797
msaa@mymsaa.org
mymsaa.org

John McCorry, Chair
Gina Murdoch, President & CEO
Lauren Hooper, Northeast Regional Director
The Multiple Sclerosis Association of America is an organization dedicated to providing the most up-to-date resources for those affected by Multiple Sclerosis, including research, publications, assistive equipment, public education, and best practices and policy for professionals working with patients.

7703   NLP Comprehensive
PO Box 348
Indian Hills, CO 80454-0348

303-987-2224
800-233-1657
FAX: 303-987-2228
learn@nlpco.com
www.nlpco.com

Tom Dotz, President
Sharon DeBault, Director of Community Relations
Jamie Reaser, PhD, Director of Professional Relations
NLP Comprehensive provides a body of publications by Steve and Connirae Andreas on the subject of NLP (Neuro-linguistic programming), as well as training.

7704   NLP University - Dynamic Learning Center
NLP University
PO Box 1112
Ben Lomond, CA 95005

831-336-3457
FAX: 503-738-9546
teresanlp@aol.com
www.nlpu.com

Robert B Dilts, Founder & Director of Training
Teresa Epstein, Coordinator
Deborah Bacon Dilts, Trainer
NLP (neuro-lingusitic programming) University seeks to create a context in which professionals of different backgrounds can develop fundamental and advanced NLP skills for applications relevant to their profession. The University provides guidance, training, certification, culture, and community support to those interested in exploring the global potential of Systemic NLP.

7705   National Alliance on Mental Illness (NAMI)
3803 N Fairfax Dr
Suite 100
Arlington, VA 22203

703-524-7600
800-950-6264
888-999-6264
FAX: 703-524-9094
info@nami.org
www.nami.org

Steve Pitman, J.D., President
Mary Giliberti, J.D., CEO
Cheri Villa, M.P.A, Chief Operating Officer
NAMI is a grassroots mental health organization working to provide people with mental health issues the technical assistance, tools and referrals to resources they need in order to manage the challenges they face.

7706   National Association for Developmental Disabilities (NADD)
12 Hurley Ave.
Kingston, NY 12401

845-331-4336
info@thenadd.org
thenadd.org

Jeanne M. Farr, CEO
Jeffrey Schmunk, Operations Manager
Michelle Jordan, Office Manager
NADD is a non-profit membership association established for professionals, care providers and families to promote understanding of and services for individuals who have developmental disabilities and mental health needs. The mission of NADD is to advance mental wellness for persons with developmental disabilities through the promotion of excellence in mental health care.

7707   National Association for Down Syndrome
1460 Renaissance Dr
Suite 102
Park Ridge, IL 60068

630-325-9112
info@nads.org
www.nads.org

Steve Connors, President
Diane Urhausen, Executive Director
Linda Smarto, Director, Programs and Advocacy
The National Association for Down Syndrome provides services and information to those with Down Syndrome and their families. The association's mission is to maintain a strong network of support systems within their own organization and with medical, educational and school service professionals who work with children and adults with Down Syndrome.

7708   National Association of Cognitive- Behavioral Therapists
102 Gilson Ave
Weirton, WV 26062

304-224-2534
800-253-0167
nacbt@nacbt.org
www.nacbt.org

Aldo R Pucci, Ph.D, President
The association's mission is to promote the teaching and practice of cognitive-behavioral psychotherapy and to support those professionals and students seeking to practice it. Some services offered by the association include educational videos, membership, CBT certification, workshops and more.

7709   National Association of Epilepsy Centers
600 Maryland Ave SW
Suite 835W
Washington, DC 20024

202-524-6767
888-525-6232
FAX: 202-484-1244
info@naec-epilepsy.org
www.naec-epilepsy.org

Nathan B Fountain, MD, President
Ellen Riker, MHA, Executive Director
Johanna Gray, MPA, Deputy Director
The National Association of Epilepsy Centers educates public and private policy makers and regulators about appropriate patient care standards, reimbursement and medical services policies. The association is designed to complement the efforts of existing scientific and charitable epilepsy organizations.

7710   National Ataxia Foundation
600 Hwy 169 S
Suite 1725
Minneapolis, MN 55426

763-553-0020
FAX: 763-553-0167
naf@ataxia.org
www.ataxia.org

William P Sweeney, President
Charlene Danielson, Treasurer
Joel Sutherland, Executive Director
The National Ataxia Foundation is a non-profit, membership-supported organization established to help improve the lives of persons affected by ataxia and their families through support, education, and research.

7711   National Autism Association
1 Park Ave
Suite 1
Portsmouth, RI 02871

401-293-5551
877-622-2884
FAX: 401-293-5342
naa@nationalautism.org
nationalautismassociation.org

Lori McIlwain, Board Chairperson
Wendy Fournier, President
Kelly Vanicek, Executive Director
The mission of the National Autism Association is to educate and empower families affected by autism and other neurological disorders, while advocating on behalf of those who cannot fight for their own rights. The association offers programs as well as educational resources.

7712   National Down Syndrome Congress
30 Mansell Ct
Suite 108
Roswell, GA 30076

770-604-9500
800-232-6372
FAX: 770-604-9898
info@ndsccenter.org
www.ndsccenter.org

Kishore Vellody, MD, President
David Tolleson, Executive Director
MaryKate Vandemark, Office Manager
The National Down Syndrome Congress provides information, advocacy and support concerning all aspects of life for individuals with Down syndrome. It is the purpose of the Congress to create a national climate in which all people will recognize and embrace the value and dignity of people with Down syndrome.

7713 National Down Syndrome Society
8 E 41st St
8th Floor
New York, NY 10017

212-460-9330
800-221-4602
FAX: 212-979-2873
info@ndss.org
www.ndss.org

Sara Weir, MS, President
Josh Hill, Executive Assistant
Ashley Helsing, Director of Government Relations
Non-profit organization dedicated to increasing public awareness about Down syndrome as well as engaging in research, education and advocacy. The organization distributes informative materials, encourages and supports the activities of local parent support groups, sponsors conferences and scientific symposiums and undertakes major advocacy efforts.

7714 National Hydrocephalus Foundation
12413 Centralia Rd
Lakewood, CA 90715-1653

562-924-6666
888-857-3434
FAX: 562-924-6666
www.nhfonline.org

Michael Fields, President & Treasurer
Debbi Fields, Executive Director
Sarah Dunn, Junior Director
The National Hydrocephalus Foundation assembles and disseminates information pertaining to hydrocephalus, its treatments and outcomes. The foundation also establishes and facilitates a communication network among affected families and individuals.

7715 Oak-Leyden Developmental Services
411 Chicago Ave
Oak Park, IL 60302

708-524-1050
FAX: 708-524-2469
info@oak-leyden.org
www.oak-leyden.org

Melissa Wyatt, President
Bertha Magana, Executive Director
Nancy Thomas, Director of Human Resources
Oak-Leyden Developmental Services works to help people with developmental disabilities meet life's challenges and reach their highest potential. Services offered by the organization include Early Intervention Program, Vocational Evaluation, Developmental Training Program, Supported Employment Program, Community Integrated Living Arrangements and Multi-disciplinary Clinic.

7716 Ontario Federation for Cerebral Palsy
104-1630 Lawrence Ave W
Toronto, ON, Canada M6L-1C5

416-244-9686
877-244-9686
FAX: 416-244-6543
info@ofcp.ca
www.ofcp.ca

Victor Gascon, President
Nilu Alizadeh, Supervisor
Cindy DeGraaff, Planning Services Manager
The Ontario Federation for Cerebral Palsy is dedicated to assisting individuals with cerebral palsy through research, financial resources, education, recreation programs, housing and life planning.

7717 Society for Cognitive Rehabilitation
668 Exton Commons
Exton, PA 19341

127-647-2369
www.societyforcognitiverehab.org

Kit Malia, President
Rita Carroll, Secretary
Pat Benfield, Treasurer
The Society for Cognitive Rehabilitation is a non-profit organization committed to the advancement of cognitive rehabilitation therapy across the globe.

7718 St. John Valley Associates
291 Newberry Dr
Suite 105
Madawaska, ME 04756

207-728-7197
800-339-9502
FAX: 207-728-3825

Robin Jackson-Eldridge, Program Director
A non-profit association with the mission of empowering adult citizens with intellectual disabilities. The association offers center-based community supports and residential supports to help members develop a sense of independence. $75.00

7719 TEACCH Autism Program
100 Renee Lynne Ct
Carrboro, NC 27510

919-966-2174
FAX: 919-966-4127
teacch@unc.edu
teacch.com

Laura G Klinger, Ph.D, Executive Director
Lauren Turner-Brown, Ph.D, Assistant Director
Rebecca Mabe, Assistant Director, Business & Operations
TEACCH Autism Program offers community-based services, training programs and research to help those with Autism Spectrum Disorder. Some programs offered by TEACCH include clinical evaluations, intervention, consultation and training, living and learning centers, supported employment and more.

7720 The Arc of North Carolina
343 E Six Forks Rd
Suite 320
Raleigh, NC 27609

919-782-4632
800-662-8706
FAX: 919-782-4634
info@arcnc.org
www.arcnc.org

John Nash, Executive Director
Melinda Plue, Director of Advocacy & Chapter Development
Nicole Kiefer, Housing Resources Coordinator
The Arc of North Carolina is committed to providing services for people with intellectual and developmental disabilities. Services include advocacy, housing, supported employment and other supports.

7721 The Arc of the United States
1825 K St NW
Suite 1200
Washington, DC 20006

202-534-3700
800-433-5255
FAX: 202-534-3731
info@thearc.org
www.thearc.org

Peter Berns, Chief Executive Officer
Ruben Rodriguez, Chief Operating Officer
Julie Ward, Senior Executive Officer, Public Policy
The Arc promotes and protects the rights of people with intellectual and developmental disabilities and actively supports their inclusion and participation in the community throughout their lifetimes. The Arc's clients include people with autism, Down syndrome, Fragile X syndrome, and various other developmental disabilities. Some services offered by The Arc include public policy advocacy, education and vocational services.

7722 The Hemispherectomy Foundation
8235 Lethbridge Rd
Millersville, MD 21108

410-987-5221
lynn@hemifoundation.org
hemifoundation.homestead.com

Kristi Hall, President, CEO & Co-Founder
Cris A Hall, Executive Director & Co-Founder
Jane Stefanik, Vice President & Chief Financial Officer
The Hemispherectomy Foundation is a non-profit organization dedicated to providing emotional, financial and educational support to individuals and their families who have undergone, or will undergo, a hemispherectomy or similar brain surgery.

7723 Tourette Association of America
42-40 Bell Blvd
Suite 205
Bayside, NY 11361
718-224-2999
FAX: 718-279-9596
support@tourette.org
www.tourette.org

Amanda Talty, President & CEO
Tracey Costikyan-Alexander, VP, Resource Development & Chapter Services
Diana Felner, VP, Public Policy
Non-profit organization with the mission of researching and controlling the effects of Tourette syndrome. Some services they offer include seminars, conferences and support groups. The association publishes brochures, flyers, educational materials and papers on treatment and research.

7724 United Cerebral Palsy
1825 K St NW
Suite 600
Washington, DC 20006
202-776-0406
800-872-5827
FAX: 202-776-0414
info@ucp.org
ucp.org

Diane Wilush, Chair
Armando Contreras, President & CEO
Ellie Collinson, Chief Program Officer
United Cerebral Palsy educates, advocates, and provides support services to ensure a life without limits for people with cerebral palsy and other disabilities. Some services offered include networking, educational information, assistive technology information, research, public policy resources and more.

Camps

7725 Adventure Learning Center at Eagle Village
4507 170th Ave
Hersey, MI 49639-8785
231-832-2234
800-748-0061
FAX: 231-832-1468
alcinfo@eaglevillage.org
www.eaglevillage.org

Cathey Prudhomme, President/CEO
Jim McCain, Director of Support Services/CFO
Craig Weidner, Director of Advancement
Offers a variety of fun camp experiences with a low staff-to-camper ratio and exciting, challenging activities. This program accepts youth, ages 5-17, who are high risk or special needs - behavioral problems, emotionally unstable or Attention Deficit. The camping experience includes canoeing, hiking, swimming and high adventure activities. Half-week, one-week, and two-week sessions June-August. Coed.

7726 CNS Camp New Connections
Mclean Hospital Child/Adolescent Program
115 Mill St
Mailstop115
Belmont, MA 02478-1064
617-855-2000
800-333-0338
FAX: 617-855-2833
mcleaninfo@mclean.harvard.edu
www.mcleanhospital.org

Roya Ostovar PhD, Center Director
Scott L. Rauch, MD., President & Psychiatrist
Joseph Gold MD, Clinical Director
Four-week summer day camp for children ages 7-17 who have pervasive developmental disorders, Asperger's Syndrome, autism spectrum disorders and non-verbal learning disabilities. The camp is designed to help children develop social skills through fun activities including: communication games, swimming, field trips, drama, and arts and crafts. *$4500.00*

7727 Camp ASCCA
Alabama's Special Camp for Children and Adults
PO Box 21
5278 Camp Ascca Dr.
Jacksons Gap, AL 36861
256-825-9226
FAX: 256-269-0714
info@campascca.org
www.campascca.org

Matt Rickman, Camp Director
John Stephenson, Administrator
Jocelyn Jones, Secretary
Camp Evoked Potential is held one week out of the year for children aged 6-18 with epilepsy at Camp ASCCA. Fully funded by The Epilepsy Foundation, persons wishing to attend the camp must apply. The camp provides a barrier free setting situated on 230 acres of wooded land at Lake Martin. The camp is staffed with medical personnel trained to care for children with all types of disabilities and provides a variety of camp activities.
1976

7728 Camp Baker
Greater Richmond ARC
7600 Beach Rd
Chesterfield, VA 23838-6513
804-748-4789
FAX: 804-796-6880
richmondarc.org

Robert L. Sommerville, Chair - Officer
Thomas G. Haskins, Vice Chair - Officer
Chriss Mumford, Secretary Officer
An organization created by families, for families that has grown to provide a continuum of programs and services for individuals with developmental disablties acroos the lifespan, helping each person achieve his or her potential and improving the quality of life for everyone in the community.

7729 Camp Buckskin
PO Box 389
Ely, MN 55731
763-432-9177
info@campbuckskin.com
www.campbuckskin.com

Tom Bauer, Camp Co-Director
Mary Bauer, Camp Co-Director
Camp is located in Ely, Minnesota. Buckskin helps children with underdeveloped social skills realize their potentials and abilities. Teaches a combination of traditional camp activities, academic activities, and social skills. Ages 6-18.

7730 Camp Candlelight
Epilepsy Foundation Arizona
941 S Park Lane
Tempe, AZ 85281
602-282-3515
800-332-1000
AZ@EFA.org
epilepsyaz.org/events/campcandlelight

Suzanne Matsumori, Executive Director
Min Skivington, Program Manager
Camp Candlelight provides children ages 8 to 17 a unique camp experience that mixes traditional summer camp with special sessions that teach campers about their seizures and gives them resources to manage the challenges that the seizures represent. Staff inclues a neurologist, several nurses, and a school psychologist, in addition to traditional camp staff who are given specialized training in responding appropriately to the needs of kids with epilepsy.

7731 Camp Civitan
Civitan Foundation
12635 N. 42nd Street
Phoenix, AZ 85032
602-953-2944
www.civitanfoundationaz.com

Dawn Trapp, Executive Director
Camp Civitan offers week long summer camp programs, and weekend programs throughout the year, to children with developmental disabilities. The camp is fully wheelchair accessible, is staffed by medical professionals and there is a 2:1 ratio of campers to staff. Camp Civitan offers campers the experience of traditional camp activities including, swimming, adaptive sports, fishing, music, arts and crafts, and talent shows.
1968

7732   **Camp Horizons**
127 Babcock Hill Rd
PO Box 323
South Windham, CT 06266- 323   860-456-1032
FAX: 860-456-4721
www.camphorizons.org

Adam Milne, Chairman
L. Sanford Rice, Treasurer
Kathleen McNAboe, VP
Bordering Lake Probus, the facilities at the camp are equipped to
accomodate a wide range of activities and programs for campers
with developmental disabilities, or other challenging emotional
and social needs. There is a 5:1 camper-counselor ratio with a
schedule of three programs in the morning and four in the
afternoon.

7733   **Camp Huntington**
56 Bruceville Rd.
High Falls, NY 12440-5100   845-687-7840
855-707-2267
FAX: 855-707-2267
www.camphuntington.com

Daniel Falk, Executive Director
Dylan Sloan, Program Director
Margaret Short, Health Director
A co-ed residential summer camp specifically designed to focus
on adaptive and therapeutic recreation. Campers include those
with learning and developmental disabilities, ADD/HD, Autism
Spectrum Disorders, Asperger's, PDD, and other special needs.
Programs focus on recreation and social skills, independence,
and participation.

7734   **Camp Krem**
Camping Unlimited
102 Brook Lane
Boulder Creek, CA 95006   831-338-3210
campkrem@campingunlimited.org
campingunlimited.org

Christina Krem DiGirolamo, Camp Director
Leon Wong, Head of Camper Services
Kristen Carter, Virtual Program Coordinator
Camp Krem - Camping Unlimited offers year-round and summer
camping programs for children and adults with developmental
disabilities. With a variety of different programs and many facilities on the campground such as a swimming pool, arts and crafts
building, amphitheater, music pavilion, and archery range, Camp
Krem provides its campers with recreation, education, and
adventure opportunities.

7735   **Camp Nissokone**
YMCA Camping Services
1401 Broadway
Suite A
Detroit, MI 48226-8929   313-267-5300
www.ymcadetroit.org

Doug Grimm, Vice President Camping Services
David Marks, Director
A six week summer resident camp program for boys and girls
whose learning and behavior styles have made successful participation in the traditional camp program difficult. All camp activities have a special emphasis on building self-esteem and peer
relationships. Strong in waterfront, nature, campcrafts and a
special arts program.

7736   **Camp Nuhop**
1077 Township Rd. 2916
Perrysville, OH 44864   419-938-7151
www.nuhop.org

Trevor Dunlap, Executive Director & CEO
Chris Clyde, Associate Director
Matt Poland, Director, Outdoor Education
A summer residential program for youth ages 6-18 with learning
disabilities, behavioral disorders, or other neuroatypical disorders. Activities include outdoor education and team-building
workshops. The staff-to-camper ratio is 3:7 or 3:8.

7737   **Camp Ramapo**
Ramapo for Children
Rt. 52/Salisbury Turnpike
PO Box 266
Rhinebeck, NY 12572   845-876-8403
FAX: 845-876-8414
office@ramapoforchildren.org
www.ramapoforchildren.org

Matthew McKnight, Camp Director
Lenora Sealey, Associate Camp Director
A residential summer camp for youth ages 6-16 with social, emo-
tional, or learning challenges.

7738   **Camp ReCreation**
9272 Madison Ave.
Orangeville, CA 95662   916-988-6835
camprecreation@outlook.com
www.camprecreation.org

Kathi Barber, Camp Director
Camp ReCreation offers residential summer camps and year
round programs for children, teens, and adults with developmental disabilities. The summer camp is held at Camp Ronald Mc-
Donald in Lassen National Forest. With a 1:1 staff to camper
ratio, Camp ReCreation offers wide variety of camp activities,
and campers wishing to participate must fill out a camper
application.
1983

7739   **Camp Royall**
250 Bill Ash Rd.
Moncure, NC 27559   919-542-1033
FAX: 919-533-5324
camproyall@autismsociety-nc.org
www.autismsociety-nc.org/camp-royall

Sara Gage, Director
A week-long overnight and day camp for children and adults with
autism. Campers participate in traditional camp activities such as
swimming, boating, hiking, and arts and crafts. Counselor-to-camper ratio is 1:1 or 1:2, depending on the campers'
needs.

7740   **Camp Ruggles**
PO Box 353
Chepachet, RI 02814   401-567-8914
campruggles@gmail.com
www.campruggles.org

Jim Field, Executive Director
Ethan Roe, Assistant Director
Camp Ruggles is located in Glocester, RI and is a summer day
camp for children with emotional and behavioral disabilities. The
camp offers 240 hours of supervised therapeutic care for children
ages 6-12.

7741   **Camp Sisol**
Jewish Community Center of Greater Rochester/JCC
1200 Edgewood Ave.
Rochester, NY 14618   585-461-2000
FAX: 585-461-0805
bettertogether@jccrochester.org
www.jccrochester.org

Josh Weinstein, Chief Executive Officer
Coed, ages 5-16. Camp Sisol accommodates children with special
needs.

7742   **Camp World Light**
Florida Baptist Convention
1230 Hendricks Ave
Jacksonville, FL 32207-8619   904-396-2351
800-226-8584
FAX: 904-396-6470
www.campworldlight.com

Anne Wilson, Camp Director
Delicia Garland, Ministry Assistant to Director
Camp is located in Marianna, Florida. One-week sessions
June-July for girls with ADD. Ages 3-12. Activities include
arts/crafts, challenge/rope courses, clowning, community service, dance, drama, drawing/painting, leadership development,
performing arts and sailing.

7743 Camp-A-Lot and Camp-A-Little
The Arc of San Diego
3030 Market Street
San Diego, CA 92102
619-685-1175
FAX: 619-234-3759
info@arc-sd.com
www.arc-sd.com

Anthony J. DeSalis, President & Chief Executive Officer
Programs of The Arc of San Diego, Camp - A - Lot (ages 18 and up) and Camp - A - Little (ages 5-17) offer recreational summer camp opportunities for individuals with physical and developmental disabilities.

7744 Casowasco Camp, Conference and Retreat Center
158 Casowasco Dr
Moravia, NY 13118-3498
315-364-8756
FAX: 315-364-7636
info@casowasco.org

Mike Huber, Executive Director
Shelly Sherboneau, CRM Coordinating Registrar
Kevin Dunn, Casowasco Assistant Director
Camp is located in Moravia, New York. Summer sessions for children with ADD. Coed, ages 6-18 and families.

7745 Center Academy at Pinellas Park
6710 86th Ave. N
Pinellas Park, FL 33782
727-541-5716
FAX: 727-544-8186
infopp@centeracademy.com
www.centeracademy.com

Mack R. Hicks, Founder & Chair
Andrew P. Hicks, Chief Executive Officer & Clinical Director
Eric V. Larson, President & Chief Operating Officer
Specifically designed for the learning disabled child and other children with difficulties in concentration, strategy, social skills, impulsivity, distractibility and study strategies. Programs offered include attention training, visual-motor remediation, socialization skills training, relaxation training, and more.

7746 Dallas Academy
950 Tiffany Way
Dallas, TX 75218
214-324-1481
FAX: 214-327-8537
www.dallas-academy.com

Elizabeth Murski, Head of School
Dallas Academy is a school for children with diagnosed learning differences such as autism, ADD/ADHD, dyslexia, and more. The academy offers a number of summer camps and programs.

7747 Eagle Hill School: Summer Program
242 Old Petersham Road
P.O. Box 116
Hardwick, MA 01037- 0116
413-477-6000
FAX: 413-477-6837
admission@ehs1.org
www.ehs1.org

Peter J. Mc Donald, Headmaster
Marilyn Waller, President
Alden Bianchi, Vice President
For children ages 9-19 with specific learning (dis)abilities and/or Attention Deficit Disorder, this summer program is designed to remediate academic and social deficits while maintaining progress achieved during the school year. Electives and sports activities are combined with the academic courses to address the needs of the whole person in a camp-like atmosphere.

7748 Englishton Park Academic Remediation
Englishton Park Presbyterian
P.O.Box 228
Lexington, IN 47138-228
812-889-2046
ThomasLisaBarnett@etczone.com
www.englishtonpark.org

Lisa Barnett, Director
Thomas Barnett, Co-Director
Camp is located in Lexington, Indiana. Two-week sessions for children with ADD. Boys and girls, ages 7-12.

7749 Florida Sheriffs Caruth Camp
Florida Sheriffs Youth Ranches
2486 Cecil Webb Place
Boys Ranch, FL 32060
386-842-5501
800-765-3797
FAX: 386-842-2429
fsyr@youthranches.org
www.youthranches.org

Roger Bouchard, President
Bill Frye, Executive Vice President
Janet Bass, Vice President of Operations
Camp is located in Inglis, Florida. One-week sessions for children with ADD. Coed, ages 10-15.

7750 Gow School Summer Programs
2491 Emery Rd.
South Wales, NY 14139
716-687-2004
FAX: 716-687-2003
summer@gow.org
www.gow.org

Matthew Fisher, Director
Co-ed summer programs for students ages 8-16 with dyslexia or similar learning disabilities. Offers a blend of morning academics, afternoon/evening traditional camp activities and weekend overnights.

7751 Hill School of Fort Worth
4817 Odessa Ave.
Fort Worth, TX 76133
817-923-9482
FAX: 817-923-4894
hillschool@hillschool.org
www.hillschool.org

Roxann Breyer, Head of School
Matt Errico, Dean, Student Success
Jimmy Cessna, Registrar
Provides an alternative learning environment for students with learning differences. Hill School caters to individuals with disabilities by offering smaller class sizes and individualized learning programs. Offers an academic summer program during the month of June.

7752 Indian Acres Camp for Boys
1712 Main St
Fryeburg, ME 04037-4327
207-935-2300
FAX: 954-349-7812
geoff@indianacres.com
www.indianacres.com

Michael Burness, Assistant Director
Mary Beth 'Bert' Wiig, Head Counselor, Camp Forest Acre
Lisa Newman, Director
Camp is located in Fryeburg, Florida. Four and seven-week sessions June-August for boys with ADD ages 7-16.

7753 Lab School of Washington
4759 Reservoir Rd NW
Washington, DC 20007-1921
200-965-6600
www.labschool.org

Katherine Schantz, Head of School
Diana Meltzer, Associate Head of School
Laurelle Sheedy McCready, Associate Head of School
The Lab School six week summer session includes individualized reading, spelling, writing, study skills and math programs. A multisensory approach addresses the needs of bright learning disabled children. Related services such as speech/language therapy and occupational therapy are integrated into the curriculum. Elementary/Intermediate; Junior High/High School.

7754 Lions Den Outdoor Learning Center
600 Kiwanis Dr
Eureka, MO 63025-2212
636-938-5245
FAX: 636-938-5289
www.wymancenter.org

David Hilliard, President
Theresa Mayberry, Executive VP
Kristine Ramsey, Sr. VP
Varied programs for developmentally disabled children, ages 6 and up, includes daily living, socialization and language skills. Sports, tent camping, crafts, and nature study are also offered. Sliding scale tuition for 2 weeks.

7755 Maplebrook School
5142 Route 22
Amenia, NY 12501   845-373-9511
                                    FAX: 845-373-7029
                      admissions@maplebrookschool.org
                            www.maplebrookschool.org
Donna Konkolics, Head of School
Roger Fazzone, President
Jennifer Scully, Assistant Head, Postsecondary Studies
A coeducational boarding school which offers a six week camp for children with learning differences and ADD.

7756 Marvelwood Summer
Marvelwood School
476 Skiff Mountain Road
PO Box 3001
Kent, CT 06757-3001   860-927-0047
                                     FAX: 860-927-0021
                                     www.marvelwood.org
Alfred C Brooks, President
Arthur F Goodearl, Jr, Head Of School
The emphasis in this summer program is on diagnosis and remediation of individual reading, spelling, writing, mathematics and study problems. Offered to ages 12-16.

7757 New Horizons Summer Day Camp
YMCA of Orange County
13821 Newport Ave.
Suite 150
Tustin, CA 92780   714-508-7616
                             newhorizons@ymcaoc.org
                         www.ymcaoc.org/new-horizons
Jeff McBride, Chief Executive Officer
New Horizons is a program by the YMCA offering day camps for adults with developmental disabilities. Outings in the community are supervised and create an environment that fosters social interaction, skill building, and friendship.

7758 New Jersey YMHA/YWHA Camps Milford
21 Plymouth St
Fairfield, NJ 07004-1686   973-575-3333
                                           800-776-5657
                                     FAX: 973-575-4188
                                     info@njycamps.org
                                     www.njycamps.org
Leonard Robinson, President
Bruce Nussman, President
Camp is located in Milford, Pennsylvania. Summer sessions for children with ADD. Coed, ages 6-17 and families.

7759 Oakland School & Camp
128 Oakland Farm Way
Troy, VA 22974   434-293-9059
                                     FAX: 434-296-8930
                          information@oaklandschool.net
                                www.oaklandschool.net
Carol Williams, Head of School
A highly individualized program that stresses improving reading ability. Subjects taught are reading, English composition, math and word analysis. Recreational activities include horseback riding, sports, swimming, tennis, crafts, archery and camping. For girls and boys, ages 7-13. Students who attend the summer camp often have a variety of learning disabilities, such as ADHD, dyslexia, visual/auditory processing disorders, and more.

7760 Outside In School Of Experiential Education, Inc.
PO Box 639
Greensburg, PA 15601   724-837-1518
                                     FAX: 724-837-0801
                                     www.myoutsidein.org
Michael C. Henkel, Executive Director
Camp programs primarily focus on substance abuse, but some services are available for special needs related to school/work. Programs are for boys ages 13-18.

7761 Phelps School Academic Support Program
583 Sugartown Rd.
Malvern, PA 19355   610-644-1754
                                     FAX: 610-540-0156
                            admis@thephelpsschool.org
                             www.thephelpsschool.org
Charles A. McGeorge, Head of School
The Phelps School is a day and boarding school for grades 6-12. They run an Academic Support Program for English, Reading, Mathematics, and Study Skills for students who have diagnosed learning differences.

7762 Quest Camp
907 San Ramon Valley Blvd.
Suite 202
Danville, CA 94526   925-743-2900
                                           800-313-9733
                                     FAX: 925-743-1937
                                     www.questcamps.com
Robert B. Field, PhD., Founder & Executive Director
Debra Forrester-Field, MA, Administrative Director
Aprilyn Artz, MA, Clinical Director
Quest Camps are designed using the Quest Camp Therapeutic System developed specifically to help and reduce a campers psychological disability. With locations in San Francisco East Bay, California, Huntington Beach, California, and Pittsburgh, Pennsylvania, camps have a 6:1 camper to staff ratio, with campers receiving sport instruction and participate in physical activity, arts, and games.
1989

7763 Raven Rock Lutheran Camp
17912 Harbaugh Valley Road
P.O.Box 136
Sabillasville, MD 21780-136   410-303-2108
                                           800-321-5824
Brenda Minnich, Executive Director
Christ-centered program for youth and developmentally disabled adults.

7764 Rimland Services for Autistic Citizens
1265 Hartrey Ave.
Evanston, IL 60202   847-328-4090
                                     FAX: 847-328-8364
                                     TTY:847-328-4090
                                     www.rimland.org
Lorraine Ganz, President
Barbara Cooper, Secretary
Services include residential living, community day services, and health and wellness programs.

7765 Rolling Hills Country Day Camp
P.O.Box 172
Marlboro, NJ 07746   732-308-0405
                                     FAX: 732-780-4726
                          info@rollinghillsdaycamp.com
                            www.rollinghillsdaycamp.com
Billy Breitner, Director
Summer sessions for children with ADD. Coed, ages 3-12.

7766 SOAR Summer Adventures
226 SOAR Lane
PO Box 388
Balsam, NC 28707   828-456-3435
                                     FAX: 801-820-3050
                                  admissions@soarnc.org
                                         www.soarnc.org
John Willson, Executive Director
A nonprofit adventure program working with disadvantaged youth diagnosed with learning disabilities in an outdoor, challenge-based environment. Focuses on esteem building and social skills development through rock climbing, backpacking, whitewater rafting, mountaineering, sailing, snorkeling, and more. Offers two week, one month, and semester programs. Locations include North Carolina, Florida, Wyoming, California, New York, Belize, Costa Rica, and the Caribbean.

7767 Sherman Lake YMCA Outdoor Center
6225 N 39th St
Augusta, MI 49012-9722 269-731-3000
FAX: 269-731-3020
shermanlakeymca@ymcasl.org
www.shermanlakeymca.org
Luke Austenfeld, Executive Director
Jean Henderson, Business Manager
Lorrie Syverson, Director of Camping, Education &
Summer camping sessions for campers with ADD and spina
bifida. Coed, ages 6-15 and families, seniors.

7768 Squirrel Hollow Summer Camp
The Bedford School
5665 Milam Rd.
Fairburn, GA 30213 770-774-8001
FAX: 770-774-8005
info@thebedfordschool.org
www.thebedfordschool.org
Betsy Box, Admissions Director
Jeff James, Head of School
Allison Day, Associate Head of School
A remedial summer program for children with academic needs
held on the campus of The Bedford School in Fairburn, Georgia.
It serves children ages 6-14.

7769 Summer@Carroll
Carroll School
25 Baker Bridge Rd.
Lincoln, MA 01773 781-259-8342
summeradmissions@carrollschool.org
www.carrollschool.org
Kristin Curry, Director
Donna Brown, Assistant Director
Summer@Carroll is a unique educational experience designed
for children with language-based learning disabilities entering
grades 1-9 in the Fall. Carroll's five-week, full-day program provides specialized reading support as well as writing and math
classes. Classes are formed according to age and skill level, typically with eight or fewer students in a class.

7770 Summit Camp
55 W 38th St.
4th Floor
New York, NY 10018 570-253-4381
info@summitcamp.com
www.summitcamp.com
Shepherd Baum, Director
Leah Love, Assistant Director
Thea Mullis, Travel Director
The camp is located in Honesdale, Pennsylvania, and is for children ages 8-19 who have a variety of developmental, social, or
learning challenges. In addition to traditional camp activities,
Summit Camp has a strong focus on social skills development and
interpersonal growth.

7771 Sunnyhill Adventures
6555 Sunlit Way
Dittmer, MO 63023 636-274-9044
sunnyhilladventures.org
Rob Darroch, Director
Summer camps and year-round programs are offered for youth
and adults of all abilities.

7772 Talisman Summer Camp
64 Gap Creek Rd.
Zirconia, NC 28790 828-697-6313
info@talismancamps.com
www.talismancamps.com
Linda Tatsapaugh, Operations Director & Owner
Robyn Mims, Admissions Director & Owner
Cory Greene, Camp Director
Talisman Summer Camp is located 40 minutes south of Asheville,
North Carolina. Offers a program of hiking, rafting, climbing,
and caving for young people with autism, ADHD and learning
disabilities. Coed, ages 6-22.

7773 Timbertop Camp for Youth with Learning Disabilities
PO Box 423
Plover, WI 54467 715-869-6262
info@timbertopcamp.org
www.timbertopcamp.org
Pete Matthai, Camp Director
Timbertop Camp is a seven-day outdoor camp for children and
youth with learning disabilities. Campers participate in traditional camp activities as well as activities that focus on enhancing
cooperative abilities, interpersonal relationships, and self-esteem. The program includes nature exploration, canoeing, arts
and crafts, archery, fishing, games, reading instruction, and
campfires.

7774 Triangle Y Ranch YMCA
YMCA of Southern Arizona
PO Box 1111
Tucson, AZ 85702 520-623-5511
FAX: 520-624-1518
www.tucsonymca.org
Dane Woll, President and CEO
Kerry Dufour, V.P. Chief Development Officer
Cathy Scheirman, Chief Financial Officer
Summer camp programs for children and young adults ages 6-17.
Camp offers horseback riding, sports, story telling, arts & crafts,
swimming, archery and nature programs.

7775 Wendell Johnson Speech And Hearing Clinic
University Of Iowa
250 Hawkins Dr
Iowa City, IA 52242-1025 319-335-3500
FAX: 319-335-8851
dorothy-albright@uiowa.edu
www.uiowa.edu
Dorothy Albright, Department Administration
Lauren Eldridge, Undergraduate Academic Programs
Mary Jo Yotty, Graduate Programs
The clinic offers assessment and remediation for communication
disorders in adults and children. The clinic also offers a Intensive
Summer Residential Clinic for school age children needing inter-
vention services because of speech, language, hearing and/or
reading problems.

Books

7776 A Miracle to Believe In
Option Indigo Press
2080 S Undermountain Rd
Sheffield, MA 01257-9643 413-229-8727
800-714-2779
FAX: 413-229-8727
Barry Neil Kaufman, Author
A group of people from all walks of life come together and are
transformed as they reach out, under the direction of the
Kaufmans, to help a little boy the medical world had given up as
hopeless. This heartwarming journey of loving a child back to life
will not only inspire you, the reader, but presents a compelling
new way to deal with life's traumas and difficulties.
379 pages
ISBN 0-449201-08-2

7777 ADD: Helping Your Child
Warner Books
1271 Avenue of the Americas
New York, NY 10020-1300 212-522-7200
FAX: 212-522-7989
Barbara Smalley, Author
Bruce Paonessa, Vice President
Elizabeth Nunuz, Manager
The definitive guide to helping children with AD/HD *$12.95*
224 pages Paperback
ISBN 0-446670-13-8

7778 **ADHD Book of Lists: A Practical Guide for Helping Children and Teens with ADDs**
Jossey-Bass
111 River St
Hoboken, NJ 7030-5773
201-748-6000
FAX: 201-748-6008
info@wiley.com
www.wiley.com

Sandra F Rief, Author
Information about Attention Deficit/Hyperactivity Disorder including strategies, supports, and interventions that have been found to be the most effective. For teachers, parents, and counselors. *$29.95*
320 pages
ISBN 0-787965-91-X

7779 **ADHD in the Schools: Assessment and Intervention Strategies**
Guilford Press
72 Spring St
New York, NY 10012-4019
212-431-9800
800-365-7006
FAX: 212-966-6708
info@guilford.com
www.guilford.com

George J DuPaul, Author
Gary Stoner, Co-Author
This landmark volume emphasizes the need for a team effort among parents, community-based professionals, and educators. Provides practical information for educators that is based on empirical findings. Chapters focus on: how to identify and assess students who might have ADHD; the relationship between ADHD and learning disabilities; how to develop and implement classroom-based programs; communication strategies to assist physicians; and the need for community-based treatments. *$36.00*
269 pages Hardcover
ISBN 0-898622-45-X

7780 **ADHD with Comorbid Disorders: Clinical Assessment and Management**
Guilford Press
72 Spring St
New York, NY 10012-4019
212-431-9800
800-365-7006
FAX: 212-966-6708
info@guilford.com
www.guilford.com

Steven R Pliszka, MD, Author
Caryn Leigh Carlson, Co-Author
James M Swanson, Co-Author
$44.00
Cloth
ISBN 1-572304-78-2

7781 **Adolescents with Down Syndrome: Toward a More Fulfilling Life**
Brookes Publishing
P.O.Box 10624
Baltimore, MD 21285-624
410-337-9580
800-638-3775
FAX: 410-337-8539
custserv@brookespublishing.com
www.brookespublishing.com

Maria Sustrova, Author
Lauren Smith, Western Region Sales Representative
Jeannine Blimline, Central Region Sales Representative
Written for health care professionals, psychologists, other developmental disabilities practitioners, educators, and parents, it covers biomedical concerns; behavioral, psychological, and psychiatric challenges; and education, employment, recreation, community, and legal concerns. *$35.95*
416 pages Paperback
ISBN 1-55766 -81-9

7782 **Adult ADD: The Complete Handbook: Everything You Need to Know About How to Cope with ADD**
Prima Publishing
P.O.Box 1260
Rocklin, CA 95677-1260
916-787-7000
800-632-8676
FAX: 916-787-7001

David B Sudderth, Author
In simple and friendly terms, the authors offer help to those leading frustrating lives. They provide coping mechanisms, both psychological and an up-to-date guide to the latest technology
$14.95
272 pages
ISBN 0-761507-96-5

7783 **All About Attention Deficit Disorders, Revised**
Parent Magic
800 Roosevelt Rd
Glen Ellyn, IL 60137-5839
630-208-0031
800-442-4453
FAX: 630-208-7366
www.parentmagic.com

Thomas Phelan, Owner
A psychologist and expert on ADD outlines the symptoms, diagnosis and treatment of this neurological disorder. *$12.95*
248 pages Paperback
ISBN 1-889140-11-2

7784 **Assistive Technology for Individuals with Cognitive Impairments Handbook**
Idaho Assistive Technology Project
University of Idaho
1187 Alturas Dr.
Moscow, ID 83843- 2268
208-885-3557
800-432-8324
FAX: 208-885-6102
idahoat@uidaho.edu
www.idahoat.org

Ron Seiler, Project Director
A handbook designed to provide resources and information on finding and acquiring assistive technology for individuals with cognitive impairments.

7785 **Attention Deficit Disorder**
Sage Publications
2455 Teller Road
Thousand Oaks, CA 91320
800-818-7243
FAX: 800-583-2665
info@sagepub.com
www.sagepub.com

Sara Miller McCune, Founder, Publisher, Chairperson
Blaise R Simqu, President & CEO
A book providing helpful suggestions for both home and classroom management of students with attention deficit disorder.

7786 **Attention Deficit Disorder and Learning Disabilities**
Books on Special Children
P.O.Box 305
Congers, NY 10920-305
845-638-1236
FAX: 845-638-0847

Barbara Ingersoll, Author
Introduces ADD and learning disabilities. This is an easy reading book. Gives definitions and discusses some effective and controverial medication, dietary, biofeedback, cognitive therapy, and many more issues. *$15.95*
246 pages Softcover
ISBN 0-385469-31-4

7787 **Attention Deficit Disorder in Adults Workbook**
Taylor Publishing Company
7211 Circle S. Road
Austin, TX 78745-5007
214-637-2800
800-225-3687
FAX: 214-819-8220
Rings@balfour.com
www.balfour.com

Don Percenti, CEO
Workbook for adults with ADD. *$17.99*
192 pages Paperback
ISBN 0-878338-50-0

7788 Attention Deficit Disorder: A Different Perception
Underwood Books
PO Box 1919
Nevada City, CA 95959-1919   800-788-3123
                                    www.underwoodbooks.com

Thorn Hartmann, Author
Supports theory linking ADD to the genetic makeup of men and
women who hunted for their food in prehestoric times. Also links
second hand smoke to disruptive behavior. *$9.95*
180 pages Paperback
ISBN 0-887331-56-4

7789 Attention Deficit Disorders: Assessment & Teaching
Brooks/Cole Publishing Company
10650 Toebben Drive
Independence, KY 41051   859-525-2230
                                    FAX: 859-282-5700
                                    www.brookscole.com

Janet W Lerner, Author
A handy resource that offers teachers, school psychologists,
councelors, social workers, administrators, and parents practical
advice for working with children who have attention deficit disorders. *$18.95*
258 pages Paperback
ISBN 0-534250-44-0

**7790 Attention-Deficit Hyperactivity Disorder: Symptoms and
Suggestons for Treatment**
Slosson Educational Publications Inc.
538 Buffalo Rd
East Aurora, NY 14052-280   716-652-0930
                                    888-756-7766
                                    FAX: 800-655-3840
                                    slosson@slosson.com
                                    www.slosson.com

Thomas W Phelan, Author
Steven Slosson, President
John Slosson, Vice President
An exhaustive review of current research and decades of experience as practicing school-based professionals, as well as being a
parent of an ADHD child, have culminated in this brief,
to-the-point, and yet informed ADHD package which has
recieved tremendous reviews. Well-grounded answers and suggestions which would facillitate behavior, learning, social-emotional functioning, and other factors in preschool and adolescence
are discussed. Answers most commonly asked questions about
ADHD/ADD. *$60.00*
61 pages

**7791 Attention-Deficit/Hyperactivity Disorder, What Every
Parent Wants to Know**
Brookes Publishing
P.O.Box 10624
Baltimore, MD 21285-0624   410-337-9580
                                    800-638-3775
                                    FAX: 410-337-8539
                                    custserv@brookespublishing.com
                                    www.brookespublishing.com

Lauren Rohe, Regional Sales Consultant
Jeff Stickler, Educational Sales Representative
Sam Schissler, Educational Sales Representative
New easy-to-understand, non-technical edition helps teachers
and parents get accessible answers to their ADHD. *$21.95*
304 pages Paperback
ISBN 1-557663-98-X

7792 Augmenting Basic Communcation in Natural Contexts
Brookes Publishing
P.O.Box 10624
Baltimore, MD 21285-0624   410-337-9580
                                    800-638-3775
                                    FAX: 410-337-8539
                                    custserv@brookespublishing.com
                                    www.brookespublishing.com

Lauren Rohe, Regional Sales Consultant
Jeff Stickler, Educational Sales Representative
Sam Schissler, Educational Sales Representative

Here you will find the techniques needed to establish a basic communication system for people of all ages with cognitive disabilities or motor sensory impairments. *$41.95*
304 pages Paperback
ISBN 1-55766 -43-6

**7793 Autism 24/7: A Family Guide to Learning at Home & in
the Community**
Autism Society of North Carolina Bookstore
505 Oberlin Rd
Suite 230
Raleigh, NC 27605-1345   919-743-0204
                                    800-442-2762
                                    FAX: 919-743-0208
                                    info@autismsociety-nc.org
                                    www.autismsociety-nc.org

David Lax, Manager
Martina Ballen, Chair
Beverly Moore, Vice Chair
Parents are encouraged to focus on skill sets and behaviors that
most negatively affect family functioning, and replacing these
behaviors with acceptable alternatives. *$19.95*

**7794 Autism Handbook: Understanding & Treating Autism &
Prevention Development**
Oxford University Press
2001 Evans Rd
Cary, NC 27513-2010   919-677-0977
                                    800-445-9714
                                    FAX: 919-677-1303
                                    custserv.us@oup.com
                                    www.oup-usa.org

Thomas Carty, Senior Vice President
Simon Li, Regional Director
Adam Glazer, Director
$25.00
320 pages
ISBN 0-195076-67-2

7795 Autism and Learning
Taylor & Francis
7625 Empire Dr
Florence, KY 41042-2919   212-695-6599
                                    800-634-7064
                                    FAX: 212-563-2269
                                    orders@taylorandfrancis.com
                                    www.taylorandfrancis.com

Rita Jordan, Author
Stuart Powell, Co-Author
This book is about how a cognitive perception on the way in
which individuals with autism think and learn may be applied to
particular curriculum areas.
160 pages Paperback
ISBN 1-853464-21-X

7796 Autism in Adolescents and Adults
Springer Publishing
11 W 42nd St
Floor 15
New York, NY 10036-8002   212-431-4370
                                    FAX: 212-460-1575
                                    service-ny@springer.com
                                    www.springerjournals.com

Eric Schopler, Editor
$63.00
456 pages
ISBN 0-306410-57-5

7797 Autism..Nature, Diagnosis and Treatment
Autism Society of North Carolina Bookstore
505 Oberlin Rd
Suite 230
Raleigh, NC 27605-1345   919-743-0204
                                    800-442-2762
                                    FAX: 919-743-0208
                                    jchampion@autismsociety-nc.com
                                    www.autismbookstore.com

David Lax, Manager
Covers perspectives, issues, neurobiological issues and new directions in diagnosis and treatment. *$49.00*

7798 **Autism: Explaining the Enigma**
Wiley Publishers
111 River St
Suite 2000
Hoboken, NJ 7030-5773

201-748-6000
FAX: 201-748-6088
info@wiley.com
www.wiley.com

Uta Firth, Author
Explains the nature of autism. *$27.95*

7799 **Autism: From Tragedy to Triumph**
Branden Books
Po Box 812094
Wellesley, MA 02482

617-734-2045
FAX: 781-790-1056
www.brandenbooks.com

Carol Johnson, Author
Julia Crowder, Co-Author
A new book that deals with the Lovaas method and includes a foreward by Dr. Ivar Lovaas. The book is broken down into two parts — the long road to diagnosis and then treatment. *$12.95*

7800 **Autism: Identification, Education and Treatment**
Routledge (Taylor & Francis Group)
7625 Empire Dr
Florence, KY 41042-2919

212-695-6599
800-634-7064
FAX: 212-563-2269
orders@taylorandfrancis.com
www.routledge.com

Dianne Zager, Editor
Jeffrey Lin, Director
Francis Chua, Manager
Chapters include medical treatments, early intervention and communication development in autism. *$36.00*
ISBN 0-805820-44-7

7801 **Autism: The Facts**
Oxford University Press
2001 Evans Rd
Cary, NC 27513-2010

919-677-0977
800-445-9714
FAX: 919-677-1303
custserv.us@oup.com
www.oup-usa.org

Simon Cohen, Author
Patrick Bolton, Co-Author
$22.50
128 pages
ISBN 0-192623-27-3

7802 **Autistic Adults at Bittersweet Farms**
Routledge (Taylor & Francis Group)
7625 Empire Dr
Florence, KY 41042-2919

212-695-6599
800-634-7064
FAX: 212-563-2269
orders@taylorandfrancis.com
www.routledge.com

Norman Giddan PhD, Author
Jane Giddan MA, Co-Author
Jefferey Lin, Director
A touching view of an inspirational residential care program for autistic adolescents and adults. Also available in softcover. *$94.95*
Hardcover
ISBN 1-560240-42-3

7803 **Be Quiet, Marina!**
Star Bright Books
13 Landsdowne St
Cambridge, MA 02139

617-354-1300
FAX: 617-354-1399
orders@starbrightbooks.com
www.starbrightbooks.com

Kirsten Debear, Author
A noisy little girl with cerebral palsy and a quiet little girl with Down Syndrome learn to play together and eventually become best friends. *$16.95*
40 pages Hardcover
ISBN 1-887734-79-1

7804 **Breakthroughs: How to Reach Students with Autism**
Aquarius Health Care Media
30 Forest Road
PO Box 249
Millis, MA 02054

508-376-1244
FAX: 508-376-1245
aqvideos@tiac.net
www.aquariusproductions.com

Leslie Krussman, President/Producer
Joseph Wellington, Distribution Coordinator
Anne Baker, Billing & Accounting
A hands-on, how-to program for reaching students with autism, featuring Karen Sewell, Autism Society of America's teacher of the year. Here Sewell demonstrates the successful techniques she's developed over a 20-year career. A separate 250 page manual ($59) is also available which covers math, reading, fine motor, self help, social adaptive, vocational and self help skills as well as providing numerous plan reproducibles and an exhaustive listing of equipment and materials resources. Video. *$99.00*

7805 **Bus Girl: Selected Poems**
Brookline Books
8 Trumbull Rd
Suite B-001
Northampton, MA 01060

617-734-6772
800-666-2665
FAX: 617-734-3952
brbooks@yahoo.com
www.brooklinebooks.com

Gretchen Josephson, Author
Lula O Lubchenco, Editor
Poems written over several decades by a young woman with Down Syndrome. *$14.95*
144 pages Paperback
ISBN 1-57129 -41-9

7806 **Change Your Brain, Change Your Life: The Breakthrough Program for Conquering Depression**
Three Rivers Press
3rd Floor
175 Broadway
New York, NY 10019

212-782-9000
FAX: 212-940-7860
www.randomhouse.com

Daniel G Amen MD, Author
Clinical neuroscientist and psychiatrist Amen uses nuclear brain imaging to diagnose and treat behavioral problems. He explains how the brain works, what happens when things go wrong, and how to optimize brain function. Five sections of the brain are discussed, and case studies clearly illustrate possible problems. *$15.00*
352 pages
ISBN 0-812929-98-5

7807 **Child and Adolescent Therapy: Cognitive-Behavioral Procedures, Third Edition**
Guilford Press
72 Spring Street
New York, NY 10012-4019

212-431-9800
800-365-7006
FAX: 212-966-6708
info@guilford.com
www.guilford.com

Chris Jennison, Publisher Emeritus, Education
Seymour Weingarten, Editor-in-Chief
Jody Falco, Managing Editor: Periodicals
Incorporating significant developments in treatment procedures, theory and clinical research, new chapters in this second edition examine the current status of empirically supported interventions and developmental issues specific to work with adolescents. *$45.00*
432 pages Cloth
ISBN 1-572305-56-8

7808 Cognitive Behavioral Therapy for Adult Asperger Syndrome
Autism Society of North Carolina Bookstore
505 Oberlin Rd
Ste 230
Raleigh, NC 27605-1345   919-743-0204
                                          800-442-2762
                                     FAX: 919-743-0208
                        jchampion@autismsociety-nc.org
                                 www.autismbookstore.com
David Lax, Manager
Text is prepared with case studies and examples from the author's own experiences working as a cognitive-behavioral therapist specializing in adults and adolescents with dual diagnosis, autism spectrum disorders, mood disorders, and anxiety disorders.

7809 Communication Development in Children with Down Syndrome
Brookes Publishing
P.O.Box 10624
Baltimore, MD 21285-0624   410-337-9580
                                          800-638-3775
                                     FAX: 410-337-8539
                        custserv@brookespublishing.com
                             www.brookespublishing.com
Lauren Rohe, Regional Sales Consultant
Jeff Stickler, Educational Sales Representative
Sam Schissler, Educational Sales Representative
This book offers an extensive, detailed explanation of communication development in children with Down syndrome relative to their advancing cognitive skills. It introduces a critical framework for assessing and treating hearing, speech, and language problems and provides explicit intervention methods and tested clinical protocols.
Paperback
ISBN 1-55766-50-5

7810 Comprehensive Guide to ADD in Adults: Research, Diagnosis & Treatment
ADD Warehouse
300 NW 70th Ave
Suite 102
Plantation, FL 33317-2360   954-792-8100
                                          800-233-9273
                                     FAX: 954-792-8545
                            websales@addwarehouse.com
                                  www.addwarehouse.com
Harvey C Parker, Owner
The first to provide broad coverage of the burgeoning field. Written for professionals who diagnose and treat adults with ADD, it provides information from psychologists and physicians on the most current research and treatment issues *$50.95*
426 pages
ISBN 0-876307-60-8

7811 Concentration Cockpit: Explaining Attention Deficits
Educators Publishing Service
P.O.Box 9031
Cambridge, MA 02139-9031   617-367-2700
                                          800-225-5750
                                     FAX: 617-547-0412
                  CustomerService.EPS@schoolspecialty.com
                                     eps.schoolspecialty.com
Rick Holden, President
Melvin D Levine, Author
This eight-page pamphlet explains the administration of The Concentration Cockpit, a newly revised poster that helps children with attention deficits gain insight into their problems and monitor their progress in grappling with these problems. *$64.50*
ISBN 0-838820-59-X

7812 Coping with ADD/ADHD
Rosen Publishing Group
29 E 21st St
New York, NY 10010-6209   212-420-1600
                                          800-237-9932
                                     FAX: 888-436-4643
                                    www.rosenpublishing.com
Jaydene Morrison, Author

At least 3.5 million American youngsters suffer from attention deficit disorder. This book defines the syndrome and provides specific information about treatment and counseling. *$16.95*
ISBN 0-823920-70-4

7813 Count Us In
Exceptional Parent Library
P.O.Box 1807
Englewood Cliffs, NJ 7632-1207   201-947-6000
                                          800-535-1910
                                     FAX: 201-947-9376
Jason Kingsley, Author
Mitchell Levitz, Co-Author
Offers information on growing up with Downs Syndrome. *$9.95*

7814 Culture and the Restructuring of Community Mental Health
Greenwood Publishing Group
130 Cremona Drive
Santa Barbara, CA 93117   805-968-1911
                                          800-368-6868
                                     FAX: 866-270-3856
                        CustomerService@abc-clio.com
                                  www.greenwood.com
William A Vega, Author
John W Murphy, Co-Author
Michael Millman, Editor, American History
Examines treatment, organizational planning and research issues and offers a critique of the theoretical and programmatic aspects of providing mental health services to traditionally underserved populations. $45.00-$52.95. *$95.00*
168 pages Hardcover
ISBN 0-313268-87-8

7815 Difficult Child
Bantam Books
1745 Broadway, 10th Floor
New York, NY 10019   212-782-9000
                                     FAX: 212-302-7985
                        BBDPublicity@randomhouse.com
                          www.randomhouse.com/bantamdell
Stanley Turecki, Author
Leslie Tonner, Co-Author
The classic and definitive work on parenting hard-to-raise children with new sections on ADHD and the latest medications for childhood disorders. *$15.95*
302 pages Paperback
ISBN 0-553380-36-2

7816 Disability Culture Perspective on Early Intervention
Through the Looking Glass
3075 Adeline Street
Suite 120
Berkeley, CA 94703-2212   510-848-1112
                                          800-644-2666
                                     FAX: 510-848-4445
                                     TTY: 510-848-1005
                                    TLG@lookingglass.org
                                   www.lookingglass.org
Megan Kirshbaum PhD, Author
For parents with physical or cognitive disabilities and their families. Available in braille, large print or cassette. *$2.00*
12 pages

7817 Down Syndrome
Aquarius Health Care Media
30 Forest Road
PO Box 249
Millis, MA 02054-1066   508-376-1244
                                          888-440-2963
                                     FAX: 508-376-1245
                                www.aquariusproductions.com
Lesile Kussmann, Owner
This is an excellent video for families who have just had a baby with Down Syndrome as well as professionals in the field of genetics and nursing. Through honest and open discussion, parents of children with Down Syndrome express the feelings and concerns they had during the early years of their child's life. Preview option available. *$150.00*
Video

7818 Driven to Distraction
Simon & Schuster/Touchstone Publishing
1230 Avenue of the Americas
Fl 11
New York, NY 10020-1513
212-698-7000
FAX: 212-698-7009
www.simonsays.com

Edward M Hallowell, MD, Author
John J Ratey, MD, Co-Author
A practical book discussing adult as well as child attention deficit disorder (ADD). Non-technical, realistic and optimistic, it is an informative how-to manual for parents and consumers. *$23.00*

7819 Dyslexia over the Lifespan
Educators Publishing Service
PO Box 9031
Cambridge, MA 02139-9031
617-367-2700
800-225-5750
FAX: 617-547-0412
eps@schoolspecialty.com
www.epsbooks.com

Margaret B Rawston, Author
Discusses the educational and career development of 56 dyslexic boys from a private school that was one of the first to have a program to detect and treat developmental language disabilities. *$18.00*
224 pages
ISBN 0-838816-70-3

7820 Embracing the Monster: Overcoming the Challenges of Hidden Disabilities
Paul H Brookes Publishing Company
PO Box 10624
Baltimore, MD 21285-624
410-337-9580
800-638-3775
FAX: 410-337-8539
www.brookespublishing.com

Veronica Crawford M.A., Author
Larry B Silver, MD, Foreword/Commentary
The author shares her experience of living with LD, ADHD and bipolar disorder to give readers an awareness of the challenges of living with hidden disabilities and what can be done to help *$24.95*
272 pages paperback
ISBN 1-557665-22-2

7821 Encounters with Autistic States
Jason Aronson
400 Keystone Industrial Park
Dunmore, PA 18512-1507
800-782-0015
FAX: 201-840-7242

Theodore Mitrani, Author
This book explores and explands the work of the late Frances Tustin, which was devoted to the psychoanalytic understanding of the bewildering elemental world of the autistic child. *$50.00*
448 pages Hardcover
ISBN 0-765700-62-

7822 Families of Adults With Autism: Stories & Advice For the Next Generation
Autism Society of North Carolina Bookstore
505 Oberlin Road
Suite 230
Raleigh, NC 27605-1345
919-743-0204
800-442-2762
FAX: 919-743-0208
books@autismsociety-nc.org
www.autismbookstore.com

Tracey Sheriff, Chief Executive Officer
Paul Wendler, Chief Financial Officer
David Laxton, Director of Communications
This book's unique point of view is that of a parent who's been there and done that and is now willing to tell the reader what it was like. *$19.95*

7823 Family Therapy for ADHD: Treating Children, Adolescents and Adults
Guilford Press
72 Spring St
New York, NY 10012-4019
800-365-7006
www.guilford.com

Craig A Everett, Author
Sandra Volgy Everett, Co-Author
Presents an innovative approach to assesing and treating ADHD in the family context. *$29.00*
Paperback
ISBN 1-572304-38-3

7824 Fighting for Darla: Challenges for Family Care & Professional Responsibility
Teachers College Press
1234 Amsterdam Ave
New York, NY 10027-6602
212-678-3929
FAX: 212-678-4149
tcpress@tc.columbia.edu

Mary Lynch, Manager
Susan M Klein, Co-Author
Samuel Guskin, Co-Author
Follows the story of Darla, a pregnant adolescent with autism. *$18.95*
161 pages
ISBN 0-807733-56-3

7825 Fragile Success
Brookes Publishing
PO Box 10624
Baltimore, MD 21285-624
410-337-9580
800-638-3775
FAX: 410-337-8539
www.brookespublishing.com

Virginia Walker Sperry, Author
A book about the lives of autistic children, whom the author has followed from their early years at the Elizabeth Ives School in New Haven, CT, through to adulthood. *$27.50*
ISBN 1-557664-58-7

7826 Getting Our Heads Together
Thoms Rehabilitation Hospital
68 Sweeten Creek Rd
Asheville, NC 28803-2318
828-274-2400
FAX: 828-274-9452

Kathi Petersen, Director Planning/Communication
Edgardo Diez MD, Medical Director Brain Injury
Kathy Price, Director Admissions
A handbook for families of head injured patients - available in Spanish as well as English. *$4.00*
40 pages Paperback

7827 Getting a Grip on ADD: A Kid's Guide to Understanding & Coping with ADD
Educational Media Corporation
1443 Old York Rd
Warmister, PA 18794
763-781-0088
800-448-9041
FAX: 215-956-9041
www.educationalmedia.com

Kim Frank Ed.S., Author
Susan Smith-Rex Ed.D., Co-Author
Free catalog of resources.
64 pages Yearly

7828 Getting the Best for Your Child with Autism
Autism Society of North Carolina Bookstore
505 Oberlin Road
Suite 230
Raleigh, NC 27605-1345
919-743-0204
800-442-2762
FAX: 919-743-0208
books@autismsociety-nc.org
www.autismbookstore.com

Tracey Sheriff, Chief Executive Officer
Paul Wendler, Chief Financial Officer
David Laxton, Director of Communications
This treatment guide helps parents navigate the complex and overwhelming world of Autism. *$16.95*

7829 Group Activity for Adults with Brain Injury
Sage Publications
2455 Teller Road
Thousand Oaks, CA 91320   805-499-0721
                                 800-818-7243
                            FAX: 805-499-0871
                            info@sagepub.com
                            www.sagepub.com

Sara Miller McCune, Founder, Publisher, Executive Chairman
Blaise R Simqu, President & CEO
Tracey A. Ozmina, Executive Vice President & Chief Operating
Officer
This manual addresses attention, memory, reasoning, and language skills in group settings. *$53.00*

7830 Guide to Successful Employment for Individuals with Autism
Brookes Publishing
P.O.Box 10624
Baltimore, MD 21285-0624   410-337-9580
                                  800-638-3775
                             FAX: 410-337-8539
                        custserv@brookespublishing.com
                        www.brookespublishing.com

Marcia Daltow Smith, Author
Ronald G Belcher, Co-Author
Patricia D Juhrs, Co-Author
Describing all aspects of job placement, this book details strategies for assessing workers, networking for job opportunities, and tailoring job supports to each individual. Also illustrates how to help individuals with autism become productive workers, and with detailed descriptions of specific jobs help provide ideas for employment. *$32.95*
336 pages Paperback
ISBN 1-55766 -71-5

7831 Handbook of Autism and Pervasive Developmental Disorders
Autism Society of North Carolina Bookstore
505 Oberlin Road
Suite 230
Raleigh, NC 27605-1345   919-743-0204
                                800-442-2762
                           FAX: 919-743-0208
                        books@autismsociety-nc.org
                        www.autismbookstore.com

David Laxton, Director of Communications
Paul Wendler, Chief Financial Officer
Tracey Sheriff, Chief Executive Officer
A list of contributors address such topics as characteristics of autistic syndromes and interventions. *$125.00*

7832 Handbook of Career Planning for Students with Special Needs
Pro- Ed Publications
8700 Shoal Creek Boulevard
Austin, TX 78757-6897   512-451-3246
                               800-897-3202
                          FAX: 512-451-8542
                          general@proedinc.com
                          www.proedinc.com

Donald D Hammill, Owner
Courtney King, Marketing Coordinator
Thomas F. Harrington, Editor
The practitioner's guide will show you how to help special needs adolescents and young adults overcome barriers to employment by identifying goals and problems, assessing interests and aptitudes, involving client families and developing communication skills. *$42.00*
358 pages

7833 Helping People with Autism Manage Their Behavior
Indiana Resource Center For Autism
2853 E 10th St
Bloomington, IN 47408-2696   812-855-6508
                               FAX: 812-855-9630
                               prattc@indiana.edu
                               www.iidc.indiana.edu

David Mank, Executive Director
Scott Bellini, Assistant Director

Covers the broad topic of helping people with autism manage their behavior. *$7.00*

7834 Helping Your Hyperactive: Attention Deficit Child
Crown Publishing Company (Random House)
1745 Broadway
New York, NY 10019-4305   212-782-9000
                                 800-632-8676
                            FAX: 212-572-6066
                            crownpublishing.com

John Taylor, Author
$19.95
ISBN 1-559584-23-8

7835 Hidden Child: The Linwood Method for Reaching the Autistic Child
Woodbine House
6510 Bells Mill Road
Bethesda, MD 20817-1636   301-897-3570
                                 800-843-7323
                            FAX: 301-897-5838
                            info@woodbinehouse.com
                            www.woodbinehouse.com

Irv Shapell, Owner
Sabine Oishi, Co-Author
Chronicle of the Linwood Children's Center's successful treatment program for autistic children. *$17.95*
286 pages Paperback
ISBN 0-933149-06-9

7836 How To Reach and Teach Children and Teens with Dyslexia
Jossey-Bass
111 River St
Hoboken, NJ 7030-5773   201-748-6000
                          FAX: 201-748-6008
                          info@wiley.com
                          www.wiley.com

Cynthia M Stowe, Author
This practical resource gives educators at all levels essential information, techniques, and tolls for understanding dyslexia and adapting teaching methods in all subject areas to meet the learning style, social, and emotional needs of students who have dyslexia. *$22.95*
340 pages
ISBN 0-130320-18-8

7837 Hyperactive Child, Adolescent, and Adult: ADD Through the Lifespan
Oxford University Press
198 Madison Ave
New York, NY 10016-4308   212-726-6000
                            www.us.oup.com/us

Paul H Wender, Author
Comprehensive general review. Update on previous research by the author, offering a basic text. Published by Connecticut Association for Children & Adults with Learning Disabilities (CACLD). *$8.75*
162 pages
ISBN 0-195113-49-7

7838 Identifying and Treating Attention Deficit Hyperactivity Disorder
Learning Disabilities Association of America
4068 Mount Royal Boulevard
Suite 224B
Allison Park, PA 15101   412-341-1515
                           FAX: 412-344-0224
                           info@ldaamerica.org
                           www.ldaamerica.org

Cindy Cipoletti, Executive Director
Tracy Gregoire, Director, Healthy Children Project
Nina DelPrato, Administrative Manager
A resource guide for families and educators on the identification and treatment of Attention Deficit Hyperactivity Disorder (ADHD).

7839 **In Search of Wings: A Journey Back from Traumatic Brain Injury**
Lash & Associates Publishing/Training
100 Boardwalk Drive, Suite 150
Youngsville, NC 27596   919-556-0300
                                            FAX: 919-556-0900
                                            orders@lapublishing.com
                                            www.lapublishing.com

Marilyn Lash, President
Bob Cluett, CEO
Bill Herrin, Director of Graphics & Design
The true story of one woman coping with traumatic brain injury after a car accident that affected her cognitive skills and memory *$14.95*
233 pages
ISBN 1-882332-00-8

7840 **In Their Own Way**
Alliance for Parental Involvement in Education
375 Hudson Street
New York, NY 10014   212-366-2000
                                            FAX: 212-366-2933
                                            ecommerce@us.penguingroup.com
                                            us.penguingroup.com

Thomas Armstrong, Author
John Makinson, Chairman and Chief Executive
Coram Williams, CFO
For the parents whose children are not thriving in school, Armstrong offers insight into individual learning styles. *$11.95*

7841 **Jumpin' Johnny Get Back to Work, A Child's Guide to ADHD/Hyperactivity**
Ste 15-5
25 Van Zant St
Norwalk, CT 6855-1729   203-838-5010
                                            FAX: 203-866-6108
                                            CACLD@optonline.net
                                            www.CACLD.org

Beryl Kaufman, Executive Director
Written primarily for elementary age youngsters with ADHD to help them understand their disability. Also valuable as an educational tool for parents, siblings, friends and classmates. Includes two pages on medication. *$12.50*
24 pages

7842 **Keys to Parenting a Child with Attention Deficit Disorder**
Barron's Educational Series
250 Wireless Blvd
Hauppauge, NY 11788-3924   631-434-3311
                                            800-645-3476
                                            FAX: 631-434-3723
                                            barrons@barronseduc.com
                                            barronseduc.com

Manuel H Barron, CEO
Francine McNamara MSW CSW, Co/Author
This book shows how to work with the child's school, effectively manage the child's behavior and act as the child's advocate. *$6.95*
160 pages Paperback
ISBN 0-812014-59-6

7843 **Keys to Parenting a Child with Downs Syndrome**
Barron's Educational Series
250 Wireless Blvd
Hauppauge, NY 11788-3924   631-434-3311
                                            800-645-3476
                                            FAX: 631-434-3723
                                            barrons@barronseduc.com
                                            barronseduc.com

Manuel H Barron, CEO
Lucy Guarino
Down Syndrome poses many challenges for children and their families. This book prepares parents and guardians to raise a child with Down Syndrome by discussing adjustment, advocacy, health and behavior, education and planning for greater independence. *$5.95*
160 pages Paperback
ISBN 0-812014-58-8

7844 **Keys to Parenting the Child with Autism**
Barron's Educational Series
250 Wireless Blvd
Hauppauge, NY 11788-3924   631-434-3311
                                            800-645-3476
                                            FAX: 631-434-3723
                                            barrons@barronseduc.com
                                            barronseduc.com

Manuel H Barron, CEO
Parents of children with autism will find a solid balance between home and practical information in this book. It explains what autism is and how it is diagnosed, then advises parents on how to adjust to their child and give the best care. *$6.95*
208 pages Paperback
ISBN 0-812016-79-3

7845 **LD Child and the ADHD Child: Ways Parents & Professionals Can Help**
1406 Plaza Dr
Winston Salem, NC 27103-1470   336-768-1374
                                            800-222-9796
                                            FAX: 336-768-9194
                                            southern@blairpub.com
                                            www.blairpub.com

Carolyn Sakowski, President
Susan H Stevens, Author
Book about learning disabilities available to parents. Stevens cuts through the jargon and complex theories which usually characterize books on the subject to present effective and practical techniques that parents can employ to help their child succeed at home and at school. New edition adds information about ADHD children. *$12.95*
201 pages Paperback
ISBN 0-895871-42-4

7846 **Let Community Employment be the Goal for Individuals with Autism**
Indiana Resource Center For Autism
2853 E 10th St
Bloomington, IN 47408-2601   812-855-9396
                                            800-825-4733
                                            FAX: 812-855-9630
                                            prattc@indiana.edu
                                            www.iidc.indiana.edu

David Mank, Executive Director
Scott Bellini, Assistant Director
A guide designed for people who are responsible for preparing individuals with autism to enter the work force. *$7.00*

7847 **Making the Writing Process Work**
Brookline Books
8 Trumbull Rd
Suite B-001
Northampton, MA 01060   617-734-6772
                                            800-666-2665
                                            FAX: 617-734-3952
                                            brbooks@yahoo.com
                                            www.brooklinebooks.com

Karen R Harris, Author
Steve Grahm, Co-Author
Making the Writing Process Work: Strategies for Composition and Self-Regulation is geared toward students who have difficulty organizing their thoughts and developing their writing. The specific strategies teach students how to approach, organize, and produce a final written product. *$24.95*
240 pages Paperback
ISBN 1-57129 -10-9

7848 **Management of Autistic Behavior**
Sage Publications
2455 Teller Road
Thousand Oaks, CA 91320   805-499-0721
                                            800-818-7243
                                            FAX: 800-583-2665
                                            info@sagepub.com
                                            www.sagepub.com

Sara Miller McCune, Founder, Publisher, Executive Chairman
Blaise R Simqu, President & CEO
Tracey A. Ozmina, Executive Vice President & Chief Operating Officer

This excellent reference is a comprehensive and practical book that tells what works best with specific problems. *$41.00*
450 pages

7849   Managing Attention Deficit Hyperactivity in Children: A Guide for Practitioners
John Wiley & Sons Inc
111 River St
Hoboken, NJ 07030-5774   201-748-6000
                                       800-825-7550
                                  FAX: 201-748-6088
                                     info@wiley.com
                                      www.wiley.com

Warren J Baker, President
Michael Goldstein, Co-Author
Matthe S Kissner, CEO
Offers information about human personality, structure and dynamics, assessment and adjustment. *$27.50*
214 pages Hardcover
ISBN 0-471121-58-9

7850   Neurobiology of Autism
Johns Hopkins University Press
2715 N Charles St
Baltimore, MD 21218-4363   410-516-6900
                                  FAX: 410-516-6968
                                   www.press.jhu.edu

William Brody, President
Thomas L Kemper, Co-Author
Margaret L Bauman, M.D., Co-Author
This book discusses recent advances in scientific research that point to a neurobiological basis for autism and examines the clinical implications of this research. *$28.00*
272 pages
ISBN 0-801880-47-5

7851   Out of the Fog: Treatment Options and Coping Strategies for ADD
Hyperion
1500 Broadway
3rd Floor
New York, NY 10036   212-563-6500
                                       800-331-3761
                                  FAX: 212-456-0176
                                www.hyperionbooks.com

Robert Miller, President
Suzanne Levert, Co-Author
Discusses the recent recognition of attention deficit disorder as a problem that is not outgrown in adolescence, and cogently summarizes the stumbling blocks this affliction creates in the pursuit of a career or attainment of a healthy family life *$14.95*
300 pages
ISBN 0-786880-87-2

7852   Overcoming Dyslexia
Vintage-Random House
3rd Fl
1745 Broadway
New York, NY 10019-4305   212-782-9000
                                  FAX: 212-302-7985
                            www.randomhouse.com/vintage
Markus Dohle, CEO
Sally Shawitz, M.D., Author
Yale neuroscientist Shaywitz demystifies the roots of dyslexia (a neurologically based reading difficulty affecting one in five children) and offers parents and educators hope that children with reading problems can be helped. *$15.00*
432 pages
ISBN 0-679781-59-5

7853   Parent Survival Manual
Springer Publishing Company
11 W 42nd St
15th Floor
New York, NY 10036   212-431-4370
                                       877-687-7476
                                  FAX: 212-941-7842
                                 cs@springerpub.com
                                  www.springerpub.com

Ursula Springer, President
Ted Nardin, CEO
Edie Lambiase, CFO
A guide to crises resolution in autism and related developmental disorders. *$39.95*

7854   Parent's Guide to Down Syndrome: Toward a Brighter Future
Brookes Publishing
PO Box 10624
Baltimore, MD 21285-0624   410-337-9580
                                       800-638-3775
                                  FAX: 410-337-8539
                        custserv@brookespublishing.com
                           www.brookespublishing.com

Siegfried Pueschel MD PhD, Author
Highlights developmental stages and shows the advances that improve a child's quality of life. Includes discussions on easing the transition from home to school and choosing integration and curricular priorities, as well as guidelines for confronting adolescent and adult issues such as social and sexual needs and independent living and vocational options. *$21.95*
352 pages
ISBN 1-557664-52-8

7855   Parenting Attention Deficit Disordered Teens
CACLD
25 Van Zant Street
Norwalk, CT 06855-1729   203-838-5010
                                  FAX: 203-866-6108
                                CACLD@optonline.net
                                        cacld.org

Beryl Kaufman, Executive Director
Detailed outline of the various problems of adolescents with ADHD. Published by Connecticut Association for Children & Adults with Learning Disabilities (CACLD). *$3.25*
14 pages

7856   Parents Helping Parents: A Directory of Support Groups for ADD
Novartis Pharmaceuticals Division
59 State Route 10
East Hanover, NJ 7936-1005   862-778-7500
                                       800-742-2422

Paulo Costa, CEO

7857   Please Don't Say Hello
Human Sciences Press
233 Spring St
New York, NY 10013-1522   212-229-2859
                                       800-221-9369
                                  FAX: 212-463-0742
                                        isbndb.com

Charles Stenken, Author
Jaroslav Chobot, Author
Zirul Evany, Author
With the support and love of his family, and through them the neighborhood children, a nine-year-old autistic boy is able to emerge from his shell. *$10.95*
47 pages Paperback
ISBN 0-89885 -99-8

7858 Preventable Brain Damage
Springer Publishing Company
11 W 42nd St
15th Floor
New York, NY 10036
212-431-4370
877-687-7476
FAX: 212-941-7842
cs@springerpub.com
www.springerpub.com

Donald L Templer, Author
Lawrence C Hartlage, Co-Author
Ursula Springer, President
Offers information on brain injuries from motor vehicle accidents, contact sports and injuries of children. *$35.95*
256 pages

7859 Reading, Writing and Speech Problems in Children
International Dyslexia Association
40 York Rd.
4th Floor
Baltimore, MD 21204
410-296-0232
FAX: 410-321-5069
info@dyslexiaida.org
dyslexiaida.org

Samuel Torrey Orton, Author
This book provides reading, reading and speech execerises for educating people with dyslexia. *$20.00*
259 pages
ISBN 0-89079 -79-1

7860 Reality of Dyslexia
Brookline Books
8 Trumbull Rd
Suite B-001
Northampton, MA 01060
617-734-6772
800-666-2665
FAX: 617-734-3952
brbooks@yahoo.com
www.brooklinebooks.com

John Osmond, Author
An informative and sensitive study of living with dyslexia which affects one in 25. He introduces the reader to the subject by sharing the difficulties of his dyslexic son. He then uses the personal accounts of other children and adult dyslexics, even entire dyslexic families, to illuminate the problems they encounter. *$14.95*
150 pages Paperback
ISBN 1-57129 -17-6

7861 Relationship Development Intervention with Young Children
Jessica Kingsley Publishers
400 Market St
Suite 400
Philadelphia, PA 19106
215-922-1161
FAX: 215-992-1417
orders@jkp.com
www.jkp.com

Steven E Gustein, Author
Rachelle Sheely, Co-Author
Social and emotional development activities for Asperger Syndrome, Autism, PDD and NLD. Comprehensive set of activities emphasizes foundation skills for younger children between the ages of two and eight. Covers skills such as social referencing, regulating behvior, conversational reciprocity, and synchronized actions. For use in therapeutic settings as well as schools and parents. *$22.95*
256 pages
ISBN 1-843107-14-7

7862 Rethinking Attention Deficit Disorder
Brookline Books
8 Trumbull Rd
Suite B-001
Northampton, MA 01060-4533
617-734-6772
800-666-2665
FAX: 617-734-3952
brbooks@yahoo.com
www.brooklinebooks.com

Miriam Cherkes-Julkowski, Author

In contrast to the common focus on behavioral symptoms of attention disorders, this book emphasizes internal factors that make attention regulation difficult. In-depth discussions of social, emotional, and academic consequences and appropriate interventions are provided. *$27.95*
250 pages Paperback
ISBN 1-571290-30-7

7863 Riddle of Autism: A Psychological Analysis
Jason Aronson
4501 Forbes Blvd
Suite 200
Lanham, MD 20706-4346
301-459-3366
800-782-0015
FAX: 301-429-5746
www.rowmanlittlefield.com

Jason Aronson, Author
James Lyons, President/CEO
Stanley Plotnick, Chairman
Dr. Victor examines the myths that cloud an understanding of this disorder and describes the meanings of its specific behavioral symptoms. *$30.00*
356 pages Paperback
ISBN 1-568215-73-8

7864 SCATBI: Scales Of Cognitive Ability for Traumatic Brain Injury
Sage Publications
2455 Teller Road
Thousand Oaks, CA 91320
805-499-0721
800-818-7243
FAX: 805-499-0871
happiness@option.org
www.sagepub.com

Sara Miller McCune, Founder, Publisher, Executive Chairman
Blaise R Simqu, President & CEO
Tracey A. Ozmina, Executive Vice President & Chief Operating Officer
Assesses cognitive and linguistic abilities of adolescent and adult parents with head injuries. *$287.00*

7865 Sex Education: Issues for the Person with Autism
Indiana Resource Center For Autism
2853 E 10th St
Bloomington, IN 47408-2696
812-855-6508
800-825-4733
FAX: 812-855-9630
iidc@indiana.edu
www.iidc.indiana.edu

David Mank, Executive Director
Scott Bellini, Assistant Director
Discusses issues of sexuality and provides methods of instruction for people with autism. *$4.00*

7866 Son-Rise: The Miracle Continues
2080 S Undermountain Rd.
Sheffield, MA 01257
413-229-2100
800-562-7171
correspondence@option.org
www.autismtreatmentcenter.org

Barry Neil Kaufman, Founder & CEO
Clyde Haberman, Senior Teacher & Director of Development
Blair Borgeson, Developmental Therapist
The center's Son-Rise Program teaches a comprehensive system of treatment and education designed to help families and caregivers enable their children to dramatically improve in all areas of learning. *$12.95*
343 pages
ISBN 0-915811-53-7

7867 Soon Will Come the Light
Future Horizons Inc
721 W Abram St
Arlington, TX 76013-6995
817-277-0727
800-479-0727
FAX: 817-277-2270
www.fhautism.com

Wayne Gilpin, Owner
Jennifer Gilpin, Vice President
Annette Vick, Manager

Offers new perspectives on the perplexing disability of autism. *$19.95*

7868 Successful Job Search Strategies for the Disabled: Understanding the ADA
Wiley Publishing
605 3rd Ave
New York, NY 10158-180

212-850-6000
FAX: 212-850-6088
www.wiley.com

Jeffrey G Allen, Author
Following a concise overview of the Americans with Disabilities Act (ADA), covers such topics as job identification, self-assessment, job leads, resumes, disability disclosure, interviewing, and accommodating specific disabilities. Includes dozen of relevant and instructive situation analyses, case examples, and answers to commonly asked questions. *$165.00*
229 pages

7869 Taking Charge of ADHD Complete Authoritative Guide for Parents
Guilford Press
72 Spring St
New York, NY 10012-4019

212-431-9800
800-365-7006
FAX: 212-966-6708
info@guilford.com
www.guilford.com

Russell A Barkley, Author
Revised and updated to incorporate the most current information on ADHD and its treatment. Provides parents with the knowledge, guidance and confidence they need to ensure that their child receives the best care possible. Also in cloth at $40.00 (ISBN# 1-57230-600-9 *$18.95*
331 pages Paperback
ISBN 1-572305-60-1

7870 Teaching Children with Autism: Strategies for Initiating Positive Interactions
Brookes Publishing
P.O.Box 10624
Baltimore, MD 21285-0624

410-337-9580
800-638-3775
FAX: 410-337-8539
custserv@brookespublishing.com
www.brookespublishing.com

Robert L. Koegel, Author
Lynn Kern Koegel, Co-Author
Robert Miller, Sales Director
Offers strategies for initiating positive interactions and improving learning opportunities. This guide begins with an overview of characteristics and long-term strategies and proceeds through discussions that detail specific techniques for normalizing environments, reducing disruptive behavior, improving language and social skills, and enhancing generalization. *$39.95*
256 pages Paperback
ISBN 1-557661-80-4

7871 Teaching and Mainstreaming Autistic Children
Love Publishing Company
9101 E Kenyon Ave
Suite 2200
Denver, CO 80237-1854

303-221-7333
FAX: 303-221-7444
www.lovepublishing.com

Stan Love, Owner
Peter Knoblock, Author
Dr. Knoblock advocates a highly organized, structured environment for autistic children, with teachers and parents working together. His premise is that the learning and social needs of autistic children must be analyzed and a daily program designed with interventions that respond to this functional analysis of their behavior. *$24.95*
ISBN 0-89108 -11-9

7872 Techniques for Aphasia Rehab: (TARGET) Generating Effective Treatment
Speech Bin
1965 25th Ave
Vero Beach, FL 32960-3062

772-770-0007
800-477-3324
FAX: 772-770-0006
store.schoolspecialty.com

Mary Jo Santo Pietro, Co-Author
Robert Goldfarb, Co-Author
TARGET is the kind of resource aphasia clinicians beg for. A practical resource that answers not only the what and how questions of treatment, but also the why. It describes dozens of treatment methods and gives you practical exercises and activities to implement each technique. It shows you how to treat all components of the disability, language disorder, overall impairment, communication problems, and the needs of the person with aphasia. *$45.00*
384 pages
ISBN 0-93785 -50-5

7873 Teenagers with ADD
Woodbine House
6510 Bells Mill Rd
Bethesda, MD 20817-1636

301-897-3570
800-843-7323
FAX: 301-897-5838
info@woodbinehouse.com
www.woodbinehouse.com

Irv Shapell, Owner
Chris A Ziegler Dendy, M.S., Author
This best selling guide to understanding and coping with teenagers with attention deficit disorder (ADD) provides complete coverage of the special issues and challenges faced by these teens. Based on current diagnostic criteria and the latest literature and research in the field, the book discusses diagnosis, medical treatment, family and school life, intervention, advocacy, legal rights, and options after high school. Parents find strategies for dealing with their teen's difficult behaviors. *$18.95*
370 pages Paperback
ISBN 0-933149-69-7

7874 Understanding Down Syndrome: An Introduction for Parents
Brookline Books
8 Trumbull Rd
Suite B-001
Northampton, MA 01060-4533

617-734-6772
800-666-2665
FAX: 617-734-3952
brbooks@yahoo.com
www.brooklinebooks.com

Cliff Cunningham, Author
Using positive and readable language, this book helps parents understand Down Syndrome. Medical details are explained in lay terms, and advice is given on working with professionals, obtaining services, and treatment techniques that help the child. Cunningham alerts families to potential problems, the prospects for the child in schooling and the passage to adulthood. Revised 1996. *$14.95*
Softcover
ISBN 1-57129 -09-5

7875 Valley News Dispatch
New York Families For Autistic Children
95-16 Pitkin Avenue
Ozone Park, NY 11417-2834

718-641-3441
FAX: 718-641-2228

Cheryl L. Marsh, Chairperson
Robert Burt, Treasurer
Education, recreation and support services for families and children with developmental disabilities.

7876 Verbal Behavior Approach: How to Teach Children with Autism & Related Disorders
Autism Society of North Carolina Bookstore
505 Oberlin Road
Suite 230
Raleigh, NC 27605-1345   919-743-0204
                                800-442-2762
                         FAX: 919-743-0208
                   books@autismsociety-nc.org
                      www.autismbookstore.com
David Laxton, Director of Communications
Paul Wendler, Chief Financial Officer
Tracey Sheriff, Chief Executive Officer
Provides full descriptions of how to teach the verbal operants that make up expressive languate which include: manding, tacting, echoing and intraverbal skills. *$19.95*

7877 Without Reason: A Family Copes with two Generations of Autism
Books on Special Children
721 W Abram St
Arlington, TX 76013-6995   817-277-0727
                                  800-489-0727
                            FAX: 817-277-2270
Wayne Tilton, President
The author discovers his son has autism. He delves into problems of the autistic person and explains reasons for their actions. *$20.95*
292 pages Hardcover

7878 Women with Attention Deficit Disorder: Embracing Disorganization at Home and Work
Underwood-Miller
708 Westover Dr
Lancaster, PA 17601-1242
Addresses the millions of withdrawn little girls and chronically overwhelmed women with ADD who go undiagnosed because they don't fit the stereotypical notion of people with ADD. *$11.95*
288 pages
ISBN 1-887424-05-9

7879 You Mean I'm Not Lazy, Stupid or Crazy?!: A Self-Help Book for Adults with ADD
Simon & Schuster
1230 Avenue Of The Americas
11th Floor
New York, NY 10020-1513   212-698-7000
                            FAX: 212-698-7099
                             www.simonsays.com
Kate Kelly, Author
Peggy Ramundo, Co-Author
Practical advice on controlling adult ADD, a straightforward guide explains how to get along in groups, become organized, improve memory, and pursue professional help. *$15.00*
464 pages
ISBN 0-684815-31-1

7880 You and Your ADD Child
Nelson Publications
1 Gateway Plz
Port Chester, NY 10573-4674   914-481-5490
                            FAX: 914-937-8950
Paul Warren MD, Author
Jody Capehart M.Ed., Co-Author
$12.99
252 pages Paperback
ISBN 0-785278-95-8

Journals

7881 Annals of Dyslexia
International Dyslexia Association
40 York Road
4th Floor
Baltimore, MD 21204   410-296-0232
                            FAX: 410-321-5069
                          info@dyslexiaida.org
               dyslexiaida.org/annals-of-dyslexia
Denise Douce, Director, Publications & Resources
IDA is a clearinghouse of scientific data and practice-based information related to dyslexia. Provides community-based referrals and information fact sheets in response to thousands of emails, calls & letters. Our annual conference attracts thousands of outstanding researchers, clinicians, parents, teachers, psychologists, educational therapists and people with dyslexia.
Tri-annual

7882 Journal of Cognitive Rehabilitation
Neuroscience Publishers
6555 Carrollton Ave
Indianapolis, IN 46220-1664   317-257-9672
                            FAX: 317-257-9674
                         neuroscience.cnter.com
Odie L Bracy, Executive Director
Publication for therapists, family and patient, designed to provide information relevant to the rehabilitation of impairment resulting from brain injury. *$50.00*
36-48 pages Quarterly

Magazines

7883 AWARE
National Fibromyalgia Association
1000 Bristol Street North
Suite 17-247
Irvine, CA 92660   714-921-0150
                            FAX: 714-921-6920
                             www.fmaware.org
Lynne Matallana, President/Founder
Mark Dobrilovic, Board of Director
John Fry, PhD, Board of Director
Magazine published three times a year with membership only.

7884 Attention
Children & Adults with ADHD
8181 Professional Place
Suite 150
Landover, MD 20785- 2264   301-306-7070
                                  800-233-4050
                            FAX: 301-306-7090
                         webmaster@chadd.org
                              www.chadd.org
Bryan Goodman, Director
A bi-monthly publication from CHADD. Free with membership.
Bi-monthly

Newsletters

7885 ADHD Report
Guilford Press
72 Spring St
New York, NY 10012-4019   212-431-9800
                                  800-365-7006
                            FAX: 212-966-6708
                            info@guilford.com
                             www.guilford.com
Russell A Barkley PhD, Editor
Presents the most up-to-date information on the evaluation, diagnosis and management of ADHD in children, adolescents and

adults. This important newsletter is an invaluable resource for all professionals interested in ADHD. *$49.95*
16 pages BiMonthly
ISSN 1065-8025

7886 Arc Connection Newsletter
Arc of Tennessee
151 Athens Way
Suite 100
Nashville, TN 37228
615-248-5878
800-835-7077
FAX: 615-248-5879
info@thearctn.org
thearctn.org

John Lewis, President
John H. Shouse, VP,Planning & Rules committee Chair
Donna Lankford, Secretary
Quarterly publication from the ARC of Tennessee. *$10.00*
12 pages Quarterly

7887 Arc Light
Arc of Arizona
5610 S Central Ave
Phoenix, AZ 85040-3090
602-268-6101
800-252-9054
FAX: 602-268-7483
thearcaz@gmail.com

Cindy Waymire, Editor
For people with intellectual and developmental disabilities.
Quarterly

7888 Autism Research Review International
Autism Research Institute
4182 Adams Ave
San Diego, CA 92116-2599
619-281-7165
FAX: 619-563-6840
br@autismresearchinstitute.com
autism.com

Steve Edelson, Executive Director
The Autism Research Institute has pubished this quarterly newsletter, Autism Research Review International (ARRI), since 1987. The ARRI has received worldwide praise for it's thoroughness and objectivity in reporting the current developments in biomedical and educational research. The latest findings are gleaned from a computer search of the 25,000 scientific and medical articles published every week. *$18.00*

8 pages Quarterly

7889 BIATX Newsletter
Brain Injury Association of Texas
316 W 12th Street
Suite 405
Austin, TX 78701-1845
512-326-1212
800-392-0040
FAX: 512-478-3370
www.texasbia.org

Judith Abner, Director
Penny Phillips, President
Donna Kuhlmann, Chairman
A online quarterly e-newsletter, as well as news and updates on the Brain Injury Association of Texas.

7890 BIAWV Newsletter
Brain Injury Association of America
PO Box 574
Institute, WV 25112-0574
304-766-4892
800-356-6443
FAX: 304-766-4940
biawv@aol.com

Peggy Brown, Director
Mike Davis, President

7891 Best Buddies Times
Best Buddies Times
907-1243 Islington Ave
Toronto, ON, Canada
416-531-0003
888-779-0061
FAX: 416-531-0325
info@bestbuddies.ca
www.bestbuddies.ca

Steven Pinnock, Director
Emily Bolyea-Kyere, Regional Program Manager
Bi-annual newsletter.

7892 Chadder
Children & Adults with Attention Deficit Disorder
4601 Presidents Drive
Suite 300
Lanham, MD 20706
301-306-7070
FAX: 301-306-7090
www.chadd.org

Michael MacKay, President
Ruth Hughes, CEO
Susan Buningh, Executive Editor
Quarterly newsletter
Quarterly

7893 Cognitive Therapy Today
Beck Institute for Cognitive Therapy & Research
One Belmont Avenue
Ste 700
Bala Cynwyd, PA 19004-1610
610-664-3020
FAX: 610-709-5336
info@beckinstitute.org
www.beckinstitute.org

Judith S Beck, Director
Aaron T Beck, President
Cognitive Therapy TodayT features articles on a wide range of topics in CBT by leading clinicians from around the world. Articles have addressed evaluating psychotherapies; CBT and special populations, such as soldiers, the elderly, or diagnoses such as schizophrenia; conceptualizing emotions; cross-cultural issues and many other issues of interest to clinicians. You will also find information on workshops, speaking engagements by Beck Institute faculty and more.

7894 Down Syndrome News
National Down Syndrome Congress
30 Mansell Court
Suite 108
Roswell, GA 30076
770-604-9500
800-232-6372
FAX: 770-604-9898
info@ndsccenter.org
www.ndsccenter.org

Jim Faber, President
Marilyn Tolbert, 1st VP
Carole J. Guess, 2nd Vice President
Must become a member to receive the newsletter.

7895 Focus Times Newsletter
Focus Alternative Learning Center
126 Dowd Avenue
PO Box 452
Canton, CT 06019-0452
860-693-8809
FAX: 860-693-0141
info@focuscenterforautism.org
www.focus-alternative.org

Marcia Bok, President
Claudia Godburn, Secretary
Rita Barredo, Treasurer
Monthly online newsletter on autism.

7896 Imagine!
Imagine!
1400 Dixon Ave.
Lafayette, CO 80026-2790
303-665-7789
imaginecolorado.org

Rebecca Novinger, Executive Director
Jeff Tucker, Director of Human Resources
Jenna Corder, Director of Client Relations

For people of all ages with cognitive, developmental, physical & health related needs, so they may live lives of independence & quality in their homes and communities.

12-16 pages quarterly

7897 NAMI Advocate
National Alliance on Mental Illness
3803 N Fairfax Dr
Suite 100
Arlington, VA 22203-3080
703-524-7600
800-950-6264
FAX: 703-524-9094
www.nami.org

Suzanne Vogel-Scibilia, President
Our mission is to provide you with the technical assistance, tools and referrals to resources you need to build organizational capacity and achieve the goals of the NAMI Standards of Excellence.

7898 NLP News
NLP Comprehensive
PO.Box 348
Indian Hills, CO 80454-648
303-987-2224
800-233-1657
FAX: 303-987-2228
www.nlpco.com

Christian Miller, Editor
Tom Dotz, President
Tom Hoobyar, Director Of Planning
An online e-newsletter on Neuro-linguistic programming.

7899 Pure Facts
Feingold Association of the US
10955 Windjammer Dr. S
Indianapolis, IN 46256
631-369-9340
help@feingold.org
www.feingold.org

Deborah Lehner, Executive Director
Relationship between foods, food additives and behaviorial or learning challenges.

7900 REACH
TEACCH
100 Renee Lynn Ct
Carrboro, NC 27510
919-966-2174
FAX: 919-966-4127
teacch@unc.edu
www.teacch.com

Dr. Laura Klinger, Director
Walter Kelly, Business Officer
Rebecca Mabe, Assistant Director of Business
Free online newsletter.

7901 Rettsyndrome.org
4600 Devitt Dr
Cincinnati, OH 45246
513-874-3020
800-818-7388
FAX: 513-874-2520
admin@rettsyndrome.org
www.rettsyndrome.org

Peter White, Chair
Gordon Rich, Chief Operating Officer
Steven Kaminsky, Ph.D, Chief Science Officer
Rettsyndrome.org offers informational resources and programs for those affected by Rett syndrome as well as their families.

7902 Weekly Wisdom
Autism Treatment Center of America
2080 S Undermountain Rd
Sheffield, MA 01257-9643
413-229-2100
877-766-7473
FAX: 413-229-3202
www.son-rise.org

Barry Kausman, Owner
Weekly Wisdom is available through a free email subscription.

Audio/Visual

7903 ADD, Stepping Out of the Dark
Child Development Media
5632 Van Nuys Blvd
Suite 286
Van Nuys, CA 91401-4602
818-989-7221
800-405-8942
FAX: 818-989-7826

Margie Wagner, Owner
A powerful, effective video, ideal for health professionals, educators and parents providing a visual montage designed to promote an understanding and awareness of attention deficit disorder. Based on actual accounts of those who have ADD, including a neurologist, an office worker, and parents of children with ADD. The DVD allows the viewer to feel the frustration and lack of attention that ADD brings to many. *$52.95*
Video

7904 ADHD in Adults
Guilford Press
72 Spring St
New York, NY 10012-4019
212-431-9800
800-365-7006
FAX: 212-966-6708
info@guilford.com
www.guilford.com

Russell A Barkley, Editor
This program integrates information on ADHD with the actual experiences of four adults who suffer from the disorder. Representing a range of professions, from a lawyer to a mother working at home, each candidly discusses the impact of ADHD on his or her daily life. These interviews are augmented by comments from family members and other clinicians who treat adults with ADHD. *$99.00*
DVD 1906
ISBN 0-898629-86-1

7905 ADHD: What Can We Do?
Guilford Press
72 Spring St
New York, NY 10012-4019
212-431-9800
800-365-7006
FAX: 212-966-6708
info@guilford.com

Russell A Barkley, Editor
A video program that introduces teachers and parents to a variety of the most effective technologies for managing ADHD in the classroom, at home, and on family outings. *$99.00*
DVD 1906
ISBN 0-898629-72-1

7906 ADHD: What Do We Know?
Guilford Press
72 Spring St
New York, NY 10012-4019
212-431-9800
800-365-7006
FAX: 212-966-6708
info@guilford.com
www.guilford.com

Bob Matloff, President
Russell A Barkley, Editor
An introduction for teachers and special education practitioners, school psychologists and parents of ADHD children. Topics outlined in this video include the causes and prevalence of ADHD, ways children with ADHD behave, other conditions that may accompany ADHD and long-term prospects for children with ADHD. *$99.00*
DVD 1906
ISBN 0-898629-71-3

7907 Around the Clock: Parenting the Delayed AD HD Child
Guilford Press
72 Spring St
New York, NY 10012-4019

212-431-9800
800-365-7006
FAX: 212-966-6708
info@guilford.com

Joan F Goodman, Editor
Susan Hoban, Editor
This videotape provides both professionals and parents a helpful look at how the difficulties facing parents of ADHD children can be handled. Video. *$150.00*
VHS 1994
ISBN 0-898629-68-3

7908 Attention Deficit Disorder: Adults
Aquarius Health Care Media
30 Forest Road
Millis, MA 02054

508-376-1244
888-440-2963
FAX: 508-376-1245
www.aquariusproductions.com

Lesile Kussmann, President/Owner
Joseph Wellington, Distribution Coordinator
Anne Baker, Billing & Accounting
Adults with ADD talk about how the disorder that went undiagnosed for so many years has affected their choice of spouses and work, and what they have found to help them. Biofeedback, which is growing as a treatment, is explained and demonstrated by its founder, Dr. Joel Lubar. Medical treatments like antidepressants and stimulants are also discussed, along with behavioral changes that can help the person with ADD and his or her spouse and family. *$149.00*
Video

7909 Attention Deficit Disorder: Children
Aquarius Health Care Media
30 Forest Rd
PO Box 249
Millisrn, MA 02054-7159

508-376-1244
888-440-2963
FAX: 508-376-1245
www.aquariusproductions.com

Lesile Kussmann, President/Owner
Everyone has been impulsive or easily distracted for different periods of time, so these symptoms that are hallmarks of Attention Deficit Disorder (ADD) have also led to criticism that too many people are being diagnosed with this biochemical brain disorder. This program examines who is being diagnosed, and what treatments are working. An innovative private school specializing in alternative education is profiled, and tips on structuring the school and home environment are included. *$149.00*
Video

7910 Autism: A World Apart
Fanlight Productions C/O Icarus Films
32 Court Street
Brooklyn, NY 11201-1731

718-488-8900
800-876-1710
FAX: 718-488-8642
info@fanlight.com
www.fanlight.com

Ben Achtenberg, Owner
Nicole Johnson, Publicity Coordinator
Anthony Sweeney, Marketing Director
In this documentary, three families show us what the textbooks and studies cannot: what it's like to live with autism day after day; to raise and love children who may be withdrawn and violent and unable to make personal connections with their families. 29 minutes. *$195.00*
VHS/DVD 1988
ISBN 1-572950-39-0

7911 Autism: the Unfolding Mystery
Aquarius Health Care Media
30 Forest Road
PO Box 249
Millis, MA 02054

508-376-1244
FAX: 508-376-1245
www.aquariusproductions.com

Lesile Kussmann, Owner
Explore what it means to be autistic, how you can recognize the signs of autism in your child, and hear about new treatments and programs to help children learn to deal with the disorder. *$145.00*
DVD 1905

7912 Biology Concepts Through Discovery
Educational Activities Software
5600 W 83rd Street
Suite 300, 8200 Tower
Bloomington, MN 55437

800-447-5286
FAX: 239-225-9299
info@edmentum.com
www.ea-software.com

Vin Riera, President/CEO
Rob Rueckel, CFO
Dave Adams, Chief Academic Officer
These videos, available in English and Spanish versions, encourage learning by presenting interactive problem solving in an effective VISUAL/AUDITORY style. *$89.00*
Video

7913 Concentration Video
Learning disAbilities Resources
6 E Eagle Road
Havertown, PA 19083

610-446-6126
800-869-8336
FAX: 610-525-8337
rcooper-ldr@comcast.net

An instructional video which provides a perspective about attention problems, possible causes and solutions. *$19.95*
Video

7914 Educating Inattentive Children
ADD Warehouse
300 Northwest 70th Avenue
Suite 102
Plantation, FL 33317-2360

954-792-8100
800-233-9273
FAX: 954-792-8545
websales@addwarehouse.com
www.addwarehouse.com

Harvey C Parker, Owner
Ideal for in-service to regular and special educators concerning the problems inattentive, elementarty and secondary students experience. *$49.00*
Video

7915 Getting Started with Facilitated Communication
Facilitated Communication Institute, Syracuse Univ
230 Huntington Hal
Syracuse, NY 13244-1

315-443-4752
FAX: 315-443-2258
thefci.syr.edu

Annegret Schubert, Director
Describes in detail how to help individuals with autism and/or severe communication difficulties to get started with facilitated communication.
Video

7916 How to Cope with ADHD: Diagnosis, Treatment & Myths
Aquarius Health Care Media
30 Forest Road
PO Box 249
Millis, MA 02054

508-376-1244
FAX: 508-376-1245
www.aquariusproductions.com

Lesile Kussmann, President/Owner
Learn how ADHD is diagnosed, clear up some of the myths, explain the treatmens that are availiable, and give you tips on how you can help your child at home. *$145.00*
DVD 1905

7917   I Just Want My Little Boy Back
Autism Treatment Center Of America
2080 South Undermountain Road
Sheffield, MA 01257

413-229-2100
800-714-2779
happiness@option.org
www.option.org

Samahria Lyt Kaufman, Co-Founder and Co-Director
Dane Griffith, Director of Administrative Services
Bears Kaufman, Co-Founder and Co-Director
A great video for parents and professionals caring for children with special needs. Join one British family and their autistic son before, during and after their journey to America to attend The Son-Rise Program at The Autism Treatment Center of America. This informative, inspirational and deeply moving story not only captures the joy, tears, challenges and triumps of this amazing little boy and his family, but also serves as a powerful introduction to the attitude and principles of the program. *$25.00*

7918   It's Just Attention Disorder
Western Psychological Services
625 Alaska Avenue
Torrance, CA 90503-5124

424-201-8800
800-648-8857
FAX: 424-201-6950
customerservice@wpspublish.com
wpspublish.com

Gregg Gillmar, VP
This ground-breaking videotape takes the critical first steps in treating attention-deficit disorder: it enlists the inattentive or hyperactive child as an active participant in his or her treatment. *$99.50*
Video

7919   Understanding ADHD
Aquarius Health Care Videos
30 Forest Road
PO Box
Millis, MA 02054

508-376-1244
FAX: 508-376-1245
www.aquariusproductions.com

Leslie Kussmann, President/Owner
A look at some of the controversies surrounding Attention Deficit Hyperactivity Disorder. This video shows how the disorder is diagnosed and presents strategies for living with a child with the disorder. Diverse and candid opinions from teachers, social workers, a behavior specialist, a pediatrician and a parent with ADHD twins. Recommended for child development students, social workers, and caregivers. Preview option available. *$120.00*
Video

7920   Understanding Attention Deficit Disorder
CACLD
25 Van Zant Street
Norwalk, CT 6855-1713

203-838-5010
FAX: 203-866-6108
CACLD@optonline.net
www.CACLD.org

Beryl Kaufman, Executive Director
Helen Bosch, President
A video in an interview format for parents and professionals providing the history, symptoms, methods of diagnosis and three approaches used to ease the effects of attention deficit disorder. Published by Connecticut Association for Children & Adults with Learning Disabilities (CACLD). *$20.00*
45 Minutes VHS

7921   Understanding Autism
Fanlight Productions C/O Icarus Films
32 Court Street
Brooklyn, NY 11201

718-488-8900
800-876-1710
FAX: 718-488-8642
info@fanlight.com
www.fanlight.com

Ben Achtenberg, Owner
Susan Newman, Editor

Parents of children with autism discuss the nature and symptoms of this lifelong disability and outline a treatment program based on behavior modification principles. 19 minutes *$199.00*
VHS/DVD 1993
ISBN 1-572951-00-1

7922   We're Not Stupid
Media Projects Inc
5215 Homer St
Dallas, TX 75206-6623

214-826-3863
FAX: 214-826-3919
mail@mediaprojects.org
www.mediaprojects.org

Fonya Naomi Mondell, Producer
We're Not Stupid is an insightful and very personal video that gives a voice to people who are struggling with learning disabilities. It was made by filmmaker Fonya Naomi Mondell, who is also living with learning differences. The filmmaker camptures the personal stories of young people from all walks of life who discuss what it's like to live with Attention Deficit Disorder and Dyslexia. Their comments are open, honest and direct, and their determination to manage their condition shines through. *$125.00*
Video

7923   Why Won't My Child Pay Attention?
ADD Warehouse
300 Northwest 70th Avenue
Suite 102
Plantation, FL 33317-2360

954-792-8100
800-233-9273
FAX: 954-792-8545
www.addwarehouse.com

Sam Goldstein, Ph.D, Author
Michael Goldstein, M.D., Co-Author
Practical and reassuring videotape, noted child psychologist tells parents about two of the most common and complex problems of childhood: inattention and hyperactivity. *$49.50*
224 pages Hardcover 1992
ISBN 0-471530-77-8

Software

7924   Cogrehab
Life Science Associates
1 Fenimore Rd
Bayport, NY 11705-2115

631-472-2111
FAX: 631-472-8146

Joann Mandriota, President
Divided into six groups for diagnosis and treatment of attention, memory and perceptual disorders to be used by and under the guidance of a professional. $95.-$1,950

Support Groups

7925   Autism Society of America
4340 East-West Highway
Suite 350
Bethesda, MD 20814

301-657-0881
800-328-8476
FAX: 301-657-0869
info@autism-society.org
www.autism-society.org

Scott Badesch, President/CEO
Jennifer Repella, VP Programs
John Dabrowski, CFO
ASA is the largest and oldest grassroots organization within the autism community, with more than 200 chapters and over 20,000 members and supporters nationwide. ASA is the leading source of education, information and referral about autism and has been the leader in advocacy and legislative initiatives for more than three decades.

7926   National Autism Hotline
Autism Services Center
929 4th Ave
PO Box 507
Huntington, WV 25701-1408   304-525-8014
                                     FAX: 304-525-8026
                              www.autismservicescenter.org

Mike Grady, CEO
Jimmie Beirne, COO
Nathel Lewis, ASC Training Coordinator
Service agency for individuals with autism and developmental
disabilities, and their families. Assists families and agencies attempting to meet the needs of individuals with autism and other
developmental disabilities. Makes available technical assistance
in designing treatment programs and more. The hotline provides
informational packets to callers and assists via telephone when
possible.

7927   National Health Information Center
Office Of Disease Prevention And Health Promotion
P.O.Box 1133
Washington, DC 20013-1133   301-565-4167
                                         800-336-4797
                                         301-468-7394
                                     FAX: 301-984-4256
                                     www.health.gov/nhic

Jessica Rowden, Sec Dept. Health Human Services
William Corr, J.D., Deputy Secretary
National health information center provides information referral
and support. NHIC links consumers and health professionals to
organizations that are best able to provide reliable health
information.

Dexterity

Associations

7928 American Amputee Foundation
1805 Wewoka Dr
North Little Rock, AR 72116   501-835-9290
                                    FAX: 501-835-9292
                                    www.americanamputee.org
Catherine J Walden, Executive Director
Serves primarily as a national information clearinghouse and referral center assisting amputees and their families. The foundation researches and gathers information including studies, product information, services, self-help publications and review articles written within the field.

7929 American Board for Certification in Orthotics, Prosthetics & Pedorthics
330 John Carlyle St
Suite 210
Alexandria, VA 22314   703-836-7114
                                    FAX: 703-836-0838
                                    info@abcop.org
                                    www.abcop.org
Eric Ramcharran, CPO, President
Catherine Carter, Executive Director
Samlane Ketevong, Director, Certification Services
The American Board for Certification in Orthotics, Prosthetics and Pedorthics is the national certifying and accrediting body for the orthotic and prosthetic professions.

7930 American Physical Therapy Association
1111 N Fairfax St
Alexandria, VA 22314-1488   703-684-2782
                                        800-999-2782
                                    FAX: 703-684-7343
                                    consumer@apta.org
                                    www.apta.org
Sharon L. Dunn, President
Matthew Hyland, Vice President
Kip Schick, Secretary
The American Physical Therapy Association fosters advancements in physical therapy practice, research and education. The association offers courses, career counceling, advocacy, publications and more.

7931 American Stroke Association
7272 Greenville Ave
Dallas, TX 75231   888-478-7653
                                    strokeconnection@heart.org
                                    www.strokeassociation.org/STROKEORG
John Warner, Presiednt
James Postl, Chairman
Nancy Brown, Chief Executive Officer
The American Stroke Association offers educational materials, seminars, conferences and transportation for those effected by strokes as well as their families, caregivers and interested professionals.

7932 Charcot-Marie-Tooth Association
PO Box 105
Glenolden, PA 19036   610-499-9264
                                        800-606-2682
                                    FAX: 610-499-9267
                                    info@cmtausa.org
                                    www.cmtausa.org
Gilles Bouchard, Chairman
Amy J Gray, CEO
Kim Magee, Director of Finance
The Charcot-Marie-Tooth Association supports the development of new drugs to treat CMT, to improve the quality of life for people with CMT and to search for a cure. The association also offers a resource center, emotional support group, treatment options, genetic testing, medication and more.

7933 Dyspraxia Foundation USA
1012 Windsor Rd
Highland Park, IL 60035   847-780-3311
                                    foundation@mail.dyspraxiausa.org
                                    www.dyspraxiausa.org
Warren Fried, President & Founder
Theresa A Bidwell, Vice President
Dyspraxia Foundation USA is a non-profit organization centered on understanding, accepting and educating on issues connected to Developmental Dyspraxia.

7934 Epilepsy Foundation
8301 Professional Place E
Suite 200
Landover, MD 20785- 2353   800-332-1000
                                    FAX: 301-459-1569
                                    ContactUs@efa.org
                                    www.epilepsy.com
Robert W Smith, Chair
Philip M Gattone, M.Ed, President & CEO
M. Vaneeda Bennett, Chief Development Officer
The Epilepsy Foundation is the national voluntary agency dedicated to the welfare of people with epilepsy in the U.S. and their families. The organization works to ensure that people with seizures are able to participate in all life experiences and to prevent, control and cure epilepsy through research, education, advocacy and services.

7935 International Parkinson and Movement Disorder Society
555 East Wells Street
Suite 1100
Milwaukee, WI 53202- 3823   414-276-2145
                                    FAX: 414-276-3349
                                    info@movementdisorders.org
                                    www.movementdisorders.org
Christopher Goetz, MD, President
Susan Fox, PhD, Secretary
Victor Fung, MBBS, PhD, FRACP, Treasurer
A professional society of clinicians, scientists, and other healthcare professionals who are interested in Parkinson's disease, related neurodegenerative and neurodevelopmental disorders, hyperkinetic movement disorders, and abnormalities in muscle tone and motor control.

7936 Lewy Body Dementia Association
912 Killian Hill Road S.W.
Lilburn, GA 30047   404-975-2322
                                    FAX: 480-422-5434
                                    www.lbda.org
Mike Koehler, CEO
Shannon McCarty-Caplan, Vice President
Christina M. Christie, President
A nonprofit organization dedicated to raising awareness of the Lewy body dementias (LBD), supporting people with LBD, their families and caregivers and promoting scientific advances.

7937 Multilingual Children's Association
20 Woodside Ave
San Francisco, CA 94127   415-690-0026
                                    FAX: 415-341-1137
                                    www.multilingualchildren.org
The Multilingual Children's Association is focused on the day-to-day joys and challenges of raising bilingual and multilingual children.

7938 National Amputation Foundation
40 Church St
Malverne, NY 11565-1735   516-887-3600
                                        516-887-3600
                                    FAX: 516-887-3667
                                    amps76@aol.com
                                    www.nationalamputation.org
Paul Bernacchio, President
William Sturges, 1st Vice President
Al Pennacchia, 2nd Vice President
Information & resources for amputees. Scholarship programs for college students with major limb amputation. Free donated durable medical equipment open to anyone in need locally-as items need to be picked up.
Quarterly

7939 National Commission on Orthotic and Prosthetic Education
330 John Carlyle Street
Suite 200
Alexandria, VA 22314- 5760
703-836-7114
FAX: 703-836-0838
info@ncope.org
www.ncope.org
Robin C Seabrook, Executive Director
Jonathan D. Day, CPO
Dominique Mungo, Residency Program Manager
The mission of NCOPE is to be recognized authority for the development and accreditation of O&P education and residency standards leading to competent patient care in the changing healthcare environment. NCOPE develops, applies, and assures standards for orthotic and prosthetic education through accreditation and approval to promote exemplary patient care.

7940 National Institute of Neurological Disorders and Stroke
National Institutes of Health
PO Box 5801
Bethesda, MD 20824
800-352-9424
www.ninds.nih.gov
Nina Schor, Deputy Director
The mission of the National Institute of Neurological Disorders and Stroke is to reduce the burden of neurological disease by supporting neuroscience research, funding and conducting training and career development programs, and disseminating scientific information on neurological health.

7941 National Stroke Association
9707 E Easter Ln
Suite B
Centennial, CO 80112-3754
303-649-9299
800-787-6537
FAX: 303-649-1328
www.stroke.org
James Baranski, CEO
Sharon Jaunchowski, Executive VP
Teran Nash, Customer Relations
The only national health organization solely committed to stroke prevention, treatment, rehabilitation and community reintegration. Provides packaged training programs, on-site assistance, physician, patient and family education materials to acute and rehab hospitals. Develops workshops; operates the Stroke Information & Referral Center and produces professional publications such as Stroke: Clinical Updates and the Journal of Stroke and Cerebrovascular Diseases.

7942 World Chiropractic Alliance
2950 N Dobson Rd
Suite 3
Chandler, AZ 85224-1819
480-786-9235
800-347-1011
FAX: 480-732-9313
www.worldchiropracticalliance.org
Terry A Rondberg, Founder/CEO
Richard Barwell, President
Dedicated to protecting and strengthening chiropractic around the world. Serving as a watchdog and advocacy organization, we place our emphasis on education and political action.

Books

7943 Carpal Tunnel Syndrome
Arthritis Foundation
1330 W Peachtree St
Suite 100
Atlanta, GA 30309
404-872-7100
800-283-7800
FAX: 404-872-0457
help@arthritis.org
www.arthritis.org
John H Klippel, President/CEO
Daniel T. McGowan, Chairman Of The Board
Rowland W. Chang, Vice Chair
The Arthritis Foundation is committed to raising awareness and reducing the unacceptable impact of arthritis, a disease which must be taken as seriously as other chronic diseases because of its devastatng consequences.

7944 Don't Feel Sorry for Paul
Harper Collins Publishing
76 Ninth Ave
New York, NY 10011
800-843-2665
www.barnesandnoble.com
Bernard Wolf, Author
Ann Ledden, Vice President
Lorna Metzler, Manager
Paul is seven but was born with deformities of both hands and feet. Paul must wear a prosthesis on both feet so that he can walk. He has a third prosthesis for his right hand. The third prosthesis has a pair of hooks Paul uses as fingers.
94 pages Hardcover
ISBN 0-39731 -88-0

7945 Functional Restoration of Adults and Children with Upper Extremity Amputation
Demos Medical Publishing
11 West 42nd Street
15th Floor
New York, NY 10036-8804
212-683-0072
800-532-8663
FAX: 212-683-0118
www.demosmedpub.com
Robert Meier III, Author
Diane Atkins, OTR, Co-Author
Provides a comprehensive reference to the surgery, prosthetic fitting, and rehabilitation of individuals sustaining an arm amputation. Covers the recent advancements in prosthetics and rehabilitation. $165.00
384 pages
ISBN 1-888799-73-0

Magazines

7946 ABC Mark of Merit Newsletter
Amer Board for Cert in Otthotics & Prosthetics
330 John Carlyle St
Suite 210
Alexandria, VA 22314-5760
703-836-7114
FAX: 703-836-0838
info@abcop.org
www.abcop.org
Timothy E. Miller, CPO
Curt A. Bertram, President Elect
James H. Wynne, CPO
An online bi-monthly newsletter.

7947 Active Living Magazine
American Amputee Foundation
PO Box 94227
North Little Rock, AR 72190
501-835-9290
FAX: 501-835-9292
www.americanamputee.org
Catherine J Walden, Executive Director
A print magazine published four times a year.

7948 Stroke Connection Magazine
American Heart Association
7272 Greenville Ave
Dallas, TX 75231-5129
214-373-6300
888-478-7653
FAX: 214-706-5231
www.strokeassociation.org/STROKEORG/
John Caswell, Editor
Debra Lockwood, Chairman
Nancy Brown, CEO
Free magazine for stroke survivors and their family caregivers.

Newsletters

7949 **Advocacy Pulse**
American Stroke Association
7272 Greenville Ave
Dallas, TX 75231-5129
214-373-6300
888-478-7653
FAX: 214-706-5231
www.strokeassociation.org/STROKEORG/

Ralph Sacco, President/Director
Debra Lockwood, Chairman
Nancy Brown, CEO

7950 **NINDS Notes**
Ntn'l Institute of Neurological Disorders & Stroke
P.O.Box 5801
Bethesda, MD 20284
301-496-5751
800-352-9424
FAX: 202-944-3295
sbaa@sbaa.org

Caroline Lewis, Executive Officer
Story C. Landis, Director
Denise Dorsey, Chief Administrative Officer
A print newsletter published three times a year.

7951 **Noteworthy Newsletter**
Ntn'l Comm on Orthotic & Prosthetic Education
330 John Carlyle Street
Suite 200
Alexandria, VA 22314- 5760
703-836-7114
FAX: 703-836-0838
info@ncope.org
www.ncope.org

Robin C Seabrook, Executive Director
Jonathan D. Day, CPO
Dominique Mungo, Residency Program Manager
The mission of NCOPE is to be recognized authority for the development and accreditation of O&P education and residency standards leading to competent patient care in the changing healthcare environment. NCOPE develops, applies, and assures standards for orthotic and prosthetic education through accreditation and approval to promote exemplary patient care.

7952 **Stroke Smart Magazine**
National Stroke Association
9707 E Easter Ln
Suite B
Centennial, CO 80112-3754
303-649-9299
800-787-6537
FAX: 303-649-1328
www.stroke.org

James Baranski, CEO
Sharon Jaunchowski, Executive VP
Teran Nash, Customer Relations
The only national health organization solely committed to stroke prevention, treatment, rehabilitation and community reintegration. Provides packaged training programs, on-site assistance, physician, patient and family education materials to acute and rehab hospitals. Develops workshops; operates the Stroke Information & Referral Center and produces professional publications such as Stroke: Clinical Updates and the Journal of Stroke and Cerebrovascular Diseases.

Hearing

Associations

7953 Alexander Graham Bell Association for the Deaf and Hard of Hearing
3417 Volta Pl. NW
Washington, DC 20007

202-337-5220
FAX: 202-337-8314
TTY:202-337-5221
info@agbell.org
agbell.org

Emilio Alonso-Mendoza, Chief Executive Officer
Lisa Chutjian, Chief Development Officer
Gayla H. Guignard, Chief Strategy Officer
The Alexander Graham Bell Association for the Deaf and Hard of Hearing (AG Bell) is the world's oldest and largest membership organization promoting the use of spoken language by children and adults who are hearing impaired. Members include parents of children with hearing loss, adults who are deaf or hard of hearing, educators, audiologists, speech-language pathologists, physicians and other professionals in fields related to hearing loss and deafness.

7954 American Academy of Audiology (AAA)
11480 Commerce Park Dr.
Suite 220
Reston, VA 20191

703-790-8466
FAX: 703-790-8631
infoaud@audiology.org
www.audiology.org

Peter E. Gallagher, Executive Director
Kathryn Werner, Chief Operating Officer
Amy Miedema, VP, Communications & Membership
The American Academy of Audiology is the world's largest professional organization for audiologists. The Academy is dedicated to providing quality hearing care services through professional development, education, research, and increased public awareness of hearing and balance disorders.

7955 American Association of People with Disabilities (AAPD)
2020 Pennsylvania Ave.
Mailbox 263
Washington, DC 20006

202-521-4316
800-840-8844
communications@aapd.com
www.aapd.com

Maria Town, President & Chief Executive Officer
Jasmin Bailey, Operations Director
Christine Liao, Programs Director
Nonprofit cross-disability member organization dedicated to ensuring economic self-sufficiency and political empowerment for Americans with disabilities. AAPD works in coalition with other disability organizations for the full implementation and enforcement of disability nondiscrimination laws, particularly the Americans With Disabilities Act (ADA) of 1990 and the Rehabilitation Act of 1973.

7956 American Cochlear Implant Alliance
P.O. Box 103
McLEAN, VA 22101-103

703-534-6146
info@acialliance.org
www.acialliance.org

Craig A. Buchman, Chair
Teresa A. Zwolan, Vice Chair
Nancy M. Young, Secretary
A not-for-profit membership organization created with the purpose of eliminating barriers to cochlear implantation by sponsoring research, driving heightened awareness and advocating for improved access to cochlear implants for patients of all ages across the US.

7957 American Society for Deaf Children
PO Box 23
Woodbine, MD 21797

800-942-2732
info@deafchildren.org
deafchildren.org

Alisha Joslyn-Swob, President
Mark Drolsbaugh, Vice President
Rachel Berman, Secretary
The American Society for Deaf Children provides information for the caretakers of deaf children so children can have full communication access in their home, school and community. The society covers areas such as visual language, audiologists, healthcare providers, assistive technology and more.

7958 American Speech-Language-Hearing Association
2200 Research Blvd
Rockville, MD 20850-3289

301-296-5700
800-638-8255
actioncenter@asha.org
www.asha.org

Gail J. Richard, President
Elise Davis-Mcfaland, President-Elect
Margot L. Beckerman, Chair
Provides information for both the general public and physicians in an easy-to-access manner. The subjects of focus are speech, hearing and language disorders.

7959 American Tinnitus Association (ATA)
PO Box 424049
Washington, DC 20042-4049

800-634-8978
ata.org

Torryn Brazell, Executive Director
David Hadley, Chair
ATA is an organization dedicated to finding cures for tinnitus and hyperacusis. ATA's research program focuses on providing seed grants for new areas of tinnitus scientific exploration.

7960 Association of Adult Musicians with Hearing Loss
AAMHL, Inc.
P.O. Box 522
Rockville, MD 20848

301-838-0443
info@musicianswithhearingloss.org
www.musicianswithhearingloss.org

Wendy Cheng, President
Jennifer Castellano, Secretary
Janice Rosen, Treasurer
The Association of Adult Musicians with Hearing Loss creates a space for adult musicians with hearing loss to discuss the challenges they face in making and listening to music. The association also offers opportunities for public performance.

7961 Association of Late-Deafened Adults
8038 Macintosh Ln
Suite 2
Rockford, IL 61107-5336

815-332-1515
TTY:815-332-1515
www.alda.org

Rick Brown, President
Cynthia Moynihan, Vice President
Matt Ferrara, Treasurer
The Association of Late-Deafened Adults supports the empowerment of late-deafened people by offering programs and information resources on a variety of topics: technology, disability laws, airline travel and more.

7962 Better Hearing Institute
1444 I St NW
Suite 700
Washington, DC 20005

202-449-1100
800-327-9355
FAX: 202-216-9646
www.betterhearing.org

Sergei Kochkin, Ph.D, Executive Director
The Better Hearing Institute is a non-profit corporation that educates the public about the neglected problem of hearing loss and what can be done about it. Its mission is to erase the stigma and end the embarassment that prevents millions of people from seeking help for hearing loss.

7963   Center for Hearing and Communication
50 Broadway
6th Floor
New York, NY 10004   917-305-7700
                                 FAX: 917-305-7888
                                 TTY:917-305-7999
                                 info@chchearing.org
                                 chchearing.org

Laurie Hanin, Executive Director
Ellen Lafargue, Co-Director Speech & Hearing Services
Kshitija Sarpotdar, Director of Finance
The Center for Hearing and Communication provides hearing
health services to people of all ages who have hearing loss. Some
of its services include free hearing screenings, complete hearing
evaluations, pediatric services and more.

7964   Communication Service for the Deaf
3520 Gateway Lane
Sioux Falls, SD 57106   866-642-6410
                                 FAX: 605-362-2806
                                 TTY:866-273-3323
                                 inquiry@c-s-d.org
                                 www.c-s-d.org

Dr. Benjamin Soukup, Founder, Chairman & CEO
Christopher Soukup, President
Brad Hermes, CFO
CSD's mission is to create greater opportunities for Deaf and hard
of hearing individuals to reach their full potential. Through
global leadership and the development of innovative technologies, CSD provides tools conducive to a positive and fully
integrated life.

**7965   Conference of Educational Administrators of Schools
and Programs for the Deaf**
PO Box 116
Washington Grove, MD 20880   202-999-2204
                                 TTY:204-866-6248
                                 ceasd@ceasd.org
                                 www.ceasd.org

Barbara Raimondo, Executive Director
Dr. David Geeslin, President
Stacey Katz Shapiro, Secretary
CEASD provides an opportunity for professional educators to
work together for the improvement of schools and educational
programs for individuals who are deaf or hard of hearing. The organization brings together a rich composite of resources and
reaches out to both enhance educational programs and influence
educational policy makers.

7966   Council of American Instructors of the Deaf (CAID)
PO Box 377
Bedford, TX 76095-0377   817-354-8414
                                 FAX: 817-354-8414
                                 caid@swbell.net
                                 www.caid.org

Keith Mousley, President
Helen Lovato, Office Manager
The CAID continues to follow the tradition begun in 1850 and
recognizes the value of bringing fellow teaching professionals
together to share experiences and ideas for the purpose of improving learning opportunities for deaf and hard of hearing children,
adolescents and young adults.

7967   Deaf REACH
3521 12th St NE
Washington, DC 20017-2545   202-832-6681
                                 FAX: 202-832-8454
                                 deaf-reach.org

Sarah E. Brown, Executive Director
Annette Reichman, President
Jonathan Tomar, Vice-President
The psychosocial rehabilitation approach, ulitzed by all
Deaf-REACH programs, provides the solid foundation to member's success. Participants are activly involved in establishing
the format and level of highly individualized service delivery that
they receive. The concept, which has achieved national acclaim,
involves teaching members necessary life skills, thus minimizing
the need for assistance from a service professional. This is part of
what distinguishes the approach at Deaf-REACH.

7968   Deaf Women United
PO Box 61
South Barre, VT 5670   info@dwu.org
                                 www.dwu.org

Alana Beal, President
Keri Darling, Vice President
Caroline Koo, Secretary
It is committed to continuing a community of support of Deaf
women from all walks of life.

7969   Deafness Research Foundation
363 Seventh Avenue,
10th Floor
New York, NY 10001-3904   212-257-6140
                                 866-454-3924
                                 FAX: 212-257-6139
                                 TTY: 888-435-6104
                       info@hearinghealthfoundation.org
                                 www.drf.org

Shari Eberts, Chairman
Mark Angelo, President
Robert Boucai, Principal
Founded in 1958, the Deafness Research Foundation is the leading source of private funding for basic and clinical research in the
hearing science. The DRF is committed to making lifelong hearing health a national priority by funding research and implementing education projects in both the government and private
sectors.

7970   Dogs for the Deaf
10175 Wheeler Rd
Central Point, OR 97502-9360   541-826-9220
                                 800-990-3647
                                 FAX: 541-826-6696
                                 TTY: 541-826-9220
                                 info@dogsforthedeaf.org
                                 dogsforthedeaf.org

Robin Dickson, CEO
Vaughan Maurice, General Manager
Janine Bol, Finance Director
Rescues dogs from shelters and professionally trains them for
people with special needs such as: deafness, autism for children,
seniors, stroke victims, cerebral palsy, etc.

7971   Ear Foundation
1817 Patterson St
Nashville, TN 37203-2110   615-329-7849
                                 800-545-4327
                                 FAX: 615-329-7935
                                 www.earfoundation.org

Suzanne Wyatt, Executive Director
National, nonprofit organization committed to integrating the
hearing and balance impaired into the mainstream of society
through public awareness and medical education. Also administers The Meniere's Network, a national network of patient support groups providing people with the opportunity to share
experiences and coping strategies.

7972   Georgiana Institute
736 Harmony Street
New Orleans, LA 70115   203-994-8215
                                 georgianainstitute@snet.net
                                 www.georgianainstitute.org

Annabel Stehli, President
The information source for Auditory Integration Training
(AIT)/Digital Auditory Aerobics (DAA).

7973   HEAR Center
301 E Del Mar Blvd
Pasadena, CA 91101-2714   626-796-2016
                                 FAX: 626-796-2320
                                 info@hearcenter.org
                                 hearcenter.org

Ellen Simon, Executive Director
Deborah Lorino, Office Manager
Berenice Castro, Accounting Supervisor
Auditory and verbal program designed to help hearing impaired
children, infants and adults lead normal and productive lives.
Seeks to develop auditory techniques to aid people who have
communication problems due to deafness. Offers diagnostic

evaluations for speech and hearing. Individual auditory, verbal training and speech-language therapy.

7974   Hearing Education and Awareness for Rockers
1405 Lyon St
San Francisco, CA 94115-2914   415-409-3277
FAX: 415-409-5683
info@hearnet.com
www.hearnet.com

Kathy Peck, Executive Director
Joseph Monatano, Chief of Audiology
Flash Gordon, Primary Care Physician
H.E.A.R.'s mission is the prevention of hearing loss and tinnitus among musicians and music fans (especially teens) through education awareness and grassroots outreach advocacy.

7975   Hearing Industries Association
1444 I Street, N.W.
Suite 700
Washington, DC 20005   202-449-1090
FAX: 202-216-9646
mjones@bostrom.com
www.hearing.org

It provides a comprehensive source of information about hearing loss - how to prevent it, identify it, evaluate it, and treat it.

7976   Hearing Loss Association of America
7910 Woodmont Ave
Suite 1200
Bethesda, MD 20814   301-657-2248
FAX: 301-913-9413
inquiry@hearingloss.org
www.hearingloss.org

Barbara Kelley, Executive Director
Lise Hamlin, Director of Public Policy
Carla Beyer-Smolin, National Chapter & Membership Coordinator
The mission of the Hearing Loss Association of America is to open the world of communication to people with hearing loss by offering information, education, resources, advocacy and training.

7977   Hearing, Speech and Deafness Center (HSDC)
1625 19th Ave.
Seattle, WA 98122   206-323-5770
888-222-5036
FAX: 206-328-6871
TTY:800-761-2821
clinics@hsdc.org
www.hsdc.org

Lindsay Klarman, Executive Director
Hearing, Speech & Deaf Center (HSDC) is a nonprofit for clients who are deaf, hard of hearing, or who face other communication barriers such as speech challenges. Their mission is to foster inclusive and accessible communities through communication, advocacy, and education.

7978   House Ear Institute
2100 W 3rd St
Los Angeles, CA 90057-1944   213-483-4431
800-388-8612
FAX: 213-484-8789
TTY: 213-484-2642
www.hei.org

James Boswell, CEO
John.W House, M.D, President
Daniel. M Graham, Executive Vice President Develop
Offers pediatric hearing tests, otologic and audiologic evaluation and treatment, rehabilitation, hearing aid dispensing, and cochlear implant services. Outreach programs focus on families with hearing impaired children.

7979   International Catholic Deaf Association
7202 Buchanan St
Landover Hills, MD 20784-2236   301-429-0697
FAX: 301-429-0698
homeoffice@icda-us.org
icda-us.org

Jean Cox, President
Kate Slosar, Vice President
T.K Hill, Secretary

An organization of Catholic deaf people and hearing people in the church working with the deaf in the united states of America.

7980   International Hearing Dog
5901 E 89th Ave.
Henderson, CO 80640-8315   303-287-3277
FAX: 303-287-3425
info@hearingdog.org
www.hearingdog.org

Valerie Foss-Brugger, President
Robert Cooley, Field Representative
Andrea Paul, Vetinary Technician
Trains and places Hearing dogs with deaf or hard-of-hearing persons, with or without multiple disabilities, nationwide, free of charge to the recipient.

7981   International Hearing Society
16880 Middlebelt Rd
Suite 4
Livonia, MI 48154   734-522-7200
FAX: 734-522-0200
interact@ihsinfo.org
ihsinfo.org

Annette Cross, BC-HIS, President
Kathleen Mennillo, MBA, Executive Director
Fran Vincent, Director, Membership & Marketing
The International Hearing Society (IHS) represents hearing healthcare professionals worldwide. Members include professionals engaged in the practice of testing human hearing and selecting, fitting and dispensing hearing instruments. IHS offers accreditation programs, advocacy, education and training in support of these services.

7982   League for the Hard of Hearing
50 Broadway
6th Fl
New York, NY 10004-3810   917-305-7700
TTY:917-305-7999
www.lhh.org

Laurie Hanin, Executive Director
Ellen Pfeffer Lafargue, Au.D, Director
Dorene Watkins, Coordinator
The Center for Hearing and Communication is a leading hearing center offering state-of-the-art hearing testing, hearing aid fitting, speech therapy and full range of services for people of all ages with hearing loss. Visit our offices in New York City and Florida for services that meet all of your hearing and communication needs.

7983   Lexington School for the Deaf: Center for the Deaf
30th Avenue and 75th St
Jackson Heights, NY 11370   718-350-3300
FAX: 718-899-9846
TTY:718-350-3056
generalinfo@lexnyc.org
www.lexnyc.org

Regina Carroll PhD, CEO/Executive Director
Philip W. Bravin, President
Gregory Hlibok, Vice President
Offers a comprehensive range of services to deaf, hard of hearing and speech impaired persons from infancy to elderly through its affiliate agencies: The Center for Mental Health Services; The Lexington Hearing and Speech Center, Lexington Vocational Services, and the Lexington School for the Deaf. The Lexington Center also provides services through its research division which houses the only federally funded Rehabilitation Engineering Center.

7984   Michigan Association for Deaf and Hard of Hearing
5236 Dumond Court
Suite C
Lansing, MI 48917-6001   517-487-0066
800-968-7327
FAX: 517-487-0202
www.madhh.org

Nancy Asher, Executive Director
Pat Walton, Office Manager
MADHH is a statewide collaboration agency dedicated to improving the lives of people who are deaf or hard of hearing through leadership in education, advocacy and services.

7985 Mississippi Speech-Language-Hearing Association
PO Box 22664
Jackson, MS 39225

800-664-6742
FAX: 601-510-7833
admin@mshausa.org
www.mshausa.org

Claudette Edwards, President
Ricki Garrett, Executive Director
The Mississippi Speech-Language-Hearing Association is the statewide organization supporting audiologists and speech-language pathologists in Mississippi by offering them resources, information, and professional development opportunities so they could better serve their clients.

7986 National Alliance of Black Interpreters
P.O. Box 90532
Washington, DC 20090-532

202-810-4451
www.naobidc.org

It provides professional training to promote excellence and empowerment in the profession of sign language interpretation.

7987 National Association of Hearing Officials
PO Box 4999
Midlothian, VA 23112-17

www.naho.org

Bonny M Fetch CALJ, President
The mission of the National Association of Hearing Officials is to improve the administrative hearing process and thereby benefit hearing officials, their employing agencies, and the individuals they serve through promoting professionalism and by providing traininf, continuing education, a national forum for discussion of issues, and leadership concerning administrative harings.

7988 National Association of Parents with Children in Special Education
3642 E Sunnydale Dr.
Chandler Heights, AZ 85142

800-754-4421
FAX: 800-424-0371
contact@napcse.org
www.napcse.org

George Giuliani, President
NAPCSE is a national membership organization dedicated to rendering all possible support and assistance to parents whose children receive special education services, both in and outside of school.

7989 National Association of Special Education Teachers
1250 Connecticut Ave., NW
Suite 200
Washington, DC 20036-2643

800-754-4421
FAX: 800-754-4421
contactus@naset.org
www.naset.org

Roger Pierangelo, Executive Director
George Giuliani, Executive Director
The National Association of Special Education Teachers (NASET) is a national membership organization dedicated to rendering all possible support and assistance to those preparing for or teaching in the field of special education. NASET was founded to promote the profession of special education teachers and to provide a national forum for their ideas.

7990 National Association of the Deaf
8630 Fenton Street
Suite 820
Silver Spring, MD 20910- 3819

301-587-1788
FAX: 301-587-1791
TTY:301-587-1789
www.nad.org

Howard A. Rosenblum, CEO
Shane H. Feldman, COO
Marc P. Charmatz, Staff Attorney
Nation's largest organization safeguarding the accessability and civil rights of 28 million deaf and hard of hearing Americans in education, employment, health care, and telecommunications. Focuses on grassroots advocacy and empowerment, captioned media deafness-related information and publications, legal assistance, and policy development.

7991 National Black Association for Speech Language and Hearing
P.O. Box 779
Pennsville, NJ 08070

877-936-6235
FAX: 877-936-6235
nbaslh@nbaslh.org
www.nbaslh.org

Cathy Runnels, Interim
Kia N. Johnson, Parliamentarian
Martine Elie, Treasurer
The mission of the National Black Association of Speech-Language and Hearing is to maintain a viable mechanism through which the needs of black professionals, students and individuals with communication disorders can be met.

7992 National Black Deaf Advocates
PO Box 32
Frankfort, KY 40602

585-475-2411
800-421-1220
FAX: 585-475-6500
president@nbda.org
www.nbda.org

Benro Ogunyipe, President
Cory Parker, VP
Sharon D. White, Secretary
The Mission of the National Black Deaf Advocate is to promote the leadership development, economic and educational opportunities, social equality, and to safeguard the general health and welfare of Black deaf and hard of hearing people.

7993 National Catholic Office of the Deaf
7202 Buchanan St
Landover Hills, MD 20784-2299

301-577-1684
FAX: 301-577-1684
TTY:301-577-4184
info@ncod.org
www.ncod.org

Consuelo Martinez Wild, Executive Director
Helps coordinate efforts of deaf or hard of hearing people who are involved in the ministry, acts as a resource center, assists bishops and pastors become available to the deaf and hard of hearing.

7994 National Cued Speech Association
1300 Pennsylvania Ave, NW
Suite 190-713
Washington, DC 20004

917-439-5126
800-459-3529
FAX: 866-269-9877
info@cuedspeech.org
www.cuedspeech.org

Anne Huffman, President
Sarina Roffe, Executive Director
Ben Lachman, Director of Development
Champions effective communication, language development and literacy through the use of cued speech.

7995 National Deaf Women's Bowling Association
9244 E Mansfield Ave
Denver, CO 80237-1915

303-771-9018
ndwbast@gmail.com

Gayle Willingham, President
Ali Martinez, VP
Holds world Deaf Bowling Torunament annually in July. Also holds Las Vegas Scratch Classic annually in October.

7996 National Hearing Conservation Association
3030 W 81st Ave
Westminster, CO 80031

303-224-9022
FAX: 303-458-0002
nhcaoffice@hearingconservation.org
www.hearingconservation.org

Jennifer Tufts, President
Beth Cooper, President Elect
Nancy Wojcik, Secretary/Treasurer
The mission of the NHCA is to prevent hearing loss due to noise and other environmental factors in all sectors of society.

7997 National Institute on Deafness and Other Communication Disorders
National Institutes of Health
31 Center Dr.
MSC 2320
Bethesda, MD 20892-2320

301-827-8183
800-241-1044
TTY:800-241-1055
nidcdinfo@nidcd.nih.gov
www.nidcd.nih.gov

Debara L. Tucci, Director
Judith A. Cooper, Deputy Director
Timothy J. Wheeles, Executive Officer
The National Institute on Deafness and Other Communication Disorders supports and conducts research to help prevent, detect and diagnose disabilities that affect hearing, balance, taste, smell, voice, speech, and communication.
1988

7998 National Student Speech Language Hearing Association
2200 Research Blvd
Suite 450
Rockville, MD 20850-3289

301-296-5650
800-498-2071
FAX: 301-296-8580
TTY: 301-296-5650
nsslha@asha.org
www.nsslha.org

Patricia A. Prelock, PhD, President
Elizabeth S. McCrea, President-Elect
Shelly S. Chabon, Immediate Past President
The American Speech-Language-Hearing Association is committed to ensuring that all people with speech, language, and hearing disorders receive services to help them communicate effectively.

7999 Registry of Interpreters for the Deaf
333 Commerce St
Alexandria, VA 22314-2801

703-838-0030
FAX: 703-838-0454
TTY:7038380459
ridinfo@rid.org
rid.org

Brenda Walke Prudhomme, President
Kelly L. Flores, VP
Dawn Whitcher, Secretary
The Registry of Interpreters for the Deaf, Inc. (RID), a national membership organization, plays a leading role in advocating for excellence in the delivery of interpretation and transliteration services between people who use sign language and people who use spoken language. In collaboration with the Deaf community, RID supports our members and encourages the growth of the profession through the establishment of a national standard for qualified sign language interpreters and transliterators, o

8000 Sight & Hearing Association
1246 University Ave. W.
Suite #226
St. Paul, MN 55104- 4125

651-645-2546
800-992-0424
FAX: 651-645-2742
mail@sightandhearing.org
www.sightandhearing.org

Kathy Webb, Executive Director
Karen Klevar, Screening Director
Bernice Burgy, Program Assistant
It is a nonprofit organization with a mission to enable lifetime learning by identifying preventable loss of vision and hearing in children.

8001 Spring Dell Center
6040 Radio Station Rd
La Plata, MD 20646-3368

301-934-4561
FAX: 301-870-2439
info@springdellcenter.org
www.springdellcenter.org

Patsy Finch, President
Badgley CPA, Treasurer
Jean Hubbard, Secretary

Since 1967, Spring Dell center has been, bridging the gap to enhance the lives of developmentally disabled people. Spring Dell's goal is to empower people in every aspect of their lives through the implementation of two programs, employment/vocational services and residential services including transportation. Spring Dell offers transportation door-to-door for persons with developmental disabilities, including day care programs, supportive environment, residential and any other transportation.

8002 Starkey Hearing Foundation
P.O. Box 41514
Minneapolis, MN 55441

866-354-3254
info@starkeyfoundation.org
www.starkeyhearingfoundation.org

Richard S. Brown, President
Brady Forseth, Executive Director
Keith Becker, Senior Director of Operations
The Starkey Hearing Foundation works to assist those with hearing impairments by offering hearing aids and aftercare services.

8003 Telecommunications for the Deaf and Hard of Hearing
8630 Fenton St
Suite 121
Silver Spring, MD 20910-3803

301-563-9122
FAX: 301-589-3797
TTY:301-589-3006
tdiforaccess.org

Claude L Stout, Executive Director
James House, Director of Public Relations
John Skjeveland, Business Manager
Promoting equal access to telecommunications and media for people who are deaf, late-deafened, hard of hearing or deaf-blind through consumer education and involvement; technical assistance and consulting; applications of exisiting and emerging technologies; networking and collaboration; uniformity of standards; and national policy development and advocacy.

8004 The Davis Center
305 White Heron Circle
Fayetteville, NY 13066

862-251-4637
ddavis@thedaviscenter.com
www.thedaviscenter.com

Dorinne S. Davis, Director
Offers sound-based therapies supporting positive change in learning, development, and wellness. All ages/all disabilities. Uses The Davis Model of Sound Intervention, an alternative approach.

8005 United States Deaf Ski & Snowboard Association
76 Kings Gate N
Rochester, NY 14617

585-286-2780
info@usdssa.org
usdssa.org

Anthony Di Giovani, Officer
It provides means for deaf people to get together to share their love for skiing and sponsor races for deaf skiers.

8006 Vestibular Disorders Association
5018 NE 15th Ave.
P.O. Box 13305
Portland, OR 97211

503-229-7705
800-837-8428
FAX: 503-229-8064
info@vestibular.org
www.vestibular.org

Sue Hickey, President
Cynthia Ryan, MBA, Executive Director
Kerrie Denner, Outreach Coordinator
The mission of the Vestibular Disorders Association is to serve people with vestibular disorders by providing access to information, offering a support network, and elevating awareness of the challenges associated with these disorders. They also aim to support and empower vestibular patients on their journey back to balance.

Camps

8007 ASD Summer Camp
Alabama Institute for Deaf & Blind
205 E South St
P.O. Box 698
Talladega, AL 35160   256-761-3214
                                   FAX: 256-761-3278
                                   TTY:256-761-3215
                            wiggins.lavina@aidb.state.al.us
                                        www.aidb.org

Paul Millard, Principal
The Alabama School for the Deaf Summer Enrichment Camp is designed especially for deaf and hard of hearing children ages 6-15. Recreation activities include swimming, skating, outdoor games, horseback riding, field trips, arts and craft. Tuition is free.

8008 Aspen Camp
4862 Snowmass Creek Rd.
Snowmass, CO 81654   970-315-0513
                                    TTY:970-315-0513
                                     hi@aspencamp.org
                                      www.aspencamp.org

Karen Immerson, Vice President
Eric Kaika, Treasurer
Open to the deaf community, including family members and friends as well as those who are deaf, deaf blind, hard of hearing, and late deafened, Camp Aspen provides year round programs for youth and adults.

8009 Camp Alexander Mack
Indiana Deaf Camps Foundation
P.O.Box 158
Milford, IN 46542   574-658-4831
                                     www.campmack.org

Galen Jay, Interim Executive Director
Lauren Carrick, Director of Development/Facility Manager
Amber Barrett, Food Service
Our program is intentionally designed to provide campers with life changing experiences that lead to a formation of personal faith within a safe faith community.

8010 Camp Bishopswood
Diocese of Maine Episcopal
143 State St
Portland, ME 04101   207-772-1953
                                        800-244-6062
                                   FAX: 207-773-0095
                                    mike@bishopswood.org
                                     www.bishopswood.org

Laurie Kazilionis, President
Robert Johnston, VP
Jeff Mansir, Treasurer
Camp is located in Hope, Maine. One to seven-week sessions for hearing impaired children June-August. Coed, ages 7-16.

8011 Camp CaPella
PO Box 552
Holden, ME 04429   207-843-5104
                                     www.campcapella.org

Deb Breindel, Director
Provides summer camp sessions for children with disabilities.

8012 Camp Chris Williams
Lions 11 B-2 and MADHH
5236 Dumond Court
Suite C
Lansing, MI 48917-6001   586-778-4188
                                   FAX: 586-285-1842
                                   TTY:586-285-1842

Nancy Asher, Executive Director
An exciting summer camp experience for deaf and hard of hearing youth and their siblings ages 8-14.

8013 Camp Comeca & Retreat Center
United Methodist Church
75670 Road 417
Conzad, NE 69130   308-784-2808
                                     www.campcomeca.com

Camp is located in Cozad, Nebraska. Summer sessions for campers with diabetes and hearing impairment. Coed, ages 6-19, families, seniors, single adults.

8014 Camp Emanuel
PO Box 752343
Dayton, OH 45475   937-477-5504
                                   crawford@campemanuel.org
                                   www.campemanuel.weebly.com

Brian Demarke, President
Stephanie Ackner, Vice President
Mary Foreman, Secretary
Camp Emanuel is a camp for hearing impaired and hearing youth. There are day sessions for children 5-14 and overnight resident sessions for children and teens 9-17. The camp aims to promote descision making, self-esteem, and acceptance by integrating non-hearing children with hearing children.

8015 Camp Grizzly
NorCal Services for Deaf & Hard of Hearing
4044 N Freeway Blvd.
Sacramento, CA 95843   916-349-7500
                                   FAX: 916-349-7578
                                   TTY:916-349-7500
                                campgrizzly@norcalcenter.org
                                     www.campgrizzly.org

Molly Bowen, Program Leader
Cheryl Bella, Program Leader
A program of NorCal Services for Deaf & Hard of Hearing, Camp Grizzly is a coed camp for children aged 7-18 who have a hearing impairment. Camp Grizzly takes place at the Camp Lodestar campground facilities and offers sporting activities, performing and creative arts, hiking, swimming, playgrounds and campfires.

8016 Camp Isola Bella
410 Twin Lakes Rd.
Salisbury, CT 06079   860-824-5558
                                   FAX: 860-824-4276
                                   TTY:860-596-0110
                                    ibdirector@asd-1817.org
                            asd-1817.org/programs/camp-isola-bella

David Guardino, Director
A camp for hearing-impaired children ages 8-17. Qualified deaf and hearing staff members with experience in education, child care and counseling are employed at the camp.

8017 Camp Joy
3325 Swamp Creek Rd
Schwenksville, PA 19473-1518   610-754-6878
                                   FAX: 610-754-7880
                                      www.campjoy.com

Angus Murray, Camp Director
A special needs camp for kids and adults (ages 4-80+) with developmental disabilities such as autism, brain injury, neurological disorder, visual and/or hearing impairments, Angelman and Down syndromes, and other developmental disabilities.

8018 Camp Juliena
Georgia Center of the Deaf and Hard of Hearing
2296 Henderson Mill Rd.
Suite 115
Atlanta, GA 30345   404-381-8447
                                        888-297-9461
                                   FAX: 404-297-9465
                                       info@gcdhh.org
                                www.gcdhh.org/camp-juliena

Jimmy Peterson, Executive Director
Andrea Alston, Coordinator, Community Outreach
A week-long residential summer camp for deaf or hard of hearing youth. Activities help campers develop leadership, team-building, social, and communication skills.

8019 Camp Mark Seven
Mark Seven Deaf Foundation
144 Mohawk Hotel Rd.
Old Forge, NY 13420   315-207-5706
                                   TTY:315-357-6089
                                    registrar@campmark7.org
                                      www.campmark7.org

Dave Staehle, Camp Director

A camp program for hard-of-hearing, deaf and hearing people. Coed, open to all ages. The camp is located on the Fourth Lake in the Adirondack Mountains.

8020   Camp Meadowood Springs
77650 Meadowood Rd.
Weston, OR 97886
541-276-2752
FAX: 541-276-7227
camp@meadowoodsprings.org
www.meadowoodsprings.org

Michelle Nelson, Camp Director
This camp is designed to help children with communication disorders and learning differences. A full range of activities in recreational and clinical areas is available.

8021   Camp Pacifica
California Lions Camp
1836 K Street
Merced, CA 95340-4818
559-373-0961
deafcamppacifica@gmail.com
camp-pacifica.org

Angelica Martinez, Camp Director
John Martinez, Assistant Director
Camp Pacifica provides a summer camp experience for children, boys and girls, aged 7-15 who have a hearing impairment. The camp is located in the foothills of Sierra on 52 acres of forested woodland. Activities include, but are not limited to, archery, canoeing, ropes course, swimming, horseback riding, and riflery. The camp costs $360, plus a registration fee.
1978

8022   Camp Ramah in the Poconos
2100 Arch St.
Philadelphia, PA 19103
215-885-8556
FAX: 215-885-8905
info@ramahpoconos.org
www.ramahpoconos.org

Rabbi Joel Seltzer, Executive Director
Rachel Dobbs Schwartz, Camp Director
Bruce I. Lipton, Director, Finance & Operations
Camp is located in Lakewood, Pennsylvania. Summer sessions for children with developmental and intellectual disabilities.

8023   Camp Shocco for the Deaf
216 North St. E
PO Box 602
Talladega, AL 35161
800-264-1225
Camp Shocco for the Deaf is a Christian Camp for children and teens with a hearing impairment, whose parents are deaf or are siblings of a person that are deaf. The camp runs for 1 week and offers a range of camp activities.

8024   Camp Taloali
15934 N Santiam Hwy. SE
PO Box 32
Stayton, OR 97383
503-400-6547
campadmin@taloali.org
www.taloali.org

Randall Smith, Camp Administrator
Summer sessions for children who are deaf, hard of hearing, or have a hearing impairment. Camp Taloali emphasizes communication, leadership, and social development.

8025   Camp Tekoa
United Methodist Camp Tekoa
PO Box 1793
Flat Rock, NC 28731-1793
828-692-6516
FAX: 828-697-3288
www.camptekoa.org

John Isley, Executive Director
Dave Bollen, Assistant Director
Karen Rohrer, Business Manager
Offers special needs camp programs for individuals with developmental disabilities.

8026   Cochlear Implant Camp
Listen Foundation
6950 E Belleview Ave.
Suite 203
Greenwood Village, CO 80111
303-781-9440
cochlearimplantcamp@gmail.com
www.listenfoundation.org/cicamp

Janette Cantwell, Camp Director
Held at the YMCA Rockies Estes Park Center, the camp offers a wide range of activities for children from 3-17 years old with cochlear implants. The camp is 4 days and 3 nights, held during the summer and also offers programs for parents and families. The cost is $800 for a family of four.

8027   Deaf Kid's Kamp
Sproul Ranch, Inc.
42263 50th Street West
Suite 610
Quartz Hill, CA 93536
661-675-3323
877-399-5449
www.deafkidskamp.com

Buffy Sproul, Executive Director
Our purpose is to meet the needs of deaf children outside of the classroom setting. These needs, as we have defined them, would include but are not limited to: social contact with peers; contact with the culture of the Deaf Community; educational and recreational programs not available in most school settings.

8028   Father Drumgoole Connelly Summer Camp
MIV: Mount Loretto
6581 Hylan Blvd
Staten Island, NY 10309-3830
718-317-2600
FAX: 718-317-2830
www.mountloretto.org

Stephen Rynn, Executive Director
Maryann Virga, Executive Assistant
Loretta Polanish, Executive Secretary
Summer sessions for children with epilepsy, hearing impairment and developmental disabilities. Coed, ages 5-13.

8029   Lions Camp Crescendo
1480 Pine Tavern Rd.
PO Box 607
Lebanon Junction, KY 40150
502-264-0120
wibblesb@aol.com
www.lccky.org

Billie J. Flannery, Administrator
Organization dedicated to enhancing quality of life for youths, including those with disabilities, through the delivery of a traditional camping experience.

8030   Lions Camp Kirby
1735 Narrows Hill Rd
Upper Black Eddy, PA 18972
610-982-5731
Alice Breon, Camp Director
Offers 2-week camps for deaf and hearing impaired children and their siblings in eastern Pennsylvania.

8031   Lions Camp Merrick
PO Box 56
Nanjemoy, MD 20662
301-870-5858
FAX: 301-246-9108
info@lionscampmerrick.org
www.lionscampmerrick.org

Heidi A. Fick, Executive Director
Donna Wadsworth, Office Administrator
This recreational camp for special needs children offers a complete waterfront program including swimming, canoeing and fishing for ages 6-16. Designed for children who are deaf, blind, or have type 1 diabetes. Also helps children to learn to deal with their special conditions.

8032   Lions Wilderness Camp for Deaf Children, Inc.
Lions Wilderness Camp Headquarters
PO Box 8
Roseville, CA 95661-9998
lionscampfordeaf@gmail.com
www.lionswildcamp.org

David Velasquez, Camp Program Director
Lions Wilderness Camp gives deaf children aged 7-15 an outdoor camp experience helping children to learn outdoor skills and enjoy nature.

8033 **Sandcastle Day Camp**
Children's Beach House
1800 Bay Ave
Lewes, DE 19958
302-645-9184
FAX: 302-645-9467
www.cbhinc.org

Martha P. Tschantz, President
Maryann Helms, Vice President
Linda M. Fischer, Secretary
Camp is located in Lewes, Delaware. Four-week sessions
June-August for Delaware children with hearing impairment or
speech/communication impairment. Coed, ages 6-12.

8034 **Sertoma Camp Endeavor**
Sertoma Camp Endeavor
P.O.Box 910
Dundee, FL 33838-0910
863-439-1300
FAX: 863-439-1300

Jeff Nunemaker, Executive Director
The intergration of deaf, hard of hearing and hearing youngsters
is a unique characteristic of our camping program. Both hearing,
deaf and hard of hearing children have the opportunity to learn
about themselves and each other in an informal and empowering
setting.

8035 **Texas Lions Camp**
PO Box 290247
Kerrville, TX 78029
830-896-8500
FAX: 830-896-3666
tlc@lionscamp.com
www.lionscamp.com

Stephen S. Mabry, President & CEO
Karen-Anne King, Vice President, Summer Camps
Milton Dare, Director, Development
Texas Lions Camp is a camp dedicated to serving children ages
7-16 in Texas with physical disabilities. While at camp, campers
will participate in a variety of activities and be encouraged to become more independent and self-confident.

8036 **YMCA Camp Fitch**
12600 Abels Rd.
North Springfield, PA 16430
814-922-3219
877-863-4824
FAX: 814-922-7000
registrar@campfitchymca.org
campfitchymca.org

Tom Parker, Executive Director
Joe Wolnik, Summer Camp Director
Brandy Duda, Outdoor Education Director
Camp is located in North Springfield, Pennsylvania. Camp pro-
grams include sessions for children with diabetes or epilepsy.

8037 **Youth Leadership Camp**
National Association of the Deaf
8630 Fenton Street
Suite 820
Silver Spring, MD 20910
301-587-1788
FAX: 301-587-1791
www.nad.org

Christopher Wagnor, President
Melissa S. Draganac-Hawk, VP
Howard A. Rosenblum, CEO
Sponsored by the National Association of the Deaf, this camp em-
phasizes leadership training for deaf teenagers and young adults.
In addition to many recreational activities and sports, there are
academic offerings and camp projects.

Books

8038 **A Basic Course in American Sign Language**
TJ Publishers
2544 Tarpley Rd
Suite 108
Carrollton, TX 75006-2288
972-416-0800
800-999-1168
FAX: 972-416-0944
customerservice@tjpublishers.com
www.tjpublishers.com

Tom Humphries, Author
Carol Padden, Co-Author
Terrence J O'Rouke, Co-Author
The first three DVDs in this series are designed to illustrate and
demonstrate each of the exercises and dialogues presented in A
Basic Course in American Sign Language. Four Deaf teachers
and three hearing students provide a variety of models for the ex-
ercises. *$35.95*
288 pages Spiral Bound
ISBN 0-932666-42-6

8039 **A Basic Course in Manual Communication**
National Association of the Deaf
8630 Fenton St.
Suite 820
Silver Spring, MD 20910
301-338-6380
FAX: 301-587-1791
TTY:301-810-3182
www.nad.org

Terrence J. O'Rourke, Author
Teachers ASL grammar and vocabulary.

8040 **A Basic Vocabulary: American Sign Languagefor
Parents and Children**
TJ Publishers
2544 Tarpley Rd
Suite 108
Carrollton, TX 75006-2288
972-416-0800
800-999-1168
FAX: 972-416-0944
customerservice@tjpublishers.com
www.tjpublishers.com

Terrence J O'Rouke, Author
Tanner Beach, Director
Carefully selected words and signs include those that children
use every day. Alphabetically organized vocabulary incorporates
developmental lists helpful to both deaf and hearing children and
over 1000 clear sign language illustrations. *$9.95*
240 pages Softcover
ISBN 0-932666-00-0

8041 **A Loss for Words**
HarperCollins Publishers
10 E 53rd St
New York, NY 10022-5244
212-207-7901
800-242-7737
FAX: 212-702-2586
spsales@harpercollins.com
www.harpercollins.com

Lou Ann Walker, Author
From the time she was a toddler, Lou Ann Walker was the ears and
voice for her deaf parents. Their family life was warm and loving,
but outside the home, they faced a world that misunderstood and
often rejected them. *$13.00*
224 pages Paperback 1987
ISBN 0-060914-25-4

8042 **Access for All: Integrating Deaf, Hard of Hearing and
Hearing Preschoolers**
Gallaudet University Bookstore
800 Florida Avenue NorthEast
Washington, DC 20002-3600
202-651-5530
FAX: 202-651-5489
gupress@gallaudet.edu
www.gallaudet.edu

Stephanie Cawthon, Ph.D., Book Review Editor
Peter V. Paul, Ph.D., Editor, Literary Issues
Ye Wang, Ph.D., Senior Associate Editor

This exciting new 90 minute videotape and manual describes a model program for integrating deaf and hard of hearing children in early education.
169 pages Book & Video

8043 Advanced Sign Language Vocabulary: A Resource Text for Educators
Charles C. Thomas
2600 S First St
Springfield, IL 62704-4730
217-789-8980
800-258-8980
FAX: 217-789-9130
books@ccthomas.com
www.ccthomas.com

Michael P. Thomas, President
Elizabeth E Wolf, Co-Author
A resource text for educators, interpreters, parents and sign language instructors. *$53.95*
202 pages Spiral Paper
ISBN 0-398057-22-0

8044 American Sign Language Handshape Dictionary
Gallaudet University Press
800 Florida Ave NE
Washington, DC 20002-3600
773-568-1550
800-621-2736
FAX: 773-660-2235
TTY: 888-630-9347
gupress@gallaudet.edu
www.gupress.gallaudet.edu

Richard A Tennant, Author
Marianne Gluszak Brown, Co-Author
Valerie Nelson-Metlay, Illustrator
The new DVD shows how each sign is formed from beginning to end. Users can watch a sign at various speeds to learn precisely how to master it themselves. Together, the new edition of The American Sign Language Handshape Dictionary and its accompanying DVD presents students, sign language teachers, and deaf and hearing people alike with the perfect combination for enhancing communication skills in both ASL and English. *$45.00*
408 pages Hardcover
ISBN 1-563680-43-2

8045 American Sign Language Phrase Book
TJ Publishers
2544 Tarpley Rd
Suite 108
Carrollton, TX 75006-2288
972-416-0800
800-999-1168
FAX: 972-416-0944
customerservice@tjpublishers.com
www.tjpublishers.com

Lou Fant, Author
Terrence O'Rourke, Principal
Tanner Beach, Director
The author provides interesting, realistic and meaningful situations. Sign language is learned through novel remarks cleverly organized around everyday topics. *$18.95*
362 pages Softcover
ISBN 0-809235-00-5

8046 American Sign Language: A Look at Its History, Structure & Community
TJ Publishers
2544 Tarpley Rd
Suite 108
Carrollton, TX 75006-2288
972-416-0800
800-999-1168
FAX: 972-416-0944
customerservice@tjpublishers.com
www.tjpublishers.com

Charlotte Baker-Shenk, Author
Carol Padden, Co-Author
Terrence O'Rourke, Principal
Answers basic questions about American Sign Language. What is it? What is its history? Who uses it? What is the Deaf community? Why is ASL important? What are the building blocks of ASL?

What is the relationship between ASL and body language? What are examples of ASL -grammar? *$4.95*
22 pages Softcover
ISBN 0-93266 -01-9

8047 At Home Among Strangers
Gallaudet University Press
800 Florida Ave NE
Washington, DC 20002-3600
773-568-1550
800-621-2736
FAX: 773-660-2235
TTY: 888-630-9347
gupress@gallaudet.edu
www.gupress.gallaudet.edu

Jerome D Schein, Author
T. Alan Hurwitz, President
Paul Kelly, Vice President Adm And Finance
At Home Among Strangers presents an engrossing portrait of the Deaf community as a complex, nationwide social network that offers unique kinship to deaf people across the country. *$36.95*
264 pages Paperback
ISBN 1-563681-41-2

8048 BPPV: What You Need to Know
Vestibular Disorders Association
5018 NE 15th Ave
Portland, OR 97211-5331
503-229-7705
800-837-8428
FAX: 503-229-8064
veda@vestibular.org
www.vestibular.org

P J Haybach, Author
Lisa Haven, Executive Director
Jerry Underwood, Managing Director
The aim of this book is to present basic information about benign paroxysmal positional vertigo (BPPV) including what it is, causes, how it is diagnosed, various treatments currently in use, and strategies for coping with the symptoms associated with BPPV. *$29.95*
207 pages Hardcover
ISBN 0-963261-14-2

8049 Ben's Story: A Deaf Child's Right to Sign
Gallaudet University Bookstore
800 Florida Avenue NorthEast
Washington, DC 20002-3600
202-651-5530
FAX: 202-651-5489
gupress@gallaudet.edu
www.gallaudet.edu

Stephanie Cawthon, Ph.D., Book Review Editor
Peter V. Paul, Ph.D., Editor, Literary Issues
Ye Wang, Ph.D., Senior Associate Editor
This is a mother's story of how she responded to the diagnosis of her son's deafness and how she struggled to have her son educated using sign language.
267 pages Softcover
ISBN 0-930323-47-5

8050 Book of Name Signs: Naming in American Sign Language
DawnSign Press
6130 Nancy Ridge Dr
San Diego, CA 92121-3223
858-625-0600
800-549-5350
FAX: 858-625-2336
info@dawnsign.com
www.dawnsign.com

Joe Dannis, President
Sam Supalla, Author
To explain how a name sign is chosen in the Deaf community, professor and researcher Sam Supalla wrote this valuable resource book. Revealing fascinating insights about the origins of ASL name signs, Supalla shows how they serve the same function as given names used in the hearing community. He also details how the history of the name sign system dates back to the early years of deaf education in America. Included for reference is a list of more than 500 name signs available for selection. *$12.95*
120 pages Paperback 1992
ISBN 0-915035-30-4

8051 Chelsea: The Story of a Signal Dog
Gallaudet University Bookstore
800 Florida Ave NE
Washington, DC 20002-3600   202-651-5855
                                   866-204-0504
                              FAX: 773-660-2235
                              TTY: 202-651-5855
                              gupress@gallaudet.edu
                              www.clerccenter.gallaudet.edu

Paul Ogden, Author
T. Alan Hurwitz, President
Paul Kelly, Vice President, Adm. & Finance
This is a story of a young deaf couple and their Belgian sheepdog,
who acts as their ears. It explains how these dogs are trained and
paired with their new owners.
169 pages

8052 Children of a Lesser God
Gallaudet University Bookstore
800 Florida Ave NE
Washington, DC 20002-3600   202-651-5855
                                   866-204-0504
                              FAX: 773-660-2235
                              TTY: 202-651-5855
                              gupress@gallaudet.edu
                              www.clerccenter.gallaudet.edu

Mark Medoff, Author
T. Alan Hurwitz, President
Paul Kelly, Vice President Adm. And Finance
The movie that won the hearts of thousands. This is a story of a
deaf woman who refuses to succumb to the hearing people's im-
age of what a deaf person should be.
91 pages Softcover
ISBN 0-822202-03-4

**8053 Choices in Deafness: A Parent's Guide to
Communication Options**
Woodbine House
6510 Bells Mill Rd
Bethesda, MD 20817-1636   301-897-3570
                                 800-843-7323
                            FAX: 301-897-5838
                            info@woodbinehouse.com
                            www.woodbinehouse.com

Irv Shapell, Owner
Sue Schwartz, PhD., Editor
A useful aid in choosing the appropriate communication option
for a child with a hearing loss. Experts present the following communication options: Auditory-Verbal Approach, Bilin-
gual-Bicultural Approach, Cued Speech, Oral Approach, and
Total Communication. This new edition explains medical causes
of hearing loss, the diagnostic process, audiological assessment,
and cochlear implants. Children and parents also offer their personal experiences. *$24.95*
400 pages Paperback
ISBN 1-890627-73-7

8054 Cochlear Implants for Kids
Alexander Graham Bell Association
3417 Volta Pl NW
Washington, DC 20007-2737   202-337-5220
                              FAX: 202-337-8314
                              info@agbell.org

Warren Estabrooks MEd, Editor
Alexander T. Graham, Executive Director
Susan Boswell, Director of Communications and Marketing
Designed to educate readers about cochlear implants, including
surgery, the importance of rehabilitation and the significance of
parents' and professionals' roles. *$12.49*
404 pages Paperback
ISBN 0-882002-08-2

**8055 Cognition, Education and Deafness: Directions for
Research and Instruction**
Gallaudet University Press
800 Florida Ave NE
Washington, DC 20002-3600   773-568-1550
                                   800-621-2736
                              FAX: 773-660-2235
                              TTY: 888-630-9347
                              gupress@gallaudet.edu

David S Martin, Editor
T. Alan Hurwitz, President
Paul Kelly, Vice President Adm. And Finance
This groundbreaking book integrates the work of 54 contributors
to the 1984 symposium on cognition, education, and deafness. It
focuses on cognition and deaf students' growth and development,
problem-solving strategies, thinking processes, language development, reading methodology, measurement of potential, and intervention programs. *$50.00*
248 pages Paperback
ISBN 1-563681-49-8

**8056 College and University Programs for Deaf and Hard of
Hearing Students**
Gallaudet & NTID
800 Florida Avenue NE
Gallaudet University
Washington, DC 20002   202-651-5000
                              800-451-8834
                         FAX: 202-651-5508
                         www.lulu.com

S. Benaissa, & L. Dunning, Co-Authors
J. DeCaro, M. Karchmer, Co-Authors
J Hochgesang, Co-Author
Compiled by Gallaudet University and the National Technical Institute for the Deaf, this publication is a guide to accessibility for
deaf and hard of hearing students in American colleges and universities. Available through LuLu Publishing. *$11.50*
240 pages Paperback
ISBN 9-998242-81-9

8057 Come Sign with Us
Gallaudet University Press
800 Florida Ave NE
Washington, DC 20002-3600   773-568-1550
                                   800-621-2736
                              FAX: 773-660-2235
                              TTY: 888-630-9347
                              gupress@gallaudet.edu
                              www.gupress.gallaudet.edu

Jan C Hafer, Author
Robert M Wilson, Co-Author
T. Alan Hurwitz, President
This fun guide for parents and educators on teaching hearing chil-
dren how to sign has been thoroughly revised with completely
new activities that provide contexts for practice. *$39.95*
160 pages Paperback
ISBN 1-563680-51-3

**8058 Comprehensive Reference Manual for Signers and
Interpreters**
Charles C. Thomas
2600 S First St
Springfield, IL 62704-4730   217-789-8980
                                    800-258-8980
                               FAX: 217-789-9130
                               books@ccthomas.com
                               www.ccthomas.com

Michael P. Thomas, President
Cheryl M. Hoffman, Author
A classic in sign language literature since its introduction over
two decades ago, this updated and expanded sixth edition of
Comprehensive Reference Manual for Signers and Interpreters
contains almost seven thousand entries, including vocabulary
and idioms, with cross-references and sign descriptions. It is intended primarily for interpreters, but it can also be used effectively by signers who have at least a working knowledge of sign
language. *$59.95*
404 pages Spiral Paper 1909
ISBN 0-398078-58-4

8059 **Comprehensive Signed English Dictionary**
Gallaudet University Press
800 Florida Ave NE
Washington, DC 20002-3600
773-568-1550
800-621-2736
FAX: 773-660-2235
TTY: 888-630-9347
gupress@gallaudet.edu
www.gupress.gallaudet.edu

Harry Bornstein, Editor
Karen L. Saulnier, Editor
Lillian B. Hamilton, Editor
The Comprehensive Signed English Dictionary is the premier volume of the Signed English series. This complete dictionary more than 3,100 signs, including signs reflecting lively, contemporary vocabulary. *$45.00*
464 pages Casebound
ISBN 0-913580-81-3

8060 **Conversational Sign Language II: An Intermediate Advanced Manual**
Gallaudet University Press
800 Florida Ave NE
Washington, DC 20002-3600
773-568-1550
800-621-2736
FAX: 773-660-2235
TTY: 888-630-9347
gupress@gallaudet.edu
www.gupress.gallaudet.edu

William J Madsen, Author
T. Alan Hurwitz, President
Paul Kelly, Vice President Adm. And Finance
This book presents English words and their American Sign Language (ASL) equivalents in 63 lessons. Part one covers 750 words and their signs. Part two deals with the interpretation of 220 English idioms (which have over 300 usages in ASL). Part three presents over 300 ASL idioms and colloquialisms prevalent in informal conversations. *$17.95*
236 pages Paperback
ISBN 0-913580-00-7

8061 **Deaf Empowerment: Emergence, Struggle and Rhetoric**
Gallaudet University Press
800 Florida Ave NE
Washington, DC 20002-3600
773-568-1550
800-621-2736
FAX: 773-660-2235
TTY: 888-630-9347
gupress@gallaudet.edu
www.gupress.gallaudet.edu

Katherine A Jankowski, Author
T. Alan Hurwitz, President
Paul Kelly, Vice President, Adm. & Finance
Employing the methodology successfully used to explore other social movements in America, this meticulous study examines the rhetorical foundation that motivated Deaf people to work for social change during the past two centuries. *$49.95*
192 pages Hardcover
ISBN 1-563680-61-0

8062 **Deaf History Unveiled: Interpretations from the New Scholarship**
Gallaudet University Press
800 Florida Ave NE
Washington, DC 20002-3600
773-568-1550
800-621-2736
FAX: 773-660-2235
TTY: 888-630-9347
gupress@gallaudet.edu
www.gallaudet.edu

John Vickrey Van Cleve, Editor
T. Alan Hurwitz, President
Paul Kelly, Vice President Adm. And Finance
Deaf History Unveiled features 16 essays, including work by Harlan Lane, Renate Fischer, Margret Winzer, William McCagg, and other noted historians in this field. Readers will discover the new themes driving Deaf history, including a telling comparison of the similar experiences of Deaf people and African Americans, both minorities with identifying characteristics that cannot be hidden to thwart bias. *$36.95*
316 pages Paperback
ISBN 1-563680-87-4

8063 **Deaf Like Me**
Gallaudet University Press
800 Florida Ave NE
Washington, DC 20002-3600
773-568-1550
800-621-2736
FAX: 773-660-2235
TTY: 888-630-9347
gupress@gallaudet.edu
www.gupress.gallaudet.edu

Thomas S Spradley, Author
James P Spradley, Co-Author
T. Alan Hurwitz, President
Deaf Like Me is the moving account of parents coming to terms with their baby girl's profound deafness. The love, hope, and anxieties of all hearing parents of deaf children are expressed here with power and simplicity. *$16.95*
292 pages Paperback
ISBN 0-930323-11-4

8064 **Deaf Parents and Their Hearing Children**
Through the Looking Glass
3075 Adeline Street
Suite 120
Berkeley, CA 94703
510-848-1112
800-644-2666
FAX: 510-848-4445
tlg@lookingglass.org
www.lookingglass.org

Maureen Block, J.D., President
Thomas Spalding, Treasurer
Alice Nemon, Secretary
The focus of this review article is on families with Deaf parents and hearing children. We provide a brief description of the Deaf community, their language, and culture; describe communication patterns and parenting issues in Deaf-parented families, examine the role of the hearing child in a Deaf family and how that experience affects their functioning in the hearing world; and discuss important considerations and resources for families, educators, and health care and service providers. *$2.00*
8 pages

8065 **Deaf in America: Voices from a Culture**
TJ Publishers
2544 Tarpley Rd
Suite 108
Carrollton, TX 75006-2288
972-416-0800
800-999-1168
FAX: 972-416-0944
customerservice@tjpublishers.com
www.tjpublishers.com

Carol Padden, Author
Tom Humphries, Co-Author
Terrence O'Rourke, Principal
Now available in paperback, this book opens deaf culture to outsiders, inviting readers to imagine and understand a world of silence. This book shares the joy and satisfaction many people have with their lives and shows that deafness may not be the handicap most hearing people think. *$15.95*
134 pages Softcover
ISBN 0-674194-24-1

8066 **EASE Program: Emergency Access Self Evaluation**
Telecommunications for the Deaf (TDI)
8630 Fenton St
Suite 604
Silver Spring, MD 20910-3822
301-589-3786
FAX: 301-589-3797
tdi-online.org

Claude L Stout, Executive Director
Gloria Carter, Executive Secretary
James House, Public Relations Director
A complete training, testing, maintenance and self evaluation program that helps emergency service providers prepare for

emergency calls from TTY users and to comply with the American with Disabilities Act. *$35.00*

48 pages

8067   Encyclopedia of Deafness and Hearing Disorders

Powell's Books
1005 W Burnside St
Portland, OR 97209-3114

503-228-4651
800-873-7323
help@powells.com
www.powells.com

Carol Turkington, Author
Michael Powell, Owner

Presents the most current information on deafness and hearing disorders in an authoritative A-to-Z compendium. *$7.50*

294 pages Hardcover
ISBN 0-816056-15-3

8068   Expressive and Receptive Fingerspelling for Hearing Adults

Gallaudet University Bookstore
800 Florida Ave NE
Washington, DC 20002-3600

202-651-5855
866-204-0504
FAX: 773-660-2235
TTY: 202-651-5855
gupress@gallaudet.edu
www.clerccenter.gallaudet.edu

LaVera M Guillory, Author
T. Alan Hurwitz, President
Paul Kelly, Vice President Adm. And Finance

Here is a new and meaningful way for adults to increase their comfort with fingerspelling. The system is based on the principles of phonetics rather than letters of the English alphabet.

42 pages Softcover
ISBN 0-875110-55-X

8069   Eye-Centered: A Study of Spirituality of Deaf People

National Catholic Office for the Deaf
7202 Buchanan St
Hyattsville, MD 20784-2236

301-577-1684
FAX: 301-577-1684
info@ncod.org
www.ncod.org

Bill Key, Author
Arvilla Rank, Executive Director
Deacon Patrick Graybill, Vice President

The findings of the five-year De Sales Project conducted by The National Catholic Office for the Deaf. *$16.70*

167 pages

8070   For Hearing People Only

Harris Communications
15155 Technology Dr
Eden Prairie, MN 55344

800-825-6758
FAX: 952-906-1099
TTY:952-388-2152
info@harriscomm.com
www.harriscomm.com

Ray Harris, CEO

For Hearing People Only answers some of the most common questions hearing people ask about Deaf culture and how Deaf people communicate and live. *$72.00*

868 pages Paperback
ISBN 9-705876-00-7

8071   From Gesture to Language in Hearing and Deaf Children

Gallaudet University Press
800 Florida Ave NE
Washington, DC 20002-3600

773-568-1550
800-621-2736
FAX: 773-660-2235
TTY: 888-630-9347
gupress@gallaudet.edu
www.gupress.gallaudet.edu

Virginia Volterra, Editor
Carol J. Erting, Editor

In 21 essays on communicative gesturing in the first two years of life, this vital collection demonstrates the importance of gesture in a child's transition to a linguistic system. *$45.95*

358 pages Paperback
ISBN 1-563680-78-5

8072   From Mime to Sign Package

TJ Publishers
2544 Tarpley Rd
Suite 108
Carrollton, TX 75006-2288

972-416-0800
800-999-1168
FAX: 972-416-0944
customerservice@tjpublishers.com
www.tjpublishers.com

Gilbert C Eastman, Author
Terrence O'Rourke, Principal
Tanner Beach, Director

More than 1,000 photographs illustrate how natural gestures, mime and facial expressions used every day can become the basis for learning sign language. *$27.95*

183 pages Softcover
ISBN 0-932666-34-5

8073   GA and SK Etiquette

Telecommunications for the Deaf
8630 Fenton Street
Suite 604
Silver Spring, MD 20910- 3822

301-589-3786
FAX: 301-589-3797
www.tdi-online.org

Claude L Stout, Executive Director
Keith Cagle, Co-Author
Roy Miller, President

Promoting equal access to telecommunications and media for people who are deaf, late-deafened, hard-of-hearing or deaf-blind through consumer education and involvement; technical assistance and consulting; applications of exisiting and emerging technologies; networking and collaboration; uniformity of standards; and national policy development and advocacy. *$11.95*

54 pages Paperback
ISBN 0-961462-17-5

8074   Gallaudet Survival Guide to Signing

Gallaudet University Press
800 Florida Ave NE
Washington, DC 20002-3600

773-568-1550
800-621-2736
FAX: 773-660-2235
TTY: 888-630-9347
gupress@gallaudet.edu
www.gallaudet.edu

Jon Mitchiner, Manager
Leonard G. Lane, Author
Jan Skrobisz, Illustrator

Features 500 of the most frequently used signs with clear illustrations and descriptions for each one. *$9.95*

218 pages Paperback
ISBN 0-930323-67-X

8075   Goldilocks and the Three Bears: Told in Signed English

Gallaudet University Press
800 Florida Ave NE
Washington, DC 20002-3600

773-568-1550
800-621-2736
FAX: 773-660-2235
TTY: 888-630-9347
gupress@gallaudet.edu
www.gupress.gallaudet.edu

Harry Bornstein, Author
Karen L Saulnier, Co-Author
T. Alan Hurwitz, President

Goldilocks and the Three Bears offers children ages 3 - 8 all of the fun their parents had when they first read about the little girl with the golden curls who turned the Bears' house upside down. *$21.95*

48 pages Hardcover
ISBN 1-563680-57-2

8076 Hearing Impaired Children and Youth with Developmental Disabilities
Gallaudet University Bookstore
800 Florida Ave NE
Washington, DC 20002-3600

202-651-5855
866-204-0504
FAX: 773-660-2235
TTY: 202-651-5855
gupress@gallaudet.edu

Evelyn Cherow, Editor
T. Alan Hurwitz, President
Paul Kelly, Vice President Adm. And Finance
The insights of 24 experts help clarify relationships between hearing impairment and developmental difficulties and propose interdisciplinary cooperation as an approach to the problems created. *$29.95*
394 pages Hardcover
ISBN 0-913580-97-X

8077 Hollywood Speaks: Deafness and the Film Entertainment Industry
University of Illinois Press
1325 S Oak St
MC-566
Champaign, IL 61820-6903

217-333-0950
FAX: 217-244-8082
uipress@uillinois.edu
www.press.uillinois.edu

Willis G. Regier, Director
John S. Schuchman, Author
Kathy O'Neill, Assistant To The Director
How deafness has been treated in movies and how it provides yet another window onto social history in addition to a fresh angle from which to view Hollywood. *$27.00*
200 pages Paperback 1999
ISBN 0-252068-50-8

8078 I Have a Sister, My Sister is Deaf
HarperCollins Publishers
10 E 53rd St
New York, NY 10022-5244

212-207-7901
800-242-7737
FAX: 212-702-2586
spsales@harpercollins.com
www.harpercollins.com

Jeanne Whitehouse Peterson, Author
Deborah Kogan Ray, Illustrator
Ann Ledden, Vice President
An emphatic, affirmative look at the relationship between siblings, as a young deaf child is affectionately described by her older sister. This Coretta Scott King Honor Award winner helps young children develop an understanding that deaf children share the same interests as hearing children. *$6.99*
32 pages Paperback 1984
ISBN 0-064430-59-6

8079 Independence Without Sight or Sound
AFB Press
2 Penn Plaza
Suite 1102
New York, NY 10121-2006

212-502-7600
800-232-5463
FAX: 888-545-8331
afbweb@afb.net
www.afb.org

Richard Obnen, Chairman Of The Board
Carl Augusto, President and CEO
Rick Bozeman, Chief Financial Officer
This practical guidebook covers the essential aspects of communicating and working with deaf-blind persons. Full of valuable information on subjects such as how to talk with deaf-blind people, adapt orientation and mobility techniques for deaf-blind travelers, and interact with deaf-blind individuals socially, this useful manual also contains a substantial resource section detailing sources of information and adapted equipment. *$39.95*
193 pages Paperback
ISBN 0-891282-46-4

8080 Innovative Practices for Teaching Sign Language Interpreters
Gallaudet University Press
800 Florida Ave NE
Washington, DC 20002-3600

773-568-1550
800-621-2736
FAX: 773-660-2235
TTY: 888-630-9347
gupress@gallaudet.edu
www.gupress.gallaudet.edu

Cynthia B Roy, Editor
Researchers now understand interpreting as an active process between two languages and cultures, with social interaction, sociolinguistics, and discourse analysis as more appropriate theoretical frameworks. Roy's penetrating new book acts upon these new insights by presenting six dynamic teaching practices to help interpreters achieve the highest level of skill. *$45.95*
200 pages Hardcover
ISBN 1-563680-88-2

8081 Intermediate Conversational Sign Language
Gallaudet University Press
800 Florida Ave NE
Washington, DC 20002-3600

773-568-1550
800-621-2736
FAX: 773-660-2235
TTY: 888-630-9347
gupress@gallaudet.edu
www.gupress.gallaudet.edu

Willard J Madsen, Author
This fully illustrated text offers a unique approach to using American Sign Language (ASL) and English in a bilingual setting. Each of the 25 lessons involve sign language conversation using colloquialisms that are prevalent in informal conversations. *$31.50*
400 pages Softcover
ISBN 0-913580-79-1

8082 Interpretation: A Sociolinguistic Model
Sign Media
4020 Blackburn Ln
Burtonsville, MD 20866-1167

301-421-0268
800-475-4756
FAX: 301-421-0270
info@signmedia.com
www.signmedia.com

Verden Ness, President
Dennis Cokely, Author
This text presents a sociolinguistically sensitive model of the interpretation process. The model applies to interpretation in any two languages although this one focuses on ASL and English. *$22.95*
199 pages
ISBN 0-932130-10-0

8083 Interpreting: An Introduction
Registry of Interpreters for the Deaf
333 Commerce St
Alexandria, VA 22314-2801

703-838-0030
FAX: 703-838-0454
TTY:703-838-0459
ridinfo@rid.org
www.rid.org

Nancy J Frishberg, Author
Shane Feldman, Executive Director
Don Roose, Director
This text is written by a practicing interpreter and includes information on history, terminology, research, competence, setting and a comprehensive bibliography. *$24.95*
249 pages Softcover
ISBN 0-916883-07-8

8084 Joy of Signing
Gospel Publishing House
1445 N Boonville Ave
Springfield, MO 65802-1894

417-862-8000
800-641-4310
FAX: 417-862-5881
www.gospelpublishing.com

Lottie L Riekehof, Author

This manual on signing includes illustrations, information on sign origins, practice sentences, and step-by-step descriptions of hand positions and movements. *$23.99*
352 pages Hardcover
ISBN 0-882435-20-5

8085 Kid-Friendly Parenting with Deaf and Hard of Hearing Children
Gallaudet University Press
800 Florida Ave NE
Washington, DC 20002-3600   773-568-1550
800-621-2736
FAX: 773-660-2235
TTY: 888-630-9347
gupress@gallaudet.edu
www.gupress.gallaudet.edu

Daria Medwid, Author
Denise Chapman Weston, Co-Author
At each chapter's beginning, experts (some deaf, some hearing), including I. King Jordan, Jack Gannon, Merv Garretson, and others, offer their insights on the subject discussed. Designed for parents with various styles, Kid-Friendly Parenting is a complete, step-by-step guide and reference to raising a deaf or hard of hearing child. *$35.95*
320 pages Paperback
ISBN 1-563680-31-9

8086 Laurent Clerc: The Story of His Early Years
Gallaudet University Press
800 Florida Ave NE
Washington, DC 20002-3600   773-568-1550
800-621-2736
FAX: 773-660-2235
TTY: 888-630-9347
gupress@gallaudet.edu
www.gupress.gallaudet.edu

Cathryn Carroll, Author
T. Alan Hurwitz, President
Paul Kelly, Vice President Adm. And Finance
In his own voice, Clerc vividly relates the experiences that led to his later progressive teaching methods. Especially influential was his long stay at the Royal National Institute for the Deaf in Paris, where he encountered sharply distinct personalities - the saintly, inspiring deaf teacher Massieu, the vicious Dr. Itard and his heartless experiments on deaf boys, and the Father of the Deaf, Abbe Sicard, who could hardly sign. *$13.95*
208 pages Paperback
ISBN 0-930323-23-8

8087 Linguistics of American Sign Language: An Introduction
Gallaudet University Press
800 Florida Ave NE
Washington, DC 20002-3600   773-568-1550
800-621-2736
FAX: 773-660-2235
TTY: 888-630-9347
gupress@gallaudet.edu
www.gupress.gallaudet.edu

Clayton Valli, Author
Ceil Lucas, Co-Author
Kristin J Mulrooney, Co-Author
Completely reorganized to reflect the growing intricacy of the study of ASL linguistics, the 5th edition presents 26 units in seven parts. Part One: Introduction presents a revision of Defining Language and an entirely new unit, Defining Linguistics. Part Two: Phonology has been completely updated with new terminology and examples. *$75.00*
560 pages Hardcover
ISBN 1-563682-83-4

8088 Literacy & Your Deaf Child: What Every Parent Should Know
Gallaudet University Press
800 Florida Ave NE
Washington, DC 20002-3600   773-568-1550
800-621-2736
FAX: 773-660-2235
TTY: 888-630-9347
gupress@gallaudet.edu
www.gupress.gallaudet.edu

David A Stewart, Author
Bryan R Clarke, Co-Author
T. Alan Hurwitz, President
Literacy and Your Deaf Child begins by introducing some common concepts, among them the importance of parental involvement in a deaf child's education. It outlines how children acquire language and describes the auditory and visual links to literacy. *$24.95*
240 pages Paperback
ISBN 1-563681-36-6

8089 Mask of Benevolence: Disabling the Deaf Community, The
DawnSign Press
6130 Nancy Ridge Dr
San Diego, CA 92121-3223   858-625-0600
800-549-5350
FAX: 858-625-2336
info@dawnsign.com
www.dawnsign.com

Joe Dannis, President
Harlan Lane, Author
Dr. Harlan Lane does not view deafness as a handicap but rather a different state from hearing. Deaf people are a societal minority and should be treasured, not eradicated. *$12.95*
360 pages Paperback 1992
ISBN 1-581210-09-5

8090 Mother Father Deaf: Living Between Sound and Silence
Harvard University Press
79 Garden St
Cambridge, MA 02138-1423   617-495-2600
800-405-1619
FAX: 617- 49- 589
contact_hup@harvard.edu
www.hup.harvard.edu

William Sisler, President
Paul Preston, Author
The book explores the intimate intersection of families like his own - families which embody the conflicts and resolutions of two often opposing world views, the Deaf and the Hearing. Although I have normal hearing, both of my parents are profoundly deaf. *$19.50*
278 pages Paperback
ISBN 0-674587-48-0

8091 My First Book of Sign
Gallaudet University Press
800 Florida Ave NE
Washington, DC 20002-3600   773-568-1550
800-621-2736
FAX: 773-660-2235
TTY: 888-630-9347
gupress@gallaudet.edu
www.gupress.gallaudet.edu

Pamela J Baker, Author
Patricia Bellan Gillen, Illustrator
T. Alan Hurwitz, President
Full-color book gives alphabetically grouped signs for 150 words most frequently used by young children. *$22.95*
80 pages Hardcover
ISBN 0-930323-20-3

8092 My Signing Book of Numbers
Gallaudet University Press
800 Florida Ave NE
Washington, DC 20002-3600

773-568-1550
800-621-2736
FAX: 773-660-2235
TTY: 888-630-9347
gupress@gallaudet.edu
www.gupress.gallaudet.edu

Patricia Bellan Gillen, Author
This full-color book helps children learn their numbers in sign language. Each two-page spread of this delightfully illustrated book has the appropriate number of things or creatures for the numbers 0 through 20. *$22.95*
56 pages Hardcover
ISBN 0-930323-37-8

8093 Nursery Rhymes from Mother Goose
Gallaudet University Press
800 Florida Ave NE
Washington, DC 20002-3600

773-568-1550
800-621-2736
FAX: 773-660-2235
TTY: 888-630-9347
gupress@gallaudet.edu
www.gupress.gallaudet.edu

Harry Bornstein, Author
Karen L Saulnier, Co-Author
Patricia Peters, Illustrator
Young readers, both hearing and deaf, will learn the special charm of rhyme while also discovering new vocabulary and new ways to experience English through signing. As they learn and memorize their favorite verses, children will also strengthen their language skills in a fun, entertaining way. *$21.95*
64 pages Hardcover
ISBN 0-930323-99-8

8094 Outsiders in a Hearing World: A Sociology of Deafness
Sage Publications
2455 Teller Rd
Thousand Oaks, CA 91320-2218

805-499-9774
800-818-7243
FAX: 805-499-0871
www.sagepub.com

Paul C Higgins, Author
An introduction to the social world of deaf people. The author gives a sociologists view of what it's like to be deaf. *$72.95*
208 pages Hardcover 1980
ISBN 0-803914-22-3

8095 Perigee Visual Dictionary of Signing
Harris Communications
15155 Technology Dr
Eden Prairie, MN 55344

800-825-6758
FAX: 952-906-1099
TTY:952-388-2152
info@harriscomm.com
www.harriscomm.com

Ray Harris, CEO
An A-to-Z guide to American Sign Language vocabulary. *$15.28*
478 pages Softcover
ISBN 9-780399-51-9

8096 Phone of Our Own: The Deaf Insurrection Against Ma Bell
Gallaudet University Press
800 Florida Ave NE
Washington, DC 20002-3600

773-568-1550
800-621-2736
FAX: 773-660-2235
TTY: 888-630-9347
gupress@gallaudet.edu
www.gupress.gallaudet.edu

Harry G Lang, Author
T. Alan Hurwitz, President
Paul Kelly, Vice President Adm. And Finance
A recount of the history of the teletypewriter, from the three deaf engineers who developed the acoustic coupler that made mass communication on TTY's feasible, through the deaf community's twenty-year struggle against the government and AT&T to have TTY's produced and distributed. *$36.50*
256 pages Hardcover
ISBN 1-563680-90-4

8097 Place of Their Own: Creating the Deaf Community in America
Gallaudet University Press
800 Florida Ave NE
Washington, DC 20002-3600

773-568-1550
800-621-2736
FAX: 773-660-2235
TTY: 888-630-9347
gupress@gallaudet.edu
www.gallaudet.edu

John V Van Cleve, Author
Barry A Crouch, Co-Author
T. Alan Hurwitz, President
Traces development of American deaf society to show how deaf people developed a common language and sense of community. Views deafness as the distinguishing characteristic of a distinct culture. *$22.95*
224 pages Paperback
ISBN 0-930323-49-1

8098 PreReading Strategies
Gallaudet University Bookstore
800 Florida Ave NE
Washington, DC 20002-3600

202-651-5855
866-204-0504
FAX: 773-660-2235
TTY: 202-651-5855
gupress@gallaudet.edu

David R Schleper, Author
T. Alan Hurwitz, President
Paul Kelly, Vice President Adm. And Finance
Here is a wealth of good advice for preparing students to understand what they read, building comprehension and enjoyment. *$14.95*
65 pages

8099 Quad City Deaf & Hard of Hearing Youth Group: Tomorrow's Leaders for our Community
Independent Living Research Utilization ILRU
2323 S Shepherd Dr
Houston, TX 77019-7019

713-520-9058
FAX: 713-520-5785
ilru@ilru.org

Lex Frieden, Director
Rose Sheperd, Manager
IICIL staff see this program as a way to develop young leaders for themovement. Emphasis is given to providing oppportunities for members of the youth group to develop skills in planning and organizing activities.

8100 Religious Signing: A Comprehensive Guide for All Faiths
TJ Publishers
P.O. Box 702701
Dallas, TX 75370

972-416-0800
800-999-1168
FAX: 972-416-0944
TTY: 301-585-4440
TJPubinc@aol.com
www.tjpublishers.com

Elaine Costello, Author
Terrence O'Rourke, Principal
Tanner Beach, Director
Contains over 500 religious signs for all denominations and their meanings illustrated by clear upper torso illustrations that show movements of hand, body and face. Includes a section on signing favorite verses, prayers and blessings. *$18.95*
219 pages Softcover
ISBN 0-553342-44-4

8101   Seeing Voices
Vintage and Anchor Books
1745 Broadway
3rd Floor
New York, NY 10019

212-782-9000
FAX: 212-572-6066
vintageanchor@randomhouse.com
www.randomhouse.com

Oliver Sacks, Author
Madeline McIntosh, President/Sales/Operations
Markus Dohle, Chairman/CEO
Well known for his exploration of how people respond to neurological impairments, Dr Sacks explores the world of the deaf and
discovers how deaf people respond to their loss of hearing and
how they develop language. A highly readable introduction to
deaf people, deaf culture and American Sign Language. *$13.95*
240 pages Softcover 2000
ISBN 0-375704-07-8

8102   Sign Language Interpreting and Interpreter Education
Oxford University Press
2001 Evans Rd
Cary, NC 27513-2009

919-677-0977
800-445-9714
FAX: 919-677-1303
custserv.us@oup.com
www.oup.com

Marc Marschark, Editor
Rico Peterson, Editor
Elizabeth A Winston, Editor
Provides a coherent picture of the field as a whole, including evaluation of the extent to which current practices are supported by
validating research. The first comprehensive source, suitable as
both a reference book and a textbook for interpreter training programs and a variety of courses on bilingual education,
psycholinguistics and translation, and cross-linguistic studies.
$65.00
328 pages Hardcover
ISBN 0-195176-94-4

8103   Signed English Starter, The
Gallaudet University Press
800 Florida Ave NE
Washington, DC 20002-3600

773-568-1550
800-621-2736
FAX: 773-660-2235
TTY: 888-630-9347
gupress@gallaudet.edu
www.gupress.gallaudet.edu

Harry Bornstein, Author
Karen L Saulnier, Co-Author
T. Alan Hurwitz, President
A first course in Signed English for adults and children, the book
is fully illustrated (several figures per page), and it is organized in
a way that leads to rewarding learning quite rapidly. The authors
of this new and exciting text believe firmly that Signed English
must be made as easy as possible if it is going to be as useful (and
used) as it can and should be. The book explains the rationale for
the Signed English system and the conventions used to teach it.
$18.50
232 pages Paperback
ISBN 0-913580-82-1

**8104   Signing Family: What Every Parent Should Know About
Sign Communication, The**
Gallaudet University Press
800 Florida Ave NE
Washington, DC 20002-3600

773-568-1550
800-621-2736
FAX: 773-660-2235
TTY: 888-630-9347
gupress@gallaudet.edu
www.gupress.gallaudet.edu

David A Stewart, Author
Barbara Luetke-Stahlman, Co-Author
T. Alan Hurwitz, President
This reader-friendly book shows parents how to create a set of
goals around the communication needs of their deaf child. Describes in even-handed terms the major signing options available,
from American Sign Language to Signed English. *$29.95*
192 pages Paperback
ISBN 1-563680-69-6

8105   Signing for Reading Success
Gallaudet University Press
800 Florida Ave NE
Washington, DC 20002-3600

773-568-1550
800-621-2736
FAX: 773-660-2235
TTY: 888-630-9347
gupress@gallaudet.edu
www.gupress.gallaudet.edu

Jan C Hafer, Author
Robert M Wilson, Co-Author
T. Alan Hurwitz, President
This booklet provides summaries of four research students on the
usefulness of signing for reading achievement. *$7.95*
24 pages Paperback
ISBN 0-930323-18-1

8106   Signing: How to Speak with Your Hands
TJ Publishers
2427 Bond Street
Suite 108
University Park, IL 60466-2288

972-416-0800
800-999-1168
FAX: 972-416-0944
customerservice@tjpublishers.com
www.tjpublishers.com

Elaine Costello, Author
Terrence O'Rourke, Principal
Tanner Beach, Director
Presents 1,200 basic signs with clear illustrations in logical topi-
cal groupings. Linguistic principles are described at the begin-
ning of each chapter, giving insight into the rules which govern
American Sign Language. *$19.95*
248 pages Softcover
ISBN 0-553375-39-3

8107   Signs Across America
Gallaudet University Press
800 Florida Ave NE
Washington, DC 20002-3600

773-568-1550
800-621-2736
FAX: 773-660-2235
TTY: 888-630-9347
gupress@gallaudet.edu
www.gupress.gallaudet.edu

Edgar H Shroyer, Author
Susan P Shroyer, Co-Author
T. Alan Hurwitz, President
A look at regional variations in ASL. Signs for selected words
collected from 25 different states. More than 1,200 signs illus-
trated in the text. *$28.95*
304 pages Paperback
ISBN 0-913580-96-1

**8108   Signs for Me: Basic Sign Vocabulary for Children,
Parents & Teachers**
TJ Publishers
2427 Bond Street
Suite 108
University Park, IL 60466-2288

972-416-0800
800-999-1168
FAX: 972-416-0944
www.tjpublishers.com

Ben Bahan, Author
Joe Dannis, Co-Author
Terrence O'Rourke, Principal
Sign language vocabulary for preschool and elementary school
children introduces household items, animals, family members,
actions, emotions, safety concerns and other concepts. *$14.95*
112 pages Softcover
ISBN 0-915035-27-8

8109 **Signs for Sexuality: A Resource Manual**
Planned Parenthood of Western Washington
2001 E Madison St
Seattle, WA 98122-2959   206-328-7715
                                          FAX: 206-328-6810
                                          www.plannedparenthood.org

Marlyn Minken, Author
Laurie Rosen-Ritt, Co-Author
Cecile Richards, President
An important book for those who want to listen to and talk with
other people about feelings, loving and caring. *$40.00*
122 pages Softcover

8110 **Signs of the Times**
Gallaudet University Press
800 Florida Ave NE
Washington, DC 20002-3600   773-568-1550
                                              800-621-2736
                                          FAX: 773-660-2235
                                          TTY: 888-630-9347
                                          gupress@gallaudet.edu
                                          www.gupress.gallaudet.edu

Edgar H Shroyer, Author
Susan P Shroyer, Illustrator
T. Alan Hurwitz, President
An excellent beginner's contact signing book that fills the gap be-
tween sign language dictionaries and American Sign Language
text. Designed for use as a classroom text. *$34.95*
448 pages Softcover
ISBN 0-913580-76-7

8111 **Silent Garden, The**
Gallaudet University Press
800 Florida Ave NE
Washington, DC 20002-3600   773-568-1550
                                              800-621-2736
                                          FAX: 773-660-2235
                                          TTY: 888-630-9347
                                          gupress@gallaudet.edu
                                          www.gupress.gallaudet.edu

Paul W Ogden, Author
T. Alan Hurwitz, President
Paul Kelly, Vice President Adm. And Finance
The author explain the broad range of hearing loss types, from minor to profound. Parents also are advised about what type of
school their child should attend and what kinds of professional
help will be best for the entire family. The book describes all
forms of communication, including choices in signing from
American Sign Language to the various manual systems based
upon English. Technological alternatives are presented also, including when and when not to consider cochler implants. *$34.95*
304 pages
ISBN 1-563680-58-0

8112 **Sing Praise Hymnal for the Deaf**
LifeWay Christian Resources
1 Lifeway Plz
MSN 146
Nashville, TN 37234-1001   615-251-2000
                                              800-458-2772
                                          FAX: 615-251-3899
                                          www.lifeway.com

Thom Rainer, President/CEO
Jerry Rhyne, CFO/ VP Finance And Buisness
Tim Vineyard, VP Technology And CIO
Designed to be used by interpreters to the deaf, sign-language
students, and deaf members of the congregation, this special
combined hymnal edition offers 234 of the most popular hymns.
$12.95
Hardcover 2000
ISBN 0-767314-09-3

8113 **TDI National Directory & Resource Guide: Blue Book**
Telecommunications for the Deaf
8630 Fenton Street
Suite 604
Silver Spring, MD 20910- 3822   301-589-3786
                                          FAX: 301-589-3797
                                          www.tdi-online.org

Claude L Stout, Executive Director

Promoting Equal Access to Telecommunications and Media for
People who are Deaf, Late-Deafened, Hard-of-Hearing or
Deaf-Blind. *$20.00*
600 pages Annual

8114 **Theoretical Issues in Sign Language Research**
University of Chicago Press
1427 E 60th St
Chicago, IL 60637-2902   773-702-7700
                                          FAX: 773-702-9756
                                          sales@press.uchicago.edu
                                          www.press.uchicago.edu

Donald A Collins, President
Susan D Fischer, Author
Patricia Siple, Co-Author
These volumes are an outgrowth of a conference held at the Uni-
versity of Rochester in 1986, dealing with the four traditional
core areas of phonology, morphology, syntax and semantics.
$29.95
348 pages Paperback 1990
ISBN 0-226251-52-7

8115 **We CAN Hear and Speak**
Alexander Graham Bell Association
3417 Volta Pl. NW
Washington, DC 20007   202-337-5220
                                          FAX: 202-337-8314
                                          TTY:202-337-5221
                                          info@agbell.org
                                          agbell.org

Carol Flexer Ph.D, Author
Catherine Richards MA, Co-Author
Written by parents for families of children who are deaf or hard of
hearing, this work describes auditory-verbal terminology and approaches and contains personal narratives written by parents and
their children who are deaf or hard of hearing. *$6.98*
184 pages Softcover

8116 **Week the World Heard Gallaudet, The**
Gallaudet University Press
800 Florida Ave NE
Washington, DC 20002-3600   202-651-5000
                                              800-621-2736
                                          FAX: 202-651-5508
                                          gupress@gallaudet.edu
                                          www.gupress.gallaudet.edu

Jack R Gannon, Author
T. Alan Hurwitz, President
Paul Kelly, Vice President Adm. And Finance
This day-to-day description of the events surrounding the Deaf
President Now movement at Gallaudet University includes full
color and black and white photographs and interviews with peo-
ple involved in the events of that week. *$49.95*
176 pages Hardcover
ISBN 0-930323-54-8

8117 **What is Auditory Processing?**
Abilitations - Speech Bin
P.O.Box 922668
Norcross, GA 30010-2668   770-449-5700
                                              800-850-8602
                                          FAX: 770-510-7290
                                          info@speechbin.com
                                          www.speechbin.com

Susan Bell, Author
What is Auditory Processing? It is and information-packed
16-page booklet created to explain auditory processing and it's
disorders and offers practical suggestions for coping with this
problem. It describes the listening process and tells how to help
children with auditory processing problems. It shows what families and teachers can do to help children who have trouble remembering and understanding what they hear and offers easy-to-use
activities and practical suggestions. *$22.69*
16 pages Softcover

8118 **You and Your Deaf Child: A Self-Help Guide for Parents of Deaf and Hard of Hearing Children**
Gallaudet University Press
800 Florida Ave NE
Washington, DC 20002-3600

773-568-1550
800-621-2736
FAX: 773-660-2235
TTY: 888-630-9347
gupress@gallaudet.edu
www.gupress.gallaudet.edu

John W Adams, Author
T. Alan Hurwitz, President
Paul Kelly, Vice President Adm. And Finance
Eleven chapters focus on such topics as feelings about hearing loss, the importance of communication in the family, and effective behavior management. Many chapters contain practice activities and questions to help parents retain skills taught in the chapter and check their grasp of the material. Four appendices provide references, general resources, and guidelines for evaluating educational programs. $29.95
224 pages Paperback
ISBN 1-563680-60-2

Journals

8119 **ADARA**
1022 7th St NE
Washington, DC 20002

301-293-8969
FAX: 301-293-9698
TTY:301-293-8969
adaraorg@gmail.com
www.adara.org

John Gournaris, Ph.D, President
Kathy Schwabeland, MA, Vice President
Denise Thew Hackett, Ph.D, JADARA Editor
ADARA's mission is to improve service excellence for those who are deaf or hard of hearing. The ADARA Update is a quarterly newsletter published by the association, offering information on events, resources, legislation, employment opportunities and other matters related to the field. JADARA is another publication by them presenting research results, articles on deafness, social services, mental health and other areas of interest.

8120 **American Journal of Audiology**
American Speech-Language-Hearing Association
2200 Research Blvd
Rockville, MD 20850-3289

240-632-2081
800-638-8255
FAX: 301-296-8580
actioncenter@asha.org
www.asha.org

Gary Dunham, Editor-in-Chief
Bridget Murray Law, Managing Editor
Carol Polovoy, Assistant Managing Editor
Articles concern screening, assesment, and treatment techniques; prevention; professional issues; supervision; administration. Includes clinical forums, clinical reviews, letters to the editor, or research reports that emphasize clinical practice.
2 x year

8121 **Hearing Professional**
International Hearing Society
16880 Middlebelt Rd
Ste 4
Livonia, MI 48154-3374

734-522-7200
800-521-5247
FAX: 734-522-0200
akovach@ihsinfo.org
www.ihsinfo.org

Kathleen Mennillo, MBA, Executive Director
Provides authoritative technical and business information that will help hearing aid specialists serve the hearing impaired.
bi-monthly

8122 **Journal of Speech, Language and Hearing Research**
American Speech-Language-Hearing Association
2200 Research Blvd
Rockville, MD 20850-3289

301-296-5700
800-638-8255
FAX: 301-296-8580
actioncenter@asha.org
www.asha.org

Gary Dunham, Editor-in-Chief
Bridget Murray Law, Managing Editor
Carol Polovoy, Assistant Managing Editor
Pertains broadly to studies of the processess and disorders of hearing, language, and speech diagnosis and treatment of such disorders.

8123 **Journal of the Academy of Rehabilitative Audiology**
Academy of Rehabilitative Audiology
PO Box 2323
Albany, NY 12220-0323

ara@audrehab.org
www.audrehab.org

Anne D. Olsen, Editor
A peer-reviewed journal published annually.

8124 **Literature Journal, The**
Gallaudet University
800 Florida Ave NE
Washington, DC 20002-3695

202-651-5488
800-621-2736
FAX: 202-651-5508
Oluyinka.Fakunle@gallaudet.edu

Charles C Welsh-Charrier, Author
T. Alan Hurwitz, President
Paul Kelly, Vice President Adm. And Finance
This book includes extensive examples of student and teacher entries taken from actual journals of deaf high school students. $12.95
44 pages Spiral Bound

8125 **Sign Language Studies**
Gallaudet University Press
800 Florida Ave NE
Washington, DC 20002-3695

202-651-5488
800-621-2736
FAX: 202-651-5508
gupress@gallaudet.edu
www.gupress.gallaudet.edu

Ceil Lucas, Editor
T. Alan Hurwitz, President
Paul Kelly, Vice President Adm. And Finance
Presents a unique forum for revolutionary papers on signed languages and other related disciplines, including linguistics, anthropology, semiotics, and deaf studies, history, and literature. $55.00
Quarterly

8126 **Volta Review**
Alexander Graham Bell Association
3417 Volta Pl. NW
Washington, DC 20007

202-337-5220
FAX: 202-337-8314
TTY:202-337-5221
vreditor@agbell.org
agbell.org

Emilio Alonso-Mendoza, Chief Executive Officer
Professionally refereed journal that publishes articles and research on education, rehabilitation and communicative development of people who have hearing impairments. Also includes subscription to Volta Voices, up-to-date magazine, bimonthly.
Biannual

Magazines

8127 Endeavor Magazine
American Society for Deaf Children
PO Box 23
Woodbine, MD 21797   800-942-2732
info@deafchildren.org
www.deafchildren.org

Tami Dominguez, Editor
ASDC's qurterly publication featuring committee reports, stories, and fun.
Quarterly

8128 Hearing Health Magazine
Deafness Research Foundation
363 Seventh Avenue
10th Floor
New York, NY 10001-3904   212-257-6140
866-454-3924
FAX: 212-257-6139
info@drf.org
www.drf.org

Andrea Boidman, Executive Director
Andrea Delbanco, Senior Editor
Yishane Lee, Editor
Serves as a source of quality information and provides the tools and resources to help people seek treatment for and manage hearing loss. Each issue features relevant and timely information on the latest research, articles written by leading authorities in the field, news about the latest technology, and human interest stories about those living with hearing loss.

8129 Hearing Life Magazine
Hearing Loss Association of America
7910 Woodmont Ave
Ste 1200
Bethesda, MD 20814-7022   301-657-2248
FAX: 301-913-9413
inquiry@hearingloss.org
www.hearingloss.org

Barbara Kelley, Executive Director
Formerly known as Hearing Loss Magazine, this official publication of the Hearing Loss Association of America helps individuals with hearing loss live a better life.
Bi-Monthly

8130 Tinnitus Today
American Tinnitus Association
PO Box 424049
Washington, DC 20042-4049   800-634-8978
ringingears.ata.org
Torryn P. Brazell, Executive Director
The magazine contains up-to-date medical and research news, feature articles on urgent tinnitus issues, questions and answers, self-help suggestions and letters to the editor from others with tinnitus. *$35.00*
28 pages 3 x year

Newsletters

8131 ASHA Leader, The
American Speech-Language-Hearing Association
2200 Research Blvd
Rockville, MD 20850-3289   301-215-6710
800-638-8255
FAX: 301-296-8580
leader@asha.org
www.asha.org

Gary Dunham, Editor-in-Chief
Bridget Murray Law, Managing Editor
Carol Polovoy, Assistant Managing Editor
Association publication containing news, notices of events and activities and information for members on issues facing the profession of audiology and speech-language pathology. *$80.00*
35 pages 2 x month

8132 American Annals of the Deaf
Gallaudet University Press
800 Florida Ave NE
Washington, DC 20002-3600   202-651-5000
800-621-2736
FAX: 202-651-5508
paul.3@osu.edu
www.gupress.gallaudet.edu

Peter V. Paul, Editor, Literary Issues
T. Alan Hurwitz, President
Paul Kelly, Vice President Adm. And Finance
Quarterly publication from the Conference of Educational Administrators Serving the Deaf. *$55.00*
Quarterly

8133 Canine Listener
Dogs for the Deaf
10175 Wheeler Rd
Central Point, OR 97502   541-826-9220
800-990-3647
800-990-3647
FAX: 541-826-6696
TTY:541-826-9220
info@dogsforthedeaf.org
dogsforthedeaf.org

Marvin Rhodes, Chair
Susan Bahr, Vice Chair
Kelly Gonzales, Development Director
Provides information on Hearing Dogs, placements, dog training, and other news about happenings at Dogs for the Deaf.
Quarterly

8134 Cochlear Implants In Children: Ethics and Choices
Gallaudet University Press
800 Florida Ave NE
Washington, DC 20002-3600   202-651-5000
800-621-2736
FAX: 202-651-5508
gupress@gallaudet.edu
www.gupress.gallaudet.edu

John B Christiansen, Author
Irene W Leigh, Co-Author
T. Alan Hurwitz, President
Designed to educate readers about cochlear implants, including surgery, the importance of rehabilitation and the significance of parents' and professionals' roles. *$55.00*
340 pages Casebound
ISBN 1-563681-16-1

8135 Communique
Michigan Association for Deaf Hard of Hearing
5236 Dumond Court
Suite C
Lansing, MI 48917-6001   517-487-0066
800-968-7327
FAX: 517-487-2586

Nancy Asher, Executive Director
Pat Walton, Office Manager
Provides leadership through advocacy and education. The association conducts leadership training for youth, information and referral services, interpreter referral, legislative advocacy, and a variety of other services.
4-8 pages Bi-annually

8136 Connect - Commmunity News
Hearing, Speech & Deafness Center (HSDC)
1625 19th Ave.
Seattle, WA 98122   206-323-5770
888-222-5036
FAX: 206-328-6871
TTY:800-761-2821
clinics@hsdc.org
www.hsdc.org

Lindsay Klarman, Executive Director
Connect is the quarterly eNews of the Hearing, Speech & Deafness Center. HSDC is is a nonprofit for clients who are deaf, hard of hearing, or who face other communication barriers such as speech challenges.
8 pages Annual

8137 Deaf Catholic
International Catholic Deaf Association
7202 Buchanan St
Landover Hills, MD 20784-2236
301-429-0697
FAX: 301-429-0698
homeoffice@icda-us.org
www.icda-us.org

Jean Cox, President
Kate Slosar, Vice President
TK Hill, Treasurer
Newsletter reporting the news of the Archdiocese, Deaf Apostolate and each of the Catholic Deaf Organizations. *$20.00*
16 pages Quarterly

8138 International Hearing Dog, Inc.
International Hearing Dog
5901 E 89th Ave.
Henderson, CO 80640-8315
303-287-3277
FAX: 303-287-3425
info@hearingdog.org

Valerie Foss-Brugger, Executive Director
Samuel Cheris, Chairman
Matt Bailey, Treasurer
International Hearing Dog, Inc. trains rescued shelter dogs for people who are deaf or hard-of-hearing, with and without disabilities, all at no cost to the recipient. Since 1979, 1300 dogs have been placed throughout all 50 states and Canada.
4-8 pages Quarterly

8139 League Letter
Center for Hearing and Communication
50 Broadway
6th Floor
New York, NY 10004-3810
917-305-7700
FAX: 917-305-7888
TTY:917-305-7999
info@chchearing.org
www.lhh.org

Laurie Hanin, Executive Director
Ellen Lafargue, Au.D., CCC, Director, Hearing Technology
Lois Kam Heymann, M.A., CCC, Director, Communication
Quarterly

8140 Listner
HEAR Center
301 E Del Mar Blvd
Pasadena, CA 91101-2714
626-796-2016
FAX: 626-796-2320
info@hearcenter.org
www.hearcenter.org

Ellen Simon, Executive Director
Berenice Castro, Accounting Supervisro
Debbie Lorino, Office Manager
Chronicals current events, spotlights pediatric and adult clients as well as community outreach events.
Semi-Quarterly

8141 NAD E-Zine
National Association of the Deaf
8630 Fenton Street
Suite 820
Silver Spring, MD 20910- 3819
301-587-1788
FAX: 301-587-1791
TTY:301-587-1789
www.nad.org

Bobbie Beth Scoggins, President
Christopher Wagner, Vice President
Includes up-to-the-minute information about the NAD, including Board news, advocacy, outreach and community activities, as well as NAD Conference and other information.

8142 NAHO News
National Association of Hearing Officials
PO Box 4999
Midlothian, VA 23112-17
701-328-3260
www.naho.org

Joy Wezelman, Editor
Janice Deshais, Editor
National Association of Hearing Officials newsletter.

8143 On the Level
Vestibular Disorders Association
5018 NE 15th Ave
Portland, OR 97211-5331
503-229-7705
800-837-8428
FAX: 503-229-8064
veda@vestibular.org
www.vestibular.org

Lisa Haven PhD, Executive Director
Jerry Underwood, Director
Vincente Honrubia, Director
Contents of each issue include information about local support groups, a calendar of conferences and training opportunities for health professionals, a list of donors, and special items indexed below. *$5.00*
12 pages Quarterly

8144 Pinnacle Newsletter
Academy of Rehabilitative Audiology
PO Box 26532
Minneapolis, MN 55426-532
952-920-0484
FAX: 952-920-6098
sherri.smith@va.gov
www.audrehab.org

John Greer Clark, Editor
Diana Derry, Co-Editor
Sherri Smith, Ph.D., Content Editor
Academy of Rehabilitative Audiology newsletter.

8145 Soundings Newsletter
American Hearing Research Foundation
8 South Michigan Avenue
Suite 1205
Chicago, IL 60603- 4539
312-726-9670
FAX: 312-726-9695
www.american-hearing.org

Sharon Parmet, Executive Director
Promote, conduct and furnish financial assistance for medical research into the cause, prevention and cure of deafness, impaired hearing and balance disorders; encourage the collaboration of clinical and laboratory research; encourage and improve teaching in the medical aspects of hearing problems; and disseminate the most reliable scientific knowledge to physicians, hearing professionals and the public.
Quarterly

8146 Spring Dell Center Newsletter
Spring Dell Center
6040 Radio Station Rd
La Plata, MD 20646-3368
301-934-4561
FAX: 301-870-2439
www.springdellcenter.org

Donna Retzlaff, Executive Director
Jody Loper, President
Brett Hamorsky, Vice President
Quarterly

8147 Vision Magazine
National Catholic Office of the Deaf
7202 Buchanan St
Hyattsville, MD 20784-2236
301-577-1684
FAX: 301-577-1684
info@ncod.org
www.ncod.org

Arvilla Rank, Editor/Executive Director
Published as a pastoral service for the deaf and hard of hearing. Provides information to members and others working in ministry.
$15.00
Quarterly

Audio/Visual

8148 **Christmas Stories**
Video Learning Library
15838 N 62nd St
Scottsdale, AZ 85254-1988

480-596-9970
800-383-8811
FAX: 480-596-9973
www.videolearning.com

Jim Spencer, Owner
Told by popular deaf story-tellers, the stories included are A Christmas Carol, Night Before Christmas, Story of the First Christmas Tree, Birth of Christ, The Great Walled City, and Little Match Girl. *$29.95*
Video/80 Mins 1986
ISBN 1-882257-02-2

8149 **Fantastic Series Videotape Set**
Gallaudet University Press
800 Florida Ave NE
Washington, DC 20002-3695

202-651-5488
800-621-2736
FAX: 202-651-5489
gupress@gallaudet.edu
www.gupress.gallaudet.edu

Rita Corey, Director
T. Alan Hurwitz, President
Paul Kelly, Vice President Adm. And Finance
These videotapes offer a blend of entertainment and information to both deaf and hearing children ages 6-10. A total of eight tapes in the series. *$254.00*
Video 8 VHS
ISBN 1-563680-12-2

8150 **Fantastic: Colonial Times, Chocolate, and Cars**
Gallaudet University Press
800 Florida Ave NE
Washington, DC 20002-3695

202-651-5488
800-621-2736
FAX: 202-651-5489
gupress@gallaudet.edu
www.gupress.gallaudet.edu

Rita Corey, Director
T. Alan Hurwitz, President
Paul Kelly, Vice President Adm. And Finance
Young viewers visit Colonial Williamsburg in Virginia to see various crafts. Other parts show chocolate being made, and films of old cars. *$39.95*
Video
ISBN 1-563680-06-8

8151 **Fantastic: Dogs at Work and Play**
Gallaudet University Press
800 Florida Ave NE
Washington, DC 20002-3695

202-651-5488
800-621-2736
FAX: 202-651-5489
gupress@gallaudet.edu
www.gupress.gallaudet.edu

Rita Corey, Director
T. Alan Hurwitz, President
Paul Kelly, Vice President Adm. And Finance
See how dogs are trained, including Fantastic's own hearing-ear dog, police dogs, plus puppies, and dogs in space? *$39.95*
Video
ISBN 1-563680-03-3

8152 **Fantastic: Exciting People, Places and Things!**
Gallaudet University Press
800 Florida Ave NE
Washington, DC 20002-3695

202-651-5488
800-621-2736
FAX: 202-651-5489
gupress@gallaudet.edu
www.gupress.gallaudet.edu

Rita Corey, Director
T. Alan Hurwitz, President
Paul Kelly, Vice President Adm. And Finance

Welcomes young viewers for a trip to a crayon factory, a jump rope tournament, and mime by actor Bernard Bragg. *$39.95*
Video
ISBN 1-563680-01-7

8153 **Fantastic: From Post Offices to Dairy Goats**
Gallaudet University Press
800 Florida Ave NE
Washington, DC 20002-3695

202-651-5488
800-621-2736
FAX: 202-651-5489
gupress@gallaudet.edu
www.gupress.gallaudet.edu

Rita Corey, Director
T. Alan Hurwitz, President
Paul Kelly, Vice President Adm. And Finance
In this video children follow the route of a letter from the mailbox through the post office to its final destination. Also, they visit dairy goats and other animals. *$39.95*
Video
ISBN 1-563680-05-X

8154 **Fantastic: Imagination, Actors, and 'Deaf Way'**
Gallaudet University Press
800 Florida Ave NE
Washington, DC 20002-3695

202-651-5488
800-621-2736
202-651-5508
FAX: 202-651-5489
gupress@gallaudet.edu
www.gupress.gallaudet.edu

Rita Corey, Director
T. Alan Hurwitz, President
Paul Kelly, Vice President Adm. And Finance
Deaf clowns, mimes, and actors display the wonders of imagination, along with performances at the international cultural celebration 'Deaf Way.' *$39.95*
Video
ISBN 1-563680-04-1

8155 **Fantastic: Roller Coasters, Maps, and Ice Cream!**
Gallaudet University Press
800 Florida Ave NE
Washington, DC 20002-3695

202-651-5488
800-621-2736
FAX: 202-651-5489
gupress@gallaudet.edu

Rita Corey, Director
T. Alan Hurwitz, President
Paul Kelly, Vice President Adm. And Finance
In this program Mike Montangino leads the way on rides at Kings Dominion, and also to see how maps are drawn, and how ice cream is made. *$39.95*
Video
ISBN 1-563680-07-6

8156 **Fantastic: Skiing, Factories, and Race Hores**
Gallaudet University Press
800 Florida Ave NE
Washington, DC 20002-3695

202-651-5488
800-621-2736
FAX: 202-651-5489
gupress@gallaudet.edu

Rita Corey, Director
T. Alan Hurwitz, President
Paul Kelly, Vice President Adm. And Finance
Snow Skiing starts this program, which continues in a factory where 'who-knows-what' is made. Also, young viewers learn about horse care, and also about the making of Oreos. *$39.95*
Video
ISBN 1-563680-08-4

8157 **Fantastic: Wonderful Worlds of Sports and Travel**
Gallaudet University Press
800 Florida Ave NE
Washington, DC 20002-3695   202-651-5488
                                    800-621-2736
                                 FAX: 202-651-5489
                              gupress@gallaudet.edu
Rita Corey, Director
T. Alan Hurwitz, President
Paul Kelly, Vice President Adm. And Finance
In this program, young viewers ride on a train, watch deaf athletes compete, and see actor Bernard Bragg perform 'The Lion and the Mouse.' *$39.95*
Video
ISBN 1-563680-02-5

8158 **Fingerspelling: Expressive and Receptive Fluency**
DawnSign Press
6130 Nancy Ridge Dr
San Diego, CA 92121-3223   858-625-0600
                                    800-549-5350
                                 FAX: 858-625-2336
                              info@dawnsign.com
                              www.dawnsign.com
Joe Dannis, President
Joyce Linden Groode, Fingerspelling Teacher
Improve your fingerspelling with this new video guide. A 24-page instructional booklet is included with fingerspelling practice suggestions. *$29.95*
120 Minutes
ISBN 1-581210-46-9

8159 **Getting Better**
Vestibular Disorders Association
5018 NE 15th Ave
Portland, OR 97211-5331   503-229-7705
                                    800-837-8428
                                 FAX: 503-229-8064
                              veda@vestibular.org
                              www.vestibular.org
Cynthia Ryan MBA, Executive Director
Tony Staser, Development Director
Vicente Honrubia, Director
Interviews with physicians, physical therapists, psychologists, social workers, and patients on Managing Symptoms, Diagnosis & Treatment, and Cognitive/Psychological Impacts. *$24.95*
Video

8160 **Helping the Family Understand**
Vestibular Disorders Association
5018 NE 15th Ave
Portland, OR 97211-5331   503-229-7705
                                    800-837-8428
                                 FAX: 503-229-8064
                              veda@vestibular.org
                              www.vestibular.org
Cynthia Ryan MBA, Executive Director
Tony Staser, Development Director
Vicente Honrubia, Director
Interviews with physicians, physical therapists, psychologists, social workers, and patients on Managing Symptoms, Diagnosis & Treatment and Cognitive/Psychological Impacts. *$24.95*
Video

8161 **Managing Your Symptoms**
Vestibular Disorders Association
5018 NE 15th Ave
Portland, OR 97211-5331   503-229-7705
                                    800-837-8428
                                 FAX: 503-229-8064
                              veda@vestibular.org
                              www.vestibular.org
Cynthia Ryan MBA, Executive Director
Tony Staser, Development Director
Vicente Honrubia, Director
Interviews with physicians, physical therapists, psychologists, social workers, and patients. on Managing Symptoms, Diagnosis & Treatment, and Cognitive/Psychological Impacts. *$24.95*
Video

Sports

8162 **American Hearing Impaired Hockey Association**
4214 W. 77th Place
Chicago, IL 60652-1618   978-922-0955
                              FAX: 312-829-2098
                              kkmm2won@aol.com
                              www.ahiha.org
Stan Mikita, President
Cheryl Hager, General Manager
Helen Tovey, Registrar, USA Hockey Reg.
The American Hearing Impaired Hockey Association provides deaf and hard of hearing hockey players the opportunity to learn about and improve their hockey skills through our program. We offer these hockey players the opportunity to be coached by a coaching staff with college, national and international experience.

8163 **USA Deaf Sports Federation**
102 N Krohn Pl
PO Box 910338
Lexington, KY 40591-0338   605-367-5760
                              FAX: 605-782-8441
                              TTY:605-367-5761
Jack C Lamberton, President
Mark Apodaca, VP Of Financial Affairs
William J Bowman, VP Of International Affairs
The USA Deaf Sports Federation's purpose was to foster and regulate uniform rules of competition and provide social outlets for deaf members and their friends; serve as a parent organization for regional sports organizations; conduct annual athletic competitions; and assist in the participation of U.S. teams in international competition.

Support Groups

8164 **Dial-a-Hearing Screening Test**
Occupational Hearing Services Inc.
300 S Chester Rd
Suite 301
Swarthmore, PA 19081-1800   610-544-7700
                              800-622-3277
                              FAX: 610-543-2802
George Biddle, President/Owner
James Biddle, Vice President
Phyllis Biddle, Treasurer
A national telephone resource providing information about hearing impairments and deafness. Dial-A-Hearing Screening Test: national test number for free telephone hearing test: 1-800-222-EARS, MON-FRI: 9:00 AM to 5:00 PM Eastern time.

Mobility

Associations

8165 Academy of Spinal Cord Injury Professionals
206 S. 6th St
Springfield, IL 62701   217-321-2488
FAX: 217-525-1271
www.academyscipro.org
Destiny Nance-Evans, Director Of Memebership Services
Kim Ruff, Director Of Education
An interdisciplinary organization dedicated to advancing the care of people with spinal cord injury/dysfunction, providing resources, research, and insights for SCI/D professionals.

8166 Academy of Spinal Cord Injury Professionals: Psychologists, Social Workers & Counselors
Academy of Spinal Cord Injury Professionals
206 S. 6th St.
Springfield, IL 62701   217-321-2488
FAX: 217-525-1271
www.academyscipro.org/
Heather Russell, President, PSWC Section
Lisa Beck, President, Academy of Spinal Cord Injury Professionals
Toby Huston, Vice President
Organizes and operates for scientific and educational purposes to advance and improve the psychosocial care of persons with spinal cord impairment, develops and promotes education and research related to the psychosocial care of persons with spinal cord injury, recognizes psychologists and social workers whose careers are devoted to the problems of spinal cord impairment.

8167 Acid Maltase Deficiency Association
P.O. Box 700248
San Antonio, TX 78270-0248   210-494-6144
FAX: 210-490-7161
TiffanyLHouse@aol.com
www.amda-pompe.org
Tiffany House, President
The Acid Maltase Deficiency Association offers resource materials to help raise awareness and provide education and insight into Pompe disease (a.k.a. Acid Maltase Deficiency), a rare genetic disease derived from the family of Lysosomal Storage Disease. The association offers information for patients, their families, as well as medical professionals.

8168 American Academy of Osteopathy
The Pyramids
3500 DePauw Blvd.
Suite 1100
Indianapolis, IN 46268-1136   317-879-1881
FAX: 317-879-0563
info@academyofosteopathy.org
www.academyofosteopathy.org
Sherri Quarles, Interim Executive Director & Accountant
Michael P. Rowane, DO, MS, FAOO, President
The mission of the American Academy of Osteopathy is to teach, advocate, and research the science, art and philosophy of osteopathic medicine, emphasizing the integration of osteopathic principles, practice and manipulative treatment in patient care.

8169 American Association of Neuromuscular & Electrodiagnostic Medicine
2621 Superior Drive NW
Rochester, MN 55901   507-288-0100
FAX: 507-288-1225
aanem@aanem.org
www.aanem.org
Shirlyn A. Adkins, JD, Executive Director
Scott Gerdes, Finance Director
Lori Nierman, Office Manager
The American Association of Neuromuscular & Electrodiagnostic Medicine (AANEM) is a nonprofit membership association dedicated to the advancement of neuromuscular (NM), musculoskeletal, and electrodiagnostic (EDX) medicine.

8170 American Back Society
St. Joseph's Professional Center
2647 E. 14th St.
Suite 401
Oakland, CA 94601   510-536-9929
FAX: 510-536-1812
www.chiroweb.com/hp/abs/index.html
Philip E. Greenman, D.O., FAAO, President
Alexander Hadjipavlou, MD, MSc, 1st Vice President
Stephen Esses, BSc, MD, 2nd Vice President
The American Back Society is a non-profit organization dedicated to providing an interdisciplinary educational forum for healthcare professionals committed to relieving pain and diminishing impairment in patients suffering from neck and back conditions through proper diagnosis and treatment.

8171 American Parkinson Disease Association
135 Parkinson Avenue
Staten Island, NY 10305   800-223-2732
FAX: 718-981-4399
apda@apdaparkinson.org
www.apdaparkinson.org
Leslie A. Chambers, President & CEO
Stephanie Paul, Vice President, Development and Marketing
Robin Kornhaber, MSW, Vice President, Programs and Services
APDA was founded in 1961 with the dual purpose to find the curefor Parkinson's disease, and to assist Americans living with Parkinson's disease live a quality life.

8172 American Spinal Injury Association
9702 Gayton Rd.
Suite 306
Richmond, VA 23238   877-274-2724
asia.office@asia-spinalinjury.org
www.asia-spinalinjury.org
Patty Duncan, Executive Director
Carolyn Moffatt, Association Manager
Kim Ruff, Administrative Assistant
Professional association for physicans and other health professionals working in all aspects of spinal cord injury.

8173 American Stroke Association
7272 Greenville Ave
Dallas, TX 75231   888-478-7653
strokeconnection@heart.org
www.strokeassociation.org/STROKEORG
John Warner, President
James Postl, Chairman
Nancy Brown, Chief Executive Officer
The American Stroke Association offers educational materials, seminars, conferences and transportation for those effected by strokes as well as their families, caregivers and interested professionals.

8174 Amytrophic Lateral Sclerosis Association
1275 K Street NW
Suite 250
Washington, DC 20005   202-407-8580
FAX: 202-464-8869
alsinfo@alsa-national.org
www.alsa.org
Barbara Newhouse, President/CEO
Calaneet Balas, Executive Vice President, Strategy
Gregory L. Mitchell, Executive Vice President, Finance & Administration
The ALS association is the only national not-for-profit health organization dedicated soley to lead the fight against ALS. The Association covers all the bases-research, patient and community services, public education, and advocacy-in providing help and hope to those facing the disease. The mission is to lead the fight to cure and treat ALS through global cutting edge research, and to empower people with Lou Gehrig's disease to live fuller lives & provide them with compassion, care and support.

8175   Arthritis Foundation
1355 Peachtree St NE
6th Floor
Atlanta, GA 30309   404-872-7100
                                                    800-283-7800
                                                    www.arthritis.org
Laurie Stewart, Secretary/Vice Chair
Rowland W. (Bing) Chang, Chair
Frank Longobardi, Treasurer
Offers information and referrals regarding educational materials
and programs, fund-raising, support groups, seminars and conferences, and aids Americans with arthritis in accessing optimal
care.

**8176   Association for Neurologically Impaired Brain Injured
Children**
61-35 220th St
Oakland Gardens, NY 11364   718-423-9550
                                                    FAX: 718-423-9838
                                                    jdebiase@anibic.org
                                                    www.anibic.org
Vincent Tancredi, Chief Financial Officer
John F DeBiase, Executive Director
Rachel Plakstis, MSC Director
ANIBIc is a voluntary, multi-service organization that is dedi-
cated to serving individuals with severe learning disabilities,
neurological impairments and other developmental disabilities.
Services include: residential, vocational, family support services, recreation (children and adults), respite (adult), in home
support services, counseling and traumatic brain injury services
(adults).

8177   Capital Area Parkinsons Society
PO Box 27565
Austin, TX 78755-2565   512-371-3373
                                                    www.capitalareaparkinsons.org
Tereasa Ford, President
Deborah Bryson, Vice President
Donna Hohm, Secretary
Founded in 1984, the Capital Area Parkinson's Society addresses
the needs for those impacted by Parkinson's disease in central
Texas. The organization offers a multitude of support groups, re-
sources, monthly meetings, exercise programs and a community
for people afflicted by Parkinson's and their care partners.

8178   Children's Hemiplegia & Stroke Association
4101 W. Green Oaks Blvd
Suite 305-149
Arlington, TX 76016   www.chasa.org
Nancy Atwood, Executive Director & Founder
Jana Smoot White, President
Patti Scrivano, Vice President
Founded in 1996, CHASA offers support and information to fam-
ilies of infants, children and young adults who have hemiplegia,
hemiparesis or hemiplegic cerebral palsy.

8179   Christopher & Dana Reeve Paralysis Resource Center
636 Morris Turnpike
Suite 3A
Short Hills, NJ 07078   973-467-8270
                                                    800-225-0292
                                                    InfoSpecialist@ChristopherReeve.org
                                                    www.christopherreeve.org
John M Hughes, Chairman
John E McConnell, Vice Chairman
Peter Wilderotter, President & CEO
The Paralysis Resource Center's goal is to provide support and
information to those living with paralysis and their caregivers.
Some programs offered include financial grants, a family support
program, advocay programs, a lending library, rehabilitation cen-
ters, a veteran program and a resource guide about paralysis.

8180   Consortium of Multiple Sclerosis Centers
3 University Plaza Dr.
Suite 116
Hackensack, NJ 07601   201-487-1050
                                                    FAX: 862-772-7275
                                                    www.mscare.org
June Halper, Chief Executive Officer
Gary Cutter, PhD, President
Lisa Skutnik, Chief Operating Officer

CMSC provides leadership in clinical research and education; develops vehicles to share information and knowledge among members; disseminates information to the health care community and
to persons affected by Multiple Sclerosis; and develops and implements mechanisms to influence health care delivery.

8181   Cure SMA
Cure SMA
925 Busse Rd
Elk Grove Village, IL 60007   800-886-1762
                                                    info@curesma.org
                                                    www.curesma.org
Jill Jarecki, Chief Scientific Officer
Kenneth Hobby, President
Richard Rubenstein, Chair
Cure SMA is the largest international organization dedicated
solely to eradicating spinal muscular atrophy (SMA) by promot-
ing and supporting research, helping families cope with SMA
through informational programs and support, and educating the
public and professional community about SMA.

8182   Dystonia Advocacy Network
One East Wacker Drive
Suite 2810
Chicago, IL 60601   dystonia-advocacy.org
Established in 2007, The Dystonia Advocacy Network (DAN) is
an organization of dystonia-affected individuals and organiza-
tions united in speaking on legislative and public policy issues
which impact the dystonia community.

8183   Epilepsy Foundation
8301 Professional Place E
Suite 200
Landover, MD 20785- 2353   800-332-1000
                                                    FAX: 301-459-1569
                                                    ContactUs@efa.org
                                                    www.epilepsy.com
Robert W Smith, Chair
Phillip M. Gattone, M.Ed, Preisdent & CEO
M. Vaneeda Bennett, Chief Development Officer
The organization works to ensure that people with epilepsy are
able to participate in all life experiences; to improve how people
with epilepsy are perceived and treated in society; and to promote
research for a cure.

8184   Friends of Disabled Adults and Children
4900 Lewis Rd
Stone Mountain, GA 30083   770-491-9014
                                                    866-977-1204
                                                    www.fodac.org
Chris Brand, President
Pam Holley, Director of Administration
Betty Felder, DME Office Manager
FODAC's mission is to provide durable medical equipment
(DME) at lost cost to the disabled and their families, and to en-
hance the quality of life for individuals with disabilities or
illnesses.

**8185   Head Injury Rehabilitation And Referral Service, Inc.
(HIRRS)**
11 Taft Court
Suite 100
Rockville, MD 20850   301-309-2228
                                                    FAX: 301-309-2278
                                                    tbi@headinjuryrehab.org
                                                    www.headinjuryrehab.org
Maggie Hunter, Director of Admissions and Quality Assurance
Robert Cousland, Director of Rehabilitation
Ricardo Hunter, President
Head Injury Rehabilitation and Referral Services, Inc. (HIRRS)
is a private not-for-profit agency that provides comprehensive
brain injury support including long-term living, daily programs,
vocational supports and services to individuals that live in the
community. The agency is located in Rockville, MD, but serves
the DC Metropolitan area.

8186   International Parkinson and Movement Disorder Society
555 East Wells St.
Suite 1100
Milwaukee, WI 53202-3823   414-276-2145
                                        FAX: 414-276-3349
                              info@movementdisorders.org
                              www.movementdisorders.org

Christopher Goetz, MD, President
Susan Fox, PhD, Secretary
Victor Fung, MBBS, PhD, FRACP, Treasurer
The International Parkinson and Movement Disorder Society
(MDS) is a professional society of clinicians, scientists, and other
healthcare professionals who are interested in Parkinson's disease, related neurodegenerative and neurodevelopmental disorders, hyperkinetic movement disorders, and abnormalities in
muscle tone and motor control.

8187   Lewy Body Dementia Association
912 Killian Hill Road S.W.
Lilburn, GA 30047   404-975-2322
                                        FAX: 480-422-5434
                                             www.lbda.org

Christina M. Christie, President
Shannon McCarty-Caplan, Vice President
Mike Koehler, CEO
The Lewy Body Dementia Association (LBDA) is a nonprofit organization dedicated to raising awareness of the Lewy body
dementias (LBD), supporting people affected by LBD, and promoting scientific advances.

8188   Mobility International USA
132 E Broadway
Suite 343
Eugene, OR 97401   541-343-1284
                                        FAX: 541-343-6812
                                         TTY:541-343-1284
                              clearinghouse@miusa.org
                                            www.miusa.org

Susan Sygall, Chief Executive Officer
Cindy Lewis, Director, Programs
A US based national nonprofit organization dedicated to empowering people with disabilities around the world through leadership development, training and international exchange to ensure
inclusion of people with disabilities in international exchange
and development programs. The National Clearinghouse on Disability & Exchange, a joint project managed by MIUSA, provides
free information and referrals.

8189   Multiple Sclerosis Association of America
375 Kings Hwy N
Cherry Hill, NJ 08034   800-532-7667
                                        FAX: 856-661-9797
                                        msaa@mymsaa.org
                                              mymsaa.org/

John McCorry, Chair
Monica Derbes Gibson, Vice Chair
Steve Bruneau, Treasurer
MSAA is a national non-profit organization dedicated to enrich-
ing the quality of life for evryone affected by Multiple Sclerosis
through vital services and support.

8190   Multiple Sclerosis Foundation
6520 N. Andrews Ave
Fort Lauderdale, FL 33309-2132   954-776-6805
                                             800-225-6495
                                        FAX: 954-938-8708
                                        admin@msfocus.org
                                            www.msfocus.org

Jules Kuperberg, Executive Director
Alan Segaloff, Co- Executive Director
Kasey Minnis, Director, Operations & Communications
A national, nonprofit organization that provides free support services and public education for persons with Multiple Sclerosis,
newsletters, toll-free phone support, information, referrals, home
care, assitive technology, and support groups.

8191   NBIA Disorders Association
2082 Monaco Ct.
El Cajon, CA 92019-4235   619-588-2315
                                        FAX: 619-588-4093
                              info@NBIAdisorders.org
                              www.nbiadisorders.org

Patricia Wood, President
Coleen Lukoff, Development Director
Melissa Woods, Social Media Director
NBIA provides support to families, educates the public and accel-
erates research with collaborators from around the world.

8192   National Association for Continence
P.O. Box 1019
Charleston, SC 29402   800-252-3337
                                        sgregg@nafc.org
                                              www.nafc.org

Katherine F. Jeter, EdD, Founder
Steven G. Gregg, PhD, Executive Director
Donna Deng, Chairperson
NAFC's mission is to educate the public about the causes, diagnosis, categories, treatment options and management alternatives
for incontinence, voiding dysfunction and related pelvic floor
disorders; to network with other organizations and agencies; to
elevate the visibility and priority given to these areas; and to advocate on behalf of consumers who suffer from such symptoms as
a result of disease or other illness.

**8193   National Center for Health, Physical Activity and
Disability**
4000 Ridgeway Dr.
Birmingham, AL 35209   800-900-8086
                                        FAX: 205-313-7475
                                        nchpad@uab.edu
                                            www.nchpad.org

James Rimmer, Principal Investigator
Angela Grant, Business Manager
Jeff Underwood, Program Director
NCHPAD promotes health for people with disability through in-
creased participation in all types of physical and social activities.
These include fitness and aquatic activities, recreational and
sports programs, adaptive equipment usage, and more.
1999

8194   National Coalition for Assistive and Rehab Technology
54 Towhee Court
East Amhurst, NY 14051   716-839-9728
                                        FAX: 716-839-9624
                                             info@ncart.us
                                              www.ncart.us

Don Clayback, Executive Director
Doug Westerdahl, President
Greg Packer, Vice President
The coalition's mission is to ensure proper and appropriate access
to complex rehab and assistive technologies.

8195   National Council on Independent Living (NCIL)
P.O. Box 31260
Washington, DC 20006   202-207-0334
                                             844-778-7961
                                        FAX: 202-207-0341
                                        TTY: 202-207-0340
                                             ncil@ncil.org
                                              www.ncil.org

Theo Braddy, Executive Director
Jenny Sichel, Director, Operations
Denise Law, Coordinator, Member Services
A national cross-disability grassroots organization, NCIL ad-
vances independent living and the rights of people with disabili-
ties through consumer-driven advocacy.

8196   National Fibromyalgia Association
3857 Birch St.
Suite 312
Newport Beach, CA 92660   nfa@fmaware.org
                                              www.fmaware.org

Lynne Matallana, President/Founder
National Fibromyalgia Association's mission is to develop and
execute programs dedicated to improving the quality of life for
people with fibromyalgia.

8197 National Mobility Equipment Dealers Association
3327 West Bearss Ave
Tampa, FL 33618 813-264-2697
866-948-8341
FAX: 813-962-8970
info@nmeda.org
www.nmeda.com

Chad Blake, President
Richard May, Vice President
Bill Koeblitz, Secretary
The National Mobility Equipment Dealers Association (NMEDA) is a non-profit trade association dedicated creating and expanding oppotunities of safe transportation for people with disabilities in vehicles modified to fit their specific needs.

8198 National Spasmodic Dysphonia Association
300 Park Blvd.
Suite 335
Itasca, IL 60143 800-795-6732
FAX: 630-250-4505
nsda@dysphonia.org
www.dysphonia.org

Charlie Reavis, President
Marcia Sterling, Treasurer
Kimberly Kuman, Executive Director
The National Spasmodic Dysphonia Association (NSDA) is a not-for-profit organization dedicated to advancing medical research into the causes of and treatments for SD, promoting physician and public awareness of the disorder, and providing support to those affected by SD through symposiums, support groups, and on-line resources.

8199 National Spasmodic Torticollis Association
9920 Talbert Ave
Fountain Valley, CA 92708 714-378-9837
800-487-8385
NSTAmail@aol.com
www.torticollis.org

Ken Price, President/Treasurer
Diane Truong, Vice President
Janelle Lazzo, Secretary
The mission of the National Spasmodic Torticollis Association is to support the needs and well being of individuals affected by Spasmodic Torticollis; to promote awareness and education; and to advance research for more treatments and a cure.

8200 Paralyzed Veterans of America
801 18th St. NW
Washington, DC 20006-3517 800-424-8200
TTY:800-795-4327
info@pva.org
www.pva.org

Charles Brown, National President
Marcus Murray, National Secretary
Carl Blake, Executive Director
A national organization serving veterans and individuals with spinal cord injury/disorder (SCI/D), as well as their family members and caregivers.

8201 Parkinson's Disease Research Society
Northwestern Medicine Central DuPage Hospital
25 N. Winfield Rd
4 North Tower
Winfield, IL 60190 630-933-4384
FAX: 630-933-3077
parkinsonsprogress.org

Carol A. Santi, President
Alex Katz, Vice President
Mitchell King, Treasurer
The PDRS mandate is to mount a concerted effort to intensify the research, both in the basic science laboratory as well as with clinical trials, to advance the diagnosis, treatment and prevention of Parkinson's disease.

8202 Simon Foundation for Continence
P.O. Box 815
Wilmette, IL 60091 847-864-3913
800-237-4666
FAX: 847-864-9758
webmaster@simonfoundation.org
www.simonfoundation.org

Cheryl B. Gartley, Founder/President
Elizabeth A. LaGro, Vice President, Communications & Education Services
Twila Yednock, Director of Special Events
The Simon Foundation is known throughout the world for its innovative educational projects and tireless efforts on behalf of people with loss of bladder and bowel control. The mission of the foundation is to remove the stigma surrounding incontinence and to provide help for people with incontinence, their families, and the healthcare professionals who provide care for people with incontinence.

8203 Society for Progressive Supranuclear Palsy
30 E. Padonia Road,
Suite 201
Timonium, MD 21093 800-457-4777
FAX: 410-785-7009
info@curepsp.org
www.psp.org

Janet Edmunson, Med, Chair
Dan Johnson, Vice-Chair
George S. Jankiewicz, CPA, CFP, Treasurer
Members of the Board of Directors of CurePSP accept the major responsibility of implementing the mission of the Foundation for PSP | CBD and Related Brain Diseases. Board members are actively involved in continually defining and redefining the mission and participating in strategic planning to review purposes, programs, priorities, funding needs, and levels of achievement.

8204 United Spinal Association
120-34 Queens Blvd
Ste 320
Kew Gardens, NY 11415 718-803-3782
FAX: 718-803-0414
www.unitedspinal.org
United Spinal Association is dedicated to enhancing the quality of life of all people living with spinal cord injuries and disorders, including veterans, and providing support and information to loved ones, care providers and professionals.

8205 Vermont Back Research Center
1 S Prospect St
Burlington, VT 05405 802-656-3131
FAX: 802-660-9243
learn@uvm.edu
www.uvm.edu
Conducts research aimed at reducing back-related disability following injury or acute pain episodes. Current research includes studies of posture, seating, vibration, materials handling, and exercise. The Center develops and tests assistive devices, and promotes employment of people with back disorders and rapid return to work after injury. The staff provides a variety of information services, including bibliographic searches and fact finding.

8206 World Chiropractic Alliance
2683 Via De La Valle
Suite G 629
Del Mar, CA 92014 480-786-9235
866-789-8073
FAX: 480-732-9313
www.worldchiropracticalliance.org

Linda Bevel, Manager
Terry A Rondberg DC, Founder/CEO
The World Chiropractic Alliance was founded in 1989 as a non-profit organization dedicated to protecting and strengthening chiropractic around the world. Since its inception, the WCA has played an important role in the global chiropractic community. In 1998, it was granted status as a Non-Governmental Organization (NGO) associated with the United Nations Department of Public Information.

Camps

8207 Camp Esperanza
Southern California Chapter
West 6th Street
Suite 1250
Los Angeles, CA 90017   323-954-5760
                               800-954-2873
                        FAX: 213-954-5790
                        jziegler@arthritis.org
                        www.arthritis.org

Jennifer Ziegler, Camp Director
Lindsey Gonzales, Regional Director, Human Resources
Manuel Loya, Chief Executive Officer
A one-week camp in August that allows children with arthritis to participate in such activities as horseback riding, swimming, etc. in a fun-filled environment.

8208 Easterseals Camp Stand by Me
Easterseals Washington
17809 S Vaughn Rd. NW
PO Box 289
Vaughn, WA 98394   253-884-2722
                        campadmin@wa.easterseals.com
                        www.easterseals.com/washington

Cathy Bisaillon, President & CEO
Angela Cox, Camp Director
Camp Stand By Me provides a safe, barrier-free environment for children and adults with any disability to experience all aspects of camp without limitations. Respite weekends offered throughout the year. Activities include campfires, fishing, swimming, sports, archery, and more.

8209 Hillcroft Services
501 W Air Park Dr.
Muncie, IN 47303   765-284-4166
                        www.hillcroft.org

Debbie Bennett, President & CEO
Abby Halstead, Chief Financial Officer
Jessica Hammett, Chief Operations Officer
Offers a summer camp program for children with autism spectrum disorders.

8210 Illinois Wheelchair Sport Camps
University of Illinois
1207 S Oak St.
Champaign, IL 61820   217-333-1970
                        FAX: 217-244-0014
                        sportscamp@illinois.edu
                        www.disability.illinois.edu/camps
Wheelchair sport programs including track, basketball, and individual skills camps. Hosted at the University of Illinois.

8211 Rising Treetops at Oakhurst
111 Monmouth Rd.
Oakhurst, NJ 07755   732-531-0215
                        FAX: 732-531-0292
                        info@risingtreetops.org
                        www.risingtreetops.org

Robert Pacenza, Executive Director
Charles Sutherland, Camp Director
Lori Schenck, Assistant Director, Services
A summer and day camp for adults and children with special needs, including autism and physical and intellectual disabilities. Campers experience traditional camp activities while gaining skills for greater independence.

8212 Twin Lakes Camp
1451 E Twin Lakes Rd
Hillsboro, IN 47949-8004   765-798-4000
                        outdoors@twinlakescamp.com
                        www.twinlakescamp.com

Jon Beight, Executive Director
Duane Bush, Guest Service
Dan Daily, Program Director
Provides a summer camp program for special needs children and young adults. Campers suffer from a wide range of maladies including crippling accidents, Spina Bifida, epilepsy, Cerebral Palsy, Muscular Dystrophy, Quadriplegia, Paraplegia, and other disabling diseases. Campers range in age from 8 to 27.

8213 YMCA Camp Fitch
12600 Abels Rd.
North Springfield, PA 16430   814-922-3219
                               877-863-4824
                        FAX: 814-922-7000
                        registrar@campfitchymca.org
                        campfitchymca.org

Tom Parker, Executive Director
Joe Wolnik, Summer Camp Director
Brandy Duda, Outdoor Education Director
Camp is located in North Springfield, Pennsylvania. Camp programs include sessions for children with diabetes or epilepsy.

Books

8214 Adapted Physical Education and Sport
Human Kinetics, Inc.
1607 N Market Street
Champaign, IL 61820-2220   217-351-5076
                               800-747-4457
                        FAX: 217-351-1549
                        info@hkusa.com
                        www.naspem.org

Joseph P Winnick EdD, Author
Scott Kimberly, Owner
Rainer Martens, President/Treasurer
Designed as a resource for both present and future physical education leaders, this book is an exceptional book for teaching exceptional children. It emphasizes the physical education of young people with disabilities. *$68.00*
592 pages Hardcover
ISBN 0-736052-16-X

8215 Arthritis Bible
Inner Traditions - Bear & Company
PO Box 388
Rochester, VT 05767-0388   802-767-3174
                               800-246-8648
                        FAX: 802-767-3726
                        customerservice@innertraditions.com
                        www.innertraditions.com

Craig Weatherby, Author
Leonid Gordin MD, Co-Author
A comprehensive guide to the alternative therapies and conventional treatments for Arthritic diseases including Osteoarthritis, Rheumatoid Arthritis, Gout, Fibromyalgia and more. *$16.95*
272 pages Paperback 1999
ISBN 0-892818-25-5

8216 Arthritis Helpbook: A Tested Self Management Program for Coping with Arthritis
Da Capo Press
44 Farnsworth Street,
Boston, MA 02210   617-252-5200
                        FAX: 617-252-5265
                        www.dacapopress.com

Kate Lorig, Author
James Fries, Co-Author
The Arthritis Helpbook is the world's leading guide to coping with joint pain, and has been used by more than 600,000 readers over its twenty years in print. It succeeds because of its tested advice, its hundreds of useful hints, and its emphasis on self-management-helping people with arthritis and fibromyalgia to achieve their own health goals. *$18.95*
Paperback
ISBN 0-738210-38-2

8217 Arthritis Sourcebook
McGraw-Hill Professional
7500 Chavenelle Rd
Dubuque, IA 52002-9655   563-584-6000
                               877-833-5524
                        FAX: 614-759-3749
                        www.mhprofessional.com

Earl J Brewer Jr MD, Author
Kathy Cochran Angel, Co-Author

A comprehensive guide to the latest information on treatments, medications, and alternative therapies for arthritis. *$16.95*
272 pages Paperback
ISBN 0-737303-81-6

8218   Arthritis, What Exercises Work: Breakthrough Relief for the Rest of Your Life
MacMillan - St. Martin's Press
175 5th Ave
New York, NY 10010-7703
646-307-5151
FAX: 212-420-9314
press.inquiries@macmillanusa.com
www.us.macmillan.com

Dava Sorbel, Author
Arthur C Klein, Co-Author
What is the most powerful arthritis treatment ever developed to help restore you to a healthy, pain-free, and vigorous life—for the rest of your life? It's exercise. Here are the right exercised for your kind of arthritis, pain-level, age, occupation, and hobbies. *$14.99*
200 pages Paperback 1995
ISBN 0-312130-25-2

8219   Arthritis: A Take Care of Yourself Health Guide
Da Capo Press
44 Farnsworth Street,
Boston, MA 02210
617-252-5200
FAX: 617-252-5265
www.dacapopress.com

James F Fries, Author
Donald M Vickery, Co-Author
In this updated book the author draws on new research to recommend exercises and new pain medications for both arthritis and fibromyalgia. *$18.95*
Paperback 1909
ISBN 0-738202-25-8

8220   Disability and Sport
Human Kinetics, Inc.
1607 N Market Street
Champaign, IL 61820-2220
217-351-5076
800-747-4457
FAX: 217-351-1549
info@hkusa.com
www.naspem.org

Karen P DePauw, Author
Susan J Gavron, Co-Author
Scott Kimberley, Owner
Provides a comprehensive and practical look at the past, present, and future of disability sport. Topics covered are inclusive of youth through adult participation with in-depth coverage of the essential issues involving athletes with disabilities. This new edition has updated references and new chapter-opening outlines that assist with individual study and class discussions. *$48.00*
408 pages Hardcover
ISBN 0-736046-38-0

8221   Fitness Programming for Physical Disabilities
Human Kinetics, Inc.
1607 N Market Street
Champaign, IL 61820-2220
217-351-5076
800-747-4457
FAX: 217-351-1549
info@hkusa.com
www.naspem.org

Patricia D Miller, Editor
Scott Kimberley, Owner
Rainer Martens, President/Treasurer
A book offering information for developing and conducting exercise programs for groups that included people with physical disabilities. A dozen authorities in exercise science and adapted exercise programming explain how to effectively and safely modify existing programs for individuals with physical disabilities. *$42.00*
232 pages Paperback
ISBN 0-873224-34-5

8222   Freedom from Arthritis Through Nutrition
Tree of Life Publications
PO Box 126
Joshua Tree, CA 92252-0126
760-366-2937
FAX: 760-366-2937
www.treelifebooks.com

Philip J Welsh DDS ND, Author
Bianca Leonardo ND, Co-Author
Reveals the results of 60 years of research on arthritis by noted nutritionist, Dr. Philip J. Welsh, D.D.S. N.D. Here you will find simple, natural, inexpensive, tested ways of coping with the various forms of arthritis, using only nutrition and other natural methods. There are no drugs or gadgets in this program. *$24.95*
255 pages Softcover

8223   Functional Electrical Stimulation for Ambulation by Paraplegics
Krieger Publishing Company
1725 Krieger Drive
PO Box 9542
Malabar, FL 32950
321-724-9542
800-724-0025
FAX: 321-951-3671
info@krieger-publishing.com
www.krieger-publishing.com

Daniel Graupe, Author
Kate H Kohn, Co-Author
FES is employed to enable spinal cord injury patients who are complete paraplegics to stand and ambulate without bracing. The text covers 12 years of amulation experience. *$49.50*
210 pages Paperback 1994
ISBN 0-894648-45-4

8224   Guide to Managing Your Arthritis
Arthritis Foundation
1330 W. Peachtree St
Suite 100
Atlanta, GA 30309
404-872-7100
800-283-7800
FAX: 404-237-8153
AFOrders@pbd.com
www.arthritis.org

Mary Anne Dunkin, Author
John Klippel, President/CEO
Cecile Perich, Chairman
Expert reviewers answer questions about basic arthritis facts, treatments, research, surgery and more. Also, specific information about six common conditions: rheumatoid arthritis, osteoarthritis, osteoporosis, fibromyalgia, lupus and gout. *$9.95*
193 pages Paperback
ISBN 0-912423-28-5

8225   How to Deal with Back Pain and Rheumatoid Joint Pain: A Preventive and Self Treatment Manua
Global Health Solutions
2146 Kings Garden Way
Falls Church, VA 22043-2593
703-848-2333
800-759-3999
FAX: 703-848-0028
information@watercure.com
www.watercure.com

Fereydoon Batmanghelidj, Author
Xiaopo Batmanjhelidj, President
Kristin Swan, Administrator
The physiology of pain production and its direct relationship to chronic regional dehydration of some joint spaces is explained: Special movements that would create vacuum in the disc spaces and draw water and the displaced discs into the vertebral joints are demonstrated. *$14.95*
100 pages Paperback
ISBN 0-962994-20-0

8226 Inclusive Games
Human Kinetics
1607 N Market Street
PO Box 5076
Champaign, IL 61825- 5076　　217-351-5076
800-747-4457
FAX: 217-351-1549
info@hkusa.com
www.humankinetics.com

Susan L Kasser, Author
Scott Kimberley, Owner
Rainer Martens, President/Treasurer
Features more than 50 games, helpful illustrations, and hundreds
of game variations. The book shows how to adapt games so that
children of every ability level can practice, play and improve
their movement skills together. The game finder makes it easy to
locate an appropriate game according to its name, approximate
grade level, difficulty within the grade level, skills required/de-
veloped, and number of players. *$17.95*
120 pages Paperback
ISBN 0-873226-39-9

**8227 Inside The Halo and Beyond: The Anatomy of a
Recovery**
WW Norton & Company
500 5th Ave
New York, NY 10110-2　　212-354-5500
FAX: 212-869-0856
www.wwnorton.com

Maxine Kumin, Author
W Drake McFeely, Chairman/President
Stephen King, VP Finance/CFO
A skilled horsewoman and lifelong athlete, poet Kumin was 73
when a riding accident left her with two broken vertebrae in her
neck. Kumin survived in the face of overwhelming odds that she
would be paralyzed for the rest of her life. Miraculously, however, she was walking again within weeks of the accident; now,
though one hand and an arm remain partially immobilized, her
life has largely resumed its normal course. Here is the journal of
her first nine months of recovery. *$13.95*
192 pages Softcover
ISBN 0-393049-00-0

8228 Life on Wheels: For the Active Wheelchair User
Patient-Centered Guides
1005 Gravenstein Highway North
Sebastopol, CA 95472　　707-827-7000
FAX: 707-829-0104
support@oreilly.com
www.oreilly.com

Gary Karp, Author
For 1.5 million Americans, life includes a wheelchair for mobility. Life on Wheels is for people who want to take charge of their
life experience. Author Gary Karp describes medical issues (paralysis, circulation, rehab, cure research); day-to-day living (exercise, skin, bowel and bladder, sexuality, home access,
maintaining a wheelchair); and social issues (self-image, adjustment, friends, family, cultural attitudes, activism). *$24.00*
565 pages Paperback 1999
ISBN 1-565922-53-0

8229 Paralysis Resource Guide
Christopher and Dana Reeve Paralysis Resource Ctr
636 Morris Turnpike
Suite 3A
Short Hills, NJ 07078　　973-467-8270
800-539-7309
FAX: 973-912-9433
information@christopherreeve.org
www.paralysis.org

John M. Hughes, Chairman
John E. McConnell, Vice Chair
Matthew Reeve, Vice Chair
A comprehensive information tool for people affected by paraly-
sis and for those who care for them. English or Spanish.
336 pages

8230 Primer on the Rheumatic Diseases
Arthritis Foundation
1330 W. Peachtree St
Suite 100
Atlanta, GA 30309-2111　　404-872-7100
800-933-7023
FAX: 404-237-8153
AFOrders@pbd.com
www.arthritis.org

Rob Shaw, President
Patience White M.D., Editor
John H. Klippel, Editor
The leading professional book about arthritis and related dis-
eases, the Primer is published by Springer and the Arthritis Foun-
dation. *$79.95*
724 pages Softcover
ISBN 0-387356-64-8

8231 Sport Science Review: Adapted Physical Activity
Human Kinetics
1607 N Market Street
Champaign, IL 61820-2220　　217-351-5076
800-747-4457
FAX: 217-351-1549
info@hkusa.com
www.naspem.org

Rainer Martens, President/Treasurer
Scott Kimberley, Owner
Jill Wikgren, COO
This issue of Sport Science Review examines the newly emerging
academic discipline of adapted physical activity. Researchers
from diverse academic backgrounds and parts of the world review the issues and controversies surrounding inclusion in physical education and sport. *$15.00*
96 pages Paperback
ISBN -073602-07-9

8232 Still Me
Random House
1745 Broadway
3rd Floor
New York, NY 10019-4305　　212-782-9000
FAX: 212-572-6066
vintageanchor@randomhouse.com
www.randomhouse.com

Christopher Reeve, Author
Markus Dohle, Chairman/CEO
Madeline McIntosh, President
The man who was Superman begins with his debilitating riding
accident, then weaves back and forth between past and present,
creating a thorough biography of Reeve's life. *$7.99*
336 pages Paperback 1999
ISBN 0-345432-41-4

8233 When Your Student Has Arthritis
Arthritis Foundation
2970 Peachtree Rd NW
PO Box 932915, Ste 200
Atlanta, GA 31193-2915　　404-237-8771
800-933-7023
FAX: 404-237-8153
aforders@arthritis.org
www.afstore.org

Rob Shaw, President
An overview of arthritis, including juvenile rhuematoid arthritis
and treatment. Also includes a school activities checklist for students, education rights, and how teachers can help.
28 pages

**8234 Yoga for Fibromyalgia: Move, Breathe, and Relax to
Improve Your Quality of Life**
Mobility Limited
PO Box 838
Morro Bay, CA 93443-0838　　805-772-3560
800-366-6038
FAX: 805-772-4717
shsh@mobilityltd.com
www.mobilityltd.com

Shoosh Lettick Crotzer, Director

The first book devoted exclusively to managing the symptoms of fibromyalgia; the comprehensive program of 26 illustrated poses, breathing techniques, and guided visualization and relaxation sessions can be practiced regardless of age or experience. The Living with Fibromyalgia section discusses lifestyle concerns. *$14.95*
128 pages 1908

Journals

8235   Topics in Spinal Cord Injury Rehabilitation
American Spinal Injury Association
9702 Gayton Rd.
Suite 306
Richmond, VA 23238   877-274-2724
                                        asia.office@asia-spinalinjury.org
                                             www.asia-spinalinjury.org
Patty Duncan, Executive Director
Carolyn Moffatt, Association Manager
Kim Ruff, Administrative Assistant
Clinical, peer-reviewed information for physiatrists, PTs, OTs, rehabilitation nurses, psychologists, neurologists, orthopedists, and others.

Magazines

8236   Arthritis Today
Arthritis Foundation
1330 W. Peachtree St.
Suite 100
Atlanta, GA 30309   404-872-7100
                                                    800-933-7023
                                               FAX: 404-237-8153
                                                  info.ga@arthritis.org
                                                    www.arthritis.org
Dan McGowan, Chairman
Rowland W. Chang, Vice Chair
Ann M. Palmer, President and CEO
Magazine for patients, physicians, public authorities and others with an interest in the field of arthritis. (Price noted paid for yearly subscription) *$12.95*
Bi-Monthly

8237   Fibromyalgia AWARE Magazine
National Fibromyalgia Association
2121 S Towne Centre Pl
suite 30
Orange, CA 92865-6124   714-921-0150
                                               FAX: 714-921-6920
                                                        fmaware.org
Lynne Matallana, Editor In Chief
Malina Anderson, CFO
Eroll Landy, Treasurer
Addresses the needs and concerns of people affected by fibromyalgia and overlapping conditions. *$35.00*
3 times a year

8238   New Mobility
Leonard Media Group
120-34 Queens Blvd.
Suite 330
Kew Gardens, NY 11415   800-404-2898
                                                www.newmobility.com
Jean Dobbs, Publisher & Editorial Director
Josie Byzek, Executive Editor
Ian Ruder, Editor
The full-service, full-color lifestyle magazine for the disability community. The award-winning magazine is contemporary, witty and candid. Produced by professional journalists and visual artists, the magazine's voice is uncompromising and unsentimental, yet practical, knowing and friendly. The magazine covers issues that matter to readers: medical news, and cure research; jobs, benefits and civil rights; sports, recreation and travel; product news, technology and innovation. *$27.95*
Monthly

8239   PALAESTRA: Forum of Sport, Physical Education and Recreation for Those with Disabilities
Challenge Publications Limited
1807 N. Federal Drive
Urbana, IL 61801   217-359-5940
                                                    800-327-5557
                                               FAX: 217-359-5975
                                                  www.palaestra.com
David P Beaver EdD, Fonding Editor
Martin.E Block, Editor-in-Chief
Julian U. Stein, Associate Editor
The most comprehensive resource on sport, physical education and recreation for individuals with disabilities, their parents and professionals in the field of adapted physical activity. Published in cooperation with US Paralympics and AAHPERD's Adapted Physical Activity Council. Informative yet entertaining and delivers valuable insights for consumers, families and professionals in the field. Published quarterly.

8240   PN/Paraplegia News
PVA Publications
2111 E Highland Ave
Suite 180
Phoenix, AZ 85016-4702   602-224-0500
                                                    888-888-2201
                                               FAX: 602-224-0507
                                                www.pn-magazine.com
Richard Hoover, Editor
Ann Santos, Assistant Editor
Packed with timely information on spinal-cord-injury research, new products, legislation that impacts people with disabilities, accessible travel, computer options, car/van adaptations, news for veterans, housing, employment, health care and all issues affecting wheelers and caregivers around the world.

8241   Spirit Magazine
Special Olympics International
1133 19th St NW
Washington, DC 20036-3604   202-628-3630
                                               FAX: 202-824-0200
                                               info@specialolympics.org
                                                www.specialolympics.org
Kathy Smallwood, Editor
Timothy P Shriver PhD, Chariman/CEO
J Brady Lum, President/COO
This magazine reflects the power of Special Olympics to build bridges between people with and without intellectual disabilities and spark personal insight, compassion and gratitude for life.
Quarterly

8242   Strides Magazine
North American Riding for the Handicapped Assoc
7475 Dakin Street
Suite 600
Denver, CO 80221-6920   303-452-1212
                                                    800-369-7433
                                               FAX: 303-252-4610
Carol Nickell, CEO
Sheila Dietrich, Executive Director
William Scebbi, CEO
This engaging magazine is a non-technical, yet accurate journal that focuses on the work of NARHA. Rider profiles, how-to articles, editorials and instructional columns seek to educate a general readership of the diverse aspects of equine facilitated therapy and activities. Each seasonal issue carries a theme.
Quarterly

8243   Stroke Connection Magazine
American Stroke Association
7272 Greenville Ave
Dallas, TX 75231-5129   214-373-6300
                                                    888-478-7653
                                               FAX: 214-706-1191
                                               www.strokeassociation.org
Ralph Sacco, President/Director
Nancy Brown, CEO
Debra Lockwood, Chairman
From in-depth information on conditions such as aphasia, central pain, high blood pressure and depression, to tips for daily living from healthcare professionals and other stroke survivors. Stroke

Connection keeps you abreast of how to cope, how to reduce your risk of stroke and how to make the most of each day.
6 issues

Newsletters

8244 A World Awaits You
Mobility International USA
132 E Broadway
Suite 343
Eugene, OR 97401
541-343-1284
FAX: 541-343-6812
TTY:541-343-1284
clearinghouse@miusa.org
www.miusa.org/away

Susan Sygall, Chief Executive Officer
Cindy Lewis, Director, Programs
Includes interviews with people with disabilities who have participated in a wide range of international exchange programs.
Annually

8245 ABS Newsletter
American Back Society
2648 International Blvd
Suite 502
Oakland, CA 94601-1547
510-536-9929
FAX: 510-536-1812
info@americanbacksoc.org
www.americanbacksoc.org

Scott Haldeman, President
Aubrey Swartz MD, Executive Director
Keeps subscribers current with timely topics on the diagnosis and treatment of a wide spectrum of painful and disabling conditions of the spine.

8246 Arthritis Foundation Great West Region
Arthritis Foundation
115 N.E. 100th St
Suite 350
Seattle, WA 98125
206-547-2707
888-391-9389
FAX: 206-547-2805
tzuehl@arthritis.org
www.arthritis.org

Scott Weaver, CEO
Kelsey Birnbaum, Vice President, Development
Deborah Genge, Vice President, Development
Offers regional updates, information on activities and events, resources and medical research for members.
Newsletter

8247 Arthritis Update
Arthritis Foundation
1330 W. Peachtree St.
Suite 100
Atlanta, GA 30309
404-872-7100
info.uny@arthritis.org
www.arthritis.org

Dan McGowan, Chairman
Rowland W. Chang, Vice Chair
Ann M. Palmer, President and CEO
Offers chapter updates, information on activities and events, resources and medical research for members.
Newsletter

8248 CurePSP Magazine
Society for Progressive Supranuclear Palsy
2648 International Blvd
Suite 502
Hunt Valley, MD 21031-1002
410-785-7004
800-457-4777
FAX: 410-785-7009
info@curepsp.org
www.psp.org

Richard Gordon Dyne DMin, President
Janet Edmunson, Chair
Dan Johnson, Vice Chair
Informs readers of findings in the area of PSP.

8249 EpilepsyUSA Magazine
Epilepsy Foundation of America
8301 Professional Pl
Landover, MD 20785-2237
301-459-3700
FAX: 301-577-2684
www.epilepsyfoundation.org

Brien J Smith, Chair
Mark E Nini, Senior Vice Chair
Richard P Denness, President/CEO
The Epilepsy Foundation's award-winning magazine, epilepsyUSA, is published online four times a year. The magazine is one of the only publications of its kind devoted entirely to news and up-to-the-minute information about epilepsy.

8250 Exchange
ALS Association
27001 Agoura Rd
Suite 250
Agoura Hills, CA 91301-5105
818-340-0182
800-782-4747
FAX: 818-880-9006
www.alsa.org

Gary A Leo, CEO
Morton Charlestein, Chairman
Andrew Soffel, Chairman
Covers a broad range of subjects including stories about the lives of ALS patients, special events, research and public policy in the ALS community.
4-6 times/year

8251 Fibromyalgia Online
National Fibromyalgia Association
2121 S Towne Centre Pl
suite 300
Ornage, CA 92865-6124
714-921-0150
FAX: 714-921-6920
www.fmaware.org

Lynne Matallana, President/Editor In Chief
Malina Anderson, CFO
Eroll Landy, Treasurer
An educational resource for patients and healthcare professionals that brings the latest news on fibrmyalgia and overlapping conditions.
Monthly

8252 Focus
Arthritis Foundation
1330 W. Peachtree St.
Suite 100
Atlanta, GA 30309
404-872-7100
info.coh@arthritis.org
www.arthritis.org

Dan McGowan, Chairman
Rowland W. Chang, Vice Chair
Ann M. Palmer, President and CEO
Offers chapter updates, information on activities and events, resources and medical research for members.
Newsletter

8253 Joint Efforts
Arthritis Foundation
1330 W. Peachtree St.
Suite 100
Atlanta, GA 30309
404-872-7100
800-464-6240
FAX: 415-356-1240
info.nca@arthritis.org
www.arthritis.org

Dan McGowan, Chairman
Rowland W. Chang, Vice Chair
Ann M. Palmer, President and CEO
Offers chapter updates, information on activities and events, resources and medical research for members.
Newsletter

8254 MIUSA's Global Impact Newsletter
Mobility International USA
132 E Broadway
Suite 343
Eugene, OR 97401
541-343-1284
FAX: 541-343-6812
TTY:541-343-1284
clearinghouse@miusa.org
www.miusa.org
Susan Sygall, Chief Executive Officer
Cindy Lewis, Director, Programs
Each issue features photos, alumni updates, highlights from recent activities, and new publications.
Quarterly

8255 Motivator
Multiple Sclerosis Association of America
706 Haddonfield Rd
Cherry Hill, NJ 8002-2652
856-488-4500
800-532-7667
FAX: 856-661-9797
jmasino@mymsaa.org
www.msassociation.org
Andrea L GriesS, Editor
Susan W Courtney, Sr Writer & Creative Director
Amanda Bednar, Contributing Writer
MSAA's 48-plus page magazine highlights and explains many vital issues of importance to our readers affected by MS. These include cover and feature stories about a variety of topics such as depression, assistive technology, the role of pets and service animals, parents with MS, and clinical trials, to name a few.
48 pages Quarterly

8256 New York Arthritis Reporter
New York Chapter of the Arthritis Foundation
122 East 42nd Street
New York, NY 10168-1898
212-984-8700
FAX: 212-878-5960
info.ny@arthritis.org
www.arthritis.org
Phyllis Geraghty, Editor
Ross Alfieri, President
Daniel T. McGowan, Chair
Provides public access to current arthritis information and resources on important health issues.
Quarterly

8257 SCI Psychosocial Process
American Assoc of Spinal Cord Injury Psych/Soc Wor
75-20 Astoria Blvd
East Elmhurst, NY 11370
718-803-3782
800-404-2898
FAX: 718-803-0414
info@unitedspinal.org
www.unitedspinal.org
David C. Cooper, Chairman
Patrick W. Maher, Vice Chairman
Joseph Gaskins, President and CEO
The purpose of this e journal is disseminating information of value to psychologists, social workers and other psychological caring for spinal cord injured persons.
2 time a year

8258 SCILIFE
National Spinal Cord Injury Association
75-20 Astoria Blvd
East Elmhurst, NY 11370
718-803-3782
800-404-2898
FAX: 718-803-0414
info@spinalcord.org
www.unitedspinal.org
David C. Cooper, Chairman
Patrick W. Maher, Vice Chairman
Joseph Gaskins, President and CEO
Filled with issue-driven articles, and news of interest to the SCI community and the larger disability community.
Bi-monthly

Audio/Visual

8259 A Wheelchair for Petronilia
Fanlight Productions C/O Icarus Films
32 Court St.
21st Floor
Brooklyn, NY 11201-1731
718-488-8900
800-876-1710
FAX: 718-488-8642
info@fanlight.com
www.fanlight.com
Bob Gliner, Director
Jonathan Miller, President
Meredith Miller, Sales Manager
Profiles a program, organized and run by Guatemalans with disabilities, which trains them to manufacture and repair cheap, sturdy wheelchairs designed for conditions in developing countries. 28 Minutes.
VHS/DVD
ISBN 1-572953-98-5

8260 Beyond the Barriers
Aquarius Health Care Videos
30 Forest Road
PO Box 249
Millis, MA 02054
508-376-1244
888-440-2963
FAX: 508-376-1245
Mark Wellman, Director
Leslie Kussmann, President/Producer
For too many years, paraplegics, amputees, quadraplegics and the blind have felt trapped by their disabilities. No more! Mark Wellman and other disabled adventurers, rock climb the desert towers of Utah, sail in British Columbia, body-board the big waves of Pipeline and Waimea Bay, scuba dive with sea lions in Mexico and hand glide the California coast. This film delivers the simple message: Don't give up, and never give in. If you can't ever lose, then you can't ever win. Preview option.
Video/47 Mins

8261 Breathing Lessons: The Life and Work of Mark O'Brien
Fanlight Productions C/O Icarus Films
32 Court St.
21st Floor
Brooklyn, NY 11201-1731
718-488-8900
800-876-1710
FAX: 718-488-8642
info@fanlight.com
www.fanlight.com
Jessica Yu, Director
Jonathan Miller, President
Meredith Miller, Sales Manager
Breathing Lessons breaks down barriers to understanding by presenting an honest and intimate portrait of a complex, intelligent, beautiful and interesting person, who happens to be disabled.
$225.00
Video/35 Mins 1996
ISBN 1-572958-41-3

8262 Complete Armchair Fitness
CC-M Productions
7755 16th St NW
Washington, DC 20012-1460
202-882-7432
800-453-6280
FAX: 202-882-7432
www.armchairfitness.com
Robert Mason, Manager
Armchair Fitness video series. 4 DVDs: Armchair Fitness Aerobic, Armchair Fitness Gentle, Armchair Fitness Strength and Armchair Fitness Yoga. *$120.00*
Video

8263   How Come You Walk Funny?
Fanlight Productions C/O Icarus Films
32 Court St.
21st Floor
Brooklyn, NY 11201-1731   718-488-8900
                                                     800-876-1710
                                              FAX: 718-488-8642
                                              info@fanlight.com
                                              www.fanlight.com

Tina Hahn, Director
Jonathan Miller, President
Meredith Miller, Sales Manager
Profiles a unique experiment in reverse integration: a school
where non disabled kids attend a kindergarten designed for chil-
dren with physical disabilities. The kids and families tackle their
differences and discover common ground through finding a way
that all can play. *$179.00*
Video/47 Mins 2004
ISBN 1-572958-84-7

8264   Key Changes: A Portrait of Lisa Thorson
Fanlight Productions C/O Icarus Films
32 Court St.
21st Floor
Brooklyn, NY 11201-1731   718-488-8900
                                                     800-876-1710
                                              FAX: 718-488-8642
                                              info@fanlight.com
                                              www.fanlight.com

Cindy Marshall, Director
Jonathan Miller, President
Meredith Miller, Sales Manager
A documentary profiling Lisa Thorson, a gifted vocalist who uses
a wheelchair. Ms. Thorson defines herself as a performer first, a
person with a disability second, and this thoughtful portrait respects that distinction. Her work as a jazz singer is at the heart of
the film, reflecting her philosophy that the biggest contribution
that she can make to the struggle for the rights of people with disabilities is doing her art the best way she can. *$149.00*
Video/28 Mins 1993
ISBN 1-572959-30-4

8265   Wheelchair Bowling
American Wheelchair Bowling Association
PO Box 69
Clover, VA 24534-69   434-454-2269
                                              FAX: 434-454-6276
                                              garyryan210@gmail.com
                                              www.awba.org

Dick Schaaf, Author
Dave Roberts, Executive Secretary Treasurer
In addition to providing historical background, it includes principles of the game from keeping score through ball drilling for the
wheelchair bowler. Through profiles of wheelchair bowlers, the
text covers ball delivery, spare making techniques and special
equipment that can be used. *$9.95*
96 pages

8266   Yoga for Arthritis
Mobility Limited
601 Morro Bay Blvd
Suite E
Morro Bay, CA 93442-2000   805-772-3560
                                                     800-366-6038
                                              FAX: 805-772-4717
                                              shsh@mobilityltd.com
                                              www.mobilityltd.com

Shoosh Crotzer, Owner/Executive Director
A yoga-based program with five separate segments, which includes breathing and relaxation techniques, stretching and
strengthening routines, and aerobic exercises. This 52-minute
program can also be performed seated. Available on DVD or
VHS; DVD includes Spanish version. *$19.95*
Video

8267   Yoga for MS and Related Conditions
Mobility Limited
601 Morro Bay Blvd
Suite E
Morro Bay, CA 93442-2000   805-772-3560
                                                     800-366-6038
                                              FAX: 805-772-4717
                                              shsh@mobilityltd.com
                                              www.mobilityltd.com

Shoosh Crotzer, Owner/Executive Director
A yoga-based program. Shows assisted versions of each exercise
for those who require it; is available with an optional Instructional Guidebook with illustrations, alternative positions, and
hints. This 48-minute program can also be performed seated.
Available on DVD or VHS; DVD includes Spanish version.
$19.95
Video

Sports

8268   Access to Sailing
423 E Shoreline Village Drive
Long Beach, CA 90802   562-901-9999
                                              www.accesstosailing.org

Duncan Milne, Founder/Executive Director
Cliff Larson, Director
Gaile Oslapas, Assistant Director
Provides therapeutic rehabilitation to disabled and disadvan-
taged children and adults, through interactive sailing outings.

8269   Achilles Track Club
42 West 38th Street
Suite 400
New York, NY 10018-6241   212-354-0300
                                              FAX: 212-354-3978

Richard Traum PhD, President/Founder
Mary Bryant, Vice President
Kathleen Bateman, Director
Organization whose goal is to guide disabled athletes into the
able-bodied community.

8270   Adaptive Sports Center
PO Box 1639
Crested Butte, CO 81224-1639   970-349-2296
                                                     866-349-2296
                                              FAX: 970-349-2077
                                              info@adaptivesports.org
                                              www.adaptivesports.org

Christopher Hensley, Executive Director
Chris Read, CTRS Program Director
Ella Fahrlander, Development Director
Year round adaptive, adventure recreation program located at the
base of Crested Butte Mountain Resort, Crested Butte ,CO. The
Adaptive Sports Centers provides adaptive downhill and cross
country ski lessons, ski rentals and snowboarding lessons in the
winter. Offers a variety of wilderness based programs in the summer including multi-day trips into the back country, extensive cycling programs, canoeing, and white water rafting.

8271   American Wheelchair Bowling Association
PO Box 69
Clover, VA 24534-69   434-454-2269
                                              FAX: 434-454-6276
                                              garyryan210@gmail.com
                                              www.awba.org

Joseph L. Fox, Chairman
Wayne Webber, Vice Chairperson
Paul Kenney, Treasurer
A non-profit organization, composed of wheelchair bowlers, ded-
icated to encouraging, developing, and regulating wheelchair
bowling and wheelchair bowling leagues.

8272 Chesapeake Region Accessible Boating
177 Defense Hwy.
Suite 9
Annapolis, MD 21401
410-266-5722
info@crabsailing.org
crabsailing.org

Brad La Tour, President
Paul Bollinger, Executive Director
Sarah Winchester, Operations Manager
Chesapeake Region Accessible Boating (CRAB) provides opportunities for the disabled and their friends to sail the Chesapeake Bay. Programs include group sails for organizations representing special guests, sailing clinics and camps, SailFree Sundays for families, and regattas for those who wish to race.

8273 Disabled Sports Program Center
Disabled Sports USA Far West
PO Box 9780
Truckee, CA 96162-7780
530-581-4161
FAX: 530-581-3127

Doug Pringle, President
Marilyn Cummings, Office Manager
Haakon Lang-Ree, Manager
Founded in 1967, Disabled Sports USA Far West is dedicated to innovative programs that provide an environment with positive therapeutic and psychological outcomes. Individuals are empowered to reach their full potential. Our programs allow individuals of all abilities to discover their own strengths and interests.

8274 Disabled Sports USA
451 Hungerford Dr
Suite 100
Rockville, MD 20850-5102
301-217-0960
FAX: 301-217-0968
www.disabledsportsusa.org

Kirk Bauer, Executive Director
Kathy Chandler, Executive Director
Kathy Celo, Operations
Provides year-round sports and recreation opportunities for people with physical disabilities, veterans and non-veterans alike, such as sanctioned regional and national events in alpine and Nordic skiing, cycling, shooting swimming, table tennis, track and field, volleyball, and weightlifting. The organization handles physical disabilities which restrict mobility, including amputations paraplegia, quadriplegia, cerebral palsy, head injury, mulitple sclerosis, muscular dystrophy, and more.

8275 Disabled Watersports Program
Mission Bay Aquatic Center
1001 Santa Clara Pl
San Diego, CA 92109
858-488-1000
FAX: 858-488-9625
mbac@sdsu.edu
www.missionbayaquaticcenter.com

Kevin Starw, Director
Kevin Waldick, Asst. director
Eric Fehrs, Maintenance Director
Devoted to providing accessible water sports and recreational opportunities for individuals with disabilities. Specially designed equipment makes water skiing, wake boarding, keelboat sailing, windsurfing, rowing, surfing, and kayaking possible for people with varying levels of mobility and ability.

8276 Galvin Health and Fitness Center
Rehabilitation Institute of Chicago
345 East Suuperior St.
Chicago, IL 60611
312-238-1000
800-354-7342
800-354-REHA
FAX: 312-238-5017
sports@ric.org
www.ric.org

Jude Reyes, Chair
Mike P. Kransy, Vice Chair
Thomas Reynolds III, Vice Chair
The RIC Sports and Fitness Program offers people with physical disabilities an on-site fitness center, specialized exercise classes and services, and adult and junior competitive and recreational sports opportunities, including the recreational/social Caring for Kids program for youth ages 7-17. Most programs are provided free of charge or for a nominal fee.

8277 Guide to Wheelchair Sports and Recreation
Paralyzed Veterans of America
801 18th St. NW
Washington, DC 20006-3517
800-424-8200
TTY:800-795-4327
info@pva.org
www.pva.org

Charles Brown, National President
Marcus Murray, National Secretary
Carl Blake, Executive Director
This guide lists descriptions of adaptive sports and recreation, activity and equipment directories, and additional resources for people with disabilities.
28 pages Booklet

8278 Handicapped Scuba Association International
Handicapped Scuba Association
1104 El Prado
San Clemente, CA 92672-4637
949-498-4540
FAX: 949-498-6128
www.hsascuba.com

Jim Gatacre, President
Patricia Derk, Vice President
A nonprofit volunteer organization dedicated to improving the physical and social well being of those with special needs through the exhilarating sport of scuba diving. An educational program for able bodied scuba instructors to learn to teach and certify people with special needs. Accessible travel opportunities.

8279 Lakeshore Foundation
4000 Ridgeway Dr
Birmingham, AL 35209-5563
205-313-7400
FAX: 205-313-7475
information@lakeshore.org
www.lakeshore.org

Jeff Underwood, President & CEO
Beth Curry, Chief Program Officer
Jen Remick, Director, Communications & Membership
Promotes independence for persons with physically disabling conditions and provides opportunities to pursue active, healthy lifestyles.

8280 National Disability Sports Alliance
25 W Independence Way
Kingston, RI 02881-1124
401-792-7130
FAX: 401-792-7132
nationaldisabilitysportsalliance.webs.

Jerry McCole, Executive Director
Serves to present disabled athletes with the opportunity to perform in many different sports. Participants range from the beginning athlete to the elite, international caliber athlete.

8281 National Skeet Shooting Association
5931 Roft Rd
San Antonio, TX 78253-9261
210-688-3371
800-877-5338
FAX: 210-688-3014
nsca@nssa-nsca.com
www.mynssa.com

Michael Hampton, Jr., Executive Director
Royce Graff, NSSA Director
Amber Schwarz, NSC Assistant Director
Offers information on sporting clay targets for the disabled hunter.

8282 National Sports Center for the Disabled
33 Parsenn Rd
PO Box 1290
Winter Park, CO 80482
970-726-1518
FAX: 970-726-4112
volunteer@nscd.org
nscd.org

Kim Easton, President & CEO
Diane Eustace, Marketing Director
Beth Fox, Outreach & Education Director
The center's mission is to provide quality outdoor sports and therapeutic recreation programs that positively impact the lives of people with physical, cognitive, emotional, or behavioral challenges. Winter programming includes alpine skiing, snowboarding, ski racing, show shoeing, and cross-country ski-

ing. Summer sports include rafting, sailing, kayaking, camping, hiking, horseback riding, fishing, and rock climbing.
6-8 pages Quarterly

8283 National Wheelchair Poolplayers Association
90 Flemons Dr
Somerville, AL 35670

256-778-0449
FAX: 703-817-1215
www.nwpainc.org

Jeffrey Dolezal, President
Bob Calderon, Secretary
Ken Force, Editor
Works together with other groups, organizations, and tournaments to update rules to include wheelchair players.

8284 Ontario Cerebral Palsy Sports Association
P.O. Box 60082
Ottawa, ON, Canada K1T-0K9

613-723-1806
866-286-2772
FAX: 613-723-6742

Amanda Fader, Executive Director
Don Sinclair, President
Lorette Dupuis, Vice President
Organization that provides, promotes and coordinates competitive opportunities as well as encourages individual excellence through sport for athletes within the cerebral palsy family. To that end, OCPSA recruits, develops and supports athletes, coaches and volunteers.

8285 Professional Association of Therapeutic Horsemanship International (PATH Intl.)
PO Box 33150
Denver, CO 80233

303-452-1212
800-369-7433
FAX: 303-252-4610
pathintl@pathintl.org
www.pathintl.org

Kathy Alm, Chief Executive Officer
Carrie Garnett, Director, Membership & Operations
Kaye Marks, Director, Marketing & Communications
A national nonprofit equestrian organization dedicated to serving individuals with disabilities by giving disabled individuals the opportunity to ride horses. Establishes safety standards, provides continuing education, and offers networking opportunities for both its individuals and center members. Produces educational materials including fact sheets, brochures, booklets, audio-visual tapes, a directory, and PATH Intl. magazine Strides.

8286 Special Olympics
1133 19th St NW
Washington, DC 20036-3604

202-393-1251
FAX: 202-715-1146
info@specialolympics.org
www.specialolympics.org

Timothy P Shriver PhD, Chariman/CEO
J Brady Lum, President/COO
Stephen M Carter, Lead Director/CEO/Vice Chair
A year-round worldwide program that promotes physical fitness, sports training and athletic competition for children and adults with intellectual disabilities.

8287 Special Olympics International
1133 19th St NW
Washington, DC 20036-3604

202-393-1251
FAX: 202-715-1146
info@specialolympics.org
www.specialolympics.org

Timothy P Shriver PhD, Chariman/CEO
J Brady Lum, President/COO
Stephen M Carter, Lead Director/CEO/Vice Chair
Provides year-round training and athletic competition in a variety of well-coached, Olympic-type sparts for persons with developmental disabilities. Offers opportunities to develop physical fitness, prepare for entry into school and community sports programs. Athletes express courage, experience joy and participate in gifts, skills and friendship with their families and other Special Olympics athletes. Local information can be provided by regional offices.

8288 US Paralympics
United States Olympic Committee
1 Olympic Plaza
Colorado Springs, CO 80909

719-866-2030
888-222-2313
FAX: 719-866-2029
www.teamusa.org/us-paralympics

Scott Blackmun, CEO
Alan Ashley, Chief of Sport Performance
Lisa Baird, Chief Marketing Officer
A division of the US Olympic Committee focused on enhancing programs, funding and opportunities for persons with physical disabilities to participate in Paralympic sports.

8289 United Foundation for Disabled Archers
20 NE 9th Ave. Glenwood,
PO Box 251
Glenwood, MN 56334- 251

320-634-3660
info@uffdaclub.com
www.uffdaclub.com

Daniel James Hendricks, President
Russ Kalk, Vice President
Debbie Kalk, Treasurer
It is the mission of the United Foundation for Disabled Archers to promote and provide a means to practice all forms of archery for any physically challenged person.

8290 Wheelchair Sports, USA
PO Box 5266
Kendall Park, NJ 08824-5266

732-266-2634
FAX: 732-355-6500

Kelly Behlmann, Owner
Gregg Baumgraten, Chairperson
Denise Hutchins, Vice-Chairperson
Initiates, stimulates and promotes the growth and development of wheelchair sports.

Support Groups

8291 Information Hotline
Arthritis Foundation, Southeast Region Inc
1330 W. Peachtree St.
Suite 100
Atlanta, GA 30309

404-872-7100
800-933-7023
FAX: 404-237-8153
info.ga@arthritis.org
www.arthritis.org

Dan McGowan, Chairman
Rowland W. Chang, Vice Chair
Ann M. Palmer, President and CEO
The mission of the Arthritis Foundation is to improve lives through leadership in the prevention, control and cure of arthritis and related diseases.

8292 Kids on the Block Programs
9385 Gerwig Lane
Suite C
Maryland, MD 21157-2893

410-290-9095
800-368-5437
FAX: 410-290-9358
www.kotb.com

Aric Darroe, President
Jane Thuman, Vice President
Christina Grogan, Marketing Manager
Features life-size puppets in educational programs that enlighten children and adults on the issues of disability awareness, medical and educational differences, and social concerns.

General Disorders

Associations

8293 AIDS United
1424 K Street, N.W.
Ste 200
Washington, DC 20005-1511
202-408-4848
888-234-2437
FAX: 202-408-1818
info@aidsunited.org
www.aidsunited.org
Jesse Milan Jr., JD, Interim President & CEO
Matthew J. Kessler, Vice President, Operations
Cody Barnett, Commuications Coordinator
AIDS United advocates for people living with or affected by HIV/AIDS and the organizations that serve them. AIDS United's mission is to end the AIDS epidemic in the United States through strategic grantmaking, capacity building, policy/advocacy, technical assistance and formative research.

8294 American Academy for Cerebral Palsy and Developmental Medicine
555 East Wells
Suite 1100
Milwaukee, WI 53202
414-918-3014
FAX: 414-276-2146
info@aacpdm.org
www.aacpdm.org
Tamara Wagester, Executive Director
Erin Trimmer, Senior Meetings Manager
Heather Schrader, Membership & Administrative Manager
Professional health academy offering multidisciplinary scientific education and promoting excellence in research and services in the area of cerebral palsy and other childhood-onset disabilities.

8295 American Academy of Allergy, Asthma & Immunology
555 E Wells St.
Ste 1100
Milwaukee, WI 53202-3823
414-272-6071
FAX: 414-272-6070
info@aaaai.org
www.aaaai.org
Thomas A. Fleisher, M.D.; FAAAAI, President
An association of medical professionals and specialists that places focus on research and treatment for allergic and immunologic diseases, as well as improved patient care.

8296 American Academy of Otolaryngology - Head and Neck Surgery
1650 Diagonal Rd
Alexandria, VA 22314-2857
703-836-4444
FAX: 703-683-5100
TTY:703-519-1585
www.entnet.org
James c. Denneny III, M.D., Executive Vice President & CEO
Sujana S. Chandrasekhar, M.D., President
Carol R. Bradford, Director, Academic
The American Academy of Otolaryngology-Head and Neck Surgery (AAO-HNS) is an organization representing specialists who treat the ear, nose, throat, and related structures of the head and neck.

8297 American Academy of Physical Medicine and Rehabilitation
9700 W Bryn Mawr Ave
Ste 200
Rosemont, IL 60018-5701
847-737-6000
877-227-6799
FAX: 847-737-6001
info@aapmr.org
www.aapmr.org
Thomas E. Stautzenbach, Executive Director & Chief Executive Officer
Gregory M. Worsowicz, President
Darryl L. Kaelin, Vice President

This national medical specialty society represents more than 6,500 physical medicine and rehabilitation physicians, whose patients include people with physical disabilities and chronic, disabling illnesses. The academy's mission is to maximize quality of life, minimize the incidence and prevalence of impairments and disability, promote societal health and enhance the understanding and development of the specialty. The organization offers information, referrals, and patient materials.

8298 American Association for Respiratory Care
9425 N. MacArthur Blvd.
Ste 100
Irving, TX 75063-4706
972-243-2272
FAX: 972-484-2720
info@aarc.org
www.aarc.org
Tom Kallstrom, Executive Director
Steve Bowden, IT, General Inquiries
AARC's mission is to advance the science, technology, ethics and art of respiratory care through research and education for its members and to teach the general public about pulmonary health and disease prevention.

8299 American Association of Cardiovascular and Pulmonary Rehabilitation
330 N. Wabash Avenue
Suite 2200
Chicago, IL 60611
312-321-5146
FAX: 312-673-6924
aacvpr@aacvpr.org
www.aacvpr.org
Adam T. deJong, President
Megan Cohen, Executive Director
Jessica Eustice, Director Of Corporate Relations
The mission of American Association of Cardiovascular and Pulmonary Rehabilitation is to reduce morbidity, mortality, and disability from cardiovascular and pulmonary diseases through education, prevention, rehabilitation, research, and aggressive disease management.

8300 American Brain Tumor Association
8550 W. Bryn Mawr Ave
Ste 550
Chicago, IL 60631-4106
773-577-8750
800-886-2282
FAX: 773-577-8738
info@abta.org
www.abta.org
Elizabeth Wilson, President & CEO
Martha Carlos, Chief Communications Officer
Kerri Mink, Chief Operating Officer
A non-profit organization founded in 1973 dedicated to the elimination of brain tumors through research and patient education services.

8301 American Diabetes Association
2451 Crystal Dr.
Suite 900
Arlington, VA 22202
800-342-2383
askada@diabetes.org
www.diabetes.org
Tracey D. Brown, Chief Executive Officer
Charlotte Carter, Chief Financial Officer
Charles Henderson, Chief Development Officer
Funds diabetes research, information and advocacy. The mission of the Association is to prevent and cure diabetes and to improve the lives of all people affected by diabetes.

8302 American Group Psychotherapy Association
25 E. 21st St.
6th Floor
New York, NY 10010-6207
212-477-2677
877-668-2472
FAX: 212-979-6627
info@agpa.org
www.agpa.org
Marsha S. Block, Chief Executive Officer
Eleanor F. Counselman, EdD; CGP, President
Nina Brown, Secretary
AGPA serves as the national voice specific to the interests of group psychotherapy. Its 4,100 members and 31 affiliate societies

provide a wealth of professional, educational and social support for group psychotherapists in the United States and around the world.

8303   American Head and Neck Society
11300 W. Olympic Blvd
Ste 600
Los Angeles, CA 90064-1663   310-437-0559
                                      FAX: 310-437-0585
                                           www.ahns.info

Dennis Kraus, MD, President
Jonathan Irish, MD, Vice President
Brian B. Burkey, MD; MEd, Secretary

AHNS is a professional organization, formed in 1998 to promote research and education in head and neck oncology. The AHNS offers clinical practice guidelines, details of events, grants, and patient information. It aims to promote and advance the knowledge of prevention, diagnosis, treatment, and rehabilitation of neoplasms and other diseases of the head and neck.

8304   American Lung Association
55 W. Wacker Dr.
Ste 1150
Chicago, IL 60601   312-781-1100
                                           800-548-8252
                                      FAX: 202-452-1085
                                          info@lung.org
                                           www.lung.org

Harold P. Wimmer, President & CEO
Sue . Swan, National Chief Development Officer
Sally Draper, National Vice President, Development

The ALA is an organization dedicated to combating tobacco use, eliminating lung diseases, and improving air quality through research, education, and advocacy. The association provides knowledge beneficial to patients, patients' families, and medical professionals and specialists.

8305   American SIDS Institute
528 Raven Way
Naples, FL 34110   239-431-5425
                                      FAX: 239-431-5536
                                         prevent@sids.org
                                           www.sids.org

Marc Peterzell, JD, Chairman
Betty McEntire, PhD, Executive Director & CEO
Nicole Dobson, MD, Board Member

American SIDS Institute is a national nonprofit health care organization that is dedicated to the prevention of sudden infant death and the promotion of infant health through an aggressive, comprehensive nationwide program of research, clinical services, education and family support.

8306   American Sexual Health Association
P.O. Box 13827
Research Triangle Park, NC 27709-3827   919-361-8400
                                      FAX: 919-361-8425
                                    info@ashasexualhealth.org

Lynn Barclay, President & CEO
Deborah Arrindell, Vice President, Health Policy

The American Sexual Health Association is a trusted source of information on sexual health, relationships, and measures to prevent adverse sexual health

8307   American Society of Pediatric Hematology/Oncology
8735 West Higgins Rd.
Ste. 300
Chicago, IL 60631   847-375-4716
                                      FAX: 847-375-6483
                                          info@aspho.org
                                           www.aspho.org

Sally Weir, Executive Director
Steve Biddle, Education Consultant
Jackie Holcomb, Education Manager

ASPHO is multidisciplinary organization dedicated to promoting optimal care of children and adolescents with blood disorders and cancer by advancing research, education, treatment and professional practice.

8308   American Thoracic Society
25 Broadway
18th Floor
New York, NY 10004-2755   212-315-8600
                                      FAX: 212-315-6498
                                        atsinfo@thoracic.org
                                          www.thoracic.org

Steve Crane, Executive Director
Nicola Black, Associate Director, Governance Activities
Jennifer A. Ian, Director, Member Services & Chapter Relations

The American Thoracic Society is dedicated to research, public health education, and patient care in relation to pulmonary disease, critical illness, and sleep disorders.

8309   Aplastic Anemia and MDS International Foundation
100 Park Ave
Ste 108
Rockville, MD 20850   301-279-7202
                                           800-747-2820
                                      FAX: 301-279-7205
                                          help@aamds.org
                                           www.aamds.org

John Huber, Executive Director
Angie Onofre, Director of Patient Programs and Services
Leigh Clark, Patient Educator

This organization, formerly known as Aplastic Anemia Foundation of America, provides a resource directory for patient assistance, produces educational material and supports research into AA and MDS.

8310   Arizona Hemophilia Association
826 North 5th Ave
Phoenix, AZ 85003   602-955-3947
                                       info@hemophiliaz.org
                                      www.arizonahemophilia.org

Cindy Komar, Chief Executive Officer
Chelsea Bolyard, Program Director
Yleana Highes, Director, Client Services

The Arizona Hemophilia Association (AHA) is a volunteer based nonprofit organization working to support, educate, and advocate for families affected by bleeding disorders in Arizona.

8311   CPATH Cerebral Palsy Awareness Transition Hope
5501A Balcones
Suite 160
Austin, TX 78731   866-742-7284
                                       info@cpathtexas.com
                                         www.cpathtexas.com

Victoria Polega, President
Marielle Deckard, Secretary
Jamie Eppele, Director, Devleopment

CPATH is a non-profit organization whose mission is to provide resources, support, and financial assistance to families and individuals living with cerebral palsy.

8312   Canadian Cancer Society
55 St. Clair Avenue W.
Ste 300
Toronto, ON, Canada M4V- 2Y7   416-961-7223
                                           888-939-3333
                                      FAX: 416-961-4189
                                      TTY:866-786-3934
                                          ccs@cancer.ca
                                           www.cancer.ca

Anne V,zina, Interim President & CEO
Martin Kabat, Chief Executive Officer
Lesley Ring, Vice President, Development & Marketing

A national community-based organization of volunteers whose mission is the eradication of cancer and the enhancement of the quality of life for people living with cancer.

8313   Canadian Diabetes Association
1400-522 University Ave
Toronto, ON, Canada M5G-2R5   416-363-3373
                                           800-226-8464
                                      FAX: 416-408-7015
                                          info@diabetes.ca
                                           www.diabetes.ca

Doug Macnamara, President & CEO
Paul Kilbertus, Senior Director, Strategic Communications

The mission of the Canadian Diabetes Association is to promote the health of Canadians through diabetes research, education, service and advocacy.

8314 Canadian Lung Association
1750 Courtwood Cres.
Ottawa, ON, Canada K2C-2B5

613-569-6411
888-566-5864
FAX: 613-569-8860
info@lung.ca
www.lung.ca

Terry Dean, President & CEO
The Canadian Lung Association is a non-profit and volunteer-based health charity, dedicated to improving lung health in the Canadian community through research, education, prevention and advocacy.

8315 Childhood Cancer Canada Foundation
21 St. Clair Ave E
Ste 801
Toronto, ON, Canada M4T-1L9

416-489-6440
800-363-1062
FAX: 416-489-9812
info@childhoodcancer.ca
www.childhoodcancer.ca

Clare Davenport, President & CEO
Natasha Bowes, Senior Manager, Fund Development
Patricia Zareba, Fund Development Manager
A national, volunteer governed, charitable organization dedicated to improving the quality of life for children with cancer. The foundation raises funds to assist with cancer research undertakings across Canada.

8316 Childhood Leukemia Foundation
807 Mantoloking Rd
Brick, NJ 08723

732-920-8860
888-253-7109
www.clf4kids.org

Barbara Haramis, Executive Director & Founder
Barb Estelle, Chief Operating Officer
Kim Wetmore, Director, Development
The CLF is a national, non-profit organization providing education, information, support, and advocacy for patients of cancer and their families. the foundation works closely with health professionals, social workers, and specialists to offer a variety of programs that aim to enrich the lives of children living with cancer.

8317 Emphysema Foundation for Our Right to Survive
PO Box 20241
Kansas City, MO 64119-0241

866-363-2673
www.emphysema.net

Linda Watson, President
Debbie Snodell, Secretary
EFFORTS is a non-profit organization that takes an active role in promoting research for more effective treatments and perhaps a cure for emphysema and related lung diseases. It also works to further education about the disease and provides a support mailing list for members.

8318 Environmental Health Center: Dallas
8345 Walnut Hill Lane
Ste 220
Dallas, TX 75231-4205

214-368-4132
FAX: 214-691-8432
contact@ehcd.com
www.ehcd.com

William J Rea, Director
Chris Rea, Business Manager
Yaqin Pan, M.D., Research Physician
Clinic providing patient care in the areas of Immunotherapy, Nutrition, Physical Therapy, Chemical Depuration, Energy Balancing, Electromagnetic Sensitivity Testing, Psychological Support Services, Family Practice Medicine and Internal Medicine. Provides services for individuals whose diseases are caused by environmental factors.

8319 Epilepsy Foundation of Alabama
3929 Airport Blvd
Suite 3-310
Mobile, AL 36609-2235

251-341-0170
800-626-1582

Donna Dodson, Executive Director
Paige Norris, Outreach & Program Director
David Toenes, Director, Client Services
The Epilepsy Foundation of Alabama provides health service programs and public education on behalf of people with seizures and epilepsy. Some of their services include emergency medication assistance, information referral, training, employer education, and camping trips.

8320 Eunice Kennedy Shriver National Institute of Child Health and Human Development (NICHD)
National Institutes of Health (NIH)
31 Center Dr.
Bldg 31, Rm 2A32
Bethesda, MD 20892-2425

301-496-5097
800-370-2943
FAX: 866-760-5947
TTY: 888-320-6942
nichdinformationresourcecenter@mail.nih.gov
www.nichd.nih.gov

Diana W. Bianchi, Director
The Eunice Kennedy Shriver National Institute of Child Health and Human Development, part of the federal National Institutes of Health, conducts and supports basic, translational, and clinical research in the biomedical, behavioral, and social sciences related to child and maternal health, in medical rehabilitation, and in the reproductive sciences.

8321 Fragile X Family
Fanlight Productions
c/o Icarus Films
32 Court Street, 21st Floor
Brooklyn, NY 11201

718-488-8900
800-876-1710
FAX: 718-488-8642
info@fanlight.com
www.fanlight.com

Ben Achtenberg, Founder, Owner
Eric Kutner, Producer
Fragile X Family takes viewers inside the lives of a developmentally disabled family who are affected by Fragile X Syndrome, an inherited chromosomal disorder. *$149.00*
VHS/VIDEO
ISBN 1-572954-14-0

8322 Herpes Resource Center
American Social Health Association
P.O. Box 13827
Research Triangle Park, NC 27709-3827

919-361-8400
800-227-8922
FAX: 919-361-8425
customerservice@ashastd.org
www.ashastd.org/stdsstis/herpes/

Lynn Barclay, President & CEO
The Herpes Resource Center (HRC) focuses on increasing education, public awareness, and support to anyone concerned about herpes.

8323 IKUS Life Enrichment Services
O-1859 Lake Michigan Dr. NW
Grand Rapids, MI 49534

616-677-5251
FAX: 616-677-2955
info@ikuslife.org
www.ikuslife.org

Scott Blakeney, Executive Director
Amy DeMott, Director, Programs & Services
Nikki Outhier, Director, Development
IKUS Life Enrichment Services helps individuals with disabilities learn new skills and experience greater freedom by providing support, recreation and educational services. IKUS also provides respite services to caregivers and families.

8324 International Academy of Biological Dentistry and Medicine
19122 Camellia Bend Circle
Suite 101
Spring, TX 77379
281-651-1745
FAX: 281-651-1745
drdawn@drdawn.net
www.iabdm.org

Dr. Dawn Ewing, Executive Director
The IABDM promotes non-toxic diagnostic and therapeutic approaches in dentistry and hosts seminars on biological diagnosis and therapy.

8325 International Academy of Oral Medicine & Toxicology
8297 ChampionsGate Blvd
Ste 193
ChampionsGate, FL 33896-8387
863-420-6373
FAX: 863-419-8136
info@iaomt.org
www.iaomt.org

Mark Wisniewski, President
Tammy DeGregorio, Executive Vice President
Kym Smith, Executive Director
A non-profit organization dedicated to funding solid peer-reviewed scientific research in the area of toxic substances used in dentistry as well as providing continuing education and carefully reviewed procedures, protocols, and methodologies to reduce the risk for patients and professionals.

8326 International Association for Cancer Victors & Friends
P.O. Box 745
Lakeport, CA 95453
408-834-5300
FAX: 408-264-9659
www.cancervictors.net
The Cancer Victors and Friends, also known as The International Association of Cancer Victors and Friends, or IACVF, is dedicated to disseminating information about alternative and complimentary methods for treating cancer and other diseases. It encompasses hundreds of clinics and practitioners as well as multiple avenues for information, including the website, printed information, chapter meetings, guest speakers, promotional videos, books, and conventions.
a.k.a. Cancer Victors & Friends

8327 International Association of Hygienic Physicians
4620 Euclid Blvd
Youngstown, OH 44512-1633
330-788-0526
FAX: 330-788-0093
www.iahp.net

Alec Burton, Co-Founder
Mark A. Huberman, Secretary/Treasurer
The International Association of Hygienic Physicians (IAHP) is a professional association for licensed, primary care physicians (Medical Doctors, Osteopaths, Chiropractors, and Naturopaths) who specialize in Therapeutic Fasting Supervision as an integral part of Hygienic Care.

8328 International Medical and Dental Hypnotherapy Association
8852 SR 3001
RR 2
Laceyville, PA 18623-9417
570-869-1021
800-553-6886
FAX: 570-869-1249
www.hypnosisalliance.com/imdha

Linda Otto, Executive Director
Robert Otto, President & CEO
Christie Boecker, Membership Services Coordinator
The association provides and encourages education programs to further, the knowledge, understanding, and application of hypnosis in complementary healthcare; encourages research and scientific publication in the field of hypnosis; and advocates for further recognition and acceptance of hypnosis as an important tool in healthcare and focus for scientific research.

8329 International Myeloma Foundation
12650 Riverside Dr
Ste 206
North Hollywood, CA 91607- 3421
818-487-7455
800-452-2873
FAX: 818-487-7454
theimf@myeloma.org
www.myeloma.org

David Girard, Executive Director
Susie Novis, President
Diane Moran, Senior Vice President, Strategic Planning
The IMF serves myeloma patients, family members, and the medical community, offering a wide range of programs in the areas of Research, Education, Support, and Advocacy.

8330 International Ventilator Users Network (IVUN)
50 Crestwood Executive Ctr.
Suite 440
St. Louis, MO 63126-1916
314-534-0475
FAX: 314-534-5070
info@ventusers.org
www.ventnews.org

Mark Mallinger, President & Chairperson
Frederick M. Maynard, Vice President
Marny K. Eulberg, Secretary
To enhance the lives and independence of individuals using ventilators by promoting education, networking and advocacy. IVUN is an affiliate of Post-Polio Health International.

8331 Leukemia & Lymphoma Society
3 International Dr
Ste 200
Rye Brook, NY 10573
914-949-5213
800-955-4572
FAX: 914-949-6691
supportservices@lls.org
www.lls.org

Louis DeGennaro, President & CEO
Piper Medcalf, Executive Director
Nancy Hallberg, Chief Marketing Officer
The Leukemia and Lymphoma Society is the world's largest voluntary health organization dedicated to funding blood cancer research, education and patient services. The society offers information and support for patients of various blood cancer types, including leukemia, lymphoma, Hodgkin's disease and myeloma. It also offers services and resources to help improve the quality of life of patients and their families.

8332 Little People of America
250 El Camino Real
Ste 218
Tustin, CA 92780
714-368-3689
888-572-2001
FAX: 714-368-3367
info@lpaonline.org
www.lpaonline.org

Joanna Campbell, Executive Director
Gary Arnold, President
April Brazier, Senior Vice President
Little People of America is a national non-profit organization that provides support and information to people of short stature and their families. Short stature is generally caused by one of the more than 200 medical conditions known as dwarfism. LPA offers information on employment, education, disability rights, adoption, medical issues, clothing, adaptive products, and the many stages of parenting a short-statured child - from birth to adult.

8333 Lowe Syndrome Association
P.O. Box 417
Chicago Ridge, IL 60415
216-630-7723
www.lowesyndrome.org

Lisa Waldbaum, President
Jane Gallery, Treasurer
Tiffany Johnson, Director, Medical & Scientific Affairs
The organization aims to foster communication, provide education, and support research into Lowe Syndrome.

8334   Lymphoma Canada
Formerly The Lymphoma Foundation Canada
6860 Century Ave
Ste 202
Mississauga, ON, Canada L5N-2W5   905-858-5967
                                         866-659-5556
                                         info@lymphoma.ca
                                         www.lymphoma.ca
Robin Markowitz, Chief Executive Officer
Lorna Warwick, National Director, Education & Services
Charlene Ragin, Marketing & Communications
Lymphoma Canada provides, at no cost and in both official languages: electronic and print materials on the Hodgkin lymphoma, non-Hodgkin lymphoma and CLL, peer and caregiver support groups, educational forums and advocacy on behalf of patients. Lymphoma Canada also funds Canadian research.

8335   Merrimack Hall Performing Arts Center
3320 Triana Blvd SW.
Huntsville, AL 35805   256-534-6455
                                         info@merrimackhall.com
                                         www.merrimackhall.com
Merrimack Hall Performing Arts Center is a nonprofit organization offering an array of programs including camps, classes, and social events, for children and adults with special needs. More than 500 individuals with special needs participate in Merrimack Hall's Happy Programs which are designed to provide participants with visual and performing arts education, as well as cultural activities.

8336   Myositis Association
1940 Duke St.
Suite 200
Alexandria, VA 22314   800-821-7356
                                         tma@myositis.org
                                         www.myositis.org
Bob Goldberg, Executive Director
Theresa Reynolds Curry, Communications Manager
Aisha Morrow, Operations Manager
The aim of TMA's programs and services is to provide information, support, advocacy and research for those concerned about myositis, as well as serving those affected by these diseases. Support groups offer members the chance to share and discuss their concerns with people in similar situations.

8337   National Association for Children of Alcoholics
10920 Connecticut Ave
Ste 100
Kensington, MD 20895-3007   301-468-0985
                                         888-554-2627
                                         FAX: 301-468-0987
                                         nacoa@nacoa.org
                                         www.nacoa.org
Sis Wenger, President & CEO
Steve Hornberger, Program Director
National non-profit membership and affiliate organization working on behalf of children of alcohol and drug dependent parents to help eliminate the adverse impact of drug use on children through public awareness, policy, advocacy, education, and support.

8338   National Association for Home Care & Hospice
228 7th St SE
Washington, DC 20003-4306   202-547-7424
                                         FAX: 202-547-3540
                                         webmaster@nahc.org
                                         www.nahc.org
Val J. Halamandris, President
Lucy Andrews, Vice Chair
Karen Marshall Thompson, Secretary
This is a non-profit trade association representing various home care, hospice and health aid organizations. With services aimed at assiting the chronically ill and disabled, the NAHC offers information on how to choose a home care provider and a zip code driven locator for home care and hospice.

8339   National Association for Medical Direction of Respiratory Care
8618 Westwood Center Dr
Ste 210
Vienna, VA 22182-2273   703-752-4359
                                         FAX: 703-752-4360
                                         www.namdrc.org
Phillip Porte, Executive Director
Vickie Parshall, Director, Member Services
Karen Lui, RN, Associate Executive Director
NAMDRC's primary mission is to improve access to quality care for patients with respiratory disease by removing regulatory and legislative barriers to appropriate treatment.

8340   National Association for Proton Therapy
1155 15th St NW
Ste 500
Washington, DC 20005   202-495-3133
                                         FAX: 202-530-0659
                                         info@proton-therapy.org
                                         www.proton-therapy.org
Leonard Arzt, Executive Director
The National Association for Proton Therapy (NAPT) is registered as an independent, non-profit, public benefit corporation providing education and awareness for the public, professional and governmental communities. It promotes the therapeutic benefits of proton therapy for cancer treatment in the U.S. and abroad.

8341   National Association of Anorexia Nervosa and Associated Disorders
750 E Diehl Road
Ste 127
Naperville, IL 60563   630-577-1333
                                         FAX: 847-433-4632
                                         anadhelp@anad.org
                                         www.anad.org
Laura Zinger, Executive Director
Deb Prinz, Director, Community Relations
A non-profit organization that seeks to alleviate the problems of eating disorders, especially anorexia nervosa and bulimia nervosa, by promoting eating disorder awareness, prevention and recovery through supporting, educating, and connecting individuals, families and professionals.

8342   National Association of Chronic Disease Diseases
325 Swanton Way
Decatur, GA 30030   770-458-7400
                                         FAX: 770-458-7401
                                         jrobitscher@chronicdisease.org
                                         www.chronicdisease.org
John W. Robitscher, Chief Executive Officer
Namvar Zohoori, President
John Patton, Director, Communications
A national public health association founded in 1988 to link the chronic disease program directors of each state and U.S. territory to provide a national forum for chronic disease prevention and control efforts. NACDD aims to mobilize national efforts to reduce chronic diseases and the associated risk factors.

8343   National Association to Advance Fat Acceptance
P.O. Box 4662
Foster City, CA 94404-0662   916-558-6880
                                         FAX: 916-558-6881
                                         www.naafaonline.com
Founded in 1969, the National Association to Advance Fat Acceptance (NAAFA) is a non-profit, all volunteer, civil rights organization dedicated to protecting the rights and improving the quality of life for fat people. NAAFA works to eliminate discrimination based on body size and provide fat people with the tools for self-empowerment through advocacy, public education, and support.

8344 National Cancer Institute
9609 Medical Center Dr.
Rockville, MD 20850   800-422-6237
                                                        TTY:800-332-8615
                                                         nciinfo@nih.gov
                                                          www.cancer.gov

Norman E. Sharpless, Director
Douglas R. Lowy, Principal Deputy Director
James Doroshow, Deputy Director, Clinical & Translational
Research
The National Cancer Institute conducts and supports research,
training, health information dissemination, and programs related
to cancer, cancer rehabilitation, and the care of cancer patients.
1975

8345 National Diabetes Information Clearinghouse
NI of Diabetes and Digestive and Kidney Diseases
31 Center Dr.
Bethesda, MD 20892   800-860-8747
                                                        TTY:866-569-1162
                                                     healthinfo@niddk.nih.gov
                                                   www.diabetes.niddk.nih.gov

Griffin P. Rodgers, Director
Gregory G. Germino, Deputy Director
Camille Hoover, Executive Officer
An information and referral service of the National Institute of
Diabetes and Digestive and Kidney Diseases, one of the National
Institutes of Health. The clearinghouse responds to written inquiries, develops and distributes publications about diabetes, and
provides referrals to diabetes organizations, including support
groups. The NDIC maintains a database of patient and professional education materials, from which literature searches are
generated.

8346 National Digestive Diseases Information Clearinghouse
NI of Diabetes and Digestive and Kidney Diseases
31 Center Dr.
Bethesda, MD 20892   800-860-8747
                                                        TTY:866-569-1162
                                                     healthinfo@niddk.nih.gov
                                                   www.digestive.niddk.nih.gov
Griffin P. Rodgers, Director
Gregory G. Germino, Deputy Director
Camille Hoover, Executive Officer
Information and referral service of the National Institute of Diabetes and Digestive and Kidney Diseases. A central information
resource on the prevention and management of digestive diseases, the clearinghouse responds to written inquiries, develops
and distributes publications about digestive diseases, provides
referrals to digestive disease organizations and support groups,
and maintains a database of patient and professional education
materials from which literature searches are generated.

8347 National Fibromyalgia Association
3857 Birch St.
Suite 312
Newport Beach, CA 92660   nfa@fmaware.org
                                                         www.fmaware.org

Lynne Matallana, Founder
National Fibromyalgia Association's mission is to develop and
execute programs dedicated to improving the quality of life for
people with fibromyalgia.

8348 National Hemophilia Foundation
7 Penn Plaza
Suite 1204
New York, NY 10001   212-328-3700
                                                           888-463-6643
                                                        FAX: 212-328-3777
                                                      info@hemophilia.org
                                                         www.hemophilia.org
Leonard Valentino, President & CEO
Dawn Rotellini, Chief Operating Officer
Kevin Mills, Chief Scientific Officer
The National Hemophilia Foundation is dedicated to finding
better treatments and cures for bleeding and clotting disorders
and to preventing the complications of these disorders through
education, advocacy and research. Established in 1948, the National Hemophilia Foundation has chapters throughout the
country.

**8349 National Kidney and Urologic Diseases Information
Clearinghouse**
NI of Diabetes and Digestive and Kidney Diseases
31 Center Dr.
Bethesda, MD 20892   800-860-8747
                                                        TTY:866-569-1162
                                                     healthinfo@niddk.nih.gov
                                                   www.kidney.niddk.nih.gov
Griffin P. Rodgers, Director
Gregory G. Germino, Deputy Director
Camille Hoover, Executive Officer
NKUDIC was established in 1987 to increase knowledge and un-
derstanding about diseases of the kidneys and urologic system
among people with these conditions and their families, health
care professionals, and the general public.

**8350 National Organization for Albinism and
Hypopigmentation**
P.O. Box 959
East Hampstead, NH 03826-0959   603-887-2310
                                                           800-473-2310
                                                        FAX: 800-648-2310
                                                        info@albinism.org
                                                         www.albinism.org

Michael McGowan, Executive Director
Diana McCown, Vice-chair
Kris Baker, Secretary
Organization offering information and support to people with al-
binism, their families and the prodessionals who work with them.

8351 National Organization for Rare Disorders
55 Kenosia Ave
Danbury, CT 06810   203-744-0100
                                                        FAX: 203-263-9938
                                                     orphan@rarediseases.org
                                                          rarediseases.org

Marshall Summar, MD, Chairman
Peter Saltonstall, President & CEO
Pamela Gavin, Chief Operating Officer
The National Organization for Rare Disorders (NORD) is an organization serving individuals with rare diseases and the organizations that serve them. NORD offers educational programs,
advocacy, research and patient services.

8352 National Organization on Fetal Alcohol Syndrome
1200 Eton Ct NW
3rd Fl
Washington, DC 20007-3239   202-785-4585
                                                           800-666-6327
                                                        FAX: 202-466-6456
                                                     information@nofas.org
                                                           www.nofas.org

Tom Donaldson, President
Kathleen Tavenner Mitchell, Vice President
Andy Kachor, Communications Director
Dedicated to eliminating birth defects caused by alcohol con-
sumption during pregnancy and improving the qualtiy of life for
those individuals and families affected.

8353 Post-Polio Health International
50 Crestwood Executive Ctr.
Suite 440
St. Louis, MO 63126   314-534-0475
                                                        FAX: 314-534-5070
                                                        info@post-polio.org
                                                         www.post-polio.org

Mark Mallinger, President
Frederick M. Maynard, Vice President
Brian M. Tiburzi, Executive Director
To enhance the lives and independence of polio survivors, home
ventilator users, their caregivers and families, and health profes-
sionals through education, networking, and advocacy.

8354   Prader-Willi Syndrome Association USA
8588 Potter Park Dr
Ste 500
Sarasota, FL 34238   941-312-0400
                                                      800-926-4797
                                              FAX: 941-312-0142
                                                    www.pwsausa.org
Ken Smith, Executive Director
Jack Hannings, Development Director
Donny Moore, Development & Communications Specialist
National, nonprofit public charity that works for the benefit of individuals with Prader-Willi syndrome and their families. Dedicated to serving individuals affected by Prader-Willi syndrome (PWS) their families, and interested professionals, providing information, education, and support services to its members.

8355   Simonton Cancer Center
P.O. Box 6607
Malibu, CA 90264-6607   818-879-7904
                                                      800-459-3424
                                              FAX: 310-457-0421
                                    simontoncancercenter@msn.com
                                            www.simontoncenter.com
Dr. O. Carl Simonton, Founder
Edward Gilbert, MD, Medical Director
Karen Smith Simonton, Executive / Program Director
The Simonton Cancer Center is a non-profit organization dedicated to improving the health and lives of cancer patients and their families through psycho-social oncology.

8356   Special Care Dentistry Association
330 N. Wabash Avenue
Ste 2000
Chicago, IL 60611-4245   312-527-6764
                                              FAX: 312-673-6663
                                                  scda@scdaonline.org
                                                  www.scdaonline.org
Kristin Dee, Executive Director
Miriam Robbins, President
Jeffrey Hicks, President-Elect
The Special Care Dentistry Association serves as a resource to all oral health care professionals who serve or are interested in serving patients with special needs through education and networking to increase access to oral healthcare for patients with special needs.

8357   Spina Bifida Association
1600 Wilson Blvd
Ste 800
Arlington, VA 22209   202-944-3285
                                                      800-621-3141
                                              FAX: 202-944-3295
                                                     sbaa@sbaa.org
                                     www.spinabifidaassociation.org
Sara Struwe, President & CEO
Lee Towns, National Director, Communications & Outreach
Elizabeth Merck, National Director, Development
Non-profit organization whose mission is to promote the prevention of spina bifida and to enhance the lives of all affected. Addresses the specific needs of the spina bifida community and serves as the national representative of almost 60 chapters. Services include Toll free 800 information and referral service, as well as legislative updates.

8358   Spina Bifida and Hydrocephalus Association of Canada
167 Lombard Ave
Suite 472
Winnipeg, MB R3B 0T6,   204-925-3650
                                                      800-565-9488
                                              FAX: 204-925-3654
                                                    info@sbhac.ca
                                                    www.sbhac.ca
Susana Scott, President
Linda Randall, Vice President
Bonnie Hidlebaugh, National Manager, Communications & Development Coordinator
The Spina Bifida and Hydrocephalus Association of Canada has been working on behalf of people with spina bifida and/or hydrocephalus and their families.

8359   Sunburst Projects
Sunburst Projects United States Headquarters
2143 Hurley Way
Suite 240
Sacramento, CA 95825   916-440-0889
                                              FAX: 916-440-1208
                                         admin@sunburstprojects.org
                                           www.sunburstprojects.org
Jacob Bradley-Rowe, Executive Director
Sunburst Projects is a international organization that works to keep families together by providing services and support for youth who are infected or affected by HIV/AIDS.

8360   Taking Control of Your Diabetes (TCOYD)
990 Highland Dr
Suite 312
Solana Beach, CA 92075   858-755-5683
                                                      800-998-2693
                                              FAX: 858-755-6854
                                                      info@tcoyd.org
                                                      www.tcoyd.org
Steven Edelman, MD, Founder & Director
Sandra Bourdette, Co-Founder & Executive Director Emeritus
Jennifer Braidwood, Director of Marketing & Special Projects
Taking Control of Your Diabetes works to educate and motivate people with diabetes to take a more active role in managing their condition. The organization also offers continuing education programs for medical professionals caring for people with diabetes.

8361   United Brachial Plexus Network, Inc.
32 William Rd
Reading, MA 01867   781-315-6161
                                                    ubpn@ubpn.org
                                                      www.ubpn.org
Richard Looby, President
Dan Aldrich, Co- Vice President & Traumatic BPI Group
The United Brachial Plexus Network, Inc. provides education, information, and assistance for those affected by Brachial Plexus Palsy by offering information, contacts, resources, parent matching, and assistance developing chapters or support groups throughout the United States and the world.

8362   World Service Office of Overeaters Anonymous
6075 Zenith Crt NE
Rio Rancho, NM 87144-6424   505-891-2664
                                              FAX: 505-891-4320
                                                        info@oa.org
                                                         www.oa.org
Sarah Armstrong, Managing Director
OA aims to provide physical, emotional, and practical support for those seeking to improve their dietary habits. OA encourages members to develop a food plan with a health care professional and a sponsor.

Camps

8363   ADA Camp GranADA
American Diabetes Association
55 E Monroe St.
Suite 3420
Chicago, IL 60603   312-346-1805
                                          illinoiscamps@diabetes.org
                                                   www.diabetes.org
Camp GranADA is an American Diabetes Association resident camp located in Monticello, Illinois at the 4H Memorial Campground. For children with diabetes, ages 8-16.

8364   ADA Camp Needlepoint
American Diabetes Association
375 Bishops Way
Brookfield, WI 53005   414-778-5500
                                            campsupport@diabetes.org
                                                   www.diabetes.org
Becky Barnett, Camp Director
Camp Needlepoint is a summer camp for children who have type 1 diabetes. Coed, ages 8-16. The camp takes place at the YMCA Camp St. Croix in Hudson, Wisconsin.

8365 ADA Teen Adventure Camp
American Diabetes Association
55 E Monroe St.
Suite 3420
Chicago, IL 60603   312-346-1805
                            illinoiscamps@diabetes.org
                            www.diabetes.org
Paula Williams, Contact
Camping for teenagers with diabetes. Coed, ages 14 to 17. Camp
dates are early in August. Located at the YMCA Camp Duncan in
Ingleside, Illinois.

8366 ADA Triangle D Camp
American Diabetes Association
55 E Monroe St.
Suite 3420
Chicago, IL 60603   312-346-1805
                            illinoiscamps@diabetes.org
                            www.diabetes.org
Triangle D Camp is a resident camp program located at the YMCA
Camp Duncan in Ingleside, Illinois. Activities include swim-
ming, row boating, canoeing, camp games, sports, and diabetes
education. For children ages 9-13 with diabetes.

8367 Adam's Camp
56 Inverness Drive East
Suite 250
Englewood, CO 80112   303-563-8290
                            contact@adamscamp.org
                            www.adamscampcolorado.org
Brian Conly, Executive Director
Paige Heydon, Director, Finance & Development
Adam's Camp is a nonprofit organization, with multiple locations
across the United States, providing therapeutic programs and rec-
reational camps for children, and the families of children with
special needs and developmental delays.

8368 Adventure Day Camp
3480 Commission Ct
Lake Ridge, VA 22192   703-491-1444
                            office@princewilliamacademy.com
                            www.princewilliamacademy.com
Dr. Samia Harris, Founder & Executive Director
Rebecca Nykwest, Communications Director
Lindsay Chickering, Office Manager
Camping for children with asthma/respiratory ailments and can-
cer. Coed, ages 2-13.

8369 Agassiz Village
238 Bedford St
Suite B
Lexington, MA 02420-3477   781-860-0200
                            FAX: 781-860-0352
                            www.agassizvillage.org
Cliff Simmonds, Executive Director
Thomas Semeta, Camp Director
Warren Soar, Facility Director
Agassiz Village offers a variety of activities for all campers, boys
and girls, younger camper and teens, and programs for physically
challenged children and teens. By participating in daily activi-
ties, campers build a cooperative and positive community of different races, ages, ethnic and cultural backgrounds while
enhancing confidence and individuality. Camp is located in
Poland, Maine. For ages 8-17.

8370 Arizona Camp Sunrise
American Cancer Society
PO Box 27872
Tempe, AZ 85285   602-952-7550
                                     800-865-1582
                            FAX: 602-404-1118
                            www.azcampsunrise.org
Barbara Nicholas, Director
Leigh Ansley, Manager
Melissa Lee, Camp Director
Provides one-week summer camping sessions to children aged
8-16 who have had, or currently have, cancer. The classes range
from sports and outdoor games to dance and drama, arts, crafts,
and cooking. Other activities planned for the campers include
horseback riding, a trip to a lake, a dance, and learning to make
friendship bracelets.

8371 Bearskin Meadow Camp
Diabetic Youth Families
5167 Clayton Rd
Suite F
Concord, CA 94521   925-680-4994
                            FAX: 925-680-4863
                            info@dyf.org
                            www.dyf.org
Davey Warner, Executive Director
Kaylor Glassman, Director, Programs
*Marissa Clarke-Howard, Director, Development & Communica-
tions*
Bearskin Meadow Camp, is a camp program offered by the Diabe-
tes Youth Families organization to children (7-13), teens (14-17),
and families who are affected by type 1 diabetes. The camp has
traditional camp activities as well as educational opportunities
for campers.

**8372 Becket Chimney Corners YMCA Camps and Outdoor
Center**
748 Hamilton Rd
Becket, MA 01223   413-623-8991
                            FAX: 413-623-5890
                            cburke@bccymca.org
                            www.bccymca.org
Drew Lipsher, Chair
David Smith, Vice Chair
Christine Kalakay, Chief Financial Officer
Half-week and one-week sessions for campers with asthma/respi-
ratory ailments. Coed, ages 3 and up, families, seniors, single
adults.

8373 Breckenridge Outdoor Education Center
PO Box 697
Breckenridge, CO 80424   970-453-6422
                                     800-383-2632
                            FAX: 970-453-4676
                            boec@boec.org
                            www.boec.org
Sonya Norris, Executive Director
Karen Skruch, Finance Director
Jeff Inouye, Ski Program Director
Breckenridge Outdoor Education Center (BOEC) provides year
round educational outdoor experiences to individuals with physical and intellectual disabilities. Some programs BOEC offer include, Adaptive Ski and Ride School, Wilderness Programs and
adaptive programs for individuals with brain injuries, multiple
sclerosis, and Parkinson's Disease.
1976

8374 Bright Horizons Summer Camp
Sickle Cell Disease Association of Illinois
8100 S. Western Avenue
Chicago, IL 60620   773-526-5016
                                     866-798-1097
                            FAX: 773-526-5012
                    sicklecelldisease-illinois@scdai.org
Darryl H. Armstrong, Chair
TaLana Hughes, Executive Director
Anquineice Brown, Outreach Coordinator
Camping for children with blood disorders, ages 7-13. The joys
of learning include instruction in first aid, swimming and water
safety, boating, horseback riding and bowling plus arts and crafts.
In addition, there is a traditional menu of camp pleasures, like
hayrides, cookouts, nature hikes and sing-a-longs.

8375 Camp ASCCA
Alabama Easter Seal Society
PO Box 21
5278 Camp Ascca Dr.
Jacksons Gap, AL 36861   256-825-9226
                            FAX: 256-269-0714
                            info@campascca.org
                            www.campascca.org
Matt Rickman, Camp Director
John Stephenson, Administrator
Jocelyn Jones, Secretary
Camp ASCCA is for children and adults with disabilities or health
impairments. Camp ASCCA strives to help these individuals

achieve equality, independence and dignity in a safe environment.
1976

8376   Camp Aldersgate
2000 Aldersgate Road
Little Rock, AR 72205

501-225-1444
FAX: 501-225-2019
hello@campaldersgate.net
www.campaldersgate.net

Sonya S. Murphy, Chief Executive Officer
Shelley Myers, Chief Operating Officer & Chief Financial Officer
Brooke Wilson, Director, Communications

Camp Aldersgate is a nonprofit organization, offering summer, weekend camps, and year-round social service programs to children, teens and adults with special needs. The camp promotes outdoor recreation and socialization in a completely accessible environment.

8377   Camp Alpine
Alpine Alternatives
2518 E. Tudor Road
Ste 105
Anchorage, AK 99507-1105

907-561-6655
800-361-4174
FAX: 907-563-9232
alpinealternatives@arctic.net
www.alpinealternatives.org/programs.html

Margaret Webber, Executive Director
LaVerne Lee, Day Outings Director & Camp Alpine Director

Offers programs aimed at helping disabled youth expand their horizons, master new skills, make new friends, and increase motor coordination. Most importantly, participants experience growth in self-confidence and independence that affects all aspects of an individual's life. Camp services are open to all, regardless of type of disability or age. Activities include canoeing, hiking, swimming, outdoor games, sports, nature identification and much more.

8378   Camp Anuenue
250 Williams St. NW
Atlanta, GA 30303

808-595-7500
888-227-2345
FAX: 808-595-7502
www.cancer.org

Pamela K. Meyerhoffer, Chair
Robert E. Youle, Vice Chairman
Douglas K. Kelsey, Board Scientific Officer

(1 week) June, children with or recovered from cancer.

8379   Camp Beausite NW
PO Box 1227
Port Hadlock, WA 98339

360-732-7222
campbeausitenw.org

Raina Baker, Executive Director

The camp is located in Chimacum, Washington. Campers range from 7-65 in age and includes those with developmental disabilities, cerebral palsy, autism, Down syndrome, and other physical or mental disabilities. The camp offers five week-long overnight summer camp sessions for adults and children.

8380   Camp Beyond The Scars
Burn Institute
8825 Aero Drive
Suite 200
San Diego, CA 92123-2269

858-541-2277
FAX: 858-541-7179
ccoppenrath@burninstitute.org
www.burninstitute.org/camp-beyond-the-scar s

Susan Day, Executive Director
Tessa Haviland, Director, Marketing & Events
Benjamin Hemmings, Director, Operations

Camp Beyond the Scars, is a weeklong sleepaway summer camp for children aged 8-17 who have survived a burn injury. Staffed by adult burn survivors, healthcare professionals, and off-duty firefighters, the camp provides an inclusive environment for burn survivors to participate in activities including, swimming, basketball, volleyball, archery, golf, and arts and crafts. The camp is free of charge, and is hosted at a camp facility in Romano, California.
1987

8381   Camp Boggy Creek
30500 Brantley Branch Rd.
Eustis, FL 32736

352-483-4200
866-462-6449
FAX: 352-483-0589
info@campboggycreek.org
www.boggycreek.org

June Clark, President & CEO
Lisa Hicks, Chief Development Officer
David Mann, Camp Director

Year-round sessions for children with a variety of chronic or life-threatening illnesses including cancer, hemophilia, epilepsy, heart defects, HIV, spina bifida and respiratory ailments. Coed, ages 7-16.

8382   Camp Bon Coeur
300 Ridge Rd.
Suite K
Lafayette, LA 70506

337-233-8437
FAX: 337-233-4160
info@heartcamp.com
www.heartcamp.com

Susannah Craig, Executive Director
Chelsea Doyle, Summer Program Coordinator
Jessica Becnel, Family Support Group Coordinator

A week-long summer camp program for children ages 7-16 with heart defects. Activities include canoeing, swimming, archery, art, sports, and teambuilding and personal development activities.

8383   Camp Breathe Easy
American Lung Association
2452 Spring Rd. SE
Smyrna, GA 30080

Camp Breathe Easy is a summer camp for children ages 6-13 with asthma. Campers learn asthma self-management techniques and coping strategies as well as participate in activities such as swimming, fishing, canoeing, sports, and arts and crafts. The camp is operated by the Georgia Chapter of the American Lung Association and held at Camp Twin Lakes in Rutledge, GA.

8384   Camp Can Do
Administrative Office
3 Unami Trail
Chalfont, PA 18914

717-273-6525
campcandoforever.org

Tom Prader, Director, Patient Camp
Stephanie Cole, Director, Patient Camp
Caitlyn McLarnon, Director, Sibling Camp

Camp Can Do is for children ages 8-17 who have been diagnosed with cancer in the last five years. The camp also offers a session for siblings of children with cancer.

8385   Camp Carefree
American Diabetes Association
Lions Camp Pride
154 Camp Pride Way
New Durham, NH 03855

campsupport@diabetes.org
www.diabetes.org

Phyllis Woestemeyer, Director

Camp Carefree is a American Diabetes Association summer camp for children with diabetes. The camp is located at Lions Camp Pride in New Durham, New Hampshire.

8386   Camp Catch-a-Rainbow
American Cancer Society
250 Williams St. NW
Atlanta, GA 30303

808-595-7500
888-227-2345
FAX: 808-595-7502
www.cancer.org

Pamela K. Meyerhoffer, Chair
Robert E. Youle, Vice Chairman
Douglas K. Kelsey, Board Scientific Officer

Camp Catch-a-Rainbow's programs are available completely free to any child in MI or IN who has or has had cancer, between the ages of 4 and 20, with their doctor's approval. Family Camp is reserved for those campers who have attended camp during that year's summer sessions and their families. Day, week, adult retreat, and family camp are available options.

8387 Camp Cheerful
Achievement Centers For Children
15000 Cheerful Lane
Strongsville, OH 44136-5420
440-238-6200
FAX: 440-238-1858
www.achievementcenters.org

Sally Farwell, President & CEO
Scott Peplin, Executive Vice President & CFO
Deborah Osgood, Vice President, Development & Marketing
Camp Cheerful provides a number of day and overnight camping options for children and adults who have disabilities. The camp hosts traditional camp activities as well as year-round therapeutic horseback riding sessions and an accessible high ropes challenge course during the summer. The focus of activities is to increase the quality of life while encouraging confidence and independence.

8388 Camp Christmas Seal
American Lung Association of Oregon
102 W McDowell Rd
Phoenix, AZ 85003-1213
602-258-7505
FAX: 202-452-1805
info@lungoregon.org
www.lungoregon.org

Kathryn A. Forbes, Chairman
John F. Emanuel, Vice Chair
Harold Wimmer, President/CEO
Camp is located in Sisterhood, Oregon. Sessions for children with asthma/respiratory ailments. Coed, ages 8-15.

8389 Camp Classen YMCA
YMCA of Greater Oklahoma City
10840 Main Camp Rd
Davis, OK 73030
580-369-2272
FAX: 580-369-2284
www.itsmycamp.org

Ford C. Price, Chair
Tricia Everest, Vice Chairman
Mike Grady, President & CEO
Camp is located in Davis, Oklahoma. Sessions for children and adults with diabetes. Coed, ages 8-17, families, seniors and single adults.

8390 Camp Conrad Chinnock
Diabetes Camping And Educational Services, Inc.
2400 E. Katella Ave.
Suite 800
Anaheim, CA 92806
844-744-2267
FAX: 909-752-5354
info@diabetescamping.org
www.diabetescamping.org

Rocky Wilson, Executive Director
Ryan Martz, Development & Program Director
Dale Lissy, Camp Manager
Camp Conrad Chinnock offers year round recreational, social, and educational opportunities for children and families with type 1 diabetes.

8391 Camp Courage North
True Friends
37569 Courage North Dr.
Lake George, MN 56458
952-852-0101
800-450-8376
FAX: 952-852-0123
info@truefriends.org
www.truefriends.org

John Leblanc, President & CEO
Conor McGrath, Senior Director, Camp & Operations
Jon Salmon, Director, Programs
Camp Courage North provides summer camp sessions for individuals with disabilities.

8392 Camp Discovery - Illinois
American Diabetes Association
55 E Monroe St.
Suite 3420
Chicago, IL 60603
312-346-1805
illinoiscamps@diabetes.org
www.diabetes.org

Camp Discovery is a day camp program for children ages 4-9 with diabetes. The camp is held at HealthTrack Sports and Wellness in Glen Ellyn, Illinois.

8393 Camp Discovery Kansas
American Diabetes Association
608 W Douglas Ave.
Wichita, KS 67203
316-684-6091
campsupport@diabetes.org
www.diabetes.org

Camp is located at Rock Springs 4-H Center in Junction City. For children and teens ages 8-16 with diabetes.

8394 Camp Echoing Hills
36272 County Rd. 79
Warsaw, OH 43844
740-327-2311
www.ehvi.org

Lauren Unger, Camp Administrator
Summer camp for children and adults with physical, intellectual and developmental disabilities.

8395 Camp Eden Wood
True Friends
6350 Indian Chief Rd.
Eden Prairie, MN 55346
952-852-0101
800-450-8376
FAX: 952-852-0123
info@truefriends.org
www.truefriends.org

John Leblanc, President & CEO
Conor McGrath, Senior Director, Camp & Operations
Jon Salmon, Director, Programs
Offers resident camp programs for children, teenagers and adults with developmental, physical or multiple disabilities. Fishing, creative arts, golf, sports and other activities are available. Respite care weekend camps year round for children, teenagers and adults. Guided vacations for teens and adults with developmental disabilities or other unique needs.

8396 Camp Floyd Rogers
PO Box 541058
Omaha, NE 68154
402-885-9022
director@campfloydrogers.com
www.campfloydrogers.com

Dylan Helberg, Camp Director
Carrie Busing, Operations Director
A camp for diabetic children. Coed, ages 8-18. Campers enjoy activities, participate in special events, engage in evening programs, and they meet other children their own age with diabetes.

8397 Camp Glengarra
Girl Scouts - Foothills Council
33 Jewett Pl
Utica, NY 13501-4715
315-733-1909
FAX: 315-733-1909

Natalie Brown, Executive Director
Karen Lubecki, Director
Camp Glengarra is located on 500+ acres of fields and forests, about eight miles west of Camden. This Girl Scout Camp hosts a myriad of programs throughout the year as well as summer day and resident camp. Summer sessions for girls 5-17 with ADD or asthma/respiratory ailments.

8398 Camp Glyndon
American Diabetes Association
800 Wyman Park Dr
Suite 110
Baltimore, MD 21211-2837
410-265-0075
800-342-2383
FAX: 410-235-4048
askada@diabetes.org
www.childrenwithdiabetes.com

Heather Magoon, Director
Camp is located in Nanjemoy, Maryland. One and two-week sessions July-August for children with diabetes and their families. Coed, ages 8-16.

8399   **Camp H.U.G.**
Arizona Hemophilia Association
826 North 5th Ave
Phoenix, AZ 85003   602-955-3947
info@arizonahemophilia.org
www.arizonahemophilia.org/camp-programs

Leigh Goldstein, Executive Director
Vickie Parra, Programs & Conferences Manager
Jessica Jackson, Finance Manager

Camp H.U.G (Hemophilia Uniting Generations) is a weekend camp program of the Arizona Hemophilia Association. The camp is for families who have a member with hemophilia, WWD, and/or other bleeding disorders.

8400   **Camp Harkness**
The Arc Eastern Connecticut
125 Sachem St.
Norwich, CT 06360   860-889-4435
FAX: 860-889-4662
info@thearcect.org
thearcect.org/camp-harkness

Kathleen Stauffer, Chief Executive Officer

A week-long summer camp program for individuals with intellectual and developmental disabilities. The camp is held at Camp Harkness in Waterford, CT.

8401   **Camp Heartland**
One Heartland
26001 Heinz Rd.
Willow River, MN 55795   888-216-2028
helpkids@oneheartland.org
www.oneheartland.org

Patrick Kindler, Executive Director
Katie Donlin, Operations Manager
Kadien Bartels-Merkel, Program Director

A program of One Heartland, a nonprofit organization working to provide camping programs for children with serious illnesses or experiencing social isolation, Camp Heartland is a weeklong summer camp for children, ages 7-15, who are infected or affected by HIV/AIDS. The camp is held in Willow River, Minnesota.

8402   **Camp Hertko Hollow**
4200 University Ave.
Suite 320
Des Moines, IA 50266   515-471-8523
855-502-8500
FAX: 515-288-2531
www.camphertkohollow.com

Jessica Thornton, Executive Director
Deb Holwegner, Camp Director

Camp Hertko Hollow is an educational and recreational summer camp program for children and teens ages 6-17 with diabetes. Campers participate in traditional camp activities and learn about living with diabetes.

8403   **Camp Hickory Hill**
PO Box 1942
Columbia, MO 65205   573-445-9146
camphickoryhill@gmail.com
www.camphickoryhill.com

Jessica Bernhardt, Camp Director

Educates diabetic children concerning diabetes and its care. In addition to daily educational sessions on some aspects of diabetes, campers participate in swimming, sailing, arts and crafts and overnight camping. Coed, ages 7-17.

8404   **Camp Ho Mita Koda**
14040 Auburn Rd.
Newbury, OH 44065   440-739-4095
info@camphomitakoda.org
www.camphomitakoda.org

Ian Roberts, Executive Director
Eric Brown, Camp Director

Camp Ho Mita Koda is a summer camp for children with type 1 diabetes. The camp aims to provide outdoor activities while also educating and building life skills for children with diabetes. Offers overnight camp, family camp, specialty camp, and leadership development programs.

8405   **Camp Hodia**
Idaho Diabetes Youth Programs, Inc.
5439 W Kendall St.
Boise, ID 83706   208-891-1023
info@hodia.org
www.hodia.org

Lisa Gier, Executive Director
Morgan Coenen, Director, Programs
Ciera Miller, Director, Marketing

Offers a variety of educational camp programs for children and teens with type 1 diabetes.

8406   **Camp Hollywood HEART**
One Heartland
26001 Heinz Rd.
Willow River, MN 55795   888-216-2028
FAX: 612-824-6303
helpkids@oneheartland.org
www.oneheartland.org

Patrick Kindler, Executive Director
Katie Donlin, Operations Manager
Kadien Bartels-Merkel, Program Director

A program of One Heartland, a nonprofit organization working to provide camping programs for children with serious illnesses or experiencing social isolation. Camp Hollywood HEART is a weeklong summer camp for youths, ages 15-20, who are infected or affected by HIV/AIDS. The camp is held in Malibu, California and is partnership camp between One Heartland and Hollywood Heart.

8407   **Camp Honor**
Arizona Hemophilia Association
826 North 5th Ave
Phoenix, AZ 85003   602-955-3947
info@arizonahemophilia.org
www.arizonahemophilia.org/camp-programs

Leigh Goldstein, Executive Director
Vickie Parra, Programs & Conferences Manager
Jessica Jackson, Finance Manager

Camp Honor offers a week long summer camp to children affected by an inherited bleeding disorders. The cost of the camp is $35 for a single camper and $50 dollars for a family (2 or more campers). Camp Honor offers children the chance to partcipate in outdoor activities and educational opportunities. In order to attend the camp there is an application process.

8408   **Camp Independence**
National Kidney Foundation
30 East 33rd Street
New York, NY 10016   770-452-1539
800-622-9010
FAX: 212-689-9261
info@kidney.org
www.kidneyga.org

Gregory W. Scott, Chair
Beth Piraino, President
Bruce Skyer, CEO

Camp Independence is Georgia's a overnight, week-long summer camp providing essential medical care, treatment & fun for kids with kidney disease and transplants. Camp Independence recognizes that campers are normal children but have special needs providing these children with opportunities for development & individual growth, peer support & normal life experiences. Activities include swimming, arts & crafts, fishing and horsebackriding, in addition to archery, games and sports, and ceramics.

8409   **Camp Jened**
United Cerebral Palsy Association New York
P.O.Box 483
Rock Hill, NY 12775-483   845-434-2220
FAX: 845-434-2253

Michael Branam, Executive Director

Camp is located in Rock Hill, New York. Sessions for adults with severe developmental and physical disabilities. Coed, ages 18-99.

8410 **Camp John Warvel**
American Diabetes Association
8604 Allisonville Rd.
Suite 140
Indianapolis, IN 46250   317-352-9226
campsupport@diabetes.org
www.diabetes.org
A camp program for children and teens ages 7-17 with diabetes.
The camp is held at Camp Crosley in North Webster, Indiana.

8411 **Camp Joslin**
The Barton Center for Diabetes Education, Inc.
30 Ennis Rd.
PO Box 356
North Oxford, MA 01537-0356   508-987-2056
FAX: 508-987-2002
info@bartoncenter.org
www.bartoncenter.org

Lynn Butler-Dinunno, Executive Director
Jenna Dufresne, Director, Health Services
Sarah Balko, Director, Camps & Programs
Camp for boys ages 6-16 with diabetes. This program offers active summer sports and activities, supplemented by medical treatment and diabetes education.

8412 **Camp Joy**
3325 Swamp Creek Rd
Schwenksville, PA 19473-1518   610-754-6878
FAX: 610-754-7880
www.campjoy.com

Robert G Griffith, President
A special needs camp for kids and adults (ages 4-80+) with developmental disabilities such as autism, brain injury, neurological disorder, visual and/or hearing impairments, Angelman and Down syndromes, and other developmental disabilities.

8413 **Camp Ko-Man-She**
Diabetes Dayton
2555 S Dixie Dr.
Suite 112
Dayton, OH 45409   937-220-6611
FAX: 937-224-0240
admin@diabetesdayton.org
www.diabetesdaytoncamp.com

Susan McGovern, Executive Director
Camp Ko-Man-She is located in Bellefontaine, Ohio, and is held annually for children with diabetes. The camp's goal is for children to socialize with other children who also have diabetes and to have fun outdoors in a medically supervised setting. Co-ed, ages 8-17.

8414 **Camp Kweebec**
157 Game Farm Rd.
Schwenksville, PA 19473   610-667-2123
FAX: 610-667-6376
info@kweebec.com
www.kweebec.com

Les Weiser, Owner/Director
Maddy Weiser, Owner/Director
Rachel Weiser, Associate Director, Director of
Camp is located in Schwenksville, Pennsylvania. Sessions for children and adults with diabetes. Coed, ages 6-16, families, seniors and single adults.

8415 **Camp L-Kee-Ta**
940 Golden Valley Drive
Bettendorf, IA 52722   319-752-3639
800-798-0833
FAX: 319-753-1410
www.gseiwi.org

Teresa Colgan, Chair
Jill Dashner, 1st Vice chiar
Anna Gibney, Development Manager
Camp is located in Danville, Iowa. Half-week and one-week sessions June-August for children with asthma/respiratory ailments. Girls, ages 7-18 and families.

8416 **Camp Latgawa**
Oregon-Idaho Conference Center
13250 S Fork Little Butte Creek Rd
Eagle Point, OR 97524- 5593   541-826-9699
camplatgawa@hotmail.com
latgawa.gocamping.org/

Eva LaBonty, Director
Camp Latgawa provides year round hospitality for groups up to 90 people. The bunk/dormitory style facilities are heated and have restrooms and showers either in the cabin or nearby.

8417 **Camp Libbey**
Maumee Valley Girl Scout Center
2244 Collingwood Blvd
Toledo, OH 43620-1147   419-243-8216
800-860-4516
FAX: 419-245-5357
www.girlscoutsofwesternohio.org

Jody Wainscott, Chair
Ellen Iobst, 1st Vice Chair
Susan Gantz Matz, 2nd Vice Chair
Camp for girls 7-18 with asthma/respiratory ailments, diabetes, epilepsy and muscular dystrophy is located in Defiance, Ohio.

8418 **Camp MITIOG**
Share, Inc
7615 N. Platte Purchase Drive
Kansas City, MO 64118   816-221-4450
877-221-4450
FAX: 816-221-1420
midlands@midlandsmc.org
www.midlandsmc.org

Mike Hale, President/Financial Officer
Pam Mathena, Adm. Assistant to MMC Financial Officer
Donna Fletcher, Congregational Consultant
Camp is located in Excelsior Springs, Missouri. One-week summer sessions for children with spina bifida. Coed, ages 6-16.

8419 **Camp Magruder**
17450 Old Pacific Hwy.
Rockaway Beach, OR 97136   503-355-2310
FAX: 503-355-8701
troy@campmagruder.org
www.campmagruder.org

Troy Taylor, Camp Director
Hope Montgomery, Program Director
Rik Gutzke, Facilities Manager
Camp is located in Rockaway Beach, Oregon. Sessions for teens and adults with developmental disabilities through Camp Hope.

8420 **Camp Nejeda**
Camp Nejeda Foundation
910 Saddlebrook Road
P.O. Box 156
Stillwater, NJ 07875   973-383-2611
FAX: 973-383-9891
info@campnejeda.org

Ernest Post, MD, Secretary
Scott Ross, President
Bill Vierbuchen, Executive Director
For children with diabetes, ages 7-15. Provides an active and safe camping experience which enables the children to learn about and understand diabetes. Activities include boating, swimming, fishing, archery, as well as camping skills.

8421 **Camp Not-A-Wheeze**
2689 E Michelle Way
Gilbert, AZ 85234   602-336-6575
FAX: 602-336-6576
info@campnotawheeze.org
campnotawheeze.org

Alan Crawford, Camp Director
Week-long summer camp for children aged 7-14 with moderate to severe asthma living in Arizona. Campers attending Camp Not-A- Wheeze, participate in a wide range of activities such as horseback riding, hiking, canoeing, and fishing as well as an asthma education class. Those wishing to attend must fill out and send in a camper application.

8422 **Camp Okizu**
Okizu Foundation
83 Hamilton Dr.
Suite 200
Novato, CA 94949-5755
415-382-9083
FAX: 415-382-8384
info@okizu.org
www.okizu.org

Suzie Randall, Executive Director
Heather Ferrier, Director, Family Services
Sarah Uldricks, Director, Marketing & Special Events
Camp Okizu offers a variety of medically supervised, residential camp programs for families who have a child diagnosed with cancer. Programs are offered throughout the year free of charge.

8423 **Camp Paivika**
PO Box 3367
Crestline, CA 92325
909-338-1102
FAX: 909-338-2502
camppaivika@abilityfirst.org
www.abilityfirst.org/camp-paivika

Kelly Kunsek, Camp Director
Lauren Wilson, Program Director
Tina Ronning-Fraynd, Coordinator, Camper Services
As a program of AbilityFirst, Camp Paivika offers overnight summer programs for children, teens and adults with developmental and physical disabilities. The camp is completely accessible and the staff is trained to provide any assistance or personal care a camper needs. Located in San Bernardino National Forest, Camp Paivika provides a traditional summer camp experience in a safe and fun environment.
1947

8424 **Camp Pelican**
PO Box 10235
New Orleans, LA 70181
888-617-1118
FAX: 866-295-3803
camppelican@gmail.com
www.camppelican.org

A week-long overnight summer camp for children with pulmonary disorders, including severe asthma and cystic fibrosis, living in the state of Louisiana.

8425 **Camp Rainbow**
Phoenix Childrens Hospital
1919 E Thomas Rd
Phoenix, AZ 85016
602-933-1000
888-908-5437
camprainbow@phoenixchildrens.com
www.phoenixchildrens.org

Emilie Jarboe, Camp Director
Camp Rainbow is for children aged 7-17 who have or had cancer or a chronic blood disorder. The camp is offered for one week during the summer, held at camp Friendly Pines in Prescott, Arizona. Campers must be patients of Phoenix Children's Hospital's Center for Cancer and Blood Disorders, with the camp offering participants the opportunity to experience traditional camp activities including but not limited to, horseback riding, canoeing, fishing, swimming, and archery.

8426 **Camp Reach for the Sky**
The Seany Foundation
3530 Camino del Rio N
Suite 101
San Diego, CA 92108
858-551-0922
www.theseanyfoundation.org

Amy Robins, Co-Founder, The Seany Foundation
Paula Lutzky, Chief Financial Officer
Emily Brody, Director, Marketing & Media
Previously run by the American Cancer Society, Camp Reach for the Sky (CR4TS) is now run by The Seany Foundation and provides an opportunity for children with cancer and their siblings to attend a free summer camp. Camp Reach for the Sky offers a multiple programs, including a Resident Oncology Camp, a Sibling Camp and Day Camps.

8427 **Camp Ronald McDonald at Eagle Lake**
2555 49th Street
Sacramento, CA 95817
916-734-4230
FAX: 916-734-4238
info@rmhcnc.org
www.campronald.org

Catherine Ithurburn, Chief Executive Officer
Pip Pipkins, Camp Manager
Camp Ronald McDonald at Eagle Lake collaborates with other nonprofit organizations to provide week long summer camp opportunities for children with special medical needs, financial hardship and/or emotional, developmental or physical disabilities. The camp is fully accessible.

8428 **Camp Ronald McDonald for Good Times**
4560 Fountain Avenue
Los Angeles, CA 90029
323-666-6400
FAX: 626-744-9969
www.campronaldmcdonald.org

Erica Mangham, Executive Director
Brian Crater, Associate Executive Director
Chad Edwards, Program Director
Free year-round residential camping for children with cancer and their families.

8429 **Camp Sawtooth**
Oregon-Idaho Conference Center
P.O.Box 68
Fairfield, ID 83327-68
800-593-7539
sawtooth@gocamping.org
www.gocamping.org

David Hargreaves, Director
Camp located 35 miles north of fairfield, centrally located for all of southern Idaho.

8430 **Camp Seale Harris**
Southeastern Diabetes Education Services
500 Chase Park S.
Ste 104
Birmingham, AL 35244
205-402-0415
FAX: 205-402-0416
info@campsealeharris.org
www.campsealeharris.org

Rhonda McDavid, Executive Director
John Latimer, Director, Camp & Community Programs
Shelby Harrison, Manager, Communications & Events
Offering overnight, family, day and community program camps, Camp Seale Harris is a nonprofit organization that offers residential camps for children and teens with diabetes. With multiple programs in Alabama, the volunteer camp counselors are trained adults living with diabetes, to better help the camp attendees gain independence in learning to manage their diabetes. Camp programs run all year round.
1949

8431 **Camp Setebaid**
Setebaid Services, Inc.
PO Box 196
Winfield, PA 17889-0196
570-524-9090
FAX: 570-523-0769
info@setebaidservices.org
www.setebaidservices.org

Mark Moyer, Executive Director
Camping sessions for children with diabetes. The camp also hosts a family day for children with diabetes and their families.

8432 **Camp Smile-A-Mile**
Smile-A-Mile Place
1600 2nd Ave. S.
Birmingham, AL 35233
205-323-8427
FAX: 205-323-6220
info@campsam.org
www.campsam.org

Bruce Hooper, Executive Director
Kellie Reece, Chief Operating Officer
Katie Langley, Special Events Director
Camp Smile-A-Mile offers 7 different educational camp opportunities for children and their families who have been affected by childhood cancer in Alabama. The programs run all year long, in a variety of formats.

8433 Camp Sunburst
Sunburst Projects United States Headquarters
2143 Hurley Way
Suite 240
Sacramento, CA 95825   916-440-0889
                                  FAX: 916-440-1208
                          admin@sunburstprojects.org
                          www.sunburstprojects.org
Jacob Bradley-Rowe, Executive Director
Camp Sunburst is a youth oriented leadership camp that promotes and creates an environment to help youth learn self confidence to change negative social patterns and break cycles of HIV/AIDS infections. Activities campers will participate in include, boating, swimming, art, dance, and sports.

8434 Camp Sunrise
Johns Hopkins Hospital
600 North Wolfe Street
CMSC 800
Baltimore, MD 21287-5904   410-955-5311
Sherryce Robinson, Mission Delivery Manager
Kira Elring, Regional Mission Director
Gloria Jetter, Regional Executive Director
Week long summer camp in White Hall, MD., for children ages 6-18 who have been diagnosed with or have survived cancer. Camp sunrise also has a 'day camp' program available for children ages 4-5. Camp activities include sports & games, swimming, arts & crafts, and nature hikes.

8435 Camp Sunshine Dreams
PO Box 28232
Fresno, CA 93729-8232   stephanie@campsunshinedreams.org
                          www.campsunshinedreams.com
Stephanie Scharbach, Contact
Pam Aiello, Contact
Camp Sunshine Dreams provides a summer camp experience to children aged 8-15 with cancer and their siblings.

8436 Camp Sweeney
PO Box 918
Gainesville, TX 76241   940-665-2011
                                  FAX: 940-665-9467
                          info@campsweeney.org
                          www.campsweeney.org
Ernie Fernandez, Camp Director
Bob Cannon, Program Director
Billie Hood, Business Manager
Camp Sweeney teaches self-care and self-reliance to children ages 5-18 with type 1 diabetes. Campers participate in activities such as swimming, fishing, horseback riding and arts and crafts while learning how to self manage their diabetes.

8437 Camp Tall Turf
816 Madison SE
Grand Rapids, MI 49507   616-452-7906
                                  FAX: 616-452-7907
                          info@tallturf.org
                          www.tallturf.org
Eric Brown, Chair
Ed Van Poolen, Vice Chair
Miriam DeJong, Director of Programs
Camp is located in Walkerville, Michigan. Summer camping sessions for youth with asthma/respiratory ailments and ADD. Coed, ages 8-16.

8438 Camp Taylor
Camp Taylor, Inc.
8224 West Grayson Rd.
Modesto, CA 95358-9094   209-545-3853
                          camp@kidsheartcamp.org
                          www.kidsheartcamp.org
Kimberlie Gamino, Founder & Executive Director
With several programs, Camp Taylor provides youth, teens, and the families of children with heart disease the opportunity to go to a free medically supervised summer sleepaway camp. Campers are able to enjoy activities such as, swimming, snorkeling, horseback riding, rock-wall, skits, archery, and heart education.
Founded in 2002.

8439 Camp Vacamas
256 Macopin Rd
West Milford, NJ 07480   973-838-0942
                                  877-428-8222
                          www.vacamas.org
Felix A. Urrutia, Executive Director
Kristin Short, Camp Director
Karen Wendolowski, Executive Secretary
Disadvantaged children with asthma or sickle cell anemia, ages 8-16, are offered special programs in canoeing, backpacking, camping, music and leadership training. Sliding scale tuition. Year round programs for youth at risk groups. Conference center facility open for group rentals.

8440 Camp Waziyatah
530 Mill Hill Rd
Waterford, ME 04088-4011   207-583-2267
                                  FAX: 509-357-2267
                          info@wazi.com
                          wazi.com
Gregg Parker, Owner/Director
Mitch Parker, Owner/Director
Camp is located in Waterford, Massachusetts. Three, four and seven-week sessions June-August for campers with cancer and diabetes. Coed, ages 8-15 and families, single adults.

8441 Camp WheezeAway
YMCA Camp Chandler
880 South Lawrence Street
Montgomery, AL 36104   334-229-4362
                          jikner@ymcamontgomery.org
                          ymcamontgomery.org/camp/wheezeaway
Jennifer Ikner, Contact
For children ages 8-12 with moderate to severe asthma, Camp WheezeAway offers week long summer camp programs that foster confidence building skills. The camp is free and managed by medical professionals. Those with children wishing to attend must apply to the camp and complete a selection process.

8442 Camp del Corazon
11615 Hesby St
North Hollywood, CA 91601-3620   818-754-0312
                                  FAX: 818-754-0377
                          info@campdelcorazon.org
                          www.campdelcorazon.org
Kevin Shannon, President & Medical Director
Chrissie Endler, Executive Director
Kristina Caberto Wallace, Director of Development & Operations
Camp del Corazon, is a nonprofit corporation offering a no cost summer camp and other programs to children aged 7-17 living with heart disease. Campers or their guardians must fill out a camp application, with acceptance into the camp dependant upon a nurse review of the parent and cardiology portions of the application.
1995

8443 Camps for Children & Teens with Diabetes
Diabetes Society
1165 Lincoln Ave
Suite 300
San Jose, CA 95125-3052   408-287-3785
                                  800-989-1165
                                  FAX: 408-287-2701
                          info@diabetessociety.org
Sharon Ogbor, Executive Director
Thomas Smith, Director
Since 1974, sponsors up to 20 day camps, family camps and resident camps for children 4 through 17. These camps provide an opportunity for children with diabetes to go to camp, meet other children and gain a better understanding of their diabetes. The total experience can help campers develop more confidence in their abilities to control their diabetes effectively while enjoying the traditional camp experience. Camps are located throughout CA and parts of Nevada.

8444 **Cedar Ridge Camp**
4120 Old Routt Road
Louisville, KY 40299   502-267-5848
                                                   FAX: 502-267-0116
                                             info@cedarridgecamp.com
                                             www.cedarridgecamp.com

Andrew Hartmans, Executive Director
Half-week, one and two-week sessions for children with diabetes, developmental disabilities and muscular dystrophy. Coed, ages 6-17.

8445 **Children's Hospital Burn Camps Program**
13123 E 16th Ave.
PO Box 580
Aurora, CO 80045   720-777-8295
                                                   FAX: 720-777-7270
                                          learnmore@noordinarycamps.org
                                             www.noordinarycamps.org
Trudy Boulter, Camp Director
Tim Schuetz, Outreach Coordinator
The Children's Hospital Colorado Burn Camps Program provides rehabilitation and reintegration opportunities for children, teens, adults, and families who have been affected by burn injuries. The Camps Program has partnerships with 7 hospitals across the United States and offers year round programs.

8446 **Clara Barton Camp**
The Barton Center for Diabetes Education, Inc.
30 Ennis Rd.
PO Box 356
North Oxford, MA 01537-0356   508-987-2056
                                                   FAX: 508-987-2002
                                                info@bartoncenter.org
                                                 www.bartoncenter.org
Lynn Butler-Dinunno, Executive Director
Jenna Dufresne, Director, Health Services
Sarah Balko, Director, Camps & Programs
Camp for girls ages 6-16 with diabetes. Campers participate in traditional camp activities and receive diabetes education. Activities include swimming, boating, sports, dance, music and arts and crafts.

8447 **Diabetes Camp**
Tanager Place
1614 W Mount Vernon Rd.
Mount Vernon, IA 52314   319-363-0681
                                                   FAX: 319-365-6411
                                             campmail@tanagerplace.org
                                                 www.camptanager.org
Donald Pirrie, Camp Director
Provides recreational activities for children and teens with diabetes. The camp has on-site 24-hour physician and nursing staff. Ages 6-17.

8448 **Dr. Moises Simpser VACC Camp**
Nicklaus Children's Hospital
3200 SW 62nd Ave.
Suite 203
Miami, FL 33155-4076   305-662-8222
                                                   FAX: 786-268-1765
                                              bela.florentin@mch.com
                                                  www.vacccamp.com
Bela Florentin, Camp Coordinator
Tania Diaz, Camp Clinical Coordinator
VACC Camp is a week-long overnight camp program for ventilation-assisted children and their families. The program includes sailing, swimming, field trips to local attractions, campsite entertainment, structured games, free play, and more. Parents have formal and informal opportunities to network among themselves.

8449 **Dream Street**
Dream Street Foundation
324 S. Beverly Dr.
Suite 500
Beverly Hills, CA 90212   424-333-1371
                                                   FAX: 310-388-0302
                                          www.dreamstreetfoundation.org
Patty Grubman, Founder
Run by The Dream Street Foundation, Dream Street Camps provide camping programs for children (aged 4-14) and young adults (18-24) with chronic and life threatening illnesses. The kids program runs in California, with the young adults program running in Arizona. The programs are free of charge, and campers can participate in different activities such as, swimming, arts and crafts, sports, horseback riding, and archery.

8450 **EDI Camp**
Wyman Center
600 Kiwanis Dr
St. Louis, MO 63025-2212   636-938-5245
                                                   FAX: 636-938-5289
                                                 www.wymancenter.org
David Hilliard, President
Theresa Mayberry, Senior Vice President
Youngsters with diabetes learn how to care for themselves while participating in a wide variety of outdoor activities and trips. The camp, managed and financed by the American Diabetes Association Greater St. Louis Affiliate, offers camperships to children from the Greater St. Louis area, ages 7-16, but nonresidents may also apply.

8451 **Easterseals Camp ASCCA**
PO Box 21
5278 Camp Ascca Dr.
Jacksons Gap, AL 36861   256-825-9226
                                                   FAX: 256-269-0714
                                                info@campascca.org
                                                  www.campascca.org
Matt Rickman, Camp Director
John Stephenson, Administrator
Jocelyn Jones, Secretary
Easterseals Camp ASCCA is Alabama's Special Camp for Children and Adults, offering therapeutic recreation for children and adults with both physical and intellectual disabilities. The camp is located on 260 acres of barrier free woodland on Lake Martin and campers experience a wide variety of educational and recreational activities, including but not limited to: horseback riding, fishing, tubing, swimming, environmental education, arts, canoeing, and zip-lining. 1 week camp fees are $750.00.
1976

8452 **FCYD Camp Utada**
Foundation for Children and Youth with Diabetes
1995 W 9000 S
West Jordan, UT 84088   801-566-6913
                                              www.fcydcamputada.org
Dave Okubo, MD, Co-Founder & Trustee
Elizabeth Elmer, Co-Founder & Trustee
Nathan Gedge, Co-Founder & Trustee
Camping for children with diabetes. Coed, ages 1-18 and families.

8453 **Father Drumgoole Connelly Summer Camp**
MIV Mount Loretto
6581 Hylan Blvd
Staten Island, NY 10309-3830   718-317-2600
                                                   FAX: 718-317-2830
                                                www.mountloretto.org
Stephen Rynn, Executive Director
Maryann Virga, Executive Assistant
Loretta Polanish, Executive Secretary
Summer sessions for children with epilepsy, hearing impairment and developmental disabilities. Coed, ages 5-13.

8454 **Florida Diabetes Camp**
Florida Camp for Children & Youth with Diabetes
PO Box 14136
Gainesville, FL 32604-2136   352-334-1321
                                                   FAX: 352-334-1326
                                          www.floridadiabetescamp.org
Gary Cornwell, Executive Director
Chris Stakely, Assistant Director
Janet Silverstein, Medical Director
Camp is located in Florida. Offers weekend and summer camps for children with type 1 diabetes.

8455 Friends Academy Summer Camps
Duck Pond Rd
Locust Valley, NY 11560   516-393-4207
                                       FAX: 516-465-1720
                                          camp@fa.org
                                   www.fasummercamp.org

Rich Mack, Camp Director
Summer sessions for children with diabetes. Coed, ages 3-14, families.

8456 God's Camp
Episcopal Church of Hawaii
68-729 Farrington Hwy
Waialua, HI 96791-9314   808-637-6241
                                            808-637-5505
                                       FAX: 808-637-5505
                                   www.campmokuleia.org

Debbie Alemeda, Manager
Episcopal Church tent camping, 5 nights, July. Church groups, family reunions, weddings, other organizations.

8457 Growing Together Diabetes Camp
ETMC
1000 S. Beckham
Tyler, TX 75701   903-597-0351
                                            800-232-8318
                                          info@etmc.org
                                          www.etmc.org

Marty Wiggins, Development Director
Vicki Jowell, Director
Elmer G. Ellis, President
A summer camp for youths ages 6 to 15 with Type 1 or Type 2 diabetes.

8458 Happiness Is Camping
62 Sunset Lake Rd.
Hardwick, NJ 07825   908-362-6733
                                       FAX: 908-362-5197
                               rich@happinessiscamping.org
                                  www.happinessiscamping.org

Laura San Miguel, President
Julie McMahon, Secretary
Beth Fuchs, Treasurer
Happiness Is Camping is a camp for children with cancer and their siblings, ages 6-16.

8459 Happy Camp
Merrimack Hall Performing Arts Center
3320 Triana Blvd SW.
Huntsville, AL 35805   256-534-6455
                                   info@merrimackhall.com
                         www.merrimackhall.com/happy-headquarters
For ages 3-12, Happy Camp is Merrimack Hall's annual half-day performing arts camp for children with special needs. Open to children with a wide range of physical or intellectual disabilities at any art level, activities include: music, theater, dance, and visual art. Happy Camp has a 1:1 staff-to-camper ratio. Camp time is from 9am - 12pm every day of the week.

8460 Hemophilia Camp
Tanager Place
1614 W Mount Vernon Rd.
Mount Vernon, IA 52314   319-363-0681
                                       FAX: 319-365-6411
                                  campmail@tanagerplace.org
                                    www.camptanager.org

Donald Pirrie, Camp Director
A six-day camp for children with hemophilia and other bleeding disorders. The camp has onsite 24-hour physician and nursing staff.

8461 Kiwanis Camp Wyman
Wyman Center
600 Kiwanis Dr
Eureka, MO 63025-2212   636-938-5245
                                       FAX: 636-938-5289
                                    www.wymancenter.org

Keat Wilkins, Chairman
Dave Hilliard, President/CEO
Tom Etzkorn, VP,Executive Resource Officer

Summer sessions for youth with diabetes. Coed, ages 8-16, run in conjunction with the American Diabetes Association. Call for program description.

8462 Kota Camp
Junior League Of Little Rock
401 South Scott Street
Little Rock, AR 72201   501-375-5557
                                          info@jllr.org
                              www.jllr.org/community/kota-camp/

Maradyth McKenzie, President
Tabitha McNulty, President Elect
Jenna Martin, Treasurer
Kota Camp is offered to children aged 6-16 with disabilities or medical conditions. Kota derived from a word used by the Quapaw Native American Tribe indigenous to Arkansas, means friend, and reflects the goals of the camp. Children with a disability bring a sibling or friend without a disability, to create a environment of inclusion, participate in camp activities, and promote an understanding of those with special needs. The camp is held at Camp Aldersgate in Little Rock.

8463 Lions Camp Tatiyee
5283 W White Mountain Blvd
Lakeside, AZ 85929   480-380-4254
                                      pam@camptatiyee.org
                                       camptatiyee.org

Richard Page, President
Lions Camp Tatiyee is the only organization in Arizona providing a week long summer camp for individuals with special needs. There is no cost for the camp and all of the programs are adaptable. Some activities that campers can participate in are, go-karting, fishing, art, games, cooking, rock wall, swimming, dances and campfires.

8464 Makemie Woods Camp
Presbytery of Eastern Virginia
P.O.Box 39
Barhamsville, VA 23011   757-566-1496
                                            800-566-1496
                                       FAX: 757-566-8803

Mike Burcher, Director
Sherri Egerton, Program Director
Karen Broughman, Office Manager
Residential Christian camp that tailors each group and individual goals. Counselors serve as teachers, friends and activity leaders. For children 8-18 with diabetes.

8465 Makemie Woods Camp/Conference Retreat
Presbytery of Eastern Virginia
P.O.Box 39
Barhamsville, VA 23011   757-566-1496
                                            800-566-1496
                                       FAX: 757-566-8803

Mike Burcher, Director
Sherri Egerton, Program Director
Karen Broughman, Office Manager
Counselors serve as teachers, friends and activity leaders. The individual is important within the small group. No camper is lost in the crowd, but is an integral partner in the group process. Residential Christian Camp and conference center. Summer camp for children 8-18 and special camp for children with diabetes.

8466 Marist Brothers Mid-Hudson Valley Camp
PO Box 197
Esopus, NY 12429   845-384-6620
                               info@maristbrotherscenter.org
Amy Reinwald-Earle, Camp Director, Special Children
Brother Owen Ormsby, Executive Director
Scott Kuhner, Director of Operations
The camp provides week-long summer sessions for children who have a variety of special needs/illnesses, such as cancer, HIV, deaf or mental disabilities. Each session is specific to the special need/illness.

8467   MedCamps of Louisiana
102 Thomas Rd.
Suite 615
West Monroe, LA 71291
    318-329-8405
    FAX: 318-329-8407
    info@medcamps.com
    www.medcamps.com

Caleb Seney, Executive Director
Kacie Hobson, Camp Director
Offers camp programs for children with chronic illnesses and physical or developmental disabilities.

8468   Mountaineer Spina Bifida Camp
534 New Goff Mountain Rd.
Charleston, WV 25313
    info@drewsday.org
    www.drewsday.org

Suzie Humphreys, Contact
A summer camp for individuals with spina bifida. Campers can participate in activities such as swimming, wheelchair hockey, baseball, and more.

8469   Muscular Dystrophy Association Free Camp
222 S. Riverside Plaza
Suite 1500
Chicago, IL 60606
    907-276-2131
    800-572-1717
    FAX: 907-276-0946
    www.mdausa.org

R. Rodney Howell, MD, Chairman
Steven M. Derks, President/CEO
Julie Faber, EVP/CFO
MDA Camp provides a wide range of activities for those who have limited mobility or are in wheelchairs. The camp offers may outdoor sporting activities, art's & crafts and talent shows.

8470   NeSoDak
Lutherans Outdoors in South Dakota
2001 S Summit Ave.
Sioux Falls, SD 57197
    605-947-4440
    800-888-1464
    nesodak@losd.org
    www.losd.org/nesodak

Vicki Foss, Director
Located in Waubay, South Dakota, NeSoDak provides camp programs for a range of ages. Hosts Camp Gilbert, a summer camp program for children with diabetes.

8471   Open Hearts Camp
The Edward J. Madden Open Hearts Camp
250 Monument Valley Rd.
Great Barrington, MA 01230
    413-528-2229
    hearts@openheartscamp.org
    www.openheartscamp.org

David Zaleon, Executive Director
Camp program for children who have had and are fully recovered from open heart surgery or a heart transplant. Four two-week sessions by age group. Small camp - around 15 campers per session.

8472   Phantom Lake YMCA Camp
S110W30240 YMCA Camp Rd.
Mukwonago, WI 53149
    262-363-4386
    office@phantomlakeymca.org
    www.phantomlakeymca.org

Karin Mulrooney, Chair
Sara Hacker, Secretary
Bill Canfield, Treasurer
Phantom Lake Camp offers day and residential camping sessions for children ages 3-17. All programs are open to individuals with disabilities.

8473   Rapahope Children's Retreat Foundation
205 Lambert Ave.
Suite A
Mobile, AL 36604
    251-476-9880
    info@rapahope.org
    www.rapahope.org

Melissa McNichol, Executive Director
Roz Dorsett, Assistant Director
Rapahope is an organization that offers a one week long summer camp for children who have, or who have had cancer. For children ages 7-17, the camp offers a wide range of summer camp activi-

ties, including but not limited to, swimming, kayaking, horseback riding, and arts. The camp is offered at no cost to campers or their families.

8474   Roundup River Ranch
8333 Colorado River Rd.
Gypsum, CO 81637
    970-524-2267
    FAX: 888-524-2477
    info@roundupriverranch.org
    www.roundupriverranch.org

Ruth B. Johnson, President & Chief Executive Officer
Sterling Nell Leija, Director of Operations
Kendra Perkins, Camp Director
Roundup River Ranch provides traditional camp experiences for children and their families with chronic and serious illnesses. The Ranch is located in Gypsum, Colorado, with all programs offered free of charge.

8475   STIX Diabetes Programs
PO Box 8308
Spokane, WA 99203
    509-484-1366
    FAX: 509-955-1329
    stix@stixdiabetes.org
    www.stixdiabetes.org

Tonya Kobluk, Director, Administration & Camps
Cindy Schneider, Director, Community Outreach
Jill Strom, Director, Development
STIX Diabetes Programs is a non-profit organization providing camp experiences for children and teens with diabetes. STIX offers a three-day non-residential day camp for children ages 6-8; a week-long residential camp for youth ages 9-16; and an excursion-based Adventure Camp for teens ages 16-19.

8476   Shady Oaks Camp
16300 Parker Rd.
Homer Glen, IL 60491
    708-301-0816
    FAX: 708-301-5091
    soc16300@sbcglobal.net
    www.shadyoakscamp.org

Scott Steele, Executive Director
Katie Clark, Camp Director
Gary Schaid, Assistant Director
Shady Oaks Camp provides summer camp programs for children and adults with cerebral palsy and similar disabilities.

8477   Sherman Lake YMCA Summer Camp
Sherman Lake YMCA Outdoor Center
6225 N 39th St
Augusta, MI 49012
    269-731-3000
    FAX: 269-731-3020
    shermanlakeymca@ymcasl.org
    www.shermanlakeymca.org

Luke Austenfeld, Executive Director
Jean Henderson, Business Manager
Lorrie Syverson, Director,Camping, Education & Retreat Services
Summer camping sessions for campers with ADD and spina bifida. Coed, ages 6-15 and families, seniors.

8478   Strength for the Journey
Oregon-Idaho Conference Center
1505 SW 18th Ave
Portland, OR 97201-2524
    503-226-7931
    800-593-7539
    suttlelake@gocamping.org
    www.gocamping.org

Jane Petke, Suttle Lake Camp Director
Geneva Cook, Camping Registrar
Camp is located near Sisters, Oregon at Suttle Lake Camp. Strength for the Journey is a program for adults living with HIV/AIDS.

8479 Summer Camp for Children with Muscular Dystrophy
Muscular Dystrophy Association - USA
222 S. Riverside Plaza
Suite 1500
Chicago, IL 60606

520-529-2000
800-572-1717
FAX: 520-529-5300
mda@mdausa.org
www.mdausa.org

R. Rodney Howell, MD, Chairman
Steven M. Derks, President/CEO
Pete Morgan, EVP/COO
Offers a wide range of activities such as adaptive sports, swimming, fishing, archery, scavenger hunts, dances & talent shows, art's & crafts, karaoke, and campfires.

8480 Suttle Lake Camp
29551 Suttle Lake Rd.
Sisters, OR 97759

541-595-6663
suttlelake@gocamping.org
suttlelake.gocamping.org

Daniel Petke, Co-Director
Jane Petke, Co-Director
Offers a variety of camp programs, including sessions for individuals with HIV/AIDS.

8481 TSA CT Kid's Summer Event
Tourette Syndrome Association of Connecticut (TSA)
c/o Massachusetts Chapter
39 Godfrey Street
Taunton, MA 02780

617-277-7589
www.tsact.org

Tom Meehan, Chairman
Peter Tavolacci, Vice-Chairman
Paul Nazario, Treasurer
TSA of Connecticut sponsors summer events for children with TS/Tourette Syndrome activities of which include minature golf in addition to an Annual Conference. The kids' program at this annual conference provides children who have TS a unique opportunity to meet other children like them who also struggle with TS. Entertainment includes puppeteers, magicians, learning karate from the experts, getting face paintings and more.
uniqu pages

8482 Texas Lions Camp
PO Box 290247
Kerrville, TX 78029

830-896-8500
FAX: 830-896-3666
tlc@lionscamp.com
www.lionscamp.com

Stephen S. Mabry, President & CEO
Karen-Anne King, Vice President, Summer Camps
Milton Dare, Director, Development
Texas Lions Camp is a camp dedicated to serving children ages 7-16 in Texas with physical disabilities. While at camp, campers will participate in a variety of activities and be encouraged to become more independent and self-confident.

8483 The Hole in the Wall Gang Camp
565 Ashford Center Rd.
Ashford, CT 06278

860-429-3444
info@holeinthewallgang.org
www.holeinthewallgang.org

James H. Canton, Chief Executive Officer
Padraig Barry, Chief Strategy Officer
Kevin Magee, Chief Financial Officer
The Hole in the Wall Gang Camp offers summer and weekend camp experiences for children and the siblings of children with serious illnesses. Located in Ashford, Connecticut, campers are able to participate in traditional camp activities in a medically safe environment.

8484 Twin Lakes Camp
1451 E Twin Lakes Rd
Hillsboro, IN 47949-8004

765-798-4000
outdoors@twinlakescamp.com
www.twinlakescamp.com

Jon Beight, Executive Director
Dan Daily, Program Director
Duane Bush, Guest Service

Provides a summer camp program for special needs children and young adults. Campers suffer from a wide range of maladies including crippling accidents, Spina Bifida, epilepsy, Cerebral Palsy, Muscular Dystrophy, Quadriplegia, Paraplegia, and other disabling diseases. Campers range in age from 8 to 27.

8485 Wisconsin Lions Camp
Wisconsin Lions Foundation
3834 County Rd. A
Rosholt, WI 54473

715-677-4969
877-463-6953
FAX: 715-677-4527
info@wisconsinlionscamp.com
www.wisconsinlionscamp.com

Evett Hartvig, Executive Director
Andrea Yenter, Camp Director
Phillip Potter, Assistant Camp Director
Provides camp programs for youth and adults in Wisconsin with disabilities, including autism, intellectual disabilities, diabetes, epilepsy, visual impairments, and hearing impairments. ACA accredited, located in central Wisconsin, near Stevens Point.

8486 Y Camp
YMCA of Greater Des Moines
1192 166th Drive
Boone, IA 50036

515-432-7558
FAX: 515-432-5414
ycamp@dmymca.org
www.y-camp.org

David Sherry, Executive Director
Mike Havlik, Program Director- Environmental
Alex Kretzinger, Program Director- Summer Camp
Camp is located in Boone, Iowa. Year-round one and two-week sessions for boys and girls with cancer, diabetes, asthma, cystic fibrosis, hearing impaired and other disabilities. Coed, ages 6-16 and families.

8487 YMCA Camp Fitch
12600 Abels Rd.
North Springfield, PA 16430

814-922-3219
877-863-4824
FAX: 814-922-7000
registrar@campfitchymca.org
campfitchymca.org

Tom Parker, Executive Director
Joe Wolnik, Summer Camp Director
Brandy Duda, Outdoor Education Director
Camp is located in North Springfield, Pennsylvania. Camp programs include sessions for children with diabetes or epilepsy.

8488 YMCA Camp Ihduhapi
Minneapolis YMCA Camping Services
15200 Hanson Blvd.
Andover, MN 55304

763-230-9622
info@campihduhapi.org
campihduhapi.org

Kerry Pioske, Camp Executive
Josh Cobb, Overnight Camp Director
Devin Hanson, Day Camp Director
Camp is located in Loretto, Minnesota. Summer sessions for campers with asthma/respiratory ailments and epilepsy. Coed, ages 7-16.

8489 YMCA Camp Jewell
YMCA of Greater Hartford
6 Prock Hill Road
P.O. Box 8
Colebrook, CT 06021

860-379-2782
888-412-2267
FAX: 860-379-8715
camp.jewell@ghymca.org
www.ghymca.org

Eric Tucker, Executive Director
Camp is located in Colebrook, Connecticut. Two-week sessions for children with cancer. Coed, ages 8-16. Also families.

8490 YMCA Camp Kitaki
Lincoln YMCA
570 Fallbrook Blvd.
Suite 210
Lincoln, NE 68521

402-434-9200
FAX: 402-434-9208
info@ymcalincoln.org
www.ymcalincoln.org

Barb Bettin, President/CEO
J.P. Lauterbach, COO
Misty Muff, Chief Administrative Officer
Camp is located in Louisville, Nebraska. Summer sessions for children with cystic fibrosis. Coed, ages 7-17 and families.

8491 YMCA Camp Shady Brook
YMCA of the Pikes Peak Region (PPYMCA)
316 N. Tejon Street
Colorado Springs, CO 80903

719-329-7227
FAX: 719-272-7026
campinfo@ppymca.org
www.campshadybrook.org

Sonny Adkins, Executive Director
Laura Petersen, Program Director
Patrick Casey, Facility Director
Camp is located in Sedalia, Colorado. One-week sessions for campers with HIV. Boys and girls 7-16. Also families, seniors and single adults.

8492 YMCA Camp of Maine
305 Winthrop Center Rd
P.O. Box 446
Winthrop, ME 04364

207-395-4200
FAX: 207-395-7230
info@maineycamp.org
www.maineycamp.org

Tom Christensen, CVO
Rebecca Henry, Vice CVO
Marty Allen, Treasurer
Activities include arts and crafts, nature study, hiking, and overnight camping, dancing, and singing. Summer session dates run from June through August; for ages 8-16.

8493 YMCA Outdoor Center Campbell Gard
4803 Augspurger Road
Hamilton, OH 45011

513-867-0600
FAX: 513-867-0127
camp@gmvymca.org
www.ccgymca.org

Pete Fasano, Executive Director
Katie Depew, Summer Program Director
Tom Andrews, Facilities and Properties Manager
Camp is located in Hamilton, Ohio. Camping sessions for children and young adults with developmental disabilities. Runs overnight and day sessions for ages 7-22 and families.

Books

8494 A Woman's Guide to Living with HIV Infection
Johns Hopkins University Press
2715 N Charles St
Baltimore, MD 21218-4363

410-516-6900
800-548-1784
FAX: 410-516-6998
jwehmueller@press.jhu.edu
www.press.jhu.edu

Rebecca A Clark M.D., PhD, Author
Robert T Maupin Jr. M.D. FACOG, Co-Author
Jill Hayes Hammer PhD, Co-Author
A resource for women with HIV that discusses coping with the diagnosis, finding a physician, recognizing symptoms, and preventing complications. Explains the latest treatment options and advice on coping with gynecologic infections. *$18.00*
328 pages Hardback

8495 ABC of Asthma, Allergies & Lupus
Global Health Solutions
2146 Kings Garden Way
PO Box 3189
Falls Church, VA 22043-2593

703-848-2333
800-759-3999
FAX: 703-848-0028
information@watercure.com
www.watercure.com

Fereydoon Batmanghelidj MD, Author
Xiaopo Batmanghelidj, President
Kristin Swan, Administrator
This book introduces new approaches in preventing and treating asthma, allergies and lupus without toxic chemicals. It also offers new insight on how to prevent and treat children's asthma. *$17.00*
240 pages
ISBN 0-962994-26-x

8496 AIDS Sourcebook
Omnigraphics
615 Griswold Street
Suite 520
Detroit, MI 48226

610-461-3548
800-234-1340
FAX: 800-875-1340
contact@omnigraphics.com
www.omnigraphics.com

Peter Ruffner, Co-Founder
Fred Ruffner, Co-Founder
Basic consumer health information about the Human Immunodeficiency Virus (HIV) and Acquired Immunodeficiency Syndrome (AIDS), including facts about its origins, stages, types, transmission, risk factors, and prevention, and featuring details about diagnostic testing, antiretroviral treatments, and co-occurring infections. *$85.00*
600 pages 5th Edition 1911
ISBN 0-780811-47-8

8497 AIDS and Other Manifestations of HIV Infection
Elsevier Inc
30 Corporate Dr
Suite 400
Burlington, MA 01803-4252

781-313-4700
800-545-2522
FAX: 800-568-5136
usbkinfo@elsevier.com
www.elsevier.com

Gary Wormser MD, Editor
A comprehensive overview of the biological properties of this etiologic viral agent, its clinicopathological manifestations, the epidemiology of its infection, and present and future therapeutic options. *$249.95*
1000 pages 2004
ISBN 0-127640-51-7

8498 AIDS in the Twenty-First Century: Disease and Globalization
Palgrav Macmillan
175 5th Ave
New York, NY 10010-7703

888-330-8477
FAX: 800-672-2054
onlinesupportusa@palgrave.com
www.palgrave-usa.com

Gabriella Georgiades, Editor
Alan Whiteside, Author
Tony Barnett, Co-Author
The authors — exprets in the field for over 15 years — argue that it is vital to not only look at AIDS in terms of prevention and treatment, but to also consider consequences which affect households, communities, companies, governments, and countries. This is a major contribution toward understanding the global public health crisis, as well as the relationship between poverty, inequality, and infectious diseases. *$32.00*
464 pages
ISBN 1-403997-68-5

8499 Adult Leukemia: A Comprehensive Guide for Patients and Families

O'Reilly Media Inc
1005 Gravenstein Hwy N
Sebastopol, CA 95472-2811

707-827-7000
800-998-9938
FAX: 707-829-0104
order@oreilly.com
www.oreilly.com

Linda Lamb, Editor
Barb Lackritz, Author

For the tens of thousands of Americans with adult leukemia, Adult Leukemia: A Comprehensive Guide for Patients and Families addresses diagnosis, medical tests, finding a good oncologist, treatments, side effects, getting emotional and other support, resources for further study, and much more. The book includes real-life stories from those who have battled leukemia themselves. *$29.95*
536 pages Paperback
ISBN 0-596500-01-7

8500 Advanced Breast Cancer: A Guide to Living with Metastic Disease

O'Reilly Media Inc
1005 Gravenstein Hwy N
Sebastopol, CA 95472-2811

707-827-7000
800-998-9938
FAX: 707-829-0104
order@oreilly.com
www.oreilly.com

Linda Lamb, Editor
Musa Mayer, Author

This is the only book on breast cancer that deals honestly with the realities of living with metastic disease, yet offers hope and comfort. All aspects of facing the disease are covered, including: coping with the shock of recurrence, seeking information and making treatment decisions, communicating effectively with medical personnel finding support, and handling disease progression and end-of-life issues. A comprehensive guide, it also provides updated resources and treatment developments. *$24.95*
532 pages Paperback 1998
ISBN 1-565925-22-X

8501 Allergies Sourcebook

Omnigraphics
615 Griswold Street
Suite 520
Detroit, MI 48226

610-461-3548
800-234-1340
FAX: 800-875-1340
contact@omnigraphics.com
www.omnigraphics.com

Peter Ruffner, Co-Founder
Fred Ruffner, Co-Founder

Basic comsumer health information about the immune system and allergic disorders, including rhinitis (hay fever), sinusitis, conjunctivitis, asthma, atopic dermatitis, and anaphylaxis, and allergy triggers such as pollen, mold, dust mites, animal dander, chemicals, foods and additives, and medications; along with facts about allergy diagnosis and treatment, tips on avoiding triggers and preventing symptoms, a glossary of related terms, and directories of resources for additional help and info. *$95.00*
608 pages 4th Edition 1911

8502 Allergies and Asthma: What Every Parent Needs to Know (2nd Edition)

American Academy of Pediatrics
345 Park Blvd.
Itasca, IL 60143

800-433-9016
FAX: 847-434-8000
www.aap.org

Mark Del Monte, Chief Executive Officer & Executive Vice President
Christine Bork, Chief Development Officer & Sr. Vice President, Development
Roberta Bosak, Chief Administrative Officer & Sr. Vice President, HR

Consumer resource for parents who need answers and information about their children's allergies and asthma. Covers advice on identifying allergies and asthma, preventing attacks, minimizing triggers, understanding medications, explaining allergies to young children, and helping children manage symptoms. *$14.95*
174 pages Paperback; eBook available 1910
ISBN 1-581104-45-6

8503 Alternative Approach to Allergies

Harper Collins Publishers
10 E 53rd St
New York, NY 10022-5244

212-207-7901
800-242-7737
FAX: 212-702-2586
spsales@harpercollins.com
www.harpercollins.com

Theron G Randolph M.D., Author
Ralph W Moss PhD, Co-Author

Here is the book that revolutionized the way allergies and other common illnesses were diagnosed and treated.
ISBN 0-060916-93-1

8504 Alzheimer Disease Sourcebook

Omnigraphics
615 Griswold Street
Suite 520
Detroit, MI 48226

610-461-3548
800-234-1340
FAX: 800-875-1340
contact@omnigraphics.com
www.omnigraphics.com

Peter Ruffner, Co-Founder
Fred Ruffner, Co-Founder

Alzheimer Disease Sourcebook, Fifth Edition provides updated information about causes, symptoms, and stages of AD and other forms of dementia, including mild cognitive impairment, corticobasal degeneration, dementia with Lewy bodies, frontotemporal dementia, Huntington disease, Parkinson disease, and dementia caused by infections. *$95.00*
600 pages 1911
ISBN 0-780811-50-8

8505 Alzheimer Disease Sourcebook, 4th Edition

Omnigraphics
615 Griswold Street
Suite 520
Detroit, MI 48226

610-461-3548
800-234-1340
FAX: 800-875-1340
contact@omnigraphics.com
www.omnigraphics.com

Peter Ruffner, Co-Founder
Fred Ruffner, Co-Founder

Basic consumer health information about alzheimer disease, other dementias, and related disorders, including multi-infarct dementia, dementia with lewy bodies, frontotemporal dementia (pick disease), Wernicke-Korsakoff syndrome (alcohol-related dementia), AIDS dementia complex, Huntington disease, Creutzfeldt-Jacob disease, and delirium. *$84.00*
603 pages
ISBN 0-780810-01-3

8506 Amyotrophic Lateral Sclerosis: A Guide for Patients and Families

Demos Medical Publishing
11 West 42nd Street
15th Floor
New York, NY 10036

212-683-0072
800-532-8663
FAX: 212-683-0118
support@demosmedical.com
www.demosmedpub.com

Richard Winters, Executive Editor
Beth Kaufman Barry, Publisher
Noreen Henson, Executive Director of Demos Heal

This comprehensive guide covers every aspect of the management of ALS. Beginning with discussions of its clinical features of the disease, diagnosis, and an overview of symptom management, major sections deal with medical and rehabilitative management, living with ALS, managing advanced disease and

end-of-life issues, and reources that can provide support and assistance. *$29.95*
470 pages 2001
ISBN 1-888799-28-5

8507 **Arthritis Sourcebook.**
Omnigraphics
615 Griswold Street
Suite 520
Detroit, MI 48226
610-461-3548
800-234-1340
FAX: 800-875-1340
contact@omnigraphics.com
www.omnigraphics.com

Peter Ruffner, Co-Founder
Fred Ruffner, Co-Founder
Basic consumer health information about osteoarthritis, rheumatoid arthritis, other rheumatic disorders, infectious forms of arthritis, and diseases with symptoms linked to arthritis, and facts about diagnosis, pain management, and surgical therapies. *$84.00*
567 pages 2nd Edition
ISBN 0-780806-67-2

8508 **Asthma Sourcebook.**
Omnigraphics
615 Griswold Street
Suite 520
Detroit, MI 48226
610-461-3548
800-234-1340
FAX: 800-875-1340
contact@omnigraphics.com
www.omnigraphics.com

Peter Ruffner, Co-Founder
Fred Ruffner, Co-Founder
Provides information about asthma, including symptoms, remedies and research updates. *$84.00*
581 pages 2nd Edition
ISBN 0-780808-66-9

8509 **Asthma and Allergy Answers: A Patient Education Library**
Asthma and Allergy Foundation of America
8201 Corporate Dr
Suite 1000
Landover, MD 20785
202-466-7643
800-727-8462
FAX: 202-466-8940
info@aafa.org
www.aafa.org

Amy Patterson, Senior Director of Administration & Governance
Jacqui Vok, Director of Programs and Services
William McLin, M.Ed., President/CEO
This resource contains 50 reproducible fact sheets for patients on a variety of popular asthma and allergy topics. Information is written in a patient-friendly question and answer format and packaged in a durable binder for easy storage and use. *$50.00*

8510 **Back & Neck Sourcebook.**
Omnigraphics
615 Griswold Street
Suite 520
Detroit, MI 48226
610-461-3548
800-234-1340
FAX: 800-875-1340
contact@omnigraphics.com
www.omnigraphics.com

Peter Ruffner, Co-Founder
Fred Ruffner, Co-Founder
Basic consumer health information about back and neck pain, spinal cord injuries, and related disorders, such as degenerative disk disease, osteoarthritis, scoliosis, sciatica, spina bifida, and spinal stenosis, and featuring facts about maintaining spinal health, self-care, rehabilitative care, chiropractic care, spinal surgeries, and complementary therapies. *$84.00*
607 pages 2nd Edition
ISBN 0-780807-38-9

8511 **Being Close**
National Jewish Health
1400 Jackson St
Denver, CO 80206-2761
303-398-1002
877-225-5654
FAX: 303-398-1125
allstetterw@njc.org
www.nationaljewish.org

Michael Salem M.D., President/CEO
William Allstetter, Director Media/External Relation
A booklet offering information to patients suffering from a respiratory disorder such as emphysema, asthma or tuberculosis, that discusses sexual problems and feelings.

8512 **Bittersweet Chances: A Personal Journey o f Living and Learning in the Face of Illness**
PublishAmerica
PO Box 151
Frederick, MD 21705-151
301-695-1707
FAX: 301-631-9073
support@publishamerica.com
www.publishamerica.com

Dana Selenke Broehl, Author
Recounts Doug and Dana Broehl's journey of growth through the darkness of cystic fibrosis and the renewed hope of a double lung transplant. *$24.95*
189 pages Softcover
ISBN 1-413713-24-6

8513 **Blood and Circulatory Disorders Sourcebook**
Omnigraphics
615 Griswold Street
Suite 520
Detroit, MI 48226
610-461-3548
800-234-1340
FAX: 800-875-1340
contact@omnigraphics.com
www.omnigraphics.com

Peter Ruffner, Co-Founder
Fred Ruffner, Co-Founder
Blood and Circulatory Disorders Sourcebook, Third Edition offers facts about blood function and composition, the maintenance of a healthy circulatory system, and the types of concerns that arise when processes go awry. It discusses the diagnosis and treatment of many common blood cell disorders, bleeding disorders, and circulatory disorders, including anemia, hemochromatosis, leukemia, lymphoma, hemophilia, hypercoagulation, thrombophilia, atherosclerosis, blood pressure irregularities, coronary *$84.00*
634 pages 2nd Edition
ISBN 0-780807-46-4

8514 **Blooming Where You're Planted: Stories From The Heart**
Meeting Life's Challenges
9042 Aspen Grove Lane
Madison, WI 53717-2700
608-824-0402
FAX: 608-824-0403
help@MeetingLifesChallenges.com
www.makinglifeeasier.com

Shelley Peterman Schwatz, Editor
Author Shelley Peterman Schwarz takes you on her journey of self-discovery and change following her diagnosis of multiple sclerosis in 1979. Her personal stories are warm and humorous, and insightful. This 138-page book will motivate and inspire you to rise above life's challenges and live life to its fullest. *$12.95*
138 pages 1998
ISBN 0-891854-01-1

8515 **Brain Allergies: The Psychonutrient and Magnetic Connections**
McGraw-Hill

William Philpott PhD, Author
Dwight Keating PhD, Author
Linus Pauling PhD, Author
A complete overview of the concept of brain allergies - the theory that exposure to certain foods and other substances triggers men-

tal disorders in people so predisposed, and that such disturbances can be cured by eliminating these substances. *$16.95*
ISBN 0-658003-98-1

8516   Brain Disorders Sourcebook
Omnigraphics
615 Griswold Street
Suite 520
Detroit, MI 48226

610-461-3548
800-234-1340
FAX: 800-875-1340
contact@omnigraphics.com
www.omnigraphics.com

Peter Ruffner, Co-Founder
Fred Ruffner, Co-Founder
Brain Disorders Sourcebook, Third Edition provides readers with updated information about brain function, neurological emergencies such as a brain attack (stroke) or seizure, and symptoms of brain disorders. It describes the diagnosis, treatment, and rehabilitation therapies for genetic and congenital brain disorders, brain infections, brain tumors, seizures, traumatic brain injuries, and degenerative neurological disorders such as Alzheimer disease and other dementias, Parkinson disease, and am *$84.00*
600 pages 2nd Edition
ISBN 0-780807-44-0

8517   Breast Cancer Sourcebook
Omnigraphics
615 Griswold Street
Suite 520
Detroit, MI 48226

610-461-3548
800-234-1340
FAX: 800-875-1340
contact@omnigraphics.com
www.omnigraphics.com

Peter Ruffner, Co-Founder
Fred Ruffner, Co-Founder
Breast Cancer Sourcebook, Fourth Edition, provides updated information about breast cancer and its causes, risk factors, diagnosis, and treatment. Readers will learn about the types of breast cancer, including ductal carcinoma in situ, lobular carcinoma in situ, invasive carcinoma, and inflammatory breast cancer, as well as common breast cancer treatment complications, such as pain, fatigue, lymphedema, hair loss, and sexuality and fertility issues. Information on preventive therapies, nutrition *$84.00*
600 pages 3rd Edition
ISBN 0-780810-30-3

8518   Breathe Free
Lotus Press
P.O. Box 325
Twin Lakes, WI 53181

262-889-8561
800-824-6396
FAX: 262-889-8591
lotuspress@lotuspress.com
www.lotuspress.com

Daniel Gagnon, Author
Amanda Morningstar, Author
An expose on respiratory diseases and their natural treatment. Learn how you can heal and/or manage common colds/flu, earaches/asthma, allergies/hay fever, pleurisy/pneumonia, coughs/sore throats, bronchitis/emphysema, AIDS and ARC related respiration infection. Covers information you wish your doctor would share with you such as what is happening to your body. *$14.95*
179 pages
ISBN 9-780914-95-5

8519   Cancer Sourcebook
Omnigraphics
615 Griswold Street
Suite 520
Detroit, MI 48226

610-461-3548
800-234-1340
FAX: 800-875-1340
contact@omnigraphics.com
www.omnigraphics.com

Peter Ruffner, Co-Founder
Fred Ruffner, Co-Founder

Cancer Sourcebook, Sixth Edition provides updated information about common types of cancer affecting the central nervous system, endocrine system, lungs, digestive and urinary tracts, blood cells, immune system, skin, bones, and other body systems. It explains how people can reduce their risk of cancer by addressing issues related to cancer risk and taking advantage of screening exams. *$84.00*
1105 pages 5th Edition
ISBN 0-780809-47-5

8520   Cancer Sourcebook for Women
Omnigraphics
615 Griswold Street
Suite 520
Detroit, MI 48226

610-461-3548
800-234-1340
FAX: 800-875-1340
contact@omnigraphics.com
www.omnigraphics.com

Peter Ruffner, Co-Founder
Fred Ruffner, Co-Founder
Cancer Sourcebook for Women, Fourth Edition offers updated information about gynecologic cancers and other cancers of special concern to women, including breast cancer, cancers of the female reproductive organs, and cancers responsible for the highest number of deaths in women. It explains cancer risks-including lifestyle factors, inherited genetic abnormalities, and hormonal medications-and methods used to diagnose and treat cancer. *$84.00*
687 pages 5th Edition
ISBN 0-780808-67-6

8521   Cardiovascular Diseases and Disorders Sourcebook, 3rd Edition
Omnigraphics
615 Griswold Street
Suite 520
Detroit, MI 48226

610-461-3548
800-234-1340
FAX: 800-875-1340
contact@omnigraphics.com
www.omnigraphics.com

Peter Ruffner, Co-Founder
Fred Ruffner, Co-Founder
Cardiovascular Diseases and Disorders Sourcebook, Third Edition, provides information about the symptoms, diagnosis, and treatment heart diseases and vascular disorders. It includes demographic and statistical data, an overview of the cardiovascular system, a discussion of risk factors and prevention techniques, a look at cardiovascular concerns specific to women, and a report on current research initiatives. *$84.00*
687 pages Hard cover
ISBN 0-780807-39-6

8522   Childhood Cancer Survivors: A Practical Guide to Your Future
O'Reilly Media Inc
1005 Gravenstein Hwy N
Sebastopol, CA 95472-2811

707-827-7000
800-998-9938
FAX: 707-829-0104
order@oreilly.com
www.oreilly.com

Linda Lamb, Editor
Nancy Keene, Author
Wendy Hobbie, Co-Author
More than 250,000 people have survived childhood cancer - a cause for celebration. Authors Keene, Hobbie, and Ruccione chart the territory of long-term survivorship: relationships; overcoming employment or insurance discrimination; maximizing health; follow-up schedules; medical late effects. The stories of over sixty survivors - their challenges and triumphs - are told. Includes medical history record-keeper. *$27.95*
464 pages Paperback 1906
ISBN 0-596528-51-5

8523 Childhood Cancer: A Parent's Guide to Solid Tumor Cancers
O'Reilly Media Inc
1005 Gravenstein Highway North
Sebastopol, CA 95472
707-827-7000
800-889-8969
FAX: 707-829-0104
order@oreilly.com
www.oreilly.com
Childhood Cancer: A Parent's Guide to Solid Tumor Cancers features a wealth of resources for parents of children with solid tumor cancers, plus many stories of veteran parents. Parents will encounter medical facts simply explained, practical advice to ease their daily lives, and tools to be strong advocates for their child. Includes a passport to record patient's medical history. *$29.95*
560 pages Paperback
ISBN 0-596500-14-9

8524 Childhood Diseases and Disorders Sourcebook, 2nd Edition
Omnigraphics
615 Griswold Street
Suite 520
Detroit, MI 48226
610-461-3548
800-234-1340
FAX: 800-875-1340
contact@omnigraphics.com
www.omnigraphics.com
Peter Ruffner, Co-Founder
Fred Ruffner, Co-Founder
Basic consumer health information about medical problems often encountered in pre-adolescent children, including respiratory tract ailments, ear infections, sore throats, disorders of the skin and scalp, digestive and genitourinary diseases, infectious diseases, inflammatory disorders, chronic physical and developmental disorders, allergies, and more. *$84.00*
600 pages Hard cover
ISBN 0-780810-31-0

8525 Childhood Leukemia: A Guide for Families, Friends & Caregivers
O'Reilly Media Inc
1005 Gravenstein Hwy N
Sebastopol, CA 95472-2811
707-827-7000
800-998-9938
FAX: 707-829-0104
order@oreilly.com
www.oreilly.com
Linda Lamb, Editor
Nancy Keene, Author
The second edition of this comprehensive guide offers detailed and precise medical information for parents that includes day-to-day practical advice on how to cope with procedures, hospitalization, family and friends, school, and social, emotional, and financial issues. It features a wealth of tools for prents and contains significant updates on treatments and procedures. *$29.95*
528 pages 4th Edition 1910
ISBN 0-596500-15-7

8526 Children with Cerebral Palsy: A Parents' Guide
Woodbine House
6510 Bells Mill Road
Bethesda, MD 20817-1636
301-897-3570
800-843-7323
FAX: 301-897-5838
info@woodbinehouse.com
www.woodbinehouse.com
Irvin Shapell, Owner
Beth Binns, Special Marketing Manager
Sarah Glenner, Office Receptionist;
A classic primer for parents that provides a complete spetrum of information and compassionate advice about cerebral palsy and its effect on their child's development and education. *$18.95*
481 pages
ISBN 0-933149-82-4

8527 Chronic Fatigue Syndrome: Your Natural Gu ide to Healing with Diet, Herbs and Other Methods
Random House Publishing
1745 Broadway
3rd Floor
New York, NY 10019-4305
212-782-9000
FAX: 212-572-6066
ecustomerservice@randomhouse.com
www.randomhouse.com
Susanna Porter, Editor
Michael T Murray N.D.
Explains specific measures sufferers can take to improve stamina, mental energy, and physical abilities. *$15.00*
208 pages
ISBN 1-559584-90-6

8528 Coffee in the Cereal: The First Year with Multiple Sclerosis
Pathfinder Publishing
520-647-0158
800-977-2282
bill@pathfinderpublishing.com
www.pathfinderpublishing.com
Moorhead recounts the experience of her first year with multiple sclerosis with a vitality unique in the often gloomy world of personal medical histories. *$14.95*
96 pages
ISBN 0-934793-07-7

8529 Colon & Rectal Cancer: A Comprehensive Guide for Patients & Families
O'Reilly Media Inc
1005 Gravenstein Hwy N
Sebastopol, CA 95472-2811
707-827-7000
800-998-9938
FAX: 707-829-0104
order@oreilly.com
www.oreilly.com
Linda Lamb, Editor
Lorraine Johnston, Author
The fourth most common cancer, colon and rectal cancer is diagnosed in 130,000 new cases in the United States each year. Patients and families need uo-to-date and in-depth information to participate wisely in treatment decisions (e.g., knowing what sexual and fertility issues to discuss with the doctor before surgery). This book covers coping with tests and treatment side effects, caring for ostomies, finding supportt, and other practical issues. *$24.95*
544 pages Paperback 1999
ISBN 1-565926-33-1

8530 Colon Health: Key to a Vibrant Life
Norwalk Press
P.O.Box 190526
Boise, ID 83719-526
928-445-5567
FAX: 928-445-5567
Norman Walker MD, Editor
Includes complete glossary of terms and index of referrals.

8531 Complementary Alternative Medicine and Multiple Sclerosis
Demos Medical Publishing
11 West 42nd Street
15th Floor
New York, NY 10036
212-683-0072
800-532-8663
FAX: 212-683-0118
support@demosmedical.com
www.demosmedpub.com
Richard Winters, Executive Editor
Beth Kaufman Barry, Publisher
Noreen Henson, Executive Director of Demos Heal
Offers reliable information on the relevance, safety, and effectiveness of various alternative therapies that are not typically considered in discussions of MS management, yet are in widespread use. *$24.95*
304 pages
ISBN 1-932603-54-9

8532 **Conquering the Darkness: One Story of Recovering from a Brain Injury**
Paragon House
1925 Oakcrest Avenue
Suite 7
Saint Paul, MN 55113-2619   651-644-3087
800-447-3709
FAX: 651-644-0997
info@paragonhouse.com
www.paragonhouse.com

Rosemary Yokoi, Publicity Director
Gordon Anderson, Executive Director
Deborah Quinn, Author
The course of recovery from a brain injury by a woman who lived through it. *$15.95*
276 pages 1998
ISBN 1-557787-63-8

8533 **Coping with Cerebral Palsy**
Rosen Publishing
29 East 21st Street
New York, NY 10010   800-237-9932
FAX: 888-436-4643
www.rosenpublishing.com

Laura Anne Gilman, Author
This second edition book provides parents of children and adults with cerebral palsy the answers to more than 300 questions that have been carefully researched. It represents 40 years of experience by the author and is presented in a highly readable, jargon-free manner. *$31.95*
ISBN 0-823931-50-1

8534 **Curing MS: How Science is Solving the Mysteries of Multiple Sclerosis**
Random House Publishing
1745 Broadway
3rd Floor
New York, NY 10019-4305   212-782-9000
FAX: 212-572-6066
www.randomhouse.com

Howard L Weiner M.D., Author
Founder-director of the Multiple Sclerosis Center at Mass General Hospital discusses what ends up as a deconstruction of the last 30 years of his own and general MS research and of experience in treating patients with the puzzling disorder. Weiner summarizes what is currently known about treatments and the potential for a cure. *$14.95*
352 pages 1905
ISBN 0-307236-04-8

8535 **Cystic Fibrosis: A Guide for Patient and Family**
Lippincott Williams & Wilkins
16522 Hunters Green Parkway
PO Box 1620
Hagerstown, MD 21741-1620   301-223-2300
800-638-3030
FAX: 301-223-2400
orders@lww.com
www.lww.com

David M Orenstein MD, Author
Text is designed specifically for patients with cystic fibrosis and their families. Explains the disease process, outlines the fundamentals of diagnosing and screening, and addresses the challenges of treatment for those living with CF. Includes new material on carrier testing, infection control, and more. *$51.50*
448 pages 3rd Edition
ISBN 0-781741-52-1

8536 **Diabetes Sourcebook.**
Omnigraphics
615 Griswold Street
Suite 520
Detroit, MI 48226   610-461-3548
800-234-1340
FAX: 800-875-1340
contact@omnigraphics.com
www.omnigraphics.com

Peter Ruffner, Co-Founder
Fred Ruffner, Co-Founder

Diabetes Sourcebook, Fourth Edition contains updated information for people seeking to understand the risk factors, complications, and management of diabetes. It discusses medical interventions, including the use of insulin and oral diabetes medications, self-monitoring of blood glucose, and complementary and alternative therapies. *$84.00*
627 pages 4th Edition
ISBN 0-780810-05-1

8537 **Digestive Diseases & Disorders Sourcebook**
Omnigraphics
615 Griswold Street
Suite 520
Detroit, MI 48226   610-461-3548
800-234-1340
FAX: 800-875-1340
contact@omnigraphics.com
www.omnigraphics.com

Peter Ruffner, Co-Founder
Fred Ruffner, Co-Founder
Digestive Diseases and Disorders Sourcebook provides basic information for the layperson about common disorders of the upper and lower digestive tract. It also includes information about medications and recommendations for maintaining a healthy digestive tract in addition to a glossary of important terms and a directory of digestive diseases organizations are also provided. *$84.00*
323 pages Hard cover
ISBN 0-780803-27-5

8538 **Duchenne Muscular Dystrophy**
Oxford University Press
198 Madison Ave
New York, NY 10016-4308   212-726-6000
800-445-9714
FAX: 919-677-1303
custserv.us@oup.com

William Lamsback, Editor
Alan Emery, Author
Francesco Muntoni, Co-Author
Identification of the genetic defect responsible for Duchenne Muscular Dystrophy and isolation of the protein dystrophin have led to the development of new theories for the disease's pathogenesis. This title incorporates these advances from the field of molecular biology, and describes the resultant opportunities for screening, prenatal diagnosis, genetic counselling and management. *$135.00*
282 pages 3rd Edition 2003
ISBN 0-198515-31-6

8539 **Ear, Nose, and Throat Disorders Sourcebook**
Omnigraphics
615 Griswold Street
Suite 520
Detroit, MI 48226   610-461-3548
800-234-1340
FAX: 800-875-1340
contact@omnigraphics.com
www.omnigraphics.com

Peter Ruffner, Co-Founder
Fred Ruffner, Co-Founder
Ear, Nose and Throat Disorders Sourcebook, Second Edition, provides consumers with updated health information on the most common disorders of the ear, nose, and throat. The book also includes descriptions of current diagnostic tests, discussion of common surgical procedures, including cosmetic surgery on the nose and ears, a glossary of related medical terms, and a directory of sources for further help and information. *$84.00*
631 pages 2nd Edition
ISBN 0-780808-72-0

8540 **Eating Disorders Sourcebook.**
Omnigraphics
615 Griswold Street
Suite 520
Detroit, MI 48226

610-461-3548
800-234-1340
FAX: 800-875-1340
contact@omnigraphics.com
www.omnigraphics.com

Peter Ruffner, Co-Founder
Fred Ruffner, Co-Founder
Provides general imformation, causes and treatments of eating disorders. *$84.00*
557 pages 2nd Edition
ISBN 0-780809-48-2

8541 **Educational Issues Among Children with Spina Bifida**
Spina Bifida Association of America
1600 Wilson Boulevard
Suite 800
Arlington, VA 22209

202-944-3285
800-621-3141
FAX: 202-944-3295
sbaa@sbaa.org
www.sbaa.org

Ana Ximenes, Chair
Sara Struwe, President & CEO
Mark Bohay, National Web Initiatives & Development Manager
Children with spina bifida/ hydrocephalus often show unique learning strengths and weaknesses that affect their schoolwork. Parents and schools need to work together to help the young people meet their physical, social, emotional, and academic goals.

8542 **Epilepsy, 199 Answers: A Doctor Responds to His Patients' Questions**
Demos Medical Publishing
11 West 42nd Street
15th Floor
New York, NY 10036

212-683-0072
800-532-8663
FAX: 212-683-0118
support@demosmedical.com
www.demosmedpub.com

Richard Winters, Executive Editor
Beth Kaufman Barry, Publisher
Noreen Henson, Executive Director of Demos Heal
An epilepsy specialist answers questions about the causes, diagnosis, and treatments, and how to live and work with this brain disorder. Includes an epilepsy history timeline, patient health record form, resources, and a glossary. *$19.95*
180 pages
ISBN 1-932603-35-2

8543 **Epilepsy: Patient and Family Guide**
Demos Medical Publishing
11 West 42nd Street
15th Floor
New York, NY 10036

212-683-0072
800-532-8663
FAX: 212-683-0118
support@demosmedical.com
www.demosmedpub.com

Richard Winters, Executive Editor
Beth Kaufman Barry, Publisher
Noreen Henson, Executive Director of Demos Heal
A guide for adults with epilepsy and for parents of children with the disorder explains the nature and diversity of seizures, the risks and benefits of the various antiepileptic drugs, and medical and surgical therapies. *$16.95*
408 pages
ISBN 1-932603-41-7

8544 **Ethnic Diseases Sourcebook**
Omnigraphics
615 Griswold Street
Suite 520
Detroit, MI 48226

610-461-3548
800-234-1340
FAX: 800-875-1340
contact@omnigraphics.com
www.omnigraphics.com

Peter Ruffner, Co-Founder
Fred Ruffner, Co-Founder
Ethnic Diseases Sourcebook provides health information about genetic and chronic diseases that affect ethnic and racial minorities in the United States. Information about mental health services, women's health, and tips for improving health are also included, along with a glossary and a list of resources for additional help and informatio methods, treatment options, and current research initiatives. *$84.00*
648 pages Hard cover
ISBN 0-780803-36-7

8545 **From Where I Sit: Making My Way with Cerebral Palsy**
Scholastic
557 Broadway
New York, NY 10012-3962

124-484-2800
FAX: 212-343-6934
www.scholastic.com

Dick Robinson, Chairman & CEO
Maureen O'Connell, Executive Vice President, Chief
Kyle Good, Senior Vice President, Corporate
An autobiographical account of a young woman explores how it feels to live with cerebral palsy while struggling to have a full life despite the challenges facing her every day. *$13.00*
136 pages
ISBN 0-590395-84-X

8546 **Genetics and Spina Bifida**
Spina Bifida Association of America
1600 Wilson Boulevard
Suite 800
Arlington, VA 22209

202-944-3285
800-621-3141
FAX: 202-944-3295
sbaa@sbaa.org
www.sbaa.org

Ana Ximenes, Chair
Sara Struwe, President & CEO
Mark Bohay, National Web Initiatives & Development Manager
Spina bifida is a birth defect involving incomplete formation of the spine.

8547 **Growing Up with Epilepsy: A Pratical Guide for Parents**
Demos Medical Publishing
11 West 42nd Street
15th Floor
New York, NY 10036

212-683-0072
800-532-8663
FAX: 212-683-0118
support@demosmedical.com
www.demosmedpub.com

Richard Winters, Executive Editor
Beth Kaufman Barry, Publisher
Noreen Henson, Executive Director of Demos Heal
Developed to help parents with the uniques challenges that this disorder presents *$19.95*
168 pages
ISBN 1-888799-74-9

8548 **Guide to Living with HIV Infection: Developed at the Johns Hopkins AIDS Clinic**
Johns Hopkins Universty Press
2715 N Charles St
Baltimore, MD 21218-4363

410-516-6900
800-548-1784
FAX: 410-516-6998
webmaster@jhupress.jhu.edu
www.press.jhu.edu

William Brody, President
John G Bartlett, M.D., Author
Ann K Finkbeiner, Co-Author

A handbook and reference for people living with HIV infection and their families, friends, and caregivers. *$19.95*
408 pages 6th Edition
ISBN 0-801884-85-6

8549   Handbook of Chronic Fatigue Syndrome
John Wiley & Sons
1 Wiley Dr.
Somerset, NJ 08875-1272   732-469-4400
                                           800-225-5945
                                       FAX: 732-302-2300
                                 onlinelibrary.wiley.com

Leonard A. Jason, Editor
Discusses diagnosis and treatment as well as the history, phenomenology, symptomatology, assessment, and pediatric and community issues. Introduces phase-based therapy and nutritional approaches. *$110.00*
794 pages 2003
ISBN 0-471415-12-1

8550   Handbook of Epilepsy
Lippincott, Williams & Wilkins
Philadelphia, PA 19106-3713   215-521-8300
                                           800-777-2295
                                       FAX: 301-824-7390

J Lippincott, CEO
Pocket-sized reference provides concise, up-to-date, clinically oriented reviews of each of the major areas of diagnosis and management of epilepsy. *$42.95*
272 pages
ISBN 0-781743-52-4

8551   Healthy Breathing
National Jewish Health
1400 Jackson St
Denver, CO 80206-2761   303-270-2708
                                           877-225-5654
                                       FAX: 303-398-1125
                            physicianline@njhealth.org
                                www.nationaljewish.org

Richard A. Schierburg, Chair
Robin Chotin, Vice Chair
Don Silversmith, Vice Chair
Offers patients with lung or respiratory disorders information on exercise and healthy breathing.

8552   Heart of the Mind
New World Library
14 Pamaron Way
Novato, CA 94949   415-884-2100
                                           800-972-6657
                                       FAX: 415-884-2199
                               ami@newworldlibrary.com
                                www.newworldlibrary.com
Provides common NLP problems and several new techniques.
208 pages
ISBN 1-577311-56-6

8553   Hepatitis Sourcebook
Omnigraphics
615 Griswold Street
Suite 520
Detroit, MI 48226   610-461-3548
                                           800-234-1340
                                       FAX: 800-875-1340
                              contact@omnigraphics.com
                                 www.omnigraphics.com

Peter Ruffner, Co-Founder
Fred Ruffner, Co-Founder
Hepatitis Sourcebook provides basic consumer health information about hepatitis A, hepatitis B, hepatitis C, and other types of hepatitis, including autoimmune hepatitis, alcoholic hepatitis, nonalcoholic steatohepatitis, and toxin-induced hepatitis. It gives the facts about risk factors, prevention, transmission, screening and diagnostic methods, treatment options, and current research initiatives. *$84.00*
570 pages Hard cover
ISBN 0-780807-49-5

8554   Hip Function & Ambulation
Spina Bifida Association of America
1600 Wilson Boulevard
Suite 800
Arlington, VA 22209   202-944-3285
                                           800-621-3141
                                       FAX: 202-944-3295
                                          sbaa@sbaa.org
                                           www.sbaa.org

Ana Ximenes, Chair
Sara Struwe, President & CEO
Mark Bohay, National Web Initiatives & Development Manager
The ability to walk is important in our society, despite recent advances in wheelchair design and wheelchair accessibility. It also is a desire of children with spina bifida.

8555   Hydrocephalus: A Guide for Patients, Families & Friends
O'Reilly Media Inc
1005 Gravenstein Hwy N
Sebastopol, CA 95472-2811   707-827-7000
                                           800-998-9938
                                       FAX: 707-829-0104
                                      order@oreilly.com
                                         www.oreilly.com

Linda Lamb, Editor
Chuck Toporek, Author
Kellie Robinson, Author
Hydrocephalus is a life-threatening condition often referred to as, water on the brain, that is treated by surgical placement of a shunt system. Hydrocephalus: A Guide for Patients, Families and Friends educates families so they can select a skilled neurosurgeon, understand treatments, participate in care, know what symptoms need attention, discover where to turn for support, keep records needed for follow-up treatments, and make wise lifestyle choices. *$19.95*
379 pages Paperback 1999
ISBN 1-565924-10-X

8556   Hypertension Sourcebook
Omnigraphics
615 Griswold Street
Suite 520
Detroit, MI 48226   610-461-3548
                                           800-234-1340
                                       FAX: 800-875-1340
                              contact@omnigraphics.com
                                 www.omnigraphics.com

Peter Ruffner, Co-Founder
Fred Ruffner, Co-Founder
This Sourcebook describes the known causes and risk factors associated with essential (or primary) hypertension, secondary hypertension, prehypertension, and other hypertensive disorders. The book also provides information about blood pressure management strategies, including dietary changes, weight loss, exercise, and medications. *$84.00*
588 pages Hard cover
ISBN 0-780806-74-0

8557   Immune System Disorders Sourcebook.
Omnigraphics
615 Griswold Street
Suite 520
Detroit, MI 48226   610-461-3548
                                           800-234-1340
                                       FAX: 800-875-1340
                              contact@omnigraphics.com
                                 www.omnigraphics.com

Peter Ruffner, Co-Founder
Fred Ruffner, Co-Founder
Immune System Disorders Sourcebook provides information about inherited, acquired, and autoimmune diseases including primary immune deficiency, acquired immunodeficiency syndrome (AIDS), lupus, multiple sclerosis, type one diabetes, rheumatoid arthritis, and Graves' disease. Tips for coping with an immune disorder, caregiving, and treatments are presented along with a glossary and directory of additional resourcesories of additional resources. *$84.00*
643 pages 2nd Edition
ISBN 0-780807-48-8

8558 Informed Touch; A Clinician's Guide To The Evaluation Of Myofascial Disorders
Inner Traditions/Bear And Company
One Park Street
PO Box 388
Rochester, VT 05767-0388 802-767-3174
800-246-8648
FAX: 802-767-3726
customerservice@innertraditions.com
www.innertraditions.com
Rob Meadows, VP Sales/Marketing
Jessica Arsenault, Sales Associate
Donna Finando, LAc, LMT, Author
A Clinician's guide to the evaluation and treatment of myofascial disorders. *$30.00*
224 pages
ISBN 0-892817-40-5

8559 Injured Mind, Shattered Dreams: Brian's Survival from a Severe Head Injury
Brookline Books
8 Trumbull Rd,
Northampton, MA 01060-4533 413-584-0184
800-666-2665
FAX: 413-584-6184
brbooks@yahoo.com
www.brooklinebooks.com
Brian, headed for normal adulthood, crashes his car and suffers a severe head injury. This book speaks to the issues in his recovery and the victory a family can achieve through caring advocacy and faith. *$17.95*
Paperback
ISBN 0-91479 -95-6

8560 Interdisciplinary Clinical Assessment of Young Children with Developmental Disabilities
Brookes Publishing
P.O.Box 10624
Baltimore, MD 21285-0624 410-337-9580
800-638-3775
FAX: 410-337-8539
custserv@brookespublishing.com
www.brookespublishing.com
Paul H. Brookes, Chairman
Jeffrey D. Brookes, President
Melissa A. Behm, Executive Vice President
Offers insight from veteran team members on interdisciplinary team assessments. Professionals organizing a team as well as students preparing for practice will find advice on how practitioners gather information, approach assessment, make decisions, and face the challenges of their individual fields. Includes case studies and appendix of photocopiable questionnaires for clinicians and parents. *$44.95*
796 pages Hardcover
ISBN 1-557664-50-1

8561 Introduction to Spina Bifida
Spina Bifida Association of America
1600 Wilson Boulevard
Suite 800
Arlington, VA 22209 202-944-3285
800-621-3141
FAX: 202-944-3295
sbaa@sbaa.org
www.sbaa.org
Ana Ximenes, Chair
Sara Struwe, President & CEO
Mark Bohay, National Web Initiatives & Development Manager
An aid for parents, family and nonmedical people who care for a child with spina bifida. *$7.00*

8562 It's All in Your Head: The Link Between Mercury Amalgams and Illness
Avery Publishing Group
299 W. Houston Street
New York, NY 10014 212-859-1100
FAX: 212-859-1150
info@programexchange.com
Dr. Higgins's critique of the use of mercury, a toxic element and environmental hazard, in dentistry. For those suffering mercury poisoning, the book examines a number of conventional and alternative treatments.
208 pages

8563 Joslin Guide to Diabetes: A Program for Managing Your Treatment
Joslin Diabetes Center
1 Joslin Pl
Boston, MA 02215-5306 617-732-2400
FAX: 617-732-2452
www.joslin.org
Richard S Beaser, M.D., Author
Amy Campbell,Ms, RD, CDE, Co-Author
Ralph M. James, Chairperson of the Board
Discusses the causes of diabetes, the role of diet and exercise, meal planning and complications. Also provide information on drawing blood, mixing and injecting insulin, special challenges, living with diabetes. *$16.95*
352 pages Revised Edition

8564 Journey to Well: Learning to Live After Spinal Cord Injury
Altarfire Publishing
1835 Oak Terrace
Newcastle, CA 95658
Margie Williams, Author
The author's close-up view of what life is like during and after such an incident, including her experience with institutional medicine and insurance companies (for better and for worse), and her determined - and ultimately successful - effort to rehabilitate herself and reconstruct her life. *$15.95*
251 pages
ISBN 0-965555-82-8

8565 Ketogenic Diet: A Treatment for Children and Others with Epilepsy
Demos Medical Publishing
11 West 42nd Street
15th Floor
New York, NY 10036 212-683-0072
800-532-8663
FAX: 212-683-0118
support@demosmedical.com
www.demosmedpub.com
Richard Winters, Executive Editor
Beth Kaufman Barry, Publisher
Noreen Henson, Executive Director of Demos Heal
Patient education reference on the use of the ketogenic diet to conrol epilepsy in children. *$24.95*
328 pages Paperback
ISBN 1-932603-18-2

8566 Latex Allergy in Spina Bifida Patients
Spina Bifida Association of America
1600 Wilson Boulevard
Suite 800
Arlington, VA 22209 202-944-3285
800-621-3141
FAX: 202-944-3295
sbaa@sbaa.org
www.sbaa.org
Ana Ximenes, Chair
Sara Struwe, President & CEO
Mark Bohay, National Web Initiatives & Development Manager
The Spina Bifida Association (SBA) serves adults and children who live with the challenges of Spina Bifida.

8567 Learning Among Children with Spina Bifida
Spina Bifida Association of America
1600 Wilson Boulevard
Suite 800
Arlington, VA 22209 202-944-3285
800-621-3141
FAX: 202-944-3295
sbaa@sbaa.org
www.sbaa.org
Ana Ximenes, Chair
Sara Struwe, President & CEO
Mark Bohay, National Web Initiatives & Development Manager

The Spina Bifida Association (SBA) serves adults and children who live with the challenges of Spina Bifida.

8568   Let's Talk About Having Asthma
Rosen Publishing
29 E 21st St
New York, NY 10010-6209

212-420-1600
800-237-9932
FAX: 888-436-4643
www.rosenpublishing.com

Marianna Johnstone, Co-Author
Elizabeth Weitzman, Co-Author
Kelly Chambers, Marketing Assistant
Many kids suffer from asthma, which can overtake them suddenly, causing them terror as they struggle for breath. This book talks about the causes and treatments for asthma, as well as precautions sufferers should take. *$21.95*
ISBN 0-823950-32-8

8569   Leukemia Sourcebook
Omnigraphics
615 Griswold Street
Suite 520
Detroit, MI 48226

610-461-3548
800-234-1340
FAX: 800-875-1340
contact@omnigraphics.com
www.omnigraphics.com

Peter Ruffner, Co-Founder
Fred Ruffner, Co-Founder
This Sourcebook provides health information about adult and childhood leukemias focusing on the diagnosis and treatments for leukemia, including chemotherapy, radiation, drug therapy, and transplantation of peripheral blood stem cells or marrow. Also included are tips for nutrition, pain and fatigue control, and recognizing possible long-term and late effects of leukemia treatment, along with a glossary and directories of additional resources. *$84.00*
564 pages Hard cover
ISBN 0-780806-27-6

8570   Life After Trauma: A Workbook for Healing
Guilford Press
72 Spring St
New York, NY 10012-4019

212-431-9800
800-365-7006
FAX: 212-966-6708
info@guilford.com
www.guilford.com

Denaour Rosenbloom, Author
Mary Beth Williams, Co-Author
Barbar E Watkins, Co-Author
A self-help book on how to deal with trauma. *$19.95*
300 pages Paperback 1910
ISBN 1-606236-08-6

8571   Life Line
National Hydrocephalus Foundation
12413 Centralia St
Lakewood, CA 90715-1653

562-402-3523
888-857-3434
888-260-1789
FAX: 562-924-6666

Debbi Fields, Executive Director
Michael Fields, President/Treasurer
Jaynie Dunn, Secretary
National Hydrocephalus Foundation quarterly newsletter. *$35.00*
12 pages Quarterly

8572   Lipomas & Lipomyelomeningocele
Spina Bifida Association of America
1600 Wilson Boulevard
Suite 800
Arlington, VA 22209

202-944-3285
800-621-3141
FAX: 202-944-3295
sbaa@sbaa.org
www.sbaa.org

Ana Ximenes, Chair
Sara Struwe, President & CEO
Mark Bohay, National Web Initiatives & Development Manager
The Spina Bifida Association (SBA) serves adults and children who live with the challenges of Spina Bifida.

8573   Liver Disorders Sourcebook
Omnigraphics
615 Griswold Street
Suite 520
Detroit, MI 48226

610-461-3548
800-234-1340
FAX: 800-875-1340
contact@omnigraphics.com
www.omnigraphics.com

Peter Ruffner, Co-Founder
Fred Ruffner, Co-Founder
Liver Disorders Sourcebook contains basic consumer health information about the liver, how it works, and how to keep it healthy through diet, vaccination, and other preventive care measures. Readers will learn about the symptoms and treatment options for such diseases as hepatitis, primary biliary cirrhosis, Wilson's disease, hemochromatosis, liver failure, cancer of the liver, and disorders related to drugs and other toxins. *$84.00*
580 pages Hard cover
ISBN 0-780803-83-1

8574   Living Beyond Multiple Sclerosis: A Woman's Guide
Hunter House
PO Box 2914
Alameda, CA 94501-914

510-865-5282
800-266-5592
FAX: 510-865-4295
www.hunterhouse.com

Judith Lynn Nichols, Author
Lily Jung, Foreword
This collection of e-mail conversations provides anecdotal and personal information contributed by women with multiple sclerosis. *$14.95*
256 pages
ISBN 0-897932-93-6

8575   Living Well with Asthma
Guilford Press
72 Spring St
New York, NY 10012-4019

212-431-9800
800-365-7006
FAX: 212-966-6708
info@guilford.com
www.guilford.com

Cynthia L Divino, Author
Michael R Freedman, Co-Author
Samuel J Rosenberg, Co-Author
Meeting the needs of a growing clinical population, this reader-friendly, practical book offers a lifeline to asthma patients attempting to understand and cope with the psychological ramifications of their illness and its treatment. *$15.95*
213 pages Paperback
ISBN 1-572300-51-4

8576   Living Well with Chronic Fatigue Syndrome and Fibromyalgia
Harper Collins Publishers
10 E 53rd St
New York, NY 10022-5244

212-207-7901
800-242-7737
FAX: 212-702-2586
spsales@harpercollins.com
www.harpercollins.com

Mary J Shomon, Author

From the author of Living Well With Hypothyroidism, a comprehensive guide to the diagnosis and treatment of chronic fatigue syndrome and fibromyalgia—vital help for the millions of people suffering from pain, fatigue, and sleep problems. *$14.95*
416 pages 2004
ISBN 0-060521-25-2

8577 Living Well with HIV and AIDS
Bull Publishing
PO Box 1377
Boulder, CO 80306-1377   303-545-6350
                                          800-676-2855
                                     FAX: 303-545-6354
                                          www.bullpub.com

David Sobel, MPH, Author
Virginia Gonzalez MPH, Co-Author
Daina Laurent MPH, Co-Author
New drugs and drug combinations have turned HIV/AIDS into a long-term illness rather than a death sentence. Practical advice on mental adjustments and physical vigilance is outlined. *$18.95*
245 pages 3rd Edition
ISBN 0-923521-52-6

8578 Living With Spinal Cord Injury Series
Fanlight Productions C/O Icarus Films
32 Court St.
21st Floor
Brooklyn, NY 11201   718-488-8900
                                          800-876-1710
                                     FAX: 718-488-8642
                                          info@fanlight.com
                                          www.fanlight.com

Barry Corbet, Producer
Jonathan Miller, President
Meredith Miller, Sales Manager
The producer, himself injured in a helicopter crash, brings a unique perspective to this classic three-part series on coming to terms with spinal cord injury. These films offer enduring proof that a tough break doesn't have to mean a ruined life. *$210.00*
VHS 1973

8579 Living with Brain Injury: A Guide for Families
Delmar Cengage Learning
PO Box 6904
Florence, KY 41022-6904   800-354-9706
                                     FAX: 800-487-8488

Richard C Senelick MD, Author
Karla Dougherty, Co-Author
A consumer text to aid people living with brain-injured survivors, includes facts on neuroplasticity, experimental rehabilitation research, and the process of rehabilitation itself. *$19.95*
225 pages Softcover 2001
ISBN 1-891525-09-3

8580 Living with Spina Bifida: A Guide for Families and Professionals
University of North Carolina at Chapel Hill
116 S Boundary St
Chapel Hill, NC 27514-3808   919-966-3561
                                          800-848-6224
                                     FAX: 919-962-2704
                                          uncpress@unc.edu
                                          www.uncpress.unc.edu

Adrian Sandler MD, Author
A handbook that addresses patients' biopsychosocial and developmental needs from birth through adolescence and into adulthood. Sandler's holistic approach encourages families to focus more on the child and less on the disability while providing abundant information about this condition. *$20.95*
296 pages 2004
ISBN 0-807855-47-8

8581 Lung Cancer: Making Sense of Diagnosis, Treatment, and Options
O'Reilly Media Inc
1005 Gravenstein Hwy N
Sebastopol, CA 95472-2811   707-827-7000
                                          800-998-9938
                                     FAX: 707-829-0104
                                          order@oreilly.com
                                          www.oreilly.com

Linda Lamb, Editor
Lorraine Johnston, Author
Straightforward language and the words of patients and their families are the hallmarks of this book on the number one cancer killer in the US. Written by a widely respected author and patient advocate, Lung Cancer: Making Sense of Diagnosis, Treatment, & Options has been meticulously reviewed by top medical experts and physicians. Readers will find medical facts simply explained, advice to ease their daily life, and tools to be strong advocates for themselves or a family member. *$27.95*
530 pages Paperback 2001
ISBN 0-596500-02-5

8582 Lung Disorders Sourcebook
Omnigraphics
615 Griswold Street
Suite 520
Detroit, MI 48226   610-461-3548
                                          800-234-1340
                                     FAX: 800-875-1340
                                          contact@omnigraphics.com
                                          www.omnigraphics.com

Peter Ruffner, Co-Founder
Fred Ruffner, Co-Founder
Lung Disorders Sourcebook offers information about specific types of lung disorders, including diagnosis, treatment, and prevention issues. The book offers advice for preventing some types lung disorder that are acquired by asbestos, radon, and other environmental exposures. *$84.00*
657 pages Hard cover
ISBN 0-780803-39-8

8583 Lupus: Alternative Therapies That Work
Inner Traditions
One Park St.
Rochester, VT 05767   800-246-8648
                                          802-767-3726
                                     TTY:customerserv
                                          info@innertraditions.com
                                          www.innertraditions.com

Sharon Moore, Author
A comprehensive guise to noninvasive, nontoxic therapies for lupus - written by a lupus survivor. *$14.95*
256 pages 2000
ISBN 0-892818-89-1

8584 MAGIC Touch
MAGIC Foundation for Children's Growth
6645 North Ave
Oak Park, IL 60302-1057   708-383-0808
                                          800-362-4423
                                     FAX: 708-383-0899
                                          mary@magicfoundation.org
                                          www.magicfoundation.org

Mary Andrews, CEO
Dianne Kremidas, Executive Director
Pam Pentaris, Office Manager
Provides support and education regarding growth disorders in children and related adult disorders, including adult GHD. Dedicated to helping children whose physical growth is affected be a medical problem by assisting families of afflicted children through local support groups, public education/awareness, newsletters, specialty divisions and programs for the children.
36-40 pages Quarterly

8585 Management of Autistic Behavior
Sage Publications
2455 Teller Road
Thousand Oaks, CA 91320   805-499-0721
                                 800-818-7243
                                 FAX: 805-499-0871
                                 info@sagepub.com
                                 www.sagepub.com

Sara Miller McCune, Founder, Publisher, Executive Chairman
Blaise R Simqu, President & CEO
Tracey A. Ozmina, Executive Vice President & Chief Operating Officer
Comprehensive and practical book that tells what works best with specific problems. *$51.00*
450 pages Paperback
ISBN 0-890791-96-1

8586 Management of Genetic Syndromes
John Wiley & Sons
111 River St
Hoboken, NJ 07030-5774   201-748-6000
                                201-748-6088
                                info@wiley.com

Suzanne B Cassidy, Editor
Judith E Allanson, Editor
Edited by two of the field's most highly esteemed experts, this landmark volume provides: A precise reference of the physical manifestations of common genetic syndromes, clearly written for professionals and families, Extensive updates, particularly in sections on diagnostic criteria and diagnostic testing, pathogenesis, and management, A tried-and-tested, user-friendly format, with each chapter including information on incidence, etiology and pathogenesis, diagnostic criteria and testing, and d *$204.95*
720 pages 3rd Edition
ISBN 0-470191-41-5

8587 Managing Post Polio: A Guide to Living Well with Post Polio
ABI Professional Publications
PO Box 149
St Petersburg, FL 33731-149   727-556-0950
                                     800-551-7776
                                     FAX: 727-556-2560
                                     www.abipropub.com

Lauro S Halstead MD, Editor
Edited by Lauro S. Halstead, M.D., Managing Post-Polio, 2nd Edition, provides a comprehensive overview dealing with the medical, psychological, vocational, and many other challenges of living with post-polio syndrome. With contributions from over 15 healthcare professionals, the majority of whom are polio survivors themselves, Managing Post-Polio distills and summarizes the wealth of information presented from over the past 20 plus years.
256 pages
ISBN 1-886236-17-8

8588 Meniere's Disease
Vestibular Disorders Association
5018 NE 15th Avenue
Portland, OR 97211   800-837-8428
                            FAX: 503-229-8064
                            info@vestibular.org
                            www.vestibular.org

P. Ashley Wackym, Chair
Cynthia Ryan MBA, Executive Director
Tony Staser, Development Director
VEDA's website contains a wealth of information on the symptoms, diagnosis and treatment of various types of vestibular disorders. *$5.00*

8589 Menopause without Medicine
Hunter House
PO Box 2914
Alameda, CA 94501-914   510-865-5282
                               800-266-5592
                               FAX: 510-865-4295
                               www.hunterhouse.com

Linda Ojeda PhD, Author

Menopause Without Medicine provides complete information on the symptoms of menopause - hot flashes, fatigue, sexual changes, depression and osteoporosis - and how to alleviate them. *$18.95*
304 pages 5th Edition
ISBN 0-897934-05-3

8590 Movement Disorders Sourcebook
Omnigraphics
615 Griswold Street
Suite 520
Detroit, MI 48226   610-461-3548
                           800-234-1340
                           FAX: 800-875-1340
                           contact@omnigraphics.com
                           www.omnigraphics.com

Peter Ruffner, Co-Founder
Fred Ruffner, Co-Founder
This Sourcebook provides health information about neurological movement disorders, their symptoms, causes, diagnostic tests, and treatments. Readers will learn about Essential Tremor, Parkinson's Disease, Dystonia, and many other early-onset and adult-onset movement disorders. Information about mobility and assistive technology aids is included, along with a glossary and a listing of additional resources. *$84.00*
600 pages Hard cover
ISBN 0-780810-34-1

8591 Multiple Sclerosis and Having a Baby
Inner Traditions
PO Box 388
Rochester, VT 05767-0388   802-767-3174
                                  800-246-8648
                                  FAX: 802-767-3726
                                  customerservice@innertraditions.com
                                  www.innertraditions.com

Judy Graham, Author
Everything you need to know about conception, pregnancy and parenthood. *$12.95*
160 pages 2001
ISBN 0-892817-88-7

8592 Multiple Sclerosis: 300 Tips for Making Life Easier
Demos Medical Publishing
11 West 42nd Street
15th Floor
New York, NY 10036   212-683-0072
                            800-532-8663
                            FAX: 212-683-0118
                            support@demosmedical.com
                            www.demosmedpub.com

Richard Winters, Executive Editor
Beth Kaufman Barry, Publisher
Noreen Henson, Executive Director of Demos Heal
This latest book in the Making Life Easier series features tip, techniques and shortcuts for conserving time and energy so you can do more of the things you want to do. These tips should help increase the number of good days you have while encouraging you to develop your own techniques for making life easier. *$16.95*
128 pages
ISBN 1-932603-21-2

8593 Multiple Sclerosis: A Guide for Families
Demos Medical Publishing
11 West 42nd Street
15th Floor
New York, NY 10036   212-683-0072
                            800-532-8663
                            FAX: 212-683-0118
                            support@demosmedical.com
                            www.demosmedpub.com

Richard Winters, Executive Editor
Beth Kaufman Barry, Publisher
Noreen Henson, Executive Director of Demos Heal
Guide for living and coping with multiple sclerosis. *$24.95*
256 pages
ISBN 1-932603-10-7

8594 Multiple Sclerosis: A Guide for the Newly Diagnosed
Demos Medical Publishing
11 West 42nd Street
15th Floor
New York, NY 10036

212-683-0072
800-532-8663
FAX: 212-683-0118
support@demosmedical.com
www.demosmedpub.com

Richard Winters, Executive Editor
Beth Kaufman Barry, Publisher
Noreen Henson, Executive Director of Demos Heal
A must-have title for anyone who has recently been diagnosed with MS and a good idea for family members and friends. *$19.95*
256 pages
ISBN 1-932603-27-1

8595 Multiple Sclerosis: The Guide to Treatment and Management
Demos Medical Publishing
11 West 42nd Street
15th Floor
New York, NY 10036

212-683-0072
800-532-8663
FAX: 212-683-0118
support@demosmedical.com
www.demosmedpub.com

Richard Winters, Executive Editor
Beth Kaufman Barry, Publisher
Noreen Henson, Executive Director of Demos Heal
A current guide to modern therapies. *$24.95*
216 pages
ISBN 1-932603-15-4

8596 Muscular Dystrophies
Oxford University Press
198 Madison Avenue
New York, NY 10016

212-726-6000
800-445-9714
FAX: 919-677-1303
custserv.us@oup.com
www.oup.com

Alan E.H. Emery, Author
Describes the opportunities for management of more than 30 types of MD through respiratory care, physiotherapy and surgical correction of contractures, and examines the potential for effective treatment utilizing the new techniques of gene and cell therapy *$165.00*
330 pages
ISBN 0-192632-91-4

8597 Muscular Dystrophy in Children: A Guide for Families
Demos Medical Publishing
11 West 42nd Street
15th Floor
New York, NY 10036

212-683-0072
800-532-8663
FAX: 212-683-0118
support@demosmedical.com

Richard Winters, Executive Editor
Beth Kaufman Barry, Publisher
Noreen Henson, Executive Director of Demos Heal
Defines the available medical options at every stage of the disease and offers guidance even when it may seem that little or nothing can be done. Includes a glossary and suggestions for furhter reading. *$19.95*
144 pages Paperback
ISBN 1-888799-33-1

8598 Muscular Dystrophy: The Facts
Oxford University Press
198 Madison Avenue
New York, NY 10016

212-726-6000
800-445-9714
FAX: 919-677-1303
custserv.us@oup.com
www.oup.com

Peter Harper, Author

A good first book for individuals and families faced with the likelihood or reality of a muscular dystrophy diagnosis. *$22.50*
178 pages
ISBN 0-192632-17-5

8599 My House is Killing Me! The Home Guide for Families with Allergies and Asthma
Johns Hopkins University Press
2175 N Charles St
Baltimore, MD 21218-4363

410-516-6900
800-548-1784
FAX: 410-516-6968
webmaster@jhupress.jhu.edu
www.press.jhu.edu

Jeffrey C May, Author
Jonathan M Samet, M.D., Foreword
Kathleen Keane, Director
Chemical consultant May describes where and how the various parts of a residence can cause temporary or chronic illness for those with allergies or other sensitivities. *$20.95*
352 pages
ISBN 0-801867-30-9

8600 Neuropsychiatry of Epilepsy
Cambridge University Press
100 Brookhill Dr
West Nyack, NY 10994

845-353-7500
845-353-4141
www.cambridge.org

Michael R Trimble, Editor
Bettina Schmitz, Editor
Covers the practical implications of ongoing research, and offers a diagnostic and management perspective. Topics include cognitive aspects, nonepileptic attacks, and clinical aspects. For professionals treating epileptic patients. *$104.00*
232 pages 2nd Edition 1911
ISBN 0-521154-69-7

8601 Nick Joins In
Spina Bifida Association of America
1600 Wilson Boulevard
Suite 800
Arlington, VA 22209

202-944-3285
800-621-3141
FAX: 202-944-3295
sbaa@sbaa.org
www.sbaa.org

Ana Ximenes, Chair
Sara Struwe, President & CEO
Mark Bohay, National Web Initiatives & Development Manager
When Nick, who is in a wheelchair, enters a regular classroom for the first time, he realizes that he has much to contribute. *$17.00*

8602 No More Allergies
Random House
1745 Broadway
3rd Floor
New York, NY 10019-4305

212-782-9000
FAX: 212-572-6066
www.randomhouse.com

Markus Dohle, CEO
Gary Null PhD, Author
Null redefines a health problem that afflicts 40 million Americans: More than mere hay fever, contemporary allergic reactions include chronic fatigue syndrome, Alzheimer's disease, and even HIV infection. These conditions, he explains, occur when our immune systems break down. This ground-breaking book now prescribes effective solutions. *$23.00*
464 pages 1992
ISBN 0-679743-10-1

8603 No Time for Jello: One Family's Experience
Brookline Books
8 Trumbull Rd,
Northampton, MA 01060-4533

413-584-0184
800-666-2665
FAX: 413-584-6184
brbooks@yahoo.com
www.brooklinebooks.com

One family's story of their attempts to remediate and cure the effects of a cerebral palsied condition the oldest son was born with. The Bratts traveled traditional routes, through distinguished medical centers in Boston, and nontraditional routes in a search for treatments that would help their son. *$17.95*
Softcover
ISBN 0-91479 -56-5

8604   Nocturnal Asthma
National Jewish Health
1400 Jackson Street
Denver, CO 80206   303-270-2708
                                        877-225-5654
                                   FAX: 303-398-1125
                                    allstetterw@njc.org
                                      nationaljewish.org

Rich Schierburg, Chair
Robin Chotin, Vice Chair
Michael Salem, M.D., President and CEO
Offers information to patients about how to understand and manage asthma at night.

8605   Obesity
Spina Bifida Association of America
1600 Wilson Boulevard
Suite 800
Arlington, VA 22209   202-944-3285
                                        800-621-3141
                                   FAX: 202-944-3295
                                        sbaa@sbaa.org
                                        www.sbaa.org

Ana Ximenes, Chair
Sara Struwe, President & CEO
Mark Bohay, National Web Initiatives & Development Manager
The Spina Bifida Association (SBA) serves adults and children who live with the challenges of Spina Bifida. *$8.00*

8606   Obesity Sourcebook
Omnigraphics
615 Griswold Street
Suite 520
Detroit, MI 48226   610-461-3548
                                        800-234-1340
                                   FAX: 800-875-1340
                                 contact@omnigraphics.com
                                    www.omnigraphics.com

Peter Ruffner, Co-Founder
Fred Ruffner, Co-Founder
Discusses diseases and other problems associated with obesity. *$78.00*
376 pages
ISBN 0-780803-33-6

8607   Occulta
Spina Bifida Association of America
1600 Wilson Boulevard
Suite 800
Arlington, VA 22209   202-944-3285
                                        800-621-3141
                                   FAX: 202-944-3295
                                        sbaa@sbaa.org
                                        www.sbaa.org

Ana Ximenes, Chair
Sara Struwe, President & CEO
Mark Bohay, National Web Initiatives & Development Manager
The Spina Bifida Association (SBA) serves adults and children who live with the challenges of Spina Bifida. *$8.00*

8608   Official Patient's Sourcebook on Bell's Palsy
Icon Group International
9606 Tierra Grande Street
Suite 205
San Diego, CA 92126   FAX: 858-635-9414
                                 orders@icongroupbooks.com
                                    www.icongroupbooks.com
Provides patients with guidance on where and how to look for information covering virtually all topics related to bell's palsy (also Antoni's Palsy; facial nerve palsy; facial palsy; facial paralysis; idiopathic facial palsy; idiopathic facial paralysis), from the essentials to the most advanced areas of research. *$24.95*
ISBN 0-597835-20-9

8609   Official Patient's Sourcebook on Cystic Fibrosis
Icon Group International
9606 Tierra Grande Street
Suite 205
San Diego, CA 92126   FAX: 858-635-9414
                                 orders@icongroupbooks.com
                                      icongroupbooks.com
For parents who have decided to make education and research an integral part of the treatment process. Although it also gives information useful to doctors, caregivers and other health professionals, it tells paretns where and how to look for information covering virtually all topics related to cystic fibrosis (also fbrocystic disease of pancreas; mucosis; mucoviscidosis; pancreatic fibrosis), from the essentials to the most advanced areas of research. *$28.95*
356 pages
ISBN 0-597831-46-7

8610   Official Patient's Sourcebook on Muscular Dystrophy
Icon Group International
9606 Tierra Grande Street
Suite 205
San Diego, CA 92126   FAX: 858-635-9414
                                 orders@icongroupbooks.com
                                      icongroupbooks.com
Created for patients who have decided to make education and research an integral part of the treatment process. Although it also gives information useful to doctors, caregivers and other health professionals, it tells patients where and how to look for information covering virtually all topics related to muscular dystrophy. *$24.95*
268 pages
ISBN 0-597832-10-2

8611   Official Patient's Sourcebook on Osteoporosis
Icon Group International
9606 Tierra Grande Street
Suite 205
San Diego, CA 92126   FAX: 858-635-9414
                                 orders@icongroupbooks.com
                                      icongroupbooks.com
Provides patients with guidance on where and how to look for information covering virtually all topics related to bell's palsy (also Antoni's Palsy; Facial Nerve Palsy; Facial palsy; Facial Paralysis; Idiopathic Facial Palsy; Idiopathic facial paralysis), from the essentials to the most advanced areas of research. *$34.95*
ISBN 0-597833-04-4

8612   Official Patient's Sourcebook on Post-Polio Syndrome: A Revised and Updated Directory
Icon Group International
9606 Tierra Grande Street
Suite 205
San Diego, CA 92126   FAX: 858-635-9414
                                 orders@icongroupbooks.com
                                      icongroupbooks.com
A sourcebook created for patients who have decided to make education and Internet-based research an integral part of the treatment process. Although it gives information useful to doctors, caregivers and other health professionals, it also tells patients where and how to look for information covering virtually all topics related to post-polio syndrome, from the essentials to the most advanced areas of research. *$28.95*
124 pages
ISBN 0-597835-31-4

8613   Official Patient's Sourcebook on Primary Pulmonary Hypertension
Icon Group International
9606 Tierra Grande Street
Suite 205
San Diego, CA 92126   FAX: 858-635-9414
                                 orders@icongroupbooks.com
                                      icongroupbooks.com
Provides patients with guidance on where and how to look for information covering virtually all topics related to primary pulmonary hypertension (also familial primary pulmonary hypertension; idiopathic pulmonary hypertension; primary obliterative pulmonary vascular disease; primary pulmonary vas-

cular disease; and pulmonary hypertension), from the essentials to the most advanced areas of research. *$24.95*
ISBN 0-597831-54-8

8614 Official Patient's Sourcebook on Pulmonary Fibrosis
Icon Group International
9606 Tierra Grande Street
Suite 205
San Diego, CA 92126   FAX: 858-635-9414
                                   orders@icongroupbooks.com
                                   icongroupbooks.com
Provides patients with guidance on where and how to look for information covering virtually all topics related to idiopathic pulmonary fibrosis (also alveolocapillary block; cryptogenic fibrosing alveolitis; diffuse fibrosing alveolitis; fibrosing alveolitis; Hamman-Rich syndrome; and idiopathic diffuse interstitial pulmonary fibrosis), from the essentials to the most advanced areas of research. *$24.95*
ISBN 0-597831-65-3

8615 Official Patient's Sourcebook on Scoliosis
Icon Group International
9606 Tierra Grande Street
Suite 205
San Diego, CA 92126   FAX: 858-635-9414
                                   orders@icongroupbooks.com
                                   icongroupbooks.com
Provides patients with guidance on where and how to look for information covering virtually all topics related to scoliosis (also Idiopathic scoliosis; Kyphoscoliosis; Paralytic scoliosis; Sciatic scoliosis), from the essentials to the most advanced areas of research. *$28.95*
ISBN 0-597829-90-X

8616 Official Patient's Sourcebook on Sickle Cell Anemia
Icon Group International
9606 Tierra Grande Street
Suite 205
San Diego, CA 92126   FAX: 858-635-9414
                                   orders@icongroupbooks.com
                                   icongroupbooks.com
Provides patients with guidance on where and how to look for information covering virtually all topics related to sickle cell anemia (also Hb S disease; Hemoglobin S disease; Hemoglobin SS disease; sickle cell disease; sickle cell trait), from the essentials to the most advanced areas of research. *$28.95*
ISBN 0-597831-57-2

8617 Official Patient's Sourcebook on Ulcerative Colitis
Icon Group International
9606 Tierra Grande Street
Suite 205
San Diego, CA 92126   FAX: 858-635-9414
                                   orders@icongroupbooks.com
                                   icongroupbooks.com
Provides patients with guidance on where and how to look for information covering virtually all topics related to ulcerative colitis (also Chronic Non-Specific Ulcerative Colitis; Colitis Gravis; Idiopathic Non-Specific Ulcerative Colitis; Idiopathic proctocolitis; Inflammatory bowel disease (IBD); Nonspecific ulcerative colitis), from the essentials to the most advanced areas of research. *$34.95*
ISBN 0-597834-09-1

8618 One Day at a Time: Children Living with Leukemia
Gareth Stevens Publishing
111 East 14th Street
Suite #349
New York, NY 10003   800-542-2595
                                   FAX: 877-542-2596
                                   customerservice@gspub.com
                                   www.garethstevens.com
Focus on Hanna, two years old, and 3 year old Frederick. Both diagnosed with Leukemia and follows them as they are treated for their illness. Includes such daily routines as eating breakfast, washing and playing. *$16.95*
56 pages Hardcover
ISBN 1-55532 -13-6

8619 Options: Revolutionary Ideas in the War on Cancer
People Against Cancer
P.O.Box 10
604 East Street
Otho, IA 50569   515-972-4444
                                   800-662-2623
                                   FAX: 515-972-4415
                                   info@PeopleAgainstCancer.org
                                   www.peopleagainstcancer.com
Frank D. Wiewel, Executive Director/Founder
Publication of People Against Cancer, a nonprofit, grassroots public benefit organization dedicated to 'New Directions in the War on Cancer.' We help people to find the best cancer treatment. We are a democratic organization of people with cancer, their loved ones and citizens working together to protect and enhance medical freedom of choice.

8620 Osteoporosis Sourcebook
Omnigraphics
615 Griswold Street
Suite 520
Detroit, MI 48226   610-461-3548
                                   800-234-1340
                                   FAX: 800-875-1340
                                   contact@omnigraphics.com
                                   www.omnigraphics.com
Peter Ruffner, Co-Founder
Fred Ruffner, Co-Founder
Discusses causes, risk factors, treatments and traditional and non-traditional pain management issues concerning osteoporosis. *$84.00*
568 pages Hard cover
ISBN 0-780802-39-1

8621 Parent's Guide to Allergies and Asthma
Allergy & Asthma Network Mothers of Asthmatics
Ste 150
PO Box 7474
Fairfax Station, VA 22039-7474   703-323-9170
                                   800-756-5525
                                   FAX: 703-323-9173
                                   custsvc@parent-institute.com
                                   www.parent-institute.com
John H Wherry, Ed.D, President
A up-to-date, easy-to-read resource offering essential information on asthma and allergies.

8622 Partial Seizure Disorders: A Guide for Patients and Families
O'Reilly Media Inc
1005 Gravenstein Hwy N
Sebastopol, CA 95472-2811   707-827-7000
                                   800-998-9938
                                   FAX: 707-829-0104
                                   order@oreilly.com
                                   www.oreilly.com
Linda Lamb, Editor
Mitzi Waltz, Author
Partial Seizure Disorders helps patients and families get an accurate diagnosis of this condition, understand medications and their side effects, and learn coping skills and other adjuncts to medication. It walks readers through developmental and school issues for young children; adult issues such as employment and driving; working with an existing health plan; and getting further help through advocacy and support organizations, articles, and online resources. *$19.95*
288 pages Paperback
ISBN 0-596500-03-3

8623 Penitent, with Roses: An HIV+ Mother Reflects
University Press of New England
1 Court St
Ste 250
Lebanon, NH 03766-1358   603-448-1533
                                   800-421-1561
                                   FAX: 603-448-7006
                                   www.upne.com
Paula W Peterson, Author
Peterson, a married, middle-class, Jewish mother, was diagnosed with full-blown AIDS four years into her marriage and 11 months

after her son was born. In seven poignant autobiographical essays and a collection of letters to her uninfected, four-year-old son, the author maintains an upbeat tone and describes her unsuccessful attempts to find the source of her infection (her husband tested negative), her relationships with her doctors, and her work as an HIV activist. *$26.95*
256 pages 2001
ISBN 1-584651-28-4

8624 Plan Ahead: Do What You Can
Spina Bifida Association of America
1600 Wilson Boulevard
Suite 800
Arlington, VA 22209   202-944-3285
                                    800-621-3141
                              FAX: 202-944-3295
                                    sbaa@sbaa.org
                                    www.sbaa.org

Ana Ximenes, Chair
Sara Struwe, President & CEO
Mark Bohay, National Web Initiatives & Development Manager
Folic aciid information for women at risk for recurrence. *$15.00*

8625 Post-Polio Syndrome: A Guide for Polio Survivors and Their Families
Yale University Press
PO Box 209040
New Haven, CT 6520-9040   203-432-0960
                                   203-432-0948
                     language.yalepress@yale.edu

Julie K Silver M.D., Author
Laro S Halstead, M.D., Foreword
A guide for polio survivors, their families, and their health care providers offers expert advice on all aspects of post-polio syndrome. Based on the author's experience treating post-polio patients, Silver discusses issues of critical importance, including how to find the best medical care, deal with symptoms, sustain mobility, manage pain, approach insurance issues, and arrange a safe living environment. *$19.50*
304 pages 2002
ISBN 0-300088-08-3

8626 Prader-Willi Syndrome: Development and Manifestations
Cambridge University Press
32 Avenue of the Americas
New York, NY 10013-2473   212-924-3900
                                   212-691-3239
                                   www.cambridge.org
Joyce Whittington, Author
Tony Holland, Co-Author
Seeks to identify and provide the latest findings about how best to manage the complex medical, nutritional, psychological, educational, social and therapeutic needs of people with PWS. *$130.00*
230 pages 2004
ISBN 0-521840-29-3

8627 Preventing Secondary Conditions Associated with Spina Bifida or Cerebral Palsy
Spina Bifida Association of America
1600 Wilson Boulevard
Suite 800
Arlington, VA 22209   202-944-3285
                                    800-621-3141
                              FAX: 202-944-3295
                                    sbaa@sbaa.org
                                    www.sbaa.org
Ana Ximenes, Chair
Sara Struwe, President & CEO
Mark Bohay, National Web Initiatives & Development Manager
This report is for health professionals, parents and teachers. *$3.00*

8628 Prostate and Urological Disorders Sourcebook
Omnigraphics
615 Griswold Street
Suite 520
Detroit, MI 48226   610-461-3548
                                   800-234-1340
                             FAX: 800-875-1340
                     contact@omnigraphics.com
                          www.omnigraphics.com

Peter Ruffner, Co-Founder
Fred Ruffner, Co-Founder
Prostate and Urological Disorders Sourcebook provides information about prostate cancer and other prostate problems, such as prostatitis and benign prostatic hyperplasia. A glossary of andrological terms and a directory of resources for additional help and information are also included. *$84.00*
604 pages Hard cover
ISBN 0-780807-97-6

8629 Protecting Against Latex Allergy
Spina Bifida Association of America
1600 Wilson Boulevard
Suite 800
Arlington, VA 22209   202-944-3285
                                    800-621-3141
                              FAX: 202-944-3295
                                    sbaa@sbaa.org
                                    www.sbaa.org

Ana Ximenes, Chair
Sara Struwe, President & CEO
Mark Bohay, National Web Initiatives & Development Manager
Because awareness and proper action may help prevent an allergic reation, learning about latex allergy is especially important for parents, health care workers and anyone who is exposed to latex regulary. *$20.00*

8630 Questions and Answers: The ADA and Personswith HIV/AIDS
US Department of Justice
950 Pennsylvania Ave. NW
Washington, DC 20530   202-307-0663
                                  800-514-0301
                            FAX: 202-307-1197
                            TTY: 800-514-0383
                                  www.ada.gov

Rebecca B. Bond, Chief
Anne Raish, Principal Deputy Chief
Christina Galindo-Walsh, Deputy Chief
A 16-page publication explaining the requirements for employers, businesses and nonprofit agencies that serve the public, and state and local governments to avoid discriminating against persons with HIV/AIDS.

8631 Raynaud's Phenomenon
Arthritis Foundation
1330 W. Peachtree Street
Suite 100
Atlanta, GA 30309   404-872-7100
                                   800-283-7800
                             FAX: 404-872-0457
                                   arthritis.org

Daniel T. McGowan, Chair
Michael V. Ortman, Vice Chair
Ann M. Palmer, CEO/President
The Arthritis Foundation is the largest national nonprofit organization that supports the more than 100 types of arthritis and related conditions. Founded in 1948, with headquarters in Atlanta, the Arthritis Foundation has multiple service points located throughout the country.

8632 Reaching the Autistic Child: A Parent Training Program
Brookline Books
8 Trumbull Rd,
Northampton, MA 01060-4533   413-584-0184
                                   800-666-2665
                             FAX: 413-584-6184
                             brbooks@yahoo.com

Detailed case studies of social and behavioral change in autistic children and their families show parents how to implement the principles for improved socialization and behavior. *$15.95*
Softcover
ISBN 1-571290-56-7

8633 Respiratory Disorders Sourcebook
Omnigraphics
615 Griswold Street
Suite 520
Detroit, MI 48226

610-461-3548
800-234-1340
FAX: 800-875-1340
contact@omnigraphics.com
www.omnigraphics.com

Peter Ruffner, Co-Founder
Fred Ruffner, Co-Founder
Respiratory Disorders Sourcebook provides up-to-date information about infectious, inflammatory, occupational, and other types of respiratory disorders. Tips for managing chronic respiratory diseases and suggestions for ways to promote lung health are presented, and the book concludes with a glossary of related terms and a list of additional resources. *$84.00*
638 pages Hard cover
ISBN 0-780810-07-5

8634 SPINabilities: A Young Person's Guide to Spina Bifida
Spina Bifida Association of America
1600 Wilson Boulevard
Suite 800
Arlington, VA 22209

202-944-3285
800-621-3141
FAX: 202-944-3295
sbaa@sbaa.org
www.sbaa.org

Ana Ximenes, Chair
Sara Struwe, President & CEO
Mark Bohay, National Web Initiatives & Development Manager
A cool and practical book for young adults becoming independent. *$22.30*

8635 Seizures and Epilepsy in Childhood: A Guide
John Hopkins University Press
2715 N Charles St
Baltimore, MD 21218-4363

410-516-6900
800-548-1784
FAX: 410-516-6998
webmaster@jhupress.jhu.edu
www.press.jhu.edu

Kathleen Keane, Director
Eileen P G Vining MD, Co-Author
Diana J Pillas, Co-Author
The award-winning Seizures and Epilepsy in Childhood is the standard resource for parents in need of comprehensive medical information about their child with epilepsy. *$54.00*
432 pages 3rd Edition
ISBN 0-801870-51-4

8636 Sexuality and the Person with Spina Bifida
Spina Bifida Association of America
1600 Wilson Boulevard
Suite 800
Arlington, VA 22209

202-944-3285
800-621-3141
FAX: 202-944-3295
sbaa@sbaa.org
www.sbaa.org

Ana Ximenes, Chair
Sara Struwe, President & CEO
Mark Bohay, National Web Initiatives & Development Manager
Dr Sloan foucuses on sexual development, sexual activity and other important issues. *$11.00*

8637 Sinus Survival: A Self-help Guide
Penguin Group
375 Hudson St
New York, NY 10014-3658

212-366-2372
FAX: 212-366-2933
insidesales@penguingroup.com
us.penguingroup.com

Robert S Ivker, Author

Self-help manual for sufferers of bronchitis, sinusitis, allergies, and colds. *$15.95*
336 pages Paperback 2000
ISBN 1-101798-02-6

8638 Social Development and the Person with Spina Bifida
Spina Bifida Association of America
1600 Wilson Boulevard
Suite 800
Arlington, VA 22209

202-944-3285
800-621-3141
FAX: 202-944-3295
sbaa@sbaa.org
www.sbaa.org

Ana Ximenes, Chair
Sara Struwe, President & CEO
Mark Bohay, National Web Initiatives & Development Manager
Examines how spina bifida and hydrocephalus may influence development and learning social skills.

8639 Solving the Puzzle of Chronic Fatigue
Essential Science Publishing
1216 S 1580 W
Ste A
Orem, UT 84058-4906

801-224-6228
800-336-6308
FAX: 801-224-6229
info@essentialscience.net
www.essentialsciencepublishing.com

Michael Rosenbaum, Author
Murray Susser, Co-Author
Although primarily a book about CFS, this comprehensive study also provides a detailed overview of candidiasis, including its causes and best approaches for treatment. *$14.95*
190 pages
ISBN 0-943685-11-7

8640 Son Rise: The Miracle Continues
New World Library
14 Pamaron Way
Novato, CA 94949

415-884-2100
800-972-6657
FAX: 415-884-2199
ami@newworldlibrary.com
www.newworldlibrary.com

Barry Neil Kaufman, Author
Documents Raun Kaufman's astonishing development from a lifeless, autistic child into a highly verbal, lovable youngster with no traces of his former condition. Details Raun's extraordinary progress from the age of four into young adulthood, also shares moving accounts of five families that successfully used the Son-Rise Program to reach their own special children. *$14.96*
372 pages
ISBN 0-915811-53-7

8641 Steps to Independence: Teaching Everyday Skills to Children with Special Needs
Spina Bifida Association of America
1600 Wilson Boulevard
Suite 800
Arlington, VA 22209

202-944-3285
800-621-3141
FAX: 202-944-3295
sbaa@sbaa.org
www.sbaa.org

Ana Ximenes, Chair
Sara Struwe, President & CEO
Mark Bohay, National Web Initiatives & Development Manager
A guide to help parents teach life skills to their disabled child. *$34.25*

8642 Stroke Sourcebook
Omnigraphics
615 Griswold Street
Suite 520
Detroit, MI 48226
610-461-3548
800-234-1340
FAX: 800-875-1340
contact@omnigraphics.com
www.omnigraphics.com

Peter Ruffner, Co-Founder
Fred Ruffner, Co-Founder
Basic Consumer Health Information about Stroke, Including Ischemic, Hemorrhagic, and Mini Strokes, as Well as Risk Factors, Prevention Guidelines, Diagnostic Tests, Medications and Surgical Treatments, and Complications of Stroke.

8643 Stroke Sourcebook, 2nd Edition
Omnigraphics
615 Griswold Street
Suite 520
Detroit, MI 48226
610-461-3548
800-234-1340
FAX: 800-875-1340
contact@omnigraphics.com
www.omnigraphics.com

Peter Ruffner, Co-Founder
Fred Ruffner, Co-Founder
Stroke Sourcebook, Second Edition provides updated information about stroke, its causes, risk factors, diagnosis, acute and long-term treatment, and recent innovations in poststroke care. Information on rehabilitation therapies, prevention strategies, and tips on caring for a stroke survivor is also included, along with a glossary of related terms and a directory of organizations that offer additional information to stroke survivors and their families. *$84.00*
626 pages Hard cover
ISBN 0-780810-35-8

8644 Succeeding With Interventions For Asperger Syndrome Adolescents
Autsim Society of North Carolina Bookstore
505 Oberlin Road
Suite 230
Raleigh, NC 27605-1345
919-743-0204
800-442-2762
FAX: 919-743-0208
books@autismsociety-nc.org
www.autismbookstore.com

Tracey Sheriff, Chief Executive Officer
David Laxton, Director of Communications
Paul Wendler, Chief Financial Officer
This book includes a very useful outline of all the therapy sessions, which can be used as a template by a practitioner for creating their own interaction therapy intervention for adolescents.

8645 Symptomatic Chiari Malformation
Spina Bifida Association of America
1600 Wilson Boulevard
Suite 800
Arlington, VA 22209
202-944-3285
800-621-3141
FAX: 202-944-3295
sbaa@sbaa.org
www.sbaa.org

Ana Ximenes, Chair
Sara Struwe, President & CEO
Mark Bohay, National Web Initiatives & Development Manager
The Spina Bifida Association (SBA) serves adults and children who live with the challenges of Spina Bifida.

8646 Taking Charge
Spina Bifida Association of America
1600 Wilson Boulevard
Suite 800
Arlington, VA 22209
202-944-3285
800-621-3141
FAX: 202-944-3295
sbaa@sbaa.org

Ana Ximenes, Chair
Sara Struwe, President & CEO
Mark Bohay, National Web Initiatives & Development Manager
Teenagers talk about life and physical disabilities. *$7.95*

8647 Ten Things I Learned from Bill Porter
New World Library
14 Pamaron Way
Novato, CA 94949
415-884-2100
800-972-6657
FAX: 415-884-2199
ami@newworldlibrary.com
www.newworldlibrary.com

Shelly Ackerman, Author
Bill Porter worked for the Watkins Corp, selling household products door-to-door in one of Portland's worst neighborhoods. Afflicted with cerebral palsy and burdened with continual pain, Porter was determined not to live on government disability and went on to become Watkin's top-grossing salesman in Portland, the Northwest, and the US. This book was written by the woman who worked as Porter's typist and driver and later became his friend and cospeaker. *$20.00*
192 pages
ISBN 1-577312-03-1

8648 Thyroid Disorders Sourcebook
Omnigraphics
615 Griswold Street
Suite 520
Detroit, MI 48226
610-461-3548
800-234-1340
FAX: 800-875-1340
contact@omnigraphics.com
www.omnigraphics.com

Peter Ruffner, Co-Founder
Fred Ruffner, Co-Founder
Thyroid Disorders Sourcebook provides essential information about thyroid and parathyroid function, diseases, and treatments. Also presented are symptoms, risk factors, diagnosis, treatments, thyroid effects on the body, and the impact of environmental conditions on the thyroid. *$84.00*
573 pages Hard cover
ISBN 0-780807-45-7

8649 Tourette Syndrome: The Facts
Oxford University Press
198 Madison Avenue
New York, NY 10016
212-726-6000
800-445-9714
FAX: 919-677-1303
custserv.us@oup.com
www.oup.com

Mary Robertson, Co-Editor
Andrea Cavanna, Co-Editor
Johnathan Keats, Author
The causes of the syndrome, how it is diagnosed, and the ways in which it can be treated. *$35.00*
122 pages
ISBN 0-198523-98-X

8650 Tourette's Syndrome: Finding Answers and Getting Help
O'Reilly Media Inc
1005 Gravenstein Hwy N
Sebastopol, CA 95472-2811
707-827-7019
800-889-8969
FAX: 707-824-8268
order@oreilly.com
www.oreilly.com

Tourette's Syndrome is a neurological disorder usually diagnosed in childhood and characterized by tics, physical jerks, and involuntary vocalizations. Tourette's can be a devastating disability. The good news is that it's very treatable. Tourette's Syn-

drome helps you secure a diagnosis, understand medical interventions, get healthcare coverage, and manage Tourette's in family life, school, community, and workplace. *$24.95*
416 pages Paperback
ISBN 0-596500-07-6

8651 Tourette's Syndrome: Tics, Obsessions, Compulsions: Developmental Psychopathology
John Wiley & Sons
111 River Street
Hoboken, NJ 07030-5774 201-748-6000
FAX: 201-748-6088
www.wiley.com

Peter Booth Wiley, Chairman
Stephen M. Smith, President & CEO
John Kitzmacher, EVP, CFO
Contains 21 contributions compromising the work of researchers associated with the Yale Child Study Center, which has been at the forefront of research on Tourette's syndrome and associated disorders. *$85.00*
600 pages
ISBN 0-471113-75-1

8652 Treating Epilepsy Naturally: A Guide to Alternative and Adjunct Therapies
McGraw-Hill Company
P.O.Box 182605
Columbus, OH 43218 800-338-3987
FAX: 609-308-4480
customer.service@mheducation.com
www.mcgraw-hill.com

David Levin, President and CEO
Patrick Milano, Chief Administrative Officer & CFO
Stephen Laster, Chief Digital Officer
Offers alternative treatments to replace and to complement traditional therapies and sound advice to find the right health practitioner. *$15.95*
288 pages
ISBN 0-658013-79-3

8653 Understanding Asthma
National Jewish Health
1400 Jackson Street
Denver, CO 80206 303-270-2708
877-225-5654
FAX: 303-398-1125
allstetterw@njc.org
nationaljewish.org

Rich Schierburg, Chair
Robin Chotin, Vice Chair
Michael Salem, M.D., President and CEO
Offers a brief introduction to asthma and then goes into the physiology of asthma, the triggers of asthma, and diagnosis and monitoring of asthma.
27 pages

8654 Understanding Asthma: The Blueprint for Breathing
Allergy & Asthma Network Mothers of Asthmatics
8229 Boone Boulevard
Suite 260
Vienna, VA 22182 800-878-4403
FAX: 703-288-5271
www.aanma.org

Michael Amato, Chair
Tonya Winders, President & CEO
Brenda Silvia-Torma, Project Manager
A layman's guide to asthma facts based on a presentation from the first national asthma patient conference.

8655 Understanding Cystic Fibrosis
University Press of Mississippi
3825 Ridgewood Road
Jackson, MS 39211-6492 601-432-6205
800-737-7788
FAX: 601-432-6217
press@ihl.state.ms.us
www.upress.state.ms.us

Leila W. Salisbury, Director
Craig Gill, Assistant Director/Editor-in-Chief
Anne Stascavage, Managing Editor

A reference for CF patients and their families. *$14.00*
128 pages
ISBN 0-878059-67-9

8656 Understanding Multiple Sclerosis
University Press of Mississippi
3825 Ridgewood Road
Jackson, MS 39211-6492 601-432-6205
800-737-7788
FAX: 601-432-6217
press@ihl.state.ms.us
www.upress.state.ms.us

Melissa Stauffer, Author
Craig Gill, Assistant Director/Editor-in-Chief
Anne Stascavage, Managing Editor
Two psychologists discuss their roles with a member who has multiple sclerosis. Includes chapters on adolescents with multiple sclerosis, employment, and research. *$14.00*
136 pages
ISBN 1-578068-03-7

8657 Urologic Care of the Child with Spina Bifida
Spina Bifida Association of America
1600 Wilson Boulevard
Suite 800
Arlington, VA 22209 202-944-3285
800-621-3141
FAX: 202-944-3295
sbaa@sbaa.org

Ana Ximenes, Chair
Sara Struwe, President & CEO
Mark Bohay, National Web Initiatives & Development Manager
The Spina Bifida Association (SBA) serves adults and children who live with the challenges of Spina Bifida.

8658 Usher Syndrome
NI on Deafness & Other Communication Disorders
31 Center Dr.
MSC 2320
Bethesda, MD 20892-2320 301-827-8183
800-241-1044
TTY:800-241-1055
nidcdinfo@nidcd.nih.gov
www.nidcd.nih.gov

Debara L. Tucci, Director
Judith A. Cooper, Deputy Director
Timothy J. Wheeles, Executive Officer
Explains what is Usher Syndrome, who is affected by Usher syndrome, what causes Usher syndrome, how is Usher syndrome treated, and what research is being conducted on Usher syndrome.

8659 What Everyone Needs to Know About Asthma
Allergy & Asthma Network Mothers of Asthmatics
8229 Boone Boulevard
Suite 260
Vienna, VA 22182 800-878-4403
FAX: 703-288-5271
www.aanma.org

Michael Amato, Chair
Tonya Winders, President & CEO
Brenda Silvia-Torma, Project Manager
Offers information and facts on gaining control of asthma, asthma triggers and monitoring asthma disorders.

8660 When the Road Turns: Inspirational Stories About People with MS
Health Communications
3201 SouthWest 15th Street
Deerfield Beach, FL 33442 954-360-0909
800-441-5569
FAX: 954-360-0034
An inspiring collection of stories written by people living with multiple sclerosis. *$10.36*
300 pages
ISBN 1-558749-07-1

8661 Young Person's Guide to Spina Bifida
Spina Bifida Association of America
1600 Wilson Boulevard
Suite 800
Arlington, VA 22209

202-944-3285
800-621-3141
FAX: 202-944-3295
sbaa@sbaa.org

Ana Ximenes, Chair
Sara Struwe, President & CEO
Mark Bohay, National Web Initiatives & Development Manager
Gives practical tips and suggestions for becoming independent
and managing your health. *$19.00*

8662 Your Child and Asthma
National Jewish Health
1400 Jackson Street
Denver, CO 80206

303-270-2708
877-225-5654
FAX: 303-398-1125
allstetterw@njc.org
nationaljewish.org

Rich Schierburg, Chair
Robin Chotin, Vice Chair
Michael Salem, M.D., President and CEO
A booklet offering information to parents and family about their
child with asthma. Offers information on diagnosis, treatments,
triggers and family concerns.

8663 Your Cleft Affected Child
Hunter House Inc. Publisher
PO Box 2914
Alameda, CA 94501-914

510-865-5282
800-266-5592
FAX: 510-865-4295
www.hunterhouse.com

Carrie T Gruman Trinker, Author
The book also provides in-depth information, guidance, and support on a wide variety of relevant topics, from feeding to surgery
to helping a child cope until his/her cleft has been fully corrected.
$16.95
288 pages Paperback
ISBN 0-897931-85-4

8664 Your Guide to Bowel Cancer
Oxford University Press
2001 Evans Road
Cary, NC 27513

919-677-0977
800-445-9714
FAX: 919-677-1303
www.us.oup.com

Offers information and public awareness on the disease of bowel
cancer. *$18.95*
ISBN 0-340927-46-1

Journals

**8665 AIDS: The Official Journal of the International AIDS
Society**
Lippincott Williams & Wilkins
2 Commerce Square
2001 Market St.
Philadelphia, PA 19103

215-521-8300
FAX: 215-521-8902
customerservice@lww.com
lww.com

JA Levy, Co Editor
B. Autran, Co Editor
R. A Coutinho, Co Editor
The latest groundbreaking research on HIV and AIDS. *$433.00*
18 per year

8666 American Journal of Orthopsychiatry
American Psychological Association
750 1st Street NorthEast
Washington, DC 20002-4242

202-336-5500
800-374-2721
FAX: 202-336-5502
TTY: 202-336-6123
www.apa.org

Nadine J. Kaslow, President
Norman B. Anderson, PhD, CEO & EVP
Bonnie Markham, Treasurer
Mental health issues from multidisciplinary and
interprofessionals perspectives: clinical, research and expository
approaches. *$45.00*
160 pages Quarterly

8667 Annals of Otology, Rhinology and Laryngology
Annals Publishing Company
4507 Laclede Ave
Saint Louis, MO 63108-2103

314-367-4987
FAX: 314-367-4988
www.annals.com

Ken Cooper, President
Richard J. Smith, Editor
Monica L. Bergers, Editor's Assistant
Original, peer-reviewed articles in the fields of otolaryngology -
head and neck medicine and surgery, broncho-esophagology, audiology, speech, pathology, allery, and maxillofacial surgery. Official journal of the American Laryngological
Association/American Broncho-Esophagological Association.
$170.00
112 pages Monthly

8668 Archives of Neurology
American Medical Association
P.O.Box 10946
Chicago, IL 60654

312-670-7827
800-262-2350
FAX: 312-464-4184
subscriptions@jamanetwork.com
jamanetwork.com

Margaret Vanner, Manager
Mission is to publish scientific information primarily important
to those physicians caring for people with neurologic disorders,
but also for those interested in the structure and function of the
normal and diseased nervous system. *$235.00*
198 pages Monthly

8669 Cleft Palate-Craniofacial Journal
American Cleft Palate-Craniofacial Association
2455 Teller Rd.
Thousand Oaks, CA 91320

800-818-7243
FAX: 800-583-2665
journal@acpa-cpf.org
www.cpcjournal.org

Jack C. Yu, Editor
A peer-reviewed, interdisciplinary, international journal dedicated to current research on etiology, prevention, diagnosis, and
treatment in all areas pertaining to craniofacial anomalies. Publishes 10 issues a year.

8670 Developmental Medicine & Childhood Neurology
American Academy for Cerebral Palsy/Dev. Medicine
555 East Wells
Suite 1100
Milwaukee, WI 53202

414-918-3014
FAX: 414-276-2146
info@aacpdm.org
www.aacpdm.org

Tamara Wagester, Executive Director
Clinical research into the wide range of neurological conditions
and disabilities that affect children.

8671 Journal of Head Trauma Rehabilitation
Lippincott, Williams & Wilkins
P.O.Box 1620
Hagerstown, MD 21740
301-223-2300
800-638-3030
FAX: 301-223-2400
orders@lww.com
www.lww.com

John D Corrigan PhD, ABPP, Editor
Scholarly journal designed to provide information on clinical management and rehabilitation of the head-injured for the practicing professional. Published bimonthly. *$113.96*

Magazines

8672 Coping with Cancer Magazine
Media America
P.O.Box 682268
Franklin, TN 37068-2268
615-790-2400
FAX: 615-794-0179
copingmag.com
Provides knowledge, hope and inspiration, its readers include cancer patients (survivors) and their families, caregivers, healthcare teams and support group leaders. *$19.95*
53 pages 6 x year

8673 CurePSP Magazine
Society for Progressive Supranuclear Palsy
Suite 201
30 E. Padonia Road
Timonium, MD 21093
410-785-7004
800-457-4777
FAX: 410-785-7009
info@curepsp.org
www.psp.org

John T. Burhoe, Chair
Everett R. Cook, Vice Chair
Richard Gordon Zyne, President-CEO
Quarterly newsletter. The society's mission is to promote and fund research into finding the cause and cure for progressive supranuclear palsy (PSP). Provides information, support and advocacy to persons diagnosed with PSP, their families and caregivers. Educates physicians and allied health professionals on PSP and how to improve patient care.

8674 EpilepsyUSA
Epilepsy Foundation
8301 Professional Place
Landover, MD 20785-2353
301-459-3700
800-332-1000
FAX: 301-459-1569
ContactUs@efa.org
epilepsyfoundation.org

Warren Lammert, Chair
Phil Gattone, President and CEO
May J. Liang, Secretary
Magazine reporting on issues of interest to people with epilepsy and their families. *$15.00*
22 pages Bi-Monthly

8675 MSFOCUS Magazine
Multiple Sclerosis Foundation
6520 North Andrews Avenue
Fort Lauderdale, FL 33309-2130
954-776-6805
888-673-6287
FAX: 954-351-0630
support@msfocus.org
www.msfocus.org

Jules Kuperberg, Executive Director
Alan Segaloff, Executive Director
Natalie Blake, Program Services Director
Contemporary national, nonprofit organization that provides free support services and public education for persons with Multiple Sclerosis, newsletters, toll-free phone support, information, referrals, home care, assistive technology and support groups.
48 pages Quarterly

8676 Orthotics and Prosthetics Almanac
American Orthotic & Prosthetics Association
330 John Carlyle Street
Suite 200
Alexandria, VA 22314
571-431-0876
FAX: 571-431-0899
info@aopanet.org
www.aopanet.org

Anita L. Lampear, President
Charles H. Dankmeyer, Vice President
Thomas F. Fise, JD, Executive Director
Features articles covering current professional, patient care, government, business and National Office activities affecting the orthotics and prosthetics profession and industry. *$40.00*
80 pages Monthly
ISSN 1061-46 1

8677 PDF News
Parkinson's Disease Foundation
1359 Broadway
Suite 1509
New York, NY 10018
212-923-4700
800-457-6676
FAX: 212-923-4778
info@pdf.org
www.pdf.org

Howard D. Morgan, Chair
Woodruff Atwell, Ph.D., Vice Chair
Stephen Ackerman, Treasurer
8-12 pages Quarterly

8678 POZ Magazine
212 W 35th St
New York, NY 10001
212-242-2163
800-973-2376
FAX: 212-675-8505
website@poz.com
poz.com
A health magazine written for individuals who are HIV+, their friends and families. POZ provides the latest treatment information, investigative journalism and survivor profiles.

8679 SCI Life
National Spinal Cord Injury Association
11300 Rockville Pike
Suite 803
Rockville, MD 20852
301-468-3902
FAX: 301-468-3904
info@ilcreations.com
ilcreations.com
SCI/LIFE is dedicated to the presentation of news concerning people with spinal cord injuries caused by trauma or disease.
Quarterly/Free

8680 Spine
Lippincott, Williams & Wilkins
530 Walnut St
Philadelphia, PA 19106-3603
215-521-8300
FAX: 215-521-8411
customerservice@lww.com

James N Weinstein DO MSc, Editor
Publishes original papers on theoretical issues and research concerning the spine and spinal cord injuries. *$9.00*
26 Issues Year

Newsletters

8681 ACPOC News
Assoc of Children's Prosthetic-Orthotic Clinics
6300 N River Rd
Suite 727
Rosemont, IL 60018-4226
847-698-1637
FAX: 847-823-0536
acpoc@aaos.org
www.acpoc.org

David B. Rotter, CPO, President
Jorge A. Fabregas, Vice President
Hank White, PT, PhD, Secretary-Treasurer

Quarterly publication from the Association of Children's Prosthetic/Orthotic Clinics. Included with membership.
40 pages Quarterly

8682   AID Bulletin
Project AID Resource Center
P.O. Box 5190
Kent, OH 44242-0001

330-672-3000
FAX: 330-672-4724
info@kent.edu
www.kent.edu/

Beverly Warren, President
Todd A. Diacon, Provost & SVP
Gregg S. Floyd, Sr. Vice President
Has the latest news on upcoming conferences, literature, developments in programs and/or services for disabled persons who are substance abusers. Offers articles on their experiences, ideas and questions of others in this field which includes providers and consumers. *$7.50*

8683   AIDS Alert
AHC Media LLC
PO Box 550669
Atlanta, GA 30355

404-262-5436
800-688-2421
FAX: 404-262-5560
www.ahcpub.com/

Joy Daughtery Dickinson, Senior Managing Editor
Source of AIDS news and advice for health care professionals. Covers up-to-the-minute developments and guidance on the entire spectrum of AIDS challenges, including treatment, education, precautions, screening, diagnosis and policy. *$499.00*
Monthly

8684   Adaptive Tracks
Adaptive Sports Center
P.O.Box 1639
Crested Butte, CO 81224

970-349-2296
866-349-2296
FAX: 970-349-2077
info@adaptivesports.org
www.adaptivesports.org

Christopher Hensley, Executive Director
Chris Read, CTRS, Program Director
Ella Fahrlander, Development Director
The Adaptive Sports Center (ASC) of Crested Butte, Colorado is a non-profit organization that provides year-round recreation activities for people with disabilities and their families. The ASC provides adaptive snowboarding downhill skiing, cross country skiing as well as backcountry trips. Summer activities include a variety of wilderness-based programs, multi-day trips into the back country, extensive cycling programs, canoeing, and white water rafting.
6 pages Quarterly

8685   Arthritis Self-Management
Rapaport Publishing, Inc.
150 W 22nd St
Ste 800
New York, NY 10011-2421

212-989-0200
FAX: 212-989-4786
ASMcustserv@cdsfulfillment.com
www.arthritisselfmanagement.com

Richard A Rapaport, President
Maryanne Schott Turner, Director of Manufacturing
Richard Boland, Art Director
Arthritis Self-Management publishes practical 'how-to' information for the growing number of people with arthritis who want to know more about managing their condition. We focus on the day-to-day and long-term aspects of arthritis in a positive and upbeat style, giving our subscribers up-to-date news, facts, and advice to help them make informed decisions about their health.
$9.97
BiMonthly

8686   Breaking Ground
Tennessee Council on Developmental Disabilities
404 James Robertson Pkwy
Suite 130
Nashville, TN 37243- 0228

615-532-6615
FAX: 615-532-6964
TTY:615-741-4562
tnddc@tn.gov
www.tn.gov/cdd

Stephanie Brewer Cook, Chair
Roger D. Gibbens, Vice Chair
Wanda Willis, Executive Director
Newsletter
20 pages 6 x Year

8687   Breaking New Ground News Note
Purdue University
225 West University Street
West Lafayette, IN 47907

765-494-4600
800-825-4264
FAX: 765-496-1356
engineering.purdue.edu/

Paul Jones, Project Manager
Bill Field, Project Director
Denise Heath, Project Asst.
News, practical ideas and success stories of and for farmers and other agricultural workers with physical disabilities.
2 pages Quarterly

8688   Diabetes Self-Management
Rapaport Publishing, Inc.
150 W 22nd St
Ste 800
New York, NY 10011-2421

212-989-0200
FAX: 212-989-4786
www.diabetesselfmanagement.com

Richard A Rapaport, President
Maryanne Schott Turner, Director of Manufacturing
Richard Boland, Art Director
Publishes practical how-to information, focusing on the day-to-day and long-term aspects of diabetes in a positive and upbeat style. Gives subscribers up-to-date news, facts and advice to help them maintain their wellness and make informed decisions regarding their health. *$9.97*
BiMonthly

8689   Directions
Families of Spinal Muscular Dystrophy
925 Busse Road
Elk Grove Village, IL 60007

847-367-7620
800-886-1762
FAX: 847-367-7623
info@fsma.org
www.fsma.org

Richard Rubenstein, Chair
Kenneth Hobby, President
Sue Kovach, Director of Finance
$35.00
60-70 pages Quarterly

8690   IAL News
International Association of Laryngectomees
925B Peachtree Street NE
Suite 316
Atlanta, GA 30309

866-425-3678
www.larynxlink.com

Wade Hampton, President
Susan Reeves, Administrative Manager
Jodi Knott, Director, Voice Institute
Focuses on rehabilitation and well-being of persons who have had laryngectomy surgery.

8691 Informer
Simon Foundation
P.O.Box 815
Wilmette, IL 60091

847-864-3913
800-237-4666
FAX: 847-864-9758
info@simonfoundation.org
simonfoundation.org

Cheryle Gartley, President and Founder
Elizabeth T. LaGro, VP, Communications & Education
Twila Yednock, Director of Special Events
Publishes items of interest to people with bladder or bowel incontinence, including medical articles, helpful devices, publications and a pen pal list. Quarterly newsletter.
Quarterly

8692 Moisture Seekers
Sjogren's Syndrome Foundation
6707 Democracy Boulevard
Suite 325
Bethesda, MD 20817

301-530-4420
800-475-6473
FAX: 301-530-4415
tms@sjogrens.org
www.sjogrens.org

Kenneth Economou, Chair
Steven Taylor, CEO
Sheriese DeFruscio, VP of Development
Newsletter of the organization for lay people and professionals interested in Sjogren's Syndrome. Contains medical news, current research, and essential tips for daily living. *$25.00*
15-16 pages Monthly

8693 Momentum
National Multiple Sclerosis Society
Ste 6
421 New Karner Rd
Albany, NY 12205-3838

518-464-0850
800-344-4867
FAX: 518-464-1232
nyr@nmss.org
www.nationalmssociety.org

Eli Rubenstein, Chair
Cynthia Zagieboylo, President & CEO
Sherri Giger, EVP, Marketing
News and information on research progress, medical treatments, patient services, therapeutic claims and activities.

8694 Options
People Against Cancer
P.O.Box 10
604 East Street
Otho, IA 50569

515-972-4444
800-662-2623
FAX: 515-972-4415
info@PeopleAgainstCancer.org
www.peopleagainstcancer.com

Frank D. Wiewel, Executive Director/Founder
Publication of People Against Cancer, a nonprofit, grassroots public benefit organization dedicated to 'New Directions in the War on Cancer.' We help people to find the best cancer treatment. We are a democratic organization of people with cancer, their loved ones and citizens working together to protect and enhance medical freedom of choice.
8 pages Quarterly

8695 PDF Newsletter
Parkinson's Disease Foundation
1359 Broadway
Suite 1509
New York, NY 10018

212-923-4700
800-457-6676
FAX: 212-923-4778
info@pdf.org
www.pdf.org

Howard D. Morgan, Chair
Woodruff Atwell, Ph.D., Vice Chair
Stephen Ackerman, Treasurer

The Parkinson's Disease Foundation (PDF) is a leading national presence in Parkinson's disease research, education and public advocacy.
12-16 pages Quarterly

8696 Parkinson Report
National Parkinson Foundation
200 SE 1st Street
Suite 800
Miami, FL 33131

800-473-4636
www.parkinson.org

John L. Lehr, President & CEO
Leilani Pearl, SVP & Chief Communications Officer
Articles, reports and news on Parkinson's disease and the activities of the National Parkinson Foundation.
32 pages Quarterly

8697 Post-Polio Health
Post-Polio Health International
50 Crestwood Executive Ctr.
Suite 440
St. Louis, MO 63126

314-534-0475
FAX: 314-534-5070
editor@post-polio.org
www.post-polio.org

Brian M. Tiburzi, Editor
Post-Polio Health supports Post-Polio Health International's educational, research, and advocacy efforts. Offers information about relevant events. Published in February, May, August and November.
12 pages Quarterly

8698 Prader-Willi Alliance of New York Newsletter
244 5th Avenue
Suite D-110
New York, NY 10001

800-442-1655
alliance@prader-willi.org
www.prader-willi.org

Rachel Johnson, Executive Director
The Prader-Willi Foundation is a national, nonprofit public charity that works for the benefit of individuals with Prader-Willi syndrome and their families. *$20.00*
Quarterly

8699 Quality Care Newsletter
National Association for Continence
P.O.Box 1019
Charleston, SC 29402-1019

843-352-2559
800-BLA-DER
FAX: 843-352-2563
memberservices@nafc.org
www.nafc.org

Donna Deng, Chairman
Nancy Hicks, Vice Chaiperson
Steven Gregg, Executive Director
Newsletter from NAFC. By donating $25 and becomming a Quality Care donor, you may receive our quarterly newsletter. *$25.00*
14-16 pages Quarterly

8700 Rasmussen's Syndrome and Hemispherectomy Support Network Newsletter
55 Kenosia Avenue
Danbury, CT 06810

203-744-0100
FAX: 203-798-2291
www.rarediseases.org/rare-disease-info

Ronald J. Bartek, Chair
Sheldon M. Schuster, Vice Chair
Peter L. Saltonstall, President & CEO
National, not-for-profit organization dedicated to providing information and support to individuals affected by Rasmussen's Syndrome and hemispherectomy. Publishes a periodic newsletter and disseminates reprints of medical journal articles concerning Rasmussen's Syndrome and its treatments. Maintains a support network that provides encouragement and information to individuals affected by Rasmussen's Syndrome and their families.

8701 **SCI Psychosocial Process**
Amer Assn of Spinal Cord Injury Psych & Soc Wks
75-20 Astoria Blvd
East Elmhurst, NY 11370   718-803-3782
                                       800-404-2898
                                  FAX: 718-803-0414
                                  info@unitedspinal.org
                                  www.unitedspinal.org/

David C. Cooper, Chairman
Patrick W. Maher, Vice Chairman
Joseph Gaskins, President and CEO
Quarterly newsletter.

8702 **Special Care in Dentistry**
Blackwell Publishing
350 Main St
Malden, MA 02148   781-388-0200
                                  FAX: 781-388-8210
                            www.blackwellpublishing.com

Peter Booth Wiley, Chairman
Stephen M. Smith, President & CEO
John Kitzmacher, EVP, CFO
$125.00
48 pages BiMonthly

8703 **TSA Newsletter**
Tourette Syndrome Association
42-40 Bell Boulevard
Bayside, NY 11361   718-224-2999
                                       800-237-0717
                                  FAX: 718-279-9596
                                  ts@tsa-usa.org
                                  www.tsa-usa.org

Stephen M. McCall, President
National non-profit membership organization whose mission is
to identify the cause of, find the cure for, and control the effects of
this disorder. A growing number of local chapters nationwide
provide educational materials, seminars, conferences and support groups for over 35,000 members.
Quarterly

8704 **Teens & Asthma**
American Lung Association
530 7th St SE
Washington, DC 20003   202-546-5864
                                  FAX: 202-546-5607
                                  www.epa.gov/

Rolando E Bates Jr, CEO
Tips from other teens with asthma to help those having it get on
with the serious business of having fun with the rest of their lives.
Online/Free

8705 **Tethering Cord**
Spina Bifida Association of America
PO Box 5801
Bethesda, MD 20824   800-352-9424
                                  www.ninds.nih.gov

Nina Schor, Deputy Director
Tethered spinal cord syndrome is a neurological disorder caused
by tissue attachments that limit the movement of the spinal cord
within the spinal column. Attachments may occur congenitally at
the base of the spinal cord (conus medullaris) or they may develop near the site of an injury to the spinal cord.

8706 **Tourette Syndrome Association Children's Newsletter**
42-40 Bell Boulevard
Bayside, NY 11361   718-224-2999
                                       800-237-0717
                                  FAX: 718-279-9596
                                  ts@tsa-usa.org
                                  tsa-usa.org

Stephen M. McCall, President
National, nonprofit membership organization. Mission is to identify the cause of, find the cure for, and control the effects of this
disorder. A growing number of local chapters nationwide provide
educational materials, seminars, conferences and support groups
for over 35,000 members.

8707 **Ventilator-Assisted Living**
International Ventilator Users Network
50 Crestwood Executive Ctr.
Suite 440
St. Louis, MO 63126-1916   314-534-0475
                                  FAX: 314-534-5070
                                  info@ventusers.org
                                  www.ventnews.org

Brian M. Tiburzi, Editor
Articles for home mechanical ventilator users, health profession-
als and industry professionals.
Bi-monthly

8708 **Voice of the Diabetic**
NFB Diabetes Action Network
200 E. Wells St.
at Jernigan Place
Baltimore, MD 21230   410-659-9314
                                  FAX: 410-685-5653
                                  nfb@nfb.org
                                  www.nfb.org

Newsletter containing personal stories and practical guidelines
by blind diabetics and medical professionals, medical news, resource column and a recipe corner.

Sports

8709 **National Sports Center for the Disabled**
33 Parsenn Rd
PO Box 1290
Winter Park, CO 80482   970-726-1518
                                  FAX: 970-726-4112
                                  volunteer@nscd.org
                                  nscd.org

Kim Easton, President & CEO
Diane Eustace, Marketing Director
Beth Fox, Outreach & Education Director
Organization providing year-round recreation for children and
adults with disabilities. Winter programming includes alpine skiing, snowboarding, ski racing, show shoeing, and cross-country
skiing. Summer sports include rafting, sailing, kayaking, camping, hiking, horseback riding, fishing, and rock climbing.

8710 **Rehabilitation Institute of Chicago's Virginia
Wadsworth Sports Program**
345 East Suuperior St.
Chicago, IL 60611   312-238-1000
                                       800-354-7342
                                       800-354-REHA
                                  FAX: 312-238-5017
                                  sports@ric.org
                                  www.ric.org

Jude Reyes, Chair
mike P. Kransy, Vice Chair
Thomas Reynolds III, Vice Chair
RIC's Center for Health and Fitness is a full service fitness center
for individuals with disabilities and the administrative offices for
RIC's Wirtz Sports Program. Eighteen different sport and recreation programs are offered free of charge. The facility is adjacent
to RIC's main building and also is the location of a branch of The
National Center for Physical Activity and Disability (NCPAD), a
joint project operated by the University of Illinois-Chigcago.

8711 **Special Hockey International (SHI)**
93 Bell Farm Rd.
Suite 120B
Barrie, ON, Canada L4M-5G1   specialhockeyinternational.org
Mike Dwyer, President
Bill Weishuhn, Treasurer
The organization has teams throughout North America and Eu-
rope, attracting over 70 teams to its annual tournament.

Support Groups

8712 AAN's Toll-Free Hotline
Allergy and Asthma Network Mothers of Asthmatics
8229 Boone Boulevard
Suite 260
Vienna, VA 22182   800-878-4403
                                                  FAX: 703-288-5271
                                                  www.aanma.org

Michael Amato, Chair
Tonya Winders, President & CEO
Brenda Silvia-Torma, Project Manager
Offers answers to questions regarding allergies and asthma, provides referrals and support to assist the patient and his or her family.

8713 Breaking New Ground Resource Center
Purdue University
225 S University St
West Lafayette, IN 47907   765-494-5088
                                                    800-825-4264
                                                  FAX: 765-496-1356
                                                  bng@ecn.purdue.edu
                                                  engineering.purdue.edu/

Bill Field, Project Director
Paul Jones, Project Manager
Steve Swain, Rural Rehab Specialist
A resource center devoted to helping farmers and ranchers with physical disabilities. Resource materials and a free newsletter are available to anyone.

8714 Clearinghouse on Disability Information: Office Special Education & Rehabilitative Service
U S Department of Education
400 Maryland Ave SW
Washington, DC 20202-1   202-245-7549
                                                    800-872-5327
                                                  FAX: 202-245-7614
                                                  www.ed.gov

Arne Duncan, Secretary Of Education
Tony Miller, Deputy Secretary
Martha Kanter, Under Secretary
Provides information to people with disabilities or anyone requesting information, by doing research and providing documents in response to inquiries. The information provided includes areas of federal funding for disability-related programs. Information provided may be useful to disabled individuals and their families, schools and universities, teacher's and/or school administrators, and organizations who have persons with disabilities as clients.

8715 Compassionate Friends, The
P.O.Box 3696
Oak Brook, IL 60522   630-990-0010
                                                    877-969-0010
                                                  FAX: 630-990-0246
                                        nationaloffice@compassionatefriends.org
                                                  compassionatefriends.org

Patrick O'Donnell, President
Georgia Cockerham, Vice President
Lisa Corrao, COO
Peer support for bereaved parents, grandparents and siblings, offering over 600 chapters in the United States. The organization also offers a quarterly magazine, We Need Not Walk Alone, and TCF resources of brochures, DVDs, and memorial wristbands for the bereaved parent, grandparent and sibling.

8716 Cornerstone Services
777 Joyce Rd.
Joliet, IL 60436   815-741-7600
                                                    877-444-0304
                                                  FAX: 815-723-1177
                                                  cornerstoneservices.org

Ben Stortz, President & Chief Executive Officer
Kim Hudgens, Vice President & Chief Operating Officer
Ken Mihelich, Vice President & Chief Financial Officer
Cornerstone Services provides progressive, comprehensive services for people with disabilities, promoting choice, dignity and the opportunity to live and work in the community. Established in 1969, the agency provides developmental, vocational, residential and behavior health services.
1969

8717 Disability Network
Ste 54
3600 S Dort Hwy
Flint, MI 48507   810-742-1800
                                                  FAX: 810-742-2400
                                                  TTY:810-742-7647
                                                  tdn@disnetwork.org
                                                  www.disnetwork.org

Bruce Chargo, Chairman
Diane Brown, Treasurer/ Vice Chairman
Mike Zelley, President & CEO
The Disability Network's mission is to realize consumer empowerment, self determination, full inclusion and participation of all people in the communities through independent living philosophy and the unequivocal implementation of the Americans with Disabilities Act

8718 Disability and Health: National Center for Birth Defects and Developmental Disabilities
Centers for Disease Control and Prevention
1600 Clifton Road
Atlanta, GA 30333   404-498-3012
                                                    800-232-4636
                                                    800-CDC-INFO
                                                  FAX: 404-498-3060
                                                  cdcinfo@cdc.gov
                                                  www.cdc.gov/ncbddd/dh

Dr. Tom Frieden, Director
Sherri A. Berger, COO
Carmen Villar, Chief of Staff
Located within the new CDC, National Center for Birth Defects and Developmental Disabilities, the Disability and Health section, operates a ralatively small program that primarily supports: data collection on the prevalence of people with disabilities & their health status and risk factors for poor health and well-being; research on measures of disability, functioning and health; health promotion intervention studies; and dissemination of health information.

8719 Easterseals
141 W Jackson Blvd.
Suite 1400A
Chicago, IL 60604   312-726-6200
                                                    800-221-6827
                                                  FAX: 312-726-1494
                                                  info@easterseals.com
                                                  www.easterseals.com

Catherine Georges, Chair
Nicole Cooper, First Vice Chair
Joan Rockey, Treasurer
Easterseals provides services, education, outreach and advocacy for people with disabilities, veterans, senior citizens and their families. Programs include early intervention, workforce development, adult day care, adult services, mental health services, and more.

8720 Epilepsy Foundation
8301 Professional Place E
Suite 200
Landover, MD 20785- 2353   800-332-1000
                                                  FAX: 301-459-1569
                                                  ContactUs@efa.org
                                                  www.epilepsy.com

Robert W Smith, Chair
Philip M Gattone, M.Ed, President & CEO
M. Vaneeda Bennett, Chief Development Officer
Offers information, referrals and support groups for those diagnosed with epilepsy.

8721 Family Support Project for the Developmentally Disabled
3424 Kossuth Ave
Bronx, NY 10467-2410   718-519-5000
                                                  FAX: 718-519-4902
                                        www.nyc.gov/html/hhc/ncbh/home.html

William Walsh, Vice President
Sheldon McLeod, COO

8722   Head Injury Hotline
Brain Injury Resource Center
P.O.Box 84151
Seattle, WA 98124-5451

206-621-8558
FAX: 206-329-0912
brain@headinjury.com
www.headinjury.com

Hugh R. MacMahon, Neurology
Constance Miller, Founder
Paul M. Kuroiwa, Performance management consultant
Disseminates head injury information and provides referrals to facilitate adjustment to life following head injury. Organizes seminars for professionals, head injury survivors, and their families.

8723   International Braille and Technology Center for the Blind
National Federation of the Blind
200 E. Wells St.
at Jernigan Place
Baltimore, MD 21230

410-659-9314
FAX: 410-685-5653
nfb@nfb.org
nfb.org/programs-services

John Berggren, Executive Director, Operations
World's largest and most complete evaluation and demonstration center of all assistive technology used by the blind from around the world. Includes all braille, synthetic speech, print-to-speech scanning, internet and portable devices and programs. Available for tours by appointment to blind persons, employers, technology manufacturers, teachers, parents and those working in the assistive technology field.

8724   Lung Line Information Service
National Jewish Health
1400 Jackson Street
Denver, CO 80206

877-225-5654
877-225-5654
FAX: 303-398-1125
allstetterw@njc.org
nationaljewish.org

Rich Schierburg, Chair
Robin Chotin, Vice Chair
Michael Salem, M.D., President & CEO
A free information service answering questions, sending literature and giving advice to patients with immunologic or respiratory illnesses. The Line is an educational service and not a substitute for medical care. Diagnosis or suggested treatment will not be provided for a caller's specific condition.

8725   NCI's Contact Center
National Cancer Institute
9609 Medical Center Dr.
Rockville, MD 20850

800-422-6237
TTY:800-332-8615
nciinfo@nih.gov
www.cancer.gov

Norman E. Sharpless, Director
Douglas R. Lowy, Principal Deputy Director
James Doroshow, Deputy Director, Clinical & Translational Research
The NCI Contact Center provides accurate, up-to-date information on cancer to patients and their families, health professionals and the general public. The Contact Center can provide specific information in understandable language about particular types of cancer, as well as information on second opinions and the availability of clinical trials.

8726   National AIDS Hotline
Centers for Disease Control and Prevention
1600 Clifton Road
Atlanta, GA 30333

404-639-3311
800-232-4636
800-CDC-INFO
FAX: 404-498-3060
www.cdc.gov

Dr. Tom Frieden, Director
Sherri A. Berger, COO
Carmen Villar, Chief of Staff

Offers free confidential information and publications on HIV infection and AIDS.

8727   PPAL Support Groups
Parent Professional Advocacy League
77 Rumford Ave.
Waltham, MA 02453

866-815-8122
FAX: 617-542-7832
info@ppal.net
www.ppal.net

Pam Sager, Executive Director
Meri Viano, Associate Director
Candice Gabrey, Program Manager, Juvenile Justice
The Parent Professional Advocacy League (PPAL) provides family support services and support groups for parents and families of children with emotional, behavioral, and mental health needs.

8728   PXE International
Ste 404
4301 Connecticut Ave NW
Washington, DC 20008- 2369

202-362-9599
FAX: 202-966-8553
info@pxe.org
www.pxe.org

Patrick F. Terry, President
Sharon Terry, CEO
Terry M. Dermaid, Executive Director
Provides support for individuals and families affected by psukdoxanthoma elasticum (PXE), and resources for healthcare professionals. PXE causes select elastic tissue to mineralize, and effects the skin, eyes, cardiovascular, and GI systems.

8729   Parent Assistance Network
Good Samaritan Hospital
10 E. 31st Street
Kearney, NE 68847

308-865-7100
800-235-9905
FAX: 308-865-2924
sheilameyer@catholichealth.net

Randy DeFreece, President
Kent Barney, Chairman
Mary Henning, Vice Chairman
Provides information and emotional support to all parents and especially to parents of children with disabilities in the central Nebraska area. Ongoing activities include parent support group meetings, parent-to-parent networking and referrals and Respite Care provider trainings.

8730   Post-Polio Support Group
Adventist Hinsdale Hospital
120 N Oak St
Hinsdale, IL 60521-3829

630-856-9000
FAX: 630-856-6000
www.keepingyouwell.com

David Crane, President
Information and support for polio patients and their families; meets the fourth Wednesday of each month.

8731   Prevent Child Abuse America
288 South Wabash Avenue
10th floor
Chicago, IL 60604

312-663-3520
800-244-5373
800-CHI-DREN
FAX: 312-939-8962
mailbox@preventchildabuse.org
preventchildabuse.org

Fred M. Riley, Chair
David Rudd, Vice Chair
James Hmurovich, President & CEO
Through public education, community partnerships and support services, PCAMW helps everyone play a role in prevention. We share information on prevention stategies and effective parenting at community forums and events and advocate for polices and services that keep children safe. We operate PhoneFriend, a telephone support line for children at home without adult supervision and conduct personal safety workshops in schools, camps and libraries.

8732   Son-Rise Program
2080 S Undermountain Rd.
Sheffield, MA 01257-9643   413-229-2100
                                            877-766-7473
                                       FAX: 413-229-8931
                             www.autismtreatmentcenter.org

Barry Neil Kaufman, Founder & CEO
Clyde Haberman, Senior Teacher & Director of Development
Blair Borgeson, Developmental Therapist

The center's Son-Rise Program teaches a comprehensive system
of treatment and education designed to help families and caregivers enable their children to dramatically improve in all areas of
learning.

8733   Special Children
1306 Wabash Ave
Belleville, IL 62220-3370   618-234-6876
                                       FAX: 618-234-6150
                                        specialchildren.net

Kathleen Cullen, Administrator

A nonprofit agency serving children with developmental disabilities ages birth to 6 years

8734   Support Works
1607 Dilworth Rd W
Charlotte, NC 28203-5213   704-331-9500
                                        www.supportworks.org

Joel Fisher, Manager

SupportWorks helps people find and form support groups. An 8
page publication Power Tools, clearly walks new group leaders
through steps of putting together a healthy self-help group.
SupportWorks also has a telephone conference program which allows people with similar diseases or other nonprofit issues to
meet by phone conference for free or at very low cost.

8735   Toll-Free Information Line
Asthma and Allergy Foundation of America
8201 Corporate Drive
Suite 1000
Landover, MD 20785   202-466-7643
                                            800-727-8462
                                            800-7 A-THMA
                                       FAX: 202-466-8940
                                            info@aafa.org
                                                aafa.org

Lynn Hanessian, Chair
Yolanda Miller, SVP & COO
Lynda Mitchell, VP, Food Allergies

The Asthma and Allergy Foundation of America (AAFA) provides practical information, community based services and support through a national network of chapters and support groups.
AAFA develops health education, organizes state and national
advocacy efforts and funds research to find better treatments and
cures.

8736   Visiting Nurse Association of America
2121 Crystal Drive
Suite 750
Arlington, VA 22202   571-527-1520
                                            888-866-8773
                                       FAX: 571-527-1527
                                        webadmin@vnaa.org
                                                vnaa.org

Mary B. DeVeau, Chair
Linnea Windel, Vice Chair
Tracey Moorhead, President & CEO

The VNAA is the official national association for not-for-profit,
community based home health organizations known as the Visiting Nurse Associations (VNA's). They created the profession of
home health care more then 100 years ag. They have a united mission to bring compassionate, high-quality and cost-effective
home care to individuals in their communities.

Speech & Language

Associations

8737 Academic Language Therapy Association
14070 Proton Rd.
Suite 100
Dallas, TX 75244   972-233-9107
                                               FAX: 972-490-4219
                                               office@altaread.org
                                               www.altaread.org

Janna Curry-Dobbs, President
Jo Ann Handy, VP Membership
Susan Louchen, VP Public Relations
The Academic Language Therapy Associationr (ALTA) is a non-profit national professional organization with the purpose of establishing, maintaining, and promoting standards of education, practice and professional conduct for Certified Academic Language Therapists. Academic Language Therapy is an educational, structured, comprehensive, phonetic, multisensory approach for the remediation of dyslexia and/or written-language disorders.
1986

8738 American Speech-Language-Hearing Association
2200 Research Blvd.
Rockville, MD 20850-3289   301-296-5700
                                                    800-638-8255
                                               actioncenter@asha.org
                                               www.asha.org

Gail J. Richard, President
Elise Davis-Mcfaland, President-Elect
Margot L. Beckerman, Chair
The American Speech-Language Association is the professional, scientific, and credentialing association for members and affiliates who are speech-language pathologists, audiologists, and speech, language, and hearing scientists in the United States and internationally. ASHA provides information for the public, professionals, students, and the research community related to hearing, balance, speech, language and swallowing disorders.

8739 Aphasia Hope Foundation
P.O. Box 79701
Houston, TX 77279   855-764-4673
                                               jstradinger@comcast.net
                                               www.aphasiahope.org

Sandy Caudell, Program Diretor
Judi Stradinger, Executive Director
Aphasia Hope Foundation is a nonprofit foundation whose mission is to promote research into the prevention and cure of aphasia and to ensure that all survivors of aphasia and their caregivers are aware of and have access to the best prossible tratments.

8740 Association of Language Companies
9707 Key West Ave.
Suite 100
Rockville, MD 20850   240-404-6511
                                               FAX: 301-990-9771
                                               info@alcus.org
                                               www.alcus.org

Christopher Carter, President
Rick Antezana, Vice President
Lenani P. Craig, Treasurer
The Association of Language Companies (ALC) is a national trade association representing businesses that provide translation, interpretation, localization, and language training services.

8741 Autism Research Institute
4182 Adams Ave.
San Diego, CA 92116-2599   866-366-3361
                                               www.autism.com

Stephen Edelson, Executive Director
Rebecca McKenney, Office Manager
Christopher Flynn, Treasurer
Conducts research on the causes, diagnosis, and treatment of autism and publishes a quarterly newsletter that reviews worldwide research. Literature on causes and treatment available. Refers patients and families to health care professionals and clinics.

8742 Autism Services Center
929 4th Ave.
P.O. Box 507
Huntington, WV 25701-0507   304-525-8014
                                               FAX: 304-525-8026
                                               www.autismservicescenter.org

Jimmie Beirne, Chief Executive Officer
Jodi Fields, Director
Barbara Bragg, Director
Provides developmental disabilities services with a specialty in autism. Services include case management, residential, personal care, assessments and evaluations, supported employment, independent living and family support.

8743 Autism Treatment Center of America
2080 S Undermountain Rd.
Sheffield, MA 01257-9643   413-229-2100
                                                    877-766-7473
                                               FAX: 413-229-8931
                                               correspondence@option.org
                                               www.autismtreatmentcenter.org

Barry Neil Kaufman, Founder & CEO
Clyde Haberman, Senior Teacher & Director of Development
Blair Borgeson, Developmental Therapist
The Autism Treatment Center of America provides innovative training programs for parents and professionals caring for children challenged by Autism, Autism Spectrum Disorders, Pervasive Developmental Disorders (PDD) and other development difficulties. The center's Son-Rise Program teaches a comprehensive system of treatment and education designed to help families and caregivers enable their children to dramatically improve in all areas of learning.

8744 Carl and Ruth Shapiro Family National Center for Accessible Media
WGBH Educational Foundation
1 Guest St.
Boston, MA 02135-2016   617-300-3400
                                               FAX: 617-300-1035
                                               TTY:617-300-2489
                                               ncam@wgbh.org
                                               ncam.wgbh.org

Donna Danielewski, Director
Geoff Freed, Director of technology projects and Web media standards
Madeleine Rothberg, Senior Subject Matter Expert
The Carl and Ruth Shapiro Family National Center for Accessible Media (NCAM) is a research and development facility dedicated to addressing barriers to media and emerging technologies for people with disabilities in their homes, schools, workplaces, and communities.

8745 Childhood Apraxia of Speech Association
416 Lincoln Ave.
2nd Fl.
Pittsburgh, PA 15209   412-343-7102
                                               www.apraxia-kids.org

Mary Sturm, President
Michele R. Atkins, Executive Director
Joshua Zellers, Treasurer
The Childhood Apraxia of Speech Association is a nonprofit publicly funded charity whose mission is to strengthen the support systems in the lives of children with apraxia so that each child is afforded their best opportunity to develop speech and communication.

8746 Deafness and Communicative Disorders Branch of Rehab Services Administration Office
Special Education and Rehab Services
400 Maryland Ave., SW
Washington, DC 20202   800-872-5327
                                               www.ed.gov

Kimberly Richey, Secretary Of Education
Promotes improved rehabilitation services for deaf and hard of hearing people and individuals with speech or language impairments. Provides technical assistance to public and private agencies and individuals.

8747 **Dysphagia Research Society**
2800 West Higgins Rd.
Suite 440
Hoffman Estates, IL 60169
888-775-7361
FAX: 847-885-8393
info@dysphagiaresearch.org
www.dysphagiaresearch.org
Gary H. McCullough, President
Sudarshan R. Jadcherla, President Elect
Susan Langmore, Secretary/Treasurer
The Dysphagia Research Society is a nonprofit organization with
the purpose of enhancing and encouraging research pertinent to
normal and disordered swallowing, to promote the dissemination
of knowledge related to normal and disordered swallowing, and
to provide a multidisciplinary forum for presentation of research
into normal and disordered swallowing.

8748 **Hearing, Speech and Deafness Center (HSDC)**
Hearing, Speech & Deafness Center (HSDC)
1625 19th Ave.
Seattle, WA 98122
206-323-5770
888-222-5036
FAX: 206-328-6871
TTY:800-761-2821
clinics@hsdc.org
www.hsdc.org
Lindsay Klarman, Executive Director
Hearing, Speech & Deaf Center (HSDC) is a nonprofit for clients
who are deaf, hard of hearing, or who face other communication
barriers such as speech challenges. Their mission is to foster inclusive and accessible communities through communication, advocacy, and education.

8749 **International Cluttering Association**
705 Tilbury Court
Sun City Center, FL 33573
elanouette@tampabay.rr.com
associations.missouristate.edu/ica
Charley Adams, Ph.D., Chair
Susanne Cook, Chair Elect
Katarzyna Wesierska, Secretary
They work to increase awareness of the communication disorder
of cluttering worldwide among speech-language thera-
pists/logopedists, healthcare professionals, people with cluttering, and the public.

8750 **International Fluency Association**
Northern Illinois University
Dept. of Communicative Disorders
DeKalb, IL 60115-2899
www.theifa.org
Elaine Kelman, President
Nan Bernstein Ratner, President Elect
Shelly Jo Kraft, Treasurer
The International Fluency Association is a not-for-profit, inter-
national, interdisciplinary organization devoted to the under-
standing and management of fluency disorders, and to the
improvement in the quality of life for persons with fluency
disorders.

8751 **Lindamood-Bell Home Learning Process**
CA
805-541-3836
800-233-1819
www.lindamoodbell.com
Nanci Bell, Founder/Director
Patricia C. Lindamood, Founder/Director
Lindamood-Bell Learning Process is dedicated to enhancing human learning. Lindamood-Belll programs teach children and
adults to read, spell, comprehend, and express language.
1986

8752 **Myositis Association**
1940 Duke St.
Suite 200
Alexandria, VA 22314
800-821-7356
tma@myositis.org
www.myositis.org
Bob Goldberg, Executive Director
Linda Kobert, Communications Director
Aisha Morrow, Operations Manager
The aim of TMA's programs and services is to provide information, support, advocacy and research for those concerned about
myositis, as well as serving those affected by these diseases. Sup-

port groups offer members the chance to share and discuss their
concerns with people in similar situations.

8753 **National Aphasia Association**
P.O. Box 87
Scarsdale, NY 10583
800-922-4622
naa@aphasia.org
www.aphasia.org
Darlene S. Williamson, President
Daniel Martin, Vice President Strategic Planning
Barbara Kessler, Vice President Community Outreach & Education
The National Aphasia Association (NAA) is a nonprofit organization that promotes public education, research, rehabilitation
and support services to assist people with aphasia and their
families.

8754 **National Association of Special Education Teachers**
1250 Connecticut Ave., NW
Suite 200
Washington, DC 20036-2643
800-754-4421
FAX: 800-754-4421
contactus@naset.org
www.naset.org
Roger Pierangelo, Executive Director
George Giuliani, Executive Director
The National Association of Special Education Teachers
(NASET) is a national membership organization dedicated to rendering all possible support and assistance to those preparing for
or teaching in the field of special education. NASET was founded
to promote the profession of special education teachers and to
provide a national forum for their ideas.

8755 **National Black Association for Speech-Language and
Hearing**
P.O. Box 779
Pennsville, NJ 08070
877-936-6235
FAX: 877-936-6235
nbaslh@nbaslh.org
www.nbaslh.org
Cathy Runnels, Interim Chair
Kia N. Johnson, Parliamentarian
Martine Elie, Treasurer
The mission of the National Black Association of Speech-Lan-
guage and Hearing is to maintain a viable mechanism through
which the needs of black professionals, students and individuals
with communication disorders can be met.

8756 **National Cued Speech Association**
1300 Pennsylvania Ave, NW
Suite 190-713
Washington, DC 20004
917-439-5126
800-459-3529
FAX: 866-269-9877
info@cuedspeech.org
www.cuedspeech.org
Anne Huffman, President
Sarina Roffe, Executive Director
Ben Lachman, Director of Development
The association champions effective communication, language
development and literacy through the use of cued speech. Families are informed about Cued Speech along with other communication options.

8757 **National Fragile X Foundation**
2100 M St., NW
Suite 170, P.O. Box 302
Washington, DC 20037-1233
800-688-8765
www.fragilex.org
Tony Ferlenda, Chief Executive Officer
Linda Sorensen, Chief Operating Officer
Jayne Dixon Weber, Director of Education & Support Services
Unites the fragile X community to enrich lives through educational and emotional support, promote public and professional
awareness and advance research toward improvemed treatments
and cure for fragile X syndrome.

8758 National Spasmodic Dysphonia Association
300 Park Blvd.
Suite 335
Itasca, IL 60143
800-795-6732
FAX: 630-250-4505
NSDA@dysphonia.org
www.dysphonia.org

Charlie Reavis, President
Marcia Sterling, Treasurer
Kimberly Kuman, Executive Director
The National Spasmodic Dysphonia Association (NSDA) is a not-for-profit organization dedicated to advancing medical research into the causes of and treatments for SD, promoting physician and public awareness of the disorder, and providing support to those affected by SD through symposiums, support groups, and on-line resources.

8759 National Stuttering Association
119 W. 40th St.
14th Fl.
New York, NY 10018
212-944-4050
800-937-8888
FAX: 212-944-8244
info@westutter.org
www.westutter.org

Gerald Maguire, Chairman
Evan Sherman, Vice Chairman
Bob Wellington, Treasurer
A nonprofit organization dedicated to bringing hope, dignity, support, education, and empowerment to children and adults who stutter and their families, and the professionals who serve them.

8760 National Tourette Syndrome Association
42-40 Bell Blvd.
Suite 205
Bayside, NY 11361
888-4TO-URET
www.tsa-usa.org

John Miller, President & CEO
Diana Felner, VP Public Policy
Sonji Mason-Vidal, VP Finance & Administration
The Tourette Association is dedicated to making life better for all people affected by Tourette and Tic Disorders.

8761 Providence Speech and Hearing Center
1301 Providence Ave.
Orange, CA 92868-3892
714-923-1521
855-901-7742
FAX: 714-639-2593
pshc@pshc.org
www.pshc.org

Bruce May, President
Kevin Timone, Vice President - Fund Development
Randy Free, Vice President - Finance
Mission is to provide the highest quality services available in the identification, diagnosis, treatment and prevention of speech, language and hearing disorders for persons of all ages.

8762 Scottish Rite Center for Childhood Language Disorders
1733 16th St., NW
Washington, DC 20009-3103
202-323-3579
FAX: 202-464-0487
council@scottishrite.org
www.scottishrite.org

Bill Sizemore, Executive Director
Offers speech-language evaluations and treatment, hearing screening and consultations to children ages birth through adolescence. Bilingual services are also available.

8763 Stern Center for Language and Learning
183 Talcott Rd.
Suite 101
Williston, VT 05495-9209
802-878-2332
learning@sterncenter.org
www.sterncenter.org

Blanche Podhajski, President
Michael Shapiro, Chief Operating Officer
Moneer Greenbaum, Director of Development
The Stern Center is a nonprofit learning center dedicated to helping children and adults reach their full potential. Stern Center professionals evaluate and teach all kinds of learners, including

those with learning disabilities such as dyslexia or attention deficit disorders.

8764 Stuttering Foundation of America
1805 Moriah Woods Blvd.
Suite 3
Memphis, TN 38117
901-761-0343
800-992-9392
FAX: 901-761-0484
info@stutteringhelp.org
www.stutteringhelp.org

Jane Fraser, President
Dennis Drayna, Director
Joseph R. G. Fulcher, Director
Provides resources, services, and support to those who stutter and their families, as well as support for research into the causes of stuttering.

8765 Texas Speech-Language-Hearing Association
2025 M St., NW
Suite 800
Washington, DC 20036-2342
855-330-8742
888-729-8742
FAX: 512-463-9468
staff@txsha.org
www.txsha.org

Judy Rudebusch Rich, President
Erin Bellue, VP of Educational & Scientific Affairs
Shannon Butkus, VP of Social & Governmental Policy
Mission is to encourage and promote the role of the speech-language pathologist and audiologist as a professional in the delivery of clinical services to persons with communications disorders. Encourages basic scientific study of processes of individual human communication with reference to speech, hearing and language.

8766 The Cherab Foundation
2301 NE Savannah Rd
Suite 1771
Jensen Beach, FL 34957
772-335-5135
help@cherab.org
cherabfoundation.org

Lisa Geng, Founder & President
Jolie Abreu, Vice President
The Cherab Foundation is a world-wide nonprofit organization working to improve the communication skills and education of all children with speech and language delays and disorders. The Cherab Foundation is committed to assisting with the development of new therapeutic approaches, preventions, and cures to neurologically-based speech disorders.

8767 The Davis Center
305 White Heron Circle
Fayetteville, NY 13066
862-251-4637
ddavis@thedaviscenter.com
www.thedaviscenter.com

Dorinne S. Davis, Director
Offers sound-based therapies supporting positive change in learning, development, and wellness. All ages/all disabilities. Uses The Davis Model of Sound Intervention, an alternative approach.

8768 Wendell Johnson Speech And Hearing Clinic
University Of Iowa
Iowa City, IA 52242-1025
319-335-8736
FAX: 319-335-8851
TTY:319-335-8736
speech-path-aud@uiowa.edu
clas.uiowa.edu/comsci/clinical-services

Ann Fennell, Clinical Coordinator
The clinic offers assessment and remediation for communication disorders in adults and children. The clinic also offers a Intensive Summer Residential Clinic for school age children needing intervention services because of speech, language, hearing and/or reading problems.

Camps

8769 CNS Camp New Connections
Mclean Hospital Child/Adolescent Program
Mailstop115
115 Mill Street
Belmont, MA 02478   617-855-2000
800-333-0338
FAX: 617-855-2833
mcleaninfo@partners.org
mcleanhospital.org
Scott L. Rauch, MD, President & Chief Psychiatrist
Blaise Aguirre, Clinical Staff
Alan Barry, Clinical Staff
Four-week summer day camp for children ages 7-17 who have pervasive developmental disorders, Asperger's Syndrome, autism spectrum disorders and non-verbal learning disabilities. The camp is designed to help children develop social skills through fun activities including: communication games, swimming, field trips, drama, and arts and crafts. *$4500.00*

8770 Camp Meadowood Springs
77650 Meadowood Rd.
Weston, OR 97886   541-276-2752
FAX: 541-276-7227
camp@meadowoodsprings.org
www.meadowoodsprings.org
Michelle Nelson, Camp Director
This camp is designed to help children with communication disorders and learning differences. A full range of activities in recreational and clinical areas is available.

8771 Camp Royall
250 Bill Ash Rd.
Moncure, NC 27559   919-542-1033
FAX: 919-533-5324
camproyall@autismsociety-nc.org
www.autismsociety-nc.org/camp-royall
Sara Gage, Director
A week-long overnight and day camp for children and adults with autism. Campers participate in traditional camp activities such as swimming, boating, hiking, and arts and crafts. Counselor-to-camper ratio is 1:1 or 1:2, depending on the campers' needs.

8772 Camp Sisol
Jewish Community Center of Greater Rochester/JCC
1200 Edgewood Ave.
Rochester, NY 14618   585-461-2000
FAX: 585-461-0805
bettertogether@jccrochester.org
www.jccrochester.org
Josh Weinstein, Chief Executive Officer
Coed, ages 5-16. Camp Sisol accommodates children with special needs.

8773 Childrens Beach House
100 West 10th Street
Suite 411
Wilmington, DE 19801-1674   302-655-4288
FAX: 302-655-4216
www.cbhinc.org
Martha P. Tschantz, President
Mary Helms, Vice President
Richard T Garrett, Executive Director
Camp is located in Lewes, Delaware. Four-week sessions June-August for Delaware children with hearing impairment or speech/communication impairment. Coed, ages 6-12.

8774 New Horizons Summer Day Camp
YMCA of Orange County
13821 Newport Ave.
Suite 150
Tustin, CA 92780   714-508-7616
newhorizons@ymcaoc.org
www.ymcaoc.org/new-horizons
Jeff McBride, Chief Executive Officer
New Horizons is a program by the YMCA offering day camps for adults with developmental disabilities. Outings in the community

are supervised and create an environment that fosters social interaction, skill building, and friendship.

8775 Sequanota Lutheran Conference Center and Camp
PO Box 245
Jennerstown, PA 15547   814-629-6627
contact@sequanota.com
www.sequanota.com
Rev. Nathan Pile, Executive Director
Angie Pile, Director, Business Management
Ann Ferry, Director, Hospitality
Runs Camp Bethesda, a summer camp for adults with developmental and intellectual disabilities. For ages 18 and up.

8776 Talisman Summer Camp
64 Gap Creek Rd.
Zirconia, NC 28790   828-697-6313
info@talismancamps.com
www.talismancamps.com
Linda Tatsapaugh, Operations Director & Owner
Robiyn Mims, Admissions Director & Owner
Cory Greene, Camp Director
Talisman Summer Camp is located 40 minutes south of Asheville, North Carolina. Offers a program of hiking, rafting, climbing, and caving for young people with autism, ADHD and learning disabilities. Coed, ages 6-22.

8777 Wendell Johnson Speech & Hearing Clinic
University Of Iowa
250 Hawkins Dr
Iowa City, IA 52242-1025   319-335-8736
FAX: 319-335-8851
kathy-miller@uiowa.edu
www.uiowa.edu
Chuck Wieland, President
Hans Hoerschelman, Vice President
Josh Smith, Budget Officer
The clinic offers assessment and remediation for communication disorders in adults and children. The clinic also offers a Intensive Summer Residential Clinic for school age children needing intervention services because of speech, language, hearing and/or reading problems.

8778 YMCA Camp Fitch
12600 Abels Rd.
North Springfield, PA 16430   814-922-3219
877-863-4824
FAX: 814-922-7000
registrar@campfitchymca.org
campfitchymca.org
Tom Parker, Executive Director
Joe Wolnik, Summer Camp Director
Brandy Duda, Outdoor Education Director
Camp is located in North Springfield, Pennsylvania. Camp programs include sessions for children with diabetes or epilepsy.

Books

8779 Autism 24/7: A Family Guide to Learning at Home & in the Community
Autism Society of North Carolina Bookstore
Ste 230
505 Oberlin Rd
Raleigh, NC 27605-1345   919-743-0204
800-442-2762
FAX: 919-743-0208
jchampion@autismsociety-nc.org
www.autismsociety-nc.org/
Sharon Jeffries-Jones, Chair
Elizabeth Phillippi, Vice Chair
Tracey Sheriff, Chief Executive Officer
Parents are encouraged to focus on skill sets and behaviors that most negatively affect family functioning, and replacing these behaviors with acceptable alternatives. *$19.95*

8780 Autism Handbook: Understanding & Treating Autism & Prevention Development
Oxford University Press
2001 Evans Road
Cary, NC 27513
919-677-0977
800-445-9714
FAX: 919-677-1303
www.oup.com/us/
Oxford University Press USA is the US branch of Oxford University Press in Oxford, England (OUP UK), which is a department of Oxford University and is the oldest and largest continuously operating university press in the world. *$25.00*
320 pages
ISBN 0-195076-67-2

8781 Autism and Learning
Taylor & Francis
37-41 Mortimer St
London, UK W1T 3
www.informatandm.com
Stuart Powell, Author
Rita Jordan, Editor
This book is about how a cognitive perception on the way in which individuals with autism think and learn may be applied to particular curriculum areas.
160 pages Paperback
ISBN 1-853464-21-X

8782 Autism in Adolescents and Adults
Springer Publishing
233 Spring St
New York, NY 10013
877-283-3229
ainy@aveda.com
aveda.edu/new-york
Eric Schopler, Editor
Gary B. Mesibov, Editor
This book is a great history lesson in the development of understanding about autism spectrum disorders, and is a testament to how far research and services in the field have come. This book contains lots of information about what general thinking and services used to be like, in an era when still little was understood about these disorders. *$63.00*
456 pages
ISBN 0-306410-57-5

8783 Autism..Nature, Diagnosis and Treatment
Autism Society of North Carolina Bookstore
Ste 230
505 Oberlin Rd
Raleigh, NC 27605-1345
919-743-0204
800-442-2762
FAX: 919-743-0208
www.autismsociety-nc.org/
Sharon Jeffries-Jones, Chair
Elizabeth Phillippi, Vice Chair
Paul Wendler, Chief Financial Officer
Covers perspectives, issues, neurobiological issues and new directions in diagnosis and treatment. *$49.00*

8784 Autism: Explaining the Enigma
Wiley Publishers
111 River Street
Hoboken, NJ 07030-5774
201-748-6000
FAX: 201-748-6088
as.wiley.com
Peter Booth Wiley, Chairman
Stephen M. Smith, President & CEO
John Kitzmacher, EVP, CFO
Explains the nature of autism. *$27.95*

8785 Autism: From Tragedy to Triumph
Branden Publishing Company
17 Station St
Brookline, MA 2445-7995
617-730-5757
www.yogainthevillage.com
Karen Wenc, Teaching Staff
Veronica Wolff, Teaching Staff
Annie Hoffman, Teaching Staff
A new book that deals with the Lovaas method and includes a foreward by Dr. Ivar Lovaas. The book is broken down into two parts — the long road to diagnosis and then treatment. *$12.95*

8786 Autism: Identification, Education and Treatment
Routledge (Taylor & Francis Group)
270 Madison Ave
New York, NY 10016-601
212-576-1411
books.google.co.in/books/about/Autism.
Dianne Zager, Editor
Chapters include medical treatments, early intervention and communication development in autism. *$36.00*
ISBN 0-805820-44-7

8787 Autism: The Facts
Oxford University Press
2001 Evans Road
Cary, NC 27513
919-677-0977
800-445-9714
FAX: 919-677-1303
www.oup.com/us/corporate/contact/?view
Simon Baron-Cohen, Co-Author
Patrick Bolton, Co-Author
$22.50
128 pages
ISBN 0-192623-27-3

8788 Autistic Adults at Bittersweet Farms
Routledge (Taylor & Francis Group)
12660 Archbold-Whitehouse Rd.
Whitehouse, OH 43571
419-875-6986
www.bittersweetfarms.org/
Robert St. Clair, President
Matt Anderson, VP
Jan Toczynski, Secretary
A touching view of an inspirational residential care program for autistic adolescents and adults. Also available in softcover. *$94.95*
Hardcover
ISBN 1-560240-42-3

8789 Beyond Baby Talk: From Sounds to Sentences, a Parent's Guide to Language Development
Prima Publishing
P.O.Box 1260
Rocklin, CA 95677-1260
916-787-7000
800-632-8676
FAX: 916-787-7001
Fernando Bueno, Editor in Chief
Julie Asbury, Managing Editor
Christopher Buffa, Sr. Editor
The authors discuss the best ways to help your child develop the all-important skill of communication and to recognize the signs of language development problems. *$15.95*
224 pages
ISBN 0-761526-47-1

8790 Breaking the Speech Barrier: Language Develpment Through Augmented Means
Brookes Publishing
P.O.Box 10624
Baltimore, MD 21285-0624
410-337-9580
800-638-3775
FAX: 410-337-8539
custserv@brookespublishing.com
readplaylearn.com
Paul Brookes, Owner
This resource describes the creation of the System for Augmenting Language (SAL) for school-age youth with developmental disabilities and offers important insights into the language development of children who are not learning to communicate typically. *$39.95*
224 pages Paperback
ISBN 1-557663-90-0

8791   Breakthroughs: How to Reach Students with Autism
Aquarius Health Care Media
Ste 230
505 Oberlin Rd
Raleigh, NC 27605-1345   919-743-0204
                                       800-442-2762
                                  FAX: 919-743-0208
                    jchampion@autismsociety-nc.org
                        www.autismtreatmentcenter.org

Sharon Jeffries-Jones, Chair
Elizabeth Phillippi, Vice Chair
Tracey Sheriff, CEO
A hands-on, how-to program for reaching students with autism,
featuring Karen Sewell, Autism Society of America's teacher of
the year. Here Sewell demonstrates the successful techniques
she's developed over a 20-year career. A separate 250 page manual ($59) is also available which covers math, reading, fine mo-
tor, self help, social adaptive, vocational and self help skills as
well as providing numerous plan reproducibles and an exhaustive
listing of equipment and materials resources. Video. *$99.00*

8792   Childhood Speech, Language & Listening Problems
Wiley Publishing
605 3rd Ave
New York, NY 10158-180   212-850-6000
                                  FAX: 212-850-6088
                books.google.co.in/books/about/Childho
Patricia McAleer Hamaguchi
Language pathologist Hamaguchi employs her 15 years of expe-
rience to show parents how to recognize the most common
speech, language, and listening problems. *$16.95*
224 pages Paperback
ISBN 0-471387-53-3

**8793   Cognitive Behavioral Therapy for Adult Asperger
Syndrome**
Autism Society of North Carolina Bookstore
Ste 230
505 Oberlin Rd
Raleigh, NC 27605-1345   919-743-0204
                                       800-442-2762
                                  FAX: 919-743-0208
                    jchampion@autismsociety-nc.org
                        www.autismsociety-nc.org

Sharon Jeffries-Jones, Chair
Elizabeth Phillippi, Vice Chair
Tracey Sheriff, CEO
Text is prepared with case studies and examples from the author's
own experiences working as a cognitive-behavioral therapist
specializing in adults and adolescents with dual diagnosis, autism spectrum disorders, mood disorders, and anxiety disorders.

**8794   Communication Development and Disorders in African
American Children**
Brookes Publishing
P.O.Box 10624
Baltimore, MD 21285-0624   410-337-9580
                                       800-638-3775
                                  FAX: 410-337-8539
                    custserv@brookespublishing.com

Paul Brooks, Owner
Research, Assessment, and Intervention. This text presents research on communication disorders and language development in
African American children. Also addresses multicultural aspects
of service delivery and intervention and discusses issues in assessing, diagnosing, and treating communication disorders.
$39.00
400 pages Paperback
ISBN 1-55766 -53-3

**8795   Communication Development in Children with Down
Syndrome**
Brookes Publishing
P.O.Box 10624
Baltimore, MD 21285-0624   410-337-9580
                                       800-638-3775
                                  FAX: 410-337-8539
                    custserv@brookespublishing.com

Paul Brooks, Owner

This book offers an extensive, detailed explanation of communication development in children with Down syndrome relative to
their advancing cognitive skills. It introduces a critical framework for assessing and treating hearing, speech, and language
problems and provides explicit intervention methods and tested
clinical protocols.
Paperback
ISBN 1-55766 -50-5

8796   Coping for Kids Who Stutter
Speech Bin
P.O.Box 1579
Appleton, WI 54912   419-589-1425
                                       888-388-3224
                                  FAX: 888-388-6344
                          info@speechbin.com
                          www.speechbin.com

James R. Henderson, Chairman
Joseph M. Yorio, President & CEO
Rick Holden, EVP, Educators Publishing Service
Informative book for children and adults about stuttering and
how to manage it. *$15.95*
32 pages
ISBN 0-93785 -43-2

**8797   Disorders of Motor Speech: Assessment, Treatment, and
Clinical Characterization**
Brookes Publishing
P.O.Box 10624
Baltimore, MD 21285-0624   410-337-9580
                                       800-638-3775
                                  FAX: 410-337-8539
                    custserv@brookespublishing.com

Paul Brooks, Owner
This book provides a probing examination of normal, dysarthric,
and apraxic speech. Great for speech-language pathologists, neurologists, physical or occupational therapists, and physiatrists.
$47.00
400 pages Hardcover
ISBN 1-55766 -23-1

**8798   Employment for Individuals with Asperger Syndrome or
Non-Verbal Learning Disability**
Jessica Kingsley Publishers
400 Market Street
Suite 400
Philadelphia, PA 19106-2513   215-922-1161
                                       866-416-1078
                                  FAX: 215-922-1474
                          orders@jkp.com
                          www.jkp.com

Laurie Schlesinger, VP Of Sales & Marketing
Yvona Fast, Author
Most people with Non-Verbal Learning Disorder (NLD) or
Asperger Syndrome (AS) are underemployed. This book sets out
to change this. With practical and technical advice on everything
from job hunting to interview techniques, from 'fitting in' in the
workplace to whether or not to disclose a diagnosis, this book
guides people with NLD or AS successfully through the employment mine field. There is also information for employers, agencies and careers counsellors on AS and NLD as 'invisible'
disabili *$22.95*
272 pages
ISBN 1-843107-66-X

8799   Encounters with Autistic States
Jason Aronson
400 Keystone Industrial Park
Dunmore, PA 18512-1507   800-782-0015
This book explores and explands the work of the late Frances
Tustin, which was devoted to the psychoanalytic understanding
of the bewildering elemental world of the autistic child. *$50.00*
448 pages Hardcover
ISBN 0-765700-62-

8800 Kitten Who Couldn't Purr
William Morrow & Company
1350 Avenue of the Americas
New York, NY 10019-4702   212-261-6500
FAX: 212-261-6925
www.goodreads.com/book/show/2319648.Th
Otis Chandler, CEO & Co-Founder
Eve Titus, Author
Jonathan the kitten doesn't know how to purr to say thank you, so he sets off to find someone to teach him. *$12.95*
32 pages

8801 Language Disabilities in Children and Adolescents
McGraw-Hill School Publishing
PO Box 182605
Columbus, OH 43218   800-338-3987
FAX: 609-308-4480
customer.service@mheducation.com
mcgraw-hill.com
David Levin, President and CEO
Patrick Milano, Chief Administrative Officer & CFO
Stephen Laster, Chief Digital Officer
A comprehensive review of research in language disabilities.

8802 Late Talker: What to Do If Your Child Isn't Talking Yet
St Martin's Griffin
175 5th Ave
New York, NY 10010-7703   646-307-5151
888-330-8477
FAX: 212-674-6132
customerservice@mpsvirginia.com
Marilyn C Agin, Author
This handbook offers advice on ways to identify the warning signs of a speech disorder, information on how to get the right kind of evaluations and therapy, ways to obtain appropriate services through the school system and health insurance, at-home activities that parents can do with their child to stimulate speech, benefits of nutritional supplementation, and advice from experienced parents who've been there on what to expect and what you can do to be your child's best advocate. *$13.95*
256 pages Paperback
ISBN 0-312309-24-4

8803 Let Community Employment be the Goal for Individuals with Autism
Indiana Resource Center For Autism
1905 North Range Road
Bloomington, IN 47408-9801   812-855-6508
800-825-4733
FAX: 812-855-9630
iidc@indiana.edu
www.iidc.indiana.edu/irca
Cathy Pratt, Director
Catherine Davies, Educational Consultant
Pamela Anderson, Outreach/Resource Specialist
A guide designed for people who are responsible for preparing individuals with autism to enter the work force. *$7.00*

8804 Lollipop Lunch
Speech Bin-Abilitations
P.O.Box 1579
Appleton, WI 54912-1579   419-589-1425
888-388-3224
FAX: 888-388-6344
info@speechbin.com
www.speechbin.com
James R. Henderson, Chairman
Joseph M. Yorio, President & CEO
Rick Holden, EVP, Educators Publishing Service
Cleverly illustrated stories and activities for phonological and language development. *$19.95*
128 pages
ISBN 0-937857-54-8

8805 Management of Autistic Behavior
Sage Publications
2455 Teller Road
Thousand Oaks, CA 91320   805-499-0721
800-818-7243
FAX: 805-499-0871
info@sagepub.com
www.sagepub.com
Sara Miller McCune, Founder, Publisher, Chairperson
Blaise R Simqu, President & CEO
Tracey A. Ozmina, Executive Vice President & Chief Operating Officer
This excellent reference is a comprehensive and practical book that tells what works best with specific problems. *$41.00*
450 pages

8806 Motor Speech Disorders
WB Saunders Company
14 Main Street
Southampton, NY 11968-2822   631-283-5050
800-523-1649
FAX: 631-283-2290
info@saunders.com
www.wbsaunders.com
Joseph R Duffy PhD, Author
Professional text on rehabilitation techniques for motor speech disorders. *$74.00*
592 pages
ISBN 0-323024-52-5

8807 Neurobiology of Autism
Johns Hopkins University Press
National Library of Medicine
Building 38A
Bethesda, MD 20894   410-516-6900
888-346-3656
888-FIN- NLM
FAX: 410-516-6998
info@ncbi.nlm.nih.gov
www.ncbi.nlm.nih.gov/pubmed/17919129
Pardo CA, Co-Author
Ebarhat CG, Co-Author
This book discusses recent advances in scientific research that point to a neurobiological basis for autism and examines the clinical implications of this research. *$28.00*
272 pages
ISBN 0-801880-47-5

8808 Nonverbal Learning Disabilities at Home: A Parent's Guide
Jessica Kingsley Publishers
400 Market Street
Suite 400
Philadelphia, PA 19106   215-922-1161
866-416-1078
FAX: 215-922-1474
hello.usa@jkp.com
www.jkp.com
Jessica Kingsley, Chairman & Managing Director
Jemima Kingsley, Director
Octavia Kingsley, Production Director
Explores the variety of daily life problems children with NLD may face, and provides practical strategies for parents to help them cope and grow, from preschool age through their challenging adolescent years. *$19.95*
272 pages Paperback
ISBN 1-853029-40-0

8809 Parent Survival Manual
Springer Publishing Company
11 West 42nd Street
8th Floor
New York, NY 10036   212-355-1501
FAX: 212-355-7370
christieseducation@christies.edu
www.christieseducation.com
Craig Lickliter, Manager
A guide to crises resolution in autism and related developmental disorders. *$39.95*

8810 Perspectives: Whole Language Folio
Gallaudet University Bookstore
PO Box 35009
Charlotte, NC 28235-5009
202-651-5750
800-995-0550
FAX: 202-651-5744
www.cpcc.edu/disabilities

Edwin A. Dalrymple, Chairman
Judith N. Allison, Vice Chair
Tony Zeiss, President
The 19 articles in this collection offer practical help to teachers seeking to emphasize whole language strategies in their classroom. *$9.95*
64 pages

8811 Please Don't Say Hello
Human Sciences Press
233 Spring St
New York, NY 10013
877-283-3229
ainy@aveda.com
aveda.edu/new-york

Phyllis Terri Gold, Author
With the support and love of his family, and through them the neighborhood children, a nine-year-old autistic boy is able to emerge from his shell. *$10.95*
47 pages Paperback
ISBN 0-89885 -99-8

8812 Promoting Communication in Infants and Young Children: 500 Ways to Succeed
Speech Bin-Abilitations
P.O.Box 1579
Appleton, WI 54912-1579
419-589-1425
888-388-3224
FAX: 888-388-6344
info@speechbin.com
www.speechbin.com

James R. Henderson, Chairman
Joseph M. Yorio, President & CEO
Rick Holden, EVP, Educators Publishing Service
This practical reference for parents, caregivers and professional service providers how to promote communication development in infants and young children. Gives down-to-earth information and activities to help your youngest children succeed. It provides step-by-step suggestions for stimulationg children's speech and language skills. Paperback. *$14.95*
ISBN 0-937857-72-6

8813 Reading, Writing and Speech Problems in Children
International Dyslexia Association
40 York Rd.
4th Floor
Baltimore, MD 21204
410-296-0232
FAX: 410-321-5069
info@dyslexiaida.org
dyslexiaida.org

Samuel Torrey Orton, Author
This book provides reading, reading and speech execerises for educating people with dyslexia. *$20.00*
259 pages
ISBN 0-89079 -79-1

8814 Relationship Development Intervention with Young Children
Taylor & Francis Group
73 Collier St.
London, N1 9BE
44- 0 -0 78
FAX: 44- 0 -0 78
hello.usa@jkp.com
www.jkp.com/jkp/distributors.php

Jessica Kingsley, Chairman
Jemima Kingsley, Director
Octavia Kingsley, Production Director
Social and emotional development activities for Asperger Syndrome, Autism, PDD and NLD. Comprehensive set of activities emphasizes foundation skills for younger children between the ages of two and eight. Covers skills such as social referencing, regulating behvior, conversational reciprocity, and synchronized

actions. For use in therapeutic settings as well as schools and parents. *$22.95*
256 pages
ISBN 1-843107-14-7

8815 Riddle of Autism: A Psychological Analysis
Jason Aronson
Ste 200
4501 Forbes Blvd
Lanham, MD 20706
301-459-3366
800-462-6420
FAX: 301-429-5746
customercare@nbnbooks.com
www.nbnbooks.com

Jason Brockwell, Sales Staff
Michael Sullivan, Sales
Mark Cozy, Sales Staff
Dr. Victor examines the myths that cloud an understanding of this disorder and describes the meanings of its specific behavioral symptoms. *$30.00*
356 pages Paperback
ISBN 1-568215-73-8

8816 Self-Therapy for the Stutterer
Stuttering Foundation of America
1805 Moriah Woods Blvd.
Suite 3
Memphis, TN 38117
901-761-0343
800-992-9392
FAX: 901-761-0484
www.stutterhelp.org

Jane Fraser, President
Jean Gruss, Journalist
Robert M. Kurtz, Chairman & CEO
A guide to help adults who stutter overcome the problem on their own. *$3.00*
191 pages Paperback
ISBN 0-933388-32-2

8817 Sex Education: Issues for the Person with Autism
Indiana Resource Center For Autism
1905 North Range Road
Bloomington, IN 47408-9801
812-855-6508
800-825-4733
FAX: 812-855-9630
www.iidc.indiana.edu/irca

Cathy Pratt, Director
Catherine Davies, Educational Consultant
Pamela Anderson, Outreach/Resource Specialist
Discusses issues of sexuality and provides methods of instruction for people with autism. *$4.00*

8818 Son-Rise: The Miracle Continues
2080 South Undermountain Road
Sheffield, MA 01257
413-229-2100
800-714-2779
sonrise@option.org
www.option.org

Samahria Lyt Kaufman, Co-Founder and Co-Director
Dane Griffith, Director of Administrative Services
Bears Kaufman, Co-Founder and Co-Director
Part One is the astonishing record of Raun Kaufman's development from an autistic child into a loving, brilliant youngster who shows no traces of his former condition. Part Two follows Raun's development after the age of four, teaching the limitless possibilities of the Son-Rise Program. Part Three shares moving accounts of five other ordinary families who became extraordinary when they used the Son-Rise Program to reach their own unreachable children. *$12.95*
343 pages
ISBN 0-915811-53-7

8819   Sound Connections for the Adolescent
Speech Bin
P.O.Box 1579
Appleton, WI 54912-1579   419-589-1425
                                                        888-388-3224
                                                   FAX: 888-388-6344
                                                 info@speechbin.com
                                                  www.speechbin.com

James R. Henderson, Chairman
Joseph M. Yorio, President & CEO
Rick Holden, EVP, Educators Publishing Service
A resource to help older elementary and secondary students understand their sound systems an how it functions. It targets skills critical for academic achievement: phonological awareness, phonemic relationships, phonemic processing, listening and memory and teaches linguistic rules they need to succeed. *$19.95*
Paperback

8820   Stuttering
NI on Deafness & Other Communication Disorders
31 Center Dr.
MSC 2320
Bethesda, MD 20892-2320   301-827-8183
                                                        800-241-1044
                                                   TTY:800-241-1055
                                               nidcdinfo@nidcd.nih.gov
                                                   www.nidcd.nih.gov

Debara L. Tucci, Director
Judith A. Cooper, Deputy Director
Timothy J. Wheeles, Executive Officer
Describes how speech is produced, treatments for stuttering and research supported by the federal government.

8821   Talkable Tales
Speech Bin-Abilitations
P.O.Box 1579
Appleton, WI 54912-1579   419-589-1425
                                                        888-388-3224
                                                   FAX: 888-388-6344
                                                  www.speechbin.com

James R. Henderson, Chairman
Joseph M. Yorio, President & CEO
Rick Holden, EVP, Educators Publishing Service
Read-a-rebus stories and pictures targeting most consonant phonemes for K-5 children. *$25.95*
128 pages
ISBN 0-93783 -44-0

8822   Teaching Children with Autism: Strategies for Initiating Positive Interactions
Brookes Publishing
P.O.Box 10624
Baltimore, MD 21285-0624   410-337-9585
                                                        888-337-8808
                                                   FAX: 410-337-8539
                                             custserv@healthpropress.com
                                                www.healthpropress.com

Melissa A. Behm, President
Mary Magnus, Director
Stategies for initiating positive interactions and improving learning opportunities. This guide begins with an overview of characteristics and long-term strategies and proceeds through discussions that detail specific techniques for normalizing environments, reducing disruptive behavior, improving language and social skills, and enhancing generalization. *$32.95*
256 pages Paperback
ISBN I-55766 -80-4

8823   Teaching and Mainstreaming Autistic Children
Love Publishing Company
9101 East Kenyon Avenue
Suite 2200
Denver, CO 80237   303-221-7333
                                                   FAX: 303-221-7444
                                                www.lovepublishing.com/

Peter Knoblock, Author
Dr. Knoblock advocates a highly organized, structured environment for autistic children, with teachers and parents working together. His premise is that the learning and social needs of autistic children must be analyzed and a daily program designed with in-

terventions that respond to this functional analysis of their behavior. *$24.95*
ISBN 0-89108 -11-9

8824   Techniques for Aphasia Rehab: (TARGET) Generating Effective Treatment
Speech Bin
P.O.Box 1579
Appleton, WI 54912-1579   419-589-1425
                                                        888-388-3224
                                                   FAX: 888-388-6344
                                                  www.speechbin.com

James R. Henderson, Chairman
Joseph M. Yorio, President & CEO
Rick Holden, EVP, Educators Publishing Service
Practical treatment manual for use by aphasia clinicians. *$45.00*
384 pages
ISBN 0-93785 -50-5

8825   Understanding & Controlling Stuttering: A Comprehensive New Approach Based on the Valsa Hyp
National Stuttering Association
119 West 40th Street
14th Floor
New York, NY 10018   212-944-4050
                                                        800-937-8888
                                                   FAX: 212-944-8244
                                                  info@westutter.org
                                                   www.nsastutter.org

Kenny Koroll, Chair
Tammy Flores, Executive Director
Stephanie Coopen, Family Programs Administrator
Demonstrates how physical and psychological factors may interact to stimulate and perpetuate stuttering through a Valsalva-Stuttering cycle. *$25.00*
176 pages
ISBN 7-929773-01-3

8826   Verbal Behavior Approach: How to Teach Children with Autism & Related Disorders
Autism Society of North Carolina Bookstore
Ste 230
505 Oberlin Rd
Raleigh, NC 27605-1345   919-743-0204
                                                        800-442-2762
                                                   FAX: 919-743-0208
                                             www.autismsociety-nc.org

Sharon Jeffries-Jones, Chair
Elizabeth Phillippi, Vice Chair
Tracey Sheriff, CEO
Provides full descriptions of how to teach the verbal operants that make up expressive languate which include: manding, tacting, echoing and intraverbal skills. *$19.95*

8827   Without Reason: A Family Copes with two Generations of Autism
Books on Special Children
721 W Abram St
Arlington, TX 76013-6995   817-277-0727
                                                        800-489-0727
                                                   FAX: 817-277-2270
                                                   www.fhautism.com/

R. Wayne Gilpin, President
Jennifer Gilpin Yacio, Vice President and Editorial Director
David Reasor, CPA and Administrative Director
The author discovers his son has autism. He delves into problems of the autistic person and explains reasons for their actions. *$20.95*
292 pages Hardcover

Journals

8828 American Journal of Speech-Language Pathology
American Speech-Language-Hearing Association
2200 Research Boulevard
Rockville, MD 20850-3289

301-296-5700
800-638-8255
FAX: 301-296-8580
nsslha@asha.org
www.asha.org

Elizabeth S. McCrea, PhD, CCC-SLP, President
Barbara K. Cone, PhD, CCC-A, Vice President for Academic Affairs in Audiology
Carolyn W. Higdon, EdD, CCC-SLP, Vice President for Finance
This is a quarterly journal of clinical practice for speech-language pathologists and language researchers. This journal will be online only beginning January 2010.

8829 Journal of Speech, Language and Hearing Research
American Speech-Language-Hearing Association
2200 Research Boulevard
Rockville, MD 20850-3289

301-296-5700
800-638-8255
FAX: 301-296-8580
nsslha@asha.org
www.asha.org

Elizabeth S. McCrea, PhD, CCC-SLP, President
Barbara K. Cone, PhD, CCC-A, Vice President for Academic Affairs in Audiology
Carolyn W. Higdon, EdD, CCC-SLP, Vice President for Finance
This bimonthly journal contains basic, as well as applied research in normal and disordered communication processes. It will be available online only beginning January 2010.

8830 Language, Speech, and Hearing Services in Schools
International Fluency Association
Northern Illinois University
Dept. of Communicative Disorders
DeKalb, IL 60115-2899

www.theifa.org

David Shapiro, President
Norimune Kawat, Secretary
Rachel Everard, Treasurer
This is a quarterly journal focusing on research appropriate to speech-language pathologists and audiologists in schools. The journal will only be available online beginning in January 2010.

Magazines

8831 Communication Outlook
Artificial Language Laboratory
220 Trowbridge Road
East Lansing, MI 48824

517-353-8332
FAX: 517-353-4766
artling@msu.edu
www.msu.edu

Lou Anna K. Simon, President
Satish Udpa, EVP for Administrative Services
Bill Beekman, VP & Secretary
Communication Outlook (CO) is an international quarterly magazine, which focuses on the techniques and technology of augmentative and alternative communication. CO provides information on technological developments for persons experiencing communication handicaps due to neurological, sensory or neuromuscular conditions. *$18.00*
32 pages Quarterly

Newsletters

8832 Access Academics & Research
American Speech-Language-Hearing Association
2200 Research Boulevard
Rockville, MD 20850-3289

301-296-5700
800-638-8255
FAX: 301-296-8580
nsslha@asha.org
www.asha.org

Elizabeth S. McCrea, PhD, CCC-SLP, President
Barbara K. Cone, PhD, CCC-A, Vice President for Academic Affairs in Audiology
Carolyn W. Higdon, EdD, CCC-SLP, Vice President for Finance
Dedicated to the specific needs of academic and clinical faculty, PhD students and researchers. The e-newsletter was developed as part of the Focused Initiative on the PhD Shortage in Higher Education.

8833 Access Audiology
American Speech-Language-Hearing Association
2200 Research Boulevard
Rockville, MD 20850-3289

301-296-5700
800-638-8255
FAX: 301-296-8580
nsslha@asha.org
www.asha.org

Elizabeth S. McCrea, PhD, CCC-SLP, President
Barbara K. Cone, PhD, CCC-A, Vice President for Academic Affairs in Audiology
Carolyn W. Higdon, EdD, CCC-SLP, Vice President for Finance
Dedicated to the specific needs of all professionals interested in hearing, balance, and the field of audiology. Each issue spotlights a specific topic of interest and relevance to audiologists.

8834 Access SLP Health Care
American Speech-Language-Hearing Association
2200 Research Boulevard
Rockville, MD 20850-3289

301-296-5700
800-638-8255
FAX: 301-296-8580
nsslha@asha.org
www.asha.org

Elizabeth S. McCrea, PhD, CCC-SLP, President
Barbara K. Cone, PhD, CCC-A, Vice President for Academic Affairs in Audiology
Carolyn W. Higdon, EdD, CCC-SLP, Vice President for Finance
An e-newsletter dedicated to the specific needs of speech-language pathologists in healthcare settings. Each issue of Access SLP Health Care features recent legislative activity impacting SLPs and provides information on clinical issues, continuing education opportunities, and ASHA web-based resources.

8835 Access Schools
American Speech-Language-Hearing Association
2200 Research Boulevard
Rockville, MD 20850-3289

301-296-5700
800-638-8255
FAX: 301-296-8580
nsslha@asha.org
www.asha.org

Elizabeth S. McCrea, PhD, CCC-SLP, President
Barbara K. Cone, PhD, CCC-A, Vice President for Academic Affairs in Audiology
Carolyn W. Higdon, EdD, CCC-SLP, Vice President for Finance
Dedicated to the specific needs of school-based speech-language pathologists. Each Access Schools e-newsletter features recent legislative activity impacting school SLPs and provides information on clinical issues, continuing education opportunities, and ASHA web-based resources.

8836 Autism Research Review International
Autism Research Institute
4182 Adams Avenue
San Diego, CA 92116-2599   619-281-7165
                                  866-366-3361
                             FAX: 619-563-6840
                                     autism.com

Stephen Edelson, Executive Director
Jane Johnson, Managing Director
Valerie Paradiz, Director
Provides clearly written summaries of articles selected from computer searches. *$18.00*
8 pages Quarterly

8837 Communicologist
Texas Speech-Language-Hearing Association
Ste 200
918 Congress Ave
Austin, TX 78701-2342   512-494-1128
                               888-729-8742
                          FAX: 512-494-1129

Judith Keller, President
Larry Higdon, Director
Melanie McDonald, President Elect
A forum for distributing current information relevant to the practices of speech-language pathology and audiology across the state. Provides TSHA membership with the latest news from the Executive Board and Task Forces, as well as information about regional associations, distinguished service providers, the TSHA Annual Convention, and committee honors and nominations. Also contains advertisements of interest to the field.

8838 Connect
Hearing, Speech & Deafness Center (HSDC)
1625 19th Ave.
Seattle, WA 98122   206-323-5770
                           888-222-5036
                      FAX: 206-328-6871
                      TTY:800-761-2821
                          clinics@hsdc.org
                            www.hsdc.org

Lindsay Klarman, Executive Director
A newsletter that addresses concerns of those affected by speech and language disorders. HSDC is a nonprofit for clients who are deaf, hard of hearing, or who face other communication barriers such as speech challenges.
8 pages Quarterly

8839 NSSLHA Now
Ntn'l Student Speech Language Hearing Association
2200 Research Boulevard
Rockville, MD 20850-3289   301-296-5700
                                  800-638-8255
                             FAX: 301-296-8580
                                 nsslha@asha.org
                                   www.asha.org

Elizabeth S. McCrea, PhD, CCC-SLP, President
Barbara K. Cone, PhD, CCC-A, Vice President for Academic Affairs in Audiology
Carolyn W. Higdon, EdD, CCC-SLP, Vice President for Finance
Published three times per year.

8840 On Cue
National Cued Speech Association
1300 Pennsylvania Avenue, NW
Suite 190-713
Washington, DC 20004   301-915-8009
                              800-459-3529
                          www.cuedspeech.org

Shannon Howell, President
Penny Hakim, 1st Vice President
John Brubaker, VP Fundraising
Published several times a year and mailed to members of the Association.

8841 Stuttering & Your Child: Help For Parents
Stuttering Foundation of America
18005 Moriah Woods Blvd
PO Box 11749, Suite 3
Memphis, TN 38111-0749   901-761-0343
                                800-992-9392
                           FAX: 901-761-0484
                            info@stutteringhelp.org
                            www.StutteringHelp.org

Jane Fraser, President
Dennis Drayna, Director
Joseph R. G. Fulcher, Director
The Stuttering Foundation provides resources, services and support to those who stutter and their families, as well as support research into the cause of stuttering. The Stuttering Foundation provides a referral list of speech-language pathologists and referrals to other information including research on stuttering, intensive workshops and camps. *$10.00*

8842 Stuttering Foundation Newsletter
Stuttering Foundation of America
P.O.Box 11749
Memphis, TN 38111-0749   901-761-0343
                                800-992-9392
                           FAX: 901-761-0484
                            info@stutteringhelp.org
                            www.stutteringhelp.org

Jane Fraser, President
Jean Gruss, Journalist
Robert M. Kurtz, Chairman & CEO

8843 Voice
Providence Speech and Hearing Association
1301 Providence Avenue
Orange, CA 92868   714-923-1521
                          855-901-7742
                     FAX: 714-744-3841
                          pshc@pshc.org
                           www.pshc.org

Lewis Jaffe, President
Bret Rathwick, Vice President - Finance
Casey Immel, Treasurer
People of all ages with speech and hearing problems by providing specialized products and services.

Audio/Visual

8844 Autism: A World Apart
Fanlight Productions
c/o Icarus Films
32 Court Street, 21st Floor
Brooklyn, NY 11201   718-488-8900
                            800-876-1710
                       FAX: 718-488-8642
                            info@fanlight.com
                            www.fanlight.com

Ben Achtenberg, Owner, Founder
Nicole Johnson, Publicity Coordinator
Anthony Sweeney, Marketing Director
In this documentary, three families show us what the textbooks and studies cannot: what it's like to live with autism day after day; to raise and love children who may be withdrawn and violent and unable to make personal connections with their families. 29 minutes.
VHS/DVD
ISBN 1-572950-39-0

8845 Autism: the Unfolding Mystery
Aquarius Health Care Media
18 N Main St
Sherborn, MA 1770-1066   508-650-1616
Lesile Kussmann, Owner
Explore what it means to be autistic, how you can recognize the signs of autism in your child, and hear about new treatments and programs to help children learn to deal with the disorder. *$145.00*
DVD

8846   Getting Started with Facilitated Communication
Facilitated Communication Institute, Syracuse Univ
370 Huntington Hall
Syracuse, NY 13244-1   315-443-9657
                                          FAX: 315-443-9218
Annegret Schubert, Producer
Describes in detail how to help individuals with autism and/or severe communication difficulties to get started with facilitated communication.
Video

8847   I Just Want My Little Boy Back
Autism Treatment Center Of America
2080 South Undermountain Road
Sheffield, MA 01257   413-229-2100
                                               800-714-2779
                                         happiness@option.org
                                            www.option.org
Samahria Lyt Kaufman, Co-Founder and Co-Director
Dane Griffith, Director of Administrative Services
Bears Kaufman, Co-Founder and Co-Director
A great video for parents and professionals caring for children with special needs. Join one British family and their autistic son before, during and after their journey to America to attend The Son-Rise Program at The Autism Treatment Center of America. This informative, inspirational and deeply moving story not only captures the joy, tears, challenges and triumps of this amazing little boy and his family, but also serves as a powerful introduction to the attitude and principles of the program. *$25.00*

8848   Understanding Autism
Fanlight Productions
c/o Icarus Films
32 Court Street, 21st Floor
Brooklyn, NY 11201   718-488-8900
                                               800-876-1710
                                          FAX: 718-488-8642
                                            info@fanlight.com
                                            www.fanlight.com
Ben Achtenberg, Owner, Founder
Nicole Johnson, Publicity Coordinator
Anthony Sweeney, Marketing Director
Parents of children with autism discuss the nature and symptoms of this lifelong disability and outline a treatment program based on behavior modification principles. 19 minutes
VHS/DVD
ISBN 1-572951-00-1

Support Groups

8849   Autism Society of America
4340 East West Highway
Suite 350
Bethesda, MD 20814-3067   301-657-0881
                                               800-328-8476
                                          FAX: 301-657-0869
                                          www.autism-society.org
Mary Beth Collins, Director of Programs
Tonia Ferguson, Senior Director of Content
Scott Badesch, President/Chief Executive Officer
ASA is the largest and oldest grassroots organization within the autism community, with a nationwide network of chapters and over 20,000 members and supporters nationwide. ASA is the leading source of education, information and referral about autism and has been the leader in advocacy and legislative initiatives for more than four decades.

8850   Friends: National Association of Young People who Stutter
38 S Oyster Bay Rd
Syosset, NY 11791-5033   866-866-8335
                                           lcaggiano@aol.com
                                        www.friendswhostutter.org
Lee Caggiano, President
A national organization created to provide a network of love and support for children and teenagers who stutter, their families, and the professionals who work with them.

8851   National Health Information Center
US Department of Health
P.O.Box 1133
Washington, DC 20013-1133   301-565-4167
                                               800-336-4797
                                               301-468-7394
                                          FAX: 301-984-4256
                                         healthypeople@hhs.gov
                                          www.healthypeople.gov
Jonathan Fielding, Chair
Shirika Kumanyika, Vice Chair
A health information referral service that puts health professionals and consumers who have health questions in touch with those organizations that are best able to provide answers.

8852   Speech Pathways
410 Meadow Creek Drive
Suite 206
Westminster, MD 21158   410-374-0555
                                               800-961-2724
                                          FAX: 410-374-8620
                                       kim.bell@speechpathways.net
                                          speechpathways.net
Kimberly A. Bell, Owner
Karie Hadley, Therapist
Erica Hamilton, Therapist
We realize that parent and family support is critical to a child's success, in therapy as well as in life. We offer support at local and regional levels along with traditional speech and language services, and a wide variety of specialized pediatric programs. Our support groups/services are open to the larger community as well as to our clients.

8853   The Cherab Foundation
2301 NE Savannah Rd
Suite 1771
Jensen Beach, FL 34957   772-335-5135
                                            help@cherab.org
                                          cherabfoundation.org
Lisa Geng, Founder & President
Jolie Abreu, Vice President
The Cherab Foundation is a world-wide nonprofit organization working to improve the communication skills and education of all children with speech and language delays and disorders.

Visual

Associations

8854 American Academy of Ophthalmology
655 Beach St
San Francisco, CA 94109   415-561-8540
                                             866-561-8558
                                        FAX: 415-561-8575
                              customer_service@aao.org
                                                  aao.org

Cynthia Ann Bradford, MD, President
David W Parke II, MD, CEO
Maria M Aaron, MD, Secretary for Annual Meeting
The American Academy of Ophthalmology is an association of
doctors who provide comprehensive eye care, including medical,
surgical and optical care. The academy is dedicated to advancing
the profession of ophthalmology through programs, public
education, courses and advocacy.

8855 American Action Fund for Blind Children and Adults
1800 Johnston St.
Baltimore, MD 21230-4914   410-659-9315
                              actionfund@actionfund.org
                                    www.actionfund.org
Barbara Loos, President
Ramona Walhof, Vice President
Sandra Halverson, Second Vice President/Medical Transcriptionist
A service agency which specializes in providing to blind people
help which is not readily available to them from government programs or other existing service systems. The services are planned
especially to meet the needs of blind children, the elderly blind,
and the deaf-blind.

8856 American Council of Blind Lions
148 Vernon Ave.
Louisville, KY 40206   502-897-1472
                              carla40206@gmail.com
                              www.acb.org/affiliate-ACBL
Carla Ruschival, President
The American Council of Blind Lions (ACBL) works to educate
members of local Lions Clubs about the needs and concerns of
blind or visually impaired people. The ACBL is open to members
from across the United States and encourages blind persons to
join their local clubs and participate in civic projects.

8857 American Council of the Blind
1703 N Beauregard St
Suite 420
Alexandria, VA 22311   202-467-5081
                                             800-424-8666
                                        FAX: 703-465-5085
                                             info@acb.org
                                                www.acb.org
Eric Bridges, Executive Director
Tony Stephens, Director, Advocacy & Governmental Affairs
The American Council of the Blind (ACB) is an association working to increase the independence, security, and opportunity for all
blind or visually impaired individuals. The Council primarily focuses on developing and maintaining policies to implement the
services needed for the blind or visually impaired.

8858 American Council of the Blind Radio Amateurs
19821 Vineyard Ln.
Saratoga, CA 95070   408-257-1034
                                             acbra@acb.org
                                        www.acbhams.org
John Glass, President
A special interest affiliate of the American Council of the Blind,
the American Council of the Blind Radio Amateurs (ACBRA)
promotes the interest of FCC licensed amaetur radio operators.
The ACBRA is made up of legally blind and fully sighted radio
amateurs.

8859 American Foundation for the Blind
2 Penn Plaza
Suite 1102
New York, NY 10121   800-232-5463
                                                  www.afb.org
Kirk Adams, President & CEO
Darren M. Davis, Executive Administrator Executive Office
The American Foundation for the Blind (AFB) is a national non-
profit that is dedicated to removing barriers, creating solutions,
and expanding possibilities for the blind and visually impaired.
The AFB is focused on spreading access to technology, elevating
the quality of information and tools for professional who serve
people with vision loss, and the promotion of independent living
for those with vision loss.

8860 American Optometric Association
243 N Lindbergh Blvd
Floor 1
St. Louis, MO 63141-7881   800-365-2219
                                                  www.aoa.org
Christopher J. Quinn, O.D, President
Barbara L. Horn, O.D, Vice President
William T. Reynolds, O.D, Secretary-Treasurer
The American Optometric Association (AOA) advocates for im-
proving the quality and availability of eye and vision care. The
AOA represents more than 44,000 doctors of optometry,
optometric professionals, and optometry students and works to
set professional standards, lobby government and organizations
on behalf of the profession, and provide research and education
leadership.

8861 American Printing House for the Blind
American Printing House for the Blind, Inc.
1839 Frankfort Ave.
Louisville, KY 40206-0085   502-895-2405
                                             800-223-1839
                                        FAX: 502-899-2284
                                             info@aph.org
                                                www.aph.org
The American Printing House for the Blind (APH) is the world's
largest nonprofit organization creating educational and independent living products for blind and visually impaired individuals. APH promotes independence through the manufacturing of
specialized materials and products for blind persons. The APH is
the official supplier of educational materials in the United States
below a college level.

8862 Associated Services for the Blind and Visually Impaired
919 Walnut Street
Philadelphia, PA 19107-5237   215-627-0600
                                        FAX: 215-922-0692
                                             asbinfo@asb.org
                                                www.asb.org
Karla S. McCaney, President & CEO
Beth Deering, Chief Program Officer
Sylvia Purnell, Director of Learning & Development
Associated Services for the Blind and Visually Impaired (ASB),
is a private, nonprofit organization working to provide services,
education, training, and resources to promote self-esteem, independence, and self determination in people who are blind or visually impaired. In addition, ASB advocates for the rights of blind
and visually impaired persons through community actions and
public education.

**8863 Association for Education & Rehabilitationof the Blind
& Visually Impaired**
5680 King Centre Dr.
Suite 600
Alexandria, VA 22315   703-671-4500
                                        FAX: 703-671-6391
                                             aer@aerbvi.org
                                                www.aerbvi.org
Neva Fairchild, President
Sergio Oliva, Secretary
Jennifer Wheeler, Treasurer
The Association for Education and Rehabilitation of the Blind
and Visually Impaired (AER) is an international, nonprofit mem-
bership organization that supports professionals who provide education and rehabilitation services to people with visual
impairments. The AER provides professional development and

growth opportunities for its members and advocates to maintain specialized blind services.

8864   Association for Macular Diseases
The Association for Macular Diseases, Inc.
210 E 64th St
New York, NY 10065   212-605-3719
                                        association@retinal-research.org
                                                          macula.org
Bernard Landou, President
The Association for Macular Diseases provides support and assistance to individuals with macular disease, their caregivers, and professional community.

8865   Association for Research in Vision and Ophthalmology
1801 Rockville Pike
Suite 400
Rockville, MD 20852-5622   240-221-2900
                                                FAX: 240-221-0370
                                                     arvo@arvo.org
                                                     www.arvo.org
The Association for Research in Vision and Ophthalmology (ARVO) advances research and understanding of the visual system and the preventing, treating, and curing visual disorders. ARVO is an international organization of 12,000 researches from 75 countries performing both clinical and basic research.

8866   Association for Vision Rehabilitation and Employment
174 Court St
Binghamton, NY 13901   607-724-2428
                                                FAX: 607-771-8045
                                                 avreinfo@avreus.org
                                                     www.avreus.org
Ken Fernald, President & CEO
Jenn Small, Chief Operating Officer
Anthony Saccento, Chief Financial Officer
The Association for Vision Rehabilitation and Employment, Inc. (AVRE) is a private, nonprofit organization providing rehabilitation and employment services for people who are blind or visually impaired in the Twin Tiers of New York and Pennsylvania. Services include Low Vision, Early Intervention, Orientation and Mobility, Vision Rehabilitation Therapy, and employment preparation and placement.

8867   Association of Blind Citizens
PO Box 246
Holbrook, MA 02343   781-961-1023
                                                FAX: 781-961-0004
                                          president@blindcitizens.org
                                                  www.blindcitizens.org
The Association of Blind Citizens (ABC) is a membership organization advocating for, and advancing opportunities in education, employment, cultural, and recreational activities for blind and visually impaired persons.

8868   Blind Children's Center
4120 Marathon St
Los Angeles, CA 90029-3584   323-664-2153
                                       info@blindchildrenscenter.org
                                          www.blindchildrenscenter.org
Sarah E. Orth, Chief Executive Officer
Fernanda Armenta-Schmitt, Director, Education & Family Services
A nonprofit organization working to foster the development and education of children from birth to the 2nd grade who are blind or visually impaired. The Blind Children's Center serves about 100 children a year through a variety of family centered programs including the infant, preschool, and elementary.

8869   Blind Information Technology Specialists
8761 E Placita Bolivar
Tucson, AZ 85715-5650   520-232-2100
                                                     www.bits-acb.org
Tom L. Jones, President
Earlene Hughes, Vice President
David Tanner, Secretary
The Blind Information Technology Specialists (BITS) is a nonprofit organization fostering the career development of computer professionals, promoting the use of computer technology and improved information access for people who are blind or visually impaired.

8870   Blinded Veterans Association
1001 King St.
Suite 300
Alexandria, VA 22314   800-669-7079
                                                      bva@bva.org
                                                      www.bva.org
Thomas Zampieri, National President
Joseph D. McNeil, Sr., National Vice President
Donald D. Overton, Jr., Executive Director
The Blinded Veterans Association locates blinded veterans who need assistance, guides them through the rehabilitation process and acts as advocates for them before Congress and the Department of Veterans Affairs in securing the benefits they have earned through their service to the nation. The association also promotes access to technology, practical use of the latest research as well as offering programs for blinded veterans.

8871   Braille Institute of America
741 N Vermont Ave.
Los Angeles, CA 90029-3594   323-663-1111
                                                     800-272-4553
                                                FAX: 323-663-0867
                                              la@brailleinstitute.org
                                                www.brailleinstitute.org
Peter A. Mindnich, President
Gloria Coulston, Vice President, Program Delivery
Nancy N. Neibrugge, Vice President, Program Content
The Braille Institute is a nonprofit organization providing assistance to blind and visually impaired individuals. The institute offers a variety of free programs, classes, and services at 5 regional centers in Southern California.

8872   California State Library Braille and Talking Book Library
PO Box 942837
Sacramento, CA 94237-0001   916-654-0640
                                                     800-952-5666
                                              btbl@library.ca.gov
                                                  www.btbl.ca.gov
A division of the California State Library, the Braille and Talking Book Library (BTBL) is a free service offering braille and audiobook to readers in Northern California who cannot read due to a visual or physical disability. The BTBL is an affiliate of the National Service for the Blind and Physically Handicapped.

8873   Canine Helpers for the Handicapped
Canine Helpers for the Handicapped, Inc.
5699 Ridge Rd.
Lockport, NY 14094   716-433-4035
                                                  chhdogs@aol.com
A nonprofit organization dedicated to training dogs in order to assist people with disabilities and promote independence.

8874   Caption Center
Media Access Group at WGBH
One Guest St.
Boston, MA 02135   617-300-3600
                                                FAX: 617-300-1020
                                                  access@wgbh.org
Pat McDonald, Director
The Caption Center was the world's first captioning agency providing access to television for viewers who are visually impaired and/or hard of hearing. The Center develops new solutions and uses closed captioning and descriptive video to promote access to technology .

8875   Central Association for the Blind & Visually Impaired
507 Kent St.
Utica, NY 13501   315-797-2233
                                                     877-719-9996
                                                     www.cabvi.org
Edward P. Welsh, Chair
Kenneth C. Thayer, Vice Chair
Richard Evans, Treasurer
It assists people who are blind or visually impaired to achieve their highest levels of independence.

8876 Chicago Lighthouse for People who are Blind and Visually Impaired
1850 W Roosevelt Rd
Chicago, IL 60608-1298
312-666-1331
FAX: 312-243-8539
TTY:312-666-8874
www.chicagolighthouse.org

Bruce R. Hague, Chairman
Sandra C. Forsythe, Vice Chairman
Janet P. Szlyk, President

A non profit agency committed to providing the highest quality educational, clinical, vocational, and rehabilitation services for children, youth and adults who are blind or visually impaired, including deaf blind and multi disabled. Also respects personal dignity and partners with individuals to enhance independent living and self sufficiency. This agency is a leader, innovator and advocate for people who are blind or visually impaired, enhancing the quality of life for all individuals.

8877 Clovernook Center for the Blind and Visually Impaired
7000 Hamilton Ave
Cincinnati, OH 45231-5240
513-522-3860
888-234-7156
FAX: 513-728-3946
TTY:513-522-3860
contact@clovernook.org
www.clovernook.org

Alfred J. Tuchfarber, Chair
Wilbert F. Schwartz, Vice Chair
Mark Jackson, Treasurer

Mission is to promote independence and foster the highest quality of life for people with visual impairments, including those with additional disabilities. We provide comprehensive program services including training and support for independent living, orientation and mobility instruction, vocational training, job placement, counseling, recreation, and youth services. Meaningful employment opportunities are also provided to individuals who are blind or visually impaired.

8878 Clovernook Printing House, The Clovernook Center for the Blind and Visually Impaired
7000 Hamilton Ave
Cincinnati, OH 45231-5240
513-522-3860
888-234-7156
FAX: 513-728-3946
contact@clovernook.org
www.clovernook.org

Alfred J. Tuchfarber, Chair
Wilbert F. Schwartz, Vice Chair
Mark Jackson, Treasurer

Clovernook also offers Braille Transcription Services including: Literary Books, Literary Magazines, Religious Materials, Instructional Manuals, ADA Conformance Materials, Literary Textbook Materials, Menus, Braille Alphabet Cards, and Forms. In addition, our Business Operations provide meaningful employment opportunities for individuals who are blind or visually impaired, while at the same time manufacturing high-quality products for customers across the country. *$145.00*
591 pages
ISBN 1-930956-48-7

8879 College of Optometrists in Vision Development
215 W Garfield Rd
Ste 200
Aurora, OH 44202-7884
330-995-0718
888-268-3770
FAX: 330-995-0719
info@covd.org
www.covd.org

David A. Damari, President
Kara Heying, Vice President
Christine Allison, Secretary-Treasurer

The College of Optometrists in Vision Development (COVD) is an international membership association of eye care professionals including optometrists, optometry students, and vision therapists. Members of COVD provide developmental vision care, vision therapy and vision rehabilitation services for children and adults.

8880 College of Syntonic Optometry
2052 W Morales Dr.
Pueblo West, CO 81007
719-547-8177
877-559-0541
FAX: 719-547-3750
Syntonics@q.com
www.collegeofsyntonicoptometry.com

Hans Lessmann, O.D, FCOVD, President
Robert Fox, O.D, FCOVD, FCSO, Vice President
Larry Wallace, O.D, Ph.D, Education Director

The College of Syntonic Optometry is an international organization dedicated to furthering Phototherapy in the treatment of the visual system. Members of the college include optometrists, and health care professionals.

8881 Columbia Lighthouse for the Blind
1825 K St. NW
Suite 1103
Washington, DC 20006
202-454-6400
FAX: 202-955-6401
info@clb.org
www.clb.org

Tony Cancelosi, President & CEO
Jocelyn Hunter, Senior Director, Communications
Toya Horten, Director, Administrative Operations

Columbia Lighthouse for the Blind (CLB) helps blind and visually impaired individuals in Washington, DC. CLB's services include training and consultation in assistive technology, employment skills, career placement, low vision care, and counseling and rehabilitation services.

8882 DeafBlind Division of the National Federation of the Blind
200 E. Wells St.
at Jernigan Place
Baltimore, MD 21230
410-659-9314
FAX: 410-685-5653
nfb@nfb.org
www.nfb.org

Alice Eaddy, Division President

The nation's largest and most influential membership organization of blind persons, with a two-fold purpose: to help blind persons achieve self-confidence and self respect and to act as a vehicle for collective self-expression by the blind. The NFB improves blind people's lives through advocacy, education, research, technology, and programs encouraging independence and self-confidence. It is the leading force in the blindness field today and is the voice of the nations blind.

8883 Desert Blind & Handicapped Association
Desert Blind and Handicapped Association, Inc.
777 E Tahquitz Canyon Way
Suite 200
Palm Springs, CA 92262
760-969-5025
info@desertblind.org

Thomas Samulski, Executive Director
George Holliday, Treasurer

The Desert Blind & Handicapped Association provides free transportation for individuals who are blind or have a disability.

8884 Eye Bank Association of America
1101 17th St NW
Suite 400
Washington, DC 20036
202-775-4999
FAX: 202-429-6036
www.restoresight.org

Kevin P. Corcoran, CAE, President & CEO
Bernie Dellario, Director, Finance
Stacey Gardner, Director, Education

The Eye Bank Association of America (EBAA) is a nonprofit organization advocating the restoration of sight by advancing donation, transplantation, and research. The EBAA is the oldest transplant association in the United States.

8885 Fidelco Guide Dog Foundation
103 Vision Way
Bloomfield, CT 06002
860-243-5200
FAX: 860-769-0567
admissions@fidelco.org
www.fidelco.org

Karen C. Tripp, Chair
G. Kenneth Bernhard, Esq., Vice Chair
Gregg Barratt, Chief of Staff
The Fidelco Guide Dog Foundation creates increased freedom and independence for men and women who are blind by providing them with guide dogs.

8886 Fight for Sight
381 Park Ave S
Suite 809
New York, NY 10016
212-679-6060
FAX: 212-679-4466
Arthur@fightforsight.org
www.fightforsight.org

Arthur Makar, Executive Director
Janice Benson, Associate Director
Fight for Sight is a nonprofit charity working to support eye and vision research through the providing of funds to scientists starting their careers.

8887 Foundation Fighting Blindness
7168 Columbia Gateway Dr.
Suite 100
Columbia, MD 21046
410-423-0600
800-683-5555
TTY:410363713951
info@FightBlindness.org
www.blindness.org

William T. Schmidt, Chief Executive Officer
Valerie Navy-Daniels, Chief Development Officer
Stephen M. Rose, PhD, Chief Research Officer
The Foundation Fighting Blindness (FFB) works to promote research in order to prevent, treat and restore vision. FFB is currently the world's leading private funder of retinal disease research, funding over 100 research grants and 150 researchers.

8888 Guide Dogs for the Blind
PO Box 151200
San Rafael, CA 94915
800-295-4050
information@guidedogs.com
www.guidedogs.com

Christine Benninger, Chief Executive Officer & President
Cathy Martin, Chief Financial Officer & Treasurer
Brent Ruppel, Vice President, Community Operations
Guide Dogs for the Blind empowers lives by creating exceptional partnerships between people, dogs, and communities. All of their services provided free of charge to their clients, including personalized training and extensive post-graduation support, plus financial assistance for veterinary care, if needed.

8889 Guiding Eyes for the Blind
611 Granite Springs Rd
Yorktown Heights, NY 10598-3499
914-245-4024
800-942-0149
FAX: 914-245-1609
info@guidingeyes.org
www.guidingeyes.org
Thomas Panek, President & Chief Executive Officer
Guiding Eyes for the Blind is a nonprofit organization providing guide dogs for individuals who are blind or visually impaired.

8890 Horizons for the Blind
125 Erick St.
A103
Crystal Lake, IL 60014
815-444-8800
800-318-2000
FAX: 815-444-8830
mail@horizons-blind.org
www.horizons-blind.org

Camille Caffarelli, Executive Director
Jeff T. Thorsen, First Vice President & Treasurer
Keith Myers, Second Vice President
Horizons for the Blind is a nonprofit organization working to improve the quality of life for people who are blind or visually im-

paired by increasing access to consumer products, services, culture, arts, education, and recreation.

8891 Independent Visually Impaired Entrepreneurs
818-238-9321
abazyn@bazyncommunications.com
www.ivie-acb.org
Ardis Bazyn, President
The Independent Visually Impaired Entrepreneurs (IVIE) is a national organization for visually impaired business owners. The IVIE offers an annual convention, planning a program of interest for business owners.

8892 Institute for Families
1300 N Vermont Ave.
Suite 1004
Los Angeles, CA 90027
323-361-4649
FAX: 323-665-7869
info@instituteforfamilies.org
instituteforfamilies.org

Gary Huffaker, Chairperson
Institute for Families is a nonprofit organization providing support and information for families of children with vision loss. The Institute provides guidance through a resource and referral network; referring families to organizations specializing in meeting the needs of children with specific vision loss problems.

8893 International Association of Audio Information Services
800-280-5325
iaaismember@gmail.com
www.iaais.org

Marjorie Moore, President
Maryfrances Evans, Vice-President
The International Association of Audio Information Services (IAAIS) is a membership organization that works to turn text into speech and providing information through broadcast, telephone or internet. IAAIS connects and supports organizations that deliver equal access information for people with disabilities worldwide.

8894 Jewish Braille Institute International
JBI International
110 E 30th St
New York, NY 10016-7393
212-889-2525
800-433-1531
FAX: 212-689-3692
admin@jbilibrary.org
www.jbilibrary.org

Dr. Ellen Isler, President & Chief Executive Officer
Israel A. Taub, Vice President & Chief Financial Officer
The Jewish Braille Institute (JBI) International is a nonprofit organization working to meet the Jewish and general cultural needs of the blind and visually impaired.

8895 Keystone Blind Association
3056 East State St.
Hermitage, PA 16148
724-347-5501
FAX: 724-347-2204
info@keystoneblind.org
www.keystoneblind.org

Jonathan Fister, President/CEO
Karen Anderson, Board Member
Sam Bellich, Board Member
The Keystone Blind Association works to education, and employ individuals with vision loss. Headquartered in Hermitage, the Association has offices in Meadville and New Castle, Pennsylvania.

8896 Lighthouse Guild
250 West 64th Street
New York, NY 10023
800-284-4422
www.lighthouseguild.org

Calvin W. Roberts, President & CEO
James M. Dubin, Chairman
Lawrence E. Goldschmidt, Vice Chairman & Treasurer
Lighthouse Guild is a not-for-profit vision & healthcare organization, addressing the needs of people who are blind or visually impaired, including those with multiple disabilities or chronic medical conditions.

8897 Lions Clubs International
300 W 22nd St
Oak Brook, IL 60523-8842
630-571-5466
FAX: 630-571-8890
TTY:630-571-6533
lions@lionsclubs.org
www.lionsclubs.org

Benedict Ancar, Director
Jui-Tai Chang, Director
Jaime Garcia Cepeda, Director
Our 46,000 clubs and 1.35 million members make us the world's largest service club organization. We're also one of the most effective. Our members do whatever is needed to help their local communities. Everywhere we work, we make friends. With children who need eyeglasses, with seniors who don't have enough to eat and with people we may never meet.

8898 Macular Degeneration Foundation
PO Box 531313
Henderson, NV 89053-1313
702-450-2908
888-633-3937
liz@eyesight.org
www.eyesight.org

Liz Trauernicht, President/Director of Communications
Julie Zavala, VP/Asst Director of Operations
David Seftel, M.D., MBA, Executive Vice President/Director of Research Development
The Macular Degeneration Foundation is dedicated to those who have and will develop macular degeneration. We offer this growing community the latest information, news, hope and encouragement.

8899 National Alliance of Blind Students NABS Liaison
American Council of the Blind
1155 15th St NW
Ste 1004
Washington, DC 20005-2706
202-467-5081
800-424-8666
FAX: 202-467-5085
info@acb.org
www.acb.org

Jill Gaus, President
Lynn Jansen, Vice President
Debby Lieberman, Secretary
A student affiliate of the American Council of the Blind which is a national organization of blind and visually impaired high school and college students who believe that every blind and visually impaired student has the right to an equal and accessible education. Also encourages blind and visually impaired students to challenge their limits and reach their potential.

8900 National Association for Parents of Children with Visual Impairments (NAPVI)
PO Box 317
Watertown, MA 02471-317
617-972-7441
800-562-6265
FAX: 617-972-7444
spedex.com@gmail.com
www.spedex.com

Susan LaVenture, Executive Director
Julie Urban, President
Venetia Hayden, Vice President
A non profit organization of, by and for parents committed to providing support to the parents of children who have visual impairments . Also a national organization that enables parents to find information and resources for their children who are blind or visually impaired including those with additional disabilities. NAPVI also provides leadership, support, and training to assist parents in helping children reach their potential.

8901 National Association for Visually Handicapped (NAVH)
111 E 59th S
Fl 6
New York, NY 10022-1202
212-889-3141
800-829-0500
FAX: 212-821-9707
TTY: 212-821-9713
info@lighthouse.org
www.lighthouse.org

Alan R. Morse, President & CEO
Lawrence E. Goldschmidt, Deputy Chair & Secretary
Himanshu R. Shah, CFO
NAVH is unique in the services it offers to the hard of seeing™ worldwide and is the only non-profit organization solely dedicated to providing assistance to this population. NAVH runs senior support groups, provides individual consultations, informational materials, training in the use of visual aids, and numerous other tools to ensure that the visually impaired can remain independent and lead fulfilling lives.

8902 National Association of Blind Educators
National Federation of the Blind
200 E. Wells St.
at Jernigan Place
Baltimore, MD 21230
410-659-9314
FAX: 410-685-5653
nfb@nfb.org
www.nfb.org

Cayte Mendez, Division President
Membership organization of blind teachers, professors and instructors in all levels of education. Provides support and information regarding professional responsibilities, classroom techniques, national testing methods and career obstacles. Publishes The Blind Educator, national magazine specifically for blind educators.

8903 National Association of Blind Lawyers
National Federation of the Blind
200 E. Wells St.
at Jernigan Place
Baltimore, MD 21230
410-659-9314
FAX: 410-685-5653
nfb@nfb.org
www.nfb.org

Scott LaBarre, President
Membership organization of blind attorneys, law students, judges and others in the law field. Provides support and information regarding employment, techniques used by the blind, advocacy, laws affecting the blind, current information about the American Bar Association and other issues for blind lawyers.

8904 National Association of Blind Merchants (NABM)
National Federation of the Blind
7450 Chapman Hwy.
Suite 319
Knoxville, TN 37920
888-687-6226
president@merchants-nfb.org
blindmerchants.org

Nicky Gacos, President
Ed Birmingham, First Vice President
Michael Colbrunn, Second Vice President
Serving as an advocacy and support group, NABM is a membership organization of blind persons employed in self-employment work or the Randolph-Sheppard Vending Program. The organization provides information on issues affecting blind merchants, including rehabilitation, social security, and tax.

8905 National Association of Blind Rehabilitation Professionals
National Federation of the Blind
200 E. Wells St.
at Jernigan Place
Baltimore, MD 21230
410-659-9314
FAX: 410-685-5653
nfb@nfb.org
www.nfb.org

Amy Porterfield, Division President
Membership organization.

8906 National Association of Blind Students
National Federation of the Blind
200 E. Wells St.
at Jernigan Place
Baltimore, MD 21230   410-659-9314
                                   FAX: 410-685-5653
                                        nfb@nfb.org
                                        www.nfb.org

Trisha Kulkarni, Division President

For over 30 years this national organization of blind students has provided support, information, and encouragement to blind college and university students. NABS leads the way in offering resources in issues such as national testing, accessible textbooks and materials, overcoming negative attitudes about blindness from school personnel, developing new techniques of accomplishing laboratory or field assignments, and many other college experiences.

8907 National Association of Blind Teachers
American Council of the Blind
1155 15th St NW
Ste 1004
Washington, DC 20005-2706   202-467-5081
                                        800-424-8666
                                   FAX: 202-467-5085
                             johnbuckley25@hotmail.com
                                     www.blindteachers.net

Jill Gaus, President
Lynn Jansen, Vice President
Debby Lieberman, Secretary

Works to advance the teaching profession for blind and visually impaired people, protects the interest of teachers, presents discussions and solutions for special problems encountered by blind teachers and publishes a directory of blind teachers in the US.

8908 National Association of Blind Veterans
PO Box 784957
Winter Garden, FL 34778   321-948-1466
                                      president@nabv.org
                                        www.nabv.org

Dwight Sayer, President
Gene Huggins, 1st Vice President
Larry Ball, 2nd Vice President

A nationwide organization of blind and visually impaired veterans striving to serve fellow veterans who have lost their sight in the service of country or have lost their sight after serving country.

8909 National Association of Guide Dog Users
National Federation of the Blind
1003 Papaya Dr
Tampa, FL 33619-4629   813-626-2789
                                        800-558-8261
                                        888-624-3841
                                     president@nagdu.org
                                        www.nagdu.org

Marion Gwizdala, President

Provides information and support for guide dog users and works to secure high standards in guide dog training. Addresses issues of discrimination of guide dog users and offers public education about guide dog use. Biennial newsletter available: Harness Up!

8910 National Association to Promote the Use of Braille
National Federation of the Blind
39481 Gallaudet Dr
Apt 127
Fremont, CA 94538   510-248-0100
                                        877-558-6524
                                   FAX: 818-344-7930
                             mwillows@sbcglobal.net
                                        www.nfbcal.org

Nadine Jacobson, President
Robert Jaquiss, Vice President
Linda Mentink, Second Vice President

Dedicated to securing improved Braille instruction, increasing the number of braille materials available to the blind and providing information of braille in securing independence, education and employment for the blind.

8911 National Beep Baseball Association
1501 41st NW
Apt G1
Rochester, MN 55901   866-400-4551
                                        www.nbba.org

Stephen A. Guerra, Secretary

It facilitates and provides the adaptive version of America's favorite pastime for the blind, low vision and legally blind.

8912 National Braille Association
95 Allens Creek Rd
Bldg 1 Ste 202
Rochester, NY 14618- 3252   585-427-8260
                                   FAX: 585-427-0263
                             nbaoffice@nationalbraille.org
                                   www.nationalbraille.org

David Shaffar, Executive Director
Jan Carroll, President
Whitney Gregory-Williams, Vice President

The only national organization dedicated to the professional development of individuals who prepare and produce braille materials.

8913 National Braille Press
88 Saint Stephen St
Boston, MA 02115-4312   617-266-6160
                                        888-965-8965
                                        888-965-8965
                                   FAX: 617-437-0456
                                        contact@nbp.org
                                        www.nbp.org

Brian A. Mac Donald, President
Kimberley Ballard, Vice President
Tony Grima, Vice President of Braille Publications

The guiding purposes of National Braille Press are to promote the literacy of blind children through braille, and to provide access to information that empowers blind people to actively engage in work, family, and commuity affairs.

8914 National Center for Vision and Child Development
Lighthouse Guild
250 West 64th Street
New York, NY 10023   800-284-4422
                                     www.lighthouseguild.org

Calvin W. Roberts, President & CEO
James M. Dubin, Chairman
Lawrence E. Goldschmidt, Vice Chairman & Treasurer

The worldwide leader in helping people of all ages who are blind or partially sighted overcome the challenges of vision loss.

8915 National Diabetes Action Network for the Blind
National Federation of the Blind
200 E. Wells St.
at Jernigan Place
Baltimore, MD 21230   410-659-9314
                                   FAX: 410-685-5653
                             bernienfb75@gmail.com
                                        www.nfb.org

Debbie Wunder, Division President

Leading support and information organization of persons losing vision due to diabetes. Provides personal contact and resource information with other blind diabetics about non-visual techniques of independently managing diabetes, monitoring glucose levels, measuring insulin and other matters concerning diabetes. Publishes Voice of the Diabetic, the leading publication about diabetes and blindness.

8916 National Eye Institute
National Institutes of Health
31 Center Dr.
MSC 2510
Bethesda, MD 20892-2510   301-496-5248
                                        2020@nei.nih.gov
                                        www.nei.nih.gov

Michael F. Chiang, Director
Santa Tumminia, Deputy Director
Melanie Reagan, Acting Executive Officer

To conduct and support research for blinding eye diseases, visual disorders, mechanisms of visual function, and the preservation of sight.

8917 National Federation of the Blind
200 E. Wells St.
at Jernigan Place
Baltimore, MD 21230   410-659-9314
                              FAX: 410-685-5653
                                  nfb@nfb.org
                                  www.nfb.org

Mark A. Riccobono, President
John Berggren, Executive Director, Operations
Anil Lewis, Executive Director, Blindness Initiatives
The National Federation of the Blind (NFB) works to help blind
people achieve self-confidence, self-respect and self-determination and to achieve complete integration into society on a basis of
equality. The Federation provides public educations, information
and referral services, scholarships, literature and publications,
adaptive equipment, advocacy services, legal services,
employment assistance and more.

8918 National Industries for the Blind
1310 Braddock Pl
Alexandria, VA 22314-1691   703-310-0500
                              FAX: 703-998-8268
                                  info@nib.org
                                  www.nib.org

Gary J. Krump, Chairperson
Ronald Tascarella, Vice Chairperson
A nonprofit organization that represents over 100 associated industries serving people who are blind in thirty-six states. These
agencies serve people who are blind or visually impaired and help
them to reach their full potential. Services include job and family
counseling, job skills training, instruction in Braille and other
communication skills, children's programs and more.

**8919 National Library Service for the Blind and Physically
Handicapped (NLS)**
1291 Taylor St NW
Washington, DC 20011   202-707-5100
                                            800-424-8567
                              FAX: 202-707-0712
                                  nls@loc.gov
                                  www.loc.gov/nls
Administers a national library service that provides Braille and
recorded books and magazines on free loan to anyone who cannot
read standard print because of visual or physical disabilities.
Annual

8920 National Organization of Parents of Blind Children
National Federation of the Blind
200 E. Wells St.
at Jernigan Place
Baltimore, MD 21230   410-659-9314
                              FAX: 410-685-5653
                                  nfb@nfb.org
                                  www.nfb.org

Carlton Walker, Division President
Support information and advocacy organization of parents of
blind or visually impaired children. Addresses issues ranging
from help to parents of a newborn blind infant, mobility and
braille instruction, education, social and community participation, development of self-confidence and other vital factors
involved in growth of a blind child.

8921 New Eyes for the Needy
549 Millburn Avenue
PO Box 332
Short Hills, NJ 07078-332   973-376-4903
                              FAX: 973-376-3807
                       neweyesfortheneedy@verizon.net
                              www.neweyesfortheneedy.org
Susan Dyckman, Executive Director
Marianne Muench Busby, Vice President
Barbara Daney, Treasurer
New Eyes provides new prescription glasses for poor children
and adults in the U.S. through a voucher system.

8922 Prevent Blindness America
211 W Wacker Drive
Suite 1700
Chicago, IL 60606   312-363-6001
                                            800-331-2020
                              FAX: 312-363-6052
                           info@preventblindness.org
                              www.preventblindness.org

James E. Anderson, Chair
Kira Baldanado, Director
Arzu Bilazer, Creative Director
The nation's leading volunteer eye health and safety organization
dedicated to fighting blindness and saving sight. Also touches the
lives of millions of people each year through public and professional education, advocacy, certified vision screening training,
community and patient service programs and research.

8923 Seeing Eye, The
10 Washington Valley Rd
PO Box 375
Morristown, NJ 07963-0375   973-539-4425
                              FAX: 973-539-0922
                                  info@seeingeye.org
                                  www.seeingeye.org

Peggy Gibbon, Director of Canine Development
James A Kutsch Jr, President/CEO
Dolores Holle, VMD, Director of Canine Medicine & Surgery
An organization that concentrates on its mission to enhance the
independence, dignity, and self confidence of blind people
through the use of seeing eye dogs. The Seeing Eye will be an organization that concentrates on its mission to enhance the independence, dignity, and self confidence of blind people through
the use of Seeing Eye dogs, and on improving its ability to fulfill
this mission. We will maintain and nuture the spirit of our founders and adhere to the highest standards of respect

8924 Society for the Blind
1238 S St.
Sacramento, CA 95811   916-452-8271
                              FAX: 916-492-2483
                          info@societyfortheblind.org
                              societyfortheblind.org

Shari Roeseler, Executive Director
Shane Snyder, Director of Programs
Serving 26 counties in Northern California, Society for the Blind
is a full service, nonprofit, agency providing services and programs for people who are blind or have low vision. services include the Low Vision Clinic, Braille Classes, computer training,
support groups, living skills instruction, mobility training, and
the Products for Independence Store.

8925 United States Association of Blind Athletes
1 Olympic Plaza
Colorado Springs, CO 80909-3508   719-866-3224
                              FAX: 719-866-3400
                                  mlucas@usaba.org
                                  www.usaba.org

Mark A. Lucas, Executive Director
Ryan Ortiz, Assistant Executive Director
John Potts, Goalball High Performance Director
USABA is a Colorado-based 501(c) (3) organization that provides life-enriching sports opportunities for every individual
with a visual impairment. A member of the U.S. Olympic Committee, USABA provides athletic opportunities in various sports
including, but not limited to track and field, nordic and alpine skiing, biathlon, judo, wrestling, swimming, tandem cycling,
powerlifting and goalball (a team sport for the blind and visually
impaired).

8926 United States Blind Golfers Association
125 Gilberts Hill Rd
Lehighton, PA 18235   615-679-9629
                                  info@usblindgolf.com
                                  www.usblindgolf.com

Jim Baker, President
Diane Wilson, Vice President
Tony Schiros, Board Member
It encourages and enhances opportunities of blind and visually
impaired golfers to compete in golf.

8927 **United States Braille Chess Association**
1881 N. Nash St.
Unit 702
Arlington, VA 22209 516-223-8685
www.americanblindchess.org

LA Pietrolungo, President
Alan Dicey, Vice President
Jay Leventhal, Secretary

It is dedicated to encourage and assist in the promotion and advancement of correspondence and over-the board chess among chess enthusiasts who are blind or visually impaired.

8928 **Vermont Association for the Blind and Visually Impaired**
60 Kimball Ave
South Burlington, VT 05403 802-863-1358
800-639-5861
FAX: 802-863-1481
general@vabvi.org
www.vabvi.org

James Mooney, President
Thomas Chase, Vice President
Debbie Balserus, Secretary

The Vermont Association for the Blind and Visually Impaired (VABVI), a non-profit organization founded in 1926, is the only private agency to offer free training, services and support to visually impaired Vermonters. Each year we serve hundreds of children from birth to age 22 and adults age 55 and over.

8929 **Vision Forward Association**
912 N. Hawley Road
Milwaukee, WI 53213 414-615-0100
855-878-6056
FAX: 414-256-8748
www.vision-forward.org

Terri Davis, Executive Director
Jacci Borchardt, Program Director
Jacque Cline, Human Resources Director

Its mission is to empower, educate, and enhance the lives of individuals impacted by vision loss through all of life's transitions.

8930 **Vision World Wide**
Apt 302
5707 Brockton Dr
Indianapolis, IN 46220-5481 317-254-1332
800-431-1739
FAX: 317-251-6588
www.visionww.org

Patricia L Prince, President

A non profit organization dedicated to improving the lives of the vision impaired through direct interaction and indirectly through the caregiving community. Also serve both the totally blind and those with various degrees and forms of vision loss.

8931 **Visions Center on Blindness (VCB)**
111 Summit Park Rd.
Spring Valley, NY 10977 845-354-3003
888-245-8333
info@visionsvcb.org
www.visionsvcb.org

Nancy D. Miller, Executive Director & CEO
Natalia S. Young, Chief Operating Officer
Carlos Cabrera, Chief Financial Officer

VISIONS VCB is a 35-acre year round residential rehabilitation and training center in Rockland County, New York. VCB offers comprehensive overnight training and vision rehabilitation facilities.

8932 **Visually Impaired Veterans of America**
American Council of the Blind
1155 15th St NW
Ste 1004
Washington, DC 20005-2706 202-467-5081
800-424-8666
FAX: 202-467-5085
www.acb.org

Jill Gaus, President
Lynn Jansen, Vice President
Debby Lieberman, Secretary

Maintain, promote and foster the well bring and rehabilitation of all visually Impaired Veterans of the Armed Forces of the United States of America who are eligible to receive from the Veterans Administration; develops and encourages the practice of high standards of personal professional conduct among Visually Impaired Veterans; maintain, promote, and foster public confidence and awareness In Visually Impaired Veterans.

8933 **Washington Ear**
12061 Tech Rd.
Silver Spring, MD 20904 301-681-6636
FAX: 301-625-1986
information@washear.org
www.washear.org

Terry Pacheco, President
Amir Rahimi, Secretary
John F. Anderschat, Treasurer

A nonprofit organization providing reading and information services for blind, visually impaired and physically disabled people who cannot effectively read print, see plays, watch television programs and films, or view museum exhibits. Ear free services strive to substitute hearing for seeing, improving the lives of people with limited or no vision by enabling them to be well-informed, fully productive members of their families, their communities and the working world.

Camps

8934 **Camp Barakel**
P.O.Box 159
Fairview, MI 48621-0159 989-848-2279
FAX: 989-848-2280
info@campbarakel.org
www.campbarakel.org

Paul Gardner, Camp Director
Hannah Gardner, Music Coordinator
Jon Ford, Head Lifeguard

Five-day Christian camp experience in mid-August for campers ages 18-55 who are physically disabled, visually impaired, upper trainable mentally impaired or educable mentally impaired, bus transportation provided from locations in Lansing, Flint and Bay City, Michigan.

8935 **Camp Bloomfield**
Wayfinder Family Services
5300 Angeles Vista Blvd.
Los Angeles, CA 90043 323-295-4555
FAX: 323-296-0424
JLucas@WayfinderFamily.org
www.wayfinderfamily.org

Miki Jordan, Chief Executive Officer
Jay Allen, President & Chief Operating Officer
Fernando Almodovar, Chief Financial Officer

Camp Bloomfield is a summer camp with week long sessions for children and youth who are blind, visually impaired or multi-disabled. The 45 acre campground offers campers a variety of activities, specifically designed to meet the needs of the children, with campers attending at no cost.

8936 **Camp Challenge**
8914 US Highway 50 East
Bedford, IN 47421 812-834-5159
info@gocampchallenge.com
www.gocampchallenge.com

Brian , Executive Director
Maria , Director of Engagement

One and two-week sessions for campers with developmental and or physical disabilities, hearing impairment and the blind/visually impaired. Ages 6-99 and families.

8937 **Camp Lawroweld**
288 West Side Rd.
Weld, ME 04285 207-585-2984
bchase@nnec.org
www.camplawroweld.org

Trevor Schlisner, Director

Camp is located in Weld, Maine. Offers various camp sessions, including a week-long camp for individuals who are blind or visually impaired.

8938   Camp Lighthouse
Columbia Lighthouse for the Blind
1825 K St. NW
Suite 1103
Washington, DC 20006   202-454-6400
                                         FAX: 202-955-6401
                                              info@clb.org
                                               www.clb.org

Tony Cancelosi, President & CEO
Jocelyn Hunter, Senior Director, Communications
Toya Horten, Director, Administrative Operations
Camp Lighthouse is a one week day camp program for children
ages 6-12 with visual impairments. Activities include games, rec-
reation, arts and crafts, field trips, and braille activities.

8939   Camp Lou Henry Hoover
Girl Scouts of Washington Rock Council
201 East Grove Street
Westfield, NJ 07090   908-518-4400
                                         FAX: 908-232-4508
                                         girlscouts@gshnj.org
                                              www.gshnj.org

Samantha Basek, Field Executive
Susan Brooks, CEO
Camp is located in Middleville, New Jersey. Sessions for girls
who are blind/visually impaired, ages 7-18.

8940   Camp Merrick
PO Box 56
Nanjemoy, MD 20662   301-870-5858
                                         FAX: 301-246-9108
                                       info@lionscampmerrick.org
                                        www.lionscampmerrick.org
Heidi A. Fick, Executive Director
Donna Wadsworth, Office Administrator
Programs offered April-January for children who are blind/visu-
ally impaired, hearing impaired or diabetic. Coed, ages 6-16.

8941   Camp Winnekeag
257 Ashby Road
Ashburnham, MA 01430   978-827-4455
                                         FAX: 978-827-4551
                                     sneconference@sneconline.org
                                          www.campwinnekeag.com
Frank Tochterman, Religious Leader
Camp is located in Ashburnham, Massachusetts. Camping ses-
sions for blind/visually impaired children. Coed, ages 8-16.

8942   Enchanted Hills Camp for the Blind
Lighthouse for the Blind
1155 Market St.
10th Floor
San Francisco, CA 94103   415-431-1481
                                         FAX: 415-863-7568
                                         info@lighthouse-sf.org
                                           www.lighthouse-sf.org

W. Brandon Cox, Chief Operating Officer
Michelle Knapik, Chief Financial Officer
Enchanted Hills Camp for the Blind is located on 311 acres of
land on Mt. Veeder, offering programs for children, teens, adults,
deaf-blind, seniors, and families of the blind. The camp gives
campers the experience of traditional summer camp but is
adapted to meet the needs of the campers.

8943   Highbrook Lodge
Cleveland Sight Center
1909 E 101st St.
Cleveland, OH 44106   216-791-8118
                                         FAX: 216-791-1101
                                         TTY:216-791-8119
                                    info@clevelandsightcenter.org
                                     www.clevelandsightcenter.org
Larry Benders, President & CEO
Kevin Krencisz, Chief Financial & Administrative Officer
Jassen Tawil, Director, Business Development & Customer Success
Camp is located in Chardon, Ohio. Summer sessions for children,
adults and families who are blind or have low vision. Sessions
inclide a wide range of outdoor camp activities. Camp activities
focus on gaining independent skills, mobility, orientation and
self-confidence in an accessible and traditional camp setting.

8944   Indian Creek Camp
Kentucky Tennessee Conference
150 Cabin Circle Drive
Liberty, TN 37095   615-548-4411
                                         FAX: 615-548-4029
                                        www.indiancreekcamp.com

Ken Wetmore, Director
Marty Sutton, Asst. Director
Toni Stephens, Program Director
Camp is located in Liberty, Tennessee. Summer sessions for chil-
dren and adults who are blind/visually impaired. Coed, ages 7-17,
families and seniors.

8945   Kamp A-Komp-Plish
9035 Ironsides Rd
Nanjemoy, MD 20662-3432   301-870-3226
                                                301-934-3590
                                         FAX: 301-870-2620
                                       recreation@melwood.org

Jonathan Rondeau, Chief Program Officer
Bekah Carmichael, Director
Doria Fleisher, Associate Director
Camp is located in Nanjemoy, Maryland. Half-week, one-week
and two-week sessions for blind/visually impaired children and
those with developmental disabilities and mobility limitation.
Coed, ages 8-16.

8946   Kamp Kaleo
46872 Willow Springs Rd.
Burwell, NE 68823   308-346-5083
                                        kampkaleo@gmail.com
                                          www.kampkaleo.com

David Butz, Camp Administrator
Offers an overnight summer camp for individuals with developmental disabilities. In addition to regular camp activities, there is
a strong focus on religious education.

8947   National Camps for Blind Children
Christian Record Services
5900 S 58th St.
Suite M
Lincoln, NE 68516   402-488-0981
                                         FAX: 402-488-7582
                                        info@christianrecord.org
                                         www.christianrecord.org
Diane Thurber, President
Lonnie Kreiter, Vice President, Finance
Christian Record Services runs National Camps for Blind Chil-
dren, summer camps for individuals who are considered legally
blind.

8948   Texas Lions Camp
PO Box 290247
Kerrville, TX 78029   830-896-8500
                                         FAX: 830-896-3666
                                         tlc@lionscamp.com
                                           www.lionscamp.com
Stephen S. Mabry, President & CEO
Karen-Anne King, Vice President, Summer Camps
Milton Dare, Director, Development
Texas Lions Camp is a camp dedicated to serving children ages
7-16 in Texas with physical disabilities. While at camp, campers
will participate in a variety of activities and be encouraged to be-
come more independent and self-confident.

8949   VISIONS Vacation Camp for the Blind (VCB)
VISIONS Center on Blindness
111 Summit Park Rd.
Spring Valley, NY 10977   845-354-3003
                                                888-245-8333
                                         info@visionsvcb.org
                                           www.visionsvcb.org
Krystal Findley-Jones, Director
A nonprofit agency that promotes the independence of people of
all ages who are blind or visually impaired. Camp offers Braille
classes, computers with large print and voice output, support
groups, discussions, cooking classes, personal and home management training, and large print and Braille books.

8950 Wendell Johnson Speech And Hearing Clinic
University Of Iowa
250 Hawkins Dr
Iowa City, IA 52242-1025   319-335-8736
                                  FAX: 319-335-8851
                                  kathy-miller@uiowa.edu
                                  www.uiowa.edu
Chuck Wieland, President
Hans Hoerschelman, Vice President
Josh Smith, Budget Officer
The clinic offers assessment and intervention for communication disorders in adults and children as well as an audiology clinic. The clinic also offers several summer programs for children with hearing, speech, language, autism and/or reading disorders, including a summer residential program for teens who stutter.

8951 YMCA Camp Chingachgook on Lake George
Capital District YMCA
1872 Pilot Knob Rd.
Kattskill Bay, NY 12844   518-656-9462
                                 FAX: 518-656-9362
                                 chingachgook@cdymca.org
                                 www.lakegeorgecamp.org
Jine Andreozzi, Executive Director
Mike Obermayer, Director, Summer Program
Carol Lewis, Office Manager
Offers sailing programs for people with disabilities.

Books

8952 A Christian Approach to Overcoming Disability: A Doctor's Story
Routledge (Taylor & Francis Group)
711 Third Ave.
New York, NY 10017   212-216-7800
                            FAX: 212-564-7854
                            orders@taylorandfrancis.com
                            www.routledge.com
Dr. Elaine Leong Eng, M.D.
A personal account of Dr. Elaine Leong Eng and her career move from obstetrician/gynecologist to full-time mom, as she faces the diagnosis of impending visual impairment. Dr. Eng offers personal experience and faith-based, psychological techniques for coping with disability.
142 pages Hardcover

8953 AFB Directory of Services for Blind and Visually Impaired Persons in the US and Canada
American Foundation for the Blind/AFB Press
2 Penn Plaza
Suite 1102
New York, NY 10121   212-502-7600
                            800-232-5463
                            FAX: 888-545-8331
                            afbinfo@afb.net
                            www.afb.org
Carl Augusto, President & Chief Executive Officer
Rick Bozeman, Finance Director, Chief Financial Officer
Kelly Bleach, Chief Administrative Officer
Comprehensive print resource containing more that 2,500 local, state, regional, and national services throughout the US and Canada for persons who are blind or visually impaired. *$79.95*
624 pages Paperback/onlin
ISBN 0-891288-05-3

8954 About Children's Eyes
National Association for Visually Handicapped
111 East 59th Street
New York, NY 10022-1202   212-821-9384
                                 800-829-0500
                                 FAX: 212-821-9707
                                 info@lighthouse.org
                                 lighthouse.org/navh
Mark G. Ackermann, President/CEO
How to identify the child with a visual problem. LightHouse acquired NAVH.

8955 About Children's Vision: A Guide for Parents
National Association for Visually Handicapped
111 East 59th Street
New York, NY 10022-1202   212-821-9384
                                 800-829-0500
                                 FAX: 212-821-9707
                                 info@lighthouse.org
                                 lighthouse.org/navh
Mark G. Ackermann, President/CEO
Offers a better understanding of the normal and possible abnormal development of a child's eyesight. LightHouse acquired NAVH. *$.50*

8956 Access to Art: A Museum Directory for Blind and Visually Impaired People
American Foundation for the Blind/AFB Press
2 Penn Plaza
Suite 1102
New York, NY 10121   212-502-7600
                            800-232-5463
                            FAX: 888-545-8331
                            afbinfo@afb.net
                            www.afb.org
Carl R. Augusto, President & Chief Executive Officer
Rick Bozeman, Finance Director, Chief Financial Officer
Kelly Bleach, Chief Administrative Officer
Details the access facilities of over 300 museums, galleries and exhibits in the United States. Also included are organizations offering art-related resources such as, art classes, competitions and traveling exhibits. *$19.95*
144 pages Large Print
ISBN 0-891281-56-8

8957 African Americans in the Profession of Blindness Services
Mississippi State University
P.O.Box 6189
Mississippi State, MS 39762   662-325-2001
                                     FAX: 662-325-8989
                                     TTY:662-325-2694
                                     nrtc@colled.msstate.edu
                                     www.blind.msstate.edu
Jacqui Bybee, Research Associate II
Douglas Bedsaul, Research and Training Coordinator
Anne Carter, Research and Training Coordinator
This study investigated the level of participation by African Americans in vocational rehab. (VR) services to persons who are visually impaired. Using surveys and interviews with all state VR directors, national census data and national RSA data, it was found nationally that African Americans are substantially under-represented in the service provider ranks, yet over-represented as clients. *$20.00*
61 pages Paperback

8958 Age-Related Macular Degeneration
National Association for Visually Handicapped
111 East 59th Street
New York, NY 10022-1202   212-821-9384
                                 800-829-0500
                                 FAX: 212-821-9707
                                 info@lighthouse.org
                                 lighthouse.org/navh
Mark G. Ackermann, President/CEO
A large booklet offering information and up-to-date research on Macular Degeneration. Also available in Russian. Revised in 2007. LightHouse acquired NAVH. *$5.00*

8959 American Anals of the Deaf Reference
800 Florida Ave NE
Washington, DC 20002-3600   202-651-5530
                                   FAX: 202-651-5489
                                   gupress@gallaudet.edu
                                   gupress.gallaudet.edu/annals
Stephanie Cawthon, Ph.D., Book Review Editor
Peter V. Paul, Ph.D., Editor, Literary Issues
Ye Wang, Ph.D., Senior Associate Editor
The controlled scope of GUPress operations allows the continuance of a highly focused commitment to individual titles that has contributed significantly to its 20 years of leadership in publishing on Deaf issues. Gallaudet University Press brings unmatched

experience and knowledge to the marketplace for books on and for the Deaf community, its advocates, and scholars invested in the study of deaf society.

8960 Americans with Disabilities Act Guide for Places of Lodging: Serving Guests Who Are Blind
US Department of Justice
950 Pennsylvania Ave. NW
Washington, DC 20530

202-307-0663
800-514-0301
FAX: 202-307-1197
TTY: 800-514-0383
www.ada.gov

Rebecca B. Bond, Chief
Anne Raish, Principal Deputy Chief
Christina Galindo-Walsh, Deputy Chief
A 12-page publication explaining what hotels, motels, and other places of transient lodging can do to accommodate guests who are blind or have low vision.

8961 Art and Science of Teaching Orientation and Mobility to Persons with Visual Impairments
American Foundation for the Blind/AFB Press
2 Penn Plaza
Suite 1102
New York, NY 10121

212-502-7600
800-232-5463
FAX: 888-545-8331
afbinfo@afb.net
www.afb.org

Carl R. Augusto, President & Chief Executive Officer
Rick Bozeman, Finance Director, Chief Financial Officer
Kelly Bleach, Chief Administrative Officer
Comprehensive decription of the techniques of teaching orientation and mobility, presented along with considerations and strategies for sensitive and effective teaching. Hardcover. Paperback also available. *$48.00*
200 pages
ISBN 0-891282-45-9

8962 Awareness Training
Landmark Media
3450 Slade Run Drive
Falls Church, VA 22042

703-241-2030
800-342-4336
FAX: 703-536-9540
info@landmarkmedia.com

Michael Hartogs, President
Peter Hartogs, VP New Business & Development
Richard Hartogs, VP Acquisitions
Covers disabilities of various types — vision, hearing, speech disorders, loss of limbs, loss of mobility, or mental/emotional limitations and how to integrate such individuals into various business and educational settings. It is a 4-part series designed to identify and enable others to interact effectively with those suffering such disabilities. *$495.00*
Set of 4

8963 Babycare Assistive Technology
Through the Looking Glass
3075 Adeline Street
Suite 120
Berkeley, CA 94703

510-848-1112
800-644-2666
FAX: 510-848-4445
tlg@lookingglass.org
www.lookingglass.org

Maureen Block, J.D., President
Thomas Spalding, Treasurer
Alice Nemon, Secretary
Available in braille, large print or cassette. Provides an overview of the baby care assistive technology work at Through The Looking Glass including a discussion of TLG's intervention model, the impact of babycare equipment and guidelines for equipment development. *$2.00*
8 pages

8964 Babycare Assistive Technology for Parents with Physical Disabilties
Through the Looking Glass
3075 Adeline Street
Suite 120
Berkeley, CA 94703

510-848-1112
800-644-2666
FAX: 510-848-4445
tlg@lookingglass.org
www.lookingglass.org

Maureen Block, J.D., President
Thomas Spalding, Treasurer
Alice Nemon, Secretary
Examines the provision of babycare equipment through the lens of ithe infant/parent relationship, the lens of the family system, and through the lens of culture. Availiable in braille, large print or cassette. *$2.00*
7 pages

8965 Basic Course in American Sign Language
TJ Publishers
P.O. Box 702701
Dallas, TX 75370

972-416-0800
800-999-1168
FAX: 972-416-0944
TTY: 301-585-4440
TJPubinc@aol.com
www.tjpublishers.com/

Tom Humphries, Author
Carol Padden, Co-Author
Terrance J O'Rourke, Co-Author
Accompanying videotapes and textbooks include voice translations. Hearing students can analyze sound for initial instruction, or opt to turn off the sound to sharpen visual acuity. Package includes the Basic Course in American Sign Language text, Student Study Guide, the original four 1-hour videotapes plus the ABCASI Vocabulary videotape. *$139.95*
280 pages

8966 Behavioral Vision Approaches for Persons with Physical Disabilities
Optometric Extension Program Foundation
7754 Braegger Road
Three Lakes, WI 54562

714-250-0176
Info@depf.org
www.depf.org

Kristin R. Jungbluth, President
Eric J. Lindberg, VP
Barbara Kuntz, Secretary
A discussion of the behavioral vision/neuro-motor approach to providing directions for prescriptive and therapeutic services for the visually handicapped child or adult. *$49.50*
197 pages

8967 Belonging
Dial Books
375 Hudson St
New York, NY 10014-3657

212-366-2000
FAX: 212-414-3394
www.penguin.com/

Deborah Kent, Author
Meg attended special schools for the blind until she was ready for high school. She decided that she wanted to go to a regular high school. She and her mother practiced her walks to school and studied the layout of the building prior to school starting, but Meg was unprepared for the trip when there were 1,500 students. She adjusted quickly to the crowds and the pace of the new school.
200 pages Hardcover
ISBN 0-80370 -30-1

8968   Berthold Lowenfeld on Blindness and Blind People
American Foundation for the Blind/AFB Press
2 Penn Plaza
Suite 1102
New York, NY 10121   212-502-7600
                                            800-232-5463
                                        FAX: 888-545-8331
                                          afbinfo@afb.net
                                              www.afb.org
Carl R. Augusto, President & Chief Executive Officer
Rick Bozeman, Finance Director, Chief Financial Officer
Kelly Bleach, Chief Administrative Officer
These writings of the pioneering educator, author and advocate
range over a forty-year period include various ground-breaking
papers for the blind educator, a rememberance of Helen Keller
and other essays on education, sociology and history. *$21.95*
254 pages Paperback
ISBN 0-891281-01-0

8969   Blind and Vision-Impaired Individuals
Mainstream
Ste 830
3 Bethesda Metro Ctr
Bethesda, MD 20814-6301   301-961-9299
                                            800-247-1380
                                        FAX: 301-654-6714
Charles Moster
Mainstreaming blind individuals into the workplace. *$2.50*
12 pages

**8970   Blindness and Early Childhood Development Second
Edition**
American Foundation for the Blind/AFB Press
2 Penn Plaza
Suite 1102
New York, NY 10121   212-502-7600
                                            800-232-5463
                                        FAX: 888-545-8331
                                          afbinfo@afb.net
                                                 afb.org
Carl R. Augusto, President & Chief Executive Officer
Rick Bozeman, Finance Director, Chief Financial Officer
Kelly Bleach, Chief Administrative Officer
A review of current knowledge on motor and locomotor develop-
ment, perceptual development, language and cognitive pro-
cesses, and social, emotional and personality development.
Paperback. *$34.95*
384 pages
ISBN 0-891281-23-8

**8971   Blindness: What it is, What it Does and How to Live with
it**
American Foundation for the Blind/AFB Press
2 Penn Plaza
Suite 1102
New York, NY 10121   212-502-7600
                                            800-232-5463
                                        FAX: 888-545-8331
                                          afbinfo@afb.net
                                              www.afb.org
Carl R. Augusto, President & Chief Executive Officer
Rick Bozeman, Finance Director, Chief Financial Officer
Kelly Bleach, Chief Administrative Officer
A classic work on how blindness affects self-perception and so-
cial interaction and what can be done to restore basic skills, mo-
bility, daily living and an appreciation of life's pleasures. *$15.95*
396 pages Paperback
ISBN 0-891282-05-

8972   Books are Fun for Everyone
Nat'l Lib Svc/Blind And Physically Handicapped
1291 Taylor Street North West
Washington, DC 20011   202-707-5100
                                        FAX: 202-707-0712
                                       TTY:202-707-0744
                                            nls@loc.gov
                                          www.loc.gov/nls
Karen Keninger, Director

8973   Books for Blind & Physically Handicapped Individuals
Nat'l Lib Svc/Blind And Physically Handicapped
1291 Taylor Street North West
Washington, DC 20011   202-707-5100
                                        FAX: 202-707-0712
                                       TTY:202-707-0744
                                            nls@loc.gov
                                          www.loc.gov/nls
Karen Keninger, Director
A free national library program of braille and recorded materials
for blind and physically handicapped persons.

8974   Books for Blind and Physically Handicapped Individuals
Nat'l Lib Svc/Blind And Physically Handicapped
1291 Taylor Street North West
Washington, DC 20011   202-707-5100
                                        FAX: 202-707-0712
                                       TTY:202-707-0744
                                            nls@loc.gov
                                          www.loc.gov/nls
Karen Keninger, Director
A free national library program of braille and recorded materials
for blind and physically handicapped persons is administered by
the National Library Service for the Blind and Physically Handicapped Library of Congress.
Annual

8975   Braille Book Bank, Music Catalog
National Braille Association
95 Allens Creek Road
Building 1, Suite 202
Rochester, NY 14618   585-427-8260
                                        FAX: 585-427-0263
                                nbaoffice@nationalbraille.org
                                        www.nationalbraille.org
Jan Carroll, President
Cindi Laurent, Vice President
David Shaffer, Executive Director
Offers hundreds of musical titles in print form, braille and on cas-
sette.
62 pages

8976   Braille: An Extraordinary Volunteer Opportunity
Nat'l Lib Svc/Blind And Physically Handicapped
1291 Taylor Street North West
Washington, DC 20011   202-707-5100
                                        FAX: 202-707-0712
                                       TTY:202-707-0744
                                            nls@loc.gov
                                          www.loc.gov/nls
Karen Keninger, Director

8977   Burns Braille Transcription Dictionary
American Foundation for the Blind/AFB Press
2 Penn Plaza
Suite 1102
New York, NY 10121   212-502-7600
                                            800-232-5463
                                        FAX: 888-545-8331
                                          afbinfo@afb.net
                                                 afb.org
Carl R. Augusto, President & Chief Executive Officer
Rick Bozeman, Finance Director, Chief Financial Officer
Kelly Bleach, Chief Administrative Officer
A handy, portable guide that is a quick reference for anyone who
needs to check print-to-braille and braille-to-print meanings and
symbols. Paperback. *$21.95*
96 pages 96 pages
ISBN 0-891282-32-7

8978 Can't Your Child See? A Guide for Parents of Visually Impaired Children
Sage Publications
2455 Teller Road
Thousand Oaks, CA 91320   805-499-0721
                                  800-818-7243
                             FAX: 805-499-0871
                             info@sagepub.com
                             www.sagepub.com

Sara Miller McCune, Founder, Publisher, Executive Chairman
Blaise R Simqu, President & CEO
Tracey A. Ozmina, Executive Vice President & Chief Operating Officer
This second edition offers parents optimistic, practical guidelines for helping visually impaired children reach their full potential. *$26.00*
279 pages Paperback

8979 Career Perspectives: Interviews with Blindand Visually Impaired Professionals
American Foundation for the Blind/AFB Press
2 Penn Plaza
Suite 1102
New York, NY 10121   212-502-7600
                                  800-232-5463
                             FAX: 888-545-8331
                                  afbinfo@afb.net
                                  afb.org

Carl R. Augusto, President & Chief Executive Officer
Rick Bozeman, Finance Director, Chief Financial Officer
Kelly Bleach, Chief Administrative Officer
Profiles of 20 successful archivers who describe in their own words what it takes to pursue and attain professional success in a sighted world. Available in large print, cassette and braille. *$19.95*
96 pages
ISBN 0-891281-70-2

8980 Careers in Blindness Rehabilitation Services
Mississippi State University
P.O.Box 6189
Mississippi State, MS 39762   662-325-2001
                             FAX: 662-325-8989
                             TTY:662-325-2694
                             nrtc@colled.msstate.edu
                             www.blind.msstate.edu

Jacqui Bybee, Research Associate II
Douglas Bedsaul, Research and Training Coordinator
Anne Carter, Research and Training Coordinator
In a follow-up study in a series examining the substantial under-representation of African Americans as professionals in blindness services, researchers questioned college students about their knowledge, opinions and interests in blindness services. *$15.00*
54 pages Paperback

8981 Cataracts
National Association for Visually Handicapped
111 East 59th Street
New York, NY 10022-1202   212-821-9384
                                  800-829-0500
                             FAX: 212-821-9707
                             info@lighthouse.org
                             lighthouse.org/navh

Mark G. Ackermann, President/CEO
A booklet offering information about Cataracts, diagnosis and treatment of this common condition. LightHouse acquired NAVH. *$4.00*

8982 Characteristics, Services, & Outcomes of Rehab. Consumers who are Blind/Visually Impaired
Mississippi State University
P.O.Box 6189
Mississippi State, MS 39762   662-325-2001
                             FAX: 662-325-8989
                             TTY:662-325-2694
                             nrtc@colled.msstate.edu
                             www.blind.msstate.edu

Jacqui Bybee, Research Associate II
Douglas Bedsaul, Research and Training Coordinator
Anne Carter, Research and Training Coordinator
Issues regarding the efficacy of separate state agencies providing specialized vocational rehabilitation (VR) services to consumers who are blind have generated spirited discussions within the rehabilitation community throughout the history of the state-federal program. In this monograph, RRTC researches report results of their investigation of services provided to blind consumers in separate and general (combined) rehabilitation agencies. *$20.00*
45 pages Paperback

8983 Childhood Glaucoma: A Reference Guide for Families
NAPVI
1 North Lexington Avenue
White Plains, NY 10601   617-972-7441
                                  800-562-6265
                             FAX: 617-972-7444
                             napvi@guildhealth.org
                             www.napvi.org

Julie Urban, President
Venetia Hayden, Vice President
Susan LaVenture, Executive Director
A vaulable tutorial and resource covering all aspects from genetics through diagnosis, sibling relationships and more.
36 pages

8984 Children with Visual Impairments: A Guide For Parents
American Foundation for the Blind/AFB Press
105 East 22nd Street
New York, NY 10010   212-949-4800
                             childrensaidsociety.org

William D. Weisberg, Ph.D., President & CEO
Drema Brown, VP of Education
Katherine Eckstein, Chief of Staff
Written by parents and professional, this book presents a comprehensive overview of the issues that are crucial to the healthy development of children with mild to severe visual impairments. It also offers insight from parents about coping with the emotional aspects of raising a child with special needs. *$16.95*
416 pages
ISBN 0-933149-36-0

8985 Classification of Impaired Vision
National Association for Visually Handicapped
111 East 59th Street
New York, NY 10022-1202   212-821-9384
                                  800-829-0500
                             FAX: 212-821-9707
                             info@lighthouse.org
                             lighthouse.org/navh

Mark G. Ackermann, President/CEO
Designed to provide a foundation for a better understanding of teaching reading, writing, and listning skills to students with visual impairments from preschool age through adult levels. LightHouse acquired NAVH. *$57.95*
322 pages
ISBN 0-398066-93-2

8986 Communication Skills for Visually Impaired Learners
Charles C. Thomas
2600 S First St
Springfield, IL 62704-4730   217-789-8980
                                  800-258-8980
                             FAX: 217-789-9130
                             books@ccthomas.com
                             www.ccthomas.com

Michael P. Thomas, President
Randall Harley, Author
Mila Truan, Author

This book has been designed to provide a foundation for a better understanding of teaching reading, writing, and listening skills to students with visual impairments from preschool age through adult levels. The plan of the book incorporates the latest research findings with the practical experiences learned in the classroom. *$57.95*

322 pages Paperback
ISBN 0-398066-93-2

8987 Comprehensive Examination of Barriers to Employment Among Persons who are Blind or Impaire
Mississippi State University
P.O. Box 6189
Mississippi State, MS 39762   662-325-2001
                                      FAX: 662-325-8989
                                      TTY: 662-325-2694
                                      nrtc@colled.msstate.edu
                                      www.blind.msstate.edu

Jacqui Bybee, Research Associate II
Douglas Bedsaul, Research and Training Coordinator
Anne Carter, Research and Training Coordinator
A multi-phase research project designed to: identify barriers to employment; identify and develop innovative successful strategies to overcome these barriers; develop methods for others to utilize these strategies; disseminate this information to rehabilitation providers; replicate the use of selected strategies in other settings. *$20.00*

90 pages Paperback

8988 Contrasting Characteristics of Blind and Visually Impaired Clients
Mississippi State University
P.O. Box 6189
Mississippi State, MS 39762   662-325-2001
                                      FAX: 662-325-8989
                                      TTY: 662-325-2694
                                      nrtc@colled.msstate.edu
                                      www.blind.msstate.edu

Jacqui Bybee, Research Associate II
Douglas Bedsaul, Research and Training Coordinator
Anne Carter, Research and Training Coordinator
This report examines cases in the National Blindness and Low Vision Employment Database to identify and profile environmental and personal characteristics of clients who are blind or visually impaired and who were achieving successful and unsuccessful retention of competitive jobs. A total of 787 cases were analyzed. *$15.00*

44 pages Paperback

8989 Dancing Cheek to Cheek
Blind Children's Center
4120 Marathon Street
Los Angeles, CA 90029-3584   323-664-2153
                                      info@blindchildrenscenter.org
                                      www.blindchildrenscenter.org

Laura Meyers, Co-Author
Pamela Lansky, Co-Author
Beginning social, play and language interactions. *$10.00*
23 pages

8990 Development of Social Skills by Blind and Visually Impaired Students
American Foundation for the Blind/AFB Press
2 Penn Plaza
Suite 1102
New York, NY 10121   212-502-7600
                                      800-232-5463
                                      FAX: 888-545-8331
                                      afbinfo@afb.net
                                      www.afb.org

Carl R. Augusto, President & Chief Executive Officer
Rick Bozeman, Finance Director, Chief Financial Officer
Kelly Bleach, Chief Administrative Officer
Offers an examination of the social interactions of blind and visually impaired children in mainstreamed settings and the community that highlights the need to teach social interaction skills to children and provide them with support. Paperback. *$45.95*

232 pages
ISBN 0-891282-17-4

8991 Diabetic Retinopathy
National Association for Visually Handicapped
111 East 59th Street
New York, NY 10022-1202   212-821-9384
                                      800-829-0500
                                      FAX: 212-821-9707
                                      info@lighthouse.org
                                      lighthouse.org/navh

Mark G. Ackermann, President/CEO
A booklet offering information about Diabetic Retinopathy. LightHouse acquired NAVH.

8992 Diversity and Visual Impairment: The Influence of Race, Gender, Religion and Ethnicity
American Foundation for the Blind
2 Penn Plaza
Suite 1102
New York, NY 10121   212-502-7600
                                      800-232-5463
                                      FAX: 888-545-8331
                                      afbinfo@afb.net
                                      www.afb.org

Carl R. Augusto, President & Chief Executive Officer
Rick Bozeman, Finance Director, Chief Financial Officer
Kelly Bleach, Chief Administrative Officer
Cultural, social, ethnic, gender, and religious issues can influence the way an individual perceives and copes with a visual impairment. *$45.95*

480 pages
ISBN 0-891283-83-8

8993 Do You Remember the Color Blue: The Questions Children Ask About Blindness
Viking Books
375 Hudson Street
New York, NY 10014-3657   212-366-2000
                                      FAX: 212-366-2933
                                      ecommerce@us.penguingroup.com
                                      www.us.penguingroup.com

John Makinson, Chairman & CEO
The author answers thirteen thought-provoking questions that children have asked her over the years about being blind.
78 pages
ISBN 0-670880-43-4

8994 Don't Lose Sight of Glaucoma
National Eye Institute
2020 Vision Place
Building 31 Room 6a32
Bethesda, MD 20892-3655   301-496-5248
                                      800-869-2020
                                      FAX: 301-402-1065
                                      2020@nei.nih.gov
                                      www.nei.nih.gov

Provides information about glaucoma for people at higher risk, answers questions about causes and symptoms, and discusses diagnosis and types of treatment.

8995 Early Focus: Working with Young Children Who Are Blind or Visually Impaired & Their Families
American Foundation for the Blind/AFB Press
2 Penn Plaza
Suite 1102
New York, NY 10121   212-502-7600
                                      800-232-5463
                                      FAX: 888-545-8331
                                      afbinfo@afb.net
                                      www.afb.org

Carl R. Augusto, President & Chief Executive Officer
Rick Bozeman, Finance Director, Chief Financial Officer
Kelly Bleach, Chief Administrative Officer
Describes early intervention techniques used with blind and visually impaired children and stresses the benefits of family involvement and transdisciplinary teamwork. Paperback. *$32.95*

176 pages
ISBN 0-891282-15-7

8996 **Encyclopedia of Blindness and Vision Impairment Second Edition**
Facts on File
132 West 31st Street
17th Floor
New York, NY 10001
800-322-8755
FAX: 800-678-3633
CustServ@InfobaseLearning.com
www.factsonfile.com

Jill Sardenga, Author
Susan Shelly, Co-Author
Alan Shelly MD, Co-Author
Designed to provide both laymen and professionals with concise, practical information on the second most common disability in the U.S. *$65.00*
340 pages Hardcover
ISBN 0-816042-80-2

8997 **Equals in Partnership: Basic Rights for Families of Children with Blindness**
NAPVI
1 North Lexington Avenue
White Plains, NY 10601
617-972-7441
800-562-6265
FAX: 617-972-7444
napvi@guildhealth.org
www.napvi.org

Julie Urban, President
Venetia Hayden, Vice President
Susan LaVenture, Executive Director
A comprehensive compilation of educational advocacy materials to help parents better understand the special needs of their children with visual impairments and to assist them in accessing appropriate services for their children.

8998 **Eye Research News**
Research to Prevent Blindness
645 Madison Avenue
Floor 21
New York, NY 10022-1010
212-752-4333
800-621-0026
FAX: 212-688-6231
www.rpbusa.org

Diane S. Swift, Chair
Brian F. Hofland, PhD, President
David H. Brenner, VP & Secretary
Yearly publication from Research to Prevent Blindness. Free.
4 pages Yearly

8999 **Eye and Your Vision**
National Association for Visually Handicapped
111 East 59th Street
New York, NY 10022-1202
212-821-9384
800-829-0500
FAX: 212-821-9707
info@lighthouse.org
lighthouse.org/navh

Mark G. Ackermann, President/CEO
A large booklet offering information, with illustrations, on the eye. Includes information on protection of eyesight, how the eye works and vision disorders. Available in Russian and Spanish also. LightHouse acquired NAVH. *$5.00*

9000 **Eye-Q Test**
National Association for Visually Handicapped
111 East 59th Street
New York, NY 10022-1202
212-821-9384
800-829-0500
FAX: 212-821-9707
info@lighthouse.org
lighthouse.org/navh

Mark G. Ackermann, President/CEO
Five questions and answers to assist in knowing more about vision. Also available in Spanish and Russian. LightHouse acquired NAVH.

9001 **Family Context and Disability Culture Reframing: Through the Looking Glass**
Through the Looking Glass
3075 Adeline Street
Suite 120
Berkeley, CA 94703
510-848-1112
800-644-2666
FAX: 510-848-4445
tlg@lookingglass.org
www.lookingglass.org

Maureen Block, J.D., President
Thomas Spalding, Treasurer
Alice Nemon, Secretary
This article provides an overview of the issues and guiding perspectives underlying 'Through the Lookinglass' eighteen years of work with families. Available in braille, large print or cassette.
$2.00
5 pages

9002 **Family Guide to Vision Care (FG1)**
American Optometric Association
243 North Lindbergh Boulevard
Floor 1
Saint Louis, MO 63141-7881
800-365-2219
aoa.org

David A. Cockrell, OD, President
Andrea P. Thau, OD, Vice President
Barry Barresi, Executive Director
Offers information on the early developmental years of your vision, finding a family optometrist and how to take care of your eyesight through the learning years, the working years and the mature years.

9003 **Family Guide: Growth & Development of the Partially Seeing Child**
National Association for Visually Handicapped
111 East 59th Street
New York, NY 10022-1202
212-821-9384
800-829-0500
FAX: 212-821-9707
info@lighthouse.org
lighthouse.org/navh

Mark G. Ackermann, President/CEO
Offers information for parents and guidelines in raising a partially seeing child. LightHouse acquired NAVH. *$.60*

9004 **Fathers: A Common Ground**
Blind Children's Center
4120 Marathon Street
Los Angeles, CA 90029-3584
323-664-2153
info@blindchildrenscenter.org
www.blindchildrenscenter.org

Paula Schmitt, Co-Author
Fernanda Armenta-Schmitt, Co-Author
Exploring the concerns and roles of fathers of children with visual impairments. *$10.00*
50 pages

9005 **Fighting Blindness News**
Foundation Fighting Blindness
7168 Columbia Gateway Drive
Suite 100
Columbia, MD 21046
410-423-0600
800-683-5555
FAX: 410-363-2393
TTY: 800-683-5551
info@FightBlindness.org
www.blindness.org

Offers information on medical updates, donor programs, assistive devices, resources and clinical trial information for persons with visual impairments, blindness and retinal degenerative diseases.
2x Year

9006 **First Steps**
Blind Children's Center
4120 Marathon Street
Los Angeles, CA 90029-3584   323-664-2153
                                       info@blindchildrenscenter.org
                                       www.blindchildrenscenter.org
Tanni L. Anthony, Co-Author
Fernanda Armenta-Schmitt, Co-Author
A handbook for teaching young children who are visually impaired. Designed to assist students, professionals and parents working with children who are visually impaired. Visit our website for many publications addressing training very young children who are blind or visually impaired. *$35.00*
203 pages

9007 **Foundations of Orientation and Mobility**
American Foundation for the Blind/AFB Press
2 Penn Plaza
Suite 1102
New York, NY 10121   212-502-7600
                                           800-232-5463
                                       FAX: 888-545-8331
                                           afbinfo@afb.net
                                              www.afb.org
Carl R. Augusto, President & Chief Executive Officer
Rick Bozeman, Finance Director, Chief Financial Officer
Kelly Bleach, Chief Administrative Officer
This text has been updated and revised and includes current research from a variety of disciplines, an international perspective, and expanded contents on low vision, aging, multiple disabilities, accessibility, program design and adaptive technology from more that 30 eminent subject experts. *$79.95*
775 pages
ISBN 0-891289-46-3

9008 **Foundations of Rehabilitation Counseling with Persons Who Are Blind or Visually Impaired**
American Foundation for the Blind/AFB Press
2 Penn Plaza
Suite 1102
New York, NY 10121   212-502-7600
                                           800-232-5463
                                       FAX: 888-545-8331
                                           afbinfo@afb.net
                                              www.afb.org
Carl R. Augusto, President & Chief Executive Officer
Rick Bozeman, Finance Director, Chief Financial Officer
Kelly Bleach, Chief Administrative Officer
Rehabilitation professionals have long recognized that the needs of people who are blind or visually impaired are unique and requie a special knowledge and expertise to provide and corrdinate rehabilitation services. *$59.95*
477 pages
ISBN 0-891289-45-3

9009 **General Facts and Figures on Blindness**
Prevent Blindness America
211 West Wacker Drive
Suite 1700
Chicago, IL 60606   800-331-2020
                                       info@preventblindness.org
                                       www.preventblindness.org
Paul G. Howes, Chairman
Hugh R. Parry, President & CEO, Prevent Blindness America
Jerome Desserich, Vice President & Chief Financial Officer

9010 **Get a Wiggle On**
American Alliance for Health, Phys. Ed. & Dance
1900 Association Drive
Reston, VA 20191-1598   703-476-3400
                                           800-213-7193
                                       FAX: 703-476-9527
                                              aahperd.org
Dolly D. Lambdin, President
E. Paul Roetert, CEO
Marybell Avery, Director

Gives teachers and parents practical suggestions for helping blind and visually impaired infants grow and learn like other children. *$5.00*
80 pages
ISBN 0-88314 -77-2

9011 **Gift of Sight**
RP Foundation Fighting Blindness
1401 W Mount Royal Ave
Baltimore, MD 21217-4245   410-225-9409
                                           800-683-5555
                                       FAX: 410-225-3936
A pamphlet offering information on the Retina Donor Program, which studies diseased, human retinal tissue in their search for a cure of retinal degenerative diseases.

9012 **Glaucoma**
Glaucoma Research Foundation
251 Post Street
Suite 600
San Francisco, CA 94108   415-986-3162
                                           800-826-6693
                                       FAX: 415-986-3763
                                       question@glaucoma.org
                                              glaucoma.org
Andrew L. Iwach, MD, Chair
Robert L. Stamper, MD, Vice Chair
Thomas M. Brunner, President and CEO
Offers information on what glaucoma is, the causes, treatments, types of glaucoma, eye exams and prevention.

9013 **Glaucoma: The Sneak Thief of Sight**
National Association for Visually Handicapped
Fl 6
22 W 21st St
New York, NY 10010-6943   212-242-4438
                                           800-3 C-NCOS
                                       FAX: 631-736-0371
                                       customerservice@cancos.com
                                              cancos.com
Denise Green, Owner
A pamphlet describing the disease, treatment and medications. Also available in Russian and Spanish. Revised in 1999. *$3.50*

9014 **Guidelines and Games for Teaching Efficient Braille Reading**
American Foundation for the Blind/AFB Press
2 Penn Plaza
Suite 1102
New York, NY 10121   212-502-7600
                                           800-232-5463
                                       FAX: 888-545-8331
                                           afbinfo@afb.net
                                              www.afb.org
Carl R. Augusto, President & Chief Executive Officer
Rick Bozeman, Finance Director, Chief Financial Officer
Kelly Bleach, Chief Administrative Officer
Based on research in the areas of rapid reading and precision teaching, these guidelines represent a unique adaptation of a general reading program to the needs of braille readers. Paperback. *$24.95*
116 pages Paperback
ISBN 0-891281-05-4

9015 **Guidelines for Comprehensive Low Vision Care**
National Association for Visually Handicapped
111 East 59th Street
New York, NY 10022-1202   212-821-9384
                                           800-829-0500
                                       FAX: 212-821-9707
                                       info@lighthouse.org
                                       lighthouse.org/navh
Mark G. Ackermann, President/CEO
A description of the proper method to conduct a low vision evaluation.LightHouse acquired NAVH. *$.50*

9016 Handbook for Itinerant and Resource Teachers of Blind Students
National Federation of the Blind
200 East Wells St
Baltimore, MD 21230-4914 410-659-9314
nfb@iamdigex.net

Doris Willoughby, Author
Sharon L Monthei, Co-Author
The Handbook provides help to teachers, school administrators or other school personnel that have experience with blind or visually impaired students. The Handbook devotes 45 pages to Braille and how to teach Braille for parents and teachers. There are other chapters offering information on the law, physical education, fitting in socially, testing and evaluation, home economics, daily living skills and more. *$23.00*
533 pages Softcover
ISBN 0-962412-20-1

9017 Handbook of Information for Members of the Achromatopsia Network
P.O.Box 214
Berkeley, CA 94701-214 510-540-4700
FAX: 510-540-4767
www.achromat.org

9018 Health Care Professionals Who Are Blind or Visually Impaired
American Foundation for the Blind
2 Penn Plaza
Suite 1102
New York, NY 10121 212-502-7600
800-232-5463
FAX: 888-545-8331
afbinfo@afb.net
afb.org

Carl R. Augusto, President & Chief Executive Officer
Rick Bozeman, Finance Director, Chief Financial Officer
Kelly Bleach, Chief Administrative Officer
This resource is essential reading for older students and young adults who are blind or visually impaired, their families, and the professionals who work with them. *$21.95*
160 pages
ISBN 0-891283-88-9

9019 Heart to Heart
Blind Children's Center
4120 Marathon Street
Los Angeles, CA 90029-3584 323-664-2153
info@blindchildrenscenter.org
www.blindchildrenscenter.org

Nancy Chernus-Mansfield, Co-Author
Dori Hayashi, Co-Author
Parents of children who are blind and partially sighted talk about their feelings. *$10.00*
12 pages

9020 Heartbreak of Being A Little Bit Blind
National Association for Visually Handicapped
111 East 59th Street
New York, NY 10022-1202 212-821-9384
800-829-0500
FAX: 212-821-9707
info@lighthouse.org
lighthouse.org/navh

Mark G. Ackermann, President/CEO
Summary of what it means to have impaired vision; includes illustrations. LightHouse acquired NAVH.

9021 Helen Keller National Center Newsletter
141 Middle Neck Road
Sands Point, NY 11050 516-944-8900
800-225-0411
FAX: 516-944-7302
hkncinfo@hknc.org
www.hknc.org

Joseph McNulty, Executive Director
The center provides evaluation and training in vocational skills, adaptive technology and computer skills, orientation and mobility, independent living, communication, speech-language skills, creative arts, fitness and leisure activities.

9022 Helping the Visually Impaired Child with Developmental Problems
Teachers College Press
1234 Amsterdam Avenue
New York, NY 10027 212-678-3929
800-575-6566
FAX: 212-678-4149
tcpress@tc.columbia.edu
www.teacherscollegepress.com

Mary Lynch, Manager
Brian Ellerbeck, Executive Acquisitions Editor
Marie Ellen Larcada, Senior Acquisitions Editor
This book aims to explore the human consequences of severe visual problems combined with other handicaps. The application of child development research to educational interventions, the need for educational and rehabilitative services that serve the human and the special needs of children and their families and the promise of technology in helping to expand communicative possibilities are also discussed. *$18.95*
216 pages Paperback
ISBN 0-807729-02-7

9023 History and Use of Braille
American Council of the Blind
2200 Wilson Boulevard
Suite 650
Arlington, VA 22201-3354 202-467-5081
800-424-8666
FAX: 703-465-5085
info@acb.org
acb.org

Kim Charlson, President
Jeff Thom, 1st Vice President
Melanie Brunson, Executive Director
A system of touch reading and writing for blind persons in which raised dots represent the letters of the alphabet.

9024 How to Thrive, Not Just Survive
American Foundation for the Blind/AFB Press
2 Penn Plaza
Suite 1102
New York, NY 10121 212-502-7600
800-232-5463
FAX: 888-545-8331
afbinfo@afb.net
www.afb.org

Carl R. Augusto, President & Chief Executive Officer
Rick Bozeman, Finance Director, Chief Financial Officer
Kelly Bleach, Chief Administrative Officer
Practical, hands-on guide for parents, teachers, and everyone involved in helping children develop the skills necessary for socialization, orientations and mobility, and leisure and recreational activities. Some of the subjects covered are eating, dressing, personal hygiene, self-esteem and etiquette. *$24.95*
104 pages Paperback
ISBN 0-89128 -48-7

9025 Hub
SPOKES Unlimited
1006 Main Street
Klamath Fals, OR 97601 541-883-7547
FAX: 541-885-2469
spokesunlimited.org

Wendy Howard, Executive Director
Celeste Wolf, Clerical Support Specialist II
Newsletter on rehabilitation, peer counseling, blindness, visual impairments, information and referral.

9026 If Blindness Comes
National Federation of the Blind
200 E. Wells St.
at Jernigan Place
Baltimore, MD 21230 410-659-9314
FAX: 410-685-5653
nfb@nfb.org
www.nfb.org

Kenneth Jerrigan, Editor
An introduction to issues relating to vision loss and provides a positive, supportive philosophy about blindness. It is a general information book which includes answers to many common ques-

tions about blindness, information about services and programs for the blind and resource listings. Contact the Materials Center.

9027 If Blindness Strikes Don't Strike Out
2600 South 1st Street
Springfield, IL 62704

217-789-8980
800-258-8980
FAX: 217-789-9130
books@ccthomas.com
www.ccthomas.com

Bob Stork, Owner

9028 Imagining the Possibilities: Creative Approaches to Orientation and Mobility Instructio
American Foundation for the Blind
2 Penn Plaza
Suite 1102
New York, NY 10121

212-502-7600
800-232-5463
FAX: 888-545-8331
afbinfo@afb.net
afb.org

Carl R. Augusto, President & Chief Executive Officer
Rick Bozeman, Finance Director, Chief Financial Officer
Kelly Bleach, Chief Administrative Officer
Innovative and varied approaches to O&M techniques and teaching and dynamic suggestions on how to analyze learning styles are just some of the important topics included. *$49.95*
378 pages
ISBN 0-891283-82-X

9029 Increasing Literacy Levels: Final Report
Mississippi State University
P.O.Box 6189
Mississippi State, MS 39762

662-325-2001
FAX: 662-325-8989
TTY:662-325-2694
nrtc@colled.msstate.edu
www.blind.msstate.edu

Jacqui Bybee, Research Associate II
Douglas Bedsaul, Research and Training Coordinator
Anne Carter, Research and Training Coordinator
This study is composed of three research projects to identify and analyze the appropriate use of and instruction in Braille, optical devices and other technologies as they relate to literacy and employment of individuals who are blind or visually impaired. *$20.00*
148 pages Paperback

9030 Information on Glaucoma
Glaucoma Research Foundation
251 Post Street
Suite 600
San Francisco, CA 94108

415-986-3162
800-826-6693
FAX: 415-986-3763
question@glaucoma.org
www.glaucoma.org

Andrew L. Iwach, MD, Chair
Robert L. Stamper, MD, Vice Chair
Thomas M. Brunner, President and CEO

9031 Intervention Practices in the Retention of Competitive Employment
Mississippi State University
P.O.Box 6189
Mississippi State, MS 39762

662-325-2001
FAX: 662-325-8989
TTY:662-325-2694
nrtc@colled.msstate.edu
www.blind.msstate.edu

Jacqui Bybee, Research Associate II
Douglas Bedsaul, Research and Training Coordinator
Anne Carter, Research and Training Coordinator
This study investigated the methods by which an individual can retain competitive employment after the onset of a significant vision loss. Interviews were conducted with 89 rehabilitation counselors across the US Strategies that contribute to successful job retention were identified as well as best rehabilitation practices in job retention. *$15.00*
60 pages Paperback

9032 Know Your Eye
American Council of the Blind
2200 Wilson Boulevard
Suite 650
Arlington, VA 22201-3354

202-467-5081
800-424-8666
FAX: 703-465-5085
info@acb.org
acb.org

Kim Charlson, President
Jeff Thom, 1st Vice President
Melanie Brunson, Executive Director

9033 Large Print Loan Library
National Association for Visually Handicapped
111 East 59th Street
New York, NY 10022-1202

212-821-9384
800-829-0500
FAX: 212-821-9707
info@lighthouse.org
lighthouse.org/navh

Mark G. Ackermann, President/CEO
A huge large print catalog of all the publications, fiction and non-fiction, cassette tapes, books-on-tape and videos available for the visually impaired from the loan library of the National Association for the Visually Handicapped. LightHouse acquired NAVH.

9034 Large Print Loan Library Catalog
National Association for Visually Handicapped
111 East 59th Street
New York, NY 10022-1202

212-821-9384
800-829-0500
FAX: 212-821-9707
info@lighthouse.org
lighthouse.org/navh

Mark G. Ackermann, President/CEO
Listing of over 7,000 commercially published and NAVH large print books available through NAVH on a loan basis. Includes a limited selection of titles available for purchase. LightHouse acquired NAVH.

9035 Large Print Recipies for a Healthy Life
123601 Wilshire
Los Angeles, CA 90025

310-826-8280
800-481-EYES
FAX: 310-458-8179

Judith Caditz PhD, Author
$21.95
283 pages
ISBN 0-962236-82-9

9036 Learning to Play
Blind Children's Center
4120 Marathon Street
Los Angeles, CA 90029-3584

323-664-2153
info@blindchildrenscenter.org
www.blindchildrenscenter.org

Susan L. Recchia, Co-Author
Presenting play activities to the pre-school child who is visually impaired. *$10.00*
12 pages

9037 Let's Eat
Blind Children's Center
4120 Marathon Street
Los Angeles, CA 90029-3584

323-664-2153
info@blindchildrenscenter.org
www.blindchildrenscenter.org

Jill Brody, Co-Author
Lynne Webber, Co-Author
Feeding a child with visual impairment. *$10.00*
28 pages

9038 Library Services for the Blind
South Carolina State University
300 College Street NorthEast
P.O. Box 7491
Orangeburg, SC 29117
803-536-7045
FAX: 803-536-8902
reference@scsu.edu
library.scsu.edu

Adrienne C. Webber, Dean, Library/Information Services
Ramona S. Evans, Administrative Specialist
Ruth A. Hodges, Reference & Information Specialist
News and information on developments in library services for readers who are blind and physically disabled.

9039 Lifestyles of Employed Legally Blind People
Mississippi State University
P.O.Box 6189
Mississippi State, MS 39762
662-325-2001
FAX: 662-325-8989
TTY:662-325-2694
nrtc@colled.msstate.edu
www.blind.msstate.edu

Jacqui Bybee, Research Associate II
Douglas Bedsaul, Research and Training Coordinator
Anne Carter, Research and Training Coordinator
Results from a telephone survey show that visually impaired respondents are involved in a wide variety of activities with little restrictions on their range of activities. Sighted respondents tended to spend more time in child care, obtaining goods and services, attending to self-care activities and engaging in social activities, while visually impaired respondents spent more time in education and passive activities. This report is a study of expenditures and time use. *$10.00*
193 pages Paperback

9040 Lion
Lion's Clubs International
300 West 22nd Street
Oak Brook, IL 60523-8842
630-571-5466
FAX: 630-571-8890
TTY:630-571-6533
www.lionsclubs.org/

Joseph Preston, International President
Jitsuhiro Yamada, 1st Vice President
Robert E. Corlew, 2nd Vice President
Publication for the blind.

9041 Living with Achromatopsia
P.O.Box 214
Berkeley, CA 94701-214
510-540-4700
FAX: 510-540-4767
www.achromat.org

Frances Futterman, Author
Consists entirely of comments from persons who know firsthand about living with achromatopsia.

9042 Low Vision Questions and Answers: Definitions, Devices, Services
American Foundation for the Blind/AFB Press
2 Penn Plaza
Suite 1102
New York, NY 10121
212-502-7600
800-232-5463
FAX: 888-545-8331
afbinfo@afb.net
afb.org

Carl R. Augusto, President & Chief Executive Officer
Rick Bozeman, Chief Financial Officer
Kelly Bleach, Chief Administrative Officer
What does low vision mean? What do low vision services cost? What diseases cause low vision? Answers to these and other questions are presented in a comprehensive format with accompanying photographs. $50.00/pack of 25.
21 pages Pamphlet
ISBN 0-891281-96-7

9043 Low Vision: Reflections of the Past, Issues for the Future
American Foundation for the Blind/AFB Press
2 Penn Plaza
Suite 1102
New York, NY 10121
212-502-7600
800-232-5463
FAX: 888-545-8331
afbinfo@afb.net
www.afb.org

Carl R. Augusto, President & Chief Executive Officer
Rick Bozeman, Chief Financial Officer
Kelly Bleach, Chief Administrative Officer
Background papers and a strategies section are used to identify the shifting needs of visually impaired persons and the resources that may be needed to address them. Paperback. *$34.95*
Paperback
ISBN 0-891282-18-1

9044 Mainstreaming and the American Dream
American Foundation for the Blind/AFB Press
2 Penn Plaza
Suite 1102
New York, NY 10121
212-502-7600
800-232-5463
FAX: 888-545-8331
afbinfo@afb.net
www.afb.org

Carl R. Augusto, President & Chief Executive Officer
Rick Bozeman, Chief Financial Officer
Kelly Bleach, Chief Administrative Officer
Based on in-depth interviews with parents and professionals, this research monograph presents information on the needs and aspirations of parents of blind and visually impaired children. Paperback. *$34.95*
256 pages Paperback
ISBN 0-891281-91-7

9045 Mainstreaming the Visually Impaired Child
NAPVI
1 North Lexington Avenue
White Plains, NY 10601
617-972-7441
800-562-6265
FAX: 617-972-7444
napvi@guildhealth.org
www.napvi.org

Julie Urban, President
Venetia Hayden, Vice President
Susan LaVenture, Executive Director
A unique, informative guide for teachers and educational professionals that work with the visually impaired. *$10.00*
121 pages Paper

9046 Making Life More Livable
American Foundation for the Blind
2 Penn Plaza
Suite 1102
New York, NY 10121
212-502-7600
800-232-5463
FAX: 888-545-8331
afbinfo@afb.net
www.afb.org

Carl R. Augusto, President & Chief Executive Officer
Rick Bozeman, Chief Financial Officer
Kelly Bleach, Chief Administrative Officer
Shows how simple adaptations in the home and environment can make a big difference in the lives of blind and visually impaired older persons. The suggestions offered are numerous and specific, ranging from how to mark food cans for greater visibility to how to get out of the shower safley. Large print. *$24.95*
128 pages
ISBN 0-891283-87-0

9047 **Meeting the Needs of People with Vision Loss: Multidisciplinary Perspective**
Resources for Rehabilitation
22 Bonad Road
Winchester, MA 01890
781-368-9080
FAX: 781-368-9096
orders@rfr.org
www.rfr.org

Susan L Greenblatt, Editor
Written by rehabilitation professionals, physicians, and a sociologist, this book discusses how to provide appropriate information and how to serve special populations. Chapters on the role of the family, diabetes and vision loss, special needs of children and adolescents, adults with hearing and vision loss. *$29.95*
ISBN 0-929718-07-0

9048 **Model Program Operation Manual: Business Enterprise Program Supervisors**
Mississippi State University
P.O.Box 6189
Mississippi State, MS 39762
662-325-2001
FAX: 662-325-8989
TTY:662-325-2694
nrtc@colled.msstate.edu
www.blind.msstate.edu

Jacqui Bybee, Research Associate II
Douglas Bedsaul, Research and Training Coordinator
Anne Carter, Research and Training Coordinator
This monograph serves as a Model Program Operation Manual for Business Enterprise Program Supervisors who administer Randolph-Sheppard vending facilities under the Randolph-Sheppard Act. A wide variety of topics are covered including the role of the State Committee of Blind Venders, the role and responsibilities of the Vending Facility Operator, model qualification, for potential Facility Managers, guidelines for location of vending facilities and policies for closing vending facilities. *$20.00*
199 pages Paperback

9049 **More Alike Than Different: Blind and Visually Impaired Children**
American Foundation for the Blind/AFB Press
2 Penn Plaza
Suite 1102
New York, NY 10121
212-502-7600
800-232-5463
FAX: 888-545-8331
www.afb.org

Carl R. Augusto, President & Chief Executive Officer
Rick Bozeman, Chief Financial Officer
Kelly Bleach, Chief Administrative Officer
Offers photographs of blind and visually impaired children around the world learning to read and write, travel independently and performing basic living skills. Covers the most recent technological advances and demonstrates the universality of educational needs and goals. Paperback. $100.00/pack of 25.
ISBN 0-891281-69-0

9050 **Mothers with Visual Impairments who are Raising Young Children**
American Foundation for the Blind/AFB Press
2 Penn Plaza
Suite 1102
New York, NY 10121
212-502-7600
800-232-5463
FAX: 888-545-8331
afbinfo@afb.net
www.afb.org

Carl R. Augusto, President & Chief Executive Officer
Rick Bozeman, Chief Financial Officer
Kelly Bleach, Chief Administrative Officer
Available in braille, large print or cassette. *$2.00*
16 pages

9051 **Move With Me**
Blind Children's Center
4120 Marathon Street
Los Angeles, CA 90029-3584
323-664-2153
info@blindchildrenscenter.org
www.blindchildrenscenter.org

Doris Hug, Co-Author
Nancy Chernus-Mansfield, Co-Author
A parent's guide to movement development for babies who are visually impaired. *$10.00*
12 pages

9052 **National Eye Institute**
National Institute of Health
31 Center Dr.
MSC 2510
Bethesda, MD 20892-2510
301-496-5248
2020@nei.nih.gov
www.nei.nih.gov

Michael F. Chiang, Director
Santa Tuminia, Deputy Director
Melanie Reagan, Acting Executive Officer
To conduct and support research for blinding eye diseases, visual disorders, mechanisms of visual function, and the preservation of sight.

9053 **Orientation and Mobility Primer for Families and Young Children**
American Foundation for the Blind/AFB Press
2 Penn Plaza
Suite 1102
New York, NY 10121
212-502-7600
800-232-5463
FAX: 888-545-8331
afbinfo@afb.net
www.afb.org

Carl R. Augusto, President & Chief Executive Officer
Rick Bozeman, Chief Financial Officer
Kelly Bleach, Chief Administrative Officer
Practical information for helping a child learn about his or her environment right from the start. Covers sensory training, concept development and orientation skills. Paperback. *$14.95*
48 pages
ISBN 0-891281-57-6

9054 **Out of the Corner of My Eye: Living with Vision Loss in Later Life**
American Foundation for the Blind/AFB Press
2 Penn Plaza
Suite 1102
New York, NY 10121
212-502-7600
800-232-5463
FAX: 888-545-8331
www.afb.org

Carl R. Augusto, President & Chief Executive Officer
Rick Bozeman, Chief Financial Officer
Kelly Bleach, Chief Administrative Officer
A personal account of students' vision loss and subsequent adjustment that is full of practical advice and cheerful encouragement, told by an 87 year old retired college teacher who has maintained her independence and zest for life. Available in paperback or on audio cassette. *$23.95*
120 pages
ISBN 0-891281-82-1

9055 **Out of the Corner of My Eye: Living with Macular Degeneration**
American Foundation for the Blind/AFB Press
2 Penn Plaza
Suite 1102
New York, NY 10121
212-502-7600
800-232-5463
FAX: 888-545-8331
afbinfo@afb.net
www.afb.org

Carl R. Augusto, President & Chief Executive Officer
Rick Bozeman, Chief Financial Officer
Kelly Bleach, Chief Administrative Officer
A personal account of students' vision loss and subsequent adjustment that is full of practical advice and cheerful encourage-

ment, told by an 87 year old retired college teacher who has maintained her independence and zest for life. *$29.95*
168 pages Paperback
ISBN 0-891238-31-2

9056 **Pain Erasure: the Bonnie Prudden Way**
Ballantine Books
1540 Broadway
New York, NY 10036-4039   212-751-2600
     FAX: 212-572-4949

Bonnie Prudden, Author
Revolutionary breakthrough in pain relief involves trigger points-tender areas where muscles have been damaged from falls, childhood ailments, poor posture, and the stresses of daily life.

9057 **Patient's Guide to Visual Aids and Illumination**
National Association for Visually Handicapped
111 East 59th Street
New York, NY 10022-1202   212-821-9384
     800-829-0500
     FAX: 212-821-9707
     info@lighthouse.org
     lighthouse.org/navh

Mark G. Ackermann, President/CEO
A reference booklet offering information on aids for the visually impaired. LightHouse acquired NAVH. *$.75*

9058 **Pediatric Visual Diagnosis Fact Sheets**
Blind Children's Center
4120 Marathon Street
Los Angeles, CA 90029-3584   323-664-2153
     info@blindchildrenscenter.org
     blindchildrenscenter.org

Sarah E. Orth, CEO
Collection of fact sheets addressing commonly encountered eye conditions, diagnostic tests and materials. *$10.00*
10 pages

9059 **Perkins Activity and Resource Guide: A Handbook for Teachers**
Perkins School for the Blind
175 North Beacon Street
Watertown, MA 02472   617-924-3434
     FAX: 617-972-7363
     info@perkins.org
     www.perkins.org

Frederic M. Clifford, Chair of the Board
Philip L. Ladd, Vice Chair of the Board
Leslie Nordon, Secretary
This is a comprehensive, two volume guide with over 1,000 pages of activities, resources and instructional strategies for teachers and parents of students with visual and multiple disabilities. *$80.00*

9060 **Personal Reader Update**
Personal Reader Department
9 Centennial Dr
Peabody, MA 01960-7906   978-977-2000
     800-343-0311
     FAX: 978-977-2409
Offers information on new services, assistive devices and technology for the blind.

9061 **Preschool Learning Activities for the Visually Impaired Child**
NAPVI
1 North Lexington Avenue
White Plains, NY 10601   617-972-7441
     800-562-6265
     FAX: 617-972-7444
     napvi@guildhealth.org
     www.napvi.org

Julie Urban, President
Venetia Hayden, Vice President
Susan LaVenture, Executive Director
This guide for parents offers games and activities to keep visually impaired children active during the preschool years. *$8.00*
91 pages Paperback

9062 **Reaching, Crawling, Walking.. Let's Get Moving**
Blind Children's Center
4120 Marathon Street
Los Angeles, CA 90029-3584   323-664-2153
     info@blindchildrenscenter.org
     www.blindchildrenscenter.org

Susan S. Simmons, Co-Author
Sharon O'Mara Maida, Co-Author
Orientation and mobility for preschool children who are visually imapired. *$10.00*
24 pages

9063 **Reading Is for Everyone**
Nat'l Lib Svc/Blind And Physically Handicapped
1291 Taylor Street North West
Washington, DC 20011   202-707-5100
     FAX: 202-707-0712
     TTY:202-707-0744
     nls@loc.gov
     www.loc.gov/nls

Karen Keninger, Director

9064 **Reading with Low Vision**
Nat'l Lib Svc/Blind And Physically Handicapped
1291 Taylor Street North West
Washington, DC 20011   202-707-5100
     FAX: 202-707-0712
     TTY:202-707-0744
     nls@loc.gov
     www.loc.gov/nls

Karen Keninger, Director

9065 **Recording for the Blind & Dyslexic**
20 Roszel Road
Princeton, NJ 08540   800-221-4792
     FAX: 609-987-8116
     Custserv@LearningAlly.org
     www.learningally.org/

Brad Grob, Chairman
Harold J. Logan, Vice Chairman
Andrew Friedman, President & CEO
Provides recorded and computerized textbooks, library services and other educational resources to people who cannot effectively read standard print because of visual impairment, dyslexia or other physical disability. RFB&D is now Learning Ally.

9066 **Reference and Information Services From NLS**
Nat'l Lib Svc/Blind And Physically Handicapped
1291 Taylor Street North West
Washington, DC 20011   202-707-5100
     FAX: 202-707-0712
     TTY:202-707-0744
     nls@loc.gov
     www.loc.gov/nls

Karen Keninger, Director

9067 **Resource List for Persons with Low Vision**
American Council of the Blind
2200 Wilson Boulevard
Suite 650
Arlington, VA 22201-3354   202-467-5081
     800-424-8666
     FAX: 703-465-5085
     info@acb.org
     acb.org

Kim Charlson, President
Jeff Thom, 1st Vice President
Melanie Brunson, Executive Director

9068 **Rose-Colored Glasses**
Human Sciences Press
233 Spring St
New York, NY 10013-1522   212-229-2859
     800-221-9369
     FAX: 212-463-0742
After a vacation, Deborah was excited about going back to school. Renewing old friendships, she met a classmate who seemed stuck up. Deborah learned that Melanie was in a recent accident resulting in impaired vision. She did not wish to wear her glasses, which were rose-colored and very funny looking. With Deborah's help, Miss Davis, the teacher showed a blurry film and

then had Melanie speak about her impaired vision. When Melanie began to participate in the class they accepted her. *$16.95*
30 pages Hardcover
ISBN 0-87705 -08-8

9069   **See A Bone**
Facts on File
132 West 31st Street
14th Floor
New York, NY 10001   212-967-8800
                                                       800-683-5433
                                                  FAX: 212-760-0862
                                                info@northernleasing.com
                                                   northernleasing.com

Mark Donnell, President
$65.00
352 pages
ISBN 0-816042-80-2

9070   **See What I Feel**
Britannica Film Company
345 4th Street
San Francisco, CA 94107   415-928-8466
                                                  FAX: 415-928-5027
Dave Bekowich, Owner
A blind child tells her friends about her trip to the zoo. Each experience was explained as a blind child would experience it. A teacher's guide comes with this video.
Film

9071   **Selecting a Program**
Blind Children's Center
4120 Marathon Street
Los Angeles, CA 90029-3584   323-664-2153
                                                info@blindchildrenscenter.org
                                                www.blindchildrenscenter.org
Deborah Chen, Co-Author
Mary Ellen McCann, Co-Author
A free guide for parents of infants and preschoolers with visual impairments.
28 pages

9072   **Show Me How: A Manual for Parents of Preschool Blind Children**
American Foundation for the Blind/AFB Press
2 Penn Plaza
Suite 1102
New York, NY 10121   212-502-7600
                                                       800-232-5463
                                                  FAX: 888-545-8331
                                                    afbinfo@afb.net
                                                       www.afb.org
Carl R. Augusto, President & Chief Executive Officer
Rick Bozeman, Chief Financial Officer
Kelly Bleach, Chief Administrative Officer
A practical guide for parents, teachers and others who help preschool children attain age-related goals. Covers issues on playing precautions, appropriate toys and facilitating relationships with playmates. Paperback. *$12.95*
56 pages
ISBN 0-891281-13-4

9073   **Sign of the Times**
Fanlight Productions
c/o Icarus Films
32 Court Street, 21st Floor
Brooklyn, NY 11201   718-488-8900
                                                       800-876-1710
                                                  FAX: 718-488-8642
                                                   info@fanlight.com
                                                    www.fanlight.com
Ben Achtenberg, Owner, Founder
Profiles a public school in the heart of Los Angeles - an American microcosm where over 300 languages are spoken, and where cultures and races collide. Fairfax High, publicized as the site of gang activity and murder, has long been a focus for bad press. But something very right is going on in this school. A Sign of the Times offers a positive example of how the American dream and American education are still alive

9074   **Special Technologies Alternative Resources**
210 McMorran Boulevard
Port Huron, MI 48060   810-987-7323
                                                     877-987-READ
                                                  star@sccl.lib.mi.us
Arnold H. Larson, Chairman
Kathleen J. Wheelihan, Vice Chairman
Arlene M. Marcetti, Board Member
Addresses the needs of a very unique diverse group of people by offering a full range of library services for people who cannot read standard print. Provides reading material in specialized formats that permit individuals with disabilities to have access to the written word, delivering to customer's mailboxes free of charge. Talking Book Machines, recorded books and magazines, descriptive videos, large print editions and braille books and magazines.

9075   **Standing on My Own Two Feet**
Blind Children's Center
4120 Marathon Street
Los Angeles, CA 90029-3584   323-664-2153
                                                info@blindchildrenscenter.org
                                                www.blindchildrenscenter.org
Lorie Lynn LaPrelle, Author
A guide to constructing mobility devices for children who are visually impaired. *$10.00*
38 pages

9076   **Starting Points**
Blind Children's Center
4120 Marathon Street
Los Angeles, CA 90029-3584   323-664-2153
                                                info@blindchildrenscenter.org
                                                www.blindchildrenscenter.org
Deborah Chen, Co-Author
Jamie Dote-Kwan, Co-Author
Basic information for the clasroom teacher of 3 to 8 year olds whose multiple disabilities include visual impairment. *$35.00*
157 pages
ISBN 0-891280-61-8

9077   **Step-By-Step Guide to Personal Management for Blind Persons**
American Foundation for the Blind/AFB Press
2 Penn Plaza
Suite 1102
New York, NY 10121   212-502-7600
                                                       800-232-5463
                                                  FAX: 888-545-8331
                                                    afbinfo@afb.net
                                                       www.afb.org
Carl R. Augusto, President & Chief Executive Officer
Rick Bozeman, Chief Financial Officer
Kelly Bleach, Chief Administrative Officer
A manual of techniques in the areas of hygiene, grooming, clothing, shopping and child care. *$19.95*
136 pages Spiralbound
ISBN 0-891280-61-8

9078   **Student Teaching Guide for Blind and Visually Impaired College Students**
American Foundation for the Blind/AFB Press
2 Penn Plaza
Suite 1102
New York, NY 10121   212-502-7600
                                                       800-232-5463
                                                  FAX: 888-545-8331
                                                    afbinfo@afb.net
                                                       www.afb.org
Carl R. Augusto, President & Chief Executive Officer
Rick Bozeman, Chief Financial Officer
Kelly Bleach, Chief Administrative Officer
A comprehensive resource designed to enable the student to enter the classroom of a university or college with confidence. Large print. *$14.95*
52 pages
ISBN 0-891281-42-8

9079 Survey of Direct Labor Workers Who Are Blind & Employed by NIB
Mississippi State University
P.O.Box 6189
Mississippi State, MS 39762
662-325-2001
FAX: 662-325-8989
TTY:662-325-2694
nrtc@colled.msstate.edu
www.blind.msstate.edu

Jacqui Bybee, Research Associate II
Douglas Bedsaul, Research and Training Coordinator
Anne Carter, Research and Training Coordinator
This report is a follow-up to surveys by National Industries for the Blind in 1983 and 1987 and summarizes the results of a national survey of approximately 500 legally blind direct labor workers. *$10.00*
101 pages Paperback

9080 Talk to Me
Blind Children's Center
4120 Marathon Street
Los Angeles, CA 90029-3584
323-664-2153
info@blindchildrenscenter.org
www.blindchildrenscenter.org

Nancy Chernus-Mansfield, Co-Author
Linda Kekelis, Co-Author
A language guide for parents of children who are visually impaired. *$10.00*
11 pages

9081 Talk to Me II
Blind Children's Center
4120 Marathon Street
Los Angeles, CA 90029-3584
323-664-2153
FAX: 323-665-3828
info@blindchildrenscenter.org
www.blindchildrenscenter.org

Nancy Chernus-Mansfield, Co-Author
Linda Kekelis, Co-Author
A sequel to Talk to Me *$10.00*
15 pages

9082 Talking Books & Reading Disabilities
Nat'l Lib Svc/Blind And Physically Handicapped
1291 Taylor Street North West
Washington, DC 20011
202-707-5100
FAX: 202-707-0712
TTY:202-707-0744
nls@loc.gov
www.loc.gov/nls

Karen Keninger, Director

9083 Talking Books for People with Physical Disabilities
Nat'l Lib Svc/Blind And Physically Handicapped
1291 Taylor Street North West
Washington, DC 20011
202-707-5100
FAX: 202-707-0712
TTY:202-707-0744
nls@loc.gov
www.loc.gov/nls

Karen Keninger, Director

9084 Teaching Orientation and Mobility in the Schools: An Instructor's Companion
American Foundation for the Blind
2 Penn Plaza
Suite 1102
New York, NY 10121
212-502-7600
800-232-5463
FAX: 888-545-8331
afbinfo@afb.net
www.afb.org

Carl R. Augusto, President & Chief Executive Officer
Rick Bozeman, Chief Financial Officer
Kelly Bleach, Chief Administrative Officer
This book, with its useful forms, checklists, and tips, will help O&M instructors and teachers of visually impaired students master the arts of planning schedules, organizing equipment and work routines, working with school personnel and educational team members, and effectively providing instruction to children with diverse needs. *$45.95*
176 pages
ISBN 0-891283-91-1

9085 Teaching Visually Impaired Children
Charles C. Thomas
2600 S First St
Springfield, IL 62704-4730
217-789-8980
800-258-8980
FAX: 217-789-9130
books@ccthomas.com
www.ccthomas.com

Michael P. Thomas, President
A comprehensive resource for the classroom teacher who is working with a visually impaired child for the first time, as well as a systematic overview of education for the specialist in visual disabilities. It approaches instructional challenges with clear explanations and practical suggestions, and it addresses common concerns of teachers in a reassuring and positive manner. Also available in cloth. *$49.95*
352 pages Paper 2004
ISBN 0-398074-77-7

9086 Textbook Catalog
National Braille Association
95 Allens Creek Road
Building 1, Suite 202
Rochester, NY 14618
585-427-8260
FAX: 585-427-0263
nbaoffice@nationalbraille.org
www.nationalbraille.org

Jan Carroll, President
Cindi Laurent, Vice President
David Shaffer, Executive Director
Lists hundreds of scholarly, college and professional textbooks offered in large print, braille or on cassette for visually impaired readers.
80 pages

9087 Three Rivers News
Carnegie Library of Pitts. Library for the Blind
4724 Baum Boulevard
Pittsburgh, PA 15213
412-687-2440
800-242-0586
FAX: 412-687-2442

Kathleen Kappel, Executive Director
Loans recorded books/magazines and playback equipment, large print books and described videos to western PA residents unable to use standard printed materials due to a visual, physical, or physically-based reading disability.
12 pages Quarterly

9088 To Love this Life: Quotations by Helen Keller
American Foundation for the Blind/AFB Press
2 Penn Plaza
Suite 1102
New York, NY 10121
212-502-7600
800-232-5463
FAX: 888-545-8331
www.afb.org

Carl R. Augusto, President & Chief Executive Officer
Rick Bozeman, Chief Financial Officer
Kelly Bleach, Chief Administrative Officer
Inspirational work that offers the penetrating observations of Helen Keller, the beloved deaf-blind champion of the rights of people with disabilities. Also available on cassette at $21.95 (ISBN# 0-89128-348-X) *$21.95*
144 pages Hardcover
ISBN 0-891283-47-1

9089 **Touch the Baby: Blind & Visually Impaired Children As Patients**
American Foundation for the Blind/AFB Press
2 Penn Plaza
Suite 1102
New York, NY 10121

212-502-7600
800-232-5463
FAX: 888-545-8331
afbinfo@afb.net
www.afb.org

Carl R. Augusto, President & Chief Executive Officer
Rick Bozeman, Chief Financial Officer
Kelly Bleach, Chief Administrative Officer
A how-to manual for health care professionals working in hospitals, clinics and doctors' offices. Teaches the special communication and touch-related techniques needed to prevent blind and visually impaired patients from withdrawing from the healthcare workers and the outside world. $25.00/pack of 25.
13 pages
ISBN 0-891281-97-5

9090 **Transition Activity Calendar for Students with Visual Impairments**
Mississippi State University
P.O.Box 6189
Mississippi State, MS 39762

662-325-2001
FAX: 662-325-8989
TTY:662-325-2694
nrtc@colled.msstate.edu
www.blind.msstate.edu

Jacqui Bybee, Research Associate II
Douglas Bedsaul, Research and Training Coordinator
Anne Carter, Research and Training Coordinator
The Transition Activity Calendar guides the student with a visual disability through the maze of college preparation. Beginning in junior high school, clearly written steps are listed for each grade level. Students planning to enter college after high school graduation can check-off their accomplishments each step of the way. The calendar helps students focus on their goals while providing reminders of tasks yet to be completed. It can be used in a self-directed manner or in a group format. *$4.25*
16 pages Paperback

9091 **Transition to College for Students with Visual Impairments: Report**
Mississippi State University
P.O.Box 6189
Mississippi State, MS 39762

662-325-2001
FAX: 662-325-8989
TTY:662-325-2694
nrtc@colled.msstate.edu
www.blind.msstate.edu

Jacqui Bybee, Research Associate II
Douglas Bedsaul, Research and Training Coordinator
Anne Carter, Research and Training Coordinator
A report offering results from telephone interviews of college students with visual impairments and mail surveys of college officials which examines the transition experience of successful college students. General domains in the study include demographics, educational history, computers, specialized and adaptive equipment, resources, college preparation, problems adjusting to college and O&M skills. A literature review covers preparing for college, task timelines,and classroom, labs and tests. *$20.00*
151 pages Paperback

9092 **Unseen Minority: A Social History of Blindness in the United States**
American Foundation for the Blind/AFB Press
2 Penn Plaza
Suite 1102
New York, NY 10121

212-502-7600
800-232-5463
FAX: 888-545-8331
abfinfo@abf.org
www.afb.org

Carl R. Augusto, President & Chief Executive Officer
Rick Bozeman, Chief Financial Officer
Kelly Bleach, Chief Administrative Officer

A lively narrative, with anecdotes, that recounts how the blind overcame discrimination to gain full participation in the social, educational, economic and legislative spheres. Hardcover.
$59.95
573 pages Paperback
ISBN 0-891288-96-1

9093 **Vision Enhancement**
UN Printing
122
1790 E 54th St
Indianapolis, IN 46220-3454

317-254-1332
800-431-1739
FAX: 317-251-6588
www.visionww.org

Patricia L Price, Managing Editor
Designed to encourage and support individuals with vision loss, family members, and caregivers. *$25.00*
72-78 pages Quarterly

9094 **Visual Impairment: An Overview**
American Foundation for the Blind/AFB Press
2 Penn Plaza
Suite 1102
New York, NY 10121

212-502-7600
800-232-5463
FAX: 888-545-8331
afbinfo@afb.net
www.afb.org

Carl R. Augusto, President & Chief Executive Officer
Rick Bozeman, Chief Financial Officer
Kelly Bleach, Chief Administrative Officer
An overall look at the most common forms of vision loss and their impact on the individual. Includes drawings as well as photographs that stimulate how people with vision loss see. Paperback.
$19.95
56 pages
ISBN 0-891281-74-0

9095 **Visual Impairments And Learning**
Sage Publications
2455 Teller Road
Thousand Oaks, CA 91320

805-499-0721
800-818-7243
FAX: 805-499-0871
info@sagepub.com
www.sagepub.com

Sara Miller McCune, Founder, Publisher, Executive Chairman
Blaise R Simqu, President & CEO
Tracey A. Ozmina, Executive Vice President & Chief Operating Officer
The major focus of this new, third edition is to present a new way of thinking about individuals with visual impairment so that they are viewed as participating members of a seeing world despite their reduced visual functioning. *$40.00*
213 pages
ISBN 0-890798-68-3

9096 **Walking Alone and Marching Together**
National Federation of the Blind
200 E. Wells St.
at Jernigan Place
Baltimore, MD 21230

410-659-9314
FAX: 410-685-5653
nfb@nfb.org
www.nfb.org

Floyd Matson, Author
The history of the organized blind movement, this book spans more than 50 years of civil rights, social issues, attitudes and experiences of the blind. Published in 1990, it has been read by thousands of blind and sighted persons and is used in colleges, libraries and programs across the country as an important tool in understanding blindness and it's impact on both personal lives and the society at large.

9097 **What Do You Do When You See a Blind Person- and What Don't You Do?**
American Foundation for the Blind/AFB Press
2 Penn Plaza
Suite 1102
New York, NY 10121   212-502-7600
                            800-232-5463
                    FAX: 888-545-8331
                        afbinfo@afb.net
                               afb.org

Carl R. Augusto, President & Chief Executive Officer
Rick Bozeman, Chief Financial Officer
Kelly Bleach, Chief Administrative Officer
Examples of real-life situations that teach sighted persons how to interact effectively with blind persons. Topics covered include how to help someone across the street, how not to distract a guide dog and how to take leave of a blind person. *$25.00*
8 pages
ISBN 0-891281-95-5

9098 **What Museum Guides Need to Know: Access for the Blind and Visually Impaired**
American Foundation for the Blind/AFB Press
2 Penn Plaza
Suite 1102
New York, NY 10121   212-502-7600
                            800-232-5463
                    FAX: 888-545-8331
                        afbinfo@afb.net
                           www.afb.org

Carl R. Augusto, President & Chief Executive Officer
Rick Bozeman, Chief Financial Officer
Kelly Bleach, Chief Administrative Officer
Explains how blind and visually impaired museum-goers experience art and offers pointers on greeting people, asking if help is needed and teaching about a specific work of art. Contains information on access laws, resources, training guides and guidelines for preparing large print, cassette and braille materials. *$14.95*
64 pages Paperback
ISBN 0-891281-58-4

9099 **Work Sight**
Lighthouse Guild
250 West 64th Street
New York, NY 10023   800-284-4422
                    www.lighthouseguild.org

Calvin W. Roberts, President & CEO
James M. Dubin, Chairman
Lawrence E. Goldschmidt, Vice Chairman & Treasurer
Intended for employers and employees who have concerns about vision loss and job performance. *$25.00*

9100 **World Through Their Eyes**
Lighthouse Guild
250 West 64th Street
New York, NY 10023   800-284-4422
                    www.lighthouseguild.org

Calvin W. Roberts, President & CEO
James M. Dubin, Chairman
Lawrence E. Goldschmidt, Vice Chairman & Treasurer
Intended to help nursing home staff understand how residents with impaired vision perceive the world. Concrete suggestions help staff provide better care to visually impaired residents. *$25.00*

9101 **You Seem Like a Regular Kid to Me**
American Foundation for the Blind/AFB Press
2 Penn Plaza
Suite 1102
New York, NY 10121   212-502-7600
                            800-232-5463
                    FAX: 888-545-8331
                        afbinfo@afb.net
                           www.afb.org

Carl R. Augusto, President & Chief Executive Officer
Rick Bozeman, Chief Financial Officer
Kelly Bleach, Chief Administrative Officer
An interview with Jane, a blind child, tells other children what it's like to be blind. Jane explains how she gets around, takes care of herself, does her school work, spends her leisure time and even pays for things when she can't see money.
16 pages
ISBN 0-891289-21-6

Journals

9102 **Journal of Visual Impairment and Blindness**
Sheridan Press,
450 Fame Ave
Hanover, PA 17331-1585   717-632-3535
                                800-352-2210
                        FAX: 717-633-8929
                    www.sheridanreprints.com

Sharon Shively, Editor
Published in braille, regular print and on ASC II disk and cassette, this journal contains a wide variety of subjects including rehabilitation, psychology, education, legislation, medicine, technology, employment, sensory aids and childhood development as they relate to visual impairments. $130 annual individual subscription, $180 annual institutional subscription.
64 pages Monthly
ISSN 0145-48 x

Magazines

9103 **Braille Forum**
American Council of the Blind
2200 Wilson Boulevard
Suite 650
Arlington, VA 22201-3354   202-467-5081
                                  800-424-8666
                          FAX: 703-465-5085
                              info@acb.org
                              www.acb.org

Kim Charlson, President
Jeff Thom, 1st Vice President
Melanie Brunson, Executive Director
Offered in print, braille, cassette, IBM computer disk and e-mail. $25 per format per year for companies and non-US residents.
48 pages Magazine

9104 **Braille Montior**
National Federation of the Blind
200 E. Wells St.
at Jernigan Place
Baltimore, MD 21230   410-659-9314
                      FAX: 410-685-5653
                    nfbpublications@nfb.org
                           www.nfb.org

Gary Wunder, Editor
The Braille Monitor is the leading publication of the National Federation of the Blind. It covers the events and activities of the NFB and addresses the many issues and concerns of the blind. *$40.00*
11 times a year

9105 **Dialogue Magazine**
Blindskills Inc.
P.O. Box 5181
Salem, OR 97304-0181   503-581-4224
                              800-860-4224
                      FAX: 503-581-0178
                    info@blindskills.com
                    www.blindskills.com

Marja Byers, Executive Director
B.T. Kimbrough, Editor
Publishes quarterly magazine in braille, large-type, cassette and email of news items, technology and articles of special interest to visually impaired youth and adults. Annual subscription cost $35 for braille, large print or cassette, $20 for email. *$35.00*
Quarterly

9106 Future Reflections
Deaf-Blind Division of the Ntn'l Fed of the Blind
200 E. Wells St.
at Jernigan Place
Baltimore, MD 21230
410-659-9314
FAX: 410-685-5653
nfbpublications@nfb.org
www.nfb.org

Deborah Kent Stein, Editor
A magazine for parents and teachers of blind children.

9107 Guide Magazine
The Seeing Eye
P.O.Box 375
10 Washington Valley Road
Morristown, NJ 7963
973-539-4425
FAX: 973-539-0922
info@seeingeye.org
seeingeye.org

James A. Kutsch, Jr., Ph.D., President & CEO
Robert Pudlak, CFO & Director of Administration & Finance
Glenn Cianci, Director of Facilities Management
The Guide offers stories of inspiration from our graduates and news of the latest program developments.

9108 JBI Voice
Jewish Braille Institute of America
110 Est 30th Street
New York, NY 10016
212-889-2525
800-433-1531
FAX: 212-689-3692
admin@jbilibrary.org
www.jbilibrary.org

Judy E. Tenney, Chairman
Thomas G. Kahn, Vice Chairman
Dr. Ellen Isler, President and CEO
Monthly recorded magazine emphasizing Jewish current events and culture.

9109 Jewish Braille Review
Jewish Braille Institute of America
110 Est 30th Street
New York, NY 10016
212-889-2525
800-433-1531
FAX: 212-689-3692
admin@jbilibrary.org
www.jbilibrary.org

Judy E. Tenney, Chairman
Thomas G. Kahn, Viec Chairman
Dr. Ellen Isler, President and CEO
The JBI seeks the integration of Jews who are blind, visually impaired and reading disabled into the Jewish community and society in general. More than 20,000 men, women and children in 50 countries receive a broad variety of JBI services.

9110 Musical Mainstream
Nat'l Lib Svc/Blind And Physically Handicapped
1291 Taylor Street North West
Washington, DC 20011
202-707-5100
FAX: 202-707-0712
TTY:202-707-0744
nls@loc.gov
www.loc.gov/nls

Karen Keninger, Director
Articles selected from print music magazines.
Quarterly

9111 Opportunity
National Industries for the Blind
1310 Braddock Place
Alexandria, VA 22314-1691
703-310-0500
FAX: 703-998-8268
services@nib.org
www.nib.org

The Honorabl Krump, Esq., Chairman
Louis J. Jablonski, Jr., Vice Chairman
Kevin A. Lynch, President and Chief Executive Officer
Offers information and articles on the newest technology, equipment, services and programs for blind and visually impaired persons.
Quarterly

9112 Providing Services for People with Vision Loss: Multidisciplinary Perspective
Resources for Rehabilitation
22 Bonad Road
Winchester, MA 01890-1302
781-368-9080
FAX: 781-368-9096
orders@rfr.org
www.rfr.org

Susan L Greenblatt, Editor
A collection of articles by ophthalmologists and rehabilitation professionals, including chapters on operating a low vision service, starting self-help programs, mental health services, aids and techniques that help people with vision loss. *$19.95*
136 pages
ISBN 0-929718-02-0

Newsletters

9113 AFB News
American Foundation for the Blind/AFB Press
2 Penn Plaza
Suite 1102
New York, NY 10121
212-502-7600
800-232-5463
FAX: 888-545-8331
afbinfo@afb.net
www.afb.org

Carl R. Augusto, President & Chief Executive Officer
Rick Bozeman, Chief Financial Officer
Kelly Bleach, Chief Administrative Officer
National newsletter for general readership about blindness and visual impairments featuring people, programs, services and activities.
12 pages Quarterly

9114 ASB Visions Newsletter
ASB
919 Walnut Street
Philadelphia, PA 19107-5237
215-627-0600
FAX: 215-922-0692
asbinfo@asb.org
www.asb.org

Karla S. McCaney, President & CEO
Beth Deering, Chief Program Officer
Sylvia Purnell, Director of Learning & Development
Newsletter associated services for the blind and visually impaired.

9115 Adaptive Services Division
District of Columbia Public Library
901G St NW,
Rm 215
Washington, DC 20001-4531
202-727-2142
FAX: 202-727-0322
TTY:202-559-5368
lbph.dcpl@dc.gov
www.dclibrary.org

Venetia Demson, Chief, Adaptive Services
DC Regional Library for the blind, deaf and physically handicapped. Provides adaptive technology and training programs.
8 pages Quarterly

9116 Alumni News
Guide Dogs for the Blind
P.O.Box 151200
San Rafael, CA 94915-1200
415-499-4000
800-295-4050
FAX: 415-499-4035
guidedogs.com

Bob Burke, Chairman
Stuart Odell, Vice Chairman
Chris Benninger, President and CEO
Restricted to graduates only.

9117   Annual Report/Newsletter
National Accreditation Council for Agencies/Blind
Rm 1004
15 E 40th St
New York, NY 10016-401   212-683-5068
                                    FAX: 212-683-4475
Ruth Westman, Executive Director
Provides standards and a program of accreditation for schools
and organizations which serve children and adults who are blind
or vision impaired.

9118   Association for Macular Diseases Newsletter
210 East 64th Street
New York, NY 10065   212-605-3719
                                    FAX: 212-605-3795
                            association@retinal-research.org
                                            macula.org

Bernard Landou, President
Mary Fern Breheny, Board Member
Patricia Dahl, Board Member
Not-for-profit organization promotes education and research in
this scarcely explored field. Acts as a nationwide support group
for individuals and their families endeavoring to adjust to the restrictions and changes brought about by macular disease. Offers
hotline, educational materials, quarterly newsletter, support
groups, referrals and seminars for persons and families affected
by macular disease.

9119   Awareness
NAPVI
1 North Lexington Avenue
White Plains, NY 10601   617-972-7441
                                          800-562-6265
                                     FAX: 617-972-7444
                                   napvi@guildhealth.org
                                         www.napvi.org
Julie Urban, President
Venetia Hayden, Vice President
Susan LaVenture, Executive Director
Newsletter offering regional news, sports and activities, confer-
ences, camps, legislative updates, book reviews, audio reviews,
professional question and answer column and more for the visu-
ally impaired and their families.
Quarterly

9120   BTBL News
Braille and Talking Book Library
P.O. Box 942837
Sacramento, CA 94237-0001   916-654-0261
                                          800-952-5666
                                     FAX: 916-654-1119
                                      btbl@library.ca.gov
                                        www.btbl.ca.gov

Janet Coles, Editor
Christopher Berger, Senior Librarian
Olena Bilyk, Web Developer
BTBL News, the quarterly newsletter of the California Braille
and Talking Book Library, features articles on topics of interest to
library customers, including information about new services, existing services, events, staff and more.

9121   Canes and Trails
Guide Dogs for the Blind
P.O.Box 151200
San Rafael, CA 94915-1200   415-499-4000
                                          800-295-4050
                                     FAX: 415-499-4035
                                            guidedogs.com

Bob Burke, Chairman
Stuart Odell, Vice Chairman
Chris Benninger, President and CEO
A quarterly newsletter for orientation and mobility specialists, re-
habilitation professionals, teachers, and service providers in the
field of blindness and visual impairment.

9122   Community Connection
Guide Dogs for the Blind
P.O.Box 151200
San Rafael, CA 94915-1200   415-499-4000
                                          800-295-4050
                                     FAX: 415-499-4035
                                            guidedogs.com
Bob Burke, Chairman
Stuart Odell, Vice Chairman
Chris Benninger, President and CEO
A newsletter produced for our volunteers and other friends of
Guide Dogs.

9123   DVH Quarterly
University of Arkansas at Little Rock
2801 S University Ave
Little Rock, AR 72204-1000   501-569-3000
Bob Brasher, Editor
Mary Boaz, Manager
Offers information on upcoming events, conferences and work-
shops on and for visual disabilities. Book reviews, information
on the newest resources and technology, educational programs,
want ads and more.
Quarterly

9124   Deaf-Blind Perspective
National Consortium on Deaf-Blindness
345 North Monmouth Avenue
Monmouth, OR 97361   503-838-8391
                                          800-438-9376
                                     FAX: 503-838-8150
                                     TTY: 800-854-7013

Ingrid Amerson, Child Development Center
Lyn Ayer, Center on Deaf & Blindness
Robert Ayres, Evaluation and Research
A free publication with articles, essays, and announcements
about topics related to people who are deaf-blind. Published two
times a year (Spring and Fall) by the Teaching Research Institute
of Western Oregon University, its purpose is to provide information and serve as a forum for discussion and sharing ideas.

9125   Fidelco
Fidelco Guide Dog Foundation
103 Vision Way
Bloomfield, CT 06002   860-243-5200
                                     FAX: 860-769-0567
                                        info@fidelco.org
                                            fidelco.org

Karen C. Tripp, Chairman
G. Kenneth Bernhard, Vice Chairman
Eliot D. Matheson, CEO
A newsletter published by Fidelco Guide Dog Foundation.

9126   Focus
Visually Impaired Center
1422 W Court St
Flint, MI 48503-5008   810-767-4014
                                     FAX: 810-767-0020

Charles Tommasulo, Executive Director
Newsletter offering information for the visually impaired person
in the forms of legislative and law updates, ADA information,
support groups, hotlines, and articles on the newest technology in
the field.
Quarterly

9127   Gleams Newsletter
Glaucoma Research Foundation
2345 Yale Street
2nd Floor
Palo Alto, CA 94306   650-328-3388
                                          800-826-6693
                                     FAX: 415-986-3763
                                    info@glaucoma.org

Tom Brunner, CEO
Offers updated medical & research information on glaucoma. Included are glaucoma treatment and coping tips, legislative information, professional articles and book reviews.
6 pages Quarterly

9128   Guide Dog News
Guide Dogs for the Blind
P.O.Box 151200
San Rafael, CA 94915-1200   415-499-4000
                                              800-295-4050
                                         FAX: 415-499-4035
                                            guidedogs.com

Bob Burke, Chairman
Stuart Odell, Vice Chairman
Chris Benninger, President and CEO
Read about changes to our teaching techniques, our new Adult
Learning Program, vet tips, and find news about our graduates.

9129   Guideway
Guide Dog Foundation for the Blind
371 East Jericho Turnpike
Smithtown, NY 11787-2976   631-930-9000
                                              800-548-4337
                                         FAX: 631-930-9009
                                         info@guidedog.org
                                           www.guidedog.org

James C. Bingham, Chairman
Alphonce J. Brown, Jr., Vice Chairman
Wells B. Jones, CEO
Offers updates and information on the foundation's activities and
guide dog programs. In print form but is also available on
cassette.
Monthly

9130   Guild Briefs
Catholic Guild for The Blind
65 East Wacker Place
Suite 1010
Chicago, IL 60601   312-236-8569
                                         FAX: 312-236-8128
                                      www.guildfortheblind.org

Brett Christenson, President
Laura Rounce, Vice President
David Tabak, Executive Director
Monthly publication for individuals who are blind or visually impaired. It contains articles on topics such as service programs,
scholarships, education, seniors, research, and government.
12 pages monthly

9131   IAAIS Report
Int'l Association of Audio Information Services
3920 Willshire Dr
Lawrence, KS 66049-3673   412-434-6023
                                              800-280-5325
                                              www.iaais.org

Stuart Holland, President
Marjorie Williams, 1st Vice President
Linda Hynson, Secretary
Newsletter for persons interested in radio reading services. *$7.00*
Quarterly

9132   Insight
Eye Bank Association of America
Ste 1010
1015 18th Street NorthWest
Washington, DC 20036   202-775-4999
                                         FAX: 202-429-6036
                                         info@restoresight.org
                                         www.restoresight.org

Colleen Bayus, Communications Manager
An electronic newsletter.

9133   LampLighter
Columbia Lighthouse for the Blind
1825 K St. NW
Suite 1103
Washington, DC 20006   202-454-6400
                                         FAX: 202-955-6401
                                              info@clb.org
                                               www.clb.org

Tony Cancelosi, President & CEO
Jocelyn Hunter, Senior Director, Communications
Toya Horten, Director, Administrative Operations
Columbia Lighthouse for the Blind's monthly newsletter. Pro-
vides information on community news and events.

9134   Library Users of America Newsletter
American Council of the Blind
2200 Wilson Boulevard
Suite 650
Arlington, VA 22201-3354   202-467-5081
                                              800-424-8666
                                         FAX: 703-465-5085
                                               info@acb.org
                                                www.acb.org

Kim Charlson, President
Jeff Thom, 1st Vice President
Melanie Brunson, Executive Director
Published twice yearly, the newsletter contains much information
about library services of particular interest to blind and visually
impaired patrons, and is available in the following formats:
Braille, audiocassette, large print and e-mail.

9135   Light the Way
Blind Children's Center
4120 Marathon Street
Los Angeles, CA 90029-3584   323-664-2153
                                    info@blindchildrenscenter.org
                                        blindchildrenscenter.org

Sarah E. Orth, CEO
Newsletter of the Blind Childrens Center, a family-centered
agency which serves young children with visual impairments.
The center-based and home-based services help the children to
acquire skills and build their independence. The center utilizes its
expertise and experience to serve families and professionals
worldwide through support services, education and research.

9136   Lighthouse Publication
Chicago Lighthouse
1850 West Roosevelt Road
Chicago, IL 60608-1298   312-666-1331
                                         FAX: 312-243-8539
                                          TTY:312-666-8874
                              publications@chicagolighthouse.org
                                www.thechicagolighthouse.org
Janet P. Szlyk, Ph.D., President & Chief Executive Officer
Mary Lynne Januszewski, Executive Vice President/CFO
Melanie M. Hennessy, SVP

9137   Lights On
Fight for Sight
Ste 809
391 Park Ave S
New York, NY 10016-8806   212-679-6060
                                         FAX: 212-679-4466

Mary Prudden, Executive Director
A newsletter published by Fight for Sight.

9138   Listen Up
Recording for the Blind & Dyslexic
20 Roszel Rd
Princeton, NJ 8540-6206   609-452-0606
                                              866-732-3585
                                         FAX: 609-520-7990
                                          www.learningally.org

John Kelly, CEO
RFB&D's bi-monthly electronic newsletter for members.

9139   Long Cane News
American Foundation for the Blind/AFB Press
2 Penn Plaza
Suite 1102
New York, NY 10121   212-502-7600
                                              800-232-5463
                                         FAX: 888-545-8331
                                             afbinfo@afb.net
                                                www.afb.org

Carl R. Augusto, President & Chief Executive Officer
Rick Bozeman, Chief Financial Officer
Kelly Bleach, Chief Administrative Officer
SemiAnnual

9140 Magnifier
Macular Degeneration Foundation
P.O.Box 531313
Henderson, NV 89053

702-450-2908
888-633-3937
liz@eyesight.org
www.eyesight.org

Liz Trauernicht, President & Director of Communications
Julie Zavala, VP & Asst. Director of Operations
David Seftel, EVP & Dircetor, R & D
The Magnifier is the distributed without charge via email and by regular mail to those without access to the Internet. It features breaking news, clinical trails, clarifies recent reports in the media, announces new Internet resources and informs the public of important additions to the web site.

9141 NAVH Update
National Association of Visually Handicapped
111 East 59th Street
New York, NY 10022-1202

212-821-9384
800-829-0500
FAX: 212-821-9707
info@lighthouse.org
lighthouse.org/navh

Mark G. Ackermann, President/CEO
A newsletter published by the National Association of Visually Impaired. LightHouse acquired NAVH.

9142 NBA Bulletin
National Braille Association
95 Allens Creek Road
Building 1, Suite 202
Rochester, NY 14618

585-427-8260
FAX: 585-427-0263
nbaoffice@nationalbraille.org
www.nationalbraille.org

Jan Carroll, President
Cindi Laurent, Vice President
David Shaffer, Executive Director
Published quarterly and included int he price of the regular and student NBA membership.

9143 NLS News
Nat'l Lib Svc/Blind And Physically Handicapped
1291 Taylor Street North West
Washington, DC 20011

202-707-5100
FAX: 202-707-0712
TTY:202-707-0744
nls@loc.gov
www.loc.gov/nls

Karen Keninger, Director
Newsletter on current program developments.
Quarterly

9144 NLS Newsletter
Nat'l Lib Svc/Blind And Physically Handicapped
1291 Taylor Street North West
Washington, DC 20011

202-707-5100
FAX: 202-707-0712
TTY:202-707-0744
nls@loc.gov
www.loc.gov/nls

Karen Keninger, Director
Newsletter on the service's volunteer activities.
Quarterly

9145 PBA News
Prevent Blindness America
211 West Wacker Drive
Suite 1700
Chicago, IL 60606

800-331-2020
info@preventblindness.org
www.preventblindness.org

Paul G. Howes, Chairman
Hugh R. Parry, President & CEO, Prevent Blindness America
Jerome Desserich, Vice President & Chief Financial Officer
Newsletter is filled with the information you need to protect your eyes, preserve your sight, and educate yourself about your own eye condition or that of a family member. Publication offered three times yearly.
3 times yearly

9146 Planned Giving Department of Guide Dogs for the Blind
Guide Dogs for the Blind
P.O.Box 151200
San Rafael, CA 94915-1200

415-499-4000
800-295-4050
FAX: 415-499-4035
guidedogs.com

Bob Burke, Chairman
Stuart Odell, Vice Chairman
Chris Benninger, President and CEO
A newsletter published by Guide Dogs for the Blind.

9147 Playback
Recording for the Blind & Dyslexic
20 Roszel Road
Princeton, NJ 08540

800-221-4792
FAX: 609-987-8116
Custserv@LearningAlly.org
www.learningally.org/

Brad Grob, Chairman
Harold J. Logan, Vice Chairman
Andrew Friedman, President & CEO
A publication dedicated to our unit's family of members, volunteers, supporters and staff. RFB&D is now Learning Ally.
3x Year

9148 Quarterly Update
National Association for Visually Handicapped
111 East 59th Street
New York, NY 10022-1202

212-821-9384
800-829-0500
FAX: 212-821-9707
info@lighthouse.org
lighthouse.org/navh

Mark G. Ackermann, President/CEO
Quarterly newsletter offering information on new products for the visually impaired, advances in medical treatments, new books available in the NAVH large print loan library and any new/updated booklets. Free. LightHouse acquired NAVH.

9149 RP Messenger
Texas Association of Retinitis Pigmentosa
P.O.Box 8388
Corpus Christi, TX 78468-8388

361-852-8515
FAX: 361-852-8515
tarp@homebiz101.com

Dorothy Steifel, Executive Director
A bi-annual newsletter offering information on Retinitis Pigmentosa. *$15.00*
BiAnnual

9150 SCENE
Braille Institute
527 North Dale Avenue
Anaheim, CA 92801

714-821-5000
800-272-4553
FAX: 714-527-7621
oc@brailleinstitute.org
brailleinstitute.org

Lester M. Sussman, Chairman
Peter A. Mindnich, President
Jon K. Hayashida, OD, FAAO, Vice President, Programs & Services
Offers information on the organization, question and answer column, articles on the newest technology and more for visually impaired persons.

9151 STAR
Special Technologies Alternative Resources
210 McMorran Boulevard
Port Huron, MI 48060

810-987-7323
877-987-READ
star@sccl.lib.mi.us
www.sccl.lib.mi.us

Arnold H. Larson, Chairman
Kathleen J. Wheelihan, Vice Chairman
Arlene M. Marcetti, Board Member
A newsletter published by Special Technologies Alternative Resources.

9152 Seeing Eye Guide
The Seeing Eye
P.O.Box 375
10 Washington Valley Road
Morristown, NJ 07963
973-539-4425
FAX: 973-539-0922
info@seeingeye.org
seeingeye.org

James A. Kutsch, Jr., Ph.D., President & CEO
Randall Ivens, Director of Human Resources
Robert Pudlak, CFO & Director of Adninistration & Finance
A quarterly publication from Seeing Eye.
Quarterly

9153 Shared Visions
Vista Center for the Blind & Visually Impaired
413 Laurel St
Santa Cruz, CA 95060-4904
831-458-9766
800-705-2970
FAX: 831-426-6233
information@vistacenter.org

Pam Brandin, Executive Director
A quarterly publication for Blind and Visually Impaired individuals from Vista Center for the Blind and Visually Impaired.

9154 Sharing Solutions: A Newsletter for Support Groups
Lighthouse Guild
250 West 64th Street
New York, NY 10023
800-284-4422
www.lighthouseguild.org

Calvin W. Roberts, President & CEO
James M. Dubin, Chairman
Lawrence E. Goldschmidt, Vice Chairman & Treasurer
A newsletter for members and leaders of support groups for older adults with impaired vision. The letter provides a forum for support groups members to network and share information, printed in a very large type format.

9155 Sightings Newsletter
Schepens Eye Research Institute
20 Staniford Street
Boston, MA 02114
617-912-0100
FAX: 617-912-0110
www.schepens.harvard.edu

Michael Gilmore, Director
Mary E. Leach, Director of Public Affairs
Frances Ng, Director of Human Resources
Publication of prominent center for research on eye, vision, and blinding diseases; dedicated to research that improves the understanding, management, and prevention of eye diseases and visual deficiencies; fosters collaboration among its faculty members; trains young scientists and clinicians from around the world; promotes communication with scientists in allied fields; leader in the worldwide dispersion of basic scientific knowledge of vision.

9156 Smith Kettlewell Rehabilitation Engineering Research Center
2318 Fillmore Street
San Francisco, CA 94115
415-345-2000
FAX: 415-345-8455
rerc@ski.org
ski.org

John Brabyn, Ph.D., CEO/Executive Director
Ruth S. Poole, COO
Arthur Jampolsky, Director
Reports on technology and devices for persons with visual impairments.

9157 Student Advocate
National Alliance of Blind Students NABS Liaison
Ste 1004
1155 15th St NW
Washington, DC 20005-2706
202-467-5081
800-424-8666
FAX: 202-467-5085
www.blindstudents.org

Melanie Brunson, Executive Director
A newsletter created by members of NABS and for any interested parties.

9158 TBC Focus
Chicago Public Library Talking Books Center
400 South State Street
Chicago, IL 60605
312-747-4300
800-757-4654
FAX: 312-747-1609
www.chipublib.org

Linda Johnson Rice, President
Christopher Valenti, VP
Christina Benitez, Secretary
Published quarterly by the Chicago Public Library Talking Book Center. Free of charge.
4 pages Quarterly

9159 Talking Books Topics
Nat'l Lib Svc/Blind And Physically Handicapped
1291 Taylor Street North West
Washington, DC 20011
202-707-5100
FAX: 202-707-0712
TTY:202-707-0744
nls@loc.gov
www.loc.gov/nls

Karen Keninger, Director
New recorded books and program news
Bi-monthly

9160 Upstate Update
New York State Talking Book & Braille Library
222 Madison Avenue
Albany, NY 12230-1
518-474-5935
800-342-3688
FAX: 514-474-5786
TTY: 518-474-7121
nyslweb@mail.nysed.gov
www.nysl.nysed.gov

Bernard A. Margolis, State Librarian & Asst. Commissioner for Libraries
Loretta Ebert, Research Library Director
Liza Duncan, Technical Services & Systmes
Books on audio cassette, cassette players, braille books, summer reading programs, braille writer, magnifiers, closed-circuit T.V., large-print photocopier, cassette books and magazines, children's books on cassette, reference materials on blindness and other handicaps.
4 pages Quarterly

9161 Visual Aids and Informational Material
National Association for Visually Handicapped
111 East 59th Street
New York, NY 10022-1202
212-821-9384
800-829-0500
FAX: 212-821-9707
info@lighthouse.org
lighthouse.org/navh

Mark G. Ackermann, President/CEO
A complete listing of the visual aids NAVH carries such as magnifiers, talking clocks, large print playing cards, etc. LightHouse acquired NAVH. $2.50
65 pages

9162 Voice
Vermont Assn for the Blind & Visually Impaired
60 Kimball Avenue
South Burlington, VT 05403
802-863-1358
800-639-5861
FAX: 802-863-1481
General@vabvi.org
vabvi.org

Thomas Chase, President
Stephen Pouliot, Executive Director
Kathleen Quinlan, Director of Operations
The Voice is a newsletter published by Vermont Association for the Blind and Visually Impaired.

9163 Voice of Vision
GW Micro
725 Airport North Office Park
Fort Wayne, IN 46825
260-489-3671
FAX: 260-489-2608
www.gwmicro.com

Dan Weirich, Owner

Offers product reviews, product announcements, tips for making systems or applications more accessible, or explanations of concepts of interest to any computer user or would-be computer user. This association newsletter is available in braille, in large print, on audio cassette and on 3.5 or 5.25 IBM format diskette.
Quarterly

Audio/Visual

9164   Aging and Vision: Declarations of Independence
American Foundation for the Blind/AFB Press
2 Penn Plaza
Suite 1102
New York, NY 10121   212-502-7600
                                                     800-232-5463
                                                FAX: 888-545-8331
                                                   afbinfo@afb.net
                                                      www.afb.org
Carl R. Augusto, President & Chief Executive Officer
Rick Bozeman, Chief Financial Officer
Kelly Bleach, Chief Administrative Officer
A very personal look at five older people who have successfully coped with visual impairment and continue to lead active, satisfying lives. Their stories are not only inspirational, but also provide practical, down-to-earth suggestions for adapting to vision loss later in life. 18 minute video tape. Also available in PAL, $52.95, 0-89128-276-9. *$42.95*
VHS
ISBN 0-891282-20-3

9165   Blindness, A Family Matter
American Foundation for the Blind/AFB Press
2 Penn Plaza
Suite 1102
New York, NY 10121   212-502-7600
                                                     800-232-5463
                                                FAX: 888-545-8331
                                                   afbinfo@afb.net
                                                      www.afb.org
Carl R. Augusto, President & Chief Executive Officer
Rick Bozeman, Chief Financial Officer
Kelly Bleach, Chief Administrative Officer
A frank exploration of the effects of an individual's visual impairment on other members of the family and how those family members can play a positive role in the rehabilitation process. Features interviews with three families whose 'success stories' provide advice and encouragement, as well as interviews with newly blinded adults currently involved in a rehabilitation program. 23 minute video tape. Also available in PAL, $49.95, 0-89128-271-8. *$43.95*
VHS
ISBN 0-891282-22-X

9166   Building Blocks: Foundations for Learning for Young Blind and Visually Impaired Children
American Foundation for the Blind/AFB Press
2 Penn Plaza
Suite 1102
New York, NY 10121   212-502-7600
                                                     800-232-5463
                                                FAX: 888-545-8331
                                                   afbinfo@afb.net
                                                      www.afb.org
Carl R. Augusto, President & Chief Executive Officer
Rick Bozeman, Chief Financial Officer
Kelly Bleach, Chief Administrative Officer
Presents the essential components of a successful early intervnetion program, including collaboration with family members, positive relationships between parents and professionals, public education, and attention to important programming components such as space exploration, braille readiness, orientation and mobility, play, cooking and music. Includes interviews with parents. Available in English or Spanish. 10 minute video tape. Also available in PAL, $33.95, 0-89128-268-8. *$26.95*
VHS
ISBN 0-891282-14-9

9167   Choice Magazine Listening
85 Channel Drive
Port Washington, NY 11050   516-883-8280
                                                     888-724-6423
                                                     888-724-6423
                                                FAX: 516-944-5849
                                                 choicemag@aol.com
                                    www.choicemagazinelistening.org
Pamela Loeser, Editor in Chief
Ann Schlegel-Kyrkostas, Associate Editor
David Graham Pade, Associate Editor
A free audio anthology is available bi-monthly to visually impaired/physically disabled or dislexic persons nationwide. Playable on the special free 4-track cassette playback equipment which is provided by the Library of Congress through the National Library Service. Each issue features eight hours of unabridged magazine articles, short stories, poetry and media selections from over 100 sources. College level and older. Bimonthly distribution.
Bi-Monthly

9168   Heart to Heart
Blind Children's Center
4120 Marathon St
Los Angeles, CA 90029-3584   323-664-2153
                                          info@blindchildrenscenter.org
                                          www.blindchildrenscenter.org
Nancy Chernus-Mansfield, Co-Author
Dori Hayashi, Co-Author
Parents of blind and partially sighted children talk about their feelings. *$35.00*
VHS/DVD

9169   Juggler
Beacon Press
24 Farnsworth Street
Boston, MA 02210   617-742-2110
                                                FAX: 617-723-3097
                                                       beacon.org
Helene Atwan, Executive Director
Andre was the young son of a wealthy, early Quebec fur trader. Because he was almost totally blind, he was overly protected by his family, and his movement outside his home was very limited.
Film

9170   Let's Eat Video
Blind Children's Center
4120 Marathon Street
Los Angeles, CA 90029-3584   323-664-2153
                                          info@blindchildrenscenter.org
                                              blindchildrenscenter.org
Jill Brody, Co-Author
Lynne Webber, Co-Author
Babies and toddlers with visual impairments lack one major avenue of exploration, and this significantly infulences their awareness, perceptions, and anticipation of the food which is presented to them. *$35.00*
VHS/DVD

9171   Look Out for Annie
Lighthouse Guild
250 West 64th Street
New York, NY 10023   800-284-4422
                                                www.lighthouseguild.org
Calvin W. Roberts, President & CEO
James M. Dubin, Chairman
Lawrence E. Goldschmidt, Vice Chairman & Treasurer
Depicts an older woman coping with her vision loss. It focuses on the emotional issues surrounding vision loss and conveys the idea that both the person with the vision disorder and their family and friends will need to make adjustments. *$25.00*
Video

9172 Not Without Sight
American Foundation for the Blind/AFB Press
PO Box 1020
Sewickley, PA 15143-920

412-741-1142
800-232-3044
FAX: 412-741-0609
www.afb.org

Carl R Augusto, President/CEO
Tracy Charlovich, Css
This video describes the major types of visual impairment and their causes and effects on vision, while camera simulations approximate what people with each impairmant actually see. Also demonstrates how people with low vision make the best use of the vision they have. 20 minute video tape, $49.95. *$42.95*
VHS 17 min
ISBN 0-891282-27-3

9173 Out of Left Field
American Foundation for the Blind/AFB Press
2 Penn Plaza
Suite 1102
New York, NY 10121

212-502-7600
800-232-5463
FAX: 888-545-8331
afbinfo@afb.net
afb.org

Carl R. Augusto, President & Chief Executive Officer
Rick Bozeman, Chief Financial Officer
Kelly Bleach, Chief Administrative Officer
Illustrates how youngsters who are blind or visually impaired integrated with their sighted peers in a variety of recreational and athletic activities. 17 minute video tape. Also available in PAL, $33.95, 0-89128-270-X. *$29.95*
VHS 17 minutes
ISBN 0-891282-28-0

9174 See What I'm Saying
Fanlight Productions
c/o Icarus Films
32 Court Street, 21st Floor
Brooklyn, NY 11201

718-488-8900
800-876-1710
FAX: 718-488-8642
info@fanlight.com
www.fanlight.com

Ben Achtenberg, Founder, Owner
The documentary follows Patricia, who is deaf and from a Spanish-speaking family, through her first year at the Kendall Demonstration Elementary School of Gallaudet University.
VHS/DVD

9175 See for Yourself
Lighthouse Guild
250 West 64th Street
New York, NY 10023

800-284-4422
www.lighthouseguild.org

Calvin W. Roberts, President & CEO
James M. Dubin, Chairman
Lawrence E. Goldschmidt, Vice Chairman & Treasurer
This video features older adults with impaired vision who have been helped by vision rehabilitation. *$50.00*

9176 Shape Up 'n Sign
Harris Communications
15155 Technology Dr
Eden Prairie, MN 55344-2273

952-906-1180
800-825-6758
FAX: 952-906-1099
info@harriscomm.com

Robert Harris, Owner
An aerobic exercise tape introducing the basic sign language for deaf and hearing children ages six to ten. *$29.95*
30 Minutes DVD

9177 Sight by Touch
Landmark Media
3450 Slade Run Drive
Falls Church, VA 22042

703-241-2030
800-342-4336
FAX: 703-536-9540
info@landmarkmedia.com

Michael Hartogs, President
Peter Hartogs, VP New Business & Development
Beverly Weisenberg, Sales Rep
This video features the life and importance of Louis Braille. Vision-impaired performers and teachers demonstrate how Braille has benefitted their lives, and how improvements are constantly being made. *$195.00*
Video

9178 Taping for the Blind
3935 Essex Lane
Houston, TX 77027

713-622-2767
FAX: 713-622-2772
www.afb.org

Carl R. Augusto, President & Chief Executive Officer
Rick Bozeman, Chief Financial Officer
Robin Vogel, VP, Resource Development
An independent non profit educational organization funded by corporations, listeners and individuals, with a mission to turn sight into sound, enriching the lives of individuals with visual, physical and learning disabilities. Founded in 1967 to read materials not availiable through other sources onto standard audio cassettes in our custom recording division. In 1978, Houston Taping fFor The Blind signed on the air. Reading several dozen popular magazines and best selling books on the air.

9179 We Can Do it Together!
American Foundation for the Blind/AFB Press
2 Penn Plaza
Suite 1102
New York, NY 10121

212-502-7600
800-232-5463
FAX: 888-545-8331
afbinfo@afb.net
afb.org

Carl R. Augusto, President & Chief Executive Officer
Rick Bozeman, Chief Financial Officer
Kelly Bleach, Chief Administrative Officer
This video illustrates a transdisciplinary team orientation and mobility program for students with severe visual and multiple impairments, covering both adapted communication systems used to teach mobility skills and basic indoor mobility in the school. For mobility instructors, administrators, teachers of the visually and severely handicapped, occupational, physical and speech therapists and parents. Discussion guide included. 10 minute video tape. Also available in PAL, $33.95, 0-89128-267-X. *$26.95*
VHS
ISBN 0-891282-13-0

Sports

9180 American Blind Bowling Association
1209 Somerset Road
Raleigh, NC 27610

919-755-0700
www.abba1951.org

Thomas Lester, President
A.J. Inglesby, 1st Vice President
James Benton, 2nd Vice President
Promotes blind bowling throughout the US and Canada by sanctioning blind bowling leagues and conducting a National Tournament. Current membership exceeds 2,000 people in the United States and Canada.

9181 **Basketball: Beeping Foam**
Maxi Aids
42 Executive Blvd.
Farmingdale, NY 11735-4710

631-752-0521
800-522-6294
FAX: 631-752-0689
TTY: 631-752-0738
sales@maxiaids.com
www.maxiaids.com

Elliot Zaretsky, Founder, President & CEO
This sound-making basketball enables the visually impaired to play basketball and other games. *$36.95*

9182 **Blind Outdoor Leisure Development**
P.O.Box 6639
Snowmass Village, CO 81615

970-923-0578
FAX: 970-923-7338
challengeaspen.org

Jimmy Yeager, President
Jack Kennedy, VP
Grayson Stover, Secretary
Outdoor recreation for the blind. Winter program of skiing with guides plus numerous summer programs for the visually impaired.

9183 **Challenge Golf**
otivation Media
1245 Milwaukee Ave
Glenview, IL 60025-2400

847-827-9057
FAX: 847-297-6829

Dorothy Bauer, Coordinator
A plain-language video, Challenge Golf is packed with information for beginners or veterans. Peter Longo covers 5 handicaps (one-arm, one-leg, in a seated position, blind, and arthritis) clearly and concisely, on how to play golf with a physical disability. In color, complete with special effects, graphs and real handicapped golfers at play. *$38.95*
Home Edition

9184 **US Association of Blind Athletes**
1 Olympic Plaza
Colorado Springs, CO 80909

719-630-0422
FAX: 719-630-0616
www.usaba.org

Mark A. Lucas, MS, Executive Director
Ryan Ortiz, Assistant Executive Director
John Potts, Goalball High Performance director
Provides athletic opportunities and training in competitive sports for visually impaired and blind individuals throughout the US Competitions indlcude local, regional and national events, internation events, and the Winter and Summer Paralympic Games.

9185 **United States Blind Golf Association**
3094 Shamrock St N
Tallahassee, FL 32309-2735

520-648-1088
info@usblindgolf.com
www.blindgolf.com

Dick Pomo, President
Provides blind and vision impaired gold tournaments to members.

Support Groups

9186 **Braille Institute Orange County Center**
527 North Dale Avenue
Anaheim, CA 92801

714-821-5000
800-272-4553
FAX: 714-527-7621
oc@brailleinstitute.org
brailleinstitute.org

Lester M. Sussman, Chairman
Peter A. Mindnich, President
Jon K. Hayashida, OD, FAAO, Vice President, Programs & Services
Offers services, publications, information and programs free of charge to blind and visually impaired persons of all ages.

9187 **Consumer and Patient Information Hotline**
Prevent Blindness America
211 West Wacker Drive
Suite 1700
Chicago, IL 60606

800-331-2020
info@preventblindness.org
www.preventblindness.org/

Paul G. Howes, Chairman
Hugh R. Parry, President & CEO, Prevent Blindness America
Jerome Desserich, Vice President & Chief Financial Officer
A toll-free line offering free information on a broad range of vision, eye health and safety topics including sports eye safety, diabetic retinopathy, glaucoma, cataracts, children's eye disorders and more.

9188 **Department of Ophthalmology Information Line**
Eye & Ear Infirmary
1855 W Taylor St
Chicago, IL 60612-7242

312-996-6590
FAX: 312-996-7770
eyeweb@uic.edu
www.uic.edu

Jospeh White, President
Offers eye clinic and physician referrals to persons suffering from vision disorders as well as offers emergency information.

9189 **Lighthouse International Information and Resource Service**
111 East 59th Street
New York, NY 10022-1202

212-821-9384
800-829-0500
FAX: 212-821-9707
info@lighthouse.org
lighthouse.org

Mark G. Ackermann, President/CEO
Provides information about eye diseases, low vision, age-related vision loss, adaptive technology, optical devices, large print and braille publishers, helps people find low vision services, vision rehabilitation services, and support groups across the U.S.; offers large selection of consumer products.

9190 **National Association for Parents of Children with Visual Impairments (NAPVI)**
1 North Lexington Avenue
White Plains, NY 10601

617-972-7441
800-562-6265
FAX: 617-972-7444
napvi@guildhealth.org
www.napvi.org

Julie Urban, President
Venetia Hayden, Vice President
Susan LaVenture, Executive Director
In 1979, a group of parents responding to their own needs founded NAPVI, the National Association for Parents of the Visually Impaired, Inc. Never before was there a self-help organization specific to the needs of families of children with visual impairments. Since that time, NAPVI has grown and helped families across the US and in other countries.

9191 **VUE: Vision Use in Employment**
Carroll Center for the Blind
770 Centre Street
Newton, MA 02458-2597

617-969-6200
800-852-3131
FAX: 617-969-6204
www.carroll.org

Joseph Abely, President
Brian Charlson, Director of Technology
Diane M. Newark, Chief Development Officer
Provides engineering solutions plus training to help people keep jobs despite their vision loss.

9192 **Washington Connection**
American Council of the Blind
1703 N. Beauregard St
Ste 420
Alexandria, VA 22311

202-467-5081
800-424-8666
FAX: 703-465-5085
info@acb.org
www.acb.org/wc

Kim Charlson, President
Jeff Thom, 1st Vice President
Eric Bridges, Executive Director
Coverage of issues affecting blind people via legislative information, participates in law-making, legislative training seminars and networking of support resources across the US.

2023 Annual Disability Statistics Compendium

List of Tables

Population and Prevalence

Employment

Table 1.1 Resident Population – States: 2018 to 2021

Geography	2018	2019	2020	2021	Geography	2018	2019	2020	2021
U.S.	327,167,439	328,239,523	329,504,815	331,893,745	MO	6,126,452	6,137,428	6,160,572	6,168,187
AL	4,887,871	4,903,185	4,922,663	5,039,877	MT	1,062,305	1,068,778	1,070,633	1,104,271
AK	737,438	731,545	725,368	732,673	NE	1,929,268	1,934,408	1,910,229	1,963,692
AZ	7,171,646	7,278,717	7,439,168	7,276,316	NV	3,034,392	3,080,156	3,159,862	3,143,991
AR	3,013,825	3,017,804	3,020,858	3,025,891	NH	1,356,410	1,359,711	1,369,826	1,388,992
CA	39,557,045	39,512,223	39,273,649	39,237,836	NJ	8,908,520	8,882,190	8,866,369	9,267,130
CO	5,695,564	5,758,736	5,801,720	5,812,069	NM	2,095,428	2,096,829	2,103,947	2,115,877
CT	3,572,665	3,565,287	3,561,894	3,605,597	NY	19,542,209	19,453,561	19,342,277	19,835,913
DE	967,171	973,764	986,302	1,003,384	NC	10,383,620	10,488,084	10,634,814	10,551,162
DC	702,455	705,749	708,050	670,050	ND	760,077	762,062	762,179	774,948
FL	21,299,325	21,477,737	21,777,656	21,781,128	OH	11,689,442	11,689,100	11,696,589	11,780,017
GA	10,519,475	10,617,423	10,735,354	10,799,566	OK	3,943,079	3,956,971	4,004,290	3,986,639
HI	1,420,491	1,415,872	1,408,226	1,441,553	OR	4,190,713	4,217,737	4,235,391	4,246,155
ID	1,754,208	1,787,065	1,845,631	1,900,923	PA	12,807,060	12,801,989	12,808,018	12,964,056
IL	12,741,080	12,671,821	12,559,183	12,671,469	RI	1,057,315	1,059,361	1,064,254	1,095,610
IN	6,691,878	6,732,219	6,755,447	6,805,985	SC	5,084,127	5,148,714	5,215,144	5,190,705
IA	3,156,145	3,155,070	3,167,157	3,193,079	SD	882,235	884,659	904,399	895,376
KS	2,911,510	2,913,314	2,917,100	2,934,582	TN	6,770,010	6,829,174	6,909,363	6,975,218
KY	4,468,402	4,467,673	4,477,027	4,509,394	TX	28,701,845	28,995,881	29,354,409	29,527,941
LA	4,659,978	4,648,794	4,636,548	4,624,047	UT	3,161,105	3,205,958	3,264,928	3,337,975
ME	1,338,404	1,344,212	1,333,280	1,372,247	VT	626,299	623,989	624,318	645,570
MD	6,042,718	6,045,680	6,039,168	6,165,129	VA	8,517,685	8,535,519	8,565,201	8,642,274
MA	6,902,197	6,892,503	6,893,349	6,984,723	WA	7,535,591	7,614,893	7,697,393	7,738,692
MI	9,995,915	9,986,857	10,005,488	10,050,811	WV	1,805,832	1,792,147	1,790,562	1,782,959
MN	5,611,179	5,639,632	5,637,415	5,707,390	WI	5,813,568	5,822,434	5,838,186	5,895,908
MS	2,986,530	2,976,149	2,949,108	2,949,965	WY	577,737	578,759	574,367	578,803

Citation: Paul, S., Rogers, S., Bach, S., & Houtenville, A. (2023). Annual Disability Statistics Compendium: 2023 (Table 1.1). Durham, NH: University of New Hampshire, Institute on Disability. Note: Authors' calculations using the U.S. Census Bureau, American Community Survey, Public Use Microdata Sample, 2018-2021, which is subject to sampling variation.

Table 1.2 State Resident Population – Projections: 2015 to 2030

State	2015	2020	2025	2030
U.S.	322,365,787	335,804,546	349,439,199	363,584,435
AL	4,663,111	4,728,915	4,800,092	4,874,243
AK	732,544	774,421	820,881	867,674
AZ	7,495,238	8,456,448	9,531,537	10,712,397
AR	2,968,913	3,060,219	3,151,005	3,240,208
CA	40,123,232	42,206,743	44,305,177	46,444,861
CO	5,049,493	5,278,867	5,522,803	5,792,357
CT	3,635,414	3,675,650	3,691,016	3,688,630
DE	927,400	963,209	990,694	1,012,658
DC	506,323	480,540	455,108	433,414
FL	21,204,132	23,406,525	25,912,458	28,685,769
GA	10,230,578	10,843,753	11,438,622	12,017,838
HI	1,385,952	1,412,373	1,438,720	1,466,046
ID	1,630,045	1,741,333	1,852,627	1,969,624
IL	13,097,218	13,236,720	13,340,507	13,432,892
IN	6,517,631	6,627,008	6,721,322	6,810,108
IA	3,026,380	3,020,496	2,993,222	2,955,172
KS	2,852,690	2,890,566	2,919,002	2,940,084
KY	4,351,188	4,424,431	4,489,662	4,554,998
LA	4,673,721	4,719,160	4,762,398	4,802,633
ME	1,388,878	1,408,665	1,414,402	1,411,097
MD	6,208,392	6,497,626	6,762,732	7,022,251
MA	6,758,580	6,855,546	6,938,636	7,012,009
MI	10,599,122	10,695,993	10,713,730	10,694,172
MN	5,668,211	5,900,769	6,108,787	6,306,130
MS	3,014,409	3,044,812	3,069,420	3,092,410
MO	6,069,556	6,199,882	6,315,366	6,430,173
MT	999,489	1,022,735	1,037,387	1,044,898
NE	1,788,508	1,802,678	1,812,787	1,820,247
NV	3,058,190	3,452,283	3,863,298	4,282,102
NH	1,456,679	1,524,751	1,586,348	1,646,471
NJ	9,255,769	9,461,635	9,636,644	9,802,440
NM	2,041,539	2,084,341	2,106,584	2,099,708
NY	19,546,699	19,576,920	19,540,179	19,477,429
NC	10,010,770	10,709,289	11,449,153	12,227,739
ND	635,133	630,112	620,777	606,566
OH	11,635,446	11,644,058	11,605,738	11,550,528
OK	3,661,694	3,735,690	3,820,994	3,913,251
OR	4,012,924	4,260,393	4,536,418	4,833,918
PA	12,710,938	12,787,354	12,801,945	12,768,184
RI	1,139,543	1,154,230	1,157,855	1,152,941
SC	4,642,137	4,822,577	4,989,550	5,148,569
SD	796,954	801,939	801,845	800,462
TN	6,502,017	6,780,670	7,073,125	7,380,634
TX	26,585,801	28,634,896	30,865,134	33,317,744
UT	2,783,040	2,990,094	3,225,680	3,485,367
VT	673,169	690,686	703,288	711,867
VA	8,466,864	8,917,395	9,364,304	9,825,019
WA	6,950,610	7,432,136	7,996,400	8,624,801
WV	1,822,758	1,801,112	1,766,435	1,719,959
WI	5,882,760	6,004,954	6,088,374	6,150,764
WY	528,005	530,948	529,031	522,979

Citation: Paul, S., Rogers, S., Bach, S., & Houtenville, A. (2023). Annual Disability Statistics Compendium: 2023 (Table 1.2). Durham, NH: University of New Hampshire, Institute on Disability. Note: Sourced from the U.S. Census Bureau, 2005, Interim State Population Projections, Table 6, which is subject to sampling variation.

Table 1.3 Civilians Living in the Community for the United States and States, by Disability Status: 2021

State	Total	Disability [1] Count	%	No Disability Count	%
U.S.	326,942,778	42,601,999	13.0	284,340,779	87.0
AL	4,956,828	805,849	16.3	4,150,979	83.7
AK	703,612	99,194	14.1	604,418	85.9
AZ	7,175,530	970,430	13.5	6,205,100	86.5
AR	2,975,548	517,723	17.4	2,457,825	82.6
CA	38,725,651	4,342,499	11.2	34,383,152	88.8
CO	5,715,351	643,030	11.3	5,072,321	88.7
CT	3,558,663	427,144	12.0	3,131,519	88.0
DE	987,806	129,543	13.1	858,263	86.9
DC	659,722	77,882	11.8	581,840	88.2
FL	21,466,906	2,911,135	13.6	18,555,771	86.4
GA	10,602,297	1,373,134	13.0	9,229,163	87.0
HI	1,382,959	168,163	12.2	1,214,796	87.8
ID	1,879,742	263,115	14.0	1,616,627	86.0
IL	12,496,616	1,491,750	11.9	11,004,866	88.1
IN	6,708,961	919,332	13.7	5,789,629	86.3
IA	3,149,081	397,179	12.6	2,751,902	87.4
KS	2,880,194	386,050	13.4	2,494,144	86.6
KY	4,428,085	783,699	17.7	3,644,386	82.3
LA	4,518,879	724,218	16.0	3,794,661	84.0
ME	1,358,182	210,432	15.5	1,147,750	84.5
MD	6,060,990	687,347	11.3	5,373,643	88.7
MA	6,915,688	808,474	11.7	6,107,214	88.3
MI	9,951,051	1,394,304	14.0	8,556,747	86.0
MN	5,652,521	679,462	12.0	4,973,059	88.0
MS	2,885,638	522,842	18.1	2,362,796	81.9
MO	6,062,846	883,553	14.6	5,179,293	85.4
MT	1,087,247	158,746	14.6	928,501	85.4
NE	1,935,685	249,584	12.9	1,686,101	87.1
NV	3,104,854	402,166	13.0	2,702,688	87.0
NH	1,373,423	166,037	12.1	1,207,386	87.9
NJ	9,163,354	962,714	10.5	8,200,640	89.5
NM	2,077,492	336,557	16.2	1,740,935	83.8
NY	19,599,249	2,359,842	12.0	17,239,407	88.0
NC	10,346,220	1,413,633	13.7	8,932,587	86.3
ND	754,481	92,470	12.3	662,011	87.7
OH	11,613,352	1,659,146	14.3	9,954,206	85.7
OK	3,903,265	675,799	17.3	3,227,466	82.7
OR	4,206,193	637,679	15.2	3,568,514	84.8
PA	12,767,247	1,764,274	13.8	11,002,973	86.2
RI	1,080,868	150,612	13.9	930,256	86.1
SC	5,107,451	730,813	14.3	4,376,638	85.7
SD	877,125	111,536	12.7	765,589	87.3
TN	6,874,621	1,030,224	15.0	5,844,397	85.0
TX	29,072,523	3,518,171	12.1	25,554,352	87.9
UT	3,309,480	345,490	10.4	2,963,990	89.6
VT	638,559	85,969	13.5	552,590	86.5
VA	8,415,775	1,040,435	12.4	7,375,340	87.6
WA	7,620,111	996,933	13.1	6,623,178	86.9
WV	1,755,575	328,527	18.7	1,427,048	81.3
WI	5,829,031	690,024	11.8	5,139,007	88.2
WY	570,250	77,135	13.5	493,115	86.5

Citation: Paul, S., Rogers, S., Bach, S., & Houtenville, A. (2023). Annual Disability Statistics Compendium: 2023 (Table 1.3). Durham, NH: University of New Hampshire, Institute on Disability. Note: Authors' calculations using the U.S. Census Bureau American Community Survey, Public Use Microdata Sample, 2021, which is subject to sampling variation. [1] The U.S. Census uses a series of six questions to identify persons with vision, hearing, cognitive, ambulatory, selfcare, and independent living disabilities. The cognitive, ambulatory, and self-care related questions are not asked of individuals less than five years old and the independent living related question is not asked of individuals less than 15 years old. See glossary for more information.

Table 1.4 Civilians Living in the Community for the United States and States – Hearing Disability: 2021

State	Total	Disability	Hearing [1] Count	Hearing [1] % Total	Hearing [1] % Disability
U.S.	326,942,778	42,601,999	11,632,358	3.6	27.3
AL	4,956,828	805,849	207,189	4.2	25.7
AK	703,612	99,194	33,375	4.7	33.6
AZ	7,175,530	970,430	298,498	4.2	30.8
AR	2,975,548	517,723	142,320	4.8	27.5
CA	38,725,651	4,342,499	1,140,178	2.9	26.3
CO	5,715,351	643,030	213,309	3.7	33.2
CT	3,558,663	427,144	112,461	3.2	26.3
DE	987,806	129,543	37,741	3.8	29.1
DC	659,722	77,882	13,979	2.1	17.9
FL	21,466,906	2,911,135	810,461	3.8	27.8
GA	10,602,297	1,373,134	346,313	3.3	25.2
HI	1,382,959	168,163	50,879	3.7	30.3
ID	1,879,742	263,115	90,163	4.8	34.3
IL	12,496,616	1,491,750	383,922	3.1	25.7
IN	6,708,961	919,332	257,714	3.8	28.0
IA	3,149,081	397,179	124,015	3.9	31.2
KS	2,880,194	386,050	118,671	4.1	30.7
KY	4,428,085	783,699	214,491	4.8	27.4
LA	4,518,879	724,218	192,346	4.3	26.6
ME	1,358,182	210,432	63,516	4.7	30.2
MD	6,060,990	687,347	167,484	2.8	24.4
MA	6,915,688	808,474	210,822	3.0	26.1
MI	9,951,051	1,394,304	366,589	3.7	26.3
MN	5,652,521	679,462	194,595	3.4	28.6
MS	2,885,638	522,842	125,051	4.3	23.9
MO	6,062,846	883,553	246,560	4.1	27.9
MT	1,087,247	158,746	56,619	5.2	35.7
NE	1,935,685	249,584	76,336	3.9	30.6
NV	3,104,854	402,166	116,057	3.7	28.9
NH	1,373,423	166,037	50,257	3.7	30.3
NJ	9,163,354	962,714	238,066	2.6	24.7
NM	2,077,492	336,557	104,951	5.1	31.2
NY	19,599,249	2,359,842	552,138	2.8	23.4
NC	10,346,220	1,413,633	388,826	3.8	27.5
ND	754,481	92,470	32,689	4.3	35.4
OH	11,613,352	1,659,146	439,895	3.8	26.5
OK	3,903,265	675,799	202,444	5.2	30.0
OR	4,206,193	637,679	186,034	4.4	29.2
PA	12,767,247	1,764,274	464,568	3.6	26.3
RI	1,080,868	150,612	34,735	3.2	23.1
SC	5,107,451	730,813	186,477	3.7	25.5
SD	877,125	111,536	36,846	4.2	33.0
TN	6,874,621	1,030,224	296,498	4.3	28.8
TX	29,072,523	3,518,171	953,033	3.3	27.1
UT	3,309,480	345,490	102,867	3.1	29.8
VT	638,559	85,969	27,757	4.3	32.3
VA	8,415,775	1,040,435	287,261	3.4	27.6
WA	7,620,111	996,933	298,587	3.9	30.0
WV	1,755,575	328,527	100,380	5.7	30.6
WI	5,829,031	690,024	207,540	3.6	30.1
WY	570,250	77,135	28,855	5.1	37.4

Citation: Paul, S., Rogers, S., Bach, S., & Houtenville, A. (2023). Annual Disability Statistics Compendium: 2023 (Table 1.4). Durham, NH: University of New Hampshire, Institute on Disability. Note: Authors' calculations using the U.S. Census Bureau American Community Survey, Public Use Microdata Sample, 2021, which is subject to sampling variation.
[1] The hearing disability question asks people of all ages, "Is this person deaf or does he/she have serious difficulty hearing?" See glossary for more information.

Table 1.5 Civilians Living in the Community for the United States and States – Vision Disability: 2021

State	Total	Disability	Vision [1] Count	Vision [1] % Total	Vision [1] % Disability
U.S.	326,942,778	42,601,999	8,086,147	2.5	19.0
AL	4,956,828	805,849	152,903	3.1	19.0
AK	703,612	99,194	17,333	2.5	17.5
AZ	7,175,530	970,430	180,033	2.5	18.6
AR	2,975,548	517,723	106,351	3.6	20.5
CA	38,725,651	4,342,499	851,920	2.2	19.6
CO	5,715,351	643,030	122,784	2.1	19.1
CT	3,558,663	427,144	78,822	2.2	18.5
DE	987,806	129,543	26,133	2.6	20.2
DC	659,722	77,882	13,812	2.1	17.7
FL	21,466,906	2,911,135	560,304	2.6	19.2
GA	10,602,297	1,373,134	278,422	2.6	20.3
HI	1,382,959	168,163	26,257	1.9	15.6
ID	1,879,742	263,115	51,278	2.7	19.5
IL	12,496,616	1,491,750	266,069	2.1	17.8
IN	6,708,961	919,332	167,290	2.5	18.2
IA	3,149,081	397,179	62,009	2.0	15.6
KS	2,880,194	386,050	66,628	2.3	17.3
KY	4,428,085	783,699	164,556	3.7	21.0
LA	4,518,879	724,218	169,253	3.7	23.4
ME	1,358,182	210,432	27,817	2.0	13.2
MD	6,060,990	687,347	118,299	2.0	17.2
MA	6,915,688	808,474	140,372	2.0	17.4
MI	9,951,051	1,394,304	222,080	2.2	15.9
MN	5,652,521	679,462	94,546	1.7	13.9
MS	2,885,638	522,842	125,866	4.4	24.1
MO	6,062,846	883,553	164,246	2.7	18.6
MT	1,087,247	158,746	27,513	2.5	17.3
NE	1,935,685	249,584	47,541	2.5	19.0
NV	3,104,854	402,166	87,917	2.8	21.9
NH	1,373,423	166,037	27,428	2.0	16.5
NJ	9,163,354	962,714	187,546	2.0	19.5
NM	2,077,492	336,557	65,600	3.2	19.5
NY	19,599,249	2,359,842	412,122	2.1	17.5
NC	10,346,220	1,413,633	272,365	2.6	19.3
ND	754,481	92,470	21,181	2.8	22.9
OH	11,613,352	1,659,146	288,275	2.5	17.4
OK	3,903,265	675,799	154,835	4.0	22.9
OR	4,206,193	637,679	105,807	2.5	16.6
PA	12,767,247	1,764,274	315,443	2.5	17.9
RI	1,080,868	150,612	25,882	2.4	17.2
SC	5,107,451	730,813	145,896	2.9	20.0
SD	877,125	111,536	18,220	2.1	16.3
TN	6,874,621	1,030,224	213,375	3.1	20.7
TX	29,072,523	3,518,171	790,067	2.7	22.5
UT	3,309,480	345,490	61,251	1.9	17.7
VT	638,559	85,969	13,221	2.1	15.4
VA	8,415,775	1,040,435	200,609	2.4	19.3
WA	7,620,111	996,933	165,503	2.2	16.6
WV	1,755,575	328,527	59,409	3.4	18.1
WI	5,829,031	690,024	108,157	1.9	15.7
WY	570,250	77,135	15,601	2.7	20.2

Citation: Paul, S., Rogers, S., Bach, S., & Houtenville, A. (2023). Annual Disability Statistics Compendium: 2023 (Table 1.5). Durham, NH: University of New Hampshire, Institute on Disability. Note: Authors' calculations using the U.S. Census Bureau American Community Survey, Public Use Microdata Sample, 2021, which is subject to sampling variation.
[1] The vision disability question asks people of all ages, "Is this person blind or does he/she have serious difficulty seeing even when wearing glasses?" See glossary for more information.

Table 1.6 Civilians Living in the Community for the United States and States – Cognitive Disability: 2021

State	Total	Disability	Cognitive [1] Count	Cognitive [1] % Total	Cognitive [1] % Disability
U.S.	326,942,778	42,601,999	16,599,667	5.1	39.0
AL	4,956,828	805,849	303,033	6.1	37.6
AK	703,612	99,194	39,606	5.6	39.9
AZ	7,175,530	970,430	369,923	5.2	38.1
AR	2,975,548	517,723	206,428	6.9	39.9
CA	38,725,651	4,342,499	1,712,140	4.4	39.4
CO	5,715,351	643,030	254,558	4.5	39.6
CT	3,558,663	427,144	166,693	4.7	39.0
DE	987,806	129,543	46,976	4.8	36.3
DC	659,722	77,882	30,292	4.6	38.9
FL	21,466,906	2,911,135	1,076,234	5.0	37.0
GA	10,602,297	1,373,134	546,355	5.2	39.8
HI	1,382,959	168,163	66,027	4.8	39.3
ID	1,879,742	263,115	106,890	5.7	40.6
IL	12,496,616	1,491,750	549,698	4.4	36.8
IN	6,708,961	919,332	353,085	5.3	38.4
IA	3,149,081	397,179	149,823	4.8	37.7
KS	2,880,194	386,050	158,696	5.5	41.1
KY	4,428,085	783,699	310,223	7.0	39.6
LA	4,518,879	724,218	287,217	6.4	39.7
ME	1,358,182	210,432	89,492	6.6	42.5
MD	6,060,990	687,347	258,281	4.3	37.6
MA	6,915,688	808,474	330,417	4.8	40.9
MI	9,951,051	1,394,304	559,323	5.6	40.1
MN	5,652,521	679,462	297,295	5.3	43.8
MS	2,885,638	522,842	206,183	7.1	39.4
MO	6,062,846	883,553	343,318	5.7	38.9
MT	1,087,247	158,746	59,594	5.5	37.5
NE	1,935,685	249,584	93,400	4.8	37.4
NV	3,104,854	402,166	147,340	4.7	36.6
NH	1,373,423	166,037	65,789	4.8	39.6
NJ	9,163,354	962,714	339,110	3.7	35.2
NM	2,077,492	336,557	131,267	6.3	39.0
NY	19,599,249	2,359,842	915,086	4.7	38.8
NC	10,346,220	1,413,633	542,557	5.2	38.4
ND	754,481	92,470	29,973	4.0	32.4
OH	11,613,352	1,659,146	674,455	5.8	40.7
OK	3,903,265	675,799	251,841	6.5	37.3
OR	4,206,193	637,679	278,753	6.6	43.7
PA	12,767,247	1,764,274	706,857	5.5	40.1
RI	1,080,868	150,612	62,031	5.7	41.2
SC	5,107,451	730,813	265,152	5.2	36.3
SD	877,125	111,536	39,187	4.5	35.1
TN	6,874,621	1,030,224	406,639	5.9	39.5
TX	29,072,523	3,518,171	1,344,974	4.6	38.2
UT	3,309,480	345,490	155,866	4.7	45.1
VT	638,559	85,969	34,335	5.4	39.9
VA	8,415,775	1,040,435	393,213	4.7	37.8
WA	7,620,111	996,933	419,649	5.5	42.1
WV	1,755,575	328,527	128,927	7.3	39.2
WI	5,829,031	690,024	269,201	4.6	39.0
WY	570,250	77,135	26,265	4.6	34.1

Citation: Paul, S., Rogers, S., Bach, S., & Houtenville, A. (2023). Annual Disability Statistics Compendium: 2023 (Table 1.6). Durham, NH: University of New Hampshire, Institute on Disability. Note: Authors' calculations using the U.S. Census Bureau American Community Survey, Public Use Microdata Sample, 2021, which is subject to sampling variation. [1] The cognitive disability question asks people 5 years and older "Because of a physical, mental, or emotional condition, does this person have serious difficulty concentrating, remembering, or making decisions?" See glossary for more information.

Table 1.7 Civilians Living in the Community for the United States and States – Ambulatory Disability: 2021

State	Total	Disability	Ambulatory [1] Count	Ambulatory [1] % Total	Ambulatory [1] % Disability
U.S.	326,942,778	42,601,999	20,448,062	6.3	48.0
AL	4,956,828	805,849	433,949	8.8	53.8
AK	703,612	99,194	37,497	5.3	37.8
AZ	7,175,530	970,430	453,010	6.3	46.7
AR	2,975,548	517,723	259,230	8.7	50.1
CA	38,725,651	4,342,499	2,099,892	5.4	48.4
CO	5,715,351	643,030	261,633	4.6	40.7
CT	3,558,663	427,144	197,903	5.6	46.3
DE	987,806	129,543	63,757	6.5	49.2
DC	659,722	77,882	41,130	6.2	52.8
FL	21,466,906	2,911,135	1,481,110	6.9	50.9
GA	10,602,297	1,373,134	674,615	6.4	49.1
HI	1,382,959	168,163	83,894	6.1	49.9
ID	1,879,742	263,115	109,517	5.8	41.6
IL	12,496,616	1,491,750	739,147	5.9	49.5
IN	6,708,961	919,332	441,531	6.6	48.0
IA	3,149,081	397,179	175,521	5.6	44.2
KS	2,880,194	386,050	171,378	6.0	44.4
KY	4,428,085	783,699	404,136	9.1	51.6
LA	4,518,879	724,218	358,951	7.9	49.6
ME	1,358,182	210,432	92,603	6.8	44.0
MD	6,060,990	687,347	328,989	5.4	47.9
MA	6,915,688	808,474	362,258	5.2	44.8
MI	9,951,051	1,394,304	672,683	6.8	48.2
MN	5,652,521	679,462	260,132	4.6	38.3
MS	2,885,638	522,842	277,244	9.6	53.0
MO	6,062,846	883,553	423,878	7.0	48.0
MT	1,087,247	158,746	69,887	6.4	44.0
NE	1,935,685	249,584	109,030	5.6	43.7
NV	3,104,854	402,166	202,209	6.5	50.3
NH	1,373,423	166,037	66,978	4.9	40.3
NJ	9,163,354	962,714	480,831	5.2	49.9
NM	2,077,492	336,557	162,446	7.8	48.3
NY	19,599,249	2,359,842	1,202,021	6.1	50.9
NC	10,346,220	1,413,633	706,606	6.8	50.0
ND	754,481	92,470	37,402	5.0	40.4
OH	11,613,352	1,659,146	784,960	6.8	47.3
OK	3,903,265	675,799	328,345	8.4	48.6
OR	4,206,193	637,679	278,294	6.6	43.6
PA	12,767,247	1,764,274	832,427	6.5	47.2
RI	1,080,868	150,612	66,451	6.1	44.1
SC	5,107,451	730,813	371,492	7.3	50.8
SD	877,125	111,536	49,754	5.7	44.6
TN	6,874,621	1,030,224	521,845	7.6	50.7
TX	29,072,523	3,518,171	1,668,948	5.7	47.4
UT	3,309,480	345,490	130,302	3.9	37.7
VT	638,559	85,969	35,880	5.6	41.7
VA	8,415,775	1,040,435	500,099	5.9	48.1
WA	7,620,111	996,933	433,107	5.7	43.4
WV	1,755,575	328,527	172,888	9.8	52.6
WI	5,829,031	690,024	297,736	5.1	43.1
WY	570,250	77,135	32,536	5.7	42.2

Citation: Paul, S., Rogers, S., Bach, S., & Houtenville, A. (2023). Annual Disability Statistics Compendium: 2023 (Table 1.7). Durham, NH: University of New Hampshire, Institute on Disability. Note: Authors' calculations using the U.S. Census Bureau American Community Survey, Public Use Microdata Sample, 2021, which is subject to sampling variation.

[1] The ambulatory disability question asks people 5 years old or older, "Does this person have serious difficulty walking or climbing stairs?" See glossary for more information.

Table 1.8 Civilians Living in the Community for the United States and States – Self-Care Disability: 2021

State	Total	Disability	Self-Care [1] Count	Self-Care [1] % Total	Self-Care [1] % Disability
U.S.	326,942,778	42,601,999	7,834,854	2.4	18.4
AL	4,956,828	805,849	136,419	2.8	16.9
AK	703,612	99,194	13,508	1.9	13.6
AZ	7,175,530	970,430	161,027	2.2	16.6
AR	2,975,548	517,723	94,650	3.2	18.3
CA	38,725,651	4,342,499	972,305	2.5	22.4
CO	5,715,351	643,030	94,972	1.7	14.8
CT	3,558,663	427,144	80,190	2.3	18.8
DE	987,806	129,543	25,609	2.6	19.8
DC	659,722	77,882	13,354	2.0	17.1
FL	21,466,906	2,911,135	544,644	2.5	18.7
GA	10,602,297	1,373,134	245,530	2.3	17.9
HI	1,382,959	168,163	33,317	2.4	19.8
ID	1,879,742	263,115	44,922	2.4	17.1
IL	12,496,616	1,491,750	280,612	2.2	18.8
IN	6,708,961	919,332	156,480	2.3	17.0
IA	3,149,081	397,179	62,640	2.0	15.8
KS	2,880,194	386,050	62,610	2.2	16.2
KY	4,428,085	783,699	148,686	3.4	19.0
LA	4,518,879	724,218	139,532	3.1	19.3
ME	1,358,182	210,432	31,491	2.3	15.0
MD	6,060,990	687,347	117,631	1.9	17.1
MA	6,915,688	808,474	153,052	2.2	18.9
MI	9,951,051	1,394,304	246,506	2.5	17.7
MN	5,652,521	679,462	117,460	2.1	17.3
MS	2,885,638	522,842	92,448	3.2	17.7
MO	6,062,846	883,553	149,152	2.5	16.9
MT	1,087,247	158,746	24,736	2.3	15.6
NE	1,935,685	249,584	36,902	1.9	14.8
NV	3,104,854	402,166	75,975	2.4	18.9
NH	1,373,423	166,037	24,079	1.8	14.5
NJ	9,163,354	962,714	199,915	2.2	20.8
NM	2,077,492	336,557	64,872	3.1	19.3
NY	19,599,249	2,359,842	504,153	2.6	21.4
NC	10,346,220	1,413,633	253,636	2.5	17.9
ND	754,481	92,470	11,369	1.5	12.3
OH	11,613,352	1,659,146	278,148	2.4	16.8
OK	3,903,265	675,799	101,921	2.6	15.1
OR	4,206,193	637,679	117,549	2.8	18.4
PA	12,767,247	1,764,274	299,947	2.3	17.0
RI	1,080,868	150,612	26,742	2.5	17.8
SC	5,107,451	730,813	136,974	2.7	18.7
SD	877,125	111,536	16,426	1.9	14.7
TN	6,874,621	1,030,224	184,867	2.7	17.9
TX	29,072,523	3,518,171	633,740	2.2	18.0
UT	3,309,480	345,490	47,294	1.4	13.7
VT	638,559	85,969	13,723	2.1	16.0
VA	8,415,775	1,040,435	197,955	2.4	19.0
WA	7,620,111	996,933	167,576	2.2	16.8
WV	1,755,575	328,527	67,876	3.9	20.7
WI	5,829,031	690,024	119,704	2.1	17.3
WY	570,250	77,135	10,028	1.8	13.0

<u>Citation</u>: Paul, S., Rogers, S., Bach, S., & Houtenville, A. (2023). Annual Disability Statistics Compendium: 2023 (Table 1.8). Durham, NH: University of New Hampshire, Institute on Disability. Note: Authors' calculations using the U.S. Census Bureau American Community Survey, Public Use Microdata Sample, 2021, which is subject to sampling variation.
[1] The self-care disability question asks people 5 years old or older, "Does this person have difficulty dressing or bathing?" See glossary for more information.

Table 1.9 Civilians Living in the Community for the United States and States – Independent Living Disability: 2021

State	Total	Disability	Independent Living [1] Count	Independent Living [1] % Total	Independent Living [1] % Disability
U.S.	326,942,778	42,601,999	15,145,689	4.6	35.6
AL	4,956,828	805,849	282,975	5.7	35.1
AK	703,612	99,194	28,946	4.1	29.2
AZ	7,175,530	970,430	314,644	4.4	32.4
AR	2,975,548	517,723	181,562	6.1	35.1
CA	38,725,651	4,342,499	1,748,365	4.5	40.3
CO	5,715,351	643,030	203,871	3.6	31.7
CT	3,558,663	427,144	157,234	4.4	36.8
DE	987,806	129,543	44,988	4.6	34.7
DC	659,722	77,882	23,100	3.5	29.7
FL	21,466,906	2,911,135	1,011,720	4.7	34.8
GA	10,602,297	1,373,134	478,422	4.5	34.8
HI	1,382,959	168,163	67,642	4.9	40.2
ID	1,879,742	263,115	80,613	4.3	30.6
IL	12,496,616	1,491,750	552,951	4.4	37.1
IN	6,708,961	919,332	313,845	4.7	34.1
IA	3,149,081	397,179	132,829	4.2	33.4
KS	2,880,194	386,050	132,766	4.6	34.4
KY	4,428,085	783,699	286,201	6.5	36.5
LA	4,518,879	724,218	248,856	5.5	34.4
ME	1,358,182	210,432	79,961	5.9	38.0
MD	6,060,990	687,347	235,056	3.9	34.2
MA	6,915,688	808,474	301,867	4.4	37.3
MI	9,951,051	1,394,304	515,106	5.2	36.9
MN	5,652,521	679,462	241,184	4.3	35.5
MS	2,885,638	522,842	180,910	6.3	34.6
MO	6,062,846	883,553	298,329	4.9	33.8
MT	1,087,247	158,746	49,421	4.5	31.1
NE	1,935,685	249,584	73,463	3.8	29.4
NV	3,104,854	402,166	134,078	4.3	33.3
NH	1,373,423	166,037	57,260	4.2	34.5
NJ	9,163,354	962,714	370,795	4.0	38.5
NM	2,077,492	336,557	122,127	5.9	36.3
NY	19,599,249	2,359,842	974,518	5.0	41.3
NC	10,346,220	1,413,633	483,601	4.7	34.2
ND	754,481	92,470	22,289	3.0	24.1
OH	11,613,352	1,659,146	556,566	4.8	33.5
OK	3,903,265	675,799	219,042	5.6	32.4
OR	4,206,193	637,679	230,735	5.5	36.2
PA	12,767,247	1,764,274	631,164	4.9	35.8
RI	1,080,868	150,612	55,598	5.1	36.9
SC	5,107,451	730,813	251,665	4.9	34.4
SD	877,125	111,536	30,477	3.5	27.3
TN	6,874,621	1,030,224	360,872	5.2	35.0
TX	29,072,523	3,518,171	1,158,453	4.0	32.9
UT	3,309,480	345,490	110,445	3.3	32.0
VT	638,559	85,969	30,712	4.8	35.7
VA	8,415,775	1,040,435	358,026	4.3	34.4
WA	7,620,111	996,933	344,150	4.5	34.5
WV	1,755,575	328,527	119,054	6.8	36.2
WI	5,829,031	690,024	233,597	4.0	33.9
WY	570,250	77,135	23,638	4.1	30.6

Citation: Paul, S., Rogers, S., Bach, S., & Houtenville, A. (2023). Annual Disability Statistics Compendium: 2023 (Table 1.9). Durham, NH: University of New Hampshire, Institute on Disability. Note: Authors' calculations using the U.S. Census Bureau American Community Survey, Public Use Microdata Sample, 2021, which is subject to sampling variation. [1] The independent living disability question asks people 15 years old or older, "Because of a physical, mental, or emotional condition, does this person have difficulty doing errands alone such as visiting a doctor's office or shopping?" See glossary for more information.

Table 3.1 Employment – Civilians with Disabilities Ages 18-64 Years Living in the Community for the United States and States: 2021

State	Total	Employed Count	% [1]	State	Total	Employed Count	% [1]
U.S.	21,375,164	8,705,513	40.7	MO	455,483	188,557	41.4
AL	427,044	138,077	32.3	MT	75,444	32,744	43.4
AK	57,446	26,466	46.1	NE	127,695	67,109	52.6
AZ	462,266	203,672	44.1	NV	203,594	86,496	42.5
AR	270,410	95,322	35.3	NH	86,205	40,316	46.8
CA	2,094,680	825,876	39.4	NJ	442,236	177,976	40.2
CO	334,153	166,776	49.9	NM	172,088	60,122	34.9
CT	210,733	93,481	44.4	NY	1,137,516	419,234	36.9
DE	63,108	29,787	47.2	NC	721,213	277,731	38.5
DC	45,567	18,345	40.3	ND	47,057	27,321	58.1
FL	1,294,357	508,919	39.3	OH	844,365	333,629	39.5
GA	718,796	279,071	38.8	OK	355,773	146,090	41.1
HI	70,655	28,568	40.4	OR	337,722	143,668	42.5
ID	129,963	65,530	50.4	PA	862,692	340,244	39.4
IL	738,699	307,531	41.6	RI	79,542	33,737	42.4
IN	475,999	193,235	40.6	SC	371,131	132,959	35.8
IA	200,714	94,631	47.1	SD	54,749	28,037	51.2
KS	201,587	87,877	43.6	TN	536,506	191,440	35.7
KY	425,527	143,193	33.7	TX	1,812,286	832,902	46.0
LA	382,524	130,691	34.2	UT	194,928	105,165	54.0
ME	111,109	39,764	35.8	VT	44,065	16,705	37.9
MD	347,449	158,268	45.6	VA	525,816	233,508	44.4
MA	390,447	162,885	41.7	WA	515,893	216,240	41.9
MI	717,556	267,500	37.3	WV	171,095	50,814	29.7
MN	346,254	176,096	50.9	WI	361,742	167,399	46.3
MS	283,513	94,106	33.2	WY	37,772	19,703	52.2

Citation: Paul, S., Rogers, S., Bach, S., & Houtenville, A. (2023). Annual Disability Statistics Compendium: 2023 (Table 3.1). Durham, NH: University of New Hampshire, Institute on Disability. Note: Authors' calculations using the U.S. Census Bureau American Community Survey, Public Use Microdata Sample, 2021, which is subject to sampling variation.

[1] The percentage of people with disabilities employed.

Table 3.2 Employment – Civilians without Disabilities Ages 18-64 Years Living in the Community for the United States and States: 2021

State	Total	Employed Count	% [1]	State	Total	Employed Count	% [1]
U.S.	177,527,241	135,973,591	76.6	MO	3,177,937	2,522,505	79.4
AL	2,547,331	1,899,619	74.6	MT	564,962	444,601	78.7
AK	370,838	277,926	74.9	NE	1,014,311	860,434	84.8
AZ	3,777,370	2,870,362	76.0	NV	1,690,271	1,241,872	73.5
AR	1,491,911	1,145,914	76.8	NH	770,904	629,599	81.7
CA	22,007,153	16,185,950	73.5	NJ	5,176,776	3,962,777	76.5
CO	3,274,242	2,616,988	79.9	NM	1,047,810	745,883	71.2
CT	1,991,370	1,560,234	78.3	NY	10,983,027	8,106,176	73.8
DE	520,770	397,392	76.3	NC	5,562,607	4,250,394	76.4
DC	404,964	315,232	77.8	ND	408,160	339,211	83.1
FL	11,356,405	8,662,175	76.3	OH	6,129,834	4,822,544	78.7
GA	5,805,086	4,413,612	76.0	OK	1,962,381	1,497,352	76.3
HI	729,300	547,871	75.1	OR	2,232,682	1,709,490	76.6
ID	971,484	772,549	79.5	PA	6,848,016	5,338,737	78.0
IL	6,917,512	5,322,567	76.9	RI	600,499	468,122	78.0
IN	3,564,936	2,805,974	78.7	SC	2,671,976	2,011,413	75.3
IA	1,668,525	1,384,786	83.0	SD	453,506	379,204	83.6
KS	1,507,357	1,219,446	80.9	TN	3,641,442	2,804,589	77.0
KY	2,242,246	1,704,911	76.0	TX	15,981,386	12,052,171	75.4
LA	2,309,022	1,666,937	72.2	UT	1,789,229	1,435,856	80.2
ME	709,211	567,913	80.1	VT	348,202	276,147	79.3
MD	3,371,887	2,663,784	79.0	VA	4,629,055	3,648,494	78.8
MA	3,981,891	3,138,799	78.8	WA	4,199,025	3,236,407	77.1
MI	5,301,641	3,997,617	75.4	WV	863,113	615,831	71.3
MN	3,065,749	2,558,927	83.5	WI	3,165,531	2,594,584	82.0
MS	1,426,633	1,040,372	72.9	WY	299,765	241,341	80.5

Citation: Paul, S., Rogers, S., Bach, S., & Houtenville, A. (2023). Annual Disability Statistics Compendium: 2023 (Table 3.2). Durham, NH: University of New Hampshire, Institute on Disability. Note: Authors' calculations using the U.S. Census Bureau American Community Survey, Public Use Microdata Sample, 2021, which is subject to sampling variation.
[1] The percentage of people without disabilities employed.

Table 3.3 Employment – Civilians with Hearing Disabilities Ages 18-64 Years Living in the Community for the United States and States: 2021

State	Total	Employed Count	% [1]	State	Total	Employed Count	% [1]
U.S.	3,986,839	2,199,414	55.1	MO	83,902	46,457	55.3
AL	77,652	40,599	52.2	MT	17,665	9,887	55.9
AK	16,161	8,489	52.5	NE	30,618	21,815	71.2
AZ	92,617	50,667	54.7	NV	39,244	22,507	57.3
AR	47,909	25,269	52.7	NH	17,348	11,082	63.8
CA	365,481	190,961	52.2	NJ	69,444	40,683	58.5
CO	77,248	47,477	61.4	NM	35,694	16,234	45.4
CT	38,726	22,650	58.4	NY	180,387	94,758	52.5
DE	11,573	6,524	56.3	NC	135,362	72,110	53.2
DC	6,590	3,116	47.2	ND	13,864	10,710	77.2
FL	229,910	123,990	53.9	OH	150,061	78,985	52.6
GA	122,542	65,074	53.1	OK	75,961	42,724	56.2
HI	14,285	8,127	56.8	OR	65,423	38,946	59.5
ID	30,151	19,328	64.1	PA	147,567	79,274	53.7
IL	130,549	74,605	57.1	RI	11,732	7,165	61.0
IN	94,795	52,903	55.8	SC	63,240	32,945	52.0
IA	42,307	24,611	58.1	SD	13,941	9,541	68.4
KS	45,597	27,547	60.4	TN	109,517	53,002	48.3
KY	85,492	39,949	46.7	TX	361,517	212,980	58.9
LA	73,199	28,165	38.4	UT	40,281	28,734	71.3
ME	18,610	8,710	46.8	VT	8,133	4,582	56.3
MD	58,476	36,976	63.2	VA	107,319	61,469	57.2
MA	62,778	35,503	56.5	WA	102,560	59,645	58.1
MI	129,355	68,819	53.2	WV	33,291	15,453	46.4
MN	67,374	44,220	65.6	WI	73,772	42,424	57.5
MS	50,519	25,044	49.5	WY	9,100	5,979	65.7

Citation: Paul, S., Rogers, S., Bach, S., & Houtenville, A. (2023). Annual Disability Statistics Compendium: 2023 (Table 3.3). Durham, NH: University of New Hampshire, Institute on Disability. Note: Authors' calculations using the U.S. Census Bureau American Community Survey, Public Use Microdata Sample, 2021, which is subject to sampling variation.
[1] The percentage of people with hearing disabilities employed .

Table 3.4 Employment – Civilians with Vision Disabilities Ages 18-64 Years Living in the Community for the United States and States: 2021

State	Total	Employed Count	% [1]	State	Total	Employed Count	% [1]
U.S.	4,198,571	2,013,445	47.9	MO	89,950	42,477	47.2
AL	85,135	31,203	36.6	MT	13,291	4,540	34.1
AK	9,079	5,296	58.3	NE	26,430	14,622	55.3
AZ	91,441	52,208	57.0	NV	45,283	21,174	46.7
AR	55,297	21,805	39.4	NH	14,175	6,791	47.9
CA	440,277	211,178	47.9	NJ	93,308	48,559	52.0
CO	66,208	35,577	53.7	NM	32,792	14,988	45.7
CT	40,603	21,894	53.9	NY	206,577	94,198	45.5
DE	13,099	6,066	46.3	NC	143,324	65,782	45.8
DC	9,703	4,536	46.7	ND	11,957	8,115	67.8
FL	259,705	126,129	48.5	OH	151,355	65,583	43.3
GA	149,327	69,295	46.4	OK	86,238	40,769	47.2
HI	12,019	6,019	50.0	OR	55,212	26,142	47.3
ID	28,388	18,652	65.7	PA	160,422	67,533	42.0
IL	136,998	69,125	50.4	RI	14,398	8,369	58.1
IN	88,865	43,279	48.7	SC	70,780	33,796	47.7
IA	33,909	18,131	53.4	SD	9,761	5,222	53.4
KS	34,818	18,283	52.5	TN	116,871	51,900	44.4
KY	89,154	34,688	38.9	TX	419,128	223,337	53.2
LA	96,632	41,732	43.1	UT	33,735	19,816	58.7
ME	14,298	4,757	33.2	VT	5,703	2,147	37.6
MD	63,400	33,869	53.4	VA	99,562	52,004	52.2
MA	64,727	32,962	50.9	WA	85,945	42,099	48.9
MI	113,662	48,583	42.7	WV	30,818	8,895	28.8
MN	46,518	23,434	50.3	WI	59,657	31,240	52.3
MS	70,633	30,111	42.6	WY	8,004	4,535	56.6

Citation: Paul, S., Rogers, S., Bach, S., & Houtenville, A. (2023). Annual Disability Statistics Compendium: 2023 (Table 3.4). Durham, NH: University of New Hampshire, Institute on Disability. Note: Authors' calculations using the U.S. Census Bureau American Community Survey, Public Use Microdata Sample, 2021, which is subject to sampling variation.
[1] The percentage of people with vision disabilities employed.

881

Table 3.5 Employment – Civilians with Cognitive Disabilities Ages 18–64 Years Living in the Community for the United States and States: 2021

State	Total	Employed Count	% [1]
U.S.	9,753,745	3,282,104	33.6
AL	183,141	48,762	26.6
AK	25,998	12,130	46.6
AZ	205,949	75,494	36.6
AR	122,218	32,258	26.3
CA	955,091	304,499	31.8
CO	160,011	66,927	41.8
CT	98,619	34,627	35.1
DE	27,107	10,465	38.6
DC	20,023	7,462	37.2
FL	571,601	179,537	31.4
GA	317,397	104,957	33.0
HI	34,386	9,810	28.5
ID	61,658	26,176	42.4
IL	320,585	109,265	34.0
IN	210,353	74,394	35.3
IA	95,770	38,546	40.2
KS	99,028	37,415	37.7
KY	188,277	46,338	24.6
LA	172,153	45,150	26.2
ME	58,996	17,561	29.7
MD	152,155	57,890	38.0
MA	190,553	67,661	35.5
MI	340,394	108,610	31.9
MN	184,745	87,731	47.4
MS	123,035	27,426	22.2
MO	211,107	78,737	37.2
MT	37,919	13,857	36.5
NE	53,833	23,877	44.3
NV	83,410	28,355	33.9
NH	42,323	17,348	40.9
NJ	185,139	54,147	29.2
NM	78,495	23,076	29.3
NY	517,427	156,912	30.3
NC	325,959	105,132	32.2
ND	17,972	9,465	52.6
OH	406,879	140,473	34.5
OK	156,751	51,656	32.9
OR	174,169	58,178	33.4
PA	421,866	139,990	33.1
RI	37,602	14,106	37.5
SC	153,828	48,209	31.3
SD	24,550	10,093	41.1
TN	240,740	66,213	27.5
TX	777,206	286,503	36.8
UT	103,270	49,683	48.1
VT	22,565	5,907	26.1
VA	228,934	81,293	35.5
WA	262,075	89,370	34.1
WV	77,253	18,155	23.5
WI	176,760	73,044	41.3
WY	16,470	7,234	43.9

Citation: Paul, S., Rogers, S., Bach, S., & Houtenville, A. (2023). Annual Disability Statistics Compendium: 2023 (Table 3.5). Durham, NH: University of New Hampshire, Institute on Disability. Note: Authors' calculations using the U.S. Census Bureau American Community Survey, Public Use Microdata Sample, 2021, which is subject to sampling variation.
[1] The percentage of people with cognitive disabilities employed.

Table 3.6 Employment – Civilians with Ambulatory Disabilities Ages 18–64 Years Living in the Community for the United States and States: 2021

State	Total	Employed Count	% [1]
U.S.	8,931,748	2,358,780	26.4
AL	209,788	40,062	19.0
AK	19,632	6,285	32.0
AZ	184,450	55,124	29.8
AR	128,378	31,628	24.6
CA	820,251	205,229	25.0
CO	111,403	36,214	32.5
CT	82,289	22,383	27.2
DE	28,267	9,976	35.2
DC	20,748	6,328	30.4
FL	583,227	152,070	26.0
GA	317,098	78,986	24.9
HI	28,670	8,300	28.9
ID	46,777	15,598	33.3
IL	316,618	85,829	27.1
IN	207,877	55,673	26.7
IA	80,060	23,003	28.7
KS	75,632	21,723	28.7
KY	199,797	41,069	20.5
LA	169,940	37,982	22.3
ME	45,789	9,117	19.9
MD	144,896	45,947	31.7
MA	140,064	35,667	25.4
MI	302,686	71,152	23.5
MN	105,314	38,044	36.1
MS	139,273	28,739	20.6

State	Total	Employed Count	% [1]
MO	194,670	46,137	23.7
MT	27,961	9,639	34.4
NE	48,455	16,969	35.0
NV	89,480	27,843	31.1
NH	28,796	9,255	32.1
NJ	182,319	47,191	25.8
NM	75,291	16,803	22.3
NY	492,523	122,257	24.8
NC	326,500	79,225	24.2
ND	14,815	5,409	36.5
OH	355,265	89,733	25.2
OK	155,889	41,564	26.6
OR	121,349	33,753	27.8
PA	356,698	88,614	24.8
RI	29,001	6,805	23.4
SC	174,347	41,485	23.7
SD	20,601	5,886	28.5
TN	253,557	58,214	22.9
TX	755,709	243,067	32.1
UT	64,731	26,577	41.0
VT	14,670	3,073	20.9
VA	224,836	68,451	30.4
WA	186,399	49,053	26.3
WV	82,894	15,111	18.2
WI	131,401	39,633	30.1
WY	14,667	4,905	33.4

Citation: Paul, S., Rogers, S., Bach, S., & Houtenville, A. (2023). Annual Disability Statistics Compendium: 2023 (Table 3.6). Durham, NH: University of New Hampshire, Institute on Disability. Note: Authors' calculations using the U.S. Census Bureau American Community Survey, Public Use Microdata Sample, 2021, which is subject to sampling variation.
[1] The percentage of people with ambulatory disabilities employed.

Table 3.7 Employment – Civilians with Self-Care Disabilities Ages 18-64 Years Living in the Community for the United States and States: 2021

State	Total	Employed Count	% [1]	State	Total	Employed Count	% [1]
U.S.	3,348,374	528,149	15.7	MO	71,063	11,868	16.7
AL	61,183	6,951	11.3	MT	10,839	2,508	23.1
AK	7,973	2,198	27.5	NE	16,548	3,922	23.7
AZ	61,460	11,065	18.0	NV	30,717	4,771	15.5
AR	45,521	6,104	13.4	NH	12,970	3,434	26.4
CA	365,270	48,555	13.2	NJ	78,150	12,395	15.8
CO	41,729	7,764	18.6	NM	32,061	5,919	18.4
CT	34,724	7,212	20.7	NY	198,077	25,429	12.8
DE	11,875	2,777	23.3	NC	110,804	18,478	16.6
DC	6,452	1,077	16.6	ND	3,847	1,178	30.6
FL	212,067	37,072	17.4	OH	121,345	19,009	15.6
GA	109,603	18,763	17.1	OK	46,235	7,237	15.6
HI	11,346	1,785	15.7	OR	50,336	8,799	17.4
ID	18,078	3,136	17.3	PA	134,141	21,735	16.2
IL	122,424	19,660	16.0	RI	12,436	1,450	11.6
IN	74,327	12,268	16.5	SC	61,556	8,645	14.0
IA	28,822	5,886	20.4	SD	7,314	793	10.8
KS	29,915	3,922	13.1	TN	83,397	12,136	14.5
KY	72,281	9,185	12.7	TX	276,165	46,771	16.9
LA	65,208	9,199	14.1	UT	23,217	6,219	26.7
ME	16,038	1,339	8.3	VT	6,185	471	7.6
MD	47,933	8,675	18.0	VA	82,485	15,319	18.5
MA	58,197	9,260	15.9	WA	72,493	10,437	14.3
MI	117,444	14,862	12.6	WV	31,477	2,647	8.4
MN	46,786	12,773	27.3	WI	57,350	8,973	15.6
MS	45,760	5,101	11.1	WY	4,750	1,017	21.4

Citation: Paul, S., Rogers, S., Bach, S., & Houtenville, A. (2023). Annual Disability Statistics Compendium: 2023 (Table 3.7). Durham, NH: University of New Hampshire, Institute on Disability. Note: Authors' calculations using the U.S. Census Bureau American Community Survey, Public Use Microdata Sample, 2021, which is subject to sampling variation.
[1] The percentage of people with self-care disabilities employed .

Table 3.8 Employment – Civilians with Independent Living Disabilities Ages 18–64 Years Living in the Community for the United States and States: 2021

State	Total	Employed Count	% [1]
U.S.	7,550,579	1,526,857	20.2
AL	150,441	20,900	13.8
AK	19,396	4,180	21.5
AZ	154,822	36,283	23.4
AR	102,928	15,298	14.8
CA	783,774	150,309	19.1
CO	109,735	30,503	27.7
CT	75,964	15,758	20.7
DE	23,182	6,444	27.7
DC	11,291	2,294	20.3
FL	447,811	85,645	19.1
GA	250,740	42,353	16.8
HI	26,466	7,553	28.5
ID	39,248	8,616	21.9
IL	268,220	56,873	21.2
IN	169,871	38,130	22.4
IA	70,035	19,569	27.9
KS	75,403	17,792	23.5
KY	153,865	21,914	14.2
LA	131,666	21,904	16.6
ME	48,499	11,042	22.7
MD	106,398	23,872	22.4
MA	140,821	32,051	22.7
MI	273,744	48,070	17.5
MN	125,635	42,706	33.9
MS	99,032	12,835	12.9
MO	157,561	34,367	21.8
MT	25,317	6,560	25.9
NE	36,130	12,425	34.3
NV	64,174	13,130	20.4
NH	31,444	9,339	29.7
NJ	164,983	28,919	17.5
NM	65,059	13,126	20.1
NY	436,592	69,615	15.9
NC	255,865	44,637	17.4
ND	9,697	2,306	23.7
OH	286,282	62,336	21.7
OK	119,785	23,373	19.5
OR	124,720	30,028	24.0
PA	315,910	62,660	19.8
RI	30,055	5,898	19.6
SC	125,691	25,228	20.0
SD	15,299	3,942	25.7
TN	191,409	30,466	15.9
TX	589,083	130,871	22.2
UT	67,291	19,382	28.8
VT	16,157	3,145	19.4
VA	176,496	38,111	21.5
WA	181,137	38,126	21.0
WV	62,089	8,324	13.4
WI	131,964	34,281	25.9
WY	11,402	3,368	29.5

Citation: Paul, S., Rogers, S., Bach, S., & Houtenville, A. (2023). Annual Disability Statistics Compendium: 2023 (Table 3.8). Durham, NH: University of New Hampshire, Institute on Disability. Note: Authors' calculations using the U.S. Census Bureau American Community Survey, Public Use Microdata Sample, 2021, which is subject to sampling variation.
[1] The percentage of people with independent living disabilities employed.

Table 3.9 Employment Gap – Civilians Ages 18–64 Years Living in the Community for the United States and States, by Disability Status: 2021

State	Disability [1]	No Disability [2]	Gap (% pts) [3]	State	Disability [1]	No Disability [2]	Gap (% pts) [3]
U.S.	40.7	76.6	35.9	MO	41.4	79.4	38.0
AL	32.3	74.6	42.3	MT	43.4	78.7	35.3
AK	46.1	74.9	28.8	NE	52.6	84.8	32.2
AZ	44.1	76.0	31.9	NV	42.5	73.5	31.0
AR	35.3	76.8	41.5	NH	46.8	81.7	34.9
CA	39.4	73.5	34.1	NJ	40.2	76.5	36.3
CO	49.9	79.9	30.0	NM	34.9	71.2	36.3
CT	44.4	78.3	33.9	NY	36.9	73.8	36.9
DE	47.2	76.3	29.1	NC	38.5	76.4	37.9
DC	40.3	77.8	37.5	ND	58.1	83.1	25.0
FL	39.3	76.3	37.0	OH	39.5	78.7	39.2
GA	38.8	76.0	37.2	OK	41.1	76.3	35.2
HI	40.4	75.1	34.7	OR	42.5	76.6	34.1
ID	50.4	79.5	29.1	PA	39.4	78.0	38.6
IL	41.6	76.9	35.3	RI	42.4	78.0	35.6
IN	40.6	78.7	38.1	SC	35.8	75.3	39.5
IA	47.1	83.0	35.9	SD	51.2	83.6	32.4
KS	43.6	80.9	37.3	TN	35.7	77.0	41.3
KY	33.7	76.0	42.3	TX	46.0	75.4	29.4
LA	34.2	72.2	38.0	UT	54.0	80.2	26.2
ME	35.8	80.1	44.3	VT	37.9	79.3	41.4
MD	45.6	79.0	33.4	VA	44.4	78.8	34.4
MA	41.7	78.8	37.1	WA	41.9	77.1	35.2
MI	37.3	75.4	38.1	WV	29.7	71.3	41.6
MN	50.9	83.5	32.6	WI	46.3	82.0	35.7
MS	33.2	72.9	39.7	WY	52.2	80.5	28.3

Citation: Paul, S., Rogers, S., Bach, S., & Houtenville, A. (2023). Annual Disability Statistics Compendium: 2023 (Table 3.9). Durham, NH: University of New Hampshire, Institute on Disability. Note: Authors' calculations using the U.S. Census Bureau American Community Survey, Public Use Microdata Sample, 2021, which is subject to sampling variation.

[1] The percentage of people with disabilities employed.
[2] The percentage of people without disabilities employed.
[3] The difference in percentage points of people with and without disabilities employed .

AIDS

AHF Federation, 584
AIDS Alert, 8683
AIDS Healthcare Foundation, 585, 2644
AIDS Sourcebook, 8496
AIDS United, 8293
AIDS Vancouver, 586
AIDS and Other Manifestations of HIV Infection, 8497
AIDS in the Twenty-First Century: Disease and Globalization, 8498
AIDS: The Official Journal of the International AIDS Society, 8665
Access & Information Network, 589
Camp Heartland, 1060, 8401
Camp Hollywood HEART, 861, 8406
Camp Starlight, 1211
Camp Sunburst, 876, 8433
Caremark Healthcare Services, 6646
Children with Disabilities, 5129
CrescentCare Legal Services, 4489
FC Search, 3192
Glaser Progress Foundation, 3162
Guide to Living with HIV Infection: Developed at the Johns Hopkins AIDS Clinic, 8548
HEAL: Health Education AIDS Liaison, 1936
HIV Infection and Developmental Disabilities, 2318
Harborview Medical Center, Low Vision Aid Clinic, 7021
Health Resources & Services Administration: State Bureau of Health, 3448
Health Resources and Services Administration (HRSA), 3223
Legal Action Center, 4499
Legal Counsel for Health Jusice, 4500
Legislative Network for Nurses, 4545
Levi Strauss Foundation, 2683
Living Well with Chronic Fatigue Syndrome and Fibromyalgia, 8576
Living Well with HIV and AIDS, 8577
A Loving Spoonful, 582
Miami VA Medical Center, 5516
Michigan Association for Deaf, and Hard of Hearing, 3467
Michigan Protection & Advocacy Service, 3480
National AIDS Hotline, 8726
Penitent, with Roses: An HIV+ Mother Reflects, 8623
Questions and Answers: The ADA and Persons with HIV/AIDS, 8630
Ryan White HIV/AIDS Program, 793
Sight by Touch, 9177
Strength for the Journey, 1219, 8478
Sunburst Projects, 8359
Suttle Lake Camp, 1220, 8480
Vinfen Corporation, 6811
Visiting Nurse Association of North Shore, 6812
WORLD, 816

Aging

ADHD: What Can We Do?, 7905
ARC Of Southeast Los Angeles-Southeast Industries, 6375
Activities in Action, 7454
Administration on Aging, 3214
Advocacy Centre for the Elderly (ACE), 592
Aging & Vision News, 7587
Aging Brain, 2201
Aging Life Care Association, 7336
Aging News Alert, 7588
Aging Services of Michigan, 7337
Aging Services of South Carolina, 7338
Aging Services of Washington, 7339
Aging and Disability Services, 3754, 7340
Aging and Disability Services Division, 3528
Aging and Disability: Crossing Network Lines, 2202
Aging and Family Therapy: Practitioner Perspectives on Golden Pond, 7457
Aging and Rehabilitation II: The State ofthe Practice, 2203

Aging and Vision: Declarations of Independence, 9164
Aging in America, 7341
Aging in Stride, 7458
Aging in the Designed Environment, 7459
Aging with a Disability, 7460
Alabama Department of Senior Services, 3251
Alabama VA Benefits Regional Office - Montgomery, 5472
Alaska Commission on Aging, 3262
Albany County Department for Aging and Albany Social Services, 3572
Albany VA Medical Center: Samuel S Stratton, 5605
Aleda E Lutz VA Medical Center, 5566
Alexandria VA Medical Center, 5549
Alliance for Aging Research, 7343
Alliance for Retired Americans, 7344
Alvin C York VA Medical Center, 5662
Amarillo VA Healthcare System, 5667
American Aging Association, 7345
American Association of Retired Persons, 7347
American Geriatrics Society, 7349
American Planning Association, 7350
American Society on Aging, 7353
American Wheelchair Bowling Association, 8271
Amyotrophic Lateral Sclerosis: A Guide for Patients and Families, 8506
Area Agency on Aging of Southwest Arkansas, 7607
Area Agency on Aging: Region One, 7608
Arizona Division of Aging and Adult Services, 3274
Arkansas Division of Aging & Adult Services, 3283
Asheville VA Medical Center, 5621
Association for Gerontology in Higher Education, 7358
Association for International Practical Training, 2602
Association of Jewish Aging Services, 7359
Association on Aging with Developmental Disabilities, 7360
Atlanta Regional Office, 5519
Atlanta VA Medical Center, 5520
Attention Getter, 1556
Attention Teens, 1557
Augusta VA Medical Center, 5521
Baltimore Regional Office, 5554
Baltimore VA Medical Center, 5555
Bath VA Medical Center, 5607
Battle Creek VA Medical Center, 5567
Bay Pines VA Medical Center, 5513
Biloxi/Gulfport VA Medical Center, 5577
Blindness, A Family Matter, 9165
Boise Regional Office, 5527
Boise VA Medical Center, 5528
Boston VA Regional Office, 5560
Bronx VA Medical Center, 5608
Brooklyn Campus of the VA NY Harbor Healthcare System, 5609
Buffalo Regional Office - Department of Veterans Affairs, 5610
Building Blocks: Foundations for Learning for Young Blind and Visually Impaired Children, 9166
Butler VA Medical Center, 5643
CARF International, 649, 1915, 7363
California Department of Aging, 3291
Cambia Health Foundation, 650, 3058
Can America Afford to Grow Old?, 4511
Canandiagua VA Medical Center, 5611
Caring for Those You Love: A Guide to Compassionate Care for the Aged, 7462
Carl T Hayden VA Medical Center, 5479
Carl Vinson VA Medical Center, 5522
Castle Point Campus of the VA Hudson Valley Healthcare System, 5612
Center for Disability and Elder Law, Inc., 4486
Center for Positive Aging, 7367
Change Your Brain, Change Your Life: The Breakthrough Program for Conquering Depression, 7806
Cheyenne VA Medical Center, 5699

Children of Aging Parents, 7368
Chillicothe VA Medical Center, 5629
Cincinnati VA Medical Center, 5630
Clement J Zablocki VA Medical Center, 5694
Cleveland Regional Office, 5631
Coatesville VA Medical Center, 5644
Colmery-O'Neil VA Medical Center, 5542
Colorado Association of Homes and Services for the Aging, 7369
Colorado Department of Aging & Adult Services, 3306
Colorado Springs Independence Center, 3905
Colorado/Wyoming VA Medical Center, 5499
Columbia Foundation, 2845
Columbia Regional Office, 5657
Communication Skills for Working with Elders, 2256
Complementary Alternative Medicine and Multiple Sclerosis, 8531
Connecticut Commission on Aging, 3315
Coping and Caring: Living with Alzheimer's Disease, 7464
Court-Related Needs of the Elderly and Persons with Disabilities, 4518
CurePSP Magazine, 8673
DSHS/Aging & Adult Disability Services Administration, 3763
Dayton VA Medical Center, 5632
DeafBlind Division of the National Federation of the Blind, 8882
Delaware Department of Health and Social Services, 3322
Delaware VA Regional Office, 5506
Denver VA Medical Center, 5500
Des Moines VA Medical Center, 5537
Des Moines VA Regional Office, 5538
District of Columbia Office on Aging, 3331
Duchenne Muscular Dystrophy, 8538
Durham VA Medical Center, 5623
Dwight D Eisenhower VA Medical Center, 5543
East Orange Campus of the VA New Jersey Healthcare System, 5600
Edith Nourse Rogers Memorial Veterans Hospital, 5561
Edward Hines Jr Hospital, 5529
Ehrman Medical Library, 4792
El Paso VA Healthcare Center, 5669
Elder Abuse and Mistreatment, 7465
Elder Visions Newsletter, 7593
ElderLawAnswers.com, 4528
Elgin Training Center, 6661
Employment for Individuals with Asperger Syndrome or Non-Verbal Learning Disability, 8798
Enabling News, 7594
Erie VA Medical Center, 5645
Eugene J Towbin Healthcare Center, 5482
Explore Your Options, 7466
Facilitating Self-Care Practices in the Elderly, 2306
Falling in Old Age, 7467
Family Intervention Guide to Mental Illness, 7468
Family-Guided Activity-Based Intervention for Toddlers & Infants, 5258
Fanlight Productions, 24
Fargo VA Medical Center, 5627
Fayetteville VA Medical Center, 5483, 5624
Films & Videos on Aging and Sensory Change, 5261
Florida Adult Services, 3346
Fort Howard VA Medical Center, 5556
Foundations of Orientation and Mobility, 9007
Gainesville Division, North Florida/South Georgia Veterans Healthcare System, 5514
Georgia Department of Aging, 3361
The Gerontological Society of America, 7450
Gerontology: Abstracts in Social Gerontology, 7486
Getting Better, 8159
Golf Xpress, 448
Grand Island VA Medical System, 5588
Grand Junction VA Medical Center, 5501
Hampton VA Medical Center, 5680
Handbook of Assistive Devices for the Handicapped Elderly, 7469

St. Louis VA Medical Center, 5583
St. Paul Regional Office, 5575
St. Petersburg Regional Office, 5517
Start-to-Finish Library, 1689
Stickybear Typing, 1706
Storybook Maker Deluxe, 1625
Strategies for Teaching Students with Learning and Behavior Problems, 2438
Strides Magazine, 8242
Successful Models of Community Long Term Care Services for the Elderly, 7481
Syracuse VA Medical Center, 5616
Teaching Special Students in Mainstream, 1979
Tennessee Commission on Aging and Disability, 3696
Tennessee Hospital Association, 7449
Texas Department on Aging, 3721
Therapeutic Activities with Persons Disabled by Alzheimer's Disease, 7482
Togus VA Medical Center, 5553
Tomah VA Medical Center, 5695
Tomorrow's Promise: Language Arts, 1695
Tomorrow's Promise: Spelling, 1697
Tompkins County Office for the Aging, 7617
Tourette Syndrome: The Facts, 8649
Triangle J Council of Governments Area Agency on Aging, 7618
US Administration on Aging, 7451
US Department of Veterans Affairs National Headquarters, 5470
University of California Memory and Aging Center, 7619
Utah Department of Aging and Adult Services, 3734
Utah Division of Veterans Affairs, 5676
V.A. Montana Healthcare System, 5585
VA Ann Arbor Healthcare System, 5571
VA Boston Healthcare System: Brockton Division, 5563
VA Boston Healthcare System: Jamaica Plain Campus, 5564
VA Boston Healthcare System: West Roxbury Division, 5565
VA Central California Health Care System, 5494
VA Connecticut Healthcare System: Newington Division, 5504
VA Connecticut Healthcare System: West Haven, 5505
VA Greater Los Angeles Healthcare System, 5495
VA Illiana Health Care System, 5532
VA Montana Healthcare System, 5586
VA Nebraska-Western Iowa Health Care System, 5591
VA North Indiana Health Care System: Fort Wayne Campus, 5535
VA Northern California Healthcare System, 5496
VA Northern Indiana Health Care System: Marion Campus, 5536
VA Pittsburgh Healthcare System, Highland Drive Division, 5653
VA Pittsburgh Healthcare System, University Drive Division, 5652
VA Puget Sound Health Care System, 5688
VA Salt Lake City Healthcare System, 5677
VA San Diego Healthcare System, 5497
VA Sierra Nevada Healthcare System, 5594
VA Southern Nevada Healthcare System, 5595
VA Western NY Healthcare System, Batavia, 5619
VA Western NY Healthcare System, Buffalo, 5620
Vermont Department of Aging, 3746
Vermont Department of Disabilities, Aging and Independent Living, 3748
Vermont Division of Disability & Aging Services, 3752
Vermont VA Regional Office Center, 5678
Veteran Benefits Administration - Anchorage Regional Office, 5478
Visiting Nurse Association of America, 8736
Visually Impaired Seniors as Senior Companions: A Reference Guide, 7483
WG Hefner VA Medical Center - Salisbury, 5625
Waco Regional Office, 5674
Washington County Disability, Aging and Veteran Services, 3649

Washington DC VA Medical Center, 5512
We Can Do it Together!, 9179
West Palm Beach VA Medical Center, 5518
West Texas VA Healthcare System, 5675
West Virginia Department of Aging, 3779
Wilkes-Barre VA Medical Center, 5654
William Jennings Bryan Dorn VA Medical Center, 5659
William S Middleton Memorial VA Hospital Center, 5696
Wilmington VA Medical Center, 5507
Winston-Salem Regional Office, 5626
Wisconsin Bureau of Aging, 3789
Wisconsin VA Regional Office, 5697
Work, Health and Income Among the Elderly, 7484
Wyoming Department of Aging, 3797
Wyoming/Colorado VA Regional Office, 5701
Yoga for Fibromyalgia: Move, Breathe, and Relax to Improve Your Quality of Life, 8234
Young Person's Guide to Spina Bifida, 8661

Alternative Therapies

The ACNM Foundation, Inc., 2858
Academy for Guided Imagery, 2564
Academy of Integrative Health & Medicine (AIHM), 588
Accreditation Commission for Acupuncture & Herbal Medicine, 590
Accreditation Commission for Midwifery Education (ACME), 591
American Academy of Medical Acupuncture, 597
American Academy of Osteopathy, 8168
American Acupuncture Council, 601
American Association of Acupuncture and Oriental Medicine (AAAOM), 602
American Association of Neuromuscular & Electrodiagnostic Medicine, 8169
American College of Advancement in Medicine (ACAM), 612
American College of Nurse Midwives (ACNM), 613
American Herb Association Newsletter, 4945
American Migraine Foundation, 1911, 2926
American Sexual Health Association, 8306
American Society for the Alexander Technique (AmSAT), 624
American Society of Clinical Hypnosis (ASCH), 625
Aromatherapy Book: Applications and Inhalations, 4952
Aromatherapy for Common Ailments, 4953
Association for Applied Psychophysiology and Biofeedback (AAPB), 632
Ayurvedic Institute, 2569
Bach Flower Therapy: Theory and Practice, 4958
Bastyr Center for Natural Health, 642
Beliefs, Values, and Principles of Self Advocacy, 4960
Brain Allergies: The Psychonutrient and Magnetic Connections, 8515
Center for Mind-Body Medicine, 658
Chinese Herbal Medicine, 4978
Chronic Fatigue Syndrome: Your Natural Gu ide to Healing with Diet, Herbs and Other Methods, 8527
Colon Health: Key to a Vibrant Life, 8530
Council of Colleges of Acupuncture & Oriental Medicine, 670
Creating Wholeness: Self-Healing Workbook Using Dynamic Relaxation, Images and Thoughts, 4986
Curing MS: How Science is Solving the Mysteries of Multiple Sclerosis, 8534
The Davis Center, 804, 8004, 8767
Designing and Using Assistive Technology: The Human Perspective, 2270
Disabled Athlete Sports Association (DASA), 682
Divided Legacy: A History of the Schism in Medical Thought, The Bacteriological Era, 2285
Dr. Ida Rolf Institute (DIRI), 689
Environmental Health Center: Dallas, 8318
Esalen Institute, 695

Everybody's Guide to Homeopathic Medicines, 5005
Feldenkrais Guild of North America (FGNA), 703
Flying Manes Therapeutic Riding, Inc., 704
Handbook of Chronic Fatigue Syndrome, 8549
Healing Herbs, 5019
Health Action, 714
Heart of the Mind, 8552
Herb Research Foundation, 5348
Homeopathic Educational Services, 718
Imagery in Healing Shamanism and Modern Medicine, 5027
Informed Touch; A Clinician's Guide To The Evaluation Of Myofascial Disorders, 8558
International Association of Hygienic Physicians, 8327
International Association of Yoga Therapists (IAYT), 725
International Childbirth Education Association, 1939
International Clinic of Biological Regeneration (ICBR), 728
It's All in Your Head: The Link Between Mercury Amalgams and Illness, 8562
JoanBorysenko.Com, 5353
Journal of Midwifery & Women's Health (JMWH), 2119
Living Beyond Multiple Sclerosis: A Woman's Guide, 8574
Living an Idea: Empowerment and the Evolution of an Alternative School, 1854
Long Beach Department of Health and Human Services, 3299
Los Angeles County Department of Health Services, 3300
Lupus: Alternative Therapies That Work, 8583
National Association for Holistic Aromatherapy (NAHA), 748
National Association to Advance Fat Acceptance, 8343
National Center for Homeopathy, 1949
National Certification Commission for Acupuncture and Oriental Medicine, 761
National Guild of Hypnotists (NGH), 766
National Headache Foundation, 2807
National University of Natural Medicine (NUNM), 771
Nothing is Impossible: Reflections on a New Life, 5069
Nutritional Desk Reference, 5070
Nutritional Influences on Illness:, 5071
Optometric Extension Program Foundation, 2856
Our Own Road, 5282
Pacific Institute of Aromatherapy, 779
Pain Erasure, 5151
Pain Erasure: the Bonnie Prudden Way, 9056
Professional Association of Therapeutic Horsemanship International (PATH Intl.), 789, 8285
Small Wonder, 1886
Solving the Puzzle of Chronic Fatigue, 8639
Structural Integration: The Journal of the Rolf Institute, 2141
Therapeutic Touch International Association (TTIA), 808
Tourette's Syndrome: Tics, Obsessions, Compulsions: Developmental Psychopathology, 8651
United States Trager Association, 811
Upledger Institute International (UII), 813
Weiner's Herbal, 5115

Amputation

American Amputee Foundation, 7928
Amputee Coalition, 628
Baylor Institute for Rehabilitation, 6982
Botsford Center For Rehabilitation & Health Improvement-Redford, 6815
Breaking New Ground Resource Center, 8713
Camp No Limits California, 864
Camp No Limits Connecticut, 921
Camp No Limits Florida, 932
Camp No Limits Idaho, 959

Autism

Camp Catch-A-Rainbow, 1044
Camp Catch-a-Rainbow, 8386
Camp Courage, 1057, 1228, 1258
Camp Debbie Lou, 1259
Camp Dream Street, 1070, 1105
Camp Enchantment, 1119
Camp Firefly, 946
Camp Good Days and Special Times, 1129
Camp Goodtimes, 1330
Camp Hobe, 1308
Camp Little Red Door, 985
Camp Mak-A-Dream, 1083
Camp Millennium, 1210
Camp Okizu, 865, 8422
Camp Okizu: Family Camp, 866
Camp Okizu: Oncology Camp, 867
Camp Okizu: SIBS Camp, 868
Camp Okizu: Teens-N-Twenties Camp, 869
Camp One Step, 971
Camp Quality Arkansas, 852
Camp Quality Central Missouri, 1076
Camp Quality Greater Kansas City, 1077
Camp Quality Heartland, 1087
Camp Quality Illinois, 972
Camp Quality Kansas, 1002
Camp Quality Kentuckiana, 988, 1004
Camp Quality Louisiana, 1011
Camp Quality New Jersey, 1110
Camp Quality North Michigan, 1048
Camp Quality Northwest Missouri, 1078
Camp Quality Ohio, 1185
Camp Quality Ozarks, 1079
Camp Quality South Michigan, 1049
Camp Quality Texas, 1292
Camp Rainbow, 848, 1293, 8425
Camp Rainbow Gold, 960
Camp Reach for the Sky, 873, 8426
Camp Ronald McDonald for Good Times, 875, 8428
Camp Smile-A-Mile, 826, 8432
Camp Smile-A-Mile: Jr./Sr. Camp, 827
Camp Smile-A-Mile: Off Therapy Family Camp, 828
Camp Smile-A-Mile: On Therapy Family Camp, 829
Camp Smile-A-Mile: Sibling Camp, 830
Camp Smile-A-Mile: Teen Weeklong Camp, 831
Camp Smile-A-Mile: Young Adult Retreat, 832
Camp Smile-A-Mile: Youth Weeklong Camp, 833
Camp SunSibs, 1023
Camp Sunrise, 1024, 8434
Camp Sunshine, 853, 951, 1017
Camp Sunshine Dreams, 877, 8435
Camp Ukandu, 1213
Camp Wapiyapi, 903
Canadian Cancer Society, 8312
Cancer Care, 2956
Cancer Clinical Trials: A Commonsense Guide to Experimental Cancer Therapies and Trials, 5177
Cancer Research Institute, 5330
Cancer Sourcebook, 8519
Cancer Sourcebook for Women, 8520
Candlelighters Childhood Cancer Foundation, 2842
Childhood Cancer Canada Foundation, 8315
Childhood Cancer Survivors: A Practical Guide to Your Future, 8522
Childhood Cancer: A Parent's Guide to Solid Tumor Cancers, 8523
Childhood Leukemia Foundation, 8316
Colon & Rectal Cancer: A Comprehensive Guide for Patients & Families, 8529
Conquering the Darkness: One Story of Recovering from a Brain Injury, 8532
Coping with Cancer Magazine, 8672
Damon Runyon Cancer Research Foundation, 5332
Desert Regional Medical Center, 6415
Double H Ranch, 1143
Eastern Idaho Regional Medical Center, 7090
Fannie E Rippel Foundation, 2933
First Descents, 914
Foundation for Advancement in Cancer Therapy, 2977
Genetic Nutritioneering, 5014
Happiness Is Camping, 1113, 8458

Healthsouth Rehabilitation Hospital of Greater Pittsburgh, 6250
The Hole in the Wall Gang Camp, 924, 8483
International Association for Cancer Victors & Friends, 8326
International Myeloma Foundation, 8329
Jane Coffin Childs Memorial Fund for Medical Research, 2728
Jane Phillips Medical Center, 6234
John Muir Medical Center Rehabilitation Services, Therapy Center, 6440
Kids Cancer Alliance, 1005
Leukemia & Lymphoma Society, 8331
Leukemia Sourcebook, 8569
Liver Disorders Sourcebook, 8573
Lung Cancer: Making Sense of Diagnosis, Treatment, and Options, 8581
Lymphoma Canada, 8334
Madonna Rehabilitation Hospital, 7149
Marist Brothers Mid-Hudson Valley Camp, 1150, 8466
Methodist Hospital Rehabilitation Institute, 6157
Multiple Sclerosis National Research Institute, 5361
NCI's Contact Center, 8725
National Association for Proton Therapy, 8340
National Cancer Institute, 3224, 8344
Northwest Hospital Center for Medical Rehabilitation, 6310
One Day at a Time: Children Living with Leukemia, 8618
Options, 8694
Options: Revolutionary Ideas in the War on Cancer, 8619
Parma Community General Hospital Acute Rehabilitation Center, 6226
Prostate and Urological Disorders Sourcebook, 8628
Psychology and Health, 5088
RA Bloch Cancer Foundation, 2914
Rapahope Children's Retreat Foundation, 837, 2633, 8473
Seany Foundation, 2698
Simonton Cancer Center, 8355
Society for Post-Acute and Long-Term Care Medicine (AMDA), 795
St. Anthony's Hospital, 7079
Sumner Regional Medical Center, 6270
V Foundation for Cancer Research, 5380
Victory Junction, 1169
YMCA Camp Jewell, 8489
Your Guide to Bowel Cancer, 8664

Cerebral Palsy

American Academy for Cerebral Palsy and Developmental Medicine, 1729, 8294
CPATH Cerebral Palsy Awareness Transition Hope, 8311
Camp CPals, 1283
Cerebral Palsy Associations of New York State, 7686
Cerebral Palsy Foundation (CPF), 659
Cerebral Palsy: North County Center, 6402
Children with Cerebral Palsy: A Parents' Guide, 8526
Coping with Cerebral Palsy, 8533
Developmental Medicine & Childhood Neurology, 8670
From Where I Sit: Making My Way with Cerebral Palsy, 8545
No Time for Jello: One Family's Experience, 8603
Ontario Cerebral Palsy Sports Association, 8284
Ontario Federation for Cerebral Palsy, 7716
Preventing Secondary Conditions Associated with Spina Bifida or Cerebral Palsy, 8627
Ten Things I Learned from Bill Porter, 8647
Treating Cerebral Palsy for Clinicians by Clinicians, 2475
United Cerebral Palsy, 1958, 7724
United Cerebral Palsy of Texas, 3729

Chiropractics

American Chiropractic Association (ACA), 611
International Chiropractors Association (ICA), 727

Chronic Disabilities

Access to Health Care, 2191
Broken Dolls: Gathering the Pieces: Caringfor Chronically Ill Children, 5127
Camp Boggy Creek, 931, 8381
Camp Discovery, 917, 967, 1229, 1269, 1285
Camp Holiday Trails, 1322
Camp Kindle, 862, 1086
Caring for Children with Chronic Illness, 2234
The Center for Courageous Kids, 1007
Comprehensive Care Coordination for Chronically Ill Adults, 4908
Counseling Parents of Children with Chronic Illness or Disability, 5207
Developing Cross-Cultural Competence:Guideto Working with Young Children & Their Families, 2271
Dream Oaks Camp, 936
Dream Street, 888, 8449
Dream Street Foundation, 2664
Family Interventions Throughout Disability, 5140
Flying Horse Farms, 1189
Living with a Brother or Sister with Special Needs: A Book for Sibs, 5144
National Association for Home Care and Hospice, 7418
National Association of Chronic Disease Diseases, 8342
The Painted Turtle, 898
Roundup River Ranch, 915, 8474
Screening in Chronic Disease, 5096

Cleft Palate

Camp About Face, 982
Cleft Palate-Craniofacial Journal, 8669
Nasometer, 1657
Your Cleft Affected Child, 8663

Cognitive Disorders

ADHD Book of Lists: A Practical Guide for Helping Children and Teens with ADDs, 7778
ADHD in the Schools: Assessment and Intervention Strategies, 2189, 7779
Academy of Cognitive Therapy, 7662
Adult ADD: The Complete Handbook: Everything You Need to Know About How to Cope with ADD, 7782
Albert Ellis Institute, 7664
American Academy of Child & Adolescent Psychiatry, 7665
American Delirium Society, 7666
Arc Connection Newsletter, 4951, 7886
Arc Light, 7887
Assistive Technology for Individuals with Cognitive Impairments Handbook, 7784
Augmenting Basic Communciation in Natural Contexts, 7792
Be Quiet, Marina!, 7803
Beck Institute for Cognitive Behavior Therapy, 7678
Biologically Inspired Cognitive Architectures Society, 7680
Biology Concepts Through Discovery, 7912
Camp Nissokone, 7735
Child and Adolescent Therapy: Cognitive-Behavioral Procedures, Third Edition, 7807
Children and Adults with Attention-Deficit Hyperactivity Disorder, 7688
Cognitive Neuroscience Society, 7689
Cognitive Science Society, 7690
Cognitive Science Student Association, 7691
Concentration Video, 7913
Count Us In, 7813
Devereux Advanced Behavioral Health California, 6416
Difficult Child, 7815

Cystic Fibrosis

Dementia

Dental Issues

Depression

Developmental Disabilities

Diabetes

Diet & Nutrition

Down Syndrome

Dyslexia

Education & Counseling

Classroom GOALS: Guide for Optimizing Auditory Learning Skills, 1814

Classroom Notetaker: How to Organize a Program Serving Students with Hearing Impairments, 1815

Closed Caption Decoder, 176

Cochlear Implant Camp, 912, 8026

Cochlear Implants In Children: Ethics and Choices, 8134

Cochlear Implants for Kids, 8054

Cognition, Education and Deafness: Directions for Research and Instruction, 8055

College and University Programs for Deaf and Hard of Hearing Students, 8056

Come Sign with Us, 8057

Communication Service for the Deaf, 7964

Communique, 8135

Comprehensive Reference Manual for Signers and Interpreters, 8058

Comprehensive Signed English Dictionary, 8059

Conference of Educational Administrators of Schools and Programs for the Deaf, 7965

Connect, 8838

Connect - Commmunity News, 8136

Connect Hearing, 367

Conversational Sign Language II: An Intermediate Advanced Manual, 8060

Council of American Instructors of the Deaf (CAID), 7966

Custom Earmolds, 260

Deaf Camps, Inc., 1025

Deaf Catholic, 8137

Deaf Children Signers, 5252

Deaf Culture Series, 5253

Deaf Empowerment: Emergence, Struggle and Rhetoric, 8061

Deaf History Unveiled: Interpretations from the New Scholarship, 8062

Deaf Kid's Kamp, 8027

Deaf Like Me, 8063

Deaf Parents and Their Hearing Children, 8064

Deaf REACH, 7967

Deaf in America: Voices from a Culture, 8065

Deafness Research Foundation, 7969

Deafness and Communicative Disorders Branch of Rehab Services Administration Office, 8746

Dial-a-Hearing Screening Test, 8164

Digital Hearing Aids, 261

Division for Communication, Language, and Deaf/Hard of Hearing (DCD), 1923

Do You Hear That?, 5254

Door Knock Signaler, 410

Doorbell Signalers, 411

Duracell & Rayovac Hearing Aid Batteries, 262

EASE Program: Emergency Access Self Evaluation, 8066

Ear Foundation, 7971

Education and Auditory Research Foundation, 3109

Education of the Handicapped: Laws, Legislative Histories and Administrative Document, 4527

Educational Audiology for the Limited Hearing Infant and Preschooler, 2294

Effectively Educating Handicapped Students, 2299

Electronic Amplified Stethoscopes, 249

Enchanted Hills Camp for the Blind, 891, 8942

Encyclopedia of Deafness and Hearing Disorders, 8067

Evaluation and Educational Programming of Students with Deafblindness & Severe Disabilities, 2302

Expressive and Receptive Fingerspelling for Hearing Adults, 8068

Eye-Centered: A Study of Spirituality of Deaf People, 8069

Fantastic Series Videotape Set, 8149

Fantastic: Colonial Times, Chocolate, and Cars, 8150

Fantastic: Dogs at Work and Play, 8151

Fantastic: Exciting People, Places and Things!, 8152

Fantastic: From Post Offices to Dairy Goats, 8153

Fantastic: Imagination, Actors, and 'Deaf Way', 8154

Fantastic: Roller Coasters, Maps, and Ice Cream!, 8155

Fantastic: Skiing, Factories, and Race Hores, 8156

Fantastic: Wonderful Worlds of Sports and Travel, 8157

Fingerspelling: Expressive and Receptive Fluency, 8158

For Hearing People Only, 8070

Free Hand: Enfranchising the Education of Deaf Children, 2310

From Gesture to Language in Hearing and Deaf Children, 8071

From Mime to Sign Package, 8072

GA and SK Etiquette, 8073

Gallaudet Survival Guide to Signing, 8074

Gallaudet University Press, 1992, 5345

Georgiana Institute, 7972

Goldilocks and the Three Bears: Told in Signed English, 8075

HEAR Center, 7973

Harc Mercantile, Ltd., 178

Harris Communications, 263

Healing Dressing for Pressure Sores, 250

Hearing Aid Batteries, 264

Hearing Aid Battery Testers, 265

Hearing Aid Care Kit, 266

Hearing Education and Awareness for Rockers, 7974

Hearing Health Foundation (HHF), 715, 2982

Hearing Health Magazine, 8128

Hearing Impaired Children and Youth with Developmental Disabilities, 8076

Hearing Loss Association of America, 7628, 7976

Hearing, Speech and Deafness Center (HSDC), 7977, 8748

Helen Keller National Center Newsletter, 9021

Hollywood Speaks: Deafness and the Film Entertainment Industry, 8077

Home Alerting Systems, 419

House Ear Institute, 7978

How to Thrive, Not Just Survive, 9024

I Can't Hear You in the Dark: How to Lean and Teach Lipreading, 2333

I Have a Sister, My Sister is Deaf, 8078

I Heard That!, 2334

I Heard That!2, 2335

Independence Without Sight and Sound: Suggestions for Practitioners, 7641

Independence Without Sight or Sound, 8079

Indiana Deaf Camp, 994

InfoLoop Induction Receiver, 179

Innovative Practices for Teaching Sign Language Interpreters, 8080

Intermediate Conversational Sign Language, 8081

International Catholic Deaf Association, 7979

International Hearing Dog, 7980

International Hearing Dog, Inc., 8138

International Hearing Society, 7631, 7981

Interpretation: A Sociolinguistic Model, 8082

Interpreting: An Introduction, 8083

Invisible Children, 5272

Jason & Nordic Publishers, Inc., 5039

Journal of the Academy of Rehabilitative Audiology, 8123

Journal of the American Academy of Audiology (JAAA), 7488

Joy of Signing, 8084

Kid-Friendly Parenting with Deaf and Hard of Hearing Children, 8085

Language Learning Practices with Deaf Children, 2356

Laurent Clerc National Deaf Education Center, 737

Laurent Clerc: The Story of His Early Years, 8086

Learning American Sign Language, 1849

Learning to See: American Sign Language asa Second Language, 2363

Learning to Sign in My Neighborhood, 1851

Legal Right: The Guide for Deaf and Hard of Hearing People, 4542

Lexington School for the Deaf: Center for the Deaf, 7983

Linguistics of American Sign Language: An Introduction, 8087

Lions Camp Kirby, 8030

Lions Wilderness Camp for Deaf Children, Inc., 893, 8032

Listen Foundation, 2717

Literacy & Your Deaf Child: What Every Parent Should Know, 8088

Literature Journal, The, 8124

A Loss for Words, 8041

Mainstreaming Deaf and Hard of Hearing Students: Questions and Answers, 2367

Mask of Benevolence: Disabling the Deaf Community, The, 8089

Meniere's Disease, 8588

Michigan Association for Deaf and Hard of Hearing, 3466, 7984

Michigan Commission for the Blind, 3471

Michigan Commission for the Blind - Gaylord, 3470

Michigan Commission for the Blind Training Center, 3472

Michigan Commission for the Blind: Escanaba, 3473

Michigan Commission for the Blind: Flint, 3474

Micro Audiometrics Corporation, 268

Microloop III Basic, 182

Miracle-Ear Children's Foundation, 2854

Mississippi Speech-Language-Hearing Association, 7985

Mother Father Deaf: Living Between Sound and Silence, 8090

Mushroom Inserts, 269

My First Book of Sign, 8091

My Signing Book of Numbers, 8092

MyAlert Body Worn Multifunction Receiver, 183

NAD Broadcaster, 4556

National Association of Blind Educators, 8902

National Association of Blind Lawyers, 8903

National Association of Blind Rehabilitation Professionals, 8905

National Association of Hearing Officials, 7987

National Association of Special Education Teachers, 7989, 8754

National Association of the Deaf, 7990

National Black Association for Speech Language and Hearing, 7991

National Black Association for Speech-Language and Hearing, 8755

National Black Deaf Advocates, 7992

National Catholic Office of the Deaf, 7993

National Deaf Women's Bowling Association, 7995

National Hearing Conservation Association, 7996

National Institute on Deafness and Other Communication Disorders, 3233, 7997

National Student Speech Language Hearing Association, 7998

New Jersey Speech-Language-Hearing Association, 2058

News from Advocates for Deaf-Blind, 7656

Nursery Rhymes from Mother Goose, 8093

On the Level, 8143

Outsiders in a Hearing World: A Sociology of Deafness, 8094

Oval Window Audio, 270

PLA240 Room Loop System, 184

Parents and Teachers, 2386

People with Disabilities Who Challenge the System, 5082

Perigee Visual Dictionary of Signing, 8095

Personal FM Systems, 185

Phone Ringers, 186

Phone Strobe Flasher, 187

Phone of Our Own: The Deaf Insurrection Against Ma Bell, 8096

Place of Their Own: Creating the Deaf Community in America, 8097

Pocketalker Personal Amplifier, 188

PreReading Strategies, 8098

Products for People with Disabilities, 391

Quad City Deaf & Hard of Hearing Youth Group: Tomorrow's Leaders for our Community, 8099

Reading and Deafness, 2407

Registry of Interpreters for the Deaf, 7999

Religious Signing: A Comprehensive Guide for All Faiths, 8100

Room Valet Visual-Tactile Alerting System, 432
See What I'm Saying, 9174
Seeing Voices, 8101
Sertoma Camp Endeavor, 941, 8034
Shape Up 'n Sign, 9176
Show Me How: A Manual for Parents of Preschool Blind Children, 9072
Sign Language Interpreting and Interpreter Education, 8102
Sign Language Studies, 8125
Sign of the Times, 9073
Signaling Wake-Up Devices, 434
Signed English Schoolbook, 2427
Signed English Starter, The, 8103
Signing Family: What Every Parent Should Know About Sign Communication, The, 8104
Signing Naturally Curriculum, 1885
Signing for Reading Success, 8105
Signing: How to Speak with Your Hands, 8106
Signs Across America, 8107
Signs for Me: Basic Sign Vocabulary for Children, Parents & Teachers, 8108
Signs for Sexuality: A Resource Manual, 8109
Signs of the Times, 8110
Silent Garden, The, 8111
Sing Praise Hymnal for the Deaf, 8112
Smoke Detector with Strobe, 435
Sonic Alert, 191
Sonic Alert Alarm Clock with Bed Shaker, 166
Sound & Fury, 5296
Soundings Newsletter, 8145
Speech Adjust-A-Tone Basic, 192
Speech and the Hearing-Impaired Child, 2433
Starkey Hearing Foundation, 272, 8002
Store @ HDSC Product Catalog, 395
Strobe Light Signalers, 438
TDI National Directory & Resource Guide: Blue Book, 8113
TTYs: Telephone Device for the Deaf, 194
Telecommunications for the Deaf and Hard of Hearing, 8003
Test of Early Reading Ability Deaf or Hard of Hearing, 2554
Texas School of the Deaf, 2075
Theoretical Issues in Sign Language Research, 8114
There's a Hearing Impaired Child in My Class, 2472
Thinklabs One Stethoscope, 256
To Love this Life: Quotations by Helen Keller, 9088
Toward Effective Public School Program for Deaf Students, 2473
USA Deaf Sports Federation, 8163
Ultratec, 273
Usher Syndrome, 8658
Vestibular Disorders Association, 8006
Vision Magazine, 8147
Volta Review, 8126
We CAN Hear and Speak, 8115
Week the World Heard Gallaudet, The, 8116
Weitbrecht Communications, Inc. (WCI), 397
What is Auditory Processing?, 8117
You and Your Deaf Child: A Self-Help Guidefor Parents of Deaf and Hard of Hearing Children, 8118
Youth Leadership Camp, 8037
iLuv SmartShaker 2, 167

Hemophilia

Arizona Hemophilia Association, 8310
Bright Horizons Summer Camp, 8374
Camp Ailihpomeh, 1278
Camp Brave Eagle, 983
Camp H.U.G., 845, 8399
Camp High Hopes, 1130
Camp Honor, 846, 8407
Camp Hot-to-Clot, 1231
Camp Klotty Pine, 1340
Camp Little Oak, 1133
Hemophilia Camp, 8460
National Hemophilia Foundation, 2995, 8348

Herbal Medicine

American Botanical Council (ABC), 609
American Herbalists Guild (AHG), 618
HerbalEGram, 2159
HerbalGram, 2107

Human Interaction Disabilities

Camp Akeela, 1225
Camp Buckskin, 1055, 7729
Camp Connect, 1098
Eagle Hill School: Summer Program, 1032, 7747
Taking Part: Introducing Social Skills to Young Children, 2551

Immune Deficiencies

IDF National Conference, 1746
Immune Deficiency Foundation, 721, 2852
POZ Magazine, 8678
YMCA Camp Shady Brook, 8491

Incontinence

Duraline Medical Products Inc., 246
Informer, 8691
Kleinert's, 380
MOMS Catalog, 384
National Association for Continence, 8192
Quality Care Newsletter, 8699
Simon Foundation for Continence, 8202
Specialty Care Shoppe, 1386

Language Disorders

Academic Language Therapy Association, 8737
American Speech-Language-Hearing Association, 7958, 8738
Association of Language Companies, 8740
Beyond Baby Talk: From Sounds to Sentences, a Parent's Guide to Language Development, 8789
International Fluency Association, 8750
Language Arts: Detecting Special Needs, 2355
Language Disabilities in Children and Adolescents, 8801
Language and Communication Disorders in Children, 2357
Lindamood-Bell Home Learning Process, 8751
OWLS: Oral and Written Language Scales LC/OE & WE, 2530
PAT-3: Photo Articulation Test, 2531
Peabody Early Experiences Kit (PEEK), 2532
Peabody Language Development Kits (PLDK), 2534
Perspectives: Whole Language Folio, 8810
Preventing Academic Failure - Teachers Handbook, 2398
RULES: Revised, 2542
Receptive-Expressive Emergent-REEL-2 Language Test, 2nd Edition, 2543
Teaching Language-Disabled Children: A Communication/Games Intervention, 2451
Teaching Reading to Disabled and Handicapped Learners, 2456
Test of Language Development: Primary, 2555
Test of Phonological Awareness, 2558
Woodcock Reading Mastery Tests, 2561

Learning Disabilities

AEPS Child Progress Record: For Children Ages Three to Six, 1797
AEPS Child Progress Report: For Children Ages Birth to Three, 2488
AEPS Curriculum for Birth to Three Years, 2190
AEPS Curriculum for Three to Six Years, 1798
AEPS Data Recording Forms: For Children Ages Birth to Three, 2489
AEPS Data Recording Forms: For Children Ages Three to Six, 1799
AEPS Family Interest Survey, 1800

AEPS Family Report: For Children Ages Birth to Three, 4933
AEPS Measurement for Birth to Three Years, 2490
AEPS Measurement for Three to Six Years, 2491
AIR: Assessment of Interpersonal Relations, 2492
AVKO Educational Research Foundation, 1908
Academic Therapy Publications, 1981
Activity-Based Approach to Early Intervention, 2nd Edition, 2192
Adaptive Education Strategies Building on Diversity, 2196
Adaptive Mainstreaming: A Primer for Teachers and Principals, 3rd Edition, 2494
Advanced Language Tool Kit, 1802
Ages & Stages Questionnaires, 2495
All Kinds of Minds, 1803
Alphabetic Phonics Curriculum, 2204
Alternative Educational Delivery Systems, 2205
American College Testing Program, 2496
American School Counselor Association, 1912
Arkansas Department of Special Education, 2016
Assessing Students with Special Needs, 2497
Assessment Log & Developmental Progress Charts for the CCPSN, 2213, 2498
Assessment of Learners with Special Needs, 2499
Assessment: The Special Educator's Role, 2219
Assistive Technology, 174
Association of Educational Therapists (AET), 635
Association on Higher Education & Disability (AHEAD), 640, 1914
BOSC: Directory of Facilities for People with Learning Disabilities, 1960
Beacon Therapeutic Diagnostic and Treatment Center, 6643
Beginning Reasoning and Reading, 1810
Behind Special Education, 2227
Benchmark Measures, 2500
BroadFutures, 7684
Buy!, 1812
CAI, Career Assessment Inventories for the Learning Disabled, 2233
CEC Catalog, 2087
CEC Pioneers Division (CEC-PD), 1916
CREVT: Comprehensive Receptive and Expressive Vocabulary Test, 2502
Camp Nuhop, 1182, 7736
Camp Starfish, 1031
Carolina Curriculum for Infants and Toddlers with Special Needs (3rd Edition), 2235
Carolina Curriculum for Preschoolers with Special Needs, 2236
Catalyst, 2090
Center Academy, 7685
Center Academy at Pinellas Park, 934, 7745
Charis Hills Camp, 1299
Chemists with Disabilities Committee - American Chemical Society, 5225
Children's Understanding of Disability, 4885
Christian Approach to Overcoming Disability: A Doctor's Story, 4979
Clovernook Printing House, The Clovernook Center for the Blind and Visually Impaired, 8878
Cognitive Approaches to Learning Disabilities, 2250
College Internship Program at the Berkshire Center, 6792
Colorado Department of Education: Special Education Service Unit, 2018
Communicating with Parents of Exceptional Children, 2254
Complete Handbook of Children's Reading Disorders: You Can Prevent or Correct LDs, 2258
Complete Learning Disabilities Resource Guide, 1962
Complete Resource Guide for Pediatric Disorders, 1964
Complete Resource Guide for People with Chronic Illness, 1965
Computer Access/Computer Learning, 2259
Conference of the Association on Higher Education & Disability (AHEAD), 1742, 4981
Council for Educational Diagnostic Services (CEDS), 1919

Lowe's Syndrome

Lung Disorders

Massage Therapy

Mental Disabilities

Multiple Disabilities

Multiple Sclerosis

Muscular Dystrophy

Neurological Impairments

Obesity

Obsessive Compulsive Disorders

Orthopedical Disabilities

Pain Management

Parkinson Disease

National Association of Blind Merchants (NABM), 749, 8904
National Association of Blind Students, 8906
National Association of Blind Teachers, 8907
National Association of Guide Dog Users, 8909
National Association to Promote the Use of Braille, 8910
National Braille Association, 8912
National Braille Press, 8913
National Camps for Blind Children, 1090, 8947
National Center for Vision and Child Development, 8914
National Eye Institute, 3227, 8916, 9052
National Eye Research Foundation, 2805
National Federation of the Blind, 2855, 7635, 8917
National Industries for the Blind, 8918
National Organization of Parents of Blind Children, 8920
Nebraska Commission for the Blind & Visually Impaired, 3521
Nevada Bureau of Vocational Rehabilitation, 3530
New England Eye Center - Tufts Medical Center, 6805
New Eyes for the Needy, 8921
New Jersey Commission for the Blind and Visually Impaired (CBVI), 3553, 5967
New Mexico Commission for the Blind (NMCFTB), 3563, 5980
New York State Commission for the Blind, 3581
North Carolina Division of Services for the Blind, 5992
North Dakota Vocational Rehabilitation Agency, 5999
North Georgia Talking Book Center, 4658
Oklahoma Department of Rehabilitation Services, 3639, 6003
Opportunity, 9111
Oregon Health Sciences University, 5638
Orientation and Mobility Primer for Families and Young Children, 9053
Out of Left Field, 9173
Out of the Corner of My Eye: Living with Vision Loss in Later Life, 9054
PBA News, 9145
PXE International, 8728
Patient's Guide to Visual Aids and Illumination, 9057
Pearle Vision Foundation, 3139
Pediatric Visual Diagnosis Fact Sheets, 9058
Pennsylvania Bureau of Blindness & Visual Services, 3654
Perkins Electric Brailler, 450
Personal Reader Update, 9060
Pet Partners, 426
Playback, 9147
Preschool Learning Activities for the Visually Impaired Child, 9061
Prevent Blindness America, 8922
Psychoeducational Assessment of Visually Impaired and Blind Students, 2405
Quantum Technologies, 5374
Quarterly Update, 9148
RP Messenger, 9149
Reaching, Crawling, Walking... Let's Get Moving, 9062
Reading Is for Everyone, 9063
Reading with Low Vision, 9064
Reference and Information Services From NLS, 9066
Rehabilitation Resource Manual: VISION, 2413
Reizen RL-350 Braille Labeler, 452
Research to Prevent Blindness, 3003

Resource List for Persons with Low Vision, 9067
Robert Ellis Simon Foundation, 2695
SCENE, 9150
Say What Clothing Identifier, 238
SciPlus 3200 Low Vision Scientific Vision, 453
See A Bone, 9069
See What I Feel, 9070
See for Yourself, 9175
Seeing Eye Guide, 9152
Seeing Eye, The, 8923
Selecting a Program, 9071
Self-Therapy for the Stutterer, 8816
Services for the Blind Branch, 5832
Services for the Blind and Visually Impaired, 3671
Shared Visions, 9153
Sightings Newsletter, 9155
Smith Kettlewell Rehabilitation Engineering Research Center, 9156
Society for the Blind, 8924
SourceAmerica, 6045
Special Technologies Alternative Resources, 9074
Standing on My Own Two Feet, 9075
State Library of Kansas, 4698
State Library of Ohio: Talking Book Program, 4820
Step-By-Step Guide to Personal Management for Blind Persons, 9077
Stretch-View Wide-View Rectangular Illuminated Magnifier, 505
Student Teaching Guide for Blind and Visually Impaired College Students, 9078
TBC Focus, 9158
Tactile Braille Signs, 439
Tactile Checkers Set, 5415
Tactile Thermostat, 440
Talk to Me, 9080
Talk to Me II, 9081
Talking Calculators, 196
Talking Digital Cooking Thermometer, 254
Talking Digital Thermometer, 255
Talking Food Cans, 293
Talking Watches, 197
Taping for the Blind, 9178
Teaching Orientation and Mobility in the Schools: An Instructor's Companion, 9084
Teaching Visually Impaired Children, 9085
Technology Assistance for Special Consumers, 1493
Technology for the Disabled, 5298
Texas Commission for the Blind, 3717
Texas Workforce Commission: Vocational Rehabilitation Services, 6030
Textbook Catalog, 9086
Tic Tac Toe, 5417
Touch the Baby: Blind & Visually Impaired Children As Patients, 9089
Touch-Dots, 456
Transition Activity Calendar for Students with Visual Impairments, 9090
Transition to College for Students with Visual Impairments: Report, 9091
US Association of Blind Athletes, 9184
Unisex Low Vision Watch, 506
United States Association of Blind Athletes, 8925
United States Blind Golf Association, 9185
Unseen Minority: A Social History of Blindness in the United States, 9092
Upstate Update, 9160
Utah Division of Services for the Disabled, 3737
Utah State Library Division: Program for the Blind and Disabled, 4847
VIP Newsletter, 2179

VISIONS Vacation Camp for the Blind (VCB), 1156, 8949
VUE: Vision Use in Employment, 9191
Vermont Association for the Blind and Visually Impaired, 8928
Vermont Division for the Blind & Visually Impaired, 3751
Veteran's Voices Writing Project, 5471
Virginia Department for the Blind and Vision Impaired (DBVI), 3756, 6046
Vision Enhancement, 9093
Vision Foundation, 2874
Vision World Wide, 8930
Visions Center on Blindness (VCB), 8931
Vista Center for the Blind & Visually Impaired, 6504
Visual Aids and Informational Material, 9161
Visual Impairment: An Overview, 9094
Visual Impairments And Learning, 9095
Visually Impaired Veterans of America, 8932
Vocational Rehabilitation Agency: Oregon Commission for the Blind, 3648
Vocational Rehabilitation Services for the Blind, 5936
Voice of Vision, 9163
Volunteer Transcribing Services, 1904
WP and HB White Foundation, 2816
Walking Alone and Marching Together, 9096
Washington Connection, 9192
Washington Ear, 8933
Wayfinder Family Services, 2706
What Do You Do When You See a Blind Person - and What Don't You Do?, 9097
What Museum Guides Need to Know: Access for the Blind and Visually Impaired, 9098
When You Have a Visually Impaired Student in Your Classroom: A Guide for Teachers, 2483
Work Sight, 9099
Working with Visually Impaired Young Students: A Curriculum Guide for 3 to 5 Year Olds, 2486
World Through Their Eyes, 9100

Women

The Advocacy Centre, 802
Fos Feminista, 706
National Women's Health Network (NWHN), 773
A Woman's Guide to Living with HIV Infection, 8494
Women to Women Healthcare, 817
Women with Visible & Invisible Disabilitiees: Multiple Intersections, Issues, Therapies, 5222

Emory University Laboratory for Ophthalmic Research, 4653
Fair Housing and Equal Employment, 5823
Florence C and Harry L English Memorial Fund, 2766
Georgia Library for the Blind and Physically Handicapped, 4654
Georgia Power, 2767
Goodwill Career Centers, 5824
Griffin Area Resource Center, 5825
Hall County Library: East Hall Branch and Special Needs Library, 4655
Harriet McDaniel Marshall Trust in Memory of Sanders McDaniel, 2769
John H and Wilhelmina D Harland Charitable Foundation, 2771
Lettie Pate Whitehead Foundation, 2772
Living Independence for Everyone (LIFE), 3965
Macon Library for the Blind and Physically Handicapped, 4656
Multiple Choices Center for Independent Living, 3966
National Center on Birth Defects and Developmental Disabilities, 4657
New Ventures, 5826
North District Independent Living Program, 3967
North Georgia Talking Book Center, 4658
Oconee Regional Library, 4659
Rome Subregional Library for the Blind and Physically Handicapped, 4660
South Georgia Regional Library-Valdosta Talking Book Center, 4661
Southeastern Paralyzed Veterans of America, 5523
Southwest District Independent Living Program, 3968
Squirrel Hollow Summer Camp, 955
Statewide Independent Living Council of Georgia, 3969
SunTrust Bank, Atlanta Foundation, 2774
Talking Book Center Brunswick-Glynn County Regional Library, 4662
Vocational and Rehabilitation Agency, 5827
Walton Options for Independent Living, 3970

Hawaii

Arc of Hawaii, 2775
Assets School, 5828
Assistive Technology Resource Centers of Hawaii (ATRC), 4663
Atherton Family Foundation, 2776
Camp Anuenue, 956
Camp Taylor: Family Camp, 879, 957
Center For Independent Living- Kauai, 3971
GN Wilcox Trust, 2777
Hawaii Center For Independent Living, 3972
Hawaii Center for Independent Living-Maui, 3973
Hawaii Centers for Independent Living, 3974
Hawaii Community Foundation, 2778
Hawaii Fair Employment Practice Agency, 5829
Hawaii State Library for the Blind and Physically Handicapped, 4664
Hawaii Vocational Rehabilitation Division, 5830
Hilo Vet Center, 5524
Honolulu VBA Regional Office, 5525
Kauai Center for Independent Living, 3975
Lanakila Rehabilitation Center, 5831
McInerny Foundation Bank Of Hawaii, Corporate Trustee, 2779
Pacific Islands Health Care System, 5526
Pacific Rim International Conference on Disability And Diversity, 1756
Services for the Blind Branch, 5832
Sophie Russell Testamentary Trust Bank Of Hawaii, 2780

Idaho

American Falls Office: Living Independently for Everyone (LIFE), 3976
Boise Regional Office, 5527
Boise VA Medical Center, 5528
Camp Hodia, 958

Camp No Limits Idaho, 959
Camp Rainbow Gold, 960
Cristo Vive International: Idaho Camp, 961
Dawn Enterprises, 3977
Disability Action Center NW, 3978
Disability Action Center NW: Coeur D'Alene, 3979
Disability Action Center NW: Lewiston, 3980
Idaho Assistive Technology Project, 4665
Idaho Commission for Libraries: Talking Book Service, 4666
Idaho Commission for the Blind & Visually Impaired, 5833
Idaho Department of Labor, 5834
Idaho Division of Vocational Rehabilitation, 5835
Idaho Falls Office: Living Independently for Everyone (LIFE), 3981
Idaho Governor's Committee on Employment of People with Disabilities, 5836
Idaho Human Rights Commission, 5837
Living Independence Network Corporation, 3983
Living Independence Network Corporation: Twin Falls, 3984
Living Independence Network Corporation: Caldwell, 3985
Living Independent for Everyone (LIFE): Pocatello Office, 3986
Living Independently for Everyone (LIFE): Blackfoot Office, 3987
Living Independently for Everyone: Burley, 3988
National Association for Holistic Aromatherapy (NAHA), 748
ROW Adventures, 5452
Southwestern Idaho Housing Authority, 3989

Illinois

ADA Camp GranADA, 962
ADA Teen Adventure Camp, 963
ADA Triangle D Camp, 964
ATIA Conference, 1727
Access Living of Metropolitan Chicago, 3990
Ada S. McKinley Community Services, Inc., 5838
Alzheimer's Association, 2781
American Academy of Pediatrics (AAP), 600
American Massage Therapy Association (AMTA), 619
Amerock Corporation, 2783
Anixter Center, 5839
Arc of Illinois, 2784
Assistive Technology Industry Association (ATIA), 631
Benjamin Benedict Green-Field Foundation, 2785
Blowitz-Ridgeway Foundation, 2786
C-4 Work Center, 5840
Camp "I Am Me", 965
Camp Callahan, 966
Camp Discovery, 917, 967, 1229, 1229, 1269, 1285
Camp FRIENDship, 968
Camp Little Giant, 969
Camp One Step, 971
Camp Quality Illinois, 972
Camp Red Leaf, 973
Center for Creative Arts Therapy, 655
Center on Deafness, 3991
Chaddick Institute for Metropolitan Development, 2787
Chicago Community Trust, 2788
Chicago Community Trust and Affiliates, 2789
Chicago Public Library Talking Book Center, 4667
Clearbrook, 5841
Community Foundation of Champaign County, 2790
Community Residential Alternative, 3992
Cornerstone Services, 5842
Courier Travel, 5443
Department of Ophthalmology and Visual Science, 4668
Division of Rehabilitation Services, 3964, 3993
Dr Scholl Foundation, 2791
DuPage Center for Independent Living, 3994
Duchossois Foundation, 2792
Easterseals, 691

Edward Hines Jr Hospital, 5529
Evenston Community Foundation, 2793
Family Resource Center on Disabilities, 696
Field Foundation of Illinois, 2794
Fite Center for Independent Living, 3995
Francis Beidler Charitable Trust, 2795
Fred J Brunner Foundation, 2796
Fulton County Rehab Center, 5843
George M Eisenberg Foundation for Charities, 2797
Glenkirk, 5844
Grover Hermann Foundation, 2798
Guild for the Blind, 4669
Horizons for the Blind, 4670
Illinois Department of Rehab Services, 3996
Illinois Early Childhood Intervention Clearinghouse, 4671
Illinois Life Span Program, 5845
Illinois Machine Sub-Lending Agency, 4672
Illinois Regional Library for the Blind and Physically Handicapped, 4673
Illinois Valley Center for Independent Living, 3997
Illinois Wheelchair Sport Camps, 974
Illinois and Iowa Center for Independent Living, 3998
Impact Center for Independent Living, 3999
Jacksonville Area CIL: Havana, 4000
Jacksonville Area Center for Independent Living, 4001
Jewish Vocational Services, 5846
John D and Catherine T MacArthur Foundation, 2799
Kennedy Job Training Center, 5847
Kreider Services, 5849
LIFE Center for Independent Living, 4002
LINC-Monroe Randolph Center, 4003
Lake County Center for Independent Living, 4004
Lambs Farm, 5850
Land of Lincoln Goodwill Industries, 5851
Les Turne Amyotrophic Laterial Sclerosis Foundation, 2800
Life Center for Independent Living: Pontiac, 4005
Lions Clubs International, 2615
Little City Foundation, 2801
Living Independently Now Center (LINC), 4006
Living Independently Now Center: Sparta, 4007
Living Independently Now Center: Waterloo, 4008
Lowe Syndrome Conference, 1747
MAGIC Foundation for Children's Growth, 2802
MDA Summer Camp, 975
Marion VA Medical Center, 5530
McDonald's Corporation Contributions Program, 2803
Michael Reese Health Trust, 2804
Mid-Illinois Talking Book Center, 4674
Muscular Dystrophy Association USA (MDA), 747
National Eye Research Foundation, 2805
National Eye Research Foundation (NERF), 4675
National Foundation for Ectodermal Dysplasias, 2806
National Headache Foundation, 2807
National Lekotek Center, 4676
North Chicago VA Medical Center, 5531
Northwestern University Multipurpose Arthritis & Musculoskeletal Center, 4677
Nothern Suburban Special Recreation Association Day Camps, 976
OMRON Foundation OMRON Electronics, 2808
Opportunities for Access: A Center for Independent Living, 4010
Options Center for Independent Living: Bourbonnais, 4011
Options Center for Independent Living: Watseka, 4012
Orchard Village, 5852
PACE Center for Independent Living, 4013
Patrick and Anna M Cudahy Fund, 3184
Peoria Area Community Foundation, 2810
Polk Brothers Foundation, 2811
Progress Center for Independent Living, 4014
Progress Center for Independent Living: Blue Island, 4015
Regional Access & Mobilization Project, 4016

Regional Access & Mobilization Project: Belvidere, 4017

Regional Access & Mobilization Project: DeKalb, 4018

Regional Access & Mobilization Project: Freeport, 4019

Retirement Research Foundation, 2812

Rimland Services for Autistic Citizens, 977

Ronald McDonald House Charities (RMHC), 792

Rotary Youth Exchange, 2620

Sears-Roebuck Foundation, 2813

Sertoma Centre, 5853

Shady Oaks Camp, 978

Shirley Ryan AbilityLab, 794

Shore Training Center, 5854

Siragusa Foundation, 2814

Skokie Accessible Library Services, 4678

Soyland Access to Independent Living (SAIL), 4020

Soyland Access to Independent Living: Charleston, 4021

Soyland Access to Independent Living: Shelbyville, 4022

Soyland Access to Independent Living: Sullivan, 4023

Springfield Center for Independent Living, 4024

Square D Foundation, 2815

Stone-Hayes Center for Independent Living, 4025

The Workshop, 5855

Thresholds, 809, 5856

Timber Pointe Outdoor Center, 979

University of Illinois at Chicago: Lions of Illinois Eye Research Institute, 4679

VA Illiana Health Care System, 5532

Vocational Rehabilitation Services, 5743, 5857

Voices of Vision Talking Book Center at DuPage Library System, 4680

WP and HB White Foundation, 2816

Washington County Vocational Workshop, 5858

Washington Square Health Foundation, 2817

West Central Illinois Center for Independent Living, 4026

West Central Illinois Center for Independent Living: Macomb, 4027

Wheat Ridge Ministries, 2818

Will Grundy Center for Independent Living, 4028

Indiana

ADEC Resources for Independence, 5859

Allen County Public Library, 4681

American Camp Association (ACA), 610

Anderson Woods, 980

Arc Northwest Indiana, 5860

Arc of Indiana, 2819

Assistive Technology Training and Information Center (ATTIC), 4029

Association of Independent Camps, 636

BI-County Services, 5861

Ball Brothers Foundation, 2820

Bartholomew County Public Library, 4682

CHAMP Camp, 981

Camp About Face, 982

Camp Brave Eagle, 983

Camp John Warvel, 984

Camp Little Red Door, 985

Camp Millhouse, 986

Camp PossAbility, 987

Camp Red Cedar, 989

Camp Riley, 990

Carey Services, 5862

Community Foundation of Boone County, 2821

DAMAR Services, 4030

Elkhart Public Library for the Blind and Physically Handicapped, 4683

Evansville Association for the Blind, 5863

Everybody Counts Center for Independent Living, 4031

Feingold Association of the US, 702

Four Rivers Resource Services, 4032, 5864

Future Choices Independent Living Center, 4033

Gateway Services/JCARC, 5865

Goodwill of Central & Southern Indiana, 5866

Happiness Bag, 991

Hillcroft Services, 992

Hoosier Burn Camp, 993

Independent Living Center of Eastern Indiana (ILCEIN), 4034

Indiana Association for Home and Hospice Care (IAHHC), 722

Indiana Civil Rights Commission, 5867

Indiana Deaf Camp, 994

Indiana Disability Employment Initiative, 5868

Indiana Resource Center for Autism, 4684

Indiana University: Multipurpose Arthritis Center, 4685

Indianapolis Regional Office, 5533

Indianapolis Resource Center for Independent Living, 4035

John W Anderson Foundation, 2822

Lake County Public Library Talking Books Service, 4686

League for the Blind and Disabled, 4036

Martin Luther Homes of Indiana, 4037

New Hope Services, 5869

New Horizons Rehabilitation, 5870

Noble of Indiana, 5871

Paladin, 5872

Putnam County Comprehensive Services, 5873

Richard L Roudebush VA Medical Center, 5534

Ruben Center for Independent Living, 4038

SILC, Indiana Council on Independent Living (ICOIL), 4039

Southern Indiana Center for Independent Living, 4040

Southern Indiana Resource Solutions, 5874

Special Services Division: Indiana State Library, 4687

St. Joseph Hospital Rehabilitation Center, 4688

Sycamore Rehabilitation Services, 5875

Talking Books Service Evansville Vanderburgh County Public Library, 4689

VA North Indiana Health Care System: Fort Wayne Campus, 5535

VA Northern Indiana Health Care System: Marion Campus, 5536

Wabash Independent Living Center & Learning Center (WILL), 4041

Iowa

Access, Inc., 5876

Arc of Iowa, 2823

Black Hawk Center for Independent Living, 4042

Camp Albrecht Acres, 995

Camp Courageous of Iowa, 996

Camp Hertko Hollow, 997

Camp Sunnyside, 998

Camp Tanager, 999

Central Iowa Center for Independent Living, 4043

Des Moines VA Medical Center, 5537

Des Moines VA Regional Office, 5538

Evert Conner Rights & Resources CIL, 4044

Hall-Perrine Foundation, 2824

Hope Haven, 4045

Iowa Career Connection, 5877

Iowa City VA Medical Center, 5539

Iowa Civil Rights Commission, 5878

Iowa Department for the Blind Library, 4690

Iowa Economic Development Authority, 5879

Iowa Registry for Congenital and Inherited Disorders, 4691

Iowa Valley Community College, 5880

Iowa Vocational Rehabilitation Services, 5881

Knoxville VA Medical Center, 5540

League of Human Dignity, Center for Independent Living, 4046

Library Commission for the Blind, 4692

Mid-Iowa Health Foundation, 2825

New Focus, 5882

Principal Financial Group Foundation, 2826

Siouxland Community Foundation, 2827

South Central Iowa Center for Independent Living, 4048

Universal Pediatrics, 812

VA Central Iowa Health Care System, 5541

Kansas

Advocates for Better Living For Everyone (A.B.L.E.), 4050

Arc of Kansas, 2828

Camp Discovery Kansas, 1000

Camp Planet D, 1001

Camp Quality Kansas, 1002

Camp Sweet Betes, 1003

Center for Independent Living SW Kansas: Liberal, 4051

Center for Independent Living Southwest Kansas, 4052

Center for Independent Living Southwest Kansas: Dodge City, 4053

Center for the Improvement of Human Functioning, 4693

Central Kansas Library Systems Headquarters (CSLS), 4694

Coalition for Independence, 4054

Colmery-O'Neil VA Medical Center, 5542

Cowley County Developmental Services, 4055

Dwight D Eisenhower VA Medical Center, 5543

Hutchinson Community Foundation, 2829

Independence, 4056

Independent Connection, 4057

Independent Connection: Abilene, 4058

Independent Connection: Beloit, 4059

Independent Connection: Concordia, 4060

Independent Living Resource Center, 3875, 4061

Kansas Human Rights Commission, 5883

Kansas Services for the Blind & Visually Impaired, 4062

Kansas VA Regional Office, 5544

Kansas Vocational Rehabilitation Agency, 5884

LINK: Colby, 4063

Living Independently in Northwest Kansas: Hays, 4064

Manhattan Public Library, 4695

Northwest Kansas Library System Talking Books, 4696

Prairie IL Resource Center, 4065

Prairie Independent Living Resource Center, 4066

Resource Center for Independent Living: Emporia, 4069

Resource Center for Independent Living: Arkansas City, 4070

Resource Center for Independent Living: Burlington, 4071

Resource Center for Independent Living: Coffeyville, 4072

Resource Center for Independent Living: El Dorado, 4073

Resource Center for Independent Living: Ft Scott, 4074

Resource Center for Independent Living: Ottawa, 4075

Resource Center for Independent Living: Overland Park, 4076

Resource Center for Independent Living: Topeka, 4077

Richard W Higgins Charitable Foundation, 2830

Robert J Dole VA Medical Center, 5545

South Central Kansas Library System, 4697

Southeast Kansas Independent Living (SKIL), 4078

Southeast Kansas Independent Living: Independence, 4079

Southeast Kansas Independent Living: Chanute, 4080

Southeast Kansas Independent Living: Columbus, 4081

Southeast Kansas Independent Living: Fredonia, 4082

Southeast Kansas Independent Living: Hays, 4083

Southeast Kansas Independent Living: Pittsburg, 4084

Southeast Kansas Independent Living: Sedan, 4085

Southeast Kansas Independent Living: Yates Center, 4086

State Library of Kansas, 4698

Three Rivers Independent Living Center, 4087

Three Rivers Independent Living Center: Clay, 4088

Bureau of Vocational Rehabilitation, 5942
Camp Buck, 1091
Camp Lotsafun, 1092
CampCare, 1093
Carson City Center for Independent Living, 4238
Discovery Day Camp, 1094
EL Wiegand Foundation, 2921
Las Vegas Veterans Center, 5592
Las Vegas-Clark County Library District, 4779
Nell J Redfield Foundation, 2922
Nevada Equal Rights Commission, 5943
Nevada Governor's Council on Developmental
  Disabilities, 5944
Nevada State Library and Archives, 4780
Northern Nevada Center for Independent Liv ing:
  Fallon, 4239
Reno Regional Office, 5593
Rural Center for Independent Living, 4240
Southern Nevada Center for Independent Living:
  North Las Vegas, 4241
Southern Nevada Center for Independent Living:
  Las Vegas, 4242
VA Sierra Nevada Healthcare System, 5594
VA Southern Nevada Healthcare System, 5595
William N Pennington Foundation, 2923

New Hampshire

Adam's Camp: New England, 1095
Agnes M Lindsay Trust, 2924
Camp Allen, 1096
Camp Connect, 1098
Camp Inter-Actions, 1099
Camp Sno Mo, 1100
Camp Wediko, 1101
Camp Yavneh: Yedidut Program, 1102
Foundation for Seacoast Health, 2925
Granite State Independent Living Foundation,
  4243
Manchester Regional Office, 5596
Manchester VA Medical Center, 5597
National Guild of Hypnotists (NGH), 766
New Hampshire Bureau of Vocational Rehabil
  itation, 5945
New Hampshire Commission for Human Rights
  (FEPA), 5946
New Hampshire Employment Security, 5947
New Hampshire State Library: Talking Book
  Services, 4781
New Hampshire Veterans Centers, 5598

New Jersey

ARC of Hunterdon County, The, 5948
ARC of Mercer County, 5949
ARC of Monmouth, 5950
Abilities Center of New Jersey, 5951
Abilities of Northwest New Jersey Inc., 5952
Alliance Center for Independance, 4244
Alliance Center for Independence (ACI), 5953
American Migraine Foundation, 2926
Arc of Bergen and Passaic Counties, 5954
Arc of New Jersey, 2927
Arnold A Schwartz Foundation, 2928
Autism New Jersey, 4782
Avis Rent A Car System, LLC, 5459
Camden City Independent Living Center, 4245
Camp Chatterbox, 1103
Camp Deeny Riback, 1104
Camp Dream Street, 1070, 1105
Camp Jaycee, 1106
Camp Jotoni, 1107
Camp Merry Heart, 1108
Camp Nejeda, 1109
Camp Quality New Jersey, 1110
Camp Sun'N Fun, 1111
Campbell Soup Foundation, 2929
Career Opportunity Development of New Jersey,
  5955
Center for Educational Advancement New Jersey,
  5956
Center for Independent Living: Long Branch, 4246
Center for Independent Living: South Jersey, 4247

Children's Hopes & Dreams Wish Fulfillment
  Foundation, 2930
Children's Specialized Hospital Medical Library -
  Parent Resource Center, 4783
Christopher & Dana Reeve Foundation, 4784
Community Foundation of New Jersey, 2931
DAWN Center for Independent Living, 4248
Dial: Disabled Information Awareness & Living,
  4249
Disability Rights New Jersey, 4250
Disabled American Veterans: Ocean County, 5599
East Orange Campus of the VA New Jersey
  Healthcare System, 5600
Easterseals New Jersey, 5957
Eden Autism, 5958
Edison Sheltered Workshop, 5959
Explorer's Club Camp, 1112
Eye Institute of New Jersey, 4785
FM Kirby Foundation, 2932
Family Resource Associates, 4251
Fannie E Rippel Foundation, 2933
Fund for New Jersey, 2934
Goodwill Industries of Southern New Jersey, 5960
Happiness Is Camping, 1113
Harbor Haven Summer Program, 1114
Heightened Independence and Progress:
  Hackensack, 4252
Heightened Independence and Progress: Jersey
  City, 4253
Hudson Community Enterprises, 5961
Inroads to Opportunities, 5962
Jersey Cape, 5963
Jewish Vocational Service (JVS) - East Orange,
  5964
Jewish Vocational Service (JVS) - Livingston,
  5965
Jewish Vocational Service (JVS) - Montclair, 5966
Lyons Campus of the VA New Jersey Healthcare
  System, 5601
Mane Stream, 1115
Martin Luther Homes of Iowa, 4047
Merck Company Foundation, 2935
Mycoclonus Research Foundation, 4786
Nabisco Foundation, 2936
New Jersey Commission for the Blind and Visually
  Impaired (CBVI), 5967
New Jersey Division of Vocational Rehabilitation
  Services (DVRS), 5968
New Jersey Institute for Disabilities (NJID), 5969
New Jersey Library for the Blind and Handicapped,
  4787
Newark Regional Office, 5602
Occupational Training Center of Burlington
  County (OTCBC), 5970
Occupational Training Center (OTC), 5971
Ostberg Foundation, 2937
Pathways to Independence, Inc., 5972
Progressive Center for Independent Living, 4254
Progressive Center for Independent Living:
  Flemington, 4255
Project Freedom, 4256
Project Freedom: Hamilton, 4257
Project Freedom: Lawrence, 4258
Prudential Foundation, 2938
Rising Treetops at Oakhurst, 1116
Robert Wood Johnson Foundation, 2939
Round Lake Camp, 1117
Somerset Community Action Program, Inc., 5973
St. John of God Community Services Vocational
  Rehabilitation, 5974
The Arc Gloucester, 5975
Total Living Center, 4259
United Cerebral Palsy Associations of New Jersey,
  5976
Verizon Foundation, 3014
Victoria Foundation, 2940

New Mexico

ADA Camp 180, 1118
Ability Center, 4260
Adelante Development Center, 5977
Arc of New Mexico, 2941
CHOICES Center for Independent Living, 4262

Camp Enchantment, 1119
Camp Rising Sun, 1120
Dental Amalgam Syndrome (DAMS) Newsletter,
  4603
Frost Foundation, 2942
Goodwill Industries of New Mexico, 5978
LifeROOTS, 5979
McCune Charitable Foundation, 2943
Native American Disability Law Center, 774
New Mexico Commission for the Blind
  (NMCFTB), 5980
New Mexico State Library for the Blind and
  Physically Handicapped, 4788
New Mexico State Veterans' Home, 5603
New Mexico Technology Assistance Program,
  4263
New Mexico VA Healthcare System, 5604
New Mexico Workforce Connection, 5982
New Vistas, 4264
San Juan Center for Independence, 4265
Santa Fe Community Foundation, 2944
Southwest Conference On Disability, 1759
Tohatchi Area of Opportunity & Services, 5983

New York

ADA Camp Aspire, 1121
AFB Center on Vision Loss, 2945
AIM Independent Living Center: Corning, 4266
AIM Independent Living Center: Elmira, 4267
ARISE, 4268
ARISE: Oneida, 4269
ARISE: Oswego, 4270
ARISE: Pulaski, 4271
Abilities, Inc., 587
Access to Independence of Cortland County , Inc.,
  4272
Action Toward Independence: Middletown, 4273
Action Toward Independence: Monticello, 4274
Adult Career and Continuing Ed Services -
  Vocational Rehabilitation (ACCESS-VR), 5984
Advocates for Children of New York (AFC), 593
Albany VA Medical Center: Samuel S Stratton,
  5605
Albany Vet Center, 5606
Altman Foundation, 2946
Ambrose Monell Foundation, 2947
American Chai Trust, 2948
American Foundation for Suicide Prevention
  (AFSP), 617, 2949
American Foundation for the Blind, 2950
American-Scandinavian Foundation, 2599
Andrew Heiskell Braille and Talking Book Library,
  4789
Annual Conference on Dyslexia and Related
  Learning Disabilities, 1733
Arthur Ross Foundation, 2951
Artists Fellowship, 2952
Autism Summer Respite Program, 1122
AutismUp: YMCA Summer Social Skills Program,
  1123
BRiDGES, 4275
Basic Facts on Study Abroad, 2603
Bath VA Medical Center, 5607
Bodman Foundation, 2953
Brain & Behavior Research Foundation, 646, 2954
Bronx Independent Living Services, 4276
Bronx VA Medical Center, 5608
Brooklyn Campus of the VA NY Harbor
  Healthcare System, 5609
Brooklyn Center for Independence of the
  Disabled, 4277
Brooklyn Home for Aged Men, 2955
Buffalo Regional Office - Department of Veterans
  Affairs, 5610
Buffalo State (SUNY), 2605
Burton Blatt Institute (BBI), 648
Camp Abilities Brockport, 1124
Camp Adventure, 1125
Camp Anne, 1126
Camp COAST, 1127
Camp EAGR, 1128
Camp Good Days and Special Times, 1129
Camp High Hopes, 1130

North Carolina

Oregon Department of Human Services Vocational Rehabilitation (DHS VR), 6008
Oregon Health Sciences University, 5638
Oregon Health Sciences University, Elks' Children's Eye Clinic, 4824
Oregon Talking Book & Braille Services, 4825
Portland Regional Office, 5639
Portland VA Medical Center, 5640
Postpartum Support International (PSI), 787
Progressive Options, 4342
Roseburg VA Medical Center, 5641
SPOKES Unlimited, 4343
Southern Oregon Rehabilitation Center & Clinics, 5642
Strength for the Journey, 1219
Sundial Special Vacations, 5453
Suttle Lake Camp, 1220
Swindells Charitable Foundation Trust, 2731
Talking Book & Braille Services Oregon State Library, 4826
Trips Inc., 5455
Umpqua Valley Disabilities Network, 4344
University of Oregon, 2625
Upward Bound Camp, 1221
World of Options, 2628
www.workability.one, 4922, 5233, 5388, 5388

Pennsylvania

Abilities in Motion, 4345
Accessible Journeys, 5441
Aces Adventure Weekend, 1222
Air Products Foundation, 3062
American Organization for Bodywork Therapies of Asia (AOBTA), 621
Anthracite Region Center for Independent Living, 4346
Arc of Pennsylvania, 3063
Arcadia Foundation, 3064
Associated Services for the Blind and Visually Impaired, 4827
Beaver College, 2604
Brachial Plexus Palsy Foundation, 3065
Brian's House, 4347
Butler VA Medical Center, 5643
Camp AIM, 1223
Camp Achieva, 1224
Camp Akeela, 1225
Camp Amp, 1226
Camp Can Do, 1227
Camp Freedom, 1230
Camp Hot-to-Clot, 1231
Camp Lee Mar, 1232
Camp Lily Lehigh Valley, 1233
Camp Orchard Hill, 1234
Camp Ramah in the Poconos, 1235
Camp STAR, 1236
Camp Setebaid, 1237
Camp Spencer Superstars, 1238
Camp Victory, 1239
Camp Wesley Woods: Exceptional Persons Camp, 1240
Camp Woodlands, 1241
Carnegie Library of Pittsburgh Library for the Blind & Physically Handicapped, 4828
Coatesville VA Medical Center, 5644
Columbia Gas of Pennsylvania Corporate Giving, 3066
Community Resources for Independence, 4348
Community Resources for Independence, Inc., Bradford, 4349
Community Resources for Independence: Lewistown, 4350
Community Resources for Independence: Altoona, 4351
Community Resources for Independence: Clarion, 4352
Community Resources for Independence: Clearfield, 4353
Community Resources for Independence: Hermitage, 4354
Community Resources for Independence: Lewisburg, 4355

Community Resources for Independence: Oil City, 4356
Community Resources for Independence: Warren, 4357
Community Resources for Independence: Wellsboro, 4358
Connelly Foundation, 3067
Dolfinger-McMahon Foundation, 3068
Dragonfly Forest Summer Camp, 1242
Elwyn, 692
Erie VA Medical Center, 5645
Free Library of Philadelphia: Library for the Blind and Physically Handicapped, 4829
Freedom Valley Disability Center, 4359
Handi Camp, 1243
Heinz Endowments, 3069
Henry L Hillman Foundation, 3070
Innabah Camps, 1244
Institute on Disabilities At Temple Univ., 4360
International University Partnerships, 2612
James E Van Zandt VA Medical Center, 5646
Jewish Healthcare Foundation of Pittsburgh, 3071
Juliet L Hillman Simonds Foundation, 3072
Learning Disabilities Association of America (LDA), 738
Lebanon VA Medical Center, 5647
Lehigh Valley Center for Independent Living, 4361
Liberty Resources, 4362
Life and Independence for Today, 4363
Mainstay Life Services Summer Program, 1245
Northeastern Pennsylvania Center for Independent Living, 4364
Oberkotter Foundation, 3073
Office of Vocational Rehabilitation (OVR), 6009
Outside In School Of Experiential Education, Inc., 1246
PECO Energy Company Contributions Program, 3074
PNC Bank Foundation, 3075
Pennsylvania College of Optometry Eye Institute, 4830
Pennsylvania Department of Labor and Industry (DLI), 6010
Pennsylvania Governor's Cabinet Committee for People With Disabilities, 6011
Pennsylvania Human Relations Commission Agency, 6012
Pennsylvania Veterans Centers, 5648
Phelps School Academic Support Program, 1247
Philadelphia Foundation, 3076
Philadelphia Regional Office and Insurance Center, 5649
Philadelphia VA Medical Center, 5650
Pittsburgh Foundation, 3077
Pittsburgh Regional Office, 5651
Reading Rehabilitation Hospital, 4831
Sequanota Lutheran Conference Center and Camp, 1248
Shenango Valley Foundation, 3078
South Central Pennsylvania Center for Independence Living, 4365
Staunton Farm Foundation, 3079
Stewart Huston Charitable Trust, 3080
Teleflex Foundation, 3081
The Guided Tour, Inc., 5454
Three Rivers Center for Independent Living: New Castle, 4366
Three Rivers Center for Independent Living: Washington, 4367
Three Rivers Center for Independent Living, 4049, 4368
Tri-County Patriots for Independent Living, 4369
USX Foundation, 3082
VA Pittsburgh Healthcare System, University Drive Division, 5652
VA Pittsburgh Healthcare System, Highland Drive Division, 5653
Variety Club Camp and Developmental Center, 1249
Voices for Independence, 4370
West Penn Burn Camp, 1250
Wilkes-Barre VA Medical Center, 5654
William B Dietrich Foundation, 3083

William Talbott Hillman Foundation, 3084
William V and Catherine A McKinney Charitable Foundation, 3085
YMCA Camp Fitch, 1251

Rhode Island

Arc South County Chapter, 3086
Arc of Blackstone, 4371
Arc of Blackstone Valley, 3087
Arc of Northern Rhode Island, 3088
Camp Mauchatea, 1252
Camp Ruggles, 1253
Canonicus Camp & Conference Center, 1254
Champlin Foundations, 3089
CranstonArc, 3090
Down Syndrome Society of Rhode Island, 3091
Frank Olean Center, 3092
Franklin Court Assisted Living, 4372
Groden Network, 6013
Hasbro Children's Hospital Asthma Camp, 1255
Horace A Kimball and S Ella Kimball Foundation, 3093
IN-SIGHT Independent Living, 4373
James L. Maher Center, 3094
Ocean State Center for Independent Living, 4374
Office Of Library & Information Services for the Blind and Physically Handicapped, 4832
Office of Rehabilitation Services, 4375, 6014
PARI Independent Living Center, 4376
Providence Regional Office, 5655
Providence VA Medical Center, 5656
Rhode Island Arc, 3095
Rhode Island Foundation, 3096
Rhode Island Services for the Blind and Visually Impaired, 6015
Talking Books Plus, 4833
The Steve Fund, 807

South Carolina

Arc of South Carolina, 3097
Burnt Gin Camp, 1256
Camp Adam Fisher, 1257
Camp Courage, 1057, 1228, 1258, 1258
Camp Debbie Lou, 1259
Camp Luv-A-Lung, 1260
Camp Spearhead, 1261
Center for Disability Resources, 656, 3098
Colonial Life and Accident Insurance Company Contributions Program, 3099
Columbia Disability Action Center, 4377
Columbia Regional Office, 5657
DREAMMS for Kids, 4791
Disability Action Center, 4378
Disability Research and Dissemination Center, 676
Graham Street Community Resources, 4379
Medical University of South Carolina Arthritis Clinical/Research Center, 4834
Ralph H Johnson VA Medical Center, 5658
South Carolina Commission for the Blind (SCCB), 6016
South Carolina Department of Employment and Workforce (DEW), 6017
South Carolina Governor's Committee on Employment of the Handicapped, 6018
South Carolina Independent Living Council, 4380
South Carolina State Library, 4835
South Carolina Vocational Rehabilitation Department (SCVRD), 6019
Walton Options for Independent Living: North Augusta, 4381
William Jennings Bryan Dorn VA Medical Center, 5659

South Dakota

Adjustment Training Center, 4382
Black Hills Workshop & Training Center, 4383
Camp Friendship, 1262
Camp Gilbert, 1263
Native American Advocacy Program for Persons with Disabilities, 4385

NeSoDak, 1264
Prairie Freedom Center for Independent Living: Sioux Falls, 4386
Prairie Freedom Center for Independent Living: Madison, 4387
Prairie Freedom Center for Independent Living: Yankton, 4388
Royal C Johnson Veterans Memorial Medical Center, 5660
Sioux Falls Regional Office, 5661
South Dakota Assistive Technology Project: DakotaLink, 4389
South Dakota Department of Human Services, 6020
South Dakota Department of Human Services: Div. of Service to the Blind & Visually Impaired, 6021
South Dakota State Library, 4836
South Dakota State Vocational Rehabilitati on, 6022
South Dakota Workforce Investment Act Training Programs, 6023
Western Resources for dis-ABLED Independence, 4390

Tennessee

ACM Lifting Lives Music Camp, 1265
All Days Are Happy Days Summer Camp, 1266
Alvin C York VA Medical Center, 5662
American Board of Disability Analysts (ABDA), 606
American Board of Disability Analysts Annual Conference, 1732
American Board of Medical Psychotherapists and Psychodiagnosticians, 607
American Board of Professional Disability Consultants, 608
Arc of Anderson County, 3100
Arc of Davidson County, 3101
Arc of Hamilton County, 3102
Arc of Tennessee, 3103
Arc of Washington County, 3104
Arc of Williamson County, 3105
Arc-Diversified, 3106
Benwood Foundation, 3107
Bill Rice Ranch, 1267
Camp Conquest, 1268
Camp Joy, 1179, 1270
Camp Koinonia, 1271
Camp Oginali, 1272
Camp Okawehna, 1273
Camp Sugar Falls, 1274
Camp Wonder, 1275
Case Management Society of America (CMSA), 654
Center for Independent Living of Middle Tennessee, 4391
Community Foundation of Greater Chattanooga, 3108
DisAbility Resource Center: Knoxville, 4392
Easterseals Tennessee Camping Program, 1276
Education and Auditory Research Foundation, 3109
International Paper Company Foundation, 3110
Jackson Center for Independent Living, 4393
Jackson Independent Living Center, 4193
LeBonheur Cardiac Kids Camp, 1277
Memphis Center for Independent Living, 4394
Memphis VA Medical Center, 5663
Mountain Home VA Medical Center - James H Quillen VA Medical Center, 5664
Nashville Regional Office, 5665
Nashville VA Medical Center, 5666
National Association of Blind Merchants (NABM), 749
Tennessee Department Human Services: Vocational Rehabilitation Services, 6024
Tennessee Department of Labor and Workforc e Development, 6025
Tennessee Human Rights Commission, 6026
Tennessee Library for the Blind and Physically Handicapped, 4837

Tennessee Technology Access Program (TTAP), 4395
Tri-State Resource and Advocacy Corporation, 4396
Vision Foundation, 2874

Texas

AADB National Conference, 1717
ABLE Center for Independent Living, 4397
Abell-Hangar Foundation, 3112
Ability Connection, 6027
Access & Information Network, 589
Albert & Bessie Mae Kronkosky Charitable Foundation, 3113
Amarillo VA Healthcare System, 5667
Amarillo Vet Center, 5668
American Academy of Environmental Medicine (AAEM), 596
American Academy of Environmental Medicine Annual Conference, 1731
American Botanical Council (ABC), 609
American Express Foundation, 3114
Arc of Texas, The, 3115
Army and Air Force Exchange Services, 2601
Attention Deficit Disorders Association, Southern Region: Annual Conference, 1736
Austin Resource Center for Independent Living, 4398
Austin Resource Center: Round Rock, 4399
Austin Resource Center: San Marcos, 4400
BA and Elinor Steinhagen Benevolent Trust, 3116
Baylor College of Medicine Birth Defects Center, 4838
Baylor College of Medicine: Cullen Eye Institute, 4839
Brazoria County Center For Independent Living, 4401
Brown Foundation, 3117
Brown-Heatly Library, 4840
CH Foundation, 3118
Camp Ailihpomeh, 1278
Camp Aranzazu, 1279
Camp Be An Angel, 1280
Camp Blessing, 1281
Camp CAMP, 1282
Camp CPals, 1283
Camp Can-Do, 1284
Camp John Marc, 1286
Camp Neuron, 1287
Camp New Horizons North, 1288
Camp New Horizons South, 1289
Camp No Limits Texas, 1290
Camp NoLoHi, 1291
Camp Quality Texas, 1292
Camp Rainbow, 848, 1293
Camp Sandcastle, 1294
Camp Spike 'n' Wave, 1295
Camp Summit, 1296
Camp Sweeney, 1297
Camp for All, 1298
Center for Research on Women with Disabilities, 4841
Centre, The, 4402
Charis Hills Camp, 1299
Christian Education for the Blind, 4842
Cockrell Foundation, 3119
Communication Service for the Deaf: Rapid City, 4384
Communities Foundation of Texas, 3120
Community Foundation of North Texas, 3121
Concentra, 6028
Cristo Vive International: Texas Camp Conroe, 1300
Cristo Vive International: Texas Camp Rio Grande Valley, 1301
Crockett Resource Center for Independent Living, 4403
Cullen Foundation, 3122
Curtis & Doris K Hankamer Foundation, 3123
Dallas Academy, 1302
Dallas Foundation, 3124
David D & Nona S Payne Foundation, 3125
Easy Access Travel, 5447

El Paso Natural Gas Foundation, 3126
El Paso VA Healthcare Center, 5669
Epilepsy Foundation of Southeast Texas, 3127
Epilepsy Foundation: Central and South Texas, 3128
Hanger, Inc., 713
Harris and Eliza Kempner Fund, 3129
Hill School of Fort Worth, 1303
Hillcrest Foundation, 3130
Hoblitzelle Foundation, 3131
Hogg Foundation for Mental Health, 717, 3132
Houston Center for Independent Living (HCIL), 4404
Houston Endowment, 3133
Houston Public Library: Access Center, 4843
Houston Regional Office, 5670
Independent Living Research Utilization Project, 4406
John G & Marie Stella Kennedy Memorial Foundation, 3134
John S Dunn Research Foundation, 3135
Kamp Kaleidoscope, 1304
LIFE/Run Centers for Independent Living, 4407
LIFE: Fort Hall, 3982
Lisle, 2616
Lola Wright Foundation, 3136
Meadows Foundation, 3137
Michael E. Debakey VA Medical Center, 5671
Moody Foundation, 3138
NADR Conference, 1749
National Association of Disability Representatives (NADR), 752
Office for Students with Disabilities, University of Texas at Arlington, 4408
Palestine Resource Center for Independent Living, 4409
Panhandle Action Center for Independent Living Skills, 4410
Pearle Vision Foundation, 3139
REACH of Dallas Resource Center on Independent Living, 4411, 4412
REACH of Fort Worth Resource Center on Independent Living, 4413
RISE-Resource: Information, Support and Empowerment, 4414
SAILS, 4415
San Antonio Area Foundation, 3140
Shell Oil Company Foundation, 3141
South Texas Charitable Foundation, 3142
South Texas Veterans Healthcare System, 5672
Sterling-Turner Foundation, 3143
TLL Temple Foundation, 3144
Talking Book Program/Texas State Library, 4844
Texas Department of Assistive and Rehabilitative Services, 4416
Texas Lions Camp, 1305
Texas Workforce Commission (TWC), 6029
Texas Workforce Commission: Vocational Rehabilitation Services, 6030
University of Texas Southwestern Medical Center/Allergy & Immunology, 4845
University of Texas at Austin Library, 4846
VA North Texas Health Veterans Affairs Care System: Dallas VA Medical Center, 5673
VOLAR Center for Independent Living, 4417
Valley Association for Independent Living (VAIL), 4418
Valley Association for Independent Living: Harlingen, 4419
Waco Regional Office, 5674
West Texas VA Healthcare System, 5675
William Stamps Farish Fund, 3145
World Federation for Mental Health, 818

Utah

Action X-Treme Camp, 1306
Active Re-Entry, 4420
Active Re-Entry: Vernal, 4421
Camp Giddy-Up, 1307
Camp Hobe, 1308
Camp ICANDO, 1309
Camp Kostopulos, 1310
Camp Nah-Nah-Mah, 1311

Central Utah Independent Living Center, 4422
Discovery Camp, 1312
FCYD Camp Utada, 1313
Kids Rock The World Day Camp, 1314
Marriner S Eccles Foundation, 3147
National Care Planning Council, 755
OPTIONS for Independence, 4423
OPTIONS for Independence: Brigham Satellit e, 4424
Overnight Camps, 1315
Pathfinders Camp, 1316
Questar Corporation Contributions Program, 3148
Red Rock Center for Independence, 4425
Utah Assistive Technology Program (UTAP) Utah State University, 4427
Utah Department of Human Services: Division of Services for People with Disabilities, 6031
Utah Division of Veterans Affairs, 5676
Utah Employment Services, 6032
Utah Governor's Committee on Employment for People with Disabilities (GCEPD), 6033
Utah Independent Living Center, 4428
Utah Independent Living Center: Minersville, 4429
Utah Independent Living Center: Tooele, 4430
Utah State Library Division: Program for the Blind and Disabled, 4847
Utah State Office for Rehabilitation (USOR), 6034
Utah State Office of Rehabilitation: Vocational Rehabilitation, 6035
Utah State Office of Rehabilitation: Service s for the Blind and Visually Impaired, 6036
VA Salt Lake City Healthcare System, 5677
Veterans Support Center (VSC), 6037

Vermont

Camp Thorpe, 1317
National Center for PTSD, 4848
Silver Towers Camp, 1318
Vermont Assistive Technology Program, 4431
Vermont Center for Independent Living: Bennington, 4432
Vermont Center for Independent Living: Chittenden, 4433
Vermont Center for Independent Living: Montpelier, 4434
Vermont Community Foundation, 3149
Vermont Department of Disabilities, Aging and Independent Living (DAIL), 6038
Vermont Department of Labor, 6039
Vermont Department of Libraries - Special Services Unit, 4849, 4850
Vermont Division of Vocational Rehabilitation, 6040
Vermont VA Regional Office Center, 5678
Vermont Veterans Centers, 5679

Virginia

ACA Annual Conference, 1720
ADA Annual Scientific Sessions, 1721
AER Annual International Conference, 1722
ASIA Annual Scientific Meeting, 1726
Access Independence, 4435
Access Services, 4851
Alexandria Library Talking Book Service, 4852
American Academy of Audiology (AAA), 595
American Academy of Audiology Conference, 1730
American Chiropractic Association (ACA), 611
American Counseling Association (ACA), 614
American National Bank and Trust Company, 2782
Appalachian Independence Center, 4436
Arc of Virginia, 3150
Arlington County Department of Libraries, 4853
Beacon Tree Foundation, 643, 3151
Blinded Veterans Association National Convention, 1738
Blue Ridge Independent Living Center, 4437
Blue Ridge Independent Living Center: Christianburg, 4438
Blue Ridge Independent Living Center: Low Moor, 4439

Braille Circulating Library for the Blind, 4854
Brain Injury Association of America (BIAA), 647
Camp Dickenson, 1320
Camp Easterseals UCP, 1321
Camp Foundation, 3152
Camp Holiday Trails, 1322
Camp Jordan, 1323
Camp Loud And Clear, 1324
Campagna Center, 6041
Camps for Children & Teens with Diabetes, 1325
Central Rappahannock Regional Library, 4855
Civitan Acres, 1326
Clinch Independent Living Services, 4440
Community Foundation of Richmond & Central Virginia, 3153
Council for Exceptional Children (CEC), 669, 4856
Council for Exceptional Children Annual Convention and Expo, 1743
Didlake, 6042
Disability Funders Network (DFN), 675
Disability Resource Center, 3949, 4441
Disability:IN, 681
ENDependence Center of Northern Virginia, 4442
Equal Access Center for Independence, 4443
From the State Capitals: Public Health, 3204
Hampton VA Medical Center, 5680
Hunter Holmes McGuire VA Medical Center, 5681
Independence Empowerment Center, 4444
Independence Resource Center, 4445
Independent Living Center Network: Department of the Visually Handicapped, 4446
International Chiropractors Association (ICA), 727
International Student Exchange Programs (I SEP), 2611
James Branch Cabell Library, 4857
John Randolph Foundation, 3154
Junction Center for Independent Living, 4447
Junction Center for Independent Living: Duffield, 4448
Loudoun County Adaptive Recreation Camps, 1327
Lynchburg Area Center for Independent Living, 4449
March of Dimes, 743
Mental Health America (MHA), 745
NEXT Conference & Exposition, 1751
National Association of State Directors of Developmental Disabilities Services (NASDDDS), 753
National Council on the Aging Conference, 1753
National Rehabilitation Association (NRA), 770
National Right to Work Legal Defense Foundation, 3155
National Vaccine Information Center (NVIC), 772
Newport News Public Library System, 4858
Norfolk Foundation, 3156
Northern Virginia Resource Center for Deaf and Hard of Hearing Persons, 4859
Oakland School & Camp, 1328
Peidmont Independent Living Center, 4450
Peninsula Center for Independent Living, 4451
Piedmont Independent Living Center, 4452
Resources for Independent Living, 3890, 4453
RespectAbility, 791
Richmond Research Training Center (RRTC), 6043
Roanoke City Public Library System, 4860
Roanoke Regional Office, 5682
Robey W Estes Family Foundation, 3157
Salem VA Medical Center, 5683
ServiceSource Disability Resource Center, 6044
SourceAmerica, 6045
Staunton Public Library Talking Book Center, 4861
University of Virginia Health System General Clinical Research Group, 4862
Valley Associates for Independent Living (VAIL), 4454
Valley Associates for Independent Living: Lexington, 4455
Virginia Autism Resource Center, 4863
Virginia Beach Foundation, 3158
Virginia Beach Public Library Special Services Library, 4864
Virginia Chapter of the Arthtitis Foundation, 4865

Virginia Department for the Blind and Vision Impaired (DBVI), 6046
Virginia Department of Veterans Services, 5684
Virginia State Library for the Visually and Physically Handicapped, 4866
Volunteers of America (VOA), 815
Woodrow Wilson Rehabilitation Center Training Program, 4456

Washington

ADA National Network, 583
Alliance for People with Disabilities: Sea ttle, 4457
Alliance of People with Disabilities: Redmond, 4458
Arc of Washington State, 3159
Bastyr Center for Natural Health, 642
Ben B Cheney Foundation, 3160
Business Enterprise Program (BEP), 5734, 6047
Camp Beausite NW, 1329
Camp Goodtimes, 1330
Camp Killoqua, 1331
Camp Korey, 1332
Camp Sealth, 1333
Community Foundation of North Central Washington, 3161
Community Services for the Blind and Parti ally Sighted Store: Sight Connection, 4459
Department of Services for the Blind (DSB), 6048
Department of Social & Health Services: Division of Vocational Rehabilitation, 6049
Department of Social & Health Services: Developmental Disabilities Administration (DDA), 6050
DisAbility Resource Connection: Everett, 4460
Easterseals Camp Stand by Me, 1334
Glaser Progress Foundation, 3162
Greater Tacoma Community Foundation, 3163
Inland Northwest Community Foundation, 3164
International Academy of Independent Medical Evaluators, 724
Jonathan M Wainwright Memorial VA Medical Center, 5685
Kitsap Community Resources, 4461
Medina Foundation, 3165
Meridian Valley Clinical Laboratory, 4867
Norcliffe Foundation, 3166
Ophthalmic Research Laboratory Eye Institute/First Hill Campus, 4868
Prime Time, Inc., 1335
SL Start Washington, 6051
STIX Diabetes Programs, 1336
Seattle Regional Office, 5686
Spokane Center for Independent Living, 4462
Spokane VA Medical Center, 5687
Stewardship Foundation, 3167
Tacoma Area Coalition of Individuals with Disabilities, 4463
VA Puget Sound Health Care System, 5688
Washington Talking Book and Braille Library, 4869
Western Washington University, 2626
Weyerhaeuser Company Foundation, 3168
Wheelchair Getaways, 5463

West Virginia

Appalachian Center for Independent Living, 4464
Appalachian Center for Independent Living: Spencer, 4465
Arc Of West Virginia, The, 3169
Bernard McDonough Foundation, 3170
Cabell County Public Library/Talking Book Department/Subregional Library for the Blind, 4870
Division of Rehabilitation Services: Staff Library, 4871
High Technology Foundation, 716, 3171
Huntington Regional Office, 5689
Huntington VA Medical Center, 5690
Job Accommodation Network (JAN), 734
Kanawha County Public Library, 4872
Louis A Johnson VA Medical Center, 5691

Brigham Manor Nursing and Rehabilitation
  Center, 7135
Bright Horizons Summer Camp, 8374
Brighten Place, 6242
BrightFocus Foundation, 7361
Brike International, 447
Bringing Out the Best, 5246
Britannica Film Company, 5255, 5307, 9070
BroadFutures, 7684
Broadmead, 4119
Broadview Multi-Care Center, 7189
Broken Dolls: Gathering the Pieces: Caring for
  Chronically Ill Children, 5127
Bronx Continuing Treatment Day Program, 6879
Bronx Independent Living Services, 4276
Bronx VA Medical Center, 5608
Brookdale Center for Healthy Aging, 7362
Brooke Publishing, 2452
Brookes Publishing, 1797, 1798, 1799, 1800, 1871,
  1895, 1985, 2190, 2192, 2207, 2213, 2196,
  2217, 2219, 2225, 2235, 2236, 2239, 2243,
  2246, 2252, 2253, 2255, 2270, 2271, 2273,
  2289, 2290, 2292, 2293, 2307, 2318, 2324,
  2327, 2340, 2342, 2358, 2366, 2378, 2393,
  2419, 2439, 2443, 2458, 2481, 2485, 2488,
  2489, 2490, 2491, 2495, 2498, 2503, 2514,
  2516, 4890, 4919, 4921, 4933, 4941, , 4985,
  4991, 5004, 5006, 5046, 5082, 5101, 5105,
  5120, 5121, 5129, 5132, 5133, 5134, 5150,
  5160, 5166, 5176, 5186, 5187, 5206, 5212,
  5228, 5229, 5258, 5293, 5299, 7781, 7791,
  7792, 7809, 7825, 7830, 7830, 7854
Brookings Institution, 4511, 7479, 7484
Brookline Books, 8, 14, 22, 1854, 1857, 1858,
  1897, 1898, 1986, 2215, 2232, 2251, 2268,
  2272, 2277, 2301, 2338, 2420, 2423, 2441,
  2444, 2449, 2451, 2464, 2468, 4960, 4996,
  5001, 5048, 5052, 5054, 5090, 5125, 5128,
  5131, 5141, 5156, 5173, 5190, 5193, 7805,
  7847, 7860, 7862, 7874, 8559, 8603, 8632
Brookline Books Publications, 2288
Brooklyn Bureau of Community Service, 6880
Brooklyn Campus of the VA NY Harbor
  Healthcare System, 5609
Brooklyn Center for Independence of the
  Disabled, 4277
Brooklyn Home for Aged Men, 2955
Brooks Memorial Hospital Rehabilitation Center,
  6556
Brooks Rehabilitation Hospital, 2570
Brooks/Cole Publishing Company, 1987, 2263,
  7789
Brotman Medical Center, 6387
Brotman Medical Center: RehabCare Unit, 6073,
  6387
Broward County Talking Book Library, 4631
Brown County Library, 4878
Brown Foundation, 3117
Brown-Heatly Building, 3724
Brown-Heatly Library, 4840
Bruno Independent Living Aids, 305
Bruno Independent Living Aids, Inc., 76, 301, 303,
  305, 307, 310, 316, 317, 318, 328, 331, 336
Bryn Mawr Rehabilitation Hospital, 6958
BTBL News, 9120
Buck & Buck, 1352, 1353, 1355, 1356, 1358,
  1359, 1361, 1362, 1364, 1365, 1366, 1367,
  1370, 1372, 1373, 1374, 1375, 1376, 1377,
  1379, 1380, 1381, 1382, 1383, 1384, 1387,
  1390, 1391, 1392, 1393, 1394
Buck and Buck Clothing, 1354
Budget Cotton/Poly Open Back Gown, 1355
Budget Flannel Open Back Gown, 1356
Buena Vida, 7509
Buffalo Hearing and Speech Center, 6881
Buffalo Regional Office - Department of Veterans
  Affairs, 5610
Buffalo State (SUNY), 2605
Build Rehabilitation Industries, 6388
Builders of Skills, 6139
Building Blocks: Foundations for Learning for
  Young Blind and Visually Impaired Children,
  9166
Building Bridges: Including People with
  Disabilities in International Programs, 2606

Building Owners & Managers Association, 1781
Building Owners and Managers Association
  International, 1765
Building Skills for Independence in the Ma
  instream, 2230
Building Skills for Success in the Fast-Pa ced
  Classroom, 2231
Building the Healing Partnership: Parents,
  Professionals and Children, 2232, 5128
Bull Publishing, 8577
Bulletin of the Association on the Handicapped,
  4969
Burbank Rehabilitation Center, 6787
Bureau of Elderly & Adult Services, 3546
Bureau of Employment Programs Division of
  Workers' Compensation, 3774
Bureau of Exceptional Education And Student
  Services, 3342
Bureau of Labor and Industries (BOLI), 6005
Bureau of Rehabilitation Services, 5789, 5896
Bureau of Rehabilitations Services, 4620
Bureau of Services for Blind Persons Train ing
  Center, 6816
Bureau of Vocational Rehabilitation, 5942
Bureau of Vocational Rehabilitation (BVR), 6000
Burger School for the Autistic, 4742
Burke Rehabilitation Hospital, 6214
Burn Institute, 856, 8380
Burn Program at Arkansas Children's, 853
Burnett Foundation, 2895
Burns Braille Transcription Dictionary, 8977
Burns-Dunphy Foundation, 2655
BurnsBooks Publishing, 1988
Burnt Gin Camp, 1256
Burton Blatt Institute (BBI), 648
Bus Girl: Selected Poems, 7805
Bushrod H Campbell and Ada F Hall Charity Fund,
  2864
Business as Usual, 5247
Business Enterprise Program (BEP), 5734, 6047
Business Publishers, 3212, 4545, 4552
Business Publishers, Inc., 7501, 7563
Butler Adult Training Center, 5705
Butler Mobility Products, 306
Butler VA Medical Center, 5643
Butlers Wheelchair Lifts, 306
Button Aid, 233
Buy!, 1812
Buying Time: The Media Role in Health Care,
  5248
Bye-Bye Decubiti (BBD), 221
Bye-Bye Decubiti Air Mattress Overlay, 159

C

C D Publications, 7588
C&C Software, 1536
C-4 Work Center, 5840
CA Health and Human Services Agency Dept of
  Rehab, 3297
Cabell County Public Library/Talking Book
  Department/Subregional Library for the Blind,
  4870
Cabinet for Health Services, 3428
CACLD, 5265, 7855, 7920
Cadinal Hill Medical Center, 6738
Caglewood, Inc., 944
Cahaba Media Group, 2108
CAHSA Connecting, 7589
CAI, Career Assessment Inventories for the
  Learning Disabled, 2233
California Community Care News, 4906
California Community Foundation, 2656
California Department of Aging, 3291
California Department of Education: Special
  Education Division, 2017
California Department of Fair Employment &
  Housing, 5749, 4525, 4526, 4529
California Department of Handicapped Children,
  3292
California Department of Rehabilitation, 3293
California Elwyn, 6389
California Endowment, 2657
California Eye Institute, 6390

California Financial Power of Attorney, 4971
California Foundation For Independent Living
  Centers, 3839
California Foundation for Independent Living
  Centers, 3840
California Governor's Committee on Employment
  of People with Disabilities, 3294
California Lions Camp, 870, 8021
California Protection & Advocacy: (PAI) A
  Nonprofit Organization, 3295
California School of Professional Psychology,
  4609
California State Council on Developmental
  Disabilities, 3296
California State Independent Living Counci l
  (SILC), 3841
California State Library Braille and Talki ng Book
  Library, 4601, 8872
Cambia Health Foundation, 650, 3058
Cambridge Career Products Catalog, 364
Cambridge Educational, 364, 1611
Cambridge University Press, 4905, 7502, 8600,
  8626
Camden City Independent Living Center, 4245
Camden Healthcare and Rehabilitation Center,
  7208
Camiccia-Arnautou Charitable Foundation, 2752
Camp "I Am Me", 965
Camp Abilities Brockport, 1124
Camp Abilities Tucson, 842
Camp About Face, 982
Camp Achieva, 1224
Camp Adam Fisher, 1257
Camp Adventure, 1125
Camp Ailihpomeh, 1278
Camp AIM, 1223
Camp Akeela, 1225
Camp Akeela Winter Address, 1225
Camp Albrecht Acres, 995
Camp Aldersgate, 851, 8376
Camp Alexander Mack, 8009
Camp Allen, 1096
Camp Alpine, 8377
Camp Amigo, 930
Camp Amp, 1226
Camp Anne, 1126
Camp Anuenue, 956, 8378
Camp Aranzazu, 1279
Camp Arye, 1171
Camp ASCCA, 823, 7727, 8375
Camp AZDA, 841
Camp Baker, 7728
Camp Barakel, 8934
Camp Barefoot, 1043
Camp Barnabas, 1071
Camp Be An Angel, 1280
Camp Beausite NW, 1329, 8379
Camp Beyond The Scars, 856, 8380
Camp Bishopswood, 8010
Camp Blessing, 1281
Camp Bloomfield, 857, 8935
Camp Boggy Creek, 931, 8381
Camp Bon Coeur, 1008, 8382
Camp Brave Eagle, 983
Camp Breathe Easy, 943, 8383
Camp Buck, 1091
Camp Buckskin, 1055, 7729
Camp Caglewood, 944
Camp Callahan, 966
Camp Callahan, Inc., 966
Camp CAMP, 1282
Camp Can Do, 1227, 8384
Camp Can-Do, 1284
Camp Candlelight, 843, 7730
Camp CANOE, 1200
Camp CaPella, 1014, 8011
Camp Carefree, 1097, 1160, 8385
Camp Carolina Trails, 1161
Camp Catch-A-Rainbow, 1044
Camp Catch-a-Rainbow, 8386
Camp Challenge, 1009, 8936
Camp Chatterbox, 1103
Camp Cheerful, 1172, 8387
Camp Chris Williams, 1045, 8012
Camp Christian Berets, 858

Camp Tall Turf, 8437
Camp Taloali, 1212, 8024
Camp Tanager, 999
Camp Taylor, 878, 8438
Camp Taylor, Inc., 878, 879, 880, 881, 882, 883, 957, 8438
Camp Taylor: Family Camp, 879, 957
Camp Taylor: Leadership Camp, 880
Camp Taylor: Teen Camp, 881
Camp Taylor: Young Adult Program, 882
Camp Taylor: Youth Camp, 883
Camp Tekoa, 1166, 8025
Camp Thorpe, 1317
Camp Thunderbird, 933
Camp Tiponi, 1187
Camp Tova, 1139
Camp Tuolumne Trails, 884
Camp Twin Lakes, 952, 948
Camp Twin Lakes: Rutledge, 953
Camp Twin Lakes: Will-A-Way, 954
Camp Ukandu, 1213
Camp Vacamas, 8439
Camp Venture, Inc., 1140
Camp Victory, 1239
Camp Wapiyapi, 903
Camp Waziyatah, 8440
Camp Webber, 839
Camp Wediko, 1101
Camp Wesley Woods: Exceptional Persons Camp, 1240
Camp WheezeAway, 834, 8441
Camp Whitman on Seneca Lake, 1141
Camp Winnekeag, 8941
Camp Wonder, 1275
Camp Woodlands, 1241
Camp World Light, 7742
Camp Yavneh: Yedidut Program, 1102
Camp-A-Lot and Camp-A-Little, 886, 7743
Campagna Center, 6041
Campaign Math, 1531
Campbell Soup Foundation, 2929
CampCare, 1093
Camping Unlimited, 863, 7734
Campobello Chemical Dependency Recovery Center, 6392
Camps for Children & Teens with Diabetes, 1325, 8443
Can America Afford to Grow Old?, 4511
Can't Your Child See? A Guide for Parents of Visually Impaired Children, 8978
Can-Do Products Catalog, 141
Canadian Art Therapy Association (CATA), 651
Canadian Cancer Society, 8312
Canadian Deafblind Association, 7625
Canadian Diabetes Association, 8313
Canadian Lung Association, 8314
Canandiagua VA Medical Center, 5611
Cancer Care, 2956
Cancer Clinical Trials: A Commonsense Guide to Experimental Cancer Therapies and Trials, 5177
Cancer Research Institute, 5330
Cancer Sourcebook, 8519
Cancer Sourcebook for Women, 8520
Candlelighters Childhood Cancer Foundation, 2842
Candler General Hospital: Rehabilitation Unit, 6132
Canes and Trails, 9121
Canine Companions for Independence (CCI), 652
Canine Helpers for the Handicapped, 653, 8873
Canine Helpers for the Handicapped, Inc., 653, 8873
Canine Listener, 8133
Canonicus Camp & Conference Center, 1254
CANPFA-Line, 7590
CAPCO Capability Corporation, 1653
Cape Coral Hospital, 7069
Cape Organization for Rights of the Disabled (CORD), 4131
Capital Area Center for Independent Living, 4151
Capital Area Parkinsons Society, 8177
Capital District Center for Independence, 4278
Capital District YMCA, 1159, 8951
Capitol Focus, 7591
Caprice Care Center, 7190
Capron Rehabilitation Center, 6506

Capsule, 7592
Caption Center, 4734, 8874
Captus Press, 4914
Car Builder Deluxe, 1562
Car Cane with Transfer Swivel Cushion, 79
Cardinal Hill Rehabilitation Hospital, 6169, 6738
Cardiovascular Diseases and Disorders Sourcebook, 3rd Edition, 8521
Cards: Musical, 5399
Cards: UNO, 5400
Care Center East Health & Specialty Care Center, 7196
Care Master Medical Services, 6624
Care-One, 6874
Career Development and Transition for Exceptional Individuals, 2088
Career Opportunity Development of New Jersey, 5955
Career Perspectives: Interviews with Blind and Visually Impaired Professionals, 8979
Career Success for Disabled High-Flyers, 4916
CAREERS & the disABLED Magazine, 5205
Careers in Blindness Rehabilitation Services, 8980
Caremark Healthcare Services, 6646
Carendo, 204
Carex Health Brands, 365, 365
Carey Services, 5862
CARF International, 649, 1915, 7363
Carilion Health System, 7014
Carilion Rehabilitation: New River Valley, 7010
Caring and Sharing Center for Independent Living, 3934
Caring and Sharing Center: Pasco County, 3935
The Caring Community of CT, 5793
Caring for America's Heroes, 4972
Caring for Children with Chronic Illness, 2234
Caring for Persons with Developmental Disabilities, 5249
Caring for Those You Love: A Guide to Compassionate Care for the Aged, 7462
Carl and Ruth Shapiro Family National Center for Accessible Media, 6788, 8744
Carl T Hayden VA Medical Center, 5479
Carl Vinson VA Medical Center, 5522
Carnegie Library of Pitts. Library for the Blind, 9087
Carnegie Library of Pittsburgh Library for the Blind & Physically Handicapped, 4828
Caro: Blue Water Center for Independent Living, 4152
Carolina Computer Access Center, 1451
Carolina Curriculum for Infants and Toddlers with Special Needs (3rd Edition), 2235, 5186
Carolina Curriculum for Preschoolers with Special Needs, 2236, 2503
Carolyn's Low Vision Products, 366, 1357
Carondelet Brain Injury Programs and Services (Bridges Now), 6346
Carpal Tunnel Syndrome, 7943
Carrie Estelle Doheny Foundation, 2658
Carroll Center for the Blind, 6789, 9191
Carroll School, 1035, 7769
Carson City Center for Independent Living, 4238
Cary Library, 4710
Casa Colina Centers for Rehabilitation, 6393, 6395
Casa Colina Padua Village, 6394
Casa Colina Residential Services: Rancho Pino Verde, 6395
Casa Colina Transitional Living Center, 6396
Casa Colina Transitional Living Center: Pomona, 6397
Casa Colinas Centers for Rehabilitation, 6074
CASA Inc., 4261
Case Management Society of America (CMSA), 654
Case Manager Magazine, 2089
Case Western Reserve University, 4814
Case Western Reserve University Northeast Ohio Multipurpose Arthritis Center, 4815
Casey Eye Institute, 4824
Casiano Communications, 7509
Casowasco Camp, Conference and Retreat Center, 7744
Casper Vet Center, 5698

Castle Point Campus of the VA Hudson Valley Healthcare System, 5612
Catalog for Teaching Life Skills to Persons with Development Disability, 1813
Catalyst, 2090
The Catalyst, 2090
Cataracts, 8981
Catholic Charities, 6750
Catholic Charities Disability Services, 1173, 1177
Catholic Guild for The Blind, 9130
Catholic Medical Center, 6860
Catholic Southwest, 6583
Catskill Center for Independence, 4279
Cave Spring Rehabilitation Center, 6618
CC-M Productions, 8262
CCARC, Inc., 5790
CD Publications, 3189, 7500
CDR Reports, 4970
CEC Catalog, 2087
CEC Pioneers Division (CEC-PD), 1916
Cecil R Bomhr Rehabilitation Center of Nacogdoches Memorial Hospital, 6272
Cedar Ridge Camp, 8444
Cedar Spring Health and Rehabilitation Center, 7243
Cedars of Marin, 6398
Cengage Learning, 2332, 4910
Centegra Northern Illinois Medical Center, 6647
Centennial Medical Center Tri-Star Health System, 7209
Center Academy, 7685
Center Academy at Pinellas Park, 934, 7745
Center for Accessible Living, 4098
Center for Accessible Living: Murray, 4099
Center for Accessible Technology, 1452
Center for Applied Special Technology, 1453
Center for Assistive Technology & Inclusive Education Studies, 1454
Center for Benefits Access, 7364
Center for Best Practices in Early Childhood, 1563
Center for Community Alternatives, 4280
Center for Comprehensive Services, 6648
The Center for Courageous Kids, 1007
Center for Creative Arts Therapy, 655
Center for Development and Disability, 1120
Center for Disabilities & Development, 3411
Center for Disabilities Studies, 3726
Center for Disability and Elder Law, Inc., 4486
Center for Disability Resources, 656, 3098, 2069
Center for Disability Rights, 3915
Center for Disability Services, 1142
Center for Educational Advancement New Jersey, 5956
Center for Health Research: Eastern Washington University, 4973
Center for Healthy Aging, 7365, 7428
Center for Hearing and Communication, 7963, 8139
Center for Human Potential, 2505
Center for Inclusive Design and Innovation, 657, 1917
Center for Independence, 3901
Center for Independence of the Disabled, 3842
Center for Independence of the Disabled of New York, 4281
Center for Independence of the Disabled of New York, 4282
Center for Independence of the Disabled of Daly City, 3843
Center for Independent Living, 3844
Center for Independent Living in Central Florida, 3936
Center for Independent Living of Mid-Michigan, 4153
Center for Independent Living of Broward, 3937
Center for Independent Living of Central Nebraska, 4231
Center for Independent Living of Florida Keys, 3938
Center for Independent Living of Middle Tennessee, 4391
Center for Independent Living of N. Florida, 3939
Center for Independent Living of North Central Florida, 3941, 3942

E

F

G

I

T

U

V

Titles from Grey House

Visit www.GreyHouse.com for Product Information, Table of Contents, and Sample Pages.

Opinions Throughout History

Opinions Throughout History: Church & State
Opinions Throughout History: Conspiracy Theories
Opinions Throughout History: The Death Penalty
Opinions Throughout History: Diseases & Epidemics
Opinions Throughout History: Drug Use & Abuse
Opinions Throughout History: The Environment
Opinions Throughout History: Free Speech & Censorship
Opinions Throughout History: Gender: Roles & Rights
Opinions Throughout History: Globalization
Opinions Throughout History: Guns in America
Opinions Throughout History: Immigration
Opinions Throughout History: Law Enforcement in America
Opinions Throughout History: Mental Health
Opinions Throughout History: Nat'l Security vs. Civil & Privacy Rights
Opinions Throughout History: Presidential Authority
Opinions Throughout History: Robotics & Artificial Intelligence
Opinions Throughout History: Social Media Issues
Opinions Throughout History: The Supreme Court
Opinions Throughout History: Voters' Rights
Opinions Throughout History: War & the Military
Opinions Throughout History: Workers Rights & Wages

This is Who We Were

This is Who We Were: Colonial America (1492-1775)
This is Who We Were: 1880-1899
This is Who We Were: In the 1900s
This is Who We Were: In the 1910s
This is Who We Were: In the 1920s
This is Who We Were: A Companion to the 1940 Census
This is Who We Were: In the 1940s (1940-1949)
This is Who We Were: In the 1950s
This is Who We Were: In the 1960s
This is Who We Were: In the 1970s
This is Who We Were: In the 1980s
This is Who We Were: In the 1990s
This is Who We Were: In the 2000s
This is Who We Were: In the 2010s

Working Americans

Working Americans—Vol. 1: The Working Class
Working Americans—Vol. 2: The Middle Class
Working Americans—Vol. 3: The Upper Class
Working Americans—Vol. 4: Children
Working Americans—Vol. 5: At War
Working Americans—Vol. 6: Working Women
Working Americans—Vol. 7: Social Movements
Working Americans—Vol. 8: Immigrants
Working Americans—Vol. 9: Revolutionary War to the Civil War
Working Americans—Vol. 10: Sports & Recreation
Working Americans—Vol. 11: Inventors & Entrepreneurs
Working Americans—Vol. 12: Our History through Music
Working Americans—Vol. 13: Education & Educators
Working Americans—Vol. 14: African Americans
Working Americans—Vol. 15: Politics & Politicians
Working Americans—Vol. 16: Farming & Ranching
Working Americans—Vol. 17: Teens in America
Working Americans—Vol. 18: Health Care Workers
Working Americans—Vol. 19: The Performing Arts

Grey House Health & Wellness Guides

Addiction Handbook & Resource Guide
The Autism Spectrum Handbook & Resource Guide
Autoimmune Disorders Handbook & Resource Guide
Cardiovascular Disease Handbook & Resource Guide
Dementia Handbook & Resource Guide
Depression Handbook & Resource Guide
Diabetes Handbook & Resource Guide
Nutrition, Obesity & Eating Disorders Handbook & Resource Guide

Consumer Health

Complete Mental Health Resource Guide
Complete Resource Guide for Pediatric Disorders
Complete Resource Guide for People with Chronic Illness
Complete Resource Guide for People with Disabilities
Older Americans Information Resource
Parenting: Styles & Strategies
Teens: Growing Up, Skills & Strategies

General Reference

American Environmental Leaders
Constitutional Amendments
Encyclopedia of African-American Writing
Encyclopedia of Invasions & Conquests
Encyclopedia of Prisoners of War & Internment
Encyclopedia of the Continental Congresses
Encyclopedia of the United States Cabinet
Encyclopedia of War Journalism
The Environmental Debate
Financial Literacy Starter Kit
From Suffrage to the Senate
The Gun Debate: Gun Rights & Gun Control in the U.S.
Historical Warrior Peoples & Modern Fighting Groups
Human Rights and the United States
Political Corruption in America
Privacy Rights in the Digital Age
The Religious Right and American Politics
Speakers of the House of Representatives, 1789-2021
US Land & Natural Resources Policy
The Value of a Dollar 1600-1865 Colonial to Civil War
The Value of a Dollar 1860-2019

Business Information

Business Information Resources
Complete Broadcasting Industry Guide: TV, Radio, Cable & Streaming
Directory of Mail Order Catalogs
Environmental Resource Handbook
Food & Beverage Market Place
The Grey House Guide to Homeland Security Resources
The Grey House Performing Arts Industry Guide
Guide to Healthcare Group Purchasing Organizations
Guide to U.S. HMOs and PPOs
Guide to Venture Capital & Private Equity Firms
Hudson's Washington News Media Contacts Guide
New York State Directory
Sports Market Place

Grey House Publishing | Salem Press | H.W. Wilson | 4919 Route, 22 PO Box 56, Amenia NY 12501-0056

Grey House Imprints

Visit www.GreyHouse.com for Product Information, Table of Contents, and Sample Pages.

Grey House Titles, continued

Education

Complete Learning Disabilities Resource Guide
Digital Literacy: Skills & Strategies
Educators Resource Guide
The Comparative Guide to Elem. & Secondary Schools
Special Education: Policy & Curriculum Development

Statistics & Demographics

America's Top-Rated Cities
America's Top-Rated Smaller Cities
The Comparative Guide to American Suburbs
Profiles of America
Profiles of California
Profiles of Florida
Profiles of Illinois
Profiles of Indiana
Profiles of Massachusetts
Profiles of Michigan
Profiles of New Jersey
Profiles of New York
Profiles of North Carolina & South Carolina
Profiles of Ohio
Profiles of Pennsylvania
Profiles of Texas
Profiles of Virginia
Profiles of Wisconsin

Canadian Resources

Associations Canada
Canadian Almanac & Directory
Canadian Environmental Resource Guide
Canadian Parliamentary Guide
Canadian Venture Capital & Private Equity Firms
Canadian Who's Who
Cannabis Canada
Careers & Employment Canada
Financial Post: Directory of Directors
Financial Services Canada
FP Bonds: Corporate
FP Bonds: Government
FP Equities: Preferreds & Derivatives
FP Survey: Industrials
FP Survey: Mines & Energy
FP Survey: Predecessor & Defunct
Health Guide Canada
Libraries Canada

Weiss Financial Ratings

Financial Literacy Basics
Financial Literacy: How to Become an Investor
Financial Literacy: Planning for the Future
Weiss Ratings Consumer Guides
Weiss Ratings Guide to Banks
Weiss Ratings Guide to Credit Unions
Weiss Ratings Guide to Health Insurers
Weiss Ratings Guide to Life & Annuity Insurers
Weiss Ratings Guide to Property & Casualty Insurers
Weiss Ratings Investment Research Guide to Bond & Money Market
    Mutual Funds
Weiss Ratings Investment Research Guide to Exchange-Traded Funds
Weiss Ratings Investment Research Guide to Stock Mutual Funds
Weiss Ratings Investment Research Guide to Stocks

Books in Print Series

American Book Publishing Record® Annual
American Book Publishing Record® Monthly
Books In Print®
Books In Print® Supplement
Books Out Loud™
Bowker's Complete Video Directory™
Children's Books In Print®
El-Hi Textbooks & Serials In Print®
Forthcoming Books®
Law Books & Serials In Print™
Medical & Health Care Books In Print™
Publishers, Distributors & Wholesalers of the US™
Subject Guide to Books In Print®
Subject Guide to Children's Books In Print®

Grey House Publishing | Salem Press | H.W. Wilson | 4919 Route, 22 PO Box 56, Amenia NY 12501-0056

SALEM PRESS

Titles from Salem Press

Visit www.SalemPress.com for Product Information, Table of Contents, and Sample Pages.

SALEM PRESS

LITERATURE

Critical Insights: Authors

Louisa May Alcott
Sherman Alexie
Isabel Allende
Maya Angelou
Isaac Asimov
Margaret Atwood
Jane Austen
James Baldwin
Saul Bellow
Roberto Bolano
Ray Bradbury
The Brontë Sisters
Gwendolyn Brooks
Albert Camus
Raymond Carver
Willa Cather
Geoffrey Chaucer
John Cheever
Joseph Conrad
Charles Dickens
Emily Dickinson
Frederick Douglass
T. S. Eliot
George Eliot
Harlan Ellison
Ralph Waldo Emerson
Louise Erdrich
William Faulkner
F. Scott Fitzgerald
Gustave Flaubert
Horton Foote
Benjamin Franklin
Robert Frost
Neil Gaiman
Gabriel Garcia Marquez
Thomas Hardy
Nathaniel Hawthorne
Robert A. Heinlein
Lillian Hellman
Ernest Hemingway
Langston Hughes
Zora Neale Hurston
Henry James
Thomas Jefferson
James Joyce
Jamaica Kincaid
Stephen King
Martin Luther King, Jr.
Barbara Kingsolver
Abraham Lincoln
C.S. Lewis
Mario Vargas Llosa
Jack London
James McBride
Cormac McCarthy
Herman Melville
Arthur Miller
Toni Morrison
Alice Munro
Tim O'Brien
Flannery O'Connor
Eugene O'Neill
George Orwell
Sylvia Plath
Edgar Allan Poe
Philip Roth
Salman Rushdie
J.D. Salinger
Mary Shelley
John Steinbeck
Amy Tan
Leo Tolstoy
Mark Twain
John Updike
Kurt Vonnegut
Alice Walker
David Foster Wallace
Edith Wharton
Walt Whitman
Oscar Wilde
Tennessee Williams
Virginia Woolf
Richard Wright
Malcolm X

Critical Insights: Works

Absalom, Absalom!
Adventures of Huckleberry Finn
The Adventures of Tom Sawyer
Aeneid
All Quiet on the Western Front
All the Pretty Horses
Animal Farm
Anna Karenina
The Awakening
The Bell Jar
Beloved
Billy Budd, Sailor
The Book Thief
Brave New World
The Canterbury Tales
Catch-22
The Catcher in the Rye
The Color Purple
The Crucible
Death of a Salesman
The Diary of a Young Girl
Dracula
Fahrenheit 451
The Grapes of Wrath
Great Expectations
The Great Gatsby
Hamlet
The Handmaid's Tale
Harry Potter Series
Heart of Darkness
The Hobbit
The House on Mango Street
How the Garcia Girls Lost Their Accents
The Hunger Games Trilogy
I Know Why the Caged Bird Sings
In Cold Blood
The Inferno
Invisible Man
Jane Eyre
The Joy Luck Club
Julius Caesar
King Lear

The Kite Runner
Life of Pi
Little Women
Lolita
Lord of the Flies
The Lord of the Rings
Macbeth
The Merchant of Venice
The Metamorphosis
Midnight's Children
A Midsummer Night's Dream
Moby-Dick
Mrs. Dalloway
Nineteen Eighty-Four
The Odyssey
Of Mice and Men
The Old Man and the Sea
On the Road
One Flew Over the Cuckoo's Nest
One Hundred Years of Solitude
Othello
The Outsiders
Paradise Lost
The Pearl
The Plague
The Poetry of Baudelaire
The Poetry of Edgar Allan Poe
A Portrait of the Artist as a Young Man
Pride and Prejudice
A Raisin in the Sun
The Red Badge of Courage
Romeo and Juliet
The Scarlet Letter
Sense and Sensibility
Short Fiction of Flannery O'Connor
Slaughterhouse-Five
The Sound and the Fury
A Streetcar Named Desire
The Sun Also Rises
A Tale of Two Cities
The Tales of Edgar Allan Poe
Their Eyes Were Watching God
Things Fall Apart
To Kill a Mockingbird
War and Peace
The Woman Warrior

Critical Insights: Themes

The American Comic Book
American Creative Non-Fiction
The American Dream
American Multicultural Identity
American Road Literature
American Short Story
American Sports Fiction
The American Thriller
American Writers in Exile
Censored & Banned Literature
Civil Rights Literature, Past & Present
Coming of Age
Conspiracies
Contemporary Canadian Fiction
Contemporary Immigrant Short Fiction
Contemporary Latin American Fiction
Contemporary Speculative Fiction

Grey House Publishing | Salem Press | H.W. Wilson | 4919 Route, 22 PO Box 56, Amenia NY 12501-0056

SALEM PRESS

Titles from Salem Press

Visit www.SalemPress.com for Product Information, Table of Contents, and Sample Pages.

Crime and Detective Fiction
Crisis of Faith
Cultural Encounters
Dystopia
Family
The Fantastic
Feminism Flash Fiction
Gender, Sex and Sexuality
Good & Evil
The Graphic Novel
Greed
Harlem Renaissance
The Hero's Quest
Historical Fiction
Holocaust Literature
The Immigrant Experience
Inequality
LGBTQ Literature
Literature in Times of Crisis
Literature of Protest
Love
Magical Realism
Midwestern Literature
Modern Japanese Literature
Nature & the Environment
Paranoia, Fear & Alienation
Patriotism
Political Fiction
Postcolonial Literature
Power & Corruption
Pulp Fiction of the '20s and '30s
Rebellion
Russia's Golden Age
Satire
The Slave Narrative
Social Justice and American Literature
Southern Gothic Literature
Southwestern Literature
Survival
Technology & Humanity
Truth & Lies
Violence in Literature
Virginia Woolf & 20th Century Women Writers
War

Critical Insights: Film

Bonnie & Clyde
Casablanca
Alfred Hitchcock
Stanley Kubrick

Critical Approaches to Literature

Critical Approaches to Literature: Feminist
Critical Approaches to Literature: Moral
Critical Approaches to Literature: Multicultural
Critical Approaches to Literature: Psychological

Literary Classics

Recommended Reading: 600 Classics Reviewed

Novels into Film

Novels into Film: Adaptations & Interpretation
Novels into Film: Adaptations & Interpretation, Volume 2

Critical Surveys of Literature

Critical Survey of American Literature
Critical Survey of Drama
Critical Survey of Long Fiction
Critical Survey of Mystery and Detective Fiction
Critical Survey of Poetry
Critical Survey of Poetry: Contemporary Poets
Critical Survey of Science Fiction & Fantasy Literature
Critical Survey of Shakespeare's Plays
Critical Survey of Shakespeare's Sonnets
Critical Survey of Short Fiction
Critical Survey of World Literature
Critical Survey of Young Adult Literature

Critical Surveys of Graphic Novels

Heroes & Superheroes
History, Theme, and Technique
Independents & Underground Classics
Manga

Critical Surveys of Mythology & Folklore

Creation Myths
Deadly Battles & Warring Enemies
Gods & Goddesses
Heroes and Heroines
Love, Sexuality, and Desire
World Mythology

Cyclopedia of Literary Characters & Places

Cyclopedia of Literary Characters
Cyclopedia of Literary Places

Introduction to Literary Context

American Poetry of the 20th Century
American Post-Modernist Novels
American Short Fiction
English Literature
Plays
World Literature

Magill's Literary Annual

Magill's Literary Annual, 2023
Magill's Literary Annual, 2022
Magill's Literary Annual, 2021
Magill's Literary Annual (Backlist Issues 2020-1977)

Masterplots

Masterplots, Fourth Edition
Masterplots, 2010-2018 Supplement

Notable Writers

Notable African American Writers
Notable American Women Writers
Notable Mystery & Detective Fiction Writers
Notable Writers of the American West & the Native American
 Experience
Notable Writers of LGBTQ+ Literature

Grey House Publishing | Salem Press | H.W. Wilson | 4919 Route, 22 PO Box 56, Amenia NY 12501-0056

SALEM PRESS

Titles from Salem Press

Visit www.SalemPress.com for Product Information, Table of Contents, and Sample Pages.

SALEM PRESS

HISTORY
The Decades
The 1910s in America
The Twenties in America
The Thirties in America
The Forties in America
The Fifties in America
The Sixties in America
The Seventies in America
The Eighties in America
The Nineties in America
The 2000s in America
The 2010s in America

Defining Documents in American History
Defining Documents: The 1900s
Defining Documents: The 1910s
Defining Documents: The 1920s
Defining Documents: The 1930s
Defining Documents: The 1950s
Defining Documents: The 1960s
Defining Documents: The 1970s
Defining Documents: The 1980s
Defining Documents: American Citizenship
Defining Documents: The American Economy
Defining Documents: The American Revolution
Defining Documents: The American West
Defining Documents: Business Ethics
Defining Documents: Capital Punishment
Defining Documents: Civil Rights
Defining Documents: Civil War
Defining Documents: The Constitution
Defining Documents: The Cold War
Defining Documents: Dissent & Protest
Defining Documents: Domestic Terrorism & Extremism
Defining Documents: Drug Policy
Defining Documents: The Emergence of Modern America
Defining Documents: Environment & Conservation
Defining Documents: Espionage & Intrigue
Defining Documents: Exploration and Colonial America
Defining Documents: The First Amendment
Defining Documents: The Free Press
Defining Documents: The Great Depression
Defining Documents: The Great Migration
Defining Documents: The Gun Debate
Defining Documents: Immigration & Immigrant Communities
Defining Documents: The Legacy of 9/11
Defining Documents: LGBTQ+
Defining Documents: Manifest Destiny and the New Nation
Defining Documents: Native Americans
Defining Documents: Political Campaigns, Candidates & Discourse
Defining Documents: Postwar 1940s
Defining Documents: Prison Reform
Defining Documents: Secrets, Leaks & Scandals
Defining Documents: Slavery
Defining Documents: Supreme Court Decisions
Defining Documents: Reconstruction Era
Defining Documents: The Vietnam War
Defining Documents: U.S. Involvement in the Middle East
Defining Documents: Workers' Rights
Defining Documents: World War I
Defining Documents: World War II

Defining Documents in World History
Defining Documents: The 17th Century
Defining Documents: The 18th Century
Defining Documents: The 19th Century
Defining Documents: The 20th Century (1900-1950)
Defining Documents: The Ancient World
Defining Documents: Asia
Defining Documents: Genocide & the Holocaust
Defining Documents: Human Rights
Defining Documents: The Middle Ages
Defining Documents: The Middle East
Defining Documents: Nationalism & Populism
Defining Documents: The Nuclear Age
Defining Documents: Pandemics, Plagues & Public Health
Defining Documents: Renaissance & Early Modern Era
Defining Documents: Revolutions
Defining Documents: Women's Rights

Great Events from History
Great Events from History: American History, Exploration to the Colonial Era, 1492-1775
Great Events from History: The Ancient World
Great Events from History: The Middle Ages
Great Events from History: The Renaissance & Early Modern Era
Great Events from History: The 17th Century
Great Events from History: The 18th Century
Great Events from History: The 19th Century
Great Events from History: The 20th Century, 1901-1940
Great Events from History: The 20th Century, 1941-1970
Great Events from History: The 20th Century, 1971-2000
Great Events from History: Modern Scandals
Great Events from History: African American History
Great Events from History: The 21st Century, 2000-2016
Great Events from History: LGBTQ Events
Great Events from History: Human Rights
Great Events from History: Women's History

Great Lives from History
Great Athletes
Great Athletes of the Twenty-First Century
Great Lives from History: The 17th Century
Great Lives from History: The 18th Century
Great Lives from History: The 19th Century
Great Lives from History: The 20th Century
Great Lives from History: The 21st Century, 2000-2017
Great Lives from History: African Americans
Great Lives from History: The Ancient World
Great Lives from History: American Heroes
Great Lives from History: American Women
Great Lives from History: Asian and Pacific Islander Americans
Great Lives from History: Autocrats & Dictators
Great Lives from History: The Incredibly Wealthy
Great Lives from History: Inventors & Inventions
Great Lives from History: Jewish Americans
Great Lives from History: Latinos
Great Lives from History: The Middle Ages
Great Lives from History: The Renaissance & Early Modern Era
Great Lives from History: Scientists and Science

Titles from Salem Press

Visit www.SalemPress.com for Product Information, Table of Contents, and Sample Pages.

History & Government

American First Ladies
American Presidents
The 50 States
The Ancient World: Extraordinary People in Extraordinary Societies
The Bill of Rights
The Criminal Justice System
The U.S. Supreme Court

Innovators

Computer Technology Innovators
Fashion Innovators
Human Rights Innovators
Internet Innovators
Music Innovators
Musicians and Composers of the 20th Century
World Political Innovators

SOCIAL SCIENCES

Civil Rights Movements: Past & Present
Countries, Peoples and Cultures
Countries: Their Wars & Conflicts: A World Survey
Education Today: Issues, Policies & Practices
Encyclopedia of American Immigration
Ethics: Questions & Morality of Human Actions
Issues in U.S. Immigration
Principles of Sociology: Group Relationships & Behavior
Principles of Sociology: Personal Relationships & Behavior
Principles of Sociology: Societal Issues & Behavior
Racial & Ethnic Relations in America
Weapons, Warfare & Military Technology
World Geography

HEALTH

Addictions, Substance Abuse & Alcoholism
Adolescent Health & Wellness
Aging
Cancer
Community & Family Health Issues
Integrative, Alternative & Complementary Medicine
Genetics and Inherited Conditions
Infectious Diseases and Conditions
Magill's Medical Guide
Nutrition
Parenting: Styles & Strategies
Psychology & Behavioral Health
Teens: Growing Up, Skills & Strategies
Women's Health

Principles of Health

Principles of Health: Allergies & Immune Disorders
Principles of Health: Anxiety & Stress
Principles of Health: Depression
Principles of Health: Diabetes
Principles of Health: Nursing
Principles of Health: Obesity
Principles of Health: Occupational Therapy & Physical Therapy
Principles of Health: Pain Management
Principles of Health: Prescription Drug Abuse

SCIENCE

Ancient Creatures
Applied Science
Applied Science: Engineering & Mathematics
Applied Science: Science & Medicine
Applied Science: Technology
Biomes and Ecosystems
Digital Literacy: Skills & Strategies
Earth Science: Earth Materials and Resources
Earth Science: Earth's Surface and History
Earth Science: Earth's Weather, Water and Atmosphere
Earth Science: Physics and Chemistry of the Earth
Encyclopedia of Climate Change
Encyclopedia of Energy
Encyclopedia of Environmental Issues
Encyclopedia of Global Resources
Encyclopedia of Mathematics and Society
Forensic Science
Notable Natural Disasters
The Solar System
USA in Space

Principles of Science

Principles of Aeronautics
Principles of Anatomy
Principles of Astronomy
Principles of Behavioral Science
Principles of Biology
Principles of Biotechnology
Principles of Botany
Principles of Chemistry
Principles of Climatology
Principles of Computer-aided Design
Principles of Computer Science
Principles of Digital Arts & Multimedia
Principles of Ecology
Principles of Energy
Principles of Fire Science
Principles of Forestry & Conservation
Principles of Geology
Principles of Information Technology
Principles of Marine Science
Principles of Mathematics
Principles of Mechanics
Principles of Microbiology
Principles of Modern Agriculture
Principles of Pharmacology
Principles of Physical Science
Principles of Physics
Principles of Programming & Coding
Principles of Robotics & Artificial Intelligence
Principles of Scientific Research
Principles of Sports Medicine & Exercise Science
Principles of Sustainability
Principles of Zoology

Grey House Publishing | Salem Press | H.W. Wilson | 4919 Route, 22 PO Box 56, Amenia NY 12501-0056

SALEM PRESS

Titles from Salem Press

Visit www.SalemPress.com for Product Information, Table of Contents, and Sample Pages.

SALEM PRESS

CAREERS

Careers: Paths to Entrepreneurship
Careers in Archaeology & Museum Services
Careers in Artificial Intelligence
Careers in the Arts: Fine, Performing & Visual
Careers in the Automotive Industry
Careers in Biology
Careers in Biotechnology
Careers in Building Construction
Careers in Business
Careers in Chemistry
Careers in Communications & Media
Careers in Cybersecurity
Careers in Education & Training
Careers in Engineering
Careers in Environment & Conservation
Careers in Financial Services
Careers in Fish & Wildlife
Careers in Forensic Science
Careers in Gaming
Careers in Green Energy
Careers in Healthcare
Careers in Hospitality & Tourism
Careers in Human Services
Careers in Information Technology
Careers in Law, Criminal Justice & Emergency Services
Careers in the Music Industry
Careers in Manufacturing & Production
Careers in Nursing
Careers in Physics
Careers in Protective Services
Careers in Psychology & Behavioral Health
Careers in Public Administration
Careers in Sales, Insurance & Real Estate
Careers in Science & Engineering
Careers in Social Media
Careers in Sports & Fitness
Careers in Sports Medicine & Training
Careers in Technical Services & Equipment Repair
Careers in Transportation
Careers in Writing & Editing
Careers Outdoors
Careers Overseas
Careers Working with Infants & Children
Careers Working with Animals

BUSINESS

Principles of Business: Accounting
Principles of Business: Economics
Principles of Business: Entrepreneurship
Principles of Business: Finance
Principles of Business: Globalization
Principles of Business: Leadership
Principles of Business: Management
Principles of Business: Marketing

Grey House Publishing | Salem Press | H.W. Wilson | 4919 Route, 22 PO Box 56, Amenia NY 12501-0056

Titles from H.W. Wilson

Visit www.HWWilsonInPrint.com for Product Information, Table of Contents, and Sample Pages.

The Reference Shelf

Affordable Housing
Aging in America
Alternative Facts, Post-Truth and the Information War
The American Dream
Artificial Intelligence
The Business of Food
Campaign Trends & Election Law
College Sports
Democracy Evolving
The Digital Age
Embracing New Paradigms in Education
Food Insecurity & Hunger in the United States
Future of U.S. Economic Relations: Mexico, Cuba, & Venezuela
Gene Editing & Genetic Engineering
Global Climate Change
Guns in America
Hacktivism
Hate Crimes
Immigration
Income Inequality
Internet Abuses & Privacy Rights
Internet Law
LGBTQ in the 21st Century
Marijuana Reform
Mental Health Awareness
Money in Politics
National Debate Topic 2014/2015: The Ocean
National Debate Topic 2015/2016: Surveillance
National Debate Topic 2016/2017: US/China Relations
National Debate Topic 2017/2018: Education Reform
National Debate Topic 2018/2019: Immigration
National Debate Topic 2019/2021: Arms Sales
National Debate Topic 2020/2021: Criminal Justice Reform
National Debate Topic 2021/2022: Water Resources
National Debate Topic 2022/2023: Emerging Technologies & International Security
National Debate Topic 2023/2024: Economic Inequality
New Frontiers in Space
Policing in 2020
Pollution
Prescription Drug Abuse
Propaganda and Misinformation
Racial Tension in a Postracial Age
Reality Television
Renewable Energy
Representative American Speeches, Annual Editions
Rethinking Work
Revisiting Gender
The South China Sea Conflict
Sports in America
The Supreme Court
The Transformation of American Cities
The Two Koreas
UFOs
Vaccinations
Voting Rights
Whistleblowers

Core Collections

Children's Core Collection
Fiction Core Collection
Graphic Novels Core Collection
Middle & Junior High School Core
Public Library Core Collection: Nonfiction
Senior High Core Collection
Young Adult Fiction Core Collection

Current Biography

Current Biography Cumulative Index 1946-2021
Current Biography Monthly Magazine
Current Biography Yearbook

Readers' Guide to Periodical Literature

Abridged Readers' Guide to Periodical Literature
Readers' Guide to Periodical Literature

Indexes

Index to Legal Periodicals & Books
Short Story Index
Book Review Digest

Sears List

Sears List of Subject Headings
Sears List of Subject Headings, Online Database
Sears: Lista de Encabezamientos de Materia

History

American Game Changers: Invention, Innovation & Transformation
American Reformers
Speeches of the American Presidents

Facts About Series

Facts About the 20th Century
Facts About American Immigration
Facts About China
Facts About the Presidents
Facts About the World's Languages

Nobel Prize Winners

Nobel Prize Winners: 1901-1986
Nobel Prize Winners: 1987-1991
Nobel Prize Winners: 1992-1996
Nobel Prize Winners: 1997-2001
Nobel Prize Winners: 2002-2018

Famous First Facts

Famous First Facts
Famous First Facts About American Politics
Famous First Facts About Sports
Famous First Facts About the Environment
Famous First Facts: International Edition

American Book of Days

The American Book of Days
The International Book of Days

Grey House Publishing | Salem Press | H.W. Wilson | 4919 Route, 22 PO Box 56, Amenia NY 12501-0056